CONCISE DICTIONARY OF WORLD HISTORY

Compiled by BRUCE WETTERAU

CONCISE DICTIONARY
·OF WORLD HISTORY·

ROBERT HALE · LONDON

First published in Great Britain 1984

ISBN 0 7090 1380 9

Robert Hale Limited
Clerkenwell House
Clerkenwell Green
LONDON EC1

Printed in the United States of America

Contents

STAFF

Compiled and edited by	Bruce Wetterau
Senior editors	Ray Hand, Jr. Kenneth Whitehead
Contributors	Lina Accurso Lilian Barrington Diana Healy Constance Murphy Linda Palmer
Associate editors	Lilian Brady Gloria Cestaro
Research Assistants	Joy Aquilino Laura Ball Roxanne Basmaci Christopher Carruth Karen Cestaro Laurie Paleo
Editorial Assistants	Ellie Aquilino Dolores Margarita Andrew Mason Robert Mason Robin Michelson

Notes to the Reader

The following explanatory notes are intended to help readers get the full measure of usefulness from the *Concise Dictionary of World History*.

- *The two types of entries.* This dictionary includes both textual entries and chronologies. Textual entries give essential information about a particular topic. Chronologies cover selected broad topics, such as countries and major wars. Both kinds of entries are positioned alphabetically under the topic name.

  The two types of entries complement each other and make it possible for the reader to locate many kinds of information by name or by date. Items listed in chronologies tend to be short, without the details about specific events already covered in textual entries. For instance, a reader who has turned to the chronology for the United States, and who wants to know more about the War of 1812, will find full details in the textual entry for that war. Conversely, the reader who has looked up the textual entry for the Stamp Act can consult the United States chronology to see how the Act fits in with the other major events leading up to the American Revolution.

- *Cross-references.* In any given entry, readers are directed by cross-references to other entries that have a significant amount of amplifying information. In most cases *(q.v.)* is used after the name of an important related entry where more information can be found. At times, *See also* is used as well. However, so many entries are interrelated (and therefore have some sort of amplifying information) that if all cross-references had been noted, the text of the book would have bristled with them. To avoid this problem, an effort was made in writing entries to use specific names of events, people, etc., as they appear in this dictionary. Thus, if readers come across an unfamiliar name, they will be able to turn to the entry under that name for more information.

  In the case of biographical names, an additional aid to the reader has been provided. Whenever a person's first initial and last name are given in an entry, it means the dictionary contains a separate entry for that individual. A first name given in full, along with the last name, indicates there is no other separate entry.

- *Variant names.* A special effort has been made to include variant spellings of names, alternate names, and pseudonyms. These variants appear inside angle brackets—⟨ ⟩—after the boldfaced entry name and will be helpful to readers, should they have occasion to do further research on the topic. Other sources may list information under one of the variant forms, and in such cases it is necessary to know what they are. On the other hand, the reader may have or remember only a variant form of a name when turning to this dictionary; for this situation, cross-references to the main entry itself have been provided for each variant name.

Key to Abbreviations

b	born	*orig.*	originally
c.	circa (approximately)	pop.	population
d.	died	*pseud.*	pseudonym
fl.	flourished	*q.v.*	which see
m.	married		

Preface

The *Concise Dictionary of World History* is a new and comprehensive basic reference for world history, complete in one volume. It is both a convenient sourcebook and a guide to a vast accumulation of facts, including thousands of people, places, events, and other items of historical import. Indeed, the amount of information contained in this dictionary is staggering, and ranges across the entire course of recorded human history. In all, there are some 10,000 alphabetically arranged entries, plus 7,000 chronologically arranged items, covering world history from the beginnings of civilization to the present day. This broad scope, and the straightforward alphabetical format, make the dictionary an invaluable reference for any reader with an appreciation of history, for students, for writers and editors, and, of course, for historians and other scholars.

The prime consideration in organizing this dictionary was to provide maximum accessibility to specific bits of historical information. Other sources, to one degree or another, may contain related information. For example, a reader in search of a certain fact or date might consult a multivolume encyclopedia, a chronology, or a commentary on the history of a country or of a period. But all too often readers are forced to resort to an index to find the particular information they want; then, after skimming a page or two of text, they may find nothing more than a passing mention.

The problem of ready access to historical information for reference uses provided the idea for this book: to create an index to world history. Thus, the *Concise Dictionary of World History* is a compilation of names and terms in world history arranged in alphabetical order, with significant information relating to each entry name given immediately after it. The entries focus on the significant historical details connected with the entry name. This "index" approach has made it possible to cover a very wide range of names and terms in a single, compact volume.

In addition, there are chronologies for selected broad topics (major countries, major wars, and other types of entries) that are located alphabetically by entry name. Items in a chronology contain the name of an event or a person, a brief explanatory note, and the related date.

The chronologies serve two purposes. First, they provide invaluable cross-references to alphabetically arranged textual entries. Many of the names of events and people that are treated in textual entries appear in the chronologies. Thus, for example, readers who want to look up an event that occurred in French history during the nineteenth century, but who cannot remember the name of the event, have only to refer to the appropriate section of the chronology for France. And then, after locating the name, they can turn to the textual entry for further information.

Second, the chronologies also provide an element of continuity by placing specific events within the larger framework of a country's history or, in the case of a battle, within the war. Further, the chronologies cover historically significant events that do not have names, such as important elections, changes in government, or acquisition of new territories by a country.

The *Concise Dictionary of World History* does focus on the political history of the world's great nations and ancient states. But the object was, as nearly as possible, to bring together in a single volume all types of information related to the study and appreciation of history, and the scope extends well beyond the province of political history to the arts, religion, science, and other areas. Readers will find geographical entries helpful, especially those for ancient places and historic regions. The many biographical entries on literary figures, artists, scientists, religious and biblical figures, social reformers, and others identify important individuals and their major contributions. Religion, a major force in shaping both society and history, is covered in numerous entries on religious groups and movements. Other entries cover major social, intellectual, and artistic movements. In addition, the *Concise Dictionary of World History* offers a potpourri of other useful reference information, including definitions of historical terms, entries for major buildings and monuments, and even a selection of mythical and legendary figures.

The *Concise Dictionary of World History* was compiled from a wide range of reference works and other sources, including general encyclopedias, historical references, biographical dictionaries, geographical dictionaries, and commentaries on world history, national history, and historical periods. In most cases at least three sources were used in compiling each entry, and the material from these sources was cross-checked to insure both accuracy and completeness. Disagreements among sources arose, to be sure, and considerable time was spent in resolving these differences. In a number of cases, areas of general uncertainty or major disagreement were noted, but it was not possible to dwell on questions of debate or interpretation among historians.

Compiling this dictionary was a long and demanding process, necessarily involving many people. Each one deserves a special measure of thanks for his or her contribution and concern for doing the best job possible. Those who were involved directly in preparing the manuscript are listed on the staff page. The staff at Macmillan also deserves recognition for the work they did in bringing a large and unwieldy manuscript through production to this handsome, finished book. Charles Levine, director of General Reference Books, handled the inevitable problems of a project of this size with aplomb and good humor. His able and efficient assistant, Glady Villegas, helped keep things running smoothly. Copy editing supervisor Lorraine Steurer and her assistant Jane Low, and copy editors Louise and Edward Lindemann, Mary Donchez, Dominick Anfuso, and Felice Sabbagh did a fine job of weeding out inconsistencies of style and giving the manuscript a final polish. Proofreader Lorraine Veach did an admirable job of reading and correcting typographical errors in the mass of galleys that made up this book.

Finally, I want to thank the Macmillan Publishing Company for giving me the opportunity to compile this new reference for world history.

BRUCE WETTERAU

The Hudson Group
Pleasantville, New York

· CONCISE DICTIONARY ·
· OF WORLD HISTORY ·

A

Aaron Biblical first high priest of the Israelites, traditional ancestor of the priests of Israel, and brother of Moses. Aaron helped Moses to lead the Israelites out of Egypt but later became his rival.

Aasen, Ivar Andreas 1813–96. Norwegian philologist. He devised (1853) a new Norwegian language (Landsmaal) by standardizing existing dialects.

Abahai *See* **Chung Te**

Abailard, Peter *See* **Abelard, Peter**

Abano, Pietro d' 1250?–1316? Italian doctor and philosopher. Abano sought to reconcile Arabian medical theory and Greek philosophy in his *Conciliator differentiarium*. Though he established Padua as a center for medical study, he was twice denounced by the Inquisition.

Abbadides ⟨Abbadids⟩ Arab Muslim dynasty that briefly ruled (1023–91) Seville, Spain. They were in power from the collapse of the caliphate of Córdoba to the occupation of Seville by the Almoravides.

Abbadids *See* **Abbadides**

Abbas I ⟨Abbas the Great⟩ 1557–1628? Shah of Persia (1587–1628). He defeated the Uzbeks and Turks, regained Persian territory, and established Isfahan as Persia's capital. Under his reign, the arts, public works, and trade flourished.

Abbas II ⟨Abbas Hilmi Pasha⟩ 1874–1944. Last Egyptian khedive (1892–1914), successor to his father, Tewfik Pasha. He unsuccessfully opposed British control of Egypt and was deposed at the beginning of WW I, when Britain made Egypt a protectorate.

Abbas, Ferhat 1899–. Algerian statesman and nationalist movement leader. He was the first president of the Algerian provisional government (1958) and president of the Constituent Assembly when Algeria gained independence from France (1962–63).

Abbas Hilmi Pasha *See* **Abbas II**

Abbasid ⟨Abbaside⟩ ⟨Abbasside⟩ Dynasty of Muslim caliphs who ruled the Empire of the Caliphate (750–1258), successors to the Umayyad caliphs (*q.v.*). The line was established (750) when Abu Muslim revolted and defeated the last Umayyad caliph, Marwan II (*d.* 750). During the reign of the 37 Abbasid caliphs, the capital was moved from Damascus to Baghdad. The caliphs' real power declined, the empire slowly disintegrated into petty kingdoms, and finally fell to the Mongols (1258). The caliphate was subsequently removed to Egypt. (*See also* Caliphate, Empire of.) Notable Abbasid caliphs included:

ABU-AL-ABBAS	750–754
AL-MANSUR	754–775
HARUN AL-RASHID	786–809
AL-MAMUN	813–833
AL-MUTASIM	833–842

Abbasside *See* **Abbasid**

Abbas the Great *See* **Abbas I**

abbey Usually a self-contained religious community of monks or nuns, consisting of several buildings, including a church, living quarters, and work spaces. Important to the development of the Benedictine order (*q.v.*), abbeys became centers for learning and the arts, as well as worship, in medieval times.

Abbey Theatre Irish theater and theatrical company formed by the Irish National Theatre Society. The society was founded (1902) by J.M. Synge, W.B. Yeats, and others. Since then many leading actors and playwrights have been associated with the theater.

ABC Powers Collective name for Argentina, Brazil, and Chile, which arose from their joint action on Latin American affairs in the early 20th cent.

Abdali Sultanate Former quasi-independent territory, a part of Yemen (southern) since 1967. The sultanate won its freedom from Yemen in 1728 and was ruled independently until 1839. Thereafter, by treaties with the British, it became part of the Aden Protectorate and ultimately of Yemen (southern).

Abd al-Kadir 1807–83. Algerian rebel leader. From 1832 to 1844 he struggled against French rule in Algeria. His army was finally driven into Morocco, was defeated (1844) at Isly, Morocco, and forced to surrender (1847).

Addallah *See* **Abdullah**

Abd Allah ⟨Khalifa, the⟩ ⟨Abdullah et Taaisha⟩ 1846–99. Sudanese rebel leader. The successor to Muhammad Ahmed, he led Sudanese independence forces to many victories against Egypt. He was decisively defeated by the British at Omdurman (1898).

Abd al-Malik ⟨Abdul-Malik⟩ c646–705. An Umayyad caliph (685–705), successor to his father, Marwan I. He conquered rival caliphs and thus unified Islam. He instituted monetary and postal reforms and made Arabic the official language.

Abd'al-Medjid *See* **Abdul Mejid**

Abd-al-Mumin ⟨Abdul-Mumin⟩ 1094?–1163. A Berber Muslim leader, founder of the Almohade Empire *(q.v.)*. A disciple of Almohade leader Muhammad ibn Tumart, he defeated (1147) the Almoravides, established Marrakesh as his capital, and extended his empire through North Africa and Muslim Spain.

Abd-ar-Rahman *See* **Abd-er-Rahman**

Abd-el-Krim 1882?–1963. Moorish rebel leader. He successfully fought the French and Spanish in Morocco, only to be defeated by their combined forces (1926).

Abd-er-Rahman ⟨Abdu-r-Rahman⟩ ⟨Abd-ar-Rahman⟩ 1778–1859. Sultan of Morocco and Fez (1822–59). His efforts to expand his influence in Algeria led to defeat in war with France (1844). Activities of Moroccan pirates led to conflict with other European nations.

Abd er-Rahman I ⟨Abd-ar-Rahman I⟩ 731–788. First Umayyad emir of Córdoba (756–788) in Muslim Spain. The only survivor of the Abbasid massacre of his family in 750, he seized power in Córdoba. He later repulsed Charlemagne's invasion at Roncesvalles (778), in defense of his emirate.

Abd er-Rahman III ⟨Abd ar-Rahman⟩ 891–961. Umayyad emir of Córdoba (912–929) in Muslim Spain and its first caliph (929–961). Under his rule the city's military and cultural importance was greatly enhanced.

Abdul-Aziz 1830–76. Ottoman sultan (1861–76). His repudiation (1875) of the interest on loans from European nations led to foreign takeover of Ottoman finances. Revolts and independence movements further shook the Ottoman Empire and he was deposed by Midhat Pasha.

Abdul-Hamid I 1725–89. Ottoman sultan (1774–89), successor to his brother, Mustafa III. During his reign, Ottoman power dwindled through two of the Russo-Turkish Wars *(q.v.)*, which established Russian supremacy in the Crimea.

Abdul-Hamid II 1842–1918. Ottoman sultan (1876–1909), successor to Murad V. His reign saw the continuing decline of the Ottoman Empire, the Russo-Turkish War (1897), and Armenian massacres (1894–96). His despotic rule was curbed (1908) by a revolt of the Young Turks.

Abdullah ⟨Abdallah⟩ 545?–c570. Muslim patriarch, father of Muhammad.

Abdullah ⟨Abdullah ibn Hussein⟩ 1882–1951. First king (1946–51) of newly independent Jordan. During the Arab-Israeli War (1948–49), he took the West Bank of the Jordan River and subsequently annexed the territory. He was assassinated (1951).

Abdullah et Taaisha *See* **Abd Allah**

Abdullah ibn Hussein *See* **Abdullah**

Abdul-Malik *See* **Abd al-Malik**

Abdul Mejid ⟨Abd al-Medjid⟩ 1823–61. Ottoman sultan (1839–61), successor to his father, Mahmud II. He introduced short-lived reforms (1839, 1856), ended, with European aid, Muhammad Ali's revolt, and fought Russia in the Crimean War (1853–56).

Abdul-Mumin *See* **Abd-al-Mumin**

Abdul Rahman, Tunku 1903–73. A Malaysian statesman. He headed the nationalist party, negotiated Malaysian independence from Britain (Aug. 31, 1957), and became first prime minister (1957–70). The Federation of Malaysia was formed (1963) during his administration.

Abdu-r-Rahman ⟨Abdurrahman⟩ d. 732. Governor of Muslim Spain (721–732). He was killed by Charles Martel in the famous Battle of Tours (732).

Abdu-r-Rahman *See* **Abd-er-Rahman**

Abednego *See* **Three Holy Children**

Abeilard, Peter *See* **Abelard, Peter**

Abel Biblical son of Adam and Eve, killed by his older brother Cain.

Abelard, Peter ⟨Abailard, ~⟩ ⟨Abeilard, ~⟩ 1079–1142. French theologian and philosopher. A teacher of wide reputation at Notre Dame in Paris, he applied Aristotelian logic to questions of faith. He secretly married a student, Héloïse, and was subsequently mutilated by thugs hired by her angry uncle. Abelard then became a monk at Saint Denis and Héloïse became a nun. Then his *Theologica*, an analysis of the Trinity, was condemned as heresy (1121), and he was thereafter hounded by charges of heresy.

Abell, Kjeld 1901–61. Danish playwright noted for his innovations in stage technique.

Abensberg-Eckmuhl, Battles of Victory for Napoleon (Apr. 23, 1809) over Austrian forces during the Napoleonic Wars (1803–15). The Austrians, under Archduke Charles Louis (1771–1847), sought to take advantage of Napoleon's difficulties in the Peninsular War to liberate occupied German states. To that end Charles launched (Apr. 10) an attack into Bavaria with a force of nearly 200,000 soldiers, while also calling for a general revolt by German states. He was met by nearly 180,000 allied French troops under Napoleon. In the ensuing battles at Abensberg, Eckmuhl, and Landshut (Apr. 19–23), Napoleon split the Austrian force and compelled it to retreat southward. Though he failed to decisively defeat the Austrians, Napoleon nevertheless prevented a general rebellion of German states.

Abercromby, Sir Ralph   1734–1801. British general. He served in the Seven Years' War (1756–63) and distinguished himself in Holland while commanding a British retreat during the French Revolutionary Wars (1792–1802). He was killed while leading an expedition against the French in Egypt.

Aberdeen, George Hamilton-Gordon, 4th earl of 1784–1860. British statesman who served twice as foreign secretary (1834–35, 1841–46), and as prime minister (1852–55). As foreign secretary, he settled two boundary disputes between the US and Canada by concluding the Webster-Ashburton Treaty (1842) and the Oregon Treaty (1846). As prime minister, he was unable to prevent British involvement in the Crimean War (1853–56).

Aberhart, William   1878–1943. Canadian politician who advocated Social Credit, or cash payments to citizens by the government. He helped to organize the Social Credit party in Alberta and served as Alberta's premier (1935–43), but was unable to implement his programs.

Abiathar   Biblical high priest of Israel. He survived the massacre of his family by Doeg, and later was a loyal supporter of David.

Abigail   Biblical wife of Nabal and David. She persuaded David not to take vengeance upon Nabal, and, after his death, married David.

Abijah ⟨Abijam⟩ *fl. c*915 BC. Second king of Judah, successor to his father, Rehoboam, and grandson of Solomon. During his brief reign, he warred against Jeroboam I.

Abijam   *See* **Abijah**

Abiram   *See* **Korah**

Abjuration, Act of   *See* **Act of Abjuration**

Abo Treaty of   Treaty (Aug. 7, 1743) between Sweden and Russia, following the Russo-Swedish War (1741–43). By its terms Sweden ceded to Russia part of southeastern Finland.

abolition   Worldwide movement for an end to slavery, and an important issue in US history. Abolition was an outgrowth of the concern for human rights that arose during the Enlightenment of the 18th cent. In Britain, the abolition movement began in the late 18th cent. and brought about laws ending slavery throughout the British Empire by the early 19th cent. British abolitionists, such as W. Wilberforce, first won passage of laws (1807) against the trading of slaves and then, by the Abolition Act of 1833, succeeded in having slavery itself abolished throughout the empire. At about the same time in South America, former Spanish colonies were establishing their independence and, as they did so, abolished slavery within their respective borders.

In the US, however, a system of slavery had become an integral part of the southern plantation economy and abolition was stubbornly resisted by southern states. By 1820, the political debate between antislavery (northern) and proslavery (southern) states had resulted in the Missouri Compromise. This compromise plan sought to keep the number of antislavery and proslavery states (and thus the number of Senate seats) equal. But keeping the balance was difficult at a time when new states were being added to the Union.

The abolitionist movement (as distinct from moderate antislavery elements) began in the North in the 1830s, through the efforts of such men as C. Finney, T. Weld, and W. Garrison. The abolitionists were generally extremists, and, though their fiery campaigns were at first unpopular even in the North, they gained strength and spurred the political debate over slavery. By 1850, the doctrine of maintaining an equal number of antislavery and proslavery states had proved unworkable. It was replaced by a new compromise formula called Popular Sovereignty *(q.v.)* This doctrine was embodied in two bills, the Compromise of 1850 and the Kansas-Nebraska Act *(q.v.)*, and seemed to resolve the issue for a time in the 1850s. But the conflict between extremist abolitionists and southern slaveholders only worsened. Violence erupted in Bleeding Kansas and the Harper's Ferry raid *(q.v.)* and, finally, the newly formed Republican Party adopted an openly antislavery platform. The election (1860) of A. Lincoln, a Republican and antislavery moderate, provoked southern states into secession and civil war. Though it was not without tremendous cost, the American Civil War *(q.v.)* finally ended slavery in the US (formally accomplished by the Emancipation Proclamation and the 13th Amendment). By the end of the 19th cent., the spread of antislavery sentiment had resulted in the abolition of slavery in most other parts of the world. Slavery continues to exist in parts of Asia and Africa.

Abominations, Tariff of   *See* **Tariff of Abominations**

Aboukir, Battle of 1. ⟨Nile, Battle of the⟩ British naval victory (Aug. 1–2, 1798) over a French fleet during the French Revolutionary Wars (1792–1802). Adm. H. Nelson commanded British forces in this battle at Aboukir Bay, Egypt. **2.** Victory for Napoleon (July 25, 1799) over the Ottoman Turks, during the French Revolutionary Wars (1792–1802). Napoleon's army of 7,700 met some 18,000 Turkish troops, led by Mustafa IV, at the village of Aboukir, Egypt. French losses were 900, Turkish were 12,000 killed and 3,000 captured.

Abraham ⟨Abram⟩ Biblical figure, regarded as the father of the Hebrew people. He journeyed from Ur to Canaan, at God's call, to found a new nation. He figures prominently in three religions—Judaism, Christianity, and Islam.

Abram *See* **Abraham**

Absalom Biblical figure, the favorite son of King David. He revolted against his father but was killed by Joab.

Absalon ⟨Axel⟩ c1128–1201. Danish archbishop and statesman. An adviser to Danish kings, he helped establish Denmark's independence from the Holy Roman Empire. He also figured in the introduction of canon law into Denmark and in the founding of Copenhagen.

absolutism Government by authority of the king alone. This form of government was prevalent in Europe from the 15th to 18th cent. It evolved gradually as monarchs overcame limits on their personal power (imposed by the church and the nobility). Absolute monarchies, typified by the rule of French King Louis XIV, were largely brought to an end in Europe by the upheavals of the French Revolution and post-Napoleonic years.

abstract expressionism ⟨New York School⟩ Artistic movement. Developed in New York in the 1940s, it was the first major artistic movement in which Americans played a dominant role. Among the early abstract expressionists were M. Rothko, W. de Kooning, and J. Pollock.

Abu-Abdallah *See* **Boabdil**

Abu al-Abbas ⟨~ as-Saffah⟩ c722–754. Muslim caliph (750–754), founder and first caliph of the Abbasid dynasty. He overthrew the Umayyad caliph (749) and massacred members of the Umayyad family.

Abubacer *See* **Ibn Tufail**

abu Bakr 573–634. Father-in-law of Muhammad, and his closest follower. As successor to Muhammad and first caliph (632–634), he began the expansion of the Empire of the Caliphate (q.v.).

Abukir, Battle of *See* **Aboukir, Battle of**

Abulfaraj *See* **Bar-Hebraeus, Gregorius**

Abu Muslim, Revolt of Muslim rebellion (747–750) led by an Iranian, Abu Muslim, against the Umayyad rulers. This revolt enabled Abu al-Abbas to overthrow the Umayyads.

Abu Nasr al-Farabi *See* **Farabi**

Abydos Ancient town, now in northwest Turkey. Here Xerxes and his army crossed the Dardanelles on a bridge of boats during an invasion of Greece (480 BC). Abydos is also associated with the legend of Hero and Leander (q.v.).

Abydos, Table of *See* **Table of Abydos**

Abyssinia *See* **Ethiopia**

Academy Ancient Greek school near Athens, founded (c387 BC) by Plato. Here Plato taught, and his followers continued teaching Platonic philosophy for 900 years. The school was finally closed by the emperor Justinian I (529).

Académie Française *See* **French Academy**

Acadia Former French colony in North America. It included what are now the coastal Canadian provinces of Nova Scotia, New Brunswick, and Prince Edward Island, as well as parts of Maine. The French founded their first permanent settlement at Port Royal (1605) and, soon after, the territory began passing back and forth between France and England. Following the War of Spanish Succession (1701–14), most of the territory came under permanent English control (by the Peace of Utrecht, 1713). British distrust of the French settlers led to mass resettlement (1755, 1758) in other colonies. The last French possessions in Acadia passed to the English by the Treaty of Paris (1763).

Acarya *See* **Bhascara**

Achaea ⟨Achaia⟩ Historic region of ancient Greece located in the north Peloponnesus. Though Achaea is said to have once extended over most of the Peloponnesus and southeast Thessaly, it was only a small territory in the north from the 6th to 4th cent. BC. During this period, and near the end of Macedonian domination (4th-3d cent. BC), towns of this region formed the Achaean League. Following the Roman conquest of Greece, Achaea was made part of a Roman province (146 BC).

Achaean League Two confederations of Greek cities, the second being regarded as an ancient model of federal government. The first (5th-4th cent. BC) was formed by Achaean towns for defense against pirates. The second (280–146 BC) was originally made up of Achaean cities allied to overthrow Macedonian rulers. By 227 BC other Greek cities, including Athens, had joined the league, and in that year Sparta declared war on the league. The league was forced to give up resistance to Macedonian control in return for help against Sparta. During the Macedonian War, however, the league sided with the Romans and subsequently came to control most of the Peloponnesus. However, the Romans became suspicious of Achaean designs and in 146 BC ended the confederation, creating a Roman province in its place.

Achaemenes *See* **Achaemenidae**

Achaemenidae ⟨Achaemenids⟩ Ancient Persian dynasty founded in the 7th cent. BC by King Achaemenes. The line includes the founder of the Persian Empire, Cyrus the Great, and provided kings of the empire during its ascendancy (from 550 BC). The last king of the dynasty was Darius III, killed during the conquest of Persia by Alexander the Great (330 BC).

CYRUS THE GREAT	550–529 BC
CAMBYSES II	529–522
DARIUS I	521–485
XERXES I	485–465
ARTAXERXES I	465–425
XERXES II	424
DARIUS II	424–404
ARTAXERXES II	404–359
ARTAXERXES III	359–338
ARSES	338–336
DARIUS III	336–330

Achaemenids *See* **Achaemenidae**

Achaia *See* **Achaea**

Acheson, Dean Gooderham 1893–1971. A presidential adviser and US secretary of state (1949–52) influential in implementing the Marshall Plan and in establishing the North Atlantic Treaty Organization. He also developed the policy of "containment" of communism.

Achilles Mythical Greek hero, the leading Greek warrior during the Trojan War. His mother had attempted to make him immortal by dipping him in the river Styx, but failed to bathe the heel by which she held him. During the Trojan War, Paris shot Achilles in the heel and killed him (thus, "Achilles' heel").

Achinese War War (1873–1904) between Dutch colonial forces and the Muslim kingdom of Achin in northern Sumatra. By the Sumatra Treaty (1871), the British recognized Dutch hegemony over Sumatra in return for Dutch claims to the Gold Coast, Africa. The Dutch subsequently moved against the Achinese (1873), who had long resisted Dutch control and were actively engaged in piracy. The Dutch defeated the sultan of Achin that year, but local leaders carried on a protracted and costly guerrilla war, which lasted until 1904.

ACLU *See* **American Civil Liberties Union**

Acre ⟨Akko⟩ City of ancient Palestine, now located in northwest Israel. Founded before 1500 BC, it is mentioned in the Bible and was an important port under the Romans. Conquered by the

Arabs (AD 638), it subsequently was held by the crusaders (AD 1104–87, 1191–1291). The Ottoman Turks controlled the city from 1517 to 1918, when it was captured by the British. The Israelis annexed the city (1949) after the Arab-Israeli War (1948).

Acre, Battle of 1. Victory for crusaders (July 12, 1191) during the Third Crusade (1189–92). Acre, defended by Saladin, was forced to surrender after a long siege (1189–91) by Christian forces. English king Richard I massacred nearly 3,000 Muslim prisoners. **2.** Muslim victory (May 18, 1291) that marked the end of Christian crusaders' presence in the Holy Land. In April, 1291, Egyptian Mamelukes laid siege (with 160,000 troops) to Acre, then one of the few remaining Christian strongholds. Despite efforts to reinforce the city, it fell, and its surviving defenders were killed. Within a few months, the last of the crusaders had been killed or driven out of the Holy Land.

Acropolis The citadel, or elevated portion, of ancient Greek cities, usually reserved for defensive or religious purposes. The best known acropolis is that of Athens, built during the 5th cent. BC. Its remains are considered one of the architectural treasures of the world and include such famous buildings as the Parthenon and Erechtheum.

Act in Restraint of Appeals to Rome English law nullifying the pope's authority in England. It was passed (Jan., 1533) by Parliament to permit King Henry VIII to annul his marriage to Catherine of Aragon and to marry A. Boleyn.

Action Française *See* **French Action**

Actium, Battle of Decisive naval battle fought (Sept. 2, 31 BC) off the west coast of Greece, in which Octavian defeated Antony and Cleopatra. By his victory, Octavian became sole ruler of the Roman Empire. The battle was brought on by Antony's dalliance with Cleopatra. Though both sides had deployed land and sea forces, Antony engaged Octavian at sea. Routed by Octavian's fleet, Antony and Cleopatra managed to escape and returned to Egypt.

Act of Abjuration Dutch declaration of independence (July 26, 1581). Following years of revolt, the Dutch finally declared their independence from Spain and its Hapsburg king, Philip II. The act listed grievances against Philip and asserted that he had forfeited rights to rule the Dutch United Provinces.

Act of Settlement British act (June 12, 1701) establishing line of succession for the crown. Following the death of the last Stuart heir to the throne, Parliament by this act passed the crown to the House of Hanover (to the granddaughter of James I, Sophia, or her heirs). In addition, the act excluded Catholics from succession and further stipulated that the monarch belong to the Church of England, that he not leave Britain without permission from Parliament, that he not involve Britain in wars to defend his foreign territories, that he not appoint foreigners to government posts, and that he appoint judges for life (or until they were found guilty of misconduct).

Act of Six Articles Series of laws passed by the English Parliament (1539) at the instigation of Henry VIII, concerning the doctrine of the Church of England. The acts upheld transubstantiation, condemned clerical marriage and Communion under both species, and sanctioned private masses and confession. They were repealed in the subsequent reign of Edward VI.

Act of Supremacy Two acts of Parliament that gave the English king supreme authority over the Church of England and thus broke ties with Rome. The first, in 1534, made Henry VIII head of the church in England, and the second, in 1559, vested this authority in Elizabeth I.

Act of Union **1.** Act (effective 1536) that united Wales with England. **2.** Act (effective May 1, 1707) that united Scotland with England. **3.** Act (effective Jan. 1, 1801) that united Great Britain and Ireland. The union with Ireland was dissolved by Anglo-Irish treaty (Dec. 6, 1921), which gave Ireland dominion status and created Northern Ireland as a separate state under British control. **4.** British act (effective 1841) that united Upper and Lower Canada. It preceded the British North America Act *(q.v.)*.

Acton, John Emerich Edward Dalberg-Acton, 1st Baron 1834–1902. English historian, who planned and began work on the *Cambridge Modern History*.

Acton, Sir John Francis Edward 1736–1811. A Neapolitan statesman. As prime minister of Naples (1785–1806), he allied it with England and Austria against France. He fled during the French occupation of Naples (1798–99), participated in reprisals against the Parthenopean Republic *(q.v.)*, and went into exile after Napoleon captured Naples (1806).

acupuncture Chinese medical technique involving the insertion of fine needles at specified points on the body. This ancient practice was developed by the Chinese before 2500 BC and is still used today to control pain and cure a variety of ailments.

Adam Biblical first man, who lived with Eve in the Garden of Eden. He is an important theological figure in the Jewish and Christian faiths. Expelled with Eve from the garden for eating an apple from the tree of knowledge of good and evil,

he was said to have lived 930 years and to have fathered Cain, Abel, and other offspring.

Adams, Abigail Smith 1744–1818. Wife of Pres. J. Adams (m. 1764) and mother of Pres. J.Q. Adams. Her letters are a colorful and detailed source of political and social history.

Adams, Brooks 1848–1927. American historian, son of C. F. Adams. He advanced his theory of the growth and decay of civilization according to lines of commerce in *The Law of Civilization and Decay*. He predicted the supremacy of the US and Russia in world affairs.

Adams, Charles Francis 1807–86. An American diplomat, son of Pres. J.Q. Adams. He played a key role in maintaining England's neutrality during the American Civil War and in negotiating the Alabama Claims *(q.v.)* with England.

Adams, Henry Brooks 1838–1918. American historian, son of C. F. Adams. His works have earned him a major place in American letters. Among them are: *History of the United States of America*, *Mont-Saint-Michel and Chartres*, and *The Education of Henry Adams*.

Adams, James Truslow 1878–1949. American historian. Adams wrote many books on American history including *The Founding of New England*, which won the Pulitzer Prize (for history) in 1922, and *The Adams Family*. He was editor of the *Dictionary of American History*.

Adams, John 1735–1826. 2nd US president (1797–1801), successor to G. Washington, and 1st vice-president (1789–97). A leading Massachusetts patriot and political theorist in the years before independence, he was a delegate to the First and Second Continental Congress, recommended G. Washington as commander of the Continental Army, helped draft the Declaration of Independence, carried out diplomatic missions in Europe, and helped negotiate the Treaty of Paris (1783), which ended the American Revolution. Serving as Washington's vice-president, Adams aligned himself with the Federalists *(q.v.)*, who advocated a strong central government. Adams' term as president saw near war with France, brought about by the American rapprochement with Britain, and a bitter struggle between Federalists and Jeffersonian Republicans. Events during his administration included: the XYZ Affair (1797); the Treaty of 1800 (or Treaty of Mortefontaine, Sept. 30, 1800), which ended the American alliance with France formed in 1778; passage of the Alien and Sedition Acts (1798); the Kentucky and Virginia Resolutions (1798–99); and Fries's Rebellion (1799). Adams was defeated by T. Jefferson in the election of 1800, sometimes also referred to as the Revolution of 1800.

Adams, John Quincy 1767–1848. 6th US president (1825–29), successor to J. Monroe. The son of former Pres. J. Adams, he served in various diplomatic posts from 1794, became a Federalist senator (1803–08), helped negotiate the Treaty of Ghent (1814), and became secretary of state (1817–25) under Pres. J. Monroe. In this last post he was involved in the purchase of Florida from Spain (1819) and was instrumental in formulation of the Monroe Doctrine (1823). Adams won the presidential election of 1824, though the four-way race was decided in the House of Representatives. Outraged Jacksonian Democrats (A. Jackson had won the popular vote) waged a bitter feud with Adams for the next four years and thereby greatly reduced the effectiveness of his administration. He was also involved in a controversy over the American System *(q.v.)* for protective tariffs, which resulted in passage of the Tariff of Abominations and the rise of the nullification controversy. Adams, defeated by Jackson in 1828, served as a congressman (1831–48) and became an anti-slavery spokesman.

Adams, Samuel 1722–1803. American statesman during the Revolutionary War era. He led radical opposition to British taxation in the American colonies, played a leading role in the Boston Tea Party, and served in the Continental Congress (1774–81). He signed the Declaration of Independence.

Adams-Onis Treaty *See* **Transcontinental Treaty**

Adana *See* **Aden**

Addams, Jane 1860–1935. American social reformer. With Ellen Gates Starr, she founded (1881) Hull House, a settlement house in Chicago and one of the first in the US. A leader of the woman suffrage and pacifist movements, she was awarded the Nobel Peace Prize (with Nicholas Murray Butler) in 1931.

Addis Ababa Capital of Ethiopia (pop. 1,196,300). It was named by Menelik II as the capital of his kingdom of Shoa, and in 1886 became the capital of Ethiopia. The Organization of African Unity (OAU) is located here.

Addison, Joseph 1672–1719. English essayist, poet, and statesman, best known for his contributions to such periodicals as the *Tattler* (founded by R. Steele) and the *Spectator* (founded with Steele). He is noted for the clarity and brilliance of his prose.

Addresses to the German Nation German nationalist speeches. J. Fichte delivered these highly nationalistic lectures at the University of Berlin in 1807–08. He called for an end to French domination of Germany and a regeneration of German spirit.

Aden ⟨Adana⟩ Port city and capital of Yemen (pop. 271,600), located on the Gulf of Aden. An important strategic and trading center since ancient times, it came under Turkish control in the 16th cent. and British control in the early 19th cent. Aden and surrounding territory were made into a British colony (Aden Protectorate) in 1937, and the city became capital of independent Yemen (southern) in 1968.

Adler, Alfred 1870–1937. Austrian psychiatrist who founded a school of psychiatry based on analysis of an individual's inferiority feelings. An associate of S. Freud from 1902 to 1911, he came to reject Freud's emphasis on sex. Instead, he developed a psychotherapy based on the premise that neurosis develops from feelings of inferiority, brought about by conflict between the environment and need for self-assertion.

Adler, Felix 1851–1933. American educator and social reformer who founded the New York Society for Ethical Culture (1876) and the Ethical Culture Movement *(q.v.)*.

Admetus In Greek mythology, the suitor of Alcestis. With Apollo's help, he won her hand by coming for her in a chariot pulled by a lion and a wild boar. She later offered to forfeit her life to save Admetus, and thereby saved them both.

Admiral Graf Spee Famous German pocket battleship of WW II. Operating in South American waters, the battleship was hunted down and engaged in battle by three British cruisers. Later bottled up in Montevideo harbor, it was scuttled by the Germans (Dec. 17, 1939).

Admonition to the Parliament, An English Puritan reform proposal. Sent anonymously to Parliament (1572), the proposal urged strict reform of the Anglican church according to Calvinistic doctrines. R. Hooker opposed the reforms.

Adonis Beautiful youth in Greek mythology, loved by both Aphrodite and Persephone. On Adonis' death, Zeus decided he should spend part of his time underground with Persephone and part aboveground with Aphrodite. This gave rise to the yearly cycle of plants, with which Adonis is associated.

Adoptionism Christian heresy, similar to Nestorianism. It originated in the 2d and 3d cents. and reappeared in Spain in 782. Adoptionists maintained that Jesus was born human and assumed divinity only after baptism and "adoption" by God. Adoptionist views were also advanced (12th cent.) by P. Abelard.

Adrian I *d.* 795. Roman Catholic pope (772–795), successor to Stephen IV. He called upon Charlemagne to defeat the Lombards (773), then threatening Rome. Thereafter, the pope maintained a close alliance with Charlemagne, and Charlemagne established a protectorate over papal lands. Adrian confirmed decrees of the Second Council of Nicaea (787).

Adrian IV   *d.* 1159. The only English pope (1154–59), born Nicholas Breakspear, successor to Anastasius IV. He crowned Frederick I (1155) Holy Roman Emperor but later came into conflict with him. Adrian's supposed donation of Ireland to Henry II of England is disputed.

Adrianople ⟨*now* Edirne⟩ City (pop. 46,000) located in northwest Turkey. It was founded by Emperor Hadrian (AD *c*125) and suffered many conquests because of its strategic location. It was variously conquered by the Visigoths, crusaders, and Ottoman Turks, and figured in the Russo-Turkish Wars (captured from the Turks, 1829, 1878) and Balkan Wars (captured from the Turks, 1813). It was restored to Turkey in 1923. *See also events below.*

Adrianople, Battle of ⟨Hadrianople, ~⟩ **1.** Victory (July 3, AD 323, at Adrianople, now in Turkey) for Constantine I, ruler of the Western Roman Empire, during the Roman Civil Wars. Constantine defeated Licinius, emperor of the East. Roughly 50,000 soldiers were involved on each side and some 20,000 were killed. **2.** Major Visigoth victory (Aug. 9, AD 378) over the Romans at Adrianople, now in Turkey. The Visigoths, under their chief, Fritigern, routed a force of 30,000 Romans under Emperor Valens. Valens and 20,000 Romans were killed. Emperor Theodosius I was subsequently forced to come to terms with the Visigoths (382).

Adrianople, Treaty of ⟨Edirne, ~⟩ Treaty (Sept. 14, 1829, at Adrianople, now in Turkey) between Russia and Turkey, ending the Russo-Turkish War (1828–29). By its terms, Russia won possession of territories along the Black Sea (including the mouth of the Danube); the Dardanelles and other Turkish waters were opened to Russian merchant ships; autonomy was recognized for Serbia, Moldavia, and Wallachia; and Greece was granted almost complete independence.

Adullamites   British political faction. The Adullamites were Liberals in Parliament who joined with Conservatives (1866) to defeat the Reform Bill of 1866. The bill would have expanded the electorate and thus stirred fears of the evils of democracy among the Adullamites.

Adventists   Protestant churches that preach the second coming of Jesus and the formation of his 1,000-year (millennial) kingdom. The origins of the Adventist churches can be traced to the teachings of an American, W. Miller, who preached the coming of the end of the world in 1843. Miller's

followers formally adopted (1845) their belief in the second coming of Christ, and in subsequent years organized various Adventist sects. The largest, the Seventh-Day Adventists, was formed officially in 1863 and is dedicated to missionary work.

Aeëtes   Mythical Greek king of Colchis, father of Medea and guardian of the Golden Fleece. Jason obtained the Golden Fleece with Medea's help and later married her.

Aegean civilization   Name for Bronze Age cultures in the region of the Aegean Sea from *c*3000 to *c*1000 BC. Aegean cultures include the Minoan on the island of Crete, the Mycenaean on the Greek mainland, and also that of the inhabitants of the Cyclades Islands. The Minoan culture (*fl.* *c*3000–*c*1500 BC) was dominant throughout the Aegean until the conquest of the Minoans (*c*1500), apparently by the Mycenaeans. The Mycenaean culture then predominated, until it was in turn destroyed by invasions from the north (*c*1100 BC).

Aegean Sea   A part of the Mediterranean Sea, lying between Greece and Asia Minor (west and east) and between Crete and the Dardanelles (south and north). The sea was called Archipelago in ancient times, thus the general term for an island group. Among the many islands within its boundaries are Samos, Lesbos, Thasos, Euboea, Dodecanese, the Aegean, and the Cyclades.

Aegaeon   *See* **Briareus**

Aegeus   Mythical Greek king of Athens, father of Theseus. He mistakenly believed his son had been killed while trying to slay the Minotaur and drowned himself in the sea, thereafter known as the Aegean.

Aegisthus   *See* **Orestes**

Aegnina, Paul of   *See* **Paul of Aegnina**

Aegospotami, Battle of   The Spartans, under Lysander, defeated the Athenians, under Conan (*d.* *c*390 BC), in the final naval battle (405 BC) of the Peloponnesian War. Athens surrendered the next year.

Aeneas   Legendary Greek hero, a Trojan, and the son of Anchises and Aphrodite. His descendants were said to have founded Rome. He is the subject of the *Aeneid* by Virgil.

Aeolia   *See* **Aeolis**

Aeolian Islands   *See* **Lipari Islands**

Aeolis ⟨Aeolia⟩ Ancient territory (now in Turkey) surrounding a number of cities on the western coast of Asia Minor. The cities were founded *c*11th cent. BC by the Aeolians, a Hellenic people.

Aeolus   Greek wind god, who lived on the island of Aeolia and who aided Ulysses in his journey. Aeolus is human in Homer's works but later appears as a god.

Aeschylus 525–456 BC. Greek poet of Athens, called the father of Greek tragedy. He is known to have fought at the battles of Marathon and Salamis (490, 480 BC), and later won a prize for his play *The Persians* (c484). Thereafter, he gained a wide reputation and made many important innovations in Greek theater, including the introduction of a second actor and the use of scenery and costumes. Among his other extant works are *Seven Against Thebes, Prometheus Bound,* and the great *Oresteia* trilogy (*Agamemnon, The Choëphoroe,* and *The Eumenides*).

Aesculapius *See* **Asclepius**

Aesop *fl.* 6th cent. BC. Famous Greek fable writer and possibly only a legendary figure. Fables attributed to him include *The Fox and the Grapes* and *The Hare and the Tortoise*. His fables are noted for their wit and moral instruction.

aesthetics ⟨esthetics⟩ In philosophy, the study of the nature of beauty in works of art. Ancient Greek philosophers, such as Plato and Aristotle, were concerned with the nature of art and beauty. But aesthetics as a distinct study began about the 15th cent. AD, when art evolved from a craft into a profession. Two basic positions on the nature of beauty are: the objective view, in which beauty is inherent in the work; and the subjective view, in which beauty is a matter of pleasing the individual observer.

Aeterni Patris Catholic encyclical issued by Pope Leo XIII on Aug. 4, 1879. It established the dominance of Thomism, the teachings of Saint Thomas Aquinas, in the Roman Catholic church.

Aethelbald *d.* 757. The King of Mercia (716–757). Aethelbald controlled most of England from the Humber River to the English Channel and styled himself "King of Britain" after 736.

Aethelbert *c*552–616. King of Kent (c560–616). Aethelbert became Anglo-Saxon England's first Christian ruler after his conversion by Saint Augustine of Canterbury. His legal code is the earliest extant code of Anglo-Saxon laws.

Aethelbert *d.* 865. King of Wessex (860–865). Aethelbert was the brother of Aethelred and Aethelbald. His brief reign was plagued by Danish invasions.

Aethelflaed ⟨Aethelfleda⟩ *d.* 918. Mercian ruler (911–918) called "Lady of the Mercians." With her brother Edward the Elder, she drove the Danes from eastern England. Mercia was united with Wessex after her death.

Aethelfrith *d.* 616. King of Northumbria (c593–616). Aethelfrith incorporated the northern kingdoms of Bernicia and Deira into Northumbria, and later warred successfully against both the Scots and the Welsh.

Aethelred *d.* 871. King of Wessex and Kent (c865–871). He began organizing forces to resist the Danish invaders but died before making significant territorial gains. He was succeeded in the task by his brother, Alfred the Great.

Aethelred *c*968–1016. King of England (978–1016). Nicknamed "the Unready," he was unable to stop raids and invasions by the Danes. An invasion by the Danish king Sweyn (1013) forced him to flee to Normandy until 1014. His sons were Edmund Ironside and Edward the Confessor.

Aethelstan *See* **Athelstan**

Aethelwulf *d.* 858. King of Wessex (839–856), successor to his father, Egbert, and father of Alfred the Great.

Aëtius *See* **Châlons, Battle of**

Aetolia Ancient region of west central Greece. Its major cities included Calydon and Thermum, and it became important in Greek history with formation of the Aetolian League (*q.v.*). It became a Roman possession after the league had collapsed (189 BC).

Aetolian League Confederation of cities in ancient Greece, similar in nature to the Achaean League. Organized by Aetolian cities in 4th cent. BC, it resisted Macedonian conquest late in that century. Then, as an ally of Macedonia (280 BC), the league extended its control over central Greece, including Boeotia. Attacks on the Achaean League (220 BC) brought war with Macedonia and defeat of the Aetolians by the Macedonians. The league next sided with the Romans against Macedonia (200–197). A dispute with the victorious Romans, however, led to war (192) and final defeat of the league (189) by the Romans.

Afars and Issas *See* **Djibouti**

Affair of the Diamond Necklace Famous scandal (1785–86) in the court of French king Louis XVI that helped precipitate the French Revolution. A prominent French nobleman, Cardinal de Rohan (1734–1803), was tricked by a young adventuress into believing that Queen Marie Antoinette wanted to purchase an expensive diamond necklace secretly. Hoping to curry favor with the queen, Cardinal de Rohan purchased the necklace on credit and gave it to the adventuress. The scandal broke when the jeweler attempted to collect. The cardinal was eventually acquitted, the adventuress escaped, and the king and queen were thoroughly disgraced by the incident.

Affair of the Spanish Marriages A political affair surrounding the marriages (1846) of Spanish queen Isabella II (to her cousin Francisco de Asís [1822–1902], duke of Cadiz) and of Isabella's sister Luisa Fernanda (to Antoine, duke of Montpensier

[1824–90], son of French Bourbon king Louis-Philippe). The marriages violated agreements (1843, 1845) between England and France that Isabella would marry within the Neapolitan and Spanish branches of the Bourbon house and that her sister would not marry a French prince until after Isabella had married and borne children. The matches were a result of Spanish distrust of British intentions in Spain, notably about possible support of the Progresistas, who sought to reinstate the Constitution of 1812. The affair was protested by British viscount H. Palmerston, who declared them contrary to provisions of the Treaty of Utrecht. The marriages caused a serious breach in British-French relations.

Affonso *See* **Alfonso**

Afghanistan Republic located in south central Asia. Afghanistan is strategically located on the main route to India and has thus been invaded and conquered many times. Great Britain and Russia vied for control of the region in the 19th cent., with Britain gaining the advantage until 1919, when its weakening colonial position in Asia led to Afghan independence. In 1978, a Communist government was established by a *coup d'état* and thus fostered close ties with the Soviets. In the late 1970s, the Soviets invaded Afghanistan, ostensibly to support the government. The Soviet occupation led to a prolonged guerrilla war by Afghan rebels. Key dates in the history of Afghanistan include:

C6TH CENT. BC   Region conquered by Persian king Darius I.

c330–327 BC   Region conquered by Alexander the Great.

3D CENT. BC–7TH CENT. AD   Afghanistan came under control of various rulers, including the Kusana and Sassanidae.

7TH CENT.   Arabs began conquest of region.

977–1186   Ghaznavids, an Islamic dynasty, ruled vast areas in Afghanistan, Iran, and northern India.

13TH CENT.   Genghis Khan conquered Afghanistan.

14TH CENT.   Tamerlane conquered Afghanistan.

16TH CENT.   Baber conquered Afghanistan, then advanced into India to establish the Mogul Empire.

1730s   Persian leader Nadir Shah conquered Afghanistan.

1747–73   Ahmad Shah became ruler in Afghanistan after death (1747) of Nadir Shah; united Afghan tribes, expanded his domain, and established an independent Afghan state.

1826–63   Dost Muhammad ruled; became emir (1835); conflicts with Britain led to his ouster

during first Afghan War (1838–42); restored, he ruled Afghanistan until his death (1863).

1863–79   Shere Ali reigned; policies led to outbreak of second Afghan War (1878–80) with Britain.

1880–1901   Abd ar-Rahman Khan reigned; rule marked by settlement of various border disputes.

1901–19   Habibullah Khan reigned; began program of modernization; kept Afghanistan neutral during WW I.

1907   Anglo-Russian convention ended long rivalry between Britain and Russia for control of Afghanistan; Afghan independence under British influence recognized.

1919–29   Amanullah Khan reigned; invaded India (third Afghan War, 1919) to end British influence in Afghanistan; secured Afghan independence by Treaty of Rawalpindi (Aug. 1919); proclaimed himself king (1926); instituted reform program that led to his overthrow.

1929–33   King Nadir Shah reigned, succeeding after period of turmoil; promoted plan of modernization; assassinated.

1933–73   Muhammad Zahir Shah reigned; maintained Afghan neutrality in WW II.

1947   Relations with Pakistan strained following Afghan support for creation of independent Pathan tribal state within Pakistan.

1956   Government signed agreements with US and Soviet Union for massive economic-aid program.

1963   Government began policy to lessen dependence on US and Soviet Union.

1964   New constitution approved, firmly establishing constitutional monarchy.

1973   King Muhammad Zahir Shah deposed (July 17) in coup led by Muhammad Daud Khan, his brother-in-law.

1973–78   Afghanistan proclaimed a republic; Muhammad Daud Khan in office as president.

1978   Coup ended in murder of Pres. Muhammad Daud Khan (Apr.); pro-Communist Nur Muhammad Taraki in power.

1979   Muslim extremists rebelled against Marxist government; kidnapped US ambassador Adolph Dubs; Dubs killed (Feb.) in police shootout, which Soviet advisers refused to discourage.

1979   Hafizullah Amin in control of the government (Sept.).

1979   Soviet-directed coup (Dec. 27) put Babrak Karmal in power; Soviet invasion of Afghanistan under way.

1980–   Rebellion broke out against presence of tens of thousands Soviet troops in Afghanistan, resulting in a prolonged guerrilla war.

Afghan Wars *See* **Anglo-Afghan Wars**

AFL–CIO *See* **American Federation of Labor–Congress of Industrial Organizations**

Africanus, Sextus Julius *fl.* AD 221. Christian historian, author of a chronology of the world. It covered history from the creation, dated at 5499 BC, to AD 221.

Afrikaans Germanic language spoken in South Africa. It is derived from the Dutch language spoken by 17th-cent. settlers of South Africa and is now considered a separate language.

Afrika Korps German military unit during WW II. Led by Field Marshal E. Rommel, the unit conquered much of North Africa in early 1942. The drive by the Afrika Korps into Egypt was finally turned back (1942) by British Gen. B. Montgomery after the Battle of el-Alamein. The unit finally surrendered (May 1943).

Afrikaner Bond South African political party. The first political party in the (then) colony, it was founded in 1879, sought independence from the British, and backed the Boers in the Boer War. It merged with other parties to form the South African party (1910).

Agade *See* **Akkad**

Agadir incident Incident (July, 1911) in which Germany challenged the French hegemony in Morocco by sending the gunboat *Panther* to Agadir harbor. The incident resulted in an accord (Nov., 1911) between the two countries.

Aga Khan Hereditary title of the leader of the Ismaili Muslim sect. Followers of the sect are numerous in India, Pakistan, central Asia, and East Africa. The current leader (since 1957) is Aga Khan IV (1936–   ), grandson of Aga Khan III.

Aga Khan III 1877–1957. Indian statesman and leader of the Ismaili Muslim sect from 1885. He worked to gain Muslim support for Britain during WW I, played an important role in conferences to reform the constitution of India (1930–32), and became president of the League of Nations General Assembly in 1937.

Agamemnon Mythical king of Mycenae (Argos) and leader of the Greeks in the Trojan War. After the Greek victory, Agamemnon returned home and was murdered by his wife, Clytemnestra, and her lover, Aegisthus.

Aga Muhammad Khan *See* **Agha Muhammad Khan**

Agar *See* **Hagar**

Agassiz, Jean Louis Rodolphe 1807–73. American naturalist, geologist, and educator. His research expeditions, writings, and lectures influenced the development of the natural sciences in the 19th cent.

Agee, James 1909–1955. American writer. Agee was an influential film critic and scriptwriter. His novel *A Death in the Family* won a posthumous Pulitzer Prize (1957).

Agenor **1.** Mythical Greek king, the father of Europa, Cadmus, Phoenix, and Cilix. When Europa was carried off by Zeus, he sent his three sons to retrieve her. **2.** Mythical Trojan warrior who fought Achilles in single combat.

Ager Bruttius *See* **Bruttium**

Agesilaus II *c*444–360 BC. Spartan king (399–360 BC), successor to Agis I. Although he was a brilliant soldier, he was unable to thwart the rise of Thebes and the decline of Sparta. His reign saw war against Persia, the Corinthian War (395–387), the King's Peace, and Spartan defeat at the Battle of Leuctra (371).

Agha Muhammad Khan ⟨Aga Muhammad Khan⟩ 1742–97. Shah of Persia (1794–97). He founded the Kajar dynasty, unified Persia, and invaded the Russian province of Georgia (1795). His cruelty in repressing internal dissent led to his assassination.

Agiad dynasty *See* **Agis I**

Agincourt, Battle of Important English victory over the French (Oct. 25, 1415), at Agincourt, France) during the Hundred Years' War (1337–1453). English king Henry V, claiming the French throne, had invaded France and, after some fighting, decided to withdraw to Calais. His force of 14,000 lightly equipped archers was intercepted by the French constable Charles d'Albret and 50,000 heavily armored soldiers. Bogged down by a muddy battlefield, the French became easy targets for the archers. Losses were 5,000 French to 200 Englishmen. Henry went on to Calais, but the battle opened the way for later English conquests in France.

Agis I *c*11th cent. BC. King of Sparta and, according to legend, founder of the Agiad dynasty. The Agiad line was one of two (with the Eurypontids) important dynasties of Spartan kings.

Agis II *d. c*399 BC. King of Sparta (*c*427–399 BC). Agis commanded the Spartan army during the Peloponnesian War (431–404 BC) and won a major victory against Argos at the Battle of Mantinea (418 BC).

Agis IV *d. c*240 BC. Spartan king (*c*244–240 BC). He attempted to strengthen Sparta through several unsuccessful reforms, for which he was tried and executed.

Agnes, Saint *fl.* 4th cent. AD. Roman Christian girl martyred at 13. She revealed her Christian faith by refusing marriage and was subsequently murdered during persecutions ordered by Diocletian.

Agnew, Spiro Theodore 1918–. An American politician, 39th US vice-president (1969–73). Noted for his speeches attacking radicals and liberals, Agnew was reelected with Pres. R. Nixon in 1972. Amid the Watergate crisis, however, Agnew came under fire for alleged corruption (during his time in Maryland politics). He resigned (Oct. 10, 1973) and pleaded no contest to charges of income tax evasion.

Agni Hindu fire god who also ruled the sun and lightning. He was second in importance only to Indra in the *Vedas*.

agnosticism Belief that one can never prove or disprove the existence of God. It is distinct from atheism, which rejects the existence of God. The term "agnostic" was coined (1869) by T.H. Huxley and implies a skepticism of man's ability to know the true nature of the world. "Agnostic" can also be used in a nonreligious sense. Among proponents of forms of agnosticism were H. Spencer, A. Comte, and I. Kant.

agrarian laws Ancient Roman laws to regulate land ownership and ensure just distribution of the considerable public lands that came into Roman hands by conquest. In 367 BC C. Licinius attempted to limit the holdings of any single owner. This law was a dead letter by the time T. and G. Gracchus sought to allow greater plebeian ownership (133–121 BC). The edict of Domitian (AD 82), confirming existing land titles, marked the end of efforts at just distribution of land.

Agrarian party ⟨*now* Centre party⟩ Finnish political party. This party was founded (1866) by Count Arvid Posse (1820–1901) to demand new methods of taxation and military quartering.

Agrarian Reform Act ⟨Stolypin Land Reform⟩ Reform measures allowing individual Russian peasant families to own land that formerly belonged to peasant communes (mirs). Decreed by Prime Minister P. Stolypin (Nov. 22, 1906) and confirmed and expanded by the Duma (1910–11), they were designed to create an independent, landowning peasantry that would support the czarist autocracy.

Agreement of the People *See* **Levelers**

Agricola ⟨Gnaeus Julius ~⟩ AD c37–93. Roman soldier and statesman. He conquered much of Britain and served as its governor (AD 78?–84?).

Agricola, Georgius ⟨Bauer, Georg⟩ 1494–1555. German mineralogist known as the father of mineralogy for his pioneering work in geology and in classification of minerals.

Agricola, Gnaeus Julius *See* **Agricola**

Agricola, Johann ⟨*or* Johannes⟩ 1494–1566. German Protestant reformer. A friend of Luther, he played a key role in the founding of Protestantism. From 1536 he opposed Luther by espousing antinomianism *(q.v.)* and helped draw up the Augsburg Interim *(q.v.)*.

Agrippa, Marcus Vipsanius c63–12 BC. Roman general and close friend of Octavian (later Augustus). Commanding Octavian's forces, he defeated Pompey (36 BC) and played a major role in Octavian's decisive victory over Antony and Cleopatra at the Battle of Actium (31 BC).

Agrippina I ⟨Agrippina the Elder⟩ d. AD 33. Granddaughter of Augustus and wife of Germanicus Caesar. When her husband died (AD 19), she became involved in a struggle with Tiberius. He banished her, and she died of starvation. Her son became the emperor Caligula.

Agrippina II ⟨Colonia Agrippina⟩ d. AD 59. Sister of the emperor Caligula. She married her uncle Claudius I and is believed to have murdered him to ensure the ascendency of her son Nero. Nero, in turn, had her put to death for her intrigues.

Agrippina, Colonia *See* **Agrippina II**
Agrippina the Elder *See* **Agrippina I**

Aguinaldo, Emilio 1869–1964. Filipino revolutionary. He led the uprising against Spain (1896–98) and fought against the US (1899–1901) as head of a short-lived Philippine republic. In 1901 he swore allegiance to the US.

Aguirre, Lope de c1508–1561. Spanish adventurer and rebel. He is said to have murdered (1560) the leaders of an expedition in search of El Dorado in South America, to have attempted to usurp Spanish control in Panama, and to have murdered his daughter just before his capture by Spanish authorities.

Ahab Great king (c874–c853 BC) of the north kingdom of Israel, successor to his father, Omri. He was allied with Jehoshaphat, king of the south kingdom of Judah. He succeeded in resisting Assyrians in two wars but was killed in a third against Benhadad. His wife, Jezebel, introduced Phoenician elements to the Hebrew culture, including the worship of Baal.

Ahaz d. c727 BC. King of Judah (c731–27 BC). He overcame the combined forces of Israel and Syria by allying Judah with Assyria. This action was criticized by Isaiah and cost Judah its independence.

Ahaziah d. c851 BC. **1.** King of Israel (c853–851 BC), successor to his father, Ahab. **2.** King of Judah (844? BC), slain (with King Jehoram of Israel) by Jehu.

Ahithopel Biblical counselor to King David. He supported Absalom in a revolt against David and killed himself when Absalom disregarded his advice.

Ahmad Mirza *See* **Ahmed**
Ahmad Shah Durrani *See* **Ahmed Shah**
Ahmed ⟨Ahmad Mirza⟩ 1898–1930. Shah of Persia (1909–25), successor to his father, Muhammad Ali. The last of the Kajar dynasty, he was overthrown by Reza Shah Pahlevi and fled to Paris.
Ahmed I 1589–1617. Ottoman sultan (1603–17), successor to his father, Muhammad III. Under his reign, the Ottoman Empire was weakened by war and uprisings. He signed the Treaty of Szitvatorok (1606) with Austria, which further diminished Ottoman influence and prestige.
Ahmed III 1673–1736. Ottoman sultan (1703–30), successor to his brother Mustafa II. He protected Charles XII of Sweden after the latter's defeat at Poltava (1709), and was thus drawn into the Northern War against Russia. Turkish involvement ended favorably with the Treaty of Pruth (1711). Ahmed later seized and lost the Peloponnesus, and signed the Treaty of Passarowitz (1718). Overthrown by the Janissaries, he died in prison.
Ahmed Bey Zogu *See* **Zog I**
Ahmed Fuad Pasha *See* **Fuad I**
Ahmed Shah ⟨Ahmad Shah Durrani⟩ c1724–73. Afghan ruler (1747–73), founder of the Durrani dynasty, and considered founder of Afghanistan. A cavalry commander under Nadir Shah (of Persia), he formed the Afghan kingdom of Kandahar after Nadir Shah's death. He extended his rule over a large area, invaded India several times (1747–69) during his reign, and sacked Delhi (1757).
Ahmose *See* **Amasis I**
Aigun, Treaty of Treaty (May 16, 1858) by which China settled its northeast border with Russia. It gave Russia territory on the Amur River. This agreement was followed by further concessions in the Treaty of Peking (*q.v.*).
Aiken, Conrad 1889–1973. American poet and novelist, whose works, such as the short story *Silent Snow, Secret Snow*, reflect his interest in the workings of the human psyche. His *Selected Poems* (1929) won a Pulitzer Prize (1930).
Ain Jalut, Battle of *See* **Ayn Jalut, Battle of**
Aix, Battle of *See* **Aquae Sextiae, Battle of**
Aix-la-Chapelle, Congress of *See* **Congress of Aix-la-Chapelle**
Aix-la-Chapelle, Treaties of Two treaties concluded at Aix-la-Chapelle, now Aachen, Germany. **1.** Treaty (May 2, 1668) ending the War of Devolution. It was arranged between France and the nations of the Triple Alliance, including England, Sweden, and the Dutch Republic. By the treaty, France retained conquered towns in Flan-

ders, while returning other territories taken from Spain. **2.** Treaty (Oct. 18, 1748), ending the War of Austrian Succession. It provided for mutual restitution of all conquered territories except Silesia (ceded to Prussia) and Parma, Piacenza, and Guastalla (ceded to Spain). The treaty also confirmed the Pragmatic Sanction of 1713 and the succession of the Protestant Hanovers in Britain.
Ajax In Greek mythology, the son of Telamon and a hero in the Trojan War, second only to Achilles. He rescued the body of Achilles from the Trojans and killed himself when Achilles' armor was awarded to Ulysses. From his blood sprang the hyacinth.
Akbar 1542–1605. Great Mogul emperor (1556–1605) of India. He subdued revolts and expanded Mogul control over all of North India (by 1592) and, later, into the Deccan. An able administrator, he adopted a policy of tolerating non-Muslims, reformed finances and taxes, and built his capital at Fatehpur Sikri.
Akhenaton *See* **Ikhnaton**
Akkad Ancient region occupying what was later the northern part of Babylonia and what is now part of Iraq. Akkad rose to prominence in the 3d millennium BC with the conquests of Sargon, who briefly united Akkadian and other cities (notably of Sumer) into an empire. The capital of the empire was Akkad (*anc.* Agade) and the language spoken was Akkadian, a Semitic dialect. The empire declined and fell (3d millennium BC) to invading tribes a century after Sargon's unification.
Akko *See* **Acre**
Alabama State in the US South, the 22d state. Alabama was first explored by the Spanish under H. de Soto (1540) and first permanently settled by the French at Mobile (1711). The region passed to Britain (1763) and then was divided between Spain and the newly created US (1783). The rest of the territory was obtained as part of the Louisiana Purchase (1803). Alabama became a state (1819) and seceded (1861) during the Civil War. Slavery was abolished in 1865. The present state constitution was adopted in 1901.
Alabama Claims US government claims against Britain. The damages claimed were caused by Confederate cruisers, notably the *Alabama*, that had been built during the American Civil War in neutral Britain. After the Civil War, the US sought payment for damages from Britain for direct and indirect losses caused by the ships. By the Treaty of Washington (1871), the British submitted to arbitration. The tribunal disallowed claims for indirect losses but awarded the US $15.5 million for direct losses (1872). The settlement helped define the role of a neutral.

Alabama Platform Plan advanced by southern political leader W. Yancey (1848), in opposition to the Wilmot Proviso. It called for protection of slavery in lands ceded to the US by Mexico and would have forbidden territorial legislatures to outlaw slavery.

Alam al-Halfa, Battle of ⟨Alam Halfa, ~⟩ British victory (Aug. 31–Sept. 4, 1942) in Egypt during WW II. The British, under Gen. B. Montgomery, turned back an attack by German Field Marshal E. Rommel's Afrika Corps.

Alamanni *See* **Alemanni**

Alamein, battles of El- 1. WW II battle (July, 1942) in which British forces stopped a German sweep across Egypt (led by Field Marshal E. Rommel from May, 1942,) and thereby saved Egypt from German conquest. **2.** WW II battle (Oct. 23–Nov. 4, 1942), in which British Gen. B. Montgomery forced the Germans under Rommel to withdraw from Egypt into Libya.

Alamo Historic fort in San Antonio, Texas. Originally a chapel, it became a symbol of resistance in Texas to Mexican domination when fewer than 200 Americans tried unsuccessfully to defend it against Santa Anna's army of thousands. The Americans occupied the fort in Dec., 1835, and held out against Santa Anna from Feb. 24 to March 6, 1836. Among the Americans slain there were D. Crockett and J. Bowie.

Alani ⟨Alans⟩ Nomadic people. The Alani were a warlike people thought to have originated in the Black Sea region before the 1st cent. AD. Forced westward by the Huns (4th cent.), many of the Alani joined with the Vandals in their invasions of Gaul and Spain.

Alans *See* **Alani**

Alarcos, Battle of Muslim victory over Spanish Christians (July 18, 1195). The Almohades, responding to an invasion by Christian forces, decisively defeated Alfonso VIII of Castile in southern Spain. Thereafter the Almohades were able to raid Alfonso's territories without opposition.

Alaric I AD c370–410. King of the Visigoths (AD 395–410), who sacked Rome in 410. Alaric commanded Visigothic troops under Roman emperor Theodosius I and became their king on the emperor's death (395). He invaded Greece, demanded subsidies from Rome, quarreled with Emperor Flavius Honorius, and laid siege to and finally sacked Rome.

Alaric II *d.* 507. Visigoth king (484–507), successor to his father, Euric. He ruled Spain and southern Gaul, and issued the *Breviary of Alaric (q.v.)*. He was defeated and killed by Frankish king Clovis I at Vouillé.

Alaric, Breviary of *See* **Breviary of Alaric**

Alaska 49th US state. Alaska was first explored (1741) by the Russians under V. Bering, and they established the first settlement on Kodiak Island (c1783). Control of the region was granted to the Russian American Fur Company (1799–1861), and in 1824 the Russians agreed to set the present southern boundary at 54° 40′ N latitude. Sec. of State W. Seward arranged (1867) for the US purchase of Alaska (nicknamed Seward's Folly) for $7.2 million. Largely ignored until the gold rush of the 1890s, Alaska did not become a territory until 1912. Alaska's Aleutian Islands were attacked by the Japanese in WW II. Alaska became a state in 1959, and its constitution dates from 1956. Since the 1970s, it has been an important oil-producing state.

Alaskan boundary dispute US-Canadian border dispute involving Canada's border with Alaska. A commission established the boundary (1903), in accordance with US claims, at the original boundary line (54° 40′ lat.) set in 1825.

Alaungpaya ⟨Alompra⟩ ⟨Aungzeya⟩ 1711–60. King of Burma (1753?–60) and founder of the Konbaung dynasty, which ruled Burma until the British takeover (1886). He led opposition to domination by the Mon kingdom and created a unified kingdom of Burma.

Alba, Fernando Alvarez de Toledo, duke of ⟨Alva, ~⟩ 1507?–82. Spanish soldier and statesman, adviser to King Philip II. As governor of The Spanish Netherlands (1567–73), he attempted to put down the Dutch rebellion for independence. His administration was marked by cruelty and was noted for the special court Alba established, called the Court of Blood, which executed thousands. Alba later led the Spanish invasion of Portugal (1580).

Al-Bah-Rayn *See* **Bahrain**

Alba Longa Ancient city in central Italy, southeast of Rome. According to legend, it was founded by Ascanius, son of Aeneas, and was the birthplace of Romulus and Remus *(q.v.)*. It was razed (c600 BC) by Tullus Hostilius, king of Rome.

Albani, Giovanni Francesco *See* **Clement XI**

Albania ⟨People's Socialist Republic of Albania⟩ Albania is a Communist republic located on the western coast of the Balkan Peninsula in southeastern Europe. Its capital is Tirana. Key dates in the history of Albania include:

C3D CENT. BC Coastal region dominated by Greek colonies; independent kingdom flourished inland.

1ST CENT. AD Kingdom came under Roman influence.

535 Byzantines took control of Albania after the fall of Rome.

1082 Normans under R. Guiscard invaded Albania.

1272 Charles I of Naples proclaimed king of the territory.

15TH CENT. Invasions by Ottoman Turks.

1444–66 Skanderbeg became a national hero by turning back 13 Turkish invasions.

1478–1912 Albania, finally conquered, made part of the Ottoman Empire.

1877 Russian victory in Russo-Turkish War ended in Treaty of San Stefano, giving much Albanian territory to other Balkan nations.

1912 First Balkan War fought.

1912 Albania proclaimed its independence; its boundaries established by international control commission.

1913 Second Balkan War; Serbia occupied Albania.

1913 European powers restored Albanian autonomy but ceded much territory to Montenegro, Serbia, and Greece; Prince William of Wied named as king (1914).

1914–18 WW I broke out; King William fled; Albania the scene of fighting between rival Balkan states seeking to dismember it, as well as of invasions by major European powers.

1918 Italy announced protectorate over Albania.

1920 Italy and other European powers occupying Albania after WW I agreed to evacuate; Albanian independence recognized.

1925 Albania became a republic under the presidency of Ahmed Zogu.

1928 Albania made a democratic monarchy; Zogu proclaimed himself King Zog I.

1939 WW II began; Italy occupied Albania (Apr. 7), uniting it with the Italian crown; Zog exiled.

1940 Albania, under Italian control, declared war on the Allies.

1940–41 Italy launched attack on Greece from Albania; Greece counterattacked into Albania but was finally forced to surrender troops in Albania.

1943–44 Anti-Fascist guerrillas led by Enver Hoxha (1908–), a Communist, resisted Italian occupation.

1944 Germans withdrew from Albania; Hoxha and his partisans established a provisional government.

1946 Republic proclaimed; constitution adopted; Hoxha became premier to 1954 of a Communist-dominated government.

1948 Albania came under Soviet domination.

1955 Entered Warsaw Pact.

1961 Albania, opposed to Soviet destalinization policy and rapprochement with Tito, broke

with the Soviet Union; allied itself with Communist China.

1968 Withdrew from Warsaw Pact.

1971 Resumed relations with Greece and Yugoslavia.

1973–76 Large-scale purge of officials.

1978 China cut aid to Albania after Albania criticized government in power after Mao Tsetung's death; Albania's alliance with China ended.

Albany Congress Meeting held (June 19–July 11, 1754) at Albany, New York, to win the Iroquois Confederacy over to the British side in the impending French and Indian Wars. The meeting, attended by delegates from seven American colonies and by 150 tribal members, failed to produce an effective alliance with the Indians. It was notable, however, as the forum for B. Franklin's Albany Plan, a planned union of the colonies. The scheme was later rejected by colonial legislatures.

Albany Plan *See* **Albany Congress**

Albany Regency New York State political machine run by Democrats (1820–c1850) and generally regarded as one of the first effective political machines in the US. The organization was developed by M. Van Buren and was centered in Albany, New York. Its decline began in the 1840s with the appearance of factions in the Democratic party, notably the Hunkers.

Albee, Edward Franklin 1928–. American playwright. Albee is known for such works as *Who's Afraid of Virginia Woolf?*, *Zoo Story*, and *A Delicate Balance*, for which he won a Pulitzer Prize (1967).

Alberoni, Giulio 1664–1752. Italian cardinal and statesman. As de facto prime minister of Spain (c1714–19), he arranged the marriage of Philip V to Elizabeth Farnese. His aggressive policies promoting Spanish interests in Italy resulted in formation of the Quadruple Alliance (1718) and a brief war against Spain. He was banished in 1719.

Albert (of Saxe-Coburg-Gotha) 1819–61. Prince consort of British queen Victoria. At first unpopular, his diligence and diplomatic ability brought him great admiration. His moderating influence in the Trent Affair (1861) may have prevented war between Britain and the US.

Albert I c1250–1308. German king (1298–1308), a Hapsburg and son of King Rudolf I. After Rudolf's death (1291), Adolf of Nassau was made king, in an attempt to keep the crown from becoming a Hapsburg title. Albert overthrew him (1298) and was confirmed king (1303) by Pope Boniface VIII.

Albert I 1875–1934. Belgian king (1909–34), successor to his uncle Leopold II. He led the Belgian army against the Germans in WW I, played a leading role in the reconstruction of Belgium after the war, and instituted such political and social reforms as universal male suffrage.

Albert II 1397–1439. Holy Roman Emperor (1438–39), successor to his father-in-law, Sigismund. He sought to prevent internal warfare in Germany and to improve its administrative organization, became embroiled in the Hussite Wars, and died while fighting the Turks. He was the first of the hereditary Hapsburg emperors.

Albert of Brandenburg 1490–1568. First Duke of Prussia (1525–68) and last grand master of the Teutonic Knights (1511–25). A Protestant, he heeded M. Luther's advice and created (1525) the secular dukedom of Prussia, ending the Teutonic Knights' rule over the territory. The territory remained under Polish suzerainty.

Albert the Bear *c*1100–1170. First margrave of Brandenburg. He led campaigns against the Wends and by treaty inherited (1150) Brandenburg from Prince Pribislav, the last Wendish prince. During his rule he expanded German influence in Eastern Europe by promoting colonization.

Albert the Great, Saint *See* **Albertus Magnus, Saint**

Albertus Magnus, Saint (Albert the Great, Saint) *c*1200–1280. Scholastic theologian and philosopher. He helped introduce the works of Aristotle in Europe, promoted the study of natural science, and advanced the use of the scientific method. One of his students was Thomas Aquinas.

Albigenses Christian heretical sect that flourished (12th–13th cents.) in southern France. Named for the city of Albi, the Albigenses were predominantly Cathari *(q.v.).* Extreme ascetics, they believed in the Manichaean dualism of good and evil. The Albigensian Crusade was mounted against them (1208). Following this, the medieval Inquisition was instituted (1233) against them, and with it began a century-long persecution that finally eliminated the sect.

Albigensian Crusade Crusade (1208–13) against heretics in southern France. The crusade was largely directed against the Cathari and Waldenses, reformist sects that had arisen in opposition to church corruption and that then enjoyed the favor of noblemen in southern France. Pope Innocent III proclaimed the crusade (1208), which amounted to an invasion of southern France by the barons of northern France under S. Montfort. In 1209 Montfort massacred some 20,000 inhabitants of Beziers and, by his victory (1213) at Muret, broke the power of the heretics. Fighting continued, however, and Monfort died (1218) at the siege of Toulouse. The conquest was completed by French king Louis IX, who, by the Peace of Paris (1229), acquired Toulouse. The subsequent medieval Inquisition eliminated heretical sects in southern France by the 14th cent.

Albion Ancient name for England, still used in literary references. It is derived from the Latin *albus,* or "white," for the white chalk cliffs of Dover.

Alboin *d.* 572? Lombard king (*c*562–572) who greatly expanded the Lombard kingdom. He began by conquering Germanic tribes (Gepidae) to the east of his lands, then located in Austria and west Hungary. He next invaded Italy (568), and eventually took all of north Italy from the Byzantines.

Albornoz, Gil Álvarez Carrillo de 1310?–67. A Spanish soldier and cardinal. He restored papal authority over the Papal States through military and diplomatic means, thus allowing return (1368) of the popes from Avignon to Rome. He prepared (1357) a constitution for the Papal States, which remained in effect until 1816.

Albrecht *See* **Albert**

Albuquerque, Alfonso de 1453–1515. A Portuguese viceroy of the Indies (1506–15), a principal founder of Portugal's empire in the East. As viceroy, he conquered Goa in India (1510) and made it a center of Portuguese power. He went on to conquer other eastern territories, including Ceylon and Malacca on the Malay Peninsula. He twice took Ormuz (1507, 1515) to control the Arab spice trade.

Alcaçovas, Treaty of Treaty (Mar. 6, 1480) between Portugal and the kingdom of Castile. By its terms Castile received the Canary Islands, while Portugal was given West Africa and Guinea. Portugal also renounced claim to the Castilian throne.

Alcaeus *d. c*580 BC. Greek lyric poet. A contemporary of Sappho, he invented Alcaic verse, which was later adapted by Horace. Of his ten books, only fragments survive.

Alcalá Zamora, Niceto 1877–1949. A Spanish statesman. He led the Spanish revolution (1931) that established the republic, and served as its first president (1931–36). Deposed because of his moderate policies, he died in exile.

Alcamenes *fl. c*440 BC. Greek sculptor, believed to have been the pupil and later rival of Phidias. His works include the sculptures *Aphrodite of the Gardens* and *Hermes Propylaios.*

Alcazarquivir, Battle of *See* **Three Kings, Battle of**

Alcibiades *c*450–404 BC. Athenian statesman and military leader. Regarded as both brilliant and unscrupulous, he rose to prominence during the Peloponnesian War (431–404 BC), when Athenian power was declining. Opposing the Peace of Nicias (421), he rallied the Athenians to an alliance against Sparta and a disastrous campaign in Sicily (415). Falsely charged with defacing sacred statues, he fled to Sparta. He aided the Spartans until forced to flee to Persia (411). Recalled to Athens (411), he led the Athenian fleet to victories against the Spartans and recovered Byzantium (408). But when the Athenian fleet was defeated by Lysander (406), he was exiled. He was subsequently killed on Lysander's orders.

Alciphron *fl.* 2d or 3d cent. AD. Greek writer. He fabricated a series of about 100 letters, supposedly written by the common people. They provide a useful picture of 4th-cent. Athenian life.

Alcmaeon Greek mythical figure. He led the Epigoni *(q.v.)* against Thebes.

Alcmaeonidae Athenian family. They influenced Athenian politics at intervals from the 7th to 5th cents. BC. Among its members were Cleisthenes, Pericles, and Alcibiades.

Alcott, Louisa May 1832–88. American novelist. Her best known work is *Little Women*.

Alcyone *See* **Halcyone**

Alden, John c1599–1687. English colonist, one of the Pilgrim founders of Plymouth Colony. According to legend, he courted Priscilla Mullens for his friend M. Standish, though she finally married Alden. Alden was assistant to the governor of Massachusetts (1633–41, 1650–86) and twice deputy governor.

Aldobrandini, Ippolito *See* **Clement VIII**

Aldrich, Nelson Wilmarth 1841–1915. American politician and financier. As US senator (1881–1911), he worked for the Aldrich-Vreeland Currency Act of 1908. His study of banking reform helped establish the Federal Reserve System.

Aldrin, Edwin Eugene, Jr. ⟨Aldrin, Buzz⟩ 1930–. American astronaut. As a member of the Apollo 11 mission (July, 1969), he was the second person to set foot on the moon.

Alekseyev, Konstantin Sergeyevich *See* **Stanislavsky, Konstantin**

Alemán, Miguel 1902–. Mexican statesman. As president of Mexico (1946–52), he worked to modernize industry and agriculture and to improve living conditions.

Alemanni ⟨Alamanni⟩ Loose confederation of Germanic tribes that had settled in what is now southern Germany by the 3d cent. AD. The Alemanni came into conflict with the Romans and by the 5th cent. AD occupied Baden, Alsace, and parts of Switzerland. Frankish king Clovis I defeated them (496), and in the 6th cent. they became subjects of Frankish kings.

Alembert, Jean le Rond d' 1717–83. A French mathematician and philosopher. A major figure of the Enlightenment in France, he was coeditor, with Diderot, of the *Encyclopédie*. His works include an important treatise on dynamics.

Alep *See* **Aleppo**

Aleppo ⟨Alep⟩ Historic city in northern Syria. Founded before the 2d millennium BC, it was on the main caravan route from Syria to Baghdad. It has been under the control of various peoples, including the Persians, Romans, Byzantines, Arabs, and Turks. Its importance declined (19th cent.) with construction of the Suez Canal.

Alessandri Palma, Arturo 1868–1950. Chilean politician, twice president of Chile (1920–25, 1932–38). He led the Liberal Alliance in Chile and was able in his second term to achieve political and economic reforms. He helped write a new constitution (1925), which included provisions for universal male suffrage.

Alessandri Rodríguez, Jorge 1895–1970. President of Chile (1958–64).

Alexander *See* **Paris**

Alexander ⟨Alexander of Battenberg⟩ 1857–93. Prince of Bulgaria (1879–86). With czarist support, he became first prince of the new autonomous state of Bulgaria. His annexation of Eastern Rumelia led to war with Serbia (1885) and to his forced abdication in 1886.

Alexander 1888–1934. Yugoslavian king (1921–34). He played a major role in unifying Yugoslavia at the end of WW I. The regent of Serbia, he created an unstable kingdom (1918) embracing the rival ethnic groups of Serbs, Croats, and Slovenes. A constitutional monarchy was established in 1921, but increasing disorders forced him to abolish it (1929) in favor of a dictatorship. He instituted a new constitution in 1931. Alexander was assassinated by a Croatian terrorist in 1934.

Alexander 1876–1903. King of Serbia (1889–1903), successor to his father, Milan. His authoritarianism, his suspension (1894) of the liberal constitution, and his scandalous marriage led to his assassination by the military.

Alexander 1893–1920. King of Greece (1917–20), successor to his father, Constantine I, when the latter was forced to abdicate by the Allies during WW I. The government was actually run by Venizelos, his premier.

Alexander I 1078?–1124. King of Scotland (1107–24), successor to his brother Edgar. He ruled the northern part of Scotland, while his brother David ruled the south. He suppressed a clan rebellion (1115).

Alexander I 1777–1825. Russian czar (1801–25), successor to his father, Paul I. After defeats at Austerlitz and Friedland, he submitted to Napoleon's Continental System, under the Treaty of

Tilsit (1807). But he later repulsed Napoleon's invasion of Russia (1812), marched into Paris (1814), and, by his defeat of Napoleon, became one of the most important rulers in Europe. In his early years, he instituted many liberal reforms. After 1814, however, he was influenced by the Pietism of J. Krüdener. This led to his formation of the Holy Alliance and support for conservative and reactionary policies, especially those of C. Metternich.

Alexander II 1818–81. Russian czar (1855–81), successor to his father, Nicholas I. Shortly after his accession, he negotiated an end to the Crimean War (1853–56) and instituted many liberal reforms, including the Edict of Emancipation (1861) and the limited local government of the Zemstvo (q.v.). His reforms, however, failed to prevent the rise of the populist Narodniki movement in the 1860s, and his attempts to suppress it led to his assassination. During his reign he brutally suppressed a Polish rebellion (1863), formed the Three Emperors' League, extended Russian territories in central Asia, and engaged in the Russo-Turkish Wars (1877–78).

Alexander III   *See* **Alexander the Great**

Alexander III ⟨Orlando Bandinelli⟩ *d.* 1181. Italian-born pope (1159–81), successor to Adrian IV. With help from the Lombard League, he managed to assert papal authority over Holy Roman Emperor Frederick I and forced him to sign the Treaty of Vienna (1177). He also opposed Henry II of England, canonized Thomas à Becket, and received Henry's penance for Becket's murder.

Alexander III 1241–86. King of Scotland (1249–86), successor to his father, Alexander II (1198–1249). He married a daughter of English king Henry III and resisted Henry's attempt to control Scotland. During his reign, Scotland finally won from Norway the permanent control of the Hebrides and the Isle of Man (1266).

Alexander III 1845–94. Russian czar (1881–94), successor to his father, Alexander II. He became czar after his father's assassination and instituted reactionary policies that included an increase in police repression and censorship. The power of the Zemstvos was sharply curtailed, national minorities were forced to undergo Russification, and religious minorities were persecuted.

Alexander VI 1431?–1503. Spanish-born pope (1492–1503), successor to Innocent VIII, and a symbol of papal corruption during the Renaissance. A member of the Borgia family, he is said to have won election to the papacy through bribery. As pope, he proclaimed division of Spanish and Portuguese possessions in the New World (1493) (*see* Treaty of Tordesillas), successfully resisted an invasion of Italy by French king Charles VIII (1494), ordered the execution of G. Savonarola (1498), and began a censorship of books (1501). Throughout his reign he pursued the aggrandizement of his family's fortunes.

Alexander Balas *d.* 145 BC. King of Syria (150–145 BC), who came to power by slaying Demetrius I, the Seleucid king. He named Jonathan Maccabaeus governor of Palestine and was later killed in battle by Demetrius II, son of Demetrius I.

Alexander, Harold Rupert Leofric George, 1st Earl of Tunis 1891–1969. British field marshal who directed the British evacuation at Dunkirk (1940) during WW II. He subsequently led British forces in Burma, North Africa, Sicily, and southern Italy, and was made commander in chief of British Mediterranean forces in 1944.

Alexander Nevsky *c*1220–63. Russian prince and military hero. He defeated the Swedes at the Battle of the Neva (1240) and the Teutonic Knights at the Battle of Lake Peipus (1242).

Alexander of Battenberg   *See* **Alexander**

Alexander of Hales *d.* 1245. English theologian and philosopher. A Franciscan, he taught at the University of Paris. His teachings contained elements of Aristotle's philosophy and influenced Franciscan scholasticism.

Alexander Severus AD 208?–235. Roman emperor (AD 222–235), successor to his cousin Heliogabalus. Considered a just ruler, he stopped persecution of the Christians during his reign and successfully fought against Persia (232).

Alexander the Great ⟨Alexander III⟩ 356–323 BC. Macedonian king (336–323 BC), successor to his father, Philip II. One of the world's greatest conquerors, he created a vast empire extending from Greece to northern India, and, by his conquests, helped spread Greek civilization throughout the ancient world. Soon after becoming king, Alexander crushed revolts in Thrace, Illyria, and Thebes. His rule in Greece thus established, he began his epic military expedition (334–324 BC) with some 37,000 soldiers and the initial objective of conquering Persia. He met and defeated the Persians at the battles of Granicus (334) and Issus ([in Syria] 333), laid siege to and finally took Tyre (332) to complete conquest of Phoenicia, marched unopposed into Egypt (332–331), and there founded the great city of Alexandria (332). He again defeated the Persians at the Battle of Gaugamela (331), sent Persian king Darius III into flight, and sacked the Persian capital of Persepolis (331). He continued eastward to Media (330) and central Asia, where he conquered the Scythians (329). Despite open discontent in his army (over his acceptance of Persian manners), Alexander invaded India

(327). After the Battle of Hydaspes (326), he took control of Punjab and, his men unwilling to go farther, returned to Persia (324). He subsequently consolidated Macedonian control of his conquests and attempted to integrate Greeks and Persians by, among other things, ordering his soldiers to marry Persian women. The hero of these great conquests, and such legendary feats as cutting the Gordian Knot (q.v.), died shortly after a prolonged banquet in 323. (See also Macedonia.)

Alexandra 1844–1925. Queen consort of English king Edward VII (m. 1863) and mother of King George V.

Alexandra Feodorovna 1872–1918. Last czarina of Russia, consort of Nicholas II (1894–1918). Her unfailing loyalty to the hated Rasputin and her disastrous meddlings in politics helped bring about the Russian Revolution. A Hessian princess, she came under Rasputin's sway when he seemed able to control her son's hemophilia. While Nicholas was at the front in WW I, she took control of the government (1915) and began replacing government ministers with favorites of Rasputin. This discredited the government and opened the way for the October Revolution (1917). She was shot, with Nicholas and her children, by revolutionaries.

Alexandria Egypt's second largest city (pop. 2,318,700) and a major center for cotton and other manufactures and exports. Founded in 332 BC by Alexander the Great, it became one of the largest and greatest cities of antiquity. The Ptolemies (q.v.) ruled their Egyptian-based empire from there (323–30 BC), and it became a principal center of both Hellenistic and Jewish culture. It attracted scholars such as Aristarchus of Samothrace, who collated Homer's texts; the geometer Euclid; and the astronomer Claudius Ptolemy, originator of the Ptolemaic System (q.v.). The Greek Septuagint (Old Testament) was translated there. Alexandria boasted antiquity's best libraries, as well as the tall lighthouse considered one of the Seven Wonders of the World. The city was captured by J. Caesar (47 BC) and incorporated into the Roman Empire by Augustus (30 BC). In Christian times it was the seat of one of the four major patriarchates, and great churchmen such as Saint Athanasius were bishops there. Alexandria declined after Arab conquerers moved Egypt's capital to Cairo (AD 969). The city was captured in modern times by Napoleon (1798), then by the British (1801), and afterward began to regain its former importance.

Alexandria, Appian of See **Appian of Alexandria**
Alexandria, Catherine of See **Catherine of Alexandria**

Alexandria, Clement of See **Clement of Alexandria**
Alexandria, Heron of See **Heron of Alexandria**
Alexandria, Saint Cyril of See **Cyril of Alexandria, Saint**
Alexandria, School of See **Alexandrian School**
Alexandrian School Egyptian Christian school. Founded at Alexandria in the mid-2d cent. AD, it was the first Christian institution of higher learning and philosophy. It sought to reconcile Christianity with Greek culture and to advance orthodox Christian teachings.

Alexis 1629–76. Russian czar (1645–76), successor to his father, Michael. Alexis established a legal code that recognized serfdom, warred against Poland (1654–67) and Sweden (1656–61) (see Northern War), acquired part of the Ukraine and Kiev, approved the schismatic reforms of Nikon (q.v.), and put down S. Razin's peasant revolt (1670–71).

Alexius I Comnenus 1048–1118. Byzantine emperor (1081–1118), successor to Nicephorus III by his overthrow, and first of the Comnenian rulers. Alexius restored the crumbling Byzantine empire that, when he took power, was threatened by invasions and internal dissent. He defended against Norman invasions (1081–85), contained the Seljuk Turks, repulsed invasions by a tribe of nomadic Turks (1091), and put down rebellions in Crete and Cyprus. His request for aid from the West against the Turks resulted in proclamation of the First Crusade (1096).

Alexius III Angelus d. 1210. Byzantine emperor (1195–1203) who deposed his brother Isaac II. Following the overthrow, crusaders (see Fourth Crusade) attacked the Byzantine capital of Constantinople (1203) and reinstated Isaac II. Isaac's son, Alexius IV, was installed as coemperor, and Alexius III died in exile.

Alexius V d. 1204. Byzantine emperor (1204), son-in-law of Alexius III Angelus. He overthrew coemperors Isaac II and Alexius IV. The army of the Fourth Crusade (q.v.) deposed him, sacked Constantinople (1204), and established the Latin kingdom of Constantinople (q.v.).

Alfarabius See **Farabi, al-**
Al Fatah See **Palestine Liberation Organization**
Alfonsine Tables ⟨Alphonsine ∼⟩ Astronomical data on the planets. This updating of Ptolemy's work was commissioned by Alfonso X and was completed in 1252. T. Brahe later proved them incorrect.

Alfonso I 693?–757. Christian king of Asturias (739–757). When the Berbers rebelled (741) in Muslim Spain, Alfonso was able to conquer Galicia, León, and Santander.

Alfonso I ⟨~ the Battler⟩ *d.* 1134. Christian king of Aragon and Navarre (1104–34). Noted for warring against the Moors, he captured Saragossa (1118) and led a raid into Andalusia (1125). He encouraged Christian settlement in his kingdom.

Alfonso I ⟨~ Henriques⟩ 1111?–1185. First king of Portugal (1139–85). The son of Henry of Burgundy, Count of Portugal, he engaged in wars (1128–39) against the Moors and rulers of León and Castile to establish an independent kingdom. He was crowned after his victory over the Moors at Ourique (July 25, 1139). He continued fighting and captured Lisbon in 1147.

Alfonso II ⟨~ the Fat⟩ 1185–1223. King of Portugal (1211–23), successor to his father, Sancho I. He helped defeat the Moors at Las Navas de Tolosa (1212). He quarreled with the church and was excommunicated by Honorius III.

Alfonso III ⟨~ the Great⟩ 838?–911? Christian king of Asturias (866–911?), who fought numerous battles against the Moors and greatly extended his kingdom.

Alfonso III 1210–79. Portuguese king (1248–79), successor to his brother, Sancho II. He completed the unification of Portugal by driving the Moors from Algarve (1249). He instituted political, financial, and commercial reforms.

Alfonso IV 1291–1357. King of Portugal (1325–57), successor to his father, Diniz. He aided Alfonso XI of Castile in his victory over the Moors at Tarifa (1340). But his approval of the murder of his daughter-in-law, I. Castro, led to a revolt by his son (later Pedro I).

Alfonso V ⟨~ the Noble⟩ 994?–1027. Spanish king of León (999–1027), successor to his father, Bermudo II. Under his reign, the city of León passed from Moorish to Spanish control.

Alfonso V ⟨~ the Magnanimous⟩ 1396–1458. King of Aragon and Sicily (1416–58), successor to his father, Ferdinand I. He conquered Naples and made himself its king in 1442. Thereafter, he held court in Naples and became involved in Italian affairs.

Alfonso V ⟨~ the African⟩ 1432–81. Portuguese king (1438–81), husband of Juana la Beltraneja. He won major victories against the Moors in North Africa but failed to advance his wife's claim to Castile. He was decisively defeated by rival claimants, Queen Isabella and King Ferdinand, at the Battle of Toro (1476).

Alfonso VI 1030–1109. Christian king of León (1065–1109) and Castile (1072–1109). His advances into Muslim territories brought about the takeover of Muslim Spain by the Almoravids. El Cid was active during Alfonso's reign.

Alfonso VI 1643–83. Portuguese king (1656–83), successor to his father, John IV. Mentally impaired, he let Count Castelho Melhor rule. He was ousted by his wife and his brother, later Peter (Pedro) II. During Alfonso's reign, Spain recognized (1668) Portugal's independence.

Alfonso VII 1104–57. King of León and Castile (1126–57). He warred frequently against the Muslims but was unable to prevent Alfonso I from establishing an independent Portugal (1139).

Alfonso VIII ⟨~ the Noble⟩ 1155–1214. Spanish king of Castile (1158–1214), successor to his father, Sancho III. In 1195, he was defeated by Muslim Almohades, and Castile was invaded by León and Navarre. He recovered and later led allied Spanish forces to a major victory over the Moors at Las Navas de Tolosa (1212).

Alfonso X ⟨~ the Wise⟩ 1221–84. Spanish king of Castile and León (1252–84), successor to his father, Ferdinand III. He conquered Cádiz and Cartagena from the Moors, sought unsuccessfully to become Holy Roman Emperor (1257–75), and encouraged culture and learning. He promulgated the Siete Partidas, a great compilation of laws.

Alfonso XI ⟨~ the Avenger⟩ 1311–50. Spanish king of Castile and León (1312-50), successor to his father, Ferdinand IV. Made king at age one, he assumed power in 1325. He led the Spanish to victory over the Moors at the Battle of Algeciras, now in Morocco (1344).

Alfonso XII 1857–85. Spanish king (1874–85), son of Isabella II. Forced into exile (1868) by a revolution, he was proclaimed king in 1874. He returned to Spain (1875), restored order, and consolidated the power of the monarchy.

Alfonso XIII 1886–1941. King of Spain (1886–1931), successor to his father, Alfonso XII. His reign was marked by political and social instability. He supported the military coup of Primo de Rivera (1923) and went into exile (1931) with the establishment of the Second Republic.

Alfonso Henriques   *See* **Alfonso I**
Alfonso the African   *See* **Alfonso V**
Alfonso the Avenger   *See* **Alfonso XI**
Alfonso the Battler   *See* **Alfonso I**
Alfonso the Fat   *See* **Alfonso II**
Alfonso the Great   *See* **Alfonso III**
Alfonso the Magnanimous   *See* **Alfonso V**
Alfonso the Noble   *See* **Alfonso V, Alfonso VIII**
Alfonso the Wise   *See* **Alfonso X**

Alfred ⟨~ the Great⟩ 849–899. Saxon king (871–899) of Wessex, England, and successor to his brother Aethelred. He is the hero of English resistance to the Danish invasions in the 9th cent. Following his brother's death in war against the Danes, he at first resorted to payment of Danegeld, then defeated the Danes at Edington (878) and London (886). Alfred repulsed renewed Danish invasions from 892 to 896. During his reign, he brought about a revival of learning, issued a code of laws, and consolidated his powers as monarch.

Algeciras, Battle of See **Alfonso XI**

Algeciras Conference Meeting of European powers (Jan.-Apr., 1906) in Algeciras, Morocco. Germany sought unsuccessfully to reduce French and Spanish influence in Morocco. By the agreement here, France and Spain received increased authority and control of Moroccan financial, commercial, and police affairs.

Alger, Horatio 1834–99. American author of more than 100 books for boys, featuring poor youths who, through hard work, clean living, and a stroke of luck, achieve success. His books were immensely popular in the late 19th cent.

Algeria Republic located in northwest Africa. Its capital is Algiers. Originally inhabited by Berbers, Algeria successively came under control of the Carthaginians, Romans, Byzantines, and Ottoman Turks. By the 17th cent. it was a center of pirate activity (see Barbary States), which continued until the French invaded Algeria and made it a colony. Its Muslim heritage, and rising nationalistic sentiment, contributed to a major struggle in the 1950s between the ruling European colonists and the Muslim majority. It ended with establishment of the Republic of Algeria in 1962. Key dates in the history of Algeria include:

9TH–5TH CENTS. BC Algeria (roughly ancient Numidia) came under domination of Carthage.

206 BC Numidians allied with Romans against Carthage during the Second Punic War; thereafter Rome gradually took control of Numidia.

AD 396–430 St. Augustine was bishop at Hippo.

AD 429 Algeria devastated by invasion of Vandals from Spain.

6TH CENT. Byzantine Empire established rule over northern Algeria.

7TH CENT. Muslim Caliphate Empire captured region; Berber tribesmen converted to Islam and adopted Arabic language and customs.

10TH CENT. Fatimid Muslim dynasty began its climb to power in northeastern Algeria.

15TH CENT. Spain conquered coastal Algeria; Turkish pirates aided Algerians against the Spanish.

16TH CENT. Turkish pirates, with Ottoman aid, drove out the Spanish; Algeria came under Ottoman rule.

1671 Dey of Algiers became autonomous ruler of Algeria; region became center for piracy and slave trade in the Mediterranean.

1816 Continued acts of piracy led British to bombard Algiers.

1830–37 French invaded Algeria and gained control of coastal Algeria; the Berber leader Abd al-Kadir continued resistance in the country's interior.

1847 Abd al-Kadir forced to surrender to French.

1848 Algeria made French territory; Europeans began large-scale colonial settlement.

1900 Algeria gained self-government in administrative and financial matters; European colonists controlled the government.

1920s–1940s Rise of nationalistic sentiment among discontented Muslims.

1942 Algeria became a center for Allied operations in North Africa during WW II.

1945 Muslim nationalist uprising led to severe repression by French; thousands of Muslims killed.

1947 Statute of Algeria passed by French national assembly, granting greater autonomy to Algerian Muslims; many of its articles were never implemented.

1954 National Liberation Front (FLN) formed by Muslims; launched (Nov. 1) an armed revolt against French rule.

1957 French military cleared the cities of FLN terrorists; Muslim resistance continued.

1958 Demonstrations against concessions to Muslims staged by French colonials and military in Algeria; this led to political crisis in France and contributed to C. de Gaulle's return to power.

1958 FLN established the rebel Provisional Government of the Algerian Republic (GPRA); F. Abbas named prime minister.

1962 Accord signed by French government and GPRA, calling for cease-fire and eventual Algerian independence under Muslim majority rule.

1962 Secret Army Organization (OAS) formed by elements of French army in Algeria; mounted a brief and unsuccessful terrorist campaign against Algerian independence; European community (some one million persons) left Algeria.

1962 Algerians voted (July 1) for independence; France recognized Algeria as an independent state.

1963 A. Ben Bella became president; consolidating power, he began implementing leftist programs.

1965 Ben Bella deposed by Houari Boumédienne, who established a revolutionary council to govern the country.

1971 Boumédienne nationalized French petroleum interests in Algeria.

1974–76 Algeria established closer relations with the US; became a major oil and gas exporter to US.

1978 Boumédienne died (Dec.) in office; Chadli Bendjedid, a leading Algerian political official, succeeded to the presidency (1979).

1980–81 Algeria, as intermediary, played a deciding role in negotiations during the hostage crisis in Iran.

Algiers Algerian capital (pop. 2,200,000) and a major North African port. Founded by Muslims (10th cent.) on the site of a Phoenician city called Icosium, it became important under the Ottoman Turks as a base for the Barbary pirates. Several military expeditions were sent against the city (16th–19th cents.), including an American force under S. Decatur (1815). French conquest of Algeria began there (1830). The city figured in WW II as an Allied headquarters and in the revolt (1958) that ended the French Fourth Republic.

Alhambra Moorish palace and fortress overlooking Granada, Spain, and built during the 13th and 14th cents. The finest example of Moorish architecture in Spain, it was damaged after the Moors were expelled from Spain (1492). Restoration began in 1828.

Ali 600?–661. Fourth Muslim caliph (656–661), successor to Uthman and son-in-law of Muhammad. He was the husband of Fatima, but his right to succeed to the caliphate was disputed. This resulted in the great split between Shiite supporters of Ali and the Sunnite Muslims. A devoted follower of Muhammad, he was challenged after his accession by Muawiya and was murdered by fanatics. (*See also* Muslim Civil Wars.)

Alien and Sedition Acts Four laws passed (1798) by US Congress. Ostensibly passed to control French aliens at a time when the French revolutionary government was becoming increasingly belligerent, the laws were an attempt by the Federalist party to stifle opposition from Jeffersonian Republicans. The Jeffersonians were sympathetic to the French Revolution and relied heavily on votes of recent immigrants. The alien laws raised to 14 years the residence needed for naturalization, and gave Pres. J. Adams power to arrest and deport aliens. The sedition act forbade criticism of the government. It resulted in the conviction of 10 Republicans and precipitated the Kentucky and Virginia Resolutions.

Alien Registration Act of 1940 *See* **Smith Act**

Ali Pasha 1741?–1822. Turkish governor of Janina in Greece (from 1788). Called "The Lion," he conquered much of Albania and was alternately the ally of France and England. His court was described by Byron in *Childe Harold's Pilgrimage.*

Aljubarrota, Battle of Important battle (Aug. 14, 1385) in Portuguese history, in which Portuguese independence from the Spanish kingdoms was confirmed. With the aid of English troops, John I, regent of Portugal, defeated armies under John I of Castile near the village of Aljubarrota, in Portugal.

Al-Khowarizmi Arab mathematician. The word "algebra" is said to derive from a work of his. His writings, translated into Latin, provided much of medieval Europe's mathematical knowledge.

Al-Kindi *See* **Kindi**

Al-Kufa *See* **Kufah**

Allah Arabic name of God. It is most closely identified with the Islamic faith, though it is also used by Arabs of the Christian faith.

Allen, Ethan 1738–89. American Revolutionary War hero and leader of the Green Mountain Boys. He formed the Green Mountain Boys in the years prior to the revolution to defend claims of Vermont settlers against rival claims of New Yorkers. During the war he led his unit at the Battle of Ticonderoga (1775) and participated in an abortive mission to take Montreal (1775), during which he was taken prisoner.

Allenby, Edmund *See* **Megiddo, Battle of**

Allende Gossens, Salvador 1908–73. Chilean politician. Allende founded the Chilean Socialist party (1933) and became the Western Hemisphere's first freely elected Marxist president (1970). Overthrown in 1973, he was said to have committed suicide.

Alliance for Progress Inter-American economic assistance program. The US established this aid program (1961) to bolster South American countries against communism and to effect social and economic reforms. Funding was sharply reduced after 1971.

Allied powers ⟨Allies⟩ WW I and WW II allies. The original Allied Powers in WW I were Britain, France, and Russia, and they opposed the German-dominated Central Powers. As the war progressed, 18 other countries joined the original Allied Powers. In WW II, the principal allies were Britain, the US, France, the USSR, and China and included numerous other countries.

Allies *See* **Allied Powers**

All-India Muslim League *See* **Muslim League**

Alma, Battle of the Victory (Sept. 20, 1854) for the French and British over the Russians during the Crimean War (1853–56). The allies threw some 26,000 troops into battle at this river near

Sevastopol. Russian losses were 1,200 killed, 4,000 captured, to allied losses of 4,000 casualties. The Russians retreated to Sevastopol.

Almagro, Diego de c1475–1538. Spanish conquistador, a leading figure in the conquest of Peru (16th cent.). He later fought Pizarro for the city of Cuzco, was defeated and executed.

Almagro, Diego de (the Younger) *See* **Castro, Cristobal Vaca de**

al Mansur *See* **Mansur**

Almohades ⟨Almohads⟩ Muslim sect and dynasty of Berber Muslims that ruled Morocco and Muslim Spain (12th–13th cents.). This puritanical sect was founded (c1120) in Morocco by Ibn Tumart (1078?–1130) in opposition to the ruling Almoravides (q.v.). By 1174, Ibn Tumart's successors had ousted the last of the Almoravide rulers. The decline of Almohade power began in the 13th cent., when they lost Muslim Spain to the Spanish and Portuguese at the Battle of Las Navas de Tolosa (1212). They were ousted from power in Morocco (1269).

Almohads *See* **Almohades**

Almoravides ⟨Almoravids⟩ Berber Muslim dynasty, rulers of an empire in North Africa and Muslim Spain (11th–12th cents.). The dynasty was founded by Abd Allah ibn Yasin (d. 1058?), who began by converting tribesmen in the Sahara to his zealous reform of Islam. The Almoravides attacked Morocco (c1054), and by 1092 they ruled Morocco, parts of Algeria, and Muslim Spain. They established their capital at Marrakesh (1062). The Almoravides were overthrown by the Almohades (q.v.) (12th cent.).

Almoravids *See* **Almoravides**

Alompra *See* **Alaungpaya**

Alp Arslan *See* **Seljuks**

Alphonsine Tables *See* **Alfonsine Tables**

Alphonso *See* **Alfonso**

Alsace Region and former province of eastern France. It came under French control by the Treaty of Westphalia (1648) but was annexed (1871) by Germany after the Franco-Prussian War. Returned to France after WW I, it was reoccupied by Germany for the duration of WW II.

Altenheim, Battle of *See* **Sasbach and Altenheim, Battles of**

Althaus, Johannes *See* **Althusius, Johannes**

Althing Parliament of Iceland. First convened in 930, it is the oldest parliamentary body in Europe, although it was inactive for a time in the 19th cent. In 1944 it voted for Iceland's independence from Denmark.

Althusius, Johannes ⟨Althaus, ~⟩ 1557–1638. German jurist. Sometimes called "the father of

federalism," he advanced the theory that all human associations (from families to nations) are based on an implied contract made by free peoples.

Altmark, Truce of Treaty (Sept. 25, 1629) between Sweden and Poland, setting up a six-year truce in their long war of succession (1600–60). Poland gave up most of its Livonian and Prussian territories, and Polish king Sigismund III gave up his claim to the Swedish throne.

Altranstadt, Treaties of Two treaties between Poland and Sweden signed in Saxony. In the first (Sept. 24, 1706), Polish king Augustus II was forced to give up the throne to Stanislaus I. In the second (Aug. 31, 1707), Holy Roman Emperor Joseph I granted Protestants of Silesia religious freedom.

Alva, Fernando Alvarez de Toledo, duke of *See* **Alba, Fernando Alvarez de Toledo, duke of**

Alvarado, Pedro de 1486?–1541. Spanish conquistador, chief lieutenant of H. Cortes in the conquest of Mexico (1519–21). He was in command of Tenochtitlan (now Mexico City) when the Aztecs forced a temporary evacuation of the city (July 1, 1520), an incident called "The Sad Night" (La Noche Triste). In 1523 he conquered Guatemala and Salvador for Cortes and was made governor of Guatemala.

Alvarez Quintero, Joaquín 1873–1944. Spanish playwright, who collaborated on more than 100 plays with his brother, Serafín Alvarez Quintero (1871–1938).

Alvarez Quintero, Serafín *See* **Alvarez Quintero, Joaquín**

Amadeo, Ferdinando Maria di Savoia *See* **Amadeus**

Amadeus ⟨Amadeo, Ferdinando Maria di Savoia⟩ 1845–90. Spanish king (1870–73), successor to Isabella II. He came to power at a time of republican-inspired unrest and was forced to abdicate after the outbreak of the Second Carlist War.

Amadeus VIII 1383–1451. Antipope Felix V, the last of the antipopes, and duke of Savoy (1416–51). He was elected antipope (1439) in opposition to Eugene IV by the Council of Basel but resigned in 1449, when Nicholas V became pope.

Amalasuntha ⟨Amalasontha⟩ d. 535. Queen and regent of the Ostrogoths (526–534), daughter of Theodoric the Great. As regent, her policy of friendship with Byzantine emperor Justinian made her many enemies, and she was banished and murdered in 535.

Amalek Biblical figure, the grandson of Esau and forerunner of the Amalekite tribe.

Amalric I ⟨Amaury I⟩ c1135–74. King of the Latin kingdom of Jerusalem (1162–74), successor to his brother Baldwin III. He sought unsuccessfully to gain control of Egypt.

Amalric II ⟨Amaury II⟩ c1155–1205. King of Cyprus (1194–1205) and of the Latin kingdom of Jerusalem (1197–1205). He gained the latter by his marriage to Isabella, daughter of Amalric I.

Aman See **Haman**

Amana Church Society See **Amana colonies**

Amana colonies Seven communal villages on the Iowa River in east Iowa. Founded (1855) by German Pietists who emigrated (1842) to escape persecution, the Amana colonies were among the most successful communes in the US. In 1932, religious and business functions were divided. This resulted in the formation of the Amana Church Society and a separate cooperative corporation.

Amanollah Khan See **Amanullah Khan**

Amanullah Khan ⟨Amanollah Khan⟩ 1892–1960. Amir of Afghanistan (1919–29), successor to his father, Habibollah. He won independence from Britain (1919), but his social reforms, including the emancipation of women, led to his overthrow.

Amasis I ⟨Ahmose⟩ d. c1546 BC. King of ancient Egypt (c1570–46 BC). He drove the Hyskos from Egypt and established the 18th dynasty. He extended Egyptian control into Nubia and the eastern Nile delta and invaded Palestine.

Amati Italian family of violin makers from Cremona, whose violins date from 1564. The family includes Andrea (c1520–c1578) and Nicolò (1596–1684), who was a teacher of A. Stradivari.

Amaury I See **Amalric I**

Amaury II See **Amalric II**

Amaziah d. c780 BC. King of Judah (c798–c780 BC), successor to his father, Jehoash. He conquered Edom but was defeated and imprisoned after attacking King Jehoash of Israel.

Amazon Mythical Greek woman warrior, member of a race said to have lived near the Black Sea. One of Hercules' labors was to retrieve the girdle of the Amazon queen Hippolyte. Amazons, led by Queen Penthesilea, fought against the Greeks at Troy.

Amboina Massacre Execution (Feb., 1623) of a group of English merchants by Dutch authorities on Amboina, an island in eastern Indonesia. The Dutch governor believed the English were conspiring with Japanese mercenaries to attack the Dutch garrison there.

Amboise, Conspiracy of See **Conspiracy of Amboise**

Amboise, Peace of French religious compromise (1563). French Catholics agreed to allow Huguenots (Protestants) limited rights of worship, specifically in the homes of nobility and in certain towns.

Ambrose, Saint AD 339?–397. Roman bishop of Milan (AD 374–392?) and noted opponent of Arianism. He persuaded Gratian, Roman emperor of the West, to ban all heresies (379). In dealing with the emperors Valentinian II and Theodosius (whom he excommunicated in 390), he laid the basis for medieval church-state relations. He wrote many hymns and is credited with introducing Eastern choral music to the Western church (Ambrosian chant). The great Ambrosian library at Milan (founded 1609) is named after him.

Ambrosian library See **Ambrose, Saint**

Ameixial, Battle of Portuguese victory (June 8, 1663) over a much larger Spanish force led by John of Austria. The battle, fought in Portugal, was part of Portugal's successful drive for independence from Spain.

Amen See **Amon**

Amenemhet I d. c1970 BC. King of ancient Egypt (c2000–c1970 BC), founder of the 12th dynasty. During his reign, trade and art flourished in Egypt. His son, Sesostris I, became coregent in 1980 BC.

Amenemhet III d. c1801 BC. An Egyptian king (1849–01 BC), successor to his father, Sesostris II. He constructed massive irrigation and land reclamation projects and promoted trade, bringing the Middle Kingdom period to a peak of influence and prosperity.

Amenhotep I ⟨Amenophis I⟩ d. 1526 BC. King of ancient Egypt (c1546–c1526 BC) and successor to his father, Amasis I. He expanded Egyptian territories in Nubia and invaded Libya.

Amenhotep II ⟨Amenophis II⟩ d. 1425 BC. King of ancient Egypt (c1450–c1425 BC), successor to his father, Thutmose III. He led successful campaigns in Asia and maintained Egyptian control over Nubia.

Amenhotep III ⟨Amenophis III⟩ d. 1379 BC. King of ancient Egypt (c1417–1379 BC), successor to his father, Thutmose IV. He consolidated gains of previous kings and inaugurated a massive building program at Thebes and elsewhere, including colossal statues at Memnon and additions to the temple at Karnak.

Amenhotep IV See **Ikhnaton**

Amenophis I See **Amenhotep I**

Amenophis II See **Amenhotep II**

Amenophis III See **Amenhotep III**

America Name for the two continents of the Western hemisphere, North America and South America, and used more specifically to refer to the US. The term was coined (1507) by the German teacher Martin Waldseemüller in memory of Amerigo Vespucci.

American Anti-Slavery Society Abolitionist organization founded (1833) by W. Garrison. The group grew rapidly in the North during the 1830s. It split (1839) over Garrison's radical policies, including his denunciation of the Constitution, though local-level groups carried on into the 1850s.

American Bill of Rights *See* **Bill of Rights**

American Civil Liberties Union 〈ACLU〉 American legal-action group. Founded in 1920, the ACLU has involved itself in controversial law cases over such civil rights as freedom of speech and assembly. Notable cases include the Scopes Trial and Brown vs. Board of Education.

American Civil War Sectional conflict (1861–65) in the US, fought between the southern agricultural states, whose plantation economies were dependent upon Negro slave labor, and the industrial North with its strong antislavery sentiment. Many complex issues contributed to the outbreak of war, but chief among them were the question of slavery, the authority of the federal government, and states' rights. (For events leading up to the war, *see* UNITED STATES, 1820–60.) The war took some 600,000 lives and caused great destruction and hardship. But it forced an end to slavery and preserved the Union. Key events in the Civil War include:

1860   A. Lincoln elected president (Nov. 6).

1860   South Carolina seceded from the Union (Dec. 20) as a result of Lincoln's election.

1861   Crittenden Compromise, a final attempt at preserving the Union, failed.

1861   Confederates fired on Union supply ship, attempting to relieve Fort Sumter in Charleston (South Carolina) Harbor (Jan. 9); Union ship withdrew.

1861   Mississippi seceded (Jan. 9), followed by Florida (Jan. 10), Alabama (Jan. 11), Georgia (Jan. 19), Louisiana (Jan. 26), and Texas (Feb. 1).

1861   A congress convened (Feb. 4) by representatives of seceding states, at Montgomery, Alabama; created provisional government of Confederate States of America and elected J. Davis its president.

1861   Confederate president Davis called for 20,000 volunteers for the Confederate army (Apr. 8).

1861   Confederate forces under Gen. P. Beauregard fired on Fort Sumter, forcing its surrender and opening hostilities of the Civil War (Apr. 12–14).

1861   Lincoln made a call for 75,000 Union volunteers (Apr. 15) and ordered a blockade of ports of the seceding states (Apr. 19); maintained throughout the war, the blockade seriously hampered but never completely stopped the flow of goods from overseas.

1861   Virginia seceded from the Union (Apr. 17), followed by Arkansas (May 6), North Carolina (May 20), and Tennessee (June 8).

1861   Confederate forces under generals Beauregard and J. Johnston routed the Union army at First Battle of Bull Run (July 21), in northern Virginia.

1861   Bull Run dashed Union hopes for a speedy victory; new Union strategy included continuing the naval blockade of the South, taking control of the Mississippi River (to split the Confederacy), and capturing Richmond, the Confederate capital.

1861   Confederates captured Springfield, Missouri, after winning the Battle of Wilson's Creek (Aug. 10).

1861   Gen. G. McClellan named (Nov.) commander of the Union army; he formed the Army of the Potomac.

1861   Trent Affair involving British steamer stopped (Nov. 8) by Union naval ship; US came to brink of war with Britain over seizure of Confederate envoys.

1862   Union campaign in the West began with fight to take key states of Kentucky and Tennessee; Union advance into Kentucky began with victory at Battle of Mill Springs (Jan. 19); Gen. Grant's forces then captured key Confederate defensive positions of Fort Henry and Fort Donelson (Feb. 6–16); Confederates abandoned Nashville and eventually retreated across Tennessee toward Shiloh.

1862   Legal Tender Act passed for issue of $150 million in greenbacks.

1862   Fight to keep Missouri secure for the Union won at Battle of Elkhorn Tavern, Arkansas (Mar. 7–8), as Union forces continued successful advance; upper Mississippi secured by Union victories at New Madrid (Mar. 13) and Island Number 10 (Apr. 8) in Missouri.

1862   Union ironclad *Monitor* fought Confederate ironclad *Merrimac* to a draw at Hampton Roads, Virginia (Mar. 9); engagement proved the value of ironclad warships.

1862   Grant's forces, pursuing the retreating Confederates in southern Tennessee, were badly bloodied but victorious at the Battle of Shiloh (Apr. 6–7); Confederates lost key leader, Gen. A. Johnston, in the battle; Union forces next captured Corinth, northern Mississippi, and forced the Confederates eastward; Memphis, Tennessee, fell to Union armies next (June 6).

1862 In the east, Union's Peninsular Campaign (Apr.–July) to capture the Confederate capital of Richmond, Virginia, proved unsuccessful; Union troops led by Gen. McClellan reached the outskirts of Richmond but were outmaneuvered by Gen. R.E. Lee's Confederate forces: Lee made commander of the Army of Northern Virginia (June); Union forces withdrawn to Washington.

1862 Admiral D. Farragut's Union fleet captured New Orleans (Apr. 28) from the Confederates; this victory capped a series of successful Union naval operations in which strategic points on the Confederate coastline were captured; fall of New Orleans also meant Confederates along Mississippi could be pressured from both north and south.

1862 New Union army advance toward Richmond defeated at second Battle of Bull Run (Aug. 29–30); Lee advanced into Maryland and threatened Washington, D.C., until suffering a bloody defeat at the Battle of Antietam (Sept. 17); Lee retreated into Virginia and, after delays, Union armies engaged him at the Battle of Fredericksburg (Dec. 13); Union forces were badly defeated and went into winter quarters.

1862–63 Vicksburg Campaign in Mississippi (Nov.–July); led by Gen. Grant, Union forces captured last Confederate positions on the Mississippi River and thus cut the Confederacy in two; the victory (July 4) marked a major turning point in the war.

1862–63 Also, in the west, Union and Confederate forces fought to a draw at Battle of Murfreesboro, Tennessee (Dec. 21, 1862–Jan. 2, 1863).

1863 Lincoln issued the Emancipation Proclamation (Jan. 1).

1863 New Union advance in the east, led by Gen. J. Hooker, halted at Battle of Chancellorsville, Virginia (May 2–4); Confederate Gen. Stonewall Jackson fatally wounded; Union troops retreated to Fredericksburg.

1863 Gen. Lee invaded the North, crossing into Pennsylvania (June).

1863 Battle of Gettysburg, Pennsylvania (July 1–3); Union forces under Gen. G. Meade were victorious in what is considered the decisive battle of the war; Lee forced to withdraw to Virginia.

1863 Draft riots in New York City (July).

1863 In the west, after Grant's victory at Vicksburg (July 4), fighting was centered around Chattanooga, in eastern Tennessee; Union forces took Chattanooga (Sept. 9) but were defeated at the Battle of Chickamauga, Georgia (Sept. 19–20); forced to retreat to Chattanooga, they were besieged by Confederates under Gen. B. Bragg; but Gen. Grant was finally victorious in the Battle of Chattanooga (Nov. 23–25), thus securing Tennessee for the Union and setting the stage for an invasion of Georgia.

1864 Gen. Grant named commander in chief of all Union armies (Mar.); Gen. Sherman made commander in the west; Grant was to attack Lee's army in Virginia while Sherman was to attack Gen. J. Johnston and take Atlanta.

1864 Battle of the Wilderness in Virginia (May 5–6) opened Grant's campaign against Lee; defeated by the Confederates, Grant moved southeastward, where he was again repulsed in bloody fighting at Spotsylvania Courthouse (May 8–21); Grant continued south toward Richmond and again suffered heavy losses at the Battles of Cold Harbor (June 1–June 12).

1864 Atlanta Campaign; led by Gen. Sherman, Union forces invaded Georgia (May 7) and marched for Atlanta; despite delaying tactics of Gen. J. Johnston, Sherman forced the Confederates to give up Atlanta (Sept. 2).

1864 Union troops defeated (June 10) by Confederate raiders at the Battle of Brice's Cross Roads in Mississippi.

1864 Petersburg Campaign begun (June 15) by Gen. Grant; after Cold Harbor, Grant attempted to bypass Lee's army and attack Petersburg, which defended the south approach to Richmond; Lee was barely able to move to defend Petersburg and the battle degenerated to a 10-month siege by Union armies.

1864 Gen. J. Early dispatched (July) by Lee to conduct raids behind Union lines; Early threatened Washington briefly; Union Gen. P. Sheridan was victorious against Early in battles in the Shenandoah Valley, Virginia, including Winchester, Fisher's Hill, and Cedar Creek (Sept. 19–Oct. 19); Early was thereafter forced to withdraw from the strategic Shenandoah Valley.

1864 Admiral D. Farragut defeated Confederate fleet (Aug. 5) at the Battle of Mobile Bay.

1864 Confederates raided Vermont town of St. Albans from Canada (Oct. 19).

1864 President Lincoln reelected (Nov.), partly because of Sherman's capture of Atlanta.

1864–65 Sherman's March to the Sea (Nov. 15–Dec. 21); leading 60,000 Union soldiers, Sherman marched southeast across Georgia, laying waste to all in his path; Savannah was taken (Dec. 21); Sherman then turned north, took Columbia, South Carolina (Feb. 17, 1865) and Goldsboro, North Carolina (Mar. 19, 1865).

1865 Thirteenth Amendment, abolishing slavery in the US, passed by Congress (Feb. 1); ratified (Dec.).

1865 Hampton Roads Peace Conference (Feb. 3), unsuccessful attempt to negotiate an end to the war.

1865 Lee made overall Confederate commander (Feb. 6).

1865 Final phase of the Petersburg Campaign; Gen. P. Sheridan defeated Confederates at Battle of Five Forks (Apr. 1), crippling Confederate position at Petersburg, Virginia.

1865 Grant captured Petersburg, Virginia (Apr. 2), and occupied Richmond (Apr. 3).

1865 Appomattox Courthouse (Apr. 9); pursued by Grant, Gen. Lee was finally surrounded and forced to surrender at Appomattox Courthouse, effectively ending the war.

1865 Lincoln assassinated (Apr. 14).

American Colonization Society An organization founded in the US (Dec., 1816) to transport Negro freedmen to Africa. The society's colonization efforts led to the founding of Liberia. Organized chiefly by Robert Finley (1772–1817), the society established a successful colony (1821) at what was to become Monrovia, Liberia, and subsequently transported several thousand Negro freedmen to Africa. By the 1830s, however, such resettlement plans had become unpopular in the US and the society declined after 1840.

American Expeditionary Force The collective name for American soldiers who fought in Europe during WW I. Commanded by Gen. J. Pershing, they entered combat Oct., 1917, and left France Aug., 1919.

American Federation of Labor–Congress of Industrial Organizations ⟨AFL–CIO⟩ Important US labor-union federation formed by the merger of the AFL and the CIO in 1955. The AFL was formed (1886) as a federation of autonomous national and local craft unions. It opposed the socialism and political activism of the Knights of Labor, and under the leadership of S. Gompers significantly improved the lot of US workers. In the 1930s a split developed over the old system of organizing workers by craft (rather than by industry) and, in 1937, ten unions were expelled from the AFL. These unions formed the CIO, which soon became a powerful new federation of industrial unions. G. Meany was named AFL–CIO president (1955) when the two federations merged.

American Fur Company Fur company (incorporated in 1808) by J. J. Astor to compete with British chartered companies in the Great Lakes region, Canada, and the American Northwest. The company helped open the Great Lakes region and the West to settlers and became one of the first American trusts.

American Indians See separate entries under names of indian tribes and nations.

American Labor party Short-lived US political party founded (1936) in New York by labor leaders and liberals. The party generally supported national and local candidates who favored New Deal social legislation, and until the early 1940s it figured in New York politics. The party split (1944) over its Communist element. The anti-Communist faction formed the Liberal Party (1944) and effectively broke the party, which disbanded in 1956.

American Party *See* **Know-Nothing Party**

American Revolution ⟨War of Independence⟩ Military conflict (1775–83) between Britain and its American colonies that resulted in American independence and creation of the United States. The military phase of this great rebellion was the culmination of a gradual split between Britain and the colonies that had been growing for decades over political and economic issues. (For events leading up to the war, *see* United States 1750–75.) The American victory in the war meant the loss of a major element in the British colonial empire, but Britain compensated for it by gaining control of India. The revolution had far-reaching international repercussions as well. A functioning democracy was established and it thus provided some impetus for other revolutionary struggles, notably in France and later in Spanish America. Key events in the war include:

1775 P. Revere's ride (Apr. 18).

1775 Battles of Lexington and Concord (Apr. 19) outside Boston, the opening hostilities of the American Revolution.

1775 Fort Ticonderoga in New York captured (May 10) by E. Allen and B. Arnold.

1775 Second Continental Congress convened (May 10); appointed (June 15) G. Washington commander of Continental Army.

1775 Battle of Bunker Hill near Boston, first major battle of the revolution (June 17); British took position but at great cost; British failed to break colonials' siege of Boston.

1775 T. Gage resigned as British commander following the Battle of Bunker HIll, succeeded by Gen. W. Howe.

1775 In Canada, American forces captured Montreal (Nov. 12).

1775–76 Quebec campaign in Canada; Continental forces unable to capture Quebec.

1776 T. Paine published *Common Sense*, calling for American independence.

1776 American colonials defeated (Feb. 27) Loyalists in the Battle of Moore's Creek Bridge; British occupation of North Carolina thwarted.

1776 G. Washington took Dorchester Heights overlooking Boston (Mar. 16); Colonial siege finally forced British evacuation (Mar. 17) of Boston.

1776 Battle of Charleston, South Carolina (June 28); colonials repulsed British attackers.

1776 Declaration of Independence proclaimed (July 4) by Congress; colonies now committed to seeking full independence.

1776 British landed on Long Island, New York; won Battle of Long Island (Aug. 27); Washington retreated to Manhattan.

1776 Battle of Harlem Heights (Sept. 16); colonials successfully delayed advance of Howe's troops up the Hudson.

1776 Washington forced to withdraw following indecisive Battle of White Plains (Oct. 28); retreated across New Jersey into Pennsylvania.

1776–77 Washington launched his surprise raid into New Jersey; crossed Delaware (Dec. 25) and took 918 prisoners in victory at the Battle of Trenton (Dec. 26); routed by British column at the Battle of Princeton (Jan. 3); took up winter quarters at Morristown, New Jersey, forcing British to withdraw to New York.

1777 British plan to cut the colonies in two during 1777; Gen. Burgoyne and Lieut. Col. St. Leger to mount two-pronged attack from Canada, linking up at Albany, New York, from the east and west.

1777 Gen. Burgoyne's forces, marching south from Montreal, captured Fort Ticonderoga (July 5); continued southward advance.

1777 Gen. Howe meanwhile left New York (July 23) and struck westward to capture Philadelphia, the colonials' capital.

1777 Americans halted St. Leger's forces at Fort Schuyler in central New York (Aug. 3–23); St. Leger forced to return to Canada without having linked up with Burgoyne.

1777 Raiding party from Burgoyne's column badly defeated (Aug. 16) at the Battle of Bennington, Vermont.

1777 Battle of Brandywine (Sept. 11) near Philadelphia; Gen. Howe defeated Washington's Colonial forces; British captured Philadelphia soon after (Sept. 26).

1777 First Battle of Saratoga fought (Sept. 19); colonials successful in holding lines against Burgoyne's forces at Freeman's Farm.

1777 Battle of Germantown (Oct. 4), unsuccessful attack by Washington on British near Philadelphia.

1777 Second Battle of Saratoga (Oct. 7); American victory at Bemis Heights ended the British attempt to split the colonies in two; Gen. Burgoyne surrendered (Oct. 17); marked a turning point in the war.

1777 Articles of Confederation passed (Nov. 15) by Congress.

1777–78 Washington wintered with troops at Valley Forge under conditions of severe hardship; Gen. von Steuben drilled the soldiers into an efficient fighting force.

1778 American victory at Saratoga convinced French to openly support American cause (from Feb. 1778); troops, supplies, and war fleet to be sent.

1778 Carlisle Commission, unsuccessful British peace mission (Apr. 12).

1778 Sir H. Clinton became British commander in chief; concerned about the arrival of the French, he evacuated Philadelphia (June 18) and marched for New York City.

1778 Gen. Washington attacked Clinton's troops in New Jersey, but the Battle of Monmouth (June 28) was indecisive; Clinton withdrew to New York City.

1778 Wyoming Massacre (July 3), bloody defeat of American settlers by superior British force in Pennsylvania.

1778 Cherry Valley Raid (Nov. 11) in New York by Tories and Indians.

1778 British shifted their offensive to the south; Savannah, Georgia, captured (Dec. 28).

1779 Spain entered war against Britain (June).

1779 Capt. John Paul Jones captured the British ship *Serapis* (Sept. 23).

1780 British Gen. C. Cornwallis launched Carolina campaign, initially successful attempt to gain control of these southern colonies.

1780 Battle of Charleston, South Carolina (May 12), led to British occupation.

1780 Plot by B. Arnold to turn West Point over to the British uncovered (Sept.); Arnold fled to the British side.

1780 Battle of Camden (Aug. 16), one of the worst American defeats of the war; enabled the British to invade North Carolina.

1780 Battle of Kings Mountain, North Carolina (Oct. 7), victory of American over British troops.

1781 Mutinies by colonial troops in Pennsylvania and New Jersey put down.

1781 Articles of Confederation ratified (Feb.)

1781 British defeated N. Greene's forces (Apr. 25) at the Battle of Hobkirk's Hill, South Carolina.

1781 N. Greene victorious (Sept. 8) at the Battle of Eutaw Springs; British driven back to Charleston, South Carolina.

1781 Yorktown campaign (Sept. 28–Oct. 19), final campaign of the war; Continental forces aided by a French fleet trapped British forces under Lord G. Cornwallis at Yorktown, Virginia, and compelled Cornwallis's surrender; marked virtual end of military conflict in colonies.

1782 British Parliament sanctioned opening of negotiations (Mar. 5); B. Franklin, J. Jay, and J. Adams negotiated for the Americans and won very favorable terms (Nov. 30) in a preliminary treaty (incorporated in the Treaty of Paris).

1783 Treaty of Paris signed (Sept. 3), formally ending war and recognizing US independence.

1783 British troops evacuated (Nov. 25) from New York City.

American Revolution, Daughters of the *See* **Daughters of the American Revolution**

American Samoa US Pacific island territory, the eastern half of the Samoan Islands. The US has administered the territory since 1899. It has a local legislature and judiciary, and a new constitution was promulgated in 1967.

American System H. Clay proposed this program (1824) for American economic self-sufficiency and internal improvements. It included road and canal construction, high tariffs to protect American industry from foreign imports, and development of American agriculture.

Ames, Oakes *See* **Credit Mobilier of America**

Amherst, Jeffrey Amherst, 1st Baron 1717–97. A British general. His campaigns against the French in Canada during the last French and Indian War (1758–60) led to British control of Canada.

Amiens, Mise of *See* **Mise of Amiens**

Amiens, Treaty of Peace treaty (Mar. 27, 1802) ending the War of the Second Coalition and the French Revolutionary Wars. Signed at Amiens, France, by Great Britain and France (and her allies, Spain and the Batavian Republic), the treaty restored all conquered territory except Ceylon and Trinidad. The British, suspicious of Napoleon, eventually refused to return Malta. War resumed in 1803.

Amin, al- *See* **Muslim Civil Wars**

Amin, Idi 1925–. Ugandan general and dictator. The armed forces commander from 1966, he overthrew the government of Pres. Milton Obote (1925–) in 1971. His dictatorship was marked by extreme cruelty, and in 1972 he ordered the expulsion of Asian residents from Uganda. He was overthrown on Apr. 11, 1979.

amir *See* **emir**

Amistad Affair Controversy (1841) in which African slaves aboard the Spanish slaver *Amistad* mutinied (1839) and sailed to America. J.Q. Adams successfully defended them before the Supreme Court as freedmen, not pirates, in a case involving salvage of the *Amistad*.

Amman Jordanian capital city (pop. 711,900), located in north-central Jordan. Occupied since before the 3d millennium BC, it was once the great capital of the biblical Ammonites and was renamed Philadelphia by Egyptian conquerors. The city disappeared entirely in the 14th cent. and was not resettled until the 19th. It became the capital of Transjordan (1921) and capital of Jordan (1946).

Ammianus Marcellinus c330–c395. Greek soldier in Roman service, and historian. Of his 31-volume history of Rome, only volumes covering AD 353–378 survive. Written in the tradition of Tacitus, they are considered a reliable source.

Ammon *See* **Amon**

Amon ⟨Ammon⟩ ⟨Amun⟩ ⟨Amen⟩ Egyptian deity, at one time patron god of Thebes but later (as Amon-Ra) considered king of the gods. He was sometimes represented as a man with a ram's head.

Amor Roman love god, also known as Cupid, usually represented as a winged child. He is identified with the Greek Eros.

Ampère, André Marie 1775–1836. French physicist and mathematician noted for his work in electromagnetism. The ampere is named for him.

Amphissean War *See* **Sacred War (Fourth)**

Amphitrite Greek sea goddess, wife of Poseidon and mother of Triton.

Amphitryon In Greek mythology, husband of Alcmene. While he was off fighting, Zeus took his form and visited Alcmene. Upon Amphitryon's return, Alcmene bore twin sons, Hercules, son of Zeus, and Iphicles, son of Amphitryon.

Amram ben Scheschna ⟨Amram Gaon⟩ d. 875. Hebrew scholar. Amram wrote the oldest surviving Jewish prayer book, the *Seder Rab Amram*. He was an expert on Judaic laws and customs.

Amritsar, Massacre of *See* **Massacre of Amritsar**

Amritsar, Treaty of Treaty (Apr. 25, 1809) between the British East India Company and Sikh leader Ranjit Singh. It defined the territories of each in the Punjab region.

Amsterdam Netherlands capital (pop. 958,000) and a major European port and commercial center. Originally a fishing village, it was chartered (1300) and joined the Hanseatic League (1369). It took part in the Protestant revolt against Spanish rule (1578) in The Netherlands and prospered as a result of the decline of Ghent and Antwerp (16th cent.). By the 17th cent., it was a major naval and commercial center of the Dutch Empire and after 1795 became the capital of Napoleon's kingdom of The Netherlands. It became the capital of independent Netherlands in 1814. It was occupied by the Germans (1940–45) in WW II.

Amun *See* **Amon**

Amundsen, Roald 1872–1928. Norwegian explorer, first to reach the South Pole (Dec. 14, 1911). With Umberto Nobile (1885–1978), he was also one of the first to fly over the North Pole (1926).

Anabaptists Christian sects that arose in Europe during the 16th-cent. Protestant Reformation. Anabaptists generally rejected infant baptism in favor of adult baptism, favored separation of the church and state, and opposed the use of force. The movement is said to have begun (c1520) in Zurich, Switzerland, and, despite persecutions by both Catholics and Protestants, spread rapidly. A sect in Moravia gave rise to the Hutterites, and a sect in The Netherlands became Mennonites.

anarchism Theory that advocates complete individual freedom, especially from control by government or other outside authority. Based on the belief that such restrictions corrupt mankind, philosophic anarchism, advanced (19th cent.) by P. Proudhon, seeks nonviolent evolution toward an anarchistic society. Extreme anarchists, beginning with the Russian revolutionary M. Bakunin, have favored terrorism to advance their cause. This violent aspect became commonly associated with anarchism after a series of violent acts (such as the Haymarket Square riot, 1886) and political assassinations, including those of French president M. Carnot (1894), Italian king Humbert I (1900), US pres. W. McKinley (1901), and Greek king George (1913).

Anastasius I AD c430–518. Byzantine emperor (AD 491–518), successor to Zeno. He drove the Isaurians from Constantinople, built a wall for defense against the Slavs and Bulgars, and instituted tax and social reforms. His adherence to Monophysitism was opposed by Rome.

Anatolia Asian section of Turkey, the peninsular region also identified as Asia Minor.

Anaxagoras c500–428 BC. Greek philosopher who taught in Athens. Among his students were Pericles and, it is believed, Socrates. He was banished for his teachings on the physical nature of the universe.

Anaximander c611–c547 BC. Greek philosopher whose teachings are said to prefigure the development of astronomy and the theory of evolution. One of the earliest Western philosophers, he attempted to provide a systematic explanation of the nature of the universe and all things in it.

Anaximenes fl. 6th cent. BC. Greek philosopher. He held that air was the primary substance of the universe and that all matter was composed of air but differed in density. He is considered, with Thales and Anaximander, to be one of the first Western philosophers.

ancien régime Term for the political and social order in France up to the outbreak of the French Revolution, in 1789.

ancient Germans Germanic (or Teutonic) people of uncertain origins who were located in the region encompassing southern Sweden, Denmark, and part of northern Germany at the time of the decline of the Celtic civilization in Europe (1st cent. BC). In subsequent migrations, Germanic tribes spread through Northern, Central, and Western Europe. The Goths settled in France and environs (4th cent. AD), the Angles and Saxons in England (5th cent. AD), the Vandals in Spain and North Africa (5th cent.), and the Franks in northern France (5th cent.). The first contact between Germanic tribes and the Romans dates from the 2d cent. BC, and in c102 BC the Cimbri and Teutones were wiped out by Roman armies. Thereafter, the various Germanic tribes gained in strength and, by their relentless attacks during the 3d to 4th cent. AD, figured in the fall of the Roman Empire.

Ancients and Moderns, Quarrel of See **Perrault, Charles**

Ancon, Treaty of Treaty (Oct. 20, 1883) between Peru and Chile ending the War of the Pacific. Peru ceded to Chile the provinces of Tarapaca, Tacna, and Arica.

Ancyra See **Ankara**

Andalusia Historic region in southern Spain. Originally the kingdom of Tartessus (2d millennium BC), it was conquered by the Phoenicians (480 BC), who had established the colony of Gadir (modern Cadiz) there (c1100 BC). Following Roman conquest (3d cent. BC), it flourished as a cultural center. Under the Moors (AD 711–1492), Andalusia was divided into the kingdoms of Córdoba, Seville, Jaén, and Granada and became a great Muslim center of commerce and culture. Christian kings of Spain completed conquest of the region in 1492. The region declined with Spain after the 16th cent.

Andersen, Hans Christian 1805–75. A Danish writer best known for such fairy tales as *The Little Match Girl*, *The Ugly Duckling*, *The Emperor's New Clothes*, and *The Snow Queen*. He also wrote novels, poetry, and books of travel sketches.

Anderson, Carl David 1905–. American physicist noted for discovery (1932) of the positron. He also helped to discover the meson. He was awarded the Nobel Prize in Physics in 1936.

Anderson, Elizabeth Garrett 1836–1917. English physician. Barred from medical schools, she trained with private physicians and was licensed to practice in 1865. She helped open the medical profession to women.

Anderson, Maxwell 1888–1959. An American dramatist best known for his tragedies in verse. Much of his work deals with modern moral and social questions. His dramatic works include *What Price Glory?*, *Winterset*, and *Barefoot in Athens*. He won the Pulitzer Prize for Drama in 1933.

Anderson, Sherwood 1876–1941. An American writer best known for *Winesburg, Ohio*, a novel dealing with the inhabitants of a small Ohio town.

Andorra Tiny principality (pop. 35,000) located in the Pyrenees Mountains, between France and Spain. Its origins can be traced back to Carolingian times. Emperor Charles II is said to have granted overlordship (9th cent.) of Andorra to the Spanish bishop of Urgel, a claim contested by French nobles until the present arrangement of joint suzerainty was agreed to in 1278. French king Henry IV inherited French rights to Andorra, which subsequently passed to French presidents. The people of Andorra speak Catalan and are governed by a semifeudal system.

Andrada e Silva, José Bonifácio de ⟨José Bonifácio⟩ 1763?–1838. Brazilian statesman considered the father of Brazilian independence. He supported independence from Portugal and establishment (1822) of a Brazilian monarchy under Pedro I. He served (1822–23) as prime minister.

Andrássy, Count Guyla (Julius) 1823–90. Hungarian statesman and a principal figure in formation of the Dual Monarchy (1867). A leader of the abortive Hungarian revolt against Austria (1848–49), he eventually sought the compromise of the Dual Monarchy and became Hungary's first prime minister (1867–71). Later, as foreign minister of Austria-Hungary (1871–79), he was responsible for the unpopular occupation of Bosnia and Herzegovina (1878) and arranged the important Dual Alliance (1879) between Germany and Austria-Hungary.

André, John 1751–80. British army officer during the American Revolution. He conspired with B. Arnold to arrange the surrender of West Point to the British. Captured (1780) before the plan could be accomplished, he was hanged as a spy.

Andrew, Saint One of the twelve apostles, brother of Saint Peter. He is said to have been martyred on an X-shaped cross. He is patron saint of Russia and Scotland.

Andrew II *d.* 1235. King of Hungary (1205–35), and son of Bela III. During his reign, he was forced by rebellious nobles to issue the Golden Bull (1222), considered the Hungarian Magna Carta.

Andrews' Raid ⟨Great Locomotive Chase⟩ Raid (Apr. 12, 1862) during the American Civil War (1861–65). Twenty-two Union soldiers, led by James J. Andrews, attempted to knock out the railway between Chattanooga, Tennessee, and Atlanta, Georgia. They stole a locomotive in Georgia but were caught by the Confederates after a ninety-mile chase.

Andreyev, Leonid Nikolayevich 1871–1919. A Russian writer. His enormous early popularity declined as his work turned from realism to the metaphysical and symbolic. His works include *The Red Laugh* and *The Seven Who Were Hanged*.

Andromache In Greek legend, wife of the Trojan Hector. After the fall of Troy, she was allotted to Achilles' son, Neoptolemus. When Neoptolemus died, she became wife of Helenus, Hector's brother.

Andromeda Princess in Greek mythology. Poseidon, angered by her mother, Cassiopeia, had her chained to a rock near the sea. She was rescued by Perseus, whom she married.

Andrusov, Treaty of ⟨Andrussovo, ~⟩ Treaty (Jan. 20, 1667) concluded between Russia and Poland, ending the Thirteen Years' War (1654–67). The treaty settled the basic issue of control of the Ukraine and, by its terms, Russia won the province of Smolensk and the east Ukraine, including Kiev.

Andrussovo, Treaty of See **Andrusov, Treaty of**

Angelico, Fra ⟨Pietro, Guido di⟩ *c*1400–55. Florentine painter whose works are noted for their religious themes. He joined the Dominican order (*c*1420–25), and was called Angelico ("the angelic") after his death.

Angelus Byzantine family. This family produced the Byzantine emperors Isaac II Angelus, Alexius III Angelus, Alexius IV Angelus, and their descendant Michael VIII Palaeologus.

Angevin **1.** Another name for the Plantagenet kings of England (1154–1399), the first three of whom were also counts of Anjou (thus Angevin). Ties between the French and English lines began with the marriage (1129) of Goeffry IV, count of Anjou, and Matilda, daughter of English king Henry I. Their son became Henry II, king of England and count of Anjou. With this dual title, King Henry II, Richard I, and John successfully ruled England and large domains on the Continent as well. These domains, including Brittany, Normandy, Anjou, Aquitaine, Maine, and Touraine, were almost entirely lost to the French by the end of King John's reign (1216). **2.** Name for rulers who were descendants of the French House of Anjou in several collateral lines. They ruled variously over Hungary, Poland, Naples, and parts of France (13th–15th cents.).

Angkor Thom Ancient capital of the Khmer Empire in northwest Cambodia. Constructed (*c*1200) after the sacking of nearby Angkor Wat, it was the Khmer capital until 1434, when Phnom Penh became the capital.

Angkor Wat   Ancient capital of the Khmer Empire in northwest Cambodia, built (12th cent.) by Khmer king Suryavarman II (d. c1150). It was sacked and ruined (c1177) and a new capital, Angkor Thom, was established nearby. Its ruins are considered a Cambodian architectural treasure.

Anglican church   See **Church of England**

Anglican Communion   A worldwide union of churches that subscribe to the beliefs and liturgy of the Church of England, as defined in the Book of Common Prayer.

Anglo-Afghan Wars ⟨Afghan Wars⟩   **1.** First ~ War (1838–42) in which the British invaded Afghanistan from India, deposed the Afghan ruler Dost Muhammad and installed their puppet. A rebellion against the British broke out (1841), forced their retreat from Kabul, and ended in a massacre of British troops (1842). Dost Muhammad was restored (1842). **2.** Second ~ War (1878–80) between Britain and Afghanistan. Concerned about Russia's increasing influence in Afghanistan, the British again invaded from India and forced the Afghan ruler to accept the Treaty of Gandamak (1879). A rebellion against the British broke out (Sept. 3, 1879). A new emir quelled the rebellion and, though he did not challenge the 1879 treaty, he continued to counter British influence by befriending Russia. **3.** Third ~ War (May 10–Aug. 8, 1919) in which the Afghans attempted to invade British India. Hoping to end British influence in Afghanistan, Afghan emir Amanullah launched a religious war. His plan to provoke Muslims in India to an uprising against the British failed, and his forces were soon forced out of India. Amanullah succeeded, however, in negotiating the Treaty of Rawalpindi (Aug. 8), by which the British recognized Afghan independence.

Anglo-American Conference   See **Trident Conference**

Anglo-Burmese Wars   See **Burma Wars**

Anglo-Dutch Wars   See **Dutch Wars**

Anglo-Egyptian Condominium   Name for the government of eastern Sudan (1899–1956). Britain and Egypt jointly ruled there: Egypt nominated its governor, who was then approved by the British.

Anglo-Egyptian Sudan   See **Sudan**

Anglo-Egyptian Treaty   Treaty (Aug. 26, 1936) whereby Britain granted Egypt conditional independence. The agreement created a military alliance between Egypt and Britain and provided for a withdrawal of British troops, except those needed to protect the Suez Canal.

Anglo-Russian Convention   Pact (Aug. 31, 1907) between Britain and Russia settling their claims to Tibet, Afghanistan, and Persia. Both nations feared growing German power, and this agreement became a basis for their alliance in WW I.

Anglo-Saxons   Germanic peoples that ruled England from 5th cent. AD, following the decline of Rome, to 1066, the time of the Norman conquest. Both the Angles and Saxons were originally located in the region around Schleswig (in north Germany and Denmark). Both arrived in the British Isles late in the 5th cent. and established small kingdoms there. "Anglo-Saxon" has also been used as a general term for the English since the time of the Norman conquest. See also Anglo-Saxon Heptarchy.

Anglo-Saxon Heptarchy   The seven Anglo-Saxon kingdoms (5th–9th cents.) that arose in England after the Teutonic invasions. Their domains included all of south England (except parts of Wales) by the 8th cent. They were conquered by the Danes (9th cent.). The seven were Essex, Wessex, Sussex, Kent, East Anglia, Mercia, and Northumbria.

Anglo-Soviet Agreement   Treaty (May 26, 1942) between Britain and the USSR, a twenty-year agreement uniting the two nations against Nazi Germany and its allies.

Angola (People's Republic of Angola)   Angola is an independent state located in coastal southwest Africa. Its capital is Luanda. Long a Portuguese colony, Angola was once a major source of slaves used in Portuguese Brazil. Significant development of the colony began after WW II and Angola was the last of Portugal's African possessions to win independence (1975). Subsequently a Soviet-backed faction gained control of the country, though guerrilla resistance continues. Key dates in the history of Angola include:

1482   Northern coast discovered by Portuguese navigator Diogo Cão.

1575   Permanent colony established by Portuguese at Luanda; region became a prime source of slaves for Portugal's colonies in Brazil.

1641–48   Dutch briefly controlled Angola.

1885   Borders of Portugal's colony established by Treaty of Berlin.

1902   Portugal gained control of the interior by conquering the native Mbundu kingdom.

1951   Angola made a Portuguese overseas province; industrial development and immigration encouraged.

1961   Native resistance to colonial government began; various groups engaged in guerrilla warfare and established competing governments in exile.

1972 Angola made an autonomous state under Portuguese supervision; guerrilla resistance continued.

1973 Legislative elections for new government held.

1974 New government in Portugal (1964) ceased fighting against rebels in Angola; ordered Angolan independence.

1975 Angolan independence declared (Nov. 11); struggle for control of government between US-backed and Soviet-backed rebel groups.

1976 Soviet-backed Movement for Liberation of Angola (MPLA) gained control (with help of Cuban troops, from Oct. 1975); resistance by rival groups continued, however.

1976 US military aid to rebel forces in Angola ended.

1977–78 Refugees from Zaire launched invasions from Angola; Soviet-backed regime denied involvement.

1982 Diplomatic contacts with Western powers (Portugal and US) reported.

Angora *See* **Ankara**

Angoulême, Louis Antoine de Bourbon, duke of 1775–1844. Last dauphin of France and eldest son of King Charles X. He failed to stop Napoleon on his return from Elba (1814) and led the French invasion of Spain (1823). He went into exile (1830) after his father was forced to abdicate.

Ångström, Anders Jonas 1814–74. A Swedish physicist noted for his work in spectrum analysis. The angstrom unit, used to measure the wavelength of light, is named after him.

animatism *See* **animism**

animism Belief that spirits dwell within all things, living and nonliving. Common as a central concept among primitive religions, animism postulates the existence of an individual spirit within each object. This is distinct from *animatism* in what are regarded as earlier, more primitive religions. This form of belief holds that all things share an undifferentiated spiritual power.

Anjala League Conspiracy (1788–89) by Scandinavian nobles and army officers against Swedish king Gustavus III. Opposed to the Russo-Swedish War (1788–90), the conspirators attempted to settle the war themselves by communicating directly with the Russians. The offer was refused, the conspirators were discovered, and most were imprisoned.

Anjou Historic region and former province located in western France. Made a countship (9th cent.) by Charlemagne, it was prominent (11th–12th cents.) as the seat of the Angevin family *(q.v.)*. Anjou became a hereditary domain of English Angevin kings (1151–1204), until it was

taken by the French king Philip II and made part of French domains.

Anjou, Margaret of *See* **Margaret of Anjou**

Ankara ⟨Ancyra⟩ ⟨Angora⟩ Capital (pop. 2,600,000) of Turkey. An important commercial center since ancient times, it became capital of a Roman province in the 1st cent. AD. Tamerlane defeated Sultan Bajazet I here in 1402. Ankara became the center of nationalist government in 1920 and capital of Turkey in 1923.

Ankara, Battle of Mongol victory (July, 1402) at Ankara, Turkey, over the forces of Ottoman sultan Bajazet I. Tamerlane led the Mongols in this battle, in which Bajazet was captured.

Anna *See* **Hannah**

Anna Comnena 1083–1148? Byzantine princess, daughter of Alexius I. Frustrated in her attempts to obtain the imperial crown, she turned to the writing of the *Alexiad*, a classic on the life of her father.

Anna Ivanovna 1693–1740. Empress of Russia (1730–40), daughter of Ivan V, and successor to her cousin Peter II. Made empress by the supreme privy council, she ruled as an autocrat, and her reign was marked by repression and terror. She relied largely upon Ernst Johann Biron (1690–1772) to rule the country. The War of the Polish Succession and the Russo-Turkish War (1736–39) took place during her reign.

Annam Historic region and ancient kingdom in central Vietnam, with origins in the 2d millennium BC. The territory became a Chinese kingdom (111 BC), and the Chinese were not driven out until AD 939. In 1472 the Champa kingdom to the south was added to Annam. From the 16th to 18th cent., the kingdom was divided between the Le and Nguyen dynasties. It was reunited, with French help (1802), as the empire of Vietnam and by 1884, Annam had become a French protectorate. In 1887 it became part of the French Union of Indochina.

Annapolis Convention US convention (Sept. 11, 1786) at Annapolis, Maryland, attended by delegates from Delaware, New Jersey, New York, Pennsylvania, and Virginia. Called to discuss commercial difficulties created by the Articles of Confederation, the convention led to the Constitutional Convention (1787), which drafted the US Constitution.

Anne 1665–1714. English queen (1702–07) and queen of Great Britain and Ireland (1707–14), successor to William III. The last Stuart monarch and the daughter of James II, she acquiesced in the overthrow of her father in the Glorious Revolution. Throughout her reign, which saw intense rivalry between Tories and Whigs, she was influenced by Sarah Jennings (1660–1774), duchess of Marlborough, and (after 1710) by A. Masham. During her reign, Great Britain was formed by the Act of Union with Scotland (1707), the succession of the Hanoverian kings was ensured by the Act of Settlement (1701), and England became embroiled in the War of Spanish Succession (1701–14).

Anne, Saint   *fl.* 1st cent. BC. Wife of Saint Joachim and mother of the Virgin Mary. She is the patron saint of Brittany and of Quebec, Canada, and of women in labor.

Anne of Austria   1601–66. French queen, wife of King Louis XIII (*m.* 1615), and daughter of Spanish king Philip III. On her husband's death (1648), she became regent for her son, Louis XIV, with Cardinal Mazarin as minister. Her regency was marked by rebellions of the Fronde (*q.v.*).

Anne of Brittany   1477–1514. Duchess of Brittany and queen consort to French kings Charles VIII (1491–98) and Louis XII (1499–1514). As sole heir to Brittany (1488), she tried desperately to guarantee its independence from France but was forced to marry first Charles, then Louis. During her lifetime she did maintain Brittany's independence, but her daughter's marriage to Francis I finally resulted in its annexation by France (1532).

Anne of Cleves   1515–57. Fourth queen consort of Henry VIII of England. Henry married her in Jan., 1540, to form an alliance with the Protestant Schmalkaldic League to forestall an attack on England by Catholic powers. The attack failed to materialize, and the marriage was dissolved in July, 1540.

annexation   Act by which a nation or state declares sovereignty over territory formerly outside its borders. Usually accompanied by military conquest or threat of it, annexation is distinct from cession, in which a state acquires territory by treaty or purchase.

Anouilh, Jean   1910–. A French playwright. Anouilh's internationally popular plays include *Antigone, Waltz of the Toreadors, Becket,* and *The Lark.*

Anschluss   German term, meaning connection or union. It was used especially to describe the incorporation of Austria into the German Reich on Mar. 11, 1938, a union that had been sought often by German nationalists after WW I.

Anselm, Saint   *c*1033–1109. Archbishop of Canterbury, Doctor of the Church, and founder of scholasticism (*q.v.*). He advanced a theory of the atonement of Christ and originated the ontological proof of God's existence.

Antaeus   In Greek mythology, the son of Poseidon and Gaea. A giant, he was invincible as

long as he touched the earth. Hercules killed him by lifting him into the air and crushing him.

Antarctica   The 5th largest continent, located almost entirely within the Antarctic Circle. Antarctica was not discovered until modern times. The British captain J. Cook was the first to sail within the Antarctic Circle (1772–75). American, British, and Russian expeditions all claim the first actual sighting (1820) of Antarctica. In subsequent years of the 19th cent., the coastal regions of the continent were explored by many, including the Scotsman J. Ross (1839–43). The Norwegian R. Amundsen reached the South Pole first (Dec. 14, 1911), followed a month later by British R. Scott (Jan. 17, 1912), whose party perished returning. The American admiral R. Byrd conducted important investigations in the 1930s. During the International Geophysical Year (1957–58), scientists from 56 nations exhaustively studied the continent. Twelve nations established stations there, and, in 1959, signed the Antarctic Treaty (*q.v.*).

Antarctic Treaty   International agreement (1959) by which twelve nations designated Antarctica an independent, demilitarized, scientific research zone. The US and the USSR were among the signatories of the 30-year treaty.

antebellum period   In general, a term used to refer to the period prior to a war. It is often used in connection with the social and political institutions of the US South that existed before the American Civil War (1861–65).

Anthony, Marc   *See* **Antony**

Anthony, Saint   (Anthony the Great, Saint) AD 251?–*c*350. Egyptian hermit and monk, also known as Saint Anthony of Egypt. The first Christian monk, he organized a monastic community in Egypt that became a model for later monastic societies in the East. He is regarded as the father of Christian monasticism.

Anthony, Susan Brownell   1820–1906. American reformer and woman-suffrage-movement leader. A pioneering figure in the feminist movement (from *c*1854), she led the struggle to secure voting rights for women, finally granted by the Nineteenth Amendment (1920).

Anthony of Egypt, Saint   *See* **Anthony, Saint**

Anthony of Padua, Saint   1195–1231. Portuguese monk and noted follower of the Franciscan order. He preached with great ability in France and Italy. He is the patron saint of Portugal and his name is invoked by Roman Catholics to find lost objects.

Anthony the Great, Saint   *See* **Anthony, Saint**

Anti-Comintern Pact   Agreement (Nov. 25, 1936) by which Germany and Japan vowed to oppose the

Communist International. They were later joined by Italy, Spain, and others.

Anti-Corn-Law League An organization formed (1839) in England to repeal the Corn Laws, grain import duties that kept the price of bread high. Under the leadership of R. Cobden and others, the league organized support among farmers and workers and eventually won Prime Minister R. Peel to their cause. Parliament repealed the Corn Laws in 1846.

Antietam, Battle of ⟨Sharpsburg, ~⟩ Bloody victory (Sept. 17, 1862) for Union forces during the American Civil War (1861–65). The battle turned back a Confederate invasion of the North that threatened Washington, D.C. The Confederates, numbering 65,000 soldiers under Gen. R.E. Lee, crossed the Potomac into Maryland shortly after the Second Battle of Bull Run. They were defeated (Sept. 17) at Antietam Creek (near Sharpsburg) by 85,000 Union soldiers under Gen. G. McClellan, following preliminary engagements (Sept. 14–15). Union casualties numbered about 12,000, while Confederate losses ranged variously from 9,000–14,000.

Anti-Federalists American political group, opponents of a strong central government. Initially they opposed adoption of the Constitution in 1789, and afterward favored strict interpretation of it. After 1793 they became known as the Jeffersonian Republican party, then as the Democratic-Republicans.

Antigone In Greek legend, the daughter of Oedipus. She buried the body of her brother Polynices, against orders given by her uncle Creon. In Sophocles' play *Antigone* she was buried alive for her disobedience.

Antigonids A dynasty that ruled ancient Macedonia and parts of Greece from 276 and 168 BC. It was established by Antigonus II, a grandson of Alexander the Great's general, Antigonus I. The dynasty prevailed until clashes with Rome resulted in defeat of the last of the dynasty, Perseus, at Pydna (168 BC).

Antigonus I ⟨Antigonus Cyclops⟩ 382?–301 BC. Macedonian general under Alexander the Great, founder of the Antigonids, and important figure in the Wars of the Diadochi (*q.v.*). He was made governor of Phrygia in 333 BC and, after Alexander's death, expanded his domains throughout Asia Minor, Syria, and Mesopotamia. He pronounced himself king (306), and was killed at the Battle of Ipsus (301).

Antigonus II ⟨Antigonus Gonatas⟩ 319?–239 BC. Macedonian king (276–239 BC), grandson of Antigonus I. He seized control of Macedonia (276), withstood attacks by Pyrrhus and Ptolemy II, won

the Chremonidean War (266–262), and briefly united Greek territories under Macedonian control.

Antigonus III ⟨Antigonus Doson⟩ *d.* 221 BC. King of Macedonia (227–221 BC). He was regent for Philip V, son of Demetrius II, and in 227 declared himself king. Siding with the Achaean League, he defeated Spartan king Cleomenes III at Sellasia (222). He formed a Hellenic League (224) to further Macedonian hegemony in Greece.

Antigonus Cyclops *See* **Antigonus I**
Antigonus Doson *See* **Antigonus III**
Antigonus Gonatas *See* **Antigonus II**

Anti-Masonic party First American third party, formed (1826) to oppose election of Freemasons to public office. The disappearance and presumed murder of a writer who was planning to reveal secrets of the fraternal order of Freemasons caused a major scandal. The Freemasons' refusal to cooperate in the investigation resulted in the founding of the Anti-Masonic party in New York, and, in 1832, the party won many congressional seats. By 1834, however, Anti-Masons had been absorbed into the new Whig party. The Anti-Mason national nominating convention at Baltimore (1831) was the first ever held and became the model for such political conventions in America.

Antinoüs AD *c*110–130. Favorite of Emperor Hadrian and his constant companion. After Antinoüs drowned in the Nile, Hadrian founded the city of Antinoöpolis and built many temples in his honor.

antinomianism Doctrine that some Christians, by virtue of their special faith, do not have to obey the moral laws of the Old Testament. The Antinomian controversy first appeared during the 16th-cent. Protestant Reformation as a doctrinal dispute involving one of M. Luther's fellow reformers, J. Agricola. Opposed by M. Luther, Agricola recanted by 1540. Subsequently, some radical Anabaptists and several sects in 17th-18th–cent. England were accused of antinomianism.

Antioch Historic city in what is now southeast Turkey. Founded by the Syrians (*c*300 BC), the city was located on important trade routes. It was conquered by the Romans (64 BC), and under them became a cultural center. The city became one of the three original patriarchates and was important in the early history of the Christian church. From the 6th cent. to the 16th, the city was conquered by various powers and figured in the Crusades. When it fell to the Ottoman Turks (1516), it was of little importance. It was made part of Syria in 1920 and was restored to Turkey in 1939.

Antioch, Principality of *See* **Principality of Antioch**

Antioch, Saint Ignatius of *See* **Ignatius of Antioch, Saint**

Antiochus I ⟨~ Soter⟩ *c*324–*c*261 BC. Seleucid king of Syria (280–*c*261 BC), successor to his father, Seleucus I. His reign was troubled by internal strife, attacks by the Gauls, and the first Syrian War *(q.v.)*, in which he lost Phoenicia and other territories. He is noted as a great builder of cities.

Antiochus II *c*287–247 BC. Seleucid king of Syria (*c*261–247 BC), successor to his father, Antiochus I. He waged the second Syrian War *(q.v.)*, a continuation of wars against Egypt that began under his father's reign. He secured peace and recovered much lost Syrian territory, however, by marrying Berenice, daughter of his enemy, Ptolemy II.

Antiochus III ⟨~ the Great⟩ 242–187 BC. Seleucid king of Syria (223–187 BC), successor to his brother Seleucus III. He waged the fourth Syrian War *(q.v.)*, extended the Seleucid Empire eastward into India, but was defeated in a struggle with Rome. After invading Greece, he was defeated by the Romans at Thermopylae (191) and Magnesia (190) and thus lost all territories west of Mount Taurus.

Antiochus IV ⟨~ Epiphanes⟩ *d.* 163 BC. Seleucid king of Syria (175–163 BC), successor to his brother Seleucus IV. He conquered most of Egypt (169–168) but was forced to withdraw by Rome. His efforts to introduce Greek institutions and religion in Judaea led to the revolt of the Maccabees *(q.v.)*.

Antiochus Epiphanes *See* **Antiochus IV**

Antiochus Soter *See* **Antiochus I**

Antiochus the Great *See* **Antiochus III**

Antipater *d.* 319 BC. Macedonian general who served as regent in Macedonia (334–323 BC) during the Asian campaign of Alexander the Great. As regent after Alexander's death, he defeated rebellious Greek city-states in the Lamian War *(q.v.)*. He maintained the last vestiges of central authority in the Macedonian Empire until his death, which was followed by the Wars of the Diadochi.

antipope Pope of the Roman Catholic church elected in opposition to the legitimate pope. Antipopes were elected for a variety of reasons, including doctrinal disputes, power struggles between the church and secular rulers, and historic divisions within the church (i.e., Babylonian captivity, Great Schism). Antipopes were elected as early as AD *c*217 (Hippolytus) and the last was elected 1439 (Felix V).

Antirent War ⟨Helderberg War⟩ Rebellion (1839–46) by tenant farmers in upper New York State against a system of perpetual leases (the patroon system). The revolt was provoked by the Van Rensselaer family's attempt to collect $400,000 in back rent and finally resulted in an end to the patroon system.

Anti-Saloon League American temperence organization founded (1893) at Oberlin, Ohio, and established as a national organization in 1895. It sought legislative prohibition of the sale of liquor and became a major factor in the passage of the Eighteenth Amendment.

anti-Semitism Historically persistent prejudice (or open hostility) toward Jews. This prejudice at first stemmed from religious differences between Jews and Christians, but from the late 19th cent. it was largely based on supposed racial differences. Anti-Semitism in this form became the basis for A. Hitler's systematic extermination (1939–45) of six million Jews during WW II. Arab hatred of the Israelis, ostensibly based on political grounds, has brought hatred of the Jews into the post-WW II, modern era.

Antisthenes *d.* 365 BC. Greek philosopher. Antisthenes was a follower of Socrates and founded the Greek school of Cynics *(q.v.)*.

Antoine, André 1858–1943. French actor, manager, and critic, influential in French theater. He founded the Théâtre Libre in Paris (1887) and there presented naturalistic plays. He also opened the Théâtre Antoine (1897) and later was director of the Odéon in Paris.

Antoine, duke of Montpensier *See* **Affair of the Spanish Marriages**

Antonescu, Ion 1882–1946. Romanian general and dictator. Made premier by King Carol (1940), he assumed dictatorial powers and forced Carol's abdication (1940). He allied Romania with Germany during WW II, declared war on the USSR (1941), and was arrested in a coup in 1944.

Antoninus, Marcus Aurelius *See* **Marcus Aurelius**; *see also* **Caracalla**

Antoninus Pius ⟨Titus Aurelius Fulvus Boinonius Arrius Antoninus⟩ AD 86–161. Roman emperor (AD 138–161), successor to Hadrian. One of the "five good emperors," he continued the period of general prosperity and built the Antonine Wall.

Antonius, Marcus *See* **Antony**

Antony ⟨Antonius, Marcus⟩ ⟨Marc Antony⟩ *c*83–30 BC. Roman soldier, political leader, and ally of J. Caesar. His love affair with Cleopatra *(q.v.)* is near legendary. A courageous soldier, he served with Caesar in Gaul (54 BC), became a tribune (49), and joined Caesar in the civil war against Pompey (notably at the Battle of Pharsalus [48], in which Pompey was defeated). He became consul with Caesar (44) and, after Caesar's assassination, forced the conspirators to flee Rome. Antony for a time opposed both the Senate and Caesar's heir,

Octavian (later Augustus Caesar). But after gaining the support of Lepidus, Antony came to terms with Octavian, and the three (Octavian, Antony, and Lepidus) formed the Second Triumvirate, with Antony ruling Asia. There followed the murders of hundreds of senators and the Battle of Philippi (42), resulting in the deaths of Cassius and Brutus. Antony then began (c42) his affair with Cleopatra, was forced to leave Egypt (40), and at Rome married Octavian's sister. He soon returned to Egypt and Cleopatra, however, and, by his dissolute life-style, alienated both Octavian and the Senate. Octavian attacked and defeated Antony at Actium (31), and, when Octavian pursued him to Alexandria, both Antony and Cleopatra committed suicide (30).

Antwerp Belgian city (pop. 197,000), a commercial center and important European port. A Norman fort in the 9th cent., it was chartered in 1291 and rose to prominence (15th cent.), when it replaced Bruges as a center for the cloth trade. By the 16th cent., it was the most important commercial and financial center in Europe. By the mid-17th cent., however, the city had suffered a number of reverses, including conquest by Spain and the closing of its port by the Peace of Westphalia (1648), and it declined quickly. Napoleon reopened the port (1795), and in the 19th cent. it again began to prosper. The Germans captured it in WW I (1914–18) and WW II (1940–44).

Anu Ancient Babylonian god, the leading member of a triad of gods with Enlil and Ea. They were the gods of heaven, earth, and water, respectively.

Anvari ⟨Anwari⟩ c1126–c1189. Persian poet. Anvari was renowned for both his lyric and satirical skills. His works are collected in the *Divan*.

Anvil, Operation ⟨Operation Dragoon⟩ Allied invasion of southern France (Aug. 15, 1944) during WW II. This landing by the American Seventh Army and the French First Army met little resistance and quickly linked up with Gen. G. Patton's forces in Switzerland.

Anville, Jean Baptiste Bourguignon d' 1697–1782. French geographer and cartographer whose maps of ancient and medieval geography are noted for their accuracy. His work led to great improvements in mapmaking.

Anwari *See* **Anvari**

ANZAC Combined Australian and New Zealand Army Corps that saw action during WW I. The unit was noted for its efforts in the Battle of Gallipoli (1915) and in later battles in France.

Anzio Historic town in central Italy. A Roman resort in ancient times, it was the birthplace of Caligula and Nero. In WW II, the Allied landings (Jan., 1944) here and at Nettuno met stiff German resistance, which stalled the drive to Rome.

Apache Indians American Indian tribes of the US Southwest. Apaches were farmer-warriors and are believed to have migrated to the Southwest from Canada about AD 1000. Some tribes, however, were also driven south from the Midwest plains by the Comanche and Ute as late as the 18th cent. Apaches attacked Spanish colonials from the 17th cent. and engaged in the bloody Apache and Navaho wars against Americans in the 19th cent. The Apaches formerly consisted of many subgroups, including Jicarilla, Chiricahua, Coyotero, and Kiowa.

apartheid Racial segregation policy enforced by the white supremacist government of the Republic of South Africa. White domination of native Africans has been part of government policy since creation of the South African state (1910). But apartheid, aiming at complete physical separation of the races, was articulated by the Afrikaner National Party government in 1948. Since then the government has resettled part of the native black population in rural "homelands," designated for blacks only, and otherwise strictly regulates them. South Africa was forced out of the British Commonwealth (1961) because of its apartheid policies.

Apelles *fl.* 4th cent. BC. Greek painter, considered the greatest of his time. He was court painter to Philip II and Alexander the Great. None of his works survives and he is known only because of his great reputation.

Aphrodite Greek goddess of love, fertility, and beauty, identified with the Roman Venus. Aphrodite won the apple of discord from Paris, and this led to the Trojan War. She was mother of Aeneas and a lover of Adonis.

Apocalypse, Four Horsemen of the *See* **Four Horsemen of the Apocalypse**

Apocrypha Collection of 14 books appended to the authorized (King James) version of the Old Testament, considered uncanonical by Jewish and Protestant faiths. They do not appear in the Hebrew version of the Bible but are included in the Septuagint (Greek) and Vulgate (Latin) versions.

Apollinaire, Guillaume 1880–1918. French poet, a leading figure in the Paris avant-garde movement. His poetry was experimental and his only play, *Les Mamelles de Tirésias*, was an early experiment in surrealism.

Apollinarianism Christian heresy that began with Apollinarius of Laodicea (d. AD 390?). Apollinarius taught that because of Jesus' divine nature, he was not truly human and therefore did not possess both perfectly human and perfectly divine natures. This heresy was condemned by the Council of Constantinople (AD 381).

Apollo ⟨Phoebus Apollo⟩ Greek god, one of the leading gods of Olympus. He was the god of archery, healing, music, and prophecy, and was also known in Roman religion as Apollo. His chief temple was at Delphi, and, as Phoebus Apollo, he was the god of light. He was later identified by the Greeks with Helios, the sun god.

Apollodorus *fl.* 5th cent. BC. Athenian painter. He is believed to have introduced the technique of shading light and color in painting. None of his works survives.

Apollonius of Perga *fl.* 3d cent. BC. Greek mathematician. His treatise on conic sections is a major mathematical work of antiquity. It contains first use of the terms "parabola," "hyperbola," and "ellipse."

Apollo program US program to land a man on the moon. Inaugurated May, 1961, by Pres. J. Kennedy, the program included a number of preliminary missions and several moon landings. Apollo 8 was the first manned moon orbit (Dec., 1968), and Apollo 11 was the first moon landing (July 20, 1969). In the latter, Astronaut N. Armstrong became the first man to walk on the moon. Apollo 17 (Dec., 1972) was the last flight of the program. (*See also* Space Exploration.)

apostle One of the twelve disciples chosen by Jesus to act as the principal missionaries of Christianity. The twelve are Peter, Andrew, John, James (son of Zebedee), James (son of Alphaeus), Philip, Bartholomew, Thomas, Thaddaeus, Matthew, Simon, and Matthias (who replaced Judas Iscariot). Early Christian missionaries, who were primarily responsible for founding the church in a country, are also referred to as apostles. Thus, Saint Patrick is the apostle of Ireland.

Apostolic Constitutions A compilation of early Christian ecclesiastical law. At first thought to be the work of the apostles, they are now believed to have been written by a 4th-cent. Syrian author. They provide valuable insight into the practices of the early Christians.

apostolic succession Christian doctrine holding that the special powers of the apostles have passed through each of their successors to the present-day bishops of the church. The doctrine is accepted by the Roman Catholic, Eastern Orthodox, Anglican, and other churches.

Appeals to Rome, Act in Restraint of *See* **Act in Restraint of Appeals to Rome**

appeasement policy British policy toward Nazi Germany from 1937 to 1939. The British, under Prime Minister N. Chamberlain, attempted to avoid war by offering Germany territorial concessions, a policy that proved both unpopular in Britain and ultimately unsuccessful.

Appian of Alexandria *fl.* 2d cent. AD. Greek-born Roman historian. He wrote a 24-volume history of Roman conquests, from the founding of Rome to the reign of Trajan. Less than half survives.

Appian Way Roman road built (312 BC) to connect Rome with Capua. It was later extended to Brindisi and was over 350 miles long, becoming the main road to the East.

Appleseed, Johnny *See* **Chapman, John**

Appomattox Courthouse Site in central Virginia where, on Apr. 9, 1865, Gen. R.E. Lee surrendered Confederate forces under his command to Gen. U.S. Grant, thereby effectively ending the Civil War. Lee's westward retreat (after the Battle of Five Forks) had been blocked by surrounding Union armies, and he was thus forced to surrender.

Apries *d.* 569 BC. Egyptian king (c588–570 BC), successor to his father, Psamtik II. He engaged in unsuccessful wars against the Babylonians under Nebuchadnezzar.

April Laws *See* **March Laws**

April Theses Plan, formulated by the Russian revolutionary N. Lenin, to replace the bourgeois provisional government of Russia with one controlled by Bolshevik-dominated soviets. Having returned to Russia after the March Revolution, Lenin first outlined his plan Apr. 17, 1917. It was adopted by the Bolsheviks after some early resistance and was carried out during the November Revolution. In addition to the takeover of power, the plan called for an end to Russian participation in WW I, distribution of land to peasants, nationalization of banks, and soviet control of manufacturing and distribution.

Apuleius, Lucius ⟨Apuleius of Madaura⟩ *fl.* 2d cent. AD. Latin philosopher and writer whose romance *Metamorphoses*, or *The Golden Ass*, had a major influence on later novelists.

Apuleius of Madaura *See* **Apuleius, Lucius**

Aquae Sextiae, Battle of ⟨Aix, ~⟩ Roman victory (102 BC) over invading Gallic tribes, the Teutones. The Romans, under G. Marius, decimated the Teutones at Aquae Sextiae, in what is now southern France, and later defeated the Cimbri, allies of the Teutones.

Aquila Ponticus *fl.* 2d cent. AD. Jewish translator of the Old Testament from Hebrew into Greek. His literal translation was used by the Hebrews for centuries.

Aquitaine Region of southwestern France. Conquered by Caesar (56 BC), it was made a kingdom by Charlemagne. The marriages of Eleanor of Aquitaine (12th cent. AD) resulted in a long struggle between England and France for possession of the kingdom. France acquired complete control by the end of the Hundred Years' War (1337–1453).

Aquitaine, Eleanor of *See* **Eleanor of Aquitaine**

arabesque Decorative style important in Muslim cultures. Derived by Muslim craftsmen from an earlier Hellenistic decorative style, it is characterized by intricately entwined vines, leaves, and other flowing lines.

Arabia ⟨Arabian Peninsula⟩ Peninsular region in the Mideast. Earliest known civilization in the region centered around the ancient Sabaean, Minaean, and Himyarite kingdoms. The birthplace of Islam (7th cent. AD), Arabia is today one of the world's most important oil-producing regions. It includes the modern countries of Saudi Arabia, Yemen (Aden), Yemen (Sana), Oman, Kuwait, United Arab Emirates, Qatar, and Bahrain.

Arabian Peninsula *See* **Arabia**

Arab-Israeli War **1.** First ∼ War (1948–49) between Israeli and allied Arab states (Egypt, Syria, Transjordan, Iraq, and Lebanon). War broke out after the creation of the Israeli state (May 14, 1948). The Arabs at first gained territories in the southeast and captured Old Jerusalem. A four-week UN-negotiated truce (June, 1948) was followed by Israeli offensives and finally a cease-fire (Jan. 7, 1949), by which time the Israelis had regained most of the lost territories. Separate armistice agreements (not formal treaties) were negotiated with the Arab states in early 1949. As a result of the war, some 400,000 Palestinian Arabs from the former Palestine fled to neighboring Arab countries. These refugees gave impetus to renewed Arab-Israeli conflicts and creation of the Palestine Liberation Organization. **2.** Second ∼ War (Oct.-Nov., 1956) between Israel and Egypt. Taking advantage of international tensions created by G. Nasser's nationalization of the Suez Canal *(q.v.)*, Israeli forces, led by M. Dayan, invaded (Oct. 29) the Sinai Peninsula. In five days of fighting, up to the Nov. 6 cease-fire, the Israelis captured nearly all the Sinai east of the canal. The Israelis turned the captured territories over to UN forces (1957), accepting guarantees of Israeli access to the Gulf of Aqaba. **3.** Third ∼ War ⟨Six-Day War⟩ (June 5–10, 1967) between Israel and the Arab states of Egypt, Syria, and Jordan. Provoked by border incidents and Egypt's closing of Israeli access to the Gulf of Aqaba, the Israelis attacked the Arab countries (June 5). They knocked out the Arab air capability, then took the Sinai, the West Bank, Old Jerusalem, and the Golan Heights. The war ended June 10, though no treaties were negotiated. **4.** Fourth ∼ War (Oct. 6–25, 1973) between Israel and allied Arab states (Egypt and Syria, supported by Iraq, Libya, and Jordan). In a surprise move on the Jewish holiday of Yom Kippur the Egyptians attacked across the Suez Canal and the Syrians attacked from the north. The Israelis fell back initially but pushed back the Arabs on both fronts, finally even gaining a foothold on the east bank of the Suez. Though fighting continued sporadically on the Syrian front (ending May 31, 1974), the Israelis agreed (Jan 18, 1974) to limited withdrawal and establishment of a UN peacekeeping force.

Arab League Loose federation of Arab countries founded (1945) to promote Arab unity and interests. Frequently rendered impotent in political matters because of internal divisions, the league has been more successful in economic and administrative affairs. It failed (1948) to prevent formation of Israel, instituted a mutual defense pact (1950), and since then has been largely ineffective in the crises brought on by Arab-Israeli wars. The original members include Egypt, Syria, Lebanon, Jordan, Saudi Arabia, Iraq, and Yemen. Since 1945, other Arab nations and the PLO have joined. Egypt was ousted (Mar., 1979) after signing peace accords with Israel.

Arab Socialist Renaissance party *See* **Ba'th party**

Arachne In Greek mythology, a maiden who challenged the goddess Athena to a contest in weaving. Athena destroyed Arachne's weaving, and the girl hanged herself. Athena then turned her into a spider and the rope into a cobweb.

Arafat, Yasir *See* **Palestine Liberation Organization**

Aragon, Catherine of *See* **Catherine of Aragon**

Aragon, kingdom of Medieval kingdom in what is now northeast Spain. Created as a kingdom (1035) by Sancho III for his son Ramiro I, Aragon eventually became one of the great medieval Spanish kingdoms. Ramiro and Alfonso I greatly expanded the original domains southward and, in 1137, added Catalonia. Many territories, including Valencia, Sardinia, the Two Sicilies, and Naples, were added from the 13th to 15th cent. It was united with Castile (1479) by Ferdinand V and Isabella I to form the basis of the modern Spanish state.

Arai Hakuseki 1657–1725. Japanese scholar, historian, and philosopher. He was noted for his writings on Confucianism.

Arakcheyev, Aleksey Andreyevich 1769–1834. Russian general. He counseled czars Paul I and Alexander I. One of Czar Alexander's most trusted advisers, he helped to reorganize the Russian army.

Araki Sadao 1877–1966. Japanese general, war minister (1931–33), and education minister

(1937–39). An ultranationalist faction leader, Araki urged Japanese world domination. He was sentenced to life imprisonment as a war criminal after WW II.

Aram   Ancient country in what is now Syria. The Aramaean people established a number of kingdoms in the region after 1200 BC. The Aramaeans unsuccessfully attacked Israel during King David's reign and later established themselves as kings of Babylonia. Western Aramaean kingdoms fell to the Assyrians (720 BC), while eastern kingdoms became part of the Chaldean Empire (7th cent.).

Arango, Doroteo   *See* **Villa, Francisco**

Aranjuez, Revolt of   Spanish rebellion (Mar. 17–19, 1808) at Aranjuez, in central Spain. Rioting here forced the dismissal of Prime Minister M. Godoy and the abdication of Charles IV during Napoleon's invasion of Spain (1807–08).

Araucanian Wars   Warfare (16th cent.) between Spanish conquistadors and the fierce Araucanian Indians in Chile. Outbreaks of violence began in the 1530s, and, in 1541, P. Valdivia fended off Araucanian attacks and founded Santiago. The Indians again threatened Santiago after massacring (1553) Valdivia's expedition farther south. Spanish forces ultimately forced the Indians southward but never conquered them. The Araucanians rose again (19th cent.) when settlers threatened these homelands in the south. They were finally defeated (1870) by the Chilean Army.

Ararat   Mountain at the eastern frontier of Turkey, traditionally considered the resting place of Noah's Ark. The kingdom of Ararat, roughly equivalent to what became Armenia, flourished from the 9th to 7th cent. BC.

Arausio, Battle of   Victory (Oct. 6, 105 BC) for Gallic tribes, the Cimbri and Teutones, over the Romans at this town in what is now southern France. Roman losses were heavy.

Arbela, Battle of   *See* **Gaugamela, Battle of**

Arbogast   d. AD 394. Frankish general in Roman service. A commander under Theodosius I, he defeated the rebel Maximus (AD 388). He failed in his attempt to install Eugenius as emperor of the West (392), and was defeated by Theodosius at Frigidus (Sept. 5–6, 394), now in northern Italy.

Arcadia   Region of ancient Greece in the central Peloponnesus, largely isolated from the rest of Greece. Its major city was Megalopolis. Arcadian cities sporadically fought against the Spartans and formed the short-lived Arcadian League (370–362 BC), with Theban support, to resist Sparta.

Arcadia Conference   First major WW II council involving the US, held in Washington, D.C. (Dec. 22, 1941–Jan. 14, 1942). It was attended by Pres. F. Roosevelt and Prime Minister W. Churchill and resulted in the first UN declaration and plans for coordinating the military effort.

Arcadian League   *See* **Arcadia**

Arcadius   AD c377–408. First Roman emperor of the East (AD 395–408). On the death of his father, Emperor Theodosius I, the Roman Empire was permanently divided into Eastern and Western empires. Arcadius' brother, Honorius, ruled the West. Arcadius was an ineffectual ruler, left the government to his ministers (including Rufinus), and was controlled by Eudoxia (d. 404), his wife.

Arc de Triomphe de l'Étoile   Triumphal arch in Paris at the end of the Champs Elysées. Built (1806–36) to commemorate the victories of Napoleon, it is a symbol of French military honor.

Arce, Manuel José   1783?–1847. Central American leader, first president of the Central American Confederation (1825–29).

archaeology   The study of past human cultures through the recovery and analysis of material remains. Archaeology is broadly divided into the study of prehistoric and historic cultures and is also divided into particular periods or cultures, such as Egyptian, Greek, and Roman. Archaeology as a science began with the 15th-cent. interest in Greek sculpture. Since then, such important discoveries as Pompey and Troy, the deciphering of Egyptian hieroglyphics, and the finding of the Dead Sea Scrolls have contributed greatly to archaeologists' knowledge of ancient cultures. Archaeologists now employ sophisticated methods for excavating and dating artifacts and draw on a wide variety of scientific disciplines in the analysis of their finds.

archangels   Chief angels in heaven. Archangels are recognized in Christian, Judaic, Islamic, and other faiths. The four most important are Michael, Gabriel, Raphael, and Uriel (principally Judaic).

archbishop   In Christian ecclesiastical hierarchy, a bishop with certain supervisory powers over the bishops of a province. The title came into use in the Western church during the 7th cent.

archduke   Title of nobility, primarily used by the Austrian Hapsburgs. It was first conferred (1453) by Hapsburg Holy Roman Emperor Frederick III and since then has been a hereditary title of male Hapsburg heirs.

Archer, William   1856–1924. A Scottish critic, playwright, and translator. His translations of H. Ibsen's works influenced the development of British and American drama.

Archidamian War   War (431–421 BC) between Sparta and Athens. It was the opening phase of the

Peloponnesian War *(q.v.)*. The first Spartan invasions of Attica in the war were led by King Archidamus II *(d. 427 BC)*.

Archidamus II *See* **Archidamian War**

Archimedes 287–212 BC. Greek mathematician and inventor noted for his contributions to the fields of geometry, mechanics, and hydrostatics. Among his discoveries were the principle of buoyancy (Archimedes' principle), a water pump known as Archimedes' screw, and the principle of the lever.

archons Magistrates in ancient Greece. Originally they had political, religious, and military powers in the city-states (especially Athens), but by the 5th cent. BC their roles had been reduced to judicial functions. The first archons were chosen from among the aristocracy. As the office declined in importance, however, eligibility was extended to other classes, and, in the 5th cent. BC, all citizens were eligible to hold the office.

Arctic Region surrounding the North Pole, including northern parts of North America, Europe, and Asia. The first known exploration of the region may have been by the Greek Pytheas (4th cent. BC). Subsequently Irish monks (9th cent. AD) and Norse Vikings (10th cent. AD) were in Iceland. Following the voyages of J. Cabot, European exploration began in earnest, stimulated largely by the search for Northeast and Northwest passages to Asia. Other explorers followed, including M. Frobisher, V. Bering, H. Hudson, J. Franklin, F. Nansen, and R. Amundsen. R. Peary became the first to reach the Pole (1909), and R. Byrd flew over it (1926). In 1958, the nuclear submarine *Nautilus* made the first voyage under the polar icecap.

Ardashir I ⟨Artaxerxes⟩ *d. AD c241.* King of Persia (AD *c226–c241*), who founded the Sassanidae dynasty. He overthrew the Parthian king, established Zoroastrianism as the state religion, expanded his empire, and warred against Roman emperor Alexander Severus (AD 231–233).

Ardennes, Battle of the *See* **Bulge, Battle of the**

Arendt, Hannah 1906–1975. A German-born American political scientist. A fugitive from Nazi Germany, she is noted for her studies of totalitarianism. Among her works are *Origins of Totalitarianism*, *The Human Condition*, and *Eichmann in Jerusalem*.

Areopagus Council of elders in ancient Athens. Formed sometime after 1000 BC and composed of former archons (magistrates) of Athens, the Areopagus functioned as a legislative body and guardian of Athenian laws. Under Draco, the council had judicial powers in murder cases, and, under Solon, its judicial powers were broadened (594 BC).

However, Solon reduced its legislative functions and instituted the Boule, or Council of 400, for these functions.

Ares Greek god of war and one of the chief gods of Olympus. He is identified with the Roman god Mars.

Argentina Republic located in southern South America. Its capital is Buenos Aires. First colonized by the Spanish in the 16th cent., Argentina gained its independence in 1816, overcame years of political turmoil, and by the late 19th cent. had become a leading nation of South America. Key events in the history of Argentina include:

1516   Río de la Plata, major coastal river delta region, discovered by Juan Díaz de Solís.

1536   Spanish established settlement at what is now Buenos Aires.

1776   Buenos Aires made seat of a viceroyalty that ruled regions of Argentina, Paraguay, Bolivia, and Uruguay.

1806–7   British force attacked and occupied Buenos Aires, forcing the viceroy to flee; Argentine forces expelled the British the following year and repelled a second British force.

1810   Argentine revolutionaries refused to recognize Spanish king Joseph Bonaparte, installed by Napoleon; revolutionaries deposed the viceroy (May 25) and established a ruling junta; the rebels later broke with representatives of deposed King Ferdinand VII, thereby instigating war with the royalists.

1810–13   Revolutionaries tried unsuccessfully to liberate all of viceroyalty; royalist forces retained control of what is now Uruguay, Paraguay, and Bolivia, however.

1816   Congress of Tucuman declared complete independence from Spain (July 9); United Provinces of Río de la Plata formed from liberated territories.

1819–20   Civil war between leaders from Buenos Aires, who wanted strong central government, and leaders from other provinces, who favored federal system of government; political turmoil continued into the 1830s.

1825–27   Argentina successfully aided Uruguayans in war against Brazil; this led to Uruguay's independence.

1835   J. Rosas assumed dictatorial powers as governor of Buenos Aires Province; rapidly extended his control over other Argentine provinces through reign of terror; united Argentina under his firm control until 1852.

1852   Rosas overthrown by J. Urquiza.

1853   Argentine constitution adopted; Argentine Republic proclaimed; Urquiza became first president.

1854–59 Buenos Aires Province seceded from the republic; defeated and forced to return five years later.

1862 Buenos Aires made capital of Argentina.

1864–70 War of the Triple Alliance with Paraguay.

1880–86, 1896–1904 Julio Argentino Roca became president; rapid development of Argentina during his presidencies.

1902 Long-standing border dispute with Chile settled.

1914–18 Argentina remained neutral during WW I.

1916–22, 1928–30 Radical party led by H. Irigoyen came to power; instituted many reforms but provoked growing opposition.

1930 Pres. H. Irigoyen overthrown by conservatives, led by Gen. José Uriburu, as economic problems caused by the Great Depression mounted.

1938 Radicals under Roberto Ortíz returned to power; kept Argentina neutral during WW II though fascist groups were active.

1943 Military coup; ruling military junta included Col. Juan Perón.

1946–55 J. Perón established popular dictatorship; regime marked by reduction of civil and political liberties.

1949 Perón secured new constitution allowing him to succeed himself as president.

1955 Military forced ouster of Perón; new government faced serious economic problems as well as the problem of dealing with Perón's followers (Peronistas).

1966 Military seized power to prevent Peronistas from gaining office; Gen. Juan Carlos Ongania in office as president (1966–70).

1971 Ban on political parties (since 1966) ended.

1972 Juan Perón returned to Argentina (Nov. 17) after 17-year exile.

1973 First elections since 1965; Héctor J. Cámpora, a Peronista, won presidency.

1973 President Cámpora resigned (July 13) to allow Perón to run for presidency.

1973–74 President J. Perón in office as elected president; his wife Isabel elected vice-president.

1974 Mass arrests (May) in Tucuman province begun to counter left-wing opposition to the Perón government.

1974 Perón died in office (July); his wife succeeded him as president.

1974 President Isabel Perón declared (Nov.) a state of siege following outbreak of numerous terrorist attacks.

1976 President Perón overthrown (Mar.) and arrested in military coup; Lieut. Gen. Jorge Rafaél Videla became new president.

1977 Inflation reported near 350% for previous year.

1981 Former president I. Perón left the country (July) for Spain.

1981–82 Gen. Leopoldo Galtieri in office as president.

1982 Falkland Islands War (Apr.–June); Argentine invasion force driven off islands by British troops.

1982 Galtieri ousted (June) after Argentina lost Falkland Islands War.

Arginusae, Battle of Sea battle during the Peloponnesian War. The Spartan Navy, under Callicratidas, was defeated by the Athenians, under Conon, off the Arginusae Islands in the Aegean Sea (406 BC.). Callicratidas was killed and over half of the Spartan ships were sunk.

Argolis Region of ancient Greece in the northeast Peloponnesus. Its most important city was Argos.

Argonaut In Greek legend, a member of the crew that sailed with Jason aboard the ship *Argo* in search of the Golden Fleece.

Argos *See* **Argus**

Argos City of ancient Greece, in northeast Peloponnesus. Inhabited since the early Bronze Age, it was a major power, and enemy of Sparta, in the Peloponnesus from the 7th cent. BC. It joined the Achaean League in 229 BC and was captured by Rome in 146 BC. Argos was a center of worship of the goddess Hera.

Argus ⟨Argos⟩ In Greek mythology, the many-eyed creature that guarded Io.

Argyll *See* **Campbell, earls of Argyll**

Ariadne In Greek mythology, the daughter of King Minos of Crete. She loved Theseus and helped him to slay the Minotaur. Later abandoned by Theseus, she wedded the god Dionysus.

Arianism Christian heresy (4th cent. AD) concerning the nature of Christ in relation to God. Arianism was the subject of a great controversy in the East, provoked (c318) by an Alexandrian priest, Arius (d. 336). Arius' teachings, which held that Christ was not of the same divine nature as God, were condemned at the First Council of Nicaea (1st ecumenical). The controversy continued, however, and a number of factions arose in opposition to the orthodox Christian Nicene party. These factions were supported by Constantius II, Roman ruler in the East, and, when he became sole emperor (350), he imposed Arianism throughout the empire. The accession of orthodox Christian rulers in the West (Gratian) and East (Theodosius I) brought an end to the controversy within the empire. The First Council of Constantinople (381) was convened and affirmed the Nicene formula. Arianism survived among Germanic tribes until the mid-7th cent.

Arius *See* **Arianism**

Arias de Ávila, Pedro ⟨Pedrarias Dávila⟩ ⟨Pedro Arias Dávila⟩ c1440–1531? Spanish soldier and colonial administrator noted for his cruelty. He replaced V. Balboa as governor in Panama (1514–26) and was involved in Balboa's execution. He expanded Spanish colonial rule and founded Panama City (1519).

Arimathea, Saint Joseph of *See* **Joseph of Arimathea, Saint**

Arion Legendary Greek poet and musician, said to have lived in the 7th cent. BC at Corinth. Reputed to be the inventor of the dithyramb.

Ariosto, Ludovico 1474–1533. Italian epic and lyric poet. His major work, the *Orlando Furioso*, an epic based on the story of Roland, is considered a Renaissance masterpiece.

Aristarchus of Samos *fl.* 3d cent. BC Greek astronomer believed to have been the first to maintain that the earth revolves around the sun. He is also said to have deduced that night and day are caused by the earth's rotation.

Aristides *d.* c468 BC. Athenian general and statesman, a commander at the Battle of Marathon, for which he was made chief archon. Later ostracized for opposition to Themistocles, he returned to fight with Athens at Salamis (480 BC) and Plataea (479). He was founder of the Delian League (478).

aristocracy Government by a special or privileged class of people, often the landed or very wealthy, considered especially worthy of ruling. It is theoretically distinct from oligarchy, in that power is wielded for the best interests of the state, not for personal gain. In modern times the term is often used to denote the privileged class itself. The governments of Athens (to the 5th cent. BC), Sparta, and Rome (during the Republic) are examples of government by aristocrats.

Aristogiton *See* **Harmodius and Aristogiton**

Aristophanes c448–c388 BC. Athenian dramatist, considered the greatest writer of ancient Greek comedy. Little is known of Aristophanes' life, but his comedies provide a revealing picture of the society, the literature and the politics of his day. His plays range from an attack on the Peloponnesian War to a satire on Socrates. He is believed to have written about 40 plays, of which 11 survive. They include *The Birds*, *The Frogs*, *Lysistrata*, *The Clouds*, *The Acharnians*, and *The Knights*.

Aristotelianism The great body of Aristotle's teachings and subsequent additions and interpretations that have accrued to it since Aristotle's lifetime (4th cent. BC). Aristotelianism flourished within and greatly influenced many cultures outside Greece. Many of Aristotle's fundamental doctrines continue to be influential in modern times. Aristotelianism spread from Greece to Rome, and, after the fall of Rome, Aristotle's teachings were lost in the West. Aristotelianism flourished (from 9th cent. AD) among the Arabs, however, and was reintroduced to the West by Muslim and Jewish scholars (12th and 13th cents.). Through the works of Saint Thomas Aquinas (13th cent.), who synthesized Aristotelian rationalism and Christian thought, Aristotelianism greatly influenced the course of medieval scholasticism and Roman Catholic theology. (*See also* Aristotle.)

Aristotle 384–322 BC. Macedonian Greek philosopher and scientist, one of the great thinkers of all time. His works in philosophy, science, ethics, and esthetics had a major influence on the development of civilization in the West. Aristotle studied (367–347 BC) under Plato at the Academy in Athens and later tutored (342–335?) Alexander the Great. Returning to Athens in 335, he opened a school (the Lyceum) and taught there until just before his death. His works, lost in the West after the fall of Rome, were reintroduced by Arab scholars in the 9th cent. and formed the basis of scholasticism (*q.v.*). In his time, Aristotle and his followers, known as Peripatetics, stressed the importance of observation, the necessary correlation of theory to fact, and the value of logic. Aristotle's works, actually compiled from lecture notes two centuries after his death, include *Organon*, on logic; *Nicomachean Ethics*, on moral philosophy; *Metaphysics*, on fundamental metaphysical concepts; *Politics*; *Poetics*, on esthetics; *Constitution of Athens*, on Athenian government; and works in the sciences. (*See also* Aristotelianism.)

Arizona US state (pop. 2,717,900) in the Southwest. Originally inhabited by Pueblo, Apache, and Navaho Indians, the region was explored by the Spanish in 1539. Although Indians successfully prevented permanent settlements in the region until the 18th cent., it was ruled as part of New Spain (1598–1821) and part of independent Mexico (1821–48). By the Treaty of Guadalupe Hidalgo and the Gadsden Purchase (1848, 1853), it became US territory. The defeat of the Apaches (late 19th cent.) brought a rise in ranching operations there, and in 1912 Arizona became the 48th state. The state constitution was passed in 1911.

Arkansas 25th US state (pop. 2,285,500), located in the south-central part of the country. The region was explored by the Spanish (1541), and the first permanent settlement, Arkansas Post (1682), was established by the French. Settled for a time under the Mississippi Scheme (c1720), the region changed hands between the French and Spanish before the US bought it in the Louisiana Purchase (1803). It was established as a separate territory (1819), and then became a state (1836). The region was settled in the early 1800s, and during the Civil War it joined the Confederacy (1861). Resistance to enfranchisement of Negroes held up readmission to the Union until 1868. The current state constitution was passed in 1874.

Arkansas Post *See* **Arkansas**

Arkwright, Sir Richard 1732–92. English inventor of the cotton spinning frame and other power-driven weaving devices. He was a major figure in the development of the factory system of textile production in England.

Arles, Council of Roman Catholic church council (AD 314). Constantine I convened this council in Gaul to deal with the Donatists *(q.v.)*. It again condemned the Donatists and affirmed the supremacy of Rome.

Arlington, Henry Bennet, 1st earl of 1618–85. An English statesman. As secretary of state (1662–74) under King Charles II, he became a leading member of the Cabal *(q.v.)*. In 1674 he was impeached for corruption and pro-Catholicism. Acquitted, he resigned.

Armada *See* **Spanish Armada**

Armageddon Biblical place where, at the end of the world, the forces of evil on earth will war against the forces of God. It is believed that the ancient city of Megiddo, Palestine, site of numerous battles, was the model for Armageddon.

Armagnacs Faction of French noblemen whose war with the Burgundians (1411–18) for control of France figured in the Hundred Years' War. The Armagnac faction was formed by Bernard VII, count of Armagnac, following the murder of Louis d'Orléans (1407) in a struggle for control of the French throne. A Burgundian, John the Fearless, was in power when civil war broke out (1411) between the two factions. The Armagnacs seized control in 1413 but became embroiled in the defense of France against an invasion by English king Henry V. John the Fearless was subsequently able to regain control of the government (1418) and thereupon massacred the Armagnacs. John was assassinated (1419) and King Charles VII came to power. Charles' alliance with the Burgundians (1435) assured the Armagnacs' final decline. (*See also* Burgundians.)

Armenia Region and former kingdom of Asia Minor, located in northeast Turkey and southwest Russia. The Armenian people settled the area before the 6th cent. BC, and Armenia became an independent kingdom in 189 BC. The Romans soon conquered it (69–67 BC). Armenia was first to adopt Christianity as a state religion (AD 303), and in the 4th–5th cents. AD suffered persecutions at the hands of the Zoroastrian Persians. Armenia was subsequently conquered by many different peoples until the 16th cent., when the Ottoman Turks took over the region. From 1894 to 1915, Armenians suffered sporadic massacres by the Turks. During WW I, they revolted and established an independent Armenia (1918). By 1921, however, Armenian territory had been divided and annexed by the USSR and Turkey.

Armenian church ⟨*also called* the Gregorian church⟩ Eastern Christian sect and Armenian national church. Founded (AD 303) in the kingdom of Armenia, it was the first Christian state church. It broke with Rome after the Council of Chalcedon (451) in a dispute over Monophysitism. The church, though it has renewed ties with Rome, maintains a largely autonomous status.

Arm-in-Arm Convention *See* **National Union Convention**

Arminianism Christian theological movement. Begun (c1603) by Dutch religious reformer J. Arminius, the movement opposed Calvinists' extreme belief in predestination. Instead, the Arminians asserted free will was fully compatible with God's sovereignty over man. Arminians issued (1610) the Remonstrance, a statement of their position, and were condemned by the Dutch Synod of Dort (1618–19). Arminianism, however, later influenced J. Wesley and Methodist doctrine.

Arminius *d.* AD c19. Chief of German tribes, once a Roman citizen. He disgraced the Roman Empire when his forces surprised and decimated a Roman army (AD 9) commanded by Varus in the Teutoburg Forest, east of the Rhine River. Arminius was later badly beaten in battle (AD 16) against Germanicus Caesar.

Arminius, Jacobus ⟨Jacob Harmensen⟩ 1560–1609. Dutch theologian who opposed the Calvinist view of predestination and whose doctrines became known as Arminianism *(q.v.)*.

armistice A temporary halt in fighting, mutually agreed upon by belligerents. Strictly speaking, a general armistice does not end the state of war. This is technically accomplished by a peace treaty. In fact, however, armistices ended both WW I (Nov. 11, 1918) and the Korean War (July 27, 1953) and each was a form of peace treaty.

Armory Show *See* **Eight, The**

Armour, Philip Danforth 1832–1901. American meat-packer. He headed the Chicago-based Armour and Company (1875–99) and was responsible for innovations in meat-packing techniques. A noted philanthropist, he was charged in 1898–99 with selling tainted beef.

Arms, Assize of   *See* **Assize of Arms**

Armstrong, John   1758–1843. American general, politician, and diplomat. He authored the *Newburgh Letters* (1783), anonymous letters written during the American Revolution demanding payment of soldiers' back pay. Later, as secretary of war (1813–14), he was blamed for military reverses in the War of 1812, including the British capture of Washington, D.C.

Armstrong, Neil Alden   1930–. American astronaut. On July 20, 1969, Armstrong became the first man to set foot on the moon. As part of the Apollo 11 flight, he and E. Aldrin remained on the moon's surface for twenty hours, collecting samples and data.

Army of the Green Standard   Army in China established during the Ch'ing dynasty (1644–1912). At one time it numbered 600,000 men (stationed throughout the empire) and acted as a supplementary army to the military force established by the Banner System. It deteriorated in strength, however, and proved ineffective against rebels in the Taiping Rebellion (1860–65).

Arnauld ⟨Arnault⟩ ⟨Arnaut⟩   French family whose members were leaders of Jansenism. They include Antoine Arnauld (1612–94), his sister Jacqueline Marie Arnauld (1591–1661), and his brother Robert Arnauld d'Andilly (c1588–1674).

Arnault   *See* **Arnauld**

Arnaut   *See* **Arnauld**

Arnhem, Battle of   German victory (Sept. 17–25, 1944) in WW II. During the Allied drive across Europe, British and Polish airborne troops made a heroic but unsuccessful attempt to seize control of a bridge across the Rhine at Arnhem, The Netherlands.

Arnold, Benedict   1741–1801. US general and notorious traitor during the American Revolution. His brilliant campaigns at Lake Champlain (1776) and at Saratoga (1777) did not earn him the recognition he coveted. Disaffected, he attempted (1780) to surrender West Point to the British. The plot was uncovered; his accomplice, Major J. André, was executed; and Arnold fled to the British.

Arnold, Matthew   1822–88. English poet and critic, one of the great English literary figures of his day. An inspector of schools (1851–86) and an Oxford professor (1857–67), he published his first volume of poetry in 1849. He subsequently published collected works, such as *Other Poems* and *New Poems*, and works of literary and social crit-

icism, such as *Essays in Criticism* and *Culture and Anarchy*.

Arnold, Thomas   1795–1842. English educator. His reforms as headmaster of the Rugby School influenced the English system of public education. He was the father of Matthew Arnold.

Arnold of Brescia   c1090–1155. Italian monk and religious reformer. Opposed to church wealth and corruption, he supported a republican uprising in Rome, and in 1155 was arrested, tried, and executed.

Arnulf   c850–899. King of the East Franks (887–899) and Holy Roman Emperor (896–99). He overthrew his uncle, Holy Roman Emperor Charles III, and became king of the Germans, defeated the Normans (891), invaded Italy at Pope Formosus' invitation, and captured Rome (895). He was crowned emperor by the pope (896) and was the last Carolingian emperor.

Aroostook War   US-Canadian border controversy. Residents of Maine and New Brunswick were involved in a dispute over rival claims to the Aroostook Valley in 1838–39, though there was no actual bloodshed. The question was settled by the Webster-Ashburton Treaty (1842).

Árpád   c840–907. Magyar chief and Hungarian national hero. He led his people from Asia into what is now Hungary (c890) and founded the line of Hungarian kings known as the Árpád dynasty (ruled 997–1301).

Arras, Battle of   **1.** French victory (Aug. 24–25, 1654) at Arras, France, over Spanish forces in the last years of the Thirty Years' War. The French broke a Spanish siege of Arras, killing some 3,000 soldiers. **2.** Unsuccessful British offensive (Apr. 9–May 3, 1917) at Arras, France, during WW I. The offensive, intended to draw German forces northward, was commanded by British Field Marshal D. Haig. Losses were 75,000 Germans and 84,000 British.

Arras, Treaty of   **1.** In 1435, French king Charles VII and Philip the Good, duke of Burgundy, concluded a treaty that reconciled the Burgundians with the monarchy and ended the Burgundian alliance with England (under the Treaty of Troyes). **2.** In 1482, French king Louis XI signed a treaty with Maximilian I (later Holy Roman Emperor), providing for the marriage of his son to Maximilian's daughter. France got Artois and Franche-Comté, which it returned (1493) when the marriage was called off.

Arriaga, Manuel José de   1842–1917. Portuguese politician. A leader in the revolt (1910) that deposed King Manuel II, he was the first president (1911–15) of the republic. He resigned (1915), following royalist uprisings.

Arsacidae ⟨Arsacids⟩ ⟨Arshakuni⟩ Dynasty of Parthian rulers. Founded by Arsaces I (c250 BC), who overthrew the Seleucids, the dynasty ruled over Persia and Mesopotamia. The Arsacidae kings ruled until the Sassanidae conquest (AD c226). Noted rulers of the dynasty were Mithradates I and II (reigned 171–138 BC, 123–88 BC).

Arsacids *See* **Arsacidae**

Arshakuni *See* **Arsacidae**

Artaxerxes *See* **Ardashir I**

Artaxerxes I *d.* 425 BC. Persian king (465–425 BC), successor to his father Xerxes I. He put down revolts in Egypt and Bactria, and fought the Athenians. He is noted for his toleration toward Judaism.

Artaxerxes II *d.* c359 BC. Persian king (404–c359 BC), successor to his father, Darius II. Under his rule Persia lost control of Egypt, and his brother Cyrus the Younger led an unsuccessful uprising (ending 401 at Cunaxa) against him. Conflicts with the Greek city-states also erupted, and Persian hegemony in Greece was established by the King's Peace (386 BC).

Artaxerxes III *d.* 338 BC. Persian king (c359–338 BC), successor to his father, Artaxerxes II. He won power by murdering many of his relatives, and his reign was marked by cruelty and bloodshed. He conquered Egypt (343 BC) and checked the decline of the Persian Empire.

art deco Decorative style. Art deco is the style of art, architecture, and jewelry that developed in the 1920s. It is characterized by a streamlined look, achieved by the use of long, sleek, stylized lines.

Artemis Greek goddess of the hunt, hunters, and wildlife, identified with the Roman Diana. She was the daughter of Zeus and Leto, and sister of Apollo.

Artevelde, Jacob van c1290–1345. A Flemish statesman who, at the outset of the Hundred Years' War between England and France, allied himself with Edward III of England and became ruler (c1337) of the city of Ghent. Though Ghent was dependent on the English wool trade, Artevelde's extreme pro-English policies led to his murder.

art for art's sake *See* **Gautier, Théophile**

Arthur I 1187–1203? Duke of Brittany. On the death of his uncle, English king Richard I, his claim to the throne was usurped by his uncle, King John. Arthur was imprisoned (1202) by John, who is also believed to have murdered him.

Arthur, Chester Alan 1830–86. US president (1881–85), the 21st, successor to Pres. J. Garfield following his assassination (1881). A prominent New York lawyer, he was early identified as a machine politician because of his association with New York Republican party boss Sen. Roscoe Conkling (1829–88). Although he had been allied with the Stalwarts faction (q.v.), Arthur became the Republican nominee for vice-president, as running mate to Garfield, and entered office with him (1881). There was concern Arthur might corrupt the national government with machine politics. But when he became president (Sept. 19, 1881), he reassured an anxious public and governed with integrity throughout his tenure. During his presidency, the Pendleton Civil Service Act (1883) was passed and the Star Route Frauds came to trial. He did not seek reelection and died soon after he left office.

Arthurian legend The exploits of the legendary British King Arthur and his Knights of the Round Table, as developed in medieval romances and adventure stories. Prominent elements of the legend include Arthur's life and conquests; the legend of Merlin; Sir Lancelot's affair with Arthur's wife, Queen Guinevere; the quest for the Holy Grail and the exploits of Sir Galahad, Parsifal, and others; Arthur's death from wounds sustained in battle with Mordred (his nephew and enemy); and the final ruin of Camelot. The legends are thought to derive from Celtic myths. Among the major works in the Arthurian cycle are *Historia Regnum Britanniae* (c1135) by Geoffrey of Monmouth, *Roman de Brut* (c1155) by Wace, works by Chrétien de Troyes, and *Morte d'Arthur* by Sir T. Malory.

Articles of Confederation First Constitution of the US (1781–89), which established a confederation of the original thirteen states. Though a central government was created by the articles, real power resided with the states. The ultimate failure of this system led to creation of a strong federal government. The articles were drafted (1776) by J. Dickinson, were passed (Nov. 15, 1777) by the Continental Congress, and became effective Mar. 1, 1781. They kept the Continental Congress as the confederation's central government and theoretically gave it power to control national and international affairs. But the Congress lacked enforcement powers, and by 1786 it was clear a new form of government was needed. The articles were superseded (1789) by the Constitution, drafted at the Constitutional Convention (1787).

Articles of Schwabach Seventeen Protestant articles of faith drawn up (1529) by M. Luther and others at Schwabach, Bavaria. These articles subsequently formed the basis of the Augsburg Confession (q.v.).

Artigas, José Gervasio 1764–1850. Uruguayan revolutionary leader and national hero. He fought in the revolution (1811) against Spain and then against the junta governing the United Provinces. He established control over areas now in Uruguay and Argentina (1814–20) but was forced into exile by a Portuguese invasion from Brazil.

art nouveau Artistic style. Art Nouveau developed in the late 19th cent. and early 20th cent. as a reaction against the excesses of Victorian art. It emphasized the use of lines, as typified by works of P. Gauguin and H. Toulouse-Lautrec.

Arundel, Thomas Howard, earl of *See* **Howard, Thomas, 13th earl of Arundel**

Arval Brothers In Roman religion, a college of 12 priests, chosen from the highest Roman families, which presided over rites to promote fertility of the fields.

Aryabhata AD *c*476–550. Hindu mathematician and astronomer. He was one of the first to use algebra. He also explained solar and lunar eclipses and the earth's rotation on its axis.

Aryan Name once used for the Indo-European peoples who spread through south Asia and northern India in ancient times. J. Gobineau spread (19th cent.) a popular but false notion concerning the existence of a superior Aryan race. This notion later formed the basis for Nazi claims that they were a "master race" and was used to justify programs to exterminate Jews and other "inferior" races.

Asa *d.* 875 BC. Third king of Judah (*c*915–875 BC), successor to his father, Abijah. He opposed idolatry and recaptured territory from the Israelites.

Asante, Empire of *See* **Ashanti, Empire of**

Asbury, Francis 1745–1816. English-born American Methodist missionary. Asbury came to America (1771) and became the first Methodist bishop in America (1784). He inaugurated the circuit-rider system for frontier missionary work.

asceticism Doctrine that calls for self-denial of material and sensual pleasures in order to develop spiritual or inner powers. It has figured in the development of both philosophy and religion. It was advocated by the Cynics and Stoics in ancient Greece and was important in the development of monasticism.

Asclepius ⟨Aesculapius⟩ Greek god of medicine, son of Apollo. Taught by the centaur Chiron, Asclepius became so skillful that Zeus feared he would make men immortal and killed him.

Asculum, Battle of ⟨Ausculum⟩ **1.** Victory (279 BC) for Pyrrhus, king of Epirus, over the Romans in what is now southeast Italy. Some 40,000 soldiers under Pyrrhus defeated an equal force of Romans at great cost. Casualties numbered 6,000 Epirots to 3,500 Romans, giving rise to the expression "Pyrrhic victory." **2.** Victory (89 BC) for

Rome in the Social War *(q.v.)*. The revolt against Rome led by the Marsi and other tribes centered, in the south, at Asculum and was marked by a massacre of Roman citizens there (90 BC). The Romans retook the city (89 BC) and soon after ended the war by extending citizenship to the rebellious tribes.

Ashanti, Empire of ⟨Asante, ~⟩ African kingdom in what is now central Ghana. The Ashanti people occupied the region by the 13th cent. and, in the second half of the 17th, King Osei Tutu created the empire, with his capital at Kumasi. The Ashanti continued to expand their empire, supplying (18th cent.) the British and Dutch with slaves from conquered peoples. Wars with the British in the 1820s, 1860s, and 1870s led first to a British takeover (1896), then annexation to the British Gold Coast colony (1901).

Asher In the Old Testament, the eighth son of Jacob. His name was given to the tribe of Israel that lived in northwestern Palestine.

Ashikaga shogunate *See* **Muromachi period**

Ashley, William *See* **Sunday, Billie**

Ashurbanipal ⟨Assurbanipal⟩ ⟨Asurbanipal⟩ *d. c*626 BC. Last of the great Assyrian kings (*c*669–*c*626 BC) and successor to his father, Esarhaddon. He was unable to keep rebellious Egypt (660 BC) within the empire, though he crushed a rebellion in Babylon (*c*648 BC) and conquered the Elamites. During his reign the empire reached the height of its splendor. At Ninevah Ashurbanipal organized a famous royal library whose 22,000 clay tablets have become a prime source of knowledge about the Mesopotamian world.

Ashurnasirpal II *d.* 859 BC. Assyrian king (884–859 BC). A ruthless conqueror, he greatly expanded his empire, extending it westward to the Mediterranean. He centralized authority by installing governors in conquered lands and moved his capital from Ninevah to Calah.

Asia, Seven Churches in *See* **Seven Churches in Asia**

asiento de negros Spanish slave contracts. They were drawn up between Spain and a company or nation providing African slaves to Spain's American colonies. The most famous was made with the British South Sea Company (1713) and figured in the outbreak of the War of Jenkins' Ear.

Asís, Francisco de, duke of Cadiz *See* **Affair of the Spanish Marriages**

Askia Muhammad I *See* **Songhai, Empire of**

Asoka *d. c*232 BC. Indian emperor (273–232 BC) of the Maurya dynasty. A great conqueror, he unified much of India for the first time, bringing it under his control. Then, remorseful of the suffering he had caused, he made Buddhism the state religion and did much to ensure its spread throughout India.

Aspadana *See* **Isfahan**

Aspern-Essling, Battle of Battle (May 21–22, 1809, near Vienna) during the Napoleonic Wars. Austrian archduke Charles Louis, commanding 80,000 soldiers, defeated Napoleon's army of 80,000 men. Austria lost 24,000 men, the French over 20,000, including Marshal J. Lannes. It was Napoleon's most serious defeat up to that time.

Asquith, Herbert Henry, 1st earl of Oxford and Asquith 1852–1928. British statesman and prime minister (1908–16), successor to H. Campbell-Bannerman. A liberal member of Parliament from 1886, he became an influential party spokesman and helped return the liberals to power in 1905. He was chancellor of the exchequer (1905–08). As prime minister, he instituted old-age pensions (1908) and unemployment insurance (1911). Following a crisis over the budget, he won passage of the Parliament Act of 1911, by which the House of Lords lost its veto powers. Asquith's advocacy (1912) of Irish Home Rule precipitated a crisis in Ireland. Britain entered WW I under his guidance but military setbacks led to his ouster in 1916. He continued as Liberal Party leader until 1926.

Assad, Hafiz al- 1928–. Syrian general and president (1971–). Assad was a defense minister who became Syria's president (Feb. 22, 1971) after leading a coup d'état. He is considered a strong supporter of the PLO.

Assandum, Battle of Victory (Oct. 18, 1016) for the invading Danes, led by Canute, over the English, led by Edmund Ironside, in what is now Essex, England.

Assassin Member of secret Muslim order that, by its practice of murdering all enemies of the order, terrorized the Muslim world (11th–13th cents.). It was founded (c1090) by Hasan ibn al-Sabbah (d. 1124) after the capture of Almut, a fort in Persia (now Iran). From this base the order, an offshoot of the Ismaili sect of Islam, spread throughout Persia and into Syria. Its followers in Persia were said to have murdered caliphs, generals, and statesmen of the Abbassid caliphate before the order fell to Mongol invaders (1256). The Syrian branch fell (1272) to the Mamelukes of Egypt.

Assembly of Notables French assembly called (Feb., 1787) in the years prior to the French Revolution (1789–99). It was convoked by Finance Minister Charles Calonne (1734–1802) to approve a land tax needed to keep the government out of bankruptcy. The assembly refused to give its approval, as had the Parliament, and forced Calonne's ouster. The assembly was dissolved May, 1787.

Assisi, Saint Francis of *See* **Francis of Assisi, Saint**

assize Term meaning a session of a court of law, as in the case of Bloody Assizes (q.v.). The term was also used in reference to ordinances, as in Assize of Arms (q.v.).

Assize of Arms English ordinance issued by King Henry II (1181), ordering knights and freemen to acquire arms according to income and rank.

Assize of Clarendon English judicial reforms (1166). Henry II instituted these reforms, which included changes in criminal law and established the first organized code for judge and jury selection.

Assouan *See* **Aswan**

Assuan *See* **Aswan**

Assurbanipal *See* **Ashurbanipal**

Assyria An ancient Near Eastern empire that, at its height (9th–7th cents. BC), included lands in present-day Arabia, Egypt, Iran, Iraq, Syria, Palestine, and Turkey. Assyria's original capital, Ashur —named after the city's principal god—was located on the upper Tigris River as early as the 3d millennium BC. From Ashur Assyrians expanded by means of successive military conquests. Innovative and effective soldiers and organizers of what they conquered, they were legendary in antiquity for their cruelty. Their greatest expansion began with Tiglath-Pileser III, who subdued Babylonia. Sargon II defeated Israel (722 BC) and deported the inhabitants. The wars of his successor, Sennacherib, with his vassal, Hezekiah of Judah, are mentioned in the Bible. Under Ashurbanipal, Assyria reached its height (7th cent. BC). The cuneiform library collected about this time, and excavated from the ruins of the Assyrian capital at Ninevah, constitutes one of the best sources of knowledge about the ancient Near East. Early in the reign of Ashurbanipal, Egypt broke away from the empire in a revolt led by Psamtik I. Thereafter the decline was rapid. The Medes and the Babylonians conquered Ninevah itself in 612 BC.

Aston, Francis William 1877–1945. An English physicist. He developed the mass spectrograph and discovered a number of isotopes. He was awarded the Nobel Prize in Chemistry in 1922.

Astor, John Jacob 1763–1848. American merchant, financier, and founder of the Astor family fortune. In 1808, he formed the American Fur Company (q.v.), which came to monopolize US fur trade and is considered the first American trust.

Astor, Nancy Witcher Langhorne, Viscountess Astor 1879–1964. A British politician. She was the first woman to sit in the House of Commons (1919–45) and was identified with the "Cliveden set," a group of British leaders who sought to appease fascist powers in the 1930s.

Asturias, Kingdom of Former Spanish kingdom (718–910) located in northwestern Spain. Fleeing the Muslim invasion of Spain, Visigothic nobles formed this northern kingdom as the last Christian stronghold in Spain. In succeeding centuries it served as the starting point for the Christian reconquest of Spain and became known as the kingdom of León and Asturias.

Astyages *fl.* 6th cent. BC. Last king of the Median Empire (584–*c*550 BC). He was overthrown by Cyrus the Great, who thereby founded Persia.

Asunción Capital (pop. 435,000) of Paraguay. It was founded 1536 or 1537 and was the major city in the Rio de la Plata region until the rise of Buenos Aires.

Asurbanipal *See* **Ashurbanipal**

Aswan ⟨Assuan⟩ ⟨Assouan⟩ Egyptian city (pop. 217,000) in Upper Egypt. Called Syene in ancient times, it was once a trading center and stone quarry, supplying stone for the great works of the Pharaohs. Nearby are the Aswan Dam (completed 1902) and the Aswan High Dam (completed 1970).

Atahaulpa *d.* 1533. Last Inca ruler before the Spanish conquest of Peru. He overthrew his brother Huascar (1532) and made himself ruler of the Inca Empire in Peru. He was captured (1532) and executed by the Spanish conquistadors under F. Pizarro.

Atalanta In Greek mythology, a beautiful huntress who challenged her suitors to beat her in a footrace. Hippomenes won by dropping golden apples, which Atalanta stopped to retrieve. The two were changed into lions after defiling a shrine of Cybele.

Atatürk, Kemal 1881–1938. Turkish soldier, statesman, and president (1923–38), considered the founder of modern Turkey. He was a leading figure in the Young Turks and other nationalist groups from 1908. By 1921 he headed a nationalist army, which repulsed a Greek invasion (1919–22) and subsequently overthrew the sultan (1922). He abolished the sultanate (Nov. 1, 1922), and, during his long term as president of the republic, he instituted many reforms aimed at westernizing Turkey.

Athaliah *fl.* 9th cent. BC. In the Old Testament, the wife of Jehoram and mother of Ahaziah. She succeeded Ahaziah and became queen of Judah, slaying all the royal children but Jehoash. An uprising resulted in her death and the succession of Jehoash.

Athanagild *d.* 567. Visigothic king of Spain (554–567). He became king by an alliance with Byzantine emperor Justinian I and restored peace within his domains by ending persecution of Catholics. He was father of Frankish queens Brunhilda and Galswintha.

Athanasius, Saint AD *c*293–373. Patriarch of Alexandria (AD 328–373) and Doctor of the Church. He attended the First Council of Nicaea and became the chief defender of Nicene orthodoxy against Arianism. He was several times exiled for his beliefs.

atheism Philosophical doctrine. Atheists deny the existence of God or any other supernatural power. The term was used by the ancient Greeks, though atheism did not become significant in the Western world until the 18th cent. Among the noted exponents of atheism are P. Holbach, L. Feuerback, and R. Ingersoll.

Athelstan ⟨Aethelstan⟩ *d.* 939. Saxon king (924–39), successor to his father, Edward the Elder. He defeated a confederation of his opponents at Brunanburh (937) and became the first Saxon ruler of all England.

Athena ⟨Pallas Athena⟩ Greek goddess, the goddess of wisdom, arts and crafts, and war. She was protectress of cities, especially Athens, which was named for her. She is identified with the Roman Minerva.

Athenian League, Second. Another name for the second period (378–338 BC) of the Delian League (*q.v.*), an alliance of Greek city-states dominated by Athens.

Athens Historic city (pop. 867,000), capital of Greece. Athens was a focal point of ancient Greek culture, noted as a center of the arts and learning. Many of the temples and other buildings of the ancient city remain as classic works of architecture. The democratic form of government developed in the city-state of Athens is considered the forerunner of modern democracy. Great philosophers (Socrates, Plato, Aristotle) taught there and the masters of Greek drama (Aeschylus, Sophocles, Euripides, and Aristophanes) were all Athenians. Inhabited before 3000 BC, Athens rose as a dominant city-state in ancient Greece during the 5th cent. BC. Its power was broken by its archrival, Sparta, during the Peloponnesian War at the end of the 5th cent. Athens continued for a time as a cultural center, but it never again attained its former greatness. (*See also* Greece.) Key events in the history of Athens include:

   *c***700** BC   Athens became leader of 12 towns in Attica.

683 BC   Hereditary kingship abolished in Athens; archons to serve one year.

621 BC   Draco's law code; first Athenian law code established harsh system of justice.

594 BC   Solon made archon amid grave social crisis; Draconian code reformed; involuntary servitude for debt (serfdom) abolished; reforms laid basis for democracy.

561–527 BC   Pisistratus in power as tyrant; rapid expansion of city begun; temple construction started.

508 BC   Cleisthenes instituted his reforms; established Athenian democracy.

490–479 BC   Persian Wars; Athens and the other city-states ultimately repulsed the Persian invaders.

490–480 BC   Themistocles in power; built up Athenian navy and (in 478 BC) rebuilt the city's fortifications.

c480–c380 BC   Greek drama flourished at Athens during this period.

480 BC   Athens destroyed by Persian king Xerxes; rebuilt soon after.

480 BC   Athenian navy won a great victory over the Persians at Salamis.

478 BC   First Delian League formed by Athens to protect against Persians.

460–429 BC   Pericles in power; fostered Athenian golden age and made Athens the political and cultural center of Greece.

454 BC   Treasury of the Delian League transferred to Athens; Athens dominated other city-states of the league.

447 BC   Construction of the Acropolis began.

431–404 BC   Peloponnesian War against Sparta; victorious Spartans forced Athens to tear down its defenses; imposed rule of Thirty Tyrants (404 BC); Athens never regained former power.

403 BC   Athenians overthrew the Thirty Tyrants; rebuilt defenses.

399 BC   Socrates forced to poison himself.

395–387 BC   Corinthian War; Athens defeated Sparta.

c387 BC   Plato founded the Academy at Athens.

378 BC   The Second Delian League formed by Athens.

357–355 BC   Social War; Athens forced to recognize independence of allies it had once dominated.

338 BC   Battle of Chaeronea; Macedonians conquered Athens.

c335 BC   Aristotle opened his school, the Lyceum, at Athens.

323–322 BC   Lamian Wars; unsuccessful revolt against Macedonian rule; Athens reduced to a provincial city; became a center of Hellenic culture.

197 BC   Athens came under Roman control, after Romans defeated Macedonians.

86 BC   Roman general Sulla sacked Athens, after Athenians opposed Rome in the Mithridatic War.

FROM AD 395   Visigoths captured city (AD 395) as Roman power declined; Athens entered a long period of obscurity in which it passed to Byzantines and later the Turks (15th cent.)

1687–88   Parthenon badly damaged in war between Ottoman Turks and Venice.

1834   Athens became capital of independent Greek kingdom; city largely rebuilt in following years.

1941–1944   German occupation of city during WW II.

Athens, Timon of   *See* **Timon of Athens**

Athos, Mount   *See* **Mount Athos**

Atkinson, Sir Harry Albert   1831–92. A British-born prime minister (1876–77, 1883–84, 1887–90) of New Zealand. While serving as prime minister and in other government posts, he encouraged local farming and industry, abolished provincial governments, and established a centralized government.

Atlanta   Capital (pop. 425,000) of Georgia, in the US South, founded 1837. A major commercial center, it was a strategic supply and rail center during the Civil War. Captured (Sept. 2, 1864), the city was burned (Nov. 15, 1864) before Gen. W. Sherman's march to the sea. It became the permanent state capital in 1877.

Atlanta, Battle of   *See* **Atlanta Campaign**

Atlanta Campaign   Series of battles (May 7–Sept. 2, 1864) fought by Union forces to capture Atlanta, Georgia, during the American Civil War (1861–65). Atlanta's capture was an important factor in the reelection of Pres. A. Lincoln. Gen. W. Sherman began moving his 100,000-man army from Chattanooga toward Atlanta on May 7. He was opposed in a long series of battles by Gen. J. Johnston (replaced by Gen. J. Hood, July 17), commanding a smaller Confederate force. These battles included engagements at Kennesaw Mountain (June 27), Peachtree Creek (July 20), Atlanta (July 22), and Ezra Church (July 28). Thereafter Sherman began heavy bombardment of the city and gradually extended Union positions around it. Sherman forced Gen. Hood to abandon the city, and occupied it Sept. 2, 1864.

Atlanta Compromise   Plan for racial harmony. In a speech given (1895) at Atlanta, Georgia, black spokesman B.T. Washington advocated friendly but separate social existences for America's blacks and whites. Whites applauded the speech, but disapproving blacks later founded the Niagara Movement (1905).

Atlantic, Battle of the Prolonged contest for control of the Atlantic during WW II. The German Navy, far smaller than the British and French navies at the outset of the war, soon resorted to submarine warfare. Allied losses of cargo shipping were heavy during the early part of WW II. But, by mid-1943, the Allies were clearly winning the battle against German submarine wolf packs, by using the convoy system and antisubmarine warfare techniques.

Atlantic Charter WW II declaration (Aug. 14, 1941) by British prime minister W. Churchill and US pres. F. Roosevelt that outlined a program for world peace. The principles of the Atlantic Charter were later incorporated (1942) into the UN Charter. The joint declaration resulted from meetings between the two leaders held aboard naval vessels in the Atlantic. Though the US was still officially neutral, it pledged, with Britain, to: forgo territorial gains; restore sovereignty to governments conquered by force; make basic raw materials available to all nations; promote improvement of economic and social conditions worldwide; ensure freedom from fear and want; maintain freedom of the seas; and work toward eliminating war.

Atlantis Legendary Greek island in the Atlantic Ocean, mentioned by Plato. Atlantis and its highly developed civilization supposedly sank beneath the sea after an earthquake.

Atlas In Greek mythology, a Titan *(q.v.)*, the son of Iapetus and Clymene, and brother of Prometheus. He led the Titans in unsuccessful war against the gods and was condemned to hold the heavens upon his shoulders.

atomic bomb Weapon of great destructive power, using energy that results from the splitting of atoms. It was developed by the US in a crash program (Manhattan Project, from 1940) during WW II. The first atomic bomb was exploded (July 16, 1945) at the New Mexico testing grounds. Two bombs were subsequently dropped on Japan (Hiroshima, Aug. 6, and Nagasaki, Aug. 9, 1945), which forced Japan's surrender and opened the age of nuclear warfare.

atomism Scientific doctrine. Atomism holds that the universe is composed of individual particles that arc invisible and indestructible. First put forward by such ancient Greek thinkers as Leucippus and Democritus, the theory gained importance among European scientists from the 17th cent. on.

atomists Early school of Greek philosophy, adherents of atomism *(q.v.)*.

Aton ⟨Aten⟩ Egyptian god. Aton was worshiped as a sun god and sole creator of the world during the rein of Egyptian king Ikhnaton. One of the earliest recorded instances of monotheism, this worship of the single god Aton ended with the restoration of the god Amon after Ikhnaton's death.

Atreus In Greek mythology, king of Mycenae and father of Agamemnon and Menelaus. Rivalry with his brother, Thyestes, over the Mycenaean throne resulted in the seduction of Atreus' wife by Thyestes and the murder of Thyestes' sons by Atreus. Atreus was later killed by Thyestes' last son, Aegisthus.

Attalid (dynasty) *See* **Pergamum**

Attalus *See* **Pergamum**

Attica Region surrounding Athens in ancient Greece, located in what is now east-central Greece. The early history of the region is uncertain. Greek legend tells of the unification of 12 independent Attic towns by Theseus to form the city-state of Athens. From the 13th cent. BC onward, Athens was the preeminent city of Attica, and, from the 5th cent. BC, the region came under Athenian control. Other Attic cities include Marathon and Eleusis.

Attila AD 406?–453. King of the Huns (AD 434–53), notorious as the leader of savage barbarian hordes from central Asia that attacked the Roman Empire. Called the "Scourge of God," he became ruler of the Huns with his brother Bleda in 434. Though East Roman emperor Theodosius II had agreed (AD 434) to pay the Huns tribute, Attila and Bleda nevertheless attacked (441) the eastern Roman provinces. They ravaged the countryside and finally agreed (443) to a treaty that trebled monies paid by the Romans. After murdering Bleda (445), Attila became sole ruler of the Huns and again attacked (447–50) the Romans. In 450, Roman emperors Marcian and Valentinian III refused Attila his tribute. Attila, with an army of some 500,000 barbarians, invaded Gaul (451), unsuccessfully laid siege to Orléans, and was defeated (451) at the Battle of Châlons by the Romans and Visigoths. He withdrew to Hungary, then ravaged northern Italy (452), and was forced to break off the invasion before reaching Rome. He died a short time later.

Attlee, Clement Richard, 1st Earl 1883–1967. British statesman and prime minister (1945–51). A social worker and member of the Fabian Society in his early years, he headed the British Labour party (1935–55). As prime minister, he instituted many important Socialist reforms, including founding of the National Health Service and nationalization of the Bank of England, utilities, and basic industries. His administration also saw Britain's granting of independence to India (1947), Pakistan (1947), Burma (1948), Palestine (1948), and Ceylon (1948, now Sri Lanka).

Attucks, Crispus　*See* **Boston Massacre**

Auckland　Major city (pop. 149,000) and port in New Zealand, situated on the North Island. Founded in 1840, it was the capital of New Zealand until 1865.

Auden, Wystan Hugh　1907–73. A British-born American poet, considered a major 20th cent. literary figure. During the 1930s, he was one of a group of left-wing writers whose works reflected their concern for social issues.

audiencia　Court of Spain during the late medieval period. It had administrative and judicial powers, and figured prominently in Spain's American colonies, where it helped check abuses of authority by colonial government officials.

Audubon, John James　1785–1851. American ornithologist and artist, best known for his drawings of North American birds in *The Birds of America.*

Augean stables　*See* **Augeas**

Augeas　In Greek mythology, the owner of the Augean stables, in which he kept vast herds of cattle. Hercules' sixth task was to clean the stables, unaided, in a day. This he did by diverting a river through them.

Augsburg, Diet of　Meeting convened (Apr. 8, 1530) by Holy Roman Emperor Charles V to convince rebellious Lutheran noblemen to help turn back a Turkish invasion of the empire. The meeting failed to win over the Lutherans. The Augsburg Confession *(q.v.)* was presented during this council. Other diets held at Augsburg include those of 1547–48 (*see* Augsburg Interim) and 1555 (*see* Augsburg, Peace of).

Augsburg, League of　Pact formed (July 9, 1686) against France by Holy Roman Emperor Leopold I and his allies prior to the War of the Grand Alliance (1688–97). Leopold entered into the defensive alliance with Holland, Sweden, Spain, Bavaria, the Palatinate, and Saxony. The league was replaced (1689) by the Grand Alliance.

Augsburg, Peace of　A convention established (Sept. 25, 1555) at Augsburg, Bavaria, providing for an end to religious conflicts of the Reformation within the Holy Roman Empire. The settlement allowed individual states to decide whether Catholicism or Lutheranism was to be practiced in their territories and determined that Catholics and Lutherans should migrate to states where their faith had been adopted. Though Calvinists were not included in the agreement, the settlement halted religious conflicts in the empire for some 50 years.

Augsburg Confession　A statement of the basic doctrines of the Lutheran church, presented (1530) at the Diet of Augsburg. The creed was largely written by P. Melanchthon and remains the authoritative statement of the Lutheran faith. The 28 articles were drawn up to provide a statement of principles that could be accepted by the Holy Roman Empire's Roman Catholics and that would put an end to false claims about Lutheran doctrine.

Augsburg Interim　Provisional settlement issued (May 15, 1548) by Holy Roman Emperor Charles V in an unsuccessful attempt to halt disputes between Catholics and Lutherans within the empire. Lutherans, however, objected to the terms and adopted (1548) a counterproposal, the Leipzig Interim.

augur　A Roman prophet who interpreted omens and signs believed to be warnings from the gods. Augurs were held in high esteem until Theodosius abolished the College of Augurs (AD *c*391).

Augusta　US city (pop. 22,000), capital of Maine. Founded as a trading settlement in the 17th cent., it was incorporated in 1797. It became the state capital in 1831.

Augusta, Treaty of　Treaty (1773) between the colony of Georgia and the Cherokee and Creek Indians. The Indians gave up two tracts of land, the sale of which was to pay off debts to white merchants.

Augustan Age　Period of great literary flowering in Rome (usually, 27 BC–AD 14; also 43 BC–AD 17). With the preceding Ciceronian Period, it forms the Golden Age of Roman literary history. During this period, many of the greatest figures in Latin literature wrote under the patronage of Emperor Augustus and his adviser Maecenas. Among the classics completed in this age are Vergil's *Aeneid,* parts of Horace's *Odes* and *Epistles,* Propertius' elegies, Livy's *History of Rome,* and Ovid's *Metamorphoses.* By extension, Augustan Age also refers to a literary flowering in other nations (i.e., 18th-cent. England and 17th-cent. France).

Augustine, Saint　AD 354–430. Great Christian thinker and a Father of the Church. He first became a follower of Manichaeanism, was converted to Christianity by Saint Ambrose (AD 387), and subsequently became bishop of Hippo in Africa (AD 396). A Neoplationist, his teachings brought together Christian religion and Greek philosophical traditions. Among his important works are attacks on Manichaeanism, Donatism, and Pelagianism. His most famous works include *Confessions* and *The City of God.*

Augustine of Canterbury, Saint　*d. c*605. Italian, first archbishop of Canterbury, known as the

Apostle of England. He and forty other Benedictine monks went to England (597) and there converted King Aethelbert. Augustine established a church and monastery at Canterbury.

Augustinians Broadly, name applied to religious orders in the Roman Catholic church that follow the Rule of Saint Augustine (concerning monastic life). More specifically, it refers to three religious orders: Augustinian Canons, an order of Roman Catholic clerics (formed 11th cent.); Augustinian Hermits, formed (1256) by the unification of autonomous Italian monasteries; and the Augustinian Recollects, a reformist offshoot (16 cent.) of the Augustinian Hermits.

Augustus ⟨orig. Gaius Octavius⟩ ⟨*adopted name* Gaius Julius Caesar Octavianus⟩ ⟨*sometimes called* Octavian⟩ 63 BC–AD 14. First Roman emperor (27 BC–AD 14). A grandson of J. Caesar's sister, he became Caesar's adopted son and heir (44 BC). After Caesar's assassination (44 BC), he began a long struggle for power. He formed the Second Triumvirate (43) with M. Antony and M. Lepidus and became ruler in the West. He then avenged Caesar's death by defeating M. Brutus and C. Cassius at Philippi (42) and Pompey at Mylae (36). He eliminated Lepidus (32) and defeated M. Antony (31) at Actium, and thus became sole ruler of the empire. He maintained the outward republican forms and ruled as "first citizen" until 27, when he accepted the title Augustus. His reign was marked by prosperity and stability, administrative reforms, consolidation of power in Rome, and the establishment of Pax Romana. The month August and the Augustan Age are both named after him.

Augustus II ⟨Augustus the Strong⟩ 1670–1733. King of Poland (1697–1733) and elector of Saxony (1694–1733). He provoked the Northern War (1700–21) with Sweden to gain possession of Livonia and, defeated, was forced to abdicate (1706) by the Treaty of Altranstadt. He was restored (1709) after Russia, an ally, defeated Sweden.

Augustus III 1696–1763. King of Poland (1734–63) and elector of Saxony (1733–63), successor to his father, Augustus II. A patron of the arts, he left affairs of state to his ministers. He supported Austria in the War of the Austrian Succession and the Seven Years' War.

Augustus the Strong *See* **Augustus II**

Aulic Council Court and advisory council of the Holy Roman Empire. Established (c1498) by Maximilian I, it was intended to assist the emperor in executive matters. It eventually became a powerful judicial court of appeals, however, and functioned until the fall of the empire (1806).

Aungzeya *See* **Alaungpaya**

Aurangzeb ⟨Aurungzebe⟩ 1618–1707. Mogul emperor of India (1658–1707), successor to his father, Shah Jehan. A fanatical Muslim, he brought the Hindu-Muslim Mogul Empire to the height of its power. Though his reign brought great prosperity, his persecution of the Hindus brought about numerous rebellions among the Sikhs, Rajputs, Jats, and especially the Marathas. The empire broke up shortly after his death.

Aurelian ⟨Aurelianus, Lucius Domitius⟩ AD c212–275. Roman general and emperor (AD 270–275), successor to Claudius II. One of the great Roman emperors, he briefly restored the disintegrating empire. Though forced to give up Dacia to the Goths, he stopped the barbarian advance at the Danube, reestablished Roman rule in the East (272) by capturing Zenobia and Palmyra, and restored Roman rule over Europe by defeating Tetricus (274), his rival for control of the region. He was assassinated while on a military campaign against the Persians. Aurelian's Wall, a 12-mile-long defensive fortification around Rome, was begun by him.

Aurelian's Wall *See* **Aurelian**

Aurelianus, Lucius Domitius *See* **Aurelian**

Aurelius, Marcus *See* **Marcus Aurelius**

Auriol, Vincent 1884–1966. French statesman. A socialist deputy from 1914, he served as first president of the French Fourth Republic from 1947 to 1954.

Aurora Latin name for Eos, the Greek goddess of the dawn.

Aurungzebe *See* **Aurangzeb**

Auschwitz ⟨*properly,* Auschwitz-Birkenau⟩ Notorious German concentration camp established (1940) by the Nazis. Some 4 million people, mostly Jews, are believed to have been exterminated there during WW II.

Ausculum, Battle of *See* **Asculum, Battle of**

Ausgleich Facilitating agreement (Feb., 1867) that created the Austro-Hungarian Dual Monarchy. Following Austria's defeat in the Austro-Prussian War (1866), negotiations between the two monarchies (in progress since 1864) were stepped up. The compromise agreement was finally reached. By its terms, the two states maintained separate ministries and parliaments, shared military and foreign-policy responsibilities and common expenses. Austrian king Francis Joseph was crowned king of Hungary (June 8, 1867).

Austen, Jane 1775–1817. English novelist famous for her comedies of manners. Her novels treat middle-class English life and are noted for their sharp insights into character and society. Her works include *Sense and Sensibility, Pride* *and Prejudice, Mansfield Park, Emma,* and *Persuasion.*

Austerlitz, Battle of ⟨The Battle of the Three Emperors⟩ Great victory by Napoleon (Dec. 2, 1805) over the combined Russian and Austrian forces during the Napoleonic Wars. It was the first battle of the War of the Third Coalition. Napoleon, with 68,000 soldiers, engaged the 83,000-man force under Czar Alexander I and Emperor Francis II near Austerlitz (now Slavkov, Czechoslovakia). By his brilliant plan and its execution, Napoleon crushed and scattered the superior force. Austro-Russian losses, including prisoners, were some 26,000 to Napoleon's 9,000 casualties. The defeat forced Russia to withdraw from Austria, and Austria to sign the Treaty of Pressburg (1805).

Austin US city (pop. 345,000) and capital of Texas. It was made capital of the republic of Texas in 1839 and became capital of the state in 1870.

Austin, Stephen Fuller 1793–1836. An American pioneer who founded Anglo-American settlements in Texas in the 1820s, when the region was under Mexican jurisdiction. He is known as the Father of Texas.

Australasia Term sometimes used to denote certain islands in the South Pacific, including Australia, New Zealand, New Guinea, and other islands in the region. It is also used as an equivalent term for Oceania.

Australia ⟨Commonwealth of Australia⟩ Australia is the smallest continent and is located between the Pacific and Indian Oceans. Its capital is Canberra. The Commonwealth is made up of the states New South Wales, Victoria, Queensland, South Australia, Western Australia, and Tasmania, and two territories, the Northern Territory and the Australian Capital Territory. Long a member of the British Commonwealth, Australia was originally settled by the British as a penal colony. Key dates in the history of Australia include:

1601 Portuguese sailor Manuel Godhino de Eredia believed to have sighted Australia.

1606 Spaniard Luis Vaez de Torres believed to have sighted Australia.

1606 Dutch explorers aboard the ship *Duyfhen* sighted Queensland.

1633 A. Tasman discovered Tasmania.

1688 Englishman W. Dampier explored western coast and landed at King Sound.

1770 Captain J. Cook explored Botany Bay; claimed eastern Australian coast for Britain.

1788 First British penal colony established at present-day Sydney.

1804–30 European settlers nearly eliminated Tasmanian aborigines in Black War.

1824 Brisbane founded as a penal colony.

1829–50 Britain claimed entire continent (1829); Australian Colonies Government Act granted limited self-government (1850).

1851 Gold strike in Victoria brought rush of new immigrants and marked beginning of period of rapid development.

1862 Explorer John McDouall Stuart became first to cross the continent.

1897–98 Constitution drafted.

1901 Constitution put into effect; Australian colonies federated.

1902 Immigration Restriction Act limited influx of non-Europeans.

1913 Construction of capital, Canberra, begun.

1931 United Australia Party formed.

1939–45 World War II; Australia joined the Allies; Allied victories in Coral Sea and elsewhere forestalled possible invasion of Australia by Japanese.

1950–53 Korean War; Australia sent troops to bolster UN forces.

1954 Australia joined SEATO.

1965–75 Vietnam War; Australian troops joined US and South Vietnamese forces in the fight against the Communists.

1972 Political crisis over continuing economic problems of inflation and recession.

1975 Governor-general Sir John Kerr dissolved parliament (Nov.) and called for new elections amid continuing fiscal difficulties.

1975 Malcolm Fraser takes office as prime minister.

1975 Australian trust territory of Papua New Guinea granted independence.

1980 Prime Minister Fraser instituted government spending cutbacks and incentives for the private sector; economic problems nevertheless continued into the 1980s.

Austrasia East Frankish kingdom from 6th to 8th cent., roughly consisting of parts of eastern France, western Germany, and The Netherlands. It was formed (511) when King Clovis I divided the Merovingian Empire between his sons. There followed a long series of wars between rulers of Austrasia and neighboring Neustria, especially between queens Brunhilda and Fredegunde, that gradually eroded royal power in Austrasia. Following the reign of Dagobert I, real power rested with the mayor of the palace in the Austrasian capital of Metz. As mayor, Pepin III seized power (751) from the Merovingians and thus founded the Carolingian line of kings.

Austria Republic located in central Europe. Its capital is Vienna. Austria's history began with

Charlemagne's establishment (8th cent.) of an Eastern March (Österreich) in the region. Later elevated to a duchy within the Holy Roman Empire, it came under the rule of the House of Hapsburg. Austria dominated the government of the Holy Roman Empire *(q.v.)* from the 15th cent. and became the leading power of Europe for a time. Austria played a pivotal role in the outbreak of WW I, but by that time control over its vast, ethnically mixed empire had greatly declined. The history of modern Austria began at the end of the war, when the empire was dissolved and a republic, greatly reduced in size, was established. Key dates in the history of Austria include:

LATE 8TH CENT. Charlemagne established Eastern March in region of what is modern Austria.

1156 Austria made a duchy by Holy Roman Emperor Frederick I.

1282 House of Hapsburg gained possession of Austria; Hapsburgs greatly increased Austria's power, importance, and holdings.

1438 Albert II, a Hapsburg, became Holy Roman Emperor; thereafter, Hapsburgs controlled the imperial crown until just before the empire was dissolved (1806).

1526 Austria gained control of Bohemia and much of Hungary, uniting these lands under the Austrian crown within the Holy Roman Empire.

1529 Ottoman emperor Suleiman the Magnificent laid siege to Vienna for the first time, thus beginning long period of military rivalry with Austria.

FROM **1517**. Protestant Reformation and attempts to halt its spread resulted in period of instability.

1524–26 Peasants' War sparked by Protestantism.

1591–1606 Fifteen Years' War fought with the Ottoman Empire.

1618–48 Thirty Years' War.

1648 Peace of Westphalia ended Thirty Years' War and reduced powers of the Holy Roman Emperor over states in the empire; Hapsburg Austria began its rise as a major power.

1682–99 Austro-Turkish War fought between Austria and her allies and the Ottoman Empire.

1701–14 War of the Spanish Succession.

1713 Austria gained control of the Spanish Netherlands by the Peace of Utrecht.

1733–35 War of the Polish Succession; Austria gained accession of Frederick Augustus II and Augustus III.

1736–39 Austria joined Russia in Russo-Turkish War.

1740 Maria Theresa succeeded to rule of the Hapsburg domains through the Pragmatic Sanction; her succession led to the War of the Austrian Succession (1740–48).

1756–63 Seven Years' War.

1772, 1793, 1795 Austria gained eastern lands through the Partitions of Poland.

1787–92 Austrians joined Russians in Russo-Turkish War.

1791 Declaration of Pillnitz issued (Aug. 27) by Austria and Prussia; contributed to outbreak of the French Revolutionary Wars.

1792–1815 Austria embroiled in French Revolutionary Wars and Napoleonic Wars.

1804 Collapse of Holy Roman Empire imminent; Francis II became the first emperor of Austria, as Francis I, and gave up the imperial crown; Holy Roman Empire dissolved two years later.

1815 Congress of Vienna established Austria as the leading power in the German Confederation replacing the Holy Roman Empire.

1815–1848 C. von Metternich, Austrian foreign minister, flourished as the leading European statesman; helped promote era of conservatism and repression of liberal nationalistic movements in post-Napoleonic Europe.

1848 Hapsburg rule threatened by revolutions of 1848; Hapsburgs were able to restore authority throughout the empire.

AUG. **14, 1865** Convention of Gastein gave Austria control of Holstein; Prussia got Schleswig.

1866 Austro-Prussian War fought (June 15–Aug. 23); led to Austria's defeat and exclusion from the German Confederation; established Prussia's dominance over German states after long rivalry with Austria.

1867 Ausgleich agreement made possible the formation of the Dual Monarchy, creating two theoretically separate kingdoms, Austria and Hungary under one king; political unrest within the empire mounted in subsequent years, however.

1914 Archduke Ferdinand, Austrian heir apparent, assassinated by Serbian nationalist at Sarajevo; subsequent Austrian demands on Serbia led to outbreak of WW I.

1914–18 World War I; Austria allied with Central Powers.

1916–18 Charles I reigned as last Austro-Hungarian emperor.

1919 Treaty of Saint-Germain concluded (Sept. 10) by Allied powers; established republic of Austria and abolished Austro-Hungarian monarchy; Austrian territory greatly reduced; union with Germany forbidden.

1920 M. Hainisch became first president of the newly formed republic of Austria.

1920s Economic disasters following WW I led to rising political turmoil, notably between Socialists and monarchists; ascendancy of National Socialists began late in the decade.

1932 Engelbert Dollfuss became chancellor; opposed Nazism and union with Germany but adopted elements of fascism in the government.

1934 Dollfuss assassinated by Austrian Nazis.

1934–38 Kurt von Schuschnigg in office as chancellor (1934); unable to resist growing Nazi pressure for Anschluss (union) with Germany; resigned.

1938 German troops occupied Austria (Mar.); Hitler made Austria part of the Third Reich.

1939–45 World War II.

1945 Austria occupied by Allied forces at end of WW II and divided into zones of occupation.

1945–50 Karl Renner served as president of the Austrian government.

1955 Allied occupation ended (May 15) by Austrian State Treaty; Austrian sovereignty recognized by major powers.

1970– Bruno Kreisky, a Socialist, in office as chancellor; Socialists now dominant party, after long rivalry with conservative People's party.

Austria, Anne of *See* **Anne of Austria**

Austria, John of *See* **John of Austria**

Austria, Margaret of *See* **Margaret of Austria**

Austria, Marie Therese of *See* **Marie Therese of Austria**

Austrian Netherlands *See* **Netherlands, Spanish and Austrian**

Austrian State Treaty Treaty (May 15, 1955) between Austria and the WW II Allies. The treaty ended the Allied occupation of Austria and halted discussions on plans for dividing it.

Austrian Succession, War of the (1740–48.) This complex war involved the major European powers in a general and largely indecisive conflict. The war broke out after the death of Holy Roman Emperor Charles VI (1740), a member of the powerful Hapsburg family. It was fought over succession to the vast Hapsburg family domains (centered on Austria), although other political rivalries were involved (notably between France and Britain). Long before his death, Charles had issued the Pragmatic Sanction of 1713, naming his daughter, Maria Theresa, as heir to the Hapsburg lands (but not the imperial title). During his lifetime, Charles labored tirelessly to win general support in Europe for her succession. But on Charles's death, Maria was seen as too weak to retain control of the domains, and rival claimants disputed her succession. When war broke out, France, Prus-

sia, Spain, Bavaria, and Saxony took up arms against Austria, ruled by Maria. Britain under George II sided with Austria. An ongoing war between Britain and Spain (War of Jenkins' Ear) merged into the general conflict, which also spread to French and British colonies (King George's War in North America) and later to Britain (second revolt of the Jacobites). Exhaustion, not decisive victory, eventually ended the war. Maria was recognized as heir to Hapsburg domains and her husband, Francis I, was elected Holy Roman Emperor. Prussia (the real winner) won Silesia from Austria and emerged as a major power. Key events include:

1740–42 Frederick the Great of Prussia started the war by invading and occupying the Austrian territory of Silesia (First Silesian War).

1741 Charles Albert of Bavaria, a rival claimant to Maria's Hapsburg domains, led his forces against Austria and captured Prague in Bohemia.

1741 Charles Albert elected Holy Roman Emperor Charles VII.

1741 Britain, fearing the French would gain control in Europe if Austria collapsed, sided with Austria.

1742 Austria conquered Bavaria and pushed into Bohemia; Prussia withdrew from the war after Austria ceded a large part of Silesia to it.

1743 French retreat (1742–43) was capped by British king George's victory over the French at the Battle of Dettingen (June 27); Saxony made peace with Austria.

1744–45 King Frederick of Prussia, fearing a too powerful Austria, joined Emperor Charles VII and France against Austria (called Second Silesian War); Prussia soon put on the defensive, however.

1745 Bavaria forced out of war following the death of Emperor Charles VII.

1745 Battle of Fontenoy (May 11) in Flanders; France defeated Austria and her allies and began to invade the Austrian Netherlands.

1745 Britain concluded peace with Prussia; Maria Theresa's husband became Holy Roman Emperor Francis I.

1745 Treaty of Dresden (Dec. 25) ended war with Prussia; Prussia recognized Francis I as emperor and Austria confirmed Prussian possession of Silesia.

1746 Britain forced to withdraw troops to contend with French-backed revolt of the Jacobites; France completed conquest of the Austrian Netherlands.

1748 Treaty of Aix-la-Chapelle signed (Oct.); provided for end of war and mutual restitution of most conquered territory, though Prussia retained Silesia.

Austro-Hungarian Monarchy *See* **Dual Monarchy**

Austro-Prussian War ⟨Seven Weeks' War⟩ War (June 15–Aug. 23, 1866) between Prussia (with Italy) and Austria (with Hanover, Bavaria, and most other German states). The war resulted in Austria's exclusion from the German Confederation (reorganized as the North German Confederation, *q.v.*) and thus opened the way to the eventual unification of Germany under Prussian domination. The war was precipitated by Prussian chancellor O. Bismarck to gain those ends for Prussia. Bismarck first provoked a crisis with Austria over administration of the Schleswig-Holstein region in spring, 1866 and, claiming Austrian violation of the Convention of Gastein *(q.v.)*, sent (June 6) Prussian troops into Holstein. In subsequent fighting the Italians lost to Austrian forces opposing them in Italy, but the Prussians displayed remarkable military efficiency and quickly defeated Austrian forces in the north. One Prussian army took Hanover (June 27–29) and, on another front in Bohemia, delivered the final crushing blow (July 3) to Austria at the Battle of Sadowa *(q.v.)*. The war was formally ended by the Treaty of Prague, which, in addition to providing for the North German Confederation, ended Austrian hegemony in Italy.

Austro-Turkish War A war (1682–99) between Austria (and her allies) and the Ottoman Empire. Taking advantage of unrest in Hungarian territories, the Turks invaded Austria and besieged Vienna (July-Sept., 1683). Poland and other states of the Holy League (formed 1684) joined the war against Turkey. Despite reverses, they won notable victories against the Turks, including the Battle of Zenta (1697). The Turks sued for peace and agreed (1699) to the Treaty of Karlowitz *(q.v.)*.

authoritarianism Political system based on blind submission of individuals to a central authority, either a single leader or small group of them.

autocracy System of government in which a single ruler has absolute power over the entire government.

auto-da-fé During the Inquisition, a public ceremony in which judges read the sentences imposed on those convicted of religious infidelity. Such ceremonies, often very elaborately staged, were held from 1481 to as late as 1815.

Autumn Harvest Uprising Chinese peasant revolt inspired by Communist forces (Sept., 1927). Mao Tse-tung was among the leaders of the revolt, which involved peasants and Communist regulars in the Hunan-Kiangsi region. Though it failed, Mao gained both experience and the conviction of the importance of peasant discontent to the Communist movement.

Avalon In Arthurian legend, the island to which King Arthur, mortally wounded in his last battle, was taken. It is sometimes identified with Glastonbury in Somerset, England.

Avars Nomadic Asian peoples. The Avars seem to have come from the Caucasus. They conquered and occupied large areas of Russia and Hungary, forming a powerful empire (c6th to 8th cent.). They were defeated by Charlemagne (805).

Aventine secession Italian political crisis. On June 10, 1924, 150 non-Fascist members withdrew from the Chamber of Deputies to protest B. Mussolini's Fascist government. Reacting to the Matteoti Crisis *(q.v.)*, the deputies demanded an end to the use of violence in suppressing dissent.

Avenzoar *See* **Ibn Zuhr**

Averescu, Alexandru 1859–1938. Romanian politician and general. Averescu fought against the Ottoman Turks (1877–78) and against the Central Powers during WW I. As prime minister (1918), he conducted Romania's post–WW I peace negotiations. He was prime minister again in 1920–21 and 1926–27.

Avernus Ancient name for Averno, a small crater lake in southern Italy. Volcanic gases arising from it were said to kill birds flying over it, and ancient Romans believed it to be the entrance to hell.

Avicenna 980–1037. Muslim philosopher and doctor. He authored over one hundred works on medicine and philosophy, including the famous *Canon of Medicine*. His works were influenced by Aristotelian and Neoplatonic teachings.

Avignon City in southeast France. It was the papal see from 1309 to 1378, during the Babylonian captivity, and served as the seat of antipopes until the end of the Great Schism (1417).

Avignon Papacy *See* **Babylonian captivity**

Avila, Saint Theresa of *See* **Theresa of Avila, Saint**

Avila Camacho, Manuel 1897–1955. A Mexican general and politician. Avila fought in the revolution of 1914 and was president from 1940 to 1946. A moderate, he inaugurated a period of consolidation of the social reforms resulting from the Mexican Revolution.

Avogadro, Amadeo 1776–1856. Italian physicist who developed (1811) Avogadro's Law, which holds that equal volumes of gases at the same temperature and pressure contain an equal number of molecules. This concept was a major contribution to the development of chemistry and physics.

Axel *See* **Absalon**

Axis Powers WW II coalition, headed by Germany, Italy, and Japan, that opposed the Allied powers. The alliance began (Oct. 25, 1936) with a pact between Germany and Italy and the Anti-Comintern Pact (Nov. 25, 1936) between Germany and Japan. The three later signed (Sept. 27, 1940) the Berlin (or Tripartite) Pact.

Ayacucho, Battle of Battle near the city of Ayacucho, Peru. On Dec. 9, 1824, revolutionary forces under A. Sucre defeated superior Spanish colonial forces, thereby securing the independence of Peru. The Spanish lost 2,000 men.

Aybak *See* **Mamelukes**

Ayer, Alfred Jules 1910–. British philosopher. Ayer was an important exponent of logical positivism. He wrote such books as *Language, Truth and Logic; The Foundations of Empirical Knowledge;* and *The Concept of a Person.*

Ayn Jalut, Battle of ⟨Ain Jalut, ~⟩ Great victory (Sept. 3, 1260, near the Sea of Galilee) for the Egyptian Mamelukes over the invading Mongols. The battle marked the end of the Mongols' westward invasion (under Hulagu). The Mamelukes later captured Syria from them.

Ayub Khan, Muhammad 1907–1974. Pakistani politician, president (1958–69). He encouraged land reform and a system of local governments called "basic democracies." However, an unsuccessful two-week war with India (1965) and internal unrest forced his resignation (Mar., 1969).

Ayyubids Muslim dynasty of Egyptian rulers. A Sunni Muslim dynasty founded (1169) by Saladin, it ruled Egypt, Iraq, Syria, and Yemen until 1250. Under Ayyubite rule, Egypt became the leading Muslim power and successfully opposed the crusaders. The dynasty was overthrown by the Mamelukes.

Ayutthaya *See* **Ramathibodi I**

Azaña, Manuel 1880–1940. Spanish statesman. He served as prime minister (1931–33) under Pres. A. Zamora and was president (1936–39) of the republic during the Spanish Civil War.

Azariah *See* **Uzziah**

Aztec Empire Empire of the Aztecs, a relatively civilized American Indian people, once located in central Mexico. At the time of the conquest of Mexico by H. Cortes (1519–21), the chief Aztec city was Tenochtitlán (founded c1325). The Aztecs migrated to this region from the north (c11th cent.) and, through a series of alliances and conquests (12th–16th cents.), gained control over neighboring peoples. Their economy was based on the cultivation of corn, they were skilled builders and craftsmen, they had a system of picture-writing, and their religion pervaded all aspects of life. They practiced human sacrifice and their chief god was Huitzilopochtli, a god of war. The Spaniards were able to conquer the numerically superior Aztec forces, led by Montezuma, because the Spanish possessed guns and horses, because they found willing allies among native peoples of the region, and because the Aztecs regarded the Spanish as descendants of the god Quetzalcoatl. (*See also* Cortes, Hernando.)

B

Baal Canaanite fertility god and king of the gods, mentioned frequently in the Bible. The worship of Baal was not limited to the Canaanites. He was worshiped in various forms as a local god in Semitic communities throughout the Near East, as well as in Egypt, Greece, and Phoenicia. In the early history of Israel, worship of Baal conflicted with the worship of the one true god, Yahweh, and was condemned by the Hebrew prophets.

Baal Shem-Tob ⟨Eliezer, Israel ben⟩ *c*1700–60. Russian-born founder of the Hasidim, a Jewish sect.

Baashaa *d. c*888 BC. King of Israel (911–*c*888 BC). He gained the throne by murdering Nadab, and made war against Asa of Judah.

Ba'ath party *See* **Ba'th party**

Bab, the ⟨Mirza Ali Muhammad⟩ 1819–50. Arab religious leader. The founder (1844) of Babism, he had a charismatic personality that, with his claims to divinity, led to his execution by the Shi'ite Muslims. He is considered one of the founders of Bahaism.

Babar *See* **Baber**

Babbage, Charles 1792–1871. English mathematician and inventor. A founder of the Royal Astronomical Society, he spent many years working on a mechanical calculator, the forerunner of modern calculating machines.

Babel, Tower of *See* **Tower of Babel**

Baber ⟨Babar⟩ ⟨Babur⟩ ⟨*orig.* Zahir ud-Din Muhammad⟩ 1483–1530. Mongol soldier, poet, and founder of the Mogul Empire in India. Descended from Genghis Khan and Tamerlane, he first tried unsuccessfully to take Samarkand from the Uzbeks. He was, however, successful in Afghanistan and established a kingdom there (1504). In 1525–26 he led a small invasion force into India and, following the capture of Delhi (1526), proceeded to conquer most of northern India. These conquests formed the Mogul Empire *(q.v.)*.

Babeuf, François Noël 1760–97. French revolutionary of the late 18th cent. whose ideas of economic egalitarianism foreshadowed modern socialism. He is sometimes called the first social-ist theorist. Seeking economic justice, he organized a secret society to overthrow the Directory (1796), but his "conspiracy of equals" was discovered and he was executed.

Babington, Anthony 1561–86. English conspirator. He joined a plot (1586) to murder Queen Elizabeth I and place Mary, Queen of Scots, on the throne. The plot was discovered and Babington was executed. Evidence of Mary's complicity led to her execution.

Babism Originally a sect of Shi'ite Muslims that flourished briefly during the 19th cent. and gave rise to Bahaism *(q.v.)*. An ascetic doctrine, it fused elements of various teachings, including Shi'ite, Gnostic, and Sufi doctrines. It spread throughout Persia, following proclamation of the arrival (1844) of the prophet, or Bab, in the person of Mirza Ali Muhammad. Persecution of Babists soon began (1845) and the Babists withdrew from the Islamic fold (1848). Uprisings against the Persian shah finally resulted in a massacre of Babists at Teheran and the execution of the Bab (1850). A successor, Baha Allah, fled Teheran and by 1863 formed Bahaism as an offshoot of Babism.

Babur *See* **Baber**

Babylon Ancient city of Mesopotamia and one of the most important cities of antiquity. Established by the 3d millennium BC, it gained importance in the early 2d millennium BC when Hammurabi made it the capital of the kingdom of Babylonia. During this period, it became the commercial center of the region. Destroyed (*c*689 BC) by Sennacherib, it was rebuilt and reached its height in the 7th–6th cents. BC, under the rule of Nebuchadnezzar II. Babylon became famous for its splendor, and its Hanging Gardens were one of the Seven Wonders of the World. Babylon fell (538 BC) to the Persians under Cyrus the Great and was later conquered (331 BC) by Alexander the Great. In the early 3d cent. BC its importance was largely eclipsed by the rise of Seleucia as commercial center of the region.

Babylon, Hanging Gardens of *See* **Hanging Gardens of Babylon**

Babylonia Term sometimes used collectively to refer to the city-state civilizations that flourished as early as the 3rd millennium BC in the valley of the Tigris and the Euphrates. More specifically, it refers to the empires centered on the city of Babylon. The first great empire was that of Hammurabi (c1830–1530 BC), which saw the issuance of the Code of Hammurabi and the appearance of the Babylonian ziggurat, or step-towered temple. Babylonia was then dominated by the Kassites (c1530–1150 BC), the Aramaeans (c1100–1000 BC), and, from the 10th cent., by the Empire of Assyria (q.v.). A Babylonian ruler, Nabopolassar, ended Assyrian rule (625 BC) and joined the Medes in the capture of Assyria's capital, Nineveh (612 BC). His son Nebuchadnezzar defeated the Egyptians at the great Battle of Carchemish in 605 BC, and a new Babylonian Empire, sometimes called the Chaldaean Empire, was formed. It included Mesopotamia, Syria, Palestine, and Cilicia. These were the days of legendary Babylonian glory when the Hanging Gardens were built. It was during this period that the Jews were deported from Judah to Babylon (the Babylonian captivity). Cyrus the Great of Persia began his attacks on Babylonia around 547 BC and Babylon fell to the Persian Empire in 538 BC.

Babylonian captivity ⟨Exile⟩ ⟨Captivity⟩ Name of important periods in the history of Israel and the Roman Catholic church. **1.** In the history of Israel, the mass deportation of prominent Jews to Babylon, following Nebuchadnezzar's conquest of Jerusalem and destruction of the temple (586 BC). When Cyrus the Great overthrew the Babylonian Empire (c538 BC), he allowed the Jews to return. Many thousands, but not all of them, did so. The end of the 70-year captivity prophesied in the Bible was marked by completion of the new temple (516 BC). **2.** In the history of the Roman Catholic church, the Avignon papacy, the period (1309–76) during which the popes resided at Avignon, in what now is France. The first pope to make his residence at Avignon was Clement V, who sought a better location from which to conduct the papacy. The seventh and last Avignon pope, Gregory XI, left Avignon (1376) to reestablish the papacy at Rome (1377). The Great Schism (see Schism) followed.

Bacchus Roman god of wine and fertility, corresponding to the Greek Dionysus. Worship of Bacchus frequently took the form of orgies.

Bacchylides fl. 5th cent. BC. Greek lyric poet. The nephew of Simonides of Ceos, he was a contemporary of Pindar. Fragments of his epicinian odes were discovered in 1896.

Bach, Alexander 1813–93. Austrian minister of justice (1848) and of the interior (1849–59). He instituted the Bach system of centralized authority, characterized by both police repression and social and economic reforms.

Bach, Karl Philipp Emanuel 1714–88. German composer, son of J. S. Bach.

Bach, Johann Christian 1735–82. German composer, the son of J. S. Bach. Bach's musical style influenced later composers, including W. Mozart.

Bach, Johann Christoph See **Bach, Johann Sebastian**

Bach, Johann Sebastian 1685–1750. German composer, the most illustrious member of a celebrated musical family and one of the great composers of all time. Orphaned by the age of 19, Bach showed his musical talents early under the tutelage of his brother Johann Christoph Bach (1671–1721). After serving variously as an organist, concertmaster, and musical director, he became musical director of the church and music school of St. Thomas in Leipzig, where he spent the rest of his life. In his lifetime he composed a vast number of works, including instrumental and vocal pieces and a large body of religious compositions. Among his best-known works are *The Well-Tempered Clavier, St. Matthew Passion, Mass in B Minor,* the *Goldberg Variations,* and the *Brandenburg Concertos.*

Bach, Wilhelm Friedemann 1710–84. A German composer. The eldest son of J. S. Bach, he was a celebrated composer and organist in his day, but wrote down few of his compositions.

Bacon, Francis 1561–1626. English philosopher, statesman, and essayist. He is credited with making important advances in inductive logic, which later encouraged the general advancement of science. In his day Bacon was noted for both his meanness and his great intelligence. His public career as a member of Parliament (from 1584) and lord chancellor (1618–21) ended with his conviction for taking bribes. His most important works include *De Augmentis Scientiarum, Novum Organum,* and *The New Atlantis.*

Bacon, Roger 1214?–1294? English philosopher and Franciscan monk. He was an important proponent of experimental science and wrote many descriptions of experiments, including one that revealed the formula for gunpowder for the first time in Europe. Bacon's interests ranged over all branches of science, including alchemy and astronomy, and he wrote an important encyclopedic work on science, *Opus Majus.* This work, however, was condemned by the Franciscans, and Bacon was imprisoned (1277?) for ten years.

Bacon's Rebellion Uprising in colonial Virginia (1676) led by Nathaniel Bacon (1647–76). The rebellion was provoked by Gov. W. Berkeley's colonial policies, including his refusal to protect colonists from attacks by Indians, with whom he had a lucrative fur trade. Bacon raised an army of 300 colonists and defeated the Indians. Declared a rebel by the governor, Bacon marched on Jamestown, captured it, and forced the governor to flee. A short time later, however, Bacon died of malaria and the rebels disbanded. Gov. Berkeley returned to exact a bloody revenge on the colonists.

Bactria Ancient country, located in what now are northern Afghanistan and southern USSR. An important focal point for trade between Western and Eastern civilizations, it was conquered by the Persians c545 BC. Conquered next by Alexander the Great (328 BC), it was made part of the Seleucid Empire. It became an independent Greek kingdom (256 BC) and during the next century expanded to include parts of Afghanistan, Pakistan, and central Asia. After 130 BC, Bactria fell to various conquerors and never again rose to power.

Bad Axe River, Battle of *See* **Black Hawk War**

Baden Former state located in southwest Germany. Baden played a role in the formation of the German Empire. It was divided between France and Germany after WW II.

Baden, Treaty of *See* **Rastatt and Baden, Treaties of**

Baden-Powell of Gilwell, Robert Stephenson Smyth Baden-Powell, 1st Baron 1857–1941. British army officer. He founded (1908) the Boy Scouts and, with his sister Agnes (1858–1945), the Girl Guides (1910).

Badoglio, Pietro 1871–1956. Italian field marshal. As head of a new government after B. Mussolini's fall in 1943, he negotiated an armistice with the Allies, but opposition led him to resign in 1944.

Badr, Battle of Battle (Mar., 624) at Badr, near Medina. Muhammad, leading 300 Muslims, attacked and defeated a Meccan force of 1,000 accompanying a caravan returning from Syria. The raid was Muhammad's first military victory and served to strengthen his movement.

Baduila *See* **Totila**

Baeda, Saint *See* **Bede, Saint**

Baedeker, Karl 1801–59. German publisher and founder of the series of Baedeker guidebooks for travelers.

Baekeland, Leo Hendrik 1863–1944. American chemist and inventor of Velox photographic paper and Bakelite, the first thermosetting plastic.

Baer, Karl Ernst von 1792–1876. Estonian biologist. A pioneer in the study of embryology, he discovered the mammalian egg and the notochord, and presented a theory of embryonic development.

Báez, Buenaventura c1810–1884. ˙ Dominican statesman. Several times president of the Dominican Republic, he sought unsuccessfully to have his country annexed by the U. S. (1869–70).

Bagdad *See* **Baghdad**

Bagehot, Walter 1826–77. English social scientist, economist, and editor (1860–77) of *The Economist*. He wrote *The English Constitution* (1867), a classic study, and *Physics and Politics* (1872), which applied physical principles to politics.

Baghdad ⟨Bagdad⟩ Iraqi capital city (pop. 3,205,600) and the nation's industrial center. The site of important cities since Mesopotamian times, the present city was founded (762) as the capital of the Abbasid caliphs. During the 8th and early 9th cents., Baghdad reached the height of its commercial and cultural prosperity as one of the greatest Islamic cities. Its decline began in the 9th cent. and was completed by successive conquests. Part of the Ottoman Empire (1638–1917), it was taken by the British (1917) and became the capital of the new kingdom of Iraq (1920). The Iraqi republic was established by a coup in Baghdad in 1958.

Baha Allah ⟨Baha Ullah⟩ 1817–92. Persian religious leader. A disciple of the Bab, he declared himself the Promised One and successor to the Bab, and founded (1863) Bahaism.

Bahaism Religion founded (1863) by Baha Allah and now practiced throughout the world. Bahaism is an offshoot of Babism, of which Baha Allah was once a follower. After persecution and exile of the Babists by the Persians, Baha Allah declared himself (1863) the Promised One, or manifestation through which men could know God. The religion was spread throughout the world by his son and successors. Among its major tenets are that God is knowable only through his manifestation; the unity of all religions; the need for world peace; and universal government.

Bahamas (*properly* Commonwealth of the Bahamas) Island chain and independent nation (pop. 240,000) in the Atlantic, southeast of Florida. The Bahamas were the site of C. Columbus' first landing (1492) in the New World (probably at San Salvador). The islands were first settled by the English in the mid-1600s. Long a base for pirates such as Blackbeard, the Bahamas were not freed of them until the early 1700s. Spanish claims to the islands were relinquished to England by the

Treaty of Paris (1783). The Bahamas were a base for blockade runners during the Civil War and rum runners during Prohibition. The islands were granted independence in 1973.

Baha Ullah *See* **Baha Allah**

Bahrein *See* **Bahrain**

Bahrain ⟨Al-Bah-Rayn⟩ ⟨Bahrein⟩ Sheikhdom (pop. 370,000) in the Persian Gulf. An oil-rich archipelago, Bahrain was ruled by the Portuguese from the 1500s to 1602, when it passed into Persian control. Since 1783 it has been ruled by a sheikh of a Kuwait family and was a British protectorate from 1861 until 1971, when it became independent.

Baïf, Jean Antoine de 1532–89. French poet, born in Venice. A learned and imaginative poet, he was one of the seven members of the Pléiade.

Bailey, James A *See* **Barnum, Phineas Taylor**

Bailly, Jean Sylvain 1736–93. French astronomer and politician, noted for his study of the moons of Jupiter. As mayor of Paris (1789–91), he allowed the national guard to fire on a mob (July, 1791), for which he was later executed.

Bainbridge, William 1774–1833. American naval officer. During the Tripolitan War he commanded the frigate *Philadelphia*, which was captured in the harbor of Tripoli. He later commanded the *Constitution* in the War of 1812.

Bain, Alexander 1818–1903. Scottish philosopher. He applied scientific principles to the study of psychology and emphasized the importance of the will.

Baird, John Logie 1888–1946. Scottish inventor and pioneer in television. He demonstrated the first television system in 1926 and demonstrated color television in 1928.

Bajazet I ⟨Beyazid I⟩ 1347–1403. Ottoman sultan (1389–1402), successor to his father, Murad I. He conquered most of Asia Minor and besieged Constantinople for ten years but was defeated by Tamerlane at Ankara (1402).

Bajazet II ⟨Beyazid II⟩ 1447–1513. Ottoman sultan (1481–1512), successor to his father, Muhammad II. He fought wars with Venice and Egypt, and completely rebuilt Constantinople after the 1509 earthquake.

Baji Rao I *d.* 1740. Second Peshwa (1720–40) of the Maratha state of India, successor to his father Balaji Vishvanath (*d.* 1720). He organized the Marathas against Muslims threatening from the north, and formed an alliance with the Rajputs against the Mogul Empire (1739).

Baji Rao II *See* **Bassein, Treaty of**

Baker, Isaac *See* **Scribner, Charles**

Baker, Norma Jean *See* **Monroe, Marilyn**

Baker, Ray Stannard ⟨*pseud.* David Grayson⟩

1870–1946. American muckraking journalist and author, whose eight-volume biography of Woodrow Wilson (1927–39) won a 1940 Pulitzer Prize.

Baksar, Battle of ⟨Buxar, ~⟩ Battle (Oct. 23, 1764) at Baksar, India, in which a British and native force of 7,000 defeated an army of 40,000, thus reestablishing British control in Bengal.

Bakufu ⟨Shogunate⟩ Name for the Japanese military government of a shogun, or hereditary military ruler. The first shogun came to power in 1192, and the Bakufu, or shogunate, ruled Japan until the 19th cent. Technically, the Japanese emperor held authority over the Bakufu, but the shogun held the true power.

Bakunin, Mikhail 1814–76. Russian revolutionary and anarchist leader. His views led to his expulsion from the Communist First International in 1872 and caused a rift in the Communist movement.

Balaam Biblical prophet called upon by Balak, king of Moab, to curse the Israelites. Rebuked by the ass on which he rode, Balaam blessed the Israelites instead.

Balaclava *See* **Balaklava, Battle of**

Balaji Vishvanath *See* **Baji Rao I**

Balakirev, Mili Alekseyevich 1837–1910. Russian composer and leader of the group called The Five. His work influenced other composers, including Tchaikovsky.

Balaklava, Battle of ⟨Balaclava⟩ Battle of the Crimean War, fought between allied forces and Russia in Oct., 1854. It is noted chiefly as the site of the British cavalry charge celebrated in *The Charge of the Light Brigade* by A. Tennyson.

Balanchine, George 1904–. American choreographer and director, since 1948, of the New York City Ballet.

Balboa, Vasco Núñez de *c*1475–1519. Spanish explorer and conquistador who discovered the Pacific Ocean in 1513.

Balder ⟨Baldur⟩ Norse god of light, the son of Odin and Frigg. Frigg obtained promises not to harm Balder from all things, except for mistletoe, with which Balder was slain by Hoder.

Baldur *See* **Balder**

Baldwin I 1058?–1118. Latin king of Jerusalem (1100–18). A leader in the First Crusade, he consolidated and strengthened Latin control in the East.

Baldwin I 1171–1205? First Latin emperor of Constantinople. A leader of the Fourth Crusade, he was proclaimed emperor in 1204 but was defeated by the Bulgarians at Adrianople (1205).

Baldwin II *d.* 1131. Latin king of Jerusalem (1118–31), successor to his cousin Baldwin I. He expanded the strength and territory of Jerusalem.

Baldwin II 1217–73. Last Latin emperor of Constantinople (1228–61), successor to his brother Robert of Courtenay. He fled to Italy when the Greeks under Michael VIII captured Constantinople in 1261.

Baldwin III 1130?–62. Latin king of Jerusalem (1143–62), son of and successor, with his mother, to King Fulk, assuming sole rule c1152. His reign saw the failure of the Second Crusade and the fall of Damascus (1154.).

Baldwin IV ⟨Baldwin the Leper⟩ c1161–85. Latin king of Jerusalem (1174–85), successor to his father, Amalric I. He spent most of his reign in conflict with Saladin.

Baldwin V d. 1186. Latin king of Jerusalem (1185–86), successor to his uncle, Baldwin IV. Raymond of Tripoli (c1140–87) acted as his regent.

Baldwin, James (Arthur) 1924–. American author. Baldwin is noted for his powerful descriptions of the black American experience in such volumes as *Another Country* and *The Fire Next Time.*

Baldwin, Robert 1804–58. Canadian statesman. A Reform party leader in Upper Canada, he supported the union of Canada and cabinet government. He formed, with L. Lafontaine, coalition governments in 1842–43 and 1847–51, the latter noted for its numerous reforms.

Baldwin, Stanley 1867–1947. British statesman. As prime minister (1923–24, 1924–29, 1935–37) he obtained passage of the Trade Disputes Act (1927), which limited the power of unions, and played a role in the abdication of Edward VIII in 1936. He opposed British rearmament in the face of the increasing German military threat.

Baldwin the Leper *See* **Baldwin IV**

Balewa, Sir Abubakar Tafawa 1912–66. Nigerian statesman, the first prime minister of independent Nigeria (1960–66).

Balfour, Arthur James, 1st earl of 1848–1930. A British statesman, prime minister (1902–05). As foreign secretary (1916–19), he issued the Balfour Declaration *(q.v.).*

Balfour Declaration British foreign-policy statement issued (Nov. 2, 1917) by A. Balfour and expressing British sympathy for the establishment of a Jewish national home in Palestine. This was a major step in the eventual founding of the state of Israel.

Baline, Israel *See* **Berlin, Irving**

Baliol, Edward de ⟨Balliol, ~⟩ d. 1363. King of Scotland and son of John de Baliol. With English support he invaded Scotland (1332), defeated David II, and was made king. He soon after lost his crown, regaining it with the support of Edward

III, to whom he ceded several Scottish counties and, in 1356, his title.

Baliol, John de ⟨Balliol, ~⟩ 1249–1315. King of Scotland (1292–96). Gaining the crown through the support of Edward I, he swore fealty to Edward but later allied with France (1295), renounced his fealty (1296), and was defeated by Edward.

Balkan Entente Mutual defense agreement (1934) between Greece, Romania, Turkey, and Yugoslavia, to provide protection from other Balkan countries. It was voided by German aggression in WW II.

Balkan Peninsula Peninsula in southeastern Europe, roughly bounded by the Adriatic, Aegean, and Black seas. Occupied by Ottoman Turks in the 14th and 15th cents., the area was the site of struggles for independence in the late 19th cent. and was the setting for the Balkan Wars and the events leading to WW I.

Balkan War **1.** First ~ War (Oct. 18, 1912–May 30, 1913) between the Ottoman Empire and the Balkan League (Bulgaria, Greece, Montenegro, and Serbia). Taking advantage of Ottoman involvement in war with Italy (Tripolitan War), the Balkan League declared war on the Ottomans and, in a rapid series of victories, overran nearly all Ottoman domains in Eastern Europe. Fighting was halted by an armistice (Dec. 3, 1912), then resumed (Jan., 1913) when peace negotiations broke down. Hostilities continued until early May, and the war was brought to a close by the Treaty of London (May 30, 1913). In the treaty, the Ottomans lost all but a small part of their European territories, which were divided among members of the league and the newly formed state of Albania. The treaty, however, did nothing to ease international tensions that led to the outbreak of WW I. **2.** Second ~ War (June 29–July 30, 1913) between Bulgaria and Serbia (soon joined by Romania, Greece, and the Ottomans). The Treaty of London left Serbia disgruntled because territories it wanted were joined to the newly formed Albania. Serbia thereupon quarreled with Bulgaria, hoping to gain part of the Macedonian territory awarded to Bulgaria by the treaty. Bulgaria retaliated by launching a surprise attack (June 29, 1913) against Serbia and its ally, Greece. Romania and the Ottomans entered the war and in a brief war helped to utterly defeat Bulgaria. By the Treaty of Bucharest (Aug. 10, with Serbia, Romania, and Greece) and by the Treaty of Constantinople (Sept. 29, with the Ottomans), Bulgaria was stripped of most of the territories it had won in the previous war. This war heightened further international tensions that led to WW I.

Balkis *See* **Sheba**

Ball, John *d.* 1381. English priest and social reformer. Excommunicated in 1376, he was a leader in the peasant revolt of Wat Tyler (1381) and was executed.

Ballet Russe *See* **Diaghilev, Sergei**

Balliol *See* **Baliol**

Balmaceda, José Manuel 1840–91. Chilean president (1886–91). He instituted wide reforms but caused a civil war between congress and the president. He was ousted and shot himself.

Balsamo, Giuseppe *See* **Cagliostro, Alessandro, Conte**

Balthazar *See* **Magi**

Baltic Entente Pact (Sept. 12, 1934) signed by Lithuania, Latvia, and Estonia. The three states sought mutual defense against Nazi Germany.

Baltic States Name for former countries of Lithuania, Latvia, and Estonia, which were located east of the Baltic Sea. The territory was under Russian rule from the 1700s. After WW I and the Baltic War of Liberation, the three independent countries were formed (1918) but were retaken by Russia in 1940 and incorporated into the USSR. The term "Baltic States" sometimes includes Finland and Poland.

Baltic War of Liberation War (1918–20) in which the Baltic States (Lithuania, Latvia, and Estonia) repulsed attacks by both the Russians and Germans and thereby maintained their newly won independence. All three Baltic states declared independence from Russia after the revolution of 1917 and soon after became embroiled in warfare. Lithuania declared independence (Feb. 16, 1918) and, with German aid, was able to defeat the invading Bolsheviks. The short-lived Treaty of Brest-Litovsk (Mar., 1918) ended fighting until Germany collapsed at the end of WW I. The Bolsheviks again invaded Lithuania (after Nov., 1918) and were again defeated, this time with Polish aid. By the Treaty of Moscow (1920), Lithuanian independence was recognized. In Latvia, German occupying forces prevented formation of a national government and army immediately after the Russian Revolution. After Germany's defeat in WW I, however, Latvia proclaimed independence (Nov. 18, 1918) and was invaded (Jan., 1919) by the Bolsheviks. The Bolsheviks were soon forced out by a combined German-Latvian force. The Germans then made an unsuccessful attempt to take over and were defeated by Latvian forces. By the Treaty of Riga (1920), Russia recognized Latvian independence.

Estonia proclaimed independence (Nov. 28, 1917) and soon came under Bolshevik attack. Germany occupied Estonia (Dec., 1917) to stop the Russian advance and, by the Treaty of Brest-Litovsk (1918), the Russians recognized Estonian independence. At the close of WW I, however, the Germans withdrew (Nov., 1918) from Estonia and the Russians again invaded (Nov. 22, 1918). They were driven out, with British help (Jan., 1919) and, by the Treaty of Tartu (Feb., 1920), Russia recognized Estonian independence.

Baltimore City (pop. 786,800) in northern Maryland. The largest city in Maryland, it was founded in 1729. The defense of Fort McHenry here during the War of 1812 inspired *The Star-Spangled Banner* by F. Key.

Baltimore, George Calvert, 1st Baron *See* **Calvert, George, 1st Baron Baltimore**

Baltimore incident US-Chilean incident (Oct. 16, 1891) shortly after the Chilean civil war. Crew members of the USS *Baltimore*, on leave in Valparaiso, were attacked, and two crewmen were killed. Chile agreed to pay an indemnity, and war was avoided.

Balts Peoples of the eastern coast of the Baltic Sea, including the Latvians and the Lithuanians.

Balzac, Honoré de 1799–1850. French writer and one of the world's greatest novelists. He labored in poverty for some ten years before publishing his first successful novel, *Les Chouans* (1829). He wrote voluminously for the next 20 years, though he was never able to elude the debts that plagued him. In 1834 he devised *The Human Comedy*, the overall scheme for his novels, which were collectively to depict human society. Among his masterpieces are *Eugénie Grandet*, *Le Père Goriot*, and *Le Cousin Pons*.

Bamboo Annals Ancient Chinese records. Written on bamboo paper, they date to the Chin state, which was destroyed in the 5th cent. BC. The papers were discovered in AD 281 but have been lost.

Bancroft, George 1800–91. American historian and statesman, and author of the 10-volume *A History of the United States*. As secretary of the navy (1845–46) he established the U.S. Naval Academy at Annapolis.

Bancroft, Hubert Howe 1832–1918. American historian. He compiled a 39-volume history of the Pacific Coast of North America, largely the work of assistants.

Bandaranaike, Mrs. Sirimavo *See* **Sri Lanka**

Bandaranaike, S.W.R.D. *See* **Sri Lanka**

Bande Nere, Giovanni delle *See* **Medici, Giovanni de'**

Bandinelli, Orlando *See* **Alexander III**

Bandung Conference Meeting of 29 African and Asian nations (1955), held at Bandung, Indonesia. Led by Communist China, it sought to promote mutual friendship and oppose colonialism.

Bangkok Capital city (pop. 4,178,000) and largest city of Thailand. An important commercial and cultural center, it became capital of Siam (later named Thailand) in 1782.

Bangladesh ⟨*formerly* East Pakistan⟩ South Asian republic (pop. 88,660,000) on the Bay of Bengal. With India and Pakistan, it was part of the Mogul Empire (1526–1857), then became a part of British India (1857–1947). In 1947, Bangladesh became East Pakistan, the eastern province of Pakistan. In 1971 East Pakistan declared its independence, which it achieved following war between India and Pakistani forces in East Pakistan (Dec., 1971). Pakistan recognized Bangladesh in 1974. Coups in 1975, 1981, and 1982 shook the government and brought the military to power.

Bangorian Controversy Religious controversy over powers of the Church of England. The controversy stemmed from a sermon delivered (1717) before King George I by the bishop of Bangor (Wales), Benjamin Hoadly (1676–1761). In it Hoadly challenged the disciplinary and judicial powers of the church. Supporters of the church's authority and Hoadly's defenders published some 200 pamphlets over a period of several years, disputing the issue.

Banks, Nathaniel Prentiss 1816–94. American politician and Union general during the Civil War. He commanded Union forces at New Orleans (1862) and captured Port Hudson (1863), thereby helping Gen. U. Grant to open the Mississippi.

Banner System Manchu army system in which tribal warriors were grouped into units under distinctive banners (1601). These companies, stationed all over China, enabled the Manchus to conquer China and establish the Ch'ing dynasty.

Bannockburn, Battle of Battle (June 23–24, 1314) at Bannockburn, Scotland. Here Scottish forces under Robert the Bruce defeated the army of English king Edward II, thereby establishing Scottish independence.

Banting, Sir Frederick Grant 1891–1941. Canadian physician. With John J. R. Macleod (1876–1935) and Charles H. Best (1899–1978), he isolated insulin, for which he and Macleod received the Nobel Prize (1923).

Bantu A diverse people of Africa, related primarily by similarities in their languages. Bantus occupy almost all of southern Africa below the Congo River. It is believed that Bantus originally occupied homelands in east-central Africa and spread (c1st cent. BC?) south from there. Bantu tribes include Ashanti, Basutos, Kaffirs, Matabele, Swahilis, and Zulus.

Banville, Théodore de 1823–91. A leading French poet of his day and a member of the Parnassian movement. He is said to have influenced later symbolist poets.

Bao Dai ⟨Nguyen Vinh Thuy⟩ 1913–. Last Vietnamese emperor (1925–45). He initially attempted reform in Vietnam but was thwarted by French colonial rule. Forced to abdicate (1945) by Ho Chi Minh, he returned in 1949 to rule, but his authority was eclipsed by his weak rule and the growing strength of the Viet Minh.

Baptists Protestant Christian denomination. Baptists permit baptism of believers only (as opposed to infant baptism) and practice baptism by immersion. The Baptist churches originated amid members of the English Separatist (Independents) movement and began (c1608) with the teachings of John Smyth, or Smith (c1570–1612). Baptists soon formed two distinct groups: the General Baptists, following J. Arminius' doctrines of the general atonement of Christ; and the Particular Baptists, following the stricter teachings of J. Calvin. The two groups merged in 1891. The first Baptist church in America was founded (1639) at Providence, Rhode Island, by R. Williams, who had been banished from Massachusetts for opposing infant baptism. The subsequent spread of Baptist churches in America was greatly accelerated during the Great Awakening. Baptist sects include the Seventh Day Baptists, who observe Calvinist doctrine and celebrate the seventh day of the week as the Sabbath.

Bar, Confederation of *See* **Confederation of Bar**

Barabbas In the Bible, a thief imprisoned at the same time as Jesus. When Pontius Pilate offered the release of either Barabbas or Jesus, the crowds chose Barabbas.

Baradaeus, Jacob *See* **Syrian Orthodox church**

Barbados Island nation (pop. 279,000) in the West Indies, off the coast of South America. Believed to have been discovered by the Portuguese (16th cent.), it was first settled by the English (c1627). Under British rule, it was a major producer of sugar until 1834, when slavery was abolished. It was the headquarters of the colonial government of the Windward Islands (1833–85) and gained independence in 1966.

Barbara, Saint *fl.* 3d or 4th cent. Virgin martyr, patron saint of artillerymen. According to legend, her father killed her for professing Christianity, and was then struck down by lightning.

Barbarelli, Giorgio *See* **Giorgione**

barbarian Greek term for a stranger or foreigner, later applied by the Romans to Germanic tribes.

barbarian invasions Name given to the conquest of portions of the Western Roman Empire by tribes from the north. By the 4th cent. AD Rome's power had declined, allowing Germanic tribes to seize and settle in northern Roman provinces. The Visigoths crossed the Danube (AD 376) and, led by Alaric, sacked Rome (410). His successor, Ataulf, sought to fuse Roman elements into a Visigothic kingdom. Rome was nearly sacked (451) by the Huns under Attila, and was sacked (455) by the Vandals under Gaiseric. The Germanic tribes under Odoacer deposed (476) Romulus Augustulus, last Roman emperor of the West, and the Western Empire ceased to exist. Other groups to seize Roman territory included the Ostrogoths, Burgundians, and the Franks.

Barberini, Maffeo *See* **Urban VIII**

Barbarossa II ⟨Khair ed-Din⟩ 1466?–1546. Turkish corsair who seized Algiers (1518) from Spain, conquered Tunis (1534), and raided the coasts of Greece, Spain, and Italy.

Barbary States Name for the North African states of Tripoli, Morocco, Tunis, and Algeria during the 16th to 19th cents. A notorious center for pirates, the region was also called the Barbary Coast. Despite a major military campaign mounted (1541) by Holy Roman Emperor Charles V, Algeria, Tunis, and Tripoli fell to the Ottoman Turks in the 16th cent. Semi-independent states within the empire, they became a haven for privateers, the Barbary pirates, who raided ships and coastal towns for booty and slaves. Morocco also became a pirate base. Attacks by European powers and the US (*see* Tripolitan War) on the Barbary States brought its decline. Piracy ended with the French conquest of Algeria (from 1830).

Barbizon school School of realistic French landscape painting (19th cent.) founded by Théodore Rousseau (1812–67) and Jean François Millet (1814–75). It contributed to the development of realism in French painting.

Barbo, Pietro *See* **Paul II**

Barbon, Praise-God *See* **Barebone, Praise-God**

Barcelona Spain's second largest city (pop. 1,745,142), the main city of Catalonia and capital of Barcelona province. Founded by Hamilcar Barca (3rd cent. BC), it has been ruled by Romans, Visigoths, Moors, and Franks. Charlemagne made Barcelona the capital of the Spanish March (801), and it subsequently became the capital of Aragon (12th cent.). Long a center for Catalonian separatism, Barcelona was the capital of the Catalan autonomous government (1932–39) and the Loyalist capital (1938–39) during the Spanish Civil War.

Barclay de Tolly, Mikhail, Prince 1761–1818. Russian field marshal of Scottish descent, whose policy of retreat before Napoleon's army (1812) proved ultimately a successful tactic. Defeated at Smolensk (1812), he was replaced by M. Kutuzov, who continued his tactic.

Bardeen, John 1908–. American physicist, twice cowinner of the Nobel Prize in Physics. He received the prize (1956) with Walter H. Brattain (1902–) and William Shockley (1910–) for development of the transistor; and (1972) with Leon N. Cooper (1930–) and John Schrieffer (1931–) for the theory of superconductivity.

Barebone, Praise-God ⟨Barbon, ∼⟩ 1596?–1679. English preacher and leather merchant. As a member of O. Cromwell's Nominated Parliament (1653), he lent it the nickname Barebones Parliament.

Barebones Parliament ⟨Little Parliament⟩ ⟨Nominated Parliament⟩ Parliament assembled by O. Cromwell (July, 1653) following his dissolution of the Rump Parliament. Named after a member, Praise-God Barebone, it resigned its powers to Cromwell, who established the Protectorate.

Bar-Hebraeus, Gregorius ⟨Abulfaraj⟩ 1226–86. Syrian scholar known best for his chronicle of the world, written in Syriac.

Bari, Council of Religious council called (1098) by Pope Urban II in an attempt to reconcile the Eastern and Western churches.

Baring British family of financiers, including Sir Francis Baring (1740–1810), chief founder (1763) of John and Francis Baring and Company, which helped to finance British military operations against the French in the Napoleonic Wars. Many family members have also served in government.

Baring, Sir Francis *See* **Baring**

Barkley, Alben W(illiam) 1877–1956. Vice-president of the United States (1949–53) under H. Truman. A member of the House (1913–27) and Senate (1927–49, 1954–56), he played a major role in forming the New Deal.

Bar Kokhba, Simon ⟨Simon Bar Cochba⟩ *d.* AD 135. Hebrew leader who led a major revolt against Roman emperor Hadrian (AD 132–135) until his defeat by J. Severus (AD 135).

Barlaam and Josaphat Popular medieval legend. Josaphat, the son of an Indian king, is converted to Christianity by the monk Barlaam. Upon his succession to the throne, he abdicates for the religious life. Some see in this story elements of the history of Buddha.

Barlow, Joel 1754–1812. American writer and diplomat, one of the Connecticut Wits. Appointed ambassador to France (1811), he was caught in Napoleon's retreat from Moscow and died from exposure.

Barnabas, Saint ⟨*originally* Joses, or Joseph⟩ *d.* AD c61. Christian apostle from Cyprus. A founder of the church at Antioch, he accompanied Paul on his first missionary journey to Cyprus.

Barnard, Christiaan Neething 1922–. South African surgeon. Barnard introduced open-heart surgery to his country and performed the first human heart transplant (Dec. 3, 1967).

Barnard, George Grey 1863–1938. American sculptor, noted for a controversial statue of A. Lincoln (1917). His private collection of Gothic and medieval art was the foundation for the Cloisters museum in New York City.

Barnard, Henry 1811–1900. American educator. With H. Mann, he led the movement to improve the US educational system and became the first US commissioner of education (1867).

Barnave, Joseph 1761–93. French revolutionary. A Jacobin leader, he helped to return the fleeing King Louis XVI to Paris (1791). Breaking with the Jacobins, he joined the Feuillants, and his advocacy of a constitutional monarchy led to his execution.

Barnburners Radical faction of New York Democrats (1842–48) opposed to their conservative counterparts, the Hunkers. Largely an antislavery group, Barnburners supported the Wilmot Proviso. The faction split from the state Democratic party (1847) and, barred from the national convention (1848), it nominated M. Van Buren for president. By splitting the Democratic vote, it helped Z. Taylor to victory. The faction broke up after the election, some members joining the Free-Soil Party. Barnburners were named after a legendary farmer who burned his barn to clear it of rats.

Barnet, Battle of Battle (Apr. 14, 1471) fought at Barnet, England, during the War of the Roses. The battle resulted in a major Yorkist victory for Edward IV over the Lancastrians, led by Henry VI.

Barnum, Phineas Taylor 1810–91. American showman. Barnum introduced sensational exhibits to his museum in New York, and with James A. Bailey (1847–1906) formed the Barnum and Bailey Circus (1881).

Baroja y Nessi, Pío 1879–1956. Basque-born writer, one of the major Spanish novelists of the 20th cent.

Baronius, Caesar 1538–1607. Italian ecclesiastical historian, author of *Annales Eccliastici*, a history of the church to the year 1198.

Barons' War Rebellion (1263–67) by English barons against the arbitrary rule of King Henry III. Henry precipitated the uprising by refusing to abide by the Provisions of Oxford and of Westminster. Led by S. de Montfort, the barons at first forced Henry's submission (1263). Fighting was renewed (1264) after the barons rejected the Mise of Amiens, arbitration in favor of Henry. Victorious at the Battle of Lewes (1264), Montfort became virtual ruler of England and summoned (1265) a representative parliament that was a model for the House of Commons. Montfort was defeated and slain by Prince Edward at the Battle of Evesham (1265), and baronial resistance ended in 1267.

baroque Artistic and architectural style, which flourished in Europe and England in the 17th and 18th cents. It was characterized by fluidity of movement and grandness of scale. It arose in Italy (c1600) and thereafter spread throughout Europe, taking on distinctive national characteristics in each area. Among the leading artists and architects in this period were (in Italy) Caravaggio and G. Bernini; (in France) N. Poussin; (in Flanders) P. Rubens; (in Holland) Rembrandt and Vermeer; (in Spain) Velasquez and (in England) Van Dyck and C. Wren. The term baroque also applies to a musical style developed in this period.

Barrackpore Mutiny Mutiny (Nov. 2, 1824) of Indian troops at Barrackpore, India, during the first Burma War (1824–26). Indian troops, holding serious grievances against British commanders, refused to obey orders and were subsequently fired upon by European troops. The massacre fostered deep resentment that contributed to the Indian Mutiny (1857–58).

Barras, Paul François Jean Nicolas, vicomte de 1755–1829. French revolutionary. An early Jacobin, he helped overthrow M. Robespierre and, with the aid of Napoleon, established the Directory (1795). He was overthrown by Napoleon in 1799.

Barrès, Maurice 1862–1923. French novelist and politician whose influential works reflected his ardent nationalism and individualism.

Barrie, Sir James Matthew 1860–1937. Scottish novelist and dramatist, known best for his play *Peter Pan*.

Barrier Treaty Treaty (Nov. 15, 1715) signed at Antwerp by Great Britain, Austria, and The Netherlands, ceding to the Dutch fortresses along the frontier with France, for protection from French attack.

Barry, John 1745–1803. US naval officer in the American Revolution. He captured the British tender *Edward*, the first British ship taken by a commissioned American naval vessel.

Barrymore, Ethel 1879–1959. American actress. The sister of J. and L. Barrymore, she was a leading figure in early 20th-cent. theater.

Barrymore, John 1882–1942. American actor, the brother of E. and L. Barrymore. He is noted for his Shakespearean roles, notably Hamlet, and for many films.

Barrymore, Lionel 1878–1954. American actor. The brother of E. and J. Barrymore, he was an outstanding character actor on stage, screen, and radio.

Bart, Jean 1650–1702. French naval officer and privateer noted for his naval exploits during the War of the Grand Alliance.

Barth, Karl 1886–1968. Swiss theologian. Barth's philosophy, called dialectical theology, stressed the word of God and his revelation in Jesus Christ as the central means of understanding man's relationship to God.

Bartholdi, Frederic Auguste 1834–1904. French sculptor whose works include the *Statue of Liberty* and the *Lion of Belfort* monument at Belfort, France.

Bartholomew, Saint One of the twelve disciples of Jesus Christ, usually identified with Nathanael. He is believed to have preached in or near India and to have been martyred in Armenia.

Bartlett, John 1820–1905. American publisher and editor, known best as compiler of *Familiar Quotations.*

Bartók, Béla 1881–1945. Hungarian composer, a major figure in 20th-cent. music. His works, striking and original, reflect his study of Hungarian folk music.

Bartolommeo, Fra ⟨Baccio della Porta⟩ 1475–1517. Italian painter. A master of the Florentine school of Renaissance painting, he was influenced by Raphael.

Barton, Clara 1821–1912. American humanitarian whose nursing services during the Civil War earned her the title Angel of the Battlefield. She founded the American Red Cross (1881).

Barton, Elizabeth 1506?–34. English servant woman known as the Nun of Kent or the Maid of Kent. Her prophecies warning against Henry VIII's marriage to Anne Boleyn were exposed as fraudulent, and she was executed.

Bartram, John 1699–1777. American botanist. He founded, near Philadelphia, the first botanical garden in the US.

Bärwalde, Treaty of ⟨Brandenburg, ~⟩ French-Swedish treaty (January 13, 1631) by which French king Louis XIII agreed to pay annual subsidies to Swedish king Gustavus II Adolphus to support an army against the Hapsburgs in the Thirty Years' War.

Barzun, Jacques 1907–. American writer and educator whose books include *Darwin, Marx, Wagner* and *The Teacher in America.*

Bascio, Matteo da *See* **Capuchins**

Basel ⟨Basle⟩ Swiss city. Founded by the Romans, Basel is now the chief railroad junction in Switzerland. It became an episcopal see (7th cent.) and joined the Swiss Confederation (1501). Basel is a major economic and cultural center.

Basel, Confession of Name of two statements of Reformation doctrine. **1.** First ~. Statement drafted by J. Oecolampadius (1531) and revised by Oswald Mycanius (1488–1552). **2.** Second ~. Name sometimes applied to the first Helvetic Confession, written (1536) by Heinrich Bullinger (1504–75) and others and adopted by the Swiss Reformed church.

Basel, Council of Council of the Roman Catholic church convened (1431–49) at Basel, noted for its struggle with Pope Eugene IV over the issue of conciliarism vs papal supremacy. The council made a number of reforms and by the Compactata of Prague (1436) found a settlement for the Hussite question. Eugene, after attempting to come to terms with the conciliarists by making numerous concessions, summoned the Council of Ferrara-Florence (1437) to deal with other church matters. The few bishops remaining at Basel declared Eugene a heretic and replaced him (1439) with antipope Felix V. The struggle continued until Pope Nicholas V, successor to Eugene, was recognized as the legitimate pope. Felix abdicated (1449) and the council at Basel was dissolved.

Basel, Peace of *See also* **Basel, Treaties of**

Basel, Treaty of **1.** ⟨~, Peace of⟩ Treaty (Sept. 22, 1499) between Holy Roman Emperor Maximilian I and the Swiss Confederation, ending a series of conflicts and effectively granting Swiss independence. **2.** Treaty (Apr. 5, 1795) between France and Prussia, ending Prussia's participation against France in the French Revolutionary Wars (1792–1802). France relinquished control of the right bank of the Rhine in return for Prussia's recognition of French claims to the left bank. **3.** Treaty (July 22, 1795) between France and Spain, ending Spain's participation against France (1793–95) in the French Revolutionary Wars (1792–1802). France returned conquered territories in exchange for Santo Domingo.

Basil I ⟨Basil the Macedonian⟩ c813–86. Byzantine emperor (867–86). He assassinated (867) his coruler, Michael III, and proclaimed himself emperor. He founded the Macedonian dynasty and his reign marked a golden age in Byzantine history.

Basil II ⟨surnamed Bulgaroktonos⟩ c958–1025. Byzantine emperor (976–1025), nominal successor (963) to his father, Romanus II, with his brother, Constantine VIII (960?–1028). Coming to power in 976, he incorporated the kingdom of Bulgaria into the empire (1018) after a series of conflicts with the Bulgarians.

Basil IV Shuisky *See* **Time of Troubles**

Basil, Saint ⟨Basil the Great, Saint⟩ AD c330–c379. Greek bishop of Caesarea (from AD 370).

One of the great Fathers of the Greek church, he supported orthodox belief against Arianism. (*See also* Basilians.)

Basil the Great, Saint *See* **Basil, Saint**

Basil the Macedonian *See* **Basil I**

Basilians Members of the religious order founded (AD 358) by Saint Basil the Great and including many of the monks of the Eastern church. A Basilian order was also established in France in 1822.

Basilides *See* **Gnosticism**

Baskerville, John 1706–75. English printer and designer of the Baskerville typefaces.

Basle *See* **Basel**

Basques An ethnic group inhabiting northern Spain and southern France from ancient times. Converted to Christianity (5th cent.), Basques largely resisted conquest by the Romans, Visigoths, Moors, and Franks. French Basques finally submitted to the Franks (9th cent.). The Basque kingdom of Navarre resisted Spanish kings until 1512. The Spanish Civil War (1936–39) divided the Basques politically, and the region was a site of fierce fighting. The Basque Separatist movement flourishes today.

Bassein, Treaty of Anglo-Indian treaty (Dec. 31, 1802). The Maratha leader Peshwa Baji Rao II (*d.* 1852) entered into an alliance with the British East India Company, trading independence for protection. The treaty gave Britain a foothold in the area and led eventually to the Second Maratha War and the downfall of the Maratha Confederacy.

Bassianus, Varius Avitus *See* **Heliogabalus**

Bastian, Adolf 1826–1905. German anthropologist. His theory, that certain ideas common to all mankind differ in form according to culture, influenced later anthropologists and psychologists.

Bastille French fortress and later (17th–18th cents.) a notorious prison in Paris, France. Built (*c*1370) by Charles V, it became a symbol of arbitrary royal powers because prisoners (from 17th cent.) detained by the king's *Lettre de Cachet* were held there. The storming of the prison (July 14, 1789) symbolized the end of the *Ancien Régime* for French revolutionaries, although the rioters were after munitions stored there, and just seven prisoners were in the jail that day. Bastille Day (July 14) is a French national holiday.

Basutoland *See* **Lesotho**

Bataan Death March Forced march (beginning Apr. 9, 1942) of 75,000 Americans and Filipinos captured by the Japanese at Bataan, Philippines, during WW II. The brutal conditions were such that only 54,000 survived the 60-mile trek. The march was commanded by Gen. Masaharu

Homma (1888?–1946), who later was hanged as a war criminal.

Batavian Republic Name given to The Netherlands after conquest (1795) by Napoleon in the French Revolutionary Wars. It became the kingdom of Holland in 1806.

Bates, Henry Walter 1825–92. English naturalist and explorer. His study of the effect of natural selection in animal mimicry supported C. Darwin's theory of evolution.

Bath English city noted since ancient times for its hot springs. The Romans founded a town (AD 1st cent.) and built extensive baths there. Destroyed in Saxon times, Bath was later restored (18th cent.)

Bathory, Elizabeth *d.* 1614. Hungarian countess, said to have slain more than six hundred young girls and to have bathed in their blood in order to restore her youth.

Bathory, Sigismund 1572–1613. Prince of Transylvania (1581–99). A vassal of Holy Roman Emperor Rudolf II, Bathory provoked a civil war in Transylvania through his policies against the Ottoman Turks.

Ba'th party ⟨Ba'ath ∼⟩ ⟨Arab Socialist Renaissance party⟩ Arab political party (founded 1943), especially influential in Syria and Iraq. The party advocates creation of a unified Arab socialist state. In Syria, the party was important in the formation (1958) of the United Arab Republic and Syria's subsequent withdrawal from it (1961). It was involved in coups (Mar., 1963; Feb., 1966), and in the latter radical left-wing Bathists took power in Syria. In Iraq, the party came to power briefly after a coup (Feb., 1963) and returned to power by a coup in July, 1968. Bathist opposition was chiefly responsible for blocking a planned union (1963) between Egypt, Syria, and Iraq.

Bath-sheba Biblical wife of David and mother of Solomon. David seduced her, had her husband Uriah the Hittite killed, and then married her.

Batista y Zaldívar, Fulgencio 1901–73. Cuban dictator. He took part in the overthrow of G. Machado (1933) and served as president from 1940 to 1944. In 1952 he seized power and ruled as dictator until overthrown by F. Castro (1959).

Batlle y Ordóñez, José 1856–1929. President of Uruguay (1903–07, 1911–15). A leader of the liberal Colorado party, he introduced numerous political and social reforms and influenced the writing of the Uruguayan constitution of 1918.

Baton Rouge American city (pop. 219,000), the capital of Louisiana. Founded by the French (1719), it was ceded to Britain (1763), occupied by Spain (1779), and annexed by the US (1810). A major Mississippi port, it is noted for its oil and petrochemical industries.

Battle Above the Clouds *See* **Chattanooga, Battle of**; *see under names inverted, as in* **Atlantic, Battle of the**

Batu Khan d. 1255. Mongol leader, a grandson of Genghis Khan. He established the Kipchak khanate, also known as the Golden Horde *(q.v.)*.

Baudelaire, Charles 1821–67. French poet and critic whose writings had a major influence on the development of the symbolist movement. His best-known collection is *Les Fleurs du mal.*

Baudouin 1930–. Belgian king (1951–), successor to his father, King Leopold III.

Bauer, Georg *See* **Agricola, Georgius**

Bauhaus School of design founded (1919) at Weimar, Germany. Originally headed (1919–28) by architect W. Gropius, the school sought to overcome divisions between the arts, crafts, and modern industry. To do this, students were given multidisciplinary training. The economical, geometric designs that became associated with the school proved unpopular with the Nazis, who closed the school (1933). Gropius and other Bauhaus associates, including L. Mies van der Rohe and L. Moholy-Nagy then carried the Bauhaus movement to the US, where Bauhaus design had been well received.

Baum, Lyman Frank 1856–1919. American writer known best for his children's book *The Wizard of Oz.*

Bautzen, Battle of Battle (May 20–21, 1813) in the Napoleonic Wars fought at Bautzen (now in East Germany). Napoleon's French army of 140,000 troops defeated a Russo-Prussian army of some 90,000. Though a victory for Napoleon I, French losses were greater than Russo-Prussian casualties.

Bavaria West German state. Originally inhabited by Celts, it was conquered by the Romans (1st cent. BC), then by Germanic peoples ending with the Franks. In 788 it became part of Charlemagne's empire. One of the main duchies of the Holy Roman Empire in medieval Germany, Bavaria passed in 1180 to the house of Wittelsbach, which held it until 1918. It became a kingdom (1806) under Maximilian I and joined the German empire in 1871. Bavaria became a socialist republic (1918) and joined the Weimar Republic, but lost its independence with the rise (1933) of Nazi Germany. In 1949 Bavaria became part of the German Federal Republic.

Bavaria, Isabeau of *See* **Isabeau of Bavaria**

Bavarian Succession, War of the ⟨Potato War⟩ Dispute (1778–79) in which Prussia prevented Austria from taking over Bavarian lands. Charles

Theodore, successor to the extinct line of Bavarian electors of Wittelsbach, precipitated the conflict by ceding Lower Bavaria to Holy Roman Emperor Joseph II of Austria. Frederick II (the Great), however, feared increased Austrian influence in southern Germany, and with Saxony raised an army against the Austrians. There were no major engagements and the brief war was ended by the Treaty of Teschen (1779).

Bayard, Pierre du Terrail, seigneur de c1473–1524. French soldier, called "the knight without fear and without blame." He halted an invasion of central France by Holy Roman Emperor Charles V at Mézières (1521) and distinguished himself in the Italian Wars (1494–1529).

Bayer, Johann 1572–1625. German astronomer and author of the *Uranometria* (1603), the first complete star chart. He also was the first to designate stars by Greek letters according to their magnitudes.

Bayinnaung Burmese ruler (1551–81). A fierce warrior, he conquered much surrounding territory and unified Burma. He twice invaded Siam, and maintained a puppet ruler there for fifteen years.

Bayle, Pierre 1647–1706. French philosopher. An advocate of tolerance and skepticism, he greatly influenced philosophers of the Enlightenment. His major work is the *Dictionnaire historique et critique.*

Bay of Islands War War (1844–47), usually considered part of the first Maori War *(q.v.)*, between European settlers and Maori natives in New Zealand. After the massacre of Europeans at Wairu (1843), a native rebellion began (1844) in the Bay of Islands region of northern New Zealand. Led by Maori chief Hone Heka, some 1,000 natives took part in the rebellion, caused by the natives' anger at declining profits from trade. They attacked settlements in the north (from 1845) until their revolt was quashed (1847) by Gov. Sir George Grey (1812–98).

Bay of Pigs invasion Unsuccessful invasion (Apr. 17, 1961) of Cuba by Cuban exiles. Organized by the US CIA, the invasion was a major embarrassment to the newly elected Kennedy administration and was an important event leading up to the Cuban missile crisis (1962). Planned (from May, 1960) under the Eisenhower administration and approved by Kennedy shortly after his inauguration, the invasion was an outgrowth of worsening relations between the US and Cuba's F. Castro. Some 1,500 Cuban exiles took part in the invasion (along Cuba's southern coast), which was intended to spark a general uprising. The invasion failed, in part because Kennedy apparently refused to allow air cover. Many of the invaders were captured, and 1,113 survivors were ransomed back to the US by the Cubans for food and medicine (1962).

Bay Psalm Book First book published in the American colonies. Published in Cambridge, Massachusetts, in 1640, its complete title is *The Whole Book of Psalms Faithfully Translated into English Metre.*

Bean, Roy c1825–1903. American frontier judge, known as the "law west of the Pecos." Bean changed the name of Vinegaroon, Texas, to Langtry in honor of the English actress Lily Langtry (1853–1929). There he dispensed his own form of frontier justice and became a figure of western folklore.

bearbaiting ⟨bullbaiting⟩ Medieval entertainment in which dogs were set upon a bear (or bull) tied to a stake or otherwise made immobile. Popular in England and Europe for centuries, it was outlawed by Parliament in the 19th cent.

Beard, Charles A(ustin) 1874–1948. American historian noted for his emphasis on the importance of economic forces in the shaping of American history.

Beatrix *See* **Juliana**

Beauchamp, Thomas de, earl of Warwick d. 1401. English statesman. One of the governors of Richard II during his minority, he later opposed Richard and was imprisoned, then exiled. He was restored by Henry IV.

Beauclerc, Henry *See* **Henry I**

Beaufort, Margaret, countess of Richmond and Derby 1443–1509. English noblewoman, mother of Henry VII. She founded professorships of divinity at Oxford and Cambridge and endowed Christ's College and St. John's College at Cambridge.

Beaufort, Pierre Roger de *See* **Gregory XI**

Beauharnais, Hortense de 1783–1837. French noblewoman. Queen of Holland from 1806–10, she was the wife of L. Bonaparte and mother of Napoleon III.

Beaumarchais, Pierre Augustin Caron de 1732–99. French playwright. His comedies *Le Barbier de Séville* (1775) and *Le Mariage de Figaro* (1784) inspired operas by G. Rossini and W. Mozart. He lost his fortune supplying arms to the US during the American Revolution.

Beauregard, Pierre Gustave Toutant 1818–93. Confederate general. He ordered the firing on Fort Sumter in 1861, thus beginning the Civil War, and fought at the first battle of Bull Run (1861) and at Shiloh (1862).

Beauvoir, Simone de 1908–. French existentialist writer, long associated with J. Sartre. Her books include *The Blood of Others* and *The Second Sex.*

Beaverbrook, William Maxwell Aitken, 1st Baron 1879–1964. Canadian-born financier, British politician, and newspaper owner. He served in Parliament, and in the cabinets of Lloyd George (1918) and Winston Churchill (1940–42), advocating free trade within the British Empire.

Bebel, August 1840–1913. German socialist leader. Drawn to socialism by W. Liebknecht, he helped to found the Social Democratic party of Germany (1869), which he led for many years.

Beccaria, Cesare Bonesana, marchese di 1738–94. Italian writer. His essay opposing capital punishment, *Dei delitti e delle pene* (1764), had a great influence on penal reform in Europe.

Bechuanaland *See* **Botswana**

Becket, Thomas à *See* **Thomas à Beckett**

Beckmann, Max *See* **expressionism**

Becquerel, Antoine Henri 1852–1908. French scientist. He discovered radioactivity in uranium and shared with the Curies the 1903 Nobel Prize in Physics.

Bede, Saint ⟨Baeda, ~⟩ 673?–737. English historian and Benedictine monk, called the Venerable Bede. His *Ecclesiastical History of the English People* is a main source for English history to the year 731.

Bedlam English hospital properly named Bethlehem Royal Hospital. Originally a priory (founded c1247) in London, it was later used for confinement of the mentally ill. Its name was slurred in common use to "bedlam," a word now used to describe any scene of uproar. The hospital was one of the first mental institutions in Europe, and the first in England.

Bedouin Arabic-speaking nomadic peoples of the Middle East, constituting about 10 percent of the population of the region. Many Bedouin have been forced by modern events to give up their nomadic way of life.

Beebe, Charles William 1877–1962. American naturalist, explorer, and writer. In 1934 he descended in the sea, using a bathysphere, to a record depth of 3,028 feet (923 meters).

Beecher, Henry Ward 1813–87. American Congregational preacher and brother of Harriet Beecher Stowe. As pastor (1847–87) of Plymouth (Congregational) Church in Brooklyn, New York, he was an influential opponent of slavery and supporter of woman suffrage and the theory of evolution. A sensational court trial for adultery (1875) tarnished his career, although the evidence was inconclusive.

Beelzebub Biblical demon referred to in the New Testament as the prince of demons. Beelzebub appears as a fallen angel and companion of Lucifer in J. Milton's *Paradise Lost.*

Beerbohm, Sir Max 1872–1956. English writer and caricaturist noted for his humorous parodies, essays, and caricatures.

Beer Hall Putsch *See* **Munich Putsch**

Beethoven, Ludwig van 1770–1827. German composer, one of the greatest composers of all time. Beethoven was tutored first by W. Mozart and then by F. Haydn (1792–94) in Vienna, then the center of the music world. Beethoven soon rose to be the preeminent composer of his day. His personal life, however, was marked by the onset of his deafness (c1801) and his stormy relationship with his nephew, then his ward. Beethoven, through his brilliant and emotional compositions, transcended the limitations set by classical style and set the stage for the works of the later Romantic period. Among his greatest works are his nine symphonies, including No. 3, the *Eroica*, originally written by him to honor Napoleon, and No. 9, which includes a choral finale based on F. von Schiller's *Ode to Joy*. His major works also include the *Moonlight Sonata, Missa Solemnis*, and the opera *Fidelio*.

Beghards Semimonastic religious associations of Catholic men, similar to the Beguines. They flourished in Europe in the 13th cent. Condemned at the Council of Vienne (1311) as a heretical sect, they gradually disappeared.

Begin, Menachem 1913–. Israeli politician and prime minister (1977–   ). A member of the right-wing underground military organization Irgun prior to Israeli independence (1948), Begin later led the Herut (Freedom) party, and then the Likud Bloc. A critic of earlier Labor party governments, he nevertheless became the Israeli prime minister who concluded formal peace with Egypt (Mar. 26, 1979). He received the 1978 Nobel Peace Prize along with Egyptian pres. A. Sadat. He was later seriously criticized for air attacks on an Iraqi nuclear reactor and for the annexation (1981) of the Golan Heights (taken from Syria in the 1967 war). The Israelis were also successful in a war against the PLO in Lebanon (1982) during his administration.

Beguines Religious communities of women that flourished in Europe in the 12th and 13th cents. Semimonastic orders, they devoted themselves to charitable works and preaching. Though condemned by the Council of Vienne (1311), they still survive in Belgium and The Netherlands.

Beham, Barthel 1502–40. German painter and engraver. He was a member of the group of engravers known as the Little Masters, whose works were influenced by A. Dürer.

Beham, Hans Sebald 1500–50. German painter and engraver, and brother of B. Beham. A member of the Little Masters, he is known for his miniature engravings.

behaviorism Psychological theory. Introduced by J. Watson (1913), behaviorism maintains that animal and human actions are physical responses to environmental stimuli. Contributors to behaviorist theory include I. Pavlov and B.F. Skinner.

Behistun Inscription ⟨Bisitun Inscription⟩ Carving in an elevated rock face near Behistun, western Iran. The inscription, ordered (c6th cent. BC) by Persian king Darius I, appears in Assyrian, Old Persian, and Elamite, and greatly facilitated decipherment of ancient Babylonian and Elamite texts.

Behrens, Peter 1868–1940. German architect noted for his influence on the development of modern architecture and industrial design.

Behring, Emil Adolph von 1854–1917. German bacteriologist and pioneer in serum therapy. With S. Kitasato he developed antitoxins for diphtheria and tetanus, and in 1901 received the first Nobel Prize in Medicine.

Behring, Vitus Jonassen *See* **Bering, Vitus Jonassen**

Beirut ⟨Beyrouth⟩ Lebanese city (pop. 702,000) and capital of Lebanon since 1920. A Phoenician city (2d millennium BC), it became a major Mediterranean trading center (after 1500 BC), and flourished under the Romans, who established a noted school of law (AD 3d cent.) there. Captured by the Arabs (635), it was recaptured by Baldwin I in the Crusades (1110) and was part of the Latin kingdom of Jerusalem until 1291. It later came under the control of the Druses, who controlled it until the 19th cent. In modern times it was the scene of a siege (1982) by Israeli forces seeking to force the PLO out of Lebanon.

Béjard *See* **Béjart**

Béjart ⟨Béjard⟩ French family of actors who performed with J. Molière. Its members included Madeleine Béjart (1618–72), Molière's mistress, and Armande Béjart (c1642–1700), Molière's wife. After Molière's death, their company merged with a rival group to become the Comédie Française.

Bel One of the major ancient Babylonian gods, whose name is cognate with Baal.

Bela IV 1206–70. King of Hungary (1235–70), successor to his father, Andrew II. During his reign, much of Hungary was devastated by Mongol invasions. Most of his rule was spent in rebuilding and repopulating Hungary, and warring against King Ottocar II of Bohemia.

Belaúnde Terry, Fernando 1912–. Peruvian architect and statesman. As president of Peru (1963–68), he instituted many social and economic reforms, but his pro-US policies led to his ouster (Oct., 1968) in a military coup.

Belfast Capital (pop. 357,600) of Northern Ireland. Northern Ireland's main port, Belfast became a center for the linen industry with the arrival (17th cent.) of French Huguenots, following revocation of the Edict of Nantes (1598), and now is the center for Irish linen manufacture. Since the 19th cent. Belfast has often been the site of violent confrontations between Protestant and Catholic groups.

Belgian Congo See **Zaire**

Belgium Constitutional monarchy located in northwestern Europe. Its capital is Brussels. Once part of the Roman province of Belgica, the region came under Frankish, Burgundian, Hapsburg, Spanish, Austrian, and French control before gaining independence in 1831. Due to its strategic importance, Belgium was guaranteed perpetual neutrality (1839) by the major European nations. Belgium's neutrality was broken twice by Germany, during both world wars. Key events in the history of Belgium include:

3D CENT. AD Franks entered region; Belgian territory eventually became part of Carolingian empire.

9TH CENT. Belgian lands became part of duchy of Lower Lorraine after division of Carolingian empire.

12TH–15TH CENTS. Lower Lorraine broke up into small duchies; region became center of wool trade and other commerce.

15TH CENT. Territory came under control of dukes of Burgundy.

1477 Control of region passed to Hapsburg family by the marriage of Mary of Burgundy to Maximilian I.

1555 Region passed to Spanish Hapsburgs and became part of the Spanish Netherlands.

1578 Revolt of the Netherlands against harsh Spanish rule; southern, predominantly Catholic part (now Belgium and Luxembourg) eventually reconquered by Spain.

1714 Territory passed to Austria by the Peace of Utrecht; constituted part of the Austrian Netherlands.

1794 Austrian Netherlands conquered by French during the French Revolutionary Wars.

1797 France acquired Belgian territories by Treaty of Campo Formio.

1815 Congress of Vienna divided former Austrian Netherlands; Grand Duchy of Luxembourg created from part of territory while remainder was united with the Netherlands.

1831 Revolt in former Austrian Netherlands (1830); independent Belgium created.

1831–65 Leopold I ruled as first king of Belgium; reign marked by extensive industrial growth.

1839 Belgian neutrality guaranteed by major European powers at the London Conference.

1865–1909 Leopold II reigned; Belgium became major industrial and colonial power; annexed Belgian Congo (1908).

1909–34 Albert I reigned.

1914 Belgium invaded by German forces (Aug. 4) at outbreak of WW I; most of Belgium occupied by Germans by end of Nov.; Belgian resistance hindered German invasion of France.

1925 Locarno Pact guaranteed the post-WW I borders of the Rhineland, Belgium, France, and Germany.

1930 Administrative division of Belgium into Flemish (Dutch-speaking) and Walloon (French-speaking) provinces under different administrations.

1934–51 Leopold III reigned.

1940 Belgium invaded by German forces (May 10) in WW II; Leopold III surrendered (May 28); Belgian government voted to rescind Leopold's power to rule; Belgian government-in-exile established in London (Oct.).

1944 Belgian forces operating with Allies in WW II liberated Belgium (Sept.).

1947 Benelux customs union established by Belgium, The Netherlands, and Luxembourg.

1949 Belgium became founding member of NATO (Apr. 4).

1951 Leopold III abdicated; his son Baudouin became king.

1957 Belgium became member (Mar. 25) of newly organized European Economic Community.

1960s Belgian Congo (now Zaire) became independent (1960); Belgium suffered period of political and social turmoil.

1972 Political crisis over readjustment of Fleming and Walloon territories.

1980 Prime Minister Wilfried Martens resigned after failing to win division of Belgium into three administrative regions based on linguistic groups.

1980 Limited autonomy granted (Aug. 5) for Flanders and Wallonia, Belgium's two major linguistic regions.

1981 Mark Eyskens in office as prime minister, following the resignation of W. Martens over financial crisis; Eyskens instituted a temporary price freeze.

1981 W. Martens returned to power as prime minister after coalition government of M. Eyskens collapsed.

Belgrade Capital (pop. 1,300,000) city of Yugoslavia. An early Roman port city, Belgrade has been occupied many times and was a key European stronghold of the Ottoman Turks (15th to 19th cents.). It became (1882) capital of the kingdom of Serbia and (1918) of the kingdom (now the republic) of Yugoslavia.

Belgrade, Treaties of Two peace treaties (Sept., 1739) by which the Ottoman Empire ended wars with both Russia and Austria. Austria ceded northern Serbia and Little Walachia to the Ottomans, while Russia retained Azov but agreed not to build a fleet on the Black Sea.

Belinsky, Vissarion Grigoryevich 1811–48. Russian writer. His view that literature had social and political responsibilities greatly influenced the development of Soviet literary criticism.

Belisarius c505–565. Byzantine general under Justinian I. He suppressed the Nika Riot in Constantinople (532), defeated the Vandals in Africa (533–34), and recaptured parts of Italy from the Ostrogoths (535–40).

Belize ⟨formerly British Honduras⟩ Commonwealth country and former British colony (pop. 144,700) in Central America. Much of its economy is based on forest products. Originally part of the Mayan civilization, it was settled by English timber cutters from Jamaica (17th cent.). Spain contested English possession until 1798. Guatemala has claimed the territory periodically since the early 19th cent. Belize was granted internal self-government in 1965 and became an independent commonwealth Sept. 21, 1981.

Bell, Alexander Graham 1847–1922. Scottish-born American inventor of the telephone. Bell, a teacher of a "visible speech" technique for the deaf, moved to Boston (1872), where he opened a training school for teachers of the deaf. At the same time he worked on his inventions and by 1876 developed a working model of his telephone. The Bell Telephone Company was formed the next year. Bell opened the Volta Laboratory in Washington, D.C., and continued his researches there. Among his inventions are the graphophone, similar to T. Edison's phonograph, and the photophone, for transmitting sound via a light beam.

Bell, Andrew 1753–1832. British educator. At Madras, India, he developed the monitorial system, which uses students in the teaching process.

Bell, Sir Charles 1774–1842. Scottish anatomist and surgeon who distinguished between motor and sensory nerves. His works include *The Nervous System of the Human Body.*

Bell, John 1797–1869. American statesman. A Whig leader in Tennessee, he delayed the state's secession from the Union until the beginning of the Civil War. He was an unsuccessful candidate for president on the Constitutional Union party ticket (1860).

Bellamy, Edward 1850–98. American novelist, author of the Utopian romance *Looking Backward, 2000–1887* (1888).

Bellarmine, Saint Robert ⟨b. Bellarmino, Roberto Francesco Romolo⟩ 1542–1621. Italian theologian. One of the foremost defenders of the Roman Catholic church in the 16th cent., he played a role in the trial of Galileo.

Bellarmino, Roberto Francesco Romolo *See* **Bellarmine, Saint Robert**

Belleau, Rémy 1528–77. French poet and scholar, and member of the literary group known as the Pleiad.

Belle-Isle, Charles Louis Fouquet, duc de 1684–1761. Marshal of France. By supporting the election of Charles Albert of Bavaria as Holy Roman Emperor Charles VII, he helped to involve France in the War of the Austrian Succession (1740–48).

Bellerophon Mythical Greek hero. With the help of the winged horse Pegasus, he slew the monster Chimera. He attempted to ride Pegasus to Mt. Olympus but fell and was crippled and blinded.

Bellini, Giovanni c1430–1516. Venetian painter. He was a leading Renaissance painter; his religious paintings and landscapes helped make Venice a center of Renaissance art.

Bellona Mythical Roman goddess of war, usually depicted as the sister or wife of Mars.

Bellow, Saul 1915–. American novelist whose works deal with individuals and their struggles within modern society. He was awarded the Nobel Prize in Literature (1976).

Belorussia ⟨White Russia⟩ Region of western USSR, now a constituent republic known as the Belorussian SSR. Formerly part of Poland, it was acquired by Russia in the Partitions of Poland (1772, 1793, 1795). Its population is composed largely of White Russians, one of the major Slavic groups in the Soviet Union.

Below, Count Otto von *See* **Caporetto, Battle of**

Belshazzar Biblical king, the son of Nebuchadnezzar, and the last king of Babylon. At a feast, his impending defeat by Cyrus and his death were foretold by handwriting on the wall, which was interpreted by Daniel.

Bemis Heights, Battle of *See* **Bunker Hill, Battle of**; *see also* **Saratoga campaign**

Bemis Heights, First Battle of *See* **Freeman's Farm, Battle of**

Benavente y Martinez, Jacinto 1866–1954. Spanish dramatist, winner of the Nobel Prize in Literature (1922). His major work, *Los intereses creados*, is in the style of the Italian commedia dell'arte.

Ben Bella, Ahmed 1918–. Algerian statesman. A leader of the Algerian nationalist movement against the French after WW II, he became Algeria's first president (1963–65).

Benchley, Robert Charles 1889–1945. American humorist and journalist whose books include *My Ten Years in a Quandary* and *Benchley Beside Himself.*

Benedek, Ludwig August von *See* **Königgratz, Battle of**

Benedict XIII (antipope) *See* **Luna, Pedro de**

Benedict XIV ⟨*b.* Prospero Lambertini⟩ 1675–1758. Italian-born pope (1740–58), successor to Clement XII. He encouraged science, learning, and the arts.

Benedict XV ⟨*b.* Giacomo della Chiesa⟩ 1854–1922. Italian-born pope (1914–22), successor to Pius X. He maintained strict neutrality during WW I, made great efforts to aid war victims, and attempted to mediate an end to the war.

Benedict, Saint *d.* c547. Italian monk. He founded the Benedictine order and the monastery at Monte Cassino. The Rule of St. Benedict is the basis of Western monasticism. (*See also* Benedictines.)

Benedictines ⟨Order of Saint Benedict⟩ Roman Catholic monks, followers of the rule of St. Benedict. Established by St. Benedict (early 6th cent.), the rule forms a traditional basis for western monasticism. It provides for a practical, well-balanced communal existence, stressing worship, study, and manual labor. St. Benedict patterned the rule after his now famous monastery founded (c529) at Monte Cassino. With the aid of Pope Gregory I, St. Augustine, and others, the rule of St. Benedict was spread throughout Western Europe and England. Thereafter, Benedictine abbeys remained predominant until the 12th cent., declined for a time, and almost disappeared during the Reformation (16th cent.). The Benedictine abbeys in their ascendency served not only to spread Christianity throughout Europe but also to preserve Latin culture (Benedictines faithfully copied books as part of their duties) in a period of great instability. The Cluniac order and Cistercians are outgrowths of Benedictine reform movements.

Benelux Name of the European economic union formed (1948) by Belgium, The Netherlands, and Luxembourg.

Beneš, Eduard 1887–1948. Czechoslovakian statesman. A founder of the Little Entente (1920–21), he served as Czech president (1935–38) but resigned after German annexation of the Sudetenland. He headed the Czech government-in-exile during WW II and served again as president (1946–48).

Benét, Stephen Vincent 1898–1943. American poet, short-story writer, and novelist. Interested in military history early in his life, Benét is known best for his narrative poem of the Civil War, *John Brown's Body.* In addition to many volumes of collected poems, Benét wrote novels, such as *Jean Huguenot,* and short stories, such as *The Devil and Daniel Webster.* He was twice awarded the Pulitzer Prize (1929, 1944).

Benét, William Rose 1886–1950. American poet, and brother of Stephen Vincent Benét. His volume *The Dust Which Is God* (1941) received the Pulitzer Prize for Poetry (1942).

Bengal Region and former province in northeast India. The Maurya and Gupta empires were centered there and the region later came under control of the Moguls. It later became a presidency (1699) under British control. It was divided between East Pakistan (Bangladesh) and India (1947).

Bengal, Partition of Administrative division of Bengal, India, ordered (July 19, 1905) by the British colonial government. It resulted in widespread protest by Bengalis and marked a turning point in the Indian nationalist movement. British viceroy of India Lord G. Curzon executed the partition to simplify administration of the region. The partition split Bengal into eastern and western parts, united them with other adjacent areas, and sparked nationalist opposition, which included boycotts and terrorist activities. The partition was rescinded (Dec., 1911) by King George V.

Bengal famine Indian disaster (1770) in which a famine destroyed one-third of the population of Bengal. Neither the British overseers nor local authorities moved to alleviate the suffering.

Bengali Indo-Aryan langauge spoken by people of eastern India and Bangladesh.

Bengal System *See* **Cornwallis Code**

Ben-Gurion, David ⟨*b.* David Grün, or Gruen⟩ 1886–1973. Israeli statesman. A leader in the founding (1948) of Israel, he served as its first prime minister (1948–53) and again in 1955–63.

Benhadad *d.* c841 BC. King of Damascus. He repulsed the Assyrian king Shalmaneser III at Karkar (853 BC), killed King Ahab of Israel in battle, and was overthrown and murdered by Hazael.

Benin ⟨People's Republic of Benin⟩ ⟨formerly Dahomey⟩ Small coastal republic in west-central Africa (est. pop. 2,800,000). In precolonial times, the region was dominated by warring tribal kingdoms, such as Great Ardra, Little Ardra, and Abomey (later called Dahomey). These wars produced, and later were often fought to produce, slaves that were sold to European slave traders. A part of what was called the Slave Coast *(q.v.)*, the region was supplying some 20,000 slaves a year by the end of the 17th cent. and continued to be important in slave trade until the 19th cent. The French were firmly established in the region by 1863 and conquered the kingdom of Dahomey (1892–93). Subsequently the French ruled the territory as a protectorate until 1899, when it was made part of French West Africa *(q.v.)*. It was made a French overseas territory (1946), an autonomous member state of the French Community (1958), and an independent state (Aug. 1, 1960). The country was torn by social and economic problems as well as by numerous changes of government. A military coup in 1963 was followed by several short-lived governments (1965, 1967, 1969), by two unsuccessful attempts at elections (1968, 1970), and finally by an 11-man military government (after a coup in 1972). Stability was restored with the installation of Lt. Col. Mathieu Kerekou (ruled 1972–   ). He renamed the country Benin in 1975.

Benin, Kingdom of Former West African kingdom located in what is now Nigeria. A powerful kingdom even before the advent of Portuguese exploration of Africa (13th cent.), it began trade with Portugal (late 15th cent.) and remained a power in the region until the 18th cent., when it began its decline. The kingdom fell to British control in the late 19th cent.

Benjamin Biblical figure, the youngest son of Jacob and Rachel, and ancestor of one of the twelve tribes of Israel.

Benjamin, Judah Philip 1811–84. American lawyer and politician. He served in the US Senate (1852–60) and in the Confederate Cabinet during the Civil War, notably as secretary of state (1862–65).

Bennett, James Gordon 1795–1872. American newspaper publisher and editor. He founded (1835) and edited the *New York Herald* and introduced innovations that greatly influenced modern journalism.

Bennett, Richard Bedford 1870–1947. Canadian statesman. As prime minister (1930–35), he presided over the Imperial Conference (1932) at Ottawa, which produced a number of preferential trade agreements within the British Empire.

Bennington, Battle of Battle of the American Revolution, at Bennington, Vermont (Aug. 16, 1777). Some 1,600 Americans under J. Stark successfully defended the town's military supplies from a British force of 800, thus further hindering British Gen. J. Burgoyne's campaign in the North.

Bentham, Jeremy 1748–1832. English philosopher, jurist, and economist who was a principal figure in the founding of utilitarianism. A qualified lawyer, he chose not to practice but to pursue a scientific analysis of law, ethics, and economics. Out of this came his utilitarian arithmetic for calculating the greatest happiness for the greatest number of people. His theories, as set forth in works such as *Introduction to the Principles of Morals and Legislation*, influenced 19th-cent. legal and political reforms.

Bentley, Richard 1662–1742. English scholar, one of the greatest of classical scholars. His *Dissertation upon the Epistles of Phalaris* is his best-known work.

Benton, Thomas Hart 1782–1858. American politician. As senator (1821–51) and congressman (1853–55), he opposed slavery but supported westward expansion. His support of hard currency earned him the nickname "Old Bullion." His grandnephew, Thomas ~ (1889–1975) was a noted painter.

Bentonville, Battle of Civil War battle (Mar. 19, 1865) at Bentonville, North Carolina. Here a Confederate force of about 24,000 under Gen. J. Johnston was defeated by a Union force under Gen. W. Sherman.

Benz, Carl Friedrich 1844–1929. German engineer credited as the builder of the first automobile powered by an internal combustion engine (demonstrated in 1885 and patented in 1886).

Ben-Zvi, Itzhak 1884–1963. Israeli statesman. A founder of Israel (1948), he served as president (1952–63).

Beowulf English epic poem, author unknown, probably composed in the 8th cent. A literary masterpiece, it is based largely on Scandinavian history and mythology.

Beranger, Pierre Jean de 1780–1857. French poet. His lyrics, favoring republicanism, led twice to his imprisonment, but their popularity earned him wide respect.

Berbers Muslim peoples of North Africa, comprising a large part of the populations of Algeria, Libya, and Morocco.

Berceo, Gonzalo de 1180?–1247? Earliest known Castilian poet, noted for his poems on religious themes.

Berchtold, Leopold, count von 1863–1942. Austro-Hungarian statesman. As foreign minister (1912–15), he sent to Serbia (July, 1914) the ultimatum that precipitated WW I.

Berengar II d. 966. Italian king (950–961). His intrigues with Pope John XII against Otto I of Germany led to his imprisonment and death in Bavaria.

Berengar of Tours c999–1088. French theologian noted for his opposition to the doctrine of transubstantiation of the eucharist.

Beresteczko, Battle of Polish-Cossack battle (summer, 1651) at Beresteczko, Ukraine. Polish forces under King John II defeated the Cossack army of B. Chmielnicki, thereby crippling the Ukrainian struggle for independence and leading eventually to Russian control of the Ukraine.

Berezina River in Belorussia, western Russia. Crossing the Berezina (Nov. 26–29, 1812) under fire, Napoleon lost 20,000 troops but saved his Grand Army from capture by the Russians.

Berg, Alban 1885–1936. Austrian composer and leading figure in 20th-cent. music. A student of A. Schoenberg, he is noted for his successful fusion of atonal and traditional elements in his music. Among his most important works is the atonal opera *Wozzeck*.

Bergara, Convention of *See* **Convention of Vergara**

Bergerac, Peace of French treaty (Sept. 17, 1577) ending the 6th War of Religion between the French Huguenots and Catholics. The Huguenots had been defeated but received favorable terms.

Bergerac, Savinien Cyrano de *See* **Cyrano de Bergerac, Savinien**

Bergman, Ingmar 1918– . Swedish filmmaker. A leading figure in cinematography, he is internationally renowned for such films as *Wild Strawberries* and *Cries and Whispers*.

Bergman, Ingrid 1915–82. Swedish actress, known best for her roles in such motion pictures as *Intermezzo* and *Casablanca*, and such stage plays as *Hedda Gabler* (1962).

Bergson, Henri 1859–1941. French philosopher. His highly imaginative philosophical works challenged scientific determinism and proved very popular. In *Creative Evolution*, his best-known work, he argues that *élan vital* (the life force), not natural selection, provides the basis for evolution. He was awarded the 1927 Nobel Prize in Literature.

Bering, Vitus Jonassen ⟨Behring, ~⟩ 1681–1741. Danish navigator. In the service of Peter the Great of Russia he explored the Siberian coast north to the Arctic and discovered Alaska for the Russians (1741), though he died during the expedition. Bering Sea and Bering Strait are named in his honor.

Bering Sea Dispute Incident (1886) between the US and Canada over pelagic, or open-sea, sealing in the Bering Sea. The US claimed jurisdiction through the purchase of Alaska from Russia, and seized several Canadian ships. An international tribunal (1893) denied the US claim, but an international agreement (1911) prohibited pelagic sealing in the Bering Sea.

Berkeley, George 1685–1753. Irish philosopher and Anglican bishop. He developed a philosophy of subjective idealism based on the principle of *esse est percipi*, the notion that material things exist only in being perceived by the mind. His thinking influenced other important philosophers, such as D. Hume and I. Kant. Among his important works are *Essay Towards a New Theory of Vision* and *Three Dialogues Between Hylas and Philonous*.

Berkeley, Sir William 1606–77. English-born governor of Virginia (1641–c1651, 1660–76). His unpopular policies led to Bacon's Rebellion.

Berkman, Alexander *See* **Goldman, Emma**

Berlin Former capital of Germany, divided in 1945 into East Berlin and West Berlin (pop.: East, 1,111,400; West, 1,926,800). West Berlin is a nonincorporated state of West Germany. Berlin was formed by the merger (1307) of two Wendish villages, Berlin and Kölln. It became the capital of the German Empire (1871–1918), the Weimer Republic (1919–32), and Nazi Germany (1933–45). After WW II the city was divided into sectors by British, French, American, and Russian occupation forces. Disagreement with Soviet authorities led to division of the city into two districts, the Russian section becoming (1949) East Berlin, and the western section West Berlin (1950).

Berlin, Congress of *See* **Congress of Berlin**

Berlin, Irving ⟨b. Israel Baline⟩ 1888– . American songwriter. Among his best-known songs are *Alexander's Ragtime Band* and *God Bless America*.

Berlin, Treaty of *See* **Congress of Berlin**

Berlin airlift ⟨*and* ~ blockade⟩ US and British effort to supply the western sectors of Berlin, Germany (June 1948–Sept. 1949) with food and fuel. The airlift broke a Soviet blockade of the city and represented an important victory for the US early in the Cold War. The result of worsening disputes between Soviet and Western powers over administration of divided Germany, the Soviet blockade began as the Western powers instituted programs for integration of their zones of occupation. The airlift began June 26, 1948, and continued until Sept. 30, 1949, although the blockade had been lifted May 4. The airlift delivered over two million tons of supplies to the beleaguered city.

Berlin Conference ⟨Berlin–West Africa Conference⟩ Meeting (Nov. 15, 1884–Feb. 26, 1885) at Berlin to resolve disputes between colonial powers in the Congo region of Africa. Attended by the European powers and the US, the conference was under the leadership of German chancellor O. Bismarck. Representatives agreed on the following for the Congo region: abolition of slavery, freedom of trade and nagivation on waterways, designation of the Congo as a neutral region, and principles for partitioning the Congo. The powers also sanctioned what was to become the Congo Free State. (*See also* Potsdam Conference.)

Berlin Decree   Order issued (1806) by Napoleon at Berlin, instituting the commercial blockade of Britain and inaugurating the Continental System. Napoleon issued the decree in response to the British blockade of commercial ports under French control. In it he also ordered the arrest of all Englishmen and confiscation of their property within French domains.

Berlin Pact   *See* **Axis Powers**

Berlin Wall   Fortified wall dividing East and West Berlin, constructed (Aug., 1961) by the East German government to stop the defection of East Germans to the West.

Berlin–West Africa Conference   *See* **Berlin Conference**

Berlioz, Hector   1803–69. French composer, considered to be the greatest French Romantic composer. His treatise on orchestration influenced later composers.

Bermuda   British crown colony (pop. 55,000), consisting of some 300 islands in the western Atlantic Ocean. Discovered (1515) by Spanish navigator Juan de Bermúdez, Bermuda was first settled by English colonists (1609). Bermuda was granted self-government in 1968.

Bermúdez, Juan de   *See* **Bermuda**

Bern   〈Berne〉 Swiss city (pop. 146,000). Founded (1191) by Berthold V of Zähringen, Bern joined the Swiss Confederation (1353) and soon became its leader. It became capital of the Swiss Confederation in 1848. Bern is the headquarters of numerous international agencies, including the Universal Postal Union and International Copyright Union.

Bernadette, Saint   〈*b.* Marie Bernarde Soubirolls〉 1844–79. French visionary. As a girl she claimed to have seen (1858) visions of the Virgin Mary in a grotto at Lourdes. She was canonized in 1933.

Bernadotte, Count Folke   1895–1948. Swedish diplomat and humanitarian. He arranged the release of thousands of concentration camp victims during WW II. He was assassinated while serving as UN mediator in Palestine.

Bernadotte, Jean Baptiste Jules   *See* **Charles XIV**

Bernanos, Georges   1888–1948. French novelist and polemicist. His *Diary of a Country Priest*, one of his best novels, reflects his opposition to modern materialism.

Bernard of Clairvaux, Saint   1090–1153.   French cleric, a mystic, and in his day one of the most prominent figures in the Roman Catholic church. A Cistercian monk, he founded the monastery at Clairvaux (1115) and spent the rest of his life as its abbot. Nevertheless, he gained great influence in the church by his eloquence, his widespread reputation as a pious and devoted churchman, and his influence with the popes of the day. He opposed the rationalist philosophy of P. Abelard and promoted the Second Crusade. He was canonized in 1174.

Bernardone, Giovanni Francesco   *See* **Francis of Assisi, Saint**

Berne   *See* **Bern**

Bernhardt, Sarah   1844–1923.   French actress whose voice and versatile acting ability made her a leading theatrical figure in the late 19th and early 20th cents.

Bernini, Giovanni Lorenzo   1598–1680.   Italian sculptor, architect, and painter, and the leading figure in Italian Baroque art. His works include statues of *David* and *Apollo and Daphne*.

Bernouilli, Jacob   *See* **Bernoulli, Jacob**

Bernoulli, Daniel   1700–82.   Swiss mathematician and physicist. His best-known work is the *Hydrodynamica*, dealing with the mechanical properties of fluids.

Bernoulli, Jacob   〈Bernouilli,   ~〉 1654–1705. Swiss mathematician whose work helped to develop calculus and the theory of probability. The Bernoulli numbers are named after him.

Bernoulli, Jacques   *See* **Bernoulli, Jacob**

Bernoulli, Jean   〈~, Johann〉 1667–1748. Swiss mathematician noted for his work in integral and exponential calculus.

Bernoulli, Johann   *See* **Bernoulli, Jean**

Bernstein, Eduard   1850–1932.   German socialist. After years in exile from Germany, in 1901 he returned to become a leader of revisionism, a movement opposed to certain Marxist theories.

Bernstein, Leonard   1918– .   American composer and conductor. His works include the *Mass*, the opera *Trouble in Tahiti*, and the musical *West Side Story*.

Berry, Charles Ferdinand, duke of   1778–1820. French noble, and son of Charles, count of Artous (later Charles X). His assassination led to a royalist reaction against the liberal movement in France.

Berserkers   〈Berserks〉 Mythological Norse warriors. They wore only animal skins into battle, relying on the ferocity of their attack as their protection. The name was later adopted for warriors employed to guard Scandinavian rulers.

Berserks   *See* **Berserkers**

Bertha of the Big Foot ⟨Bertrada⟩ *d.* 783. Frankish queen, the wife of Pepin the Short and the mother of Charlemagne. She is celebrated in Carolingian legend.

Berthelot, Pierre Eugène Marcelin 1827–1907. French chemist. His research and numerous writings greatly contributed to the development of modern chemistry, especially organic and thermochemistry.

Berthier, Louis Alexandre 1753–1815. Marshal of France. He served as chief of staff under Napoleon (1805–14). Upon Napoleon's return from exile in Elba, Berthier retired from France. He died, perhaps by suicide, shortly therafter.

Bethlehem, Synod of *See* **Jerusalem, Synod of**

Berthold V of Zähringen *See* **Bern**

Bertrada *See* **Bertha of the Big Foot**

Berzelius, Johan Jakob *See* **Berzelius, Jöns Jakob**

Berzelius, Jöns Jakob ⟨~, Johan Jakob⟩ 1779–1848. Swedish chemist. His accurate table of atomic weights and introduction of modern chemical symbols were major contributions to the development of modern chemistry. He also discovered the elements selenium, thorium, and cesium.

Besant, Annie ⟨*b.* Annie Wood⟩ 1847–1933. English social reformer and theosophist. She advocated Fabian socialism and other movements before adopting Theosophy (1889) and moving to India. There in 1916 she founded the Indian Home Rule League.

Bessarabia Region of southwest European USSR, now largely incorporated into the Moldavian SSR. It has frequently been a path of invasion between Europe and Asia. Contested by Russia and Romania in the 20th cent., it became part of the Soviet Union by the Romanian peace treaty of 1947.

Bessemer, Sir Henry 1813–98. English inventor of the Bessemer process for the economical production of steel.

Betancourt, Romulo 1908–. Venezuelan politician. Twice president of Venezuela (1945–48, 1959–64), Betancourt instituted such reforms as universal suffrage, land redistribution, and industrial development, while securing greater revenues from oil companies in Venezuela.

Bethel Ancient biblical city north of Jerusalem. Temporarily the resting place of the Ark of the Covenant, it later became a center of heathen worship.

Bethlehem Town in western Jordan. The birthplace of Jesus, it is one of the principal shrines of Christianity. Here Emperor Constantine erected (AD *c*330) the Church of the Nativity, where St. Jerome produced the Vulgate version of the Bible.

Bethlehem was part of the British Palestine mandate from 1922 to 1948, when it became part of Jordan. It has been occupied by Israel since the 1967 Arab-Israeli War.

Bethlen, Gabriel 1580–1629. Prince of Transylvania (1613–29) and king of Hungary (1620–21). He opposed the Holy Roman Empire in the Thirty Years' War.

Bethlen, Count Stephen 1874–1947? Hungarian statesman. As prime minister (1921–31), he sought revision of the Treaty of Trianon, secured a treaty of friendship with Italy (1927), and guided Hungary's economic recovery from WW I.

Bethmann-Hollweg, Theobald von 1856–1921. German statesman. As chancellor of Germany (1909–17), he did not want war, but his policies contributed to the outbreak of WW I. His attempts to bring about a mediated end to the war led to his forced resignation.

Betti, Ugo 1892–1953. Italian dramatist and poet. Betti's dramas are ranked in importance second only to those of Pirandello. His plays include *La Padrona, Frano allo scalo nord,* and *Il diluvio.*

Betterton, Thomas 1635?–1710. English actor and manager, considered the greatest actor of the Restoration.

Beyazid I *See* **Bajazet I**

Beyazid II *See* **Bajazet II**

Beyle, Marie Henri *See* **Stendhal**

Beyrouth *See* **Beirut**

Bhagavad-Gita Sanskrit poem, considered a major exposition of Hindu philosophy as well as a literary treasure. An anonymous work, it is one episode in the Mahabharata *(q.v.).*

Bhascara ⟨Acarya⟩ 1114–c1185. Hindu astronomer and mathematician, noted as the first to make systematic use of the decimal system in a mathematical work.

Bhil People of western India and Pakistan, numbering about two million and speaking Bhili, an Indo-European language.

Bholan Pass *See* **Bolan Pass**

Bhumibol Adulyade *See* **Chakkri dynasty**

Bhutan Himalayan kingdom (pop. 1,300,000) northwest of India. Bhutan was conquered by the Tibetans (16th cent.) and the Chinese (1720). The southern part of Bhutan was annexed by the British (1865), who agreed to an annual subsidy to Bhutan for the annexed territory. A hereditary monarchy was established in Bhutan in 1907. From 1949 Bhutan's foreign affairs have been guided by India, which defended the kingdom from Chinese encroachment following China's occupation of Tibet (1950). The independent status of Bhutan was augmented by its admittance (1971) to the UN.

Bhutto, Zulfikar Ali 1928–79. Pakistani political leader. His policies helped to cause the secession of East Pakistan and the ensuing war (1971). As president (1971–73) and prime minister (1973–77), he opposed secession and the formation of Bangladesh but was forced to recognize its independence (1974).

Biafra Nigerian secessionist state that existed from 1967 to 1970. Its population was largely of the Ibo tribe, which believed it could not survive within Nigeria. The secession, led by Lt. Col. Chukwuemeka Odumegwu Ojukwu (1933–   ), led to the Nigerian Civil War and was ended by a combination of Nigerian military advances and economic sanctions. It is believed that more than a million Biafrans died of starvation.

Bible *See* **Old Testament, New Testament, Septuagint**

Bibliothèque Nationale National archive of France and its most important library. The origins of the collection date back to the 14th cent. and the royal library of Charles V. This collection of some 900 volumes was successively added to and since 1537 it has received by law a copy of all books published in France. The collection now contains over 6½ million books and manuscripts.

bicameral system Political system by which the legislative branch of a government is divided into two chambers. Examples include the US Congress, divided into the Senate and the House of Representatives, and the British Parliament, divided into the House of Lords and House of Commons.

Bichat, Marie François Xavier 1771–1802. French anatomist and physiologist. His pioneering human tissue studies contributed to the development of modern histology.

Biddle, John 1615–62. English theologian, the founder of English unitarianism. Biddle, frequently imprisoned for heresy, died in jail.

Bidlack Treaty Treaty (1846) between the US and New Granada (later Colombia), guaranteeing New Granada sovereignty over the Isthmus of Panama and granting the US right-of-way across the Isthmus. It became important when the US sought to build the Panama Canal.

Biedermeier Artistic style and period in Germany following the Napoleonic Wars. The style became popular among the middle class in the 1820s and 1830s. It emphasized the comforts of middle-class home and family life. Biedermeier furniture was generally of simple, homey design and was made of inexpensive materials.

Bienville, Jean Baptiste le Moyne, sieur de 1680–1768. French colonial governor and colonizer of Louisiana. From 1701 he was leader of the first colonies in Louisiana and founded New Orleans in 1718.

Bierce, Ambrose Gwinnett 1842–1914? American journalist and author, known best for his sardonic short stories.

Bierstadt, Albert *See* **Hudson River School**

Big Black River, Battle of American Civil War battle (May 17, 1863) at the Black River, Mississippi. Here Confederate Gen. John Pemberton (1814–81) sought unsuccessfully to keep his army from being trapped by Gen. U.S. Grant at Vicksburg.

Big Foot, Bertha of the *See* **Bertha of the Big Foot**

Big Stick Policy Term given to the aggressive foreign policy of Pres. T. Roosevelt, who advocated massive military and naval power as an instrument of foreign diplomacy. It was derived from the saying "speak softly and carry a big stick."

Bildad In the Bible, one of the three comforters of Job.

Bilhapur, Battle of Indian battle (Apr. 1, 1731) in which the Maratha Peshwa Baji Rao I (*d.* 1740) defeated his opponents and killed his rival to become virtual ruler in the Maratha kingdom.

Billaud-Varenne, Jean Nicolas 1756–1819. French revolutionary, a Jacobin. A member of the Committee of Public Safety during the French Revolution, he helped institute the Reign of Terror and, later, to overthrow Robespierre.

Billings, Warren *See* **Mooney, Thomas J.**

Billings, William 1746–1800. American composer of hymns, one of the earliest American composers. His books included *The New England Psalm Singer*.

Bill of Rights **1.** English bill enacted 1689, one of the key documents of English constitutional law. It established the supremacy of Parliament, ending a long struggle for power with the English kings. The bill largely reiterated the terms of the Declaration of Rights (1688), drawn up at the close of the Glorious Revolution and signed by William III and Mary II as a condition for accession to the throne. The provisions stemmed from abuses of royal power under James II and included required parliamentary consent for suspension of laws, raising taxes, and maintaining an army. They also provided for the right to petition the king, the free election and operation of Parliament, and a variety of judicial reforms. Royal succession was also established and Roman Catholics barred from the throne. **2.** The first ten amendments to the Constitution of the US (all adopted 1791). Concern for the protection of basic rights of individuals sparked strong opposition to ratification of the Constitution, and amendments guaranteeing such rights were promised to win its ratification. Congress submitted (Sept. 25, 1789) twelve amendments, drafted by J. Madison, to the states for ratification and ten were adopted (Dec. 15, 1791). *See also* Constitution of the United States *for individual amendments of the Bill of Rights.*

Billy the Kid 〈Bonney, William H.〉 1859–81. American outlaw, one of the leading figures in American western lore.

Bimetallism Monetary system in which two metals, usually gold and silver, were coined without limit and valued at a fixed ratio. Adopted by many countries in the 18th and 19th cents., the system lost favor and was discarded.

Bindusara *See* **Maurya Empire**

Binet, Alfred 1857–1911. French psychologist. With Théodore Simon (1873–1961), he devised an intelligence test that, with modifications, is widely used today.

Bingham, Hiram *See* **Machu Picchu**

Birdseye, Clarence 1886–1956. American inventor. He developed the first effective process for quick-freezing food. The company he founded (1924) later became the General Foods Corporation.

Birgitta, Saint *See* **Bridget of Sweden, Saint**

Birmingham Largest city in Alabama (pop. 284,400). Founded in 1871, Birmingham is a major industrial center. It was a focal point for black civil rights drives in the South during the 1960s.

Biron, Ernst Johann *See* **Anna Ivanovna**

Biscoe, John *d.* 1848. British navigator. His voyage (1831–32) to Antarctica helped to support British claims in the area.

Bishop Hill American religious and economic colony, founded (1846) in Henry County, Illinois, by Swedish immigrants. It dissolved in 1860.

Bishops' Wars **1.** First ~ (1639). Brief war between the Scots and English king Charles I in the years prior to the English Civil War (1642–49). Charles's attempt (1637) to force Anglican liturgy on the Presbyterian Scots resulted in the Solemn League and Covenant (1638) and the seizure of Edinburgh castle (1639). The war was ended without actual fighting by the Peace of Berwick (1639), in which Charles made concessions to the Scots. **2.** Second ~ (1640). Brief war between the Scots and English king Charles I just prior to the English Civil War (1642–51). The Presbyterian Scots reaffirmed the covenant and, amid the crisis caused by the Short Parliament in England, the Scots invaded northern England (1640). Following their victory at Newburn on the Tyne (Aug. 28), they occupied Northumberland and Durham. By the Treaty of Ripon (Oct. 26), Charles ended the war and agreed to make cash payments to the Scottish army. This, however, necessitated calling of the

Long Parliament (1640), which in turn brought on the civil war.

Bisitun Inscription *See* **Behistun Inscription**

Bismarck, Otto Eduard Leopold von 〈Iron Chancellor〉 1815–98. Prussian statesman, who brought about German unification and become first chancellor of the German empire (1871–90). A member of the Prussian Diet (1847–50) and Prussian minister to the Diet of the German Confederation at Frankfurt (1851–59), he was made Prussian premier (1862). Thereafter he put into action plans for the unification (by "blood and iron") of Germany under Prussian domination. He precipitated the Austro-Prussian War (1866) and, with Austria defeated, created the North German Confederation (1866). To further unification, he provoked (by publication of the Ems Dispatch) the Franco-Prussian War (1870–71) and was named (1871) chancellor of the new German empire under King William I. He subsequently involved Germany in an intricate web of alliances (Three Emperors' League, Dual Alliance, Triple Alliance, Triple Entente) by which he became the leading European statesman. As chancellor he instituted many internal administrative reforms and, in an effort to combat the Socialists, set up the first comprehensive social security plan. He was forced to resign (1890) after the accession of William II.

Bithynia Ancient country located in what is now northwestern Turkey. The territory was originally occupied by Thracian tribes and from the 6th cent. BC it was nominally controlled by Persians and then by Macedonians. An independent kingdom after 297 BC, it flourished briefly with its capital at Nicomedia. Following its decline it became a province of Rome (74 BC).

Bizet, Alexandre César Léopold *See* **Bizet, Georges**

Bizet, Georges 1838–75. (b. Alexandre César Léopold ~) French composer. He is known best for his opera *Carmen*, based on a story by Prosper Mérimée (1803–70).

Bjorko, Treaty of German-Russian agreement. Signed (July 24, 1905) by Kaiser William II and Czar Nicholas II, it called for mutual military support in Europe should either country be attacked. It was never implemented.

Bjornson, Bjornstjerne 1832–1910. Norwegian playwright, novelist, and political leader. A major figure in 19th-cent. Norwegian literature, he was awarded the Nobel Prize in Literature (1903).

Björnsson, Sveinn 1881–1952. Icelandic statesman. He was regent of Iceland (1941–44) during the German occupation of Denmark, and became the first president of the Republic of Iceland (1944–52) upon Iceland's independence from Denmark.

Black, Hugo La Fayette 1886–1971. US Senator (1927–37) from Alabama and Associate Justice of the Supreme Court (1937–71). He was a noted defender of civil liberties.

Black and Tans Name applied to members of the British auxiliary police force sent to Ireland (1920) to make reprisals against Irish revolutionaries. Their brutality raised the anger of the Irish and the indignation of the British, and contributed to establishment of the Irish Free State (1921). They derived their name from the colors of their uniforms.

Blackbeard ⟨Edward Teach⟩ ⟨Edward Thatch⟩ *d.* 1718. English pirate. He is believed to have been an English privateer during the War of Spanish Succession (1701–14) and to have subsequently turned to piracy. He raided from the West Indies to the Virginia coast (1716–18) and was finally killed while trying to elude capture.

Black Code ⟨Code Noir⟩ French edict, issued (1685) by King Louis XIV to govern the treatment of slaves and freed blacks in the French holdings in the West Indies.

Black Codes Generally, local laws in the US that from the 17th to 19th cents. regulated the conduct and punishment of Negro slaves; and specifically, laws passed by Southern states immediately after the Civil War to regulate freed blacks. The post-Civil War laws varied, though in general they aimed at maintaining the sharp divisions between blacks and whites. Blacks were permitted to marry and own personal property but land-ownership restrictions, oppressive work laws, mandatory segregation of public facilities, and other provisions effectively blocked their emancipation. In the North the laws were regarded as disguised slavery and helped bring on the programs of Radical Republicans and the Reconstruction era.

Black Death *See* **Black Plague**

Black Earl *See* **Butler, Thomas, 10th Earl of Ormonde**

Black Flag Army Chinese army that fought against the Manchus in the Taiping Rebellion (1850–64). At the close of the rebellion, the army fled into Indochina, where it later fought the French in the undeclared Sino-French War (1883–85).

Blackfoot Indians American Indian tribes of the Algonquin family, who flourished in the Great Plains region of the US and Canada in the 18th and 19th cents. For a time successful against the encroachments of white civilization, the tribes were eventually forced to sign treaties with the US government. Reduction of the buffalo herds brought mass starvation and near destruction to the Blackfeet in the later 19th cent.

Black Friday US financial panic (Sept. 24, 1869), caused by speculators J. Gould and J. Fisk, who were attempting to corner the gold market. On discovering the scheme, President U. Grant flooded the market with government gold to break the corner. This remedy, however, precipitated a panic on the securities market and left thousands ruined. Another day of financial panic (Sept. 18, 1873) is also called Black Friday.

Black Hand Secret criminal society. Organized in Sicily, it flourished there in the late 19th cent., and spread to the US, where it became prominent for a time in the early 20th cent. The society in Sicily was ruthlessly suppressed under B. Mussolini.

Black Hawk War Brief war (1832) between the US and a band of Sac and Fox Indians led by Black Hawk. The conflict arose over the forced cession of Sac and Fox lands in Illinois to the US, called for by a disputed 1804 treaty. Black Hawk refused to leave the lands until forced to move west of the Mississippi in 1831. In 1832 he led a band of 1,000 starving warriors, women, and children back to Illinois and was met by a combined force of militia and US regulars. Pursued into Wisconsin, he was defeated in the Battle of Bad Axe River and all but 150 of his band were massacred.

Black Hole of Calcutta Prison cell for petty thieves in Calcutta, India, that became the scene of a notorious incident. According to a report by an official of the British East India Company, the company's garrison in Calcutta was attacked and taken by native rebels (June 20, 1756). The survivors, supposed to have numbered 146, were locked overnight in the 15- by 18-ft cell. Of them, only 23 were reported to have survived. The number of men locked in the cell is now believed greatly exaggerated.

Black Hundreds ⟨League of the Russian People⟩ Russian political group which flourished in the early 1900s. Composed of clergy, police, bureaucrats, and the rich, it opposed the growing Russian revolutionary movement, and conducted pogroms against the Jews.

Blackmore, Richard Doddridge 1825–1900. English novelist. His best-known novel is *Lorna Doone,* now a classic.

Black Muslims ⟨Nation of Islam⟩ American racial-religious movement, founded (1930) by Wallace D. Fard (c1877–1934?) to apply the teachings of Islam to black American life. The movement gained many followers through the teachings of Malcolm X.

Black nationalism American black political and social movement, which seeks to encourage a separate national identity among blacks in the US. It stresses the common African heritage and the experiences of American blacks. Rooted in the 19th cent., the movement came to play an important role in the 1960s and 1970s.

Black Panthers American black political movement, founded (1966) by Huey Newton (1941?–) and Bobby Seale (1936–). The movement advocated revolution to achieve equality for blacks. Black Panthers were frequently involved in incidents of violence during the 1960s.

Black Plague ⟨Bubonic plague⟩ ⟨Black Death⟩ Epidemic disease that ravaged Europe and Asia in the mid-14th cent., so called because it turns the skin of its victims black. It is caused by bacteria infesting rats or other rodents and transmitted to humans by fleas. Epidemics of the plague occurred in Athens (5th cent. BC) and Rome (3d cent. AD), but the epidemic of the 14th cent. killed an estimated one-quarter to three-quarters of the populations of Europe and Asia. Another epidemic (1665) devastated London.

Black Power Slogan that gained prominence in the US during the movement for black equality in the 1960s. It implies a sense of racial pride and an often militant desire to overcome economic and racial barriers through unified black effort.

Blackshirts *See* **SS**

Blackstone, Sir William 1723–80. English jurist. He is known best for his *Commentaries on the Laws of England*, which had a major influence on the teaching and practice of law in England and the US.

Black Thursday Name given to Thursday, Oct. 24, 1929, when nearly 13 million shares of stock were sold in a panic on the New York Stock Exchange. It marked the beginning of the stock market crash that inaugurated the Great Depression.

Black War Sporadic outbreaks of violence (1804–30) between Europeans and natives of Van Diemen's Land (Tasmania). Clashes between aborigines and European soldiers and convict settlers (sentenced to this British penal colony) began soon after the arrival of the Europeans in 1804. Competition for food and land, atrocities committed by the Europeans, and retaliatory attacks by the natives continued until 1830, by which time the native population had been nearly eliminated. The remaining 200 natives were finally resettled (1835) on Flinders Island.

Black Watch ⟨Royal Highlanders⟩ Distinguished regiment of Scottish infantrymen named for their dark tartan colors. The unit was first organized (1725) to maintain order in the Scottish Highlands. It was formally designated a regiment c1739 and is now the 42d regiment.

Blackwell, Elizabeth 1821–1910. American physician. She was the first woman to receive a medical degree in the US (1849).

Blaine, James Gillespie 1830–93. American politician. Blaine was an unsuccessful Republican candidate for president in 1884, and was twice secretary of state (1880–81, 1889–92).

Blair, Eric Arthur *See* **Orwell, George.**

Blair, Francis Preston 1791–1876. American journalist and politician. He was once an influential Democrat and member of Pres. A. Jackson's Kitchen Cabinet. His antislavery beliefs led him to help found the Republican Party. He supported A. Lincoln's candidacy (1860) and later, with his approval, arranged the Hampton Roads Conference (1865).

Blake, Robert 1599–1657. English admiral. Considered one of the greatest English admirals, he won naval engagements against the Royalists (1649–51), Dutch (1652–53), the Barbary pirates (1655), and Spain (1656–57).

Blake, William 1757–1827. Major English poet and artist, and a leading influence in the Romantic movement. Blake, a visionary, created a highly individual style and was largely unrecognized in his time. Born to a prosperous family, he first became an engraver's apprentice (1771). He continued as an engraver, painted, and illustrated books such as Dante's *Divine Comedy*. At the same time he wrote books of poetry, such as *Songs of Innocence* and *Songs of Experience*, and prophetical books such as the *The Marriage of Heaven and Hell*.

Blanc, Louis 1811–82. French Socialist and journalist. He advocated, in *Organisation du Travail*, the establishment of workshops managed by the workers. He was a member of the provisional government set up (1848) after the February Revolution *(q.v.)*.

Blanchard, François *See* **Blanchard, Jean Pierre**

Blanchard, Jean Pierre ⟨~, François⟩ 1753–1809. French balloonist. With Dr. John Jeffries (1744–1819), he made the first aerial crossing of the English Channel.

Blanche of Castile 1187?–1252. Wife of Louis VIII (m. 1200) and queen of France during his reign (1223–26). She served twice (1226–36, 1248–52) as regent for her son, Louis IX.

Blanco Fombona, Rufino 1874–1944. Venezuelan poet and essayist who was a leader of the literary movement known as Modernismo.

Bland-Allison Act Act of US Congress (1878) reestablishing the silver dollar as legal tender and providing for minimum government purchases of silver to support market prices. The act was part of the larger Free-Silver movement sparked by the discontinuation of the silver dollar (known as the

Crime of '73). The bill originally proposed by Rep. Richard P. Bland (1835–99) provided for unlimited silver coinage but was amended to allow for only $2–4 million in monthly silver bullion purchases. The act was superseded by the Sherman Silver Purchase Act (1890).

Blanqui, Louis Auguste 1805–81. French revolutionary. Blanqui figured in the major political upheavals of his day and spent much of his adult life in prison.

Blavatsky, Helena Petrovna 1831–91. Russian theosophist. She helped to found the Theosophical Society (1875) and expounded Theosophy in such works as *Isis Unveiled* and *The Secret Doctrine.*

Bleeding Kansas Name applied to the US territory of Kansas during the local war (1854–59) between proslavery and antislavery factions there prior to its admission as a state. The Kansas-Nebraska Act (1854) left to the voters the question of extending slavery into Kansas (Popular Sovereignty). Soon after its passage, Free-Soilers (antislavery "Jayhawkers") and proslavery men ("Border Ruffians") from Missouri streamed into the state. Violence between the two sides was narrowly averted in the Wakarusa War (Dec. 1855), caused by the murder of an antislavery man. However, there followed the sack (May 21, 1856) of Lawrence, Kansas by proslavery men, the Pottawatomie Massacre, and numerous other bloody skirmishes. The violence continued until the Wyandotte Constitution was adopted (1859). Kansas was admitted as a free state (1861).

Blenheim, Battle of Major Anglo-Austrian victory (Aug. 13, 1704) in the War of the Spanish Succession (1701–14). A combined Anglo-Austrian force of 52,000 (under J. Churchill, duke of Marlborough, and Eugene of Savoy) surprised and defeated some 60,000 French and Bavarian troops (under French Marshal Comte Camille de Tallard, 1652–1728) at the Bavarian village of Blenheim. Anglo-Austrian casualties numbered 12,000. Franco-Bavarian losses were some 15,000 casualties and 13,000 captured. The battle eliminated Bavaria from the war and marked the beginning of France's decline as a military power in Europe.

Blest Gana, Alberto 1830–1920. Chilean novelist. A leading Spanish-American author of the 19th cent., he wrote realistic novels of life in Chile. *Martin Rivas* and *During the Reconquest* are among his works.

Bligh, William 1754–1817. English admiral, remembered as the captain of HMS *Bounty (q.v.)* during its famous mutiny of 1789. Later, as governor of New South Wales, he was the object of yet another mutiny (1808).

Bliss, Sir Arthur Edward Drummond 1891–1975. English composer, noted early in his career for his innovative compositions. He became Master of the Queen's Music in 1953.

Bloc National French conservative coalition, which dominated politics in France from 1919–24. It stressed fiscal conservatism and strict German compliance with the treaty of Versailles.

Blitzkrieg German term, meaning "lightning war," used to describe the German battle tactic in WW II of using massive numbers of airplanes and mechanized forces in sudden assaults on opposing forces.

Bloch, Ernest 1180–1959. Swiss-American composer. His music is based on both classical and Hebraic traditions.

Blois, Charles of *See* **Charles of Blois**

Blois, treaties of Several treaties signed at Blois, France, including **1.** First ~ (1504), by which Holy Roman Emperor Maximilian I recognized the rule of French King Louis XII in Naples. **2.** Second ~ (1505), by which French King Louis XII renounced his claim to Naples, thereby surrendering control to Ferdinand II of Aragon.

Blok, Aleksandr Aleksandrovich 1880–1921. Russian poet, a leader of the Russian Symbolist movement.

Bloodless Revolution *See* **Glorious Revolution**

Blood Purge Name given the murder (June 30, 1934) of 74 Nazi leaders by order of A. Hitler. Hitler later declared the purge was in response to an alleged plot, but it was actually conducted to eliminate radical elements from the Nazi party, notably Ernst Roehm (1887–1934), leader of the Storm Troopers.

Blood River, Battle of Boer victory (Dec. 16, 1838) in Natal, South Africa, over the Zulu tribe. About 500 Boers under A. Pretorius repulsed an attack of some 10,000 Zulu, killing about 3,000 Zulu warriors. The battle broke Zulu dominance in the area and secured the Boer position in Natal.

Bloody Assizes Trials conducted in western England after an unsuccessful rebellion (1685) by the Duke of Monmouth against King James II. Presided over by the notorious Baron G. Jeffreys and four other judges, the trials of Monmouth's followers resulted in over 300 hangings, some 800 deportations to Barbados, and the flogging and imprisonment of many others.

Bloody Mary *See* **Mary I**

Bloody Omaha *See* **Omaha Beach**

Bloody shirt American political phrase. Drawn from the saying "waving a bloody shirt," it refers to the post-Civil War techniques used by radical Republicans of stirring up wartime memories and emotions for political gain.

Bloody Sunday Russian massacre (Jan. 22, 1905). Thousands of Russians, marching in St. Petersburg to present a petition of grievances to Czar Nicholas II, were fired on by czarist forces. The massacre left more than a hundred dead and several hundred wounded, and led to the Russian Revolution of 1905.

Bloody Week Bloody fighting (May 21–28, 1871) in Paris, France, that marked the downfall of the Commune of Paris *(q.v.)*. Parisian rebels had established the Paris Commune (Mar., 1871) by force and taken over the city. On May 21 government forces began a week-long battle to retake Paris and killed about 20,000 Parisian rebels.

Bloomfield, Leonard 1887–1949. American linguist. A specialist in Germanic langauges, he was among the first to apply scientific principles to the study of languages.

Bloomsbury group A group of English intellectuals that met for discussions in the Bloomsbury section of London in the early 20th cent. Its members included E.M. Forster, J. Keynes, and V. Woolf.

Blount, William 1749–1800. American political leader. Governor of the territory that became Tennesssee (1709–96), he became a senator (1796–97) from Tennessee, but was expelled when it was discovered he had plotted to help the British take over Spain's Florida territory.

Blücher, Gebhard Leberecht von 1742–1819. Prussian field marshal. He played an important role in the defeat of Napoleon at Waterloo (1815).

Blue Laws A term usually applied to laws in the US regulating business and recreational activities on the Sabbath. The term was first used (1781) to describe such laws of the Puritan colony at New Haven, which were printed on blue paper.

Blues and Greens Two Byzantine political factions, important during the 6th cent. They represented divergent popular views on various matters, as in the case of religious doctrine, in which the Blues supported Monophysitism and the Greens supported Christian orthodoxy. Both factions had widespread popular support, though the Blues also claimed the backing of the upper class. Blues and Greens joined forces in the bloody Nika Revolt (532) and in the overthrow of Emperor Maurice (602). By the 9th cent., however, their power was all but broken. The two factions derived their names from racing colors worn by charioteers at Constantinople's Hippodrome.

Blum, Léon 1872–1950. French Socialist and premier. As head of a leftist coalition known as the Popular Front government (1936–37), he instituted many Socialist reforms.

Boabdil ⟨Abu-Abdallah⟩ *d.* 1538. Last Moorish king of Granada (1482–92). His surrender to Castilian forces in 1492 marked the end of Moorish dominion in Spain.

Boadicea ⟨Boudicca⟩ *d.* AD 62. Queen of the Iceni, in what is now Norfolk and Suffolk, England. She led an unsuccessful but bloody rebellion against Roman rule.

Boanerges Biblical name given by Jesus to the disciples James and John, and meaning "sons of thunder."

Boas, Franz 1858–1942. German-American anthropologist. He is considered a leader of this field in this century, and his work has had a major influence on the science.

Boaz Biblical husband of Ruth and forebear of David.

Boccaccio, Giovanni 1313–75. Italian poet and writer. His best-known work is the *Decameron.*

Bocskay, István 1557?–1606. Hungarian nobleman. He led a rebellion, with Turkish support, in Hungary (1604–06) against the oppressive rule of Holy Roman Emperor Rudolf II. He succeeded in winning treaties that guaranteed constitutional and religious rights for Hungary.

Bodel, Jean c1165–1210. French trouvère (medieval poet). His *The Play of St. Nicholas* (c1200) is believed to be the first miracle play written in French.

Bodin, Jean 1530–96. French political philosopher. His major work, *Les Six livres de la république,* advocated limited monarchy as the ideal form of government and influenced the 17th-cent. philosopher T. Hobbes.

Bodoni, Giambattista 1740–1813. Italian printer. He designed the Bodoni typeface, which is still used today.

Boehme, Jakob ⟨Böhme, Jakob⟩ 1575–1624. German theosophist and mystic. His book *Aurora,* condemned as heretical, attempted to explain God and the world in terms of opposing elements, i.e., good and evil. His writings anticipated those of such later philosophers as G. Hegel and B. Spinoza.

Boeotia Ancient region of Greece. It became prominent with the creation of the Boeotian League (c550 BC), which under the domination of Thebes, engaged in a power struggle with Athens. Boeotia's decline began with the league's defeat by Philip of Macedon (338 BC). Boeotia was the birthplace of the poets Hesiod and Pindar.

Boeotian League In ancient Greece, a confederacy of city-states of Boeotia. Founded c550 BC, it was dominated by Thebes and ruled by a form of federal government. The league opposed Sparta in the Corinthian War (395–387 BC), allied itself with Athens to defeat Sparta (379 BC), and suffered in the Third Sacred War (355–346 BC). Defeated with Athens by the Macedonians (338 BC), it was dissolved (335 BC) by Alexander the Great after an unsuccessful revolt.

Boer Name applied to early settlers of South Africa, especially those of Dutch or Huguenot descent. Their descendants are now usually called Afrikaners. The first Boers were settled near the Cape of Good Hope (1652) by the Dutch East India Company. After British annexation of the region (1815), the Boers resisted British authority, abandoned the colony, and set out on what is known as the Great Trek. They fought the British in the Boer War (1899–1902), but their territories were finally absorbed into the Union of South Africa.

Boer War ⟨South African War⟩ War (1899–1902) between the Boers of the Orange Free State and the South African Republic (Transvaal), and Great Britain. Tensions between the Boers and the British, caused by conflicts of territorial claims in South Africa, were further aggravated by discovery (1886) of gold in the Transvaal and subsequent influx of prospectors and settlers, mainly British subjects. In order to protect their holdings, the Boers passed laws unfavorable to foreigners. The Jameson Raid *(q.v.)* of 1895 led P. Kruger, president of the South African Republic, to conclude a military alliance (Mar. 17, 1896) with the Orange Free State. The situation continued to deteriorate, and the Boers declared war (Oct. 12, 1899). The Boers claimed early victories but in 1900 heavy British reinforcements, under command of Lord H. Kitchener, began to turn the tide. Kruger fled (1900) to Europe to secure intervention on the Boers' behalf, but was unsuccessful. Great Britain annexed the Transvaal (Sept., 1900), but a vicious guerrilla war continued until 1902. The war was ended by the Treaty of Vereeniging (May 31, 1902), by which the Boers yielded to British sovereignty in return for promises of representative government in the future and indemnities for war damages.

Boethius, Anicius Manlius Severinus ⟨Boetius⟩ AD *c*475–*c*525. Roman philosopher and statesman. His translations of Aristotle kept the study of Greek philosophy alive into the Middle Ages.

Boetius *See* **Boethius, Anicius Manlius Severinus**

Boganda, Barthelemy 1910–59. African statesman. A major African nationalist leader, Boganda became the first premier of the Central African Republic (1958–59).

Bogart, Humphrey 1899–1957. American actor. One of the great film stars, Bogart is noted for such films as *Casablanca*, *The Maltese Falcon*, and *The Treasure of Sierra Madre.*

Bogomils Slavic religious cult. The Bogomils, extreme ascetics, arose in Bulgaria in the 9th cent. and flourished in the Balkan region until the 15th cent.

Bogotá The capital city of Colombia (pop. 2,836,400). Founded (1538) by Spanish explorers, it subsequently became the capital of New Granada and the center of Spain's colonial empire in South America. The city became the capital of Great Colombia following independence from Spain (1819) and capital of what is now Colombia after division of Great Colombia (1830).

Bohemia Historic kingdom, now part of Czechoslovakia. Part of the Moravian Empire, Bohemia came under the rule of the Premysl dynasty (9th cent.) and then became part of the Holy Roman Empire (10th cent.). With the succession (1355) of Holy Roman Emperor Charles IV, Bohemia reached its greatest period. Under Hapsburg rule (1526–1918) it gradually lost its independence. After WW I, Bohemia was incorporated into the new country of Czechoslovakia.

Bohemond I *c*1056–1111. Norman nobleman, a son of Robert Guiscard. A leader in the First Crusade, he declared himself prince of Antioch after aiding in its capture (1098).

Böhme, Jakob *See* **Boehme, Jakob**

Bohr, Niels Henrik David 1885–1962. Danish physicist. He made major contributions to the understanding of atomic structure and was a pioneer in the development of quantum physics. He was awarded the Nobel Prize in Physics (1922).

Bohun, Henry de, 1st earl of Hereford 1176–1220. English nobleman. He was among the group of barons who forced King John of England to sign the Magna Carta (1215).

Bohun, Humphrey V de, 2d earl of Hereford and 1st earl of Essex *d.* 1274. English nobleman, son of Henry de Bohun. He joined with the barons in the writing of the Provisions of Oxford (1258) but sided with King Henry III during the Barons' War (1263–67).

Bohun, Humphrey VII de, 3d earl of Hereford and 2d earl of Essex *d.* 1298. English nobleman, grandson of Humphrey V. He led the barons who forced King Edward I to reaffirm (1297) the Magna Carta and to agree to limitations on his powers of taxation (1297).

Bohun, Humphrey VIII de, 4th earl of Hereford and 3d earl of Essex 1276–1322. English nobleman, son of Humphrey VII de Bohun. He was one of the 21 barons who forced King Edward II to accept limitations on his powers (1311). He also joined the barons in the execution (1312) of the king's favorite, P. Gaveston.

Bolan Pass ⟨Bholan Pass⟩ A mountain pass in western Pakistan linking Asia and India. It has long been used as both a trading and invasion route to the Indian subcontinent.

Boleslaus I c966–1025. Polish ruler (992–1025), the first to designate himself Poland's king. He organized Poland's army and internal administration, expanded the kingdom, and waged war with Holy Roman Emperor Henry II.

Boleslaus III 1086–1138. Duke of Poland (1102–38). He fought Holy Roman emperors Henry V and Lothair II, enlarged his domain, and recaptured part of Pomerania.

Boleslav   *See* **Boleslaus**

Boleslaw   *See* **Boleslaus**

Boleyn, Anne ⟨Anne⟩ ⟨Bullen, Anne⟩ 1507–36. English queen (1533–36), second wife of Henry VIII (*m.* 1533) and mother of Elizabeth I. She was tried and executed for adultery and incest, upon being unable to bear Henry a male heir.

Bolingbroke, Henry St. John, 1st Viscount 1678–1751. British statesman, an influential Tory during the reign of Queen Anne. He was secretary for war (1704–08) during the War of Spanish Succession and later arranged the ouster (1714) of R. Harley as leader of the Tory ministry. He fled Britain on the accession of George I (1714). Returning some years later, he turned to writing and became an associate of Pope and Swift.

Bolívar, Simón 1783–1830. Venezuelan revolutionary and hero in the South American movement for independence from Spain. The son of wealthy parents, he took an early part in the Venezuelan revolution (1810). Following Spanish victories (1812), he led a military force that briefly recaptured Venezuela (1813). Final success came in the following years. He liberated New Granada (1819) in the Battle of Boyaca, then Venezuela (1821), Ecuador (1822), Peru (1824), and Upper Peru (later Bolivia, so named after him) (1825). In 1819 he was proclaimed president of Great Colombia (eventually including Colombia, Ecuador, and Venezuela). Though his plans for a united South America gave rise to Pan-Americanism, Bolívar was unable to hold Great Colombia together. His assumption of dictatorial powers (1828) failed to prevent secession of Venezuela and Ecuador and in 1830 he resigned.

Bolivia ⟨Republic of Bolivia⟩ Bolivia is an independent state located in west central South America. Its capital is Sucre. Bolivia was ruled by Indians and Incas until the Spanish conquests in the 1530s. Colonial rule was ended in the 1820s through the efforts of Simón Bolívar, for whom the country is named. Political unrest, rebellions, and coups have plagued Bolivia from the time of its independence. Key dates in the history of Bolivia include:

13TH CENT.   Incas conquered region from native Indians.

1538   Incan Empire conquered by H. Pizarro; Bolivia became part of the viceroyalty of Peru.

1545   Silver discovered; native Indians forced to work in mines as colonial settlers rushed to exploit the region.

1776   Region annexed to the new viceroyalty of La Plata.

1809   Uprising in Chuquisaca marked beginning of revolt against Spanish colonial rule.

1824   S. Bolívar and A. de Sucre led successful military campaign against Spanish royalists in Peru and Bolivia; Battle of Ayacucho (near Lima, Dec. 9) ended royalist resistance.

1825   Bolivia declared independence from Spain (Aug. 6).

1826   Constitution drafted by S. Bolívar adopted; Sucre became first president.

1836   A. Santa Cruz seized power in Peru and invaded Bolivia; Peru and Bolivia joined as a federal republic with Santa Cruz as leader.

1839   Chile, opposed to the federation, defeated Santa Cruz at the Battle of Yungay (Jan.) and thus ended the federation.

1866–74   Treaties established 24th parallel as Chile-Bolivian border.

1879–84   War of the Pacific with Chile; Bolivia lost all coastal territories.

1880   New constitution adopted; failed to halt political turmoil.

1899   Brazil seized rubber-rich Acre region (in eastern Bolivia) after revolt by Brazilian settlers there.

1903   Brazil received 70,000 sq. mi. of Acre region by the Treaty of Petropolis.

1904   Treaty with Chile granted Bolivia free access to the sea.

1932–35   Chaco War, undeclared border war with Paraguay over Chaco region.

1934–37   Col. David Toro in power after a series of coups; he seized Standard Oil holdings and mining company profits.

1940   Gen. Enrique Peñaranda elected president under new constitution (adopted 1938); elections followed short-lived attempt to establish totalitarian state (1939).

1943   Peñaranda joined Allies in WW II; ordered conscription of laborers to work in mines to produce strategic raw materials.

1943 National Revolutionary Movement (MNR) seized power after widespread strikes by workers protesting oppressive working conditions.

1944–46 MNR leader Gualberto Villarroel in office as president; established totalitarian state.

1946–51 Conservative elements seized power; put down MNR-backed rebellions and attempted to prevent duly-elected MNR candidate from taking office in 1951.

1952–64 V. Paz Estenssoro, MNR candidate who won elections, in office after MNR seized power.

1951–56 Estenssoro nationalized tin-company holdings, initiated agrarian reforms, and extended civil rights to Indians.

1964 Military seized power in the wake of economic problems and rise of terrorist groups.

1967 Government troops, battling guerrilla movement since 1965, killed Che Guevara.

1967 New constitution adopted.

1970 Gulf Oil Company holdings nationalized (with compensation).

1971–78 Col. Hugo Banzer Suárez in power after series of coups (1969–71).

1978–80 New round of military coups and political unrest followed contested presidential election.

1980 Gen. Luis García Meza seized power (July 17) after presidential elections failed to produce a clear winner.

1981–82 Meza's harsh rule resulted in a military takeover and rapid succession of military rulers.

Bolivian National Revolutionary Movement (MNR) Political group (founded 1941) that fostered a social revolution in Bolivia during the 1950s. Following a general rebellion (Apr. 9–11, 1952), exiled MNR leader V. Paz Estenssoro became president (1952–56) and instituted sweeping economic and social reforms. These included universal suffrage, nationalization of tin mines, land reforms, and disbanding of the army and militia. The reforms bred runaway inflation, however, and by the early 1960s the government abandoned the revolution for a program of fiscal austerity.

Bollandists Name of a group of Belgian Jesuits who are charged with the continuous updating of the *Acta Sanctorum*, the collected lives and legends of the Roman Catholic saints. The group is named after Jean de Bolland (1596–1665), the editor who completed (1643) the first volumes. Except for the period 1794–1837, Bollandists have been revising the great work continuously since 1643.

Bologna Italian city (pop. 477,000), capital of Bologna province in northern Italy. Of Etruscan origin, Bologna was one of the leading cultural centers of medieval Europe, and also scene of the Guelph-Ghibelline rivalry.

Bologna, Concordat of *See* **Concordat of Bologna**

Bologna, Giovanni 1529?–1628. Flemish sculptor. Among his most famous works are the statues *Flying Mercury* and the *Rape of the Sabines*.

Bolshevik Party Conference Name sometimes used for a congress of the Russian Social Democratic Workers party, convened (1912) at Prague by N. Lenin. In an effort to maintain the unity of his own Bolshevik faction, Lenin used the occasion to permanently split the party and forced the Menshevik faction to form a separate party organization.

Bolsheviks One of the two important factions of the Russian Social Democratic Workers' party. The faction originated under N. Lenin during the second congress of the Social Democratic Workers' party (1903) at Brussels and London. Generally, the Bolsheviks wanted to establish a dictatorship of the proletariat immediately after the revolution they anticipated would come. Their opponents, the Mensheviks, believed an intermediate stage of bourgeois rule was needed before workers took power. The split subsequently widened and in 1912 Lenin formed the Bolsheviks as a small but distinct revolutionary party. Following the February Revolution and Lenin's return to Russia (1917), the Bolsheviks became increasingly popular with the workers. By controlling the Moscow and Petrograd Soviets the Bolsheviks were able to become the ruling power in the government after the October Revolution. Lenin first shared power with other factions but gradually eliminated rival parties. Bolsheviks were officially named Russian Communist Party (Bolsheviks) in 1918 and Communist Party of the Soviet Union in 1952.

Bombay Indian city (pop. 5,968,000), capital of Maharashtra state and a major port and industrial center. Native Indian settlements date from the 12th cent. and the site of the modern city was ceded to the Portuguese c1534. The British acquired control (1661) and for nearly two centuries Bombay was Indian headquarters of the East India Company. The opening of the Suez Canal assured the city continuing prosperity.

Bona Dea Roman goddess of fertility, also known as Fauna.

Bonaparte, Charles Lucien Jules Laurent 1803–57. Naturalist, a son of Napoleon's brother Lucien. His best-known work is *American Ornithology*.

Bonaparte, Jérôme 1784–1860. Napoleon's youngest brother. King of Westphalia (1807–13), he fought in Russia and at Waterloo, and served as marshal of France under Napoleon III.

Bonaparte, Joseph 1768–1844. King of Naples (1806–08) and Spain (1808–13). The oldest brother of Napoleon, he was forced to abdicate (1813) after the Peninsular Wars.

Bonaparte, Letizia Ramolino 1750–1836. Corsican matron, the mother of Napoleon.

Bonaparte, Louis 1778–1846. Brother of Napoleon. King of Holland (1806–10), he resisted the Continental System, and was forced by Napoleon to abdicate.

Bonaparte, Lucien 1775–1840. Brother of Napoleon. As president of France's Council of Five Hundred, he helped Napoleon overthrow the Directory and seize power in 1799

Bonaparte, Mathilde 1820–1904. Daughter of Napoleon's brother Jérôme. She was a noted patroness of the arts during the Second French Empire.

Bonaparte, Napoleon *See* **Napoleon I**

Bonaparte, Napoléon Eugène Louis Jean Joseph 1856–79. French prince, the son of Napoleon III. He became pretender to the throne on his father's death (1873). He was killed while on a military expedition in Africa.

Bonaparte, Napoléon Joseph Charles Paul 1822–91. Known as Prince Napoleon. He was heir designate to the throne following the death of the son of Napoleon III.

Bonaparte, Pierre Napoléon 1815–81. French politician, son of Napoleon's brother Lucien. He was tried for the murder of a journalist in 1870, but was acquitted.

Bonaventure, Saint ⟨Bonaventura, Saint⟩ 1221–74. Italian theologian. An important church scholar, he was canonized in 1482 and made Doctor of the Church in 1587.

Boniface *See* **Bonifacius**

Boniface, Saint c675–754? English Benedictine monk and martyr, originally called Wynfrid or Wynfrith. Called the Apostle of Germany, he is noted for his missionary work among the Germanic tribes.

Boniface VIII 1235?–1303. Italian pope (1294–1303), successor to Celestine V. He fought to maintain supremacy of the church over European kings, notably Philip IV of France. The struggle with Philip eventually resulted in a papal bull (1302) in which Boniface proclaimed supremacy of the pope in temporal and religious matters. An adviser to Philip, who was by then threatening to depose the pope, captured Boniface briefly at Anagni. Though Boniface is said to have stood up to ill treatment, he died shortly after his rescue.

Bonifácio, José *See* **Andrada e Silva, José Bonifácio de**

Bonifacius ⟨Boniface⟩ d. AD 432. Roman general. As governor of the Roman province of Africa he became involved in a dispute with Emperor of the West Valentinian III. He was said to have invited the Vandals to aid against the Romans, which led to conquest of Africa by the Vandals under Gaiseric (AD 432).

Bonn Capital of West Germany (pop. 285,000). Originally a Roman frontier garrison known as Castra Bonnensia (1st cent. AD), it passed to the Franks and was destroyed by the Normans in the 9th cent. It later became the seat of the archbishops of Cologne and an electorate of the Holy Roman Empire (13th–19th cents.). Occupied by allied troops after WW I and again after WW II, it became West Germany's capital in 1949.

Bonnard, Pierre 1867–1947. French painter and lithographer, associated with the Nabis and later the Intimists.

Bonney, William H. *See* **Billy the Kid**

Bonnie Prince Charlie, the Young Pretender *See* **Stuart, Charles Edward**

Bonnivard, François de ⟨Bonivard, François de⟩ c1493–1570. Swiss patriot. Prior of St. Victor, he was imprisoned in Chillon castle for opposing the Duke of Savoy in the Revolt of Geneva, and was the subject of G. Byron's poem *The Prisoner of Chillon*.

Bonus Army ⟨∼ Marchers⟩ ⟨∼ Expeditionary Force⟩ Mass gathering of US WW I veterans (spring-summer of 1932) at Washington, D.C., during the Great Depression. The unemployed and impoverished veterans (estimated variously at 12–20,000) camped in Washington to press their demand for immediate payment of a WW I bonus of about $1,000 each (due to be paid in 1945). The Senate defeated (June 17) a bill for immediate payment and Pres. H. Hoover ordered (July 28) removal of the marchers. US Army troops under Gen. D. MacArthur drove the marchers out and burned their camps. The bonus was finally paid in 1936.

Bonus Expeditionary Force *See* **Bonus Army**

Bonus Marchers *See* **Bonus Army**

Book of Common Prayer Name of the authorized prayer book of the Church of England and its branches in other countries. Compiled by T. Cranmer (1549), it presented selected and revised versions of Catholic liturgies in English. Made mandatory that year by the Act of Uniformity, it was alternately suppressed and modified in following years. A modern version was adopted in 1928.

Book of Concord   Collection (1580) of the major documents of Lutheran faith, including the Apostles' Creed, Nicene Creed, and Augsburg Confession.

Book of the Dead   Name given to the collection of ancient Egyptian prayers, formulas, and incantations buried with the dead for use by them in the afterlife.

Boone, Daniel   1734–1820. American frontiersman and folk hero. He blazed the Wilderness Road through Kentucky, which he helped to explore and settle.

Booth, Ballington   1859–1940. English reformer, a son of W. Booth. A commander of the US Salvation Army (1887–96), he left it to found the Volunteers of America (1896).

Booth, Bramwell   1856–1929. British general of the Salvation Army. He succeeded his father W. Booth as general in 1912.

Booth, Charles   1840–1916.   English social reformer. His *Life and Labour of the People in London* contributed to the development of the modern social survey method.

Booth, Edwin   1833–93. American actor. Considered one of the great American actors, he is known best for his performances of *Hamlet.*

Booth, Evangeline Cory   1865–1950.   Britishborn daughter of William Booth. She was commander of the US Salvation Army (1904–34) and general of the international Salvation Army (1934–39).

Booth, John Wilkes   1838–65. American actor. He assassinated Abraham Lincoln at Ford's Theatre in Washington, D.C., on April 14, 1865. Injured while making his escape, Booth was treated by Dr. Samuel Alexander Mudd (1833–83). Mudd later was imprisoned for helping Booth. Booth was captured and killed (Apr. 26) and his body identified, but rumors arose that he had escaped.

Booth, Junius Brutus   1796–1852. English actor. The father of E. and J. Booth, he emigrated to the US in 1821.

Booth, William   1829–1912.   English minister, the founder (1878) and first general of the Salvation Army.

Booth-Tucker, Emma Moss   1860–1903. English reformer, a daughter of W. Booth. With her husband Frederick St. George de Latour Booth-Tucker (1853–1929), she commanded the US Salvation Army (1896–1903).

bootlegging   Usually, illegal trafficking in alcohol, especially in the US during Prohibition (1920–33). Though the illegal manufacture and sale of alcohol was known before Prohibition, it became a burgeoning industry during the Prohibition years. Bootlegging involved smuggling from foreign countries, illegal manufacture within the US, and distribution through illegal "speakeasies." The profits from these lucrative operations helped to establish organized crime in the US and spawned widespread police and political corruption. Activities of bootleggers and the general disregard for dry laws forced the repeal of Prohibition (1933).

Borah, William Edgar   1865–1940. American politician. An isolationist US Senator (1907–40), he opposed the Versailles Treaty and US entry into the League of Nations but supported international disarmament and the Kellogg-Briand Pact.

Bordeaux   French seaport (pop. 226,000) and a center of the French wine trade. Known to the Romans as Burdigala, it became the seat of the dukes of Aquitane (11th cent.), prospered under English rule (1154–1453), and served several times (1870, 1914, 1940) as the seat of provisional French governments.

Bordeaux Assembly   French National Assembly gathered (Feb. 13, 1871) at Bordeaux, France, following France's defeat in the Franco-Prussian War and the subsequent overthrow of the French Empire.

Borden, Lizzie Andrew   1860–1927. American woman, tried for the brutal ax murders of her father and stepmother (1892). She maintained her innocence and, after a sensational trial, was acquitted.

Borden, Sir Robert Laird   1854–1937. Canadian statesman. Prime minister from 1911–20, he led Canada through WW I, and helped win independent representation for British dominions in the League of Nations.

Border, the   Name given to the border region between England and Scotland. Celebrated in the literature of both peoples, it was the site of many historic battles between the English and Scots until the 17th cent.

Bordet, Jules   1870–1961.   Belgian immunologist, a leader in the study of immune systems. With Octave Gengou he discovered the whooping cough bacillus (1906). For his study of immunity factors in blood he was awarded the Nobel Prize in Medicine (1919).

Bordone, Paris   1500–71. Venetian painter during the Renaissance. A student of Titian, he was noted for his portraits. *Fisherman Presenting the Ring of St. Mark to the Doge* is one of his most famous works.

Boreas   Ancient Greek personification of the north wind. He was revered by the Athenians for having saved Athens by wrecking the invading fleet of Persian king Xerxes.

Borel, Joseph Pierre   *See* **Borel, Petrus**

Borel, Petrus ⟨Borel, Joseph Pierre⟩ 1809–59. French novelist and poet, one of the leading figures of the French Romantic movement. His works include the verse collection *Rhapsodies.*

Borghese, Camillo   *See* **Paul V**

Borgia, Cesare 1476–1507. Italian soldier and political leader, son of Pope Alexander VI. Ruthless and opportunistic, he is said to have reflected the qualities of N. Machiavelli's *Prince.* He strengthened the position of the papacy.

Borgia, Lucrezia 1480–1519. Italian Renaissance noblewoman, daughter of Pope Alexander VI, and sister of C. Borgia. As duchess of Ferrara, she was a noted patroness of the arts and letters, but she is known best through legends of her family's vices and crimes.

Borglum, Gutzon 1867–1941. American sculptor. Among his best-known works is the Mount Rushmore National Memorial.

Boris I *d.* 907. Bulgarian ruler (852–89). He converted to Christianity (865) and is credited with introducing and spreading Byzantine Christianity throughout Bulgaria.

Boris III 1894–1943. King of Bulgaria (1918–43). Possessing virtually dictatorial powers in the last years of his reign, he supported the Axis Powers in WW II. He died under mysterious circumstances shortly after a confrontation with A. Hitler.

Borja, Alfonso de   *See* **Calixtus III**

Borman, Frank 1928–. American astronaut. He was a crew member of the Apollo 8 space mission, which made the first manned orbit of the moon (Dec., 1968).

Born, Max 1882–1970. German-born British physicist noted for his contributions to the theory of relativity and quantum theory. With Walter Bothe (1891–1957) he received the 1954 Nobel Prize in Physics.

Borobudur A pyramid-like structure in Java, considered one of the greatest of all Buddhist monuments. It was built early in the 9th cent. by adherents of Mahayana Buddhism.

Borodin, Alexander   *See* **Igor**

Borodino, Battle of Narrow victory (Sept. 7, 1812) for Napoleon during the Russian invasion of the Napoleonic Wars. In the battle some 120,000 retreating Russian troops under Gen. M. Kutuzov made their last defense of Moscow at the village of Borodino. The Russians managed to hold off Napoleon's force of 130,000 soldiers in the daylong battle but retreated during the night. The French suffered 30,000 casualties and the Rus-

sians 45,000. After the battle Napoleon was able to march unopposed into Moscow, but he had lost his chance to destroy the Russian army.

Bosch, Hieronymus ⟨Jerom Bos⟩ *c*1450–1516. Dutch painter, noted for the bizarre and grotesque. His works include *The Crowning with Thorns* and *The Garden of Earthly Delights.*

Bosnia and Herzegovina Historic region, now part of Yugoslavia. Once part of the Roman province of Illyricum, it was settled by Serbs and Croatians (7th cent.). After the 12th cent. it came under Hungarian domination. By the late 15th cent. the region had fallen to the Turks, who controlled it until the Bosnian Rebellion (1875). After the Russo-Turkish War, Austria-Hungary occupied the region (1878), then annexed it (1908), thereby precipitating the Bosnian Crisis. The assassination (1914) of Archduke Ferdinand in Sarajevo led to WW I, after which the territory was annexed (1918) to Serbia. In 1946 it became one of the six constituent republics of Yugoslavia.

Bosnian crisis International crisis caused by Austria-Hungary's annexation (Oct. 6, 1908) of Bosnia and Herzegovina. The incident contributed to tensions that led to WW I, by straining relations between Austria-Hungary and Russia and by arousing Serbian nationalism. Austria-Hungary had occupied the territories since the Russo-Turkish War (1877–78). When Austria-Hungary announced formal annexation, Russia sided with Serbians in protest. Germany supported Austria-Hungary and threatened war, and Russia, humiliated, backed down.

Bosnian Rebellion Revolt (1875) in Bosnia against Ottoman rule. The uprising, which began in nearby Herzegovina, gained support from Serbia, and culminated in the Serbo-Turkish War of 1876–78.

Bossuet, Jacques Bénigne 1627–1704. French bishop and orator, considered one of the great French orators. He attacked F. Fenelon and Quietism, and figured in the Gallican controversy.

Boston US city, (pop. 563,000) the capital of Massachusetts. Established in 1630 by J. Winthrop, Boston played a leading role before and during the American Revolution. It was the site of the Boston Massacre (1770), the Boston Tea Party (1773), the Battle of Bunker Hill (1775), and the siege of Boston (1775–76), which forced British evacuation. A cultural and educational center, it is called the "Athens of America."

Boston, Siege of American military victory (1775–76) during the American Revolution. Shortly after the battles of Lexington and Concord (Apr. 19, 1775), Colonial forces began a siege of Boston, then held by the British. Installation by the Continental Army of artillery on Dorchester Heights (Mar., 1776) forced British evacuation of the city (Mar. 17).

Boston Massacre Incident (Mar. 5, 1770) leading up to the American Revolution (1775–83), in which British troops fired into a crowd of rioting colonials in Boston. The Townshend Acts, and the quartering of British troops in Boston to enforce them, led to frequent harassment of the soldiers by Boston colonials. On Mar. 5, a group of nine soldiers was threatened by a crowd of 50–60 angry colonials. The soldiers opened fire and killed five, including Crispus Attucks (1723?–70), who is sometimes called the leader of the mob. The soldiers were later tried and acquitted on charges of murder, though two were found guilty of manslaughter, and most of the Townshend Acts were repealed.

Boston Tea Party Famous incident (Dec. 16, 1773) leading up to the American Revolution. American colonists had protested the tea tax imposed by British Parliament in the Townshend Acts and had blocked delivery of tea at New York and Philadelphia. At Boston, however, Gov. T. Hutchinson demanded payment of the tax. A group of some 50 colonists, disguised as Indians and including S. Adams and P. Revere, boarded three British ships in Boston harbor and threw their cargoes of tea overboard. Parliament responded with the Intolerable Acts, closing the port of Boston.

Boswell, James 1740–95. Scottish author, diarist and famous biographer of S. Johnson. A lawyer from 1776, he sought to befriend the great men of his time and first met Johnson in 1763. He became famous with publication of his *Account of Corsica* (1768) and joined Johnson's literary club (1773). His classic *Life of Samuel Johnson* was published in 1791. Boswell's literary reputation was further strengthened by discovery (1927) of his voluminous journals, in Ireland.

Bosworth Field, Battle of Tudor victory (1485) over the Yorkists, ending the Wars of the Roses in England. Some 5,000 rebel troops under Henry Tudor (later Henry VII) engaged 15,000 Yorkists under King Richard III. Treachery and disorganization led to Richard's defeat and death in battle. Henry thus gained the throne and founded the Tudor dynasty.

Botha, Louis 1862–1919. South African soldier and statesman. A Boer, he was the first prime minister of the Union of South Africa (1910–19).

Bothe, Walter *See* **Born, Max**

Bothwell, James Hepburn, earl of c1536–1578. Scottish nobleman and third husband of Mary

Queen of Scots (*m.* 1567). Their marriage led to a revolt (1567) of the Scottish nobles. Bothwell fled, dying a prisoner in Denmark.

Botswana 〈Bechuanaland〉 Landlocked South African republic (pop. 820,000). The British occupied Bechuanaland (1884) to prevent incursions from the Boers and Germans, incorporating the southern area into Cape Colony. In the 20th cent. the Union of South Africa sought several times to annex the Bechuanaland protectorate. Britain granted the territory independence on Sept. 30, 1966. Recent discovery of major mineral deposits have increased Botswana's strategic and economic importance.

Botticelli, Sandro 〈*b.* Allesandro di Mariano Filipepi〉 c1444–1510. Florentine painter of the early Renaissance. His works include the *Birth of Venus* and illustrations for Dante's *Divine Comedy.*

Boudicca *See* **Boadicea**

Bougainville, Louis Antoine de 1729–1811. French navigator. He made the first French circumnavigation of the world (1766–69).

Bouillon, Godfrey of *See* **Godfrey of Bouillon**

Boulanger, Georges Ernest Jean Marie 1837–91. French general and political figure, the instigator of Boulangism, a nationalist movement seeking revenge against Germany. Though for a time he threatened to topple the Third Republic, he was finally forced to flee to Belgium, where he committed suicide.

Boulangism *See* **Boulanger, Georges Ernest Jean Marie**

Boule *See* **Areopagus**

***Bounty*, HMS** English ship aboard which occurred the celebrated mutiny on Apr. 28, 1789. The ship, under the command of Capt. W. Bligh, was carrying a cargo of breadfruit trees from Tahiti to the West Indies. Led by the mate Fletcher Christian (*fl.* late 18th cent.), the crew mutinied and set the captain and 18 others adrift. The remainder of the crew is believed by some to have founded a colony at Pitcairn Island.

Bourbon Powerful French royal family whose descendants were rulers of France, Spain, Kingdom of Two Sicilies, and Parma. The family can be traced back to a 9th-cent. French nobleman, Adhemar (or Aimar). The founder of the royal line was Robert of Clermont (1256–1318), a son of French King Louis IX. Robert married (1272) the Bourbon heiress, Beatrice. The elder line thus formed became extinct (1527) with the death of Charles, duke of Bourbon. But a collateral line, Bourbon-Vendôme, produced Henry IV (ruled 1589–1610), the first of a long line of Bourbon kings of France. King Louis XIV's brother, Phi-lippe, duke of Orleans (1640–1701), founded the Orléans (Bourbon) line and Louis' grandson, Philip, duke of Anjou, founded the Bourbon-Spain line as King Philip V. Bourbon rule of France was uninterrupted until the French Revolution (1789–99), when King Louis XVI was deposed (1792) and guillotined. During the Bourbon Restoration, Louis XVI's brother ruled as Louis XVIII. His successors, Charles X and Louis Philippe (Bourbon-Orléans) were the last Bourbon kings of France. Thereafter claims to the throne by royal pretenders of the Bourbon line continued until extinction of the line with the death (1883) of H. Chambord. Royal claims then passed to the Orléans line. (*See also* Bourbon-Spain, Bourbon-Sicily, Bourbon-Parma.) Bourbon Kings of France were:

Henry IV	1589–1610
Louis XIII	1610–43
Louis XIV	1643–1715
Louis XV	1715–74
Louis XVI	1774–92
Louis XVII	1793–95 (never ruled)
Louis XVIII	1814–24
Charles X	1824–30
Louis Philippe	1830–48 (Bourbon-Orléans)

Bourbon, Charles, duke of Bourbon 1490–1527. Constable of France under Francis I. He supported Holy Roman Emperor Charles V against Francis in the Italian Wars.

Bourbon-Parma A branch of the Bourbon family of French royalty. The line was established as a branch of Bourbon-Spain in 1748 when Philip, a son of Spanish king Philip V, was made duke of Parma and Piacenza. The line survived until 1859 when Robert, 5th duke of Parma, lost his title.

Bourbon-Sicily Line of rulers in southern Italy, a branch of the French Bourbon family. Established by Ferdinand I, who was made king of Naples (1759) and ruled the Kingdom of the Two Sicilies (1816–25), it lasted until 1860, when the kingdom was incorporated into Italy.

Bourbon-Spain Line of rulers in Spain, a branch of the French Bourbon family. Established with the sucession (1700) of King Philip V, the grandson of French King Louis XIV, it has continued, with interruptions, to the present as the royal family of Spain. The rulers are:

Philip V	1700–24
Louis I	1724
Philip V	1724–46 (restored)
Ferdinand VI	1746–59
Charles III	1759–88
Charles IV	1788–1808
Ferdinand VII	1808
Ferdinand VII	1814–33 (restored)
Isabella II	1833–68
Alfonso XII	1874–85
Alfonso XIII	1886–1931
Juan Carlos I	1975–

bourgeoisie Originally, French merchants and craftsmen in medieval times, who, as a class, occupied the economic and social middle ground between landowners and peasants. With the breakup of feudal society, the rise of capitalism and the advent of the Industrial Revolution, the bourgeoisie came to include a wide range of groups of entrepreneurs, such as bankers, factory owners, merchants, and professionals. By K. Marx's theory of class struggle, society consists of the capitalist bourgeoisie pitted against the wage-earning workers, or proletariat (*q.v.*).

Bourges, Pragmatic Sanction of *See* **Pragmatic Sanction of Bourges**

Bourne, Randolph Silliman 1886–1918. American pacifist and essayist. His articles in opposition to US participation in WW I were collected in *Untimely Papers*.

Bouvines, Battle of Battle (July 27, 1214) at Bouvines, France, in which 10,000 French led by Philip II of France defeated a coalition army of 15,000 led by King John of England and Holy Roman Emperor Otto IV. Philip thus gained control of most of the French lands formerly held by the English (Angevin domains).

Bowditch, Nathaniel 1773–1838. American mathematician and navigator. He corrected and revised J. Moore's *The Practical Navigator* and in 1802 issued his famous *The New American Practical Navigator*.

Bowdler, Thomas 1754–1825. English editor. His expurgated edition of W. Shakespeare's plays, *The Family Shakespeare*, gave rise to the term "bowdlerize."

Bowie, James ⟨Jim⟩ 1799–1836. American frontiersman, credited with invention of the Bowie knife. He died at the Alamo during the Texas war for independence.

Boxer Rebellion Widespread uprising (1900) in northern China against foreigners and foreign influence. Increased foreign domination of China led to the rise of the nationalist, secret organization I Ho Ch'uan, or Boxers, and by 1898 the group had the support of the Dowager Empress Tz'u Hsi. In early June, 1900, rebellion broke out. Some 140,000 Boxers occupied Peking and began burning foreign buildings and churches and killing Chinese Christians. The Dowager Empress repulsed a small relief force (June 13), declared war, and ordered all foreigners killed. However, a force of 18,000 foreign soldiers finally overcame the Boxers (Aug. 14), and took control of Peking. China was forced subsequently to make new commercial concessions and to pay reparations, by the Boxer protocol (Sept. 7, 1901).

Boyacá, Battle of Victory (Aug. 7, 1819) for South American revolutionaries fighting for independence from Spain. With Gen. Francisco de Paula Santander (1792–1840), S. Bolívar led some 3,000 rebels across flooded plains and through the high passes of the Andes to surprise a 5,000-man Spanish force outside Bogotá. The engagement near the Boyacá River resulted in the capture of the Spanish commander and 1,800 prisoners, and the independence of New Granada.

Boyar Title given to Russian landowning nobles who were influential in Russia from the 10th to 17th cents. The title was abolished by Peter I.

boycott Concerted refusal by groups or nations to deal economically, politically, or socially with an individual, group, or nation. Its purpose is to protest or change actions or policies.

Boyle, Richard, 1st earl of Cork 1566–1643. English-born Irish administrator, noted for his encouragement of trade and industry in Ireland.

Boyle, Robert 1627–91. Irish-English physicist and chemist. He advanced (1662) Boyle's Law, which explains the relationship of the pressure of a gas to its volume.

Boyne, Battle of the A victory (July, 1690) in Ireland for English King William III over the Jacobite armies of former King James II. Some 35,000 Protestants under William defeated about 25,000 Catholics (French and Irish) at the Boyne River, forcing James to flee to France.

Bozzaris, Marco ⟨~, Markos⟩ c1788–1823. Greek patriot, an important leader in the War of Greek Independence.

Bozzaris, Markos See **Bozzaris, Marcos**

Brabant Revolution Brief rebellion (1789–90) against the rule of Holy Roman Emperor Joseph II in the Belgian provinces of the Austrian Netherlands. The revolt fostered the subsequent drive for Belgian independence.

Bradford, William 1590–1657.   English-born American colonist. First elected governor of Plymouth Colony in 1621, he was reelected thirty times. He wrote the *History of Plymouth Plantation*.

Bradford, William 1663–1752. English-born colonial printer. He published the first *American Book of Common Prayer* and the first New York newspaper, the *New York Gazette*.

Bradley, Omar Nelson 1893–1981. US general. A top commander in North Africa and Europe in

WW II, he was made general of the army (1950) and chairman of the joint chiefs of staff (1949–53).

Bradstreet, Anne Dudley c1612–1672. English-born Colonial poet, considered the first important woman writer in America.

Brady, James Buchanan ⟨Diamond Jim ~⟩ 1856–1917. American financial speculator. A flamboyant, self-made millionaire, he was noted for wearing numerous diamonds and other gems.

Brady, Matthew B. c1823–96. American photographer. A pioneer in photography, he was noted for his many photographs of the US Civil War.

Braga, Teófilo 1843–1924. Portuguese poet and political leader. He was the first president (1910–11) of the new republic of Portugal, and served again in 1915. He wrote an important history of Portuguese literature.

Braganca See **Braganza**

Braganza ⟨Bragança⟩ Ruling house of Portugal (1640–1910) and Brazil (1822–89). The family was founded by Alfonso (d. 1451), the illegitimate son of Portuguese King John I. The first member of the royal line was John IV, who ruled the newly independent Portugal (1640–56). The line of rulers lasted until the ouster of Manuel II (1910) and formation of the republic. The Braganza family also provided rulers of Brazil for a time in the 19th cent. They were Pedro I, son of Portuguese King John VI, and Pedro II, who was ousted in 1889. The Braganza kings of Portugal were:

John IV	1640–56
Alfonso VI	1656–83
Peter II	1683–1706
John V	1706–1750
Joseph	1750–77
Maria I	
(with Peter III)	1777–86
Maria I	1786–1816
John VI	1816–26
Peter IV	1826
Maria II	1826–28
Miguel	1828–34
Maria II	1834–53
Peter V	1853–61
Louis I	1861–89
Carlos I	1889–1908
Manuel II	1908–10

Braganza, Catherina of See **Catherine of Braganza**

Bragg, Braxton 1817–76. Confederate general in the US Civil War. He led Confederate forces to victory in the battle of Chickamauga (1863), the bloodiest battle of the war.

Brahe, Tycho 1546–1601. Danish astronomer. His careful astronomical observations challenged the Aristotelian idea of a fixed universe, and contributed to the growth of modern astronomy.

Brahma One of the three major gods, with Vishnu and Shiva, of Hinduism. He is usually depicted with four heads and four arms and is often shown riding a swan. In the early period of Hinduism, he was revered as the sole creator of the earth. His importance as a deity has declined over the centuries, and he now plays a minor role in Hindu worship.

Brahman Supreme being of the early Vedic texts, infinite, eternal, the spiritual essence of the universe. In later Hindu theology it is one of the three major gods (with Vishnu and Shiva), personified as the god Brahma.

Brahman ⟨Brahmin⟩ Highest caste of the Hindu religion. Brahmans are by tradition responsible for the study and teaching of the Vedas, and performance of special religious ceremonies. *See also* **caste system.**

Brahmanism Early phase of Hinduism. Brahmanism derived (*c*700 BC) from worship of the sacred texts of the Vedas and was followed (*c*500 BC) by the classical period of Hinduism. Brahmanism was developed by the Brahmans, or priests, who oversaw worship of the Vedic texts. Among its characteristic features were an increasing concern for philosophical speculations (as in the Upanishads), increased elaboration of ceremonies (especially sacrifices), the emergence of the caste system, and development of the concept of transmigration of the soul. The rise of Buddhism and Jainism brought about the evolution of Brahmanism into classical Hinduism.

Brahmin *See* **Brahman**

Brahms, Johannes 1833–97. German composer of the romantic period, one of the world's great composers. Brahms rejected what was then the revolutionary romanticism of R. Wagner and F. Liszt and created compositions that combined a restrained romanticism with classical forms. A gifted musician in his youth, Brahms became friends with R. Schumann, who helped establish Brahms's reputation as a composer. Brahms settled in Vienna after 1863 and there composed the bulk of his works, including *German Requiem, Violin Concerto in D*, and his four great symphonies.

Braille, Louis 1809?–52. French teacher and inventor of the Braille system of writing for the blind.

Braintree Resolutions Resolutions passed (Sept. 24, 1765) by the town of Braintree, Massachusetts, calling for legal resistance to the Stamp Act.

Brain Trust Advisers to F. Roosevelt during his presidential campaign (1932) and the early period of his first administration. The group played a role in formulation of New Deal policies.

Bramante, Donato 1444–1514. Italian painter and architect, noted for his buildings in the High Renaissance style. His major work was his plan for the rebuilding of St. Peter's church in Rome.

Brancusi, Constantin 1876–1957. Romanian sculptor, a leading sculptor of the modern abstract school. His work focused on the simplified forms of objects.

Brandenburg Ancient region divided since WW II between East Germany and Poland. It was conquered by Albert the Bear (12th cent.), whose descendants, the Ascanians, ruled it until 1320. Made an electorate of the Holy Roman Empire, it passed to Frederick I of Hohenzollern. After the Thirty Years' War, it became a military power under the rule (1640–88) of Frederick William, the Great Elector, who conquered East Pomerania and freed Prussia from Polish rule. His son Frederick III took the title Frederick I, King of Prussia (1701), by which name it was known thereafter.

Brandenburg, Albert of *See* **Albert of Brandenburg**

Brandenburg, Treaty of *See* **Bärwalde, Treaty of**

Brandt, Willy ⟨Frahm, Karl Herbert⟩ 1913–. German statesman. Brandt served as mayor of West Berlin (1957–66) and chancellor of the German Federal Republic (1969–74). He was awarded the Nobel Peace Prize (1971).

Brandy Station, Battle of Battle (June 9, 1863) of the American Civil War. At Brandy Station (now Brandy), Virginia, a force of federal cavalry attacked and was repulsed by Confederate cavalry commanded by Gen. J. Stuart.

Brandywine, Battle of British victory (Sept. 11, 1777) over Colonial forces during the American Revolution (1775–83). The victory led to the capture of the Colonial capital of Philadelphia (Sept. 27). Gen. G. Washington, commanding some 11,000 colonials, hoped to block the British advance from New York to Philadelphia. He met the British force of some 15,000 soldiers, commanded by Gen. W. Howe, at Brandywine Creek just south of Philadelphia but was eventually forced to withdraw. British casualties were about 600 to American casualties of some 1,000.

Brant, Joseph 1742–1807. Mohawk Indian chief. He joined the British side during the American Revolution and did much to win Indians to their cause. He led Indian forces at the Battle of Oriskany (1777) and in the Cherry Valley Raid (1778).

Branting, Karl Hjalmar 1860–1925. Swedish statesman, a founder of the Swedish Social Democratic Party. As premier (1920, 1921–23, 1924–25), he helped to promote social reforms. He was awarded the Nobel Peace Prize (1921).

Braque, Georges 1882–1963. French painter, one of the leading painters of the 20th cent. With P. Picasso he developed cubism.

Braschi, Giovanni Angelo See **Pius VI**

Brasidas d. 422 BC. Spartan general who won fame during the Peloponnesian War. He defeated the Athenians under Cleon at Amphipolis, but both he and Cleon were killed during the battle (422 BC).

Bratianu, Ion See **Bratianu, John**

Bratianu, John ⟨~, Ion⟩ 1864–1927. Romanian statesman. Premier of Romania (1909–11, 1914–18, 1922–26), he brought Romania into WW I against the Central Powers, and represented Romania at the Paris Peace Conference (1919).

Brattain, Walter H. See **Bardeen, John**

Braun, Eva 1912–45. German woman, the mistress of A. Hitler. Hitler kept their relationship a secret, and she played no role in his career. She and Hitler were married (Apr. 29, 1945) one day before their joint suicide.

Braun, Wernher von 1912–77. German-American engineer. He helped to develop rockets for the German military during WW II. After the war he went to the US and played a major role in the development of the American space program.

Brazza, Pierre Paul François Camille Savorgnan de 1852–1905. Italian-born French explorer. He established a protectorate over what became the French Congo, founded Brazzaville, and helped to build the French empire in Africa.

Breakspear, Nicholas See **Adrian IV**

Breasted, James Henry 1865–1935. American archaeologist noted for his contributions to the understanding of Egyptian history. His works include *A History of Egypt*.

Brébeuf, Saint Jean de 1593–1649. French Jesuit missionary in Canada. A missionary among the Huron Indians in New France (1625–29, 1634–49), he was captured and tortured to death in an Iroquois raid.

Brecht, Bertolt 1898–1956. German playwright and poet, and leading figure in 20th-cent. drama. His plays and experimental epic theater emphasized the role of social comment in modern drama.

Breckinridge, John Cabell 1821–75. American politician. He served as vice-president (1857–61) under J. Buchanan and was an unsuccessful presidential candidate (1860). He served as a Confeder-ate officer and secretary of war (1865) during the American Civil War.

Breda, Compromise of Document signed (1566) by Dutch and Flemish noblemen in the Spanish Netherlands to protest the Inquisition and loss of liberties under Spanish rule. The document is important in the events leading up to the Netherlands revolt against the Spanish. Largely written by Philip van Marnix (1538–98), it was signed by 2,000 Catholic and Protestant noblemen and was presented to Margaret of Parma, the Spanish regent, at Brussels. The nobles, later known as Gueux, were given some satisfaction but sentiment for revolt was only briefly abated.

Breda, Declaration of Document signed (Apr. 4, 1660) by Charles II of England promising concessions in return for his restoration to the English throne. After the failure of the Protectorate and earlier republican experiments, the Convention Parliament was convened and Charles was invited to return to the throne. He was required only to sign the declaration, which promised amnesty to his former enemies, religious toleration, and back pay owed the army.

Breda, Treaty of Treaty signed (July 31, 1667) by England, The Netherlands, and her allies, France and Denmark, ending the Second Dutch War (1664–67). The English Navigation Acts were changed in favor of Dutch traders and possession of conquered territories by the warring nations was confirmed. The English received the Dutch colonies of New York and New Jersey and regained possessions in the West Indies. The French regained Acadia and retained French Guiana.

Breed's Hill, Battle of See **Bunker Hill, Battle of**

Brehon laws ⟨Feinechus⟩ Ancient Irish legal system, supervised by hereditary judges known as brehons. The system existed in Ireland until the 17th cent., and is noted for its completeness and detail.

Breitenfeld, Battles of Two Swedish victories in the Thirty Years' War (1618–48) at the village of Breitenfeld (now in Germany). **1.** In 1631 Swedish King Gustavus Adolphus, leading a 47,000-man army of Swedes and Saxons, defeated Count J. Tilly and his 40,000-man army of the Holy Roman Empire. The battle was the first major Protestant victory and marked the rise of Sweden as a major power. **2.** In 1642 the Swedish force invading Saxony under Gen. L. Torstensson surprised and defeated armies of the Holy Roman Empire under Archduke Leopold William (1614–62). Soon after this battle the Swedes captured Leipzig.

Brescia Italian city of ancient origins, now a commercial, manufacturing, and cultural center.

Originally a Celtic town, it was conquered by the Romans (225 BC), sacked by Attila the Hun (AD 452), and by the 11th cent. became a powerful Lombard city. It became part of Italy in 1860.

Brescia, Arnold of *See* **Arnold of Brescia**

Brest-Litovsk, Treaty of Short-lived peace treaty signed (Mar. 3, 1918) by Russia and the Central Powers. This treaty ended war between Russia and the German allies but was rendered void by the defeat of Germany and the general armistice ending WW I late in 1918. Russia, weakened by revolution, and now under N. Lenin's leadership, was forced to accept humiliating terms. By the treaty Russia gave up Poland, the Baltic States, and part of Belorussia, and recognized the independence of Finland, the Ukraine, and Georgia.

Brazil Republic located in eastern South America. Its capital is Brasilia. Brazil was colonized and settled by the Portuguese and was seat of the Portuguese monarchy from 1808 to 1821. Brazil became an independent empire in 1822. Development of the country was largely accomplished by slave labor imported from Africa. Although the monarchy established a plan for gradual emancipation, the abolition of slavery (1888) by Isabel, daughter of the emperor, alienated the planters and led to the establishment of the Republic of Brazil in 1889. Key dates in the history of Brazil include:

1500 P. Cabral claimed Brazil for Portugal.

1521–57 Portuguese king John III expanded Portuguese influence in Brazil.

1532 First permanent Portuguese colony established at São Vicente.

1555 French Huguenot settlement established in Rio de Janeiro Harbor.

1567 Portuguese forced Huguenots out and founded Rio de Janeiro.

1633 Dutch West India Company gained control of northeastern Brazil.

1654 Settlers from Rio de Janeiro forced the Dutch to leave Brazil.

1708–09 War of the Emboabas, civil war between established and new settlers.

1763 Rio de Janeiro became capital of Brazil.

1789 Tiradentes Conspiracy, to overthrow Portuguese rule, uncovered.

1807–08 In Europe, Napoleon invaded Portugal in the Peninsular War; Portuguese king John VI fled to Brazil (1807); established Rio de Janeiro as his capital (1808).

1822 John VI returned to Portugal (1821), his son remaining to govern in Brazil; son declared Brazilian independence (Sept. 7) and became Brazilian emperor Pedro I.

1827 Brazilian troops defeated (Feb. 20) at Battle of Ituzaingo in fight to keep control of Uruguayan territories.

1831–39 Pedro I abdicated; his son Pedro II succeeded (1831); reign marked by expansion of economy, construction of roads and railroads, and influx of new settlers from Europe.

1852 Brazil fought war with Argentina.

1865–70 War of the Triple Alliance against Paraguay.

1889 Isabel, daughter of Pedro II, abolished slavery in Brazil during the absence of her father (1888); action led to overthrow of the monarchy, and establishment of a republic (1889).

1889–91 M. Fonseca in office as first president.

1917 Brazil entered WW I against Germany (Oct.)

1930 Julio Prestes elected to presidency (Mar. 11).

1930 Revolution in Brazil (Oct.) broke out before Prestes' inauguration; Getulio Vargas made acting president; Vargas moved to block Prestes and his supporters, the Paulistas, from gaining power.

1932 Paulistas staged unsuccessful revolt against Vargas' rule.

1934 Brazilian National Constituent Assembly passed new constitution and made Vargas president.

1937 New constitution issued by Vargas, who took personal control of the government; federal power greatly increased.

1942 Brazil entered WW II on the side of the Allies.

1945 Vargas overthrown (Oct.).

1946 New constitution passed (Sept.).

1950–54 Vargas elected president; presidency marked by economic and political turmoil; forced to resign.

1955–60 Juscelino Kubitschek in office as elected president (1955); began the construction of Brasilia.

1961–64 João Goulart in office as president; parliamentary government instituted (1961–63) during his presidency but presidential government restored in 1963; military forced Goulart's resignation (1964).

1964–67 Gen. Humberto Castelo Branco served as president; exercised special powers and dissolved all political parties; new constitution passed (1967).

1967–74 Period of political unrest; government dominated by succession of military leaders; outbreaks of terrorism by leftists increased.

1974–79 Gen. Ernesto Geisel in office as president.

1977 Government canceled US military aid, charging interference in its domestic affairs.

1977 President Geisel suspended Congress to stifle growing opposition.

1978 Constitutional reforms gave limited freedoms to people, though military government left many restrictions in force.

1979– Gen. João Baptista da Figueiredo in office as president; economic problems (especially high inflation) and pressure for return to democracy continued into 1982.

Brétigny, Treaty of ⟨Calais, ~⟩ Treaty (May 8, 1360) between France and England temporarily ending the Hundred Years' War (1337–1453). The treaty was a result of the French defeat at the Battle of Poitiers (1356), in which French King John II had been taken prisoner. By the treaty John was released on payment of 3 million gold crowns. France also ceded territories to England, including Aquitane, Gascony, and Calais. In return English King Edward III dropped claims to the French throne. The peace was short-lived and within 13 years France reconquered nearly all territories lost in the treaty.

Breton, André 1896–1966. French poet, essayist and critic, a founder of the movement known as surrealism.

Breton Succession, War of the Dynastic struggle in Brittany (1341–65) during the Hundred Years' War. It was ended by the Treaty of Guérande (Apr. 12, 1365), which reestablished rule of the Montfort line in Brittany.

Bretton Woods Conference Name applied to the United Nations Monetary and Financial Conference, held (July 1–22, 1944) at Bretton Woods, New Hampshire. The conference was called to consider how best to cope with the expected financial problems of the post-WW II world. Its recommendations led to the creation (1945) of the International Bank for Reconstruction and Development, designed for long-term financial aid; and the International Monetary Fund, designed to help stabilize exchange rates and promote international monetary cooperation.

Breuer, Josef 1842–1925. Austrian physician. He is considered a forerunner of S. Freud. His use of hypnosis and other techniques for the treatment of mental disorders was later developed by Freud and others into psychoanalysis.

Breuer, Marcel Lajos 1902–. Hungarian-born American architect and furniture designer. Associated with the Bauhaus, he later worked in partnership with W. Gropius.

Breughel, Jan See **Bruegel, Jan**

Breughel, Pieter See **Bruegel, Pieter**

Breviary of Alaric Compilation of laws, issued (AD 6th cent.) by Visigothic King Alaric II, and binding upon his Roman subjects. Visigoths were ruled by a separate code.

Brewster, William 1567–1644. English Puritan and an influential leader of the Pilgrims at Plymouth Colony. He helped organize the first party of Pilgrims to sail for America and accompanied them aboard the *Mayflower* (1620).

Brezhnev, Leonid Ilich 1906–82. Russian Communist leader. He and A. Kosygin became joint leaders of the USSR after the ouster of N. Khrushchev (1964). Brezhnev joined the Communist Party in 1931 and later became a protégé of Khrushchev. He was a member of the party Central Committee, first in 1952–53 and again from 1956. He then became chairman of the Supreme Soviet (1960–64), second secretary of the Central Committee (1964), and finally first secretary (Oct., 1964) after Khrushchev's fall from power. During his term he set forth the Brezhnev Doctrine (1968) in conjunction with the Russian invasion of Czechoslavakia and was instrumental in arranging closer ties with the West, a policy known as détente.

Brezhnev Doctrine Russian foreign policy statement. Issued (Sept., 1968) by L. Brezhnev, it defended the Russian invasion (Aug., 1968) of Czechoslovakia by stating that Warsaw Pact members had the right to intervene in the affairs of member nations whenever common Socialist interests were threatened.

Brian Boroimhe See **Brian Boru**

Brian Boru ⟨Brian Boroimhe⟩ 926–1014. Irish King (1002–14). By force of arms he became high king of Ireland, but was killed after his army defeated a coalition of Irish and Danish forces at the Battle of Clontarf (1014).

Briand, Aristide 1826–1932. French Socialist statesman. Eleven times French premier, and foreign minister from 1925 to 1932, he supported the League of Nations and was a key formulator of the Locarno Pact (1925) and the Kellogg-Briand Pact (1928). He was awarded the Nobel Peace Prize (1926).

Briareus ⟨Aegaeon⟩ Mythical Greek monster with one hundred arms and fifty heads. He was the son of Uranus and Ge.

Brice's Cross Roads, Battle of American Civil War battle (June 10, 1864) at Brice's Cross Roads, Mississippi. Some 7,800 Union troops under Gen. Samuel Sturgis were defeated by 3,500 Confederate cavalry under Gen. N. Forrest. Union casualties were 617 dead and wounded, 1,623 captured, and Confederates losses were 491.

Bridge of Sighs Stone bridge in Venice, Italy, connecting the Doge's palace, where criminals were tried, with the prison. Built c1600, it received its name from the lamentations of convicted criminals.

Bridger, James ⟨Jim⟩ 1804–81. American fur trader. One of the Mountain Men, from 1822 he ranged over the Northwest as a trapper, fur trader, and guide and was said to be the first white man to reach the Great Salt Lake, Utah (1824).

Bridget, Saint ⟨Brigid, Saint⟩ 453?–523? One of the three patron saints of Ireland. She founded Ireland's first nunnery at Kildare.

Bridget of Sweden, Saint ⟨Birgitta, Saint⟩ 1303?–1373. Swedish visionary and the patron saint of Sweden. Her account of her visions had a wide influence during the Middle Ages.

Bridgewater, Battle of *See* **Lundy's Lane, Battle of**

Brienne, John of *See* **John of Brienne**

Brigid, Saint *See* **Bridget, Saint**

Brill, Paul 1554–1626. Flemish painter. His landscape paintings influenced the development of Italian art in the 16th and 17th cents.

Brindisi Italian seaport. Mention of the port can be found in Greek legends. After 226 BC it became an important Roman naval station, located at one end of the Appian Way. It later became the port of embarkation for crusaders and was an Italian naval base in WW I.

Brisbane Australian seaport (pop. 1,101,700) and capital of Queensland. Founded (1824) as a penal colony, it first became a town (1834) and then officially ceased to be a penal colony (1842). It became capital of Queensland in 1859.

Brissot de Warville, Jacques Pierre 1754–93. French revolutionary and writer. A leader of the Girondists in the French Revolution, he urged war against Austria (1792). He was executed after a power struggle between the Girondists and the Jacobins.

Bristol Major English seaport (pop. 416,300). Bristol was chartered in 1155 and the harbor was built nearly a century later. The port thrived in the 17th and 18th cents. as a center for slave and colonial trade. The city was badly damaged in WW II.

Britain In modern usage, another name for Great Britain. Britain is the Anglicized form of Britannia, the Roman name for its territories on the British Isles. The term is also specifically applied as a name for the region prior to the Anglo-Saxon invasions of the 5th cent. AD.

Britain, Battle of German bombing raids over Britain (1940–41) during WW II. The raids originally were intended to destroy the Royal Air Force preparatory to the projected invasion of Britain, called Operation Sea Lion. Intensive German air raids began in summer, 1940, and by September the bombing of London and other cities had begun. German aircraft, numbering 1,000 at times, bombed London for 57 consecutive nights. German losses, however, were heavy and by October it became apparent that the Luftwaffe could not gain air supremacy over Britain. By April, 1941, the Germans had given up their invasion of Britain and the air raids had tapered off. The battle was the first major German setback and saw the first use of radar in combat.

British Cameroon *See* **Cameroon**

British Columbia Canadian province on the Pacific coast (pop. 2,687,000). Explored and claimed for Great Britain by J. Cook (1778). G. Vancouver mapped the area (1792–94). Explorers such as A. Mackenzie crossed to the Pacific and posts were established in New Caledonia, as the area was known, by fur traders. It became part of the Hudson's Bay Company (1821). Part of the region, known as the Oregon Country, was ceded (1846) to the US. With the discovery of gold in the Fraser River basin, population increased and it became (1858) a British crown colony. It became a Canadian province in 1871.

British Commonwealth of Nations Association of Great Britain, its dependencies, and many of its now independent former dependencies. It was established by the Statute of Westminster (Dec. 11, 1931). Its members were originally part of the British Empire but now maintain autonomous governments. The member states enjoy special trade agreements.

British East Africa Collective name of territories once under British control, including Kenya, Uganda, Zanzibar, and Tanganyika. All but Tanganyika became British protectorates between 1890 and 1895. Britain acquired Tanganyika from Germany (1919). The four countries won their independence in the 1960s.

British East India Company British trading company that controlled (18th–19th cents.) commercial and political affairs in India. Chartered (1600) by Queen Elizabeth I to gain a share of the Asian spice trade, the company focused on India after the Amboina Massacre (*q.v.*) in Indonesia (1623). In India, the company defeated the Portuguese (1612) and was granted (1668) political powers by Charles II. It became the United Company (1708) by a merger with a rival British trading company. The French were finally expelled from India (1751–60) by R. Clive and the company took control (1765) of Bengal, making it the dominant power in India. British government intervention in India was effected by the Regulating Act (1773) and the East India Act (1784). The government took over all administrative functions after the

Indian Mutiny (1857–58). The United Company was legally dissolved in 1873.

British Empire *See* **Great Britain**

British Expeditionary Force Name given to British forces sent from England to fight in foreign regions other than those held by the British Empire, and specifically to the British forces in Europe during WW I and WW II.

British Guiana *See* **Guyana**

British Honduras *See* **Belize**

British Isles General term for the islands of Great Britain and Ireland, and several thousand small islands, forming an archipelago off western Europe.

British New Guinea *See* **Papua New Guinea**

British North America Act Legislation (Mar. 29, 1867) by which the British Parliament united Upper and Lower Canada (Ontario and Quebec), Nova Scotia, and New Brunswick to form the Dominion of Canada. The act also provided a constitutional framework for governing the dominion until Apr., 1982, when constitutional power was formally transferred to Canada.

British Somaliland ⟨Somaliland Protectorate⟩ Former British protectorate in eastern Africa. Under British control from the 1880s, it was joined (1960) with Italian Somaliland to form the republic of Somalia.

Britons Name given to the native Celtic-speaking people who inhabited England at the time of the Roman invasion (1st cent. BC).

Brittany Historic region of northwestern France. Settled (AD c500) by Britons driven from Britain by the Anglo-Saxons, Brittany fought for its independence for centuries, from the Franks, the counts of Anjou, from England, and from France. It was finally united with France through the marriage (1491) of Anne of Brittany to King Charles VIII, and formally incorporated into France in 1532.

Brittany, Anne of *See* **Anne of Brittany**

Britten, Benjamin 1913–76. English composer, considered the most important British composer since H. Purcell. His works include the operas *Peter Grimes* and *Billy Budd*.

Brock, Sir Isaac 1769–1812. British general. As British military commander in Canada (1806–12), he became famous for capturing American forces at Detroit in the War of 1812. He was killed in a later battle.

Brod, Max *See* **Kafka, Franz**

Broglie, Jacques Victor Albert, duc de Broglie 1821–1901. French historian and statesman. He was twice premier (1873–74, 1877) during the French Third Republic.

Broglie, Victor François, duc de Broglie 1718–1804. French soldier, and marshal of France. He distinguished himself in the War of the Austrian Succession (1740–48) and the Seven Years' War (1756–63), and led the counterrevolutionary army against the French Revolution.

Bronstein, Lev Davidovich *See* **Trotsky, Leon**

Brontë, Anne 1820–49. English novelist. Her novels were *Agnes Grey* and *The Tenant of Wildfell Hall.*

Brontë, Charlotte 1816–55. English novelist, whose best-known novel, *Jane Eyre*, is considered a classic.

Brontë, Emily Jane 1818–48. English novelist, whose best-known novel, *Wuthering Heights* (1847), is considered a classic.

Bronze Age Stage in the development of civilization following the Stone Age when metal replaced stone for tools and weapons. Dating varies according to region and culture. The early part of the Bronze Age is sometimes referred to as the Copper Age and dates from c3500 BC, when copper came into general use in the Near East. Early cultures, such as the Sumerian, Mesopotamian, Minoan, and Mycenaean, developed around the mining, trading, smelting, and casting of metals in following centuries. Bronze did not come into general use until after 2000 BC. The Bronze Age was followed by the Iron Age (*q.v.*)

Brooke, Alan Francis, Viscount Alanbrooke 1883–1963. British general. He served with distinction in WW I, and became an expert on artillery and antiaircraft weaponry. During WW II he supervised British defenses during the evacuation at Dunkirk, served as chief of the Imperial Staff.

Brooke, Sir Charles Anthony Johnson 1829–1917. Englishman, the 2d white rajah of Sarawak, Borneo (1868), and successor to his uncle, J. Brooke. He completed the pacification of native tribes and developed the territory into a prosperous state.

Brooke, Sir James 1803–68. Englishman and 1st white rajah (1841–68) of Sarawak, a province in Borneo. He was named rajah after helping the Sultan of Borneo to put down a native revolt. He created a government for Sarawak, outlawed headhunting and suppressed piracy in the region.

Brooke, Rupert 1887–1915. English poet. The author of two volumes of poetry, he served in the Royal Navy and died during WW I.

Brook Farm Short-lived experimental community, founded (1841) at West Roxbury, Massachusetts, by G. Ripley, and including among its members and guests such notable literary figures as R. Emerson, M. Fuller, and N. Hawthorne.

Brooks, Van Wyck 1886–1963. American critic, biographer, and literary historian. Brooks received a Pulitzer Prize (1937) for *The Flowering of New England,* a volume in his *Makers and Finders* series on American literary history.

Broschi, Carlo *See* **Farinelli, Carlo**

Brothers of the Sword, Order of the *See* **Livonian Knights**

Broun, Heywood Campbell 1888–1939. American newspaper columnist. He began his liberal column *It Seems to Me* in the 1920s at the New York *World* and continued writing it for other newspapers until his death. He was a founder and first president of the American Newspaper Guild (1933–39).

Browder, Earl Russell 1891–1973. American Communist Party leader. A party member from 1919, he was secretary general (1930–44) and candidate for US president (1936, 1940). He was expelled from the party (1946) for supporting free enterprise in the US.

Brown, Charles Brockden 1771–1810. American novelist. The author of *Wieland* and other novels, he is sometimes called the first professional American novelist.

Brown, George 1818–80. Canadian statesman and journalist. The founder (1844) of the Toronto *Globe,* he was elected to the Canadian legislature (1851) and led the Clear Grits party. He supported Canadian federation, secularization of the Clergy Reserves, and purchase of the Northwest Territories.

Brown, John 1880–1859. American abolitionist. Believing himself divinely appointed to lead southern slaves to freedom, he led the unsuccessful raid on the US arsenal at Harpers Ferry (Oct. 16, 1859). His composure during his subsequent imprisonment and trial helped establish him as a leading martyr for the antislavery cause.

Brown, Robert 1773–1858. Scottish botanist. He described Brownian movement, the continuous motion of particles in solution, and discovered the plant cell nucleus.

Browne, Robert *See* **Congregationalism; Brownists**

Browning, Elizabeth Barrett 1806–61. English poet, and wife of R. Browning. Her *Sonnets from the Portuguese* is considered her best work.

Browning, Robert 1812–89. English poet, a leading figure in 19th-cent. English poetry. His major work is the four-volume epic *The Ring and the Book.*

Brownists Group advocating separation from the established church in England during the 16th–17th cents. The movement is considered an early form of Congregationalism. Brownists were followers of Robert Browne (c1550–1633), who published tracts (1582) outlining the principles of the movement. The group believed in local, self-governing churches and regulation of their daily lives by covenant. Browne, reconciled to the English church (1591), was denounced by his followers.

Brownsville Affair American racial incident (1906) at Brownsville, Texas. A night shooting raid on the town, resulting in the death of a citizen, was blamed on black soldiers from nearby Ft. Brown. The guilty parties could not be determined, and may not have been the soldiers. Nonetheless, President T. Roosevelt issued a directive giving dishonorable discharges to 167 soldiers. In 1972 the order was reversed by the army and the discharges changed to honorable discharges.

Brown vs. Board of Education of Topeka, Kansas US Supreme Court decision (May 17, 1954) unanimously overturning an 1896 ruling allowing "separate but equal" facilities for blacks and whites. American public schools thus were forced to integrate racially.

Bruce ⟨Brus⟩ Famous Scottish royal family. The family traces its origins to Robert de Bruce (or Brus) (*fl.* 11th cent.), who helped William I conquer England (1066). The most famous of the family is Robert I (1274–1329), known as Robert the Bruce. The line ended with the death of David II (1371), when the crown passed to the first Stuart king, Robert II.

Bruce of Melbourne, Stanley Melbourne Bruce, Viscount 1883–1967. Australian statesman. He served as prime minister (1923–29) and as high commissioner for Australia in London (1933–45).

Bruckner, Anton 1824–96. Austrian composer, known best for his masses and symphonies. He is considered one of the greatest Austrian composers of the 19th cent.

Bruegel, Jan ⟨Brueghel, ~⟩ ⟨Breughel, ~⟩ 1568–1625. Flemish painter, called Velvet Bruegel, and known best for his still life and landscape paintings.

Bruegel, Pieter ⟨~ the Elder⟩ ⟨Brueghel, ~⟩ ⟨Breughel, ~⟩ c1525–69. Flemish painter of landscapes and peasant scenes, considered the greatest of 16th-cent. Flemish painters. He was the head of a long line of painters. His works include *Peasant Wedding* and *Fall of Icarus.*

Bruegel, Pieter the Elder *See* **Bruegel, Pieter**

Brueghel, Jan *See* **Bruegel, Jan**

Brueghel, Pieter *See* **Bruegel, Pieter**

Bruges ⟨Brugge⟩ Flemish city (pop. 118,000) in northwest Belgium, capital of West Flanders province. Founded in the 9th cent., it became a major port of the Hanseatic League (13th cent.) and was a major center for the Flemish wool industry. The silting up of its harbor and the falling off of the cloth industry led to its decline (15th cent.) until extensive harbor repairs were initiated (1895).

Brugge *See* **Bruges**

Brumaire Name of the second month in the French Revolutionary Calendar. On 18 Brumaire (1799) the Directory, composed of revolutionaries, was overthrown and replaced by the Consulate, under Napoleon's control.

Brummell, Beau *See* **Brummell, George Bryan**

Brummell, George Bryan ⟨Brummell, Beau⟩ 1778–1840. English dandy. Called Beau Brummell, he was a friend of the Prince of Wales (later George IV) and arbiter of English fashion for a time.

Brunanburh, Battle of *See* **Athelstan**

Brundisium, Treaty of Roman agreement (40 BC), in which Mark Antony agreed to rule of the eastern provinces of the Roman Empire, while Octavian ruled the western provinces except for Africa, which remained under control of Lepidus.

Brunechaut *See* **Brunhilda**

Brunelleschi, Filippo 1377–1446. Florentine architect, one of the greatest of Italian Renaissance architects. His works include the dome for the cathedral at Florence.

Brunei Sultanate British protectorate (pop. 213,000) in northwest Borneo. A powerful sultanate controlling all of Borneo in the 16th cent., it was first visited by Magellan's ships (1521). Military expeditions by colonial powers quickly reduced Brunei's power and by the 19th cent. it controlled more than modern Brunei and Sarawak. Sarawak became a separate sultanate under the British soldier J. Brooke, who quashed a rebellion in Brunei (1841). Brunei became a British protectorate in 1888. A constitution, granted in 1959, returned control of internal affairs to the sultan. Agreements set 1983 as the date for full independence.

Brunhild ⟨Brünnehilde⟩ ⟨Brynhild⟩ Warrior-princess of German mythology and literature. She appears as the queen of Iceland in the epic poem *Nibelungenlied*, and as a Valkyrie in R. Wagner's *The Ring of the Nibelungs*.

Brunhilda ⟨Brunechaut⟩ 534?–613. Frankish queen, the wife of Sigebert I of Austrasia (*m.* 561). Her regency of Austrasia (575–613) was marked by a bloody rivalry with Fredegunde *(q.v.)*, wife of Chilperic I of Neustria. She seized Neustria, but was defeated and killed by Clotaire II, son of Chilperic I.

Brüning, Heinrich 1885–1970. German statesman. His unpopular policies as chancellor (1930–

32) failed to ease Germany's political and economic problems, and he was forced to resign shortly before A. Hitler's rise to power.

Brünnehilde *See* **Brunhild**

Bruno, Saint *c*1030–1101. German monk and founder of the Carthusian order.

Bruno, Giordano 1548–1600. Italian philosopher. His opposition to religious and scientific dogma led to his being burned as a heretic. His ideas influenced later philosophers, notably G. Leibniz and B. Spinoza.

Bruno of Egisheim *See* **Leo IX, Saint**

Brunswick, Caroline of *See* **Caroline of Brunswick**

Brus *See* **Bruce**

Brusa *See* **Bursa**

Brussels Capital (pop. 1,000,000) and largest city of Belgium. A commercial, administrative, and cultural center, it is the seat of the European Economic Community and NATO. Dating to *c*7th cent., it became a center of the cloth industry (13th cent.), and the capital of the Spanish Netherlands (15th cent.) and later of the Austrian Netherlands (18th cent.). It became the capital of independent Belgium in 1830 and was occupied by the Germans in WW I and WW II.

Brut ⟨Brute⟩ ⟨Brutus⟩ Legendary founder of New Troy (now London, England) and first king of the Britons. A Trojan and a descendant of Aeneas, he appears in the works of Geoffrey of Monmouth, Layamon, and Wace (*fl.* 12th cent.).

Brute *See* **Brut**

Bruttium ⟨Ager Bruttius⟩ ⟨Calabria⟩ Ancient region located at the southern tip of Italy. It was colonized by the Greeks (8th cent. BC) and conquered by the Romans (3d cent. BC). Renamed Calabria (its modern name) by the Byzantines, who controlled it after the Romans, it became part of the Kingdom of Naples (13th cent.) and part of Italy in 1860.

Brutus *See* **Brut**

Brutus, Decimus Junius *d.* 43 BC. Roman general. The governor of Gaul, he was, with M. Brutus and others, an assassin of J. Caesar (44 BC). He was killed by M. Antony.

Brutus, Lucius Junius *fl.* 509 BC. Roman historical figure, said to have led the Romans in driving the Tarquins from Rome and to have founded the Roman republic.

Brutus, Marcus Junius 85–42 BC. Roman soldier and leader. He sided with Pompey in the civil war with J. Caesar, and later joined with Cassius in Caesar's assassination. Defeated by M. Antony and Octavian at Philippi, he committed suicide.

Bryan, William Jennings 1860–1925. American political leader. A gifted orator, he became a leader in the Populist and Free Silver movements and was three times defeated for the presidency of the United States (1896, 1900, 1908). He gave his famous "Cross of Gold" speech at the Democratic convention in 1896. In later years he supported Fundamentalism and was involved in prosecuting the Scopes trial. Bryan served in Congress (1891–95), and as secretary of state (1913–15) under W. Wilson.

Bryan-Chamorro treaty US-Nicaraguan treaty (Aug. 14, 1914), by which the US purchased exclusive rights to build a canal across Nicaragua. The canal was never built.

Bryant, William Cullen 1794–1878. American poet and editor. His early poems, such as *Thanatopsis*, made him a leading American poet. Editor and part owner of the New York *Evening Post* (1829–78), he helped to found the Republican party.

Bryce, James Bryce, Viscount 1838–1922. British historian and statesman. A leader of the Liberal party, he was a popular and successful ambassador to the United States (1907–13). His works include *The American Commonwealth*.

Brynhild *See* **Brunhild**

Buber, Martin 1878–1965. Vienna-born Jewish philosopher. His major works deal with the relationship of man and God, and include *I and Thou*.

Bubonic plague *See* **Black Plague**

buccaneers Bands of adventurers of English, French, and Dutch descent that preyed upon the Spanish ships and settlements in the Caribbean and along the South American coast from 1630 to 1690. They became widely known for their exploits under such leaders as H. Morgan. The buccaneers disappeared toward the end of the 17th cent. when many enlisted in the War of the Grand Alliance (1689–97) as privateers.

Bucephalus The favorite horse of Alexander the Great. Alexander built the ancient city of Bucephala, near the present Jhelum, Pakistan, to commemorate the death of the horse (326 BC).

Buchanan, Franklin 1800–74. American naval officer. An organizer and first superintendent (1845–47) of the US Naval Academy, he became the senior naval officer of the Confederacy (1862–64) during the American Civil War. He was captured at the Battle of Mobile Bay (1864).

Buchanan, James 1791–1868. 15th US president (1857–61), successor to F. Pierce. The American Civil War (1861–65) broke out in the last months of his administration. Prior to his election, he was a congressman (1821–31), a senator (1834–45), secretary of state (1845–49) and (variously) a US diplomat. Though personally against slavery, he advocated maintaining the balance between slave and free states. To that end he supported such measures as the Compromise of 1850 and helped formulate the controversial Ostend Manifesto (1854). His part on the latter won him the backing of the South and the presidential election in 1856 as a Democrat. As president he enraged Northern abolitionists by supporting enforcement of the Fugitive Slave Laws and the pro-slavery Lecompton Constitution in the Bleeding Kansas controversy. The Harpers Ferry Raid (1859) increased North-South tensions and, with the Democratic party split, A. Lincoln won the election (1860). In the last months of his administration, Buchanan opposed South Carolina's secession (Dec., 1860) and the seizure of federal forts, but took no decisive action.

Bucharest Capital city (pop. 1,807,000) of Romania and a major industrial and commercial center. The modern history of the city dates from the 15th cent., when it became the residence of the Walachian rulers. It became capital of Romania (1862) and was later occupied by the Germans in WW I and WW II. It fell to the USSR in 1944.

Bucharest, treaties of 1. Treaty (1812) between Russia and Turkey ending the Russo-Turkish War (1806–12). Russia, concerned about the possibility of invasion by Napoleon, sought peace with Turkey. By the treaty's terms, Russia kept Bessarabia and returned Walachia and part of Moldavia. **2.** Treaty (1886) ending war between Serbia and Bulgaria over Bulgaria's annexation of E. Rumelia. Serbia, defeated, conceded the takeover. **3.** Treaty (Aug., 1913) ending Second Balkan War. Defeated Bulgaria received only a small part of territories taken from the Turks in the First Balkan War (1912–13). By the treaty, her former allies, Serbia, Greece, and Romania, divided most of the territories among themselves. **4.** Short-lived treaty (1918) between the Central Powers and defeated Romania toward the end of WW I. The concessions, including losses of territory and oil leases to the Central Powers, were voided by the Allied victory (1918).

Buchenwald Village in East Germany, site of a notorious Nazi death camp. Established after 1933, the camp later became a center for the extermination of Jews and political prisoners. It was captured by American forces in 1945.

Buchman, Frank *See* **Moral Re-armament**

Buchmanism *See* **Moral Re-armament**

Buck, Pearl Sydenstricker 1892–1973. American novelist, known best for *The Good Earth* and other novels of life in China. She was awarded a Pulitzer Prize in 1932, and received the Nobel Prize for Literature in 1938.

bucket shop Name for a type of brokerage house, now illegal, which operated in Britain and the US. The bucket-house operator would delay placing a customer's order, in hopes of making a profit through either the rise or fall of market prices.

Buckingham, George Villiers, 1st duke of 1592–1628. English statesman. He held great power during the reigns of James I and Charles I, and used it to enrich his relatives. His abuses and disastrous military adventures to Spain and France aroused the wrath of Parliament, which was dissolved by Charles. He was killed by a discontented naval officer.

Buckingham, George Villiers, 2d duke of 1628–87. English courtier and son of the 1st duke of Buckingham. He supported Charles II in the English Civil War (1642–49). After the Restoration (1660–88) he regained the estates he had lost, and became a powerful figure at court and a member of the Cabal ministry.

Buckingham Palace The British royal family residence in London since 1837. The building originally belonged to the duke of Buckingham and was bought (1761) by George III for his wife. Since the time of Queen Victoria the 600-room building has been designated a royal residence.

Buckle, Henry Thomas 1821–62. English historian. He completed only two volumes of his *History of Civilization in England*, which influenced the scientific method of writing history.

Buczacz, Peace of Short-lived Polish-Turkish treaty, negotiated (Oct. 18, 1672) to end fighting between the Poles and Ottomans in the Ukraine. When the Polish Diet refused ratification, fighting resumed.

Budaeus *See* **Bude, Guillaume**

Budapest Hungarian capital city (pop. 2,085,600), a commercial and industrial center located on the banks of the Danube River. It is noted as one of the most picturesque cities of Europe. Its origins can be traced to a 1st-cent.-AD Roman town, Aquincum, but the city's modern history begins in the 17th cent. when two ruined cities on opposite banks of the Danube, Buda and Pest, were retaken from the Turks. By 1848 Pest had become the capital of Hungary and in 1873 the two cities were united as Budapest. The city flourished as one of the two capitals of Austro-Hungary, and became the capital of independent Hungary (1919). Budapest was almost completely destroyed in WW II and was the center of the Hungarian Revolt of 1956.

Buddha *c*563–*c*483 BC. Title (Sanskrit for "enlightened one") of Siddhartha Gautama, the founder of Buddhism *(q.v.)*, one of the world's great religions. The son of Suddhodana (*fl. c*6th cent. BC), a king of the Sakya tribe in what is now Nepal, and his wife Mahamaya, Siddhartha at the age of 29 gave up a life of ease to seek the path to enlightenment. After attaining it he spent the rest of his life teaching others.

Buddhism Religion that originated with the teachings of Buddha in India during the 6th cent. BC. Buddhism arose in opposition to Hinduism, though it shares concepts of bondage in cycles of birth, suffering, and death and escape from this cycle through attainment of nirvana. Many schools of Buddhist thought sprang from Buddha's teachings, though all accept Buddha's fundamental doctrine of the Four Noble Truths (existence is suffering; suffering has a cause within the self; one may be freed of suffering; following the precepts of the Eightfold Path ends suffering and leads to nirvana). The two main schools of Buddhist thought in modern times arose from a split that developed in the 4th cent. BC. The two schools are Mahayana and Theraveda. Though Buddhism has virtually disappeared in India, it is prevalent in Japan, Korea, China, Tibet, and in Southeast Asia. *See also* Tibetan Buddhism, Pure Land Buddhism, Zen Buddhism. Key events in the spread of Buddhism include:

*c*528 BC Buddhism founded; Siddhartha, after six years of wandering in search of spiritual truth, discovered enlightenment (*c*528 BC) while meditating at Buddha Gaya (now in northeast India); articulated his Four Noble Truths in first sermon soon after; as Buddha, spent the rest of his life spreading his teachings.

*c*483 BC Buddha died; his teachings at first spread orally by his followers.

*c*340 BC Various factions among the rising Buddhist movement split into two great sects; these eventually became the Mahayana (Greater Vehicle) and the Theraveda or Hinayana (Lesser Vehicle), the major divisions of modern Buddhism.

*c*273–*c*232 BC Indian Emperor Asoka promoted the spread of Buddhist teachings; had "Rock Edicts," containing Buddhist principles, engraved on stones and pillars throughout the Maurya empire; sent Buddhist missionaries to Ceylon and elsewhere.

2D–1ST CENTS. BC Various Buddhist schools put their own versions of Buddhist teachings in written form; Pali Canon, earliest surviving example of them, written (*c*29–17 BC) by the Theraveda school (in Ceylon).

1ST CENT. BC Mahayana sutras written; marked rise of Mahayana school.

1ST CENT. AD Buddhism introduced in China.

4TH CENT. AD Buddhism spread from China to Korea.

EARLY 5TH CENT. AD Buddhaghosa, Ceylonese Buddhist scholar, wrote his famous work on Buddhist doctrines, *Way to Purity.*

6TH CENT. Centers of Buddhism in India destroyed during invasions by White Huns; Buddhism in India began to decline.

6TH CENT. Buddhism spread from Korea to Japan; won only limited following among the nobility until the 12th cent.

6TH CENT. Buddhism introduced in Burma.

6TH CENT. Rise of Zen Buddhism and Pure Land Buddhism in China; eventually became dominant schools of Buddhism there.

7TH CENT. Practices of the Tantra spread among Buddhists; magic, ritual, and spells used to attain various ends, both religious and practical.

7TH CENT. Buddhism introduced in Tibet; rise of Tibetan Buddhism began.

9TH CENT. In China, great persecution of Buddhists ordered (845) by T'ang dynasty emperor; restoration of Confucianism (neo-Confucianism) under the T'ang emperors further increased opposition to Buddhism in China.

11TH–13TH CENTS. Final decline of Buddhism in India; Buddhism was nearly eliminated in the centuries following destructive invasions by Muslims of the Ghaznavid dynasty.

12TH CENT. Zen and Pure Land Buddhism became widespread in Japan.

Budé, Guillaume ⟨Budaeus⟩ 1467–1540. French scholar. A leading Renaissance scholar, he persuaded Francis I to found the Collège de France, and assembled a library that became the Bibliothèque Nationale.

Budge, Sir Ernest Alfred Wallis 1857–1934. English archaeologist who collected and translated many ancient texts and supervised excavations in Egypt, Mesopotamia, and the Sudan for the British Museum.

Buena Vista, Battle of US victory (Feb. 22–23, 1847) over Mexican forces in the Mexican War (1846–48). US forces numbering 5,000 men under Gen. Z. Taylor were met by a Mexican force of 15,000 under Gen. A. Santa Anna near the hacienda of Buena Vista in northeastern Mexico. In the two-day battle, US forces were hard pressed but eventually won with the aid of artillery barrages. US casualties numbered some 700 to about 1,500 Mexicans.

Buenos Aires Capital city (pop. 2,982,000) of Argentina and one of the largest cities and seaports in South America. First permanently settled by Spain (1580), it became capital of the viceroyalty of Rio del Plata in 1776. The city declared independence from Spain in 1810 and became capital of Argentina in 1862.

Buffalo Bill ⟨Cody, William Frederick⟩ 1846–1917. American scout, buffalo hunter, and Indian fighter. His adventures in the West were the subject of numerous dime novels by N. Buntline and others. In 1883 he formed his celebrated Wild West Show and toured the United States and abroad. Cody, Wyoming, stands on the site of his ranch.

Buganda Former East African kingdom, located north of Lake Victoria in what now is Uganda. The leading kingdom of East Africa in the 19th cent., it was the center of a flourishing ivory trade. The kingdom came under the control (1890s) of the Imperial British East Africa Company and was incorporated into Great Britain's Uganda Protectorate. The kingdom continued to exist until 1967, when it became part of the Republic of Uganda and its monarchy was abolished.

Bukhari, al- 810–870. Arab scholar. His collection of the sayings of the Muslim prophet Muhammad, *Sahih,* is regarded by orthodox Muslims as second only to the Koran in religious importance.

Bukharin, Nikolai Ivanovich 1888–1938. Russian Communist party leader. A Bolshevik, he was a member of the ruling Communist Politburo (1924–29). Ousted (1929) from party leadership for opposing Stalin's policy of agricultural reform, he later became a victim of Stalin's Purge Trials and was executed for treason.

Bulfinch, Charles 1763–1844. American architect. As the fourth and last architect of the Capitol building in Washington, D.C., he supervised its completion (1817–30). Among his other buildings are the Massachusetts State House and the Connecticut State House.

Bulganin, Nikolai Aleksandrovich 1895–1975. Soviet political leader. With the support of N. Khrushchev he became premier in 1955. He opposed Khrushchev (1957) and was expelled from the Central Committee and replaced by Khrushchev (1958).

Bulgaria ⟨People's Republic of Bulgaria⟩ Republic in southeastern Europe, situated on the eastern part of the Balkan Peninsula on the Black Sea. Its capital is Sofia. Once part of the Roman Empire, Bulgaria was dominated for centuries by the Ottoman Turks. Bulgaria was established as an autonomous principality after the Russo-Turkish War of 1877–78. It fell to the Soviets during WW II and thereafter remained under Soviet domination. Key dates in the history of Bulgaria include:

6TH CENT. AD Thrace and Moesia (now modern Bulgaria) settled by Slavic tribes.

7TH CENT. Bulgars invaded the region and merged with the Slavs.

680–1018 First Bulgarian Empire; established by Khan Asparuhk; Bulgarians thereafter repeatedly threatened the Byzantine Empire.

852–889 Boris I ruled; Christianity introduced.

893–927 Empire reached its zenith under Bulgarian Czar Simeon.

10TH CENT. Rise of the heretical Bogomil sect.

969–976 Byzantine Emperor John I drove the Russians out of Bulgaria soon after their forces invaded.

1018 Bulgarian Empire made part of Byzantine Empire by Basil II; remained under Byzantines to 1185.

1185–1396 Second Bulgarian Empire; established by Ivan Asen.

1218–41 Ivan II reigned in Bulgaria; conquered much of Balkan Peninsula.

1330 Bulgaria defeated by Serbs; made a tributary.

1389–96 Ottoman Turks invaded and conquered Bulgaria; centuries of Turkish domination followed.

1876 Bulgarians, led by Stefan Stambulov, revolted against Ottomans; Turks killed 15,000 in reprisals (Bulgarian Horrors); Europe aroused against Ottomans.

1877–78 Russo-Turkish War.

1878 Congress of Berlin following Russo-Turkish War; autonomous Bulgaria (under Ottoman suzerainty) created, though much smaller than that sought by Russia; Eastern Rumelia (southern part of modern Bulgaria) made autonomous province under Ottoman suzerainty; Macedonia remained under direct Ottoman control.

1879 Russian czar's nephew, Prince Alexander of Battenberg, made ruler of Bulgaria.

1885–86 Eastern Rumelia annexed by Bulgaria; led to Serbo-Bulgarian War (1885–86) in which Serbia was defeated.

1887–1918 Prince Ferdinand of Saxe-Coburg-Gotha ruled; succeeded following Alexander's abdication (1886).

1908 Ferdinand declared complete independence; made himself czar.

1912–13 First Balkan War; Bulgaria and allies defeated Ottoman Turks.

1913 Second Balkan War; Bulgaria sought larger share of conquered territories, but was defeated.

1914–18 WW I; Bulgaria sided with Central Powers (1915) in hopes of regaining territories lost in Second Balkan War; retook Macedonia and Dobruja (1916); forced to sign armistice with allies (1918).

1918–43 Boris III reigned; succeeded on his father's abdication.

1919 Treaty of Neuilly formally ended hostilities of WW I; Bulgaria lost substantial territories.

1920–23 Aleksandr Stamboliski, leader of peasant Agrarian party, in office as premier; overthrown in coup (1923).

1925 Greece invaded Bulgaria but the conflict was ended by the League of Nations.

1935 Boris assumed dictatorial powers.

1940–45 WW II; Hitler forced Romania to cede southern Dobruja to Bulgaria (1940); Bulgaria joined Axis powers and was occupied by Nazis (1941); Boris assassinated after refusing Hitler's demand to break relations with Soviets (1943); Boris succeeded by his son, Simeon II; Soviets invaded Bulgaria and won immediate armistice (1944).

1946 Monarchy abolished and people's republic established (Sept.).

1946 Communist leader Vasil Kolarov became first head of state.

1947 One-party system established; farms collectivized and industry nationalized on Soviet pattern.

1950 Purge of Communist Party instituted by Vulko Chervenko.

1951–52 160,000 citizens of Turkish origin deported.

1955 Entered Warsaw Pact.

1965 Unsuccessful army coup.

1968 Aided Russian invasion of Czechoslovakia.

1971 New constitution adopted; Stanko Todorov named chairman of the Council of Ministers.

1981 Grisha Filipov named chairman of the Council of Ministers, replacing Stanko Todorov.

Bulgarian Horrors Name applied to the brutal suppression of the 1876 Bulgarian uprising against Ottoman rule. The name was derived from the title of a pamphlet by W. Gladstone which attacked B. Disraeli's pro-Ottoman foreign policy.

Bulgaroktonos *See* **Basil II**

Bulge, Battle of the ⟨Ardennes, ~⟩ Unsuccessful German counterattack (1944–45) on Allied positions in Belgium during WW II. It was the last major German offensive on the Western Front. German armored divisions under Marshal G. von Rundstedt launched their surprise attack (Dec. 16) during a period of bad weather in the Ardennes, southern Belgium, in hopes of splitting the Allied forces and of taking the strategic port of Antwerp. They drove 60 miles into Allied territory, creating a "bulge" in the lines. Allied resistance, notably the heroic stand by an American division at Bastogne under command of Gen. Anthony C. McAuliffe (1898–1975), helped to stall the Germans. Improved flying weather allowed Allied air forces to support counterattacks, forcing the Germans to retreat (Jan.).

bull In the Roman Catholic religion, the term applies to a document or pronouncement by the pope, of greater importance than a papal brief or encyclical. Papal bulls deal with such matters as canonizations, pronouncements of church doctrine, and the like. *See also* Golden Bull.

bullbaiting *See* **bearbaiting**

Bullen, Anne *See* **Boleyn, Anne**

Bullinger, Heinrich *See* **Basel, Confession of; Helvetic Confession**

Bull Moose Name given members of the first Progressive party, also known as the Bull Moose party, which was formed in the US (1912–16) to support the presidential candidacy of T. Roosevelt.

Bull Run, Battle of 〈Manassas, Battle of〉 American Civil War battles fought in northern Virginia. **1.** Confederate victory (July 21, 1861) which halted a Union drive, led by Gen. I. McDowell, from Washington toward Richmond. Some 32,000 Confederates under Gen. P. Beauregard forced the 37,000-man Union army to retreat after hard fighting. Casualties were about 3,000 Union to 2,000 Confederate. **2.** Confederate victory (Aug. 29–30, 1862). Gen. R. Lee's 56,000-man Confederate force attacked a 70,000-man Union army, led by Gen. J. Pope, at Bull Run and forced Pope to retreat to Washington. Casualties were about 9,000 Confederate to 16,000 Union.

Bülow, Bernhard Heinrich Martin, Fürst von 1849–1929. German statesman. As chancellor of Germany (1900–09) he attempted to strengthen Germany's position as a world power, but instead his policies strengthened the Triple Entente of Britain, France, and Russia.

Bulwer, Sir Henry *See* **Clayton-Bulwer Treaty**

Buoncompagni, Ugo *See* **Gregory XIII**

Bunau-Varilla, Philippe Jean 1859–1940. French engineer. Chief engineer of the French Panama Canal project, he worked to sell the project to the US after the French failure (1889), helped instigate the revolution that led to Panamanian independence, and as Panamanian minister negotiated the Hay-Bunau-Varilla Treaty (1903), which gave the US control of the Canal Zone.

Bunche, Ralph Johnson 1904–71. American diplomat. A founder of the United Nations, he worked to negotiate an Arab-Israeli truce in 1949, for which he received the 1950 Nobel Peace Prize.

Bundestag German legislature, the popularly elected lower house of the parliament of the German Federal Republic. It is responsible for election of the chancellor.

Bunin, Ivan Alekseevich 1870–1953. Russian poet and novelist, author of *The Village.* He was awarded the Nobel Prize in Literature (1933).

Bunker Hill, Battle of 〈Breed's Hill, ~〉 Victory (June 17, 1775) for American colonials over the British early in the American Revolution (1775–83). The first major battle of the war, it proved the Colonial militia could stand up to the British regulars and thus aided the cause of the revolution. The Colonial militia had laid siege to Boston soon after the war began. To block the first British attempt to break the siege, Col. W. Prescott and some 1,000 militiamen were sent (June 16) to fortify Bunker Hill, north of Colonial Boston. The following afternoon, 3,000 British troops, sent by Gen. T. Gage, attacked the fortifications (actually located on nearby Breed's Hill). The colonials, ordered by Prescott to hold fire until they saw "the whites of the enemy's eyes," withstood two British charges. Out of ammunition, they were forced to retreat on the third. The British sustained heavy casualties (about 1,000 to 450 Americans) and failed to break the siege.

Bunsen, Robert Wilhelm 1811–99. German chemist. With G. Kirchhoff he pioneered spectrum analysis and discovered the elements cesium and rubidium. He introduced the Bunsen burner.

Bunyan, John 1628–88. English preacher and author, whose Christian allegory *The Pilgrim's Progress* is a classic of English literature.

Bunyan, Paul Legendary giant lumberjack and American folk hero. Bunyan and his giant blue ox, Babe, were the subjects of numerous tall tales, told among lumberjacks. His adventures were first published as stories in the early 1900s.

Burbage, James *d.* 1597. English actor. At Shoreditch (now part of London) he built (c1576) the first English theater. Known as The Theatre, it was later moved and rebuilt as the Globe Theatre.

Burckhardt, Jacob Christoph 1818–97. A Swiss historian. His best-known work, *The Civilization of the Renaissance in Italy,* was a model for later works employing a cultural treatment of history.

Burckhardt, Johann Ludwig *See* **Burckhardt, John Lewis**

Burckhardt, John Lewis 〈~, Johann Ludwig〉 1784–1817. Swiss explorer of Africa and the Middle East. He rediscovered the ancient city of Petra (1812) and traveled to Mecca (1814).

Burger, Warren Earl 1907–. American jurist. Burger was appointed Chief Justice of the Supreme Court by R. Nixon (1969). Burger was a conservative and his decisions reflected his concern for judicial restraint.

Burgesses, House of American Colonial assembly. Established in Virginia (July 30, 1619), it was the first representative governing body in America.

Burghley, William Cecil, 1st Baron ⟨Burleigh, ~⟩ 1520–98. English statesman. Appointed secretary of state (1558) and lord high treasurer (1572), he was chief adviser to Elizabeth I for 40 years.

Burgoyne, John 1722–92. British general and dramatist. He distinguished himself during the Seven Years' War (1756–63), but was defeated at Saratoga (1777) during the American Revolution. He wrote several popular plays.

Burgundians French political faction that engaged in civil war (1411–18) against the rival Armagnacs for control of France in the 15th cent. The conflict began (1407) when John the Fearless, duke of Burgundy, murdered his rival, Louis, duke of Orléans (brother of the insane French king Charles VI), in a struggle for control of the French throne. John's opponents, the Armagnacs, were so named after their leader Bernard VII, count of Armagnac. He was the father-in-law of Charles, the new duke of Orléans. The conflict led to English intervention (1415) under Henry V, who defeated the duke of Orléans at Agincourt (Oct. 25, 1415) and reconquered Normandy. The civil war thus became part of the Hundred Years' War. The Burgundians captured Paris (1418) and massacred many Armagnacs. John the Fearless was later assassinated (1419) while negotiating with the dauphin (later Charles VII) of France. John's son, Philip the Good, then signed the Treaty of Troyes (1420), allying the Burgundians with the English and declaring English king Henry V regent of France. The ascendancy of the Burgundians came when Philip signed the Treaty of Arras (1435), by which he recognized the new king Charles VII as rightful king of France and allied with him against the English. The power of the Armagnacs declined thereafter.

Burgundy Historic region of eastern France. Settled (AD 5th cent.) by the Germanic Burgundians, it came under the rule of the Merovingians (6th cent.), and was partitioned several times before being reunited (933) as the Second Kingdom of Burgundy. It entered its period of greatest power as a duchy under the rule of Philip the Bold (1342–

1404), who received it (1364) from his father John II of France. Philip's descendents greatly increased its territories. After the death of Charles the Bold (1477), most of its possessions passed to the Hapsburgs, but the duchy itself was incorporated into France, remaining a province until its division in the French Revolution.

Burgundy, Henry of *See* **Henry of Burgundy**

Burgundy, Mary of *See* **Mary of Burgundy**

Buridan, Jean d. c1358. French philosopher. As rector of the University of Paris, he taught nominalism. The allegorical Buridan's Ass, an animal starving between two identical stacks of hay, is identified (incorrectly) with his discussion of the will and moral dilemma.

Burke, Edmund 1729–97. British statesman and political philosopher. He is considered a major British political thinker for his views on Britain's government and its policies toward Ireland, India, and the colonies. He became a member of Parliament (1765) in the Whig Party, was sympathetic to the cause of American colonials, helped bring about Lord North's resignation, and supported abolition of the slave trade. He opposed the radicalism of the French Revolution in *Reflections on the French Revolution.*

Burke, Martha Jane *See* **Calamity Jane**

Burleigh, William Cecil, 1st Baron *See* **Burghley, William Cecil, 1st Baron**

Burlingame, Anson *See* **Burlingame Treaty**

Burlingame Treaty Treaty (1868) of friendship between the US and China. It was negotiated by Anson Burlingame (1820–70), a former American diplomat who had become an envoy of the Chinese emperor. By it China recognized Western principles of international law and the US recognized China's territorial sovereignty. The treaty also opened the way for large-scale immigration of Chinese laborers to the US.

Burma ⟨Socialist Republic of Burma⟩ Republic located on the Bay of Bengal in Southeast Asia. Its capital is Rangoon. Dominated for centuries by China and Britain, Burma finally achieved independence in 1948. Key dates in the history of Burma include:

3D CENT. AD Burmese emigrated from Tibet.

1044 Smaller Burmese states were consolidated; Buddhist monarchy established by King Anawratha.

1287 Mongol dynasty of China conquered Burma; Thai Shan princes, affiliated with Mongols, ruled.

1519 Portuguese traders arrived in region.

c1550–1600 Toungoo dynasty overthrew Shan princes; ruled unified empire in Burma.

1612 British East India Company established posts near Rangoon.

1753–60 Alaungpaya founded modern Burmese state; also founded Konbaung dynasty, last dynasty of Burma; expanded empire into India and Thailand.

1824–26 First Burma War initiated by Burmese invasion of eastern territories in British India.

1826 Peace of Yandabo declared; Burma ceded Tenasserim and Arakam, gave up claims on Assam and Manipur, and paid indemnity.

1852 Second Burma War; brought on by dissension between Burmese monarchy and British traders; south part (lower Burma) came under British control.

1885–86 Third Burma War; conquest of Mandalay by Britain; marked end of Konbaung dynasty and independent Burma.

1886 Burma annexed (Jan.) by colonial government of British India.

1937 Britain separated Burma from India; granted it new constitution; Burma became self-governing crown colony.

1941–45 WW II; Burma Road, vital Allied supply line to China, made Burma a major battleground; Japanese invaded Burma (1941) and cut Burma Road (1942); Anti-Fascist People's Freedom League, led by Aung San, began resistance against Japanese; Allied forces retook Burma (Apr., 1945).

1947 Anglo-Burmese agreement; provided for elections to decide future status of Burma; Aung San's Freedom League won elections and he became premier.

1947 Aung San and other officials assassinated; Thakin Nu formed new council.

1948 Independence from Britain (Jan. 4).

1950 Socialist Freedom League government confronted by uprisings by Communists and by Karen tribesmen fighting for independent state.

1950–53 Chinese Nationalists forced into Burma by Chinese Communist armies; UN finally ordered Nationalists to leave Burma.

1958 Political crisis within Freedom League party; Premier U Nu asked Gen. U Ne Win to take over government.

1960 Civilian government restored after U Nu's faction won elections.

1962 Gen. U Ne Win overthrew civilian government; established military dictatorship; nationalized industry; kept rebel groups in check though they remained active into the 1970s.

1974 People's Assembly formally empowered (Mar. 2) under new constitution creating socialist

republic; 12-year rule by military coalition ended; U Ne Win remained in power.

1981 U San Yu replaced the aging U Ne Win as president.

Burma War ⟨Burmese War⟩ ⟨Anglo-Burmese War⟩ **1.** First ~ War (1824–26) brought on by a Burmese invasion (1823) of eastern territories in British India. The British invaded Burma (1824), and took Rangoon easily. Despite stiffening resistance, British forces moved northward and eventually defeated the Burmese army (1825). By the Treaty of Yandabo (Feb. 24, 1826), the Burmese ceded western provinces to British India, including Arakan and Assam. **2.** Second ~. War (1852) brought on by friction between the Burmese monarchy and British traders in Burma. The British invaded (1852) Burma, captured all of the south, but did not advance to the north. The British annexed (Jan., 1853) the province of Pegu and a revolution in the north brought the accession of King Mindon Min, who did not challenge the British conquests. **3.** Third ~. War (1885–86) in which the British completed their conquest of Burma and ended the rule of the Konbaung dynasty. The invasion of the remaining independent northern territories was provoked by continuing friction between British traders and the Burmese monarch, Thibaw (1858–1916, reigned 1878–85). Thibaw surrendered late in 1885 and the British formally annexed Burma (Jan. 1, 1886), though guerrilla warfare against the British continued for several years.

Burnett, Frances Eliza Hodgson 1849–1924. English-born American writer, known best as author of *Little Lord Fauntleroy.*

Burnham, Daniel Hudson 1846–1912. American architect and city planner. He designed early steel-frame "skyscrapers" such as the Chicago Masonic Temple building (1892) and devised (1907–09) a farsighted plan for the development of the city of Chicago.

Burning of the Books Chinese religious controversy (213 BC), in which Ch'in emperor Shih Huang-ti (259–210 BC) attempted to censor all writings which did not support his views. Some books were burned and several scholars executed.

Burns, John 1858–1943. British labor leader. As president of the Local Government Board (1905–14), he became the first working-class man to serve in a British Cabinet.

Burns, Robert 1759–96. Scottish national poet and one of the world's most celebrated poets. He captured and enriched the spirit of Scottish folk tradition. Though raised on a farm, he was well educated and after failing as a farmer he turned (1786) to publishing his poetry. He enjoyed immediate success with *Poems, Chiefly in the Scottish Dialect*, and thereafter devoted himself to writing poems and songs of rural Scotland. He wrote such poems as "Tam o' Shanter" and "The Jolly Beggars" and the ever-popular song "Auld Lang Syne."

Burnside, Ambrose Everett 1824–81. Union general in the US Civil War. He fought in the first battle of Bull Run and Antietam. Succeeding G. McClellan (1862) as commander of the Army of the Potomac, he was relieved following his defeat at Fredericksburg.

Burr, Aaron 1756–1836. US vice-president (1801–05) who was later charged with treason (1807). Once a US senator from New York (1791–97), Burr served as the third US vice-president under T. Jefferson. While in office he killed (1804) his political rival, A. Hamilton, in a duel. His political career finished, he sought to create an independent country in what was then Mexican territory. An associate, Gen. J. Wilkinson, betrayed him and reported that Burr had also intended to encourage the secession of western US territories. Tried (1807) for treason and acquitted, he lived out the rest of his life in obscurity.

Burroughs, Edgar Rice 1875–1950. American author of adventure novels, known best as the creator of the Tarzan stories.

Bursa ⟨Brusa⟩ ⟨Prusa⟩ Turkish city and center of the Turkish silk industry. Founded in the 3d cent. BC, it was the capital of Bithynia and was called Prusa. It was the first capital of the Ottoman Empire (1326–1413).

Burundi Republic (pop. 4,510,000) in east central Africa on Lake Tanganyika. Claimed (1890) by Germany as part of German East Africa, it was taken by Belgium in WW I and incorporated into the League of Nations mandate of Ruanda-Urundi, which became (1946) a UN trust territory. Belgium continued to rule through the native monarchical government until Burundi's independence (1962). Conflict between the country's two major ethnic groups, the Tutsi and Hutu, cost many lives after establishment of a republic (1966), and in the 1970s the Tutsi emerged as the dominant group within Burundi.

Bury, John Bagnell 1861–1927. British historian and authority on the late Roman and Byzantine empires.

Büsching, Anton Friedrich 1724–93. German geographer. His emphasis on the use of statistical data helped to establish geography as a science.

Bushido Term meaning "way of the warrior" and a code of conduct in Japan identified with Samurai

warriors. The code developed from feudal times and stressed personal honor and, above all, loyalty to the feudal lord. Formulated during the Kamakura shogunate (12th–14th cents.), it became the code of the Daimyo and Samurai in the 17th cent. In the 19th cent. the code was made the basis for fierce loyalty to the emperor and governed Japanese life until the end of WW II.

Bushman Member of an ancient indigenous African tribe, living primarily in South Africa.

Bushnell, David 1742–1824. American inventor, sometimes called the father of the submarine. His submarine, the *Turtle*, invented in 1775, is considered a forerunner of modern submarines.

Bushnell Horace 1802–76. American Congregational minister. His theological views had a major influence on the growth of religious liberalism.

bushrangers Australian bandits of the 19th cent. Originally escaped convicts, they terrorized the bush country from the late 1700s to 1880, when the last band was caught and killed. They have become part of Australian folk history.

Busta Gallorum, Battle of ⟨Battle of Taginae⟩ Battle ⟨AD 552⟩ in which Byzantine General Narses defeated the Goths in Italy and killed their leader, Totila. The battle brought much of Italy under Byzantine rule.

Butades of Sicyon *fl. c*600 BC. Greek sculptor who worked at Corinth. He is believed to have been the first to sculpt in clay.

Bute, John Stuart, 3d earl of 1713–92. British statesman who held great influence over King George III in the early years of his reign. As prime minister (1762–63) he negotiated the Treaty of Paris (1763), ending the Seven Years' War (1756–63).

Butler, Benjamin Franklin 1818–93. American politician and Union general in the American Civil War, noted for his harsh measures as military governor of New Orleans (1862). As a representative in Congress (1867–75, 1877–79), he helped lead radical Republicans in adopting reconstruction and impeaching President A. Johnson.

Butler, John 1728–96. Notorious American Loyalist commander during the 'American Revolution. His mixed force of whites and Indians, called Butler's Rangers, perpetrated the Wyoming Massacre (1778) in Pennsylvania's Wyoming Valley.

Butler, Samuel 1835–1902. An English author of the Utopian satire *Erewhon* and the autobiographical novel *The Way of All Flesh*.

Butler, Thomas, 10th earl of Ormonde ⟨Black Earl⟩ 1532–1614. Irish nobleman. He was noted for serving the English cause in putting down Irish rebellions in 1579 and 1597.

Butler, Walter 1752?–81. Notorious American Loyalist commander during the American Revolution. The son of J. Butler, he commanded Butler's Rangers during the Cherry Valley Massacre (1778).

Buxar, Battle of *See* **Baksar, Battle of**

Byzacena *See* **Roman Province of Africa**

Bye plot ⟨Surprising treason⟩ ⟨Surprise plot⟩ Conspiracy (1603) to imprison English King James I and hold him hostage until the adoption of religious reforms.

Bylini Russian term for the heroic and narrative folk poems of Russian history. Passed down through oral tradition, the Bylini have had a notable influence on Russian literature.

Byng, Julian Hedworth George, 1st Viscount Byng of Vimy 1862–1935. British general. During WW I he led the Canadian Corps in the celebrated capture of Vimy Ridge (1917), and commanded the British 3d Army (1917–18).

Byrd, Richard Evelyn 1888–1957. American admiral, polar explorer and aviator. A pioneer in polar aviation, he was the first to fly over the North Pole (1926). He established (1928) the Little America base in Antarctica, flew over the South Pole (1929), and headed US expeditions in the Antarctic until the 1950s.

Byron, George Gordon, 6th Baron 1788–1824. English poet and satirist, one of the great Romantic poets and a symbol of Romanticism personified. He was born clubfooted. Byron succeeded his eccentric father as baron in 1798. Following publication of a satire, *English Bards and Scotch Reviewers*, he won widespread fame. Divorced in 1816, he left England and lived the rest of his free-spirited life in Europe. He died while aiding Greek insurgents fighting against Turkish rule. His many important works include *A Vision of Judgment*, *Beppo*, *Don Juan* and *Childe Harold's Pilgrimage*.

Byzantine Empire The Byzantine Empire was the successor state to the Roman Empire after the fall of the Western Roman Empire (AD 476). It corresponds to the Eastern Roman Empire (created by the division of the Roman Empire into the Western and Eastern empires, AD 395). It became the last bastion of Roman and Hellenic culture. For centuries after the Western Empire collapsed, the Byzantine Empire withstood the onslaughts of such groups as the Vandals, Goths, Persians, Seljuk and Ottoman Turks, thereby insuring a relatively peaceful period for the reorganization of Europe. It preserved Roman and Greek traditions and contributions, such as the legal code *Corpus*

Juris Civilis, made a lasting imprint on Western civilization. Key dates in the history of the Byzantine Empire include:

AD 330 Roman emperor Constantine I rebuilt city of Byzantium as Constantinople, making it seat of the Roman Empire.

AD 395 Roman Empire permanently divided at death of Theodosius; his son Arcadius succeeded as emperor of the Eastern (or East Roman) Empire.

AD 476 Fall of Western Roman Empire; Eastern Empire survived as the Byzantine Empire, successor state to Roman Empire.

AD 476–477 Reign of Zeno the Isaurian (474–481) challenged by the usurper, Basiliscus.

6TH CENT. AD Rise of Blues and Greens, rival political factions, within the empire.

527–565 Justinian I reigned; one of the great rulers of the Byzantine Empire; ordered compilation of the legal code *Corpus Juris Civilis* (529–535); empire reached its height under Justinian, including in its domains Italy, part of North Africa, and southern Spain.

532 Constantinople heavily damaged in Nika Riot of Blues and Greens against Justinian; attempt to overthrow Justinian failed.

532 Construction of Hagia Sophia begun; one of the masterpieces of Byzantine architecture, it was but a part of the great building program under Justinian.

533–534 North Africa brought under Byzantine control when Byzantine general Belisarus defeated Vandals.

535 Belisarus began reconquest of Italy (from Ostrogoths), later completed by Narses.

540 Persians invaded Syria.

552–554 Byzantine general Narses defeated the Ostrogoths, led by Totila, in Italy; brought Italy under firm Byzantine control.

559 Belisarius repulsed invasion of the Huns and Slavs that had reached the outskirts of Constantinople.

568–571 Lombards invaded northern Italy, taking control of all but the Exarchate of Ravenna.

LATE 6TH CENT. Great migration of Slavs into Balkan Peninsula.

591–593 Invading Avars, threatening Constantinople, driven back.

602–610 Phocas, a soldier, reigned after seizing the throne.

610–641 Heraclius I reigned; assumed power after Phocas was overthrown.

622–627 Heraclius warred against and decisively defeated the Persians, who had intermittently threatened the empire from 540 and who had conquered much of the southern empire from 611.

626 Constantinople successfully resisted attacks by Slavs and Avars.

FROM **634** Rise of the Muslim Caliphate Empire; Muslims began rapid expansion of their empire, taking over considerable Byzantine territory.

636 Byzantine power in Syria broken by Muslim Arab victory at Battle of the Yarmuk River. (Aug. 20).

637–642 Muslim caliphs continued expanding their empire; Jerusalem fell (637) and Byzantine Egypt was lost (642).

638 Heraclius' attempt to resolve religious controversy over Monophysitism gave rise to new heresy, Monotheletism.

673–678 Muslim Arab threat to Byzantine Empire reached its height; Constantinople withstood siege by Arabs throughout the period and finally won peace settlement (678).

695–717 Period of anarchy and unrest in which the army gained power and named a succession of emperors; empire raided by Arabs and a new enemy, the Bulgars; order restored by Leo III.

698 Muslim Arab caliphs completed conquest of Byzantine territories in North Africa (begun 647).

717–741 Leo III reigned; put down revolts by army and restored order; founded Isaurian dynasty; began controversy over iconoclasm (726).

741–775 Constantine V reigned; advocated iconoclasm, lost control of Italy; warred against Bulgars (755–764).

751–756 Lombards conquered the Exarchate of Ravenna, Byzantine foothold in Italy; Franks called in by pope to aid against Lombards and thereby began alliance of popes in Rome and European monarchs.

780–797 Irene, mother of Emperor Constantine VI, held real power during his reign; overthrew him (797).

787–843 Iconoclastic controversy; temporarily ended by Council of Nicaea (787); revived again in 815; the ban on icon worship was finally rescinded in 843.

797–802 Irene reigned as first Byzantine empress; refused to recognize Charlemagne's empire as successor state to Western Roman Empire (800).

813–820 Leo V reigned; repelled Bulgar attack on Constantinople; forced Bulgars to accept peace treaty (817).

860s Saints Cyril and Methodius began their missionary work among the Slavs.

869–870 Council of Constantinople; Photius, patriarch of Constantinople and leader of Byzantine opposition to the primacy of Rome, was ex-communicated by the council; Ignatius, called to succeed him, attempted to heal growing split between Eastern and Western churches.

867–886 Basil I reigned; founded Macedonian dynasty (867–1057); introduced legal code; his reign marked a golden age in Byzantine history; Basil rebuilt Byzantine military strength; his armies and navy generally successful against Muslim Arabs.

886–912 Leo VI reigned; compiled Basilica, the Byzantine legal code; warfare against the Bulgarians (from 889).

900s Rise of feudalism in the empire; feudal revolts against the emperors in this century proved unsuccessful.

913–959 Constantine VII reigned; Bulgarians seriously threatened Constantinople; warfare with Russian princes.

969–976 John I reigned; forced the Russians out of Bulgaria and, advancing against the Muslim Arabs, took parts of Syria.

976–1025 Basil II reigned; won final submission of Bulgarians (1018) after decisive victory against them (1014).

1042–54 Constantine IX reigned with wife Zoë; Seljuk Turks began to drive Byzantines from Asia Minor; empire began to crumble.

1042 Normans began attacks on Byzantine territories in southern Italy; eventually won control of Sicily and Naples to form Kingdom of the Two Sicilies (1091).

1054 Schism between Roman and Eastern Orthodox churches became permanent.

1071 Romanus IV defeated by Seljuk Turks at Battle of Manzikert; Byzantine hold on Asia Minor seriously weakened as Seljuks advanced.

1081–1118 Alexius I Comnenus reigned; established the Comnenian dynasty (1081–1185); defended the empire against Norman invasions led by Robert Guiscard.

1096 Era of the Crusades began; Byzantine emperors, threatened by Seljuk advances, forced to contend with potentially dangerous force of European Christians sent to fight the Seljuks in the Holy Land.

1143–80 Manuel Comnenus reigned; averted war with Christians on Second Crusade; extended Byzantine hegemony over Hungary, notably after conquering Dalmatia (1168); accepted unfavorable peace after war with Venice (1176); attempted to promote ties with the Western church.

1185–95 Isaac II reigned; acceded after leading a revolt; collapse of central authority began as petty nobles gained power; Normans defeated but revolt by Bulgarians resulted in creation of a new Bulgarian kingdom (1185).

1204 Crusaders (on Fourth Crusade) captured Constantinople; Latin Empire of Constantinople established after sack of Constantinople.

1204–05 Baldwin I reigned as first Latin emperor of Constantinople.

1206 Theodore I Lascaris founded the empire of Nicaea after the fall of the empire to the crusaders.

1228–61 Baldwin II reigned as last Latin emperor of Constantinople.

1244 Mongol incursions into Asia Minor began.

1261 Michael VIII Paleologus (ruled 1261–82) reconquered Constantinople, effectively ending Latin Empire of Constantinople; Byzantine Empire reestablished.

1300s Ottoman Turks began their rise to power in northwestern Asia Minor, expanding their empire at the expense of the Byzantines.

1340s Serbs, led by Stephen Dushan, rose to power and threatened the Byzantine empire.

1341–47 War between John V and John VI for control of the empire; both Turks and Serbs called in to help; war set the stage for the final collapse of the empire; by 1391 the Turks had begun their attacks on Constantinople, the last vestige of Byzantine Empire.

1453 Constantinople fell to the Ottoman Turks; Constantine XI, last Byzantine emperor (1448–53), fell defending the city; Byzantine Empire ceased to exist.

Byzantium Ancient Greek city once located on the site of Constantinople. It gave its name to the Byzantine Empire, of which Constantinople later became capital. Founded 7th cent. BC by Megarian Greeks, it became an important commercial city. It was conquered (AD 196) by the Romans and, by order of Constantine I, the city was later rebuilt (AD 330) as Constantinople.

C

Caaba *See* **Kaaba**

Cabal An unpopular, inner group of five advisers that served (1667–73) King Charles II of England. This informal ministry dominated court policy and engaged in various intrigues until Parliament forced its dissolution (1673). Members were: Clifford of Chudleigh; Lord Shaftsbury, A. Ashley Cooper; the duke of Buckingham, G. Villiers; the earl of Arlington, H. Bennet; and the duke of Lauderdale, J. Maitland.

Cabala ⟨Cabbala⟩ A mystical interpretation of the Scriptures that arose among Jews in the 13th cent. and to a lesser degree among Christians in the 15th and 16th cents. Cabalists held that for those who knew the secrets, every word, letter, number, and accent in the Scriptures revealed mysteries about God and the universe. Cabalism influenced the development of Hasidism.

Cabarrus, Jeanne Marie Ignace, Theresa de *See* **Tallien, Theresa**

Cabbala *See* **Cabala**

Cabeca de Vaca, Álvar Núñez *See* **Cabeza de Vaca, Álvar Núñez**

Cabet, Étienne 1788–1856. French socialist and founder of the Icaria commune in America (c1849).

Cabeza de Vaca, Álvar Núñez ⟨Cabeca de Vaca, ~⟩ c1490–c1557. Spanish soldier and explorer. Tales of his trek through the unexplored American Southwest spurred exploration of the region.

Cabiri Gods of ancient Greece associated with fertility cults. They are believed to correspond with Demeter, Hermes, and Persephone.

Cabochiens Faction of Parisian tradesmen that sided with the Burgundians in the civil war against the Armagnacs (1411–18). In 1413 Cabochiens rioted and seized control of Paris. Before the uprising was quashed by the Armagnacs, Cabochiens issued their *ordonnance cabochienne*, radical reforms intended to end government corruption.

Cabot, George *See* **Hartford Convention**

Cabot, John 1450–98. Italian navigator serving England. On a voyage of discovery (1497), he landed at what may have been Cape Breton Island and explored the coastline of Nova Scotia and Newfoundland.

Cabral, Pedro Alvares ⟨Cabrera, ~⟩ c1467–c1520. Portuguese navigator. His discovery of the Brazilian coast (1500) is disputed.

Cabrera, Pedro Alvares *See* **Cabral, Pedro Alvares**

Cabrillo, Juan Rodríguez d. 1543. Portuguese soldier and explorer in the service of Spain. During an exploratory voyage, he discovered the California coast (1542).

Cabrini, Saint Frances Xavier 1850–1917. Italian-American founder of Missionary Sisters of the Sacred Heart of Jesus (1880). The first American saint, she is best known for her work among Italian immigrants in the US.

Caccini, Giulio 1550?–1618. Italian composer and singer. He was a member of a group of Florentine music theorists who composed what are considered the earliest operas.

Cade, John (Jack) *See* **Cade's Rebellion**

Cade's Rebellion In England, a brief revolt (1450) by small-property owners over political grievances and corruption in King Henry VI's government. Led by John (Jack) Cade (d. 1450), some 40,000 rebels took London and executed the king's treasurer, Lord Saye. The rebels disbanded on being promised pardons by the king.

Cadillac, Antoine de la Mothe 1658–1730. A French colonial administrator in North America and founder of Detroit (1701). He was a governor of Louisiana (1711–16).

Cadmus Founder of the city of Thebes in Greek mythology. He was also believed to have introduced the alphabet to the Greeks.

Cadoudal, Georges 1771–1804. Royalist conspirator during the French Revolution. He was a principal leader of the royalist Chouans (*q.v.*) in revolt against the revolutionary government. He was guillotined after participating in an attempt to overthrow Napoleon I.

Cadwaladr *See* **Cadwallader**

Cadwallader ⟨Caedwalla⟩ ⟨Cadwaladr⟩ *d.* 664/ 689? King of the Gwynedd in what is now North Wales.

Caedmon *fl.* 670. Earliest known English Christian poet. He was said to be an illiterate herdsman who discovered his poetic gifts through a vision.

Caedwalla   *See* **Cadwallader**

Caerleon ⟨Caerllion⟩ ⟨Isca Silurum⟩ Now a district in Wales, it was once the site of a major Roman fortress in Britain. It is also considered one of the possible locations of King Arthur's court, the legendary Camelot.

Caerllion   *See* **Caerleon**

Caesar The famous family of the Julian clan of ancient Rome and, for a time, title of Roman rulers. The line begins with Sextus Julius, who was praetor in 208 BC. Its two most famous members are Julius and Augustus Caesar. After AD 68, the name "Caesar," with "Augustus," became a title taken by emperors who were not of the family. This tradition lasted to the time of Hadrian, who adopted only the title "Augustus."

Caesar, Julius *c*102–44 BC. Great Roman statesman and general. Caesar strengthened Rome's control over the empire by replacing the Roman oligarchy with a dictatorship and by pacifying Italy and the provinces. He extended the empire throughout Gaul and devised the Julian calendar, the basis of the modern calendar. Caesar aligned himself with the popular party during his early career and, in 60 BC, sought the consulate of Rome. Frustrated by Senate opposition, he formed the First Triumvirate with Crassus and Pompey and thus became consul in 59 BC. He was then named proconsul of Gaul and Illyricum (58) and became a military hero as commander of Roman armies in the Gallic Wars (58–51). Crassus' death ended the triumvirate (53) and set Pompey, now sole consul, against Caesar. In 49, Caesar led his armies from Gaul against Pompey. Crossing the Rubicon, he marched unopposed to Rome, and was made dictator. Caesar emerged victorious from the ensuing military exploits (49–45) in the provinces against Pompey's army and in 44 was named dictator for life. But his dictatorial powers had aroused bitter resentment in Rome. On the Ides of March (Mar. 15) 44, Caesar was assassinated by a band of conspirators which included Brutus, Cassius, and Casca. (For further details on Caesar's exploits, *see* Rome, 60–44 BC; Gallic Wars.)

Caesarea, Eusebius of   *See* **Eusebius of Caesarea**

Caetano, Marcelo José das Neves Alves 1906–. Portuguese statesman, premier (1968–74), successor to A. Salazar. Though an extreme conservative, he permitted some moderate reforms before being ousted by the military.

Cagliostro, Alessandro, Conte ⟨*pseud. of* Balsamo, Giuseppe⟩ 1743–95. Italian adventurer. He was a magician and alchemist who was popular in King Louis XVI's court, until he was implicated in the Affair of the Diamond Necklace (1785).

Cagoulards French terrorist group of the 1930s. Named for the hoods worn by the members, the group supported royalist and fascist tendencies. In November, 1937, an armed revolt against the Popular Front government *(q.v.)* was forestalled by discovery of their arms caches.

Cahenslyism Late 19th-cent. movement among European Roman Catholic immigrants in the US calling for appointment of bishops and priests of their own nationality. The movement was named for a German, Peter Paul Cahensly, who with other Europeans pressed the cause at the Vatican.

Caillaux, Joseph 1863–1944. French statesman, influential in French politics between 1898 and 1939. He served several times as finance minister and once as premier (1911–12). A pacifist, he was convicted of treason in 1920, but by 1925 he had returned to office as finance minister.

Cain In the Bible, the oldest son of Adam and Eve. He killed his brother Abel in a jealous rage, after which God made him a fugitive for the rest of his life.

Cairo Egyptian capital city (pop. 5,084,500), a port and the largest city in Africa. Founded 969 by the Fatimids as the Egyptian capital, it was taken by Saladin in the 12th cent. Cairo was the capital under the Mamelukes from the 13th to 16 cents., and reached the height of its prosperity before modern times. The Ottoman Turks controlled it from the 16th to 19th cents., and after 1805 Cairo was capital of a quasi-independent country. The British maintained a military presence there from 1882 to 1946.

Cairo Conference Meeting of WW II Allies held (Nov. 22–26, 1943) at Cairo to discuss Far East policies. It preceded the Teheran Conference and was attended by US president F. Roosevelt, British prime minister W. Churchill, and Chinese general Chiang Kai-shek. Afterward, the leaders pledged to continue war against Japan until its surrender, to strip Japan of its island possessions, to grant Korea eventual independence, and to forgo territorial gains by their respective nations.

Cakste, Janis 1859–1927. Latvian statesman. During WW I, he was an important figure in securing independence for and recognition of the republic of Latvia. He was its first president, elected in 1922 and reelected 1925.

Calabria   *See* **Bruttium**

Calais French port city (pop. 74,600). Here, in 1347, following a long siege by the English under King Edward III, six town burghers volunteered their lives to save the city. They were spared, and the city was subsequently controlled by the British from 1347 to 1558. In WW II, it was the objective of Hitler's drive to the sea (1940).

Calais, Treaty of *See* **Brétigny, Treaty of**

Calamity Jane (*pseud. of* Burke, Martha Jane) *c*1852–1903. American frontier heroine. A skilled rider and markswoman who dressed in men's clothing, she gained widespread notoriety in the late 1800s for her exploits in the South Dakota Black Hills.

Calatrava, Knights of *See* **Knights of Calatrava**

Calcutta Major city and port (pop. 3,148,800). Founded (1690) as a British East India Company factory, it became the site of Fort William after 1696. It was captured briefly by the Bengalis (1756–57), and was the capital of British India (1773–1912) before Delhi.

Calcutta, Black Hole of *See* **Black Hole of Calcutta**

Calder, Alexander 1898–1976. American sculptor. He is best known as the originator of mobiles.

Calderón Bridge Bridge in west central Mexico where a rebel force under M. Hidalgo y Costilla was defeated by Spanish royalist forces (Jan. 17, 1811). It marked the end of the first attempt at Mexican independence.

Calderón de la Barca, Pedro 1600–81. Spanish dramatist and poet. He is considered one of Spain's greatest playwrights. *El divino Orfeo* and *La hija del aire* are among the many plays he wrote.

Caldwell, Erskine 1903–. American author of novels about the rural South. *Tobacco Road* and *God's Little Acre* are among his best-known works.

Caleb In the Bible, a man sent by Moses to spy in the land of Canaan.

Caledonia Roman name for the region north of their territories on the British Isles and roughly corresponding to what is now Scotland. In modern usage it refers to Scotland.

Calhoun, John Caldwell 1782–1850. American statesman, vice-president (1825–29, 1829–32), and champion of the Old South. A nationalist and supporter of the War of 1812, he became secretary of war (1817–25) and then served as vice-president under J. Q. Adams and A. Jackson. He became a supporter of states' rights, and, breaking with Jackson over the Eaton Affair *(q.v.)* and nullification *(q.v.)*, he resigned the vice-presidency. After winning passage (1832) of the controversial Ordi-

nance of Nullification in South Carolina, he served in the US Senate (1832–43, 1845–50), where he worked to protect the interests of the South and oppose abolition of slavery. His debates with D. Webster are famous.

California US state on the Pacific coast (pop. 23,668,600), the 31st state. Spanish explorer J. Cabrillo claimed the lower coast for Spain (1542), and Sir F. Drake claimed the region north of San Francisco (1579) for the English. Gaspar de Portola established a permanent settlement at San Diego (1769), and settlement by Americans did not begin until the 1840s. The Mexican governor of the region was driven out in 1845, and, during the Mexican War (1846–48), the territory was occupied by US troops. It was ceded to the US by the Treaty of Guadalupe Hidalgo *(q.v.)*. The gold rush of 1848 increased population, and California became a state in 1850. Its constitution has been in effect since 1880.

Caligula AD 12–41. Roman emperor (AD 37–41), successor to Tiberius and notorious as a despotic ruler. Though his father, mother, and two brothers were rumored to have been put to death by Tiberius, Caligula befriended and ultimately succeeded him. At first a popular figure, he is sometimes said to have gone mad after a serious illness (AD *c*38). Tales of his subsequent ruthless cruelties and eccentric behavior are legion, and he squandered the great wealth of the treasury. He was assassinated.

caliph Ruler of the Muslim state founded by the prophet Muhammad (7th cent.). The caliphate was established on Muhammad's death (632) and was invested with absolute temporal and spiritual powers. Caliphs reigned over the Empire of the Caliphate *(q.v.)* from 632 until its conquest by the Mongols in 1258. The first four caliphs, Abu Bakr, Umar, Uthman, and Ali, were descendants of Muhammad and are called the Orthodox Caliphs. Their reign was broken in 661 when Muawiya took the caliphate by force and established the Umayyad dynasty *(q.v.)*. The Abbasid line later replaced the Umayyads

Caliphate, Empire of Muslim theocracy established in western Arabia (7th cent.) by the prophet Muhammad. After Muhammad's death (632), the original Muslim state was rapidly expanded into a great empire by his successors, the caliphs, who held both temporal and spiritual powers. Two great dynasties ruled this empire, the Umayyads and their successors, the Abbasids. At its greatest extent, the Muslim Empire stretched from Afghanistan in the east, across the Mideast and North Africa, and up into Spain. But divisions among the Arab Muslims over religious and political matters, and strains caused by inclusion of so many diverse peoples within the Muslim world, seriously weakened the empire. These problems set the stage for the empire's final decline and eventual collapse before the invading Mongols (1258). Key events in the history of the empire include:

c613 Muhammad began preaching at Mecca in western Arabia.

622 Hejira (July 15–16), Muhammad's flight from Mecca to escape enemies of his teachings; marked beginning of Muslim era; Muhammad established following at Medina.

624–625 Muhammad's followers defeated a force from Mecca at Badr, but were themselves defeated at Uhud.

628 Opposed by the Jews at Medina, Muhammad condemned them and conquered the oasis of Khaibar, which they had held.

630–632 Muhammad marched into Mecca with 10,000 followers (632); tradition of pilgrimage established; Muhammad, now secure in his position as prophet, also established tradition of jihad (holy war) against nonbelievers and thus paved the way for the great expansion of the empire; raids against Byzantines to north conducted.

632 Muhammad died (June 8); caliphate established.

632–634 Abu Bakr, Muhammad's father-in-law, became first of the four patriarchal caliphs; suppressed revolts and established Muslim military power.

634–644 Umar I, second patriarchal caliph; Persian lands to north (modern Iraq) conquered (c635); Jordan, Palestine, and Syria taken from Byzantines after Battle of Yarmuk (636); northern advance stopped at edge of Byzantine Anatolia; Byzantine Egypt conquered (640–645).

644–656 Uthman, third patriarchal caliph; completed conquest of Persia (651); launched expeditions to Cyprus and North Africa; discontent within Muslim world led to his assassination.

656–661 Ali, fourth patriarchal caliph and husband of Fatima, Muhammad's daughter; first Muslim Civil War broke out when Muawiya opposed Ali's succession.

661 Hasan, Ali's son, appointed caliph after Ali was assassinated; Hasan soon after submitted to Muawiya.

661–680 Muawiya reigned as first caliph of the Umayyad dynasty (reigned 661–750); he restored order after civil war and made Damascus capital of the Muslim Empire; great expansion of the empire accomplished by his Umayyad successors.

674–680 Raids against Byzantine Empire became a protracted war in which the Muslims seriously threatened Constantinople.

680–683 Yazid I, Muawiya's son, became caliph; opposition in Arabia to domination by Syrian Muslims provoked Yazid's attacks on Medina and Mecca; set stage for second civil war.

683–692 Second Muslim Civil War.

684 Power struggle within Islamic leadership led to division of Islam into Shi'ite and Sunni (orthodox) Muslims.

685–692 Abd al-Malik succeeded as caliph; made peace with the Byzantines and then set about subduing various rebel groups involved in civil war; rival caliph (Ibn az-Zubayr) in Arabia was slain in battle at Mecca (692), thus ending the civil war.

692–705 Remainder of al-Malik's reign marked by his consolidation of power, building of the Dome of the Rock at Jerusalem (691), renewed war with the Byzantines, the capture of Carthage (698), and conquest of Byzantine North Africa.

711–714 Muslims from North Africa raided Visigothic kingdom in Iberia; quickly brought about collapse of the kingdom.

732 Muslim invaders drove Christians in Iberia far to the north (into modern northern Spain); Muslims halted by Charles Martel at Battle of Poitiers (in modern France) and never again advanced northward from Spain.

716–717 Arab Muslims mounted their last major attack on Byzantine Constantinople; attackers withdrawn after the death of Caliph Suleiman (reigned 715–717).

724–743 Hisham reigned as caliph; his reign was marked by the end of rapid territorial expansion under the Umayyad dynasty, and general peace and prosperity; Muslim Empire now extended from Afghanistan in the east, across the Arabian Peninsula and North Africa, and into Spain in the west; a Berber revolt (740–742) greatly reduced territories in North Africa that were held by the Arabs; period of decline followed Hisham's reign.

747–750 Revolt of Abu Muslim; by taking advantage of discontent among various Arab groups, Abu Muslim succeeded in fomenting a general rebellion that resulted in the overthrow of the Umayyad dynasty; Abbasid dynasty established by abu-al-Abbas as Saffan (reigned 750–54).

750–1258 Abbasid dynasty reigned; moved government from Damascus (Syria) to Baghdad

(Iraq) in 763; period marked by deepening split between Sunni (orthodox) and Shi'ite Muslims, increasing influence of Persians (later Turks) in the Muslim world, and the consequent decline in power of the old Arab ruling class; Abbasid caliphs took on a stronger religious image as imams.

750 Abd-ar-Rahman I was the only Umayyad to escape executions that followed the Abbasid takeover; he made his way to Muslim Spain and established (755) the Umayyad line there (ruled until 1031).

754–775 Al-Mansur reigned as caliph; killed Abu Muslim and thus sparked unsuccessful revolts; moved capital to Baghdad (c763), which developed into the leading Muslim city; his reign was marked by stability and prosperity.

786–809 Harun al-Rashid reigned as caliph; luxury of his court immortalized in *Thousand and One Nights*; but rebellion and unrest were common in Syria, Egypt, and in far eastern reaches of empire; Harun issued the Meccan documents (802), which set forth his ill-fated plan to divide the empire in two on his death.

809–813 Third Muslim Civil War; broke out after Harun's death, between rulers of new eastern and western empires; Abd Allah al-Mamun emerged victorious.

813–833 Al-Mamun reigned as caliph; golden age of Muslim Arab culture; al-Mamun warred against Byzantines, put down revolts in Egypt, Syria, and Armenia; ordered translation of Greek texts; attempted to heal rift between Sunni and Shi'ite Muslims.

842–847 Al-Wathiq reigned as caliph; unsuccessfully tried to halt rising influence of non-Arabs (Persians, Turks) by returning to pro-Arab orthodox Sunni policies.

861–945 Breakdown of central authority; period of widespread rebellion and unrest; provincial rulers in the east and west became largely autonomous; political and military leadership taken over by the amir (from 945); caliphs reduced to spiritual figureheads largely dependent upon the amirs.

929 Umayyad ruler Abd-ar-Rahman III took advantage of weakened Abbasid caliphate to declare himself first caliph of Muslim Spain.

945–1055 Buyids, a dynasty of Persians, in power as amirs; though they favored the Shi'ite Muslims, they nevertheless maintained the Sunni caliphs in power.

969–1171 Fatimids, an extremist Shi'ite sect vehemently opposed to the Abbasids, conquered Egypt (969) and established the Fatimid dynasty there; actively attempted to overthrow Abbasids while they remained in power.

998 Rise of the Sunni Muslim Ghaznavid Empire in Afghanistan.

1008–31 Fourth Muslim Civil War; fought in Spain, it resulted in the end of the Umayyad dynasty rule there.

1055–92 Seljuk Turks, zealous Sunni Muslims, rose to power as their eastward migration increased their numbers in the empire; led by Togrul Beg, the Seljuks ousted (1055) the Buyid amirs from power, restored Sunni power, and themselves assumed temporal powers as sultans; Seljuk power reached its zenith under Malik-shah (1072–92), and thereafter conflicts among the sultans gave increased power to the Abbasid caliphs.

1095–1291 Era of the Crusades; rise of Saladin, who suppressed the Fatimids in Egypt (1171), as the great leader of Muslim forces against the crusaders.

1258 End of the Empire of the Caliphate; Mongol conqueror Hulagu Khan overran the empire and destroyed the capital of Baghdad; last reigning caliph, al-Musta'sim (ruled 1242–58), killed.

c1261–1517 Abbasid line lived on in Egypt, but held no real power; line ended by Ottoman Turk conquest of Egypt (1517).

Calixtines *See* **Utraquists**

Calixtus II ⟨Callistus II⟩ ⟨*orig.* Guido of Vienne⟩ d. 1124. French-born pope (1119–24), successor to Gelasius II. He forced Holy Roman Emperor Henry V to accept the Concordat of Worms (1122) and thereby ended the Investiture Controversy.

Calixtus III ⟨Callistus III⟩ ⟨*orig.* Borja, Alfonso de⟩ 1378–1458. Spanish-born pope (1455–58), successor to Nicholas V. He failed in his attempts to raise a crusade against the Turks. Calixtus III was also the name of an antipope to Alexander III (1168).

Callaghan, Leonard James 1912–. British Labour party prime minister (1976–79). A conservative Labourite, he rose in the party through trade union work and served as chancellor of the exchequer (1964–67), home secretary (1967–70), and foreign secretary (1974–76). His term of office was marked by severe economic problems.

Calles, Plutarco Elias 1877–1945. Mexican revolutionary general and president (1924–28). He joined the revolution against P. Díaz (1910) and, as president, instituted unsuccessful agrarian reforms. He established the National Revolutionary party, and, until his exile in 1936, he virtually ruled Mexico.

Callias *fl.* 449 BC. Athenian statesman. He is believed to have negotiated the Treaty of Callias

(449), in which a long period of hostility between the Greeks and Persians was brought to an end. There is doubt that a written treaty ever existed, but the two peoples remained at peace for many years after his mission.

Callias, Treaty of *See* **Callias**

Callimachus Late 5th-cent.-BC Greek sculptor. He is believed to have been an Athenian and the originator of the Corinthian column.

Calliope One of the Muses in Greek mythology. She was the patroness of epic poetry and mother of Orpheus.

Callisto Nymph in Greek mythology who was Artemis' attendant. Changed into a bear by Artemis (or Hera), she was removed to the heavens by Zeus. There she became the constellation known as the Great Bear.

Callistus II *See* **Calixtus II**

Callistus III *See* **Calixtus III**

Calmette, Albert Léon Charles 1863–1933. A French bacteriologist. A student of L. Pasteur, he developed, with Camile Guerin (1872–1961), a vaccine used to inoculate infants against tuberculosis.

Calonne, Charles *See* **Assembly of Notables**

Calpurnia *fl.* 1st cent. BC. Roman woman, J. Caesar's last wife (from 59 BC). She is said to have tried to prevent his attendance at the Senate on the day of his assassination (44 BC).

Calvé, Emma 1858–1942. French operatic soprano especially noted for her performances as Carmen.

Calvert, George, 1st Baron Baltimore *c*1580–1632. British colonizer, whose efforts led to the founding (1632) of the colony of Maryland.

Calvin, John 1509–64. French theologian and, as founder of Calvinism, one of the great figures of the Protestant Reformation. Able at debating, Calvin at first studied law. He became a Protestant (1533), and was forced to leave France because of religious persecution. Later (at Basel, 1536) he completed his great theological work *Institutes of the Christian Religion*, which systemized Protestant dogma. He next went to Geneva (1536) to establish a theocracy according to his Calvinistic doctrines. Expelled from Geneva (1538) and then recalled (1541), Calvin struggled until 1555 to establish his absolute supremacy there. He was involved in noted controversies against the Lutherans and the Anabaptists, as well as in the trial and burning of M. Servetus (1553).

Calvinism **1.** The body of religious teachings advanced by J. Calvin and his followers. Calvinism arose during the 16th-cent. Reformation and differed from Lutheranism in placing the church above the state, in emphasizing predestination

and the notion of grace, and in developing a theology of the covenant (pact with God). Calvinistic doctrines were important in the development of English Puritanism, Scottish Presbyterianism, and the theocratic communities of early New England Puritans. Other noted Calvinists include J. Knox and J. Edwards. **2.** Name for the body of doctrines that form the basis of the Reformed and Presbyterian churches.

Calvo, Carlos 1824–1906. Argentine diplomat and jurist. He is best known for the Calvo Doctrine, advanced in his book *International Law of Europe and America in Theory and Practice.*

Calydon Ancient Aetolian city, whose ruins are located in what is now central Greece. According to legend, it is the place where the Calydonian boar was hunted.

Calydonian hunt Episode in Greek mythology. The god Artemis sent a monstrous wild boar to destroy Calydon. The boar was hunted by Meleagar, son of the king of Calydon, and many others. It was slain by Meleagar.

Calypso A nymph in Greek mythology. In Homer's *Odyssey*, she was Odysseus' companion for seven years on the island of Ogygia. She offered Odysseus immortality to keep him there, but he refused her and again took up his homeward journey.

Cambacérès, Jean Jacques Régis de 1753–1824. French revolutionary statesman. He was second consul under Napoleon (1799–1804), and, from 1804, archchancellor of the French empire. He played an important role in formulating the Code Napoléon.

Cambodia Republic located in Southeast Asia. Its capital is Phnom Penh. Cambodia's early history was shaped in part by early Hindu and Buddhist influences. The Khmer Empire flourished in Cambodia from the 6th to 15th cents. and at its peak made Cambodia the leading empire in the region. As the Khmer Empire declined, Cambodia suffered numerous attacks from neighboring states, and finally in the 19th cent. became a French protectorate. After achieving independence (1953), Cambodia became increasingly embroiled in the conflict in Vietnam, its traditional enemy. The Vietnam War had drastic repercussions in Cambodia, and political and social instability continued into the 1980s. Key dates in the history of Cambodia include:

c3D–5TH CENTS. AD Funan Empire flourished in Cambodia; Hinduism and other elements of Indian culture introduced.

c6TH CENT. AD Funan Empire overrun by Khmer people from the north; Khmer Empire established in Cambodia.

9TH–13TH CENTS. Khmer Empire rose to its height; extended its power through much of Southeast Asia.

12TH–13TH CENTS. Angkor Wat and Angkor Thom built.

13TH CENT. Buddhism introduced.

13TH–15TH CENTS. Khmer Empire declined; lost territories in increasing attacks from Siam in the west and Annam in the east; collapse came in 15th cent.

1863 French established protectorate over Cambodia.

1887 Cambodia made part of French colonial Indochina.

1941–55 Norodom Sihanouk reigned as king.

1940–45 WW II; Japanese troops entered Cambodia (1940) and held real power there; French Vichy government was allowed to remain until 1945, when the Japanese ousted the French from all Indochina.

1945 French reestablished control in Cambodia following WW II.

1946 Cambodia became autonomous within the French Union.

1953 Cambodia became independent.

1954 Cambodia invaded by Vietminh, Communist forces fighting against French rule in neighboring Vietnam.

1954 French withdrew troops from Indochina at the end of the French Indochina War.

1955 Norodom Sihanouk turned over Cambodian throne to his father, Prince Norodom Suramarit, and became prime minister.

1960 Sihanouk became Cambodian chief of state.

1960–75 Vietnam War; Sihanouk's attempts to keep Cambodia neutral ultimately failed as war spread from Vietnam into Cambodia.

1963–65 Sihanouk, claiming US interference in Cambodian affairs, refused further US aid (1963); diplomatic relations with US ended.

1969 US began secret aerial bombing of Communist bases in Cambodia; diplomatic relations reestablished with US soon after.

1969 Lon Nol became premier (Aug.).

1970 Sihanouk unable to get the large Vietnamese Communist force to leave Cambodia; he was overthrown (Mar. 18) in bloodless coup; Lon Nol became chief of state; Cambodian troops began fighting Vietnamese.

1970 South Vietnamese and US forces began offensives (Apr. 29–30) against Communist strongholds in Cambodia.

1970 Cambodian government forces under increasing attacks by antigovernment Khmer Rouge and Vietnamese Communists; US air strikes supported government troops.

1970 Cambodian government forces driven out of northeastern provinces by Communists; Premier Lon Nol given wartime powers (June 27).

1970 Republic proclaimed (Oct. 9).

1970 Cambodian and South Vietnamese forces began offensive (Nov. 8) south of Phnom Penh.

1971 South Vietnamese began new offensive (July 8) in Cambodian Parrot's Beak region.

1971 North Vietnamese broke through defenses north of Phnom Penh (Dec. 2).

1972 Lon Nol seized power (Mar. 10); dissolved National Assembly.

1972 Lon Nol elected (June 4) to presidency under new constitution.

1973 Highway 5, last supply route to Phnom Penh, cut (Apr. 4) by Khmer Rouge forces.

1973 Direct US participation in fighting ended (Aug. 15).

1975 Evacuation of American personnel (Apr. 11–12).

1975 Gen. Lon Nol fled Cambodia (Apr. 1) as Khmer Rouge forces closed in.

1975 Cambodian government surrendered (Apr. 17) to Khmer Rouge rebels; rebels, led by Pol Pot, instituted reign of terror; forced populace to leave cities for forced labor in countryside.

1975 Sihanouk named chief of state for life by Khmer Rouge rebels (Apr.).

1975 *Mayaguez* incident (May).

1978 Vietnamese invasion of Cambodia began after series of border incidents.

1979 Phnom Penh captured by Vietnamese-backed insurgents (Jan. 7); Pol Pot regime fell; resistance by Khmer troops continued in some areas.

1982 Sihanouk formed government in exile with Khmer Rouge rebel leaders; Vietnamese forces remained in Cambodia, fighting isolated battles against rebels.

Cambrai, Battle of Inconclusive WW I battle (Nov. 20–Dec. 3, 1917) between the British and Germans. This battle in north France saw the first important tactical deployment of (British) tanks in combat. British losses were 43,000, German 41,000.

Cambrai, League of A short-lived alliance (1508–10) between Holy Roman Emperor Maximilian I, King Ferdinand V of Aragon, King Louis XII of France, and Pope Julius II. The league was formed at Cambrai (Dec. 10, 1508) for the purpose of conquering and dividing up territories of the republic of Venice. The league collapsed (1510), having had only partial success.

Cambrai, Treaty of ⟨Ladies' Peace⟩ ⟨Paix des Dames⟩ Treaty (Aug. 3, 1529) between French king Francis I and Holy Roman Emperor Charles V which briefly halted the Italian Wars (1494–1559). It was negotiated by Francis's mother, Louise of Savoy, and Charles's aunt, Margret of Austria. By its terms, Charles surrendered claims to Burgundy, and Francis gave up claims in Italy. War soon broke out again, lasting until 1559.

Cambridge Agreement Agreement (Aug. 26, 1629) that transferred the government of the Massachusetts Bay Company from England to the Massachusetts colony. Puritan stockholders had refused to make the journey from England to the Massachusetts colony if this condition could not be met.

Cambridge Platform Essentially a constitution for governing New England Congregational churches, adopted Aug., 1648. The platform was approved as a declaration of principles for church government and doctrine at a church synod held in Massachusetts.

Cambridge Platonists Philosophical school that developed (17th cent.) at Cambridge University, England. Founded by Benjamin Whichcote (1609–83), the school arose in reaction to the teachings of T. Hobbes, and attempted to synthesize the teachings of Plato with Christian doctrines.

Cambuluc *See* **Peking**

Cambyses II *d.* 522 BC. Persian king (529–522), successor to his father, Cyrus the Great. He conquered Egypt (525 BC) but was forced to abandon plans for further conquests in Africa by a revolt at home. He died trying to quash the rebellion.

Camden, Battle of British victory (Aug. 16, 1780) over American colonials during the Carolina Campaign *(q.v.)* in the American Revolution (1775–83). One of the greatest disasters in American military history, the defeat led to the British invasion of North Carolina. Lord C. Cornwallis, commanding some 2,200 British regulars, opposed a force of about 3,000 American regulars and new recruits, led by Gen. H. Gates. The Americans, planning to attack the British-held town of Camden, South Carolina, were routed by Cornwallis. Losses were 2,000 Americans (including Gen. J. Kalb) and 324 British.

Camel, Battle of the ⟨Basra, ~⟩ Victory (Dec. 9, 656) for the caliph Ali over his opponents during the First Muslim Civil War (656–661). The rebels, led by Muhammad's widow, Aisha (611–678), his cousin Zobair (d. 656), and his companion Talha (d. 656), took control of Basra, a port city on the Persian Gulf. Ali, commanding some 29,000 soldiers, attacked the larger rebel force and finally captured Aisha.

Camelot Legendary place in England where, according to Arthurian legend, King Arthur had his court. A number of places have been thought to be the actual location of Camelot, among them Cadbury Castle and Caerleon.

Cameronians Scottish religious group. Cameronians were Covenanters and followers of Richard Cameron (d. 1681). They organized as the Reformed Presbyterians after 1681. Most Cameronians united with the Church of Scotland (1876).

Cameroon ⟨*prop.* United Republic of Cameroon⟩ ⟨*formerly* Federal Republic of Cameroon⟩ Republic of west central Africa, independent since 1960. Capital is Yaoundé. German presence in the region began in the late 19th cent., and by 1902 the territory was a German colony. Conquered by the Allies during WW I, it was divided (1919) by League of Nations mandate into French Cameroon and British Cameroon. These territories became (1946) UN trust territories. French Cameroon became independent (1960) and the south half of British Cameroon was joined to it (1961). The north sector was ceded to Nigeria.

Camillus, Marcus Furius *d.* 365? BC. Celebrated Roman general and statesman. He was elected dictator five times between 396 and 367 BC, and prevented the destruction of Rome by the Gauls (c390 BC). He is credited with several other important victories.

Camisards Protestant peasants in southern France who rebelled (1702–10) against persecutions by French Catholics. The revolt followed revocation (1685) of the Edict of Nantes by King Louis XIV and his attempts to impose Catholicism on his subjects. Led by the peasant commander J. Cavalier and others, the Camisards burned Catholic churches and used guerrilla tactics against royal armies. The government retaliated by massacring whole villages. The revolt was broken by 1705, though sporadic fighting continued until 1710.

Camoëns, Luiz Vaz de *See* **Camões, Luiz Vaz de**

Camões, Luiz Vaz de ⟨Camoëns, Luiz Vaz de⟩ 1524–80. Considered the greatest Portuguese poet. He is best known for his epic poem *The Lusiads.*

Camorra Secret society of criminals that flourished (19th cent.) in Naples, Italy. Of uncertain origins, the society was known for its involvement in robbery, smuggling, and blackmail by the early 19th cent. The Camorra operated freely under the Bourbon rulers of Naples and eventually gained considerable political power. Following the unification of Italy (1861), the government began a campaign against the Camorra. Manhunts (from 1882) and a sensational murder trial (1911), involving 20 supposed Camorra members, brought about its decline.

Campanella, Tommaso 1568–1639. Italian philosopher and Dominican monk. Imprisoned for 27 years during the Inquisition, he is best known for his work *The City of the Sun*. An account of a utopian society, it parallels Plato's *Republic*.

Campania Historic region in southern Italy noted for its productive farms. Once held by Etruscans and Greek colonists, the region came under Roman control in 340 BC. After the fall of Rome, it changed hands several times, becoming part of the kingdom of Naples (1282) and finally Italy (1861). Among the famous ancient cities in this region were Pompeii, Capua, and Cumae.

Campbell, Archibald, 8th earl and 1st marquess of Argyll 1607–61. Scottish nobleman. A leader of the Covenanters during the English Civil War, he was defeated by J. Montrose (1645). He then supported Charles II, and, in 1652, submitted to Cromwell and the Commonwealth. He was beheaded for treason during the Restoration.

Campbell, Archibald, 9th earl of Argyll 1629–85. Scottish nobleman. A Royalist during the English Civil War, he fled to Holland (1681). He later returned to take part in the Duke of Monmouth's rebellion (1685).

Campbell, John, 1st earl of Breadalbane 1635–1716. Scottish nobleman. He is said to have taken part in organizing the massacre of the MacDonald clan at Glencoe (1692).

Campbell, John, 2d duke of Argyll and duke of Greenwich 1678–1743. Scottish general. Campbell supported the union of England and Scotland, served in the War of Spanish Succession (1701–14), supported George I's accession to the throne, and quelled the Jacobite revolt of 1715.

Campbell-Bannerman, Sir Henry 1836–1908. A British statesman. He became Liberal party leader (1899) and British prime minister (1905–08). An opponent of the Boer War, he is noted for permitting self-government for the defeated Orange Free State and Transvaal (1906–07).

Campbellites *See* **Disciples of Christ**

Campion, Edmund 1540–81. English Jesuit martyr. He was arrested and tortured after distributing a pamphlet, titled *Ten Reasons* (1581), denouncing the Anglican church. He was executed on spurious charges of treason after he refused to recant.

Campi Raudii *See* **Cimbri**

Campo Formio, Treaty of Treaty (Oct. 17, 1797) between France and Austria ending the War of the First Coalition during the French Revolutionary Wars (1792–1802). The treaty, which marked Napoleon's victory over Austria, was signed at the village of Campo Formio in northern Italy, following the preliminary Peace of Loeben (Apr. 18, 1797). By its terms, France won the Belgian provinces, Lombardy, and the Ionian Islands. Austria received most of the republic of Venice, including the city of Venice, Istria, and Dalmatia.

Camus, Albert 1913–60. French author, one of the major writers of this century. Among his best-known works are *The Stranger* and *The Plague*. He won the Nobel Prize in literature in 1957.

Canaan Biblical name for ancient Palestine. In the Old Testament it was the Israelites' promised land. Following their exodus from Egypt, the Israelites conquered and settled this region.

Canada Country located in the northern part of North America. Its capital is Ottawa. Canada was explored and settled by both English and French and its history reflects the influence of both nations, as well as the struggle of French- and English-speaking Canadians to overcome their differences. Canada was threatened by invasion from the US during the American Revolution and again during the War of 1812, but since that time has had peaceful and friendly relations with the US. Created by the unification of 4 provinces in 1867, Canada has grown into a federation of 10 provinces. Key dates in the history of Canada include:

1000 Leif Ericsson, Norse explorer, believed to have landed somewhere on Canadian coast.

1497 J. Cabot explored Nova Scotia and Newfoundland.

1534–35 J. Cartier discovered Gulf of St. Lawrence, St. Lawrence River; established French claims to the area.

1583 England discovered and claimed Newfoundland.

1605 Port Royal, first permanent settlement in Canada, founded by S. de Champlain; French colony of Acadia established in following years.

1608 S. de Champlain founded Quebec.

1629–32 English took Quebec (1629); it was returned to France in 1632; fur trade exploited in subsequent years.

1663 French government dissolved Company of New France and assumed rule of French territories in Canada.

1670 Hudson's Bay Company formed by English for colonization and trade in Canada; was prominent in the early development of Canada.

1689–97 King William's War; French and English launched attacks on each other's settlements in Canada; began series of wars for control of North American colonies.

1696   France defeated the Iroquois Confederacy.

1702–13   Queen Anne's War; British captured Port Royal and other French territories.

1713   Britain acquired most of Acadia, Newfoundland, and territory around Hudson Bay through Peace of Utrecht.

1744–48   King George's War.

1755   Many French Acadians deported by British for refusing oath of loyalty to the king.

1756–63   French and Indian War fought; British defeated French on Plains of Abraham (1759) and took Quebec; Montreal fell to British (1760); conflict ended by Treaty of Paris (1763), by which all French territory in Canada passed to Britain.

1774   Quebec Act passed (June 22) by British Parliament; established permanent government in Canada, granted concessions to French-speaking people of Quebec.

1775–83   Canada remained loyal to the king during the American Revolution; Quebec later became a haven for Loyalists fleeing the US after the Revolution.

1783   North West Company founded for Canadian fur trade; later rivaled Hudson's Bay Company.

1791   Constitutional Act divided Quebec into English-speaking Upper Canada (now Ontario) and French-speaking Lower Canada (now Quebec).

1812–15   War of 1812 between the US and Britain; several invasions of Canada repulsed.

1818   Convention of 1818 established Canadian-US border.

1821   North West Company merged with Hudson's Bay Company, ending bitter competition and some violence.

1837   Unsuccessful attempt to overthrow the government by W. L. Mackenzie and some 800 followers; Mackenzie's escape to the US resulted in the *Caroline* Affair.

1839   Lord Durham's Report to British Parliament; following revolts in both Upper and Lower Canada for reform, Lord Durham investigated and recommended union of the provinces and establishment of effective government.

1841   Upper and Lower Canada united.

1846   Dispute with US over Canada's boundary in the Oregon Country settled.

1848–51   Clear Grits movement.

1854   Clergy Reserves secularized after long controversy.

1864   Charlottetown Conference held to discuss unification of all Canadian provinces.

1864   Quebec Conference held (Oct. 10–27) by delegates from provinces of British North America; drafted resolutions that were the basis for establishment of unified Canada.

1866–67   Westminster Conference in London laid basis for British North America Act.

1867   British North America Act; provinces of Quebec, Ontario, Nova Scotia, and New Brunswick unified and became the dominion of Canada.

1867–73   Sir J.A. Macdonald served as first prime minister; guided nation through crucial early years.

1867   Canada First Movement organized to promote Canadian nationalist spirit.

1869–70   Riel's Rebellion in western Canada against government.

1870   Red River Settlement joined Canada as province of Manitoba.

1873   Prince Edward Island became Canadian province.

1873   Pacific scandal helped bring down J. Macdonald's Conservative government.

1873–96   Long economic depression.

1878–91   Macdonald back in office as prime minister; instituted policy of trade protectionism to ease effects of depression; began construction of Canadian Pacific Railway.

1884–85   Riel's Rebellion in Saskatchewan against government.

1885   Canadian Pacific Railway completed; east and west coasts linked by rail.

1888   Jesuit Estates Act passed.

1890s   European immigrants began arriving in large numbers.

1896–1911   Sir W. Laurier served as first French-Canadian prime minister; wheat-producing Prairie provinces settled; economic prosperity restored.

1897   Great Klondike gold rush began.

1905   Alberta and Saskatchewan became provinces of Canada.

1911–20   Sir R. Borden served as prime minister; won independent representation for British dominions in the League of Nations (1919).

1914–18   WW I; Canada joined Allies and actively participated in war effort.

1921–30   W.L. Mackenzie King served as prime minister.

1930–40   Cooperative Commonwealth Federation, Canadian Socialist party, and Social Credit movement gained support during the Depression.

1931   British Commonwealth of Nations created; Canada gained equal status with Britain and other members of the Commonwealth; Canadian autonomy formalized.

1935–48 Mackenzie King back in office as prime minister.

1939–45 WW II; Canada joined Allies and played an active role in the war effort.

1949 Newfoundland became Canadian province.

1949 Canada became founding member of NATO.

1957–63 John G. Diefenbaker served as prime minister; brought Conservatives to power for first time since 1930s.

1959 St. Lawrence Seaway opened.

1960s French separatist movement in Quebec became major political controversy.

1963–68 Lester Pearson served as prime minister; Liberals returned to power.

1968–79 Prime Minister P. Trudeau in office; a Liberal and French-Canadian, he faced a worsening crisis over French separatism in Quebec; favored bilingualism, opposed separatism.

1970 Diplomatic relations with China established.

1970 Trudeau utilized (Oct. 16) War Measures Act to halt kidnappings by French-Canadian separatists.

1975 Prime Minister Trudeau imposed wage and price controls (1975–78) in the face of worsening economic problems.

1979 Economic problems forced Prime Minister Trudeau to dissolve Parliament (Mar. 26) and call for new elections.

1979–80 Joe Clark (Progressive Conservative) became prime minister after defeating Trudeau's Liberal faction in the elections.

1980 Trudeau restored to office of prime minister, succeeding Clark.

1980 Referendum to implement Quebec separatism defeated (June) in Quebec provincial vote; serious threat to Canadian unity averted.

1982 Constitution Act signed by Queen Elizabeth (Apr. 17); provided for legal autonomy of Canada and replaced the British North America Act as the instrument of Canadian government; Canada to remain in Commonwealth and to continue to recognize British monarch.

Canada Company British land company. At the instigation of author J. Galt, the company was organized (1826) to generate revenue to compensate settlers' losses arising from the War of 1812. The company sold government lands in northern Canada and helped promote colonization there.

Canary Islands Seven islands in the Atlantic Ocean off the northwest coast of Africa (pop. 1,275,000) which now make up two provinces of Spain. Once called the Fortunate Isles, they have long been a stopping place for travelers from many parts of the world. In 1402, they were settled by the Spanish kingdom of Castile, and they have remained under Spanish control since then.

Canaveral, Cape US space-program center and principal launch point for US rockets into outer space. Used for rocket testing since 1950, it was the launch site for the first US space satellite (Jan. 31, 1958), the first US manned space flight (May 5, 1961), and the Apollo program (q.v.) moon landing (July 20, 1969).

Candragupta See **Chandragupta**

Cannae, Battle of Great Carthaginian victory (216 BC) over the Romans during the Second Punic War (218–201 BC). The Carthaginians, led by Hannibal, encircled and decimated a Roman army of some 85,000 men, led by consuls Gaius Terentius Varro and Lucius Aemilius Paulus, near the village of Cannae, in what is now southeast Italy. Roman losses were over 50,000; Carthaginian, fewer than 6,000.

Cannon, Joseph Gurney 1836–1926. American politician. A Republican congressman for 46 years between 1873 and 1923, he wielded almost complete control over the House during his term as its Speaker (1903–11).

Cano, Juan Sebastián del d. 1526. Spanish navigator. He took command of and completed Magellan's exploratory voyage of 1519, following Magellan's death in the Philippines (1521). He thus became the first man to circumnavigate the earth (1522).

canon law System of regulations for governing the clergy and the church. The Roman Catholic church, the Eastern Orthodox church, the Anglican churches, and independent Eastern Christian churches all have accumulated bodies of canon law. The Roman Catholic canon law is by far the most extensive. It includes laws issued by popes, ecclesiastical councils, and bishops (for local matters). Canon law can be traced back to the early papal decretals (1st cent. AD). The subsequent profusion of canon laws led to efforts at systemizing them, as in Gratian's works, the corpus of canon law (*Corpus juris canonici*, 1580) and the code of canon law (*Codex juris canonici*, 1917). Canon laws of the Church of England, known as the Constitutions and Canons Ecclesiastical, were issued 1603–04. (For canon law of the Eastern churches, *see* Oriental canon law.)

canon law, Oriental See **Oriental canon law**

Canopus, Decree of See **Decree of Canopus**

Cánovas del Castillo, Antonio 1828–97. Spanish politician and historian. Cánovas was instrumental in restoring Bourbon king Alfonso XII to the throne (1875), and subsequently served as premier intermittently between 1875 and 1897.

Canterbury City and borough in southeast England and the ecclesiastical center of England. It has been an important city since Saint Augustine's mission to the British Isles, when he built a cathedral there (602). The church has since been rebuilt several times. From the time of Thomas à Becket's murder (1170) to the 16th cent., Canterbury was the site of numerous pilgrimages in his honor.

Canterbury, Saint Augustine of *See* **Augustine of Canterbury, Saint**

canton Term for a constituent state in the Swiss Confederation.

Canton Chinese port city (pop. 5,200,000), an important trading and industrial center. The city became part of the Chinese Empire in 3d cent. AD and the first port opened to European trade (16th cent.). It remained China's only port of foreign trade until 1842. It was the seat of the nationalist rebellion (1911) and was occupied by the Japanese (1938–45) in WW II. Canton was seized (1949) by the Communists, who undertook the modernization and development of the city.

Canton Commune The short-lived government formed by the Chinese Communist party in opposition to Kuomintang *(q.v.)* efforts to suppress them. The Communists captured Canton (Dec., 1927), with much bloodshed, but were quickly and ruthlessly suppressed.

Canton system Chinese trade system. From 1759 until the Treaty of Nanking (1842), foreign merchants were allowed to conduct their trade with China only in the city of Canton and were forced to deal with approved merchants (the Cohong).

Canute ⟨Cnut⟩ ⟨Knut⟩ c995–1035. Danish king of England (1016–35), Denmark (1019–35), and Norway (1028–35). He invaded England (1015), conquered Wessex and Northumbria, and, after pitched battles, divided England with Edmund Ironside. Following Edmund's death (1016), he became sole ruler, and administered his kingdom wisely. He married Aethelred's widow, Emma, and by her had his son Harthacanute. He succeeded his brother to the Danish throne (1019), and, after defeating a Norwegian invasion of Denmark (1026), he conquered Norway (1028).

Canute IV ⟨~ the Saint⟩ *d.* 1086. Danish king (1080–86). Canute built many churches and cathedrals, and attempted an invasion of England (1085). He was killed by rioters who were enraged over taxes he imposed.

Canute the Saint *See* **Canute IV**

Cape Frontier Wars ⟨Frontier Wars⟩ ⟨Kafir Wars⟩ Series of wars fought in the 18th and 19th cents. by Dutch, and later British, settlers against natives in South Africa. The major conflict occurred (1850–53) after the British annexed territory to the east of Cape Colony and established British Kaffraria there. The Xhosa were defeated and several years later suffered a famine. Renewed resistance by the Xhosa led to the last Kafir war (1877–78) and their final defeat. In the years following, their territories were absorbed by the Cape Colony.

Cape of Good Hope Cape at the southern tip of Africa, notorious among sailors for heavy seas. First rounded (1488) by Bartholomeu Diaz (1450?–1500). It was an important landmark on the sea trade route between Europe and the East. The cape itself was colonized by the Dutch (1652), passed to the British (1806), and was made part of South Africa (1910).

Čapek, Karel 1890–1938. Czech playwright, novelist, and essayist. He is best remembered for his play *R.U.R., (Rossum's Universal Robots)* from which the term "robot" derives.

Capellari, Bartolomeo Alberto *See* **Gregory XVI**

Cape St. Vincent, Battle of Naval battle (Feb. 14, 1797) off the coast of southern Portugal during the French Revolutionary Wars (1792–1802). The British forces, commanded by Sir John Jervis (1735–1823), defeated a Spanish fleet of almost twice as many ships, which were to have joined the French in an invasion of Britain.

Capet, Hugh *See* **Hugh Capet**

Capetians Dynasty of kings that ruled in France from 987 to 1328. The Capetians were descendants of Robert the Strong (*d.* 866), count of Anjou and Blois, and the first Capetian king was Hugh Capet. He replaced the last Carolingian king in 987, and at that time ruled only a small kingdom around Paris. His successors, however, gradually absorbed the surrounding kingdoms and increased the power of the monarchy, thereby laying the foundations of modern France. The Capetians were succeeded by the collateral lines of Valois and Bourbon. The Capetian kings were:

Hugh Capet	987–996
Robert II	996–1031
Henry I	1031–60
Philip I	1060–1108
Louis VI	1108–37
Louis VII	1137–80
Philip II	1180–1223
Louis VIII	1223–26
Louis IX	1226–70
Philip III	1270–85
Philip IV	1285–1314
Louis X	1314–16
John I	1316
Philip V	1317–22
Charles IV	1322–28

capitalism Economic system in which property, means of production, and financial institutions are privately owned and which is driven by the profit motive. Theoretically based on free enterprise and unregulated competition, capitalism can be traced back to the 16th cent., when mercantilism rose to replace feudalism. Capitalism flourished, however, with the coming of the Industrial Revolution (18th cent.) and spawned such notable capitalist theoreticians as A. Smith. Social inequities and theoretical weaknesses perceived by K. Marx gave rise to socialism in the 19th cent. By the 20th cent., the archetypal capitalistic notion of unregulated enterprise (never fully realized) had given way to a host of social reforms and regulatory bodies imposed by national governments.

Capitol *See* **Capitoline Hill**

Capitol Domed building in Washington, D.C., that houses the US Senate and House of Representatives. It is the symbolic center of the federal government. Begun in 1793 from plans submitted by W. Thornton, the unfinished building was burned by the British (1814) during the War of 1812. Work on it began again that year and was finally completed (1830) by C. Bulfinch, the sixth architect involved in its construction. It was subsequently enlarged (1851–65) by Thomas U. Walter (1804–87).

Capitoline Hill ⟨Capitol⟩ One of the seven hills of Rome and the historic center of the city. It is the site of the temple of Jupiter Capitolinus and the Tarpeian Rock, from which criminals were thrown to their death.

capitulations Economic concessions granted by the Ottoman empire to friendly European states. The practice was abolished (1914) on the eve of WW I. Restored after the war, they were again abolished by the Treaty of Lausanne (July, 1923).

Capo d'Istria, Count Giovanni Antonio *See* **Kapodistrias, Count Ioannes Antonios**

Capone, Alfonse 1899–1947. Notorious American gangster. He was the leader of Chicago's organized crime underworld form the mid-1920s to 1931, when he was convicted of federal income tax evasion. He subsequently died of an advanced case of syphilis.

Caporetto, Battle of ⟨Isonzo, Battle of⟩ Austro-German victory (Oct. 24, 1917) over the Italians during WW I. The battle was a major disaster for the Italians and resulted in reorganization of the army and formation of the Supreme Allied War Council for coordinating the war effort. Fifteen combined Austrian and German divisions, under German general Otto von Below (1857–1944), attacked Italian forces on the Isonzo line at Caporetto (then) in northeast Italy. Italian forces retreated some 70 miles (Oct. 24–Nov. 7), by which time some 300–600,000 Italians had been lost as casualties, prisoners, or deserters.

Capote, Truman 1924–. Noted American author. Among his novels are *Other Voices, Other Rooms* and *In Cold Blood*, a work he called a nonfiction novel.

Cappadocia Ancient region now located in eastern Turkey. Once a satrapy of Persia (*c*6th cent. BC), it evolved into an independent kingdom (3d cent. BC). Henceforth it became an ally of the Romans and finally a province (AD 17).

Captivity *See* **Babylonian Captivity**

Capua Town in southern Italy and once a prosperous city of ancient Rome. Originally an Etruscan town, it fell to the Romans (*c*340 BC) and prospered following the construction of the Appian Way. The scene of Spartacus' revolt (73 BC), it was destroyed by the Vandals (AD 456) and the Muslims (840). The modern city was built in 856 and was subsequently the scene of many battles, including heavy fighting during WW II (1943).

Capuchins Roman Catholic order of Franciscan monks, properly the Friars Minor Capuchin. The order was established (*c*1525) in Italy by Matteo da Bascio (*c*1495–1552) as a movement for reform of the Catholic church. Its friars were expected to live a life of poverty. The movement became widespread, and in subsequent years they rivaled the Jesuits in importance within the church.

Carabobo, Battle of Battle (June 24, 1821) in northern Venezuela that established Venezuelan independence from Spain. A combined force of 6,500 rebels under S. Bolívar and J. Paez attacked and crushed a smaller Spanish force, led by Gen. Miguel de la Torre. Soon afterward, Bolívar liberated the capital, Caracas.

Caracalla ⟨Marcus Aurelius Antoninus⟩ AD 188–217. Roman emperor (AD 211–217), notorious for his ruthless brutality. He and his brother Geta succeeded their father, Septimius Severus. Caracalla, however, killed Geta and ordered a massacre of some 20,000 of his brother's followers (AD 212). He also granted citizenship to all free men within the empire in order, it is believed, to increase tax revenues.

Caracas Venezuelan capital city (pop. 2,800,000). Founded (1567) by the Spanish, it became a prosperous city in Spain's American colonies. The revolution for Latin American independence from Spain began (1810) in the city and Venezuela's independence from Spain was declared there (July 5, 1811). The city passed between rebel and Spanish control until S. Bolívar took Caracas for the last time in 1821, after which it became the capital of Venezuela.

Caractacus ⟨Caratacus⟩ ⟨Caradoc⟩ *fl.* AD 50. British chieftain, a son of Cymbeline. He led the British against Roman invaders (AD 43–50) but was finally defeated and captured by Emperor Claudius' forces.

Caradoc *See* **Caractacus**

Carafa, Gian Pietro *See* **Paul IV**

Caratacus *See* **Caractacus**

Carausius, Marcus Aurelius 245?–293. Roman general. Placed in command of a Roman fleet in Gaul, he revolted and set himself up as emperor in Britain (c287–293). He was killed by one of his ministers during an invasion ordered by Roman emperor Maximian.

Caravaggio ⟨Michelangelo Merisi⟩ 1573–1610. Italian artist who influenced the development of baroque art through his naturalistic paintings. His noted works include *Death of the Virgin* and the *Fortune Teller.*

Carbonari Italian secret society formed in the kingdom of Naples in the early 19th cent. Carbonari groups came to stand for freedom from foreign rule. The lodges first appeared during, and soon opposed, the reign of J. Murat (1808–15), the Neapolitan king installed by Napoleon. The lodges spread throughout Italy and, in the post-Napoleonic years, opposed Austrian domination. By 1830, however, the Carbonari were drawn into the movement for Italian unification, the Risorgimento, and disappeared. In the 1820s, Carbonari lodges were also active in Spain and France.

Carchemish, Battle of Battle (605 BC) in which Babylonian king Nebuchadnezzar defeated the Egyptian king Necho II along the Euphrates River, in what is now Syria. The defeat cost Egypt its territories in Syria.

Cárdenas, Garcia López de *See* **Coronado, Francisco Vásquez de**

Cárdenas, Lázaro 1895–1970. Mexican soldier and president (1934–40). Cardenas fought in the 1913 revolution, and, as president, he aroused much opposition by nationalizing foreign-owned properties (including oil fields) and by breaking up large estates to give land to small farmers. The latter reform established government-owned communal farms (the Ejido system).

Cardigan, James Thomas Brudenell, 7th earl of 1797–1868. British general during the Crimean War (1853–56). He led the now famous charge of the Light Brigade at the Battle of Balaklava (1854). The disastrous cavalry maneuver is said to have been caused by a mixup in orders.

cardinal In the Roman Catholic church, an ecclesiastical rank second only to the pope. Cardinals act as advisers to and emissaries of the pope and, as members of the Sacred College of Cardinals, elect the pope.

Cardozo, Benjamin Nathan 1870–1938. American jurist and associate justice of the US Supreme Court (1932–38). He was an influential jurist, whose wide reputation stemmed from his term as a New York State appeals court judge (1914–28) and his books on jurisprudence.

Carelton, Guy, 1st Baron Dorchester 1724–1808. British general and governor of Quebec four times between 1766 and 1796. Commander of British troops in Canada during the American Revolution, he defeated the Americans during the Quebec Campaign (1775–76). He became commander of British forces in America and served to the end of the Revolution (1782–83).

Carlisle Commission ⟨Peace Commission of 1778⟩ British peace overture during the American Revolution (1775–83). Surprised by their defeat at Saratoga (1777), the British sent F. Howard, 5th earl of Carlisle, to America to offer the colonials a negotiated settlement. On June 17, however, the Continental Congress responded by demanding complete independence and withdrawal of all British forces, and thus rejected the British peace offer.

Carlism *See* **Carlists**

Carlists Supporters of Don Carlos (1788–1855) and his descendants as rightful heirs to the Spanish throne (after 1833). Carlists represented a conservative element in support of traditional monarchy and the church, and, though greatly diminished in number, they continue to be a factor in rural Spain. The movement known as Carlism began when Don Carlos claimed the throne on the death of his brother, King Ferdinand VII, by the terms of the Salic Law. Ferdinand, however, had set aside (1832) the Salic Law to ensure succession of his daughter, Isabella II. Ferdinand's death thus provoked the Carlist Wars (1833–39, 1873–76) and other lesser Carlist uprisings. The direct line of Carlist claimants ended in 1936, though Carlists supported Don Juan (1913–), son of Alfonso XIII, as his successor. Don Juan's son, Juan Carlos, became king of Spain on Gen. F. Franco's death (1975).

Carlist Wars **1.** Civil War (1833–39) in Spain, the Carlists' rebellion against the government of Queen Isabella II. Supporters of Don Carlos, a rival claimant to the throne, rebelled soon after the accession of Isabella. Their strength lay in northern rural Spain, especially the Basque Provinces and Navarre, Aragon, and Catalonia, where opposition to a liberalized and centralized monarchy was strongest. The Carlists' attempt to capture Madrid failed (1837), however, and after a mutiny, the Carlist commander joined (1839) Gen. B. Espartero, commander of government forces. The war ended with the Convention of Vegara and Don Carlos' departure from Spain. **2.** Civil war (1873–76) in Spain, a rebellion by Carlists against the newly formed republic. Following abdication of King Amadeus and creation of the republic (1873), Carlists in northern Spain again rebelled. The bloody war involved the Basque Provinces and Catalonia, Aragon, and Valencia, and ended (1876) when Don Carlos VII (1848–1909) fled Spain.

Carloman 751–771. Co-ruler of the kingdom of the Franks (768–71), successor, with his brother Charlemagne, to their father, Pepin the Short. Carloman ruled the eastern half of the kingdom, which, on his death, was seized by Charlemagne.

Carloman 828–880. German king (876–880), son of Louis the German. He was king of Bavaria and Carinthia, and of Italy (877–80), but he failed in his claim to the crown of the Holy Roman Empire.

Carloman d. 884. Co-ruler (879–882) of the West Frankish Kingdom. With his brother Louis III, he succeeded his father, King Louis II (the Stammerer), and became sole ruler on his brother's death (882).

Carlos *See also* **Charles**

Carlos VII *See* **Carlist Wars**

Carlos, Don *See* **Carlists**

Carlos de Austria, Don 1545–68. Spanish prince and son of King Philip II. Accused of conspiring to murder his father, he was tried and died soon afterward in prison. His father was rumored to have murdered him. He is the subject of Schiller's tragedy *Don Carlos.*

Carlotta 1840–1927. Empress of Mexico (1864–67), the wife of Maximilian from 1857. She was sent to Europe (1866) to seek aid for the fight against republican revolutionaries then opposing her husband. She failed, became insane, and was confined in Belgium.

Carlowitz, Treaty of *See* **Karlowitz, Treaty of**

Carlsbad Congress *See* **Carlsbad Decrees**

Carlsbad Decrees (Karlsbad ~) Measures recommended (Aug. 31, 1819) by German ministers for suppression of liberal agitation within the German Confederation. The ministers met at the Carlsbad Congress, convened (Aug. 6) by C. von Metternich, following the murder of the German writer August von Kotzebue (1761–1819) by a student. They resolved on press censorship, supervision of universities to suppress liberal student organizations, and establishment of a central committee to investigate revolutionary conspiracies. The measures failed to check the growth of liberalism.

Carlson, Evans Fordyce 1896–1947. American soldier, WW II leader of "Carlson's Raiders," a guerrilla unit famous for attacks (1942) on Makin Island and Guadalcanal.

Carlyle, Thomas 1795–1881. Scottish essayist and historian, one of the most influential social critics of his day. He gave up teaching in 1819 and, after publishing works on the German romantics, wrote *Sartor Resartus,* in which he established his characteristic literary style. He moved to London (1834) and there wrote his great *French Revolution* and other works, including *Chartism,* and *History of Frederick the Great.*

Carman, William Bliss *See* **Confederation group**

Carmathians *See* **Karmathians**

Carmelites One of the four important Roman Catholic orders of mendicant friars. The order was begun (c1155) by a group of European hermits under Saint Berthold on Mount Carmel in Palestine. Approved 1226 by Pope Honorius III, the order moved to Europe after the crusaders were forced out of the Holy Land. There the Carmelites abandoned (13th cent.) hermitism and became mendicant friars. A movement to return to a more rigorously ascetic existence was begun (1562) by Saint Theresa and Saint John of the Cross. In 1593 it became the independent order of Discalced Carmelites.

Carmona, António Oscar de Fragoso 1869–51. Portuguese president (1926–51). A general, he took part in the military coup of 1926 and became president of the provisional government that year. He was subsequently elected president and established, with A. Salazar as premier, dictatorial control of Portugal.

Carnap, Rudolf 1891–1970. A German-born American philosopher. He is noted as a leading advocate of logical positivism and for his works on the philosophy of language, including *The Logical Syntax of Language, Logical Foundations of Probability,* and *Introduction to Symbolic Logic and Its Applications.*

Carnegie, Andrew 1835–1919. Scottish-born American steel magnate and philanthropist. Between 1873 and 1900 he built the Carnegie Steel Company into one of the country's largest steel manufacturing concerns. Following its sale to US Steel Corporation (1901), he turned to philanthropy and endowed numerous libraries and educational institutions.

Carnot, Lazare Nicolas Marguerite 1753–1823. French revolutionary. He was known as the "Organizer of Victory" for his skills at organizing and directing the army during the French Revolutionary Wars. He was a member of the Committee of Public Safety and the Directory, and served in various posts under Napoleon.

Carnot, Marie François Sadi 1837–94. French president of the Third Republic (1887–94). His term was marked by troubles with G. Boulanger and the Panama Scandal (1892). He was assassinated by an Italian anarchist.

Carnot, Nicolas Léonard Sadi 1796–1832. French physicist, son of L. Carnot. A pioneer in the science of thermodynamics, he is sometimes referred to as a founder of that field.

Caro, Joseph ben Ephraim ⟨Karo, ~⟩ 1483–1575. Jewish scholar, an authority on the Talmud. He wrote *Shulhan Aruk*, an important codification of Jewish law and customs.

Carol I 1839–1914. German prince and first Romanian king (1881–1914). He won Romania's independence from the Ottoman Turks at the Congress of Berlin (1878) and, on becoming king, instituted programs to modernize the country.

Carol II 1893–1953. Romanian king (1930–40), successor to his son, Michael. After renouncing his right of succession (1925), he returned to Romania (1930), ousted his son, and had himself proclaimed king. He contested attempts by the fascist Iron Guard to take control after 1938 but was forced to abdicate in 1940.

Carolina campaign British campaign (1780–81) to subdue the Carolinas during the American Revolution. A military failure, the campaign contributed to the subsequent final British defeat (1781) at Yorktown (*q.v.*). After the capture (May, 1780) of Charleston, South Carolina, by Sir H. Clinton, British forces under Gen. C. Cornwallis moved north. At Camden, South Carolina, they routed (Aug. 16) Colonial forces under Gen. H. Gates. Gates retreated to North Carolina, but Cornwallis was defeated (Oct. 7) by guerrillas in the Battle of King's Mountain. Gates was replaced as commander in the South by Gen. N. Greene. The British suffered another defeat in the Battle of Cowpens (Jan. 17, 1781), but gained a nominal victory (Mar. 15, 1781) at Guilford Courthouse, and a victory (Sept. 8) at Eutaw Springs. Nonetheless, Cornwallis was obliged to retreat to Charleston and afterward shifted fighting to Virginia, thus setting the stage for the Yorktown campaign.

***Caroline* Affair** Destruction (Dec. 29, 1837) of an American vessel by Canadian forces during their effort to quash a rebellion by W. Mackenzie. Mackenzie and his rebels, opposed to Britain's planned union of Upper and Lower Canada, had retreated to Navy Island in the Niagara River. They were being supplied by American sympathizers via the steamer *Caroline*. On Dec. 29, Ca-

nadian forces crossed into US territory and destroyed the *Caroline*, killing one American. The incident resulted in counterthreats of war by both the US and British governments.

Caroline of Brunswick 1768–1821. Wife of English king George IV. She married George (1795) while he was still a prince, but by the next year the two were separated. She fought successfully George's attempt to end the marriage by divorce, but was nevertheless barred from the coronation. She died a few weeks later.

Carolingians Dynasty of Frankish kings that ruled the Carolingian Empire and successor states until the 10th cent. The line was founded by Pepin of Landen (*d.* 640), who was mayor of the palace of Austrasia for the Merovingian king Dagobert I. Succeeding generations continued to rule as mayors of the palace, though they in fact had the power of kings. It was not until Pepin the Short deposed (751) the last Merovingian that the Carolingians took the title of king. Pepin's son, Charlemagne, vastly expanded Austrasia and created the Carolingian Empire. Shortly after Charlemagne's death, the empire was divided (843) among his three sons into the west, the east, and Francia Media. By 870 almost all of Francia Media had been absorbed by the east and west empires and the Carolingian family was clearly divided into French and German lines.

Carolingian Mayors of the Palace

Pepin of Landen	628–640
Pepin of Heristal	687–714
Charles Martel	715–741
Carloman (with Pepin)	741–747
Pepin the Short	741–751

Imperial Kings of the Empire

Pepin the Short	751–768
Charlemagne	768–814
Louis I	814–840
Lothair I (title only)	840–855
Louis II (title only)	855–875
Charles II the Bald (title only)	875–877

Carondelet, Francisco Luis Hector, baron de c1748–1807. Spanish colonial governor of Louisiana and West Florida (1791–95). He is noted for having strained relations between the US and Spain by forming alliances with Indians against the US. He also attempted to stir up separatist movements among Kentucky frontiersmen.

Carpenter, Malcolm Scott 1925–. American astronaut. Carpenter was the second American to orbit the earth (May 24, 1962).

carpetbagger In the US South during Reconstruction (1865–77), a derisive term for politicians and adventurers from the North. Carpetbaggers were generally believed to have moved south after the Civil War (with no more possessions than fitted into a carpetbag) to take advantage of newly enfranchised Negro voters. Many northerners who went south did so to help Negros through the transition from slavery to freedom. However, numerous unscrupulous opportunists among them helped corrupt Reconstruction governments in the South.

Carpocrates *See* **Carpocratians**

Carpocratians Gnostic sect founded 2d cent. AD by the Alexandrian philosopher Carpocrates. Carpocratians rejected the divinity of Jesus and believed that all men had once been united with God. They were notorious libertines who argued that religious regulations only hindered them in attaining spiritual perfection. The sect survived to the 6th cent. AD.

Carranza, Venustiano 1859–1920. Mexican revolutionary and political leader. Carranza joined F. Madero in his revolt (1910) against P. Díaz, and then fought V. Huerta when he overthrew Madero (1913). Carranza headed the provisional government (1914–17) and during this time successfully countered uprisings by F. Villa and E. Zapata. He accepted the constitution of 1917, served as president (1917–20), and was killed after trying to prevent A. Obregón from taking office as president.

Carrera, Rafael 1814–65. Guatemalan revolutionist and dictator (1840–65). He brought the Central American Federation to an end by declaring Guatemala's independence (1838), reestablished the power of the church in Guatemala, and dominated the affairs of other Central American states.

Carrhae, Battle of Parthian victory (53 BC) over Roman invaders in what is now southern Turkey. During the wars of the First Triumvirate, Crassus invaded Parthia with a large army. His force was routed and he was killed, leaving Pompey the effective ruler of Rome.

Carrick's Ford, Battle of Union Victory (July 14, 1861) in West Virginia during the early skirmishes of the American Civil War (1861–65).

Carroll, Lewis (*pseud. of* Dodgson, Charles Lutwidge) 1832–98. English writer, mathematician. He is best known as the author of two famous children's books, *Alice's Adventures in Wonderland* and *Through the Looking Glass.*

Carson, Kit (*prop.* Christopher) 1809–68. Celebrated American frontiersman. Carson first won notoriety as a guide on J. Fremont's exploratory treks through the West (1842–45). He became a noted Indian fighter and later an Indian agent in the Southwest.

Cartagena Spanish port city (pop. 146,900) and major naval base. Founded (243 BC) by Carthaginian general Hasdrubal, it became the center of Carthaginian power in Spain and later flourished under Roman control (from 209 BC). It was held by the Moors until conquest by the Spanish Christians (13 cent.), and was developed into a major naval base by Spanish king Philip II (16th cent.).

cartel An agreement among manufacturers and suppliers of similar products to fix prices, limit supplies, and otherwise manipulate a market in order to increase profits. A cartel may be either domestic or international in scope. Cartels were important in Germany from the late 19th cent., and especially after WW I. (For domestic cartels in the US, *see* trust.)

Carter, James Earl *See* **Carter, Jimmy**

Carter, Jimmy ⟨Carter, James Earl⟩ 1924–. Thirty-ninth president of the US (1977–81). An Annapolis graduate and navy officer, he was a moderately liberal Georgia legislator (1962–66), and was elected governor of Georgia in 1970. Although almost unknown nationally and without major backing, he managed by a brilliant grassroots campaign to defeat Republican G. Ford handily in the 1976 presidential election. President Carter tried to project a populist image as president and to add the common touch to the presidency. His major achievement in office was perhaps the personally negotiated Camp David accords that led to the 1979 peace treaty between Egypt and Israel, ending a state of war lasting over 30 years. Important events during the Carter administration included the return of the Panama Canal *(q.v.)* to Panama, the continuing "energy crisis" brought about by the decision of the OPEC nations to raise oil prices (from 1974), the "nuclear accident" caused when radioactive gases escaped from the Three Mile Island plant in Pennsylvania (1978), and the Soviet invasion of Afghanistan (1979), which prompted President Carter to embargo grain and technology exports to Russia and call for US withdrawal from the Moscow Olympic games. He was criticized for his handling of the Hostage Crisis *(q.v.)* and US Mideast policy suffered as a result of this incident and the Iranian revolution that spawned it. These stresses of the late 1970s, combined with a deteriorating economy, contributed to Carter's defeat on Nov. 4, 1980, by R. Reagan.

Carteret, Philip 1639–82. English colonial governor, the first governor of New Jersey (1665–76). He became governor of East New Jersey (1676–82) after the colony was divided.

Cartesianism Philosophical doctrine first articulated by R. Descartes. It held that there is an absolute division between the mind (thinking) and the material world (matter). Mind, matter, and

God were all considered innate. Descartes's mind/ matter dualism arose from his famous proposition, "I think, therefore I am." The philosophy was further developed and modified by Nicolas de Malebranche (1638–1715), B. Spinoza, and others.

Carthage Ancient city-state of North Africa, located near modern Tunis. Founded, according to tradition, by Dido of Tyre (9th cent. BC), it rose to prominence in the 6th-5th cents. BC and established control over Sardinia, Malta, the Balearic Islands, and much of North Africa and Sicily. Rivaling Rome for control of the Mediterranean, Carthage engaged Rome in the First Punic War (264–241 BC), by which it lost Sicily. Subsequently conquering much of Spain, under Hamilcar Barca and Hasdrubal, it fought the Second Punic War (218–201 BC), and was defeated by Rome despite the brilliant campaign of Hannibal. The Third Punic War (149–146 BC) brought final destruction of Carthage and razing of the city. A new city founded by J. Caesar rose to become Rome's administrative center in Africa. Captured (AD 439) by the Vandals under Gaiseric, it was recovered (AD 553) by the Byzantines, and destroyed by the Arabs (AD 698).

Carthusians Small order of Roman Catholic monks, founded (1084) in France by Saint Bruno. Belonging to a strict and contemplative order, the monks live in private cells within their monasteries and meet with one another only during worship and communal meals. Since its founding, the order has never undergone reform.

Cartier, Sir Georges Étienne 1814–73. Canadian statesman. A leading French-Canadian advocate of federation, he became joint prime minister of Canada (1858–62) with Sir J. Macdonald (1858–62) and later served in the government of unified Canada.

Cartier, Jacques 1491–1557. His discovery and exploration of the Gulf of St. Lawrence and the St. Lawrence River (1534–35) laid the basis for French claims in Canada.

Cartwright, John 1740–1824. English reformer known as the "Father of Reform." A radical who supported the American colonists, he was noted for advocating parliamentary reform, universal manhood suffrage, and abolition of slavery.

Caruso, Enrico 1873–1921. Italian operatic tenor, one of the most famous opera singers of all time. From 1903, he appeared chiefly at New York's Metropolitan Opera House.

Carver, George Washington 1864–1943. American agricultural scientist. A former slave, he won a wide reputation as Tuskegee Institute's director of agricultural research. He is noted for discovering new uses for such crops as peanuts, soybeans, and sweet potatoes.

Carver, John c1576–1621. English Puritan and Pilgrim. He was a prosperous merchant in London who made financial arrangements for the Pilgrim colony in New England. He sailed with the *Mayflower* and became first governor of the colony at Plymouth (1620).

Casablanca Largest Moroccan city (pop. 1,371,300), a seaport and commercial center. Built by the Portuguese on the site of an earlier city, it was destroyed by an earthquake (1755). Rebuilt by the Moroccans (1757), it was developed into a prosperous commercial seaport by the French after 1912. During WW II, it was one of three landing points in the Allied invasion of North Africa (1942).

Casablanca Conference Meeting (Jan. 14–24, 1943) during WW II between US president F. Roosevelt, British prime minister W. Churchill, and others at Casablanca. Held shortly after the city's capture, the meeting resulted in a joint declaration to prosecute the war against the Axis powers until their unconditional surrender.

Casals, Pablo 1876–1973. Spanish musician, composer, and conductor who was a world-famous cellist. He was especially noted for his performances of works by J.S. Bach.

Casanova de Seingalt, Giovanni Jacopo 1725–98. Italian adventurer and world-famous womanizer. His autobiography, *Story of My Life*, celebrates his many amorous exploits.

Casca, Publius Servilius d. c42 BC. Roman politician, the first of the group of assassins to stab J. Caesar (44 BC).

Casement, Sir Roger David 1864–1916. British consular official and Irish revolutionary. He became famous for revealing mistreatment of native workers in the Congo Free State (1904). He was executed during WW I, however, for seeking German help in securing Ireland's independence.

Casimir II 1138–94. Polish king (1177–94), a member of the Piast family. He established the Polish Senate and instituted laws protecting the rights of peasants.

Casimir III ⟨Casimir the Great⟩ 1310–70. Polish king (1330–70), successor to Ladislaus I and last ruler of the Piast family. He is noted for having consolidated royal control over the kingdom and for having expanded its territories through peaceful means. He founded the University of Cracow (1364).

Casimir IV 1427–92. Polish king (1447–92) and ruler of Lithuania (1440–92), successor to his brother Ladislaus III. A member of the Jagiellon family, he emerged victorious from a long war with the Teutonic Knights (1466) and convened the first Polish Diet (1467).

Casimir the Great   *See* **Casimir III**

Caslon, William   1692–1766. English type designer. He designed the famous typeface known as Caslon.

Caspar   *See* **Magi**

Cassander   354?–297 BC. Macedonian king (305–297 BC), the son of Antipater. One of the Diadochi, who fought for control of the Greek empire after the death of Alexander the Great (323 BC), he became the dominant figure in the struggle by 318 and king in 305. He rebuilt the city of Thebes.

Cassandra   Daughter of Trojan king Priam in Greek mythology. She took the gift of prophecy from Apollo and then spurned him. Apollo, in revenge, decreed that no one should believe her prophecies.

Cassel, Battle of   Battle (1328) in which French king Philip VI defeated the rebellious communes of Flanders and reestablished French rule.

Cassini, Jean Dominique   ⟨~, Giovanni Domenico⟩ 1625–1712. Italian-born French astronomer. Among his many discoveries concerning the sun and planets was his identification of four moons of Saturn.

Cassiopeia   Mother of Andromeda in Greek mythology. She was transformed into the constellation Cassiopeia because she boasted of her daughter's beauty.

Cassirer, Ernst   1874–1945. German philosopher, a leader of the Neo-Kantian Marburg school. He studied the relationship between culture and man's symbolizing activity.

Cassius   ⟨Cassius Longinus, Gaius⟩ *d.* 42 BC. He was a principal conspirator against J. Caesar and one of his assassins (44 BC). He killed himself after his armies were defeated by M. Antony at the Battle of Philippi.

Cassius Longinus, Gaius   *See* **Cassius**

caste system   System for hereditary division and ranking of groups within a society, especially in Hindu India. An individual is born into the caste, is required to take up the caste occupation (warrior, farmer, priest), and must marry within the caste. The caste system in India dates back to the period of Brahmanism *(q.v.)* and now consists of thousands of castes based on occupation. Originally, however, there were four great castes, Brahmans (priests and scholars), Kshatriyas (rulers and warriors), Vaisyas (farmers and merchants), and Sudras (laborers, servants, and peasants). The fifth caste, considered to be outside society, was that of the Untouchables (menial laborers and outcasts). The system has thus far resisted forces opposing it, including the rise of Buddhism (a reaction against it), the period of British domination, industrialization, and the efforts of M. Gandhi. Untouchability, however, was abolished by law in 1949.

Castile, Blanche of   *See* **Blanche of Castile**

Castile, Eleanor of   *See* **Eleanor of Castile**

Castile, kingdom of   Historic Spanish kingdom, formed from territories the Christian kings captured from the Moors (8th-9th cents.). After two centuries of claims and counterclaims León was permanently united with Castile (1230). Then, in 1479, Castile was unified with Aragon under Queen Isabella and King Ferdinand. This new kingdom formed the basis of modern Spain.

Castillon, Battle of   French victory (July 17, 1453) over the English, ending the Hundred Years' War (1337–1453). French forces, responding to a revolt in Guyenne, laid siege to the town of Castillon in southwest France. English forces, some 6,000, under John Talbot, 2d earl of Shrewsbury (1413–60), were sent by English king Henry VI to take advantage of the revolt. Shrewsbury attacked the French siege force prematurely (July 17), and his army was routed. Guyenne was back in French control by Oct., 1453, the remaining British troops having left France.

Castlereagh, Robert Stewart, 2d Viscount   1769–1822. British statesman, noted for his term as foreign secretary (1812–22). He played a major role in organizing the Grand Alliance, which defeated Napoleon and was an important figure in the Congress of Vienna (1814–15), which subsequently carved up the French Empire.

Castor and Pollux   Twin brothers in Greek and Roman mythology. Castor was known as a horseman and Pollux was a boxer. Referred to as the Dioscuri, they were the patrons of sailors.

Castracani, Castruccio   1281–1328. Italian nobleman. As the lord of Lucca, he led the Ghibellines of Tuscany in successful battles against Florence. Holy Roman Emperor Louis IV created him a duke in 1327.

Castro, Cipriano   1858–1924. Venezuelan president (1901–08), successor to Ignacio Andrade. Castro seized control of the government (1899). His refusal to honor foreign debts led to a blockade (1902) by Germany, Italy, and France. He was overthrown by J. V. Gómez.

Castro, Cristóbal Vaca de   *fl.* 1540–45. Spanish colonial administrator, sent to Peru (1541) to settle the feud between F. Pizarro and Diego de Almagro (1520–42). Finding Pizarro dead, he assumed the governorship and put down Almagro's rebellion. He was succeeded (1544) by N.

Vela and then imprisoned for 12 years on false charges of embezzlement.

Castro, Fidel 1926–. Cuban premier (1959–) and central figure in the Cuban Revolution. An opponent of Cuban dictator F. Batista, he led an unsuccessful revolt (July 26, 1953), organized the 26th of July Movement *(q.v.)*, and failed again (1956) at a revolt. From his mountain bases, however, he led a guerrilla movement that finally overthrew Batista (Jan. 1, 1959). Thereafter he established a totalitarian government, instituted sweeping economic and social reforms (including nationalization of industry and collective agriculture), entered the Communist sphere, and announced a policy of exporting revolution. His rule has been marked by the Bay of Pigs Invasion, Cuban Missile Crisis, economic failures, growing isolation from other Latin American countries, the involvement of Cuban troops in African revolutionary movements, and the mass emigration (1980) of Cuban "boat people" to the US.

Castro, Inés de *d.* 1355. Spanish noblewoman. A noted beauty, she was the beloved mistress of Dom Pedro, the future Peter I of Portugal. She was murdered on orders given by his father, King Alfonso IV. The tragic incident is a recurrent theme in Portuguese literature.

Catalan Romance language. Derived from Latin, Catalan is spoken in Andorra and parts of Spain and France. There is a large body of literary works in Catalan.

Catalan Company European mercenary soldiers (14th cent.). Led by R. de Flor, the Catalans were employed by Byzantine emperor Andronicus II to fight Turkish invaders. They defeated the Turks, then ravaged the country themselves for several years.

Cateau-Cambrésis, Treaty of Treaty concluded (1559) between France, Spain, and England. It ended the long struggle for control of Italy (1494–1559). Hostilities began with the Italian Wars (1494–1559) between France and Spain, with England joining the fighting occasionally as Spain's ally. By the treaty, Spain's dominance over Italy was recognized, thus initiating a long period of control by Spain's Hapsburg rulers. France also restored Savoy to Spain, agreed to an adjustment in the border of the Spanish Netherlands, and returned Corsica to Genoa. French possession of Calais was confirmed by England.

Cathari Christian heretics of a variety of sects that once flourished in Western Europe (11th-14th cents.). Influenced by the Bogomils *(q.v.)* and Paulicians *(q.v.)*, the Cathari were exponents of Manichaean Dualism, in which God ruled over the spiritual world and Satan ruled over the material world. By the mid-12th cent., the Cathari had churches in Italy and France. In southern France, where they were most numerous, they were called Albigenses and were the object of the 13th-cent. Albigensian Crusade *(q.v.)*. This and the subsequent persecution of the Inquisition put an end to the heretical sects.

Cathay Name used to refer to China in medieval times. M. Polo established the term in popular usage through descriptions of his journey to the region. The term generally applied to what is now northern China.

Cather, Willa Sibert 1876–1947. American novelist. She is best known for her stories of frontier life, of which *O Pioneers!* and *My Ántonia* are noted examples.

Catherine I 1684?–1727. Russian empress (1725–27). The mistress of Czar Peter I (the Great), she became his second wife (1712). She was crowned empress-consort (1724), and, on her husband's death, she succeeded him on the throne (1725). The government during her reign was dominated by A. Menshikov.

Catherine II ⟨Catherine the Great⟩ 1729–96. German-born Russian empress (1762–96), successor to her husband, Peter III, by his overthrow. An able and ambitious leader, she was an important figure in Russia's emergence as a European power. She conspired with a lover, Gen. Grigori Orlov (1734–83), to usurp and murder (1762) her unpopular husband. She made many important administrative reforms, but it was her involvement in European wars and politics that most benefited Russia. She won control of Poland by installing a lover as king (Stanislaus II), and then took the lion's share of territory in the Partitions of Poland. With her lover G. Potemkin she devised the Greek Project to dismember the Ottoman Empire. After the Russo-Turkish War (1768–74), she annexed the Crimea (1783). She was a noted patron of the arts and friend of the Encyclopedists.

Catherine de Médicis 1519–89. French queen (1547–59) as wife of King Henry II and ruler of France as regent (1560–74) to her second son, King Charles IX. She became regent on the death of her first son, King Francis II (1560), and during the religious conflicts that dominated her regency, alternately allied herself with Protestants and Catholics. She took part in planning the Massacre of St. Bartholomew's Day (1572). Her third son, Henry III, succeeded to the throne in 1574.

Catherine of Alexandria, Saint *d.* AD 307? Christian martyr and virgin, of Alexandrian birth. She is said to have been condemned to death by the Roman emperor for professing her Christian faith.

In what was considered a miracle, the torture wheel broke and she was beheaded instead.

Catherine of Aragon 1485–1536. Spanish-born English queen. Catherine was the daughter of Ferdinand and Isabella of Spain, wife of Henry VIII (*m.* 1509), and mother of Mary Tudor. Henry's attempt to annul their marriage (from 1527) resulted in a break with the Roman Catholic church. This culminated in his marriage to Anne Boleyn (1533) and formation of the Church of England.

Catherine of Braganza 1638–1705. Portuguese noblewoman, wife of English king Charles II (1662–85). A Roman Catholic, she was unpopular in England and was accused (by T. Oates) of trying to poison her unfaithful husband (1678). She returned to Portugal some years after her husband's death.

Catherine of Siena, Saint 1347–80. Italian mystic and one of the influential figures of the medieval church. She gained a wide reputation for her dedication to the needy. She is said to have influenced Pope Gregory XI to end the Babylonian Captivity (1376).

Catherine of Valois 1401–37. French noblewoman and wife (*m.* 1420) of English king Henry V. She was mother of Henry VI by the king. After Henry's death (1422) she had a son by a Welsh nobleman, Owen Tudor (*d.* 1461). That son became father of Henry VII, first of the Tudor kings.

Catherine the Great   *See* **Catherine II**

Catherine the Great, Instruction of   *See* **Instruction of Catherine the Great**

Catholic church   *See* **Roman Catholic church**

Catholic Emancipation Movement in Britain to end discrimination against Catholics which was imposed by English law and which included forfeiture of inherited land and exclusion from Parliament. Reform measures were passed in the late 18th cent., and by the Catholic Emancipation Act (Apr. 13, 1829) Catholics were given nearly full equality.

Catholic Emancipation Act   *See* **Catholic Emancipation**

Catholic League ⟨League⟩ ⟨Holy League⟩ League of French Roman Catholics formed (1576) by Henry duke of Guise and aided by Spanish king Philip II, to suppress Protestantism during the French religious wars. It opposed the accession of Henry of Navarre to the French throne as Henry IV, but, weakened over the years, was unable to block Henry's coronation (1594).

Catholic Reformation ⟨Counter-Reformation⟩ Name of the 16th-cent. religious reform movement within the Roman Catholic church. Spurred by the widespread gains of the Protestant Reformation *(q.v.)* in Europe, forces within the Roman Catholic church which had long advocated reform began to exert greater influence. Decisive moves toward reform began with the convening (1545) of the Council of Trent by Pope Paul III. The council met in three different sessions (1545–47, 1551–52, 1562–63) to reformulate Catholic doctrine with greater precision and to reform abuses and corruption that had given rise to Protestantism. The council reaffirmed the Roman Catholic teaching on the seven sacraments and on the importance of church tradition alongside the Scriptures. In the practical realm, the council established the modern seminary system for training priests and thus provided the means to eliminate many of the abuses by the clergy. The council's liturgical reforms lasted virtually intact until replaced by those of the Second Vatican Council (1962–65). Great reforming popes of the Catholic Reformation included Paul III; Paul IV, who thoroughly reformed abuses in the Roman Curia; Pius IV; and Saint Pius V, who reformed the Roman missal and breviary. An important element in the Catholic Reformation was the reform of religious orders, such as that effected by Saint Theresa of Avila and Saint John of the Cross within the Carmelite order, and the founding of new orders, notably the Jesuits. These religious orders, especially the Jesuits, spread the spirit of the Catholic Reformation, founded new schools, and helped to wrest converts from Protestantism. The foreign and military policies of Catholic rulers in Europe, such as Holy Roman Emperor Charles V and his son Philip II of Spain, were often conducted according to imperatives inspired by the Catholic Reformation. But the religious and educational reforms that came out of this reform movement had more lasting effects.

Catiline *c*108–62 BC. Roman politician and conspirator. Barred from the consulship (66 BC) on charges that were later proved false, he was subsequently accused of plotting (65) a rebellion. He was acquitted and ran again (63) for the consulship against Cicero. Defeated, he organized the Conspiracy of Catiline *(q.v.)*.

Catiline, Conspiracy of   *See* **Conspiracy of Catiline**

Cato, Marcus Porcius   *See* **Cato the Elder; Cato the Younger**

Cato Minor   *See* **Cato the Younger**

Cato Street Conspiracy English assassination plot. A. Thistlewood, an anarchist, plotted the murder of British Cabinet officers but was captured with accomplices (Feb., 1820) at his arsenal on Cato Street. He was executed for treason.

Cato the Censor   *See* **Cato the Elder**

Cato the Elder ⟨Cato the Censor⟩ ⟨*name of* Marcus

Porcius ~) 234–149 BC. Roman statesman and champion of the traditional way of life in Rome. He resisted the influence of Greek civilization in Rome and promoted a return to the simple, idealistic, and moral life of old Rome. He staunchly opposed the Scipio family, an embodiment of Hellenistic influences, and as censor instituted many measures aimed at reforming Roman life. His public career included terms as consul (195 BC) and censor (184). His repeated demand for an attack on Carthage helped bring about the Third Punic War (149–146).

Cato the Younger ⟨Cato Minor⟩ ⟨*name of* Marcus Porcius ~) 95–46 BC. Roman statesman and great-grandson of Cato the Elder. He was a highly regarded leader of the Optimates, conservative aristocrats, and actively opposed J. Caesar and his allies. He joined in the armed resistance to Caesar and killed himself following Caesar's victory at the Battle of Thapsus (46 BC).

Catton, Charles Bruce 1899–1978. American historian noted for his works on the American Civil War. He won the Pulitzer Prize (1954) for his book *A Stillness at Appomattox.*

Catullus, Gaius Valerius 84?–54? BC. Roman lyric poet, regarded as the greatest of ancient Rome. He is best remembered for his love poems to a woman he named Lesbia (perhaps Clodia, *q.v.*).

Catulus, Gaius Lutatius *fl.* 3d cent. BC. Roman consul (242 BC) and general. He was commander of the Roman fleet that defeated the Carthaginians off the Aegates islands (241). The action ended the First Punic War (264–241).

Catulus, Quintus Lutatius *d.* 87 BC. Roman general and consul (102 BC). Together with co-consul Marius, Catulus defeated the Cimbri (101 BC). Marius received sole credit, however, and Catulus later supported L. Sulla against him.

Catulus, Quintus Lutatius *d. c*60 BC. Roman politician and consul (78 BC). The son of Q. L. Catulus, he helped Pompey put down a revolt by M. Lepidus (77? BC). An opponent of J. Caesar, he accused Caesar of taking part in the Conspiracy of Catiline. Caesar in turn accused him of embezzlement.

Caucasian **1.** Peoples inhabiting the Caucasus region of southwest Russia, including the Soviet Republics of Georgia, Armenia, and Azerbaijan. **2.** Term for the Caucasoid or so-called white race.

caudillo Term for a leader who is a political boss with a strong (often insurgent) military following. It is used especially in reference to such South American leaders as J. de Rosas and P. Díaz.

Caulaincourt, Armand Augustin Louis, marquis de 1772–1827. French diplomat and general. He

became Napoleon's aide-de-camp (1802), and served as ambassador to Russia (1807–11) and foreign minister (1813–14, 1815).

Cavaignac, Louis *See* **June Days**

cavalier **1.** A horseman, mounted knight, or cavalryman. **2.** Name used by royalist supporters of English king Charles I during the English Civil War (1642–49). They opposed the Roundheads, or Parliamentarians. **3.** Name of the Royalist party following Restoration (1660–88) of the monarchy in England. "Cavalier" was eventually replaced by "Tory" as the party name.

Cavalier, Jean 1681–1740. French Protestant. He was leader of the Camisards (*q.v.*) during their rebellion (1702–04). He fled the country after the treaty he arranged with the Catholics proved unacceptable to his followers.

Cavalier Parliament ⟨Long Parliament of the Restoration⟩ Parliament of the English Restoration which sat from 1661 to 1679 and which was overwhelmingly Royalist. The parliament was responsible for passage of repressive laws (*see* Clarendon Code) directed against Catholics and Puritans.

Cavalier poets English literary group. Named for their royalist sympathies, these poets flourished in the 17th cent. and included in their number R. Lovelace, R. Herrick, and J. Suckling.

Cavendish, Henry 1731–1810. English physicist and chemist. Through his experiments, he determined the composition of air, discovered the properties of what came to be known as hydrogen, and found that water was a compound of oxygen and this gas.

Cavour, Count Camillo Benso di 1810–61. Italian statesman and one of the most important figures in the Risorgimento, the unification of Italy. As premier (1852–59, 1860–61) of what was then the kingdom of Sardinia, he brought about the union of central Italy with the north (1860), encouraged G. Garibaldi to invade Sicily, and sent troops to occupy the Papal States. The unification of the kingdom of Italy under Victor Emmanuel II was completed just before his death (1861).

Caxton, William *c*1422–1491. English printer, the first in his country. He learned printing at Cologne (1471–72), printed the first book in English, *The Recuyell of the Historyes of Troye* (1475), while at Bruges. He printed the first book in England (1477) at Westminster.

Ceausescu, Nicolas 1918–. Romanian statesman, president since 1967. He pursued a policy of independence from Russia while establishing closer ties with China and the West.

Cecilia, Saint 2d or 3d cent. AD. Roman Christian martyr and the patroness of music.

Cecrops In Greek mythology, first king of Attica and founder of Athens. He was half man and half dragon and introduced to Attica such things as marriage laws, burial of the dead, and an end to human sacrifice.

Celaya, Battle of **1.** First victory (Sept. 28, 1810) for Mexican revolutionaries, led by M. Hidalgo y Castilla, over Spanish forces. **2.** Decisive victory (Apr., 1915) for forces of provisional Mexican leader V. Carranza over a rebel force led by F. Villa. Carranza's forces were led by A. Obregón.

Celestial Empire Name formerly used to refer to the Chinese Empire. The early Chinese believed their land was ruled by the "Heavenly Dynasty," and thus gave rise to the term "Celestial Empire."

Celestine I, Saint *d.* AD 432. Italian-born pope (AD 422–32), successor to Saint Boniface I. He opposed Nestorianism and approved the decision of the Council of Ephesus (AD 431). He is sometimes said to have sent Saint Patrick to Ireland.

Celestine V, Saint ⟨Murrone, Pietro del⟩ 1215–96. Italian-born pope (1294), successor to Nicholas IV. Founder of the Celestine Order (c1254), he resigned after a chaotic five-month reign. He was subsequently imprisoned by his successor, Boniface VIII, to prevent a schism in the church.

Cellini, Benvenuto 1500–71. Italian sculptor, goldsmith, and author during the Renaissance. His autobiography is considered an important account of 16th-cent. life. *Perseus with the Head of Medusa* is among his most famous sculptures.

Celsius, Anders 1701–44. Swedish astronomer who invented the centigrade (Celsius) thermometer (1742).

Celtiberian War War (134–133 BC) in which the Romans conquered the Celtiberians, descendants of Iberians and Celtic invaders in Spain. They were decisively defeated by Scipio Africanus the Younger (133 BC).

Celts ⟨Kelts⟩ Ancient people who dominated Western and Central Europe until about the 1st cent. BC. Celtic tribes are believed to have emanated from a region encompassing part of France and southern Germany (before 1200 BC). By the 5th cent. BC, their migrations had carried them into Spain, the British Isles, the Balkan region, and Asia Minor. In the early 4th cent., they even invaded and sacked Rome. The Celts were farmer-raiders with what was primarily a tribal organization. They evolved a well-developed culture (called La Tène) and religion (*see* Druids). By 1st cent. BC, the Celts succumbed to invasions of Germanic tribes and their civilization disappeared as a distinct entity.

Cenci, Beatrice 1577–99. Italian noblewoman whose cruel fate has been the subject of several literary works. Imprisoned and brutalized by her father, she arranged to have him murdered. She and the other members of the family confessed to the plot under torture and, refused leniency, were executed (1599).

centaur In Greek mythology, a creature that was half man and half horse. The offspring of King Ixion, centaurs originally inhabited Mount Pelion in Thessaly. They were generally represented as having a savage nature.

Center party German political party that figured in the Kulturkampf (1871–83). Formed to protect interests of Catholics in the newly formed imperial German state, its membership included Catholics from all classes. Though it suffered during Chancellor O. von Bismarck's Kulturkampf (*q.v.*) and was never able to attain a clear majority in subsequent years, the party remained a force in German politics until the 1930s.

Center party *See* **Agrarian Party**

CENTO *See* **Central Treaty Organization**

Central African Republic Republic located in central Africa. Its capital is Bangui. First explored and occupied (1890s) by the French, it became the French colony of Ubangi-Shari (1894). It was joined (1906) with Chad into an administrative unit and became (1910) part of French Equatorial Africa. In 1920, Chad became a separate colony. Ubangi-Shari became a French territory in 1946, and in 1958, it became autonomous as the Central African Republic. It became fully independent on Aug. 13, 1960. Its first president, David Dacko, was overthrown (1965) in a military coup headed by Col. Jean-Bédel Bokassa, who made himself emperor. Bokassa's ruthless and arbitrary rule was ended (1979) by another coup, and Dacko was reinstalled as president. Dacko was overthrown in a military coup (Sept. 1, 1981) and Gen. André Kolingba became head of state.

Central America Name of the southernmost region of North America, including part of lower Mexico, Guatemala, Honduras, El Salvador, Nicaragua, Costa Rica, and British Honduras. Though properly part of South America, Panama is generally referred to as part of Central America.

Central America, United Provinces of *See* **Central American Union**

Central American Federation *See* **Central American Union**

Central American States, Organization of *See* **Organization of Central American States**

Central American Union ⟨Central American Federation⟩ ⟨United Provinces of Central America⟩ Confederation (1823–38) of Central American states, including Guatemala, El Salvador, Nicaragua, Honduras, and Costa Rica. The states were part of the Mexican Empire (1822–23) until A. Iturbide was ousted (Feb., 1823). Soon after the union was formed, civil war broke out between liberals and conservatives, and liberal leader Francisco Morazán (1799–1842) became president (1829). He ruled until Indian rebels, led by R. Carrera, captured Guatemala City (1838) and thereby dissolved the union. Numerous subsequent attempts at reunification have failed.

Central Committee In the USSR, governing body of the Communist party. The Central Committee was formed (1912) to determine Bolshevik policy. After the Bolsheviks took control of the Russian government, the Central Committee established (1919) the Politburo and the Secretariat as well as the Orgburo (absorbed by the Secretariat, 1952). Although the Central Committee is nominally the highest governing body in the Communist party, policy-making and administrative functions have been largely taken over by the Politburo and the Secretariat.

Central Intelligence Agency (CIA) US intelligence agency. It was formed (1947) under the National Security Act and replaced the Office of Strategic Services (OSS), organized during WW II. In addition to information gathering, the agency has at times been involved in the internal affairs of foreign countries. These activities became a source of controversy in the 1960s and 1970s and included involvement in the Bay of Pigs Invasion, in the war in Laos, and in Chile during Allende's regime.

Central Powers Name applied to Germany and its allies during WW I. In addition to Germany, the Central Powers included Austria-Hungary, Bulgaria, and the Ottoman Empire.

Central Treaty Organization ⟨CENTO⟩ International organization formed in 1955 for Mideast defense. Originally known as the Middle East Treaty Organization, it was reorganized in 1959. Members included Turkey, Great Britain, Pakistan, and Iran.

Ceos, Simonides of *See* **Simonides of Ceos**

Cerberus In Greek mythology, a monstrous dog that guarded the entrance to Hades. It had three heads and a serpent's tail and was captured by Hercules as one of his 12 tasks.

Ceres Roman goddess, protectress of agriculture.

Cernan, Eugene Andrew 1934–. American astronaut. He was a crew member of Apollo 17, the last American mission to the moon (Dec., 1972).

Cerro Gordo, Battle of US victory (Apr., 1847) and first important engagement of US forces against Mexicans during the Mexican War (1846–48). About 8,500 US troops, under Gen. W. Scott,

routed some 12,000 Mexicans, under A. de Santa Anna, near Veracruz, Mexico.

Cervantes Saavedra, Miguel de 1547–1616. A Spanish novelist, poet, and playwright. He is author of *Don Quixote*, a classic novel satirizing the extravagant romances of chivalry popular in his day. Cervantes' early life was turbulent: he lost his left hand in the Battle of Lepanto (1570), was captured and enslaved by the Barbary pirates, and was finally ransomed (1580). He subsequently wrote poems and plays but did not publish Part I of *Don Quixote* until he was in his late fifties. It proved an immediate success.

Cervera y Topete, Pascual *See* **Santiago, Battle of**

Céspedes, Carlos Manuel de *See* **Ten Years' War**

cession *See* **annexation**

Ceylon *See* **Sri Lanka**

Cézanne, Paul 1839–1906. French postimpressionist painter who influenced the development of 20th-cent. art. Painting landscapes and still lifes most often, he developed a style in which he emphasized the underlying structure of a subject through his use of geometric patterns and color. His work played an important role in the development of cubism.

Chacabuco, Battle of Victory (Feb. 12, 1817) for Chilean rebels during the war for Chilean independence from Spain. Rebel forces, led by J. San Martín and B. O'Higgins, defeated the Spanish forces north of Santiago and occupied that city soon afterward. O'Higgins was then named ruler, but Chilean independence was not proclaimed until a year later.

Chaco Peace Conference *See* **Chaco War**

Chaco War Bloody war (1932–35) between Bolivia and Paraguay over possession of the Gran Chaco, a lowland plain in central South America. The war was precipitated by Bolivia's need for a coastal port and the discovery of oil in the Chaco. Sporadic fighting began (1928), and, by 1932, full-scale war had broken out. Early gains by the numerically superior Bolivian forces were wiped out by Paraguayan victories, under Lt. Col. José Estigarribia (1888–1940). Paraguay declared war formally (1933), and, after heavy fighting (1934), its forces drove (1935) into Bolivian territory. Bolivia rallied to counterattack, regained the initiative, and agreed to a truce (1935). Three years of negotiations at the Chaco Peace Conference resulted in a treaty (1938) by which Paraguay won most of the contested Chaco. Bolivia was granted a corridor to and a port on the Paraguay River. About 100,000 soldiers were killed in the war.

Chad ⟨Tchad⟩ Republic located in north central Africa. Its capital is N'Djamena. The region of modern Chad was explored by Arab traders in the 7th cent. The Muslim empire of Kanem, later known as Bornu, was established by peoples from North Africa in the 13th cent. and was dominant in the region until the rise of the rival empires of Wadai and Bagirmi (16th–17th cents.). The French began their conquest of Chad in the early 1890s and made it part of the French Congo in the early 1900s. In 1920, Chad became a separate French colony. It became a French territory in 1946 and voted (1958) for self-rule within the French Community. Chad became independent on Aug. 11, 1960. Muslim tribes in the north began (1966) a guerrilla war that continued until 1973. Chad was severely affected by a drought in the 1960s and 1970s. From 1975, Chad was in a state of turmoil with various groups fighting for control of the government. Libyan troops brought an end to the fighting in 1980, and in 1981 an international peace-keeping force had replaced the Libyans.

Chaeronea Ancient Boeotian town in what is now Greece. The birthplace of Plutarch, it was the site of two battles important in ancient times. On Sept. 1, 338 BC, Macedonian king Philip II defeated the armies of Athens and Thebes and thereby established Macedonian control over Greece. In 86 BC some 30–40,000 Romans under L. Sulla defeated the 110,000-man army of Mithridates VI during the First Mithridatic War.

Chagall, Marc 1887–. Russian-born painter. He is regarded as a forerunner of the surrealists. In addition to his paintings, which often draw on Jewish life and folklore, Chagall has also done notable murals and book illustrations.

Chain, Ernst Boris *See* **Florey, Sir Howard Walter Florey, Baron**

Chakkri dynasty ⟨Chakri ~⟩ Ruling dynasty of Thailand from 1782. The line was founded by Chao P'ya Chakkri, who was instrumental in repulsing the Burmese invasions of the late 18th cent. and who ruled as King Rama I (1782–1809). The line of Chakkri kings remains unbroken to modern times, though the king today is no more than a figurehead. Notable rulers of the dynasty include King Mongkut (Rama IV, 1851–68), King Chulalongkorn (Rama V, 1868–1910), and King Prajadhipok (Rama VII, 1925–35), who advocated creation of a constitutional government. The current Thai king is Bhumibol Adulyade (1927–   ) (Rama IX, from 1946).

Chalcedon, Council of Fourth ecumenical council (AD 451) of the early Christian church, held in Chalcedon (now in Turkey). Convened by Eastern Roman emperor Marcian, the council reversed the council of Ephesus, condemned Eutyches and his Monophysitism *(q.v.)*, proclaimed the dual nature

(human and divine) of Christ as formulated by Pope Leo I, and issued letters against Nestorius.

Chalcis ⟨Chalkis⟩ Greek city. In ancient times it was the most important city on the island of Euboea. It was settled by the Ionians, and later defeated neighboring Eretria in the Lelantine Wars (7th cent. BC). Conquered by the Athenians (c506 BC), it remained under their control until 411 BC, and later flourished under the Romans. Chalcis founded many colonies in ancient times.

Chaldaea *See* **Chaldea**

Chaldea ⟨Chaldaea⟩ Originally, the region south of Babylonia. After the Chaldean Empire (second Babylonian Empire) was established (625 BC) by Nabopolassar, Chaldea included the whole of Babylonia. The empire prospered under Nabopolassar's son, Nebuchadnezzar II, and was subsequently conquered by the Persians (538 BC). (*See also* Babylonia.)

Chaldiran, Battle of Victory (Aug. 23, 1514) for the Ottoman Turks, under Selim I, during an invasion of Persia. Selim led his force of 50,000 men into Persia against the Safavid ruler Ismail I. The invasion was part of a holy war proclaimed by Selim I against the heretical Shi'ite Muslim sect.

Chalkis *See* **Chalcis**

Challenger expedition Great oceanographic survey undertaken (1872–76) by the British. Under the direction of Sir Charles W. Thomson (1830–82) aboard the HMS *Challenger*, the expedition covered nearly 69,000 miles in the Atlantic, Indian, Antarctic, and Pacific oceans. The 50-volume report was a major contribution to the field of oceanography.

Challoner, Richard 1691–1781. English Catholic bishop. His revision of the Douay version of the Bible became the edition used by English Catholics.

Châlons, Battle of One of the decisive battles of history, fought near Châlons-sur-Marne, France, in June, AD 451. The Roman general Aëtius (AD 396?–454), allied with the Visigoths, defeated Attila the Hun and prevented his conquest of Western Europe.

Chamberlain, Arthur Neville 1869–1940. British statesman and prime minister (1937–40) in the years leading up to WW II, successor to S. Baldwin. A Conservative member of Parliament from 1918, he at first pursued a policy of appeasement toward the Fascists and Nazis by recognizing Italy's takeover of Ethiopia (1938) and acceding to Hitler in the Munich Pact (1938). He also ordered a speed-up of British rearmament, however, and when Hitler invaded Poland (1939), he declared war on Germany. The British defeat in Norway (1940) forced his resignation.

Chamberlain, Sir Austen 1863–1937. A British statesman, son of J. Chamberlain. As foreign secretary (1924–29) to S. Baldwin, he played a major role in negotiating the Locarno Pact (1925). He won the Nobel Peace Prize in 1925.

Chamberlain, Joseph 1836–1914. British statesman. As colonial secretary (1895–1903), he formulated the policy of imperial preference for colonial trade (1902). His tenure was marked by the Boer War (1899–1902).

Chamberlain's Men British theatrical company. W. Shakespeare wrote for and acted in this troupe, which was organized in 1594. It performed frequently at the Globe Theatre and was designated the King's Men by James I (c1603).

Chambers, Robert See **Chambers, William**

Chambers, Whittaker See **Hiss, Alger**

Chambers, Sir William 1726–96. English architect of the Palladian school. One of the most important English architects of his day, he designed Somerset House (1776) in England and wrote *A Treatise on Civil Architecture.*

Chambers, William 1800–83. Scottish publisher. With his brother, Robert (1802–71), he founded the publishing firm of W.R. Chambers (after 1832). The company published educational and reference works, among them *Chambers' Encyclopedia.*

Chambord, Henri Charles Ferdinand Marie Dieudonné d'Artois, count of 1820–83. French nobleman and Bourbon claimant to the throne as Henry V. After the fall of Napoleon III (1871), there was a brief movement toward restoration of the Bourbon monarchy. Chambord's outspoken hatred of the revolution, however, defeated the movement (1874), and the Third Republic was formally instituted.

Chamoun, Camille 1900–. Lebanese political leader, president (1952–58). He was a Christian and an advocate of pro-West policies. Muslim opposition to his administration resulted in the Lebanese Crisis (q.v.).

Champa Ancient kingdom (2d–17th cents.) of the Chams, located in what is now south and central Vietnam. Formed (2d cent. AD) during the disintegration of the Chinese Han dynasty, the kingdom was known to the Chinese as Lin-yi. Thereafter it came under the influence of India, was reconquered and ruled by China (5th–6th cents.), warred with neighboring Annam (q.v.) and the Khmer Empire, and succumbed to Annamese domination in the 14th cent. The kingdom was completely absorbed by Annam by the 17th cent.

Champion's Hill, Battle of Union victory (May 16, 1863) during the American Civil War (1861–65). Some 15,000 Union soldiers, led by Gen. U. Grant, defeated 17,500 Confederate soldiers, led by Gen. J. Pemberton, at this Mississippi town. Union losses were nearly 2,500, Confederate, 3,800. Grant subsequently advanced to Vicksburg.

Champlain, Samuel de 1567–1635. French explorer called the father of New France. He made his first voyage to Canada in 1603 and later founded colonies and explored the region (1604–07). He founded Quebec (1608) and was colonial governor of New France (1633–35).

Champollion, Jean François 1790–1832. French Egyptologist, the founder of Egyptology. Working with the Rosetta Stone (q.v.), he was largely responsible for finding the keys to deciphering Egyptian hieroglyphics (1821).

Chancellorsville, Battle of Confederate victory (May 2–4, 1863) over Union forces during the American Civil War (1861–65). The victory resulted in the Confederate invasion of Pennsylvania and the Battle of Gettysburg. A 130,000-man Union army, under Gen. J. Hooker, advanced (May 1) to Chancellorsville, Virginia, and was defeated there by a 60,000-man Confederate force, led by Gen. R.E. Lee. However, Confederate Gen. "Stonewall" Jackson was wounded in the battle and died later. Union losses were 17,000, Confederate 12,000.

Chandler, Raymond Thornton 1888–1959. An American author of detective stories, including *The Big Sleep* and *Farewell, My Lovely.*

Chandragupta ⟨Candragupta⟩ d. 286? BC. Indian emperor (c321–c297 BC), founder of the Maurya Empire. Through his conquests he created an empire that included most of India. He subsequently turned back an invasion by Seleucus I (305 BC) and established an effective administrative system. He is said to have abdicated in 297 to become a Jainist monk.

Chandragupta I ⟨Candragupta I⟩ d. AD 330? Indian king (AD 320–330?). He founded the Gupta dynasty, and, through marriage, vastly extended his domains in northern India.

Chandragupta II ⟨Candragupta II⟩ ⟨Vikramaditya⟩ d. AD c415. Ruler (AD c380–c415) of the Gupta kingdom in northern India. He extended his domains to the west and south by conquests. His reign marked a high point in the Hindu arts.

Chang Ch'ien d. 114 BC. Chinese minister and explorer under Han dynasty emperor Wu Ti. Sent on official missions into central Asia, he provided the Chinese with knowledge of the cultures in Bactria, Parthia, and India.

Chang Hsüeh-liang 1898–. Chinese warlord of Manchuria (1928–31). Forced to withdraw to China by the Japanese (1931), he was responsible for the Sian Incident (1936).

Chang Kuo-t'ao 1897–. Chinese political leader, a founding member of the Chinese Communist party. He lost a power struggle with Mao Tse-tung during the Long March (1935) and defected to the Chinese Nationalists.

Chang Ling AD c33–156? Founder of Taoism in China. Once a faith healer, he taught that sin is the source of bodily ills. His cult was known as the Five Pecks of Rice (q.v.).

Channing, Edward 1856–1931. American historian, author of a major work on American history, *A History of the United States.*

Chao K'uang-yin *See* **Sung**

Chaos In Greek mythology, the original, confused state of the universe, from which all things were created. There are various creation myths. In one, Gaea arose from Chaos to become the mother-creator of all things.

chapbook Inexpensive pamphlet. Chapbooks contained popular reading material and first appeared in Europe during the late 15th and early 16th cents. They were the forerunners of popular magazines, which supplanted them in the 19th cent.

Chaplin, Charles Spencer (Charlie) 1889–1977. English movie actor and director. One of the great comic actors of the silent film era, he was a founder of United Artists (1919).

Chapman, John (Johnny Appleseed) 1774–1845. American pioneer and folk hero. A tree nurseryman in Pennsylvania, he sold and gave away seedlings to westward-bound pioneers. From c1800 to 1845 he wandered in the wilderness region as far west as Ohio tending apple-tree nurseries he had planted in the forests and helping settlers with their orchards.

Chardin, Pierre Teilhard de *See* **Teilhard de Chardin, Pierre**

Chares 3d cent. BC. Greek sculptor. He created the Colossus of Rhodes, one of the Seven Wonders of the World, and is said to be the founder of the Rhodian school of sculpture.

Charlemagne (Charles the Great) (Charles I) c742–814. King of the Franks (768–814) and emperor (800–814) of the vast Carolingian Empire in Western Europe, united by his conquests. The son and successor of Pepin the Short, he first succeeded (768) with his brother Carloman as co-ruler of the Frankish domains, then became sole ruler (771) on Carloman's death. Thereafter he conquered the Lombards (773–774) in response to Pope Adrian's request for aid against them, subdued the Saxons (772–785), failed (778) in his invasion of Muslim Spain, annexed Bavaria (788), and conquered the Avars in the region of the Danube (by 798). He was crowned by Pope Leo III (Christmas Day, 800) as emperor of the (reconstituted) Western Roman Empire in return for preventing the pope's ouster by unruly Romans. His coronation formed the basis for the later creation of the Holy Roman Empire, though Byzantine emperor Michael I recognized Charlemagne (812) only as emperor of the Carolingian Empire (and not as Emperor of the Western Roman Empire). Under Charlemagne's rule an effective administrative system was developed, commerce, education, and building were promoted, and his capital at Aix-la-Chapelle became a cultural center.

Charles I (Spanish king) *See* **Charles V**

Charles I *See* **Charlemagne**

Charles I (Charles of Anjou) 1226–85. French nobleman, king of Naples and Sicily (1266–85), son of French king Louis VIII. He won the throne of Naples and Sicily by conquest and, in subsequent years, vastly extended his territories. His harsh rule, however, led to the Revolt of the Sicilian Vespers (1282).

Charles I 1288–1342. Hungarian king (1308–42), son of Charles II of Naples and founder of the Hungarian Angevin line. He reorganized the army and stimulated trade. Under his rule, Hungary regained its status as a major power.

Charles I 1600–49. English king (1625–49), successor to his father, James I. His firm belief in the divine right of kings and consequent struggles with Parliament resulted in the English Civil War (1642–49). Charles's marriage to the unpopular French Catholic Henrietta Maria and his wars against Spain and France only added to his differences with Parliament. The struggle began soon after his accession and was characterized by bold maneuvers on both sides: Parliament refused Charles money grants until he agreed to end arbitrary practices; Charles briefly relented, agreeing to the Petition of Right (1628), then dissolved Parliament (1629) and ruled without it, raising money by a variety of means. Charles rigorously pursued religious uniformity, and his attempt to impose Anglican liturgy in Scotland embroiled him in the Bishops' Wars (1639–40). This brought on a need for money and prompted calling of the Short and Long parliaments (1640), which in turn resulted in the English Civil War. Defeated, Charles was tried and executed (1649).

Charles I 1863–1908. Portuguese king (1889–1908), successor to Louis I. Charles vied with Britain and Japan for African colonial territories and contended with unrest at home. A revolt (1906) prompted him to grant Prime Minister João Franco (1855–1929) dictatorial powers. This resulted in a revolt (1908) and in his assassination.

Charles I 1887–1922. Last ruler of the Austro-Hungarian Empire (1916–18), successor to Emperor Francis Joseph. He acceded during WW I and tried to open negotiations for peace (1916). He likewise failed in a plan to keep the dual monarchy united, and in 1918 Hungary and Czechoslovakia declared independence.

Charles II (king of Hungary) *See* **Charles III of Durazzo**

Charles II ⟨Charles the Bald⟩ 823–877. King of the West Franks (France) (843–877) and emperor of the West (875–877), a son and successor to Louis I (the Pious). With Louis the German, he made the Oath of Strasbourg (842), and subsequently agreed to redivision of the empire by the Treaty of Verdun (843) and the Treaty of Mersen (870). He then succeeded to the imperial crown (875).

Charles II 1248–1309. King of Naples (1285–1309), successor to his father, Charles I (1226–85). He was defeated (1302) in the War of the Sicilian Vespers to regain Sicily (begun in his father's reign).

Charles II ⟨Charles the Bad⟩ 1332–87. King of Navarre (1349–87). He was noted in his day as a treacherous intriguer who conspired against his father-in-law, John II, among others.

Charles II 1630–85. English king (1660–85), successor (after the English Restoration) to his father, Charles I. His restoration (1660) brought a period of relative stability after the fall of the Protectorate. Following the English Civil War, by agreements with the Scots, he was crowned (1651) Charles II, and invaded England. Defeated (1651) by O. Cromwell, he fled to the Continent, where he remained until his restoration. Though he favored Catholicism and religious toleration, he was forced by public sentiment and acts of the Cavalier Parliament to accept strict laws of uniformity (Clarendon Code and Test Act) and to rescind his two declarations of indulgence (1662, 1672). Charles nevertheless continued his efforts in behalf of Catholicism, established his pro-Catholic Cabal (1667–74) ministry, and entered into secret (and unsuccessful) agreements with the French (Treaty of Dover, 1670). The Popish Plot (1678), defaming Catholics, led to an attempt by Parliament to block the succession of Charles's Catholic brother, James II. Charles dissolved Parliament (1681), ruled without it, and, after the Rye House Plot (1683), gained popularity. During his reign, Britain also entered the Triple Alliance (1668) and was involved in the Second and Third Dutch Wars.

Charles II 1661–1700. Last Spanish Hapsburg king (1665–1700), successor to his father, Philip IV. His reign was marked by the continued decline in Spain's power and the War of Devotion *(q.v.)* and the War of the Grand Alliance *(q.v.)*. His choice of Philip of Anjou (Philip V) as successor led to the War of Spanish Succession (1701–14).

Charles III ⟨Charles the Fat⟩ 839–888. Frankish emperor of the West (881–887) and king of the East (882–887). He briefly reunited Charlemagne's empire (885–887) but proved a weak ruler. His overthrow by Arnulf (887) began the final breakup of Charlemagne's empire.

Charles III ⟨Charles the Simple⟩ 879–929. French king (893–923), proclaimed king in opposition to, and successor to, King Eudes. He ended Norse raids by ceding (911) territory to them (now part of Normandy), and added Lorraine to the French kingdom (911). He was deposed in 923.

Charles III ⟨Charles of Durazzo⟩ 1345–86. King of Naples (1381–86) and Hungary (1385–86) as Charles II. A member of the Angevin line, he succeeded Joanna I in Naples by deposing her and putting her to death. He was assassinated soon after being elected to succeed King Louis I of Hungary.

Charles III 1716–88. Spanish king (1759–88), successor to Ferdinand VI. An "enlightened despot," he instituted many beneficial administrative reforms. His reign was marked by defeat in the Seven Years' War (1756–63) and Spain's participation in the American Revolution (after 1779).

Charles IV ⟨Charles the Fair⟩ 1294–1328. French king (1322–28), successor to his brother Philip V and last of the Capetian kings. He won (1327) a part of Aquitaine from the English, who then controlled the territory.

Charles IV 1316–78. German king (1346–78). Elected Holy Roman Emperor in opposition to Louis IV (1346), he succeeded him (1347) but was not crowned until 1355. He issued the Golden Bull of 1356 and thus established a constitutional basis for his rule of the empire.

Charles IV 1604–75. Duke of Lorraine. Charles attempted to resist domination by the French kings by means of plots and intrigues, and thus lost control of his domains several times. He supported Spanish involvement in the Fronde *(q.v.)*.

Charles IV 1748–1819. Spanish king (1788–1808), successor to his father, Charles III. A weak ruler, he relied on M. de Godoy to run the government. His reign was marked by two invasions by the French (1794, 1807) and domination by Napoleon. He was forced to abdicate in 1808.

Charles V ⟨Charles the Wise⟩ 1337–80. French king (1364–80), successor to his father, John II. As regent for his father (1356–60), he put down the

Jacquerie revolt. As king, he ruled France during its recovery from the early phase of the Hundred Years' War (1337–1453). He consolidated the power of the monarchy, strengthened the military, instituted reforms, and regained almost all the territories lost to the English.

Charles V 1500–58. Spanish king (1516–56, as Charles I, succeeding Ferdinand II) and Holy Roman Emperor (1519–56, as Charles V, succeeding Maximilian I). A Hapsburg, he was one of the most powerful European kings, ruling over a vast inherited empire that included much of Europe and all of Spain's New World possessions. Charles's reign was marked by involvement in the Italian Wars (1494–1559) against France and by attempts to stop M. Luther and the Protestant Reformation. In addition to the events of the Italian Wars, Charles's reign saw the brief Revolt of Comuneros (1520–21); his Diet of Worms (1521), banning Lutheranism; rebellions in Germany, such as the Peasants' War (1524–26), and the rise of the Lutheran Schmalkaldic League; war against the Ottoman Turks; the Council of Trent (1545) and the Counter-Reformation; the defeat (1547) of the Schmalkaldic League and the Diet of Augsburg (1547–48); and the unsuccessful Augsburg Interim (1548). Charles abdicated (1556) in Spain to his son Philip II and in the Holy Roman Empire to Ferdinand I.

Charles V ⟨Charles Leopold⟩ 1643–90. Duke of Lorraine. Deprived of his duchy by Louis XIV, Charles became a successful field marshal for the Holy Roman Emperor. He aided the defense of Vienna (1683) and drove the Turks from Hungary (1685).

Charles VI ⟨Charles the Well-Beloved⟩ ⟨Charles the Mad⟩ 1368–1422. French king (1380–1422), successor to his father, Charles V. He suffered fits of insanity and could not rule by himself. His reign was marked by war between the Armagnacs and Burgundians, the English invasion of France (1420), and the Treaty of Troyes (1420).

Charles VI 1685–1740. Austrian Holy Roman Emperor (1711–40), successor to his brother Joseph I and last of the direct Hapsburg line. A pretender to the Spanish throne, he precipitated the War of Spanish Succession (1700–14). His accession as emperor (1711) soon ended this conflict, though he again warred against Spain as a member of the Quadruple Alliance (1718–20). In wars with the Ottoman Empire (1716–18, 1736–39), he won and then lost territory in Hungary and Serbia. He lost the War of Polish Succession (1733–35). His attempt to ensure succession of his daughter Maria Theresa to Hapsburg domains (by the Prag-

matic Sanction of 1713) led to the War of Austrian Succession (1740–48).

Charles VII ⟨Charles the Well-Served⟩ 1403–61. French king (1422–61), successor to his father, Charles VI. From the time of the Siege of Orléans (1429) to the Battle of Castillon (1453), he gradually forced the English out of France and thus finally ended the Hundred Years' War (1337–1453). He also issued the Pragmatic Sanction (1438).

Charles VII ⟨Charles Albert⟩ 1697–1745. Holy Roman Emperor (1742–45), successor to Charles VI. On the death of Charles VI, he became embroiled in the War of Austrian Succession (1740–48) and died before peace was restored.

Charles VIII 1470–98. French king (1483–98), successor to his father, Louis XI. He initiated the Italian Wars (1494–1559) with an abortive invasion of Italy, in which he hoped to conquer the kingdom of Naples. He was defeated at the Battle of Fornovo (1495).

Charles IX 1550–74. French king (1560–74), successor to his brother, Francis II. The Wars of Religion (q.v.) began during his reign. Under pressure from his mother, Catherine de Medici, he ordered the Massacre of St. Barholomew's Day (1572), in which thousands of Huguenots were killed.

Charles IX 1550–1611. Regent of Sweden (1592–94, 1599–1604) and king (1604–11). He opposed the Catholic king Sigismund III (of Poland and Sweden), defeated him in battle (1598), and restored Lutheranism in Sweden. He precipitated a long period of wars with Poland (1600–60) and provoked the Kalmar War (1611–13).

Charles X 1757–1836. French king (1824–30), successor to King Louis XVIII. He took part in the counterrevolutionary Wars of the Vendée. As king he vainly tried to reestablish the ancien régime. His last prime minister, A. de Polignac, provoked the July Revolution (1830).

Charles X Gustavus 1622–60. Swedish king (1654–60), successor to his cousin Queen Christina. He led Sweden in the First Northern War (1655–60). He died while treaties, advantageous to Sweden, were being concluded.

Charles XI 1665–97. Swedish king (1660–97), successor to his father, Charles X Gustavus. By the Riksdag of 1682, he established an absolute monarchy in Sweden. His reign was marked by treaties concluding the First Northern War (1655–60) and by Sweden's participation in the Third Dutch War (1672–78).

Charles XII 1682–1718. Swedish king (1697–1718), successor to his father, Charles XI. He proved himself a brilliant military leader during the Second Northern War (1700–21), but his ambitious plans ultimately cost Sweden its status as a major power.

Charles XIII 1748–1818. Swedish king (1809–18) and first king of a united Sweden and Norway (1814–18). Successor to his nephew, Gustavus IV, he ruled Sweden under a constitution that limited his powers. During his reign, Finland was ceded to Russia (1809) and Sweden and Norway were united (1814).

Charles XIV John ⟨orig. Bernadotte, Jean Baptiste Jules⟩ 1763–1844. French general and king of Sweden and Norway (1818–44), successor to Charles XIII. A French marshal under Napoleon, he was elected crown prince of Sweden (1810), and from that time virtually ruled Sweden. He turned against Napoleon and helped defeat him at Leipzig (1813). He then forced Norway into union with Sweden (1814). His subsequent reign was marked by a period of relative peace.

Charles XV 1826–72. King of Sweden and Norway (1859–72), successor to his father, Oscar I. A popular ruler, he supported the creation of a bicameral legislature (1866).

Charles Albert *See* **Charles VIII**

Charles Albert 1798–1849. A Sardinian king (1831–49), a member of the Savoy family. A liberal-minded ruler during the Risorgimento, he warred against Austria twice and was defeated both times, first at Custozza (1848) and again at Novara (1849). He abdicated after his second defeat.

Charles Edward, the Young Pretender *See* **Stuart, Charles Edward**

Charles Leopold *See* **Charles V**

Charles Louis, Archduke *See* **Abensberg-Eckmuhl, Battles of**

Charles Martel ⟨Charles the Hammer⟩ 688–741. Frankish ruler (c715–741), successor to his father, Pepin of Herstal, and grandfather of Charlemagne. He became mayor of the palace of Austrasia after his father's death (714). He subsequently defeated rulers of Frankish territories, the Spanish Muslims, and a number of German tribes, to create a unified Frankish kingdom. He divided the kingdom between his sons Pepin and Carloman.

Charles of Anjou *See* **Charles I**

Charles of Blois c1319–64. Duke of Brittany. Charles was the nephew of French king Philip VI. He was a chief figure in the War of the Breton Succession (1341–65), which was ended soon after his death in battle.

Charles of Durazzo *See* **Charles III**

Charles of Valois 1270–1325. French nobleman, son of French king Philip III. Created count of

Valois by his father (1285), he was father of French king Philip VI, the first of the Valois line.

Charles the Bad *See* **Charles II**

Charles the Bald *See* **Charles II**

Charles the Bold 1433–77. Last of the powerful dukes of Burgundy (1467–77), successor to his father, Philip the Good. He was an enemy of French king Louis XI and ambitious to reestablish the kingdom of Lotharingia. His final defeat at Nancy (1477) marked the end of Burgundy's status as an autonomous state.

Charles the Fair *See* **Charles IV**

Charles the Fat *See* **Charles III**

Charles the Great *See* **Charlemagne**

Charles the Hammer *See* **Charles Martel**

Charles the Mad *See* **Charles VI**

Charles the Simple *See* **Charles III**

Charles the Well-Beloved *See* **Charles VI**

Charles the Well-Served *See* **Charles VII**

Charles the Wise *See* **Charles V**

Charleston US port city (pop. 69,510) in South Carolina. Founded (1670) by the English colonizer William Sayle (d. 1671), it was a major southern port during Colonial times. It figured in the American Revolution and Civil War (see Battles of Charleston). The attack (1861) on Fort Sumter (q.v.) in Charleston harbor marked the beginning of fighting in the Civil War.

Charleston US city (pop. 64,000), capital of West Virginia. It was incorporated in 1794 and first became the capital of the state from 1870 to 1875. In 1885 it became the permanent capital.

Charleston, Battle of **1.** American victory (June 28, 1776) over the British during the American Revolution (1775–83). American colonel W. Moultrie successfully defended his garrison on Sullivan's Island in the Charleston, South Carolina, harbor during an attack by British warships. **2.** Major British victory (May 12, 1780) during the American Revolution (1775–83). Following a six-week siege by some 16,000 soldiers under Sir H. Clinton, the British forced the surrender of Charleston, South Carolina, and some 7,000 American defenders under Gen. B. Lincoln. The British then launched their invasion of the Carolinas. They held the city until Dec. 14, 1782. **3.** ⟨Siege of Charleston⟩ Prolonged Union effort to capture this South Carolina city during the American Civil War (1861–65). Following capture of Fort Sumter (q.v.) by the Confederacy, Charleston harbor was blockaded by the Union Navy and, after 1863, was bombarded by Union forces. It did not fall to Union forces (taken Feb. 18, 1865) until Sherman's March to the Sea.

Charlottetown Conference Preliminary meeting (Sept., 1864) of delegates from Canadian provinces to discuss unification of Canada. The conference was followed by the Quebec Conference *(q.v.)*. Originally called to discuss federation of the Maritime Provinces, the conference was attended by delegates of other provinces, who promoted a plan for a general union.

Charon In Greek mythology, ferryman on the river Styx. He transported the souls of the dead across the river to the underworld. A coin placed in the mouth of the corpse before burial was his fee.

charte constitutionnelle See **Charter of 1814**

chartered companies Companies created by special government charter for the purpose of colonization and trade in foreign lands. The companies were especially important (16th-17th cents.) in the creation of Europe's vast overseas colonial empires. Chartered companies were frequently empowered to govern as well as explore and colonize these new lands and thus figured in the early history of the US, Canada, India, and Africa. Their functions, however, were eventually absorbed by the home governments. *See separate entries for the following major trading companies:*

British East India Company
Dutch East India Company
Dutch West India Company
French East India Company
Hudson's Bay Company
Massachusetts Bay Company
Muscovy Company
Virginia Company

Charter of 1814 ⟨charte constitutionnelle⟩ Constitution issued (June 14, 1814) by French king Louis XVIII, following his restoration to the throne at the end of the Napoleonic era. Louis promulgated the constitution at the urging of C. Talleyrand and other advisers. It established a constitutional monarchy with a bicameral legislature and guaranteed civil liberties and religious toleration established under Napoleon's reign. Catholicism was made the state religion. The charter was rewritten in 1830.

Charter to the Nobility Charter (May, 1785) guaranteeing the rights and prerogatives of the Russian nobility. Issued by Catharine II (the Great), the charter extended these rights to the nobility as a corporate body and eliminated earlier distinctions between old and new nobility. By its terms the nobility were granted the rights of assembly, petition of the monarch, and trial by their peers. It also gave them powers over their serfs, excluded them from mandatory service to the state, and exempted them from personal taxes.

Chartism Mass movement (1838–48) for political reform which arose among workingmen in Britain. The movement was centered around demands for reforms set forth in the People's Charter, drafted by William Lovett. They included universal male suffrage, voting by ballot, and elimination of property qualifications for members of Parliament. Spawned by a severe depression and unpopular revisions of the Poor Laws, the movement briefly became nationwide. Chartist petitions were submitted to Parliament (1838, 1840, 1848), and all were rejected. Chartist riots in May, July, and Nov., 1839 resulted in arrests of Chartist leaders and a decline in the movement. It revived briefly in 1848, but a return of prosperity brought the final decline of the movement.

Chase, Salmon Portland 1808–73. American public official and 6th chief justice of the US Supreme Court (1864–73). He was a founder of the Free Soil and Republican parties and secretary of treasury under Pres. A. Lincoln (1861–64). Chase proposed the plan for the national banking system (1863), presided over the impeachment proceedings against Pres. A. Johnson (1868), and was several times a candidate for president.

Chase, Samuel 1741–1811. American patriot, Supreme Court associate justice (1796–1811), and signer of the Declaration of Independence. T. Jefferson's failed attempt to have him impeached for political reasons (1805) helped establish the court's traditional independence from political influence.

Chateaubriand, François René, vicomte of 1768–1848. French writer and diplomat, a founder of French romanticism. His life was enmeshed with the upheavals of the French Revolution, and he variously served the monarchists, Napoleon, and the Restoration. His first great literary success, however, came (1802) with publication of *The Genius of Christianity*. His many other works include the novels *Atala* and *René*, and his memoires, *Mémoires d'outre-tombe*.

Chateauguay, Battle of British victory (Oct. 26, 1813) during the War of 1812. A small contingent of British troops intercepted and defeated the advance party of an American invasion force, led by Gen. W. Hampton, as it neared its objective of Montreal, Canada. The defeat turned back the American invasion of Canada.

Chattanooga, Battle of Union victory (1863) at Chattanooga, Tennessee, during the American Civil War (1861–65). One of the important Union victories, it was the culmination of the Chattanooga Campaign (1863) and gave the North undisputed possession of that strategic city. The Army of the Cumberland, under Gen. W. Rosecrans, was besieged (Sept., 1863) at Chattanooga by Confederate forces, under Gen. B. Bragg, after the Battle of Chickamauga Creek. By November, Gen. U. Grant had replaced Rosecrans and had mustered some 60,000 men to face Bragg's 50,000. He began the attack late in November with units under Gen. W. Sherman, Gen. J. Hooker, and Gen. G. Thomas. On Nov. 24, Hooker cleared Lookout Mountain (Battle Above the Clouds) of Confederates. On Nov. 25, Thomas moved up Missionary Ridge and routed the Confederates. Bragg was forced to retreat into Georgia and sustained losses of 7,000 men to the Union's 6,000.

Chatterton, Thomas 1752–70. English poet. Recognized as a forerunner of the romantic movement, he was largely unrecognized in his own time. He committed suicide at age 17.

Chaucer, Geoffrey 1340?–1400. Early English poet, author of *The Canterbury Tales* and one of the most important figures in English literature. Born into a middle-class family, Chaucer won the favor of King Edward III, subsequently held various court-appointed administrative posts, and even undertook a number of diplomatic missions (during the 1370s). Chaucer's literary works are usually divided into three periods. The early period (ending 1370) reflects a French influence and includes his first major work, the *Book of the Duchesse*. The middle period shows an Italian influence (Boccaccio, Dante) and includes *House of Fame*, *Parlement of Foules*, *Legend of Good Women*, and *Troilus and Criseyde*. The late period (after 1387) includes his masterpiece, *Canterbury Tales*.

Chaumette, Pierre Gaspard 1763–94. French revolutionary. As procurator general of the Commune of Paris, he instituted social reforms, including improvements in hospitals and treatment of the poor. He was executed by M. Robespierre for advocating the Cult of Reason.

Chautauqua movement Adult education system. Similar to the Lyceum, it was begun (1873) in Chautauqua, New York, by John Vincent (1832–1920) and Lewis Miller (1829–99). It supports summer lectures and classes in the arts, sciences, and humanities.

Chaykovsky, Nikolai Vasilyevich 1850–1926. A Russian Socialist. Chaykovsky established (1875) an unsuccessful utopian commune in Kansas. Returning to Russia, he opposed the Bolshevists and headed (1918–20) the counterrevolutionary, White Russian government at Archangel.

Chazars *See* **Khazars**

Checkers Speech Emotional television address on Sept. 23, 1952, in which R. Nixon preserved his position as vice-presidential candidate and won new support for the Eisenhower-Nixon ticket. Nixon answered charges that he had benefited from a fund raised by California friends by pointing to his modest personal circumstances, noting his wife's "Republican cloth coat" and his dog, Checkers.

checks and balances The principle of government whereby power is divided among executive, legislative, and judicial branches, in order to prevent excesses and abuses of power. The theory of the separation of powers was articulated in Montesquieu's *The Spirit of Laws* (1748) and was applied to government in the US Constitution *(q.v.)* in 1789.

Cheever, John 1912–1982. American novelist and short-story writer whose works depict life in 20th-cent. suburban America. Among his works are *The Wapshot Chronicle* and *Bullet Park*.

Cheka Russian secret police unit. The Cheka was organized in Dec., 1917 to combat counterrevolutionary activity. It was granted power of execution in 1918. After 1922 it was replaced by the GPU *(q.v.)*.

Chekhov, Anton Pavlovich 1860–1904. Russian playwright and short-story writer, one of Russia's great literary figures. A practicing physician until forced to retire by a chronic case of tuberculosis, he first won fame with stories such as *Ward Number Six* and *The Steppe*. From 1898 he began writing plays, which were produced by the Moscow Art Theater and which are now world famous. Among them are *The Sea Gull*, *Uncle Vanya*, and *The Cherry Orchard*.

Cheng Ch'eng-kung 1624–62. Chinese pirate and soldier. Cheng's pirates supported rulers of the Ming dynasty against the invading Manchu. Forced to abandon the mainland by the Manchu conquests, he captured Taiwan from the Dutch (1661) and established a short-lived government there.

Chennault, Claire Lee 1890–1958. American general. He organized (1941) the volunteer air-combat unit called the Flying Tigers, which fought in China, and headed conventional US air-combat units there later in WW II.

Ch'en Tu-hsiu 1879–1942. Chinese scholar and Communist leader. Ch'en, an advocate of sweeping cultural revolution, was a leader of the May Fourth Movement *(q.v.)* and a principal founder of the Chinese Communist party.

Chénier, André Marie de 1762–94. French poet, sometimes called the greatest of 18th-cent. France. He was guillotined during the Reign of Terror in France and is perhaps best known for his *Élégies*.

Cheops *See* **Khufu**

Chephren See **Khafre**

Cheribon Agreement See **Linggadjati Agreement**

Cherokee Indians North American Indian tribe once located in the US Southeast. First visited by the Spanish (mid-16th cent.), they were subsequently friendly with British settlers until the mid-18th cent. The tribal population was cut in half by a smallpox epidemic (c1750), and, after 1760, hostilities against the settlers began. During the American Revolution (1775–83), the Cherokees allied themselves with the British royalists, and engaged in sporadic warfare (1776–81). Their defeat and loss of territories in subsequent treaties began the process of their removal from the Southeast. By the Indian Removal Act, the Cherokee were forcibly removed (1838) to Oklahoma. The long trek under Chief J. Ross cost thousands of lives and was called the Trail of Tears. In Oklahoma the Cherokee became one of the Five Civilized Tribes. The tribe disbanded in 1906.

Cherry Valley Raid Raid (Nov. 11, 1778) on a village in upper New York during the American Revolution (1775–83). The Iroquois Indians, led by J. Brant, joined with W. Butler and Butler's raiders in this attack, which left the town destroyed.

Chersonese, Tauric Ancient city in the Crimea, near modern Sevastopol. Founded (6th cent. BC) by the Ionian Greeks, it was an important trading center in ancient times and continued to flourish under the Romans and Byzantines. It fell into ruin in the 14th cent.

Chersonese, Thracian ⟨Chersonesus⟩ Geographical region, known as the Gallipoli Peninsula, it is located in European Turkey. It was a major grain-producing region in ancient times and was crossed by major trade routes.

Chersonesus See **Chersonese**

cherub Form of angel. Cherubim are represented as beautiful, winged children in Christian art.

Chesapeake US frigate. On June 22, 1807, the British ship *Leopard* stopped her off the Virginia coast, searched her for British deserters, and forcibly removed four crewmen. This incident, the "*Chesapeake* Affair," increased anti-British sentiment in the US in the years before the War of 1812. When, during the War of 1812, the *Chesapeake* was attacked and boarded (June 1, 1813) outside of Boston harbor by crewmen of the British warship *Shannon*, American commander J. Lawrence uttered his famous cry, "Don't give up the ship!"

Chesapeake* Affair** See ***Chesapeake

Chesterton, Gilbert Keith 1874–1936. English author and critic. A prolific man of letters, noted for his mastery of the paradox, he wrote essays, poems, critical works, theological treatises, and even a series of detective novels.

Chevreuse, Marie de Rohan-Montbazon, duchess of 1600–79. French noblewoman. She was involved in several conspiracies against Cardinal Richelieu and Cardinal Mazarin during their terms as ministers of France. Exiled by Richelieu, she later became Mazarin's ally.

Chevrolet, Louis See **Durant, William Crapo**

Cheyenne Indians North American Indian tribe, once located in the Great Plains. Pressed by hostilities with other tribes, the Cheyenne migrated from Minnesota and, by the early 1800s, had settled in the Black Hills. By 1851, part of the tribe had moved south, and the Cheyenne were split into northern and southern tribes. Discovery of gold (1858) on tribal lands in Colorado brought on war with the whites. The southern Cheyenne were generally subdued by Gen. G. Custer after his destruction of the Washita River village (1868). The northern Cheyenne and Sioux combined to massacre Custer's forces at Little Bighorn (1876). They surrendered in 1877 and were removed to Oklahoma

Chia-ching 1507–66. Chinese emperor (1522–66). During his reign, China was plagued by Mongol invasions, raids by Japanese pirates, and rebellions. He ceded Macao to Portugal (1557).

Chia-ch'ing 1760–1820. Unpopular Chinese emperor (1796–1820), successor to his father, Ch'ien Lung. He put down the White Lotus Rebellion and suppressed piracy, but his measures to replenish the treasury proved unpopular.

Chiang Ch'ing 1914?–. Chinese Communist political leader and the wife of Mao Tse-tung. In 1966 she became a leading figure in the Cultural Revolution *(q.v.),* and remained an important political figure into the 1970s. Following Mao's death, she fell from power and was finally put on trial (Nov. 20–Dec. 29, 1980) with the Gang of Four *(q.v.)* for abuses during the Cultural Revolution.

Chiang Chung-cheng See **Chiang Kai-shek**

Chiang Kai-shek ⟨Chiang Chung-cheng⟩ 1887–1975. Chinese Nationalist general and leader, who headed the governments of China (1928–49) and of the exiled Nationalists on Taiwan (after 1949). A trained military leader, Chiang took part in the Chinese Revolution of 1911, rebellions against the government of Yuan Shih-kai, and served (from 1918) in Sun Yat-sen's Nationalist Kuomintang government. He began the Northern Expedition (1926–28), took control of the Kuomintang (Sun had died 1925), broke with the Communists (1927), warred against them in the Chinese Civil War (1927–49), and established the Nationalists as rulers of China (1928–49) until the Communist takeover. He held power under various titles, and, after being seized in the Sian Incident (1936), agreed to an alliance with the Communists against the threat of Japanese invasion. He then led a loosely united China during the Sino-Japanese War (1937–45) and WW II, but, after 1945, resumed civil war against the Communists. This time the Communists gained the upper hand, and by 1949 he and his Nationalist government had been forced into exile on Taiwan. Chiang's subsequent fortunes declined with those of his government on Taiwan. After enjoying two decades of US support, his government was expelled (1971) from the UN in favor of the Communist People's Republic of China.

Chiang Kai-shek, Madame   *See* **Soong Mei-ling**

Chiaramonte, Barnaba Gregorio   *See* **Pius VII**

Chicago   US city (pop. 3,005,100) in Illinois. A major commercial, industrial, and transportation center, it started as a trading post (17th cent.), and was the site of Fort Dearborn (1803–12). Chartered in 1837, it grew rapidly after the mid-19th cent. as a rail transportation center. The Great Fire of 1871 almost destroyed the city. Chicago was the scene of the 1886 Haymarket Square Riot and the Pullman Strike (1894), and site of the Manhattan Project (*q.v.*) facility where the first sustained nuclear chain reaction (Dec. 2, 1942) was produced.

Chicago School   American architectural school that pioneered the building of skyscrapers (late 19th cent.). Principal figures in this school were L. Sullivan, F. L. Wright, D. Burnham, and J. Root.

Chicherin, Georgi Vasilyevich   1872–1936. Russian revolutionary and diplomat. He served as foreign commisar (1918–28) after the Russian revolution and won recognition of the new government by Western European countries. He negotiated the Treaty of Rapallo (1922).

Chickamauga Creek, Battle of   Battle (Sept. 19–20, 1863) during the American Civil War (1861–65). Some 55,000 Union troops, led by W. Rosecrans, were engaged by 70,000 Confederates, led by B. Bragg, near Chattanooga. Union losses were 16,000, Confederate 18,000, making this one of the war's bloodiest battles.

Ch'ien Lung   1711–99. Chinese emperor (1735–96), fourth emperor of the Ch'ing dynasty. By his military conquests, he brought the Chinese Empire to its greatest territorial extent, adding Sinkiang in the west and establishing Chinese hegemony in Annam and Burma. The government, however, was weakened by rampant corruption.

Chiesa, Giacomo della   *See* **Benedict XV**

Chikamatsu, Monzaemon   1653–1724. Japanese dramatist, sometimes called the "Shakespeare of Japan." He wrote over one hundred plays, most of them for puppet theater.

Childebert I   *d.* 558. Merovingian Frankish king (511–558), successor with his three brothers to his father, Clovis I. Childebert received the northwestern part of the Merovingian Kingdom (in what is now France), and by various means increased his holdings at his brothers' expense.

Childebert II   570?–595. Frankish king of Austrasia (575–595), successor to his father, Sigebert. From 575 to 585, his mother Brunhilde ruled for him as regent. He subsequently engaged in wars to expand his territories and was defeated in one attempt, by Neustrian king Clotaire II.

Childeric I   AD *c*436–481. Frankish king (AD *c*457–481), one of the first of the Merovingian dynasty and father of Clovis I. He was successful in ridding his kingdom (now part of Belgium) of Visigoths (by AD 469) and Anglo-Saxon pirates.

Children's Crusade   *See* **Crusade, Children's**

Chile   Republic located on the southwestern coast of South America. Its capital is Santiago. Chile gained its independence from Spain in 1818 but its growth was slow until the late 19th and early 20th cents., when its rich deposits of nitrates and copper came under the control of foreign companies. Chile's political history has been one of struggle between conservative and liberal factions. The 20th cent. saw the rise of Communist and Socialist organizations as powers in the political scene. In 1970 Salvador Allende Gossens became the first Marxist to be elected chief executive of a government in the Western Hemisphere. He died in 1973 during a military coup. Key dates in the history of Chile include:

1540s–50s   Spanish under Pedro de Valdivia founded Santiago (1541), Concepción (1550), Valdivia (1552), and other settlements in Chile.

16TH CENT.   Conquistadors fought Araucanian Wars against Indians in central Chile.

1810–14   Unsuccessful attempt to establish Chilean independence led by Bernardo O'Higgins and Juan Martínez de Rozas.

1817   Argentine rebel José de San Martín and the Chilean rebel B. O'Higgins led rebel force from Argentina into Chile; began expulsion of Spanish royalists from Chile with victory at Battle of Chacabuco (Feb. 12); B. O'Higgins named director general.

1818   O'Higgins proclaimed Chilean independence (Feb. 12).

1818   José de San Martín defeated the Spanish in final battle of Maipú (1818); Chilean independence firmly established.

1818–23 O'Higgins governed Chile; opposition to his rule led to his resignation.

1833 New constitution adopted; led to eventual establishment of strong, centralized representative government in Chile.

1879–83 Chile emerged victorious in War of the Pacific (1879–83); conflict ended by the Treaty of Ancon (1883); Chile awarded valuable territories from Bolivia and Peru.

1883–1929 Tacna-Arica Controversy, prolonged territorial dispute with Peru; ultimately resolved along lines suggested by US Pres. H. Hoover.

1886–91 J. Balmaceda served as president; his liberal reforms caused civil war and his ouster; parliamentary dictatorship ruled until adoption of 1925 constitution.

1891 *Baltimore* Incident (Oct. 16) threatened war with US.

1920–25 A. Alessandri Palma served as president; assisted in creation of a new constitution (1925).

1927–31 Carlos Ibáñez del Campo served as president; promoted labor and educational reforms.

1930s Great Depression caused great hardship in Chile; promoted the rise of Socialist and Marxist groups that sought to alter Chilean government and economic system.

1946–52 Gabriel González Videla served as president; administration sought to solve Chile's economic ills and took measures against Communists.

1952–58 C. Ibáñez del Campo served second time as president.

1958–64 Jorge Alessandri served as president; administration marked by continuing economic trouble.

1964–70 Eduardo Frei Montalvo served as president; introduced numerous reforms; government took controlling interest in US mines in Chile.

1970–73 S. Allende, a Communist, became president; nationalized copper companies and other industries; sought to institute Socialist program in Chile.

1971 Diplomatic relations established (Jan. 5) with China.

1971 Congress blocked Allende's planned governmental reforms; measures would have created unicameral legislature and increased presidential powers.

1972 Allende imposed martial law (Oct. 12) in 13 provinces to deal with truckers' strike.

1973 Military staged unsuccessful coup (June 29) against Allende government.

1973 Military coup overthrew Allende government (Sept. 11); President Allende died under suspicious circumstances; US CIA implicated in attempts to destabilize the government.

1973 Gen. Augusto Pinochet Ugarto became president (Sept. 13); instituted right-wing dictatorship firmly opposed to Marxists.

1976 OAS accused military government of police terrorism.

1978 Government lifted state of siege in force since military takeover.

1980 New constitution adopted.

1981 Pinochet elected president under new constitution; civilian president to be elected at close of Pinochet's eight-year term.

Chilpancingo, Congress of *See* **Congress of Chilpancingo**

Chilperic I *d.* 584. Frankish king of Neustria (561–584), whose reign was marked by feuds and warfare against his brother, Sigebert, king of Austrasia. The feud became vicious when Chilperic killed his wife Galswintha, sister of Austrasian Queen Brunhilde, and eventually led to Sigebert's conquest of Neustria (575).

Chimera Greek mythological monster, a fire-breathing creature that was part lion, part goat, and part dragon. It was slain by Bellerophon, who rode the winged horse Pegasus.

Ch'in Fourth dynasty of Chinese rulers (221–207 BC). During this dynasty, warring Chinese states were unified into the first Chinese empire. The unification was effected (by 221 BC) by Emperor Shih Huang Ti *(q.v.)*, leader of a petty kingdom in the northwest that rose to power during the Chou period. As emperor, he ended feudalism and established an administrative system that became a model for succeeding dynasties. He built the Great Wall *(q.v.)*. His son, who succeeded him, was overthrown in a rebellion (207) that brought the Han dynasty *(q.v.)* to power.

Chin ⟨Tsin⟩ Name of Chinese dynasty (AD 265–419). It was founded by General Ssu-ma Yen (*d.* 290), who briefly united China after the period of the Three Kingdoms. After his death, the empire was destroyed by the Revolt of Eight Kings and by foreign incursions. The period up until the outbreak of the revolts is called the Western Chin (AD 265–317). The subsequent period, Eastern Chin (AD 317–419), saw establishment of the capital at Nanking and creation of a kingdom in southern China. The north during this period was generally ruled by barbarian invaders.

China ⟨People's Republic of China⟩ Communist republic located in east central Asia. Its capital is Peking. Archaeological evidence indicates China had an advanced civilization as early as the 3d–2d millennium BC and it seems to have spread from the Yellow River valley. Legends tell of great rulers of ancient times, notably: Fu Hsi, the mythical first ruler of China who supposedly taught people how to fish, hunt, and domesticate animals in 2900 BC; Shen Nung, the second ruler, who taught them farming skills and established an agricultural society; and Huang Ti, the third ruler, who was credited with many innovations, ranging from the introduction of mathematical calculations to the building of boats. The later Hsia dynasty of Chinese rulers remains shrouded in legend and it is with the Shang dynasty that the known history of China—backed by significant archaeological evidence—begins. Key events in the history of China include:

c2200–c1766 BC Hsia dynasty, legendary first dynasty of rulers, said to have been founded by Yü the Great.

c1766–1122 BC Shang dynasty ruled; first dynasty identified by archaeological evidence; relatively advanced civilization with extensive farming, chariots, and bronze weapons.

1122–221 BC Chou dynasty in power; classical age of Chinese literature in which Confucius, Lao-tze, and Mencius flourished; Bronze Age culture reached its height and iron was introduced; period also noted for political turmoil and development of feudalism in China.

485 BC Equal-field system established to distribute land.

481–221 BC Warring States period ended Chou dynasty rule; empire divided into petty kingdoms; frequent warfare and corruption characterized the period, which also saw the rise of Confucianism.

255–210? BC Reign of Shih Huang Ti; as ruler of the Ch'in kingdom in the northwest, he extended his control over the warring states, abolished feudalism and created (221) the first unified Chinese empire; began construction of the Great Wall.

213 BC Burning of the Books ordered by Emperor Shih Huang Ti.

202 BC–AD 220 Han dynasty reigned; restored order after death of Shih Huang Ti; empire greatly expanded, especially by Wu Ti; Chinese Examination System introduced and Confucianism was promoted; Buddhism introduced from India; silk trade developed and many cultural advances made.

2 CENT. BC Explorer Chang Ch'ien traveled through India and Greece; brought back knowledge of these cultures.

AD 9–25 Han dynasty briefly overthrown by Wang Mang, a government official.

C 1ST CENT. AD Chang Ling founded Taoism.

AD C 100 First Chinese dictionary compiled.

AD 105 Paper invented.

AD 184–204 Rebellion of the Yellow Turbans; contributed to final overthrow of Han dynasty (AD 220).

AD 220–589 Six Dynasties period followed the collapse of the Han dynasty; each of the dynasties had its capital at Nanking; period marked by warfare between petty kingdoms, rise of Buddhism and Taoism, significant cultural advances, and a resurgence of feudalism.

AD 220–264 Three Kingdoms period immediately after the fall of the Han dynasty was marked by bloody wars, intrigues, and individual heroism; empire was divided into the Wu, Wei, and Shu Han kingdoms.

AD 304–439 Ascendancy of Sixteen Kingdoms in northern border region.

589–618 Sui dynasty reigned; reunited China, began construction of Grand Canal, refortified Great Wall.

618–907 T'ang dynasty, founded by Li Yüan; Confucianism revived, printing developed, and the civil service system refined.

684–704 Wu Hou reigned as empress of China; Korea conquered (655).

712–756 T'ang Hsüan Tsung reigned; instituted reforms and fostered great prosperity.

755 T'ang dynasty nearly overthrown in revolt by An Lu-shan; rulers never regained former power.

907–960 Five Dynasties and Ten Kingdoms period; five short-lived dynasties ruled from the end of the T'ang to the rise of the Sung; marked by chaos.

960–1279 Sung dynasty in power; after order was restored, there followed a period of great cultural flowering and such innovations as printing with movable type and first use of gunpowder; commerce flourished; the dynasty finally collapsed before the Mongol invasions, begun by Genghis Khan (c1206) and completed by Kublai Khan.

1260–1368 Yüan dynasty, founded by Kublai Khan, ruled China; established capital at Peking, completed Grand Canal and made numerous other advances.

c1275–1292 Marco Polo in China during his famous journey.

1368–1644 Ming dynasty in power, last of native Chinese emperors; restored traditional Chinese culture and made many conquests (later lost these territories); Spanish and Portuguese traders entered China.

1403–24 Yung-Lo reigned; annexed Annam,

moved his capital from Nanking to Peking and brought Ming dynasty empire to its zenith.

1644 Ch'ing forces (from Manchuria) seized control of China after they were called in by Ming emperor to put down a rebellion.

1644–1912 Ch'ing dynasty (Manchu) in power, last dynasty of emperors; they greatly expanded the empire but during the 19th cent. succumbed to incursions by foreign powers and internal dissent.

1662–1722 K'ang-hsi extended China's rule to Taiwan, Tibet, and Outer Mongolia.

1673–81 Revolt of the Three Feudatories against the Manchu dynasty quashed.

1704 Pope intervened in Rites Controversy among Roman Catholic missionaries in China.

1735–96 Ch'ien-lung reigned; brought empire to its greatest extent.

1759 "Canton system" established to control activities of foreign traders in China; marked restriction of foreign trade by government that lasted into the next century.

1796–1804 White Lotus Rebellion led by Buddhist adherents against Manchu rule; contributed to ultimate collapse of Manchu dynasty.

1813 Chia-ch'ing's failure to end corruption and high taxes resulted in a siege of the palace.

1839–42 First Opium War fought against Britain; China defeated and forced to cede Hong Kong and make trade concessions to British; other European powers forced similar concessions soon after.

1850–64 Taiping Rebellion, unsuccessful but devastating uprising against Ch'ing rule; became model for later Nationalist and Communist revolts.

1856–60 Second Opium War fought against France and Great Britain; China defeated and forced to allow opium trade and make substantial concessions.

c1861–c74 Self-strengthening movement, unsuccessful attempt to modernize and Westernize China.

1870 Tientsin Massacre, 20 Frenchmen killed by mob of Chinese.

1871–81 Russia occupied Chinese territory in Ili Crisis.

1883–85 Sino-French War ended in French control of Vietnam and other Indochina domains.

1894–95 Sino-Japanese War fought with Japan over control of Korea; China defeated and forced to grant substantial concessions to Japan.

1895 Sun Yat-sen led an abortive revolution in Canton.

LATE 1890s Foreign powers established spheres of influence in China, effectively dividing the country among themselves.

1898 Short-lived Reform Movement of 1898 attempted Westernization.

1899–1900 US enunciated Open Door Policy to maintain equal trading privileges between foreign powers operating in China and to guarantee the sovereignty of the Chinese government.

1900–01 Boxer Rebellion against foreign influence.

1911 Chinese Revolution of 1911 (Oct.–Dec.) sparked by Sun Yat-sen; long rule of Ch'ing dynasty formally ended soon after (1912) with emperor's abdication.

1911 Sun named president of new government (Dec.).

1912 Boy emperor abdicated and China declared a republic (Feb. 12).

1912 Sun resigned (Feb. 15) to unite country behind new leader, Yüan Shih-kai; Yüan soon after established a repressive regime.

1915 Japan presented its Twenty-one Demands, seeking virtual domination of China; China forced to concede to most of the demands.

1917 China joined Allies in WW I.

1917–26 Rise of warlord states followed death of President Yüan; Sun Yat-sen headed the nationalist Kuomintang faction and won control of the southern provinces.

1922 Nine-Power Treaty signed; Japanese withdrew from Chinese territory.

1924–27 United Front, alliance between Chinese Communist Party and Kuomintang.

1926–28 Chiang Kai-shek, now leader of the Nationalist Kuomintang, conducted the successful Northern Expedition against warlords.

1927 Chiang split with the Communists; long civil war between nationalist Kuomintang and Communists (1927–49) began.

1927 Autumn Harvest Uprising, unsuccessful Communist peasant revolt (Sept.).

1928 Northern Expedition ended in victory; Chiang Kai-shek set up nationalist government at Nanking.

1931 Mukden Incident, pretext used by the Japanese to invade and occupy Manchuria.

1931–34 Kiangsi Soviet, the Communist opposition government to Chiang Kai-shek's nationalist Kuomintang government, set up in southwest by Mao Tse-tung and Chu Teh.

1934–35 Long March by Chinese Communists to escape nationalist Kuomintang armies; Mao Tse-tung became leader of Communist party (1935); Communists established base in northwest.

1936 Chiang Kai-shek seized (Dec. 12) in Sian Incident; agreed to alliance with Communists to fight invading Japanese.

1937–45 Second Sino-Japanese War; Japanese invasion of China itself; conflict merged into WW II.

1945 Sino-Soviet Treaty, intended to deter future Japanese aggression, signed with USSR.

1945–49 Final phase of civil war between nationalist Kuomintang and Communists broke out soon after WW II ended; Communists emerged victorious (1949); Chiang Kai-shek forced to withdraw to Taiwan, where he set up his nationalist government; US refused to recognize Communist China.

1949 Mao became chairman of the new People's Republic of China; Chou En-lai named premier.

1949 Inner Mongolia became part of China.

1950 Tibet occupied by China.

1950–53 Korean War; Chinese troops aided North Koreans.

1951–52 Three-Anti Campaign mounted by Communist Party leaders.

1953–57 Five-Year Plan; collectivization of agriculture and beginnings of industrial development with Soviet aid.

1958–60 Great Leap Forward; unsuccessful program for rapid industrialization of China.

1960 Sino-Soviet split over Communist ideology; Soviets end aid to China.

1962 Border war with India.

1964 First Chinese atomic bomb exploded.

1966–69 Cultural Revolution; government purged and radical ideology spread throughout the populace in a period of great turmoil.

1971 US Table Tennis Team visited China; marked efforts to normalize US-Chinese relations.

1971 Lin Piao, Mao's heir apparent, was killed in a plane crash (Sept. 12).

1971 Admission of China to UN approved (Oct.); Taiwan expelled.

1972 US restrictions on trade with China eased; US Pres. Nixon visited China as part of effort to normalize relations.

1976 Premier Chou En-lai died (Jan. 8); Hua Kuo-feng succeeded him as a compromise between radicals and moderates.

1976 700,000 reported dead in major earthquake in northeast China (July).

1976 Mao died (Sept. 9); Premier Hua Kuo-feng became party chairman, succeeding Mao.

1976 Chiang Ch'ing, Mao's widow, and other radicals arrested.

1978 Technical state of war ended by friendship treaty with Japan.

1979 Full diplomatic relations with US established (Jan. 1).

1979 Troops ordered across border into Vietnam to punish the Vietnamese for their involvement in Cambodia (Feb.).

1979 National People's Congress endorsed new criminal law code (first under Communist regime) and popular elections for local people's congresses.

1979 Government officially criticized the Cultural Revolution and, while not denouncing Mao, sought to end cult worship of him.

1980 Central Committee ordered removal of most images of Mao then on public display.

1980 Mao's widow and nine other radicals tried in public show trials (Nov. 20–Dec. 29) as government continued shift from radicalism.

1981 Hua Kuo-feng, Mao's hand-picked successor as party chairman, resigned; Gen. Hu Yao-pang named as Hua's successor.

1982 US agreed to limit arms sales to Taiwan in order to continue policy of friendly relations toward China.

China, Great Wall of See **Great Wall of China**

China, Nationalist See **Taiwan**

Chindits See **Wingate, Orde Charles**

Chinese Civil War War (1945–49) that culminated a long struggle between Kuomintang (Nationalist) Chinese and the Communist Chinese for control of China. The civil war is generally considered to have begun in 1945, soon after the end of WW II. But Communist and Nationalist forces had been fighting in China intermittently since 1927. In 1926–27 the Communists had helped Chiang Kai-shek's Kuomintang forces take power from the warlords (provincial military rulers). After his victory in 1927, however, Chiang Kai-shek purged Communists from the Kuomintang, formed his Nationalist government, and began military expeditions against Communist strongholds. From 1931, the Kuomintang was also forced to contend with Japanese expansionism that later resulted in the Sino-Japanese War (*q.v.*). The Kuomintang finally drove the Communists out of the region south of the Yangtze River, precipitating the Communists' famous Long March (1934–35) to strongholds in northwest Shensi province. Mao Tse-tung emerged as the Communist leader during the march. Despite their differences, Kuomintang and Communists at times organized a temporary common front against the invading Japanese, notably in 1937 when the Red Army was ostensibly incorporated into the

Chinese army. China entered WW II as an ally, but a controversy developed when US Gen. J. Stilwell urged Chiang Kai-shek to commit more of his troops to fighting against the Japanese, instead of the Chinese Communists. At the end of WW II, both Kuomintang and Communist forces moved to take over territories formerly occupied by the Japanese. US Gen. G. Marshall was dispatched to China to attempt reconciliation between the two forces (Dec., 1945). But by Apr., 1946, widespread fighting had resumed, in which the Kuomintang was initially successful. Nationalist victories culminated in the capture of the Communist capital of Yenan (Mar. 19, 1947), but the tide of the war subsequently turned in favor of the Communists. They gained control of Manchuria by the end of 1947 and captured Peking on Jan. 15, 1949. The Communists kept up the pressure and by July Chiang Kai-shek was forced to begin withdrawing the remnants of his Kuomintang forces to Taiwan. The Communists proclaimed the People's Republic of China on Oct. 1, 1949, while the Nationalists formally established their government on Taiwan on Dec. 8, 1949.

Chinese Communist party Ruling political party of the People's Republic of China. Founded (1921) by Ch'en Tu-hsiu and Li Ta-chao, it first joined the Chinese Kuomintang government but was expelled (1927) by Chiang Kai-shek. Thus there began the long struggle between the Communists and the Kuomintang, the Chinese Civil War *(q.v.)*. The party maintained a precarious existence in China and was forced to make the famous Long March into northern China. Led by Mao Tse-tung (after 1935), it thrived in the north and established its own government. It effected a truce (1936) with the Kuomintang in the face of Japanese aggression and conducted a guerrilla war against the Japanese during WW II. In 1945 it resumed war with the Nationalists, and forced them out of the mainland in 1949. Since that time the Communist party has remained the dominant power in China.

Chinese Examination System A system of civil service examinations long in use in the Chinese Empire. Candidates were tested in their knowledge of the Confucian classics. The system began around 124 BC under the Han emperor Wu Ti (156–87 BC), and was expanded in the T'ang and Sung dynasties. The system helped maintain the stability of China for over 2,000 years, and was not abolished until 1905 amid a movement to modernize China.

Chinese exclusion acts US legislation passed (1882–94) to prohibit Chinese immigration. Chinese (particularly laborers) began emigrating to the Pacific coastal region by the mid-19th cent.

The Burlingame Treaty (1868) further encouraged this influx of cheap labor until resentment among US workers came to a head. Congress passed the first exclusion act in 1882, banning Chinese immigration for 10 years. Subsequent acts (1888, 1892) violated treaties with China, and by a new treaty (1894), immigration was banned for another 10 years. The ban continued until 1924, when new immigration laws shut out all Asians. The exclusion acts were repealed in 1943.

Chinese Revolution of 1911 Uprising that succeeded in overthrowing the last (Ch'ing, or Manchu) dynasty of Chinese emperors and establishing a Chinese Republic. The revolution broke out in Wuhan on Oct. 11, 1911, after army officers were implicated in the secret revolutionary society *T'ung-meng-hui* (Combined League Society), headed by Dr. Sun Yat-sen. On being discovered, the officers forced their commander to rebel against Manchu troops and the rebellion spread from province to province. The imperial family fled (Dec., 1911), and the boy emperor, Hsüan T'ung (Pu-Yi), abdicated on Feb. 7, 1912. The government passed into the hands of a national assembly at Nanking which had elected Sun the first president of the Chinese Republic (Dec. 30, 1911). China officially became a Republic on Feb. 12, 1912. Sun soon resigned (Feb. 15, 1912) in order to unite the country behind Yüan Shih-kai, a former Manchu military leader who had come to terms with the rebels. In office, however, Yüan sought to increase his power. He was opposed by the (Nationalist) Kuomintang party (founded 1912), which favored a parliamentary system with an elected prime minister. Elections established the Kuomintang as the strongest party in the parliament (convened Apr. 8, 1913), and when Yüan attempted to consolidate his power, the Kuomintang started a second revolution (July 10). Yüan crushed the revolt and, finally, dissolved parliament (Jan. 10, 1914). Yüan ruled until his death (1916), though his power was checked somewhat by provincial military rulers. Following Yüan's death, the military rulers, who came to be called "warlords," vied for control of China. They thus prevented establishment of an effective central government until the rise of the Kuomintang, under Chiang Kai-shek's leadership, some years later. (*See also* Chinese Civil War.)

Ch'ing ⟨Manchu⟩ Last dynasty of emperors of China (ruled 1644 to 1912). The Ch'ing dynasty was founded (1636) in the Manchurian provinces. Called in (1644) by the Ming emperor to recapture Peking from the bandit Li Tzu-ch'eng, the Manchu seized power for themselves and installed Ch'ing emperor Shun Chih. By 1683 all China had been conquered and a government by Manchu and former Ming officials was in complete control. During the dynasty's long reign, China's territory and population were increased threefold. Emperor Ch'ien Lung expanded Chinese domains to their greatest point in the 18th cent., but, in the 19th cent., incursions by European powers and internal dissent began to weaken the empire. By 1912 the successful Chinese Revolution of 1911 had overthrown Emperor Pu-Yi, last of the Ch'ing rulers.

Shun Chih	1644–61
K'ang-hsi	1661–1722
Yung Chêng	1723–35
Ch'ien Lung	1735–96
Chia Ch'ing	1796–1820
Tao Kuang	1821–50
Hsien Fêng	1851–61
T'ung Chih	1862–75
Kwang-hsü	1875–1908
Hsuan T'ung	1908–12

Chinghiz Khan   *See* **Genghis Khan**

Ch'in Shih Huang Ti   *See* **Shih Huang Ti**

Chippendale, Thomas   1718–79. Noted English furniture maker. His graceful, neoclassic furniture designs drew from Chinese Gothic, and French rococo art.

Chippewa, Battle of   US victory (July 5, 1814) over the British during the War of 1812. An invasion force of some 4,000 Americans crossed the Niagara River into southern Canada and defeated a British force of about 2,000.

Chiron   In Greek mythology, a centaur. Chiron, instructed by Apollo and Diana, became a prophet, physician, and teacher of Hercules, Achilles, and Jason. At his death, Jupiter placed him in the constellation Sagittarius.

Chisholm* vs *Georgia   US Supreme Court decision (1793) that affirmed the right of a citizen to sue the government of another state in federal court. The decision was superseded by the 11th Amendment (1798).

Chislieri, Antonio   *See* **Pius V**

chivalry   Code of moral and ethical conduct that developed during feudal times in Europe (12th–15th cents.). Central to the code was the feudal knight, who exhibited the ideal qualities of piety, loyalty to his feudal lord, courtesy and courtly (platonic) affection for ladies of the court, and valor on the field of battle. Chivalry flourished in the 12th and 13th cents., especially during the Crusades. It declined as an ideal of conduct by the 15th cent., when military campaigns were more openly waged for gain than for reasons of honor or religious duty. The chivalric code was central to the popular medieval romances of the Arthurian legend (*q.v.*).

Chivington Massacre   *See* **Sand Creek Massacre**

Chlorus, Constantius   *See* **Constantius I**

Chmielnicki, Bogdan   ⟨Khmelnitsky, Bogdan⟩ 1593–1657. Zaporozhe Cossack leader. He led the rebellion of the Ukrainians against Polish domination (1648–54). With Russian aid, he successfully resisted Polish armies, and, in 1654, the Ukraine was declared an autonomous Russian protectorate.

Chocim, battles of   ⟨Khotin, ~⟩   **1.** Polish victory (Aug.-Sept., 1621) over the Ottoman Turks, ending a brief war between the two (1620–21). The war was sparked by Polish intervention in Moldavia, and, in 1621, the Turks, under Osman II, invaded Poland. Polish forces, raised by Sigismund III, met the Turks at Chocim and successfully withstood Turkish attacks for over a month. **2.** Polish victory (Nov., 1673) over the Ottoman Turks, ending a brief war between the two (1672–76). The Turks, allied with Ukrainian Cossacks (then in rebellion against Poland) invaded the Ukraine (1672) and initially forced Poland to negotiate. Polish forces regrouped under John Sobieski (later King John III) and attacked the Turks at Chocim, Moldavia. The Poles largely destroyed the 25,000-man Turkish army garrisoned there and turned the tide of the war.

Chomsky, Avram Noam   1928–.   American writer, linguist, and teacher. Chomsky developed his revolutionary theory of generative grammar in such books as *Current Issues in Linguistic Theory*, *Cartesian Linguistics*, and *Language and Mind*.

Chopin, Frédéric François   1810–49. Polish-born composer of the romantic school, famous for his compositions for the piano. A child prodigy, he first performed publicly on the piano at age eight. He left Poland permanently (1831) for Paris, and during an affair with G. Sand (1836–47) wrote his 24 preludes for the piano. Other works for the piano include numerous mazurkas, nocturnes, and polonaises.

Chou   Third dynasty of rulers (c1122 BC–c221 BC) in China and the Chinese classical age. The Chou people, dominant in the Wei River valley, invaded the Chinese Kingdom and overthrew (c1122 BC) Chou Hsin, the Shang dynasty ruler. Wu Wang became the first emperor and founder of the Chou dynasty, which lasted for nearly a millennium. The dynasty is traditionally divided into two periods. The *Western* Chou (c1122–771) lasted until the capital of Hao (near modern Sian) was overrun by local lords and their barbarian allies. The *Eastern* Chou dynasty (771–221) then established itself at Lo-yang. The Eastern Chou dynasty is subdivided into the Ch'un Ch'iu (722–481) and the Warring States (481–221) periods, and eventually fell to rulers of the Ch'in dynasty. The Chou period was a time of great cultural flowering. The Five Classics were written and Confucius, Lao-tze, and Mencius, among others, spread their teachings.

Chouan, Jean *See* **Chouans**

Chouans Peasant bands in western France that rebelled (1793) against the revolutionary government during the French Revolution (1789–99). Named after their leader, Jean Chouan (*pseud.* of Jean Cottereau, 1757–94), they later were led by G. Cadoudal and took part in the Wars of the Vendée (1793–96) and other risings. Though their guerrilla activities were largely suppressed by Napoleon, small uprisings (the "Petite Chouannerie") continued until Napoleon's downfall (1815).

Chou En-lai 1898–1976. Chinese Communist leader, premier (1949–76) and foreign minister (1949–58). A founder of the Chinese Communist party, he served (1924–27) with other Communists in the Kuomintang's nationalist revolution. During the subsequent civil war (1927–49), in which the Kuomintang turned against the Communists, he participated in the Long March. A leading Communist official thereafter, he helped bring the Communists to power in 1949. Later, as foreign minister, he headed delegations to the Geneva and Bandung conferences. He is said to have exercised a moderating influence during the Cultural Revolution and to have been responsible for the Sino-American rapprochement in the 1970s.

Chou Hsin c1154–c1122 BC. Last Shang dynasty emperor of ancient China. He was notorious for his cruelty and debauchery, and his overthrow (1122) brought the Chou dynasty to power.

Chou Kung *fl.* 12 cent. BC. Chinese statesman, brother of Emperor Wu Wang. A wise and just man, he became the model for Chinese rulers and officials of succeeding generations. He served as regent of the empire on his brother's death and wrote the *Chou Li*, a code of laws for the Chou state.

Chremonidean War War (c266–262 BC) fought by Athens and Sparta against Macedonian rule. Spurred on by promises of aid from Egyptian king Ptolemy II, the Athenians and Spartans rebelled (266 BC) against King Antigonus II. The Spartans were badly defeated (265), and the Athenians yielded (262) after a two-year siege by the Macedonians. The Macedonians subsequently established new military outposts in the region.

Chrestien de Troyes *See* **Chrétien de Troyes**

Chrétien de Troyes (Chrestien de Troyes) *fl.* 1164. French poet, one of the great medieval poets of the Arthurian romances. Among his important works are *Érec et Énide*, *Cligès*, *Lancelot*, *Yvain*, and *Perceval*. In the latter he introduced the search for the Holy Grail to the Arthurian cycle.

Christ, Churches of *See* **Churches of Christ**

Christ, Disciples of *See* **Disciples of Christ**

Christadelphians Small religious denomination (Brothers of Christ), founded in America by John Thomas (1805–71) c1848. They believe that Christ will return to establish a theocracy at Jerusalem. They refuse to vote, hold office, or engage in warfare.

Christian I 1426–81. King of Denmark and Norway (1450–81) and Sweden (1457–64), founder of the Oldenburg line. He warred against the Swedes (1451–57) to press his claim to the Swedish throne, took possession of Schleswig and Holstein (1460), and was deposed from the Swedish throne (1464). In his last attempt to retake the throne (1471), Christian was repulsed by S. Sture.

Christian II 1481–1559. Danish king of Denmark and Norway (1513–23) and Sweden (1520–23), successor to his father, King John. His reign marked the final breakup of the Kalmar Union (1523). An unpopular king, he at first succeeded in bringing rebellious Sweden back into the Union (1520). He ordered the Stockholm Bloodbath (1520), however, and, by the popular reaction against him, helped bring on Swedish independence (1523). At that time Denmark also rebelled and deposed him.

Christian III 1503–59. King of Denmark and Norway (1534–59). With Sweden, he helped break the power of the Hanseatic League (1536), established the supremacy of the Danish navy in Northern Europe, made Lutheranism the state religion in Denmark and Norway (1536), and reduced Norway's status to that of a province of Denmark.

Christian IV 1577–1648. King of Denmark and Norway (1588–1648). He strengthened the navy, industry, and commerce in his kingdom. He successfully waged the Kalmar War (1611–13), but his invasion of Germany during the Thirty Years' War (1618–48) proved disastrous. Following a defeat by the Swedes, he was forced to yield power to the nobility.

Christian V 1649–99. King of Denmark and Norway (1670–99). Popular with his people, he advanced commoners into the ranks of the nobility. Until 1676, he was largely guided by one such nobleman, P. Griffenfeld, who led him into an unsuccessful war (1675–79) with Sweden. The monarchy became absolutist during his reign.

Christian VII 1749–1808. King of Denmark and Norway (1766–1808). He was mentally unstable, and his physician, J. Struensee, largely controlled the government until his execution (1772). Thereafter, other advisers and finally Christian's son, Frederick VI, held power.

Christian VIII 1786–1848. King of Denmark (1839–48). Elected king of Norway (1814), he permitted adoption of a liberal constitution, attempted to break the union of Norway with Sweden, and was forced to abdicate (1814) by the Swedes. As Denmark's king, he reformed the penal system.

Christian IX 1818–1906. King of Denmark (1863–1906), successor to Frederick VII. His war with Austria and Prussia (1864) ended in defeat and loss of the provinces of Schleswig, Holstein, and Lauenburg. His reign was marked by agitation for liberal constitutional reforms.

Christian X 1870–1947. King of Denmark (1912–47), successor to his father, Frederick VIII. He granted women the right to vote (1915), and, by his refusal to flee the invading Nazis in WW II, became a symbol of Danish resistance.

Christian, Fletcher *See **Bounty**, HMS*

Christiania *See **Oslo***

Christian Churches *See **Disciples of Christ***

Christianity General term used to describe the religion that arose in Palestine (1st cent. AD) from the life and teachings of Jesus Christ and that has spread to nearly every part of the world. Historically, it has been the predominant religion in the West for many centuries and had an enormous influence on the development of Western civilization, especially in literature, art, architecture, and music. Christianity is based on the New Testament *(q.v.)*, which records the acts and teachings of Jesus, and the Old Testament is regarded as sacred and authoritative Scripture. Christian doctrine was further refined by a series of "creeds" promulgated in the course of early church history. Together, these beliefs attempted to reflect Jesus Christ's own revelations about God and the salvation of mankind. Apostles chosen by Jesus constituted the early leadership of the church, or "assembly" of his followers. The church perpetuated the teachings of Jesus, claimed the authority to interpret them authentically, and administered the sacraments, believed to have been established by Jesus for the spiritual benefit of the faithful. However, disagreements among Christians about Jesus' teachings occurred as early as New Testament times. Major doctrinal crises usually resulted in "little churches" that split off from the main church and maintained "heresies," such as Arianism, Monophysitism, Nestorianism, Do-

natism, and so on. These were condemned by the main tradition, and most of the dissident Eastern and African churches had split from the church by the end of the Council of Chalcedon (AD 451). Bitter disputes over such issues as Iconoclasm caused the final split (1054) between the Roman Catholic and Eastern Orthodox churches. Some centuries later, Christianity was again divided by the Protestant Reformation, which followed M. Luther's rebellion (1517) against the authority of the church. Protestantism arose from this split and became, with the Roman Catholic church and the Orthodox Eastern church, one of the three main branches of Christianity. In modern times, especially since the 1920s, adherents of the ecumenical movement have been active in attempting to overcome the differences that separate these three branches. (*See also* Roman Catholic church; Protestantism; Reformation; Orthodox Eastern church; names of sects.)

Christian mysticism *See **mysticism***

Christian Science ⟨*prop.* Church of Christ, Scientist⟩ Religion founded (1879) by M. Eddy. Christian Scientists believe the evils of the material world, such as illness, sin, and death, are mere illusions that can be overcome by faith alone. Thus, Christian Scientists have frequently gained notoriety by refusing medical help. M. Eddy experienced a miraculous healing herself (1866), and organized the mother church in Boston (1892). Since then the faith has spread to many countries around the world.

Christian Socialism Socioreligious movement that began in mid-19th-cent. England. A reaction against the social inequities of capitalism, Christian Socialists were more concerned about the sufferings of the poor in an industrial society than about expropriation of privately owned factories and property. An outgrowth of the failed Chartism movement, this form of socialism spawned a number of workingmen's associations, cooperative ventures, and some reforms during the 1850s. By the late 19th cent., the movement had spread to the US and Germany. In Germany, Christian Socialist parties became involved in anti-Semitic activities and were officially condemned there (1894).

Christians of Saint John *See **Mandaeans***

Christie, Agatha 1890–1976. English writer, one of the most successful mystery writers of all time. Among her works are *Ten Little Indians*, *The Mousetrap*, and *Witness for the Prosecution*.

Christina 1626–89. Queen of Sweden (1632–54), successor to her father, Gustavus II. An eccentric woman, she abdicated in favor of her cousin Charles X (1654). She was unsuccessful in her attempt to regain the crown after his death in 1660.

Christophe, Henri 1767–1820. Haitian rebel and ruler. Born a slave, he joined the rebellion against French rule led by F. Toussaint L'Ouverture. He became provisional leader of Haiti (1807), and then, in a subsequent civil war, formed a kingdom in the north (1811). Haiti was reunified on his death.

Christopher, Saint 3d cent. AD. Martyr whose existence is historically uncertain. He is said to have carried a small child across a river, discovering partway across that he could barely hold up the child. After the crossing, the child revealed himself as Christ, carrying the weight of the world in his hands. Christopher is the patron saint of travelers.

Chrysler's Farm, Battle of ⟨Crysler's Farm, ~⟩ Battle (Nov. 11, 1813) during the War of 1812. British forces defeated a superior American force north of the St. Lawrence and thus halted the American advance against Montreal.

Chrysostom, Saint John AD c347–407. Clergyman and one of the fathers of the Greek church. He became archbishop of Constantinople (AD 398–403) and, for a time, enjoyed wide influence and fame for his eloquence. Popular with the common people, he was banished to Armenia (404).

Chudleigh, 1st Baron, Clifford of *See* **Clifford of Chudleigh, 1st Baron**

Chu Hi *See* **Chu Hsi**

Chu Hsi, ⟨Chu Hi⟩ 1130–1200. Chinese Neo-Confucian philosopher, one of China's most important commentators on Confucianism. Until 1905, public officials were required to have a thorough knowledge of his works on Confucianism, *The Four Books*, to pass the civil service examination. Though he believed that human nature in reality was less than good, he taught that an individual's essential goodness could be brought out by study of the classics. His teachings were also influential in Japan and Korea.

Chuikov, Vasily Ivanovich 1900–82. Russian general. He commanded the stubborn Russian defense of Stalingrad (1942) during WW II, accepted the German surrender of Berlin (1945), and commanded Russian forces in Germany (1949–53).

Chu-ko Liang AD 181–234. Chinese soldier and government minister, credited with helping Liu Pei found the Shu Han dynasty (*see* Han). A military, mathematical, and organizational genius, he is celebrated in Chinese legend and literature.

Chulalongkorn ⟨Rama V⟩ 1853–1910. King of Siam (1868–1910). Educated by an English governess, he carried out the modernization programs begun by his father, King Mongkut. He abolished

slavery (1874), reorganized the government to centralize authority, and managed to maintain Siam's independence by playing the British and French against each other.

Ch'un Chiu A period in Chinese history (722–481 BC), a subdivision of the Chou dynasty (*q.v.*). Also called the "Spring and Autumn Period," it was marked by the rise of small, quarreling states.

Chung Te ⟨Abahai⟩ 1592–1643. Manchurian ruler (from 1627) and founder of the line that became the Ch'ing dynasty (*q.v.*). He began the Manchu conquest of the Ming dynasty but died before it could be completed (1644).

Churches of Christ American Protestant churches, most numerous in the American South and West. Fundamentalist and evangelical, they are an offshoot of the Disciples of Christ, and broke away from that body c1840.

Churchill, Sir Winston Leonard Spencer 1874–1965. British statesman, author, and prime minister (1940–45, 1951–55). He is regarded as one of the outstanding figures of the 20th cent. for his brilliant leadership of Britain during WW II. A soldier and well-known journalist by the time he was elected to Parliament (1900), he was a Conservative party member throughout most of his career. He served in a variety of government posts, including first lord of the admiralty (1911–15), colonial secretary (1921–22), and chancellor of the exchequer (1924–29). Churchill recognized and spoke out against the threat of Nazi Germany and was next appointed to the admiralty (1939). He became prime minister (1940) when N. Chamberlain's government was ousted for its handling of the war with Germany. During the war years, he rallied the British to the war effort, lobbied for help from the US (then neutral), and helped write the famous Atlantic Charter (1941). Subsequently, he figured in the conferences of the Allies at Casablanca (1943), Quebec (1943), Cairo (1943), Teheran (1943), Yalta (1945), and Potsdam (1945). In the postwar years, Churchill was out of power (1945–51), though he spoke vigorously against the menace of the USSR (coining the phrase "iron curtain"). Prime minister again in 1951, he retired in 1955 but continued as a member of Parliament until 1964. He received the Nobel Prize in Literature in 1953.

Church of Christ, Scientist *See* **Christian Science**

Church of England ⟨Anglican Church⟩ The Christian, national church of England and mother church of the Anglican Communion. It is headed by the king (or queen) and the archbishops of the two traditional provinces, Canterbury and York. Though the church retains much of the structure and liturgy of the Roman Catholic church (it was united with Rome until the reign of Henry VIII), its doctrines are largely an outgrowth of the Protestant Reformation. These doctrines are set forth in the Book of Common Prayer, the Thirty-Nine Articles, the Catechism, and Books of Homilies. Key dates in the history of the church are:

2d–5th cents. Christianity was established in Britain during the Roman occupation.

5th cent. Christianity declined during the Anglo-Saxon invasions that followed the Romans' departure; vestiges of Christianity survived as the Celtic church.

597 Saint Augustine began conversion of the Anglo-Saxons.

601 Saint Augustine became the first archbishop of Canterbury; first cathedral built.

735 York became an archbishopric.

1066 The Norman conquest marked the beginning of closer ties with Rome, the arrival of clerics from continental Europe, and the rise of clerical influence in secular matters.

1170 Thomas à Becket martyred after long struggle with King Henry II to maintain church prerogatives against royal authority.

c1529–34 Henry VIII brought to a head a long struggle for power between the monarchy and the pope; he demanded the pope's assent to his divorce from Catherine of Aragon.

1533 Pope Clement VIII refused his sanction to the divorce and excommunicated Henry; T. Cranmer named archbishop of Canterbury.

1534 Henry obtained passage of the Act of Supremacy in Parliament; it named him head of the English church and thus created the Church of England; no doctrinal changes were made.

1536–39 Henry seized the property of the monasteries.

1539 Henry obtained passage of the Act of Six Articles to check the spread of Lutheranism; there followed persecutions of both Lutherans and Catholics, who refused to recognize Henry as head of the church.

1547 King Edward VI repealed the Act of Six Articles and introduced Protestant doctrines in the church.

1549 Book of Common Prayer was issued; revised (1552); first Act of Uniformity passed requiring clergy to conform to rites in Book of Common Prayer; other Acts of Uniformity passed 1551, 1559, and 1662.

1552 The Forty-two Articles, concerning Anglican doctrine, were published by T. Cranmer.

1555–58 Mary I briefly restored Roman Catholicism during her reign; papal authority was reestablished in England; Protestants were persecuted.

1559 Independent national church of England reestablished by Elizabeth I; Act of Supremacy reenacted.

1563 The Thirty-nine Articles of Faith (replacing the Forty-two Articles) were published to complete Elizabeth's refounding of the church; the church thus established was a compromise and incorporated largely Protestant dogma with Catholic structure and liturgy (in English); the reforms failed to satisfy Protestant extremists and gave added impetus to such dissenters as Nonconformists, Puritans, Separatists, Brownists, Presbyterians, and Congregationalists.

1604 Hampton Court Conference (q.v.) held.

1611 King James (authorized) version of the Bible was completed.

1625–49 Reign of Charles I; Charles, an absolutist, aroused opposition among Puritans and other groups by his high-handed measures, intended to bring about religious uniformity; his attempt to impose episcopacy led to the Solemn League and Covenant (q.v.) in Scotland (1638).

1642–49 English Civil War—political and religious struggle between Royalists (Anglicans and Catholics) and Parliamentarians (Puritans and Presbyterians).

1649–60 Victorious Puritan Parliamentarians established the Commonwealth and Protectorate (q.v.); the Church of England was disestablished for a time.

1660 Charles II restored to the throne; the reaction against Puritanism began.

1661 Modern version of the Book of Common Prayer adopted.

1661–65 Clarendon Codes, harsh measures to promote uniformity with the Church of England, were enacted, giving new impetus to the Nonconformists.

1688 King James II attempted to reestablish Catholicism in England; the archbishop of Canterbury refused to read James's order of toleration in all churches; James was deposed and replaced by the Protestants, William and Mary, in the Glorious Revolution (1688).

1689 English Bill of Rights was passed, with measure excluding Catholics from the monarchy.

1701 Act of Settlement, stipulating that the monarch must belong to the Church of England, was passed.

1717 Bangorian Controversy began (during George I's reign).

c1729 Movement that resulted in the Methodist Church was begun by J. Wesley; the movement arose amid a new concern for evangelicalism in the Church of England (18th cent.)

1799 Anglican Church Missionary Society, an outgrowth of evangelicalism, was founded.

1829 Catholic Emancipation Act passed, ending long-standing restrictions on Catholics.

c1833 Rise of the Oxford Movement, which sought a return to Roman Catholic ritual and dogma in the Anglican church.

20th cent. Rise of the ecumenical movement.

1919 Church Assembly, a church legislative body, was formed.

1982 Pope John Paul II visited Britain; meetings with Anglican church leaders marked significant step in effort to reestablish ties between the English church and Rome.

Church of Scotland National church (Presbyterian) of Scotland. Movement toward a Protestant national church in Scotland began (1557) with the signing of the First Covenant by Scottish nobles. Under the guidance of J. Knox, the movement came under Calvinist influence, and Knox figured in the drafting (1560) of the *Book of Discipline,* which outlined the church's Presbyterian organization. The church's legal position was ratified (1592) by Parliament, but James VI (after 1603, English king James I) and his successors in Scotland sought to reimpose the episcopacy. This led to the resistance by the Covenanters *(q.v.)* during the 17th cent. Existence of the church was guaranteed (1707) by the union of England and Scotland. The church suffered a number of secessionist movements, notably the Free Church of Scotland (1843) and the United Presbyterian Church of Scotland (1847), which merged (1900) into the United Free Church of Scotland. The latter rejoined the Church of Scotland in 1929.

Church of the Brethren *See* **Dunkards**

Church of the New Jerusalem ⟨New Church⟩ Religious society formed by the followers of E. Swedenborg. The first church appeared in England in 1788. Followers believe in achieving self-realization through an understanding of Swedenborg's commentaries on the Scriptures.

churrigueresque Relating to a Spanish architectural style. Introduced by Charles II's royal architect, Don José Churriguera (1650–1723), it was a highly ornate adaptation of Renaissance and baroque styles.

Chu Teh 1886–1976. Leading Chinese Communist general. He participated in the Chinese Revolution of 1911, and, following the break between Nationalists and Communists (1927), he joined with Mao Tse-tung to form the Communist army. He became general of all Communist forces (1931–54) and, after the Communist victory in China (1949), served in high government posts.

Cibó, Giovanni Battista *See* **Innocent VIII**

Cicero, Marcus Tullius ⟨Tully⟩ 106–43 BC. Great Roman orator, statesman, philosopher, and man of letters. His orations, especially the *Orations Against Catiline* and the *Philippics,* are important in the study of Latin. An ardent republican, he was elected consul (63 BC) and exposed the famous Conspiracy of Catiline (63 BC). He was exiled (58) for executions he ordered as a result of the conspiracy, and was then recalled (57). He was a staunch defender of the republic during the Roman Civil Wars and opposed J. Caesar. After Caesar's assassination, he delivered the famous *Philippics* (44–43) against his enemy, M. Antony. He was put to death (43) by Octavian at Antony's insistence.

Ciceronian Period Latin literary period (70–43 BC) It marked the first great stage of Latin literature and was greatly influenced by the technique and style of Cicero. It was followed by the Augustan Age *(q.v.).*

Cid, the ⟨El Cid⟩ ⟨Cid Campeador⟩ c1040–99. Spanish soldier and hero. His real name was Rodrigo Díaz de Vivar. He fought valiantly in wars between the kingdoms of Castile and Navarre but was banished from Castile (1081). Thereafter, he was a soldier of fortune under the Moors of Saragossa and had many adventures. He conquered Valencia (1094) and ruled it until his death.

Cid Campeador *See* **Cid, the**

Cimabue, Giovanni d. c1302. Italian painter. His paintings, mostly on religious themes, reflect the change in Italian medieval painting from the once-dominant formal Byzantine style to the more natural style of later artists. He is said to have been Giotto's teacher.

Cimber, Lucius Tillius Roman conspirator, one of J. Caesar's assassins (44 BC). He distracted Caesar with a petition and then held him during the stabbing.

Cimbri Germanic tribe that invaded Rome (2d cent. BC) after being forced out of their homelands to the north. They were victorious in several engagements before being annihilated by Marius and Q. Catulus at Campi Raudii (101 BC).

Cimmerians Ancient people of the northern Black Sea region who flourished briefly in the 7th cent. BC. Mentioned by Homer, they were apparently forced (late 8th cent.) southward by the Scythians into what is now Turkey. There they conquered Phrygia and invaded Lydia (7th cent.). Defeated decisively by the Lydians late in the 7th cent., they disappeared from history.

Cimon d. 449 BC. Athenian soldier-statesman, noted for his victories against the Persians. He distinguished himself at the Battle of Salamis (480 BC). As commander of Athenian forces, he won a great victory over the Persians at Eurymedon River (466), in which he defeated both their naval and land forces. His popularity declined when he became leader of the pro-Spartan faction in Athens.

Cincinnatus *fl.* 5th cent. BC. Roman hero, consul (460 BC) and dictator (458 BC). According to traditional accounts, he was made dictator to rescue the Roman army from annihilation by the Aequi, and, once that was accomplished, gave up his power to return to farming.

Cinna, Lucius Cornelius *d.* 84 BC. Roman consul (87–84 BC) and a leader of the popular party. Elected consul under L. Sulla, he tried to rescind some of Sulla's reforms after Sulla left to fight Mithridates VI in the east. With Marius, he overcame Sulla's supporters at Rome and massacred them. He became sole consul on Marius' death (86 BC), and was murdered by his soldiers shortly before Sulla's return.

Cinq-Mars, Henri Coiffier, marquis de 1620–42. French courtier and conspirator in the court of Louis XIII. Ambitious for power, he plotted against Louis' minister, Cardinal Richelieu. One plan, which involved a secret pact with Spain, was uncovered and ended with his execution.

Cinque Ports Confederation (11th–15th cents.) of English port cities located on the English Channel. The confederation provided ships and personnel to the crown for defense of England. Its importance declined rapidly after the formation of the royal navy (late 15th cent.) under Henry VII. The original five ports were: Hastings, New Romney, Hythe, Dover, and Sandwich.

Ciompi, Revolt of the Revolt (1378) by lower-class workingmen *(ciompi)* in Florence. Government in Florence was dominated by the major guilds, which had successfully excluded such lesser guilds as that of the wool workers. Inequities and economic hardships imposed by this system sparked the revolt (July, 1378). It resulted in formation of a short-lived government in which all guilds were represented. Major guilds regained control by 1382.

Circe Sorceress in Greek mythology. Daughter of Helios, she lured sailors to her island and changed them into animals. Odysseus forced her to change his sailors back into human form.

Cisalpine Republic Republic in north Italy set up (1797) and controlled by Napoleon. It included Milan, Modena, Parma, Bologna, Ferrara, Romagna, and later Venetia. It became Napoleon's kingdom of Italy (1805), and was dissolved by the Congress of Vienna (1815).

Cistercians Order of Roman Catholic monks founded (1098) in France by Saint Robert. An out-

growth of the Benedictine order, the Cistercians were reformers. They rebelled against the laxity that had overtaken the Benedictine order by returning to the strict, ascetic life of the first Benedictines. Both Saint Stephen Harding and Saint Bernard of Clairvaux influenced the development of the order, the latter being largely responsible for its rapid spread during the 12th cent. By the 14th cent., however, it weakened and declined, and this set the stage for later reform movements in the order, notably by the Trappists. Begun (1664) at La Trappe, France, this movement fostered still stricter observance of the ascetic life and became a permanent division of the Cistercian order.

Citium, Zeno of *See* **Zeno of Citium**

Citizen Genêt *See* **Genêt, Edmond Charles Édouard**

Citizen King *See* **Louis Philippe**

city-state ⟨*Greek* polis⟩ A city and surrounding lands governed as an autonomous state by its citizens. Though city-states appeared in other civilizations, they were especially important in the history of ancient Greece. Such city-states as Athens, Sparta, and Thebes came to dominate whole regions of Greece. For purposes of mutual defense, the city-states formed confederacies, such as the Delian and Peloponnesian leagues. Ultimately, however, the city-states and their leagues were no match for the centralized power of the Macedonian and Roman empires.

civilistas South American political parties. Active in Peru and Brazil (late 19th-early 20th cents.), the civilistas were primarily made up of merchants, bankers, and landowners who opposed control of their governments by the military. The antimilitary policies of the civilistas were partly responsible for Peru's defeat in the War of the Pacific (1879–84).

Civil Rights Act Name of several US laws. **1.** Passed (1866) over Pres. A. Johnson's veto, the act gave Negroes full rights as citizens and was designed to counter Black Codes enacted by Southern states after the Civil War. The constitutionality of the act was questioned, however. Once its provisions had been confirmed by passage of the 14th Amendment, Congress reenacted the bill (1870). **2.** Passed (1871) to enforce the 14th and 15th Amendments, particularly in regard to Ku Klux Klan terrorism and discrimination in public establishments. It was ruled (1883) unconstitutional in part. **3.** Passed (1875) to require equal accommodations in public facilities. It was struck down (1883). **4.** Passed (1957) to establish a civil rights commission to investigate infringements of Negro voting rights. **5.** Passed

(1964) to end discrimination of all kinds, including religious and sex discrimination. It was a sweeping measure, though it was used first to attain civil rights for blacks. It forbade discrimination in public places, schools, and employment. **6.** Passed (1968) to end housing discrimination.

civil rights movement US social reform movement of the late 1950s and early 1960s that secured wide-ranging legal rights for American blacks (and other minorities). Among the federal acts passed as a result of this movement were the landmark Civil Rights Act of 1964, banning discrimination in employment, schools, and public accommodations; the 1965 Voting Rights Act, guaranteeing blacks the right to vote; and the 1968 housing bill, banning discrimination in housing. After the American Civil War and emancipation from slavery, blacks became the object of discriminatory laws (Jim Crow laws, *q.v.*) and practices. The Jim Crow laws created separate white and black societies in the South and elsewhere, despite passage of the 13th, 14th, and 15th constitutional amendments and the civil rights acts of the Reconstruction period. The Supreme Court established the principle of separate but equal facilities by its decision in *Plessy vs. Ferguson* (1896). The NAACP later pressed the cause of black civil rights but the basic principle of "separate but equal" stood until the 1950s, when the Supreme Court banned school segregation in its decision on *Brown vs. Board of Education of Topeka* (1954). The popular civil rights movement began a year later after a black woman, Mrs. Rosa Parks, refused to move to the back of a bus in Montgomery, Alabama (Dec. 5, 1955). Out of this incident came a nonviolent protest movement against discrimination, organized by such groups as Rev. Dr. M. L. King's Southern Christian Leadership Conference (SCLC), the Student Non-violent Coordinating Committee (SNCC), and the Congress of Racial Equality (CORE). Sit-ins, freedom rides, and other nonviolent protests culminated (1963) in the March on Washington (*q.v.*). In subsequent years these protests, and the commitment of presidents J. F. Kennedy and L. Johnson to civil rights, led to passage of the sweeping civil rights legislation of the 1960s. As this legislation was being passed, however, splits developed within the civil rights movement and began the period of its decline. By 1966 advocates of black power came to the fore to challenge the concepts of nonviolence and racial harmony that had been so important in rallying support among blacks and whites for civil rights. Rioting by blacks in major cities across the country, the assassination of Dr. King (Apr. 4, 1968), and the fanatical militancy of

such splinter groups as the Black Panthers ended the organized civil rights movement by the close of the 1960s.

Civil War *See under country names (i.e., American, English, Chinese, Russian, Mexican)*

Clairvaux, Saint Bernard of *See* **Bernard of Clairvaux, Saint**

Clapham Sect English social reformers. These wealthy, conservative Evangelical Christians were active c1790–1830. They advocated abolition of slavery, prison reform, an end to gambling and brutal sports, and missionary work. W. Wilberforce was a prominent member.

Clare, Gilbert de, 8th earl of Gloucester 1243–95. English nobleman. In the Barons' War he was at first a leader of the barons. He then turned to the royalists and helped defeat S. Montfort at Evesham (1265).

Clare, Gilbert de, 9th earl of Gloucester 1291–1314. English nobleman who was killed serving Edward II at the Battle of Bannockburn.

Clare, Richard de, 7th earl of Gloucester 1222–62. English nobleman. He was a leader of the barons who forced the Provisions of Oxford on King Henry III (1258).

Clarence, George, duke of 1449–78. English nobleman. He frequently conspired against his brother, King Edward IV. Edward finally imprisoned the duke in the Tower of London and executed him.

Clarendon, Assize of *See* **Assize of Clarendon**

Clarendon, Constitutions of *See* **Constitutions of Clarendon**

Clarendon, Edward Hyde, 1st earl of *See* **Hyde, Edward, 1st earl of Clarendon**

Clarendon, George William Frederick Villiers, 4th earl of *See* **Villiers, George William Frederick, 4th earl of Clarendon**

Clarendon Code Four laws enacted (1661–65) during the reign of King Charles II to suppress Nonconformists and other sects dissenting from the established (Anglican) Church of England. The laws were passed shortly after Charles's restoration, during the ministry of E. Hyde, 1st earl of Clarendon, though he opposed them. The acts were: Corporation Act (1661), requiring all municipal officers to be Anglican; the Act of Uniformity (1662), requiring all clergymen to accept and use the Anglican Book of Common Prayer; the Conventicle Act (1664), forbidding assembly (of more than five) for worship of faiths other than Anglican; and the Five-Mile Act (1665), forbidding Nonconformists to come within five miles of any town. Charles attempted unsuccessfully to moderate the laws by his declarations of indulgence (1662, 1672).

Clark, George Rogers 1752–1818. American Revolutionary war commander. Clark commanded volunteer units in Kentucky and environs (the Old Northwest) during the American Revolution (1775–83) and secured this frontier against British and Indian attacks. He was a brother of W. Clark.

Clark, Mark Wayne 1896–. American general. He was Fifth Army Commander in North Africa and Italy (1943–44) during WW II and commander of UN troops in Korea (1952–53).

Clark, William 1770–1838. American explorer. With his friend, M. Lewis, he undertook a three-year journey of exploration (1804–06) through the newly acquired lands of the Louisiana Purchase to the Pacific Northwest. The maps and journals compiled by Lewis and Clark contributed greatly to knowledge of the region.

Clarke, John 1609–76. English-born preacher, one of the founders of Rhode Island. Driven out of Massachusetts Bay colony for siding with A. Hutchinson and the antinomianism *(q.v.)* cause, he helped found Portsmouth (1638) and Newport (1639). With R. Williams, he returned to England and helped secure a royal charter for Rhode Island.

classical **1.** In music, the period from *c*1750 to *c*1820. The classic period was presaged by the decline of baroque forms and the appearance of rococo, or preclassical compositions, in the early 18th cent. The classic period saw the development of the sonata form, the rise of instrumental over vocal music, and evolution of the characteristic classical mediums: the symphony, string quartet, instrumental sonata, and solo concerto. Among the many notable composers of this period are W. Mozart, F. Haydn and L. Beethoven. **2.** In literature, the body of poetic, dramatic, and prose works written by ancient Greeks and Romans. The classic period in Greece ranges from about the 6th cent. to the 4th cent. BC, and in Rome from the 1st cent. BC to 2nd cent. AD.

classical revival *See* **Neoclassicism**

classicism Term applied to the imitation of the aesthetic values (such as simplicity, symmetry, and harmony of form) found in the art, architecture, and literature of ancient Greece and Rome. Revival of these values began during the Renaissance and influenced many artists, among them Michelangelo and Raphael. Classicism led to the formation of the 16th-cent. French literary group the Pléiade, and influenced such 16th- and 17th-cent. English writers as J. Dryden and A. Pope. The Napoleonic age saw the growth of classical imitation in the classical revival. Classicism also influenced art and architecture in continental Europe, England, and the US in the 19th cent. It con-

tinues to be a force in 20th-cent. architecture and the arts.

Claudian (Claudianus) *d.* 408? Alexandrian-born Latin poet. Claudian was the last of the great Latin classic poets. *The Rape of Proserpine* is one of his best-known epic poems.

Claudianus *See* **Claudian**

Claudius I (Germanicus, Tiberius Claudius Drusus Nero) 10 BC–AD 54. Roman emperor (AD 41–54), proclaimed successor to Caligula. Not considered a strong ruler, he nevertheless added Mauretania (AD 41–42) and Britain (after AD 43) to the Roman Empire.

Claudius II (Claudius, Marcus Aurelius) AD 214–270. Roman emperor (AD 268–270), successor to Galenius. He led Roman forces in an important victory over invading Goths at Naissus (AD 269).

Claudius, Marcus Aurelius *See* **Claudius II**

Clausewitz, Karl von 1780–1831. Prussian general and noted writer on military strategy. His famous book *On War* advocated "total warfare" against every possible enemy target, including civilians and private property.

Clausius, Rudolf Julius Emmanuel 1822–88. A German mathematical physicist. He is considered a pioneer in thermodynamics and introduced the concept of entropy.

Clay, Henry 1777–1852. American statesman. Three times an unsuccessful presidential candidate (1824, 1832, 1844), he was a congressman from Kentucky (1811–14, 1815–21, 1823–25), secretary of state (1825–29), and Whig party senator (1831–42, 1849–52). As a congressman he formulated his American System *(q.v.)*, helped pass the Missouri Compromise (1820), and was instrumental in J. Q. Adams' election as president. He helped end the Nullification Controversy by the Compromise Tariff of 1833, and, by the Compromise of 1850, tried to prevent civil war.

Clayton, John M. *See* **Clayton-Bulwer Treaty**

Clayton Antitrust Act US bill passed (1914) to supplement the provisions of the Sherman Antitrust Act (1890). It specified as antitrust violations corporate practices not covered in the previous bill, including rebates, interlocking directorates, intercorporate stock holdings, and price discrimination. The act exempted labor and agricultural organizations from the provisions and also included restrictions on the use of injunctions in labor disputes.

Clayton-Bulwer Treaty Treaty signed (1850) by the US and Britain guaranteeing that neither country would attempt to dominate or colonize the territories of Central America. Negotiated by US secretary of state John M. Clayton (1796–1856) and British diplomat Sir Henry Bulwer

(1801–72), the treaty was designed to maintain the neutrality of a proposed canal (later the Panama Canal) through the Central American isthmus. The treaty was both vague and highly controversial, however, and was finally superseded by the Hay-Pauncefote Treaty (1901), which made possible a US-controlled canal.

Clear Grits Political faction (1848–51) in western Canada (now Ontario). Followers demanded legislative representation by population and rejected pro-Catholic policies on the Clergy Reserves (*q.v.*). G. Brown was a leading figure in the party, which eventually merged with other groups to form the Liberal party.

Cleisthenes ⟨Clisthenes⟩ *fl.* 6th cent. BC. Athenian statesman who established democracy in Athens. A member of the politically active Alcmaeonidae family, he was chief archon in 525–524 BC. In 508 BC, he took advantage of a political crisis over Sparta to institute his reforms, which broke the power of the landed aristocrats and the tribes. A principal feature of his new system was the establishment of political districts (demes) by region rather than by social status. He is said to have instituted the practice of ostracism.

Clemenceau, Georges 1841–1929. French premier (1906–09, 1917–20). Known as "the Tiger," he rallied French forces in WW I and thereby played an important role in the Allied victory. He took part in founding the French Third Republic (1870), and later was implicated in the Panama Scandal. His first government was ousted over his handling of a miners' strike. His second government fell because he failed to press for harsh terms from Germany in negotiations for the Treaty of Versailles (1919).

Clemens, Samuel Langhorne *See* **Twain, Mark**

Clement I, Saint ⟨Clement of Rome⟩ AD 30?–100? Pope (AD 90–99 or 88?–97) and first apostolic father. One of the earliest popes, Clement is reputed to have written the Epistle to the Corinthians contained in the New Testament.

Clement III *See* **Guibert of Ravenna**

Clement V ⟨Got, Bertrand de⟩ 1264–1314. French-born pope (1305–14). Clement moved the papacy from Rome to Avignon, France, and thus began the Babylonian captivity (*q.v.*). Under pressure from French king Philip IV, he called the Council of Vienne (1311) and dissolved (1312) the Knights Templars (*q.v.*).

Clement VI ⟨Roger, Pierre⟩ 1291–1352. French-born pope (1342–52) at Avignon, France. Clement's reign was marked by the outbreak of the Black Plague, and he is remembered for his attempts to protect Jews, then being accused of causing the plague.

Clement VII (antipope) *See* **Robert of Geneva**

Clement VII ⟨Medici, Giulio de⟩ 1478–1534. Italian-born pope (1523–34). Clement was caught in the power struggle between French king Francis I and Holy Roman Emperor Charles V. In 1527, Charles invaded Italy, sacked Rome, and imprisoned Clement. Clement also refused (*c*1527) Henry VIII his divorce from Catherine of Aragon, and thus set the stage for the break between the English church and Rome.

Clement VIII ⟨Aldobrandini, Ippolito⟩ 1536–1605. Italian-born pope (1592–1605). Clement absolved French king Henry IV of excommunication after he rejected Protestantism (1593) and moderated the influence of the Spanish kings on the church.

Clement XI ⟨Albani, Giovanni Francesco⟩ 1649–1721. Italian-born pope (1700–21). Clement condemned Jansenism and, embroiled in the struggle for the Spanish throne, failed to avert the War of Spanish Succession (1701–14).

Clement XIV ⟨Ganganelli, Lorenzo⟩ 1705–74. Italian-born pope (1769–74). To avoid schism with Spain and France, he dissolved (1773) the Society of Jesus (Jesuits), then regarded by the kings as a threat to their power.

Clement, Jacques 1567–89. French monk, a Dominican. Clement assassinated (1589) French king Henry III for choosing a Protestant as his successor.

Clement of Alexandria *d.* AD *c*215. Greek Christian theologian and teacher at the Alexandrian School. He was the teacher of the Christian philosopher Origen and a prolific writer. He fled Alexandria during the persecution of Christians under Severus.

Clement of Rome *See* **Clement I, Saint**

Cleomenes I *d. c*489 BC. King of Sparta (*c*519–491 BC). He is remembered for his interference in Athenian politics (notably his attempt to oust the Athenian leader Cleisthenes to undo his democratic reforms) and for his cruelty in battle against Argos (*c*494), during which some 6,000 enemy soldiers were slaughtered.

Cleomenes III *d.* 219 BC. King of Sparta (*c*235–221 BC). He established the supreme authority of the king by abolishing the Spartan ephorate (five elected magistrates) and enacted other reforms. He was successful in warfare against the Achaean League (227–222) until the league allied itself with Macedon. His subsequent defeat (222) by Antigonus III at Sellasia marked the fall of Sparta to the Macedonians.

Cleon *d.* 422 BC. Athenian politician and soldier. Cleon began his career by opposing Pericles and is generally remembered as a demagogue. He distinguished himself in battles against the Spartans during the Peloponnesian Wars (431–404 BC) and was killed in battle.

Cleopatra 69–30 BC. Queen of Egypt (51–49, 48–30 BC), noted beauty celebrated for her love affairs with J. Caesar and M. Antony. Wedded by custom to her brother, Ptolemy XIII, she was ousted from power by him (49). Caesar, then pursuing Pompey in Egypt, fell in love with her and restored her to power (48 BC). With Ptolemy XIII dead, she nominally married another brother, Ptolemy XIV, and became Caesar's mistress, bore him a son, Cesarion, and lived with Caesar at Rome (from 46) until his assassination (44). She then met and entranced Antony (42) and they lived together until 40, when Antony was forced to return to Rome and marry the sister of Octavian (later Augustus). Cleopatra by this time had had twin children by Antony. Antony and Cleopatra again became lovers in 36 and their affair was both dissolute and unpopular in Rome. Octavian at last sent an army to destroy Antony and Cleopatra. Octavian was victorious at the Battle of Actium (31) and the two lovers fled to Alexandria. There, with Octavian approaching, she is said to have induced Antony to commit suicide. She then tried to captivate Octavian and, seeing he was unmoved and intended to display her in his triumph at Rome, killed herself.

Cleopatra's Needles Two red granite Egyptian obelisks, marked with hieroglyphics and dating from c1500 BC. They stood first in Heliopolis and then were moved (c14 BC) to Alexandria. Today one stands in London, the other in New York City.

Clergy Reserves Canadian land grants to the church. The British Constitutional Act (1791) specified that land be set aside for Protestant clergy. From the early 19th cent., however, disposition of the lands was disputed. The Anglican Protestant churches claimed all the land for themselves, while other denominations contested the claim. The land was finally redesignated for secular use (1854) and large cash payments were made to the churches (including the Roman Catholic church).

Clermont *See* **Fulton, Robert**

Clermont, Council of Church council (1095, at Clermont, France), in which Pope Urban II preached the First Crusade. The Byzantine Empire was at that time being reduced by Muslim conquests and Emperor Alexis I requested aid from the pope. At the council Urban II urged French knights to take up the cause, citing Muslim persecutions, the Muslim capture of the Holy Land, and the possible material gain of such a venture.

The response was enthusiastic and Raymond IV accepted the first of the crosses distributed by Urban.

Cleveland US port city (pop. 573,800) on Lake Erie in Ohio. Once part of the Western Reserve, Cleveland was planned in 1796 and incorporated as a village in 1814. It expanded rapidly in the 1820s as the Erie and Ohio canals opened important water routes and it soon became a major transportation and industrial center.

Cleveland, Stephen Grover 1837–1908. (*nicknamed* the Great Obstructionist) 22d and 24th US president (1885–89, 1893–97), successor to C. Arthur, B. Harrison. A former governor of New York and a reform Democrat, he was elected to his first term amid a popular movement to end corrupt government. As president, he opposed political bosses, fought "pork barrel" legislation and implemented the Pendleton Civil Service Act of 1883. The fight for lower tariffs, however, loomed as the major issue of his first administration. He subsequently lost the election (1888) to Harrison over the issue. Reelected (1892) when the Populist party split the vote, his second administration was devoted largely to ending the economic depression that resulted from the Panic of 1893 (*q.v.*). During his second term, Cleveland failed to prevent passage of the Wilson-Gorman Tariff Act (1894, raising tariffs), forced repeal of the Sherman Silver Purchase Act (1893), used federal powers to break the Pullman Strike (1894), became involved in the Venezuela Boundary Dispute (*q.v.*), and expanded powers claimed under the Monroe Doctrine as a result of it. Continuing economic problems and the rising power of the free-silver movement, resulted in his failure to win renomination (1896).

Cleves, Anne of *See* **Anne of Cleves**

Clifford of Chudleigh, Thomas Clifford, 1st Baron 1630–73. English statesman. A Catholic member of the Cabal ministry under Charles II, he was forced to resign when the Test Act (1673) banned Catholics from holding office.

Clinton, George 1739–1812. American statesman and vice-president (1805–1812), Clinton served as first governor of New York (1777–95) and first proposed the Erie Canal. He died during his (second) term as vice-president, under J. Madison.

Clinton, Sir Henry 1738?–95. British general during the American Revolution (1775–83). He served under Gen. W. Howe early in the war, then succeeded him as British commander (1778–81). He evacuated Philadelphia (1778) and later captured Charleston (1780), but his failure to provide timely support for Gen. C. Cornwallis in the

Yorktown Campaign *(q.v.)* was blamed for the final British defeat in the war. He resigned his command (1781) after Cornwallis surrendered in the South.

Clio One of the Muses in Greek mythology, the patroness of history.

Clisthenes *See* **Cleisthenes**

Clive, Robert, Baron Clive of Plassey 1725–74. British soldier and statesman who helped establish British rule in India. In the service of the British East India Company, he defeated the French in the south, conquered the native rulers of Bengal, and established himself as its first British governor (1757–60). He then defeated (1759) the Dutch in India. He again served as the Bengali governor (1765–67).

Cliveden Set *See* **Astor, Nancy Witcher Langhorne, Viscountess Astor**

Clodia *fl.* 1st cent. BC. Roman matron, noted beauty and sister of Clodius. She is thought to have been Catullus' lover, immortalized in his poems as Lesbia.

Clodius *d.* 52 BC. Roman tribune and demagogue. He figured in Cicero's exile from Rome (58 BC) and, as a rival of the tribune Milo, led a gang of thugs that tyrannized the city of Rome for several years.

Clontarf, Battle of Battle (April 23, 1014, near Dublin) in which the Irish, led by King Brian Boru, turned back an attempted invasion of Irish domains by the Danes under Sweyn.

Clotaire I *d.* 561. Merovingian king (558–561). Upon the death of his father, Clovis I, Clotaire and his three brothers divided the Frankish Kingdom. From 558 to 561, however, he reigned as sole king of the Franks. His kingdom was divided on his death. One son, Sigebert I, received Neustria and another, Chilperic I, received Austrasia.

Clotaire II 584–629? Merovingian king (584–629) of Neustria. He put Austrasian queen Brunhilde to death, seized her lands, and reunited the Frankish Empire under his rule (613–629). In 614 he was forced to concede privileges to the nobility and the clergy.

Clotho One of the three Fates in Greek mythology, she spins the thread of life.

Cloth of Gold, Field of *See* **Field of Cloth of Gold**

Clotilda, Saint AD c470–545. Frankish queen (AD 493–511). Clotilda converted her husband, Clovis I, to Christianity. After his death (511) she gave up her power to help the needy.

Clovis I c466–511. Frankish king (481–511), founder of the Merovingian Empire. He ended Roman domination in Gaul by defeating their armies at Soissons (486). Next he conquered the

Thuringians, converted to Christianity after defeating the Alemanni in 496, won notable victories against the Burgundians and Visigoths, and established his capital at Paris.

Cluniac order Medieval reformist branch of the Benedictine order, founded (910) at Cluny, France. The order sought a return to the earlier, strict observance of the Rule of Saint Benedict and rose to great power by the 11th cent. The order declined sharply in the 12th cent.

Clymene Nymph in Greek mythology, daughter of the Titan Oceanus. Among her sons were Atlas and Prometheus. She is elsewhere portrayed as the wife of Helios.

Clytemnestra Wife of King Agamemnon in Greek mythology. She and her lover, Aegisthus, killed Agamemnon after his return from the Trojan Wars. They in turn were killed by her son Orestes.

Cnidus, Eudoxus of *See* **Eudoxus of Cnidus**

Cnossus (Knossos) Ancient city and center of the Minoan Civilization *(q.v.)*. Occupied before the third millennium BC, the city was the site of a splendid palace. The city was destroyed by invaders (probably Mycenaean) about 1400 BC.

Cnut *See* **Canute**

Cobbett, William 1763?–1835. English journalist and reformer. He was a noted advocate of reforms to improve the lot of the industrial working class.

Cobden, Richard 1804–65. English politician. Cobden favored free trade and led the fight to repeal the Corn Laws. Elected to Parliament (1841), he opposed the Crimean War and urged British support for the North in the American Civil War.

Cochin China Historic region in the south of Vietnam embracing the Mekong Delta region. It was long contested by the Khmer and Champa kingdoms and was finally taken over by the kingdom of Annam (18th cent.). It became part of the French domains in Indochina (c1862–1949) and then was joined to other territories to form Vietnam. Saigon is the major city of the region.

Cochise *d.* 1874. Apache Indian chief in Arizona. He became a leader (after 1861) of Apache raiders who warred against white settlers. His band of 200 braves conducted raids until 1872, when they surrendered voluntarily.

Cockaigne *See* **Land of Cockaigne**

Cockayne *See* **Land of Cockaigne**

Cockcroft, Sir John Douglas 1897–1967. English physicist. He and E. Walton shared the Nobel Prize in physics (1951) for splitting atomic nuclei with accelerated atomic particles.

Cocteau, Jean 1889–1963. French writer, artist, and film maker. Cocteau was a leader of surrealism and the avant-garde. Among his best-known works are the films *Beauty and the Beast* and *Orphée* and the novel *Les Enfants Terribles*.

Code Civil *See* **Code Napoléon**

Code Napoléon ⟨*Code Civil*⟩ ⟨Napoleonic Code⟩ Compilation of the civil laws of France and its possessions issued by Napoleon (1804). It is still in effect, with modifications, in France today. Following the breakup of the Napoleonic Empire, the code was modified and voluntarily adopted by a number of European countries.

Code of Canon Law ⟨Codex Juris Canonici⟩ Codification of Roman Catholic canon law. Begun (1904) under Pope Pius X, it was completed and promulgated (1917) under Pope Benedict XV. (*See also* canon law.)

Code of Hammurabi A relatively sophisticated legal code written (c18th cent. BC) by Hammurabi, founder of the Babylonian Empire. One of the earliest known legal codes, it was based on the system of "an eye for an eye" and meted out punishments equal in kind and severity to the injury inflicted. The code was rediscovered in 1901.

Codex Juris Canonici *See* **canon law; Code of Canon Law**

Codomannus, Darius *See* **Darius III**

Cody, William Frederick *See* **Buffalo Bill**

Coeur, Jacques c1395–1456. French merchant and financial adviser to Charles VII. He restored order to the state finances and helped finance the military campaign that finally drove the English from Normandy. He was driven out of France (c1454) on trumped-up charges.

Coeur d'Alene Riots Strikes and riots by union miners in Idaho during the 1890s. Rioting began in 1892, when miners attacked armed guards protecting nonunion lead and silver miners. Sporadic outbreaks of violence continued, and, in 1905, the unrest became a major scandal when the governor of Idaho was murdered. A former miner, who said the union was involved in the murder, was convicted.

Coeus *See* **Titan**

Cohan, George Michael 1878–1942. American showman, writer, and composer. He wrote such famous songs as "Over There" and "I'm a Yankee Doodle Dandy" and wrote the shows *Little Johnny Jones, The Tavern,* and *Forty-Five Minutes from Broadway.*

Cohn, Ferdinand 1828–98. German botanist and bacteriologist. Cohn is often called the father of bacteriology. He aided R. Koch in his research on the disease anthrax.

Cohong. *See* **Canton system**

Coke, Sir Edward 1552–1634. English jurist, famous in English history as a defender of common law against royal prerogative. He played a major role in formulating the Petition of Right (1628). Notoriously severe as a prosecutor, he tried Sir W. Raleigh and, later, the conspirators in the Gunpowder Plot. As chief justice of common pleas (1606–13) and chief justice of the king's bench (1613–16), however, he became a champion of the supremacy of common law. Returned to Parliament, he became a leader of the opposition to James I and Charles I.

Coke, Thomas *See* **Methodism**

Colbath, Jeremiah Jones *See* **Wilson, Henry**

Colbert, Jean Baptiste 1619–83. French statesman. As comptroller of finance to Louis XIV, Colbert supported mercantilism and government economy. His policies helped make France a commercial and naval power.

Colchis Ancient country located near the Black Sea. It was thought to be the mythical land of Medea, where the Golden Fleece, sought by Jason, was kept.

Cold Harbor, Battle of Battle (June 1–12, 1864) during the American Civil War (1861–65). Fought during Gen. U. Grant's drive toward Richmond, the battle pitted over 100,000 Union soldiers against some 59,000 Confederates, led by Gen. R. E. Lee. The Confederates stopped the Union advance in stiff fighting and finally forced Grant to turn away from Richmond toward Petersburg.

Cold War Name for the international rivalry that developed between the US and the USSR after WW II. The Cold War period saw the division of the world into sharply defined Western and Communist spheres of influence, domination of world politics by the US and USSR as superpowers, East-West political and propaganda struggles, the continuing threat of nuclear war (from the 1950s), and outbreaks of limited warfare between pro-Western and pro-Communist forces. Suspicions about Stalin's designs for expansion of the Communist world were aroused after WW II by his transformation of Soviet-occupied Eastern Europe into a network of Communist satellite states. In a famous speech (Mar. 15, 1946) at Fulton, Missouri, former British prime minister W. Churchill pointed to the "iron curtain" that had descended across Europe. The following year US President H. Truman announced the Truman Doctrine (Mar. 12, 1947) to counter threatened Communist takeovers in Greece and Turkey. This was followed by announcement of the Marshall Plan to provide for the recovery of war-torn Europe and to counter Communist expansionism there. The last years of the 1940s were marked by the US-Soviet confrontation in the Berlin blockade and airlift (from 1948), formation of NATO (1949), and the Communist takeover in China (1949). The 1950s saw increased Communist activity in Southeast Asia, the Korean War, formation of the Communist Warsaw Pact (1955), a continuing US policy of "containing" Communism, the rise of the nuclear arms race and the threat of "massive retaliation." At the same time, however, possibilities of a "thaw" in Cold War tensions were seen in the death of Soviet leader J. Stalin (1953), N. Khrushchev's de-Stalinization policy, the limited successes of the Geneva Summit Conference (1955), and the exchange of official visits in 1959 (Vice-President R. Nixon to USSR; Khrushchev to US). The early 1960s brought renewed tensions, however. The building of the Berlin Wall (1961) and the Cuban Missile Crisis temporarily halted moves toward better East-West relations. But a trend of more far-reaching importance in the 1960s was the breakup of rigid divisions between pro-West and Communist-bloc countries. The Sino-Soviet split (1960) led to a deep rift in the Communist bloc (later exploited by the US). The costly and unsuccessful Vietnam War not only cost the US considerable power and prestige but it also led to divisions among Western nations. The 1970s saw a turning away from the hard-line divisions of the Cold War period in favor of a new policy of détente *(q.v.)*. The US opened relations with China, increased trade and other economic ties with the USSR, and entered into nuclear arms limitation talks. Policies of détente by no means eliminated mistrust and competition between the superpowers, however. Events of the late 1970s and early 1980s, such as the Soviet invasion of Afghanistan, the crisis over Solidarity in Poland, and the movement for a military defense buildup in the US produced a marked "chill" in US–Soviet relations.

Cole, Thomas *See* **Hudson River School**

Coleridge, Samuel Taylor 1772–1834. A leading English romantic poet and critic. Once called a "damaged archangel" by C. Lamb, Coleridge wrote his most important poems during his friendship with W. Wordsworth (1797–c1802). Together they published (1798) *Lyrical Ballads,* an important work in the English romantic movement which contained Coleridge's famous "Rime of the Ancient Mariner." Coleridge also wrote during this period the poems "Kubla Khan," "Christabel," and "Dejection: An Ode." Addicted to opium by 1800, he moved to London (1816), where the habit was brought under control and he completed his notable *Biographia Literaria.*

Colet, John 1467?–1519. British theologian. A leading humanist and scholar, he influenced such scholars as D. Erasmus and T. More, and founded (1509) St. Paul's school in London.

Colette 1873–1954. French novelist, whose works are noted for their minute observation and descriptive intensity. Among her works is the novel *Gigi.*

Coligny, Gaspard de 1519–72. Soldier and prominent French Huguenot. Fearful of Coligny's influence over the young King Charles IX, Catherine de Médicis instigated his murder in the St. Bartholomew's Day Massacre.

Coliseum *See* **Colosseum**

collectivism Economic system that advocates control of the means of production by groups of workers or the state rather than by the individual.

Collins, Michael 1890–1922. A leader of the Irish Republican Army. A member of the Sinn Fein, he negotiated a treaty (1921) with the British giving Ireland dominion status but was assassinated by extremist revolutionaries.

Collins, Michael 1930–. American astronaut. He guided the command module of the Apollo 11 mission, during which N. Armstrong and E. Aldrin became the first two men to set foot on the moon (July 20, 1969).

Collins, William Wilkie 1824–89. English author, the first Briton to write detective novels. He wrote *The Woman in White* and *The Moonstone.*

Collodi, Carlo ⟨*pseud.* of Carlo Lorenzini⟩ 1826–90. Italian author. A journalist by profession, Collodi wrote many children's tales, including the classic *Pinocchio.*

Cologne City (pop. 976,800) in West Germany on the Rhine River. Made a Roman colony (AD 50) by the emperor Claudius, it was made an archdiocese by Charlemagne and flourished as a member of the Hanseatic League. After a period of decline it was annexed to Prussia (1815) and rose to become a major commercial and cultural center. Cologne was heavily damaged during WW II.

Colombia Republic located in northwestern South America. Its capital is Bogotá. Colombia's coast was first explored (1502) by C. Columbus and Spanish settlements were established in the area soon after. In the early 18th cent. the area, known as New Granada, was incorporated into the larger viceroyalty of New Granada and in 1819 was liberated from Spanish rule by S. Bolívar's victory at Boyacá. Much of Colombia's modern history has been marked by conflict between conservative and liberal factions, which have sought to determine the nation's political character. Key dates in the history of Colombia include:

1538 G. Jiménez de Quesada conquered Colombia for Spain; founded Bogotá.

EARLY 16TH CENT. Audencia of New Granada, including area of modern Colombia, established.

1717–39 New Granada joined with areas later forming modern Ecuador, Panama, and Venezuela to form viceroyalty of New Granada.

1780–81 Revolt of the *comuneros* presaged independence movement.

1810 Uprising in Bogotá (July 20); marked beginning of New Granada's war for independence.

1819 S. Bolívar's victory (Aug. 7) in the Battle of Boyacá secured the independence of New Granada Audencia from Spanish rule.

1819 New nation of Greater Colombia (Gran Colombia) proclaimed; included New Granada, Ecuador (after 1822), Panama, and Venezuela.

1821 New Constitution adopted; Bolívar became first president of Greater Colombia.

1831 Greater Colombia dissolved (1830); New Granada, including area of modern Panama, became republic of New Granada; struggle began between conservatives, favoring strong central government and Roman Catholic church, and liberals, favoring federalism and anticlericalism.

1851–52 Slavery abolished.

1858 Provinces of New Granada reorganized as independent states within confederation known as Granadina.

1863 Civil war between liberal and conservative factions broke out (1861); victorious liberals formed United States of Colombia.

1867–80 Period of civil wars between liberal and conservative factions; conflict ended by election (1880) of R. Núñez, a moderate, as president and formation of a liberal-conservative coalition.

1885 Liberal uprising against federal government defeated.

1886 Republic of Colombia established; abolished sovereign states in favor of central government; Roman Catholic church made state church.

1899–1902 Colombia plunged into civil war; conservative faction regained power after three years of conflict.

1903 Hay-Herrán Treaty negotiated to establish US control over what was to become the Panama Canal Zone; treaty rejected by Colombian Congress.

1903 Uprising in Panama; US sent troops to aid Panamanians against Colombia; US recognized Panamanian independence and soon after completed treaty with Panamanians for Panama Canal.

1914 Thomson-Urrutia Treaty negotiated; Colombia recognized Panamanian independence and received special privileges in the Canal Zone and an indemnity from the US.

1930 Liberals in power for the first time in over two decades; held presidency until 1946 though reform programs failed to solve the social and economic problems.

1941 WW II; Colombia joined the Allies.

1948 Liberal leader Jorge Eliécer Gaitán assassinated in Bogotá (Apr. 9); led to violent conflict in Bogotá and elsewhere in Colombia.

1948–58 La Violencia; violence in Bogotá marked the beginning of period of civil unrest and repressive rule that resulted in the deaths of some 200,000 persons.

1950 Liberal party withdrew from presidential election (1949); conservative Laureano Gómez became president.

1953 G. Rojas Pinilla seized power in military coup.

1957 Military junta ousted Rojas Pinilla, ending his brutal and corrupt reign as dictator.

1957 National Front, a liberal-conservative coalition, formed; coalition formed to end unrest and was to remain in effect until 1974 with conservative and liberal presidents alternating every four years (from 1958).

1958 Alberto Lleras Camargo elected National Front president.

1966–70 National Front president Carlos Lleras Restrepo in office; his highly successful administration put through political reforms and greatly improved the economy.

1974–78 Liberal President Alfonso López Michelsen in office following first free elections in over 20 years.

1978 Liberal President Julio César Turbay Ayala in office.

1981 Government captured or killed top leaders of M-19 urban guerrilla group; offer of amnesty for followers failed.

1982 Belisario Betancur Cuartas, a Conservative, in office as president.

colonialism Policy or program by which a state seeks political or economic control over other territories. In ancient times the Phoenicians, Greeks, and Romans all established colonies to expand their trade and culture, often populating them with their own citizens. In medieval times, especially the 13th cent., Italian city-states such as Venice and Genoa followed the same pattern. During the 15th to 17th cents., Portugal, Spain, England, France, and the Netherlands all established extensive colonial empires, both in the New World and in the East. By the 18th cent., however, Britain had acquired control of India, Canada, and other territories and, despite loss of the American colonies, ranked as the greatest European colonial power. France lost one colonial empire in the 18th-cent. colonial wars with Britain and acquired another empire in Africa in the 19th cent. The efforts of Japan, Germany, and Italy to become colonial powers in the late 19th and early 20th cents. contributed to the outbreak of both WW I and WW II. In the Spanish-American War, the US acquired Caribbean territories and the Philippines. The breakup of the Spanish and Portuguese empires in South America began in the early 19th cent., when most colonies there won independence. The main period of decolonization, however, began after WW I, when colonial rule came to be considered temporary and necessary only for the development of the colony. Decolonization proceded rapidly after WW II, when colonial empires broke up and former colonies gained independence. (See also imperialism.)

Colonna, Oddone   See **Martin V**

Colorado   West central state of the US (pop. 2,888,800), the 38th state. The territory was first explored and claimed by the Spanish (18th cent.) and the French. The eastern, French portion, was sold to the US with the Louisiana Purchase (1803), and the rest was ceded by Mexico in the Treaty of Guadalupe Hidalgo (1848). Settlers came in great numbers with the discovery of gold at Cherry Creek (1858). Colorado became a territory (1861), and statehood was granted in 1876.

Colosseum ⟨Coliseum⟩   Amphitheater situated in Rome, the scene of gladiatorial combat and, by tradition, the arena for Christian martyrdom. Completed in AD 80, it could seat about 50,000.

Colossus of Rhodes   Massive bronze statue of the sun god Helios that stood in the harbor of Rhodes (Greece) (280–c225 BC). One of Seven Wonders of the World, it was destroyed by an earthquake.

Colt, Samuel   1814–62. American arms developer who invented (1835) the first successful revolving-magazine pistol, the Colt revolver.

Columba, Saint   ⟨Columcille⟩ 521–597. Irish priest and saint. He established a monastery in Scotland (563), from which he spread Christianity throughout northern Scotland.

Columbia   American city (pop. 99,300), capital city of South Carolina. Founded (1786) as the state capital, Columbia was burned by Gen. W. Sherman (1865) during the Civil War. It is a major commercial and cultural center.

Columbia   The world's first reusable space ship, called the "space shuttle." Despite minor malfunctions, it flew into earth orbit in both April and November, 1981, and glided back to safe landings at Edwards Air Force Base, California. Further successful flights were made March, July 1982.

Columbus   American city (pop. 565,000), the capital of Ohio (from 1816). Its proximity to rich agricultural areas and sources of raw materials has contributed to its growth as a major industrial and transportation center.

Columbus, Bartholomew   See **Santo Domingo**

Columbus, Christopher   1451–1506.   Genoese navigator in the service of Spain, credited with the discovery (1492) of America. Though the Vikings are believed to have previously landed (c1000) in North America, it was Columbus' voyage that opened the great epoch of European exploration and colonization in the New World. Columbus became an experienced navigator while serving the Genoese and Portuguese, and his idea of sailing west to Asia was not new. It was not until 1492, however, that the Spanish monarchs Ferdinand and Isabella agreed to finance his venture. He left Spain (Aug. 3, 1492) with three ships, (the *Santa Maria*, *Niña*, and *Pinta*) and landed on the island of San Salvador in the Bahamas Oct. 12, just over two months later. Believing he had reached islands east of Japan, he briefly explored the Caribbean and then returned to Spain later in October. Three other voyages followed (1493, 1498, 1502), on which he discovered other Caribbean islands and reached the South American coast. Unable to administer the Spanish colony in the New World, he was removed as governor (1500), and died shortly after his disastrous fourth voyage (1502–04).

Columcille, Saint   See **Columba, Saint**

Comanche Indians   North American Indian tribe. A nomadic offshoot of the northern Shoshone Indians, they moved south and established themselves (18th cent.) as the dominant group in the southern Great Plains. Noted for their excellent horsemanship and skill in combat, they successfully defended their lands against settlers for many years. They were finally defeated, and relocated on reservations in Oklahoma after several bloody engagements in the 1870s.

Combes, Émile   1835–1921.   French politician. As premier (1902–05), he brought about the separation of church and state.

Combination Acts   British antiunion laws. The Combination Acts of 1799 and 1800 outlawed trade unions and punished those who joined or aided them. The laws were repealed in 1824, restored the next year, and then ignored.

Comenius, John Amos   1592–1670. Czech clergyman and noted educational reformer. He is known best for his *Didactica magna*, which sets forth his theory of universal education for men and women.

Commager, Henry Steele 1902–. American historian. Commager's numerous works include *The American Mind*, *The Era of Reform*, *The Blue and the Gray*, and *Majority Rule and Minority Rights*.

Committee of Public Safety French revolutionary committee, set up by the National Convention (Apr. 6, 1793) to supervise the executive bodies of the Convention. From July, 1793 to July, 1794, the Committee ruled France, mobilized the nation, and instituted the Reign of Terror under the domination of its principal member, M. Robespierre. Robespierre was overthrown July, 1794, but the Committee continued, much weakened, until establishment of the Directory (1795).

Committees of Correspondence Committees set up (1763–75) by towns, cities, and legislatures in Colonial America. Formed originally to communicate with other American colonies about opposition to British laws (Sugar Act, Stamp Act), they helped promote Colonial unity and organization of the Continental Congress. Notable among them was the Boston committee, formed (1772) by S. Adams; and the Virginia committee (formed 1773), on which T. Jefferson and P. Henry served. The Boston committee directed the Boston Tea Party (1773).

Commodus AD 161–192. Roman emperor (AD 180–192), successor to his father, Marcus Aurelius. On his father's death, Commodus cut short his military campaign against the Germans and began a life of dissipation in Rome. He was strangled by an arena wrestler named Narcissus.

Commodus, Lucius Ceinoius *See* **Verus, Lucius Aurelius**

common law Term applied to the legal system prevalent in England and in other countries orginally colonized by England. It is based upon a history of judicial precedent in which court decisions were derived from common custom and reason rather than statutes.

Commonweal of Christ *See* **Coxey's Army**

commonwealth Term for an organized community that exists through consent of the governed. The term was frequently used by such 17th-cent. political theorists as T. Hobbes and J. Locke. In English history, the term "commonwealth" refers to the period (1649–60) when the English monarchy was abolished and England governed as a commonwealth. (*See also* Protectorate.)

Commonwealth of Nations, British *See* **British Commonwealth of Nations**

commune Term once applied to medieval towns that achieved self-government by rebellion or by charter. Communes were generally formed in areas where royal authority was weak.

Commune of Paris (Paris Commune) **1.** Governmental body during the French Revolution (1789–99). Originally formed (1789) as the elected city government of Paris (under Mayor Jean Sylvain Bailly, 1736–93), the Commune became a vehicle for radical extremists in the revolution. Under the leadership of J. Hébert and P. Chaumette, it vied with the Committee of Public Safety and the National Convention for control of the revolutionary government. Executions of its leaders during the Reign of Terror weakened the Commune's power, and it was finally abolished (1794) in the Thermidorian reaction. **2.** Short-lived rebel government formed (1871) in Paris. Opposed to policies of A. Thier's Government of National Defense, and particularly the humiliating peace terms accepted after the Franco-Prussian War (1870–71), Parisian workers rose in rebellion (Mar. 18, 1871). A government was formed by the revolutionaries (mostly radical republicans) and enacted some short-lived reforms. Government troops reentered the city and, in what is known as Bloody Week, crushed the revolt by May 28. More than 17,000 men, women, and children were executed and thousands of others were arrested in what amounted to reprisals against the working class by the bourgeoisie and aristocracy.

communism Political philosophy based upon the principle of collective ownership of both property and means of production. Communists view history from the perspective of class struggle and seek to establish a classless society, in its most ideal form a "dictatorship of the proletariat." The idea of a communal society, a fundamental element of communist thought, dates back to the ancient Greeks and was advanced by Plato in his philosophical work the *Republic*. T. More in his famous work *Utopia* (1516) promoted the idea of a communal society and T. Münzer, leader of the Anabaptists, advanced the ideal of a religious communal society during the unsuccessful Peasants' War (1524–25). The Industrial Revolution (*q.v.*) and the severe economic hardships suffered by workers gave rise to socialism in the late 18th and early 19th cents. Modern communism then emerged from the socialist movement (*see* Socialism), first as a radical wing of socialism and finally (early 1900s) as a separate and distinct ideology of revolution and collective ownership. The fundamental rivalry between communist and capitalist societies has been a factor in world history since the creation of the first Communist state (USSR, 1917). After WW II it led to the tensions of the Cold War (*q.v.*). *See also* Union of Soviet Socialist Republics (from 1917), Marxism, Leninism, Stalinism. Key events in the history of Communism include:

1848 *Communist Manifesto* written by K. Marx and F. Engels; introduced concept of historic necessity of revolution as a result of class struggle; initially a statement of radical Socialist principles, it became the cornerstone of communist ideology.

1864 First International formed at London; a Socialist labor federation, it was split by a power struggle between Marx and the anarchist N. Bakunin (1876).

1870s Spread of Socialist parties in Europe.

1880s–90s Split widened between advocates of gradual ("evolutionary") socialism and exponents of revolutionary socialism (communism).

1889 Second International formed at Paris; federation of Socialist and labor groups committed to eventual social revolution.

1896 Anarchists, extreme radicals, ousted from Second International; Marxist doctrine of inevitable revolution reaffirmed, however.

1898 German evolutionary Socialist E. Bernstein called for a revision of Marxist ideology and denied historical necessity of revolution.

1903 Russian Social Democratic Labor Party founded (Mar.) by Russian Marxists at Minsk.

1903 N. Lenin forced Russian Social Democratic Labor Party to split into Bolshevik (revolutionary) and Menshevik (gradualist) factions; split led to formation of the Communist party when Bolsheviks seized control of the Russian Revolution (1917).

1914 Second International collapsed as Socialist groups split along nationalist lines at the outbreak of WW I.

1915 Zimmerwald Conference of Socialists denounced WW I as imperialistic; this stand was attacked by Lenin's leftist factions, which wanted to transform the war into a civil war against the bourgeoisie.

1916 Spartacus party formed in Germany; became nucleus of German Communist party after WW I.

1917 Russian Revolution; Lenin's Bolsheviks seized power (Oct.) and thus established Russia as the first Communist state. Communist dictatorship of Russia instituted.

1918 Bolsheviks formed Communist Party in Russia; Lenin's ideology dominant under his leadership (to 1924).

1919 Communists formed Third International, or Comintern, to spread Communist revolution worldwide; break between Socialists and Communists complete.

1921 Chinese Communist party founded.

1920s Lenin died (1924); J. Stalin began to consolidate personal power in the USSR; moved party away from ideology of world revolution and began ideological struggle with L. Trotsky.

1929–38 Trotsky expelled from the USSR (1929); Stalin concentrated on establishment of model Communist state in the USSR; secured complete control of Communist party in series of purge trials (late 1930s) and thus established his totalitarian state.

1941–45 The Soviets joined Allied nations during WW II after Russia was invaded (1941) by Nazi Germany.

1943 Comintern dissolved to promote alliance with Allies during WW II.

1945 Relations between the Communists and the West deteriorated at the end of WW II; Soviets established satellite states in Eastern Europe; Cold War began.

1949 Chinese Communists came to power on Mainland China, forcing nationalists to flee to Taiwan.

1950–53 Korean War, first major armed conflict stemming from the Cold War ideological rivalry between East and West.

1956 Destalinization; Soviet premier N. Khruschchev denounced Stalinism at 20th party congress; attack contributed to uprisings against Communist regimes in Poland and Hungary.

1960 Relations between Soviets and Communist China disintegrated; led to major ideological split within Communist world.

1960–75 Vietnam War, second major conflict arising from Cold War rivalry between East and West.

1966–69 Cultural Revolution in China; ultraradical Chinese Communist factions sought to impose extremist ideology throughout government and society.

1970s Soviets joined US in promoting détente, policy aimed at lessening tensions between non-Communist and Communist nations; resulted in diplomatic and economic ties between various nations of the two blocs.

Communist Manifesto Fundamental statement of Communist revolutionary doctrine, written (1848) by K. Marx and F. Engels. It proposed that workers around the world join together and fight to put control of business and government in the hands of the proletariat. These doctrines had few international consequences until the rise of the Russian Communist party during the Russian Revolution (1917).

Communist party ⟨Communist Party of the Soviet Union⟩ Political party that rules the Soviet Union. It was founded (1903) by N. Lenin at the party congress of the Russian Social Democratic party in London. Lenin headed the Bolshevik *(q.v.)* faction, the radical wing of the party, which stood in opposition to the more moderate Mensheviks. It became the ruling party in Russia following the Russian Revolution and subsequent seizure of power by the Bolsheviks (1917). *(See also* Union of Soviet Socialist Republics [from 1917]; Communism.)

Communist Party of the Soviet Union *See* **Communist party**

Comnenus Family name of a line of Byzantine rulers, who reigned in the 11th and 12th cents. The line was founded by Manuel Eroticus Comnenus *(fl.* 11th cent.), a general under Byzantine emperor Basil II. A branch of the family later ruled the empire of Trebizond. The Comnenian rulers of the Byzantine Empire were:

Isaac I	1057–59
Alexius I	1081–1118
John II	1118–43
Manuel I	1143–80
Alexius II	1180–83
Andronicus I	1183–85

Compactata *See* **Iglau, Compact of**

Compactata of Prague *See* **Hussite Wars**

Compact of Iglau ⟨Compactata⟩ Agreement signed (1436), at Iglau (Jihlava), now in Czechoslovakia, between the Hussites and German king Sigismund

Company of the Merchants of the Staple ⟨Merchant Staplers⟩ Association of English merchants who controlled the country's wool exports from the 13th through the 16th cents. Its name came from the practice of gathering all exports into one town, called the "staple," to minimize export duties. Its influence waned with increased domestic use of wool and the resulting decline in exports.

Compostela, Saint James of *See* **James, Saint, "the Greater"**

Compromise of Breda *See* **Breda, Compromise of**

Compromise of 1850 Series of bills passed (1850) by US Congress to settle the crisis over extension of slavery into new territories. The compromise measures, arranged by H. Clay and S. Douglas and supported by D. Webster, prevented secession of the South for some years but failed to resolve the fundamental question of slavery. The crisis was brought on (1849) by California's petition to be admitted to the union as a "free" state. The compromise, intended to balance the interests of the North and South, included California's admission as a free state, the eventual admission of Utah and New Mexico with the slavery question to be determined by popular sovereignty, the abolition of slave trade in Washington, D.C., and a strict fugitive-slave law. The peace was short-lived. The doctrine of popular sovereignty contributed to the armed conflicts of Bleeding Kansas and the fugitive-slave law aroused bitter opposition in the North.

Compromise of 1867 *See* **Dual Monarchy**

Comstock, Henry Tompkins Paige *See* **Comstock Lode**

Comstock Lode Site of major US silver deposits, near Virginia City, Nevada. It was named for Henry Tompkins Paige Comstock (1820–70), who claimed (1859) sections of the lode but sold his claim before its value was discovered. It produced great amounts of silver and contributed to the settlement of Nevada and California, but was depleted and abandoned by c1898.

Comte, Auguste 1798–1857. French philosopher, founder of positivism and an important figure in the development of sociology. He described his system for attaining a stable society in the modern world in his work *The Course of Positive Philosophy.* Another important work in the development of positivism is his *System of Positive Polity.*

***Comunero* movement** Spanish republican rebellion. The uprising took place (1520–21) in the cities of Castile in reaction to the autocratic rule of Charles V. Though Charles crushed the rebellion, he subsequently modified his policies. Similar *comunero* revolts occurred later in Paraguay (1723–35) and in New Granada (1780–81).

***Comuneros,* Revolt of the** Uprising (1780–81) in New Granada, now Colombia. The revolt was in response to tax policies of the colonial government.

Comus Ancient Greek god of mirth, depicted as a youth bearing a drinking cup and a torch. He was a follower of Dionysus. He appears in the poetic masque *Comus* by J. Milton.

Comyn, John *See* **Robert I**

conciliarism Medieval religious theory. It held that a general council of the Roman Catholic church possessed greater authority than the pope and had the power to depose him. Both Vatican councils (1870, 1962–65) reaffirmed papal supremacy.

Concini, Concino *d.* 1617. Italian adventurer in France. The favorite of Queen Marie de Médicis, he held great influence in the early reign of King Louis XIII and was made marshal of France. His intrigues, however, aroused the wrath of Louis, by whose order he was assassinated.

Concord American city, the capital city of New Hampshire (since 1808). It is famous for its granite quarries.

Concord, Battle of *See* **Lexington and Concord, Battles of**

concordat Binding treaty between an ecclesiastical authority (usually the pope) and a secular one. It carries the force of international law.

Concordat of Bologna French-papal agreement, (Aug. 18, 1516) by which Pope Leo X ceded to French king Francis I extensive control over the French church.

Concordat of 1801 Agreement between Napoleon and Pope Pius VII ending the break between the Roman Catholic church and the revolutionary government of France. The church was reestablished in France, church property confiscated during the revolution was to remain in private hands, and archbishops and bishops were to be nominated (for appointment by the pope) by the French government. The concordat remained in force until 1905, when anticlericalism in France brought about legal separation of church and state.

Concordat of Worms An agreement concluded (1122) between Holy Roman Emperor Henry V and Pope Calixtus II, to end the Investiture Controversy. By its terms, the power to appoint bishops and abbots was divided between emperor and pope. Elections of bishops or abbots were to take place in the presence of the emperor or his representative. The emperor was to decide contested elections. Those elected were to be first invested with secular duties and privileges by the emperor, and then consecrated with spiritual rights and obligations by the pope. In Burgundy and Italy, however, investiture by the emperor was to follow consecration by the pope. Although the concordat gave the pope spiritual authority over the emperor, it did not end the rivalry between the two.

Condé, House of Line of French nobles. A branch of the powerful Bourbons, its members bore the title "prince of Condé," beginning in the 16th cent. with Louis I de Bourbon (1530–69), a leader of the Conspiracy of Amboise. The line became extinct in 1830.

Condé, Louis II de Bourbon, prince de (the great Condé) 1621–86. French general. Though loyal to the court at the outset of the Fronde *(q.v.)*, he fell into disfavor. He then led a rebel army during the Fronde of the princes.

Condé, Louis Joseph de Bourbon, prince de 1736–1818. French general and leader of the army of Condé, a corps of French émigrés formed to overturn the French Revolution.

Condorcet, Antoine Nicolas, marquis of 1743–94. French philosopher. His most famous work predicted the perfectibility of mankind. An active supporter of the French Revolution, he died in prison at the hands of the extremist Jacobin faction.

condottieri Italian mercenaries. Employed by medieval Italian city-states in their frequent feuds, they often changed sides to the highest bidder and proved ineffective in combat. Engagements between rival condottieri bands were noted for their lack of bloodshed.

Confederacy ⟨Confederate States of America⟩ Secessionist government of the South during the US Civil War (1861–65). A provisional government was formed (Feb., 1861) shortly after the secessions began, and a permanent government for the eleven states of the Confederacy was installed Feb., 1862. J. Davis was president and A. Stephens vice-president. The Confederate constitution was adopted Mar., 1861, and Richmond was made the capital July, 1861. The Confederacy carried on all domestic and foreign governmental functions for the duration of the war. In the foreign arena, the South failed in its attempt to force European powers into an alliance by withholding cotton exports. The failure of King Cotton as a weapon proved to be a crucial setback. At home, the largely agricultural South was at a disadvantage against the more populous, industrial North. Soon after war began, there developed manpower shortages (even with conscription), material shortages caused by the Union blockade of the South, and serious inflation caused by lack of adequate financial reserves. Despite the Confederacy's determined and often heroic military stand, it was finally forced to surrender to the North at Appomattox Courthouse (Apr., 1865). The Confederate States, with dates of their secession and reentry to the Union, are:

South Carolina	Dec., 1860–June, 1868
Mississippi	Jan., 1861–Feb., 1870
Florida	Jan., 1861–June, 1868
Alabama	Jan., 1861–June, 1868
Georgia	Jan., 1861–July, 1870
Louisiana	Jan., 1861–June, 1868
Texas	Feb., 1861–Mar., 1870
Virginia	Apr., 1861–Jan., 1870
Arkansas	May, 1861–June, 1868
North Carolina	May, 1861–June, 1868
Tennessee	June, 1861–July, 1866

Confederate States of America *See* **Confederacy**

Confederation, Articles of *See* **Articles of Confederation**

Confederation Government Confederation government of Bolivia and Peru (1836–39). The confederation was opposed by Chile and Argentina and fell after defeat of its forces by Chile at Yungay (Jan. 20, 1839).

Confederation group Canadian literary group of the late 19th cent. Its members were noted for their celebration of Canada's natural beauty, and included the poets William Bliss Carman (1861–1929) and Charles G. D. Roberts (1860–1943).

Confederation of Bar League of Polish nobles formed (1768) at Bar (then in Poland) to oppose Russian domination of Polish internal affairs. The league formed after Polish king Stanislaus II acceded to the wishes of Catherine II of Russia and granted religious equality to Poland's non-Roman Catholic minority. The nobles, among them C. Pulaski, were finally defeated by Russian armies in 1772, despite assistance from Turkey and France. The war with Russia culminated in the first Partition of Poland (1772).

Confederation of Radom League of Polish nobles. Formed (June 23, 1767) with Russia's support, it was a confederation of groups opposed to the reform measures of Polish king Stanislaus II. The league was a contributing factor in events leading up to the first Partition of Poland (1772).

Confederation of the Rhine League of German states (1806–13) organized by Napoleon. He formed the league, after defeating the Austrians at the Battle of Austerlitz (1805), to counter the two major German powers, Austria and Prussia. The league ultimately included almost all the German states except Austria and Prussia. On joining, each of the states gave up its allegiance to the Holy Roman Empire. The major states that joined the league included Bavaria, Württenberg, Baden, Hesse-Darmstadt, and Nassau. The league collapsed after Napoleon's defeat in Russia but nevertheless played a part in the later unification of modern Germany.

Conference of Genoa Meeting (Apr. 10–May 19, 1922) of 29 European nations and five British Commonwealth countries at Genoa, Italy. The conference was held to discuss resumption of trade between Europe and the new Soviet government and plans for financing post-WW I reconstruction. Other questions soon dominated the conference, however, including repayment for foreign property seized by the Soviets during their revolution, repayment of the Russian war debt, and repayment for damages inflicted by the Allied military expedition into Russia after the revolution. The Treaty of Rapallo (1922), a separate pact between Russia and Germany, forced the adjournment of the conference.

Conference of Lausanne 1. Meetings (Nov., 1923–July, 1924) between Allied powers and the Ottoman Empire, leading to the Treaty of Lausanne. **2.** Meetings (June–July, 1932) to discuss repayment of war debts from WW I. Attended by Great Britain, France, Belgium, Germany, Italy, and Japan, the conference scrapped the Young Plan for war reparations by Germany, such repayment having been made impossible by worldwide economic depression. The new plan called for repayment of a reduced sum, but was ultimately rejected (1932) by the US Congress. Germany subsequently made no payments and the Nazi government later repudiated the debt.

Conference of San Remo International conference held (Apr. 19–26, 1920) at San Remo, Italy. Representatives of Great Britain, France, Italy, Japan, Belgium, and Greece completed the draft of the later peace treaty of Sèvres with Turkey and created British mandates in Palestine and Iraq, and French mandates in Syria and Lebanon.

Confucianism Chinese moral and ethical philosophy that has played a major role in much of China's history. Confucianism is based on classical writings and precepts dating to the early period of Chinese history. These precepts were systematized by Confucius (551–479 BC) and modified and developed by later Chinese philosophers. Originally an ethical system, Confucianism adopted metaphysical elements from Buddhism, Taoism, and other systems, notably with the advent of Neo-Confucianism (10th–13th cents.). It greatly influenced the Chinese imperial government, and Confucian traditions were perpetuated by the Chinese Examination System (q.v.). Confucianism declined with the opening of China to the West (19th cent.) and has been virtually eliminated from political life by the Chinese Communists. Key dates in the history of Confucianism include:

23D–3D CENTS. BC Elements of what became Confucian thought developed during Hsia (23d–18th cents. BC), Shang (18th–12th cents. BC), and Chou (12th–3d cents. BC) dynasties.

8TH–3D CENTS. BC Chou dynasty declined under pressure from barbarian invasions; political disintegration and rise of feudalism altered traditional Chinese life.

551–479 BC Confucius lived; sought to reestablish order through traditional political and moral teachings; believed by tradition to have expanded and ordered such thought in works including *Wu Ching (Five Classics)* and *I Ching (Classic of Changes)*.

479 BC Confucius died; subsequent scholars compiled aphorisms attributed to him in *Lun yü*; some 70 disciples continued his teachings.

372–289 BC Mencius lived; advanced Confucian thought and carried on vigorous debates with opposing philosophical schools.

3D CENT. BC Hsun-tzu lived; opposed Mencius' teaching that humanity's nature was basically good and advocated strong hierarchy of society; contributed to rise of Legalists, whose teachings supported strong imperial rulers.

221–207 BC Confucian thought declined with unification of China under Ch'in dynasty, which drew upon Legalist teachings.

206 BC–AD 220 Confucianism restored during rule of Han dynasty.

156–87 BC Han emperor Wu Ti reigned; established Confucianism as official philosophical school. Chinese Examination System, based on knowledge of Confucian thought, adopted for testing civil servants.

C 1ST CENT. AD Confucianism split into two schools: the Old Text School, which placed emphasis on the original Classical texts; and the New School, which incorporated later texts and teachings, including Taoist thought.

1ST CENT. AD Shrines to Confucius constructed; Confucius became subject of veneration.

3D CENT. AD Fall of Han Dynasty (AD 220); Confucianism declined with rising political disorder in China.

3D–6TH CENTS. AD Buddhism and Taoism gained in importance as Confucianism declined.

581–907 China reunited during Sui (581–618) and T'ang (618–907) dynasties; Confucianism regained its position of importance; new edition of *Wu Ching* issued during early T'ang (7th cent.).

960–1279 Rise of Neo-Confucianism during Sung dynasty; incorporated metaphysical elements from Taoism and Buddhism.

1130–1200 Chu Hsi lived; greatest exponent of Neo-Confucian thought.

1472–1529 Wang Yang-ming lived; developed school of thought emphasizing introspection and intuition which increasingly opposed the rigid institutional form of Confucianism adopted by the Ming dynasty.

19TH CENT. Confucian traditions challenged by Western influences on Chinese life.

1858–1927 K'ang Yu-wei lived; attempted to incorporate Western thought into framework of Confucianism; sought unsuccessfully to modernize China in Hundred Days of Reform (1898).

1905 Chinese Examination System abolished in move toward modernization.

1911–12 Chinese imperial rule ended by Nationalist Revolution; Confucianism as an institution severely crippled.

1949 Communists came to power in China; Confucian teachings suppressed.

Confucius 551–479 BC. Famous Chinese philosopher whose teachings form the basis for Confucianism. Confucius was a social reformer who hoped to create a just society by his teachings on morality and government. Little is known of his life. Born to a poor family in eastern China, he educated himself and became known for his scholarship. He served in an official post for a time and then turned (c495 BC) to travel, and gathered a small circle of disciples. Through them he hoped to bring an end to the constant wars and tyrannical governments so prevalent in his time. Soon after the death of Confucius, the disciples compiled his teachings in the *Analects*, which was studied as a basic text in China for two thousand years.

Congo ⟨People's Republic of the Congo⟩ ⟨*formerly* French Congo⟩ Republic located in Equatorial Africa. Its capital is Brazzaville. The Congo's coastal region was first explored (15th cent.) by the Portuguese. In the 1870s, the region north of the Congo River was explored by Savorgnan de Brazza (1852–1905), who founded Brazzaville (1880) and established a French claim in the region. The same year he negotiated with the native Bateke and established a French protectorate over the area, which became known as the French Congo and, later, Middle Congo. In 1910, the Congo was made part of French Equatorial Africa. It became (1946) a French overseas territory and was granted autonomous rule (1958). The Congo became independent on Aug. 15, 1960, with Fulbert Youlou in office as its first president. An uprising in 1963 led to a change in government and the introduction of Communist economic and political systems. An army coup brought Maj. Marien Ngouabi to power in 1968. He was assassinated in 1977. A new constitution was adopted (1979) and a treaty with the USSR was concluded (1981).

Congo, Democratic Republic of the *See* **Zaire**

Congregationalism System of church organization in which local churches govern themselves. Congregational churches are usually Protestant and are most numerous in the US and Britain. Congregationalism arose (16th–17th cents.) in Britain as a reaction to the established Church of England and first appeared among the followers (Brownists) of Robert Browne (c 1550–1633). Congregationalists in the early 17th cent., then known as Independents, suffered persecutions until 1689, when the Act of Toleration was declared. The movement spread to America (1620) with the Pilgrims, and the first Congregational church was built (1629) at Salem, Massachusetts. Since then

Congregationalism in both the US and Britain has undergone periods of expansion and decline. From the 19th cent., groups of these churches have tended to form unions and broad fellowships while maintaining the autonomy of the local congregation.

Congress Kingdom of Poland ⟨Congress Poland⟩ Kingdom of Poland created (May 3, 1815) by the Congress of Vienna after Napoleon's fall. The Russian czar was designated ruler of the kingdom, though Congress Poland was granted a constitution, a legislative diet, and the right to maintain an army. Polish resistance to the czar's domination led to the November Insurrection (1830–31) and January Insurrection (1863–64). Both revolts were unsuccessful and resulted in severe repression and eventual reduction of the kingdom to a Russian province 1864. Poland was ultimately recreated as an independent state after WW I.

Congress of Aix-la-Chapelle Meeting (Oct.–Nov., 1818) of members of the Quadruple Alliance (Britain, Austria, Prussia, Russia) and France at Aix-la-Chapelle (now Aachen, Germany). The powers resolved (Oct. 9) to withdraw the forces occupying France since Napoleon's defeat and to restore France to full sovereignty. The congress was one of several meetings in which the major powers shaped the conservative policy (as in the Holy Alliance), which prevailed in Europe immediately after the Napoleonic era.

Congress of Berlin Meeting of European powers called (1878) to renegotiate the Treaty of San Stefano and deal with British and Austro-Hungarian dissatisfaction with terms forced on the Ottoman Empire by Russia after the Russo-Turkish War (1877–78). Headed by O. von Bismarck, the meeting resulted in the Treaty of Berlin (July 13, 1878), which cost Russia much of what it had gained in the earlier treaty. Austria-Hungary was to occupy Bosnia and Herzegovina; Britain was to occupy Cyprus; and Montenegro, Serbia, and Romania were recognized as independent. An autonomous Bulgaria (much smaller than that sought by Russia) was created under Ottoman suzerainty. Russia gained control over Ottoman territories in Asia and the Balkans.

Congress of Chilpancingo Mexican revolutionary congress (convened Sept., 1813) at Chilpancingo, Mexico. It declared Mexican independence from Spain (Nov., 1813) and promulgated Mexico's first constitution (Oct. 22, 1814).

Congress of Laibach Meeting (Jan.–May, 1821) of European powers. A continuation of the Congress of Troppau (1820), it was held at Laibach, Yugoslavia, and was attended by representatives of the Holy Alliance (Austria, Prussia, and Russia), Great Britain, France, and other, lesser states. Despite opposition by the French and British, the congress sanctioned armed intervention (by C. Metternich's Austrian forces) to put down liberal revolutions in Naples and Piedmont. The congress was a victory for Metternich's conservative policies, which supported absolutist monarchies.

Congress of Paris Conference (Feb.–Mar., 1856) of Austria, France, Great Britain, the Ottoman Empire, Russia, and Sardinia, to end the Crimean War. The congress culminated with the Treaty of Paris (q.v.).

Congress of Troppau Conference (Oct.–Dec., 1820) at Troppau, Austria (now Opava, Czechoslovakia), to consider European action against the uprisings in Spain and the Two Sicilies. The Russian and Austrian emperors attended, the latter accompanied by C. Metternich, but Britain and France sent lower-ranking representatives and refused to subscribe to the protocol threatening armed intervention against insurgents. (See also Congress of Laibach.)

Congress of Tucumán Argentine Congress that met in Tucumán and declared (July 9, 1816) Argentine independence from Spain. The Congress pursued the idea of an independent South American monarchy but was unable to impose an effective government structure. It was ultimately forced to disband (1820) by local caudillos.

Congress of the United States The legislative branch of the US government, consisting of the Senate and the House of Representatives. As established by Article I of the Constitution, Congress is empowered to "make all laws" necessary for the execution of the power "vested by [the] Constitution in the government of the United States." The Senate, the upper house, consists of two senators from each state, named by state legislatures until the 17th Amendment provided (1913) for their election by direct popular vote. Senators serve terms of six years and one-third of the members are elected every two years, making the Senate a continuing body. The vice-president of the United States is the presiding officer of the Senate and has a vote in case of a tie. When the vice-president is absent, his place is taken by a president *pro tempore*, who is fourth in line of succession to the US presidency. The House of Representatives, the lower house, consists of 435 members apportioned according to population, each state being entitled to at least one. Representatives serve for two years, and the entire body is elected anew every two years. The House is presided over by a speaker, nominated by the party currently enjoying a majority and elected by the House. The speaker is third in line of succession for the US presidency. Legislation must be approved by both houses. Money bills and impeachment proceedings originate only in the House. The Senate confirms presidential appointments (by a simple majority), ratifies treaties (by a two-thirds majority), and tries impeachment cases. Congress is required by the Constitution to hold an annual session which, since the passage of the 20th Amendment (1933), begins on Jan. 3 of each year. Legislation, once it has passed both houses, must be signed by the president within ten days, or it becomes law automatically, unless Congress adjourns in the meantime. Two-thirds majorities are needed in both houses to override a presidential veto. Since 1803 the US Supreme Court has effectively exercised a power implied, but not specified, in the Constitution, of invalidating congressional legislation on grounds that it is unconstitutional. If this occurs, Congress must redraft the bill or initiate a constitutional amendment (which must be approved by three-fourths of the states) to secure the legislation it wishes.

Congress of Verona Conference held (Oct. 20–Dec. 14, 1822) between the major European powers. The congress authorized French intervention in the Spanish revolution against Ferdinand VII, but British opposition led to failure of the congress system.

Congress of Vienna International congress (Sept., 1814–June, 1815) called to reorganize Europe following the fall of Napoleon. The agreements reached at this convention shaped Europe's political structure for much of the 19th cent. Principal nations at the congress were France, Austria, Prussia, Russia, and Great Britain, although numerous smaller nations were represented. Major settlements reached at the congress included establishment of the borders of France and confirmation of the restoration of Bourbon king Louis XVIII to the French throne; confirmation of Ferdinand VII as king of Spain; establishment of the German Confederation from the remnants of the Holy Roman Empire; the reestablishment and enlargement of the Swiss Confederation; and the restoration of the Austrian monarchy. Austria lost Belgium, the Austrian Netherlands, and other territories, but was compensated with new lands, including Lombardy-Venetia, Dalmatia, and the Tyrol. Prussia gained substantial portions of the Rhine and Saxony. Poland was divided among Austria, Prussia, and Russia, and a new Polish kingdom (Congress Kingdom of Poland) was placed under Russian

rule. A new kingdom of The Netherlands was established, and the kingdom of Sardinia restored. Sweden received Norway, Russia kept Finland, and Great Britain retained possession of Cape Colony, Ceylon, Malta, and other territories. The Papal States were restored, but the congress did nothing to advance the unification of Italy.

Congress party See **Indian National Congress**

Congress Poland See **Congress Kingdom of Poland**

Congreve, William 1670–1729. English Restoration dramatist who excelled in the comedy of manners. His best-known plays include *Love for Love* and *The Way of the World.*

Connally, John Bowden, Jr. 1917–. American politician. Connally managed the senatorial campaign (1948) of L. Johnson, served as secretary of the navy under J. Kennedy (1961–62), and as governor of Texas (1963–68). He served as secretary of the treasury (1971–72) and as special adviser to the president (1973–74) under R. Nixon.

Connecticut Compromise See **Virginia and New Jersey Plans**

Connecticut Wits (Hartford Wits) Group of American poets in and around Hartford, Connecticut, who flourished in the years immediately after the American Revolution. Largely composed of Yale instructors and students who were conservative Federalists, they collaborated to produce a number of political satires in verse. Their works, written in the style of earlier British poets, were aimed at the liberalism of Jeffersonian Democrats and included *The Anarchiad* and *The Political Greenhouse.* Leading members included J. Barlow and Timothy Dwight (1752–1817).

conquistadores Spanish military adventurers who led the Spanish exploration and conquest of the New World. Among them were F. Pizarro and H. Cortés.

Conrad I d. 918. Elected German king (911–918). His reign was marked by instability and rebellions inspired by feudal lords.

Conrad II c990–1039. Elected German king and Holy Roman Emperor (1024–39). The first of the Salian emperors, he stabilized and strengthened his domain.

Conrad III c1093–1152. Elected German king (1138–52), first of the Hohenstaufen line. His contest with Lothair II over the crown of the Holy Roman Empire led to struggles between the Guelphs and Ghibellines.

Conrad IV 1228–54. Elected German king (1237–54), son of Emperor Frederick II. One of the last Hohenstaufen rulers, he continued his father's struggle with Pope Innocent IV for control of Italy.

Conrad, Joseph 1857–1924. Polish-born author, considered one of the greatest English novelists. Once a merchant seaman, he wrote stories of adventure reflecting his maritime experiences. Among the best known are *Lord Jim* and *Heart of Darkness*.

Conrad von Hotzendorf, Franz, Graf 1852–1925. Austro-Hungarian field marshal. He served as chief of staff (1906–11, 1912–17) of Austro-Hungarian forces before and during WW I, but was dismissed during the war for opposing the peace initiatives of Emperor Charles I.

conservatism Belief in preserving the stability of the existing order. Conservatives oppose broad reforms (though not necessarily all reform) that may cause upheavals of the social or political system and thus often oppose liberalism. Conservatism of the 19th cent., a reaction against the French Revolution (1789–99), was articulated in the works of E. Burke and others. It was characterized by support for rule by the king and the propertied class and opposed liberal republicanism of the rising bourgeoisie. In modern times, conservatism has come to favor such things as freedom from the regulation of business and opposes extension of the welfare state.

Conservative party (Canada) *See* **Progressive Conservative party**

Conservative party Major British political party (formed 1832), a coalition of middle-class interests. Though it represents a conservative viewpoint, the party has traditionally favored moderate social and political reforms. The successor to the Tory party, it was formed after passage of the Reform Bill (1832). Under the leadership of Sir R. Peel, the Conservatives began courting the rising business class, and Peel's Tamworth Manifesto (1834) was written to that end. Peel headed the first Conservative government of Britain (1834–35), and thereafter Conservatives have been in and out of power up to modern times. Among the Conservative governments were: 1841–46 under Peel; 1874–80 under B. Disraeli; 1885–1905 (except 1886, 1892–95) under R. Salisbury and A. Balfour; 1922–29 (except 1924) under A. Law and S. Baldwin; 1935–40 under S. Baldwin and N. Chamberlain; 1940–45 (coalition government) under W. Churchill; 1951–64 under Churchill, A. Eden, H. Macmillan, and A. Douglas-Home; 1970–74 under E. Heath; and 1979– under M. Thatcher.

Conspiracy of Amboise Unsuccessful plot (1560) by French Protestants (Huguenots) to kidnap King Francis II and put an end to the influence of the Catholic Guise family. Led by the Bourbon prince Louis I de Bourbon Condé, they planned to seize the king and members of the Guise family at Amboise. They were discovered, however, and some 1,200 Huguenots were massacred.

Conspiracy of Catiline Abortive attempt (63–62 BC) to overthrow the Roman government during Cicero's consulship. Organized by Catiline after losing his bid (63 BC) for the consulship, the conspiracy was revealed to Cicero by Fulvia, Catiline's mistress. Cicero then denounced Catiline in the Senate in the first of four famous orations against him. Catiline fled Rome and Cicero had those conspirators remaining behind arrested and executed without due process. Cicero was later exiled for this. Catiline and his army of rebels meanwhile were caught trying to escape to Gaul. The rebels were defeated in battle and Catiline was slain.

Constable, John 1776–1837. Leading 19th-cent. English landscape artist. He strongly influenced the French Romantics.

Constance 1152–98. Wife of Holy Roman Emperor Henry VI (m. 1186). She served (1197–98) as regent for her son, and assured his accession to the throne as Emperor Frederick II.

Constance, Council of Council (1414–18) of the Roman Catholic church that ended (1417) the Great Schism. The council (part of which is called the 16th ecumenical council) also issued (1415) the Sacrosancta, which confirmed the supremacy of the church council over the pope (Conciliarism). When the council convened, there were three popes—Gregory XII, John XXIII, and Benedict XIII. After issuing the Sacrosancta, it deposed John (1415), negotiated Gregory's resignation, and deposed Benedict (1417), to end the Schism. Martin V was then elected (1417) pope. The council also declared the Hussite movement heretical and had J. Huss and Jerome of Prague burned at the stake (1415, 1416).

Constance, Peace of Peace treaty (June 12, 1446) between Zurich (and its ally, Holy Roman Emperor Frederick IV) and neighboring Swiss cantons, ending a war for control of disputed territories.

Constance, Treaty of Treaty (1183), by which Holy Roman Emperor Frederick I made peace with Pope Alexander III and with the Lombard towns. By its terms the Lombard towns gained virtual autonomy, but Frederick retained nominal suzerainty.

Constans I AD 320 or 323–AD 350. Roman emperor (AD 337–350), successor to his father, Constantine I. After the death (AD 340) of his brother Constantine II, he became sole ruler of the Western Roman Empire.

Constant de Rebecque, Benjamin   1767–1830. A Swiss-born French author and politician. A widely known liberal pamphleteer in France, he wrote *Adolphe*, an early psychological novel.

Constantine   1868–1923. Greek king (1913–17 and 1920–22). His refusal to support the Allies in WW I forced his first abdication, and his disastrous war with Turkey, the second.

Constantine I (~the Great) (*orig.* Constantinus, Flavius Valerius Aurelius) AD 280?–337. Roman emperor (AD 306–337) who helped make Rome a Christian state. On the death (AD 306) of Constantinus I, Constantine's father and co-emperor with Galerius, there followed a long struggle among rival claimants to the throne. On the eve of the Battle of Milvian Bridge (312) against his last rival, Constantine had a vision, accepted Christianity, and by his subsequent victory in battle became emperor in the West. By his Edict of Milan (313) with co-emperor Licinius, he confirmed Christianity as a lawful religion. He emerged victorious from battle with Licinius (323) and thereby became sole ruler of the Roman Empire. He convened the First Council of Nicaea (325) to resolve the dispute over Arianism and strengthen Christianity. He moved the imperial capital to Byzantium, which he rebuilt (330) as the city of Constantinople.

Constantine II   AD 316–340. Son of Constantine I and co-emperor (AD 337–340) of the Roman Empire. He was killed while trying to seize territories controlled by his brother Constans I.

Constantine IV   *d.* 685. Byzantine emperor (668–685). He halted Muslim attacks on Constantinople but was forced to give up northern territory to the Bulgars.

Constantine V   718–775. Byzantine emperor (741–775), successor to his father, Leo III. His advocacy of Iconoclasm and opposition to monasticism eventually cost the Byzantine Empire its control over Rome and the rest of Italy.

Constantine VI   *b. c*770–797. Byzantine emperor (780–797), successor to his father, Leo IV. His mother, Irene, ruled as regent (780–790) and as co-ruler (792–97) but deposed and blinded him.

Constantine VII (Porphyrogenitus, Constantine) 905–959.   Byzantine emperor (913–959) and scholar, son of Leo VI. His writings concerned the history and politics of his empire. His reign was marked by legal and land reforms, and war with Bulgarians and Russian princes.

Constantine VIII   *See* **Basil II**

Constantine XI (Palaeologus, Constantine) *d.* 1453. Last Byzantine emperor (1449–53), successor to his brother John VIII. He died during the Great Siege of Constantinople, in which the Turks completed their conquest of the Byzantine Empire.

Constantine, Donation of   *See* **Donation of Constantine**

Constantine the Great   *See* **Constantine I**

Constantinople (*now* Istanbul) Former capital of the Byzantine Empire and of the Ottoman Empire. Located in what now is Turkey, it has been named Istanbul since 1930. Known in ancient times as Byzantium, the city was renamed Constantinople (AD 330) by Constantine the Great, who established it as the capital of the Roman Empire. It became capital of the Byzantine Empire after the fall of the Western Roman Empire (AD 476). The city flourished under Byzantine rule. It was sacked by crusaders (1204) during the Fourth Crusade and became the nucleus of the Latin Kingdom of Constantinople (*q.v.*). The Ottoman Turks, under Muhammad II, conquered it and thereby overthrew the Byzantine Empire (1453). The city remained capital of the Ottoman Empire through WW I. During the subsequent occupation (1918–23) by Allied forces, the last Ottoman sultan was deposed (1922), and Ankara became capital of the new republic of Turkey.

Constantinople, Councils of   **1.** First Council of ~ (AD 381) (2d ecumenical council). Called by Roman emperor Theodosius I, the council condemned Arianism and Apollinarianism, reaffirmed the Council of Nicaea (AD 325) and the Nicene Creed, and issued a doctrinal statement on the Holy Ghost as an equal in the Trinity of the Father, Son, and Holy Ghost. **2.** Second Council of ~ (AD 553) (5th ecumenical council). Convened by Byzantine emperor Justinian I, the council condemned Nestorianism and approved Justinian's edict of 544 on the heresy. **3.** Third Council of ~ (680–681) (6th ecumenical council). Called by Byzantine emperor Constantine IV, the council condemned Monotheletism, issued a doctrinal statement on the existence of separate will and operation in both the human and divine natures of Christ, and condemned Pope Honorius I as a Monothelite. The Quinisext Council is considered part of this council in the West. **4.** Fourth Council of ~ (869–870) (8th ecumenical council in the West). Called at the recommendation of Byzantine emperor Basil I, the council excommunicated Photius, rival of Saint Ignatius of Constantinople for the patriarchy of Constantinople.

Constantinople, Latin Empire of   *See* **Latin Empire of Constantinople**

Constantinople, Saint Ignatius of   *See* **Ignatius of Constantinople, Saint**

Constantinople, Treaty of   *See* **Balkan War (2)**

Constantius I ⟨Chlorus, Constantius⟩ AD c250–306. Roman emperor (AD 305–306) and father of Constantine the Great. He put down the rebellion of Allectus in Britain (296) and defeated the Alemanni in Gaul (298).

Constantius II AD 317–361. Roman emperor (AD 337–361), son of Constantine the Great. He fought against the Persians under Shapur II. On the death of his brother Constans I (AD 350), he became sole emperor.

Constantius III d. AD 421. Roman emperor of the West (AD 421). A general of Honorius, he defeated the Visigoths, married Honorius' sister (417), and was named co-emperor by Honorius (421).

constitution See **Constitution of the United States**

Constitution, the See **Old Ironsides**

Constitution Act See **Canada (1982)**

Constitutional Union party American political party. Composed mainly of former Know-Nothings and Whigs, it nominated J. Bell as presidential candidate in the 1860 election. It carried Kentucky, Tennessee, and Virginia, but soon after disappeared as a political force.

Constitution of the United States Document empowering the federal government of the US. In addition to defining the form and system of government, it describes the basic liberties of American citizens and basic laws of the land. Drafted and signed (Sept. 17, 1787) at the Constitutional Convention *(q.v.)*, the Constitution was designed to remedy the shortcomings of the Articles of Confederation *(q.v.)*, by providing for a strong central government. The Constitution went into effect (Mar. 4, 1789), following ratification by 11 (9 required had ratified by June 21, 1788) of the original 13 states. The Bill of Rights, a set of 10 amendments to the Constitution, was passed (Sept. 25, 1789) and ratified (Dec. 15, 1791). The 2 remaining states ratified the Constitution after passage of the Bill of Rights. Amendments in the Bill of Rights are listed below. The Constitution consists of a Preamble, the following seven articles, and the Amendments to the Constitution listed below them.

Article I Describes the organization, powers, and limitations of the legislative branch.

Article II Empowers the president and executive branch *(q.v.)* and describes the duties of the president and means by which he is to be elected.

Article III Empowers the judicial branch *(q.v.)* and defines jurisdictions of the Supreme Court and lower courts.

Article IV Describes the relationship of states to the federal government, as well as to other states.

Article V Describes the method of amending the Constitution.

Article VI Declares the Constitution to be the supreme law of the land, which no state may abridge.

Article VII Describes the ratification process.

AMENDMENTS TO THE CONSTITUTION

Bill of Rights (all adopted 1791).

Amendment I guarantees freedom of religion, speech, the press, petition, and assembly.

Amendment II guarantees the right to bear arms.

Amendment III restricts quartering of soldiers.

Amendment IV protects against illegal search and seizure.

Amendment V guarantees due process and rights of the accused.

Amendment VI guarantees the accused a speedy trial and other rights during trial.

Amendment VII guarantees the right to a jury trial in civil suits.

Amendment VIII protects against imposition of excessive bail and cruel and unusual punishment.

Amendment IX reserves for the people rights not enumerated in the Constitution.

Amendment X reserves for the states or the people powers not enumerated in the Constitution.

Subsequent Amendments

Amendment XI limits the jurisdiction of federal judiciary (ratified 1798).

Amendment XII revises procedures for electing the president and vice-president (ratified 1804).

Amendment XIII abolishes slavery (ratified 1865). This and the following two amendments resulted from the Civil War.

Amendment XIV reaffirms the right of citizens to representation and equal protection under the law. It also bans insurgents (namely Confederates) from government office, and invalidates debts incurred by them (ratified 1868).

Amendment XV guarantees the right to vote, regardless of race or creed (ratified 1870).

Amendment XVI empowers the federal government to collect the income tax (ratified 1913).

Amendment XVII changes the procedure for electing senators from election by state legislatures to direct popular election (ratified 1913).

Amendment XVIII bans alcoholic beverages (ratified 1919). *See also* Prohibition.

Amendment XIX guarantees women the right to vote (ratified 1920). *See also* Woman's Suffrage.

Amendment XX revises the term of office for the president, vice-president, and Congress (to eliminate the lame duck Congress *(q.v.)* (ratified 1933). It also fixes the line of succession in the event of the president's death in office.

Amendment XXI repeals Prohibition (ratified 1933).

Amendment XXII establishes the two-term limit on the presidency (ratified 1951).

Amendment XXIII provides for voting and representation rights for the District of Columbia (ratified 1961).

Amendment XXIV bans poll taxes (ratified 1964).

Amendment XXV provides for presidential succession and replacement of the vice-president (ratified 1967).

Amendment XXVI lowers the voting age to 18 (ratified 1971).

Constitutional Convention ⟨Federal Constitutional Convention⟩ ⟨Philadelphia Convention⟩ US convention called (May 25–Sept. 17, 1787) at Philadelphia, Pennsylvania, and presided over by G. Washington. The convention was called by Congress to amend the Articles of Confederation, which had proved ineffective in dealing with the political and economic problems besetting newly independent America. Delegates from 12 states (Rhode Island sent no delegates) drafted and signed (Sept. 17, 1787) the Constitution of the United States of America after much debate (*see* Virginia and New Jersey Plan). The convention then dissolved and the Constitution was sent to the 13 states for ratification. There ensued a major struggle by the Federalist party, supporters of the Constitution, to secure its enactment into law. This came with ratification (June, 1788) by New Hampshire, the ninth state to do so.

Constitutions and Canons Ecclesiastical *See* canon law

Constitutions of Clarendon Sixteen ordinances issued (1164) by English king Henry II to limit the power of the Catholic church. These measures were opposed by Thomas à Becket, and his murder (1170) by the king's supporters forced Henry to modify the ordinances.

Constitutions of Melfi ⟨Liber Augustalis⟩ Administrative law code given (1231) to the kingdom of Sicily by Holy Roman Emperor Frederick II. One of the important legal documents of the Middle Ages, it established a strong and efficient central government in the kingdom.

consul Name given the two chief magistrates of the ancient Roman republic. Consuls wielded vir-

tually royal powers although their term of office was limited. The position was the highest achievable by private citizens.

Consulate French government (1799–1804) established after overthrow of the Directory in the *coup d'état* of 18 Brumaire. Under the Consulate, three consuls—one of whom was Napoleon—ruled France, until Napoleon's assumption (1804) of the title "emperor."

Continental Army American army during the American Revolutionary War authorized by the Second Continental Congress and placed under the command of Gen. G. Washington on June 15, 1775. This force had arisen spontaneously around Boston following the Battles of Lexington and Concord *(q.v.)*. Numbering around 20,000 at its maximum, the army was trained by Washington and led to victory (1781) over the British.

Continental Congress Legislature and interim government (1774–89) for the 13 colonies (later states) during the American Revolution and postwar years until adoption of the Constitution of the United States. The First Continental Congress, brought about by Colonial opposition to the Intolerable Acts (especially among Committees of Correspondence and the Sons of Liberty), was convened (Sept. 5–Oct. 26, 1774) at Philadelphia, with P. Randolph presiding. It opposed J. Galloway's conciliatory plan, created the Continental Assocation to halt trade with Britain, and sent a list of colonists' grievances to King George III. The Second Continental Congress was convened (May 10, 1775–Dec. 20, 1776) at Philadelphia, with Randolph (and later J. Hancock) as president. The Congress created the Continental Army (May 31, 1775), appointed G. Washington commander (June 15), rejected Lord North's plan for peaceful settlement, opened American ports in defiance of British acts, and adopted the Declaration of Independence (July 4, 1776). During the war, subsequent sessions, held at Philadelphia (except 1776–77, 1777–78), were characterized by disputes between Congress and the military. After adoption of the Articles of Confederation (1781), the inability of the congress to govern effectively led to the Annapolis and Constitutional conventions and eventual adoption of the Constitution.

Continental Divide ⟨Great Divide⟩ Continental barrier marking a division between eastward- and westward-flowing river systems. Specifically, in North America, the term refers to the Rocky Mountain chain.

Continental System French economic plan (1806–12) adopted by Napoleon (in the Berlin Decree) to freeze trade with England during the Napoleonic Wars. Russia's refusal to conform to it led to Napoleon's invasion of Russia (1812). The plan also contributed to outbreak of the War of 1812.

Contreras, Battle of Battle (Aug. 19–20, 1847) of the Mexican War. A decisive victory for American forces under Gen. W. Scott over Mexican soldiers under Gen. A. de Santa Anna, it was fought during the American drive on Mexico City.

Conventicle acts English religious acts (1593, 1664). Created to suppress dissension within the Anglican church, they were repealed by the Toleration Act (1689).

Convention of Akkerman Treaty (Oct. 7, 1826) forced on the Ottoman Turks by the Russians and signed at Akkerman, Russia. By its terms, the Turks granted Serbia autonomy, gave Russia rights to oversee the autonomy of Moldavia and Walachia, and granted Russia navigation and commercial rights in Turkish domains.

Convention of 1818 US-British border agreement (Oct. 20, 1818) establishing the 49th parallel as the US-Canadian border from the Lake of the Woods to the Rocky Mountains and providing for open occupation of Oregon territory for 10 years.

Convention of Gastein Austro-Prussian agreement (Aug. 14, 1865) settling administration of Schleswig-Holstein, seized (1864) from Denmark. Prussia administered Schleswig and Austria administered Holstein.

Convention of Kloster-Zeven Agreement signed (Sept. 8, 1757) by the duke of Cumberland near Zeven, in Hanover, following his defeat by the French in the Seven Years' War. The convention, allowing French occupation of Hanover, was repudiated by the British government.

Convention of Sintra Agreement (Aug. 30, 1808) between British and French forces in Portugal during the Peninsular War. Much criticized in Britain, it allowed the French to return home with their arms, baggage, and booty.

Convention of Vergara 〈Bergara, ~〉 Agreement (Aug. 31, 1839) ending resistance by Spanish Carlists to the rule of Queen Isabella II.

Convention Parliament English Parliament (Apr.–Dec., 1660). It restored Charles II and the Stuart monarchy to the English throne, following Charles' signing of the Declaration of Breda (q.v.), and thus began the Restoration (q.v.) period.

Conway, Thomas See **Conway Cabal**
Conway, Treaty of See **Llewelyn ab Gruffydd**
Conway Cabal American Revolutionary plot. Several dissatisfied American officers, including Gen. Thomas Conway (1735–1800?), sought unsuccessfully to replace G. Washington with H. Gates as head of the Continental Army.

Cook, James 1728–79. English navigator famed for his exploratory voyages in the Pacific and Antarctic. In command (1768–71) of the ship *Endeavour*, he discovered and charted New Zealand and the eastern coast of Australia, and circumnavigated the globe. On his second voyage (1772–75), commanding the *Resolution* and the *Adventure*, he explored the Antarctic coast and discovered New Caledonia. His third voyage (1776–79), to discover a northwest or northeast passage, ended with his murder by Hawaiian natives.

Cooke, Jay 1821–1905. American financier. He founded (1861) Jay Cooke and Company, which marketed federal bonds during the Civil War. Its failure (Sept. 18, 1873) caused the Panic of 1873.

Coolidge, Calvin 1872–1933. The 30th US president (1923–29), successor to W. Harding. Coolidge was governor of Massachusetts (1919–21) when he won national attention by using the state militia to break the Boston police strike (1919). Shortly thereafter he was nominated as the Republican vice-presidential candidate, and entered office with Pres. W. Harding. As vice-president, he was not part of Harding's inner circle and was not involved in the Teapot Dome scandal (q.v.). After Harding's death (1923) he became the president and quickly restored public confidence in government. Reelected (1924), he refused to run again in 1928. His administration was characterized by probusiness policies; presidential vetoes of farm-relief legislation; conservative fiscal policies stressing economy in government and tax cuts; and encouragement of speculative stock market booms, which finally resulted in the stock market crash of 1929.

coolie A Chinese or Indian laborer. Coolies were indentured laborers sent during the 19th cent. to work in the US, West Indies, and other places where cheap labor was needed.

Cooper, James Fenimore 1789–1851. The first major American novelist. A sailor and US naval officer (1806–11), he married (1811) and took up the life of a gentleman. He won fame with publication (1821) of his second book, *The Spy*, and thereafter began his *Leatherstocking Tales* of frontier life. This series included *The Pioneers, The Last of the Mohicans, The Prairie, The Pathfinder,* and *The Deerslayer.*

Cooper, Leon N. See **Bardeen, John**
Cooper, Leroy Gordon, Jr. 1927–. American astronaut. One of the seven original astronauts, he made the last flight of the Mercury program, aboard *Faith 7* (May, 1963).
Cooper, Peter 1791–1883. US manufacturer, inventor, and philanthropist. He constructed the

early locomotive "Tom Thumb" and founded Cooper Union, a college in New York City.

Co-operative Commonwealth Federation Canadian political party active in the 1930s and 1940s. Formed (1932) during the Depression, the party advocated creation of a socialist state by democratic means. It was strongest in the western provinces and won control (1944) of the government of Saskatchewan. The party continued to dominate Saskatchewan but declined in the other provinces after WW II.

Copenhagen Capital city (pop. 699,300) of Denmark. Denmark's commercial and cultural center, it was first fortified (1167) by Archbishop Absalon, chartered (1254), and several times attacked by the Hanseatic League. It became Denmark's capital in 1443. It was bombarded by the British (1801, 1807) during the French Revolutionary and Napoleonic Wars and was occupied by the Germans (1940–45) during WW II.

Copenhagen, Battle of British naval victory (Apr. 2, 1801) against the Danish fleet at Copenhagen. The battle stemmed from the French Revolutionary Wars. Denmark had joined (1800) the League of Armed Neutrality along with Russia, Sweden, and Prussia. In addition to proclaiming their neutrality, the four nations also agreed to ignore British rules governing maritime activities of neutrals. Though the British did not declare war, they nevertheless sent a fleet under Lord H. Nelson on a raid against the Danish. The British destroyed the Danish fleet at Copenhagen.

Copernicus, Nicholas 1473–1543. Polish astronomer, considered the founder of modern astronomy. On the basis of his observations and calculations, he advanced the then revolutionary idea that the earth rotated on its axis and that the planets, including the earth, revolved around the sun (the Copernican system). Educated in astronomy at the University of Krakow, he was appointed (1497) canon of the cathedral at Frauenburg, East Prussia. In subsequent years he began to develop his heliocentric theory, opposing the traditional, earth-centered theory. By 1530, he had largely completed his book on the theory, *On the Revolutions of the Celestial Spheres (De revolutionibus orbium coelestium)*, but delayed the start of publication until 1540. He is said to have received the first bound copy just before his death (1543).

Copland, Aaron 1900–. American composer. His works, reflecting American themes and traditions, include the ballets *Rodeo*, *A Lincoln Portrait*, and *Appalachian Spring.*

Copper Age The stage in the development of civilization when pure copper came into use. The Copper Age is considered the early part of the Bronze Age. The earliest known use of copper (*c*6500 BC) occurred in the Near East, and by *c*3500 BC copper metallurgy was well known throughout the region. Copper was in general use by *c*3000 BC, and this is commonly considered the beginning of the Bronze Age. The use of bronze began *c*2400 BC and became widespread after 2000 BC.

Copperhead Derogatory American political term applied to northern Democrats who either opposed the Civil War or sympathized with the South.

Coptic church Christian church of Egypt. The church has only a small following in a country that has been predominantly Islamic since the 7th cent. Formed in early Christian times, it adheres to Monophysitism and has been independent of the Roman Catholic church since AD 451, when the Council of Chalcedon declared Monphysitism a heresy. A still smaller church, the Catholic Coptic church, rejoined the Roman Catholic church in 1741.

Coral Sea, Battle of the US-Japanese naval and air battle (May 7–8, 1942) in the southwest Pacific during WW II. The US assembled a task force to meet a Japanese fleet involved in a planned invasion of Port Moresby, New Guinea. US carrier planes sank a Japanese carrier the first day. In a battle fought solely by carrier planes the next day, the US sustained heavy losses (including one carrier sunk) but turned back the Japanese for the first time in the war.

Corbeil, Treaty of Treaty (May 11, 1258) signed by French king Louis IX and James I of Aragon. It settled territorial claims of France and Aragon, with terms favorable to France.

Corday, Charlotte 1768–93. Frenchwoman, the assassin of French revolutionary leader J. Marat (July 13, 1793). She stabbed Marat in his bath because of his persecution of the Girondists, with whom she sympathized.

Cordeliers Political club formed (1790) during the French Revolution. Officially known as the Society of the Friends of the Rights of Man and of the Citizen, it was founded to denounce abuses of power. It soon became a formidable political power under the leadership of G. Danton and others. The Cordeliers were involved in the deposing of King Louis XVI, and later, under the more radical influence of J. Hébert and J. Marat, brought down (1792–93) the moderate Girondists. Under Hébert's leadership the club adopted extreme radicalism, and for a time Hébert rivaled M. Robespierre for power. The club dissolved when Hébert was executed (1794) during the Reign of Terror.

Córdoba ⟨Cordova⟩ Spanish city, capital of Córdoba province. Founded by the Carthaginians, it flourished as the capital of a Muslim caliphate (756–1031). It is renowned for its great Moorish mosque, later converted into a cathedral.

Córdoba, Treaty of Treaty (Aug. 24, 1821) signed by Mexican revolutionary forces and Spanish colonial authorities at Córdoba, Mexico. The treaty established Mexican independence.

Cordova *See* **Córdoba**

Corfu Declaration Proclamation (July 20, 1917) calling for creation of Yugoslavia at the end of WW I. Meeting at Corfu, Greece, representatives of the Serbian government-in-exile, the Croats, and the Slovenes put aside long-standing differences and announced a planned union of their states under Serbian king Peter I. Montenegro joined the union (Nov. 26) after the ouster of King Nicholas I, who had opposed it. The new kingdom was formally proclaimed Dec. 4, 1918.

Corinth Ancient Greek city. Settled (9th cent. BC) by Dorians, it became a major city-state in the Peloponnesus and the leading commercial center of Greece. Corinth played a major role in the Persian Wars (499–479 BC) and allied with Sparta against Athens in the Peloponnesian War (431–404 BC). It fought against Sparta in the Corinthian War (395–387 BC), and became a member of the Achaean League (243 BC). Destroyed (146 BC) by the Romans, it became a Roman colony (44 BC). Subsequently occupied by the Ottoman Turks, the Venetians, and again by the Turks, it was completely destroyed (1858) by earthquake. Modern Corinth stands northeast of the ancient site.

Corinth, Battle of Battle (Oct. 3–4, 1862) of the American Civil War, at Corinth, Mississippi. Union forces under W. Rosecrans defeated Confederate units under S. Price and E. Van Dorn in two days of heavy fighting.

Corinthian order Greek architectural style, the last of the three major styles of classical Greek architecture. An ornate style, it influenced later Roman and Renaissance styles.

Corinthian War War (395–387 BC) against Spartan domination, fought by Athens and her allies (Corinth, Argos, and Thebes). At the instigation of Persia, then at war with Sparta, the allied city-states went to war against Sparta. The Spartans won initial victories—the battles of Nemea and Coronea—but suffered a major defeat at the hands of the Persians in a naval battle at Cnidus (all 394 BC). Athens subsequently began to rebuild its former empire by taking over former Spartan possessions. Sparta thus was forced to sue for peace with the Persians, and finally accepted the King's Peace (387 BC).

Coriolanus *fl.* 5th cent. BC. Legendary Roman patrician, said to have received his surname by capturing the Volscian city of Corioli. He later led the Volscians against Rome and spared it from destruction only because of the tearful pleas of his wife and mother.

Corneille, Pierre 1606–84. French dramatist, one of the great French tragedians. His best-known work is *Le Cid.*

Cornelia *fl.* 2d cent. BC. Roman matron, the mother of Tiberius and Gaius Gracchus. To a patrician matron discussing jewelry, she is said to have pointed to her sons and said, "These are my jewels."

Cornelius, Pope *See* **Novatian**

Corn Laws Series of English laws regulating export and import of grain, to maintain a stable supply of domestic grain. Opponents of the laws formed (1839) the Anti-Corn Law League, and in 1846 Parliament, led by R. Peel, repealed the laws.

Cornwallis, Charles Cornwallis, 1st Marquess 1738–1805. British general and statesman. He led British forces in the Carolina and Yorktown campaigns (*q.q.v.*) and his surrender at Yorktown, Virginia (1781), effectively ended fighting in the American Revolution. As governor general of India (1786–93, 1805), he instituted (1793) the Cornwallis Code for governance of India.

Cornwallis Code ⟨Bengal System⟩ Administrative reforms adopted (May 1, 1793) by the British East India Company for the government of Bengal, India. The system, named after Governor General C. Cornwallis, was adopted elsewhere in India and remained in effect until 1833. By the code, administration was separated into commercial, revenue, and judicial departments. Private trade was strictly forbidden, and adequate salaries were paid to administrative personnel. Though the system introduced a measure of stability, it also excluded Indians from important posts.

Coronado, Francisco Vásquez de 1510–44. A Spanish explorer of what became the US Southwest. Seeking treasure cities, Coronado led an expedition (1540–42) north from Mexico into Texas, and from there through Oklahoma to Kansas. García López de Cárdenas led a party of Coronado's men on a side trip and discovered the Grand Canyon (1540).

Coronea, Battle of 1. Boeotian victory (447 BC) over Athens during the First Peloponnesian War. The Athenian defeat led to reestablishment of the Boeotian League. **2.** Battle (394 BC) during the Corinthian War, a Spartan victory over the coalition of city-states allied against it.

Coronel, Battle of German naval victory (Nov. 1, 1914) off Coronel, Chile, during WW I. The German squadron under Admiral Graf von Spee decisively defeated an inferior British squadron under Sir Christopher Cradock (1862–1914), who went down with his flagship.

corporative state Economic system, first employed by the Italian Fascist government of B. Mussolini. It involved government control of the national economy while retaining elements of capitalism, and was adopted in part by Nazi Germany and by Spain under F. Franco.

Corpus Juris Canonici *See* **canon law**

Corpus Juris Civilis ⟨Justinian Code⟩ Roman legal code issued (529–535) by order of Byzantine emperor Justinian I. The voluminous work provided a systematic and comprehensive code of Roman law and greatly influenced later European legal systems. It consisted of four major parts: the Codex, a compilation of existing imperial ordinances; the Digesta, or Pandecta, a collection of extracts of written legal opinions on laws; the Institutiones, a manual on Roman law; and the Novellae, a compilation of imperial laws instituted by Justinian.

Corpus of Canon law *See* **canon law**

Corregidor, Siege of Month-long Japanese siege (Apr.-May, 1942) of Corregidor Island, Philippines, during WW II. After the fall of Bataan, 11,000 US and Filipino troops under Gen. J. Wainright held out against Japanese attacks, but were forced to surrender (May 6, 1942).

Correspondence, Committees of *See* **Committees of Correspondence**

Cortes Spanish national assembly, which derives its name from the legislative assemblies formed (12th cent.) in various Spanish states.

Cortes, Hernando ⟨Cortez, ~⟩ 1485–1547. Spanish conqueror of Mexico (1519–21). He joined with D. Velázquez in conquering Cuba (1511) and was chosen by him to lead a military expedition into Mexico. Setting out (1519) with only 550 men, and ignoring Velázquez' orders for his recall, he conquered Mayan Indian tribes and then marched on the Aztec capital of Tenochtitlán (later Mexico City). By 1521 he had defeated both the Aztec Empire and the forces Velázquez had sent against him. He was, however, replaced (1526) by J. Ponce de León as governor of New Spain, a post King Charles V refused to restore to him.

Cortez, Hernando *See* **Cortes, Hernando**

Cortona, Pietro da 1596–1669 Italian painter and architect and noted master of the baroque style. *Allegory of Divine Providence* is among his works.

Corupedion, Battle of Battle in the Wars of the Diadochi *(q.v.)* fought in Asia Minor (281 BC). Se-

leucus I, ruler of the Seleucid Empire, defeated and killed Lysimachus and thus became master of Asia Minor.

Cosa Nostra *See* **Mafia**

Cossa, Baldassarre ⟨Cassa, Baltasare⟩ ⟨John XXIII (antipope)⟩ c1370–1419. Antipope (1410–15) as John XXIII, during the Great Schism. He was elected in opposition to Pope Gregory XII and antipope Benedict XIII. He was deposed (1415) by the Council of Constance.

Cossa, Baltasare *See* **Cossa, Baldassarre**

Cossacks Russian peasant-soldiers, noted as cavalrymen in the Russian imperial armies. Cossacks in the 15th cent. were escaped serfs from Poland and Russia who formed independent settlements on the Ukrainian frontier. From the 16th cent. Cossack bands were in the service of Polish and Russian sovereigns and by the 18th cent. were under Russian domination. Although they lost their traditional autonomy, they eventually became a privileged military class in the Russian Empire. By the 1900s there were some 12 Cossack units, named for the geographic regions they occupied, including the Don and Kuban Cossacks. Cossacks were frequently used to put down rebellions. They fought the Bolsheviks during the Russian Civil War (1918–22). Under the new regime they lost their special privileges and their villages were turned into Communist collectives.

Costa e Silva, Artur da 1902–69. Brazilian president (1967–69). Head of a military regime that had seized power (1964) in Brazil, he initially attempted reforms but in 1968 dissolved congress and assumed dictatorial powers.

Costa Rica Republic located in Central America, bordered on the east by the Caribbean Sea and the west by the Pacific Ocean. Its capital is San José. Originally a Spanish colony, Costa Rica has a democratic constitutional government, and has enjoyed relative political stability throughout much of its history. Key dates in the history of Costa Rica include:

1502 Columbus discovered Caribbean coast; named it Costa Rica (rich coast).

c1563 Region subdued and brought under captaincy general of Guatemala.

1821 Declared independence from Spain (Sept. 15).

1822–23 Forced to join Mexican empire under A. de Iturbide.

1823–38 Iturbide's empire collapsed; Costa Rica joined United Provinces of Central America.

1848 Republic declared.

1857 Helped to defeat the filibuster W. Walker in Nicaragua.

1874 Banana cultivation introduced; coffee previously dominated agriculture.

1896 Disputed territory on boundary with Nicaragua awarded to Costa Rica.

1899 United Fruit Company founded to exploit the banana trade.

1917–19 Frederico Tinoco in office after overthrowing elected president Alfredo Gonzáles; US opposition brought his overthrow.

1918 Entered WW I on Allied side.

1941 Joined Allies in WW II.

1948 Disputed presidential election between Otilio Ulate and Rafael Calderón Guardia resulted in brief civil war; military junta, led by Col. José Figueres Ferrer seized power; Guardia's attempted invasion failed (Dec.).

1949–53 Ulate in office as president after new constitution was adopted (1949).

1951 Attempted coup by Guardia thwarted.

1951 Costa Rica joined the Organization of American States.

1953–58 Figueres in office as elected president.

1958–62 Mario Enchadi Jiménez in office as president after UN-supervised elections.

1974–78 Daniel Oduber Quirós in office as president; ruling National Liberation Party failed to keep majority in legislature.

1978–82 Coalition leader Rodrigo Carazo Odio in office as president; serious economic problems led to inability to pay foreign debt.

Coster, Laurens Janszoon *See* **Koster, Laurens Janszoon**

Cottereau, Jean *See* **Chouans**

Cotton, John 1584–1652. English-born Puritan clergyman and grandfather of C. Mather. A leading figure in the Massachusetts Bay Colony, he advocated theocracy and helped to found the Congregational church.

Cotton Famine English industrial crisis (1861–65) caused by the withholding of cotton from English mills by events of the American Civil War. The mill workers of Lancashire were particularly affected, but Britain maintained its support of the Union.

Coty, René 1882–1962. French politician, last president (1954–59) of the Fourth Republic. He retired when C. de Gaulle became president of the Fifth Republic (1959).

Coué, Émile 1857–1926. French pharmacist and psychotherapist. He introduced (1920) autosuggestion, and is known for his formula "Every day in every way I am getting better and better."

Coulomb, Charles Augustin de 1736–1806. French physicist. He formulated Coulomb's Law.

The electrical unit of quantity, the coulomb, was named for him.

council, ecumenical *See* **ecumenical council**

Council in Trullo *See* **Quinisext Council**

Council of Four Hundred *See* **Areopagus**

Council of Ten Venetian tribunal founded (c1310) to investigate plots against the state. It soon gained vast powers in both domestic and foreign matters, and existed until abolishment (1797) of the Venetian state by Napoleon.

Council of the Republic Preparliament Russian provisional government (Oct.-Nov., 1917), headed by A. Kerensky. Largely ineffective, it was swept away by the Bolshevik seizure of power.

count European rank of nobility, equivalent to the German Graf and the English earl. The title derives from the Latin *comes*, originally an official in the Roman republic.

Count's War ⟨Feud of the Counts⟩ War of succession (1533–36) in Denmark. By confirming succession of Christian III, the war confirmed the Protestant Reformation in Denmark-Norway (then united under Christian) and established hereditary succession to the throne. On the death of King Frederick I (reigned 1523-33), Christian, a Lutheran and the legitimate heir, was opposed by Count Christopher of Oldenburg. Christian had the services of the Swedish navy, while Christopher had the support of Danish nobles and populace. The tide of the war turned in Christian's favor by 1535, when Christopher's army and naval forces were destroyed. Christopher finally surrendered (July 28, 1536) at Copenhagen.

coup d'état French term meaning "blow to the state," applied to the seizure by force of political power and the overthrow of the state.

Courtenay, Robert of *See* **Robert of Courtenay**

Court of Blood *See* **Alba, Fernando Alvarez de Toledo, Duke of**

Courtrai, Battle of *See* **Golden Spurs, Battle of the**

Cousteau, Jacques-Yves 1910–. French underwater explorer and co-inventor of the aqualung (1943). The co-author of such books as *The Silent World* and *The Living Sea*, he is one of the world's leading proponents of oceanic exploration and conservation.

Couthon, Georges 1755?–94. French revolutionary. He crushed a counterrevolution in Lyon (1793) and helped M. Robespierre conduct the Reign of Terror. He was guillotined after the *coup d'état* of 9 Thermidor (July 27, 1794).

Covenanters Scottish Presbyterians who, during crises in the 16th–17th cents., were sworn to defend their church by a solemn covenant. The first covenant was signed (1557) when Protestants opposed the Catholics in a struggle for power in Scotland. The National Covenant was signed (1638) to oppose Charles I's episcopal reforms and resulted in the Bishops' Wars (1639–40). By the Solemn League and Covenant (1643), the Scots became allies of the Parliamentarians in the early phase of the English Civil War. The Parliamentarians eventually turned against the Scots and defeated them (1650–51). After Charles's restoration (1660), renewed attempts at suppressing Presbyterianism led to rebellions and royal persecutions until the Glorious Revolution (1688).

Coward, Sir Noel 1899–1973. Playwright, actor, and composer. His sophisticated comedies included *Hay Fever*, *Private Lives*, and *Blithe Spirit*. He also produced the film *Brief Encounter*.

Cowell, Henry Dixon 1897–1965. American composer, one of the leading avant-garde American composers. He introduced the use of "tone clusters," several adjacent piano keys struck simultaneously.

Cowley, Abraham 1618–67. English poet and essayist. One of the leading poets of his day, he also served as royalist agent for English queen Henrietta Maria in France during the English Civil War.

Cowpens, Battle of Battle (Jan. 17, 1781) of the Carolina Campaign *(q.v.)*, in the American Revolution, near Cowpens, northern S. Carolina. Some 1,000 Continental troops under D. Morgan decisively defeated a British force of 1,100 under Col. Banastre Tarleton (1754–1833). The British suffered over 900 dead, wounded, or captured. The Americans lost 12 dead, 60 wounded.

Cowper, William 1731–1800. English poet. A leading poet of the 18th cent., he suffered recurrent bouts of mental illness, but managed to produce such masterpieces as the long poem *The Task* and *The Castaway*.

Cox, Jacob Dolson 1828–1900. American general and politician. Appointed a Union brigadier in the Civil War, he fought at Antietam (1862) and Atlanta (1864). He later served as governor of Ohio (1866–68) and secretary of the interior (1869–70) under Pres. U. Grant.

Coxey, Jacob S. *See* **Coxey's Army**

Coxey's Army ⟨Commonweal of Christ⟩ Band of unemployed men, led by Jacob S. Coxey (1854–1951), who marched (1894) from Massilon, Ohio, to Washington, D.C., seeking Congressional aid in relieving unemployment. Coxey failed to raise the great number of men he had hoped for, and the movement collapsed when Coxey and others were arrested in Washington (May 1, 1894) for trespassing.

Cradle of Liberty *See* **Faneuil Hall**

Cradock, Christopher *See* **Coronel, Battle of**

Craigavon, James Craig, 1st Viscount 1871–1940. Irish statesman. An opponent of home rule, he became the first prime minister of Northern Ireland (1921–40).

Crane, Stephen 1871–1900. American writer. One of the pioneers of American realism, he is known best for his Civil War novel *The Red Badge of Courage*.

Cranmer, Thomas 1489–1556. English clergyman. He aided Henry VIII in dissolving his marriage to Catherine of Aragon and was appointed (1533) archbishop of Canterbury. Subsequently, he supported Henry variously as head of the Church of England and in Henry's other divorces. He compiled the Book of Common Prayer (1549) and played a major role in writing the Forty-two Articles. On the accession of Catholic Queen Mary he was burned for heresy.

Crashaw, Richard 1612–49. English poet noted for his religious poetry. A convert to Roman Catholicism, Crashaw traveled to France (1644), then to Italy, where he was influenced by the baroque style of art. His works include the volume *Steps to the Temple*.

Crassus, Lucius Licinius 140–91 BC. Roman politician and orator. He sponsored a law banishing those who had not legally attained Roman citizenship. The law was a major cause of the Social War.

Crassus, Marcus Licinius d. 53 BC. Roman politician. One of the wealthiest Romans, he suppressed (71 BC) the slave revolt led by Spartacus, and joined with J. Caesar and G. Pompey in the first Triumvirate (60 BC). His death while fighting the Parthians led to a power struggle between Caesar and Pompey.

Crazy Horse d. 1877. American Sioux Indian chief of the Oglala tribe. He was a leader in the defeat of Gen. G. Custer at the Battle of Little Bighorn (1876).

Creasy, Sir Edward Shepherd 1812–78. English historian. Creasy's major works include *Fifteen Decisive Battles of the World* and *The History of the Ottoman Turks*.

Crécy, Battle of Battle (Aug. 26, 1346) of the Hundred Years' War, at Crécy, France. English king Edward III led a force of some 10,000 to a decisive victory over about 20,000 French led by Philip VI. The English then advanced to besiege Calais.

Crédit Mobilier of America US railroad construction company involved in a major American financial scandal (1872). The scandal revolved around construction of the Union Pacific Railroad (1865–69), partly funded by federal loans and grants and partly by a Union Pacific bond issue.

Between 1865 and 1869, directors and principal stockholders of Union Pacific allowed exorbitant payments for construction to be made to Crédit Mobilier, which they owned. Crédit Mobilier in turn paid others for actual construction and thereby realized millions in profits. Union Pacific capital was thus systematically drained off and by 1869 the company was deeply in debt. The scandal broke during the 1872 presidential election campaign, when it was revealed that US congressman Oakes Ames (1804–73) and other politicians were involved in the corrupt dealings.

Creek Indians North American Indian tribe that once inhabited parts of Georgia and Alabama. In Colonial times, the Creek generally fought alongside English settlers in wars against the Spanish and Apache Indians, formed the unsuccessful Creek Confederation, and were defeated in the Creek War (1813–14). They were moved to Indian Territory in the 1830s. There the Creek became one of the Five Civilized Tribes.

Creek War War (1813–14) between the Creek Indians and the US. The Creek, British allies in the War of 1812, were stirred up by the Shawnee chief Tecumseh and began the war by massacring (Aug. 30, 1813) about 500 Americans at Fort Mims, Georgia. Gen. A. Jackson was sent with some 5,000 soldiers to subdue the Creek. After winning initial battles, Jackson put an end to the war by his decisive victory (Mar. 27, 1814) at the Battle of Horseshoe Bend. The Creek subsequently signed the Treaty of Fort Jackson (Aug. 9, 1814), giving up most of their tribal lands.

Creon Legendary Greek figure, the uncle of Oedipus. As regent of Thebes he rewarded Oedipus's victory over the Sphinx by giving him the kingdom and the hand of Jocasta, Oedipus's mother. As king of Thebes, Creon killed Antigone for disobeying him (by burying her brother Polynices).

Crépy, Treaty of ⟨Crespy, ~⟩ Treaty (Sept. 18, 1544, at Crépy, northern France) between Holy Roman Emperor Charles V (also king of Spain) and French king Francis I, ending wars between them (1521–44). By its terms Charles gave up claims to Burgundy, and Francis relinquished claims to Naples, Flanders, and Artois.

Crespy, Treaty of *See* **Crépy, Treaty of**

Crete Greek island. Crete was the center of the Minoan civilization *(q.v.)* and one of the earliest advanced cultures. By the 16th cent. BC it had spread its culture and influence to the Greek mainland and throughout the eastern Mediterranean and had established dynastic centers at Cnossos and Phaistos, its major cities. After the fall of the Minoans (c1400 BC), Crete was resettled by Dorian Greeks. It became an important commercial center and, in the 3d cent. BC, a haven for pirates. Annexed (67 BC) by Rome, it later became part of the Byzantine Empire, passed to Venice (1204) during the Fourth Crusade, and then to the Ottoman Turks (1715). Rivalry between Greece and Turkey for control of Crete led to the Greco-Turkish War (1897) and establishment (1898) of a semiautonomous state under European occupation. Crete declared its union with Greece (1908) and was officially annexed in 1913. During WW II, it was captured (May, 1941) by the Germans in the first successful major airborne operation.

Crèvecoeur, Michel-Guillaume Jean de ⟨*pseud.* ~, J. Hector St. John⟩ 1735–1813. French-born American author and agriculturalist. He is known best for his *Letters from an American Farmer*.

Crick, Francis Harry Compton *See* **Watson, James**

Crimea Russian region, now part of the Ukrainian SSR. A peninsula extending from the Ukraine to the Black Sea, it has been conquered many times in history. It was the site of the Crimean War (1853–56).

Crimean War War in southeastern Europe (1853–56) fought by Russia against the Ottoman Turks and their allies, France, Britain, and Sardinia. A long series of Russo-Turkish Wars *(q.v.)* had resulted in Russian expansion in southeast Europe at the expense of the Turks. In the 19th cent., European powers became concerned over the dismemberment of the Ottoman Empire (*see* Eastern Question). Rivalries between France (a long-time ally of the Ottomans) and Russia finally provided the spark that led to war. British and French troops bore the brunt of fighting and the allies were ultimately victorious. The war broke Russian dominance in southeastern Europe. Key events in the Crimean War include:

1851–53 France challenged Russia's position as custodian of Christian holy places within the Ottoman Empire; it sought special considerations for Latin Christian churches from the Ottoman Turks; these were granted (1852) and the Russians, who favored Greek Orthodox Christians, were roused to action.

1853 Russian Czar Nicholas I delivered ultimatum to Turkish government (May); Russian demands refused; Russian forces occupied (July) Moldavia and Walachia (now in Romania).

1853 Ottoman Empire declared war on Russia (Oct. 23).

1854 France and Britain declared war on Russia (Mar.).

1854 Russia withdrew from Moldavia and Walachia under pressure from Austria; Austrian army moved into the region (Aug.).

1854 British and French forces landed on the Crimean Peninsula on the north coast of the Black Sea; victorious in the Battle of Alma River (Sept. 20) soon after; Russian forces withdrew to Sevastopol.

1854 Allied forces began siege of Sevastopol, key Russian position on Black Sea (Oct.).

1854 Battle of Balaklava fought (Oct. 25); Russians failed to break siege of Sevastopol but inflicted heavy casualties on the British; this battle inspired Tennyson's famous poem *Charge of the Light Brigade.*

1854 Russians defeated at Battle of Inkerman (Nov. 5); siege of Sevastopol continued.

1854–55 Military action halted during winter; severe conditions suffered by the war casualties led to Florence Nightingale's celebrated nursing efforts.

1855 Sardinia declared war against Russia (Jan.).

1855 Nicholas died (Mar.); Alexander II became Russian czar; moved to negotiate an end to the war.

1855 Russian forces marching to relieve Sevastopol defeated at Battle of Chernaya River (Aug. 16).

1855 Allied forces besieging Sevastopol captured Malakhov fortress (Sept. 8); Russians forced to evacuate Sevastopol (Sept. 11).

1856 Treaty of Paris (Mar. 30) formally ended hostilities.

Crime of '73 Name for the US government's move (1873) to stop minting the silver dollar. The action was vigorously opposed by Populists and other advocates of free silver *(q.v.).* The 1878 Bland-Allison Act *(q.v.)* restored the silver dollar as legal tender.

Cripps Mission Unsuccessful diplomatic mission (Mar. 22-Apr. 12, 1942) to India, in which the British government offered eventual independence in exchange for India's support during WW II. With India in the midst of its long drive for independence and with the Japanese threatening invasion of India from the East, the British sent Sir Stafford Cripps (1889–1952) to negotiate for India's help in fending off the Japanese. Indian leader M. Gandhi opposed the plan for phased independence after the war and the Indian National Congress rejected it (Apr. 11). The Congress later called (Aug. 8) for immediate independence. The subsequent arrest of its leaders resulted in mass demonstrations and an official ban on the Congress.

Crispi, Francesco 1819–1901. Italian statesman. He aided G. Garibaldi in the conquest of Sicily (1860) and served as Italian premier (1887–91, 1893–96).

Crispin and Crispinian, Saints *fl.* 3d cent. Christian martyrs, patron saints of shoemakers, whose trade they followed. Said to have been brothers, they were beheaded by order of Roman emperor Maximilian.

Crispus, Gaius Sallustius *See* **Sallust**

Cristofori, Bartolomeo di Francesco 1655–1731. Italian harpsichord maker, credited with invention of the hammer action employed in pianos and construction (c1710) of the first piano.

Crittenden, John J *See* **Crittenden Compromise**

Crittenden Compromise Unsuccessful legislation proposed (Dec., 1860) in a final attempt to avert the US Civil War. Put forward by Kentucky senator John J. Crittenden (1787–1863), the measures attempted to rework the Missouri Compromise (1820). Crittenden sought to continue the Fugitive Slave Laws, uphold the doctrine of Popular Sovereignty in new territories, and sanction slavery in the District of Columbia. The measure was defeated in the Senate by one vote (Mar., 1861).

Crius *See* **Titan**

Croatia Historic region now a constituent republic of Yugoslavia. Settled by Croats in the 7th cent., it formed a union with Hungary (1102). Its Westernization and acceptance of Christianity set it apart from the Slavs. It was conquered by the Turks (16th cent.) and by Napoleon (1809–13). In 1918, the Serbs, Croats, and Slovenes joined to form Yugoslavia. There has been periodic agitation in Croatia for greater autonomy.

Croato-Hungarian compromise of 1868 *See* **Nagoda**

Croce, Benedetto 1866–1952. Italian philosopher, historian, critic, and statesman. Founder (1903) of the journal *La Critica,* he strongly opposed Fascism and was a leader of the Liberal party after WW II.

Crockett, David 1786–1836. American frontiersman and politician. He fought against the Creek Indians in the War of 1812 and was a member of Congress (1827–31, 1833–35). He died at the Alamo.

Croesus *d.* 546? BC. Last king of Lydia (560–546 BC), successor to his father, Alyattes, and famed for his great wealth. He was defeated in battle by Cyrus the Great at Sardis (546).

Croker, Richard 1841–1922. Irish-born American politician. He was leader (1886–1902) of New York's Tammany Hall.

Cromwell, Oliver 1599–1658. British soldier and statesman, a hero of the English Civil War (1642–49) and head of government during the Commonwealth and Protectorate (1649–58). A leader of the Parliamentarians before the outbreak of war, he later distinguished himself as a military commander (eventually second in command of the New Model Army) at such battles as Marston Moor (1644), Naseby (1645), Preston (1648), and Worcester (1651). He ordered King Charles I's execution (1649), and on formation of the Commonwealth (1649) became its leader. He invaded and subdued Ireland (1649) and Scotland (1650–51). Taking on dictatorial powers, he dissolved (1653) the Rump Parliament and others in following years. After the failure of his Barebones Parliament, he was made (1653) Lord Protector, thus establishing the English Protectorate, but was unable in his last years to form a stable parliamentary government. Two years after his death the Convention Parliament restored (1660) the English monarchy. He failed in his attempts to form an international Protestant league, concluded the first of the Dutch Wars, and added Jamaica and Dunkirk to the English possessions.

Cromwell, Thomas, earl of Essex 1485?–1540. English statesman. He served as secretary to Cardinal Wolsey and later rose to become chief counselor to King Henry VIII. In Henry's service he played a major role in the Protestant Reformation, and arranged the king's marriage to Anne of Cleves. Henry's dissatisfaction with the match contributed to Cromwell's downfall and beheading.

Cronos *See* **Cronus**

Cronus ⟨Cronos⟩ Greek mythological figure identified with the Roman Saturn. A Titan, he overthrew his father, Uranus, to become ruler of the world, but was in turn overthrown by his son Zeus.

Crookes, Sir William 1832–1919. English physicist and chemist. He discovered (1861) the element thallium and invented the Crookes radiometer.

Cross of Gold speech Speech (July 8, 1896) by W. Bryan, a delegate at the Democratic National Convention. His speech, supporting the free-silver movement, contained the words "you shall not crucify mankind upon a cross of gold" and secured for Bryan the presidential nomination.

Croton, Milo of *See* **Milo of Croton**

Crouchback, Edmund *See* **Lancaster, Edmund, earl of**

Crusade *(See also individual crusades.)* Principally, the medieval wars undertaken (11th–13th ccnts.) by European Christians to reconquer the Holy Land from the Muslims. Brought on by Seljuk conquests in the region and appeals for aid from Byzantine emperor Alexius I, the First Crusade was preached (1095) by Pope Urban II at the Council of Clermont. Thereafter the crusades became a popular vehicle for spiritual and material gain throughout Europe and resulted in nine (including the Children's Crusade) major expeditions against the Muslims. The term "crusade" was later used in reference to military expeditions, sanctioned by the pope, against heretics and others.

Crusade, Children's Ill-fated crusade (1212) by unarmed children to free the Holy Land. Supported by church authorities after the disgrace of the Fourth Crusade, it included contingents from France and Germany. In France, some 30,000 youths, led by the visionary peasant boy Stephen of Cloyes, left by ship (Aug., 1212) from Marseilles. Those who survived passage to Alexandria were sold into slavery. The German group of 20,000 youths, led by the German boy Nicholas of Cologne, marched across the Alps to Italy. Most, however, died or deserted along the way.

Crusade, First Holy war (1096–99) by European Christians to aid the Byzantines in the recapture of the Holy Land from the Muslims (Seljuks). The only successful crusade, it resulted in formation of the Crusader States *(see below).* Wandering preachers, notably Peter the Hermit and Walter the Penniless, spread the message of the crusade in Europe and raised hordes of peasant followers. These disorganized bands marched (1096) to Constantinople, robbing villages and massacring Jews along the way. They were quickly thrown into battle against the Muslims (and killed) in Asia Minor. Organized contingents of crusader knights arrived at Constantinople (late 1096), where Byzantine king Alexis I demanded an oath of loyalty from them. Fighting against Muslims began the next year and included victories for the crusaders at Nicaea (1097), Dorylaeum (1097), and Antioch (1098). Finally, some 20,000 crusaders marched to Jerusalem, took the city (July 15, 1099), and massacred Muslims and Jews. The crusade ended with the Battle of Ashkelon (Aug. 12, 1099), when crusaders defeated an army of Egyptian Muslims near Jerusalem. The crusaders set up the Crusader States, including the Latin Kingdom of Jerusalem, the Principality of Antioch, and the counties of Edessa (under Baldwin, later Baldwin I of Jerusalem) and Tripoli (under Raymond IV).

Crusade, Second Holy war (1147–49) fought by European Christians after the Muslims captured Edessa (1144) from the crusaders. Preached by Saint Bernard of Clairvaux, the crusade involved a combined force of 140,000, led by Holy Roman Emperor Conrad III and French king Louis VII. The Germans and French departed for Constantinople (Apr., 1147), pillaged Byzantine territories along the way, and were quickly sent to Asia

Minor by Byzantine emperor Manuel I. The Germans were nearly wiped out in a surprise attack at Dorylaeum (Oct., 1147) and the French were likewise reduced by the Muslims. The remnants of the two forces combined (1148) and unsuccessfully attacked Damascus (1148). They were badly mauled in the ensuing retreat. Conrad left for Europe (1148) and Louis' departure (1149) brought the crusade to an end.

Crusade, Third   Holy war (1189–92) fought by European Christians after the capture (1187) of Jerusalem by the Egyptian sultan Saladin. Preached by Pope Gregory VIII, the crusade was led by Holy Roman Emperor Frederick I, English king Richard I, and French king Philip II. Frederick died on the way, and Richard and Philip arrived (1191) to join the siege at Acre (under way since 1189). The city was taken (July, 1191), and after a quarrel with Richard, Philip returned to France. Richard negotiated a truce (1192) with Saladin, in which the Christians retained only a small part of the former kingdom of Jerusalem and access to Jerusalem. The crusade ended with Richard's departure (Oct., 1192).

Crusade, Fourth   Holy war (1202–04) fought by European Christians, originally directed against Muslim conquerors of the Holy Land. This crusade brought the crusades into discredit and ended with the formation of the Latin Empire of Constantinople. Preached by Pope Innocent III, the crusade was led by French noblemen. Assembling at Venice (1202), they agreed, in return for passage to the Holy Land, to help Venice capture the city of Zara on the Adriatic. For this they were briefly excommunicated by the pope. The crusaders, promised money and aid, again diverted from their mission and moved to reinstate deposed Byzantine emperor Isaac II (d. 1204). The crusaders arrived at Constantinople and put Isaac (1203) on the throne, only to see him overthrown (1204) by Alexis V. The crusaders thereupon sacked the city and set up the Latin Empire (1204), ending, for a time, the existence of the Byzantine Empire.

Crusade, Fifth   Holy war (1218–21) fought by European Christians against Muslim Egypt. Preached by Pope Innocent III, the crusade was led by papal legate Cardinal Pelagius, Hungarian king Andrew II, and John of Brienne. Crusaders attacked (May, 1218) Damietta on the Nile delta and, following a long siege, captured (Nov., 1219) the city. Their long-delayed advance up the Nile (July, 1221) foundered in the rising flood waters of the river, and the crusaders were forced ultimately to evacuate Egypt (Sept., 1221).

Crusade, Sixth   Holy war (1228–29) undertaken by Holy Roman Emperor Frederick II. After failure

of the Fifth Crusade, Frederick was obliged to take some action. He set out in 1227, was excommunicated by Pope Gregory IX for delaying, and continued to Acre where he negotiated (1229) a 10-year treaty with the Egyptians without engaging in any hostilities. Despite opposition from Christian factions in Jerusalem, he was crowned king of the city (1229) and returned to Europe. Unrest between these factions ensued and Turkish and Egyptian Muslims retook the city (1244).

Crusade, Seventh   Holy war (1248–54) undertaken by French king Louis IX. With the support of Pope Innocent IV, Louis embarked (1248) and attacked Egypt (May, 1249) with a force of 15,000 soldiers. Damietta (on the Nile delta) fell to the Christians again (1249) but further advances toward Cairo (1250) met with disaster. Louis was captured (and later ransomed) and many of his soldiers were massacred. Damietta was evacuated, and Louis spent the next four years in Jerusalem (to 1254) in attempts to gain release of his captured soldiers and to better fortify Christian positions in the Holy Land.

Crusade, Eighth   Last of the holy wars (1270), undertaken by French king Louis IX. With the rise of Mameluke sultan Baybars (reigned 1260–77), the Muslims began renewed conquests of Christian territories in the Holy Land. Louis began preparations in 1267 (Antioch fell in 1268) and departed July, 1270. He landed at Tunis, but his force was struck by disease. Louis died and his army withdrew. Subsequently (in what is sometimes called the Ninth Crusade) Prince Edward (later Edward I) landed at Acre (1271), concluded a treaty (1272) with the Muslims, and withdrew. Muslim conquests continued, however, and the last Christian outpost in the Holy Land was lost (1291) at the Battle of Acre. Thereafter crusaders withdrew to Cyprus.

Crusade, Ninth   Name sometimes given to the final phase of the Eighth Crusade (q.v.).

Crysler's Farm, Battle of See **Chrysler's Farm, Battle of**

Crystal Palace   Famous English exhibition hall. Constructed of iron and glass, it was built at Hyde Park for the Great Exhibition of 1851, and was reerected near London, where it stood until razed by fire (1936).

Cuba   Island republic located in the West Indies. Its capital is Havana. First discovered (1492) by C. Columbus and colonized by Spain, it became the center for Spanish colonization in the New World and was the last Spanish stronghold to gain independence (19th cent.). Cuba came under increasing US domination after the Spanish-American War, until F. Castro's successful revolution in

1959 turned the island into a strategic Communist stronghold in the West. It became a base for the promotion of revolutions in Latin America, in the 1960s. Key dates in the history of Cuba include:

1492 C. Columbus discovered Cuba.

EARLY 1500s Spanish began colonization of Cuba; used island as base for colonial expansion in the New World.

1763 British occupied Havana (1762) during Seven Years' War; Spanish control of Cuba restored by Treaty of Paris.

1868–78 Ten Years' War against Spanish rule; revolt ended in failure.

1886 Slavery abolished.

1895 New war against Spanish rule, led by José Martí, began.

1898 US government and citizens outraged by accounts of Spanish brutality in Cuba; war fever reached height with the sinking of US battleship *Maine* in Havana harbor (Feb.).

1898 Spanish-American War; Spain defeated, Cuba made independent under US military control.

1901 In US, the Platt Amendment placed Cuba under US protection and stated that US could intervene in Cuba militarily.

1902 Estrada Palma became first president of Cuba.

EARLY 1900s Massive US investment in Cuba began; led to uprising in Cuba and US military intervention (1906–09); US again intervened in 1912, 1917.

1925–33 Gerardo Machado served as president; instituted numerous reforms but became increasingly repressive and was overthrown (1933) by Fulgencio Batista.

1933–59 Batista regime; Batista controlled Cuban politics from 1933 to 1952; seized power (1952) and established a dictatorship.

1934 US scrapped unpopular Platt Amendment.

1953 F. Castro staged unsuccessful uprising the year after Batista seized power.

1956 Castro began guerrilla war, centered in Oriente province, against Batista.

1958 US cut off military aid to Cuba.

1959 Batista fled Cuba (Jan. 1); Castro marched triumphantly into Havana, beginning Cuban revolution.

1959–61 Castro's revolution grew increasingly Communist in orientation; thousands were arrested, many executed; property, notably US holdings, was confiscated; US broke diplomatic relations (Jan., 1961).

1961 Castro openly avowed communism.

1961 Bay of Pigs invasion (Apr.) by US-backed Cuban exiles was crushed.

1962 Cuba expelled from council of Organization of American States.

1962 Cuban Missile Crisis (Oct.).

1973 Agreement with US for return of hijackers marked a shift toward better relations with the US.

1975 Cuban troops in Angola to support Marxist regime.

1977 US eased some restrictions on trade and travel to Cuba.

1978 Cuban troops in Ethiopia to aid Marxist regime there.

1978 Castro agreed to allow emigration of political prisoners to US; 50,000 others with relatives outside Cuba also allowed to leave.

1980 Cuban boat people; Castro, angered by swarms of refugees anxious to leave Cuba, opened a port to boats from US; refugees, including Cuban criminals, transported to US by tens of thousands (Apr.–Sept.).

Cuban Missile Crisis US-USSR Cold War confrontation (Oct. 22, 1962–Jan. 7, 1963) over installation of ballistic missiles in Cuba. The crisis nearly precipitated nuclear war between the US and the USSR. After the US-backed Bay of Pigs Invasion (1961), Soviet chairman N. Khrushchev authorized installation of the missiles on Cuban soil. US president J. Kennedy proclaimed a naval quarantine of Cuba (Oct. 22, 1962) after learning of the sites and publicly warned that an attack from Cuban bases would mean US retaliation against Russia itself. Khrushchev gave in to US demands for withdrawal of the missiles (Oct. 28) and the US promised not to invade Cuba. The US lifted its quarantine (Nov. 20) and, in a formal note to the UN (Jan. 7, 1963), the US and Russia announced the end of the crisis.

Cuban Revolution Phase of modern Cuban history that began on Jan. 1, 1959, with the overthrow of the regime of F. Batista by F. Castro and his band of insurgents. Castro, heading his 26th of July Movement *(q.v.)*, had earlier attempted to invade Cuba with a force of revolutionaries (Dec., 1956), but his forces had been defeated and scattered. A small band hid out in the Sierra Maestra Mountains, conducting guerrilla actions and acquiring new recruits, until Castro was finally able to take over. His immediate efforts to install a socialist government brought quick US reactions in the form of an economic and sugar boycott and, later, the disastrous Bay of Pigs Invasion *(q.v.)*. Soviet support of the Cuban Revolution brought about (Oct., 1962) the Cuban Missile Crisis *(q.v.)*, when the USSR tried to install offensive missiles there. Cuba became a virtual Soviet satellite, and over the years has pursued a policy of "exporting" revolution by its involvement in political upheavals in Latin America and even Africa (Angola). Castro's style of socialism remained highly personal despite his dependence on the Soviet bloc.

cubism Artistic movement. A reaction against realism and impressionism, cubism reduced all objects to their basic geometrical shapes. Famed cubists include P. Picasso and G. Braque.

Cuchulain Legendary Irish warrior, noted for his great strength. According to one legend, he single-handedly defended Ulster against an attack by the combined armies of Ireland.

Culpeper, John *See* **Culpeper's Rebellion**

Culpeper's Rebellion American Colonial uprising (1677–79). Led by John Culpeper (*fl.* 1677), Carolina colonists rebelled against restrictive British trade laws and established their own government (1677–79).

Cult of Reason Short-lived extremist anti-Catholic movement during the French Revolution led by P. Chaumette, J. Hébert, and others. Chaumette staged the first worship ceremony for the cult in Notre Dame Cathedral and he later ordered Paris churches closed. The cult was abolished (1794) and its leaders executed by Robspierre.

Cultural Revolution (Great Proletarian Cultural Revolution) Chinese political movement (1966–69) headed by Mao Tse-tung and intended to help purge the Chinese Communist party of bourgeois or capitalist elements. Implemented by brigades of young people known as Red Guards, the movement spread to touch every facet of life in China and seriously damaged China's cultural, industrial, and political development.

Cumae Ancient city near Naples, Italy, believed to be the oldest Greek colony in Italy. Founded (*c*750 BC) by Greek settlers, it became a Roman town (338 BC) and was destroyed AD 1205. Extensive ruins exist on its site.

Cumberland Road *See* **National Road**

Cummings, Edward Estlin 1894–1962. American writer and painter noted for his brilliantly unorthodox poetry. His novel *The Enormous Room*, a classic, is based on his experiences in France during WW I.

Cunard, Sir Samuel 1787–1865. Canadian ship-owner and merchant. He established (1839) the first regular transatlantic steamship line, which became the Cunard Line.

Cunaxa, Battle of Battle (401 BC) at Cunaxa, north of Babylon, in which Cyrus the Younger attempted to overthrow his brother, Persian king Artaxerxes II. Cyrus was killed, and the 13,000 Greek mercenaries in his army began their Retreat

of the Ten Thousand, celebrated by Xenophon in his *Anabasis*.

cuneiform writing Ancient writing system, developed (*c*4th millennium BC), probably by the Sumerians. Based on wedge-shaped symbols, it was widely used in Asia Minor and included numerous distinct systems, including Babylonian, Elamite, Hittite, and Persian.

Cupid Ancient Roman god of love, son of Mercury and Venus. He is depicted as a winged boy carrying a bow and quiver of arrows.

curia Ancient Roman political division. By tradition, Romulus divided Rome into three tribes of 10 curiae each. Each curia voted as a unit in the assembly, the Comitia Curiata. The term came to denote the meeting place of such a body, as the Roman Senate, etc.

Curie, Pierre 1859–1906 and **Curie, Marie Sklodowska** 1867–1934. French scientists and co-discoverers of radium and polonium. The Curies were married (1895), and, after A. Becquerel discovered radioactivity, Marie began her own investigations. She was joined by Pierre in 1898, and in that year they jointly isolated radium and polonium. With Becquerel they were awarded the 1903 Nobel Prize in Physics. Following Pierre's death, Marie continued work on radium and received the Nobel Prize in Chemistry (1911).

Curtis, Charles 1860–1936. American politician, vice-president of the US (1929–33) under Pres. H. Hoover. A Republican, Curtis served in the House of Representatives (1893–1907) and Senate (1907–13, 1915–29).

Curtis, Cyrus Hermann Kotzschmar 1850–1933. American publisher. He established (1890) the Curtis Publishing Company, which published the *Ladies' Home Journal* and the *Saturday Evening Post*.

Curzon, George Nathaniel, 1st Marquess Curzon of Kendleston 1859–1925. He served as viceroy of India (1898–1905) and in the cabinets of H. Asquith and D. Lloyd George during WW I. He instituted the Partition of Bengal (*q.v.*). As foreign secretary (1919–24) he presided over the Conference of Lausanne.

Curzon Line Armistice line proposed by British foreign secretary G. Curzon during the Russo-Polish War (1920). It was incorporated almost entirely as the Russian-Polish border, by treaty (Aug. 16, 1945).

Cush Ancient African kingdom. Believed to have been located in what is now the Sudan, it extended into Egypt and possibly southern Arabia and Ethiopia.

Custer, George Armstrong 1839–76. American soldier. He distinguished himself as a Union officer in the Civil War but later led more than 200 men to their deaths in the Battle of Little Bighorn.

Custer's last stand *See* **Little Bighorn, Battle of**

Custoza, battles of **1.** Battle (July 24, 1848) at Custoza, Italy, in which Austria defeated Italian rebels and Sardinian forces led by Sardinian king Charles Albert. **2.** Battle (June 24, 1866) at Custoza, in which Austria decisively defeated Italian forces seeking to liberate Venice from Austria. Nonetheless, Austria ceded Venice to France, and France ceded it (July 3) to Italy.

Cutter, Charles Ammi 1837–1903. American librarian who developed an early system for the classification of books.

Cuvier, Georges Léopold Chrétien Frédéric Dagobert, Baron 1769–1832. French naturalist. He contributed greatly to the development of comparative anatomy and paleontology.

Cuza, Alexander John 1820–73. First prince of Romania (1859–66). Elected (1859) prince in both Moldavia and Walachia, he was proclaimed prince of Romania on unification of the two states (1861), confiscated and redistributed monastic lands, freed the serfs (1864), and reformed Romanian legal and educational systems.

Cybele Ancient nature goddess, identified with the Greek Rhea. Of Asiatic origin, she was worshiped by both Greeks and Romans as the Great Mother of the gods.

Cyclades Greek islands in the Aegean Sea, so named because they form a circle around the island Delos. The islands were part of the Delian League (5th–4th cent. BC).

Cyclops Mythical Greek one-eyed giant. According to one legend, the Cyclopes, Titans, and the sons of Uranus and Gaea helped Vulcan to forge the thunderbolts by which Zeus overthrew Cronus.

Cymbeline ⟨Cunobelinus⟩ *fl.* AD *c*40. Legendary British king. W. Shakespeare's play *Cymbeline* is based only vaguely on his life.

Cynewulf ⟨Cynwulf⟩ *fl. c*750. English poet. Little is known of his life. His surviving works, chiefly religious in nature, are *Juliana, The Ascension, Elene,* and *The Fates of the Apostles.*

Cynics Philosophical school (4th cent. BC–6th cent. AD) founded in ancient Greece by Antisthenes. Originally the Cynics held that virtue was the only good and, preaching a life of self-sufficiency and ascetic poverty, came to ridicule the conventional way of life. Other famous Cynics included Diogenes of Sinope and Crates.

Cynwulf *See* **Cynewulf**

Cyprian, Saint ⟨Cyprianus, Thascius Caecilius⟩ *d.* AD *c*258. Bishop of Carthage (AD *c*248). He op-

posed Pope Stephen I on the issue of papal authority over other bishops, and disputed the validity of baptisms performed by schismatics.

Cyprianus, Thascius Caecilius *See* **Cyprian, Saint**

Cyprus Island republic (pop. 630,000) in the Mediterranean, site of Mt. Olympus. Populated since Neolithic times (*c*4000–3000 BC), its development was strongly influenced after 1500 BC by Greece. Conquered many times, including by the Ottoman Turks (1571), Cyprus was placed under British administration (1878) and was annexed by Britain (1914). It gained independence in 1960. Continuous strife between Greek Cypriots (80 percent of pop.) and Turkish Cypriots (18 percent) led to serious clashes between Greece and Turkey. A military coup (July 15, 1974) resulted in the ouster of President Makarios by rebels seeking union with Greece. Turkey invaded Cyprus (July 20) to protect the Turkish Cypriots and took half of the island. Makarios became president again (Dec. 7) and Turkish Cypriots withdrew to a sector in the north. The situation remains unresolved.

Cyrano de Bergerac, Savinien 1619–55. French satirist and fantasist, known for fighting many duels occasioned by comments about his large nose. He was the subject of the play *Cyrano de Bergerac* by E. Rostand.

Cyrenaics Ancient Greek philosophical school (4th cent. BC). They held that pleasure was the highest good, and contributed to development of the philosophy of Epicureanism.

Cyrene, Simon of *See* **Simon of Cyrene**

Cyril and Methodius, saints *d.* 869/885. Greek brothers who were apostles to the Slavs. They translated the liturgy into Slavonic and are believed to have invented the Cyrillic alphabet, upon which modern Russian and Slavic languages are based.

Cyril of Alexandria, Saint *d.* AD 444. Patriarch of Alexandria (AD 412–444) and Doctor of the Church. He expelled the Jews from Alexandria. An opponent of Nestorianism, he presided over the Council of Ephesus (AD 431).

Cyril of Jerusalem, Saint AD 315?–386? Christian theologian and bishop of Jerusalem (AD *c*350–386?). He was expelled three times from his see for his opposition to Arianism.

Cyrus the Great *d.* 529 BC. Persian king (*c*550–529 BC), founder of the Persian Empire. He overthrew the Median king Astyages (*c*550 BC), conquered Lydia (*c*546 BC) and Babylonia (538 BC), and extended his empire into Asia. He freed the Jews in Babylonia, ending the Babylonian Captivity.

Cyrus the Younger *d.* 401 BC. Persian prince, son of Darius II. After his brother Artaxerxes II became king (404 BC), Cyrus conspired against him. Raising an army against Artaxerxes, he was defeated and killed in the Battle of Cunaxa.

Czechoslovakia Federal republic located in central Europe. Its capital is Prague. Czechoslovakia was formed (1918) during the dismemberment of the Austro-Hungarian Empire at the end of WW I. Czechoslovakia included the historic regions of Bohemia, Moravia, and Slovakia as well as Ruthenia, which became part of the Soviet Union in 1945. Czechoslovakia was dismembered on the eve of WW II (1938–39) by Germany, Poland, and Hungary and was reestablished (1945) at the end of the war. Key dates in the history of Czechoslovakia include:

1916 Czechoslovak National Council formed (Jan.) for creation of independent nation.

1918 Czech National Council proclaimed itself the government in the Czech lands (Oct. 28) and formed union with Slovakia (Nov. 14); Tomáš Masaryk became first president of Czechoslovakia.

1919 Republic of Czechoslovakia recognized by Allied powers and Austria, by Treaty of St. Germain (Sept.).

1920 Treaty of Trianon (June); Hungary recognized Czechoslovakia, and Ruthenia was added to its territory.

1920–21 Little Entente, defensive pact formed by Czechoslovakia, Romania, and Yugoslavia.

1930s In Germany, rise of A. Hitler as dictator coincided with rise of German nationalist agitation in northwestern Czechoslovakia (Sudetenland) for union with Germany.

1935 Masaryk resigned as president; succeeded by Eduard Beneš.

1938 Hitler's demands in Czechoslovakia led to crisis in Europe; war temporarily averted by Munich Pact (Sept. 29); major European powers agreed to cession of Sudetenland to Germany.

1938 Beneš resigned as president (Oct. 5); succeeded by Emil Hácha; Czechoslovakia reorganized as federated republic of Czecho-Slovakia (Nov.).

1938 Poland occupied part of Czechoslovakia (Oct.).

1939 Germany and Hungary completed dismemberment of Czechoslovakia (Mar.); Germany declared protectorate over Bohemia and Moravia

and occupied Slovakia; Hungary annexed Ruthenia, renamed Carpatho-Ukraine.

1940 Beneš established Czech government-in-exile in London during WW II.

1945 Czechoslovakia reconstituted at end of WW II; Ruthenia (Carpatho-Ukraine) incorporated into Soviet Union (July); Beneš again became president of Czechoslovakia (Oct.).

1946 Communist Party became leading political party in Czechoslovakian national elections.

1948 Communists secured virtual control of Czech government (Feb.).

1948 Jan Masaryk, non-Communist foreign minister, died (Mar. 10) in fall from window; death called suicide by government.

1949 New constitution establishing Czechoslovakia as a People's Democratic Republic, modeled on Soviet lines (May 9); Beneš resigned as president (June 7); constitution signed into law (June 8) by his successor, Communist Party leader Klement Gottwald.

1950–52 Series of government and party purges instituted to consolidate Communist Party control in Czechoslovakia.

1957–68 Antonin Novotný served as president.

1968 Alexander Dubček became Communist Party leader (Jan.), replacing A. Novotný; Ludvík Svoboda made president (Mar.); Prague Spring, program of liberalization, began under Dubček's direction.

1968 Warsaw Pact forces led by Soviet army invaded Czechoslovakia (Aug. 20); most of the Prague Spring reforms instituted were reversed.

1969 Dubček ousted as party leader (Apr.).

1970 Dubček expelled from Communist Party (June).

1975 Gustav Husak in office as president.

1977 Over 200 Czech intellectuals signed a petition demanding compliance with human rights provisions of the Helsinki agreement; hundreds of others added their signatures as police began arresting those who signed (Jan. 6); sporadic arrests continued into the early 1980s.

Czechoslovak National Council Nationalist organization of Czechs and Slovaks. Formed (Jan., 1916) by T. Masaryk, E. Beneš, and others, it became the first provisional Czech government when the republic was established (Nov. 14, 1918).

Czolgosz, Leon *See* **McKinley, William**

D

Dabrowski, Jan Henryk 1755–1818. Polish general. He participated in the rebellion against Russia (1794) and led the Polish legion under Napoleon.

Dacca Capital of Bangladesh (pop. 1,730,300). It dates back to c1000 and was prominent as the Mogul capital of Bengal (17th cent.). It became the capital of Bangladesh, formerly East Pakistan, in 1971.

Dachau West German town, infamous for the Nazi concentration camp opened there in 1933. It operated until the Allied occupation (1945).

Dacia Ancient European region corresponding roughly to modern Romania. The Dacian, or Getae, people were conquered by the Romans under Trajan, and Dacia was made a Roman province (AD 107). Aurelian surrendered it to the Goths (c270).

Dada ⟨Dadaism⟩ Literary and artistic movement. Dada flourished in Europe at the end of WW I. It stressed the absurdity and unpredictability of life through flamboyant and nihilistic art and literature. It was the forerunner of surrealism.

Dadaism *See* **Dada**

Daedalus Greek mythical craftsman who built the great Cretan labyrinth for King Minos. Imprisoned on Crete, he made wax wings for himself and his son Icarus who, while escaping, flew too close to the sun, which melted his wings.

Dagobert I c612–c639. Frankish king (629–639), son of King Clotaire II. He united Austrasia, Aquitaine, and Neustria, and was the last Merovingian king to rule a united Frankish kingdom.

Dagon Near Eastern fertility god. He is mentioned in the Old Testament as one of the major gods of the Philistines.

Daguerre, Louis Jacques Mandé 1789–1851. French scene painter and photography pioneer. He invented the daguerreotype (1839), a process using copper for the photographic plate.

Dahomey, Republic of *See* **Benin**

Daigo II 1287–1339. Japanese emperor (1318–39). Daigo was exiled (1319) for attempting to re-store power to the monarchy by overthrowing the shoguns, or military rulers. Returned to the throne after a revolt, he was again ousted (1336). He then set up a rival government at Nara that survived until the end of the 14th cent.

Dáil Éireann House of Representatives of the Republic of Ireland. Though elected as members of the British Parliament (Dec., 1918), the representatives met instead at Mansion House, Dublin, proclaimed the Irish republic, and continued as an illegal body until the establishment of the Irish Free State (1921).

Daimler, Gottlieb 1834–1900. German engineer and pioneer auto-maker. He developed an internal-combustion engine (1885) and founded the Daimler Motor Company (1890).

Daimyo Japanese feudal lord. From the 8th cent., these lords owned great estates and wielded great political power as independent territorial barons. Brought under the power of the shogunate (1603), they were eventually forced to turn their lands over to the emperor (1869).

Dakar Capital and port city of Senegal (pop. 798,800). Established around a French fort (1857), Dakar became the capital of French West Africa (1902) and the capital of newly independent Senegal in 1958.

Dakota Indians *See* **Sioux Indians**

Daladier, Édouard 1884–1970. French politician, member of the Radical Socialist party. As premier (1938–40), he signed the Munich Pact (1938) to appease Nazi Germany. He was arrested and interned in Germany during WW II.

Dalai Lama Tibetan Buddhist spiritual leader. The line of Dalai Lamas was begun in the 14th cent., and each one is considered to be the reincarnation of his predecessor. The 14th in the line was installed in 1940, and fled Tibet during the abortive revolt against the Communist Chinese occupation (1959). (*See also* Tibetan Buddhism.)

Dalhousie, James Andrew Broun Ramsay, 1st marquess of 1812–60. British statesman and governor general of India (1847–56). He annexed the

Punjab (1849) and other states, began the Indian telegraph and railway systems, and instituted reforms in Hindu society.

Dali, Salvador 1904–. Spanish surrealist artist. He painted everyday objects in distorted, nightmare situations (called "paranoiac") based on his study of psychology and dreams. He wrote *The Secret Life of Salvador Dali.*

Dallas Texas city (pop. 904,000). Established in 1841, it is an industrial and commercial center. President J. F. Kennedy was assassinated there on Nov. 22, 1963.

Dallas-Clarendon Convention *See* **Dallas, George Mifflin**

Dallas, George Mifflin 1792–1864. US statesman and J. Polk's vice-president (1845–49). As minister to Great Britain (1856–61), he negotiated the Dallas-Clarendon Convention (1856), which helped settle Anglo-American rivalries over Central America, and brought an end to England's claim of a right of search.

Dalmatia Province of Yugoslavia on the Adriatic, historically part of Croatia. Once part of the Roman Empire, it was taken by Slavic tribes (7th cent.) and ruled variously by Venetians, Turks, and Austrians. Italy disputed its award to Yugoslavia after WW II but finally agreed to its cession in the Italian peace treaty (1947).

Dalton, John 1766–1844. Pioneer English scientist known for his work on atomic theory. He also studied color blindness (Daltonism) and developed the law of partial pressures, called Dalton's Law, stating that the total pressure of a mixture of gases equals the sum of the pressures of the different gases composing the mixture.

Damascus Capital (pop. 835,000) of Syria, and considered the oldest continuously inhabited city in the world. A city before the time of Abraham (c1500 BC), it was held by the Egyptians, Israelis, Hittites, Persians, Greeks, Romans and, in AD 635, was captured by the Arabs. It was ruled by the Ottoman Turks for some 400 years (from 1516). It was occupied by the British and Arabs (1918) and then was capital of the French mandate. In 1941, it became capital of independent Syria.

Damascus, Saint John of *See* **John of Damascus, Saint**

Damien, Father 1840–89. Belgian Catholic missionary. Ordained in Honolulu (1864), he worked with the lepers of Molokai, Hawaii, from 1873 until his death from the disease.

Damocles Courtier of the tyrant Dionysius the Elder of Syracuse (4th cent. BC). After praising the tyrant, he was invited by Dionysius to a banquet. Damocles was seated beneath a sword hanging by a single thread, signifying the precariousness of power.

Damon and Pythias Two friends, of ancient Syracuse, whose loyalty to each other has come to symbolize true friendship. Pythias, condemned to die by the tyrant Dionysius I of Syracuse, was allowed time to arrange his affairs only because his friend Damon pledged his own life against Pythias's return. Rather than sacrifice his friend's life, Pythias returned on schedule. Dionysius was so moved by this loyalty that he pardoned Pythias.

Dampier, William 1652–1715. English buccaneer and explorer. He was a pirate (1678–91) in Spanish-American waters, chiefly on the west coast of South America. He published his *New Voyage Round the World* in 1697, and, two years later, discovered the Dampier Archipelago and straits.

Damrosch, Walter 1862–1950. German-American conductor and composer. He formed the Damrosch Opera Company, specializing in German works, and composed the opera *Cyrano de Bergerac* (1913). He was the conductor of the New York Symphony (1903–27).

Dan In the Bible, son of Jacob and Bihah. He was the founder of one of the twelve tribes of Israel, whose best-known member was Samson.

Dana, Charles Anderson 1819–97. Crusading American journalist. After five years at Brook Farm and 15 years as New York *Tribune* editor, he became part-owner and editor of the New York *Sun*, where he became involved in exposing government corruption.

Dana, James Dwight 1813–95. American geologist and mineralogist. He was a scientist on C. Wilkes's Antarctic and South Seas expedition, wrote *A System of Mineralogy*, and co-edited the *American Journal of Science.*

Dana, Richard Henry 1815–82. American lawyer and author of the novel *Two Years Before the Mast.* He also wrote *The Seaman's Friend*, a manual on the legal rights of seamen.

Danaë In Greek mythology, the daughter of Acrisius, who imprisoned her because of the prophecy that her offspring would kill him. But Zeus visited her as a shower of gold. She bore him Perseus, through whom the prophecy was eventually fulfilled.

Danaüs In Greek mythology, son of Belus. He founded Argos and commanded his 50 daughters, the Danaïdes, to kill their husbands (his brother's sons) on the night following their joint wedding ceremony. Forty-nine complied and were condemned to Hades, where they were required to fill a sieve with water forever.

Danbury Hatters' Case US Supreme Court decision (1908). The United Hatters of North America boycotted a nonunion firm. Under the Sherman Antitrust Act, the union was declared in restraint of trade, the first time the act was applied to a labor combination.

Dandolo, Enrico c1108–1205. Doge of Venice (1192–1205), who led the crusaders in the capture of Constantinople (1203–04) on the Fourth Crusade. Earlier he was ambassador to the Byzantine court (1173) and was blinded there by order of the emperor Manuel.

Danegeld Medieval English land tax used to buy off Danish raiders, especially under King Ethelred (978–1016). It was revived under the Normans (12th cent.) who created the Domesday Book (q.v.), partly to facilitate the levy of this tax.

Danelaw Region of Anglo-Saxon England settled by the Danes (9th cent.). It extended north from the Thames, along the east coast, and Danish laws obtained there.

Daniel An Old Testament prophet, taken captive to Babylon (605 BC). He interpreted dreams for Nebuchadnezzar, became an official, and had to be delivered from the lion's den where he had been thrown by Darius for disobeying an edict.

Daniels, Josephus 1862–1948. American statesman and journalist. He was editor of the Raleigh *News and Observer*, secretary of the navy under W. Wilson, and ambassador to Mexico under F. Roosevelt.

Danilo I 1677–1735. Montenegrin leader, the last elected prince-bishop of Montenegro. The post was made hereditary to the prince-bishops' nephews thereafter. He formed a military alliance with Russia in order to help preserve Montenegrin independence against the Turks.

Danilo II 1826–60. Montenegrin prince-bishop. Danilo secularized his post, retaining his princely title but transferring his religious duties to an archbishop. He continued to fight the Turks, but his internal reforms provoked dissent and he was assassinated.

D'Annunzio, Gabriele 1863–1938. Italian poet, dramatist, novelist, and soldier. His poetry was richly sensual; in other writings he espoused Fascism. He was an Italian hero in WW I and afterward occupied Fiume for Italy (1919–21) in defiance of the Treaty of Versailles.

Dante Alighieri 1265–1321. Italian poet, and author of *The Divine Comedy*, one of the greatest masterpieces of Western literature. Dante, through his works, helped to establish the Italian vernacular as the literary language of Italy. Raised in Florence, he was exiled (1302) after a factional struggle among the Guelphs, of which he was a member. He wandered through various Italian cities until sometime after 1313, when he settled in Ravenna. *The Divine Comedy*, partly inspired by a continuing romantic devotion to a woman thought to be Beatrice Portinari, consists of three parts: Hell, Purgatory, and Paradise. In this epic poem, he journeys to each of the three, guided through the first two by Vergil (q.v.) and through heaven by Beatrice.

Danton, Georges Jacques 1759–94. A leading figure in the French Revolution, Danton was noted as a powerful orator and has been portrayed variously as a great patriot and an unscrupulous politician. He was a leader of the Cordeliers (founded 1790), and vigorously supported wars of national defense against foreign powers while serving in the Legislative Assembly (1791–92.) He claimed to have played a role (nature uncertain) in the storming of the Tuileries Palace (Aug. 1792) and subsequent overthrow of the monarchy, then arose as a leading figure in the new government. He was elected to the new National Convention (1792), voted for the execution of Louis XVI, and became leader of the Jacobin Club (Mar. 1793). He was a leader of the Committee of Public Safety (Apr.–July, 1793) and was in power when the Girondists (June) were expelled from the Convention. Excluded from the new Committee of Public Safety (soon dominated by Robespierre), Danton became a leader of forces (later called Indulgents) seeking to moderate radicalism of the revolution and excesses of the Reign of Terror. He was finally arrested by Robespierre and guillotined (Apr. 5, 1794).

Danzig (Gdańsk) Polish city (pop. 364,300) and major Baltic seaport. First mentioned in the 10th cent., it joined the Hanseatic League (13th cent.). It alternated between being a free city and a part of Prussia. A. Hitler's demand that it be returned to Germany in 1939 was the immediate cause of his invasion of Poland, precipitating WW II. The city again rose to prominence as a center of labor unrest (1980–81), fostered by Solidarity (q.v.).

Daphne In Greek mythology, a nymph, daughter of a river god. She rejected all suitors, including Apollo, and was changed into a laurel tree to escape him.

Daphnis Greek mythological shepherd, son of Hermes. Blinded for unfaithfulness to a nymph, he comforted himself with songs on the flute. He was revered for inventing bucolic poetry.

Dardanelles (Hellespont) Narrow strait between the Aegean and Marmara seas that controls navigation between the Mediterranean and Black seas.

Important in both ancient and modern times, it was called the Hellespont by the Greeks and was celebrated in the legend of Hero and Leander (q.v.). Ancient Troy was located on its western shore and it was the site of famous crossings during invasions by Xerxes I (480 BC) and Alexander the Great (334 BC). In the 19th cent., it was the object of the Straits Question (q.v.) and during WW I the scene of the Gallipoli Campaign (q.v.).

Dardanelles Campaign See **Gallipoli Campaign**

Dardanus In Greek mythology, the progenitor of the Trojan kings. A son of Zeus and the Pleiad Electra, he was the mythical ancestor of the Trojans.

Dare, Virginia b. 1587. First child of English parents born in America. She was born in Sir Walter Raleigh's Roanoke Island colony; the island was found deserted in 1591.

Dares Phrygius Trojan priest of Hephaestus, named in the *Iliad*. He was supposed to be the author of an account of the fall of Troy popular in medieval times.

Dar es Salaam Indian Ocean seaport (pop. 870,020) and capital of Tanzania since 1964. Founded in 1862 by the Sultan of Zanzibar, it was made the capital of German East Africa in 1891.

Darien Scheme Abortive Scottish attempt at colonization on the Isthmus of Panama (1698–1700). Directed by W. Paterson, it failed with enormous losses to investors.

Dario, Ruben ⟨Sarmiento, Felix Ruben Garcia⟩ 1867–1916. Nicaraguan-born poet and journalist. A leader of *Modernismo*, he strongly influenced modern Spanish-language writers with works such as *Azul* (1888).

Darius I ⟨~ the Great⟩ c549–486 BC. Persian king (521–486 BC) and successor to Cambyses II, after defeating a false claimant, Magian Gomates. Darius, a member of Achaemenid (q.v.) dynasty, proved a great ruler. He extended the Persian Empire into northern India and Europe, and in battle against the Scythians he invaded Macedonia and Thrace (515). He was, however, unsuccessful in his efforts against the Greek city-states during the Persian Wars (q.v.). Noted as a great builder and administrator, he created an effective administrative organization based on a system of satrapies.

Darius II ⟨Darius Nothus⟩ d. 404 BC. Persian king (423–404 BC), illegitimate son of Artaxerxes. He spent much time suppressing revolts, formed an alliance with Sparta against Athens (c412 BC), and lost Egypt (410 BC).

Darius III ⟨Codomannus, Darius⟩ d. 330 BC. Last king of Persia's Achaemenid (q.v.) dynasty (336–330 BC). He was defeated by Alexander the Great at Granicus (334), Issus (333), and Gaugamela (331). He fled, only to be murdered by one of his satraps, Bessus.

Darius Codomannus See **Darius III**

Darius Nothus See **Darius II**

Dark Ages A period of European history between the decline of Roman civilization and the rise of medieval Christian civilization. It is often dated from AD 476–800, or, more generally, between AD c500 and c1000. (See also Middle Ages.)

Darlan, Jean François 1881–1942. French admiral, member of H. Pétain's cabinet in the Vichy government (q.v.). He negotiated an armistice with the Allies in North Africa independently of Vichy (1942) and then was assassinated by an antifascist.

Darnley, Henry Stuart, Lord 1545–67. Scottish lord. Darnley was the second husband of Mary, Queen of Scots, and father of James I of England. After his implication in the murder of Mary's secretary David Rizzio (1533?–66), he was himself assassinated.

Darrow, Clarence Seward 1857–1938. American lawyer. He was defense counsel in controversial trials such as that for US Socialist E. Debs in the 1894 Pullman strike (q.v.); for Chicago thrill killers Leopold and Loeb (1924); and in the 1925 Scopes Trial (q.v.) on the teaching of evolution, where he was opposed by W. J. Bryan.

Dartmouth College case US Supreme Court decision (1819). The court ruled that New Hampshire could not forcibly alter the charter or character of Dartmouth College. This ruling applied the sanctity-of-contracts principle to a state-issued charter and powerfully reinforced the Constitution's contract clause as a protection of private property against state encroachment.

Darwin, Charles Robert 1809–82. English naturalist, who established Darwinism (q.v.) as the reigning scientific theory of biological evolution. Though he did not originate the concept of evolution, his many observations and explanations of the mechanisms of natural selection provided the first widely accepted basis for the theory. A grandson of E. Darwin, he first became convinced of gradual evolution while serving (1831–36) as a naturalist aboard HMS *Beagle*. He subsequently began a long period of research and observation. Prodded by the work of A. Wallace, who reached (1858) the same conclusions independently, Darwin published (1859) his famous *On the Origin of Species by Means of Natural Selection*. He supplemented this with many other works, notably *The Descent of Man*.

Darwin, Erasmus 1731–1802. English physician and grandfather both of C. Darwin and F. Galton.

In his writings such as *Zoonomia* (1794–96), he anticipated later evolutionary principles.

Darwinism Theory of biological evolution developed by C. Darwin (mid-19th cent.) and now accepted, with some modifications, as the reigning scientific theory of evolution. Though the idea of evolution was not new, Darwin's theory explained the mechanisms which established it in the scientific community. The theory posed radical implications for religious thinkers and philosophers. Darwinism supplanted the then widely accepted theory of a special creation of each species. It postulated three mechanisms: heredity, by which features of a species are passed to succeeding generations; variety (now understood as mutation), the process by which new features are developed; and natural selection (later dubbed "survival of the fittest"), through which new characteristics become dominant by being tested in the environment.

Dathan An Old Testament chieftain. Dathan was a Reubenite who joined in a conspiracy with Korah *(q.v.)*.

Daudet, Alphonse 1840–97. French writer. He was noted for his gentle, humorous portrayal of provincial life in the south of France, as in *Lettres de Mon Moulin* (1869).

Daudet, Léon 1867–1942. French writer and journalist, son of A. Daudet. He cofounded the royalist paper *L'Action Française* (1907) and was known for his polemics against his times, which he considered decadent.

Daugherty, Harry Micajah 1860–1941. American politician and US attorney general (1921–24) under W. G. Harding. He was tried but not convicted of a conspiracy to defraud the US government (1927) because of his alleged involvement in the Teapot Dome *(q.v.)* and other scandals.

Daughters of the American Revolution Patriotic society organized in 1890 in Washington, D.C. Its members are women who are descendants of those who aided the revolution.

Daumier, Honoré 1801–79. French caricaturist, painter, and lithographer. His work satirized the bourgeoisie, and he was briefly imprisoned for depicting King Louis Philippe as Gargantua, but he is considered a major realistic artist.

Daun, Leopold, Graf von 1705–66. Austrian soldier. Field marshal during the Seven Years' War (1756–63), he twice defeated Frederick the Great's Prussian army (1757 and 1758) but was defeated at Torgau (1760). He advocated a classic war of maneuver.

dauphin Title of the heir to the French throne. It was first given to the future Charles V by his grandfather Philip VI (1350) when the latter ac-

quired the southeastern province of Dauphiné from which the title was taken.

Dauphiné Former French frontier province in the southeast. Its capital was Grenoble. Formerly ruled by the counts of Vienne, it was purchased by the French crown in the mid-14th cent.

David d. *c*973 BC. Second king of Israel (*c*1013–*c*973 BC), one of the great figures in the Old Testament, and an ancestor of Jesus. A heroic figure for both Christians and Jews, David is the subject of such famous biblical narratives as the David and Goliath story. Many of the psalms are also attributed to him. David succeeded Saul as king of the Hebrews, after first serving and then warring against him. As king, David forged the confederation of Hebrew tribes into a unified kingdom and fixed his capital at Jerusalem.

David I 1084–1153. King of Scotland (1124–53), son of Malcolm III and Saint Margaret. He defended his niece Matilda's claims to the English throne against Stephen, but was defeated in 1138 at the Battle of the Standards. He introduced the Anglo-Norman feudal system into Scotland and founded many monasteries.

David II ⟨David Bruce⟩ 1324–71. King of Scotland (1329–71). Son of Robert the Bruce. When Scotland was successfully invaded by E. de Baliol, he was exiled to France (1334–41). He tried to invade England (1346) after regaining the throne but was routed at the Battle of Neville's Cross *(q.v.)*, captured, and held prisoner until 1357. Most of the rest of his reign was spent trying to pay off his ransom.

David, Jacques Louis 1748–1825. French painter, founder of the French classical school. He was court painter to Louis XVI but then supported the French Revolution. Later he was Napoleon's court painter. One of his best-known works is *The Assassination of Marat* (1793). He dominated French painting for a generation.

David, Saint d. 588? Patron saint of Wales. He founded many churches and monasteries and moved the seat of ecclesiastical government to Mynyw (Menevia), today Saint David's. The national Welsh festival is still celebrated on his feast day of Mar. 1.

David Bruce *See* **David II**

Dávila, Pedrarias *See* **Arias de Ávila, Pedro**

Dávila, Pedro Arias *See* **Arias de Ávila, Pedro**

Davis, Bette 1908–. American actress, known for playing intense, sensitive women in such films as *Of Human Bondage* and *The Little Foxes.*

Davis, David 1815–86. American jurist and statesman. Davis was frequently presiding judge when A. Lincoln practiced law, and was named by him to the US Supreme Court (1862). He later served as US senator from Illinois.

Davis, Jefferson 1808–89. American soldier, statesman, and president of the Confederacy (1861–65) during the US Civil War. A Mississippi senator (1847–51) and soldier in the Mexican War, he became US secretary of war (1853–57). Again in the Senate (1857–61), he led the Southern bloc until Mississippi seceded. As Confederate president (provisional, 1861, and elected 1862), he attempted to form a strong central government. This policy and his attempts to manage the army personally led to many disputes within the Confederate government. Davis was captured (1865) by Union soldiers after Lee's surrender and was imprisoned for two years.

Davis, John ⟨Davys, John⟩ c1550–1605. English navigator who made three voyages (1585–87) in search of the Northwest Passage (q.v.) during which he discovered Davis Strait. He discovered the Falkland Islands in 1592. He was killed by Japanese pirates while sailing near Singapore.

Davis, John William 1873–1955. American lawyer and politician. He was a West Virginia congressman (1911–13), US solicitor general (1913–18), and ambassador to England (1918–21). In 1924, he was the Democratic compromise candidate for president, chosen on the 103d ballot after a deadlocked convention; but he was easily defeated by C. Coolidge in the election.

Davis, William Morris 1850–1934. American geographer and geologist. He formulated the theory of land change through cycles of erosion, introduced the term "peneplain" to describe a rolling lowland, and wrote The Coral Reef Problem (1928).

Davout, Louis Nicolas 1770–1823. French general. He fought successfully for Napoleon at Austerlitz (1805), Auerstedt (1806), and Wagram (1809), and joined the Russian campaign (1812–13). He was Napoleon's minister of war during the Hundred Days (1815).

Davy, Sir Humphry 1778–1829. English scientist. He studied the effects of nitrous oxide (laughing gas), and isolated the elements sodium, potassium (1807), calcium, boron, magnesium, and strontium (1808) through his research in electrochemistry. He also did research in agricultural chemistry.

Dawes, Charles Gates 1865–1951. American statesman and vice-president (1925–29) under C. Coolidge. As head of the post-WW I reparations commission, he authored the Dawes Plan (q.v.), which temporarily stabilized European finances. He was Nobel Prize cowinner (peace), 1925.

Dawes Act US law (1887) that sought to integrate American Indians into the national life. Sponsored by Massachusetts senator Henry L. Dawes (1816–1903), it conferred citizenship on civilized Indians and gave land individually to those renouncing tribal holdings.

Dawes Plan Post-WW I reparations agreement. C. Dawes introduced the schedule for gradual German war reparations of almost 20 billion marks to the Allies. Though accepted in 1924, it proved impractical and was abolished and replaced by the Young Plan in 1929.

Dawson Canadian city in the Yukon Territory (pop. c750). It was a boom town during the 1898 Klondike gold rush; then it rapidly declined. Today it is a trade center and tourist attraction.

Day, Benjamin Henry 1810–89. American journalist. He founded a penny newspaper, the New York Sun (1833), the first newspaper to employ newsboys; and Brother Jonathan (1842), the first illustrated weekly in the US.

Dayan, Moshe 1915–81. Israeli general and statesman. Dayan was a brilliant military strategist as chief of staff in the Sinai Conflict (1956) and minister of defense in the Six-Day War (1967). He also served as agriculture minister and again as defense minister.

Daye, Stephen c1594–1668. English-born American printer. He had the first printing press in the colonies, in Cambridge, Massachusetts. The first piece he issued was a broadside, The Freeman's Oath (1639), followed by the famous Bay Psalm Book (1640), the first book printed in the American colonies.

D-Day June 6, 1944, the start of the WW II Normandy Invasion (q.v.). Beginning at 6:30 AM, Allied forces landed on five beaches code-named Omaha and Utah (Americans) and Gold, Juno, and Sword (British and Canadians). The worst channel weather in 25 years caused a one-day postponement of the landing from the planned June 5 disembarkment.

deacon Christian clerical rank. In the Catholic church, the deaconate is the first rank in Holy Orders and can be held by both single and married men, though only the single can advance to the priesthood. In Protestant religions, deacons serve various religious and administrative functions.

Dead Sea Scrolls Ancient manuscripts discovered (from 1947) in caves above the Dead Sea. Written between the 1st cent. BC and the first half of the 1st cent. AD, they were left by the ancient Jewish sect of Essenes and include material on their life and practices. There are fragments from nearly every book of the Old Testament—in a few cases complete books, such as the Isaiah scroll.

These scrolls contain texts virtually identical to the received biblical texts, and are nearly a thousand years older than the earliest texts previously available to scholars. The Dead Sea Scrolls are considered one of the most valuable and significant archaeological finds of all time.

Deák, Francis 1803–76. Hungarian statesman. He advocated recognition of Hungarian rights within the union with Austria. After the failure of the 1848 Hungarian Revolution, he became acknowledged leader of his country. He restored the constitution (1867) and supported the dual Austro-Hungarian monarchy.

Deakin, Alfred 1856–1919. Australian statesman. He was the first Australian attorney general (1901) and three times prime minister (1903–04, 1905–08, 1909–10). He was an advocate of the federation of Australian states.

Deakin, Arthur 1890–1955. British trade union leader. Deakin led England's powerful Transport Workers Union and later the World Federation of Trade Unions (1945–49). He withdrew from the latter because of its Communist sympathies and helped found the International Confederation of Free Trade Unions.

Dean, James 1931–55. American actor. Despite his early death in a car crash, Dean made an indelible impression in his handful of starring film roles: *East of Eden, Rebel Without a Cause,* and *Giant.*

Deane, Silas 1737–89. American Revolutionary politician; the first US foreign diplomat. He successfully negotiated aid for the Revolution, recruited C. Pulaski, Baron F. W. von Steuben, and the Marquis de Lafayette, but was later accused of profiteering and died in exile.

Dearborn, Fort *See* **Fort Dearborn**

Dearborn, Henry 1751–1829. American soldier and statesman. Dearborn fought in the American Revolution, most notably at Bunker Hill and Quebec. He was Jefferson's secretary of war, but had to be relieved of his command in the War of 1812. Fort Dearborn was named for him.

Deborah In the Bible (Judges 4 and 5), a prophetess and judge of Israel. She directed the leader of the Israeli tribes, Barak, in his victory over the Canaanites, and sang afterward the famous triumphal song believed to be one of the oldest texts in the Bible.

Debrecen The third largest Hungarian city (pop. 155,122). Founded in the 14th cent., it was an important market center. In 1849, L. Kossuth proclaimed Hungarian independence from the Hapsburgs there in a short-lived revolt.

Debs, Eugene Victor 1855–1926. US Socialist leader. He helped direct the 1894 Pullman strike

(q.v.) and ran for president as a Socialist five times (1900–20). He was imprisoned during WW I for criticizing the prosecution of persons charged with sedition under the Espionage Act (1918).

Debussy, Claude 1862–1918. French composer of impressionistic works such as *Prelude to the Afternoon of a Faun, Nocturnes,* and *La Mer.*

Decadents Name applied to 19th-century poets and authors who felt that art should be above conventional morality; they included P. Verlaine, S. Mallarmé, and O. Wilde.

Decalogue *See* **Ten Commandments**

Decatur, Stephen 1779–1820. US naval officer in the Tripolitan War (1801–05) and the War of 1812 (1812–14) and the US punitive expedition of 1815 against Algiers. He is remembered for his toast: "Our country! In her intercourse with foreign nations may she always be in the right; but our country, right or wrong."

Deccan Term used to describe peninsular India. It is mostly low tableland. It was the region of Dravidian populations not reached by the Aryan invasions (1700–1200 BC) and the scene of the British-French struggle for control of India (late 18th cent.).

Decembrist Conspiracy The first modern revolutionary uprising in Russian history. Following the death of Czar Alexander I *(q.v.)*, the Decembrists staged an uprising in St. Petersburg (Dec., 1825) to try to prevent the accession of Nicholas I *(q.v.)* and secure a constitution. Most of the conspirators were nobles and officers. Their uprising was easily quelled and 121 went on trial, of which five were executed, 31 were imprisoned, and the rest were exiled to Siberia. Although they failed, the Decembrists had established a revolutionary "tradition" which had profound effects on later Russian history.

Decius AD 201–251. Roman emperor (249–251). Sent by the emperor Philip the Arabian to put down a mutiny, he was compelled by his soldiers to become emperor, and they deposed Philip. During his brief reign he inaugurated the greatest persecution of Christians in antiquity.

Decker, Thomas *See* **Dekker, Thomas**

Declaration of *See under names inverted, as in* **Independence, Declaration of**

Declaratory Act *See* **Stamp Act Congress**

Decree of Canopus ⟨Table of Tanis⟩ Ancient Egyptian decree, written (238 BC) in Greek, demotic script, and hieroglyphics. Discovered in 1866, it provided translators with an important key to deciphering Egyptian writings, second only to the Rosetta Stone *(q.v.)*.

Deere, John 1804–86. US manufacturer of agricultural implements. In partnership, he made the first steel plow. He formed the manufacturing firm Deere & Company (1868) in Moline, Illinois.

Defence of India Act British legislation. The act was first passed in 1915 to quell German-inspired revolts in India during WW I. When it was extended after the war, M. K. Gandhi began his Non-cooperation Movement.

Defenestration of Prague An incident (May 23, 1618) in which Bohemian Protestants threw two imperial regents from the window of Hradčany Castle in Prague, to protest the closing of Protestant chapels. The two escaped with their lives, but the incident signaled the beginning of Bohemian revolt against Hapsburg rule. This marked the beginning of the Thirty Years' War.

Defoe, Daniel ⟨De Foe, ~⟩ 1660–1731. English author best known for his classic novel *Robinson Crusoe*. Defoe went bankrupt as a merchant and later as a pamphleteer, and was imprisoned (1702–03) for offending the queen. He subsequently turned to journalism and became involved in a number of publications. He did not begin writing novels until his late fifties and thereafter wrote such famous works as *Robinson Crusoe* and *Moll Flanders.*

Degas, (Hilaire Germain) Edgar 1834–1917. French artist. He is best known for his impressionistic pastels and paintings of dancers and women at their toilette, such as *The Rehearsal* and *The Tub.*

De Gasperi, Alcide 1881–1954. Italian statesman. During WW II, he organized the Christian Democratic Party. He was premier (1945–53) and led Italy into NATO (1951).

de Gaulle, Charles 1890–1970. French general and first president (1959–69) of the Fifth Republic. A WW I veteran and a brigadier general, he opposed the armistice (1940) with Germany after the fall of France and organized the Free French forces in London (1940). He became copresident (1943) with H. Giraud of the French Committee of National Liberation at Algiers and, by mid-1944, had made himself sole president. He returned to France (Aug., 1944) amid the Allied victories and served briefly as president of the provisional French government (Nov., 1945-Jan., 1946). He was recalled (May, 1958) to lead France out of the crisis over Algerian independence, and after passage (Nov. 1958) of a new constitution created the Fifth Republic, he was elected president. He supported Algerian independence, though rebellions by the French in Algeria delayed it until 1962. During his long tenure, de Gaulle sought to restore France's waning prestige. He ended French participation in NATO (1966), developed a French

nuclear-weapons program, blocked Britain's entry into the Common Market, and pursued an independent foreign policy that included establishing closer ties with China and Russia. His government survived serious student and labor unrest (May, 1968) but he was forced to resign (1969) after his referendum on political reforms was defeated.

Deirdre Heroine of Irish legend. She was the beautiful chosen wife of King Conchobar. It was prophesied of her that she would cause bloodshed, and when she eloped with a lover, Usnach, he was slain by Conchobar, and she died on his grave.

Deists Enlightenment school of religious thought. Deists believe that God exists because of the existence of the universe, nature, and reason. They eschew formal religions, revelation, and belief in miracles. Famous Deists include F.M.A. de Voltaire, J.-J. Rousseau, and T. Jefferson.

Dekker, Thomas ⟨Decker, ~⟩ 1572?–1632. English Elizabethan dramatist and pamphleteer. He wrote *The Shoemaker's Holiday* and other satiric accounts of London life.

De Kooning, Willem 1904–. Netherlands-born US artist. A leader of the abstract expressionism movement (*q.v.*), he painted, notably, a series entitled *Woman.*

Delacroix, Ferdinand Victor Eugène 1798–1863. French artist, considered the leader of the Romantic school. He painted many scenes from literature and history such as *Dante and Vergil* and *The Massacre at Chios.*

Delany, Martin Robinson 1812–85. American black leader. He founded the newspaper *Mystery* (1843) to publicize his people's problems, became a medical doctor at Harvard, advocated emigration to Africa, and served as an army physician during the American Civil War.

Delaroche, Hippolyte Paul 1797–1859. French painter of portraits and historical subjects such as *Death of Queen Elizabeth* and *Children of Edward.*

Delaware US state (pop. 595,200) in the Middle Atlantic region; the first state. Originally inhabited by the Delaware Indians, the area was explored by H. Hudson in 1609 and was settled by the Dutch (1631) and the Swedes (1638). The English took control of the region in 1664 and it was granted to W. Penn as part of Pennsylvania (1682). Delaware broke ties with Pennsylvania and became an independent state (1776) and was the first state to ratify the US Constitution (1787). Its constitution was adopted in 1897.

Delaware Indians American Indian tribe. A branch of the Algonquins, they lived mainly in the New York-New Jersey-Pennsylvania area.

They were conquered by the Iroquois (1720) and later driven westward by settlers.

De la Warr, Thomas West, Baron 1577–1618. The first English governor of Virginia (1610). Delaware Bay and the state of Delaware are named for him.

Delcassé, Théophile 1852–1923. French foreign minister (1898–1905, 1914–15). He contributed to the Entente Cordiale *(q.v.)* with England and the establishment of other European alliances in the years before WW I.

De Leon, Daniel 1852–1914. US Socialist leader and writer. He was the Socialist Labor Party candidate for New York governor (1891) and edited its journal, *The People.* He was a doctrinaire Marxist and, in 1905, helped found the Industrial Workers of the World *(q.v.).*

Delescluze, Charles 1809–71. French radical and journalist. He participated in the February Revolution of 1848, and later opposed Napoleon III. A leader of the 1871 Paris Commune *(q.v.),* he died fighting on the barricades.

Delft City in The Netherlands (pop. 86,800). Founded in the 11th cent., it flourished as a commercial center (16th and 17th cents.) and was famous for its pottery (delftware) and for paintings of it by 17th-cent. native son J. Vermeer.

Delhi ⟨Old Delhi⟩ Indian city (pop. 3,287,900) in north central India, adjacent to the city of New Delhi. Delhi came to prominence when Shah Jahan made it the capital of the Mogul Empire (1638). Extensive construction followed, including the Red Fort, within which was the famed Peacock Throne. Delhi was sacked (1739) by the Persian Nadir Shah, who removed the Peacock Throne. Occupied (1803) by the British, Delhi was a center for the Sepoy uprising of 1857. It served as the capital of India (1912–31) until the inauguration of New Delhi.

Delhi Pact 1. British-Indian agreement. On March 5, 1931, M. K. Gandhi agreed to discontinue Indian civil disobedience against Britain and join in the Round Table Conferences in return for the release of nonviolent political prisoners. **2.** ⟨Nehru-Liaqat Pact⟩ An agreement between India and Pakistan concluded on April 8, 1950, whereby refugees were allowed to move back and forth to settle property, abducted women and loot were restored, forced conversions were canceled, and minority rights guaranteed.

Delhi sultanate The first Muslim Empire in India (1192–1398). It was established by the conquest of Delhi by Mohammed of Ghor (1192). His general, Qutb ud-Din, established the "slave dynasty" (so called because he and some of his successors were former military slaves) that ruled until 1290. It

was succeeded by the Khalji dynasty, which ruled until 1320, brought almost the entire subcontinent under the Delhi sultanate's sway and steadily repulsed the Mongols. Revolts and a loss of territory began in the Tughluq dynasty (1325–98). With the capture of Delhi by Tamerlane (1398), the sultanate disintegrated. Only local rulers remained until the establishment (16th cent.) of the Mogul Empire.

Delian League League of Greek city-states originally constituted (478 BC) to oppose invasion of Greece by the Persian Empire. The league's headquarters and treasury were on the island of Delos, but Athens maintained its leadership in the league, which at its height included about 140 members. It was slowly transformed into an Athenian empire in which members attempting to secede, such as Naxos (*c*470 BC), were subdued by Athenian forces. The league's treasury was eventually transferred to Athens (454 BC). The league came to an end with the decisive defeat of Athens (404 BC) by Sparta in the Peloponnesian War *(q.v.).* It was revived as the second Athenian confederacy (378 BC) but was destroyed by Philip of Macedon's defeat of Athens (338 BC).

Delilah Old Testament woman. Delilah, a Philistine, tricked Samson into revealing that the secret of his strength was in his long hair. She then betrayed him to her people.

Delisle, Guillaume 1675–1726. French cartographer. Delisle is often called the father of modern cartography. His maps corrected many long-standing errors, and he was appointed court geographer by Louis XV.

Della-Cruscans Members of an English poetical movement. These English poets lived in Italy in the late 18th cent., publishing highly romantic, sentimental verse under Italian pseudonyms.

Della Robbia, Luca 1400?–1482. Italian Renaissance sculptor. A Florentine, Della Robbia was greatly admired for his sculpture gallery of boys and angels (*cantoria*) in the Florence cathedral. He founded a family studio famous for enameled terra cotta works.

Delorme, Philibert 1510?–1570. French Renaissance architect. He designed the Château d'Anet for Diane de Poitiers, the great gallery of Chenonceaux, and the Tuileries, commissioned by Catherine de Médicis.

Delos Greek island in the Aegean Sea and legendary birthplace of Artemis and Apollo. It was a commercial center until conquered by Mithridates VI (88 BC) and subsequently abandoned.

Delphi A town in Phocis, Greece, at the foot of Mount Parnassus. It was the seat of the Delphic oracle, which prophesied from the 7th cent. BC until it was silenced by the Christian Roman emperor Theodosius (4th cent. AD). The oracle was believed to speak for the god Apollo through a priestess in a trance.

demagogue In ancient Greece, a leader of the popular party or cause of the common people. In modern times, it refers to any political leader who plays upon the passions of the masses for personal gain.

deme Ancient Greek territorial division. A deme was a subdivision of districts or villages, smaller than a city-state.

Demeter In ancient Greek religion, goddess of agriculture, daughter of Cronus and Rhea. She was the mother of Persephone, who was abducted by Pluto.

Demetrius *See also* **Dmitri**

Demetrius I *c*337–283 BC. King of Macedon (294–288 BC), a son of Antigonus I. He commanded his father's army and helped to rebuild his empire during the wars of the Diadochi *(q.v.)*. Finally driven out by Lysimachus and Pyrrhus, he had to surrender to Seleucus I (285). His son, Antigonus II, later regained Macedon.

Demetrius I ⟨Soter, Demetrius⟩ *c*187–150 BC. King of Syria (162–150 BC). During the reign of his father, Seleucus IV, he lived in Rome as a hostage. He escaped and took the throne after killing his cousin Antiochus V, whose father, Antiochus IV, had usurped the throne from Seleucus; but he was defeated by another usurper, Alexander Balas, in league with the Maccabees.

Demetrius II *d.* 229 BC. King of Macedon (239–229 BC). Macedon was seriously weakened by his constant and losing warfare with the Aetolian League and the Achaean League. Antigonus III succeeded him.

Demetrius II ⟨Nicator, Demetrius⟩ *d. c*125 BC. King of Syria (145–139 and 129–125 BC). The son of Demetrius I, he deposed Alexander Balas, who had previously deposed his father. He was captured (139 BC) and held by the Parthians for 10 years, but was released and resumed his reign. He reaffirmed Judaean independence, freeing the Jews from Syrian taxation.

De Mille, Cecil Blount 1881–1959. American motion-picture producer who made the first US feature film, *The Squaw Man* (1913). He also produced film epics such as *The Ten Commandments* (1923, remade 1956).

democracy Form of government based on rule by the people, though that rule may be exercised in various ways. The classic example of early democracy is that of the ancient Greek city-state Athens. It was a direct democracy, in which all citizens participated in government by their vote. That

system worked because the total number of citizens was small and a large part of the populace (slaves and women) was denied citizenship. Athenian democracy, and the democratic assemblies of the early Roman republic, represented short-lived experiments in government by the people. Both gave way to imperial forms of government and it was not until the 18th–19th cent. that the democratic form of government began to flourish. Social and political concepts (representative assemblies, natural rights, and the social contract) developed from the Middle Ages onward and contributed to the development of modern democracy. The gradual ascendancy of parliamentary government in Britain, the American Revolution, and the French Revolution were important in its implementation and rapid spread during the 18th to 20th cents. Modern democracy is generally a representative democracy: government is run by representatives of the people, elected and fully accountable to them. This form of government is often accompanied by a constitution that empowers the government and enumerates the rights of the people (constitutional democracy). In the West, notions of personal freedoms and individual rights are fundamental elements of the concept of democracy. The so-called peoples' democracy of communist countries, however, is based on the contention that economic democracy (economic equality, collective ownership) is of overriding importance.

Democratic Centralists Opposition group that attempted to check the growth of bureaucratization and authoritarianism within the Russian Communist party after the Russian Revolution. The 7th Soviet Congress (Dec., 1919) ostensibly endorsed the group's aims. But when no progress was realized, Centralists presented a Declaration of Forty-six to the Politburo (Oct. 15, 1923). However, J. Stalin subsequently defeated all further opposition at the 15th Party Congress (Dec., 1927).

Democratic League Chinese political group. Founded in 1941, it sought a middle ground between the Chinese Communists and Nationalists. After WW II, its membership divided between the two groups.

Democratic party One of the two major American political parties. It was founded (1792) by T. Jefferson under the name of Democratic Republicans. It adopted its present name with the popular victory (1828) of President A. Jackson. Badly split over the slavery issue, it lost its dominant position and became the minority party from 1860 until the election (1912) of W. Wilson, except for the elections (1884, 1892) of G. Cleveland. The election (1932) of F. D. Roosevelt inaugurated a long period of Democratic dominance that usually included its control of one or both houses of Congress, even under Republican presidents. The party originally favored limited federal government and state and local rights, but this policy was completely reversed in the 20th cent., when it became the party of federal intervention and "big government." The party has been consistent throughout its history, however, in favoring populism, low tariffs, cheap money, and the perceived interests of the common man, while opposing big business, industrial concentrations, and rigid monetary and fiscal standards.

Democratic Republicans *See* **Democratic party**

Democritus *c*460–*c*370 BC. Ancient Greek materialistic philosopher who expanded on the atomic theory of his teacher Leucippus. He held that everything is composed of indestructible atoms of matter whose motion explained the creation of the universe.

Demosthenes 384?–322 BC. Athenian and the greatest Greek orator. A professional speech writer, he turned to politics in 355 BC. By his speeches he warned the Athenians against King Philip of Macedon, who was becoming a threat to their liberty. Later he struggled against the pro-Macedonian faction in Athens. He poisoned himself after taking part in an unsuccessful revolt (323) against Macedonian rule. His speeches include the three *Philippics* (against King Philip), the *Olynthiacs*, and *On the Crown*.

Deng Xiaoping *See* **Teng Hsiao-p'ing**

Denikin, Anton Ivanovich 1872–1947. Russian general. He succeeded General L. G. Kornilov (1918) as supreme commander of the White Army, which unsuccessfully fought the Bolshevik forces until its defeat in 1920.

Denis, Maurice 1870–1943. French artist. He was a leader of the Symbolist movement and a member of the Nabis group *(q.v.)* of painters, and is especially known for his religious works and murals and book illustrations.

Denis, Saint 3d cent.? Patron saint of France and traditional first bishop of Paris. He was martyred by decapitation on Montmartre during the persecution by Roman emperor Valerian, and is represented in traditional Christian art carrying his head in his hands.

Denmark Constitutional monarchy located on the northern coast of Europe. Its capital is Copenhagen. The region was inhabited by Scandinavian peoples (Norse) from prehistoric times and a ruling dynasty emerged at the end of the 8th cent. The Danes were subsequently involved in invasions of England (9th–11th cents.), helped colonize Greenland, Iceland, and Atlantic Islands, and were for a time united with neighboring Sweden and Norway. A constitutional monarchy was established in Denmark in the mid-19th cent. Key events in Denmark's history include:

9TH–11TH CENTS. Danes participated in Viking raids on Western Europe; invaded England in the reign of King Alfred (reigned 871–99).

c910–c985 Harold Bluetooth reigned; first Christian king of Denmark (after 960), who claimed to have unified kingdom.

1013 Conquest of England, by Sweyn, son of Harold Bluetooth.

1018–35 Denmark, Norway, and England united under King Canute the Great.

1080–86 Canute IV reigned; attempted an invasion of Norman England (1085).

1157–82 Waldemar I (the Great) reigned; he overcame rival claimants to the throne and restored order after a period of civil war; began eastward expansion of Danish empire at the expense of the Wends (Slavs).

1202–41 Waldemar II reigned; extended Danish control over northern Europe to Estonia in the east; initiated many domestic and legal (Jutland Code) reforms and strengthened the monarchy; divided Denmark into great feudal estates.

1282 Eric V forced by nobles to accept the Great Charter and share his power with annual parliaments and a Council of Nobles.

1320–26 Christopher II reigned; nobles forced him to agree to further limitations of royal powers.

1340–75 Waldemar IV reigned; restored Denmark as a leading power; forced to submit to the Treaty of Stralsund (1370), granting the Hanseatic League extensive commercial rights.

1380 Iceland united with Denmark.

1397 Kalmar Union formed by Queen Margaret; united Denmark, Norway, and Sweden under the Danish crown.

1448–81 Christian I founded the Oldenburg dynasty; the present ruling family traces descent to him. He united Schleswig and Holstein with the Danish crown.

1513–23 Christian II reigned; notoriously cruel, he ordered Stockholm Bloodbath of Swedish nobles; driven out of Sweden (1521) and deposed (1523) by Danes.

1523 Sweden won independence from Denmark.

1533–36 Counts' War, war of succession confirming the Protestant Reformation in Denmark-Norway.

1535–39 Christian III reigned; Lutheranism established as state religion.

1611–13 Denmark defeated Sweden in the Kalmar War.

1618–48 Thirty Years' War; Sweden rose as the dominant Scandinavian power and acquired Danish territory.

1648–70 Frederick III reigned; Denmark badly defeated in renewed war with Sweden (1657–60); in the (first) Northern War forced to accept Treaty of Copenhagen (1660), settling modern boundaries of Denmark, Sweden, and Norway; in subsequent years, Frederick instituted absolute monarchy in Denmark.

1665 P. Griffenweld wrote the King's Law, justifying absolute monarchy.

1700–21 Northern War.

1788 Serfdom abolished, and peasant ownership promoted thereafter.

1803–15 Napoleonic Wars; Denmark sided with Napoleon; lost Norway to Sweden and Pomerania to Prussia (1815).

1848–63 Frederick VII reigned; liberal movement, gaining support since the 1830s, ascendent during his rule.

1848–51 War with Prussia over status of Schleswig; Denmark forced to agree to make no efforts to increase ties with region.

1849 Liberal constitution enacted; constitutional monarchy established.

1863–1906 Christian IX reigned; liberals lost power to conservatives; industrialization begun in 1850s proceeded rapidly and, along with agrarian reforms, brought Denmark a period of great prosperity.

1864 War with Prussia and Austria; Denmark annexed Holstein (1863) and thus abrogated agreement of 1851; defeated soon after war broke out (1864), Denmark lost Schleswig and Holstein by the Treaty of Vienna.

1866 New constitution promulgated; gave conservatives more power by increasing the power of the upper house (Landsting), which became more powerful than the lower house (Folketing).

1912–47 Christian X reigned.

1914–18 Denmark neutral in WW I.

1915 Constitutional reforms enacted.

1918 Universal suffrage enacted.

1918 Iceland granted independence, though Danish monarch continued as titular head of state.

1920 Denmark joined the League of Nations.

1920 Northern part of Schleswig united with Denmark following a plebiscite.

1939 Denmark signed nonaggression pact with Nazi Germany.

1939–45 WW II; Denmark occupied by Germans (1940); Danish underground actively resisted Nazis; Danish minister in Washington put Greenland under US protection; Denmark liberated by British (1945).

1944 Iceland voted for independence from Denmark, ending a union that began in 1380.

1945 Joined UN.

FROM 1945 Social Democratic party became the leading political force in Denmark.

1947–72 Frederick IX reigned.

1949 Became founding member of NATO (Apr. 4).

1953 New constitution; established constitutional monarchy with unicameral legislature (Folketing); constitution amended to allow succession of female heir.

1972 Denmark joined the Common Market.

1972 Margrethe II succeeded to the throne.

1973–75 Social Democrats out of power; election defeat resulted from high taxes.

1975–82 Anker Jorgensen, a Social Democrat, in office as prime minister.

1982 Poul Schlüter, Conservative party leader, in office as prime minister.

Denver US city (pop. 491,400), capital of Colorado and its largest city. On the South Platte River, it is a transportation hub with mining, agricultural, and tourist industries. It was formed in 1860, becoming a boom town after the discovery of gold and silver.

Deogaon, Treaty of Indian-British treaty. In it on Dec. 17, 1803, Raghuji Bhonsla II of Maratha ceded much of his land, and almost all his power, to the British East India Company.

De Quincey, Thomas 1785–1859. English writer famous for his essays. He wrote, notably, *Confessions of an English Opium Eater.*

Derby, Edward George Geoffrey Smith Stanley, 14th earl of 1799–1869. English statesman. He supported national education for Ireland, abolished West Indian slavery as colonial secretary (1833), became a leader of the Conservative party, and was three times prime minister (1852, 1858–59, 1866–67).

dervish The friar, or male religious, of Islam. Although they form religious communities or fraternities—which were very important in the Middle Ages—they do not take vows. Some dervishes, such as howling or whirling dervishes, favor extreme practices. Others favor mystical practices.

Desargues, Gérard 1593–1662. French mathematician and a founder of modern geometry. He worked on conic sections and developed the theorem on the perspective of two triangles that is named for him.

Descartes, René 1596–1650. French philosopher, mathematician, and scientist, who is called the father of modern philosophy. By his famous proposition, "I think, therefore I am *(Cogito, ergo sum),*" he oriented philosophy toward problems of epistemology and formulated a philosophical dualism of mind and body. His thinking greatly influenced rationalist philosophers and spawned Cartesianism. In mathematics, Descartes is said to have founded analytic geometry and developed the Cartesian coordinates and Cartesian curves. His most important works are *Discourse on Method, The Meditations,* and *The Principles of Philosophy.*

Desiderius *d.* after 774. Last Lombard king of Italy. Pope Adrian I requested aid from Charlemagne after Desiderius threatened Rome. Desiderius was defeated at Pavia (774) by Charlemagne, who assumed the title "King of the Lombards" and sent Desiderius to a monastery. This event strengthened ties between the Roman Catholic Church and the Frankish kings.

Desiderius Erasmus *See* **Erasmus**

De Smet, Pierre Jean 1801–73. French Jesuit missionary who won the trust of Indians in the American midwest and later served as a mediator in disputes between Indians and settlers.

Des Moines US city (pop. 191,000), capital of Iowa. First established as Fort Des Moines (1843), it became the capital in 1857. It is a center for communication and industry in the heart of the Corn Belt.

Desmond, earls of Title of Irish nobility first given to Maurice Fitzgerald (1329). The title was last borne by Gerald Fitzgerald, the 15th earl, who rebelled against Queen Elizabeth (1579), was at large for some four years but was finally captured and killed (1583).

Desmoulins, Camille 1760–94. French revolutionist and journalist. His speech of July 12, 1789, roused the crowd to attack the Bastille two days later. He published two notable revolutionary newspapers, but during the Reign of Terror *(q.v.),* he failed to support M. Robespierre completely, and he was guillotined, with G. J. Danton, as a moderate.

De Soto, Hernando *c*1500–42. Spanish explorer. De Soto explored what is now the southern United States and is believed to be the first white man to cross the Mississippi River. He died of fever and was buried in the river.

Despenser, Hugh le *d.* 1265. Medieval justiciar, or high royal judicial officer, of England. Despenser sided with the barons in the Barons' War *(q.v.)* against Henry III (1263). He was killed at the battle of Evesham. His namesake son and grandson both served the king against the barons.

Despenser, Hugh le ⟨*called* the Elder⟩ 1262–1326. English adviser to King Edward II, created earl of Winchester. He and his son dominated the king until the uprising of the barons under R. de Mortimer and Queen Isabella. They were then hanged for rapacity.

Despenser, Hugh le ⟨*called* the Younger⟩ *d.* 1326. English courtier. He and his father supported Edward II and both were banished (1321). Upon their return, Hugh continued to provoke quarrels with R. de Mortimer and Queen Isabella, and was hanged after the latter came to power.

Dessalines, Jean Jacques *c*1758–1806. Emperor of Haiti (1804–06). Born a slave, he fought in the insurrection under F. D. Toussaint L'Ouverture (1791). He expelled the French with British help (1803) and declared himself Emperor Jacques I (1804). He was assassinated because of his cruelty.

destalinization USSR political program instituted (Feb. 24–25, 1956) by N. Khrushchev at the Communist party's 20th Congress. In his now famous Secret Speech, Khrushchev denounced the excesses of J. Stalin's regime, particularly the political purges of the 1930s, and called for moderation in party rule and an end to the political terrorism identified with Stalin's rule. The campaign destroyed the cult image of Stalin as the allwise leader of international communism and helped spark the outbreak of political and intellectual turmoil in Hungary and Poland in 1956.

détente French term meaning "relaxation," adopted as an English word in the late 1960s to describe efforts to ease Cold War tensions between the US and USSR. The Strategic Arms Limitation Talks (SALT) that began in Nov., 1969, and the resulting treaties, were major initiatives that fostered détente. The heyday of détente was 1972–78. US–Soviet relations cooled after the Soviet invasion of Afghanistan in Dec., 1979, and the repression by the Polish government in Dec., 1981, which threatened to revive the Cold War *(q.v.).*

Detroit US city (pop. 4,344,140). The largest city in Michigan, it is the "automobile capital of the world." It began (1701) as a French settlement, was captured by the British (1760), and ceded to the US (1796). In the War of 1812, it was surrendered by W. Hull (1812) to the British, but retaken by W. H. Harrison in 1813. From 1837 to 1847, it was the state capital.

Deucalion In Greek mythology, the son of Prometheus. He and his wife Pyrrha survived the flood, sent by Zeus, in an ark that landed on Mount Parnassus, whence they repopulated the earth.

Deulino, Truce of A treaty concluded in the winter of 1618–19 that brought about a 14-year truce in the fighting that broke out during Russia's Time of Troubles *(q.v.)*. The Polish king Sigismund III had taken advantage of the troubles to try to place his son on the throne of Muscovy. By this treaty, Poland retained Smolensk, while Russia received back important hostages. No final settlement was reached until the Treaty of Polianov (1634), when Poland recognized Michael Romanov as the legitimate czar.

Deuteronomic Reform Religious reform movement in the kingdom of Judah (*c*621 BC). The movement was begun by King Josiah after a law code, believed to be that contained in the biblical book of Deuteronomy, was found in the temple at Jerusalem. Reforms included elimination of pagan worship in rural areas and centralization of worship in Jerusalem.

Deuteronomy In the Bible, the last of the five books of the law (the Pentateuch). It contains a summary of the history of God's dealings with Israel; of the law believed delivered to Moses, including the Ten Commandments *(q.v.)*, songs and speeches of Moses, and the account of his death.

Deutsch-Wagram *See* **Wagram, Battle of**

De Valera, Eamon 1882–1975. Irish statesman. He was the president of Sinn Fein (1917–26), founded the extreme republican group Fianna Fáil (1924), was prime minister (1937–48, 1951–54, 1957–59) and president (1959–73) of Ireland.

Devolution, War of War (1667–68) in which the French king Louis XIV attempted to conquer the Spanish Netherlands, later The Netherlands *(q.v.)*. The war stemmed from Louis' marriage to Marie Thérèse, daughter of the Spanish king Philip IV. When Philip failed to pay her dowry, Louis claimed the Spanish Netherlands as his wife's rightful inheritance. His claim was made on the basis of an old law of "devolution." Louis' armies, under H. Turenne, overran (1667) the Spanish Netherlands and Franche-Comté. The Netherlands organized the Triple Alliance *(q.v.)* in 1668 and forced Louis' armies to retire by the Treaty of Aix-la-Chapelle *(q.v.)*. The French, however, again invaded The Netherlands in the Third Dutch War.

Devonshire, Spencer Compton Cavendish, 8th duke of 1833–1908. British statesman. Originally a Liberal, he broke with W. E. Gladstone over Irish Home Rule *(q.v.)*, and led Parliament in defeating that issue on several occasions.

Dewar, Sir James 1842–1923. British chemist and physicist. He invented the Dewar flask, which prevented heat loss, and studied the properties of matter at low temperatures. He liquefied (1898) and solidified hydrogen (1899).

De Wet, Christiaan Rudolph 1854–1922. Boer general. He wrote *The Three Years' War* (1902) about his service in the Boer War of 1899–1902 *(q.v.)*. In 1914, he led a rebellion against South Africa's entrance into WW I.

Dewey, George 1837–1917. American admiral who defeated the Spanish squadron in Manila Bay during the Spanish-American War (1898). Only eight Americans were wounded, while eight Spanish ships were destroyed.

Dewey, John 1859–1952. American philosopher and educator. A professor at Columbia and other American universities in the years from 1888 to 1930, he was an early and important exponent of pragmatism *(q.v.)*. In addition, his theories on education had an important influence on the progressive-school movement. He was a prolific writer; his works include *Essays in Experimental Logic, Experience and Nature*, and *Art as Experience*.

Dewey, Melvil 1851–1931. US librarian who founded the Dewey Decimal System for the classification of library books. This system classifies subjects using numbers from 000 through 999, designating more specific subjects with decimal points.

Dewey, Thomas Edmund 1902–71. American politician. He was governor of New York (1942–54) and ran as Republican candidate for president in 1944 and 1948, when he unexpectedly lost to H. Truman.

Dewey Decimal System *See* **Dewey, Melvil**

Dhar Town in central India. It was the capital of the Rajput dynasty of Malwa (9th–14th cents.) and a center of Hindu culture and learning. It is now a district administrative center.

dharma Hindu religious principle. Dharma expresses the religious, philosophical, ethical, and moral laws that govern the behavior and duties of each individual. In essence, it is equivalent to virtue, or right conduct. It is sacred to Hinduism, Buddhism, and Jainism *(q.v.)*.

Dharma-sastra Sanskrit legal books. From the 1st cent. BC through the 6th cent. AD, these basic books of Hindu law were written in verse by the Brahmans.

Dhiban *See* **Dibon**

Diadochi Macedonian generals who, as successors of Alexander the Great, battled each other in the wars of succession (323–281 BC) that broke up the Macedonian Empire. Called the Wars of the Diadochi, these hostilities began with a struggle for the regency and quickly became battles for the throne itself. They were continued by succeeding generations of the generals and, by 281 BC, resulted in the formation of distinct empires under the Seleucids *(q.v.)* in Asia Minor, the Ptolemys *(q.v.)* in Egypt, and Antigonids *(q.v.)* in Macedonia. Among the Diadochi were Perdiccas, Antipater, Craterus, Seleucus I, Ptolemy I, Antigonus I, Eumenes, Demetrius I, and Lysimachus.

Diaghilev, Sergei Pavlovich 1872–1929. Russian ballet producer. He founded the Ballet Russe (1909), which revolutionized the dance by integrating music and scene in its productions and worked with artists such as the composer I. Stravinsky and the choreographer V. Nijinsky.

dialectical materialism Doctrine of Marxism, or communism, which holds that all reality is independent of the human mind and is reducible to matter. History proceeds through the clash of opposing forces that become resolved into new syntheses. All human history is a class struggle characterized by exploitation on the part of those who own the means of production; but the dialectical movement of history, it is held, will eventually result in the overthrow of capitalism by the proletariat of workers, and a classless society will ensue. This philosophy was expounded through the writings of K. Marx and F. Engels. (*See also* Marxism.)

Diamond Jim Brady *See* **Brady, James Buchanan**

Diamond Necklace, Affair of the *See* **Affair of the Diamond Necklace**

Diana In Roman religion, goddess of the hunt, the forest, and the moon, and the patroness of women and childbirth. She was identified with the Greek Artemis *(q.v.)*.

Diane de Poitiers 1499–1566. Mistress of Henry II of France. She became his mistress while he was still Dauphin (1536) and had greater influence than his wife, Catherine de Médicis. Noted for her beauty, she was a patroness of (and inspiration for) the arts.

Díaz, Bartholomeu *See* **Cape of Good Hope**

Díaz, Porfirio 1830–1915. Mexican soldier and president (1877–80, 1884–1911). Born of poor parents, he served in the Mexican War *(q.v.)*, the War of Reform (1857–60), and the wars against Maximilian. In subsequent years, he led rebellions against the elected government and, after overthrowing S. Lerdo de Tejada, was elected president. In his long term of office, he established firm control over political machinery, used harsh measures to suppress insurrections, and opened Mexico to foreign exploitation. He was overthrown (1911) by F. Madero.

Dickinson, Emily 1830–86. One of the great American poets. The daughter of a Massachusetts lawyer, she spent much of her life as a recluse in her father's house. She devoted herself to writing letters and poems, ultimately completing over 1,000 poems. Of these, she allowed fewer than a dozen to be printed in her lifetime. Her genius was recognized with the posthumous publication of her poems, beginning in 1890.

Dickinson, John 1732–1808. American statesman. A member of the Continental Congress (1774–76), he was against the Declaration of Independence. He wrote the *Letters from a Farmer in Pennsylvania* (1767–68) protesting the Townshend Acts *(q.v.)*.

dictator In ancient Rome, dictators were chosen by the consuls of the Roman Republic *(q.v.)* in times of emergency. They wielded great power but were limited to six-month terms and were held accountable for their decisions. The term is applied in modern times to authoritarian leaders who assume extraordinary powers, with or without legislative sanction, such as A. Hitler or B. Mussolini.

Diderot, Denis 1713–84. French Enlightenment philosopher, editor of the great French *Encyclopédie*, and man of letters. As editor of the *Encyclopédie* (1745–72), he arranged for contributions from all the important French writers (later known as the Encyclopedists *(q.v.)* of his day and created one of the chief works of the *philosophes (q.v.)*. Diderot was also a novelist (*Rameau's Nephew*), dramatist, and innovative critic of art. His philosophical works include *Thoughts on the Interpretation of Nature* and *Elements of Physiology*.

Dido In Roman mythology, the founder of Carthage *(q.v.)*. She threw herself on a funeral pyre either to escape marrying an African king or, according to Vergil, because she was deserted by Aeneas.

Diemen, Anton van 1593–1645. Governor general of the Dutch East India Company (1636–45). He took Ceylon and Malacca from the Portuguese and extended Dutch influence in the East Indies.

Dien Bien Phu, Battle of Vietnamese victory over France (May 7, 1954) during the Indochina war. The battle concluded with the surrender of the French fortified outpost at Dien Bien Phu in a northwestern valley of Vietnam. Hoping to lure the guerrilla forces of the Vietminh *(q.v.)* into a pitched battle in which artillery would be decisive, the French general Henri Navarre concentrated some 15,000 men in a fortified camp. But the Vietnamese general V. Nguyen Giap surrounded it with some 40,000 troops, brought up his own artillery, and, after a long siege (Nov., 1953–May, 1954), left 2,293 dead, 5,134 wounded, and took more than 10,000 prisoners in all. The

French were compelled to leave Indochina after a big-power conference at Geneva in July, 1954, which partitioned Vietnam along the 17th parallel. This battle is considered one of the greatest victories ever won by a former colony over a colonial power.

Dieppe raid An experimental commando attack by the Allies during WW II (Aug. 19, 1942) on the French coastal town of Dieppe. More than two-thirds of the mostly Canadian troops were lost.

Diesel, Rudolf Christian Karl 1858–1913. German inventor and engineer. Diesel invented an internal-combustion engine (1892) and the refined diesel engine (1896) which bears his name.

Diet of See under names inverted, as in **Worms, Diet of**

Dietrich, Marlene 1904–. German-born film actress who first gained fame in the movie The Blue Angel (1930). She also made many movies in the US and entertained Allied troops during WW II.

Digby, Sir Kenelm 1603–65. English diplomat and author. He supported Charles I during the English Civil War (q.v.) and was chancellor to Queen Henrietta Maria after the Restoration (1660–64).

Diggers Groups of communal farmers who flourished (1649–51) briefly in England. Spurred on by high food prices after the English Civil War (q.v.), a small band of peasants led by Gerrard Winstanley (1609–52) occupied and cultivated common lands in Surrey. The Diggers, Puritan extremists who called themselves True Levellers, wanted an end to private ownership of land. Opposition soon mounted, however, and in 1650 they were forced to disband. Several other Digger colonies were likewise dispersed.

Dillinger, John 1902–34. American bank robber. Dillinger roamed Depression-era mid-America robbing banks and allegedly murdering 16 people. Declared "public enemy number one," he was killed by the FBI in a Chicago shoot-out.

Dinah In the Bible, the daughter of Jacob and Leah. She was raped by the Hivite prince, Shechem. Shechem wanted to marry her but was killed by her brothers, Simeon and Levi, who attacked the Hivite city to avenge the rape.

Dingley Tariff American protective tariff. This law, sponsored by Maine's Republican congressman Nelson Dingley (1832–99), imposed a high protective tariff on foreign imports from 1897 to 1909.

Dinh Bo Linh ⟨Dinh Tien Hoang⟩ d. 979. Vietnamese emperor. Dinh Bo Linh was an able soldier and organizer who created (968) a reunified empire in Vietnam, ending a period of anarchy and established independence from China.

Dinh Tien Hoang See **Dinh Bo Linh**

Diniz 1261–1325. King of Portugal (1279–1325), son of Alfonso III. He encouraged agricultural improvements, founded the University of Coimbra (1290), negotiated the first commercial treaty with England (1294), and founded the Portuguese navy (1317).

Diocletian AD 245–313. Roman soldier and emperor (AD 284–305), successor to Numerian (Emperor of the East) in 284 and Carinus (Emperor of the West) on the latter's death in 285. Diocletian instituted military, financial, and administrative reforms, including the division of the empire (AD 293) into four parts (the East; Italy and Africa; Gaul, Spain, and Britain; Illyricum and the Danube region). During his reign Britain was again made part of the empire, the Persians were conquered, and the last serious persecutions of Christians began (303). He brought a measure of stability to the empire but did not reverse the decline brought on by excessive taxation, a burdensome bureaucracy, and ongoing economic problems. He abdicated in 305.

Dio Coccelanus See **Dion Chrysostom**

Diodorus Siculus d. after 21 BC. Sicilian-born Greek historian who wrote a world history, starting with the creation and extending to Caesar's Gallic Wars.

Diogenes d. c320 BC. Greek Cynic philosopher. He rejected the comforts of life, living in a tub, and is known for going about with a lantern "looking for an honest man."

Diogenes Laërtius See **Zeno of Citium**

Diomed ⟨Diomede⟩ ⟨Diomedes⟩ **1.** In Greek legend, son of Tydeus and a Greek leader in the Trojan War. **2.** The name of a legendary Thracian king who was killed by Hercules while trying to protect his man-eating horses.

Diomede See **Diomed**

Diomedes See **Diomed**

Dion Cassius AD c155–235? Greek-born Roman historian. Cassius held many high Roman civilian and military offices, but was best known for his 80-volume History of Rome, written in Greek, of which 19 books survive intact.

Dion Chrysostom ⟨Dio Coccelanus⟩ d. after AD 112. Greek philosopher and rhetorician. He was banished from Rome by Emperor Domitian but returned under Nerva and Trajan. Of his orations, 80 still exist.

Dion of Syracuse 409?–354? BC. Syracusan philosopher and politician. He tried to set up a government according to the teachings of Plato under his nephew Dionysius the Younger but failed. He became ruler himself (356 BC) but was assassinated shortly afterward.

Dionysia See **Dionysus**

Dionysius of Halicarnassus *fl.* 1st cent. BC. Greek historian who came to Rome in 29 BC and wrote a 20-volume history of Rome, *Roman Antiquities,* of which only the first nine are extant.

Dionysius the Areopagite, Saint *fl.* 1st cent. AD. Athenian Christian converted by the apostle Paul. Tradition says he was the first bishop of Athens. In the Middle Ages, several mystical treatises that greatly influenced scholasticism *(q.v.)* were mistakenly attributed to him. These writings were actually composed around the 5th cent., and are today attributed to Pseudo-Dionysius.

Dionysius the Elder 430–367 BC. Tyrant of Syracuse (405–367 BC). He led two successful wars against Carthage (398–392) and made Syracuse the major power in Greek Italy. Later wars with Carthage were failures.

Dionysius the Younger *fl.* 368–344 BC. Tyrant of Syracuse, son of Dionysius the Elder. His uncle, Dion of Syracuse, with Plato's backing, tried to make him into a philosopher-prince but failed. He was expelled by Dion (356) and again by Timoleon (344) after the former's assassination.

Dionysus Mythical Greek fertility god, son of Zeus. Dionysus was a nature god who ruled all vegetation but was particularly honored as the god of wine. Festivals and orgies, Dionysia, were celebrated in his name. He corresponds to the Roman Bacchus.

Diophantus 3d cent. AD. Greek mathematician. He introduced a type of indeterminate algebraic equation into his work *Arithmetica;* six of the 13 books of this earliest known work on algebra are extant.

Diori, Hamani 1916–. The first president of Niger (1960–74). Diori led his country to complete independence from France (1960). He supported economic growth and mediated in the Biafran War but was overthrown by a military coup.

Dioscorides, Pedanius 1st cent. AD. Greek physician. While serving as surgeon with Nero's Roman army, he collected the pharmacological information used in his text *De Materia Medica,* used for 1,500 years.

Dioscuri *See* **Castor and Pollux**

diplomatic revolution ⟨reversal of alliances⟩ European foreign-policy conditions leading to the Seven Years' War *(q.v.)* also brought about (1756) changes in long-established alliances. The year preceding the war saw the alliance of France with Austria and Russia, and of Britain with Prussia, and the estrangement of Britain from Russia, which fought on the side of Austria and France in the war.

Dirac, Paul Adrien Maurice 1902–. English physicist. He developed a version of quantum mechanics and shared a Nobel Prize in Physics with E. Schrödinger (1933). He and E. Fermi developed the Fermi-Dirac statistics.

Directory Executive body (1795–99) of the French First Republic during the French Revolution. It consisted of five directors nominated by the Council of Five Hundred *(q.v.)* and elected by the Council of Ancients. Embroiled in struggles with the councils and plagued with infighting among the directors, the Directory succumbed first (1797) to the *coup d'état* of 18 Fructidor and finally (1799) to the coup of 18 Brumaire, in which Napoleon took power. The Directory was then replaced with the Consulate.

Dirksen, Everett McKinley 1896–1969. American statesman. Dirksen served Illinois as a Republican congressman (1933–49) and senator (1950–69). Generally a conservative, he nevertheless led Democratic President L. Johnson's fight for the Civil Rights and Voting Rights acts of 1964–65.

Disarmament Conference International conference held in Geneva (1932–37) for the purpose of preventing general rearmament. It was attended by members of the League of Nations as well as by the United States and USSR. Deadlocks ensued over the definitions of war materials and over refusal of various countries to accept parity. France refused to accept limitations. Germany, already limited in armaments by the Treaty of Versailles *(q.v.),* contended that it had a right to rearm unless other nations disarmed to an equivalent level. The conference adjourned for five months (1933). When it reassembled, Germany had passed under Nazi control and withdrew (Oct. 14) from the conference and the League of Nations. The conference was thenceforth without significance, though it met sporadically until May, 1937.

Disciples of Christ ⟨Campbellites⟩ American Protestant body, founded by former Presbyterians Thomas and Alexander Campbell *c*1810. They preached unity among all Christians, with the Bible as their only guide. They became known as the Christian Churches and officially adopted this name in 1957.

Disney, Walt 1901–66. American movie producer. He created the cartoon character Mickey Mouse (1928) and produced full-length animated and other popular films such as *Snow White and the Seven Dwarfs* (1938).

Disputations Debates in medieval universities. Students were required to defend views against attacks on them. They evolved into the modern examination system whereby degree aspirants are required to defend original theses before examining professors.

Disraeli, Benjamin, 1st earl of Beaconsfield
1804–81. British author, statesman, and Conservative prime minister (1868, 1874–80), succeeding (respectively) E. Derby and W. Gladstone. A controversial figure, Disraeli pursued an aggressive foreign policy in the interests of British imperialism. He was a noted author when he became (1837) a member of Parliament and there became a leader of the young Conservative (Tory) faction. He aggressively opposed the prime minister and member of his own party, Sir R. Peel, on the repeal of the Corn Laws (q.v.) in 1846 and thereby helped bring down Peel's government. He subsequently served as chancellor of the exchequer (1852, 1858–59), worked for passage of the Reform Bill of 1867 to enfranchise a large bloc of working-class voters, and served briefly as prime minister (1868). Though many social reforms were instituted, Disraeli's second term as prime minister (1874–80) was dominated by foreign-policy matters. These included formal annexation of Fiji (1874) and Transvaal (1877), purchase of controlling interest in the Suez Canal (1875), the Anglo-Afghan War (1878–79), and involvement in the continuing power struggle between the Ottoman Empire and Russia in the eastern Mediterranean.

District of Columbia US federal district (pop. 648,000) co-extensive with the city of Washington, on the Potomac River between Virginia and Maryland. Established by congressional acts (1790–91), the region was chosen by G. Washington as the seat of the federal government. The government moved there (June 10, 1800) from Philadelphia during the presidency of J. Adams. The town of Georgetown was consolidated with Washington (1878), which is governed by a presidential commission. Residents of the district won the right to vote in presidential elections (1961) by the 23d Amendment and the right to elect its own mayor by adopting a new charter (1974).

Divine, Father c1882–1965. American black religious leader. Born George Baker, he founded the Peace Mission movement in the Harlem section of New York City.

divine right Royalist doctrine asserting that a king's power came from God and that he was accountable only to God, not to his people. It reached its height in Europe in the 17th cent. It was largely ended by England's Glorious Revolution and the French Revolution.

Divines at Westminster, Assembly of See **Westminster Assembly**

Dix, Dorothea Lynde 1802–87. American social reformer. She crusaded for more humane treatment for the insane and the imprisoned, and was superintendent of women nurses during the American Civil War.

Dixie Name applied to the US southern states. The origin of the term is obscure, and has been attributed to memories of a kind slaveholder of that name as well as to the Mason-Dixon line (q.v.). A song, Dixie, composed (1859) for a minstrel show by Daniel Decatur Emmett (1815–1904) became the song of the Confederacy and later of the South generally.

Dixiecrats (States' Rights Democrats) American political group. In 1948, Southern Democrats refused to support their party's civil rights program, and formed their own group. Their presidential candidate was Governor Strom Thurmond of South Carolina, who carried four southern states against H. Truman.

Dixon, Jeremiah See **Mason-Dixon line**

Djakarta Indonesian city (pop. 4,576,000). Founded 1619 and formerly called Batavia by the Dutch, Djakarta is the capital (from 1949) and largest city of Indonesia. It is the center of much of Indonesia's education, trade, manufacturing, and transportation.

Djibouti (formerly Afars and Issas, French Territory of the; French Somaliland) Independent country in East Africa. Capital is Djibouti. Held by the French from 1862, it was a colony (French Somaliland) from 1896 until 1946, when it became a territory in the French Union. In 1958 it entered the French Community. It was renamed Afars and Issas in 1967 and became independent on May 8, 1977. Gouled Aptidon Hassan (in office 1977–) was first president. An underdeveloped nation with an agricultural economy, it is strategically located at the entrance to the Red Sea. The US was granted rights to establish military bases there (1980), after unrest in Ethiopia threatened Djibouti's stability.

Dmitri (Demetrius) Name of the son of Ivan IV, child heir to the Russian throne, who was murdered (1591), possibly by B. Godunov. Dmitri was also the name of three claimants (false Dmitris) to the throne who appeared shortly after Godunov succeeded to the throne. They created what is called the Time of Troubles (1604–13). The first false Dmitri appeared c1600 and may have been Yury Otrepyev, a Russian nobleman. He ruled for less than a year, after Godunov died (1605), before being assassinated. The second Dmitri (the Thief of Tushino) was active from 1607 to 1610, and the third (the Thief of Pskov) was active from 1611 until his execution in 1612.

Dobson, Frank 1888–1963. English sculptor. He developed a modernistic, nonnaturalistic style, and did many female nudes and sculpted portraits.

Docetism Early heresy in Christianity, which claimed that Jesus did not take a true human form on earth but was a phantasm. It was a form of Gnosticism (q.v.).

Doctors' Plot Russian Stalinist conspiracy. On January 13, 1953, J. Stalin announced that 10 prominent Russian doctors were American agents who were plotting to murder Communist leaders. Stalin died before the trials, and most of the accused were released.

Doctrinaires French royalist political writers who gave their name to any abstract, dogmatic thinker by the manner in which they defended the restored French monarchy (1815–30). They included, notably, F. Guizot.

Doctrine of Lapse One of the policies used by the British East India Company (19th cent.) to justify annexation of native kingdoms in India. By it, a failure in the direct royal line of succession meant that direct control of the state passed to the company. Parts of the Maratha states were annexed in this way. This doctrine was used in conjunction with the doctrine of paramountcy, by which the company justified interference in states that were being misgoverned.

Dodecanese Greek island group in the Aegean Sea (pop. 121,000). It belonged to the Ottoman Empire (16th cent. to 1912), then to Italy until 1947, when it was ceded to Greece. Rhodes is the administrative center.

Dodge City American city. Located on the Arkansas River in Kansas, Dodge City's location on the Santa Fe Trail (q.v.) made it a rowdy cowboy town in the latter half of the 19th cent. It is now a major tourist attraction.

Dodgson, Charles Lutwidge See **Carroll, Lewis**

Dondona Village in Epirus, Greece, site of the oldest of the ancient Greek oracles. It was dedicated to the chief god, Zeus.

Doeg Old Testament soldier. Doeg was Saul's chief herdsman. He slew 85 priests in the Nob massacre.

Doenitz, Karl 1891–1980. German admiral. He planned the creation of the new German submarine fleet, contrary to the terms of the Versailles Treaty (q.v.) and commanded it during WW II. As A. Hitler's designated successor, he ordered Germany's surrender (May 7, 1945).

doge Chief office in the one-time Italian republics of Genoa and Venice. The Venetian doge was the chief magistrate from 697 until 1797, though his real power was curtailed after the establishment of the Council of Ten in 1310.

Dogen 1200–1253. Japanese philosopher and teacher. Dogen was a Buddhist monk who studied Zen Buddhism (q.v.) in China and introduced it to Japan through his Soto School.

Doheny, Edward L. See **Teapot Dome**

Dole, Sanford Ballard 1844–1926. Hawaiian statesman. He served as the first president of the Republic of Hawaii (1894–1900) and as governor of the US Territory of Hawaii (1900–1903) when it was annexed.

Dolet, Étienne 1509–46. French scholar and printer of Lyon called "the martyr of the Renaissance." He was executed for heresy after publishing a work allegedly denying the soul's immortality.

dollar diplomacy Diplomatic expression. In general, this term refers to the policy of buying another country's support with loans or aid. Specifically, it refers to the foreign policy of W. H. Taft and P. C. Knox, who sought to increase US trade by supporting US enterprises abroad.

Dollfuss, Engelbert 1892–1934. Austrian statesman. He became chancellor in 1932 and declared a dictatorship along Italian Fascist lines (1934). He was assassinated by Austrian Nazis attempting a takeover.

Döllinger, Johann Joseph Ignaz von 1799–1890. German theologian and historian. Excommunicated for opposing the doctrine of papal infallibility as promulgated by the First Vatican Council (1869–70), he became a member of the Old Catholics (q.v.).

Domenico Veneziano c1400–1461. Italian Renaissance painter who created the St. Lucy Altarpiece in the Uffizi palace at Florence.

Domesday Book The record of a survey ordered by William the Conqueror (1086) to determine economic conditions in England and the ownership of land for taxation purposes.

Dominic, Saint 1170?–1221. Spanish Catholic churchman who founded the Dominicans (q.v.) in 1216, a religious order that emphasizes study and preaching. He was a Castilian; his full name was Dominic Guzmán.

Dominican Republic Independent state located on the eastern part of the Caribbean island of Hispaniola, adjacent to Haiti. Its capital is Santo Domingo. The island was governed by Spain until it was ceded to France in 1795. The republic was established in 1844 and long periods of internal disorder ensued. Key events in the Dominican Republic's history include:

    1492 Columbus discovered island of Hispaniola; claimed it for Spain; named it La Española; established his son Diego as viceroy.

    1496 Santo Domingo established.

1697 Western part, a haven for buccaneers, ceded to France.

1795 In the Treaty of Basel, Spain ceded La Española to France.

1801 Haitian black slaves, under Toussaint L'Ouverture, revolted; conquered island; French forces subsequently defeated Toussaint.

1808–09 Successful revolt against the French.

1814–21 Spanish again ruled; finally expelled (1821).

1822 Eastern part of island conquered by Haitians, led by J. Boyer.

1844 Haitian rule overthrown on east part of island; Pedro Santana established the Dominican Republic; became first president.

1861–65 Became Spanish province, after long period of unrest and frequent attacks by Haiti.

1865 Spain withdrew forces; second Dominican Republic declared (Feb.); unrest became chaotic.

1869 President Buenaventura Báez attempted annexation with US; US Senate refused to ratify treaty.

1882–99 Gen. Ulíses Heureaux served as president; was assassinated.

1905 Government finances near collapse; control of customs department turned over to US (to 1940).

1916–24 US sent marines to quell civil disorders (1916); military government established.

1922 Partial restoration of civilian government.

1930–61 Rafael Trujillo Molina in power after overthrowing Horacio Vásquez (1930); began long dictatorship.

1937–38 Border dispute with Haiti; Trujillo expelled Haitians in Dominican Republic, during which 10,000 of them were killed (1937); dispute settled (1938).

1947 Election held; Trujillo curbed opposition party, was reelected "overwhelmingly."

1947 Trujillo charged that Cuban Communists were plotting invasion.

1949 Uprising quelled; Trujillo blamed Cubans and others for revolt.

1959 Abortive coup by exiled Dominicans living in Cuba.

1960 OAS charged Trujillo with involvement in plot to kill Venezuelan president Betancourt; sanctions imposed.

1960 Trujillo named Joaquin Balaguer president.

1961 Trujillo assassinated (May 30); Balaguer subsequently attempted democratic reforms.

1962 Balaguer forced out of office by civil unrest.

1962–63 Leftist Juan Bosch in office as elected president; Bosch overthrown (Sept.) by right-wing military coup; civilian triumvirate ruled afterward.

1965 Leftist revolt (Apr.) became civil war; US Pres. L. Johnson sent marines, who effectively supported anti-Bosch forces; OAS arranged a cease-fire.

1965 Hector García Godoy became provisional president (Sept.).

1966 Balaguer elected president; OAS forces withdrawn; Balaguer was subsequently reelected, until 1978.

1978–82 Antonio Guzmán, Dominican Revolutionary party leader, in office as president; instituted land reform program.

1979 Coup attempt failed (Sept.).

Dominicans ⟨Order of Preachers⟩ Important order of Catholic friars founded (1216) in France by Saint Dominic. Sanctioned the same year by Pope Honorius III, the order began as an attempt to convert the Albigenses (q.v.). Since then the order has retained its evangelical character and is also characterized by devotion to theological studies, preaching, and teaching. The order was greatly influenced (13th cent.) by its member Saint Thomas Aquinas and since then has also been dedicated to promoting Thomism (q.v.). The order was in charge of the Inquisition (q.v.) and actively engaged in missionary work. Other noted Dominicans include Albertus Magnus and Savonarola. With the Franciscans (q.v.), it is one of the two principal Catholic orders of friars.

dominion Former name of a country in the British Commonwealth (q.v.). Prior to 1939, "dominion" referred to a self-governing country, such as Canada, which still retained ties to the British Empire. The term was abandoned because of its implied inferior status.

Domitian ⟨Domitianus, Titus Flavius⟩ AD 51–96. Roman emperor (81–96), son of Vespasian, successor to his brother Titus. The cruelty of his later years led to his assassination in a plot led by his wife, Domitia. Nerva succeeded him.

Domitianus, Titus Flavius *See* **Domitian**

Donar *See* **Thor**

Donatello c1386–1466. Italian Renaissance sculptor. A founder of realistic sculpture, as seen in his bronze *David* (Bargello palace, Florence), he was the first sculptor since antiquity to do free-standing statues independent of their surroundings.

Donation of Constantine Grant of land claimed to have been made to the papacy by the emperor

Constantine. The document supporting the alleged grant was probably forged around the 8th cent. to bolster papal claims of temporal power over central Italy. The demonstration of this forgery in the Renaissance (1440) by a papal secretary, L. Valla, was one of the first successful uses of historical critical methods that later became standard.

Donation of Pepin *See* **Pepin the Short**

Donatism North African schismatical movement (4th cent. AD). The Donatists believed that only the "pure" were true members of the church and that sacraments administered by priests who had sinned were invalid. They were condemned by the Synod of Arles (314) and declined definitively after the formidable attack on their doctrines launched by Saint Augustine in the early 5th cent.

Donatus *fl.* AD 333. Roman teacher of grammar and rhetoric. He taught Saint Jerome and wrote the *Ars grammatica*, a Latin textbook used throughout the Middle Ages.

Don Carlos *See* **Carlist Wars; Carlists**

Don Carlos *See* **Carlists**

Don Cossacks Cossacks *(q.v.)* who settled along the lower course of the Don River and founded a semi-independent republic under the suzerainty of the Russian czars (16th cent.). They lost their autonomy after a revolt (1707–08) and became a special military caste (1835). They were used by the czars to suppress revolutionary movements after 1886.

Donelson, Fort *See* **Fort Donelson**

Doniphan, Alexander William 1808–87. American soldier. As a commanding officer in the Mexican War, he marched his troops in a brilliant long march by land and sea from New Mexico to Chihuahua (Dec., 1846-Mar., 1847). He fought two victorious battles along the way, losing few men.

Donizetti, Gaetano 1797–1848. Italian opera composer of *Lucia di Lammermoor* (1835) and other romantic operas.

Donne, John 1572–1631. English poet, the foremost of the Metaphysical Poets *(q.v.)*. Donne was for a time an adventurer, a public official and, finally, was ordained as an Anglican priest (1615). Though his poetry was later neglected (until the 20th cent.), both his poetry and sermons were well recognized in his day. He is noted for his use of imagery and paradox; his works include *Songs and Sonnets*, his two *Anniversaries, Devotions upon Emergent Occasions*, and his many sermons.

Donnelly, Ignatius 1831–1901. American author and reformer. He was congressman (1863–69) from Minnesota and a founder of the Populist party (1892). He tried to prove that F. Bacon wrote

Shakespeare's plays in *The Great Cryptogram* (1888).

Donner party Group of emigrants to California (1846–47) who were trapped all winter by snow in the Sierra Nevadas. Out of 87, 47 survived only by recourse to cannibalism.

Donnybrook Irish town and county. Now part of Dublin, Donnybrook was famous for its annual fair (1204–1855) in which drunken brawling was an expected part of the festivities, making the word "donnybrook" synonymous with a brawl.

Don Pacifico affair Incident (1850) in which the British government seized Greek ships in Piraeus (Athens) harbor in support of the claims of a British subject, David Pacifico, against the Greek government. It was considered an extreme example of the bellicose foreign policy of Lord Palmerston, who was obliged to promise Queen Victoria that he would inform her of his actions after the French and Russians protested the incident.

Doppler, Christian Johann 1803–53. Austrian physicist. He discovered that the frequency of light and sound waves seems to vary according to the distance of the source from the observer, a phenomenon now called "Doppler's principle."

Doria, Andrea 1468–1560. Genoese admiral of an ancient Genoese princely family. He fought for Francis I of France between 1522 and 1528, but then switched allegiance to the emperor Charles V. He established a virtual dictatorship over Genoa (1529), and fought sea battles in alliance with the empire against both Turks and Barbary pirates. He was one of the great Italian seamen. The ocean liner *Andrea Doria* (sunk [1956] in the Atlantic) was named after him.

Dorians People of ancient Greece who settled in the Peloponnesus (c1100 BC), replacing the Achaean Greeks. They established colonies in Crete, Italy, Sicily, and Asia Minor.

Doric order Greek architectural style. Doric is the earliest style of Greek art and architecture (7th cent. BC). Its columns, which had no base, were marked by 20 sharp-edged flutes, culminating in a characteristic curved-mold capital. Doric columns predominated in such ancient structures as the Parthenon *(q.v.)* and the Colosseum *(q.v.)*.

Dornier, Claudius 1884–1969. German aircraft designer and builder. He initiated all-metal airplanes and made seaplanes such as the *Do X* (1929) which carried 169 passengers from Germany to New York on its maiden flight (1931). Dornier bombers were Luftwaffe standards in WW II.

Dorr, Thomas Wilson 1805–54. American crusader for universal manhood suffrage. During the agitation against the Rhode Island Charter, which restricted the franchise to property-owners, both Dorr's followers and their rivals called their own constitutional conventions and set up rival governments of Rhode Island (1841–42). Even after the adoption of a new constitution, Dorr was sentenced to life for treason but was later pardoned.

Dort, Synod of *See* **Arminianism; Remonstrants**

Dorylaeum, battles of **1.** First ~. Crusader victory over the Seljuk Turks fought at Dorylaeum (near modern Eskişehir, Turkey) on July 1, 1097, during the First Crusade *(q.v.)*. The first column of the Crusader army, consisting of some 10,000 men under Bohemond, was attacked by a huge Turkish army. Reinforcements arrived and the Turks were routed, suffering some 30,000 casualties to about 4,000 Crusader casualties. **2.** Second ~. Turkish victory over a German army led by Conrad III of Hohenstaufen in Oct., 1147, during the Second Crusade *(q.v.)*. Only Conrad and some knights were able to fight their way out of an ambush in which the Crusader army was decimated by Turkish archers. The defeat contributed to the failure of the Second Crusade.

Dos Passos, John Roderigo 1896–1970. American realistic author of the trilogy *U.S.A.* (1937), made up of *The 42d Parallel, 1919,* and *The Big Money.*

Dost, Muhammad 1793–1863. Emir (ruler) of Afghanistan (1826–63). His attempts to play off the Russians against the British embroiled him with the latter in the first of the Afghan Wars (1839–42), but an accommodation with the British was finally reached in 1855.

Dostoyevsky, Feodor Mikhailovich 1821–81. Russian novelist and one of the world's great writers. His *The Brothers Karamazov* is a classic. He first gained recognition (1846) as a writer with *Poor Folk* but was exiled (1849) to Siberia for his association with a radical group. On returning (1859) from Siberia, he again took up writing and completed his most important works. Among them are *Notes from the Underground, Crime and Punishment, The Idiot,* and *The Possessed.*

Doubleday, Abner 1819–93. Reputed originator of baseball and Civil War officer. A 1908 commission concluded that he indeed invented baseball as we know it, in 1839, at Cooperstown, N.Y., but its conclusions are still disputed by some.

Doughty, Charles Montagu 1843–1926. English traveler and author. He published the classic *Travels in Arabia Deserta* (1888), based on his original observations of Arab life.

Doughty, Thomas *See* **Hudson River School**

Douglas Noble family prominent in Scottish history for more than 700 years. The family figured in the border wars between Scotland and England

and members were variously earls, marquises, and dukes of Douglas, Angus, Hamilton, Queensberry, and Morton. The origins of the family are uncertain, though the Douglases were among the ancestors of the Stuart *(q.v.)* line of Scottish kings. In modern times, a descendent of the Douglas family, Sir A. Douglas-Home, was British prime minister (1963–64). Among the prominent members of the family were: William of Douglas (d. 1298), 1st lord of Douglas, a leader of J. de Baliol's forces; Sir James Douglas, lord of Douglas (1286–1330), great commander under Robert I the Bruce; William Douglas, 1st earl of Douglas (c1327–84), engaged in border wars with the English; James Douglas, 2nd earl of Douglas and Mar (c1358–88), raided across English border, was killed at the battle of Otterburn; Archibald Douglas, 3d earl of Douglas (c1328–1400), made the family the most powerful in Scotland; Archibald Douglas, 4th earl of Douglas (c1369–1424), who joined the French against the English in 1423; Archibald Douglas, 5th earl of Douglas (c1391–1439), who rose to great power under James II; William Douglas, 6th earl of Douglas (1423–1440), beheaded with his brother by James II to break the family's power; William Douglas, 8th earl of Douglas (c1425–52), murdered by James II after regaining some family lands; James Douglas, 9th earl of Douglas (1426–88), rebelled against James II and thus lost family lands to the Angus line; Archibald Douglas, 5th earl of Angus (c1449–1514), opposed James III and became chancellor under James IV; Archibald Douglas, 6th earl of Angus (c1489–1557), married Scottish dowager queen, Margaret Tudor, and for a time gained control of Scotland; Archibald Douglas, 8th earl of Angus (1555–88), joined an English-backed invasion of Scotland and forced James to restore his family lands.

Douglas, Clifford Hugh 1879–1952. English engineer and economist. He authored the theory of Social Credit *(q.v.)* and served as reconstruction adviser to the government of Alberta, Canada (1935), which was dedicated to his theories.

Douglas, David 1798–1834. Scottish botanist. He traveled early throughout North America studying its plants. The Douglas Fir which he observed (c1825) is named for him.

Douglas, Gawin 1474?–1522. Scottish poet and Bishop of Dunkeld. He is known for doing the first English translation of the Aeneid and is considered one of the greatest early Scottish poets.

Douglas, Sir James 1803–77. Canadian colonial governor. He built Fort Victoria on Vancouver Island (1843), where he became governor (1851). He was also appointed governor of British Columbia (1858–1863).

Douglas, Stephen Arnold 1813–61. American statesman, a great orator and central figure in the national debate over slavery in the years prior to the American Civil War. A Democrat from Illinois, he was a congressman (1843–47) and senator (1847–61). As a senator he was a proponent of expansionism and became chairman of the Committee on Territories. He thereby held an important position in the North-South struggle over slavery, then centered on the question of extending slavery to new US territories. He formulated the doctrine of popular sovereignty, was instrumental in passage of the Compromise of 1850 *(q.v.)*, and proposed what became the 1854 Kansas-Nebraska Act *(q.v.)*. He engaged in the notable Lincoln-Douglas debates during the senatorial election (1858), when he defeated Lincoln, but was narrowly defeated by Lincoln in the presidential election (1860).

Douglas, William Orville 1898–1980. US Supreme Court justice (1939–75). Douglas was appointed to the Supreme Court by F. D. Roosevelt. He was consistently liberal on most matters, such as civil rights, the first amendment, civil liberties, and the environment.

Douglas-Home, Sir Alexander Frederick 1903–. British statesman. He entered Parliament as a Conservative (1931), was secretary to N. Chamberlain (1937–39), foreign secretary (1960–63). On becoming prime minister (1963–64), replacing H. Macmillan, he had to renounce his Scottish peerage.

Douglass, Frederick 1817–1895. American abolitionist who escaped slavery in 1838. Taught to read by a former owner, he lectured in the US and Britain, edited an abolitionist newspaper, organized two regiments of Massachusetts Negroes in the American Civil War, and finally wrote *Life and Times of Frederick Douglass* (1882).

Douhet, Giulio 1869–1930. Italian general. He was an early advocate of strategic bombing and an independent air force whose theories influenced German and Italian tactics in the Spanish Civil War *(q.v.)*.

Doumer, Paul 1857–1932. French statesman. He was president of the French Third Republic (1931–32) until his assassination by the insane Russian émigré P. Gorgoulov. A. Lebrun succeeded him.

Doumergue, Gaston 1863–1937. French politician. He was first elected to the Chamber of Deputies (1893) as a Radical-Socialist, served in several ministries, and was elected president of the Third French Republic (1924–31). He later served briefly as a "strong man" premier (1934) as

a result of the turmoil surrounding the Stavisky Affair *(q.v.)*.

Dover American city, capital of Delaware (pop. 17,500). Founded in 1683 on order of W. Penn, it has been the capital since 1777 and is the seat of Kent county.

Dover City in New Hampshire (pop. 21,000). It was the first permanent settlement in New Hampshire (1633), and was a center of the industrial revolution in New England based on water power.

Dover, Treaty of Anglo-French secret treaty. On May 22, 1670, Charles II of England secretly agreed to aid French King Louis XIV in his plans for expanding French domains. In return, Louis was to provide money that would free Charles from financial dependence on Parliament. By this agreement, Louis XIV broke up the Triple Alliance *(q.v.)* against him and paved the way for the Third Dutch War *(q.v.)*.

Dow, Herbert Henry 1866–1930. American chemist. Dow patented many chemical processes, including the extraction of bromine and magnesium from brine. He founded the Dow Chemical Corporation.

Dowie, John Alexander 1847–1907. Scottish founder of what he called the Christian Catholic Church (1896). He preached faith healing and, in 1901, established Zion City in Illinois, where he ruled his followers as a benevolent despot until deposed (1905).

Dowson, Ernest Christopher 1867–1900. English poet. One of the Decadents *(q.v.)*, he is remembered for the lines, "I have been faithful to thee, Cynara, in my fashion."

Doyle, Sir Arthur Conan 1859–1930. English author who created the famous detective character Sherlock Holmes. The first Holmes book was *A Study in Scarlet* (1887); it introduced his friend, Dr. Watson, and his home on Baker Street.

Dozsa Rebellion Hungarian peasant revolt (1514). Gyorgy Dozsa led 100,000 peasants against the taxes and oppression of the nobility (1514). The revolt was crushed, the peasants condemned to servitude, and Dozsa executed.

Draco ⟨Dracon⟩ *fl.* 621 BC. Athenian lawgiver and politician. His laws were very severe, death being prescribed for most crimes. He also transferred responsibility for punishment of murder from the victim's family to the state. The adjective "draconian" refers to him.

Dracon *See* **Draco**

Draft riots Mass rioting (July 13–16, 1863) in New York City during the American Civil War (1861–65). The riots were provoked by a new and unpopular draft act for Union armies. Laborers especially resented a provision that allowed the rich to buy deferments and also feared that newly freed blacks would take their jobs. The rioters, mostly foreign-born Americans, ransacked draft stations, burned buildings, looted stores, and attacked Negroes. Police and state militia finally quelled the riots but not before some 500–1,000 people had been injured and $1.5-2 million worth of property was damaged.

Drago, Luis _See_ **Drago Doctrine**

Drago Doctrine International law proposal advanced by Luis Drago (1859–1921) at the Hague Conference (1907). It forbade the use of military force by one country to recover debts owed by another, but was not accepted.

Dragoon European soldier of the late 16th to early 20th cents. Dragoons were trained as both cavalry and foot soldiers.

Drake, Edwin Laurentine 1819–80. American oilman. He drilled the first oil-producing well in the US, at Titusville, Pennsylvania (1859).

Drake, Sir Francis 1540?–1596. English navigator and adventurer, regarded as the greatest of the Elizabethan seamen. From 1572, Drake undertook a number of raiding missions against Spanish colonies in the Americas, which made him rich and famous. On one such expedition (1577–80), to raid Spanish colonies on the Pacific coast of South America, he captured great riches and by his westward return became the first Englishman to circumnavigate the earth. In 1588 he served as vice-admiral against the Spanish Armada. His invasion of Portugal (1589) failed, and he died during a raid on the West Indies.

Drang nach Osten ⟨Drive to the East⟩ German phrase describing Germany's historic desire to expand eastward. It was last cited by A. Hitler to justify his aggression toward such countries as Poland, Czechoslovakia, and, ultimately, Russia.

Dravidians Group of people, living primarily in southern India, who speak the Dravidian language.

Drebbel, Cornelis Jacobszoon 1572–1634. Dutch inventor. He designed the first navigable submarine (1620).

Dred Scott Case US Supreme Court case (1857) involving Dred Scott, a slave taken from Missouri, a slave state, to Illinois, a free state, and then to a free territory. Scott argued that his residence in the free state and territory made him a free man. The court decided against Scott, stating that slaves had no legal standing in court, and that the Missouri Compromise _(q.v.)_ (1820) was unconstitutional.

Dreiser, Theodore 1871–1945. American novelist noted for such naturalistic novels as _Sister Carrie_ and _An American Tragedy._

Dresden, Battle of Battle (Aug. 26–27, 1813) of the Napoleonic Wars, at Dresden, now in East Germany. Napoleon's last major victory in Germany, it caused 10,000 French casualties to the allies' (Austrians, Prussians, Russians) 38,000 casualties.

Dresden, Treaty of Treaty (Dec. 25, 1745) between Austria and Prussia, ending the Second Silesian War. Frederick the Great of Prussia gained control of much of Saxony, retained much of Silesia, and acknowledged Francis I as Holy Roman Emperor.

Dresden Codex Mayan hieroglyphic text, one of the few pre-Columbian manuscripts to survive the Spanish conquest. It is kept in the state library at Dresden, East Germany.

Drew, Daniel 1797–1879. American railway speculator. A director of the Erie Railroad, he allied successfully with J. Fisk and J. Gould in the "Erie War" (1866–68) against C. Vanderbilt, but later went bankrupt in the Panic of 1873.

Dreyer, John Louis Emil 1852–1926. Danish astronomer. His _New General Catalogue of Nebulae and Clusters of Stars_ is a standard reference.

Dreyfus Affair Controversy over the French army's refusal to recognize the false conviction of Capt. A. Dreyfus for treason. The affair dominated French political life from Dreyfus' conviction (1894) to his final exoneration (1906). Dreyfus, an Alsatian of Jewish background, was convicted on the evidence of a document supposedly written by Dreyfus, offering military intelligence to the German military attaché. Later it was discovered that Major F. Esterhazy had written the document. Esterhazy was acquitted by a court-martial (1898), prompting E. Zola, a supporter of Dreyfus, to publish his open letter _J'Accuse,_ accusing the judges of acquitting Esterhazy in order to protect the army. In 1898 it was learned that another document apparently incriminating Dreyfus was in fact forged by Major Hubert Henry (1846–98), who confessed to the forgery and committed suicide. Dreyfus was retried, but, incredibly, was once again convicted. In order to settle the matter, Pres. E. Loubet pardoned Dreyfus (Sept., 1899), and in 1906 a court of appeals exonerated Dreyfus. He was reinstated in the army. The affair polarized French society for more than a decade. Traditionalists and Catholics tended to support the army, as did anti-Semites. Dreyfus gained the support of liberals such as E. Zola and G. Clemenceau. As a result of the affair, the anticlerical Radical party came to power in France.

Drive to the East _See_ **Drang nach Osten**

Droysen, Johann Gustav 1808–84. German historian and politician. He urged the unification of Germany under Prussia and wrote a 14-volume political history of Prussia.

Druids Ancient Celtic priests and teachers. Knowledge of them comes chiefly from Roman writers, notably J. Caesar.

Drury Lane Theatre London theater. The oldest English theater still in use, its original building opened in 1663. Its current building dates to 1812.

Druses ⟨Druzes⟩ Middle Eastern religious sect, whose members live largely in the mountain regions of Syria and Lebanon. They believe in the divinity of the sixth Fatimid caliph, al-Hakim (985–1021) and in his second coming. Their opposition to Christians, notably the Maronites, in the 19th cent. brought French intervention in the region.

Drusus Caesar d. AD 23. Roman soldier. The son and heir of Roman emperor Tiberius, he suppressed a serious mutiny in Pannonia (AD 14). He was poisoned by his wife Livilla and her lover Sejanus, the emperor's favorite.

Drusus, Marcus Livius d. 109? BC. Roman politician. Made tribune (122 BC) with C. Gracchus, he successfully undermined the liberal reforms sought by Gracchus by proposing, but failing to implement, even more liberal reforms.

Drusus, Marcus Livius d. 91 BC. Roman politician, son of the elder M. Drusus. Made tribune (91 BC), he attempted to introduce reforms but was assassinated.

Drusus Germanicus, Nero Claudius 38–9 BC. Roman soldier. The brother of Roman emperor Tiberius and father of the emperor Claudius, he was acclaimed for his successful campaigns in Germany.

Druzes See **Druses**

Dryden, John 1631–1700. English poet, dramatist, and critic. He first gained recognition (1659) with *Heroic Stanzas*, and in 1668 became poet laureate. His conversion to Catholicism (1685) and the accession (1688) of the Protestant monarchy under William and Mary, ultimately cost him the laureateship. Among his poems are *Religio Laici, The Hind and the Panther*, and *Alexander's Feast*. His many dramatic works include *All for Love, Absalom and Achitophel*, and *Marriage à la Mode*.

dualism In philosophy and religion, the division of the world into two separate components such as mind and matter in Cartesianism, and good and evil in religion and some systems of ethics.

Dual Monarchy ⟨Austro-Hungarian Monarchy⟩ System established (1867) by the Ausgleich (*q.v.*), whereby the Austrian Empire was divided into Austrian and Hungarian kingdoms. The two states were united in the person of the Austro-Hungarian king, who ruled through ministries in Austria and Hungary. Ministries of war, foreign affairs, and finance were combined, however. The system was largely worked out by F. Deak, and in accordance with it Austrian emperor Francis Joseph was crowned king of Hungary on June 8, 1867.

Duane, James 1733–97. American politician. As a member of the Continental Congress (1774–83), he helped draft the Articles of Confederation.

Duarte 1391–1438. Portuguese king (1433–38), successor to his father, John I, and father of Alfonso V. Called the "philosopher king," he is noted chiefly for his aid to and encouragement of his brother, Henry the Navigator.

Du Barry, Marie Jeanne Bécu, countess 1743–93. French mistress of King Louis XV. Though not greatly involved politically, she held a position of influence in Louis' court. She was guillotined during the French Revolution.

Dubček, Alexander 1921—. Czechoslovakian political leader whose liberal reforms led to the Soviet-sponsored invasion of Czechoslovakia (1968). Dubček fought with the Slovakian Resistance forces against the Germans in WW II. After the war he rose through Communist party ranks and in Oct., 1967, became first secretary of the party. His subsequent easing of censorship, rehabilitation of political prisoners, and program of democratization alarmed the Soviet Union, which with other Warsaw Pact countries invaded Czechoslovakia (Aug. 20–21, 1968). Dubček was forced to make political concessions to the Soviets and his reform program was gradually dismantled. Dubček became (Jan., 1970) ambassador to Turkey, and soon after disappeared from the political scene.

Dublin Capital city (pop. 566,000) of the Republic of Ireland. Captured by the Danes (9th cent.), it was conquered by the English in 1171. It was the scene of many struggles for Irish independence, notably the 1803 uprising led by R. Emmet and the Easter Rebellion of 1916.

Du Bois, William Edward Burghardt 1868–1963. American writer, educator, and civil rights leader. He was a founder (1909) of the National Association for the Advancement of Colored People (NAACP).

Ducas Byzantine family name. The dynasty included Emperor Constantine X (reigned 1059–67), Michael VII (reigned 1071–78), and Alexius V (reigned 1204).

Duccio di Buoninsegna 1255?–1319? Italian artist. He founded the Sienese school of art. His major work is the *Maesta* altarpiece in the Siena Cathedral.

Duchamp, Marcel 1887–1968. French-born American artist. A founder of Dada, he was also associated with cubism and other art movements of the 20th cent. He is known best for the cubist *Nude Descending a Staircase.*

Duchesne, André 1584–1640. French historian noted for his compilations of the sources of French and Norman histories.

Dudley, John, duke of Northumbria *See* **Edward VI**

Dudley, Thomas 1576–1653. Colonial governor of Massachusetts (1634–35, 1640–41, 1645–46, 1650–51). His strict orthodoxy led to conflict with other Puritan leaders, notably J. Winthrop.

Duer, William 1747–99. American Revolutionary leader and financier. He served in the Continental Congress (1777–79) and as assistant secretary of the Treasury (1789) under A. Hamilton. His imprisonment (1792) for debt is said to have contributed to the financial panic of 1792.

Dufay, Guillaume c1400–74. Flemish composer, the leading Burgundian composer of his day. He is noted for his innovations in four-part music and musical notation, and use of counterpoint.

Dufour, Guillaume Henri 1787–1875. Swiss general. He served in the French army under Napoleon, and later led Swiss forces against the Sonderbund (1847). He helped to found the Red Cross.

Dufy, Raoul 1877–1953. French artist. Associated for a time with the fauvists, he developed his own personal style, produced many fabric designs, and illustrated books for such writers as G. Apollinaire and A. Gide.

Du Gange, Charles du Fresne, Sieur 1610–88. French scholar known for his medieval Greek and Latin dictionaries, *Glossarium ad Scriptores Mediae et Infimae Latinitatis* and *Graecitatis.*

Du Guesclin, Bertrand c1320–1380. French soldier and constable of France, called the "eagle of Brittany" for his daring exploits against English forces during the Hundred Years' War while in the service of French kings John II, Charles V, and Henry II.

Duhamel, Georges 1884–1966. French author. His background as a surgeon was reflected in his novels *Vie des Martyrs* and *Civilisation.*

Dukas, Paul 1865–1935. French composer. His best-known work is *The Sorcerer's Apprentice.*

Dukhobors ⟨Doukhobors⟩ ⟨Christian Community of Universal Brotherhood⟩ ⟨*since 1939,* Union of Spiritual Communities of Christ⟩ Religious sect that originated in southern Russia during the 18th cent. Made up largely of peasants, the sect refused to recognize the authority of church or state and believed in individual revelation. They developed flourishing communes in the 19th cent. but were several times forcibly moved eastward in conflicts with the czarist government. Some 7,000 Dukhobors were allowed to emigrate (1898–99) to western Canada, where their eccentric beliefs (including refusal to pay taxes) caused sporadic conflicts with government authority.

Dulles, John Foster 1888–1959. US secretary of state (1953–59). A prominent international lawyer and diplomat, he was appointed secretary of state by President D. Eisenhower. Thereafter he promoted, and was identified with, America's Cold War policies. He was a proponent of collective security agreements (Southeast Asia Treaty Organization) and massive nuclear retaliation to counter the threat of communism. He also backed the National Chinese and helped formulate the Eisenhower Doctrine.

Duluth, Daniel Greysolon, Sieur ⟨Du Lhut, Daniel Greysolon, Sieur⟩ 1636–1710. French explorer in North America. He explored the Lake Superior region (1678) and northern Minnesota (1680), where the city of Duluth is named for him.

Duma Russian legislative body. Created by Czar Nicholas II after the 1905 revolution, the Duma served as the lower house of the Russian legislature until the revolution of 1917. Nicholas dissolved it several times. (*See also* Union of Soviet Socialist Republics [1905–17].)

Dumas, Alexandre ⟨Dumas père⟩ 1802–70. French novelist and dramatist, author of such popular historical novels as *The Three Musketeers* and *The Count of Monte Cristo.* A clerk in Paris in his early years, he first gained recognition (1829) with his historical plays, including *Henri III,* but it was his novels that won him enduring fame. From the 1840s on, he wrote voluminously and produced (frequently in collaboration with others) his most famous works.

Dumas, Alexandre ⟨Dumas fils⟩ 1824–95. French novelist and dramatist, the illegitimate son of Alexandre Dumas père. He was the author of *La Dame aux Camélias,* which was dramatized as *Camille.*

Du Maurier, Daphne 1907–. English author. Her novels include *Rebecca, Frenchman's Creek,* and *My Cousin Rachel.*

Dumouriez, Charles François 1739–1823. French general during the French Revolutionary Wars (1792–1802). At first successful against Prussia and Austria, he joined Austria after his defeat at Neerwinden (1793).

Dunant, Jean Henry 1828–1910. Swiss philanthropist, the moving force behind the establishment (1864) of the Red Cross. He was corecipient of the first Nobel Peace Prize (1901).

Duncan, Isadora 1878–1927. American dancer whose interpretive dancing and unconventional personal life greatly influenced the development of modern dance.

Dundee, John Graham of Claverhouse, 1st Viscount c1649–1689. Scottish soldier, known as Bonnie Dundee. He led his forces against William of Orange in an attempt to restore James II to the throne, but was killed at Killiecrankie.

Dunes, Battle of the Battle (June 14, 1658) of the Fronde, near Dunkirk, now in France. The Spanish army under Don John of Austria and Louis II de Conde was decisively defeated by the French under Vicomte H. de Turenne.

Dunkards ⟨Church of the Brethren⟩ ⟨Dunkers⟩ ⟨Tunkers⟩ German Baptist sect, so called for their baptismal practice of immersion. Originating in Germany (1708), they were forced by persecution to move to America (1719).

Dunkirk Seaport on northern coast of France near the Belgian border. It was the site of the heroic evacuation (May 29–June 4, 1940) of some 340,000 British and French troops trapped by the advancing Germans early in WW II. The two-pronged German invasion of Belgium (May) encircled the British and French divisions by May 20 and an attempted Allied breakout to the south (May 21–23) was defeated. With the Germans closing in and their only escape being to cross the English Channel, the British organized (May 29) what became a makeshift armada of transports and civilian craft, and every available boat was pressed into service. The success of the evacuation was in large part due to the Royal Air Force, which provided air cover for the evacuation. Though the evacuation proved a remarkable feat, huge stores of heavy equipment and material had to be left behind.

Dunois, Jean, comte de c1403–68. French general, natural son of Louis, duke of Orléans. During the Hundred Years' War, he served the Dauphin (later Charles VII), defended Orléans until relieved by Joan of Arc (1429), and helped to capture Paris (1436).

Duns Scotus, John d. 1308. Scottish philosopher and theologian. He founded Scotism, a school of scholasticism frequently opposed to the speculative theology of T. Aquinas.

Dupin, Amandine Aurore Lucie *See* **Sand, George**

Dupleix, Joseph François, Marquis 1697–1763. French colonial administrator. As governor of French India (1742–54), he sought to establish French supremacy in India but was thwarted by the English under R. Clive.

Duplessis, Maurice Le Noblet 1890–1959. Canadian politician. He was a founder of the Union Nationale party, which advocated French-Canadian autonomy. He was attorney general and premier of Quebec (1936–39, 1944–59).

Du Pont, Éleuthère Irénée 1771–1834. American industrialist. His gunpowder plant, built (1802) near Wilmington, Delaware, was the foundation for the E. I. Du Pont de Nemours & Co. industrial complex.

Du Pont, Pierre Samuel 1870–1954. American industrialist. He was a director of E. I. Du Pont de Nemours & Co., established by his great-grandfather, E. I. Du Pont.

Du Pont, Samuel Francis 1803–65. American naval officer. He commanded the South Atlantic fleet of the federal blockade against the South during the Civil War but was relieved of command after the Union defeat at Charleston, South Carolina (1863).

Du Pont de Nemours, Pierre Samuel 1739–1817. French economist. An adviser in the treaty negotiations following the American Revolution (1783), he participated in the French Revolution but was forced to flee (1799) to the US.

Dupplin Moor, Battle of Battle (Aug. 12, 1332) of the Scottish Civil War. Edward de Baliol, claimant to the Scottish throne, defeated Donald, earl of Mar, regent for Scottish king David II. Baliol was soon after crowned king of Scotland.

Durand, Asher Brown 1796–1886. American painter and engraver. A founder of the Hudson River school, he is noted for his engraving of J. Trumbull's painting *Signing of the Declaration of Independence*.

Durand Line Boundary line established (Nov. 12, 1893) to divide Afghanistan from British territories in India. It later became the border between Afghanistan and Pakistan.

Durant, Ariel *See* **Durant, Will**

Durant, Will ⟨~, William James⟩ 1885–1981. American philosopher and historian. With his wife Ariel (1898–1981) he wrote the 11-volume *The Story of Civilization*.

Durant, William Crapo 1861–1947. American industrialist. He founded General Motors (1908) and the Chevrolet Motor Company (1911), the latter with Louis Chevrolet (1879–1941).

Durban City (pop. 851,000) and leading seaport of the Republic of South Africa. Founded in 1824, it was named (1835) for Sir Benjamin D'Urban (1777–1849), then governor of Cape Colony.

D'Urban, Sir Benjamin *See* **Durban**

Dürer, Albrecht 1471–1528. German artist, considered one of the great artists of the German Renaissance. He adapted styles of the Italian Renaissance painters and was noted for his use of classical forms and for his technical mastery. He was famed for his woodcuts and engravings as well. Among Dürer's famous works are: the paintings *Adam and Eve* and *Four Apostles;* the altarpieces *Feast of the Rose Garlands* and *Adoration of the Trinity;* the copper engravings *Knight, Death and Devil* and *St. Jerome in His Study;* and the woodcuts *Apocalypse* and *Passion of Christ* (two cycles).

Durham, John George Lampton, 1st earl of 1792–1840. British statesman. As governor general of Canada (1838) he assumed near-dictatorial powers in dealing with French-Canadian resistance in Lower Canada. He was nominal author of the *Report on the Affairs of British North America.*

Durkheim, Émile 1858–1917. French sociologist, considered a founder of modern sociology. His works include *The Division of Labor in Society.*

Dürnkrut, Battle of *See* **Marchfeld, Battle of**

Durrell, Lawrence George 1912–. British writer, known best for his tetralogy of novels *The Alexandria Quartet.*

Duryea, Charles Edgar 1862–1938. American inventor and manufacturer. Duryea built one of the first successful automobiles (1892) and introduced the spray carburetor and pneumatic tires.

Düsseldorf West German city (pop. 607,600). A major river port and industrial center, it was heavily damaged in WW II. Its art academy was the center of the 19th-cent. Düsseldorf school of art.

Dutch Wars Three wars (1652–54, 1664–67, 1672–78) conducted principally by England and France against the United Provinces (later The Netherlands). The cause of the first two wars was the trade rivalry between England and the Dutch. The third war was the result of the expansionist aims of French king Louis XIV and ultimately involved several European powers. The war ended with the United Provinces intact and the acquisition of territories from Spain and others. Key dates include:

1652–54 First Dutch War.

1651 Navigation Act passed by English Parliament to curtail Dutch trade with English colonies; led to outbreak of war.

1652 English fleet under R. Blake engaged the Dutch (May), marking the opening of the first Dutch War.

1652 Dutch defeated the English at Dungeness (Nov.), thereby gaining control of the English Channel.

1653 Dutch concluded (Jan.) treaty with Denmark, effectively ending English trade in the region.

1653 English fleet victorious over the Dutch at Portland (Feb.); Dutch fleet withdrew.

1653 English defeated the Dutch at Gabbard's Shoal (June) and began blockade of Dutch ports.

1653 Dutch Admiral Maarten Tromp attempted unsuccessfully to break English blockade off Texel (July 31) and was killed.

1654 Treaty of Westminster signed (Apr.) between England and the United Provinces, thus ending the first Dutch War; England won favorable terms, including payment for losses.

1664–67 Second Dutch War.

1664 English attacked Dutch possessions in Africa and the North American colony of New Netherland, thus opening hostilities of the second Dutch War.

1665 England declared war on the United Provinces (Mar.).

1665 English forces defeated the Dutch at battle of Lowestoft (June).

1666 French declared war on England (Jan.) but made little effort to support the Dutch.

1666 Dutch were victorious over the English fleet at the Battle of the Downs (June 1–4).

1666 English fleet victorious over the Dutch (Aug.); began to sink Dutch merchant shipping.

1667 Dutch destroyed English fleet docked on Thames River (June); followed outbreak of plague (1665) and Great Fire of London (1666).

1667 Treaty of Breda signed (July 31), ending the second Dutch War; provisions largely favorable to the Dutch, but the English gained the colonies of New Netherland.

1672–78 Third Dutch War.

1670 Treaty of Dover concluded between English king Charles II and French king Louis XIV, thus preparing the way for third Dutch War.

1672 France invaded the United Provinces (May) from the south, opening hostilities of the third Dutch War.

1672 Dutch opened the dikes at Amsterdam, flooding the region and halting French advance.

1672 Dutch fleet victorious over the English and French at Battle of Southwold Bay.

1672 William of Orange became leader of the United Provinces after an uprising against the government.

1673 Spain, the Holy Roman Empire, and Lorraine joined the war against France (and its ally Sweden); French driven out of the United Provinces by year's end.

1674 England ceased hostilities against the Dutch; France continued the war and gained several victories.

1675 France recovered Alsace region by Marshal Turenne's victory at the Battle of Turckheim (Jan. 5).

1675 Swedes defeated in the Battle of Fehrbellin (June 28).

1675 Austrians defeated French at the battles of Sasbach and Altenheim, near the Rhine (July 27–Aug. 1); French Marshal Turenne killed. French retreated across the Rhine.

1676 Dutch and Spanish fleets defeated in battles in the Mediterranean.

1678 French captured Ghent and Ypres.

1678–79 Treaties of Nijmegen signed, ending the war; terms generally favorable to France; United Provinces gained back all its territory.

Dust Bowl US region in the southern Great Plains famous during the Great Depression. Once a fertile prairie region, the area was ravaged in the early 1930s by great dust storms that stripped off the topsoil and made farming impossible. Brought on by a combination of severe drought, poor farming practices, and the prevailing high winds in the region, the dust storms forced thousands of farmers in parts of Kansas, Oklahoma, Texas, New Mexico, and Colorado to desert their farms. Conservation measures have since greatly reduced the area susceptible to dust storms.

Dutch East India Company Dutch colonial trading company (1602–1798) that advanced and protected Dutch commercial and colonial interests from the Cape of Good Hope to the Strait of Magellan.

Dutch Guiana *See* **Surinam**

Dutch West India Company Dutch colonial trading organization (1621–1791). It fought the Portuguese for Brazil but was driven out (1654). It was driven from New Netherland (modern New York–New Jersey) by the English (1664). Reorganized (1674), it was never successful.

Dutra, Eurico Gaspar 1885–1974. Brazilian soldier and statesman. As president (1946–51), he restored Brazil to a constitutional democracy, and improved relations with the US.

Duvalier, François ⟨Papa Doc⟩ 1907–1971. Haitian dictator. Elected president (1957), he declared himself president for life (1964), and suppressed all opposition through terrorism.

Dvaravati Ancient kingdom which flourished from the 6th-13th cents. AD in what now is Thailand. It was instrumental in spreading Indian culture and influence throughout Southeast Asia.

Dvořák, Anton 1841–1904. Czech composer noted for his use of Slavic folk material in his compositions. He is known best for his symphony *From the New World.*

Dyarchy ⟨Diarchy⟩ Governmental system introduced by the British to India (1919). It gave control of certain portions of the government to local officials while keeping major control in British hands. It sought to develop India's capacity for self-rule by stages.

Dyrrhachium, Battle of Setback for J. Caesar (48 BC) during his campaign against Pompey. Caesar met a far superior army under Pompey at Dyrrhachium, in what is now Albania. After waiting some months for reinforcements, battle was joined and Caesar was defeated, at a cost of 1,000 men.

E

Ea *See* **Anu**

Eadgar *See* **Edgar**

Eakins, Thomas 1844–1916. American artist, one of the great artists of the 19th cent. His works are in the realistic style and include the *Clinic of Dr. Gross.*

Earhart, Amelia 1898–1937. Noted American aviator, first woman to fly solo across the Atlantic (1932) and first person to fly solo from Hawaii to California (1935). Her disappearance in an apparent crash somewhere over the Pacific (1937) remains a mystery.

earl British title of nobility. The oldest English noble rank, it dates from the reign of Danish king Canute. It is hereditary and ranks below duke and marquess. It corresponds in rank to a count.

Early, Jubal Anderson 1816–94. Confederate general in the American Civil War. He led the southern forces in the Shenandoah Valley (1864–65) and almost reached Washington, D.C. His eventual defeat by Gen. P. Sheridan resulted in his loss of the command and cleared the way for the Union drive toward Richmond.

East Africa Geographical area comprising the modern countries of Uganda, Kenya, and Tanzania. (Ethiopia and Somalia, and, farther south, Mozambique, are sometimes also included.) The name came into use before WW II to designate the Uganda protectorate, the Kenya colony and protectorate, and the Tanganyika territory, all under British administration.

East Anglia Early English kingdom, located in what are now Norfolk and Suffolk counties. It was one of the kingdoms of the Anglo-Saxon heptarchy *(q.v.)* and its first known king was Raedwald (6th cent.). It was conquered by the Anglo-Saxon kingdom of Mercia (7th cent.) and passed to the Danish conquerors in 878.

Easter Island Chilean island in the eastern Pacific, noted for the gigantic carved stone statues found there. Since the island was discovered (1772), numerous theories have been developed concerning the origins of the statues.

Eastern Chin *See* **Chin**

Eastern Empire *See* **Roman Empire; Byzantine Empire**

Eastern Orthodox church *See* **Orthodox Eastern church**

Eastern Question Broad term referring to the series of international conflicts and crises (19th–20th cents.) brought on by the breakup of the Ottoman Empire. Control of the Eastern European territories of the Ottoman Empire was of key importance to various European powers, notably Russia, whose interest in the region dated from the late 16th cent. In the 19th cent., competing interests and growing instability of the region led to a series of shifting alliances among European powers to take over or prevent the takeover of various parts of the region. At various times the countries involved included Russia, Austria, Prussia, Britain, France, and, later, Germany. The crises were numerous and included the Russo-Turkish Wars, the War of Greek Independence, the Crimean War, the Bosnian Rebellion, the Bosnian Crisis, and the Balkan Wars. The Eastern Question ended with WW I and the collapse of the Ottoman Empire, although the region remained unstable.

Eastern Roman Empire *See* **Roman Empire; Byzantine Empire**

Eastern Solomons, Battle of Naval battle (Aug. 23–25, 1942) in which the Americans defeated the Japanese during WW II. It was part of the battle for Guadalcanal *(q.v.).*

Easter Rebellion Revolt in Ireland (Apr. 24–May 1, 1915) against British rule. Led by P. Pearse, the rebellion broke out in Dublin, spread to other parts of Ireland, and was suppressed only after bitter fighting in the streets. The subsequent execution of Pearse and others helped bring down the H. Asquith government and paved the way for creation of the Irish Free State *(q.v.).*

East Goths *See* **Ostrogoths**

East India Act *See* **British East India Company**

East India Company, British *See* **British East India Company**

East India Company, French. *See* **French East India Company**

East Indies In modern usage, the islands of the Malay Archipelago, including Indonesia, Borneo, Sumatra, and New Guinea. In early colonial times it referred to India.

Eastman, George 1854–1932. American inventor and industrialist. He developed a process for making photographic dry plates (1880), produced the Kodak camera (1888), and founded the Eastman Kodak Company.

East Pakistan *See* **Bangladesh**

East Prussia Historic region in Eastern Europe and the homeland of the Prussians. It was conquered by the Teutonic Knights (13th cent.), accepted Polish suzerainty (16th cent.), and became part of the independent kingdom of Prussia *(q.v.)* in 1701.

Eaton, John Henry 1790–1856. American politician. He was a senator (1818–29) and secretary of war (1829–31) under President A. Jackson. The refusal by Washington society to accept his second wife led to the Eaton affair and his resignation.

Eaton, Theophilus 1590–1658. American Colonial governor. He was a founder of New Haven colony and its first governor (1639–58). He also drafted a code of laws for the colony (1656).

Eaton, William 1764–1811. US army officer. During the Tripolitan War (1801–05), he led a small American-backed force that sought to end the war by restoring Pasha Hamet to power. The war ended before the scheme could be completed.

Eaton affair Incident in which US secretary of war J. Eaton was forced to resign (1831) because Washington society refused to accept his new wife, Margaret O'Neale Eaton (1799–1879). The recent widow of a local innkeeper, she married Eaton (1828) shortly before he became secretary of war. Washington socialites, led by Vice-President J. Calhoun's wife, snubbed Mrs. Eaton. Though Eaton had President A. Jackson's support, he eventually resigned.

Eban, Abba Solomon 1915–. Israeli statesman. Eban was Israel's first UN representative and first ambassador to the US. He was foreign minister (1966–74) under Prime Minister G. Meir.

Ebert, Friedrich 1871–1925. German politician. As first president of the German republic (1919–25), he worked for acceptance of the Weimar constitution and put down uprisings (1919, 1920) from the left (Spartacus party) and right (Kapp Putsch).

Éboli, Ana de Mendoza de la Cerda, princesa de 1540–92. Spanish noblewoman and mistress of King Philip II. She was involved in court intrigues and is a character in J. Schiller's *Don Carlos.*

ecclesiastical courts Courts established by the church to judge and punish offenses against religious or canon law. During the Middle Ages, these courts came to rival the imperial or royal courts, since they had jurisdiction over all clerics; over wills; over all sacramental matters, which, by extension, included marriages, separation, legitimacy, etc.; and over widows, orphans, and other wards of the church. It was this broad responsibility of the ecclesiastical courts that made possible establishment of the Inquisition *(q.v.).* The power of the courts declined after the Reformation.

Echo In Greek mythology, a mountain nymph. Angered by Echo's chattering, the goddess Hera took away her power to speak and allowed her only the ability to repeat what others said. Rebuffed later by Narcissus, Echo pined away until only her voice remained.

Eck, Johann Maier von 1486–1543. German Roman Catholic theologian, an opponent of M. Luther and the Lutheran reform movement. He was instrumental in having Luther excommunicated (1520).

Eckehart, Meister *See* **Eckhart, Meister**

Eckhart, Meister ⟨Eckehart, ∼ ⟩ *c*1260–*c*1328. German Dominican mystic, founder of German mysticism. Though he was accused of heresy (1327) and his teachings were condemned by Pope John XXII (1329), he nevertheless influenced later religious and philosophical movements.

Eckhout, Gerbrand van den *See* **Eeckhout, Gerbrand van den**

eclecticism Philosophical doctrine that advocates the taking of usable elements from various philosophical systems, without concern for contradictions between the systems. Eclecticism arose among Greek philosophers as early as the 2d cent. BC. Cicero was among its most famous practitioners.

Ecuador Republic located on the west coast of South America. Its capital is Quito. The country has a history of political instability and has had nearly 50 presidents since it gained independence in the 19th cent. There has been a long-standing rivalry between Ecuador's two principal cities, Quito in the highlands and Guayaquil on the coast. Quito is the traditional center of the conservative faction, which favors landowners and the church. Guayaquil is home of the liberals and radical revolutionaries. Key events in the history of Ecuador include:

    1000 Indian kingdom of Quito formed; later absorbed into the Inca Empire of Peru.

1532 Spanish conquistador F. Pizarro conquered region.

1534 Spanish conquistador P. de Alvarado attempted unsuccessfully to conquer Ecuador, as discord among Spanish broke out.

1540 Pizarro's brother, Gonzalo, rebelled against Spain, ruled independently for nine years.

1548 Spanish forces reconquered the territory; executed Gonzalo Pizarro.

1563 Became a presidency (administrative district) of the Viceroyalty of Peru.

1809 First unsuccessful revolt against Spain.

1822 Rebel commander A. Sucre decisively defeated Spanish forces at the Battle of Pichincha; Ecuador gained independence; region made part of S. Bolívar's Great Colombia.

1830 Ecuador became an independent state after the breakup of Great Colombia.

1830–35 Juan José Flores, a conservative, in office as president; civil war broke out between liberals and conservatives (1833).

1832 War with Colombia; Ecuador failed to gain Colombian border territories it sought; border disputes with Colombia and Peru persisted for more than a century after.

1895 Revolution of 1895; conservatives ousted and liberals began long period of control of government; many liberal reforms enacted.

1907–11 Liberal constitutional reforms made during the second presidency of Eloy Alfaro, (1907–11).

1925 Military takeover; inaugurated a series of regimes headed by rival military juntas; 12 presidents were in office between 1931 and 1940.

1941 Border war with Peru; dispute resolved by arbitration; Peru awarded most of the territory by treaty (1944).

1944 Revolution in Guayaquil returned to office Dr. José María Velasco Ibarra (who had been deposed as president by the military in 1935); he remained in office until 1947.

1945 Ecuador joined the UN.

1948 Galo Plaza Lasso, a former ambassador to the US, elected in free elections to the presidency; remained in office to 1952.

1956–60 Camilo Ponce Enriquez in office as president; first conservative in power in over half century.

1960 Ecuador repudiated treaty (made in 1944) awarding Peru border territory.

1966 Military junta removed from power; civilian government to be installed.

1968–72 Velasco Ibarra in office as president; his fifth time in office (from 1934).

1970 President Velasco Ibarra assumed dicta-

torial powers amid prolonged fighting between students and police.

1970s Ecuador claimed 200-mile limit on its territorial waters; seized several US fishing boats; US cut off aid.

1972 President Velasco Ibarra deposed by military to prevent holding of elections scheduled for June (Feb. 15).

1975 Right-wing military coup attempt crushed (Sept. 1).

1978 New constitution restored civilian government.

1979–81 Jaime Roldós Aguilera in office as president.

1981 Two-month border war with Peru broke out (Jan. 28).

1981 US tuna boat seized for violating Ecuador's claimed 200-mile territorial limit; it was released after one month.

1981 Osvaldo Hurtado Larrea in office as president after President Aguilera was killed in a plane crash (May 24).

ecumenical council In the Roman Catholic church, a general council called by the pope (before 1123, called by the emperor) to decide doctrinal questions and other church matters. The council's decisions must be approved by the pope before the council is considered ecumenical and its findings become binding. Of the 21 councils recognized by the Roman Catholic church as ecumenical, the Orthodox Eastern church recognizes only seven of the councils (excluding the Fourth Council of Constantinople) held before the schism of 1054. The ecumenical councils are the councils of:

1. Nicaea, First (AD 325)
2. Constantinople, First (AD 381)
3. Ephesus (AD 431)
4. Chalcedon (AD 451)
5. Constantinople, Second (553)
6. Constantinople, Third (680–681)
7. Nicaea, Second (787)
8. Constantinople, Fourth (869–870)
9. Lateran, First (1123)
10. Lateran, Second (1139)
11. Lateran, Third (1179)
12. Lateran, Fourth (1215)
13. Lyons, First (1245)
14. Lyons, Second (1274)
15. Vienne (1311–12)
16. Constance (1414–18)
17. Basel & Ferrara-Florence (1431–45)
18. Lateran, Fifth (1512–17)
19. Trent (1545–63)
20. Vatican, First (1869–70)
21. Vatican, Second (1962–65)

ecumenical movement Movement seeking the unification of all the Protestant churches in the world and, eventually, the unification of all Christians. Its origins date to the 19th cent. and the formation of such groups as the Evangelical Alliance (1846). The movement became international with the establishment of the World Missionary Conference (1910), and gained momentum with the founding of the International Missionary Council (1921) and the Universal Christian Conference on Life and Work (1925). The leading force for ecumenism today is the World Council of Churches, which held its first assembly in 1948 and merged (1961) with the International Missionary Council. In the US, a number of Protestant groups have merged to form the United Church of Christ. Further dialogue among Christian churches, aimed at final reunification, was encouraged by the Second Vatican Council.

edda Ancient Icelandic literary works (13th cent.) in two parts. The *Prose Edda*, by Snorri Sturluson, is a textbook of Icelandic poetry. The *Poetic Edda* is a valuable collection of poems giving the text of Scandinavian myths.

Eddy, Mary Baker 1821–1910. American religious leader and founder of the Christian Science church *(q.v.)*. She wrote *Science and Health with Key to the Scriptures* and the *Church Manual* and founded the *Christian Science Monitor* (1908).

Eden, Garden of   *See* **Garden of Eden**

Eden, Robert Anthony 1897–. British statesman. He was prime minister (1955–57), but was forced to resign after he ordered military intervention in the Suez Canal crisis (1956).

Edgar ⟨Eadgar⟩ 943?–975. King of the English (959–975), son of Edmund I. He supported reforms of the English monasteries which brought about a return to strict observance of the Benedictine rule. He was formally crowned king (973, at Bath) in the first coronation for a king of all England.

Edgar Atheling 1050?–1130? English prince, grandson of Edmund Ironside. Chosen king after the defeat of King Harold at the Battle of Hastings, he was forced to submit to William the Conqueror (1066). After taking part in unsuccessful rebellions, he made peace (1074) with William.

Edict of Emancipation Edict issued in Russia (Mar. 3, 1861) by Alexander II, freeing the serfs. By its terms, serfs (about one-third of the Russian population) were granted personal freedom and rights to an allotment of land, to be paid for over a 49-year period. Failure of this land-allotment system helped foment the Russian Revolution. The author of the edict is believed to have been Vasily Drosodov Philaret (c1782–1867), long an advocate of the abolition of serfdom.

Edict of January   *See* **L'Hôpital, Michel de**

Edict of Milan Decree (AD 313) that granted religious toleration of Christians within the Roman Empire. Issued by Constantine, emperor of the West, and Licinius, emperor of the East, it established a lasting policy of toleration within the empire. It also ordered restoration of property confiscated from Christians.

Edict of Nantes Declaration of religious toleration in France (Apr. 13, 1598) at the close of the Wars of Religion. King Henry IV attempted to restore peace between the Protestant Huguenots and Catholics by granting Protestants greater freedom. By the edict, Huguenots were allowed the same civil and social rights as Catholics, though they were not allowed to hold religious services in Paris. The edict was denounced by the Catholics. The eventual revocation of the Edict of Nantes by Louis XIV (Oct. 18, 1685) stripped Protestants of all rights and resulted in a mass emigration of Protestants to other European countries and to America.

Edinburgh Capital city of Scotland (pop. 463,900). The city was chartered (1329) by Robert I (the Bruce) and became capital of Scotland (1436). It lost prestige when King James of Scotland succeeded (1603) to the English throne as James I and when, by the Act of Union (1707), the Scottish national government was dissolved. The city later flourished as a cultural center (18th–19th cents.).

Edinburgh, Philip Mountbatten, duke of 1921–. Consort of British queen Elizabeth II. They were married Nov. 20, 1947, and he was made a prince in 1957.

Edinburgh, Treaty of Treaty (July 6, 1560) between England, France, and Scotland, signed to ease the strife between Protestants and Catholics in Scotland. It provided for a withdrawal from Scotland of both French troops (supporting the Catholics) and English troops (supporting the Protestants).

Edington, Battle of Battle (878) in which Alfred the Great, Anglo-Saxon king of Wessex, decisively defeated the invading Danes. Wessex thus remained the only Anglo-Saxon kingdom to resist the Danes successfully and became the center from which the Anglo-Saxon kings would reconquer England (10th cent.).

Edirne   *See* **Adrianople**

Edison, Thomas Alva 1847–1931. Famous American inventor, one of the great inventors of the modern world. An industrious youth, with no formal education, he eventually held over 1,000 US patents. Among his many important inventions were the first practical phonograph (1877), the electric light bulb (1878), a complete system to supply and distribute electricity, an improved storage battery, the mimeograph, and the Kinetoscope. His discovery of the Edison effect led to the creation of the electron tube. The many companies Edison formed eventually became the General Electric Company.

Edmund, Saint 1170?–1240. English archbishop of Canterbury (1233–40). Involved in struggles with King Henry III, he managed to force concessions and reforms from Henry for a time. Ultimately, however, Henry prevailed, and Edmund resigned as archbishop (1240).

Edmund Ironside d. 1016. King of the English (1016), successor to his father, Ethelred the Unready. After his father's death, he led the resistance against the invading Danes under King Canute. Edmund was killed at the Battle of Assandun (1016).

Edo See **Tokyo**

Edom Biblical region, between the Dead Sea and the Gulf of Aqaba in what is now Jordan. It was inhabited by the descendants of Esau.

Edrisi See **Idrisi**

Edward I 1239–1307. English king (1272–1307), successor to his father, Henry III. He consolidated the power of the crown at the expense of the barons and the clergy, annexed Wales, and engaged in wars for control of Gascony and Scotland. Crowned (1274) after his return from the Ninth Crusade, he conquered and annexed Wales by the Statute of Wales (1284). From 1290 until his death, he was involved in wars to control Scotland (against J. de Baliol, W. Wallace, and Robert Bruce). He established (1303) English claims to Gascony by a treaty with Philip IV. By various statutes, he limited the authority of church courts to clerical matters, and, by the Statutes of Westminster (1275–90), he limited the power of the feudal lords. He also convened (1295) the Model Parliament.

Edward II 1284–1327. King of England (1307–27), successor to his father, Edward I. He was a weak ruler whose favorites (notably P. Gaveston) angered the barons, and he was defeated in wars for control of Scotland by Robert Bruce at the Battle of Bannockburn (1314). His wife, Isabella, with R. de Mortimer, deposed him.

Edward III 1312–77. English king (1327–77), successor to his father, Edward II. He usurped (1330) the regency controlled by his mother and R. de Mortimer, 1st earl of March, and began the long series of wars with France known as the Hundred Years' War (1337–1453). He also engaged in indecisive wars against Scotland. His reign saw the rising power of the Commons in Parliament,

the ravages of the Black Plague (1348–49, 1362, 1369), the resultant labor shortages that helped end serfdom, and enactment of laws to curb papal authority over the English church.

Edward IV 1442–83. King of England (1461–70, 1471–83), successor to Henry VI. He led the Yorkist party against the Lancastrians in the Wars of the Roses (1455–85), and, after being forced to flee England (1470), returned to depose Henry VI. Both Henry and the Lancastrian leader R. Neville, earl of Warwick, were put to death.

Edward V 1470–83. King of England (1483), successor to his father, Edward IV. He was arrested and believed murdered by his uncle, the duke of Gloucester. The duke thereupon succeeded him as Richard III.

Edward VI 1537–53. English king (1547–53), successor to his father, Henry VIII. Administration was left to his regents, E. Seymour and John Dudley (1532?–88), duke of Northumbria, who ousted Seymour in 1549. During Edward's reign, Protestant reforms were introduced to the newly created Church of England by publication of the Forty-Nine Articles (1553) and the first Book of Common Prayer (1549). Dudley arranged for Edward to name Lady J. Grey to succeed him.

Edward VII 1841–1910. English king (1901–10), successor to his mother, Queen Victoria. As king he promoted Anglo-French relations (1904).

Edward VIII 1894–1972. King of England (1936), successor to his father, George V. Edward abdicated the throne when objections within the government to his proposed marriage with the twice-divorced Wallis Warfield Simpson threatened a constitutional crisis. Thereafter known as the duke of Windsor, he married Mrs. Simpson (1937).

Edwards, Jonathan 1703–58. American Congregationalist theologian, who initiated the Great Awakening (q.v.) revival movement in America. He wrote *Freedom of the Will* (1754).

Edward the Black Prince 1330–76. Son and heir of Edward III of England. During the Hundred Years' War (1337–1453), he defeated and captured French king John II at the Battle of Poitiers. He subsequently ruled Aquitaine (1363–72), and died before his father.

Edward the Confessor d. 1066. King of England (1042–66). Raised among the Normans, he nevertheless succeeded his Danish half brother, Harthacanute. He struggled with the Dane Godwin (q.v.) because he favored the Normans during his reign. On Edward's death, Norman claims to the throne resulted in the Norman Conquest (q.v.).

Edward the Elder d. 924. Anglo-Saxon king of Wessex (899–924), successor to his father, Alfred the Great. He largely completed a campaign, begun (917) with his sister, Aethelflaed, to drive the Danes from England. At his death he controlled Mercia, East Anglia, and Northumbria.

Edward the Martyr　*d.* 978.　Anglo-Saxon king of the English (975–78), successor to his father, Edgar. He was said to have been murdered by his stepmother, Aelfrida.

Eeckhout, Gerbrand van den ⟨Eckhout, Gerbrand van den⟩ 1621–74. Dutch artist, pupil of Rembrandt. He was noted for biblical scenes and portraits.

Egbert　*d.* 839.　King of Wessex (802–839). By his victory over Mercia (825) at Ellendune, he ended Mercia's domination of Wessex and thus initiated the rise of Wessex as the dominant power in England. At his death he was recognized as overlord of Kent, Surrey, Sussex, Essex, East Anglia, and Northumbria.

Egeria　Roman goddess, a water spirit. She was associated with Diana, childbirth, and prophecy, and was counselor to her husband, King Numa Pompilius *(q.v.)*.

Eginhart　*See* **Einhard**

Egmont, Lamoral, count of　1522–68.　Flemish statesman and hero. With Count P. Hoorn, he opposed persecutions of Protestants in the Spanish Netherlands by Spanish king Philip II. Both were subsequently executed, which resulted in the outbreak of the revolt against Spanish rule in The Netherlands.

Egypt ⟨Arab Republic of Egypt⟩ Country located in northeastern Africa. Its capital is Cairo. The Nile River flows (south to north) through Egypt to the Mediterranean Sea. Civilization developed in the fertile Nile valley in extremely ancient times and had reached a high degree of organization by 3100 BC. At that time a unified kingdom was created by joining Lower Egypt (essentially, the region of the Nile delta in the north) and Upper Egypt (region south of Cairo). Ancient Egyptian civilization flourished for nearly two millennia thereafter (about 2700–1000 BC) before beginning the period of final decline. Egyptian history (up to Alexander's conquest in 332 BC) is generally divided into 30 dynasties, corresponding to the ruling dynasties reckoned to have been in power during each period. Dates, especially before 2000 BC, are at best approximations.

Alexander the Great's conquest of Egypt (332 BC) marked the beginning of continuous domination by foreign powers that lasted into the 20th cent. During that time the Egyptians absorbed first Hellenic Greek, then Roman, and finally Muslim cultural influences from their rulers. Muslim culture, which was brought to Egypt by Arab conquerors (7th cent. AD), remains dominant in modern

Egypt, which is Arabic-speaking. Modern Egypt has played an important role in Mideast affairs. Until the late 1970s it was the leading center of Arab unity and of implacable opposition to Israel. Then in 1978–79 Egypt became the first Arab nation to establish diplomatic relations and enter into formal peace agreements with Israel. Key events in the history of Egypt include:

c3400 BC　Egyptians began using primitive hieroglyphic writing.

c3100 BC　Menes united Upper and Lower Egypt under his rule; built Memphis as his capital; founded 1st dynasty, which consisted of five kings.

c3100–c2890 BC　1ST DYNASTY.

c2890–c2700 BC　2D DYNASTY; little-known period in which Hetepsekhemui reigned as first king; advances in technology, government, and the arts continued, setting the stage for the Old Kingdom; last king of dynasty, Khasekhemui, reunified Egypt after period of struggle.

c2700–c2200 BC　**Old Kingdom Period**;　first period of Egyptian greatness and the age during which the pyramids were built.

c2700–c2613 BC　3D DYNASTY; founded by Sanakht, of whom little is known.

c2650?　Zoser flourished as king; Imhotep, his minister, credited with directing the construction of the first step pyramid (of cut stone) outside Memphis; Zoser's reign also marked by advances in government and first cultural flowering; southern border established at First Cataract on the Nile.

c2613–c2500 BC　4TH DYNASTY; founded by Snefru. This was the dynasty of kings who built the first true pyramids.

c2613–c2589 BC　Snefru reigned; government administration reached high degree of refinement; raids conducted into Nubia and Libya, and the Sinai said to have been conquered; pyramid construction techniques were refined and first true pyramid built at Dahshur, near Cairo.

c2589–c2566 BC　Khufu reigned; he built the Great Pyramid at Giza, the largest of all pyramids; his reign marked a high point in the power of Egyptian kings and he was revered as both king and god.

c2555–? BC　Khafre reigned; built second great pyramid at Giza; great Sphinx believed to have been carved in Khafre's image during this period.

c2500 BC　Menkaure reigned; traditionally regarded as a just ruler; Menkaure's reign is believed to mark the beginning of the decline of the king's power; he built the smallest of the three pyramids at Giza; sculpture reached high degree of refinement.

c2500–c2345 BC 5TH DYNASTY; rise of sun worship, centered on shrine of sun god, Ra, at Heliopolis; during this period, central authority of the king weakened as provincial rulers gained power; scribes active and papyrus scrolls indicate detailed administrative organization of temples; Pyramid Texts date from this time.

c2345–c2200 BC 6TH DYNASTY; founded by King Teti; powerful local rulers continued to rise; this led to the breakup of the Egyptian kingdom at the end of the dynasty.

c2343?–c2294 BC Pepi I reigned; the son of Teti, Pepi was forced to fight a rival for the throne; he sent military expeditions to Nubia and Palestine; extensive trade with Byblos (in modern Lebanon).

c2294–c2200 BC Pepi II reigned; he succeeded to throne at age six and ruled for 94 years, according to tradition; kingdom, weakened by rise of provincial nobles, collapsed soon after his death, bringing an end to the Old Kingdom Period.

c2200–c2040 BC **First Intermediate Period**; kingdom divided among local rulers, who vied with one another to expand their domains; centers of power established at Heracleopolis (Middle Egypt) and Thebes (Upper Egypt), resulting in the ascendancy of Thebes and reunification of Egypt under its rulers.

c2200–c2130 BC 7TH–10TH DYNASTIES.

c2130–c2000 BC 11TH DYNASTY; kings ruled from Thebes and gradually expanded their power; Mentuhotep II began final struggle with Heracleopolis and by his victory (2040 BC) reunited Upper and Lower Egypt.

c2040–c1786 BC **Middle Kingdom Period**; kings ruled as feudal lords over the powerful nobles; period marked by Golden Age of Egyptian literature and art, and flourishing commerce; hieroglyphic writing system refined.

c2000–c1786 BC 12TH DYNASTY.

c2000–c1970BC Amenemhet I reigned; founded 12th dynasty by seizing power from Mentuhotep III in about 2000 BC; established capital at Ithtowe, near Memphis; conquered lower Nubia, advancing border of Egypt to Second Cataract of the Nile; developed contacts with Asiatic peoples.

c1970–1926 BC Sesostris I reigned; crushed an attempted takeover in which his father, Amenemhet I, was killed; waged successful campaigns in Nubia and Libya; brought about a period of prosperity.

c1926–c1897 BC Amenemhet II reigned; mines in Nubia and Sinai yielded gold and copper; contacts with Greek culture on Crete established.

c1897–c1878 BC Sesostris II reigned; recla-

mation of the Fayyum depression (south of Cairo) began; later became one of Egypt's most fertile agricultural regions.

c1878–c1849 BC Sesostris III reigned; a powerful ruler, he instituted administrative reforms and curbed the power of the nobles; built fortifications at Second Cataract to secure Egypt's southern border.

c1849–c1801 BC Amenemhet III reigned; prosperity reached its zenith and the arts flourished; reclamation of the Fayyum continued; extensive trade with foreign lands brought influx of foreign peoples.

c1786–c1570 BC **Second Intermediate Period** (13TH–17TH DYNASTIES); the end of the 12th dynasty (c1786 BC) marked the rise of the vizier, the king's chief officer of state, as the real ruler of Egypt; the viziers continued in power until the rise of the Hyksos, an Asiatic people that had gradually settled parts of Egypt; Hyskos ruled as kings of the 15th and 16th dynasties.

c1650–c1570 BC 17TH DYNASTY; this dynasty arose at Thebes and gradually restored control of Egypt to native rulers, thus ending the Second Intermediate Period; the final reunification of Egypt under native rule was completed by Amasis I, founder of the 18th dynasty.

c1570–c1085 BC **New Kingdom Period**; last period of Egyptian greatness, in which the ancient empire reached its height; it was marked by establishment of a law code, the building of magnificent temples, and the great military conquests of the Egyptian kings.

c1570–c1320 BC 18TH DYNASTY, the greatest of all Egyptian dynasties.

c1570–c1546 BC Amasis I reigned; expulsion of the Hyksos was completed (1570) and Egypt was again united under a single native ruler; Amasis wed his sister, following practice established by previous dynasty.

c1546–c1526 BC Amenhotep I reigned; extended Egyptian territories southward into Nubia and sent military expeditions into Asia; began New Kingdom practice of burial in the Valley of the Tombs of the Kings.

c1526–c1512 BC Thutmose I reigned; extended Egyptian control to the Fourth Cataract of the Nile in the south and sent a military expedition deep into Syria.

c1512–c1504 BC Thutmose II reigned; married his half-sister, Hatshepsut, who wielded real power during his reign; she later became regent to Thutmose III.

c1504–c1450 BC Thutmose III reigned; his conquests in Syria and the Sudan greatly increased Egyptian power and wealth.

c1450–c1425 BC Amenhotep II reigned; led successful campaigns to maintain Egypt's hold on Syria.

1425–1417 BC Thutmose IV reigned; conducted successful military expeditions into Nubia and Syria.

c1417–c1379 BC Amenhotep III reigned; built temples at Thebes and elsewhere; married Tiy, a commoner; military gained considerable influence during his reign.

c1379–c1362 BC Ikhnaton reigned; during his reign he instituted monotheistic worship of the god Aton and attempted to eliminate the traditional worship of Amon; change sparked a cultural revolution, though worship of Amon was restored soon after Ikhnaton's death.

c1361–c1352 BC Tutankhamen reigned; the boy king was forced to restore Amon worship; the capital of Egypt was reestablished at Thebes; Tutankhamen's tomb, containing great riches, was discovered virtually intact in AD 1922.

c1348–c1320 BC Horemheb reigned; appointed military men to government posts; appointed Ramses I his heir.

c1320–c1200 BC 19TH DYNASTY.

c1320–c1318 BC Ramses I reigned; founded the 19th dynasty.

1318–1304 BC Seti I reigned; conquered Libyans and invaded Syria in an attempt to check the advance of the Hittites.

c1304–c1237 BC Ramses II reigned; his long reign was marked by prosperity and unsuccessful campaigns against the Hittites; he was a noted temple-builder and was probably the king who enslaved the Hebrews.

c1288–1299 BC Battle of Kadesh, inconclusive attack by Ramses II on Hittites in Syria.

c1236–c1223 BC Merneptah reigned; defeated attacks by the Libyans and Sea Peoples; records of his reign contain the earliest mention of Israel, and many believe him to have been king at the time of the Hebrew Exodus from Egypt.

c1210–c1200 BC Seti II reigned; came to the throne after period of rule by a usurper; period of anarchy (c1210–c1200 BC) followed his death.

c1200–c1085 BC 20TH DYNASTY; founded by Setnakht (ruled 1200–1198 BC), who restored order.

c1198–c1167 BC Ramses III reigned as the last of the great Egyptian kings; successfully defeated attacks by Libyans and seaborne assaults by the Sea Peoples; other groups of Sea Peoples (Philistines) settled in Palestine, then Egyptian territory; economic decline began in Ramses' reign and, combined with the increasing power of The-

ban priests, helped erode the power of subsequent kings in the dynasty.

c1085–332 BC Period of decline and foreign domination followed the end of the New Kingdom Period (c1085 BC).

c1085–c945 BC 21ST DYNASTY; called the Tanite dynasty; the capital was located at Tanis, in the Nile delta region; priests at Thebes gained great power, and little is known of the kings that reigned in this period; Egypt lost control of its Asian empire and of Nubia.

c945–c745 BC 22D DYNASTY; called the Libyan dynasty, it was founded by Sheshonk I, member of a Libyan family in Egypt; the capital became Bubastis; attempts to foster relations with priests at Thebes were only partly successful.

c745–c712 BC 23D–24TH DYNASTIES; period of civil war and political chaos; 23d dynasty (in south) recognized by Thebes; Libyans attempted to establish control over south; invasion by Piankhi (c730 BC), a Kushite, and his withdrawal; Libyans again controlled north, maintaining capital at Sais (24th Saite dynasty) until c712.

c712–c663 BC 25TH DYNASTY; called the Ethiopian Dynasty, it was founded by Shabaka, who conquered all Egypt; the Ethiopian kings had only nominal allegiance of the Libyan and Egyptian nobles in the north, however, and could not meet the rising threat of the Assyrians.

c689–c663 BC Taharka reigned; gave support to Palestine in its revolt against Assyria; defeated (671 BC) by Esarhaddon, who drove him out of Egypt; Taharka managed to regain the south (as far as Thebes) and held it against attack by the Assyrian Ashurbanipal.

c663–c525 BC 26TH DYNASTY.

c663–c609 BC Psamtik reigned; appointed governor by the Assyrians, he launched a successful rebellion and regained Egyptian independence; established his capital at Sais, in the delta region, and reunited Egypt; encouraged influx of Greeks and thereby established Greek influence in Egypt.

c609–c593 BC Necho reigned; he took advantage of the collapse of Assyrian Empire (at the hands of the Babylonians) to conquer Syria and Palestine (c612 BC); Necho was, however, defeated by the Babylonian Nebuchadnezzar at Carchemish (605 BC) and thereafter withdrew to Egypt.

588–570 BC Apries reigned; he warred unsuccessfully against the Babylonians in Syria; an unsuccessful campaign in Libya led to a period of civil war and the overthrow of Apries.

c525–c404 BC 27TH DYNASTY; Egypt conquered by Persian king Cambyses (c525 BC), who founded the 27th dynasty; Egypt administered as a Persian satrapy (province).

c486 BC Egyptians in delta region rebelled against Persian rule; Persian king Xerxes I broke the revolt and reduced Egypt's status within the empire.

c465–c450 BC New revolt in delta region; Egyptians, with aid from Greeks, held out for some years.

404–399 BC 28TH DYNASTY; formed by successful revolt after death of Persian king Darius II; capital established at Sais.

399–380 BC 29TH DYNASTY; new dynasty came to power through power struggle; capital established at Mendes.

380–343 BC 30TH DYNASTY; founded by Nekhtnebf I, after he seized power (380 BC); he succeeded in turning back an invasion by Persia (374 BC); Persian King Artaxerxes III reconquered Egypt (343 BC) and put an end to the dynasty.

332 BC Alexander the Great conquered Egypt; Egypt began period of rule by Macedonian Greeks.

332 BC Alexandria founded by Alexander the Great; city later became a leading center of Hellenistic culture.

323 BC Ptolemy, one of Alexander's generals, became governor of Egypt on Alexander's death; friction between Alexander's heirs, among whom the Macedonian empire had been divided, led to the Wars of the Diadochi; as the wars continued, the heirs gradually assumed the role of kings in their respective domains.

321 BC Ptolemy defeated Perdiccas in the wars and thereby strengthened his position as ruler of Egypt.

312 BC Ptolemy defeated Antigonus I, his former ally, in the Wars of the Diadochi.

306 BC Demetrius defeated Ptolemy in a naval battle off Salamis, but his ally Antigonus I failed in his land invasion of Egypt.

305–285 BC Ptolemy I reigned over Egypt, Libya, and other lands after proclaiming himself king; founded the great library of Alexandria and made the city a center of Hellenistic culture and trade; founded Ptolemaic dynasty.

301 BC Battle of Ipsus; Antigonus' defeat and death in battle, in which Ptolemy I did not participate, ended serious threat to Ptolemy's rule in Egypt.

285–246 BC Ptolemy II reigned; he built the museum at Alexandria, continued to foster the arts and learning, and commissioned the translation of the Hebrew Old Testament into Greek (Septuagint); revived earlier Egyptian rulers' practice of marrying their sisters.

276–272 BC First Syrian War; Ptolemy II defeated the Seleucids under Antiochus I.

260–255 BC Second Syrian War.

246–222? BC Ptolemy III reigned; dynasty at the height of its power, with the Egyptian navy controlling the eastern Mediterranean.

245–241 BC Third Syrian War; Ptolemy gained Mediterranean coastal domains in Syria and southern Asia Minor.

221–205 BC Ptolemy IV reigned; the decline of the dynasty began with his rule.

221–217 BC Fourth Syrian War; Ptolemy IV defeated Seleucids under Antiochus I and gained Coele Syria.

205–181?BC Ptolemy V reigned; possessions in the eastern Mediterranean coastal region lost to Syria in the fifth Syrian War (201–195 BC).

180–145 BC Ptolemy VI reigned; unable to halt an invasion (170 BC) by Antiochus IV of Syria, he was forced to share power with his wife, Cleopatra, and his brother (later Ptolemy VII); a war between Ptolemy VI and his brother brought the first intervention by Rome in Egyptian affairs.

145–116 BC Ptolemy VII reigned; he seized power from Ptolemy VI, married, then drove off the widow of Ptolemy VI; after putting down a revolt led by her (130–127 BC), he ruled with great cruelty and drove the scholars out of Alexandria.

116–107 BC Ptolemy VIII reigned; he was driven out of Egypt by his brother and coruler, Ptolemy IX.

107–88 BC Ptolemy IX reigned; he held power after driving Ptolemy VIII out of Egypt; was himself overthrown by Ptolemy VIII (88 BC).

88–81 BC Ptolemy VIII reigned after regaining the throne from Ptolemy IX.

80 BC Ptolemy X; deposed by a mob at Alexandria after he murdered his stepmother (who was also coruler).

80–51 BC Ptolemy XI reigned; an ineffective and hated ruler, he was deposed by rebellious Alexandrians (58 BC); he was restored by the Romans (55 BC).

51–47 BC Ptolemy XII reigned; Ptolemy XI left Egypt to his children, Ptolemy XII and Cleopatra (VII); Ptolemy XII deposed Cleopatra (49 BC).

48 BC Cleopatra began her famous love affair with Caesar, then in Egypt; he undertook the Alexandrine War to restore her to the throne, and in the fighting her brother, Ptolemy XII, was killed (47 BC).

47–44 BC Ptolemy XIII reigned; he was married to his sister, Cleopatra, and installed on the Egyptian throne by Caesar.

44 BC Cleopatra had Ptolemy XIII murdered so that her son by Caesar could become king.

44–30 BC Ptolemy XIV reigned; he was co-ruler with his mother, Cleopatra, until he was slain by Octavian.

42–30 BC Cleopatra, hoping to advance Egypt's fortunes, pursued her love affair with Marc Antony; the liaison was unpopular in Rome, especially after Antony was married to Octavian's sister; friction between Antony and Octavian (later Augustus) mounted and led to inevitable conflict between the two leaders of the Roman world at the Battle of Actium.

31 BC Octavian defeated Antony and Cleopatra at Actium; Antony and Cleopatra committed suicide (30 BC).

30 BC Ptolemy XIV killed by Octavian; Egypt became a Roman province.

30 BC–AD 639 Egypt under Roman rule; as a major source of Rome's grain supply, Egypt retained a special status within the empire; local government remained in hands of Egyptian bureaucrats and Egypt enjoyed relative peace and prosperity, even as Rome suffered political upheavals.

2D CENT. AD Alexandrian School founded.

AD c185–c254 Origen lived; became leading theologian of the early Greek church.

c3D CENT. AD Spread of the Coptic language among Egyptians; use of Greek alphabet and borrowed Greek words to replace some earlier Egyptian words.

AD c293–373 Saint Athanasius, an Egyptian, lived; led struggle against Arianism in the Christian church.

4TH CENT. AD Land gradually became concentrated in large estates, as a result of excessive taxes imposed by Romans.

4TH CENT. AD Christianity became dominant religion of Egypt.

AD c375–44 Saint Cyril of Alexandria lived; figured prominently in struggle against Nestorianism.

AD 395 Permanent division of the Roman Empire into Eastern and Western empires; Egypt administered as part of the Eastern Empire.

AD 476 Fall of the Western Roman Empire; Roman domination of Egypt continued under the Byzantine (Eastern Roman) rulers; Christianity flourished.

616 Egypt conquered by Persians under Khosru II; reverted to Byzantines on the death of Khosru II (628).

639–642 Muslim conquest of Egypt.

642–1882 Muslim rule of Egypt began under the Arab caliphs of the Empire of the Caliphate; during this period Egypt gradually adopted Arab language, Islamic religion and culture.

661–750 Umayyad caliphs ruled Egypt as part of the Empire of the Caliphate; colonization by Arabs and incentives for those who adopted Islam gradually reduced following of Christian church.

706 Arabic made official language of Egypt, replacing Coptic language.

747–750 Revolt of Abu Muslim: general rebellion in the Empire of the Caliphate; brought the Abbasid dynasty of caliphs to power.

750–969 Abbasid caliphs ruled over Egypt.

829–830 Unsuccessful rebellion by Copts and others against Abbasid rule; subsequent repressive measures against Copts spurred conversion to Islam.

868–905 Tulunid dynasty in power; Ahmad ibn Tulun, a Turk, made governor by the Abbasid caliph; Tulun quickly asserted autonomy of Egypt and took control of Syria; Egypt prospered.

905 Muslim caliphs restored their control over Egypt.

935–969 Ikhshidid dynasty of governors reigned; reasserted Egyptian autonomy; internal unrest in Egypt beginning in 968 paved the way for the Fatimid conquest.

969–1171 Fatimid rule in Egypt; Fatimids, a Shi'ite sect of Islam, had already gained control of most of North Africa before taking Egypt; they subsequently attacked the Abbasid caliphs and took control of Syria and part of Mesopotamia.

969 Cairo founded by Fatimids; made Egypt a center of Islamic religion.

FROM 1047 Breakup of the Fatimid empire; territories in east and west gained independence.

1099 Jerusalem captured by Christians on First Crusade; marked further decline of Fatimid power.

1167–69 Syrian armies invaded Egypt to aid Fatimids in regaining control; Saladin, a Syrian commander, made vizier of Egypt by Fatimids.

1169–93 Saladin reigned in Egypt; in 1171 he ended Fatimid rule and restored Egypt to the Abbasid caliphs; founded Ayyubid dynasty in Egypt; asserted Egyptian autonomy after 1174 and brought under his control Syria, part of Mesopotamia, Yemen, the Hejaz, and after 1187 much of the Holy Land.

1169–1250 Ayyubid dynasty in power in Egypt; Saladin divided his empire among his heirs at his death; this resulted in breakdown of central authority; to meet challenge of Christian Crusaders, last of Ayyubid rulers purchased Turkish slaves, Mamelukes, to fight in his army; Mamelukes seized power in 1250.

1187 Saladin conquered Jerusalem in his campaign to drive Christians from Holy Land; this prompted the Third Crusade by Christians.

1189–92 Third Crusade; Christians ultimately negotiated truce with Saladin, in which they were granted access to Jerusalem.

1217–21 Fifth Crusade; Christian forces attacked and invaded Egypt; withdrew following defeat in attack on Cairo.

1228–29 Sixth Crusade; Egyptians concluded treaty with Holy Roman Emperor Frederick II, giving him control of Holy Land (1229).

1244 Egyptians and Turks reoccupied Jerusalem.

1248–54 Seventh Crusade; Christians invaded Egypt and were routed during advance on Cairo.

1250–1517 Mamelukes reigned in Egypt; Mamelukes, Turkish slaves in Egyptian army, took advantage of power struggle among Ayubbids to seize power; with the subsequent collapse of the Empire of the Caliphate (1258) before the Mongol invasions, Mameluke Egypt became a Muslim center.

1260–77 Baybars I reigned as Mameluke sultan of Egypt.

1260 Mamelukes defeated (Sept. 3) the Mongols at the Battle of Ayn Jalut, checking their western advance.

1261 Abbasid caliphs permitted to establish themselves in Cairo, following the Mongol conquest of the Empire of the Caliphate.

1270–72 Eighth Crusade; prompted by Mameluke conquests in the Holy Land, it ended in negotiated settlements (1271–72).

1291 Mameluke armies won the Battle of Acre, driving the last of the Crusaders from the Holy Land.

1293–1341 al-Malik an-Nasir reigned as sultan; Mamelukes concluded treaty with the Mongols (1323); period of general peace and prosperity ensued; Mameluke decline began after death of al-Malik.

1517 Ottoman sultan Selim I conquered Egypt.

1517–1882 Ottomans ruled Egypt; Egypt, reduced to a province, was exploited and declined; Mamelukes continued to wield power as beys (local rulers) under the Ottoman viceroy; the beys of Egypt gained power and eventually asserted the autonomy of Egypt.

1786–87 Ottoman troops sent to Egypt to reassert control over the Mameluke beys; troops withdrawn after failing to break power of beys.

1768–73 Ali Bey in power; called himself sultan and secured Ottoman recognition of his autonomy.

1798–1801 Napoleon launched French invasion of Egypt during the French Revolutionary Wars; campaign, which ended in disaster, had been calculated to disrupt British colonial trade and threaten India; French driven out by combined British and Ottoman force.

1799 Napoleon's troops discovered Rosetta stone.

1801–05 Ottomans failed in their attempt to reassert control in Egypt; soldier, Muhammad Ali, became viceroy after a revolt (1805) against the Ottoman viceroy.

1805–49 Muhammad Ali reigned as virtually independent viceroy of Egypt; instituted sweeping reforms, undertook economic development (beginning industrialization), and laid foundations of modern Egyptian state.

1811 Muhammad Ali ordered massacre of Mameluke leaders to break the power of this faction.

1811–18 Muhammad Ali's Egyptian troops defeated the fanatical Wahabi sect; restored the Hejaz and central Arabia to Ottoman control.

1820–21 Northern Sudan conquered; Egyptian control in region expanded under Ali's successors.

1825–28 Egyptian forces fought against rebels in Greece, following request from the Ottoman sultan for aid; Egyptian successes in campaign brought European intervention; Egyptians forced to withdraw.

1831–40 Egyptians occupied Syria; declining Ottoman Empire unable to repel invasion; European powers, concerned about the collapse of the Ottoman Empire, forced Egyptians to withdraw (1840).

1841 Hereditary right to Egyptian sultanate granted to Muhammad Ali by the Ottoman sultan.

1848–54 Abbas I reigned as Egyptian sultan; halted Westernization policy and opposed European influence.

1854–63 Muhammad Said Pasha reigned; instituted many reforms to modernize Egypt; construction of Suez Canal began (1859); reforms and canal proved costly and later ruined Egyptian finances; first foreign loan arranged through British.

1863–79 Ismail Pasha reigned; attempted to finish modernization program; undertook extensive building and floated huge loans, creating massive government debt; completed the ruin of Egypt's finances; hired Europeans to command military campaigns to conquer the Sudan (1870s).

1869 Suez Canal completed.

1875 Ismail Pasha, confronted with Egypt's worsening financial situation, was forced to sell Egypt's shares in the Suez Canal to the British, who thereby gained controlling interest.

1876 Debt commission established by British and French to manage Egyptian finances; Ismail Pasha forced to submit to this intervention by Europeans.

1878 Europeans appointed to head some government ministries.

1879 Ismail Pasha deposed, partly through influence of French and British.

1879–92 Tewfik Pasha reigned; European control firmly established, and French and British remained in government posts; nationalist uprisings against Europeans led to establishment of direct British administration of Egypt (1882).

1881–82 Nationalist uprisings led by Arabi Pasha.

1882 Nationalist riots at Alexandria (June 12); British bombarded Alexandria (July) and landed troops; nationalists defeated and Cairo occupied (Sept.); British assumed sole control over Egypt.

1883 Organic Law, reorganizing the Egyptian government, issued by British; legislative assemblies with only advisory powers created; British ruled through resident consul general.

1883–98 Revolt in the Sudan; rebels initially led by Muhammad Ahmed (the Mahdi) seized control of the Sudan; massacred Sir C. Gordon's forces at Khartoum (1885); rebels controlled Sudan until reconquest by Lord Kitchener (1896–98).

1888 Suez Canal Convention signed by European powers to guarantee neutrality of Suez Canal.

1892–1914 Abbas II reigned; failed in attempt to break British control (1893); during his reign, the nationalist movement reasserted its opposition to both British occupation and rule of Abbas II.

1898 Fashoda Crisis with France; British, completing conquest of Sudan, encountered French in region (1898); French and British subsequently reached agreement defining spheres of influence in region.

1899 Anglo-Egyptian condominium established joint British-Egyptian rule in eastern Sudan (until 1956).

1902 Aswan Dam completed.

1914–18 WW I; war declared against Ottoman Empire; British declared Egypt a protectorate (1914) and deposed Abbas II.

1917–22 Fuad I reigned as sultan; made major gains in freeing Egypt of British rule.

1918 Nationalist Wafd Party founded by Sa'd Zaghlul and others.

1919 Nationalist revolt, fueled by harsh British administration during WW I; British troops used to quell revolt.

1921 Nationalist unrest; Europeans attacked and nationalist leaders deported as talks on Eygptian independence continued.

1922 Egypt granted independence by British (Feb. 28), though continued British presence (including troops) to be negotiated.

1922 Fuad I proclaimed king of Egypt (Mar. 15); reigned to 1936.

1923 Constitution issued (Apr. 19) establishing bicameral legislature.

1924 Zaghlul, leader of Wafd nationalists, in office as first premier; his brief term was ended by conflict with Britain over the Sudan; in subsequent years Wafd party often opposed both government and British, and political situation remained unstable; ongoing negotiations with British, who continued their dominating presence in Egypt.

1936–52 Farouk I reigned; further steps toward British withdrawal brought measure of stability until last year of his reign.

1936 Anglo-Egyptian treaty signed (Aug. 26); British troops to be withdrawn, though British retained right to keep troops along Suez; Egypt and Britain made allies.

1938 King Farouk dissolved Wafd-dominated Parliament; new elections returned majority of supporters of his government.

1939–45 WW II; Egypt remained neutral; nevertheless became important base of British operations and site of battles in the North Africa campaign.

1945 Egypt became a member of the UN.

1945 Egypt joined Arab League.

1946 New Anglo-Egyptian treaty (Oct.) rejected by Egyptians because British refused to give up the Sudan to Eygpt.

1948–49 First Arab-Israeli War: Egypt joined other Arab states against newly created state of Israel; Egypt signed armistice (Feb. 24) but not permanent treaty with Israel.

1950 Wafd party gained control of elected government as political unrest increased; began struggle with King Farouk that ended with creation of Egyptian republic (1953).

1950–52 Nahas Pasha, Wafd leader, became premier; sought immediate withdrawal of all British forces; anti-British unrest increased and Egypt abrogated 1936 treaty (Aug. 6, 1951); British refused to withdraw and violence between nationalists and British broke out; King Farouk dismissed the Wafd government (Jan. 27, 1952) as violence increased.

1952 Army coup (July 23) led by Gen. Muhammad Naguib; Farouk abdicated in favor of Ahmad Fuad II, his infant son.

1952 Agrarian reforms enacted.

1953 Treaty with Britain signed (Feb. 12) granting right of self-determination in Sudan.

1953 Republic declared (June 18); monarchy abolished.

1953–54 Gen. Naguib in office as first president.

1954 Treaty with Britain signed (Oct.); British to withdraw forces from Suez Canal within 20 months; British permitted to send troops under specified conditions.

1954–70 Gamal Abdal Nasser, a military leader, in office as president (from Nov.); during his long tenure, he restored political stability and became a leading exponent of Arab nationalism.

1956 New constitution adopted.

1956 Suez Crisis; Nasser was refused loan (by US) to build Aswan High Dam, and thereupon nationalized Suez Canal (July 26); Israel, responding to long series of border clashes with Egypt, launched (Oct. 29) invasion of Egypt, beginning the Second Arab-Israeli War; Israelis captured Sinai (as far as the Suez Canal) amid Suez Crisis.

1956 British and French troops entered fighting to retake canal (Oct. 31).

1956 Cease-fire arranged (Nov. 6).

1956 UN forces occupied the canal zone (Dec.), ending Suez Crisis.

1957 Israeli forces withdrawn from Egyptian territory.

1958–61 United Arab Republic; Egypt and Syria united, with Yemen joining soon after; G. Nasser elected president; program of nationalization in Eygpt began (largely complete by 1962).

1960 Construction of Aswan High Dam begun with massive Soviet aid.

1961 Syria withdrew from the UAR following disputes with Egypt; Egypt dissolved union with Yemen.

1964 New constitution adopted.

1967 Third Arab-Israeli War (June 5–10); Israelis pushed to east bank of Suez Canal in six days; Suez blocked by wrecks, and Egyptian losses in armament were heavy; Soviets provided massive aid to Egypt to rebuild army.

1970 Thousands of Soviet soldiers in Egypt to aid in ongoing clashes with Israelis.

1970 Nasser died (Sept. 28).

1970–81 A. Sadat in office as president; after years of hostility with Israel, Sadat reversed Egyptian policy and entered in historic treaty with Israelis (1979).

1971 Aswan High Dam dedicated.

1971 Sadat crushed coup attempt (May 14).

1972 Sadat ousted (July 18) Soviet military advisers and took over Soviet bases in Egypt.

1973 Sadat took over (Mar. 26) duties of premier; made himself military governor-general of Egypt.

1973 Sadat signed agreement with Libya providing for unification of two countries in prearranged stages; agreement never implemented.

1973 Fourth Arab-Israeli War (Oct. 6–25); Israelis occupied part of west bank of Suez; Arab nations imposed oil embargo on US and other Israeli allies; cease-fire halted fighting; US secretary of state H. Kissinger negotiated pull-back from Suez Canal by both sides (Jan., 1974) and thereafter Kissinger sought to further negotiations through "shuttle diplomacy."

1973 Relations with Libya strained (Dec.) over Egypt's conduct of this fourth war.

1974 Full diplomatic relations reestablished with the US (Feb. 28).

1974 Treaty with US signed; US to provide nuclear technology for peaceful purposes.

1974 Premiership restored (Sept.); Abdel Azziz Heqazi assumed duties.

1975 Suez Canal reopened (June).

1976 Sadat announced an end to friendship treaty with the Soviets (Mar.).

1977 Cease-fire (July) ended series of border clashes with Libya.

1977 Sadat made historic state visit to Israel (Nov. 19–21) in the first of a series of peace initiatives between the two nations.

1977 Tripoli Declaration issued (Dec. 5) by Arab opponents of Sadat's peace initiatives; diplomatic relations with Egypt frozen.

1977 Israeli prime minister M. Begin visited Egypt (Dec. 24–26) to continue discussion of possible peace settlement.

1978 Sadat signed (Sept. 17) the Camp David Accords, providing a framework for peace with Israel.

1979 Sadat signed (Mar. 26) historic formal peace treaty with Israel: Israelis to pull out of Sinai in phases; Egypt and Israel to establish diplomatic relations.

1979 Arab League imposed sanctions against Egypt to protest Egyptian-Israeli treaty (Mar. 31).

1981 Sadat assassinated in Cairo by Muslim fundamentalists (Oct. 6); Hosni Mubarak succeeded him as president.

1982 Phased Israeli withdrawal from occupied Egyptian territory in the Sinai completed (Apr. 25), in accordance with treaty.

Egyptian-Israeli Peace Treaty Treaty signed (Mar. 26, 1979) by Egyptian president A. Sadat and Israeli prime minister M. Begin. The agreement formally ended the state of war that had existed between the two countries for some 30 years and established diplomatic relations. The treaty followed the signing (Sept. 17, 1978) of the Camp David accords by the two leaders. This agreement culminated a 13-day conference among US President J. Carter, Sadat, and Begin and provided for a "framework for peace" in the Mideast. Both the Camp David accords and the peace treaty were actively opposed by other Arab countries.

Ehud Old Testament hero who killed Eglon, king of the Moabites. Ehud then led Israel to victory against Moabite soldiers, ending 18 years of persecution.

Eichmann, Adolf 1906–62. German Nazi official, a principal figure in the Nazi program to exterminate Jews during WW II. He escaped to Argentina after the war, was brought back to Israel (1960), tried, and hanged.

Eiffel Tower Paris landmark, built for the Paris exposition of 1889 in the Champ-de-Mars. Designed by Alexandre Gustave Eiffel (1832–1923), it is 984 feet high.

Eight, The Group of American artists who exhibited together in New York (1908). They advocated a realistic view of their surroundings, as opposed to academism. They became part of the "ashcan" school, and were involved in the famous Armory show (1913), at which European modern art was introduced to America.

1800, Treaty of *See* **Adams, John**

1814, Charter of *See* **Charter of 1814**

1812, War of War (June 18, 1812–Jan. 8, 1815) between the US and Britain, largely provoked by British harassment of US shipping. During the prolonged conflict between Britain and Napoleonic France, both sides set up naval blockades, and American trade suffered badly. While the *Chesapeake* affair *(q.v.)* and other incidents turned Americans against the British, US response was limited to a series of ineffective trade embargo measures, including the Nonimportation Act (1806), the Embargo Act (1807), and the Nonintercourse Act (1809). Widespread suspicion that the British had provoked Indians to attack Americans at the Battle of Tippecanoe (1811) and subsequent efforts by "war hawks" *(q.v.)* in Congress led to a declaration of war by President J. Monroe (June 18). There followed a three-pronged attack on Canada. This initial attack failed and resulted in the surrender of Detroit (Aug. 16, 1812) by Gen. W. Hull. The American navy succeeded in capturing the British warships *Guerrière* and *Macedonian*, among others, in 1812, though the British soon regained control of the seas. But on Lake Erie, Commodore O. Perry captured a British fleet (Sept., 1813) and thereby made possible the Amer-

ican victory at the Battle of the Thames (Oct., 1813) and the burning of Toronto. In 1814, American victories at the battles of Chippawa and Lundy's Lane in Canada and an abortive British invasion of New York under Sir G. Prevost ended in retreat behind the respective borders. The British amphibious invasion (Aug.-Sept., 1814) in the South resulted in the capture and burning of Washington, D.C. But again, after failing to capture Fort McHenry *(q.v.)* in nearby Baltimore (Sept. 14), the British withdrew. Meanwhile, dissatisfaction with the war on both sides led to negotiations and the Treaty of Ghent *(q.v.)*, officially ending the war (Dec. 24, 1814). News of the treaty, however, arrived only after A. Jackson's decisive victory over the British at the Battle of New Orleans (Jan. 8, 1815).

Eighth Crusade *See* **Crusade, Eighth**

Eighth Route Army Chinese Communist army, formed in 1937 and led by Chu Teh. It engaged in guerrilla warfare against the Japanese invaders (1937–45) in China and worked in collaboration with the Nationalist government. The unit became part of the Communist People's Liberation Army after the war.

Einaudi, Luigi 1874–1961. Italian statesman and economist. An anti-Fascist, he was exiled (1943–45), became minister of the budget (1947), and was elected first president of the Italian republic (1948–55).

Einhard ⟨Eginhart⟩ c770–840. Frankish historian. He was a favorite in the court of Charlemagne and wrote the biography *Life of Charlemagne.*

Einstein, Albert 1879–1955. German-born American theoretical physicist, one of the most important scientists of all time, who developed the theory of relativity and made important contributions to the quantum theory. While earning a doctorate (1905) at the University of Zurich and working (1902–09) in a Swiss patent office, Einstein formulated three great theories: the special theory of relativity, in which he postulated the equivalence of mass and energy ($E = mc^2$); his theory of Brownian motion; and his theory on the photoelectric effect. He developed his general theory of relativity (1913–16), and achieved wide recognition (1919) when part of the theory was confirmed by independent observation. Forced to leave Germany (1933), he emigrated to the US, and was for the remainder of his life a member of the Institute for Advanced Study at Princeton, New Jersey. He was awarded the Nobel Prize in Physics in 1921.

Einthoven, Willem 1860–1927. Dutch physiologist. He developed the electrocardiograph (1903).

He was awarded the Nobel Prize in physiology in 1924.

Eisenhower, Dwight David 1890–1969. Thirty-fourth US president (1953–61), succeeding President H. Truman, and supreme commander of Allied forces during WW II. Eisenhower's two terms as president were marked by a period of general peace and prosperity, his conservative domestic policies, the Cold War, and a US policy aimed at "containment" of communism. Once an aide to D. MacArthur, Eisenhower rose quickly during WW II to become US commander in North Africa (1942), Allied commander in North Africa (1942–43), and supreme commander of Allied forces in Europe (1943–45). A brilliant organizer of military forces, he commanded the massive Normandy invasion (1944) and subsequent Allied drive across Europe, which brought an end to the war in Europe. In the postwar years he served in various military posts and, as first NATO commander (1950–52), organized these forces. In 1952 he ran for the presidency as a Republican and, during his first term (1953–57), ended the Korean War (1953), organized SEATO (1954), and attended the Geneva Conference (1955). His second term (1957–61) was marked by the rise of the civil rights movement (federal troops forcibly desegregated schools in Little Rock, Arkansas, in 1957), the Eisenhower Doctrine (*q.v.*), the Lebanese crisis (1958), the Cuban Revolution (1959), and the U-2 crisis (1960).

Eisenhower Doctrine Statement of US foreign policy articulated (Jan. 5, 1957) by President D. Eisenhower in the wake of the Suez crisis. In it he offered economic and military assistance to any Mideast country in need of aid to resist Communist aggression.

Eisenstein, Sergei Mikhailovich 1898–1948. Russian film director, considered a pioneer in film technique. Among his classics are *Potemkin, Ten Days That Shook the World,* and *Alexander Nevsky.*

Eisner, Kurt 1867–1919. German Socialist. He organized the revolution that overthrew the monarchy in Bavaria (1918) and became prime minister of the short-lived Bavarian republic. He was assassinated soon afterward.

ejido system *See* **Cárdenas, Lázaro**

Elam Ancient country located in present-day Iran. Its capital was Susa. Its turbulent history as an independent, warlike state extends from the 4th millennium BC to 640 BC, when it was absorbed into the Assyrian Empire.

elastic clause Name of a clause in Article I, Section 18, of the US Constitution. It gives Congress the power to make all laws necessary to execute powers specifically enumerated in the Constitution. It therefore allows Congress to decide what other powers (not set forth) are needed (thus, the "elastic" clause).

El Cid *See* **Cid, the**

El Dorado Legendary country of great riches sought, but never found, in South America by adventurers such as Pizarro (1539) and Sir W. Raleigh (1595).

Eleanor of Aquitaine 1122?–1204. Queen consort of Louis VII of France (1137–52) and Henry II of England (1152–89). For supporting her sons in revolt against Henry, she was put into confinement by Henry (1173–85). She was adviser to her sons King Richard I and King John of England.

Eleanor of Castile *d.* 1290. Queen consort of English king (*m.* 1254) Edward I and daughter of Ferdinand III of Castile. She joined Edward on a crusade (1270–72) and there prevented his death.

Eleatic school One of the important pre-Socratic schools of philosophy. It is believed to have been founded (5th cent. BC) by Parmenides, and was centered at Elea, a Greek colony in Italy. The Eleatics denied conventional notions of reality, believing instead in an infinite, changeless "Being." Principal exponents of Eleaticism were Parmenides, Zeno and Elea, Melissus of Samos (*fl.* 5th cent. BC), and Xenophanes, once thought to be the founder of the school.

electoral college In the US, the body of electors chosen from each state to select the next president. Though they usually vote for the candidate who won the majority of popular votes in their state, they are not constitutionally obliged to do so, and presidents have won elections with less than the majority popular vote. Various plans have been advanced to change the system, including election by direct popular vote.

electors Ecclesiastical and secular German princes. From the 13th cent. to the collapse of the Holy Roman Empire (1806), these princes of various German states elected the king of Germany, who then became the Holy Roman Emperor.

Electra In Greek legend, the daughter of Agamemnon and Clytemnestra. With her brother, Orestes, she avenged the murder of their father by Clytemnestra and her lover Aegisthus.

Eleusinian Mysteries In ancient Greece, an important secret religious ritual honoring Demeter and Persephone. The ritual originated in Eleusis, and after *c*600 BC was celebrated in nearby Athens. Initiation into the mysteries eventually became open to all Greek citizens. The ritual itself was divided into two parts: the Lesser Mysteries, honoring the return of Persephone, were celebrated each year in February; and the Greater

Mysteries, honoring Demeter, were held once every five years in early fall. Celebration of the Greater Mysteries involved a mass procession from Athens to Eleusia, where a secret ritual, still unknown today, was performed.

Elgar, Sir Edward William 1857–1934. English composer. His best-known works are *Dream of Gerontius* and the five *Pomp and Circumstance* marches.

Elgin, James Bruce, 8th earl of 1811–63. British statesman. He was governor of Jamaica (1842–46) and then governor-general of Canada (1847–54).

Elias *See* **Elijah**

Eliezer, Israel ben *See* **Baal Shem-Tov**

Elihu In the Old Testament, the comforter of Job, who advises Job to accept God's will.

Elijah ⟨Elias⟩ *fl. c875* BC. Biblical Hebrew prophet. He worked to end worship of the god Baal during the reign of King Ahab and his wife Jezebel.

Elijah ben Solomon 1720–97. Lithuanian Jewish scholar. Elijah opposed Hasidism *(q.v.)* as unscholarly and divisive. His teachings include commentaries on the Old Testament, Talmud, Mishnah, Midrash, cabala, and halakah.

Eliot, Charles William1834–1926. American educator, president of Harvard University (1869–1909), and editor of the *Harvard Classics.*

Eliot, George ⟨Evans, Mary Ann⟩ 1819–80. English novelist. Her psychological novels, considered among England's greatest, include *Adam Bede, The Mill on the Floss,* and *Silas Marner.*

Eliot, Sir John 1592?–1632. English parliamentary leader. Eliot championed free speech and other liberties in Parliament, brought impeachment charges against the duke of Buckingham, the king's favorite, and promoted the Petition of Right *(q.v.).* Charles I imprisoned him.

Eliot, John 1604–90. English Colonial missionary. His work with Indians in Massachusetts led to his translation of the Bible into their native language. It was the first Bible printed (1661) in North America.

Eliot, Thomas Stearns 1888–1965. American-born English poet, dramatist, and critic who was a leading modernist and one of the great poets of this century. He settled in London (1914) and there began writing his early poems while working as an editor. He became a British citizen in 1927. His works include poems, such as *The Waste Land, Ash Wednesday,* and *Four Quartets,* plays, and critical works. He was awarded the Nobel Prize in Literature in 1948.

Eliseus *See* **Elisha**

Elisha ⟨Eliseus⟩ *fl.* 875 BC. Biblical Hebrew prophet who succeeded Elijah in the task of ending the worship of Baal. By his use of moderate and diplomatic means, Elisha was able to gain many disciples for the worship of God.

Elizabeth *See* **Isabeau of Bavaria**

Elizabeth 1596–1662. Queen of Bohemia (1619–20) as wife of Frederick the Winter King (m. 1613). She was noted for beauty and for the misfortunes she suffered after Frederick was deposed.

Elizabeth ⟨Petrovna, Elizabeth⟩ 1709–62. Empress of Russia (1741–62) by her overthrow of young Ivan VI. Advised by her chancellor, Bestuzhev-Ryumin, she rid Russia of German influence and opposed Prussia in the Seven Years' War.

Elizabeth 1837–98. Empress of Austria (1854–98) and queen of Hungary (1867–98) as wife of Emperor Francis Joseph (m. 1854). She was assassinated by an Italian anarchist.

Elizabeth 1843–1916. Queen of Romania (1881–1916), wife of Carol I (m. 1869). Using the pseudonym Carmen Sylva, she wrote books in four languages, including *Pensées d'une reine* and *The Bard of Dimbovitza.*

Elizabeth I 1533–1603. English queen (1558–1603), successor to Mary I. Elizabeth's reign saw a period of increasing commercial activity, England's rise as a naval power, the beginnings of English exploration and colonization in the New World, and a period of great literary activity. The dominant aspect of her reign, however, was the restoration of Protestantism and her struggle with Catholics at home and abroad. She reestablished the Church of England by winning passage of the Act of Supremacy and the Act of Uniformity (1559) and promulgated (1563) the Thirty-Nine Articles *(q.v.)* of the Anglican faith. The subsequent Catholic rebellions and plots against Elizabeth resulted in increasingly repressive measures against them, as well as in the execution (1587) of the Catholic Mary Queen of Scots, whose accession the conspirators sought. Though Elizabeth agreed with France to a mutual military withdrawal from Scotland by the Treaty of Edinburgh (1560), she nevertheless supported Protestants against the Catholics there. Likewise, she offered support to French Protestant Huguenots and help to Protestants in the revolt of The Netherlands against Spain. Her anti-Catholic policies and encouragement of raids by English privateers on Spanish shipping finally provoked Philip II of Spain to mount an unsuccessful attempt to invade England and end Protestantism there (*see* Spanish Armada). The last years of her reign were marked by a revolt led by her favorite, R. Devereaux, 2d earl of Essex. (*See also* Great Britain [1558–1603]; Elizabethan Age.)

Elizabeth II 1926–. British queen (1952–   ), successor to her father, George VI. She entered the direct line of succession upon abdication of her unclc, Edward VIII (1936), married (1947) Philip Mountbatten (1921–), duke of Edinburgh, and was crowned June 2, 1953. Though her role is largely symbolic and ceremonial, Elizabeth enjoys great popularity with her subjects. Political events during her reign include the Suez Canal crisis (1956) and religious turmoil in Northern Ireland.

Elizabeth, Saint In the Bible, the mother of John the Baptist and cousin of the Virgin Mary.

Elizabeth, Saint 1207–31. Hungarian princess, daughter of King Andrew II, and wife of Louis IV of Thuringia. She devoted herself to the poor and sick and was canonized in 1235.

Elizabethan Age Period of English history, specifically the reign of Elizabeth I (1558–1603). England enjoyed many years of general peace and prosperity and rose as a great naval power during this period. But it was most remarkable as a golden age of English literature. W. Shakespeare, E. Spenser, and C. Marlowe all belong to this time. Early 17th-cent. literature, produced during the reign of James I, is sometimes included in this period, though it is more specifically called Jacobean.

Elizabeth of Valois 1545–68. Spanish queen (1559–68), daughter of French king Henry II. She married (1559) Philip II, though she was originally intended for his son Don Carlos.

Elkhorn Tavern, Battle of (Battle of Pea Ridge) American Civil War battle (Mar. 7–8, 1862) in northwestern Arkansas, a victory for Union forces.

Elkins, Stephen Benton 1841–1911. American statesman. He was secretary of war under President B. Harrison (1891–93) and senator from West Virginia (1895–1911). He authored the Elkins Act (1903) against railroad rebates.

Elkins Act of 1903 *See* **Elkins, Stephen Benton**

Ellenborough, Edward Law, earl of 1790–1871. British statesman, president of the Board of Control of the East India Company and governor-general of India (1841–44). He annexed Sind (1843).

Ellesmere, Thomas Egerton, Baron *c*1540–1617. English jurist, statesman, and adviser of both Elizabeth I and James I. He participated in the trials of Mary Queen of Scots (1586) and the 2d earl of Essex (1601), and was a champion of royal prerogative.

Ellis, Henry Havelock 1859–1939. English physician and author. He advocated sex education and wrote *Studies in the Psychology of Sex.*

Ellis, William 1794–1872. English missionary in the South Sea Islands (1816–24). He set up the first printing press in the South Pacific.

Ellora Village in west central India, site of Buddhist, Hindu, and Jaina cave temples dating from the 5th cent. AD. The most outstanding is the Hindu Kailasa temple (8th cent.).

Ellsworth, Lincoln 1880–1951. US explorer and engineer. With R. Amundsen and Umberto Nobile, he was on the first flight across the North Polar Basin in the dirigible *Norge* (1926). In 1935, he became the first to fly across Antarctica.

Ellsworth, Oliver 1745–1807. American statesman and jurist. As delegate to the Constitutional Convention, he co-authored the Connecticut Compromise (*see* Virginia and New Jersey Plans) (1787). He was the third chief justice of the US (1796–1800).

El Salvador Republic located in western Central America on the Pacific Coast. Capital is San Salvador. The country was ruled by Spain until 1821. Densely populated and primarily agricultural, its history has been marked by considerable internal strife. Key dates in El Salvador's history include:

1524–25 Spanish conquistador Pedro de Alvarado began conquests of El Salvador during his invasion of Central America; area later included in the captaincy general of Guatemala.

1821 Independence from Spain (Sept. 15).

1821–23 Became part of A. de Iturbide's Mexican Empire

1823–39 Joined Central American Federation after collapse of Iturbide's empire.

1839 Republic established; thereafter revolutions regularly broke out.

1886 Constitution enacted.

1931–44 Gen. Maximiliano Hernández Martínez in power as dictator; he overthrew (1931) the first freely elected president in 20 years.

1939 New constitution adopted.

1944 Martínez fled as unrest spread (1944); turmoil continued in subsequent years; Maj. Oscar Osorio in power (1949–56) after military coup.

1962–67 Julio Adalberto Rivera in office after period of continuing instability; free elections restored.

1969 Soccer War fought with Honduras.

1970 Demilitarized zone established along border with Honduras.

1972–77 National Conciliation Party candidate Arturo Armando Molina in office as president; was appointed by National Assembly after elections produced no clear winner.

1977–79 Gen. Carlos Romero in office as president; violence and charges of voting fraud during elections.

1979 Violence between government forces and leftist rebels flared; 23 killed when police fired on demonstrators outside a cathedral in San Salvador (May 8).

1979 Romero declared state of siege; constitution suspended (May 24).

1979 Romero deposed (Oct. 15) by civilian and military junta; junta failed in attempt to end violence and came under attack by both leftist and rightist extremists.

1980 Civilian junta members resigned (Jan.).

1980 Four American women missionaries murdered (Dec. 4); US suspended aid pending investigation.

1981 José Napoleón Duarte became president; US aid restored; major offensive by leftists failed.

1981 US Pres. R. Reagan sent military advisers; increased military and economic aid.

1982 Rightists gained majority in Constituent Assembly during elections; Alvaro Alfredo Magaña named president.

Elsevier, Louis See **Elzevir, Louis**

Elssler, Fanny 1810–84. Celebrated Austrian dancer known for her folk dances s s and energetic style. She made successful tours of Europe and the US (1841), and retired in 1851.

El Supremo See **Francia, José Gaspar Rodriguez**

Éluard, Paul 1895–1952. French poet, a founder of surrealism. He participated in the French Resistance. Among his works are *Poésie et vérité* and *Au rendez-vous allemand*.

Elysian fields ⟨Elysium⟩ In Greek legend, a paradise for those who had lived righteous lives.

Elysium See **Elysian fields**

El Zanjón, Peace of See **Ten Years' War**

Elzevir, Louis ⟨Elsevier, ~⟩ 1540–1617. One of a Dutch family of book publishers. He founded the business in Leiden in 1583 and it continued until 1712.

Emancipation, Edict of See **Edict of Emancipation**

Emancipation Proclamation Famous proclamation issued (Sept. 22, 1862) during the American Civil War by President A. Lincoln. It declared all slaves in the Confederacy to be free (as of Jan. 1, 1863) and was issued by Lincoln as a wartime measure in his capacity as commander in chief of the military. It did not apply to slaves outside territories held by rebels (ultimately freed by other legislation), but nevertheless granted theoretical freedom to some three million Negroes. The proclamation, brought about partly by pressure from northern abolitionists, marked a change in Lincoln's policy from simple restoration of the Union (and maintenance of the status quo on slavery) to a more definitive antislavery policy. Formal abolition of slavery in the US was finally accomplished by adoption (1865) of the 13th Amendment.

Emanuel I See **Manuel I**

Embargo Act US legislation (Dec. 22, 1807) halting all exports from the US. During the Napoleonic Wars (1803–15), both Britain and France declared blockades of each other and thereby interfered with American commerce. The Embargo Act was President T. Jefferson's attempt to use economic pressure to force both Britain and France to recognize the neutral shipping rights of American merchants. The act, even with additional legislation passed in 1808 and 1809, proved both unenforceable and economically disastrous for the US. Britain and France were largely unaffected. With New England nearing open rebellion, the Nonintercourse Act was passed (1809), resuming all foreign trade except that with Britain and France. Legislative trade restrictions were effectively ended with Macon's Bill No. 2 (Mar. 23, 1810).

Emboabas, War of the Brief civil war (1708–09) in eastern Brazil. Established settlers, called *paulistas*, fought European newcomers, called *emboabas*, who flocked to the area during a gold rush. When the *emboabas* won, the *paulistas* moved westward, and discovered new gold deposits.

Emerson, Ralph Waldo 1803–82. American poet, essayist, and lecturer who greatly influenced American thought. A Harvard student at age 14, he later traveled in Europe (1832–33), where he met such leading Romantic poets as Coleridge and Wordsworth. Returning to the US, he began writing actively (1835). He soon published his essay *Nature*, which established him as a leading exponent of Transcendentalism. In following years, he wrote, lectured widely, and was a member of the Massachusetts literary circle that included H. Thoreau and N. Hawthorne. He gained widespread recognition in the 1840s with his two volumes of essays, which included the celebrated *Self-Reliance.*

Emigrant Aid Company New England company (*active* 1854–57) formed to promote settlement of Kansas territory by antislavery settlers. Organized (1854) just before passage of the Kansas-Nebraska Act, the company was designed to ensure that Kansas would not become a slaveholding state, an issue to be decided by a popular vote (*see* popular sovereignty). The company sent over 1,000 abolitionist settlers to Kansas, who later figured in the Bleeding Kansas (*q.v.*) incident.

émigrés French royalist sympathizers who fled France during the revolution. Many joined Prince L. de Condé in setting up court at Koblenz, and most returned on restoration of the monarchy (1814).

Emin Pasa, Mehmed ⟨Schnitzer, Eduard⟩ 1840–92. German explorer. Named governor of a province in the Sudan by C. Gordon (1878), he was rescued by Sir H. Stanley during an uprising (1885) by the Mahdists.

emir ⟨amir⟩ Muslim title that was used variously for a military or naval commander, provincial governor, or other official. Though emirs who were provincial governors usually had administrative powers under the caliph, they sometimes had sufficient power to rule as virtually independent sovereigns. Muslim caliphs adopted the title amir al-muminin, or "commander of the faithful."

Emmanuel Philibert 1528–80. Duke of Savoy (1553–80). He regained his duchy from the French by the Treaty of Cateau-Cambrésis (1559). He instituted much-needed reforms to revitalize the economy and eliminated foreign influence there.

Emmet, Robert 1778–1803. Irish nationalist leader. The uprising in Ireland he had planned with French help failed in 1803 and he was hanged for treason.

Emmett, Daniel Decatur *See* **Dixie**

Empedocles *c*490–430 BC. Greek philosopher. He taught, as earlier Greeks had, that all things were composed of the elements earth, water, fire, and air and that harmony and discord caused them to variously combine and separate.

emperor Royal title, derived from the Latin *imperator*, a title given to victorious generals. Caesar and Augustus both adopted the title to mean supreme ruler, and from the time of Nero, it came into continuous use in the Roman Empire. Charlemagne reestablished use of the title in the West (9th cent.).

Empire of *See names inverted, as in* **Ashante, Empire of**

Empire style French decorative style, a neoclassic style introduced in France during Napoleon's reign. It was marked by emphasis on classic forms and imperial grandeur. Adapted variously in other countries, it spread throughout Europe and to the US.

empiricism A school of philosophy holding that all valid human knowledge is derived from experience. Although the concept of empirical knowledge has been known since ancient Greek times, the school began its classical development in Britain (18th cent.), especially in the writings of J. Locke, G. Berkeley, and D. Hume. Empiricists oppose rationalism, with its defense of intuition, innate ideas, or *a priori* knowledge. Some form of empiricism lies at the base of most modern philosophies of science.

Empson, William 1906–. English poet and critic. He wrote an influential critical work, *Seven Types of Ambiguity*. His poetry, known for its wit and intellect, includes *The Gathering Storm*.

Ems dispatch Telegram sent to Prussian chancellor O. von Bismarck by King Wilhelm I of Prussia (later German emperor Wilhelm I) on July 13, 1870. The French ambassador had sought assurances from Wilhelm that no member of his family would seek the Spanish throne. Wilhelm refused to give such an assurance and then telegraphed a report of his conversation with the ambassador to Bismarck. Bismarck, however, wanted a test of strength with France. He edited the telegram to make it appear that France had been insulted and published it. Predictably, France then declared war on July 19, thus beginning the Franco-Prussian War *(q.v.)*.

encomienda System for supplying Indian laborers in Spanish colonial America (16th–18th cents.). The encomienda (entrustment) specified that a Spanish settler would receive a certain number of Indian laborers, in return for which he would protect them and instruct them in Christianity. The system resulted in great hardships for the Indians despite attempts at reform (16th cent.).

Encyclopédie *See* **Encyclopedists; Diderot, Denis**

Encyclopédistes *See* **Encyclopedists**

Encyclopedists ⟨*Encyclopédistes*⟩ Name of group of writers who produced the *Encyclopédie*, a great French encyclopedia of science, arts, and trades, which was important in advancing the ideas of the Enlightenment *(q.v.)*. The work was edited by J. d'Alembert and D. Diderot, in France (1751–72), and contained articles by many noted writers of the Enlightenment, who subsequently became known as Encyclopedists. *(See also philosophes.)*

Endecott, John ⟨Endicott, ~⟩ *c*1588–1665. English colonist. He was a founder of the Massachusetts Bay colony and its first governor (1629–30).

Enders, John *See* **Robbins, Frederick Chapman**

Endymion In Greek legend, a shepherd loved by Selene, goddess of the moon. She visited him every night on Mt. Latmus, where he was perpetually asleep.

Enesco, Georges 1881–1955. Romanian violinist, composer, and conductor known for his Romanian folk themes. He was a teacher of Yehudi Menuhin.

Engels, Friedrich 1820–95. German Socialist philosopher who, as a collaborator with K. Marx, helped found modern communism. The son of a factory owner, he spent much of his life (especially after 1850) in England. Engels was a leading figure at the First International and Second International, and collaborated with Marx to write the *Communist Manifesto (q.v.)*. By his continuing collaboration with Marx, Engels greatly influenced Marxism and the theory of Dialectical Materialism. He edited the last two volumes of *Das Kapital* (after Marx's death), and his own work, *The Origin of the Family, Private Property, and the State*, is said to have influenced N. Lenin.

Enghien, Louis Antoine Henri de Bourbon-Condé, duke of 1772–1804. French prince, son of émigré leader L. de Condé. He was kidnapped on Napoleon's orders, accused of a conspiracy with G. Cadoudal to overthrow Napoleon, and executed.

England Constituent unit of the United Kingdom of Great Britain and Northern Ireland. It is the administrative and economic center of the United Kingdom and has the largest population. For the history of England, *see* Great Britain.

England, Church of *See* **Church of England**
England, Mary of *See* **Mary of England**
English Bill of Rights *See* **Bill of Rights**
English Civil War ⟨Great Rebellion⟩ Armed conflict (1642–49) between forces of the English Parliament and those of monarchy, under Stuart king Charles I. The war was caused by a complex of political and religious problems. The absolutism of King Charles (and of James I before him) brought an ongoing struggle for power between the king and Parliament to a head. Attempts to impose religious uniformity aroused Puritans and Independents against the government as well. In general, the war pitted the Royalists, composed of the aristocracy, the Anglicans, and Catholics, against Parliamentarians, including the gentry, merchants, and artisans. During the war O. Cromwell emerged as the leading figure of the parliamentary army and the army became a stronghold of Puritan sentiment. Cromwell became leader of the government (*see* Commonwealth *and* Protectorate) created after the monarchy was abolished. The monarchy was reestablished in 1660. (*See also* Great Britain.) Key events in the war include:

1625 Charles I succeeded to the throne; his belief in divine right of kings led to a continuation of struggle between king and Parliament which had embroiled the reign of his predecessor, James I.

1626 Parliament dissolved by Charles because it had limited his right to collect customs duties and had impeached his favorite, G. Villiers, duke of Buckingham.

1628 Charles I convened a new Parliament in order to raise needed money.

1628 Petition of Right presented to Charles by Parliament; listed his abuses of power; Charles agreed to demands to get money.

1629 Charles again dissolved Parliament; step taken after Parliament continued protests against taxation, Star Chamber proceedings, and religious restrictions.

1629–40 Charles ruled without Parliament for 11 years.

1634 Charles extended ship-money tax, a device for raising money without Parliament, from coastal towns to entire kingdom.

1638 Solemn League and Covenant signed by Scottish Presbyterians after Charles attempted to impose Anglican liturgy in Scotland.

1639 First Bishops' War; Charles warred with Scotland over his attempt to impose Anglican liturgy there; Charles forced to reconvene Parliament to get funds for war.

1640 Short Parliament convened; dissolved by Charles after it demanded reforms.

1640 Second Bishops' War with Scotland; Charles was defeated and forced to agree to monetary payments to Scots.

1640 Long Parliament convened, brought about by Charles's need for money; Parliament passed numerous fundamental reforms, including law prohibiting dissolution of Parliament without its consent; Charles agreed to reforms.

1641 Grand Remonstrance issued against Charles by Parliament; Parliament demanded control over the army, church reform, and appointment of royal ministers acceptable to it.

1642 Charles tried to have J. Pym and other leaders of parliamentary opposition arrested (Jan.); break between Parliament and Royalists nearly complete.

1642 Nineteen Propositions issued (June) by Parliament and rejected by Charles; preparations for war began on both sides, with Royalists generally concentrated in north and Parliamentarians in the south.

1642–46 First Civil War.

1642 Battle of Edgehill (Oct. 23) fought; first major battle of war proved indecisive.

1643 Parliament secured an alliance with Scotland by promising to establish Presbyterianism as the state church in England (Sept.); Scottish troops then joined fighting.

1644 Battle of Marston Moor (July 2); O. Cromwell and his regiment (called Ironsides) inflicted a disastrous defeat on the Royalists.

1645 Self-Denying Ordinance passed; all members of Parliament (except Cromwell) resigned their commands in army (Apr.).

1644–45 Parliamentary army reorganized into the New Model Army; Puritan influence became predominant in the army.

1645 Cromwell victorious over Charles in the

Battle of Naseby (June 14); Royalist resistance nearly broken.

1646 Battle of Stowe-on-the-Wold (Mar. 26); Royalists beaten in this last battle of the First Civil War.

1646 Charles surrendered himself to the Scots (May 5).

1647 Charles turned over to Parliament by the Scots (Jan.).

1647 Growing independent and Puritan religious opinion in the army made consensus impossible on the parliamentary side; Presbyterians began to turn back to royalism.

1647 Army refused order by Parliament to disband; seized King Charles (June 4); Cromwell joined rebelling army faction, which then attempted to negotiate with Charles; army occupied London (Aug. 6) to impose policies on Presbyterian members of Parliament.

1647 King Charles escaped to the Isle of Wight (Nov.); concluded agreement with Scotland, now disaffected by the radicalism of the English Parliamentarians; Scottish armies to fight for Royalist cause.

1648–49 Second Civil War, brief but complex struggle; pitted Scotland against England, Parliament against the Royalists, and Independents against Presbyterians.

1648 Parliamentary forces quelled uprisings in various parts of the kingdom.

1648 Battle of Preston; Cromwell and his parliamentary army defeated the invading Scottish army (Aug. 17–19); marked end of fighting in the Second Civil War.

1648 King Charles again seized by the army (Dec.).

1648 Pride's Purge; parliamentary army, under Cromwell's control, expelled pro-Royalist Presbyterians from Parliament (Dec.); remaining members constituted Rump Parliament.

1649 Instrument of Government (temporary) issued by army (Jan. 20).

1649 King Charles beheaded after trial (Jan. 30); monarchy abolished and Commonwealth proclaimed the day of Charles's execution; Cromwell became head of state.

enlightened despot Monarch whose power, though absolute, was theoretically based on the rule of reason. The doctrine of enlightened despotism arose during the 18th-cent. Enlightenment.

Enlightenment ⟨Age of Reason⟩ Intellectual movement of the 18th cent., centered in France but extending throughout Europe and to America. Characterized by an abiding belief in rationalism, science, and natural laws, it fostered radically new views that challenged accepted religious, politi-

cal, and social doctrines. The Enlightenment was an outgrowth of the 17th-cent. advances in science and philosophy (especially the work of J. Locke, I. Newton, and R. Descartes), and many of the ideas of the Enlightenment were embodied in the American and French revolutions. The Encyclopedists (q.v.), philosophes (q.v.), physiocrats (q.v.), and numerous individual literary and intellectual figures were important to the Enlightenment. Commonly associated with the Enlightenment were: (in France) J. Rousseau, F. Voltaire, D. Diderot, and C. Montesquieu; (in Britain) A. Smith, J. Bentham, D. Hume, and E. Gibbon; (in Germany) G. Lessing, M. Mendlessohn, and J. von Herder; (in America) T. Paine, T. Jefferson, and B. Franklin. (See also deism.)

Enlil See **Anu**

Ennius, Quintus 239–169? BC. Roman poet, called the father of Latin literature. He wrote the history of Rome in his epic poem Annales.

Enoch Biblical figure. Enoch was the eldest son of Cain, who named a city for him.

Enragés During the French Revolution (1789–99), a group of extremist Parisian workers who sacked Paris shops for food (Feb.–Mar., 1793) and forced the ouster of the moderate Girondist faction. Though they exacted further concessions from the revolutionary government, their leaders were arrested in September.

entente Agreement or understanding between two nations on matters of policy.

Entente Cordiale The "cordial understanding" reached between Britain and France (Apr. 8, 1904). By the agreement, France was given a free hand in Morocco, while British control of Egypt was recognized. Spheres of influence in Africa, Thailand, and the Pacific were better defined. Russia later joined the pact (1907), making it the Triple Entente (q.v.).

Enver Pasha 1881–1922. Turkish general. A Young Turk (q.v.), he was a leader in the 1908 revolt to restore the liberal 1876 constitution. He became minister of war, helped bring Turkey into WW I as a German ally, and, during the war, became virtual ruler of Turkey. He fled Turkey after the war.

Eos Greek goddess of dawn and the lover of Orion. She corresponds to the Roman Aurora.

Epaminondas d. 362 BC. Theban general and noted tactician. He led the Boeotians to victory over Sparta at Leuctra (371 BC), thus breaking Spartan power. He was killed in battle during a later invasion of the Peloponnesus.

Épée, Charles Michel, Abbé de l' 1712–89. French teacher. He devised a one-hand system of communication for deaf-mutes and founded a school for them in Paris.

Ephesus Ancient Greek seaport, once located near what is now Smyrna, Turkey. A leading Ionian city of great wealth in classical Greek times, it passed first to the Persians and then to the Romans. Under the Romans it prospered as the leading city of the Asian province until it was sacked by the Goths (3d cent. AD).

Ephesus, Council of Third ecumenical council called (AD 431) by Roman emperors Theodosius II (Eastern) and Valentinian III (Western) to resolve the controversy over Nestorianism (q.v.). The council, under Saint Cyril, condemned Nestorius' teachings, but did so before the arrival of the Eastern bishops, who supported him. A controversy resulted and was not settled until Pope Celestine I upheld the council, excommunicated Nestorius, and won the support of Theodosius.

ephor Name for a magistrate of Sparta and other Dorian cities. A board of five ephors was elected annually, and, though functions changed over the centuries, they shared functions of government with the dual kings of Sparta. Ephors figured in Spartan government from the 8th cent. BC. Eliminated (c227 BC) by Cleomenes III, the office was later restored.

Ephorus c405–330 BC. Greek historian who wrote a universal history of Greece, arranged by topics. Only fragments remain.

Ephraim In the Bible, the younger son of Joseph and founder of one of the 12 tribes of Israel.

Epictetus AD 55?–135?. Greek Stoic philosopher. A freed slave, Epictetus taught that salvation lay in acceptance of God's will and concern for the common welfare. He wrote nothing, and his teachings were set down by his pupil Flavius Arrian.

Epicureanism Greek school of philosophy founded (after 306 BC) by Epicurus. It held that the chief aim of life was to experience pleasure and avoid pain. Epicurus himself taught that such an end was to be achieved by prudence and moderation, but this aspect of his teaching was not always observed by his followers. Epicureanism anticipated both modern materialism and modern utilitarianism.

Epicurus 341–270 BC. Greek philosopher who taught that happiness and pleasure are the supreme moral good. However, he also advised honor and restraint, principles that were overlooked by his enthusiastic followers.

Epigoni Mythical Greek warriors. The sons of the Seven Against Thebes (q.v.), they avenged their fathers' deaths 10 years later by capturing Thebes themselves.

Epimetheus In Greek mythology, the brother of Prometheus. He was the husband of Pandora, who opened the box containing the world's evils.

Épinay, Louise de la Live d' 1726–83. French literary figure during the Enlightenment. She was a friend and patroness of D. Diderot, J. Rousseau, and others.

Epiphanes, Ptolemy V See **Ptolemy V**

Epirus Ancient Greek country on the Ionian Sea in what is now northwest Greece and southern Albania. It reached the height of its power under King Pyrrhus (3rd cent. BC), and declined after it fell to the Romans in the third Macedonian War (171–168 BC).

Episcopal church, Protestant See **Protestant Episcopal Church**

Epoch of Civil Wars In Colombian history, a period (1867–80) of civil war between liberals, who sought a democratic federal government free of clerical domination, and conservatives, who advocated a strong central government and a prominent position for the church. The struggle ended (1880) with the election of Rafael Núñez (1825–94), who formed a coalition of conservatives and moderates. As president (1880–82, 1884–94), he at first introduced liberal reforms, but he also strengthened the central government and the church's position within it.

Epstein, Sir Jacob 1880–1959. American-born sculptor. His works are massive and were often controversial: his *Strand Statues* were removed (1937) from the British Medical Building in London.

equal-field system Chinese system for land distribution and taxation established in 485 BC and later also adopted in Japan. Each adult peasant was allotted a specified amount of land, most of which reverted to the government on his death. The system disappeared in China and Japan by the 8th cent. AD.

Equal Rights Amendment See **feminism**

Equatorial Africa, French See **French Equatorial Africa**

Equatorial Guinea (formerly Spanish Guinea) West African republic (pop. 360,000) whose agricultural economy is based primarily on cocoa and coffee. Discovered by the Portuguese in 1471, the area was ceded to the Spanish in 1778. The British later settled some freed slaves there, and the Cubans set up a penal colony (19th cent.). A Franco-Spanish treaty defined the boundaries (1900) of this Spanish possession. Independence was proclaimed on Oct. 12, 1968. Lt. Col. Teodoro Obiang Nguema seized power (Aug. 3, 1979) and suspended the Constitution.

equites Originally, the Roman cavalry. The equites were chosen from the elite of Roman society and, after the 1st cent. BC, formed a distinct class charged with administrative and financial matters.

ERA *See* **feminism**

era of good feeling In US history, a term used to describe the period 1817–24, when, with the decline of the Federalist party, the Democratic Republican policies went unchallenged and sectionalism decreased. J. Monroe was president during this period.

Erasmus ⟨Desiderius ~⟩ 1466?–1536. Dutch theologian and one of the great humanist scholars. Ordained a Roman Catholic priest (1492), he soon came to oppose the pedantry of scholastic theologians. He traveled widely throughout Europe (settling in Basel after 1521) and, through his critical and satirical works, became a leading figure among the circle of humanist thinkers there. He remained within the Catholic church, however, and, after refusing to join M. Luther's movement for radical reforms, came to oppose him openly. Among Erasmus' many important works are his edition of the *New Testament*, editions of Latin and Greek classics, and his critical pieces, including *The Praise of Folly* and *Colloquies*.

Erastianism *See* **Erastus, Thomas**

Erastus, Thomas 1524–83. Swiss physician and theologian. A supporter of Zwingli, he was excommunicated briefly. A posthumously published paper arguing for secular punishment of sins (as opposed to divine excommunication) gave rise to a movement known as Erastianism. This movement effectively advocated complete domination of the church by the state.

Erato In Greek religion, the Muse of erotic poetry.

Eratosthenes c275–c195 BC. Greek scientist, astronomer, and poet. He was the first to measure the earth's circumference and tilt of its axis.

Erebus In Greek religion, son of Chaos, husband of Night, and father of Day. He was darkness personified.

Erech ⟨Uruk⟩ Ancient Mesopotamian city located in what is now Iraq. Founded about 5000 BC, it was the site of temples of the Sumerian goddess Inanna and the god Anu.

Erechtheum Ionic temple on the Athenian Acropolis. Built between 421 and 405 BC, and designed by Mnesicles, it is known for its complexity of design and the technical mastery of its detail.

Erechtheus In Greek legend, king of Athens. He is supposed to have sacrificed one of this daughters to win a war against Eleusis. He was later destroyed by Poseidon.

Eretria Ancient Greek city, once located on the island of Euboea, Greece. Eretria was destroyed by Darius (490 BC) for supporting an Ionian revolt in the years leading up to the Persian Wars *(q.v.)*. Though resettled by Athens, it never regained its previous influence.

Erfurt Parliament Meeting (Mar. 20, 1850) between Prussia and a number of lesser German states to consider Prussia's plan for a union of German states, dominated by Prussia and Austria. Austria opposed the plan, however, and Prussia was forced by threat of war to withdraw it. The withdrawal was made in the "Punctation [or humiliation] of Olmütz" (Nov. 29, 1850). This was a formal agreement signed by Prussia accepting the existing German Confederation (dominated by Austria).

Erhard, Ludwig 1897–. German statesman. He was responsible for the postwar economic recovery in West Germany and became its economics minister (1949). He succeeded K. Adenauer as chancellor (1963–66).

Eric VII ⟨Eric of Pomerania⟩ c1381–1459. King of Norway (1389–1439), Sweden (1412–39), and Denmark (1412–39). He ruled in a period of internal unrest and was deposed in all three countries (1439).

Eric IX d. 1160. King of Sweden (1150–60). He led a crusade against Finland (1157) to force the Finns to accept baptism. He was killed while there and later became patron saint of Sweden.

Eric XIV 1533–77. King of Sweden (1560–68), successor to his father, Gustavus I. An ineffective ruler, he was deposed and imprisoned by his brother, John.

Eric of Pomerania *See* **Eric VII**

Ericsson, John 1803–89. Swedish engineer. He invented the screw propeller (1836) and built the Union ironclad *Monitor*, which fought (1862) the Confederate ironclad *Merrimac* during the American Civil War.

Ericson, Leif *See* **Leif Ericson**

Eric the Red *fl.* 10th cent. Norse explorer. On being exiled from Iceland, he explored Greenland and founded the first colony there (c986), near the modern Julianehaab.

Eridu Ancient Sumerian city, south of Ur in modern Iraq. It was founded between 7000 and 5000 BC and is considered the oldest known city in Sumer. It was the seat of the water god Ea.

Erie Indians North American Indian tribe. They inhabited the Lake Erie region in the present states of New York, Pennsylvania, and Ohio. In 1656 the Erie were almost annihilated by the Iroquois, the survivors being assimilated into the Iroquois tribes.

Erik *See* **Eric**

Erinyes ⟨Furies⟩ Monstrous Greek goddesses of vengeance. They rose from the underworld to pursue and torment wrongdoers. They were: Alecto, the relentless when angered; Tisiphone, avenger of murder; and Megaera, the jealous.

Eris In Greek mythology, the goddess of strife. Not invited to the wedding of Peleus and Thetis, she threw the apple of discord among the guests, and thus precipitated the Trojan War.

Ermak *See* **Yermak**

Ernest Augustus of Hanover *See* **George V**

Ernst, Max 1891–1976. German artist. He was a follower of the Dada movement and a founder of surrealism, known for his work in collage and other mediums.

Eros Greek god of love. At first considered the son of Chaos, he was later believed to be the son of Aphrodite and Zeus.

Erskine, Thomas, 1st Baron 1750–1823. Scottish jurist, noted defense counsel during a wave of treason and sedition trials in Britain brought on by upheavals of the French Revolution. T. Paine was among his clients (1792).

Erzberger, Matthias 1875–1921. German statesman and leader of the Catholic Center party. He led the delegation that signed the armistice ending WW I (1918). He was assassinated by nationalists.

Esarhaddon King of Assyria (681–669 BC), successor to his father, Sennacherib. He conquered the Chaldaeans and the Egyptians (c670 BC) and built the great palace at Nineveh.

Esau Biblical figure, son of Isaac and the older twin brother of Jacob. Jacob tricked him out of his birthright, and Esau later settled in Edom.

Eskimo A people who are the chief inhabitants of the Arctic regions in northeast Siberia and from the Bering Sea to Greenland. They are of uncertain, but possibly Asian, origin, and had ranged as far east as Greenland by the 13th cent.

Espartero, Baldomero 1792–1879. Spanish general and statesman. He won important victories for Isabella II in the Carlist War (1833–39), became regent (1841–43), and was prime minister (1854–56).

Esperanto Artificial international language. Esperanto was invented (1887) by Ludwig Zamenhof (1859–1917). It has its roots in the Romance languages, its words are spelled phonetically, and it utilizes a simple grammatical structure.

Espy, James Pollard 1785–1860. American meteorologist. In *Philosophy of Storms* he advanced what is said to be the first valid explanation of cloud formation.

Essad Pasha 1863–1920. Albanian political leader. He joined the Young Turks and was Albanian deputy in the Turkish Parliament. During WW I, he was dictator (1914–16) of newly created Albania. He fled the country after being defeated by the Austrians in the war.

Essex, Robert Devereux, 2d earl of 1567–1601. English courtier and favorite of Elizabeth I. He was a commander in the fighting that led to the sack of Cádiz (1596). Sent to Ireland (1599) to put down a rebellion by the earl of Tyrone, he concluded a truce (against the queen's wishes) and suddenly found himself in disfavor. He made a rash attempt (1601) at ousting the queen's ministry by force, but the plot was uncovered and he was executed.

Essex Junto Extremist faction of the American Federalist party, so nicknamed by J. Hancock because most of its members came from Essex County, Massachusetts. It was prominent in the calling (1814) of the secessionist Hartford Convention *(q.v.)*.

Estaing, Charles Hector, comte d' 1729–94. French admiral. He commanded a French fleet (1778–80) in support of the colonists during the American Revolution (1775–83), and was guillotined during the French Revolution (1789–99).

Este Italian princely family that ruled Ferrara (1240–1597) and Modena (1288–1796). They were noted patrons of the arts. Azzo d'Este II (996–1097) was the founder of the line, which ended with the death of Ercole III Rinaldo (1727–1803).

Esterházy Hungarian noble family. Ferenc Zerházy (1563–94) took the name when he became baron of Galantha, and the line includes soldiers, art patrons, and diplomats. Prince Nikolaus Joseph (1714–90) was patron to J. Haydn for 30 years.

Esterhazy, Ferdinand Walsin 1847–1923. French army officer involved in the Dreyfus Affair *(q.v.)*. He sold military documents to the Germans, for which a French Jew, Capt. A. Dreyfus, was convicted. Esterhazy confessed in 1899.

Esther In the Old Testament, queen of Persia, wife of King Ahasuerus. She saved the Jews from annihilation, at the hands of Haman.

esthetics *See* **aesthetics**

Estienne, Henri II 1531?–98. French-born Swiss printer. Estienne continued his family's successful printing business. A distinguished scholar, he was renowned for his editing of classical works, particularly *Thesaurus Graecae linguae.*

Estienne, Robert 1498?–1559. French printer and scholar. Robert headed the family printing business and was royal printer to Francis I. He was especially noted for his Bibles and his editions of Greek and Roman classics.

Estigarribia, José *See* **Chaco War**

Estonia Former state and present constituent republic (pop. 1,466,000) of the USSR, located on the
Baltic Sea. The Danes conquered Estonia (1219),
and the Teutonic Knights ruled it from the 14th
to the 16th cents. Sweden subsequently controlled
the region until 1721, when Estonia passed to Russia. It became an independent republic (Feb. 24,
1918) amid the upheavals of the Russian Revolution and WW I, was involved in the Baltic Wars of
Liberation *(q.v.)*, and was reannexed by the USSR
(Aug. 3, 1940).

Estonian Revolt of 1343 *See* **St. George's Day Revolt**

Estrées, Gabrielle d' 1573–99. Mistress of King
Henry IV of France. Their three children were le-
gitimized and became the founders of the Vendôme line.

Ethical Culture movement A nonsectarian movement founded by F. Adler (1876) in New York
City. It seeks the advancement of moral systems
based on ethics rather than on religious doctrine.

ethics Branch of philosophy concerned with good
and evil as it relates to human conduct. Among
the ancient Greeks, Socrates equated virtue with
knowledge, while both Plato and Aristotle
grounded it in the nature of humanity. Aristotle
further held that virtue contributed to achievement of man's proper end and advocated following
the "golden mean" to attain it. The Judeo-Chris-
tian tradition equated the good with the will of
God, and, in the teachings of such philosophers as
Saint Thomas Aquinas (13th cent. AD), its attainment was linked with the realization of humanity's proper end. I. Kant (18th cent.), with his
categorical imperative, tried to establish an absolute ethical standard independent of religion. Philosophers of the rationalist school grounded ethics
in the human conscience, while empiricists tied
it to human experience.

Ethiopia *(formerly* Abyssinia) Ethiopia is a Socialist state located in northeast Africa, and bordered on the north by the Red Sea. Its capital is
Addis Ababa. Ethiopia has one of Africa's longest
recorded histories and by tradition traces its government back to about the 11th cent. BC and to
the rule of King Menelik I, believed to be the son
of Solomon and Sheba. The region was early dominated by Egypt and, in the 8th cent. BC, Ethiopians conquered much of Egypt and controlled it
to about the 7th cent. BC. Key dates in Ethiopia's
history include:

1ST CENT. AD Kingdom of Aksum flourished in
region; recorded history of Ethiopia began.

4TH CENT. AD Bishop Frumentius introduced
Christianity.

6TH CENT. AD Conquered what is now Yemen in

Arabia; period of commercial prosperity and cultural flowering followed.

650 Muslims drove Ethiopians from Arabia;
cut off from rest of world by Muslim conquest of
North Africa, Ethiopia sank into obscurity for a
thousand years.

1520 Portuguese visited Ethiopia.

1530–43 Portuguese aided Ethiopians in repulsing invasion by Somalis.

1855 Ethiopia reunified by King Theodore II.

1868 King Theodore imprisoned British diplomats; British invaded, Theodore committed suicide.

1889–1911 Menelik II reigned; expanded borders of Ethiopia.

1889 Addis Ababa became capital.

1895–96 Italy invaded in the Ethiopian War;
Menelik defeated Italy, and Ethiopian independence was recognized.

1916–30 Zauditi, Menelik's daughter, became empress; her cousin Ras Taffari ruled as regent.

1930 Zauditi died; Ras Taffari crowned emperor Haile Selassie I.

1931 Haile Selassie granted country a constitution and a parliament.

1934–35 Italy invaded and conquered Ethiopia in Italo-Ethiopian War; League of Nations unable to halt Italy's aggression.

1936 Haile Selassie forced into exile.

1936 Ethiopia annexed to Eritrea and Italian
Somaliland to form Italian East Africa.

1941 WW II; British forces captured Ethiopia
(1941); Haile Selassie restored.

1952 UN placed Eritrea (eastern coastal region) under Ethiopian rule.

1955 New constitution adopted.

1960 Coup attempt (Dec.); Haile Selassie restored by the army.

1969 Eritrean Liberation Front started violent
campaign for secession of Eritrea.

1970 Guerrilla activity in Eritrea resulted in
declaration of state of emergency.

1974 Serious unrest caused by long drought
and resulting famine; resignation of the cabinet;
Haile Selassie named a moderate, Endalkachew
Makonnen, prime minister; agreed to call constitutional convention.

1974 Army took control of Addis Ababa
(June).

1974 Makonnen overthrown (July), arrested,
later executed; succeeded by Michael Imru.

1974 Haile Selassie peacefully deposed
(Sept. 12); placed under palace arrest; US military
aid halted.

1974 Armed forces committee proclaimed Ethiopia a Socialist state with one political party, the Supreme Progressive Council (Dec. 20).

1975 All lands and businesses nationalized.

1975 Haile Selassie died (Aug. 27).

1975 Government troops battled Eritrean guerrillas as fighting intensified.

1977 Gen. Teferi Benti, chairman of Provisional Military Council, shot and killed during a council meeting; Lt. Col. Mengistu Haile Mariam became head of state.

1977 American diplomats ordered to leave.

1977 Heavy fighting between government troops and ethnic Somalis in southeastern Ethiopia; Somalia charged with aiding rebels.

1977 Russia ended (Oct.) military aid to Somalia, backed Ethiopia in border war.

1978 Somalis defeated (Mar.) in southeast, Ogaden region; Cuban troops aided Ethiopian victory; government reported successes against guerrillas in Eritrea; fighting against guerrillas nevertheless continued into the early 1980s.

1978 Friendship treaty signed with the Soviets.

Etruria *See* **Etruscans**

Etruscans Ancient people who established a flourishing civilization in northern Italy (Etruria) between the 8th and 4th cents. BC. They are believed to have emigrated to Italy from the Near East around the 12th cent. BC. They initiated trade with the Greeks, and their navy virtually dominated the Mediterranean for two centuries (7th–6th cents.). They ruled in Rome (6th cent.) as the legendary "Tarquin kings," but were expelled around 509 BC, according to tradition, after the king's son raped the Roman matron Lucretia. The Romans subsequently defeated them decisively in the Battle of Lake Regullus (496 BC), and began the gradual subjugation of Etruscan cities (completed by 282 BC). The Romans borrowed freely from Etruscan civilization, and the Latin alphabet is derived from the earlier Etruscan writing system.

Euboea Island on the east coast of Greece. Important ancient towns were Khalkis and Eretria. Dominated by Athens (5th cent. BC) and Macedon (from 4th cent.), it was taken by Rome (194 BC). The island passed to various conquerors after Rome's fall and was annexed to Greece in 1830.

Euclid *fl.* *c*300 BC. Greek mathematician famous for his fundamental contribution to the study of geometry and the development of mathematics. Details of his life are uncertain, but it is known that he taught at the great school of Alexandria in Egypt and that he wrote the celebrated mathematical treatise *Elements.* The work included a systematic presentation of plane geometry, which

long served as the basic text for its study, and treatments of number theory and solid geometry. It was not until the 19th cent. that fundamental departures from his system of plane geometry began to be presented.

Eudes ⟨Odo⟩ *c*860–898. French king (888–898), successor to Charles III (the Fat) in the West Frankish Kingdom. He defended Paris against the Norsemen and was succeeded by his rival, Charles III (the Simple).

Eudes of Lagery *See* **Urban II**

Eudoxus of Cnidus 408?–355? BC. Greek astronomer and mathematician known for his explanation of the motion of the planets and calculation of the length of the solar year.

Euergetes, Ptolemy III *See* **Ptolemy III**

Eugene III ⟨Montemagno, Bernardo dei Paganelli di⟩ *d.* 1153. Italian-born pope (1145–53) who was driven from Rome by Arnold of Brescia, the reformer. He preached the unsuccessful Second Crusade (1147–49) while in France.

Eugene IV 1383–1447. Italian-born pope (1431–47), successor to Martin V. His reign was marked by his dispute with the Council of Basel (*q.v.*) over conciliarism. He convened the Council of Ferrara-Florence (*q.v.*) in its stead. His opponents unsuccessfully tried to depose him and elected the antipope Felix V.

Eugene of Savoy, Prince 1663–1736. Great French-born general. A brilliant strategist in service of the Holy Roman Empire, he defeated the Turks at Vienna and later drove them from Hungary. He commanded the imperial armies during the wars of Spanish Succession (1701–14) and Polish Succession (1733–35). Among his many victories were the battles of Zenta and Blenheim.

Eugénie ⟨*in full,* Eugénia Marie de Montijo de Guzmán⟩ 1826–1920. Empress of France (1853–70) as wife of Napoleon III. She fled to England when the empire fell (1870).

Euhemerus *fl.* *c*330 BC. Greek mythographer whose work *Sacred History* sought to prove that mythological beings were based on events of historical fact.

Eulenspiegel, Till *fl.* 14th cent. German folk hero, a peasant and prankster who played wicked, often obscene, tricks on the arrogant. His escapades are the subject of numerous literary and musical works.

Euler, Leonhard 1707–83. Swiss mathematician. Called the most prolific mathematician of all time, he produced works that treated all major branches of mathematics.

Eumanes II *See* **Pergamum**

eunuch Male court official who had been castrated. Eunuchs were variously employed as harem guards, political advisers, and military leaders in many Middle Eastern, Asian, and Oriental states.

Euphrates See **Tigris and Euphrates**

Euric d. AD c484. King of the Visigoths (466–484), younger son of Theodoric I. Under Euric, the Visigothic kingdom reached its greatest extent. He ruled most of Spain and southern Gaul and established his capital at Toulouse. He wrote the first Visigothic law code.

Euripides 480?–406 BC. One of the three great tragic poets (with Sophocles and Aeschylus) of ancient Greece. He spent the greater part of his life in Athens, and there entered his tragedies in the annual competition of the festival of Dionysus. He is said to have written 92 plays (of which 18, definitely attributed to him, survive) but won first prize in only four competitions. His writing is generally considered more realistic in tone then that of the other great tragic poets. Among his extant works are *Cyclops, Orestes,* and *Electra.*

Europa In Greek mythology, daughter of Phoenix or Agenor. She was carried off by Zeus to Crete and there bore his sons Minos, Rhadamanthus, and Sarpedon.

European Economic Community ⟨Common Market⟩ West European economic association. It was formed in 1957 and its original members were Belgium, France, Italy, Luxembourg, The Netherlands, and W. Germany. Its goals were to establish the economic union of member nations and eventually to bring about political union. It has sought to eliminate internal tariffs, institute a uniform external scale of tariffs, achieve free movement of labor and capital from one nation to another, abolish obstructions to free competition, and establish collective trade and transportation policies. In 1973, Great Britain, Ireland, and Denmark joined the organization.

European Recovery Plan See **Marshall Plan**

Eurymedon River, Battle of See **Cimon**

Eusebius of Caesarea ⟨Eusebius Pamphili⟩ AD c263–339? Greek theologian and historian. He became bishop of Caesarea in Palestine (AD c314) and wrote on early Christian history in *Chronicle* and *Ecclesiastical History.*

Eusebius Pamphili See **Eusebius of Caesarea**

Eustachi, Bartolomeo ⟨Eustachio, Bartolommeo⟩ d. 1574. Italian anatomist who described the Eustachian tube connecting the ear to the pharynx, as well as other organs of the body.

Eustachio, Bartolommeo See **Eustachi, Bartolomeo**

Eutaw Springs, Battle of American Revolutionary War battle (Sept. 8, 1781), part of the Carolina Campaign *(q.v.).* Some 2,300 Americans under

N. Greene narrowly defeated 2,500 British troops under Col. Alexander Stewart, forcing them to retire to nearby Charleston, South Carolina. American casualties were 400, British 693.

Euterpe In Greek mythology, one of the nine Muses, the patroness of flute playing, joy, and pleasure.

Eutyches AD c378–c452. Archimandrite of the Eastern church in Constantinople. He founded Eutychianism, an early and extreme form of Monophysitism *(q.v.),* in reaction to Nestorianism. He was condemned for heresy, excommunicated, and banished (AD 451).

Eutychianism See **Eutyches**

Evangelical Alliance Association of Protestant evangelical Christians of various denominations founded in 1846. The alliance originated in reaction to the Oxford Movement *(q.v.)* in the Church of England and was formed during a London convention attended by some 800 delegates from evangelical churches in Europe and America. Branch organizations were created in various countries with the aim of promoting unity and the doctrines of evangelicalism. The importance of the alliance has declined in this century.

evangelicalism A term used to describe churches and groups within the Protestant fold that emphasize a strict and literal biblical faith, personal conversion experiences, and pietistic practices. Originally the Lutherans were known as Evangelicals, as distinguished from the Calvinists, who were called "Reformed." But the term was later applied to the new Protestant sects that arose (18th cent.) from Pietism *(q.v.)* in Europe, Methodism *(q.v.)* in Britain, and the Great Awakening *(q.v.)* in the United States. Today such conservative Protestant groups as the Fundamentalists prefer to be called Evangelical rather than Protestant.

Evans, Mary Ann See **Eliot, George**

Evarts, William Maxwell 1818–1901. American lawyer and statesman. He was counsel for A. Johnson in the impeachment proceedings (1868) and for the Republican party in the Hayes-Tilden dispute over the election of 1876.

Evatt, Herbert Vere 1894–1965. Australian statesman. He was justice of the high court of Australia (1930–40) and led the Australian delegation to conferences on formation of the UN. He served as president of the UN General Assembly (1948–49).

Eve Biblical first woman. She was the wife of Adam and mother of Cain and Abel. In the Bible, she was tricked by a serpent into eating the forbidden apple from the tree of knowledge. She tempted Adam to taste it as well, and thereby caused their expulsion from the Garden of Eden.

Evelyn, John 1620–1706. English author. His *Diary* (1640–1706) is considered an important source regarding 17th-cent. English life.

Everest, Sir George 1790–1866. British surveyor general of India (1830–43) for whom Mount Everest is named.

Evesham, Battle of Decisive battle (Aug. 4, 1265) that all but ended armed resistance in the Baron's War (1263–67). Edward (later Edward I) defeated and captured S. de Montfort near this town in central England and thereby restored his father, King Henry III, to power.

evolution Biological theory holding that living things have developed gradually from earlier forms. The concept appears in ancient Greek writings by Thales, Aristotle, and others. Scientific advances (17th–19th cents.) tended to support it, but it was C. Darwin's great work *On the Origin of Species* that eventually brought about its acceptance. The biological theory of evolution conflicts with the religious concept of special creation, which stipulates that God created each species separately, and has led to such controversies as the Scopes Trial (1925). The dispute, notably in the US, continues to the present day.

Ewald, George Heinrich August von 1803–75. German Orientalist and theologian. He is best known for his *Hebrew Grammar* and *History of Israel.*

Ewell, Richard Stoddert 1817–72. Confederate general during the American Civil War (1861–65). He served under Gen. S. Jackson and lost a leg at the second battle of Bull Run (1862). Taking over Jackson's command after Jackson was killed in battle, Ewell led R. E. Lee's invasion of Pennsylvania and commanded units in the Battle of Gettysburg, the Wilderness campaign, and the Petersburg campaign.

Exarchate of Italy *See* **Exarchate of Ravenna**

Exarchate of Ravenna 〈Exarchate of Italy〉 The part of Italy that was taken during the Byzantine conquest of the Ostrogoths and made part of the Byzantine Empire (6th–8th cents.). It was reduced to the area around Ravenna before finally being seized by the Lombards (752).

executive branch The branch or department of modern government, notably in the US, that executes or carries out the laws, as distinguished from the legislative branch, which enacts them, and the judicial branch, which interprets them. These distinctions stem from the theory of checks and balances *(q.v.)*, or separation of powers, whereby absolute power is denied to any single organ of government. In the US, the Constitution grants the president executive powers. However, it specifies only that he shall be commander in chief of the armed forces, that he may make treaties and appoint officers of the government (by and with the consent of the Senate, generally), and that he must report to Congress from time to time on "the state of the union." From this bare outline of presidential executive authority, the development of the power of the modern presidency has been considerable. The president and his administration now command an enormous apparatus of state that makes it possible for him to intervene effectively in nearly every aspect of the society. Presidents H. Truman and L. Johnson were even able to make war without the express consent of Congress—in Korea and Vietnam respectively—by calling these wars "police actions" or by securing only concurring "resolutions" about them from Congress. The 1970s and 1980s have witnessed a trend, arising from Vietnam and the Watergate controversies, toward curbing presidential powers.

Exile *See* **Babylonian captivity**

existentialism Modern school of philosophy concerned with human beings' relationship to the world around them and which teaches that the actual existence of humanity holds the clue to the meaning of being. Existentialism stems from S. Kierkegaard's revolt against the rationalism of G. Hegel. His work was subsequently built upon by two noted philosophers, M. Heidegger and J. Sartre.

Exodus The escape (c13th cent. BC) by the Jews from their enslavement in Egypt. It is an event of great significance in biblical history and is described in the second book (Exodus) of the Old Testament. The book narrates the flight from Egypt under Moses' guidance and includes the crossing of the Red Sea, the trek through the wilderness, and the giving of the Ten Commandments on Mt. Sinai.

Expedition of the Thousand A daring military campaign (Apr.-Oct., 1860) in which G. Garibaldi, with an army of some 1,000 scarcely trained, idealistic volunteers, conquered the Bourbon kingdom of Naples. Garibaldi undertook the campaign in the name of a unified Italian state. Impatient of the cautious diplomatic efforts at unification by Victor Emmanuel II of Piedmont-Sardinia and his minister C. Cavour, Garibaldi landed his force in Sicily on his own and conquered the island (by Aug. 20) after defeating a force of some 20,000 Bourbon troops there. He then crossed to the mainland and marched triumphantly into Naples (Sept. 7). He was prevented from marching on Rome itself by the intervention of the army of Victor Emmanuel II, and soon after turned over conquered Bourbon territories to Emmanuel.

expressionism Twentieth-cent. movement in art and literature that sought to express an inner vision or the essence of a subject by exaggerating or distorting its characteristics. The movement flourished before and after WW I, especially in Germany. The German Max Beckman (1854–1950), Austrian O. Kokoschka, Frenchman G. Rouault, and Lithuanian Chaim Soutine (1894–1943) were all considered notable expressionist painters. In literature, the Irish novelist J. Joyce, the German writer F. Kafka, and, in some of his plays, the American playwright E. O'Neill, were considered expressionist writers. The movement, though itself short-lived, was immensely influential in the subsequent development of painting and writing.

Eyck, Hubert van c1366–1425. Flemish painter, believed to be the older brother of Jan van Eyck. Little is known of his life. He is thought to have painted the altarpiece at Ghent.

Eyck, Jan van c1390–1441. Flemish painter. Van Eyck was a master of realism, rendering minute detail with great accuracy. His most famous work is *Giovanni Arnolfini and His Bride* (1434).

Eylau, Battle of Battle (Feb. 8, 1807) during the Napoleonic Wars (1803–15). Napoleon fought this indecisive battle against the combined forces of Russia and Prussia at Eylau (now Bagrationovsk, USSR). Heavy snow contributed to the confusion of battle. France suffered 15,000 casualties, the allies 18,000.

Ezechiel *See* **Ezekiel**

Ezekiel ⟨Ezechiel⟩ In the Bible, a Hebrew prophet and minister to the captive Jews of Babylon.

Ezra Hebrew scribe and priest (5th cent. BC).

Ezra Church, Battle of *See* **Atlanta Campaign**

Ezzelino da Romano 1194–1259. Ghibelline leader. The son-in-law of Holy Roman Emperor Frederick II, Ezzelino aided him against the Lombards and became the most powerful man in northern Italy. His rule there was remembered for its cruelty.

F

Fabian Society English Socialist society, founded (1883) by Frank Podmore (1855–1910) and Edward Pease (1857–1955) to gradually advance the Socialist cause from within the existing government framework. Fabians did not advocate revolutionary methods for change. They helped organize a labor-oriented committee (1900), which later became the British Labour party, with which Fabians are affiliated today. Prominent Fabians include G. Shaw and S. Webb.

Fabius Maximus Rullianus, Quintus ⟨Fabius Maximus Rullus, Quintus⟩ *d. c*290 BC. Roman general, consul (five times between 322 and 295 BC) and dictator (315 BC). He won an important victory at Sentinum (295 BC) in the third Samnite War.

Fabius Maximus Verrucosus, Quintus ⟨Cunctator, or the Delayer⟩ *d.* 203 BC. Roman general, consul (five times between 233 and 209 BC), and dictator (217 BC). The leader of Roman forces at the outset of Hannibal's invasion during the Second Punic War, he is remembered for delaying tactics in which he harassed but did not directly engage the enemy. The strategy was unpopular but was proved correct after his replacement (216) and the subsequent Roman defeat at Cannae (216).

Facta, Luigi *See* **March on Rome**

Fahrenheit, Gabriel Daniel 1686–1736. German physicist noted for the invention of the Fahrenheit temperature scale and introduction of the mercury thermometer.

Fa-Hsien *fl.* AD 399–414. Chinese monk and writer. He traveled throughout India and its neighboring regions and gathered much information about Indian culture, history, and geography. He translated Buddhist religious literature into Chinese.

Faidherbe, Louis Léon César 1818–89. French colonial governor of Senegal (1854–61, 1863–65) and soldier. He strengthened and expanded the colony during his administration.

fair Gathering of merchants and consumers. The fair had its origins in the public marketplaces of ancient Greece and Rome. It grew to be a large periodic event and the major vehicle for trade before the development of transportation. Fairs were often tied to religious festivals and occasions and became so important to both church and state that they were given special powers and privileges. With the rise of commerce and industry in the 17th and 18th cents. and the increasing ease with which people could find things to buy, fairs lost their importance. They have continued into the present in somewhat modified form.

Fairbanks, Douglas 1883–1939. American movie actor and producer. A founder (1919) of United Artists Corp., he was famous for his movie roles as a swashbuckling hero.

Fair Deal Name given (1949) by President H. Truman to the domestic program of his administration. It called for legislation to increase jobs, improve civil rights, create new housing, establish a national medical plan, and repeal the Taft-Hartley Act.

Fairfax of Cameron, Thomas, 3d Baron 1612–71. Engligh general, a leader of the Parliamentarians during the English Civil War. He succeeded R. Devereux as commander (1645), organized the New Model Army (1645), and won several important victories, including the Battle of Naseby. He resigned (1650) after formation of the Commonwealth, refusing to invade Scotland.

Fair Labor Standards Act ⟨Wages and Hours Act⟩ American labor law (1938), the first attempt to regulate the wages and working hours of American laborers. It fixed minimum-wage and overtime rates and established child-labor age limits.

Fair Oaks, Battle of *See* **Seven Pines, Battle of**

Fair of Lincoln *See* **Lincoln, Battle of**

Faisal *c*1906–75. Saudi Arabian king (1964–75), successor to his brother King Saud. A leading figure in the Arab world, he led Saudi Arabia against Israel in the Arab-Israeli War of 1967. He was assassinated by his nephew.

Faisal I ⟨Faysal I⟩ ⟨Feisal I⟩ King of Syria (1920) and Iraq (1921–33). A leader of the Arab nationalist movement, he was a key figure in the Arab revolt against Ottoman rule during WW I. Crowned king of Syria (1920), he was deposed by the French in the same year but became king of Iraq with support of the British.

Faisal II ⟨Faysal II or Feisal II⟩ 1935–58. Last king of Iraq (1939–58), successor to his father, Ghazi I. He was killed during the revolution that ended the monarchy in Iraq.

Falange Spanish political party that became the ruling party of Spain under Gen. F. Franco. Organized (1933) by José Antonio Primo de Rivera (1903–36), it became the party of Spanish fascism. Falangists took part in the Spanish Civil War (1936–39), and, after 1937, the group was taken over by Franco. Franco turned the party to his own ends, making it the official party under his dictatorship. Though its ideology was significantly altered, the party continued in power until recent times.

Falier, Marino *See* **Faliero, Marino**

Falieri, Marino *See* **Faliero, Marino**

Faliero, Marino ⟨Falier or Falieri, ~⟩ 1274–1355. Doge of Venice (1354–55). Involved in a conspiracy by plebians to assassinate the patricians, or nobles, he was executed after a trial by the Council of Ten.

Falkland, Lucius Cary, 2d Viscount *c*1610–43. English writer and Royalist during the English Civil War. A member of the Short and Long parliaments (1640), he failed in his attempts to head off the civil war. He served with Charles I, and, despairing of the war, is said to have welcomed his own death in battle.

Falkland Islands British crown colony (pop. 2,000), located southeast of Argentina. Believed to have been discovered (1592) by British navigator J. Davis, they were settled (18th cent.) by the British and French. French and British possessions were taken over by Spain, though Britain retained formal sovereignty. The islands were then claimed (early 19th cent.) by Argentina after it gained independence from Spain. Britain retook control of the islands (1833). During WW I the British destroyed a German fleet under Graf von Spee near here (Dec., 1914). Argentina unsuccessfully challenged British sovereignty over the islands in the 1982 Falkland Islands War (*q.v.*).

Falkland Islands, Battle of Naval engagement (Dec. 8, 1914) between British and German fleets, near the Falkland Islands during WW I. The battle led to the destruction of the German fleet and the death of its commander, Graf von Spee.

Falkland Islands War Brief war (1982) between Argentina and Britain over possession of the Falkland Islands. Following years of unsuccessful negotiations with Britain for possession of the islands, the Argentines invaded (Apr. 1–2, 1982) and took control of the islands. A British naval task force arrived off the islands some weeks later and the first British landings began in June. The British took several Argentine strongholds on the islands and, after surrounding the main Argentine contingent at Stanley, forced the nearly 10,000 Argentine troops to surrender (June 14).

Fall, Albert Bacon 1861–1944. US senator from New Mexico (1912–21) and secretary of the interior (1921–23). He was convicted (1929) of receiving bribes in return for leases to oil lands in the Teapot Dome scandal.

Fallen Timbers, Battle of Battle (1794) between American forces under Gen. A. Wayne and Indians of the Northwest Confederation. Fought near present-day Toledo, Ohio, it was a decisive defeat for the confederation and ended concerted Indian resistance to settlement by whites.

Fallières, (Clément) Armand 1841–1931. French statesman. He was president of the Third Republic of France (1906–13).

false decretals Forged ecclesiastical papers. Decretals are religious letters outlining binding church decisions. In the 9th cent., several anonymous French clergymen sought to end Carolingian interference in church affairs by falsifying several documents and inserting into them legitimate decretals. The false decretals, supposedly advancing religious independence from civil authority, were largely believed until the 17th cent.

False Dmitris *See* **Dmitri; Time of Troubles**

Family Compact Name of a wealthy group of Canadians who dominated the government in Upper Canada between the late 1700s and mid-1800s. Members of this group controlled both the government ministries and the Legislative Council. Popular reaction to their control centered around questions of patronage, land grants, control of the judiciary, and support for the Anglican church. Following a period of legislative conflict and the Act of Union (1840), reformers won the government. A similar group in French Lower Canada was called the Château Clique.

Family Compact Name of three treaties between the Bourbon rulers of France and Spain. **1.** The first ~ (1733) was concluded to counter British commercial supremacy and to check Austrian designs on Italy. **2.** The second ~ (1743) provided for continuation of the 1733 alliance. **3.** The third ~ (1761) was the most important of these treaties. It brought Spain into the Seven Years' War against Britain. Spain's participation (after 1762) was minimal, however.

Faneuil, Peter *See* **Faneuil Hall**

Faneuil Hall ⟨Cradle of Liberty⟩ Historic public market- and meeting place, in Boston, Massachusetts. The original hall, built (1740–42) by Peter Faneuil (1700–43), burned in 1761. Rebuilt (1763), it was the site of meetings of American revolutionaries.

Fanfani, Amintore 1908–. Italian statesman. A left-wing Christian Democrat, Fanfani held numerous government positions and was a leading force in Italian politics in the 1950s and 1960s. He was three times prime minister (Jan., 1954, 1958–59, 1960–63) and was elected life senator (1972).

Fannin, James W. *See* **Goliad Massacre**

Farabi, al- ⟨Muhammad Ibn Muhammad Ibn Tarkhān al-Farabi⟩ ⟨abu Nasr al-Fārābi⟩ ⟨Alfarabius⟩ *c*870–*c*950. Arab philosopher. He is remembered chiefly as an influential exponent of Aristotle's teachings in the Islamic world.

Faraday, Michael 1791–1867. English scientist, renowned for his contributions to the study of electricity and magnetism. He began (1813) as an assistant to Sir H. Davy, and demonstrated (1831) the principal of electromagnetic induction. Faraday's laws of induction and electrolysis are named after him.

Fard, Wallace D. *See* **Black Muslims**

Far East Term that generally refers to the eastern portion of the Asian continent. It includes eastern Siberia, Mongolia, China, Korea, and Japan and is sometimes also meant to include the countries of Southeast Asia.

Far Eastern Territory Former Russian administrative region on the Pacific Ocean from the Arctic Ocean to Korea. Organized as the Far Eastern Republic (1920), it became (1922) part of the Russian SFSR, was reorganized (1926) as the Far Eastern Territory, and was subdivided (1938).

Fargo, William George 1818–81. American pioneer in express delivery. A founder (1850) of the American Express Company, he and other partners set up the Wells, Fargo and Company (1852), linking California with the East.

Farigoule, Louis *See* **Romains, Jules**

Farinelli, Carlo ⟨Broschi, Carlo⟩ 1705–82. Italian castrato soprano, considered one of the greatest of opera singers.

Farley, James Aloysius 1888–1976. American politician. He played a major role in the presidential election campaigns (1932, 1936) of F. Roosevelt and served under Roosevelt as postmaster general (1933–40).

Farmer-Labor party Short-lived minor US political party (1919–24). Founded as the National Labor party, it became the Farmer-Labor party in 1920 and advocated a policy of nationalization. It ran a third-party presidential candidate (1920), fell

to Communist control (1923), and disappeared after 1924. A Minnesota party of the same name (1918–44) supported F. Roosevelt in 1932 and 1936.

farmers-general French financiers who in prerevolutionary France bought the right to collect taxes from the citizenry. Their unscrupulousness contributed to the French Revolution.

Farnese Italian family that ruled the duchy of Parma and Piacenza from 1545 to 1731. It was founded by Alessandro Farnese, who, as Pope Paul III, established (1545) the duchy for his natural son, Pier Luigi Farnese (1503–47). Other members included A. Farnese (*q.v.*).

Farnese, Alessandro *See* **Paul III**

Farnese, Alessandro 1545–92. Italian soldier, duke of Parma and Piacenza (1586–92), and celebrated general in the service of Spanish king Philip II. He was appointed (1578) governor of The Netherlands, and his victories over the Dutch rebels helped ensure Spain's control in the region.

Farnese, Elizabeth 1692–1766. Spanish queen, wife of Philip V (*m.* 1714). For a time the virtual ruler of Spain, her stratagems enabled her son Charles III to become king of Naples and Sicily.

Farnese, Pier Luigi *See* **Farnese**

Farouk I ⟨Faruk I⟩ 1920–65. Egyptian king (1936–52), successor to his father, Fuad I. His unpopular policies and Egypt's defeat by Israel in 1948 led to his overthrow by M. Naguib and G. Nasser.

Farragut, David Glasgow 1801–70. American naval officer during the US Civil War. He led the Union navy to major victories at New Orleans (1862) and Mobile Bay (1864). At the latter he uttered his famous "Damn the torpedoes." He was the US Navy's first vice-admiral (1864) and admiral (1866).

Farrell, James Thomas 1904–79. American novelist, known best as author of the Studs Lonigan trilogy.

Faruk I *See* **Farouk I**

fascism Political movement for totalitarian government that began in Italy (*c*1919) under the leadership of B. Mussolini. Fascism is sometimes used more restrictively to refer to the Italian movement, the parallel German movement being distinguished as National Socialism (Nazism). Fascism is characterized by subservience of the individual to the state (in the person of an exalted leader), extreme nationalism, elitism (and especially in Nazism, anti-Semitism), formation of the corporative state (*q.v.*), militarism, and imperialism. Fascism in Italy was born amid the post-WW I chaos bred by labor unrest and attempts at Communist and Socialist takeover. Mussolini organized (c1919) bands of thugs, later called Blackshirts, and, with police backing, brutally suppressed labor agitation in northern Italy. He then created the Fascist party (1921) with the backing of many conservative elements, and took control of the Italian government (Oct. 29, 1922) after the famous March on Rome (q.v.). Thereafter the Facist party remained the ruling party of Italy until the close of WW II. For the rise of fascism in Germany, see National Socialism, and in Spain, see Falange.

Fashoda Incident Diplomatic crisis (1898) between Britain and France over claims to the Sudan. Both countries sought to link their colonies on the African continent by continuous corridors of land. The Sudan represented an intersection of their aims. Defying British claims, the French sent a military contingent from the Congo and occupied Fashoda (now Kodok). The British, under Lord H. Kitchener, arrived two weeks later. The French government, fearing all-out war, withdrew its forces a month and a half later, and subsequently dropped claims to the region (1899) in return for British concessions in the Sahara.

Fastolf, Sir John   See **Herrings, Battle of the**

Fates 1. In Greek mythology, three goddesses who controlled the destiny of an individual's life. Clotho spun the thread of life, Lachesis determined its length, and Atropos cut it. **2.** In Roman mythology, the Fates (Parcae) were Nona, Decuma, and Morta.

Fathers of the Church   Term applied to the early Christian writers whose interpretations of Christian doctrine are generally considered definitive by the church.

Fatima 606?–632. Daughter of Muhammad and wife of Ali. An important figure in Islamic religion, she is by tradition the forebear of the Fatimid dynasty.

Fatimid ⟨Fatimite⟩ Muslim dynasty that ruled (909–1171) an empire in North Africa. Members of the Syrian Shiite sect, the Fatimids claimed the Muslim caliphate as descendants of Muhammad's daughter Fatima. The dynasty was founded by the Syrian Said ibn Husayn. He was proclaimed the Mahdi following rebellions in northwestern Africa and Sicily (909) and ruled there in opposition to the Abbasid caliphs. The Fatimids subsequently reached their greatest power under el-Moizz (reigned 935–975). He conquered Egypt, Palestine, and part of Syria, and built Cairo, which he made his capital. The empire began to disintegrate after his reign, giving way to internal

stresses, Norman invasions, the Crusades (11th cent.), and the Abbasids under Saladin.

Fatimite   See **Fatimid**

Fauchard, Pierre 1678–1761. French dentist, considered a founder of modern dental practices. He wrote The Surgeon Dentist, which became a standard work in the field.

Faulkner, William 1897–1962. American novelist. One of the great American writers of the 20th cent., he is celebrated for his novels chronicling life in the imaginary Yoknapatawpha County, Mississippi. Among his best works are The Sound and the Fury, As I Lay Dying, and Absalom, Absalom! He was awarded the Nobel Prize in Literature (1949) and twice was awarded the Pulitzer Prize for Fiction (1955, 1963).

Faunus   Ancient Roman god of the forests, crops, and livestock, identified with the Greek god Pan. His female counterpart was Bona Dea.

Faure, Félix 1841–99. French statesman. As president (1895–99), he improved French relations with Russia but came into conflict with Britain over the Fashoda Incident. The Dreyfus Affair occurred during his presidency, and his refusal to reopen the case contributed to friction between pro-Dreyfus and anti-Dreyfus factions.

Faust fl. 16th cent. German doctor who acquired the reputation of a magician who had sold his soul to the devil (Mephistopheles) for knowledge and power. His legend is the basis for numerous literary works, notably the dramatic poem Faust by J. Goethe.

Faust, Johann   See **Fust, Johann**

Fausta, Flavia Maximiana d. AD c326. Roman empress, wife of Constantine I (the Great), and mother of Constantine II, Constantius II, and Constans I. She is said to have been put to death by her husband after causing him to kill his oldest son, Crispus, because of her false accusations.

Faustin I   See **Soulouque, Faustin Élie**

Faustina the Younger AD c125–176. Roman empress, daughter of Antoninus Pius, and wife of Marcus Aurelius. She accompanied her husband on many campaigns, thus earning the title "Mother of the Army."

fauvism   Brief French artistic movement of the early 20th cent. characterized by bold use of color and expressionist approach. Its adherents included H. Matisse and G. Roualt, and it influenced the development of later movements, notably cubism.

Favre, Gabriel Claude Jules 1809–80. French statesman. He was leader of the republican opposition to Napoleon III's Second Empire. As vice-president and foreign minister of the Government of National Defense (1871), he negotiated the disadvantageous Treaty of Frankfurt, ending the Franco-Prussian War.

Fawcett, Dame Millicent Garrett 1847–1929. English feminist. An advocate of peaceful means to gain woman's suffrage, she opposed the militant Pankhursts.

Fay, Sidney Bradshaw 1876–1967. American historian, known best for his work on the causes of WW I, *The Origins of the World War.*

Faysal *See* **Faisal**

February Manifesto Russian proclamation (Feb. 15, 1899) declaring that the czar had the right to overrule Finland's constitution and rule by edict. Up to that time Finland was ruled as an autonomous duchy within Russia. The manifesto was revoked by Czar Nicholas II (Nov., 1905) during the Russian Revolution of 1905.

February Revolution 1. Revolution in France (1848) that brought about the abdication of King Louis Philippe and creation of the short-lived Second Republic. The king's increasingly reactionary policies, opposition to his unpopular minister F. Guizot, and widespread unemployment caused by a severe economic slump resulted in the revolt, which was precipitated by the banning (Feb. 22, 1848) of an antigovernment banquet. Rioting broke out that day, and the revolution began the next, when government troops fired on demonstrators. The king abdicated (Feb. 24), and the republic was immediately proclaimed. The provisional government was a coalition of moderate republicans, led by A. de Lamartine, and Socialist republicans, led by L. Blanc. It subsequently recognized "the right to work," created (Feb. 26), the national workshops to ease unemployment, and proclaimed universal male suffrage (Mar. 2). The workshops soon failed, however, and mass demonstrations by Socialist republicans aroused fears of a Communist takeover. Moderates were thus victorious in elections for the new National Assembly, and, in the face of new unrest, moved (Mar. 15) to dissolve the national workshops. This precipitated the bloody uprising known as June Days *(q.v.).* Gen. L. Cavaignac was installed as dictator and restored order. The assembly promulgated a new constitution (Nov. 20), and Louis Napoleon (later Napoleon III) was elected president. Soon after taking office, Napoleon seized power and founded the Second Empire (1852). **2.** ~ ⟨March Revolution⟩ The beginning phase of the Russian Revolution *(q.v.)* in 1917. It was precipitated by bread riots in Petrograd and resulted in the abdication of Czar Nicholas II on Mar. 12, 1917 (old-style dating, Feb. 27). The February Revolution was followed by the October Revolution *(q.v.),* in which Bolsheviks seized power.

Federal Constitutional Convention *See* **Constitutional Convention**

federalism The system of government whereby states or entities unite under a centralized (federal) government, while retaining a measure of autonomy. The federalist system established by the US Constitution (1789) placed foreign affairs, common defense, interstate commerce, and the like under a strong federal government. Existing autonomous governments in the various states that joined the federal union continued to function, though with reduced powers.

Federalist Papers American political essays. They were a series of 85 essays written (1787–88) by A. Hamilton, J. Madison, and J. Jay which urged the ratification of the United States Constitution and expressed the need for a strong central government. Originally written for New York State newspapers, they were collected (1788) as *The Federalist.* They were an important formative influence in the early years of America's government.

Federalist party American political party, considered America's first organized political party. Formed about the time of the Constitutional Convention (1787), it was led by A. Hamilton. The Federalists espoused a strong central government and a pro-British, anti-French foreign policy. They were opposed by T. Jefferson's Democratic Republicans. G. Washington, though officially neutral, frequently sided with the Federalists. J. Adams, the second US president, was the last Federalist party member to gain the presidency. The party's power declined rapidly after the Hartford Convention.

Fëdor I ⟨Feodor *or* Fyodor⟩ 1557–98. Russian czar (1584–98), successor to his father, Ivan the Terrible, and last czar of the Rurik dynasty. He was incompetent, and the government was run by his brother-in-law, B. Godunov.

Fëdor II ⟨Feodor *or* Fyodor⟩ 1589–1605. Russian czar (1605), successor to his father, B. Godunov. He ruled only briefly before being killed in a riot provoked by the nobles, the boyars. He was succeeded by a pretender to the throne, the first of the false Dmitris.

Fëdor III ⟨Feodor *or* Fyodor⟩ 1656–82. Russian czar (1676–82), successor to his father, Alexis. Under his reign the system of appointing noblemen to military and civil positions on the basis of social rank was abolished (1681 or 1682).

Feinechus *See* **Brehon Laws**

Feisal *See* **Faisal**

Felix V (antipope) *See* **Amadeus VIII**

Fellini, Federico 1920–. Italian film director

noted for his innovative film techniques and his juxtaposition of realism and fantasy. His films include *La Strada* and *La Dolce Vita*.

Felton, Rebecca Latimer 1835–1930. American writer and reformer. She was the first woman to serve in the Senate, serving Oct.–Nov., 1922, as interim appointee from Georgia.

feminism Women's movement to secure political, economic, and social equality with men. Though the concern for equality for women dates back to ancient times, feminism as a movement is rooted in the 18th and 19th cent. Mary Wollstonecraft's *Vindication of the Rights of Women* (1792) is considered a seminal work, and feminism as an organized movement began at a women's convention at Seneca Falls, New York (July, 1848). The feminist cause, especially in the area of woman suffrage *(q.v.)*, was subsequently carried forward in the US by the National Woman Suffrage Association (led by S. Anthony and E. Stanton) and eventually spread to Europe. By the early 1900s, feminists had gained considerable improvement in the status of women, most notably in achieving the right to vote. A resurgence of feminism in the US occurred in the 1960s, when the movement became known as Women's Liberation. The National Organization for Women (NOW) was formed in 1966 and the late 1960s and early 1970s saw the rise of militant feminism. Though feminists brought about reforms in such areas as abortion and sex discrimination in employment, their campaign in the late 1970s and early 1980s centered on the drive to ratify the Equal Rights Amendment (passed by Congress, 1972). The amendment failed to win ratification in the required number of states by the June, 1982, cutoff date.

Fénelon, François de Salignac de la Mothe 1651–1715. French theologian and writer. His support of quietism led to the condemnation (1699) by Pope Innocent XII of Fénelon's *Explanation of the Sayings of the Saints*.

Feng Yu-hsiang 1880–1948. Chinese general. Called the "Christian General," he supported Chiang Kai-shek and the Kuomintang in the 1920s but later opposed Chiang's policies.

Fenian movement Irish nationalist movement. A secret revolutionary group organized (c1858) to achieve complete Irish independence from Britain, it included groups in both Ireland and America. It actively harassed the British in Britain, Ireland, and America in the 1860s and 1870s. Its activities were frequently betrayed by spies planted within the organization's ranks. It was eventually replaced by the Sinn Fein movement.

Feodor *See* **Fëdor**

Ferber, Edna 1887–1968. American novelist and short-story writer. Among her novels are *So Big* and *Show Boat*. She was awarded the Pulitzer Prize for Fiction in 1925.

Ferdinand 1861–1948. First czar of Bulgaria (1908–18). He proclaimed Bulgaria's independence from the Ottoman Empire and fought against it in the Balkan Wars. His alliance with the Central Powers in WW I led to his abdication.

Ferdinand 1865–1927. Romanian king (1914–27). By siding with the Allies in WW I, he was able to double Romania's size through postwar peace treaties. He introduced voting and agrarian reforms.

Ferdinand I ⟨Ferdinand the Great⟩ *d.* 1065. Spanish king of Castile (1035–65) and León (1037–65). He brought much of Spain under his control and began the expulsion of the Moors from Spain, but divided his kingdom among his three sons at his death.

Ferdinand I 1345–83. Portuguese king (1367–83), successor to his father, Peter I. He waged three successive wars to gain the Castilian throne and each time suffered a humiliating defeat.

Ferdinand I 1503–64. Holy Roman Emperor (1558–64), successor to his brother Charles V. He negotiated the Peace of Augsburg (1555) and reformed the Aulic Council (1559).

Ferdinand I 1751–1825. King of the Two Sicilies (1816–25). As king of Naples, Ferdinand had been forced to flee (1799) when Napoleon established the Parthenopean Republic. Reinstated by the British (1815), he became king of the unified kingdom of the Two Sicilies (1816). His reactionary rule led to serious turmoil (1820) and the granting of constitutional government, which he soon abrogated.

Ferdinand II 1578–1637. Holy Roman Emperor (1619–37), king of Bohemia and Hungary, successor to his cousin Matthias. His reign was marked by the Thirty Years' War, in which he attempted to put down a series of rebellions by Protestants which began just after his succession to the Bohemian throne (1618).

Ferdinand II 1810–59. King of the Two Sicilies (1830–59), successor to his father, Francis I. His harsh rule earned him the enmity of many. A revolt (1848) in Palermo led to his approval of a constitution, which he soon ignored. He later bombarded the cities of Palermo and Massina, then in rebellion, and earned the name "King Bomba."

Ferdinand II 1816–85. Titular king of Portugal (1837–53). He became king consort by his marriage (1836) to Maria II, and on her death became regent to his sons Pedro V (1853–55) and Louis (1861).

Ferdinand III 1199–1252. King of Castile (1217–52) and León (1230–52). Ferdinand united Castile with León and recaptured most of Spain from the Moors. He was canonized in 1671.

Ferdinand III 1608–57. Holy Roman Emperor (1637–57), successor to his father, Ferdinand II. A series of defeats at the hands of Protestants forced him to agree to the Peace of Westphalia (1648), ending the Thirty Years' War.

Ferdinand IV 1285–1312. Spanish king of Castile and León (1295–1312), successor to his father, Sancho IV. During his reign, Gibraltar was retaken from the Moors (1309).

Ferdinand V (Ferdinand the Catholic) 1452–1516. Spanish king, king of Aragon (1479–1516), king of Castile and León (1474–1504), and regent of Castile (1504–16). Through marriage and conquest, Ferdinand pursued the unification of Spanish kingdoms into what is now modern Spain. He married Isabella I of Castile (1469) and from 1474 they ruled Castile jointly. He succeeded his father, John II, as king of Aragon (1479), and subsequently conquered Granada from the Moors (1492). He began the Italian Wars against France, conquered Naples (1504), and annexed most of the kingdom of Navarre (1512). His reign saw the voyage of C. Columbus (1492) and the acquisition of rich possessions in the New World. With Isabella, he also instituted the Inquisition and expelled the Jews (1492) and the Moors (1502). Following Isabella's death (1504), he ruled Castile as regent.

Ferdinand VI 1712?–59. Spanish king (1746–59), successor to his father, Philip V. He enacted numerous domestic reforms and ably kept Spain from involvement in the Seven Years' War.

Ferdinand VII 1784–1833. Spanish king (Mar.-May, 1808, 1814–33), successor to his father, Charles IV. He was prevented from having real power by M. de Godoy. Ferdinand forced his father's abdication (1808) but was in turn forced from the throne by Napoleon and imprisoned until 1814. Ferdinand resumed control after Napoleon's ouster from Spain, but his rule was harsh and repressive. His repeal of the Salic Law in favor of his daughter Isabella II led to the first Carlist War. During his reign, Spanish power declined and Spain lost all its possessions in the Western Hemisphere except for Cuba.

Ferdowsi *See* **Firdausi**

Ferlinghetti, Lawrence 1919–. American poet. Owner of City Lights bookshop and founder of City Lights Books (publishers), both in San Francisco, he was a leading figure in the Beat movement of the 1950s, and published the works of A.

Ginsberg and others. His collections include *A Coney Island of the Mind.*

Fermat, Pierre de 1601–65. French mathematician. He is considered the founder of the modern theory of numbers.

Fermi, Enrico 1901–54. Italian-American physicist who made major contributions to the then emerging science of nuclear physics and who worked on construction of the atom bomb. During experiments in 1934 to 1937, Fermi became the first to split uranium atoms with neutrons, though he did not know it at the time. In 1938 other scientists found that he had actually split atoms and thus discovered the previously unknown process of nuclear fission. Fermi became part of the secret Manhattan Project in the US during WW II and in Dec., 1942, produced the first controlled nuclear chain reaction. He received the Nobel Prize in Physics in 1938.

Fernandez, Manuel Felix *See* **Guadalupe Victoria**

Ferrar, Nicholas 1592–1637. English theologian who established (1626) a small utopian community at Little Gidding. Although initially successful, it was disbanded by Parliament (1647).

Ferrara-Florence, Council of Roman Catholic church council (1438–45) convened to end the schism between the Latin and Greek churches. An extension of the Council of Basel, it was opened at Ferrara but was moved to Florence (1439) because of the plague. Agreement was reached (1439) on the use of the Latin term "Filioque" *(q.v.)*, on the use of unleavened bread in the Eucharist, on the Latin definition of purgatory, and on papal supremacy. Union of the two churches was announced (1439), though many Greeks refused to recognize the union and the schism ultimately continued.

Ferry, Jules 1832–93. French statesman and public official during the Government of National Defense. His education bill (1882) established the French system of public education, free of religious influence. As premier (1880–81, 1883–85) he greatly expanded the French colonial empire in Africa and Indochina.

Fersen, Hans Axel, Count 1755–1810. Swedish soldier and marshal of Sweden. He helped in the unsuccessful attempt to get King Louis XVI and Marie Antoinette out of France at the outset of the French Revolution. Later, as marshal under Gustavus IV, he took part in the wars against Napoleon.

Fertile Crescent Ancient Middle Eastern region stretching from the Nile to the Euphrates in parts of modern Egypt, Israel, Lebanon, Syria, Jordan, and Iraq. The site of some of the earliest settlements, the region has been conquered numerous times.

Fes *See* **Fez**

Festus, Sextus Pompeius *fl.* 2d cent. AD. Roman lexicographer. His abridgment of a major glossary of Latin words by Marcus Verrius Flaccus is a primary source for the study of Roman civilization.

Fetterman Massacre Massacre of 80 US soldiers (1866) in Wyoming during the Sioux Wars. Led by Col. William Judd Fetterman (1833?–66), the soldiers ventured off a safe trail and were ambushed by a band of Chief Red Cloud's warriors.

Feud of the Counts *See* **Count's War**

feudalism Social system, based on land ownership, that was prevalent in medieval Europe (8th–14th cents.). By this system, a feudal lord granted lesser nobles (vassals) rights to lands (fiefs) within his domains and guaranteed them protection from attack. In return, the vassals swore their loyalty to the feudal lord and provided a specified number of warriors for his army. Vassals, in turn, subdivided their fiefs (subinfeudation), and thus became lords to vassals of progressively smaller fiefs. At the bottom of this complex structure was the feudal manor, which was tenanted by serfs *(q.v.),* and which by its agricultural output provided the economic base for the feudal system. The feudal system is generally thought to have arisen in Europe in the Frankish Kingdom of Charlemagne (8th–9th cents.). From there, it was spread by Frankish conquests to Spain, Italy, and Germany. It was transplanted to England by the Normans under William the Conqueror and to the Holy Land by rulers of the Crusader States. Though the feudal society at its height (13th cent.) provided a viable means of protection from outside attack, there were inherent weaknesses in the system. Hardships suffered by the serfs were legion. The system of subinfeudation fragmented authority, put the reigning king at the mercy of his vassals, and, by creating a multitude of largely independent petty kingdoms, fostered warfare among them. The rise of powerful monarchs and the growth of a new middle class (merchants and officials), among other factors, helped bring about a gradual decline of feudalism. By the 14th cent., it had largely disappeared, though European society retained vestiges of the system for centuries. Other cultures also experienced periods of feudalism, notably Japan (10th–19th cents.).

Feuerbach, Ludwig Andreas 1804–72. German philosopher. Once a student of G. Hegel, he became a proponent of naturalistic materialism. He held that god was a projection or man's inner nature.

Feuillants French political club during the French Revolution. The Feuillants, including A. Barnave, the Marquis de Lafayette, and E. Sieyès, favored a constitutional monarchy but after 1792 were suppressed by the Jacobins.

Fez ⟨Fes⟩ Moroccan city (pop. 325,300), a Muslim holy city. Founded (790) by Idris I, it rose in power as the capital of early sultans. At the height of its power in the 14th-15th cents., it declined after Marrakesh became the capital.

Fianna Fáil Irish political party. Organized under the leadership of E. de Valera in 1926, it was formed to oppose the Irish Free State (est. 1921) and to win complete independence from Britain. It has largely controlled the Irish government since 1932, though its major rival, Fianna Gael, has been in power for short periods and as of 1981 headed the government.

Fichte, Johann Gottlieb 1762–1814. German philosopher. An influential proponent of transcendental idealism in his day, he is also remembered for his patriotic discourses, *Addresses to the German Nation.*

Ficino, Marsilio 1433–99. Italian philosopher and translator of Greek classics into Latin. He was an important exponent of Platonism in his day.

fief In feudalism, land granted by a lord to a vassal in return for the vassal's knightly service and allegiance. The fief was the cornerstone of feudal society.

Field, Stephen Johnson 1816–99. American jurist, associate justice of the Supreme Court (1863–97). A conservative, he was largely responsible for early interpretations of the 14th Amendment which blocked government regulation of business for many years.

Fielding, Henry 1707–54. One of the greatest of English novelists. He is known best for his classic novel *Tom Jones.*

Field of Cloth of Gold Name given the place, near Calais, France, where in 1520 English king Henry VIII met French king Francis I to propose an alliance. Little was accomplished.

Fieschi, Sinibaldo de' *See* **Innocent IV**

Fifteen Years' War War (1591–1606) between Austria and the Ottoman Empire. After initial Turkish advances against the Austrians, S. Bathory, prince of Transylvania, allied (1595) with Holy Roman Emperor Rudolf II. The Turks invaded Transylvania but were driven out. The Hapsburgs occupied Hungary, but then S. Bocskay, with Turkish aid, fomented a revolt in Transylvania and drove the Hapsburgs from Hungary (1604–06). The war marked the ascendance of Transylvania as a political power, and demonstrated a decline in Ottoman imperial power in Europe.

fifth column Term for subversives who work from within to undermine a nation. During the Spanish Civil War, the fascist Gen. Gonzalo Queipo de Llano (1875?–1951), advancing on Madrid with four military columns, is said to have referred to supporters within the city as his "fifth column."

Fifth Crusade *See* **Crusade, Fifth**

Fifth Monarchy Men Puritan extremists in England active during the 17th cent. This sect of millenarians derived its name from belief in a fifth kingdom mentioned in the Book of Daniel. Its followers held that Jesus would return to rule this kingdom (fifth after Assyrian, Persian, Greek, and Roman empires) and that they were appointed to establish the kingdom for him by any means, including force. They rebelled briefly (1657, 1661), but the sect died out following the subsequent execution of their leader.

Fifth Republic Name given the new government of France established with the election (Dec., 1958) of C. de Gaulle as president.

Fifty-four forty or fight Slogan used by Americans who in the 1840s sought annexation of all of the Oregon Territory up to latitude 54° 40′ North, then jointly occupied by Britain and the US. It was used by the Democrats during the successful presidential campaign of J. Polk (1844).

Fiji Island group and republic in the South Pacific. Discovered (1643) by A. Tasman, the islands became a British colony (1874), were granted a constitution (1937), and became an independent republic (Oct. 10, 1970). Fiji was a strategic supply link in Allied operations during WW II.

filibuster Prolonged political debate used by legislators to obstruct passage of bills they oppose but lack the strength to defeat. In the 19th cent. the term was applied to armed adventurers who led private expeditions to Central and South American nations.

filioque Latin term meaning "and from the Son," added by the Latin church (6th cent.) to the Nicene Creed. It provoked a bitter controversy and was a main cause of the schism between the Eastern and Western churches.

Filipepi, Allesandro di Mariano *See* **Botticelli, Sandro**

Fillmore, Millard 1800–74. Thirteenth US president (1850–53), successor to Z. Taylor. A political leader in New York State, Fillmore served as US congressman (1833–35, 1837–43), and joined the Whig party in 1834. He became vice-president (1849) under Taylor, the Whig candidate, and president on Taylor's death in office (July 9, 1850). During his administration, Fillmore attempted to

steer both his policies and the Whig party on a middle course in the intensifying debate over abolition of slavery. He supported passage of the Compromise of 1850 *q.v.* and thereby helped delay civil war. But he raised a storm of protest among northern abolitionists when he sought to enforce the Fugitive Slave Act *(q.v.)*, which was part of the compromise. The Whig party was badly split over the slavery issue during the election of 1852. Fillmore failed to win renomination, and the party disintegrated soon after the election. Fillmore subsequently retired from politics except for a brief reappearance (1856) as the Know-Nothing party's presidential candidate.

Fink, Mike 1770?–1823? American frontiersman and folk hero. A celebrated Indian fighter, marksman, and brawler, he was at one time a keelboatman on the Mississippi and Ohio rivers.

Finland Republic located in northern Europe. Its capital is Helsinki. Finns took over the region by about the 8th cent. Finland came under Swedish control in the 12th cent. and remained subject to the Swedish kings until the Russians conquered the territory during the Napoleonic Wars. Russian control was ended by a successful drive for independence that coincided with the Russian Revolution of 1917. Since that time the neighboring Soviet Union has been a major factor in Finnish history. The Soviets have influenced Finnish politics in the years after WW II, but the government successfully established a neutral stance and maintains relations with both East and West. Key events in the history of Finland include:

7TH–8TH CENTS. Finns, migrating to Finland from the south, forced Lapps to move to far northern region.

1157 Territory conquered by Sweden's king Eric IX, who introduced Christianity; area ruled as part of Sweden until early 19th cent.

c1550 Protestant Reformation; Lutheranism spread throughout the country.

1581 Finland made a grand duchy; Swedish language and culture continued to dominate.

1700–21 Great Northern War; Sweden ceded parts of eastern Finland to Russia.

1808–09 Russia, as an ally of Napoleon, invaded and conquered Finland during the Napoleonic Wars; Russians allowed Finns considerable autonomy thereafter.

1812 Helsinki became the capital of Finland in place of Turku.

1863 Finnish nationalist feelings began to rise in the early 19th cent.; Finnish language finally achieved official status.

1899 Czar Nicholas II initiated policy to Russify Finland; constitution suspended by the February Manifesto (Feb. 15); Russia henceforth ruled Finland by edict.

1903–04 Russian governor-general of Finland granted dictatorial powers as Finns resisted Russification (1903); governor-general assassinated (1904).

1905 Finns joined in general strike as Revolution of 1905 broke out in Russia; Czar Nicholas II granted many concessions, including limited self-government.

1917 After the outbreak of the Russian Revolution, the Finnish Parliament declared the country's independence (Dec. 6).

1918 Finnish War of Independence; anti-Communist Finns defeated Bolshevik Finns (Jan.–May).

1919 Republic established; Kaarlo Juho Ståhlberg in office as first president. (1919–25).

1923 Finnish Communist party outlawed.

1932 Lapua Movement, fascist group, formed in 1929, attempted coup (1932); suppressed by government thereafter.

1932 Nonaggression treaty signed with USSR as part of Finnish foreign policy of maintaining neutrality.

1939–40 Russo-Finnish War broke out as WW II began; Russians victorious after hard fighting and heroic Finnish resistance; Finland forced to give up territories in the east.

1941 Germany invaded USSR; Finland aligned itself with the Germans in the hope of regaining territories lost to the USSR.

1944 Finland again defeated by Soviets; forced to make further concessions and join in effort to drive Germans out of Finland.

1946–56 Juho Kusti Passikivi in office as president; believed appeasement of the Soviets was essential for Finnish independence.

1947 Post-WW II treaty confirmed loss of eastern territories to the USSR.

1948 Treaty of cooperation signed with Soviets; power of Finnish Communist party began to decline.

1955 Joined the UN.

1956–81 Urho Kekkonen in office as president; maintained a policy of neutrality.

1966 Finnish Communists participated in coalition government.

1970 Finland concluded trade agreements with both the European Economic Community (Common Market) of the West and the Council for Mutual Economic Assistance (Comecon) of the Eastern Communist countries.

1975 Helsinki the site of the signing of a European security agreement by 35 heads of govern-

ment; established procedures for seeking international peace.

1981 Long-time president Urho Kekkonen resigned because of ill health.

1982 Mauno Koivista, a Social Democrat, elected president.

Finlay, Carlos Juan ⟨~, Charles John⟩ 1833–1915. Cuban physician who discovered (1881) that yellow fever was transmitted by mosquitoes. His findings were confirmed (1900) in experiments by a US Army commission.

Finlay, Charles John *See* **Finlay, Carlos Juan**

Fin mac cumhail ⟨Fionn mac Cumhail⟩ ⟨Finn Mac Cool⟩ Legendary Irish hero, leader of a band of heroic warriors called the Fenians that roamed Ireland in the 3d cent. His adventures are the subject of the Fenian ballads.

Finney, Charles Grandison 1792–1875. American evangelist. A lawyer turned Presbyterian minister (1924), he became famous for his highly successful revival meetings.

Finnish War of Independence Civil war (Jan.–May, 1918) fought by anti-Communist Finns with German help. The Finnish Bolsheviks were defeated and the former Russian province aligned itself with Germany in the last months of WW I.

Finn mac Cool *See* **Fin mac Cumhail**

Fionn mac Cumhail *See* **Fin mac Cumhail**

Firdausi ⟨Firdusi⟩ ⟨Ferdowsi⟩ ⟨Firdousi⟩ ⟨*pseud. of* Abul Kasim Mansur⟩ c940–1020. Persian poet, author of the *Book of Kings*, the Persian national epic. The narrative poem covers Persian history to AD 641 and the conquest by the Muslims.

Firdousi *See* **Firdausi**

Firdusi *See* **Firdausi**

fire-eaters Pejorative term applied by Americans in the North to southern extremists who advocated secession to preserve slavery.

Firestone, Harvey Samuel 1868–1938. American rubber manufacturer. He founded the Firestone Tire and Rubber Co. (1900) and built it into one of the largest rubber companies in the US.

First Helvetic Confession *See* **Basel, Confession of**

First Coalition Alliance of European nations against France that opposed the French Revolution. It was formed in 1792 and its major members included Austria, Prussia, Russia, Britain, and Spain. (*See also* French Revolutionary Wars.)

First Crusade *See* **Crusade, First**

First Punic War *See* **Punic War, First**

First Republic Spanish republic (1872–73). It was formed following the abdication of Spanish king Amadeo I but was soon overthrown, and Alfonso XII was proclaimed king.

Fischer von Erlach, Johann Bernhard 1656–1723. Austrian architect and sculptor who introduced the baroque style to Austria.

Fish, Hamilton 1808–93. American statesman. He served as governor of New York (1849–50) and US senator (1851–57). As secretary of state (1869–77) under Pres. U. Grant, he negotiated settlement of the Alabama Claims with Britain.

Fish, Hamilton 1849–1936. American politician. A son of H. Fish, he was assistant US treasurer under T. Roosevelt (1903–08) and congressman (1909–11).

Fisher, Saint John 1459–1535. English Catholic bishop and martyr. He was beheaded for refusing to acknowledge King Henry VIII as head of the church in England under the acts of Succession and Supremacy.

Fisk, James 1834–72. American financier. A flamboyant personality and unprincipled financial manipulator, in his most infamous scheme he attempted, with D. Drew and J. Gould, to corner the gold market (1869). This resulted in the financial panic called Black Friday.

Fitch, John 1743–98. American inventor. He is considered the inventor (before R. Fulton) of the first American steamboat (1787) although he failed to establish it commercially.

Fitzgerald, Edward *See* **Omar Khayyam**

Fitzgerald, Lord Edward 1763–98. Irish revolutionary. He unsuccessfully sought aid from revolutionary France for his uprising (1798) against British rule. Wounded in battle, he died in prison.

Fitzgerald, Francis Scott Key 1896–1940. American novelist and short-story writer, one of America's great writers. Fitzgerald has gained a place in American literature as the chronicler of the post-WW I "Jazz Age." His novels include *This Side of Paradise, The Beautiful and Damned, The Great Gatsby, Tender Is the Night,* and *The Last Tycoon.* Among his short-story collections are *Tales of the Jazz Age* and *All the Sad Young Men.*

Fitzgerald, Gerald, 15th earl of Desmond *d.* 1583. Irish nobleman. He rebelled against Queen Elizabeth's attempts to take over Irish lands. Declared a traitor, he was hunted down and killed.

Fitzgerald, James, 20th earl of Kildare and 1st duke of Leinster 1722–73. Irish nobleman. A member of the Irish Parliament, he is remembered for blocking a plan to hand over surplus revenues from Ireland to the British crown.

Fitzgerald, Maurice *d.* 1176. Soldier of Welsh and Norman heritage. He helped the king of Leinster, D. McMurrough, in his invasion of Ireland (1169) and thus acquired the Fitzgerald family holdings there.

Fitzgerald, Thomas, 10th earl of Kildare (called Silken Thomas) 1513–37. Irish nobleman. When his father, the lord deputy of Ireland, was rumored to have been executed by Henry VIII, Fitzgerald led the Irish in rebellion against the king (1534). He surrendered the following year, and was eventually hanged.

Five Civilized Tribes Five American Indian tribes forcibly removed from their lands in southeastern US to the West after passage of the Indian Removal Act (1830). The tribes were the Cherokee, Chickasaw, Choctaw, Creek, and Seminole.

Five Dynasties Chinese historical period between the end of the T'ang dynasty (907) and the beginning of the Sung (960). Five successive short-lived dynasties tried but failed to establish authority. Corruption and anarchy reigned instead, and northern China also suffered famine and floods. The unsuccessful dynasties were the Later Liang (907–923), Later Tang (923–936), Later Chin (936–947), Later Han (947–950), and Later Chou (950–960). Their capitals were located near the present-day Kaifeng, Honan Province.

Five Forks, Battle of Union victory (Apr. 1, 1865) in the American Civil War, at Five Forks, near Richmond, Virginia. Union forces under Gen. P. Sheridan defeated the Confederate troops of Gen. G. Pickett. The battle led to the Union capture of Petersburg and (Apr. 3) Richmond.

Five Hundred, Council of Ancient Athenian representative government. Established (508 BC) by Cleisthenes, it consisted of 50 representatives from each of 10 tribes.

Five Nations, League of *See* **Iroquois Confederacy**

Five Pecks of Rice Chinese religious movement, founded (2d cent. AD) by Chang Ling, a Taoist religious leader. Chang and his successors used the poverty and turmoil then prevalent in China to establish their own political and religious movement.

Five-Power Constitution Chinese governmental system advanced by Sun Yat-sen to replace the Chinese imperial order. It called for government by five departments—executive, legislative, judicial, examination, and control—and was implemented (1928) nominally by Chiang Kai-shek upon his accession to power.

Five-Year Plan In the USSR, name given economic programs designed to increase industrial and agricultural growth through establishment of quotas or goals. The first plan was established (1928) by J. Stalin.

Fizeau, Armand Hippolyte Louis 1819–96. French physicist. He made (1849) the first measurement of the speed of light at the earth's surface. He also studied the spectrum of the sun and applied the Doppler effect to the motion of the stars.

Flaccus, Aulus Persius *See* **Persius**

Flaccus, Quintus Horatius *See* **Horace**

flagellants Christian sects originating in 13th-cent. Europe and practicing self-punishment (whipping) as a means to avoid God's wrath. The movement was largely suppressed by the 15th cent., but flagellant sects have continued sporadically to the present.

Flagg, Ernest 1857–1947. American architect. He designed the Singer Building in New York City, which at its completion (1908) was the tallest building in the world (612 ft.).

Flaherty, Robert Joseph 1884–1951. American movie director, explorer, and writer. He directed *Nanook of the North* (1922), generally considered the forerunner of documentary motion pictures.

Flaminian Way One of the great Roman roads. Begun in 220 BC, it extended for 209 miles between Rome and Cisalpine Gaul, ending at what is now Rimini, in northern Italy.

Flamininus, Titus Quinctius *c*230–174? BC. Roman general and statesman. During the second Macedonian War, he defeated Macedonian king Philip V (197 BC) and subsequently declared (196 BC) Greece independent of Macedonian rule.

Flaminius, Gaius ⟨or Caius⟩ *d* 217 BC. Roman statesman and general. As censor (220 BC) he undertook construction of the Flaminian Way and the Circus Flaminius. He was killed leading Roman forces against Hannibal's invasion of Italy.

Flamsteed, John 1646–1719. English astronomer. The first astronomer royal (appointed 1675), he compiled a major star catalogue, the posthumously published *Historia Coelestis Britannica*.

Flanders Historic county located along the North Sea coast and now divided between Belgium and France. Flanders became a countship in 862 and, though dominated by French monarchs, enjoyed a great deal of autonomy in subsequent centuries. Flanders became the leading center of the cloth industry in Europe (13th cent.), and its major cities (Ghent, Ypres, and Bruges) prospered as free communes in manufacturing and trade. Industrialization and prosperity during the 13th and 14th cents. brought a period of rebellion against French domination, alliance with England during the Hundred Years' War, and conquest by the dukes of Burgundy. Flanders passed to the Hapsburgs (1477), came under control of the Spanish Hapsburg kings (1506), and unsuccessfully rebelled (1576–84) against Spanish rule during the revolt of the Low Countries. After 1714, parts of Flanders passed to various powers until 1830, when the final disposition between Belgium and France was completed. Flanders was the scene of heavy fighting during WW I and the British retreat at Dunkirk during WW II.

Flanders, Henry of *See* **Henry of Flanders**

Flaubert, Gustave 1821–80. French writer, considered a master of the realistic novel. His masterpiece, *Madame Bovary*, resulted in his prosecution on moral grounds, but he was acquitted.

Flavian Family of Roman emperors that ruled in the 1st cent. AD. The Flavian emperors were Vespasian and his sons Titus and Domitian.

Flavius Arrian *See* **Epictetus**

Fleet Prison Notorious English jail in London. Its inmates included religious martyrs and victims of the Star Chamber, and it later became known as a debtors' prison. Several times destroyed, it was permanently demolished in 1845–46.

Fleming, Sir Alexander 1881–1955. Scottish bacteriologist. He was codiscoverer, with Sir H. Florey, of penicillin, and was corecipient of the Nobel Prize in Physiology in 1945.

Flemish school Term applied to the tradition of art and architecture that originated in Flanders before the 12th cent. and achieved great influence in European art (15th–17th cents.). The introduction by H. and J. van Eyck of improved techniques in oil painting (15th cent.) revolutionized painting in Europe and helped make Flanders a center of artistic activity. Other notable 15th-cent. Flemish artists included H. Bosch and P. Brueghel the Elder. Flemish art again flourished in the 17th cent. with the work of P. Rubens, A. Van Dyck, and J. Brueghel.

Fleurus, battles of Three battles fought near Fleurus, Belgium. **1.** Victory (Aug. 9, 1622) of Protestant forces over an allied Catholic army of Spanish and Bavarians during the Thirty Years' War. **2.** Victory (July 1, 1690) of French king Louis XIV over allied forces during the War of the Grand Alliance. **3.** French victory (June 26, 1794) over Austria during the French Revolutionary Wars. Some 70,000 French troops defeated a force of 50,000, mostly Austrians. The battle marked a turning point in France's struggle against the First Coalition.

Fleury, André Hercule de 1653–1743. French statesman and Roman Catholic cardinal. A trusted adviser to Louis XV, he effectively ruled France from 1726 to 1743.

Flodden, Battle of Battle fought (Sept. 9, 1513) at Flodden, northern England. Some 20,000 English soldiers under T. Howard, 2d duke of Norfolk, defeated an invading Scottish army of 30,000 led by

King James IV. James was killed and his army was crushed, with losses put at 10,000.

Flor, Roger de *d. c*1306. Italian-born mercenary. He entered the service of the Byzantine emperor Andronicus II (*c*1303), but the brutal practices of his army and his apparent intention to set up his own kingdom led to his assassination.

Flora Ancient Roman goddess of flowers and spring.

Floréal, coup of 22 *See* **French Revolution (1798)**

Florence Historic city (pop. 457,800), located in central Italy. In the 14th and 15th cents. Florence was not only a great center of Renaissance art and humanist studies but also a leading banking center and a birthplace of modern capitalism. In ancient times Florence was first an Etruscan, then a Roman town, and rose to importance in the 12th cent., when it became an autonomous commune. Florence was ruled by the famous Medici (*q.v.*) family between 1434 and 1737, except for such brief interregnums as the short-lived, puritannical republic established under G. Savonarola (1494–98). In 1737, the Hapsburg-Lorraine family succeeded the Medici and ruled Florence until it was absorbed into the unified kingdom of Italy (1860). Florence served briefly as capital of the kingdom (1864–71). The city was home at one time or other for some of the world's greatest literary, intellectual, and artistic figures, including Dante, L. da Vinci, Galileo, N. Machiavelli, G. Boccaccio, Michelangelo, Raphael, B. Cellini, Donatello, Massacio, and S. Botticelli. Among its many landmarks are the Uffizi, the Pitti Palace, and the Cathedral of Santa Maria del Fiore (begun 1296), with its octagonal cupola (by F. Brunelleschi, 1434), campanile (by Giotto, 1387), and famous bronze doors (by A. Pisano and L. Ghiberti, 1330–1447). Florence's many art treasures generally survived WW II, but floods in 1966 caused considerable damage.

Flores, Venancio *See* **Triple Alliance, War of the**

Florey, Sir Howard Walter 1898–1968. British pathologist. With Ernst Boris Chain (1906–79), he purified penicillin and succeeded in producing enough for practical use. With Chain and A. Fleming (*q.v.*), who discovered penicillin, Florey was awarded the Nobel Prize in Medicine in 1945.

Florida US state (pop. 9,740,000), on the Atlantic Ocean and the Gulf of Mexico, the 27th state. Ponce de León discovered the region and claimed it for Spain (1513). Colonization began with the founding (1565) of St. Augustine. Britain gained Florida in the Treaty of Paris (1763), but it was returned to Spain in 1783. After years of conflict, it was ceded to the US (1819). Granted statehood in 1845, Florida seceded from the Union (1861) and joined the Confederacy in the US Civil War. It was readmitted in 1868, and its present constitution was adopted in 1885.

Floridablanca, José Moñino y Redondo, conde de 1728–1808. Spanish statesman. He was premier of Spain (1776–92), and president of the Central Junta (1808), the Spanish government during the French invasion of Spain in the Peninsular War.

Floyd, John Buchanan 1806–63. US secretary of war (1857–60) and Confederate general. He resigned as secretary of war under suspicion of having mismanaged finances, and subsequently became a Confederate general. He was relieved of command after his defeat at Fort Donelson (1862).

Flying Dutchman Legendary ghost ship said to sail the waters off the Cape of Good Hope. The legend of the ship, with its crew of dead men doomed to sail forever, is the basis for R. Wagner's opera *Der Fliegende Holländer.*

Foch, Ferdinand 1851–1929. French general and, in 1918, commander of Allied armies in WW I. He fought at the battles of the Marne (1914) and Somme (1916) and was largely responsible for the final defeat of the Germans in 1918.

Fokine, Michel 1880–1942. Russian-born American choreographer, considered the father of modern ballet.

Fokker, Anthony Herman Gerard 1890–1939. Javanese-born aircraft manufacturer. Fokker manufactured airplanes for Germany in WW I. He later emigrated to America, became a US citizen, and designed both commercial and military aircraft in the US.

Folger, Henry Clay 1857–1930. American businessman, known best as founder of the Folger Shakespeare Library in Washington, DC. The library is based on his personal collection of Shakespeareana.

Folk High School *See* **Grundtvig, Nikolai Frederik Severin**

Fonseca, Manuel Deodoro da 1827–92. Brazilian general and first president of Brazil (1889–91). He took part in overthrow of the monarchy and establishment of the republic (1889).

Fontaine, Pierre François Leonard 1762–1853. French architect. He and Charles Percier (1764–1838), his associate, were two of the leading architects of the Empire period. He was architect for Napoleon and, later, for kings Louis XVIII and Louis Philippe.

Fontainebleau Name applied to a school or group of artists who, in 16th-cent. France, largely during the reigns of kings Francis I and Henry II, decorated the royal palace at Fontainebleau.

Fontainebleau, Treaty of Treaty (Oct. 27, 1807) between Napoleon and Spanish king Charles IV dividing Portugal between Spain and France. The treaty was just a step in Napoleon's campaign to bring the Iberian Peninsula under French control.

Fontana, Domenico 1543–1607. Italian architect. He designed the Lateran palace (1588) and parts of the Vatican (1588). He also was responsible for setting up the Egyptian obelisk in front of St. Peter's.

Fontenelle, Bernard Le Bovier de 1657–1757. French man of letters. His works, many of which dealt with scientific subjects, helped set the stage for the Enlightenment.

Fontenoy, Battle of Battle (May 11, 1745) of the War of the Austrian Succession, at Fontenoy, near Tournai, Belgium. French count M. de Saxe, leading 50,000 French troops, defeated an equivalent force of English, Dutch, Hanoverians, and Austrians under the British duke of Cumberland. It was the last British campaign of the war.

Foote, Andrew Hull 1806–63. American naval officer. As commander of Union naval operations on the upper Mississippi in the Civil War, he distinguished himself in operations against Fort Henry, Fort Donelson, and Island No. 10.

Foot Resolution Resolution introduced (1829) into the US Congress by Samuel A. Foot calling for limitation of sale of public lands. The resolution led to the famous debate (1830) between D. Webster and R. Hayne concerning states' rights and nullification.

Foraker, Joseph Benson 1846–1917. American politician. An Ohio political boss, he was US senator (1897–1909) until a scandal involving payments from the Standard Oil Co. ended his political career.

Forbidden City Chinese fortress city located within the city of Peking, so-called because most Chinese were forbidden to enter. It was the site, from 1421 to 1911, of the emperors' palaces. After China's fall to the Communists (1949), the palaces were opened to the public as museums.

Force Bill Name given to several pieces of American legislation. **1.** Bill passed (Mar. 2, 1833) to reinforce the Tariff of 1832 over the nullification efforts of South Carolina. **2.** Bill passed (May 31, 1870) to aid in Reconstruction of the South and to protect the rights of newly freed slaves. **3.** Bill passed (Apr. 20, 1871) aimed at suppression of the Ku Klux Klan. **4.** Bill, also called the Lodge Election Bill, introduced into Congress (1890) to establish federal control of national elections for the further protection of black voters. This bill never cleared the Senate.

Ford, Edsel Bryant 1893–1943. American auto manufacturer, son of H. Ford. He was president of Ford Motor Co. (1919–43).

Ford, Ford Madox ⟨Hueffer, Ford Madox⟩ 1873–1939. English novelist, poet, and critic. As editor of the *Transatlantic Review* and *English Review*, he published works by the major writers of this century. Among his own works are *The Good Soldier* and *Parade's End*.

Ford, Gerald Rudolph, Jr. ⟨orig. King, Leslie Lynch, Jr.⟩ 1913–. Thirty-eighth US president (1974–77), successor to R. Nixon. Ford, noted for his integrity and his loyalty to the Republican party, was a US congressman from Michigan (1949–73) and House minority leader (1965–73). Appointed (Dec. 6, 1973) to replace Vice-President S. Agnew amid the emerging Watergate crisis *(q.v.)*, he became president (Aug. 9, 1974) when Nixon was forced to resign. During his brief tenure as president, Ford issued (Sept. 8, 1974) Nixon a full pardon for charges arising from Watergate, presided over the final evacuation of US personnel from Saigon (Apr. 29, 1975), and ordered a rescue operation in the Mayaguez Incident *(q.v.)*. Ford failed to win election to a full term in 1976, in part because of widespread reaction to Watergate and the Republican party.

Ford, Henry 1863–1947. American auto manufacturer who pioneered the assembly-line techniques that revolutionized modern mass production. With others he organized (1903) the Ford Motor Co., and by 1907 had won sole control of it. He introduced to America (1908) the Model T, an inexpensive car, which was produced until its replacement (1928) by the Model A.

Ford, John 1586–c1640. English dramatist, considered the major English dramatist during the reign of Charles I. His works include *'Tis Pity She's a Whore*, *The Broken Heart*, and *Love's Sacrifice*.

Ford, Worthington Chauncey 1858–1941. American statistician, historian, and editor. He edited the writings of G. Washington and J. Q. Adams, and was chief of the manuscript division of the Library of Congress (1902–09).

Foreign Legion French volunteer army unit composed mainly of foreigners. Established (1831) by King Louis Philippe to secure French control in Algeria, the legion fought in wars throughout the French colonial empire and served with distinction in WW I and WW II. Its headquarters were moved from Algeria to France in 1962.

Foreign Ministers, Council of Council of the foreign ministers of the major Allied powers, called together (1945) at the end of WW II to formulate peace settlements with nations that had been allied with the Axis. It included ministers from the US, Great Britain, the USSR, and (from 1946) France.

Foreign Wars, Veterans of *See* **Veterans of Foreign Wars**

Forester, Cecil Scott 1899–1966. British writer known best for his series of novels featuring Horatio Hornblower, a fictional naval hero of the Napoleonic era.

Formigny, Battle of Battle (Apr. 15, 1540) of the Hundred Years' War, at Formigny, northern France. A decisive French victory over the English, it marked the end of English resistance to the French recapture of northern France. Some 4,000 of the 5,000-man English force were slaughtered.

Formosa *See* **Taiwan**

Fornovo, Battle of French victory (July 6, 1495) over the forces of the League of Venice during the French invasion of Italy (1494–95) by Charles VIII during the Italian Wars *(q.v.)*.

Forrest, Edwin *See* **Macready, William Charles**

Forrest, Nathan Bedford 1821–77. Confederate general during the American Civil War. Considered a great military strategist, he led many important calvary raids behind enemy lines (1862–64). He is said to have ordered the Fort Pillow Massacre (1864).

Forrestal, James Vincent 1892–1949. American public official. He was secretary of the navy (1944–47) under President F. Roosevelt and the first secretary of defense (1947–49) upon the organization of the Department of Defense.

Forster, Edward Morgan 1879–1970. English novelist, essayist, and critic. One of the major authors of the 20th cent., he wrote, among other works, *Howards End* and *A Passage to India*.

Fort Clatsop *See* **Lewis and Clark Expedition**

Fort Dearborn American army post, established (1803) on the Chicago River and named for Secretary of War H. Dearborn. Destroyed during the War of 1812, it was rebuilt (1816–17), and, with other communities, became the city of Chicago.

Fort Donelson Confederate stronghold during the American Civil War, located on the Cumberland River at Dover, Tennessee. Its fall (Feb. 16, 1862) to Union forces under Gen. U. Grant, aided by a gunboat flotilla under Commodore A. Foote, allowed the Union army to advance on Nashville. Here Grant issued his famous reply to a request for surrender terms: "No terms except unconditional and immediate surrender can be accepted."

Fort McHenry US fort at the entrance to Baltimore Harbor. Its bombardment (Sept. 13–14, 1814) by the British during the War of 1812 inspired F. Scott Key to write *The Star Spangled Banner*

Fort Pillow Massacre Incident of the US Civil War at Fort Pillow, on the Mississippi, north of Memphis, Tennessee. The fort was stormed (Apr. 12, 1864) and taken by Confederate forces under Gen. N. Forrest, and many of its defenders, half of whom were black, were killed. Forrest was accused of allowing his men to massacre the black Union troops after they had surrendered.

Fort Stanwix, Battle of Siege (Aug. 2–23, 1777) during the American Revolution. At Fort Stanwix, near Rome, New York, 750 Americans successfully withstood a siege by a British force of 1,700 led by Gen. B. St. Leger. The relief of the fort by B. Arnold contributed to the subsequent British defeat at Saratoga.

Fort Sumter Fort in the harbor of Charleston, South Carolina, site of the first military action of the American Civil War. Following the secession of South Carolina (Dec., 1860), state officials demanded the evacuation of some 100 US Army soldiers garrisoned in the fort. When President A. Lincoln signaled his intent to resupply the fort (Apr., 1861), Confederate forces, under Gen. P. Beauregard, shelled it (Apr. 12–14) and forced its evacuation. The fort was not recaptured until 1865.

forty-niners Name given to the American gold prospectors who traveled by thousands to California in 1849 after hearing that gold had been discovered (1848) on J. Sutter's land.

Forty-two Articles *See* **Thirty-nine Articles**

forum Roman meeting place. Similar to the Greek agora, it was a large, centrally located, open-air place in which Roman citizens would gather for festivals, speeches, elections, or other public events.

Fosdick, Harry Emerson 1878–1969. American Baptist minister. A well-known leader of modernists within the church, he became embroiled in controversy with the fundamentalists in the 1920s. His sermons were aired in a national radio program (1926–46).

Foster, Stephen Collins 1826–64. American song writer. His minstrel songs and ballads, such as *Oh! Susannah, Camptown Races*, and *My Old Kentucky Home*, are among the best known of popular American songs.

Foster, William Zebulon 1881–1961. American Communist party leader and presidential candidate (1924, 1928, 1932). A labor agitator, he headed the party from 1921 to 1930 and from 1945 to 1957.

Foucault, Jean Bernard Léon 1819–68. French physicist. He developed a method to measure accurately the speed of light (1850), demonstrated the earth's rotation by means of "Foucault's pendulum" (1851), and invented the gyroscope (1852).

Fouché, Joseph 1763?–1820. French revolutionary and famed minister of police. As untrustworthy as he was shrewd, he alternately helped and intrigued against French leaders in the tumultuous years between 1792 and 1815. As police minister (1799–1802, 1804–10), he organized the French police and created a notorious spy network.

Fouqué, Friedrich Heinrich Karl, Baron de la Motte 1777–1843. German Romantic novelist and poet. He is known best for his story *Undine*.

Fouquet, Jean ⟨Foucquet, Jean⟩ c1415–c1480. French painter. A leading painter in his day, he was court painter to Louis XI and Charles VII. Among his works are the illuminations in the *Book of Hours*.

Fouquet, Nicolas ⟨Foucquet, Nicholas⟩ 1615–80. French superintendent of finance (1653–61) to King Louis XIV. He enriched himself and others at the expense of the royal treasury and was finally tried for embezzlement (1661–64) and sentenced to life imprisonment (1664).

Fouquier-Tinville, Antoine Quentin 1746–95. French revolutionary. Prosecutor for the Revolutionary Tribunal (1793–94) during the Reign of Terror, he himself fell victim to the guillotine.

Four Forest Cantons The first four Swiss cantons (Uri, Schwyz, and Unterwalden in 1291, Lucerne in 1332) to break away from Hapsburg domination. They formed the foundation of the Swiss Confederation.

Four Freedoms American policy objectives as stated by President F. Roosevelt in his State of the Union message (1941). The freedoms, to be enjoyed by the world, were: freedom of speech, freedom of worship, freedom from want, and freedom from fear.

Four Horsemen of the Apocalypse In the Bible, four horses and riders of different colors which traditionally signify war (red horse), famine (black horse), death (pale horse), and Jesus Christ (white horse).

Fourier, Charles 1772–1837. French social philosopher. He advocated the organization of society based on the phalanx, a communal unit of 1,620 people. His philosophy fostered numerous attempts at communal societies, including the Brook Farm experiment in the US.

Fourier, Jean Baptiste Joseph, Baron 1768–1830. French mathematician and physicist noted for his contributions in the field of mathematical physics.

Fournier, Pierre Simon 1712–68. French type designer and founder. He designed many new type faces and wrote the *Manuel typographique*.

Four Noble Truths *See* **Buddhism**

Four-Power Pacific Treaty International pact (Dec. 13, 1921) by which the US, Great Britain, France, and Japan agreed to respect each other's Pacific territorial rights and to confer peacefully in case of disagreement.

Fourteen Points American peace proposals advanced (Jan. 8, 1918) by US president W. Wilson as a foundation for a lasting peace after WW I. They were: the abolition of secret diplomacy; freedom of the seas; equality of trade among peaceful nations; mutual reduction of armaments; peaceful mediation of colonial disputes; self-determination for USSR possessions; restoration of Belgium; restoration of French territory in Alsace-Lorraine; readjustment of the Italian border; autonomy for the national populations within Austria-Hungary; restoration of Serbia, Montenegro, and Romania; establishment of an independent Poland; self-determination for Turkish possessions and the internationalization of the Dardanelles; and the creation of a "general association of nations" to mediate future disputes. Many of the points as enumerated by Wilson were altered or ignored by the Treaty of Versailles *(q.v.)*, but the 14th point was the foundation for the League of Nations.

Fourth Crusade *See* **Crusade, Fourth**

Fourth Republic Name given the French government established (1946) after WW II. It lasted until 1958. (*See also* France [1946–1958].)

Fowler, Henry Watson 1858–1933. English lexicographer. He compiled the classic reference work *A Dictionary of Modern English Usage*.

Fox, Charles James 1749–1806. British statesman. Acclaimed for his oratory, the liberal Fox supported both American and Irish independence and the French Revolution. He argued for religious toleration and an end to the slave trade.

Foxe, John 1516–87. English Protestant clergyman. He wrote the widely read *Book of Martyrs*, which recounted (though not always accurately) the persecution of Protestant reformers up to his time.

Fox Indians *See* **Sac and Fox Indians**

Frahm, Karl Herbert *See* **Brandt, Willy**

France ⟨French Republic⟩ Republic located in Western Europe. Its capital is Paris. France evolved from the West Kingdom of the Franks, which was formed by the division of Charlemagne's empire (843). Development of a powerful French monarchy began in the 10th cent. and culminated in the absolutism of Louis XIV in the

17th–18th cents. By then France had also become a major European power. A flourishing culture developed in France and it has significantly influenced modern civilization in the West, notably in literature and the arts. The French Revolution plunged France into chaos and, as the experiment in liberal republicanism failed, brought Napoleon to power. Under Napoleon, France briefly controlled nearly all of continental Europe. By the time of Napoleon's fall in 1815, the spirit of the French Revolution had been spread throughout Europe and gave rise to liberal, nationalistic movements that flowered in the mid-1800s. France remained politically unstable throughout much of the 19th cent. and was further weakened by the ravages of WW I and WW II. Since WW II France has followed a relatively independent foreign policy, cultivating relations with Third World countries and, in more recent years, with Soviet-bloc countries. (*See also* French Revolution, French Revolutionary Wars, Napoleonic Wars.) Key events in the history of France include:

c600 BC   Celts settled in Gaul (region roughly that of modern France).

c600 BC   Marseilles founded by Ionian Greeks as a trading colony.

58–51 BC   Romans, led by J. Caesar, conquered Gaul; prospered in subsequent years as a Roman province.

1ST CENT. AD   Christianity introduced in Gaul.

3D CENT. AD   Invasions of Gaul by Visigoths, Franks, and other barbarian peoples began.

FROM 428 AD   Salian Franks gradually took control of northern France.

481 AD   Clovis I became leader of the Salian Franks; this marked the beginning of the Merovingian Empire in Gaul.

486 AD   Battle of Soissons; Clovis I defeated armies of the last Roman governor of Gaul.

496 AD   Clovis defeated the invading Alemanni; converted to Christianity and thereafter became a staunch opponent of Arianism.

500   Clovis attacked but did not conquer Burgundy.

507   Visigoths defeated by Clovis in battle at Vouillé.

511–687   Merovingian Empire divided; on the death of Clovis (511) there followed nearly two centuries of wars and divisiveness; two Frankish kingdoms, Austrasia and Neustria, emerged but their kings had been weakened by the constant wars; the mayors of the palace, who served them, held real power.

c534   Burgundy conquered.

687   Pepin of Heristal, as mayor of the Palace of Austrasia (687–714), conquered Neustria; he thus united the Merovingian Empire under his rule, though the kings remained in title; Pepin was the first of the Carolingians.

715–741   Charles Martel, Pepin's son, became Austrasian mayor of the palace; subdued Neustria and began series of conquests that expanded Frankish domains.

732   Battle of Poitiers; Charles Martel won famous victory over Muslim force advancing from Spain; victory increased his power.

751   Carolingian kingdom founded; Pepin the Short, mayor of the palace from 741, overthrew the Merovingian king and took the crown for himself (751).

754–756   Donation of Pepin; in return for papal sanction for his overthrow of the Merovingians, Pepin aided the pope against invading Lombards in Italy; donated lands conquered from them to the church.

768–814   Charlemagne reigned; by his conquests brought the Carolingian Empire to its greatest extent, including most of modern France, Germany, northern Italy, and the Low Countries.

800   Charlemagne crowned emperor of the (reconstituted) Western Roman Empire by Pope Leo III; coronation, granted in return for aiding pope, established ties between Rome and the European monarchs.

814–840   Louis I (the Pious) reigned as the last ruler of a unified Carolingian Empire.

843   Treaty of Verdun; empire divided into three parts by Louis' heirs: West Frankish kingdom (roughly modern France), East Frankish kingdom (roughly modern Germany), and a narrow middle kingdom that included Italy; middle kingdom (except Italy) largely absorbed by other two in following years.

870   Treaty of Mersen; middle Frankish kingdom (except Italy) divided between West and East Frankish kingdoms.

843–877   Charles the Bald reigned as king of the West Franks; Charles held the imperial crown as (titular) ruler of the Carolingian Empire from 875; beginnings of feudalism appeared during his reign.

877–879   Louis II (the Stammerer) reigned.

879–884   Louis' heirs, Louis III (ruled 879–882) and Carloman (ruled 879–884), reigned in the West Frankish kingdom.

881   Louis III defeated Norse raiders at Saucourt.

881–887   Charles III (the Fat) reigned; he briefly reunited West and East Frankish kingdoms (882–887) but was overthrown; final breakup of the Carolingian Empire.

888–898 Eudes and Charles III (the Simple) chosen as rival kings of the west; Eudes was forced to defend Paris against Norse raiders and fight a civil war with Charles.

898–923 Charles III king in the west; after Eudes' death (898) he ended Norse raids by ceding parts of Normandy to their leader, Rollo (911); deposed by rebellious nobles (923).

922–923 Robert I, a Capetian, named king in opposition to Charles during the revolt; he was killed in battle.

923–936 Rudolph reigned; central authority further weakened by renewed fighting against Norsemen and rivals, as well as against Hungarian invaders.

936–954 Louis IV reigned; embroiled in wars with Hugh the Great, a leader of the nobles who was aided by German king Otto I; Louis finally emerged victorious in 950.

954–986 Lothair reigned; wars with the nobleman Hugh Capet and Holy Roman Emperors Otto II and Otto III (over Lorraine) reduced royal power to almost nothing.

987–996 Hugh Capet reigned, founding the Capetian line of French kings; his domains consisted of the region around Paris; as king of the west, he held only nominal rule over the feudal kingdoms that then comprised France (including Normandy, Brittany, Burgundy, and Aquitaine).

996–1031 Robert II reigned; excommunicated by Pope Gregory V for marrying (996) widow of Eudes; brought Burgundy under the control of French kings (1015).

1031–60 Henry I reigned; embroiled in various wars to maintain his domains and opposed interference by the church.

1060–1108 Philip I reigned; increased royal domains at the expense of feudal lords; unsuccessfully attempted to separate Normandy from English control (after 1066); opposed the reforms of Pope Gregory VII.

1108–37 Louis VI (the Fat) reigned; warred with King Henry I of England over English domains on the Continent; repulsed an invasion by the Holy Roman Emperor Henry V (1124); issued royal charters to towns then beginning a period of rapid growth.

1095 First Crusade preached at Council of Clermont, held in France; French nobleman, Raymond IV, count of Toulouse, organized the crusade.

1137–80 Louis VII reigned; forced to submit to the pope (1144); took part in the unsuccessful Second Crusade; rivaled English for control of Continental domains.

1144 Geoffrey Plantagenet, count of Anjou, conquered Normandy; later gave this powerful duchy to his son, Henry of Anjou (later Henry II of England).

1152 Louis VII annulled his marriage to Eleanor of Aquitaine; she later married Henry of Anjou and when Henry became king of England, he laid claim to Anjou, Normandy, and Aquitaine as English possessions; this led to long rivalry with expanding French state.

1180–1223 Philip II reigned; by his conquests, doubled French domains; conquered northeastern territories from feudal lords and captured Normandy, Brittany, Anjou, Maine, and Touraine from the English (1204).

1200 University of Paris founded; in following years Paris became a medieval center of learning; Albertus Magnus and Saint Thomas Aquinas did highly influential work in theology there.

1208–13 Albigensian Crusade against heretics in southern France.

1233 Medieval Inquisition began.

1214 Battle of Bouvines; Philip emerged victorious from this battle against English king John and Holy Roman Emperor Otto IV; secured possession of earlier conquests and established France as a major power.

1223–26 Louis VIII reigned; launched unsuccessful invasion of England to aid barons' revolt (1216–17); resumed fighting against Albigensians.

1226–70 Louis IX reigned; considered the ideal medieval monarch, he brought medieval France to its height; instituted administrative reforms.

1229 Raymond of Toulouse, who had supported the Albigensians, submitted to the crown; his lands, comprising much of southern France, added to royal domains.

1242 Unsuccessful rebellion by nobles in southern France, aided by invasion by English king Henry III.

1248–54 Louis' participation in the Seventh Crusade proved ruinous; captured and ransomed back to France.

1259 Treaty of Paris, settling territorial disputes with English king Henry III; included renunciation of former English territories and French suzerainty over Aquitaine.

1270–85 Philip III reigned.

1285–1314 Philip IV reigned; his attempt to tax clergy grew into dispute with the pope.

1294–98 War with England; Philip failed in his effort to take the English-held duchy of Guienne.

1302–03 Philip called the first States General (council of nobles) in connection with his dispute with the pope.

1302 Battle of the Golden Spurs (July 11); Flemish towns opposing French annexation decisively defeated French troops.

1305 Philip secured election of Pope Clement V, a supporter of his cause.

1309 Pope Clement V moved the papacy to Avignon (Babylonian captivity), increasing Philip's control of church.

1312 Pope Clement V condemned the Knights Templars at King Philip's urging; Philip then confiscated the order's considerable wealth.

1314–16 Louis X reigned.

1316 John I reigned

1317–22 Philip V reigned; Salic law invoked to justify his succession and thus established its use in France.

1322–28 Charles IV (the Fair) reigned as last of the Capetian kings.

1328–1589 Valois dynasty reigned; founded by Philip VI.

1328–50 Philip VI reigned; the Salic Law was invoked to allow for his succession.

1337–1453 Hundred Years' War; long rivalry for control of English domains on the Continent ended when French drove out all English forces (1453); victory gained at great cost, with France laid waste and its nobility decimated.

1341–65 War of the Breton Succession, dynastic struggle in Brittany.

1348–49 Black plague broke out in France.

1350–64 John II reigned; was captured during the Hundred Years' War (1356).

1358 Jacquerie, group of French peasants, revolted against increased war taxes.

1364–80 Charles V (the Wise) reigned; regained much territory from England, instituted reforms, consolidated power of the monarchy, strengthened the military.

1380–1422 Charles VI reigned; suffered fits of insanity and was unable to rule; civil war between Burgundians and Armagnacs broke out (after 1407) over which faction was to control the regency of Charles; Burgundians became allies of English.

1422–61 Charles VII reigned; English controlled north of France at outset of his rule; not crowned until after Joan of Arc inspired French troops to lift siege of Orleans; his reign saw the end of the Hundred Years' War (1453) and the capture of virtually all English territory on the Continent.

1438 Pragmatic Sanction of Bourges; issued by Charles VII to limit papal powers; asserted powers of French king in France and declared pope subject to general council (conciliarism).

1440 Praguerie, revolt by nobles against Charles VII.

1461–83 Louis XI reigned; overcame rebellious nobles and laid the basis for absolute monarchy in France.

1465 League of the Public Weal, rebel alliance formed by nobles against King Louis XI.

1477 Louis defeated Charles the Bold, duke of Burgundy; Burgundy, until then autonomous state, joined to French crown.

1480 House of Anjou became extinct; Louis added its territories (Provence, Anjou, Maine, and Bar) to possessions of French crown.

1470–98 Charles VIII reigned; his attempt to conquer Naples brought on the long Italian Wars.

1494–1559 Italian Wars for control of Italy; Spanish Hapsburgs emerged victorious after years of sporadic warfare.

1498–1515 Louis XII reigned; he was unsuccessful in the Italian Wars.

1520 Treaty of Cambrai (Ladies' Peace) with Holy Roman Emperor Charles V; it briefly halted the Italian Wars.

1515–47 Francis I reigned; continued Italian Wars against Holy Roman Emperor Charles V; his reign marked by flowering of the French Renaissance and by beginnings of Protestantism in France.

1516 Concordat of Bologna; Pragmatic Sanction of Bourges rescinded.

1520 Field of Cloth of Gold; Francis attempted to form alliance with English King Henry VIII.

1547–59 Henry II reigned; ended Italian Wars and began persecutions of French Protestants (Huguenots); increased royal powers.

1547 Brittany united to French crown.

1556–58 War between Valois and Hapsburg families won by Spanish Hapsburgs at the Battle of Gravelines, northern France.

1558 Calais captured by French; was last English territory in France.

1559–60 Francis II reigned; Catholic Guise family rose to power and dominated his reign; used their power to severely persecute Protestants.

1560 Conspiracy of Amboise, Protestant plot to break power of Guise family; foiled, it led to massacres of Protestants.

1560 Treaty of Edinburgh signed with England and Scotland; led to withdrawal of French and English troops from Scotland to ease conflict between Catholics and Protestants there.

1560–74 Charles IX reigned; he was dominated by his mother, Catherine de Médicis, throughout his reign.

1562–98 Wars of Religion; series of wars stemming from persecution of French Protestants by Catholics and complicated by struggles for political power.

1574–89 Henry III reigned; helped plan the Massacre of St. Bartholomew's Day (1572) during the continuing Wars of Religion; the last of the Valois line, he was assassinated.

1589–1610 Henry IV reigned; the leader of French Protestants, he converted to Catholicism (1593) to win support for his accession; he founded the Bourbon line.

1589–1792 House of Bourbon in power.

1598 Edict of Nantes established toleration of Protestants and ended Wars of Religion.

1610–43 Louis XIII reigned; dominated by his mother, Marie de Médicis, until 1617 and thereafter relied on his ministers.

1618–48 Thirty Years' War.

1624–42 Cardinal Richelieu in power as chief minister to Louis XIII; promoted concentration of power in monarchy at expense of nobles; helped make France the dominant European power.

1632 Company of New France formed; promoted French colonization of Acadia in eastern Canada until English permanently took over in 18th cent.

1642–61 Cardinal Mazarin in power as chief minister; succeeded Richelieu and remained in office under Louis XIV; continued Richelieu's policies; broke remaining power of nobles and helped make France leading power.

1643–1715 Louis XIV reigned; absolutism reached its height in France while his extravagance and expansionist wars wrecked French finances; built palace of Versailles.

1648 Alsace controlled by France after the Treaty of Westphalia ending the Thirty Years' War.

1648–49 Fronde of the Parlement, unsuccessful rebellion against Louis' rule.

1650–53 Fronde of the Princes, unsuccessful rebellion by nobles led by the Prince de Condé.

1659 Peace of the Pyrenees ended hostilities with Spain that continued after the Thirty Years' War; border established.

1664 French East India Company, colonial trading organization, formed to develop trade with India.

1667–68 War of Devolution; first of Louis' expansionist wars and directed at acquiring the Spanish Netherlands.

1672–68 Dutch War; Louis XIV sought to expand French domains and commerce at the expense of The Netherlands.

c1680 Poison Affair; Louis XIV's mistress accused of obtaining potions to kill rivals.

1682 Gallican Articles approved by French clergy, an important document in French movement called Gallicanism, which sought greater independence of the French church from the pope.

1685 Revocation of the Edict of Nantes; toleration of French Protestants ended, resulting in mass emigration of Protestants from France.

1688–97 War of the Grand Alliance, Louis' third expansionist war.

1700s Enlightenment, great intellectual movement devoted to rationalism, emerged in France and spread through Europe and America.

1701–14 War of the Spanish Succession; France gave up claims to Spanish throne and lost all but small part of colonial possessions in Canada.

1702–10 Revolt of the Camisards, Protestant peasants.

1715–74 Louis XV reigned; a weak and unpopular ruler, he was dominated by his mistresses; financial difficulties of his reign helped bring on French Revolution.

1720 Mississippi Scheme uncovered; financial scandal involved government.

1733–35 France supported Poland in War of the Polish succession; occupied duchy of Lorraine (1733).

1740–48 War of the Austrian Succession; France mainly fought England in the colonies.

1756 Diplomatic Revolution ended long-established European alliances.

1756–63 Seven Years' War; France lost most of colonies in India and Canada to England by the Treaty of Paris.

1771 Parlements (courts) dissolved by Louis to check their growing power; restored (1774) after move proved unpopular.

1774–92 Louis XVI reigned; tried to rule as an enlightened despot but attempts to put forward badly needed reforms failed (partly frustrated by Queen Marie Antoinette) and led to the French Revolution.

1774–76 A. Turgot, minister of finance, started ambitious program of tax and other reforms but was dismissed before it was completed.

1777–81 J. Necker in power as finance minister; enacted some reforms and was ousted (1781); he then made public the precarious state of the treasury.

1778–83 French aided colonists in American Revolution, thus further depleting royal treasury.

1783–87 C. de Calonne in office as finance minister; devised plan to save France from financial disaster by reforming land tax; plan bitterly opposed by aristocrats.

1785 Affair of the Diamond Necklace; Queen Marie Antoinette implicated, which only increased popular dislike of her.

1787 Assembly of Notables convened (Feb.); Calonne's land-tax reform submitted to it to circumvent opposition from the Parlements (courts); assembly dismissed without accomplishing reform (May).

1787–88 Brienne in office as finance minister; continued to press for Calonne's reforms and met continuing opposition from the aristocracy; forced decision to call States General; resigned (Aug.).

1788–89 Necker recalled as finance minister; States General convened (1789) and thus began the revolution.

1789–99 French Revolution; France plunged into several years of turmoil and unsuccessful experimentation with republican government; Napoleon emerged as the leader of revolutionary France and established first the Consulate (1799) and then the empire (1804) under his imperial control.

1792–1802 French Revolutionary Wars; other European powers, opposed to the revolutionary government, warred against France.

1797 XYZ Affair, attempted bribing of American diplomats by French officials; led to undeclared naval war with US.

1799–1804 Government of the Consulate in power; Napoleon seized power by the Coup of 18 Brumaire (Nov. 9); he established the Consulate with himself as dictator, restored order, and instituted reforms.

1799 Constitution of the Year VIII (Dec. 29); formally established government of the Consulate and instituted efficient administrative system.

1800 Treaty of San Ildefonso concluded between Spain and France; Spain retroceded Louisiana territory to France.

1801 Napoleon restored relations with the Roman Catholic church, severed since the early days of the revolution.

1802 French Revolutionary Wars ended; terms favorable to France.

1802 Napoleon made consul for life (Aug. 2).

1803–15 Napoleonic Wars; Napoleon's conquests gave France control of most of continental Europe for a time.

1804 Assassination plot against Napoleon discovered (Feb.); G. Cadoudal, a conspirator, executed; Napoleon used incident to justify creation of the empire.

1804 Napoleon proclaimed emperor (May 18) by Senate and Tribunate of the Consulate.

1804–14 Empire period; Napoleon crowned (Dec. 2); Napoleon created a new nobility and installed rulers in conquered territories within the empire; period marked by expansion of the empire throughout Europe during the Napoleonic Wars.

1804 Napoleon issued the famous Code Napoléon.

1807 Napoleon issued the Commercial Code.

1810 Penal code issued by Napoleon.

1810 Napoleon married Marie Louise, daughter of Austrian Emperor Francis I, after divorcing Josephine.

1814 Napoleon's first abdication (Apr. 6), following occupation of Paris by allied forces.

1814–48 Restoration period.

1814–24 Louis VIII reigned; restored to power (Apr. 6); issued Declaration of Saint-Ouen (May) as basis for new constitution.

1814 Treaty of Paris (first, May 30); returned France to boundaries of 1792.

1814 Charter of 1814 issued (June 4) as new constitution for France; retained some freedoms gained by revolution.

1815 Hundred Days; Napoleon returned from exile and entered Paris (Mar. 20); reestablished as emperor, he was defeated at Waterloo and again abdicated (June 22).

1815 Chamber Introuvable established (Aug.); ultraroyalists dominated Chamber of Deputies as persecutions of former revolutionaries and Bonapartists reached height; Chamber finally dissolved (Sept., 1816) and replaced by moderates.

1815 Treaty of Paris (second, Nov. 20); imposed harsher terms, including payment of war indemnity and military occupation by allies for three years.

1818 Military occupation of France ended after the Congress of Aix-la-Chapelle.

1820 Comte de Villèle established ministry of ultraroyalists; marked victory of ultraroyalists in struggle with moderates and liberals; ministry instituted reactionary policies.

1822 French intervention in the liberal revolt in Spain approved at the Congress of Verona; Spanish monarchy restored (1823).

1824–30 Charles X reigned; vainly tried to reestablish *ancien régime* and thereby provoked growing hostility of liberal factions; decision to install ultraroyalist ministry under A. de Polignac led to revolution.

1830 July Revolution (July–Aug.) ended in victory for bourgeois liberals; Charles abdicated and a parliamentary monarchy was created by revision of the Charter of 1814.

1830–48 Louis Philippe ("Citizen King") reigned; installed by the Chamber of Deputies, he was head of the Orléanist line of the Bourbon family; his reign was marked by workers' rebellions and struggles between Legitimists and Bonapartists.

1830 Algeria occupied by French.

1848 February revolution broke out; forced King Louis Philippe to abdicate (Feb. 24) and led to establishment of Second Republic.

1848–52 Second Republic.

1848 June Days, bloody revolt by workers in Paris (June 23–26).

1848 New constitution (Nov.) created government by strong president and unicameral legislature.

1848–51 Louis Napoleon, nephew of Napoleon I, in office as elected president.

1851 Coup by Louis Napoleon (Dec. 2); he proclaimed himself Emperor Napoleon III.

1852–60 Second Empire period.

1852–70 Napoleon III reigned; promulgated imperial constitution (Jan. 15, 1852); promoted industrialization and economic growth.

1854–56 Crimean War; France opposed Russian expansion into domains of the Ottoman Turks.

1858 Attempt to assassinate Napoleon III by Italian nationalist Felice Orsini (Jan. 14); prompted Napoleon to help Italian nationalists drive Austrians out of Italy (from May, 1859).

1860 Napoleon agreed (Nov.) to more liberal government to counter mounting opposition to his rule; legislature given new powers.

1861 French intervened in Mexico; established Mexican empire under Maximilian I, which lasted until just after French troops were forced to withdraw (1866).

1870 New constitution creating parliamentary empire forced on Napoleon by growing movement for liberalization (Apr.)

1870–71 Franco-Prussian War; France was quickly defeated and occupied, marking end of French hegemony on the Continent.

1870 Reverses in Franco-Prussian War led to political unrest; Napoleon III overthrown (Sept.).

1870–71 Government of National Defense formed (Sept. 4); capitulated to Germans (Jan. 28, 1871).

1870–1940 Third Republic.

1871–73 A. Thiers in office as head of state (Feb.) with legislative assembly (Bordeaux assembly).

1871 Commune of Paris, bloody revolt by radicals in Paris (Mar.–May).

1871 Treaty of Frankfurt (May 10) ended the Franco-Prussian War; France lost territory in Alsace and Lorraine.

1873–79 M. MacMahon in office as second president of the republic; his unsuccessful attempt to name a royalist ministry over objections of the Chamber of Deputies established power of chamber over ministry (1877).

1875 New constitution formally established republic after attempts to restore monarchy failed to gain support.

1879–87 J. Grévy in office as president; his term marked beginning of anticlerical movement in France, and of expansion of the French colonial empire in Indochina and North Africa.

1883–85 Sino-French War; France won control of Vietnam as it expanded its control in Indochina.

1884 Trade unions legalized; labor movements and socialism on the rise.

1889 Boulanger Crisis; Gen. G. Boulanger, widely popular since 1886, came close to seizing power as dictator (Jan. 1889); fled France soon after.

1892 Panama Scandal rocked French government.

c1894–1906 Dreyfus Affair, French army captain falsely accused of treason; prolonged crisis brought moderate leftists to power and advanced anticlericalism.

1898 Fashoda Incident, with Britain, resulting from French and British expansion in Africa.

1904 Entente Cordiale, informal understanding with Britain, reached to counter growing power of Germany.

1905 Separation of church and state by law.

1905 Moroccan Crisis, resulting from colonial rivalry with Germany.

1906–13 Clément Armand Fallières served as president; his term marked by rise of nationalism and spread of labor troubles.

1911 Agadir Incident, renewed troubles with Germany over Morocco.

1913–20 Raymond Poincaré in office as president; led France through war years.

1914–18 World War I; France, the primary battleground, devastated by the war; after the war, gained left bank of the Rhine, as well as mandates in Syria and Africa.

1919–24 Bloc National, a conservative coalition, dominated national politics.

1923–25 France occupied the Ruhr district when Germany failed to make war reparations payments.

1925 Locarno Pact signed with Germany, restoring relations.

1931–40 A. Lebrun in office as president; his term marked by economic troubles of the Great Depression, attempts to appease Italians and Germans, and the fall of the Third Republic (1940).

1934 Stavinsky Affair; the financial scandal resulted in a political crisis.

1935 Concessions in Africa made to Italians.

1936–38 Popular Front formed governments in France under Lebrun; front was a coalition of Socialists, radicals, and Communists led by L. Blum; instituted social reforms.

1938 Munich Pact signed to appease Nazis.

1939–45 World War II; the French, quickly defeated and occupied, nevertheless continued to resist Germans; much of France damaged in Allied drive across Europe at end of war.

1940 Vichy government under Marshal Pétain, established in unoccupied France (June).

1942 Vichy government superseded following complete German occupation of France.

1940 C. de Gaulle set up Free French government in London.

1944–46 De Gaulle established provisional government at Paris (Aug.); Vichy collaborators purged; nationalization of financial industry and utilities (1945–46).

1945 France joined the UN.

1946 France received massive US aid to rebuild war-torn economy.

1946–58 Fourth Republic; government formed with weak executive; colonial empire reorganized as the French Union.

1946–54 Indochina War; France unsuccessfully tried to reestablish its control over the region.

1947–54 Vincent Auriol in office as first president; French politics marked by rivalries between the Popular Republican Movement (MRP, moderate), Socialists, and Communists.

1949 France became founding member of NATO.

1954 Rebellion against French rule in Algeria broke out (Nov. 1); followed France's defeat in Indochina that year.

1956 Suez Crisis; France joined with Britain in opposing Egyptians.

1957 France became founding member of European Economic Community.

1958 De Gaulle recalled to power (June 1) as continuing crisis in Algeria threatened to topple French government; de Gaulle given extraordinary powers and mandate to write new constitution.

1958 Fifth Republic formed; new constitution established strong presidency; French Community replaced French Union of overseas territories.

1958–69 De Gaulle in office as first president; achieved granting of Algerian independence; pursued independent foreign policy and established strong Gaullist constituency.

1960 France exploded its first nuclear device.

1962 Algerian independence granted despite terrorist campaign by Secret Army Organization in France and Algeria.

1964 France recognized Communist China.

1966 France withdrew from NATO; US and others forced to withdraw military forces from France.

1968 Student riots (May) sparked a national political crisis; subsequent elections gave de Gaulle an absolute majority; education system reformed.

1969 De Gaulle resigned (Apr.) after his program for regional reform was rejected by voters.

1969–74 G. Pompidou in office as president; largely continued de Gaulle's policies, though he ended French opposition to Britain's membership in the Common Market.

1970 Pompidou signed agreement for political and economic cooperation with USSR.

1974 President Pompidou died in office (Apr. 2).

1974–81 Valery Giscard d'Estaing in office as president; continued Gaullist independent foreign policy.

1979 Strikes and rioting broke out after government subsidies to industry were cut.

1979 President d'Estaing's prestige damaged by rumors he had received diamonds as gifts from former Emperor Bokassa of Central African Empire; French influence in Africa diminished.

1981 François Mitterand, a Socialist, in office as president; his election victory over the Gaullist coalition marked a sharp leftward shift in French politics; Mitterand named four Communists to cabinet posts.

1981 President Mitterand began implementing his Socialist program; minimum wage raised 10% and new taxes of business and the wealthy promised.

1982 Nationalization of selected major industries became effective. (Feb. 11).

1982 French troops took part in operation to oversee evacuation of PLO from Beirut, Lebanon.

France, Anatole ⟨*pseud. of* Jacques Anatole Thibault⟩ 1844–1924. French author. One of the leading literary men of his day, he wrote *Thais* and *The Red Lily*, among other works. He was awarded the Nobel Prize in Literature in 1921.

France, Battle of German offensive (June 5–16, 1940) against France during WW II. After defeating the Belgian and Allied armies in Belgium and forcing the British and Allied armies to evacuate at Dunkirk, the Germans turned to the destruction of the French army. Outflanking the Maginot Line *(q.v.)*, the Germans moved south, taking Paris on June 14 and Verdun one day later. On June 16, French premier P. Reynaud resigned and was replaced by Marshal H. Petain, who immediately called for an armistice. France formally accepted Germany's armistice terms (June 22, 1940) at Compiègne, in the same railway car in which the Germans had accepted armistice terms in WW I.

Franche-Comté Name given to the French county of Burgundy (as distinct from the duchy of Burgundy). It became a possession of the Hapsburgs (16th cent.), and was annexed by France (1678).

Franchia Media *See* **Lotharingia; Treaty of Verdun**

Francia, José Gaspar Rodriguez ⟨El Supremo⟩ 1761?–1840. Dictator of Paraguay (1814–40). Joining the government after the bloodless revolt against Spain (1811), he became dictator (1814) and thereafter freely exercised his harsh personal rule.

Francis I 1494–1547. French king (1515–47), successor to his father-in-law, Louis XII. Much of his reign was spent in conflict with Holy Roman Emperor Charles V. Despite his failure to gain the support of English king Henry VIII at the Field of Cloth of Gold (1520), Francis engaged Charles in four wars, largely unsuccessful. During his reign the French Renaissance flowered and J. Cartier explored North America.

Francis I 1708–65. Holy Roman Emperor (1745–65). As duke of Lorraine (1729–37), he ceded his duchy to Poland to end the War of the Polish Succession. His marriage (1736) to Maria Theresa, a stronger personality and Hapsburg heiress, led to his accession as coregent of Austria and Holy Roman Emperor during the War of the Austrian Succession *(q.v.)*. The Seven Years' War (1756–63) was fought during his reign.

Francis I 1777–1830. Italian king of the Two Sicilies (1825–30), successor to his father, Ferdinand I. His reign was marked by corruption and repressive policies.

Francis I (of Austria) *See* **Francis II**

Francis II 1453–88. Duke of Brittany (1458–88), successor to his father, Arthur III. Francis struggled to remain independent of France. He joined (1465) the League of the Public Weal against Louis VI and unsuccessfully rebelled against Charles VIII, whom his daughter, Anne of Brittany, later married.

Francis II 1544–60. French king (1559–60), successor to his father, Henry II. The Guise family effectively ruled France during his short reign and used their power to persecute the Huguenots (Protestants). The unsuccessful attempt to break their power was called the Conspiracy of Amboise.

Francis II ⟨Francis I of Austria⟩ 1768–1835. Last Holy Roman Emperor (1792–1806) and king of Bohemia and Hungary, successor to his father, Leopold II. He was also first emperor of Austria (Francis I, 1804–35). A determined opponent of the French Revolution and of Napoleon, he was several times defeated by the French in battles between 1793 and 1806. In 1806 he was compelled to sign the Treaty of Pressburg, which dissolved the Holy Roman Empire.

Franciscans Originally a religious order founded in Italy (1209) by Saint Francis of Assisi and now three separate orders: Friars Minor, Friars Minor Conventual, and Friars Minor Capuchin. The order was founded on rules written by Saint Francis stressing a life of poverty, religious devotion, and dedication to helping others. Francis subsequently rewrote and moderated the rules following the rapid spread of his order. These new rules were formally approved by Pope Honorius III (1223). By the 16th cent. the order had split between the Conventuals, who adhered to the communal life, and the zealously ascetic Observants. The Observants became an independent order (1517) and subsequently gave rise to the Capuchins (1525), whose order was founded on still stricter devotion to the ascetic life. The Franciscans have been prominent in missionary and educational work.

Francis Ferdinand 1863–1914. Austrian archduke (1875–1914). The nephew of Austrian emperor Francis Joseph I, he became heir after the death (1889) of Crown Prince Rudolf. The assassination of Francis and his wife at Sarajevo (June 28, 1914) touched off WW I.

Francis Joseph 1830–1916. Emperor of Austria (1848–1916) and king of Hungary (1867–1916). An absolutist, Francis was forced to yield to constitutional reform (1867) and creation of the Dual Monarchy *(q.v.)* after a series of military reversals. He allied himself with the Central Powers in WW I.

Francis of Assisi, Saint ⟨b. Giovanni Francesco Bernardone⟩ 1182–1226. Italian monk, founder of the Franciscans and one of the great saints of the Christian church. The son of a merchant, he converted to a life of poverty and religious devotion while still in his twenties. He began preaching as a layman in 1209, and, in that year, with permission from Pope Innocent III, founded the Franciscan order based on his teachings. He made a pilgrimage to Palestine (1219–20) during the Fifth Crusade, and in 1221 gave up leadership of the Franciscans. Following a 40-day fast (1224) at Mount Alverno, he miraculously received the "stigmata," wounds likened to those suffered by Jesus at the Crucifixion. Francis died with the wounds, said to be the first instance of such stigmata. He was canonized in 1228.

Francis of Sales, Saint 1567–1622.   French Roman Catholic bishop, Doctor of the Church. He is known for his work in converting French Calvinists and for founding the Order of the Visitation for women.

Francis Xavier, Saint 1506–52.   Basque Jesuit missionary. Francis and Saint Ignatius Loyola were founding members of the Jesuits. His missionary work took him to India and Japan.

Franck, César Auguste 1822–90. Belgian-French organist and composer of the Romantic school. His best-known work is his *Symphony in D minor.*

Franco, Francisco 1892–1975. Spanish general and dictator. Made army chief of staff (1934), he took part in the military revolt (1936) at the outset of the Spanish Civil War. Later that year he became leader of the rebel government and, with the aid of German and Italian troops, brought the civil war to an end (1939). Despite the Fascist origins of his ruling Falange party, Franco kept Spain neutral during WW II and maintained a pro-Western policy in the years afterward until his death.

Franco, João *See* **Charles I (1863–1908)**

Franconia One of the five historic duchies of medieval Germany (with Saxony, Lotharingia, Swabia, and Bavaria), located in what is now southern W. Germany. Originally part of the Frankish Kingdom, it became the East Frankish or East German Kingdom on the division of the Carolingian Empire (843). It was partitioned (939), creating the duchies of Rhenish Franconia and Eastern Franconia. In subsequent centuries the duchies were further fragmented and divided. The name Franconia now survives as the name of three modern German provinces in Bavaria: Lower, Middle, and Upper Franconia.

Franco-Prussian War War (1870–71) between France and Prussia (with allied German states). The war brought about the unification of the German states under Prussian domination and thus achieved the long-sought goal of Prussian minister O. von Bismarck. Following the Austro-Prussian War (1866), France aggressively sought an opportunity to check the rising power of Prussia. Bismarck, on the other hand, was near to completing the unification of German states. Only the southern states remained outside the North German Confederation *(q.v.)* and Bismarck hoped to play on anti-French sentiment to bring them into the fold. With both sides thus primed, war was almost inevitable and fighting broke out in Aug., 1870. France suffered a humiliating defeat soon after. Consequences of the war were far-reaching: France rebelled against the monarchy and established the Third Republic (1870); Germany was unified (1871); and French hegemony over continental Europe was ended. Key dates in the war include:

1870 Prince of Prussia's ruling house (Hohenzollern-Sigmaringen) offered Spanish throne; France, concerned about growing Prussian power, threatened war if the prince took the throne; Prussians declined the throne (July 11).

1870 France demanded apology and assurances from Prussian king William I against further consideration of taking the Spanish throne; William I refused (July 13).

1870 Ems Dispatch released (July 13) by Prussian minister O. von Bismarck, contributing to tensions that ended in outbreak of war; Bismarck revised the dispatch, sent to him by King William, to help provoke war.

1870 France declared war on Prussia (July 19).

1870 France mobilized some 200,000 troops, Prussia more than 450,000; southern German states joined Prussian cause against France, as Bismarck had expected (July); Prussians invaded Alsace (Aug. 4).

1870 The Prussians defeated the French in major battles at Weissenburg (Aug. 4), at Worth (Aug. 6), and at Spichern (Aug. 6).

1870 French armies led by Marshal A. Bazaine bottled up at Metz by two German armies; attempts to break out were defeated at Vionville (Aug. 16) and Gravelotte (Aug. 18).

1870 Marching to relieve Metz, the French under Marshal M. de MacMahon and Emperor Napoleon III were surprised by the Germans and driven northward toward Sedan (late Aug.).

1870 Battle of Sedan (Sept. 1), northern France, ended in surrender of French army and downfall of the Emperor Napoleon III.

1870 Paris rebelled upon the news of defeat at Sedan; France declared a Republic; Paris surrounded and besieged by the Germans (Sept. 19).

1870 Marshal Bazaine surrendered his garrison of nearly 180,000 men at Metz (Oct. 27); Paris continued to resist despite worsening famine.

1871 German states formally unified (Jan. 18) into the German Empire; William I of Prussia became king of Germany; these events marked culmination of Bismarck's long effort to achieve unification.

1871 Paris surrendered to Germans (Jan. 28)

1871 French named A. Thiers as head of state (Feb.); preliminary peace treaty approved (Mar. 1).

1871 Commune of Paris, bloody revolt by Paris radicals (Mar.–May) against new government; loyal French troops retook city and inflicted severe reprisals.

1871 Final peace treaty signed at Frankfurt (May 10); France ceded Alsace and part of Lorraine to the German Empire and agreed to pay five billion francs in reparations.

Frankfurt ⟨Frankfurt am Main⟩ Historic German city (pop. 632,600) in West Germany. A Roman town as early as the 1st cent. AD, by the 12th cent. it was the traditional place for the coronation of German kings. A commercial center whose fairs were known throughout Europe by the 13th cent., it is today a prominent industrial, commercial, and financial center.

Frankfurt, Council of Ecclesiastical meeting. Called (794) by Charlemagne, with the approval of Pope Adrian I, to consider the acts by the Second Council of Nicaea, it condemned Adoptionism as well as the worship of graven images.

Frankfurt, Treaty of French-German treaty (May 10, 1871) ending the Franco-Prussian War. France was forced to yield disputed territories in Alsace and Lorraine, to pay a five-billion-franc indemnity, and to suffer German occupation until these terms were met.

Frankfurt am Main *See* **Frankfurt**

Frankfurter, Felix 1882–1965. Austrian-born American Supreme Court justice. Appointed (1939) by F. Roosevelt, he followed a policy of judicial restraint, particularly in criminal and civil-liberties cases.

Frankfurt Parliament *See* **Revolutions of 1848**

Franklin A short-lived, self-governing US state (1784–88) in what is now eastern Tennessee. The lands were ceded by North Carolina to the US government in 1784, but settlers in the territory were determined to enter the Union as a state. They established a government (1785), with J. Sevier as president, and until 1788 continued to press for recognition as a state. The territory was again ceded to the US (1790), and became the state of Tennessee (along with additional lands to the west) in 1796.

Franklin, Benjamin 1706–90. American publisher, author, scientist, statesman, and diplomat, whose wit and wisdom made him one of the most widely known figures of Colonial America. Largely self-educated (he left school at 10), he owned his own newspaper in Philadelphia by 1730 and there published the internationally famous *Poor Richard's Almanack* (1732–57). He subsequently invented the Franklin stove (c1744), conducted his famous experiment with lightning by means of a kite (1752), and invented bifocal eyeglasses (1784). During this period he became widely known in scientific circles for his researches and also served as deputy postmaster general for the American colonies (1753–74). He was a delegate (1754) to the Albany Congress *(q.v.)*, and, after 1757, spent a great deal of time in England serving as an agent on various matters. He returned to America (1775) just prior to the outbreak of the American Revolution, was a delegate to the Second Continental Congress, and helped draft the Declaration of Independence, which he also signed. Sent to France (1776) to win recognition for the republic, he gained a wide following there. He was in England again (1781) to help with peace negotiations to end the Revolutionary War. Once again in America, he helped arrange the compromise at the Constitutional Convention (1787) which resulted in the writing of the Constitution.

Franklin, Sir John 1786–1847. English explorer of the North American Arctic. His expedition (1845) in search of the Northwest Passage ended in disaster when his ships became icebound midway between the Atlantic and Pacific oceans.

Franks Germanic tribe that formed a powerful empire in Gaul after the fall of the Roman Empire. Believed to have originated along the Rhine River, the Franks by the 3d cent. AD had gained in strength and numbers and began a series of invasions into Gaul. Clovis I united the several Frankish tribes (5th cent. AD), adopted Christianity, and conquered much of Gaul from the Romans. He established the Frankish Empire, which flourished under the Merovingian dynasty and later the Carolingian. The Franks reached their height under the rule of Charlemagne (9th cent.), whose empire was divided and eventually became France and Germany. France derives its name from the Franks.

Fraser, James Earle 1876–1953. American sculptor. His best-known works are *The End of the Trail* and the Indian and buffalo on the US nickel.

Frazer, Sir James George 1854–1941. Scottish classicist and anthropologist. He is known best for his work *The Golden Bough.*

Fredegund *d.* 597. Frankish queen. The mistress of King Chilperic I of Neustria, she convinced the king to kill his wife, Galswintha (567), and make her queen. Galswintha, however, was sister of Brunhilda, queen of Austrasia, and the murder of

Galswintha caused a long war between Neustria and Austrasia, in which Austrasia was finally victorious.

Frederick I ⟨Frederick Barbarossa⟩ c1123–90. Holy Roman Emperor (1155–90), prominent member of the Hohenstaufen family and successor to Conrad III. His reign was marked by attempts to pacify warring German nobles and by several unsuccessful attempts to gain control over Lombardy. He was killed during the Third Crusade.

Frederick I 1372–1440. Elector of Brandenburg (1417–40) and first of the Hohenzollern line. Made elector (1417) by Holy Roman Emperor Sigismund, he secured the future of the Hohenzollern family.

Frederick I 1657–1713. First Prussian king (1701–13), son of Frederick William and his successor as elector of Brandenburg (1688–1713). By promising Prussian military aid in the oncoming War of the Spanish Succession, he won permission from Leopold I to create the kingdom of Prussia (1701).

Frederick II 1194–1250. Holy Roman Emperor (1220–50), king of Germany (1212–20), Sicily (1197–1250), and Jerusalem (1229–50). A Hohenstaufen, he was a grandson of Frederick Barbarossa, whose antipapal policies he continued. He was excommunicated several times, once for seizing the Papal States. His attempts to unify Italy and Germany, largely unsuccessful, were opposed vigorously by the Lombard League. While conducting the Fifth Crusade, he crowned himself (1229) king of Jerusalem. He later frequently referred to himself as "lord of the world." Because of his unceasing struggles with the papacy, the strength of both the Hohenstaufen family and the German nation were weakened. Powerful Italian city-states emerged soon after his death.

Frederick II ⟨Frederick the Great⟩ 1712–86. Prussian king (1740–86), successor to his father, Frederick William I. Under Frederick's leadership, Prussia evolved from a small Germanic state into an international power. A brilliant military tactician, Frederick seized portions of Silesia in the War of the Austrian Succession. Almost defeated in the Seven Years' War (1756–63), Frederick emerged victorious when his admirer Peter III assumed the Russian throne and took Russia out of the war. Frederick promulgated civil, legal, and penal reforms and internal improvements such as roads and canals. A patron of the arts, he enjoyed a long correspondence with Voltaire. Frederick increased Prussian domains through the First Partition of Poland (1772) and engaged in the War of the Bavarian Succession (1778–79) to prevent Prussia's rival, Austria, from gaining power within the Holy Roman Empire.

Frederick III 1415–93. Holy Roman Emperor (1452–93) and king of Germany (1440–93). Frederick set the stage for future Hapsburg domination by marrying (1477) his son Maximilian I to Mary of Burgundy, whereby Burgundy came under Hapsburg rule. He swore German allegiance to Rome, a move that infuriated German nobility.

Frederick III ⟨Frederick the Wise⟩ 1463–1525. Elector of Saxony (1486–1525). He founded the University of Wittenberg (1502), where M. Luther and Melanchthon became professors. He later became Luther's protector (1521) after the Diet of Worms.

Frederick III ⟨Frederick the Pious⟩ 1515–76. Elector palatine (1559–76). A convert to Lutheranism (1546) and then Calvinism (1561), he became a leading figure in the latter movement. He published the Heidelberg Catechism (1563).

Frederick III 1609–70. King of Norway and Denmark (1648–70). Frederick was forced to cede much of his territory to Swedish king Charles X following a war (1657–60). A coalition of burghers and clergy then united to curb aristocratic power, strengthen the monarchy, and help Denmark regain its vitality.

Frederick III 1831–88. Emperor of Germany and king of Prussia (1888). A liberal, Frederick ruled for only 99 days before succumbing to throat cancer.

Frederick IV 1574–1610. Elector palatine (1592–1610). An ardent Lutheran, he helped found (1608) the Protestant Union of Evangelical States and was chosen its first leader.

Frederick IV 1671–1730. King of Norway and Denmark (1699–1730). Frederick was unsuccessful in his attempts to regain southern Sweden. He established an educational system and abolished serfdom.

Frederick V 1723–66. King of Denmark and Norway (1746–66). He took little interest in state, leaving it to his foreign minister. During his reign, trade with Asia and the Americas greatly increased and his kingdom's financial affairs flourished.

Frederick VI 1769–1839. King of Denmark (1808–39) and Norway (1808–14). Frederick's alliance with Napoleon against Britain, resulting largely from the British bombardments (1801, 1807) of Copenhagen, led to the loss of Norway to Sweden through the Treaty of Kiel (1814).

Frederick VII 1808–63. Danish king (1848–63), successor to his father, Christian VIII. His reign was marked by the adoption of a constitution and creation of a constitutional monarchy. He also incorporated into Denmark much of Schleswig-Holstein (1863), thereby precipitating war with Prussia.

Frederick VIII 1843–1912. Danish king (1906–12), successor to his father, Christian IX. He served in the war against Prussia (1864) and had an uneventful reign.

Frederick IX 1899–1972. Danish king (1947–72). Frederick and his father, Christian X, imprisoned (1943–45) by the Nazis in WW II, became symbols of Danish resistance to German occupation.

Frederick Augustus I ⟨Frederick Augustus the Just⟩ 1750–1827. First king of Saxony (1806–27) and elector of Saxony (1763–1806). Defeated by Napoleon (1806), he concluded a separate peace and, as a result, became king. After Napoleon's final defeat, however, the Congress of Vienna (1815) ceded the major part of his kingdom to Prussia.

Frederick Augustus the Just   *See* **Frederick Augustus I**

Frederick Barbarossa   *See* **Frederick I**

Frederick Henry 1584–1647. Prince of Orange and stadholder of the United Provinces (1625–47). He regained many Dutch cities from Spain and finally negotiated an advantageous treaty with that country (1647).

Fredericksburg, Battle of   Battle (Dec. 13, 1862) of the American Civil War at Fredericksburg, Virginia. Some 78,000 Confederate troops under Gen. R. E. Lee decisively defeated an assault by 120,000 Union troops under command of Gen. A. Burnside, halting Burnside's advance on Richmond. Confederate casualties were 5,000, Union casualties 12,000. Burnside was relieved of command. The battle was as much a boost to Confederate hopes as it was a defeat for Union arms and morale.

Frederick the Fair   *c*1286–1330. German king (1314–22) and Austrian duke (1306–30). A disputed election (1314) for the German crown led to war between Frederick and Louis IV of Bavaria. The conflict ended in Frederick's defeat (1322) and retirement to Austria.

Frederick the Great   *See* **Frederick II**
Frederick the Great Elector   *See* **Frederick William**
Frederick the Pious   *See* **Frederick III**
Frederick the Winter King 1596–1632. King of Bohemia (1619–20) and elector palatine (1610–20). The Protestants of Bohemia, refusing to accept the Catholic Ferdinand II as their king, chose Frederick instead. He was quickly defeated and exiled. He was son-in-law to English king James I and grandfather of George I.

Frederick the Wise   *See* **Frederick III**
Frederick William   ⟨Frederick the Great Elec-

tor⟩ 1620–88. Elector of Brandenburg (1640–88). Frederick negotiated an armistice to the Thirty Years' War and built a strong army in the interim, ensuring him fair treatment in the Peace of Westphalia. He unified Prussia and secured its sovereignty through a treaty (1657) with Poland.

Frederick William 1771–1815. Duke of Brunswick (1813–15). After Napoleon seized his duchy (1806), he formed the Black Brunswickers in a brave but unsuccessful attempt (1809) to drive out the French. He finally succeeded (1813) but was killed soon after.

Frederick William I 1688–1740. Prussian king (1713–40), successor to his father, Frederick I. Considered a strong ruler, he instituted many reforms and built the Prussian army into a powerful fighting force.

Frederick William II 1744–97. Prussian king (1786–97), successor to his uncle Frederick II. Though he was not considered an exceptional leader during his reign, Prussia continued its territorial expansion, notably at the expense of Poland through the partitions of Poland.

Frederick William III 1770–1840. King of Prussia (1797–1840). A weak king, he was dominated by Napoleon, but he allied himself with Russia and declared war (1813) on France. After the Congress of Vienna he alienated his people by joining the reactionary Holy Alliance.

Frederick William IV 1795–1861. Prussian king (1840–61), successor to his father, Frederick William III. His reign was marked by a brief rebellion (1848) and by his involvement in unsuccessful plans to unify Germany. (*See* Revolutions of 1848.)

freedmen   Term applied to former slaves who were released from bondage. In ancient Rome, freedmen were accorded varying degrees of civil rights.

Freedmen's Bureau   US government bureau (1865–72) formed during Reconstruction to help former black slaves and oversee abandoned lands after the Civil War. Headed by Gen. O. Howard, the bureau provided food, medical attention, some semblance of protection, and, later, educational institutions for newly freed slaves in the war-torn South. It failed, however, in its aim to resettle blacks on the abandoned lands. Unpopular among white southerners, it was finally disbanded in 1872.

free enterprise   Economic doctrine based on the action of private individuals and companies operating in the marketplace free of government control. It is strongly identified with capitalism.

Free French   Name given the military wing of the French Committee of National Defense. It was formed (June 23, 1940) in London by C. de Gaulle to continue French opposition to German occupation after the fall of France (1940) during WW II.

Freeman's Farm, Battle of 1. ⟨Saratoga, First Battle of⟩ First engagement (Sept. 19, 1777) of the Saratoga campaign during the American Revolution. Continental forces under Gen. H. Gates repulsed British forces under Gen. J. Burgoyne, thereby delaying the British advance on Albany. **2.** ⟨Saratoga, Second Battle of⟩ ⟨Bemis Heights, Battle of⟩ Battle fought (Oct. 7, 1777) by a British reconnaissance party under Burgoyne and colonials under Gen. B. Arnold at Bemis Heights, near Freeman's Farm. The Americans were victorious.

Freemasons Secret fraternal order, one of the largest in the world. Though the order claims ancient origins, it seems to have developed from fraternities of English and Scottish stonemasons in the Middle Ages. The modern history of the organization dates from the formation of the Grand Lodge in England (1717). The movement spread rapidly throughout Europe and reached America in 1730 or 1733. Today there are independent national Masonic organizations in many countries throughout the world. In addition to their vow of secrecy, Masons generally adhere to a liberal philosophy of equality and religious toleration. They are generally opposed by the Catholic church. In America a reaction against them gave rise to the Anti-Masonic party. Many prominent people have been Freemasons, including 13 US presidents.

free silver American currency-reform movement. Adherents of free silver advocated unlimited coinage of silver as a way to increase the supply of money. Free silver was espoused by populists, progressives, and farmers, and was opposed by eastern financiers, who favored the single gold standard. This controversy led to adoption of the Bland-Allison Act (1878) and the Sherman Silver Purchase Act (1890). The free silver movement figured in American politics in the last half of the 19th and early 20th cents. W. Bryan based his unsuccessful presidential campaigns of 1896 and 1900 on the advocacy of free silver.

Free-Soil party Short-lived US political party (1848–54) organized to oppose extension of slavery into new US territories. Following the defeat of the Wilmot Proviso in Congress, antislavery Whigs, Barnburners, and members of the Liberal party met in Buffalo (1848) and formally organized the party. Their presidential candidate, M. Van Buren, failed to win (1848) but proved to be a decisive factor in the election of President Z. Taylor. Following the Compromise of 1850, the party began to dissolve, and in 1854 it became part of the newly formed Republican party.

Free Territory of Trieste Territory created (1947) after WW II. It divided the Adriatic city of Trieste and environs into zones administered by Britain and Yugoslavia. It was abolished (1954) and its holdings divided between Italy and Yugoslavia.

freethinker Term applied to one whose religious and philosophical opinions are freely arrived at by use of reason, rather than through ecclesiastical authority. The term came into use in the 18th cent. with the rise of deism.

free trade Term applied to commerce conducted without governmental interference in the form of import and export regulations. A. Smith's *Wealth of Nations* was a strong argument for free trade, which developed as a movement in the 17th and 18th cents.

free will Philosophical concept that holds that man can choose, through his own will, a given action. The concept has long been a subject of both philosophical and religious debate. It opposes the concept of determinism.

Frei Montalva, Eduardo 1911–. Chilean president (1964–70). He was a founder of the Christian Democratic party (1957) and as president introduced many democratic and economic reforms.

Freising, Otto of *See* **Otto of Freising**

Frémont, John Charles ⟨The Pathfinder⟩ 1813–90. American explorer, soldier, and an unsuccessful presidential candidate of the new Republican party (1856). He led expeditions in the Rockies (1842) and in Oregon and California (1843–44). In 1845 he took part in the revolt by Californian settlers against Mexico and set up the Bear Flag State. He subsequently became a leader in the conquest of California during the war with Mexico. He made a fortune when gold was discovered on his California property in the 1840s but eventually lost it all in unsuccessful railroad ventures. He served as commander in the West during the Civil War but was removed because of his actions regarding slavery. He was governor of the Arizona Territory (1878–83).

French, Daniel Chester 1850–1931. American sculptor known best for his statue of A. Lincoln in the Lincoln Memorial, Washington, D.C.

French Academy ⟨Académie Française⟩ French cultural society. Dating from the early 1630s and a small informal group of scholars who met weekly to discuss intellectual matters, it was formally established (1835) by Cardinal Richelieu to regulate French language and literature.

French Action ⟨Action Française⟩ French Royalist party. Organized (1898) by extreme conservatives, it supported H. Petain's government during WW

II. Postwar charges of collaboration with the Germans resulted in its decline.

French and Indian War War (1754–63) in North America that became part of the larger European conflict known as the Seven Years' War. The French and Indian War was the last in a series of wars between the British and French for control of territory in what are today Canada and the United States (For more on the earlier wars, *see* King William's War, Queen Anne's War, King George's War.) The war was sparked by rivalry over the upper Ohio Valley region. The French in the late 1740s sought to link their Canadian and Louisiana possessions by taking control of the Ohio Valley region. This, however, blocked any future westward expansion of the British colonies along the American coast and thus roused the colonists to action. Ultimately, France lost all its Canadian colonies to the British. The war also gave American colonists a sense of being able to defend themselves and contributed to their growing feelings of independence from the British crown. Key dates in the war include:

1748 Ohio Company formed by Virginians to explore Ohio Valley territory to west of American colonies.

1748–49 French built a string of forts in Canada and the Ohio Valley to secure their control of the region.

1753 French commander Marquis Duquesne led force of French troops to occupy the Ohio Valley; G. Washington sent by Virginians to tell them to leave region.

1754 French built Fort Duquesne (at modern Pittsburgh).

1754 G. Washington on military expedition from Virginia against French; built Fort Necessity but was forced to surrender it soon after.

1754 Albany Convention held (June) to coordinate defense plans to deal with French expansion in the western region.

1755 Campaign against French in the Ohio Valley (and Canada) began under British Gen. Braddock.

1755 Braddock was defeated and later died after attack on Fort Duquesne (July 9).

1756 Seven Years' War began in Europe.

1756 French under Gen. L. de Montcalm took British forts Oswego and George.

1757 British Fort William Henry taken by French.

1758 Gen. de Montcalm repulsed British attacks (July) on Fort Ticonderoga.

1758 British captured Louisburg (July 26) in eastern Canada.

1758 Fort Duquesne captured from the French (Nov. 25); renamed Fort Pitt.

1759 Fort Ticonderoga fell to British forces.

1759 Battle of the Plains of Abraham in Canada (Sept. 13); decisive engagement of the war; de Montcalm killed in battle; British captured Quebec (Sept. 18) soon after.

1760 Montreal captured (Sept. 8), ending the war in the Americas.

1763 Treaty of Paris; British possession of French territory in Canada confirmed.

French and Swedish War War (1635–48) conducted by France and Sweden against the forces of the house of Hapsburg and the Holy Roman Empire. The last phase of the Thirty Years' War (1618–48), it was ended by the Peace of Westphalia (1648).

French Cameroon *See* **Cameroon**

French Community Organization of French states overseas department, and former territories created by the constitution of the Fifth Republic (1958). Among its members are France, Corsica, French Polynesia, French Guiana, and others. It promotes economic, technical, and cultural exchanges.

French Congo Former French possession, now known as French Equatorial Africa *(q.v.)*.

French East India Company French colonial trading organization established (1664) by J. Colbert to protect French trade interests. It was successful for a time in India under J. Dupleix, less so in America, and was abolished in 1769.

French Equatorial Africa Former federation of French colonies in west central Africa, with its capital at Brazzaville. The first French settlements were established on the Gabon River (1839). French claims were extended by exploration, military ventures, and agreements with other colonial powers until 1887, when the approximate borders of what was then known as the French Congo were established. The federation of French Equatorial Africa was formed (1910), and during WW II it supported the Free French forces. The territories in the federation voted for independence (1958), and in 1960 they became the Central African Republic, and the republics of Chad, Gabon, and the Congo.

French Guiana Overseas department (pop. 63,000) of France, located on the northeast coast of South America. The first permanent settlement was established (1604) at Cayenne, by the French. The colony was captured (1676) briefly by the Dutch during the Dutch Wars, and by 1713 boundary disputes with the neighboring Portuguese were settled. In the 18th cent., Jesuits were expelled, some 14,000 Europeans died in an unsuccessful attempt to establish a new colony, and the colony saw an influx of deportees from France (many of whom died) during the French Revolution. France briefly lost the colony (1809–17) to British and Portuguese forces, and, after abolition of slavery (1848), the colony entered a period of economic decline. It was in 1852 that the first of the penal colonies was established, the most notorious of them, Devil's Island, continuing in use until 1951. The colony was made an overseas department in 1946.

French Guinea *See* **Guinea**

French Indochina *See* **Indochina, Federation of**

French Indochina War *See* **Indochina War**

French Morocco Former French protectorate in northwestern Africa. Occupied by the French in the early 1900s, the region became a French protectorate (1912). It was incorporated (1956) with Spanish Morocco and Tangier into the kingdom of Morocco.

French Polynesia French Pacific territory consisting of over one hundred Pacific Ocean islands, the largest of which is Tahiti. Acquired during the 19th cent., the islands were placed under central administration in 1903.

French Revolution Prolonged political and social struggle (1789–99) in France that surrounded the overthrow of the monarchy and establishment of the First Republic. The revolution was caused by a number of factors, chief among them resentment against the *ancien régime,* the old social order dominated by the king and his nobles, and a prolonged crisis over government finances. The ideas of the Enlightenment *(q.v.)* and the recent success of the American Revolution also helped provide a climate for the revolution. The revolution began as an attempt to create a constitutional monarchy and in this early phase the moderate bourgeoisie dominated the revolution. But by late 1792 the demands for long-overdue reforms and the sheer inertia of revolution resulted in proclamation of the republic. The republic was consumed by the violence of the revolution. Attacks by other European nations (*see* French Revolutionary Wars) only multiplied effects of the bitter factional struggles, riots, and counterrevolutionary uprisings. The chaos helped bring the extreme radicals to power and touched off the bloody Reign of Terror. The French succeeded in mustering powerful armies and were victorious against their foreign enemies. However, a succession of attempts to form a stable republican government failed and ended in creation of the Consulate, a dictatorship led by their great military leader, Napoleon. (*See also* France, Napoleon.) Key events in the revolution include:

1789 States General convened (May 5); representatives of the three estates (clergy, nobility, and commoners) met at Versailles; its intended purpose (to enact fiscal reforms) dwarfed by strong sentiment for sweeping political and social reform.

1789 Jacobins, a political club (faction) formed by delegates to the States General.

1789 Third estate (commoners) insisted it alone represented France; voted to constitute itself as the National Assembly (June 17) after a deadlock developed in the States General over voting procedures.

1789 Tennis Court Oath taken (June 20) by members of the National Assembly after they had been locked out of their meeting hall; meeting in a tennis court, they vowed not to disband until France had a constitution; individual members of other estates joined third estate.

1789 Louis XVI yielded to the National Assembly and ordered that all members of the remaining two estates should join it (June 27).

1789 King Louis concentrated troops around Paris and Versailles; Louis dismissed (July 11) his popular minister, J. Necker, and this along with fears that Louis might disband the National Assembly led to unrest in Paris.

1789 Rioting began in Paris (July 12).

1789 Paris Commune formed (July 13) as revolutionary sentiment spread in French cities; new militia formed in Paris (National Guard) and elsewhere; Lafayette commanded the Paris National Guard.

1789 Storming of the Bastille (July 14), an arsenal and prison; the Great Fear (of reprisals by royalist armies) spread through countryside as peasants refused to pay taxes and attacked estates of noblemen (July–Aug.).

1789 Feudal structure in France abolished by National Assembly (Aug. 4); legal and fiscal equality proclaimed.

1789 Declaration of the Rights of Man adopted by the National Assembly (Aug. 26).

1789 National Assembly wrote a new constitution providing for a constitutional monarchy; (Sept. 10); king's powers sharply limited, unicameral legislature provided for.

1789 Paris mob, consisting mostly of women, stormed the royal palace of Versailles (Oct. 5–6); angered by high bread prices and the king's resistance to Assembly legislation, they forced the king's removal to Paris; National Assembly removed to Paris.

1789 National Assembly confiscated church lands to overcome financial crisis. (Nov. 2); issued *assignats,* notes backed by these public lands.

1789 Public opinion swayed in favor of revolutionary action by rise of clubs such as the Jacobins and publication of inflammatory political newspapers such as J.P. Marat's *L'Ami du Peuple.*

1790 Cordeliers, political club formed to prevent abuses of power; J.P. Marat and G. Danton became leaders.

1790 Civil Constitution of the Clergy (July 12); Roman Catholic church reorganized, and clerics to be paid by the state.

1790 King Louis approved the new national constitution creating a constitutional monarchy (July 14).

1790 Assembly imposed (Nov. 27) requirement of oath by clerics as resistance to Civil Constitution of the Clergy mounted; church split over oath and many clerics who refused suffered persecutions.

1791 Reacting to rising revolutionary tide, Louis XVI attempted to flee abroad with the royal family (June 20–21); apprehended at Varennes (June 25) and brought back to Paris a virtual prisoner.

1791 Feuillants, political club formed by moderate Jacobins (June) who opposed abolition of the monarchy.

1791 Paris republicans demanded the king be deposed; massed on the Champ de Mars (July 17), they were fired on by the National Guard (on Lafayette's order) and were dispersed.

1791 Declaration of Pillnitz (Aug. 27); Prussia and Holy Roman Empire agreed to war against France to restore the monarchy, if other powers joined them; declaration angered French and paved the way for war.

1791 Constitution put in force by the Assembly (Sept. 3); King Louis swore to uphold it (Sept. 14).

1791–92 Legislative Assembly in power; convened (Oct. 1), it was initially dominated by moderate Girondists; radical Jacobins among the groups opposed to the Girondists.

1792 Legislative Assembly under Girondist influence declared war on the Austrians (Apr. 20), inaugurating the French Revolutionary Wars. French armies quickly put on defensive by Austrians.

1792 Fall of Girondist ministry (June 13); rapid spread of unrest.

1792 Austro-Prussian armies crossed into France (July 11); radicalism increased in Paris.

1792 Brunswick Manifesto (July 27); Austro-Prussian commander threatened to destroy Paris if the king was harmed; Parisians angered by manifesto.

1792 Storming of Tuileries (Aug. 10); mob instigated by radicals killed the king's Swiss Guard; Legislative Assembly "suspended" the king and formed provisional government headed by G. Danton; new assembly, the National Convention, to be formed.

1792 Lafayette, then in command of units in the revolutionary army, defected (Aug. 19) to the Austrians to escape trial by radicals.

1792 September Massacres (Sept. 2–6) in Paris; prisoners in Paris jails slaughtered as hysteria mounted over approach of Austro-Prussian armies; soon after, French armies turned tide against the enemy.

1792–95 National Convention in power; convened (Sept. 21); dominated first by Girondists, then by Jacobins.

1792 First Republic proclaimed (Sept. 22) by National Convention; monarchy abolished (Sept. 21).

1793 Louis XVI guillotined (Jan. 21) after being tried for treason by the National Convention.

1793 Britain entered war against France (Feb.) and French armies soon after again suffered reverses.

1793 Counterrevolutionary rebellion in the Vendée (western France) began (Mar.)

1793 Émigrés, French royalists who had fled revolutionary France, declared "civilly dead" by Convention; (Mar. 28) émigré property confiscated.

1793 Committee of Public Safety established by National Convention (Apr. 6); at first had limited executive functions.

1793 J. Hébert arrested (May 24) for leading disorders; arrest instigated by Girondists.

1793 Insurrection of radical *Enragés;* Convention forced to arrest 31 Girondist deputies; this gave the "Mountain" (Jacobins and other left radicals) control of the Convention (June 2), and marked fall of Girondists (moderates) from power.

1793 Girondist deputies sparked revolts in the provinces after being forced to flee Paris (June); revolutionary government restored order by year's end.

1793 New Republican constitution proclaimed (June 22); it did not really take effect because extraordinary power remained in hands of the Committee of Public Safety.

1793 Committee of Public Safety gained dictatorial powers, taking on powers from the Convention and the Paris Commune (July); the Committee thus effectively became ruling body of revolutionary France. Robespierre became Committee member July 27.

1793 C. Corday killed J.P. Marat (July 13) for his persecution of the Girondists.

1793 Universal conscription of males ordered (Aug. 23) as internal revolts and advances of the armies of the First Coalition threatened the revolutionary government; an army of nearly a million men created.

1793–1794 Reign of Terror instituted (Sept.) after sansculottes (radical workers and shopkeepers) invaded the Convention and demanded it do more to prevent counterrevolutionary activities; thousands of royalists, counterrevolutionaries and others were ultimately killed.

1793 Convention formally suspended constitution (of 1793); Committee of Public Safety to head revolutionary government until end of wars with foreign powers; Robespierre, a member of the committee since July 28, gradually took control of it by eliminating his opponents.

1793 Execution of Queen Marie Antoinette (Oct. 16).

1793 Principal Girondists guillotined (Oct. 31); executions averaged 60 per month thereafter.

1793 Anti-Christian Hébertists transformed the Cathedral of Notre Dame into a "Temple of Reason" (Nov. 7).

1793 Worship of God abolished (Nov. 10); Hébertists led anti-Christian movement and proclaimed "Cult of Reason."

1793–1805 French Revolutionary Calendar put in effect (Nov. 24); remained in use to 1805.

1793 Revolutionary dictatorship of France set up by Committee of Public Safety (Dec. 4); committee took power to appoint and dismiss even local officials.

1793 New victories by French armies drove enemy back out of France (Dec.)

1794 J. Hébert, radical leader of the anti-Christian movement, guillotined (Mar. 24) on orders from Robespierre; Hébert was a major opponent of Robespierre, who wanted a more moderate policy on religion.

1794 J. Danton, another leader of opposition to Robespierre, guillotined (Apr. 5) along with his followers; Robespierre leading power of government.

1794 Cult of the Supreme Being proclaimed by Robespierre (June), after Convention instituted a civic religion recognizing a Supreme Being (May 7).

1794 Law of 22 Prairial passed (June 10); allowed only acquittal or death in trials and eliminated most rights of accused; executions increased markedly and aroused sentiment against Robespierre.

1794 *Coup d'état* of 9 Thermidor (July 27); Convention impeached Robespierre; he was beheaded (July 28) along with his followers; moderates took power and the Thermidorian Reaction began. Terror ended and persecution of the Jacobins began; more radical revolutionary measures rescinded.

1794 Paris Commune abolished (July 27).

1794 Jacobin club closed in Paris (Nov. 12).

1795 Riots over food prices and attack on National Convention (Apr. 1) suppressed by National Guard; reprisals against radical leaders.

1795 New attack on National Convention and riots among workers in Paris (May 20) put down by National Guard; reprisals against suspected Jacobins spread (White Terror).

1795 Churches reopened (May 30).

1795 Revolutionary Tribunal, the court of the Terror, abolished (May 31); justice courts empowered to try treason.

1795 Constitution of 1795 (Aug. 22); executive power rested with five-man Directory; Council of 500 and Council of Elders established.

1795 Insurrection against the Directory suppressed (Oct. 5) by troops commanded by Gen. Napoleon Bonaparte; Napoleon named commander of the Army of the Interior.

1795–99 Directory in power; convened Nov. 2, it presided over the last years of the revolution and pursued a generally moderate course.

1796 Counterrevolutionary uprising of the Vendée and elsewhere again suppressed (Feb.)

1796 Napoleon given command of French armies in Italy; his success in the Italian campaign (from Apr.) made him a national hero.

1797 F. Babeuf executed (May 17); had led (1796) conspiracy of former Jacobins and advocates of what became Socialist doctrines.

1797 Coup of 18 Fructidor (Sept. 4) by the republicans; Directory took on dictatorial powers.

1797 Treaty of Campo Formio (Oct. 17); War of the First Coalition ended, though Britain continued hostilities.

1798 Napoleon given approval to begin what became his disastrous campaign against Egypt (beginning in May).

1798 Coup of 22 Floréal (May 11); election of new council members nullified to block seating of Jacobins; opposition to the Directory, which arranged the nullification, spread.

1799 Coup of 30 Prairial (June 18); Councils, bolstered by newly elected Jacobin members, forced the ouster of three directors; censorship of press ended and radicalism again flourished.

1799 Napoleon returned to Paris (Oct. 16) after leaving his army behind in Egypt.

1799 Coup of 18 Brumaire (Nov. 9); Napoleon, with the aid of directors E. Sieyes and Pierre Roger Ducos, and his brother Lucien, engineered the overthrow of the Directory; established Consulate under his control.

French Revolutionary Calendar Calendar established during the French Revolution, used in France from Nov. 24, 1793, to Dec. 31, 1805. It reorganized the calendar into 12 months of 30 days each. The months were divided into three 10-day "decades" instead of weeks and the five days (or six in a leap year) at the end of the year were holidays. The names of the months were:

Vendémiaire	Germinal
Brumaire	Floréal
Frimaire	Prairial
Nivôse	Messidor
Pluviôse	Thermidor
Ventôse	Fructidor

French Revolutionary Wars Series of wars (1792–1802) between France and various European powers, notably Austria and Britain. (The wars against France between 1803 and 1815 are called the Napoleonic Wars.) The French Revolutionary Wars were sparked by the European monarchs' disapproval of the new revolutionary government, by attempts to restore the monarchy in France, and by the desire of some revolutionary factions to demonstrate the strength of their new government. To defend France, the revolutionary government created what became a powerful army and the wars quickly became a vehicle for the expansion and aggrandizement of France. Britain, which became France's most stubborn enemy, retained supremacy of the seas. The wars brought Napoleon (a hero of the conflict) to power in France, gained France considerable territory and influence in Europe, and brought on the final collapse of the Holy Roman Empire (1806). (*See also* French Revolution, Napoleon, Napoleonic Wars, France.) Key dates in the wars include:

1791 Declaration of Pillnitz (Aug); Holy Roman Empire and Prussia said they would restore French king Louis XVI, if the other powers would join them.

1792 Girondists, who favored war, gained control of the government (Mar.).

1792–97 War of the First Coalition; Austria, Prussia, Britain, Spain, The Netherlands, and others joined in war against France.

1792 France declared war on Austria (Apr. 20).

1792 Brunswick Manifesto issued (July 27) by the commander of the Austro-Prussian forces; promised destruction of Paris if King Louis was harmed; increased radical sentiment against monarchy.

1792 Austrian and Prussian armies advanced against French armies; reverses aroused mobs in Paris and King Louis was "suspended" (Aug. 10).

1792 Battle of Valmy (Sept. 20), French revolutionaries defeated combined Austrian and Prussian force; first important battle of the war.

1792 French republic declared (Sept. 22); French armies advanced into foreign territories.

1792 France defeated Austria at Jemappes and occupied Austrian Netherlands (Belgium, Nov. 6).

1792 France issued (Nov.) a declaration of willingness to assist all peoples fighting for liberty.

1793 Louis XVI executed (Jan. 21); other powers of First Coalition joined the fighting soon after.

1793 French forces defeated in Holland by the Austrians (Mar. 18) and at Mainz by the Prussians (July 23).

1793 Counterrevolution in Vendée began (Mar.), increasing troubles of revolutionary government.

1793 Committee of Public Safety formed (Apr. 6) as crisis deepened; Reign of Terror began some months later.

1793 Armies of the coalition advanced into French territory (July); French revolutionary government declared (Aug.) universal conscription to deal with invasion and internal revolt.

1793 British captured Toulon (Aug. 29).

1793 Inexperienced French forces defeated Austrians at the Battle of Wattignies (Oct. 15–16), forcing them to retreat.

1793 Revolt of the Vendée put down (Oct.); harsh reprisals by revolutionary government followed.

1793 Toulon recaptured from British (Dec. 19); French armies reentered German territory soon after.

1794 Spain invaded by French forces (May).

1794 French forces defeated Austria at the Battle of Fleurus (June 26); Austrian Netherlands recaptured (July) and United Provinces invaded.

1794 Robespierre executed (July); Reign of Terror ended.

1795 Batavian Republic created (May 16) by victorious French, who joined conquered territories of the Austrian Netherlands and the United Provinces.

1795 Peace agreements (*see* Basel, Treaties of) forced on Prussia (Apr. 5) and Spain (July 22).

1795 French forces repulsed invasion (July) by British seeking to aid royalist Chouans.

1795 French mounted three-pronged attack in an effort to knock Austria out of the war; two armies attacked German states while Napoleon led southernmost army against Austrians in northern Italy.

1796 French armies advanced against German states until the new Austrian commander, Archduke Charles,. turned the tide (Aug.–Sept.) and drove them back across the Rhine.

1796 Napoleon advanced through Nice to Piedmont (Apr.); Savoy and Nice ceded to France.

1796 Napoleon victorious against the Austrians at the Battle of Lodi, in Italy (May 10).

1796 Napoleon created the Lombard republic after conquering much of Lombardy (May) from the Austrians.

1796 Treaty of San Ildefonso concluded (Aug. 19); Spain formally allied with France against Great Britain.

1796–97 Siege of Mantua, Italy, conducted by Napoleon I; Austrian surrender gave Napoleon mastery of Italy (Feb.).

1797 British defeated a French and Spanish naval force (Feb. 14) in the Battle of Cape Saint Vincent.

1797 Treaty of Tolentino concluded (Feb. 19) between Napoleon and Pope Pius VI; pope sought to halt French advance on Rome and ceded territories to France.

1797 Fighting with Austria halted by Peace of Leoben (Apr. 18).

1797 French invaded and occupied Venice (May).

1797 Cisalpine Republic created (July) from conquered territories in northern Italy.

1797 Treaty of Camp Formio (Oct.); formally ended war between Austria and France; France gained Austrian territories in The Netherlands and Italy, and the left bank of the Rhine; Austria gained part of Venice; treaty ended war of First Coalition, though Britain continued against France.

1798 French created Roman Republic (Feb.) after taking pope captive.

1798 French invaded Switzerland (Apr.) to enforce creation of the Helvetic Republic.

1798 Napoleon, now a hero to the French, began his attack on the British Empire by way of Egypt (July); government gave him permission for operation in part to get him out of country.

1798 Napoleon advanced in Egypt, captured Alexandria (July 2) and routed the Egyptian Mamelukes at the Battle of the Pyramids (July 21).

1798 Battle of the Nile; British fleet under Adm. H. Nelson destroyed Napoleon's fleet (Aug. 1).

1798 War of the Second Coalition; Russia, Britain, Austria, Ottoman Empire, Portugal and Naples joined to oppose Napoleon (Dec. 24); Russians and Austrians to attack in Italy, Austrians to attack in Germany and Switzerland, British and Russians to attack in The Netherlands.

1799 French proclaimed the Parthenopean Republic (Jan. 23) after capturing Kingdom of Naples.

1799 Napoleon attacked the Ottoman Empire in Syria (Feb.); forced to withdraw to Egypt (Mar. 20).

1799 Battle of Stockach (Mar 25); Austrians defeated French and forced them back across the Rhine.

1799 Austrians and Russians successful in northern Italy; defeated French at Magnano (Apr. 5), Cassano (Apr. 27), Trebbia (June 17–19), and Novi (Aug. 15).

1799 Battle of Zurich (June 4–7); Austrians briefly successful in Switzerland; Zurich lost to French in following Sept.

1799 Parthenopean Republic overthrown (June 20) and monarchy restored.

1799 In Egypt, Napoleon defeated Ottoman Turks at the Battle of Aboukir (July 25); situation remained hopeless for French, since they were cut off from France by the British; Napoleon returned to France (Aug. 24), leaving subordinates to extricate the army.

1799 Russians forced into retreat after being defeated by the French at Zurich (Sept. 26).

1799 Convention of Alkmaar (Oct. 18); British agreed to withdraw from The Netherlands following their unsuccessful campaign there.

1799 Russia, defeated and disgruntled with its allies, withdrew from the coalition. (Oct. 22).

1799 Napoleon seized power in France (Nov. 9); became first consul; after consolidating his position, he returned to the war.

1800 Battle of Marengo (June 14) in Italy; Napoleon defeated the Austrians and reestablished French control in Italy.

1800 British occupation of Malta (Sept.).

1800 In north, Austrians defeated at the Battle of Hohenlinden (Dec. 3); Second Coalition collapsed, though Britain carried on fighting.

1801 Treaty of Lunéville (Feb. 9) ended Austrian participation in war against France.

1801 Peace treaty with Naples (Mar. 18).

1801 Battle of Copenhagen (Apr. 2), British naval victory against the Danish fleet at Copenhagen.

1801 British forced French to surrender Egypt (Aug.).

1801 War of the Oranges; France and Spain conquered and divided Portugal (Sept.).

1802 Treaty of Amiens (Mar. 27) between Britain and France, ending the war of the Second Coalition and the French Revolutionary Wars; Britain agreed to restoration of conquered territories.

French Somaliland   *See* **Djibouti**

French Union French political organization (1946–58) that replaced the colonial system. Established by the constitution of the Fourth Republic, it brought France and its overseas territories and protectorates into a loose federation. Former colonies were granted semiautonomous status and had limited representation in the French government. In 1954, Vietnam, Laos, and Cambodia broke away from the union, and in 1958 the union was reorganized into the French Community.

French West Africa Former federation of French West African territories that included Dahomey, French Guinea, French Sudan, Ivory Coast, Mauritania, Senegal, Niger, and Upper Volta. Established in 1895, the territories became autonomous republics in 1958, and the federation was abolished in 1959.

Fréron, Louis Marie-Stanislas 1754–1802. French revolutionary. A zealous participant in the Reign of Terror, he was a leader in the successful conspiracy against M. Robespierre (1794) and took part in subsequent Thermidorian reaction against the Jacobins.

Freud, Sigmund 1856–1939. Austrian neurologist and founder of psychoanalysis. Freud pioneered the use of free association in the treatment of psychological problems and explored the effect of childhood impressions and repressed feelings on later behavior. His theories had a major influence on other scientists working in the field, including A. Adler and C. Jung. Both Adler and Jung, however, disagreed with Freud's emphasis on the importance of sexuality as a motivating force in behavior, and they developed their own followings. Freud, however, remains a major force in psychoanalysis. Among his many writings are *The Ego and the Id, Totem and Taboo,* and *A General Introduction to Psychoanalysis.*

Frey and Freyja ⟨Freyr and Freya⟩ Norse god of fertility, the sun, and rain, and his female counterpart (Freyja), the goddess of love, marriage, and fertility. Freyja is usually identified as Frey's sister.

Freyja   *See* **Frey and Freyja**

Freyr and Freya   *See* **Frey and Freyja**

Friar Lands Question US-Filipino land controversy. The Catholic church, which had been involved in Spanish rule in the Philippines, owned almost one-tenth of its improved lands. After the American takeover (1898), the US bought 410,000

acres from the church (1903), to be resold to Filipino farmers.

Friars Minor Capuchin   *See* **Capuchins; Franciscans**

Frick, Henry Clay 1849–1919. American industrialist, a key organizer of the Carnegie Steel Co. (1889) and the US Steel Corp. (1901).

Friedland, Battle of French victory (June 14, 1807) over Russia in the Napoleonic Wars. Some 86,000 French troops defeated a Russian force of 46,000 at Friedland (now Pravdinsk, Russian SFSR). The battle led to the Treaty of Tilsit.

Friedman, Milton 1912–. American economist. A prolific writer, he is a noted advocate of laissez-faire capitalism.

Friends, Society of   *See* **Society of Friends**

Fries, John   *See* **Fries's Rebellion**

Fries's Rebellion An abortive revolt (1799) by Pennsylvania German-Americans opposed to a new federal property tax levied for a potential war with France. Led by John Fries (c1750–1818), the rebels briefly took up arms against the assessors and collectors. All were eventually pardoned by Pres. J. Adams.

Frigg ⟨Frigga⟩ Norse goddess, wife of Odin and queen of the heavens. She was mother of Balder and goddess of marriage. Her name comes down to us in the word "Friday."

Frigga   *See* **Frigg**

Friuli Historic region in what is now northeastern Italy and northwestern Yugoslavia. Subjected to Roman rule (2d cent. BC), it became a Lombard duchy (6th cent. AD), then passed to the Franks (8th cent.). Thereafter it changed hands several times and was subsequently divided and fragmented. The final disposition of the region between Italy and Yugoslavia was made in a treaty (1947) following WW II.

Frobisher, Sir Martin 1535?–94. English navigator. He led three exploratory voyages (1576, 1577, 1578) to Canada's northern coast in an unsuccessful attempt to find a northwest passage.

Froebel, Friedrich Wilhelm August 1782–1852. German educator. The founder of the kindergarten system, he opened the first such school (1837) at Bad Blankenburg, Germany.

Frohman, Charles 1860–1915. American theatrical manager. He built a powerful syndicate of theaters and was noted for his ability to develop the talent of his performers.

Froissart, Jean 1333?–1400? French courtier and chronicler. His chronicles of the 14th cent. provide a valuable and lively account of the times.

Fromm, Erich 1900–1980. German-born American psychoanalyst. He is known especially for his books dealing with the isolation of man in modern society. Among his works are *Escape from Freedom* and *The Sane Society.*

Fronde Two major rebellions by French noblemen, brought about for the most part by their opposition to the growing power of the monarchy. **1.** Fronde of the Parlement (Aug., 1648–Apr., 1649). The government's need for more income led the French minister, Cardinal J. Mazarin, and Anne of Austria, regent for young King Louis XIV, to seek approval of a drastic revenue measure. The Parlement of Paris, a special court, rejected the measure, which included forfeiture of magistrates' salaries. Parlement then proposed new limitations on royal authority. This the government answered by arresting some members of Parlement, an act that provoked a popular uprising in Paris (Aug. 26, 1648). The government, then embroiled in the last months of the Thirty Years' War, acknowledged the protest and released the members. With the Thirty Years' War over, however, the government turned against the rebellious nobles. Troops under Louis II de Bourbon, prince de Condé, blockaded Paris (Jan., 1649), but he was unable to break the rebellion. The government therefore accepted (Apr. 1, 1649) the Peace of Rueil, ending the Fronde of the Parlement. **2.** Fronde of the Princes (Jan., 1650-Sept., 1653). The prince de Condé, leader of the government troops in the Fronde of the Parlement, soon fell out with the government and was arrested (Jan. 18, 1650). The nobles united for his release, however, and engaged in fighting with government troops in various provinces. Though the government succeeded in putting an end to armed resistance, an alliance of Condé's supporters in Paris won the ouster (Feb., 1651) of the hated minister, J. Mazarin, and obtained Condé's release. However, the intrigues of Anne of Austria, regent to King Louis XIV, soon provoked him to war against the government (Sept., 1651). Condé was unsuccessful in battle and was rescued from total defeat when his army was allowed to enter the city of Paris (July, 1652). Unable to win over the Parlement in Paris, and with support for the Fronde waning, Condé fled France. King Louis returned to Paris (Oct. 21, 1652), recalled Mazarin (Feb., 1653), and crushed the last of the rebels by Sept., 1653. The Fronde of the Princes was the nobles' last major rebellion against the monarchy.

Frontenac, comte de Palluau et de ⟨Louis de Buade⟩ 1620–98. French governor of New France (1672–82, 1689–98). He defeated the warring Iroquois Confederacy (1696), and during the war between England and France he successfully defended the colony against British attack.

Frontier Wars *See* **Cape Frontier Wars**

Frost, Robert Lee 1875–1963. One of the best-known American poets in the 20th cent., famous for his deeply symbolic poems of rural New England life. He was born in San Francisco and lived with his family in New England from age 10. In his early years he worked at a number of trades before leaving for England (1912). Following the immediate popularity of his first collections of poetry, *A Boy's Will* and *North of Boston*, he returned to New England. He continued to write poetry, completing several additional collections, including *Mountain Interval* and *New Hampshire*, and taught at various universities. He received the Pulitzer Prize for Poetry in 1924, 1931, 1937, and 1943.

Fructidor, coup of 18 *See* **French Revolution (1797)**

Fuad I ⟨Ahmed Fuad Pasha⟩ 1868–1936. Egyptian king (1922–36), the first to reign after Egypt's independence from Britain. He was made sultan (1917) and became king when Egypt was declared nominally independent (1922). Later faced with strong opposition from the Wafd party *(q.v.)*, he twice dissolved the parliament (1928, 1930).

Fuchs, Klaus Emil 1911–. German-born British physicist and spy for the Communists. He worked in the US on the atomic bomb project (1943–46) and thereafter continued his work in nuclear research in Britain. Exposed as a spy (1950), he admitted passing information to the Soviets from 1943.

Fugger Family of German bankers and merchants who dominated and influenced European trade and finance from the 15th to 17th cents. Their interests included the collection of church indulgences; mercury, copper, and silver mines; shipping; and real estate. Their influence and fortunes declined after their constant loans of money to finance various unsuccessful wars for the Hapsburgs.

fugitive slave laws American slave laws. Passed between 1793 and 1850, they made mandatory the return of runaway southern slaves. Frequent northern disobedience of the laws was a contributing factor to the Civil War.

Fu Hsi ⟨The Great Bright One⟩ *fl. c*2800 BC. Legendary Chinese emperor. He is said to have formulated the diagrams upon which the *I Ching* is based and to have instituted the first marriage rites and laws in China.

Fujiwara family Family of Japanese nobles that virtually ruled Japan from the 9th to 12th cents. It rose to power under Nakatomi (later Kamatari) Fujiwara (d. 669), and gained dominance under

Yoshifusa Fujiwara (804–872), but was defeated (12th cent.) by the Minamoto and Taira families.

Fujiwara, Michinaga 966–1027. Japanese regent (998–1027). Michinaga was the most powerful of the Fujiwara family, having married off daughters to four emperors and serving as regent for all of them.

Fujiwara, Nakatomi *See* **Fujiwara family**

Fujiwara, Yoshifusa *See* **Fujiwara family**

Fukuzawa, Yukichi 1834–1901. Japanese author, educator, and journalist. He became one of his century's most influential proponents of Westernization in Japan.

Fulbright, James William 1905–. US senator (1945–75). A Democratic senator from Arkansas, he was the widely known chairman of the Foreign Relations Committee from 1959 to 1974 and a strong opponent of US military intervention.

Fulk V the Young 1092–1143. Count of Anjou (1109–31) and king of Jerusalem (1131–43). He married (1129) the daughter of Baldwin II, upon whose death (1131) he became king of Jerusalem. He halted the advance of Zangi. His grandson became English king Henry II.

Fuller, Melville Weston 1833–1910. American jurist and 8th chief justice of the US Supreme Court (1888–1910). He was a skilled administrator and is considered one of the ablest chief justices in the court's history.

Fuller, Richard Buckminster 1895–83. American architect and engineer. Fuller is noted for his use of geodesic domes in building design.

Fuller, Thomas 1608–61. English clergyman, author, and noted wit. He wrote the *History of the Worthies of England*, a valuable source of biographical information.

Fulton, Robert 1765–1815. American inventor who built the first commercially successful steamboat in America. In 1802 he contracted with R. Livingston to build a steamboat for use on the Hudson River. The *Clermont* was completed and launched in 1807 and subsequently went into regular service on the river. He later designed the *Fulton*, the first steam-powered warship (1814).

Fulvia *d.* 40 BC. Wife of M. Antony (from 44 BC). After Antony became enamored of Cleopatra, she instigated a revolt (41 BC) against Octavian in hopes of drawing him back to her. Spurned by Antony, she died a short time later.

Fundamentalism American Protestant movement originating in the early 20th cent. Fundamentalists adhere to traditional interpretations of the Bible. Among its members was W. Bryan, who defended Fundamentalism in the famous Scopes evolution trial.

Fundamental Orders Legal code governing the colony of Connecticut from 1639 to 1662. It was an early step in the development of American democracy.

Funk, Casimir 1884–1967. Polish-born American biochemist. He is credited with the discovery of vitamins.

Furies *See* **Erinyes**

Fust, Johann ⟨Faust, ~⟩ 1400?–66. German moneylender and partner (1450?–55) of J. Gutenberg. He gained possession of Gutenberg's press on dissolution of their partnership and went into the business of printing books with his son-in-law.

futurism Italian artistic and literary movement. Introduced (1909) by F. Marinetti, futurism expressed the turbulent nature of the 20th cent. Its glorification of war and destruction was a precursor of facism.

futwa *See* **mufti**

Fyodor *See* **Fëdor**

G

Gable, (William) Clark 1901–60. American movie actor who during his long career (1930–60) became a symbol of the rugged yet romantic male in such roles as that of Rhett Butler in *Gone with the Wind.*

Gabon ⟨Gabon Republic⟩ Independent state located in west central Africa, on the Atlantic coast. Its capital is Libreville. Gabon's history prior to the Portuguese exploration (15th cent.) is largely unknown. Gabon's principal industries revolve around exploiting its rich oil, uranium, iron ore, and manganese deposits. Key events in Gabon's history include:

15TH CENT. Portuguese navigator Diego Cam explored region, which became a center of the slave trade (to 19th cent.).

1839 French established their first settlement.

1849 Libreville founded.

1889–1904 Governed by French as part of French Congo.

1910–57 Governed as part of French Equatorial Africa.

1913 Albert Schweitzer established hospital in region soon after control of the interior was established.

1940 Free France captured Gabon from the Vichy government during WW II.

1946 Became French overseas territory.

1958 Given status as autonomous republic within the French Community.

1960 Gabon established as independent republic (Aug. 17); Leon Mba in office as first president (1960–67).

1964 President Mba deposed in military coup; restored by France.

1967 President Omar Bongo in office; succeeded after President Mba died; pursued policies to speed exploitation of natural resources.

1973 President Bongo converted to Islam; reelected without opposition.

1980 President Bongo reelected.

Gabriel 1. In the Bible, one of the seven archangels and the principal messenger announcing God's will. He is represented as revealing to Daniel the meaning of his visions and announcing the births of John the Baptist and Jesus Christ. **2.** In the Islamic faith, he is the angel represented as revealing the sacred writings of the Koran to Muhammad.

Gabriel, Jacques Ange 1690–1782. French architect. One of the greatest French architects of his century, he became royal architect to Louis XV (1742) and designed additions to palaces and public buildings.

Gabrieli, Andrea and **Giovanni** c1510–86, 1557–1612. Italian organists and composers at St. Mark's in Venice. Giovanni became first organist at the church on his uncle's death. Both wrote masses and other choral works in addition to works for the organ.

Gad In the Bible, one of the Twelve Tribes of Israel (q.v.). It was named after Gad, son of Jacob and Zilpah. The tribe settled the region east of the Jordan River and later became one of the Lost Tribes (q.v.).

Gadsden Purchase Treaty between the US and Mexico for the purchase of a strip of territory in northern Mexico (1853). The 30,000-square-mile strip was an important part of a projected southern transcontinental railroad route, but the Mexican War had left the boundary with Mexico unsettled. The purchase of the land for $10 million was negotiated by James Gadsden (1788–1858) and narrowly approved by the Senate (1854).

Gaea ⟨Ge⟩ Goddess of the earth in early Greek mythology. She was daughter of Chaos and both mother and wife to Uranus (the heavens) and Pontus (the sea).

Gaelic Language of Celtic origins that is spoken in the Scottish Highlands, Ireland, and on the Isle of Man. In 19th-cent. Ireland, a "Gaelic Revival" attended the discovery of the means to translate Ireland's early Gaelic literature.

Gaeta, Giovanni da *See* **Gelasius II**

Gaffar Khan *See* **Red Shirt Movement**

Gagarin, Yuri Alekseyevich 1934–68. Soviet astronaut and national hero. The first man to travel in space (Apr. 12, 1961), he orbited for about one and a half hours aboard his spacecraft, *Vostok 1*, and reached a maximum orbit of 188 miles above the earth. He died in a plane crash.

Gage, Thomas 1721–87. English general during the American Revolutionary War. Appointed commander of British forces in North America (1763), he replaced T. Hutchinson as governor of Massachusetts in 1774. The colony was then on the verge of revolt and, when he ordered the munitions at Concord seized (1775), the full-scale revolution began. He resigned his command after Bunker Hill *(q.v.)* in 1775.

gag rules Rules of legislative procedure designed to prevent consideration of or debate on certain issues. Gag rules were important in US history from 1836 to 1844, when they were used to block consideration of numerous antislavery petitions in the House of Representatives. J. Q. Adams was a leading figure in the successful drive to repeal the gag rules.

Gainsborough, Thomas 1727–88. Celebrated English landscape and portrait painter, founder of the English school *(q.v.)*. Among his many famous works are *The Blue Boy* and *The Watering Place*.

Gaiseric ⟨Genseric⟩ AD *c*390–477. King of the Vandals *(q.v.)* and Alani *(q.v.)* (AD 428–477). After leading his people from Spain to Africa (429), he proceeded to conquer the Roman province of Africa and from there won Sardinia, Corsica, and Sicily. In 455 he sacked Rome.

Gaitskell, Hugh Todd Naylor 1906–63. British statesman and Labour party leader (1955–63). The most serious challenge to his leadership came in 1960 when he managed to reverse a party conference vote in favor of unilateral nuclear disarmament.

Gaius 2d cent. AD. Roman jurist. He wrote a voluminous legal text, *Institutes*, which formed the basis for the later *Institutes* of Justinian I.

Galahad, Sir Knight of the Round Table in Arthurian Legend, the noblest and purest of all the knights. He was son of Launcelot and Elaine and a hero of the quest for the Holy Grail *(q.v.)*.

Galatea A sea nymph who, when her beloved Acis was killed by a jealous rival, changed his body into the river Acis.

Galatia Ancient region of central Asia Minor, located in area around modern Ankara, Turkey. It was named for the Gauls, who took it in the 3rd cent. BC. Their expansion was stopped by Attalus I. The Romans conquered the area in 189 BC. It became a Roman province in 25 BC.

Galba, Servius Sulpicius 3 BC–AD 69. Roman emperor (AD 68–69), successor to Nero. A provincial governor, he was proclaimed emperor by his troops after an uprising against Nero (AD 68). A short time later he was killed in a rebellion (AD 69) led by his successor, Otho.

Galbraith, John Kenneth 1908–. Canadian-American economist. An influential proponent of Keynesian economics, he was an adviser to President J. Kennedy, and US ambassador to India (1961–63). Among his writings are *The Affluent Society* and *The New Industrial State*.

Galen ⟨Galenus, Claudius⟩ AD *c*130–*c*200. Greek physician. Sometimes considered the founder of experimental physiology, he was regarded as the principal medical authority well into medieval times.

Galenus, Claudius *See* **Galen**

Galerius ⟨Gaius Galerius Valerius Maximinianus⟩ *d* AD 311. Roman emperor (AD 305–310) of the Eastern Empire, successor with Constantius I (in the West) to Diocletian. A zealous persecutor of Christians, he granted an edict of toleration just before his death.

Galicia, kingdom of Spanish kingdom, located in northern Spain. It was an independent kingdom of the German Suevi in the 5th and 6th cents. AD. It was conquered in turn by Visigoths and Moors before becoming linked to Castile and León.

Galician Offensive *See* **June Offensive**

Galilee The northern region of ancient Palestine in what is now northern Israel. It is mentioned frequently in the Bible as Jesus' homeland. After the Romans destroyed Jerusalem (AD 70) it became a stronghold of Judaism. The region was resettled by Zionists late in the 19th cent. and was entirely absorbed by Israel after the Arab-Israeli War *(q.v.)* of 1948–49.

Galilee, Judas of *See* **Judas of Galilee**

Galileo ⟨*properly*, Galileo Galilei⟩ 1564–1642. Italian mathematician, physicist, and astronomer. One of the world's great scientists, he is regarded as the founder of the experimental method, which is the cornerstone of modern science. Born at Pisa, he discovered the law of pendulums as a student and first won notice by his invention of the hydrostatic balance (*c*1586). He later experimented (*c*1589–92) with falling bodies (not, as in the popular legend, by dropping objects from the tower of Pisa) and disproved the Aristotelian theory that objects of different weights fall at different speeds. This revelation (which aroused great hostility in the scholarly community), his observation of the parabolic path of a projectile, and other discoveries foreshadowed the universal laws of motion formulated by I. Newton. After constructing (*c* 1610) and perfecting a telescope (invented earlier by the Dutch), Galileo discovered that the moon shines by reflected light, that the Milky Way is composed of individual stars, and that Jupiter was orbited by four moons (12 are now known). His researches confirmed his belief in the Copernican theory (q.v.) and he openly supported (1613) this heliocentric theory. It was condemned by the church (1616) as dangerous and Galileo was warned by church authorities against supporting it. Nevertheless, he published (1632) his *Dialogue Concerning the Two World Systems*, openly supporting Copernican theory. He was subsequently tried and sentenced to house arrest by the Inquisition. He continued his scientific work, however, and discovered the librations (oscillations) of the moon before his death.

Gall *c*1840–94. American Indian, a Sioux war chief. He was a leader under Sitting Bull during the massacre of G. Custer and his men at the Battle of Little Bighorn (q.v.) in 1876. He ended his war with the whites in 1881.

Gallas, Matthias, graf von 1584–1647. Imperial general (1634–45) of the Holy Roman armies during the Thirty Years' War (q.v.). A commander under A. von Wallenstein, Gallas was involved in his removal (1634) and then succeeded him (1634) as overall commander. His drunkenness and several disastrous defeats finally led to his own removal in 1645.

Gallatin, Albert 1761–1849. Swiss-American US secretary of the treasury (1801–14). Through his insistence on sound fiscal policies he managed a significant, though temporary, reduction in the national debt. The reduction was wiped out by the War of 1812. He played a major role in negotiating the Treaty of Ghent (q.v.) in 1814, which ended the conflict.

Galle, Johann Gottfried 1812–1910. German astronomer who discovered the planet Neptune (1846).

Gallican Articles *See* **Gallicanism**

Gallicanism Movement among French Catholics for greater independence from papal authority. Gallicanism can be traced back to the Great Schism (14th cent.) and involved both secular and ecclesiastical matters. The famous Gallican Articles, issued by Louis XIV (1682) and approved by the French clergy, represent the clearest statement of Gallican aims. They proclaimed that the king was not subject to the pope, that the pope was subject to ecumenical councils, that the traditions and customs of the French church were outside the pope's authority, and that the pope's authority in doctrinal matters was binding only with approval of the whole church. Gallicanism was seriously compromised by the state's attack on the church during the French Revolution. Later, the First Vatican Council (q.v.) of 1870 con-

firmed the opposing philosophy of Ultramontanism and firmly established papal authority. Gallicanism subsequently ceased to be an active movement.

Gallic Wars Series of campaigns conducted by J. Caesar (58–51 BC) leading to the Roman conquest of Gaul. The wars began when Caesar moved against the Helvetii, who attempted to move into southern Gaul. Caesar then defeated (57 BC) the tribes in what is now Belgium, defeated the Veneti (56) in Brittany, and conducted a punitive invasion (55) into Germany. In 54 he invaded Britain (for the second time, the first being in 55) and defeated the Britons under King Cassivellaunus but returned to Gaul soon after. He subsequently put down a rebellion of all Gaul (52 BC), led by Vercingetorix, and the following year reduced all resistance to Roman authority in Gaul. The campaigns gave Caesar immense power and prestige. As commander of a strong army he was able to contest Pompey's authority as leader of Rome. The main source for information on the campaigns is Caesar's own *De bello Gallico*.

Gallieni, Joseph Simon 1849–1916. French soldier and colonial governor. He played an important role in pacifying the French Sudan and Madagascar (1870–1905). During WW I he played a critical role in the victory of the first Battle of the Marne (q.v.) in 1914.

Gallienus, Publius Licinius Valerianus Egnatius *d.* AD 268. Roman emperor, coruler with his father Valerian (AD 253–260) and successor to him (260–268). His reign was marked by the widespread revolts of the Time of the Thirty Tyrants (q.v.).

Gallipoli Campaign ⟨Dardanelles Campaign⟩ Allied military operation in Turkey during WW I. The Allies attempted to wrest control of the Dardanelles (q.v.) from Turkey in order to better supply Russia. The campaign was advocated by W. Churchill, backed by D. Lloyd George and Lord H. Kitchener, and commenced on Feb. 19, 1915. After an unsuccessful naval attempt to force the straits, British and French troops were landed on both sides of the straits, notably on the Gallipoli peninsula. The operation became a disaster in which 55,000 Allied troops were lost before the evacuation (Dec., 1915–Jan., 1916). Churchill was obliged to resign as first lord of the admiralty.

Gallitzin, Demetrius Augustine 1770–1840. American Roman Catholic clergyman born a Russian prince. From 1795 to 1840 he was a widely known frontier missionary to settlers in southwestern Pennsylvania.

Galloway, Joseph *c*1731–1803. American loyalist leader during the American Revolutionary War. As a delegate to the Continental Congress *(q.v.)* in 1774–75, he proposed a plan for peaceful settlement with Britain. His plan was narrowly defeated, and he later joined the British, becoming superintendent of the Philadelphia port under Gen. W. Howe.

Gallup, George Horace 1901–. American public opinion expert. He developed the Gallup poll, a survey of public opinion. The poll first gained wide notice when Gallup successfully predicted the reelection of President F. Roosevelt in 1936.

Galsworthy, John 1867–1933. English novelist and dramatist. Born of a wealthy family, he is best known for The Forsyte Saga, a series of novels about a well-to-do family in the late 1800s and early 1900s. He also wrote successful plays, including *Strife* and *Loyalties*. He won the Nobel Prize in Literature in 1932.

Galt, Sir Alexander Tilloch 1817–93. English-born Canadian statesman. A member of the Canadian parliament from 1849 to 1872, he became an important advocate of confederation of the provinces. Following the 1867 British North America Act *(q.v.)*, he served briefly as finance minister (1867–68) of the newly created dominion.

Galt, John 1779–1839. Scottish novelist. He is best known for his tales of Scottish country life.

Galton, Sir Francis 1822–1911. English scientist. In *Hereditary Genius*, he presented strong evidence that talent is an inherited characteristic. A grandson of E. Darwin and cousin of C. Darwin, he founded—and coined the term for—the science of eugenics.

Galuppi, Baldassare 1706–85. Italian composer of light operas who is credited with the development of the *opera buffa* style. His best-known opera is *Il Filosofo di Campagna*.

Galvani, Luigi 1737–90. Italian physiologist. His controversy with A. Volta over the source of the electricity which induced muscle contractions in frogs' legs through use of dissimilar metals stimulated important research into the nature of electricity. Some terms dealing with electricity are named after Galvani.

Gálvez, Bernardo de c1746–86. Spanish colonial governor. As Spanish governor of Louisiana (1777–83), he was largely responsible for Spain's acquisition of British territory in Florida (1783). He became viceroy of New Spain in 1785.

Gálvez, José, Marqués de la Sonora 1720–87. Spanish colonial administrator. As inspector general to New Spain (1765–72), he instituted important reforms in the administration of the colonies.

Gama, Vasco da c1469?–1524. Portuguese navigator who first made the sea voyage from Europe to India. His voyage and the trade it opened up

with India provided the foundation for the Portuguese Empire. Chosen by King Manuel I to find a route to India, he sailed with four ships in 1497. He rounded the Cape of Good Hope (already explored by 1488) and after enduring both storms and mutinies he reached Calicut in India (1498). He subsequently commanded a fleet of 20 ships on a second voyage to India (1502–03). This time he founded the Mozambique and Sofala colonies on the African coast and, after leading a naval attack, established Portuguese rule over Calicut. Sent to India as a viceroy in 1524, he died soon after arriving.

Gamaliel **1.** Jewish rabbi, *d.* about AD 50. A prominent Pharisee who taught St. Paul (Acts 22) and advised against persecuting the Apostles (Acts 5). **2.** ~ of Jabneh. Jewish rabbi, *d.* AD 115? A grandson of Hillel, and a leader of his people recognized by the Romans, he helped establish the Passover Seder ritual that was substituted for the former Temple sacrifice, interrupted by the destruction of the Temple in AD 70.

Gambetta, Leon 1838–82. French political leader. After the fall of the Second Empire *(q.v.)* in 1870, he organized a provisional government of national defense, dramatically escaped from Paris in a balloon, and was virtual dictator of France for five months (1870–71). One of the founders of the Third Republic *(q.v.)* and shapers of its constitution (1875), he served briefly as premier (1881–82).

Gambia West African republic. The smallest African nation, it extends in a narrow strip from the Atlantic along both sides of the Gambia River for about 200 miles. Peanuts are the primary product. It was discovered by the Portuguese (1455) and used by the British as an anti-slave-trade base (1800s). Gambia became a British crown colony in 1843. Periodically governed by Sierra Leone, it became independent in 1965. Pres. Dawda Kairaba Jawara, in office since 1970, was reelected again in 1982.

Gambrinus Legendary Flemish king who is supposed to have invented beer.

Gamow, George 1904–68. Russian-American nuclear physicist and author of popular books on science. He is noted for his work in explaining stellar evolution through principles of nuclear physics.

Gandamak, Treaty of Treaty signed by Amir Yakub of Afghanistan with the British on May 16, 1879, concluding the Second Afghan War *(q.v.)*. By it the British agreed to pay the amir an annual subsidy for their occupation of the Khyber Pass *(q.v.)*, the amir agreed to conduct his foreign relations only through the government of India, and British trade was to be free.

Gandhi, Indira 1917–. Indian prime minister (1966–77, 1980) and daughter of J. Nehru. She succeeded Pres. Lal Bahadur Shastri (1904–66) and presided over India's defeat of Pakistan (1971). Facing a challenge to her 1972 election, she declared a state of emergency (1975) and suspended the 1976 election. She was unseated as prime minister the following year (July 25, 1977) but after new elections she was returned to power several years later (Jan. 14, 1980).

Gandhi, Mohandas Karamchand 1869–1948. Indian political leader and national hero who became a symbol of nonviolent protest and of India's independence movement. Educated in both India and Britain, he remained overseas until 1914. On his return, he supported the British government in India during WW I, though he took an increasing interest in Indian home rule. Meanwhile he took up the life of an ascetic and began advocating abolition of the caste system (q.v.) in India. His nonviolent campaigns of civil disobedience (called *satyagraha*) against various laws soon propelled him to the leadership of the movement for Indian home rule, as well as the Congress party (q.v.). Arrested for organizing a protest against the government salt monopoly, he was released to take part (1931) in the Round Table Conference (q.v.). During the 1930s, the pattern of Gandhi's mass nonviolent protests and subsequent arrests continued. But Gandhi only gained prestige (he was called Mahatma, or "great soul") and he was able to wrest major concessions from the British rulers of India. During the early part of WW II, he began demanding India's complete independence from Britain. This he tried to achieve by refusing Indian support for the British war effort against the Japanese, a tactic that resulted in his internment until 1944. He vigorously supported Britain's postwar plans to grant India's independence, though he was unsuccessful in opposing the partition of India and creation of Pakistan (1947). He was assassinated (Jan. 30, 1948) by a Hindu fanatic during a time of disturbances between Muslims and Hindus.

Ganganelli, Lorenzo *See* **Clement XIV**

Gang of Four Four leading figures of the Cultural Revolution (q.v.) in China in 1966–69 who were put on trial (Nov. 20, 1980) along with other radicals. They were charged with a variety of abuses during the Cultural Revolution, including the deaths of some 34,000 people. The leading figure among the four was Chiang Ch'ing, Mao Tsetung's wife; the trial marked her fall from power.

GAR *See* **Grand Army of the Republic**

Garamond, Claude *d.* 1561. French type designer. His Roman type faces supplanted the Gothic type faces then in use and helped establish the Roman style as the standard in printing.

Garbo, Greta ⟨Gustafsson, Greta Lovisa⟩ 1905–. Swedish-American movie actress. A celebrated beauty and talented actress, she made films from 1922 to 1941.

Garcia Iñiguez, Calixto 1836–98. Cuban revolutionary. A commander in the rebellion called the Ten Years' War (q.v.) of 1868–78, he led Cuban forces against the Spanish in the Spanish-American War (1898).

García Lorca, Federico 1898–1936. Spanish poet and dramatist. He was one of the most important Spanish poets of this century. His works include *Gypsy Ballads* and *Lament for the Death of a Bullfighter*.

Garcilaso de la Vega 1539?–1616. Peruvian historian, best known for his commentaries on the life of the Incas and the conquest of Peru.

Garden of Eden In the Bible (Book of Genesis), the original home of Adam and Eve, the first man and woman. They were expelled for eating the forbidden fruit. The Bible appears to give Mesopotamia as its location.

Garfield, James Abram 1831–81. Twentieth US president (1881), successor to R. Hayes. A former teacher, lay preacher, and Ohio state senator, Garfield distinguished himself as a Union army major general during the American Civil War (1861–65) and served as a Republican US congressman (1863–80). He became the Republican presidential candidate (1880), breaking a deadlock between supporters of J. Blaine and U. Grant at the party convention. On taking office (Mar. 4, 1881), Garfield initiated a political struggle with a Republican faction called the Stalwarts (q.v.) by naming Blaine as secretary of state and initiating action on the Star Route Frauds. After only months in office, Garfield was mortally wounded (July 2, 1881) by a disgruntled office-seeker, Charles J. Giteau, and died Sept. 19.

Garibaldi, Giuseppe 1807–82. Italian soldier and hero of the Risorgimento (q.v.), or unification of Italy. While in his twenties, he was involved in an unsuccessful revolt (1835) in Italy and fled to South America. He became famous there as a leader of rebel forces in Uruguay (1842–46). Garibaldi returned to Italy and joined his friend G. Mazzini in establishing a revolutionary republic at Rome (1849). He became a hero for his leadership of rebel forces against the pope's armies, but was ultimately forced to retreat and flee Italy. Having given up his hopes for an Italian republic, he was willing (1860) to serve the interests of Victor Emmanuel II to further the unification of Italy. That year he undertook his famous conquest of the Kingdom of Two Sicilies with the Expedition of the Thousand *(q.v.)*. In 1861 Victor Emmanuel became king of a united Italy, except for the Papal States. Garibaldi made two reckless and abortive attacks on the Papal States (1862, 1867). In 1874, he became a member of the Italian parliament.

Garigliano, battles of Battles fought near the strategic Garigliano River in south central Italy. **1.** On Dec. 28, 1503, 15,000 men under Ferdinand V decisively defeated a French invasion force under Louis XII, forcing the latter to accede to Spanish rule over Naples. **2.** From Nov., 1943, to May, 1944, there was heavy fighting here in WW II during the Allied drive on Rome, including the battle for Cassino.

Garneau, François Xavier 1809–66. French-Canadian historian. Considered the earliest important historian of this nationality, he wrote the *History of Canada.*

Garner, John Nance 1868–1967. US vice-president (1933–41). A Democratic congressman from Texas (1903–33), he served under President F. Roosevelt during his first two terms.

Garnier, Marie Joseph François 1839–73. French explorer in Indochina. He played a major role in an expedition that ranged from Cambodia and Laos to Yunnan in China (1866–68), accurately mapping territory unknown to geographers.

Garrick, David 1717–79. English actor, theater manager, and dramatist. Considered one of England's greatest actors, he was especially known for his Shakespearean roles.

Garrison, William Lloyd 1805–79. American abolitionist. An uncompromising and often abrasive publicist for the antislavery cause, he published (1831–65) the *Liberator*, a newspaper he made famous with his views and which he continued until the abolition of slavery.

Garter, Order of the *See* **Order of the Garter**

Garvey, Marcus 1887–1940. Jamaican-born American black nationalist. Through his Universal Negro Improvement Association (from 1914), Garvey advocated the worldwide union of blacks, rejected integration, and championed a "Back to Africa" movement.

Gary, Elbert Henry 1846–1927. American lawyer and business executive. He was one of the principal organizers of the US Steel Co. (1901) and served as its chairman (1903–27). Gary, Indiana, was named for him.

Gascoigne, George 1525?–77. English poet, essayist, and dramatist, noted for his experimentation with literary forms. He was author of *Certain Notes of Instruction*, considered the first essay by an Englishman on writing verse.

Gaspar *See* **Magi**

Gasparri, Pietro 1852–1934. Italian cardinal. Under Pope Pius X, he was responsible for organizing the Code of Canon Law (1904–07), a codification of the law of the Roman Catholic church. He also played a major role in negotiating the Lateran Treaty *(q.v.)* of 1929.

Gaspee A British revenue cutter that was burned by rebellious Rhode Islanders on June 10, 1772. The names of the perpetrators were concealed and they went unpunished. Britain passed the Intolerable Acts *(q.v.)* partly in retaliation.

Gastein, Convention of *See* **Convention of Gastein**

Gates, Horatio 1728?–1806. American general in the American Revolutionary War. As commander of an army in the north, he defeated the British Gen. Burgoyne in an important victory at Saratoga, which turned the tide of the war in the Americans' favor. Subsequently embroiled in the Conway Cabal *(q.v.)*, he was transferred to the South and was disgraced in the Carolina Campaign (1780).

Gates, Sir Thomas *d.* 1621. English colonial governor of Virginia. Named in the Virginia colony charter (1606), he twice served as governor (1610, 1611–14).

Gath Ancient Philistine city mentioned in the Bible as the home of Goliath and of David's refuge from Saul. The location of its ruins has not yet been identified.

Gatling, Richard Jordan 1818–1903. American inventor. He invented the Gatling gun (1861), a crank-operated forerunner of the machine gun.

Gaudier-Brzeska, Henri 1891–1915. French sculptor. He was the leading sculptor in the movement known as vorticism *(q.v.)*.

Gaugamela, Battle of ⟨Battle of Arbela⟩ Decisive Macedonian victory (Oct. 1, 331 BC) over the Persians during Alexander the Great's wars of conquest. The battle marked the beginning of the decline of the Persian Empire. Alexander's 47,000 Macedonian troops defeated some 250,000 soldiers under Darius III on the plain of Gaugamela in the territory of ancient Assyria. Losses were 40–90,000 Persians to only 100–500 Macedonians.

Gauguin, Eugène Henri Paul 1848–1903. Famous French painter, a postimpressionist and a principal figure in the development of modern art. He did not begin painting full time until age 35, before then dividing his time between his work as a stockbroker and painting. He was associated with the impressionists until 1888, when he developed his own characteristic style, synthetism. Instead of imitating nature, he created abstracted figures from the primitive subjects and bright colors he used. Despairing of modern civilization, Gauguin went to Tahiti (1891) and thereafter lived in the South Pacific (excepting 1893–95). Among his many famous works are: *The Yellow Christ; Where Do We Come From? What Are We? Where Are We Going?;* and *Tahitian Landscape.*

Gaul Ancient name for the area once inhabited by Celts, roughly comprising modern France. Roman Gaul included also parts of northern Italy (Cisalpine Gaul). By the time of Julius Caesar, Rome already ruled the part of Transalpine Gaul that is today Provence. Caesar conquered the rest of Gaul for Rome in the Gallic Wars *(q.v.)* of 58– 51 BC, immortalizing in his account of the wars Gaul's division into "three parts"—Aquitania, Gallia, and Belgica. Gaul flourished as a center of Roman civilization until the collapse of the Western Empire (AD 476) and thereafter came under control of the Franks. Gaul formed the nucleus of the Frankish Merovingian and Carolingian empires.

Gaullists French political term. Gaullists were the supporters of the nationalistic policies of French general (later president) C. de Gaulle. The term was employed to describe de Gaulle's followers during the period of his leadership of the Free French *(q.v.)* and it was retained to describe the political party organized after 1945 and dominant after the foundation of the Fifth Republic *(q.v.).*

Gaunt, John of *See* **John of Gaunt**

Gauss, Karl Friedrich 1777–1855. German mathematician. He is regarded as one of the greatest of all mathematicians. He had begun producing notable work by the time he was 22 and went on to formulate important theories in mathematics (especially number theory), physics, and astronomy.

Gautier, Théophile 1811–72. French poet and novelist. He was an exponent of pure aestheticism and coined the term "art for art's sake" in the preface to his famous story *Mademoiselle de Maupin* (1835).

Gaveston, Piers *d.* 1312. English nobleman, a favorite of King Edward II of England and regent during his absence. An enemy to the barons by his manner and his position, he was several times exiled for short periods. On his return in 1312, however, the barons revolted and executed him.

Gawain, Sir A knight in the Arthurian Legend *(q.v.).* A nephew of King Arthur, he was at first portrayed as a model of the virtues of knighthood. In later Arthurian literature he is shown to be flawed and lacking in spiritual devotion.

Gay, John 1685–1732. English dramatist and poet, best known for his work *The Beggar's Opera.*

Gay-Lussac, Joseph Louis 1778–1850. French chemist and physicist. He made many discoveries

in chemistry and physics and is noted for his work on properties of gases. He formulated the law of combining volumes for gases (1809).

Ge *See* **Gaea**

Geary, John White 1819–73. American politician and Union general. He was governor of Kansas (1856–57) during the period when it was called Bleeding Kansas *(q.v.),* proved an able commander during the American Civil War, and later served as governor of Pennsylvania (1867–73).

Geber *See* **Jabir ibn Hayyan, Abu Musa**

Geddes, Sir Patrick 1854–1932. Scottish biologist and sociologist noted for his work in the field of town planning. His works include *City Development* and *Cities in Evolution.*

Geiger, Abraham 1810–74. German rabbi and scholar. He was an early leader of Reform Judaism *(q.v.).*

Geiger, Johannes Wilhelm 1882–1945. German physicist and inventor, with W. Müller, of what is now known as the Geiger counter (1928), a device for measuring radiation.

Gelasius I *d.* AD 496. Pope (AD 492–496). He was important in the formulation of the doctrine of papal primacy in controversies with the Byzantine emperor. His strictures against Caesaropapism helped lead to the later Western idea of the separation of church and state.

Gelasius II ⟨Gaeta, Giovanni da⟩ *d.* 1119. Italian-born pope (1118–19), successor to Paschal II. Gelasius opposed Holy Roman Emperor Henry V in the ongoing investiture controversy *(q.v.).* When Henry set up antipope Gregory VIII, Gelasius excommunicated them both. Gelasius was subsequently driven out of Rome by Henry and died at Cluny, France.

Gellius, Aulus *fl.* 2d cent. AD. Roman author of *Attic Nights,* a book containing extracts of many ancient works that are now otherwise lost.

Gelon *d.* 478 BC. Greek ruler. He made himself master of Syracuse and much of Sicily. He crushed the Carthaginians at Himera (480 BC).

Gempei War Japanese civil war (1180–85) that led to the downfall of the Taira clan as rulers of Japan. The Taira held power in Japan from 1160, after defeating the leader Minamoto Yoshitomo. In 1180 his son, Minamoto Yoritomo, organized dissident Taira clan members and the remainder of the Minamoto clan for a rebellion against Taira authority. The war culminated in the naval battle of Dannoura (1185), in which the Taira were crushed. Yoritomo remained the virtual ruler of Japan, and in 1192 was made shogun, thereby establishing the Kamakura shogunate, which ruled Japan until 1333.

Generation of '98 Spanish intellectual movement. Spain's 1898 defeat in the Spanish-American War fostered an introspective period among Spanish writers and philosophers that ultimately enriched Spanish literature. They included Miguel Unamuno y Jugo (1864–1936), José Martínez Ruiz (1874–1967), and José Ortega y Gasset (1883–1955).

Genêt, Edmond Charles Édouard ⟨Citizen Genêt⟩ 1763–1834. French diplomat. He was sent to the US to win its support in the French revolutionary government's war against Britain. He was unable to sway President G. Washington from a neutral policy and, when he attempted to rally popular support, Washington had him recalled.

Genet, Jean 1910–. French dramatist. Genet was a leading proponent of the Theater of the Absurd, portraying social outcasts in such plays as *The Maids, The Balcony,* and *The Blacks.*

Geneva City (pop. 150,100) in Switzerland, capital of Geneva canton, located on Lake Geneva and the Rhône River. A cultural and tourist center, it has often been the scene of international conferences and is known for its manufacture of watches and precision instruments. Originally a center of Celtic Allobroges, it passed through successive rulers, including Roman, Frankish, and Burgundian. It was the home of J. Calvin (16th cent.) and his theocracy, and a center of the Reformation *(q.v.).* It became a canton of Switzerland in 1815.

Geneva, Robert of *See* **Robert of Geneva**

Geneva conferences International meetings. This name refers to several peace-keeping conferences held in the Swiss city. A 1927 meeting tried but failed to achieve a reduction of naval armaments. The Disarmament conference, held primarily between 1932 and 1934, also failed to restrict offensive weaponry and fell apart when A. Hitler withdrew. A 1954 meeting discussed a Korean War armistice and partitioned Indochina, while a 1955 summit meeting among the US, France, Britain, and Russia sought to end the Cold War. A 1958 US-British-Russian meeting was the first of several held to discuss the banning of nuclear tests and nuclear arms limitation.

Geneva Conventions International agreements. From 1864 through 1949, a series of international agreements was reached at Geneva, Switzerland, to regulate and prevent abuses of war and the treatment of prisoners of war. Initiated by the Red Cross, signatory nations agreed to provide humane treatment for all prisoners as well as medical attention for the sick and wounded. Because of WW II abuses, the four conventions signed in Aug., 1949, concerning the sick and wounded, prisoners of war, and civilians in time of war are considered especially important.

Geneva Protocol League of Nations agreement. On Oct. 2, 1924, the assembly of the League of Nations unanimously agreed to make arbitration of disputes mandatory for member nations. However, the protocol became a dead letter when the British cabinet rejected the idea several months later and failed to ratify the protocol.

Geneviève, Saint *c*422–*c*500 or 512. Patron saint of the city of Paris. She is said to have predicted correctly that Paris would remain unscathed by an impending attack by Attila the Hun (451).

Genghis Khan ⟨Jenghiz ~⟩ ⟨Chinghiz ~⟩ ⟨*orig. name* Temujin⟩ 1167?–1227. Mongol conqueror, who, as leader of notoriously savage Mongol armies, created a vast Asian empire. Named chief of a Mongol tribe while still a youth, he succeeded in conquering other Mongol tribes and in organizing them (1206) into a confederacy. With his capital at Karakorum (*in modern* Mongolian People's Republic), he invaded (1213–18) and conquered northern China. From 1218 to 1224 he extended his empire in the west, conquering parts of what are now northern India, Iran, Iraq, and southern Russia. By the time of his death, the empire extended from the Korean peninsula in the east to the Black Sea in the west. The empire was subsequently divided among his sons, including Ogadai and Jagatai, and their descendants, including Batu Khan, Hulagu Khan, and Kublai Khan.

Genoa Italian city (pop. 795,000) in northwestern Italy, capital of Genoa province and Liguria. It is a major seaport on the Italian Riviera. It prospered under the Romans, then became an independent city, often involved in fighting with rivals Pisa and Venice. Admiral A. Doria expelled the French (1528) and revived the city. In 1805, Napoleon annexed Genoa to France and the Congress of Vienna joined it to the kingdom of Sardinia in 1815. The damage done during WW II has been repaired and the port modernized. Genoa is the birthplace of C. Columbus.

Genoa, Conference of *See* **Conference of Genoa**

Genseric *See* **Gaiseric**

Gent *See* **Ghent**

Gentili, Alberico 1552–1608. Italian jurist who is regarded as one of the earliest writers on international law. He is noted for his works on laws for the conduct of war.

Gentlemen's Agreement Accord (Feb. 24, 1907) between the US and Japan halting the immigration of Japanese laborers into the United States. By this agreement, brought about by pressure from West Coast states, Japan promised to stop further emigration and the US agreed to stop anti-Japanese discrimination.

Gentz, Friedrich von 1764–1832. Prussian political theorist in the Austrian service. He was influential in the realignment of the European powers after the Napoleonic Wars *(q.v.)*, and was chief secretary at the Congresses *(q.v.)* of Vienna (1814–15), Aix-la-Chapelle (1818), Troppau (1820), and Verona (1822).

Geoffrey IV ⟨Geoffrey Plantagenet⟩ 1113–51. Count of Anjou. He laid claim to and conquered Normandy (1135–44). In 1150 he turned the duchy over to his son, the future English king Henry II.

Geoffrey of Monmouth *c*1100–54. English clergyman and writer. He was author of *Historia Regum Britanniae* (*c*1135), a fanciful account of British kings that contained the first account of the legendary King Arthur and widely influenced British literature.

Geoffrey Plantagenet *See* **Geoffrey IV**

George I 1660–1727. German-born elector of Hanover and king of Great Britain and Ireland (1714–27), the first of the Hanoverian kings and successor to Queen Anne. An unpopular king, he succeeded under the 1701 Act of Settlement *(q.v.)*. Under his reign Britain entered into the Quadruple Alliance *(q.v.)* and concluded the 1713 Peace of Utrecht. The king himself was implicated in the South Sea Bubble scandal *(q.v.)*. He was the great-grandson of James I.

George I 1845–1913. Greek King (1863–1913), elected successor to Otto I. His reign was marked by the adoption of a constitution (1864), the acquisition of new territories in Thessaly and Epirus, and an unsuccessful war with the Ottoman Turks (1896–97) over Crete (Greco-Turkish War *[q.v.]*).

George II 1683–1760. German-born elector of Hanover and king of Great Britain and Ireland (1727–60), a member of the Hanover family, and successor to his father, George I. Under his reign Britain saw the last of the Jacobite rebellions (1745–46), the ouster of Sir R. Walpole, and the beginning of the Seven Years' War (1756–63).

George II 1890–1947. Greek King (1922–23, 1935–47), successor to his father Constantine I. He was forced to leave Greece (1923) and shortly thereafter a republic was proclaimed (1924). Recalled in 1935, he acquiesced to the dictatorship of J. Metaxas (1936) and, in 1941, fled from the invading Germans. He was restored to the throne in 1946, and was succeeded by his brother Paul I (1901–64).

George III 1738–1820. King of Great Britain and Ireland (1760–1820), a member of the Hanover family, and successor to his grandfather, George II. Under his reign Britain enjoyed a period of economic prosperity and cultural activity. At the same time the king's policies led to political instability at home and the American Revolution *(q.v.)* abroad. By 1784, however, he achieved his goal of breaking Whig control in Parliament with a general Tory victory in the elections. He also oversaw Britain's participation in the French Revolutionary Wars *(q.v.)*, arranged the union of the Irish and English kingdoms (1801), and refused to permit Catholic Emancipation (1801). Suffering what was believed a hereditary disease, he became insane (1810). He was elector and later king of Hanover but he never visited it.

George IV 1762–1830. King of England and Ireland (1820–30), a member of the Hanover family, successor to his father George III. He became regent for his insane father (1810) and under him the Tory party continued in power. His reign saw a marked decline in the influence of the monarchy, thanks to his dissolute ways and to the scandals that surrounded his married life. He was succeeded by his brother William IV.

George V 1819–78. German king, the last king of Hanover (1851–66) and successor to his father, Ernest Augustus (1771–1851). He allied himself with Austria during the Austro-Prussian War *(q.v.)* and following the Prussian victory his kingdom was taken over and annexed by Prussia. His father, a son of George III of England, had acceded to the throne of Hanover in 1837 when Hanover was separated from Britain at the accession of Victoria.

George V 1865–1936. King of Great Britain (1910–36), successor to his father, Edward VII. He played a moderating role in the crises during his reign and guided Britain through WW I. Among the events of this period were the 1916 Irish Sinn Fein rebellion *(q.v.)*, the 1922 Irish Free State *(q.v.)* settlement, the formation of the "national" government (1931) and the 1935 Government of India Act *(q.v.)*. A popular monarch, he changed the royal family name from Saxe-Coburg-Gotha to Windsor during WW I.

George VI 1895–1952. King of Great Britain and Northern Ireland (1936–52), successor to his brother Edward VIII. He is noted for his efforts to shore up British morale during WW II. During his reign, India was granted independence (1947). He was succeeded by his daughter Elizabeth II.

George, Henry 1839–97. American economic reformer. He developed the idea of the single tax (1871). Under this system, designed to eliminate poverty, the government would abolish all taxes except that on land itself.

George, Saint 4th cent.? Patron saint of England. A saint of the Eastern church, he may have been martyred in Palestine around AD 250 or during the great persecutions by Diocletian on Apr. 23, 303. Because of the association of his name with chivalric legends during the Middle Ages, particularly the one about his slaying of the dragon, he became very popular in story and art, was made patron of soldiers and adopted as patron by England, Aragon, and Portugal.

George of Podebrad 1420–71. Bohemian king (1458–71). A leader of the Utraquists (q.v.) in the Hussite Wars (q.v.), he took Prague (1448) and became first regent to King Ladislaus (1453–57) and then king of Bohemia. He successfully resisted a challenge to his throne by the Hungarian king Matthias Corvinus (1469).

Georgia Historic region located on the eastern shore of the Black Sea, now a constituent republic of the USSR. In ancient times the region was known as Colchis (q.v.) and Iberia and was part of the Roman Empire after 65 BC. After the 4th cent. AD the region was involved in wars between the Byzantines and Persians. The process of unifying the region began in the 7th cent. AD. Georgia reached its cultural flowering as a kingdom in the 12th and 13th cents. and then declined as a result of invasions by Mongols and Timurs and wars between the Turks and Persians. From 1801 to 1864 Russia annexed Georgian lands and, after a brief period of independence (1918–21) following the Russian Revolution, Georgia was made a republic within the USSR (1922). J. Stalin was a native of Georgia.

Georgia US state (pop. 5,464,300) and one of the original Thirteen Colonies (q.v.). Georgia was first explored by the Spanish under H. de Soto (1540). The first town, Savannah, was founded (1733) by J. Oglethorpe for the English. Rival claims to the region were settled when Oglethorpe defeated the Spanish at the Battle of Bloody Marsh (1742). Georgia was made a colony in 1754 and ratified the Constitution in 1788. Amid the Yazoo Land Claims (q.v.) controversy, Georgia turned over its western lands to the federal government and established its current boundaries (1802). The Creek and Cherokee Indians were forced to leave the state in the 1830s. The state was ravaged by Sherman's March during the US Civil War and afterward the great plantations were replaced by tenant farmers and sharecroppers. Blacks voted in the Democratic primary for the first time in 1946 and were integrated with whites in the schools after 1961. The state adopted a new constitution in 1945.

Georgian style English architectural style. This formal, neoclassic style, characterized by red brick with white woodwork, was popular in England c1715–1820. From there it was transported to colonial America.

Gerhardsen, Einar Henry 1897–. Norwegian statesman. Gerhardsen was a labor leader who was held hostage by the Nazis during WW II. He was the first (1945–51) postliberation Norwegian prime minister, a post he held twice more (1955–63, 1963–65).

Géricault, Jean Louis André Théodore 1791–1824. French painter who rebelled against the classical school and became an important figure in the transition to romanticism in French painting. The Raft of the Medusa (1819) is among his most famous paintings.

German Confederation A loose confederation (1815–66) of 35 independent German kingdoms and 4 free cities formed largely for mutual defense. It was dominated by Austria, and its history was marked by a growing rivalry between Austria and Prussia. Following the destruction of the Holy Roman Empire (q.v.) by Napoleon and the subsequent fall of his French-based empire, the German states were left largely unprotected. The German Confederation was therefore created at the Congress of Vienna (q.v.) in 1815 and a German diet under Austrian presidency was formed. The diet, briefly supplanted (1848–50) by the Frankfurt Parliament, survived until the Austro-Prussian War (q.v.) of 1866 and the formation of the North German Confederation (q.v.).

German East Africa Name of a former German colony in East Africa. The region was first explored by the Germans in 1884 and was declared a protectorate in 1885. In 1891 the German government took direct control of the colony, overcame native rebellions and developed it. Following WW I, it was divided (1919) between Britain and Belgium, becoming Tanganyika and Ruanda-Urundi respectively.

Germanic laws German tribal laws. These were the unwritten, customary laws of the Germanic peoples prior to their contact with Rome. They dealt predominantly with family and property rights and codes of justice and punishment, and were regarded as personal and tribal law, not territorial.

Germanicus, Tiberius Claudius Drusus Nero See **Claudius I**

Germanicus Caesar 15 BC–AD 19. Roman general and consul whose uncle was Emperor Tiberius. As commander of Roman armies on the Rhine, he defeated Arminius (AD 16) and his German tribes. Tiberius is said to have become jealous of his fame and, after sending him to the East, finally instigated his murder.

German Nation, Addresses to the *See* **Addresses to the German Nation**

German New Guinea *See* **Papua New Guinea**

Germans, ancient *See* **Ancient Germans**

Germantown, Battle of Battle (Oct. 4, 1777) during the American Revolution. Gen. G. Washington attacked this British stronghold near Philadelphia. Though it failed, it was a daring raid and, together with the colonial victory in the Saratoga Campaign, helped convince the French to send aid to the Americans.

Germany Country located in central Europe. It has been divided into East Germany (German Democratic Republic) and West Germany (Federal Republic of Germany) since WW II. The unified German state was formed (19th cent.) from the petty German states that were once part of the Holy Roman Empire. *(For history of Germany prior to 1801, see* Holy Roman Empire.*)* By the end of the 19th cent., Germany had emerged as a major military and industrial power. It was deeply involved in the complex series of events that led to WW I and played a major role in the fighting against the Allied powers. Germany was defeated and the harsh terms of the Treaty of Versailles helped create the climate that brought A. Hitler to power. Germany was once again defeated in WW II and the victorious Allies, determined to prevent another war, divided Germany into zones of occupation. Cold War tensions between the Soviet Union and the Western powers hardened the divisions. In the late 1940s the occupation zones of western powers became West Germany (Bonn as capital) and the Soviet zone became East Germany (East Berlin as capital). Divided Germany became a focal point for East-West tensions in subsequent years. Key events include:

1801 Treaty of Lunéville (Feb. 9); Austria and other states of the Holy Roman Empire consented to treaty after being defeated by France; treaty effectively ended the Holy Roman Empire.

1803 Austria and German states formally accepted Napoleon's plan to begin reorganization of the 300 petty states that made up the Holy Roman Empire.

1805–15 Napoleonic Wars; German states suffered much destruction in the wars; French occupation introduced liberalism and aroused German nationalism.

1806 Confederation of the Rhine created (July 12) by Napoleon; completed reorganization of German states; included Bavaria, Baden, Württemberg, and Hesse-Darmstadt.

1806 Holy Roman Empire formally dissolved (Aug. 6) by Holy Roman Emperor Francis II; he became Austrian Emperor Francis I.

1807–08 Addresses to the German Nation, nationalistic lectures delivered by J. Fichte.

1814–15 Congress of Vienna; Austria gained control over other German states as leader of a new confederation; Prussia and Bavaria enlarged by new territories.

1815–66 German Confederation; German states now reduced to about 40, united under the leadership of Austria; C. von Metternich, Austrian statesman, dominated the Confederation until mid-century and imposed his conservative policies.

1819 Carlsbad Decrees; were measures recommended for suppression of liberal agitation within the German Confederation.

1819 Zollverein, a customs union, established under the leadership of Prussia; by 1830 it included nearly all the German states except Austria and strengthened Prussia's position as leader of the states.

1830 Liberal revolt broke out, sparked by July Revolution in France; liberals suppressed by Metternich, with Prussian aid.

1832 Federal Diet of Confederation given greater powers by Six Articles; included tighter controls on press and assembly within the states.

1833 Abortive plot to seize Federal Diet at Frankfurt and create liberal, unified German state.

1837–51 Ernst Augustus succeeded to the throne of Hanover; abolished liberal constitution (1840) and established absolute monarchy.

1840–61 Frederick William IV reigned in Prussia; increased Prussia's role as leader of German Confederation.

1847 United Diet of Prussia convened by Frederick IV; aroused hopes of liberals elsewhere in the Confederation.

1848 Revolutions of 1848; Metternich fell from power (Mar. 13) and Austria was preoccupied with revolts in domains outside the Confederation; King Frederick of Prussia appeased rebels by embracing German nationalism and granting liberal constitution; other German states did the same.

1848–50 Frankfurt National Assembly convened (May 18); dominated by middle class, this parliament replaced the Diet of the Confederation and sought to form a national government of Germany.

1848–51 War over Schleswig-Holstein; Prussians intervened to prevent Danish troops from occupying region, which had large German-speaking population.

1849 Frankfurt Constitution drawn up (Mar. 27) by Frankfurt Parliament; named Prussian king Frederick emperor of a unified German state; Frederick demurred, then refused the crown and offered his own scheme, the Prussian Union.

1850 Erfurt Parliament met (Mar.); Prussian Union accepted.

1850 Austria, having quelled the liberal revolts within its domains, countered by reconstituting the German Confederation (May); threatened Prussia with war if it went ahead with the Prussian Union.

1850 Punctation of Olmütz (Nov. 29); Prussia, humiliated by Austria, agreed to reestablishment of the German Confederation.

1850–53 Prussia successfully resisted Austria's efforts to join the Zollverein and thus maintained its economic hold over the German states; period of rapid industrialization began.

1860–62 Crisis over reorganization of the Prussian army; liberals feared a large standing army would give the king too much power; reorganization carried through.

1861–71 William I reigned as king of Prussia.

1862 O. von Bismarck came to power in Prussian government; a conservative, he ultimately succeeded in uniting Germany (1871).

1863 Social Democratic Party of Germany founded.

1863 Prussians again succeeded in blocking Austrian entry to the Zollverein.

1864 War over Schleswig-Holstein; Denmark annexed the duchies, violating agreement of 1851; Prussia defeated Denmark, which ceded Schleswig-Holstein to Austria and Prussia.

1866 Austro-Prussian War; Bismarck helped provoke war over Schleswig-Holstein; Prussians won control of both duchies by their victory and organized a new confederation of German states in the north.

1866–71 North German Confederation; formed (without Austria) under the leadership of Prussia; was nucleus of subsequent German Empire.

1869 German Social Democratic Workingmen's party formed.

1870 France opposed offer of Spanish crown to Prussian prince, Leopold of Hohenzollern-Sigmaringen; after winning refusal, sought to humiliate Prussia and thereby helped bring on war.

1870 Bismarck revised and released (July 13) Ems Dispatch and thereby increased tensions with France.

1870–71 Franco-Prussian War; Bismarck, hoping to bring southern German states into the North German Confederation, helped provoke war with France; the war united the German states and ended in defeat of France.

1871 Germany unified (Jan. 18); William of Prussia created king of united Germany; Alsace and Lorraine added to German territories after war with France.

1871–88 William I reigned as German emperor; Bismarck became chancellor and leading figure of the government of the German Empire.

1871 Imperial constitution accepted by the Reichstag (Apr. 14); framed by Bismarck, it established Prussian kings as hereditary emperors of Germany; Bundestag (upper house) and Reichstag (lower house) formed.

1871–87 Bismarck instituted the Kulturkampf, cultural struggle against the Catholic church in Germany.

1871 Center Party organized to protect interests of Catholics.

1872 Bismarck arranged the Three Emperors' League (between Germany, Russia, and Austria-Hungary) to isolate France.

1873 Financial crisis; economic depression lasting some years followed.

1875 Socialists met at Gotha (May); marked rise of socialism in Germany; groups united, adopted nonviolent socialism of Ferdinand Lassalle.

1875 Central bank (Reichsbank) formed.

1878 Emperor William escaped two assassination attempts.

1878 Reichstag dissolved after Bismarck blamed Social Democrats for attempts on the emperor; Socialists suppressed (1878–90).

1879 Alliance with Austria marked restoration of relations with that state.

1879 Protective tariff enacted, ending free-trade policy; rapid industrialization and commercial prosperity followed.

1882 Triple Alliance with Italy and Austria.

1882 German Colonial League formed to promote colonial expansion.

1883–89 Model social security laws enacted as Bismarck attempted to counter Socialist influence.

1884 Southwest Africa made a German protectorate.

1884 Togoland and the Cameroons became German colonies.

1885 Germany declared German East Africa a protectorate.

1887 Reinsurance Treaty, secret agreement with Russia to maintain neutrality in each other's wars with other states.

1888 Frederick III reigned briefly before his death.

1888–1918 William II reigned as last of the German emperors; first sought to appease Socialists by instituting labor and other social reforms, then became increasingly conservative.

1890 Bismarck resigned over differences with new emperor and rising power of the Socialists.

1891 Erfurt Congress of Socialists; German Socialists adopted Marxian principles.

1897 German naval expansion began with emperor's appointment of Alfred von Tirpitz as marine minister.

1900–09 Count von Bülow in office as chancellor; considerable social legislation enacted.

1905 Moroccan crisis with France.

1911 Alsace and Lorraine made a German state.

1911 Agadir Incident, crisis with France over Morocco; France ceded Congo territory to Germany to avert war.

1912 Socialists gained control of the Reichstag; victory came after adoption of moderate (revisionist) Socialist principles.

1914 Murder of Austrian Archduke Francis Ferdinand by a Serbian nationalist (June); Austria, backed by Germany, declared war on Serbia; Russia backed Serbia and declarations of war followed; Germans put Schlieffen Plan into motion, beginning war with attack on Belgium (Aug. 4).

1914–18 World War I: Germany, a leader of the Central Powers, suffered heavy losses in the war and though it was never invaded was forced to accept an armistice (Nov. 11, 1918).

1917 Field Marshal P. von Hindenburg and Chief of Staff E. Ludendorf overthrew Chancellor Theobald Bethmann-Hollweg; held power to 1918.

1918 Mutiny at Kiel began among German navy men (Oct. 28) and quickly became nationwide uprising; Emperor William fled to Holland (Nov. 9) and a republic was proclaimed.

1918 Socialists took control of government (Nov. 10); struggle between Social Democrats and Spartacists (Communists) began.

1918 Armistice to end the war accepted by Germans (Nov. 11).

1919 Spartacist uprisings in Berlin, led by Communists, crushed (Jan.–Mar.); Communist leaders were executed.

1919 Treaty of Versailles; accepted by German government (June 23) after futile attempt to modify harsh terms; Germany stripped of colonies, forced to cede Alsace-Lorraine to France, north Schleswig to Denmark, and Polish Corridor to Poland; forced to agree to heavy war reparations and restrictions on rearmament; terms bitterly resented in Germany and contributed to outbreak of WW II.

1919–33 Weimar Republic; established by constitution (adopted July 31), it was governed by a chancellor and two houses, the Reichstag and Reichsrat.

1919–25 F. Ebert in office as first president of the new republic.

1920 Kapp Putsch, unsuccessful attempt to reestablish monarchy (Mar. 13–17).

1920 Spartacist uprising in the Ruhr crushed.

1920 Center party gained control of the government in Reichstag elections.

1921 A. Hitler reorganized German Workers' party into Nazi party; his appeal to German nationalism, hatred of Jews, and fear of Communists gradually won him a sizable following in subsequent years; Nazi storm troops used brutal force to advance party cause.

FROM **1922** Germany beset by severe economic troubles; drastic austerity measures and foreign loans averted bankruptcy.

1922 Treaty of Rapallo (Apr. 16) canceled war indemnities and normalized relations with USSR.

1923 Hitler instigated the abortive Munich Putsch (Nov. 9).

1923–30 Ruhr district occupied after Germany defaulted on war reparations.

1924 Dawes Plan for war reparations accepted.

1925–34 Von Hindenburg in office as president.

1925 Locarno Pact signed; marked rapprochement with Germany by European powers.

1925 Hitler published *Mein Kampf.*

1926 Germany admitted to League of Nations.

1927 Von Hindenburg denied German responsibility for war (Sept. 18) that was stipulated in Treaty of Versailles.

1929 Kellogg-Briand Pact for renunciation of war accepted.

1929 Young Plan revising war reparations payments adopted.

1929 Great Depression caused severe economic problems in Germany, which had just recovered from the postwar depression.

1930 President Hindenburg dissolved the Reichstag (July 16) after his budget bill was turned down.

1930 Nazi party made significant gains in elections for new Reichstag; Nazis increased their power in subsequent elections and blocked creation of effective government; violence by Nazi storm troops.

1933 Hitler named chancellor (Jan. 30) after his Nazi party effectively paralyzed government; Von Hindenburg reluctantly made appointment after being convinced Hitler could be controlled.

1933 Reichstag Fire (Feb. 27); Hitler blamed Communists and used incident to assume dictatorial powers.

1933 Enabling Act passed (Mar. 23) establishing Hitler's corporative state and his dictatorship.

1933–45 Third Reich; Hitler in power to last days and National Socialist party was only legal party; Hitler's militarism led to world war; Jews and others persecuted in the Holocaust.

1933 Gestapo (secret police) organized by Hitler lieutenant, H. Göring; terrorized populace, arrested political opponents, Jews, and members of other "inferior races" for transport to concentration camps.

1933–45 Dachau, one of the notorious Nazi concentration camps, in operation.

1933 Germany withdrew from League of Nations.

1934 Hitler ordered Blood Purge of Nazi party leaders (June 30); eliminated all opposition to his rule.

1934 Austrian Chancellor E. Dollfuss killed in unsuccessful Nazi takeover attempt.

1934 President Von Hindenburg died (Aug. 2); Hitler assumed presidency while retaining chancellorship.

1935 Hitler attacked Treaty of Versailles provision on disarmament of Germany (Mar. 16).

1935 Locarno Pact denounced; Rhineland reoccupied (Mar.) by German military.

1935 Nazis instituted (Sept. 15) Nuremberg Laws against Jews.

1936 Pact concluded with Fascist Italy (Oct.).

1936 Anti-Comintern Pact with Japan marked expansion of Axis alliance.

1936 Hitler instituted his four-year plan to turn economy into a war machine; Göring was head of program.

1938 Anschluss; Germans invaded and annexed Austria (Mar. 12–13).

1938 German occupation of the Sudetenland; Munich Pact (Sept. 29) was move by European powers to appease Hitler and allowed him to occupy region; resulted in complete dismemberment of Czech state, however.

1939 Pact of Steel with Italy (May 22) cemented Rome-Berlin axis.

1939 Nonaggression pact with the USSR (Aug.); paved way for attack on Poland.

1939 Germans invaded Poland (Sept. 1); WW II began.

1939–45 World War II; Hitler briefly established a German empire that included nearly all of Europe, but ultimately suffered total defeat; Germany devastated by Allied drive to crush Nazi war machine.

1945 Hitler committed suicide (Apr. 30), as Soviets advanced through streets of Berlin; Adm. K. Doenitz succeeded him.

1945 Doenitz signed Germany's unconditional surrender (May 7–8); German war machine dismantled and Germany divided into four occupation zones, each administered separately (by US, Britain, France, and USSR).

1945 Potsdam Conference, Allies set postwar policies (July–Aug.).

1945–46 Nuremberg Trials held to judge leaders of Nazi party for war crimes.

1945–47 War's aftermath; food shortages and severe economic conditions prevailed; 10 million Germans migrated from Soviet-occupied zones to Western zones; local administration by Germans set up; Socialist Unity party (SED), a Communist organ, dominated politics in the Soviet (Eastern) sector; Christian Democrats, Social Democrats, and others arose in the Western zones.

1947 Moscow Conference; split developed between Soviets and Western powers occupying Germany (Mar.–Apr.).

1948 Western powers instituted currency reforms (June 18) in Western zone; Soviets reacted by blockading Berlin.

1948–49 Berlin Blockade and Airlift, major test of strength in emerging Cold War.

1949 Federal Republic of Germany formed (May 23) from Western-occupied zones; Theodore Heuss became first president (1949–59), formalized division of Germany.

1949 K. Adenauer in office as first West German chancellor (1949–63).

1949 German Democratic Republic established (Oct. 7) by Soviets to govern their Eastern zone; Wilhelm Pieck named president (1949–60).

1950 East German government accepted Oder-Neisse line as boundary with Poland.

1950 Western powers eased controls imposed in West by occupation statute.

1952 Bonn Convention signed; West Germany granted nearly complete sovereignty.

1953 Soviets turned control of East Germany over to a civilian commissioner.

1955 West Germany gained full independence, though troops of occupying powers remained; joined NATO; armed forces created.

1955 East Germany entered Warsaw Pact.

1950s West German economy boomed as its industry completed recovery from war; East Germany continued to stagnate under Soviet system.

1957 Saarland turned over to West Germany by France.

1957 West Germany became charter member of the Common Market.

1960–71 In East Germany, Walter Ulbricht in office as chairman of council of state; won Soviet recognition for East German republic; economy prospered; adopted hard-line policy against West Germany to force recognition of East Germany.

1961 Berlin Wall erected by East Germans to stop the flow of refugees to the West.

1963 West Germany signed friendship treaty with France.

1963–66 Ludwig Erhard (Christian Democrat) in office as West German chancellor; poor economy and other problems forced his resignation.

1966–69 Kurt Georg Kiesinger (Christian Democrat) in office as West German chancellor; formed coalition government with Christian Socialists and Social Democrats; opened relations with East European nations.

1968 East German troops participated in the Warsaw Pact invasion of Czechoslovakia.

1968 New East German constitution adopted.

1969–74 In West Germany, Willy Brandt (Social Democrat) in office as chancellor; his *Ostpolitik* resulted in formal treaties with the Soviets and their European satellite nations.

1970 West German Chancellor W. Brandt and East German Premier W. Stoph at first meeting between leaders of these two states (Jan 19).

1970 East Germans halted traffic (Dec. 18–22) between West Berlin and West Germany for four days.

1971– In East Germany, Erich Honecker in office as chairman of the council of state; relations with West Germany significantly improved.

1973 Treaty signed (June 6) to normalize relations between East and West Germany.

1973 West and East Germany admitted to the UN.

1974 Chancellor Brandt of West Germany resigned (May 6) after one of his aides was exposed as an East German spy.

1974–82 Helmut Schmidt (Social Democrat) became West German chancellor.

1974 East Germany established diplomatic relations with US (Sept.).

1974 East Germany adopted new constitution.

1976 Communist summit held (June) in East Berlin; Soviet domination in Communist countries opposed.

1978 East German troops involved in fighting in Angola.

1980 East Germany closed border with Poland (Oct.) as crisis over Solidarity movement mounted.

1981 East German head of state Honecker spoke on possible reunification of Germany, reversing party line (Feb.).

1981 Controversy in West Germany over stationing of US nuclear missiles there; Chancellor Schmidt threatened to resign (May) over issue, but won approval.

1982 Helmut Kohl, leader of coalition of Christian Democratic Union and Christian Social Union, in office as West German chancellor.

Geronimo 1829–1909. Celebrated Apache Indian chief who steadfastly resisted attempts to confine his people to Indian reservations. He led groups of Indians away from reservations in the Southwest several times between 1876 and 1886, raiding white settlements and eluding capture. He surrendered for the last time in 1886 and was eventually settled at Fort Sill, Oklahoma (1887).

Gerry, Elbridge 1744–1814. American statesman, US vice-president (1813–14) and signer of the Declaration of Independence. He was a delegate to the Continental Congress (1776–85), a US congressman (1789–93) and was involved in the 1797 XYZ Affair (q.v.). While governor of Massachusetts (1810–12), he was accused of rearranging election districts to his party's advantage, a tactic now known as "gerrymandering."

Gerrymandering *See* **Gerry, Elbridge**

Gershonites *See* **Levites**

Gershwin, George 1898–1937. American composer. He was one of the great American composers of the 20th cent. His many popular songs contained elements of folk and jazz music. His works range from songs like *Swanee* and *Summertime* to his famous opera, *Porgy and Bess*, and his Piano Concerto in F Major.

Gerson, John (Jean de Charlier de Gerson) 1362?–1428. French theologian and church statesman. An advocate of Conciliarism (q.v.), he helped to end the Great Schism (q.v.) in the Western church at the Council of Constance (1414) with the election of a new pope, Martin V.

Gesenius, Wilhelm 1786–1842. German biblical scholar. He wrote what are considered important pioneer studies of Hebrew grammar.

Gessner, Salomon 1730–88. Swiss poet and landscape painter. He is best known for poems such as *Daphnis* and *The Death of Abel*.

Gestalt Name of a school of psychology which holds that humans perceive sights, sounds, etc., as an organized or structured whole and not as a series of individual sensations. The school had its beginnings in the experimental work of M. Wertheimer (from 1912). His work was carried forward by colleagues and students.

Gestapo Notorious Nazi secret police organization officially responsible for internal security within the Third Reich. Formed in 1933, the Gestapo had the power to arrest enemies of the state without judicial review. The Gestapo terrorized the German populace and became a primary element in A. Hitler's persecution of the Jews, sending millions of them to concentration camps where they were systematically murdered.

Gettysburg, Battle of Union victory (1863) at Gettysburg, Pennsylvania, during the American Civil War. The series of battles (July 1–3) between some 88,000 Union and 75,000 Confederate soldiers is considered the turning point of the war. Gen. R. E. Lee was forced to break off his invasion of the North (in Pennsylvania since June 17) to meet the threat of the Army of the Potomac under Gen. G. Meade. Advance elements of the two forces met accidentally just outside Gettysburg (July 1) and Union forces were pushed back to Cemetery Hill. Confederate forces did not attack again until late July 2, giving Meade time to position his army on Cemetery Ridge. Following several indecisive battles, Lee ordered a massive attack on the Union center. About 15,000 Confederates led by Gen. G. Pickett attacked Cemetery Ridge in this famous charge (July 3). The failure of this charge and the defeat of J. Stuart's cavalry marked the close of the battle. Lee began his retreat to Virginia late July 4 and Meade did not immediately order his forces to pursue. Casualties were about 23,000 Union soldiers and 20,000 Confederates.

Gettysburg Address Celebrated speech delivered by President A. Lincoln (Nov. 19, 1863) to dedicate a new national cemetery at Gettysburg, Pennsylvania. The speech was delivered just five months after the famous Battle of Gettysburg (q.v.) and begins with the famous "Four score and seven years ago our fathers brought forth on this continent a new nation, conceived in liberty . . ." and ended with the now classic characterization of the US government as a "government of the people, by the people, for the people."

Ghana (Republic of Ghana; *formerly* Gold Coast) Independent state located in western Africa on the Gulf of Guinea. Its capital is Accra. It was frequently visited (after the 15th cent.) by navigators and traders from many European coun-

tries and became a center of the slave trade. Dominated by Britain from the 19th cent. until 1960, the country has since experienced considerable political turmoil. Key events in Ghana's history include:

1482 Portuguese established first European settlement at Elmina; rich slave and gold trade soon attracted other European powers.

16TH CENT. Traders from Britain and The Netherlands arrived.

1640 Swedish traders arrived.

1821 Britain began its rule over parts of the Gold Coast.

1850–74 End of slave trade, and warfare with the Ashanti tribes, brought withdrawal of Danish and Dutch. Britain allied with the native Fanti states to defeat the Ashanti tribe (1874).

1874 British established Gold Coast as a colony, separating it from other territories it held in the region.

1896–1901 Britain again fought Ashanti tribe.

1951 Britain granted Gold Coast a new constitution.

1951 Kwame Nkrumah of the Convention People's party elected first prime minister.

1957 Ghana became independent member of the British Commonwealth.

1957 British Togoland voted to become part of Ghana.

1960 Ghana declared a republic (July 1); Nkrumah named himself president for life.

1961 Nkrumah organized Union of African States with Guinea and Mali.

1964 Opposition parties banned by referendum; Nkrumah arrested opponents.

1966 Nkrumah overthrown (Feb.) by military coup of Gen. Emmanuel Kotoka; National Liberation Council (NLC) ruled.

1967 New military coup averted, but Kotoka killed (Apr.).

1969 NLC transferred power to civilian government of Kofi Busia; new constitution established.

1972 Col. I. K. Acheampong overthrew Busia as economic problems worsened; constitution suspended, National Redemption Council (NRC) governed.

1978 Lt. Gen. Frederick Akuffo ousted Acheampong; economic problems continued.

1979 Akuffo overthrown (June 4) by Lt. Jerry Rawlings; elections promised; former leaders of government executed on charges of corruption.

1979 Return to civilian government; Hilla Limann of People's National party elected president.

1981 Limann overthrown (Dec. 31) in coup directed by Jerry Rawlings; provisional military council ruled.

Ghazali, al- 1058–1111. Islamic theologian, philosopher, and Sufi mystic. One of the greatest Islamic theologians, he did much to establish Sufism *(q.v.)* as part of Islamic orthodoxy. He opposed rationalistic philosophy that undermined orthodox doctrine and did all he could to reconcile philosophy with theology.

Ghazan, Mahmuo 1271–1304. Mongol ruler of Persia (1295–1304). Ghazan was the first Mongol ruler to convert to Islam, which he made the state religion of Persia. He extended his domains to include Syria.

Ghaznavids Turkish dynasty that ruled vast areas in modern Afghanistan, Iran, and northern India from 977 to 1186. Its most notable sultan was Mahmud (reigned 998–1030). Its first capital was Ghazni, Afghanistan, and then Lahore, India. Conquests by the Seljuk Turks (1040) brought on the decline of this empire.

Ghent ⟨Gent⟩ Belgian city (pop. 243,000), the historic capital of Flanders. It is a major port, connected to the North Sea by canals, and a commercial and manufacturing center. In existence since the 7th cent., Ghent was a center of the cloth industry and was controlled by fabric-industry guilds. It united briefly with The Netherlands (1576) in the revolt against Spanish rule. Recaptured by Spain in 1584, it remained under their control until the French Revolution. The Germans occupied it in WW I and WW II.

Ghent, Pacification of *See* **Pacification of Ghent**

Gheorghiu-Dej, Gheorghe 1901–65. Romanian statesman and Communist party leader from 1945. He served as prime minister (1952–55) and then as president of the State Council (1961–65).

Gherardesca, Ugolino della *See* **Ugolino della Gherardesca**

Ghibellines *See* **Guelphs and Ghibellines**

Ghiberti, Lorenzo c1378–1455. Florentine sculptor, a major figure in the early Renaissance. His famous bronze doors of the Baptistry of the Cathedral of Florence show his development of perspective and naturalistic forms.

Gibbon, Edward 1737–94. British historian. Gibbon's *The History of the Decline and Fall of the Roman Empire* is still considered the major historical and literary reference work dealing with that time period.

Gibraltar ⟨Rock of Gibraltar⟩ One of the ancient Pillars of Hercules, it is a British crown colony and strategic fortress at the western approach to the Mediterranean. Taken by the Moors (711), it was reconquered by the Spanish (1462). The English captured it (1704) during the War of Spanish Succession *(q.v.)* and have held it ever since. It was last besieged by a combined force of the Spanish and the French (1779–83) and was bombed but not seriously damaged in WW II. Beginning in 1966, Spain began calling upon Britain to return Gibraltar, and a UN General Assembly resolution to that effect was adopted in 1969. But a popular referendum (1967) favored continued British rule.

Gibran, Kahlil ⟨Jibran, Kahlil⟩ 1883–1931. Arab-American poet and mystic. The highly romantic Gibran, who wrote in both Arabic and English, is known for such books as *The Prophet, The Forerunner,* and *Jesus, the Son of Man.*

Gide, André 1869–1951. French writer. A controversial author, he was a cofounder of the journal *Nouvelle Revue Française* (1909). His novels include *The Immoralist* and *The Counterfeiters.* He received the Nobel Prize in Literature (1947).

Gideon Biblical hero. Gideon led the Israelites to victory over the Midianites and surpressed the idolatrous worship of Baal.

Gilbert, Sir Humphrey 1539?–83. English navigator and soldier. He reached Newfoundland (1783) on an exploratory voyage to North America and claimed it for England.

Gilbert, William 1540–1603. English scientist and physician, court physician to Queen Elizabeth I. He was first to describe the earth's magnetic field (1600), and devised the terms "electricity," "electric force," and "electric attraction." He published his studies of magnetism in *De Magnete.*

Gilbert, Sir William Schwenck 1836–1911. English playwright. He is best known for his long collaboration with Sir A. Sullivan, in which he wrote librettos for such popular operettas as *H.M.S. Pinafore, The Pirates of Penzance,* and *The Mikado.*

Gilded Age American post-Civil War historical period. Extending from approximately 1869 to 1877, this era was characterized by conspicuous materialism, dubious business and political ethics, and unbounded self-confidence. It took its name from a critical novel (1873) by Mark Twain and US man of letters Charles Dudley Warner (1829–1900).

Gilgamesh Legendary king important in Babylonian mythology who, on the death of his friend Enkidu, sought a plant that would make him immortal. The king's exploits are recounted in the *Epic of Gilgamesh.* One version was unearthed from the ruins of the library of Assyrian king Ashurbanipal, who ruled in the 7th cent. BC. This written version of the legend is thought to date from c2000 BC, and has attracted special interest because of its account of a universal flood that supposedly once engulfed mankind.

Ginsberg, Allen 1926–. American poet and leading member of the Beat movement. He is best known for his 1956 poem *Howl*.

Giolitti, Giovanni 1842–1928. Italian statesman. He was five times premier between 1892 and 1921 and universal male suffrage (1912) was among the liberal social reforms he fostered. Willing to make alliances with any group that supported his election, he provided the Fascists a firm foothold in the government (1921).

Giorgione ⟨Giorgio Barbarelli⟩ c1478–1511. Venetian painter. He was a predominant force in 16th-cent. Venetian painting. Among his works are *The Three Philosophers* and the *Tempesta*.

Giotto ⟨Giotto di Bondone⟩ 1266?–1337. Celebrated Florentine painter, sculptor, and architect. One of the greatest painters of the 14th cent., he departed from the traditional Byzantine forms to create a more powerful style of his own, foreshadowing the Renaissance. Among his many famous works are the frescoes in the Arena Chapel in Padua, including *Life of Christ*, *Life of the Virgin*, and the *Last Judgment*.

Giraud, Henri Honoré 1879–1949. French general. During WW II, he was commander (1942) of French forces during the Allied operations to secure North Africa. Following the Casablanca Conference *(q.v.)*, he became copresident (with Gen. C. de Gaulle) of the French Committee of National Liberation (1943). Differences with de Gaulle, however, forced his retirement (1944).

Girondists French political group that figured prominently in the early stages of the French Revolution *(q.v.)*. Composed of well educated, moderate republicans, the group dominated the Legislative Assembly (1791–92). The decline of the Girondists began with the overthrow of the constitutional monarchy (1792) and the formation of the revolutionary National Convention *(q.v.)*. The Convention was dominated by radical Jacobins, called Montagnards, who had the support of the working class. The Girondists' moderate policies and open opposition to the Montagnards put them in disfavor with the populace. Hostility toward Girondists culminated in the execution of many of the party's leaders, including J. Brissot de Warville and P. Vergniaud, at the outset of the Reign of Terror. (*See also* French Revolution.)

Girtin, Thomas 1775–1802. English painter. He was one of the early masters of watercolor painting and his landscapes helped establish watercolor as a distinct artistic medium.

Giscard d'Estaing, Valery 1926–. French political leader. Giscard d'Estaing served as finance minister for C. de Gaulle and G. Pompidou before becoming president (1974). He was defeated in 1981 by Socialist F. Mitterand.

Giuliano, Pedro *See* **John XXI**

Giza, Pyramids of Egyptian pyramids. These three Pyramids *(q.v.)*, built c2613–c2500 BC, are located near the city of Giza on the western banks of the Nile. They are included among the ancient Seven Wonders of the World *(q.v.)*. Khufu built the oldest (and largest, over 480 feet high), Khafre the second (over 470 feet high), and Menkaure the third (over 355 feet high).

Gizycka, Eleanor M. *See* **Patterson, Eleanor Medill**

gladiators Professional fighters of ancient Rome who were pitted against one another (or wild animals) in armed combat, often to the death. Gladiators provided a popular form of entertainment in the Roman world from about 264 BC to about AD 405 and fights were performed in arenas before large crowds. Gladiators took part in the Servile Wars *(q.v.)*.

Gladstone, William Ewart 1809–98. One of the greatest British statesman of his century and prime minister (1868–74, 1880–85, 1886, 1892–94). The son of a Liverpool merchant, he entered Parliament (1833) as a Conservative. He held a number of government posts as a Conservative before changing his affiliation and becoming Liberal party leader (1867). He was embroiled in controversies in subsequent years, including attacks on the Disraeli government for complacence in the Belgian Horrors, the failure of his own government to relieve Gen. C. Gordon at Khartoum, and the Irish Home Rule question. His many accomplishments included civil service reform, an end to paid military commissions, institution of the secret ballot, a system of national public education, and Irish land reforms.

Glass, Carter 1858–1946. American politician, US congressman (1902–18), US secretary of treasury (1918–20), and US senator (1920–46). A framer of legislation creating the Federal Reserve System (1913), he was an outspoken opponent of President F. Roosevelt's New Deal.

Glencoe, Massacre of *See* **Massacre of Glencoe**

Glenn, John Herschel, Jr. 1921–. American astronaut in the Project Mercury program. He was the first American to orbit the earth (Feb. 20, 1962), aboard the spacecraft *Friendship 7*.

Glidden, Carlos *See* **Sholes, Christopher Latham**

Glinka, Mikhail Ivanovich 1804–57. Russian composer. He is considered the founder of Russia's nationalist school of composers. He is known best for his opera *A Life for the Czar*.

Globe Theatre London theater where, after 1599, W. Shakespeare's plays were performed. Built by the actor Richard Burbage (1567?–1619) and others, it was octagonal in shape. It was rebuilt after a fire (1613) and demolished by the Puritans (1644).

Glorious Revolution ⟨Bloodless Revolution⟩ In English history the period (1688–89) that saw the overthrow of King James II, the crowning of William of Orange and his wife Mary II, and the final recognition of parliamentary supremacy. James II's Catholicism and the birth (1685) of his Catholic son and heir, James Edward, aroused a united Whig and Tory opposition to his rule. Seven of its leaders offered the English throne to the Dutch prince William and his wife Mary, James II's Protestant daughter. William landed at Torbay in England (Nov. 5, 1688) with some 14,000 men and James fled to France (Dec. 22) after his armies deserted him. The throne was offered to William and Mary under conditions set forth in the British Bill of Rights (1689). These conditions, which assured parliamentary supremacy, were accepted and the two were crowned as joint rulers (1689).

Gloucester, Gilbert de Clare, 8th earl of *See* **Clare, Gilbert de, 8th earl of Gloucester**

Gloucester, Gilbert de Clare, 9th earl of *See* **Clare, Gilbert de, 9th earl of Gloucester.**

Gloucester, Humphrey, duke of 1391–1447. English nobleman, youngest son of Henry IV. Noted as a patron of the Humanists, he was arrested (1447) after a long struggle for power with H. Beaufort, and died a few days later.

Gloucester, Richard de Clare, 7th earl of *See* **Clare, Richard de, 7th earl of Gloucester**

Gloucester, Robert earl of *d.* 1147. English nobleman and illegitimate son of Henry I. Made earl by his father (1122), he supported Matilda in her fight against Stephen to succeed Henry I.

Gloucester, Thomas of Woodstock, duke of 1355–97. English nobleman. A son of Edward III, Gloucester took control (1386) of Richard II's government. Richard asserted his authority (1389). Richard later placed Gloucester under charge of Thomas Mowbray (1366?–99), who was suspected of Gloucester's murder.

Gluck, Christoph Willibald 1714–87. German-born opera composer. He broke with the dominant Italian opera style to create operas in which words and music worked together for dramatic effect. He employed this radical new approach in such operas as *Orfeo ed Euridice* and *Iphigénie en Aulide.*

Gneisenau, August, Graf Neithardt von 1760–1831. Prussian general. The chief strategist during Prussia's war of liberation from Napoleonic France (1813–15), he played an important role in the battles at Leipzig (1813) and Waterloo.

Gneist, Rudolf von 1816–95. German jurist and politician. He was a member of the Prussian Diet (1858–93) and the German Reichstag (1867–84).

Gnosticism Religious movement, important in the early history of Christianity, which promised personal salvation through revelation of mystical knowledge. Gnosticism fused elements of many religious, philosophical, and mythical systems of the ancient world and, though the many Gnostic sects varied widely in their beliefs, they generally believed in a world-creator, religious dualism, and Docetism. Gnostic sects had incorporated many Christian ideas by the 1st cent. AD and flourished in the 2d cent. AD. Gnosticism came to be regarded as a heresy by the Christian church and by the 6th cent. most Gnostic sects had disappeared. Major Gnostic sects included those formed by Valentinus (*fl.* AD *c*135) and Basilides (*d.* AD *c*140). Important texts of the Mandaean and Coptic Gnostics were found in Egypt in the mid-20th cent.

Gobelins *See* **Le Brun, Charles**

Gobineau, Joseph Arthur, count of 1816–82. French diplomat and writer. He was an early advocate of the racial supremacy of the Aryans. His *Essay on the Inequality of Human Races* is thought to have influenced both F. Nietzsche and A. Hitler.

God Supreme being of the Christian, Judaic, and Islamic religions. In each, he is creator and ruler of the world, infinite and eternal, transcendent over the material world and immanent in it, all-seeing and all-knowing, and benevolent and supremely good. By the Old Testament, knowledge of God arose among the Hebrews, first as a tribal god and then as ruler of the world. Knowledge of God as the supreme being (and special protector of the faithful) was then adopted by Christians, and later by Muslims. In the history of the Christian church, there have been a number of important arguments for the existence of God, including: God as the first cause in a world of progressive causes and effects (cosmological argument); God as the planner in a world that operates by a grand design (teleological argument); God as the most perfect human conception, which must therefore exist, since existence is part of that perfection (ontological argument).

Goddard, Robert Hutchings 1882–1945. American physicist, sometimes called the father of modern rocketry. Goddard designed and built early high-altitude rockets, the first liquid-fuel rockets, and guidance devices.

Gödel, Kurt 1906–. Czech-American mathematician. He formulated an important theorem (1931), which states that a mathematical system can give rise to propositions that cannot be proved by the system.

Godfrey of Bouillon 1061?–1100. French crusader. A leader of the First Crusade, he became the first Latin ruler of Palestine after the fall of Jerusalem and the battle of Ascalon (1099).

Godfrey of Strasbourg *See* **Gottfried von Strassburg**

Godiva, Lady *fl.* c1040–80. Englishwoman renowned for her legendary ride through Coventry. She is said to have ridden naked through the town on a white horse in order to convince her husband, Earl Leofric, to lower an unfair tax. The story of Peeping Tom is generally regarded as a later (17th cent.) addition to the legend.

Godoy, Manuel de 1767–1851. Spanish statesman. He was twice prime minister (1792–97, 1801–08). His policies proved disastrous for Spain. The decisive defeat of the Spanish navy at Trafalgar (1805) and the furor aroused by the Treaty of Fontainebleau (1807) finally led King Charles IV to abdicate (1808).

Godwin (Godwine) *d.* 1053. English nobleman, earl of Wessex. He helped Edward the Confessor gain the throne (1042) but was later exiled by him in a dispute (1051). Godwin launched a successful invasion of England (1052), forcing Edward to restore his lands.

Godwine *See* **Godwin**

Goebbels, Paul Joseph 1897–1945. German propaganda minister in A. Hitler's Third Reich. A loyal ally to Hitler from 1926, Goebbels was instrumental in his rise to power. As propaganda minister (1933–45), he skillfully manipulated the mass media to maintain Hitler's power and to forward the planned extermination of millions of Jews.

Goering, Hermann Wilhelm *See* **Göring, Hermann Wilhelm**

Goethals, George Washington 1858–1928. American army engineer who, as chief engineer (1907–14), supervised the completion of the Panama Canal.

Goethe, Johann Wolfgang von 1749–1832. German poet, dramatist, novelist, and scientist, and one of the great figures in Western literature. A genius of great breadth, he wrote treatises on botany, biology, and physics. But it was in the field of literature that he attained his greatest fame. Early influenced by the Sturm und Drang movement, he gained his early fame (1773) with a play, *Götz von Berlichingen* and the novel *The Sorrows of Young Werther.* From 1775 he held offices in the court of Saxe-Weimar, where he met Charlotte von Stein. One of the many women with whom he was romantically involved, she became the inspiration for many of his poems. He maintained an active friendship with F. Schiller. Goethe completed two of his most famous works, *Wilhelm Meisters Lehrjahre* and *Faust,* in his later years.

Gog Biblical warlike ruler. Magog is sometimes identified as Gog's ally or as the name of his kingdom. Gog and Magog together are also used to represent the future enemies of the kingdom of God.

Gogh, Vincent van 1853–1890. Dutch painter, one of the greatest. A postimpressionist, he greatly influenced expressionism. After failures in both life and love, he took up painting (1880). He painted in The Netherlands until 1886, then lived in Paris with his beloved brother Theo until 1888. In that year he took a house at Arles and there developed his characteristic style. At Arles and after a fight with P. Gauguin, he suffered (1889) the first of what became continuing fits of insanity and cut off his ear. He was committed to the asylum at St.-Rémy (1889–90) and then lived outside Paris for three months before his suicide. Among his many famous works are *The Potato Eaters, Sunflowers, The Chair and Pipe, Starry Night,* and *Crows Over the Wheat Fields,* his last.

Gogol, Nikolai Vasilievich 1809–52. Russian novelist, short-story writer, and dramatist. Considered the founder of realism in Russian literature, he is known best for his novel *Dead Souls.*

Gogunda, Battle of (Haldishat, Battle of) Battle (June, 1576) fought in Rajasthan, northwestern India, between the army of Mogul emperor Akbar and the much smaller army of Rajput leader Pratap Singh of Mewar. The Moguls defeated the Rajputs, but the latter continued their gallant resistance for decades.

Gold Coast *See* **Ghana**

Golden Age Historical term given by the ancient Greeks and Romans to the earliest period of the world, during which mankind was peaceful and innocent and warfare nonexistent.

Golden Bull Royal edict, deriving its name from the Latin *bulla aurea* and bearing a gold seal. It was frequently used by Byzantine and Holy Roman Emperors. Notable Golden Bulls included that of 1222, issued by Hungarian king Andrew II to establish the rights of nobles and powers of the monarchy; and the Golden Bull of 1356, issued by Holy Roman Emperor Charles IV, stating the powers of the electors and the process through which emperors were to be elected.

Golden Bull of Rimini Edict (1226) by which Holy Roman Emperor Frederick II granted sovereignty over Prussia to the Teutonic Knights. He incorporated the Knights into his plans and reorganized them into agents of both Christianity and German culture.

Golden Bull of 1356   Document important in the history of the Holy Roman Empire. Issued by Emperor Charles V, it reformed procedures for electing the emperor (to a majority of seven electors), eliminated involvement of the papacy in selecting the emperor, and formally acknowledged the relatively independent status of princely states within the empire. This framework remained relatively unchanged until the empire was dissolved in 1806.

Golden Circle, Knights of the   *See* **Knights of the Golden Circle**

Golden Fleece   In Greek mythology the gold fleece of the winged ram Chrysomallus. It was kept by King Aeëtes in Colchis and guarded by a dragon. The fleece was sought and finally taken by Jason and the Argonauts.

Golden Fleece, Order of the   *See* **Order of the Golden Fleece**

Golden Horde ⟨Kipchak Khanate⟩   Mongol khanate formed by Batu Khan, a grandson of Genghis Khan and conqueror of the western Russian territories it embraced. Formed in the mid-13th cent., it included Kiev, Moscow, and Novgorod. Russian rulers were kept in power as vassals and were forced to pay heavy taxes to the khans. The khans adopted the Muslim religion and remained in power until 1395, when Tamerlane conquered the region. The empire subsequently broke up into the khanates of Crimea, Kazan, and Astrakhan.

Golden House   Roman palace. After the fire of AD 64, Nero seized many acres of land in Rome to build this magnificent palace, which included an artificial lake within its walls. Little of it remains today.

Golden Spurs, Battle of the ⟨Courtrai, Battle of⟩ ⟨Kortruk, Battle of⟩   Flemish-French battle (July 11, 1302) near Courtrai, Belgium, in which untrained Flemish townsmen defeated the professional soldiers of French king Philip the Fair. The craftsmen were opposing the French annexation of Flanders (1301). The battle was so named because after the fighting the field was littered with the gilt spurs of the French.

Goldfish, Samuel   *See* **Goldwyn, Samuel**

Goldman, Emma   1869–1940.   Notorious Russian-American anarchist. She became associated with the anarchist movement shortly after her arrival in the US (1886) and was arrested in New York City (1893) for inciting a riot. She and fellow anarchist Alexander Berkman (1870–1936) were deported to Russia (1919) for obstructing the draft.

Goldmann, Max   *See* **Reinhardt, Max**

gold rush   Term applied to the waves of prospectors and others who travel to a new region upon discovery of gold. Notable gold rushes occurred in California (1849), Australia (1850s), South Africa (1884), and the Klondike (1897–98).

Goldsmith, Oliver   1728–74.   British playwright, poet, and novelist. He is known best for his play *She Stoops to Conquer* and his novel *The Vicar of Wakefield*.

Goldwyn, Samuel ⟨Goldfish, Samuel⟩ 1882–1974.   Polish-American film producer. With C. De Mille he produced his first film (1913), *Squaw Man*, and later formed a production company that became part of Metro-Goldwyn-Mayer (1925). He went on to produce many major motion pictures, including *All Quiet on the Western Front*.

Goliad Massacre   Massacre (Mar. 27, 1836) at Goliad, Texas, of some 350 Texan fighters during the Texan war for independence (1836). The force, under Col. James W. Fannin (1804?–36), had surrendered as prisoners of war, but were executed by order of Gen. A. de Santa Anna. The massacre served to further inflame the Texan spirit for independence.

Goliath   Biblical giant, a Philistine. He challenged the Israelites to send their champion against him settle their war. David killed him with his slingshot.

Gombos, Julius   1886–1936.   Hungarian premier (1932–36) who promoted fascism in Hungary.

Gomez Castro, Laureano Eleuterio   1889–1965. Colombian politician. Earlier exiled for supporting A. Hitler and F. Franco, as president (1950–51) he declared martial law, suspended parliament, and was deposed.

Gómez, Juan Vicente   1857?–1935.   Venezuelan dictator (1908–35), successor to C. Castro. He was noted for stimulating a period of economic growth and for the ruthless tactics he used to maintain power.

Gomorrah ⟨Gomorrha⟩   In the Bible, one of the five cities of the plain (with Sodom, Admah, Zeboiim, and Zoar). Both Sodom and Gomorrah were destroyed because of their legendary wickedness.

Gomorrha   *See* **Gomorrah**

Gompers, Samuel   1850–1924.   British-born American labor leader. One of the leading figures of the labor movement in his day, he was a founder and president (1886–1924, except 1895) of the American Federation of Labor.

Gomulka, Wladyslaw   *See* **Poland (1956)**

Goncalves Dias, Antonio   1823–1864.   Brazilian poet, considered the national poet of Brazil. Of mixed racial origin, he glorified Indians and the "common people."

Goncourt, Edmond Louis Antoine and Jules Alfred, Huot de 1822–96, 1830–70. French authors and brothers who were famous for their collaboration on such novels as *Renée Mauperin, Germinie Lacerteux,* and *Madame Gervaisais.* Edmond's will established the Goncourt Academy, which awards the Goncourt Prize for fiction.

Góngora y Argote, Luis de 1561–1627. Spanish poet. His elegant style attracted a following of imitators. Their florid attempts at recreating his style became a movement called Gongorism.

Gonzaga Family of Italian noblemen which ruled Mantua and surrounding territories from 1328 to 1708. Established by Luigi Gonzaga (1267–1360), the family ruled as dukes after 1530. The direct line of succession ended in 1627 and competing claims to the dukedom resulted in the War of Mantuan Succession (1628–31). Following the death (1708) of the last of the Gonzaga line, Carlo IV, the duchy was divided and absorbed by Austria and Savoy.

Gonzaga, Luigi. *See* **Gonzaga**

Good Emperors, the Name given to the Roman emperors who reigned during the years AD 96–169. They were Nerva, Trajan, Hadrian, Antoninus Pius, Marcus Aurelius, and Lucius Aurelius Verus

Goodman, Benny ⟨Goodman, Benjamin David⟩ 1909–. American bandleader and clarinetist, celebrated as the "King of Swing." He formed his orchestra in 1934 and made it one of the most popular of the groups playing swing music.

Good Neighbor Policy US policy for improved relations with Latin America, developed during Pres. F. Roosevelt's administration. It ended the policy of US military intervention and established greater economic cooperation and mutual defense agreements.

Good Parliament English Parliament (1376), which attempted to reform the political abuses of Edward III and John of Gaunt. Its reforms were nullified by the Parliament of 1377.

Good Thief ⟨Penitent Thief⟩ Biblical thief. While being crucified with Jesus, he accepted Jesus. For this, Jesus promised him a place in heaven. He is known in the Catholic Church as St. Dismas.

Goodyear, Charles 1800–60. American inventor. He discovered the process for vulcanizing rubber (1839) but failed to capitalize on it and died in debt.

Gorboduc Legendary English king. He is said to have divided his kingdom between his sons, Ferrex and Porrex. The sons, however, made war on each other and were both killed. *Gorboduc* is the name of the first English play in blank verse

(1561), written by T. Sackville and Thomas Norton (1532–84).

Gorchakov, Aleksandr Mikhailovich, Prince 1798–1883. Russian statesman and diplomat. As foreign minister (1856–78) he nullified terms of the Treaty of Paris (1871), imposed after the Crimean War, and was unable to prevent the Russo-Turkish War (1877–78).

Gordian I AD 158–238. Roman co-emperor with his son, Gordian II, for three weeks. He and his son succeeded the tryannical Maximinus. Gordian killed himself on learning of the death of his son in battle.

Gordian II AD 192–238. Roman co-emperor with his father, Gordian I. He was slain in battle after ruling only three weeks.

Gordian III ⟨Gordianus Pius⟩ AD *c*224–44. Roman emperor (238–44). He succeeded co-emperors Balbinus and Pupienus, who were assassinated shortly after replacing his uncle, Gordian II and grandfather Gordian I. He attacked the Persians (242) but was later assassinated by his soldiers.

Gordian knot A famous knot which Alexander the Great is said to have cut with a single stroke of his sword. The knot, of great complexity, fastened a yoke to a cart in Gordium, the capital of Phrygia. When he arrived in the city, Alexander was told that whoever untied the knot would rule Asia, whereupon he cut it with his sword. This gave rise to the expression "to cut the Gordian knot."

Gordianus Pius *See* **Gordian III**

Gordius Mythical Greek king of Phrygia and founder of Gordium. The Phrygians were told by an oracle that their new king would arrive in an oxcart and when the peasant Gordius arrived in his cart, he was made king. Gordius then fastened the yoke to his cart with a knot of great complexity, called the Gordian Knot.

Gordon, Charles George 1833–85. British soldier and colonial administrator. He became famous as a military commander in China during the Taiping Rebellion (1860–65) and gained further honors in pacifying the Sudan (1873–80). In 1874 he was sent back to the Sudan and was killed in the Battle of Khartoum.

Gordon, John Brown 1832–1904. American politician and Confederate general in the American Civil War. He served with distinction during the war, then became US senator from Georgia (1873–80, 1891–97) and governor of Georgia (1886–90).

Gordon Riots ⟨No Popery Riots⟩ Mass anti-Catholic riots in London, England (1780). The riots began after a crowd said to number 50,000 persons was led by Lord George Gordon (1751–93) to the

House of Commons to demand repeal of the Catholic Relief Act of 1778. There followed a week of destructive riots in which the London prisons were forced open. Catholic churches were burned, and some 400–800 persons were killed or injured. Though a number of rioters were executed, Gordon was acquitted.

Gorges, Sir Ferdinando c1566–1647. English promoter of colonies in North America and proprietor of Maine. Though he never set foot in America, he was involved in many unsuccessful schemes to promote colonization. He eventually received a royal charter to Maine, which his grandson sold for £1,250.

Gorgons Mythical Greek monsters, traditionally three sisters named Medusa, Stheno, and Euryale. They were so ugly that anyone who looked at them was turned to stone. Medusa was slain by Perseus.

Göring, Hermann Wilhelm ⟨Goering, ~⟩ 1893–1946. German military and political leader, one of Hitler's chief lieutenants. A hero of the WW I air war, he joined Hitler in the Munich Putsch (1923), and became president of the Reichstag (1932). When Hitler came to power (1933) he was involved in the Reichstag Fire, was made prime minister and air minister, set up the Gestapo and concentration camps, and in the late 1930s mobilized Germany for war. He was designated Hitler's successor until 1943, when his Luftwaffe proved unable to prevent Allied air attacks on Germany. Tried for war crimes at Nuremberg (1945–46), he committed suicide just before his scheduled execution.

Goshen In the Bible, a fertile region located in Lower Egypt, occupied by the Israelites. Its location has not been identified in modern times.

Got, Bertrand de *See* **Clement V**

Gotham Originally, a village in England. To avoid the expense of an impending visit by King John, the townspeople made themselves appear as complete fools and thus put off the royal party. The name has since been applied to New York City.

Gothic Medieval artistic and architectural style in Europe from the 12th–15th cents. Originating in France, it supplanted the Romanesque style. Gothic art was flowing, mystical, individualistic, and tended toward the naturalistic. Architecture (and allied decorative arts) dominated the movement. Gothic architecture was characterized by height, high vaulted ceilings, tracery between large (often stained glass) windows, and flying buttresses. There was increasing emphasis on decorative detail toward the end of the movement. The most famous example of Gothic architecture is the cathedral of Notre Dame in France. The Gothic styles gave way to the Renaissance forms.

Gothic revival American and British architectural movement of the 19th cent. It revived elements of the Gothic style of architecture.

Goths Germanic tribes. An ancient Teutonic peoples, they included the Ostrogoths and the Visigoths (q.q.v.). The Ostrogoths established an empire in the region of the Ukraine. After the fall of their empire (AD c370) to the Huns, they joined the Huns in conquest. After the Huns were forced back, the Ostrogoths, when they traveled westward, invaded Italy and overthrew Odoacer (493). The Visigoths moved into the Roman Empire (4th cent. AD), sacked Rome (410), then turned westward to Gaul and Spain. In Gaul they were defeated by the Frankish king Clovis (507) and were defeated in Spain (711) by Muslim invaders from North Africa.

Gottfried von Strassburg ⟨Godfrey of Strasbourg⟩ *fl.* 13th cent. German poet. Considered one of the most important poets of medieval Germany, he wrote a famous version of *Tristan und Isolde.*

Gould, George Jay 1864–1923. American railroad magnate, son of J. Gould. He inherited his father's railroading interests (1892), but lost them following the panic of 1907.

Gould, Jay 1836–92. American financier and railroad magnate. A ruthless businessman, he was involved with J. Fisk and D. Drew in their scheme to corner the gold market. Following the Black Friday panic (1869) that resulted from the scheme, he bought up railroads and became a major operator in the Southwest.

Government of India acts British laws passed by Parliament (1773–1935) to govern India. The first acts (1773–1830), also known as the East India Company Acts, regulated the British East India Company. Later acts transferred (1858) power to the crown, and finally paved the way for Indian self-government.

Government of National Defense Interim French government established (Sept., 1870) during the Franco-Prussian War, following the defeat of Napoleon III at Sedan (q.v.) and subsequent overthrow of his government. This government continued the futile war until Jan. 28, 1871, when it surrendered. Following the peace settlement, the uprising of the Paris Commune (q.v.), and attempts at restoring the monarchy, the French Third Republic was formally established by adoption of the Constitution of 1875.

Gower, John d. 1408. English poet. Friend and contemporary of Chaucer, he was considered, with Chaucer, a leading poet in his day. His works include *Confessio Amantis*, a collection of tales.

Gowon, Yakubu 1934–. Nigerian general. Made head of the military government following two 1966 coups, he defeated the secessionist Biafrans and reunited the country (1970), but was deposed in 1975.

Goya y Lucientes, Francisco José de 1746–1828. Spanish artist, considered one of the greatest painters of his century. He began as a designer of royal tapestries and by 1786 was court painter to Spanish king Charles III. Thereafter he enjoyed widespread fame and the favor of the rulers of Spain, and painted portraits of many Spanish notables. After an illness left him deaf in 1793, he also began to do satirical and sardonic works on social evils, including *The Caprices* and *The Disasters of War*. Late in his life he produced such macabre scenes as *Saturn Devouring His Children* and a series of lithographs that included several famous bullfight scenes.

Gozzi, Carlo, Count 1720–1806. Italian dramatist. He is remembered as the author of dramatic "fairy tales" that provided the basis for later works by J. Goethe, F. Schiller, and others.

GPU Soviet secret police. Established (Feb., 1922) to replace the Cheka, it ruthlessly quelled all opposition to government policy. It was renamed OGPU in 1923 and in 1934 its functions passed to the NKVD (1934–46). After that, secret police activities successively passed to the MGB (1946–53), the MVD (1953–54), and finally the KGB (*q.v.*).

Gracchus, Caius Sempronius d. 121 BC. Roman tribune (123, 122 BC). Elected tribune on the death of his brother, Tiberius Gracchus, he continued the agrarian reforms begun by his brother. The reforms aroused opposition among the aristocrats and he was killed following his defeat for a third term as tribune.

Gracchus, Tiberius Sempronius d. 133 BC. Roman tribune (133 BC). As tribune he formulated the Sempronian Law, designed to eliminate the widespread poverty of Romans by redistributing public lands to them. Subsequent opposition to his plan in the Senate resulted in a riot in which he was killed.

Graces Greek goddesses of beauty and charm, traditionally three in number. The daughters of Zeus and Eurynome, they were Aglaia (brightness), Euphrosyne (joy), and Thalia (bloom).

Graefe, Albrecht von *See* **Gräfe, Albrecht von**

Gräfe, Albrecht von 1828–70. German ophthalmologist, sometimes called the founder of modern ophthalmology. He developed new treatments for glaucoma (1857) and cataracts (1867).

Graham, Billy ⟨Graham, William Franklin⟩ 1918–. American evangelist. A widely known preacher, he has organized highly successful revivalist crusades in the US and abroad since 1949.

Graham, Martha 1893–. American dancer, choreographer, and teacher who greatly influenced modern dance. Among her highly individualistic works are *Deaths and Entrances*, *Appalachian Spring*, and *Phaedre*.

Graham, William Franklin *See* **Graham, Billy**

Grail, Holy *See* **Holy Grail**

Granada, Kingdom of Once located in southern Spain, this kingdom was part of domains held by the Muslims during medieval times. By 1238, Spanish Christians had conquered most of the Muslim territories and the Kingdom of Granada was the last remaining Muslim stronghold on the Iberian peninsula. Spanish King Ferdinand finally conquered Granada in 1492 and added these lands to his domains.

Gran Colombia *See* **Great Colombia**

Grand Alliance *See* **Grand Alliance, War of the**

Grand Alliance, War of the ⟨League of Augsburg, War of the⟩ War (1688–97) between France and an alliance of European states. Holy Roman Emperor Leopold I, concerned about the expansionist aims of French king Louis XIV, formed the League of Augsburg (July 9, 1686) with the Palatinate, Bavaria, Saxony, Spain, Sweden, and later, Savoy (1687). While Leopold was embroiled in war against the Turks in the East, however, Louis invaded (Oct., 1688) and ravaged the Palatinate. Leopold responded by forming (May 12, 1689) the Grand Alliance against France, with members of the original league, England's King William III, and the United Provinces (The Netherlands). The war that followed, though centered in the United Provinces, resulted in largely indecisive fighting elsewhere in Europe, in colonial possessions of the belligerents (the American phase was King William's War [*q.v.*]), and on the high seas. In 1690, the French were victorious at the Battle of Fleurus (*q.v.*) and in actions in Savoy, but an invasion of Ireland ended in failure. In 1692, the English (with the allied Dutch) navy routed (May 19–23), a French fleet in the Battle of La Hogue, which proved to be the decisive naval battle of the war and which established lasting English naval supremacy over France. Soon after, however, the French were victorious at the Siege of Namur (*q.v.*) and the Battle of Steenkirk (July 24), in which the English, under William III, were routed. In 1693, the French were victorious at Neerwinden (July 29) and at Marsaglia (Oct. 4), near the Po River in Savoy. The death (1695) of the leading French commander, Marshal F. Luxembourg, and the strain of the protracted war on all parties, led to negotiated peace (Sept. 30, 1697) by the Treaty of Ryswick *(q.v.)*.

Grand Army   Name given the combined French armies (1805–12) under Napoleon. Its great size, excellent training, and organization made Napoleon master of Europe. It was virtually destroyed (1812) during Napoleon's retreat from Russia.

Grand Army of the Republic ⟨GAR⟩   Organization of US Civil War veterans who had served in the Union army or navy. Founded by J. Logan, Richard J. Oglesby (1824–99), and others (1866), the group held its first national encampment at Indianapolis, Indiana, later that year. The group, dedicated to promoting fraternal ties, passage of legislation for veterans' benefits, and service to needy veterans, reached its greatest membership of 400,000 by 1890. It was until 1900 a powerful political bloc within the Republican party, after which time its membership and influence rapidly dwindled. The group's last national encampment was held in 1949 and the organization was dissolved in 1956.

Grand Canal   Canal in China. Begun in the 6th cent. BC and completed 2,000 years later, it is the world's longest canal, extending over 1,000 miles from Peking to Hangchow.

grandee   Spanish honorary title, dating to the 13th cent. A title held by the highest rank of Spanish nobility, it conferred such privileges as the right to wear headgear in the presence of the king.

grandfather clause   Constitutional clause instituted around the turn of the 20th cent. by Southern states to circumvent the 15th Amendment to the Constitution, guaranteeing suffrage to newly freed blacks. The clause limited voting privileges to those who could vote as of Jan. 1, 1867, and their descendants, thus effectively disenfranchising blacks, who did not have the vote in 1867. The clause was declared unconstitutional in 1915.

Grand Rebel   *See* **Sivaji**

Grand Remonstrance   In English history, a list of grievances presented by the Long Parliament (Dec. 1, 1641) to King Charles I. Charles did not accept them and, in Jan., 1642, he unsuccessfully attempted to arrest leaders of the opposition in the Commons. The Remonstrance widened the rift between king and Parliament and hastened the coming of the English civil war.

Granger movement   US agrarian movement of the 19th cent., an outgrowth of a farmers' organization called the National Grange of the Patrons of Husbandry (founded 1867). Grangers sought to redress farmers' economic grievances through cooperative ventures and political pressure on state legislatures. By the time the movement began to decline (after 1876), they had established many farmers' cooperatives and won passage of Granger laws in Midwest farm states. The laws, designed to control railroads and their shipping rates, led to the famous Granger case, *Munn* vs *Illinois* (1876).

Granicus, Battle of the   Battle (334 BC) at the Granicus River, now in Turkey. There Alexander the Great won his first major victory against the Persian emperor Darius III.

Grant, Ulysses Simpson   1822–85. Commander in chief of Union armies (1863–65) during the American Civil War and 18th president of the US (1869–77), succeeding A. Johnson. He became a colonel in the Illinois volunteers (1861) at the outbreak of the Civil War and soon distinguished himself in battle. He won increasingly important commands, broke Confederate control of the Mississippi, and cut the Confederacy in half by his victory at Vicksburg (1863). Soon afterward he was named commander in chief and, by his war of attrition, forced R. E. Lee's surrender at Appomattox (1865). Joining the Radical Republicans *(q.v.)*, Grant won the presidential election of 1868 easily and was elected to a second term in 1872. He was a popular and personally honest president, but his term of office was marked by the turmoil of Reconstruction *(q.v.)* and by the many scandals of the Gilded Age, notably the Crédit Mobilier scandal *(q.v.)*, the Whiskey Ring *(q.v.)*, and the Black Friday *(q.v.)* financial panic.

Granvelle, Antoine Perrenot de   1517–86. Frenchman in the service of King Philip II of Spain. As prime minister in The Netherlands (c1560–64), he aroused hostility to the Spanish rule there by persecuting Protestants. He relinquished his post on the advice of the king.

Granville, John Carteret, 1st Earl   1690–1763. English statesman. A member of the House of Lords (1730–42), he led the opposition against R. Walpole and finally secured his ouster (1742). As chief minister (1742–44) he himself fell from favor after supporting Maria Theresa in the War of the Austrian Succession.

Grass, Günter   1927–. German writer. He is known best for his first novel, *The Tin Drum*, a milestone in the development of post-WW II German literature.

Grasse, François Joseph Paul, comte de   1722–88. French admiral. Commanding French fleet sent to aid Colonial forces during the American Revolution, he succeeded in trapping Gen. Cornwallis at Yorktown and contributed to the American victory in the Yorktown Campaign.

Gratian ⟨Flavius Gratian⟩ AD 359–383. Roman emperor of the West (AD 375–383) with his brother Valentinian II. With Saint Ambrose as his adviser, he made himself unpopular by persecuting pagans. He was defeated by the usurper Maximus and was put to death.

Gratian *fl.* 1140. Italian monk and scholar, regarded as the founder of the science of canon law. He compiled the great collection of canon law, the *Decretum Gratiani.*

Grattan, Henry 1746–1820. Irish statesman and leader in the fight for Ireland's independence from England. He won legislative independence for Ireland's parliament (1782), fought for Catholic Emancipation, and eloquently opposed the Act of Union that joined England and Ireland (1801).

Gravelines, Battle of Spanish victory (July 13, 1558) over the French, the deciding battle in the dynastic wars known as the Valois-Hapsburg Wars. Some 2,000 French troops were killed. The battle led to the Treaty of Cateau-Cambrésis (1559).

Graves, Robert Ranke 1895–. English poet and novelist. He has published collections of his poetry, novels such as *I, Claudius,* and critical works.

Gray, Thomas 1716–71. One of the great English poets of his century and author of *Elegy Written in a Country Churchyard.*

Gray Eminence *See* **Joseph, Father**

Grayson, David *See* **Baker, Ray Stannard**

Great Awakening Religious revival movement in the American colonies *c*1720–60. The American counterpart of the European quietism and Pietism movements, this evangelical movement largely affected the Calvinist sects. Revivalist preachers such as J. Edwards and G. Whitefield gained many converts by mid-century and their teachings led to splits in the established congregations between factions known as "old lights" and "new lights."

Great Bright One, the *See* **Fu Hsi**

Great Colombia ⟨Gran Colombia⟩ Former South American republic. Established (1822) by S. Bolívar, it consisted of parts of modern Colombia, Panama, Venezuela, and Ecuador. It lasted until 1830, when Venezuela and Ecuador established their independence.

Great Britain ⟨United Kingdom of Great Britain and Northern Ireland⟩ Kingdom located in western Europe. It includes England, Scotland, Wales, and Northern Ireland. The rise of Britain as a modern state dates from the Norman Conquest (1066), and by the late 16th cent. Britain had become a major European power. From the 17th cent. to 19th cent., it acquired a vast colonial empire, gave birth to the Industrial Revolution, and became the world's leading military and commercial power. Though Britain maintained its preeminence in the early 20th cent., competition from other industrialized nations (US, Germany, Japan), the breakup of its worldwide colonial empire, and the two world wars brought an end to its dominance as a world power. Britain played a crucial role in the Allied victories during World War I and World War II. In the years after 1945, Britain divested itself of almost all of its remaining colonial territories. (*See also* Scotland, Wales, colonialism.) Key events in Britain's history include:

5TH CENT. BC Celts invaded British Isles.

55–54 BC J. Caesar led Roman military expeditions to British Isles, which he called Britannia.

AD 43–84 Roman conquest of Britain; Caractus led revolt against Roman invaders (43–50); Queen Boadicea led another unsuccessful revolt; Roman soldier Agricola conquered north part of England (from AD 78).

AD c120–136 Hadrian's Wall built across Britain to protect flourishing Roman towns from attacks by tribes from the north (Scotland).

AD 410 Romans completed their withdrawal from British Isles; troops needed elsewhere to defend empire against barbarian attacks.

5TH CENT. AD Celtic culture flourished after the Roman withdrawal; attacks by Picts from north resisted; invasions by Saxons, Angles, and Jutes (Germanic tribes from the Continent) forced Celtic inhabitants westward into what is now Wales.

6TH–8TH CENTS. Rise of the Anglo-Saxon Heptarchy, group of seven small kingdoms formed by invading Anglo-Saxons; included Northumbria, Mercia, Wessex, Essex, Kent, Sussex, and East Anglia; Northumbria (founded *c*547) and Mercia (founded *c*582) chief among them. Period marked by frequent wars between the rival kingdoms.

597 Saint Augustine began Christianization of England; soon after his arrival converted Ethelbert, king of Kent; Ethelbert became first Christian Anglo-Saxon ruler in England.

664 Synod of Whitby; called to decide between Celtic Christianity, then on the rise, and Roman Christianity; decision favored Roman Christianity and thus fostered ties with Christians on the Continent.

787 First raids by the Danes.

802–839 Egbert became king of Wessex; ended supremacy of Mercia by his decisive victory in 825; accepted as king by other kingdoms in the Anglo-Saxon Heptarchy, he was the first to unify what later became modern England.

856–878 Danes launched major invasions of England.

871–899 Alfred the Great became king of Wessex; led resistance against invading Danes; revived learning; issued code of laws and consolidated his powers.

878 Alfred defeated the Danes at the Battle of Edington and thereby halted their advance in England; divided England with Danes and gave them the north part, called Danelaw.

899–921 Conquest of the Danelaw by Alfred's descendants.

925–939 Athelstan became first king to effectively rule a united England; defeated confederation of opponents at Battle of Brunanburh (939).

959–975 Edgar reigned as king of the English; crowned formally (973) at Bath in first coronation ceremony ever held for king of united England.

994–1012 Invasions by Danes, led by Sweyn, renewed; King Ethelred (reigned 978–1016) at first paid them tribute, then ordered execution of all Danes (1002); Sweyn conquered England (1012) and became king.

1013–15 King Ethelred forced to flee to Normandy (1013–14); launched invasion of England and drove out Danes (1015).

1016 Danes returned under Canute; Canute defeated Ethelred's son, King Edmund Ironside, at the Battle of Assandun.

1016–35 Canute reigned as king of England; ruled England wisely; inherited Danish crown (1018) and gained control of Norway (1028); his descendants ruled England to 1042.

1042–66 Edward the Confessor reigned; succeeded the last Danish king and thus restored Anglo-Saxon rule; however, he was raised in Normandy and appointed many French-speaking Normans to his court.

1053 Revolt led by Earl of Godwin forced exile of Edward's Norman appointees.

1063–65 Harold subjugated Wales for Edward (1063); ended rebellion in Northumbria (1065).

1066 Edward at his death named Harold his successor, though his cousin, Duke William of Normandy, claimed the crown.

1066 Battle of Hastings fought (Oct. 14); William the Conqueror defeated and killed English King Harold II; Norman Conquest largely completed.

1066–87 William the Conqueror reigned; crowned king of England in London (Dec. 25); William killed or disenfranchised Anglo-Saxon nobles, replacing them with Normans; instituted feudal system in England.

1085 William ordered compilation of Domesday Book.

1100–35 Henry I reigned; defeated attempt by older brother Robert to take throne (1101); cap-

tured Normandy from him (1106), bringing it back under English control.

1135–54 Civil war broke out after Henry's death over his successor; proved economically ruinous; Henry II chosen successor (1154).

c1135 Geoffrey of Monmouth wrote the first account of the Arthurian legend in *Historia Regnum Britanniae.*

1154–89 Henry II reigned; restored order; by his inheritance of Anjou, Normandy, and Aquitaine established the Angevin Empire on the Continent; began Plantagenet line of English kings.

1164 Henry II issued Constitutions of Clarendon, limiting power of the Catholic church in England.

1166 Henry II instituted the Assize of Clarendon, noteworthy judicial reforms.

1170 Thomas à Becket murdered; this capped a long struggle with King Henry II over his attempts to limit church powers in England.

1171 Henry began conquest of Ireland by English.

1181 Henry II issued the Assize of Arms ordering citizenry to procure weapons.

1189–99 Richard I reigned; led unsuccessful Third Crusade to retake Jerusalem.

1199–1216 King John reigned; rule marked by struggle with pope and rising power of the barons.

1204 War with Philip II of France; King John lost Normandy and other English possessions on the Continent.

1209 King John excommunicated by Pope Innocent III in controversy over investiture of archbishop of Canterbury.

1213 King John forced to accept sovereignty of the pope by Innocent III.

1215 King John forced to sign Magna Carta by his barons.

1216–72 Henry III reigned; his incompetence finally aroused the barons against him.

1217 Nobles who supported succession of a Frenchman (later Louis VIII of France) defeated at Battle of Lincoln.

1258 Henry III compelled to accept Provisions of Oxford, series of reforms imposed by barons.

1264 Mise of Amiens annulled (Jan. 23) Provisions of Oxford.

1264–67 Barons' War; S. de Montfort, baronial leader, virtually ruled England during war.

1272–1307 Edward I reigned; consolidated the power of the crown at the expense of the barons and the clergy.

1275, 1285, 1290 Statutes of Westminster promulgated by King Edward I to reform civil and criminal laws.

1284 Statute of Wales enacted (Mar. 19); Wales annexed.

1295 Model Parliament convened, a forerunner of modern British Parliament.

1307–27 Edward II reigned; unpopular, he appointed Piers Gaveston to official post and thereby aroused the barons against him; deposed by the queen and nobles.

1311 Twenty-one barons forced limitations on Edward II's powers; he did not break the barons' power until 1322.

1314 Robert I the Bruce defeated Edward at the Battle of Bannockburn and thereby ended English overlordship of Scotland.

1327–77 Edward III reigned; usurped (1330) the regency controlled by his mother and R. de Mortimer, 1st earl of March.

1337–1453 Hundred Years' War with France.

1348 Black Plague reached England; combined with ravages of Hundred Years' War to bring about major social changes, including end of feudalism; rise of Lollardry, and Peasants' Revolt (1381).

1376 Good Parliament unsuccessfully attempted to reform abuses by Edward III.

1377–99 Richard II reigned; period marked by conflicts with barons.

1381 First Navigation Act passed; government unable to implement it.

1388 Merciless Parliament impeached five of Richard II's followers for treason; action influenced Richard to more moderate course.

1399–1413 Henry IV reigned; rebelled (1399) against Richard II, defeating him and establishing the House of Lancaster.

1407 Merchants Adventurers trading company formed for English cloth trade.

1413–1422 Henry V reigned; continued fighting in the Hundred Years' War; concluded Treaty of Troyes (1420).

1422–61 Henry VI reigned; rule marked by loss of all English possessions on the Continent at the end of the Hundred Years' war (1453) and prolonged unrest.

1450 Cade's Rebellion.

1455–85 Wars of the Roses, complex dynastic struggle between the House of York and House of Lancaster; ended with accession of Henry VII.

1477 W. Caxton printed the first book in England.

1485–1509 Henry VII reigned; marked beginning of reign of Tudor kings; he suppressed Yorkist plots, promoted trade, and restored the royal treasury.

1509–47 Henry VIII reigned; attempt to secure a male heir brought conflict with Catholic church.

1513 Scottish invasion force crushed at the Battle of Flodden, northern England.

1529 Henry sought divorce from his childless wife, Queen Catherine of Aragon, to marry Anne Boleyn; permission refused by pope.

1533 Act in Restraint of Appeals to Rome passed by Parliament; Pope's authority nullified in England; Henry now able to marry A. Boleyn.

1534 First Act of Supremacy passed by Parliament; created Church of England with Henry VIII as head of the church; Henry sought to maintain Catholic character of church.

1535 Sir T. More executed for refusing to endorse Henry VIII's Act of Supremacy.

1536 Pilgrimage of Grace, uprising caused by suppression of papal authority in England; second uprising (Jan., 1537) led to martial law in northern England.

1536 Wales formally united with England.

1539 Henry had Parliament pass Act of Six Articles to oppose doctrines of the Protestant Reformation.

1547–53 Edward VI reigned; favored Protestantism; first Book of Common Prayer authorized for Church of England (1549); first Act of Uniformity passed (1549).

1553 Lady Jane Grey reigned nine days as England's queen; was overthrown and later executed.

1553–58 Mary I reigned; reinstated (1555) Catholicism and ties with Rome; persecuted Protestants.

1555 Muscovy Company founded for Russian trade; first joint-stock company.

1558–1603 Elizabeth I reigned; rule marked by England's rise as a commercial, colonial, and naval power; Elizabethan Age marked cultural flowering in England.

1559 Second Act of Supremacy passed by Parliament; reestablished Church of England and named Elizabeth I head of the church.

1560 Treaty of Edinburgh signed with France and Scotland; led to withdrawal of English and French troops from Scotland, to ease conflict between Catholics and Protestants there.

1562 J. Hawkins became first Englishman to engage in the slave trade.

1568–87 Mary Queen of Scots imprisoned by Elizabeth; finally executed after being implicated in plot by Catholics against England.

1571 Thirty-Nine Articles on doctrines of Church of England promulgated.

1583 Newfoundland discovered and claimed.

1588 Spanish Armada destroyed by English fleet; fighting with Spain resulted from England's support for revolt of Netherlands.

c1594–1616 W. Shakespeare flourished as an established playwright.

1600 British East India Company formed to gain a share of spice trade; company defeated the Portuguese in India (1612) and gradually expanded its interests there.

1603–25 James I reigned; first of the Scottish Stuart line; his accession united crowns of England and Scotland; his rule marked by arbitrary and high-handed means, as well as religious unrest and troubles with Parliament.

1603 Bye Plot to force religious reforms.

1604 Hampton Court Conference called; failed to settle differences between the Anglicans and Puritans.

1605 Gunpowder Plot, Catholic conspiracy by English Catholics to blow up Parliament and the king.

1607 Jamestown (Virginia) founded (May 14) as first permanent English settlement in North America.

1611 King James Bible issued.

1620 Pilgrims, seeking to escape persecution of religious dissenters in England, founded Plymouth Colony in New England.

1625–49 Charles I reigned; his arbitrary rule and chronic need for money led to prolonged conflict with Parliament and finally civil war.

1626–30 Unsuccessful war against France.

1628 Petition of Right, grievances issued by Parliament and presented to Charles I (May).

1629 Charles dissolved Parliament and ruled for 11 years without it.

1637 Charles attempted to force Anglican liturgy on Scotland; Scottish Presbyterians aroused.

1639–40 Bishops' Wars fought by Charles against Scottish Covenanters.

1640 Short Parliament convened by Charles I; refused Charles's aid for war against Scottish Covenanters.

1642 Charles I refused to accept Parliament's Nineteen Propositions.

1642–49 English Civil War; forces of Parliament defeated royalists and established Commonwealth.

1643 Westminster Assembly convened to fix doctrine of Church of England; members all Calvinist.

1649 Commonwealth proclaimed (Jan. 30) after King Charles's execution at the end of the English Civil War; O. Cromwell, leader of the victorious parliamentary army, became head of state; Rump Parliament sat after Pride's Purge (1648).

1649–52 Revolts by Scots and Irish put down by Cromwell; Irish harshly treated.

1651 Navigation Act passed to control Dutch shipping; resulted in first Dutch War.

1653 Rump Parliament dissolved; "Barebones Parliament" convened by O. Cromwell.

1653 Protectorate established by new Instrument of Government; first detailed written constitution of a European state; Cromwell given broad powers as Lord Protector.

1657 Humble Petition and Advice drawn up by Parliament (Mar.); modified and superseded Instrument of Government; O. Cromwell continued as protector.

1658–60 Cromwell died (1658); dissatisfaction with government of Protectorate (and Puritan reforms enacted) brought England to near anarchy by 1660.

1660 Convention Parliament convened; Charles II restored to throne by Parliament.

1660–85 Charles II reigned; marked beginning of English Restoration period (1660–88).

1660 Revolt of Fifth Monarchy Men put down.

1661–79 Royalist Cavalier Parliament convened; rise of Whig and Tory parties.

1661–65 Clarendon Code passed; four harsh laws designed to suppress any religious sects dissenting from the established Church of England.

1664 Navigation Act passed to control passage of goods to English colonies through England; led to great unrest and contributed to American Revolution.

1665–67 Second Dutch War.

1668 England joined Triple Alliance against France.

1670 Charles II signed the secret Treaty of Dover with France.

1670 Hudson's Bay Company founded; did much to promote colonial and commercial development of Canada.

1672–78 Third Dutch War.

1672 Declaration of Indulgence issued by Charles II; granted religious toleration for Nonconformists; voided by Parliament, suspicious of James's Catholic sympathies.

1678 Fictitious Popish Plot; revelations resulted in hysteria and persecution of Catholics.

1683 Rye House Plot, abortive Whig plan to assassinate King Charles II and the duke of York.

1685–88 James II reigned; his arbitrary rule and sympathies for Catholicism led to his overthrow.

1685 Duke of Monmouth's revolt; James captured Monmouth at Battle of Sedgemoor.

1687 Declaration of Indulgence issued by James II; granted toleration of Nonconformists and Catholics; aroused widespread sentiment against James.

1688 Glorious Revolution; James deposed; Protestants William and Mary became rulers of England (reigned 1689–1702) after agreeing to abide by provisions of the English Bill of Rights.

1689 English Bill of Rights enacted; established supremacy of Parliament, ending long power struggle with monarchy.

1689 Nonconformists granted religious freedom by Act of Toleration.

1689–97 War of the Grand Alliance fought to oppose expansionism of Louis XIV; American phase called King William's War.

1690 James's attempt to retake the throne, with French and Irish aid, defeated by King William at the Battle of the Boyne.

1694 Bank of England instituted.

1701 Act of Settlement passed by Parliament; provided for royal succession and limited royal powers.

1701–14 War of the Spanish Succession, fought on the Continent and in the colonies (as Queen Anne's War).

1704 Gibraltar taken from Spain.

1702–14 Queen Anne reigned; last of Stuart monarchs.

1707 Act of Union uniting England and Scotland as Great Britain (May 1).

1713 Treaty of Utrecht, ending War of the Spanish Succession; Britain gained considerable colonial territories from France, including Acadia, Newfoundland, and Hudson Bay region.

1714–27 George I reigned; founded the Hanoverian line of English monarchs (reigned to 1837); his rule marked by rise of prime minister as leader of government and by rise of Whigs as dominant party.

1715 Revolt of the Jacobites, supporters of King James and his heirs, failed.

1716 Septennial Act passed by Parliament; extended life of a Parliament from three to seven years.

1718 Britain joined in Quadruple Alliance.

1719 Revolt of the Jacobites put down.

1720 South Sea Bubble, stock scheme involving the South Sea Company; its collapse ruined thousands.

1721–42 R. Walpole in power; usually regarded as first prime minister.

1727–60 George II reigned; Walpole continued in office and was relied on to handle most of the responsibilities of government.

1739 War of Jenkins' Ear with Spain broke out.

1740–48 War of Austrian Succession; colonial rivalry with France continued, in North America as King George's War.

1745–46 Jacobite revolt led by Charles Edward (Bonnie Prince Charles); last serious Jacobite rising, it ended in failure.

1756 Diplomatic Revolution ended long-established alliances in Europe.

1756–63 Seven Years' War; war in America called French and Indian War.

1760–1820 George III reigned; often controversial, he became insane in his later years.

MID-1700s Industrial Revolution began; starting in Britain, it later spread to other European nations.

1763 Treaty of Paris ending Seven Years' War; Britain gained mastery of Canada and India; treaty marked Britain's rise as the dominant colonial power.

1765 Stamp Act and Quartering Act passed by Parliament; resulted in opposition in American colonies.

1767 Townshend Acts passed to reassert authority in American colonies; led to increased resistance to English rule.

1774 Second Quartering Act passed by Parliament after Boston Tea Party.

1775–83 American Revolution broke out in the colonies; resulted in loss of America, a major part of Britain's colonial empire; American colonies replaced by expansion of British interests elsewhere, notably India.

1780 Gordon Riots led by Lord George Gordon to protest for repeal of the Catholic Relief Act of 1778.

1783–1801 W. Pitt the Younger served as prime minister; strengthened office of prime minister and led Britain through the long wars with France; a revived Tory party coalesced around his leadership.

1793–1802 Britain joined in French Revolutionary Wars against France.

1799–1800 Combination Acts banning trade unions passed.

1801 Act of Union; Great Britain and Ireland united, creating the United Kingdom (Jan. 1).

1803–15 Napoleonic Wars; Britain played a leading role in the wars against Napoleon; immediate postwar years marked by severe economic problems and social unrest.

1807 Britain abolished slave trade.

1811–16 Rise of the Luddites, bands of workingmen angered by low wages and unemployment.

1811–20 Regency period; George, Prince of Wales, ruled as regent for his father, King George III.

1812–15 War of 1812 fought with US.

1815 Corn Law passed; prevented import of foreign grain and thereby raised price of bread; working class especially hard hit.

1819 Peterloo massacre; British cavalry attacked demonstrators seeking reforms.

1820 Cato Street Conspiracy, an anarchist assassination plot against cabinet officers, uncovered.

1820–30 George IV reigned; proved an incapable ruler.

1824 Combination Acts, banning unions, repealed; later restored, then ignored.

1829 Catholic Emancipation Act removed most penalties imposed on English Catholics (by Penal Laws); Catholics finally readmitted to Parliament.

1830–37 William IV reigned.

1832 Reform Bill of 1832 passed; doubled size of electorate and transferred power to industrialized cities; reforms marked the end of the Tory party, which was reformed as the Conservative party (1832).

1833 Oxford Movement within the Church of England begun by sermon delivered by J. Keble at Oxford.

1833 Slavery abolished throughout the British Empire.

1837–1901 Victoria reigned, British Empire reached its zenith; period of her reign known as the Victorian Age.

1838–48 Rise of Chartism, mass movement among workingmen for effective political reform.

1839–42 First Opium War in China; Britain won trading concessions in China.

1841–46 R. Peel served as prime minister; brought his newly formed Conservative party to power and effected repeal of the controversial Corn Laws.

1846 Corn Laws repealed.

1849, 1854 Navigation Acts repealed.

1850 Don Pacifico Affair with Greece.

1853–56 Crimean War.

1856–60 Second Opium War with China; Britain won further trading privileges and forced China to legalize opium trade.

1857–59 Indian Mutiny; native revolt against British East India Company rule resulted in transfer of governing authority to the British crown.

1861 Trent Affair with US; brief dispute that stemmed from the American Civil War.

1867 Reform Bill of 1867; doubled electorate and redistributed parliamentary seats.

1867 Parliament passed British North America Act, establishing Canada as a self-governing dominion; marked start of Britain's withdrawal from direct rule within the colonial empire.

1868 B. Disraeli served as prime minister.

1868–94 W. Gladstone rose to power; served as prime minister during much of this period as a Liberal Party leader; considered one of Britain's great statesmen, he instituted many reforms.

1872 San Juan Boundary Dispute with US settled; US awarded San Juan Islands southeast of Vancouver, B.C.

1874–80 B. Disraeli again served as prime minister; his term marked by an aggressive foreign policy.

1875 Disraeli negotiated purchase of Suez Canal stock; British thereby gained controlling interest and began involvement in Egypt.

1878–80 Second Anglo–Afghan War; Britain invaded Afghanistan from India to check rise of Russian influence there.

1882 Phoenix Park murders by Irish extremists opposed to British rule.

1884 Reform Bill of 1884 established virtual universal male suffrage.

1885 Battle of Khartoum (Sudan); famous battle in which Lord Gordon was defeated and killed.

1886 Unsuccessful attempt to pass Home Rule Bill for Ireland; sentiment for bill had been building in the 1880s as other attempts at reform failed to appease the Irish; Gladstone backed the bill and was forced out of office (until 1892) in the controversy.

1899 Venezuela boundary dispute with US.

1899–1902 Boer War; ruinous conflict in South Africa won by Britain at great cost.

1901–10 Edward VII reigned.

1904 Entente Cordiale, informal understanding with France, reached to counter growing power of Germany.

1905–15 Liberals in power; many reforms enacted, notably under Prime Minister H. Asquith.

1906 Labour party founded by coalition of Socialists and trade unions.

1907 Anglo-Russian Convention settled disputes with Russia over Persia, Afghanistan, and Tibet; strengthened relations.

1908 Fashoda Incident, crisis over claims to the Sudan.

1910–36 George V reigned.

1911 Parliament Act passed eliminating House of Lords' veto power over parliamentary legislation.

1912 British ocean liner *Titanic* sank (Apr. 14).

1914–18 World War I; Britain played a major role in opposing the Central Powers.

1915 Easter Rebellion in Ireland against British rule

1916–22 D. Lloyd George (Liberal) in office as prime minister.

1917 Balfour Declaration supported creation of a Jewish state.

1918 Women granted right to vote.

1919 Third Anglo–Afghan War.

1920 Britain became a founding member of the League of Nations; awarded mandates over Iraq and Palestine (formerly part of the Ottoman Empire) and over South West Africa and German East Africa.

1920 Government of Ireland Act created Northern Ireland and provided for Irish Home Rule.

1921 Irish Free State formed after Home Rule failed to end unrest in Ireland.

1922 Protectorate over Egypt ended, though British involvement in Egypt continued.

1924 J.R. MacDonald served briefly as prime minister; marked first time Labour party held power.

1929 Great Depression began; Britain suffered during the worldwide economic crisis; abandoned the gold standard (1931).

1931 British Commonwealth of Nations formed (Dec. 11) by Statute of Westminster.

1931–35 MacDonald again served as prime minister.

1936 Edward VIII reigned; abdicated soon after his succession to marry American divorcee.

1936–52 George VI reigned.

1937–39 British prime minister N. Chamberlain pursued policy of appeasement toward Nazi Germany; Munich Pact concluded (1938); preparations for war begun.

1939–45 World War II; Britain suffered heavy losses, both through combat and through extensive German air attacks on its cities (Battle of Britain).

1940–45 W. Churchill served as prime minister; led Britain through most of WW II.

1945–51 C. Attlee (Labour) in office as prime minister; many Socialist reforms insituted; industry nationalized, socialized medicine introduced (1948); rapid withdrawal from colonialism began as former colonies granted independence.

1945 Britain became a founding member of the UN.

1947 Independence granted to India and Pakistan.

1948 Britain accepted US aid through Marshall Plan to rebuild war-torn economy.

1948 Burma, Ceylon, and Palestine granted independence.

1951–55 W. Churchill (Conservative) served second term as prime minister; denationalized industries and Bank of England; Conservatives held power to 1964.

1952– Queen Elizabeth II reigned.

1957 Conservative Prime Minister A. Eden (1955–57) forced to resign over British intervention in Suez Crisis.

1957–63 M. H. Macmillan was prime minister; Conservatives retained power.

1964–70 H. Wilson (Labour) in office as prime minister; first Labour government since 1951; his attempts to join EEC frustrated by C. de Gaulle.

1963 Nuclear Test Ban Treaty signed (Aug. 5).

1965 Racial discrimination in public places banned.

1965 Rhodesia unilaterally declared its independence, thereby beginning the protracted Rhodesian crisis.

1967 Steel industry nationalized.

1969 Violence in Northern Ireland between Roman Catholics and Protestants, increasing since 1966, reached serious proportions.

1970–74 E. Heath (Conservative) in office as prime minister; strikes (dock, 1970; postal, 1971; coal, 1974) worsened Britain's growing economic problems; violence in Northern Ireland continued.

1970 Britain admitted to Common Market.

1971 Decimal currency system instituted.

1971 British troops sent to Northern Ireland to reinforce security forces and maintain border controls.

1972–74 Direct British rule imposed in Northern Ireland; Ulster Parliament ordered suspended.

1973 Britain proclaimed state of emergency to counter economic difficulties resulting from labor disputes, trade deficits, and fuel shortages.

1974–76 H. Wilson (Labour) in office as prime minister.

1974 Three-day work week and state of emergency ended.

1974 IRA bomb damaged houses of Parliament (June 17); 11 injured.

1974 Antiterrorist laws enacted following rise in terrorism; IRA outlawed.

1975 First oil pumped from North Sea oil fields.

1976–79 J. Callaghan (Labour) in office as prime minister.

1976 Government imposed new austerity measures in the face of continuing economic crisis.

1978 First "test-tube" baby born in Lancashire.

1979 Voters in Scotland and Wales rejected referendum for home rule.

1979– M. Thatcher (Conservative) in office as Britain's first woman prime minister; sought to curb Britain's worsening economic crisis by tough deflationary policies.

1979 IRA terrorist bomb killed British WW II hero, Lord Mountbatten.

1980 Rhodesian crisis resolved through intervention of British government.

1981 Marriage of Prince Charles and Lady Diana (July 20); became an event of worldwide proportions.

1982 Falkland Islands War against Argentina; Argentine invasion force driven off islands by British.

1982 Pope John Paul made historic visit to Britain; marked major step in efforts to reestablish ties between the Church of England (independent national church since 1534) and Rome.

1982 IRA terrorist bombs exploded in London (July); 10 persons killed.

Great Company, the   See **Hudson's Bay Company**

Great Condé   See **Condé, Louis II de Bourbon, prince of Condé**

Great Depression Name given the worldwide economic collapse following the US stock market crash of 1929. The stock market failure of 1929 marked the end of the US economic boom of the 1920s, and led to mass failures of businesses and the simultaneous rise of vast unemployment both in the US and in Europe. In the US the Depression reached its lowest point in the early 1930s, and slackened with the New Deal *(q.v.)* reforms inaugurated by President F. Roosevelt. Full economic recovery did not occur until the opening of WW II. In Europe, the economic failure contributed to the rise of the Nazi party in Germany. (*See also* United States [1929–39].)

Great Fear Name given to panics (July-Aug., 1789) among the rural peasants in France during the early phase of the French Revolution (1789–99). Peasants, who had stopped paying taxes to local landed aristocrats, were overcome by unfounded rumors that the aristocrats had hired brigands to attack them. This prompted a series of peasant revolts that brought an end to the taxes.

Great Fire of London   See **London**

Great Interregnum   See **Interregnum**

Great Leap Forward Chinese Communist campaign (1958–59) to increase agricultural and industrial output by reorganizing the populace into communes. The government hoped to take advantage of China's great manpower reserves by this new system. The program ended in failure (1960).

Great Moravia   See **Moravia**

Great Peloponnesian War   See   **Peloponnesian War**

Great Proletarian Cultural Revolution   See **Cultural Revolution**

Great Rebellion   See **English Civil War**

Great Schism   See **Schism**

Great Society Name for the legislative program adopted by President L. Johnson during his elected term (1965–69). This program of liberal social reforms included his "war on poverty," civil rights reforms, and federal educational, medical, and housing programs.

Great Trek Emigration (1835–40), by 14,000 Afrikaners (Boers) from Cape Colony into the African interior. Opposed to British policies, especially those favoring natives, the Afrikaners moved northward, battled with native peoples, and finally established the Afrikaner republic of Natal (1839).

Great Wall of China Celebrated defensive wall built (214–204 BC) by Ch'in dynasty emperor Shih Hwang-ti and added to by succeeding rulers. The 1,500-mile-long, 25-foot-high wall failed to prevent invasions from the north.

Greco, El ⟨*pseud. of* Domenicos Theotocopoulos⟩ c1514–1614. Greek-born Spanish painter, one of the great painters of all time. A student of Titian, he was in Toledo, Spain, by 1577, and there became an artist of some reputation. His characteristically distorted figures and use of color, however, did not receive wide recognition until this century. Among his many famous works are *Assumption of the Virgin, Burial of Count Orgaz, Crucifixion, Resurrection,* and *View of Toledo.*

Greco-Turkish Wars   **1.** War (Apr.-May, 1897) between Greece and Turkey over control of the island of Crete, then under Turkish rule. A rebellion on Crete (1896) and a call for union with Greece led to Greek military intervention (1897) on the island. Halted by a blockade established by the European powers, Greece then attacked Turkey (Apr., 1897). After one month of war and several severe defeats, Greece accepted an armistice. **2.** War (1921–22) between Greece and Nationalist Turks, led by Kemal Ataturk, who refused to recognize terms of the Treaty of Sèvres (1920) between Greece and the Ottoman Turkish government. Greece invaded Anatolia and, after initial Greek victories, the Turks under Ataturk drove the Greeks out. The was was ended by the

Treaty of Lausanne (1923). Greece gave up eastern Thrace, and the two countries exchanged minority populations.

Greece ⟨Hellenic Republic⟩ Country located in southeastern Europe and occupying the southern part of the Balkan Peninsula. Its capital is Athens. Greece is divided into two geographic regions: northern mainland Greece and the southern Peloponnesus. The two are connected by a narrow isthmus. The culture of ancient Greece, which flourished during the 1st millennium BC, has had enormous impact on the development of Western civilization. Greek philosophers, poets, dramatists, scientists, artists, and architects made many fundamental contributions to their respective fields and are still admired in modern times. These great accomplishments were made despite the nearly constant wars between the many Greek city-states that evolved in ancient Greece. These rivalries, notably between Athens and Sparta, finally cost the Greeks their independence, however. The Roman conquest of Greece (2d cent. BC) began a period of decline and foreign domination that lasted until the 19th cent. AD, when the modern Greek state was created. Key events in Greek history include:

3000–1000 BC Aegean civilizations flourished.

c2200–c1400 BC Minoan civilization flourished on the island of Crete.

c1600–c1200 BC Mycenaean civilization flourished on mainland Greece.

14TH–13TH CENT. BC Achaeans arrived in the Peloponnesus.

c1200 BC Trojan War, legendary conflict recounted in Homer's *Iliad*, fought with Troy.

11TH CENT. BC Dorians invaded the Peloponnesus; Aeolians and Ionians consequently established colonies in western Asia Minor.

9TH CENT.? BC Lycurgus reformed Spartan society; created rigid, militaristic system to produce warriors.

FROM 9TH CENT. BC Rise of the Greek city-states.

c800 BC Sparta, in extreme southeastern Greece, gained hegemony over surrounding region, Laconia.

c800 BC Corinth, on the eastern coast between Sparta and Athens, developed a thriving commerce.

c800 BC Homer believed to have lived; *Iliad* and *Odyssey* attributed to him.

c800 BC Hesiod lived.

8TH–6TH CENT. BC Period of colonization; Greeks established colonies in southern Italy, Sicily, North Africa, and Spain.

776? BC First Olympic games held at Olympia.

735–715 BC First Messenian War; Sparta conquered Messenia, to the west.

7TH CENT. BC The city of Argos briefly dominated the Peloponnesus.

c700 BC Athens, on the eastern coast of the Greek mainland, gained control over the surrounding region, Attica.

c650–c600 BC Second Messenian War; Sparta put down a revolt by the Messenians.

625–585 BC Periander reigned as tyrant of Corinth.

c621 BC Draco established severe laws, the Draconian code, in Athens.

c600 BC Thebes, in region of Boeotia (north of Attica), formed Boeotian League.

594 BC Solon instituted his reforms at Athens amid grave social crisis; reforms laid basis for democracy.

c590 First Sacred War fought by league of city-states to protect the shrine at Delphi.

c582–507 BC Pythagoras lived; founded school at Crotona, Italy; greatly influenced Western civilization.

c570 BC Levantine War.

561–527 BC Peisistratus in power as tyrant of Athens; began temple construction and rapid expansion of the city.

MID–6TH CENT. BC Sparta formed the Peloponnesian League, consisting of all the city-states on the Peloponnesus.

c546 BC Persians conquered Ionian Greek colonies in western Asia Minor.

c522–443 BC Great poet Pindar lived.

520–490 BC Cleomenes reigned in Sparta; maintained Sparta's position as dominant power in the Peloponnesus; intervened in Athenian politics.

508 BC Cleisthenes instituted his reforms; established Athenian democracy.

507 BC Spartans invaded Attica in order to oust Cleisthenes and restore the aristocracy in Athens; Athenians drove off the Spartans.

506 BC Athens, in war with Boeotian League, defeated Thebes and Euboea.

5TH–4TH CENT. BC First Achaean League formed to defend against pirates.

499–493 BC Ionian Greek colonies rebelled unsuccessfully against Persian rule; Athenians sent aid, thus provoking the Persians to invade Greece later (490).

c496–c406 BC Sophocles, one of the greatest of tragic poets, lived.

490–480 BC Themistocles in power in Athens; built up Athenian naval strength.

490–479 BC Persian Wars: Greek city-states successfully resisted large-scale invasions by Persians.

478 BC Delian League formed by city-states to oppose invasion by Persia; became basis of Athenian power in Greece.

464–461 BC Helots of Messenia rebelled against Spartan rule.

467 BC Athens conquered Naxos when it attempted to withdraw from Delian League; thereafter Athens remained in firm control of the league.

466 BC Cimon, Athenian statesman and military leader, won Battle of Eurymedon River in new fighting against Persians.

460–445 BC Peloponnesian War (first); Athenians engaged in war with the Peloponnesian League, and at the same time aided a revolt against the Persians in Egypt.

460–429 BC Pericles came to power in Athens; Athens underwent great cultural flowering and became intellectual and political center of Greece.

c460–400 BC Thucydides, great historian of ancient Greece, lived.

c460–c370 BC Hippocrates, father of medicine, lived.

458 BC Athenians defeated the Peloponnesians and captured Aegina.

457 BC Sparta joined the Peloponnesians in war against Athens; invaded Boeotia, defeating Athens at the Battle of Tanagra; withdrew from Boeotia, leaving it to Athens.

457 BC Defensive walls built between Athens and the Pireus.

455 BC Athenians captured Achaea, on the northern part of the Peloponnesus.

454 BC Athenian forces routed in Egypt by the Persians.

454 BC Treasury of Delian League transferred to Athens; marked ascendancy of Athens in Greece.

451 BC Peace of Callias ended hostilities with Persia.

451 BC Athens and Sparta agreed to five-year peace.

448 BC Second Sacred War.

447 BC Pericles began the construction of the magnificent Athenian acropolis.

447 BC Bocotia rcbcllcd and withdrew from the Delian League.

446 BC Revolt by Euboea; Athens put down the rebellion after reaching an agreement with the Peloponnesian League, which had invaded Megara, an Athenian ally.

445 BC Thirty Years' Peace ended the first Peloponnesian War.

440–439 BC Athenians subjugated rebellious Samos.

c434–c355 BC Xenophon, historian, lived.

431–404 BC Peloponnesian War (Great); Athens ultimately defeated by Sparta and never regained former power in Greece; Spartans briefly ascendant in Greece.

404 BC Athenians forced by victorious Spartans to accept rule of Thirty Tyrants.

403 BC Athenians overthrew the Thirty Tyrants; rebuilt city's defenses.

399 BC Socrates, renowned philosopher, forced to poison himself at Athens.

395–387 BC Corinthian War was fought against Spartan domination by Athens and her allies, Corinth, Argos, and Thebes.

c387 BC Plato, great philosopher of ancient Greece, founded his Academy at Athens.

378 BC Second Delian League formed by Athens; warred against Sparta until 371.

371 BC Thebes defeated Sparta at the Battle of Leuctra.

370 BC Arcadian League formed by Epaminondas of Thebes; Thebes ascendant on Greek mainland until league broke up (362).

359 BC Philip II became king of Macedon in northern Greece; in subsequent years subdued rebellious peoples of Macedon and then extended his control over Greece.

355–346 BC Third Sacred War; in the general war between Greek city-states, Philip gained control over a large part of the Greek mainland.

339–338 BC Fourth Sacred War; by his victory at Chaeronea, Philip of Macedon gained control over all Greece; formed Hellenic League under Macedonian hegemony.

336 BC Alexander the Great became king of Macedon; put down revolt by Greek city-states, destroying Thebes (335).

c335 BC Lyceum founded at Athens by Aristotle, one of the world's greatest philosophers.

334–324 BC Alexander's epic journey of conquest began with conquest of Persia, and soon after a vast, but short-lived, empire was created that stretched from India to Greece and Egypt; Macedonian conquests spread Greek culture, inaugurating the Hellenistic Age.

332 BC Alexandria founded in Egypt by Alexander; later became center of Hellenistic culture.

323 BC Alexander died; Antipater, Craterus, and Perdiccas became regents of the Macedonian Empire; breakup of the empire began.

323–322 BC Lamian War, unsuccessful attempt by Athens and other city-states to overthrow Macedonian rule.

321–281 BC Wars of the Diadochi (Alexander's generals); resulted in partition of the empire, creation of dynasties of Macedonian rulers in each, and spread of Hellenistic influence.

301 BC Battle of Ipsus; Diadochi, after some years of war, agreed to partition of the empire; Macedon fell to Cassander, son of Antipater.

c300 BC Voyages of Pytheas to British Isles and possibly Iceland.

c300 BC Stoicism established at Athens by Zeno.

290 BC Aetolian League formed in west part of Greek mainland.

280–146 BC Second Achaean League; gradually gained control of the Peloponnesus.

279–276 BC Gauls (Celts) invaded northern Greece, ravaging Macedon.

276 BC Antigonus II Gonatus gained control of Macedon; founded Antigonid line of Macedonian kings and warred against Pyrrhus of Epirus.

c266–262 BC Chremonidean War fought by Athens and Sparta against Macedonian rule.

235–222 BC Cleomenes III reigned in Sparta; instituted much needed reforms and abolished ephors.

222 BC Antigonus III defeated Sparta and forced it to become an ally; Cleomenes driven out and ephors restored.

221–178 BC Philip V reigned as king of Macedon.

214–205 BC Macedonian king Philip V successful in First Macedonian War against Rome.

200–196 BC Second Macedonian War; Macedonia forced to pay Rome tribute.

171–168 BC Third Macedonian War with Rome; Macedonia defeated and divided into four republics.

149–148 BC Fourth Macedonian War; Macedonia defeated and reduced to a Roman province.

146 BC Rome dissolved the Achaean League; Greece thereafter administered by Roman governor of Macedon.

146 BC–AD 395 Greece under Roman rule; economy generally declined though Hellenistic culture continued to flourish and influence Roman culture; Byzantine culture developed under Greek influences.

88–85 BC Greece invaded by Romans under Sulla after supporting Mithridates in the Mithridatic War; Greece ravaged.

AD 67 Nero granted Greece independence; move rescinded by his successors.

AD 117–138 Revival in Greece fostered by Roman Emperor Hadrian, who rebuilt many Greek cities.

AD 267–268 Goths invaded Greece; repulsed by Romans.

AD c393 Olympic games abolished by the Romans.

AD 395 Roman Empire permanently divided into Western and Eastern (Byzantine) empires.

AD 395–1204 Greece under Byzantine control; general decline of Greece.

AD 395–396 Greece ravaged in new invasions by Goths.

529 Nine-hundred-year-old Greek Academy closed by Justinian I.

6TH–8TH CENTS. Slavs invaded northern regions of Greece.

1204 Byzantine Empire conquered by Christians on Fourth Crusade; Latin Empire of Constantinople created; Greece divided into feudal duchies, including French-controlled duchy of Athens; Venetians took control of islands and some Greek coastal regions.

1261–1453 Byzantines reestablished their empire; reconquered part of Greece; Duchy of Athens and other territories remained under European control.

1456–1829 Ottoman Turks controlled Greece; their rule over the territory was challenged variously in wars with Venice, Austria, and Russia; Greece in period of decline.

1566 Ottomans captured island of Chios from Genoa.

1571 Battle of Lepanto; European Christians defeated Ottoman fleet in battle for Cyprus.

1669 Ottomans captured Crete from Venice.

1718 Treaty of Passarowitz, ending Austro-Turkish War and war with Venice; Ottoman control of Greece recognized in exchange for other territories.

1769 Unsuccessful revolt against Ottoman rule led by Russian Count Orlov.

1797 Ottomans took Ionian Islands from Venice.

1815 Friendly Association, secret society, founded by Greek nationalists.

1821 Abortive revolt led by the Russian Alexander Ypsilanti; sparked general uprising.

1821–32 War of Greek Independence fought; led to Greek independence from Ottoman Empire.

1824–26 Muhammad Ali, Ottoman viceroy of Egypt, invaded Greece to reestablish Ottoman control.

1827 European powers became involved in conflict over Greek independence; Russians subsequently waged Russo-Turkish War (1828–29).

1829   Treaty of Adrianople; treaty ended Russo-Turkish War and Ottomans relinquished control of Greece.

1830   London Protocol (Feb. 3); Europeans established Greece as a kingdom, much smaller than sought by nationalists.

1832   Otto I named king by London Conference; instituted autocratic and unpopular rule; financial problems of new kingdom increased in subsequent years and led to increasing involvement by European powers.

1843   Otto forced to grant constitution; bicameral legislature set up.

1850   British blockaded coast in Don Pacifico Affair.

1862   Otto I deposed.

1863–1913   George I reigned.

1864   New constitution adopted by King George I.

1897   Greco-Turkish War fought (Apr.–May) with Ottoman Turks over control of Crete; Greece, defeated in several engagements, accepted an armistice.

1912–13   Balkan Wars; Greece participated in the wars and gained much of Macedonia and Thrace, former Ottoman domains.

1913   Crete united with Greece.

1913–17   Constantine I reigned.

1914–18   WW I; Greece became a battleground in the Salonica campaign; gained additional territories at end of war.

1917   Constantine refused to support Allies in WW I; was forced to abdicate.

1917–20   Alexander reigned.

1920–22   Constantine I restored to Greek throne.

1921–22   Greco-Turkish War fought with Turkey after Greek invasion of Anatolia; Kemal Atatürk drove the Greeks from Anatolia.

1922–23   George II reigned; forced to abdicate.

1923   Greek republic proclaimed.

1934   Greece joined Balkan Entente, reversing former anti-Turkish policy.

1935   Monarchy reinstated in Greece after years of economic problems and political chaos.

1935–41   George II reigned after restoration of the monarchy.

1936–41   J. Metaxas established as dictator with support of king.

1939–45   WW II; Italian invasion from Albania repulsed (1939–40); occupied by Nazi Germans (1941–44), Greece fell into economic ruin; beginning of civil war between pro-royalists and pro-Communist guerrilla groups; British restored Greek government (1944).

1944–49   Greek Civil War; British and American aid helped Greek government put down Communist insurrection.

1946–47   George II restored to the throne.

1947–64   Paul I reigned as king, succeeding after George died.

1947   Truman Doctrine announced by US Pres. Truman to provide aid against Communists in continuing Greek Civil War.

1951   New constitution adopted; marked return to political stability.

1951   Greece joined NATO.

1955–63   National Radical Union Party in power under Constantine Karamanlis; period marked by economic recovery and rising tensions over Cyprus.

1964–73   Constantine II reigned; political unrest mounted during his reign.

1967   Military coup (Apr. 21) by right-wing military officers following a succession of political crises; repressive regime instituted, ostensibly to prevent Communist takeover.

1967   Constantine left Greece; military officer made regent.

1968   New constitution adopted; increased powers of prime minister at the expense of the monarchy.

1970   Relaxation of government controls imposed in 1967; some constitutional rights restored.

1973   Unsuccessful coup by navy (May).

1973   Greece proclaimed a republic (June 1); monarchy abolished.

1973   Georgios Papadopoulos made first president of new Greek republic.

1973–74   Pres. Phaidon Gizikis in office following a bloodless coup (Nov. 25).

1974   Military junta resigned (July 23) after Turkey invaded Cyprus; civilian government to be formed.

1974   Prime Minister Karamanlis reinstated; new constitution adopted.

1974   Greece withdrew from NATO to protest Turkish invasion of Cyprus.

1980   Greece rejoined NATO.

1981   Greece admitted to Common Market.

1981   Andreas Papandreou, a Socialist, in office as prime minister.

Greece, Seven Wise Men of   *See* **Seven Wise Men of Greece**

Greek Civil War   Civil war (1944–49) between Communist and rightist factions in Greece. Following the withdrawal of Nazi occupation forces (fall, 1944), Communist guerrillas attacked both rightist guerilla forces and the British occupation army. By the Varkizoi Agreement (Jan. 14, 1945), a short-lived government was established. Government instability and widespread unrest, however, led to new fighting (May, 1946). The Communist faction was finally defeated, with American and British aid, by Oct., 1949.

Greek fire Flammable substance used by the Byzantines in warfare from the 7th cent. This secret mixture ignited on contact with water and was used effectively against Arab fleets in naval battles.

Greek Independence, War of The Greek revolt (1821–32) against the Ottoman Empire. After centuries of Turkish domination, Greeks in the Peloponnesus rebelled (Mar. 25, 1821) and proclaimed Greek independence (Jan., 1822). The revolt spread, attracting popular support in Europe and such volunteers as Lord Byron, and the Turks were forced to seek aid from Egypt (1824). The Egyptians and Turks soon occupied much of the southern Peloponnesus, but their advance was slowed by intervention of European powers: first at the Battle of Navarino (Oct., 1827), in which the Egyptian naval forces were routed; then by the outbreak of the Russo-Turkish War (1828–29). The London Conference (1830–31) of European powers set the final terms of Greek independence in the London Protocol (Feb. 3), and Otto I was designated king (1832) by the Treaty of London. The Ottoman Turks recognized the independent kingdom of Greece by the Treaty of Constantinople (1832).

Greek Project Secret plan formulated (1782) by Russia's Catherine the Great for the conquest and dismemberment of the Ottoman Empire. Part of the plan called for creation of a new kingdom of Dacia out of Ottoman domains. The plan won Austrian approval but was never implemented.

Greeley, Horace 1811–72. Celebrated American newspaper editor. He founded the *New Yorker* (1834) and the *New York Tribune* (1841). He wielded great influence as editor of the *Tribune* and after 1850 he became an outspoken critic of slavery. Following the American Civil War he was an unsuccessful opponent of U. Grant in the 1872 presidential elections. He is often remembered for the expression "Go west, young man."

Green, Duff 1791–1875. American journalist. As owner of the *United Telegraph*, a Washington, D.C., newspaper, he backed A. Jackson for president (1828) and became a member of the Kitchen Cabinet. He later broke with Jackson and supported H. Clay for president (1832).

Green, Hetty 1835–1916. American financier. Green inherited $10 million and increased it to $100 million through astute management. She

was considered the wealthiest woman in the world.

greenback Nickname for legal-tender notes issued by the US government during the American Civil War (1861–65). It was not backed by gold and contributed to inflation during the war years. Greenbacks were backed by gold reserves after 1879. (*See also* Greenback party.)

Greenback party US political party (1874–88) made up largely of farmers who opposed a return to the gold standard. Greenbackers feared that discontinuation of legal-tender notes (greenbacks) and resumption of the gold standard would mean deflation and financial hardship. The party formed after the Panic of 1873 and ran presidential candidates in 1876, 1880, and 1884, though only once polled more than a million votes. With resumption of the gold standard (1879), Greenbackers joined the Free Silver movement and the party declined rapidly.

Greene, Graham 1904–. English novelist and playwright. He is the author of both thrillers and more serious novels, of which *Orient Express* and *The Power and Glory* are examples.

Greene, Nathanael 1742–86. American general in the American Revolution. A strategist considered by many to be second only to G. Washington, he figured in the battles at Trenton (1775), Brandywine (1777), and Germantown (1777). From 1780, he was commander in the South. After reorganizing the army there, he led it to victory in the Carolina Campaign.

Greene, Robert 1558?–92. English dramatist, a contemporary of Shakespeare, who wrote a variety of plays, including the comic romance *Friar Bacon and Friar Bungay.*

Greenland World's largest island, located in northeastern North America and nominally controlled by the Danish government. It was discovered (c982) and colonized by the Norseman Eric the Red. Later, his son Leif Ericsson probably visited North America (Vinland) while sailing to Greenland (c1000). Between the 12th and 16th cents., a European colony flourished there and became a Catholic bishopric (c1100). The colony subsequently declined and colonists merged with the Eskimo population. Greenland was recolonized from 1721 by the Norwegians and Danes. Denmark got possession of the colony at the Congress of Vienna (1815) and subsequently took greater interest in developing the island. The US established bases there during WW II (some still remain) and in 1953 Greenland was given representation in the Danish parliament. Greenland subsequently won the right of home rule (May 1, 1979) and organized its own parliament.

Green Mountain Boys A militia unit first organized by E. Allen (1770) to protect settlers in the Green Mountains (now Vermont) from speculators who held British grants to their land. From 1775 on, they figured in the revolution. They captured Ticonderoga (1775) and won the Battle of Bennington (1777).

Greens, Blues and *See* **Blues and Greens**

Green Standard, Army of the *See* **Army of the Green Standard**

Gregorian calendar Reformed calendar, instituted by Pope Gregory XIII (Oct., 1582). A reformation of the Julian calendar, it established the 365-day year with a leap year of 366. Its effective date of Oct. 5, 1582, according to the Old Style (Julian), thus became Oct. 15, 1582, by the New Style.

Gregorian church *See* **Armenian church**

Gregorian Reform Term applied to the program of Roman Catholic religious reform advanced by Pope Gregory VII. The reforms notably included attempts to halt lay investiture, the granting of ecclesiastical authority by temporal rulers. Gregory's policies brought him into fierce conflict with Holy Roman Emperor Henry IV.

Gregory I, Saint ⟨Gregory the Great⟩ *c*540–604. Italian-born pope (590–604), successor to Pelagius II. A Doctor of the Church, he was a celebrated church administrator, noted for his reforms in both church organization and liturgy. He promoted spiritual supremacy of the pope, established the authority of the pope in temporal matters, began the Christianization of Britain (596), and encouraged the spread of monasticism. The Gregorian chant is traditionally ascribed to him.

Gregory VII, Saint ⟨*orig.* Hildebrand⟩ *c*1020–1085. Italian-born pope (1073–85), successor to Alexander II and one of the great church reformers. In the face of powerful opposition, Gregory undertook reforms to end widespread church corruption. In 1073 he called reform synods, condemned clerical marriage and simony, and appointed legates to oversee enforcement of church laws. His battle for reform focused on lay investiture, which he banned in 1075 and which set German emperor Henry IV against him. He twice excommunicated Henry. In retaliation, Henry appointed antipope Clement III, attacked Rome (1081–83), and forced Gregory to retreat to Salerno (where he died).

Gregory IX ⟨Segni, Ugolino di⟩ 1147?–1241. Italian-born pope (1227–41), successor to Honorius III. A pope of forceful disposition, he twice excommunicated Holy Roman Emperor Frederick II (1227, 1239), organized the office of the Inquisi-

tion (1233), and ordered the collection of the *Decretals,* which furthered codification of canon law.

Gregory XI ⟨Beaufort, Pierre Roger de⟩ 1330–78. French-born pope (1370–78), successor to Urban V. The last of the French popes, he ended the Babylonian captivity by moving the papacy from Avignon to Rome (1377).

Gregory XII ⟨Correr, Angelo⟩ *c*1327–1417. Venetian-born pope (1406–15) during the Great Schism in the Western church, successor to Innocent VII. He was elected to oppose antipope Benedict XIII and was deposed at the Council of Pisa (1409). He resisted the deposition until after the Council of Constance (1415) was convened and Martin V was elected pope.

Gregory XIII ⟨Buoncompagni, Ugo⟩ 1502–85. Italian-born pope (1572–85), successor to St. Pius V. He reformed the Julian calendar, establishing the modern Gregorian calendar *(q.v.)* in its place, and promoted education of the clergy.

Gregory XVI ⟨Capellari, Bartolomeo Alberto⟩ 1765–1846. Italian-born pope (1831–46), successor to Pius VIII. He was a conservative and proponent of Ultramontanism. He put down a rebellion by the Carbonari (1832) within the Papal States.

Gregory Nazianzus, Saint ⟨Gregory Theologus⟩ AD *c*329?–389. Cappadocian theologian and bishop. One of the four fathers of the Eastern church, he is remembered for his discourses on the Holy Trinity.

Gregory of Nyssa, Saint *d.* AD 394. Cappadocian theologian and bishop. One of the four Fathers of the Eastern church, he was a leading proponent of orthodoxy at the first Council of Constantinople (AD 381).

Gregory of Tours, Saint 538?–93. French historian and bishop. He wrote the *History of the Franks,* still regarded as an important historical resource.

Gregory the Great *See* **Gregory I, Saint**

Gregory Theologus *See* **Gregory Nazianzus, Saint**

Grenville, George 1712–70. British statesman. As chief minister (1763–65) under King George III, he put through the Revenue Act of 1764 and the Stamp Act of 1765, both of which served to stir up sentiment for rebellion in the American colonies.

Grenville, George Nugent Temple, 1st marquess of Buckingham 1753–1813. British statesman, son of G. Grenville. He was lord lieutenant of Ireland (1782–83, 1787–89).

Grenville, Sir Richard 1541?–91. Celebrated English naval hero. His ships carried the first colonists to Roanoke Colony (1585), but he is best remembered as captain of the *Revenge.* During an abortive raid on Spanish treasure ships off the Azores, the *Revenge* battled against 15 Spanish warships for a full day before being taken. Grenville died of wounds after the battle.

Grenville, William Wyndham, Baron 1759–1834. British statesman, a son of G. Grenville (1712–70). A leading advocate of Catholic Emancipation, he organized the coalition government known as the Ministry of All Talents (1806–07). British slave trade was abolished under this ministry (1807).

Grévy, Paul Jules 1807–91. French statesman and president (1879–87) during the Third Republic, successor to M. Macmahon. He was forced to resign because of a scandal that broke shortly after his election to a second term.

Grey, Albert Henry George, 4th Earl 1851–1917. British colonial administrator. He was administrator of Rhodesia (1896–97) and governor general of Canada (1904–11).

Grey, Charles, 2nd Earl 1764–1845. British statesman. He was a Whig party leader in the House of Commons and prime minister (1830–34). He obtained passage of the Reform Bill of 1832.

Grey, Sir George *See* **Bay of Islands War**

Grey, Lady Jane 1537–54. English queen for nine days (1553), successor to Edward VI. Soon after being crowned, she acceded to Mary I's claim to the throne and was later sentenced for treason. She was executed after her father, H. Grey, duke of Suffolk, took part in Sir T. Wyatt's rebellion.

Grey, Zane 1875–1939. American author who wrote many popular western novels, including *Riders of the Purple Sage.*

Grey of Fallodon, Edward Grey, 1st Viscount 1862–1933. British statesman. A liberal member of Parliament (1885–1916), he served as foreign secretary (1905–16) and helped guide Britain through the early phase of WW I. He arranged completion of the Triple Alliance (1907) and the Treaty of London (1915).

Grieg, Edvard Hagerup 1843–1907. Norwegian composer who created a distinctive national style.

Grierson, John 1898–1972. British film producer, noted as a leading figure in British documentary films.

Griffenfeld, Peder Schumacher, Count 1635–99. Danish statesman. He wrote the King's Law (1665), which justified Denmark's absolute monarchy, and under Christian V he became chancellor of Denmark (1673–76).

Griffith, Arthur 1872–1922. Irish statesman and president of the Irish Republic (1922). He founded the Sinn Fein (1905) and was a leader in negotiations to establish the Irish Free State (1921).

Griffith, David Lewelyn Wark 1875–1948. American movie director, a pioneer in the field. He introduced many new techniques and was a founder of United Artists (1919). *The Birth of a Nation* and *Intolerance* are among his most important films.

Grillparzer, Franz 1791–1872. Austrian dramatist and poet, sometimes called Austria's greatest playwright. *The Ancestress* and *A Dream Is Life* are among his successful plays.

Grimké, Sarah Moore and **Angelina Emily** 1792–1873, 1805–79. American abolitionists and advocates of women's rights. The daughters of a Southern slaveholder, they first spoke out against slavery in 1835 and for women's rights in 1838. They are sometimes regarded as the first to raise the issue of women's rights in America.

Grimm, Jakob and **Wilhelm** 1785–1863, 1786–1859. German folklorists and philologists. Though they did much original work in the study of the Germanic languages and folklore, they are best known for their collection of tales, *Grimm's Fairy Tales.*

Grimoard, Guillaume de *See* **Urban V**

Grivas, Georgios Theodoros 1898–1974. Greek Cypriot general. Grivas headed EOKA, which led the struggle for freedom from Britain. However, he opposed independence and sought union with Greece. He fled Cyprus when his troops killed several Turkish Cypriots (1967).

Grolier de Servières, Jean, vicomte d'Aguisy 1479–1565. French bibliophile. He collected what became a famous library of 3,000 specially bound books. The collection was finally broken up in 1675.

Gromyko, Andrei Andreyevich 1909–. Soviet foreign minister (1957–) and member of Soviet Central Committee (1956–). He became a diplomat (1939) following The Great Purge of 1938 and was appointed US ambassador (1943–46). He became deputy foreign minister (1946) and delegate to the UN in 1946. As foreign minister, he pursued Cold War policies against Western powers. During the 1970s he played an important part in the Nixon-Brezhnev summit talks.

Groote, Gerhard ⟨Groot, Gerhard⟩ 1340–84. Dutch religious reformer and preacher who opposed scholastic theologians and founded the Roman Catholic order Brethren of the Common Life (c1374).

Gropius, Walter 1883–1969. German-American architect, a famous exponent of modern architectural style and founder of the Bauhaus school (*q.v.*).

Grosseteste, Robert c1170–1253. English theologian and scholar. He was a prolific writer on scholarly subjects and, as bishop of Lincoln (1235–53), he both defended church privileges against Henry III and criticized corruption within the Curia.

Grote, George 1794–1871. English historian. His 12-volume *History of Greece* is considered a classic.

Grotefend, Georg Friedrich 1775–1853. German philologist who became famous for deciphering the Persian Cuneiform script.

Grotius, Hugo 1583–1645. Dutch jurist. He wrote *On the Laws of War and Peace* (1625), generally considered to be the foundation of international law. In it he contends that nations, as well as individuals, are subject to natural law.

Grouchy, Emmanuel, marquis de 1766–1847. French general. Sometimes said to be responsible for Napoleon's defeat at Waterloo (1815), he failed to keep the main Prussian force from reaching Waterloo.

Groves, Leslie R. *See* **Manhattan Project**

Gruen, David *See* **Ben-Gurion, David**

Grundtvig, Nikolai Frederik Severin 1783–1872. Danish educator, theologian, and writer. He founded the Danish Folk High School (1844), a system of adult education that briefly became popular in European countries.

Grünewald, Mathias ⟨*pseud. of* Neithart, Mathias Gothardt⟩ *fl.* 1500–30. German artist, sometimes considered the greatest of the German Gothic painters. The Isenheim altarpiece is among his greatest works.

Guadalajara, Battle of Battle (Mar., 1937) during the Spanish Civil War (1936–39). Spanish Nationalists with a large contingent of allied Italian troops (some 50,000 soldiers in all) began a drive toward Guadalajara in an effort to surround nearby Republican-held Madrid. In subsequent fighting (Mar. 15–18), the Italians were routed by Spanish Republican armies and the Nationalist offensive was halted.

Guadalcanal, Battle of First major Allied counteroffensive (Aug., 1942–Feb., 1943) against the Japanese during WW II. The battle, fought by both land and sea forces, began with the landing of some 16,000 US marines (Aug. 7, 1942) and establishment of a beachhead on the island of Guadalcanal, in the Solomon Islands. Bloody fighting on the island at times saw the marines outnumbered 10 to one, as the Japanese poured reinforcements into the fighting. The naval battles, fought to stem the tide of these reinforcements, continued from Aug. 9 to Nov. 30, when the Allies established naval supremacy. The battle for Guadalcanal ended when the Japanese evacuated some 14,000 troops from the island (Feb. 7–9). Japanese losses were 23,000 dead or missing and 1,000 captured. US losses were 1,600 killed and many thousands more, casualties of battle and disease.

Guadalupe Hidalgo, Treaty of Treaty concluded (Feb. 2, 1848) between the US and Mexico ending the Mexican War (1846–48). According to the treaty, signed at the Mexican town of Guadalupe Hidalgo, the US paid $15 million in return for what was then roughly half of Mexico. It set the US boundary at the Rio Grande and included what are now Texas, California, Arizona, New Mexico, Nevada, Utah, and western Colorado. In ratifying the treaty (1848), the Senate rejected a move to add the Wilmot Proviso (*q.v.*) and thereby fueled the growing debate over the extension of slavery.

Guadalupe Victoria ⟨*b.* Fernandez, Manuel Felix⟩ 1786?–1843. Mexican general, the first president of Mexico (1824–29). He supported the government of A. de Iturbide and the Plan of Iguala (1821), by which Mexico became independent, but in 1823 joined A. de Santa Anna's revolt against Iturbide.

Guarantees, Law of Italian law (May 13, 1871) which attempted to establish the relationship between the Italian government and the papacy. It guaranteed religious and diplomatic freedom to the papacy, and established an annual income for the pope, but did not restore papal authority to the territories that had been incorporated into Italy. Pope Pius IX did not accept it, and relations between Italy and the papacy were not formalized until the promulgation of the Lateran Treaty of 1929.

Guatemala ⟨Republic of Guatemala⟩ Independent state located in western Central America on the Pacific coast. Its capital is Guatemala City. Guatemala was the home of the ancient Mayan-Quiche civilization, which was conquered by Spain (1523–24). Since its independence in 1821, Guatemala has had a history marked by military dictatorships, coups, border warfare, poverty, and natural disasters. Key events in Guatemala's history include:

1523–24 P. de Alvarado conquered region during military expedition from what is now Mexico; captaincy general of Guatemala established, including most of Central America.

1821 Guatemala declared independence from Spain (Sept. 15).

1821–23 A. de Iturbide made Guatemala part of his Mexican Empire.

1823 Guatemala joined Central American Federation.

1838 R. Carrera declared independence from Central American Federation.

1840–65 R. Carrera reigned as dictator.

1859 Treaty set boundary with British Honduras, but Guatemala later disputed terms and laid claim to that territory.

1873–85 Justo Rufino Barrios became president; invaded El Salvador to reestablish Central American Federation; was killed.

1898–1920 Manuel Estrada Cabrera reigned as dictator.

1906 Gen. Manuel Barillas revolted against Cabrera; embroiled most of Central America in warfare; armistice arranged by T. Roosevelt and P. Díaz.

1920 Revolution broke out, forcing Cabrera's resignation; unrest continued over next decade.

1931–44 Gen. Jorge Ubico ruled as dictator; ruled repressively, but ended peonage of Indians and campaigned successfully against corruption.

1945–51 Leftist Dr. Juan José Arévalo in office as president; implemented land and labor reform.

1945 Guatemala renewed its long-standing claims to British Honduras.

1951–54 Jacobo Arbenz Guzmán in office; expropriated large estates, including those of the United Fruit Company.

1954–57 Col. Carlos Castillos Armas in office after leading revolt with secret US help; Guzmán fled to Cuba.

1957 Castillos assassinated; series of coups followed in 1960s.

1960–61 Cuban exiles, to be used later at Bay of Pigs, trained in Guatemala.

1967 Leftist and rightist factions instituted campaign of terrorist violence.

1968 US Ambassador John Gordon Mein killed.

1970–74 Conservative Col. Carlos Araña Osorio in office as president; imposed state of siege to deal with terrorists.

1974–78 Gen. Kjell Langerud García in office as president.

1976 Almost 100,000 killed or injured in major earthquake (Feb. 4).

1977 Britain offered independence to Belize (formerly British Honduras); Guatemala threatened invasion to make good its claim to this territory in long dispute over 1859 treaty.

1978–82 Gen. Fernando Romeo Lucas García in office as president; instituted corrupt and brutal regime; US military aid halted (1978).

1981 Guatemala agreed to recognize independent Belize and negotiate territorial claims.

1982 Gen. José Efraín Ríos Montt in power following military coup (Mar. 23); Montt began brutal war against Leftist guerrillas.

Guatemala City Capital city (pop. 1,000,000) of Guatemala, the largest city in Central America. Founded by the Spanish in 1527, it became a colonial capital in 1776 and capital of the independent republic of Guatemala in 1839. Earthquakes greatly damaged the city in 1917 to 1918 and again struck the region around the city in 1976.

Guayaquil Conference Strategy meeting (July 26–27, 1822) between leaders of the South American independence movement. S. Bolívar and J. San Martín met at this Ecuadorian coastal city to discuss joining forces against Spain. They failed to reach an agreement and Bolívar continued to fight alone.

Guelphs and Ghibellines Two opposing political factions prominent during the struggle for control of northern and central Italy (13th–15th cents.) The Guelphs supported the pope and the Ghibellines the German Holy Roman Emperors. The rivalry led to numerous local wars during this period and in Florence a long civil war that ended (1266) with the expulsion of the Ghibellines. By the 14th cent., after the power of Holy Roman Emperors declined in Italy and the papacy was removed to France, the rivalry was important only in local political struggles. (*See also* Welf.)

Guérande, Treaty of *See* **Breton Succession, War of the**

Guèrin, Camille *See* **Calmette, Albert Léon Charles**

Guerrero, Vicente 1783?–1831. Mexican revolutionary and president (1829). From 1810 he led revolutionary forces and became a celebrated guerrilla fighter. After 1822, he joined forces with A. Santa Anna in toppling A. de Iturbide and became vice-president under Guadalupe Victoria. Guerrero was overthrown (1829) by his vice-president, Anastasio Bustamente.

Gueux Dutch revolutionaries. In 1566, Dutch and Flemish nationals petitioned (1566) the ruling Spanish government for redress of grievances by the Compromise of Breda *(q.v.)*, but were dismissed as "ces gueux," (beggars). Adopting the name "Gueux" as a badge of pride, they organized under William the Silent and successfully harassed Spanish shipping, notably at the siege of Leiden (1574).

Guevara, Che (Guevara de la Serna, Ernesto) 1928–67. Argentinian-born Communist revolutionary leader. An important figure in F. Castro's Cuban revolution (1959), he became a renowned leader of revolutionary movements in Latin America. He was captured and killed while leading a guerrilla war in Bolivia (1966–67).

Guevara, de la Serna, Ernesto *See* **Guevara, Che**

Guggenheim, Simon 1867–1941. American philanthropist and US senator from Colorado (1907–13). He founded the John Simon Guggenheim Memorial Foundation (1925), which provides fellowships in the arts.

Guibert of Ravenna ⟨Clement III⟩ *d.* 1100. Italian antipope (1080–1100) to Gregory VII. He was enthroned when Henry IV captured Rome (1084) and in turn crowned Henry Holy Roman Emperor.

Guicciardini, Francesco 1483–1540. Italian historian and statesman. He wrote *Storia d'Italia*, which is considered the most important history written in the 16th cent.

Guido Aretinus   *See* **Guido d'Arezzo**

Guido d'Arezzo ⟨Guido Aretinus⟩ *c*990–1050. Italian Benedictine monk who made important modifications in the system of musical notation. He is said to have developed the musical staff.

Guido of Vienne   *See* **Calixtus II**

guilds ⟨gilds⟩ Medieval European merchant and craft associations. Guilds originated in Europe (11th cent.) as merchants' associations, formed to protect traveling merchants from bandits. Merchants' guilds became powerful, both economically and politically (12th–13th cents.). They were completely displaced, however, by the rise of the craft guilds and disappeared by the 14th cent. The craft guilds, composed of workers in a particular craft, declined in the 15th cent. as a result of internal disputes and other problems. They disappeared with the rise of capitalism (16th–17th cents.).

guild socialism Movement, centered in Britain, advocating state-owned, worker-controlled industry. It arose briefly in Britain during the early 20th cent. and called for creation of national guilds. Through these guilds, workers were to operate companies while the government was to retain actual ownership. The movement declined rapidly in the early 1920s.

Guilford Court House, Battle of American victory (Mar. 15, 1781) over the British during the Carolina Campaign *(q.v.)* of the American Revolution (1775–83). The battle was fought at Guilford, North Carolina, between some 4,400 Americans under Gen. N. Greene and 2,200 British under Gen. C. Cornwallis. Losses were light in the five-hour battle, but the engagement is said to have led Cornwallis to abandon the Carolinas to the Americans.

Guinea Name once used by Europeans to refer to the western coastal region of Africa.

Guinea ⟨Republic of Guinea⟩ ⟨*formerly* French Guinea⟩ Republic located on the coast of West Africa. Capital is Conakry. In precolonial times, the region was divided variously between tribal states, including empires of Mali, Ghana, and Ful-

ani. Portuguese explorers arrived in the 15th cent., and in subsequent centuries the region supplied slaves to the Portuguese, British, and French. In the 19th cent., the French sought to protect trade in agricultural products and declared a protectorate (1849) over part of the region. They gradually expanded their control and established it as a separate colony (1891), though fighting with natives continued until the end of the century. From 1893 to 1895, the colony was known as French Guinea and after 1895 it was administered as part of French West Africa. Then a major bauxite producer, it became an overseas territory of France (1946) and, after voting against joining the French Community *(q.v.)* in 1958, it achieved full independence. Under Sékou Touré (1922–), president of Guinea since its independence, Guinea first pursued closer relations with Russia and then with the Western powers (from late 1960s). In 1970, Touré successfully repulsed an invasion, launched from Guinea-Bissau, aimed at his overthrow.

Guinea-Bissau ⟨*formerly* Portuguese Guinea⟩ Coastal West African country. Capital is Bissau. First discovered (1446) by the Portuguese, the region became a center for the slave trade in the 17th and 18th cents. It came under Portuguese control, and its boundaries were established through agreement with France (1886). An independence movement began in Portuguese Guinea in the early 1960s under the leadership of A. Cabral. Rebel forces gained control of parts of the country and in 1973 declared the independence of Guinea-Bissau. Portugal granted independence Sept. 10, 1974. The government was overthrown in a military coup (Nov. 14, 1980).

Guinegate, Battle of   *See* **Spurs, Battle of the**

Guinevere Wife of King Arthur in the Arthurian Legend. She had an adulterous love affair with one of Arthur's knights, Sir Lancelot, joined a convent, and eventually died there.

Guinness, Sir Alec 1914–. British actor, noted for his versatility. Among his many famous roles were those he played in *The Lavender Hill Mob* and *The Bridge on the River Kwai.*

Guiscard, Robert   *See* **Robert Guiscard**

Guise French Roman Catholic family that played a major role in French politics (16th and 17th cents.). It was founded by Claude de Lorraine (1496–1550), 1st duke of Guise. His daughter, Mary of Guise, was the mother of Mary Queen of Scots. His sons François de Lorraine (1519–63), 2d duke of Guise, and Charles de Guise (1524–74) gained great power in France under Francis II. Their persecution of the Huguenots (Protestants) and rivalry with the Bourbons led to the Conspiracy of Amboise (1560), which they ruthlessly suppressed. Their massacre (1562) of Huguenots at Vassy led to the Wars of Religion (1562–98). François' son, Henri de Lorraine (1550–88), 3d duke of Guise, aided in planning and execution of the Massacre of St. Bartholomew's Day (1572) and formed the Catholic League (1576), which continued persecution of the Huguenots. The line ended with François Joseph de Lorraine, 7th duke of Guise (d. 1675).

Guise, Charles de, Cardinal of Lorraine 1524–74. French Catholic cardinal, son of Claude I, 1st duke of Guise. He and his brother, François, 2d duke of Guise, were the most influential men in the court of Francis II. He is said to have brought the Inquisition to France and is noted for persecution of Protestants.

Guise, Claude de Lorraine, 1st duke of 1496–1550. French Catholic nobleman and soldier. He founded the Guise family, which rose to power in France during the 16th cent. He was created duke of Guise by Francis I in 1527.

Guise, François de Lorraine, 2d duke of 1519–63. French Catholic nobleman and soldier, son of Claude I, 1st duke of Guise. He shared the power of government under Francis II with his brother Charles de Guise and took part in the persecution of French Protestants (Huguenots). Following Catherine de Medici's rise to power, he joined with others in opposing tolerance toward the Huguenots. His troops are said to have sparked the Wars of Religion by a massacre of Huguenots at Vassy (1562).

Guise, François Joseph de Lorraine, 7th duke of See **Guise**

Guise, Henri de Lorraine, 3d duke of 1550–88. French Catholic nobleman and soldier, a son of F. de Lorraine. He fought the Huguenots in the Wars of Religion, took part in planning the massacre of St. Bartholomew's Day (1572), and formed the Catholic League (1576).

Guise, Henri de Lorraine, 5th duke of 1614–64. French Catholic nobleman, a grandson of H. de Lorraine. He joined the opposition to Cardinal Richelieu (1641) and was forced to flee France until 1654.

Guise, Louis II de Lorraine 1555–88. French cardinal. Louis was the younger brother of H. de Lorraine. He was assassinated by the Royal Guard.

Guise, Mary of See **Mary of Guise**

Guizot, François Pierre Guillaume 1787–1874. French statesman and historian. After 1840 he became chief minister in the government of Louis Philippe, formed after the July Revolution (1830). He was ousted during the February Revolution (1848).

Gujrat, Battle of Battle (Feb. 21, 1849) between British troops under Lord Gough, and some 50,000 Sikhs, led by Sher Singh. The British victory ended the Second Sikh War and resulted in annexation of the Punjab by the British.

Gulf of Tonkin Resolution Resolution passed by the US Congress (Aug. 7, 1964) in support of President L. Johnson's involvement of US military forces in Vietnam. It came as a direct result of the Gulf of Tonkin incident, in which North Vietnamese PT boats attacked (Aug. 4) US destroyers in the gulf. The US retaliated by bombing North Vietnam, and Johnson, requesting congressional approval for such attacks, won passage of the resolution.

Gulistan, Treaty of Treaty (Oct. 12, 1813) between Russia and Persia, at Gulistan, now in Azerbaijan SSR. Persia ceded to Russia much of what became Azerbaijan, and gave up claims to Georgia, Dagestan, and other areas in the region.

Gundahar. See **Gunther**

Gundicar See **Gunther**

Gundicarius See **Gunther**

Gunnar See **Gunther**

Gunpowder Plot Conspiracy by English Catholics to blow up Parliament and King James I (1605). Angered by King James's failure to order greater religious toleration of Catholics, five conspirators planned to provoke a general Catholic uprising. They hid a number of barrels of gunpowder in a basement under Parliament in anticipation of the day the king was to attend. The plot was discovered and one conspirator, Guy Fawkes, was caught in the cellar. The four accomplices, in addition to others who had been involved, were caught and executed.

Guntharius See **Gunther**

Gunther ⟨Gundahar⟩ ⟨Gundicar⟩ ⟨Gundicarius⟩ ⟨Gunnar⟩ ⟨Guntharius⟩ d. AD 437. Burgundian king (AD 413–437). Gunther was the first king of Burgundy. He led his people across the Rhine (413) to establish his kingdom and later died in battle against Attila.

Gupta dynasty Dynasty of rulers of India (AD c320–550). Guptas ruled over an empire that at one time included northern and parts of central India. The dynasty was founded by Chandragupta I and the empire was greatly expanded by Samudragupta. Chandragupta II was the greatest of all Gupta rulers. Indian art and commerce flourished under the Guptas until the empire was overrun by White Huns (5th cent.).

Gurkhas See **Nepal**

Gustavian Enlightenment See **Swedish Enlightenment**

Gustav line In WW II, the German line of defense in southern Italy, stretching from Pescara to Gaeta. The Allies finally broke through it during their attack on Rome (May 1944).

Gustavus I 1496–1560. Swedish king (1523–60), first of Vasa dynasty. Following the Stockholm Bloodbath, he raised an army of Swedes against the Danish rulers of Sweden and defeated them. He was elected king (1523) and the Kalmar Union (*q.v.*) was dissolved. He consolidated the power of the monarchy and in 1544 royal succession was made hereditary.

Gustavus II 〈Gustavus Adolphus〉 1594–1632. Swedish king (1611–32), successor to his father, Charles IX. With help from his chancellor, A. Oxenstierna, he pacified the nobles and restored order to Swedish government. He ended the Kalmar War (1613), successfully waged wars against Russia (1613–17) and Poland (1621–29), and proved a skilled leader of Protestant troops in the Thirty Years' War. He was killed at the Battle of Lutzen (1632).

Gustavus III 1746–92. Swedish king (1771–92). His reign is sometimes referred to as the Swedish Enlightenment. He renewed the authority of the monarchy and restored order, instituted important reforms, and entered into a costly war with Russia (1788–90).

Gustavus IV 〈Gustavus Adolphus〉 1778–1837. Swedish king (1792–1809), successor to his father, Gustavus III. He was an unpopular ruler, and his foreign policies proved disastrous for Sweden. He lost Finland to Russia (1808) and was finally overthrown (1809). His heirs were forbidden to succeed him.

Gustavus V 1858–1950. Swedish king (1907–50), successor to his father, Oscar II. He proved to be a popular and able constitutional monarch who maintained Sweden's neutrality through WW I and WW II.

Gustavus VI 1882–1973. Swedish king (1950–73), successor to his father, Gustavus V. During his reign the Swedish Riksdag passed legislation reducing the king's role to that of a figurehead.

Gutenberg Johann *c*1400–68?. German generally regarded as the inventor (in the West) of the method of printing with movable type. Few details of Gutenberg's life are certain but he is thought to have invented his printing method (*c*1438) while living in Strasbourg. Later, in Mainz, he entered a partnership (1450) with a goldsmith, J. Fust, and began printing the Mazarin Bible. He lost his press and type following a suit by Fust (1455). It is believed that Chinese and Korean printing techniques, invented earlier and

similar to Gutenberg's, were unknown to Europeans.

Guyana 〈*formerly* British Guiana〉 Independent republic in northeast South America. Capital is Georgetown. The Dutch founded the first settlement (*c*1620) at Essequibo and in the following century both Britain and France founded colonies there. During the Dutch Wars, England captured the region, but the Dutch regained possession by the Treaty of Breda (1667). The region changed hands frequently during the French Revolutionary and Napoleonic Wars, though Britain ultimately gained control of it at the Congress of Vienna (1815). British Guiana was formally created in 1831 and the discovery of gold (1879) there led to an international controversy, known as the Venezuela Boundary Dispute (*q.v.*), over claims to part of the territory. The movement for independence began after WW II, and a constitution, providing for elections, was adopted in 1952. Britain suspended the constitution (1953) when a pro-Communist government was elected, but new elections in 1957 returned a more moderate government. Despite unrest during the 1960s, elected governments remained in power, and full independence was granted May 26, 1966. A major crisis was averted (1970) when a 12-year truce was negotiated with Venezuela and Surinam over claims to territory in Guyana. Guyana became a republic that same year.

Guyon, Jeanne Marie de la Motte 1648–1717. French mystic and author. An important figure in the religious movement known as quietism, she became embroiled in the controversy surrounding it. She was eventually imprisoned in the Bastille (1695–1702) for her writings.

Guzmán Blanco, Antonio 1829–99. Venezuelan dictator. He was vice-president (1863–68) and following overthrow of the government, he led a counterrevolution. He was subsequently elected president (1870) and, until his overthrow in 1888, he ruled with dictatorial powers.

Gwinnett, Button *c*1735–1777. American patriot and signer of the Declaration of Independence. He was a delegate to the Continental Congress (1776–77) and was president of the State of Georgia (1777).

Gwyn, Eleanor *See* **Gwyn, Nell**

Gwyn, Nell 〈Gwyn, Eleanor〉 〈Gwynn, Eleanor〉 1650–87. English actress and mistress to Charles II (after 1669). A lively and spirited lady of humble background, she was a popular public figure in her day, as well as a favorite of the king.

Gwynn, Eleanor *See* **Gwyn, Nell**

Gypsies Nomadic people of uncertain origins that are today found throughout the world. Gypsies speak a language called Romany and are thought to have originated in northern India. They appeared in Persia as a nomadic people (c1000), in Europe (c1500) and North America (late 1800s). Traditionally Gypsies are craftsmen, entertainers, fortune-tellers, and travel in caravans. As outsiders in settled lands, they have been the object of persecutions, most notably the execution of 400,000–500,000 of them in Hitler's concentration camps.

H

Haakon I ⟨Haakon the Good⟩ *c*914?–61. Norwegian king ⟨*c*935–961⟩. An able ruler, he attempted to introduce Christianity to Norway.

Haakon IV ⟨Haakon the Old⟩ ⟨Haakon Haakonsson⟩ 1204–63. Norwegian king ⟨1217–63⟩. Under his reign medieval Norway began its golden age. He added Greenland and Iceland to his realm, made important legal reforms, and encouraged the arts.

Haakon VII 1872–1957. Norwegian king ⟨1905–57⟩, a son of Danish King Frederick VIII. He was elected king by parliament on the dissolution of the union between Norway and Sweden. He ruled in exile at London during the Nazi occupation ⟨1940–45⟩.

Haakon Haakonsson *See* **Haakon IV**

Haakon the Good *See* **Haakon I**

Haakon the Old *See* **Haakon IV**

habeas corpus Writ issued by a court to one who has imprisoned another, calling for the person detained to be produced before the court for a specific purpose. It is used largely to prevent false imprisonment.

Habibullah Khan 1872–1919. Amir of Afghanistan ⟨1901–19⟩. He established friendly relations with the British in India, maintained neutrality in WW I, and introduced many reforms.

Hades Mythical Greek god of the underworld (also called Pluto), also the name of his kingdom. A brother of Zeus, he reigned with Persephone over this land for spirits of the dead. It was bounded by five rivers, including the Styx and Lethe.

Hadith Muslim term, meaning "tradition," applied specifically to stories of the life and technique of Muhammad. They are sacred to Islam.

Hadrian AD 76–138. Roman emperor ⟨AD 117–138⟩. An energetic ruler, Hadrian fortified the empire's boundaries, built Hadrian's Wall, and suppressed the revolt of Bar Kokba.

Hadrianople, Battle of *See* **Adrianople, Battle of**

Hadrian's Wall Defensive stone wall built by the Romans to protect the northern border of their territories in Britain against invading tribes. Built largely under the reign of Emperor Hadrian, it stretches 73.5 miles across a narrow point in the island of Britain. Large sections of the wall are still standing.

Haeckel, Ernst Heinrich 1834–1919. German biologist and evolutionist. His speculations on biological evolution, based on Darwin's theory, stimulated interest in evolutionary theory.

Hafiz ⟨*pseud. of* Shams ud-din Muhammad⟩ *d.* 1389? One of the greatest of Persian poets, he was a member of the Sufi sect and is perhaps most widely known for his collection of poetry, the *Divan.*

Hagar ⟨Agar⟩ In the Old Testament, handmaiden to Abraham's wife, and mother of his oldest son Ishmael. Eventually forced out into the wilderness with her son, she was rescued by God.

Hagia Sophia ⟨Santa Sophia⟩ Former cathedral at Constantinople, considered a masterpiece of Byzantine art and one of the world's most magnificent buildings. Built as a Christian church by Byzantine emperor Justinian I, it became a mosque ⟨1453⟩ after the Turks conquered Constantinople and now is a museum.

Hague, The Capital of The Netherlands ⟨pop. 468,000⟩. Originally a town that grew up around a palace built by Count William of Holland ⟨*c*1250⟩, it became one of the important diplomatic centers of Europe by the 17th cent. Since the first Hague Conference ⟨1899⟩, the city has been associated with advancement of international justice. The International Court of Justice is located here.

Hague Conferences ⟨~ Conventions⟩ **1.** First ~ ⟨International Peace Conference of 1899⟩, held at the Hague in The Netherlands ⟨May 18-July 29, 1899⟩. Called by Russia, it was attended by 26 countries, including the US. Though the major question of arms limitations went unresolved, the conference set up the Hague Tribunal ⟨Permanent Court of Arbitration⟩, and banned poison gas, "dumdum" (expanding) bullets, and aerial bombing from balloons. **2.** Second ~ ⟨International Peace Conference of 1907⟩ held at the Hague ⟨June 15–Oct. 18, 1907⟩. Convened by Russia, it was attended by 44 countries. Again the conference made no resolution on arms limitation, though agreement was reached on rights of neutral shipping, general conventions on land and sea warfare, and a ban on submarine mines. The outbreak of WW I forced cancellation of a third conference (1915), but the conferences nevertheless laid the basis for such international organizations as the League of Nations and the United Nations.

Hague Conventions *See* **Hague Conferences**

Hague Tribunal Permanent Court of Arbitration, an international court. Established (1899) at The Hague, in The Netherlands, as a forum to settle international disputes, it was superseded by the World Court (1921).

Hahn, Otto 1879–1968. German scientist. In 1938, with Fritz Strassmann, he demonstrated nuclear fission by bombarding uranium with neutrons. He received the Nobel Prize for Chemistry (1944).

Haidar Ali *See* **Mysore Wars**

Haig, Douglas, 1st Earl 1861–1928. British field marshal in WW I who commanded British forces in France after 1915. His strategy of fighting a "war of attrition" cost the British heavy casualties and aroused a public controversy. Nevertheless, he led the Allied assault that finally broke German resistance (1918).

Haile Selassie ⟨Tafari Makonnen⟩ ⟨Ras Tafari⟩ 1891–1975. Emperor of Ethiopia (1930–74) who worked to modernize his country and bring it into the world political arena. He led the unsuccessful defense against the invading Italian army (1935) and with British help regained his throne (1941). He was deposed (1974) in a military coup.

Hainisch, Michael Arthur Josef Jakob 1858–1940. Austrian statesman. Though he favored union with Germany, he was elected first president of the newly formed federal republic of Austria (1920–28).

Haiphong Port city and industrial center in northern Vietnam (pop. 1,515,000). Its harbor, built (1874) by the French, developed into an important Southeast Asian commercial center. During the Vietnam War it became a prime target for US bombers (1965–68) and toward the end of the war the US mined the harbor (1972–73).

Haiti Republic in the West Indies on Hispaniola Island. Latin America's most densely populated nation, it was ceded by Spain to France (1697), and in the late 18th and early 19th cents. was the scene of numerous revolts against French rule, notably that of Toussaint L'Ouverture. It became independent (1804), and its history became one of frequent political turmoil. It was occupied (1915–34) by US Marines. Its recent history was marked

by conflict with the neighboring Dominican Republic and the tyrannical rule (1957–71) of François ("Papa Doc") Duvalier. Duvalier's son, Jean-Claude, succeeded in 1971. Continued economic problems led to the exodus of Haitian "boat people" to the US in 1980.

Hakka Chinese people living in southern China. A distinct group, their name means "guest people." It is believed they migrated (12th–13th cents.) from northern China.

Hakluyt, Richard 1552?–1616. English geographer. His many books on voyages of discovery helped promote exploration and colonization of North America by the English.

Halcyone ⟨Alcyone⟩ In Greek mythology, the daughter of Aeolus. After her husband Ceyx drowned, the gods took pity and changed them both into kingfishers, granting them a week of winter calm. This winter lull has come to be known as the "halcyon days."

Haldighat, Battle of *See* **Gogunda, Battle of**

Haldimand, Sir Frederick 1718–91. British general and administrator. During the French and Indian War he served in the Montreal expedition (1760) led by J. Amherst. As governor of Quebec province, he curbed French-Canadian support for the American Revolution.

Hale, Edward Everett 1822–1909. American author and clergyman, known best for his short novel *The Man Without a Country*.

Hale, George Ellery 1868–1938. American astronomer. He organized and directed the Yerkes and Mount Wilson observatories and is noted for discovering magnetic fields in sunspots.

Hale, Nathan 1755–76. American Revolutionary War officer and hero who is said to have spoken the famous words "I only regret that I have but one life to lose for my country." Originally a Connecticut militiaman, he volunteered for a dangerous spy mission behind British lines on Long Island. He was caught while returning and was hanged as a spy the next day.

Halepa, Pact of *See* **Pact of Halepa**

Hales, Alexander of *See* **Alexander of Hales**

Half-Breeds US political term applied in the 1870s and 1880s to Republicans who supported liberal Democratic policies. They were opposed within the Republican party by the conservative Stalwarts. The Half-Breeds' leaders included J. Blaine and J. Garfield.

Half-Way Covenant A church doctrine formulated by Puritans in New England in the mid-17th cent. Originally a personal experience of conversion was required for full membership in the Congregational church, though children of members were baptized and enjoyed nearly all church privileges. A controversy arose over the question of baptizing (and admitting to membership) the offspring of these children, many of whom had grown up without a conversion experience. The doctrine of extending privileges to these offspring was adopted at a church synod (1662), but the issue remained highly controversial.

Halicarnassus, Dionysius of *See* **Dionysius of Halicarnassus**

Halidon Hill, Battle of English victory (July 19, 1333) over the Scottish forces of King David II. English king Edward III, besieging Berwick for E. de Baliol, decisively defeated a Scottish relief force led by Sir A. Douglas, regent for David II.

Halifax, Charles Montague, earl of 1661–1715. English statesman. A Whig party member, he instituted borrowing schemes that created the British national debt (1692), and adopted plans that created the Bank of England (1694).

Halifax, Edward Frederick Lindley Wood, 1st earl of 1881–1959. English statesman. He was viceroy of India (1926–31), foreign secretary (1938–40) and ambassador to the US (1941–46). As foreign secretary he was a staunch supporter of N. Chamberlain's appeasement policy toward the Nazis.

Hall, Charles Martin 1863–1914. American chemist who discovered the first practical process for manufacturing aluminum (1886). With the backing of the Mellon family, he founded a company that eventually became the Aluminum Company of America.

Hall, Granville Stanley 1844–1924. American psychologist and educator. Sometimes called the founder of educational and child psychology, he also originated the *American Journal of Psychology* (1887).

Halleck, Henry Wager 1815–72. Union general in the American Civil War. Although an able administrator, he was an indecisive strategist. He served as general-in-chief of all Union armies (1862–64) until replaced by U. Grant.

Haller, Albrecht von 1708–77. Swiss physiologist, anatomist, and botanist. Sometimes called the father of experimental physiology, he is known best for his *Physiological Elements of the Human Body.*

Halley, Edmund 1656–1742. English astronomer and mathematician. Though noted for a variety of discoveries relating to heavenly bodies, he is known best for calculating accurately the return (1758) of the comet now named after him.

Hals, Frans *c*1580–1666. Dutch painter, now ranked among the great portrait painters of his time. He painted both group and individual portraits and during his career developed a characteristic looseness and freedom of style. Among his

works are *Banquet of the Officers of the St. George Militia, The Governors of the Almshouse,* and *Lady Regents of the Almshouse.*

Halsey, Bull *See* **Halsey, William Frederick, Jr.**

Halsey, William Frederick ⟨Bull ∼⟩ 1882–1959. American admiral in WW II. An aggressive commander of carrier task forces, he was an important figure in many of the island campaigns against the Japanese. He became commander of South Pacific naval forces (1942–44) and commander of the US Third Fleet (1944–45).

Ham One of the three sons of Noah, said to be the progenitor of the Hamitic races.

Hama ⟨Hamath⟩ Syrian city. An ancient city mentioned in the Bible, its origins date to prehistoric times. Once controlled by the Hittites, it thereafter fell variously to the Assyrians, Persians, Romans, Byzantines, Arabs, and Turks, among others. It became part of Syria in 1941.

Haman ⟨Aman⟩ Persian minister mentioned in the Old Testament. His plan to massacre the Jews of Persia was blocked by the intercession of Esther.

Hamath *See* **Hama**

Hamburg Major port city in West Germany (pop. 1,680,300). Founded in the 9th cent., it rose in importance to rival the other great port cities of Europe by the 19th cent. It joined the German Confederation in 1815. Destroyed by bombing raids at the end of WW II, the city has since returned to commercial importance.

Hamelin, Pied Piper of *See* **Pied Piper of Hamelin**

Hamilcar Barca *d.* 229 or 228 BC. Carthaginian general, father of Hannibal. He fought ably in Sicily during the First Punic War, put down a revolt by mercenaries at Carthage (241–238 BC), and made extensive conquests in Spain.

Hamilton, Alexander 1757?–1804. American statesman and a leading Federalist in the early years of the republic. A delegate to the Continental Congress (1782–83), he worked to establish a strong, centralized federal system of government. At the Annapolis Convention (1786), he proposed the convening of the Philadelphia Convention (1787). He made major contributions to the Federalist Papers, which played an important role in gaining ratification of the Constitution. As first US secretary of the treasury (1789–95), he formulated fiscal policy and established the Bank of the US (1791). A leader with J. Adams of the Federalists in their opposition to the Jeffersonian Republicans, he came to oppose Adams. His political maneuvering against his enemy A. Burr led to the famous duel in which he was shot and killed by Burr.

Hamilton, James, 2d Baron Hamilton and 1st earl of Arran *See* **Hamilton family**

Hamilton, James, 2d earl of Arran *See* **Hamilton family**

Hamilton, James, 3d earl of Arran *See* **Hamilton family**

Hamilton, James, 3d marquess and 1st duke of 1606–49. Scottish nobleman. A royalist, he led a 24,000-man army against the Parliamentarians during the English Civil War. Defeated by O. Cromwell at Preston, he was hanged shortly thereafter.

Hamilton, John, 1st marquess of 1532–1604. Scottish nobleman. A supporter of Mary Queen of Scots, he participated in the murder of J. Stuart and fled to England.

Hamilton, William, 2d duke of *See* **Hamilton family**

Hamilton, Sir William 1788–1856. Scottish philosopher, noted for his work in the fields of metaphysics and logic.

Hamilton family Noble family prominent in Scottish history for more than 300 years. Members of the family were variously barons, earls, dukes, and marquises of Hamilton, Arran, Belhaven, Claneboye, Haddington, and Orkney. Among the prominent members of the family were: James Hamilton, 2d baron Hamilton and 1st earl of Arran (1477?–1529), member of the council of regency during the minority of James V; James Hamilton, 2d earl of Arran (d. 1575), regent to Mary Queen of Scots during her minority; James Hamilton, 3d earl of Arran (1530–1609), proposed as suitor to both English Queen Elizabeth I and Mary Queen of Scots, later confined for insanity; and William Hamilton, 2d duke of Hamilton (1616–51), supported Charles II in the English Civil War.

Hamlin, Hannibal 1809–91. American statesman. An opponent of slavery, as a member of the US House of Representatives (1843–47) he supported the controversial Wilmot Proviso (1846). He also served in the Senate (1848–57, 1869–81), was an early member of the Republican party, and was 15th vice-president of the US (1861–65) under President A. Lincoln.

Hammarskjöld, Dag 1905–61. Swedish statesman and UN secretary general (1953–61). He held various posts in the Swedish government (1930–53) and (1951–53) was a delegate to the UN. Noted as an able and active peacemaker, he played an important role in easing the Suez Crisis (1956) and in maintaining Mideast stability during the crisis in Lebanon (1958). He was killed in an airplane crash while attempting to mediate an end to the civil war that broke out (1960) in the Congo.

Hammerstein, Oscar 1847?–1919. German-American operatic manager. He arranged the first American appearances of many noteworthy European opera productions and singers in the early 1900s.

Hammerstein, Oscar 2d 1895–1960. American lyricist and librettist. He is known best for his collaboration with R. Rodgers, on such hit musicals as *Oklahoma!, The King and I,* and *The Sound of Music.*

Hammett, Samuel Dashiell 1894–1961. American author, noted as the originator of the hard-boiled detective novel. His works include *The Maltese Falcon* and *The Thin Man.*

Hammond, James Henry 1807–64. American statesman. An early supporter of southern secession, he served in the US House of Representatives (1835–36) and as governor of South Carolina (1842–44). A member of the Senate (1857–60), he delivered a celebrated speech in which he declared that "cotton is king." (*See* King Cotton.)

Hammurabi *fl. c*1792–50 BC. Babylonian king. Credited with bringing Mesopotamia under one rule, he is known best for his comprehensive legal code covering economic, familial, criminal, and civil codes of conduct. Considered advanced, humane, and civilized for its era, the code was discovered in 1901.

Hammurabi, Code of *See* **Code of Hammurabi**

Hampden, John 1594–1643. English parliamentary leader. He became a hero of Parliamentarians when he challenged the right of King Charles I to levy ship-money taxes (1637). His near arrest along with four other members of Parliament (1642) helped bring on the English Civil War.

Hampton, Wade 1818–1902. American statesman and Confederate general in the American Civil War. A wealthy planter, he raised "Hampton's Legion" and served well in many important battles. After the war, he became a noted South Carolina politician, elected governor (1876–78) and senator (1879–90).

Hampton Court Conference English religious conference (Jan., 1604) called by King James I to settle the differences between the Anglicans and the Puritans. Its only positive result was the King James Bible.

Hampton Roads Peace Conference American Civil War peace conference (Feb. 3, 1865) aboard the steamer *River Queen* near Hampton Roads, Virginia. The conference failed to negotiate an end to the war.

Hamsun, Knut (*pseud. of* Knut Pedersen) 1859–1952. Norwegian novelist. An influential naturalist writer in the early 20th cent., he is known best for *Hunger* and *The Growth of the Soil*. He was awarded the 1920 Nobel Prize for Literature.

Hancock, John   1737–93. American Revolutionary War patriot, first signer of the Declaration of Independence. A Boston merchant, Hancock became involved in opposition to British taxation when his ship was seized in the Liberty Affair (1768). He served as president of the Provincial Congress (1774–75), a member of the Continental Congress (1775–80), and as its president (1775–77).

Hancock, Winfield Scott   1824–86. Union general and unsuccessful Democratic presidential candidate in 1880. He fought well in several major battles, notably at Gettysburg. His evenhanded treatment of Southerners after the war helped him win the Democratic nomination against J. Garfield.

Hand, Learned   1872–1961. US Federal Court of Appeals judge. As US district judge (1909–24) and appellate court judge (1924–51), he was a widely respected jurist.

Handel, George Frederick   1685–1759. German-born English composer, one of the foremost baroque composers. He produced his first operas in Hamburg, next went to Italy (1707–09), and made his first visit to London (1710). He became a British citizen (1726). In England he composed his many famous Italian operas, oratorios, concertos, and occasional pieces. Among his works are the operas *Berenice* and *Serse*, the oratio *Messiah*, the orchestral piece *Water Music*, and what is now the British coronation theme, *Zadok the Priest*.

Handy, William Christopher   1873–1958. American composer and bandleader. He popularized the blues idiom in American jazz music and is perhaps best known for his *St. Louis Blues*.

Han dynasty   Chinese dynasty. Founded by Liu Pang (later known as Han Kao Tsu, (d. 195 BC), it succeeded the Ch'in dynasty and ruled China from 202? BC to AD 220. Many characteristic features of Chinese culture were established in this period. The Han unified China, repealed many harsh laws, promoted education and culture, and spread Confucianism. A paid bureaucracy and the Chinese Examination System were instituted during this period, and a distinctive artistic style also emerged. Wu Ti was one of the most notable rulers. Wang Mang briefly interrupted the reign of the Han (AD 9–23) by his revolt.

Han-fei-tzu   d. 233 BC. Chinese philosopher. His advocacy of authoritarianism and complete obedience to the emperor gained great influence in the Ch'in dynasty.

Hang-chou   *See* **Hangchow**

Hangchow   ⟨Hang-chou⟩ Chinese city (pop. 1,100,000), an industrial and cultural center. Founded (606), it has been famous as a center of silk production for centuries. The city reached the height of its importance as the capital of the Southern Sung dynasty (12th cent.) and was largely rebuilt after the Taiping Rebellion (1861).

Hanging Gardens of Babylon   Ancient gardens built (probably in the 6th cent. BC) at Babylon. A series of terrace gardens, they were one of the Seven Wonders of the World.

Hanna, Marcus Alonzo   ⟨Mark Hanna⟩ 1837–1904. American businessman and politician. A successful Ohio businessman and a power in the Republican party, he played a key role in W. McKinley's successful campaigns for governor of Ohio (1891, 1893) and for president (1896).

Hanna, Mark   *See* **Hanna, Marcus Alonzo**

Hannah   ⟨Anna⟩ Biblical mother of Samuel.

Hannibal   247–182? BC. Carthaginian general during the Second Punic War (218–201 BC). The son of Hamilcar Barca, he became (221 BC) commander of Carthaginian forces in Spain and, by his attack on a city allied to Rome, precipitated (218) the Second Punic War. In one of history's most celebrated military maneuvers, he led an army of 40,000 soldiers (with a supply train of elephants) out of Spain and across the Alps to invade Rome itself. He gained major victories over the Romans at Lake Trasimeno (217) and Cannae (216) but was unable to take the city. Recalled (203) to defend Carthage from Roman attack, he was defeated at Zama (202). He later joined Syrian king Antiochus in wars against Rome, but was defeated (182) and poisoned himself.

Hanno   *fl.* 5th cent. BC. Carthaginian navigator who led a fleet of ships along the west coast of Africa for the purpose of establishing new colonies. He eventually founded seven colonies and may have reached Sierra Leone.

Hannover, House of   *See* **Hanover, House of**

Hanoi   Capital of Vietnam (597,000). The city has been the capital of the Vietnamese or their conquerors throughout much of their history. It was capital for their Chinese rulers in the 6th or 7th cent. AD, for Vietnamese rulers from the 11th to the 17th cent., for the French (1887–1954), and capital of North Vietnam (1954–76). It was heavily bombed during the Vietnam War (1965–68, 1972).

Hanover, House of   ⟨Hannover, ~⟩ German ruling family of Hanover. Descended from the Guelphs, the line acceded to the British throne, through the Act of Settlement (1701), through George I. Succeeding Hanoverian rulers of England were George II, George III, George IV, and William IV. Upon the accession (1837) of Queen Victoria the two kingdoms were separated, Victoria being unable by Hanoverian law to accede to the throne of Hanover.

Hanseatic League Once powerful federation of cities (13th–17th cents.), mainly located in what is now northern Germany. It sought to establish trade monopolies and protect its concerns against piracy, robbery, and intervention by foreign governments. The cities of Lübeck and Hamburg founded (1241) the league. It eventually included over 100 others and virtually controlled trade in the Baltic and North Sea regions. The league established great trading depots, including the Steelyard in London, Bruges, Bergen, and Novgorod. The league reached the zenith of its power with conquest of the Danes and the Treaty of Stralsund (1370). The league gradually declined thereafter, due to being unable to resist the Dutch in the Baltic region, the growing power of other European kingdoms, internal struggles among member cities, and the change in trading patterns brought about by the discovery of the New World. The last meeting of the league was held in 1669.

Hansen, Hans Christian Svane 1906–60. Danish statesman. As foreign minister (1953–60) and prime minister (1955–60) he played a key role in Denmark's economic growth and in its emergence as a major force within NATO.

Hanson, John 1721–83. American Revolutionary War patriot and political leader. Sometimes referred to as the first US president, he was actually a presiding legislative officer called the "president" (1781–82) under the Articles of Confederation.

Hansson, Per Albin 1885–1946. Swedish statesman. As prime minister (1932–46) in the critical Depression and WW II years, he encouraged public works, agricultural projects, and social welfare, and kept Sweden neutral during the war.

Han Wên-kung *See* **Han Yu**

Han Yu ⟨Han Wên-kung⟩ 768–824. Chinese official, essayist, and poet. A Confucian, he was an outspoken critic of Taoism and Buddhism, and was once exiled from the emperor's court for his views. His writings earned him the title "Prince of Letters."

Hapsburg (Habsburg) One of the major dynasties of European rulers (13th-20th cents.) Members of the Hapsburg house became rulers of Austria, the Holy Roman Empire, and Spain. The line can be traced back to the 11th-cent. counts of Hapsburg, and in 1273 Rudolf I founded the imperial line. Elected king of the Germans in 1273, he acquired Austria (1278) and made it a hereditary possession (1282). The Hapsburgs ruled as kings of the Germans (rulers not crowned as "emperor" by the

pope) with interruptions until 1452, when Frederick III was crowned Holy Roman Emperor. Thereafter the title remained in the family until the empire succumbed to Napoleon (1806). By advantageous marriages and inheritance of family domains, Hapsburg rulers vastly increased their holdings and reached the height of their power (16th cent.) under Emperor Charles V, who was also Spanish King Charles I. The Hapsburg line was divided on his death into Spanish (rulers 1504–1700) and Austrian lines. The Austrian line (known as Hapsburg-Lorraine after 1740) ruled the Holy Roman Empire to 1806 and Austria, Hungary, and Bohemia until 1918.

Hapsburg Kings & Holy Roman Emperors

Rudolf I	1273–91
Albert I	1298–1308
Albert II	1438–39
Frederick III	1440–93
Maximilian I	1493–1519
Charles V	1519–56
Ferdinand I	1556–64
Maximilian II	1564–76
Rudolf II	1576–1612
Matthias	1612–19
Ferdinand II	1619–37
Ferdinand III	1637–57
Leopold I	1658–1705
Joseph I	1705–11
Charles VI	1711–40

Hapsburg-Lorraine Holy Roman Emperors

Francis I	1745–65
Joseph II	1765–90
Leopold II	1790–92
Francis II	1792–1806

(Francis II becomes Francis I of Austria, 1804)

Spanish Hapsburg Monarchs

Holy Roman Emperor Charles V, as Charles I	1516–56
Philip II	1556–98
Philip III	1598–1621
Philip IV	1621–65
Charles II	1665–1700

Austrian Hapsburg Monarchs

Maria Theresa	1740–80
Joseph II	1780–90
Leopold II	1790–92
Francis II	1792–1804
Francis II, as Francis I	1804–35
Ferdinand I	1835–48
Francis Joseph I	1848–1916
Charles I	1916–18

Hapsburg, Rudolf of *See* **Rudolf I**

Hapsburg-Lorraine *See* **Hapsburg**

Hara, Kei ⟨Hara, Takashi⟩ 1856–1921. Japanese statesman and prime minister (1918–21). He built his Seiyukai party into a Western-style political machine and became the first Japanese prime minister to form a cabinet according to parliamentary principles.

Hara, Takashi *See* **Hara, Kei**

Hardecanute *See* **Harold Harefoot**

Hardenberg, Prince Karl August von 1750–1822. Prussian statesman. As chancellor from 1810, he guided Prussia through the turbulent years of the Napoleonic Wars and was responsible for many political and social reforms.

Harding, Warren Gamaliel 1865–1923. Twenty-ninth US president (1921–23), successor to W. Wilson. Harding's administration was notorious for the Teapot Dome (*q.v.*) scandal. A newspaper publisher and Republican politician in Ohio, he later became a US senator (1915–21). His term as senator was undistinguished, though his congenial manner won him influential friends. Finally, at the deadlocked Republican convention of 1920, Harding was nominated as the compromise candidate for president. He campaigned on a return-to-"normalcy" platform that gained wide appeal in post-WW I America and he won the election easily. Though he was personally an honest man, he surrounded himself with political appointees who proved to be unscrupulous and corrupt. The first years of his administration were marked by a single major administration initiative, the convening of the Washington Conference (1922) for international reduction of naval armament. But in 1923 rumors of scandal began to spread. Harding died while on a tour of the West (Aug. 2, 1923), apparently after receiving reports of the impending revelations. In following months, his appointees in various departments, including Interior, Justice, the Veterans' Bureau, and others, were charged with corruption and negligence. Of the scandals uncovered, Teapot Dome was the worst.

Hardy, Thomas 1840–1928. English novelist and poet, a leading author of the 19th cent. Among his best-known works are *Tess of the D'Urbervilles* and *Jude the Obscure*.

Haremhab *See* **Harmhab**

Hargreaves, James *d.* 1778. English inventor who devised the spinning jenny (*c*1764).

Harlan, John Marshall 1833–1911. Associate justice of the US Supreme Court (1877–1911). A noted dissenter and considered a strict constructionist, he dissented in the Supreme Court's decision (1896) upholding "separate but equal" treatment of blacks.

Harlem Heights, Battle of Series of skirmishes (Sept. 16, 1776) in northern Manhattan, New York, during the American Revolution. The skirmishes slowed the British advance north after the Battle of Long Island, and helped Colonial forces to prepare for the coming Battle of White Plains.

Harley, Robert, 1st earl of Oxford 1661–1724. British statesman and leader of the Tory ministry (1710–14) under Queen Anne. As speaker of the house (1701–05) and secretary of state (1704–08) he exercised considerable influence in the government, and with others oversaw British involvement in the War of Spanish Succession. He was made leader of the Tory ministry (1710) by the queen's favor and during his time in power concluded the Peace of Utrecht (1713). Harley was finally ousted through the efforts of his rival, Henry St. John, 1st Viscount Bolingbroke.

Harmensen, Jacob *See* **Arminius, Jacobus**

Harmhab ⟨Haremhab⟩ Egyptian pharaoh (*c*1350–1315 BC) and founder of the 19th dynasty. He restored worship of the traditional god Amon and brought about a return of prosperity.

Harmodius and **Aristogiton** *d. c*514 BC. Athenian tyrannicides. They attempted to assassinate the tyrant Hippias and his brother Hipparchus. The plot failed, though Hipparchus was killed. Harmodius was killed immediately and Aristogiton was killed later. Hippias continued his rule for several years more, but after his overthrow Harmodius and Aristogiton were honored.

Harmonists *See* **Harmony Society**

Harmony Society ⟨Harmonists⟩ 19th-cent. Protestant religious sect. Founded in Germany by George Rapp (1757–1847), it practiced celibacy, asceticism, and communal sharing. It founded the villages of Harmony, Pennsylvania (1806), and New Harmony, Indiana (1814). In 1825 it sold its Indiana holdings to R. Owen and moved back to Pennsylvania. It was disbanded in 1906.

Harmsworth, Alfred Charles William, 1st Viscount Northcliffe *See* **Harmsworth, Harold Sidney, 1st Viscount Rothermere**

Harmsworth, Harold Sidney, 1st Viscount Rothermere 1868–1940. English publisher. With his brother, Alfred Charles William, 1st Viscount Northcliffe (1865–1922), he built a newspaper publishing empire in Britain that included the *Evening News*, the *Daily Mail*, and the *Daily Mirror*.

Harnack, Adolph von 1851–1930. German theologian. An important church historian, he wrote the influential work *The History of Dogma*.

Harold I ⟨Harold the Fair-haired⟩ *c*850–*c*933. Norwegian king (*c*860–*c*933). Son of Halfdan the Black, Harold conquered much of Norway and became its first king. During his reign large numbers of Norsemen migrated to Iceland.

Harold II 1022?–66. Last Saxon king of England (1066). Chosen heir by Edward the Confessor, Harold ruled less than a year before his defeat by William, duke of Normandy, at the Battle of Hastings, in which he was killed.

Harold III ⟨Harold the Stern⟩ ⟨Harold Hardrada⟩ d. 1066. Norwegian king (c1047–66), successor to Magnus I. He joined with Earl Tostig in an invasion of northern England (1066) and fell with him in battle at Stamford Bridge.

Harold Bluetooth d. c985. Danish king. Harold attempted to impose Danish suzerainty over Norway but was defeated. Forced to accept Christianity, he introduced it to Denmark. He was killed in battle by his son Sweyn I.

Harold Hardrada See **Harold III**

Harold Harefoot d. 1040. English king (1037–40). The illegitimate son of King Canute, he spent much of his reign fighting Canute's legitimate son Hardecanute (1019?–42) for the throne.

Harold the Fair-haired See **Harold I**

Harold the Stern See **Harold III**

Harpers Ferry Raid Raid (Oct. 16–18, 1859) on a federal arsenal at Harpers Ferry, Virginia (now West Virginia), carried out by J. Brown and 21 other abolitionists. Brown and his men captured the arsenal as part of a plan to start a general slave uprising in the South. Their base at Harpers Ferry was to be the nucleus of a new state in the surrounding mountains, where escaping slaves could find refuge. In fact, the raid was a failure and the arsenal was easily recaptured by combined federal troops and local militia. Brown and six of his followers were hanged. However, the incident had a profound effect on the South, which became convinced the abolitionists would stop at nothing. Even though his direct action was generally disapproved, Brown became a martyr of the antislavery cause, as attested by the marching song, *John Brown's Body*. The incident was a contributing factor in the election of A. Lincoln, the subsequent secession of the slave states of the South, and thus the American Civil War.

Harpy Mythical Greek monster, half woman and half bird.

Harriman, Edward Henry 1848–1909. American railroad magnate and financier. Once a New York City stockbroker, he built a combination of western railroad lines that made him one of the most powerful men in 19th-cent. American railroading.

Harriman, William Averell 1891–. American statesman and diplomat, son of E. H. Harriman. He served in various diplomatic posts since the early 1940s and was chief US negotiator of the

Nuclear Test Ban Treaty (1963). Harriman also served as governor of New York (1955–58).

Harris, Joel Chandler 1848–1908. American writer and humorist famous for his Uncle Remus stories.

Harris, Roy 1898–1979. American composer whose symphonies are noted for their American themes.

Harris, Townsend See Harris Treaty

Harrisburg American city (pop. 53,300), capital city of Pennsylvania. Settled in the early 18th cent., it is located in an area rich in iron and coal and is a major steel, rail, and industrial center.

Harrison, Benjamin 1833–1901. Twenty-third US president (1889–93), successor to G. Cleveland. He was a Union officer during the American Civil War and a US senator from Indiana (1881–87). The Republican presidential nominee in 1888, he defeated G. Cleveland in the Electoral College, though Cleveland had almost 100,000 more popular votes. During his administration, the US expanded its influence abroad while at home the economy weakened, setting the stage for the financial Panic of 1893. The first Inter-American Conference was held (fostering the Pan-American movement), and the US participated in the Berlin Conference (1889). Legislation affecting the economy at home included the Sherman Anti-Trust Act (1890), the high, protective McKinley Tariff Act (1890), and the inflationary Sherman Silver Purchase Act (1890).

Harrison, William Henry 1773–1841. Ninth US president (Mar. 4–Apr. 4, 1841), successor to M. Van Buren. Harrison, who caught pneumonia at his inauguration ceremony, was the first president to die in office. He was a leading figure in the development of the Old Northwest (q.v.) and served as governor of the Indiana Territory (1800–12). Harrison became a national figure by defeating Indian chief Tecumseh, then at war against white settlers, at the famous Battle of Tippecanoe (1811). Later, in the War of 1812, he took command of the Old Northwest and reestablished American control of the region, by recapturing Detroit (Sept., 1813) and by his victory at the Battle of Thames River (1813). He then became a US congressman (1816–19), US senator (1825–28), and finally Whig party candidate for president (1840). His successful campaign, best remembered for the slogan "Tippecanoe and Tyler Too," evaded the issues and instead promoted Harrison as the image of a rugged westerner.

Harris Treaty Treaty between the US and Japan signed on July 29, 1858. It provided for unsupervised trade and residence at five Japanese ports, a tariff, and the prohibition of imports of opium. It was negotiated by Townsend Harris (1804–78), first US consul general (1855), and later minister (1859), to Japan.

Harsa, Harshavardhana *See* **Harsha**

Harsha ⟨Harsa, Harshavardhana⟩ 590?–647?. Indian ruler (606–47). An able commander, he united all of northern India into an empire that lasted throughout his reign.

Hart, Larry *See* **Hart, Lorenz**

Hart, Lorenz ⟨Hart, Larry⟩ 1895–1943. American lyricist noted for his collaboration with R. Rodgers on such popular Broadway shows as *Connecticut Yankee, The Boys from Syracuse,* and *Pal Joey.*

Hart, Moss 1904–61. American playwright. His many successful productions include the musicals *Lady in the Dark* and *My Fair Lady.* He frequently collaborated with G. Kaufman. Their comedy *You Can't Take It with You* was awarded the 1937 Pulitzer Prize for Drama.

Harte, Francis Bret(t) 1836–1902. American writer, known best for his vivid sketches of California life.

Hartford Convention Meeting of New England Federalist party members held (Dec. 15, 1814–Jan. 4, 1815) in Hartford, Connecticut, during the War of 1812. The convention was brought on by widespread dissatisfaction with the war in New England. Presided over by George Cabot (1752–1823), the meeting was held in secrecy and included delegates from Massachusetts, Connecticut, New Hampshire, Vermont, and Rhode Island. Though the convention rejected outright secession, its final report generally adopted a states' rights position and attacked President J. Madison's policies on trade embargoes and the war. The air of secrecy and the timing of the convention (the war ended soon afterward) aroused popular suspicions of treason and thereby contributed to the downfall of the Federalist party.

Harun-al-Rashid ⟨Harun ar-Rashid⟩ *c*764–809. Fifth Abbasid caliph (786–809) and most famous of the dynasty. A son of Mahdi, he reigned during the height of the Islamic empire, which then included southwestern Asia and northern Africa. His exploits and the splendor of his court at Baghdad are celebrated in *The Thousand and One Nights.*

Harvey, William 1578–1657. English physician who was first to identify correctly the function of the heart and blood circulation. He published his findings in 1628.

Hasan ⟨Hassan⟩ *c*624–*c*669. Islamic ruler, the 5th caliph (661), and a grandson of Muhammad. He was proclaimed caliph on the death of his father Ali but soon relinquished the title to Muawiyah, who challenged his succession.

Hasan ibn al-Sabbah *See* **Assassin**

Hasdrubal *d.* 207 BC. Carthaginian general, son of Hamilcar Barca and brother of Hannibal. As commander in Carthaginian Spain he fought successfully against the Romans. He was killed while trying to join his forces with those of Hannibal in Italy.

Hasdrubal *d.* 221 BC. Carthaginian general. Son-in-law of Hamilcar Barca, he succeeded Barca as commander in Spain and added to Carthaginian conquests there.

Hasidim ⟨Assideans⟩ Name given to members of two specific movements in Jewish history. **1.** Group (also known as Assideans) which flourished *c*300–175 BC. It strictly observed the Talmud and rejected the influence of other cultures. **2.** Group which evolved in Poland *c*1750, led by Israel ben Eliezer (or Ba'al Shem Tov). Followers believed in miracles as manifestations of God's love and presence, and felt that goodness of heart was more important than scholarship. The sect continues today.

Hasmoneans *See* **Maccabees**

Hassan *See* **Hasan**

Hassan II 1929–. Moroccan king (1961–). Hassan suspended Morocco's constitution (1965), but continued unrest forced him to yield to reforms (1971) and a larger role for the parliament.

Hastings, Battle of English-Norman battle (Oct. 14, 1066) in which English king Harold II was defeated and killed by the invading forces of William (the Conqueror), duke of Normandy. William moved on to London, where he was crowned king (Dec. 25). This battle is widely regarded by historians as the most important event in British history, marking the start of Norman influence in England.

Hastings, Warren 1732–1818. British colonial governor. As governor general of India (1774–84), Hastings successfully protected British interests. Upon his return to England he was charged with extortion and mismanagement, but was eventually acquitted.

Hatch acts American laws (1939, 1940). Proposed by Senator Carl Hatch (1889–1963), they limited campaign contributions from individuals and committees and forbade federal employees from campaigning for candidates.

Hatshepsut *d. c*1481 BC. Egyptian queen, wife of Thutmose II. A woman of unusually great power, she ruled Egypt during the reign of her husband, and also as regent for Thutmose III. She brought a period of peace to Egypt.

Hauptmann, Bruno Richard 1899–1936. German-American carpenter, convicted kidnapper of the C. Lindbergh baby. Arrested (1934) after passing some of the $50,000 ransom money paid two years earlier, Hauptmann was convicted after a sensational trial, and was electrocuted (1936).

Hauptmann, Gerhart 1862–1946. German dramatist, novelist and poet, considered a leading figure in German literature. His many works include the plays *Before Dawn* and *The Weavers*. He was awarded the 1912 Nobel Prize for Literature.

Hausa States ⟨Haussa States⟩ Group of former African states located in what now is northern Nigeria. Conquered many times during their history, they were taken over (early 20th cent.) by the British and incorporated into the Protectorate of Nigeria.

Haushofer, Karl 1869–1946. German geographer and leading exponent of Geopolitics. His theories had an early influence on A. Hitler and Haushofer later became a political adviser to Hitler.

Haussmann, Georges Eugene, Baron 1809–91. French official and city planner who, under Napoleon III, redesigned the city of Paris.

Havana Capital of Cuba (pop. 1,008,500) and commercial center. Originally called San Cristóbal, it was founded (c1515) by Spanish colonists. A key to Spain's New World possessions, it became the capital of Cuba (16th cent.) and continued to grow in importance to the 19th cent.

Hawaii US island state (pop. 965,000), the 50th state. First settled (c8th cent.) by Polynesians, the islands were discovered by Capt. J. Cook (1778) and called the Sandwich Islands. The accession (1810) of Hawaiian king Kamehameha I was accompanied by increased foreign trade and growing Western influence. The islands' last ruler, Queen Liliuokalani, was deposed in 1893 and Hawaii was annexed to the US in 1898. The surprise attack (Dec. 7, 1941) on the US naval base at Pearl Harbor led to US entry into WW II. Hawaii became a state in 1959.

Hawkesbury, Baron *See* **Liverpool, Robert Banks Jenkinson, 2d earl of**

Hawkins, Sir John ⟨Hawkyns, Sir John⟩ 1532–95. English seaman and admiral. The first Englishman to engage in the slave trade (1562), he directed reconstruction of the English fleet and took part in battle against the Spanish Armada.

Hawkyns *See* **Hawkins, Sir John**

Hawthorne, Nathaniel 1804–64. American novelist and short-story writer, one of the first great American authors. After 12 years of working in enforced seclusion (from 1825), he produced an unsuccessful first novel and a number of short stories (collected as *Twice-Told Tales*) that won him some recognition. He married (1842) and thereafter completed his most famous novels, *The Scarlet Letter* and *The House of the Seven Gables*. *The Scarlet Letter* is considered the first American psychological novel.

Hay, John 1838–1905. American statesman and author. Private secretary to A. Lincoln (1861–65), he was secretary of state under presidents W. McKinley and T. Roosevelt (1898–1905). He is chiefly remembered as negotiator of the Open Door Policy and the Hay-Pauncefote Treaty.

Haya de la Torre, Victor Raúl 1895–. Peruvian political leader and founder (1924) of the Apra Party, a popular radical party in Peru. He was twice an unsuccessful presidential candidate (1931, 1962).

Hay-Bunau-Varilla Treaty The treaty concluded (Nov. 18, 1903) between the US and newly independent Panama, establishing the US-controlled Panama Canal Zone. Shortly after Colombia rejected (Aug. 12, 1903), the Hay-Herrán Treaty, Panamanian rebels declared Panama's independence (Nov. 3) from Colombia. Two weeks later the US concluded the treaty for the Canal Zone. Terms, negotiated by US Secretary of State J. Hay, were nearly the same as had been offered to Colombia, including a $10-million payment and $250,000 annuity.

Haydn, Franz Joseph 1732–1809. Austrian composer, one of the most important masters of classical music. He made fundamental advances in the symphonic form, the string quartet, and the sonata and thereby profoundly influenced the development of classical music. He wrote most of his great works under the patronage (1761–90) of the Austrian noble house of Esterhazy, and gained recognition throughout Europe. Haydn was known to have influenced his friend W. Mozart and taught L. Beethoven. He wrote over 100 symphonies, including his great *Symphony No. 102 in B Flat Major*, numerous string quartets, operas, piano concertos, and masses.

Hayes, Helen ⟨Brown, Helen Hayes⟩ 1900–. American actress. An actress since childhood, she has starred in stage, motion picture, television, and radio productions.

Hayes, Rutherford Birchard 1822–93. Nineteenth US president (1877–81), successor to U. Grant. He distinguished himself in the American Civil War and became a congressman (1865–67), governor of Ohio (1868–72), and Republican presidential candidate in 1876. The election, which saw the return of former Confederate states to participation in national politics, appeared to favor Hayes's opponent, S. Tilden. Disputes over returns in four states, however, put the election in the hands of a congressional electoral commission, which ultimately decided the election in Hayes's favor. (*See also* United States [1876].) Once in office, Hayes worked to end Reconstruction (1865–77). He removed the remaining federal troops from southern states, appointed southerners to government posts, and generally adopted a policy of reconciliation. His attempts at ending civil service corruption embroiled him in a bitter feud with the Stalwart (*q.v.*) Republican Senator Roscoe Conkling. In the controversy over silver coinage, (*see* Free Silver), Hayes attempted to block passage of the Bland-Allison Act (*q.v.*), but his veto was overridden (1878).

Hay-Herrán Treaty Treaty negotiated (1903) between Colombia and the US to establish control over what was to become the Panama Canal Zone. Colombia, then in control of the region, ultimately refused (Aug. 12, 1903) to ratify the treaty. Terms of the treaty negotiated by US secretary of state J. Hay, included a $10-million payment and a $250,000 annuity in return for rights over the canal route. The US soon afterward concluded the Hay-Bunau-Varilla Treaty with the newly formed independent Panamanian government.

Haymarket Square riot American labor riot (May 4, 1886) in Chicago, Illinois. A bomb, exploding at a labor demonstration, killed seven policemen and four civilians, and wounded over 100 others. Eight anarchists were convicted in connection with the bombing. Four were hanged and one committed suicide, and the remaining three were pardoned in 1893.

Hayne, Robert Young 1791–1839. US senator (1823–32) and spokesman for the South. He was D. Webster's opponent in the famous debate (1830) over issues then dividing the North and South.

Hay-Pauncefote Treaty Treaty signed (Nov. 18, 1901) by the US and Britain, which enabled the US to control the proposed Panama Canal. The treaty superseded the Clayton-Bulwer Treaty (1850) with Britain in which the US agreed to joint control of such a canal. Negotiated by US Secretary of State J. Hay, the treaty provided for a canal under US jurisdiction and equal treatment for shipping of all nations, and tacitly permitted fortification of the Canal Zone by the US.

Hays, Arthur Garfield 1881–1954. American lawyer, noted as defense attorney in civil liberties cases. He was defense counsel in the Scopes Trial and in the Sacco-Vanzetti Case.

Hazael *fl.* 840 BC. King of Damascus who, according to biblical accounts, killed Benhadad and

succeeded him. He later conquered Israel and Judah.

Hazlitt, William 1778–1830. English essayist and critic. He was an important literary critic and a master of the essay. Among his best-known works are the collected essays *Table Talk* and *The Plain Speaker.*

Hearn, Lafcadio 1850–1904. Greek-born writer who became an American (1869) and then Japanese (1895) citizen. He is known best for his books on Japanese culture.

Hearst, William Randolph 1863–1951. American newspaper publisher. He built a newspaper and magazine publishing empire using the sensationalism and mass-appeal journalism for which he is best remembered.

Heath, Edward Richard George 1916– . British politician. A Conservative, Heath entered Parliament (1950) and held a variety of posts in the governments of A. Eden, H. Macmillan and A. Douglas-Home. As prime minister (1970–74), he succeeded in gaining British entry into the Common Market (1972). However, increasing economic troubles and conflict in Northern Ireland led to his defeat.

heaven In religion, that place or state of existence in which the just, after death, find eternal bliss through the revelation of God.

Hebe Ancient Greek goddess of youth. Daughter of Zeus and Hera, she was the wife of Hercules.

Hébert, Jacques René 1755–94. French journalist and revolutionary. A Jacobin and a leader of the sansculottes after his political newspaper became popular with the lower classes, he was involved in the storming of Tuileries Palace (1792) and the overthrow of the monarchy. Soon after he became a member of the Commune of Paris, and was arrested (May, 1793) for aiding the radical movement to oust the (moderate) Girondists from the National Convention. His sansculotte supporters won his release soon after, however, and in June, 1793 Hébert was involved in the riot by working-class radicals that forced the expulsion of Girondists from the National Convention. With the Jacobins now in power, Hébert attempted to force the revolution into ever more extreme measures through his control of the sansculottes, who had forced (Sept., 1793) institution of the Reign of Terror. Hébert, with P. Chaumette, was a leader in the radical de-Christianization program and establishment of the Cult of Reason (*q.v.*). He was opposed (from mid-1793) by G. Danton and Robespierre, and in Mar., 1794 Hébert was arrested and guillotined along with other Hébertists.

Hebron City in western Jordan, since 1967 part of the Israeli-occupied West Bank. A holy city for both Jews and Muslims, it was settled even before biblical times. It was capital of David's kingdom before Jerusalem and is the burial site of Abraham, Isaac, and Jacob.

Hecate Greek goddess of magic and witchcraft who had powers over the sky, earth, and sea. She is sometimes depicted with three bodies set back to back.

Hector Trojan hero. The son of Priam, he slew the Greek Patroclus in the Trojan War, and was in turn slain by Achilles.

Hecuba In Greek legend, the wife of Trojan King Priam, taken by Odysseus after the fall of Troy. The mother of Paris and Hector, she blinded Thracian King Polymestor and killed his children for the murder of her youngest son, Polydorus.

Hedonism Philosophical doctrine, derived in part from the Greek Cyrenaics, that that holds that human pleasure is the highest good. Today it implies the gratification of all sensual desires.

Hedwig *See* **Jadwiga**

Heem, Jan Davidszoon de ⟨Heem, Johannes de⟩ 1606–1683 or 1684. Dutch artist, considered one of Holland's greatest still-life painters.

Hegel, Georg Wilhelm Friedrich 1770–1831. German idealistic philosopher, one of the most influential 19th-cent. thinkers. He was a professor at Jena, Heidelberg, and, from 1818, at Berlin. Hegel held ultimate reality to be absolute spirit or mind, and hence held that "whatever is rational is real and whatever is real is rational." All things tend to the complete and perfect design of mind by a logical process which Hegel called the "dialectic." In this process an original tendency, or "thesis," gives rise to its opposite tendency, an "antithesis." Both are then resolved into a higher unity, a "synthesis." Hegel analyzed all reality in terms of this dialectic, and it became a favorite tool of subsequent philosophers. K. Marx and F. Engels rejected Hegel's idealism in favor of materialism but nevertheless based Marxism *(q.v.)* on Hegelian dialectic. Many other philosophers retained Hegel's idealism, however. Hegel's philosophy is set forth in such works as *Phenomenology of Mind* and, especially, *Encyclopedia of the Philosophical Sciences.* Hegel's thought was sometimes used by disciples to support a philosophy of extreme German nationalism.

hegira ⟨hejira⟩ Name for Muhammad's forced departure (622) from Mecca and journey to Medina, a pivotal event in the history of Islam. Under a system developed by Omar, 2d caliph, all events of the Muslim era are dated from the beginning of the lunar year (July 16, 622) in which the hegira occurred. Muhammad was driven from Mecca for opposing the local religion (polytheistic) and, once

in Medina, established himself in that city. (*See also* Muhammad.)

Heian-kyo *See* **Kyoto**

Heian period Period of Japanese history (794–1185) marked by the rise of Buddhism, development of the manorial system, and control of the imperial court by the Fujiwara clan.

Heidegger, Martin 1889–1976. German philosopher. Influenced by E. Husserl and S. Kierkegaard, he published (1927) his important work *Being and Time,* in which he discussed the meaning of "being." Though he denied any connection to existentialism, his investigations of the sense of being, and his identification of the loss of it as the central problem of Western civilization, greatly influenced the existential philosopher J. Sartre.

Heidelberg German city (pop. 122,000). Internationally known for its castle ruins and for its university, the oldest in Germany. It was the residence of the electors' palatinate until 1720.

Heidelberg Catechism Calvinist document. Written (1563) at the request of elector Frederick III the Pious, it was widely adopted by Reformed churches.

Heike *See* **Taira family**

Heine, Heinrich 1797–1856. German lyric poet. After briefly trying careers in business and law, he turned to poetry and established (1827) an international reputation with publication of *The Book of Songs.* Soon afterward he was forced (1831) to leave Germany because of his liberal social ideals and settled in Paris. There he became identified with the Young Germany literary movement and, in addition to his poems, wrote prose satires. His poems were frequently set to music by such noted composers as R. Schumann, F. Schubert, and F. Mendelssohn. The best known of them is *Die Lorelei.*

Heinkel, Ernst Heinrich 1888–1958. German aircraft manufacturer and engineer who built the first turbojet aircraft.

Heisenberg, Werner 1901–76. German physicist who made major contributions to the Quantum Theory. He formulated the matrix theory of quantum mechanics and the uncertainty principle.

Hejaz Historic region in western Saudi Arabia. It lies on the Red Sea coast and was occupied as early as Babylonian times.

hejira *See* **hegira**

Hel Norse mythical goddess of the dead, and daughter of Loki. Hel also refers to her underworld kingdom.

Helderberg War *See* **Antirent War**

Helen ⟨Helen of Troy⟩ Celebrated beauty in Greek mythology who was the cause of the Trojan

War. The wife of Spartan king Menelaus, she was taken by Paris (or fled with him) to Troy. Troy was besieged by an army of Greeks and, after its fall, Helen was reconciled with her husband.

Helena, Saint AD c248–c328. Mother of Constantine I. She was said to have discovered, while on a pilgrimage to Jerusalem (AD c327), the cross upon which Jesus Christ was crucified.

Helen of Troy *See* **Helen**

Helgoland Bight, Battle of ⟨Heligoland Bight, Battle of⟩ British naval victory over Germany (Aug. 27, 1914) in WW I, the first major naval engagement of the war. Meeting the German fleet off the coast of northwestern Germany, the British fleet sank three cruisers and one destroyer and severely damaged three other cruisers, losing no ships of its own.

Heligoland Bight, Battle of *See* **Helgoland Bight, Battle of**

Heliodorus *fl.* 175 BC. Ancient Syrian statesman. He was treasurer of Seleucus IV, murdered him (175 BC), and unsuccessfully attempted to take the throne. According to the Bible, he entered the Temple at Jerusalem but was prevented from carrying away the treasure by three angels.

Heliogabalus ⟨Bassianus, Varius Avitus⟩ AD 204–222. Roman emperor (AD 218–222), successor to Caracalla. Proclaimed emperor by the soldiers, he was killed after a short reign marked by debauchery.

Heliopolis ⟨*biblical* On⟩ Ancient Egyptian city, once located near what is now Cairo. It was the seat of worship of the sun god Ra in earliest times and a center of learning until eclipsed by Alexandria (332 BC). Cleopatra's Needles were located there.

Helios Ancient Greek sun god. He drove his chariot from east to west each day. The center of his worship was Rhodes. His position as sun god was gradually assumed by Apollo.

hell Theological term for the place of suffering and punishment for those who lived evil lives on earth, and a place of eternal damnation. It is also called the dwelling place of the Devil.

Hellen Mythical Greek king, the ancestor of the Hellenes, or the Greeks. His sons Dorus and Aeolus, and grandsons Ion and Achaeus, were the progenitors respectively of the Dorian, Aeolian, Ionic, and Achaean Greeks.

Hellenic League League of Greek city-states (all but Sparta), formed (338 BC) by Philip of Maccdonia. After Philip's death (336), several of these cities rebelled, only to be suppressed (335) by Alexander the Great. After Alexander's death (323), Athens led in creating a new league, which was destroyed (322) by the Macedonians under

Antipater. Later Hellenic Leagues were revived (303) by Demetrius I and (c224) by Antigonus III.

Hellenism Name applied to the culture of the ancient Greeks, especially that of Athens at its height (5th cent. BC). It is also applied to the works of those who later adopted Hellenic values and principles. The Hellenistic Age, a time when Greek culture spread throughout the eastern Mediterranean, is generally dated from the death of Alexander the Great to the rise of Augustus in Rome (323–30 BC).

Hellespont *See* **Dardanelles**

Hellman, Lillian 1905–. American playwright whose works include *The Children's Hour*, *The Little Foxes*, and *Watch on the Rhine*.

Helmholtz, Hermann, Ludwig Ferdinand von 1821–94. German physiologist, physicist, and mathematician. Much of his work was connected with sense perception. He is noted for his study of the conservation of energy.

Helmont, Jan Baptist van 1577?–1644. Flemish chemist, physicist, and physician. He discovered carbon dioxide and introduced the term "gas" into scientific vocabulary.

Helots Spartan slaves. Considered state property, they were assigned to both agricultural and military tasks. Because of their huge numbers, Helot revolts were greatly feared by the Spartans.

Helsinki Finnish city (pop. 496,300), the capital and cultural and commercial center of Finland. It was founded (1550) by Swedish king Gustavus I.

Helvetia Roman term for a region in what is now western Switzerland. The name comes from the Celtic people (Helvetii) who occupied the region in Caesar's time and is sometimes used to refer to Switzerland.

Helvetic Confession 1. First ~. *See* Basel, Confession of (second). **2.** Theological statement written (1562) by Heinrich Bullinger (1504–75) and considered one of the most important statements of Reformation doctrine. It was adopted (1566) by the Swiss cantons and was well received elsewhere in Europe.

Helvetius, Claude Adrien 1715–71. French philosopher. His book *De l'esprit* contended that all human actions are based on self-interest.

Hemingway, Ernest 1898–1961. American novelist and short-story writer, a leading American writer of this century. He is noted for his terse literary style and the recurrent themes of courage and virility that pervade his works. After graduation from high school (1917), he became a newspaper reporter and later an ambulance driver in WW I. He worked in Paris as a correspondent after the war and established himself with publication (1926) of *The Sun Also Rises*. Thereafter he wrote such major works as *A Farewell to Arms, For Whom the Bell Tolls,* and *The Old Man and the Sea.* He was awarded the Nobel Prize for Literature in 1954.

Henderson, Arthur 1863–1935. British statesman. A leader and organizer of the Labour Party, he played a leading role in British politics from 1903. He was awarded the Nobel Peace Prize in 1934.

Hengist and **Horsa** Legendary Germanic brothers, said to have led the Jutish invasion of England (c5th cent.) and to have founded the kingdom of Kent. By tradition, they were invited by King Vortigern to help the Britons in war against the Picts and Scots.

Henri, Robert 1865–1929. American painter. One of the original members of The Eight or "ashcan school," he was an influential teacher of art in the US.

Henrietta Maria 1609–69. French wife (*m.* 1625) of King Charles I of England, and daughter of French King Henry IV and Marie de Médicis. Both her Roman Catholic faith and intrigues with foreign governments on her husband's behalf were factors in the outbreak of the English Civil War.

Henry I ⟨Henry the Fowler⟩ 876?–936. German king (919–936), successor to Conrad I and founder of the Saxon line. He added Lotharingia (Lorraine) to the German kingdom (925), put an end to Magyar raids, and reasserted the authority of the monarchy.

Henry I 1008–1060. Capetian king of France (1031–60). He put down various rebellions and later warred unsuccessfully against William, duke of Normandy.

Henry I ⟨Henry Beauclerc⟩ 1068–1135. King of England (1100–35), successor to his brother, William II. Henry obtained the crown while his older brother, Robert, duke of Normandy, was away on crusade. Henry subsequently defended the crown against an invasion (1101) of England by Robert and later took Normandy from Robert (1106). As king, Henry became embroiled in the investiture controversy (*q.v.*) with St. Anselm, and a compromise was reached (1107). Henry's efforts to arrange the succession of his daughter, Matilda, resulted in a civil war during the reign of his successor, Stephen.

Henry II 973–1024. Holy Roman Emperor (1014–24) and German king (1002–24). The last Saxon emperor, he recaptured most of the German land taken by Polish king Boleslaus I and extended his influence throughout Italy. He was canonized (1146).

Henry II 1133–89. King of England (1154–89), successor to King Stephen. The grandson of Henry

I, son of Matilda and husband of Eleanor of Aquitaine, Henry founded the Plantagenet line. He restored order to strife-torn England, reformed its laws, and established the supremacy of royal courts over local justices. He defined church-state relations with the Constitutions of Clarendon, but his arguments with Thomas à Becket led indirectly to the latter's murder. Henry consolidated English holdings in northern England, Ireland, and Scotland. He was the father of Richard I and John I.

Henry II ⟨Henry of Trastamara⟩ 1333?–79. King of Castile and Leon (1369–79). The illegitimate son of Alfonso XI, he fought his half-brother Peter the Cruel for the throne, and ultimately killed Peter (1369). Henry supported the French in the Hundred Years' War.

Henry II 1519–59. King of France (1547–59), son of and successor to Francis I. Regarded as a weak ruler, he instituted repressive measures against Protestants, added Calais to French domains (1558), and negotiated an end to the Italian Wars (*q.v.*).

Henry III ⟨Henry the Black⟩ 1017–56. German king and Holy Roman Emperor (1046–56), son and successor of Conrad II. His reign marked the height of the Holy Roman emperor's power. His efforts to reform the church, however, did not succeed.

Henry III 1551–89. French king (1574–89), successor to his brother Charles IX. As duke of Anjou, he aided his mother Catherine de Médicis in planning the St. Bartholomew's Day Massacre (1572). His reign was marked by the Wars of Religion that raged in France between the Catholics and Huguenots, and by the War of the Three Henrys (1585–89).

Henry IV 1050–1106. Holy Roman Emperor (1056–1106), successor to his father, Henry III. His reign was marked by a long and unsuccessful struggle with the pope over lay investiture On gaining his majority (1065), Henry moved to restore authority of the crown in the duchies (notably Saxony). His struggle with the church began (1075) when he appointed a number of bishops. Condemned by Pope Gregory VII for the action, Henry declared the pope deposed (1076), only to be himself declared deposed by the pope. Faced with a rebellion against the crown, Henry was forced to submit to the pope and was absolved after doing penance at Canossa (Jan., 1077). However, the German nobles elected Rudolf of Swabia as antiking and a civil war ensued (1077–80), from which Henry emerged victorious. Gregory in the meantime again deposed Henry, who in turn made Clement III antipope. Henry then invaded Italy

(1081–83) and drove Gregory into exile, where he died. The reforming popes who succeeded Gregory supported revolts against Henry (from 1093). In one, Henry was entrapped (1105) by his rebellious son (later Henry V), but he escaped and died the next year. (*See also* Investiture Controversy.)

Henry IV ⟨Henry of Bolingbroke⟩ ⟨Henry of Lancaster⟩ 1367–1413. English king (1399–1413), a son of John of Gaunt and the first of three kings of the House of Lancaster. He led a successful rebellion against King Richard II (1399), after which he claimed the crown for himself. His reign was marked by rebellions, including those in Wales and Scotland, and the crown's worsening financial troubles.

Henry IV 1553–1610. First Bourbon king of France (1589–1610), successor to Henry III. His reign marked the end of the Wars of Religion (1562–98). Henry was raised a Protestant and, as Henry of Navarre, became nominal leader of the Protestants (Huguenots) in the Wars of Religion after 1569. His subsequent marriage (1572) to Margaret of Valois, sister of Catholic King Charles IX, during a brief peace in the wars nearly proved disastrous. The marriage was opposed by both sides and only days afterward there occurred the Massacre of Saint Bartholomew's Day *(q.v.)* against Protestants. Henry, who thereupon renounced Protestantism to prevent his own death, was confined at Charles's court (1572–76) until he could effect an escape. Afterward he resumed command of Protestant forces and, in 1584, he became heir to the French throne (by the accession of Henry III and death of his heir). However, the Catholic League *(q.v.)* bitterly opposed the possible accession of a Protestant, and provoked the War of the Three Henrys *(q.v.)*. Henry was successful in this war and, in 1589, became king by the death of Henry III. The Catholic League warred against him, however, and by its alliance with Spain ultimately forced Henry to once again embrace Catholicism (1593). With that, opposition to Henry began to dissolve and he entered Paris in 1594. He then instituted a policy of reconciliation that resulted (1598) in the Edict of Nantes *(q.v.)*, establishing religious toleration. Henry's subsequent reign was marked by a period of general stability and rebuilding.

Henry V 1081–1125. Holy Roman Emperor (1106–25), successor to his father, Henry IV, and last of the Salian dynasty. After leading a near-successful revolt against his father, Henry succeeded him and began to consolidate his power in the empire. But he soon fell out with Pope Paschal II over the investiture controversy *(q.v.)*, which had plagued his father's reign. In 1111 he captured pope and cardinals at Rome and thereby forced the pope to grant him the right of investiture. The struggle over investiture continued, however, and when Henry lost the support of his bishops, as well as the nobles, he was forced to accept (1122) a compromise measure, the Concordat of Worms *(q.v.)*.

Henry V 1387–1422. English king (1413–22). Allying England with the Burgundians, Henry reopened the Hundred Years' War and led the English to victory in the Battle of Agincourt (1415). He conquered Normandy and Rouen and concluded the Treaty of Troyes (1420), by which he agreed to marry Catherine of Valois, daughter of French king Charles VI. Charles acknowledged him rightful heir to the French throne.

Henry VI 1421–71. King of England (1422–61, 1470–71), the last Lancastrian king of England. Henry, while still an infant, succeeded his father Henry V as king of England and his maternal grandfather Charles VI as king of France. Completely unfit to rule, he lost all English territories in France except for Calais. A period of insanity (1453–54) led to the appointment of Richard, duke of York, as lord protector, and his recovery led to the long struggle for the throne between the houses of York and Lancaster, the Wars of the Roses *(q.v.)*. Richard succeeded in defeating Henry and imprisoning him, and in being named heir apparent to the throne (1460). Richard was killed soon after and his son claimed the throne as Edward IV. Henry fled to Scotland but was restored briefly (1470–71). Captured by Edward's forces, he was imprisoned in the Tower of London, where he was murdered.

Henry VII ⟨*orig.* Henry Tudor⟩ 1457–1509. English king (1485–1509), founder of the Tudor dynasty, and successor to Richard III. During the period of civil war called the Wars of the Roses, Henry went into exile (1471) in Brittany. The succession (1483) of the unpopular Yorkist, Richard III, made Henry (of the House of Lancaster) a leading contender for the throne. Henry landed in England (1485), defeated Richard at Bosworth Field, and was crowned (1486). By his marriage (1486) to Edward IV's daughter, Elizabeth, he united the houses of York and Lancaster and founded the Tudor line. This also ended the Wars of the Roses. Thereafter Henry foiled Yorkist plots by L. Simnel and P. Warbeck and, despite several attempts at rebellion, generally restored peace after the civil wars. His reign saw the beginnings of English overseas exploration and institution of Poyning's Law (1495).

Henry VIII 1491–1547. English king (1509–47), successor to his father, Henry VII. The early years of Henry's reign were marked by participation with the Holy League (from 1511) in war against France and by the defeat of invading Scottish armies at the Battle of Flodden (1513). When relations with Holy Roman Emperor Charles V soured, Henry briefly attempted reconciliation with the French at the Field of Cloth of Gold (q.v.). But by 1522 Henry was back at war with France. In the meantime, Henry received (1521) the title "Defender of the Faith" from Pope Leo X for his book, written in answer to M. Luther and the emerging Protestant movement. By 1529, however, Henry fell afoul of the church through his efforts to divorce his first wife, Catherine of Aragon. The struggle continued for some years and included Henry's secret marriage to his new love, A. Boleyn (1533), Henry's excommunication (1534), and finally passage of the Act of Supremacy (q.v.), creating the Church of England. In subsequent years, Henry dealt ruthlessly with any opposition, Catholic or Protestant, to his position as supreme head of the church in England. Events of this period included the beheading of his former minister, Sir T. More, and many others, confiscation of monastery lands, suppression of the Pilgrimage of Grace (q.v.), and passage of the Act of Six Articles (q.v.). Events of Henry's later reign included the continuing struggle with the French, a defeat of Scottish forces that resulted in the death of King James V, and a series of new wives that brought the total to six by the time of his death. Edward VI, Elizabeth I, and Mary Tudor were his children.

Henry, Joseph 1797–1878. American physicist. He built the first electric motor (1829) and discovered electrical induction independently of M. Faraday. The henry, the electrical unit of inductance, is named for him.

Henry, O. (William Sydney Porter) 1862–1910. American short-story writer whose stories are noted for their use of irony and surprise endings.

Henry, Patrick 1736–99. American Revolutionary War patriot and orator famous for the words "Give me liberty or give me death," uttered in a speech (Mar., 1775), urging colonists to prepare defenses. A delegate to the Continental Congress (1774–76) and twice governor of Virginia (1776–79, 1784–86), he was an ardent supporter of individual liberties. He played a major role in winning passage of the Bill of Rights.

Henry of Bolingbroke See **Henry IV**

Henry of Burgundy d. 1112 or 1114. French nobleman and father of Alfonso I, first king of Portugal. He was made count of Portugal by Alfonso VI of León and Castile in return for his help in fighting the Spanish and the Moors.

Henry of Flanders c1174–1216. Second Latin emperor of Constantinople (1205–16), successor to his brother, Baldwin I. Considered the most competent of the Latin emperors, he defeated invading Bulgarians.

Henry of Lancaster See **Henry IV**

Henry the Black See **Henry III**

Henry the Fowler See **Henry I**

Henry the Lion 1129–95. German prince, duke of Saxony and Bavaria. With the aid of Holy Roman Emperor Frederick I, he recovered Bavaria (1155) and other family territories taken by the Hohenstaufens. When he refused to help Frederick (1176) in a war against the Italians, Frederick stripped him of his holdings.

Henry the Navigator 1394–1460. Portuguese prince. The success of the exploratory voyages along the African coast, which he sponsored, laid the foundation for the Portuguese colonial empire.

Henry the Proud c1108–39. Duke of Bavaria (1126–38) and Saxony (1137–38). Henry aided his father-in-law, Holy Roman Emperor Lothair II, against the Hohenstaufens. After Conrad of Hohenstaufen succeeded Lothair as Conrad III (1138), Henry lost his duchies. He reconquered Saxony but died soon after.

Henry Tudor See **Henry VII**

Hepburn, Katharine 1909–. American stage and screen actress. A noted movie actress since 1932, she has won four Academy Awards.

Hepburn Act US law (June 29, 1906) empowering the Interstate Commerce Commission to regulate railroad rates. It allowed the commission to lower excessive rates and prohibited certain practices.

Hephaestus Ancient Greek god of fire and divine metalsmith, identified with the Roman god Vulcan.

Hepworth, Dame Jocelyn Barbara 1903–75. English sculptor. She is considered an influential non-figurative sculptor.

Hera Ancient Greek goddess, the wife of Zeus and queen of the Olympian gods. She was the protector of women and is often portrayed as Zeus' angry or jealous wife.

Heraclea Ancient Greek city located in what is now southern Italy. Site of one of two battles from which the expression "Pyrrhic victory" derives. Here (280 BC) and at Asculum (279 BC) King Pyrrhus of Epirus was victorious in battle with the Romans, but with such heavy losses that the victory was questionable.

Heracles See **Hercules**

Heraclitus c535–c475 BC. Greek philosopher, an early proponent of a metaphysical philosophy. He believed permanence an illusion and the only reality was constant change.

Heraclius I *c*575–641. Byzantine emperor (610–41) who deposed the tyrant Phocas. During his reign the empire came under attack from several quarters. He defeated the Avars and Bulgars, and then the Persians (622–627), but lost Syria and Egypt to the Muslims (636–642).

Herakles *See* **Hercules**

herald   Name applied to an officer of a medieval court who was charged with delivering messages (such as declarations of war or peace) from one military commander or sovereign to another.

heraldry   Medieval system involving the display of a hereditary symbol, or charge, on shields for purposes of identification. Dating to the 12th cent., the practice soon spread throughout Europe.

Herat   City in northwestern Afghanistan (pop. 150,000). An important city in ancient times, it lies on trade routes from China to Europe and Persia to India. It has been attacked and conquered many times and in 1881 became a part of Afghanistan.

Herbert, George   1593–1633. English poet and clergyman. He was one of the metaphysical poets.

Herbert, Victor   1859–1924. Irish-born American composer and conductor. He is known best for his many operettas, which include *Babes in Toyland* and *Naughty Marietta*.

Hercules   (Heracles or Herakles) Hero of great strength and courage in Greek and Roman mythology, son of Zeus and Alcmene. Hercules undertook his famous 12 tasks to repent the murder of his wife and children, committed in a fit of madness. The tasks were: kill the Nemean lion (1) and Lernean hydra (2); capture the Arcadian hind (3) and the Erymanthian boar (4); clean the Augean stables (5); slaughter the Stymphalian birds (6); capture the Cretan bull (7) and man-eating mares of Diomedes (8); fetch the golden girdle of Hippolyte (9), the red oxen of Geryon (10), and the golden apples of the Hesperides (11); and bring back from the underworld the guardian of its gates, the dog Cerberus (12).

Hercules, Pillars of   *See* **Pillars of Hercules**

Herder, Johann Gottfried von   1744–1803. German critic, clergyman, and philosopher. He played an important role in the Sturm und Drang literary movement in Germany.

Heredia, José-María de   *See* **Parnassians**

Heristal, Pepin of   *See* **Pepin of Heristal**

Herkimer, Nicholas   *See* **Oriskany, Battle of**

Hermandad   In Spain, local organizations with police powers. Originating in the 12th cent., these units were raised by federations of towns in the kingdoms of Castile, Aragon, and León and provided protection against petty criminals and lawless noblemen. King Ferdinand and Queen Isabella organized (1496) the Holy Hermandad (Santa or Neuva ~), which eventually became a national police unit. The Hermandad had the power to arrest, try, and penalize criminals. It was eventually replaced by a civil guard, though local units survived to 1835.

Hermaphroditus   Ancient Greek deity with both male and female attributes. The son of Hermes and Aphrodite, he was so loved by the nymph Salmacis that she prayed to be united with him in one body.

Hermes   Ancient Greek god. Usually identified as messenger of the gods, he was first a god of fertility. Later he had many functions, including being god of roads and travelers, luck and wealth, merchants and commerce. His Roman counterpart is Mercury.

Hermetic Books   Ancient Egyptian texts dealing with such subjects as astronomy, astrology, and magic. They were said to have been written by Thoth, the god of wisdom.

Hermitage   Russian museum, located in Leningrad. Constructed (1765) as a palace by Catherine II, it contains one of the largest collections of art treasures from all nations and periods.

Herndon, William Henry   1818–91. American lawyer and biographer. A. Lincoln's law partner, he wrote a biography of Lincoln that gave rise to the legendary Ann Rutledge romance.

Hero   *See* **Heron of Alexandria**

Hero and Leander   Mythical Greek lovers. According to legend, Leander swam the Hellespont nightly to see his beloved Hero. When he drowned one night, Hero likewise drowned herself.

Herod Antipas   *See* **Salome**

Herodotus   484?–425 BC. Greek historian. Herodotus traveled widely throughout the known world, settling in southern Italy. He is known best for his richly detailed history of the Persian Wars, and is often called the "father of history."

Herod the Great   73?–4 BC. King of Judaea (37–4 BC), son of Antipater and best known of the Idumaean rulers (reigned 1st cent. BC–1st cent. AD). Herod was made king of Judaea by the Roman M. Antony in 39 BC and took possession of the kingdom two years later. He put down revolts in the early part of his reign and in succeeding years Judaea enjoyed a period of great prosperity. He constructed many public buildings and, though he had converted to Judaism, he promoted Hellenism. Suffering fits of insanity, he became tyrannical and notoriously brutal toward the end of his reign. According to the Bible, he was in power at the time of Jesus' birth and ordered the massacre of the Innocents.

Heron of Alexandria ⟨Hero⟩ AD 3d cent. or earlier. Greek mathematician and inventor. He devised a formula to find the area of a triangle and invented a crude steam engine.

Herophilus *fl.* 300 BC. Greek anatomist at Alexandria. Sometimes called the father of anatomy, he dissected and described many organs of the body.

Herrick, Robert 1591–1674. English clergyman and poet. One of the Cavalier Poets, he is remembered for the simplicity and sensuousness of his poetry.

Herrings, Battle of the Incident during the English siege of Orléans in 1429. The French attacked an English supply column, led by Sir John Fastolf (1378?–1459), and, in turning back the enemy, the English fought from behind barrels of herring that were among the supplies.

Herriot, Édouard 1872–1957. French statesman. He headed the Radical (Socialist) party from 1919 until his death and was premier three times (1924–5, 1926, 1932).

Herschel, Sir John Frederick William 1792–1871. English astronomer, son of Sir William Herschel. He continued his father's work, discovered numerous celestial bodies, and made advances in applying photography to astronomy.

Herschel, Sir William 1738–1822. English astronomer. He discovered Uranus (1781), using a reflecting telescope of his own devising, and catalogued hundreds of new double stars, nebulae, and star clusters.

Hersey, John 1914–. American author. His best-known books include *A Bell for Adano* and *Hiroshima*. He was awarded the Pulitzer Prize for Fiction in 1945.

Hertz, Heinrich Rudolph 1857–94. German physicist. He discovered radio waves (c1886) and thereby proved J. Maxwell's electromagnetic theory of light and heat. The unit of frequency, the hertz, is named for him.

Hertzog, James Barry Munnik 1866–1942. Boer War guerrilla leader and premier of South Africa (1924–39). His policies included independence from Britain and increased racial segregation.

Herzegovina *See* **Bosnia and Herzegovina**

Herzen, Aleksandr Ivanovich 1812–70. Russian radical and writer. Living outside Russia after 1847, he published journals and wrote books on socialism and revolution.

Herzl, Theodor 1860–1904. Austrian-born founder of modern Zionism. The Dreyfus case convinced Herzl that acceptance of Jews in Europe was impossible. He subsequently wrote *The Jewish State*, a pamphlet in which he advocated creation of a separate Jewish state.

Hesiod *fl.* c8th cent. BC. One of the great early Greek poets. He is known best for two works, *Theogony* and *Works and Days*. The Hesiodic school of ancient Greek poetry is named after him.

Hesperides Three maidens in Greek mythology who, along with a dragon, guarded a tree bearing golden apples. Hercules was charged with taking the apples in his eleventh task.

Hess, Rudolf 1894–. German Nazi leader and A. Hitler's confidant. He created a sensation in 1941 when on his own initiative he flew to Scotland apparently for the purpose of negotiating peace between Britain and Germany. He was sentenced to life imprisonment during the Nuremberg trials.

Hesse West German state. In 1567, the lands of Philip of Hesse were divided among his four sons and eventually formed the two holdings of Hesse-Kassel and Hesse-Darmstadt. Hessian mercenaries came from these regions. Hesse-Kassel became Electoral Hesse and was annexed by Prussia (1868). Hesse-Darmstadt joined the German Empire in 1871 and the Republic in 1918. These two regions form the basis of modern Hesse.

Hesse, Hermann 1877–1962. German novelist and poet. He was noted for his interest in human conflicts, psychology, and Oriental mysticism, expressed in such novels as *Demian*, *Siddhartha*, and *Steppenwolf*. He was awarded the 1946 Nobel Prize for Literature.

Hestia Ancient Greek goddess of the hearth. She was the daughter of Cronus and Rhea.

Heuss, Theodor 1884–1963. West German politician and publisher, and first president of the German Federal Republic (1949–59). As leader of the Free Democratic Party after WW II, he was instrumental in the creation of West Germany's new constitution.

Heyerdahl, Thor 1914–. Norwegian anthropologist and adventurer. His *Kon-Tiki* expedition (1947), in which a balsa raft was used to cross the Pacific, showed that Polynesians could have migrated from South America.

Hezekiah 740?–692? BC. King of Judah (720?–692? BC), successor to his father Ahaz. His reign was marked by reforms in religious practices and by two invasions by the ruling Assyrians.

Hiawatha *fl.* c1450. Legendary Onondaga Indian chief believed to be the founder of the Iroquois Confederacy. He was the hero of H. Longfellow's poem *The Song of Hiawatha*.

Hickok, James Butler ⟨Wild Bill Hickok⟩ 1837–76. American soldier, scout, and deputy US marshal. Known as "the fastest gun in the West," he was noted for his gunfight with the McCanles gang (1861) and for cleaning up the Kansas frontier towns of Hays (1869) and Abilene (1871). He was shot and killed by Jack McCall during a poker game.

Hickok, Wild Bill *See* **Hickok, James Butler**

Hicks, Elias 1748–1830. American Quaker preacher and early abolitionist. His opposition to evangelicalism led to a split (1827) within the Society of Friends. His followers were called Hicksites.

Hidalgo y Costilla, Miguel 1753–1811. Mexican priest and national hero. He organized and led (1810–11) an army of Mexicans in a nearly successful rebellion against Spanish rule (defeated at Calderón Bridge). His revolt marked the opening of the Mexican Revolution.

Hideyoshi ⟨Toyotomi, ~⟩ 1536?–98. Japanese soldier and, as the emperor's chief minister, dictator (1585–98). He completed unification of Japan (1590), instituted numerous civil reforms, and launched an unsuccessful invasion of China (1592).

Hiero I ⟨Hieron I⟩ d. 466 BC. Greek tyrant of Syracuse, successor to his brother Gelon. Though a patron of literature, he ruled as a despot.

Hiero II ⟨Hieron II⟩ d. c215 BC. Greek tyrant of Syracuse (c270–215 BC). He concluded a treaty with Rome which recognized his rule over southeast Sicily. In return he supplied Rome with money and soldiers during the Punic Wars.

hieroglyphics A system of picture-writing used by the ancient Egyptians from c3400 BC. Hieroglyphic writing died out by AD 500, and its meaning was lost until discovery (1799) and decipherment (early 19th cent.) of the Rosetta Stone.

Hieron I *See* **Hiero I**

Hieron II *See* **Hiero II**

Higginson, Thomas Wentworth 1823–1911. American author and Unitarian minister. He was an early abolitionist and commanded the first black regiment during the Civil War.

Highlands, The ⟨Scottish Highlands⟩ The mountainous northern region of Scotland where the Gaelic language and customs survive even today. Highland clansmen played an active role in the Jacobite rebellions of 1715 and 1745.

Hilbert, David 1862–1943. German mathematician. His work included important advances in the theory of numbers, theory of invariants, and the axiomization of geometry.

Hilgard, Ferdinand Heinrich Gustav *See* **Villard, Henry**

Hill, Ambrose Powell 1825–65. Confederate general during the American Civil War. His infantry unit figured in the Seven Days' Battles, Second

Battle of Bull Run, Antietam and Gettysburg. He was killed in the Petersburg Campaign.

Hill, Daniel Harvey 1821–89. Confederate general in the American Civil War. He fought in several Virginia campaigns and commanded a corps at Chickamauga.

Hill, James Jerome 1838–1916. American railroad builder. As president of the Great Northern Railway (1882–1907), Hill directed most of the US and Canadian northwestern rail traffic. He was called "the Empire Builder."

Hillary, Sir Edmund Percival 1919–. New Zealand mountain climber. With the Sherpa Tenzing Norgay (c1914–), he was the first to climb Mount Everest (1953).

Hillel fl. 30 BC–AD 9. Jewish scholar born in Babylonia, considered one of the great interpreters of the Hebrew scriptures.

Hilliard, Nicholas 1537–1619. First important English miniature painter. He did portraits of many in Queen Elizabeth's court.

Hillman, Sidney 1887–1946. American labor leader. One of the founders of the Congress of Industrial Organizations (CIO), he helped extend the scope of union benefits.

Himera, Battle of Battle (480 BC) between Carthage and Syracuse in Sicily. Carthage, responding to requests from the Sicilian city-state Himera for aid against Agrigentum, was decisively defeated by Syracuse. The Carthaginian general Hamilcar was killed, and Syracuse gained dominance in Sicily.

Himmler, Heinrich 1900–45. German National Socialist leader and one of the most powerful men in A. Hitler's Third Reich. Notorious for his ruthlessness and cruelty, he headed the SS (state police unit) and the Gestapo (secret police) and ran the concentration camps in which millions died.

Hinckley, John W., Jr. *See* **Reagan, Ronald Wilson**

Hincks, Sir Francis 1807–85. Irish-born Canadian journalist and statesman. As premier of united Canada (1851–54), he negotiated a reciprocal trade agreement with the US and pushed for railroad construction.

Hindemith, Paul 1895–1963. German composer and violist. One of the leading composers of the 20th cent., he is known best for his opera *Mathis der Maler.*

Hindenburg, Paul von 1847–1934. German field marshal and president of the Weimar Republic (1925–34). The commander of German armies during WW I, he emerged as a national hero despite Germany's defeat. In failing health by 1933, he appointed A. Hitler as his chancellor and thus opened the way for Hitler's takeover of the German government.

Hindi Indo-Aryan language. A written variation of Hindustani, Hindi is the official language of India and is spoken by more than 150 million people. It has an extensive literature.

Hinduism Religion practiced by the majority of the people of India. Hinduism in its modern form evolved in stages from ancient Vedism (c1500 BC) to Brahmanism, and finally (c2d cent. BC) to early Hinduism. During its long development Hinduism has absorbed doctrines, rites, and practices from numerous other religions and sects and has spawned a great number of Hindu sects. Generally, however, Hinduism is characterized by acceptance of the Vedas (sacred texts), by adherence to the caste system (q.v.), by belief in cycles of life, death, and rebirth of the individual, and by the promise of escape from this cycle through enlightenment. Key dates in the development of Hinduism include:

c2000–1000 BC Harappa civilization flourished in Indus Valley; developed early religious traditions later incorporated into Vedism, Brahmanism, and ultimately Hinduism.

c1500 BC Aryans invaded India from region of Iran; brought new elements to traditional Indian religion and began Vedic period (1500–700 BC).

c900 BC Rig-Veda, compiled over a long period, reached its final form; became a sacred Hindu text.

c800–500 BC Upanishads written over extended period; these philosophic texts advanced concepts of reincarnation and karma.

c700–c500 BC Rise of Brahmanism; priestly class of Brahmins gained power; promoted elaborate rituals, philosophical speculations, and eventually the caste system.

c600–100 BC Sutras written; established rigid order of conduct and religious ritual and divided society into four classes; caste system arose during this period.

c500 BC Buddhism, Jainism, and various sects emerged to challenge traditional Brahmanism, which had lost its hold on the populace; in reaction, elements of Brahmanism, Jainism, and Buddhism were merged; concept of four stages of life introduced during this period.

c500 BC–AD c100 Mahabharata and Ramayana, great Hindu epics, written (exact dates unknown); period marked beginning of Hinduism as distinct from earlier Brahmanism.

3D–2D CENT. BC Mauryan empire flourished; Buddhism spread at the expense of Brahmanism.

2D CENT. BC Beginnings of Hinduism; rise of sects revering Vishnu and Shiva (Siva) as devotional deities.

4TH CENT. AD Hinduism began period of growth with rise of Gupta empire.

4TH–8TH CENTS. AD Puranas, verse texts dedicated to devotion of individual deities, written during Gupta rule.

7TH–11TH CENTS. Growth of sects devoted to Shiva and Vishnu (devotional Hinduism) contributed to decline of Buddhism in India.

c788–c820 Sankara, considered leading Hindu philosopher, lived; his teachings formed basis of modern Hinduism.

FROM c12TH CENT. Muslim incursions into India brought new Islamic influence to region; Islam incorporated superficially into Hinduism, but Hindu philosophy greatly influenced development of Islam in India.

c13TH–15TH CENTS. Bhakti, movement marked by emotional devotion to a personal deity, arose.

19TH CENT. Western influence on Hinduism began as British East India Company took control of India.

1897 Ramakrishna Mission founded by Vivekananda, a disciple of Ramakrishna; mission advanced a simplified form of Hinduism that encouraged social reform and denied the caste system.

1869–1948 M. Gandhi lived; merged traditional Hindu concepts and values into rising Indian nationalist movement; became the leading symbol of Hindu religion in the 20th cent.

1947 India became independent; government of India instituted numerous reforms in subsequent years, among them the outlawing of the caste system.

Hindustan Term meaning "land of the Hindus" and sometimes used to refer to all of India. More often, however, it means the northern part of India. "The Deccan" refers to the southern portion of India.

Hindustani Language group that includes the spoken languages of India (Hindi) and Pakistan (Urdu).

Hipparchos See **Hipparchus**

Hipparchus ⟨Hipparchos⟩ fl. 2d cent. BC. Important early Greek astronomer. He is believed to have compiled the first star catalogue and discovered subtle changes in the equinoxes caused by the wobble in the earth's rotation.

Hippias 6th–5th cent. BC. Tyrant of Athens (527–510 BC). After the murder (514 BC) of his brother Hipparchus by Harmodius and Aristogiton, Hippias became an even more repressive ruler. He was overthrown (510 BC) by the Alcmaeonidae and exiled to Persia.

hippies Young nonconformists of the youth counterculture in the US during the 1960s. They claimed to be searching for a nonmaterialistic way of life and experimented with unconventional dress and behavior to set themselves apart from the American middle class. Characteristic of the hippie lifestyle were worn and flamboyant clothing, long hair, use of marijuana and other drugs, and belief in free love and communal living.

Hippocrates *c*460–*c*370 BC. Greek physician, frequently called the "father of medicine." Though little is known of his life, Hippocrates appears to have been a medical writer and teacher of great scientific skill and high moral standards. The Hippocratic Oath, still administered to all new physicians, reflects his medical ethics.

Hippodamus ⟨Hippodamus of Miletus⟩ *fl.* 5th cent. BC. Greek architect. He planned Pireaus and the city of Rhodes.

Hippodamus of Miletus *See* **Hippodamus**

Hippolyte Amazon queen in Greek mythology. She wore a golden girdle that Hercules took from her as one of his 12 labors.

Hippolytus Son of Theseus in Greek mythology. He spurned the advances of his stepmother, Queen Phaedra, who then turned his father against him and killed herself. Before he realized his son's innocence, Theseus had Hippolytus killed by Poseidon.

Hippolytus, Saint ⟨~ of Rome⟩ AD *c*160–235. Italian theologian, martyr, and the first antipope. He broke with Rome over the question of heresy and became antipope (AD 217–235). The *Canons of Saint Hippolytus* are believed to be a later revision of his *Apostolic Tradition* by an unknown author.

Hippolytus of Rome *See* **Hippolytus, Saint**

Hiram ⟨Huram⟩ 989?–936 BC. Phoenician king of Tyre. A friend of David and Solomon, he helped with the construction of the Temple at Jerusalem.

Hirohito 1901–. Emperor of Japan since 1926, the son and successor to Taisho. His reign was marked by wars against China from the 1930s and Japan's participation in WW II. He accepted unconditional surrender to the US (1945) and a new constitution making him constitutional monarch (1946).

Hiroshima Japanese city, the target of the first atomic bomb (Aug. 6, 1945). The bombing virtually destroyed the city, hastened the end of WW II, and marked the beginning of the age of nuclear warfare.

Hiss, Alger 1904– US State Department official accused of spying for the Russians. Named by former Communist party member Whittaker Chambers (1901–61) as a conspirator in a Russian spy ring, Hiss was tried and convicted for perjury (1950). R. Nixon figured prominently in the Hiss

investigation and the sensational trial was exploited by Senator J. McCarthy.

historiography The study of methods of historical investigation and of writing history.

Hitchcock, Alfred Joseph 1899–1980. British-American film director, famous for such suspense thrillers as *North by Northwest, Psycho*, and *The Birds*.

Hitler, Adolf 1889–1945. Austrian-born German dictator (1933–45) and founder of the National Socialist party (Nazis). Hitler's perverse schemes for German world-domination and creation of an ethnically pure "master race" resulted in the outbreak of WW II and the extermination of millions of Jews and other minority groups. A failed artist, Hitler served in WW I and later joined (1919) the German Workers' Party in Bavaria, Germany. He reorganized it (1921) into the National Socialist party *(q.v.)* and turned it into a nationalistic, paramilitary group. He failed (1923) in his attempt to seize power in Bavaria (Munich Beer Hall Putsch) and, during his short term in prison, started writing *Mein Kampf (q.v.)*, in which he outlined his plans for the Nazi party. The party grew rapidly during the Great Depression, largely because of Hitler's ability to play on hatred of the Jews and Communists in the name of German nationalism. The party's strength in the Reichstag increased greatly as a result, though Hitler lost the 1932 presidential election to P. von Hindenburg. Hindenburg named Hitler (Jan. 30, 1933) as his chancellor, however, and Hitler soon after began to consolidate his power. He succeeded in gaining emergency powers, and in banning the Communists, by blaming the Reichstag Fire *(q.v.)* on them. He then won passage of the Enabling Act (Mar. 23, 1933), which established the Third Reich *(q.v.)*. Following Hindenburg's death (1934), Hitler became sole ruler of Germany and embarked on his program of expanding German power. He occupied the Rhineland (1936), annexed Austria (1938), occupied Czechoslovakia (1939), and invaded Poland (1939). The last action provoked the outbreak of WW II *(q.v.)*. Despite his remarkable early successes, the tide of the war was clearly against him by 1944. With the Russians entering Berlin the following year, he committed suicide (Apr. 30, 1945) with his wife and former mistress, E. Braun.

Hitotsubashi *See* **Tokugawa Keiki**

Hittite Empire Once powerful kingdom in Asia Minor (*c*1600–*c*1200 BC). The Hittites are believed to have discovered the technique of tempering iron and thus figure in the beginnings of the Iron Age *(q.v.)*. The Hittite peoples first appeared (*c*1800 BC) in what is now central Turkey in a migration from the East. They established the Old Kingdom (1600–1400 BC) and during this period Hittite rulers gradually expanded their domains throughout Turkey and into northern Syria. The Hittite ruler Mursilis I even attacked Babylon (c1590) and thereby ended the rule of the Amorite kings. The empire reached its greatest power (especially under Suppiluliumas I, [c1380–c1340]) during the New Kingdom (1400–1200), when it dominated Asia Minor. Toward the end of this period, Hittites under Muwatallis (c1306–c1282) engaged the Egyptians for control of Syria. This resulted in the famous Battle of Kadesh (1288) and a treaty. Sometime around 1200 BC invasions by Phrygian, Thracian, and Assyrian peoples caused the sudden collapse of the Hittite empire. By c700 BC the Assyrians had absorbed the last vestiges of the Hittite empire.

Hoban, James c1762–1831. Irish-American architect. He designed and built the White House and was a supervisor in the construction of the Capitol building.

Hobbes, Thomas 1588–1679. British philosopher. A theorist in both natural and political philosophy, he was a friend of such notables as Galileo and B. Jonson. He formulated a mechanistic view of human actions, and his writings on free will and the social contract had an enormous influence on the development of political philosophy. His works include *Human Nature* and *Leviathan.*

Hobkirk's Hill, Battle of Battle of the American Revolution (Apr. 25, 1781), in which a force of 900 British troops defeated some 1500 Americans under Col. N. Greene, near Camden, South Carolina.

Ho Chi Minh ⟨*pseud. of* Nguyen That Thanh⟩ 1890?–1969. Vietnamese Communist leader, one of the foremost Communists of the 20th cent. He left Vietnam in 1911 and until WW II stayed variously in the US, Britain, France, China, and the USSR. He founded the Indochinese Communist party (1930) and was sought by the French soon thereafter as a leader of revolutionary Vietnamese nationalists. During WW II he organized the Viet Minh movement for Vietnamese independence and his guerrilla units fought the Japanese. After the war he proclaimed (1945) Vietnam a republic, of which he became president (1945–54). He was soon embroiled in the Indochina War (1946–54) and the republic was divided into South and North Vietnam. President of the northern sector (1954–69), he organized the National Liberation Front and the Vietcong guerrilla armies, which fought in the south during the protracted Vietnam War (1960–75).

Ho Chi Minh Trail Network of jungle and mountain trails connecting North Vietnam with South Vietnam, Laos, and Cambodia during the Vietnam War. Much of the network came into use from WW II on, in fighting against the Japanese, French, and the Americans and South Vietnamese. Neither land assaults nor strategic bombing of segments (from 1965) succeeded in preventing the use of the trail to supply the North Vietnamese-Vietcong war effort.

Hofer, Andreas 1767–1810. Austrian patriot. Attempting to keep his native Tyrol under Austrian rule, he led a peasant rebellion that withstood Bavarian and French forces from 1809 to 1810.

Hoffmann, Ernest Theodor Amadeus 1776–1882. German author and composer, known best for his Gothic horror stories.

Hofmannsthal, Hugo von 1874–1929. Austrian poet and dramatist, famous for his librettos to R. Strauss operas, including *Der Rosenkavalier* and *Electra.*

Hogarth, William 1697–1764. English painter and engraver. He is known best for "morality pictures," of which *Marriage à la Mode* is considered his masterpiece.

Hohenheim, Theophrastus Bombastus von *See* **Paracelsus**

Hohenlinden, Battle of Battle (Dec. 3, 1800) of the French Revolutionary Wars, at Hohenlinden, southern Germany. Some 110,000 French troops led by J. Moreau defeated an Austrian force of 130,000 under Archduke John, brother of Holy Roman Emperor Francis II. The last major engagement of the War of the Second Coalition, it left only England in opposition to Napoleon.

Hohenstaufen Family of German nobles and rulers of the Holy Roman Empire (1138–1254). The family originated in the 11th cent. with a Swabian count, Frederick (d. 1105). The first Hohenstaufen emperor was Conrad III, crowned 1138. The Hohenstaufen rulers were opposed by the Guelphs and, by their involvement in Italy, eventually brought about the downfall of the family. The family became extinct by the death (1254) of Conrad IV, the execution of Conradin (1268), and the execution of Frederick's illegitimate son, Enzio (1272).

Rulers of the Holy Roman Empire

Conrad III	(king of the Germans, 1138–52)
Frederick I Barbarossa	(emperor, 1155–90)
Henry VI	(emperor, 1191–97)
Philip of Swabia	(king of the Germans, 1198–1208)

| Frederick II | (emperor, 1220–50) |
| Conrad IV | (king of the Germans, 1250–54) |

Hohenzollern Family of German nobles that provided rulers of Prussia (1415–1871), brought about a united Germany (1871–1918), and created a line of Romanian kings (1866–1947). The family was begun by the 11th-cent. counts of Zollern. Following the death of Frederick of Hohenzollern (c1200), the family split into Franconian and Swabian lines. The fortunes of the Franconian line grew around control of Brandenburg, of which Frederick I became elector (1417). Thereafter the line increased its power and domains and in 1701 Frederick I was crowned king of the new kingdom of Prussia. After the unification of Germany (1871), the Franconian rulers ruled as German kaisers until establishment of the Weimar Republic (1918). The Swabian line, later split into the Hohenzollern-Hechingen and Hohenzollern-Sigmaringen lines. The latter division produced princes and then kings of Romania (1866–1947).

German Kaisers

William I	(1871–88)
Frederick III	(1888)
William II	(1888–1918)

Romanian Kings

Carol I	(prince 1866–81; king 1881–1914)
Ferdinand I	(1914–27)
Michael	(1927–30, 1940–47)
Carol II	(1930–40)

Hojo Family of Japanese feudal nobles. As regents for a line of weak Shoguns and puppet emperors, they were in effect the rulers of Japan between about 1219 and 1333. Among them were Hojo Yasutoki (1183–1242), who consolidated power in the regency, and Hojo Tokimune (1215–84), who repulsed an invasion of Japan by Kublai Khan.

Hojo Tokimune *See* **Hojo**

Hojo Yasutoki *See* **Hojo**

Hokusai 1760–1849. Japanese artist, considered one of the great color-print designers. A prolific artist, he produced many works, including the 15-volume *Ten Thousand Sketches.*

Holbach, Paul, Henri Thiry, baron d' 1723–89. French philosopher. An outspoken materialist and naturalist, he attacked religion in several philosophical works.

Holbein, Hans, the Elder 1465–1524. German portrait and religious painter, known especially for his altarpieces and for his silverpoint drawings.

Holbein, Hans, the Younger 1497–1543. German Renaissance portrait and religious painter. The most famous of a family of painters, he is known for his altarpieces, portraits done as court painter to English King Henry VIII, and paintings of religious subjects.

Holberg, Ludvig, Baron 1684–1754. Norwegian-born Danish poet, playwright, historian, and philosopher. His collected works are regarded as the foundation of Danish literature.

Holderlin, Friedrich 1770–1843. German poet. A protégé of F. von Schiller, Holderlin combined classical Greek form with the energy of the Sturm und Drang movement. He is considered a bridge between the classic and romantic schools of poetry.

Holiday, Billie ⟨Holiday, Eleanora⟩ 1915–59. American jazz singer, also known as Lady Day, one of the great figures of American jazz. Her fame and fortune did not compensate for a disastrous personal life and she died of drug addiction.

Holiday, Eleanora *See* **Holiday, Billie**

Holland Former county of the Holy Roman Empire that is now divided into two provinces of The Netherlands. Established in 1018, it passed to the house of Wittelsbach (14th cent.) and then to Burgundy (1433). Holland was a leader in commerce, shipbuilding, and the cloth industry in the 16th cent. and led in the fight for Dutch independence.

Hollywood Suburb of Los Angeles, California, and symbolic center of the US movie industry. Hollywood was incorporated in 1903 and the first films were shot there in 1910–11. From the 1920s to 1940s, during the golden age of film, it became the home of movie studios and playground for the stars who worked in them. Major studios began closing after the 1940s, and Hollywood has since become a center for production of radio and television shows.

Holmes, John Haynes 1879–1964. American clergyman and writer. He championed many social causes and was a founder of both the American Civil Liberties Union and National Association for the Advancement of Colored People.

Holmes, Oliver Wendell, Sr. 1809–94. American poet and writer and father of O.W. Holmes, Jr. He is known best for his poems *Old Ironsides* and *The Chambered Nautilus* and his series of prose works called the "Breakfast-Table" sketches.

Holmes, Oliver Wendell, Jr. 1841–1935. American jurist and US Supreme Court associate justice (1902–32). Appointed to the court by T. Roosevelt, he became known as the "Great Dissenter" for his dissenting opinions in cases in which the court struck down new laws passed by Congress. Despite his advocacy of such judicial restraint, he developed the "clear and present danger" concept in regard to restrictions on freedom of speech.

Holmes, Sherlock *See* **Doyle, Sir Arthur Conan**

Holocaust Name given to the Nazis' systematic attempt to exterminate European Jews (and others) during WW II. A. Hitler established the first concentration camps in Germany soon after taking power in 1933. Originally intended for Hitler's political opponents, they were soon after used to imprison Jews and other groups. After WW II broke out, Hitler began his notorious "final solution" and some of these camps (Dachau, Auschwitz, Buchenwald, and Treblinka among them) became extermination centers. Some 6 million Jews and many others, including other ethnic groups, nationalities, and political opponents, were murdered in these centers. It is estimated that in all the Nazi camps (including POW camps) some 18 to 26 million persons died.

Holowczyn, Battle of Battle (July 4, 1708) in the Northern War at Holowczyn, Russia. The Swedish army under Charles XII defeated the Russian army under Gen. Aleksandr Menshikov during the Swedish invasion of Russia. The Russian scorched-earth policy, however, forced Charles to abandon his march east and move south to the Ukraine.

Holst, Gustav 1874–1934. English composer. He was inspired by such European composers as R. Strauss and I. Stravinsky. His works include the orchestral suite *The Planets.*

Holy Alliance League formed (Sept. 26, 1815) by Russian czar Alexander I, Austrian king Francis I, and Prussian king Frederick William III. The league was largely an agreement in which the monarchs swore to uphold Christian principles in their kingdoms. A part of the general European realignment after the fall of Napoleon's empire, it was eventually joined by all Christian European rulers except British king George IV. The alliance itself had little direct impact, but it became a symbol of conservative reactionary policies by which monarchs maintained social order and which characterized European politics until the mid-19th cent.

Holy Ghost (Holy Spirit) Third person of the Trinity (Father, Son, and Holy Ghost) in Christian doctrine. At the First Council of Constantinople (AD 381), the Holy Ghost was held to be a distinct entity, coequal with the Father and the Son.

Holy Grail Legendary cup used by Jesus at the Last Supper. Saved by Joseph of Arimathea after Jesus' crucifixion, it was said to have been taken to Britain, where it was subsequently lost. As the object of religious quests, it is a central theme of the Arthurian Legend *(q.v.).*

Holy Land Name applied to the middle, eastern region of Palestine. It is so called because of its historical associations with the Christian, Islamic, and Jewish religions.

Holy League **1.** Holy League of 1495 formed to repel an invasion (1494) of Italy by French king Charles VIII. Joined by Pope Alexander VI, Holy Roman Emperor Maximilian I, Ferdinand and Isabella of Spain, and the cities of Venice and Milan, the league forced Charles to retreat (1496) from Naples. **2.** Holy League of 1511 formed to drive French king Louis VII out of Italy during the Italian Wars. It was joined by Pope Julius II, English king Henry VIII, Spanish king Ferdinand V, and the city of Venice, and succeeded in expelling (1512) the French from Milan. The French persisted, however, and the allies eventually made separate peace agreements with France. **3.** Holy League of 1526 formed to force Holy Roman Emperor Charles V out of Italy. It was joined by Pope Clement VII, French king Francis I, and the cities of Venice and Milan, and was defeated by Charles. **4.** Holy League of 1538 formed to oppose the Schmalkaldic League. It was joined by Holy Roman Emperor Charles V and other German Catholic noblemen. **5.** Holy League of 1576 (Catholic League) formed to oppose Protestantism in France during the Wars of Religion. It was first proclaimed by Henri, 3d duc de Guise, in protest to concessions granted the Protestants by King Henry III. Disbanded by Henry after a Protestant uprising, it was re-formed (1585) to oppose Protestant heir to the throne, Henry IV. During the War of the Three Henrys the league controlled France's cities, and, on Henry III's assassination (1589), Henry IV was forced to accept Catholicism (1593) to end the league's resistance.

Holy Roman Empire. Political entity in central Europe from the 10th to 19th cents., which gave rise to the modern states of Germany and Austria. Its history is complex and begins with the Carolingian Empire of Charlemagne. Charlemagne's empire was (from 800) considered the successor state to the Western Roman Empire (defunct since 476) and embraced much of Europe. But it was divided in 843 and central authority soon died out in the two major divisions, the eastern kingdom (roughly, modern Germany) and the western kingdom (roughly, modern France). Otto I restored control in the east and in 962 was crowned emperor of the Romans by the pope. The Holy Roman Empire was thus founded as the reconstituted Western Roman Empire. Otto's coronation also marked the beginning of the often troubled alliance between the emperors and the Roman Catholic popes. In subsequent centuries the empire was torn by struggles with the popes and by the rising power of the princes. In the 13th cent.

the Holy Roman emperors gave up their claims to control Italy and in the 14th cent. they lost effective control over the princely states within the empire. They had direct rule over only their personal domains, though in the case of the Hapsburg emperors (ruled from the 15th cent.) this amounted to considerable territory. The Protestant Reformation, wars with the Ottoman Turks and with France further weakened the empire in the next centuries. Its final collapse was brought on by the French Revolutionary Wars at the end of the 18th cent. (For subsequent history of the region, *see* Germany, Austria; *also* Reformation.) Key events in the history of the Holy Roman Empire include:

771–814 Charlemagne reigned as king of the Franks; asserted Frankish control in Italy and expanded the Carolingian Empire eastward, subduing the German tribes.

800 Charlemagne crowned emperor by Pope Leo III; this was taken as revival of the Western Roman Empire, which had collapsed in 476.

814–840 Louis I (the Pious) reigned over the empire; his heirs began struggle that would lead to division of empire.

840–855 Lothair I reigned as emperor; though he retained title of emperor, the Carolingian Empire was divided soon after his accession.

843 Treaty of Verdun; Carolingian Empire divided; Louis the German gained the East Frankish Empire, Charles the Bald gained the West Frankish kingdom, and Lothair received the imperial title (with no sovereignty over other kingdoms), Italy, and a narrow middle section of the Carolingian domains (Lotharingia).

843–876 Louis the German reigned over the East Frankish kingdom (roughly modern Germany).

855–875 Imperial crown passed to Louis II, son of Lothair I; he inherited direct control over Italy only.

870 Treaty of Mersen; Louis the German and Charles the Bald divided the middle kingdom (except Italy), thus bringing East and West Frankish kingdoms to a common border.

875–877 Imperial crown passed to the West Frankish king, Charles II (the Bald), on the death of Louis II.

876 Louis the German died; his East Frankish kingdom divided among his heirs.

881–887 Charles III (the Fat) reigned as imperial emperor, succeeding after period of strife; reunited east under his rule (882).

884–887 Charles III (the Fat) next succeeded (884) to West Frankish throne; Carolingian Empire thus briefly reunited; Charles unable to repulse invasion by Norsemen; deposed in east and west.

887 Arnulf deposed Charles III in the east.

887–899 Arnulf reigned as king of the East Franks; repulsed invasions by Norsemen and Slavs.

896–899 Arnulf reigned as emperor; crowned after pacifying Italy (895) at the pope's request; was last of the Carolingian line of emperors, and no emperor was crowned again until 962.

899–911 Louis the Child reigned as king of the East Frankish kingdom; Magyar raids (from 900) broke down central authority and increased power of feudal lords.

911–918 Conrad I reigned as elected king of east; continuation of Magyar raids, and feuds and rebellions by feudal lords nearly caused complete breakup of eastern kingdom; Lorraine became part of western kingdom.

919–936 Henry I (the Fowler) reigned as elected king of the eastern kingdom; as duke of Saxony he had been ar archfoe of the king; but during his reign he reestablished royal authority in the east; regained Lorraine and decisively defeated the Magyars (933).

936–973 Otto I reigned as German king; completed reestablishment of central authority; regarded as first emperor of the Holy Roman Empire (after 962).

951 First invasion of Italy by Otto; he assumed the title of King of the Lombards.

955 Otto I decisively defeated the Magyars at the Battle of Lechfeld.

960 Otto I subdued the Slavs.

961 Second invasion of Italy by Otto I; he quickly defeated Italian king Berengar II at the request of Pope John XII.

962 Otto crowned emperor by the grateful pope; this marked the beginning of the Holy Roman Empire and the second revival of the Western Roman Empire.

962 Privilegium Ottonianum, agreement concluded (Feb. 13) between Otto and the pope to regulate relations between them; marked the beginning of the long, often troubled relationship between Holy Roman emperors and the popes.

963 Pope John deposed by Otto; Leo VIII installed in his place.

965 John XIII named pope by Otto after Leo VIII died; Romans refused to accept him.

966–972 Otto invaded Italy a third time; subdued the Romans and had some successes against the Byzantines in southern Italy.

973–983 Otto II reigned; imperial control in Italy weakened; Danes revolted in the north and Slavs launched invasions of the empire.

974–978 Revolt by Bavaria (led by Henry the Wrangler); Otto ultimately defeated Henry.

980 Otto defeated French king Lothair, who was attempting to take the duchy of Lorraine.

981–982 Campaign by Otto against Arabs in southern Italy failed.

983–1002 Otto III reigned; installed two popes (Gregory V and Sylvester II) and tried to make Rome capital of the empire; driven out by rebellious Romans in 1001.

1002–24 Henry II reigned as last of the Saxon emperors; crowned 1014; warred against king Boleslaus of Poland and reasserted control over Italy (1021–22).

1024–39 Conrad II reigned as first of the Salian rulers; elected German king after the extinction of the Saxon line, he was forced to put down revolts in Germany and Italy; crowned emperor (1027).

1024–1125 Salian dynasty of emperors in power.

1039–56 Henry III reigned; crowned emperor 1046; imperial power at its height; established border with Hungary that remained fixed for centuries; supported the Cluniac Order and failed in his attempt to reform the church.

1046 Synods of Sutri and Rome; Henry reasserted imperial right to nominate popes and named Clement II in place of three rivals claiming papacy.

1056–1106 Henry IV reigned, crowned emperor 1084; his reign marked the beginning of the Investiture Controversy and the rise of the power of the popes.

1075–76 Reformer Pope Gregory VII condemned Henry for appointing a number of bishops, thus beginning the Investiture Controversy; Henry deposed the pope (1076), while the pope deposed Henry.

1077 Henry forced to submit to the pope and do penance at Canossa to avoid revolt within the empire.

1077–80 Civil war within the empire; Henry victorious against the antiking Rudolf of Swabia.

1081–84 Henry marched against Rome as struggle with Pope Gregory was renewed; crowned emperor by antipope Clement III, whom he installed; Normans, allies of pope, drove Henry out of Rome.

1106–25 Henry V reigned; crowned emperor 1111; he accepted the Concordat of Worms (1122), which ended the Investiture Controversy but not the rivalry between popes and the imperial emperors.

1125–37 Lothair II reigned; elected king (with support of clergy) over rival claimant with hereditary ties to royal line.

1125–35 Civil war between the Welfs (Lothair's supporters) and Waiblingers (supports of the Hohenstaufen family, which claimed the throne on the basis of heredity); the war, won by Lothair, marked the beginning of the long struggle between these factions for control of the throne.

1133 Lothair II crowned emperor after invading Italy (1132–33) to support Pope Innocent II against a rival.

1138–52 Conrad III reigned as first king of the Hohenstaufen line; elected king by German nobles, he was never crowned emperor.

1138–42 Civil war between Conrad and the Welfs; defeated Welfs agreed to peace, but rivalry between Welf and Waiblinger factions continued throughout century.

1147–49 Conrad joined in the Second Crusade; meanwhile the struggle with the Welfs spread disorder throughout the German domains.

1152–90 Frederick I Barbarossa reigned; crowned emperor 1155, he opposed the growing power of the papacy and sought to reimpose imperial control over Italy (launched six invasions of Italy); attempted to check the power of the princes in the empire.

1155 Holy Roman Empire made official name of empire by Frederick.

1156 Austria created as an independent duchy.

1167 Lombard League formed by Lombard cities in northern Italy against Holy Roman Emperor Frederick I.

1189–90 Frederick joined the Third Crusade and died in Asia Minor.

1190 Order of Teutonic Knights formed at Acre during Third Crusade; later became a power in Prussia.

1190–97 Henry VI reigned; crowned emperor 1191; his reign was marked by continuing struggles with the Welfs and by restoration of order in Sicily.

1192–94 English king Richard I held captive by Henry; Richard forced to accept suzerainty of Holy Roman Empire over England and pay a large ransom to obtain his release.

1197–1211 Civil war over succession; Waiblinger Philip of Swabia and Welf Otto IV vied for control; Philip killed (1208) and Otto was deposed after a brief reign.

1212–50 Frederick II reigned; a Hohenstaufen, he opposed the Welfs and continued the struggle with the papacy; imperial control of northern Italy declined.

1214 Battle of Bouvines; Frederick, allied with French king Philip II, defeated the Welf leader Otto IV.

1226 By issuing the Golden Bull of Rimini, Frederick II granted the Teutonic Knights sovereignty over Prussia.

1246 Antiking of Germans named by Pope Innocent IV, who sought to break power of Hohenstaufens and gain control of Italy; warfare in Italy and Germany followed.

1250–54 Conrad IV succeeded his father, but was never crowned emperor; continued struggle with Innocent IV and died as he was about to renew war in Italy.

1254–73 Great Interregnum followed death of Conrad IV; nobles gained power; no recognized German king during this period.

1273–91 Rudolf I reigned as king; he ended the Great Interregnum and founded the Hapsburg line; never crowned emperor; imperial powers declined sharply.

1278 Rudolf defeated Bohemian king Ottocar II and thereby gained core of Hapsburg domains (Austria, Styria, Carniola) that remained in family until the 20th cent.

1279 Papal sovereignty over Papal States recognized by Rudolf; followed recognition of papal sovereignty in southern Italy (1275).

1291 Four Forest Cantons formed league against the Hapsburgs and thus began the struggle for independence of Switzerland.

1292 Adolphe of Nassau elected king of the Germans to prevent crown from becoming hereditary Hapsburg title.

1300s Rise of the Hanseatic League, a league formed by German towns to safeguard and promote commerce as imperial authority declined; league remained powerful until the 15th cent.

1314–47 Louis IV reigned; fought Frederick the Fair (1314–22) for German crown.

1327–30 Louis intervened in Italy, declared emperor by Roman laity (1328).

1338 Declaration at Rhense; German electors eliminated papal confirmation for naming of emperor; declared election of German king by them automatically conferred imperial crown; practice of papal confirmation nevertheless continued.

1347–78 Charles IV reigned; received papal confirmation in 1355 and brought end to long struggle with papacy over Italy.

1348 Black Plague began spreading throughout the empire.

1356 Golden Bull of 1356 issued by Charles; formal constitution for empire which confirmed decentralization of authority and created a federation of sovereign states; emperors never again exercised real control over empire, only personal domains; papal confirmation of election of emperor effectively eliminated.

1376–88 First Swabian League formed by German principalities to oppose Charles' increased taxes on cities.

1378–1400 Wenceslaus reigned as king; he was a weak ruler; his reign was marked by warfare between the princes and the imperial cities; deposed in favor of Rupert (ruled 1400–10).

1410–37 Sigismund reigned; was also king of Hungary (1387–1437).

1410 Battle of Tannenberg fought; victory of Polish and Lithuanian forces, who halted eastern advance of Teutonic Knights.

1414 Council of Constance convened at Sigismund's urging; brought Great Schism to an end (1417).

1415 Bohemian religious reformer J. Huss executed for heresy.

1419–34 Hussite Wars, struggle between followers of J. Huss and imperial forces.

1428 Sigismund's campaign failed against the Turks advancing in the east.

1438–39 Albert II reigned; following his election as emperor, the imperial crown became hereditary in the Hapsburg family.

1440–93 Frederick III reigned; last emperor crowned at Rome (1452); obtained Burgundy by marrying his son, Maximilian, to Mary of Burgundy (1477) and thus set stage for great expansion of Hapsburg hereditary domains.

1488–1534 Second Swabian League formed by German principalities.

1493–1519 Maximilian reigned; greatly expanded Hapsburg domains, often at the expense of the empire; attempts to reform administration of empire proved only partly successful as princes sought to maintain their power.

1494–1559 Italian Wars; Maximilian involved the empire in wars there; fought France to regain Burgundian territories in Italy, which he had inherited.

1495 Diet of Worms instituted limited constitutional reforms.

c1498 Aulic Council, emperor's personal council, established by Maximilian I.

1499 Switzerland gained independence from the empire.

1508 Maximilian joined the League of Cambrai in war against Venice, gaining some of its territory.

1513 Maximilian joined Holy League against France.

1516 Hungary and Bohemia added to Hapsburg domains through marriage.

1516 Maximilian's grandson succeeded to the Spanish throne, thus adding Spain and the New World to Hapsburg domains.

1517 Reformation began (Oct.) when M. Luther posted his demands for church reform.

1519–58 Charles V reigned; as king of Spain and Holy Roman Emperor he ruled vast domains but continuing Italian Wars and revolts connected with the Reformation diminished his power.

1521 M. Luther called before imperial Diet of Worms; refused to recant his Protestant teachings.

1522–23 Knight's War, unsuccessful rebellion by knights to ensure ancient privileges against the Reformation.

1524–25 Peasants' War, unsuccessful uprising of peasants and townsmen; denounced by M. Luther and crushed.

1525 Teutonic Knights dissolved by Grand Master Albert of Brandenburg.

1526–29 War with advancing Ottoman Turks, who were successful in Hungary and laid siege to Vienna (1529).

1531 Schmalkaldic League formed by Protestant nobles to oppose the emperor's threats to end Lutheranism by force.

1532 Religious Peace of Nuremberg.

1535 Charles successfully attacked Turkish-held Tunis.

1544–47 Schmalkaldic War against German Protestant powers.

1545–63 Council of Trent; marked beginning of the Counter-Reformation.

1548 Augsburg Interim proclaimed by Diet of Augsburg; Charles V attempted to force a settlement of strife between Catholic and Protestant nobles in the empire.

1555 Peace of Augsburg provided formula for ending conflict between Catholics and Protestants within the empire.

1556 Charles V abdicated Spanish throne to his son Philip.

1556 Charles V abdicated German throne in favor of his brother Ferdinand; Ferdinand subsequently lost control of much of Hungary to the Turks.

1568 Truce concluded with Ottoman Turks by Emperor Maximilian II (reigned 1564–76); emperor agreed to pay tribute to Turks in return for control of part of Hungary.

1576–1612 Rudolf II reigned; Catholic Reformation actively supported, opening way to Thirty Years' War.

1604–06 Hungarians, led by S. Bocksay, revolted against attempts to impose Catholicism in Hungary.

1608–21 Protestant Union formed by Protestant princes to prevent imperial government from reimposing Catholicism.

1612–19 Matthias reigned; failed to ease conflicts between Catholics and Protestants; outbreak of Thirty Years' War.

1618–48 Thirty Years' War; Emperor Ferdinand II (reigned 1619–37) unable to put down revolt by Protestant nobles in Bohemia; war became general European war of religion that seriously weakened the Holy Roman Empire.

1648 Treaty of Wesphalia ending the war; Emperor Ferdinand III (reigned 1637–57) forced to agree to terms that effectively ended central authority of imperial crown; thereafter emperors really controlled only hereditary Hapsburg domains.

1658–1705 Leopold I reigned; empire embroiled in wars.

1672–78 Third Dutch War; Leopold joined coalition against French King Louis XIV.

1682–99 Austro-Turkish War; Ottoman Turks forced to withdraw from almost all of Hungary.

1689–97 War of the Grand Alliance against France.

1701–14 War of the Spanish Succession over claims to the Spanish throne; French Bourbon line succeeded in Spain; Austrian Hapsburgs gained the Austrian Netherlands and Spanish territories in Italy.

1701 Frederick I created the Kingdom of Prussia.

1711–40 Charles VI reigned; tried to ensure succession of his daughter, Maria Theresa, to Hapsburg domains; wars with Turks proved indecisive.

1713 Emperor Charles VI issued the Pragmatic Sanction of 1713 to ensure succession of his daughter, Maria Theresa.

1733–35 War of the Polish Succession.

1740–48 War of the Austrian Succession; Maria Theresa ultimately retained Hapsburg domains and her husband became Holy Roman Emperor Francis I (reigned 1745–65); Prussia, under Frederick II (the Great), emerged as a major power during the war.

1756–63 Seven Years' War; Austrian Hapsburgs failed to regain territories from Prussia while Prussian power increased in Europe.

1765–90 Joseph II reigned; an enlightened despot, he attempted to institute many reforms, but many proved to be short-lived.

1778–79 War of the Bavarian Succession; Joseph thwarted in plan to annex Bavaria to Austria.

1781 Serfdom abolished.

1781 Edict of Toleration issued by Joseph.

1787–92 Austrian participation in the Russo-Turkish War proved fruitless.

1790–92 Leopold II reigned; repealed many of Joseph's reforms.

1792 Declaration of Pillnitz; Leopold joined Prussia in this proclamation against revolutionaries in France.

1792–1806 Francis II reigned as the last emperor of the Holy Roman Empire.

1792–1802 French Revolutionary Wars; Emperor Francis defeated by French.

1801 Treaty of Lunéville, ending wars between the Holy Roman Empire and France; Francis forced to consent to the virtual dissolution of the empire and reorganization of German states.

1804 Francis II became Austrian emperor Francis I.

1804–15 Napoleonic Wars; Austria quickly defeated by Napoleon and forced to consent to the Treaty of Pressburg (1805).

1806 Holy Roman Empire formally dissolved.

Holy Sepulcher Church in Jerusalem built over what are traditionally believed to be the sites of Jesus' crucifixion and tomb. Completed in AD 336, the building was originally a rotunda. It has been destroyed, rebuilt, and remodeled several times. The modern structure dates from 1810.

Holy Spirit *See* **Holy Ghost**

holy war A war fought for the advancement or defense of a religion, such as the Crusades, or, in Islam, a Jihad. The Jihad provided the impetus for conquest (of non-believers) that led to the rapid expansion of the Muslim Empire of the Caliphate in the 7th cent.

Homer Ancient Greek poet who is generally regarded as the author of two of the greatest epic poems in Western literature, the *Iliad* and the *Odyssey.* Homer was revered in ancient times, though the details of his life are largely a matter of legend and conjecture. Even his authorship of the two great epics has been contested (the "Homeric question"). He is thought to have lived in a Greek colony in Asia Minor in the 9th or 8th cent. BC and, according to one legend, was blind. What is certain, however, is that the two epics profoundly influenced ancient Greek culture and the subsequent development of Western literature.

Homer, Winslow 1836–1910. A leading American artist, he is known best for his paintings of the sea.

Home Rule Irish movement for self-government. Formed (1870) by Isaac Butt (1813–79) and led by C. Parnell (to 1890), the movement included demands for a separate Irish parliament and land reform (*see* Irish Land Acts). Two Home Rule bills

(1886, 1893) were backed by W. Gladstone's British Liberal party, but they failed to overcome Conservative opposition in Parliament. A third Home Rule bill was finally passed (1912), but implementation was delayed by the outbreak of WW I. During the war, radical Irish Republicans came to the fore, and, with the declaration of Irish independence by the Dail Eireann (1918), the Irish Republican Army went into armed rebellion against the British government. The Irish Free State (later the Republic of Ireland) was created in 1921.

Homestead Act US law (passed 1862). The act granted 160 acres of public land to a settler after a five-year occupancy. The movement for land grants to settlers gained momentum after 1835, when land sales were no longer needed to eliminate the public debt. Of great interest to the developing western states, such land grants were promoted by the Free-Soil Party and opposed by the South. By the 1850s the issue of land grants had become related to extension of slavery in the new western territories. It was not until after the secession of southern states and the outbreak of the Civil War (1861–65) that the act passed Congress.

Homestead strike Famous US labor dispute (1892). Following the breakdown of wage negotiations with the Carnegie Steel Company at Homestead, Pennsylvania, members of the Amalgamated Association of Iron and Steel Workers went on strike. Company manager H. Frick, however, hired strikebreakers and some 300 Pinkerton detectives to protect them. Strikers shot at the detectives (July 6), and a gun battle broke out in which several were killed and wounded. The state militia was called out to restore order, and the plant was reopened. The strike was officially ended Nov. 20.

Homma, Masaharu *See* **Bataan Death March**

Homo habilis *See* **Leakey, Louis Seymour Bazett**

Honduras (Republic of Honduras) Independent state located in northern Central America. Its capital is Tegucigalpa. A Mayan culture once flourished in the area (from 4th cent. AD) but by the time Columbus discovered Honduras (1502) it had already declined. Like other Central American republics, Honduras has experienced considerable political turmoil since gaining independence from Spain in 1521. There have been well over 100 coups since that time. Key dates in the history of Honduras include:

1502 Columbus discovered coastal region of Honduras.

1524 P. de Alvarado established coastal settlements.

1539 Honduras became part of the captaincy general of Guatemala.

1821 Honduras proclaimed independence from Spain.

1821–23 Became part of Iturbide's Mexican Empire.

1825–38 Joined Central American Federation.

1838 Became a republic; subsequent history marked by political instability, the struggle between liberals and conservatives, and interference by neighboring countries.

1860 American adventurer and filibusterer William Walker captured in Honduras while on an expedition aimed at Nicaragua.

1863 Alliance with Nicaragua and El Salvador ended in warfare with them.

1874–83 Marco Aurelio Soto in office as president (except 1876); his administration marked by stable government and enactment of reforms.

1883–1911 Long period of unrest and revolution; US Marines finally intervened (1911) during a revolt, led by Manuel Bonilla, and restored order.

1924 Civil war broke out after liberal president López Gutiérrez (1919–24) attempted to hold office after his term; US intervened.

1933–49 Tiburcio Carías Andino in office as president; rebellion put down (1937).

1957 New constitution promulgated.

1957–63 Liberal leader Ramón Villeda Morales in office as president.

1961 Dispute over southeastern border with Nicaragua settled by International Court of Justice.

1963 Villeda Morales overthrown by military junta led by Osvaldo López Arellano.

1965 Twelfth constitution adopted; López Arellano elected president.

1969 Soccer War fought with El Salvador.

1971–75 Ramón Ernesto Cruz elected president (1971); López Arellano ousted Cruz (1972) and held power to 1975.

1975 Bloodless coup (Apr. 22) by Col. Juan Alberto Melgar Castro followed bribery scandal.

1978 Military coup (Aug. 7), by Gen. Policarpo Paz Garcia, ousted Melgar Castro.

1980 Military allowed election of a Constitutional Assembly (Apr.); Paz Garcia formally transferred power to the Assembly (July).

1982 Paz Garcia relinquished power to elected president, Roberto Suazo Córdovo, ending military rule.

Hong Kong British crown colony (pop. 4,900,000) in southeastern China, comprised of Hong Kong Island, Kowloon Peninsula, and the New Territories. Victoria, its capital, is site of one of the

world's best harbors. Hong Kong is a major trade and commercial center in the Far East. China ceded Britain the island (1841) and the peninsula (1860), and leased it the New Territories for 99 years (1898). Hong Kong was occupied by the Japanese during WW II.

Honolulu US city (pop. 365,000), capital of Hawaii, on Oahu Island. It is a major seaport and tourist and economic center. Its harbor was discovered (1794) by English captain William Brown. Honolulu was the capital of the kingdom of Hawaii (19th cent.), and later of the territory and (1959) the state of Hawaii. The Japanese bombing of the US naval base there at Pearl Harbor (Dec. 7, 1941) brought about the US entry into WW II.

Honorius I *d.* 638. Italian pope (625–638), successor to Boniface V. His failure to condemn Monothelitism outright as heresy led to his own posthumous condemnation as a heretic at the Council of Constantinople (680). This in turn led to a controversy over papal infallibility.

Honorius II ⟨Scannabechi, Lamberto⟩ *d.* 1130. Italian pope (1124–30), successor to Calixtus II. As cardinal, he brought an end to the Investiture Controversy by the Concordat of Worms (1122).

Honorius III ⟨Savelli, Cencio⟩ *d.* 1227. Roman pope (1216–27), successor to Innocent III. Considered an able administrator, he confirmed the orders of the Dominicans (1216), the Franciscans (1223), and the Carmelites (1226).

Honorius, Flavius AD 384–423. Roman emperor of the West (AD 395–423). A weak ruler, he inherited the western half of the Roman Empire on the death of his father, Theodosius I. During his reign his empire was invaded by Visigoths, who captured Rome (AD 409).

Hood, Thomas 1799–1845. English poet. Though he wrote much in a humorous vein, he is perhaps best remembered for such serious poems as *The Song of the Shirt* and *The Bridge of Sighs.*

Hooke, Robert 1635–1703. English physicist and inventor. He is credited with discovering the law of elasticity in solids (c1660), now called Hooke's law, and with being the first to use the biological term "cell" (1667).

Hooker, Joseph 1814–79. Union general in the American Civil War. Nicknamed "Fighting Joe," he succeeded (1863) A. Burnside in command of the Army of the Potomac. Following a major defeat at Chancellorsville (1863) and only days before the Battle of Gettysburg, Hooker resigned as commander of the army.

Hooker, Richard 1554?–1600. English theologian. An Anglican clergyman, he wrote *Of the Laws of Ecclesiastical Polity*, a closely reasoned defense against the arguments of Catholics and Puritans.

Hooker, Thomas 1586–1647. Puritan clergyman born in England. One of the founders of Hartford (1636), he was pastor of the colony until his death.

Hoorn, Philip de Montmorency, count of 〈Horn, ~〉 1518–68. Flemish nobleman and soldier. Though loyal to the Spanish rulers of The Netherlands, he opposed the Inquisition and was beheaded.

Hoover, Herbert Clark 1874–1964. Thirty-first US president (1929–33), successor to C. Coolidge. A mining engineer by profession, he became known for his work as head of the US-backed relief agencies in Europe during and after WW I. He next served as US secretary of commerce (1921–29) and in that capacity brought about construction of the Hoover Dam and St. Lawrence Seaway. Picked by the Republican party to succeed Coolidge, he defeated the Democratic contender, A. Smith, in the 1928 election. Only months after he took office, however, inherent weaknesses in the US economy, fostered by his predecessor's policies, culminated in the stock market crash of Oct., 1929 (Black Thursday). As the economic crisis widened into the Great Depression, Hoover maintained an abiding faith in business to restore the economy and private charity to aid the needy. This policy was both unsuccessful and much criticized as the number of unemployed grew to unprecedented proportions. Though Hoover firmly opposed direct federal aid to the unemployed and public works programs, he nevertheless did institute the Federal Farm Board and the Reconstruction Finance Corporation (1932). The failure of his policies to check the worsening depression, his expulsion of the Bonus Army *(q.v.)* from Washington, and the rising tide of bankruptcies, mortgage foreclosures, and bank failures contributed to his defeat by F. Roosevelt in 1932. Thereafter he remained out of politics until after WW II, when he headed two Hoover commissions (1947–49, 1953–55) to investigate government inefficiency.

Hoover, John Edgar 1895–1972. American public official. A sometimes controversial director of the Federal Bureau of Investigation (from 1924 to his death), Hoover is credited with turning it into a model law enforcement agency.

Hoover Commission *See* **Hoover, Herbert Clark**

Hopi Indians 〈Moki〉 Tribe of Pueblo Indians *(q.v.)* located in northeastern Arizona.

Hopkins, Gerard Manley 1844–89. English poet and Jesuit priest whose poetry has had an important influence on the poets of the 20th cent.

Hopkins, Johns 1795–1873. American financier and philanthropist. Originally a grocer, he amassed a large fortune in banking and left three million dollars to found Johns Hopkins University in Baltimore.

Hopkins, Stephen 1707–85. American politician and signer of the Declaration of Independence. He served as Colonial governor of Rhode Island six times from 1755 to 1768 and was a member of the Continental Congress (1774–76).

Hopkinson, Francis 1737–91. American patriot, writer, musician, and signer of the Declaration of Independence. His pamphlets and songs helped win support for the American Revolution. He was a delegate to the Continental Congress in 1776.

Hor *See* **Horus**

Horace 〈Flaccus, Quintus Horatius〉 65–8 BC. Roman poet, one of the great lyric poets of all time. His works reflect the temper of the Augustan Age and his mastery of poetic form. A freedman's son, he was schooled in Rome and Athens. After the Roman Civil War, in which he served, Horace worked under the patronage of his friend Maecenas. By 35 BC he had produced his first book of *Satires* and thereafter wrote his *Odes, Epistles, Ars Poetica,* and other works.

Horae Mythical Greek goddesses of the seasons, usually identified as children of Zeus and Themis. Hesiod tells of three goddesses, Eunomia (Order), Dike (Justice), and Eirene (Peace), though the number varies from two to four.

Horatius 〈Cocles〉 Legendary hero of Rome who singlehandedly defended the Siblican bridge outside Rome against the attacking Etruscan army of Lars Porsena. He gave Roman forces time to cut the bridge behind them and saved Rome.

Horeb In the Bible, another name for Mount Sinai, where the Law was given to Moses and the place where the golden calf was made. Elijah also fled there.

Horney, Karen 1885–1952. American psychiatrist. She broke with Freudian doctrines on the causes of neuroses, emphasizing environmental and social factors instead of biological drives.

Horowitz, Vladimir 1904–. World-famous Russian-American pianist. Celebrated for his technical mastery, he performed regularly in concerts from the 1920s to the early 1950s.

Horsa *See* **Hengist and Horsa**

Horseshoe Bend, Battle of *See* **Creek War**

Horthy, Miklós von Nagybánya 1868–1957. Hungarian admiral and head of state (1920–44). He defeated the Communist revolutionaries and was named regent to the deposed emperor, Charles I. Horthy later refused to allow Charles to retake the throne and himself ruled Hungary until he was arrested by A. Hitler.

Horus ⟨Hor⟩ Egyptian sky god. He was usually represented as a falcon and his eyes were the sun and the moon. He was the god of goodness and light, and Egyptian kings were believed incarnations of him.

Hoshea Last king of Israel, son of Elah. He assassinated and succeeded Pekah (732? BC). His alliance with Egypt against the Assyrians led to the conquest of Israel by the Assyrians (722? BC).

hostage crisis ⟨American hostage crisis⟩ International crisis (from Nov. 4, 1979) in which Iranian militants seized the US Embassy in Teheran, Iran, and held 52 Americans hostage for 444 days. Following the overthrow (Jan., 1979) of Shah R. Pahlavi in the Iranian revolution, anti-American sentiment in Iran was whipped to a fever pitch. The embassy seizure itself was sparked by the shah's arrival in the US for medical treatment. Militants, suspecting a plot to return the shah to power, captured the embassy (Nov. 4) and took 90 hostages. They later released all but 52 Americans. Their demands included return of the shah and his wealth to Iran, and they threatened to try the hostages as spies. President J. Carter ordered the freezing of Iranian assets in the US (Nov. 14). The seizure had the support of Ayatollah R. Khomeini, who used the incident to consolidate his control over the revolution and publicly humiliate the US. Carter was thwarted in attempts to negotiate the hostages' release, and a military rescue attempt (Apr. 24, 1980) failed, leaving eight US servicemen dead. The shah died (July 27), and negotiations dragged through the 1980 presidential election. Negotiators finally reached an accord (Jan. 19, 1981), but the hostages were not released until a few minutes after R. Reagan was sworn in as US president (Jan. 20).

Hottentots A South African people who controlled a large part of South Africa before the arrival of European settlers. They now are divided among several tribes, and their pastoral culture is largely dispersed.

Houdini, Harry ⟨pseud. of Ehrich Weiss⟩ 1874–1926. American magician who became world-famous for his escape tricks.

Houdon, Jean Antoine 1741–1828. Leading 18th-cent. French sculptor. He is considered a master of portrait sculptures.

Houphouët-Boigny, Felix See **Ivory Coast**

House, Edward Mandell 1858–1938. American diplomat and President W. Wilson's adviser. Known as "Colonel" House, he helped Wilson negotiate terms for the Treaty of Versailles and the Covenant of the League of Nations at the close of WW I.

House of See under family names, as in **Bourbon; Hapsburg**

Housman, Alfred Edward 1859–1936. English poet and classical scholar, known best for his collection of poetry *A Shropshire Lad.*

Houston, Samuel 1793–1863. American frontiersman, soldier, and political official who played a major role in the Texas war for independence. A US congressman (1823–27) and Tennessee governor (1827–29), he lived (1829–33) with the Cherokee Indians after his wife left him. By 1835, however, Houston had become involved in the struggle between American settlers and the Mexicans for control over what is now Texas. As commander of American forces, he eventually routed the Mexicans at San Jacinto (1836) and thereby won Texas' independence. He was president of the territory (1836–38, 1841–44) and, after statehood (1845), became senator (1846–59). Elected governor (1859), he opposed secession and was forced out of office (1861).

Howard Leading English family of noblemen. The duke of Norfolk, who heads the family, is hereditary earl marshal and premier duke of England. The family has a number of cadet branches, including earldoms of Arundel, Northampton, Nottingham, Suffolk, Surrey, Norwich, and Carlisle. The line was founded by William Howard (d. 1308) and gained title (1483) to Norfolk through the marriage of Robert Howard (d. before 1436) to the daughter of T. Mowbray, the first duke of Norfolk. Prominent members of the family include:

John Howard, 1st duke of Norfolk
Thomas Howard, 2d duke of Norfolk
Thomas Howard, 4th duke of Norfolk
Henry Howard, 1st earl of Northampton
Charles Howard, 1st earl of Nottingham
Charles Howard, 1st earl of Carlisle
Frederick Howard, 5th earl of Carlisle

Howard, Bronson Crocker 1842–1908. American playwright whose successes helped spark the development of American drama. Among his best-known plays are *Saratoga* and *Shenandoah.*

Howard, Catherine 1521?–42. Fifth queen of English king Henry VIII. Married to the king shortly after his divorce from Anne of Cleves (1540), she was convicted of adultery the following year and was beheaded.

Howard, Charles, 1st earl of Carlisle 1629–85. English statesman. A supporter of O. Cromwell, he nevertheless continued to serve after the Restoration of Charles II (1660).

Howard, Charles, 1st earl of Nottingham 1536–1624. English nobleman. He served as ambassador to France (1559), lord high admiral (1585–1618), and lord lieutenant general of England

(1599–1619). He was in command of the expedition that defeated the Spanish Armada (1588).

Howard, Sir Ebenezer 1850–1928. English city planner. He was the leading founder of the English garden city movement, which aimed at relieving urban congestion by building self-sufficient towns surrounded by open spaces.

Howard, Frederick, 5th earl of Carlisle. 1748–1825. English statesman. Howard was unsuccessful in his attempt (1778) to reconcile the American colonies (1778). He later served as viceroy of Ireland (1780–82) and as guardian to Lord G. Byron, the poet.

Howard, Henry, earl of Northampton 1540–1614. English noble. He served as lord privy seal under King James I and was a commissioner at the trials of W. Raleigh and G. Fawkes.

Howard, Henry, earl of Surrey c1517–47. English poet. Howard translated two books of Vergil's *Aeneid*, thus introducing blank verse to England. He also introduced the Petrarchean sonnet.

Howard, John, 1st duke of Norfolk 1430?–85. English noble. John served under Edward IV and Richard III. He died fighting for Richard at the Battle of Bosworth Field.

Howard, Oliver Otis 1830–1909. Union general in the American Civil War. A capable military leader, he is better known as chief commissioner of the Freedmen's Bureau (1865–74) and as a founder and president of Howard University (1869–74).

Howard, Robert *See* **Howard**

Howard, Thomas, 2d duke of Norfolk 1443–1524. English noble. The son of J. Howard, he was wounded in the Battle of Bosworth Field (1485) and was imprisoned. He later defeated the Scots at Flodden Field (1513) and his father's lands and titles were restored to him.

Howard, Thomas, 4th duke of Norfolk 1536–72. English noble. Queen Elizabeth I placed him in charge of investigating Mary Queen of Scots, but he was imprisoned for planning to marry her. His plot to aid Spanish king Philip II in an invasion led to his execution.

Howard, Thomas, 13th earl of Arundel c1586–1646. British art patron, noted for his great art collection, particularly his ancient statuary, the Arundel marbles.

Howard, William *See* **Howard**

Howe, Julia Ward 1819–1910. American author and social reformer. She is known best as the author of *The Battle Hymn of the Republic*.

Howe, William, 5th Viscount Howe 1729–1814. English commander of British forces (1775–78) during the American Revolution. He played an important role in the Battle of Bunker Hill and soon after succeeded Gen. T. Gage as overall commander in America. In subsequent battles he occupied New York City (1776) and Philadelphia (1777) but failed to capture Gen. G. Washington's army. This led to the major British defeat at Saratoga (1777) and his subsequent resignation.

Howells, William Dean 1837–1920. American novelist and literary critic. Sometimes called the champion of realism in literature, he is said to have influenced S. Crane, M. Twain, H. James, and others. He wrote *A Modern Instance* and *The Rise of Silas Lapham*.

Hoxha, Enver *See* **Albania** (1943–46)

Hoyle, Edmond 1672–1769. English writer and authority on games. His *Short Treatise on the Game of Whist*, published in 1742, was gradually expanded to include many other games and established him as an authority on game rules.

Hsia Legendary first dynasty in traditional Chinese history which is said to have reigned c1994–c1523 BC (c2205–c1766 BC, by traditional dating). It was succeeded by the Shang dynasty. Archaeological evidence indicates the existence of an early Hsia state in the Yellow River valley in northeastern China. The potter's wheel, bronze weapons, and chariots are believed to have been in use during the Hsia period. Yu is the legendary founder of the dynasty.

Hsia Kuei *fl.* 1195–1224. Chinese painter during the Sung dynasty. Cofounder with Ma Yüan of the Ma-Hsia landscape-painting school, he is regarded as a master of the genre.

Hsiang Army *See* **Hunan Army**

Hsiung-nu Asian people who established (3d cent. BC) an empire in Manchuria, Mongolia, and Siberia. They raided northern China for several centuries and established several dynasties, but declined in importance by the 5th cent. AD. The Great Wall of China was completed (3d cent. BC) to control their advance.

Hsüan-tsang 602–664. Chinese scholar. A Buddhist monk, he traveled throughout India and translated Sanskrit religious literature into Chinese. His notes on Asiatic religion, archaeology, and anthropology are invaluable.

Hsüan T'ung ⟨P'u-yi, Henry⟩ 1905–67. Last emperor of China (1908–12). He ruled under the name of Hsüan T'ung, and was later emperor of the Japanese Manchurian puppet state of Manchukuo under the name of K'ang Tê.

Hsün-tzu c298–c230 BC. Chinese philosopher. He promoted the teachings of Confucius and stressed the benefits of culture in overcoming man's basic evil nature.

Huang Hsing 1871–1916. Chinese general. As Sun Yat-sen's representative in China during the 1911 revolution, he played a key role in the toppling of the Chinese imperial dynasty. He served as Sun's prime minister and was a founding member of the Kuomintang.

Huang Ti ⟨Yellow Emperor⟩ ⟨Shen Yen Huang Ti⟩ The third of China's legendary early emperors who, according to tradition, reigned in the third millennium BC. Many fundamental elements of China's civilization are credited to him, including mathematical calculations, the calendar, money, the use of bamboo, and the study of medicine, among others. He is, with Lao-tze, considered the founder of Taoism, and his wife is believed to be the discoverer of the uses of the silkworm.

Huascar d. 1533. Emperor of the Incas in Peru. On his father's death (1525), he succeeded to the larger portion of an empire divided between his brother Atahualpa and himself. He lost the empire to his brother (1532) and was later secretly murdered by him.

Huayna Capac See **Inca**

Hubertusburg, Treaty of Treaty (Feb. 15, 1763) between Prussia and Austria ending the Seven Years' War. It guaranteed Prussia's possession of Silesia and its role as a major power in Germany.

Hudaybiyah, Pact of al- Treaty (628) between Muhammad and the rulers of Mecca permitting Muhammad and his followers to enter Mecca for the rite of 'umrah (pilgrimage).

Hudson, Henry d. 1611. English navigator in English and Dutch service. Seeking the Northwest Passage for the Dutch East India Co., he explored the Hudson River (1609). On another attempt financed by Englishmen, he discovered and explored what became known as Hudson Bay (1610).

Hudson River school Group of American landscape painters and an early school of painting native to America. The school, which stemmed from the European Romantic movement, flourished from 1825 to 1875. It is characterized by but not limited to the dramatic landscapes of the Hudson River region. Among the artists of this school are Thomas Cole (1801–48), Albert Bierstadt (1830–1902), and Thomas Doughty (1793–1856).

Hudson's Bay Company ⟨The Great Company⟩ Chartered corporation (from 1670) that figures prominently in the early development of Canada. Licensed for trade, settlement, and exploration of a vast and vaguely specified region surrounding the Hudson Bay, the company eventually expanded its holdings to the Pacific Coast. It had governmental control and a monopoly over the lucrative fur trade in its domains. Early clashes with the French traders ended with recognition of British sovereignty in Canada (Treaty of Paris, 1763), and bloody conflicts with the rival British North West Company were ended by a merger of the companies (1821). Following the unification of Canada (1869), nearly all the company territory was turned over to the Canadian government, and the company thereafter became a powerful retail and manufacturing concern. It was broken up into Canadian and British organizations in 1930.

Hueffer, Ford Madox See **Ford, Ford Madox**

Huerta, Victoriano ⟨Huerta, Vicente Garcia de la⟩ 1854–1916. Mexican general who overthrew President F. Madero and became military dictator (1913–14). After seizing power, Huerta was faced with numerous attempts at counterrevolution as well as the opposition of US President W. Wilson. Huerta finally fled Mexico and was later jailed in the US.

Hugh Capet c938–96. French king (987–996), son of Hugh the Great and first of the Capetian kings. Inheritance of his father's extensive territories (956) gave him great power, and, after the death of King Louis V, last of the direct Carolingian line, he was elected king.

Hughes, Charles Evans 1862–1942. American statesman and jurist. An associate justice of the Supreme Court (1910–16), he was narrowly defeated by W. Wilson for president (1916). He thereafter served as secretary of state (1921–25) and chief justice of the Supreme Court (1930–41).

Hughes, Howard Robard 1905–76. Controversial American businessman and reclusive billionaire. Hughes built his financial empire around his father's company, the Hughes Tool Co., and eventually held interests in airplane manufacturing, motion pictures, a major airline, and gambling casinos.

Hugh of Avalon See **Hugh of Lincoln, Saint**

Hugh of Lincoln, Saint ⟨Hugh of Avalon⟩ 1135?–1200. English bishop. A Carthusian monk, he is noted for his skill and courage in defending church prerogatives against the designs of English monarchs.

Hugh of Saint Victor 1096?–1141. French or German scholar and mystical theologian. Under his guidance the monastery school of Saint Victor in Paris became one of medieval France's most important intellectual centers.

Hugh the Great d. 956. French duke, son of Robert I and father of Hugh Capet. Excluded from the succession, he supported the succession of the Carolingian king Louis IV and attempted to rule through him.

Hugo, Victor 1802–85. French writer. Hugo's poetry, plays, and novels occupy a major place in

French Romantic literature. His drama *Hernani* caused riots between classicists and romanticists in 1830, but today he is best remembered for his novels *The Hunchback of Notre Dame* and *Les Misérables*. A political republican and member of the National Assembly, Hugo was forced into exile by Napoleon III but returned to Paris in triumph after Napoleon's ouster (1870).

Huguenots French Protestants, important in French history during the 16th and 17th cents. Followers of J. Calvin, Huguenots first suffered persecution at the hands of the French Catholic monarchy shortly after the beginning of the Protestant Reformation (1517). Despite executions and massacres, the movement spread to the French nobility, where it became interrelated with the struggle for political power. Bitter rivalry led to such events as the Conspiracy of Amboise (1560), the St. Bartholomew's Day Massacre (1572), and the Wars of Religion (1562–98). A period of toleration followed the Edict of Nantes (1598) and ended with Huguenot uprisings in the 1620s when King Louis XIII attempted to suppress Protestantism. By the Peace of Alais (1629), Huguenots lost their political power, and, under Louis XIV, the Edict of Nantes was revoked (1685). This led to a mass exodus of most Huguenots from France. Civil rights of Huguenots were not restored until 1787. By the Declaration of the Rights of Man (1789) they were granted religious equality.

Hui-neng 638–713. Chinese priest and sixth patriarch of Zen Buddhism. He is known for his introduction of the doctrine of satori, or "sudden enlightenment."

Huitzilopochtli War god, sun god, and chief deity of the Aztecs. It was to this god that the Aztecs made human sacrifices, usually of war prisoners or slaves.

Hukbalahap Rebellion Revolt (1946–54) by Communist-led guerrillas in the Philippines. The Hukbalahap, or People's Anti-Japanese party, proved a highly successful resistance group during the Japanese occupation, and after WW II went into open rebellion against Pres. M. Roxas' government. Their guerrilla war grew into a widespread peasant rebellion by 1950 that finally ended with the surrender of guerrilla leader Luis Taruc in 1954.

Hulagu Khan ⟨Hulegu or Hulaku⟩ 1217–65. Mongol ruler, grandson of Genghis Khan and founder of the Il-Khan dynasty. Sent to put down a revolt by the Persians, he defeated and executed Caliph Mustasim, destroyed the Islamic capital of Baghdad (1258), and set up his khanate, which lasted until 1335.

Hulaku *See* **Hulagu Khan**

Hulegu *See* **Hulagu Khan**

Hull, Cordell 1871–1955. American statesman and US secretary of state (1933–44). As President F. Roosevelt's secretary of state, he did much to stimulate trade with other nations through reciprocal trade agreements and played an important role in establishing the UN. He was awarded the Nobel Peace Prize in 1945.

Hull, William 1753–1825. American general and governor of the Michigan Territory (1805–12). During the War of 1812, he was in command of Detroit, and surrendered it to the British without resistance (1812). He was court-martialed for cowardice, but his death sentence was commuted.

Hull House *See* **Addams, Jane**

humanism Philosophy or attitude that places mankind and human values, welfare, and creativity at the center of consciousness. Humanism was the philosophy that, beginning in the 14th cent., was a central feature of the Renaissance *(q.v.)* in Italy, and spread over the rest of Europe in the following three centuries. It represented a shift from the medieval view of the world as an adjunct to God's creation and fostered a new emphasis on the study of man and the world as objects in themselves. It favored a new Platonism *(q.v.)* over Aristotelianism *(q.v.)* and Scholasticism *(q.v.)*. It also looked to Greek and Roman models in art, literature, and thought. One of the major results of the early Renaissance in Italy was an intensive search for and study of ancient manuscripts. The Turkish conquest of Constantinople (1453), which drove many Greek-speaking scholars to seek refuge in Italy, gave added impetus to this interest in the ancient world. The great early Renaissance humanists included F. Petrarch, G. Boccaccio, L. Valla, and the host of Italian painters led by Michelangelo and L. da Vinci. Erasmus and T. More were outstanding later humanists. In modern times, humanism has come to mean an agnostic philosophy that regards man as "the measure of all things," as opposed to religious beliefs.

Human Rights, Universal Declaration of *See* **Universal Declaration of Human Rights**

Humbert I ⟨Umberto I⟩ 1844–1900. Italian king (1878–1900) who succeeded his father, Victor Emmanuel II. Under his reign Italy joined in the Triple Alliance (1882) and prosecuted the Ethiopian War (1887–96).

Humbert II ⟨Umberto II⟩ 1904–. Last king of Italy (1946), successor to his father, Victor Emmanuel III. A referendum held shortly after his succession created a republic and stripped him of his powers.

Humble Petition and Advice English constitution advanced (Mar., 1657) by Parliament during the Protectorate. Superseding the Instrument of Government *(q.v.)*, it established an upper house of Parliament and named O. Cromwell king, with the power to choose his successor. Cromwell declined to be named king, and, after subsequent modifications, the Humble Petition was passed. Cromwell was named lord protector.

Humboldt, Baron Alexander von 1769–1859. German scientist and explorer. His discoveries made while on scientific expeditions, notably one to Central and South America (1799–1804), helped stimulate the study of earth sciences.

Hume, David 1711–76. Scottish philosopher and historian. Hume developed a skeptical philosophy that restricted knowledge to actual experience and rejected most theology as an unprovable matter of belief. Among his many writings are *An Enquiry Concerning Human Understanding* and *History of England.* The latter was long a major reference work. (*See also* empiricism.)

Humiliation of Olmütz *See* **Erfurt Parliament**

Humphrey, Hubert Horatio 1911–78. US vice-president (1965–69). As a Democratic senator from Minnesota (1949–65), he was a noted orator, liberal leader, and staunch defender of civil rights. While serving as vice-president under L. Johnson, Humphrey defended escalation of the Vietnam War. This was a contributing factor in his narrow loss to R. Nixon in the presidential race of 1968. He was reelected to the Senate (1970) and tried unsuccessfully to win the Democratic presidential nomination in 1972.

Hunan Army (Hsiang Army) Chinese regional army organized (1852) in the province of Hunan by Tsêng Kuo-fan. Its purpose was to help bring an end to the Taiping Rebellion. At its peak the force numbered approximately 125,000 men.

Hundred Days **1.** Period in French history (Mar. 20-June 28, 1815) during which Napoleon returned from exile and attempted to reestablish his empire. Escaping exile on the island of Elba, he landed in the south of France (Mar. 1, 1815) and marched north with a small force. By the time he reached Paris (Mar. 20, 1815), he had rallied France behind him and forced King Louis XVIII to abdicate. Once again emperor, he was opposed (from Mar. 25) by a new coalition of nearly all the other European nations. Following the coalition victory over J. Murat at Tolentino (May 3) and subsequent capture of the kingdom of Naples, Napoleon launched an attack (June 14) into Belgium. Napoleon's forces were victorious in the battles of Ligny and Quatre Bras (June 16), but were completely crushed at the great Battle of Waterloo

(June 18). Soon after, Napoleon surrendered to the British, and King Louis was restored (June 28), ending the Hundred Days period. (*See also* Waterloo; Napoleonic Wars.) **2.** Period in US history (from Mar. 4, 1933) marking the first months of President F. Roosevelt's administration. Roosevelt was inaugurated (Mar. 4) during the Great Depression, amid economic disaster, great unemployment, and numerous bank failures. During the Hundred Days period his administration initiated much of the legislation for his first New Deal *(q.v)* program. The term "Hundred Days" has also been applied to the early months of other presidential administrations.

Hundred Years' War Series of related wars (1337–1453) between England and France. The conflict stemmed from English claims to the French throne (based on descent from the Norman conquerer, William I) and the long rivalry over territories on the Continent that were then English possessions. Just before war broke out, France and England were vying for the lucrative wool and cloth trade of Flanders, and English king Edward III was concerned about protecting the English-held duchy of Guienne (in modern France). Edward touched off the war by invading France to take the crown by force. The protracted war that followed was fought mainly in France and devastated the country. The outbreak of the Black Plague only added to the loss of life on both sides. The consequences of the war were far-reaching: English presence on the Continent was all but ended; and the ravages of war contributed to the decline of feudalism, the rise of a middle class, and the emergence of a strong monarchy. Key dates in the history of the war include:

1337 English king Edward III proclaimed himself king of France in opposition to French king Philip VI.

1339 English invaded France through the Low Countries; land war indecisive.

1340 English gained control of the Channel by their victory (June 24) in the naval battle of Sluis.

1345 New English invasion of northern France began.

1346 Battle of Crécy fought (Aug. 26); major English victory over the French.

1346–47 English besieged and captured Calais; victory followed by lull in fighting (to 1355).

1355 English forces led by Edward the Black Prince conquered Bordeaux in southwest France; thereafter English conducted raids in southern France.

1356 Battle of Poitiers (Sept. 19); English routed French forces and captured King John II, who had succeeded to the French throne.

1360 Treaty of Brétigny, ending first period of the Hundred Years' War; England gained Calais and much of Aquitaine from France; French king John returned for a large ransom.

1369–86 Fighting resumed; new French king Charles VI attacked English (1369) using guerrilla war tactics; by 1386 the French had retaken much of the territory held by England.

1396 England and France agreed to a truce, to last for 30 years.

1415 English king Henry V resumed the war by invading France; France embroiled (from 1407) in civil war between Burgundians (pro-English) and Armagnacs over control of the French throne; subsequent alliance between Burgundians and English seriously weakened French position.

1415 Henry V defeated French at Battle of Agincourt; French suffered heavy losses.

1415–19 Normandy conquered; Rouen captured (1419); English gained control of most of northern France.

1420 Treaty of Troyes signed (May 20); by its terms French king Charles VI accepted English king Henry V as heir to the French throne.

1422 Both Henry and Charles died; the French dauphin, Charles's son, declared himself French king Charles VII; the English held that Henry's son, Henry VI, was king; Henry VI controlled the north, Charles VII the south.

1428 English invaded southern France; laid siege to French stronghold of Orléans (Oct.).

1429 French fortunes at low ebb; young visionary Joan of Arc convinced Charles VII to give her command of force to relieve Orléans.

1429 Joan's forces lifted (May) siege of Orléans; tide of war turned in favor of the French; English forces pushed northward.

1429 French won major victory at Battle of Patay (June 18); La Hire routed Shrewsbury's English troops in northern France.

1429 Charles VII crowned (July 17) at Rheims after being encouraged by Joan of Arc.

1430 Joan of Arc captured by Burgundians (then allied with the English); ransomed to the English, she was burned at the stake (1431) as a witch.

1435 Treaty of Arras signed between France and Burgundy, ending the alliance between Burgundy and England and greatly strengthening the French position.

1436 French forces captured Paris from the English; lull in fighting ensued.

1444 Truce of Tours (May 28); fighting halted until 1449.

1449 French began final offensive of war; attacked English in Normandy and Guienne.

1450 Battle of Formigny in northern France (Apr. 15), a decisive French victory.

1450 French completed reconquest of Normandy.

1451 French took duchy of Guienne, except for Bordeaux, from the English.

1453 French captured Bordeaux, marking end of the war; English territories on the Continent (once extensive) now reduced to the city of Calais, which England held until 1558.

Hungarian Revolution of 1956 Brief but bloody rebellion (Oct. 23-Nov. 14, 1956) against Russian domination in Hungary. The revolt was caused by a series of factors, including the movement for reform in Poland, the denunciation of Stanlinism by N. Khrushchev, and the Soviet-aided ouster (July, 1956) of the repressive regime of Matyas Rakosi in Hungary. The revolt was sparked (Oct. 23) when Hungarian forces fired on people demonstrating in Budapest in support of Polish reform and in opposition to Soviet presence in Hungary. Soon the entire country was in revolt. I. Nagy, who as premier had earlier (1953–55) introduced reforms in Hungary, was restored to power (Oct. 24), and János Kádár (1912–) became new head of the Communist party. Nagy immediately instituted liberal reforms, called for Soviet withdrawal from Hungary, took Hungary out of the Warsaw Pact, and sought aid from the UN to secure Hungary's neutrality. Meanwhile Kádár formed a countergovernment and called for Soviet assistance. Russian forces entered Hungary and on Nov. 4 began operations against the revolt. The rebellion was crushed by Nov. 14 and Kádár was installed as the new head of the government. Nagy and others, tricked by promises of safe conduct, were captured, sent to Romania, and executed.

Hungary Republic located in central Europe. Its capital is Budapest. The region of present-day Hungary was part of the Roman provinces of Pannonia and Dacia and was subsequently occupied by Germanic tribes, Huns, Avars, and ultimately the Magyars (9th cent.), who profoundly shaped the history of Hungary. A kingdom from the early 11th cent., Hungary later fell under Ottoman and Austrian Hapsburg domination. Hungarian resistance to Austrian hegemony led to formation (1867) of the Dual Monarchy, or Austro-Hungarian Monarchy. Hungary finally became independent with the collapse of the Austro-Hungarian Empire at the end of WW I and, in 1949, became a People's Republic, modeled along Soviet Communist lines. Key dates in the history of Hungary include:

2D CENT. AD Germanic tribes invaded region; later displaced by the Huns.

5TH—8TH CENT. AD   Avars occupied region.

c890   Arpad led Magyars from Asia to Hungary; established Arpad dynasty.

955   Holy Roman Emperor Otto I defeated the Magyars on the Lechfeld; marked the end of Magyars' westward expansion.

1001–38   Stephen I reigned as first crowned king of Hungary; established Christianity in the kingdom.

1077–95   Ladislaus I, a national hero, reigned; conquered Croatia.

1222   King Andrew II (reigned 1205–35) issued the Golden Bull, known as the "Magna Carta of Hungary"; marked rise of powerful magnates (nobles).

1235–70   Bela IV reigned; rule marked by devastating Mongol invasion (1241) and conflict with Austria.

1301   Andrew III, last of the Arpad dynasty, died; period of unrest and civil war.

1308–42   Charles Robert of Anjou reigned as Hungarian King Charles I; strengthened the monarchy, curbed the power of the nobles, and founded the Angevin line in Hungary.

1342–82   Louis I (the Great) reigned; conducted wars against Venice (1346, 1357–58, 1381) and by the Treaty of Turin (1381) gained all of Dalmatia; succeeded to the Polish throne (1370) and thereby made Hungary one of the largest kingdoms in Europe; promoted administrative reforms and commercial prosperity.

1387–1437   Sigismund reigned; began period of rule by foreign kings; his crusade against the Ottoman Turks advancing on fringes of the kingdom failed (1396); elected emperor of the Holy Roman Empire (1411); suppressed the Hussites.

1456   John Hunyadi, Hungarian hero, ended Ottoman siege of Belgrade.

1458–90   Matthias Corvinus reigned; successful against the Turks; conquered Bohemia, Lusatia, Moravia, and Silesia, reorganized the government, and made Hungary the dominant power in central Europe.

1490–1526   Period of unrest followed death of Matthias Corvinus; nobles sought to regain power; Zapolya family gained control of Transylvania; Doza Rebellion by peasants broke out (1514); kingdom unable to check continuing advance of Turks.

1526   Battle of Mohacs, Turkish victory over Louis II of Hungary; led to more than 150 years of Turkish domination of central Hungary, Hapsburg domination in the west, and ascendancy of noblemen in Transylvania.

1572–1608   Rudolph II (later Holy Roman Emperor) reigned as king of Hungary; Protestantism had spread among Magyars as a result of the Reformation (especially in Transylvania) and Rudolph began imperial policy of imposing the Catholic Counter-Reformation in Hungary and elsewhere.

1604–06   S. Bokskay led rebellion against Hapsburgs of Holy Roman Empire, then controlling western Hungary; won constitutional and religious rights for Protestants by Peace of Vienna.

1618–48   Thirty Years' War; Hungarian nationalists used opportunities to oppose domination by Hapsburg Holy Roman Empire.

1682–99   Austro-Turkish War; Austrian Hapsburgs gradually pushed Turks out of Hungary; their claim to the Hungarian throne recognized by Hungarian nobles (1687); finally won control of Turkish domains in Hungary (then including Transylvania).

1703–11   Francis Rákóczy led unsuccessful rebellion against Hapsburg rule in Hungary; Hapsburgs then promoted settlement of Hungary by Germans and Slavs.

1740–48   War of Austrian Succession; Hungary supported claims of Maria Theresa to Hapsburg domains.

1806   Holy Roman Empire dissolved as a result of defeat in Napoleonic Wars; power of Austrian Hapsburgs reduced in subsequent post-Napoleonic period; Austrian Hapsburgs retained control over Hungary.

FROM 1815   Rise of liberal nationalist movement began in the post-Napoleonic period.

1848–49   March Laws instituted liberal constitutional monarchy under Hapsburg domination following outbreak of Revolutions of 1848 in Europe; Austrian troops sent into Hungary; L. Kossuth proclaimed Hungary a republic (Apr., 1849).

1849   Austrians victorious (with Russian aid) at the Battle of Temesvar (Aug. 9); battle ended short-lived Hungarian Republic.

1866–67   Austrian power seriously weakened by Austro-Prussian War (1866); Magyar nationalists forced compromise agreement, Ausgleich, establishing Dual Monarchy of Austria-Hungary (1867).

1867–1916   Francis Joseph reigned as king of Austria and Hungary; Austria and Hungary theoretically equal under separate governments; unrest grew among the Hungarian national minorities (Croats, Serbs, and Rumanians).

1873   The cities of Buda and Pest were united.

1914–18   WW I; Hungary, as part of the Austro-Hungarian empire, fought with the Central Powers; hardships of war aroused discontent and brought collapse of the Dual Monarchy (Nov. 11, 1918).

1918 Hungarian People's Republic proclaimed (Nov. 16) at close of WW I; Michael Károlyi became first president.

1919 B. Kun seized power after new government proved unable to check unrest among minorities; he established short-lived, Communist soviet republic of Hungary. (Mar. 21–Aug. 1); invasion by Czechs and Romanians ended the Soviet government.

1919–44 Nicholas Horthy de Nagybanya in power; harsh reprisals against leftists (White Terror) began; he was named regent of a vacant monarchy (1920).

1920 Treaty of Trianon signed (June 4) by Allied Powers after WW I; established new Hungarian state but greatly reduced territory; this later led to alliance with fascist Germany in effort to regain lands.

1932–36 Premier J. Gambos in office; promoted fascism.

1939–45 WW II; Hungary became an ally of Germany; Germany occupied Hungary when it attempted to end participation in war (1943); Soviet forces drove out Germans and occupied the country (Oct., 1944–Apr., 1945) after hard fighting.

1946 Following national elections (1945), a new constitution was adopted.

1947–49 Minority Communist party consolidated its control within the Hungarian government; aided by Soviet forces, it conducted campaigns against anti-Communists and the church.

1948 Cardinal Mindszenty, Roman Catholic primate of Hungary, arrested and convicted in trial staged by Communists; imprisoned until 1956.

1949 Communists gained control of Hungarian government; new constitution adopted (Aug. 10) establishing the Hungarian People's Republic, modeled on Soviet lines.

1949–53 Mátyás Rákosi ruled as premier; his pro-Stalinist policies caused wide unrest and political and economic turmoil.

1953–55 Imre Nagy made premier; moderated Hungary's economic programs but was removed from office.

1955 Hungary joined Warsaw Pact (May 14).

1955–56 Rákosi back in power.

1956 Hungarian Revolt (Oct. 23–Nov. 14), unsuccessful uprising against Russian domination; I. Nagy led new government; declared Hungarian neutrality and withdrew it from Warsaw Pact; revolt crushed by invasion of Russian and other Warsaw Pact forces.

1956 Cardinal Mindszenty, released from prison during revolt, took refuge in US embassy until 1971, when he was allowed out of Hungary.

1956–65 János Kádár in power as premier; led opposition to liberal government of Hungarian Revolution; instituted reforms and purged Stalinist party leaders.

1958 Nagy executed.

1964 Kádár established agreement with Roman Catholic church to improve relations.

1965 Gyula Kallai became premier; Kádár remained in power as party secretary of the Hungarian Socialist Workers party; policies of reform and relaxation of controls continued.

1968 Economic reforms established more liberal economic policies and led to increases in production.

1975 György Lazar in office as premier.

1978 WW II war-debt claims with US settled; US authorities returned Saint Stephen's Crown and other national treasures to Hungary.

Hunkers Faction of New York State Democrats in the 1840s, conservatives who opposed the radical faction called the Barnburners. They followed a line consistent with President J. Polk's policies, favored chartering of state banks and opposed agitation against slavery. They split openly with the Barnburners in the 1846 gubernatorial election. In the 1848 presidential election, antislavery Barnburners joined with the Free-Soil party to support M. Van Buren. This split the Democratic party vote and helped Z. Taylor win the presidency.

Huns Nomadic people of Asia, notorious for their military skills and savagery, who for a time (5th cent. AD) threatened the Roman Empire. The Huns, of uncertain origins, were at times identified with Hsuing-Nu, White Huns, Magyars, and others. Skilled horsemen and archers, they appeared in Eastern Europe AD *c*370, and, fighting in roving bands (hordes), they conquered the Alani, Ostrogoths, and Visigoths. Victories over the latter two peoples caused great migrations eastward. In the 5th cent. AD the Huns occupied Eastern and Central Europe and had reached the borders of the Eastern Roman Empire. By AD 432 a single king of the Huns, Rugilas (Rua or Roas), was exacting tribute from the Romans. His successor, Attila the Hun, launched three invasions into the empire (441, 447, 451). On the first he advanced into the Eastern Empire and threatened Constantinople. On the second he again attacked the Eastern Empire and passed through the Balkans into Greece. On the third he attacked the Western Empire and unsuccessfully attempted to take Gaul. After he was defeated by a combined force of Romans and Visigoths at the Battle of Chalons (451), however, he invaded and briefly ravaged Italy. His death (453) was soon followed by disintegration of his kingdom and the Huns as a unified people.

Hunter's Lodges Secret organizations established (after 1837) in the US along the border with Canada, to overthrow British rule in Canada. They made two notable attacks (Prescott, Ontario, Nov. 11, 1838; Windsor, Ontario, Dec. 4, 1838) but were quickly repulsed.

Huntington, Collis Potter 1821–1900. American railroad magnate. He and his business partners made the first transcontinental railroad possible by organizing and building the Central Pacific Railroad (1863–69). He later became president of the Southern Pacific (1890), a railroad he helped form.

Hunyadi, John ⟨Hunyady, Janos⟩ c1387–1456. Hungarian general and hero of the resistance to Turkish conquest. He defeated the Turks in many battles, including his "Long Campaign" (1443–44) and the storming of Belgrade (1456). He also served as elected governor of Hungary (1446–52).

Hunyady, Janos *See* **Hunyadi, John**

Huram *See* **Hiram**

Huran ar-Rashid *See* **Harun-al-Rashid**

Huron Indians A group of North American Indian tribes that, in the 17th cent., were located in the Great Lakes region. Bitter enemies of the Iroquois Confederacy, the Huron were mercilessly attacked (1648–50) and nearly wiped out by the Iroquois. Some of the surviving Huron settled in Ohio, where they sided with the British in the Revolutionary War and the War of 1812. They were subsequently resettled in Oklahoma.

Husayn ibn-'Ali *See* **Husein ibn-Ali**

Husein ⟨Husayn ibn-'Ali⟩ c626–680. Shi'ite Muslim saint, a son of the fourth caliph 'Ali, and Fatima, daughter of Muhammad. He is revered by the Shi'ites as the true heir of the prophet Muhammad. He was killed (680) while trying to claim the caliphate after Muawiyah's death.

Husein ibn-Ali ⟨Husayn ibn-'Ali⟩ 1856–1931. Arabian king (1917–24). Amir of Mecca (1908–16) under the Turks, he led the Arab revolt against them (1916) during WW I and proclaimed himself king of Arabia in 1917. He was defeated in a war with Ibn Saud (1924) and went into exile.

Hu Shih 1891–1962. Chinese philosopher and statesman. He was primarily responsible for the change from classical written Chinese to the vernacular as the official written language in China (1922).

Huss, John 1369–1415. Czech religious reformer. A Catholic priest, he was excommunicated and later burned at the stake for advocating the teachings of J. Wyclif. His death led to Hussite Wars (1419–34).

Hussar Name given to units of light cavalry in European armies of the 18th and 19th cents. They were named after the Hungarian cavalry corps organized (15th cent.) by King Mathias Corvinus.

Hussein ibn Talal 1935–. Jordanian king (1953–), successor to his father, King Talal. During his reign he has maintained a generally moderate stance in the Arab-Israeli conflicts, though he joined with the Arabs in the war of 1967. He successfully put down a revolt by Palestinian guerrillas in Jordan (1970).

Husserl, Edmund 1858–1938. German philosopher who founded the school of thought called phenomenology.

Hussites Followers of J. Huss in Bohemia and Moravia who were involved in a 15th-cent. rebellion against the authority of the Roman Catholic church. Following the execution (1415) of Huss as ordered by the Council of Constance, Hussites split into two groups, the moderate Calixtines, or Utraquists, and the radical Taborites. Despite differences they were allied in seeking approval of the Four Articles of Prague, which called for freedom to preach, communion in both bread and wine, the expropriation of church property, and punishment of mortal sins by civil authorities. They fought together in the Hussite Wars (1415–36) until the church won over the Utraquists with promises of concessions. After the defeat of the Taborites (1434), Utraquists were granted reforms in an agreement known as the Compactata of Prague (1436). The Utraquists eventually split (16th cent.), with one faction joining the evolving Lutheran church and the other the Roman Catholic church.

Hussite Wars Series of wars (1415–36) fought between Hussites and forces of the Holy Roman Empire. Precipitated by the death (1415) of J. Huss and the succession (1419) of the German Holy Roman Emperor Sigismund as king of Bohemia, the wars involved Hussite demands for religious reforms and Bohemian nationalism. Led by J. Zizka, Hussite forces defeated the emperor's armies (1420, 1422). He was succeeded by Procopius the Great (1424), who led the successful resistance to the crusades against them (1426, 1427, 1431) and commanded invasions into Silesia and Saxony (1425–26) and into Franconia (1429–30). The rift between Utraquists and Taborites widened during the wars, however, and in 1433, Utraquists opened negotiations with the Catholic church at the Council of Basel. Utraquists turned against the Taborites (led by Procopius), who refused concessions offered by the church, and civil war broke out in Bohemia. The Taborites were completely defeated (1434) at the Battle of Lipany, ending the wars. Concessions granted to the Hussites were formalized (1436) in the Compactata of Prague, which granted Utraquists the right to communion in both kinds, the right to retain church lands, and the establishment of a separate Bohemian church.

Hutchinson, Anne   c1591–1643.   English-born American religious reformer. Expelled (1637) from Massachusetts Bay colony by the Puritans for opposing the rigidity of their beliefs, she became one of the founders of Rhode Island.

Hutchinson, Thomas   1711–80. Unpopular Colonial governor of Massachusetts (1771–74). His rigorous enforcement of Colonial laws, notably the Stamp Act, led to the Boston Tea Party (1773). He was replaced by Gen. T. Gage in 1774.

Hutten, Ulrich von   1488–1523. German poet, humanist, and patriot. His satiric *Little Conversation Book* was written to aid M. Luther.

Hutterian Brethren   *See* **Hutterites**

Hutterites   ⟨Hutterian Brethren⟩   Communal sect with Anabaptist roots which adheres to the primitive-communist doctrine. It was founded by the Tyrolian Jacob Hutter (d. 1536), and its members endured persecution until their settlement in the US in the 19th cent.

Hutton, James   1726–97. Scottish geologist. He developed the theory of uniformitarianism (1785), which holds that the same geological processes have been at work throughout much of earth's history. The theory is fundamental to modern geology.

Huxley, Aldous Leonard   1894–1963.   English author. Among his many works is the widely read *Brave New World*.

Huxley, Thomas Henry   1825–95. English biologist. An outspoken critic of nonscientific thought, he became the leading advocate of Darwinism in England.

Huygens, Christiaan   1629–95. Dutch physicist. He discovered Saturn's rings (1655) and polarization of light (1678). He devised the pendulum for clocks (1657) and formulated a wave theory of light.

Hydaspes, Battle of the   ⟨Jhelum, ~⟩   Last battle fought (326 BC) by Alexander the Great during his campaign in Asia. Alexander defeated the Indian king Porus near the Hydaspes, now the Jhelum, a tributary of the Indus. Indian losses were 12,000, compared to 980 Macedonian dead.

Hyde, Edward, 1st earl of Clarendon   1609–74. English statesman and historian. A member of Parliament, he originally opposed, then joined Charles I in the period of the English Civil War. He later helped to restore Charles II. His *History of the Rebellion and Civil Wars in England* is still considered an invaluable historical document.

Hydra   Mythical Greek monster with nine heads. Whenever one of the heads was cut off, two new ones grew out of the neck. Hercules finally killed the monster by burning the necks.

Hyksos   Name for Egyptian kings who were of a Semitic people (sometimes also called Hyksos) that invaded and conquered Egypt during the Middle Kingdom. They ruled c1675–c1550 BC and introduced the horse and chariot to Egypt. The Hyksos kings were finally defeated (c1570 BC) by Amasis I.

Hymen   ⟨Hymenaeus⟩   A youth of great beauty, the personification of marriage in Greek mythology.

Hymenaeus   *See* **Hymen**

Hypatia   d. AD 415. Neoplatonic philosopher, mathematician, and celebrated beauty. A teacher of philosophy at Alexandria, she was cruelly murdered by rioting monks, said to be instigated by Saint Cyril, archbishop of Alexandria.

Hyperboreans   A mythological Greek people who worshiped Apollo and lived in a paradise far to the north. The term has come to be applied to northern peoples in general.

Hyperion   One of the Titans of Greek mythology. He was son of Uranus and Gaea, and father of Helios, Selene, and Eos.

Hypnos   Ancient Greek god of sleep. The brother of Thanatos (Death) and father of Morpheus, he was identified with the Roman Somnus.

I

Iamblichus *d. c330.* Syrian philosopher, and leading figure in the development of Neoplatonism *(q.v.)*. He combined the teachings of Plato and Pythagoras with mystical and magical ideas into a religious type of philosophy.

Iapetus In Greek mythology, a Titan, the son of Uranus and Gaea, and the father of Atlas, Epimetheus, Menoetius, and Prometheus (and therefore ancestor of the human race).

Iasi, Treaty of *See* **Jassy, Treaty of**

Ibáñez (del Campo), Carlo 1877–1960. President of Chile (1927–31). He was popular in the pre-Depression era for implementing labor and education reforms.

Iberia 1. Ancient name for Spain; after the Iberian people who once dwelled there. The Iberian peninsula, occupied by Spain and Portugal, is named for them. **2.** Ancient country. Iberia was located in what is now eastern Georgia in the USSR. The Iberians were allied with Rome and later became part of the Byzantine Empire.

Iberian Gates Mountain pass in the Caucasus mountains. It has been an invasion route since ancient times, and is also called the Daryal Pass.

Iberville, Pierre le Moyne, sieur d' 1661–1706. A French-Canadian explorer who founded the first settlement in the Territory of Louisiana and discovered the mouth of the Mississippi River.

Ibn al-'Arabi 1165–1240. Spanish-born Muslim mystical philosopher and poet. He joined Muslim religious teachings with uplifted mystical expression in such works as *The Meccan Revelation* and *The Interpreter of Desire*.

Ibn Batuta 1304?–78? Muslim traveler and writer. He visited countries from Morocco (his birthplace) to China from around 1325, describing his travels in detail in his book *Rihlah (Travels)*. He is considered one of the most reliable authorities on his times.

Ibn Khaldun 1334–1406. Arab historian, philosopher, and statesman. Born in Tunis, he served as a Muslim judge in Cairo. Considered the greatest of the Arab historians, he provided a description of Arab culture in his *Muqaddimah (Introduc-*

tion), as well as a philosophy of history explaining the rise and fall of civilizations.

Ibn Saud *c1880–1953.* Saudi Arabian king and founder (1932) of the modern Saudi state. Raised in exile with his family in Kuwait, he began (c1900) his campaign to reconquer the family domains in the Nejd. By 1922 he had firm control of the Nejd and then conquered the Hejaz (1924–25), of which he became king in 1926. In 1932 he changed the name of this kingdom to Saudi Arabia. He introduced a stable, nationalistic form of government and put an end to tribal wars. His decision to open the country to oil exploration led to the discovery of one of the world's largest oil fields.

Ibn Taymiyah 1263–1328. Arab Islamic theologian. An ardent conservative and traditionalist, he suffered imprisonment (1306–07) as a result of his teachings, which were thought to be too anthropomorphic.

Ibn Tufail ⟨Abubacer⟩ 12th cent. Arab philosopher and physician, born in Spain. He was the author of a romantic philosophical work, *The History of Havy Ibn-Yaqzan*, about a hermit on an island who attained knowledge of the divine.

Ibn Tumart ⟨Muhammad ~⟩ 1078?–1130. Arab reformer. He founded the Almohade *(q.v.)* sect among Berber tribes in North Africa.

Ibn Zuhr ⟨Avenzoar⟩ *c1090–1162.* Islamic physician, born in Seville, and a leading medical authority of his day. His writing, translated into Hebrew and Latin, attempted to combat quackery.

Ibrahim Pasha 1789–1848. Egyptian general. He was the conquerer of Arabia and Syria for his father Muhammad Ali, the ruler of Egypt; but was obliged to evacuate some of his conquests when Western powers came to the aid of a faltering Ottoman Empire *(q.v.)*. He briefly succeeded his father as Viceroy of Egypt before his death.

Ibsen, Henrik 1828–1906. Norwegian writer. Ibsen was a poet and playwright whose dramas established him as one of the world's foremost realistic writers. He explored the depth of emotions beneath society, and his opinions were often far in advance of his time. Among his major works are *The Wild Duck, A Doll's House, Hedda Gabler,* and *An Enemy of the People.*

Icarus *See* **Daedalus**

Iceland ⟨Republic of Iceland⟩ Island republic located in the North Atlantic near the Arctic Circle. Capital is Reykjavik. Iceland was settled (9th cent.) by Norsemen. A legislative assembly, the Althing, was established (930), Christianity was introduced (c1000), and Iceland recognized Norwegian suzerainty (1264). Iceland then came under Danish control (by the union of Denmark and Norway) in 1380 and, in the mid-16th cent., the Danes imposed Lutheranism. Iceland declined in the 17th and 18th cents., suffering economic exploitation, pirate raids, and a series of volcanic eruptions. It revived in the following century and an independence movement, led by J. Sigurdsson, eventually (1874) resulted in the granting of a constitution and some home rule. Sovereignty was granted in 1918, though by the terms of the Act of Union Iceland remained in personal union with the king of Denmark. The collapse of Denmark in WW II brought occupation by the British and the Americans and, on June 17, 1944, Iceland became an independent republic. In subsequent years, Iceland joined the UN (1946), concluded an agreement (1951) allowing the US to maintain bases there, and engaged in disputes with Britain over fishing rights and territorial waters (1958–61, 1973–76).

Ickes, Harold LeClaire 1874–1952. American politician and social reformer of President Franklin Roosevelt's New Deal (*q.v.*) era. He was secretary of the interior (1933–46).

Iconoclastic Controversy Religious dispute. The Iconoclasts of the Byzantine Empire opposed the use of images (icons) in religious worship (sanctioned 7th cent.), on the grounds that icons were sacrilegious. Emperor Leo III denounced the use of icons (726) and in subsequent years icon worshippers and iconoclasts were alternately persecuted. The controversy raged throughout the 8th and 9th cents., and was denounced (787) by the Second Council of Nicaea (*q.v.*), which decreed that icons could be venerated but not worshipped. The controversy was ended (843) with the restoration of icon worship during the reign of Emperor Michael III.

Ictinus Highly acclaimed Greek architect of the 5th cent. BC. He was a chief designer of the Parthenon (*q.v.*).

Idaho Northwestern state of the US (pop. 943,900), the 43rd state. White men first entered the region with the Lewis and Clark expedition (*q.v.*) of 1805, and the fur traders soon followed.

Idaho was held jointly by the US and Great Britain until 1846, and it became part of the Oregon Territory in 1848. The discovery of gold (1860) and silver (1863) brought many settlers who built up what are ghost towns today. The Idaho constitution was adopted in 1889, and statehood came in 1890. The state is famous for its potatoes, grown in the arid but fertile plateau watered by federal reclamation projects on the Snake River.

idealism Term in ethics, art, and philosophy. In ethics it is a doctrine that recognizes moral or intellectual ideals as superior to materialistic concerns and seeks perfection in attaining these ideals. In art the aesthetic ideal, the way the subject should appear, is the standard of perfection, and not the mere copying of reality. In philosophy, it refers to schools of thought in which the real world is believed to be nothing more than ideas perceived by the intellect. It is opposed to materialism (*q.v.*). Idealism has been espoused in one form or another since the times of Plato. Plato held that the ideas were an unchanging reality that existed independently of one's mind. In more recent times, it was held that these ideas (and thus the real world) were created by the mind itself. Noted proponents of idealism in various forms are Plato, G. Berkeley, I. Kant, and G. Hegel.

Ides of March March 15 by the Roman calendar. J. Caesar was assassinated on this day in 44 BC.

Idomeneus In Greek legend, a king of Crete, who fought with the Greeks in the Trojan War (*q.v.*). On his way home he vowed to Poseidon during a storm to sacrifice the first living thing he met on his return, and was thus forced to sacrifice his own son.

Idris I 1890–. The king of Libya from its independence (1951), until he was deposed by a *coup d'état* in 1969. He was a leader of the Senussi sect in Cyrenaica before being made king.

Idrisi ⟨Edrisi⟩ *b.* 1099? Arab scientist and geographer at the Court of Roger II of Sicily, the compiler of one of the most significant works of medieval geography (1154).

Ieper *See* **Ypres**

Ieyasu *See* **Iyeyasu**

Ifni Former Spanish territory, now part of southwest Morocco, and noted for its fisheries. Ceded by Morocco to Spain in 1860, it was returned to Morocco in 1969.

Iglau, Compact of *See* **Compact of Iglau**

Iglau, Compactata of *See* **Compact of Iglau**

Ignatius of Antioch, Saint *d.* AD c107. Syrian Catholic bishop. Ignatius was sent to Rome for execution. En route he wrote seven letters which defined and clarified Catholic beliefs, and are invaluable testimonies to early Christian beliefs.

His writings contain history's first mention of the name "Catholic church," which he describes as ruled by bishops.

Ignatius of Constantinople, Saint 800–877. Greek Catholic patriarch. Ignatius, son of Emperor Michael I, opposed the Iconoclasts in the Iconoclastic Controversy *(q.v.)*. He was ousted by Photius but restored by the Fourth Council of Constantinople *(q.v.)*.

Ignatius of Loyola, Saint 1491–1556. Spanish religious leader. Of noble birth, he entered military service, and was wounded at Pamplona (1521). While convalescing he conceived (from reading lives of the saints) the idea of becoming a soldier for Christ. At the University of Paris he formed the nucleus of the Jesuits, or Society of Jesus *(q.v.)*, a religious order for men organized along military lines. After approval by the pope (1540), the Jesuits with Ignatius as their first general organized the most effective Catholic response to the Reformation *(q.v.)*, dominated and revolutionized European education, and became the largest religious order of modern times.

Igor *c*877–945. Duke of Kiev (912–45), succeeding Oleg. He was the son of Rurik, founder of the first dynasty of Russian czars. He concluded a treaty with the Byzantium (945) after his attempt at conquest was thwarted.

Igor 1150–1202. Russian prince and legendary hero. His defeat in a battle in 1185 inspired the first work of Russian literature, *The Song of Igor's Campaign* (*c*1187), rendered in a modern English translation by V. Nabokov (1960). It also inspired the famous opera *Prince Igor* (1869) by Russian composer Alexander P. Borodin (1834–87).

Iguala, Plan de *See* **Plan de Iguala**

IGY *See* **International Geophysical Year**

Ikeda, Hayato 1899–1965. Moderate Japanese statesman who was prime minister (1960–1964). He played a large part in Japan's amazing economic recovery following WW II.

Ikhnaton ⟨Akhenaton⟩ ⟨Amenhotep IV⟩ *d. c*1362 BC. Egyptian pharaoh (*c*1379–*c*1362) of the XVIIIth dynasty, successor to his father Amenhotep III. He is renowned for having instituted monotheism in Egypt by forcibly converting his kingdom to the worship of the sun god Aton *(q.v.)* Despite resistance from the priesthood, he attempted to eradicate all reference to other gods, including Amon *(q.v.)*, and founded a new capital at Akhetaton (now Tel El Amarna). His conversion sparked revolutionary changes in Egyptian art and literature but Ikhnaton's preoccupation with it is believed to have resulted in the loss of extensive territory in the provinces. His successor, Tutankhamen, was forced to restore worship of the old gods. Ikhnaton's reign is referred to as the Amarna Age.

Île-de-France *See* **Mauritius**

Île-de-France French region and former province located around Paris. It was the center of the French monarchy's lands from which the modern nation of France evolved.

Iliad and **Odyssey** Two celebrated Greek epic poems, believed to have been written (*c*9th cent. BC) by Homer. In ancient Greece they were revered as sources for moral and spiritual guidance. In modern times they are considered among the greatest masterpieces of Western literature. The *Iliad* tells the story of the Trojan War *(q.v.)*, fought to return Helen to her husband, the Spartan King Menelaus. The *Odyssey* narrates the adventures of Odysseus, a Greek hero, "a man who was never at a loss," during his return to Ithaca after the Trojan War.

Ili crisis Dispute between Russia and China, centering on Ili province in Chinese Turkestan. Russia invaded Ili (1871) to control the advance of a local ruler, Yakub Beg (1820–77). After Yakub Beg's death, Russia restored most of Ili to China (1881), through the Treaty of St. Petersburg *(q.v.)*.

Il-Khan Mongol dynasty that reigned (1258–1353) in Persia (modern Iran). Between 1253 and 1258, the Mongol Hulagu Khan conquered this territory, including the Islamic capital of Baghdad, and founded the Il-Khan dynasty. The dynasty reached its height under Mahmud Ghazan (1295–1304), who became the first Mongol to convert to Islam (Sunni). In subsequent years internal unrest broke the Il-Khan's power and brought their rule to an end by 1353.

Illinois State in the north central US (pop. 11,418,500), the 21st state. French explorers, Marquette and Jolliet, first explored the region (1673), and in 1680 La Salle built Fort Crèvecoeur. The French ceded the area to Great Britain in 1763 after the French and Indian Wars *(q.v.)*. In 1787, the region became part of the Northwest Territory. Illinois became a state in 1818, and the Indians were driven out after the 1832 Black Hawk War *(q.v.)*. The present state constitution was adopted in 1970. The capital is at Springfield. The state's prairie lands constitute one of the country's agricultural heartlands, but it is also one of the principal industrial states.

Illuminati Rationalistic type of religious society founded in Bavaria in 1776 by Adam Weishaupt (1748–1830). It claimed enlightened religious views, but was banned in Bavaria in 1785. The term "illuminati" was also used for other rationalistic-type and anticlerical religious sects from the 16th to 18th cents.

Illyria and **Illyricum** Illyria was an ancient region on the Adriatic coast, roughly corresponding to parts of Yugoslavia and Albania. The early Illyrians frequently practiced piracy, until they were conquered by the Romans (between 2d and 1st cent. BC). The Romans established it as the province Illyricum, which eventually sent many legionnaires and emperors (Claudius II and Diocletian) to Rome. Illyricum was divided into the provinces of Dalmatia *(q.v.)* and Pannonia after AD 9.

Illyrian Wars Two successful wars fought by the Romans (229–28, 219 BC) to suppress Illyrian pirates. In gratitude the Greeks admitted the Romans to the Eleusinian Mysteries and Isthmian Games, marking the official recognition by the Greeks of Rome as a civilized power.

Illyricum *See* **Illyria** and **Illyricum**

Imagists American and English poetry school. These early 20th-century poets opposed the excessive sentimentality of the 19th century. They stressed clearly defined images and verbal precision, and included E. Pound, D. H. Lawrence, and A. Lowell.

imam Islamic leader. "Imam" is a term of high respect in Muslim countries, although the actual duties and honor attached to the name vary. Most typically, the imam leads the Friday prayers at the mosque.

Imhotep *c*2980–2950 BC. Egyptian sage. Imhotep was revered as the architect of the first step pyramid, as a doctor, and adviser to 3d-dynasty kings. He was elevated to deity status after his death.

Immigration Restriction Act Legislation passed in 1901 by the Commonwealth of Australia restricting the immigration of non-Europeans into the country. One of the first pieces of Australian legislation, it remains in effect but with notable modifications since WW II.

impeachment Process of formal accusation of public officials for misconduct in office. Developed from the 14th cent. in the English system, the right of impeachment in the US is vested in the Congress by the US Constitution. President A. Johnson and Supreme Court Justice S. Chase were impeached but subsequently acquitted. A congressional committee voted to ask Congress to impeach President R. M. Nixon over Watergate *(q.v.)* but he resigned first.

Imperial Conferences Meetings of delegates from dominions within the British Empire (and later, the Commonwealth) held variously between 1907 and 1937. The conferences were called to discuss economic and mutual-defense concerns, though their resolutions were nonbinding until enactment of the 1931 Statute of Westminster *(q.v.)*. After WW II the formal conferences were replaced by policy meetings between prime ministers of Commonwealth countries. Imperial Conferences were held 1907, 1911, 1917–18, 1921, 1923, 1926, 1930, 1932, 1936, 1937. Before 1907 such meetings were called Colonial Conferences and were held 1887, 1897, 1902.

imperialism In general, the rule over or control of one state by another. More specifically, "imperialism" is used in either of two ways, referring to ancient and modern forms. Ancient imperialism is the process by which early empires were created. This involved military conquest and, to one degree or another, political domination. Ancient imperialism led to creation of the Macedonian, Persian, Roman, Chinese, and numerous other empires. Modern imperialism is the policy by which nations built colonial empires (beginning in 15th–16th cents.). Modern imperialism was at first spurred on by the rewards of increased trade and mineral riches in the Americas, the Indies, and later Africa. However, the industrial age brought new motivations. The great colonial empires of the 18th and 19th cents. were exploited for raw materials and also served as ready markets for the vast quantities of finished goods produced by the industrial nations. Competition between the great colonial powers, notably the British, French, Dutch, Portuguese, and later the Germans, led to instability and frequent wars during the 19th cent. In the 20th cent., however, the rise of nationalism brought new resistance to this form of imperialism and resulted in independence movements within the colonies. The years after WW I, and especially those following WW II, saw the breakup of colonial empires as most former colonies won their independence.

impressionism French school of painting (*c*1872–1886) whose radical innovations profoundly influenced the development of the visual arts. Reacting against then current standards regarding the primacy of subject matter in painting, a small group of French painters led by E. Manet and C. Monet began experimenting with new techniques. Though members of the group developed highly individualistic styles, they generally created works in which color and form, not the subject matter, predominated. Impressionists exhibited as a group eight times (1874–86) before disbanding and remained out of favor in established art circles until the 1920s. Among the impressionists were E. Manet, C. Monet, C. Pissaro, A. Renoir, and E. Degas.

Inca South American Indian people and their vast empire in the Andes region, which at the time of the Spanish conquest (16th cent.) extended from Ecuador to northern Chile. According to legend, the empire was founded (AD c1100) by Manco Capac at what is now Cuzco, Peru. It expanded slowly until the early 15th cent., when a period of rapid conquests began. The empire reached its zenith under the rule of Huayna Capac (1493–1525), who divided the empire between his sons, Atahualpa *(q.v.)* and Huáscar *(q.v.)*. The two subsequently warred against each other and, when the Spanish conquistador F. Pizarro arrived in South America (1532), Atahualpa had just defeated his brother. After being received by Atahualpa on friendly terms, Pizarro captured and executed him (1533), entered Cuzco, and with his small force easily subjugated this empire of 10–12 million people. At the time of the Spanish conquest the Incas had a well advanced civilization organized in a rigid hierarchy, over which the emperor ruled with absolute (and divine) authority. Inca society was based on agricultural production and its religion centered on sun worship. They were great builders and constructed magnificent cities, such as Machu Picchu, and a system of roads, irrigation, and mountainside terraces. There was also extensive mining and advanced metallurgy. Under the Spanish, the Inca religion was forcibly suppressed, a colonial government was installed, and the native population was drawn away from agriculture for work in the mines and colonial towns.

incunabula Bibliographical term. Taken from the Latin word for "cradle," the term refers to the earliest of printed books, those dating from before 1500. They include books from the presses of J. Gutenberg, W. Caxton, and so on.

Independence, Declaration of The document in which the 13 American colonies proclaimed their freedom from Britain. Following the initial battles of the American Revolution, it became clear to members of the Second Continental Congress that a negotiated settlement with Britain was no longer feasible. Consequently, R. H. Lee called on the Congress (June 7, 1776) to adopt a statement proclaiming independence. Largely drafted by T. Jefferson, it was formally adopted by Congress on July 4, 1776 (having already been passed on July 2). J. Hancock, president of the Congress, was first of the 56 delegates to sign the document. The day of adoption (July 4) is celebrated as US Independence Day.

Independence, War of *See* **American Revolution**

Independence Hall Building in Philadelphia from which, on July 4, 1776, the Declaration of Independence was proclaimed. Both the Continental Congress *(q.v.)* and the US Constitutional Convention met there. It is now a museum.

Independents ⟨Separatists⟩ 17th-cent. term given to those English Christians who believed that local congregations should have control of their own church affairs, free from civil or ecclesiastical control. The Pilgrims *(q.v.)* who founded Plymouth in Massachusetts (1620) were Independents. The Puritans who founded the Massachusetts Bay *(q.v.)* colony (1630) became separatists in New England after they abandoned their attempts to reform the Church of England. Both groups eventually espoused Congregationalism *(q.v.)*. In England, Independents enjoyed their greatest influence during the Commonwealth and Protectorate and were suppressed in subsequent years.

Independent Treasury American treasury system, adopted in 1846, by which public revenues were kept at and disbursed from the Treasury and subtreasury buildings, without using private or state banks. The system ended with passage of the Federal Reserve Act (1913).

India ⟨Republic of India⟩ Country located on the Indian subcontinent in southern Asia. Its capital is New Delhi. India has one of the world's oldest cultures, and such religions as Hinduism, Buddhism, and Jainism were begun in India. India was first unified (4th cent. BC) under the Mauryan dynasty and later empires under the Guptas (4th-6th cent. AD,) and Muslim Moguls (16th–18th cent.) also brought much of India under one ruler. Except for these periods, Indian history was characterized by disunity and warfare between petty states, a fact that enabled the British to gain control over the Indian subcontinent in the 18th–19th cent. The movement for independence from Britain began in the late 19th cent. After a long series of nonviolent protest campaigns led by M. Gandhi, India finally became independent in 1947. Conflicts between the Hindu majority and the considerable Muslim population, however, resulted in creation of two separate states (India and Pakistan) when independence was granted. Key dates in the history of India include:

c2500–c1500 BC Indus Valley civilization flourished along the Indus River in the northwest (modern Pakistan).

c1500 BC Aryans invaded India; swept through Indus Valley and settled in northern Punjab region and along northern Ganges River.

1500–700 BC Vedic period; Vedism, the religion of the Aryans, was evolved and refined; Rig-Veda, which later became sacred Hindu text, reached final form.

c800–c500 BC Upanishads written; advanced

such fundamental religious doctrines as reincarnation and karma.

c700–c500 BC Brahmanic period; priestly class of Brahmans gained hold over religious community; promoted elaborate rituals, philosophical speculations, and eventually the establishment of the caste system.

c6TH–c5TH CENT. BC Period of social, religious ferment; warrior class revolted against Brahman (priestly) class; rise of new religions and sects in opposition to Brahmanism, which was losing its hold on the populace.

c6TH–2D CENT. BC Sutras written; established rigid order of conduct and religious ritual and divided society into four classes, giving rise to caste system.

6TH CENT. BC Magadha kingdom founded in northeastern India as first important Aryan state; became nucleus of later Mauryan kingdom.

557 BC Vardhamana Mahavira achieved enlightenment and thus founded Jainism; Jainism arose in opposition to Brahmanism in the period of ferment, 6th–5th cent. BC.

c528 BC Buddha achieved spiritual enlightenment at Buddha Gaya, in northeastern India; Buddhism founded.

517–509 BC Persians under Darius I conquered Indus Valley region in the northwest.

327–326 BC Alexander the Great conquered northwestern region that had fallen to Persians; Battle of Hydaspes River.

c322–c185 BC Mauryan Empire; first great Indian empire; founded in northeastern India, it eventually included nearly all of India and part of Afghanistan; native Indian culture flourished.

c322–297 BC Chandragupta reigned; seized power (c322) in Magadha, drove out the Macedonian Greeks, united the north and created the great Mauryan Empire.

c305 BC Chandragupta defeated Seleucus I Nicator; extended empire westward into modern Afghanistan.

302 BC Alliance concluded with Seleucids; thereafter Greek culture had influence in northern India.

297–273 BC Bindusara reigned over the Mauryan Empire; believed to have conquered Deccan (southern India).

273–232 BC Asoka reigned in Mauryan Empire; brought empire to its greatest extent (including most of India); then renounced conquest by force and actively promoted Buddhism, making it the state religion.

2D CENT. BC Beginnings of Hinduism; earlier Brahmanism adopted elements of Buddhism, Jainism, and other competing religious systems; Hin-

duism eventually became the dominant religion of India.

185–73 BC Sunga dynasty ruled northern India; Mauryan dynasty overthrown; Hinduism replaced Buddhism as state religion and Buddhists were persecuted.

FROM c185 BC Tamil kingdoms ascendant in the south; included Chola, Pandyas, and Ceras; conducted trade with the Romans and peoples of Southeast Asia, spreading Hindu culture among them.

c128 BC–AD 450 Yueh-chih people controlled an empire in the northwest.

c50 BC–AD 450 Kushan kingdom; descendants of Yueh-chih, ruled a kingdom in northwestern India that eventually included Afghanistan and parts of central Asia; traded with Rome and spread Buddhism to central Asia and China.

AD 320–c500 Gupta Empire in northern India; eventually included north, parts of central and western India; period of peace and prosperity; golden age of Indian culture; Hinduism enjoyed period of growth.

AD 320–330 Chandragupta I reigned; founded Gupta dynasty after conquering states surrounding the Magadha kingdom.

AD 330–c380 Samudragupta reigned; completed conquest of the north.

AD c380–413 Chandragupta II reigned; an able ruler, he extended the empire westward and southward; cultural flowering reached its height.

AD 405–411 Fa-hsien, Chinese Buddhist, visited India.

LATE 5TH–6TH CENT. White Huns invaded India and occupied northern India; Gupta Empire collapsed; Huns' power finally broken in wars against Turks and Sassanids.

606–647 Harsha reigned; reunited northern India under a native ruler for last time; his empire disintegrated into petty states at his death; period of warfare and disunity followed.

7TH CENT. Rise of the Rajput warrior class in northwestern India; they remained powerful until the 16th cent.

888–1267 Chola dynasty, ruling in southeast India, became a major power in the south; Rajaraja I (ruled 985–1014) gained hegemony over Deccan; Chola rulers invaded Sri Lanka (11th cent.); conquered by Muslims.

977–1186 Rise of the Muslim Ghaznavid dynasty in Afghanistan; raids by Muslims into India began.

1186–94 Muhammad of Ghor, a Muslim, destroyed the Ghaznavids and conquered northern India (by 1194).

1192–1398 Delhi Sultanate, first Muslim kingdom in India established after capture of Delhi by Muslims (1192); Muhammad of Ghor and succeeding rulers (Slave dynasty) conquered most of India; Jagirdar revenue system established; Buddhism in India began rapid decline.

1398–99 Tamerlane the Mongol conqueror invaded India; Delhi Sultanate ended after Tamerlane sacked Delhi and massacred citizens.

1414–51 Sayyid dynasty ruled the kingdom of Delhi.

1451–1526 Lodi dynasty; Bahlol, an Afghan, deposed the Sayyid rulers, took Delhi, and founded the Lodi dynasty; domains expanded beyond immediate area of Delhi.

1498 Portuguese explorer V. da Gama reached India; first European fort in India established on southwest coast at Cochin (near Bombay) in 1503.

1510 Portuguese established headquarters at Goa, on southwest coast.

c1520 Sikh faith founded by Nanak in the northwest Punjab region.

1526–1761 Mogul Empire; Muslim rulers established control over much of India, uniting it for the first time in centuries; Mogul rulers proved able administrators and sought to integrate Muslim and Hindu peoples; distinctive Mogul culture evolved.

1526–30 Baber reigned as first Mogul emperor; defeated Lodi ruler at Battle of Panipat (Apr. 20, 1526); completed conquest of kingdom of Delhi in north.

1556–1605 Akbar reigned as Mogul emperor; subdued revolts in Punjab, Rajputana, and Gujarat; added Bengal, Kashmir, Sind, and parts of the Deccan, thereby creating a strong Indian empire.

1613 British East India Company established trading colony at Surat after defeating Portuguese.

1628–58 Shah Jahan reigned as Mogul emperor; Mogul culture reached its zenith; Taj Mahal built (1632–53).

1658–1707 Aurangzeb reigned as Mogul emperor; his harsh reign weakened Mogul power in India; attempted to impose Muslim faith and persecuted Hindus, provoking numerous revolts.

1661 British East India Company gained control of Bombay.

1664 Maratha Empire founded in southwestern India and later expanded into central India; led by Sivaji, a champion of Hinduism, the Marathas created an independent empire; warred against Mogul emperor Aurangzeb and, by weakening Moguls, paved the way for the rise of the British.

1674 Pondicherry established by French on extreme southeastern coast of India; became center of French domains in India.

1691 Calcutta founded by British.

1707 Death of Aurangzeb; Mogul Empire split up; Maratha Empire expanded into central India and dominated the south as the most powerful single kingdom.

1708–12 Religious order of Sikhs transformed to military order; defeated by Bahadur Shah, ruler of the crumbling Mogul Empire, who drove them into Punjab in the north (1712).

1724 Hyderabad established as independent kingdom in south central India; came under rule of Nizam dynasty after decline of Mogul Empire (of which it was part).

1739 Persians under Nadir Shah invaded India and sacked Delhi; invaders withdrew, taking fabulous wealth with them, including Peacock Throne and Koh-i-noor diamond.

1746–63 Rivalry between British and French for control of India.

1746–48 French, led by J. Dupleix, captured Madras (1746) from British while War of the Austrian Succession raged in Europe; Madras restored (1748).

1751 British soldier R. Clive captured Arcot in ongoing rivalry with French for control of southern India.

1756 Black Hole of Calcutta incident followed capture of British-held Calcutta by Nawab of Bengal (eastern India); British recaptured Calcutta (1757).

1756–63 British successful in fighting against French in India as Seven Years' War raged in Europe; Clive virtually destroyed French power in India by victory in Battle of Plassey (1757), in which British gained control of Bengal.

1756–64 Afghan emir Ahmad Shah invaded India; captured Delhi; Marathas and Sikhs defeated in Battle of Panipat (1761); after Afghans withdrew, surviving Indian kingdoms were unable to resist expansion of British power.

1761 Muslim leader Haidar Ali seized power in Mysore (south central India).

1764 British put down native rebellion in Bengal at the Battle of Baksar.

1765–67 R. Clive served as administrator of Bengal; began expanding British control over native states.

1767–69 Haidar Ali conducted first Mysore War against British East India Company.

1770 Bengal famine killed one third of population; British authorities made no attempt to help.

1773 Regulating Act, reorganizing British

East India Company, passed; first British government intervention in rule of India.

1774 Rohilla War conducted by the Nawab of Oudh, aided by the British East India Company, against the Afghan Rohillas.

1775–82 First Maratha War; led to British acquisition of Salsette Island.

1780–84 Haidar Ali conducted second Mysore War against British.

1790–92 Tipu Sahib, son of Haidar Ali, defeated in third Mysore War against British; forced to cede half his territory.

1798 Ceylon (now Sri Lanka) became a British colony.

1799 Tipu Sahib defeated and killed in fourth Mysore War; British restored native monarchy in Mysore.

1803–05 Second Maratha War fought between British and Maratha Confederacy.

1806 Vellore Mutiny against British by Sepoy troops.

1809 Treaty of Amritsar defined spheres of British and Sikh influence in the Punjab (north).

1814–16 War with the Nepalese Gurkhas.

1817–18 Third Maratha War fought between British and Marathas; resulted in destruction of Maratha Confederacy and British domination of most of India; Sind and Punjab still independent.

1824 Barrackpore Mutiny among native Indian troops quashed by British; set stage for 1857 mutiny.

1824–26 First Burma War; British gradually increased control over Burma through a series of wars.

1829 British banned practice of suttee.

1833 British East India Company lost China trade monopoly by revision of charter.

1839–42 First Anglo-Afghan War; British attached the Afghan state from India; marked first in series of wars for control of Afghanistan.

1843 Sind armies defeated by small British force at the Battle of Miani, Pakistan.

1843 Britain annexed the Sind.

1845–46 British victorious in First Sikh War in the northwest Punjab region.

1848–49 British victorious in Second Sikh War; annexed Punjab (1849).

1848–56 Unpopular Doctrine of Lapse used by governor-general, Earl of Dalhousie, to acquire direct control of native kingdoms.

1852 Second Burma War.

1857–59 Indian Mutiny; major revolt by Indian troops (Sepoys) against British rule; surviving remnant of the Mogul Empire dissolved.

1858 British government took direct control of administration of India, ending British East India Company involvement (Sept. 1); numerous reforms enacted.

1861 Native Indians appointed to legislative and executive councils.

1877 Queen Victoria crowned Empress of India.

1878–81 Second Anglo-Afghan War.

1885 Third Burma War; British gained all of Burma.

1885 Indian National Congress party formed; Indian nationalists used as a vehicle for the Indian independence movement; failed to gain support of Muslims and thus became Hindu nationalist movement.

1905–11 Partition of Bengal by British Viceroy, Lord Curzon (ruled 1898–1905); created Muslim majority in East Bengal and sparked protest and violence among nationalists.

1906 Muslim League founded to advance interests of Muslims.

1909 Indian Councils Act; legislation increased Indian self-government.

1914–18 WW I; many native Indian troops used by British in fighting Central Powers; war weakened British control in India.

1915 Defence of India Act passed in Britain to quell wartime native revolts; its extension after the war sparked Gandhi's Noncooperation Movement.

1917 Montagu declaration promised development of self-government in India.

1918–19 Millions died in influenza epidemic.

1918 Montagu-Chelmsford report promised limited self-government; inadequacies of plan attacked by Indian National Congress.

1919 Rowlatt Acts passed (Feb.) extending British government's wartime powers; Gandhi led protest against the acts.

1919 Amritsar Massacre (Apr.); British troops fired on unarmed natives in the Punjab; anti-British sentiments intensified.

1919 Government of India Act (Dec. 23); Britain instituted system of dyarchy as step toward self-rule for India.

1920–22 Noncooperation Movement (satyagraha) organized by Gandhi to protest British rule.

1927 Simon Commission formed by British to study working of Indian constitution; its 1930 report boycotted by Indian National Congress.

1930–31 Gandhi launched second noncooperation campaign after British announced willingness to discuss dominion status for India (1929); radicals wanted full independence.

1930 Red Shirt Movement, anti-British movement supporting Indian National Congress, launched in northwestern India by A. Khan.

1931 Gandhi agreed (Mar.) to Delhi Pact, ending second noncooperation campaign.

1935 Government of India Act; provided for creation (in 1937) of elected provincial legislatures and a federal legislature.

1937 Constitution and government established by Government of India Act (1935) in effect.

1939–45 WW II; British viceroy declared war on Axis powers without consulting Indian leaders; radicals thereupon demanded complete independence as price for their support.

1940 Gandhi began another noncooperation campaign; thousands arrested in 1940 and 1942.

1942 National Congress party suppressed.

1942 Cripps Mission; unsuccessful attempt by British to offer eventual Indian independence in exchange for support during WW II.

1944 Brief, unsuccessful Japanese invasion of India (from Burma).

1945 India became member of the UN.

1945–46 British government first offered, then insisted on complete independence for India; plan for independent government held up by disagreements between Hindu Indian Nationalist Congress and Muslim League (which wanted separate Muslim state); clashes between Hindus and Muslims increased.

1947 India gained formal independence (Aug. 15) as a British dominion; partitioned into India proper and West and East Pakistan (in north), where Muslims were concentrated; independence followed by violence between Hindus and Muslims and migrations by millions between Hindu and Muslim territories.

1947–64 J. Nehru in office as India's first prime minister.

1947–48 Lord L. Mountbatten served as last British viceroy.

1947 Punjab partitioned; Muslim west joined to Pakistan; Hindu east joined to India.

1948 Gandhi assassinated (Jan.) by Hindu fanatic as disorders continued.

1948 Hyderabad, princely state in central India, forced to join in dominion of India.

1948–49 India-Pakistani war over Kashmir.

1950 India became a republic (Jan. 26), ending ties with British; Rajendra Prasad in office as first president (1950–62); Nehru continued as prime minister.

1956 Government acquired French settlement of Pondicherry.

1961 India annexed Portuguese settlements (Goa and others).

1962 Chinese invaded (Oct.) northeastern border region and occupied territory disputed since 1957.

1965–68 India-Pakistani conflict over Rann of Kutch.

1966–77 Indira Gandhi in office as prime minister.

1969 Indian National Congress party split after suffering election reverses; I. Gandhi formed New Congress party and won major victory in 1971 elections.

1970 I. Gandhi dissolved Parliament (Dec.) after it opposed her reform measures.

1971 India-Pakistani war (Dec.) over Bangladesh independence.

1973 Agreement for cooperation (Nov.) with USSR signed.

1974 India exploded its first nuclear device.

1975 Prime minister I. Gandhi convicted (June) of election fraud; her resignation called for.

1975 Gandhi declared (June) state of emergency; ordered mass arrest of opponents; press censorship imposed.

1976 Constitutional rights suspended (Jan.) and elections postponed; Prime Minister Gandhi given new powers.

1976 Diplomatic relations resumed with Pakistan.

1977 Gandhi's Congress party defeated (Apr.) in elections; Morarji Desai, Janata Party leader, became prime minister.

1977 Gandhi arrested (Oct.) on charges of corruption.

1979 Charran Singh in office as prime minister following Morarji Desai's resignation.

1979 Political crisis continued; Singh resigned.

1980 Gandhi returned to power as prime minister after her faction of the Congress Party won the Jan. elections.

Indiana State in the north central US, (pop. 5,490,000), the 19th state. The area was explored by the French, including R. La Salle, who arrived in 1679. Vincennes was the first settlement. In 1763, the Treaty of Paris ceded the territory to England as part of the Northwest Territory *(q.v.)*. After the Revolutionary War (1783), it was ceded to the US, which began to force the Indians out of the region. It became a state in 1816 and adopted its constitution in 1851.

Indian Councils Act British reform act for the government of India enacted on Nov. 15, 1909. It provided for increased Indian self-government in the form of a representative legislature. An earlier act of the same name (1861) reorganized India's executive administration.

Indian Mutiny ⟨Sepoy Rebellion⟩ Widespread revolt (1857–58) by native Indian troops (sepoys) serving in the British East India Company army. The revolt brought about the transfer of authority in India from the company to the British crown (Sept. 1, 1858) and later became a symbol for Indian nationalists. Resentment against East India Company rule had been building for some time, particularly over the company's annexation of native lands and its failure to respect native customs. Hindus and Muslims alike were offended by the introduction of cartridges greased with cow and pig fat and this sparked the mutiny. Indian troops rebelled (May 10, 1857) at Meerut and the bloody revolt (involving massacres of British army officers and European civilians) spread rapidly throughout northern and central India. British forces retook Delhi (Sept. 1857) and Lucknow (Mar. 1858). The revolt was effectively crushed in 1858, though some fighting continued into 1859. As a result of the uprising, the (titular) ruler of the Mogul Empire, Bahadur Shah II, was banished by the British. This formally ended the existence of the Mogul Empire.

Indian National Congress ⟨Congress party⟩ Political party in India. Founded in 1885, it became a vehicle for the Indian independence movement in the early 20th cent. The party was taken over (1917) by militants such as B. Tilak and A. Besant and, under the leadership of M. K. Gandhi, it organized the passive-resistance campaigns (satyagraha) against British domination that continued to the 1940s. The party was disbanded (1942) by the British but reorganized (1945) and became the ruling party of independent India (1947). It was led (1947–64) by J. Nehru until his death and continued as the ruling party under I. Gandhi. Opposition to I. Gandhi, however, finally split (1969) the party into the New Congress Party, supporting I. Gandhi, and the Old Congress Party, supporting Morarji R. Desai, who succeeded Mrs. Gandhi as prime minister between 1977 and 1980 under the banner of a new Janata party. In 1980, Mrs. Gandhi was returned to power as prime minister, at the head of her faction of the Congress Party.

Indian Removal Act US law (1830) implemented by President A. Jackson. It called for the removal of Indian tribes east of the Mississippi and their resettlement in the western territories. During the 1830s some 60,000 Indians were forced to move. Those who resisted were marched under such conditions that, of some 11,000 Cherokees moved, over 4,000 died (1838).

Indian Reorganization Act ⟨Wheeler-Howard Act⟩ US legislation enacted (1934) to improve the economic conditions on American Indian reservations and promote their assimilation into the American mainstream.

Indians, American *See under tribal names*

Indian Territory US lands set aside (1834) for resettlement of Indian tribes in the West. It once occupied nearly all of what is now Oklahoma. Government policy of removing Indian tribes from the US Southeast was formalized by the Indian Removal Act *(q.v.)* of 1830. By the Indian Intercourse Act (1834) the western territories were set aside for them. Though the territory became the home of a number of tribes displaced by white settlers, westward expansion eventually forced the government to open even this territory to settlers. The western part was opened in 1889 and, on the admission (1907) of Oklahoma as a state, the territory was abolished.

India-Pakistani Wars Conflicts between India and Pakistan in the years after the British partition of the Indian subcontinent (Aug. 15, 1947). **1.** Kashmir clashes. Partition brought on both rival claims to Kashmir and armed conflict. A UN cease-fire negotiated on Jan. 1, 1949, gave India two-thirds, Pakistan one-third, of Kashmir. **2.** Rann of Kutch clashes. Fighting in 1965 along the West Pakistan-Gujarat border led to an international arbitration commission award of 90 percent of the Rann of Kutch to India, 10 percent to Pakistan, on Feb. 19, 1968. **3.** India-Pakistani War of 1971. Indian aid to East Pakistan's successful effort to achieve independence as Bangladesh *(q.v.)* led to a full-scale war between India and Pakistan that broke out on Dec. 3, 1971. Pakistan agreed to a cease-fire in the east on Dec. 16, and in the west on Dec. 17. On July 3, 1972, the two countries signed a treaty providing for withdrawal of troops and a commitment to seek peaceful solutions.

Indochina, Federation of ⟨French Indochina⟩ Former federation of states in Southeast Asia including Cochin China, a French colony, and the French protectorates of Annam, Cambodia, Laos, and Tonkin. France had originally gained control in these areas between 1863 and 1894. The Japanese took control during WW II and the French tried to reestablish sovereignty from 1945. However, nationalist groups in Annam, Cochin China, and Tonkin sought independence as the republic of Vietnam from 1945, and plunged the area into war (Indochina War, *q.v.*). The Geneva Conference *(q.v.)* of 1954 marked the end of the federation, since it marked the end of French control of the area.

Indochina War ⟨French Indochina War⟩ War (1945–54) fought by Vietnamese Communists and nationalists against occupying armies, most notably the French. Following the Japanese defeat

(1945) in WW II, British and Chinese forces occupied the region. At the same time, however, Communist nationalist leader Ho Chi Minh proclaimed the Democratic Republic of Vietnam and began a war against the British and Chinese. French troops reoccupied Indochina (1946) and, after the breakdown of an agreement granting the Vietnamese republic a large measure of autonomy, fighting resumed (late Dec. 1946). This time it was between the French and the Communist nationalist (Vietminh) forces under Vo Nguyen Giap. Heavy fighting continued through 1947. After failing to come to terms with Ho Chi Minh, the French supported creation of an independent Vietnam (within the French Union) with Bao Dai as emperor (Mar. 8, 1949). The Vietminh continued fighting, however, drove the French from northern Vietnam (Oct. 1950), conquered parts of Laos (1953), and broke French military strength (1954) at Dien Bien Phu *(q.v.)*. Geneva Conference accords (signed July 21, 1954) ended the war, provided for partition of Vietnam, and promised elections for reunification by 1956. The US, which had been aiding the Bao Dai regime since 1950, did not sign the accord and thus opened the way for its involvement in the Vietnam War *(q.v.)*, sometimes called the Second Indochina War.

Indo-European Name applied to the large family of languages of Europe and southern and southwestern Asia, believed to have evolved from a common parent language, Proto-Indo-European, spoken sometime before 2000 BC. Indo-Iranian languages such as Persian and Sanskrit are members, as well as the Celtic, Germanic, Greek, Romance, and Slavic languages of Europe.

Indonesia (Republic of Indonesia, *formerly* Dutch East Indies) Country consisting of islands (Sumatra, Borneo, Java, and others) in the Malay Archipelago in the South Pacific. Its capital is Djakarta (on Java). Most Indonesians are descended from Malay and Papuan peoples. The islands were long under the influence of other cultures, notably the Chinese, Indian, and Muslim (from 14th–15 cent.). The period of European colonial domination began with the arrival of the Portuguese in the 16th cent. Key dates in the history of Indonesia include:

16TH CENT. Portuguese traders arrived to exploit the spice trade; established trading posts (from 1511).

1596–1600 Dutch and English traders arrived.

EARLY 17TH CENT. Dutch succeeded in driving out Portuguese and English; Dutch East India Company controlled region for next two centuries.

1623 Amboina massacre; English settlers executed by Dutch authorities.

1799 Dutch government assumed control of colony from the Dutch East India Company.

1811–16 British seized the territory during the Napoleonic Wars; restored to Dutch control afterward.

1916 Volksraad, an advisory council, formed by Dutch colonial government.

1922 Indonesia incorporated into the Dutch kingdom.

1927 Indonesian Nationalist party formed under Achmed Sukarno; marked rise of nationalist movement.

1942–45 WW II; Japan occupied Indonesia; nominal self-government.

1945 Sukarno took control (Aug.) of islands of Sumatra and Java; he and Muhammad Hatta proclaimed independent republic.

1945–49 War for independence.

1949 Dutch agreed to creation of the Republic of Indonesia; Sukarno elected president, Hatta premier.

1949 Independence granted (Dec. 27).

1956 Hatta fought with Sukarno and resigned.

1958 Unsuccessful revolts in Sumatra, Celebes, and other islands.

1960 Sukarno dissolved Parliament; took firm control of government.

1962 Sukarno seized control of Dutch New Guinea; UN negotiated transfer pending referendum.

1963 Dutch New Guinea transferred to Indonesia as West Irian.

1963–66 War with newly formed Federation of Malaysia; Sukarno launched sporadic guerrilla raids into territory.

1965 Indonesia withdrew from UN as Sukarno developed closer ties with Communist countries; Communist party in Indonesia gained strength.

1965 Communist coup attempted (Sept.) against army, which had powerful voice in government; Gen. Suharto blocked the coup and began taking control of government; relations with West later reestablished.

1965 Widespread massacres of Communists; hundreds of thousands killed (Oct.-Dec.).

1967 Sukarno forced out of office (Mar.) by National Assembly.

1967 Suharto began long term as president; restored order and began aggressive program to rebuild Indonesian economy; his pro-West policies resulted in substantial foreign aid.

1969 West Irian formally annexed.

1976 Pertamina, state-owned oil company, went bankrupt as Indonesian economic problems worsened.

1977 Release of 10,000 political prisoners jailed in 1965.

1978 Government crackdown against opposition criticism (Jan.); newspapers closed, university activity restricted.

1978 Suharto elected to third five-year term as president.

1979 Indonesia established center for Vietnamese "boat people"; provided services on temporary basis only.

indulgence Catholic theological term for the pardon and remission of temporal punishment due to sin. In the early church, severe penances were imposed upon penitent sinners. As time went on, the church relaxed the actual penalty, granting an "indulgence" instead by which the penitent received the same merit as if he had actually performed the penance. The church claims to be able to do this by drawing upon the storehouse of merit already acquired in the sight of God by the sacrifice of Jesus and by the virtue and penances of the saints. Indulgences are now granted for specific good works performed or prayers said. Abuses which crept into the granting of indulgences, specifically the buying and selling of them, was one of the issues which led to the revolt of M. Luther (1517) at the time of the Reformation *(q.v.)*.

Indulgence, Declaration of 1. A proclamation (1672) by the English king Charles II granting religious toleration for Nonconformists *(q.v.)*. Parliament, however, refused to accept terms of the declaration and voided it. **2.** Proclamation (1687) by the English king James II granting religious toleration for Catholics as well as Nonconformists. The resentment this proclamation aroused was one of the causes of the Glorious Revolution *(q.v.)* of 1688.

Indus Main river of Pakistan, rising in the Himalayas in Tibet and flowing southwest across Pakistan to the Arabian Sea. The use of its waters has been the cause of conflict between India and Pakistan. The prehistoric Indus valley civilization grew up along its banks.

Indus civilization ⟨Mohenjo-daro civilization⟩ Ancient civilization that flourished in the Indus river valley (*c*2500 BC–1500 BC). Excavations at Mohenjo-daro and Harappa in modern Pakistan have revealed a civilization as advanced as those of ancient Egypt and Mesopotamia.

Industrial Revolution Period that saw industry become the predominant force in European economic and social life (18th-19th cents.). This era was marked by the shift from agricultural and cot-

tage-industry forms of production to the factory system, the great increase in the use of machinery for production, a population shift that created great urban centers, and the marked dependence of laborers on their employers. The Industrial Revolution began in the British cotton textile industry and is generally dated from 1750 to 1850. Though the use of machinery was not unknown and though some factories were operating before 1750, this period saw the gradual changeover to an industrial society in Britain. Traditionally, certain inventions are associated with the beginning of industrialism, including J. Watt's steam engine, J. Kay's flying shuttle, J. Hargreaves' spinning jenny, S. Crompton's spinning mule, and Edmund Cartwright's power loom (all between 1733 and 1785). In succeeding years the Industrial Revolution spread to other countries: France after 1830; Germany after 1850; and the US principally after 1860.

industrial union A union or workers' organization known as a "vertical" union because of its acceptance of all types of workers in a given industry, whether skilled or unskilled, and regardless of specialization. Previously unions of a particular craft such as carpenters or fitters had been the norm. Industrial unions developed in Britain in the latter half of the 19th cent.

Industrial Workers of the World ⟨IWW⟩ ⟨Wobblies⟩ Radical labor union active mainly in the US. Founded (1905) in Chicago to promote syndicalism *(q.v.)*, the union was dedicated to the overthrow of capitalism and advocated general strikes and other tactics to gain this end. Composed largely of unskilled industrial workers, it conducted some 150 strikes in the early 1900s. The union's radical aims and opposition to US participation in WW I led to federal government prosecutions (1917–18) and to harassment during the Red Scare (1919). The organization ceased to be important in the 1920s, when its major concern was opposition to the new US Communist party. Leaders of the IWW included E. Debs (1855–1926), William ("Big Bill") Haywood (1869–1928) and D. De Leon (1852–1914).

Ingersoll, Robert Green 1833–99. An American humanistic philosopher, politician, and orator. He was a leading proponent of agnosticism and a critic of the Bible and Christianity.

Ingres, Jean Auguste Dominique 1780–1867. A French painter, one of the leading figures in French classical painting in the 19th cent.

Inkerman, Battle of Battle of the Crimean War *(q.v.)*, fought on November 5, 1854, at Inkerman, east of Sevastopol. There the English and French defeated the Russians, who had unexpectedly attacked the English camp.

Inner Mongolia ⟨Inner Mongolian Autonomous Region⟩ Autonomous region of the present People's Republic of China, located in the steppe region of northeastern China. It is the traditional home of nomadic Mongol tribes.

Inner Mongolian Autonomous Region *See* **Inner Mongolia**

Inness, George 1825–94. American landscape painter, whose works were influenced by the Hudson River and Barbizon schools of painting *(qq.v.).*

Innocent I, Saint *d.* 417. Italian pope (401–417), who upheld Saint John Chrysostom and condemned Pelagianism *(q.v.).* Rome was sacked by Alaric I during his pontificate (410).

Innocent II ⟨Papareschi, Gregorio⟩ *d.* 1143. Roman pope (1130–43). Elected by a minority of cardinals to succeed Honorius II, he was forced to flee Rome. He regained his office in 1138, convened the Second Lateran Council *(q.v.)* of 1139, and condemned P. Abelard and Arnold of Brescia.

Innocent III ⟨*orig.* Lotario di Segni⟩ 1161–1216. Italian-born pope (1198–1216), successor to Celestine III. Under Innocent's reign, the papacy achieved its greatest power. Continuing the policies of Gregory VII regarding supremacy of the pope over secular rulers, Innocent became involved in struggles with European kings to enforce his authority. He vied with Holy Roman Emperor Otto IV, excommunicated him (1210), and finally crowned Frederick II in his place (1215). In England, he forced acceptance of his favorite as archbishop of Canterbury and thereby began a struggle with King John. He excommunicated John (1209), ultimately forcing John in 1213 to accept the sovereignty of the pope and to agree to pay him tribute. In addition to asserting papal authority over these and other European sovereigns, Innocent also preached the Fourth Crusade *(q.v.),* which resulted in the creation of the Latin Empire of Constantinople *(q.v.);* promoted the Albigensian Crusade *(q.v.);* called the great Fourth Lateran Council *(q.v.);* and gave papal approval to the missions of both the Franciscans and Dominicans.

Innocent IV ⟨Fieschi, Sinibaldo de'⟩ *d.* 1254. Pope (1243–54), who convened the First Council of Lyons *(q.v.)* in 1245 and fought to maintain papal sovereignty distinct from the Holy Roman Empire and the Hohenstaufen *(q.v.)* emperors.

Innocent VIII ⟨Cibó, Giovanni Battista⟩ 1432–92. Pope (1484–92), who authorized the Inquisition to bring charges against witches in Germany (1484). He maintained peace with the Ottoman Empire and temporarily halted the Turkish advance into

Europe by keeping the brother and rival of Sultan Beyazid II prisoner.

Innocent XI ⟨Odescalchi, Benedetto⟩ 1611–89. Pope (1676–89). Personally saintly, Innocent quarreled with Louis XIV of France over the latter's claim to be able to administer vacant church sees. As a result, the king convoked a synod and issued (1673) the famous four articles on Gallicanism *(q.v.).* The two also clashed over the king's 1685 revocation of the Edict of Nantes, since Innocent believed that the Protestants had to be tolerated. He also condemned quietism *(q.v.).*

Inquisition Name of two historic Roman Catholic tribunals. **1.** The medieval Inquisition was established (1233) by Pope Gregory X in response to the spread of heretical sects, such as the Albigenses and Waldenses in northern Italy, southern France, and Germany. Judges of the Inquisition were chosen from among the Dominicans to try and judge cases of heresy, then considered intolerable by civil and ecclesiastical authorities alike. If found guilty of heresy, the heretic was turned over to secular authorities for punishment. Though burning at the stake was the ultimate penalty for unrecanted heresy, this penalty was uncommon in medieval times. The usual punishment was penance, fine, or imprisonment. Torture was used in the civil courts of the time and was also admitted in trials for heresy by Innocent IV (1252), despite earlier papal denunciations of torture. During the Catholic Reformation, the functions of the medieval Inquisition were assigned to the Holy Office (1542). Called the Roman Inquisition, it was active against Protestantism and heard charges of heresy against Galileo in what became a famous trial. Its typical function in modern times was the examination of theological writings. The Holy Office was replaced by the Roman Congregation for the Doctrine of the Faith in 1965. **2.** Spanish Inquisition. This was a quasi-ecclesiastical tribunal established in 1478 by King Ferdinand and Queen Isabella primarily to examine converted Jews, and later converted Muslims, and punish those who were insincere. Pope Sixtus IV reluctantly approved the Spanish Inquisition, which was largely controlled by the Spanish monarchs. The Grand Inquisitor was always a Dominican, however, and the first and most notorious was T. de Torquemada. The Spanish Inquisition was much harsher than the medieval Inquisition and the death penalty was more often exacted, sometimes in mass *autos-da-fé.* It judged cases of polygamy, seduction, usury, and other crimes, and was active in Spain and her colonies. Estimates of its victims have ranged from less than 4,000 to more than

30,000 during its existence. By the 17th cent. the harshness of the Inquisition was greatly reduced and it was abolished altogether in 1834.

Instruction of Catherine the Great ⟨Nakaz⟩ Document written (1767) by Catherine the Great of Russia, containing her political views, largely borrowed from C. de Montesquieu, to guide a commission convened (1768) to reform the Russian government. The commission did not produce any meaningful reforms.

Instrument of Government English constitution under which O. Cromwell ruled England as lord protector between Dec., 1653 and May, 1657. It vested executive authority in the lord protector and a council of state, created a unicameral Parliament, and disenfranchised all Catholics and rebels. The unwillingness of Parliament to ratify it led to its replacement by the Humble Petition and Advice *(q.v.)*, but it is notable as the first written constitution of a modern European state.

Insull, Samuel 1859–1938. English-born American public-utilities magnate. He worked as secretary to inventor T. A. Edison, and later managed Edison's growing electrical equipment empire. He headed a giant Midwest utility complex until 1932, when economic reverses caused its collapse.

integration *See* **segregation**

intelligentsia Term applied to the group of 19th-cent., middle-class Russians who were educated and influenced by Western ideas, and who sought social and political reform. The intelligentsia influenced the development of 20th-cent. revolutionary movements in Russia.

International **1.** First (1864–81): Socialist labor federation (founded at London, Sept. 28, 1864) that quickly came under the domination of K. Marx. It was called the International Workingmen's Association. While its express purpose was to foment a Socialist workers' revolution, it failed to play an active role in labor unrest of the period. Split (1876) by a power struggle between Marx and the anarchist M. Bakunin, it was largely defunct by 1881. **2.** Second (1889–1914): Loose federation of Socialist groups and labor unions (founded at Paris, 1889). Though committed to an eventual Socialist revolution, the group generally supported parliamentary democracy. The anarchists were formally ousted (1896). The chief aim of the international, however, was its opposition to war, and the outbreak of WW I split the organization along national lines. **3.** Third ⟨Communist International⟩ ⟨Comintern⟩ (1919–43): Organization of Communist parties (founded at Moscow, Mar., 1919), following the Russian revolution. Formed by Russian Communist leader N. Lenin, the group was intended to oppose other Socialist factions

and to foment worldwide revolution. The Comintern, under Soviet domination, became involved in ideological struggles and, in 1943, J. Stalin dissolved the Comintern to ensure Allied support in the fight against Nazi Germany.

International Confederation of Free Trade Unions *See* **labor unions**

International Court of Justice UN judicial body organized in 1945 and superseding the Permanent Court of International Justice, the judicial arm of the League of Nations. The idea for an international court stemmed from the Permanent Court of Arbitration, set up (1899) at the Hague Conference *q.v.)*, to provide a peaceful means for settling international disputes. A number of cases were settled by the organization in the years prior to WW I, and in 1921 the Permanent Court of International Justice (World Court) was organized under the auspices of the League of Nations. This court was created to exercise judicial functions (albeit limited by consent of the nations involved) rather than simply offering a forum for negotiation and arbitration. The International Court of Justice replaced this court (1945) after the UN was created and is likewise referred to as the World Court. The court is based at The Hague and consists of 15 judges selected by the UN Security Council and the General Assembly.

International Federation of Trade Unions *See* **labor unions**

International Geophysical Year ⟨IGY⟩ 18-month period from July, 1957, through Dec., 1958, devoted to the cooperative study of the earth and its environment by some 66 participating nations. During the IGY, the USSR launched its first satellite, the Van Allen radiation belt was discovered by a US satellite, and important discoveries about the ocean floor were made, as were many new discoveries about Antarctica *(q.v.)*. A 12-nation cooperative agreement on Antarctica was signed as a result of the IGY.

International Monetary Fund International organization, conceived in 1944 at the Bretton Woods Conference *(q.v.)* and associated with the United Nations as a specialized agency (1945) to help provide stability of international exchange rates and aid member nations in international transactions.

International Peace Conference of 1899 *See* **Hague Conferences**

International Peace Conference of 1907 *See* **Hague Conferences**

International Style Architectural movement. Popular in Europe and America in the 1920s, it employed modern materials, emphasized smooth, light lines and walls of glass with steel supports.

Among its adherents were W. Gropius and Le Corbusier.

International Workingmen's Association *See* **International (First)**

Interregnum, The Great The period in the history of the Holy Roman Empire between the death of the last Hohenstaufen *(q.v.)* emperor, Conrad IV, in 1254, and the election of the first Hapsburg *(q.v.)* emperor, Count Rudolf of Hapsburg, in 1273. There was no recognized ruler of Germany during this period, and it was characterized by a growth in the power of the princes.

Intolerable Acts Restrictive acts passed by the British Parliament in 1774 in retaliation for the Boston Tea Party *(q.v.)*. Four acts closed Boston harbor until restitution had been made for the tea destroyed; revoked the Massachusetts charter and established military government; removed British Colonial officials from the jurisdiction of Colonial courts; and provided for the quartering of British troops in occupied dwellings. A fifth act, the Quebec Act, which had been under consideration before, placed the territory between the Ohio and the Mississippi under the jurisdiction of the province of Quebec. These Intolerable Acts led directly to the convening to the First Continental Congress *(q.v.)* later in the same year.

Inukai, Ki Tsuyoshi 1855–1932. Japanese politician, president of the Seiyukai party (1929–32), and prime minister (Jan.–May, 1932). His assassination marked the rise of military and end of party control of Japanese government.

Investiture Controversy Power struggle (11th–12th cents.) between the Holy Roman Empire and the papacy. The controversy centered on the rift (from 1075) between Emperor Henry IV and Pope Gregory VII over "lay investiture" and was not finally settled until issue of the Concordat of Worms *(q.v.)* of 1122. At the time of the controversy, bishops and other clerics had both secular and clerical powers over ecclesiastical domains. Both the emperor and the pope were involved in their installation (investiture), a practice known as lay investiture. The practice led to abuses of the clerical offices and, reacting to a movement for reform, Pope Gregory abolished (1075) lay investiture. In the struggle that followed, Henry was excommunicated, civil war between factions of rebellious nobles broke out (over this and other issues) within the Holy Roman Empire, and Henry attacked Rome (1081–82). Under Emperor Henry V, the controversy continued until a compromise was finally arranged (1122) with Pope Calixtus II in the Concordat of Worms.

Invincible Armada *See* **Spanish Armada**

Io Greek mythological daughter of King Inachus of Argos. Beloved of Zeus, she was changed into a heifer by his jealous wife Hera and placed under the watch of the 100-eyed Argus. She is identified with the Egyptian Isis *(q.v.)*, and the Ionian Sea was named for her.

Ion *fl.* 5th cent. BC. Greek poet. Only fragments of his poems and plays remain, but he was once awarded third prize in a drama competition won by Euripides.

Ionesco, Eugene 1912–. Romanian-born French playwright. In plays such as *The Bald Prima Donna* (1950) and *Rhinoceros* (1960) he is considered to have written the purest and most characteristic works in the modern Theater of the Absurd *(q.v.)*.

Ionia Ancient district of Asia Minor on the Aegean Sea in modern western Turkey. Colonized by the Ionian Greeks (c1000 BC), it was taken by Croesus (6th cent. BC) and then by the Persians under Cyrus the Great. The Ionian revolt against Persia resulted in the Persian Wars *(q.v.)*. The Ionian cities fell to Alexander the Great (334 BC) and later to Rome, and were destroyed as Greek cities by the Ottoman conquest (15th cent. AD).

Ionian School Early school of Greek philosophy, composed of philosophers who were active (6th–5th cents. BC) in Ionia. They held divergent views, though in general they attempted to explain the world around them in terms of matter and physical forces. Among the thinkers of this school were Thales, Anaximander, Anaximenes, Anaxagoras, Heracleitus, and Diogenes of Apollonia.

Ionic order Greek architectural style. The Ionic is one of the major styles of early Greek architecture. It is characterized by slender fluted columns topped by a scroll-shaped capital, and had developed by the 6th cent. BC.

Iowa State in the north central US (pop. 2,913,400), the 29th state. Originally inhabited by the Sioux Indians, the area was explored by Père J. Marquette (1637–1675), Louis Jolliet (1645–1700), R. de La Salle (1643–87), and Julien Dubuque (1762–1810), who formed the first settlement, Dubuque, in 1833. Iowa was acquired by the US in the Louisiana Purchase *(q.v.)* of 1803 and became the Iowa Territory in 1838. The rich prairie soil attracted many settlers, and Iowa became a state in 1846. The state constitution was adopted in 1851. Iowa is noted for its abundant corn and other grains. Des Moines is the capital and largest city.

Iphigenia In Greek legend, the daughter of Agamemnon and Clytemnestra, sacrificed by her father at Aulis to save the Greek fleet, becalmed on its way to Troy. In another legend she is saved and carried off to Tauris. Euripides wrote famous plays on both legends.

Ipsus, Battle of Battle fought at Ipsus, in Phrygia, Asia Minor, in 301 BC, in which Antigonus I was slain by Lysimachus and Seleucus. The battle marked the end of Alexander's empire.

Iqbal, (Sir) Muhammad 1873–1938. Indian poet, philosopher, and political leader. He urged the establishment of an independent Muslim state, and is considered the spiritual father of modern Pakistan (q.v.).

IRA See **Irish Republican Army**

Irala, Domingo Martínez de d. 1556 or 1557. Spanish soldier and first governor of Paraguay (1537–42, 1544–56). He was the first governor in the Americas elected by a free vote of the colonists.

Iranian revolution See **Iran** (1978)

Iran Republic, located in the Mideast between Iraq and Afghanistan. Its capital is Teheran. "Iran" is the modern name of Persia (since 1935) and its emergence as a modern nation may be said to have begun with the overthrow of the Kajar dynasty (1925) by Reza Shah Pahlavi. Iran has inherited Persian cultural traditions and has long been a center of the Shi'ite sect of the Islamic religion. Under the Pahlevi dynasty, programs to modernize Iran were actively pursued. However, the pace of modernization, as well as discontent with repressive rule by the shahs, led to the Iranian revolution of 1979. Radical Muslim fundamentalists seized control of the government, attacked Western and modernist influences, and set about reviving traditional Muslim society. (For history prior to 1925, see Persia.) Key events in Iranian history are:

1921 Reza Pahlavi, a soldier, took power in a coup ending British control over Iran (then a League of Nations mandate); led military dictatorship.

1925 Reza Pahlavi elected hereditary shah; founded Pahlavi dynasty (in power 1925–79).

1925–41 Reza Shah Pahlavi in power; instituted reforms, promoted industrialization and advance of education.

1935 Name of the country officially changed from Persia to Iran by Reza Shah Pahlavi.

1936 Modernization begun; shah's wife and daughters appeared in public without veils, breaking tradition.

1937 Treaty with Iraq; ceded control of the strategic Shatt al Arab River to Iraq.

1941–45 WW II, Iran occupied by Britain and USSR.

1941 Reza Shah Pahlavi, forced out because of his German ties, abdicated in favor of his son Mohammed Reza Shah Pahlavi (Sept. 16).

1941–79 Mohammed Reza Shah Pahlavi reigned.

1943 Teheran Conference (Nov.); US, USSR, and Britain agree to guarantee independence of Iran after the war.

1945–46 Short-lived Soviet republics formed in Azerbaijan and Kurdistan, as a result of agitation by USSR.

1946 Soviet troops withdrawn from Iran, following Iranian demands at the UN for their departure; Soviets were granted oil concessions.

1951 Premier Gen. Ali Razmara, an opponent of movement to nationalize oil industry, assassinated (Mar. 7); succeeded by Muhammad Mosaddegh.

1951 Premier Mosaddegh, with aid of his National Front movement, nationalized oil industry (Apr.); created National Iranian Oil Company (NIOC).

1952 British blockade nearly brought NIOC operations to a halt; Mosaddegh first ousted, then returned to power, whereupon the shah fled, leaving Mosaddegh in control.

1953 Mosaddegh forced from office (Aug.); shah returned with aid of Western powers; operation of the NIOC placed in the hands of a Western consortium.

1955 Joined Baghdad Pact, organized against Soviet expansion; received considerable US aid during 1950s and 1960s.

1960s Shah instituted White Revolution reform movement; aimed especially at land reform.

1960 Iran became a founding member of OPEC.

1963 Shah's modernization plans approved in a referendum; women received right to vote; unrest among some religious groups, alienated by reform movement.

1965 Attempted assassination of the shah (Jan.).

1969 Iran renounced 1937 treaty with Iraq as tensions mounted between the two countries; border clashes occurred sporadically.

1971 Program to bolster Iran's military capabilities began after Britain withdrew from Persian Gulf (1971); US and British aid increased and soon made Iranian military strongest in Mideast.

1971 2,500th anniversary of Persian Empire celebrated in Iran (Oct. 12).

1973 Shah fully nationalized oil industry in Iran (Mar 20); Western consortium agreed in return for long-term oil contracts (May).

1973 Iran did not participate in Arab oil embargo; used increased profits to finance modernization.

1976 Iran became a leader of OPEC members that raised oil prices.

1978 Muslim fundamentalists, opposed to government reforms, sparked riots in Teheran; called for removal of shah (May 11).

1978 Martial law was imposed in many cities (Sept. 8).

1978 Shah yielded to continuing unrest; named Shahpur Bakhtiar prime minister of a civilian government (Dec. 27); opposition by Muslim fundamentalists continued.

1979 Shah fled Iran, leaving behind Bakhtiar's caretaker government (Jan. 16).

1979 Ayatollah Khomeini, leader of the Muslim fundamentalist rebels, returned to Iran after 15-year exile (Feb. 1).

1979 Khomeini formed opposition government in defiance of Prime Minister Bakhtiar (Feb. 5).

1979 Khomeini supporters toppled the Bakhtiar government after days of armed clashes; imperial palace invaded and some army officers executed (Feb. 11).

1979 Khomeini instituted puritanical and repressive Islamic fundamentalist regime; industry and financial institutions nationalized; Islamic traditions revived and most Western cultural influences banned.

1979 Unrest among the Kurds in northwestern Iran; Khomeini government granted concessions to Kurds (Mar. 18).

1979 Khomeini government executed 21 officials accused of plotting against the government (Aug. 8).

1979 Exiled shah arrived in US for medical treatment (Oct. 22).

1979–81 Hostage Crisis; self-styled Iranian "students" seized US Embassy and held Americans as prisoners; Khomeini government exploited incident to inflame anti-Americanism and thus strengthen its hold on Iran.

1979 Mehdi Bazargan, head of provisional government, pledged to establish an Islamic republic, resigned.

1979 Islamic constitution adopted; Shi'ite Islam became state religion and Ayatollah Khomeini was designated religious and political leader (Dec. 3).

1979 Exiled shah left the US for Panama (Dec. 15).

1980 Abolhassan Bani-Sadr in office as first president elected under the Islamic regime (Feb.).

1980 Exiled shah left Panama for Egypt (Mar. 23).

1980 US military mission to rescue hostages failed (Apr. 25).

1980 Military coup foiled (July 10).

1980 Shah died in exile in Egypt (July 27).

1980 Months of Iranian-Iraqi border clashes led to an all-out attack by Iraq on Iranian airfields; Iraq advanced in the Gulf area toward Abadan (Sept. 22).

1980 Iran-Iraq war extended to the northern provinces; Iraq invaded Iranian Kurdistan (Dec. 26).

1981 Iranian Army mounted a counteroffensive against Iraq (Jan. 5).

1981 Khomeini ousted President Bani-Sadr, as tensions increased between moderates and radical Muslim fundamentalists (June 22).

1981 Top Islamic government officials killed by bomb in Teheran (June 28).

1981 Bomb explosion killed the newly elected president, Muhammad Ali Raja'i, the prime minister, and three other top government officials (Aug. 30); Marxist opposition group blamed.

1981 Hojutolislam Ali Khomeini in office as president (Oct. 2), second president in three months.

1982 Iran claimed to have expelled all Iraqi troops (May) from Iranian territory as war with Iraq continued; Iran counterattacked into Iraq.

Iraq ⟨Republic of Iraq⟩ Country located in the Mideast and lying between the Caspian Sea and the Persian Gulf. Its capital is Baghdad. Modern Iraq occupies roughly the region of ancient Mesopotamia, known as the "Cradle of Civilization." The Sumerian, Akkadian, Babylonian, and Assyrian cultures all arose in this region. Later, the area was famous as a center of Arab Muslim civilization and Baghdad became the capital of the Empire of the Caliphate *(q.v.)* under the Abbasid dynasty of caliphs. The region was controlled by the Ottoman Turks in the 16th–20th cent. The British took it during WW I and began the exploitation of Iraq's oil resources, eventually making the country one of the world's major oil producers. Key events in Iraqi history include:

1831 Ottoman Province of Iraq established, subdivided into the three vilayets of Mosul, Baghdad, and Basra.

1901 British obtained concession to begin exploitation of Iraq's oil wealth.

1918 WW I; British invaded and occupied region of Iraq during war with Ottoman Empire.

1920 Iraq made a British League of Nations mandate at San Remo Conference (Apr.); mandate confirmed by the Treaty of Sèvres.

1920 Armed rebellion against British rule (July); quelled at great cost.

1921 Organized as a kingdom; Faisal I confirmed as king in a plebiscite (Aug.).

1921–33 Faisal I reigned as king in Iraq.

1924 Twenty-year treaty of alliance signed between Iraq and Britain (Oct.), providing for continued British bases.

1925 First Iraqi parliamentary elections (Mar.).

1930 Treaty of alliance with Britain for 25 years; Britain to support Iraq's admission to the League of Nations.

1931 Iraq Petroleum Company, a consortium of American, British, Dutch, and French interests, obtained concession to exploit Mosul oil fields; pipeline to the Mediterranean opened three years later.

1932 Iraq became a member of the League of Nations (Oct.).

1933–39 King Ghazi I reigned; succeeded his father, Faisal I.

1936–41 Period of political turmoil; seven coups staged.

1939 King Ghazi killed in an automobile accident (Apr.); succeeded by his infant son, Faisal II, under a regent.

1939–58 Faisal II reigned.

1941 Rashid Ali al-Ghailani, leader of a pro-Nazi group, seized power (Apr. 4); routed by British troops, he fled and British control was restored (May 31).

1943 Rise of Ba'ath ("Renaissance"), Arab nationalist-Socialist party.

1944 Pro-British premier, Gen. Nuri es-Said, proposed a new country, "Greater Syria," to be made up of Iraq, Jordan, Palestine and Syria (Aug.).

1945 Iraq joined the Arab League.

1948 Arab-Israeli War; Iraq joined in Arab attack on newly created Israeli state (May 15); Iraq declined to sign any truce with Israel.

1954 All political parties dissolved by Nuri es-Said.

1955 Baghdad Pact signed, forming alliance that later became the Central Treaty Organization.

1958 Arab Union formed (Feb.); Iraq and Jordan joined in federation.

1958 Republic declared after coup (Feb. 14); King Faisal II killed and Arab Union dissolved.

1958–63 Gen. Abdul Karim Kassem, leader of the coup, in power as premier; established ties with Soviets, pressed Iraqi claim to Kuwait and Iranian Shatt-al-Arab.

1959 Iraq withdrew from Baghdad Pact.

1962 Kurdish revolt led by Mustafa al-Barzani gained control of much of northern Iraq; autono-

mous Kurdistan sought; fight continued sporadically in the 1960s and 1970s.

1963 Overthrow and execution of Kassem by Ba'ath-dominated coup led by Col. Abdul Salam Aref (Feb.); Aref later instituted purely military rule (Nov.).

1966 President Abdul Salam Aref killed in an airplane crash; succeeded by his brother Abdul Rahman Aref (Apr.).

1968 President Abdul Rahman Aref forced out by Gen. Ahmad Hassan al-Bakr in a bloodless coup (July).

1968–79 Ahmad Hassan al-Bakr in power.

1970 Right-wing coup attempt blocked by government (Jan. 20).

1972 Treaty of friendship with USSR signed.

1972 Iraq Petroleum Company nationalized by government (June 1).

1973 Unsuccessful coup attempt.

1973 Fourth Arab-Israeli War fought between Israel and allied Arab states (Oct.); joined in oil embargo against Israel's allies.

1974 Border war with Iran.

1974 Kurdish rebels took control of territory along border with Turkey.

1975 Government troops crushed revolt by Kurds (Mar. 22) after withdrawal of Iranian support.

1979 Bombing of Kurdish villages in Iran in retaliation for continued resistance against the central government.

1979 Saddam Hussein in office as president after ill health forced Ahmad Hassan al-Bakr to resign (July 16).

1980– Full-scale war with Iran broke out; Iraqi troops crossed border into Iran (Sept. 22) after bombing Teheran and Iranian airfields.

1981 Israeli fighters destroyed a nuclear reactor being constructed near Baghdad (June 7).

1982 Iraqi troops driven from Iran (May) as the Iraq-Iran war continued.

Ireland ⟨Republic of Ireland; *formerly* Irish Free State, Eire⟩ Independent country located in the western part of the British Isles and occupying all but the northeastern section (Northern Ireland) of a large island. Invaded by the Celts in the 4th cent. BC, Ireland was subjected to raids by the Norsemen from the 9th–11th cent. The English took control of Ireland in the 12th cent. and thus began the long struggle between the Irish and their English overlords. The Irish finally gained independence from Britain in 1922. However, the long-standing hatred of the British has found new expression in the movement to unite Protestant Northern Ireland (created in 1920) with the Catholic Republic of Ireland. The movement began in the 1960s and since then the Irish Republican Army (IRA) has waged a brutal terrorist campaign aimed at Irish Protestants and the British. Key dates in the history of Ireland include:

c400 BC Ireland inhabited by Celtic tribes.

AD c430 St. Patrick introduced Christianity.

c500–800 Golden Age of Irish culture; native Gaelic arts and literature developed; Gaelic culture spread to Scotland; monasteries established and Irish missionaries sent abroad.

c524–528 Saint Bridgit of Ireland founded the first nunnery at Kildare.

9TH–11TH CENT. Norse invasions.

1002–14 Brian Boru ruled as high king of Ireland.

1014 B. Boru defended Dublin and destroyed the power of the Norse invaders at the Battle of Clontarf (Apr. 23).

11TH–12TH CENT. Period of warfare between rival clans.

1155 Henry II of England authorized to take possession of Ireland by order of papal bull; document may have been forged.

1169 English conquest of Ireland began; soldiers sent to restore deposed Irish king of Leinster.

1171 Henry II led a large army into Ireland; his overlordship recognized by some; began period of English rule, based at Dublin; feudalism introduced; wars with Irish opposed to British rule began.

13TH CENT. An Anglo-Irish Parliament established; native Irish were excluded from it.

1315 Scots invaded Ireland; led by Edward Bruce, they allied with local chieftans; undermined English rule.

14TH–15TH CENT. English power effectively limited to an area around Dublin called the Pale (where Irish law and customs were forbidden).

1455–85 Anglo-Norman noblemen of the Pale of Ireland participated in Wars of the Roses; their power in Ireland further weakened by the wars.

1494 Tudor king Henry VII renewed efforts to control Ireland; sent a new English governor, Sir Edward Poynings.

1495 Poyning's Law passed by Irish Parliament; Irish Parliaments thereafter to be subject to English Parliament.

1541 Henry VIII created a Protestant "Church of Ireland," but most of the inhabitants remained Catholic; Catholic monasteries abolished.

16TH–17TH CENT. Penal laws passed to prohibit practice of Roman Catholicism in Britain and Ireland.

16TH–17TH CENT. Large-scale colonization of Ireland by Protestants; many Catholics driven off

their lands; confiscation of Irish lands during 17th cent. created Irish tenant farm system, with lands held by absentee landlords.

1603 Tyrone's rebellion crushed; Ulster and Munster counties devasted.

1650 O. Cromwell ruthlessly crushed an Irish rebellion that had begun in 1641; many thousands killed; more Irish lands confiscated.

1690 Battle of the Boyne near Dublin; English king James II, a Catholic who was deposed during the Glorious Revolution (1688), was defeated by his successor, William III; James was supported by French and Irish Catholics.

1782 H. Grattan won independence for Ireland's Parliament with repeal of Poyning's Law, but Catholics were denied the right to hold office.

1798 Rebellion by Irish Protestant Wolfe Tone; revolt failed despite aid from revolutionary France.

1801 George III and Prime Minister W. Pitt promoted the Union of Ireland and England to solve Irish problem; abolition of the Irish Parliament and legislative union in a United Kingdom of Great Britain and Ireland effected.

1829 Catholic Emancipation Act; penal laws directed against Catholics repealed.

1845–49 Great Potato Famine; hundreds of thousands starved to death; nearly two million emigrated to the US.

c1858 Fenian movement organized; attempted to secure Irish independence; eventually superseded by Sinn Fein.

1869 Anglican church in Ireland formally dissolved.

FROM 1870 Rise of the Home Rule movement for self-government: Home Rule became a major controversy (from late 1800s); opposed by Irish Protestants.

1870–1903 Irish Land Acts passed by British Parliament to aid tenant farmers.

1899 Sinn Fein, nationalist political party, founded by A. Griffith to secure Irish independence.

1916 Irish Republican Army (IRA) formed.

1916 Easter Rebellion broke out; suppressed after fierce fighting; leaders executed, but rebellion led to fall of the government of H. Asquith and eventual establishment of the Irish Free State.

1916 R. Casement executed for seeking German aid in establishing Irish independence.

1918 Dail Eireann (Irish assembly) created by Sinn Fein members who had been elected to British Parliament and who had refused to take their seats; Irish republic proclaimed.

1919–21 Guerrilla war between Irish rebels and British government forces.

1920 British Black and Tans employed brutal measures against Irish revolutionaries.

1922 Irish Free State established (Jan.) as dominion in the British Commonwealth; northern counties of Ulster remained united with Britain.

1922–32 William T. Cosgrave in office as first president of the executive council.

1926 Fianna Fail party founded to sever all ties with Britain.

1937 Independence (as "Eire") declared, though ties with the British Commonwealth were retained.

1937–48 Eamon de Valera in office as first prime minister of Eire.

1939–45 WW II; Eire remained neutral.

1949 The Republic of Ireland proclaimed, replacing Eire; withdrawal from the British Commonwealth and final independence from Britain (Apr. 18).

1955 Ireland joined the UN.

1959–73 E. de Valera served as president of Ireland.

1960s IRA terrorism began in earnest in an effort to unite Northern Ireland to the Republic of Ireland.

1966–73 John Lynch in office as prime minister; moved against IRA terrorists.

1972 Emergency powers for government approved by legislature in face of increased terrorism in Ireland (Dec. 2).

1976 More stringent antiterrorist laws passed by the republic after the assassination of the British ambassador.

1977–79 Lynch in office as prime minister; advocated unification with Northern Ireland (1978).

1979 Charles J. Haughey in office as prime minister, following resignation of John Lynch (Dec.).

1981 IRA prisoners in Northern Ireland's Maze Prison began fasts to the death in order to dramatize the cause of Irish unity.

1981 Garret FitzGerald in office as prime minister.

1982 Haughey returned to office as prime minister.

Ireland, John 1838–1918. US Catholic leader and first archbishop of St. Paul, Minn. (1888–1918). Ordained in 1861, he became a spokesman for Catholic immigrants, encouraging their integration and westward migration. He favored government support for Catholic schools, and was a spokesman for liberal Catholicism.

Ireland, William Henry 1777–1835. English forger of documents and manuscripts of William Shakespeare. His forgeries were discovered (1796), and he admitted to the hoax.

Irenaeus, Saint AD 125–c202. Early Catholic theologian. Irenaeus was bishop of Lyons and a Father of the church. He opposed Gnosticism (q.v.) eloquently in his work *Against Heresies,* one of the earliest Christian writings to treat doctrine systematically and one of the most important early witnesses to the ancient primacy of Rome over other Christian churches.

Irene c752–803. Byzantine empress. She served as regent for her son Constantine VI from 780 to 790 and in 797 deposed him and had him blinded. She opposed the Iconoclasts, and restored use of icons in the Eastern church. She was deposed in 802.

Ireton, Henry 1611–51. English soldier and Parliamentarian. The son-in-law of O. Cromwell, Ireton signed Charles I's death warrant. He later assisted Cromwell in dispossessing the Irish and establishing English settlers.

Irigoyen, Hipólito 1850?–1933. Argentine political leader. As head of the Radical party, he worked for electoral reform, and served as president from 1916 to 1922. Reelected in 1928, he was overthrown in 1930.

Iris Mythological Greek goddess of the rainbow, and messenger of the gods.

Irish Free State Name used by the Republic of Ireland from 1922 to 1937; that is, during the period that Ireland had dominion status within the British Empire. (*See also* Ireland [1922–1937].)

Irish Land Acts Legislation passed (1870–1903) for the benefit of Irish tenant farmers. The acts, initiated by W. E. Gladstone, were designed to curtail landlord abuse and provide incentives for peasant proprietorship.

Irish Republican Army ⟨IRA⟩ Irish nationalist organization dedicated to the creation of a single unified Irish state. Organized from the elements dispersed during the Easter Rebellion (q.v.) of 1916, it became the political arm of the Sinn Fein (q.v.) party, and opposed dominion status after the creation of the Irish Free State in 1922. It declined after its former supporter E. de Valera took over the Irish government and because of its opposition to the Allies in WW II, and was eventually outlawed by both Irish governments. In 1969, it launched new terrorist measures in Northern Ireland which the British government was not able to quell after a dozen years. However, the IRA was by then split into "officials," advocating a Socialist Ireland by democratic means, and the "provisionals," advocating terrorism.

Iron Act British law passed (1750) to limit the growth of the iron industry in the American colonies. It prohibited construction of slitting and plating mills and steel furnaces. It aimed to increase the export of iron ore from the colonies to Britain but had only a limited success.

Iron Age Period in the development of human culture in which iron came to be used predominantly for making tools and weapons. The Iron Age, which succeeded the Bronze Age *(q.v.)*, began at various times in various locations. Widespread use of iron is generally thought to have begun in the Near East and it was the Hittites *(q.v.)* who are credited with discovering the technique of tempering iron. Following the breakup of the Hittite Empire (*c*1200 BC), ironworking techniques were spread through Europe and Asia Minor. By the 5th cent. BC, the use of iron was well established in Europe.

Iron Chancellor *See* **Bismarck, Otto Eduard Leopold von**

ironclad Warship built during the mid-19th cent. fitted with iron plates. This type of ship was first used by the French during the Crimean War and later employed by both sides in the US Civil War. Ironclads were replaced at the end of the century by all-metal warships.

iron curtain Name applied to the Soviet Union's policy of limiting Western information and influence within its borders and those of its Eastern European satellites after WW II. The term was coined by W. Churchill and used in a speech at Fulton, Missouri (Mar. 6, 1946).

Iron Guard Romanian fascist group, founded 1924. Organized in military fashion by Corneliu Zelea-Codreanu (1899?–1938), the group assassinated the Romanian premier (1933). Officially banned thereafter, it continued as the "All-for-the-Fatherland" party. In 1938 King Carol II arrested Zelea-Codreanu and other leaders. The group then helped I. Antonescu take power (1940) in Romania, but they soon turned against him and rebelled (1941). Following suppression of the group by Antonescu and the fall of Germany in WW II, the group disappeared.

Iron Mask, Man in the *See* **Man in the Iron Mask**

Iroquois Confederacy ⟨Iroquois League⟩ ⟨League of Five Nations⟩ Confederation of Indian tribes important in US Colonial history. It was composed of five tribes (a sixth, the Tuscarora, joined *c*1722) which occupied Northeast woodlands from Maine to the Great Lakes region. Formed sometime in the 16th cent., the Confederacy was well organized and proved highly effective in warfare. In the 17th cent., it drove off rival tribes, including the Huron, Neutral Nation, and Erie *(qq.v.)*. In the French and Indian Wars (17th–18th cents.) they generally served British interests against the

French. During the American Revolution, the Confederacy split, with most tribes taking the British side. They took part in the Battle of Oriskany, the Wyoming Massacre, and Cherry Valley Raid *(qq.v.)*, but were finally defeated (1779) in New York by an American retaliatory force. Thereafter the Confederacy ceased to be important. The six tribes of the Confederacy were: Mohawk, Seneca, Onondaga, Oneida, Cayuga, and Tuscarora.

Iroquois League *See* **Iroquois Confederacy**

irredentism Originally an Italian nationalist movement that aimed to add to Italy all territories inhabited by Italian-speaking people not included at the time of the unification of Italy (1870–71). This was considered *terra irredenta* ("unredeemed land"), and included the Trentino, Trieste, Istria, Fiume, and parts of Dalmatia, most of which Italy finally acquired after WW I. But the term "irredentism" has since been applied to any nationalist movement seeking to incorporate territory on the basis of historical, ethnic, and geographic considerations.

Irving, Edward 1792–1834. Scottish minister, whose writings and religious teaching led to the establishment of what he called the Catholic Apostolic Church (Irvingites), which sought to prepare for the second coming of Christ.

Irving, Washington 1783–1859. American author. Irving was one of the first native American writers, and is often called the inventor of the short-story form. His *History of New York by Diedrich Knickerbocker* was one of America's first comic works. His *Sketchbook* includes the famous short stories "Rip Van Winkle" and "The Legend of Sleepy Hollow."

Irvingites *See* **Irving, Edward**

Isaac In the Bible, the only son of Abraham and Sarah, husband of Rebecca, and father of Jacob and Esau. He was about to be offered as a sacrifice to God by Abraham, but was spared because of Abraham's unquestioning obedience and faith.

Isaac I ⟨Isaac Comnenus⟩ *c*1005–61. Byzantine emperor (1057–59), successor to Michael VI, whom he deposed. He abdicated in 1059 because of ill health and retired to a monastery. He was the first of the Comneni emperors.

Isaac II ⟨Isaac II Angelus⟩ Byzantine emperor (1185–95) and co-emperor (1203–04). He was deposed and blinded in 1195 by his brother, who became Alexius III; but his son, later Alexius IV, appealed to the Latins of the Fourth Crusade, and the two were briefly restored as co-emperors. Their overthrow by Alexius V led to the storming and sacking of Constantinople by the Crusaders (1204).

Isaac Comnenus   *See* **Isaac I**

Isaac II Angelus   *See* **Isaac II**

Isabeau of Bavaria ⟨Elizabeth⟩ 1371–1435. French queen (1389–1422?). When her husband Charles VI became insane (1392), Isabeau ruled as regent. She sided with the British in the Hundred Years' War and promoted the Treaty of Troyes *(q.v.)*. She was the mother of Catherine of Valois, who married Henry V of England.

Isabel 1846–1921. Princess and regent of Brazil. Her abolition of slavery in 1888 helped lead to the fall of the Brazilian Empire in 1889 by alienating the large slave-holding landowners. She followed her father Pedro II into exile.

Isabella 1292?–1358. French-born queen of England. With her lover, Roger de Mortimer, she ousted her husband Edward II (1327) and installed her son Edward III. She had her husband murdered; later her son executed Mortimer and jailed her.

Isabella I ⟨Isabella the Catholic⟩ 1451–1504. Queen of Spain. Queen of Castile, with her husband Ferdinand V *(q.v.)*, she united most of Spain, instituted the Inquisition, expelled the Jews (1492), and drove the Moors from Granada (1492). She financed the expedition of C. Columbus that discovered the Americas (1492).

Isabella II 1830–1904. Queen of Spain (1833–68), successor to her father Ferdinand VII. Her succession over her uncle, Don Carlos, led to rebellion by the Carlists, who refused to recognize any female succession. Her policies caused political turmoil and she was deposed in 1868.

Isabella the Catholic   *See* **Isabella I**

Isaiah ⟨Isaias⟩ *fl.* 8th cent. BC. Hebrew prophet who began to prophesy in the reign of King Uzziah (*c*740 BC) and continued to *c*701 BC. Considered the greatest of the prophets, he warned against entangling alliances, preached redemptive suffering, prophesied the fall and later redemption of Israel, and proclaimed the coming of a Messiah. The book of the Old Testament attributed to him contains some of the Bible's most beautiful passages. Most scholars consider Chapters 40–46 of the Book of Isaiah to have been written by a later, postexilic prophet whom they designate Deutero-Isaiah.

Isaias   *See* **Isaiah**

Isauria Ancient district in south-central Asia Minor. Its warlike people were legendary, though defeated by Servilius in 76 BC; it became part of the Roman province of Galatia. It was the birthplace of the Byzantine emperor Zeno, among others.

Isaurian Dynasty of Byzantine emperors that ruled from 717 to 802. The line was founded by Leo III and the last reigning member of the line was the empress Irene, who was forced to abdicate in 802. The Isaurian rulers were:

Leo III	717–741
Constantine V	741–775
Leo IV	775–780
Constantine VI	780–797
Irene	797–802

Isca Silurum   *See* **Caerleon**

Isfahan ⟨Ispahan⟩ ⟨Aspadana⟩ Iranian city. Located in west-central Iran, Isfahan is an ancient city famed for its architecture, mosques, rugs and other textiles. It was the capital of Persia from the 16th to 18th cents.

Ishbosheth In the Bible, the son of Saul, whom he succeeded as king of Israel. He was murdered, and David executed his killers and became king.

Ishmael Son of the biblical Abraham by his wife's handmaid Hagar. The Arabs claim descent from Ishmael, thus distinguishing themselves from the descent claimed by the Jews from his half-brother Isaac.

Ishtar Leading goddess of the ancient Assyrian and Babylonian religions. She was revered as the goddess of love, sex, and war, and as the Earth Mother, or Mother Goddess.

Isidore of Seville, Saint *c*560–636. Bishop of Seville (600–636) and prolific writer. His *Etymologiae*, especially *De Natura Rerum*, and other works were very influential. His encyclopedic learning was the means of transmitting much classical learning to the Middle Ages.

Isis Egyptian goddess. Isis was the goddess of nature and fertility. Her worship spread throughout the entire Mediterranean region and was practiced as late as the sixth cent. AD.

Islam One of the world's three great monotheistic religions, with Christianity and Judaism. Islam is the newest of the three and was founded by the prophet Muhammad *(q.v.)* in the 7th cent. AD. Muslims believe Muhammad was the last of the prophets (ie., Adam, Noah, Abraham, Moses, and Jesus) sent by Allah (God). They exult in their submission to and praise of Allah. The Islamic faith, derived from the earlier Judaic and Christian faiths, is based on the Koran *(q.v.)*, the revelations of Allah to Muhammad; the Sunna, collections of sayings of Muhammad (compiled in the 9th cent.); and the principle called Ijma, by which long-established practices are simply accepted as legitimate. The prophet Muhammad during his lifetime laid the foundations of the great Muslim theocratic state, the Empire of the Caliphate *(q.v.)*. After his death, the empire was rapidly expanded to include domains stretching from India, across the Mideast, and into North Africa and served to spread the Muslim faith throughout these regions. A dispute over the succession of the caliph (ruler of the Muslim theocracy) in the 7th cent. gave rise to the two main divisions in the Muslim world: the Sunni (orthodox) and Shi'ite sects *(qq.v.)*. The Shi'ites gave rise to other sects, including the Fatimids, Assassins, Karmathians, and Druses *(qq.v.)*.

Islamabad Pakistani capital; site was chosen as Pakistan's capital in 1959. It was planned as a blend of traditional Islamic architecture and modern urban style. Construction began in 1960.

Ismail I 1486–1524. Shah of Persia, 1502–24, founder of Safavid dynasty. Established the Shi'ite form of Islam as the state religion, thus incurring the special enmity of the Sunni Turks and Uzbeks, with whom he warred unceasingly. Succeeded by his son Tahmasp I, father of Ismail II.

Ismail II 1551–77. Shah of Persia, 1576–77. (*See also* Ismail I.)

Ismail Pasha 1830–95. Egyptian ruler under Ottoman suzerainty (1863–79). The Suez Canal was completed during his rule, but his improvement schemes plunged Egypt into debt, and he was forced to sell his canal shares to Britain (1875) and put Egypt's finances under the control of foreign bondholders (1876). He was also known as the Khedive Ismail.

Isocrates 436–338 BC. Athenian orator and rhetorician. A pupil of Socrates, he was perhaps the leading teacher of his day. His 21 surviving discourses are valuable sources of information about Greek life.

isolationism Policy of noninvolvement in the affairs of other nations. In the US, isolationists often cited the warning of G. Washington (in his farewell address) against "entangling alliances." Isolationist policies generally prevailed in the US during the 19th cent., and especially between WW I and WW II. Enough senators favored isolationism to prevent Senate ratification of the Treaty of Versailles *(q.v.)*, which would have meant an active US role in the League of Nations *(q.v.)*, as proposed by W. Wilson. International aggression, however, forced the US to abandon isolationist policies even before the country's entry into WW II.

Isonzo, Battle of *See* **Caporetto, Battle of**
Ispahan *See* **Isfahan**

Israel Republic located on the eastern Mediterranean coast. Its capital is Jerusalem. The history of modern Israel begins with its creation in 1948, but the movement to establish a Jewish state in Palestine dates to the late 19th cent. and the beginnings of the Zionist movement. Since its creation, Israel has had to contend with hostile Arab

neighbors, frequent wars, and in more recent years terrorist attacks by guerrillas of the Palestine Liberation Organization (PLO). Friction between Arabs and Israelis has been one of the factors contributing to Mideast instability. US efforts to settle the differences bore first fruit with the normalization of relations between Egypt (first Arab state to do so) and Israel in the 1970s. (*For history of the region prior to 1948, see* Palestine; *also* Israel, Kingdom of; Judah, Kingdom of.) Key dates in the history of modern Israel include:

1897 T. Herzl led first Zionist council at Basel, Switzerland.

1917 Balfour Declaration (Nov. 3) announced British support for a Jewish "National Home" in Palestine.

1922 League of Nations made Palestine a mandate territory of Britain.

1947 UN Special Committee on Palestine issued plan to divide Palestine into separate Arab and Jewish states and establish Jerusalem and environs as an international zone; plan passed (Nov. 29) by UN General Assembly.

1948 Israeli state created (May 14); Tel Aviv became capital.

1948–63 D. Ben-Gurion served as Israel's first prime minister.

1948–49 Arab-Israeli War broke out upon creation of the Israeli state (May 14); 400,000 Palestinian refugees fled from Israel to neighboring Arab states.

1949 Israel admitted to UN (May 11).

1950 Jerusalem officially became capital of Israel (Jan. 23).

1950 Law of Return enacted; provided for automatic citizenship for all immigrant Jews.

1956 Arab-Israeli War (Oct.-Nov.); Israelis invaded Sinai amid Suez Crisis; captured Sinai territory turned over to UN peace-keeping force.

1956 Israeli forces withdrew from the Sinai peninsula (Nov.); UN peace-keeping forces were subsequently moved into area.

1957 Israeli forces completed withdrawal from Gaza strip (Mar.); UN forces moved into area.

1963–69 Levi Eshkol in office as prime minister.

1964 PLO organized; dedicated to reclaiming lands occupied by Israel.

1967 Egyptian president G. Nasser mobilized Egyptian forces (May) and blocked Israeli access to the Gulf of Aqaba.

1967 Arab-Israeli War (June 5–10); Israelis victorious in Six-Day War; Sinai recaptured and the West Bank and Golan Heights taken.

1969 Prime minister L. Eshkol died (Feb. 26).

1969–74 G. Meir in office as prime minister.

1972 Palestinian terrorists killed 11 members of the Israeli Olympic team (Sept. 25) in attack on Olympic Village at Munich, Germany.

1973 Arab-Israeli War (Oct. 6–25); Israelis repulsed attacks by Egyptians and Syrians.

1974 Israeli forces pulled back from front lines in Syrian and Egyptian territory seized in 1973 war; UN forces established a buffer zone.

1974–77 Yitzhak Rabin in office as prime minister.

1976 Entebbe Raid (July 3–4) in Uganda to rescue passengers in airliner hijacked by Palestinians.

1977– M. Begin in office (June 21) as prime minister.

1977 Egyptian president Sadat made a historic state visit to Israel (Nov. 19–21) in the first of a series of peace initiatives between the two nations.

1977 Begin visited Egypt (Dec. 24–26) to continue discussion on possible peace settlement.

1978 Prime Minister Begin signed Camp David Accords (Sept. 17), providing a framework for peace with Egypt.

1979 Begin signed historic formal peace treaty with Egypt (Mar. 26); Israelis to pull out of occupied Sinai in phases (completed 1982).

1981 Israeli fighter planes sent into Iraq (June 7) to destroy a nuclear reactor under construction near Baghdad.

1981 Israel annexed occupied territory of the Golan Heights (Dec. 14).

1982 Lebanese War; Israelis invaded Lebanon (June 6) after long series of PLO attacks launched from inside Lebanon; PLO pushed north and encircled in Beirut; PLO, defeated (Aug.), was allowed to withdraw to various Arab countries.

1982 Massacre of hundreds of Palestinian refugees in Beirut, Lebanon, by Lebanese Christian militia; failure of Israeli occupation force to prevent massacre caused political crisis in Israeli government; the defense minister was ultimately forced to resign (1983).

Israel, kingdom of Originally, the Old Testament kingdom of the Hebrews ruled by Saul, David, and Solomon. Following the rebellion (c933 BC) by Jeroboam I, the kingdom was divided. The northern part, which was thereafter called Israel, included lands of the 10 northern tribes. The southern part, called Judah (q.v.), included the lands of the tribes of Benjamin and Judah. The kingdom of Israel was overrun (c722) by Assyrians (q.v.) under Sargon II, and many of the inhabitants were carried off. They became known as the Ten Lost Tribes (q.v.).

Issachar Son of Jacob and Leah. He gave his name to one of the 12 tribes of Israel, which ultimately settled west of the Jordan River.

Issus, Battle of Decisive victory (333 BC) for Alexander the Great over the Persians under Darius III during the Macedonian conquest of the Persian Empire. In an effort to check the invasion, Darius led an unsuccessful attack upon the Macedonians on the Issus plain in present-day southern Turkey. The Macedonians reputedly lost 450 men versus tens of thousands of slain Persians.

Istanbul ⟨Constantinople⟩ Turkish city (pop. 3,900,000), capital of Istanbul province, on both sides of the Bosporus. Turkey's chief city, it is a major seaport and commercial center. It began as Byzantium (c660 BC) and Constantine changed its name to Constantinople (q.v.) in 330 AD. It was the Turkish capital until 1922, when it was occupied by the Allies and the Ottoman sultan was deposed. In 1930, the name officially became Istanbul. It is one of the world's great historic cities.

Isthmian Games Greek athletic events. These games were held on the Isthmus of Corinth from 582 BC to the 4th cent. AD in honor of Poseidon. They consisted of both athletic and musical competitions.

Itagaki, Taisuke 1837–1919. Japanese statesman. He played a major role in the 1868 Meiji Restoration (q.v.), founded the Jiyuto (Liberal) party, and worked to bring constitutional reforms to the government.

Italian East Africa Italian African colonies. This was the name given (1936) to the federation of Italian-controlled colonies in Africa composed of Eritrea, Ethiopia, and Italian Somaliland. Italy lost them after WW II.

Italian Wars Series of destructive wars (1494–1559) for control of Italy. The wars, largely fought by France and Spain, resulted in the domination of Italy by the Spanish Hapsburgs. Fighting began with an invasion (1494) of Italy by French king Charles VIII. He took Naples but was forced out of Italy by an alliance of the Holy Roman Empire, Spain, and the pope. French king Louis XII launched another invasion (1499) and took Milan, Genoa, and Naples but was driven out of Naples (1503) by the Spanish. Pope Julius II then organized (1508) the League of Cambrai (q.v.) against Venice. By 1510, however, he had turned against France and formed the Holy League (q.v.) against it. Following some years of fighting, a peace was arranged (1516) by which the French held Milan and Spain kept Naples. Fighting again erupted (1521) between Holy Roman Emperor

Charles V and the new French king, Francis I. In the course of battle, Francis was captured (at the Battle of Pavia) and forced to sign the Treaty of Madrid (1526). On being freed, Francis renounced the treaty and formed a new alliance with England, the pope, Venice, and Florence. In this phase of the wars, Charles sacked Rome (May 1527) and forced the pope to come to terms, the French failed in their siege of Genoa, and Francis finally gave up all claims to Italy in the Treaty of Cambrai (1529). Francis fought two other unsuccessful wars against the Spanish outside Italy. By the Treaty of Cateau-Cambrésis (1559), Spain was confirmed as the dominant power in Italy.

Italo-Ethiopian War War (1935–36) in which Italy took control of the independent African state of Ethiopia. It contributed to international tensions that led up to WW II. Following a border incident (Dec. 5, 1934) between Ethiopia and Italian Somaliland, the Italian dictator B. Mussolini ordered an invasion (Oct. 2, 1935). Ignoring calls for arbitration as well as League of Nations sanctions, the Italians advanced slowly against the Ethiopians in the rough terrain. After taking the fortress of Makallé (Nov. 8), they advanced to the capital, Addis Ababa. Troops under Gen. P. Badoglio took the capital (May 5, 1936) and thus ended the war. Italy's disregard for the League of Nations sanctions, and France's and Great Britain's failure to back the sanctions, severely damaged the League's prestige.

Italo-Turkish War ⟨Tripolitan War⟩ War (1911–12) in which Italy established a Libyan colony on the North African coast. As part of its policy of colonial expansion, Italy sought a North African colony and had won approval of its plans from major European powers. In the wake of the Moroccan Crisis (q.v.) of 1911, Italy declared war (Sept. 29, 1911) on Turkey and invaded the province of Tripoli. Tripoli and other coastal towns were taken quickly by forces under Gen. Carlo Caneva (1845–1922), but resistance by the Libyans forestalled a complete conquest. The Italian navy carried hostilities to other Turkish possessions in the Mediterranean, closing the Dardanelles (Apr.–May) and taking Rhodes (May 16) and the Dodecanese Islands (May). Threat of war in the Balkans forced the Turks to negotiate and, by the Treaty of Lausanne (q.v.), the war was ended (Oct. 18) in Italy's favor.

Italo-Yugoslav Treaty Agreement between Italy and Yugoslavia concluded Jan. 27, 1924. By its terms, the city of Fiume (Rijeka), constituted a free city by the Treaty of Rapallo (1920), was incorporated into Italy. Yugoslavia occupied the city in 1945 and Italy ceded it to Yugoslavia in 1947.

Italy (Italian Republic) Country located in southern Europe on the Mediterranean Sea. Its capital is Rome. Italy's history begins with the Romans and for many centuries it was the center of the vast empire of the Romans. After the fall of the Western Roman Empire (5th cent. AD), the Italian peninsula suffered many centuries of divisiveness, wars, and foreign domination. It nevertheless gave birth to the great flowering of Western civilization, the Renaissance. Rome, as the seat of the Roman Catholic popes, was also the spiritual center of Europe for many centuries. The movement for unification of Italy (Risorgimento) began early in the 19th cent. and in 1861 the modern state of Italy achieved unification. Italy fell under the sway of Fascism in the 1920s and was defeated by the Allies in WW II. Italy since the war has had numerous governments and the 1960s and 1970s saw the rise of leftist and Communist factions among Italian voters. (*For history of Italy before the 5th cent., see* Rome.) Key events in Italian history include:

AD 476–493 Odoacer ruled Italy; deposed last Western Roman emperor, Romulus Augustus (AD 476); virtual ruler until his assassination; Ravenna the capital.

AD 488 Theodoric the Ostrogoth invaded Italy, slew Odoacer, and ruled until his death in 526.

526 Byzantine emperor Justinian I sent forces (led by Belisarius and Narses) to expel the Goths from Italy.

552 Byzantines defeated Goths in Italy at Battle of Busta Gallorum; Goth king Totila killed and Byzantines briefly ruled Italy.

568 Invasion of Italy by the Lombards, another Germanic people, who conquered much of Italy; Byzantines held Exarchate of Ravenna and some other parts of Italy; Lombards did not take Rome, due to the efforts of Pope Gregory the Great.

568–774 Italy under the Lombards; Lombards allowed bishops temporal powers in localities; meanwhile the split between the Eastern church and Rome grew; the Byzantines renewed attempts to drive the Lombards from Italy.

751 Lombards captured the Byzantine capital of Ravenna.

753 Lombards threatened Rome; seeking to consolidate their hold on Italy, they advanced on Rome; Pope Stephen II appealed to the Frankish ruler Pepin the Short for aid against the Lombards.

754–756 Pepin the Short invaded Italy and defeated the Lombards.

756 Donation of Pepin; Pepin gave the pope lands about Rome that he had conquered from the Lombards; the donation became the basis of the

Papal States and established the alliance between the pope and the kingdoms of Western Europe.

774 Charlemagne conquered the Lombards, who had again threatened Rome; Charlemagne became king of the Lombards after Desiderius surrendered at the siege of Pavia.

800 Pope crowned Charlemagne emperor of the Romans, thereby reconstituting the Western Roman Empire under Carolingian rule; thus formed alliance between European monarchs and popes.

9TH CENT. Carolingian Empire divided by Treaties of Verdun and Mersen; two great Frankish kingdoms created, East (German) and West (French); a third part, including Italy, later became contested.

9TH–10 CENT. Control of Italy passed to weak rulers; rise of petty kingdoms and frequent wars between them.

917 Arab Muslims conquered Sicily and pillaged Italy.

961–962 Otto I, then asserting his rule over the German states, aided Pope John XII against King Berengar II.

962 Otto I crowned emperor by the pope; Holy Roman Empire (eastern part of former Carolingian empire) then became the successor state to the Western Roman Empire; alliance formed between Otto I and the pope led to years of struggle for control of Italy, over which the popes claimed sovereignty.

11TH CENT. Normans conquered southern Italy and Sicily from the Byzantines and Arabs; these lands, later known as the Kingdom of the Two Sicilies, remained under relatively strong rule thereafter and developed independently of the north; northern Italy, ravaged by wars, broke up into petty kingdoms and city-states.

1075–1122 Investiture Controversy, long struggle between reforming popes and the emperors of the Holy Roman Empire; ended by Concordat of Worms.

1130–54 Roger II reigned in the south; consolidated conquered lands, adding Capua, Naples and the Abruzzi; ruled one of the most advanced unified kingdoms of the time; feudal system firmly established there, but not in northern Italy.

12TH CENT. Hohenstaufen rulers of the Holy Roman Empire gained control of southern Italy as successors to the Normans.

12TH–13TH CENT. Lombard League opposed attempts by Holy Roman emperors to force submission of Lombard communes in northern Italy.

1183 Lombard League forced the church and Holy Roman Emperor to recognize its autonomy by the Treaty of Constance.

13TH–14TH CENT. Struggle between Guelphs (supporters of papal control in Italy) and Ghibellines (supporters of Hohenstaufen Holy Roman emperors); strife led to breakdown of central authority in north and central Italy, and the rise of local rulers in the cities; coincided with struggle between popes and Hohenstaufen emperors.

1279 German king Rudolf I, a Hapsburg, ended long struggle between popes and Holy Roman Empire over papal sovereignty in Italy; recognized papal sovereignty in Papal States and in south.

1266 Kingdom of the Two Sicilies conquered by Charles of Anjou, brother of France's king Louis IX.

1282 Angevin rule overthrown by the Sicilian Vespers and Sicily came under the power of the Spanish House of Aragon.

14TH CENT. Babylonian Captivity (1309–78); papacy removed to Avignon, France; control of the Papal States broke down and gave rise to independent cities and merchant republics (Venice and Genoa); French and Spanish warred for control in the south.

1348 The Black Death (bubonic plague), introduced by Genoese sailors coming from the East, ravaged Italy and spread to the rest of Europe.

14th–15th cent. Ruling families came to power in northern Italian cities—Medici in Florence, Visconti and Sforza in Milan, Este of Ferrara, Gonzaga of Mantua, Scala of Verona, etc.; presided over the Renaissance, which began in Italy.

1442 Spanish House of Aragon won complete control of southern Italy (Sicily and Kingdom of Naples) after driving out the French.

1478 Pazzi Conspiracy, abortive attempt to depose L. de Medici from power in Florence.

15TH–18TH CENT. Popes gradually established their authority over the Papal States and extended domains to include most of central Italy.

1494 Charles VIII of France invaded the peninsula, marking the beginning of the Italian Wars.

1494–1559 Italian Wars fought for control of Italy; Spanish Hapsburgs won after years of sporadic warfare.

1508–10 League of Cambrai formed by Holy Roman Empire, Spain, France, and the pope to conquer the Republic of Venice.

1511 Holy League of erstwhile enemies, Spain, Venice, and the pope, founded to drive Louis XII of France out of Italy.

1529 In the Peace of Cambrai, France renounced all territorial claims in Italy.

1559 By the Treaty of Le Cateau-Cambrésis, Spain gained control of both Milan and the Kingdom of the Two Sicilies.

1720 Kingdom of Sardinia created; formed by Savoy, Piedmont, and island of Sardinia under House of Savoy.

MID-18TH CENT. Naples, Sicily, Parma, and Piacenza passed to Spanish Bourbons; Milan, Mantua, Tuscany, and Modena, to Austria.

1792–1802 French Revolutionary Wars; Italy, scene of much fighting, fell to Napoleon.

1797 By the Treaty of Campo Formia, Napoleon established the Cisalpine Republic (Milan) and the Ligurian Republic (Genoa).

1798–99 Roman Republic, a short-lived republic established at Rome.

1805 Napoleon, crowned emperor in 1804, made himself king of an "Italy" consisting of the Cisalpine Republic, Emilia-Romagna, and Venetia.

1806 Joseph Bonaparte made king of Naples.

1808 Joachim Murat, Napoleon's brother-in-law, succeeded as king of Naples.

1808–30 Rise of the Carbonari society in Naples to oppose French domination; later became early supporters of liberal nationalist movement.

1809 Napoleon annexed the Papal States to France.

1815 Congress of Vienna after Napoleon's fall; Papal States restored; Spanish and Austrian rule restored in other parts of Italy.

1815–61 Rise of the nationalist movement (Risorgimento) for unification of Italy.

1816 Kingdom of the Two Sicilies formally created by unification of Sicily and Naples under one crown.

1831 Young Italy movement formed by Italian nationalist G. Mazzini.

1846 Pius IX elected pope; began a series of reforms in the Papal States.

1848–49 Revolutions of 1848; abortive revolts in Rome, Venice, Florence, Naples, and Savoy.

1849–61 Victor Emmanuel II reigned as king of Sardinia, which became the nucleus of the unified Italian state.

1852 Count C. Cavour became Sardinian prime minister.

1859–60 King Victor Emmanuel II, with French aid, drove Austrians out of Lombardy in north; he gained Lombard territories but ceded Savoy and Nice to France.

1860 Garibaldi and his Expedition of the Thousand conquered the Kingdom of the Two Sicilies (May–Sept.); territory turned over to Victor Emmanuel II in the name of a united Italy.

1861 Kingdom of Italy formally proclaimed (Mar. 17).

1861–78 Victor Emmanuel II reigned as first king of a united Italy; Venetia, Rome, and part of Papal States still outside the Italian kingdom in 1861.

1861 First Italian parliament convened in Turin by Victor Emmanuel II.

1866 Austro-Prussian War; Italy joined Prussia and thereby gained control of Venetia, formerly Austrian domain.

1870 Victor Emmanuel II seized Rome, then in pope's control; beginning of Roman Question; Italian unification substantially completed.

1878–1900 Humbert I reigned as king of Italy.

1895–96 Italy prosecuted the Ethiopian War, establishing an East African colony.

1900–46 Victor Emmanuel III reigned as king of Italy.

1911–12 Italo-Turkish War; Italy established a Libyan colony on the North African coast.

1912 Universal male suffrage granted.

1915 Italy entered WW I after gaining territorial concessions in the secret Treaty of London.

1919 Italy gained control of former Austrian domains at the end of WW I; was awarded Trieste, southern Tyrol, Istria, and other territories.

1921 Fascist party organized by B. Mussolini.

1922 March on Rome conducted by Fascist followers of B. Mussolini; failure of King Victor Emmanuel III to oppose the movement led to Mussolini's rise to power.

1922 B. Mussolini and Fascist party took control of the Italian government (Oct. 29).

1922 Italian government voted B. Mussolini dictatorial powers for one year to restore order (Nov. 25).

1924 Matteotti Crisis resulted in the Aventine Secession by non-Fascist deputies (June 10); Mussolini suspended constitution and further consolidated power.

1926 Mussolini instituted the Corporative State in Italy.

1929 Lateran Treaty; agreement between Italy and the papacy settling the Roman Question; created Vatican City as an independent enclave under direct papal control.

1935–36 Italo-Ethiopian War; Italy took control of the independent African state of Ethiopia.

1936 Mussolini formally annexed Ethiopia in defiance of League of Nations efforts to secure Italian withdrawal.

1936 Italy established an alliance with Germany, the Rome-Berlin Axis (July).

1937 Italy, Germany and Japan in the Anti-Comintern Pact (Sept.).

1938 Munich Pact; agreement providing for the German annexation of the Czechoslovakian territory of Sudetenland.

1939 Pact of Steel concluded, cementing alliance with Germany (May 22); followed by Italian occupation of Albania.

1939–45 WW II; Italy joined Axis Powers (1940) but continuing military reverses led to Mussolini's overthrow (1943) as Allies invaded Italy; Italy signed armistice (Sept., 1943) and joined Allies against Germany; Germans then unsuccessfully opposed Allies in Italy.

1945 Mussolini and his mistress captured by partisans and summarily executed (Apr.).

1946 Humbert II became last king of Italy; monarchy abolished and republic established shortly thereafter (June 10).

1947 Formal treaty ending the war; Italy lost some territory to Yugoslavia and control over its colonial domains.

1948 New republican constitution in effect (Jan. 1).

1948 Christian Democrats won control of government, defeating leftist coalition led by Communists; Christian Democrats dominated postwar Italian politics.

1948–55 L. Einaudi in office as first president of the new Italian Republic.

1949 Italy became founding member of NATO (Apr. 4).

1954 Trieste divided between Italy and Yugoslavia.

1955 Italy joined UN.

1957 Became a member of newly organized European Economic Community.

1962 A. Fanfani inaugurated first of several Christian Democratic governments "opening to the left" in alliance with Socialists; there followed a succession of political crises and new governments in the 1960s and 1970s.

1963–68 A. Moro premier.

1972–73 G. Andreotti formed government after political crisis.

1974 Italian voters supported continuation of divorce law (May 13).

1974 Political crisis ended when A. Moro formed minority government (1974–76).

1976–79 Andreotti again in power as premier; governed with support of growing Communist faction.

1976 Communist gains in Italy; party member named speaker of the Chamber of Deputies (July 5).

1977 Roman Catholicism no longer state religion of Italy by new agreement between government and Vatican.

1978 Former premier A. Moro kidnapped and eventually killed by terrorists (Mar. 16).

1978– Alessandro Pertini in office as Italy's first Socialist president.

1979–80 Francesco Cossiga, Christian Democrat, in office as premier; government collapsed after Communists were barred from government posts.

1979 Palace of Senators in Rome badly damaged by terrorist bomb (Apr. 20).

1980–81 Arnaldo Forlani, Christian Democrat, in office as premier.

1981 Hundreds of government officials named as members of a secret Masonic society seeking to undermine the parliamentary government; Premier Arnaldo Forlani's coalition government collapsed as a result of the scandal (May 26).

1981 Giovanni Spadolini (Republican party) became new premier following the scandal (June 28); ended long rule by Christian Democrats.

1982 Terrorists kidnapped (Jan.) US Gen. James Dozier, a NATO commander; released him unharmed some six weeks later.

Ito, Hirobumi, Prince 1841–1909. Japanese statesman and premier (1886–88, 1892, 1898, 1900–01). He tried to introduce Western ideas learned while on government missions to the US and Europe, and drafted the constitution of Japan in 1889. He was assassinated while serving as resident-general in Korea.

Iturbide, Agustín de 1783–1824. Mexican military leader. He led in the Mexican independence movement and, as Agustin I, ruled as emperor from May 1822 to March 1823.

Ituzaingo, Battle of Decisive Argentine-Uruguayan victory over Brazil, fought in what is now northeastern Argentina on February 20, 1827. Both Argentina and Brazil had claimed what is now Uruguay when they became independent from Spain and Portugal respectively. As a result of this battle, Uruguay was founded as an independent buffer state (1828).

Ivan III ⟨Ivan the Great⟩ 1440–1505. Grand duke of Moscow (1462–1505). He broke the power of Novgorod, exploited divisions between the Tatars of the Golden Horde (q.v.), and captured part of the Ukraine from Lithuania. He laid the groundwork for a strong Russian monarchy.

Ivan IV ⟨Ivan the Terrible⟩ 1530–84. Grand duke of Moscow (from 1533) and first czar of Russia (1547–84). Notorious for cruelty and erratic behavior later in his reign, he nevertheless greatly expanded Russian domains and consolidated the power of the monarchy at the expense of the Boyars. He succeeded (1533) his father, Vasily III, as grand duke and ended his regency (1547) by taking the title of czar. He summoned (1566) the first national assembly, began Russia's expansion to the east by conquering Kazan (1552) and Astrakhan (1556), taking them from the Tatars, and engaged in the long, unsuccessful Livonian War *(q.v.)* of 1557–82. Siberia was also conquered (1581–83). In 1565 he split the empire, taking part of it as his personal domain (the *oprichniki*), and then instituted a reign of terror. He executed and exiled Boyars, led a massacre of the inhabitants of Novgorod (1570), and murdered his own son Ivan (1580).

Ivan V 1666–96. Czar of Russia (1682–96). Physically and mentally unfit to rule, he was nominal coruler with Peter I under his sister Sophia's regency. He retained his title after Peter's succession (1689) but never actively ruled.

Ivan VI 1740–64. Czar of Russia (1740–41). A nominal ruler, he was deposed as an infant by Elizabeth, daughter of Peter I, and imprisoned until his assassination more than 20 years later.

Ivan the Great *See* **Ivan III**

Ivan the Terrible *See* **Ivan IV**

Ivory Coast ⟨Republic of Ivory Coast⟩ Republic located in coastal West Africa. Capital is Abidjan. European traders established settlements in the region from the 16th cent. and for a time trade in slaves and ivory flourished. The French made the coastal region a protectorate in 1842 and created the colony of the Ivory Coast (1893), even though native resistance in the interior had not yet been completely broken. Made part of French West Africa (1895), it was held by Vichy government forces in WW II and became a French territory (1946). Ivory Coast next became an autonomous republic (1958) within the French Community. It achieved complete independence (Aug. 7, 1960).

Since that time the republic has been under the leadership of President Felix Houphouët-Boigny (1905–   ), who has maintained a pro-Western policy.

Iwo Jima, Battle of US conquest (Feb. and Mar., 1945) of the principal island of the Volcano Islands, during WW II. Three US Marine divisions assaulted the entrenched Japanese on Feb. 9 after heavy bombardment and killed some 21,000 of them, taking 1,259 prisoners when the fighting ended on March 17. Americans killed totaled 4,189 and there were 15,749 wounded. The raising of the flag on Mount Suribachi on February 23 was considered one of the most memorable incidents of the war in the Pacific.

IWW *See* **Industrial Workers of the World**

Ixion Mythological king of the Lapithae, and father of the Centaurs. For attempting to seduce his wife, Hera, Zeus bound him forever to a fiery revolving wheel.

Iyeyasu ⟨Tokugawa, ~⟩ ⟨Ieyasu⟩ 1542–1616. Japanese soldier and ruler. Iyeyasu aided Hideyoshi's unification of Japan. He subsequently made himself daimyo and shogun, and virtual ruler of Japan. He was the founder of the Tokugawa *(q.v.)* shogunate, which ruled Japan until 1867.

Izmir ⟨*formerly* Smyrna⟩ Capital of Izmir (province), western Turkey (pop. 1,700,000). A leading Turkish seaport, it was founded in the 3d millennium BC, and became a leading commercial center by *c*1000 BC. Controlled by the Ionian Greeks from the 7th cent. BC and later (after 1424) by the Ottoman Turks, it has been contested by both Greece and Turkey. It was awarded to Turkey by the 1923 Treaty of Lausanne *(q.v.)*. As Smyrna it was an important center of early Christianity and scene of the martyrdom of St. Polycarp (AD 155).

J

Jabesh-Gilead Ancient city in Palestine (presently Jordan), burial place of Saul and his three sons. It is referred to in the Old Testament as suffering retribution from the Israelites.

Jabir ibn Hayyan, Abu Musa ⟨Geber⟩ c721–c815. Arab alchemist and physician. Numerous writings attributed to him, on the nature of matter, influenced the development of medieval alchemy and chemistry.

Jabneh, Gamaliel of *See* **Gamaliel**

Jackson, Andrew 1767–1845. Seventh US president (1829–37), successor to J. Q. Adams. A military hero, frontiersman, and populist, he became the symbol of the movement known as Jacksonian Democracy. A Tennessee lawyer, he rose to prominence as a military commander in the War of 1812. He defeated the Creek Indians in the Battle of Horseshoe Bend (Mar., 1814) in Alabama and won (1815) a decisive victory over the British at the Battle of New Orleans *(q.v.)*. Later, commanding a military force in the first Seminole War (1817–18), he crossed into Spanish-held Florida and provoked an international incident. He served in the US Senate, first in 1797 to 1798, and then from 1823 to 1825. During the latter term, he was an unsuccessful presidential candidate (1824), but by 1828 he had gained sufficient strength to win election to two terms (1828, 1832). Jackson's administration was marked by institution of the spoils system *(q.v.)*; the rise of the Kitchen Cabinet *(q.v.)* and the Eaton affair that helped break it up; opposition to a protective tariff (favoring the eastern industrialists), which resulted in the nullification doctrine and the resignation (1832) of Vice-President J. Calhoun; the retiring of the public debt (1835); and Jackson's opposition to the Bank of the United States. In this last struggle, Jackson campaigned (1832) against rechartering the bank. On retaking office, he ordered transfer (1833) of federal funds from the central bank to designated state banks. This fueled a land speculation boom in the West. Jackson tried to curb it by ordering (1836) the purchase of all public lands in gold and silver. But the resultant drain on the banks, and mistrust of their bank notes already in circulation, finally led to the financial Panic of 1837.

Jackson, Robert Houghwout 1892–1954. American jurist, who served from 1941 to 1954 as associate justice of the US Supreme Court. He also served as US counsel at the Nürnberg Trials *(q.v.)*.

Jackson, Stonewall *See* **Jackson, Thomas Jonathan**

Jackson, Thomas Jonathan ⟨Stonewall Jackson⟩ 1824–63. Confederate general and noted strategist during the American Civil War. Made a brigadier general (May, 1861) under Gen. J. Johnston; Jackson's steadfastness earned him his nickname at the first battle of Bull Run (1861). He further distinguished himself in fighting in the Shenandoah Valley (1862) and then served under Gen. R.E. Lee in the Seven Days' Battles, the second Battle of Bull Run, and Antietam. Made lieutenant commander, he fought at Fredericksburg, and Chancellorsville *(qq.v.)*. He was accidentally killed by his own troops at Chancellorsville.

Jacksonian Democracy Term applied to the political developments accompanying the presidency of A. Jackson (1829–37), including the spoils system *(q.v.)*, universal white male suffrage, and party conventions.

Jack the Ripper *fl.* 19th cent. English murderer who killed six or seven women in London between Aug. and Nov., 1888. The murders caused a sensation and, despite an exhaustive investigation, his identity has never been satisfactorily proven.

Jacob Biblical patriarch and brother of the disinherited Esau. After wrestling with an angel, his name was changed to Israel. His descendants formed the Twelve Tribes of Israel *(q.v.)*.

Jacobins Political club that rose to prominence as a faction during the French Revolution (1789–99). Centered in Paris, the club at its height of power (1793) had thousands of branch groups throughout France. Under the leadership of M. Robespierre, the group dominated the revolutionary government for a time (1793–94) and was responsible for the Reign of Terror. The club began (1789) as a group of moderate deputies to the National Assembly, though by 1790 bourgeois moderates had swelled their ranks and made the club an important pressure group. Following the overthrow of the king (1792), the club admitted Montagnards (q.v.), and began to espouse more democratic, then radical, revolutionary aims. They opposed and ousted (1793) the Girondists (q.v.) over the prosecution of the French Revolutionary Wars, set up the revolutionary dictatorship, and oversaw the Reign of Terror. The Jacobins fell from power with Robespierre's overthrow on 9 Thermidor (July 27, 1794) and thereafter the club was suppressed.

Jacobite church   See **Syrian Orthodox church**

Jacobites   Supporters of English king James II (and his heirs in the Stuart line) after the Glorious Revolution (q.v.) of 1688. Considerable support for James remained after his exile (1688) and was kept alive (1688–1746) by Roman Catholics and disaffected Tories. Jacobites were especially active in Scotland and two unsuccessful rebellions were organized there (1715, 1745). The first Jacobite rebellion ("the fifteen") broke out when George I succeeded to the English throne. Led by J. Erskine, 6th earl of Mar, the Jacobites hoped to install James's son, James Francis Edward Stuart (the Old Pretender), but they were soundly defeated. The second Jacobite rebellion broke out in Scotland. It was led by James's grandson, Charles Edward Stuart (Bonnie Prince Charlie) and was aided by the French, then at war with Britain in the War of Austrian Succession (q.v.). After early victories, Charles's advance into England stalled. His subsequent retreat turned into a rout of the Jacobites at Culloden Moor (Apr. 16, 1746) and thus ended Jacobite resistance.

Jacquard, Joseph Marie   1752–1834. French weaver and inventor. He invented the Jacquard loom, the first machine to weave in patterns.

Jacquerie   Revolt (May–June, 1358) by French peasants during the Hundred Years' War (1337–1453). Peasants in northern France rebelled when French nobles demanded increased taxes despite the fact that the countryside had recently been pillaged by English mercenary soldiers. Led by Guillaume Cale (d. 1358) and E. Marcel, the peasants sacked and burned castles. They were defeated less than a month later, however, and thousands were massacred by the vengeful nobles.

Jade Emperor   Chinese Taoist supreme deity of the universe believed to inhabit a jade palace.

Jadwiga   (Hedwig) 1371–99. Queen of Poland (1384–99). She inherited Poland (and her sister,

Hungary) from her father, Louis I. She married Jagiello, grand duke of Lithuania, uniting the two kingdoms. She is a canonized Catholic saint.

Jaffa   ⟨Joppa⟩ Mediterranean seaport city, since 1950 incorporated with Tel Aviv (q.v.), Israel. It was prominent in biblical history, during the Crusades, during the Napoleonic Wars, and during WW I, and changed hands many times.

Jaffna, kingdom of   Former Tamil kingdom in northern Sri Lanka (Ceylon). It was well established by the 14th cent. and lasted until it was conquered by the Portuguese in the 17th cent. The Tamils, a Dravidian people from India, had settled on the island as early as c200 BC.

Jagatai   d. 1242. Mongol conqueror and a son of Genghis Khan. He joined in his father's great wars of conquest and, following the death of Genghis Khan, did not oppose the succession of his younger brother, Ogadai, as grand khan. In the division (1227) of the Mongol empire among the heirs of Genghis Khan, Jagatai gained vast domains corresponding roughly to Turkistan and Afghanistan.

Jagello   See **Jagiello**

Jagellon   See **Jagiello**

Jagiello   ⟨Jagello⟩ ⟨Jagellon⟩ Dynasty that ruled in Bohemia, Hungary, Lithuania, and Poland in the 14th–16th cents. (in Poland from 1386 to 1572). The dynasty was founded by Jagiello, duke of Lithuania, who took the name Ladislas II of Poland and was a major force in European affairs.

jagirdar system   Indian feudal system introduced (13th cent.) by the sultans of Delhi by which officials received the right to collect revenues from estates in lieu of salaries. The system weakened central authority but survived until Indian independence.

Jahn, Friedrich Ludwig   1778–1852. German teacher and nationalist who founded the Turnverein gymnastic movement, through which he sought to free Germany from Napoleonic rule and instill in young Germans a sense of strength and national identity.

Jainism   Indian religion. Arising in the 6th cent. BC as a reaction to the rigidity of the Vedic religion, Jainism was by tradition established by 24 saints, or religious figures, the last being Vardhamana Mahavira. It taught a rigid form of asceticism, a reverence for all living things, and the performance of good acts as means for escaping the cycle of rebirth and achieving Nirvana. At first quite distinct from Hinduism, Jainism eventually incorporated elements of Hinduism. Today many prominent Indians practice Jainism.

Jajau, Battle of   Battle fought (June 12, 1707) at Jajau, India, by Bahadur Shah and his brother

Azam Shah, over succession to the Mogul throne in India. Bahadur Shah was victorious, and his brother was killed in battle.

Jalal ad-Din ar-Rumi *c*1207–1273. Great Persian Sufi (mystical) poet and founder of an order of dervishes. In the West, his disciples were called whirling dervishes.

Jamaica Island republic in the West Indies, noted as a tourist attraction and source of bauxite. It was discovered by C. Columbus in 1494 and controlled by Spain until captured by the British in 1655. Sugar was a major product until the abolition of slavery (1833). There have been many Negro insurrections. Independence was finally gained Aug. 6, 1962. From 1972–80, Prime Minister Michael Manley pursued a policy of instituting a socialist economy. However, the election of Edward Seaga (1980) brought a return to pro-West, capitalistic orientation.

James I ⟨James the Conqueror⟩ 1208–76. King of Aragon (1213–76). James conquered the Balearic Islands (1229–35), drove the Moors from Valencia (1238), and enabled Castile to recapture Murcia from the Moors (1266).

James I 1394–1437. King of Scotland (1406–37), successor to his father, Robert III. By breaking the power of the nobility and the Highland clans, James established strong monarchical rule in Scotland. He was assassinated by a group of nobles.

James I ⟨James VI⟩ 1566–1625. Scottish king of England (1603–25), successor to Elizabeth I and first of the Stuart line in England. James first succeeded (1567) his mother, Mary Queen of Scots, to the Scottish throne (under a regency) and then succeeded to the English throne. During his reign in England, war with Spain was ended, the Hampton Court Conference *(q.v.)* was called (1604), the Gunpowder Plot *(q.v.)* was exposed (1605), and relations between James and the Parliament deteriorated seriously. This last helped bring on the English Civil War some years later. In addition, English colonies at Jamestown and Plymouth were founded (1607, 1620) and the King James Bible was commissioned (1604). The throne of England passed to him by virtue of his descent from Margaret Tudor, daughter of Henry VII.

James II 1430–60. King of Scotland (1437–60), successor to his father, James I. He reestablished the strong monarchy created by his father and attacked English outposts (1460).

James II 1633–1702. English king (1685–88), successor to his brother Charles II. His overthrow during the Glorious Revolution *(q.v.)* of 1688 established the supremacy of the Parliament in England. James served under his brother Charles

after the restoration (1660) and converted to Catholicism (1668). Shortly after being crowned, he put down a rebellion by the Duke of Monmouth (1685) and instituted the Bloody Assizes *(q.v.)*. His penchant for autocratic methods and efforts to promote Catholicism, notably his declarations of indulgence *(q.v.)*, prepared the way for the Glorious Revolution. But it was the birth (1688) of his son and (Catholic) heir that finally precipitated the revolt. James was succeeded by his daughter Mary and her Protestant husband, William III. His attempt to retake the throne was foiled at the Battle of the Boyne *(q.v.)* in 1690, though Jacobites *(q.v.)* carried on the cause for him and his heirs until 1746.

James III 1451–88. King of Scotland (1460–88), successor to his father, James II. A weak ruler, he was unable to control his nobles, who rebelled. They defeated and killed James at Sauchieburn.

James IV 1473–1513. King of Scotland (1488–1513), successor to his father, James III. He unified Scotland and allied it with France against Henry VIII of England. He and many of his nobles died in the Battle of Flodden *(q.v.)*.

James V 1512–42. King of Scotland (1513–42), successor to his father, James IV. Assuming power after 1528, he supported Catholicism in Scotland, and allied himself with France against his uncle Henry VIII.

James VI *See* **James I**

James, Epistle of *See* **James, Saint, "the Lesser"**

James, Henry, Sr. 1811–82. American philosophical and theological writer and the father of novelist H. James, Jr., and philosopher W. James.

James, Henry 1843–1916. American author, who lived most of his adult life in England. His novels reflect the impact of the older, more sophisticated European society, as in *The American, The Ambassadors,* and *The Golden Bowl.*

James, Jesse Woodson 1847–82. American outlaw leader of a legendary gang of train and bank robbers in the 1860s and 1870s. James was murdered by Robert Ford, a gang member, for the reward.

James, Saint, "the Greater" *d.* AD *c*44. One of the Apostles, brother of John and son of Zebedee. He and his brother were called Sons of Thunder because of their zeal. Traditionally he preached Christianity in Spain, where he is venerated as Saint James of Compostela, whose feast (July 25) has for centuries been one of Europe's greatest festivals. According to tradition, he returned to Judaea, where he was martyred.

James, Saint, "the Lesser" *d.* AD *c*62. One of the Apostles, traditionally identified as the kinsman of Jesus, who became bishop of Jerusalem and is supposed to have been the author of the Epistle of James in the New Testament. According to Josephus, he was stoned to death.

James, William 1842–1910. American philosopher and psychologist, brother of H. James. He published his major work, *The Principles of Psychology*, in 1890. He was an advocate of the theory of pragmatism *(q.v.)* and a member of the Harvard faculty until 1907. His other important works include *The Will to Believe* (1897) and *The Varieties of Religious Experience* (1902).

Jameson, Sir Leander Starr   *See* **Jameson Raid**

Jameson Raid Unsuccessful attempt to overthrow (1895) the Boer government of Transvaal. Led by Sir Leander Starr Jameson (1853–1957), the controversial raid was part of a broader scheme to bring all of South Africa under British control. The plan was hatched by C. Rhodes and Jameson and counted on starting a general uprising of Uitlanders, non-Boer foreigners, in Transvaal. To that end Jameson and some 500 armed men invaded Transvaal (Dec. 29, 1895). They were quickly overpowered by Boer forces at Krugersdorp, however, and surrendered (Jan. 2, 1896).

James the Conqueror   *See* **James I**

Jamestown First North American permanent British settlement. Situated in Virginia on the James River, the former village was founded by the London Company on May 14, 1607. Although repeatedly ravaged by fire, Jamestown was the capital of Virginia until 1699.

Jami 1414–92. Persian poet, considered the last great Persian poet and noted for his writings on Sufi philosophy.

Jammu and Kashmir   *See* **Kashmir**

Janáček, Leoš 1854–1928. Czech composer whose works reflect his intense interest in Czech folk music. His best-known work was his opera *Jenufa*.

Janissaries ⟨Janizaries⟩ A special elite corps of the army of the Ottoman Empire, noted for its military successes (15th–16th cents.). Members of the corps were procured by taking the children of Ottoman Christian subjects and training them. By the 18th cent. they had become involved in Ottoman politics. Opposing reform, they revolted (1826), were defeated, and the organization was dissolved.

Janizaries   *See* **Janissaries**

Jansen, Cornelis 1585–1638. Dutch bishop and theologian. His four-volume work *Augustinus* (1640) was a major influence in the development of Jansenism.

Jansenism Religious movement (*fl.* 17th–18th cents.) in the Roman Catholic church, centered in France. Characterized by its emphasis on the doc-

trines of divine grace and predestination and by its opposition to the Jesuits, Jansenism sought a return to the severity of early Christianity. The movement stemmed from the posthumous publication (1642) of *Augustinus*, a controversial work by C. Jansen based on the teachings of Saint Augustine. Papal condemnation of Jansenist doctrines began (1653) with Innocent X, and thereafter defense of the movement became a facet of the larger conflict, known as Gallicanism *(q.v.)*, between the pope and French Catholics. Jansenists were finally suppressed (1730) in France, however, when Louis XIV joined the pope in opposing them. Noted Jansenists were Antoine Arnauld, B. Pascal, and P. Quesnel.

January Insurrection ⟨Second Polish Revolution⟩ Revolution by Poles (1863–64) against Russian domination of the Congress Kingdom of Poland. Despite the liberalization of Russian rule in Poland by Czar Alexander II, Polish radicals (mainly students) continued political agitation. When the Polish government sought (Jan., 1863) to draft them into the Russian army, they fled to the countryside and began an armed insurrection. Although badly outnumbered and poorly armed, they gained popular support through their promises of land reform. The revolt thus spread to Lithuania and Belorussia. Receiving only diplomatic support from European powers and unable to institute their reforms, the rebels soon lost popular support. Russia crushed the insurrection, reinstituted direct administration of Poland, and reintroduced harsh measures.

Janus Roman god of beginnings and guardian of doors and archways. He is usually represented as having two faces. The month of January is named after him.

Japan Island country located off the east coast of Asia. Its capital is Tokyo. Throughout much of its early history, Japan was strongly influenced by Chinese culture. A feudal system of government, in which shoguns, or military leaders, held real power, evolved in Japan in the 12th cent. and continued well into the 19th cent. With the 19th-cent. Meiji Restoration, the emperor again held real power and the feudal system was abolished. Japan was rapidly modernized and, by the beginning of the 20th cent., was already a major industrial and military power. Militarists gradually gained control of government, however, and Japan joined the Axis Powers in WW II. Japan was forced to surrender after the US used atomic bombs against it. In the postwar era, Japan again rose as an industrial power and today ranks among the leading industrial nations. Key events in Japanese history include:

660 BC Legendary Emperor Jimmu supposedly founded Japanese Empire; all Japanese emperors traditionally believed descended from him.

AD 360 Legendary Empress Jingo supposedly led an army to invade Korea; contacts with the mainland stimulated the development of Japanese civilization.

AD 430 First imperial court records appear in (then) recently adopted Chinese script.

FROM 5TH CENT. Japan ruled under loose feudal system; Chinese cultural influence strong.

c552 Buddhism brought to Japan from Korea.

604 First Japanese constitution; established administration of imperial domains and created a council.

621 Imperial edict established Buddhism as the official religion of Japan.

794–1185 Heian period; Fujiwara family dominated government as regents; arts flourished.

794 Kyoto made imperial residence; remained capital for almost entire period to 1869.

966–1027 Dictatorship of Michinaga, greatest of the Fujiwaras, considered classical period of Japanese literature and culture.

1156 Hogen War; Minamoto and Taira clans gained power.

1180–85 Gempei War, civil war leading to downfall of Taira clan and rise of Minamoto clan as ruling family in Japan.

1192 Great Minamoto leader, Yoritomo, took the title of shogun, inaugurating military dictatorship and establishing military capital at Kamakura on Tokyo Bay.

1192 Shoguns, military rulers, established as actual rulers in Japan while emperors continued as nominal rulers; system of government continued to 1867, when emperor regained power.

13TH CENT. Zen Buddhism introduced by Dogen.

13TH CENT. Shinran flourished; he founded True Pure Land sect.

1219–1333 Hojo family served as virtual rulers of Japan (in post of regent); period marked by frequent civil wars.

1274 Mongols attempted invasion of Japan.

1281 Mongols again unsuccessful in attempt to invade Japan; fleet broken up by typhoon, which gave rise to kamikaze ("divine wind").

1331–33 Emperor Daigo II (reigned 1318–39) unsuccessfully attempted to break power of shoguns and restore imperial authority; Hojo family, driven out by Daigo, replaced by Ashikaga family.

1338–1578 Muromachi period; Ashikaga shoguns ruled with their capital at Kyoto; period marked by frequent wars between feudal lords; Buddhist church became powerful political and military force; arts flourished; commercial prosperity.

1542 Portuguese made first contact with Japanese.

1549 Saint Francis Xavier began Christian missionary work in Japan.

1568–82 Nobunga, warrior of the Taira clan, gained control of the government and broke the power of the Buddhist church.

1590 Hideyoshi unified Japan under his control as dictator; reorganized the feudal nobility and their lands.

1592, 1596 Hideyoshi twice invaded Korea.

1603 Tokugawa shogunate founded by Ieyasu; capital moved from Kyoto to (modern) Tokyo.

1603–1867 Tokugawa period; capital at Tokyo; rigid feudal system instituted; rise of the samurai, feudal loyalties, and Confucianism; commercial prosperity and the rise of the merchant class.

1612 Persecution of Christians began

1624 Period of isolationism began; travel to and from Europe forbidden; only Dutch traders allowed use of one port, Nagasaki.

1637–38 Shimabara Rebellion by Japanese Catholics.

1720 Ban on European books ended; subsequent years marked by increasing contact with Europeans.

1841–43 Tempo Reforms introduced by Tokugawa shogunate in unsuccessful attempt to return to feudal agricultural society.

1854 US Commodore M. Perry forced Japan to officially end isolation and sign Treaty of Kanagawa (Mar. 3).

1858 Harris Treaty signed, opening five ports to US trade (July 29).

1867 Imperial courtiers allied with landowners forced resignation of last shogun and "restored" the boy emperor Meiji, or Mutsuhito (reigned 1867–1912).

1867–1912 Meiji Restoration; power of emperor restored; period of modernization and Westernization in Japan, during which time Japan rapidly developed its industry and became a world power.

AFTER 1868 Rise of the Zaibatsu, family-controlled cartels.

1871 Feudal fiefs abolished by imperial decree; merchant families ascendant.

1876 Samurai warrior class abolished by imperial decree after system of universal military service was established.

1877 Satsuma Rebellion, unsuccessful revolt by samurai warriors.

1889 Constitution drafted by Prince H. Ito, establishing limited constitutional monarchy with bicameral legislature.

1894–95 Sino-Japanese War fought with China over control of Korea; Japan emerged victorious and gained substantial Chinese concessions; marked beginning of Japanese imperialism.

1899 Rights of extraterritoriality in Japan abandoned by major powers.

1904–05 Russo-Japanese War fought; victorious Japan emerged as a world power; first defeat of European by an Asian power.

1905 Treaty of Portsmouth ended the Russo-Japanese War (Sept. 5); Japan maintained foothold in Manchuria.

1908 "Gentlemen's Agreement" with US by which Japan restricted emigration of laborers.

1910 Japan annexed Korea (Aug.).

1912–26 Emperor Taisho reigned.

1914 WW I; Japan occupied Tsingtao and the German-held Marshall, Caroline, and Mariana islands.

1915 Twenty-one Demands presented to China; sought virtual control of China.

1918–22 Japanese forces played major role in Allied military expedition against revolutionary Red Army in Siberia during Russian Civil War.

1921 Four-Power Treaty signed.

1922 Nine-Power Treaty signed.

1925 Universal manhood suffrage instituted.

1926– Emperor Hirohito reigned.

1929 Japan hard-hit by Great Depression; gave impetus to militarist movement.

1931 Japan overran Manchuria following the Mukden Incident, deliberately provoked by its army there (Sept. 18); soon after, created puppet state of Manchukuo.

1932 Prime minister T. Inukai assassinated; rise of militarists in the Japanese government.

1933 Japan withdrew from League of Nations after a commission criticized its Manchurian policy.

1936 Anti-Comintern Pact signed; was a German-Japanese agreement to oppose the Communist International.

1936 Militarists unsuccessfully attempted coup.

1937–45 Second Sino-Japanese War; culminated in gradual expansion of Japanese influence in China.,

1938 National Mobilization bill passed; gave government control over industry and finance; created Japanese war machine.

1940 Political parties dissolved, following period of increasing police repression.

1940 WW II, Japan joined the Rome-Berlin Axis (Sept.).

1940 "Greater East Asia Co-Prosperity Sphere" proclaimed; Japanese troops dispatched to occupy French Indochina.

1941 Neutrality pact signed with Soviets (Sept.).

1941 Gen. H. Tojo became prime minister; militarists thus gained complete control of the government (Oct.).

1941–45 Japan a major participant in WW II; engaged US in Pacific theater, beginning with Pearl Harbor attack (Dec. 7); after initial gains, Japanese were slowly driven back and defeated; final surrender came after US dropped atomic bombs on Hiroshima (Aug. 6) and Nagasaki (Aug. 9).

1945–52 American occupation; forces under Gen. D. MacArthur in complete control; instituted a demilitarization and democratization process; economy recovered slowly.

1946 Emperor Hirohito acceded to a new constitution and the role of constitutional monarch (May).

1948 War crimes trials of militarists concluded.

1951 Peace treaty concluded at San Francisco between Japan and most of her wartime enemies, including the US (Sept.).

1951 Security treaty with the US (renewed 1960, 1970); US to defend Japan against attack; allowed US troops to be stationed there.

1952 Japan regained full sovereignty (Apr. 28).

AFTER 1955 Liberal Democratic party became dominant in Japan.

1958 Japan became a member of the UN.

1960 Widespread protest against US-Japanese security treaty forced Prime Minister Kishi Nobusuke to resign.

1972 US restored Okinawa to Japan (May 15).

1972 Agreement signed in China formally ended state of war between Japan and China (begun Sept. 25, 1937); relations with China resumed.

1974 Liberal Democrat Kakuei Tanaka resigned as prime minister (in office 1972–74).

1976 Tanaka jailed for accepting money in Lockheed scandal; Liberal Democratic party narrowly retained control of government.

1976–78 Prime Minister Takeo Fukuda in office; Japan entered period of economic prosperity; began negotiations with US and other countries to reduce her trade surplus.

1978–80 Masayoshi Ohira in office as prime minister; economic prosperity continued.

1980– Zenko Suzuki in office as prime minister, successor to Ohira, who died in office (June 12).

1982 Japan's continuing economic growth and favorable balance of payments led to US demands for easing of restrictions on imports to Japan and limitations on auto exports to the US.

Japheth In the Bible, the son of Noah and ancestor of the peoples who inhabited Europe and Asia Minor.

Jaques-Delacroze, Émile 1865–1905. Swiss composer. He developed eurhythmics, the expression of musical rhythms through bodily movement.

Jason Mythological Greek leader of the Argonauts (q.v.), who sailed to obtain the Golden Fleece.

Jaspers, Karl 1883–1969. German philosopher and psychopathologist and a leading figure in the modern existential movement of philosophy.

Jassy, Treaty of ⟨Iasi⟩ Agreement signed between Russia and Turkey on Jan. 9, 1792, at the end of the Russo-Turkish War (1787–92). The Ottomans regained Moldavia, Walachia, and Bessarabia, while Russia gained a portion of the Black Sea coast and saw her annexation of the Crimea recognized.

Jaurès, Jean 1859–1914. French Socialist leader who helped to found the unified French Socialist party (1905). He opposed the imminent French-German military confrontation of WW I and was assassinated by a fanatical nationalist.

Java Sea, Battle of the Japanese naval victory (Feb. 27–Mar. 1, 1942) during WW II over an Allied force in the Java Sea. A fleet of 14 Dutch, British, Australian, and American ships, under Dutch command, was routed by a superior Japanese force. The Japanese sank all Allied ships but four American destroyers and sustained minimal losses. The victory opened the way to their subsequent conquest of Java.

Jay, John 1745–1829. American founding father. He was president of the Continental Congress (1778). With B. Franklin and J. Adams, he negotiated peace with Britain after the American Revolutionary War. He favored a strong central government and was one of the authors of the Federalist Papers (q.v.). As the first chief justice, he held the states to be subordinate to the federal government in Chisholm vs Georgia (1793)—a decision that provoked the passage of the 11th Amendment, denying authority to the federal courts in suits brought by citizens against states. He negotiated Jay's Treaty (q.v.), the unpopularity of which ruined his chances for the presidency. He later served two terms as governor of New York (1795–1801).

Jayewardene, Junius Richard See **Sri Lanka**

Jay's Treaty Treaty concluded Nov. 10, 1794, between the US and Great Britain. Though the US won most of the important concessions it sought, the treaty nevertheless aroused a heated controversy in the US and was denounced as a surrender to the British. Negotiated by J. Jay (US) and Lord Grenville (Brit.), the treaty was intended to forestall another war with Britain. It provided for British evacuation of the Northwest Territory, settlement of boundaries between the US and British holdings in North America, compensation for attacks on US shipping, and removal of most restrictions on US commerce within British territories. Restrictions on US trade with the British West Indies were among the provisions that fueled the controversy.

Jeanne d'Arc See **Joan of Arc**

Jeans, Sir James Hopwood 1877–1946. English mathematical physicist and astronomer. He contributed to the dynamical theory of gases and the tidal theory of planetary evolution and wrote many popular books on astronomy.

Jedda See **Jidda**

Jefferson, Thomas 1743–1826. Third US president (1801–09), successor to J. Adams. His administration, a victory for the Jeffersonian Republicans, saw the decline of the Federalist party. Earlier, Jefferson was active in the events leading up to the American Revolution. He was a leader in the House of Burgesses (q.v.) in Virginia, helped organize the Committees of Correspondence (q.v.), was a delegate to the Second Continental Congress (1775–76), and wrote the draft of the Declaration of Independence (q.v.). In following years he served as governor of Virginia (1779–81), delegate to the Continental Congress (1783–84), and as secretary of state (1790–93). In the latter post he became the center of the anti-Federalist faction and quarreled with Federalist leader A. Hamilton. Support for his opposition faction, which came to be called the Jeffersonian Republicans, grew in intervening years, and in 1796 Jefferson was elected vice-president (1797–1801). During this period he drafted the Kentucky Resolutions (q.v.) in response to passage of the Alien and Sedition Acts, which were at least partly directed at Jeffersonian Republicans. His support increased, and he became president (election decided in House of Representatives) in 1801 and was reelected in 1804. His term was marked by US participation in the Tripolitan War (q.v.), the Louisiana Purchase (q.v.), the Lewis and Clark expedition (q.v.), prohibition of the slave trade in the US, A. Burr's trial on charges of treason, and conflicts with Britain over attacks on US shipping. Incidents such as that involving the Cheaspeake (q.v.), were an outgrowth of war between Britain and Napoleon, and Jefferson tried unsuccessfully to impose trade embargoes (see Embargo Act) to put a stop to them. The failure of these measures later contributed to the outbreak of the War of 1812 with Britain.

Jeffersonian Republicans First opposition political party in US history and direct ancestor of the present Democratic party (q.v.). Organized in the 1790s around opposition to Federalism (q.v.), it held power nationally between 1801 and 1825 under the presidencies of T. Jefferson, J. Madison, and J. Monroe. It advocated limited government.

Jeffreys of Wem, George Jeffreys, 1st Baron 1645?–1689. English judge under James II, notorious for his vicious and corrupt conduct during the Bloody Assizes, following the 1685 rebellion of James Scott, duke of Monmouth.

Jeffries, Dr. John See **Blanchard, Jean Pierre**

Jehoahaz ⟨Joahaz⟩ d. c804 BC. King of Israel, son and successor to Jehu. The Bible reports that under him the northern kingdom reached one of its lowest points because he did what was evil (II Kings 13:1–9).

Jehoash ⟨Joash⟩ **1.** King of Judah (837?–798? BC). Rescued from death at the hands of Jehu and made king at seven, he reigned 40 years before being assassinated. **2.** King of Israel (800?–785? BC). He was son and successor to Jehoahaz, and his reign was supported by the prophet Elisha. At Beth Shemesh he defeated and reduced Judah to vassalage.

Jehoiachin fl. c598 BC. King of Judah, successor to his father, Jehoiakim. He ruled only a few months before being captured (597?) by Nebuchadnezzar, carried to Babylon with 10,000 of his people, and imprisoned until the emperor's death.

Jehoiakim fl. c600 BC. King of Judah (609–598) and son of Josiah. He deposed his brother with the support of Pharaoh Necho. He later rebelled against the Babylonian Nebuchadnezzar, and died before the Babylonian capture of Jerusalem. Jeremiah prophesied the destruction of Jerusalem and the Temple during his reign.

Jehoram ⟨Joram⟩ d. c843 BC. King of Israel and son of Ahab. With aid from the king of Judah, he suppressed a revolt in Moab. The death of Jehoram and his family at the hands of Jehu marked the end of the family of Ahab.

Jehoshaphat ⟨Josaphat⟩ fl. 9th cent. BC. King of Judah, successor to his father, Asa. He allied himself with Ahab, king of Israel, and was killed in the latter's expedition to capture Ramoth-Gilead from Syria.

Jehovah's Witnesses Religious sect founded in the US by Charles Taze Russell (1852–1916) during the late 19th cent. The Witnesses are noted for their belief in Christ's imminent Second Coming and in their rejection of national allegiances. The

members promote their views through the publications The Watchtower, Awake!

Jehu King of Israel (842–815 BC) and legendary chariot driver. He led the revolt against Ahab and his wife, Jezebel, which resulted in their murder because they introduced Baal worship. He also slew kings Jehoram and Ahaziah of Israel and Judah, and was anointed king of the former by the prophet Elijah.

Jellicoe, John Rushworth Jellicoe, 1st Earl 1859–1935. British naval officer who led the British fleet against the German navy at the WW I Battle of Jutland (q.v.) in 1916.

Jemappes, Battle of Battle of the French Revolutionary Wars (q.v.), fought on Nov. 6, 1792, at Jemappes, in southern Belgium. The French defeat of the Austrian army led to French occupation of Belgium.

Jena-Auerstedt, Battles of French victories in related battles fought on Oct. 14, 1806, in the Napoleonic Wars. **1.** At Jena, Napoleon flanked and defeated several Prussian and Saxon forces totaling some 48,000 men, with his army totaling some 56,000. Napoleon lost about 5,000 men and pushed on to Weimar; German casualties were 11,000 killed and wounded and 15,000 captured. **2.** North, in Auerstedt, on the same day, a 26,000-man French force under Marshal L. N. Davout assaulted a 63,000-man Prussian force. The French lost 8,000 men but killed or wounded 12,000 of the enemy.

Jenghiz Khan See **Genghis Khan**

Jenkins's Ear, War of War (1739–c1743) between England and Spain. The war was soon absorbed by the larger conflict of the War of the Austrian Succession (q.v.). Exclusion of English traders from Spain's American colonies led to smuggling and to a growing resentment against the Spanish. Matters came to a head (1738) when Capt. Robert Jenkins (fl. 1731–39) appeared before Parliament. There he exhibited the remains of his ear, which he claimed the Spanish had cut off (1731) after boarding his ship in the West Indies. War was declared (1739), despite Sir R. Walpole's reluctance. In addition to English attacks (1739–40) on Spanish cities in the Caribbean, there were two attacks (1740, 1743) on St. Augustine (Florida), led by J. Oglethorpe, and a Spanish attack (1742) on Georgia. By 1743, however, hostilities in the Americas had become part of King George's War (q.v.), which was itself a part of the War of the Austrian Succession.

Jenner, Edward 1749–1823. English physician. From 1796 he pioneered the use of vaccination to prevent smallpox, a major step in the development of the science of immunology.

Jennings, Sarah, duchess of Marlborough *See* **Anne, queen of England**

Jeremiah ⟨Jeremias⟩ *c*650–*c*570 BC. One of the major Hebrew prophets, whose activities and prophecies are recorded in the Old Testament book named for him. He claimed to have received a divine call to be a prophet in the 13th year of King Josiah (627–626 BC). He preached social justice, warned against Egypt, and counseled the leaders of Judah to accept Babylonian vassalage. He prophesied the fall of Jerusalem and the Temple in the reign of King Jehoiakim (609–598 BC), ascribing these coming calamities to the people's apostasy from God. After the Babylonian captivity (586 BC), he was taken to Egypt, where he died. A personal feature of the prophecies of Jeremiah are his laments at being obliged to preach a message so unpopular that he was constantly threatened with imprisonment and death.

Jeremias *See* **Jeremiah**

Jericho Ancient city in Palestine, west of the Jordan River. It was captured and destroyed (*c*1400–1200 BC) by the Israelites under Joshua, according to the Bible. Modern archaeological excavations have shown that the city was several times destroyed and rebuilt during a history of continuous occupation dating back to *c*8000 BC.

Jeroboam I *fl.* 10th cent. BC. First king of the divided northern kingdom of Israel. He is noted for encouraging idolatry in his kingdom, after successfully leading the revolt against Solomon's successor, Rehoboam (933 BC), which left only the southern kingdom to the house of David.

Jeroboam II *fl.* 8th cent. BC. King of Israel, successor to his father, Jehoash. He was the last great king of an independent Israel. The prophets Amos and Hosea appeared during his reign.

Jerom Bos *See* **Bosch, Hieronymus**

Jerome, Saint AD *c*347–419? Christian scholar and monastic leader. After retreating to the desert for study, he was ordained in AD 378 and became secretary to Pope Saint Damasus (382). From 386, he lived in a Bethlehem monastery, where he wrote several theological works, corresponded with Saint Augustine and other church leaders, and did his monumental translation of the Bible from the original Greek and Hebrew into Latin. This Latin version of the Bible, called the Vulgate *(q.v.)*, remained the official version of the Bible in the Western Catholic church until it was finally replaced by an updated Latin version in 1979.

Jerome of Prague *c*1365–1416. Czech religious reformer who supported the doctrines of J. Wyclif and defended J. Huss at the Council of Constance *(q.v.)*. He was burned as a heretic.

Jerusalem Israeli capital city (pop. 376,000), located in central Israel. Historically, it is important to the Jewish people as the capital of their ancient kingdom of Israel; to the Christians as the site of the Last Supper, the crucifixion, and the resurrection of Christ; and to the Muslims as the place where Muhammad ascended to heaven. Inhabited from the 2d millennium BC (and perhaps earlier), the ancient city was conquered by King David (*c*1000 BC) and became the capital of the kingdom of Israel *(q.v.)*. His son, King Solomon, built the Temple (*c*970 BC) and thereby established the city's importance to the Jewish religion. It was conquered variously in succeeding centuries until 586 BC, when the Babylonian king Nebuchadnezzar took the city, destroyed the Temple, and instituted the Babylonian captivity *(q.v.)*. Persian king Cyrus returned the city to the Hebrews some years later, and the Temple was rebuilt by 515 BC. From the 2d cent. BC, under the Maccabees *(q.v.)*, the city rose to great prominence and, after the Roman conquest in 65 BC, the city flourished as the capital of the Roman client king, Herod the Great. This period of Roman control was marked by the crucifixion of Christ, the Jewish Revolts *(q.v.)*, destruction of the city and Temple by the Romans (AD 70), and the rebuilding of the city by Emperor Hadrian. With toleration of Christianity established within the empire, Jerusalem became a Christian center (4th cent. AD). It was conquered (AD 637) by the Muslims (who constructed the Dome of the Rock mosque, *q.v.*), by the crusaders (who made it the capital of the Latin kingdom of Jerusalem, *q.v.*), and by the Muslim conqueror Saladin (1187). Thereafter the city declined until the 19th cent. During WW I, it was captured (1917) by the British and made the capital of their territory of Palestine. The UN plan for creation of the Israeli state set Jerusalem aside as an internationally administered city, but, during the 1948 Arab-Israeli War, the Arabs occupied the Old City and the Israelis took the New City (made the Israeli capital in 1950). In the 1967 Arab-Israeli War, the Israelis occupied the Old City and annexed it (June, 1967).

Jerusalem, Council of Conference convened by the Apostles in Jerusalem (AD *c*50) concerning the rights of gentile Christians. In the interests of church harmony, it was ruled that the gentiles were exempted from the Mosaic Law observed by the Judaic Christians. Paul and Barnabas pleaded for exemption for the gentile Christians, and Peter agreed. The entire proceedings are described in Acts 15.

Jerusalem, Latin kingdom of *See* **Latin kingdom of Jerusalem**

Jerusalem, Saint Cyril of *See* **Cyril of Jerusalem, Saint**

Jerusalem, Synod of ⟨Bethlehem, Synod of⟩ Council held in Bethlehem (1672) by the Eastern Orthodox church to denounce Calvinist and Lutheran doctrine and defend the memory of Cyril Lucaris (1572?–1638), patriarch of Constantinople (1621), from the accusations of Protestantism lodged against him.

Jervis, Sir John *See* **Cape Saint Vincent, Battle of**

Jesse In the Bible, the father of David. He is represented as the first member of the genealogical line leading to Jesus Christ.

Jesuit Estates Act Law passed in 1888 by the Quebec legislature; this law was controversial because of Protestant objections. The act awarded the Society of Jesus $400,000 as partial restitution for property appropriated by the British government following temporary suppression of the Jesuit order (1773).

Jesuits *See* **Society of Jesus**

Jesus ⟨Jesus Christ⟩ *c*8/6 BC–AD *c*29. Founder of Christianity, recognized by Christians as the Son of God and the Messiah whose coming was prophesied. His life, as set forth in the four Gospels, began with his miraculous birth (celebrated Dec. 25) to Mary at Bethlehem. Jesus was a Jew and was raised in his father's trade of carpentry. He grew up in a period of unrest among the Jews, then chafing under Roman rule. Following his baptism by John the Baptist *(q.v.)*, Jesus realized his divine calling and retired into the wilderness to meditate. Gathering his disciples about him, Jesus then undertook missions to Galilee. The success of these and other missions, the power of his miracles, and his attacks on the Pharisees made Jesus a threat to the governmental and religious authorities of Jerusalem. Thus, when he went to Jerusalem for the last time and created a sensation by ousting the money-changers from the Temple, the authorities sought to eliminate him. After the Last Supper *(q.v.)*, Jesus was betrayed by Judas Iscariot, arrested, and crucified. Blame for the death of Jesus has been a major controversy within the Christian church, some holding the Jewish people accountable, while others (especially in recent times) believe it was the Roman officials. He was entombed that day, and some days later his resurrection (celebrated as Easter) became known in Jerusalem. Thereafter his disciples went forth to spread his teachings, and thus began the Christian era.

Jesus, Society of *See* **Society of Jesus**

Jesus Christ *See* **Jesus**

Jethro In the Bible, a priest of the Midianites and father-in-law of Moses. He advised Moses to appoint deputies to help govern the people.

Jewish Agency An international political group evolved from the World Zionist Organization. Founded by C. Weizmann (1929), the agency was the primary institution responsible for the establishment of a Jewish state in Palestine (1948). It sought world support and oversaw the settlement of Jews in Palestine and functioned as a kind of "government" of the Jews settled there, dealing with the British Mandate authorities.

Jewish Revolts Revolts of ancient Palestine Jews against Roman rule. **1.** The first revolt (AD 66–73) resulted in the capture of Jerusalem and the destruction of the Jewish Temple by the Roman general (later emperor) Titus in AD 70. **2.** The second revolt (AD 132–135), led by S. Bar Kokhba, was bloodily suppressed by Hadrian, who converted Jerusalem to Aelia Capitolina and forbade any Jew to live in it.

Jews Term generally used to refer to individuals who are either of Jewish parentage or who are followers of the Judaic religion. Within the Jewish community some groups apply stricter limitations on the use of the term. Jew, Hebrew, and Israelite are frequently used interchangeably, but these terms properly refer to peoples of specific historic periods. Hebrew usually refers to the nomadic people who were ancestors of the Jews. Israelite refers to the Hebrews and their descendants who inhabited the Holy Land. It applies to these peoples in the period from their entry into the Holy Land until the end of the Babylonian captivity in 538 BC. Israelites who survived the captivity are called Jews, and this applies to their descendants into modern times. (For history, *see* Palestine, Judaism, Israel.)

Jezebel *fl.* 9th cent. BC. In the Bible, Phoenician princess who became the wife of King Ahab of Israel. She encouraged the worship of Baal and was a bitter opponent of the prophet Elijah, who prophesied her downfall. This in fact came about when Jehu triumphed over the house of Ahab; Jezebel was thrown from her window and killed, and her body was eaten by dogs. Her name is used to describe any wicked woman.

Jhelum, Battle of *See* **Hydaspes, Battle of the**

Jibran, Khalil *See* **Gibran, Kahlil**

Jidda ⟨Jedda⟩ Seaport city (pop. 561,100) in western Saudi Arabia. A major commercial center, it is the port of entry for pilgrims traveling to Mecca and for most nonpetroleum commerce with the Kingdom of Saudi Arabia. The modern city was founded in the 1600s about 12 miles north of Old

Jidda, which was founded around AD 646 by the caliph Uthman.

jihad *See* **holy war**

Jim Crow laws Laws passed by states in the US South legalizing racial segregation. In the 1880s, following Reconstruction *(q.v.)*, statutes were devised separating blacks from whites in transportation facilities and excluding blacks entirely from specific establishments (housing, schooling, etc.) serving whites. In 1896, the US Supreme Court, in *Plessy* vs *Ferguson*, ruled separate but equal facilities constitutional, and the Jim Crow laws were not successfully challenged until after WW II. It wasn't until the ruling in the 1954 *Brown* vs *Board of Education of Topeka* case *(q.v.)* declaring separate educational facilities to be unconstitutional that the doctrine began to be reversed. In 1963, the March on Washington *(q.v.)* helped lead to the civil rights acts *(q.v.)* of the 1960s, which effectively outlawed Jim Crow laws and customs. The name is believed to have been taken from a character in a popular minstrel show.

Jimenez de Cisneros, Francisco ⟨Ximenes, Cardinal⟩ 1436–1517. Spanish prelate and statesman. An austere Franciscan, he was confessor to Queen Isabella (1492) and later archbishop of Toledo (1495) and cardinal. He was regent of Spain after the death of Ferdinand (1516) and faced down the nobles while preparing for the accession of Charles I (later the emperor Charles V). A patron of learning, he founded the University of Alcalá (1508) but was also a severe inquisitor general (named 1507).

Jimenez de Quesada, Gonzalo *c*1500–79. Spanish conquistador who conquered Colombia and founded Bogotá (1538).

Jimmu Tenno *fl.* 660 BC. Legendary first emperor of Japan. Believed to have been a direct descendant of the Sun Goddess, he is regarded as founder of the dynasty of Japanese emperors that still reigns today.

jingoism Term used to describe advocates of extreme nationalistic fervor. It was first applied to those who wanted Britain to intervene on the side of Turkey in the Russo-Turkish War of 1877–78 and came from a line in a popular song, "We don't want to fight, but, by jingo, if we do, we've got the ships, we've got the men, we've got the money too."

Jinnah, Muhammad Ali 1876–1948. Indian Muslim statesman. He served as head of the Muslim League from 1934 to 1948, led the struggle to establish Pakistan *(q.v.)*, and served as its first governor-general (1947–48).

Joab Old Testament soldier. A nephew of David, he commanded David's army. He was notably brutal in the deaths of Abner, Amasa, and Absalom. He was executed by Solomon.

Joachim, Joseph 1831–1907. Hungarian violinist and composer, noted for his interpretation and performance of works for violin.

Joahaz *See* **Jehoahaz**

Joanna II 1371–1435. Last Angevin queen of Naples. Her reign (1414–35) was marked by numerous intrigues and love affairs and a power struggle between the houses of Anjou and Aragon for control of Naples.

Joan of Arc ⟨Jeanne d'Arc⟩ *c*1412–31. French saint and heroine during the Hundred Years' War *(q.v.)*. A visionary, the young girl became convinced she had a divine mission to aid the French dauphin Charles (later Charles VII) against his opponents, the English and the Burgundians. After persuading Charles to give her troops, she raised the Siege of Orleans *(q.v.)* in 1429 and won the Battle of Patay *(q.v.)*. Shortly after Charles's coronation, however, she failed in her siege of Paris and was captured by the Burgundians. Turned over to an ecclesiastical court, she was tried as a heretic and was burned at the stake (May 30, 1431). She was canonized in 1920.

Joash *See* **Jehoash**

Job Biblical figure. Job, the faithful servant of God, maintains his faith despite incredible trials and the loss of everything he values in his life. Eventually he is restored by God to happiness. The book of Job in the Bible is considered one of the world's most profound attempts to explain why the innocent suffer while the wicked prosper.

Jodl, Alfred 1890–1946. German general. Jodl was Hitler's chief of the armed forces operation staff and a key adviser. He was condemned to death at the Nürnberg Trials *(q.v.)* for his shooting of hostages and prisoners of war.

Joel *c*5th cent. BC. Old Testament prophet. One of the minor prophets, he foretells the establishment of Jerusalem as a fertile, holy city upon the people's full acceptance of God.

Joffre, Joseph Jacques Césaire 1852–1931. French general and marshal of France. He was commander in chief of the army in WW I (1914–16), and his tactics led to the French victory at the 1914 Battle of the Marne *(q.v.)*.

Johanan ben Zaccai *fl.* 1st cent. AD. Leader of the Pharisees at Jerusalem. After the destruction of Jerusalem by the Romans (AD 70), he founded the academy at Jabne (Jamnia), thus assuring the survival of traditional Judaism.

Johannesburg Largest city (pop. 1,441,000) and commercial center of the Republic of South Africa. Founded in 1886, it is the mining center of the Witwatersrand gold fields in Transvaal province.

John 1167?–1216. King of England (1199–1216). The youngest son of Henry II, he succeeded his older brother, Richard I. He quarreled with the church and saw his kingdom placed under a papal interdict in 1208. He abused feudal custom and was forced by his barons to sign the Magna Carta (q.v.), England's first grant of general liberties, in 1215. During his reign England lost most of its domains on the continent (Angevin empire).

John I c925–976. Byzantine emperor (969–976). He recaptured Bulgaria from the Russians and extended Byzantine rule over parts of Syria.

John I ⟨John the Posthumous⟩ 1316. King of France and posthumous son of Louis X. He lived only five days and was succeeded by Louis's brother, Philip V.

John I 1350–95. King of Aragon (1387–95), successor to his father, Peter IV. He was a patron of education, and he adopted a friendly policy toward French politics and customs.

John I ⟨John the Great⟩ 1357–1433. Portuguese king (1385–1433), successor to his half-brother, Ferdinand I, and an illegitimate son of Pedro I. He opposed Castilian claims to the Portuguese throne during the interregnum (1383–85) that followed Ferdinand's death. Following an invasion (1384) by Castilian armies, John was crowned (1385) and went on to win the Battle of Aljubarrota (q.v.) in 1385. This victory marked the turning point in the hostilities (ended formally, 1411) and thus secured Portugal's independence. During his subsequent reign, John concluded an alliance with England (1386) and began the period of Portuguese overseas colonization. One of John's sons was Prince Henry the Navigator.

John I 1358–90. Spanish king of Castile and León (1379–90). He had to defend his throne against a claim by John of Gaunt and ended up marrying off his son and successor to the latter's daughter. He tried to unite the Portuguese and Castilian crowns but was twice defeated by the Portuguese, notably at the Battle of Aljubarrota (q.v.) in 1385.

John I ⟨John Zápolya⟩ 1487–1540. King of Hungary (1526–40) and governor of Transylvania (1511–26). His reign as king was marked by conflict with Ferdinand of Austria, who claimed the throne.

John II ⟨John Comnenus⟩ 1088–1143. Byzantine emperor (1118–43). John occupied himself with regaining lost Byzantine lands and influence. He was successful against the Magyars, Serbs, Petchenegs, and Roger II of Sicily, but was forced to yield trading privileges to Venice.

John II ⟨John the Good⟩ 1319–64. King of France (1350–64), successor to his father, Philip VI. Captured by the English in the Battle of Poitiers (1356) during the Hundred Years' War, he was released in return for hostages. When one hostage escaped, John returned voluntarily to England, where he died.

John II 1397–1479. King of Aragon (1458–79) and Navarre (1425–79), successor in Aragon to his brother Alfonso V. His reign was troubled by civil war and rebellion.

John II 1405–54. Spanish king of Castile (1406–54), successor to Henry III. A patron of the arts, he left governing to a favorite. He was the father of Isabella I.

John II ⟨John the Perfect⟩ 1455–95. King of Portugal (1481–95), successor to his father, Alfonso V. He curbed the power of the nobility, made peace with Spain, and sponsored colonizing expeditions. Bartholomew Dias rounded the Cape of Good Hope (1488) during his reign.

John II 1609–72. King of Poland (1648–68). His reign was called "the Deluge" because of incessant warfare with the Cossacks, Russia, and Sweden. In 1655, Charles X of Sweden nearly overran Poland. After ceding the Ukraine to Russia, John retired to a monastery.

John III ⟨John Ducas Vatatzes⟩ d. 1254. Byzantine emperor of Nicaea (1222–54). John was left only the region of Nicaea by his father-in-law and predecessor, Theordore I Lascaris. John managed to recapture much lost territory but could not regain Constantinople from the Latins.

John III ⟨John the Fortunate⟩ 1502–57. King of Portugal (1521–57). Portuguese influence in Brazil, India, Macao, and the Spice Islands was expanded during John's reign. Domestically, he instituted the Inquisition and involved the Jesuits in higher education. The Portuguese overseas empire reached its apogee during his reign.

John III ⟨John Sobieski⟩ 1624–96. King of Poland (1674–96). John was commander in chief of the Polish army prior to his election as king. His reign was marked by constant warfare with the Turks. For raising the Turkish siege of Vienna (1683) he became known as the champion of Christendom.

John IV d. 1656. King of Portugal (1640–56). John expelled the Spanish from Portugal (1640) and became king. He also ousted the Dutch from Brazil (1654) and allied himself with France against Spain in order to protect his interests. He was the first king of the Braganca (q.v.) line.

John V ⟨John Palaeologus⟩ 1332–91. Byzantine emperor (1341–91), successor to his father, Andronicus III. He was forced to recognize the suzerainty of the Ottoman Turks, who had captured large parts of the empire. He tried to heal the Christian schism between East and West in order to secure Western help against the Turks.

John V 1689–1750. King of Portugal (1706–50). John inherited the War of the Spanish Succession *(q.v.)* but eventually made peace with France and Spain. Enriched by gold from Brazil, his court was an elegant center of culture. He increased Catholic influence in secular affairs.

John VI ⟨John Cantacuzenus⟩ 1292–1383. Byzantine emperor (1347–54). He was chief adviser to Andronicus III and claimed the regency after the latter's death (1341). He fought and later became coregent with John V through the aid of the Ottoman Turks, thus helping the Turks to gain more power over the empire. He abdicated (1354) and retired to a monastery, where he wrote a history of the period.

John VI 1769–1826. King of Portugal (1816–26). Regent from 1799 for his insane mother, Maria I, he was forced to rule from Brazil (1807–21) because of the Napoleonic Wars and French occupation. He was also forced to recognize Brazilian independence (1825) under his son Dom Pedro I.

John VIII d. 882. Pope (872–882). John opposed Ignatius of Constantinople and supported Photius. He allowed the Slavs to use their own languages in liturgy. He was forced to pay tribute to the Saracens for Rome's protection. Overall he was the strongest pope of the 9th cent.

John VIII ⟨John Palaeologus⟩ 1390–1448. Byzantine emperor (1425–48). John was left only the city of Constantinople at his accession. He unsuccessfully sought to safeguard his remaining domains by agreeing (1439) to a union of Eastern and Western churches at the Council of Florence.

John XII ⟨Octavian⟩ c937–964. Pope (955–964). He crowned Otto I Holy Roman Emperor (962), and, after conspiring against him, was deposed by a synod of 50 German and Italian bishops organized by Otto.

John XXI ⟨Giuliano, Pedro⟩ d. 1277. Pope (1276–77). John was the only Portuguese pope. He was the author of both medical and scholastic philosophical texts, including the *Compendium of Logic.*

John XXII 1244–1334. Pope (1316–34), who reigned at Avignon. He condemned the spiritual Franciscans, improved church administration, and struggled with Holy Roman Emperor Louis IV over papal authority in the empire.

John XXIII ⟨Roncalli, Angelo Giuseppe⟩ 1881–1963. Italian pope (1958–63), successor to Pius XII and a highly popular figure in the history of the modern church. Born to a poor family, he was ordained (1904) and later served in Vatican diplo-

matic posts. As pope, he was noted for promoting peace and social reforms to aid the poor, especially in such acclaimed encyclicals as *Mater et Magistra* and *Pacem in Terris* (both 1961); seeking cooperation with other religious denominations; and convening the Second Vatican Council *(q.v.).*

John XXIII (antipope) *See* **Cossa, Baldassarre**

John, Saint *fl.* 1st cent. AD. One of the Apostles. Brother of James, he was, with Peter, closest to Jesus and was the "disciple whom Jesus loved." Traditionally held to be the author of the fourth Gospel, three epistles, and the Book of Revelation, he was also held to have lived to an advanced age in Ephesus, dying there AD c100.

John Baptist de la Salle, Saint 1651–1719. French priest and educator and founder of the Christian Brothers teaching order. He spent his life teaching the children of the poor. In order to train his teachers, he founded (1685), at Rheims, what is considered the first normal school.

John Birch Society US organization devoted to exposing Communist subversion in the US and abolishing liberal legislation. Founded in 1958, it was briefly one of the foremost right-wing groups operating in the US.

John Cantacuzenus *See* **John VI**

John Capistran, Saint ⟨John of Capistrano, Saint⟩ 1385?–1436. Italian Franciscan priest. John preached against the Hussites *(q.v.)* in Germany and unsuccessfully led a band of crusaders to Belgrade in order to try to oust the Turks.

John Comnenus *See* **John II**

John Damascene, Saint *See* **John of Damascus, Saint**

John Ducas Vatatzes *See* **John III**

John Frederick I ⟨John Frederick the Magnanimous⟩ 1503–54. Elector (1532–47) and duke (1547–54) of Saxony, last elector of the Ernestine branch of the house of Witten. A leader of the Schmalkaldic League *(q.v.),* he warred against Emperor Charles V, and lost his electorship.

John Frederick the Magnanimous *See* **John Frederick I**

John Lackland *See* **John**

John Maurice of Nassau 1604–79. Dutch general and colonial governor. John conquered much of Brazil from Portugal for the Dutch West India Co. *(q.v.)* and seized Portuguese settlements on the coast of Guinea. He was governor of Brazil (1636–43).

John Mark *See* **Mark, Saint**

John of Austria 1547–78. Spanish soldier and naval hero who led Spanish forces to victory over the Turks in the 1571 Battle of Lepanto *(q.v.).* He was the natural son of Emperor Charles V.

John of Austria 1629–79. Spanish general, illegitimate son of Philip IV of Spain. He served as prime minister to Charles II from 1677 to 1679, having overthrown the regency of the Queen Mother Maria.

John of Brienne c1148–1237. French crusader. A leader in the Fifth Crusade (q.v.), he became titular king of Jerusalem (1210–25) and regent and co-emperor of Constantinople (1228–37) during the minority of Baldwin II.

John of Capistrano, Saint See **John Capistran, Saint**

John of Damascus, Saint ⟨Saint John Damascene⟩ c675–749. Syrian theologian and Doctor of the Eastern church, noted especially for his theological work *The Fountain of Wisdom* and for his writings against iconoclasm.

John of Gaunt 1340–99. Duke of Lancaster (from 1362) and son of Edward III of England. In effect, he ruled in England during the last years of his father's reign and during the early reign of Richard II. He was the ancestor of the Tudor (q.v.) kings.

John of Lancaster 1389–1435. English nobleman. John, son of Henry IV and brother of Henry V, was regent of France for his infant nephew, Henry VI. He attempted to solidify English rule in France, but his allowance of Joan of Arc's execution helped undermine his support.

John of Leiden c1509–36. Dutch leader of the Anabaptists (q.v.), who led a rebellion in Münster in 1534 and ruled briefly as "king." The lawlessness of his reign harmed the Anabaptist movement.

John of Salisbury c1115–80. English scholastic writer and philosopher. He served as bishop of Chartres (1176–80), wrote books on the church and Aristotelian philosophy, and was author of a biography of his friend Thomas à Becket.

John of the Cross, Saint 1542–91. Spanish mystic and poet, Doctor of the Church and founder of the Discalced Carmelites. His works are considered masterpieces of Spanish literature as well as of Catholic mystical theology.

John Palaeologus See **John V**

John Palaeologus See **John VIII**

John Paul II ⟨b. Wojtyla, Karol⟩ 1920–. Polish-born pope (1978–), successor to John Paul I, who died after only 34 days in office. John Paul II was the first non-Italian pope to be elected in nearly half a century. He has made notable journeys abroad, including the first papal visit to England (May 28, 1982) since the Church of England split from the Roman Catholic Church in 1534. He was wounded in an assassination attempt (May 14,

1981) at St. Peter's Square, Rome by a Muslim fanatic named Mehmet Ali Agca.

John Sobieski See **John III**

Johnson, Andrew 1808–75. Seventeenth US president (1865–69), successor to A. Lincoln on his assassination. A political leader in Tennessee, Johnson became a US congressman (1843–53) and senator (1857–62) and was the only southern senator to remain loyal to the Union during the American Civil War. In return, President A. Lincoln first appointed him military governor of Tennessee (1862–64) and then made Johnson his running mate in 1864. Johnson served as vice-president from March to April, 1865, when Lincoln was assassinated. A war Democrat, with no formal schooling, Johnson was unpopular in Congress from the outset. His attempts to promote a conciliatory Reconstruction program in the South, however, inflamed radical Republicans in Congress. Seeking to ensure equal rights still being denied Negroes in parts of the South, Congress passed the Civil Rights Act of 1866 (q.v.) over Johnson's veto. Then, in a bitter war against him, Congress passed other acts of Reconstruction despite his veto. Finally, when Johnson ousted his secretary of war, E. Stanton, radical Republicans won a House resolution for his impeachment (Feb. 24, 1868). The Senate tried Johnson (Mar. 5–May 26, 1868) on charges that his dismissal of Stanton violated the Tenure of Office Act (passed over his veto) but failed by a slim margin to convict him. Johnson did not seek reelection.

Johnson, Guy c1740–88. Irish-born American Loyalist leader. Johnson was England's superintendent of Indian affairs. He organized the Indians against the American colonists during the American Revolution.

Johnson, Hiram Warren 1866–1945. American political leader and governor of California (1910–17). He helped to found the Progressive party (1912) and ran unsuccessfully as vice-presidential candidate with Theodore Roosevelt. As US senator (1917–45), he was a leading isolationist.

Johnson, James Weldon 1871–1938. American poet. The first black admitted to the Florida bar (1897), Johnson helped to found and was secretary (1916–30) of the National Association for the Advancement of Colored People.

Johnson, Lyndon Baines 1908–73. Thirty-sixth US president (1963–69), successor to the presidency on J. Kennedy's assassination. His administration was marked by the passage of wide-ranging social legislation, ill-fated involvement in the Vietnam War (q.v.), and major outbreaks of social and political unrest. A Democrat and New Deal supporter, Johnson rose under the influence of President F. Roosevelt. He became US congressman from Texas (1937–49) and senator (1949–61). As Senate majority leader (from 1955), he demonstrated great political skill and was elected vice-president (1960) under Kennedy. On Kennedy's assassination (Nov. 22, 1963), he assumed office and was subsequently elected president by a wide margin in 1964. In the first years of his presidency, Johnson oversaw passage of bills instituting sweeping social reforms. In 1964, he won passage of legislation advanced under Kennedy, including the Civil Rights Act of 1964 *(q.v.)* and a major tax cut. He pressed for and got legislation for his Great Society *(q.v.)* program, which included the Voting Rights Act, aid to education, funding for antipoverty programs, and a Medicare program. His involvement in the Vietnam War, which increased dramatically after the 1964 elections, undermined his social programs, however. Antiwar protests as well as riots by blacks in cities across America increased to fever pitch by 1968, and Johnson declined to run for another term. (*See also* United States [1963–69].)

Johnson, Reverdy 1796–1876. American lawyer and politician. He served as council for the defense in the Dred Scott case *(q.v.)*, helped to keep his native Maryland in the Union during the Civil War, and supported the Reconstruction policies of Pres. A. Johnson.

Johnson, Richard Mentor 1780–1850. Vice-president of the United States (1837–41) under Martin Van Buren. Johnson was the first vice-president to be chosen by the Senate, following a deadlock in the Electoral College.

Johnson, Samuel 1709–84. English literary figure who was renowned for his conversation as well as for his writings. After a brief career as a teacher, he came to London in 1737 and began writing journalistic works. His pioneering *Dictionary of the English Language* was published in 1755. In 1763, he began his association with his most famous biographer, J. Boswell.

Johnson, Sir William 1715–74. British Colonial merchant and landowner whose friendly relations with the Mohawk Indians and the Iroquois nation greatly helped the British during the French and Indian Wars *(q.v.)*.

Johnson, William 1771–1834. American jurist, who served as associate justice of the US Supreme Court (1804–34).

Johnston, Albert Sidney 1803–62. Confederate general in the American Civil War. An able general, he led Confederate forces against U. S. Grant at the Battle of Shiloh *(q.v.)*, in which he was killed.

Johnston, Joseph Eggleston 1807–1901. Confederate general in the American Civil War. He was one of the most able officers of the Confederacy, but his policy of defensive warfare during Sherman's Atlanta Campaign angered J. Davis, who relieved him of command. He was restored to command by Gen. R. E. Lee toward the end of the war.

John the Baptist, Saint d. AD c30. Jewish prophet and the forerunner of Jesus Christ. He baptized his followers, including his kinsman Jesus, but indicated that he merely anticipated the Messiah "who is to come." He denounced the tetrarch Herod Antipas for incestuously marrying his own niece, Herodias, daughter of his brother's wife. Herodias' revenge came when her daughter Salome pleased Herod with dancing and was told she could have whatever she desired. At Herodias' instigation, Salome asked for the head of John the Baptist on a platter. The incident of John's meeting his end in this manner has been a favorite theme of Christian art.

John the Fortunate *See* **John III**
John the Good *See* **John II** (1319–64)
John the Great *See* **John I** (1357–1433)
John the Perfect *See* **John II** (1455–95)
John the Posthumous *See* **John I** (1316)
John Zápolya *See* **John I** (1487–1540)

Joinville, Jean, sire de 1224?–1317? French historian whose biography of Louis IX of France is a valuable account of the life of Louis and of the Seventh Crusade *(q.v.)*.

Jolliet, Louis *See* **Marquette, Jacques**

Jolson Al ⟨Yoelson, Asa⟩ 1886–1950. American singer and entertainer, famous for his stage performances and hit songs. He appeared in *The Jazz Singer* (1927), the first major film to use sound.

Jona *See* **Jonah**

Jonah ⟨Jonas⟩ ⟨Jona⟩ In the Bible, a Hebrew prophet sent by God to reform Nineveh. He set sail to avoid his mission, was swallowed by a whale, but emerged unscathed. Eventually he did preach to Nineveh, whose people repented. But Jonah proved to be less than happy when God decided to shower mercy upon repentant Nineveh. The story is told in the book of Jonah.

Jonas *See* **Jonah**

Jonathan In the Bible, the son of Saul and friend of David. Jonathan protected David from Saul's anger. He died in the battle at Mt. Gilboa.

Jones, Alfred Ernest 1897–1958. Welsh psychoanalyst. An associate and biographer of S. Freud, Jones played a key role in the introduction of psychoanalysis to Britain, Canada, and the United States.

Jones, Inigo 1573–1652. English architect. He introduced the Renaissance Palladian (neoclassical) style into England in such buildings as the Queen's House in Greenwich (1616) and the Banqueting Hall in Whitehall (1619–22).

Jones, John Luther See **Jones, Casey**

Jones, John Paul 1747–92. Scottish-born American naval hero. John Paul added "Jones" to his name and settled in America to avoid a trial springing from his improper handling of a ship's mutiny. During the American Revolution he plagued British shipping off the coasts of both England and North America. His most famous victory (1779) was aboard the *Bonhomme Richard.* Ordered to surrender by the British ship *Serapis,* he replied, "I have not yet begun to fight."

Jones, Robert Edmond 1887–1954. American scenic designer. He designed imaginative sets for such plays as E. O'Neill's *The Iceman Cometh* and Marc Connelly's *The Green Pastures* and for such films as the early color film *La Cucaracha* (1933).

Jones, Sir William 1746–94. English Orientalist and jurist who was influential in fostering the study of Oriental literature and language in Western Europe. He was the first to point out the resemblance of Sanskrit *(q.v.)* to Latin and Greek (1787).

Jonestown Former communal settlement founded by the Rev. Jim Jones and followers of his US-based People's Temple cult. Over 900 persons died (Nov. 19, 1978) after Jones ordered a mass suicide of his followers.

Jongleurs French medieval entertainers. The jongleurs were wandering minstrels whose specialties were comic songs and stories, juggling, and acrobatics.

Jonson, Ben 1572–1637. English Elizabethan playwright, critic, and poet. Considered to be the second-ranking English playwright after his friend W. Shakespeare, Jonson was also England's first unofficial poet laureate. Among his many satiric, innovative plays are *Every Man in His Humour,* *Every Man Out of His Humour, Volpone,* and *The Alchemist.*

Joppa See **Jaffa**

Joram See **Jehoram**

Jordan Kingdom located in the Middle East. Its capital is Amman. Formerly known as Transjordan, it became part of Great Britain's League of Nations mandate territory of Palestine after WW I. The history of modern Jordan begins in 1946 when it became independent as the Hashemite Kingdom of Transjordan. (*For history of the region prior to 1946, see* Palestine.) Key dates in the history of Jordan include:

1920 Transjordan became part of British mandate territory of Palestine.

1921 Transjordan made separate from Palestine; Abdullah ibn Hussein became ruler in Transjordan under British control.

1946 Transjordan granted independence (May 25) as Hashemite Kingdom of Transjordan.

1948–49 First Arab-Israeli War broke out after creation of Israeli state; Jordanian forces seized territory on West Bank of Jordan River.

1949 Transjordan became known as Jordan (Apr.).

1950 Jordan annexed territory on West Bank of Jordan River occupied during 1948–49 war.

1951 King Abdullah was assassinated; succeeded by his son Talal.

1952 Talal removed as mentally unfit; his son Hussein became king.

1958 Jordan joined (Feb.) with Iraq to form Arab Federation; revolution in Iraq overthrew the Iraqi monarchy (July) and Jordan withdrew from the federation (Aug.).

1967 Third Arab-Israeli War (Six-Day War) fought between Israel and Arab states (June 5–10); Israelis drove Jordanian forces across Jordan River and occupied West Bank.

1968 Palestine Liberation Organization (PLO) guerrillas in Jordan clashed with government troops; PLO sought West Bank as nucleus of new Palestinian state, while King Hussein wanted it restored to Jordan.

1970 Renewed fighting between PLO and government troops (Sept.); Syrian troops crossed into Jordan to aid PLO.

1970 King Hussein formed new military-civilian government (Sept. 26) following cease-fire with PLO.

1970 Hussein again formed a new government (Oct. 28) after renewed fighting with PLO commandos.

1971 Jordanian troops engaged PLO commandos in fierce fighting (Jan.) near Amman.

1971 Government troops attacked PLO commando bases in north (July 13); PLO bases destroyed; Palestinian guerrillas driven out of Jordan to Lebanon, where they established new bases.

1971 PLO guerrillas assassinated Jordanian prime minister Wasfi al-Tal (Nov. 28).

1972 Hussein wounded in unsuccessful assassination attempt (Dec.) by Palestinian.

1973 Fourth Arab-Israeli War fought (Oct. 6–25) between Israel and allied Arab states; Jordan remained effectively neutral, but sent some units to fight in Syria.

1974 Hussein joined in Arab summit resolution backing the PLO as the sole representative of

Palestinians and calling for independent Palestinian state.

1979 King Hussein and PLO leader Yasir Arafat issued joint statement condemning imminent peace settlement between Egypt and Israel (Mar. 17).

1980 Jordan announced its support for Iraq in its war against Iran (Sept.).

Josaphat *See* **Jehoshaphat**

Joseph *See* **Barnabas, Saint**

Joseph In the Bible, the son of Jacob and Rachel. Sold into slavery in Egypt by his brothers, Joseph became an important personage in Pharaoh's court. He proved to be the salvation of his family when famine drove them from Canaan to Egypt.

Joseph 1715–77. King of Portugal (1750–77). Joseph was completely dominated by his chief minister, the marquês de Pombal, who reformed the government and expelled the Jesuits.

Joseph c1840–1904. American Indian chief of the Nez Percé Indians (q.v.), who, in 1877, led his people on an unsuccessful retreat toward Canada after being forced to give up tribal lands.

Joseph I 1678–1711. Holy Roman Emperor (1705–11), successor to his father, Leopold I, and king of Hungary (1687–1711). In the War of the Spanish Succession, he successfully fought France but unsuccessfully supported the claim of his brother Charles (later Charles VI) to the Spanish throne.

Joseph II 1741–90. Holy Roman Emperor (1765–90), successor to his father, Francis I, and first of the Hapsburg-Lorraine line. An enlightened despot, Joseph initiated many social and administrative reforms, although most did not last beyond his reign. Dominated by his mother, Maria Theresa, during the first years of his reign, he undertook a broad plan to modernize the empire after her death (1780). He abolished (1781) serfdom and granted peasants basic rights; abolished monasteries, reduced the clergy, and issued (1781) the Edict of Toleration; and attempted to centralize government of the diverse territories within the empire. This last reform led to revolts in Hungary and the Austrian Netherlands. His reign also saw the War of the Bavarian Succession, territorial acquisitions from the first Partition of Poland, and participation of Austrian forces in the Russo-Turkish War of 1787–92 (q.v.).

Joseph, Father ⟨Gray Eminence⟩ ⟨b. François Leclerc du Tremblay⟩ 1577–1638. French Capuchin monk, religious reformer, and confidential agent of Cardinal Richelieu. His activities as Richelieu's agent helped lead France into the Thirty Years' War.

Joseph, Saint *fl.* 1st cent. AD. New Testament figure. Joseph was a Galilean carpenter, descendant of King David and husband of Mary. He was regarded as the young Jesus' earthly protector.

Joséphine ⟨Marie Josèphe Rose Tascher de la Pagerie⟩ 1763–1814. Empress of France and wife of Napoleon Bonaparte (1796–1809).

Joseph of Arimathea, Saint Secret follower of Jesus who received Jesus' body after the crucifixion and buried it in his own tomb. He figures in many later stories.

Josephus, Flavius c37–c100 AD. Jewish historian and soldier, noted for his works on Jewish history, including *The History of the Jewish Wars*, an account of the revolt of Judaea (AD 66–70), in which the Jewish Temple was destroyed.

Joses *See* **Barnabas, Saint**

Joshua ⟨Josue⟩ In the Bible, the successor to Moses as leader of the Hebrews, whom he led in the actual conquest of Canaan. His name is given to one of the books of the Bible.

Josiah ⟨Josias⟩ d. c609 BC. King of Judah, successor to his father, Amon. He led religious reforms that made Jerusalem the center of worship of Yahweh. The great event of his reign came in its 18th year when the "book of the law," apparently the book of Deuteronomy, was discovered in the Temple.

Josias *See* **Josiah**

Josquin des Prés c1445–1521. Flemish composer, considered the greatest Renaissance composer of his day. He is noted for his masses, motets, and chansons.

Josue *See* **Joshua**

Jouhaux, Léon 1879–1954. French Socialist and trade union leader long associated with the International Labor Organization. He was awarded the Nobel Peace Prize in 1951.

Joule, James Prescott 1818–89. English physicist, noted for his discovery of the law of conservation of energy. The electrical unit of work is named after him.

Jourdan, Jean Baptiste 1762–1833. French revolutionary marshal of France. He gained a decisive victory over the Austrians in the 1794 Battle of Fleurus (q.v.). and introduced the first law that allowed general conscription (1798).

Jovian ⟨Jovianus, Flavius Claudius⟩ AD c331–364. Roman emperor (363–364), successor to Julian the Apostate. He made an unpopular treaty with the Persians, and restored Christianity to the position granted by Constantine and annulled by Julian.

Jovianus, Flavius Claudius *See* **Jovian**

Jowett, Benjamin 1817–93. English classical scholar, noted for his translation of the *Dialogues of Plato* (1871) and, as master of Balliol College, Oxford, for his influence on education.

Joyce, James 1882–1941. Irish author whose novel *Ulysses* (1922), with its innovative style, is considered a 20th-cent. literary masterpiece. Joyce left Ireland in 1904 and lived as an expatriate on the Continent. Two of his works are the semi-autobiographical *A Portrait of the Artist as a Young Man*, published in 1916, and *Finnegans Wake*, a vast experimental novel, published in 1939.

Juan Carlos I 1938–. Spanish king (1975–), successor to Gen. F. Franco. The son of the Carlist (*q.v.*) pretender Don Juan, he was designated (1954) by Franco as the next ruler of Spain. Juan Carlos succeeded to the throne Nov. 22, 1975, after Franco's death. He withstood an attempted military coup (Feb. 23–25, 1981), in which Spanish Civil Guardsmen stormed the Parliament and took many of the country's leaders hostage.

Juana la Beltraneja 1462–1530. Castilian princess and daughter of Henry IV of Castile. She contested the throne of Castile with Isabella. After Isabella's succession (1479), Juana retired to a convent.

Juárez, Benito 1806–72. Mexican national hero and president (1858–61, provisional; 1861–72), successor to I. Comonfort. He took part in the overthrow of Santa Anna, and, as minister of justice, reduced the power of the church and army in what is called the *Ley Juárez*. He became acting president on Comonfort's resignation and emerged victorious in the War of the Reform (1858–61). He then led the opposition government during the brief reign of Emperor Maximilian (1864–67) and, after Maximilian's fall, he was elected president (1867–72) twice. Juárez died while a revolt by P. Díaz was under way.

Juba I *c*85–46 BC. King of Numidia. He supported Pompey against Julius Caesar in North Africa. Defeated, he committed suicide.

Juba III *d.* AD *c*20. King of Numidia. Protégé of Augustus, he married Cleopatra Selene, daughter of Antony and Cleopatra. He was made king of Numidia and then Mauretania, and was a noted historian.

Jubal Old Testament figure. According to the book of Genesis, Jubal, son of Lambech and Adah, invented stringed and wind instruments and is considered the founder of music.

Judaea ⟨Judea⟩ Roman name for the southernmost division of ancient Palestine, called Judah (*q.v.*) in the Old Testament.

Judah Fourth son of Jacob and Leah. His name was given to one of the Twelve Tribes of Israel (*q.v.*) and to the area of southern Palestine in which two of the tribes settled.

Judah Southern part of the kingdom of Israel, a separate Israelite kingdom after the northern part seceded (*c*933 BC). The tribes of Judah and Benjamin had originally settled this southern region of the kingdom of Israel. In the unstable period after King Solomon's death, the north revolted against King Rehoboam and broke away. Jerusalem then became the capital of Judah. Judah became the sole Jewish national state after the Assyrians conquered the northern kingdom (*c*721) and dispersed its inhabitants. Judah also came under Assyrian domination, then passed to the Egyptians and finally to the Babylonians. Revolts against the Babylonians brought harsh reprisals by King Nebuchadnezzar (586), marked by the destruction of the Temple at Jerusalem and the Babylonian captivity (*q.v.*). After the Persians conquered the Babylonians, the Jews were allowed to return to Jerusalem and rebuild the Temple (516). Alexander the Great's conquests ended Persian rule and Judah subsequently passed to the Seleucids. The Jews successfully rebelled (168–142) against the Seleucids (*see* Maccabees), and a new independent Jewish kingdom, Judaea, was established (142). Independence was short-lived, however, and after a period of religious strife between Pharisees and Sadducees Judaea came under Roman control (from 63 BC). Revolts against Roman rule led to the destruction of Jerusalem in AD 70. (*See also* Palestine.)

Judah I AD *c*135–*c*220. Patriarch of the Jews in Palestine and president of the Sanhedrin. He compiled the Mishna (*q.v.*), a compendium of religious and social law.

Judaism One of the world's three great monotheistic religions. Modern Judaism is actually rabbinic Judaism, which developed (from 1st cent. AD) from the religion of the Jews of ancient Palestine. This forerunner of Judaism also gave rise to Christianity. Rabbinic Judaism arose after the destruction of the second Temple at Jerusalem. Rabbis (teachers) replaced the priests as religious leaders, the autonomous synagogues replaced the Temple as the center of worship, and prayer and study of the Torah were substituted for the sacrificial rites of the Temple. The Judaic tradition evolved by the rabbis governed both religious and secular life and preserved Jewish culture during the many centuries in which the Jews were dispersed in various foreign lands. (*See also* Palestine; Israel.) Key dates in the history of Judaism include:

C16TH?–13TH CENT.? BC   Hebrews arrived in Palestine; practiced polytheistic religion; era of the patriarchs, Abraham, Isaac, and Jacob, and acceptance of Yahweh (Jehovah).

c13TH CENT. BC Exodus under the guidance of Moses; Ark of the Covenant, the Law, given to Moses; Israelites became the chosen people and settled in the promised land (Palestine).

c940 BC First Temple constructed at Jerusalem under King Solomon; practices of sacrificial worship.

8TH CENT.? BC Period of the prophets, including Isaiah, Jeremiah, Elijah, Amos, Hosea, and Micah; opposed the priests and worship of false gods.

722 BC Exile of many of the inhabitants (Ten Lost Tribes) of the Northern Kingdom of Israel after the Assyrian conquest.

c622? BC Deuteronomic reform; foreign cults purged; Temple dedicated solely to worship of Yahweh, and worship concentrated at the Temple.

586 BC Babylonian conquest of the Kingdom of Judah; first Temple at Jerusalem destroyed; beginning of the Babylonian captivity.

586–538 BC Babylonian captivity; Israelites conducted prayer meetings to maintain their faith during foreign captivity.

538 BC Return to Palestine began; building of the second Temple completed (516), reestablishing a center of worship.

FROM 5TH CENT. BC Ezra began period of religious reforms; introduced the Torah (written Law), formalizing religious doctrine and observances; scribes (Sopherim) assumed leadership from priests; beginnings of oral Law as exposition of written Law; Babylonian prayer meetings outside the Temple continued, laying basis for synagogues.

5TH–2ND CENT. BC The Hebrew Bible ("the Old Testament") compiled from sacred writings, divided into the Law (Torah), the Prophets, and the Writings; exact versions edited by scholars called Masoretes.

FROM 2D CENT. BC Rise of the Sadducees (priestly class adhering strictly to the written Law) and Pharisees (adhering to the written Law and oral Law).

FROM 63 BC Palestine under Roman rule; Great Sanhedrin (Jewish court with religious and political functions) at the Temple in Jerusalem (until AD 70).

30 BC–AD 9 Hillel flourished; great biblical commentator and interpreter of Jewish tradition; devised "Seven Rules of Hillel" for interpreting the Bible.

AD 70 Second Temple at Jerusalem destroyed by Romans; from this time began the development of modern Judaism, with the ascendancy of the rabbinic tradition and decentralized worship in the synagogues; sacrificial worship replaced by prayer service and study.

AFTER AD 70 Johanan ben Zakkai flourished; a noted sage, he set up an academy after the destruction of the Temple and helped lay the foundations of rabbinic Judaism.

AD 40–135 Akiba ben Joseph lived; a chief founder of rabbinic Judaism.

2ND CENT. AD Jews, exiled from Jerusalem after the second Jewish Revolt (132–135), began to disperse to other areas of Near East; rabbinic Judaism devoted to preserving Jewish community and eventual return to promised land.

AD 3D CENT. Mishna codified in final form; collection of oral Laws begun in time of Ezra.

AD 500 Talmud, a collection of the opinions and decisions of the rabbis, compiled; with the Torah (Law), the Talmud became one of the twin pillars of Judaism.

9TH CENT. Seder Rab Amram, oldest surviving prayer book, written.

10TH CENT. Religious study centers, originally founded in Babylon, moved to Spain.

1040–1105 Rashi lived; famous for his commentaries on the Bible and Talmud.

1135–1204 Maimonides lived; the leading figure in medieval Judaism, he compiled a great code of Jewish Law and wrote important philosophical works.

13TH CENT. Rise of Cabala, a form of Jewish mysticism.

18TH CENT. Systematic modern study of rabbinic literature introduced by Elijah ben Solomon of Wilna (1720–97).

1720–97 Elijah ben Solomon lived; noted authority on Jewish culture; opposed Hasidism.

c1740 Hasidim movement founded in Poland: emphasized a mystical approach to God; opposed to rigorous doctrinal literalism; founded by Baal Shem Tov (c1700–60).

1783 Plea for religious tolerance advanced by Enlightenment philosopher M. Mendelssohn.

19th CENT. Rise of Reform Judaism, movement to make Judaism compatible with the modern world.

1810–74 Abraham Geiger lived; principal leader in the Reform Judaism movement.

19TH CENT. Haskala movement among Jews of Eastern and Central Europe; called for assimilation of Jews into European culture through reform of Jewish traditions and breakup of the Jewish ghettos.

19TH CENT. Orthodox Judaism reaffirmed its rigorous adherence to the totality of Jewish law and tradition; Rabbi Samson Raphael Hirsch (1808–85) among noted leaders.

19TH CENT. Conservative Judaism arose as middle position between Reform and Orthodox Judaism; divisions between various groups continue to present day.

1897 Zionism founded by Theodore Herzl; Zionists sought restoration of Jewish homeland in Palestine.

1948 Israel created; Jewish national state re-established in Palestine for the first time in many centuries.

Judas, Saint *See* **Jude, Saint**

Judas Iscariot One of the Apostles of Jesus Christ. He betrayed Jesus for 30 pieces of silver at the Garden of Gethsemane. Repenting his act, he killed himself.

Judas of Galilee *fl.* AD 6. Ancient Jewish zealot leader. He fomented a revolt against the Roman census for taxation purposes in AD 6 on the grounds that only God was the rightful ruler of Israel. He was killed for his part in this revolt. (Acts 5:37).

Jude, Saint ⟨Saint Judas⟩ One of the Apostles of Jesus Christ. He was also called Lebbaeus and Thaddeus. According to tradition, he suffered martyrdom in Persia with Saint Simon.

Judea *See* **Judaea**

judicial branch Branch of government vested with authority to interpret the laws and administer the courts. Based on the theory of the separation of powers, Article III of the US Constitution vests judicial power in a Supreme Court and lower courts established by Congress. Although not specifically provided for in the US Constitution, the power of judicial review of executive and legislative acts has become a marked feature of US government. Judicial review is considered to have started with the 1803 decision of the Supreme Court in *Marbury* vs *Madison (q.v.)*, in which the court claimed power to invalidate acts of Congress.

Judith Jewish heroine who saved the people of her city from an attack by Holofernes, general of Nebuchadnezzar, by stealing into his camp and killing him. The incident has been a favorite subject for painters.

judo *See* **jujitsu**

Jugurtha *d.* 104 BC. King of Numidia (118–104 BC), successor to his uncle, Micipsa. Jugurtha's reign was marked by conflict with Rome. He was eventually captured and put to death in Rome.

jujitsu Oriental weaponless system of defense that aims to utilize an opponent's weight and strength against him by applying pressure to sensitive parts of his body, often by means of blows with the side of the hand (an allied system was developed as karate). Jujitsu was developed over a period of some 2,000 years by Buddhist monks in Japan, China, and Tibet as a means of self-defense not in conflict with nonviolent religious principles. Judo was created in the late 1880s in Japan by modifying jujitsu holds too dangerous to be used in sport.

Julia *d.* 54 BC. Daughter of Julius Caesar and wife of Pompey, who helped maintain peace between the two leaders while she lived.

Julia 39 BC–AD 14. Roman matron. Julia was the daughter of Augustus and wife of Tiberius, but she was banished by her father for her infidelities, and died of starvation soon after Tiberius became emperor.

Juliana 1909–. Queen of The Netherlands (1948–80), successor to her mother, Queen Wilhelmina. She stepped down in favor of her daughter Beatrix (1938–), who became queen in April, 1980.

Julian calendar Calendar instituted (46 BC) by Julius Caesar, dividing the year into 12 months and making it 365 days, 11 hours in length. It was superseded by the Gregorian calendar *(q.v.)* in most of Europe in 1582, although the change was not made in England until 1752 and in Russia until after 1917.

Julian the Apostate AD 331?–363. Roman emperor (AD 361–363), successor to Constantius II. Raised a Christian, he converted to paganism and unsuccessfully sought to restore it in the empire; hence his name.

Julius I, Saint *d.* AD 352. Pope (AD 337–352), successor to Pope Saint Mark. He supported Athanasius against the followers of Arianism by convoking a synod at Rome (AD 340), which cleared Athanasius of all the Arians' charges against him. Julius explicitly claimed jurisdiction over the other churches.

Julius II 1443–1513. Pope (1503–13), successor to Pius III. He returned the Papal States to church control and joined in the Holy League against France. He was a great patron of the arts, commissioning his own portrait by Raphael, the initial building of St. Peter's (1506) by Bramante, and the Creation frescoes on the ceiling of the Sistine Chapel *(q.v.)* by Michelangelo.

July Offensive *See* **June Offensive**

July Revolution Rebellion (July, 1830) in France that resulted in the forced abdication of Charles X and the crowning of Louis-Philippe. A victory for the upper bourgeoisie over the aristocracy, the rebellion was brought about by Charles's attempt to restore the absolutist Ancien Régime *(q.v.)*. It was sparked by his selection of the unpopular Ultra-royalist J. de Polignac to head the government. To overcome opposition to Polignac in the Chamber of Deputies, Charles issued the July Ordinances (July 26), dissolving the chamber, changing the electoral system (to his advantage), and imposing press censorship. Riots broke out in Paris (July 27–29), Charles abdicated, and Louis-Philippe was chosen king (Aug. 9) by the deputies. The reign of Louis-Philippe was thus called the July Monarchy after the revolt.

June Days   Revolt (June 23–26, 1848) by workers in Paris, France, during the early months of the Second Republic *(q.v.)*. Though workers had supported the February Revolution (1848), unemployment and failure of the work-relief program (national workshops) failed to ease the workers' discontent. A mass protest in which workers briefly took over (May 15) the National Assembly, resulted in the decision to dismantle the national workshops. The ensuing revolt engulfed Paris in bloody street fighting and brought down the interim government. Gen. Louis Cavaignac (1802–57) was granted dictatorial powers to restore order, and finally put an end to the fighting.

June Offensive ⟨July Offensive⟩ ⟨Summer Offensive⟩ ⟨Kerensky Offensive⟩ ⟨Galician Offensive⟩   Russian offensive (June–July, 1917) during WW I. After the overthrow of the czar in the February Revolution (1917), the provisional government, headed by A. Kerensky, continued to prosecute the war and launched a major offensive in Galicia (July 1). After initial gains, the offensive came to a standstill, and Russian forces were routed by the German counterattack (July 19). The failure of the offensive caused mass desertion and contributed to the Bolshevik seizure of power in Nov., 1917.

Jung, Carl Gustav   1875–1961. Swiss psychiatrist. One of his early works, *The Psychology of Dementia Praecox* (1906), led to a collaboration with S. Freud. Jung broke with Freud in 1913 after publishing *The Psychology of the Unconscious* in 1912. He developed the theory of personality types, extroverted and introverted, and of the collective unconscious.

Junges Deutschland   *See* **Young Germany**

Junius, Franciscus   1589–1677.   German-born scholar, noted for his studies of ancient, Anglo-Saxon, and Gothic literature.

Juno   Chief goddess in the Roman religion, wife and sister of Jupiter and guardian of women and marriage. She corresponds to the Greek goddess Hera.

junta   Governmental committee. A junta is a council that exercises administrative powers, usually in a political emergency or after the over-

throw of a government. From Spanish *juntar*, "to join."

Jupiter   Chief god in the Roman religion, also called Jove. He corresponds to the Greek god Zeus.

Jurchen   *See* **Sung**

Justin I   AD *c*450–527. Byzantine emperor (AD 518–527), successor to Anastasius I and uncle of Justinian I. Justin established close ties with the church in Rome, persecuted Monophysitism *(q.v.)*, and relied largely upon others to govern the empire.

Justinian I   AD 483–565. Byzantine emperor (AD 527–565), successor to his father, Justin I. One of the great rulers of the late empire, he is especially remembered for the legal codex, *Corpus Juris Civilis (q.v.)*, compiled at his direction. His reign was marked by the conflict between the Blues and Greens in the Nika Riot (532); his call for the Second Council of Constantinople (553) and his involvement in the controversy over Monophysitism *(qq.v.)*; and his expansion of the empire, including reconquest of Africa from the Vandals (533–548) and Italy from the Ostrogoths (535–554). Many public buildings were constructed during his reign, including the Hagia Sophia *(q.v.)*.

Justinian Code   *See* **Corpus Juris Civilis**

Justin Martyr, Saint   AD *c*100–165. Christian religious philosopher and apologist who combined Christian belief with Platonic philosophy. He was one of the first intellectual apologists for Christianity and is an invaluable source for our knowledge of early Christian doctrines.

Jutes   Ancient Germanic people, possibly from the area near the mouth of the Rhine, who invaded England in the 5th cent. AD and settled in Kent and on the Isle of Wight.

Jutland, Battle of ⟨Skagerrak, ~⟩   Indecisive WW I naval battle (May 31–June 1, 1916) off the coast of Denmark. It was the only important sea battle between the British and German navies during the war. The German High Seas Fleet, under Admiral R. Scheer, was lured into battle (May 31) with the superior force of the British Grand Fleet, under Admiral J. Jellicoe. Though outnumbered, the Germans inflicted the greater losses on the British before managing to escape the trap. The Allied North Sea blockade, however, was not tested again by German surface warships.

Juvenal ⟨Decimus Junius Juvenalis⟩   1st–2d cent. AD. Leading Roman satirical poet whose 16 verse satires described the follies and vices of Roman life and served as models for later writers.

Juvenalis, Decimus Junius   *See* **Juvenal**

K

Kaaba ⟨Caaba⟩ Sacred shrine in the Great Mosque at Mecca and the major site of pilgrimage for the followers of Islam. Muslims face toward it when praying.

Kabul Afghan city (pop. 800,000), the capital and largest city of Afghanistan. Strategically located on the main routes to the Khyber Pass, it has been conquered many times since the time of Alexander the Great. It became Afghanistan's capital in the 18th cent. and figured in the Anglo-Afghan wars of the 19th cent.

Kadar, Janos *See* **Hungarian Revolution of 1956**

Kadesh, Battle of Inconclusive battle (*c*1288 BC) between the Egyptians under King Ramses II and the Hittites. The Egyptians launched the attack on Kadesh, in Syria, in an attempt to halt the Hittite encroachment on the Egyptian Empire.

Kadet ⟨Constitutional Democratic party⟩ Russian political party founded in 1905. A party of moderation, it was continually undermined by more radical groups and ceased to function after 1917.

Kaffirs *See* **Kafirs**

Kafirs ⟨Kaffirs⟩ Term originally applied by Muslims to all unbelievers. Adopted by the European settlers of South Africa, it was applied to the Bantu-speaking native peoples of the area.

Kafir Wars *See* **Cape Frontier Wars**

Kafka, Franz 1883–1924. Czech-born Austrian author. Kafka published little in his lifetime and supported himself by working in an insurance office. His friend Max Brod (1884–1968) published his three novels, *The Trial, The Castle,* and *Amerika* posthumously. These works on the alienation of modern man greatly influenced later existentialist authors and marked Kafka as one of the great writers of the 20th cent.

Kaganovich, Lazar Moiseyevich 1893–. Russian Communist leader who was instrumental in the rise to power of J. Stalin. Kaganovich played a key role in the development of Russian transportation and heavy industry.

Kagawa, Toyohiko 1888–1960. Japanese Christian evangelist, social reformer, and writer. He was prominent in the Japanese labor and social-welfare movements of the 1920s and 1930s.

K'ai Feng Jews Religious group that practiced Judaism at K'ai Feng, Honan province, China, from about the 12th to 19th cent.

Kailas Tibetan mountain peak, the highest point of the Kailas range in the Himalayas. It is believed by pilgrims to be the dwelling place of the Hindu god Shiva.

Kairouan ⟨Qairwan⟩ City in northern Tunisia, a holy city of Islam. Founded in 670, it was a major Islamic political, religious, and cultural center until the rise of Tunis in the 11th cent.

Kaiser-Wilhelmsland *See* **Papua New Guinea**

Kalb, Johann 1721–80. German officer in the French army. As a general in the Continental Army during the American Revolution, he served with G. Washington at Valley Forge (1777), and was killed in the Carolina Campaign.

Kalevala National epic of Finland. It was compiled and edited by E. Lönnrot, who used Finnish folk verses to produce a unified work.

Kali Hindu goddess, also known as the Black One. The consort of Shiva, she was goddess of death and destruction and was worshiped by the Thugs *(q.v.).*

Kalidasa *fl.* AD 5th cent.? Indian dramatist, considered to be the greatest Sanskrit writer and perhaps the greatest writer in India's history. His drama *Sakuntala* is his best-known work.

Kalinin, Mikhail Ivanovich 1875–1946. Russian politician. Official head of the Soviet Union from 1919 to 1946, he was chairman of the Soviet central executive committee (1919–38) and of the Presidium (1938–46).

Kalmar Union Scandinavian union (1397) of Denmark, Norway, and Sweden, joined under one crown at Kalmar, Sweden. Sweden withdrew (1523) with the accession of Gustavus I, though Denmark and Norway remained united until 1814.

Kalmar War War (1611–13) between Sweden and Denmark for the possession of Norway's north coast and the dominance of the Baltic. Danish king Christian IV defeated Sweden under Charles IX. Denmark achieved a position of dominance over Sweden and exacted a tribute for the return of the port of Älvsborg.

Kalmucks ⟨Kalmycks⟩ Nomadic people of Mongolian stock occupying the region of the lower Volga River in the USSR. The Kalmucks migrated to the region (17th cent.) from Chinese Turkistan and were at first allies of the expanding Russian empire. In the 18th cent. they were made vassals, however, and Russian oppression forced the bulk of the Kalmucks into their disastrous journey back to China (1771). Of the 300,000 that began the trek, the majority were killed in attacks by Russians and the Kazakh and Kirghiz peoples. Those that reached Chinese Turkistan were settled in Sinkiang, northwestern China. The remaining Kalmucks in Russia were exiled to Siberia after WW II for collaborating with the Germans. They were released from exile in 1957.

Kalmycks *See* **Kalmucks**

Kamakura shogunate Period in Japanese history (1192–1333) when members of the Minamoto clan ruled Japan as shoguns. Minamoto Yoritomo, operating from Kamakura (north of Kyoto) crushed the rival clans of Taira (1185) and Fujiwara (1189) and was named shogun by the emperor in 1192. Yoritomo thus established the long period of rule by the shoguns and the warrior class. Imperial administration was quickly undermined during the Kamakura period and replaced by that of the shoguns. Following Yoritomo's death in 1199, however, the Hojo clan came to power as regents and became effective rulers under the Minamoto shoguns. The Hojo clan (and the Kamakura shogunate) remained in power until Emperor Daigo II led a successful revolt (1333) in which he ended the Kamakura rule. He reigned until 1336, when he in turn was ousted and there began a period of wars that brought the Ashikaga shoguns to power. During the Kamakura shogunate, the feudal system was established (formalized by the Joei Formulary, 1232), foreign trade flourished, the Zen and Pure Land sects of Buddhism were introduced to Japan, and there was a cultural flowering as well. The No Theater was developed during this period.

Kamehameha I ⟨Kamehameha the Great⟩ 1758?–1819. Hawaiian king who united and ruled all the Hawaiian Islands (1810–19) and established the Kamehameha dynasty of Hawaiian rulers.

Kamehameha the Great *See* **Kamehameha I**

Kamenev, Lev Borisovich 1883–1936. Russian Communist leader. He was a member, with J. Stalin and G. Zinoviev, of the triumvirate that suc-ceeded N. Lenin and opposed L. Trotsky. He was executed (1936) in the Stalinist purge of the 1930s.

Kamiakin *See* **Yakima Indian Wars**

Kamikaze Japanese word meaning "divine wind." It was originally applied to the typhoon that destroyed (1281) a Mongol invasion fleet. In WW II it was applied to the Japanese suicide pilots who tried to fly their bomb-loaded planes into US ships.

Kammu 737–806. Emperor of Japan and founder of Kyōto, the capital of Japan until 1868. A strong ruler, he diminished the power of the Buddhists and brought peace to Japan's northern borders.

Kanagawa, Treaty of ⟨Perry Convention⟩ Treaty (Mar. 31, 1854) between Japan and the US. The treaty was secured by Commodore M. Perry, who had sailed to Japan (1853–1854) with a fleet of US warships to end Japanese isolationism. It secured good treatment for US sailors, opened two ports to US trade, and established a US consulate at Shimoda. It was the model for later treaties with other Western powers.

Kandinsky, Wassily 1866–1944. Russian painter and theorist, considered the founder of abstract art. He was a founder of the influential Munich art group, the Blau Reiter.

Kandy, kingdom of *See* **Sri Lanka**

Kanem-Bornu African empire that flourished in the region around Lake Chad from the 9th to 19th cent. It reached its height in the 16th–17th cents.

K'ang-hsi 1654–1722. Chinese emperor (1661–1722). He extended China's rule to Taiwan, Tibet, and Outer Mongolia, and encouraged the teaching of Western mathematics and astronomy.

K'ang Sheng 1899–1975. Chinese political leader. An active Communist since the 1920s, he was a member of the Central Committee and the Politburo and was one of the most powerful leaders in China.

K'ang Yu-wei *See* **Reform Movement of 1898**

Kanishka *See* **Kaniska**

Kaniska ⟨Kanishka⟩ AD 78?–103? Chinese ruler of northern India and founder of the Kusana empire *(q.v.)*. He was an ardent Buddhist and may have introduced the belief to China. Trade with the Romans was fostered during his reign.

Kano Japanese family of painters who dominated art in Japan between the 15th and 17th cents. For seven generations they set painting style and their influence persisted well into the 19th cent.

Kansas Central US state (pop. 2,363,200), the 34th state. First explored (1541) by the Spanish explorer Francisco Coronado (1510–54), it was later claimed by France and acquired by the US in the Louisiana Purchase (1803). Kansas was at first considered too barren for settlement, but the controversy between pro- and antislavery groups seeking to establish a majority increased the population and led to passage of the Kansas-Nebraska Act *(q.v.)* and the civil war known as Bleeding Kansas *(q.v.).* Kansas became a state in 1861.

Kansas-Nebraska Act US bill enacted (May 30, 1854) to establish Kansas and Nebraska as separate territories and, more important, to provide a compromise on the extension of slavery into the territories. Sponsored by Senator S. Douglas, the act helped bring on the American Civil War. Slavery had been barred from the region by the Missouri Compromise (1820), but Douglas' bill introduced the doctrine of Popular Sovereignty, by which inhabitants of the region would decide the issue of slavery. Unpopular with antislavery groups, the act fostered creation of the antislavery Republican party and led to Bleeding Kansas *(q.v.).*

Kant, Immanuel 1724–1804. German philosopher. As a teacher at Königsberg University, he began his writings partly in reaction to his studies of G. Leibniz. His metaphysical work *Critique of Pure Reason* expressed his theories of what man could know. His *Critique of Practical Reason* (1788) gave his ethical beliefs, and his *Critique of Judgment* (1790) combined and completed his philosophies. Kant's writings have established him as one of the great philosophers of all time. He engineered a revolution in philosophy by focusing on what the human mind could subjectively know rather than upon what was objectively "out there."

Kantipur *See* **Kathmandu**

Kao Kang *c*1902–55. Chinese Communist leader. He was one of the most powerful political figures in the Communist government until his purge (Apr., 1955) from the party and subsequent suicide.

Kao Tsu ⟨Liu Pang⟩ 256–195 BC. Chinese emperor (202?–195 BC). Originally a peasant named Liu Pang, he seized power when the Ch'in dynasty collapsed. He established the Han dynasty, which created the administrative system that characterized Chinese rule until 1911.

Kapodistrias, Ioannes Antonios, Count ⟨Capo d'Istria, Giovanni Antonio⟩ 1776–1831. Greek president (1828–31). A former adviser to Russian czar Alexander I, he supported Greek independence. His autocratic measures made him an unpopular president, however, and he was assassinated.

Kappel, Battle of *See* **Kappel Wars**

Kappel Wars Name applied to two wars (1529, 1531) between Swiss Protestants and Catholics during the Swiss Reformation. During the second,

the Swiss religious reformer U. Zwingli was killed at the Battle of Kappel (Oct. 11, 1531).

Kapp Putsch Unsuccessful reactionary uprising in Berlin (1920), named after its leader, Wolfgang Kapp (1858–1922). It sought to overthrow the Weimar Republic and restore the German monarchy.

Karachi Largest city (pop. 3,498,600) in Pakistan. It was Pakistan's capital from 1947 to 1959.

Karadžić, Vuk Stefanović ⟨Karajich, Vuk Stephenovich⟩ 1787–1864. Serbian scholar. He developed a simplified Cyrillic alphabet to reflect the Serbian language more closely and compiled collections of Serbian folk songs and tales.

Karageorge ⟨*b.* George Petrovic⟩ 1766?–1817. Serbian patriot who led the Serbian uprising against the Turks (1804). He was named hereditary leader of the Serbs (1808), and founded the Karageorgevich dynasty.

Karageorgevich Serbian dynasty, descended from the patriot leader Karageorge. It ruled Serbia from 1842 to 1858, and the kingdom of Serbs, Croats, and Slovenes (later Yugoslavia) from 1903 to 1945.

Karaites Jewish religious sect, said to have been founded in Persia in the 8th cent. It rejected Talmudic interpretation of the Bible and accepted only the Bible as the source of religious law. Its importance declined after the 12th cent., but it has inspired much biblical scholarship.

Karajich, Vuk Stephenovich *See* **Karadžić, Vuk Stefanović**

Karakhan, Lev *See* **Karakhan Manifesto**

Karakhan Manifesto Russian manifesto issued (July 15, 1919) by Lev Karakhan (1889–1937), then a member of the newly formed foreign ministry of the USSR. The manifesto renounced czarist rights and privileges in China. It made a tremendous impression in China as the first such renunciation by a former imperialist power and helped lead to the foundation of a Chinese Communist party (1921).

Karamanlis, Constantine 1907–. Greek statesman and prime minister (1955–63, 1974–). He was instrumental in resolving the crisis in Cyprus in 1960. Karamanlis was returned to power in 1974, following the collapse of the military junta that had taken control in 1967.

karate *See* **jujitsu**

Karens Members of several Sino-Thai tribal groups living in southern Burma and constituting a major minority. The Karens have resisted Burmese political rule since Burma's independence in 1948.

Karlowitz, Treaty of ⟨Carlowitz, Treaty of⟩ Treaty (Jan. 26, 1699) between the Ottoman Turks and Austria and her allies of the Holy League (Poland,

Russia, and Venice), ending the Austro–Turkish War (1682–99). The treaty's provisions made Austria the major power in Eastern Europe. By its terms Austria gained most of Hungary, Transylvania, Croatia, and Slavonia. Poland won Podolia, and Venice received Dalmatia and Morea. Russia continued hostilities until it gained Azov.

Karman, Theodore von 1881–1963. American aeronautical engineer noted for his contributions in the field of mathematics to the development of aerodynamics.

Karmathians ⟨Carmathians⟩ Muslim reformist sect prominent from the 9th to 10th cent. Founded (c890) by the peasant prophet Karmat, the sect was centered in lower Mesopotamia and set up a communistic community there. From this base they fostered wars and rebellions against the Abbasid caliphate, and in the 10th cent. conquered Yemen. In c930 the Karmathians attacked Mecca and carried off the sacred Muslim Black Stone of the Kaaba. They ransomed it back (952); thereafter they declined from power quickly.

Karnak Egyptian village. Karnak occupies the northern half of the ancient site of Thebes; Luxor, the southern half. Karnak is famed for its ancient ruins and temples, especially the Temple of Amon, with its vast hall containing 134 massive columns arranged in 16 rows, the finest construction of the 18th dynasty.

Karo, Joseph ben Ephraim *See* **Caro, Joseph ben Ephraim**

Károlyi, Mihály, Count 1875–1955. Hungarian statesman who sought Hungarian autonomy within the Austro-Hungarian Empire. After World War I, he briefly served as president of the Hungarian republic (1919) before the rise of B. Kun.

Kashmir ⟨Jammu and Kashmir⟩ Former princely state, now divided between Pakistan and India. It includes the Indian state of Jammu and Kashmir (54,000 sq. mi.) and Pakistani-controlled Azid Kashmir (32,000 sq. mi.). It was included in the Mogul Empire in 1587, and, after changing rulers several times, became part of British India in 1846. There was a Muslim revolt there after the 1947 partition of India. India and Pakistan have both made claims on the entire territory.

Kassem, Abdul Karim 1914–63. Iraqi political and military leader. After leading a successful revolt (1958) against the Iraqi monarchy, he became the first premier of the Iraqi republic, but was overthrown and executed by the Baath party in Feb., 1963.

Kassites Ancient people, possibly originating in western Iran, who conquered Babylonia and ruled there from the 18th to 12th cent. BC.

Kastrioti, George *See* **Skanderbeg**

Kathmandu ⟨Katmandu⟩ ⟨Kantipur⟩ Ancient city (pop. 150,400), capital of Nepal. It has long been a religious center and the seat of the ruling family of the Gurkha peoples (q.v.).

Katmandu *See* **Kathmandu**

Katō, Kōmei *See* **Kato, Takaakira**

Kato, Takaakira ⟨Katō Kōmei⟩ 1860–1926. Japanese statesman, and foreign minister when Japan presented the Twenty-One Demands (q.v.) to China (1915). He organized and headed the conservative Kenseikai party (1913).

Katyn Village in western USSR, near Smolensk. The nearby Katyn Forest was the site of a massacre (1943) of Polish officers during WW II, committed by either Russian or German forces. The Russians have consistently accused the Germans, but in 1952 a US congressional investigating committee claimed to have established that the massacre was carried out under Soviet auspices.

Kaufman, George S. 1889–1961. American playwright, collaborator on many very popular musicals and plays, including the Pulitzer Prize-winning *Of Thee I Sing* (1931) and *You Can't Take It with You* (1936).

Kaunda, Kenneth (David) 1924–. Zambian political leader who led the Zambian independence movement and became Zambia's first president (1964–).

Kaunitz, Wenzel Anton, Fürst von 1711–94. Austrian statesman. He allied Austria with France and Russia in a coalition against Prussia that led to the Seven Years' War (q.v.).

Kautsky, Karl Johann 1854–1938. German Socialist leader and Marxist theorist. He was the main contributor to the Erfurt program, which committed the German Social Democratic party to a Marxist program.

Kay, John 1704–64. English inventor of the fly shuttle (1733), a major advance in the development of mechanical weaving.

Kazan Capital city (pop. 870,000) of the Tatar Autonomous Soviet Socialist Republic, on the Volga River. A major commercial center, it was capital of an independent Tatar khanate from the 15th cent. until its capture by Ivan IV (1552). It became the capital of the Volga region in 1708 and was an outpost for Russian colonization of the East.

Kean, Edmund 1789–1833. English actor whose dynamic performances in such roles as Iago, Shylock, and Othello revolutionized English acting style and made him famous as one of England's greatest actors.

Kearny, Philip 1814–62. American Union general. A nephew of S. W. Kearny, he fought in the

Mexican War and with the French in Europe. He was a dashing commander in the Peninsular Campaigns and was killed in action reconnoitering Confederate lines.

Kearny, Stephen Watts 1794–1848. American general in the Mexican War. He captured New Mexico, established a civil government there, and helped to capture California, where he was military governor for a time.

Keats, John 1795–1821. English poet, considered one of England's greatest Romantic poets. He gave up a career as a medical student in 1816 to write poetry. Despite his tragically short life and the lack of recognition of his work, Keats produced a number of works renowned for their sensuous imagery. Among his best-known poems are the odes *On Melancholy, To a Nightingale, On a Grecian Urn*, and *To Psyche*.

Keble, John 1792–1866. English clergyman and poet whose sermon *National Apostacy* is considered the origin of the Oxford movement within the Anglican church.

Keita, Modibo *See* **Mali**

Keitel, Wilhelm 1882–1946. German field marshal and chief of staff of the German high command during WW II. He was convicted at Nürnberg for war crimes and was executed.

Keith, George 1693?–1778. Scottish Jacobite leader. A brother of J. Keith, he took part in the abortive Jacobite uprising of 1715, and then escaped to the Continent, where he eventually rose high in the service of Prussia.

Keith, James Francis Edward 1696–1758. Scottish Jacobite leader in the Jacobite rebellion of 1715. He later served as field marshal in the Prussian army during the Seven Years' War.

Keller, Helen Adams 1880–1968. American author and public figure. Blind and deaf from infancy, she overcame her handicaps and became a noted writer and lecturer.

Kellermann, François Christophe 1735–1820. French general and marshal of France, his defeat of the Prussian army at the Battle of Valmy (1792) saved the revolutionary government in France.

Kelley, Oliver Hudson 1826–1913. American agriculturalist. He was one of the founders (1867) of the National Grange and became a leader of the Granger movement.

Kellogg, Frank Billings 1856–1937. American statesman. As US secretary of state (1925–29), he formulated the Kellogg-Briand Pact, for which he received the Nobel Peace Prize in 1929.

Kellogg-Briand Pact ⟨Pact of Paris⟩ International agreement (Aug. 27, 1928) declaring an end to war as an instrument of national policy. Initiated by US secretary of state F. Kellogg and French foreign minister A. Briand, the pact was originally signed at Paris by 15 nations and ultimately was subscribed to by 62. The pact was rendered ineffective by the lack of means of enforcement and by provisions that allowed defensive wars and wars to defend allies. In the following years it was ignored by the Japanese (Manchurian invasion, 1931) and others.

Kelts *See* **Celts**

Kelvin, William Thomson, 1st Baron 1824–1907. Scottish mathematician and physicist, noted especially for his contributions to the fields of thermodynamics and electricity. The scale of absolute temperature is named for him.

Kendall, Amos *See* **Kitchen Cabinet**

Kennedy Prominent American political family from Massachusetts. The founder, Joseph P. Kennedy (1888–1969), acquired a large fortune and served as F. Roosevelt's ambassador to London (1937–40). Three of his sons have gained prominence as American political leaders: J. Kennedy; R. Kennedy; and Edward Kennedy (1932–   ), US senator from Massachusetts from 1962.

Kennedy, Edward M. *See* **Kennedy Family**

Kennedy, John Fitzgerald 1917–63. Thirty-fifth US president (1961–63), successor to D. Eisenhower. A Democrat and US congressman from Massachusetts (1947–53), he served in the Senate from 1953 to 1960 and there established himself politically. In the 1960 elections he successfully opposed R. Nixon and became the youngest president (and first Catholic) ever elected to the office. As president, he sought enactment of legislation, which became stalled in Congress, for his New Frontier *(q.v.)* program; instituted the Alliance for Progress (1961) program; and started the Peace Corps program. Kennedy put the federal government squarely behind the civil rights movement in the South and used both federal troops and federal pressure to promote school desegregation there. In foreign affairs, Kennedy quickly became embroiled in a series of clashes with the Communists, including the embarrassing failure of the Bay of Pigs Invasion *(q.v.)*, the crisis over the Berlin Wall *(q.v.)*, the Cuban missile crisis *(q.v.)*, and increasing involvement in the war against the Communists in Vietnam. He also concluded the Nuclear Test Ban Treaty of 1963. Kennedy was assassinated (Nov. 22, 1963) in Dallas, Texas, by Lee Harvey Oswald (1939–63). Oswald was in turn shot and killed by Jack Ruby (1911–67), a local citizen. Despite findings of the Warren Commission that Oswald acted alone, rumors of a second gunman and of various conspiracies persisted for years.

Kennedy, Joseph P. *See* **Kennedy**

Kennedy, Robert F. 1925–68. American politician, younger brother of President J. Kennedy. He was attorney general under presidents Kennedy and L. Johnson (1961–64). As US senator from New York (1964–68), he ran for the Democratic presidential nomination in 1968 but was assassinated on June 5, 1968.

Kennedy Round Series of tariff negotiations conducted (1964–67) by 50 countries responsible for 80 percent of world trade. They agreed to tariff reductions of up to 50 percent on many industrial goods and to substantial reductions on other tariffs.

Kennesaw Mountain, Battle of *See* **Atlanta Campaign**

Kensett, John Frederick 1818–72. American painter, one of the group of painters known as the Hudson River school.

Kensington Rune Stone Controversial stone found (1898) on a farm near Kensington, Michigan. It bears runic inscriptions supposedly carved by Norse explorers in 1362.

Kent, kingdom of Ancient English kingdom. Founded by the Jutes (5th cent. AD), it rose to power (6th cent.) under Aethelbert, but in the 9th cent. became part of the kingdom of Wessex. The kingdom contained the bishopric of Canterbury, established during Aethelbert's rule.

Kent State Massacre Incident at Kent State University in Kent, Ohio, on May 4, 1970. Ohio National Guardsmen called out against a Vietnam War protest rally fired on protesters, killing four students. The incident provoked a nationwide protest against repression and redoubled sentiment against the war.

Kentucky Central state of the US (pop. 3,661,400), the 15th state. Kentucky was first settled in the 1760s. D. Boone opened the Wilderness Road from Tennessee to Kentucky and founded the first settlement, Boonesborough (1775). Made a county of Virginia (1776), Kentucky was the first territory west of the Appalachians to become a state (1792). Federal adoption of the Alien and Sedition Acts (1798) led to passage of the Kentucky and Virginia Resolutions. Kentucky was a border state during the American Civil War. Although it remained in the Union, many Kentuckians fought for the Confederacy.

Kentucky and Virginia Resolutions Resolutions passed (Nov., Dec., 1798) by legislatures in the two states to oppose the Alien and Sedition Acts (1798). The ideas these resolutions put forward laid the basis for states' rights and the nullification controversy. Written by T. Jefferson (Kentucky) and J. Madison (Virginia), the resolutions

amounted to a reply by Jeffersonian Republicans to the Federalist party interpretation of federal government powers. Essentially, Jefferson put forward the idea of a compact between the federal government and states established by the Constitution. Further, the states had the power to nullify federal laws they deemed unconstitutional.

Kenya ⟨Republic of Kenya, *formerly* British East Africa⟩ Republic located on the east coast of Africa. Its capital is Nairobi. The region of Kenya was early dominated by the Arabs. Control then passed to the Portuguese, back to the Arabs, and finally to the British. Kenya became independent in 1963. Key dates in the history of Kenya include:

8TH CENT. Arabs settled coast, establishing autonomous colonies.

c1000 Bantu tribes arrived in region.

16TH CENT. Portuguese arrived (from 1498) and gradually gained control of Kenyan coastal region.

1729 Arabs drove out Portuguese and took control of region.

1886 Britain and Germany set up "spheres of influence" in region; most of Kenya went to Britain.

1888 British East Africa Company given royal charter.

1895 British government took control; East Africa Protectorate established.

FROM 1903 European settlers arrived, taking control of highlands region.

1920 Kenya divided into British crown colony (coast) and protectorate (interior).

1952–56 Native Mau-Mau uprising against European domination.

1961 Black Africans gained majority control in Kenya's legislative council for the first time; Jomo Kenyatta, nationalist leader, freed from exile.

1963 Independence declared (Dec. 12); unicameral legislature established by constitution; Kenya African Union became sole political party.

1963–68 Border war with Somali Democratic Republic.

1964 Republic declared; Kenyatta first president (in office 1964–78).

1967 Kenya, Uganda, and Tanzania established East African trading community.

1969 Tom Mboya, Kenyatta's probable successor, assassinated.

1976 Hostilities with Uganda ended by formal peace agreement.

1978 Kenyatta died (Aug. 22); Daniel Arap Mori elected president.

Kenyatta, Jomo c1894–1978. Kenyan political leader and statesman. He was a leader in the Kenyan independence movement and became first president of the Republic of Kenya (1964–78).

Kepler, Johannes 1571–1630. German astronomer, author of three laws describing planetary motion, now known as Kepler's laws. Kepler's work contributed to the later work of I. Newton.

Kerensky, Aleksandr Feodorovich 1881–1970. Russian revolutionary. He took part in the February Revolution (1917) that toppled the czarist government, and served as premier of the Provisional Government from July until the Bolshevik October Revolution.

Kerensky Offensive *See* **June Offensive**

Kern, Jerome 1885–1945. American composer noted for his scores for many musicals. His musical *Show Boat* had a major influence on later musicals.

Kerouac, Jack ⟨~, Jean-Louis⟩ 1922–69. American novelist. A leader of the Beat movement, Kerouac is known best for his novel *On The Road*.

Kerouac, Jean-Louis *See* **Kerouac, Jack**

Kesselring, Albert 1887–1960. German field marshal, one of A. Hitler's top commanders. He led air operations in Poland, Russia, and the West, and was commander in chief of operations in Italy (1943) during WW II.

Key, Francis Scott 1779–1843. American poet, author of *The Star-Spangled Banner.* Key's poem, inspired by the British attack on Ft. McHenry (1814) during the War of 1812, was set to music and became the US national anthem (1931).

Keynes, John Maynard, 1st baron of Tilton 1883–1946. British economist whose views have influenced the economic policies of many governments, notably F. Roosevelt's New Deal *(q.v.).* He wrote *The General Theory of Employment, Interest, and Money,* which advocated government intervention in solving the unemployment problem. A delegate to the Bretton Woods Conference (1944), he played a key role in establishing the International Monetary Fund.

KGB Russian political security police force. Created in 1954, it functions as an espionage agency as well as a force against internal subversion and domestic dissidence. (*See also* GPU.)

Khafre ⟨Chephren⟩ c2555–? BC. Ancient Egyptian king of the 4th dynasty. He built the second great pyramid at Giza.

Khair ed-Din *See* **Barbarossa II**

Khalifa, the *See* **Abd Allah**

Khalji Dynasty *See* **Delhi Sultanate**

khanate of Khiva Former khanate in south-central Asia, ruled by the Uzbeks. It flourished from the 16th cent. until its conquest by Russia (1873). The area is now part of the Turkmen and Uzbek Soviet Socialist Republics.

Khanbalik *See* **Peking**

Khartoum, Battle of Battle (1885) between British forces and the forces of the Mahdi, at Khartoum, Sudan. The British were besieged at Khartoum and were finally (Jan. 26) overwhelmed, and British general C. Gordon and all his garrison were killed. The battle is one of the great military engagements of British history.

Khazars ⟨Chazars⟩ Turkic people who ruled a powerful empire (c6th–10th cents.) located west of the Volga and north of the Black Sea in what is now southeastern USSR. With its capital at Itil, at the mouth of the Volga, the Khazar empire controlled trade between Byzantium and the East and between the Arab Empire and Slavic peoples to the north. By the 8th cent., the Khazar ruling class had embraced Judaism and entered into close relations with the Byzantines. The empire fell (965) to invading Russian armies of Sviatoslav, duke of Kiev, and thereafter ceased to be a power.

Khedive Ismail *See* **Ismail Pasha**

Khmelnitsky, Bogdan *See* **Chmielnicki, Bogdan**

Khmer Empire Ancient empire of southeast Asia located in what are now Cambodia and Laos. Established in the 6th cent., it rose to prominence in the 9th to 15th cents., during which time Buddhism, Hinduism, Sanskrit literature, and other elements of Indian culture flourished in the region. The empire reached its height in the 12th and 13th cents., when the cities of Angkor Wat and Angkor Thom were built. Its decline began (14th cent.) with repeated invasions by Annamese and Thais. The capture (15th cent.) of Angkor Thom by the Thais marked the end of Khmer power in the region.

Khmer Rouge ⟨Red Cambodians⟩ Cambodian Communists. Supported by the Viet Cong, the insurgent group overthrew the government of Lon Nol (1975), and, after a bloody rule, was in turn overthrown by a Vietnamese-backed faction (1978).

Khomeini, Ruhollah, Ayatollah 1901–. Iranian religious leader, a Muslim fundamentalist, and virtual dictator of Iran from Jan. 31, 1979 as a result of the Iranian revolution. Long exiled in Iraq and France during the regime of Shah Muhammad Reza Pahlevi, he returned to tumultuous popular acclaim in Iran after nearly a year of massive violent protests had resulted in the shah's abdication and departure (Jan. 16, 1979). It soon became clear that successive governments and officials acted only on the sufferance of the Ayatollah, even when pledged to the idea of an Islamic republic. He instituted a puritanical and repressive regime, increasingly dominated by religious leaders. Declining to take responsibility for actual government, even though his power was absolute, he contributed to increasing turmoil and chaos, especially after Iraq's military attack on Iran on Sept. 22, 1980. Khomeini's approval of mob violence led to the seizure by Iranian militants of the US Embassy (Nov. 4, 1979) and the hostage crisis (q.v.).

Khorezm Region of ancient Persia, now part of Soviet Turkistan. Once part of Cyrus the Great's empire, it became independent in the 12th cent. It was conquered by Genghis Khan (1220), Tamerlane (1378), and by the Uzbeks (16th cent.), who established an independent Uzbek state called the khanate of Khiva (q.v.).

Khosru I d. 579. Persian king (531–579). He expanded his empire east to the Indus River, and conquered parts of the Byzantine Empire. He encouraged culture and instituted reforms.

Khosru II d. 628. Persian king (590–628). After being usurped, Khosru regained the throne with the aid of Byzantine emperor Maurice. After Maurice's murder (602), Khosru turned against the Byzantines, but was defeated by Heraclius I.

Khrushchev, Nikita Sergeyevich 1894–1971. Russian Communist leader, first secretary of the Communist Party of the Soviet Union (1953–64) and premier (1958–64). He joined (1918) the Communist party and rose through the ranks to serve J. Stalin in the Great Purge. A member of the ruling Politburo from 1959, he won the power struggle that erupted after Stalin's death (1953) and that year replaced Malenkov as the party's first secretary. His long tenure during the Cold War era was marked by his de-Stalinization program (1956), Russian intervention in the Hungarian Revolution (1956), erection of the Berlin Wall (1961), the U-2 incident, failed Five-Year Plans, and the Cuban missile crisis (1962). His ouster (Oct., 1964) was brought on by failures in the Cuban crisis and agricultural production, as well as deteriorating relations with China.

Khufu (Cheops) c2589–c2566 BC. Ancient Egyptian king of the 4th dynasty. He built the great pyramid at Giza.

Khwarazm See **Khorezm**

Khyber Pass Steep mountain pass on the border of Pakistan and Aghanistan. It has long been a commercial route to India as well as an invasion route for such conquerors as Alexander the Great and Tamerlane. It also was used by British forces during the Anglo–Afghan Wars.

Kiangsi soviet Independent Chinese Communist government set up (1931) in Kiangsi province after the split between Nationalists and Communists. It was from Kiangsi that the Long March (1934) to Shansi province began.

Kickapoo Indians North American Indian tribe, once located in the northern Midwest. After the massacre (c1765) of the Illinois Indians, in which the Kickapoo took part, they occupied lands in Illinois. They aided the British in the American Revolution, fought with Chief Tecumseh against the Americans in the War of 1812, and, after ceding their lands to the US, took part in the Black Hawk War (1831–32). Forced to leave Illinois, they resettled in Kansas.

Kid, Thomas See **Kyd, Thomas**

Kidd, William c1645–1701. British privateer and pirate, known as Captain Kidd. Through numerous legends and stories he has come to be a leading figure in pirate lore.

Kido Koin (Kido Takayoshi) 1833–77. Japanese statesman. He helped to overthrow the Japanese shogunate (1868) and restore imperial rule. He subsequently helped to end feudalism in Japan and institute constitutional government.

Kido Takayoshi See **Kido Koin**

Kiel, Treaty of Peace settlement (Jan. 14, 1814) between Denmark and Sweden during the Napoleonic Wars. Denmark, an ally of France, was forced to surrender Norway to Sweden, thus further declining as a European power.

Kierkegaard, Sören 1813–55. Danish philosopher and religious writer whose works had a tremendous influence on the development of modern existentialism. Kierkegaard opposed the philosophical system of the dialectic advanced by G. Hegel and held that man's existence must be governed by his own conscious choice. He also advanced the theory that in religion "truth is subjectivity." His works include *Either/Or, Philosophical Fragments,* and *Works of Love.*

Kiesinger, Kurt Georg 1904–. German politician. As chancellor of West Germany (1966–69), he continued the pro-West policies of K. Adenauer and L. Erhard.

Kiev Russian city (pop. 2,144,000), capital of Kiev oblast and Ukrainian SSR and third largest Russian city. Originally a trading center between Scandinavia and Constantinople, it was conquered (9th cent.) by the Varangians, then rose in the 11th cent. to become capital of Kievan Russia. Destroyed (1240) by the Mongols, it passed to Lithuania (14th cent.), Poland (1569), and Russia (1686). Occupied by the Germans during WW II, the city was heavily damaged.

Kimhi, David 1160?–1235? Hebrew scholar believed to have lived and died in Narbonne, France. His grammar and lexicon were the leading works in their field for centuries.

Kim Il-sung ⟨Kim Song Ju⟩ 1912–. Leader of the Democratic People's Republic of Korea (North Korea) since 1948.

Kimitake Hiraoka   *See* **Mishima Yukio**

Kim Song Ju   *See* **Kim Il-sung**

Kindi ⟨Al-Kindi⟩ *fl.* 9th cent. Arab philosopher. He translated Aristotle's work into Arabic and attempted to reconcile Aristotelian and Neoplatonist thought. His extensive writings dealt with medicine, astrology, and mathematics.

king   Designation given to the male ruler of a nation or state. The title is generally hereditary.

King, Martin Luther, Jr. 1929–68. American civil rights leader renowned for his use of nonviolent resistance in the fight for racial equality. A minister in Montgomery, Alabama, he led a successful boycott opposing segregated city buses (1956), and organized the Southern Christian Leadership Conference. One of the leading figures in the black civil rights movement, he led the massive March on Washington, D.C. (1963). King was awarded the Nobel Peace Prize in 1964. He was assassinated in 1968 in Memphis, Tennessee.

King, William Lyon Mackenzie 1874–1950. Canadian Liberal party leader and prime minister (1921–26, 1926–30, 1935–48). A specialist on labor, he was first elected to Parliament in 1908 and became Liberal party leader in 1919. During his long tenure as prime minister, he guided Canada through WW II, entered into defense alliances with the US by the Ogdensburg Declaration (1940) and Hyde Park Declaration (1941), and took part in the United Nations Charter conferences (1945).

King Cotton   Term once used in the US South to express the value, both political and economic, of the southern cotton crop in the years before the American Civil War. Believers in the notion of King Cotton held that the importance of cotton would guarantee the South's success if it were ever forced to secede from the Union. Senator J. Hammond made it the subject of a famous speech before the US Senate (Mar. 4, 1858).

kingdom of   *See under names inverted, as in* **Castile, kingdom of**

King George's War (1744–48). American phase of the War of the Austrian Succession in Europe. It was an outgrowth of colonial rivalries between France and Britain, both of which then had interests in North America, and it was the third of four so-called French and Indian Wars *(q.v.).* The French began hostilities by capturing a British fort located off Nova Scotia. Spurred on by colonists in Massachusetts, the northern British colonies mustered an army of 4,000 militiamen. With the aid of British warships, they captured the heavily defended French fort at Louisburg, Nova Scotia

(1745). Two subsequent attempts (1746, 1747) by French fleets failed to retake Nova Scotia. The French and their Indian allies launched raids into the British colonies, while the British were successful against the French in the West Indies. The war was ended by the Treaty of Aix-la-Chapelle (1748), which restored conquered territories.

King Philip's War   War (1675–76) between New England colonists and Indian tribes in the region. The bloody war cost the lives of hundreds of colonists and resulted in the dispersal of New England tribes to the West. Relations between colonists and Indians were seriously eroded by the Pequot War (1637) and expansion of white settlements on Indian lands. The Indians formed a confederacy under King Philip, son of the Indian leader Massasoit, but they maintained peaceful relations until colonials executed three Wampanoag tribesmen. War broke out with an Indian raid (June, 1675) on a border settlement. Thereafter dozens of Colonial settlements from Connecticut to Maine were raided and burned. The Colonial militia retaliated in kind against Wampanoag, Narragansett, and Nipmuck villages. The war ended with the death (Aug., 1676) of King Philip.

King's law   *See* **Griffenfeld, Peder Schumacher, Count**

Kingsley, Charles 1819–75. English author and clergyman whose novels reflected his concern for social issues of the day. He was a leading figure in the Christian Socialism movement.

King's Men   *See* **Chamberlain's Men**

Kings Mountain, Battle of   Battle (Oct. 7, 1780) of the Carolina Campagin *(q.v.)* in the American Revolution, at Kings Mountain, South Carolina. A decisive American victory over Loyalist forces, it contributed to the final British defeat.

King's Peace ⟨Peace of Antalcidas⟩ Peace agreement (387 BC) between Sparta and Persia. Sparta, simultaneously fighting a war against Persia and against an alliance of Greek city-states (Corinthian War, 395–387 BC), negotiated this peace with Persian king Artaxerxes II. By its terms, Greek cities in the west were declared to be autonomous, while those in Asia Minor were to belong to Persia. Sparta forced (386) Athenian acceptance of the peace by a naval blockade, and thereafter dominated the region as it had before the Corinthian War. This led to new rebellions and Sparta's eventual defeat (371) by Thebes.

Kingston   Capital city (pop. 111,900) of Jamaica since 1872. Founded in 1693, Jamaica has become one of the commercial, industrial, and tourist centers of the West Indies and is noted for its deepwater harbor.

King William's War American Colonial war (1689–97) fought by Britain against France in North America. An extension of the War of the Grand Alliance against French king Louis XIV, it is considered the first of the French and Indian Wars. War began with a naval attack on Quebec (1690) by the British. The French and their Indian allies, led by Count Frontenac, then launched attacks on Schenectady, New York, Salmon Falls, New Hampshire, and Casco Bay, in Maine. The New England colonies in turn raised a militia, led by Sir W. Phips, which captured (May 11, 1690) Port Royal in French Acadia. British colonists subsequently attacked Quebec, but were unable to take it. Thereafter, the French and British and their respective Indian allies conducted raids on border settlements. The Treaty of Ryswick ended the war and provided for restoration of all conquered territories.

Kinsey, Alfred Charles 1894–1956. American zoologist, known best for his studies of human sexual behavior.

Kinshasa ⟨Leopoldville⟩ Capital city (pop. 2,008,400) of Zaire. Founded (1881) by H. Stanley, it is Zaire's commercial and cultural center.

Kioto *See* **Kyoto**

Kipchak khanate *See* **Golden Horde**

Kipling, Rudyard 1865–1936. English author, one of England's leading writers in the late 19th and early 20th cents. Much of his work reflects England's history as a colonial empire. He was awarded the Nobel Prize for Literature in 1907.

Kirby-Smith, Edmund *See* **Smith, Edmund Kirby**

Kircher, Athanasius 1601?–80. German Jesuit and scientist. His work with microscopes led him to believe that disease was caused by invisible bodies. He is credited with the invention of the magic lantern.

Kirchhoff, Gustav Robert 1824–87. German physicist, noted for his contributions to spectrum analysis, thermodynamics, and electricity. With R. Bunsen, he discovered the elements cesium and rubidium.

Kirchner, Ernst Ludwig 1880–1938. German painter and graphic artist. He was one of the founders of Die Brücke, a German expressionist art movement.

Kirke, Sir David 1596?–1654? English trader and adventurer. He captured Quebec (1629) and served as governor of Newfoundland.

Kirov, Sergei Mironovich 1888–1934. Russian Communist leader. His assassination marked the beginning of the Stalinist purges of the 1930s.

Kisfaludy, Károly 1788–1830. Hungarian dramatist, considered the founder of Hungarian national drama. Among his best-known works is the play *Tatars in Hungary*.

Kish Ancient Mesopotamian city in Iraq, east of Babylon. According to ancient legend, it was the site of the first Sumerian capital after the Great Flood.

Kishi Nobusuke 1896–. Japanese prime minister (1957–60). His support of a controversial US-Japanese security treaty caused widespread protest and led to his resignation.

Kissinger, Henry Alfred 1923–. American political scientist, US secretary of state (1973–77) under presidents R. Nixon and G. Ford. He figured prominently in the Nixon administration's efforts to find a solution to the Vietnam War. Following the Arab-Israeli War (1973), Kissinger instituted his so-called shuttle diplomacy, in which he traveled between the Egyptian and Israeli capitals in an attempt to negotiate an agreement between the two countries. He was awarded the Nobel Peace Prize in 1973.

Kitasato, Shibasaburo 1852–1931. Japanese physician and bacteriologist. He developed an antitoxin for tetanus (with E. Behring) and identified ,independently of A. Yersin, the bacillus causing bubonic plague (1894).

Kit-Cat Club London club of the early 18th cent. It was founded by leading Whigs and included well-known literary personages among its members.

Kitchen Cabinet Group of unofficial advisers to US president A. Jackson during his first term of office (1829–33). Composed of editors of important newspapers and Jackson's political associates, the group came to replace regular Cabinet officers and advisers in formulating Jackson's policies. Of diminished importance after the Cabinet reorganization (1831), the group included Amos Kendall (1789–1869), Francis P. Blair (1791–1876), Duff Green (1791–1875), William B. Lewis, John H. Eaton (1790–1856), Isaac Hill, and M. Van Buren.

Kitchen Debate Widely publicized exchange between US vice-president R. Nixon and Soviet premier N. Khrushchev that took place (1959) while the two men were visiting an American exhibit of a model American kitchen. The two vigorously argued the merits of the American and Soviet systems before the accompanying reporters and media representatives. Nixon later instanced this impromptu "debate" as proof of his ability to deal with the Soviets.

Kitchener, Horatio Herbert Kitchener, 1st earl 1850–1916. British field marshal and statesman. He conquered the Sudan and reoccupied Khartoum (1898), and was chief of staff in the South

African War. As secretary of war (1914–16), he greatly expanded Britain's military forces.

Kittredge, George Lyman 1860–1941. American scholar and educator. An authority on Shakespeare, Chaucer, and Malory, he taught at Harvard (1888–1936) and had a great influence on the teaching of English.

Kitty Hawk Village in northeastern North Carolina. Nearby is Kill Devil Hill, where the Wright brothers made their first successful powered flight (1903).

Kléber, Jean Baptiste 1753–1800. French general. He campaigned in the French Revolutionary Wars, suppressed the Royalist rebellion in the Vendée (1793), and commanded French forces in Egypt.

Klee, Paul 1879–1940. Swiss abstract artist, whose many works are noted for their innovative style, subtle humor, and use of color.

Kleist, Heinrich von 1777–1811. German poet and dramatist, considered one of the great German dramatists of the 19th cent.

Klemperer, Otto 1885–1973. One of the leading German orchestral conductors of the 20th cent. He is noted for introducing new works of I. Stravinsky and others and for his interpretations of the works of L. Beethoven and G. Mahler.

Klondike Region of the Yukon Territory in northwestern Canada. Discovery of gold here in 1896 led to the gold rush (1897–99).

Kloster-Zeven, Convention of *See* **Convention of Kloster-Zeven**

Kluck, Alexander von *See* **Marne, Battle of the**

KMT *See* **Kuomintang**

Knickerbocker American Colonial term for Dutch colonists in New York State. They were so named after the Herman Knickerbocker family, which settled near Albany (c1674).

Knights Hospitalers ⟨Knights of St. John⟩ ⟨Knights of Jerusalem⟩ ⟨*in full* Order of the Hospital of St. John of Jerusalem⟩ Important religious and military order founded (c1099) in Jerusalem. The order was created by Gerard de Martignes and confirmed (1153) by Pope Eugenius III. Dedicated to the healing and protection of pilgrims to the Holy Land, the order grew rich and powerful during the Crusades. Grateful knights, healed at the order's hospital, made bequests of money and land, while the knights of the order undertook military operations in its name. The misfortunes of the Crusades and the rise of Turkish power, however, forced the order to relocate several times after the fall of Jerusalem (1187): to Acre (1189); to Cyprus (1291); to Rhodes (1310), which they conquered; and to Malta (1530). The order declined in importance after being driven out of Rhodes. Napoleon's conquest of Malta (1798) effectively brought the order to an end. In 1879 it was reorganized and revived as a charitable organization.

Knights of Calatrava Oldest Spanish military and religious order. Established by Cistercian monks to protect the city of Calatrava against the Moors (1158), the order subsequently gained control of large territories. It remained powerful until King Ferdinand and Queen Isabella took control of it (1493) under the authority of the crown.

Knights of Jerusalem *See* **Knights Hospitalers**

Knights of Labor US labor organization, founded (1869) in Philadelphia. Originally a secret organization under the leadership of Uriah S. Stephens (1821–82), it included workers of all kinds (as opposed to craft organizations) and sought to replace capitalism with workers' cooperatives. Secrecy was abolished (1881), and under the leadership of Terence V. Powderly (1849–1924) the group reached its greatest membership, some 700,000. In 1886, after a wave of strikes in the US and the disastrous Haymarket Square Riot, membership in the group began a rapid decline. By the end of the century, it was largely replaced by the American Federation of Labor, and was disbanded in 1917.

Knights of Saint Crispin Early US trade union. Founded (1867) to organize shoemakers, a major union in the US. By 1878, however, most of its members had joined the Knights of Labor.

Knights of St. John *See* **Knights Hospitalers**

Knights of the Golden Circle Secret order of supporters of the South during the American Civil War. Founded (1854) in Ohio as a proslavery group, it turned to supporting the Confederacy after the outbreak of war. Active mainly in Ohio, Illinois, Indiana, Missouri, and Kentucky, the group was composed largely of Democrats who wanted to end the war (called Copperheads). In 1864, the group became known as the Sons of Liberty.

Knights of the Temple of Solomon *See* **Knights Templars**

Knights Templars ⟨Templars⟩ ⟨Knights of the Temple of Solomon⟩ Important religious military order founded (c1119) during the Crusades. Organized by Hugh de Payens at Jerusalem to protect Christian pilgrims from Muslim attacks, the order was confirmed (1128) by Pope Honorius III. It subsequently grew into a powerful army in service against the Muslims and, through bequests, gained considerable wealth and lands in Europe. After the failure of the Crusades, the Templars became a powerful banking group and thereby aroused opposition by the European nobility. French king Philip IV, with consent of Pope Clement V, began persecutions (1307) of the Templars. By 1314, its property had been confiscated, and the order ceased to exist.

Knights' War Unsuccessful rebellion of German knights (1522–23) during the Reformation. The knights, led by F. von Sickengen, supported the Reformation and sought to ensure their ancient privileges.

Knossos *See* **Cnossus**

Know-Nothing party ⟨American party⟩ Short-lived US political party active in the mid-1800s. Originally a secretive group, members answered questions about its activities by saying they knew nothing (hence the name). Its major aim, however, was promotion of American nativism, in reaction to the rising tide of European immigration. The party became a national organization (1845) and made significant gains in the 1854 elections in New York, Massachusetts, and other states. The secretive elements were abolished in 1855, but the party split the same year over the slavery issue. It declined rapidly during the remainder of the decade, and its presidential candidate, M. Fillmore, carried only Maryland in 1856.

Knox, Frank ⟨Knox, William Franklin⟩ 1874–1944. American newspaper publisher. He was unsuccessful Republican vice-presidential candidate (1936), but served as US secretary of the navy (1940–44) under President F. Roosevelt in a Democratic administration.

Knox, Henry 1750–1806. American officer in the American Revolution. He directed the removal of artillery from Fort Ticonderoga to Boston, where it was used to force British evacuation. Knox served as first US secretary of war (1785–94).

Knox, John c1514–72. Scottish reformer and founding father of the Church of Scotland. After the execution (1546) of his mentor, G. Wishart, he joined a group of Scottish Presbyterian conspirators who had avenged Wishart's death. Eventually captured by Catholic forces, he was rescued from slavery and thereafter served the Protestant cause in England and on the Continent. With the beginning of the Scottish Reformation (1557), Knox returned to Scotland (1559) to lead the fight against Catholic armies. Following the establishment of the Church of Scotland, Knox and others wrote the *First Book of Discipline*, setting forth the basic organization of the church. Knox lost many supporters with the accession (1561) of Mary Queen of Scots. He continued to uphold his beliefs and resolutely opposed Mary. His efforts were rewarded when the Protestant nobles forced her abdication (1567).

Knox, Philander Chase 1853–1921. American politician. As US attorney general (1901–04), he led government prosecution of trusts. As secretary of state (1909–13), he defended American financial interests abroad through what has been termed "dollar diplomacy."

Knox, William Franklin *See* **Knox, Frank**

Knut *See* **Canute**

Kobo-Daishi *See* **Kukai**

Koch, Robert 1843–1910. German bacteriologist, a leading figure in the founding of bacteriology. His contributions include the discovery of the organisms causing anthrax (1876) and those causing tuberculosis (1882).

Koffka, Kurt 1886–1941. German psychologist. With W. Köhler and M. Wertheimer, he founded the school of Gestalt psychology.

Koguryŏ Ancient Korean kingdom, founded c2d–1st cents. BC. In 668 BC, it was overrun by the Chinese T'ang and Korean Silla dynasties, and was incorporated into the kingdom of Silla.

Kohathites *See* **Levites**

Köhler, Wolfgang 1887–1967. Estonian-born psychologist who, with K. Koffka and M. Wertheimer, founded the Gestalt school of psychology.

Kokoschka, Oskar 1886–1980. Austrian painter and writer and leading figure in expressionism. He is noted for his expressionist landscapes and dramas.

Kolchak, Aleksandr Vasilyevich 1874–1920. Russian admiral and leader (1918–20) of anti-Bolshevik forces in Siberia during the Russian civil war.

Kolin, Battle of Austro-Prussian battle (June 18, 1757) during the Seven Years' War, at Kolin, now in Czechoslovakia. A force of 53,000 Austrians under L. von Daun defeated some 60,000 Prussians under Frederick the Great, raising the Prussian siege of Prague and forcing Frederick to evacuate Bohemia.

Konbaung dynasty *See* **Alaungpaya**; **Burmese War** (third)

Königgrätz, Battle of ⟨Sadowa, ~⟩ Decisive battle (July 3, 1866) near Königgrätz, now in Czechoslovakia, ending the Seven Weeks' War between Prussia and Austria. Prussian troops commanded by H. von Moltke defeated the Austrian army under Ludwig August von Benedek (1804–81). Austrian casualties were about 40,000, compared to Prussian losses of fewer than 15,000. The victory gave Prussia dominance over Germany.

Königsmark, Countess Maria Aurora 1668?–1728. Swedish noblewoman, mistress of King Augustus II of Poland and Saxony, and mother of Maurice, Comte de Saxe.

Konoye, Fumimaro, Prince 1891–1945. Japanese statesman. As premier of Japan (1937–39, 1940–41) he helped to form the Axis alliance with Germany and Italy.

Koowescoowe *See* **Ross, John**

Korah Biblical Hebrew leader who led an unsuccessful revolt against Moses and Aaron. He was swallowed up by the earth with Dathan, Abiram, and 250 others.

Koran ⟨Quran⟩ The sacred book of Islam. A compilation of the revelations received by Muhammad during his lifetime, it is one of the world's most influential books and the major unifying force in the Islamic religion. The authorized version was written (*c*650) by Muhammad's secretary, Zaid ibn Thabit, by order of the caliph Uthman. Divided into 114 chapters (suras), the Koran sets forth religious doctrine and codes concerning conduct of the followers of Islam. Accepted as the word of God, the Koran is above doubt or criticism in the Islamic world.

Korea Country occupying a large peninsula in eastern Asia, divided after WW II into North Korea (Democratic People's Republic of Korea, capital at Pyongyang) and South Korea (Republic of Korea, capital at Seoul). Korea has been influenced by neighboring China since ancient times and was reduced to a Chinese vassal state in the 17th cent. Control of Korea passed to the Japanese in the early 1900s and they held it until the end of WW II. The Soviets and the US established zones of occupation in 1945 and North and South Korea have been under separate governments ever since. Since the Korean War *(q.v.)* there have only been limited and largely fruitless talks on reunification. Key events in the history of Korea include:

12TH CENT. BC Ki Tse, Chinese feudal lord, founded first known kingdom in Korea; had fled China after overthrow of Shang dynasty.

1ST CENT. BC–7TH CENT. AD Three Kingdoms period: rise of three separate native kingdoms (Koguryo, Silla, Paekche) on Korean peninsula.

4TH CENT. AD Buddhism introduced.

670–935 Kingdom of Silla gained control over peninsula and formed first unified Korean kingdom; Confucianism and other elements of Chinese culture introduced.

935–1392 Koryo kingdom established control over Korea; distinct Korean culture developed.

13TH CENT. Korea invaded by Mongols from China; Mongols gained control over Korea.

1392 Yi Songgye founded Yi dynasty in Korea (ruled until 1910); established capital at Seoul, ended Mongol control, and established Confucianism.

1592–98 Japanese emperor Hideyoshi unsuccessfully attempted to conquer Korea; Koreans drove out Japanese with Chinese help.

1637 Chinese reduced Korea to vassal state following series of invasions.

17TH–19TH CENT. Korea entered period of extreme isolationism; Hermit Kingdom, as it was called, permitted only Chinese influence.

1876 Japan forced Korea to agree to a commercial treaty, thus ending period of Korean isolation; opened Korea to trade agreements with US and other Western nations.

1894–95 First Sino-Japanese War fought; led to increasing Japanese influence over Korea.

1904–05 Japanese forces occupied Korea during Russo-Japanese War, thus increasing Japan's hold on Korea.

1905 Korea declared a Japanese protectorate.

1910–45 Korea part of Japanese empire; annexed in 1910, it was thereafter exploited by Japanese; underwent rapid industrialization.

1945 Korea divided at end of WW II into two sectors; Soviet troops occupied sector north of 38th parallel; US forces occupied territory in south; plans called for reunification within five years.

1948 Soviet opposition to moves for reunification resulted in establishment (May 1) of People's Republic of Korea in north and (Aug. 15) Republic of Korea in south.

1948–60 Syngman Rhee in office as first elected president of Republic of Korea.

1948–72 Kim Il-sung (Kim Song Ju) premier in North Korea.

1949 US and Soviets withdrew troops from Korea.

1950 North Korean forces invaded south (June 25), instigating Korean war (1950–53).

1953 South Korea signed mutual defense treaty with US.

1958 Chinese completed withdrawal of troops from North Korea.

1960 Protest march (Apr. 19) in South Korea led to bloodbath as police shot at student demonstrators; civil unrest spread throughout South Korea, forcing Syngman Rhee to resign.

1961 Military junta seized power (May) in South Korea in bloodless coup; Gen. Park Chung Hee became leader of military government.

1963–69 Park Chung Hee president in South Korea; fostered economic growth and buildup of military.

1968 North Koreans seized US intelligence ship *Pueblo* (Jan. 23), provoking international incident.

1972 Pres. Park imposed martial law in South Korea (Oct. 17); National Assembly dissolved; political activities banned.

1972 Constitutional revisions adopted (Nov. 21); gave Pres. Park unlimited power and term of office.

1972 Kim Il Sung elected president of North Korea (Dec. 28); remained in office into early 1980s; new constitution promulgated.

1974 Pres. Park ordered measures to stifle growing opposition (Jan 8) in South Korea.

1974 Unsuccessful assassination attempt against Pres. Park in Seoul (Aug.).

1977 US announced intention of withdrawing US troops from Korea; opposition to move later ended in reversal of plan.

1977 North Koreans shot down US helicopter that had accidentally crossed over into the north.

1977 South Koreans implicated in scandal involving bribery of US congressmen.

1979 Talks on reunification with north held (Jan.-Mar.), though little progress was made.

1979 South Korean President Park assassinated (Oct. 26) by head of the Korean intelligence agency; martial law imposed.

1979–80 Choi Kyu Hah installed as South Korean president; some political restrictions rescinded; forced to resign (1980) as unrest mounted.

1980 Antigovernment unrest resulted in imposition (May 18) of total martial law in south.

1980 South Korean troops crushed antigovernment revolt in city of Kwangju (June 21).

1980 Chun Doo Hwan in office (Sept. 1) as president of South Korea.

1980 Major purge of government officials (July 9) directed at ending corruption in South Korea.

1980 New constitution approved by South Korean voters (Oct. 22); would limit presidential powers and lift ban on political parties.

1981 Martial law lifted (Jan. 24) by Pres. Chun Doo Hwan.

Korean War War (1950–53) between the North Koreans, backed by the Communist Chinese, and the South Koreans, backed by UN peace forces (principally US troops). Korea was ravaged by the war and there were some 4 million casualties (2 million of them civilians). The war was caused by various factors, including the Communists' desire to reunite Korea under their rule and the rise of Cold War tensions between Communist and non-Communist nations. Korea had been divided at the end of WW II, with Soviet forces occupying the territory north of the 38th parallel, and US forces to the south of it. Plans to reunite the country were never instituted. A Communist government was established in the north and a pro-Western government evolved in the south. Thus the Communist invasion of the south in 1950 became a part of the larger Cold War (q.v.) between the Communists and the US and its Western allies. In this context the war was a major test of the US policy of "containing" communism. Key events in the war include:

1950 Communist forces from North Korea mounted full-scale invasion of south (June 25); UN called for measures to aid South Korea against the invasion.

1950 US Pres. H. Truman ordered US military to aid South Korea as part of UN police action (June 30).

1950 South Korean and US forces driven to small zone around Pusan, southeastern Korea (early Sept.).

1950 US Gen. D. MacArthur, commander of UN forces, launched amphibious landing at Inchon (Sept. 15), well to the north; forced North Koreans to retreat.

1950 Seoul retaken by UN forces (Sept. 26).

1950 UN forces followed retreating North Korean forces across 38th parallel; captured Pyongyang, North Korean capital (Oct. 19).

1950 UN forces occupied most of Korea and advanced to Yalu River, Korean border with China, despite warnings by Chinese; Chinese launched invasion into Korea (Nov. 26).

1951 Chinese forces captured Seoul (Jan. 4).

1951 UN forces recaptured Seoul (Mar. 14) after Communist advance faltered.

1951 Communists pushed back to lines roughly along the 38th parallel; Gen. MacArthur openly advocated new invasion across 38th parallel, and was removed (Apr. 11) as supreme commander by President Truman; MacArthur was succeeded by Gen. M. Ridgway.

1951 Communist spring offensive (from May 15) failed.

1951 Peace talks began (July 10) at Kaesong; reconvened at Panmunjom (Oct. 25).

1953 Armistice signed (July 27).

Kornilov, Lavr Georgyevich 1870–1918. Russian general, made commander in chief by A. Kerensky after the February Revolution (1917). He was dismissed, then arrested, for sending troops against Kerensky, and later led anti-Bolshevik forces.

Kortruk, Battle of *See* **Golden Spurs, Battle of the**

Koryo Korean kingdom (935–1392) from which the name Korea is derived. During its existence the Korean peninsula was unified and its capital established at Songjong (modern Kaesong).

Korzybski, Alfred ⟨Habdank⟩ 1879–1950. Polish-born American scientist who founded the linguistic system known as general semantics.

Kosciusko, Thaddeus 1746–1817. Polish general and champion of Polish independence. He fought with distinction against the British in the American Revolution, then fought unsuccessfully in Poland against the Russians (1792–93). After the second Partition of Poland (1793), he led a rebellion (1794) against both Russian and Prussian forces. This led to the third Partition of Poland and his imprisonment (1794–96). Thereafter he lived in the US, France, and Switzerland.

Kosovo, Battle of   **1.** Battle (June 20, 1389; by tradition, June 15) at Kosovo, now in Yugoslavia, in which the Ottoman forces of Murad I defeated a confederation of Slavic forces under Serbian prince Lazar I (*d.* 1389). Both Murad and Lazar were killed. **2.** Battle (Oct. 16–17, 1448) at Kosovo, now in Yugoslavia, in which the Ottoman forces under Murad II defeated the Hungarian army of J. Hunyadi.

Kossuth, Lajos   *See* **Kossuth, Louis**

Kossuth, Louis ⟨~, Lajos⟩ 1802–94. Hungarian revolutionary, one of the leading figures in the Hungarian Revolution of 1848. He led the republic of Hungary briefly (1849), but was forced to resign in the face of Russian and Austrian intervention.

Koster, Laurens Janszoon ⟨Coster, Laurens Janszoon⟩ *c*1370–*c*1440. Dutch sexton, credited by some as being the inventor of printing with movable type. The controversy over whether he or J. Gutenberg first used movable type continues.

Kosygin, Aleksey Nikolayevich 1904–80. Russian statesman who succeeded N. Khrushchev as premier (1964–80). He joined the Communist party in 1927 and held various government positions under J. Stalin and Khrushchev. He played a major role in Soviet economic planning. As premier, he shared power with L. Brezhnev for a time but was gradually overshadowed.

Kowait   *See* **Kuwait**

Krebs, Sir Hans Adolf 1900–. German-born English biochemist. With F. A. Lipmann, he received the Nobel Prize in Physiology and Medicine in 1953 for his studies of the metabolic reaction process known as the citric acid, or Krebs, cycle.

Kremer, Gerhard   *See* **Mercator, Gerardus**

Kremlin Triangular citadel in Moscow, once a fortress and now the seat of the government of the USSR. Originally constructed in 1156 and modified considerably thereafter, the Kremlin is surrounded by a wall topped by twenty towers. Inside are numerous buildings that were once cathedrals, armories, and palaces, now used for government

purposes. The center of czarist government until 1712, when Peter the Great made St. Petersburg capital, it became the seat of the revolutionary government in 1918. Within the Kremlin walls is the famous Great Bell (Czar Bell), the world's largest. Red Square is located on the east side of the Kremlin.

Kreuger, Ivar 1880–1932. Swedish financier who attempted to build a world monopoly of the production of matches. The worldwide Great Depression caused his speculative venture to fail, and he committed suicide.

Kreutzer, Rodolphe 1766–1831. French composer and violinist noted for his 40 études for the violin. L. Beethoven dedicated his *Kreutzer Sonata* to him.

Krishna One of the leading Hindu divinities, the eighth incarnation of Vishnu.

Krishnamurti, Jiddu 1895–. Indian religious philosopher. With Annie Besant, he founded the World Order of the Star, in which he was proclaimed the incarnation of the messianic Buddha. He renounced the claim and dissolved the order. Since 1969 he has headed the Krishnamurti Foundation.

Kroeber, Alfred Louis 1876–1960. American anthropologist and authority on the Indians of southwestern US, Mexico, and Peru. His work is a major contribution to modern anthropology.

Kronos   *See* **Cronus**

Kronstadt Rebellion Russian revolt (Mar., 1921), the first major revolt against Bolshevik rule after the Russian civil war. Headed by sailors from the Kronstadt naval base near Leningrad, it sought measures to ease the economic hardships caused by the civil war and Bolshevik rule. Though suppressed, it led to the institution of the New Economic Policy.

Kropotkin, Peter Alekseyevich, Prince 1842–1921. Russian anarchist and author, a leading figure in the development of anarchist theory.

Krüdener, Barbara Juliane von, Baroness 1764–1824. Russian novelist and mystic who for a time had great influence over Czar Alexander I. She claimed to have inspired Alexander to conclude the Holy Alliance.

Kruger, Oom Paul   *See* **Kruger, Stephanus Johannes Paulus**

Kruger, Stephanus Johannes Paulus ⟨Kruger, Oom Paul⟩ 1825–1904. South African statesman. Leader of the Transvaal independence movement, he served as president of the Transvaal (1883–1900) until the Boer defeat in the Boer War.

Kruger telegram Communication (Jan. 3, 1896) from German kaiser William II to Paulus Kruger, president of the Transvaal Republic, congratulating him on his victory over the British in the Jameson Raid *(q.v.)*. The telegram greatly angered the British people.

Krupp, Alfred 1812–87. German steel magnate. He introduced modern production methods to Germany and manufactured heavy guns for Prussia in the Franco-Prussian War.

Krupp, Alfred Krupp von Bohlen und Halbach 1907–67. German industrialist, son of G. Krupp. During WW II, he employed concentration-camp victims as slave labor in Krupp factories, and confiscated property in the Nazi-occupied nations. He was imprisoned after the war (1948–51).

Krupp, Friedrich 1787–1826. German steel manufacturer. He founded the steel works at Essen (c1810) which later grew into the massive Krupp armaments and munitions empire.

Krupp, Friedrich Albert (Fritz) 1854–1902. German industrialist, son of A. Krupp. He greatly expanded the scope of Krupp interests.

Krupp, Gustav Krupp von Bohlen und Halbach 1870–1950. German industrialist. He adopted the name Krupp upon his marriage to Bertha Krupp, daughter of F. Krupp. He made Krupp the leading armaments manufacturer during WW I, supported the rise of A. Hitler, and helped Germany to rearm for WW II.

Krutch, Joseph Wood 1893–1970. American author and critic, noted for his drama criticism and for his writing on nature.

Krylov, Ivan Andreyevich 1768–1844. Russian fabulist. His fables in verse satirized contemporary Russian figures and attitudes and have had a lasting influence on Russian culture.

Kshatriya caste *See* **caste system**

Kuala Lumpur Capital and largest city (pop. 452,000) of Malaysia. It was founded (1857) as a mining town by the Chinese, who constitute the majority of the city's population. It became the capital of the Federated Malay States (1895) and of independent Malaya (1957).

Kuan Ti Chinese god of war. Originally a Chinese scholar, who was executed in the 3d cent. AD, he was later deified as the god of war and became a favorite deity of the Chinese people.

Kublai Khan c1215–94. Mongol emperor (1260–90), successor to his brother Mangu Khan, and grandson of Genghis Khan. He was founder of the Mongol Yüan dynasty in China. Following his election as emperor, he attacked northern China, and thus completed (1279) Mongol conquest (and reunification) of China. With his capital at Khanbalik, or Cambuluc (modern Peking), he ruled China and nominally controlled a vast Mongol empire that stretched across Asia. His military ex-

peditions against Korea and Burma were successful, but he failed in his attacks on Japan (1274–81) and Java (1293). He was a great builder, and the splendor of his court was recorded by M. Polo.

Kuchuk Kainarji, Treaty of Treaty (July 21, 1774) between Russia and the Ottoman Empire, ending the Russo-Turkish War of 1768–74. The treaty gave Russia Black Sea ports in the Crimea, opened Turkish waters to Russian ships, and gave Russia rights to represent Christians within the Ottoman Empire. The latter provision allowed Russia to proclaim itself protector of orthodox Christians there and facilitated the eventual takeover of Ottoman territories. In addition to ceding Crimean territories to Russia, the treaty made the Ottoman khanate of Crimea independent, and restored Walachia and Moldavia to the Ottomans.

Kufah ⟨Al-Kufa⟩ Former Arab city located south of Baghdad. Founded (638) by Caliph Omar I, it became seat of the Abbasid caliphate for a time (8th cent.) and rose to become a major seat of Muslim culture. Repeatedly attacked from the 10th cent. on, it had practically disappeared by the 14th cent.

Kukai ⟨Kobo-Daishi⟩ 774–835. Japanese Buddhist priest and scholar. Kukai evolved the "True Word" Buddhist philosophy. He is credited with inventing the style in which Japanese is written.

Ku Klux Klan Secret terrorist organization formed (1867) in the US South to oppose Reconstruction and maintain white supremacy. The Klan originated in Tennessee under the leadership of Gen. N. Forrest and later was responsible for attacks on blacks and carpetbaggers. Forrest disbanded the Klan (1869), and the Force Bill (1870, 1871) effectively suppressed it. Reformed (1915) by William J. Simmons, the new Klan promoted anti-Catholic, anti-Semitic and white supremacist views and after WW I rose to power in many states, including those outside the South. The Klan declined (after 1925) and died out during the Depression. Revived again (1960s) under Robert Shelton, the Klan carried out attacks on civil rights workers in the South.

Kulikovo, Battle of Russian victory (Sept. 8, 1380) over forces of the Golden Horde. Though the Tatars later reconquered the Russians, the battle marked the turning point in the struggle against Tatar domination (from 1240). The Russians, led by Dmitri Ivanovich, prince of Moscow, met the Tatars, led by Mamay, leader of the western part of the Golden Horde, at Kulikovo, on the upper Don River. There were great losses on both sides, but the Tatars were forced to retreat, and did not return until 1382.

Kulturkampf German Chancellor O. Bismarck's struggle (1871–83) to assert government control over the Roman Catholic church. Precipitated by the declaration (1870) of papal infallibility (which expanded papal powers at the expense of secular leaders), conflict between the church and state governments broke out in Germany and other European countries. In Germany, Bismarck had, by 1872, taken steps to limit Catholic influence, including expulsion of the Jesuits. He instituted the May, or Falk, Laws (May, 1873), which further limited church powers, and then mandated (1875) civil marriage services. Resistance by German clergymen and the Catholic Center party's 1878 election victory forced Bismarck to moderate. Some years after the death of Pope Pius IX (1878), he reached an accommodation with Pope Leo XIII.

Kun, Béla 1886–c1939. Hungarian Communist leader who briefly headed a Soviet republic in Hungary (1919). Later a leader of the Comintern, he became a victim of the Stalinist purges of the 1930s.

Kunersdorf, Battle of Austro-Russian victory (Aug. 12, 1759) over Prussia during the Seven Years' War, at Kunersdorf, Poland. The battle left the Prussian army of Frederick the Great in complete disarray, but the allies failed to follow up their victory.

Kuomintang ⟨KMT⟩ Chinese nationalist political party, the ruling party in China from 1928 to 1949. Following the Communist takeover (1949) on the mainland, the KMT formed the opposition government in Taiwan. Organized (1912) as a political party after the Chinese Revolution of 1911, it was led by Sun Yat-sen and called for parliamentary government. Banned (1913), the party organized (1917–23) opposition governments under Sun and then joined (1923) with the Chinese Communist party (CCP). The KMT launched (1926) the Northern Expedition and, by 1928, after breaking with the CCP (1927), took control of the government. Civil war between the Nationalists and the Communists raged almost continuously thereafter until the CCP expelled the KMT in 1949.

Kurdistan Mountain region including parts of Iran, Iraq, Syria, Turkey, and Soviet Armenia. Inhabited primarily by Kurds, it has been conquered successively by the Arabs, Seljuk Turks, Mongols, and Ottoman Turks. After WW I, the region was taken from Ottoman rule, and the Treaty of Sèvres (1920) called for establishment of a new Kurdish state. The Treaty of Lausanne (1923), which superseded the Treaty of Sèvres, made no such provision, and the region has since been the site of several Kurdish revolts.

Kurds *See* **Kurdistan**

Kuropatkin, Aleksey Nikolayevich 1848–1925. Russian general. He fought in the Russo-Turkish War of 1877–78, served as minister of war (1898), and unsuccessfully commanded Russian troops in Manchuria (1904–5) in the Russo-Japanese War.

Kusana ⟨Kushana⟩ ⟨Kushan⟩ Descendants of the Yüeh-chi, who established a ruling dynasty over much of northern India, Afghanistan, and territories to the north from AD c78–220. They declined at about the time of the rise of the Sassanidae.

Kushan *See* **Kusana**

Kushana *See* **Kusana**

Kutuzov, Mikhail Ilarionovich 1745–1813. Russian field marshal who commanded Russian forces during Napoleon's invasion of Russia (1812–13). He fought the French at Borodino, and defeated Napoleon through a policy of retreat and minor engagement.

Kuwait ⟨Kowait⟩ Independent Arab emirate, at the head of the Persian Gulf between Saudi Arabia and Iraq. Originally settled (18th cent.) by Arab tribes, Kuwait passed under nominal Ottoman rule (late 18th to early 19th cent.). By agreement with the sheik of Kuwait (Jan. 23, 1899), it became a British protectorate, remaining so until its independence (June, 1961). Oil was discovered in Kuwait (1938), and the emirate has since become a major exporter of oil. Its ruling family, in power since the 18th cent., governs through a constitutional monarchy. Kuwait had the world's highest per capita income in 1981.

Kwang Hsu 1872–1908. Emperor of China (1875–1908), successor to his aunt, Tz'u Hsi. After assuming authority (1889), he issued several edicts to institute reform in China during the "hundred days of reform." His aunt soon resumed the regency, ending Kwang's rule.

Kyd Thomas ⟨Kid, Thomas⟩ 1558–94. English dramatist, whose play *The Spanish Tragedy* was the model for the Elizabethan revenge tragedy. He may also have written an earlier version of *Hamlet*.

Kyongsong *See* **Seoul**

Kyoto ⟨Kioto⟩ Japanese city (pop. 1,465,000). Founded (794) as Heian-kyo and made capital of Japan, it was the imperial residence until 1868, when Tokyo became the capital. It is a major center of Japanese art and culture.

L

labor unions Organizations of workers for improvement of pay, benefits, and working conditions. Unions are the chief manifestation of the labor movement, which rose in response to the new economic and social order brought about by the Industrial Revolution. Early unions in Europe date from the 18th cent. and were at first suppressed by law. During the 19th cent., unions generally won legal recognition and greatly increased their memberships. In 1901, the first international labor union federation, what became known as the International Federation of Trade Unions (IFTU), was formed by the Second Socialist International. By 1919, the IFTU included about half the world's union members, but splits caused by formation of a separate Communist union federation (1921) and internal disputes resulted in the breakup of the IFTU (1945). It was replaced (1945) by the World Federation of Trade Unions (WFTU), with Communist unions participating. By 1949, however, the WFTU split along Communist/non-Communist lines, and in that year the non-Communist unions organized the International Confederation of Free Trade Unions (ICFTU). Since then, both the ICFTU and WFTU have been active in promoting union growth in underdeveloped countries. In the US, the union movement began in earnest with formation of the first national federation of unions, the National Labor Union (1866–72), which was followed by the Knights of Labor (1869–1917) and the American Federation of Labor (1886–   ). The late 1800s saw a period of major strikes and attempts to suppress unions by violent means. The early 1900s were marked by the activities of the militant Industrial Workers of the World (IWW). Nevertheless union membership steadily increased and important benefits were won. The New Deal legislation of the Depression years included many acts favoring both labor and unions. A longstanding division in the US labor movement, the rivalry between the American Federation of Labor and the Congress of Industrial Organizations, was ended (1955) by a merger in which the AFL-CIO was formed.

Labour party British political party, founded (1900) by a coalition of trade unions with participation by members of the Fabian Society (q.v.). Though openly committed to Socialist ideals since 1918, the party has traditionally favored specific legislative programs over ideology. The party formed its first government (1922–24) under R. MacDonald, who again led the government (1929–31). The Labour party joined the coalition government under W. Churchill during WW II and, after a major victory at the polls in 1945, formed the government of C. Attlee (1945–51). During Attlee's ministry, major Socialist programs were enacted, including nationalization of railroads, banks, mines, and utilities, and establishment of a national health plan. Ousted by the Conservatives, the Labour party returned to power under H. Wilson (1964–70, 1974–76) and under J. Callaghan (1976–79).

Labrador Largely unpopulated peninsular region in northeastern Canada. It was explored by Norsemen and rediscovered by J. Cabot (1497).

La Bruyère, Jean de 1645–96. French writer, known for his moralistic work *Les Caractères ou les moeurs de ce siècle* (1688), considered a classic of French literature.

Lacedaemon *See* **Laconia**

La Chaise, François d'Aix de 1624–1709. French Jesuit priest. From 1675 until his death he was the confessor of Louis XIV and wielded great influence.

Laclede, Pierre c1724–78. French fur trader and pioneer in America. The trading post and village he founded along the Mississippi (1764) became St. Louis, Missouri.

Laconia ⟨Lacedaemon⟩ In ancient Greek geography, a region in the southern Peloponnesus. Its capital and chief city was Sparta, which was for years involved in a struggle with Athens for leadership in Greece.

Ladd, William 1778–1841. American pacifist, writer, and crusader for international peace. He founded the American Peace Society (1828) and popularized its cause through many writings.

Ladies' Peace *See* **Cambrai, Treaty of**

Ladislaus ⟨Lancelot⟩ *c*1379–1414. King of Naples (1386–1414), successor to his father, Charles III of Anjou. He warred (1387–99) against his rival for the throne, Louis II, and sacked Rome (1413).

Ladislaus I 1040–95. King of Hungary (1077–95). One of Hungary's national heroes, he defended the country against the Poles, Russians, and Tatars and conquered Croatia. He was canonized as a Catholic saint.

Ladislaus I 1260–1333. Duke (1306–20) and king (1320–33) of Poland. He restored the Polish kingdom, which had been divided (1305–12). He took Danzig as the ally of the Teutonic Knights but later fought and won a six-year war against the order.

Ladislaus II ⟨~ Jagiello⟩ 1350?–1434. King of Poland (1386–1434). Ladislaus, grand duke of Lithuania, married the Polish queen Jadwiga, became king, and thereby founded the Jagiello dynasty. During his reign, he warred against the Teutonic Knights and, by his victories (notably the Battle of Tannenberg, 1410), made Poland a great power.

Ladislaus III 1424–44. King of Poland (1434–44) and of Hungary (as Ladislaus V, 1440–44). He led two crusades against the Turks. The first won him Walachia (1443). He was killed in battle at Varna (in Bulgaria) during the second.

Ladislaus V ⟨Ladislaus Posthumus⟩ 1440–57. King of Hungary (1444–57) and Bohemia (1453–57). Prevented from leaving the court of his guardian, Holy Roman Emperor Frederick III, until 1452, he was then unable to wrest power from his regents, J. Hunyadi (Hungary) and George of Podebrad (Bohemia).

Ladislaus Jagiello *See* **Ladislaus II**

Ladislaus Posthumus *See* **Ladislaus V**

Lady of the Lake In Arthurian legend, an enchantress who lived in a castle in an underwater kingdom. She gave the sword Excalibur to Arthur, kidnapped Sir Launcelot as a youth and brought him up.

Laënnec, René Théophile Hyacinthe 1781–1826. French physician. He invented the stethoscope and made major contributions to the diagnosis of chest diseases.

Laertes In Greek legend, the king of Ithaca and father of Odysseus. He was one of the Argonauts.

La Farge, John 1835–1910. American artist, noted for his murals and stained-glass windows, many of which were executed for churches and chapels.

Lafayette, Marie Joseph Paul Yves Roch Gilbert du Motier, marquis de ⟨La Fayette, ~⟩ 1757–1834. French soldier and political leader, a hero of the American Revolution and the early French Revo-lution. A volunteer general in the American Revolution, he distinguished himself at the battles of Brandywine (1777) and Yorktown (1780) and convinced the French to aid the American cause. During the French Revolution, he was a prominent member of the bourgeois faction; served in the Assembly of Notables (1787), the States-General (1789) the National Assembly (vice-president, 1789); and drafted the Declaration of the Rights of Man (1789). He fell from prominence when, frightened by the growing extremism of the revolution, he ordered the Paris National Guard to fire on a mob (July 17, 1791). Under threat of trial for his opposition to radical republicanism, he defected (1792) to Austria. Returned to France (1799) by Napoleon, he lived quietly until the July Revolution (1830), when he helped install King Louis Philippe.

Laffite, Jean ⟨Lafitte, ~⟩ *c*1780–1826? French privateer and smuggler. He and his men helped the Americans defeat the British in the Battle of New Orleans (1815), during the War of 1812.

Lafitte, Jean *See* **Laffite, Jean**

La Follette, Robert Marion 1855–1925. American politician, US senator (1906–25), and a leader of the Progressive party. He was the unsuccessful Progressive candidate for president in 1924.

La Fontaine, Jean de 1621–95. French poet, author of *Fables choises, mises en vers* (1668–94), consisting of more than 200 fables in verse and considered a literary masterpiece.

LaFontaine, Sir Louis Hippolyte 1807–64. Canadian statesman who served as joint prime minister with R. Baldwin of a united province of Canada (1842–43, 1848–51). Their ministries introduced reforms and established responsible parliamentary government in Canada.

Lagash ⟨Shirpurla⟩ Ancient city in Sumeria, located in southern Mesopotamia between the Tigris and Euphrates rivers. Inhabited as early as the 6th millennium BC, the city rose to importance in the 3d millennium BC and was conquered by the Akkadian ruler, Sargon, during this period.

Lagos, Battle of Naval battle (Aug. 7–18, 1759) of the Seven Years' War. A British fleet under Admiral Edward Boscawen (1711–61) defeated a French naval force off Lagos, Portugal, and thus headed off a major French invasion of England.

Lagrange, Joseph Louis, Comte 1736–1813. French mathematician, considered the leading mathematician of his day. His major work was *Mécanique analytique*, a mathematical analysis of mechanics.

La Hire ⟨*pseud. of* Vignoles, Etienne de⟩ *c*1390–*c*1443. French commander during the Hundred Years' War (1337–1453). He was a loyal companion of Joan of Arc and helped her defeat the English at Orléans and Patay. He continued in command during the decade following her death.

La Hogue, Battle of *See* **Grand Alliance, War of the**

Laibach, Congress of *See* **Congress of Laibach**

laissez-faire Economic theory popular during the 18th and 19th cents., which assumed an underlying natural order in economic systems. Thus, it was believed, individuals left to their own initiative (i.e., free from government regulation) would naturally produce the greatest good for themselves and society as a whole. The theory was advanced by the French Physiocrats *(q.v.)* (18th cent.) as a reaction against mercantilism *(q.v.)* and they emphasized the basic tenet of freedom from government regulation. A. Smith (the "invisible hand" of unregulated competition) and J. S. Mill became the leading exponents of the doctrine in Britain, where it appealed to the commercial interests of the Industrial Revolution. The laissez-faire doctrine was also applied to politics, in a more limited fashion. The doctrine was largely out of favor by the end of the 19th cent.

Lake Chudskoye, Battle of *See* **Peipus, Battle of Lake**

Lake Regillus, Battle of *See* **Etruscans**

Lally, Thomas Arthur, compte de French general, who led a French expeditionary force in India during the Seven Years' War. His forced surrender to the British at Pondicherry (Jan., 1761) marked the end of French power in India and led to his execution by French authorities for treason.

Lama A Tibetan Buddhist holy man. (*See also* Tibetan Buddhism.)

Lamar, Lucius Quintus Cincinnatus 1825–93. American statesman. He supported the Confederacy during the American Civil War (1861–65) and later served as congressman and senator from Mississippi (1873–75), as secretary of the interior (1885–88), and as associate justice of the Supreme Court (1888–93).

Lamarck, Jean Baptiste Pierre Antoine de Monet, chevalier de 1744–1829. French biologist. He is known for his theory of evolution (proved incorrect by C. Darwin), which held that acquired characteristics are hereditary.

Lamartine, Alphonse Marie Louis de 1790–1869. French poet and politician. He is known best for his volume of poetry, *Méditations poétiques,* which influenced the Romantic movement.

Lamb, Charles 1775–1834. Great English essayist, poet, and critic. Among his noted works were *Essays of Elia* and (written with his sister Mary) the children's book *Tales from Shakespeare.*

Lambertini, Prospero *See* **Benedict XIV**

lame duck An officeholder who has failed to be reelected but who remains in office until his successor is sworn in. The Twentieth Amendment to the US Constitution (Jan. 23, 1933) abolished the former lame duck sessions of Congress by requiring a new Congress to convene on Jan. 3 after the November in which it was elected.

Lamennais, Felicité Robert de ⟨La Mannais, ~⟩ 1782–1854. French priest and liberal Catholic apologist. He promoted both papalism and Christian democracy in France. He broke with church authorities on doctrinal issues and died an unrepentant excommunicate.

Lamia In classical mythology, a female demon who murdered and devoured children after the goddess Hera murdered her children.

Lamian War ⟨Greek War⟩ War (323–322 BC) against Macedonian rule in Greece, fought after the death of Alexander the Great. Athens, at the head of a league of Greek city-states, waged war against the Macedonian general Antipater and succeeded in besieging him at the city of Lamia. The arrival of Macedonian reinforcements (322 BC) allowed Antipater to lift the siege and defeat Athens and its allies. He then imposed an oligarchical government (controlled by him) on Athens.

Lancaster English noble family founded (1267) by E. Lancaster, second son of Henry III. Lancastrian kings of England were Henry IV, Henry V, and Henry VI. Lancastrians warred against the Yorkists in the War of the Roses *(q.v.).*

Lancaster, Edmund, earl of ⟨Crouchback, Edmund⟩ 1245–96. Second son of Henry III of England, brother of Edward I. He held the title King of Sicily (1255–63), fought in the crusades (1271), and founded the House of Lancaster.

Lancaster, John of *See* **John of Lancaster**

Lancaster, Thomas, earl of c1277–1322. English nobleman, leader of the barons who opposed Edward II and his favorites, notably P. Gaveston and the Despensers. Though he gained great power under Edward for a time, he was eventually defeated and beheaded during warfare against the king.

Lancelot *See also* **Ladislaus**

Lancelot, Sir ⟨Launcelot⟩ Knight important in Arthurian legend. Kidnapped as a youth and raised by the Lady of the Lake, he became a knight of King Arthur's Round Table and lover of the king's wife, Guinevere. He was father of Sir Galahad.

Land, Edwin Herbert 1909–. American inventor and physicist, inventor of the Polaroid camera. He also devised range-fingers, night-sight lenses, and anti-aircraft sights for use in WW II.

Land Acts, Irish *See* **Irish Land Acts**

Landen, Pepin of *See* **Carolingians**

Land of Cockaigne ⟨Land of Cockayne⟩ Imaginary land in medieval lore, where idleness and gluttony prevailed.

Land of Nod Biblical place. Cain fled to this land east of Eden after killing his brother Abel.

Landon, Alfred Mossman 1887–. American politician. A banker and oil executive, Landon was governor of Kansas (1933–37). The Republican presidential candidate in 1936, he was soundly defeated by F. Roosevelt.

Landsmaal *See* **Aasen, Ivar**

Landsteiner, Karl 1868–1943. Viennese-born American pathologist. He won the Nobel Prize (1930) for his discovery of human blood types, and later identified the RH Factor (1940).

Lane, Sir Ralph c1530–1603. English adventurer and governor of the ill-fated Lost Colony *(q.v.)* in Roanoke, Virginia.

Lanfranc d. 1089. Italian priest who became archbishop of Canterbury (1070–89) during the reign of William I. He served as adviser to the king and crowned his successor, William II (1087).

Langdon, John 1741–1819. American Revolutionary War leader. He provided financial backing for the New Hampshire militia, and was president of New Hampshire (1785–86, 1788–89), a delegate to the Constitutional Convention, and US senator (1789–1801).

Langland, William c1330–1400. English author, believed to have written the allegorical poem *The Vision of Piers Plowman*. It is considered a classic of medieval literature.

Langtry, Lily *See* **Bean, Roy**

Lannes, Jean 1769–1809. French marshal. He served under Napoleon in the Italian (1796) and Egyptian (1798–99) campaigns, won an important victory at Montebello (1800), and was killed in the battle at Essling.

La Noche Triste *See* **Alvarado, Pedro de**

Lansdowne, Henry Charles Keith Petty-Fitzmaurice, 5th marquis of 1845–1927. British statesman. He was governor general of Canada (1883–88) and of India (1888–94), secretary of war (1895–1900) during the Boer War, and foreign secretary (1900–05).

Lansing US city (pop. 130,400), capital of Michigan, and a manufacturing center. It was settled c1837 and became capital in 1847.

Laocoön In Greek mythology, a priest of Apollo. During the Trojan War he warned the Trojans not to allow the wooden horse, left by the Greeks, into the city. But when he and his sons were strangled by serpents, the Trojans decided to ignore his admonition.

Lao Country *See* **Pathet Lao**

Laodicean War *See* **Syrian War** (third)

Lao-Dong ⟨Vietnam Workers party⟩ Vietnamese Communist party established in 1951 by Ho Chi Minh. It succeeded the Viet-Minh as the ruling political party of the Democratic Republic of Vietnam.

Laos ⟨Lao People's Democratic Republic⟩ Communist state located in Southeast Asia, on the northwest Indochina peninsula. Its capital is Vientiane. The people are believed to be descendants of the Thai. Long dominated by France, Laos was (after 1950) torn by a bitter struggle between the Western-backed royalists and the Communist-backed Pathet Lao. The Pathet Lao gained complete control in 1975.

MID-14TH CENT. Lan Xang kingdom founded by Fa Ngoun; Buddhism introduced.

17TH CENT. Lan Xang kingdom extended control over much of Indochina.

1707 Lan Xang kingdom divided into Luang Prabang and Vientiane kingdoms; constant warfare for next century.

19TH CENT. Siam dominated region.

19TH CENT. French arrived in region.

1893 Laos became French protectorate, incorporated into French Indochina.

1942–45 WW II; occupied by Japan; encouraged to declare independence from France under rule of king of Luang Prabang.

1946 France reestablished control; made king of Luang Prabang constitutional monarch.

1949 Laos granted semi-autonomous status within French Union.

1950 Nationalist, Communist Pathet Lao formed by Prince Souphanouvong to oppose French domination.

1953 Vietnamese Communist Viet Minh and Pathet Lao power established in north as French Indochina War spread to Laos.

1954–55 Geneva agreement gave northern provinces to Pathet Lao, remainder to royalists.

1954 Laos gained full sovereignty (Dec. 29).

1957 Prince Souvanna Phouma, royalist premier, and Pathet Lao leader Souphanouvong formed unified government.

1959–62 Civil war resumed, soon becoming conflict between Communists, neutralists, and pro-West factions; neutralist Souvanna Phouma driven into Cambodia.

1962 Geneva Conference arranged for unified coalition government under Souvanna Phouma.

1963 Renewed civil war with Pathet Lao, aided by North Vietnam.

1964 Right-wing military coup attempt against Souvanna Phouma.

FROM 1965 Vietnam War intensified; North Vietnamese established Ho Chi Minh Trail through eastern Laos and gradually increased troop strength there.

1970 Laotian government troops lost Plain de Jarres to North Vietnamese.

1970 CIA activity in Laos revealed.

1971 South Vietnamese troops backed by US air support invaded Laos (Jan.-Mar.) as Vietnam War spread to region.

1971 North Vietnamese and Pathet Lao forces advanced against government positions.

1973 Pathet Lao and Souvanna Phouma concluded (Feb. 21) peace agreement.

1973 Government and Pathet Lao reached (July 29) general agreement on political and military settlement.

1973 Right-wing military coup put down (Aug.).

1974 Coalition government formed with Pathet Lao; Souvanna Phouma remained as premier, Souphanouvong as president of National Political Council.

1975 Pathet Lao abolished coalition government and monarchy (Dec. 2).

1975– President Souphanouvong in power in new government.

1979 Vietnamese and Laotian forces invaded Cambodia from Laos and overthrew Pol Pot regime.

Lao-tze ⟨Lao-tzu⟩ c604–531 BC. Chinese classical philosopher. The reputed founder of Taoism (q.v.), he preached conformity to the Tao, or eternal spirit of right conduct, and is considered one of the great figures of Chinese history.

Lao-tzu See **Lao-tze**

La Pérouse, Jean François de Galup, comte de 1741–c1788. French navigator. He explored the Pacific islands while searching for the Northwest Passage and discovered La Pérouse Strait (1787).

Laplace, Pierre Simon, marquis de 1749–1827. French astronomer and mathematician. He made important discoveries concerning planetary motions.

Lapland North European region that lies almost entirely within the Arctic Circle and is divided between Norway, Sweden, Finland, and Russia. Its indigenous inhabitants, the Laplanders, are nomadic.

Lapse, Doctrine of See **Doctrine of Lapse**

Lapua movement Fascist organization (1929–32) in Finland. Strongly opposed to Russia and communism, the group rose to power briefly and forced a government ban on the Communist party. However, an attempt (1932) to overthrow the government, led by Gen. Kurt M. Wallenius, miscarried and resulted in a ban on the Lapua movement.

Lardner, Ringgold Wilmer ⟨~, Ring⟩ 1885–1933. American writer. He was known for his humorous short stories about ordinary people. His works include *You Know Me, Al* and *How to Write Short Stories*.

Lares and **Penates** Ancient Roman deities, worshiped at the crossroads and in the household. The Lar originally was a god of the field. He later evolved into a household god as well and was worshiped, with the Penates, or household gods, as protectors of the home.

Largo Caballero, Francisco 1869–1946. Spanish Socialist leader whose radical polemics helped bring on the Spanish Civil War (1936–39). He served briefly as prime minister and war minister (1936–37) before being ousted by the Communists.

La Rochefoucauld, François, duc de 1613–80. French writer famous as the author of maxims, such as those collected in *Réflexions ou sentences et maximes morales*.

Larousse, Pierre Athanase 1817–75. French grammarian, lexicographer, and encyclopedist, who compiled a number of the leading reference works of 19th-cent. France, including the *Grand Dictionnaire universel du XIX siècle*.

Larsa Ancient city of Babylonia, near what is now Uruk, Iraq. It is mentioned in the Bible (Genesis) and flourished under the Elamites from c2000 BC to 1760 BC.

Lars Porsena ⟨Lars Porsenna⟩ Legendary Etruscan king of Clusium who conquered Rome (6th cent. BC).

Lars Porsenna See **Lars Porsena**

La Salle, Robert Cavelier, sieur de 1643–87. French explorer in North America. He claimed the Mississippi Valley region for France (1682) and named it Louisiana.

Lascaris, Theodore See **Nicaea, Empire of**

Las Casas, Bartolomé de 1474–1566. Spanish missionary and historian. He worked to improve the treatment of South American Indians by the Spanish, helped bring about the New Laws (1542), and wrote the *Historia de las Indias*.

Lassalle, Ferdinand 1825–64. German Socialist and labor leader. He participated in the revolution of 1848 and was a founder of the German Social Democratic party.

Lasso, Orlando di ⟨orig. Roland Delattre⟩ c1530–94. Belgian composer. He is considered one of the greatest Renaissance composers and is especially noted for his motets. As a youth he was kidnapped three times for choirs because his voice was so beautiful.

Last Supper In the Bible, the last meal taken by Jesus and his disciples before his arrest and crucifixion. Jesus there established the sacrament of the Eucharist and told of the future betrayal by one of them (Judas Iscariot).

La Téne culture *See* **Celts**

Lateran Name of a complex of church buildings in southeastern Rome, built on land donated to the Catholic church by Emperor Constantine. Among them are the Basilica of St. John Lateran, the cathedral church of Rome, and the Lateran Palace (16th cent.)

Lateran Councils Councils of the Roman Catholic church at Rome. **1.** First (9th ecumenical): Convened by Pope Calixtus II (1123), it reaffirmed decisions of the Concordat of Worms *(q.v.)* regarding the Investiture Controversy *(q.v.)*. It was the first church council convened in the West. **2.** Second (10th ecumenical): Convened (1139) by Pope Innocent II, it ended the schism created by election of antipope Anacletus II (reigned 1130–38), condemned the teachings of Arnold of Brescia, and forbade marriage by monks, nuns, and other clerics. **3.** Third (11th ecumenical): Convened (1179) by Pope Alexander III, it came after restoration of peace between the pope and Holy Roman Emperor Frederick I. The council ordered that the pope be elected solely by the college of cardinals (by a two-thirds majority) and proclaimed the Albigensian Crusade *(q.v.)*. **4.** Fourth (12th ecumenical): Convened (1215) by Pope Innocent III, it is considered one of the great councils. It instituted many lasting organizational and procedural reforms, proclaimed the crusades *(q.v.)* to recover the Holy Land, defined the doctrine of transubstantiation, and established the Easter Duty. **5.** Fifth (18th ecumenical): Held (1512–17) under popes Julius II and Leo X, the council opposed attempts to revive conciliarism *(q.v.)* and issued the Concordat of 1516, providing for a settlement of disputes between the pope and French king Louis XII.

Lateran Synod Roman Catholic synod (1059) that established the procedure by which the pope was to be elected. It called for election by a college of cardinals, thus eliminating the powers of both the Holy Roman Emperor and the Roman clergy in the selection of popes.

Lateran Treaty Agreement (Feb. 11, 1929) between Italy and the papacy, settling the Roman Question. During the unification of Italy (Risorgimento), the kingdom of Italy seized control of the Papal States and the city of Rome (1860, 1870). The new government offered (Law of Guarantees, 1871) the pope compensation for the territories taken and rights to the Vatican and Lateran. But the pope refused and thus created the Roman Question. Negotiations began in 1926 and the final agreement was signed by B. Mussolini, for King Victor Emmanuel III, and Cardinal P. Gaspari, for Pope Pius XI. It provided for creation of Vatican City as an independent state, establishment of Roman Catholicism as the state religion in Italy, and a large financial compensation to the church for loss of the Papal States.

later Le dynasty Vietnamese dynasty (1428–1788). During its existence the kingdom of Annam *(q.v.)* gained its independence from China and greatly increased its territorial control.

Lathyrus, Ptolemy VIII *See* **Ptolemy VIII**

Latimer, Hugh *c*1485–1555. English Protestant martyr. He supported King Henry VIII in his divorce from Catherine of Aragon, then opposed by the Roman Catholic church, and actively preached the Reformation. Under Catholic Mary Tudor, however, he was convicted of heresy and burned at the stake.

Latin America Term used to refer to the Spanish and Portuguese-speaking countries south of the southwest border of the US, including Mexico and the nations of Central America and South America. *(See individual countries.)*

Latin Empire of Constantinople Feudal empire centered at Constantinople (1204–61). It was established by leaders of the Fourth Crusade *(q.v.)*, after they captured the Byzantine capital of Constantinople (1204) and divided various Byzantine lands among themselves and their Venetian bankers. Viewed as a Western intrusion, in Eastern lands, it began to decline soon after its creation. The empire suffered the hostility of the local population, incursions of the Bulgars and Turks, and resistance by the Byzantine emperors, who retired across the Bosporus to form the empire of Nicaea. The empire lapsed after Byzantine emperor Michael VIII retook Constantinople in 1261. However, some Greek islands remained in Venetian hands, Athens passed under Catalan rule, and part of mainland Greece remained in the Frankish Villehardouin family for a longer period.

Latin Fathers *See* **Fathers of the Church**

Latin Kingdom of Jerusalem Kingdom established (1099) in Palestine and Syria by leaders of the First Crusade *(q.v.)*. A feudal kingdom, it included the cities of Jerusalem, Acre, and Tyre and controlled Antioch, Edessa, and Tripoli. Among its rulers were Baldwin I, Baldwin II, Fulk, Amalric I, and Baldwin V. Subsequent crusades were unsuccessful against the Muslims, and Jerusalem fell (1187) to Saladin. Thereafter Muslim armies made further conquests and expelled the last Christian forces from the region by the capture

(1291) of Acre. Although the kingdom itself ceased to exist in fact, the title "King of Jerusalem" continued in use for centuries.

Latins Ancient people that inhabited Latium, a plain in what is now central Italy. Romans were Latins and Rome was one of the early Latin cities established in the region (as were Alba Longa, Tusculum, and others). The cities formed confederations to resist the Etruscans and Samnites (Samnite Wars, *q.v.*,) and Rome gradually emerged as the dominant power. Rome established complete control by her victory in the Latin War (340–338 BC).

Latin Wars Wars (340–338 BC) in which a number of Italian cities sought equality with Rome. With their defeat by Rome, some of these states were made into colonies, others into states dependent upon Rome, and others ceded land for settlement by the Romans.

La Tremoille, Louis de la *See* **Novara, Battles of**

Latrobe, Benjamin Henry 1764–1820. American architect. He introduced the Greek Revival style in America and directed the rebuilding of the Capitol after it was burned by the British in 1814.

Latter-Day Saints, Church of Jesus Christ of *See* **Mormons**

Lattimore, Owen 1900–. American Orientalist and writer. He spent many years overseas in China and served as the US political adviser to Chiang Kai-shek. He was unjustly charged (1950) by Senator J. McCarthy with being a major Communist spy in the US and was not completely cleared until 1955.

Latvia Historic region and constituent republic of Russia, located along the Baltic Sea. Taken by the Livonian Brothers of the Sword (13th cent.), the area was subsequently divided and controlled variously by Poland, Sweden, and Russia. Latvia became an independent state (1918) during the Baltic Wars of Liberation, but by 1940 it had been annexed by Russia.

Laud, William 1573–1645. Archbishop of Canterbury (1633–45). He persecuted the Puritans and Calvinists and supported Charles I in his conflict with Parliament. Impeached by the Long Parliament (1640), he was beheaded.

Lauderdale, John Maitland, duke of 1616–82. Scottish statesman. As secretary of state for Scotland and member of the Cabal *(q.v.)* ministry, he was notorious for his harsh rule in Scotland.

Laudon, Gideon Ernst Freiherr von 〈Loudon, ~〉 1717–90. Austrian field marshal. He fought in the service of the Hapsburgs and distinguished himself in the War of Austrian Succession, the Seven Years' War, and the Austro-Turkish War.

Lancelot, Sir *See* **Launcelot, Sir**

Laura de Noves 1308?–40. Woman believed to be the inspiration for Petrarch's love poems.

Laurens, Henry 1724–92. American statesman, president of the Continental Congress (1777–78). He was captured (1780) by the British while taking a proposed treaty to The Netherlands. The treaty later precipitated war between England and The Netherlands.

Laurier, Sir Wilfrid 1841–1919. Canadian statesman and first French-Canadian prime minister (1896–1911). A leader of the Liberal party, he worked to develop the Canadian west.

Lausanne, Conference of *See* **Conference of Lausanne**

Lausanne, Treaty of **1.** Treaty (Oct. 18, 1912) concluding the Italo-Turkish War. The treaty called for Turkey's withdrawal from Tripoli. **2.** Treaty (July 24, 1923) that formally ended hostilities of the Greco-Turkish War (1920–22) and modified terms of the Treaty of Sèvres *(q.v.)*. By it Turkey regained control of the Dardanelles, eastern Thrace, and other territories, including Smyrna.

Laval, François Xavier de 〈Laval-Montmorency, François Xavier〉 1623?–1708. French cleric, the first Catholic bishop in Canada. He founded the seminary of Quebec (1663), which became Laval University.

Laval, Pierre 1883–1945. French politician. As premier of the Vichy government during WW II (1942–44), he instituted forced labor and other harsh measures in France. He was executed for treason after the war.

Lavalleja, Juan Antonio *c*1786–1853. Uruguayan revolutionary. He led a group, known as the Thirty-three Immortals, and declared Uruguayan independence from Brazil (1825). He later led the Blancos party in Uruguay.

Laval-Montmorency, François Xavier *See* **Laval, François Xavier de**

Laveran, Charles Louis Alphonse 1845–1922. French physician. He discovered the parasite that causes malaria (1880). Awarded Nobel Prize (Physiology and Medicine) in 1907.

Lavoisier, Antoine Laurent 1743–94. French chemist. He explained the role of oxygen in combustion and thereby disproved the phlogiston theory.

Law, Andrew Bonar 1858–1923. British statesman. He succeeded A. Balfour as Conservative party leader in the House of Commons (1911–15), where he opposed Irish Home Rule. He became prime minister (1922–23).

Law, John 1671–1729. Scottish financier. He organized the ill-fated Mississippi Scheme *(q.v.)* in France for the exploitation of Louisiana colonies.

Law of Guarantees Italian law (May 13, 1871) that attempted to establish the relationship between the Italian government and the papacy. It guaranteed religious and diplomatic freedom to the papacy, and established an annual income for the pope, but did not restore papal authority to the territories that had been incorporated into Italy during unification. Pope Pius IX did not accept it, and relations between Italy and the papacy were not formalized until signing of the Lateran Treaty of 1929.

Lawrence, Abbott 1792–1855. US manufacturer and politician. He was a founder of the textile city Lawrence, Massachusetts, and was US minister to Great Britain (1849–52).

Lawrence, Amos Adams 1814–86. American philanthropist. He supported abolitionist movements and contributed to the establishment of a college in Lawrence, Kansas, that became the University of Kansas.

Lawrence, Charles 1709–60. British general and governor of Nova Scotia (1756–60). He was largely responsible for the deportation of French colonials from Acadia (in Canada) after the British took over this French colony.

Lawrence, David Herbert 1885–1930. British author. Lawrence was one of the most influential writers in the 20th cent. His work includes the novels *Sons and Lovers, Women in Love, The Rainbow,* and *Lady Chatterley's Lover.*

Lawrence, Ernest Orlando 1901–58. American physicist. Lawrence invented the cyclotron. He also introduced the use of neutron beams in cancer treatment and patented a color television tube. Awarded Nobel Prize in physics 1939.

Lawrence, James 1781–1813. American naval officer. He commanded the *Hornet* and the *Chesapeake (q.v.)* during the War of 1812. It was aboard the latter that he uttered his famous cry "Don't give up the ship!"

Lawrence, Sir Thomas 1769–1830. English painter, the leading portrait painter of his day. Among his works is the noted portrait of Queen Charlotte.

Lawrence, Thomas Edward ⟨Lawrence of Arabia⟩ 1888–1935. English soldier and author. During WW I, he led the Arab troops of Faisal I in revolt against the Turks and described his adventures in *The Seven Pillars of Wisdom* (1926).

Lawrence of Arabia *See* **Lawrence, Thomas Edward**

Laxness, Halldór Kiljan 1902–. Icelandic novelist. His works include *The Weaver of Cashmere* and *Independent People.* He received the Nobel Prize in literature in 1955.

Layamon *fl. c*1200. Middle English poet whose work, *Brut,* makes the first mention in English of the Arthurian legend and introduced Lear, Cymbeline, and Merlin.

lay investiture *See* **investiture controversy**

Lazarus In the Bible, the brother of Mary and Martha of Bethany. He was raised from the dead by Jesus after four days.

League *See* **Catholic League**

League of *See under names inverted, as in* **Augsburg, League of**

League of Augsburg, War of *See* **Grand Alliance, War of**

League of the Russian People *See* **Black Hundreds**

Leahy, William Daniel 1875–1959. American naval officer. He served in the Spanish-American War and in WW I. He became chief of staff under President F. Roosevelt (1942) and continued in that post under President H. Truman until 1949.

Leakey, Louis Seymour Bazett 1903–72. British archaeologist and anthropologist. He is noted for his controversial interpretations of extremely ancient humanoid fossils, which indicated that forerunners of man were much older than previously thought. His wife, Mary Leakey, discovered (1959) the noted Zinjanthropus fossil remains (believed 1,750,000 years old) in the Olduvai Gorge, Tanzania. Leakey subsequently discovered (1961) what he called a more direct ancestor of man, the *Homo habilis.*

Leander *See* **Hero and Leander**

Leaning Tower of Pisa Tower constructed (1174–1350) at Pisa, Italy. It leans about 17 feet from the perpendicular due to settling, and is a noted attraction for tourists. Numerous attempts have been made to halt the settling, which threatens to topple the structure.

Lear Legendary king of Britain. Geoffrey of Monmouth apparently adapted the story of Lear and his three daughters from Celtic mythology. W. Shakespeare made the story the basis of his tragedy *King Lear.*

Lebanese Crisis US intervention in a Lebanese civil war. US marines were landed in Lebanon by President D. Eisenhower (July, 1958), in pursuance of the Eisenhower Doctrine *(q.v.),* after opposition to the pro-Western government of C. Chamoun broke out into open rebellion. The marines helped to stabilize the situation. The crisis was resolved by the election of Gen. F. Chebab, who had refused to commit the Lebanese army to either side during the fighting.

Lebanese War *See* **Lebanon** (1982)

Lebanon ⟨Republic of Lebanon⟩ Country located in the Mideast and occupying the mountainous coastal region of the eastern Mediterranean. The Lebanese coast was originally the home of Phoenician traders and from the 6th cent. BC various powers had control of the region. Later the mountains of Lebanon offered refuge to religious groups seeking to escape persecution. The Maronite Christians arrived first (7th cent. AD) and were followed by the heretical Muslim sect, the Druses. Orthodox Muslims also arrived in the region. In modern times conflict between these diverse factions has resulted in instability and war. Traditional rivalries were further complicated in the 1970s as PLO guerrillas, Syrian troops, and UN peace-keeping forces occupied various parts of the country. Effective control of the country became virtually impossible. The Israelis finally crushed the Palestine Liberation Organization (PLO) in Lebanon during the 1982 Lebanese War but many obstacles to the creation of a stable government remained. Key events in Lebanese history include:

c25TH–6TH CENT. BC Phoenicians controlled region; established cities in coastal region (modern Sidon, Tyre, Beirut, and others) which served as a base for their commercial empire.

6TH–4TH CENT. BC Persians took control of territory.

4TH–1ST CENT. BC Alexander the Great conquered the area (332 BC) and thereafter the area was controlled by successor states in the region.

64 BC Romans took control of area; Christianity later introduced.

5TH CENT. AD Byzantines maintained control over area after the collapse of the Western Roman Empire.

7TH CENT. AD Maronite Christians established themselves in the Lebanese mountains seeking refuge from persecution by the Byzantine emperor.

7TH CENT. Arab Muslim conquest; Maronites in mountain regions resisted Islam and thus began the historic split between Christians and Muslims in surrounding territories.

11TH CENT. Members of the Muslim Druse sect, fleeing Orthodox Muslim persecution, established an emirate in southern Lebanon.

16TH–20TH CENT. Ottoman Empire controlled region; Lebanon enjoyed considerable autonomy.

FROM 1516 Maronites in religious communion with the Catholic church in Rome.

1860 Druse massacre of Christians led to active French intervention.

1861–1914 Greater Lebanon, governed by a Christian, created by Ottomans; made relatively autonomous under Ottoman control.

1920 France given League of Nations mandates over Lebanon and Syria.

1926 Lebanese Republic organized by French as separate from Syria.

1941 Vichy forces ousted by Allies during WW II; Free French declared it independent (1941), though troops remained to 1946.

1943 Unwritten "National Compact" allotted Lebanese presidency to a Maronite Christian; prime minister to be a Sunni Muslim, assembly speaker a Shi'ite Muslim, foreign minister an Orthodox Christian, etc.

1945 Lebanon became a fully independent republic (Jan. 1).

1945 Became a member of the UN.

1945 Joined the Arab League.

1948–49 Arab-Israeli War; Lebanon joined in Arab attack on newly created Israeli state.

1952–58 C. Chamoun served as president; established relations with Western powers.

1958 US Marines landed in Lebanon (July) to halt civil war against pro-Western Maronite government of C. Chamoun; crisis ended with election of Gen. Fuad Chebab.

1958–64 Chebab in office as president; fostered closer relations with Arab states.

1962 Military coup attempt crushed.

1964–70 Charles Helou in office as president.

1967 Lebanon did not participate in Arab-Israeli War.

1969 Fighting broke out (Oct.) between Palestine Liberation Organization (PLO) guerrillas and Lebanese troops.

1970–76 Suleiman Franjieh in office as president. PLO guerrillas, driven out of Jordan, established headquarters in Lebanon; tensions with Israel increased as PLO guerrillas launched attacks on Israelis.

1972 PLO guerrillas and Lebanese troops clashed.

1973 Lebanese Prime Minister Saeb Salam resigned (Apr.) after Israelis raided PLO buildings in Beirut.

1973 Lebanon neutral in fourth Arab-Israeli War.

1975–76 Lebanese civil war pitted Muslims allied with Palestinians and PLO against the Phalangists, a military organization of the Maronites, which dominated the other Christian forces.

1976 Cease-fire agreement reached (Jan.) through Syrian involvement; Muslims gained greater voice in government.

1976 Elias Sarkis elected to presidency by parliament (May), after the ouster of Franjieh.

1976 15,000 Syrian troops entered Lebanon to help halt the civil war (May).

1976 Syrian troops occupied Beirut (Nov. 10) as part of Arab League plan to restore peace there.

1978 Israelis invaded southern border region (Mar.) to clear out PLO guerrilla strongholds there; turned over many strategic points to Christian militia as they withdrew to Israel.

1981 Fighting broke out (Apr. 2) in Beirut and surrounding area; Syrian troops involved in the fighting against Christian militia while Israeli jets attacked Syrians.

1981 Syrian antiaircraft missile emplacements moved into Bekáa Valley after Israeli air attacks.

1981 Downing of Israeli aircraft by Syrian antiaircraft missile led to Israeli demand to withdraw emplacements (May).

1981 Special envoy Philip C. Habib dispatched to Middle East by US President R. Reagan to arrange peaceful settlement.

1981 Israeli air raids conducted in Lebanon in retaliation for PLO attacks on Israel; US suspended shipment of aircraft to Israel (July 20).

1981 Cease-fire between Israelis and the PLO in Lebanon arranged by US special envoy P. Habib (July 24).

1981 Bomb explosions kill dozens in Sidon (Sept. 1) and in Beirut (Oct. 1).

1982 Lebanese War; major invasion of southern Lebanon by Israel began (June 6); Israelis said they would halt advance at 25 miles into Lebanon.

1982 Syrian antiaircraft missile sites in Bekáa Valley destroyed by Israeli air attacks.

1982 Israeli forces drive to within sight of Beirut (June 10); PLO trapped in Beirut between Israelis and Phalangists.

1982 Siege of Beirut (June–Aug.); Israelis gradually advanced to positions surrounding PLO-controlled west Beirut; began shelling and bombing of sector as neotiations with PLO and others were continued by US envoy P. Habib.

1982 PLO agreed in principle to evacuate Beirut; President Reagan declared end to violence was crucial (Aug. 2) as conditions in west Beirut worsened.

1982 Habib plan for evacuation accepted by Israel (Aug. 15); US, France, and Italy agreed to contribute troops to oversee evacuation of PLO forces, thus ending Israeli siege of Beirut (Aug. 19).

1982 Last PLO guerrillas evacuated from Beirut (Aug. 21–Sept. 1).

1982 President-elect Bashir Gemayel and other Christian Phalangists killed by terrorist bomb (Sept. 14).

1982 Beirut Massacre revealed (Sept.); hundreds of Palestinians massacred in refugee camp by Christian militiamen; Israeli occupation forces criticized for failing to prevent massacre.

1982 Amin Gemayel named president (Sept.).

Lebrun, Albert 1871–1950. French statesman, last president of the Third Republic (1931–40). He surrendered to Marshal H. Pétain, head of the pro-German Vichy government.

Le Brun, Charles 1619–90. French artist. Court painter to King Louis XIV (from 1662) and thereafter he dominated French art. He was director of the Gobelins, a company producing furnishings for French royalty, and designed much of the interior at Versailles, including the Galerie des Glaces.

Lechfeld, Battle of Decisive victory (Aug. 10, 955) over the Magyars by Otto I, German king (later emperor). The battle, which took place near Augsburg, Germany, put an end to the Magyars' westward expansion.

Leclerc, Charles Victor Emmanuel 1772–1802. French general, Napoleon's brother-in-law. He died of yellow fever contracted while putting down a revolt in Haiti led by P. Toussaint L'Ouverture.

Leclerc, Jacques Philippe 1902–47. French general during WW II. He led a force of Free French troops stationed in Equatorial Africa on a 1,500-mile march to join the British in Tripoli (1942–43). He was also a commander in the Normandy invasion.

Lecompton Constitution Proslavery constitution adopted (1857) by the Territory of Kansas prior to its admission as a state. S. Douglas led congressional opposition to acceptance of the constitution and admission of Kansas as a proslavery state. This forced a vote (1858) by inhabitants of Kansas, and the Lecompton Constitution was rejected. Kansas was admitted (1861) as a free state.

Leconte de Lisle, Charles *See* **Parnassians**

Le Corbusier ⟨*pseud.* of Jeanneret, Charles Édouard⟩ 1887–1965. Swiss-born French architect whose work helped revolutionize 20th-cent. architectural design. He pioneered the use of ferro-concrete and modular housing designs and was an advocate of artistic purism.

Leda In Greek mythology, the wife of Tyndareus, king of Sparta. She was mother of Castor and Pollux, Helen of Troy, and Clytemnestra. Legends vary as to the children's father, some accounts saying Ledo was seduced by Zeus.

Ledru-Rollin, Alexandre Auguste 1807–74. French politician. He took part in the Revolution of 1848 and advocated universal suffrage. After an unsuccessful insurrection against Louis Napoleon (1849), he fled to England.

Le dynasty, later *See* **later Le dynasty**

Lee, Ann 1736–84. English mystic. Called Mother Ann, she became a leader of the Shaking

Quakers and introduced the Shaker sect to the US (1774) at Watervliet, New York.

Lee, Arthur 1740–92. American diplomat. In France with B. Franklin and S. Deane to obtain aid for the colonials during the American Revolution, he became involved in disputes with Deane and Franklin. Both Deane and Lee were eventually recalled.

Lee, Charles 1731–82. English-born American army officer during the American Revolution. As second-in-command to G. Washington, he constantly criticized and disobeyed him. He conspired with Lord Howe, prevented an American victory at Monmouth (1778), and was ousted in disgrace (1780).

Lee, Fitzhugh 1835–1905. Confederate general in the American Civil War, nephew of R. E. Lee. A cavalry commander, he figured in battles at Antietam, Chancellorsville, and Gettysburg and in the Wilderness and Shenandoah Valley campaigns. He later became governor of Virginia (1886–90).

Lee, Francis Lightfoot 1734–97. American Revolutionary War leader. He was a delegate to the Continental Congress (1775–79) from Virginia and signed the Declaration of Independence.

Lee, Henry ⟨Lee, Light-Horse Harry⟩ 1756–1818. American Revolutionary cavalry officer, father of R. E. Lee. He was a member of the Continental Congress (1785–88) and governor of Virginia (1792–95). He eulogized G. Washington as "first in war, first in peace, and first in the hearts of his countrymen."

Lee, Light-Horse Harry *See* **Lee, Henry**

Lee, Richard d. 1664. English colonist in Virginia. A wealthy landowner, he held various public offices and founded the Lee family, which was prominent in Virginia.

Lee, Richard Henry 1732–94. American statesman and signer of the Declaration of Independence, which he vigorously supported in the Continental Congress. He helped arrange the Committees of Correspondence *(q.v.)* and was a Virginia delegate to the Continental Congress (1774–79, 1784–89). His opposition to a strong federal government created by the Constitution helped bring about passage of the Bill of Rights.

Lee, Robert Edward 1807–70. Confederate commander during the American Civil War (1861–65) and military hero of the Confederacy. A Virginian and West Point graduate, he distinguished himself during the Mexican War (1846–48), served as a cavalry commander in Texas (1857–61), and led federal troops (1859) against J. Brown in the Harpers Ferry Raid *(q.v.)*. He resigned from the military (1861) when Virginia seceded from the Union, and organized Virginia's military forces. He then served as J. Davis' military adviser (1861–62) and, in mid-1862, took command of the Army of Northern Virginia. It was in this command that Lee proved his brilliance as a military commander and seriously challenged the better-equipped Union armies. He blocked a Union drive toward Richmond (1862), launched a Confederate invasion of the North (checked at Antietam, 1862), turned back new Union offensives at Fredericksburg and Chancellorsville (1862, 1863), and began his second invasion of the North. Badly defeated at Gettysburg (1863) in this campaign, he skillfully conducted defensive operations (1864–65) against U. Grant's forces for the remainder of the war. Named overall Confederate commander (Feb. 6, 1865), he was at last forced to surrender at Appomattox Courthouse (Apr. 9, 1865) and thereby effectively ended the Civil War.

Lee, William 1739–95. American diplomat. His proposed commercial treaty between the American colonies and The Netherlands was discovered by the British and became the cause of war between England and The Netherlands (1780).

Lee Kuan Yew 1923–. First prime minister of the Republic of Singapore (1959–   ).

Leeuwenhoek, Antony van 1632–1723. Dutch scientist. Using microscopes he made himself, he became the first to describe accurately bacteria, protozoa, red corpuscles, spermatozoa, striped muscle, and many other microscopic cells and organisms.

Legal Tender Act US congressional act (1862) authorizing the issue of $150 million in paper (Greenback) notes without gold backing to help finance the Civil War. After the war the act was declared unconstitutional by the Supreme Court (1870). The court reversed itself in 1871.

Léger, Fernand 1881–1955. French artist, noted for his use of modern industrial images in his "machine art."

legion Unit of the Roman army. It was in use from about 400 BC to the time of the German invasions and, though its composition and organization varied through this period, generally consisted of 4,000–6,000 infantrymen arranged in eight ranks. Other units, such as cavalry, were also part of the legion.

Legislative Assembly Name of the national representative body of revolutionary France (Oct. 1, 1791–Sept. 20, 1792). Dominated by the moderate Girondists, it was replaced by the National Convention after the overthrow of the monarchy. During the Second Republic, the name was revived for the assembly, which sat for two years (1849–51).

It was dissolved by Napoleon III as a prelude to the dissolution of the Second Republic itself.

legislative branch   Name for the branch of government that makes or changes laws. It is generally representative and is often composed of two houses (upper and lower). (*See also* Congress of the United States.)

Legitimists   In French history, the supporters (19th cent.) of the head of the senior Bourbon line as rightful French king. They opposed the claims of the Orleanists and the Bonapartists.

Leguia, Augusto Bernardino   1863–1932. President of Peru (1908–12, 1919–30). He settled long-standing disputes with Bolivia, Brazil, and Chile. Though he encouraged modernization, his ruthless treatment of opponents led to his ouster in 1930.

Leibnitz, Gottfried Wilhelm, baron von   *See* **Leibniz, Gottfried Wilhelm, baron von**

Leibniz, Gottfried Wilhelm, baron von ⟨Leibnitz, ~⟩ 1646–1716. German philosopher and mathematician. Leibniz developed new notations for calculus and a theory of infinitesimal calculus that predated I. Newton's findings by three years. He actively sought a reconciliation of Catholicism and Protestantism and professed an optimistic belief in a divine plan of the universe that was ridiculed by Voltaire in *Candide*. Leibniz' work influenced, among others, I. Kant and B. Russell.

Leicester, Robert Dudley, earl of   1532?–88. English courtier who won the favor of Queen Elizabeth I but did not succeed in marrying her. A member of the Puritan sect, he opposed Catholics in England and advocated war with Spain.

Leiden ⟨Leyden⟩   City in southwest Netherlands. The University of Leiden (1575) is the oldest in The Netherlands. Originally a Roman settlement, the city became a textile manufacturing center in the 16th cent. A center of the revolt against Spanish rule in the Low Countries, Leiden was nearly reduced by a long siege. It was saved when William the Silent opened the dikes and flooded the surrounding countryside (1574).

Leiden, John of   *See* **John of Leiden**

Leif Ericsson   *fl.* 1000. Norse explorer, son of Eric the Red. Raised among the Norse colonists in Greenland, he was converted to Christianity while visiting Norway. Sent back to Greenland to convert the colonists, he apparently went off course and landed somewhere in North America, which he called Vinland. He wintered there and then went on to Greenland. By another account, he first went to Greenland and then sailed westward on a voyage of discovery.

Leipzig   City (pop. 565,000) in East Germany. Chartered in the 12th cent., it hosted annual trade fairs and was the scene of one of M. Luther's debates (1519). It was a leading cultural center of Europe from the 17th to early 20th cents. and many important figures in German music and literature resided there. The city was heavily damaged in WW II.

Leipzig, Battle of ⟨Nations, ~⟩   Major defeat (Oct. 16–19, 1813) for Napoleon during the Napoleonic Wars. The battle resulted in the loss of Germany and Poland. Prior to the battle, the allies forced Napoleon to concentrate his 180,000-man army at Leipzig and, after a preliminary battle (Oct. 16), massed some 300,000 troops to oppose him. The main attack was launched (Oct. 18) and included Austrian, Russian, Prussian, and Swedish troops. By the early hours of Oct. 19, Napoleon's retreat was under way. Allied losses were 55,000. The French lost 38,000 and some 30,000 were taken prisoner.

Leipzig Debate   Famous debate (July, 1519) between M. Luther and J. Eck held in Leipzig (now in East Germany). Luther was called upon to defend his then emerging Protestant doctrine and his opposition to indulgences (*q.v.*). Both Luther and Eck, a Catholic theologian, claimed to have won.

Leipzig Interim   *See* **Augsburg Interim**

Leisler, Jacob   *See* **Leisler's Rebellion**

Leisler's Rebellion   Insurrection (1689–91) in the British colony of New York. The ouster of the Catholics and accession of Protestant King William (1688) precipitated uprisings in the colonies against Catholic officials. Jacob Leisler (1640–91) set himself up as governor of southern New York in one such outbreak. In 1691, his supporters skirmished with British troops sent to restore order, though Leisler surrendered later that year. He was subsequently executed.

Lemaître, Georges   1894–1966. Belgian astrophysicist who postulated the "big bang" theory of the creation of the universe.

Lemercier, Jacques   *c*1585–1654. French architect. Royal architect (from 1618), he completed the Louvre and designed the Sorbonne and the Palais Richelieu (which became the Palais Royal).

Lenclos, Ninon de   1620?–*c*1705. French courtesan whose lovers included La Rochefoucauld and the Great Condé. Her salon attracted the leading society of her day.

lend-lease   Program used by the US during WW II to provide Allies with war materials and supplies. Congress narrowly passed (Mar. 1941) the Lend-Lease Act just prior to US entry into the war, initially to aid Britain. This aid was soon extended to China, Russia and, by war's end, some 35 other allied nations. A reverse lend-lease program was set up in 1942, by which nations could repay lend-lease debts by providing US forces with supplies and services. When the program ended (Aug. 1945), some $50 billion in aid had been provided.

L'Enfant, Pierre Charles 1754–1825. French-born American architect and engineer. He drew up plans for the capital city of Washington, D.C., but was dismissed in 1792. His plans were ignored until 1901, when they were used in the remodeling of the city.

Lenin, Nikolai ⟨*pseud. of* Ulyanov, Vladimir Ilich⟩ 1870–1924. Russian Communist leader, a central figure in the Russian Revolution, and founder of the Bolsheviks *(q.v.)*. Lenin embraced Marxism in 1889 and was eventually arrested and exiled to Siberia (1897–1900). Leaving Russia, he became prominent in the Social Democratic Labor party and, at a party meeting (1903), began the division of the group into two factions, the Mensheviks and (his) Bolsheviks. On the outbreak of the Russian Revolution of 1917, Lenin's return to Russia in the famous "sealed train" (Apr.) was arranged by the Germans, who were counting on the revolution to eliminate Russia from participation in WW I. In Russia, Lenin opposed the provisional government, advocating instead a dictatorship of the proletariat. Lenin's Bolshevik faction gradually gained control of the Soviets in ensuing months and finally ousted the provisional government (1917) in the October Revolution *(q.v.)*. Lenin became dictator and, aided by J. Stalin, L. Trotsky, and others, arranged the Treaty of Brest-Litvosk (1918) with Germany, turned Russian factories over to workers, ended private ownership of land, nationalized banks, and introduced other radical reforms. Consolidating his position, Lenin successfully opposed attempts at counter-revolution (1918–21) and crushed his political opponents. He established (1919) the Third International *(q.v.)* and introduced (1921) his New Economic Policy *(q.v.)* to revive the economy. By the time of his death in 1924, he ruled virtually without opposition and had succeeded in laying the foundations of the Russian Communist state.

Leningrad ⟨*formerly* St. Petersburg⟩ Russian city (pop. 4,073,000), located in the northeast on the Gulf of Finland. It is a major seaport and industrial center. The city was founded (1703) as St. Petersburg by Peter the Great as a "window into Europe," and made the Russian capital in 1712. The scene of revolutionary movements in 1825, 1905, and 1917, it was replaced as capital by Moscow in 1918. The city was renamed Petrograd (1914) and Leningrad (1924). During WW II, it was besieged and heavily damaged by Germany (Sept. 1941–Jan. 1944).

Leninism Term applied to the political, economic, and social theories advanced by N. Lenin. His theories were built on the teachings of K. Marx and included a new perception of imperialism. Lenin held that imperialist powers would, in their exploitation of underdeveloped regions, come into conflict with each other and thereby sow the seeds of their own destruction. Leninism was also marked by its authoritarian temper, especially in its concept of the revolutionary party as an elite, highly disciplined organization.

Lenôtre, André ⟨Le Nôtre,~⟩ 1613–1700. French landscape architect who designed the gardens of Versailles, Chantilly, Fontainebleau, and others.

Leo I *d.* AD 474. Roman emperor of the East, (457–474), successor to Marcian. He organized the disastrous attack on the Vandals, under Gaiseric, in North Africa (468).

Leo I, Saint AD *c*400–461. Italian-born pope (440–461), one of the important popes of the early church. He actively opposed heresy, including Manichaeanism, Pelagianism, Nestorianism, and Eutychianism. His doctrines regarding the two natures of Jesus in one person were adopted at the Council of Chalcedon *(q.v.)*.

Leo III, Saint *d.* 816. Italian-born pope (795–816), successor of Adrian I. He crowned Charlemagne as Roman emperor in 800, thus re-creating the Roman Empire in the West and establishing the tradition by which the pope conferred imperial authority on the emperor.

Leo III ⟨~ the Isaurian⟩ *c*680–741. Byzantine emperor (717–41) and founder of the Isaurian dynasty. He defeated the last Arab siege of Constantinople (717–18) and began the long controversy over iconoclasm (726).

Leo V *d.* 820. Byzantine emperor (813–20), successor to Michael I. He halted the Bulgar attacks on Constantinople. He also precipitated a resurgence of the iconoclastic controversy and deposed the patriarch Nicephorus.

Leo VI ⟨Leo the Wise⟩ ⟨Leo the Philosopher⟩ 866–912. Byzantine emperor (886–912) whose compilation of imperial law, the *Basilica*, was adopted as the Byzantine Empire's legal code.

Leo IX, Saint ⟨Bruno of Egisheim⟩ 1002–54. German-born pope (1049–54). A clerical reformer. His unsuccessful battle with the Normans in Sicily (formerly dominated by the Byzantines) led to quarrels and excommunication (July 16, 1054) of the patriarch of Constantinople. This in turn precipitated the Schism *(q.v.)* between the Eastern and Western churches.

Leo X ⟨Medici, Giovanni de⟩ 1475–1521. Italian-born pope (1513–21), successor to Julius II. His main interest was in the arts. He excommunicated M. Luther (1521) for initiating a protest against the sale of indulgences (1517) during his reign and thus figured in the beginning of the Protestant Reformation.

Leo XIII ⟨Pecci, Gioacchino⟩ 1810–1903. Italian-born pope (1878–1903), successor to Pius IX . He helped end the anti-Catholic Kulturkampf *(q.v.)* in Germany and worked to end friction between the papacy and secular governments elsewhere. He supported the scientific and religious theories of Thomas Aquinas and pointed out flaws in both capitalism and socialism in his *Rerum novarum* (1891).

Leo Africanus c1485–c1554. Arab traveler and author. Captured by pirates and sold as a slave to Pope Leo X, he converted to Christianity and wrote his famous work, *Description of Africa.*

Leonardo da Vinci 1452–1519. Italian painter, sculptor, architect, engineer, and scientist who was one of the greatest figures of the Renaissance and who is today remembered as the archetypal "Renaissance man" for his multifaceted genius. Born in Florence, he studied art as an apprentice and in 1478 painted his early masterpiece *Adoration of the Kings.* Thereafter he enjoyed the patronage of a succession of nobles, including Ludovico Sforza at Milan (1482–99), Cesare Borgia (1502) at Florence, Louis XII of France (1506), and Francis I (from 1516). During his lifetime he completed such famous works as the *Last Supper, Madonna and Child with St. Anne,* the *Mona Lisa,* and *St. John the Baptist.* He is considered an influential pioneer in Renaissance painting and is noted as a master of light and shade and for his technique of sfumato, by which he added a delicately hazy quality to the blending of color. None of his sculptures survive, but he is known to have worked on, among others, a monument to Francesco Sforza. In his lifetime, Da Vinci was also employed as an architect and military engineer and was deeply involved in studies of human anatomy (especially as it related to art) and the natural world. The full extent of his interests, however, was revealed only in his notebooks, which range from details of his scientific investigations to drawings of a man-powered flying machine.

Leonidas d. 480 BC. King of Sparta (c491–480 BC), successor to his half-brother Cleomenes I. He became a Spartan hero when he led the unsuccessful defense of the pass of Thermopylae (480 BC) against invading Persians during the Persian Wars. He and his force of 300 Spartans were killed in the battle.

Leopardi, Giacomo 1798–1837. Italian poet. An invalid from his youth, he became a leading Ital-

ian lyricist. His poems, pessimistic in tone, include *Canzoni* and *Canti.*

Leopold I 1640–1705. Holy Roman Emperor (1658–1705), successor to his father Ferdinand III. His reign was marked by participation in the Austro-Turkish War (1682–99), the War of the Grand Alliance (1689–97), the third Dutch War (1672–78), and the start of the War of the Spanish Succession (1701–14).

Leopold I 1676–1747. Prince of Anhault-Dessau (1693–1747). Leopold served Prussia as a field marshal in the War of the Spanish Succession (1701–14) and the War of the Austrian Succession (1740–48).

Leopold I 1790–1865. First king of independent Belgium (1831–65). He refused the Greek throne before finally accepting that of Belgium. He was noted for his diplomacy, and his reign was marked by a period of peace and stability.

Leopold II 1747–92. Holy Roman Emperor (1790–92), successor to his brother, Joseph II. An enlightened despot, he repealed many of his brother's reforms, which were then precipitating rebellion in Hapsburg domains. He subsequently joined Prussia in the Declaration of Pillnitz *(q.v.),* a cause of the French Revolutionary Wars (1792–1802). He died just before war began.

Leopold II 1835–1909. King of Belgium (1865–1909), successor to his father Leopold I. He sent explorer H. Stanley to the Congo, which he later used to base his claim on the region. The Congo Free State was recognized to be under his personal control (1885) until reports of his ruthless exploitation of the natives forced the Belgian government to take it over (1908).

Leopold III 1901–. King of Belgium (1934–51), successor to his father, Albert I. He led the Belgian Army against the German invaders during WW I, surrendered (May 28, 1940), and was held prisoner until 1945. Opposition to his restoration after the war forced his abdication (1950).

Leopoldville *See* **Kinshasa**

Leo the Isaurian *See* **Leo. III**

Leo the Philosopher *See* **Leo VI**

Leo the Wise *See* **Leo VI**

Leovigild d. 586. Visigothic king of Spain (568–86), successor to his brother, Athanagild. He warred successfully against the Suevi in the north and the Byzantines in the south and thus came to control most of what became modern Spain.

Lepanto, Battle of Naval victory (Oct. 7, 1571) for Christian allies of the Holy League over the Ottoman navy. Little more than a temporary setback for the Ottoman Turks, the battle marked the first major defeat of the Turks by Christian forces. The allied Christian fleet was formed after the Turks invaded (1570) Cyprus, controlled by Venice. It consisted of some 200 ships sent by Spain, Venice, and the pope. The fleet, commanded by John of Austria, engaged the Ottoman navy of some 200 ships, commanded by Ali Pasha, off Lepanto, Greece. In a matter of hours the Ottoman navy was destroyed and only about 40 ships escaped capture or sinking. The Turks rapidly rebuilt their navy (by 1572) and ultimately took Cyprus (1573).

Lepidus, Marcus Aemilius   *d.* 77 BC. Roman statesman and consul (78 BC). As consul he opposed Sulla's reforms and tried unsuccessfully to reverse them. He marched on Rome (77) after being denied the consulship for 77 and, after losing in battle at Milvian Bridge was decisively defeated by Pompey.

Lepidus, Marcus Aemilus   *d.* 13 BC. Roman statesman. With Mark Antony and Octavian, a member of the second triumvirate (43–36 BC) that ruled Rome after the assassination of J. Caesar. He was forced from power (36 BC) after attempting a revolt (in Sicily) against Octavian.

Lerdo de Tajada, Sebastián   1825–89. President of Mexico (1872–76). He succeeded B. Juárez as president and was overthrown by P. Díaz.

Lerma, Francisco Gómez de Sandoval y Rojas, duque de   1552?–1625. Spanish politician. Lerma was prime minister (1598–1618) to Philip II, over whom he exerted great influence. He expelled the Moriscos and was finally driven from office for financial corruption.

Lermontov, Mikhail Yurevich   1814–41. Russian poet and novelist. An influential Romantic, he is known for his novel *A Hero of Our Time* and such poems as *The Demon, Borodino,* and *Ismail-Bey.*

Le Sage, Alain René   1668–1747. French novelist and dramatist, an exponent of realism noted as the author of the novel *Gil Blas* and the play *Turcaret.*

Lesbos   Greek island, located in the Aegean Sea. A Bronze Age civilization flourished there and the island was later settled by Aeolians (end of 2d millennium BC). It rose as a center of Greek culture (7th–6th cent. BC) and was home to the poets Sappho and Alcaeus and the philosopher Theophrastus.

lese majesty ⟨leze majesty⟩   A crime against the state or the ruler of a state. Important in medieval times, the concept can be traced back to the Roman republic, when it was used to refer to violations of basic laws of the state. During the time of the Roman Empire, the term was extended to cases involving acts against the emperor himself.

Lesotho (*formerly* Basutoland)   Kingdom in South Africa, lying within the borders of the Republic of South Africa. The kingdom was formed (*c*1800) by elements of various Bantu peoples forced out of their homelands by the Zulus. These peoples defended the kingdom against the Zulus and later the Boers. It became a British protectorate in 1868 and a colony in 1884. After successfully resisting annexation by South Africa, Lesotho became an independent kingdom (Oct. 4, 1966).

Lespinasse, Julie de   1732–76. Hostess of a noted Parisian salon. She began in the literary salon of Madame Du Deffand and then opened her own (1764) with the philosopher J. d'Alembert as her leading guest.

Lesseps, Ferdinand Marie, vicomte de   1805–94. French diplomat and engineer. He originated the idea of the Suez Canal and directed its construction (1859–69). His Panama Canal project (begun 1881) ended in scandal and a French government inquiry.

Lessing, Doris   1919–. British author. Lessing's work, which reflects the political and social upheaval of the modern era, includes *The Grass Is Singing, The Children of Violence,* and *The Golden Notebook.*

Lessing, Gotthold Ephraim   1729–81. German critic, philosopher, and dramatist. Lessing introduced Shakespeare to German literature, assisted in the formation of the German national theater, published theological essays espousing freedom of thought, and wrote the plays *Miss Sara Sampson, Minna von Barnhelm,* and *Nathan the Wise. Laokoon* is among his critical works.

Le Tellier, Michel   1603–85. French statesman. As minister of war (1643–66), he organized the first French royal army and was appointed chancellor (1677–85) by Louis XIV.

Lethe   In Greek mythology, a river in Hades that caused forgetfulness in those who drank from it.

Leto   In Greek mythology, a daughter of the Titans. Hera, jealous of Leto's relationship with Zeus, sent the serpent Python to drive her away. Leto stopped at Delos, where she gave birth to Apollo and Artemis.

lettres de cachet   French warrants. These secret letters were used to imprison or exile personal enemies of the king or nobility (from 17th cent.). They were outlawed by the National Assembly (1789).

Leucippus   5th cent. BC. Greek philosopher, thought by some to have originated the theory of atoms, usually credited to his pupil Democritus.

Leuctra, Battle of   Battle (371 BC) in which the Spartans were decisively beaten by the military tactics of the Thebans, led by Epaminondas. The battle marked the beginning of the brief Theban ascendancy over Greece.

Leutze, Emanuel 1816–68. American painter, known for his *Washington Crossing the Delaware*.

Levant Term used for those countries on the eastern shore of the Mediterranean, from Egypt to Greece. It sometimes also refers to the former French Levant states, Syria and Lebanon.

Levelers Extremist English Puritan sect and political group active (c1647–50) during the English Civil War and Commonwealth. Levelers favored total religious and political equality and advocated a written constitution, universal male suffrage, an end to the monarchy, and abolition of economic and social privileges. Unable to advance their cause in the Long Parliament *(q.v.)*, Levelers organized followers in O. Cromwell's New Model Army. In the Putney debates (Oct. 1647), Levelers forced the army command to consider a proposed constitution, called *Agreement of the People*. It was rejected by Gen. H. Ireton and later mutinies (1649) by Levelers resulted in suppression of the group. Prominent Levelers included J. Lilburne, Richard Overton (*fl.* mid-17th cent.), and William Walwyn (*fl.* mid-17th cent.)

Leverrier, Urbain Jean Joseph 1811–77. French astronomer who, along with the Englishman J. C. Adams, discovered the planet Neptune (1846).

Leviathan Biblical sea monster variously depicted as a whale, snake, or crocodile. It usually symbolizes evil or destruction.

Lévi-Strauss, Claude 1908–. French social anthropologist famous for his works defining structural anthropology. His first major work was titled *The Elementary Structures of Kinship.*

Levites Ancient Hebrew religious functionaries. Drawn from the male population of the tribe of Levi, Levites were originally temple servants and later became teachers of the Law. The tribe of Levi is sometimes said to be named after Jacob's third son, by Leah. Three families make up the tribe of the Levites: the Gershonites, Merarites, and Kohathites.

Lewes, Battle of Battle (May 14, 1264) during the Barons' War *(q.v.)*. The barons, led by S. de Montfort, defeated the royal army, captured both King Henry III and Prince Edward (later Edward I), and thereby forced concessions from the king.

Lewes, George Henry 1817–78. English philosopher, critic, and author. He founded *The Fortnightly Review* and wrote the *Life of Goethe* (1855). He lived with G. Eliot from 1854.

Lewis, Clive Staples 1898–1963. English author of *The Screwtape Letters* and the children's fantasies, the *Chronicles of Narnia*.

Lewis, John Llewellyn 1880–1969. American labor leader. He was president of the United Mine Workers of America (1920–60) and founder of the Committee for Industrial Organization (CIO) in 1935.

Lewis, Meriwether 1774–1809. American explorer. With W. Clark, he led the famous Lewis and Clark expedition *(q.v.)* to the Pacific Northwest.

Lewis, Percy Wyndham 1886–1957. British author and artist. He founded the vorticist magazine *Blast* (1914) with E. Pound, wrote satirical and autobiographical novels, and painted works in a variety of styles.

Lewis, Sinclair 1885–1951. American author. His satiric novels of American provincialism include *Main Street, Babbitt, Arrowsmith, Elmer Gantry,* and *Dodsworth.*

Lewis and Clark expedition Famous overland expedition (1804–06) in the US Far West. The expedition charted an overland route to the Pacific and provided valuable scientific and practical information about the largely unexplored region. Initiated by T. Jefferson and sponsored by the government, the expedition consisted of about 40 men under the leadership of M. Lewis and W. Clark. The party left from St. Louis (May 14, 1804) and followed the Missouri River to its headwaters (recruiting the Indian guide Sacajawea along the way), crossed the Continental Divide, and then followed in succession the Clearwater, Snake, and Columbia rivers to the Pacific Ocean. They built Fort Clatsop on the coast and, after spending the winter there, returned (Sept. 23, 1806) to St. Louis.

Lexington and Concord, Battle of Opening hostilities (Apr. 19, 1775) of the American Revolution (1775–83). The British governor of Massachusetts, Gen. T. Gage, sparked the battle by sending a column of infantrymen from Boston to destroy a colonial supply depot at Concord, Massachusetts. Word was sent ahead of the British, however, by P. Revere and others. The British were met at Lexington Green by 50 colonial militiamen (Minutemen), under Capt. John Parker (1729–75), and seven Americans were killed in a brief battle. The British continued to Concord and destroyed what supplies remained there. Part of the British force was attacked at Concord bridge by some 400 Minutemen, and the British began their retreat to Boston. Along the way the Minutemen, using guerilla tactics, harried the British column and eventually killed 273. American losses were 95.

Leyden *See* **Leiden**

Ley Juárez *See* **Reforma, La**

Ley Lerdo *See* **Reforma, La**

Leyte Gulf, Battle of ⟨Philippine Sea, Battle of⟩ Major WW II victory for the US in battle against the Japanese (Oct. 23–25, 1944). Considered one of the greatest sea and air battles, the victory enabled the US to reconquer the Philippines. The battle was provoked by US landings (Oct. 20) on Leyte, in the Philippines. The Japanese (in "Sho-Go," or Victory Operation) planned to draw the US 3d Fleet northward by means of a decoy fleet and to crush the US landing force in a three-pronged attack. One of the three Japanese attack elements was located and damaged (Oct. 23) by US subs. On Oct. 25, all three were engaged by naval and air units of the US 7th Fleet and were largely destroyed.

leze majesty *See* **lese majesty**

L'Hôpital, Michel de ⟨L'Hospital, ~⟩ *c*1505–73. French statesman, until 1568 chief counselor to Catherine de Médicis. He urged a policy of religious tolerance toward Protestants (Huguenots), won passage of the Edict of January (1562) granting them religious freedoms, and was dismissed (1568) during the Wars of Religion (1562–98).

Liao-yang, Battle of Japanese victory in battle (Aug. 25–Sept. 3, 1904) during the Russo-Japanese War (1904–05). The Russian Gen. A. Kuropatkin was forced to retreat after bitter fighting near this town in northeastern China.

Liaquat Ali Khan 1895–1951. The first prime minister (1947–51) of newly formed Pakistan. He was assassinated.

Libby, Willard Frank 1908–. American chemist who developed the radioactive carbon-14 dating method, an important research tool for archaeologists, anthropologists, and historians. He received the Nobel Prize in Chemistry in 1960.

Libby Prison Notorious Confederate prisoner-of-war camp in Richmond, Virginia, originally a tobacco warehouse. Conditions were bad, and many captured Union soldiers died there between 1863 and 1865.

Liber Ancient Roman god of wine and fertility. His female consort was Libera and he later became identified with Bacchus and the Greek Dionysius.

liberalism Generally, a philosophy that advocates maintaining the freedom of individuals from outside restraints. It is characterized by a belief in the fundamental goodness and rationality of mankind, and belief in continuing change as a means to perfect the order of things. Thus it often arises in opposition to conservatism. Fueled by ideas of the Enlightenment, liberalism flourished in the 18th–19th cents. as a movement toward greater personal liberty, toward restrictions on government powers, and toward such persuasive doctrines as laissez-faire economics. By the 20th cent., however, the focus of liberalism had been changed by disparity between industrialists' wealth and the lot of the worker. Thus in modern times, liberalism became concerned with freeing the individual from economic and social restraints. To do this, liberals have sought to institute government programs to provide basic protections for the individual, such as social security, welfare, and other minimum-maintenance programs. (*See also* Liberal party.)

Liberal party **1.** British party that, with the Conservative party, was one of the two major parties in that country between 1832 and 1931. Formed from the Whig party after the Reform Bill of 1832, the Liberal party embraced many progressive social-reform causes including extension of the franchise and Home Rule for Ireland. At the same time, it favored laissez-faire capitalism and free trade. The party placed many prime ministers in office, such as W. Gladstone, H. Asquith, and, during WW I, D. Lloyd-George. The party declined from the 1920s vis-à-vis the Labour party because of its adherence to laissez-faire doctrines. It finally split in 1931 and thereafter became a minor party. A revival in the 1970s brought back to it the votes of about 15 percent of the electorate. **2.** New York State party founded (May, 1944) by elements of the American Labor Party, who charged that the latter had become Communist-dominated. It has sometimes held the balance of power in elections between the major parties. From around 1970 it has been counterbalanced by the New York Conservative party. **3.** Name given to a number of continental parties generally believing in laissez-faire capitalism and opposed to growing trends toward government regulation of the economy.

Liberal Republican party Short-lived party created (1872) by insurgent Republicans. It was formed largely in reaction to corruption in President U. Grant's first administration, and the party platform included civil service reform and a more moderate program of Reconstruction in the South. The party nominated (1872) H. Greeley for president and, though it had the support of the Democratic party, Greeley was easily beaten by U. Grant in his bid for a second term. The party disappeared shortly thereafter. Leaders included C. Sumner, C. Schurz, and C. F. Adams.

Liberal Union British political party formed (1886) by disaffected members of the Liberal party. They opposed the policies of W. Gladstone.

Liberia ⟨Republic of Liberia⟩ Republic located in coastal West Africa. The capital is Monrovia. Liberia was founded (1821) as a home for freed slaves by the American Colonization Society (*q.v.*). Between 1822 and the beginning of the American Civil War (1861–65), thousands of American Negro colonists were transported there and in 1847 Liberia became an independent republic.

The country's subsequent history in the 19th cent. was marked by clashes with native populations in the interior, loss of territory to European powers colonizing West Africa, a rebellion that resulted in overthrow of the government (1871), and a growing national debt. The government finally went bankrupt in 1909, though in following years new foreign loans and leases to the Firestone Company for a vast rubber plantation helped the national economy. In 1930, confirmed reports of slavery in Liberia forced the resignation of the government, though by 1936 slavery was effectively eliminated. During the long tenure (1944–71) of President W. Tubman, Liberia was opened to foreign investment, and exploitation of its natural resources was begun. William Tolbert, Jr., served as president (1971–80) until his overthrow by army sergeant Samuel Doe (Apr., 1980). Doe suspended the constitution and established military rule.

Liberius *d.* AD 366. Italian-born pope (AD 352–366), successor to Julius I. He was banished by Emperor Constantius II (355) for his stand against Arianism *(q.v.)*, returned in 358 and later reaffirmed the Nicene faith.

liberty Freedom from restraint of choice or limitation of action, especially in reference to an individual. It is generally conceded that complete personal freedom (anarchy) is untenable and that, in a society, some restraints must be imposed on individuals by government or other outside authority. However, the character of government and the balance between restraints and liberties has been a cause of debate and rebellion throughout the evolution of human civilization. The Magna Carta, Declaration of Independence and Declaration of the Rights of Man, among others, are all expressions of the drive toward individual liberty, as are the philosophical writings of J. Locke and J. Rousseau.

Liberty, Sons of *See* **Sons of Liberty**

Liberty, Statue of *See* **Statue of Liberty**

Liberty Affair Incident in Boston harbor in which British customs officials seized (June 10, 1768) J. Hancock's sloop, *Liberty*, which was smuggling Madeira wine. The popular outcry caused the officials to take refuge and call for infantry support.

Liberty Bell Bell, symbolic in American history, which hung in Independence Hall, Philadelphia, from 1753. According to traditional accounts, it was rung on the signing of the Declaration of Independence (July 4, 1776) in Philadelphia. It cracked beyond repair in 1846.

Liberty Poles ⟨Liberty Trees⟩ In Colonial America, poles erected (1765–66) as symbols of opposition to unpopular British policies and officials. The first Liberty pole was located in Boston.

Liberty party First US political party (1840–48) organized to promote abolition of slavery. Led by James G. Birney (1792–1857) and Gerrit Smith (1797–1874), the party was formed (1840) in New York by members of the American Antislavery Society, who were opposed to the society's policy against political action. It nominated Birney as its presidential candidate (1840, 1844). In 1844 it indirectly helped elect J. Polk to the presidency by splitting antislavery support for the Whig party candidate, H. Clay. The party merged (1848) with antislavery Whigs and Democrats prior to the 1848 presidential election, forming the Free-Soil party *(q.v.)*.

Liberty Trees *See* **Liberty Poles**

Libya Republic located in northern Africa, bordering Egypt on the west. Its capital is Tripoli. The region comprising modern Libya came under Ottoman control in the 16th cent. but maintained relative autonomy during the period 1711–1835. The Italians seized control of the region during war with the Ottomans in the early 1900s. After WW II Libya came under UN control (1949) and gained independence in 1951. Since 1969, when Muammar al-Qaddafi seized power, Libya has been a radical and revolutionary influence in the Middle East. Key dates in the history of Libya include:

7TH CENT. BC Phoenicians founded colonies in Tripolitania; region later became eastern part of Carthaginian domains.

7TH CENT. BC Cyrenaica settled by Greek colonists.

1ST CENT. BC Cyrenaica passed to Romans; made a province with Crete.

46 BC Romans conquered Tripolitania during Numidian War; annexed it to African province.

7TH CENT. AD Tripolitania and Cyrenaica overrun by Arab Muslims.

16TH CENT. Tripolitania and Cyrenaica conquered by Ottomans and merged into administrative regency of Tripoli.

1711 Ahmad Karamanli became dey of Tripoli; killed Ottoman governor and secured the governorship, thus established hereditary Karamanli rule of Tripoli (until 1835).

18TH–19TH CENT. Tripoli became center for pirates, chief source of revenue for the day; led to Tripolitan war with US (1801–05) and operations by European countries to destroy the pirates; Ottoman Empire resumed governorship of Tripoli (1835).

1911–12 Italo-Turkish War; Italy occupied northern Tripoli.

1912–14 Italy conquered the rest of Tripoli.

1930s Development of Libya began; influx of Italian colonists.

1934 Italy established Libya as a colony.

1940–43 WW II; Libya was site of fierce fighting during North Africa campaigns; after Axis forces were defeated (1943) in region, Libya came under Allied administration.

1949 Administration of Libya passed to UN (1949), which called for Libyan independence by 1952.

1951 Independence granted (Dec. 24); Libya became United Kingdom of Libya, a federated state composed of Cyrenaica, Tripolitania, and Fezzan, a southwest desert region.

1951–69 Idris I reigned as king of Libya.

1953 Libya joined the Arab League.

1953–54 Treaties for establishment of British and US military bases signed.

1955 Became member of the UN.

1958 Oil discovered in Libya; economic situation improved in following years.

1963 Government reorganized by royal decree; provincial governments abolished in favor of central government.

1964 Treaty with Britain terminated; British troops to be withdrawn.

1969 Military coup; Muammar al-Qaddafi seized power (Sept. 1) from King Idris I.

1969– Qaddafi in power as head of state; though he later relinquished some government posts, he retained ultimate control and aligned Libya with radical elements in Mideast and elsewhere.

1969 Unsuccessful attempt to overthrow Qaddafi (Dec.).

1970 Libya closed US bases; confiscated Italian and Jewish property.

1970 Unsuccessful attempt to overthrow Qaddafi (July).

1973 Qaddafi instituted purge of political opponents (Apr. 15).

1973 Qaddafi signed (Aug. 29) agreement with Egypt providing for unification of the two countries in prearranged stages; plan never enacted.

1973 Libya nationalized majority holdings of foreign oil companies in the country (Sept. 1).

1973 Relations with Egypt strained (Dec. 1) over Egypt's conduct of Arab-Israeli War.

1975 Major arms sale secured from Soviet Union; Russia agreed to supply Libya with nuclear reactor.

1977 Four-day border war with Egypt broke out (July 21); cease-fire arranged through mediation of Algerian President Houari Boumediène (July 24).

1979 Libyan troops sent in unsuccessful attempt to aid Ugandan dictator Idi Amin; Amin granted asylum in Libya.

1980 Formal agreement signed calling for unification of Libya and Syria (Sept. 10); plan subsequently tabled.

1980 Libyan troops intervened in Chad to end civil war there (Dec. 16).

1981 Libyan diplomats expelled (May 6) from the US for supporting terrorist activities.

1981 Two Libyan fighters shot down (Aug. 19) in dogfight with US fighters off the Libyan coast.

Lichnowsky, Karl Max, Fürst von 1860–1928. German diplomat. Unauthorized publication of a pamphlet he wrote describing his vain efforts to prevent the outbreak of WW I resulted in his ouster (1918) from the Prussian legislature.

Licinian Rogations *See* **Licinius Calvus Stolo, Caius**

Licinius d. AD 325. Roman emperor (AD 308–24) who ruled jointly with Galerius (AD 308–11) and who defeated Emperor Maximinus (314), thereby taking control of the East. He was defeated by Constantine (AD 324), exiled, and executed.

Licinius Calvus Stolo, Caius *fl.* 375 BC. Roman tribune. He is said to have introduced the Licinian Rogations, which advanced rights of the plebians.

Lidice Village in Czechoslovakia, near Prague. It was "liquidated" by the Germans (1942) in reprisal for the assassination of the Nazi governor, Reinhard Heydrich.

Lie, Jonas Lauritz Idemil 1833–1908. Norwegian novelist. His novels treat Norwegian life in a realistic way, as in *The Pilot and His Wife* and *The Family at Gilje.*

Lie, Trygve Halvdan 1896–1968. Norwegian statesman. The first secretary-general of the United Nations (1946–52), he resigned because of Russian objections to his support for UN participation in the Korean War.

Liebig, Justus, baron von 1803–73. German chemist. He established the first chemical teaching laboratory and was a founder of agricultural chemistry.

Liebknecht, Wilhelm 1826–1900. German Socialist and journalist. After participating in the Revolution of 1848, he lived in exile in England (1849–62) and worked with K. Marx. In 1869 he founded the Social Democratic Labor party.

Liechtenstein Small European principality located in the Alps between Austria and Switzerland. It was created in 1719 by the joining of Schellenberg and Vaduz counties in the Holy Roman Empire. It became independent of the German Confederation in 1866 and is a member of a Swiss customs union (1924).

Liège Belgian city (pop. 224,000). It is an industrial and transportation center located in eastern Belgium. In existence since the 6th century, it became a cultural center in the Middle Ages. Napoleon made it part of France from 1794 to 1815, when it was joined to The Netherlands by the Congress of Vienna. It joined the revolt of 1830 and was made part of Belgium. It was held by the Germans in WW I and WW II.

Ligne, Charles Joseph, prince of 1735–1814. Austrian field marshal. An adviser of Holy Roman Emperor Joseph II and friend of Catherine II of Russia, he is chiefly remembered for his correspondence with European dignitaries.

Ligny, Battle of Early battle (June 16, 1815) of the Waterloo campaign, fought in Ligny, Belgium, during the Napoleonic Wars (1803–15). Napoleon defeated the Prussian force under Marshal G. Blücher.

Liguria Historic region in northwestern Italy along the Ligurian Sea and including the Italian Riviera, the Maritime Alps, and the Ligurian Apennines. Conquered by the Romans (2d cent. BC), the region eventually came under Genoese control (by 16th cent.) and became part of Italy during its unification (1860).

Ligurian Republic French satellite state. Napoleon gave this name to the republic of Genoa in 1797 and incorporated it into France in 1805. It became part of Sardinia after Napoleon's fall.

Li Hung-chang 1823–1901. Chinese statesman. He commanded forces against the Taiping Rebellion (1861–64), founded the Chinese navy, and became the dominant figure in Chinese foreign affairs (from c1872). He worked to improve relations with the West and to modernize China.

Lilburne, John 1614?–57. English leader of the Leveler (q.v.) faction. Though imprisoned several times, he continued to distribute Puritan pamphlets and agitate for more democratic rule. In 1655, while in prison, he became a Quaker.

Li Li-san c1900–. Chinese Communist leader. He dominated the Chinese Communist party during the late 1920s. He was eventually replaced by Mao Tse-tung when his strategy of inciting urban labor rebellions (Li Li-san line) failed.

Lilith In Talmudic folkore, a female demon who was supposed to be Adam's first wife. She is a night creature, associated with child-killing and lust.

Liliuokalani 1838–1917. Queen of the Hawaiian Islands (1891–93). She succeeded her brother King Kalakaua and was deposed for trying to resist changes in the constitution.

Lima Peruvian capital city (pop. 2,833,600), port city, and a cultural and industrial center. Founded by F. Pizarro (1535), it became the capital of the Spanish Viceroyalty of Peru. It was badly damaged (1746) in an earthquake.

Lima, Saint Rose of *See* **Rose of Lima, Saint**

Liman von Sanders, Otto 1855–1929. German general. He commanded the Turkish armies at Gallipoli (1915) and forced the Allied withdrawal. As German commander in Palestine, he was defeated in 1918.

Lincoln US city (pop. 171,900), capital of Nebraska. Founded in 1864, it became the capital in 1867 and is a railroad and commercial center.

Lincoln, Abraham 1809–65. American national hero, 16th US president (1861–65), successor to J. Buchanan, and Union leader during the American Civil War (q.v.). Born to a poor family and raised on the Illinois frontier, he educated himself, worked at various jobs (his rail-splitting days are often remembered), and became a lawyer in 1836. Though he had been involved in politics in the 1830s and 1840s, his rise to prominence did not begin until he became embroiled in the slavery question (1850s). As a Republican (from 1856), he unsuccessfully opposed S. Douglas for the US Senate (1858). But in the seven now famous Lincoln-Douglas debates, held during that campaign, Lincoln established himself as a leader of the moderate opposition to slavery. Lincoln became the Republican presidential candidate (1860) and, with the Democratic party split over slavery, won the election. Southern states began seceding soon after his election and just over a month after he took office, hostilities between the North and South broke out at Fort Sumter and the Civil War began. In succeeding years, Lincoln instituted wartime measures, some of which were challenged; meddled in military matters and went through a succession of commanders, finally settling on U. Grant (1863); and maintained his steady, moderate course despite reverses in the war and bitter disputes between radical abolitionists and conservative factions. However, the Emancipation Proclamation (q.v.) and the Gettysburg Address (q.v.) are by far the best-known events connected with Lincoln's wartime administration. With the war going in the North's favor, Lincoln won reelection to a second term in 1864. Then came R. Lee's surrender and an end to the war. But, tragically, less than a week afterward Lincoln was shot and killed (Apr. 15, 1865) at Ford's Theater by J. Booth (q.v.).

Lincoln, Battle of ⟨Fair of Lincoln⟩ Royalist victory (May 20, 1217) which ended a rebellion by English barons in alliance with Prince Louis of France, pretender to the English throne. Some 400 knights led by the regent of King Henry III, William Marshal (earl of Pembroke), defeated approximately 600 Frenchmen and barons at the town of Lincoln.

Lincoln, Benjamin   1733–1810. American Revolutionary War army officer. He was forced to surrender Charleston, South Carolina, to the British (1780), served as secretary of war (1781–83), and put down Shays' Rebellion (1787).

Lincoln, Mary Todd   1818–82. Wife of A. Lincoln (m. 1842). After losing three of her four sons and seeing her husband shot, she was committed (1875) to an asylum. She was released the next year.

Lincoln, Robert Todd   1843–1926. American lawyer, son of A. Lincoln. He was secretary of war (1881–85), US minister to England (1889–93), and president of the Pullman Company (1897–1911).

Lincoln, Saint Hugh of   *See* **Hugh of Lincoln, Saint**

Lindbergh, Ann Spencer Morrow   1907–. American author, wife of C.A. Lindbergh (m. 1929). Among her works are *North to the Orient, Gift from the Sea,* and *The Unicorn and Other Poems.*

Lindbergh, Charles Augustus   1902–74. American aviator, the first man to fly alone and nonstop across the Atlantic Ocean (May 20–21, 1927). Virtually unknown when he left the US aboard his plane *Spirit of St. Louis,* he was an international celebrity by the time he reached Paris. He married Anne Morrow (1929) and they lived quietly until their child was kidnapped and murdered (1932) in one of the most sensational crimes of this century. The public later turned against Lindbergh, however. An isolationist, he was convinced of the invincibility of Nazi air power and his speeches for the America First Committee against US intervention in WW II were called pro-Nazi. During the war, however, he distinguished himself by flying combat missions with the US air force.

Lines of Torres Vedras   Three lines of defensive fortification in Portugal, extending from the Tagus River to the ocean. They were constructed to protect allied forces, under the Duke of Wellington, from French attack during the Peninsular War (1808–14). The lines were never seriously attacked and thereby halted the French invasion of Portugal.

Linggadjati Agreement   〈Cheribon Agreement〉 Agreement (Nov. 25, 1946) in which The Netherlands formally recognized Indonesia as the de facto government of Java, Sumatra, and Madura.

Linlithgow, Victor Alexander John Hope, 2d marquess of   1887–1952. British statesman who, as viceroy of India (1936–43), maintained British authority in India during the crucial early years of WW II.

Linnaeus, Carolus   〈orig. Linné, Carl von〉 1707–78. Swedish botanist. Linnaeus is considered the father of modern botany, primarily for his system of classification and nomenclature of plants and animals. He published over 180 works during his lifetime; among them were *Flora Lapponica, Systema Naturae,* and *Species Plantarum.*

Linné, Carl von   *See* **Linnaeus, Carolus**

Lin Piao   1907–71. Chinese Communist general and politician. After the Long March (1934–35), he became commander of Communist forces in the northeast against Chiang Kai-shek's Nationalist army. He became heir apparent to Mao Tsetung after replacing Liu Shao-ch'i (1966) as second-in-command of the Chinese Communist party. He died in a plane crash under suspicious circumstances.

Linton, Ralph   1893–1953. American anthropologist, author of *The Study of Man, The Cultural Background of Personality,* and *The Tree of Culture.*

Lipari Islands   〈Aeolian Islands〉 Group of volcanic islands north of Sicily. The legendary home of the wind god, Aeolus, they were used by the Fascists for holding political prisoners.

Li Po   〈Li Tai Po〉 c700–762. Chinese T'ang dynasty poet, considered one of China's greatest. A romantic, he is said to have gotten drunk, reached for the moon's reflection in a river, and drowned.

Lippi, Fra Filippo   c1406–69. Italian Renaissance painter. He was under the patronage of Cosimo de Medici and did the frescoes in the cathedral choir at Prato.

Lippmann, Walter   1899–1974. US journalist and author. He wrote the influential political column *Today and Tomorrow* (1931–67) and several books, including *Public Opinion.*

Lisbon   Portuguese capital city (pop. 829,900) and port. Originally settled by the ancient Iberians, it was taken by the Romans (205 BC), the Moors (AD 716) and by the Christian kings (AD 1147). It subsequently rose to prosperity (16th cent.) as the commercial center of the Portuguese colonial empire. It was badly damaged (1755) in a severe earthquake.

Lister, Joseph 1st Baron   1827–1912. English surgeon, founder of antiseptic surgery. After studying Pasteur's theories on bacteria, he developed (1865) the use of carbolic acid as an antiseptic.

Liszt, Franz   1811–86. Hungarian composer and pianist, foremost concert pianist of his day. He originated the symphonic poem form, of which *Les Préludes* and *Mazeppa* are examples. He revolutionized the sonata form by introducing the device of the leitmotiv. Among his many works for the piano are his Hungarian rhapsodies.

Li Tai Po *See* **Li Po**

Lithuania Former European state in the Baltic Sea region, located in what is now western USSR. Organized as a duchy (13th cent.) to resist attacks by the Livonian Brothers and the Teutonic Knights, Lithuania for a time became a powerful medieval state with domains extending to the Black Sea. It came into personal union with Poland (1386) by royal marriage and was forced by the threat of Russian domination (under Ivan IV) to accept the Union of Lublin (1569) with Poland. Russia gained control of Lithuanian territories by the three Partitions of Poland (18th cent.). Lithuania again became an independent state after the Baltic Wars of Liberation *(q.v.)*, only to be annexed by the USSR (Aug. 3, 1940).

Little, Malcolm *See* **Malcolm X**

Little America US base in the Antarctic, on Ross Ice Shelf. It was established by R. E. Byrd (1928–30) as a base for his Antarctic exploration. He reestablished the base (1933, 1939) during subsequent expeditions.

Little Bighorn, Battle of ⟨Custer's last stand⟩ Famous massacre (June 25, 1876) of Gen. G. Custer and his cavalry unit by Sioux and Cheyenne Indians. Custer, leading the advance element of a large cavalry force sent against the Sioux, discovered an Indian camp on the Little Bighorn River near what is now Hardin, Montana. He launched an immediate attack on what he thought was a small force but the Indians, led by Chief Sitting Bull, had hidden the bulk of their warriors. When Custer advanced, they surrounded and massacred the entire force of over 250 men.

Little Entente Alliance between Czechoslovakia, Romania, and Yugoslavia formed by treaties (1920–21). The major aim of the alliance was to maintain boundaries of the three countries (as set by treaties after WW I) against German or Hungarian encroachments. The alliance proved ineffectual against the expansionist designs of A. Hitler, however. It ended when Germany, by the terms of the Munich Pact (1938), was permitted to occupy the Czechoslovakian territory of Sudetenland.

Little Parliament *See* **Barebones Parliament**

Little Rock US city (pop. 158,500), the capital of Arkansas. Founded in 1821, it was made the capital of Arkansas Territory that year and became the state capital (1836) when the territory became a US state. President D. Eisenhower sent federal troops to the city (1957) to enforce school desegregation.

Littre, Maximilien Paul Émile 1801–81. French philosopher and lexicographer, a leader of the pos-

itivist school. He is known for his *Dictionary of the French Language.*

Liturgical movement Movement among Christian churches to develop new interest for the church liturgy among their followers. Though rooted in the 19th cent., the movement in the Roman Catholic church was greatly advanced by the Second Vatican Council (1962–65), which introduced use of vernacular translations of Latin texts and fostered greater involvement in the services by the laity. Among Protestant churches, the movement focused on revising texts to eliminate archaic expressions and on changing the form of services.

Litvinov, Maxim Maximovich 1876–1951. Russian Communist diplomat. As commissar of foreign affairs (1930–39), he sought cooperation with Western nations against the Axis Powers. He was ambassador to the US (1941–43).

Li Tzu-ch'eng 1605–45. Chinese rebel leader instrumental in the collapse of the Ming dynasty (1644). He organized a rebel government, took Peking, and forced the remaining Ming forces into an alliance with the Manchus. The Manchus first defeated his forces and then took control of China for themselves.

Liu Shao-ch'i 1898–1974. Chinese Communist leader. A recognized authority on party organization, he was head of state (1959–68) and heir apparent under Mao Tse-tung. He was ousted during the Cultural Revolution.

Liutprand d. 744. Lombard king (712–744). His reign brought the Lombard kingdom to its greatest power. He centralized authority, instituted a just code of law, and conquered Byzantine territories in Italy.

Liverpool, Robert Banks Jenkinson, 2nd earl of ⟨Hawkesbury, Baron⟩ 1770–1828. English statesman. He was prime minister (1812–27) during the War of 1812 with the US and the last phase of the Napoleonic Wars.

Livia Drusilla *c*55 BC–AD 29. First Roman empress, wife of Augustus. She married Octavian (Augustus) in 38 BC, before he became emperor. She had two sons, Tiberius and Drusus (Germanicus) by her previous marriage, and she later conspired to ensure Tiberius' succession as emperor.

Livingston, Edward 1764–1836. American lawyer and statesman. A noted jurist in his day, he was secretary of state (1831–33) under President A. Jackson and formulated the president's reply (1832) to the nullification doctrine.

Livingston, Robert 1654–1728. Colonial leader in New York. Livingston had extensive land holdings, served in the New York provincial assembly

(1709–11, 1716–25), and was secretary of Indian affairs (1695–1728).

Livingston, Robert R. 1746–1813. American statesman. A New York delegate to the Continental Congress, he served on the committee that drafted the Declaration of Independence. As Pres. T. Jefferson's ambassador to France, he helped negotiate the Louisiana Purchase. He later financed R. Fulton's steamboat, the *Clermont.*

Livingston, William 1723–90. American Revolutionary leader. Livingston served in the Continental Congress and became the first governor of independent New Jersey (1776), a post he held until his death.

Livingstone, David 1813–73. Scottish missionary and explorer. Arriving in Africa as a medical missionary (1841), Livingstone explored its interior, and his discoveries included Victoria Falls and the Zambezi River. He was feared lost on an 1866 expedition to the source of the Nile River. Found by H. Stanley (1871), he refused to leave Africa and died of disease while continuing his search for the Nile headwaters.

Livingstone, Philip 1716–78. American Revolutionary War leader and philanthropist. A moderate, he opposed the Stamp Act, signed the Declaration of Independence, and was a member of the Continental Congress from New York.

Livius Andronicus *fl.* 3d cent. BC. Roman poet, known as the founder of Roman drama. A freed Greek slave, he translated the *Odyssey* and Greek plays into Latin.

Livland *See* **Livonia**

Livonia ⟨Livland⟩ Former state located on the east shore of the Baltic Sea. Beginning in the early 13th cent., the Germanic Livonian Knights conquered the region from the native people, the Livs. These Christian knights formed a confederation out of their domains that flourished during the 15th cent. However, internal struggles among the knights and the spread of the Protestant Reformation weakened the state and, during the Livonian War (1558–83), the order disbanded (1561). Portions of the territory passed to or were conquered by Lithuania, Denmark, Poland, Sweden, and Russia. Russia gradually gained control of the region through conquests in the Second (Great) Northern War (1700–21) and Partitions of Poland (18th cent.).

Livonian Knights ⟨Brothers of the Sword, Order of the⟩ German religious order founded (1202) to conquer and Christianize Baltic lands. The order created Livonia *(q.v.)* from conquered territories. The order disbanded (1561) after being defeated by the Russians during the Livonian War *(q.v.).*

Livonian War Unsuccessful war (1558–82) waged by Russian Czar Ivan IV for control of Livonia and access to the Baltic Sea. Russian attacks against Livonia first led to the dissolution (1561) of the ruling order, the Livonian Knights *(q.v.).* Livonia was then divided among Poland, Lithuania, Sweden, and Denmark, but Russia continued its attempt to conquer the region. Initially successful, it suffered a series of losses to Poland's king, Stephen Bathory, and ultimately was forced (1582) to accept a peace settlement by which it renounced its claims over Livonia.

Livy 59 BC–AD 17. Great Roman historian. Sponsored by Emperor Augustus, Livy wrote the collection of 142 books known as the *Annals of Rome,* which cover the history of Rome from its founding in 753 BC to 9 BC. Thirty-five books are extant and fragments and summaries of all but two remain.

Li Yüan 565–635. Chinese emperor (618–27) and founder of the T'ang dynasty. An official in the Sui dynasty government, he led a revolt (617) that put him in power.

Llewelyn ab Gruffydd *d.* 1282. Welsh prince and ruler (1246–82), nephew and successor of David II. Though he sided with S. de Montfort in the unsuccessful Barons' War (1263–67), he nevertheless came to control most of Wales during Henry III's reign. Wars with Edward I, however, led to subjugation of Wales by the Treaty of Conway (1277).

Lloyd George, David, 1st earl of Dwyfor 1863–1945. Controversial, Welsh-born, British statesman and Liberal prime minister (1916–22). He first entered Parliament (1890) as a Liberal. As Chancellor of the Exchequer under H. Asquith, he proposed (1909) his famous People's Budget, which provided social insurance by taxing the wealthy. The bill brought on a major political crisis and cost the House of Lords its veto power (by the Parliament Act of 1911). In 1911 he sponsored legislation for health and unemployment insurance programs. After ousting Asquith, he became prime minister and, during his term of office, helped bring the US into WW I, played a major role in negotiating the Treaty of Versailles (1919), and set up the Irish Free State (1922).

Lloyd's Famous London insurance corporation founded in the late 17th cent. Its main business is marine insurance but it handles many other types of insurance risks on an international basis.

Lobachevsky, Nikolai Ivanovich 1793–1856. Russian mathematician. He was a founder of non-Euclidean geometry.

Lobengula *See* **Matabele War**

Locarno Pact Agreement signed (Oct. 16, 1925) at Locarno, Switzerland, by Germany and other European powers, guaranteeing the post-WW I borders of the Rhineland, Belgium, France, and Germany. A major step in Germany's reentry to postwar world affairs, the agreement was preceded by several treaties between individual signators and eventually led to Germany's acceptance into the League of Nations. The pact was denounced by A. Hitler and was finally broken when the Germans remilitarized (Mar. 7, 1936) the Rhineland. Other signators of the pact were Britain, France, Italy, Belgium, Czechoslovakia, and Poland.

Locke, John 1632–1704.   English philosopher who founded British empiricism. His doctrines on natural rights influenced the writing of the Declaration of Independence and the Constitution of the United States. In his *Essay Concerning Human Understanding,* he described the human mind and the process by which it acquires knowledge through the five senses. Natural rights, he believed, included the rights of property, the pursuit of happiness, and religious toleration. Locke held that governments were social compacts and should be based on natural laws. His philosophy greatly influenced the thinking of the 18th-cent. Enlightenment and provided a philosophical basis for the American and French revolutions.

Locofoco party   *See* **Locofocos**

Locofocos ⟨Locofoco party⟩   Nickname for a faction (and short-lived party) of radical Jacksonian Democrats that appeared (1835) in the US. Largely a phenomenon of the Northeast, the Locofocos advocated an end to the national bank and other monopolies. Locofocos split (1835) with regular Democrats in New York and formed (1836) the Equal Rights Party. President M. Van Buren eventually took up many of their policies and the Locofocos rejoined the Democratic Party (by 1838).

Lod   *See* **Lydda**

Lodge, Henry Cabot 1850–1924. American politician. He served as senator from Massachusetts (1893–1924) and, as a leading isolationist, headed opposition to US entry to the League of Nations.

Lodge, Henry Cabot, Jr. 1902–. American politician. He was senator from Massachusetts (1937–44, 1947–53), US representative to the UN (1953–60), and made an unsuccessful bid for the vice-presidency, running with R. Nixon (1960).

Lodi, Battle of   French victory (May 10, 1796) over the Austrians in Italy, during the French Revolutionary Wars (1792–1802). Napoleon, commander of the French forces, distinguished himself during the battle and was nicknamed the "Little Corporal." In the battle, Napoleon attacked Lodi Bridge with 5,000 soldiers and forced the 10,000 Austrian defenders to retreat.

Loeben, Peace of   *See* **Campo Formio, Treaty of**

Logan, John Alexander 1826–86. Union general in the American Civil War, senator from Illinois (1871–77, 1879–86), and founder of Memorial Day (1868).

Logos   Greek philosophical term used to describe the force of reason and order in the cosmos. The concept, advanced by Heraclitus (6th cent. BC), came to represent a link between God and man.

Lohengrin   In German legend, the knight of the swan and the Holy Grail. He rescued a princess and married her on the condition that she never ask his true identity. When she finally asked, he left her forever.

Loisy, Alfred Firmin 1857–1940.   French theologian who founded Modernism in the Catholic church. He was excommunicated for his views in 1908.

Loki   In Norse mythology, the god of evil. He was punished for the murder of Balder but will lead his evil forces when the world ends.

Lollardry ⟨Lollardy⟩   English church reform movement that began (14th cent.) at Oxford. Some Lollard doctrines are said to have presaged those of the Reformation. Formed (late 14th cent.) by J. Wycliffe at Oxford, the movement spread throughout England. Persecutions began (1399) under Henry IV and, after two rebellions were suppressed (1414, 1431), the movement went underground, surviving until the rise of the 16th-cent. Reformation. Lollard doctrines, as set forth in their *Twelve Conclusions* (1395) and elsewhere, include: condemnation of the papacy; belief in primacy of the Scriptures; denial of transubstantiation; opposition to war; and condemnation of sacramentals, confession, pilgrimages, clerical celibacy, and other practices of the Catholic church.

Lollardy   *See* **Lollardry**

Lombard League   Alliance formed (1167) by Lombard cities in northern Italy against Holy Roman Emperor Frederick I (Barbarossa). Following attempts by Frederick to enforce his authority over the cities, they formed the league (with the support of Pope Alexander III) and successfully resisted Frederick's armies. By the Peace of Constance (1183), Frederick guaranteed the cities their freedom and the league ceased to be important. It was reactivated (1226) to defend against attacks by Holy Roman Emperor Frederick II. Cities in the league included Milan, Venice, Mantua, Padua, and Brescia.

Lombardo   Italian architects and sculptors. Pietro Lombardo (c1435–1515) and his sons Antonio (c1458–1516) and Tullio (c1455–1532) worked on such noted Venetian structures as the Doge's palace, Dante's tomb, and the Church of Santa Maria dei Miracoli.

Lombards, Kingdom of Kingdom in Italy formed (6th cent.) by Germanic tribes known as the Lombards. Led by Alboin, these tribes migrated south and conquered (568–572) most of the north and parts of central and southern Italy. After a period of initial instability, the kingdom flourished (7th–8th cent.) with its center at Pavia. Frankish conquest of the kingdom was provoked by Lombard invasions of the Papal States. The Franks, under Pepin the Short, invaded Lombard domains (c751) to aid Pope Stephen II. When Lombard King Desiderius again attacked Rome (772), Charlemagne completely conquered the Lombard kingdom and ended its existence as an independent state.

Lombardy Leading industrial region of modern Italy. Once a Roman province, it became the center of the Lombard kingdom (q.v.). It passed to Charlemagne (774) and, in medieval times, its cities flourished as independent communes (see Lombard League). The region eventually came under control of the duchy of Milan (14th cent.) and was controlled by various powers before being absorbed into the unified kingdom of Italy (19th cent.).

Loménie de Brienne, Étienne Charles 1727–94. French statesman and ecclesiastic. As minister of finance, he convoked the States-General of 1789. He died in prison during the French Revolution.

Lomonosov, Mikhail Vasilyevich 1711–65. Russian scientist and author. He reformed the Russian literary language, bringing to it a more energetic, idiomatic style.

London Great Britain's capital city (pop. 7,028,200), located in southeastern England. One of the world's greatest cities, it is Britain's cultural and commercial center. London's history dates from Roman times and, in AD c60, the Roman settlement was attacked by Queen Boadicea (q.v.). After the fall of Rome, London received (AD 597) the Christian missionary St. Augustine. It was established as a city of some importance by AD 886, when Alfred the Great took it from the Danes and refortified it. London's growth began in the centuries following the Norman Conquest (1066) and, during the reign of Elizabeth I (16th cent.), it prospered as a commercial (with the rise of trading companies), political, and cultural center. The city later figured as a stronghold of Parliamentary forces in the English Civil War (1642–49), suffered the ravages of plague (1665), and was largely destroyed in the great fire of London (Sept. 2–5, 1666). Rebuilt, it rose to worldwide prominence as the seat of Britain's great colonial empire. Though it suffered some raids during WW I, Lon-

don was a chief objective of German airborne raids in the Battle of Britain (q.v.) in WW II. Today London is the site of such famous structures as Westminster Abbey (q.v.), Buckingham Palace (q.v.), and the Tower of London (q.v.). (See also London, Treaties of and London conferences.)

London, Declaration of Proposed (1909) international regulations for naval warfare. The declaration was a result of the London Naval Conference (1908), attended by Great Britain and other European powers, the US, and Japan. It attempted to formalize wartime conventions for blockades, war prizes, contraband, and other matters. The declaration failed to win ratification by the participating nations and an attempt to gain voluntary compliance during WW I was rejected.

London, Jack ⟨London, John Griffith⟩ 1876–1916. American author of adventure stories, such as Call of the Wild, The Sea-Wolf, and White Fang.

London, John Griffith See **London, Jack**

London, Tower of See **Tower of London**

London, Treaties of 1. Treaty (Mar. 17, 1824) between The Netherlands and Britain defining their respective spheres of influence in Malaysia. The British gained control of Malacca. 2. Treaty (July 6, 1827) between Britain, France, and Russia, in which they agreed to force the Ottoman Turks and Greek independence fighters to accept mediation. The powers used military force to intervene after Turkey rejected the plan. 3. Treaty (Nov. 15, 1831) between major European powers, settling matters relating to the Belgian war for independence from The Netherlands. 4. Treaty (1832) between Britain, France, and Bavaria, granting the newly created Greek throne to Otto I. 5. Treaty (May 11, 1867) between major European powers, establishing Luxembourg as an independent and neutral state. 6. Treaty (Mar. 13, 1871) in which signators to the Treaty of Paris (1856) acceded to Russian demands to end the neutral status of the Black Sea. 7. Treaty (May 30, 1913) ending the first Balkan War. It stripped Turkey of its domains on the Balkan Peninsula. Disputes among Balkan states over division of this territory resulted in the Second Balkan War. 8. Secret treaty (Apr. 26, 1915) between Italy, Britain, France, and Russia, granting Italy territorial concessions in return for its entry in WW I. The lands included Trieste, south Tyrol, and part of Dalmatia.

London Bridge Bridge over the Thames River in London, England. Once a structure complete with stores and houses, it was damaged, redesigned, and rebuilt many times between 1176 and 1831. It was rebuilt again in the 1960s.

London Company London-based company of stockholders that joined with the Plymouth Company to found colonies in the United States under a charter given by James I (1606). The company established the Jamestown, Virginia, colony, the first permanent English settlement in America.

London conferences Meetings between representatives of international powers, held in London (19th–20th cents.). These conferences included that of 1830–31, which established Greek independence (1831) and attempted to resolve the war between the Belgians and Dutch over Belgian independence; 1838–39, which settled the division of The Netherlands and newly independent Belgium; 1852, which attempted to resolve conflicts between the Danes and the German Confederation over administration of Schleswig-Holstein; 1908, which resulted in the Declaration of London (*q.v.*) on naval armament; 1930 (London Naval Conference), which established regulations on submarine warfare and limited construction of new battleships; 1933, which unsuccessfully attempted international financial reforms to end the Great Depression; 1945, which saw the beginnings of the postwar rift between Russia and the other WW II Allies.

Long, Crawford Williamson 1815–78. American physician. He was the first physician to use ether in surgery (1842).

Long, Huey Pierce 1893–1935. Notorious American politician (called "the kingfish"). He was governor of Louisiana (1928–31) and US senator (1931–35), and was known as the leader of a corrupt political machine that controlled his state. He gained nationwide attention with his "Share-the-Wealth" plan.

Longchamp, William of d. 1197. English prelate and statesman. As chancellor to Richard I, he ruled the country while the king was on the Third Crusade (1190). Unpopular, he was ousted by Richard's brother, John (1191).

Longfellow, Henry Wadsworth 1807–82. Famous American poet who wrote about the history and legends of America. Among his many popular poems are *The Wreck of the Hesperus*, *The Village Blacksmith*, *Evangeline*, *The Song of Hiawatha*, *The Courtship of Miles Standish*, and *Paul Revere's Ride*. He also wrote a translation of Dante's *Divine Comedy*.

Longinus c213–273. Greek philosopher. He advised Queen Zenobia, ruler of the eastern kingdom of Palmyra, to revolt against Rome. When the revolt failed, he was executed by Emperor Aurelian as a traitor. Longinus was long thought to be the author of *On the Sublime*.

Long Island, Battle of British victory (Aug. 27, 1776) over the Americans during the American Revolution. After evacuating Boston, the British

(under Gen. W. Howe) occupied Staten Island. Intending to take New York City, some 20,000 British landed (Aug. 22) at Gravesend, on Long Island. After several days' delay, they engaged and defeated an equal number of American soldiers, under G. Washington, at Brooklyn Heights, Long Island. Washington withdrew (Aug. 29), first to Manhattan and then northward toward White Plains.

Long March Heroic march (1934–35) by the remnants of the Chinese Communist army during the Chinese Civil War. When Chinese Nationalists surrounded their base in southeast China, about 100,000 Communist soldiers broke out of the trap (Oct. 15, 1934). During their subsequent 6,000-mile march to a new base in Shensi province (northwest China), the Communists crossed rugged terrain and were harried by Nationalist forces. Mao Tse-tung became leader of the Chinese Communist party during the march (at Tsunyi, Jan., 1935), and, by the time the Communists reached Shensi (Oct., 1935), over half had died or been killed.

Long Parliament Name for the English Parliament that sat (Nov. 3, 1640–Mar. 16, 1660) during the English Civil War period. Called by Charles I to raise money, the Parliament refused, and civil war broke out soon after. After Charles's defeat, the parliament became the object (1648) of Pride's Purge (*q.v.*). Reduced to 60 members, it thereafter became known as the Rump Parliament. Later Charles I was tried and executed by the Parliament, which was twice dissolved for intervals by O. Cromwell and was succeeded by the Convention Parliament (*q.v.*).

Long Parliament of the Restoration *See* **Cavalier Parliament**

Longstreet, James 1821–1904. Confederate Army general in the American Civil War. His slowness to attack at Gettysburg (1863) is generally considered the reason for that Confederate defeat.

Longworth, Nicholas 1869–1931. American legislator. A congressman from Ohio, Longworth was Speaker of the House from 1925 to 1931.

Lon Nol 1913–. Cambodian military leader. He was premier (1966–67), and took control of the government after overthrowing Prince Sihanouk (1970). Reverses in the civil war with Communist Khmer Rouge guerrillas eventually drove him from office (1975).

Lönnrot, Elias 1802–84. Finnish philologist who gathered the oral folklore of his country and published it in the *Kalevala*.

López, Francisco Solano 1826?–70. Dictator of Paraguay (1862–70). He warred unsuccessfully against Brazil, Argentina, and Uruguay in the War of the Triple Alliance *(q.v.)* and was killed during fighting.

López, Narciso 1798–1851. Spanish-American soldier and revolutionary. He led three unsuccessful military expeditions against Spanish Cuba (1849, 1850, 1851), and was killed in the third.

López de Legaspi, Miguel *d.* 1572. Spanish explorer. He conquered the Philippines for the Spanish (1564) and founded the city of Manila (1571).

Lord Dunmore's War War (Jan.–Oct., 1774) between Shawnee Indians and the Virginia militia. It was prompted by white encroachments on Indian lands and Virginia's seizure of western Pennsylvania. The war, culminating in the Shawnees' defeat at the Battle of Point Pleasant (Oct. 10), opened Kentucky and the Ohio Valley to Colonial expansion.

Lorelei A cliff above the Rhine River in Germany where, according to legend, a siren lures sailors to their death by her singing.

Lorentz, Hendrik Antoon 1853–1928. Dutch physicist. He and Pieter Zeeman received the Nobel Prize in Physics in 1902 for their explanation of the Zeeman Effect, concerning electromagnetic radiation.

Lorenz, Konrad 1903–. Austrian zoologist. Lorenz established the discipline of ethology, the scientific study of patterns of animal behavior, especially as related to aggression. With Karl von Frisch and Nikolaas Tinbergen, he was awarded the Nobel Prize in Physiology and Medicine in 1973.

Lorenzini, Carlo *See* **Collodi, Carlo**

Los Alamos Site (and now a town) in New Mexico where the US government produced and tested atomic bombs. Opened in 1942 as part of the Manhattan Project *(q.v.)*, the facility there constructed the world's first atomic bombs and conducted the earliest test explosion on July 16, 1945.

Los Angeles US city (pop. 2,966,700) located in southern California. Founded as a Spanish settlement (1781), it passed from Spanish to Mexican control and was captured (1846) by the US during the Mexican War (1846–48). Growth was rapid thereafter, as the gold rush, the arrival of railroads from the East (1870s, 1880s), and the discovery of oil (1890s) all brought waves of new settlers. From the early 1900s, Los Angeles has been famous as the center of the movie industry *(see* Hollywood).

Lost Battalion American army unit in WW I. Several American companies, led by Major Charles Whittlesey, were cut off by German forces in the Argonne Forest (Oct., 1918). They were rescued after heroically resisting German attacks for five days.

"lost colony" ⟨Roanoke Colony⟩ English settlement established (July, 1587) on Roanoke Island (now in North Carolina). The 117 colonists vanished mysteriously, leaving behind only the carved word "Croatan." The cause of the disappearance has never been discovered.

Lost Dauphin *See* **Louis XVII**

"lost generation" Name applied to a group of American writers whose lives and works were greatly influenced by the events of WW I. Among them were F. S. Fitzgerald and E. Hemingway. The term derives from G. Stein's remark, "You are all a lost generation," which Hemingway used as the epigraph to his novel *The Sun Also Rises.*

Lost Tribes of Israel Ten tribes of Israel that were exiled from there by the Assyrian king Sargon (*c*722 BC). Their fate is unknown, but several theories assert that they became the ancestors of various peoples, including the Anglo-Saxons, American Indians, and Ethiopians. The ten tribes were those of Asher, Dan, Ephraim, Gad, Issachar, Manasseh, Naphtali, Reuben, Simeon, and Zebulun. (*See also* Twelve tribes of Israel.)

Lot In the Bible, son of Haran, Abraham's brother. His wife was turned into a pillar of salt when disobeying God's warning not to look back at the destruction of Sodom.

Lotario di Segni *See* **Innocent III**

Lothair 835–869. Carolingian king of Lotharingia (855–869). The son of Lothair I (emperor of the West), he became involved in a lengthy dispute with Pope Nicholas I over his divorce and subsequent marriage to his mistress.

Lothair 941–986. Carolingian king of France (954–986), successor to his father, Louis IV. He was dominated throughout most of his reign by Hugh the Great and later by Archbishop Bruno of Cologne. His efforts to obtain control of Lorraine led to conflict with Holy Roman Emperor Otto II.

Lothair I 795–855. Carolingian emperor in title (840–855), a successor to his father, Louis I, and grandson of Charlemagne. His defeat at Fontenoy (841) marked the end of his attempts to reunite the Carolingian Empire under his rule. By the Treaty of Verdun (843), he became ruler of Lotharingia, the middle portion of the divided empire.

Lothair II 1075–1137. Holy Roman Emperor (1133–37). He was elected to succeed Henry V, and his was the first case in which an elective monarchy came to power over a rival, hereditary claimant.

Lotharingia Kingdom created by the division of the Carolingian Empire into three parts. Lotharingia (then also called Francia Media) was the middle of the three kingdoms established by the Treaty of Verdun (843) and was first ruled by Emperor Lothair I. At its greatest extent, it included what are now The Netherlands, Belgium, Luxembourg, the region of Lorraine in France, and Italy. It was divided (870) by the Treaty of Mersen (*q.v.*).

Lotophagi *See* **lotus-eaters**

lotus-eaters ⟨Lotophagi⟩ In Greek legend and the *Odyssey*, a people of Africa who ate the lotus plant, which caused forgetfulness and idleness.

Loudon, Gideon Ernst, Freiherr von *See* **Laudon, Gideon Ernst, Freiherr von**

Louis I ⟨Louis the Pious⟩ 778–840. Carolingian emperor (814–840), successor to his father, Charlemagne. His reign was marked by revolts by his sons over his plans to divide the empire among them. They deposed (and later restored) him twice, once in 830 and again in 833. His reign marked the end of the unified Carolingian Empire.

Louis I ⟨Louis the Great⟩ 1326–82. King of Hungary (1342–82) and Poland (1370–82). Louis conducted several wars against Venice, acquiring control of Dalmatia. He also drove the Turks and Tatars from his lands.

Louis I 1339–84. King of Naples (1382–84). Louis was the son of French king John II. Joanna I of Naples made Louis heir to Naples. He was overthrown by a rival claimant, Charles of Durazzo (Charles III).

Louis I 1786–1868. King of Bavaria (1825–48), son of Maximilian I. He made Munich a cultural center, but his conservative policies and his liaison with L. Montez led to his forced abdication during the Revolution of 1848.

Louis I 1838–89. Portuguese king (1861–89), successor to his brother Peter V. His reign was marked by political unrest and numerous changes of ministries. Under his rule, slavery was abolished in Portuguese colonies.

Louis II d. 875. Frankish king of what is now Italy (844–875), nominal emperor of the Carolingian empire. Louis spent most of his reign holding the invading Arabs in check in southern Italy.

Louis II ⟨Louis the Stammerer⟩ 846–879. Frankish king (877–879) of the West (France) Frankish kingdom, successor to his father, Charles II (the Bald).

Louis II 1377–1417. Claimant to the throne of Naples. The son of Louis I, he inherited his father's claim to the kingdom, though he actually held it only from 1390 to 1399. He was driven out by Lancelot.

Louis II 1506–26. King of Hungary and Bohemia (1516–26). Louis was the last of the Jagiello dynasty. He was unable to prevent the Turkish conquest of his Hungarian lands, and died at the Battle of Mohács.

Louis II 1845–86. King of Bavaria (1864–86), successor to his father, Maximilian II. He was the patron of R. Wagner, and he built extravagant palaces. Declared insane in 1886, he drowned himself.

Louis III c863–882. Frankish king (879–882) of the West (France), a son of Louis II. He ruled jointly with his brother Carloman, and turned back the Norman invasion at Saucourt (881).

Louis III 1403–34. Rival for the throne of Naples (1417–34). The son of Louis II, he fought Joanna II and her ally Alfonso V of Aragon for the throne. When Alfonso fell out with Joanna, she made Louis her heir (1421) instead.

Louis IV ⟨Louis d'Outremer⟩ 921–954. King of France (936–954), son of Charles III (the Simple) and successor to Rudolph. His reign was marked by strife with his vassal Hugh the Great.

Louis IV ⟨Louis the Bavarian⟩ 1287?–1347. Holy Roman Emperor (1328–47). Louis fought Frederick the Fair (1314–22) in order to secure his claim. Following defeat of Frederick, Pope John XXII still refused Louis the imperial crown. Pope John steadfastly opposed Louis in ensuing years, and in 1338 the German electors ruled against the papacy. They declared that their election of the emperor automatically conferred the imperial crown.

Louis V 967–987. King of France (986–987), successor to Lothair. The last Carolingian king of France, he was succeeded by Hugh Capet, founder of the Capetian (*q.v.*) line.

Louis VI ⟨Louis the Fat⟩ 1081–1137. King of France (1108–37), successor to his father, Philip I. He fought several wars with King Henry I over English territories on the Continent and strengthened royal authority.

Louis VII ⟨Louis the Young⟩ c1120–80. King of France (1137–80), successor to his father, Louis VI. He annulled his marriage to Eleanor of Aquitaine (1152), who subsequently married Henry II of England. This gave rise to Henry's claims to Aquitaine and a long series of wars between Louis and Henry. Louis aided Henry's sons in a revolt against their father (1173–74) but gained no territories from it.

Louis VIII 1187–1226. King of France (1223–26), successor to his father, Philip II. He invaded England at the invitation of the barons, then rebelling against King John (1216), but withdrew (1217) after the accession of Henry III eroded his support among them.

Louis IX ⟨Saint Louis⟩ 1214–70. King of France (1226–70), successor to his father, Louis VIII. His mother, Blanche of Castile, was his regent (to 1234) and, later, his close adviser. He was defeated and captured on the Seventh Crusade *(q.v.)* and settled territorial disputes with Henry III of England (by the Treaty of Paris, 1259). His reign was marked by a period of peace and prosperity.

Louis X 1289–1316. King of France (1314–16), successor to his father, Philip IV. He was forced to grant charters to the nobles to gain their support. He was dominated by Charles of Valois.

Louis XI 1423–83. French king (1461–83), successor to his father, Charles VII. As king, he succeeded in overcoming the rebellious nobles and thereby laid the basis for an absolute monarchy in France. Louis engaged in many revolts against his father, notably the Praguerie (1440), and, as king, succeeded in putting down a revolt (1465) by the League of the Public Weal *(q.v.)*. He took Normandy from his brother Charles. In 1467 he began a long war with Charles the Bold (duke of Burgundy) and his allies Francis II (duke of Brittany) and English king Edward IV. Louis ultimately won Burgundy by the Treaty of Arras (1482), and, with the extinction of the Anjou line, also acquired their territories for the crown.

Louis XII 1462–1515. King of France (1498–1515), successor to his cousin Charles VIII, known as "the Father of the People" for his benevolent rule. His foreign policy was dominated by attempts to conquer parts of Italy in the Italian Wars *(q.v.)*.

Louis XIII 1601–43. French king (1610–43), successor to his father, Henry IV. His reign was marked by the strong leadership of his ministers, Cardinal de Richelieu and J. Mazarin, who centralized royal authority and laid the foundation for absolutism in France. Rebellions by French Protestants (Huguenots) were quelled and France joined in the Thirty Years' War (from 1635).

Louis XIV ⟨The Sun King⟩ 1638–1715. French king (1643–1715), successor to his father, Louis XIII. Louis' reign marked the height of absolutism in France, and, by his expansionist policies, he embroiled the country in a costly series of wars. During Louis' minority, France was weakened by the ongoing Thirty Years' War (1618–48) and rebellions known as the Fronde (1648–53). Louis took power (1661) on the death of the powerful minister Cardinal Mazarin, continued the process of centralizing authority in his own hands, and fostered a period of commercial prosperity. With the royal finances restored and the army strengthened, Louis set out on the first of his wars to enlarge French domains, the War of Devolution (1667–78). This was followed by the Third Dutch War (1672–78), the War of the Grand Alliance (1689–97), and, finally, the War of Spanish Succession (1701–14). This last war left France seriously weakened financially. Within France, Louis' reign was marked by his arbitrary use of the *lettre de cachet (q.v.)*, his growing intolerance of Protestants (Huguenots), which ended in his revocation (1685) of the Edict of Nantes *(q.v.)*, and his support of Gallicanism *(q.v.)*. Louis was a lavish patron of the arts, and his reign is sometimes referred to as the Augustan Age of French literature. He likewise maintained a splendid court (in part to keep the nobles in check) and built the magnificent palace of Versailles.

Louis XV 1710–74. French king (1715–74), successor to his great-grandfather, Louis XIV. Louis was a weak and (at his death) unpopular ruler. The financial difficulties that arose during his reign helped bring on the French Revolution (1789–99). Made king at five, he attained his majority in 1723. The government, however, was largely run (1726–43) by A. Fleury . Thereafter Louis was influenced by a succession of mistresses, notably Mmes. de Pompadour and Du Barry. Louis' reign was marked by: the War of Polish Succession (1733–35); acquisition of the duchy of Lorraine (1735); the War of Austrian Succession (1740–48); the disastrous Seven Years' War (1756–63), which cost France her Canadian and Indian colonies; suppression of the Jesuits (1764); dissolution of Parlement (1771); and a belated attempt at fiscal and legal reforms.

Louis XVI French king (1774–92), successor to his grandfather, Louis XV. He was overthrown during the French Revolution. Louis was an ineffective ruler and failed in attempts at fiscal and administrative reform, put forward by such ministers as A. Turgot and J. Necker, and was often opposed by Queen Marie Antoinette and the royal court. The extravagance of the court and French support (1778–81) for the American Revolution helped bring the government to near bankruptcy. Thereafter, Louis' reign was swept up in the events of the French Revolution, including: convening of the Assembly of Notables (1787) to approve new taxes; convening of the States-General (1789); legislative rebellion by the third estate and creation of the National Assembly (1789); the storming of the Bastille (1789), provoked by the king's ouster of Necker; transfer (1789) of the king and family from Versailles to Tuileries palace in Paris; an unsuccessful attempt at escape (1791) by the king and family; institution (1791) of a constitutional monarchy; establishment (1792) of the republic; trial and execution (1793) of Louis for suspected conspiracy with foreign powers.

Louis XVII 1785–95? Titular king of France during the French Revolution. The son of Louis XVI, he was imprisoned with the royal family in 1792.

After his father's execution, Louis was for a time the symbol of royalist hopes. He died in prison.

Louis XVIII 1755–1824. French king (1814–24), crowned after the fall of Napoleon. Following the outbreak of the French Revolution, he fled France (1791) and actively promoted counterrevolutionary plots. He was made king of France (1814), partly through the efforts of C. Talleyrand. His reign began the Restoration (1814–30) and included such events as the Hundred Days (1815) and the rise of the Ultraroyalists *(q.v.).*

Louis, Saint *See* **Louis IX**

Louis de Bourbon *See* **Condé**

Louis de Buade *See* **Frontenac, comte de Palluau**

Louis d'Outremer *See* **Louis IV**

Louise 1776–1810. Queen of Prussia, wife of Frederick William III. She is remembered for her courage in the face of Prussian defeats in the Napoleonic Wars.

Louise of Savoy 1476–1531. Mother of French king Francis I and regent during her son's Italian expeditions (1515–16 and 1525–26). In 1529, she negotiated the Treaty of Cambrai.

Louisiana State (pop. 4,204,000) in the US South, the 18th state. Louisiana and environs were claimed for France by LaSalle in 1682. The first settlement in Louisiana was New Orleans (founded 1718), and Louisiana passed to the US by the Louisiana Purchase of 1803. The Territory of Orleans became the state of Louisiana in 1812. Louisiana seceded (1861) from the Union during the Civil War, and was readmitted in 1868. The present state constitution was passed in 1921.

Louisiana Purchase US acquisition (May 2, 1803) of French-held territory extending westward from the Mississippi River to the Rocky Mountains. The purchase doubled the size of the US and guaranteed use of the commercially important Mississippi River. The territory (at first French, then Spanish) reverted to French control (1800) after Napoleon conquered Spain. US president T. Jefferson, fearful that Napoleon might close New Orleans to US commerce, sent (Apr., 1803) R. Livingston to France to buy the city. Some weeks later, with J. Monroe taking part, negotiations were opened by French minister C. Tallyrand for the purchase of the whole Louisiana territory (over 800,000 sq. mi.). The agreement was signed in May (dated Apr. 30, 1803), and the total price, with interest, came to just over $27 million.

Louis Philippe (Citizen King) 1773–1850. King of the French (1830–48), successor to Charles X by the July Revolution (1830). Once a liberal supporter of the French Revolution, Louis Philippe lived in exile (from 1793) until the Restoration (1814–30). He joined the liberal opposition to the monarchy, and was later chosen king by A. Thiers, M. Lafayette, and other bourgeois leaders of the July Revolution. Though it began in a liberal spirit, his reign gradually became absolutist. Workers' rebellions, demands for enfranchisement of the lower bourgeoisie, and the struggles between Legitimists and Bonapartists eventually culminated in the February Revolution (1848). The king abdicated (Feb., 1848) and fled to England.

Louis the Bavarian *See* **Louis IV**

Louis the Child 893–911. Frankish king (899–911) of the East (Germany), successor to Arnulf. Louis was the last German Carolingian ruler. Invasions by the Magyars from the east eventually broke down the authority of the monarchy in the east.

Louis the Fat *See* **Louis VI**

Louis the German c804–876. Frankish king (843–876) of the East (Germany). He was allotted a portion of the divided Carolingian Empire by his father, Louis I. Louis joined with his brother, Charles the Bald, to block Lothair I's attempt to reunite the Carolingian Empire under his rule. Louis and Charles forced Lothair to accept the divided empire by the Treaty of Verdun (843).

Louis the Great *See* **Louis I**

Louis the Pious *See* **Louis I**

Louis the Stammerer *See* **Louis II**

Louis the Young *See* **Louis VII**

Louis the Younger d. 882. Frankish king (876–882) of the East (Germany), successor to his father, Louis the German. He expanded his domains by conquering western Lotharingia from Charles the Bald (876). He later acquired eastern Lotharingia.

Lourdes Town in southwestern France famous for its shrine at the spot where Saint Bernadette was said to have seen visions of the Virgin. Millions make pilgrimages there each year.

Lourenço Marques *See* **Maputo**

Louvois, Michel Le Tellier, marquis de 1639–91. French war minister. Under Louis XIV, he instituted reforms that made the French army the most powerful in Europe, encouraged and ruthlessly enforced the revocation of the Edict of Nantes *(q.v.),* and became notorious for the destructiveness of his armies during the War of the Grand Alliance.

Louvre Museum in Paris, France. The original structure was started by Francis I in 1546 and was added to by succeeding rulers. The vast art collection includes the *Mona Lisa* and the *Venus de Milo.*

Lovejoy, Elijah Parish 1802–37. American journalist and abolitionist martyr. He was killed in Alton, Illinois, defending his printing press against a proslavery mob. His death increased sympathy for the abolitionist cause.

Lovell, James Arthur, Jr. 1928–. US astronaut, crew member on the first manned flight to orbit the moon, the Apollo 8 mission (launched Dec. 21, 1968). He was also aboard the ill-fated Apollo 13 moon flight, aborted because of equipment malfunction.

Lowell, Amy 1874–1925. American poet and critic, a leader of the imagists. Her most famous poems are *Lilacs* and *Patterns*.

Lowell, Francis Cabot 1775–1817. American textile manufacturer. He was a founder of the Boston Manufacturing Co., the first factory to convert raw cotton into finished cloth.

Lowell, James Russell 1819–91. American poet, essayist, and critic. He was editor of the *Atlantic Monthly* and the *North American Review* and was an influential figure in 19th-cent. New England literary circles. Among his many works was *The Bigelow Papers.*

Lowell, Percival 1855–1916. American astronomer. He founded (1894) the Lowell Observatory in Flagstaff, Arizona, and predicted the discovery of the planet Pluto.

Lowell, Robert Traill Spence 1917–77. American poet. His works include *In Lord Weary's Castle, Life Studies, The Dolphin,* and *Near the Ocean.*

Lower Canada Name applied (1791–1841) to the Canadian region comprising present-day Quebec. Settled primarily by the French, it was joined with Upper Canada by the Act of Union (1841) and became known as Canada East. With the confederation of Canada (1867) it became the province of Quebec.

Lower Egypt Region of Egypt usually considered to include the Nile delta and valley north of latitude 30° N. A rich, fertile region, it was united with Upper Egypt by Egyptian king Menes (*c*3100 BC).

Lowie, Robert Harry 1883–1957. American anthropologist. He studied North American Indians and wrote the influential *Primitive Society* and *Social Organization.*

Loyalists ⟨Tories⟩ American colonists who remained loyal to Britain during the American Revolution (1775–83). Loyalists, often government officials and professionals, were centered in New York, Pennsylvania, Georgia, and the Carolinas. Loyalist raids, notably those by W. and J. Butler, roused bitter hatred toward them among the Colonial patriots and led to passage of laws confiscating their property. A large number of the Loyalists, seeking the protection of the British, migrated to Canada.

Lo-yang Historic city (pop. 750,000) in north-central China. Founded during the Chou dynasty, it was the capital of that dynasty (from 771 BC) and was the capital at various intervals of succeeding dynasties, including the Han, Northern Wei, and Sui.

Loyola, Saint Ignatious of *See* **Ignatius of Loyola, Saint**

Lübeck Historic city (pop. 240,000) and major port located in northeastern West Germany. Founded 1143, it became a free city in 1226. It rose as a commercial center of medieval Europe and was headquarters (from 1358) of the Hanseatic League *(q.v.).* The city declined in the 16th cent.

Lublin, Union of Agreement (July 1, 1569) between Poland and Lithuania, merging the two kingdoms into a federated state under a single monarch. King Sigismund II, king of Poland and Lithuania, pressured Lithuanian nobles into accepting formal unification, which lasted to the end of the 18th cent.

Lucan AD 39–65. Roman poet who wrote *Bellum Civile* (often called *Pharsalia*), on the civil war between Caesar and Pompey. He was compelled to kill himself when his part in a conspiracy against Nero was discovered.

Lucania Ancient region of southern Italy. Once inhabited by Greeks and Lucanians, it was devastated by wars with Rome in the 3rd cent. BC.

Lucaris, Cyril of *See* **Jerusalem, Synod of**

Lucca Historic city (pop. 95,000) in north-central Italy. Founded by the Romans (2d cent. BC), it prospered from the 12th cent., when it became a free commune. The city was a center for the arts (12th–15th cents.), became a republic (15th cent.), and retained its freedom until the French conquest (1799). It became part of unified Italy in 1860.

Luce, Clare Boothe 1903–. American playwright and politician. Her plays include *The Women,* and *Kiss the Boys Goodbye.* She served as congresswoman from Connecticut (1943–47) and was ambassador to Italy (1953–56).

Luce, Henry Robinson 1898–1967. American publisher. He cofounded the weekly news magazine *Time* (1923), then founded *Fortune* (1930), *Life* (1936), and *Sports Illustrated* (1954).

Lucian *fl.* 2d cent. AD. Greek satirical author who wrote *Dialogues of the Gods* and *Dialogues of the Dead.*

Lucifer In Greek mythology, the planet Venus as the morning star. In the Bible, it is a name for Satan.

Lucilius, Gaius *See* **Lucillius, Caius**

Lucillius, Caius ⟨Lucilius, Gaius⟩ *c*180–102? BC. Latin poet. As the originator of Latin satire, he influenced Horace, Persius, and Juvenal.

Luckner, Felix, Graf von   1886–1966. German naval officer. He was known as the "Sea Devil" for his raids on commercial vessels during WW I. He destroyed more than $25 million worth of Allied shipping.

Lucrece ⟨Lucretia⟩ Legendary Roman matron known for her virtue. After being raped by Sextus Tarquinius, she killed herself. The incident was said to have provoked the Romans to revolt and drive out the Tarquin rulers.

Lucretia   *See* **Lucrece; Etruscans**

Lucretius ⟨Titus Lucretius Carus⟩ *c*99–*c*55 BC. Roman poet. Lucretius is renowned for his work *On the Nature of Things*, which is a poetic treatment of the philosophies and scientific theories of Epicurus and Democritus.

Lucullus *c*110–56 BC. Roman general. Serving under Sulla, he defeated Mithridates VI and made other conquests in Asia Minor.

Luddites   Bands of workingmen in England who attempted (1811–12, 1816) to destroy textile machinery. Fostered by low wages and unemployment, the movement began (1811) in Nottingham with night raids on textile factories to destroy equipment. The movement spread to other industrial areas, supposedly under the leadership of a mythical King Ludd (or Ned Ludd), and in 1812 harsh repressive measures were enacted to put an end to it. A brief resurgence of the movement was similarly dealt with.

Ludendorff, Erich von   1865–1937. German general. He was P. von Hindenburg's chief of staff during WW I and participated in A. Hitler's "beerhall putsch" (1923). He was a fanatic in his Aryan racist views.

Ludford Bridge, Battle of   *See* **Roses, Wars of the**

Luis   *See* **Louis**

Luke, Saint   Traditionally, author of the Third Gospel and the Acts of the Apostles. He is thought to have been a physician and was a companion of Saint Paul.

Lull, Ramon ⟨Lully, Raymond⟩ *c*1236–*c*1315. Catalan mystic and philosopher. He tried to convert the Muslims of North Africa to Christianity, and was said to have been stoned to death at Bougie.

Lully, Jean Baptiste   1632–87. French composer. He was composer to King Louis XIV and head of the Académie Royale de Musique. He developed the French overture form.

Lully, Raymond   *See* **Lull, Ramón**

Lumière, Louis Jean and **Auguste Marie Louis Nicolas**   1864–1948, 1862–1954. French brothers who invented the cinematograph for photographing and projecting movies.

Lumumba, Patrice Hemery   1925–61.   Political leader of Zaire (then called the Congo). He worked for its independence from Belgium and was its first prime minister (1960). He was murdered after being deposed in the unrest that followed independence.

Luna, Pedro de   1328–1423. Spanish ecclesiastic, antipope as Benedict XIII at Avignon (1394–1417) during the Great Schism. He proved able but was unwilling to relinquish his office to end the Great Schism. He was deposed (1417) by the Council of Constance (*q.v.*).

Lundy's Lane, Battle of ⟨Niagara, ~⟩ ⟨Bridgewater, ~⟩   Bloody but indecisive battle (July 25, 1814) during the War of 1812. Some 2,000–3,000 Americans, under Gen. W. Scott, advanced into southern Ontario, Canada, and at Lundy's Lane met 4,500 British soldiers, under Gen. Gordon Drummond. The battle raged into the night, when, with both sides exhausted, the Americans withdrew to Fort Erie.

Lunéville, Treaty of   Treaty (Feb. 9, 1801) between Austria and France, ending Austria's participation in the French Revolutionary Wars. It provided for the division of territories in Italy. It also restored Pope Pius VII to Rome and Ferdinand IV to Naples.

Lusitania   Ancient Roman province, including what is modern Portugal and part of western Spain. It was named for the Lusitani people, who resisted the Romans (2d cent. BC).

Lusitania   British ship that was torpedoed and sunk by a German submarine (May 7, 1915), with a loss of 1,195 lives. This incident was a factor in the US entry into WW I.

Lutetia ⟨Lutetia Parisiorum⟩ Roman name for what is now Paris, France.

Lutetia Parisiorum   *See* **Lutetia**

Luther, Martin   1483–1546.   German religious leader, father of the Protestant Reformation (*q.v.*) and founder of Lutheranism (*q.v.*). An Augustinian friar, he was ordained (1507), and subsequently was a professor (1511–46) at the University of Wittenberg, in Saxony. In ensuing years, he arrived at his fundamental doctrine of personal salvation through faith alone. This doctrine ultimately put him in conflict with the church practice (then widespread) of selling indulgences (*q.v.*), and, on Oct. 31, 1517, he nailed his famous Ninety-five Theses (*q.v.*) to the door of the church in Wittenberg to protest the practice. Thereafter Luther found wide support for his protest, refused to recant (1518), debated the Catholic

J. Eck (1519) in the famous but inconclusive Leipzig Debate, burned a papal bull condemning his views (1520), was thereupon excommunicated, and was called (1521) before the Diet of Worms (q.v.). During this period, he expanded the scope of reforms he sought, as set forth in three treatises: *Address to the Christian Nobility of the German Nation,* calling for German control of the German church; *The Babylonian Captivity of the Church,* attacking papal authority and denying the office of the priesthood as a link between God and man; and *The Freedom of a Christian Man,* reaffirming the doctrine of justification by faith alone. After the Diet of Worms ordered his arrest, Luther was given protection (1521–22) by the Elector Frederick III. He returned to Wittenberg, however, to try to prevent splits within the growing Reformation movement. The remainder of his years were spent in voluminous writing and in disputes with leaders of new sects spawned by his beliefs, including H. Zwingli and J. Calvin.

Lutheranism The branch of Protestant Christianity based on the teachings of M. Luther. Lutheranism stems from Luther's famous Ninety-five Theses (q.v.), which sparked the Protestant Reformation, though its doctrine is more conservative than that of Calvinist Reformed churches. Luther's doctrine stressed that man's salvation comes from faith alone, through the redeeming sacrifice of Jesus Christ; that the Scriptures constitute the one necessary guide to truth; and that the sacraments are valid only as aids to faith. The principal Lutheran statements of faith were the Augsburg Confession (q.v.), and Luther's two catechisms. These and other Lutheran documents were collected in the definitive Book of Concord (1580). Luther denied the sacrificial character of the Catholic Mass, and the Lutheran churches formed according to his doctrines abolished clerical celibacy, had communion administered under both kinds (bread and wine), and retained only the two sacraments of Baptism and the Lord's Supper. The Lutheran churches, organized around individual local congregations, were at first established state churches in the German principalities. Lutheranism also became the established church in Denmark, Finland, Norway, and Sweden. The Prussian state attempted to merge Lutheran churches forcibly with Reformed churches and this led to the first free Lutheran church (1817). This was the typical form Lutheranism assumed in North America, where it was first brought to Manhattan by Dutch settlers (1625) and to Fort Christina (modern Wilmington, Delaware) by Swedish settlers (1638). (*See also* Luther, Martin; Reformation.)

Lutzen, Battle of 1. Swedish victory (Nov. 16, 1632) in Saxony during the Thirty Years' War (1618–48). Swedish king Gustavus II, in an effort to aid German Protestant allies, attacked and defeated the army of the Holy Roman Empire, led by Count A. Wallenstein. **2.** Inconclusive battle (May 2, 1813) in the Napoleonic Wars (1803–15). Napoleon forced the allies to withdraw but did so at a cost of 20,000 casualties.

Luxembourg ⟨Luxemburg⟩ European grand duchy lying between Belgium, France, and Germany. Once a county of the Holy Roman Empire, it was made a duchy (1354) by Emperor Charles IV. It was subsequently ruled by the Spanish and Austrian Hapsburgs, was occupied by France (1794), and became a part of The Netherlands by the Congress of Vienna (1815). In 1867, it was declared a neutral, independent territory, although the Germans occupied it during WW I and WW II. Constitutional revisions (1948) ended Luxembourg's official neutral status.

Luxembourg, François Henri, duke of 1628–95. French general. He served under his cousin, the Great Condé, in the Fronde and led successful campaigns in Flanders during the War of the Grand Alliance (q.v.), defeating William of Orange at Steenkerke (1692) and Neerwinden (1693).

Luxemburg *See* **Luxembourg**

Luxemburg, Rosa 1870?–1919. German revolutionary. She was a founder of the Spartacus party (q.v.), which became the German Communist party. Arrested after WW I, she was murdered by soldiers.

Luynes, Charles d'Albert, duke of 1578–1621. French statesman. He was the favorite and chief adviser of Louis XIII and conspired with him to kill C. Concini and to exile Louis' mother, Marie de Médici. He worked to check the influence of nobles and Protestants.

Lvov Russian city (pop. 553,000) located in the Ukraine. Founded (1256) by a Ukrainian nobleman, it became an important medieval trading center. Austria assumed control of the city by the first Partition of Poland (1772), and, after serving as capital of the Ukrainian Republic (1918–1919), it was annexed by Poland (1921). Russia occupied it (1939), lost it to the Germans in WW II, and formally annexed it (1945).

Lvov, Prince Georgi Yevgenyevich 1861–1925. Russian statesman. A member of the first Duma (1905), he was head of the revolutionary Provisional Government from March to July, 1917. He resigned in favor of A. Kerensky.

Lyautey, Louis Hubert Gonzalve 1854–1934. French statesman and marshal. He was resident general of Morocco (1912–16, 1917–25), holding it against the Germans in WW I.

Lyceum Ancient Athenian school where Aristotle taught (founded 335 BC). He and his students were called Peripatetics because they strolled about the school grounds during lessons. The school declined soon after Aristotle's death.

Lycurgus In Greek tradition, the Spartan leader whose reforms of Spartan government and society created the characteristically militaristic Spartan way of life. He may have ruled in the 7th cent. BC.

Lydda ⟨Lod⟩ City in modern Israel mentioned in the Bible as the site of Peter's miracle. Traditionally, it is the home of England's patron saint, Saint George.

Lydia Ancient country of Asia Minor in what is now northwest Turkey. The tyrant Cyges founded the Mermnadae dynasty (685–546 BC), which built a powerful Lydian empire of great wealth. The Lydians are believed to have originated the use of coined money during this time. Croesus, the last ruler of independent Lydia, was defeated by Cyrus the Great of Persia (546 BC). Lydia later became a province under the Romans.

Lyell, Sir Charles 1797–1875. English geologist. He wrote *Principles of Geology* and *Elements of Geology* and was a leading exponent of uniformitarianism, the doctrine that the earth's surface was shaped by processes that continue to the present day.

Lyons City (pop. 457,400) in eastern France. Founded (43 BC) by the Romans, it was an early center of Christianity in Gaul. It was made part of the Holy Roman Empire (1032), saw the rise of the Waldenses *(q.v.)* in the 12th cent., and became part of French royal domains (1312). A center of the silk industry in the West from the 15th cent., Lyons suffered during the French Revolution. During WW II, it was a stronghold of the French Resistance.

Lyons, Councils of **1.** First (13th ecumenical council): Called (1245) by Pope Innocent IV during his struggle with Holy Roman Emperor Frederick II. With Rome under siege by Frederick, the pope used the session to excommunicate and depose Frederick. **2.** Second (14th ecumenical council): Called (1274) by Pope Gregory X to act on a pledge by Byzantine emperor Michael VIII to unite the Eastern church with the West. After concessions on the Filioque were made by delegates from the Greek church, the union was proclaimed. It was largely ignored, however, and was later repudiated by Andronicus II. The council also established procedures for election of the pope by cardinals, and ended the Interregnum by recognizing Rudolf I as Holy Roman Emperor.

Lyons, Joseph Aloysius 1879–1939. Australian statesman. He was a founder of the United Australia party (1931), and as prime minister (1931–39) brought about a period of economic stability.

Lysander d. 395 BC. Spartan military leader. He was admiral of the Spartan fleet that defeated Athens at Notium (407 BC) and that ended the Peloponnesian War by taking Athens in 404 BC.

Lysenko, Trofim Denisovich 1898–1976. Russian agronomist and biologist. As president of the Academy of Agricultural Sciences (1938–56, 1958–62), he tried to develop high-yield crops and to advance his unorthodox views of genetics.

Lysias c459–c380 BC. Greek orator and speech writer. His simple, unembellished and yet effective style had an important influence on Attic Greek prose.

Lysimachus c355–281 BC. Macedonian general under Alexander the Great. After Alexander's death, he took part in the Wars of the Diadochi *(q.v.)* and thereby became ruler of Thrace (and later Macedonia). He was killed in battle against Seleucus.

Lysippos *See* **Lysippus**

Lysippus ⟨Lysippos⟩ Greek sculptor in 4th cent. BC who changed the style of rendering the human figure, making the head smaller and the body more slender. He was a favorite of Alexander the Great.

M

Mabillon, Jean 1632–1707. French scholar. A Benedictine monk, he wrote *De re diplomatica*, which established the science of diplomatics, the study of historical sources.

Mabovitch, Goldie *See* **Meir, Golda**

Macao ⟨Macau⟩ Portuguese province (pop. 282,000) at the mouth of the Canton River in China. Settled by Portugal (1557), it was a major port until the rise of Hong Kong (19th cent.).

McAdoo, William Gibbs 1863–1941. American politician. As US secretary of the treasury (1913–18), he founded and was first chairman of the Federal Reserve Board (1913).

MacArthur, Douglas 1880–1964. American general. He was Allied commander of the Southwest Pacific during WW II and administrator of the Allied occupation of Japan. He was dismissed as commander of the UN forces in Korea by Pres. H. Truman (1951) after he publicly advocated a second drive into North Korea.

Macau *See* **Macao**

Macaulay, Thomas Babington 1800–54. English historian. His best-known work is *The History of England from the Accession of James the Second*.

McAuliffe, Anthony C. *See* **Bulge, Battle of the**

Macbeth d. 1057. Scottish king (1040–57). He killed his cousin Duncan to gain the throne and was himself killed and succeeded by Duncan's son Malcolm Canmore. His story was the basis for W. Shakespeare's play.

Maccabees ⟨Hasmoneans⟩ Family of Jewish rulers and patriots that ruled Palestine (2d-1st cent. BC). In reaction to suppression and persecution of Jewish religious observances by Seleucid king Antiochus IV, a Jewish priest named Mattathias (d. c166 BC) began (c168) a guerrilla war called the Revolt of the Maccabees. His third son, Judas Maccabeus (d. c161 BC), defeated Seleucid armies and expelled them (164) from Jerusalem. He then rededicated the Temple (commemorated by Hanukkah) and was killed during a subsequent Seleucid invasion. He was succeeded by his brother, Jonathan (d. 143 BC), who was successful against the Seleucids and became the Jewish high priest. Killed by the Seleucids, he was succeeded by Simon (d. 135 BC), who negotiated (142) independence for Judaea (southern Palestine) and was made high priest and governor. He was assassinated, and was succeeded by John Hyrcanus (d. 104 BC), his son, under whose rule Judaea reached its height. Later Judaean history was marked by the religious struggle between the Sadducees and the Pharisees. The last Maccabees to rule were the brothers Hyrcanus II (d. 30 BC) and Aristobulus II (d. 48 BC), who engaged in civil war against each other. The war was ended by the Roman general Pompey the Great, who conquered Jerusalem (63 BC), reduced Hyrcanus to religious rule, and established Roman political control over Judaea.

McCarthy, Eugene Joseph 1916–. US senator (1958–70). An opponent of the Vietnam War, he made an unsuccessful bid for the Democratic presidential nomination (1967).

McCarthy, Joseph Raymond 1909–57. American politician. US senator from Wisconsin (1947–57). As chairman of the Senate's Government Operations Committee, he ruined many careers by accusing government officials (and others) of Communist affiliations. He was censured by the Senate in 1954. His tactics gave rise to the term "McCarthyism."

McClellan, George Brinton 1826–85. Union general in the American Civil War. Made commander in chief (Nov., 1861), he stopped the Confederate advance at Antietam but was removed from command (Nov., 1862) because of his reluctance to engage the enemy. In 1864 he was an unsuccessful Democratic candidate for the presidency.

McClernand, John Alexander 1812–1900. Union general in the American Civil War. He fought at the Battle of Shiloh and commanded the Vicksburgh Campaign (1863) until superseded by Gen. U. Grant, and relieved of command for insubordination.

McClure, Sir Robert John Le Mesurier 1807–73. British naval officer. As commander of a ship in an Arctic expedition (1850–54), he was the first to complete a Northwest Passage, culminating the long search for a sea route from the Atlantic to the Pacific Ocean by way of the Arctic.

McClure, Samuel Sidney 1857–1949. American editor and publisher. He established the first US newspaper syndicate (1884) and founded (1893) *McClure's Magazine.*

McCormick, Cyrus Hall 1809–84. American inventor and manufacturer. He designed the McCormick reaper (1831). His company merged with others to form the International Harvester Company.

McCormick, Robert Rutherford 1880–1955. American editor and publisher. As editor and publisher of the *Chicago Tribune* (1920–55), he became a leader in conservative journalism. He opposed labor unions, the New Deal, and international involvement.

McCormick, Ruth Hanna 1880–1945. US politician. The daughter of M. Hanna, she served as Republican national committeewoman (1924–28) and congresswoman from Illinois (1929–31).

McCrae, John 1872–1918. Canadian physician and poet. A surgeon in the British Army in WW I, he wrote the famous poem *In Flanders Fields.*

McCulloch vs **Maryland** US Supreme Court decision (1819) confirming the powers of Congress to establish a federal bank. Chief Justice J. Marshall's ruling enhanced the powers of the federal government.

Macdonald, Alexandre 1765–1840. French general. He fought in the French Revolutionary Wars and was made marshal by Napoleon. He later served Louis XVIII.

Macdonald, Flora 1722–90. Scottish Jacobite heroine. She aided in the escape of Prince Charles Edward Stuart after his defeat at Culloden Moor (1746).

MacDonald, James Ramsey 1866–1937. English statesman, first British Labour party prime minister (1924, 1929–31, 1931–35).

Macdonald, Sir John Alexander 1815–91. Canadian statesman. He played a major role in the union of the Canadian provinces (1867) as the Dominion of Canada and was its first prime minister (1867–73, 1878–91).

Macdonough, Thomas 1783–1825. American naval officer. He defeated a superior British fleet (Sept. 11, 1814) on Lake Champlain in the War of 1812. His victory remains one of the great events of US naval history.

McDougall, Alexander 1731–86. American Revolutionary War general. He distinguished himself in the battles of White Plains and Germantown, and became commander of West Point (1780) after B. Arnold's plot to surrender West Point to the British failed. He was a member of the Continental Congress (1781–82, 1784–85).

MacDowell, Edward Alexander 1861–1908. American composer, known best for his symphonic poems and piano pieces.

McDowell, Irvin 1818–85. Union general in the American Civil War. He commanded at the first Battle of Bull Run (1861) and was superseded by Gen. G. McClellan. He was relieved of command after the second Battle of Bull Run (1862).

Macedonia European region on the Balkan Peninsula consisting of parts of Greece, Yugoslavia, and Bulgaria. Under Philip II (359–336 BC), ancient Macedon came to dominate Greece. Seat of the Macedonian Empire under Alexander the Great, it later was conquered by the Roman, Byzantine, and Ottoman empires. Various claims to the region led to the Balkan Wars (1912–13) and the division of the region, largely between Greece and Yugoslavia.

Macedonia, Kingdom of Ancient country located in northern Greece. Though the region was colonized by Greeks in the 8th cent. BC, Macedonia did not become a major power until the 4th cent. BC, when Philip II (q.v.) made his kingdom the dominant power in Greece. His conquests set the stage for the spectacular reign of his son, Alexander the Great (q.v.), who created a vast, but short-lived, Hellenistic empire (4th cent. BC) that extended as far east as India. Following Alexander's death (323), his generals fought against each other in the Wars of the Diadochi (q.v.) and eventually carved up that empire into a number of successor states. Macedonia proper, weakened by the wars, was restored (3d cent. BC) during the reigns of Cassander, Antigonus II, and Antigonus III. Under Philip V, however, it was defeated by Rome in the first two Macedonian Wars (q.v.). After the Third Macedonian War Rome divided up the kingdom and, in 146 BC, made it the first Roman province.

Macedonianism Religious heresy advanced by Macedonius (*fl.* AD 360), Bishop of Constantinople. It held that the Holy Spirit was not equal to the Father and the Son. Macedonianism was condemned by the Council of Constantinople (AD 381).

Macedonian Wars Four wars between the Kingdom of Macedonia (q.v.) and Rome that resulted in the complete domination of Greece by Rome. **1.** First (214–205 BC): King Philip V (q.v.) allied himself with Carthage against Rome during the Second Punic War, and the resultant conflict with Rome was the First Macedonian War. The war ended to Philip's advantage. **2.** Second (200–196 BC): This war was brought on by Philip V's attempts to expand his domains. The terms imposed by the victorious Romans were harsh and included subjugation by Rome and payment of tribute. **3.** Third (171–168 BC): Philip's son, Perseus, provoked the third war with Rome by trying to expand Macedonian control in Greece. Rome defeated him and divided Macedonia into four republics. **4.** Fourth (149–148 BC): The Romans this time put down a Macedonian revolt against their rule. Macedonia was thereafter reduced to a Roman province.

McGillivray, Alexander 1759–93. American Indian chief. A leader of the Creek Indians, he supported the British during the American Revolution. Later, with Spanish assistance, he successfully resisted American claims to Creek lands.

McGovern, George Stanley 1922–. American politician, US congressman (1957–61) and senator (1963–81) from South Dakota. A leader of the movement to end the Vietnam War, he was unsuccessful Democratic candidate for president (1972).

McGuffey, William Holmes 1800–73. American educator. He compiled the famous McGuffey Eclectic Readers, which were used in American schools for generations.

McHenry, Fort See **Fort McHenry**

Machado, Gerardo 1871–1939. Cuban political leader. As Cuba's president (1925–33), he attempted internal reforms, but his brutal suppression of opposition led to his downfall.

Machado de Assis, Joaquim Marie 1839–1908. Brazilian author, considered Brazil's greatest writer. His novels include *Memórias póstumas de Braz Cubas, Quincas Borba,* and *Dom Casmurro.*

Machiavelli, Niccolò 1496–1527. Italian statesman, author, and philosopher. A Florentine diplomat, he was imprisoned briefly by the Medici when they regained power (1512). After his release he turned to writing. His best-known work, *The Prince,* contains Machiavelli's thoughts on the methods by which a prince may acquire and make use of political power. It is thought that he used C. Borgia as the model for his cynical, ruthless prince.

Machu Picchu Ancient Incan city, located in the Andes mountains of Peru. First discovered (1911) by Hiram Bingham (1875–1956), it is one of the major pre-Columbian archaeological sites.

Mackenzie, Sir Alexander 1764?–1820. Canadian explorer. He charted the course of the Mackenzie River (1789) and made the first transcontinental journey across America north of Mexico (1793).

Mackenzie, William Lyon 1795–1861. Canadian journalist and political insurgent. He led an unsuccessful attempt (1837) to take over the government in Toronto

McKinley Tariff Act See **Harrison, Benjamin**

McKinley, William 1843–1901. Twenty-fifth US president (1897–1901), successor to G. Cleveland. He distinguished himself in the American Civil War, became a Republican congressman (1877–83, 1885–91) from Ohio and championed the establishment of high protective tariffs. He secured passage of the McKinley Tariff Act of 1890 but was defeated for reelection. Returning to Ohio, McKinley received the support of M. Hanna and the Ohio Democratic party, and became governor (1892–96). Chosen the Republican presidential candidate in 1896, he supported the party's gold platform and defeated the Democratic candidate, W. Bryan, who campaigned for free silver *(q.v.).* During McKinley's first term the US engaged in the Spanish-American War *(q.v.),* from which it emerged a world power and gained possession of Cuba and the Philippines. McKinley also presided over the annexation of Hawaii, and supported the Open Door policy in China. McKinley again opposed Bryan in the 1900 election and was reelected. He altered his stand on tariffs and began to support commercial reciprocity. He spoke on the subject at the Pan-American Exposition in Buffalo (Sept. 5, 1901), and the next day was shot by an anarchist, Leon Czolgosz. He died Sept. 14 and was succeeded by his vice-president, T. Roosevelt.

Mack von Leiberich, Baron Karl See **Ulm, Battle of**

MacLeish, Archibald 1892–. American poet, three times winner of the Pulitzer Prize (1933, 1953, 1959). He served as an adviser to President F. Roosevelt and as librarian of Congress (1939–44).

McLuhan, Herbert Marshall 1911–. Canadian educator and author. He is noted for his books on the effects electronic media have on society. Among them are *Understanding Media: The Extensions of Man* and *The Medium Is the Message: An Inventory of Effects.*

MacMahon, Marie Edmé Patrice Maurice de 1808–93. French marshal and statesman. A monarchist, he was the second president (1873–79) of the French Third Republic (1870–1940).

Macmillan, Daniel and **Macmillan, Alexander** 1813–57; 1818–96. Scottish booksellers and publishers. They founded (1844) the publishing firm of Macmillan and Company.

MacMillan, Maurice Harold 1894–. British statesman. As prime minister (1957–63), he sought to improve relations with the US after the

Suez Canal crisis, but failed to gain Great Britain's entry into the Common Market.

McNaughton, Andrew George Latta 1887–1966. Canadian army officer. He was commander of Canadian forces in England during WW II.

Macon, Nathaniel 1758–1837. American politician, US congressman (1791–1815) and senator (1815–28) from North Carolina. He was a strong supporter of T. Jefferson and states' rights.

Macon's Bill No. 2 *See* **Embargo Act**

Macready, William Charles 1793–1873. English actor and manager of Covent Garden theatre (1837–39) and of Drury Lane (1841–43). His rivalry with American actor Edwin Forrest (1806–72) sparked violence (May 10, 1849) at New York's Astor Place opera hall. In the ensuing riot more than 20 were killed.

McReynolds, James Clark 1862–1946. American jurist. Appointed associate justice to the Supreme Court (1914–41) by President W. Wilson, he was a strong opponent of the New Deal legislation.

Macrobius *fl.* AD *c*400. Latin author and philosopher. He wrote the *Saturnalia*, a series of dialogues.

Madagascar ⟨Democratic Republic of ~; *formerly* Malagasy Republic⟩ Island republic (pop. 8,740,000) located on Madagascar, off the southeast coast of Africa. Capital is Tananarive. First settled by Africans and Indonesians, Madagascar was discovered by the Portuguese (1500), and the French established tentative settlements on the island (1642 to late 18th cent.). Several independent kingdoms were once formed on Madagascar, but in the 18th cent. the Merina people began to establish their control over the island with British aid. During this period Christian missionaries and foreign trade were alternately encouraged and opposed by Merina rulers, until the reign (1868–83) of Queen Ranavalona II, who converted to Christianity. The last Merina ruler was Queen Ranavalona III (reigned 1883–96). The French declared a protectorate over Madagascar (1882), which was recognized by Britain and Germany (1890). The Merina resisted, heavy fighting broke out (1894–96), and the monarchy was abolished (1897). Madagascar was occupied by the British (1942) during WW II. In 1958 it became the Malagasy Republic, an autonomous state within the French Community, and on June 26, 1960, it became independent. Following the resignation of the president (1975) over continuing economic problems, Commander Didier Ratsiraka was installed (June, 1975) as president. Ratsiraka then began a program of nationalization.

Madero, Francisco Indalecio 1873–1913. Mexican president (1911–13). He was a leader in the revolution (1911) against Pres. P. Díaz. Unsuccessful as a reform president, he was arrested and murdered by order of V. Huerta.

Madison American city (pop. 170,600), capital city of Wisconsin. Founded in 1836, it is a major commercial and governmental center and seat of the University of Wisconsin.

Madison, Dolly 1768–1849. Wife of President J. Madison and famous Washington, D.C., hostess. Her letters and memoirs are a valuable source for early US history.

Madison, James 1751–1836. Fourth US president (1809–17), successor to T. Jefferson. An early opponent of British colonial policies, Madison served in the Virginia Convention (1776) and in the Continental Congress (1780–83), then served in the Virginia legislature (1784–86). As a delegate to the Annapolis Convention (*q.v.*) in 1786 he supported the call to convene the Federal Constitutional Convention (1787). There he became, with A. Hamilton, the leading force in the drafting of the Constitution. After the convention, he joined Hamilton and J. Jay in writing the Federalist Papers, which argued for adoption of the Constitution. As a congressman from Virginia (1789–97), he next supported establishment of the Bill of Rights and opposed the conservative policies followed by Hamilton and others. With T. Jefferson, he drafted the Virginia Resolutions (*see* Kentucky and Virginia Resolutions) in response to the Alien and Sedition Acts (*q.v.*). On Jefferson's election as president, Madison became secretary of state (1801–09). His support of a trade embargo against Britain (*see* Embargo Act) contributed to the outbreak of the War of 1812, which was fought during his terms as president (1809–17). Discontent with Madison's policies and his conduct of the war led in New England to the Hartford Convention (*q.v.*).

Madison, Marbury vs *See* **Marbury** vs. **Madison**

Madjapahit Empire *See* **Majapahit Empire**

Madoc ⟨Madog⟩ *fl.* 1170? Legendary Welsh prince said to have discovered America before C. Columbus.

Madog *See* **Madoc**

Mad Parliament *See* **Oxford, Provisions of**

Madras Indian city (pop. 2,469,400), located in southeastern India. Founded (1639) by the British East India Company, it is a major commercial and cultural center.

Madrid Capital city (pop. 3,520,300) of Spain and of Madrid province. Originally a Moorish fortress, it was captured (1083) by Alfonso VI of Castile and became the Spanish capital (1561) under King

Philip II. The scene of a revolt against the French (1808) during the Peninsular War, Madrid was a Loyalist stronghold against the forces of F. Franco during the Spanish Civil War until its fall (1939).

Madrid, Treaty of Treaty (Jan. 14, 1526) between Hapsburg emperor Charles V and his prisoner, French King Francis I, temporarily ending the Italian Wars *(q.v.)* between France and Spain. The treaty was never ratified, and Francis subsequently renounced its provisions.

Maecenas *d.* 8 BC. Roman statesman. He was adviser to Emperor Augustus and a noted patron of the arts. Among his friends were Horace and Vergil.

Maerlant, Jacob van *c*1235–*c*1300. A Flemish poet. He wrote didactic poetry, the most famous being *Spiegel Historiael*, an adaptation of Vincent of Beauvais' *Speculum Historiale*.

Maeterlinck, Maurice 1862–1949. Belgian symbolist poet and dramatist. His play *Pelléas et Mélisande* (1892) was the inspiration for C. Debussy's opera. He was awarded the Nobel Prize for Literature in 1911.

Mafia *(in recent times*, Cosa Nostra) Notorious crime organization that originated in Sicily. Currently active in the US, S. America, and elsewhere, the group is involved in illegal and quasilegal (business) ventures. The Mafia dates from the 13th cent. and operated in Sicily (18th–19th cent.) as autonomous bands of criminals. Noted for their use of terrorism, bloody vendettas, and vows of secrecy, the Mafia bands resisted government campaigns to suppress them (late 19th, early 20th cent.). The group spread to the US in the last years of the 19th cent. Using tactics of their forebears and aided by widespread evasion of the law during Prohibition, organized Mafia "families" built a nationwide crime syndicate that now dominates organized crime in the US.

Magdeburg, sack of Destruction (May 20, 1631) of the city of Magdeburg, now in East Germany, during the Thirty Years' War. Imperial forces under J. Tilly successfully stormed the city and killed its defenders. Fires broke out, and virtually the whole city was destroyed.

Magellan, Ferdinand *c*1480–1521. Portuguese navigator and explorer. Sponsored by Spanish king Charles I (later Holy Roman Emperor Charles V), Magellan set out (1519) to find a western sea route to the Molucca Islands (Spice Islands). He sailed the strait that bears his name, and discovered the Philippines. Though he died in the Philippines (1521), his expedition continued west, under J. Cano, becoming the first to circumnavigate the globe.

Magenta, Battle of French-Piedmontese victory (June 4, 1859) over Austria near Milan, Italy. The Austrian loss advanced the cause of Italian unity.

Magi Members of a priestly caste in ancient Persia. They became priests of the Zoroastrian religion and were considered wise men. The word "magic" comes from "magi." In Christian tradition, the Magi (or Three Kings) brought gifts to the newborn Jesus Christ. The three were Caspar, Melchior, and Balthazar.

Maginot, André *See* **Maginot Line**

Maginot Line Network of fortifications on the French-German frontier. Named for war minister André Maginot (1877–1932), who supervised its construction, it was supposedly impregnable to any German assault. During WW II the Germans bypassed the line, attacking through Belgium and thus rendering the line useless.

Magliabechi, Antonio 1633–1714. Italian bibliophile. He was court librarian (1673–1714) to Cosimo III de Medici, grand duke of Tuscany. His 30,000-volume library is now part of the National Library in Florence.

Magna Carta (Magna Charta) English charter, important in the development of British constitutional law and a symbol (mainly by later interpretations) of basic liberties. Angered by King John's heavy taxation and abuses of power, the barons and the church united to force him (by threat of civil war) to sign the document at Runnymede on June 19, 1215. Originally written to guarantee rights of the nobility, it contained provisions for church freedom, trial by jury, habeas corpus, and matters of minor import. John later attempted to void the charter and died in the resulting civil war. However, it was reaffirmed by his son, Henry III, in 1216, 1217, and 1225.

Magna Charta *See* **Magna Carta**

Magna Graecia Ancient Greek colonies in southern Italy. Established in the 8th cent. BC, they thrived in the 7th and 6th cents. BC, but soon after began their decline.

Magnesia, Battle of *See* **Antiochus III**

Magnetius *See* **Mursa, Battle of**

Magnus I (Magnus the Good) 1024–47. King of Norway (1035–47) and Denmark (1042–47), son of Olaf II. He succeeded Danish king Harthacanute (1042), thereby joining Norway and Denmark. He attempted to press Harthacanute's claim to the English throne but was unsuccessful.

Magnus VI 1238–80. Norwegian King (1263–80), son of Haakon IV. He established a comprehensive system of law in Norway.

Magnus VII 1316–73. King of Sweden (1319–63) and Norway (1319–55), successor to his grandfather Haakon V. A weak ruler, he lost the

Norwegian crown to his son Haakon VI and the Swedish throne to his nephew Albert, duke of Mecklenburg (1340?–1412), who ruled as Albert III.

Magnus the Good *See* **Magnus I**

Magruder, John Bankhead 1810–71. Confederate general in the American Civil War. He defeated Gen. B. Butler at Big Bethel (June 1861) and later commanded Confederate forces in the Peninsular Campaign (1862).

Magyars People, living primarily in Hungary, who speak the Hungarian language of the Finno-Ugric family. Descended from nomadic peoples who migrated from the Urals (5th cent.), they also include groups living in Romania, Yugoslavia, Czechoslovakia, and the Ukraine.

Mahabharata One of the two great Sanskrit epics (with the Ramayana) of ancient India. The 18-book work, composed between 200 BC and AD 200, is a complex merging of Indian history and Hindu religious lore. The Mahabharata contains the Bhagavad-Gita, the most important single religious text in Hinduism.

Mahadi, Muhammad Ahmed 〈Muhammad Ahmed〉 1843?–85. Muslim leader who claimed he was the Mahdi. He led a successful revolution against the Egyptian occupation of the Sudan, and defeated the British at Khartoum (1885).

Mahamaya *See* **Buddha**

Mahan, Alfred Thayer *See* **Sea Power**

Maharashtra, Kingdom of *See* **Marathas, Kingdom of**

Mahavira 〈Vardhamana〉 c599–527 BC. Last of the 24 tirthankaras (saints) who founded the Indian religion of Jainism. He established a monastic order that practiced asceticism and respect for all life.

Mahayana A leading form of Buddhism, practiced in China, Japan, Korea, and Tibet, and noted for its more liberal treatment of Buddhist doctrine.

Mahdi In Islam, a leader who will appear at the end of the world to save true believers. Although this is not mentioned in the Koran, there have been several claimants to the title.

Mahican Indians 〈Mohican ~〉 North American Indian tribe that lived in the upper Hudson Valley. They were dispersed in the mid-17th cent. as a result of wars with the Mohawks. A number of Mohicans settled in Stockbridge, Mass.

Mahler, Gustav 1860–1911. Austrian composer and conductor. He is known best for his nine symphonies and his unfinished tenth symphony.

Mahmud II 1784–1839. Ottoman sultan (1808–39). During his reign, territory was lost to Russia,

Syria was ceded to Egypt, and Greece became independent.

Mahone, William 1826–95. Confederate general in the American Civil War and US politician. As US senator from Virginia (1881–87), he was a powerful leader in Virginia politics after Reconstruction.

Mahrattas, Kingdom of *See* **Marathas, Kingdom of**

Maia In Greek mythology, the eldest of the Pleiades, daughters of Atlas. She was the mother of Hermes by Zeus.

Maida, Battle of Battle (July 4, 1806) at Maida, southern Italy, during the Napoleonic Wars. Some 5,000 British troops under Gen. John Stuart defeated a French force led by Gen. Jean Reynier (1771–1814), thereby halting the French advance south.

Mailer, Norman 1923–. American writer, noted for his incorporation of factual material within a fictional framework. Among his books are *The Naked and the Dead, The Deer Park, The Armies of the Night,* and *The Executioner's Song.*

Maillol, Aristide 1861–1944. French artist. Originally a painter and tapestry designer, he became famous for his massive statues of female nude figures.

Maimonides 〈Maimun, Moses ben〉 1135–1204. Spanish-born Jewish philosopher, considered one of the greatest influences on Jewish thought. He wrote a commentary on the Mishna, the *Mishneh Torah,* and a *Guide for the Perplexed.*

Maimun, Moses ben *See* **Maimonides**

Maine Northeastern US state (pop. 1,124,700), the 23rd state. The Maine coast had long been known to mariners of various countries, and the entire region was granted to the Plymouth Company in 1606. The first English settlement failed (1607), but there were several successful settlements by the time Maine was annexed to Massachusetts (1652). Conflict with the French and Indians slowed the area's development, and there was dissatisfaction with Massachusetts rule. Maine was admitted to the Union in 1820. The Aroostook War *(q.v.)* led to the Webster-Ashburton Treaty settling the US boundary with Canada.

Maine US battleship whose destruction in the harbor of Havana (Feb. 15, 1898) precipitated US entry into the Spanish-American War.

Maintenon, Françoise d'Aubigné, marquise de 1635–1719. Second wife of King Louis XIV of France. She was governess for his illegitimate children and married him morganatically (1685?).

Maipu, Battle of Battle (Apr. 5, 1818), near Santiago, Chile. Here J. de San Martin defeated Spanish royalist forces and gained independence for Chile.

Maitland, William 1528?–73. Scottish statesman. A supporter and adviser of Mary Queen of Scots, he worked for the unification of England and Scotland under her rule.

Majapahit Empire ⟨Madjapahit ~⟩ ⟨Modjopahit ~⟩ Hindu kingdom that flourished in Java (1315th cents.). The Majapahit period is regarded as a golden age in the history of Java. The kingdom was centered in eastern Java, though its extent at the height of its power is uncertain. Founded (1292) by King Vijaya, the kingdom reached its zenith under Vijaya's grandson, King Hayam Wuruk (1350–89), and his minister Gajah Mada. Muslim states that emerged in northern Java conquered the Majapahit kingdom in the late 15th cent.

Majorian d. AD 461. Roman emperor of the West (AD 457–461). He became emperor with the support of Ricimer and worked to reform tax laws. After his defeat by Gaiseric (AD 460), he abdicated and was murdered on Ricimer's orders.

Makarios III ⟨Mouskos, Mihail Christodoulou⟩ 1913–77. Archbishop of the Orthodox Church of Cyprus. A leader in the enosis movement for union with Greece, he became first president of independent Cyprus (1959–77). His ouster in 1974 was followed by the crisis in Cyprus *(q.v.)* and his return to power that year.

Malacca ⟨Melaka⟩ Malayan state. Malacca has in turn been ruled by the Portuguese, Dutch, English, and Japanese. It became part of Malaysia in 1963.

Malachy, Saint 1095–1148. Irish archbishop and church reformer. He established territorial hierarchy in the Irish church and founded (1142) Mellifont, the first Cistercian abbey in Ireland.

Malagasy Republic *See* **Madagascar**

Malan, Daniel François 1874–1959. South African statesman. As prime minister (1948–54), he established apartheid laws for the separation of the races.

Malatesta Italian family which ruled Rimini and the area around it from the 13th to 16th cents. Prominent members were Malatesta da Verucchio (d. 1312), a leader of the Guelphs, and Sigismondo Pandolfo Malatesta (1417–68).

Malatesta, Sigismondo Pandolfo *See* **Malatesta**

Malawi ⟨ Republic of Malawi; *formerly* Nyasaland⟩ Republic in southeast Africa. First explored (1859) by D. Livingstone, the region was annexed by Britian (1891) as the British Central African Protectorate. Renamed Nyasaland, it became (1953) part of the Federation of Rhodesia and Nyasaland. Opposition to the Federation formed

in Nyasaland, and it was abolished (1963). Nyasaland became independent as Malawi (1964) and became a republic (1966).

Malaya Peninsula of Southeast Asia, now divided between Malaysia and Singapore.

Malaysia Constitutional monarchy located in Southeast Asia. It is divided into two parts: West Malaysia, on the Malay peninsula, and East Malaysia, on the island of Borneo. Its capital is Kuala Lumpur. Key dates in the history of Malaysia include:

1511 Portugal occupied Malacca on the Malay peninsula.

1641 Dutch captured Malacca.

1786 British East India Company given rights to the island of Penang.

1800 Sultan of Kedah gave British rights to Province of Wellesley on the mainland.

1816 Siam, extending control into region, acquired Perah.

1819 Britain founded Singapore.

1821 Siam acquired Kedah.

1824 Treaty of London defined British and Dutch spheres of influence; Britain acquired Malacca; Straits Settlement created joint administration for Penang, Malacca, and Singapore.

1874 Pankor Engagement; marked beginning of British domination of Malay states following period of unrest, civil wars, and piracy.

1896 Federated Malay states created; British resident general named.

1909 Britain gained control of additional territory from Siam.

1940–45 Japan occupied Malaya for duration of WW II.

1946–48 Britain resumed control; created unpopular Union of Malaya (1946), replaced (Feb. 1, 1948) by Federation of Malaya.

1948–50 Communist insurrection ("The Emergency"); 500,000 Chinese residents resettled because most Communists involved were Chinese.

1957 Malaya gained independence; joined the British Commonwealth; admitted to UN.

1963 Singapore, Sabah, and Sarawak joined (Sept. 16) federation, establishing Federation of Malaysia; federation opposed by Indonesia, which mounted guerrilla war (1963–65).

1965 Singapore (with large ethnic Chinese population) seceded from the federation.

1969 Violence followed Chinese electoral gains; parliament suspended.

1970–76 Tun Abdul Razak in office as prime minister.

1976–81 Datuk Hussein bin Onn in office as prime minister.

1978 "Boat people" fleeing Vietnam poured into Malaysia.

1978 Official ban on "boat people" ended (Nov.) when several hundred drowned off Malaysian coast.

1981– Datuk Seri Mahathir bin Muhammad in office as prime minister.

Malchus *See* **Porphyry**

Malcolm III ⟨Malcolm Canmore⟩ d. 1093. Scottish king (1057–93), successor to Macbeth, whom he killed in battle. He gave refuge to Edgar the Aetheling and married Edgar's sister, Saint Margaret. He was killed on a raid into England.

Malcolm Canmore *See* **Malcolm III**

Malcolm X ⟨Little, Malcolm⟩ 1925–65. American black leader. A militant Black Muslim, he preached separation from whites, but later came to believe that blacks and whites might be able to live together. He became involved in a struggle within the Black Muslim movement and was assassinated.

Malebranche, Nicolas de *See* **Cartesianism**

Malenkov, Georgi Maksimilianovich 1901–. Soviet statesman and Communist leader. He became premier and party secretary (briefly, in 1953) after the death of J. Stalin (1953) but was forced to resign as premier, following a policy struggle with N. Khrushchev and others.

Malevich, Casimir *See* **suprematism**

Mali ⟨Republic of Mali; *formerly* French Sudan, Sudanese Republic⟩ Independent republic located in western Africa. Capital is Bamako. Many early African empires flourished in the region, including the Mali Empire, which reached its peak in the 14th cent., and the Songhai Empire of the 15th and 16th cents. A period of warfare and invasion ensued until the rise of new Muslim states (19th cent.). The French conquered much of the region by 1898, and Mali, as French Sudan, became part of French West Africa. Rising nationalism in the 20th cent. led to formation of the Sudanese Union, which soon became Mali's leading political party. Under Modibo Keita (1915–) the party campaigned for independence. In 1958 French Sudan became autonomous, within the French Community, as the Sudanese Republic, and in 1960 it became independent as the Republic of Mali. Keita, its first president, followed a Socialist course until his overthrow (1968). Gen. Moussa Traoré subsequently became head of state (1968–). In the early 1970s Mali was devastated by a severe drought and famine.

Malik Shah *See* **Seljuks**

Malinowski, Bronislaw 1884–1942. Polish-born anthropologist. He formulated the functional theory of social anthropology.

Mallarmé, Stéphane 1842–98. French poet. He was an early symbolist. His best-known poem, *L'Après-Midi d'un faune,* inspired C. Debussy's musical composition of the same name.

Mallon, Mary *See* **Typhoid Mary**

Malone, Edmund 1741–1812. English scholar and editor. He produced an important chronology of the works of W. Shakespeare and exposed the Shakespearean forgeries of W. Ireland.

Malory, Sir Thomas d. 1471. English author of the medieval prose romance *Morte d'Arthur.* This account of King Arthur and his Round Table is considered one of the greatest prose works in the English language.

Malpighi, Marcello 1628–94. Italian physician noted for his studies of anatomy and his early use of the microscope for animal and plant study.

Malplaquet, Battle of Battle (Sept. 11, 1709) of the War of the Spanish Succession. The allied army of English, Dutch, and Austrians under J. Churchill, duke of Marlborough, and Prince Eugene of Savoy, forced the French to withdraw. Casualties were so heavy, however, that the allies were obliged to halt their advance on Paris.

Malraux, André 1901–. French author and political figure. Active in the political struggles of his time, he used his experiences in such novels as *La Condition humaine* and *L'Espoir.*

Malta Independent island state in the Mediterranean, comprising the islands of Malta, Gozo, and Comino, and several islets. Occupied by the British from 1800, it was the scene of fierce bombing by the Germans and Italians during WW II. It became independent in 1964 and a republic (Dec. 13, 1974), within the British Commonwealth. British military presence was ended in 1979.

Malthus, Thomas Robert 1766–1834. English economist. His *An Essay on the Principle of Population* contended that population would always increase faster than means of subsistence.

Malvinas Islands Argentine name for Falkland Islands *(q.v.).*

Mamelukes Warrior class that provided rulers of Egypt from 1250 until the conquest by Ottoman Turks (1517). Of Asian stock, Mamelukes were first used as slaves and then as warriors by the Muslim rulers of Egypt. The Bahrite dynasty of Mameluke sultans (1250–1382) was founded by Aybak (d. 1257), and their rule was characterized by internal dissent and frequent rebellions. Nevertheless, the Bahrite Mamelukes halted the Mongol advance (1260) in Syria and crushed the powerful Assassin sect. During the bloody reign of the Burjite dynasty of Mamelukes (1382–1517), the Egyptians warred against Tamerlane, expelled Christian knights from Cyprus, and finally succumbed (1517) to the Ottoman Turks under Selim I. Under the Turks, the Mamelukes retained their lands and many government posts and eventually regained considerable autonomy. They retained power in Egypt until 1811, when they were virtually exterminated by the Egyptian ruler Muhammad Ali.

Mamun, al- 786–833. Seventh Abbassid caliph (813–33), son of Harun ar-Rashid and successor to his brother al-Amin. A Mutazilite, he tried to impose that sect's rationalistic beliefs on his subjects.

Managua Capital (pop. 398,500) and largest city of Nicaragua. Made capital (1857), it was largely destroyed by earthquake and fire (1931), and again by earthquake (1972).

Manassas, Battle of *See* **Bull Run, Battle of**

Manchu *See* **Ch'ing**

Manchukuo Puppet state established (1932) in Manchuria by the Japanese. Its nominal ruler was Henry Pu Yi, last Ch'ing emperor. It ceased to exist (1945) when Manchuria was returned to China after WW II.

Manchuria Major industrial region, northeastern China. Home of the Manchus, who established the Manchu (Ch'ing) dynasty in China (1644–1912), it has been the object of struggles between China, Russia, and Japan. Russia and Japan fought for control of it in the Russo-Japanese War (1904–05). Japan occupied Manchuria (1931–32) and set up the puppet state of Manchukuo (1932–45). Returned to China (1945), it became a Chinese Communist stronghold by 1948.

Mancini, Pasquale Stanislao 1817–88. Italian political leader. A liberal and anticlerical, he introduced numerous reforms. As minister of foreign affairs (1881–85) he negotiated the Triple Alliance (1882) with Austria and Germany.

Manco Capac *d.* 1544. Inca ruler. Kept prisoner by F. Pizarro, he escaped (1536), raised an army, and laid seige to Cuzco. Defeated, he continued to fight in the mountains, but was murdered by followers of another rebel leader, D. de Almagro.

Mandaeans ⟨Christians of Saint John⟩ Religious group of Iran and Iraq. They revere John the Baptist and place emphasis on the rite of baptism and fertility worship.

Mandarin Formerly, a Chinese imperial official. The dialect spoken by Chinese officials was known as Mandarin Chinese and in its modern form is the most widely used dialect in China.

mandate Designation for a colonial territory placed under the control of another power by the League of Nations. The system of mandates was used after WW I to provide for those former German and Turkish territories (including Iraq, Palestine, Syria, and Southwest Africa) that were deemed unable to govern themselves. Mandates still in effect in 1946 became UN trusteeships.

Mandeville, Sir John *fl.* 14th cent. English author. He wrote *The Travels of Sir John Mandeville*, a romanticized travel account that gained great popularity. It was based largely on the travels of such figures as M. Polo. Little is known of the author.

Manet, Édouard 1832–83. French artist. His paintings, such as *Déjeuner sur l'herbe*, influenced the development of impressionism. Manet painted realistic subject matter and developed a characteristic use of color and brush technique that challenged the then conventional academic style. His first showings met with protest and criticism from established art circles, but he was soon joined by other emerging impressionist painters of his day. His other noted works include *Olympia, Bar at the Folies-Bergère*, and *At the Café*.

Manfred c1232–66. Sicilian king (1258–66), natural son of Holy Roman Emperor Frederick II. He opposed papal authority over Sicily, but was killed in battle against the forces of Charles of Anjou, who claimed the throne.

Manhattan Project US project inaugurated (1942) to develop the atomic bomb during WW II. Placed (Aug., 1942) under command of Gen. Leslie R. Groves (1896–1970), the project scientists created the first self-sustaining nuclear chain reaction (at Chicago, Dec. 2, 1942) and exploded the first nuclear device (July 16, 1945) near Alamogordo, New Mexico. The project produced the bombs dropped on Hiroshima (Aug. 6) and Nagasaki (Aug. 9). By hastening the Japanese surrender it saved countless American lives, but its success ushered in a new age, in which total war is unthinkable.

Manichaeanism *See* **Manichaeism**

Manichaeism ⟨Manichaeanism⟩ Religious sect founded in 3d cent. AD Persia, on the teachings of Mani (*fl.* 3d cent.). It drew on Gnosticism, Zoroastrianism, and Christianity. Manichaeism was a dualistic religion which held the universe was divided into the forces of God and light and the forces of Satan and evil. Man had both, the spirit being light and goodness, the body itself being evil. The sect spread rapidly for a time, though by the 6th cent. it had largely disappeared in the West.

Manifest Destiny Historical expression used to justify US expansion in the 1840s. It held that America was chosen by God to establish its dominion from sea to sea, and was used to support American annexation of Texas and territories in the West and Mexico.

Manila Filipino city (pop. 1,438,300), former capital and leading city of the Philippines. The Battle of Manila Bay (q.v.) was fought here during the Spanish-American War. Manila was occupied by the Japanese during WW II.

Manila Bay, Battle of US naval victory (May 1, 1898) during the Spanish-American War, at Manila. The US fleet under Commodore G. Dewey completely destroyed the Spanish Pacific fleet, thereby securing the Philippines from Spanish control.

Manin, Daniele 1804–57. Venetian statesman. He helped to free Venice from Austrian rule. Made president of the Venetian republic (1848), he unsuccessfully opposed union with Sardinia. He led a valiant but fruitless struggle against Austrian forces until Venice's fall (Aug., 1849).

Man in the Iron Mask Anonymous French prisoner, held captive and masked in the Bastille from 1698 until his death in 1703. His identity remains unknown.

Manitoba Canadian province. First settled (17th cent.) by the Hudson's Bay Company, it was contested by the British and French in the French and Indian Wars, and was ceded to Britain by the Treaty of Paris (1763). It became a province in 1870.

Maniu, Iuliu 1873–1951. Romanian statesman. Leader of the Romanian National Peasants' party and prime minister (1928–30, 1932–33), he was convicted of treason (1947) by the Communists and died in prison.

Manlius Capitolinus, Marcus d. 384? BC. Roman consul (392 BC). Awakened one night by the cackling of geese, he discovered and repulsed an attack on Rome by the Gauls (390).

Manlius Imperiosus Torquatus, Titus fl. 4th cent. BC. Roman dictator and consul. He fought against the Gauls and Latins, and put his son to death for disobeying orders not to engage the enemy in single combat.

Mann, Horace 1796–1859. American educator. As the first secretary of the Massachusetts state board of education (1837–48), he developed theories and practices that greatly influenced the development of public education in the US.

Mann, Thomas 1875–1955. German novelist, considered one of the preeminent writers of the 20th cent. Awarded the Nobel Prize in 1929, Mann was forced to flee Germany (1933) by the rise of A. Hitler. He became a US citizen in 1944. Among his works are *Death in Venice, The Magic Mountain*, and *Doctor Faustus*.

Mann Act US law (1910) which prohibits the transportation of women across state lines for immoral purposes.

Mannerheim, baron Carl Gustav Emil von 1867–1951. Finnish military leader and statesman. He established the Mannerheim Line (q.v.) and commanded Finnish forces in the Russo-Finnish War. He later served as president of Finland (1944–46).

Mannerheim Line Finnish fortification across the Karelian Isthmus. Built under the direction of C. Mannerheim to prevent Soviet aggression, it fell to Russian forces (1940) in the Russo-Finnish War.

mannerism European art style of the 16th cent., characterized by exaggeration, and the disconcerting use of color, form, and spatial relationships. Arising as a reaction to High Renaissance art, it was in turn replaced by the baroque style.

Mannheim, Karl 1893–1947. German sociologist. His book *Ideologie und Utopie* explored the role of individual thought processes and their relation to social conflict.

manorial system ⟨Seigniorial system⟩ Medieval economic system in which a lord gave a peasant the right to tend land on his estate in return for a fixed payment. The system, derived from feudalism, flourished in Europe in the 11th-15th cents., and similar systems arose elsewhere, notably in Japan.

Mansard, François *See* **Mansart, François**

Mansart, François ⟨Mansard, François⟩ 1598–1666. French architect. He is noted for his incorporation of classical elements into baroque architecture. The mansard roof is named after him.

Mansfeld, Peter Ernst, Graf von 1580?–1626. Mercenary in the Thirty Years' War (1618–48). He supported the Protestants, notably Elector Palatine Frederick V.

Mansur ⟨Al Mansur⟩ d. 775. Second Abbasid caliph (754–75), successor to his brother Abu al-Abbas. He founded the city of Baghdad (762).

Mansur ⟨al-Mansur⟩ 934–1002. Regent of Córdoba under the caliph Hisham II. Assuming complete control, he led many victorious campaigns against Christian cities, and temporarily restored Ummayyad influence in Spain.

Mantegna, Andrea 1431–1506. Italian painter. One of the greatest artists of his day, he is especially noted for his frescoes in Padua, Milan, and Verona.

Mantua, Siege of French campaign (July, 1796–Feb., 1797) of Napoleon Bonaparte against an Austrian army besieged at Mantua, Italy. Napoleon held off four separate Austrian relief attempts, and Mantua ultimately surrendered (Feb. 2), leaving Napoleon virtual master of Italy.

Mantuan Succession, War of the Conflict during the Thirty Years' War in which France and the Hapsburgs both sought control of the Italian duchy of Mantua. The Treaty of Cherasco (Apr.

26, 1631) awarded the duchy to Charles of Nevers, a member of the French Gonzaga family.

Manu Hindu mythical figure, the first man, from whom all humanity descends. He was, by tradition, author of the Sanskrit code of law.

Manuel ⟨Manuel I Comnenus⟩ 1120–80. Byzantine emperor (1143–80), successor to his father John II. He hoped to rebuild the Roman Empire but was defeated by the Turks at Myriocephalon (1176).

Manuel I ⟨Emanuel I⟩ 1469–1521. Portuguese king (1495–1521), successor to John II. During his reign, Portugal became a major commercial power through the voyages of discovery of V. da Gama and P. Cabral.

Manuel I Comnenus See **Manuel**

Manuel II Palaeologus 1350–1425. Byzantine emperor (1391–1425), successor to his father John V Palaeologus. He sought aid from the kingdoms of Europe to fight the Turks but was unsuccessful. In 1422 he was forced to pay tribute to Murad II.

Manuel II 1889–1932. Portuguese king (1908–10), son of Charles I. He succeeded to the throne after his father and brother were assassinated and was deposed by the republican revolution.

Manx Language of the Goidelic group of the Celtic subfamily, once spoken on the Isle of Man but now practically extinct.

Manzikert, Battle of Byzantine-Turkish battle (1071) at Manzikert, now in Turkey. Some 70,000 Seljuk Turks destroyed an army of 40,000 under Byzantine emperor Romanus IV. The battle led to the fall of Asia Minor to the Turks.

Maoism Ideology of revolutionary communism developed by Mao Tse-tung. Mao's thinking is generally considered allied with, but distinct from, Russian communism. Mao early on perceived the value of mobilizing China's peasant class, ignored by traditional Marxists in favor of the proletariat as a source of revolution. By arousing a martial spirit (a fundamental element of Maoist doctrine), Mao succeeded in bringing Chinese peasants to revolution. Once in power, Mao turned away from the traditional Communist pathway to economic development. He opposed formation of a bureaucratic elite and instituted his Great Leap Forward (q.v.), which fostered labor-intensive, backyard industries. When this program failed, he again resorted to the martial spirit to purge the party of bureaucrats and elitists, this time with the disastrous Cultural Revolution (q.v.).

Maori Wars Wars (1860–72) between Maoris, native inhabitants of New Zealand, and British settlers seeking Maori lands on the North Island of New Zealand. As a result of the Maori King Movement, the natives on the North Island elected a king (1858) and adopted a general policy of refusing to sell native-owned lands to the settlers. A breach of that policy resulted in the first phase of the Maori Wars (1860–61), which ended in a truce. Officials of the British government provoked the second phase of fighting (1863–64), which embroiled the whole North Island in war. The settlers emerged victorious, only to find themselves in another war (1864–72) against more fanatical elements of the Maori tribes. Peace was finally established (1872), with large portions of Maori lands in the possession of the settlers. An earlier uprising (1843–48) is sometimes called the First Maori War.

Mao Tse-tung 1893–1976. Chinese Communist leader, founder and first chairman (1949–59) of the People's Republic of China. Born to a peasant family in Hunan province, Mao became a founding member of the Chinese Communist Party. After the split between the Nationalist Kuomintang and the Communists, Mao lead an abortive peasant revolt known as the Autumn Harvest Uprising (1927). Continuing to oppose the Kuomintang, Mao helped to set up the Kiangsi Soviet (q.v.) in southeastern China and became its chairman (1931). Nationalist military successes against the Communists forced the Red Army to make its famed Long March (q.v.) of some 6,000 miles to Shensi province in northwestern China (1934–35). There, Mao established Communist control in the region and began the long struggle against nationalist Kuomintang (see Chinese Civil War) and the invading Japanese (1937–45) during WW II. The last phase of the civil war with the nationalists broke out soon after WW II, and in 1949 the Communists established control over China.

Mao, who had become chairman of the Chinese Communist Party (CCP) in 1935, became chairman of the new People's Republic of China (1949). In following years Mao sought to establish communism in China independently of the Russian model and sought to adapt Marxist ideology to Chinese society. During this period China entered the Korean War (q.v.). In order to build the Chinese economy, Mao instituted the Great Leap Forward (1958), a disastrous economic experiment that led to the rise of Liu Shao-ch'i (q.v) as chairman of the republic. Mao retained his position as chairman of the CCP. The struggle between Liu and Mao led to the Cultural Revolution (q.v.) in 1966, and by 1970 Mao was once again undisputed leader of China, remaining so until his death. Mao's writings, especially those dealing with the revolutionary movement and guerrilla tactics, achieved a tremendous influence in China and in other countries, especially among radicals in the developing nations.

Maputo ⟨*formerly* Lourenço Marques⟩ Capital of Mozambique and port city (pop. 750,000). Founded in the late 18th cent., it was incorporated in 1887 and began to develop after 1895, when railroad lines reached the city. It became the capital in 1907.

Maquis French guerrilla forces that fought against German occupation forces during WW II.

Mar, John Erskine, 1st earl of *d.* 1572. Scottish noble. He served as guardian of James VI, son of Mary Queen of Scots.

Mar, John Erskine, 2nd earl of 1558–1634. Scottish noble. He succeeded his father as guardian of Scottish king James VI (James I of England) and was treasurer of Scotland (1616–30).

Mar, John Erskine, 6th earl of 1675–1732. Scottish noble, known as "Bobbing John" for his changes of allegiance. He led the unsuccessful Jacobite rebellion of 1715, which sought to secure the English throne for James, the Old Pretender.

Marat, Jean Paul 1743–93. French Revolutionary leader. He edited the journal *L'Ami du peuple,* in which he waged a verbal war against the moderate Girondists. He was stabbed to death in his bath by C. Corday.

Maratha kingdom ⟨Mahrattas, ~⟩⟨Maharashtra, ~⟩ Kingdom in west-central India that rose to power in the period between the fall of the Mogul Empire and British conquest of India (c18th-19th cents.). A small state overshadowed by Mogul power in the early 17th cent., it was greatly expanded by the conquests (1647–80) of Sivaji. Following the death (1707) of the Mogul emperor Aurangzeb, the Marathas extended their control in the southern peninsula. Under Baji Rao, they defeated Mogul armies and (after 1739) took control of the government of the failing empire. With the death (1740) of Baji Rao, central control of the empire declined rapidly. From 1772, it was ruled by five chieftains in what was known as the Maratha Confederacy. The confederacy fell to the British (1818) in the Maratha Wars.

Maratha Wars Series of three wars (1775–1818) in India between the British and the Maratha Confederacy, resulting in the fall of the Maratha Confederacy and British domination in India. **1.** The first war (1775–76, 1778–82) was ended by the Treaty of Salbai (1782), by which the British gained Salsette Island, near Bombay. **2.** The second war (1803–05) was sparked by the granting of British protection to Peshwa Baji Rao II through the Treaty of Bassein (1802). **3.** The third war (1817–18) was sparked by a British invasion of the Maratha Confederation in an attempt to defeat the Pindari tribes, which had been raiding the British territories. The war ended (1818) with the defeat and dissolution of the Maratha Confederation.

Marathon, Battle of Battle (490 BC) in which Athenian and Plataean forces under Miltiades defeated the Persian army of Darius I. This great battle of the Persian Wars *(q.v.)* ended the first Persian expedition against the Greek mainland.

Marbury vs **Madison** US Supreme Court decision (1803). Handed down by Chief Justice J. Marshall, it was the first decision to declare an act of Congress to be unconstitutional. It helped to establish the Supreme Court's right of judicial review over acts of Congress.

Marc Antony *See* **Antony**

Marcel, Etienne *d.* 1358. French leader. As provost of the merchants of Paris, he secured expanded powers for the States-General from King John II in exchange for funds to continue the Hundred Years' War. After John's capture by the English, he allied with Charles the Bad of Navarre against the dauphin (later Charles V), but was assassinated.

Marcel, Gabriel Honoré 1889–1973. French philosopher and writer, considered an early existentialist. His philosophy held that experience is more important than metaphysics.

Marcellus, Marcus Claudius *c*268–208 BC. Roman general. Five times consul of Rome, he was called "the sword of Rome." He conquered Syracuse (212 BC), and died while fighting against Hannibal.

Marches, the Mountainous region in central Italy. The region passed (8th cent.) to nominal papal control, but by the 10th cent. independent imperial provinces (marches) were established. Eventually (14th-17th cents.) restored to the Papal States, it joined the kingdom of Italy (1860).

Marchfeld, Battle of ⟨Dürnkrut, Battle of⟩ Battle (1278) at Dürnkrut, on the Marchfeld, Austria. Here Rudolph I, count of Hapsburg, defeated the Bohemian king Ottokar II.

March Laws ⟨April Laws⟩ Hungarian reform measures adopted during the 1848 Revolution. They provided for establishment of an independent Hungarian state under only nominal Austrian control. Austria refused to recognize the March Laws after it defeated the revolutionaries.

March on Rome Fascist insurrection (Oct.-Nov. 1922) led by B. Mussolini, by which Fascism came to power in Italy. Fascist forces threatened to seize power in Rome and elsewhere and began massing their followers for the insurrection, planned for Oct. 28. After King Victor Emmanuel III refused to declare martial law, Prime Minister Luigi Facta

(1861–1930) resigned, crippling the Italian government. Mussolini then was asked (Oct. 29) to form a government by the king to avert a civil war. Mussolini's new government gave him (Nov. 25) dictatorial powers until Dec. 31, 1923.

March on Washington **1.** Mass civil rights demonstration (Aug. 28, 1963). Some 200,000 blacks and their supporters, led by Dr. M. King, rallied in Washington, D.C., to press their demands for equal rights. During the rally, Dr. King uttered his famous words "I have a dream. . . ." **2.** Mass antiwar demonstration (Nov. 15, 1969) held in Washington, D.C. Led by a coalition of moderate and radical antiwar groups, some 250–400,000 protesters gathered for a largely nonviolent demonstration to press their demands for an end to the Vietnam War. The demonstration marked the high point of Vietnam antiwar protest in the US.

Marcian AD c390–457. Eastern Roman emperor (AD 450–57), successor to Theodosius II. He refused to pay tribute to Attila the Hun, avoided wars, and assembled the Council of Chalcedon (451).

Marcion fl. AD 144. Early Christian who founded (AD 144) the heretical Marcionite sect. He said there were two Gods and rejected the Old Testament.

Marconi, Guglielmo, Marchese 1874–1937. Italian physicist. He pioneered wireless telegraphy and was the first to transmit radio signals across the Atlantic (1901).

Marcos, Ferdinand Edralin 1917–. President of the Philippines (1966–). Pursuing a policy of close ties with America and hostility to communism, he declared martial law (1972), and maintains strict authoritarian control of his country.

Marcus Antonius See **Antony**

Marcus Aurelius ⟨orig. Marcus Aurelius Antoninus⟩ AD 121–180. Roman emperor (AD 161–80) and famous exponent of Stoicism. Though he ordered persecutions of Christians, his rule was otherwise considered wise and humane. He ruled (161–169) with his brother Lucius Verus (d. 169) and was sole emperor thereafter. His reign was marked by his successes against rebellions and barbarian invasions (by Parthians, Germans, and others). In one such victory (AD 174) a German tribe was confused by a fierce thunderstorm and thus fell to the emperor's troops, thereafter called the "Thundering Legion." Marcus Aurelius is known best, however, for his great philosophical work, *Meditations*.

Marcuse, Herbert 1898–. German-born American political philosopher, known best for his studies of the failings of modern industrial society. His works, which influenced the radical intellec-

tual movements of the 1960s, include *One-Dimensional Man*.

Marcus Vitruvius Pollio *See* **Vitruvius**

Marcy, William Learned 1786–1857. American politician. As US senator (1831–32) he made the remark "to the victor belong the spoils of the enemy" in defense of patronage. This gave rise to the term "spoils system."

Marduk Ancient Babylonian god. God of all Babylonia, he was also the leading god of the city of Babylon.

Marengo, Battle of Battle (June 14, 1800) in which the French under Napoleon defeated the Austrians under Baron Michael von Melas (1729–1806) at Marengo, Italy. The victory secured northern Italy for France during the French Revolutionary Wars.

Mareth Line German defensive line in Tunisia during WW II. Established by Field Marshal E. Rommel after the 1,500-mile retreat of the Afrika Korps across Libya, it was overcome by Allied forces (Mar., 1943).

Margaret 1353–1412. Queen of Denmark, Norway, and Sweden, daughter of Danish king Waldemar IV. She married (1363) Norwegian king Haakon VI, overthrew Swedish King Albert (1389), and established (1397) the Kalmar Union. Though her nephew Eric VII of Pomerania (ruled 1389–1429) was nominal king, she held the power.

Margaret Maid of Norway 1283–90. Queen of Scotland (1286–90), and successor to Scottish king Alexander III. She was betrothed to Edward, son of English king Edward I. Her death resulted in civil war and Edward I's claim to the rule of Scotland.

Margaret of Angoulême *See* **Margaret of Navarre**

Margaret of Anjou 1430?–82. Queen consort to English king Henry VI (m. 1445). She was a leader of the Lancastrians against the Yorkists during the Wars of the Roses.

Margaret of Austria 1480–1530. Hapsburg princess, daughter of Emperor Maximilian I. She was regent of The Netherlands (1507–15, 1519–30) for her nephew Charles (later Holy Roman Emperor Charles V).

Margaret of Navarre ⟨Margaret of Angoulême⟩ 1492–1549. Queen consort (m. 1527) of King Henry II of Navarre and sister of French king Francis I. She took an active interest in religious reforms and the arts and was the author of the *Heptaméron*.

Margaret of Parma 1522–86. Natural Daughter of Holy Roman Emperor Charles V and mother of A. Farnese. She served ably as regent of The Netherlands (1559–67).

Margaret of Scotland, Saint *d.* 1093. Queen consort (*m. c*1070) of Scottish king Malcolm III and sister of Edgar Atheling. She helped to advance Roman Catholic church practices in Scotland.

Margaret of Valois 1553–1615. Queen of Navarre, daughter of French king Henry II, and wife (*m.* 1572) of Henry IV. Her marriage was annulled (1599), allegedly because of her promiscuity.

Margaret Tudor 1489–1541. Queen consort of Scottish king James IV (*m.* 1503) and daughter of English king Henry VII. Temporarily regent for her son James V, she lost the regency through her marriage (1514) to A. Douglas, 6th earl of Angus.

Marggraf, Andreas Sigismund 1709–82. German chemist. His discovery of sugar in beets (1747) contributed to the formation of the sugar industry.

Maria I 1734–1816. Portuguese queen (1777–1816), daughter of Portuguese king Joseph I, and wife (*m.* 1760) of Peter III. She and Peter secured the downfall of the hated minister S. Pombal and released many prisoners of his rule. She fled to Brazil (1807) after Napoleon's invasion of Portugal.

Maria II ⟨Maria da Gloria⟩ 1819–53. Portuguese queen (1826–28, 1834–53), daughter of Brazilian king Pedro I. Her reign was marked by civil strife, including civil war and the usurping of the throne by Miguel.

Maria Christina 1806–78. Queen consort of Spanish king Ferdinand VII. She prompted her husband to allow their daughter, Isabella, to succeed him, thus causing the Carlist Wars.

Maria Christina 1858–1929. Queen consort (*m.* 1879) of Spanish king Alfonso XII. While she served as regent (1886–1902) for their son Alfonso XIII, Spain lost the last of its empire in the Americas during the Spanish-American War.

Maria da Gloria *See* **Maria II**

Maria Luisa 1751–1819. Spanish queen, wife (*m.* 1765) of Spanish king Charles IV. She and her lover M. de Godoy actually ruled the country, ruined its finances, and set the stage for Napoleon's takeover (1808).

Mariamne *d.* 29 BC. Jewish princess, wife of Herod. She was executed by Herod after being falsely accused of adultery by Salome.

Maria Theresa 1717–80. Austrian archduchess and queen of Hungary and Bohemia (1740–80), consort (*m.* 1736) of Holy Roman Emperor Francis I. She succeeded her father Charles VI as ruler of Austrian Hapsburg domains by the law of pragmatic sanction. Her succession resulted in the War of the Austrian Succession (1740–48).

Marie 1875–1938. Romanian queen (1914–27), granddaughter of English queen Victoria, and wife (*m.* 1893) of Romanian king Ferdinand I. She helped persuade Ferdinand to join the Allies in WW I.

Marie Antoinette 1755–93. French queen (1774–93), wife of King Louis XVI (*m.* 1770), and an important figure in events leading to the French Revolution. She was the daughter of Austrian Holy Roman Emperor Francis I. Her unpopularity in France helped undermine the credibility of the monarchy. This was due in part to her Austrian heritage, her extravagance, her association with dissolute courtiers, and her influence over her indecisive husband. Her reputation became notorious in the prerevolutionary times, and scandals, often exaggerated or untrue, surrounded her (such as her supposed remark, "If they have no bread, let them eat cake," and involvement in the Affair of the Diamond Necklace). Removed (1789) with Louis from Versailles to the Tuileries palace, she was taken prisoner during the storming of Tuileries (1792). She was guillotined (Oct. 16, 1793) some months after Louis.

Marie de Médicis 1573–1642. Queen consort (*m.* 1600) of French king Henry IV of France and regent (1610–17) for their son, Louis XIII. She depleted the treasury and formed an alliance with Spain before being exiled by her son.

Marie Louise 1791–1847. Empress of France (1810–15), second wife (*m.* 1810) of Napoleon I, mother of Napoleon II, and daughter of Holy Roman Emperor Francis II.

Marie Thérèse of Austria 1638–83. Queen consort (*m.* 1660) of French king Louis XIV. Daughter of Spanish king Philip IV, she renounced her claim to the Spanish throne in return for a substantial dowry. Louis, claiming never to have received it, seized part of the Spanish Netherlands in the War of Devolution.

Marignano, Battle of Battle (Sept. 13–14, 1515) during the Italian Wars, at Marignano, Italy. Here the Franco-Venetian forces under French king Francis I defeated the forces of the Swiss Confederation, forcing the Swiss to retreat. The victory led to the French conquest of Milan.

Marinetti, Filippo Tommaso 1876–1944. Italian author. Considered the founder of futurism, he also supported fascism.

Marion, Francis *c*1732–95. American Revolutionary general, known as the Swamp Fox for his guerrilla tactics against the British in South Carolina.

Maritime Provinces Name for the Canadian Atlantic provinces of New Brunswick, Nova Scotia, and Prince Edward Island.

Maritime Territory ⟨Primorski Krai⟩ Easternmost territory of the USSR. Vladivostock, its capital, is eastern terminus of the Trans-Siberian railway.

Maritsa River, Battle of the Decisive Ottoman victory (Sept. 26, 1371) over Serbia, at Maritsa River, near Adrianople. A force of 70,000 Serbs led by King Vukâsin attempted to halt Turkish expansion in the Balkans, but were overwhelmed by an inferior Turkish force, under Murad I.

Marius, Gaius c155 BC–86 BC. Roman general. He fought with distinction in Africa and in Gaul, and served as consul seven times between 108 and 101.

Mark, Saint ⟨John Mark⟩ Apostle and traditional author of the Second Gospel. He was a companion to saints Paul and Barnabas.

Markiewicz, Constance Georgine Gore-Booth, Countess 1876–1927. Irish nationalist. Sentenced to death for her role in the Easter Rebellion (1916), she was released in 1917. The first woman to be elected to the British Parliament (1918), she declined her seat, and later served in the Dail Eireann.

Marlborough, John Churchill, 1st duke of 1650–1722. English general, noted for his victories during the War of the Spanish Succession. Instrumental in putting down the rebellion by the Duke of Monmouth (1685), he shifted his allegiance from James II to William III during the Glorious Revolution (1688) and commanded William's forces against rebels in Ireland (1689–91). Out of favor (1692), he was restored under Queen Anne, who was an intimate friend of his wife, the Duchess of Marlborough. He won great fame for his service in the War of the Spanish Succession, notably in the battles of Blenheim (1704), Ramillies (1706), Oudenarde (1708), and Malplaquet (1709). Out of favor (1711) when Queen Anne switched allegiance to A. Masham, he was again restored under King George I.

Marlowe, Christopher 1564–93. English dramatist and poet, considered England's greatest pre-Shakespearean playwright. Among his plays are *Tamburlaine, Dr. Faustus, The Jew of Malta,* and *Edward II.* He also appears to have written parts of W. Shakespeare's *Titus Andronicus* and *Henry VI.* He wrote numerous poems, among them "The Passionate Shepherd to His Love."

Marmont, Auguste Frédéric Louis Viesse de 1774–1852. Marshal of France who served with Napoleon. His surrender of Paris (1814) forced Napoleon to abdicate.

Marmousets Advisers to French King Charles V, who, though reliable, were unpopular with the nobility because of their humble origins. They also served for a time under Charles VI.

Marne, Battle of the **1.** Allied victory (Sept. 5–9, 1914) over German forces advancing on Paris during WW I. The battle marked the failure of the German Schlieffen Plan. The Germans, commanded by Gen. Alexander von Kluck (1846–1934), marched toward Paris with little opposition until they reached the Marne River. French Gen. J. Joffre rushed his troops out of Paris to the river and there attacked the Germans. Though the battle itself was indecisive, the Germans ultimately withdrew. **2.** Allied victory (July 15–Aug. 7, 1918) over German forces during WW I. The battle marked the turning point of WW I in favor of the Allies. German forces, under Gen. E. Ludendorff, attacked (July 15) Allied positions near Reims and crossed the Marne River to the west of it. French Gen. F. Foch counterattacked (July 18) and forced the Germans to retreat.

Marnix, Philip van *See* **Breda, Compromise of**

Maronites Lebanese religious community. Formed (7th cent.) during the Monothelitism controversy, they were attacked by the Druses (19th cent.), and subsequently became autonomous under French protection.

Marprelate Controversy Pamphlet war (1588–89) waged by anonymous Puritans against the Anglican church. The original pamphlets were directed against Bishop John Whitgift (1530?–1604) and the authoritarianism of the Anglican church. They were attributed to a pseudonymous author, "Martin Marprelate," and were not sanctioned by Puritan leaders. The Anglicans replied with pamphlets of their own, and in the early 1590s government suppression of the Marprelate pamphleteers succeeded in ending the controversy. The author (or authors) of the pamphlets is still unknown.

Marquand, John Phillips 1893–1960. American author, noted for his novels dealing with upper-class life in New England. His novel *The Late George Apley* was awarded a Pulitzer Prize (1938).

Marquette, Jacques 1637–75. French missionary explorer. He and Louis Jolliet (1645–1700) discovered and charted the course of the Mississippi River (1673).

Mars Ancient Roman god of war, identified with the Greek god Ares. He was the father of Romulus and Remus.

Marsaglia, Battle of *See* **Grand Alliance, War of the**

Marseilles French city (pop. 912,100), in southeastern France on the Mediterranean Sea. Settled by Greeks (c600 BC), it is France's second largest city and a major port.

marshal Military rank. Marshal denotes the highest army rank in such countries as Britain, France, Germany, Russia, and China. It derives from the Frankish word for the keeper of the king's horses.

Marshall, George Catlett 1880–1959. American general and statesman. He was army chief of staff during WW II. As secretary of state (1947–49) he originated the postwar European Recovery Program (Marshall Plan). He was awarded the Nobel Peace Prize (1953).

Marshall, James Wilson 1810–85. American pioneer. His discovery (Jan. 1848) of gold at J. Sutter's mill in California led to the Gold Rush of 1849.

Marshall, John 1755–1835. American jurist. A Federalist, and one of the American diplomats involved in the XYZ Affair, he was elected to Congress (1799) and served as secretary of state (1800–01). He was appointed by J. Adams to the Supreme Court as chief justice (1801–35). Marshall's decisions in such cases as *Marbury* vs *Madison* and the Dartmouth College case helped to establish the Supreme Court's right of judicial review and also helped to strengthen the authority of the federal government.

Marshall, Thomas Riley 1854–1925. American politician, vice-president of the US (1913–21) under W. Wilson. He is remembered for his remark, "What this country needs is a really good five-cent cigar."

Marshall, Thurgood 1908–. American jurist. As head of the legal staff of the NAACP, he successfully argued before the Supreme Court the landmark civil rights case *Brown* vs *Board of Education of Topeka* (1954). He became the first black to be appointed to the Supreme Court (1967–).

Marshall Islands Pacific islands, since 1947 part of the US Trust Territory of the Pacific Islands. Scene of heavy fighting during WW II, they were later the site of US nuclear weapons tests.

Marshall Plan ⟨European Recovery Program⟩ US program (1948–52) that successfully aided the recovery of Western European nations after WW II. Outlined (1947) by US Secretary of State G. Marshall, the program provided massive economic aid (more than $12 billion) and a basis for integration of European economies. The program, also aimed at containing the rising influence of Communist parties in war-torn Europe, was accepted by Western European nations (also Turkey and Iceland). The US Congress, by the Foreign Assistance Act of 1948, created the Economic Cooperation Administration (ECA) to administer the program. The participating countries in turn created (1948) a coordinating agency, the Organization for European Economic Cooperation (renamed the Organization for Economic Cooperation and Development). The program was completed in 1952.

Marsilius of Padua *d.* c1342. Italian political philosopher. His *Defensor pacis* held that political (and ecclesiastical) power comes from the people. This concept had an immense influence on medieval political philosophy.

Marston Moor, Battle of First significant victory (July 2, 1644) of the parliamentary forces over the Royalists during the English Civil War. The Royalists under Prince Rupert were decisively defeated by forces under O. Cromwell, T. Fairfax, and others, near York.

Marsyas In Greek mythology, Phrygian figure who unsuccessfully challenged Apollo to a musical contest. He played the lute, and Apollo the lyre.

Martel, Charles *See* **Charles Martel**

Martens, Frederick ⟨Martens, Fyodor Fyodorovich⟩ 1845–1909. Russian diplomat. An authority on international law, he served as arbitrator at many conferences, including the Hague Conferences. He was awarded the Nobel Peace Prize (1902).

Martens, Fyodor Fyodorovich *See* **Martens, Frederick**

Martha In the Bible, the sister of Mary and Lazarus of Bethany. She is a symbol of the active life, whereas Mary symbolizes the contemplative life.

Martí, José 1853–95. Cuban writer and patriot. Founder (1892) of the Cuban Revolutionary party, he was killed by Spanish forces in Cuba.

Martial AD c40–c104. Roman poet. He is noted for his witty epigrams, which became the models for the contemporary epigram.

Martignac, Jean Baptiste Sylvère Gay, vicomte de 1778–1832. French statesman. He was minister of the interior (1828–29) under French king Charles X, but his policies of compromise with liberals alienated the king. He was replaced by Charles with the royalist J. Polignac.

Martin I, Saint *d.* 655. Pope (649–55). He convoked the Lateran Council (649), which condemned Monothelitism. For opening the controversy to debate he was banished to the Crimea by Byzantine Emperor Constans II.

Martin IV *d.* 1285. Pope (1281–85). His excommunication of Byzantine emperor Michael VIII caused a break between the Eastern and Western churches.

Martin V ⟨Colonna, Oddone⟩ 1368–1431. Catholic pope (1417–31). Martin's unanimous election at the Council of Constance ended the Great Schism. He was less successful in his reconciliation attempts with the Eastern church and in controlling the Hussites.

Martin, Saint AD c316–397? French bishop of Tours (c371), and patron saint of France. He founded the monastery at Marmoutier and was noted for his piety.

Martin vs **Hunter's Lessee** *See* **Story, Joseph**

Marvell, Andrew 1621–78. English poet. One of the leading satirists of his day, he is known for his wit and lyricism in such poems as *To His Coy Mistress.*

Marwan II *See* **Muslim Civil Wars**

Marx, Karl 1818–83. German economist and philosopher, considered the founder and premier theorist of modern socialism and international communism. Marx studied at the universities of Bonn and Berlin but abandoned law to take up the study of history and philosophy. Adopting elements of the philosophies of G. Hegel and L. Feuerbach, among others, Marx became an ardent supporter of socialism. He became editor of the *Rheinische Zeitung* in 1842, but his radicalism led to the paper's suppression (1843). Moving to Paris, Marx met F. Engels, who became his friend and collaborator, and with whom he wrote *The German Ideology*, which dealt with Marx's concept of dialectical materialism *(q.v.)* as the operating human force in human history. Joining the Communist League (1847), Marx wrote (with Engels) what has become known as the *Communist Manifesto.*

The failure of the 1848 revolutions in Europe led Marx to move to London (1849), where he spent the remainder of his life in poverty, only partly eased by the efforts of Engels and others. Marx made a prodigious study (at the British museum) of the principles of capitalism and wrote his massive work, *Das Kapital*, which remained unfinished at his death. Marx was a leading figure in the establishment of the First International *(q.v.)*. His writings, especially the *Communist Manifesto* and *Das Kapital*, greatly influenced the radical movements of the late 19th and early 20th cents., notably the Russian Communist movement headed by N. Lenin. His writings form a theoretical foundation for modern Communist ideology and embody an important and controversial system of political and economic thought.

Marx, Wilhelm 1863–1946. German statesman. As chancellor (1923–24) he supported acceptance of the Dawes Plan for war reparations. He served again as chancellor (1926–28).

Marx Brothers US movie and stage comedians. The best-known brothers were Groucho (Julius, 1895–1977), Harpo (Arthur, 1893–1964) and Chico (Leonard, 1891–1961). Their classic slapstick films include *Animal Crackers* and *Duck Soup.*

Marxism Collective term applied to the political, economic, and social theories advanced by K. Marx and F. Engels in such works as the *Communist Manifesto* and *Das Kapital.* Marx's theories greatly influenced the Socialist movement of the late 19th cent. and are considered the theoretical foundation for modern international communism. In his writings, Marx advanced the doctrine of dialectical materialism, the idea that the history and structure of civilization have been determined by economic systems operating during each stage of development. As each system developed, he asserted, new economic forces arose and inevitably led to the system's replacement. Thus feudalism was replaced by capitalism, and capitalism was fated to be replaced by socialism and, ultimately, communism.

A key element of Marxist doctrine is the view of all history as the history of class struggle, of the ruling elite pitted against the working class. According to Marx, this would eventually lead to crisis, in which the working class would rise up against the capitalist order, seize the means of production, and establish communal ownership through a "dictatorship of the proletariat." With the abolition of the ruling class, all class struggle, hence all history, would come to an end. Finally, when a rational economic system was evolved, the structure of the political state would wither away.

Marx's theories had a profound influence on the development of Socialist movements and were the basis for the Bolshevik political movement led by N. Lenin. The Bolsheviks' success in establishing the first Communist state in Russia (1917) contradicted Marx's conviction that the first Communist uprising would take place in a modern industrialized nation. The massive political bureaucracy created under Lenin, and J. Stalin, also contradicted Marxist doctrine. Subsequent modifications of capitalism, such as the workers' vastly higher standard of living and the rise of a managerial class, have also brought some of Marx's principal tenets into question. Nonetheless, Marxism as a body of political thought remains, in name if not in practice, the official political dogma of the world's Communist nations.

Mary Mother of Jesus and principal saint of the Roman Catholic church. There are many biblical references to her and these include: her betrothal to Joseph, a carpenter of Nazareth; the annunciation of the birth of Jesus; Mary's visit to her cousin, Elizabeth, mother of John the Baptist; the birth of Jesus and purification at the Temple; the arrival of the Magi and the journey to Egypt; and her presence at the crucifixion. Church dogma relating to Mary includes the doctrines of Mary, the Virgin Mother; Mary, the Mother of God; Mary's freedom from original sin (Immaculate Conception); and Mary's assumption directly into heaven (the Assumption).

Mary   *See* **Mary Queen of Scots**

Mary 1867–1953. Queen consort (m. 1893) of English king George V. She was the mother of kings Edward VIII and George VI.

Mary I 〈Mary Tudor〉 〈Bloody Mary〉 1516–58. English Queen (1553–58), daughter of Henry VIII and Catherine of Aragon. Her marriage (1554) to Spanish King Philip II caused great opposition. She briefly reestablished Roman Catholicism in England (1555–59) and persecuted Protestants.

Mary II 1662–94. English queen (1689–94), daughter of James II. After James was forced into exile by the Glorious Revolution (1688), Mary became joint sovereign with her husband William of Orange (William III).

Maryland US Middle Atlantic state (pop. 4,216,400), the 7th state. English king Charles I granted the colony to G. Calvert, 1st Baron Baltimore (1632), and it was first settled (1634) by Catholics and Protestants seeking religious freedom. Its northern border is the Mason-Dixon line, drawn (1767) to settle a boundary dispute with Pennsylvania. During the US Civil War Maryland remained in the Union but its citizens fought on both sides. One of the war's major engagements was fought here at Antietam (1862).

Maryland, McCulloch vs *See* **McCulloch vs Maryland**

Mary Magdalen 〈Mary Magdalene〉 Biblical disciple of Jesus, who cast out the evil spirits possessing her. She witnessed both Jesus' crucifixion and his resurrection.

Mary Magdalene *See* **Mary Magdalen**

Mary of Burgundy 1457–82. Duchess of Burgundy, daughter of Charles the Bold and heiress to The Netherlands. Her marriage (1477) to Maximilian of Austria (later Holy Roman Emperor Maximilian I) gave the Hapsburgs control of The Netherlands.

Mary of England 〈Mary of France〉 〈Mary Tudor〉 1496–1533. Queen consort (1514–15) of French king Louis XII and daughter of English king Henry VII. She was the grandmother of Lady Jane Grey.

Mary of France *See* **Mary of England**

Mary of Guise 1515–60. Queen consort (m. 1538) of Scottish king James V. The daughter of C. de Lorraine, 1st duke of Guise, she was regent (1554–59) for her daughter Mary Queen of Scots.

She was removed from the regency for her opposition to J. Knox.

Mary of Modena 1658–1718. Queen consort (m. 1673) of English king James II of England. The birth (1688) of her son, James Francis Edward, ensured a Catholic succession and provoked the Glorious Revolution.

Mary Queen of Scots 〈Stuart, Mary〉 1542–87. Scottish queen (1542–68), a Catholic of the Stuart family and a celebrated beauty. Her life was marked by controversy and intrigue. She was named queen shortly after birth. Her early life was spent in France. She returned (1561) to Scotland and married (1565) her unpopular cousin, Lord Darnley, to strengthen her claims to the English throne. The couple became disaffected and, after her husband's murder, generally attributed to the Earl of Bothwell, she married Bothwell (1567). This led to a Scottish revolt, Mary's forced abdication (June 15, 1567), and her escape to England (1568). As an heir to the throne and a threat to Queen Elizabeth, Mary was kept under guard in England. After several plots by Catholics to overthrow Elizabeth in favor of Mary, Mary was implicated in a scheme by A. Babington and was beheaded. Mary's son became King James I.

Mary Tudor *See* **Mary of England**

Masaccio 1401–28? Italian painter, one of the leading figures in Italian Renaissance painting. His works influenced many later artists, including Michelangelo and Raphael.

Masada Israeli fortress on a mountain overlooking the Dead Sea. It was the last Zealot stronghold against Rome (AD 66–73). Here the Zealots withstood a two-year Roman siege, but, faced with imminent defeat, virtually all chose death over capture by the Romans.

Masaniello 1620–47? Neapolitan insurrectionist. A fisherman, he led a successful revolt against Spanish rule in Naples. He was murdered soon after.

Masaryk, Jan 1886–1948. Czech statesman and diplomat. He became (1940) foreign minister in the government in exile in London during WW II, and remained in office after the Communist takeover (1948). Soon afterward, he allegedly committed suicide.

Masaryk, Thomas Garrigue 1850–1937. A founding father of Czechoslovakia and its first president (1918–35). He was a leader of pro-Slovak interests in the Austro-Hungarian Empire and fled the country at the outbreak of WW I. With E. Beneš, he organized a de facto government of Czechoslovakia, which won the support of the Allies. When independent Czechoslovakia was formed after WW I, Masaryk was elected president

(1918, 1920, 1927, 1934) and instituted a major land-reform program.

Mashhad *See* **Meshed**

Masinissa c238–149 BC. Numidian king in East Africa. He switched allegiance (c206 BC) from Carthage to Rome in the Second Punic War and was rewarded with Carthaginian territory.

Maskelyne, Nevil 1732–1811. English astronomer. He published the *Nautical Almanac* and introduced the determination of longitude by the moon's position.

Mason, Charles *See* **Mason-Dixon line**

Mason, George 1725–92. American Revolutionary statesman. A member of the Constitutional Convention (1787), he refused to sign the Constitution because of its compromise on slavery and its provision for strong federal government. The changes he called for influenced the drafting of the Bill of Rights.

Mason, John 1586–1635. English colonist. A founding member (1629) of the Laconia Company, he founded New Hampshire.

Mason-Dixon line Boundary line between Maryland and Pennsylvania surveyed (1763–67) by Charles Mason (1730–87) and Jeremiah Dixon (*fl.* 1763–67). Once the line between free and slave states, it is now the traditional border between the North and South.

Masora (Massorah) Hebrew text of the Old Testament. Compiled (mainly c6th–c10th cents.) by Hebrew scholars (Masoretes), the work represents an effort to reconstruct the Hebrew Old Testament in its original form. The Masora contains critical notes and a system for the proper pronunciation of the text.

Maspero, Gaston 1846–1916. French Egyptologist. He established the French Institute of Oriental Archaeology, discovered the royal mummies at Dayr al-Bahri (1881), and directed many excavations.

Massachusetts Northeast US state (pop. 5,737,000), the 6th state. The first permanent settlement was founded by the Pilgrims at Plymouth (1620). The Massachusetts Bay Company governed the colony (1629–84), which included the province of Maine. Massachusetts became a leader in the Colonial resistance to British rule and was the site during the American Revolution of the battles of Lexington, Concord, and Bunker Hill (1775). The state constitution was adopted in 1780 and Massachusetts became a state in 1788.

Massachusetts Bay Company English colonizing company chartered (1620) by English king Charles I. Originally intended for trade, it was used by the Puritans to establish a theocracy in Massachusetts. Its charter was annulled (1684).

Massacre of Amritsar Massacre (Apr. 13, 1919) at Amritsar, India. There, troops under British command fired on unarmed Indian nationalist protesters, killing some 400 and wounding about 1,200. The massacre did much to strengthen the anti-British movement in India.

Massacre of Glencoe Massacre (Feb. 13, 1692) of the Scottish Macdonald clan by the rival Campbell clan. The Campbells, led by J. Campbell and J. Dalrymple, 1st earl of Stair, were sent to Glencoe to secure the Macdonalds' oath of allegiance to English King William III. Instead, the Campbells killed some 38 Macdonalds.

Massacre of Saint Bartholomew's Day Massacre of French Protestants (Huguenots) that started in Paris (Aug. 24, 1572) and marked the beginning of renewed fighting in the Wars of Religion (*q.v.*). The massacre was a result of the continuing religious and political rivalry between Protestants and Catholics (led by the Guise family). The Guise family and Catherine de Médicis, mother of King Charles IX, sought to check the rising influence of Adm. G. Coligny, a Protestant. When an attempt to assassinate Coligny failed (Aug. 22), Catherine persuaded King Charles to order the death of Huguenot leaders then in Paris for the wedding of Henry of Navarre (later Henry IV). Following the initial bloodshed (Henry of Navarre and Prince de Condé escaped death), a general massacre of Protestants broke out in Paris and spread to the countryside. Thousands were killed by the time the persecution was halted in October.

Massacre of Vassy *See* **Guise, François of Lorraine, 2d duke of Guise**

Massasoit c1580–1661. Chief of the Wampanoag Indians. He signed (1621) a treaty of friendship with the Plymouth colonists and aided the settlers in their first years in New England. His son was King Philip.

Massena, André 1758–1817. French general. He served under Napoleon Bonaparte. His defeat of the Russians at Zurich (1799) saved France from invasion.

Massenet, Jules 1842–1912. French composer. He is known best for his operas *Manon* and *Le Cid.*

Massorah *See* **Masora**

Mastai-Ferretti, Giovanni M. *See* **Pius IX**

Masters, Edgar Lee 1879–1950. American poet, known best for his *Spoon River Anthology*, a collection of epitaphs exploring the lives of the former residents of a small midwestern town.

Masudi d. 956. Arab historian. He wrote the 30-volume *Annals*, a history of the world. It was abridged as *Meadows of Gold and Mines of Gems.*

Matabele War Brief war (July 1894–Jan. 1895) between British colonial forces in South Africa and the Matabele tribes. The Matabele, an offshoot of the Zulu tribes, had settled in their Rhodesian homelands by c1837. Hostilities with white settlers broke out into open war (July 1894) between the British South Africa Company and the Matabele, led by Lobengula (1870–94). The British quickly won the war and thereafter governed the Matabele territory. One final rebellion by the Matabele in 1896 was unsuccessful.

Mata Hari ⟨Zelle, Margaretha Geertruida⟩ 1876–1917. Dutch dancer and spy. She was executed by the French after being found guilty of spying for the Germans during WW I.

Match King See **Kreuger, Ivar**

Mater et Magistra See **John XXIII**

materialism Philosophical doctrine. Materialism as a theory has existed in various forms from ancient times among the Greek Epicureans to present-day communism (dialectical materialism). Essentially, materialism argues that all aspects of reality (including consciousness) can be explained in terms of bits of matter, or their motion. It is opposed to philosophical idealism and is often in conflict with religion, because it places "matter" over "mind." Materialist philosophers include D. Diderot, T. Hobbes, K. Marx and F. Engels.

Mather, Cotton 1663–1728. American Puritan minister and author, son of I. Mather. One of the leading religious and intellectual figures of his day, he is noted for his involvement in the Salem witchcraft trials (1692).

Mather, Increase 1639–1723. American Puritan minister, son of R. Mather. He was pastor of North Church, Boston (1664–1723) and president of Harvard College (1685–1701). His *Cases of Conscience Concerning Evil Spirits* helped to stem the witchcraft hysteria of the 1690s.

Mather, Richard 1596–1669. English Puritan minister. He emigrated to Massachusetts in 1635 and was the pastor of Dorchester until his death. He helped to draft the Cambridge Platform (1648).

Mathew, Theobald 1790–1856. Irish temperance missionary. A Capuchin priest, he campaigned for temperance in Ireland, England, and the US.

Mathura See **Muttra**

Matilda 1046–1115. Countess of Tuscany, a supporter of the papacy in its conflict with the Holy Roman Emperors. It was at her castle that Holy Roman Emperor Henry IV did penance to Pope Gregory VII (1077).

Matilda ⟨Maud⟩ 1102–67. Holy Roman Empress, as wife (*m*. 1114) of Henry V. Daughter of English king Henry I, she was, by her second husband, Geoffrey of Anjou (*m*. 1128), the mother of the future English king Henry II.

Matisse, Henri 1869–1954. French artist. A leader of the art movement known as fauvism, he is noted for his use of bold primary colors.

matriarchy Social system in which family descent is traced through the mother's lineage. Such societies have been observed in Pacific islands, African tribes, and in some American Indian cultures.

Matsuoka, Yosuke 1880–1946. Japanese statesman. As foreign minister (1940–41) he helped establish the Axis alliance with Germany and Italy (1940).

Mattaniah See **Zedekiah**

Matteo da Bascio See **Capuchins**

Matteotti Crisis Crisis (1924) that marked the beginning of B. Mussolini's Fascist dictatorship in Italy. The incident began with a stinging denunciation of the Fascists (May 30) before the Chamber of Deputies, delivered by Socialist deputy Giacomo Matteotti (1885–1924). Matteotti was then kidnapped (June 10) and killed by Fascist thugs. A massive popular reaction against Fascists ensued and opposition deputies walked out in protest (the Aventine Secession). The deputies, however, proved unable to oust Mussolini. He thereupon seized the opportunity to establish the political controls by which he became dictator.

Matthew, Saint One of the twelve Apostles of Jesus. He was originally a tax collector, but little else is known of his life. He is the traditionally acknowledged author of the First Gospel.

Matthew of Paris See **Paris, Matthew**

Matthias 1557–1619. Holy Roman Emperor (1612–19), son of Maximilian II and successor to his brother Rudolf II. His failure to establish an accord between Catholics and Protestants resulted in the Thirty Years' War.

Matthias, Saint Christian apostle. Matthias was chosen by lot to replace Judas Iscariot as one of the twelve Apostles of Jesus.

Matthias Corvinus 1443?–90. Hungarian king (1458–90). He waged war against the Turks and Holy Roman Emperor Frederick III, and was a patron of Renaissance culture.

Maud See **Matilda**

Maugham, William Somerset 1874–1965. English author, known best for his novels and short stories. His novels include *Of Human Bondage* and *The Moon and Sixpence*.

Maupassant, Henri René Albert Guy de 1850–93. French author, considered a master of the short story.

Maupeou, René Nicolas de 1714–92. French chancellor (1768–74) under Louis XV. In an attempt to reform the government, he dissolved the Parlement (1771), but it was restored under Louis XVI.

Maurepas, Jean Frédéric Phélippeaux, comte de 1701–81. French statesman, minister of state under French king Louis XV. He was banished (1749) for offending Mme. de Pompadour. He returned (1774) under Louis XVI and aided the American colonies against Britain during the American Revolution.

Mauretania ⟨Mauritania⟩ Ancient region of northwest Africa, comprising parts of present-day Morocco and Algeria. It fell under Roman influence and was formally annexed (AD 42). It fell to the Vandals AD c429.

Mauriac, François 1885–1970. French author. He is known best for his novels dealing with Roman Catholicism, among them *The Desert of Love* and *Thérèse*. He was awarded the Nobel Prize for Literature (1952).

Maurice c539–602. Byzantine emperor (582–602), successor to Tiberius II. An able and successful ruler, he made peace with Persia and defeated the Avars but was murdered by mutinous troops under Phocas.

Maurice 1521–53. Duke (1541–47) and elector (1547–53) of Saxony. He gained the electoral title by aiding Holy Roman Emperor Charles V against the Schmalkaldic League. He later supported the German Protestant princes against Charles.

Maurice of Nassau 1567–1625. Prince of Orange (1618–25), son of William the Silent. He drove the Spanish from the United Provinces and concluded (1609) a 12-year truce with Spain.

Mauritania ⟨Islamic Republic of Mauritania⟩ Independent state located in northwest Africa on the Atlantic coast. Its capital is Nouakchott. Mauritania is largely a desert region, and many of its people (among them Arabs, Berbers, and Moors) are nomadic. It gained independence in 1960 after nearly a hundred years of French rule. Key dates in the history of Mauritania include:

11TH CENT. Almoravide movement established among the Muslim Berbers.

14TH–15TH CENT. Mali Empire dominated southeast Mauritania.

15TH CENT. Portuguese navigators explored coast.

FROM 17TH CENT. European traders active in region.

1860s France gained control of southern Mauritania.

1903 Became French protectorate ruled by colonial government in Senegal.

1904 Became part of French West Africa.

1920 Became a colony of French West Africa, separate from Senegal.

1946 Became French overseas territory.

1957 Nouakchott became administrative center.

1958 Became autonomous republic within the French Community.

1960 Fully independent under Makhtar Ould Daddah (Nov. 28).

1961 Joined UN; Morocco, which claimed Mauritania, objected. Mauritania occupied the southern part of Spanish Sahara (Morocco took the north); the Polisario Front, a Saharan independence group, opposed takeover.

1978 Bloodless coup ousted longtime president Makhtar Ould Daddah; military provisional government set up.

1979 Lt. Col. Muhammad Mahmoud Ould Louly installed as head of state.

1979 Fighting with Morocco, over part of former Spanish Sahara, ended (Aug.); Mauritania withdrew from the region.

1980 Military junta installed Lt. Col. Mohamed Khouna Ould Haidala as head of state; he remained in power into the early 1980s.

Mauritius ⟨Île de France⟩ Island country in the Indian Ocean. Discovered (16th cent.) by the Portuguese, it was held in turn by the Dutch (1598–1710), French (1715–1810), and British (1810–1968). It gained independence on Mar. 12, 1968.

Maurocordátos, Aléxander *See* **Mavrocordátos, Aléxander**

Maury, Matthew Fontaine 1806–73. American naval officer and hydrographer. He charted the Atlantic, Pacific, and Indian oceans and wrote *Physical Geography of the Sea*, the first modern oceanographic work.

Maurya Empire Ancient Indian empire (*fl.* 4th–2d cent. BC) of the Maurya dynasty rulers. The first great Indian empire, it united nearly the whole Indian subcontinent (and part of Afghanistan) and saw the development of a flourishing native Indian culture. The empire was founded by Chandragupta I, who overthrew (c322 BC) the ruler of the Magadha kingdom in eastern India and conquered (c305) domains of Seleucus Nicator to the west. The kingdom reached its greatest expansion under the rule of Asoka, who added to conquests made by his predecessor, Bindusara (*d.* c272). Asoka established Buddhism as the state religion. Following his reign, the empire entered into decline and by c185 had broken up into petty kingdoms. (*See also* India [322–185 BC].)

Mausolus *d.* 353 BC. Persian satrap, ruler of Caria (376–353 BC). He is known for his monumental tomb at Halicarnassus, known as the Mausoleum.

Mavrocordátos, Aléxander ⟨Maurocordátos, Aléxander⟩ 1791–1865. Greek statesman. He was a leader in the revolution against Turkey (1821), president of the first national assembly (1822), and twice premier.

Maxentius d. AD 312. Roman emperor (AD 306–312). Maxentius became emperor after his father, Emperor Maximian, and Emperor Diocletian abdicated. Maximian supported him against Severus. After a quarrel, however, Maximian refused to help him against Constantine, who defeated him in battle (312) at Milvian Bridge (q.v.).

Maximian d. AD 310. Roman emperor with Diocletian (AD 286–305). He ruled the empire in the West until his abdication (305). He later helped his son Maxentius to become emperor, then broke with him and supported Constantine.

Maximilian 1832–67. Austrian archduke and emperor of Mexico (1864–67). Unpopular with the Mexicans, he was opposed by B. Juárez. Supported for a time by French troops sent by Napoleon III, he refused to abdicate after their withdrawal (1867), and was captured and shot.

Maximilian I 1459–1519. Holy Roman Emperor (1493–1519), successor to his father Frederick III. He greatly expanded the hereditary Hapsburg domains, often at the expense of the interests of the Holy Roman Empire. Prior to his accession, he added Burgundian lands (Burgundy, The Netherlands, and Luxembourg) to Hapsburg possessions by his marriage (1477) to Mary of Burgundy. Burgundy was lost (by the Treaty of Arras, 1483) in wars with the French, and Maximilian undertook the Italian Wars (1494–1559) to regain Burgundian lands there. Though Switzerland was able to win (1499) independence from the empire, Maximilian added Hungary and Bohemia to the Hapsburg possessions by the marriage (1516) of his grandson and granddaughter to heirs of King Ladislaus II. He also ensured Hapsburg succession in Spain by the marriage of his son Philip to heiress Joanna (Charles V was their son).

Maximilian I ⟨Maximilian the Great⟩ 1573–1651. Duke (1597–1651) and elector (1623–51) of Bavaria. He was a key founder (1609) of the Catholic League, which opposed the Protestant Union in the Thirty Years' War (1618–48).

Maximilian I 1756–1825. King (1806–25) and elector (1799–1806) of Bavaria. He gained the crown by allying himself with Napoleon and ruled as an enlightened monarch. He championed Bavarian independence and opposed the unification of Germany.

Maximilian II 1527–76. Holy Roman Emperor (1564–76), successor to his father, Ferdinand I. A nominal Catholic, he was tolerant of the Protestants in his realm. He concluded a truce (1568) with Turkish sultan Selim II.

Maximilian II 1811–64. Bavarian king (1848–64), successor to his father, Louis I. His reign was liberal and devoted to the arts and learning. He tried to form a union of small German states led by Bavaria to balance the influence of Austria and Prussia.

Maximilian the Great See **Maximilian I**

Maximin d. AD 238. Roman emperor (AD 235–238). He spent much of his reign campaigning against the invading Germans. He was assassinated by his own soldiers.

Maximin d. AD 313. Roman emperor (AD 308–313). He persecuted the Christians and attempted to revitalize paganism. He was defeated by Licinius.

Maximus d. AD 388. Roman emperor of the West (AD 383–388). He defeated Gratian and drove Valentinian II from Italy. He was defeated and put to death by Eastern emperor Theodosius I.

Maxwell, James Clerk 1831–79. Scottish physicist. He is noted for his *A Treatise on Electricity and Magnetism* and for his important theory of electromagnetic radiation. He has been ranked with I. Newton in his contributions to modern science.

Maya Group of related Central American Indian tribes, living in the Yucatan peninsula, southern Mexico, Guatemala, and Belize. The origin of the Maya is uncertain, but by the 1st millennium BC they had already begun to establish an advanced culture. The Mayan civilization was based on agriculture, and each community retained political independence under the rule of a local hierarchy of priests and political chieftains. Mayan cities centered around royal houses and religious temples built on pyramidal structures. The Maya devised an extremely accurate calendar, a vigesimal (base 20) number system, a complex pantheon of gods and religious ceremonies, and a system of hieroglyphic writing that has yet to be deciphered. Their culture is noted for its advances in the arts, architecture, astronomy, and mathematics. Their cities included Chichén Itzá, Uxmal, and Mayapán, which formed the League of Mayapán (13th cent AD). The league was rent by civil war, and the cities eventually abandoned. Mayan civilization had passed its peak by the time of the Spanish conquest (16th cent.) The Spanish accelerated the Mayan decline, abolished much of the Mayan religion, and destroyed virtually all of the Mayan records. A few survive, such as the Dresden Codex *(q.v.)* and the Popol Vuh *(q.v.),* a later text based on original Mayan sources.

Mayaguez Incident Seizure (May 12, 1975) of the US cargo ship *Mayaguez* by Cambodian authorities. Within two weeks after US forces were evacuated from Vietnam, Cambodians boarded the *Mayaguez* and took 39 crewmen hostage. President G. Ford ordered their rescue, during which 38 Americans were killed.

Mayakovsky, Vladimir 1893–1930. Russian poet, leading poet of the Russian Revolution. Among his best-known poems are *A Cloud in Trousers* and *The Backbone Flute,* both written before the revolution.

Mayapán, League of *See* **Maya**

Mayenne, Charles de Lorraine, duc de 1554–1611. French general, brother of Henry of Guise. He headed the Catholic League against French king Henry IV but refused to place the Spanish Catholic infanta Isabella on the throne.

Mayflower English ship upon which the Pilgrims sailed from England to Plymouth, Massachusetts (Sept.–Nov. 1620). The Pilgrims arrived off Cape Cod in November, and landed at Plymouth Dec. 26. (*See also* Pilgrims.)

Mayflower Compact An agreement, signed (Nov. 21, 1620) by the Pilgrims aboard the ship *Mayflower.* By it the settlers agreed to form a "civil body politic," which would form a government with binding laws. It was the basis for the government in Plymouth.

May Fourth Movement Mass movement in China (early 20th cent.) sparked by intellectuals who sought government reform and modernization of Chinese society. The movement, beginning as early as 1915, was precipitated by the government's inability to check Japanese expansionism. But among intellectuals it fostered a broad attack on traditional Chinese society and culture and helped to introduce Western ideologies. The intellectual movement was translated to mass protests by the events of 1919. The post-WW I Versailles Peace Conference transferred (Apr. 28) German concessions in Shantung province, China, to Japan. Some 3,000–5,000 students in Peking began (May 4) a series of mass protests against the decision, and over the weeks these spread to other cities and spawned a boycott of Japanese goods. China subsequently refused to sign the Treaty of Paris, but more important results were the rising political power of intellectuals, the further decline of traditional culture, the spread of the vernacular in written Chinese, and greater freedoms for women. Among the leading figures in the movement were Ch'en Tu-hsiu and Hu Shih.

Mayo, Charles Horace and **William James** 1865–1939; 1861–1939. American surgeons. They established the Mayo Clinic in Rochester, Minnesota, and founded (1915) the Mayo Foundation for Medical Education and Research.

Mazarin, Jules ⟨Mazarini, Giulio⟩ 1602–61. French cardinal and statesman. He succeeded (1642) Cardinal Richelieu as minister of France under King Louis XIII and remained powerful during the regency of Anne of Austria.

Mazarin Bible First known book printed (c1455) from movable type. Printed by J. Gutenberg, it was so named for its discovery (1760) in the library of Cardinal Mazarin.

Mazarini, Giulio *See* **Mazarin, Jules**

Mazepa, Ivan Stepanovich 1644?–1709. Cossack hetman (leader) in the Russian Ukraine. He fought with the Swedes under Charles XII against Russia, but was defeated at Poltava (1709).

Mazurian Lakes, Battles of the Military campaigns on the Russian front during WW I. **1.** Battle (Sept. 9–14, 1914) in which the Germans drove the Russians from East Prussia, inflicting casualties of 125,000 (against some 10,000 German casualties). **2.** Battle (Feb. 7–21, 1915) in which the Germans attempted a knockout blow at Russia. They inflicted 200,000 Russian casualties, but without decisive results.

Mazzini, Giuseppe 1805–72. Italian revolutionary and political writer. He campaigned for a united Italy under a republican government, founded the Young Italy Movement (1831), and was a leader in the short-lived Roman republic of 1849. He aided Garibaldi in his efforts to unify Italy and later refused to take part in the monarchical government established in 1861.

Mboya, Thomas Joseph *See* **Mboya, Tom**

Mboya, Tom ⟨Mboya, Thomas Joseph⟩ 1930–69. Kenyan political leader. A leader in the Kenyan independence movement, he held several ministerial positions in the government of J. Kenyatta before being assassinated.

Mc *For names beginning with Mc, see under* **Mac**

Mead, George Herbert 1863–1931. American philosopher. He emphasized the importance of language in social interaction. His *Mind, Self, and Society* was published posthumously.

Mead, Margaret 1901–78. American anthropologist, noted especially for her studies of the people and cultures of Oceania. Her books included *Coming of Age in Samoa, Growing Up in New Guinea,* and *Male and Female.*

Meade, George Gordon 1815–72. Union general in the American Civil War. He fought with distinction at Antietam (1862), Fredericksburg

(1862), and Chancellorsville (1863), and defeated Gen. R. E. Lee at Gettysburg (1863).

Meany, George 1894–1980. US labor leader. Originally a plumber, he rose to become (1952) president of the American Federation of Labor (AFL) and of the AFL-CIO (1955).

Mecca Saudi Arabian city (pop. 366,800), the birthplace of Muhammad (570) and the Holy City of Islam. It is the site of the Great Mosque and the Kaaba. Mecca was conquered by the Ottoman Turks (1517), the Wahabis (1803–13), and Ibn-Saud (1924), who founded Saudi Arabia. (*See also* Muhammad.)

Mecklenburg Former East German state (until 1952) and historic region on the Baltic. First settled in the 6th cent., it became (14th cent.) a duchy within the Holy Roman Empire. Divided (1701) into Mecklenburg-Schwerin and Mecklenburg-Strelitz, it was reunited (1934).

Mecklenburg Declaration of Independence American declaration (May 20, 1775) severing ties with Britain, said to have been made by the citizens of Mecklenburg, North Carolina. Although these citizens did adopt anti-British resolutions around that time, the declaration is probably not authentic.

Medea Mythological Greek sorceress. She helped Jason to obtain the Golden Fleece from her father, Aeëtes, king of Colchis.

Media Ancient Asian country of indeterminate boundaries in what is now roughly northwestern Iran. Under Cyaxares, Media won its independence from the Assyrian Empire, taking much of its territory. The Persian king Cyrus conquered (*c*550 BC) Media from Astyages, and it remained a part of the Persian Empire until the time of Alexander the Great.

Medici Italian family, rulers of Florence (15–18th cents.) and world-famous patrons of the arts who transformed Florence into a treasure house of European art. Though the family can be traced back to the 12th cent., the huge family fortune was founded by Giovanni di Bicci de' Medici (1360–1429). From his sons stem the two major branches: the Elder Branch, by Cosimo (1389–1464); and the Younger Branch, by Lorenzo (1395–1440). The Elder Branch controlled Florence by means of influence until 1531, when Alessandro (1511–37) became hereditary duke. On his death the extinct Elder Branch was replaced by the Younger. It ruled Florence until the death of Gian Gastone (1671–1737). Prominent members of the family include Pope Leo X, Pope Clement VII, Pope Leo XI, Catherine de Médicis, and Marie de Médicis.

Medici, Alessandro de' 1511–37. Duke of Florence (1532–37). Made duke by his father-in-law, Holy Roman Emperor Charles V, he was hated for his tyrannical rule. His assassination by L. de' Medici ended the Elder Branch of the Medici line.

Medici, Cosimo de' 1389–1464. Florentine ruler and banker. He used his wealth and influence to encourage the arts and scholarship.

Medici, Cosimo I de' 1519–74. Duke of Florence (1537–69). Although a cruel ruler, he increased the wealth and size of his territories, and defeated and incorporated Siena (1555). He was made duke of Tuscany (1569).

Medici, Cosimo II de' 1590–1620. Grand duke of Tuscany (1609–21), successor to his father, Ferdinand I de' Medici. He was a patron of Galileo.

Medici, Ferdinand I de' 1549–1609. Grand duke of Tuscany (1587–1609). He strengthened the duchy.

Medici, Gian Gastone de' 1671–1737. Grand duke of Tuscany (1723–37). He was the last male member of the Medici family. After his death the now impoverished duchy passed to Francis of Lorraine, later Holy Roman Emperor Francis I.

Medici, Giovanni Angelo de' *See* **Pius IV**

Medici, Giovanni de' (Bande Nere, Giovanni delle) 1498–1526. Italian general known as John of the Black Bands. He fought for both sides in the Italian Wars and was mortally wounded in battle.

Medici, Giovanni de' *See* **Leo X**

Medici, Giulio de' *See* **Clement VII**

Medici, Ippolito de' 1511–35. Italian cardinal. He and his cousin, Alessandro de' Medici, ruled Florence under Pope Clement VII. While on a mission to Holy Roman Emperor Charles V he died, possibly poisoned by order of Alessandro.

Medici, Lorenzo de' 1449–92. Florentine statesman known as "the Magnificent." Son of P. de' Medici, he ruled Florence (1478–92) and was a noted writer and patron of the arts.

Medici, Lorenzo de' 1492–1519. Duke of Urbino (1516–19) and son of P. de' Medici. His tomb in Florence was created by Michelangelo. He was the father of Catherine de Médicis.

Medici, Piero de' 1414–69. Florentine merchant prince, successor to his father, C. de' Medici, as ruler of Florence. The father of L. de' Medici, he was known as "the Gouty" because of his ill health.

Medici, Piero de' 1471–1503. Florentine merchant prince, son of L. de' Medici (the Magnificent). He ruled Florence (1492–94) until expelled by Savonarola during the invasion of Tuscany by French king Charles VIII.

medieval *See* **Middle Ages**

Medieval Inquisition *See* **Inquisition (1)**

Medina Saudi Arabian city (pop. 100,000). It holds the tomb of Muhammad and is Islam's second most holy city. Muhammad made his hegira (flight) here from Mecca in 622. It was ruled successively by the Ottoman Turks, Egyptians, Wahabis and again by the Turks until taken by Ibn-Saud (1924).

Medina-Sidonia, duke of *See* **Spanish Armada**

Mediterranean Sea World's largest inland sea, between southern Europe, North Africa, and western Asia. A number of the world's oldest civilizations developed in the Mediterranean region.

Medusa In Greek mythology, one of the Gorgons. She had hair of snakes and a gaze that transformed onlookers into stone. She was slain by Perseus. Chrysaor and Pegasus sprang from her blood.

Megalopolis Ancient Greek city. Founded (*c*370 BC) in Arcadia as an anti-Spartan outpost, it was destroyed (222 BC) by Cleomenes III.

Mégara Town in central Greece. The ancient capital of Megaris, it prospered under the Dorians and was the birthplace of Euclid.

Megarian school of philosophy A Greek philosophy founded by Euclid of Megara. It held that good was a single quality, though known by different names.

Megiddo, Battle of Battle (Sept. 19, 1918) of WW I at Megiddo, now in Israel. Here the British under Gen. Edmund Allenby (1861–1936) defeated the Ottoman Turks and began their northward thrust through Palestine. The Ottomans were forced to sign an armistice the next month.

Mehemet Ali *See* **Muhammad Ali**

Meigs, Fort *See* **Fort Meigs**

Meiji *See* **Mutsuhito**

Meiji restoration Period of modernization and Westernization in Japan (1868–1912). During this period Japan developed its industry and became a world power. The period began with restoration of power to the emperor, Mutsuhito (reign name, Meiji), after the centuries-long rule by Tokugawa shoguns. The emperor abolished feudalism (1868–69), made Tokyo capital (1869), modernized government administration (1885), and acceded to a new constitution (1889). The government thereafter consisted of an upper and lower (elected) house, a premier, and a group of elder statesmen (Genro). During this period, which ended (1912) with Meiji's death, Japan engaged in the Sino-Japanese War (1894–95) and Russo-Japanese War (1904–05).

Mein Kampf Political publication by A. Hitler. Written by Hitler during his imprisonment after the Munich Putsch, it outlined National Socialism and its program for German expansion and world domination.

Meir, Golda ⟨Mabovitch, Goldie⟩ ⟨Myerson, Goldie⟩ 1898–1978. Israeli political leader and prime minister (1969–1974). She was a founder of Israel, and as prime minister she made a concerted though unsuccessful effort to achieve peace in the Middle East. The Fourth Arab-Israeli War was fought during her administration.

Meitner, Lise 1878–1968. Austrian physicist. With O. Hahn she discovered protoactinium, and accomplished uranium fission (1938) with Hahn and Fritz Strassman (1902–).

Melaka *See* **Malacca**

Melanchthon, Philip 1497–1560. German religious scholar. He worked with Luther, published the *Loci Communes* (1521), setting forth Reformation principles, and wrote the Augsburg Confession. He attempted to moderate differences between Catholics and Protestants in order to avoid war and played a significant role in reforming the German educational system.

Melas, Baron Michael von *See* **Marengo, Battle of**

Melba, Dame Nellie ⟨Armstrong, Helen⟩ 1861–1931. Australian operatic soprano. One of the most popular opera singers of her day, she appeared throughout Europe and the US.

Melbourne, William Lamb, 2d Viscount 1779–1848. British statesman. As prime minister (1834, 1835–41) he was a friend and adviser to the young Queen Victoria. His wife, Lady Caroline, had an affair with Lord G. Byron.

Melchior *See* **Magi**

Melchisedec *See* **Melchizedek**

Melchites Christian group of the Middle East headed by the patriarch of Antioch. They are in communion with the pope, but their rites are performed in Arabic.

Melchizedek ⟨Melchisedec⟩ Biblical king and priest of Salem. He blessed Abraham, who gave him tithes. He is considered a precursor of a Christ figure.

Meleager Mythological Greek hero, son of Calydonian king Oeneus. He killed the boar that Artemis had sent to ravage his country because his father had not sacrificed to her.

Melfi, Constitutions of *See* **Constitutions of Melfi**

Melissus of Samos *See* **Eleatic school**

Mellon, Andrew William 1855–1937. American financier. As secretary of the treasury (1921–32), he introduced (1920) tax reforms that helped reduce the national debt. He donated his art collection and gave funds to form the National Gallery of Art.

Melpomene *See* **Muses**

Melville, Andrew 1545–1622. Scottish Presbyterian scholar and successor to J. Knox. He improved the Scottish universities, wrote much of the *Second Book of Discipline,* and was sent to the Tower of London (1607–11) by English king James I for his criticisms of the Anglican church.

Melville, Herman 1819–91. American author, known best for his classic novel *Moby Dick.* Melville used his experiences as a seaman (1841–44) in such books as *Typee, Omoo, Mardi, Redburn,* and *White Jacket.* After a period of popularity and literary success, Melville drifted into a life of anonymity and spent his later years as a customs official in New York City (1866–85). He died virtually unknown, but today is considered one of America's great writers.

Memnon In Greek mythology, Ethiopian king, son of Eos (Dawn). He fought against the Greeks in the Trojan War and was killed by Achilles. Zeus made him immortal.

Memphis American city (pop. 646,000), the largest city in Tennessee. A major port on the Mississippi, it was founded (1819) by A. Jackson and others. It fell (1862) to Union forces during the Civil War and was a major Union supply center during the war.

Memphis Capital of the Old Kingdom of ancient Egypt, located at the apex of the Nile delta. It was said to have been established by Menes and was dedicated to the god Ptah.

Menahem *d. c*738 BC. King of Israel (*c*744–738 BC). He killed Shallum for the throne and ruled cruelly. He paid tribute to Assyria for protection.

Menander 342?–291? BC. Greek comic dramatist. He was considered the best of the New Comedy writers and wrote more than 100 plays, which were based on love plots.

Mencius 371?–288? BC. Chinese Confucian philosopher who had a major role in the development of Confucianism. He is called the second sage, after Confucius. His *Book of Mencius* states that man is innately good, holds family duty to be the foundation of society, and stresses the need for rulers to be concerned for the common people. The book later became a classic Confucian text.

Mencken, Henry Louis 1880–1956. American journalist and critic noted for his iconoclastic criticisms of literature and middle-class American life. Among his works is the classic study *The American Language.*

Mendel, Gregor Johann 1822–84. Austrian biologist. An Augustinian monk, he conducted his experiments on hybrid plants in his monastery garden. He formulated Mendel's Law on dominant and recessive genes, and discovered the male cell's role in fertilization. His studies, ignored in his lifetime, were later rediscovered and form the basis for modern genetics.

Mendeleev, Dmitri Ivanovich *See* **Mendelejeff, Dmitri Ivanovich**

Mendelejeff, Dmitri Ivanovich ⟨Mendeleev, ~⟩ ⟨Mendeleyev, ~⟩ 1834–1907. Russian chemist. He formulated the periodic law and established a table for the classification of the elements.

Mendeleyev, Dmitri Ivanovich *See* **Mendelejeff, Dmitri Ivanovich**

Mendelssohn, Jakob Ludwig Felix ⟨Mendelssohn-Bartholdy, Felix⟩ 1809–47. German composer, grandson of M. Mendelssohn. He was one of the leading composers of the 19th cent.

Mendelssohn, Moses 1729–86. German Jewish philosopher. He advocated assimilation of the Jews into the German culture and was the model for G. Lessing's play *Nathan the Wise.*

Mendès-France, Pierre 1907–82. French statesman. A Radical Socialist, he was premier (1954–55) when France declared an armistice with Indochina. He was forced from office because of his liberal policy toward Algeria.

Mendoza, Antonio de 1490?–1552. Spanish colonial administrator and first viceroy of New Spain (1535–50). His 15-year administration was just and fair to the Indians and helped stabilize the Mexican territory.

Mendoza, Pedro de 1487?–1537. Spanish soldier and explorer. Commissioned by Holy Roman Emperor Charles V to colonize the Rio de la Plata area, he founded Buenos Aires (1536).

Menelaus Mythical Greek king of Sparta. He was the husband of Helen, whose abduction was the cause of the Trojan War. He fought under his brother, Agamemnon.

Menelik II 1844–1913. Ethiopian emperor (1889–1913). He crushed an Italian invasion attempt (1895–96), expanded Ethiopia's territory, and worked to modernize his empire.

Menendez de Aviles, Pedro 1519–74. Spanish sailor and colonizer. Menendez founded St. Augustine, Florida (1565), and led the massacre (1565) of French Huguenot colonists at Fort Caroline, Florida.

Menes *fl.* 3100 BC. Egyptian king. He united Upper and Lower Egypt and founded the 1st dynasty. He also is said to have founded the ancient capital of Memphis.

Menkure ⟨Mycerinus⟩ *fl. c*2500 BC. Egyptian king of the 4th dynasty. He built the smallest of the three pyramids at Giza.

Mennonites Protestant Christian sect. Mennonites, now most numerous in the US and Canada, believe in adult baptism, refuse to bear arms, and seek a simplified existence free of worldly concerns. The sect originated in Europe as an outgrowth of the Anabaptists and was largely formed aound the work of the Dutch reformer Menno Simons (1496–1561), for whom it is named. The elements of the Mennonite doctrine were set forth (1632) in the Dordrecht Confession of Faith. Mennonite settlements were founded in America as early as 1683. The Mennonite church has split into many smaller sects, including the Amish sects.

Menotti, Gian-Carlo 1911–. Italian composer. His operas have been extremely popular in the US, to which he emigrated in 1927. He is twice winner of the Pulitzer Prize for Music (1950, 1955).

Mensheviks Russian revolutionary party. The Mensheviks, opposed to N. Lenin's Bolsheviks, sought to form a party of the masses (rather than a revolutionary elite), believed there was a necessary transition period before creating the socialist state, and were willing to work with bourgeois elements during this time to achieve their goal. The Mensheviks were formed by a split (caused by N. Lenin, 1903) in the Russian Social Democratic Workers' party and were first led by L. Martov (1873–1923). The Social Democratic party was permanently split into two factions in 1912 and thereafter the Mensheviks were often divided by internal dissent. They dominated the provisional government of Russia after the February Revolution of 1917 (q.v.), were ousted from power by the Bolsheviks in the October Revolution (q.v.), and were officially suppressed by the Bolsheviks after 1922.

Menshikov, Aleksandr Danilovich 1672–1729. Russian field marshal and statesman. Adviser to Peter the Great, he helped secure the throne for Peter's widow, Catherine I. He ruled Russia during her reign.

Mentor In Greek mythology, a friend of Odysseus and tutor to his son Telemachus. His name has come to mean "wise adviser."

Mentuhotep II ⟨Nebhapetre⟩ Egyptian king (2060–10 BC), a ruler of the 11th dynasty. His reign marked the ascendancy of Thebes and under his leadership Upper, Middle, and Lower Egypt were reunited (c2039 BC).

Menzies, Robert Gordon 1894–. Australian statesman. As prime minister (1939–41, 1949–66) he followed a pro-American, anti-Communist policy.

Mephistopheles Personification of the devil who figured in the medieval German legend of J. Faust. Faust is said to have sold his soul to him. Mephistopheles appears in works by C. Marlowe, J. Goethe, and T. Mann.

Merarites *See* **Levites**

mercantilism Economic policy and theory that dominated European financial and governmental thinking from the 16th–18th cents. It argued that governmental regulation of a nation's industry and trade was necessary; that exports were preferable to imports or to equal trade; that large populations and armies were beneficial to a nation; that a country's true wealth was determined by its possession of gold and silver. Mercantilism was attacked by Adam Smith in *Wealth of Nations* (1776), a book advocating the laissez-faire (q.v.) doctrines that replaced mercantilism in the 18th cent.

Mercator, Gerardus ⟨Kremer, Gerhard⟩ 1512–94. Flemish cartographer. He invented the Mercator projection (1568) for navigator's maps and started work on a great atlas, which was finished (1594) by his son.

Merchants Adventurers English company (1407–1807) established by merchants dealing in foreign trade. Their major market, until 1564, was in the Spanish Netherlands, where finished English cloth was in demand.

Merchants of the Steelyard In medieval England, German merchants of the Hanseatic League (q.v.). They conducted their trading operations out of the Steelyard, a section of London along the Thames that served as English headquarters of the league. Special privileges granted these merchants (by royal order) aroused resentment among the English. But the privileges were continued because the trade was economically valuable. With the rise of the English carrying trade in the 16th cent., the German merchants ceased to be important and Queen Elizabeth expelled them (1598).

Merchant Staplers *See* **Company of the Merchants of the Staple**

Mercia, kingdom of Ancient Anglo-Saxon kingdom comprising much of central England. Settled (6th cent.) by Angles, it was overcome and divided (886) by invading Danes in the east and Alfred of Wessex in the west.

Merciless Parliament ⟨Wonderful Parliament⟩ In English history, the parliamentary session (1388) which impeached five of King Richard's supporters on broadly construed charges of treason. The incident stemmed from Richard's ongoing struggle for power with Parliament and forced him to take a more moderate course for some years.

Mercury Ancient Roman god of commerce, identified with the Greek god Hermes.

Meredith, George 1828–1909. English novelist, noted for his intellectual and psychological novels. Among his best-known novels are *The Ordeal* of *Richard Feverel, The Egoist,* and *The Amazing Marriage.*

Merezhkovsky, Dmitri Sergeyevich 1865–1941. Russian novelist and critic. He wrote the trilogy of historical novels *Christ and Antichrist,* and was an influential figure in the Russian religious and intellectual movements of the early 20th cent.

Mergenthaler, Ottmar 1854–99. German-born American inventor of the Linotype machine. Patented in 1884, it greatly advanced the printing industry.

Mérimée, Prosper *See* **Bizet, Georges**

Merlin Magician and sage of Celtic mythology and Arthurian legend. He was counselor to King Arthur and his father, Uther Pendragon.

Mermaid Tavern Historical English meeting place in London. The Friday Street Club regularly gathered there. Its members included W. Shakespeare, B. Jonson, and J. Donne.

Merneptah d. c1223 BC. Ancient Egyptian king (c1236 BC–c1223 BC), successor to his father Ramses II. He repelled an invasion by the Libyans. The earliest mention of Israel is on one of the steles commemorating this victory. It is thought the Exodus occurred during his reign.

Merope Name of several women of Greek mythology, including **(1)** one of the Pleiades, the wife of Sisyphus and **(2)** the foster mother of Oedipus.

Merovech *See* **Merovingians**

Merovingians Frankish dynasty and empire (5th–8th cents.) in Western Europe. The dynasty was founded (5th cent.) by the kings of the Salian Franks, one of whom was Merovech (reigned 448–457). The rise of the Merovingians from their kingdom on the Rhine began with the rule of Clovis I (481–511). He united the Salian and Ripuarian Franks, accepted Christianity (496), and, by his conquests, created a vast empire that included most of Gaul. His empire was divided by his four sons at his death, united again by Clotaire I (reigned 558–561) and redivided into Austrasia (q.v.), Neustria (q.v.), and Burgundy (under Austrasian control). Merovingian territories were briefly united again under the rule of Clotaire II and Dagobert I (613–639, inclusive). Already weakened by the many bitter internal wars, the Merovingian rulers after Dagobert lost all real power to the noblemen. Called the "do-nothing" kings, these kings ruled in name only and the mayors of the palace (supposedly in the king's service) held actual power. Charles Martel greatly expanded his power as mayor of the palace, and his son, Pepin the Short, finally overthrew the last Merovingian king, Childeric III, in 751. He thus founded the Carolingian Empire (q.v.). (See also France [481–751].)

Merrimack *See* **Monitor and Merrimack**

Mersen, Treaty of Treaty (870) dividing Lotharingia, one of the three kingdoms formed by division of the Carolingian Empire in 843. The treaty, formulated on the death (869) of Lotharingian king Lothair, was signed by Charles II ("the Bald") and Louis the German (all three were sons of Louis I). Lotharingia lay between Charles' kingdom of the Western Franks and Louis' kingdom of the Eastern Franks, and the two monarchs divided the territory between themselves. Thus a common border was established between the two kingdoms, later to become the states of France and Germany.

Meshed ⟨Mashhad⟩ Iranian city, capital of Khorasan province. An agricultural and trading center and a place of pilgrimage, it contains the shrine of Imam Ali Riza, a Shi'ite Muslim religious figure.

Mesolithic *See* **Stone Age**

Mesopotamia Historic region located in what is now Iraq. An important center of early civilization, the area is the fertile plain surrounding the Tigris and Euphrates rivers. The earliest towns in the region were located in the north (5th millennium BC), though the first important cultures eventually rose in the south, notably Sumer (q.v.). There followed the dynasty of Ur (q.v.), the Akkadian Empire (q.v.), the first and second Babylonian Empires (q.v.), and the Assyrian Empire (q.v.). Thereafter the region succumbed to other powers, beginning with the Persians, Macedonians, and Romans.

Messenia Ancient Greek region in the Peloponnesus, and site of the present Messinias. Its citizens frequently rebelled against Sparta's domination, notably in the Messenian Wars (q.v.).

Messenian Wars Two wars (c735–c715 BC, c650–c600 BC) waged by Sparta against Messenia. The first led to Spartan victory over Messenia. The second, prompted by an uprising in Messenia, was a prolonged struggle and ended with complete Spartan domination of Messenia.

Messerschmitt, Willy 1898–. German aviation designer and manufacturer. He founded the Messerschmitt aircraft manufacturing works and built planes for the Luftwaffe during WW II.

Messiaen, Olivier-Eugène-Prosper-Charles 1908–. French composer and organist. His work is noted for its originality and religious mysticism.

Messiah ⟨Messias⟩ In religion, especially Christianity and Judaism, a redeemer who would come from God to save humanity. In Islam, the Mahdi is a messianic figure.

Messias *See* **Messiah**

Messina Italian city, capital of Messina province,

Sicily. Founded (8th cent. BC) by settlers from Chalcis, it was destroyed by the Carthaginians (396 BC) and later rebuilt by rulers of nearby Syracuse. Thereafter, it figured in the struggles between the tyrants of Syracuse and the Carthaginians. Messina allied itself with Rome (264 BC) and this brought on the First Punic War between Rome and Carthage. It was later taken by the Goths, Byzantines, and Arabs, before being taken by the Normans, who made it part of their kingdom of Sicily. Centuries later, the capture of Messina during WW II marked the fall of Sicily to the Allies (1943).

Metacomet *See* **Philip** (*d.* 1676)

metaphysical poets Group of 17th-cent. English lyric poets whose works were noted for their contrasting imagery and intellectual brilliance or wit. The term was coined by S. Johnson, and a leading figure of the group was J. Donne.

Metaurus, Battle of the Battle (207 BC) of the Second Punic War, at the Metaurus River, northeast of Rome. Roman forces under the consuls Marcus Livius Salinator and Claudius Nero decisively defeated the Carthaginians under Hasdrubal, thus saving Rome from invasion and assuring Hannibal's eventual defeat.

Metaxas, John ⟨Metaxas, Yanni⟩ 1871–1941. Greek general and statesman. A royalist, as premier (1936–41) he assumed dictatorial powers. He repelled the Italian invasion of Greece (1940) during WW II.

Metaxas, Yanni *See* **Metaxas, John**

Metchnikoff, Èlie 1845–1916. Russian microbiologist and zoologist. He discovered that certain blood cells engulf foreign bodies, a process called phagocytosis. For his work in immunology he was awarded, with P. Ehrlich, the Nobel Prize for Physiology and Medicine (1908).

Metellus Macedonicus, Quintus Caecilus *d.* 115 BC. Roman general. He gained Roman victories in Macedonia and Greece. As censor (131 BC), he advocated compulsory marriage to increase the birthrate.

Metellus Numidicus, Quintus Caecilius *d.* 91? BC. Roman general. He defeated the Numidians under Jugurtha (109 BC) but was exiled for opposing the reforms of Lucias Appuleius Saturninus.

Metellus Pius, Quintus Caecilius *d. c*63 BC. Roman general who served under Sulla. He was commander of the war in Spain against Sertorius and consul (80 BC) with Sulla.

Methodism Protestant Christian religious movement in Britain and America, based largely on the teachings of J. Wesley. The movement began (1729) in Oxford, England, when Wesley, his brother Charles (1707–88), G. Whitefield, and others began to hold meetings for religious study. Adopting elements advanced by the Moravian church, the group began a program of evangelism, and by their actions were barred from participation within the Church of England. Whitefield, opposing Wesley's support of the doctrines of J. Arminius, separated from the group (*c*1741) and formed the Calvinistic Methodists. In 1784 Wesley ordained Thomas Coke (1747–1814) and F. Asbury superintendents of the movement in America, which had grown steadily through the 18th cent. After Wesley's death (1791), the movement in Britain formally separated from the Church of England as the Wesleyan Methodist Church. Methodist factions formed in both America and Britain in the 19th cent., and some subsequently were rejoined. A merger of churches in the US (1939) formed the Methodist Church. This in turn joined (1968) with the Evangelical United Brethren Church to form the United Methodist Church, the largest Methodist group in the world.

Methodius, Saint *See* **Cyril and Methodius, Saints**

Methuselah Biblical figure, son of Enoch. He was the longest-living patriarch, said to have lived 969 years.

Methven, Battle of *See* **Robert I**

Metternich, Prince Klemens Wenzel Nepomuk Lothar von 1773–1859. Austrian statesman, the leading European statesman (1815–48), whose conservative policies helped maintain political stability in post-Napoleonic Europe. As Austrian foreign minister (1809–48), he helped form the Quadruple Alliance, which finally defeated Napoleon (1813). Thereafter he sought to maintain the balance of power in Europe and to preserve the stability of the monarchies against liberal movements. He made Austria the dominant power in the German Confederation, helped create the Holy Alliance, took part in formulating the Carlsbad Decrees, and was a leading figure at the congresses of Vienna (1814–15), Troppau (1820), Laibach (1821), and Verona (1822). Metternich was forced out of power by the liberal revolutions of 1848, brought on in part by the repressive measures he advocated to maintain order.

Mexican Revolution Period of political and social turmoil in Mexico following the overthrow (May, 1911) of P. Díaz by F. Madero. Madero subsequently headed a popular movement that sought to implement reforms in Mexico. But his rule was ineffective and he was in turn overthrown and murdered (Feb., 1913) by Gen. V. Huerta. Huerta's reactionary rule led to revolts headed by V. Carranza, F. Villa, and E. Zapata, and he was forced from office (1914). Carranza became president, though his rule was challenged by Villa and Zapata, who continued armed resistance. Villa's raid into the US (Mar. 1916) provoked a US expedition into Mexico, headed by Gen. J. Pershing, but Villa successfully evaded it. Under Carranza, Mexico established the Constitution of 1917, which called for separation of church and state, agrarian reform, and nationalization of foreign holdings and mineral rights. Reform came slowly, however, and Mexico remained politically volatile for many years.

Mexican War War (May, 1846–Feb., 1848) between the US and Mexico. It resulted in US acquisition of vast territories in the West, including California, Nevada, Utah, New Mexico, and Arizona. The war was a result of US expansionist policies and accumulated tensions between the two countries. Following admission (1845) of Texas (which had rebelled against Mexican rule) to the Union, relations with Mexico became strained. The US attempted to buy California and New Mexico, but J. Slidell's mission failed. President J. Polk then ordered US troops into disputed territory along the Rio Grande (July, 1845). The Mexicans responded in kind and, on Apr. 25, 1846, fighting broke out between the two armies. The US declared war (May 12, 1846), but by this time US forces under Gen. Z. Taylor had already forced the Mexicans to retreat across the Rio Grande. Gen. S. Kearny invaded New Mexico (June–Aug. 1846), secured it for the US, and then entered California (Dec., 1846), which had already been taken over for the US by Pacific Naval Commander John Drake Sloat (1781–1867) and Capt. J. Frémont. Meanwhile US forces under Taylor and others pushed into Mexico. Taylor won an important victory over A. de Santa Anna (now Mexican president) at the Battle of Buena Vista (Feb., 1847). Gen. W. Scott landed some 12,000 US troops at Veracruz (Mar., 1847), took the city, and began the march to Mexico City. Scott won a rapid succession of victories at Cerro Gordo, Contreras, and Chapultepec (a fortress defending Mexico City), and entered Mexico City on Sept. 14, 1847. The Treaty of Guadalupe Hidalgo (q.v.) brought the war to an end and, among its other provisions, provided for the purchase of captured Mexican territory for $15 million.

Mexico Republic, the southernmost country of North America. Its capital is Mexico City. The region comprising Mexico saw the rise and development of a number of indigenous civilizations, among them the Toltec, Maya, and Aztec. Conquered (16th cent.) by the Spanish and made part of the viceroyalty of New Spain, Mexico became independent in 1821. Since then its history has

been marked by periods of political struggle, notably the Mexican Revolution (q.v.), which laid the basis for modern Mexican society. Key dates in the history of Mexico include:

8TH–11TH CENT. Toltecs flourished in central Mexico.

14TH–15TH CENT. Aztecs flourished in Mexico.

1517 Francisco Fernández de Córdoba explored Yucatán; was first European to explore region.

1519–21 H. Cortés began conquest of Mexico.

1528 Juan de Zumarraga became first bishop of Mexico; in subsequent years the Roman Catholic church forcibly Christianized native Indians and gained great landholdings in Spanish Mexico.

1535 Viceroyalty of New Spain created; Mexico City established as capital amid ruins of Aztec capital of Tenochtitlán.

16TH CENT. *Repartimiento* system established: Spaniards given title to vast tracts of lands and native Indian peoples living on them; gave rise to oppressive system of forced labor and helped preserve social divisions between Spanish landowners, Indians, and mestizos (racially mixed persons).

1540s Spanish explored and laid claim to modern US Southwest region, including California, Arizona, New Mexico, and Texas.

1541 Mixton War, unsuccessful Indian revolt against Spanish rule.

1680 Pueblo Rebellion, Indian revolt in New Mexico that halted Spanish colonization in that region for a decade.

1786 Reforms enacted by Viceroy Jose de Gálvez to end long-standing corruption and abuses of power by Spanish colonial government.

1808 Army of French emperor Napoleon occupied Mexico; Joseph Bonaparte made king.

1810 Miguel Hidalgo y Costilla issued (Sept. 16) the *Grito de Dolores*, a call to rebellion to secure social and economic equality; Indians and mestizos rose in revolt.

1810 Hidalgo y Costilla marked his first victory at the Battle of Celaya.

1811 Rebel force under Hidalgo y Costilla crushed by Spanish royalists at Calderón Bridge (Jan. 17).

1813–14 Congress of Chilpancingo proclaimed (1813) a constitutional republic; main rebel forces defeated (1814) by royalist general A. de Iturbide; V. Guerrero carried on guerrilla war.

1820 Spanish Revolution of 1820; conservatives in Mexico (former royalists) decided in favor of independence from Spain.

1821 Guerrilla leader V. Guerrero and conservative general A. de Iturbide formulated (Feb.) Plan of Iguala, calling for Mexican independence as a monarchy.

1821 Spain recognized Mexican independence by the Treaty of Córdoba (Aug. 24).

1822–24 De Iturbide seized power and declared himself emperor (1822); overthrown (1823) by Antonio López de Santa Anna; republic declared and Guadalupe Victoria became its first president (1824–29).

1833–36 Santa Anna in office as president.

1836 Santa Anna humiliated by Texas revolution; lost the presidency.

1838 Pastry War: brief conflict with France.

1839–44 Santa Anna returned to power.

1845–48 Mexican War fought against US; defeated, Mexico lost California and the Southwest to US; Santa Anna ruled and commanded armies (1846–47).

1853–55 Santa Anna ruled as dictator; overthrown by a liberal revolution (begun 1854) led by Benito Juárez and others.

1854–76 *La Reforma*, period of liberal reforms.

1857 New liberal constitution adopted.

1858–61 War of Reform; Juárez served as provisional president; nationalized church property (1859) and began policy of reform in Mexico.

1861 Juárez elected president; policies of reform led to resentment by conservatives and European intervention; France moved to establish colonial empire in Mexico.

1863 French invaders defeated Mexican forces at the Battle of Puebla (May 17); Mexico City captured soon after.

1864–67 Austrian archduke Maximilian ruled as emperor of Mexico.

1865–67 French withdrew troops from Mexico (1865); Juárez forces launched successful campaign against Maximilian, who was captured and executed.

1867–72 Juárez in office as president; put down revolts; succeeded at his death by Sebastián Lerdo de Tejada.

1876 P. Díaz overthrew S. Lerdo de Tejada.

1876–1911 Díaz in power (except 1880–84); promoted economic development, but favored rich landowners at expense of poor; peonage increased and church again came back in favor.

1911 Mexican Revolution began (May) with overthrow of P. Díaz by F. Madero.

1913 F. Madero overthrown and murdered (Feb.) by Gen. V. Huerta.

1914 Vera Cruz incident; US Marines occupied the city (Apr.–Nov.).

1914 V. Huerta forced from office by uprisings led by V. Carranza, F. Villa, and E. Zapata.

1914–20 Carranza served as president; restored order but there was continued resistance by F. Villa and E. Zapata.

1915 Gen. A. Obregón defeated F. Villa at the Battle of Celaya.

1916 F. Villa's raid on Columbus, New Mexico, led to US military expedition into Mexico; Villa evaded capture.

1917 Constitution established; provided for separation of church and state; communal lands restored to Indians; labor and other reforms.

1920–24 Gen. Á. Obregón overthrew Carranza (1920) and served as president.

1924–28 Plutarco Elias Calles served as president.

1928 Obregón reelected president; assassinated before he could take office.

1929 Calles founded National Revolutionary party, Mexico's most powerful political party.

1934–40 L. Cardenas served as president; instituted many reforms; improved lot of Indians, distributed lands under ejido system, nationalized railroads, and expropriated foreign oil holdings.

1940–46 Manuel Avila Camacho served as president; followed more conservative domestic policy; brought Mexico into WW II against the Axis (1942).

1945 Became a member of the UN.

1946 National Revolutionary party renamed the Institutional Revolutionary party.

1946–52 M. Alemán served as president; worked at modernization of agriculture and improvement of living conditions.

1948 Became a member of OAS.

1952–58 Adolfo Ruiz Cortines in office as president.

1958–64 Adolpho López Mateos in office as president.

1964–70 Gustavo Díaz Ordaz in office as president; reforms enacted to aid poor, including seizure of some large estates.

1970–76 Luis Escheverría Alvarez in office as president; promoted ties with underdeveloped Third World countries.

1976–82 José López Portillo in office (Dec. 1) as president; increased Mexican oil output and thereby eased economic problems; world oil glut in 1981 brought new economic crisis.

1981 Portillo met with US President R. Reagan to discuss growing problem of illegal Mexican aliens in US; new US immigration program to be established.

1982 Portillo devalued the peso as economic problems worsened.

1982 Mexican-owned banks nationalized (Sept.) as economic crisis worsened.

Mexico City Capital (pop. 8,988,200) and largest city of Mexico. Originally the Aztec capital, Tenochtitlán, it was captured (1521) by H. Cortés during the Spanish conquest of Mexico, and became the capital of New Spain (1521–1821). It was captured (1821) by rebels during the war for independence and later by Gen. W. Scott (1847) during the Mexican War.

Meyer, Adolf 1866–1950. Swiss-born American psychiatrist. He originated the term "mental hygiene" and held that the cure of mental illness lay in dealing with the whole personality.

MGB *See* **GPU**

Miani, Battle of British victory (Feb. 17, 1843) over the forces of the mirs of Sind. The British victory led to annexation of most of Sind into British India.

Micah ⟨Micheas⟩ Old Testament prophet, author of the book of Micah, the sixth of twelve books of the minor prophets.

Michael Archangel of the Christian, Jewish, and Muslim religions. He is represented as leading the angels in the battle against evil spirits.

Michael 1596–1645. Russian czar (1613–45), founder of the Romanov dynasty. His election ended the Time of Troubles. During his reign Russia made peace with Sweden and Poland.

Michael 1921–. Romanian king (1927–30, 1940–47), son of Carol II. He overthrew the dictatorship of I. Antonescu (1944) and supported the Allies in WW II. He was forced into exile by the Communist takeover (1947).

Michael I ⟨Michael I Rhangabe⟩ *d.* c845. Byzantine emperor (811–813). He supported the orthodox faith against the iconoclasts.

Michael I Rhangabe *See* **Michael I**

Michael II *d.* 829. Byzantine emperor (820–829). He took the throne after his supporters assassinated his predecessor, Leo V. He was tolerant of both sides in the religious dispute between iconoclasts and orthodoxy.

Michael III 839–867. Byzantine emperor (842–867), last of the Amorian-Phrygian line. The controversy over iconoclasm was ended during his reign (843). He warred successfully against the Arabs and Slavs.

Michael VIII ⟨Michael Palaeologus⟩ 1224–82. Byzantine emperor (1259–82). He recovered Constantinople (1261) from the Latins and formed a union with Pope Gregory X against Charles of Anjou. Its failure led to the massacre called the Sicilian Vespers (1282).

Michael the Brave *d.* 1601. Romanian prince of Walachia (1593–1601). He captured and declared himself prince of Transylvania (1599) and Moldavia (1600), thereby uniting Romania under his rule. His realm was divided after his death, but he is considered a Romanian national hero.

Micheas *See* **Micah**

Michelangelo (Buonarroti) 1475–1564. Italian artist, one of the towering figures of the Italian Renaissance. A gifted poet, painter, and sculptor, he is celebrated for such masterpieces as his statues of David and Moses, and the Pietà (1497). His painting of the Sistine Chapel took four years to complete (1508–12).

Michelet, Jules 1798–1874. French historian. He wrote the *Histoire de France,* an emotional and nationalistic work.

Michelin, André and **Édouard** 1853–1931; 1856–1940. French industrialists. Brothers, they invented and produced removable pneumatic tires and established the Michelin tire company.

Michelson, Albert Abraham 1852–1931. American physicist. He measured the speed of light, using an interferometer of his own design. The results of the Michelson-Morley experiment, conducted with Edward Williams Morley (1838–1923), contributed to A. Einstein's theory of relativity. He was awarded the Nobel Prize (1907).

Michener, James Albert 1907–. American author. He was awarded a Pulitzer Prize (1948) for his *Tales of the South Pacific.* Among his novels are *Hawaii* and *Centennial.*

Michigan State in the north-central US (pop. 9,258,300), the 26th state. Michigan was first explored and settled by the French (17th cent.). It was ceded to Britain after the French and Indian War (1754–63), and was scene of the Indian revolt known as Pontiac's Rebellion (1763–66). It was ceded to the US (1783) and became part of the Northwest Territory (1787). After settlement of a boundary dispute with Ohio, Michigan became a state in 1837.

Mickiewicz, Adam 1798–1855. Polish poet. A romantic and patriot, he is known best for the epic *Pan Tadeusz.*

Micon *fl.* c460 BC. Greek painter and sculptor. He collaborated with Polygnotus on *The Greeks and the Amazons* and the mural on the Stoa Poikile at Athens.

Midas Mythical Greek king of Phrygia. Dionysus granted him the ability to turn whatever he touched to gold.

Middle Ages Period in European history (c5th–15th cents.) between the fall of the Roman Empire and the discovery of the New World by Columbus (1492). It was the transition period from the ancient cultures to those of the modern world, and its beginning phase is sometimes referred to as the

Dark Ages *(q.v.)*. The Middle Ages were marked by the rise of the church, by the spread and collapse of feudalism, and by the formative stages of many of the modern European states.

Middle East Term denoting the countries of southwestern Asia and northeastern Africa, including parts of Turkey, Syria, Israel, Jordan, Iraq, Iran, Lebanon, all of the Arabian peninsula, Egypt, and Libya.

Middle English Name given the language of medieval England and also a period in English literature *(c*1100–*c*1500). Middle English language replaced Old English and can be divided into three developmental periods: Early Middle English *(c*1100–*c*1250); Central Middle English *(c*1250–*c*1400); and Late Middle English *(c*1400–*c*1500). Middle English literature includes works by W. Langland, Sir T. Malory, G. Chaucer, and J. Gower.

Middle Kingdom Period in ancient Egyptian history, lasting from the latter half of the 11th dynasty to the 12th dynasty *(c*2000 BC–*c*1786 BC). It followed the First Intermediate Period, began with the rule of Amenemhet I and ended with the rule of Amenemhet IV. Egypt enjoyed commercial prosperity during this period, which also saw rule of the pharaohs as feudal lords, the transfer of the capital from Thebes to Ithtowe, the conquest of lower Nubia, and a golden age of Egyptian literature and arts. The Middle Kingdom was followed by the Second Intermediate Period and the coming of the Hyksos.

Middleton, Thomas 1570?–1627. English dramatist. He wrote tragedies and satirical comedies on the mores of his time, usually in collaboration. Among his works are *Women Beware Women* and *The Changeling.*

Middle West (Midwest) American geographical designation, the collective name for the north central states of the US.

Midgard In Old Norse mythology, the middle earth, the home of the human race. It was formed by the body of the giant, Ymir, the first living creature.

Midhat Pasha 1822–84. Turkish statesman. As grand vizier (1872, 1876–77), he was instrumental in obtaining the first constitution (1876) for the Ottoman Empire.

Midianites Biblical nomadic tribe of northern Arabia, related to the Israelites through Abraham. Moses married the daughter of the Midian priest Jethro.

Midrash An interpretation of Hebrew Scriptures, using rabbinical commentaries.

Midway, Battle of US naval victory over the Japanese (June 3–6, 1942), during WW II. The battle was fought by carrier-based planes on both sides and marked the turning point for the US in the Pacific War. A Japanese task force, assembled to take US-held Midway Island, was intercepted (June 3) off Midway by aircraft of a US carrier force. The Japanese counterattacked with their aircraft, and the battle raged until June 6. Japanese losses included three carriers, 275 planes, one heavy cruiser, and three destroyers. US losses included one carrier, 150 planes, and a destroyer.

Mieris, Frans van 1635–81. Dutch painter, known for his small genre and portrait paintings.

Mies van Der Rohe, Ludwig 1886–1969. German-American architect. He was director of the Bauhaus in the 1930s. As professor of architecture (1938–58) at the Illinois Institute of Technology, he pioneered construction of functional glass-and-steel buildings.

Mifflin, Thomas 1744–1800. American Revolutionary leader. He was quartermaster general in the Revolutionary army and was involved in the Conway Cabal. He was first governor of Pennsylvania (1790–99).

Miguel 1802–66. Pretender to the Portuguese throne, son of John VI. An absolutist, he contested the succession of his brother Pedro, and later of Pedro's daughter Maria. He renounced his claim in 1834 after having ruled from 1828. (*See also* Portugal [1828–33].)

Mikhailovich, Draja 1893?–1946. Serbian soldier. He led a guerrilla force against German occupation during WW II, then fought against the Communists. He was executed by Tito's forces.

Mikoyan, Anastas Ivanovich 1895–1978. Russian Communist statesman. A member of the Central Committee (1923–1978), he held cabinet positions under J. Stalin and N. Khrushchev and was chairman of the Presidium of the Supreme Soviet (1964–65).

Milan 1854–1901. Prince (1868–82) and king (1882–89) of Serbia. By allying with Russia in the Russo-Turkish Wars, he gained Serbia's independence (1878) from the Ottoman Empire.

Milan Italy's financial center and second largest city (pop. 1,706,300), capital of Lombardy and of Milano province. A Gallic city, it was conquered by Rome (222 BC) and later by the Huns and Goths. Under the Visconti as dukes of Milan (1349–1447), the city reached its peak of importance. Subsequently held by the Spanish, French, and Austrians, it was incorporated into Italy in 1860.

Milan, Edict of *See* **Edict of Milan**

Milan Decree Decree issued (Dec. 17, 1807) by Napoleon, as part of the Continental System. It stated that ships trading with Great Britain lost their neutrality.

Miletus Ancient Greek city in Caria now in Turkey. Once a prosperous Ionian seaport, it led in the Ionian revolt against Persia (c499 BC). The Persians sacked the city (494 BC).

Milhaud, Darius 1892–1974. French composer, a pioneer in the use of polytonality. His works include the opera *Christophe Colomb* and the ballet *La Création du Monde.*

military-industrial complex Collective term for the US defense establishment, including arms development, manufacturing and procurement. At the end of his term of office, President D. Eisenhower warned against its growing power and it continues to wield great influence, especially in promoting costly new weapons systems. During the Vietnam War the military-industrial complex was the target of numerous protests. The end of the war and the cutback in defense contracts during the late 1970s curtailed its power for a time.

Militia Ordinance Bill passed (1642) by the English Parliament that caused the break between Parliament and King Charles I, just prior to the start of the English Civil War (1642). Following Charles' attempt (Jan., 1642) to seize five members of the House of Commons, Parliament passed the Militia Ordinance, giving it control over the militia. Charles rejected (Mar.) the measure, and his supporters in Parliament joined him at York. The Rump Parliament at London then delivered (June 2) its Nineteen Propositions, which included the ordinance, to the king.

Mill, James 1773–1836. British philosopher, historian, and economist. He adopted and contributed to the principles of his friend J. Bentham, the founder of utilitarianism. He wrote a *History of British India.*

Mill, John Stuart 1806–73. British philosopher and political economist, son of J. Mill. He further developed the utilitarian doctrines established by J. Bentham and the elder Mill, and formulated principles of inductive reasoning. His works include *A System of Logic* and *On Liberty.*

Millais, Sir John Everett 1829–96. English painter. He was a founder (1848) of the Pre-Raphaelite brotherhood. His works include the controversial *Christ in the House of His Parents.*

Millay, Edna St. Vincent 1892–1950. American poet, one of the leading poets of the 20th cent. She was awarded the Pulitzer Prize (1923) for *The Ballad of the Harp Weaver.*

millennialism Christian belief in the millennium, a period of 1,000 years before the end of the world during which Christ and the saints will rule on earth.

millennium Period of one thousand years. In Christianity, the millennium refers to the time when Jesus will reappear and rule on earth.

Miller, Arthur 1915–. American playwright, twice winner of the Pulitzer Prize (1950, 1956). His plays include *Death of a Salesman, The Crucible,* and *A View from the Bridge.*

Miller, Henry 1891–1980. American author. His books *Tropic of Cancer* and *Tropic of Capricorn,* banned in the US until the 1960s because of their sexual content, influenced the development of modern literature and helped to break traditional literary barriers.

Miller, William 1782–1849. American religious leader. As founder of the Second Adventists, or Millerites, he predicted the Second Coming of Christ in 1843. His movement evolved into the Adventist church (*q.v.*).

Millerand, Alexandre 1859–1943. French statesman. He was minister of war (1912–13, 1914–15) and president of France (1920–24). He was forced from office by a coalition of the political left.

Milligan, ex parte US Supreme Court decision (1866) that military tribunals could judge civilians only in the absence of civil courts. The decision limited presidential, congressional, and military powers over civilians in wartime.

Millikan, Robert Andrews 1868–1953. American physicist, noted for his work on the photoelectric effect and for measuring the charge on the electron. He was awarded the Nobel Prize (1923) and discovered cosmic rays (1925).

Mill Springs, Battle of Union victory (Jan. 19, 1862) over the Confederates in the American Civil War, at Mill Springs, Kentucky. The battle was the first major Union victory in the West.

Milne, Alan Alexander 1882–1956. English author, famous for his children's books, *Winnie-the-Pooh* and *The House at Pooh Corner.*

Milner, Alfred Milner, 1st Viscount 1854–1925. British statesman. He was a high administrator in South Africa (1897–1905), and his inflexible stand furthered tensions leading to the South African (Boer) War (1899–1902).

Milo 95–47 BC. Roman politician. His rivalry with Clodius led to Clodius' murder and Milo's exile to Massilia. Milo's advocate, Cicero, too afraid to speak at his trial, later published his oration *Pro Milone.*

Milon *See* **Milo of Croton**

Milo of Croton ⟨Milon⟩ *fl.* late 6th cent. BC. Greek athlete, renowned for his wrestling skill and feats of strength at the Olympic and Pythian games.

Milos *See* **Milosh**

Milosh ⟨Milos⟩ 1780–1860. Serbian prince

(1817–39, 1858–60) and founder of modern Serbia. He led the revolt against the Turks and was named hereditary prince (1827). He founded the Obrenović dynasty.

Miltiades d. 489 BC. Greek general. As commander of the Athenian forces, he defeated the Persians at Marathon (490 BC).

Milton, John 1608–74. English poet. Milton began his career as a poet while still at Cambridge University. Though acclaimed for his pastoral poem *Lycidas*, he spent much of his time writing essays supporting the movement to reform the Church of England. His support of the Commonwealth caused him political trouble after the Restoration. Though blind from 1652, Milton dictated the works for which he is known best, *Paradise Lost* and *Paradise Regained*.

Milvian Bridge Roman bridge, constructed (109 BC) over the Tiber as part of the Flaminian Way. Here Constantine defeated Maxentius (AD 312) and thus became sole ruler in the Western Roman Empire. Here, too, he saw the vision of a cross in the sky that led him to adopt Christianity. Constantine soon after brought about toleration of Christianity in the empire.

Minamoto Yoritomo 1147–99. Japanese shogun (1192–99), founder of the Kamakura shogunate. He participated in the rebellion against the Taira clan and later set up the feudal system, the shogunate, by which Japan was ruled until the 19th cent.

Minden, Battle of Battle (Aug. 1, 1759) between the French and allied Prussian and British troops during the Seven Years' War (1756–63). Some 45,000 Prussian and British soldiers routed 60,000 French soldiers in this battle at Minden (now located in West Germany).

Mindon Min 1814–78. Burmese king (1853–78) and founder of Mandalay. During his reign he was forced to grant large concessions to the British.

Mindszenty, Jozseph 1892–1975. Hungarian Roman Catholic clergyman, primate of Hungary (1946–74). Arrested (1948) for treason, he was freed during the 1956 revolution, then took asylum in the US embassy until 1971, when he left Hungary.

Minerva Ancient Roman goddess of handicrafts and the arts. She was identified with the Greek goddess Athena.

Ming Dynasty of native Chinese emperors (1368–1644) who greatly expanded the Chinese empire. Under its rulers the empire came to include all or parts of Vietnam, Burma, Turkistan, Korea, and Mongolia. Hung-Wu, founder of the dynasty, came to power (1368) and ousted (by 1371) the Mongols of the Yüan dynasty. During the long reign of the Ming emperors the Chinese civil service system was reinstituted; Confucianism was state-supported; exploratory voyages (1405–33) as far west as Arabia were made; European settlements were established (16th cent.) at Canton and Macao; Christian missionaries arrived; and the arts, especially ceramics and architecture, flourished. A succession of weak rulers, heavy taxes, and dissent among factions in government led to peasant revolts and the fall of the dynasty (1644) to the Ch'ing (Manchu) dynasty.

Ministry of All Talents See **Grenville, William Wyndham**

Minnesota North-central US state (pop. 4,077,200), the 32d state. First explored by the French (17th cent.), it became an important fur-trading region. The part of Minnesota east of the Mississippi was part of the Northwest Territory, and that west of the Mississippi was ceded to the US by the Louisiana Purchase (1803). Minnesota was admitted to the Union (1858) and fought for the Union in the Civil War. It was a center for the growth of the Granger movement, and also for the Populist party movement of the 1890s.

Minoan civilization Bronze Age culture that developed on Crete (c3000 BC–1000 BC). One of the ancient Greek Aegean civilizations, it was for a time a major maritime power in the Mediterranean. By 1500 BC the Minoans had a well-developed written language and had become skilled in working ceramics and bronze. The Minoan capital at Cnossus with its luxurious palace, was twice destroyed (and rebuilt) in the second millennium BC, possibly by earthquakes and/or invasions by the Myceneans. The palace was destroyed a last time (c1400) and, soon after, the Minoan civilization disappeared. This civilization is generally divided into three periods: Early Minoan (c3000 BC–c2200 BC); Middle Minoan (c2200 BC–c1500 BC); and Late Minoan (c1500 BC–c1000 BC). The Mycenaean civilization predominated after the fall of the Minoans.

Minos In Greek mythology, the son of Zeus and Europa, and the king of Crete. His wife, Pasiphaë, was the mother of the Minotaur.

Minotaur In Greek mythology, a monster with a bull's head and a man's body. It was kept in a labyrinth on Crete and King Minos sacrificed Athenian youths to it. Theseus, one of its intended victims, killed the creature.

Minseito Japanese political party formed in 1927. A centrist party, it had ties with Japanese business interests and sought better relations with the West. The Minseito, formed from the earlier Kenseito party, was a major party in the years before WW II. The party was dissolved in 1940 after the militarists came to power. A new Democratic party formed after WW II absorbed much of the Minseito party's membership.

Minsk Russian city (pop. 1,262,000), capital of the Belorussian Soviet Republic and an industrial center (since late 19th cent.). Its rise began in the 11th cent. and, after being joined to Lithuania (1326), it flourished as a commercial center (15th cent.). Control of Minsk passed to Poland (1569) and then to Russia (1793). It was occupied by the Germans in both WW I and WW II and was largely destroyed in the latter war. It was recaptured by the Russians in 1944.

minstrel In medieval Europe, a musician, singer, juggler, or other kind of entertainer. While many traveled, others were employed as court entertainers.

Minuit, Peter c1580–1638. Dutch colonial governor of New Netherland who purchased Manhattan Island from the Indians for $24 worth of trinkets in 1626. He founded New York City (then New Amsterdam) by building a fort at the south end of the island. Later, in Swedish service, he founded New Sweden (1638) on the Delaware.

mir Peasant community in Russia. The mir was self-governing until the 17th cent. and thereafter controlled peasant lands in its locality. The mirs were abolished (1917) after the Russian Revolution.

Mirabeau, Honoré Gabriel Riquetti, comte de 1749–91. French revolutionary politician. Imprisoned by his father during his reckless youth, he later became a popular and powerful orator in the early days of the revolution. In the National Assembly he unsuccessfully advocated establishment of a constitutional monarchy.

Mirabeau, Victor Riquetti, marquis de 1715–89. French political economist, father of H. Mirabeau. His physiocratic philosophy was set forth in *The Friend of Man, or Treatise on the Population*.

Miramón, Miguel 1832–67. Mexican general. Miramón opposed the leader of liberal forces, B. Juárez, and served as chief marshal to Emperor Maximilian, with whom he was captured and executed.

Miranda, Francisco de 1750–1816. Venezuelan revolutionary. He fought the Spanish, briefly gained Venezuelan independence (1810), and ruled with dictatorial powers. He was forced to surrender to the counterattacking Spanish (1812) and died in prison.

Miriam In the Bible, sister of Moses and Aaron. She led the song of Miriam.

Miró, Joan 1893–1974. Spanish artist. A surrealist painter, he used pure colors and abstract shapes in his fantasies, such as *Dog Barking at the Moon*.

Mirza Ali Muhammad *See* **Bab, The**

Mise of Amiens Arbitrated agreement by which the Provisions of Oxford (*q.v.*) were annulled (Jan. 23, 1264). English king Henry III, after disputes with his barons, took the question of the provisions to French king Louis IX for mediation. Louis ruled in favor of Henry.

Mishima Yukio (Kimitake Hiraoka) 1925–70. Japanese writer best known for his novels concerning the conflict between Eastern and Western cultural influences in Japanese life. The decline of Japanese values and traditions is the major theme of his last work, *The Sea of Fertility*.

Mishna Collection of Jewish oral laws, divided into six orders: seeds (Zeraim), festivals (Moed), women (Nashim), damages (Nezikim), sacrifices (Kodashim), purifications (Tohorot). With commentaries included in the Gemara, it constitutes the Talmud (*q.v.*).

Mississippi US state in the Southeast, (pop. 2,520,600), the 20th state. The first settlement was established at Biloxi by the French in 1699. The area was held by the British and the Spanish after 1763 and was ceded to the US in 1783. The Mississippi Territory was created in 1798 and included the present states Mississippi and Alabama. The western section became the state of Mississippi in 1817, and its constitution was adopted in 1890. It was the second state to secede in the American Civil War (1861) and was readmitted in 1870. Mississippi was a focal point of the drive to win civil rights for blacks during the 1960s.

Mississippi Bubble *See* **Mississippi Scheme**

Mississippi Scheme (Mississippi Bubble) Plan to exploit the lower Mississippi valley and other French colonial territories. French comptroller general J. Law bought up (1717) colonization rights to the Mississippi Territory and in subsequent financial manipulations won control over other French possessions. His Mississippi Company, which attempted to finance the French national debt in 1720, promoted a speculative boom that ended in financial disaster (Oct., 1720).

Missouri State (pop. 4,346,300) in the central US, the 24th state. J. Marquette and Louis Jolliet first explored the area (1673, 1683), which was claimed by the French as part of the Louisiana Territory. In 1803, it became part of the US by the Louisiana Purchase (*q.v.*), and the Missouri Territory was created in 1812. The dispute over whether to admit territories as slave states resulted (1820) in the Missouri Compromise (*q.v.*), and Missouri was admitted as a slave state in 1821. The present constitution was adopted in 1945.

Missouri Compromise US legislation passed (1820–21) to maintain the balance between slaveholding and free states. This compromise between the proslavery South and the abolitionists in the North was largely engineered by Rep. H. Clay. It remained in force until replaced (1850) by the Compromise of 1850, which established the doctrine of popular sovereignty *(q.v.)*. The issue was first raised (1819) when Missouri applied for admission to the union as a slave state. With states then equally balanced (11 each) between slave and free, the Senate rejected the measure (Feb., 1819). The final compromise measure (passed Mar., 1820), however, provided for the admission of Maine as a free state, Missouri as a slave state, and banned slavery in the Louisiana Purchase territory north of Arkansas. Separate legislation requiring the Missouri constitution to guarantee rights of Negro freedmen (Mar., 1821) held up admission of Missouri until Aug., 1821.

Mistral, Frédéric 1830–1914. French poet. He was a founder of the Félibrige, an association for the promotion of the Provençal language, and wrote a Provençal-French dictionary.

Mitchell, Margaret 1900–49. American novelist, who wrote one book, *Gone With the Wind*, an immediate and lasting success. She won the Pulitzer Prize (1937).

Mitchell, William Lendrum 1879–1936. American army general and pilot. He advocated creation of an independent air force and increased use of air power in wartime. He was court-martialed (1925) for his criticism of military leadership.

Mithra In Persian mythology, the god of light and wisdom. Mithraism *(q.v.)* spread into the Roman Empire and rivaled Christianity until the 3rd cent.

Mithradates VI ⟨Mithridates VI⟩ *c*131 BC–63 BC. King of Pontus (120–63 BC). He waged the three Mithradatic Wars *(q.v.)* against the Romans and was finally defeated by Pompey.

Mithradatic Wars **1.** First (88–84 BC). War between Mithradates VI, king of Pontus, and Rome. Taking advantage of unrest in the Roman province of Asia and the upheavals brought about by the Social War (91–88 BC), Mithradates overran the province. While the struggles for power continued at Rome, Roman armies, under L. Sulla, met Mithradates' armies (87) in Greece. By the battles of Chaeronea (86) and Orchomenos (85), Sulla forced the invaders out of Greece and later (84) forced Mithradates to give up all his conquests. **2.** Second (83–81 BC). War between Mithradates VI and Rome. The Romans, under Murena, attacked Cappadocia and Pontus. It ended with the restoration of territories Mithradates lost during the war. **3.** Third (74–63). War between Mithradates VI, his son, and Rome. Mithradates' son, Armenian king Tigranes I, took over Cappadocia and Syria. Roman consul L. Lucullus won early victories against Mithradates and Tigranes (73) but was forced to break off fighting (68) when his troops mutinied. Under command of Pompey (66–63), the Romans completed the conquest and annexed Pontus to the Asian province.

Mithraism Major religion of the ancient world, widespread within the Roman empire shortly before adoption of Christianity (3d cent. AD). Roman Mithraism, which in some ways resembled Christianity, was concerned with the battle between good and evil, and held out the promise of immortality to its followers. Worship of the god Mithras flourished in Persia (5th cent. BC) and subsequently spread throughout the Mediterranean world. In Greece it became one of the Mystery religions and in Rome it flourished by the 2d cent. AD. With the official adoption of Christianity, Mithraism was suppressed in the Roman empire and soon disappeared.

Mithridates VI *See* **Mithradates VI**

Mitre, Bartolomé 1821–1906. Argentine statesman and general. Mitre helped to overthrow J. de Rosas (1861) and became president (1862–68). He succeeded in uniting the country and brought about a period of prosperity.

Mitterand, François 1916–. French president (1981–). A Socialist, Mitterand won a clear victory over former President V. d'Estaing and, in subsequent elections for the National Assembly, his party's candidates won by wide margins. In office, Mitterrand increased taxes to business and the wealthy and raised the minimum wage by 10 percent.

Mnemosyne In Greek mythology, the goddess of memory, daughter of Titans Uranus (heaven) and Ge (earth). She was mother of the nine Muses by Zeus.

Moabites Ancient Semitic people from the Transjordan plateau east of the Dead Sea. Their kingdom, Moab, is mentioned in the Old Testament. It ceased to exist after conquest by the Assyrians (8th cent. BC).

Moabite stone Ancient inscriptions. This ancient slab dates from 850 BC. Written by the Moabite Mesha in Hebrew, it describes his victory against Israel.

Mobile Bay, Battle of Union victory (Aug. 5, 1864) in a naval battle during the American Civil War (1861–65). Seeking to neutralize the Confederate port at Mobile Bay, Union land forces attacked (Aug. 3) and captured forts at the entrance to the bay. The Union fleet, commanded by Admiral D. Farragut, then broke through a minefield, entered the bay (Aug. 5), and forced the Confederate fleet to surrender. It was during this battle that Farragut uttered his famous order to continue the attack, "Damn the torpedoes."

Mobutu Sese Seko ⟨Mobutu, Joseph Désiré⟩ 1930–. President (1967–) of the Republic of Zaire (formerly the Congo).

Moctezuma   *See* **Montezuma**

Model Parliament   Two representative bodies that figured in the development of the British Parliament. **1.** Assembly convened (1265) during the Barons' War (1263–67) by S. de Montfort. Present were two citizens (burgesses) from each city and two knights from each shire in England. **2.** Assembly convened (1295) by King Edward I. Representatives of the higher clergy, knights, burgesses, and lower clergy attended.

Modena, Mary of   *See* **Mary of Modena**

modern art   Revolution in Western art that began in the late 19th cent. with impressionism *(q.v.)* and continues into the present with such schools as abstract expressionism *(q.v.)* and Op art *(q.v.)*. The art is generally characterized by the unconventional use of color, imagery, spontaneity, and the artist's personal vision of the subject matter.

Modernism   Modern religious movement (19th–20th cents.) that interpreted traditional Christian doctrines in a way believed more compatible with the teachings of modern philosophy and the findings of modern science. A school of thought of this name among Roman Catholics was condemned as heretical by Pope Pius X (1907).

Modernismo   Movement among Spanish poets. It began in Latin America (late 19th cent.) with publication of *Azul* (1888), a collection by R. Dario. The movement that grew out of this work was largely a rebellion against the Romantic and naturalistic traditions in Spanish poetry and involved exotic imagery and unconventional meter and rhythm.

Modestinus, Herennius   *fl.* *c*250 BC. Roman jurist. Modestinus was a student of Ulpian and was one of Rome's most distinguished and influential judges.

Modigliani, Amedeo   1884–1920. Italian modernist painter and sculptor. He is known for his characteristic elongation of form and use of muted color in his paintings.

Modjopahit Empire   *See* **Majapahit Empire**

Moesia   Ancient province of the Roman Empire (from AD 15), situated in what is today southern Serbia and northern Bulgaria. It was later divided into Upper and Lower Moesia.

Mogul   ⟨Mughal⟩ Muslim dynasty that ruled in India from the 16th to 19th cents. The Mogul Empire was at its height from the 16th to the early 18th cents. and was noted for its efficient administrative organization and for its great contributions in the fields of art, architecture, and literature. The Mogul Empire was founded by Baber, who established Mogul power in India by victory in the battle of Panipat (1526). Baber (ruled 1526–30) was succeeded by his son Humayun (ruled 1530–56). Other notable Mogul rulers were Akbar (ruled 1556–1605), who greatly expanded Mogul power; Jahangir (ruled 1605–27), his son; Shah Jahan (ruled 1628–58), who expanded Mogul power into the Deccan by conquering Bijapur and Golconda, and who built the Taj Mahal at Agra; and Aurangzeb (ruled 1658–1707), under whose rule the Mogul Empire reached its height and began its decline. Aurangzeb was unable to halt the rising strength of the Marathas, and after his death (1707) the empire began to divide into a group of provinces. In the 18th cent. British influence in the region also began to increase, and the empire was further weakened. Its last ruler, Bahadur Shah II (ruled 1837–57) was emperor in title only. After the failure of the Indian Mutiny (1857), he was deposed by the British and the empire ceased to exist.

Mohács, Battle of   Battle (Aug. 29, 1526) in which Sulayman I of Turkey defeated and killed Louis II of Hungary. This led to more than 150 years of Turkish domination in Hungary.

Mohammed   *See* **Muhammad**

Mohegan Indians   North American Indian tribe important in Colonial New England. Following the Pequot War *(q.v.)*, the Mohegans became a powerful tribe in southern New England. The tribe gradually sold off its lands to white settlers and thereafter lived on a reservation in Connecticut.

Mohican   *See* **Mahican Indians**

Moholy-Nagy, László   1895–1946. Hungarian painter, designer, photographer, and teacher. He taught at the Bauhaus school (1923–29) in Germany and founded a school of design in Chicago (1939).

Moki   *See* **Hopi Indians**

Molay, Jacques de   1243?–1314. Last grand master of the Knights Templars *(q.v.)*. Philip IV of France had Molay and his followers arrested (1307) for heresy in a move to break the order's power. Molay confessed under torture, then recanted, and was burned at the stake.

Moldavia   Historic former principality now located in modern Romania. It won independence from the Hungarian monarchy (*c*1349) and resisted the Ottoman Turks until the 16th cent. Thereafter it remained under their control until after the Russo-Turkish War (1828–29). By the Treaty of Adrianople, Moldavia came under the protection of Russia, though it continued to recognize Turkish suzerainty. Following the Crimean War (1853–56), Moldavia became largely independent and, in 1861, it formally united with neighboring Wallachia to form the modern state of Romania (q.v.).

Molech ⟨Moloch⟩ Ancient Canaanite deity, worshiped during the reigns of kings Ahaz and Manasseh. Children were sacrificed to him.

Molière ⟨*pseud. of* Jean Baptiste Poquelin⟩ 1622–73. Great French playwright. Originally an actor, Molière headed his own touring company. However, he is remembered for his brilliant comedies that satirized the characters and society of his times. Among his many works are *Tartuffe*, *The School for Husbands*, *The School for Wives*, *The Doctor in Spite of Himself*, and *The Misanthrope*.

Molina, Luis 1535–1600. Spanish Jesuit who wrote *Concordia liberi arbitrii cum gratiae donis*. In it he articulated his doctrine of Molinism, which sought to reconcile free will and divine grace.

Molinism *See* **Molina, Luis**

Molinos, Miguel de 1640–97. Spanish priest who founded quietism (q.v.), spiritual passiveness. In 1685, he was condemned by the Inquisition and died in prison.

Molly Maguires Irish-American terrorist group active (1860s–1870s) in the Pennsylvania coal-mining regions. Reacting against poor working and living conditions there, this secret group intimidated and murdered mine company officials and engaged in acts of sabotage. Pinkerton detectives suppressed the group in 1877.

Molnár, Ferenc 1878–1952. Hungarian novelist and playwright. He wrote the novel *The Paul Street Boys* and the plays *Liliom* and *The Swan*.

Moloch *See* **Molech**

Molotov, Vyacheslav Mikhailovich ⟨*orig.* Skriabin, ~⟩ 1890–. Russian statesman. As foreign minister, he was chief Russian spokesman for international affairs during and after WW II. A hard-line Stalinist, he tried unsuccessfully to depose N. Khrushchev (1957) and was expelled from the Communist party (1964).

Moltke, Helmuth von 1800–91. Prussian field marshal. As chief of the general staff (1858–88), he was responsible for Prussian successes in the war against Denmark (1864), the Austro-Prussian War (1866), and the Franco-Prussian War (1870–71).

Moltke, Helmuth von 1848–1916. German army chief of general staff (1906–14). He changed the Schlieffen Plan (q.v.) at the outbreak of WW I, thereby weakening the offensive against France and prolonging the fighting.

Mommsen, Theodor 1817–1903. German historian known for his *History of Rome*. He received the Nobel Prize for literature in 1902.

Momos *See* **Momus**

Momus ⟨Momos⟩ Greek mythical figure, the personification of censure, ridicule, insult, and humiliation.

Monaco Independent principality located near the border between France and Italy on the Mediterranean coast. Believed to have been settled by the Phoenicians, it became an independent state in the 13th cent. It was annexed by France (1793–1814), came under the protection of Sardinia (1815–60), and was ceded back to France (1860), which restored its sovereignty under French protection. A constitution was promulgated in 1911 and the current one was adopted in 1962. The principality has been ruled by Prince Rainier III (1923–) since 1949.

monarchianism Christian heresy (2d–3d cents. AD). It held that God the Father and Jesus are one, as opposed to two beings in one person. Two forms of Monarchianism developed, dynamic and modalistic, both of which were opposed by the church.

monasticism Religious movement in which individuals seek spiritual perfection by living apart from the general society. Monks generally live communally in their monasteries (though in some monastic movements they live as hermits). Their lives are strictly regulated by the monastic rule (often ascetic) and worship is the central focus of their existence. Monasticism has been a part of various religions, including Christianity (Western and Eastern), Hinduism, Buddhism, Islam, and Jainism. In the Western Christian church, monasticism generally arose (6th cent.) and acquired its characteristic form from the teachings of St. Benedict. Thereafter, monasticism spread throughout Europe and spawned many important orders (*see* Benedictines, Carthusians, and Cistercians). Further, these orders were of great importance as centers of learning in an otherwise unstable medieval European society and, by their work as copyists, preserved many of the ancient classics.

Monck, George, 1st duke of Albemarle ⟨Monk, ~⟩ 1608–70. English general. A Royalist at the outbreak of the English Civil War, he was captured by the Parliamentarians (1644). After the fall of Charles I, he served under O. Cromwell in fighting in Ireland and Scotland. He later played a central role in making arrangements for the restoration of the monarchy under Charles II.

Mondale, Walter Frederick 1928–. US vice-president (1977–81) under President J. Carter. He was early identified with liberal Democratic politics in Minnesota and became US senator (1964–77) from the state.

Mondrian, Piet 1872–1944. Dutch artist. He was a founder of the De Stijl movement in abstract art and developed an abstract style called neoplasticism.

Monet, Claude 1840–1926. French artist, a founder of impressionism *(q.v.)*. Noted especially for his many landscapes, Monet developed a characteristic style using color to emphasize the effects of light. Among his many important works are *Water Lilies, Haystacks,* and *Rouen Cathedral.*

Mongkut *See* **Chakkri dynasty**

Mongol Empire Great Asian empire founded (13th cent.) by the Mongol conqueror Genghis Khan *(q.v.)*. After uniting the Mongol tribes under him (1206), Genghis Khan invaded northern China and subdued Korea. He next led his fierce bands westward, conquered Khorezm, the region of modern Iran and Iraq, and part of Russia, and raided northern India. On his death in 1227, Genghis' son Ogadai became the imperial ruler (great khan), and each of his other sons ruled a part of the empire (khanate). In the west, Mongols under Batu Khan conquered Russia and there established (1241) the Khanate of the Golden Horde *(q.v.)*, or Kipchak Empire, that ruled Russia until the 15th cent. In Persia, the Mongol conqueror Hulagu Khan established the Il-Khan dynasty, which ruled there (1258–1353). Kublai Khan became great khan in 1260 and moved the Mongol capital to China, where he built a splendid city. He founded the Yüan dynasty, which ruled China until the rise of the Ming dynasty (1368). Under Tamerlane (reigned 1360–1405), the Mongols of the Timurid *(q.v.)* Empire, in central Asia, rose to importance for a time. Finally the Mongol conqueror Baber established the Mogul *(q.v.)* dynasty in India (1526–1707). From the 15th cent., however, the history of the empire was one of decline and power struggles between tribal factions. Finally Mongolia itself was conquered by the Manchus (17th–18th cents.).

Mongolia Historic region located in east-central Asia, to the north of China proper. It is divided today between the Mongolian People's Republic (Outer Mongolia) and Inner Mongolia, now part of China. From ancient times it was the home of nomadic peoples who regularly threatened the Chinese Empire from the north. The region rose to prominence in the 13th cent. as the seat of Genghis Khan's Mongol Empire *(q.v.)*. The decline of the Mongol Empire brought Chinese control over both Inner (southern) and Outer (northern) Mongolia (by the 17th cent.). Outer Mongolia regained its independence (1921) as the Mongolian People's Republic *(q.v.)*. The Japanese captured parts of Inner Mongolia in the 1930s, during the Second Sino-Japanese War, but these territories were restored to China following WW II.

Mongolian People's Republic *(formerly* Outer Mongolia) Republic located between north-central China and the USSR, in east-central Asia. This part of the historic region of Mongolia *(q.v.)* became an independent kingdom under the "Living Buddha" during the Chinese Revolution of 1911. The Chinese reoccupied the territory (1919) but were driven out by White Russians (1921) at the close of the Russian Civil War. Russian Communist troops in turn drove out the White Russians, and Mongolia was proclaimed an independent state under the Living Buddha. After the death of the Living Buddha, Mongolia was proclaimed a republic (1924) and came under the control of Communists. Imposition of the Communist system and persecution of Buddhist priests resulted in the exodus of priests, leading thousands of followers and much livestock, to China (Lama Rebellion, 1932). Mongolia entered into a formal alliance with the USSR in 1936 and remains a Soviet satellite state in modern times. It was admitted to the UN in 1961 and supported the Soviets in their ideological conflict with the Chinese (from the 1960s). A 20-year friendship treaty with the USSR was signed in 1966 and an agreement for Soviet economic aid was completed in 1970.

Mongols Nomadic Asian people. They rose to importance in the 13th cent. under Genghis Khan, who founded the vast Mongol Empire *(q.v.)*. His descendants founded successor states, such as those of the Chinese Yüan dynasty, the Russian Golden Horde, the Timur Empire and the Mogul Empire. Present-day Mongolia is divided between Russia (Outer Mongolia) and China (Inner Mongolia).

Monitor and **Merrimack** Two ironclad warships during the American Civil War that fought the first battle (Mar. 9, 1862) between armored warships. The Union *Monitor*, commanded by Lt. John L. Worden (1818–97), and the Confederate *Merrimack*, then named the *Virginia* and commanded by Lt. Catesby Jones (1821–77), engaged in battle at Hampton Roads, Virginia. After an inconclusive battle, both ships withdrew and never fought again. The *Monitor* foundered and sank (Dec., 1862) and the *Merrimack* was destroyed (May, 1862) to prevent its capture.

Monmouth, Battle of ⟨Monmouth Courthouse, ~⟩ Indecisive battle (June 28, 1778) during the American Revolution (1775–83). British troops, then retreating from Philadelphia under Gen. H. Clinton's command, were being pursued by Gen. G. Washington's forces. Washington ordered an attack on the British rear at Monmouth, New Jersey. But the action was mishandled by Gen. C. Lee and only the arrival of Washington's main force prevented defeat. That night the British withdrew and eventually arrived safely in New York. Casualties numbered 300 to 400 on both sides.

Monmouth, James Scott, duke of 1649–85. English nobleman, illegitimate son of Charles II and rival of the duke of York (later James II) for the throne. The favorite of anti-Catholic factions in England, he became involved in the Rye House Plot *(q.v.)*. After the accession of James II, Monmouth attempted a rebellion against him. Monmouth's small force was defeated at Sedgemoor (July 6, 1685) and he was beheaded.

Monmouth Courthouse, Battle of *See* **Monmouth, Battle of**

Monmouth's Revolt *See* **Monmouth, James Scott, duke of**

Monnet, Jean 1888–. French political economist and statesman. He drafted the Monnet Plan (1947) for the rebuilding of postwar French economy, the Schuman Plan that resulted in the European Coal and Steel Community, and headed the Action Committee for the United States of Europe (from 1956).

Monocacy, Battle of American Civil War battle (July 9, 1864) fought near Frederick, Maryland. Some 6,000 federal troops, under Gen. L. Wallace, were defeated by the 14,000-man army of Gen. J. Early. The action, however, delayed Early's advance on Washington and thus gave Gen. U. Grant time to strengthen the capital's defenses.

Monophysitism Controversial doctrine of the early Christian church contending that Jesus had but one nature (divine) and not two (human and divine). The concept had its beginnings in 4th-cent. Apollinarianism and developed as a reaction to the extreme dualism of Nestorianism. Monophysitism was denounced as a heresy by the Council of Chalcedon (AD 451), though the council's attempt to formulate a compromise doctrine failed. Proponents of Monophysitism, such as Eutyches, continued the dispute and a schism soon developed between the Western church and the Monophysite Eastern Church. The schism was of-

ficially ended (519) by Emperor Justin I, who upheld the Council of Chalcedon. Nevertheless Monophysites persisted and, though persecuted, eventually formed the Coptic, Jacobite, and Armenian churches (all Monophysite).

monotheism Religious doctrine. Monotheism holds that there is only one God, as opposed to polytheism, which recognizes many gods. For the history of the world's major monotheistic religions, *see* Judaism, Christianity, and Islam.

Monothelitism Controversial doctrine of the early Christian church contending that Jesus had two natures (human and divine) but only one will (divine). The doctrine was a 7th-cent. attempt to provide an acceptable compromise to the dispute over Monophysitism. It was put forward (622) and promulgated (638) as official doctrine within the Byzantine Empire by Heraclius I. The compromise, however, created a furor. Opposed by popes in the Western church, Monothelitism was condemned (649) by a Lateran Council called by Pope Saint Martin I. Emperor Constans II seized and exiled the pope in retaliation and it was not until the accession of Constantine IV (668) that attempts were made to settle the controversy. Constantine called the Third Council of Constantinople (680), which subsequently denounced the doctrine as a heresy. Monothelitism, though briefly revived (711–13), thereafter died out.

Monroe, James 1758–1831. Fifth US president (1817–25), successor to J. Madison. Monroe distinguished himself during the American Revolution and he was wounded in the Battle of Trenton. After the war he was elected to the Virginia legislature (1782) and the Continental Congress (1783–86). A supporter of states' rights, he opposed the centralized government set up by the Constitution. As US senator (1790–94), he supported T. Jefferson against the Federalists. He served (1794–96) as US minister to France and as governor of Virginia (1799–1802). Appointed (1802) special envoy to France, he helped R. Livingston negotiate the Louisiana Purchase (1803). He served as secretary of state (1811–17) and of war (1814–15) under President J. Madison, and succeeded Madison as president (1817). He was reelected handily in 1820. His terms in office saw the Seminole War, US acquisition of Florida from Spain (1819), passage (1820) of the Missouri Compromise *(q.v.)*, and issuance (1823) of what is now called the Monroe Doctrine *(q.v.)*. His years as president were called the Era of Good Feeling *(q.v.)* and were marked by significant westward migrations. Monroe supported the colonization of Liberia, whose capital, Monrovia, is named for him.

Monroe, Marilyn ⟨Baker, Norma Jean⟩ 1926–62. American actress and famous sex symbol of American film. Major films include *Bus Stop, Some Like It Hot,* and *The Misfits.*

Monroe Doctrine Guiding principle of US foreign policy in North and South America (19th–20th cents.). Enunciated by President J. Monroe (Dec. 2, 1823), the new policy declared that the US would henceforth oppose European powers in any attempt to colonize or interfere with affairs of states in the Americas. It also restated the US policy of nonintervention in European affairs (and existing European colonies). The declaration was prompted by Russian expansionist policies in Alaska and the possible takeover of newly independent South American states. Restated by Pres. J. Polk (1845, 1848), the doctrine was largely ignored by European powers in the 19th cent. Pres. T. Roosevelt added the Roosevelt Corollary (1904) in response to the Venezuela Claims *(q.v.)* incident, thus including possible US intervention to maintain the peace in any South American country. Increasing resentment by South American nations toward US domination in the 20th cent. has led to greater US involvement in such multilateral organizations as the OAS. Exceptions to this trend include the Cuban Missile Crisis and US intervention in the Dominican Republic (1965).

Monrovia Capital city (pop. 171,700) of Liberia, founded by the American Colonization Society *(q.v.)* for freed slaves (1822) and named for J. Monroe. It is a major African seaport on the Atlantic.

Montagnards *See* **Mountain, the**

Montaigne, Michel Eyquem de 1533–92. Great French essayist. A courtier to French King Charles IX and once the mayor of Bordeaux, Montaigne was noted for his three books of essays. In them he revealed a spirit of humanism, skepticism of knowledge, and mastery of style. He greatly influenced French and English literature.

Montalembert, Charles Forbes, count of 1810–70. French political leader and historian. A leader of liberal Catholics, he was editor of the newspaper *L'Avenir* and an opponent of Emperor Napoleon III.

Montana State (pop. 786,700) in the US Northwest, the 41st state. Montana was acquired (1803) by the US in the Louisiana Purchase *(q.v.)* and first explored by Lewis and Clark in their expedition of 1804–06. Fur traders set up trading posts in succeeding years, and the discovery of gold in 1852 resulted in several mining settlements. In 1864, the Montana Territory was organized, and after wars with the Sioux Indians (including the Battle of Little Bighorn) the territory saw an increase in ranching. The coming of the railroads brought new settlements and, in 1889, Montana became a state. A new constitution was adopted in 1973.

Montanism Christian movement (2d cent. AD), which was started in Phrygia by Montanus (*fl.* 2d cent.) and his followers, the illuminati. Extreme ascetics who said the end of the world was near, Montanists believed Montanus' teachings to be divine prophecies and held their sect to be superior to the orthodox church. The movement was largely suppressed in the 2d cent., though it persisted until the 9th cent. in some areas.

Montcalm, Louis Joseph de 1712–59. French general. He was commander of the French forces in Canada during the French and Indian War *(q.v.)*. He successfully defended French territories against the British until his defeat and death at the Battle of the Plains of Abraham.

Monte Carlo Town and world-famous resort in the Mediterranean principality of Monaco. It is noted for its gambling casino, opened in 1861 and now operated by the government (since 1967).

Monte Cassino *See* **Benedictines**

Montecuccoli, Raimondo, count of *See* **Montecucculi, Raimondo, count of**

Montecucculi, Raimondo, count of ⟨Montecuccoli, ~⟩ 1609–80. Italian-born general of the Holy Roman Empire. A brilliant tactician, he was successful in the Thirty Years' War and against the Turks (1664) and the French (1672–75).

Montefiore, Sir Moses Haim 1784–1885. British Jewish leader and philanthropist. He was sheriff of London (1837) and traveled throughout Europe and the Middle East trying to alleviate the oppression of Jews.

Montejo, Francisco de *c*1479–*c*1548. Spanish conquistador who took part in the conquest of Mexico under H. Cortés.

Montemagno, Bernardo dei Paganelli di *See* **Eugene III**

Montenegro Former independent kingdom located in what is now southern Yugoslavia. A mountainous region, it was first settled by Serbs (1389) after their homelands were conquered by the Turks. They warred against the Turks in the 18th and 19th cents. (allied with Russia) and after the Russo-Turkish War (1876–78) secured recognition of independence. Montenegro figured in the Balkan Wars *(q.v.)*, supported Serbia in WW I, and joined the Kingdom of Serbs, Croats, and Slovenes after WW I. It was a center of resistance under J. Tito during WW II and became part of Yugoslavia in 1946.

Montesquieu, Charles de Secondat, baron de la Brède et de 1689–1755. French political philosopher. His most important work was *The Spirit of*

Laws, which theorized on the way external conditions determine the form government takes and advocated the balance of power between government and individuals.

Montessori, Maria 1870–1952. Italian educator. She was the first woman recipient of a medical degree in Italy and originated the Montessori system of children's education (based on self-motivation and spontaneity).

Monteverdi, Claudio 1567–1643. Italian composer. His first madrigals were published when he was 15, and he went on to compose works that are important in the early history of opera. Among them are *Orfeo* and *L'Arianna.*

Montevideo Uruguayan capital city (pop. 1,500,000). It was founded (1726) by the Spanish. Its early history was marked by rivalry between colonial powers for its control. Made capital of Uruguay in 1830, it again suffered during the civil wars of that century. Its port was opened in 1901.

Montez, Lola 1818–61. Irish adventuress. As mistress of Louis I of Bavaria, she antagonized the Jesuits with her liberalism and was forced to leave (1848). She died in the US.

Montezuma ⟨Moctezuma⟩ 1480?–1520. Aztec emperor (c1502–20). A despotic and unpopular ruler, he was taken hostage by the Spanish under H. Cortés. He was killed during the Aztec uprising against the Spanish (June, 1520).

Montfort, Simon de c1160–1218. Norman crusader. He led the Albigensian Crusade *(q.v.)* in southern France and was killed at the siege of Toulouse.

Montfort, Simon de, earl of Leicester 1208–65. English statesman and soldier. Formerly an adviser to Henry III and leader of his forces during revolts in Gascony, Montfort broke with the king and became leader of the barons during the Barons' War *(q.v.).* Following his victory at Lewes (1264), he became virtual ruler of England and summoned the Model Parliament *(q.v.).* He was finally defeated and captured at the Battle of Evesham *(q.v.).*

Montgolfier, Jacques Etienne 1745–99. French inventor. He and his brother, Joseph Michel, designed and constructed the first practical balloon. It was inflated with hot air and first ascended (unmanned) in 1783.

Montgomery Alabama city (pop. 178,200). Incorporated in 1819, it became an important river port and state capital (1847). The Confederacy was formed here (Feb., 1861) at the start of the American Civil War, and it served as the first capital of the Confederate States (until May, 1861). It was captured by the Union in 1865.

Montgomery, Bernard Law, 1st viscount Montgomery of Alamein 1887–1976. Noted British field marshal during WW II. He defeated Rommel's forces at el-Alamain in Africa (1942) and forced their surrender (1943), took part in the invasion of Sicily (1943) and Italy, and played a major role in the Normandy invasion (1944) and subsequent Allied drive to Germany.

Montgomery, Richard 1738–75. Irish-American Revolutionary War general. He was second-in-command of the Montreal expedition and was killed while attacking Quebec.

Monticello T. Jefferson's Virginia estate, located near Charlottesville, Virginia. Designed by Jefferson, it was completed in 1772. He and his family are buried here. It became a national monument in 1926.

Montini, Giovanni Battista *See* **Paul VI**

Montmorency, Anne, duke of 1493–1567. Marshal (1522) and constable of France (1537). He served in the Italian Wars under Francis I. Under Charles IX, he fought in the Wars of Religion and was killed in battle.

Montmorency, Mathieu, baron of c1174–1230. Constable of France (1218). He served under Philip II and under Louis VIII against the English and supported the regency of Blanche of Castile.

Montpensier, Louise d'Orléans, duchess of 1627–93. French princess and soldier. Niece of Louis XIII, she commanded rebel troops in the Fronde of the Princes *(q.v.)* and saved the Great Condé's army at the Battle of the Faubourg Sainte-Antoine (1652).

Montreal Canadian city (pop. 2,798,000) and important river port. First settled by the French (1642), it became a fur-trading center and starting point for expeditions of the Canadian interior. It passed to the British (1760) and was occupied by American colonials (1775–76) during the American Revolution. Its growth in the 19th cent. began with completion of canals to the Great Lakes and it was capital of Canada (1844–49).

Montreux Convention Agreement (July 20, 1936) revising the Straits Convention of 1923. It abolished the International Straits Commission and gave Turkey authority to close the Dardanelles to shipping during wartime.

Montrose, James Graham, 5th earl and 1st marquess of 1612–50. Scottish general. Originally a Covenanter, Montrose supported Charles I during the English Civil War (1642–49). He won important victories in Scotland before being decisively defeated at Philiphaugh.

Monts, Pierre du Guast, comte de 1560–1630. French explorer. Monts was S. de Champlain's patron. Together they explored the St. Lawrence

River and the American coast to Cape Cod. Monts founded the first French colony at Port Royal (1605).

Mooney, Thomas J. 1883–1942. American radical labor leader. Mooney and Warren Billings (1893–1973) were convicted for the bombing at the San Francisco Preparedness Parade (July 22, 1916) in which ten were killed. His death sentence was commuted (1918) and both were pardoned (1939).

Moore, George Edward 1873–1958. British philosopher. A friend of B. Russell, Moore was a realist whose major work, *Principia Ethica*, opposed philosophical idealism.

Moore, Henry 1898–. British artist and sculptor, he is an internationally known sculptor, noted for the characteristic organic form of his sculptures. He also completed a famous series of drawings of bomb shelter scenes during WW II.

Moore, Sir John 1761–1809. British general, noted for his service during the Peninsular War (1808–14). He led his troops on a famous retreat through the mountains to La Coruña, where he defeated the French. He was mortally wounded in the battle.

Moore's Creek Bridge, Battle of Battle (Feb. 27, 1776) during the American Revolutionary War, fought near Wilmington, North Carolina. Colonial patriots defeated a Loyalist force of 1,800 men and thereby checked British plans for occupation of North Carolina.

Moors Originally, a mixed Arab and Berber people living in the Roman province of Mauretania. They became (8th cent. AD) zealous converts to Islam and, led by Tarik (ibn Ziyad), invaded the Iberian peninsula (711). There they conquered the Visigoths and ranged into France, where their advance was checked (732) by C. Martel at Poitiers. All of Spain, save the northern Christian part, was subsequently constituted as a Muslim caliphate under Abd ar-Rahman I. With its capital at Córdoba, the caliphate prospered and many centers of commerce and Muslim culture were established. The government, however, was weak and fell to the Almoravids (1086) and then the Almohads (1174). The Moors were slowly driven from the Iberian peninsula in the Reconquista, the Christian reconquest (11th–15th cents.), and many Moors resettled in (North) Africa. Those that remained in Spain were persecuted under the Inquisition and were finally expelled (1609). The term "Moors" sometimes refers to Muslims in general.

Moral Re-armament ⟨Buchmanism⟩ ⟨Oxford Group⟩ International evangelistic organization begun by Frank Buchman (1878–1961) in 1922.

The movement is nondenominational and aims at a spiritual revitalization of the individual and attainment of the four moral absolutes: purity, unselfishness, honesty, and love. The movement has been most successful among Protestant denominations.

Morat, Battle of Battle (June 22, 1476) in the war between the Swiss Confederation and Burgundy (1474–76). Some 35,000 Swiss infantrymen routed 20,000 mercenaries in the service of Charles the Bold of Burgundy at this town (now in western Switzerland). Charles was forced to retreat.

Moravia Historic region and former kingdom, located in what is now central Czechoslovakia. Moravia was settled by the Slavs (6th cent.), rose to become a powerful kingdom (Great Moravia) in the 9th cent. and was converted to Christianity by Cyril and Methodius (863). It was taken by the Magyars (10th cent.) and then became part of the kingdom of Bohemia, ruled by the Hapsburgs. In 1918 it was made part of Czechoslovakia and, with Silesia, formed the province of Moravia and Silesia (1927). Taken by Germany during WW II, the region was restored in 1945.

Moravia, Alberto ⟨Pincherle, Alberto⟩ 1907–. Italian writer, Moravia's novels of alienation in the modern world include *The Indifferent Ones*, *The Conformist*, and *The Woman of Rome*.

Moravian Church ⟨Renewed Church of the Brethren⟩ ⟨Unitas Fratrum⟩ A small Protestant evangelical denomination founded (c1457) by a group of Hussites. Persecution of the Unitas Fratrum, as it was first called, began (c1460) and eventually drove its members out of Bohemia and Moldavia. But a few of the Moravians were left when, in 1727, the church was revived in Saxony. From this new Moravian community at Herrnhut, the church began sending out missionaries to the Americas, Africa, and Asia. From 1735, they founded new Moravian settlements in America. Most members of the church now live in the US.

Moray, James Stuart, 1st earl of *See* **Murray, James Stuart, 1st earl of**

Morazan, Francisco *See* **Central American Union**

More, Sir Thomas 1478–1535. English author, statesman, and Roman Catholic saint. More wrote his famous *Utopia* and served as lord chancellor (1529–32) to Henry VIII. His refusal to endorse Henry's Act of Supremacy *(q.v.)*, creating the Church of England, led to his resignation and eventual execution.

Morea *See* **Peloponnesus.**

Moreau, Jean Victor 1763–1813. French general. He supported Napoleon in the coup of 18 Brumaire and, as one of Napoleon's generals, won the signal victory at the Battle of Hohenlinden (1800).

Napoleon grew jealous and had him banished in 1804. Moreau died fighting for the Royalist cause against Napoleon.

Morelos y Pavón, José María 1765–1815. Mexican priest and hero of the movement for independence from Spain. He fought under and then succeeded M. Hidalgo y Castilla and was successful in his early campaigns against the Spanish. He was later captured and shot, however.

Moreno, Mariano 1778–1811. Argentine revolutionary and intellectual leader. His publications attacking the Spanish colonial administration set the stage for the revolution (May, 1810) that ousted the Spanish viceroy. As a member of the revolutionary government, he established the national library and the government newspaper.

Morfontaine, Treaty of See **Adams, John**

Morgan, Daniel 1736–1802. American Revolutionary War general. Morgan defeated the British at the Battle of Cowpens (1781). After the war, he quelled the Whiskey Rebellion (1794) and served in Congress (1797–99.)

Morgan, Sir Henry 1635?–88. Welsh buccaneer. Morgan was a privateer in English service; his daring acts of piracy had the tacit approval of the British government and included brutal attacks on Spanish possessions in the Caribbean. He became lieutenant governor of Jamaica in 1674.

Morgan, John Hunt 1825–64. Confederate general. Morgan was known for his daring raids (1862) behind Union lines in Kentucky, Indiana, and Ohio. Finally captured, he escaped and was later killed at Greenville, Tennessee.

Morgan, John Pierpont 1837–1913. American financier and a leading figure in the early 20th-cent. financial world. The son of J. S. Morgan, he reorganized some of the major US railroads, took over US government financing after the Panic of 1873, and in 1901 financed formation of the United States Steel Corporation. He became the target of congressional investigations into money trusts in 1912.

Morgan, Junius Spencer 1813–90. American financier. Morgan's British-based firm, J. S. Morgan and Company, lent $50 million to France during the Franco-Prussian War.

Morgan, Thomas Hunt 1866–1945. American scientist. Hunt won the Nobel Prize in Physiology and Medicine in 1933 for his work with the fruit fly (Drosophila), which confirmed the action of chromosomes and genes in heredity.

Morganfield, McKinley See **Waters, Muddy**

Morgarten, Battle of Decisive victory (Nov. 15, 1315) of the Swiss Confederation over the Austrian Hapsburgs. The Austrians, under Leopold I, invaded the canton of Schwyz, a member of the confederation. They were ambushed in Morgarten Pass and some 1,500 Austrians were killed.

Morgenthau, Henry Jr. 1891–1967. US statesman. As treasury secretary (1934–45) under President F. Roosevelt, he supervised America's WW II economy, including massive taxation and government spending programs.

Moriscos Moriscos were Moors in Spain who were forcibly converted to Catholicism after 1492. Many practiced Islam secretly, however, and all were deported in 1609.

Morison, Samuel Eliot 1887–1976. American historian, writer, and teacher. Morison won Pulitzer prizes for *Admiral of the Ocean* and *John Paul Jones*. Among his many other works is *The Growth of the American Republic* (with H. Commager).

Morley, Edward Williams See **Michelson, Albert Abraham**

Mormons (Latter-Day Saints, Church of Jesus Christ of) Religious denomination founded (1830) in New York. Mormonism is characterized by an emphasis on revelation, the interdependence of spiritual and daily life, and concern for the church community. Mormons were noted as polygamists until the practice was banned (1890). The church was founded by J. Smith after he translated into the Book of Mormon the golden tablets he said were delivered to him in a revelation. In 1831 Smith moved the church to Ohio, then to Missouri (1831), and was driven to Illinois (1839). There Smith was killed (1844) by an angry mob. Under B. Young the Mormons moved west and settled (1847) Salt Lake City, Utah. After Utah became a US territory (1850), friction between Mormon and non-Mormon settlers developed and led to the Mormon War (1857). Mormons, however, were in firm control of the territory when it became a state (1896) and since then have spread their faith worldwide.

Mormon War (Utah War) Hostilities (1857–58) between Mormon settlers in Utah and US government troops. When a non-Mormon was appointed by the US government as governor of the Utah Territory (1857), Mormon governor B. Young instituted martial law. US troops, sent there to restore order, were fired upon by Mormons in sporadic raids that lasted until a peace was negotiated (June, 1858). The federal appointee then replaced Young as governor.

Mornay, Philippe de, seigneur du Plessis-Marly 1549–1623. French diplomat and Protestant (Huguenot) leader during the Wars of Religion. Mornay wrote tracts in support of the Protestant cause and reconciled the Protestant leader, Henry of Navarre (later Henry IV), with the Catholic king Henry III.

Morny, Charles, duc de 1811–65. French statesman. He helped organize the coup (Dec. 1851) that made his half-brother, Napoleon III, dictator of France.

Moro, Aldo 1916–78. Italian statesman and prime minister (1963–68). As prime minister, he formed a coalition government with the Socialists, though Italy's serious economic problems prevented him from instituting reforms he wanted. He was premier (1974–76) and was kidnapped (Mar., 1978) and killed by left-wing terrorists.

Morocco Kingdom located on the northwest coast of Africa at the entrance to the Mediterranean Sea. Its capital is Rabat. In the 8th cent. Morocco was the base for the Arab conquest of Spain. After the Moors were expelled from Spain (15th cent.), Morocco came under attack by Spain and Portugal. In the late 19th cent., Morocco became the object of rivalry among the European imperial powers, and both Spain and France established (1912) protectorates there. Morocco was reestablished as an independent kingdom in 1956. Key dates in the history of Morocco include:

1ST CENT. BC Kingdom of Mauretania in region of modern Morocco constituted as Roman province of Mauretania.

5TH CENT. AD Vandals conquered region.

LATE 7TH CENT. Arabs entered Morocco; introduced Islam to Berbers in region.

8TH CENT. Berbers and Arabs launched invasion of Spain.

c788–900 Idris I and descendants established Morocco as unified and independent kingdom.

11TH CENT. Almoravides conquered region, ending period of tribal rule and strife between Umayyad and Fatimid Muslim factions.

12TH CENT. Almohades conquered the Almoravides.

16TH CENT. Spain and Portugal conquered coastal Morocco.

1554 Saadian (first Sherifian) dynasty founded in Morocco.

1578 Portuguese ended attempts to conquer Morocco following defeat in Battle of the Three Kings (Aug. 4).

1660 Alawite (second Sherifian) dynasty founded.

17TH–19TH CENT. Alawites reconquered much of Morocco; kingdom became center for Barbary pirates.

1822–59 Abdu-r-Rahman reigned; attempted to expand influence into Algeria; was defeated by French, who had invaded Algeria.

1860 Spain invaded Morocco.

1880 Madrid Conference; major powers agreed to respect Morocco's independence; agreement proved short-lived as commercial rivalries intensified.

1906 France and Spain received authority over Moroccan internal affairs at the Algeciras Conference (Jan.–Apr.).

1911 Germany challenged French hegemony in Morocco in the Agadir Incident (July); forced to concede French and Spanish hegemony.

1912 France and Spain established protectorates over Morocco; France received the bulk of the territory (Mar. 30); Spain established (Nov. 27) Spanish Morocco and a Southern Protectorate that became part of Spanish Sahara; Tangier became an international zone.

1921–26 Rif War, unsuccessful revolt against colonial rule, led by Abd-el-krim.

1936 In Spanish Morocco, F. Franco began revolt that marked the beginning of the Spanish Civil War.

1937 Unsuccessful nationalist revolt against French rule.

1942 WW II; Morocco occupied (Nov.) by Allies.

1952 Nationalist Istiglal party declared illegal by French authorities.

1953 Sultan Sidi Muhammad, who supported the Moroccan nationalist movement, deposed by the French.

1955 Sidi Muhammad restored as sultan by the French as unrest spread in Morocco.

1956 France gave up its protectorate (Mar.); Spain renounced its protectorate over Spanish Morocco (Apr.); Morocco was awarded international zone of Tangier (Oct.).

1957 Sidi Muhammad became Moroccan King Muhammad V.

1958 Spain surrendered its Southern Protectorate to Morocco.

1961 Muhammad V died (Feb. 26); succeeded by his son Hassan II.

1962 Hassan II issued constitution establishing parliamentary government in Morocco.

1965 Political turmoil in Morocco came to a head; Hassan II declared state of emergency (June) and assumed personal rule.

1969 Ifni ceded to Morocco by Spain.

1970 New constitution approved (July 25); five-year state of emergency ended.

1971 Unsuccessful attempt to overthrow government (July 10).

1972 King Hassan's proposed constitution approved in nationwide vote (Mar. 1).

1972 Unsuccessful assassination attempt against Hassan II (Aug.).

1975 Some 350,000 Moroccans took part in a march into Spanish Sahara (Nov. 6–9) to press claim that northern section belonged to Morocco; fighting between Moroccans, Mauritanians, and Algerians over region continued; cease-fire established in 1981.

1977–78 Moroccan troops fought in Zaire against guerrilla forces.

Morpheus Greek god, a son of Hypnos, god of sleep. Morpheus brought dreams of human beings, as opposed to animals or symbols.

Morrill, Justin Smith 1810–98. American legislator. Morrill was a founder of the Republican party in Vermont, served 43 years (1855–98) in both houses of Congress, and established land grant colleges by the Morrill Act (1862).

Morrill Act *See* **Morrill, Justin Smith**

Morris, Gouverneur 1752–1816. American statesman. Morris was a member of the Continental Congress (1778–79) and the Constitutional Convention (1787), and put the draft of the Constitution in final form. He planned the decimal system of coinage used in America and was minister to France (1792–94).

Morris, Lewis 1671–1746. Colonial jurist and statesman. Morris was chief justice of New York, was instrumental in the separation of New York and New Jersey (1738) into two colonies, and served as New Jersey's first governor (1738–46).

Morris, Robert 1734–1806. American financier and patriot. A signer of the Declaration of Independence, he was called the "financier of the Revolution." He controlled government financing efforts, including those for the army. He later served as a US senator (1789–95) and died in debt.

Morris, William 1834–96. English poet, Socialist, and decorative artist who was an important figure in the Victorian era. Early in his career he was active in the decorative arts and crafts. His major collections of poetical works include *The Defence of Guenevere and Other Poems, The Life and Death of Jason, The Earthly Paradise,* and *Three Northern Love Songs.* He also wrote prose romances, such as *News from Nowhere* and *The Well at the World's End.*

Morse, Jedidiah 1761–1826. American geographer. Morse was a minister whose geography textbooks earned him the name "father of American Geography." His son was S. Morse.

Morse, Samuel Finley Breese 1791–1872. An American painter and inventor. Morse was a portrait painter who developed the telegraph (from 1832) and the Morse code.

Mortimer, Edmund de, 3d earl of March and 1st earl of Ulster 1351–81. English nobleman. Edmund's marriage to Philippa, daughter of Edward III's son, formed the basis to the York *(q.v.)* family claim to the English throne.

Mortimer, Edmund de, 5th earl of March and 3d earl of Ulster 1391–1425. English nobleman. Edmund was heir presumptive of Richard II. He was jailed after Henry IV took the throne. Released by Henry V, Mortimer served Henry faithfully, resisting plots to put himself on the throne.

Mortimer, Roger de, 1st earl of March 1287?–1330. English nobleman. Roger and Queen Isabella, his lover, deposed (1327) and murdered her husband, Edward II, and ruled England together. Isabella's son, Edward III, had him tried and executed.

Mortimer, Roger de, 4th earl of March and 2d earl of Ulster 1374–98. English nobleman. The son of E. de Mortimer, he was declared heir presumptive by the childless Richard II, but died in battle. His great-grandson became Edward IV.

Mortimer's Cross, Battle of Battle (Feb. 2, 1461) during the Wars of the Roses *(q.v.),* Edward, Duke of York, defeated the House of Lancaster. He proclaimed himself king as Edward IV, though the Lancastrians continued to contest his power.

mortmain From the French word for "dead hand," mortmain implies perpetual ownership of land, especially by a church. Such land was exempt from taxes and, from feudal times in England, efforts were made to limit or ban such holdings and figured in the conflict between church and state.

Morton, James Douglas, 4th earl of *c*1516–81. Scottish nobleman. Morton was lord chancellor (1563–66) to Mary Queen of Scots. He participated in the deaths of her secretary David Rizzio (1566) and her husband, Lord Darnley. He later forced her abdication (1567) and flight to England.

Morton, Thomas *fl.* 1622–47. English colonial trader. Morton was an Anglican and a fur trader who came into conflict with the early Puritan settlers in New England. They had him arrested and exiled several times.

Morton, William Thomas Green 1819–68. An American dental surgeon. Morton demonstrated the use of ether for surgical anesthesia (1846) and gained general acceptance for its use in medicine. C. Long was the first to use ether in surgery (1842).

Mosaddegh, Muhammad 1880–1967. Iranian statesman. As premier (1951–53), he nationalized Iran's oil industry (1951). This move alienated the West. Amid a major political crisis in Iran, he forced (1953) the shah to flee the country. However, the shah had Western support and soon forced Mosaddegh out of power.

Mosby, John Singleton 1833–1916. Confederate ranger. During the American Civil War Mosby led a small group called "Mosby's Rangers." They specialized in swift, daring raids behind Union lines, and effectively harassed Union military operations.

Moscow Capital city (pop. 7,831,000) of the USSR, located in west-central USSR. One of the world's major cities, it is the Soviet Union's largest city and its commercial and cultural center. Inhabited from Neolithic times, Moscow was first mentioned as site of a village in 1147. It became the seat of the grand dukes of Moscow and was, from the 14th cent., seat of the metropolitan (later called the patriarch) of the Russian Orthodox Church. Moscow was destroyed several times by the Tatars but rose to defeat the Tatars and gain dominance over all of Russia. In 1547, Grand Duke Ivan IV first took the title "czar of Russia." Czar Peter I moved Russia's capital to St. Petersburg (now Leningrad) in 1712. Moscow was virtually destroyed by fire (1812) during Napoleon's occupation and subsequent retreat. It became capital of the USSR (1918) after the Russian Revolution, and was the prime objective of the German invasion (1941) during WW II. The Kremlin (q.v.) is located there.

Moscow Conferences World War II meetings between the Allies (Britain, Russia, and the US) to discuss war and postwar strategies. In the first (1941), America and Britain agreed to lend-lease aid for Russia, and in the second (1942) they discussed the creation of a second European theater of war. At the third meeting (1943), they agreed to the formation of the United Nations, and at the fourth (1944) they discussed the problems of Poland, Bulgaria, and Yugoslavia. A 1947 conference (including France) was less successful in deciding the postwar status of Germany.

Moscow Declaration Agreement (Oct. 30, 1943) by the Soviet Union, Britain, the United States, and China on the need to establish an international peace-keeping organization. It was one of the preliminary agreements that led to formation of the UN.

Moseley, Henry Gwyn Jeffreys 1887–1915. English physicist. By his research on the X-ray spectra of elements, he made important discoveries concerning atomic structure, including the link between atomic number and the charge of its nucleus.

Moses fl. c14th–13th cent. BC. Great Hebrew prophet and religious leader. Knowledge of his life is based on biblical accounts, according to which he was raised in the Egyptian court. He fled Egypt after intervening between an Egyptian and a Hebrew slave and, after becoming a shepherd, received his call from Yahweh (God) to rescue the Hebrews. He returned to Egypt and, demanding that the pharaoh (possibly Ramses II) release his people, caused the plagues of Egypt. Moses finally led his people out of Egypt (see Exodus) and across the desert to Mt. Sinai, where he received the Ten Commandments. He then led the Hebrews on the 40-year journey to the Holy Land (Canaan), during which there was much hardship and dissent. When the Hebrews reached the edge of the Holy Land at the Jordan river, Moses climbed Mt. Pisgah to view it and then disappeared. Moses is traditionally regarded as the author of the first five books of the Old Testament (Genesis, Exodus, Leviticus, Numbers, and Deuteronomy), known collectively as the Pentateuch.

Moses, Anna Mary Robertson ⟨Moses, Grandma⟩ 1860–1961. American painter. She took up painting in her seventies and quickly established herself as an American folk artist.

Moses, Grandma See **Moses, Anna Mary Robertson**

Moslem See **Muslim**

Mosley, Sir Oswald Ernald 1896–. British politician. He founded (1932) the British Union of Fascists. He conducted an anti-Jewish campaign and supported the Nazis, which resulted in his confinement from 1940 to 1943.

mosque Islamic temple, traditionally built facing Mecca and generally including an open courtyard and a minaret (tower). The first mosques were patterned after Muhammad's courtyard at Medina. Among the many famous mosques are the Dome of the Rock (q.v.) and the Blue Mosque in Istanbul.

most-favored-nation clause Provision in treaties for international trade. It stipulates that the two participating nations will grant each other all commercial concessions (such as favorable import duties) that have been extended to other nations.

Most Serene Republic of San Marino See **San Marino**

Mother Lode Popular name of the gold-bearing region located in the western Sierra Nevada Mountains of California.

Mo Ti See **Mo-tzu**

Mott, Lucretia Coffin 1793–1880. American feminist and abolitionist. Together with E. Stanton she organized the first US women's rights convention at Seneca Falls, New York (1848).

Mo-tzu ⟨Mo Ti⟩ 470?–391? BC. Chinese philosopher. Mo-tzu taught that people should love each other as they love their own families. For a time this doctrine of universal love rivaled the popularity of Confucianism.

Moultrie, William 1730–1805. American Revolutionary War general. Moultrie defeated a British attack at Sullivan's Island (now Fort Moultrie) and was taken prisoner in the fall of Charleston (1780). He later served as governor of South Carolina.

Mountain, the ⟨Montagnards⟩ French extremist faction in the National Convention (q.v.) during the French Revolution. They were so named because they occupied a raised part of the legislative hall. They opposed (and eventually defeated) the more moderate Girondists (q.v.). They eventually took control of the Jacobins and became the controlling force behind the Reign of Terror (q.v.). Principal figures in the group were M. Robespierre and G. Danton.

Mountain Meadows massacre Massacre of 137 settlers (Sept., 1857) in Utah, provoked by disputes between Mormon and non-Mormon settlers in Utah. Mormons were charged with inciting the attack, carried out by a mixed band of Paiute Indians and white settlers, apparently led by Mormon John D. Lee (1812–77). Their victims were only passing through Utah on their way to California, and only a few children were spared. Lee was tried and executed (1877).

Mount Athos Mountain located in northeastern Greece. It is noted as the site of numerous monasteries of the Orthodox Eastern Church, the first of which was founded there c963.

Mountbatten, Louis, 1st earl Mountbatten of Burma 1900–79. British admiral and statesman. As supreme Allied commander in Southeast Asia (1943–46), Mountbatten defeated the Japanese in Burma. He was last viceroy of India (1947) and chairman of the chiefs of defense staff (1959–65). He was assassinated by Irish terrorists.

Mount Rushmore Mountain in the Black Hills of western South Dakota. The heads of T. Jefferson, A. Lincoln, G. Washington, and T. Roosevelt, carved out of the face of the mountain by G. Borglum, are a national monument.

Mount Sion *See* **Zion**

Mount Vernon Virginia estate of G. Washington from 1747 until his death in 1799. It is the burial place of the Washington family and is located near Alexandria, Virginia.

Mousgorgsky, Modest Petrovich *See* **Musorgsky, Modest Petrovich**

Mouskos, Mihail Christodoulou *See* **Makarios III**

Mozambique ⟨People's Republic of Mozambique, *formerly* Portuguese East Africa⟩ Independent state located in coastal southeast Africa. Its capital is Maputo. It gained independence in 1975

after nearly five centuries of Portuguese colonial rule. Key dates in Mozambique's history include:

10TH CENT. Arabs and Swahili traders settled coastal region.

1498 Vasco da Gama visited region.

1505 Portuguese began colonization.

16TH–17TH CENT. Portuguese gradually took control of the interior; *prazeros* (owners of large estates) forced natives to work lands.

FROM MID-17TH CENT. Slave trade flourished.

1752 Colonial government established.

1891 Treaty established border between Mozambique and British territories.

1910 Status changed from province to colony.

1917 Firm control by Portugal over native population secured after nearly two decades of fighting.

1951 Mozambique became a Portuguese overseas province.

EARLY 1960s Reform laws passed; ended forced labor and improved conditions for native blacks.

1963 National Front for the Liberation of Mozambique (FRELIMO) organized.

1964–74 War for independence; FRELIMO guerrillas slowly gained control of much of Mozambique.

1974 New Portuguese military government arranged cease-fire in Mozambique (July); agreed to independence for Mozambique.

1975 Independence granted (June 25); President Samora Moises Machel, a Maoist, took office and remained in power into the early 1980s. Marxist government established.

1976 Mozambique closed border with white-ruled Rhodesia.

1980 Reopened border after native blacks came to power in Zimbabwe (Rhodesia).

Mozarabs Christians in Muslim Spain (8th–11th cents.) who adopted the Muslim language and culture while retaining their Christian faith. They lived in largely autonomous communities.

Mozart, Wolfgang Amadeus 1756–91. Great Austrian musical genius of the classical period who composed works in every genre. He began composing when he was five and went on a concert tour through Europe at age six. His most famous operas are *The Marriage of Figaro* and *Don Giovanni*. In spite of the brilliance of his many symphonies, concertos, and his last opera, *The Magic Flute*, he died in poverty.

Muawiya d. 680. He once served as Muhammad's secretary and later became governor of Syria. In the first Muslim Civil War (q.v.), he contested the succession of Ali to the caliphate and, after Ali's death (661), deposed his successor,

Hasan. Muawiya thus founded the Umayyad *(q.v.)* dynasty.

Mubarak, Hosni Egyptian president (1981—   ), successor to A. Sadat on his assassination. By his visit (June, 1982) to Saudi Arabia, Mubarak established the first high-level contact with that country since the split between Egypt and its Arab neighbors over the Camp David accords.

muckrakers In US journalistic history, reporters who exposed corruption in business and politics during the early 1900s. They included I. Tarbell, L. Steffens, and U. Sinclair.

Mudd, Samuel Alexander *See* **Booth, John Wilkes**

Mudéjar Name for the Spanish Muslims (later called Moriscos) who were allowed to remain in Spain after the Christian reconquest of Muslim territories there. They lived in protected communities and developed a unique artistic style, which influenced Spanish architecture. They were forced to leave Spain in 1614.

mufti Muslim lawyers who advise judges on Islamic law. Their opinion papers are called *futwa* and are binding in matters of marriage, divorce, and inheritance.

Mughal *See* **Mogul**

mugwumps In US history, Republicans who deserted (1884) party presidential candidate J. Blaine to support Democrat candidate G. Cleveland, who was subsequently elected.

Muhammad 570?–632. Arabian prophet and religious leader, founder of Islam *(q.v.)*. The son of Abdallah, a merchant of Mecca, Muhammad was raised by his uncle after his father's early death. At the age of 24, Muhammad married Khadija, a prosperous widow many years his senior; of their children only one, Fatima, had children. Muhammad became a successful merchant in Mecca. However, he came to feel called upon by God to preach among the Arabian people, to dispel their ignorance and superstition, and to provide the Arab world with its own prophet. According to Islamic teaching, he was favored by a revelation from God through the archangel Gabriel.

At first Muhammad preached only to a small circle, including members of his family, Ali, his son-in-law, and Abu Bakr, his friend. He taught that there was one true God, and that key elements of the struggle toward God's mercy were fasting, almsgiving, and prayer. After several years he felt called upon to preach in public, but his exhortations against the pagan rituals practiced in Mecca made him many enemies. An attempt on his life was planned in 622 but Muhammad was warned and fled to Yathrib, later called Medina. This flight, known as the Hejira, traditionally marks the beginning of the Muslim era.

At Medina, Muhammad found increased support and made many new converts. He continued to elaborate his teachings and accounts of his revelations, which formed the basis of the Koran *(q.v.)*. However, the growing strength of Islam brought Muhammad into conflict with the Meccans. Muhammad's followers defeated a superior Meccan force at Badr (624) but were defeated at Uhud (625). The strength of Islam continued to rise, however, and in 630 Muhammad marched into Mecca leading 10,000 faithful. At Mecca he instituted the tradition of the pilgrimage. He spent his last years at Medina in the company of his several wives, among them his favorite, Aisha (Ayeshah), daughter of Abu Bakr. By his death virtually all of Arabia had come under the control of Islam and the theocratic state *(see* Caliphate, Empire of*)* he had established.

Muhammad II 1430–81. Ottoman sultan (1451–81), called the Conqueror, successor to his father, Murad II. He captured Constantinople (1453), bringing the Byzantine Empire to an end. He made Constantinople his capital, and took Greece, most of Serbia, and the Aegean Islands.

Muhammad IV 1641–92. Ottoman sultan (1648–87), son of Sultan Ibrahim, who had been deposed and murdered. Order was restored under the viziers of the Kuprili family (after 1656). He was unable to prevent Algerian independence (1669), however, and he was deposed after military reverses in the Austro-Turkish War *(q.v.)*.

Muhammad V 1844–1918. Ottoman sultan (1909–18). He succeeded his brother, Abdul-Hamid II, who was overthrown by the Young Turks. Muhammad's reign saw the loss of most of the Ottoman Empire's European possessions in the Balkan Wars *(q.v.)* and its ruinous WW I alliance with the Central Powers.

Muhammad VI 1861–1926. Last Ottoman sultan (1918–22), successor to his brother, Muhammad V. He came to power at the close of WW I, submitted to the harsh terms of the Treaty of Sèvres *(q.v.)*, and was deposed (Nov. 3, 1922) by the Turkish nationalist K. Atatürk, who established the republic.

Muhammad Ahmad *See* **Mahadi, Muhammad Ahmed**

Muhammad Ali ⟨Mehemet Ali⟩ ⟨Muhammad Ali Pasha⟩ 1769–1849. Egyptian viceroy (1805–48), considered the founder of the modern Egyptian state. After unsuccessfully opposing Napoleon in Egypt, he became viceroy of Egypt, then under Ottoman rule. He massacred Mameluke *(q.v.)* leaders in Egypt and thereby established undisputed power, defeated the Wahabis in Arabia (by 1818), invaded the Sudan, sent troops to aid the Ottoman sultan in the War of Greek Independence *(q.v.)*, and went to war against the sultan (in Syria). By his victories against the sultan, he gained (1841) virtual independence for Egypt under nominal Ottoman suzerainty. The viceroyalty of Egypt was made hereditary.

Muhammad Ali Pasha *See* **Muhammad Ali**

Muhammad of Ghor *See* **Taraori, Battles of**

Muhammad Reza Shah Pahlevi 1919–80. Shah of Iran (1941–79), successor to his father, Reza Shah Pahlevi. He succeeded after his father was deposed by British and Soviet military intervention and, amid nationalist unrest, was forced to leave the country briefly in 1953. He was restored with US and British help and subsequently attempted to promote social and economic reforms. Criticized for his pro-Western policies and brutal treatment of dissenters, he was forced out of Iran (Jan. 16, 1979) by a Muslim fundamentalist revolution in Iran that brought Ayatollah Khomeini to power. In ill health and resisting attempts to return him to Iran for trial (notably the hostage crisis), the former shah died in exile in Egypt.

Muhlenberg, Frederick Augustus Conrad 1750–1801. American clergyman. Muhlenberg served in the Continental Congress (1779–80) and was a member (1789–97) and first speaker of the House of Representatives.

Muhlenberg, Heinrich Melchior 1711–87. German-American clergyman. He organized (1748) the first Lutheran synod in America and is regarded as the founder of American Lutheranism.

Muhlenberg, John Peter Gabriel 1746–1807. American clergyman, soldier, and politician. Muhlenberg served as brevet major general in the American Revolution, and was later a congressman and senator from Pennsylvania.

Mukden Incident Incident (Sept. 18, 1931) used by Japan as a pretext for its invasion of Manchuria. Following an attempt to sabotage the Japanese-controlled South Manchurian Railway, Japanese troops occupied (Sept. 18) nearby Mukden. With the arrival (Sept. 21) of more troops from Korea, the Japanese army began to actively take over the territory. Chiang Kai-shek's nationalist armies, then occupied in civil war with the Communists, were unable to oppose the Japanese, and by February conquest of Manchuria was complete. Thereupon the Japanese created (Feb. 18) the puppet state of Manchukuo *(q.v.)*.

Müller, Hermann 1876–1931. German statesman and political leader in the Weimar Republic. He was chancellor (1920, 1928–30) and, during his second term, negotiated the Young Plan *(q.v.)* and brought an end to French occupation of the Rhineland (1929).

Muller, Johannes *See* **Regiomontanus**

Muller, Johannes Peter 1801–58. German physiologist and anatomist. Muller was famed for research in such fields as physiology, pathology, and comparative anatomy.

Mumford, Lewis 1895–. American educator, author, and social critic. Mumford's works range from city planning to cultural history and treat the larger thesis that humanity must counter dehumanizing tendencies of the modern technological world. This is to be accomplished by restoring cultural emphasis on human and moral values. Among his notable works are *Technics and Civilization*, *The City in History*, and *The Pentagon of Power*.

Munda, Battle of Battle (Mar. 17, 45 BC) that marked the end of resistance within the Roman Empire to J. Caesar's rule. Following Caesar's victory at Thapsus, Pompey's sons, Gnaeus Pompey (75?–45 BC) and Sextus Pompey (75–35 BC), organized a rebellion against Caesar in the Roman province of Spain. Though outnumbered, Caesar met and defeated the rebel force at Munda, an ancient town in southern Spain. It was Caesar's last military victory.

Munich City (pop. 1,314,000) located in southern West Germany, in a commercial and manufacturing center. Founded in 1158, it became (1255) the seat of the dukes of Bavaria (Wittelsbach line), capital of the kingdom of Bavaria (1806), and an important cultural center (19th cent.). In the next century, Munich became headquarters of A. Hitler's National Socialist (Nazi) movement, the scene of the Munich Putsch *(q.v.)* and the Munich Pact *(q.v.)*. Rebuilt after suffering heavy damage in WW II, Munich was the site of the 1972 Summer Olympics, at which 11 Israeli athletes were killed by Palestinian terrorists.

Munich Agreement *See* **Munich Pact**

Munich Pact ⟨~ Agreement⟩ Pact (Sept. 30, 1938) between Germany and other European powers providing for the German annexation of the western Czechoslovakian territory of Sudetenland. A. Hitler had entered into a dispute with Czechoslovakia earlier in 1938 over the territory, which was predominantly German. After several months of negotiations between the major powers, a complex plan for the phased occupation of the territory was worked out and agreed to (at Munich) by Germany, France, Great Britain, and Italy. The pact was rendered meaningless when Hitler invaded (Mar., 1939) Czechoslovakia.

Munich Putsch ⟨Beer Hall Putsch⟩ A. Hitler's unsuccessful attempt (Nov. 9, 1923) to seize power in Bavaria and, ultimately, to take control of the Weimar Republic. As leader of the National

Socialist (Nazi) party, Hitler joined with the extremist Gen. E. Ludendorff in a badly organized attempt to incite a right-wing revolution in Munich. Hitler had hoped to capitalize on Germany's severe economic crisis, but his plan soon failed. Arrested and tried, Hitler was sentenced to five years in prison. He served only eight months and during this time wrote his seminal work, *Mein Kampf (q.v.).*

Muñoz Marin, Luis 1898–. Puerto Rican statesman and governor (1948–64). He founded (1938) the Popular Democratic party and, as the first elected governor, implemented social and economic reforms.

Munsey, Frank Andrew 1854–1925. American publisher, who bought and consolidated competing newspapers and magazines. Among his holdings were the *New York Sun* and the *New York Herald.*

Münster, Sebastian 1489–1552. German theologian and geographer. Münster edited a Hebrew Bible and wrote (1544) *Cosmographia,* the first detailed geography of the world written in the German language.

Münzer, Thomas *c*1489–1525. German radical reformer, often considered to be among the Anabaptists. Münzer saw the Protestant Reformation as a social and political revolution, as well as a religious revolt. He broke with M. Luther and became a leader in the Peasants' War *(q.v.).* He was captured and beheaded.

Murad I 1326?–89. Ottoman sultan (*c*1360–89). By his conquests, he made the Byzantine Empire a vassal state, consolidated Ottoman control over Anatolia, extended Ottoman domains into the Balkans, and established (1362) the Ottoman capital at Edirne (formerly Adrianople). He laid the foundations of the administrative system of the later Ottoman Empire and formed the military corps known as the Janissaries *(q.v.).*

Murad II 1403–51. Ottoman sultan (1421–51). He overcame rival claimants to the throne and, by 1425, had firm control of the empire. He took Salonika (1430) in northern Greece during a war with Venice and won important victories at Varna (1444) and Kosovo (1448) in fighting against the Hungarians and Poles.

Murad IV *c*1612–40. Ottoman sultan (1623–40). By means of brutal force, he broke the power of rebellious military leaders (including those of the Janissaries), restored the authority of the central government, and successfully concluded a war with Persia, in which he captured Baghdad (1638).

Murad V 1840–1904. Ottoman sultan (1876), successor to his uncle, Abd al-aziz. He was declared insane after three months and was deposed in favor of his brother Abd al-Hamid II.

Murasaki Shikibu *c*978–*c*1031. Japanese writer. She wrote *Tales of Genji,* one of the first great novels written in Japanese.

Murat, Joachim 1767–1815. French marshal and king of Naples (1808–15). Murat was one of Napoleon's most able cavalry commanders and distinguished himself in Napoleon's Italian, Egyptian, Peninsular, and Russian campaigns. He helped Napoleon seize power in the coup of 18 Brumaire and again joined him in the Hundred Days' campaign.

Muratori, Ludovico Antonio 1672–1750. Italian historian. As archivist and librarian at Modena, he discovered early Christian writings (AD 2d cent.) that listed the books of the New Testament.

Murdoch, Jean Iris ⟨Bayley, J. O.⟩ 1919–. British novelist and philosopher. Murdoch's writings include the novels *A Severed Head* and *The Flight from the Enchanter.*

Muret, Battle of Victory for the French Catholic nobles (Sept., 1213) during the Albigensian Crusade *(q.v.).* Forces of the noblemen of northern France, led by S. de Montfort, decisively defeated those of the Albigensian leader Raymond VI at this town in southern France. Raymond's ally, King Pedro II of the Spanish kingdom of Aragon, was killed in the battle. Spanish influence in southern France was thus ended.

Murfreesboro, Battle of *See* **Stones River, Battle of**

Murillo, Bartolomé Esteban 1617?–82. Spanish baroque painter. Murillo was noted for his portraits and religious subjects, including the *Vision of St. Anthony.* He was a founder and first president of the Seville Academy (1660).

Muromachi period ⟨Ashikaga period⟩ In Japanese history, the period in which the Ashikaga shoguns ruled (1338–1578). Their capital was located at Kyoto. Though the era was marked by the rise of the power of feudal lords and frequent warfare (especially in the first and last centuries), it nevertheless saw commercial prosperity, increased foreign trade, contacts with China, the predominance of Zen Buddhism, and a cultural flowering.

Murphy, Frank 1893–1949. American politician and associate justice of the Supreme Court (1940–49). Known for his liberalism, he delivered a dissenting opinion opposing the confinement of Japanese-Americans during WW II.

Murray, James 1722–94. British general and colonial administrator. He distinguished himself in the Seven Years' War (1756–63), served as governor of Quebec (1760), Canada (1763–66) and Minorca (1774–82).

Murray, Sir James Augustus Henry 1837–1915. Scottish-born English lexicographer. Murray became editor (1879) of the Oxford English Dictionary (completed 1928), editing over half of it himself and establishing its organization.

Murray, James Stuart, 1st earl of ⟨Moray, ~⟩ c1531–70. Scottish nobleman. A Protestant, he at first supported the rule of his sister, the Catholic Mary Queen of Scots. Later, however, his support of the Calvinist J. Knox resulted in a break with Mary and Murray's unsuccessful attempt (1565) at rebellion. After Mary's fall from power (1567), he became regent, resisted her attempts to regain power, and promoted the Protestant Reformation in Scotland.

Murrone, Pietro del See **Celestine V, Saint**

Murrow, Edward Roscoe 1908–65. Noted American broadcast journalist. Murrow was renowned for his vivid WW II radio reports from England. He pioneered television journalism with his programs See It Now and Person to Person.

Mursa, Battle of Battle fought (Sept. 28, AD 351) during the Roman civil wars. Roman emperor Constantius II, with an army of 40,000, defeated the usurper Magnetius, leading some 50,000 troops, in a bloody battle at Mursa (now in Yugoslavia). Combined losses totaled 25,000 men.

Mursilis I See **Hittite Empire**

Muscovy Company ⟨Russia Company⟩ English joint-stock trading company founded in 1555. The company enjoyed a monopoly on the Russian trade until 1698.

Muses Collective name for nine mythical Greek goddesses. They were daughters of Zeus and patronesses of the arts: Clio (history), Euterpe (music), Thalia (comedy), Melpomene (tragedy), Terpsichore (dance), Erato (love poems), Polymnia (sacred poems), Urania (astronomy), and Calliope (eloquence and epic poems).

Muslim civil wars Political upheavals that significantly altered the course of Muslim history. The first (656–61) was caused by the assassination of Uthman, the third caliph, and involved a struggle for the caliphate between Ali (600?–661), fourth caliph, and Muawiya leader of the Umayyads (q.v.). Ali was assassinated and Muawiya thereupon established the Umayyad dynasty of caliphs. This event marked the beginning of the long Umayyad rule and also caused the fundamental schism within the Islamic world: the Shi'ites (q.v.) supported Ali (and his successors) as the only rightful heirs to the caliphate, while the orthodox Sunni (q.v.) Muslims supported the Umayyads. The second (683–92) was caused when Abd Allah ibn az-Zubayr sought the caliphate after the death of Yazid I (d. 683). The civil war ended with the defeat and death of az-Zubayr and the rise of Marwan II (d. 750) as unchallenged leader of the Muslim world. A third civil war divided the Abbasid caliphate after the death (809) of Harun al-Rashid. The struggle was initiated by his son al-Amin (785?–813), his designated successor, and another son, Abd Allah al-Mamun (786–833), who was proclaimed caliph in Persia. The war ended (813) with al-Amin's defeat and death and the ascendancy of al-Mamun. A final civil war (1008–31) in Córdoba, Spain, ended with the elimination of the Umayyad caliphate in Spain (1031).

Muslim League ⟨orig. All-India Muslim League⟩ Political organization founded (1906) in India. Formed by Aga Khan III for the protection of Muslim's rights, the group broke away from the predominantly Hindu Indian National Congress and demanded (1940) a separate Muslim state. Led by (Muhammad Ali) Jinnah, it won the creation (1947) of Pakistan and became the dominant political party in the new state. The league had split into factions by the 1960s and declined after the 1970 elections.

Musorgsky, Modest Petrovich ⟨Moussorgski, ~⟩ 1839–81. Russian composer. He is best known for his opera, Boris Godunov, and his piano suite, Pictures at an Exhibition.

Mussolini, Benito 1883–1945. Italian Fascist dictator and WW II ally of A. Hitler. The preeminent leader of Italian Fascism, he organized the first Fascist group (1919) and party (1921). He orchestrated the Fascist militia's march on Rome (Oct. 1922) and by it became head of the Italian government. Thereafter his rule was marked by the institution of his dictatorship and the following events: the Matteoti Crisis (1924); abolition of parliamentary government (1928); the Lateran Treaty (1929); the Italo-Ethiopian War (1935–36); intervention in the Spanish Civil War; occupation of Albania (1939); and participation and defeat in WW II. Ousted from power (1943), he headed a German-backed opposition government until his execution in 1945.

Mutanabbi, al- 915–965. Great Arab poet, author of collected poems known as the Divan.

Mutasim, al- See **Abbasid**

Mutsuhito ⟨reign name, Meiji⟩ 1852–1912. Japanese emperor (1867–1912), successor to the shogun rulers of Japan. His reign is known as the Meiji Restoration (q.v.). It saw the end of feudalism and the transformation of Japan into a modern industrial state. He introduced many reforms, including a judicial code, a constitution (1889, providing for a legislature), and the Western calendar (1873). In addition to extensive Westernization, his reign was marked by the Satsuma Rebellion (1877), the Sino-Japanese War (1894–95) and the Russo-Japanese War (1904–5).

Muttra ⟨Mathura⟩ This city, located in north-central India, is the reputed birthplace of Krishna. It is one of the seven sacred Hindu cities.

Muwatallis *See* **Hittite Empire**

Mycale, Battle of Greek naval victory (Sept., 479 BC) over the Persians in the Aegean. With the victory at Plataea it was instrumental in ending the Persian invasion of Greece.

MVD *See* **GPU**

Mycenae Ancient Greek city, once located in northeastern Greece. It was the center of the Mycenaean civilization (q.v.).

Mycenaean civilization Ancient Aegean civilization that flourished on the Greek mainland (c1600–1200 BC). The Mycenaeans entered Greece from the north in c2000 BC. They were in regular contact with Minoans (q.v.) on Crete, and they incorporated many elements of Minoan civilization into their own culture. The period of their cultural and commercial domination of the region lasted from 1400 to 1100 BC, when the Dorian Greeks displaced the Mycenaeans. The epics of Homer are now regarded as giving a vivid picture of Mycenaean civilization at its height.

Mycerinus *See* **Menkure**

Myconius, Oswald *See* **Basel, Confession**

Myerson, Goldie *See* **Meir, Golda**

Mylae, Battle of Important Roman victory in a naval battle (260 BC), off southern Italy against the Carthaginians in the First Punic War (264–241 BC).

Myrdal, Gunnar 1898–. Swedish economist and sociologist. Myrdal's *An American Dilemma* (1944) was an important study of racial problems and their effect on American democracy. He received the Nobel Prize in Economics in 1974.

Myriocephalon, Battle of Decisive battle (1176) in wars between the Byzantines and Seljuk Turks. Byzantine forces under Murad I Comnenus attempted to recapture territory then occupied by the Turks. The Turks, under Kilij Arslan II, overwhelmed them at a mountain pass near the Myriocephalon fortress in Phrygia. The victory established the Turks in Anatolia.

Myrmidons Mythical Greek tribe. This warlike group from Thessaly was led by Achilles in the siege of Troy.

Myron 5th cent. BC. Greek sculptor. Myron was renowned for his statues of athletes in action, the most famous of which was his *Discus Thrower (Discobolus)*.

Mysia *See* **Pergamum**

Mysore Wars Series of four wars (1767–99) fought in India against British rule. In 1761 the Muslim leader Haidar Ali (1722–82) seized power in Mysore and began to increase his control over the region. He waged the first war (1767–69) against the East India Company, but gained little. In the second war (1780–84), he fought the British with French aid. Upon his death (1782) his son Sahib Tipu (d. 1799) became ruler and continued the struggle. In the third war (1790–92), Tipu was defeated by the British under Lord C. Cornwallis and lost half his territory. The fourth war (1799) ended in the death of Tipu and restoration of the native monarchy in Mysore.

Mysteries Ancient religious cults that supplemented the official Greco-Roman paganism. The best-known Mystery cults were the Eleusinian (q.v.), Orphic (q.v.), and Dionysiac. They usually included initiation into secret "knowledge," including rites of purification and the reenactment of sacred dramas.

mysticism Religious doctrine. Mysticism is the belief that a person can attain direct communication with God through spiritual, intuitive, or transcendental means. This communion of a person's spirit with God results in a feeling of being at one with the universe and is often accompanied by spiritual ecstasy. Mysticism has been an element in many religions, including Christianity.

N

Nabataeans Ancient Arabian people. The Nabateans were a Semitic people who lived on the trade route between Syria and Arabia. This strategic position enabled them to become wealthy by charging trade duties. The Roman emperor Trajan put an end to Nabataean autonomy in AD 105 and formed the Roman province Arabia Petraea.

Nabis Group of French artists of the 1890s, including Pierre Bonnard (1867–1947) and M. Denis, who derived their name from the Hebrew word for prophet. They are characterized by their use of bold colors over flat areas and a common dislike of impressionism *(q.v.)*.

Nabokov, Vladimir 1899–1977. Russian-born American writer. Nabokov is best known for his novels *Lolita* and *Pale Fire*, his vivid and expressive style, and his often bizarre subject matter.

Nabonidus d. 583? BC. Last king of Babylonia (c556–538 BC). Nabonidus coruled with his son Belshazzar. He allied himself unsuccessfully with Croesus of Lydia against Cyrus the Great of Persia.

Naboplassar *fl.* 7th cent. BC. Babylonian king (625–605 BC). He ended Assyrian control of Babylonia and thus founded (625) the Chaldaean Empire. He warred against Necho II of Egypt.

Naboth Old Testament figure. When Naboth would not give King Ahab his vineyard, Ahab's wife, Jezebel, had him slain. The term "Naboth's vineyard" is thus used to describe property wrongfully coveted by another.

Nabu ⟨Nebo⟩ Middle Eastern mythical god. Nabu was the god of learning and patron of writing in both the Assyrian and Babylonian cultures, and hence was the patron of priests and scribes.

Nadab In the Old Testament, the son of Aaron. He was a priest slain with his brother Abihu for offering "strange fire" in sacrifice (Leviticus 10).

Nader, Ralph 1934–. US lawyer and consumer advocate. His publication *Unsafe at Any Speed* (1965), attacking the auto industry, not only prompted legislation on auto safety but launched him on a highly active career as a consumer advocate and critic of government.

Nader Shah *See* **Nadir Shah**

Nadir Shah ⟨Nader Shah⟩ 1688–1747. Shah of Persia (1736–47). Originally a soldier, he usurped the throne, successfully warred with the Turks, sacked Delhi and Lahore, and seized the Koh-i-noor diamond and the Peacock Throne. He is considered the last of the great Asian conquerers.

Näfels, Battle of Battle in the Austrian-Swiss Wars, fought on April 9, 1388. The Swiss ambushed and defeated the much larger Austrian invasion force at this central Swiss town. It helped lead to a 20-year truce that virtually assured the independence of the Swiss cantons under the Holy Roman Empire.

Nagano, Osami 1880–1947. Japanese admiral. Nagano ordered and organized the 1941 Japanese attack on Pearl Harbor *(q.v.)*, which brought America into WW II. He was indicted as a war criminal and died while on trial.

Nagarjuna AD c150–c250. Indian Buddhist philosopher. Nagarjuna founded the Madhyamika (Middle Path) school of Buddhism, and was especially noted for his concept of "emptiness."

Nagasaki Japanese city (pop. 421,100), one of Japan's most important ports and a steel and shipbuilding center. Much of it was destroyed by the second atomic bomb, dropped Aug. 9, 1945, which ended WW II.

Nagoda Compromise agreement (Sept., 1868) by which Croatia was rejoined with Hungary in the Austro-Hungarian Dual Monarchy. Croatia, independent of Hungary since 1848, was granted a large measure of autonomy in return for accepting union with Hungary and a governor named by Hungary. The agreement remained in force until WW I.

Naguib, Muhammad 1901–. Egyptian general and political leader. He took part in the Egyptian revolution (July 23, 1952) that deposed King Farouk I and became premier of the new, military regime. In 1954 he was removed from power and replaced by G. A. Nasser.

Nagy, Imre 1896–1958. Hungarian Communist premier. Nagy was premier (1953–55) but was forced out by Soviet pressure. He was recalled during the 1956 Hungarian Revolution *(q.v.)* but was executed when the USSR put down the rebellion.

Nagyvarad, Peace of Short-lived agreement concluded on Feb. 24, 1538, dividing Hungary between Ferdinand of Hapsburg and John Zápolya, who contended for the Hungarian throne following the death of King Louis II (1526) at the Battle of Mohacs.

Nahas Pasha, Mustafa el- 1876–1965. Egyptian politician. He led the nationalist Wafd party *(q.v.)* and was prime minister five times between 1928 and 1952.

Nairobi Capital and largest city (pop. 818,000) of Kenya. It is linked by road to the rest of the country and is particularly famous for Nairobi National Park, a major wildlife sanctuary. Beginning as a waterhole for the pastoral Masai tribe, Nairobi became the capital of the British East African Protectorate in 1905.

Naismith, James A. 1861–1939. American athletic director. While a physical education instructor, Naismith invented the game of basketball in 1891.

Nakaz *See* **Instruction of Catherine the Great**

Namur, sieges of Important battles fought at Namur in south-central Belgium, at the confluence of the Meuse and Sambre rivers. **1.** In the War of the Grand Alliance *(q.v.)*, Namur resisted for 26 days before surrendering on June 5, 1692, to a French force that lost 2,600 men against twice that number of casualties in the city. On Sept. 1, 1695, the Dutch retook Namur after a two-month siege, losing 18,000 men to half that number of French casualties. **2.** In WW I, 37,000 Belgian defenders held out for five days against 100,000 Germans before surrendering on Aug. 25, 1914.

Nanak 1469–1539. Indian religious leader and founder of the Sikhs *(q.v.)*. Born a Hindu, he came to regard some Hindu practices and beliefs as superstitious, especially when compared to those of the Muslims, by whom he was influenced. He founded the Sikhs as a bridge between the two religions.

Nanking Chinese city (pop. 1,420,000), located in east-central China on the Yangtze River and serving several times as China's capital. It was the seat of the puppet government (1938–45) established by the Japanese after their capture of the city in 1937, which was followed by the brutality known as "the rape of Nanking." Sun Yat-sen is buried there.

Nansen, Fridtjof 1861–1930. Norwegian explorer and statesman who promoted the separation of Norway from Sweden. His arctic expeditions furnished much valuable information about the North Pole. He won the Nobel Peace Prize in 1922 for Russian relief work.

Nantes, Edict of *See* **Edict of Nantes**

Naphtali Son of Jacob. He was the father of one of the Twelve Tribes of Israel. Its territory was located near the Sea of Galilee.

Napier, John 1550–1617. Scottish mathematician. Napier invented the logarithm. He introduced Napier's rods for use in counting and decimal points for writing fractions.

Napier of Magdala, Robert Cornelis, 1st Baron 1810–90. British soldier. Napier fought in the Sikh Wars *(q.v.)* and the Indian Mutiny, captured Magdala in Ethiopia, and was commander in chief in India (1870–76).

Naples Italian city (pop. 1,225,300) located in southwestern Italy, on the Bay of Naples. It is one of Italy's busiest ports. Settled *c*600 BC by Greeks, Naples has been successively dominated by Romans, Byzantines, Muslims, Normans, Goths, Austrians, and the French. Mount Vesuvius stands nearby, as do the excavations of ancient Pompeii *(q.v.)* and Herculaneum. The famous San Carlo Opera House has functioned there since 1737.

Naples, kingdom of Former kingdom in Italy. The kingdom of Naples, often united with Sicily, dominated southern Italy from the Middle Ages until 1860. Roger II unified the region and declared himself king of Sicily and Apulia (1130). Because the area was of strategic naval and commercial importance, it became the focus of frequent power struggles. At various times the region was ruled by the Normans, the Hohenstaufens, the Angevins, the Spanish, and the Bourbons. Napoleon overthrew the latter, renaming Naples the Parthenopian Republic (1799). The Bourbons were restored by Admiral H. Nelson later that year but were routed again by Napoleon in 1806. The Bourbons again resumed the throne in 1816, renaming it the Kingdom of the Two Sicilies *(q.v.)*. The area was united with the rest of Italy by G. Garibaldi (1860).

Napoleon I (Napoleon Bonaparte) 1769–1821. Emperor of the French (1804–14). One of the great conquerors of all time and a gifted administrator as well, Napoleon created a short-lived French empire that included virtually all of continental Europe. By his conquests, he helped to spread liberal reforms instituted in France and thereby affected the subsequent development of modern Europe. Napoleon was born in Corsica, became an artillery officer in the French Army (1785), and served with the republican army during the French Revolutionary Wars *(q.v.)*. Napoleon was given command of the republican army in Italy

(1796). He quickly reorganized the units under his command into an effective fighting force, and his Italian campaign (1796–97) was overwhelmingly successful.

Napoleon's campaign in Egypt (1798–99) proved disastrous. At the same time, France's armies on the Continent suffered serious reverses, and the revolutionary government was on the verge of collapse. Napoleon returned to France and, with the aid of his brother, Lucien Bonaparte, and Joseph Sieyes, overthrew the Directory (Nov. 9, 1799). Napoleon was given dictatorial powers as head of the Consulate (q.v.). He consolidated his position and from 1800 to 1802 brought the French Revolutionary Wars to a successful conclusion.

In following years he instituted reforms in education, law—notably the Code Napoleon (q.v.)—and government. He also restored relations with the church (1801), severed during the French Revolution. Napoleon seized on the opportunity presented (1804) by an assassination plot against him (by G. Cadoudal and others) and made himself emperor. He was crowned by the pope (Dec. 2) at Paris. With the empire (q.v.) thus established, Napoleon set about creating a nobility and a court. He ultimately named rulers to various states (notably Spain, Holland, Naples, and Sweden). But when he made himself king of Italy (1805), the British (already at war with him) and other powers organized against him and the Napoleonic Wars (q.v.) broke out.

Napoleon enjoyed his greatest military successes during these wars (notably at the Battle of Austerlitz), and by about 1808 he had extended French control throughout the Continent. But his invasion of Russia proved disatrous. Napoleon marched into Russia (June, 1812) with some 500,000 troops and hardly managed to escape (Nov., 1812) with fewer than 50,000 troops. The defeat cost Napoleon his empire. One by one former allies joined the coalition of powers against him and by Mar., 1814, the Napoleonic Wars had come to a close. Napoleon abdicated (Apr. 11, 1814) and was exiled to the island of Elba.

Napoleon's final defeat did not come until 1815, however. In that year he returned to France and triumphantly entered Paris (Mar. 20). Thus began his famous Hundred Days (q.v.) in which he attempted to reestablish his empire. Defeated utterly at Waterloo, Napoleon again abdicated (June 22, 1815) and lived out the rest of his life in exile on the island of St. Helena.

Napoleon II 1811–32. Titular king of Rome. He was the son of Napoleon and Marie Louise. After his father's 1815 abdication, he was brought to his mother's land, Austria, where he remained a vir-

tual prisoner until he died of tuberculosis. He was used as a pawn by C. von Metternich in bargaining with France.

Napoleon III 1808–73. Emperor of the French, nephew of Napoleon I and son of L. Bonaparte. After two unsuccessful attempts to seize power, he was elected French president in 1848. He proclaimed himself emperor in 1852 and inaugurated the Second Empire (q.v.). His foreign and domestic policies were popular until 1860, when he was forced to liberalize his government. He was captured during the Franco-Prussian War (1870–71), deposed, and died in exile.

Napoleonic Code *See* **Code Napoleon**

Napoleonic Wars Wars fought (1803–15) by Napoleon I of France against various European powers. The Napoleonic Wars followed an earlier series of wars (1792–1802), the French Revolutionary Wars (q.v.). The French Revolutionary Wars had helped bring Napoleon to power and made France the most powerful nation on the European continent. But Napoleon was unable to match the British navy, and the British remained a continuing threat to his dominance of Europe. Mutual distrust finally resulted in declaration of war (1803) between France and Britain and, in the years following, various coalitions of European states tried unsuccessfully to defeat Napoleon. Napoleon soon extended his French empire across nearly all of continental Europe. But his ill-fated invasion (1812) of Russia, a former ally, proved to be his undoing. Defeated (1814), Napoleon was forced into exile. He returned to power briefly during his famous Hundred Days (q.v.), only to meet his final defeat at Waterloo. Key events in the Napoleonic Wars include:

1803 Britain and France again at war (May); British, suspicious of Napoleon's designs, refused to evacuate Malta (by the Treaty of Amiens) and thus provoked war.

1803 British, with superior navy, captured French overseas colonies; Napoleon, with superior land army, cut British trade with continental Europe and began assembling forces to invade Britain.

1804 British secured informal agreement with Russia for coalition against Napoleon.

1804 French empire proclaimed; Napoleon crowned himself emperor (Dec. 2).

1805 Napoleon proclaimed himself King of Italy and annexed Genoa and the Ligurian Republic; brought Austria into coalition against France.

1805 Third Coalition formed; Russia joined Britain (Apr. 11) and Austria then joined both (Aug. 9); Spain allied itself with France.

1805 Battle of Trafalgar: Adm. H. Nelson destroyed (Oct. 21) the 33-ship combined Spanish-French fleet; Nelson killed but Napoleon's invasion of Britain henceforth impossible.

1805 Battles of Ulm (Oct. 20) and of Austerlitz (Dec. 3): Napoleon crushed superior Austrian-Russian forces.

1805 Treaty of Pressburg: Austria yielded Venice and Dalmatian coast to France, and Tirol and Vorarlberg to Bavaria (Dec. 26); Austria forced out of the coalition.

1806 Joseph Napoleon installed as king of Naples (southern Italy); former Bourbon rulers forced to flee to Sicily, where the British gave them protection.

1806 Confederation of the Rhine, composed of German states organized by Napoleon, formally ended the Holy Roman Empire.

1806 Napoleon created the kingdom of Holland.

1806 British halted attempted French invasion of Sicily at the Battle of Maida (July 4).

1806–12 Russo-Turkish War; Ottoman Turks turned against the Russians at French urging.

1806 Fourth Coalition: Prussia, now allied with Russia, declared war on France (Oct. 8).

1806 Napoleon was victorious over superior Prussian armies at Jena-Auerstadt (Oct. 14); Napoleon occupied Berlin, the Prussian capital.

1806–12 Napoleon instituted Continental System, forbidding all to trade with Britain; established by Berlin Decree (Nov. 21, 1806).

1807 Battle of Eylau proved inconclusive (Feb. 8) as Russians attempted to aid Prussia.

1807 Napoleon defeated a large Russian force at the Battle of Friedland in East Prussia; victory led to the Treaties of Tilsit. (June 14).

1807 Treaties of Tilsit; Russia made an ally of France, and Prussia forced to join Continental System (July 7–9), among other concessions.

1807 Grand Duchy of Warsaw created by Napoleon.

1807 Napoleon created the kingdom of Westphalia from Prussian and Hanoverian lands.

1807 British attacked Copenhagen (Sept.); Denmark declared war against Britain.

1807 Treaty of Fontainebleau (Oct. 27); Spanish government allowed French troops to cross Spain to invade Britain's ally Portugal.

1807 Portugal occupied by French; Portuguese court removed to Brazil (Nov.).

1807 Orders in Council issued (Nov.-Dec.) by British, instituting a blockade of Napoleonic Europe.

1807 Milan Decree issued (Dec. 17) by Napoleon; ships that dealt with Great Britain lost their neutrality.

1808 Revolt by Spanish at Aranjuez (Mar.) led to dismissal of Godoy and abdication of Charles IV (May).

1808 Napoleon appointed his brother, Joseph, king of Spain (June); French troops occupied Madrid (July 20); Spanish rebelled and sent the French into retreat.

1808 Congress of Erfurt (Sept.); meeting between Napoleon and Russian czar Alexander I to reaffirm alliance.

1808–14 Peninsular War; Napoleon led a new invasion of Spain, while the British invaded Portugal; in the long campaign that followed, the French were finally driven out of Portugal and Spain.

1809 Fifth Coalition; Austria, allied with Britain, renewed the war on land in the east (Apr.).

1809 Napoleon defeated Austrian forces at Battle of Abensberg-Eckmühl (Apr. 23).

1809 Napoleon annexed the Papal States.

1809 Napoleon suffered his first major military defeat at the Battle of Aspern-Essling in Austria (May 21–22).

1809 Napoleon victorious in the bloody Battle of Wagram in Austria; prevented formation of new coalition against him (July 5–6).

1809 Pope Pius VII arrested (July) by Napoleon; the pope had excommunicated him for annexing the Papal States.

1809 Peace of Schönbrunn concluded by Napoleon with Austria; France gained some 32,000 square miles of Austrian territory (Oct. 14).

1810 Napoleon married Marie Louise, daughter of Austrian emperor Francis II, after divorcing Josephine.

1810 Napoleon annexed Holland.

1810 Czar Alexander I withdrew from the Continental System (Dec. 31).

1812 War of 1812, between the US and Britain, broke out (June 18); US Commerce had suffered as a result of French and British harassment of neutral shipping; war against Britain lasted to 1815.

1812 Napoleon assembled some 600,000 men in the Grand Army and invaded Russia (June 24); Russians, led by M. Kutuzov and Prince Barclay de Tolly, adopted scorched-earth policy as they retreated eastward before Napoleon's army.

1812 Battle of Borodino (Sept. 7); narrow victory for Napoleon; enabled Napoleon to march unopposed into Moscow (Sept. 14).

1812 Russians burned Moscow (Sept. 15–19).

1812 Napoleon remained at Moscow (Sept.–Oct.), waiting for Russians to come to terms; his overtures rejected.

1812 Napoleon ordered the retreat from Moscow (Oct. 19); Grand Army harassed by Russian forces throughout the retreat.

1812 Onset of the Russian winter hampered French retreat; cold weather, constant attacks by Russians, and lack of supplies seriously weakened Napoleon's army; French suffered heavy losses.

1812 Berezina River Crossing (Nov. 26–28); Napoleon's forces suffered heavy losses while crossing this Russian river; French retreat became a rout. Napoleon abandoned his troops and made for Paris (Dec. 5); only some 30,000 of his troops survived his retreat.

1813–14 War of Liberation; Prussia, Russia, Sweden, Austria, and Britain eventually participated in defeating Napoleon.

1813 Prussia, again allied with Russia, declared war on France (Mar.).

1813 Napoleon defeated (May 2) Prussians and Russians at the Battle of Lutzen, in Saxony.

1813 Battle of Bautzen; Russians and Prussians defeated by Napoleon (May 20–21).

1813 Sixth Coalition; Austria joined allies (Aug. 12); for the first time, Napoleon now faced Austria, Britain, Prussia, and Russia at the same time.

1813 Napoleon won his last major battle, at Dresden; fought against allied Austrian, Russian, and Prussian troops (Aug. 27).

1813 Battle of the Nations: the allies defeated Napoleon at Leipzig (Oct. 16–19).

1813–14 Invasion of France by the allies (Dec.); Paris occupied (Mar. 31).

1814 Napoleon abdicated (Apr. 11); Louis XVIII restored to French throne; Napoleon exiled to Elbe.

1814 Treaty of Paris formally ended hostilities after Napoleon's defeat; terms not harsh (May 30); boundaries restored to what they were in 1792; some colonies restored.

1814–15 Congress of Vienna in session; restored legitimate monarchs in Austria, Prussia, Spain, and in Italian kingdoms; created the kingdom of The Netherlands, kingdom of Poland (ruled by Russia), and the German Confederation; reestablished independent Switzerland; reached agreement to hold regular congresses to maintain peace.

1815 Hundred Days; Napoleon returned to Paris (Mar. 20) from exile and attempted to reestablish his empire (Mar.-June).

1815 King Louis XVIII fled and the French rallied to Napoleon; Napoleon instituted a liberal constitution; forced to fight by a new coalition against him, he invaded Belgium (June).

1815 French forces victorious at the Battle of Quatre Bras (June 16).

1815 Battle of Waterloo fought; marked Napoleon's final defeat (June 18).

1815 Abdication of Napoleon (June 22); Napoleon exiled to St. Helena in the south Atlantic; Louis was restored.

1815 Treaty of Paris formally ended hostilities after Napoleon's defeat; France submitted to loss of territories, payment of an indemnity, and occupation by allied armies (Nov. 20).

Nara Japanese city and prefecture (pop. 210,000), located on Honshu just north of Osaka. Nara is one of Japan's most historic and religious centers and was the first permanent capital of Japan. It has a 53-foot-high statue of Buddha, the largest in the world. It is also the resting place of Jimmu Tenno, the first Japanese emperor.

Narcissus Mythical character. Indifferent to the love of Echo, he was doomed by Nemesis to fall in love with and pine away for his own image, which he saw reflected in a pool.

Narodniki (Populists) Russian populist movement of the 19th century which advocated land for the peasants. Prevented by the police from active work in the villages, adherents of the movement formed a secret Land and Liberty society in 1876; the latter became dominated by its terroristic wing, the People's Will, which, in 1881, assassinated Czar Alexander II.

Narottama *See* **Norodom**

Narragansett Indians North American Indians whose language was of the Algonquian-Wakashan stock and who occupied present-day Rhode Island. One of their chiefs sold R. Williams the land on which he founded Providence. They were allied with the colonists in the 1637 Pequot War *(q.v.)* but declined in power along with other Indians after the 1638 King Philip's War *(q.v.)*.

Narses AD *c*478–*c*573. Byzantine general and statesman. Narses conquered the Ostrogoths *(q.v.)* under Totila in AD 522. He served as prefect of Italy from 554 to 567, when he was removed by Justin II.

Narvaez, Ramon Maria 1800–68. Spanish general and statesman. He was a strong military supporter of Isabella II against the Carlists, and later overthrew B. Espartero. With brief intervals, he served as Isabella's premier from 1844 to 1851 and several times thereafter.

Naseby, Battle of English Civil War battle fought near Naseby in central England on June 14, 1645. Charles I's Cavalier army of around 7,000 engaged the Puritans' newly organized New Model Army *(q.v.)* of about 14,000 men, commanded by Sir T. Fairfax, with O. Cromwell commanding the cavalry. The Puritans routed the Cavaliers, whose infantry (some 3,500) were killed or captured.

Nash, Ogden 1902–71. American writer. Nash was best known for his humorous and satirical verses and for the lyrics of the Broadway musical *One Touch of Venus.*

Nash, Thomas *See* **Nashe, Thomas**

Nashe, Thomas (Nash, Thomas) 1567–1601. English dramatist and satirist, a master of scurrilous invective, Nash's anti-Puritanism plunged him into the Marprelate Controversy *(q.v.).* He and co-writer B. Jonson were imprisoned for their play *The Isle of Dogs.*

Nashville American city (pop. 455,700), the capital of Tennessee. It is a river port, as well as an agricultural and industrial city. It was founded 1779 and became state capital in 1843. The Hermitage, the residence of A. Jackson, is there.

Nashville, Battle of American Civil War battle. On Dec., 15–16, 1864, the Union army of Gen. G. Thomas defeated the Confederates, in the last major battle of the Civil War. Union losses were 400 killed and 1,740 wounded against total Confederate losses of around 15,000.

Naso, Publius Ovidius *See* **Ovid**

Nassau Former German duchy. Located in central West Germany, Nassau occupied parts of the present Hesse and Rhineland-Palatinate. It contributed future rulers to The Netherlands and Luxembourg, including the line of William I (the Silent) of Orange, who was also the ancestor of kings of England. Nassau was incorporated into Prussia (1866) after the Austro-Prussian War *(q.v.).*

Nassau Bahama city (pop. 120,000), located on New Providence Island in the Caribbean, and the capital of the Bahama Islands. Its healthful, temperate climate has made it an international tourist attraction. It was founded in the 1600s and for a period was a rendezvous for pirates.

Nassau, John Maurice of *See* **John Maurice of Nassau**

Nassau, Maurice of *See* **Maurice of Nassau**

Nasser, Gamal Abdel 1918–70. Egyptian statesman. Nasser assisted the 1952 *coup d'état* that ended the monarchy. He also ousted Gen. M. Naguib (1954), naming himself prime minister. He was elected and served as president of Egypt (1956–58) and of the United Arab Republic (1958–70). Strongly Muslim and nationalistic, he seized control of the Suez Canal (1956) provoking the Suez crisis *(q.v.),* established an alliance with the USSR, and fought the June, 1967, war against Israel. During his tenure he was the foremost sym-

bol of Arab nationalism and resistance to Western domination.

Natal South African province, located in the eastern coastal region. Inhabited by the Zulus, it was discovered by V. da Gama in 1497 and was settled by the Boers in 1837 after their Great Trek. It became a British colony (1843) and, after the Boer War, it became part of South Africa (1910).

Nathan Biblical figure, a Hebrew prophet who lived during the time of Solomon and David. He rebuked David for the abduction of Bathsheba with a parable ("Thou art the man"), and his advice saved the kingdom for Solomon.

Nathanael Biblical figure. Nathanael was a disciple of Jesus and is believed to be an alternate name for Bartholomew, one of the Twelve Apostles.

Nation, Carry 1846–1911. American temperance crusader. Brandishing an ax, she smashed saloons, and endured countless beatings and over thirty arrests for her temperance movement activities *(q.v.).*

National Assembly The legislative assembly into which the States General constituted themselves June, 1789, during the French Revolution. The aim was to prepare a constitution (hence it is also called the Constituent Assembly). The National Assembly ultimately brought about creation of a constitutional monarchy (1791) and was superceded by the Legislative Assembly. (*See also* French Revolution [1789–91].)

National Association for the Advancement of Colored People (NAACP) Organization formed in 1909 to counteract the lynching of blacks by whites. Its first black leader was W. E. B. DuBois. Today it conducts legal and political civil rights activities. In the 1970s, with a membership of more than 400,000 in more than 1,500 local units, it maintained its position as the leading US civil rights organization. It was primarily responsible for bringing about the landmark 1954 US Supreme Court antisegregation decision *Brown* vs *Board of Education of Topeka (q.v.).*

National Convention French legislative body (Sept. 21, 1792–Oct. 25, 1795), successor to the Legislative Assembly *(q.v.)* during the French Revolution. Convened after the suspension of King Louis XVI, the National Convention established the republic and condemned Louis to death. It came under the control of the Jacobins, and then of M. Robespierre, who promoted the Reign of Terror *(q.v.).* The Thermidorian reaction in the Convention brought this bloody period to an end. The National Convention was replaced by the Directory *(q.v.).*

National Covenant Bond or engagement instituted by Scottish Presbyterians (Feb. 28, 1638) to observe and maintain their 1581 Confession of Faith. It was the result of England's King Charles I's efforts to impose the English liturgy upon the Scots. (*See also* Covenanters.)

National Front for the Liberation of the South *See* **National Liberation Front**

nationalism Political or social movement in which an individual's primary loyalty is given to the state. Arising with the formation of modern nation-states, nationalism became a major influence in the history of Europe in the 17th and 18th cents. Later it became a driving force in movements by national groups against imperial rule, such as in Ireland (19th cent.) and colonial states in Africa and Asia (20th cent.). Extreme nationalism also contributed to the rise of Fascism in Italy and National Socialism (Nazism) in Germany.

Nationalist China *See* **Taiwan**

National Labor Union *See* **labor unions**

National Liberation Front ⟨National Front for the Liberation of the South⟩ ⟨NLF⟩ Political and military organization formed (Dec. 20, 1960) to overthrow the South Vietnamese government and reunite North and South Vietnam. Reacting to abuses under the Diem regime in the South, both Communist and non-Communist Vietnamese joined the NLF, though the organization was clearly dominated by Communists. During the Vietnam War *(q.v.)*, the NLF military forces, the Vietcong, proved highly successful in guerrilla operations against US and South Vietnamese forces. The NLF established a provisional rebel government in June, 1969, and secured the final conquest of the South in 1975.

National Prohibition Act *See* **Volstead Act**

National Republican party US political party (*c*1825–*c*1836). National Republicans were supporters of J. Q. Adams and nominated him in 1828 to oppose A. Jackson. In 1832, the party nominated H. Clay to oppose Jackson, and, after Clay's defeat, it went into decline. Party members included those connected with business, farm, and labor interests who supported high tariffs and a national bank. By 1836 they had merged with other anti-Jackson forces to create the Whig party *(q.v.)*.

National Road ⟨Cumberland Road⟩ Major US highway to the Old Northwest, linking Cumberland, Maryland, and St. Louis, Missouri. Construction began with federal financing in 1811, and by 1833 the road extended to St. Louis. The highway was of major importance in settlement of the American West.

National Security Act US legislation enacted on July 24, 1947 (and amended on Aug. 10, 1949) that unified the US armed services, with joint chiefs of staff, under a single department headed by a secretary of defense at cabinet level. It established within the executive office of the president the National Security Council, with the president, vice-president, secretaries of state and defense, and others designated by the president as members. And it authorized and established the US Central Intelligence Agency (CIA).

National Socialism ⟨Nazism⟩ Political movement in Germany, the German counterpart of fascist movements that arose in Europe and elsewhere after WW I. National Socialism shared with other fascist movements the characteristics of extreme nationalism, militarism, determination to create a totalitarian state, formation of an elitist class, unswerving obedience to a single leader, and nationalistic expansionism. A. Hitler, leader of the German fascists, outlined many of the doctrines of National Socialism in his book, *Mein Kampf.* Racism was a particularly strong element in the German movement and centered on a fanatical belief in the existence of a "master race," composed of Germanic peoples.

It was the duty of the master race, Hitler preached, to dominate the world and eliminate so-called inferior races (particularly Jews and blacks). Hitler and others used this master race theory skillfully to play on popular fears (of Jews, of Communists) and to arouse German nationalistic spirit at a time when Germany was in the midst of political and economic crisis. Indeed, HItler's fanatical rhetoric (and effective political organization) won a large following for the National Socialism movement and gave Hitler control of the government. But his fanaticism had horrifying consequences. His militant nationalism led directly to WW II and the loss of millions of lives in bloody combat. His attempts to impose the "final solution" to purify the races led to mass extermination of millions of Jews and others (*see* Holocaust) in concentration camps. Germany's defeat in WW II effectively ended the National Socialism movement. (*See also* Nazi party; fascism.)

National Socialist German Workers' party *See* **Nazi party**

National Union Convention ⟨Arm-in-Arm Convention⟩ Meeting (Aug. 14–16, 1866) in Philadelphia of supporters of President A. Johnson to organize opposition to Radical Republicans *(q.v.)*. Its candidates were soundly defeated by Radical Republicans in the 1866 congressional elections.

National Workshops *See* **February Revolution**

Nation of Islam *See* **Black Muslims**

Nations, Battle of *See* **Leipzig, Battle of**

Nations League of International organization (1919–46) formed to maintain peace and security in the post-WW I world. Though the league generally failed in its aims during the 1930s, it provided a foundation for the UN organization that succeeded it. Provided for by the Paris Conference of 1919 (largely due to US President W. Wilson's efforts) and the Treaty of Versailles (1919), the league consisted of a secretariat, council, assembly, and the Permanent Court of International Justice. Original members included the WW I Allies and neutral nations, which were later joined by other nations. The US, however, did not join because of isolationist sentiment in Congress. This and the provision for unanimous assent in both the assembly and council seriously weakened the league. Though it was generally successful in social and economic matters, it failed to effectively promote disarmament. Then, beginning with Japan's occupation of Manchuria (1931), the inability of the league to prevent armed aggression became apparent. Other wars of aggression by Japan, Italy, and Germany followed in the 1930s and with the outbreak of WW II, the league collapsed. It was officially dissolved Jan., 1946.

naturalism Modern philosophical movement that seeks to explain all phenomena in natural, empirical terms, rejecting any metaphysical or supernatural casuality. The literary movement of the same name aims to present human life in similar objective, empirical terms, rejecting free will and spiritual factors, and is best exemplified in the novels of E. Zola.

natural rights Philosophical concept. Natural rights are inherent rights that cannot be taken away by a government. They are expressed in the Declaration of the Rights of Man and the Declaration of Independence *(qq.v.)*, and, in the writings of such thinkers as J. Locke and T. Paine.

Navaho Indians ⟨Navajo Indians⟩ American Indian tribe of the Athapascan family of Indian languages. Originally nomadic, they settled in the American Southwest in the 17th cent. They pillaged settlements until subdued by K. Carson (1863–64), who destroyed their sheep and fruit trees. They were granted a 3.5 million-acre reservation in Arizona, New Mexico, and Utah in 1878. By the 1970s they numbered more than 120,000 and hence were America's largest Indian tribe.

Navajo Indians *See* **Navaho Indians**

Navarino, Battle of Naval battle in the Greek War of Independence, fought on Oct. 20, 1827, in the Peloponnesian harbor of Navarino (now Pylos). Britain, France, and Russia sent 24 ships to the aid of Greece after the Turkish sultan Mahmud II had secured the help of an Egyptian fleet under Ibrahim Pasha to help quell the Greek re-

volt. The Egyptian-Turkish ships were bottled up in the harbor and more than 50 were sunk, with an allied loss of only 300 men against defenders' casualties of over 4,000. This was the last pitched battle fought between wooden sailing ships.

Navarre, kingdom of Spanish province. It was originally a Basque kingdom on both sides of the Pyrenees; the Spanish portion was annexed by Ferdinand the Catholic in 1515, while the French part was incorporated into France when Henry III of Navarre became Henry IV of France (1589). The historic kingdom reached its apex when its king, Sancho III, married the heiress of Castile and ruled over most of Christian Spain (1000–35).

Navarre, Margaret of *See* **Margaret of Navarre**

Navas de Tolosa, Battle of Las Important victory (1212) for the Spanish over the Almohads (North African Muslims) during the Christian reconquest of Spain. The Spanish, led by King Alphonso VIII of Léon and Castile, overwhelmed the Almohads on the plain of Las Navas de Tolosa in southern Spain.

Navigation Acts English legislation (14th and 19th cents.) designed to limit carrying trade to ships of England and English colonies. The first Navigation Act was passed in 1381 but could not be implemented because of a lack of ships. The era of an effective act dates from 1651, when a law aimed primarily at Dutch shipping began the practice of "enumerating" goods that could be shipped to England or its possessions only in their own ships. It contributed to the outbreak of the first Dutch War (1652–54). Enforcement of the acts, especially the 1664 act, by which English colonies could receive European goods shipped only via England, also contributed to unrest in the American colonies. These laws were especially effective during the 17th and 18th cents., and English carrying trade tonnage increased during this period. The acts were all eventually repealed (1849 and 1854).

Nayler, James 1618–60. English Quaker leader. His followers acclaimed him in the words, "Holy, holy, holy, Lord God of Israel," as he rode into Bristol (1656). He was then imprisoned, pilloried, whipped, and branded for blasphemy (1656) in spite of his explanation that they were only worshiping the "Christ within him."

Nazareth Israeli city. Nazareth, in lower Galilee, is revered as the town in which Jesus spent his formative years. Its major industries today are tourism, agriculture, and textiles.

Nazi party ⟨National Socialist German Workers' party⟩ German political party, the instrument of A. Hitler's rise to power and the organ through which he exercised totalitarian control of the German state (1933–45). Founded (1919) as the German Worker's party, it was renamed and reorganized by Hitler along paramilitary lines (by creating the SA, or Nazi storm troops). He took complete control of it in 1921, and, with the aid of H. Goering, R. Hess, and (later) P. Goebbels, began to establish the Nazi themes (see National Socialism) of belligerent nationalism, anticommunism, and anti-Semitism. Hitler's first attempt (1924) to take power, the Munich Putsch (q.v.), failed, and, after a short jail term, he returned to lead the party. The decisive factor in the rise of the Nazi party was the economic collapse and Depression that began in 1929. The Nazis made significant gains in the Reichstag elections of 1930 and 1932, and, in Jan., 1933, Hitler was appointed chancellor. The Reichstag Fire (q.v.), in Feb., 1933, gave Hitler the pretext to suppress the Communists and other opponents. In late 1933, Hitler established the corporative state and made the Nazis the official ruling party. Then, by his Blood Purge (q.v.) of certain elements of the Nazi party, he established (1934) totalitarian control of the party and the state. Thereafter the party's history, marked by its involvement in WW II and the staggering loss of human life, was that of Germany until 1945. Among the organs of the Nazi party were the SS (Black Shirts, q.v.); the SD (Security Service), for espionage and control of the concentration camps; the Gestapo (q.v.); and the Hitler Youth organization.

Nearchus *fl.* 324 BC. Macedonian general. Nearchus was a friend of Alexander the Great and commanded a fleet of his on a voyage from the Indus River to the Persian Gulf in 325–324 BC. He later wrote an account of his journey.

Near East Term sometimes applied to the areas around the eastern Mediterranean, the southwestern parts of Asia, and northeast Africa. Today it is more often designated as the Middle East (q.v.).

Nebhapetre *See* **Mentuhotep II**

Nebo *See* **Nabu**

Nebraska State in the central US, the 37th state (pop. 1,570,000). The Spanish and French first visited the area, which was included in the Louisiana Purchase (q.v.) of 1803. Lewis and Clark explored the region, and fur traders set up the first settlements. It became a territory through the Kansas-Nebraska Act (q.v.) in 1854, and obtained its present boundaries in 1863. The Homestead Act (1862) and the railroad brought settlers and farmers, and, in 1867, it was admitted as a free state. The state constitution was adopted in 1875.

Nebuchadnezzar c630–562 BC. King of Babylon (605–562 BC), successor to his father, Nabopolassar. In 586 BC, he destroyed Jerusalem while putting down a revolt there and exiled most of its inhabitants to Babylon (Babylonian captivity, q.v.). He rebuilt most of the temples in his land and made Babylon, with its Hanging Gardens (q.v.), one of the most beautiful cities in the ancient world.

Necho *d.* 593 BC. Egyptian pharaoh (609–593 BC) of the 26th dynasty. After the fall of Ninevah (612 BC), he sought to aid the Assyrians against the Babylonians and conquered Syria and Palestine, defeating Josiah at Megiddo (608 BC). But he was himself defeated by Nebuchadnezzar at Carchemish in 605 BC. His defeat spelled the doom of Assyria. Forced to retire to Egypt, he repulsed an attempted invasion and later commissioned a Phoenician naval expedition that apparently circumnavigated Africa.

Necker, Jacques 1732–1804. Swiss-born French statesman and financier. As director of finances and the treasury in prerevolutionary France he tried but failed to restore fiscal soundness to the old regime. He was one of those who recommended calling the States General (q.v.), and his dismissal by Louis XVI was one of the causes of the seizure of the Bastille on July 14, 1789. His daughter was the writer Mme. G. de Staël.

Neerwinden, Battle of *See* **Grand Alliance, War of the**

Nefertiti c1372–50 BC. Egyptian queen. She was the wife of Ikhnaton and influenced his religious reforms. A famous limestone bust depicting her head, found in 1912, is now in the Berlin Museum.

Negro Ethnic and racial term. Negro, meaning "black," is the name given by ethnologists to the brown-skinned peoples who originated in the regions of Africa south of the Sahara. From the 16th to 19th cents., European colonial powers used Negroes taken from Africa as slaves in their colonies. The movement to end slavery (q.v.) began in the late 17th cent. and was largely completed in the 19th cent (see abolition). During the civil rights movement (q.v.) of the 1960s in the US, the term "black" came into general use in preference to "Negro."

Nehemiah *fl.* 5th cent. BC. Ancient Jewish leader. He obtained permission from the Persians as governor extraordinary of Judaea to rebuild the walls of Jerusalem (444 BC). He also instituted religious reforms that became characteristic features of postexilic Judaism, as recounted in the Old Testament Book of Nehemiah.

Nehru, Jawaharlal 1889–1964. Indian statesman, a leader in the movement for India's independence, and India's first prime minister (1947–64). Nehru studied in England and was admitted to the bar (1912). Returning to India, he joined (1919) the nationalist movement for Indian independence from Britain led by M. Gandhi. With Gandhi's help, he became president (1929) of the Indian National Congress, and was reelected three times. During WW II he refused to support the British war effort and was imprisoned. When Indian independence was granted (1947), he became prime minister and minister of foreign affairs. He adopted a policy of nonalignment in international matters and promoted a domestic program of industrialization and socialization. He sought reorganization of the separate Indian states along linguistic lines. His administration was marked by conflict with Pakistan over Kashmir and by a Chinese invasion of India (1962).

Nehru-Liaqat Pact *See* **Delhi Pact**

Nekhtnebf I Ancient Egyptian pharaoh (380– 361 BC) and founder of the 30th dynasty. He decisively repelled a Persian invasion force (374 BC).

Nelson, Horatio Nelson, Viscount 1758–1805. English admiral and national hero. His ships destroyed the French fleet (1798) at the Battle of the Nile (q.v.), stranding Napoleon's army in Egypt. At Trafalgar (q.v.), in 1805, his fleet annihilated a numerically superior French-Spanish fleet, ending Napoleon's hopes of subduing Britain. Nelson was killed at Trafalgar. He is celebrated by the Nelson Column in Trafalgar Square, London.

Nemea, Battle of *See* **Corinthian War**

Nemesis Greek mythical goddess. Nemesis was the avenging goddess of just retribution.

Nemirovich-Danchenko, Vladimir Ivanovich 1858–1943. Russian author and director. Together with Stanislavsky, he founded the Moscow Art Theater, which influenced European and American as well as Russian theater standards.

neoclassicism ⟨classic revival⟩ Artistic and architectural movement. The classic revival centered in Europe and America in the late 18th and early 19th cents. It was based on a reappreciation of the cultures of Greece and Rome. Examples of its architecture are the Washington Monument and the US Capitol.

Neolithic *See* **Stone Age**

Neoplatonism Philosophical school developed especially by Plotinus in Alexandria and Rome in the 3rd cent. AD. Based on Plato's teachings and containing elements of Oriental philosophy and mysticism, it was the last of the great pagan schools of thought. It taught belief in the One, a comprehensive deity, who gave the Logos (divine word) to individuals through emanation. Porphyry and Iamblichus were important exponents of Neoplatonism. Its influence declined after Justinian closed the Academy at Athens in AD 529, but it influenced both medieval and modern philosophy.

Neoptolemus Greek mythological warrior. Also called Pyrrhus, he was the son of Achilles and a hero of the Trojan War, in which he slew Priam at the altar of Zeus. He was later slain by Orestes at Delphi.

Neo-Pythagoreanism Philosophical movement that developed in the 1st cent. AD. It incorporated elements of the philosophy advanced (6th cent. BC) by Pythagoras, greatly emphasizing the mystical elements while borrowing from Jewish and Hellenistic philosophy.

Nepal Independent Himalayan kingdom situated between Tibet in the north, and India in the south and west. Located in Nepal is Mt. Everest, the highest peak in the world. Nepal's population includes a number of ethnic groups, among them the Sherpas, noted as mountain climbers and guides, and the Gurkhas, who became renowned as fighters in the British army. The Gurkhas gained prominence in Nepal, and in the 18th cent. invaded Tibet. Their invasion was defeated (1792) by the Tibetans and Chinese, and a subsequent treaty favored Tibet. A Gurkha invasion of India led to war (1814–16) with Great Britain. Again defeated, the Gurkhas were obliged by treaty to withdraw to roughly what has become Nepal's southern border. Great Britain affirmed Nepal's independence by treaty (1923). Nepal was ruled by a monarchy until 1951, when a constitutional monarchy was established. India maintained considerable influence in Nepal until the 1960s, when Nepal began to establish relations with China as well. A Sino-Nepalese treaty (1961) defined Nepal's border with Tibet. The country has been ruled since 1972 by King Birendra Bir Bikram Shah.

Neptune Roman mythical god. Neptune was the god of the sea and corresponds to the Greek god Poseidon. He is represented with a beard and carrying a trident.

Nerchinsk, Treaty of Agreement signed in 1689 between czarist Russia and the Manchu Empire of China involving trade concessions and territorial disputes. Russia gained trade access to Peking but lost her Amur Basin trading outposts. It was China's first settlement with a European power, and it governed basic Russo-Chinese relations until the mid-19th cent.

Nero ⟨Claudius Caesar⟩ AD 37–68. Roman emperor (AD 54–68), successor to Claudius I, who had married Nero's mother, Agrippina II, great-granddaughter of Augustus. His reign went well until his cruelty, vanity, and instability surfaced and he murdered his mother (AD 59) and his wife (AD 62). He blamed the Christians for the fire that destroyed much of Rome (64) (for which he was popularly believed responsible), and he began their persecution. He rebuilt the city, creating the mammoth Golden House (q.v.) as his palace. A plot against Nero (Pisonian conspiracy led by Gaius Piso) was uncovered in AD 65 and led to widespread execution, resulting in the deaths of Seneca and Lucan, among others. In 68, the legions and the Praetorian Guard revolted, and Nero committed suicide.

Neruda, Pablo 1904–73. Chilean poet and diplomat. A surrealist, he was an influential Spanish-language poet. Among his works are *Twenty Love Poems and a Song of Despair, A New Decade,* and *Toward the Splendid City.* He was awarded the Nobel Prize in Literature in 1971.

Nerva AD c30–98. Roman emperor (AD 96–98). He was consul in AD 71 and 90, was banished by Domitian, but succeeded to the throne after the latter's murder. He was a just ruler who accomplished reforms in laws and taxation; he adopted Trajan to be his successor.

Nervi, Pier Luigi 1891–1979. Italian architect and engineer. Nervi pioneered the use of "ferrocement," concrete-reinforced steel. Among his many well-known designs are the UNESCO building (Paris), the George Washington Bridge Bus Terminal (New York), and the Olympic Stadium (Rome).

Nesselrode, Karl Robert, Count 1780–1862. Russian statesman and diplomat. Guiding czarist foreign policy for some 40 years, he strongly favored the Holy Alliance (q.v.). He dispatched Russian troops to crush the Hungarian revolt of L. Kossuth (1849), but was unable to avert the Crimean War (q.v.).

Nestorianism Christian movement (5th cent. AD) that held Jesus Christ had two distinct personalities—divine and human—linked by a moral union. Advanced by Nestorius, this view was condemned by the Council of Ephesus (AD 431), which held that Jesus had both human and divine natures but was one person. Though Nestorianism declined in the West, it spread through the Middle East, Persia, India, and China, and there reached its height (7th–10th cents.) in the form of the Nestorian church. The church rapidly declined in these regions (13th and 14th cents.) following the failure of the Crusades and the ensuing persecution by Tamerlane of Christians in the East. Some Nestorians rejoined the Roman Catholic church (16th cent.) and became known as Chaldaeans.

Netherlands, The (Kingdom of The Netherlands) Country located in northwestern Europe on the coast of the North Sea. Its capital is Amsterdam; seat of government, The Hague. Originally part of the Carolingian Empire, the region of The Netherlands first passed to the Holy Roman Empire, and then to the personal domains of the Hapsburg family. The Netherlands at this time formed the northern part of the Low Countries (q.v.). The Netherlands gained independence (as the United Provinces) in the 16th cent. and in the 17th cent. formed a great commercial empire. Dutch culture also flourished in this period. In the 18th cent., Dutch power declined as a result of rivalries and wars with England and France. The modern kingdom of The Netherlands was created in 1815. Key dates in the history of The Netherlands include:

4TH–8TH CENT. Area subdued by the Franks; conversion to Christianity under Charlemagne.

9TH CENT. Break-up of the Carolingian Empire; area passed into the eastern (German) possessions of Lothair I, and hence eventually became a part of the Holy Roman Empire.

14TH–15TH CENT. Low Countries, including present-day Belgium, Luxembourg, and The Netherlands, came under the rule of the dukes of Burgundy.

1477 Marriage of Mary of Burgundy to Archduke Maximilian of Austria (May); this brought the Low Countries under the control of the Hapsburg family.

1555 Hapsburg Holy Roman Emperor Charles V presented the Low Countries to his son King Philip II of Spain.

1550s–60s Calvinism began to make inroads in the prosperous northern provinces—the area of the present-day Netherlands.

1560s Spanish attempted to impose Inquisition and thereby gain firm control over Low Countries, then agitating for more freedom.

1568 Revolt, led by William I the Silent, broke out in the northern provinces.

1572–74 Spanish driven out of the Low Countries.

1576 Pacification of Ghent; Low Countries united under William I's leadership.

FROM 1578 Spanish reconquered southern provinces of the Low Countries and reestablished Catholicism there.

1579 Union of Utrecht brought together the seven northern provinces (most of the present-day territory) as the United Provinces of The Netherlands; southern provinces became the Spanish Netherlands.

1581 Dutch declared independence from Spain by the Act of Abjuration (July 26).

1584 William of Orange assassinated; succeeded by his son Maurice of Nassau.

1585 England joined the United Provinces in the struggle against Spain.

1602 Dutch East India Company founded as a colonial trading company that would be the basis of the Dutch overseas empire.

1609–22 Twelve Years' Truce concluded with Spain; assured *de facto* independence to the United Provinces.

1618–48 The Low Countries became the principal theater of the Thirty Years' War.

1619–67 Dutch took control of Cape of Good Hope, Java, Sumatra, and the other islands of the Malay Archipelago (modern Indonesia).

1621 Dutch West India Company founded for colonizing and trade in the New World.

c1636 Dutch seized Ceylon and Malacca from the Portuguese.

1648 Treaty of Westphalia; Spain recognized the independence of the United Provinces at the end of the Thirty Years' War.

17TH CENT. Golden Age of Dutch culture, especially art and philosophy.

1652–54 First Dutch War with England, stemming from commercial rivalries.

1652–72 J. de Witt served as head of state.

1664–67 Second Dutch War with England; colony of New Amsterdam (later New York City) was lost but possession of Surinam was confirmed.

1667–68 War of Devolution; Netherlands invaded by France; Netherlands joined Triple Alliance against Louis XIV of France, thereby forcing Louis to end the War of Devolution.

1672–78 Third Dutch War; Louis XIV of France invaded the United Provinces; his French advance was halted when Dutch opened dikes around Amsterdam (1672); French driven out by 1673.

1672 William III of Orange made stadholder (ruler) of the United Provinces during the Third Dutch War; came to power after J. de Witt was murdered for attempting to negotiate with French invaders.

1688–97 War of the Grand Alliance; Dutch opposed France.

1689 William III of Orange became king of England.

1701–14 War of the Spanish Succession; Dutch opposed France.

1715 Treaty of Barrier established forts along Dutch border to contain France.

1747 William IV of Orange became hereditary stadholder (ruler), displacing republican party that had ruled from 1702.

1794 United Provinces overrun by French during French Revolutionary Wars.

1795–1806 Batavian Republic established by French revolutionaries.

1806–10 Kingdom of Holland established by Napoleon, who made his brother Louis its king.

1810 United Provinces annexed by France after King Louis was overthrown.

1815 Kingdom of The Netherlands formed by the Congress of Vienna; house of Orange provided rulers; part of Austrian Netherlands (roughly modern Belgium) joined to kingdom; the other part became the Grand Duchy of Luxembourg.

1815–40 William I reigned.

1830–31 Revolt in former Austrian Netherlands (1830); independent Belgium created.

1839 London Conference recognized Belgian independence.

1840–49 William II reigned.

1848 New liberal constitution promulgated.

1849–90 William III reigned; rapid industrialization of The Netherlands and spread of unions accompanied period of commercial prosperity.

1873–1904 Achinese War; Dutch colonial forces pacified northern Sumatra.

1890–1948 Wilhelmina reigned.

1899 First International Peace Conference held at The Hague; convened to resolve rules of war and the question of arms limitations.

1907 Second International Peace Conference; unsuccessful in resolving arms limitation; agreements reached on other aspects of land and sea warfare.

1914–18 WW I; Netherlands remained neutral.

1940 WW II; German surprise invasion (May); Rotterdam destroyed by air attacks.

1940–45 German occupation; reign of terror instituted by Germans; mass executions used in retaliation for resistance by Dutch underground; nearly all Dutch Jews killed in concentration camps.

1945 The Netherlands became a member of the UN.

1948–80 Queen Juliana reigned, following abdication of her mother, Queen Wilhelmina.

1949 The Netherlands became founding member of NATO.

1949 Indonesia granted its independence after a four-year war.

1954 Surinam and Netherlands Antilles granted political equality with The Netherlands.

1957 Became a member of newly organized European Economic Community.

1963 Dutch ceded the western half of New Guinea ("West Irian") to Indonesia.

1975 Surinam granted independence (Nov. 25), leaving the Netherlands Antilles as the only remaining possession of the once vast Dutch Empire.

1976 Queen Juliana's husband, Prince Bernhard, disgraced in scandal over dealings with Lockheed Aircraft Corp.

1980 Queen Beatrix crowned (Apr. 30), following the abdication of her mother, Queen Juliana.

Netherlands, Spanish and Austrian Region corresponding approximately to modern Luxembourg and Belgium. The region came under control (15th cent.) of the Hapsburgs as part of their domains known as the Low Countries (Netherlands, Belgium, and Luxembourg). The northern provinces of the Low Countries gained independence as the United Provinces (later called The Netherlands) during the revolt of 1581. The southern part remained under control of the Spanish Hapsburgs and thenceforth became known as the Spanish Netherlands. In 1714, however, the area was ceded to Austria by the Peace of Utrecht. It was called the Austrian Netherlands from that time until it was conquered by the French (1794), during the French Revolutionary Wars. In 1815, after Napoleon's downfall, the Grand Duchy of Luxembourg was created from a part of this territory and the remainder was united with The Netherlands. But the union was short-lived and, following a rebellion against The Netherlands, independent Belgium was formed (1831).

Neuilly, Treaty of This treaty between Bulgaria and the Allies was signed Nov. 27, 1919, after WW I. Bulgaria ceded lands to Yugoslavia, Greece, and Romania, paid reparations, and limited its army to 20,000 men.

Neumann, John von 1903–57. Hungarian-born American mathematician. Neumann worked on the atomic bomb, designed computers, and co-wrote *The Theory of Games and Economic Behavior.*

Neustria Western part of the Merovingian Frankish kingdom, located in what is now northwestern France and including Paris. Formed by Clovis I (6th cent.) when he divided his domains among his descendants, Neustria was involved in dynastic wars with the neighboring Frankish kingdom of Austrasia *(q.v.).* The continuing struggle between the monarchs permitted the mayors of the palace to exercise real power, and, in 687, the Austrasian mayor of the palace, Pepin of Heristal, permanently united Neustria with Austrasia. *(See also* Merovingians.)

Neutrality Act Act of the US Congress approved on August 31, 1935, and amended in 1936, 1937, and 1939. The aim of this legislation was to keep the US out of war by prohibiting the sale or transport of war goods or the travel of Americans in belligerent countries or on belligerent carriers.

These acts had become a dead letter even before the US entry into WW II in 1941.

Neutral Nation North American Indians inhabiting the northern shore of Lake Erie. This branch of the Iroquois attempted to remain neutral in the Huron-Iroquois War. But in 1649, when some Hurons joined them, the Iroquois Confederacy destroyed them all.

Neuve-Chapelle, Battle of British offensive (Mar. 10–13, 1915) on the Western Front during WW I. Under the over-all command of British field marshal Sir John French, the British unleashed one of the war's first mass artillery barrages against German positions around the town of Neuve-Chapelle in northern France. British forces then took the town, but their offensive was soon contained by the Germans.

Neva, Battle of the Battle fought July 15, 1240 on the Neva River, near what is now Leningrad, in which Alexander, prince of Novgorod, decisively defeated a Swedish invasion. For this he received the surname Nevsky.

Nevada US western state (pop. 799,184), the 36th state. Although the area was crossed by many on their way to California, it was first really explored by J. C. Frémont (1843–45). It was ceded to the US by Mexico (1848) after the Mexican War *(q.v.)* and became part of the Utah Territory (1850). The discovery of gold and silver in the Comstock Lode resulted in several new settlements, and Nevada became a separate territory in 1861. In 1864, it adopted its present constitution and was admitted to the Union. Mostly semi-arid, the state is noted for its mineral wealth and legalized gambling.

Neville, Ralph, 1st earl of Westmorland 1364–1425. English nobleman. Neville supported his brother-in-law Henry IV against Richard II (1399) and put down the revolts of H. Percy, in 1403, and Richard Scrope (1350–1405), in 1405. His grandsons were kings Edward IV and Richard III.

Neville, Richard, earl of Warwick 1428–71. English nobleman, grandson of Ralph Neville. Called "the Kingmaker," he aided the Yorks in the Wars of the Roses *(q.v.),* but turned against Edward IV. He was killed aiding George, duke of Clarence.

Neville's Cross, Battle of English victory in the English-Scottish wars, fought near Durham, England, on Oct. 17, 1346. David II of Scotland invaded England while Edward III was in France, but the English overwhelmed the invaders with archers and spearmen. David himself was captured and held for ransom.

New Amsterdam Dutch colonial settlement in present-day New York State. The Dutch colonized the area at the mouth of the Hudson River (1624–64). It served as the capital of New Netherland until it was captured by Britain (1664) and renamed New York.

Newburgh Letters *See* **Armstrong, John**

New Brunswick Eastern Canadian province (pop. 709,100), one of the Maritime Provinces. Although explored in 1525 by the Portuguese, it was settled by the French under S. de Champlain and the sieur de Monts in 1604. Under the French, the area of Nova Scotia and New Brunswick was called Acadia *(q.v.)*, and when the British gained control after the French and Indian Wars *(q.v.)*, both territories were known as Nova Scotia. Many Loyalists from New England settled there after the American Revolution, and it became a separate province in 1784. In 1867, it joined with other provinces to form the Dominion of Canada. The province is known for its agriculture, forests, and fishing.

Newcastle, Thomas Pelham-Holles, duke of 1693–1768. English prime minister. Newcastle's weakness during the Seven Years' War *(q.v.)* with France forced his resignation in 1756, but he returned the next year in a political coalition with W. Pitt. He was ineffective in office but skilled in the use of patronage in gaining majorities for Pitt, R. Walpole, and others.

New Church *See* **Church of the New Jerusalem**

New Deal Name for the program of sweeping social and economic reforms initiated (1933–39) by US Pres. F. Roosevelt during the Depression years. The fundamental premise of the New Deal, that federal government intervention to protect the social and economic welfare of the people was justified, represented a major shift in US government policy and resulted in a trend toward social reform legislation that continued long after the Depression years. Nevertheless, the rapidly worsening Depression demanded new solutions. When Roosevelt took office (1933), he called a special session of Congress which (during Roosevelt's famous Hundred Days) enacted a plethora of reform legislation. Among the measures passed were the Emergency Banking Relief Act (Mar. 9), to prevent the complete collapse of the US banking system; the act creating the Civilian Conservation Corps (CCC) (Mar. 31), to provide 250,000 jobs; the act abandoning the gold standard (Apr. 19); the Agricultural Adjustment Act (AAA) (May 12), to provide farm subsidies; the act creating the Tennessee Valley Authority (TVA) (May 18); the Home Owners Refinancing Act (June 13); and the National Industrial Recovery Act (NIRA) (June 16), to aid business and labor. Reform measures passed after the Hundred Days included the repeal of Prohibition (Dec. 5, 1933); the act creating the Securities and Exchange Commission (SEC) (June 6, 1934); and the act creating the Federal Housing Authority (FHA) (June 28, 1934). This completed what is traditionally considered the First New Deal (1933–34). Roosevelt's Second New Deal (1935–39) was marked by still more reform legislation and by growing judicial and political opposition to his programs. The Supreme Court struck down some of Roosevelt's programs (AAA, NIRA) in the years 1935 to 1937 and this gave rise to Roosevelt's abortive plan to "pack" the court with his appointees (1937). But the great bulk of New Deal legislation remained in force. Among the reforms of the Second New Deal were the act creating the Works Progress Administration (WPA) (Apr. 8, 1935), that ultimately employed 8.5 million Americans; the National Labor Relations Act (July 5, 1935), guaranteeing workers the right to organize and bargain collectively; the Social Security Act (Aug. 14, 1935); and the Fair Labor Standards Act (June 25, 1938), guaranteeing a 40-hour work week and minimum wage. Despite initial opposition, much of the New Deal legislation has survived and has been added to in succeeding generations. The impact of these reforms on modern American society and politics has been enormous.

New Economic Policy Russian Communist economic policy that allowed limited free enterprise such as small businesses and sale of surpluses by peasants. Instituted by N. Lenin in Mar., 1921, to relax tensions and gain support for the regime, it followed the earlier period of "war communism" characterized by forced requisitions of goods, confiscation of capital, nationalization, etc. The NEP was replaced by the first Five-Year Plan *(q.v.)* in 1928.

New Empire *See* **New Kingdom**

New England Name given to the northeastern area of the United States. It includes the states of Maine, Vermont, New Hampshire, Massachusetts, Connecticut, and Rhode Island.

New England Confederation Confederation formed in 1643 between the colonies of Massachusetts Bay, Plymouth, Connecticut, and New Haven. It was formed to provide for common interests and defense. The first experiment in federation in America, it was dissolved with the revocation of the Massachusetts charter in 1684.

Newfoundland Island off the eastern coast of Canada, which with Labrador forms the tenth Canadian province (pop. 583,600). It was discovered in 1497 by J. Cabot and became the major fishery, which it remains today. It became a province in 1949.

New France North American territory colonized by France (c1600–1763). The major settlements were in Canada, along the St. Lawrence, with Montreal and Quebec as the principal ones. Part of Maine and sections along the Mississippi and Great Lakes basins were also settled and claimed.

New Freedom US political term. It was coined for the presidential campaign of W. Wilson, the winning candidate (1912). It called for a renewed emphasis on individual economic initiative and competition.

New Frontier US campaign term employed by J. F. Kennedy during his presidency (1961–63) to encourage a spirit of challenge and greater opportunity to the American people.

Newgate Once a London guardhouse, Newgate became a famous prison and an execution site from the 15th cent. It was the scene of many riots and fires before it was demolished in 1902.

New Granada New Granada was a Spanish colonial viceroyalty in South America. It included what is now Colombia, Equador, Panama, and Venezuela. Originally part of the viceroyalty of Peru, it was created as the separate viceroyalty of New Granada in the 18th cent.

New Guinea, Territory of See **Papua New Guinea**

New Hampshire Northeastern US state. One of the New England states (pop. 920,610), the 9th state. It was originally explored by Martin Pring (1603); the first settlements were at Dover and Portsmouth. The area was governed by Massachusetts (1641–43), and, even when made a separate colony (1679), New Hampshire was under the Massachusetts governor until 1741. In 1782, it gave up its claim to Vermont, and the population increased as lumber camps were established. The first colony to declare its independence, New Hampshire became a state in 1788 and adopted its constitution in 1792. It was one of the cradles of the Industrial Revolution in the US. Its early presidential primary makes the state an important arena for aspiring presidential candidates, and national electoral trends often become evident there.

New Hampshire Grants Land claimed by both New York and New Hampshire colonies. E. Allen and his Green Mountain Boys (q.v.) established its independence as Vermont in 1777.

New Harmony See **Harmony Society**

Ne Win, U ⟨Thakin Shu Maung⟩ 1911–. Burmese military and political leader. As a military commander he played a leading role in achieving Burma's independence from Britain (1948). In 1962 he overthrew the government of U Nu and established a military junta that dominated Burmese politics in the next decades. He remained in power until 1981.

New Jersey US eastern state (pop. 7,364,200), the 3d state. The Dutch and Swedes established the first colonies in the region, which was taken by the English in 1664. It was under proprietary rule until it was made a royal province in 1702. It was ruled by the governor of New York until 1738. In 1776, New Jersey declared itself a state and was the scene of several important battles in the American Revolution, especially at Princeton and Trenton. It ratified the US Constitution in 1787 and adopted its present state constitution in 1947. It is a major industrial region and transportation hub.

New Jerusalem, Church of the See **Church of the New Jerusalem**

New Kingdom ⟨New Empire⟩ Period of ancient Egyptian history (1580–1085 BC), which included the 18th–20th dynasties. The New Kingdom began after the overthrow of the Hyksos (q.v.). Thebes was made capital. The pharaohs centralized power in their own hands and by their conquests brought the Egyptian empire to its greatest extent (parts of Asia included). During this period such pharaohs as Thutmose I and Thutmose III proved themselves great conquerors. Many temples were built and the pharaoh Ikhnaton briefly established a monotheistic religion in Egypt. After the reign of Ramses III (c1198–67), the priests at Thebes gained power and thus brought about ancient Egypt's decline. The New Kingdom was followed by a period of domination by various foreign peoples that led finally to the reduction of Egypt to a Roman province. (See also Egypt [1580–1085 BC].)

Newman, John Henry 1801–90. English churchman and writer. He was a founder of the Oxford movement (q.v.), which sought closer correspondence between the beliefs and practices of Christian antiquity and those of the Church of England. He held in his Tract 90 (1841) that the Thirty-Nine Articles (q.v.) of the Church of England were consistent with Catholicism. His own bishop repudiated this position, however, and Newman converted and was received into the Catholic church (1845). His spiritual autobiography, Apologia pro vita sua (1864), is considered a masterpiece both of Christian apologetics and English literature. He was made a cardinal in 1879.

New Mexico US state in the Southwest (pop. 1,300,000), the 47th state. Originally inhabited by the Pueblo and Apache Indians, the area was first explored by the Franciscan missionary Fray Marcos de Niza (d. 1558) in 1539 and then by Francisco Vasquez de Coronado (1510–54), who discovered the Grand Canyon while in search of a fabled golden city, Quivira. The early Spanish settlements were destroyed by the Indians but reestablished by 1692. The region was a province of Mexico until it was ceded to the US (1848) in the Treaty of Guadalupe Hidalgo *(q.v.)*. Terminus of the Santa Fe Trail *(q.v.)* and later the railroad, it became a territory in 1850 but remained troubled by the Indian conflict and disputes between ranchers and homesteaders. It became a state and passed its constitution in 1912. In 1943 the US established its atomic research facility at Los Alamos, and the first atomic bomb was exploded at the White Sands Proving Ground on July 16, 1945.

New Model Army English parliamentary army that successfully concluded the English Civil War. It was originally commanded by Sir T. Fairfax but later came under the leadership of O. Cromwell. It was organized by Parliament (1645) to replace the private armies of parliamentarians. By the Self-Denying Ordinance of April, 1645, parliamentary leaders were supposed to be denied commands. Cromwell was the notable exception, and, in fact, by its success the highly trained New Model Army became his power base, eclipsing even Parliament.

New Nationalism US political ideology promoted by T. Roosevelt during his unsuccessful presidential campaign against W. Wilson (1912). Emphasizing a paternalistic approach, Roosevelt's program called for a strong federal government to institute social reforms and protect human rights.

New Netherland Dutch colony in America. Captured by the British in 1664, it was divided into New York and New Jersey. The first permanent Dutch settlement was Fort Orange on the Hudson (now Albany, New York), established in 1624; New Amsterdam (later New York City) was founded soon after.

New Orleans American city (pop. 557,500). New Orleans is the largest city in Louisiana. Located at the mouth of the Mississippi River, it is a major American port. Settled by the French (c1718), it was ceded to the US with the Louisiana Purchase in 1803 and served as Louisiana's capital (1812–49).

New Orleans, Battle of American victory in the War of 1812 *(q.v.)*, fought near New Orleans on Jan. 8, 1815, two weeks after the Treaty of Ghent *(q.v.)* ending the war. Gen. A. Jackson, unaware the war had been ended, lost only eight killed and thirteen wounded, in the battle, while killing over two thousand British, including their commander, Sir Edward Pakenham (1778–1815). The battle restored American prestige and vaulted Jackson to fame.

New Spain Spanish viceroyalty (1535–1821) consisting of Mexico, what is now the US Southwest, and Central America south to Panama. Spain's possessions among the Caribbean Islands, Florida, and the Philippines were also once administered at part of the viceroyalty. New Spain ceased to exist after Mexico won its independence (1821).

New Sweden Swedish colonial settlement. New Sweden was Sweden's only American colony. It was located in present-day Pennsylvania, New Jersey, and Delaware. Founded in 1638, it was absorbed by the Dutch (1655), after its conquest by P. Stuyvesant.

New Testament The Christian portion of the Bible, relating to the life and teachings of Jesus Christ and the activities and teachings of some of the apostles chosen by Jesus to carry on his work. It consists of 27 books: 4 accounts of the life of Jesus, called "Gospels" ("good news"), ascribed to Matthew, Mark, Luke, and John; an account of the activities of the apostles, especially Paul; 21 epistles, or letters, written in apostolic times and ascribed to Paul, Peter, James, John, and Jude; and an apocalypse, or The Book of Revelations, ascribed to John. The earliest books of the New Testament are thought to have been written around AD 50. Although some say that parts were written later, current scholarship tends to accept the tradition that all of the books were written in the second half of the 1st cent. The canon, or list of approved New Testament books, was not approved by the Catholic church until the 4th cent. A festal epistle of St. Athanasius of Alexandria (AD 367), as well as a contemporary decree of Pope St. Damasus in Rome (381), constitute the evidence that the canon had finally been fixed in its contemporary form. Although the New Testament authors wrote according to no established plan, Christians have traditionally believed they were inspired and divinely protected from error in what they wrote.

New Thought American philosophical and religious movement. "New Thought," an outgrowth of transcendentalism *(q.v.)*, was popular in America in the late 19th and early 20th cents. It stressed optimism, idealism, and the mind's creative power.

Newton, Huey *See* **Black Panthers**

Newton, Sir Isaac 1642–1726. English mathematician and physicist. During 1664–66, his university, Cambridge, was closed because of plague, and Newton in this time discovered laws of motion and universal gravitation, calculus, and the variations of the light spectrum. His findings were published in the *Principia* (1687) and *Opticks* (1704). Today Newton and Leibniz share the credit for the discovery of calculus, but Newton's laws of motion and universal gravitation are considered among the greatest syntheses in the history of human thought. They dominated science until replaced by the theory of A. Einstein in the 20th cent. Newton was the greatest and culminating figure of the 17th-cent. scientific revolution, and was president of the Royal Society from 1703 until his death. In his last years he turned to theology and alchemy.

New York Middle Atlantic state (pop. 18,557,300) of the US and the 11th state. Originally inhabited by the Algonquian and Iroquois Indians, the area was first explored (1524) by Giovannida Verrazano (1485–1528) and H. Hudson (1609). The Dutch established the New Netherland colony (1624), which was taken by the English in 1664 and granted to the duke of York. During the American Revolution, the British held New York City, and several important battles were fought in the territory. New York became a state in 1788 and adopted its current constitution in 1894. Called the Empire State, New York is highly industrialized throughout, yet has a rich agriculture with orchards and vineyards. The completion of the Erie Canal (1825) as well as the building of railroads (from 1831) made New York the principal locus of east-west travel and commerce in the 19th and early 20th cents.

New York City US port city (pop. 7,071,000) in southeastern New York State, one of the world's great cities. The area was visited by H. Hudson (1609), and the city's history began with the establishment (1624) of the Dutch colony of New Netherland. New Amsterdam, at the tip of Manhattan Island, was its capital. Manhattan was, according to traditional accounts, bought by P. Minuit for $24 in trinkets (1626). During the Dutch Wars, the British captured the colony (1664) and renamed it New York, after the duke of York. Development of the city (given a royal charter, 1686) began under British rule. However, local government was at times harsh and provoked unrest, including Leisler's Rebellion (q.v.) of 1689–91. During the American Revolution, the British captured (1776) New York City and used it as a base of operations until the end of the war. The city was nearly destroyed by fires during the occupation, but by 1790 it was already the country's largest city.

New York City was first capital of the US (1785–90) and President G. Washington was inaugurated there (Apr. 30, 1789). The opening of the Erie Canal (1825) made the city a center of transportation to the Great Lakes region and, although much of the city was destroyed by fire in 1835, it underwent a new period of growth. By the mid-1800s it was the nation's leading port. During the American Civil War it was the scene of bloody Draft Riots (1863). After the war, New York City was rapidly industrialized and became the port of entry for millions of immigrants (arriving until the early 1900s), many of whom stayed in the city's slum districts (such as Hell's Kitchen) and worked in its factories. In 1898 the city limits were expanded beyond Manhattan to include the boroughs of the Bronx, Brooklyn, Queens, and Staten Island. The early 1900s marked the beginning of the construction of the modern city. The first skyscrapers went up, bridges were constructed, and work on the vast subway system began. By the 1920s New York City was not only a booming commercial and financial center but was also being transformed into a world metropolis.

New York school *See* **abstract expressionism**

New Zealand Island country in the South Pacific, composed of North Island, South Island, and numerous smaller islands. The capital is Wellington. First discovered (1642) by the Dutch captain A. Tasman, it was visited several times (1769–77) by J. Cook, and was first settled by the British (1840). That year saw the signing of the Treaty of Waitangi (Feb. 6, 1840), by which the Maoris maintained possession of their land but acknowledged British sovereignty. Friction between the colonists and Maoris led to the Maori Wars (q.v.) and subjugation of the Maoris in the 1870s. In 1852 New Zealand was divided into six provinces and granted self-government. It became a dominion (1907), and by the Statute of Westminster (1931) became independent. However, New Zealand did not ratify the statute until the 1940s. New Zealanders distinguished themselves in combat during WW I, WW II, and the Vietnam War.

Ney, Michel 1769–1815. French marshal. Ney, long a supporter of Napoleon, urged him to abdicate after the disastrous losses of the Napoleonic Wars. After briefly serving Louis XVIII, Ney again joined Napoleon during the Hundred Days, was defeated with him at Waterloo (q.v.), and was executed.

Nez Percé Indians American Indian tribe of the Sahaptin-Chinook linguistic family. They occupied the northwestern part of America before they were overrun by gold prospectors in the 1860s and 1870s. This led to an unsuccessful revolt by their Chief Joseph in 1877.

Ngo Dinh Diem 1901–63. Vietnamese political leader and prime minister (1954–63). Following the French defeat in Indochina, he emerged as the strong man in South Vietnam, and seemed to have built a solid regime as virtual dictator, enjoying US support. But his authoritarianism and favoritism to Catholics rather than Buddhists led to growing unrest among Communists and non-

Communists alike in South Vietnam. He was overthrown in a military coup in 1963 that was engineered with apparent US complicity. He was murdered after being overthrown.

Nguyen Cao Ky 1930–. South Vietnamese military and political leader. He served as commander of the US-backed South Vietnam air force (1963–65). In 1967 he became vice-president under Nguyen van Thieu, whom he unsuccessfully attempted to oppose in the 1971 elections. He emigrated to the US after South Vietnam's defeat (1975).

Nguyen dynasty Vietnamese dynasty, founded (1802) by Nguyen Anh (d. 1820). The dynasty nominally ruled after the French occupation of Indochina, until 1945.

Nguyen That Thanh *See* **Ho Chi-minh**

Nguyen van Thieu 1923–. South Vietnam (Republic of Vietnam) political leader. President (1967–75) during the years of major US involvement in the Vietnam War, he was unable to check the Communist advance following the US withdrawal in 1973. He resigned and went into exile after the fall of South Vietnam.

Niagara, Battle of *See* **Lundy's Lane, Battle of**

Niagara movement Organization of American black intellectuals and professionals, organized (1905) by W. E. B. Du Bois and others to advance black civil rights. Largely ineffective, the movement dissolved in 1910, and some members, including Du Bois, joined in forming the NAACP.

Nibelungenlied This Middle High German epic poem (early 13th cent.) is by an unknown author. It is taken from the oral tradition of Siegfried and involves the gold of the Nibelungen, an evil family. The modern operatic tetralogy the *Ring*, by R. Wagner, is based on the saga.

Nicaea Ancient city. Nicaea, now Iznik, Turkey, was founded in the 4th cent. BC. Across the Bosporus from Constantinople, it was the site of important Catholic church councils (AD 325 and 787) before its capture by the Turks (1330).

Nicaea, Councils of Councils of the Catholic church, both held in the ancient city of Nicaea, across the Bosporus from present-day Istanbul. **1.** (1st ecumenical): Convened in AD 325 by the Roman emperor Constantine, it condemned Arianism (q.v.) and established the Nicene Creed (q.v.). **2.** (7th ecumenical): Convened by the Byzantine empress Irene (AD 787) to consider the question of Iconoclasm, raised when her predecessor, Leo III, issued a decree forbidding the "worship" of images (726). The council decided that images could be venerated but not worshiped. It was the last council recognized as ecumenical by both Eastern and Western churches.

Nicaea, Empire of State founded (1206) by Theodore Lascaris (d. 1222) to the southeast of Constantinople and lasting until 1261. It was one of the small states formed by the Byzantines after the crusaders conquered Constantinople and set up the Latin Empire of Constantinople (q.v.). It was from Nicaea that the Byzantines launched the successful military conquest of the Latin Empire (1261). The Byzantine Empire was reestablished under Michael VIII.

Nicaragua Independent state located in Central America. Its capital is Managua. Nicaragua's main exports are cotton, coffee, and sugar cane. It is Central America's largest, but most sparsely populated, country and has a long history of dictatorship and political repression.

1522 First visited by Spaniards under Gil Gonzalez Davila; settlements established.

16TH–19TH CENT. Ruled under captaincy general of Guatemala.

1821 Declared independence from Spain.

1821–25 Became part of De Iturbide's Mexican empire.

1825–38 Joined Central American Federation.

1838 Liberals (based in the city of León) and conservatives (in Granada) fought for control; liberals declared Nicaraguan independence and withdrew from the federation.

1848 Britain seized San Juan del Norte in move to control Mosquito Coast.

1855 Capital established at Managua, between León and Granada.

1855 American filibuster William Walker was employed by liberals to head army; captured and sacked Granada.

1856 Walker became president of Nicaragua.

1856–57 Walker seized holdings of C. Vanderbilt in Nicaragua; Vanderbilt backed conservatives, forcing Walker to flee.

1863–93 Conservatives in control of the government.

1893–1909 Liberal revolt brought José Santos Zelaya to power; ruled as dictator.

1907 Zelaya attempted to revive Central American Federation; warred against Honduras and El Salvador; Central American Conference ended hostilities.

1909 Conservatives overthew Zelaya with US support.

1912 Unsuccessful coup; US Marines occupied Nicaragua (1912–25).

1927–33 Marines reoccupied Nicaragua after internal strife resumed; compromise negotiated between factions ended immediate crisis.

1937–56 Anastasio Somoza García, National Guard general, overthrew the government and established military dictatorship.

1939 Constitution revised; Somoza, reelected, visited US and obtained aid.

1947 A. Somoza defeated in elections by Leonardo Arguello; but Somoza became chief of National Guard and forced Arguello to resign.

1956–67 Luis Somoza ruled after his father was assassinated.

1960 Border dispute with Honduras settled; International Court of Justice ruled against Nicaragua.

1967–72 Maj. Gen. Anastasio Somoza-Debayle became president following the death of Luis Somoza.

1972 Somoza-Debayle resigned (May 1) from presidency; interim government to rule until 1974 elections; Somoza retained control of the country.

1972 Earthquake devastated (Dec. 23) Managua.

1973 Somoza-Debayle declared martial law after leftists kidnapped 14 officials.

1974 Somoza-Debayle resigned from army; won presidential election.

1978 Widespread rioting (Jan. 10) in Managua after leading opponent of Somoza-Debayle was assassinated.

1978 National strike (Jan. 23–30) renewed antigovernment unrest.

1978 Sandinista guerrillas seized (Aug. 22) National Palace.

1979 Sandinista guerrillas began (May) civil war; Somoza-Debayle ordered massive bombings, alienating many civilians; resisted American and OAS appeals to step down.

1979 Somoza-Debayle resigned, fled country (July 17); Sandinista guerrillas entered Managua, took control of government, capping seven-week civil war.

1979 Country ruled by five-member junta, including two non-Sandinistas.

1981 Nicaragua charged with supplying arms to Salvadoran rebels; US president R. Reagan suspended aid (Jan.).

Nicator, Demetrius *See* **Demetrius II.**

Nicene Creed ⟨Niceno-Constantinopolitan Creed⟩ This is the summation of the basic tenets of Christianity, accepted by Roman Catholicism, Eastern Orthodox, Anglican and most other Protestant churches. It was drawn up at the Council of Nicaea (AD 325) in order to state the true faith of the church as against the beliefs advanced by Arianism *(q.v.).* But a few elements were added later by the First Council of Constantinople (381), when it assumed substantially the form in which

it is recited today. The filioque clause *(q.v.)* was added still later in the West (from the 9th cent.). Though sanctioned by the authority of the Roman Catholic church, the filioque has always been rejected by the Eastern church.

Niceno-Constantinopolitan Creed *See* **Nicene Creed**

Nicephorus I *d.* 811. Byzantine Emperor (802–811). He deposed the empress Irene, whom he had served as treasurer. He arranged boundary treaties with Charlemagne (803, 810) establishing the boundaries between the Eastern and Western empires. He was killed by invading Bulgarians.

Nicephorus II ⟨Nicephorus II Phocas⟩ *c*913–969. Byzantine emperor (963–969). His continuous warfare and heavy taxes made him unpopular. He was murdered by his wife, Theophano, and her lover, his nephew John Tzimisces, who succeeded him as John I.

Nicephorus II Phocas *See* **Nicephorus II**

Nicholas I, Saint *c*825–867. Pope (858–867). Nicholas mediated both secular and religious matters. He prevented the divorce of Lothair of Lorraine and supported St. Ignatius of Constantinople against Photius for the see of Constantinople. He upheld the right of bishops to appeal to Rome over their archbishops. He was one of the popes traditionally called "the Great."

Nicholas I 1796–1855. Czar of Russia (1825–55). Acceding despite the Decembrist Conspiracy *(q.v.),* Nicholas suppressed the Polish uprising (1830–31) and helped Austria subdue Hungary (1849). His attempt to expand into Ottoman domains led to the Crimean War *(q.v.).*

Nicholas I 1841–1921. Prince and king of Montenegro. He obtained European recognition of Montenegro's independence in the 1878 Treaty of Berlin. He opposed the union of Montenegro with Serbia into Yugoslavia and was deposed in 1918.

Nicholas II 1868–1918. Last Russian czar (1894–1917), successor to his father, Alexander III. An ineffective and autocratic ruler, Nicholas was greatly influenced by his wife Alexandra, who was in turn dominated by Rasputin *(q.v.).* Russia's defeat in the Russo-Japanese War (1904–05) led to the Revolution of 1905 *(q.v.),* and Nicholas was forced to establish a duma (1906). He took command of the army in WW I (1915), leaving Alexandra (with Rasputin) to govern. Under Alexandra, government at home became chaotic and this, with failures in the war, led to the Russian Revolution of 1917 *(q.v.).* Nicholas and his family were shot by revolutionaries (1918).

Nicholas III ⟨Orsini, Giovanni Gaetani⟩ *d.* 1280. Pope (1277–80). Nicholas successfully managed to keep civil rulers such as Charles I of Anjou and

Rudolf I of Germany from interfering in church affairs. His efforts to effect a reunion with Constantinople ultimately failed.

Nicholas V ⟨Parentucelli, Tommaso⟩ 1397–1455. Pope (1447–55). Nicholas ended a schism when antipope Felix V submitted to him. He was a patron of the arts and is the virtual founder of the Vatican library.

Nicholas V ⟨antipope⟩ *See* **Rainalducci, Pietro**

Nicholas, Saint *fl.* 4th cent. Catholic bishop of Myra in Lycia. Though little is known of his life, he is the subject of many legends and is the patron of Russia, Greece, Sicily, children, and sailors. Legend has transformed his generosity into the Christmas character "Santa Claus," a corruption of his name.

Nicholas of Cusa 1401–64. German humanist and scholar, and from 1448 Roman Catholic cardinal. He worked for monastic reform, and carried out extensive diplomatic missions for Nicholas V. He proposed the hypothesis that the earth revolves around the sun before Copernicus and calendar reform a century before the Gregorian reform. He attacked decadent scholasticism in *De Docta Ignorantia*, "Of Learned Ignorance" (1440).

Nicias *d.* 413 BC. Athenian statesman and general during the Peloponnesian War. Nicias defeated the Spartans and Corinthians (427–426 BC) and made peace with Sparta (421). He opposed the siege of Syracuse (415) but was made commander along with Alcibiades and Lamachus. The expedition proved a disaster, and he was captured by the Syracusans and executed.

Nicodemus New Testament figure. Since Nicodemus was a member of the Sanhedrin, he visited Jesus secretly at night. He helped to bury him after the crucifixion.

Nicopolis, Battle of Decisive victory (Sept. 25, 1396) by Ottoman Turks over a European army of crusaders. King Sigismund of Hungary organized the crusaders in a response to the Turkish threat to Constantinople. The Turks, under Sultan Bayazid I, overwhelmed the crusaders at Nicopolis in Bulgaria, thus ending any effective European resistance to Ottoman expansion. Thousands were killed and some 10,000 taken prisoner. Only Tamerlane's invasion saved Europe from further Turkish conquests at this time.

Niebuhr, Reinhold 1892–1971. American Protestant theologian. He advanced his theory of applied Christianity in such books as *Moral Man and Immoral Society* and *The Nature and Destiny of Man*. Niebuhr preached "conservative idealism" against facile American optimism, emphasizing the reality of sin in human affairs.

Niemcewicz, Julian Ursyn 1757–1841. Polish writer and patriot. He aided T. Kosciusko in the 1794 Polish revolt and was jailed with him. He was exiled in 1831 for additional revolutionary activity.

Niemoller, Friedrich Gustav Emil Martin 1892–. German anti-Nazi theologian. Originally a Nazi advocate, he opposed Hitler's takeover of the Lutheran church. He spent the years 1937–45 in a concentration camp.

Nien Rebellion Chinese revolt. The Nien, a secret society of rebel guerrillas, staged uprisings from 1853 against the Ch'ing dynasty during and after the Taiping Rebellion *(q.v.)*. They were destroyed in 1868.

Nietzsche, Friedrich Wilhelm 1844–1900. German philosopher who proposed new values in place of what he regarded as the decadent slave morality of Christianity in *Beyond Good and Evil* (1886). One of his new values involved the "superman" who would achieve by asserting a "will to power." Nietzsche developed this idea in *Thus Spake Zarathustra* (1883–85). He predicted the "death of God" in his *Joyful Wisdom* (1910), among other works. His ideas influenced the Nazis, although Nietzsche was an anti-state individualist and not anti-Semitic.

Niger ⟨Republic of Niger⟩ Independent state located in west-central Africa in the Sahara region. Its capital is Niamey. The country is largely arid, and most of the population is engaged in subsistence farming. A drought (1968–75) almost devastated the country. Key events in the history of Niger include:

16TH CENT. Songhai Empire controlled large parts of the territory.

16TH CENT. Bornu Empire established by Berbers after the fall of the Songhai Empire.

19TH CENT. Fulani tribe gained southern part.

1884–85 Conference of Berlin placed Niger within French sphere of influence.

1893 Sudanese warriors destroyed Bornu Empire.

1896 Became part of French West Africa.

1922 Became separate colony within French West Africa.

1926 Niamey replaced Zinder as capital.

1946 Became a member of the French Union; gained limited self-government.

1958 Became an autonomous republic in the French Community.

1959 Constitution adopted.

1960 Withdrew from French Community, proclaiming complete independence (Aug. 3).

1960–74 Hamani Diori in office as first president.

1968–75 Drought brought severe economic problems and famine; US relief (1974) aided recovery.

1974 Military coup (Apr. 15); Lt. Col. Seyni Kountché suspended constitution, ruled by decree.

1976 Kountché formed civilian-dominated government; Kountché remained in power into the early 1980s.

Nigeria (Federal Republic of Nigeria) Independent state located in western Africa on the Gulf of Guinea. Its capital is Lagos. The land is rich in oil, making Nigeria among the wealthiest of African nations. Originally populated by such tribes as the Hausa, Fulani, Yoruba, and Ibo, Nigeria was for many years a British colony until 1960.

15TH CENT. Portuguese visited region; slave trade established.

1795–96 Mungo Park explored the Nigerian interior.

1830–31 Richard and John Lander explored the interior.

1861 Britain took control of Lagos; began expanding control in region.

1886 Royal Niger Company chartered; gained control of all trading companies on the Niger River and in the north.

1885 Britain established supremacy over southern Nigeria at the Conference of Berlin.

1897 Kingdom of Benin added to Nigeria.

1900 Protectorate established over southern Nigeria; northern sector pacified and established as a separate protectorate.

1914 Colony and protectorate of Nigeria established by British; economic development began.

1947 Britain granted constitution giving native Nigerians more involvement in government.

1954 New constitution granted after 1947 and 1951 constitutions proved unworkable.

1960 Nigeria became independent (Oct. 1); Abubaka Tafawa Balewa became prime minister (1960–66).

1963 Nigeria became a republic.

1963–66 Bitter disputes between tribal groups and regional governments.

1966 Balewa and other officials killed (Jan.) in coup by Ibo army; Major Gen. Johnson Ironsi became head of military government; abolished constitution.

1966–75 Lt. Col. Gowon in power after coup (July) by Hausa army; Supreme Military Council reigned.

1966 Muslim Hausa tribe massacred (Sept.) Christian Ibos in the north; Ibos fled to eastern region.

1967 Eastern region withdrew (May) from the federation of Nigeria to become Biafra; bloody civil war ensued.

1970 Biafra surrendered (Jan. 12) to Nigerian government troops, ending nearly three years of war.

1973–74 Famine devastated the area.

1975 Increasing unrest resulted (July 29) in bloodless coup; Muritala Rufai Muhammad installed as head of government.

1976 Muhammad assassinated by seven officers who failed in coup attempt; Supreme Military Council chose Lt. Col. Olusegun Obasanjo as president.

1977 Local government councils elected National Constituent Assembly.

1978 Ban on political parties, in effect since 1966, lifted.

1979 Alhaji Shehu Shagari in office; first civilian president in over a decade. Shagari remained in office into the early 1980s.

Nightingale, Florence 1820–1910. English nurse. Nightingale introduced strict standards of sanitation to army hospitals during the Crimean War *(q.v.)* and founded a training school for nurses. She was the first woman to receive the Order of Merit.

nihilism Nineteenth-century movement among the Russian intelligentsia that advocated the overthrow of all order and authority. Given its name in the novel by I. Turgenev, *Fathers and Sons* (1861), the movement embraced both those who wanted to overthrow existing governments by force and terror and those who sought to throw off personal moral restraints.

Nijinsky, Vaslav 1890–1950. Russian ballet dancer and choreographer. Nijinsky revolutionized dance as a member of S. Diaghilev's Ballet Russe. He choreographed such classics as *The Afternoon of a Faun* and *The Rite of Spring*.

Nijmegen, treaties of Series of European treaties. France ended the Dutch Wars (1672–78) with The Netherlands and Spain by these treaties, signed in the Dutch town of Nijmegen (1678–79). The Netherlands regained all its conquered territories, while France gained Franche-Comte, Artois, and towns in Flanders from Spain.

Nika Riot Riot and abortive revolt (532) in Constantinople. The Blues and Greens *(q.v.)*, two popular parties in the Byzantine Empire, were normally opposed to each other. But they united to demand that Emperor Justinian oust two hated officials. Justinian complied but this failed to appease what had become an angry mob. In the ensuing riot, Constantinople was burned, the empress Theodora thwarted an attempt to overthrow her husband, and the emperor's general, Belisarius, restored calm by slaughtering some 30,000 rioters. The incident marked the end of popular party power in the empire.

Nike ⟨Victoria⟩ Greek goddess. She was the winged goddess of victory in both war and athletic events. The Nike, or *Winged Victory* of Samothrace (3d cent. BC), in the Louvre in Paris is one of the best-known ancient works of art. It was discovered on the Greek island of Samothrace in 1863.

Nikolsburg, Treaty of Treaty concluded on Dec. 12, 1621, between Ferdinand II of Austria and Gabriel Bethlen, king of Hungary (1619–21) during the Thirty Years' War *(q.v.)* Hungarian Protestants' rights were guaranteed by the Hapsburgs, and Ferdinand regained the Hungarian crown, renounced by Bethlen.

Nikon 1605–81. Russian patriarch. Nikon was patriarch of the Russian Orthodox church (1652–66). His reforms and resistance to state interference led to widespread opposition and to his removal. His reforms were eventually adopted.

Nile, Battle of the *See* **Aboukir, Battle of**

Nimitz, Chester William 1885–1966. American five-star admiral. Nimitz commanded the US Pacific Fleet during WW II and received the Japanese surrender aboard his ship, the battleship *Missouri.* He was chief of naval operations (1945–47).

Nin, Anaïs 1903–77. American writer. Nin was famed for her letters and diaries as well as such fiction as *Under a Glass Bell* and *Ladders of Fire.*

Nine-Power Treaty Two treaties resulting from the Washington Conference (Nov. 12, 1921–Feb. 6, 1922). The first (Feb. 4, 1922) guaranteed China its territorial sovereignty. The second (Feb. 6, 1922) gave it authority to set trade tariffs. The conference was attended by the US, Britain, France, Belgium, The Netherlands, Portugal, Italy, Japan, and China.

Nineteen Propositions A group of demands presented (1642) by the Long Parliament *(q.v.)* to Charles I of England. Charles rejected these demands, designed to limit his rule, and this led to the English Civil War *(q.v.)* The propositions included demands that the Parliament be allowed to choose ministers, control the army, and enforce the laws against Catholics.

Ninety-five Theses Martin Luther's historic document posted on the church door in Wittenberg, Germany, on Oct. 31, 1517, a date that is now considered the beginning of the Protestant Reformation. The theses not only protested the selling of indulgences in the Roman Catholic church, but advanced Luther's opinions on doctrines of the faith, which proved to be unacceptable to church authority. Originally the theses were posted only to invite debate from other Catholic theologians. They later came to be considered the inauguration of the Reformation.

Nineveh Ancient city. Nineveh was the capital of the Assyrian empire, located near modern Mosul, Iraq. Sennacherib and Ashurbanipal greatly contributed to its glory by their buildings and sculptures. The fabulous royal library of Nineveh was organized by Ashurbanipal *(q.v.).* The city fell to a coalition of Babylonians, Medes, and Scythians in 612 BC. Its fall is celebrated in the Old Testament book of the prophet Nahum.

Ninth Crusade *See* **Crusade, Ninth**

Niobe Greek mythical queen of Thebes. Niobe boasted of her six sons and six daughters, who were then killed by Apollo and Artemis. She fled to Mount Sisyphus, where she wept till she was turned to a weeping stone image by Zeus.

Nirvana In Buddhism and Hinduism *(qq.v.),* Nirvana represents the final state of bliss and freedom to which all aspire. In Hinduism it involves release from the perpetual cycle of rebirths. In Buddhism it is the state achieved by enlightenment (knowledge) in which the individual is released from all desire, anger, or pain. Some sages hold it to be equivalent to extinction or annihilation of the personality. The Sanskrit word refers to the going out of a flame after the exhaustion of its fuel.

Nixon, Richard Milhous 1913–. Thirty-seventh US president (1969–74), successor to L. Johnson. After practicing law for five years, Nixon served in the navy during WW II. He began his political career in 1946 with his election as a Republican to Congress. As a member of the House Committee on Un-American Activities, he gained national attention through the investigation of A. Hiss. In 1950 he was elected to the Senate and in 1952 was elected vice-president under D. Eisenhower. As vice-president (1953–61) he made numerous trips abroad. In Venezuela (1958) he was nearly trapped in violent demonstrations, and while visiting Russia (1959) he participated in the Kitchen Debates *(q.v.)* with N. Khrushchev.

Chosen Republican candidate for president (1960), he was defeated by J. Kennedy and, following his defeat (1962) for the governorship of California, he retired to private life. In 1968 he again received the Republican presidential nomination, this time defeating the Democratic candidate (H. Humphrey). As president, Nixon began the withdrawal of US troops from Vietnam, but the order to invade Cambodia (1970) and Laos (1971) provoked widespread protest. In foreign policy, Nixon sought to ease tensions between the West and the Communist bloc through a policy of detente *(q.v.)*, and he visited China in 1972 to mark the US reapproachment with the Communist state. That year he was reelected, defeating the Democratic candidate G. McGovern in a landslide. Nixon obtained a cease-fire with North Vietnam (1973) effectively ending US participation in the Vietnam War *(q.v.)*. Soon after his reelection, however, revelations concerning the Watergate affair *(q.v.)* began to emerge. His vice-president, S. Agnew, was forced to resign (1973) and was succeeded by G. Ford. Nixon was in turn forced to resign (Aug. 9, 1974) under threat of impeachment. He was succeeded by Ford, who granted him a pardon. (*See also* United States [1968–74].)

Niza, Fray Marcos de *See* **New Mexico**

Nkrumah, Kwame 1909–72. Ghanaian statesman. Nkrumah led strikes against British domination of Ghana, which achieved independence under his leadership. He later became its first prime minister (1951) and president (1960).

NKVD *See* **GPU**

NLF *See* **National Liberation Front**

Noah Old Testament patriarch. Because of his goodness, God spared Noah, his family, and two animals of each specie from the Deluge. God instructed Noah to build the Ark as a refuge, as recounted in the Book of Genesis.

Noailles, Maurice, duc de 1678–1766. Marshal of France under Louis XV. He distinguished himself in the wars of the Austrian, Polish, and Spanish succession *(qq.v.)*.

Nobel, Alfred Bernhard 1833–96. Swedish inventor and industrialist. Nobel invented dynamite, though he was a pacifist. With his fortune he established the coveted Nobel prizes, awarded yearly to scientists, writers, and peacemakers.

Nobile, Umberto *See* **Amundsen, Roald**

nobiles *See* **patricians**

Nobility, Charter to the *See* **Charter to the Nobility**

Nod, Land of *See* **Land of Nod**

Nogi, Maresuke, Count 1849–1912. Japanese general. He fought in the Sino-Japanese War *(q.v.)*, captured Port Arthur in the Russo-Japanese War *(q.v.)*, and outflanked the Russians at Mukden.

nominalism Philosophical doctrine, important in medieval times, which held that universals (abstractions) do not exist and that only specific objects have real existence (ie., a man exists but humanity, the abstract concept of all men, does not or is unknowable). Nominalists thus opposed the scholastic philosophers and challenged fundamental tenets of Christian theology (ie., the Holy Trinity was unknowable). The philosopher Roscellinus (*d.* after 1220) is said to have held the nominalist view in the extreme form. An intermediate position (Conceptualism) held that universals exist in the mind as concepts but have no substantive reality in the world outside the mind. This middle position was adopted by William of Ockham *(q.v.)*.

Nominated Parliament *See* **Barebones Parliament**

Nonconformists Term used to describe those who decline to subscribe to the established state religion. It came into use in English history to describe those Protestants who rejected the established Church of England, particularly those who separated from it around the time of the 1660 Restoration *(q.v.)* of the monarchy and passage (1662) of the Act of Uniformity *(q.v.)*. It has been applied to Baptists, Congregationalists, Presbyterians, Methodists, and Unitarians, as well as independent groups such as the Brownists, Quakers, and Plymouth Brethren. In Scotland this term, or "dissenters," was used to refer to those who separated from the established Presbyterianism, and included the Anglicans.

Noncooperation movement Indian protest movement organized between Sept., 1920 and Feb., 1922 by M. K. Gandhi as a reaction to a British Amritsar Massacre *(q.v.)* in 1919. The movement involved boycotting British institutions and goods. An outbreak of violence brought the movement to an end though Gandhi later used nonviolent protests (satyagraha) against the British to gain India's independence.

Nonpartisan League US alliance of farmers formed in 1915. Its purpose was to apply political pressure to achieve the farmers' demands for state control of storage and distribution centers. It spread rapidly through the wheat belt from Wisconsin to Washington and the Southwest. It declined after WW I.

Nonproliferation Treaty Treaty (July 1, 1968) in which nuclear powers agreed to prevent the spread of nuclear-weapons technology to nations that did not then possess such capabilities. The treaty was signed by the US, Britain, USSR, and numerous other nonnuclear countries. Reports of new weapons-development programs persist, however, notably in Pakistan, Libya, and South Africa.

Nootka Sound controversy In 1789 Spain and Britain almost went to war over Nootka Sound, a natural harbor on the coast of Vancouver Island. The Nootka Sound Convention of 1790 granted both nations fishing and settlement rights and ended Spain's exclusive claims to the west coast of North America.

No Popery Riots *See* **Gordon Riots**

Nordenskjold, N.A.E. *See* **Northeast Passage**

Nordlingen, battles of **1.** Decisive victory for the Holy Roman Empire (Sept. 5–6, 1634) during the Thirty Years' War (1618–48). A combined force of Imperial and Spanish troops, led by Archduke Ferdinand (later Ferdinand III), routed a Swedish force near this Bavarian town. The victory forced France to join the war (May, 1635) and ended Swedish influence in southern Germany. **2.** Victory for the French (Aug. 3, 1645) during the Thirty Years' War (1618–48). French troops, led by the Great Condé, defeated a combined force of the Holy Roman Empire and Bavaria at Nordlingen. The victory was gained at great cost, however, and brought about a lull in fighting.

Norfolk, Thomas Mowbray, 1st duke of *c*1366–99. English nobleman. Norfolk was a "lord appellant" who dominated Richard II from 1387 to 1389. Uneasy after Richard regained power, he quarreled with Bolingbroke (later Henry IV) and both he and Bolingbroke were banished.

Norman Conquest English historical period inaugurated in 1066. One of the formative eras in English history, it began with the defeat of the English king Harold II by William the Conqueror, duke of Normandy, at the Battle of Hastings *(q.v.)*. Thereafter the customs, laws, and language of the Normans were introduced in England. William replaced the English nobles with his Norman followers and established the feudal system in England.

Normandy Historic region of France on the English Channel. The Norseman Rollo was proclaimed the first duke of Normandy by Charles III of France (911). Duke William (the Conqueror) united Normandy with England by his conquest of England in 1066. It was taken by France under Philip II in 1204, retaken by England in 1417, and again by France in 1450. The beaches of Normandy were the scene for the Allied invasion during WW II (1944). Rouen is the historic capital.

Normandy invasion ⟨Operation Overlord⟩ World War II Allied invasion. On D-Day, June 6, 1944, Allied land, naval, and air troops invaded the northern shores of Nazi-held France. They established beachheads (Utah, Omaha, Gold, Juno, Sword) in five key areas by the next day, opening the area for other Allied troops. The invasion signaled the beginning of the end of the Nazi war effort. The invasion, the largest amphibious landing in history, was overseen and executed by Gen. D. Eisenhower, and some 800,000 combat troops had been massed in Britain for the operation. Over

4,000 ships, under the command of British admiral Sir Bertram Ramsay, were used in the invasion; and about 5,000 fighters and almost 6,000 bombers were used to provide air support. British Field Marshal B. Montgomery was in command of Allied ground forces during the invasion.

Normans *See* **Norsemen**

Norns Norse mythical goddesses. The Norns were three Fates who wove the web of life: Urth (past), Verthandi (present) and Skuld (future).

Norodom ⟨Narottama⟩ 1834–1904. Cambodian king (1860–1904) who brought an end to his country's independence by accepting a French protectorate (1864).

Norodom Sihanouk 1922–. Cambodian king (1941–55). Following the French withdrawal from Indochina (1954), he established the People's Socialist Community, abdicated the throne in favor of his father (Prince Norodom Suramarit) and became prime minister. He became head of state again after his father's death (1960) but was unsuccessful at maintaining neutrality during the Vietnam War and was overthrown in 1970 by a rightist coup.

Norris, Frank 1870–1902. American writer. Norris was a naturalist and was influenced by E. Zola. His works include *McTeague*, *The Octopus*, and *The Pit*, and often intended to expose corruption and exploitation.

Norris, George William 1861–1944. American legislator. Norris was both a congressman (1903–13) and senator (1913–43). He opposed US entry into WW I, established the Tennessee Valley Authority *(q.v.)*, and introduced the 20th (Lame Duck) Amendment to the Constitution, which was enacted in 1933.

Norsemen ⟨Northmen⟩⟨Normans⟩ Scandinavian Vikings who, from the 8th cent., raided and colonized such diverse territories as England, Ireland, France, and Russia. Vikings also colonized Iceland and Greenland and even visited "Vinland" (North America). Norseman from what is now Denmark were called Danes and attacked England as early as 787. The major assault by Norsemen on France came c845. In 912, French king Charles III gave the Norseman Rollo the area around Rouen. This was the beginning of the duchy of Normandy. Later, Christianized Normans of Normandy established (10th cent.) kingdoms in southern Italy and Sicily and, under William the Conqueror, invaded and conquered England (1066). In Russia, the Norsemen were known as Varangians, and one of them, Rurik, established at Novgorod (862) the dynasty that ruled in Russia until 1598. In the same period, strong rulers such as Harold I and Canute began to organize Norse homelands into the Scandinavian nations of Norway, Denmark, and Sweden.

North, Frederick, 2d earl of Guilford and 8th Baron North 1732–92. English statesman. Lord North was George III's prime minister (1770–82) during the American Revolution. His acquiescence to the king's harsh policies in the years leading up to the American Revolution led to the loss of the American colonies. He did not fully support the war and remained in office at the king's insistence until 1782 and the British defeat at Yorktown.

North Africa Geographical designation. This term identifies the African countries south of the Mediterranean and north of the Sahara desert. It generally includes Morocco, Algeria, Tunisia, Libya, and, sometimes, Egypt.

North Africa, campaign of Series of military actions in North Africa (1940–43) during WW II. Following Italy's entry into the war (1940), Italian forces began an invasion of Egypt (Sept., 1940). The British counterattacked (Dec.) and drove them back some 500 miles into Libya (Feb., 1941). This brought German intervention and two major German offensives. Gen. E. Rommel, commanding the Afrika Korps, attacked the British (Apr., 1941) and advanced into Egypt. The British counterattacked and drove Rommel back through Libya to El Agheila (Jan., 1942). Rommel opened a new counteroffensive (May, 1942) and again pushed into Egypt. The turning point came (Oct., 1942) in the Battle of El Alamein *(q.v.)*. The British, now under command of B. Montgomery, forced Rommel to retreat. Outwitting British attacks, he fell back to southern Tunisia. New Allied forces, commanded by Gen. D. Eisenhower, landed in the west (Nov., 1942) in Algeria. They pushed into Tunisia and guaranteed the German defeat, but only after heavy fighting. When the Axis forces finally surrendered (May, 1943) more than 250,000 troops were taken prisoner. The Axis defeat in North Africa was a major victory for the Allies.

Northampton, Battle of *See* **Roses, Wars of the**

North Atlantic Treaty Organization ⟨NATO⟩ Alliance formed after WW II by the Atlantic nations of Europe and North America to counter potential Soviet bloc threats. The treaty was originally signed Apr. 4, 1949, and members included Belgium, Canada, Denmark, France, Great Britain, Iceland, Italy, Luxembourg, The Netherlands, Norway, Portugal, and the United States. Greece and Turkey joined in 1952 and West Germany in 1955.

North Carolina State (pop. 5,874,500), in the US Southeast, the 12th state. Sir W. Raleigh's colony on Roanoke Island (1580s) was unsuccessful, and

the region was granted by Charles II to eight members of his court. It reverted to the court in 1729 and became a royal colony. During the American Revolution, the Mecklenburg Declaration of Independence *(q.v.)* was drawn up (1775) calling for independence. North Carolina was the scene of fighing in the American Revolution and ratified the US Constitution in 1789 and relinquished its claims to Tennessee in 1790. During the Civil War, it seceded in 1861 and rejoined the Union in 1868. The present amended state constitution was adopted in 1868. North Carolina leads the nation in the production of tobacco, textiles, and furniture.

Northcliffe, Alfred Charles William Harmsworth, Viscount 1865–1922. English journalist and publisher. He was considered the most successful publisher in English history, having either founded or salvaged such papers as the *Daily Mail*, the *London Observer* and the London *Times*.

North Dakota North central US state (pop. 652,700), the 39th state. The French explorer Pierre de la Verendrye and his sons explored the region in the mid-1700s, and the fur trade brought in others. The US acquired half of the area with the Louisiana Purchase (1803) and the other half from the British in 1818. In 1861, the Dakota Territory was formed, including North Dakota, South Dakota, Montana, and Wyoming, but it was sparsely settled until the late 1800s because of the conflict with the Indians. North Dakota adopted its constitution and became a state in 1889. It is one of the world's premier wheat-growing regions.

Northeast Boundary Dispute US-Canadian border controversy. Due to the vagueness of the 1783 Treaty of Versailles, the border between Maine and New Brunswick was unclear. Several points were clarified in the Jay Treaty and the Treaty of Ghent *(qq.v.)* After the Aroostook War *(q.v.)*, America and Britain decided to settle the matter permanently through the Webster-Ashburton Treaty of 1842 *(q.v.)*.

Northeast Passage Sea route to the Pacific along the northern coasts of Russia and Siberia. Navigators attempted to open such a route from the 16th cent. but it was not opened until 1878–79, when N. A. E. Nordenskjold (1832–1901) of Sweden accomplished this. The Soviet Union today maintains the route with the help of icebreakers and patrol planes.

Northern Expedition Military campaign in China (1926–28) conducted by the nationalist Kuomintang and led by Chiang Kai-shek. Planned by Sun Yat-sen, the operation was launched (1926) to overcome the warlords, local military rulers who were preventing establishment of an effective central government. The nationalists quickly won control of the south and, as the campaign proceeded, the historic purge of Communists from the Kuomintang began (Apr. 1927). Peking was captured (June 1928) and, with the capital secured, Chiang Kai-shek became ruler of a unified China. His authority was never secure, however, and after the Chinese Civil War *(q.v.)* the Communists finally gained control of China (1949).

Northern Ireland ⟨Ulster⟩ Division (pop. 1,540,000) of the United Kingdom, located in northeastern Ireland. The capital is Belfast. It includes six of the nine counties of the historic English province of Ulster and hence is frequently called Ulster. The English seized much of the land in the area (17th cent.) after suppressing a rebellion in Ireland. Ulster was subsequently settled by English and Scottish Protestants. The political rivalry between Catholics and Protestants (the latter comprising the majority of the population) dates to the 19th cent. and W. Gladstone's proposal for Home Rule *(q.v.)* in Ireland. The Protestants, fearing Catholic domination from the south, opposed Home Rule. The Government of Ireland Act (1920) established Northern Ireland as a separate province, but the Republic of Ireland refused to acknowledge the division. Frequent clashes continued which, in the late 1960s, erupted into civil war between a wing of the IRA and a Protestant group, the Ulster Defense Association. In 1972 Britain assumed control of government in Northern Ireland. Subsequently, a coalition of Northern Ireland's Social Democratic and Labour parties gained control of a reconstituted assembly, formed an 11-member Northern Ireland Executive, and planned a Council of Ireland, which would seek cooperation between Catholic and Protestant factions. Continued terrorism by both the IRA and Protestants hampered efforts to resolve the conflict, and a general strike in Ulster (May, 1974) led to resumption of governmental control by Britain. The bloody terrorist war continued in the 1980s.

Northern Rhodesia ⟨Zambia⟩ African country. Located in south-central Africa, this was the former name of Zambia from 1911 to its establishment as a republic (1964). The name comes from the British empire-builder C. Rhodes.

Northern Sung *See* **Sung**

Northern Territories Australian region. This is a sparsely settled area of northern Australia bounded by the Timor and Arafura seas on the north and Queensland on the east. Its chief industries are mining and cattle raising.

Northern War (First) War (1655–60) between Sweden and Poland and its allies (Austria, Den-

mark, and Russia) sparked by Sweden's attempt to expand its Baltic domains. Swedish king Charles X invaded Poland and won a major victory at Warsaw (1656) before being forced to withdraw. In 1658, Charles invaded Denmark and nearly captured Copenhagen. The war with Poland was formally ended (1660) by the Treaty of Oliva *(q.v.)* and the Treaty of Copenhagen with Denmark, in which Sweden gained Danish territory in southern Sweden.

Northern War ⟨Great ~⟩ War fought (1700–21) by Sweden under Charles II and Russia under Peter I (the Great). Russia was supported by Denmark, Saxony, Poland, Prussia, and Hanover. The original belligerents (Russia, Poland, and Denmark) sought to break Swedish hegemony in the Baltic region. Charles prolonged the war by proving a far better warrior than expected, but Sweden was ultimately defeated. The Northern War, concurrent with the War of the Spanish Succession in southern Europe, marked the rise of Russian power in the Baltic.

1699 Peter I of Russia, Frederick IV of Denmark, and Augustus II of Poland and Saxony joined in secret alliance against Sweden.

1700 Poland invaded Swedish Livonia; Denmark invaded Schleswig.

1700 Denmark forced out of the war by Charles's surprise invasion near Copenhagen; Treaty of Travendal signed (Aug.).

1700 Charles defeated Russia at Narva (Nov. 30); broke Polish seige of Riga.

1701–02 Charles invaded Poland, took Warsaw and Cracow; fighting continued in Poland for next few years.

1704 Charles forced election of Stanislaus I as rival king of Poland (to Augustus).

1706 Charles pursued Augustus into Saxony; forced Augustus to withdraw from the Russian alliance; Stanislaus recognized as Polish king by the Treaty of Altranstadt.

1706 Russian czar Peter occupied Ingermanland and Livonia.

1707 Charles attacked Russia, invading the Ukraine.

1708 Russians defeated Swedish support troops at Lesnaya (Oct.).

1709 Russia defeated the Swedes' main army at Poltava; Charles fled to Bessarabia, in the Ottoman Empire.

1709 Augustus II invaded Poland, expelled Stanislaus; Russia, Denmark, Poland, and (soon after) Hanover, Saxony, and Prussia then began the conquest of Sweden's Baltic territories.

1710 Ottoman sultan declared war on Russia at Charles' urging.

1711 Russia launched unsuccessful attack against the Ottomans; forced to sign Treaty of the Pruth, relinquishing Azov; Ottomans ceased hostilities.

1714 Charles returned to Sweden; continued the futile struggle against the full coalition.

1718 Charles invaded Danish Norway; was killed in action.

1718 Frederick I of Sweden began peace negotiations with all belligerents except Russia.

1719 First Treaty of Stockholm signed (Nov.); Sweden ceded Bremen and Verdun to England-Hanover.

1720 Second Treaty of Stockholm signed (Feb.); Sweden sold parts of Pomerania and the port of Stettin to Prussia.

1720 Treaty of Fredericksbourg (June) restored Danish conquests to Sweden.

1721 War ended by Treaty of Nystad with Russia; Sweden ceded Livonia, Estonia, part of Karelia, and Ingermanland to Russia; retained Finland.

North German Confederation An alliance of 22 German states north of the Main River under the leadership of Prussia. Formed (1866) after the Austro-Prussian War *(q.v.)*, it succeeded the German Confederation *(q.v.)* which had been dominated by Prussia's rival, Austria. The new confederation lasted between 1866 and 1871, when Prussian minister O. von Bismarck achieved his goal of creating a unified empire of all German states under Prussian domination (and excluding Austria). Bismarck thereby created the modern German state.

Northmen   *See* **Norsemen**

Northumberland, earls of   *See* **Percy**

Northumberland, John Dudley, duke of   *c*1502–53. English soldier and politician. He ruled England during the minority of Edward VI and persuaded him to transfer the throne from Mary and Elizabeth I to his own daughter-in-law, Lady Jane Grey. He was subsequently beheaded.

Northumbria, kingdom of Anglo-Saxon kingdom of England, formed by uniting the kingdoms Deira and Bernicia. During the 7th cent., the kingdom accepted Christianity and became the major power in England. Mercia gradually became more powerful, but the entire York area was overrun and ruled by the Danes, until they were beaten by Harold II of England (1066).

North West Company Canadian fur-trading company founded in 1783. It carried on a vigorous and often violent competition with the Hudson's Bay Co. until a merger of the two in 1821.

Northwest Ordinances Legislation passed (1784–87) under the Articles of Confederation to settle the state of western territory (the Northwest Territory, *q.v.*) ceded to the central government by the states after the American Revolution. The principal ordinance was passed on July 13, 1787, and is sometimes called the Ordinance of 1787; it established territories and provided the conditions under which they could become states. It also provided for education, religious freedom, and land division, and it prohibited slavery in the territories as well. This legislation was the most significant accomplishment of the government under the Articles of Confederation.

Northwest Passage Sea route from the Atlantic to the Pacific through the Arctic above North America. From the 16th cent. on, the quest for such a passage gave enormous impetus to the exploration of the North American Arctic, but the actual existence of such a route was not demonstrated until the 1850s, and it was not traveled by a commercial ship until the ice-breaking tanker SS *Manhattan* accomplished the feat in 1969.

Northwest Territory ⟨Old Northwest⟩ Region that was the first US territory, comprised of the present states of Ohio, Indiana, Illinois, Michigan, Wisconsin, and part of Minnesota. The area was first explored by French traders and missionaries and was taken by the British in the French and Indian Wars (1763). The Treaty of Paris (1783), ending the Revolution, gave the land to the US. Territorial government was established by the Northwest Ordinance (1787) and the area was divided (1800) into the Indiana Territory and Northwest Territory (including then only Ohio and some adjoining regions).

Norton Thomas   *See* **Sackville, Thomas, 1st earl of Dorset**

Norway ⟨Kingdom of Norway⟩ Kingdom located in northern Europe and occupying the western part of the Scandinavian peninsula. Long a seafaring people, Norwegians were among the Scandinavian Norsemen who raided Europe and colonized Iceland and Greenland between the 9th and 11th cent. Norway was united with neighboring powers for much of its history. From the 14th to 19th cent. it was under Danish control and during the 19th cent. it passed to Sweden. Norway gained independence in 1905 and today possesses one of the world's great merchant marine fleets. Key dates in Norwegian history include:

9TH CENT.   Mountain valleys and fjords of Norway divided into local *fylker* (counties) ruled by petty kings.

860–933 Harold I (the Fairhaired) reigned; conquered and unified most of Norway by 872 and became its first king; also conquered Orkneys and Shetlands.

860–1000 Vikings from Norway intensified seaborne conquests; colonization of Iceland (874), Normandy (911), and Greenland (974).

935–961 Haakon I reigned; briefly reunited kingdom, divided since Harold's death.

995–1000 Olaf I reigned; Christianity introduced; defeated and killed at Svöld in fighting against Sweden and Denmark.

1000 Norway divided between Denmark and Sweden after Olaf's defeat.

1016–28 Olaf II reigned after ending foreign rule; Christianity established; aroused opposition of nobles.

1028 King Canute (of England and Denmark), aided by disaffected nobles, conquered Norway.

1035–47 Magnus I reigned, following Canute's death; ruled as king of Norway and Denmark (from 1042).

1184–1202 Sverre reigned in Norway; gained throne after period of dynastic warfare; created strong monarchy with support of peasants; asserted supremacy of monarchy over church and thereby provoked Crosier War (1196–c1202) against bishops and followers.

1217–63 Haakon IV reigned; Norway enjoyed peace and prosperity; Greenland and Iceland united with crown (1262).

1263–80 Magnus VI reigned; prosperity continued; Magnus instituted administrative and ecclesiastical codes.

1319–43 Magnus II of Sweden inherited Norwegian throne; forced to abdicate in 1343.

1343–80 Haakon VI reigned.

1380–87 Margaret of Denmark, Haakon's wife, exercised real power in Norway as regent for her son, Olaf V.

1387–97 Margaret held power in both Norway and Denmark after her son died without heirs.

1389–97 Margaret conquered Sweden with the aid of disaffected nobles.

1397 Kalmar Union formed; united Denmark, Norway, and Sweden under one crown; Norway subsequently dominated by Denmark.

14TH CENT. Black Death (plague) ravaged Norway.

1523 Sweden withdrew from Kalmar Union; for the next three centuries. Norway, governed as a Danish province.

1534–59 Christian III of Denmark reigned. Lutheranism introduced as Norwegian state religion.

1814 Treaty of Kiel; Denmark, an ally of the defeated Napoleon, was forced to cede Norway to Sweden.

1815 Swedish army forced Norway to accept Sweden's Charles XIII, but Norway was recognized as an independent kingdom united with Sweden through the king.

1821 Norwegian Storting (parliament) abolished the Danish-created nobility.

AFTER 1850 Golden Age of Norwegian literature and music, with such writers as H. Ibsen and K. Hamsun and such composers as E. Grieg.

1884 Norwegian government made responsible to the Storting, despite Swedish opposition.

1905 Union with Sweden dissolved by Storting (Aug.) after conflict over separate consular service to assist growing Norwegian merchant fleet; ratified by Sweden (Oct.).

1905–57 Haakon VII reigned as king of Norway.

1914–18 Norway neutral in WW I.

1920s Labor party (Socialist) rose as dominant power in Norwegian politics; much social legislation passed in 1930s.

1940 WW II; Nazi Germany invaded and occupied Norway (Apr. 8–9), a neutral.

1940–45 German occupation; V. Quisling, head of Norwegian Nazis, took over government while the king set up government in exile in Britain.

1945 Norway became charter UN member.

1945–51 E. Gerhardsen (Labor party) in office as prime minister; brought about Norway's rapid postwar economic recovery.

1949 Norway became founding member of NATO.

1955–65 Gerhardsen again in office as prime minister; retirement and social welfare programs instituted.

1957– King Olaf V reigned.

1965 Labor party out of power in Norway for first time in three decades.

1971 Scandal forced resignation of prime minister Per Borten's government (Mar.).

1972 Entry into the EEC rejected by voters.

1972 Lars Korvald installed as new prime minister; government crisis over rejection of European Economic Community (EEC) membership ended.

1973 Prime Minister Trygve Bratteli installed following resignation of Lars Korvald.

1976 Government set up national oil company in the wake of North Sea oil discoveries.

1981 Gro Harlem Brundtland became first woman prime minister of Norway.

1981 Käre Willoch, a conservative, in office as prime minister following ouster of the Labor Party.

Noske, Gustav 1868–1946. German politician. As minister of defense he surpressed many radical insurrections, most notably the Berlin Spartacus Revolt (1919). He resigned after the 1920 Kapp Putsch *(q.v.)*.

Nostradamus ⟨Notredame, Michel de⟩ 1503–66. French physician and astrologer. His symbolic rhymes have come to be regarded by some as prophecies for the world's future and its ending.

Notredame, Michel de *See* **Nostradamus**

Notre Dame de Paris Cathedral begun in 1163 regarded as a classic example of Gothic architecture. One of the best-known churches in the world, its twin towers were completed around 1245, and it was finally completed in the 14th cent. and restored in the 19th. V. Hugo used it as the setting of his famous romantic novel of the same name (1831).

Notus Greek god of the south wind, son of Astraeus and Eos.

Novara, Battles of **1.** Battle in which a 13,000-man Swiss army, fighting on behalf of the League of Cambrai *(q.v.)*, defeated (June 6, 1513) a 10,000-man French army commanded by Louis de la Tremoille (1460–1525). Fighting near Novara in the Italian Piedmont, the Swiss pikemen suffered heavy casualties but inflicted 50 percent casualties on La Tremoille. The defeat forced French king Louis XII to withdraw from Italy. **2.** Battle in which 100,000 raw troops of Sardinia-Piedmont were defeated (Mar. 23, 1849) by a numerically inferior but better trained army of Austrian regulars near Novara. The battle was fought during the Italian war of independence. Field Marshal J. Radetzky inflicted the crushing defeat that led to Charles Albert's abdication and saddled Piedmont-Sardinia with a 65-million-franc indemnity.

Nova Scotia One of the Maritime Provinces of eastern Canada (pop. 856,100). Originally inhabited by Algonquian Indians, the area may have been explored by J. Cabot (1497). The French founded the first settlement in 1605, but there was constant conflict with the English for control of the area known as Acadia *(q.v.)*. In 1755, England gained control and expelled the French Acadians; the incident was described in H. W. Longfellow's *Evangeline*. Many US Loyalists and Scottish immigrants settled there, and the colony of Nova Scotia entered the Canadian Confederation in 1867. The province is noted for fishing, forestry, mining, and tourism.

Novatian *fl.* AD 250. Early Christian heresiarch and antipope. A Roman priest, he denied that those Christians who had lapsed during the persecution of Decius (AD 250) could be readmitted to the church. When Pope Cornelius (251–53) de-

creed indulgence towards the lapsed, Novatian started his own rigorist sect that lasted until the 6th cent.

November Insurrection Unsuccessful Polish rebellion (1830–31) against Russian domination of the Congress Kingdom of Poland *(q.v.)*. It began (Nov. 29, 1830) after the French July Revolution and rebels seized control of Warsaw. Czar Nicholas was deposed as king of Poland (Jan. 25, 1831) and the numerically superior Russian army advanced into Poland (Feb.). The Russians attacked Warsaw (Sept.) after several battles and the Polish army withdrew to Prussia, where it surrendered (Oct. 5).

November Revolution *See* **October Revolution**

Novgorod Russian city (pop. 128,000). Novgorod, located in northwest Russia, is one of Russia's oldest cities. Its position on the trade route made it a major commercial and cultural center. The foundation of the Russian state dates from 862 when the inhabitants of Novgorod asked Rurik to rule them. At its height in the 14th cent., Novgorod boasted rich fairs, factories, and churches. It came under the control of Moscow in 1478. It was a member of the Hanseatic League *(q.v.)*. Its churches and museums suffered at Nazi hands in WW II.

Noyes, John Humphrey 1811–86. American religious reformer. In 1848, Noyes established the Oneida Community *(q.v.)*, which believed in the "perfectionism" of man through communion with Jesus, the practice of polygamy, and communal living.

Nubia Ancient region of northeastern Africa that was for many centuries ruled by Egypt. By the 8th century BC, Nubia had become independent and conquered Egypt. The Negro tribe Nobatae formed the next powerful kingdom of the area and converted to Christianity. After the Muslim takeover (14th cent.), the area became divided into small states.

Nuclear Nonproliferation Treaty *See* **Nonproliferation Treaty**

Nuclear Test-Ban Treaty Treaty signed in Moscow (Aug. 5, 1963) between the US, Britain, and the USSR, banning nuclear-weapons tests in the atmosphere, in outer space, and under water. It provided for no international enforcement machinery, nor, since France did not sign, did it include all nuclear powers.

nullification The states' rights doctrine in US history holding that a state had the authority to remedy federal abuses of power by nullifying federal laws within its borders. The Kentucky and Virginia Resolutions *(q.v.)* of 1798–99 had argued that the union was a voluntary compact and that the federal government had no authority not specifically delegated to it by the Constitution. The issue of a protective tariff, which hurt the South, brought the conflict to a head in the 1820s, and the theory of nullification was articulated (1824) by J. C. Calhoun. His home state, South Carolina, passed an Ordinance of Nullification (1832), declaring the federal tariff act invalid. A. Jackson obtained a force bill allowing him to use military force to collect the tariff in Charleston but, through the efforts of H. Clay, sought a compromise tariff. South Carolina then rescinded its nullification (1833). The issue was not raised again until 1861, when South Carolina seceded from the Union, precipitating the American Civil War *(q.v.).* The Union victory in the war ultimately settled the issue by establishing federal supremacy over the states.

Numa Pompilius *c*715–672 BC. Legendary second king of Rome. Numa is thought to have succeeded Romulus, to have established religious and civil laws, and to have been loved for his wisdom.

Numidia Ancient North African country, situated roughly in modern Algeria. Masinissa became ruler after allying himself with Rome in the Punic Wars *(q.v.)* and was the leader during Numidia's golden age. Under King Juba I, Numidia fell to Rome (46 BC) but enjoyed a long period of prosperity until the invasion of the Vandals in 428. It was later conquered by the Muslims.

Nunez Vela, Blasco *d.* 1546. First Spanish viceroy of Peru (1544–46), sent to enforce the "New Laws" of B. de Las Casas. He antagonized nearly everybody and a revolt against the "New Laws" led by G. Pizarro brought about an altercation in which the viceroy murdered a man. He was arrested, and executed when he tried to raise forces to quell the rebellion and avoid trial in Spain.

Nuremberg *See* **Nürnberg**

Nureyev, Rudolf 1938–. Russian ballet dancer. Nureyev defected from Russia in 1961 and became in the West a major international ballet star.

Nurhachi 1559–1626. Manchurian tribal chief and founder of China's Ch'ing (Manchu) dynasty (1644–1912). After uniting Manchuria, he began the conquest of the Chinese empire, which his son, Dorgon, completed.

Nürnberg, Religious Peace of *See* **Religious Peace of Nürnberg**

Nürnberg Laws Two racial laws passed by the German Nazi party on Sept. 15, 1935. German Jews were denied German citizenship and forbidden to marry or have sexual relations with non-Jews.

Nürnberg Standstill *See* **Religious Peace of Nürnberg**

Nürnberg Trials War-crimes trials held after WW II in Nuremberg, Germany, for the purpose of trying leaders of the Nazi party. Authorized by the Allies' London Agreement (Aug. 8, 1945), the trials were conducted by a special international tribunal. Twenty-four Nazi leaders were indicted, including H. Göring, W. Keitel, J. von Ribbentrop, A. Rosenberg, R. Hess, and H. Schacht. The tribunal held 403 public sessions (Nov. 20, 1945–Oct. 1, 1946), heard hundreds of witnesses, and utilized captured German documents to prove the charges of war crimes and crimes against peace and humanity (notably the slaughter of the Jews). Twelve defendants were sentenced to be hanged, while the others were either imprisoned or acquitted. Two defendants, including H. Göring, committed suicide. The trials were controversial, but the tribunal argued that all the violations were of international laws recognized prior to WW II and that Nazi crimes against the Jews required a unique response.

Nyasaland *See* **Malawi**

Nyerere, Julius 1922–. First president of the United Republic of Tanzania (from 1964). He founded the Tanganyika National Union political party (1954), became the first prime minister and then president when Tanganyika became independent (1961), and effected the union of Tanganyika and Zanzibar as Tanzania (1964).

nymph Greek mythical female divinities. These beautiful maidens were identified with nature; there were wood nymphs, tree nymphs, sea nymphs, and mountain nymphs.

Nyssa, Saint Gregory of *See* **Gregory of Nyssa, Saint**

Nystad, Treaty of Treaty concluded between Russia and Sweden in 1721 ending the Northern War *(q.v.).* Sweden retained Finland but ceded Livonia, Estonia, Ingria, and part of Karelia to Russia, and Russia obtained her "window" on the Baltic.

O

OAS *See* **Organization of American States**

Oates, Titus 1649–1705. English conspirator who caused a flurry of anti-Catholic hysteria and judicial murder of 35 Catholics with his fabricated story of the Popish Plot *(q.v.)* to kill Charles II so the Catholic James II could succeed. He was convicted of perjury in 1685 and imprisoned, but was freed and pensioned after the Glorious Revolution *(q.v.)* in 1688.

Oath, Charter of *See* **Charter of Oath**

Oath of Strasbourg Oath sworn (842) by Charles II (the Bald) and Louis II (the German) confirming their joint alliance against their brother, Emperor Lothair I. One of the versions in which this oath was recorded is considered to be the earliest written example of the French language.

Obed Old Testament figure. Obed was the son of Ruth and Boaz and the grandfather of King David.

Obote, Milton *See* **Amin, Idi**

Obregón, Álvaro 1880–1928. Mexican general and president (1920–24). Obregón supported V. Carranza against V. Huerta, F. Villa, and E. Zapata, but eventually deposed Carranza. As president, he advocated education and land reforms and improved relations with the US.

O'Brien, William Smith 1803–64. Irish revolutionary. The Protestant O'Brien first supported the cause of Irish independence in Parliament. When his Young Ireland group later failed in an 1848 insurrection, he was sentenced to death, but was banished instead.

O'Casey, Sean 1884–1964. Irish playwright. O'Casey is best known for his satiric tragicomedies written for the Abbey Theatre *(q.v.)*. They include *The Shadow of a Gunman*, *Juno and the Paycock*, and *The Plow and the Stars*.

Occam, William of *See* **Ockham, William of**

occultism Supernatural belief in unseen, extraordinary forces that cannot be explained by ordinary scientific means. Occult fields include astrology, alchemy, spiritualism, and theosophy.

Oceania ⟨Oceanica⟩ Pacific Islands. This is the collective name for the thousands of islands in the central and South Pacific Ocean. Ethnically they are divided into Australasia, Melanesia, Micronesia, and Polynesia.

Oceanica *See* **Oceania**

Ochs, Adolph S. 1858–1935. American publisher. Ochs fought yellow journalism *(q.v.)* in his newspapers the *New York Times*, which he converted into a world-famous newspaper dedicated to objective reporting, the Chattanooga *Times*, and the Philadelphia *Times Ledger*. He financed the *Dictonary of American Biography*.

Ockham, William of ⟨Occam, ∼⟩ c1285–c1349. English Franciscan philosopher. He opposed the Aristotelian realism of T. Aquinas, holding that universal ideas exist only in the thinking mind. He is remembered for his principle of economy in thought, called "Ockham's Razor." In philosophy he was a nominalist whose ideas contributed to the decline of scholasticism *(q.v.)* and eventually to the Protestant Reformation.

O'Connell, Daniel 1775–1847. Irish political leader. Nicknamed "The Liberator," O'Connell attempted to gain Irish freedom through political agitation. He founded the Catholic Association (1823) and was first Catholic lord mayor of Dublin (1841) since the reign of James II. His election to Parliament in 1828 provoked the passage of the Catholic Emancipation Act *(q.v.)* to enable him to take his seat without the usual oaths. He supported the Whigs in Parliament and tried to break up the union of Britain and Ireland. Losing support in later years, he died a broken man in Italy.

O'Connor, Frank ⟨O'Donovan, Michael⟩ 1903–66. Irish writer. O'Connor's short stories illuminate many aspects of Irish life. He directed for the Abbey Theatre and translated Gaelic literature into English.

O'Connor, Rory Roderick 1116?–98. Last high king of Ireland (1166–75). O'Connor was king of Connaught before he seized the high kingship (1166). He was forced to submit (1175) to Henry II of England in the Treaty of Windsor *(q.v.)*.

Octavia *d.* 11 BC. Roman matron. Octavia was the beautiful and virtuous sister of Augustus and wife (from 40 to 30 BC) of Marc Antony, and kept peace between them for a time. Antony deserted her for Cleopatra.

Octavia AD 42–62. Roman empress. Octavia was the daughter of Claudius and the wife of Nero, who divorced her. She was exiled and executed because of the jealousy of Nero's third wife, Poppaea.

Octavian *See* **Augustus**

Octavian *See* **John XII**

Octavianus, Gaius Julius Caesar *See* **Augustus**

Octavius, Gaius *See* **Augustus**

October Manifesto Manifesto issued on Oct. 30, 1905, by Russian czar Nicholas II. Issued in response to the Russian Revolution of 1905 *(q.v.)*, it guaranteed civil liberties and called for establishment of a duma, which would have the power to confirm all legislation. The manifesto would have turned the Russian government into a constitutional monarchy, but it was only partially enacted.

October Revolution ⟨November Revolution⟩ The *coup d'état* of Oct. 24–25, 1917 (new style, Nov. 6–7), by which the Bolsheviks *(q.v.)*, under the leadership of N. Lenin, took control of the Russian Revolution *(q.v.)*. The revolution began with the February Revolution *(q.v.)*, the abdication of Czar Nicholas II (March 15, 1917), and the formation of a provisional government dominated by Socialists (eventually headed by A. Kerensky). In April, however, Lenin and other Bolshevik leaders returned to Russia. They called for Russia's withdrawal from WW I and establishment of a program of land distribution, and managed to gain increasing support. On the night of Nov. 6–7 (old style, Oct. 24–25), supported by Red Guards and the sailors of Kronstadt, the Bolsheviks, led by L. Trotsky, seized all government buildings and the Winter Palace in Petrograd. The Council of People's Commissars was then set up, with Lenin as chairman, and the Communist regime in Russia began. (*See also* Union of Soviet Socialist Republics [1917]; Russian Revolution.)

Octobrists ⟨Union of October 17⟩ Russian conservative political party. It sought enactment of constitutional reforms based on the October Manifesto *(q.v.)* issued by Czar Nicholas II. Formed in 1906, the party was dissolved during the 1917 Russian Revolution.

Oda Nobunaga 1534–82. Japanese military leader, son of Daimyo. He was the first Japanese commander to arm his troops with muskets. With his allies Hideyoshi Toyotomi and Ieyasu, he unified most of Japan.

Oder-Neisse Line Polish-German frontier established by the USSR, Great Britain, and the US at the 1945 Potsdam Conference *(q.v.)*. Poland was compensated at Germany's expense for the Soviet acquisitions on her eastern border. These controversial borders were not recognized by West Germany until 1971.

Odescalchi, Benedetto *See* **Innocent XI**

Odets, Clifford 1906–63. American playwright. Odets reflected a strong social conscience in such plays as *Waiting for Lefty*, *Awake and Sing*, *Golden Boy*, and *The Country Girl*.

Odo *See* **Eudes**

Odoacer ⟨Odovacar⟩ AD *c*435–493. German chieftain and mercenary in Roman service who deposed the last Western Roman emperor, Romulus Augustus, in AD 476. A member of the Sciri or Rugian tribe, he was the virtual ruler of Italy until assassinated by an Ostrogothic king, Theodoric, acting for the Byzantines.

O'Donnell, Leopoldo 1809–67. Spanish general and statesman. O'Donnell supported Isabella II against the Carlists *(q.v.)*, overthrew B. Espartero, and served several times as premier.

O'Donovan, Michael *See* **O'Connor, Frank**

Odo of Lagery *See* **Urban II**

Odovacar *See* **Odoacer**

Odysseus ⟨Ulysses⟩ Greek mythical king and warrior. His adventures in the Trojan War were related in Homer's *Iliad*, and his long trip back to Ithaca recounted in Homer's *Odyssey*. He was noted for his wisdom and cunning and for being "never at a loss."

Odyssey *See* **Iliad** and **Odyssey**

Oecolampadius, Johannes 1482–1531. German theologian and reformer. He helped D. Erasmus edit the Greek New Testament, but came under M. Luther's influence (1522). He carried the Reformation to Basel, later siding with U. Zwingli. He drafted the First Confession of Basel (1531).

Oedipus Greek mythical king. Oedipus was abandoned in infancy when an oracle predicted that he would kill his father, Laius, king of Thebes, and marry his mother, Jocasta. He survived and unwittingly returned to fulfill the prophecy by killing Laius, encountered as a stranger at a crossroads, and going on to Thebes, where he married Laius' widow, Jocasta. He blinded himself when he discovered his crimes.

Oenone Greek mythical nymph. Oenone, wife of Paris, was a skilled healer. When Paris deserted her for Helen, and was mortally wounded at Troy, Oenone refused him aid. She committed suicide after his death.

Offa d. 796. King of Mercia (757–796). Offa made his kingdom the most powerful in Anglo-Saxon England. He introduced the coinage system used in England for centuries thereafter, and negotiated (with Charlemagne) the first commercial treaty in English history.

Offenbach, Jacques 1819–80. German-born French composer. Offenbach created a popular, elegant style of French operetta, but is today best remembered for his full-scale opera *Tales of Hoffmann*.

Og Biblical king of Bashan. Og was an Amorite of huge size. He was defeated by the Israelites on their entrance into Canaan.

Ogadai 1185–1241. Mongol ruler (1229–41), successor to his father, Genghis Khan. He conquered northern China (1234) and sent armies, under Batu Khan, westward into Russia, where they sacked Kiev (1240) and thereby ended Russian resistance. The armies then overran Poland and Hungary, and only Ogadai's death prevented their advance into Western Europe. Ogadai built the Mongol capital city of Karakorum.

Oglesby, Richard J. *See* **Grand Army of the Republic**

Oglethorpe, James Edward 1696–1785. English philanthropist. Oglethorpe was involved with penal reform and the treatment of debtors. He founded the American colony of Georgia (1733) as an asylum for debtors.

OGPU *See* **GPU**

O'Higgins, Bernardo 1778–1842. Chilean soldier and statesman. He became leader of the revolutionary forces in Chile (1813) and helped defeat the Spaniards at Chacabuco *(q.v.)* in 1817. He was named supreme dictator and proclaimed Chilean independence on Feb. 12, 1818. He was the first president of Chile, until 1823, when he was deposed for his reforms. He died in exile in Peru.

Ohio State (pop. 10,797,500) in the north central US, the 17th state. Prehistoric Mound Builders inhabited Ohio, and the Erie and Iroquois Indians were later major tribes there. La Salle claimed the region for France, but the British gained control in the French and Indian War (1754). It was ceded to the US after the American Revolution in the Treaty of Paris (1783). Ohio became part of the Northwest Territory in 1787, and Marietta was its first settlement (1788). It became a state in 1803, and adopted its present constitution in 1851.

Ohio Company Organization of Virginia and Maryland colonists interested in western settlement. A British royal charter in 1749 granted it 200,000 acres around the forks of the Ohio River. Activities of the company helped provoke the French and Indian War *(q.v.)*, since it encroached on territory then claimed by France. The company was the first organized American Colonial effort to settle territory west of the Alleghenies.

Ohio Company of Associates American Colonial settlers. New Englanders formed this settlement group in Boston (1786). The next year they purchased and colonized the land that became the city of Marietta, Ohio, under the Northwest Ordinance of 1787.

Ohm, Georg Simon 1787–1854. German physicist. His research into electrical current resistance resulted in the formation of Ohm's law, the basic law of current flow. The unit measure of electric resistance, the ohm, was named in his honor.

Ojibwa Indians North American Indian tribe. Also called the Chippewa, the Ojibwa were a major branch of the Algonquin Indians, and lived in the Great Lakes region. They supported the French in their many colonial wars against the English, but sided with Britain against America in the American Revolution and the War of 1812. They were known for their pictograph form of writing.

Okinawa Japanese island. Okinawa was the scene of a bloody WW II battle between America and Japan (Apr. 1–June 21, 1945). America won despite casualties of some 48,000, one-third of them fatal. The Japanese lost some 110,000 of their 120,000-man garrison before surrendering on June 21, 1945. Okinawa remained under US military control until May, 1972, when it was returned to Japan.

Oklahoma US state (pop. 3,025,300) in the Southwest, the 46th state. Originally inhabited by various tribes of Plains Indians, the area was explored by the Spanish and French, beginning in the 16th cent. It became part of the US with the Louisiana Purchase of 1803 and, as the Indian Territory *(q.v.),* was made the home of displaced Indians. Agitation by land-hungry settlers opened the territory for settlement in 1889. The Indian Territory and the western section known as the Oklahoma Territory merged to form the state of Oklahoma in 1907, and the state constitution was adopted in that year.

Oklahoma City US city (pop. 403,200). Located in the central part of Oklahoma, it was settled during the 1889 land rush. It became the state capital in 1910.

Okubo, Toshimichi 1832?–78. Japanese statesman. Okubo, a member of the Satsuma clan, played a major role in restoring the emperor (1868) (Meiji Restoration) and westernizing Japan. He opposed his kinsmen's 1877 Satsuma rebellion and was assassinated by them the next year.

Okuma, Shigenobu, Marquis 1838–1922. Japanese statesman. Okuma opposed the feudal aristocracy of H. Ito, supported constitutional reforms, served as prime minister (1898, 1914–16), and founded Waseda University (1892).

Olaf I c963–1000. King of Norway (995–1000). He tried to convert Norway to Christianity, and commissioned Leif Ericson to carry Christianity to Greenland. He was killed in battle against the Danes and the Swedes, who then divided his lands.

Olaf II c995–1030. King of Norway (1015–28). Olaf attempted to unite Norway religiously and politically but provoked internal dissension instead. He was deposed and killed at the Battle of Stiklestad. He is the patron saint of Norway, and completed the Christianization of the country begun by Olaf I.

Olaf V 1903–. King of Norway (1957–). Olaf served as commander in chief of the Norwegian armed forces against the Nazi occupation of Norway in WW II. He returned to Norway in 1945.

Old Believers Russian religious dissenters within the Russian Orthodox church who opposed the liturgical reforms made by Nikon, patriarch of Moscow (1652–58). Persecuted through the 17th and 18th cents., they split into several sects, some of which still exist and are now officially recognized.

Oldcastle, Sir John d. 1417. English soldier and leader of Lollardry (q.v.) He performed valuable military service for Henry IV in Wales. His devotion to the teachings of J. Wycliffe led to his condemnation for heresy. Shakespeare's character Sir John Falstaff may have been modeled on him.

Old Catholics Schismatic Catholic sect that was formed in Germany in protest against the dogmatic definition of the pope's infallibility issued in 1870 by the First Vatican Council (q.v.). The group acquired a bishop consecrated by a Dutch Jansenist bishop in Holland. Mass was said in the vernacular and priests were allowed to marry. The Old Catholics established intercommunion with the Church of England in 1931.

Old Delhi See **Delhi**

Oldenbarneveldt, Jan van 1547–1619. Dutch statesman. Oldenbarneveldt aided William the Silent in driving Spain from The Netherlands and helped negotiate the Treaty of Utrecht (q.v.) He was executed by religious opponents.

Old English Language of the early period (5th–11th cents.) in the development of modern English. It was essentially the language of the 5th-cent. Teutonic invaders of England (Celtic influence was minimal) and had four dialects: Northumbrian, Mercian, Kentish, and West Saxon. The literature of the Old English period is predominantly West Saxon and dates primarily from the reign of Alfred the Great. The best-

known work from this period is the epic poem *Beowulf*.

Old Ironsides ⟨Constitution⟩ Famous US warship, a 44-gun frigate. Built (1798) for service against French privateers, it saw action during the Tripolitan War and during the War of 1812. In the latter war, the ship was victorious in battle against the British ships *Guerrière* (Aug. 19, 1812) and *Cyane* and *Levant* (Feb. 20, 1815). The ship was rebuilt in 1833, 1877, and 1925 and was the subject of O. W. Holmes' poem *Old Ironsides*.

Old Kingdom ⟨Pyramid Age⟩ One of the three great divisions of ancient Egyptian history (with the Middle and New kingdoms), the period during which the great pyramids were built. Generally this period may be taken to include dynasties 3d–6th, though sources vary (1st–6th and 3d–8th are also given). Dates vary as well, though c2700–c2200 BC is a good guideline. The Egyptian capital was at Memphis. Among the notable rulers of this period are Zoser, Snefru, Khufu, Menkaure, and Pepi.

Old Northwest See **Northwest Territory**

Old Testament Christian term for the older, Hebrew portion of the Bible. It begins with an account of the creation of the world, recounts the calls by God to such figures as Abraham, Isaac, Jacob, Moses, and David, and through them treats the covenant established by God with the Jewish people. It also promises the coming of the Messiah. The Jews adopted the present canon of approved books (considered inspired) around AD 100. They divided them into: **1.** The Law, consisting of the Pentateuch, or first five books: Genesis, Exodus, Leviticus, Numbers, and Deuteronomy. **2.** The Prophets, another group of books: Joshua, Judges, I and II Samuel, I and II Kings, Isaiah, Jeremiah, Ezekiel, and the Twelve (Minor) Prophets. **3.** The Writings (Hagiographa), consisting of heterogeneous books: Psalms, Proverbs, Job, Song of Solomon, Ruth, Lamentations, Ecclesiastes, Esther, Daniel, Ezra, Nehemiah, and I and II Chronicles. This Jewish version was based on the Masora (q.v.). The Christians used a different canon, based on a 3rd-cent. BC Greek translation called the Septuagint (q.v.). They considered the following additional books (regarded by the Jews only as pious writings) to be inspired Scripture: Tobias, Judith, Wisdom, Ecclesiasticus, Baruch, and I and II Maccabees. The Christian canon was approved in the 4th cent. AD and stabilized in the Latin Vulgate (q.v.). At the Reformation, the books not included in the Jewish canon were set aside by the Protestants as uninspired Apocrypha (q.v.). The so-called higher criticism of the 19th cent. tended to impugn both the authorship and historicity of the books of the Old Testament. Later research, including archaeological evidence, goes further toward confirming religious traditions, but there is no general agreement concerning Old Testament authorship and chronology. A series of editors and sacred authors from the 10th cent. BC no doubt composed the books from written and oral traditions. However, in both Christian and Jewish religious traditions, the belief is that God protected them from error in communicating these texts.

Oleg *d.* 912. Early Russian ruler. He was a Viking (Varangian) leader and the reputed founder of Kievan Russia. Oleg expanded his realm of Novgorod, inherited from Rurik, to include Kiev, which then became the capital of a Kievan-Novgorodian state (882). His treaties with the Byzantine Empire (907, 911) opened Russia to Greek Christian and cultural penetration.

Oliva, Peace of Treaty between Poland and Sweden (May 3, 1660) ending the First Northern War. King John II of Poland renounced his claim to the Swedish throne and ceded Livonia. West Prussia was confirmed as Polish, but the sovereignty of the elector of Brandenburg over it was recognized.

Olivares, Gaspar de Guzman, conde de 1587–1645. Spanish statesman. He was prime minister to Philip II (1621–43), but his policies of constant warfare and heavy taxation led to revolts by Catalonia and Portugal, and he was removed.

Olivier, Lord Laurence 1907–. English actor. Olivier is considered one of the world's great actors of stage and screen. Among his many notable films are *Hamlet* and *Richard III*.

Ollivier, Émile 1825–1913. French statesman. Napoleon III called upon him to help create the "Liberal Empire," which instituted many reforms. However, Ollivier's decision to lead France into the Franco-Prussian War (1870) forced his dismissal.

Olmütz, Punctation of *See* **Erfurt Parliament; Revolutions of 1848**

Olney, Richard 1835–1917. American statesman. As attorney general (1893–95), he broke the Pullman strike *(q.v.)*, and, as secretary of state (1895–97), he declared that America had the right to arbitrate the Venezuala Boundary Dispute *(q.v.)*.

Olympia Ancient Greek plain. Olympia was a religious center and site of festivals and athletic contests honoring Zeus. It was the site of the Olympic games *(q.v.)*, and its statue of Zeus by Phidias was one of the ancient Seven Wonders of the World *(q.v.)*.

Olympiad Greek time measurement. An Olympiad was the four-year period between Olympic games, each Olympiad being marked from the beginning of the games. The first Olympiad was reckoned to have begun in 776 BC.

Olympian In Greek mythology, one of twelve gods who dwelt on Mount Olympus. These included Zeus and his wife, Hera; Zeus' brothers, Poseidon and Pluto; his sister, Hestia; and the children of Zeus—Ares, Hermes, Apollo, Hephaestus, Athena, Aphrodite, and Artemis.

Olympias *d.* 316 BC. Macedonian queen. She was the wife of Philip of Macedon, and the mother of Alexander the Great, over whom she had great influence. She executed Alexander's successor, Antipater, and was in turn executed by Antipater's son, Cassander.

Olympic games Religious athletic games. These ancient Greek games were held (776 BC–AD 393) at Olympia once every four years and were called an Olympiad *(q.v.)* to honor Zeus. They were revived in 1896, and are now held in a different world city every four years.

Olynthus Ancient Greek city. Olynthus was a coastal city and frequent target of Athens and Sparta. It was destroyed by Philip II of Macedon in 347 BC.

Omaha Beach 〈Bloody Omaha〉 WW II beachhead. One of the five landing points used during the Allied invasion of France on D-Day (June 6, 1944). The American forces landing at this point suffered the fiercest resistance.

Oman Oil-rich Middle Eastern sultanate (pop. 890,000) on the southeastern Arabian Peninsula, on the Arabian Sea. It was ruled by the Portuguese (1508–1648) and by the Turks (1659–1741) before being taken by the founder of the present ruling family from Yemen, Ahmad ibn Said. Oman developed strong ties with Great Britain (18th cent.) and was the most powerful Arab state in the early 19th cent. Sultan Qabus bin Said deposed his father in 1970, promising to use oil revenues for modernization.

Omar 〈Umar〉 581–644. Second Muslim caliph. A father-in-law of the prophet Muhammad, he at first opposed Islam, but was converted by 618. He chose Abu Bakr as the first caliph to succeed to the authority of the prophet (632), and succeeded him (634). During his caliphate, Arab armies advanced into Syria, Egypt, and Persia. He established the administration and taxation of the subsequent empire.

Omar Khayyám *fl.* 11th cent. Persian poet, astronomer, and mathematician. Khayyám reformed the Muslim calendar and wrote an algebra textbook. However, he is best known for his epigrammatic poems *The Rubáiyát*, especially as translated into English (1859) by Edward Fitz-Gerald (1809–83).

Omdurman, Battle of British defeat and capture of the Mahdist capital at Omdurman, in the central Sudan (Sept. 2, 1898). An Anglo-Egyptian force of about 26,000, led by Sir (later Lord) H. Kitchener, defeated a poorly armed Mahdist force of 40,000 and destroyed the state established by the Mahdi *(q.v.)* in 1881. It began British dominance in the Sudan.

Omphale Greek mythical queen. Omphale was queen of Lydia. The Delphic Oracle forced Hercules to serve her for three years to atone for his murder of the sons of Neleus, king of Pylos. She dressed him in women's clothes and made him spin wool with her maids.

Omri *d. c874* BC. King of Israel (887–875 BC). Omri moved the capital of Israel to Samaria and had close ties to the Syrians. He married his son Ahab to Jezebel, a Phoenician.

On *See* **Heliopolis**

Oñate, Juan de *d.*1624? Spanish explorer. Oñate took possession of much of the American Southwest for Spain, and was first governor of what is now New Mexico.

Oneida Community Religious commune in America in 19th cent. It was established by J. H. Noyes, a Perfectionist, in New York State (1847). It practiced communal living, and permitted polygamy. In 1881, it was reorganized as a joint stock company and its social experiments were abandoned.

O'Neill, Eugene Gladstone 1888–1953. American playwright. O'Neill won the Nobel Prize in Literature (1936). *Beyond the Horizon* won the first of his three Pulitzer Prizes. Other works include *Anna Christie, Long Day's Journey into Night,* and *The Iceman Cometh.*

O'Neill, Shane *c*1530–67. Irish chieftain. O'Neill fought for the chieftainship against his British-backed illegitimate half brother, Matthew. Though Shane won acknowledgment from Elizabeth I, he turned against England, was defeated, and was slain by a rival clan.

Ontario East-central Canadian province (pop. 8,600,500). The area was first explored by the French (early 17th cent.), although settlement (by Britain and France) was delayed because of wars with the Iroquois Indians. British claims to the region were upheld by the Treaty of Paris (1763), and Ontario was joined to the province of Quebec (1774). Loyalists from the US settled there during the American Revolution, and battles were fought there during the War of 1812. Ontario and Quebec entered the Dominion of Canada as separate provinces in 1867.

Op art ⟨optical art⟩ Artistic style of the 20th cent. characterized by repetition of form and specific color combinations to create the illusion of movement.

OPEC *See* **Organization of Petroleum Exporting Countries**

Open Door International diplomatic term applied to the policy of a country that trades with all other nations on an equal basis. The term was first used in the 1890s by the US, which sought to trade with China at a time when such nations as Britain, Russia, France, Japan, Italy, and Germany all demanded special trade concessions from the Chinese. The policy was advanced (1899–1900) to the major nations by US secretary of state J. Hay. Hay declared it to be in effect in 1900.

Operation Dragoon *See* **Anvil, Operation**

Operation Overlord *See* **Normandy invasion**

Operation Sea Lion *See* **Britain, Battle of**

Opium War Name given two 19th-cent. wars between China and European powers. **1.** The first war (1839–42) began when China attempted to enforce its ban on the importation of opium and seized British-owned opium in Canton. Britain soon defeated China and forced it to cede Hong Kong to Britain, open several ports to British trade, and pay an indemnity. **2.** The second war (1856–60) began after Chinese boarded the British ship *Arrow.* France joined Britain in a new war against China. Soon defeated, China agreed to the Treaty of Tientsin (1858), which opened a number of new ports to European trade and secured rights of interior travel in China, rights for Christian missionaries, residence in Peking for foreign diplomats, and legalization of the opium trade. China's opposition to the agreements led to new conflict and the occupation (1860) of Peking and burning of the imperial summer palace. The conflict ended with the Conventions of Peking (1860), which granted still further concessions.

Oporto ⟨Porto⟩ Portugal's second largest city (pop. 335,700). Dating to Roman times, it was captured by the Moors (716) and recaptured by the Christians (997). It has long been a center of republican and revolutionary thought.

Oppenheimer, J. Robert 1904–67. American physicist. He was a leading figure in the Manhattan Project *(q.v.)* and made important contributions to the construction of the first atomic bomb, but after WW II he became a leading advocate of civilian and international control of atomic energy.

oprichniki *See* **Ivan IV**

Ops Ancient Roman goddess of the harvest, plenty, and fertility. The wife of Saturn, she is identified with the Greek goddess Rhea.

optical art *See* **Op art**

Optimates *See* **Cato the Younger**

oracle Ancient Greek religious prophet. Oracles were priests and priestesses who gave the gods' answers to questions posed by humans. The most famous oracle was dedicated to Apollo at Delphi.

Orange Free State South African province. First settled (1820s) by the Boers, it was annexed by Britain (1848). It became independent (1854), but continued conflict in the region led to the Boer War (1899–1902) and its reannexation. It became part of the Union of South Africa in 1910.

Orangemen Irish Protestant political group. It was founded in 1795, and its members sought to maintain Protestant dominance over the Catholics in Ireland.

Oranges, War of the Brief war (1801) in which France and Spain invaded and defeated Portugal. After Portugal's surrender, the country was divided between France and Spain.

Orcus Ancient Roman god. He ruled the underworld and the dead, and is identified with the Greek god Hades.

Order of Preachers *See* **Dominicans**

Order of Saint Benedict *See* **Benedictines**

Order of the Garter Order of knighthood in England founded by King Edward III and formally established in 1350. The order was originally limited to 26, including the king, but its membership was enlarged by later kings. According to tradition, its motto, *Honi soit qui mal y pense* (roughly, Shame on him who thinks evil of it) is a remark attributed to Edward III. While dancing with a countess, he picked up a garter she had dropped, and, returning it to her, made the comment to bystanders.

Order of the Golden Fleece Order of knighthood founded (1430) by Philip the Good, duke of Burgundy. Through intermarriage with the Hapsburg family, the order passed to Spain and Austria. It takes its symbol from Jason and the Argonauts.

Order of the Hospital of St. John of Jerusalem *See* **Knights Hospitalers**

Ordinance of 1787 *See* **Northwest Ordinances**

ordonnance cabochienne *See* **Cabochiens**

Oregon US state (pop. 2,632,700) in the Northwest, the 33d state. It was first explored (16th cent.) by Spanish, British, and Russians, who set up fur-trading posts along its coast. Robert Gray (1755–1806) claimed the area along the Columbia River for the US (1792), and the Lewis and Clark expedition explored farther inland in 1805. As part of the Oregon country, it was held jointly by England and the US from 1818 until England gave up its claims (1846). Oregon's constitution was adopted in 1857, and it was admitted to the Union in 1859.

Oregon Question Dispute between Britain and the United States over the US-Canadian northwest border. The Convention of 1818 had provided for joint occupation west of the Rockies between 42° and 54° 40′. A treaty (June, 1846) established the border along the 49th parallel.

Oregon Trail American pioneer route stretching from Independence, Missouri to the Columbia River in Oregon. It was one of the main paths of pioneer travel to the West from the 1840s to the 1870s and extended for some 2,000 miles through the wilderness.

Orestes Greek mythical figure. He was the son of Clytemnestra and Agamemnon, and the brother of Iphiginea and Electra. He slew his mother and her lover, Aegisthus, to avenge their murder of his father.

Orestes *d.* AD 476. Roman general. He used barbarian help in deposing (AD 475) Western Roman emperor Julius Nepos and installing his own son Romulus Augustulus the last emperor of the Western Roman Empire.

Organization of African Unity Organization of independent African states, established (1963) to promote African unity and mutual cooperaiton in defense and development.

Organization of American States ⟨OAS⟩ International organization, founded (1948) to promote military, economic, and cultural cooperation. Its member nations include the United States and most of the nations of Latin America. Cuba was expelled from the OAS in 1962.

Organization of Central American States Central American association, organized (1951) to promote regional and economic unity. Its member states include Costa Rica, El Salvador, Guatemala, Honduras, and Nicaragua.

Organization of Petroleum Exporting Countries ⟨OPEC⟩ International group formed (1960) to promote the interests of countries that supply the world market with oil. When the group was founded, member nations were largely at the mercy of the great international oil companies, which controlled all-important (in times of plentiful supply) systems of distribution and marketing. But as oil consumption began to outstrip production in the late 1960s, producing countries began to get the upper hand. By cutting back their production, OPEC members found they could effectively force the great industrial powers to pay any price for oil they demanded. The huge price increases it put into effect (Dec., 1973) signaled the ascendancy of OPEC as a dominant force in the world oil industry. Membership now includes oil-producing countries in the Middle East, Africa, and South America. An oversupply of oil developed in the early 1980s, forced OPEC members to agree to reduced prices and production quotas.

Orgetorix *d.* 60? BC. Helvetian chieftain at the time of J. Caesar's Gallic Wars *(q.v.).*

Oriental canon law Ecclesiastical laws concerning the government of Eastern Christian churches. Rudimentary collections of such laws can be traced back to the 5th cent. AD, and a major compilation, important to the canon law of the Eastern Orthodox church, was completed by Photius *c*880. The various churches in the East do not share a common code of canon law.

Origen AD 185?–254? Christian philosopher. Origen wrote over 800 works seeking to explain and justify Christianity in terms of Greek thought, especially Neoplatonism and Stoicism. He instituted biblical textual criticism at his famous school in Alexandria.

Orion Greek mythical figure. A giant hunter, he was the subject of several legends. At his death he was transformed into the constellation Orion.

Oriskany, Battle of Battle (Aug. 6, 1777) of the American Revolution, in northern New York State. American militiamen under Gen. Nicholas Herkimer (1728–77) were ambushed and defeated by British troops led by Barry St. Leger (1737–89) as the Americans were attempting to relieve Fort Stanwix (now Rome, New York).

Orlando, Vittorio Emmanuele 1860–1952. Italian statesman. As premier (1917–19), he was one of the "Big Four" at the Versailles Peace Conference (1919), which formally ended WW I.

Orléanists French supporters of King Louis Philippe of the Orléans branch of the Bourbon line. Louis Philippe came to the throne after the July Revolution (1830). The Orléanists supported his monarchy against both republican and Bonapartist forces.

Orléans The cadet (younger) branch of the French Valois and Bourbon royal houses. The line has played a leading role in French history. The title "duke of Orléans" was first given (1344) to Philippe (1336–75), son of Valois French king Philip VI. In 1392, King Charles VI gave the title to his brother Louis, a key figure in the struggles between the Armagnacs and Burgundians *(q.v.).* Other members included Charles of ~, a cocommander at the Battle of Agincourt *(q.v.)* and father of French king Louis XII; Philippe I of ~, son of King Louis XIII and brother of King Louis XIV; his son, Philippe II of ~, regent of France during the minority of King Louis XV; Louis Philippe Joseph of ~, who sided with the revolutionists during the French Revolution; and his son, French king Louis

Philippe. Louis Philippe Albert of ~ (1838–94) became count of Paris; and his son, Louis Philippe Robert of ~, became pretender to the French throne upon extinction (1883) of the elder Bourbon line.

Orléans, Charles, duke of 1391–1465. French prince and poet, son of Louis, duke of Orléans. He tried to avenge the murder of his father by joining the Armagnacs against the Burgundians. He was captured in the Battle of Agincourt (1415) and taken to England. Ransomed in 1440, he spent the rest of his life as a literary personage.

Orléans, Gaston, duke of 1608–60. French prince, son of French king Henry IV and younger brother of Louis XIII. He was involved in several unsuccessful conspiracies against Cardinal Richelieu, and was exiled (1652) from Paris for leading the Fronde.

Orléans, Louis, duke of 1372–1407. French nobleman, chief counselor to his brother, French king Charles VI. Louis' conflict with his uncle, Philip the Bold of Burgundy, precipitated the long power struggle between the Armagnacs and the Burgundians. He was killed by Philip's son John the Fearless.

Orléans, Louis Philippe Albert, duke of *See* **Orléans**

Orléans, Louis Philippe Joseph, duke of 1747–93. French revolutionary. In 1789, he and other liberal nobles joined the third estate. He changed his title to "Citizen Égalité," and voted for the execution of his cousin Louis XVI. His son became King Louis Philippe.

Orléans, Louis Philippe Robert, duke of 1869–1926. French nobleman, pretender to the French throne during the Third Republic.

Orléans, Philippe I, duke of 1640–1701. French nobleman and soldier. The brother of King Louis XIV, he fought in the Dutch Wars and won the Battle of Cassel. He founded the house of Bourbon-Orléans.

Orléans, Philippe II, duke of 1674–1723. French nobleman and soldier. He was successful in the War of the Grand Alliance and the War of the Spanish Succession. As regent for King Louis XV (1715–23), he presided over the failure (1720) of the Mississippi Scheme *(q.v.).*

Orléans, Siege of Historic siege of Orléans, France, (Oct., 1428–May, 1429) by the English during the Hundred Years' War. The English, supporting the claims of English king Henry VI to the French throne, laid siege to Orléans, controlled by the supporters of the French dauphin Charles VII. The English brought the city to near surrender when Joan of Arc, who had gained the permission of Charles to raise an army, entered the city and lifted the siege. The English defeat marked the turning point in the Hundred Years' War.

Orleans, Territory of *See* **Territory of Orleans**

Orlov, Grigory *See* **Catherine II**

Ormonde, James Butler, 2d duke of 1665–1745. Anglo-Irish soldier. A grandson of the first duke, he served as lord lieutenant of Ireland and as commander in chief (1711–14) during the War of the Spanish Succession. Impeached (1715) under George I, he fled to the Continent and joined the Jacobites.

Ormonde, James Butler, 12th earl and 1st duke of 1610–88. Anglo-Irish statesman. He was the principal Irish supporter of the Stuarts during the English Civil War and was twice lord lieutenant of Ireland after the Restoration.

Orozco, José Clemente 1883–1949. Mexican painter, considered one of the 20th-cent. masters of the mural and fresco. Many of his works depict scenes from the Mexican Revolution.

Orpheus Mythical Greek musician. He was permitted to lead his dead wife, Eurydice, from Hades, providing he did not look back at her during their return trip. He looked back, and she vanished forever.

Orphic Mysteries Ancient Greek cult. Dating to the 6th cent. BC, it was said to have been founded by Orpheus. Its adherents followed an ascetic code of life.

Orsini Roman family that from the 12th cent. held great political and religious power in Rome and Italy. Its members included popes Celestine III, Nicholas III, and Benedict XIII. It supported the Guelph faction in the long struggle between the Guelphs and Ghibellines (*q.v.*).

Orsini, Giovanni Gaetani *See* **Nicholas III**

Ortega y Gasset, José 1883–1955. Spanish philosopher and writer. His books made him the most influential author of pre-Franco Spain. One of his best-known works is *Revolt of the Masses.*

Orthodox church of Russia Largest of the Orthodox Eastern churches. The origins of the Russian church go back to the introduction of Christianity in Russia by Byzantine missionaries. Christianity was made the state religion of Kiev in 988 and the church was governed from Constantinople. In 1439 the Union of Florence briefly reunited Russian Christians with the Roman Catholic church; soon after failure of the union, the Russian church declared itself autocephalous (autonomous and independent). The patriarchate of Moscow was given formal status in 1589, but in 1712 Czar Peter the Great abolished the patriarchate and put the church under strict state control. The patriarchate was reestablished just before the Russian Revolution of 1917 but, during both Lenin's and Stalin's regimes, the church suffered severe persecutions. In 1943, as part of Stalin's new policies during WW II, the church was revived and encouraged to expand. The church endured yet another period of persecutions (1959–64) under N. Khrushchev. In the 1960s, the church opened relations with the Roman Catholic church (following the Second Vatican Council) and joined the World Council of Churches.

Orthodox Eastern church Collective name for the family of Christian churches that exist largely in the Middle East, Eastern Europe, and Russia. All the Orthodox churches accept the authority of the first seven ecumenical councils of the Catholic church but do not accept later councils. They also do not recognize the authority of the Roman Catholic pope as supreme head of the church nor the practice of mandatory celibacy for priests. The origins of the Orthodox church can be traced to the late Roman Empire. As the empire weakened and was divided into the Western Empire and the Eastern Empire, so too did the early Christian church suffer a growing division.

The Western church developed along Latin lines and adapted Roman political and civil patterns, while the Eastern church retained a traditional Greek heritage. The separation between the two parts of the Christian world occurred slowly from the 5th to 11th cents. and became a complete schism in 1054, when Pope Leo IX excommunicated Michael Cerularius, patriarch of Constantinople, and all his followers. The primary disagreement between the Eastern and Western churches was the incorporation of the term *filioque*, meaning "and from the son," into the Nicene Creed. The introduction of the filioque occurred in the Western church after centuries of controversy over the nature of the Holy Trinity, the supremacy of the Father, and the nature of the Son as a being with a divine and human nature. The Eastern churches also refused to accept the spiritual supremacy of the pope, as they do not recognize one person as the leading spiritual figure.

Eastern churches are largely autonomous, and the major divisions of the church are known as patriarchates. Chief among these are the patriarchates of Constantinople, Alexandria, Antioch, and Jerusalem, all formed in the early history of the Christian church. From these, through missionary work and emigration, sprang numerous other Orthodox churches in Eastern Europe. The greatest of these was the Orthodox church of Russia (*q.v.*), which was originally governed through the patriarchate of Constantinople. It became an independent patriarchate in 1589. In recent years there have been renewed efforts at reconciling the Roman and Orthodox churches, and several Orthodox representatives were invited as observers to the Second Vatican Council *(q.v.). (See also* Roman Catholic church *for history to 1054.)*

Orwell, George ⟨Blair, Eric Arthur⟩ 1903–50. British novelist, essayist, and critic, one of the leading political writers of his day. He is known best for his novels *Animal Farm* and *1984.*

Osborne, John James 1929–. English playwright, considered the leading "angry young man" of British drama. His plays include *Look Back in Anger* and *The Entertainer.*

Osborne, Thomas, 1st earl of Danby 1631–1712. English statesman. He served under King Charles I, but his staunch Anglicanism led him to oppose James II. He arranged the marriage of Princess Mary to William of Orange.

Oscar I 1799–1859. King of Norway and Sweden (1844–59). Oscar pursued liberal policies. He championed fiscal and penal reforms and freedom of the press.

Oscar II 1829–1907. King of Sweden (1872–1907) and Norway (1872–1905). During his reign, Norway severed its union with Sweden (1905). Oscar was a noted writer and a patron of the arts.

Osceola c1800–38. Seminole Indian leader. He conducted a successful guerrilla campaign against US forces in the Second Seminole War (1835–37). Arriving for a truce talk, he was arrested and imprisoned. He died soon after.

Osei Tutu d. 1712. West African leader, founder and first ruler of the Ashanti nation. The nation was created from a confederacy of West African kingdoms in what is now Ghana.

Osiris Ancient Egyptian god. Osiris brought agriculture and civilization to earth. Killed by his envious brother Set, he then became god of the underworld.

Osler, Sir William 1849–1919. Canadian-born British physician, noted for his studies of blood platelets and his numerous books on medical history. His *Principles and Practice of Medicine* has long been a leading reference work.

Oslo Capital and leading city (pop. 461,400) of Norway. Founded (c1050) by King Harold III, it was destroyed by fire (1624), then rebuilt as Christiania, and renamed Oslo in 1924. It was occupied by the Germans (1940–45) during WW II. Oslo was the site of the 1952 Olympic games.

Osman I ⟨Othman I⟩ 1259–1326. Turkish leader, founder of the Ottoman Empire. Declaring himself emir (c1299), Osman greatly extended his holdings, largely through conquest of territory from the Byzantine Empire.

Osmeña, Sergio 1878–1961. Filipino statesman. Osmeña was vice-president (1935–44) when the Philippines fell to Japan in WW II. He fled with President M. Quezon, whom he succeeded as president (1944–46).

Ostend Manifesto Document formulated (Oct., 1854) at Ostend, Belgium, calling for US acquisition of Cuba. Drawn up by the US ministers to France (John Y. Mason, 1799–1859), Great Britain (J. Buchanan), and Spain (P. Soule), it suggested that Cuba should be taken by force if necessary. It caused such an uproar that Secretary of State W. Marcy disavowed it.

ostracism Greek political banishment imposed by Athenians on those disrupting local stability. The banishment lasted ten years.

Ostrogoths ⟨East Goths⟩ Germanic tribe. The Ostrogoths were the eastern tribes of the Goths, the Visigoths being their western counterparts. They were believed to have originated in southern Russia. After being conquered by the Huns (AD c370), they joined with them against the Visigoths and pushed westward into the Roman Empire. After Attila's death (AD 453), many Ostrogoths settled in Hungary. Others continued into Italy, where their leader, Theodoric, defeated Odoacer and became king (493). They were finally subjugated by the Byzantine general Narses (552) and were absorbed into other cultures.

Oswald, Lee Harvey *See* **Kennedy, John F.**

Oswiu *See* **Oswy**

Oswy ⟨Oswiu⟩ d. 670. Northumbrian king (c642–670). By war or marriage, he united most of England under him. He advanced Christianity in England and, at the Synod of Whitby *(q.v.),* favored Roman religious practices over the Celtic.

Othman I *See* **Osman I**

Otho I *See* **Otto I**

Otho, Marcus Salvius AD 32–69. Roman emperor (AD 69). Otho helped Galba overthrow Nero. Subsequently he overthrew Galba and proclaimed himself emperor. After ruling for three months, he was in turn defeated by Vitellius.

Otis, James 1725–83. American Colonial statesman. Otis resigned his office of advocate general in Massachusetts (1756–61) after refusing to enforce the Writs of Assistance. He later served in the Stamp Act Congress.

Ottawa Canadian capital city (pop. 626,000). Founded in 1827, it was designated as the capital (1858) by Queen Victoria.

Ottawa Indians North American Indian tribe. A branch of the Algonquian linguistic family, they lived north of the Great Lakes. They sided with the French in the French and Indian Wars, and later with the British in the American Revolution and the War of 1812. The Indian leader Pontiac was an Ottawa Indian.

Otterburn, Battle of *See* **Douglas family**

Otto I ⟨Otto the Great⟩ 912–973. German king (936–973) and Holy Roman Emperor (962–973). Otto became king at the end of a period in which the east Frankish kingdom—created by the Treaty of Verdun *(q.v.)*—had broken up into petty states. Central authority was then beginning to reemerge under the leadership of the kingdom of Saxony. As German king, Otto succeeded in extending his authority over rebellious German dukes by force of arms and by using the church to strengthen his rule ("Ottonian" system). He further reinforced his position by defeating the invading Magyars (955) and by subduing the Slavs (960). He intervened in the west Frankish kingdom (France) over possession of Lorraine and in 951 marched into Italy and assumed the title king of the Lombards. In 961, he again invaded Italy to aid Pope John XII against Berengar II. The pope crowned Otto emperor (962), a title that had lapsed at the end of the 9th cent., and concluded an agreement to regulate relations between the pope and the emperor. Otto's coronation is thus usually taken as the beginning of the Holy Roman Empire *(q.v.)* and its long, often troubled alliance with the church. In 963, Pope John turned against Otto, fearing he had become too powerful. Otto deposed John, installed Leo VIII as pope, and soon after suppressed a revolt by the Romans. After Leo's death in 965, the Romans again revolted and Otto was forced to invade Italy again (966–972).

Otto I ⟨Otho I⟩ 1815–67. Greek king (1832–62). The son of Louis I of Bavaria, he was selected to be the king of Greece by the London Conference, after the War of Greek Independence. Autocratic and ambitious, he was unpopular and was finally deposed.

Otto I 1848–1916. Bavarian king (1886–1913), successor to his brother Louis II. He became insane in 1872, and his uncle Luitpold served as his regent (1886–1912). He was deposed by parliament and Luitpold's son became Louis III.

Otto II 955–983. Holy Roman Emperor (973–983) and German king (961–983), successor to his father, Otto I. He repulsed attacks from Bavaria and Denmark but was badly defeated by the Arabs in southern Italy (982).

Otto III 980–1002. Holy Roman Emperor (996–1002) and German king (983–1002), successor to his father, Otto II. He installed his cousin as Pope Gregory V and his tutor as Pope Sylvester II. He attempted to make Rome his capital but was forced out. He was preparing to retake the city when he died.

Otto IV 1182?–1218. Holy Roman Emperor (1209–15) and German king. He contested the throne with Philip of Swabia, and became emperor after Philip's death. He was excommunicated for attacking Italy, and Frederick II was made rival king (1212). Otto was defeated by French king Philip II at Bouvines (1214), and was deposed (1215).

Ottocar I ⟨Ottocar, Premysl I⟩ ⟨Ottokar I⟩ d. 1230. Bohemian king (1198–1230). Otto car won Bohemia's autonomy from Philip of Swabia (1198).

Ottocar II ⟨Ottocar, Premysl II⟩ ⟨Ottokar II⟩ d. 1278. Bohemian king (1252–78). He added Austria, Styria, Carinthia, and Carniola to his empire but failed to become Holy Roman Emperor. He opposed Holy Roman Emperor Rudolf I and was defeated and killed at the Battle of Marchfeld.

Ottocar, Premysl *See* **Ottocar**

Ottokar *See* **Ottocar**

Ottoman Empire Former empire established in the 13th cent. by the Osmanli (Ottoman) Turks. Formed from the territories once ruled by the Seljuk Turks, the empire expanded its holdings at the expense of the Byzantine Empire. The Ottoman conquest of Constantinople (1453) marked the end of the Byzantine Empire. The Ottomans then advanced into Europe, creating an empire that stretched from the Balkans (southeast Europe), across the Near East and into North Africa. By the early 18th cent. the empire began to disintegrate, and during the 19th cent. the Eastern Question *(q.v.)* became a major concern of European powers. The empire was finally dismembered at the end of WW I. *(For subsequent history, see* Turkey.*)* Key dates in the history of the Ottoman Empire include:

c1299–1326 Osman I reigned; founded Ottoman Empire in northwest Anatolia by absorbing neighboring states as the power of the Seljuk Turks declined; attacked domains of Byzantine Empire.

1326 City of Bursa, conquered by Osman, became first capital of Ottoman Empire.

1326–59 Orkhan reigned as second Ottoman ruler; expanded control over western Anatolia, taking Byzantine and neighboring Turkmen states; began Ottoman expansion in the Balkans (southeast Europe).

1359–89 Murad I reigned; empire rapidly expanded eastward into Byzantine domains and westward into Balkans; Byzantines forced to recognize Ottoman suzerainty.

1361 Ottomans conquered Adrianople; city subsequently became capital of the empire.

1371 Murad I decisively defeated the Serbs (Sept. 26) at the Battle of Maritsa River, near Adrianople.

1386 Battle of Konya; Turkmen states, allied to halt Ottoman expansion eastward, defeated by Murad I.

1389 Christian Slavs defeated (June) at the Battle of Kosovo, now in southern Yugoslavia; Ottoman advance in Balkans continued.

1389–1403 Bajazet I reigned; continued Ottoman advance in Balkans, arousing Europeans against him; his annexation of Turkmen states in Anatolia ended in ruinous conflict with Tamerlane.

1391–98 Bajazet blockaded Constantinople.

1394 Salonika captured.

1395–96 Bajazet invaded Hungary; defeated force of Hungarian, French, English, Polish crusaders at Nicopolis (1396), in Bulgaria.

1402 Tamerlane invaded the empire; Bajazet defeated at the Battle of Ankara (July) and taken captive.

1413–21 Muhammad I reigned after struggle to reunite empire.

1421–51 Murad II reigned: expansion of empire renewed.

1444 Battle of Varna fought (Nov. 10); Murad II destroyed invading Hungarian army, thus maintaining control of Eastern Europe.

1451–81 Muhammad II reigned; called "the Conqueror," he greatly expanded Ottoman domains.

1453 Ottomans captured Constantinople and thus ended the Byzantine Empire; Ottomans made Constantinople their capital.

1456 Ottoman siege of Belgrade lifted after victory by Hungarian J. N. Hunyadi.

1456–58 Serbia subjugated and annexed to empire.

1461 Trebizond Empire, a remnant of Byzantine Empire in Greece, conquered; Ottomans extended control over Greece.

1463–79 First major war with Venice, which the Turks won.

1468 Albania conquered after series of defeats at the hands of Scanderbeg.

1475 Tatar khanate of Crimea forced to recognize Ottoman suzerainty.

1480 Ottomans established foothold in southern Italy with capture of Otranto.

1480–81 Siege of Rhodes, last Christian stronghold in eastern Mediterranean; Turks repulsed.

1512–20 Selim I reigned; in addition to his conquests, Selim I proclaimed himself successor to the Muslim Arab caliphs; Ottomans thus became leaders of the Muslim world.

1514 Selim I victorious (Aug. 23) over a Persian army at the Battle of Chaldiran in Armenia.

1515 Selim annexed parts of Persia.

1516 Syria conquered.

1517 Selim I conquered Egypt.

1518 Algiers conquered.

1520–66 Suleiman I reigned; made notable legal reforms, encouraged arts and greatly expanded empire; also built up Ottoman navy.

1521 Belgrade conquered.

1522 Rhodes conquered.

1526 Battle of Mohacs; Turkish victory over Hungarian king Louis II; eventually led to Turkish domination of Hungary.

1529 Turks laid siege to Vienna; forced to withdraw.

1530s Ottomans conquered Iraq and other territories from Persia.

1535 Alliance with France against Hapsburgs formed; continued in subsequent centuries.

1540 Ottoman control extended into southern Hungary.

1541 Buda taken; much of Hungary fell under Ottoman rule.

1551 Ottomans conquered Tripoli.

1566–74 Selim II reigned; Cyprus conquered and Tunisia reconquered; reign marked by beginning of decline in sultan's powers as the Muslim clergy and Janissaries gained strength.

1571 Battle of Lepanto, victory of the Christian Holy League over the Ottoman navy; marked first check of Ottoman expansionism.

1571 Cyprus conquered from Venice.

1574–95 Murad III reigned; parts of Armenia conquered, taken from Persia.

1591–1606 Fifteen Years' War fought with Austria.

1603–17 Ahmed I reigned; empire weakened by Treaty of Szitvatorok (1606); commercial concessions granted to European powers.

1605–23 Persians warred against Ottomans, finally capturing Baghdad.

1620–21 Poles victorious at Battle of Chocim.

1623–40 Murad IV reigned; reconquered territories lost to Persia and captured Baghdad (1638); decline of empire, due to corruption, maladministration, and internal unrest, accelerated after his death; grand viziers rose to power.

1645–64 War with Venice in which weakness of Ottoman Empire was revealed.

1676–81 Russo-Turkish War; Russians gained most of Turkish Ukraine.

1682–99 Austro-Turkish War fought; Ottomans lost Hungary, Transylvania, Croatia, Slavonia, Dalmatia, and Podolia.

1695–96 Russo-Turkish War; Russians captured Azov.
earlier success of Persia in Transcaucasus (1730).

1710–11 Russo-Turkish War; Ottomans attacked Russia, regaining Azov as the Northern War raged in the Baltic region.

1736–39 Russo-Turkish War; Russians retook Azov.

1743–46 War with Persia proved indecisive; earlier success of Persia in Transcaucasus (1730).

1768–74 Russo-Turkish War; Russians victorious and greatly increased influence in Crimea; Russians established as protectors of Christians in Ottoman domains; war ended by Treaty of Kuchuk Kainarji.

1787–92 Russo-Turkish War; Russia generally successful in war, caused by its annexation of the Crimea (1783).

1789–1807 Selim III reigned; forced to abdicate during a revolt caused by his attempts at reform.

1806–12 Russo-Turkish War; Russia acquired Bessarabia.

1808–39 Mahmud II reigned; attempted to reestablish power of sultanate.

1821–31 Greek War of Independence; Ottomans lost Greek domains.

1826 Convention of Akkerman signed (Oct. 7); Serbia granted autonomy; Russia to oversee autonomy of Moldavia and Walachia.

1826 Revolt of the Janissaries quashed; their power broken.

1828–29 Russo-Turkish War; Russia penetrated deeply into the Balkans.

1831–33 War with Egypt; Muhammad Ali of Egypt gained Syria; European powers intervened to halt further conflict.

1839–61 Abdul-Mejid reigned; his reforms were opposed by Muslim reactionaries; continued existence of Ottoman state largely dependent on European powers.

1839–40 Ottomans unsuccessfully attacked Egyptians in Syria; Europeans forced Egyptian ruler Muhammad Ali to return Syria to Ottomans; Muhammad Ali made hereditary ruler of Egypt, under Ottoman suzerainty.

1853–56 Crimean War; European powers opposed Russia's expansion into Ottoman domains; Eastern Question became major diplomatic concern in following years.

1861–76 Abd-al-Aziz reigned; liberal movement led by Midhat Pasha gained momentum dur-

ing his rule; Midhat played key role in his overthrow.

1875 Bosnia and Herzegovina rebelled against Ottoman rule; uprisings led to Serbo-Turkish War (1876–78).

1876 Bulgarian Horrors; Christians massacred.

1876–78 Serbo-Turkish War; Serbs joined rebels in Bosnia and Herzegovina and declared war on the Ottomans; conflict merged with the Russo-Turkish War.

1877 Midhat Pasha secured passage of constitution establishing parliamentary rule in the empire; parliament soon dissolved by sultan Murad V.

1877–78 Russo-Turkish War; victorious Russians advanced to just outside Constantinople.

1878 Congress of Berlin; Russian gains in Russo-Turkish War reduced but Ottomans nevertheless lost much of the Balkans.

1883 British took control of Egypt.

1894–96 Massacres of rebellious Armenians.

1897 Greco-Turkish War fought (Apr.–May) with Greece over control of Crete; Turks gained several victories and Greece accepted an armistice.

1908 Rebellion by Young Turks forced restoration of constitutional government.

1908 Bulgaria became independent; Bosnia and Herzegovina passed to Austro-Hungarian empire.

1911–12 Italo-Turkish War; Italy gained Tripoli and the area that became Libya.

1912–13 Balkan Wars; Ottoman rule in Europe virtually ended.

1913 Young Turks, led by Enver Pasha, seized control of government.

1914–18 Ottomans joined Central Powers during WW I; Arab revolts and Allied drive from Egypt through Palestine further reduced Ottoman power; Allied victory guaranteed the ultimate dissolution of the empire.

1918–22 Muhammad VI, last Ottoman sultan, reigned.

1920 Treaty of Sèvres signed with Allies; formally ended existence of Ottoman Empire; Turkish nationalists refused to recognize treaty.

1922 Muhammad VI overthrown by nationalists; Republic of Turkey established.

Otto of Freising *d.* 1158. German historian and bishop of Freising. The uncle of Holy Roman Emperor Frederick I, he is known best for *The Two Cities*, a history of the world to the year 1146.

Otto the Great *See* **Otto I**

Oudenaarde, Battle of ⟨Audenarde, ~⟩ Allied victory over the French (July 11, 1708) during the

War of the Spanish Succession, at Oudenaarde, now in Belgium. Some 80,000 allied troops under J. Churchill, duke of Marlborough, and Prince Eugene of Savoy defeated about 100,000 French under the command of Louis Joseph, duke of Vendôme.

Ourique, Battle of   *See* **Alfonso I, king of Portugal**

Outer Mongolia   *See* **Mongolia**

Outer Space Treaty   Treaty sponsored (1966) by the UN. Signed (1967) by more than sixty nations, it sought to control the use of outer space for military purposes and promoted international cooperation in space activities.

Overland Trail   Name applied to any of several routes used by American pioneers to travel to the West from the Mississippi in the 19th cent. It applies especially to the Oregon Trail *(q.v.)*

Overton, Richard   *See* **Levelers**

Ovid   (Naso, Publius Ovidius) 43 BC–AD 18. Roman poet, considered one of the great poets of antiquity. Among his many works are *The Art of Love, Metamorphoses,* and *Fasti.* After his banishment by Augustus (AD 8), he wrote *Tristia,* poems of exile.

Owen, Robert   1771–1858. British manufacturer and reformer. A successful textile manufacturer, he instituted reforms in child employment, education, health, and hygiene. His progressive ideas were adopted by several experimental communities, including one at New Harmony, Indiana *(q.v.).*

Owens, Jesse   1913–80. American athlete, a black who won four gold medals for the US at the 1936 Olympics at Berlin. His outstanding performance was a severe blow to A. Hitler's myth of Aryan supremacy.

Oxenstierna, Count Axel Gustavsson   1583–1654. Swedish statesman. He virtually ruled Sweden for King Gustavus II during the Thirty Years' War, and served as guardian for Queen Christina.

Oxford, Provisions of   *See* **Provisions of Oxford**

Oxford and Asquith, Herbert Henry, 1st earl of   *See* **Asquith, Herbert Henry, 1st earl of Oxford and Asquith**

Oxford Group   *See* **Moral Rearmament**

Oxford movement   Movement among 19th-cent. Anglican clergymen at Oxford University to renew the faith and worship of the Church of England *(q.v.)* by returning to early Christian sources. The movement sought to establish that the Anglican church was a branch of the ancient undivided Catholic church by virtue of apostolic succession, and did not derive ecclesiastical authority from king or parliament. It also sought to revive ancient Catholic teachings. The movement is usually dated from 1833, when J. Keble preached an Oxford sermon on England's "national apostasy." J. Newman edited and wrote many of a series of pamphlets, *Tracts for the Times,* propagating the movement's ideas and inspiring the name Tractarians for its adherents. The third principal leader was E. Pusey, who inspired another name, Puseyites, for the group. The movement is considered to have ended (1845) with the conversion of Newman and some other members to Catholicism, but its main themes and ideas have continued to influence the Church of England.

Oxmal   *See* **Uxmal**

Ozaki, Yukio   1859–1954. Japanese statesman. A newspaper editor and leading liberal, he was elected to every diet between 1890 and 1952. He advocated universal suffrage and opposed militarism and was jailed during both world wars.

P

Paasikivi, Juho Kusti 1870–1956. Great Finnish statesman, prime minister (1918, 1944–46) and president (1946–56). As both prime minister and president he pursued a policy of appeasement toward Russia as the only way to ensure Finnish independence.

Pacem in Terris *See* **John XXIII**

Pacific, War of the War (1879–84) between Chile and the neighboring states of Bolivia and Peru. The war erupted over disputed coastal territories located along the border between Chile and Bolivia. Chile first occupied the Bolivian coastal province of Antofagasta (from Feb. 14, 1879), and then Peru was drawn into the conflict. Chile declared war on them both (Apr., 1879) and, after completing its occupation of Bolivia's coastal territory, attacked Peru. Chile made extensive conquests in Peru and finally occupied the capital city of Lima in Jan., 1881. With the Peruvian government on the verge of collapse, Peru and Chile signed (1883) the Treaty of Ancon *(q.v.)*, by which Chile won mineral-rich Peruvian lands. Chile and Bolivia then signed the Treaty of Valparaiso (Apr. 4, 1884), by which Bolivia ceded its entire coastline to Chile.

Pacification of Ghent Religious truce and union (Nov. 8, 1576) agreed to by Protestant and Catholic provinces of the Spanish Netherlands, then in rebellion against rule by the Spanish Hapsburgs. The agreement was intended to put aside religious differences between the Calvanistic (northern) provinces and the Catholic (southern) provinces for the purposes of driving out Spanish troops sent to put down their revolt. This document was followed (1879) by the Union of Utrecht *(q.v.)*, by which the northern provinces declared complete independence.

Pacific Islands, Trust Territory of the UN trust territory administered by the US. Capital is Saipan. It consists of the Caroline, Marshall, and Mariana (except Guam) island groups. German possessions until WW I, the islands became Japanese territories by League of Nations mandate (1922). They were taken by the US during WW II and became US trust territories in 1947.

Pacific Scandal Canadian political scandal (1873). Prime Minister J. Macdonald was charged with awarding the contract for the Canadian Pacific Railway to a syndicate headed by Sir Hugh Allan, in return for campaign contributions by Allan. The scandal contributed to the downfall of Macdonald's Conservative administration.

Pacific Treaty, Four-Power *See* **Four-Power Pacific Treaty**

pacifism Ethical, philosophical, or moral opposition to war or violence. Pacifism may take the form of either individual or organized action. Its development has been greatly influenced by religion, and doctrines of nonviolence may be found in the teachings of Buddhism, Christianity, and Judaism, as well as in the tenets of such sects as Quakers and Mennonites. In modern history, pacifism was a factor in M. Gandhi's policies of nonviolent resistance against British rule in India, in the civil rights movement in the US (1950s and early 1960s), and, for a time, in the opposition to the US conduct of the Vietnam War.

Pact of Halepa ⟨Khalepa, Treaty of⟩ After quelling an insurrection in Crete, the ruling Turks through this pact granted (Oct., 1878) Greek Christians on the island a majority of seats in the assembly, as well as a large measure of self-government.

Pact of Paris *See* **Kellogg-Briand Pact**

Pact of Steel Treaty (May 22, 1939) between Germany and Italy, confirming the German-Italian alliance. The treaty obligated each to enter any war in which the other was engaged. Thus Italy joined A. Hitler in WW II (June 10, 1940) and ultimately broke the treaty by reaching a separate peace with the Allies on Sept. 3, 1943.

Paderewski, Ignace Jan 1860–1941. Polish pianist, composer, and patriot. A world-famous pianist, Paderewski donated much of his fortune made from piano concerts to Polish charities. He served briefly as Poland's prime minister in 1919.

Padilla, Juan de 1490–1521. Spanish revolutionary. Padilla led a revolt by the Communeros *(q.v.)* against Holy Roman Emperor Charles V but was captured and executed.

Padua Historic city (pop. 235,000), located in northern Italy. A rail and commercial center, it has many historic buildings, adorned with works by Giotto, Titian, Donatello, and others. Mentioned as early as 302 BC, it later flourished under Roman control. It rose to prominence again (11th–13th cents.) as a free commune. The city passed to Venice (1405–1797) and played a role in the unification of Italy. The University of Padua was a noted intellectual center in medieval times.

Padua, Marsilius of *See* **Marsilius of Padua**

Padua, Saint Anthony of *See* **Anthony of Padua, Saint**

Paean Greek god. Paean was the god of healing and the physician to the other gods.

Paeonius *fl.* 5th cent. BC. Greek sculptor. Paeonius is thought to have sculpted the famed statue of Nike *(Winged Victory)* that was discovered in 1875.

Páez, José Antonio 1790–1873. Venezuelan revolutionary and statesman. He aided S. Bolívar in the fight for South American independence from Spain. Later, however, he led the movement to separate (1831) Venezuela from Bolívar's Great Colombia *(q.v.)*. Páez was president (1831–35, 1839–43) and dictator (1861–63) of Venezuela.

Paganini, Niccolò 1782–1840. Great Italian violinist and composer. Paganini revolutionized violin technique, making extensive use of harmonics.

Pagerie, Marie Joséphine Rose Tascher de la *See* **Joséphine**

Paget, Sir James 1814–99. British surgeon. He discovered the parasite that causes trichinosis and was noted for his work on cancers and bone diseases.

Pahlavi ⟨Pehlevi⟩ Iranian branch of the Indo-European languages. Pahlavi was the middle stage (3d–10th cent. AD) in the evolution from the old to modern Persian language and was the official language of the Sassanid dynasty.

Paine, Thomas 1737–1809. English-born American patriot, pamphlet writer, and political theorist. He emigrated to America in 1774 and quickly became active in the revolutionary cause. His famous pamphlet *Common Sense* (Jan. 1776) argued for independence from Britain and his series of pamphlets, *The Crisis* (1776–83), advanced the patriot cause during the war years. Returning to England, he wrote *The Rights of Man* in support of the French Revolution. Convicted of treason in England, he went to France and took part in the revolution, until he was imprisoned (1793–94) during the Reign of Terror. While there he wrote *The Age of Reason*, promoting deism *(q.v.)*. Returning to the US (1802), he was met with disfavor and died in obscurity.

Painlevé, Paul 1863–1933. French mathematician and statesman. Painlevé promoted aviation in France and served twice as premier (1917, 1925). He was renowned for his writings on higher mathematics.

Paiute Indians North American Indian tribe, a branch of the Shoshone tribe. They were divided into the northern Paiute (in parts of California, Oregon, and Nevada) and the southern Paiute (in parts of Nevada, Utah, and Arizona). The Ghost Dance religion arose among the Paiutes during the late 19th cent.

Paix des Dames *See* **Cambrai, Treaty of**

Pakenham, Sir Edward *See* **New Orleans, Battle of**

Pakistan ⟨Republic of Pakistan⟩ Muslim state bordering northwestern India in southern Asia. Its capital is Islamabad. The early history of Pakistan was largely that of India, and it was not until 1947 that the modern state was created (by the partition of India into Hindu and Muslim homelands). Muslim Pakistan once also included a separate area (East Pakistan), bordering on northeastern India. The two were governed as one nation until 1971, when the eastern part gained independence as Bangladesh. The Indus Valley in Pakistan long served as a route for invading India and was crossed by the Aryans, Persians, Arabs, and Turks. Key dates in the history of Pakistan include:

2500–c1500 BC Indus Valley civilization flourished in Pakistan; succumbed to Aryan invaders.

AD 700–900 Muslim Arabs conquered northwestern India (including Pakistan).

c1200 Turkish invaders occupied Bengal; converted Hindus to Islam.

16TH–19TH CENTS. Eastern (Bangladesh) region controlled by Indian (Muslim) Mogul Empire.

1730s Persia captured western region.

18TH CENT. Afghanistan ruled Sind and Punjab in west.

1780–1839 Sikhs (under Ranjit Singh) ruled the Punjab.

1840s British, expanding their domains in India, began conquest of region of Pakistan (proper); captured Sind and Punjab but were unable to completely subdue tribes in region.

1901 Britain created North-West Frontier Province of India to administer Pakistan (proper).

1906 Nationalist Muslim League founded as Indian nationalist movement, dominated by Hindus, failed to hold Muslim support.

1930 Concept of Muslim nation separate from India promulgated by Muhammad Iqbal.

1940 Muhammad Ali Jinnah demanded creation of Muslim state in areas of large Muslim population in India.

1947 Britain created India and Pakistan as separate independent states (Aug. 15).

1947 Capital established at Karachi; Jinnah in office as first governor-general (1947–48); Liaquat Ali Khan in office as first prime minister (1947–51).

1947–48 Violence between Hindus and Muslims in India and newly created Pakistani states resulted in migrations by millions between Hindu and Muslim-controlled lands.

1948–49 India-Pakistan War over Kashmir.

1951 Prime minister Liaquat Ali Khan assassinated.

1955 West Pakistan reorganized into new administrative districts; eastern region officially named East Pakistan.

1956 Constitution adopted; Pakistan became member of the British Commonwealth.

1956–58 Iskander Mirza in office as first president.

1958–69 Army general Muhammad Ayub Kahn held power as head of state; given dictatorial powers (1958) in wake of continuing economic problems and unrest.

1959 Islamabad made capital.

1965 India-Pakistan conflict over Kashmir and Rann of Kutch.

1968–69 Strikes and riots in East Pakistan led to Ayub Khan's resignation; Gen. Agha Muhammad Yahya Khan installed; declared martial law.

1970 Elections for National Assembly to write new constitution; East Pakistan separatist movement (Awami League) gained majority.

1971 Yahya canceled assembly, banned Awami League.

1971 Bangladesh (East Pakistan) declared independence (Mar. 26).

1971 Bloody civil war (Mar.–Dec.) between Pakistan and Bangladesh; India joined fighting (Dec.) in support of Bangladesh and invaded West Pakistan; Pakistan surrendered (Dec. 16).

1971–73 Ali Bhutta took control as president of Pakistan.

1976 Pakistan and India resumed diplomatic relations.

1978 Military coup (July 5) following contested election.

1978– Gen. Muhammad Zia ul-Haq in office as military-backed president; suppressed political opposition; opposed Soviet occupation of Afghanistan.

1981 US military aid program approved.

1982 Zia continued ban on political activity and postponed scheduled 1982 elections.

Palaemon Greek god, a sea god who was the special protector of ships. He corresponds to the Roman god Portunus.

Palaeologus Byzantine ruling dynasty. This Greek family ruled the Byzantine Empire from 1261 to 1453, when the Turks brought the empire to an end. Emperor Michael VIII became the first ruler of the line when he ousted the crusader kings of the Latin Empire of Constantinople and thereby restored the Byzantine Empire. The last ruler of the family, Constantine XI, was killed defending Constantinople against the Turks. The family became extinct in the 16th cent. Byzantine rulers were:

Michael VIII	1261–82
Andronicus II	1282–1328
Michael IX (co-ruler)	1295–1320
Andronicus III	1328–41
John V	1341–47
John VI	1347–54
John V	1354–76
Andronicus IV	1376–79
John V	1379–91
John VII (co-ruler, 1398–1412)	1390
Manuel II	1391–1425
John VIII	1425–48
Constantine XI	1449–53

Palaeologus, Constantine *See* **Constantine XI**

Palamedes Greek mythical hero. Palamedes is considered the inventor of numbers, measures, coinage, and the alphabet. He also fought in the Trojan War.

Palatinate Historic region located in southwestern West Germany, consisting of the Lower Palatinate (in the state of Rhineland-Palatinate) and the Upper Palatinate (in Bavaria). The areas were in the control of the counts palatine, a title given (1156) by Emperor Frederick I to his brother, Conrad, whose descendants became electors palatine (1356) and the leading princes of the Holy Roman Empire. The region passed to the Wittelsbach (*q.v.*) family (1214–1777), underwent many divisions and unifications, and was ravaged during the Thirty Years' War (1618–48) and the War of the Grand Alliance (1689–97). A part of the Palatinate was ceded to France for a time (1801–15) but was recovered after Napoleon's fall.

pale A specified district that is subject to certain restrictions or to a separate governing body. The Pale in Ireland (12th–16th cents.) centered around Dublin, was ruled by England, and lasted until conquest of Ireland was complete. The Pale of Settlement was created (1792) by Russian empress

Catherine II as the only region in which Russian Jews were allowed to settle and travel. It initially consisted of territories ceded by Poland and was greatly enlarged in subsequent years. It was eliminated by the Russian Revolution of 1917.

Pale of Settlement *See* **pale**

Paleolithic *See* **Stone Age**

Palermo stone Inscribed stone, part of a year-by-year record of events of Egyptian dynasties I-V (3d–2d millennium BC). It is an important source of historical information for this period.

Palestine Historic region on the east coast of the Mediterranean, including modern Israel and the part of Jordan east of the Jordan River. Palestine is considered a Holy Land by the Jews, Christians, and Muslims, and the historic center of the region is Jerusalem. Palestine, inhabited since very ancient times, is the scene of many of the events recounted in the Bible. The region was controlled by various powers of the ancient world, though it remained a Jewish homeland until late in the Roman era. Palestine subsequently fell to the Muslims (7th cent. AD) and Jerusalem, already a holy city to the Jews and Christians, became a Muslm holy city as well. Palestine remained in Muslim hands until the 20th cent., though by the end of the 19th cent. Jews had already begun again to colonize the region. The movement to create a Jewish homeland in Palestine after WW I resulted in serious clashes between Arabs and Jews there. The conflict between Arabs and Israelis continued after creation of Israel in 1948 and contributed to Mideast instability into the 1980s. (*For history of the region after 1948, see* Israel.) Dates prior to 500 BC are in many cases approximate. Key events in the history of Palestine include:

3D MILLENNIUM BC Formation of towns and cities in region.

c2100 BC Amorites, a Semitic people, invaded region.

c18TH–16TH CENT. BC Hyksos invasion; Egypt ruled by Hyksos.

16TH?–13TH? CENT. BC Hebrews believed to have arrived in Palestine; time of the Patriarchs, Abraham, Isaac, and Jacob; Hebrews settled variously (in modern Israel, Jordan, and northeast Egypt).

c1500–c1450 BC Egyptians, led by Thutmose III, conquered Palestine after driving out Hyksos; region known as Canaan.

14TH CENT. BC Egyptians lost control over Palestine during the reign of Ikhnaton.

EARLY 13TH CENT. BC Egyptian king Ramses II reestablished control over Palestine during wars with the Hittites.

c1270?–c1230? BC Exodus; Moses led the Hebrews enslaved in Egypt out of Egypt to the edge of the promised land (Canaan) in Palestine.

1231 BC Egyptian king Merneptah attacked Hebrews in Canaan (probably those already living there).

c1230? Joshua, leading the Hebrews (Joseph tribes), crossed the Jordan River and conquered Canaan; Jericho believed to be first city they conquered.

c1200 BC Invasions by Sea Peoples occupied Egypt, breaking its hold on Palestine; Philistines, one of the Sea Peoples, settled on southern coast of Palestine.

11TH CENT. BC Philistines began expanding into domains of the Israelites.

c1028?–1013? BC Saul became king of the Israelites; formerly led by Judges, tribal leaders, the Israelites were forced to unite by the increasing pressure from the Philistines; after early victories, Saul was defeated and died at Mount Gilboa.

1013–973 BC David reigned; as leader of the tribe of Judah conquered the Philistines, established the Israelite capital at Jerusalem, and conquered the Moabites, Ammonites, and Edomites; established unified kingdom of Israel; put down revolts by Absalom and Sheba.

973–933 BC Solomon reigned; kingdom further expanded and a thriving commerce developed; renowned for the splendor of his court, Solomon built many buildings and constructed the first Temple at Jerusalem.

933 BC Rehoboam succeeded Solomon; refused to lessen heavy taxes imposed on northern tribes during Solomon's reign.

933 BC Jeroboam led the Ten Tribes of Israel in a revolt against Rehoboam; formed the northern Kingdom of Israel; capital at Samaria.

933 BC Rehoboam formed the kingdom of Judah (in the south) from the tribes of Judah and Benjamin; conducted wars against kingdom of Israel.

c874–853 BC Ahab reigned as king of Israel in the north; his reign marked by wars with Assyria and rise in worship of Canaanite god Baal, promoted by Jezebel, Ahab's wife; time of Elijah's struggle against Baal-worship.

842–816 BC Jehu reigned as king of Israel; led revolt against Baal-worship and slew (843) Ahaziah, king of Judah, and Jehoram, king of Israel; gained control over kingdom of Judah; massacred Baal-worshipers, including Jezebel; paid tribute to Assyrians.

780–740 BC Uzziah reigned as king of Judah; kingdom of Judah reached height of its power;

time of prophet Isaiah began in last years of Uzziah's reign.

732?–722 BC Hoshea reigned as last king of Israel; assassinated Pekah and seized power; allied Israel with Egypt and thus brought on the Assyrian conquest.

731–727 BC Ahaz reigned in Judah; allied Judah with Assyria against Israel and Syria; lost Judah's independent status.

722 BC Kingdom of Israel in north destroyed by Assyrian king Sargon; capital of Samaria taken after long siege; Israelites of the north exiled from their lands and thus became the Ten Lost Tribes; colonies of Aramaeans settled northern kingdom.

720?–692? BC Hezekiah reigned as king of Judah; rebelled unsuccessfully against rule of Assyrian king Sennacherib.

c640–609 BC Josiah reigned as king of Judah; decline of Assyrian power gave him relative autonomy; Book of Law discovered in the Temple at Jerusalem (c622); gave rise to Deuteronomic Reform, in which foreign cults were purged, the Temple was dedicated solely to worship of Yahweh, and worship was concentrated at Jerusalem.

609 BC Josiah killed at the Battle of Megiddo during fighting with the Egyptians; Egyptian king Necho took control of the kingdom of Judah.

605 BC Nebuchadnezzar defeated the Egyptians at the Battle of Carchemish; kingdom of Judah passed to the Babylonians.

598 BC Revolt against Babylonian rule failed.

597–586 BC Zedekiah reigned as last king of Judah; installed by the Babylonians, he rebelled (588–586) and was defeated; Nebuchadnezzar destroyed the Temple and city of Jerusalem and carried off many of the Judahites to Babylon; kingdom of Judah ceased to exist.

586–538 BC Babylonian captivity ended by Persian defeat of Babylonians; Cyrus the Great permitted Jews to return to Palestine.

538–332 BC Persians ruled Palestine; region administered as part of the satrapy of Syria; districts (under own governors) included Judah, Samaria, and others.

516 BC Second Temple at Jerusalem completed, formally ending the captivity and reestablishing a center of Jewish worship.

458? BC Ezra became religious leader of the Jews; established the Law (Torah) as central to Judaism and the Jewish community.

FROM 445 BC Nehemiah, governor of Judaea, rebuilt city and its walls; introduced reforms.

c428 BC Samaritans built their own temple at Mount Gerizim, north of Jerusalem, as a result of Jews' opposition to their sect.

332 BC Alexander the Great conquered Palestine.

323–198 BC Ptolemies, Macedonian rulers of Egypt, controlled Palestine; Greek influences reached Palestine.

198–168 BC Seleucids controlled Palestine, following campaigns of Antiochus III.

2D CENT. BC Nabateans began expanding into Syria as Seleucid power waned; eventually ruled domains that bordered on Palestine; became Roman allies by 1st cent. BC.

EARLY 2D CENT. BC First appearance of the Pharisees, who upheld both the oral tradition and the written Law of the Torah.

175–163 BC Antiochus IV reigned as Seleucid ruler; declared Judaism illegal and began persecution (168) that sparked revolt by the Maccabees in Palestine.

168 BC Mattathias, a Jewish priest, began revolt of the Maccabees in Palestine.

c164 BC Judas Maccabeus expelled the Seleucids from Jerusalem after defeating their armies; rededicated the Temple at Jerusalem (commemorated by Hanukkah).

164–161 BC Judas continued wars, even though Seleucids granted Jews religious freedom; he was killed in fighting.

161–143 BC Jonathan Maccabeus continued wars against Seleucids; killed in battle.

142 BC Simon negotiated independence of Judaea.

142–135 BC Simon served as high priest and governor of the newly independent Jewish national state, Judaea; assassinated.

135–104 BC John Hyrcanus reigned; Judaea reached its height.

104 BC Aristobulus I reigned; adopted title of king and conquered part of (modern) Lebanon.

103–76 BC Alexander Jannaeus reigned; supported the Sadducees and persecuted the Pharisees.

76–67 BC Salome Alexandra reigned; the widow of Alexander Jannaeus, she favored the Pharisees during her reign.

67–63 BC Civil war between Aristobulus II and John Hyrcanus II; Romans under Pompey intervened and took control of Judaea.

63 BC–AD 67 Palestine administered as part of the Roman province of Syria.

63 BC–AD 395 Romans controlled Palestine.

40–37 BC Antigonus, Aristobulus' son, led abortive revolt (with Parthian support) against Roman rule; executed (37 BC).

37–4 BC Herod the Great ruled Palestine under Roman authority; practiced Judaism and promoted Hellenism; became ruthless and cruel toward end of reign.

8?–6? BC Jesus of Nazareth born; raised as a Jew.

4 BC Massacre of the Innocents; Herod ordered all infants in Bethlehem murdered.

4 BC–AD 39 Herod Antipas ruled Galilee under Roman authority; married his niece, Herodias, and was thus criticized by John the Baptist; ordered execution of John at behest of Salome.

AD 26–36 Pontius Pilate, Roman procurator of Judaea, alienated the Jews.

AD 27? Jesus baptized by John the Baptist; Jesus began his public ministry in which he spread his teachings and aroused the opposition of the Pharisees.

AD 30 Last Supper; Jesus arrested at Jerusalem as a threat to religious and political authorities; Herod Antipas refused to pass judgment on Jesus and returned him to Pontius Pilate, who acceded to demands and ordered Jesus' execution.

AD 30 Jesus crucified at Jerusalem; his martyrdom and the subsequent missionary work by his disciples marked the beginning of the Christian era.

AD 36 Pontius Pilate recalled to Rome; subsequent Roman procurators continued to alienate Jews.

AD 66–73 First Jewish revolt; Zealots, a radical Jewish faction, rose against Roman rule; Romans retook Jerusalem and destroyed the Temple (AD 70); Jerusalem destroyed and Jewish state dissolved.

AD 132–135 Second Jewish revolt; led by S. Bar Kokba, the Jews failed to end Roman rule; Emperor Hadrian built Aelia Capitolina on site of Jerusalem and refused to allow Jews to live there; thereafter Jews remained centered in Mideast until medieval times, when large numbers of them migrated to Europe.

4TH CENT. AD Palestine made a center of Christianity after Romans ended persecutions of Christians; many Jews left the region and settled elsewhere in Mideast.

5TH–7TH CENT. Palestine under Byzantine rule.

614 Persians conquered Palestine.

628 Byzantine Emperor Heraclius recovered Palestine.

640 Muslim Arabs completed conquest of Palestine; subsequently became Muslim Holy Land.

691 Dome of the Rock built in Jerusalem by Muslims; became site of Muslim pilgrimage.

9TH–11TH CENT. Palestine controlled by the Fatimids, Muslims based in Egypt and rivaling the Abbasid caliphs for control of the Muslim world; Christians and Jews in Palestine persecuted; control of Palestine contested by other Muslim factions.

11TH–13TH CENT. Era of the Crusades; European Christians briefly established control over the Palestinian Holy Land.

1099–1291 Latin Kingdom of Jerusalem; Christian kingdom in Palestine founded during the First Crusade; the kindgom ceased to exist after Acre fell (1291) to the Mamelukes (Muslim rulers of Egypt).

13TH–16TH CENT. Mamelukes controlled Palestine.

16TH–20TH CENT. Ottoman Turks ruled Palestine; after defeating the Mamelukes (1516) the Ottomans administered Palestine as a part of the province of Syria; general decline of region continued.

1831 Muhammad Ali, Ottoman viceroy of Egypt, seized Palestine in rivalry with Ottoman sultan; Egyptians held region until 1840; led to period of settlement by Europeans, notably Jews.

1870 European Jews began colonization of Palestine; first Jewish settlement founded (1878).

FROM 1882 Russian Jews, fleeing the pogroms in Russia, began arriving in Palestine.

1897 Zionist movement founded for creation of a Jewish national state in Palestine; Ottoman government turned down Zionist plan, though Zionists actively supported colonization by Jews (from 1906).

1917 British occupied Palestine during the course of their offensive against the Ottoman Turks in WW I.

1917 Balfour Declaration (Nov. 2); British, at the urging of Zionist leaders, declared support for creation of Jewish national state in Palestine.

1920 Britain received preliminary approval from League of Nations for its mandate in Palestine; plan for creation of Jewish state approved.

1921 Anti-Jewish riots by Palestinian Arabs, then the majority population in Palestine.

1922 British League of Nations mandate over Palestine and Transjordan approved.

1922 British White Paper recommended that Jewish state exist within Palestine; proposed limits on immigration by Jews.

1923 Transjordan split off from Palestine; organized as an autonomous state.

1928 Rioting between Arabs and Jews over the Wailing Wall in Jerusalem.

1929 Widespread attacks by Arabs against Jews.

1930 British White Paper recommended limiting Jewish immigration and banning new purchases of land by Jews.

1930s Immigration of Jews to Palestine increased manyfold as Nazi persecutions in Germany began; opposition to British rule in Palestine mounted among Arabs and Jews alike as situation became increasingly intractable.

1936 Widespread riots by Arabs against Jews.

1936–37 Jews formed underground armies in response to Arab attacks; Haganah (1936) adopted solely defensive policy; Irgun Zvai Leumi conducted retaliatory raids (1937) against Arabs and eventually fought British forces as well.

1937 Peel Commission Report; recommended partitioning Palestine into Jewish, Arab, and British sectors.

1937–39 Period of near open war and terrorism with Arabs, Jews, and British battling for control.

1939 British White Paper abandoned partition scheme in favor of limiting Jewish immigration and land purchases; eventual independence to be granted; outbreak of WW II brought temporary halt to serious violence.

1945 Arab League formed.

1945–47 Waves of illegal immigrants entered Palestine as horrors of the Nazi Holocaust created new pressure for creation of Jewish national state; intense fighting between Jews, Arabs, and British.

1947 London Conference; British unable to solve Palestinian problem, put question before UN.

1947 UN approved (Nov.) plan to partition Palestine into Jewish, Arab, and International (Jerusalem) zones; Arabs denounced plan; renewed fighting in Palestine.

1948 State of Israel created as British occupation force completed withdrawal; immediately attacked by Arabs in first Arab-Israeli War.

Palestine Liberation Organization ⟨PLO⟩ Arab political and terrorist organization. Founded in 1964, the PLO is made up of various Arab guerrilla groups dedicated to reclaiming Palestinian homelands now occupied by Israel. The group has been involved in a bitter guerrilla war with the Israelis, and their activities have contributed greatly to Mideast instability in recent times. Their activities have included airplane hijackings, terrorist bombings, massacres of Israeli civilians, and skirmishes with Israeli military forces. The PLO actively supported Muslims in the civil war with Christians in Lebanon and used Lebanon as a staging area for raids on Israel until the Lebanese War (see Lebanon [1982]). Since 1964 the PLO has been headed by Yasir Arafat (1929–), whose guerrilla organization (Al Fatah) dominates the PLO. The PLO was formally recognized by the UN in 1974.

Pali Indo-European language. Thought to be the language of Buddha, Pali is still employed in the liturgical literature of Buddhists in Sri Lanka, Burma, and Thailand.

Palikao, Charles Guillaume Cousin-Montauban, count of 1796–1878. French general. His title was bestowed after his victory at Palikao while on an Anglo-French military expedition in China (1860). He briefly served as premier (1870) during the collapse of the French Second Empire.

Palladianism Architectural style developed during the Renaissance by A. Palladio. It incorporated elements of classical Roman architecture. Palladianism was influential in England (17th–18th cents.) and was introduced there by I. Jones.

Palladio, Andrea 1508–80. Famous Italian architect of the Renaissance. Palladio rebelled against excessive ornamentation, adapted classic Roman styles, and created the style known as Palladianism. He is considered the founder of modern Italian architecture.

Palladium Sacred image of Athena in Greek religion. It was said that Zeus caused it to protect the city of Troy. It was stolen by Odysseus and Diomedes, after which Troy fell to the Greeks.

Pallas Mythical Greek giant who, according to one legend, was killed by Athena when he tried to rape her.

Pallas Athena See **Athena**

Palmerston, Henry John Temple, 3d Viscount 1784–1865. British statesman who played an important role in foreign affairs in the 19th cent. He served as secretary of war (1809–28), foreign minister (1830–34, 1835–41, 1846–51), and prime minister (1855–58, 1859–65). A Whig party member, he played a role in arranging Belgian independence (1831), orchestrating European intervention against Muhammad Ali to prevent the break-up of the Ottoman Empire (1841), the Affair of the Spanish Marriages (1846), the Don Pacifico Affair (1850), and the overthrow of French Emperor Napoleon III. His terms as prime minister were marked by British involvement in the Crimean War (1853–56) and the Indian Mutiny (1857–58) and by Britain's neutral support for Italian unification and its stance in the American Civil War.

Palmyra ⟨Tadmor⟩ Ancient Syrian city. Palmyra was supposedly founded by Solomon and was an important trade center after its takeover by Rome. It subsequently became the nucleus of a powerful, quasi-independent eastern empire under Roman domination. The ambitions of its queen, Zenobia, led to destruction of the city (AD 273) by Aurelian.

Palo Alto, Battle of First major battle of the Mexican War (1846–48), fought at this Texas city on May 8, 1846. American forces under Gen. Z. Taylor defeated the Mexican army in the first of several successful engagements against it.

Pan Greek god. Half man and half goat, Pan was considered the god of fertility and nature.

Pan-African congresses International conferences to promote interests of black peoples and nations. Blacks from America and the West Indies met in London in 1900 to protest white oppression in Africa. W. Du Bois emerged as a leading figure here and in the subsequent meetings of 1919, 1921, 1923, and 1927. The congress in 1945 called for independence of all African states from colonial powers.

Panama ⟨Republic of Panama⟩ Independent state in Central America, located on the Isthmus of Panama that connects Central and South America. Its capital is Panama City. Panama is bisected by the Panama Canal Zone, currently under US jurisdiction. Panama was ruled by Spain until 1821 and was part of Colombia until independence was proclaimed in 1903, following a successful revolution. Key events in Panama's history include:

1502 Columbus visited the coastal region on his fourth voyage.

1513 V. de Balboa, Spanish governor, explored the region; crossed the isthmus to the Pacific Ocean.

1519 P. Arias de Villa founded Panama City.

16TH CENT. Region administered as part of the viceroyalty of Peru; main route to rich Spanish colonies in Peru passed across the Isthmus of Panama.

1717 Administrative control passed to viceroyalty of New Granada.

1821 Joined Colombia in revolt against Spain; was governed subsequently as part of Colombia.

1881 F. de Lesseps began construction of Panama Canal; his company went bankrupt (1889), however.

1903 Colombia refused US rights to build canal; US backed Panamanian revolt against Colombia gained Panama its independence.

1903 Hay-Bunau-Varilla Treaty concluded between US and newly independent Panama; established the US-controlled Panama Canal Zone; canal construction began (1904).

1904 Constitution adopted.

1914 Panama Canal opened (Aug. 15).

1939 New treaty provided for equal rights and responsibilities in the Canal Zone.

1941 Pro-German president Harmodio Arias ousted and exiled.

1968 Dr. Arnulfo Arias elected president; overthrown by military coup; two-man junta

reigned; overthrown by Gen. Omar Torrijos, head of the National Guard.

1969–78 Demetrio Basilio Lakas Bahas in office as military-backed president; Gen Torrijos held real power.

1972 New constitution promulgated; National Assembly established.

1977 US and Panama signed treaty (Sept. 7) giving Panama control of canal in 1999.

1978– Aristides Royo in office as president.

1978 US Senate approved transfer of Canal Zone to Panama.

1981 Gen. Torrijos, de facto military ruler, killed in plane crash.

1982 President Aristides Royo resigned (July 30) as disunity between factions mounted; Ricardo de la Espriella made president.

Panama Canal Man-made waterway extending 51 miles across the Isthmus of Panama in Central America. Originally proposed as early as Spanish colonial times and actively pursued by the US since about the mid-1800s, the canal was begun (1881) by the Frenchman F. de Lesseps (builder of the Suez Canal). De Lesseps's firm went bankrupt (1889) as a result of construction problems and outbreaks of tropical disease. The US again took an interest in the project and settled a long dispute with the British over US control of the proposed canal (by the Hay-Pauncefote Treaty, 1901). The US for a time considered a canal through Nicaragua, but under President T. Roosevelt made arrangements to take over the French project in Panama. Colombia (then in control of Panama) refused to ratify a treaty for construction of the canal. The US soon after supported a revolution in Panama. Panama gained independence (Nov., 1903) and on Nov. 17 the US concluded the Hay-Bunau-Varilla Treaty with the new government. Construction work began in 1904 and was completed under the supervision of Col. G. Goethals by 1914. In recent times Panama sought control of the canal and the US agreed (1978) to effect the transfer in 1999.

Panama Canal Zone Area of Panama, extending five miles on either side of the Panama Canal, and administered by the United States from 1903. The US Senate, after a heated controversy, enacted (1978) legislation to return the canal to Panama in 1999.

Panama City Capital city (pop. 439,400) of Panama, located at the southeastern terminus of the Panama Canal. Founded in 1519 by Pedrarius, it was destroyed by the buccaneer H. Morgan, rebuilt in 1673, and designated capital in 1903.

Panama Scandal Scandal (1892) involving the government of the French Third Republic and the failed French Panama Canal Company. The company, in financial trouble because of mismanagement and corruption, floated a new loan in 1888. To get approval from the Chamber of Deputies for the loan, the company's directors bribed many of the deputies. An investigation some years after the company failed (1889) revealed the bribery and toppled the government.

Pan-American conferences ⟨Inter-American ~⟩ Meetings (from 1826) held between various South American states and the US to discuss mutual economic and defense concerns. Conferences up to 1889 (1826, 1847, 1856, 1864) were concerned largely with matters of defense. The First International Conference of American States (1889–90), largely initiated by the US, established what became the Pan-American Union (q.v.) and led to treaties covering trade, arbitration of disputes, and international administrative matters. Additional conferences in 1936, 1938, 1939, 1940, and 1945 worked out mutual-defense agreements. In 1948, the Ninth International Conference formed the Organization of American States (q.v.).

Pan American Union Organization founded in 1890 and composed of republics in North and South America. The union promoted technical, commercial, and cultural interchange among its member nations. It became part of the Organization of American States on formation of that body in 1948.

Pandit, Vijaya Lakshmi 1900–. Indian diplomat. Sister of J. Nehru, she led the Indian delegation to the UN and served as ambassador to both Russia and the US.

Pandora The first woman in Greek mythology. Given a box the gods warned must never be opened (Pandora's box), she nevertheless became curious and looked inside. By so doing, she released all the evils upon the world. Only hope remained in the box.

Pan-Germanism German nationalist movement, organized in 1894. It called for the political unification of all German-speaking people. The movement was used to justify Germany's expansionist policies and after WW I figured in A. Hitler's National Socialist program.

Pangkor Engagement British agreement (Jan., 1874) with the local ruler of Perak, a state in northern Malaya. In exchange for accepting a British resident with authority, the Perak chief was assured of British support. The treaty led to the eventual British domination of the Malay states.

Panic of 1837 US financial panic that began in the spring of 1837, shortly after President M. Van Buren took office. A land speculation boom in the West during A. Jackson's administration was fueled by the many banknotes of inflated value issued by state banks. Jackson's Specie Circular (issued 1836) required payment for public lands (in the West) in hard currency, and thus undermined the value of these notes. A financial collapse followed in 1837, first in the western land market and then spreading to commodities and other markets.

Panic of 1869 *See* **Black Friday**

Panic of 1873 US financial panic (sometimes also called Black Friday) that began on Sept. 18. It was caused by the failure of Jay Cooke and Company, a financial house that had marketed federal bonds during the Civil War.

Panic of 1893 US financial panic brought on by a withdrawal of British investment capital from the US. British capital had fueled a boom in railroad building in the late 19th cent. A worldwide Depression, however, caused British investors to withdraw from the American market and resulted in a collapse of the railroad boom and a flow of gold out of the US. President G. Cleveland sought repeal of the Sherman Silver Purchase Act (q.v.) as a remedy, which he won (1893).

Panipat, Battles of Three battles fought by the Moguls at Panipat, in India. **1.** On Apr. 20, 1526, Baber and his force of some 2,000 Moguls defeated the Afghans and thus established the Mogul dynasty that ruled until 1761. **2.** On Nov. 3, 1556, the third Mogul emperor, Akbar the Great, headed an army of 20,000 and defeated a much larger force of Hindus. **3.** On Jan. 14, 1761, the Afghan Emperor Ahmad Shah Durrani defeated an army of Marathas during his invasion of India; left Indian kingdoms weakened and paved the way for the British takeover.

Pankhurst, Emmeline Goulden 1857–1928. British feminist, who founded (1903) the Women's Social and Political Union to promote woman suffrage. A militant, she was frequently jailed. English women received the vote just before her death.

Panmunjom Korean village where peace was negotiated (1951–53) between UN forces and the North Koreans and Chinese during the Korean War (1950–53). The village is located just south of the 38th parallel. The armistice ending the war was signed there July 27, 1953.

Pannonia Ancient Roman province. Pannonia was located south of the Danube River and included parts of what are now Austria, Hungary, and Yugoslavia. The territories were conquered by the Roman Empire in AD 9.

Pan-Slavism Slavic unity movement. This movement arose in the 19th cent. and stressed the common culture and history of the various Slavic peoples, then divided between Austrian and Ottoman empires. Pan-Slavism figured in Russian imperial policy, contributed to the outbreak of the Russo-Turkish War (1877–78), and was a factor in Russia's alliance with Serbia against the Austrians in the years before WW I.

Pantaléon, Jacques   *See* **Urban IV**

pantheism   Religious term for the belief that God and the universe are one. Pantheism has been a factor in both religion (notably Hinduism, in which Brahman is all things in the universe) and philosophy.

Pantheon   Roman temple. Built by Agrippa (27 BC) at Rome to honor all gods, it was rebuilt (2d cent. AD) by Hadrian. It is now a Christian church (from 609).

Paoli, Pasquale   1725–1807.   Corsican patriot. Paoli rebelled against Genoese and, later, French domination of Corsica. As governor (1755–69, 1791–93) he instituted political reforms. He drove out the French with British help (1794).

papacy   The system of government of the Roman Catholic Church, which is headed by the pope (bishop of Rome), who is considered the successor to St. Peter and vicar of Christ. The pope is considered infallible by the Roman Catholic Church in matters of faith or morality and is head of independent Vatican City. Early popes played an important role in the spread of the Christian church and in resolving the many doctrinal disputes of that era. In medieval times popes were the central figures in the great struggles for power between the church and European monarchs. Later they instituted the Catholic Reformation (*q.v.*) and, gradually forced to relinquish their secular powers, came to focus on spiritual concerns. In modern times, the popes have been especially active in adapting the church to the rapidly changing modern world (*see* Second Vatican Council). (*See also* Roman Catholic Church; Papal States.)

Papal States   Former territory over which the pope had direct temporal rule (756–1870). The size of the territory varied throughout its history but at its greatest extent it included a wide swath across central Italy. From the 4th cent. the pope had control of lands in Rome (the Patrimony of St. Peter) but the existence of the sovereign state is dated from the Donation of Pepin (756). Pepin the Short, in return for papal recognition of his accession as king of the Franks, aided the pope against the invading Lombards and donated lands taken from them (around Ravenna) to the pope. The popes remained sovereign during the Middle Ages but real control of the territories was frustrated by feudal nobles and struggles with the Holy Roman emperors (11th–14th cents.). While the papacy was located at Avignon during the Babylonian captivity, effective control passed to the local nobles. From the 15th to 18th cents., the popes gradually established central authority and brought papal domains to their greatest extent. The Papal States were conquered by Napoleon (1796) and restored to the pope by the Congress of Vienna (1815). Almost all papal domains were lost during the unification of Italy (1860) and, in 1870, Italian king Victor Emmanuel II seized Rome as well. The pope thereupon declared himself a "prisoner" in the Vatican and the Roman Question over rights to the Papal States was not resolved until the signing of the Lateran Treaty (1929).

Papareschi, Gregorio   *See* **Innocent II**

Papen, Franz von   1879–1969.   German politician. As P. Hindenburg's chancellor, he facilitated the rise of the Nazi party by lifting the ban on their paramilitary troops and later helped bring A. Hitler to power.

Paphlagonia   Ancient country in Asia Minor. Bounded on the north by the Black Sea, it was absorbed by Rome in 65 BC.

Papineau, Louis Joseph   1786–1871.   French-Canadian political leader. He stirred his followers in Lower Canada to rebellion against British rule (1831), shortly before the revolt led by W. Mackenzie broke out. He escaped to the US, then returned in 1844.

Papinian   *d.* AD 212.   Roman jurist. The friend and counselor of Emperor Severus, he was considered one of the great Roman jurists. He was executed by Caracalla.

Pappus   *fl.* AD c300.   Greek mathematician. His book *Synagogue* (*Collection*) records the teachings of earlier mathematicians whose original works have been lost.

Papua New Guinea (*formerly* New Guinea, Territory of)   Country consisting of the eastern part of New Guinea and adjacent islands. Capital is Port Moresby. Europeans reached New Guinea in the 15th cent. and the southeastern part of the island became (1884) the British protectorate of British New Guinea. It came under control of Australia (1905) and was renamed Papua. The northeastern part of the island was incorporated into the German possession of German New Guinea (1884) and was known as Kaiser-Wilhelmsland. Occupied (1914) by Australia during WW I, it became an Australian mandate (1920) as the Territory of New Guinea. In 1949 Papua and the Territory of New Guinea were merged, and became independent (Sept. 16, 1975) as Papua New Guinea.

papyrus   Reed plant once widely cultivated by the ancient Egyptians and used by them to make writing paper.

Paracelsus ⟨Hohenheim, Philippus Aureolus Theophrastus Bombastus von⟩ 1493–1541. Swiss alchemist and physician. Paracelsus defied (then) conventional ideas of medicine and introduced the use of particular chemicals to cure specific diseases.

Paraclete *See* **The Holy Ghost**

Paraguay ⟨Republic of Paraguay⟩ Landlocked country located in the south-central part of South America. Its capital is Asunción. Since its independence in 1811, Paraguay has been ruled almost continuously by a succession of dictators.

1526–29 Sebastian Cabot explored Paraguay for Spain.

1538 Asunción founded.

1608 Jesuit order established in region.

1617 Hernando Arias de Saavedra set up separate administrations for Paraguay and Argentina.

1721–35 Revolt of the *comuneros;* independence from Spain sought.

1767 Jesuits expelled.

1776 Region became part of the viceroyalty of the Rio de la Plata.

1811 Paraguay independent after bloodless rebellion against Spain.

1814–40 J. Francia (El Supremo) in power as first of three early dictators; instituted harsh rule.

1844–62 Carlos Antonio López in power as dictator.

1862–70 Francisco Solano López succeeded his father.

1864–70 War of the Triple Alliance against Uruguay, Brazil, and Argentina; over a million Paraguayans killed.

1870 New constitution promulgated.

1932–35 Chaco War with Bolivia over border region.

1935–38 Buenos Aires Peace Conferences granted most of Chaco region to Paraguay.

1940–48 Higinio Moringio in power as dictator.

1948 Juan Natalicio González elected president.

1949 Revolts (Jan.–Apr.) against Gonzáles and his successor; Federico Cháves assumed power.

1949–54 Cháves in power.

1953 Cháves reelected.

1954 Cháves ousted by military coup.

1954– Gen. Alfredo Stroessner in power; suppressed opposition during his long reign that continued into the early 1980s.

1965 Stroessner relaxed siege imposed when he took power; exiles returned.

1967 Constitution revised.

1978 Work begun on Itaipú dam and hydroelectric power plant (the world's largest); joint project with Brazil to be completed 1988.

Parcae *See* **Fates**

Parentucelli, Tommaso *See* **Nicholas V**

Paris ⟨Alexander⟩ In Greek mythology, son of Trojan king Priam and Hecuba. Abandoned as a baby because a prophecy warned he would bring the destruction of Troy, Paris was raised by shepherds. Paris returned to Troy and was then chosen to mediate a dispute between Aphrodite, Athena, and Hera over possession of the Apple of Discord. He gave it to Aphrodite, who in turn helped him abduct the Spartan beauty Helen, wife of King Menelaus. This sparked the Trojan War and conquest of Troy.

Paris France's capital city (pop. 2,296,900), located in north-central France. One of the great cultural and intellectual centers of the world, Paris is the commercial and industrial hub of France. Originally a Gallic village, it was conquered by J. Caesar (52 BC) and prospered under Roman influence. Paris became the capital of several Merovingian kings, notably Clovis I. Hugh Capet, duke of Paris, became king of France (AD 987), and under his influence and that of his successors the city became the capital of France, and a center of trade, learning, and culture. French King Louis XIV moved the capital to Versailles (1682). Paris was a site of struggle between the Armagnacs and Burgundians *(q.v.)* during the Hundred Years' War, and was occupied by the English (1420–36). It was the center of the massacre of St. Bartholomew's Day *(q.v.)* in 1572. Paris played a major role in the French Revolution and was occupied by allied armies (1814) after the fall of Napoleon. It was also the scene of the revolutions of 1830 and 1848. During the Franco-Prussian War (1870–71) it was occupied by the Germans, and subsequently became the site of the Commune of Paris *(q.v.)*. The Germans made an unsuccessful drive to capture Paris during WW I but occupied the city (1940–44) during WW II. In 1968 Paris was the scene of severe political disorder. It was the site of the US-Vietnam peace negotiations (1968–73).

Paris, Commune of *See* **Commune of Paris**

Paris, Congress of *See* **Congress of Paris**

Paris, Matthew ⟨Matthew of Paris⟩ d. 1259. Noted English writer of Latin chronicles of the 13th cent. A monk of St. Albans, he wrote *Chronica Majora,* a history of the world to 1259, and *Historia Anglorum,* a history of England.

Paris, Treaty of 1. Treaty (1229) between French king Louis IX and the nobleman Raymond VII of Toulouse, ending the last of the fighting sparked by the Albigensian Crusade *(q.v.)*. Louis gained the county of Toulouse and agreed to certain marriage arrangements. **2.** Treaty (Feb. 10, 1763) between Britain, France, and Spain ending the Seven Years' War (1756–63) and the subsidiary French and Indian War in the colonies. The treaty marked the ascendancy of Britain as the leading colonial power. By its terms Britain received French holdings in Canada, America (east of the Mississippi), Grenada, the Grenadines, and Senegal. Britain received Florida from Spain and returned Cuba and the Philippines to Spain, while Spain got all of the Louisiana Territory west of the Mississippi from France. Britain gave France Guadeloupe, Martinique, Miquelon, and St. Pierre. Britain also restored some French possessions in India. **3.** Treaty (Sept. 3, 1783) between the US, Britain, and other European powers ending the American Revolution (1775–83). It was negotiated by B. Franklin, J. Jay, and J. Adams for the US. By its terms Britain recognized US independence, US boundaries were fixed (at the Mississippi in the West), Spain reacquired Florida and Minorca from Britain, and France got Senegal and Tobago. The US was granted fishing rights in areas off the British-Canadian coast and was to prevent abuses against former loyalists. **4.** Treaty (May 30, 1814) between France and the allied powers who had defeated Napoleon. The terms of the treaty were not harsh and included a return of France to her borders of 1792, restoration to France of most of her colonies taken by Britain, and the loss of Malta to Britain. No indemnity was imposed and a congress was to be held at Vienna to work out final arrangements. **5.** Treaty (Nov. 20, 1815) between France and the victorious European allies after Napoleon's defeat at the end of his Hundred Days *(q.v.)*. Harsher terms were imposed and included a large indemnity, a return to the borders of 1790, and payment of expenses for an army to occupy northern France. **6.** Treaty (Mar. 30, 1856) between Russia and the allies (Ottoman Turks, Britain, France, and Sardinia) ending the Crimean War. Russia returned Kars and regained Sevastopol, ceded the mouth of the Danube and part of Bessarabia, and abandoned claims to protect Christians within the Ottoman empire. The Black Sea was declared neutral. **7.** Treaty (Dec. 10, 1898) between the US and Spain ending the Spanish-American War (1898). In return for $20 million, Spain gave up Cuba and ceded to the US the territories of the Philippines, Guam, and Puerto Rico.

Paris Peace Conference Conference (1919–20) of Allied leaders at the end of WW I to determine peace terms to be imposed on Germany and the other Central Powers—Austria, Hungary, Bulgaria, and Turkey. It resulted in the Treaty of Versailles (signed, with protest by Germany June 28, 1919), the Treaty of Saint-Germain (signed by Austria, Sept. 10) and the Treaty of Neuilly (signed by Bulgaria, Nov. 27). At the outset of the conference (Jan. 18, 1919) Allied leaders met in the Council of Ten (two representatives for each of five powers) to oversee the activities of a number of commissions charged with various aspects of the settlements (reparations, territorial questions, the League of Nations, etc.). G. Clemenceau served as president of the council. By Mar., 1919, however, a Council of Four had been formed to direct the peace conference. This council consisted of Clemenceau (France), D. Lloyd George (Britain), V. Orlando (Italy), and W. Wilson (US). A major deadlock was broken (Apr. 7) when Wilson threatened to leave the conference, and compromises on such issues as the status of the Rhineland and Danzig were reached. The League of Nations Covenant was approved (as part of the Treaty of Versailles) by the conference Apr. 28, 1919. The conference closed (Jan. 16, 1920), leaving terms of treaties with Hungary and Turkey unresolved.

Park Chung Hee 1917–79. South Korean president (1963–79). He rose to power through the military and participated in the 1961 military coup against the civilian government. Elected president in 1963, he subsequently consolidated his power and instituted a police state in Korea. During his administration, border clashes with North Korea subsided, the economy improved, Korean officials were implicated (1976–77) in charges of attempting to bribe US congressmen, and the US announced plans (1977, never implemented) to withdraw troops stationed there. Park was assassinated (Oct. 26, 1979).

Parker, Dorothy 1893–1967. American writer. Noted for her acerbic wit, she wrote short stories such as *Big Blonde,* screenplays such as *A Star Is Born,* and poetry collections such as *Enough Rope* and *Death and Taxes.*

Parker, Sir Hyde 1739–1807. British admiral. Parker's second in command at the Battle of Copenhagen *(q.v.)*, H. Nelson, was in charge of actual fighting (1801). In a famous incident during the battle, Nelson ignored Parker's order to withdraw and went on to victory. Nelson replaced Parker as commander soon after.

Parker, Capt. John *See* **Lexington and Concord, Battle of**

Parkes, Sir Henry 1815–96. Australian statesman. Parkes fought to end the practice of transporting British criminals to Australia. He was also active in promoting free trade and educational and civil service reforms.

Parkman, Francis 1823–93. American historian. Parkman lived with the Sioux, traveled the Oregon Trail, and wrote many works on American history, including *The California and Oregon Trail, A Half-Century of Conflict,* and *Montcalm and Wolfe.*

Parlement A French royal court under the Ancien Régime. There were parlements in Paris and 14 provincial cities. They combined the functions of a department of justice and appellate court, had no legislative powers, but did enjoy a certain "right of remonstrance" against royal acts.

Parlement, Fronde of the *See* **Fronde**

Parliament Legislative assembly. In Britain, Parliament consists of the reigning monarch, the House of Lords, and the House of Commons. Power rests largely with the House of Commons, the monarch being sovereign in name only and the House of Lords having lost much of its power in 1911. The prime minister is elected from the Commons. British Parliament, the oldest surviving parliament, provided the model for parliaments that were established in British dominions throughout the world. The origins of the British Parliament can be traced to the 13th-cent. royal feudal council, the Curia Regis, which gave rise to the House of Lords and to the irregular assemblages of the knights and burgesses, which gave rise to the House of Commons. Though a forerunner of Parliament (King Edward III's Model Parliament) was convened in 1295, the basic structure of Parliament did not appear until the 14th cent. Thereafter, Parliament began a long struggle for supremacy over the English monarchs, usually relying on its control of finances to force concessions. This struggle resulted in the English Civil War *(q.v.)*, in which Parliament deposed (and executed) the king and then some years later reinstituted the monarchy.

Parliament finally established its supremacy over the monarchs by the Glorious Revolution *(q.v.)* of 1688, and thereafter the monarchs' involvement in government steadily diminished. In the 18th cent., Sir R. Walpole established the prime minister as effective head of government, and in the 19th cent. the party system was firmly rooted in Parliament. The ascendancy of the House of Commons came in 1911 when, after a political crisis, the House of Lords lost its veto power over legislation (Parliament Act).

Parliament, An Admonition to the *See* **Admonition to the Parliament, An**

Parliament Act British act (1911) by which the House of Lords lost its veto power over parliamentary legislation. It was passed amid a political crisis caused by the opposition by the House of Lords to a proposed tax on the wealthy to fund a social insurance program. The bill was advanced (1909) by D. Lloyd George.

Parma, Margaret of *See* **Margaret of Parma**

Parmenides *fl.* 5th cent. BC. Greek philosopher. Parmenides was a founder and leading member of the Eleatic school. He taught that all being was one reality and that change and motion were but illusions of the senses.

Parnassians French school of poetry prominent during the 19th cent. Parnassians sought technical perfection and emotional detachment in their works, in reaction to the Romantic movement. Noted members of this school include Charles Leconte de Lisle (1818–94), S. Prudhomme, José-María de Heredia (1842–1905), and P. Verlaine.

Parnassos *See* **Parnassus**

Parnassus ⟨Parnassos⟩ Mountain located in central Greece. The ancient Greeks believed it to be the favorite haunt of Apollo, the Muses, and Dionysus.

Parnell, Charles Stewart 1846–91. Leading figure in the Irish Home Rule movement in the late 19th cent. He was elected to Parliament (1875) as a Home Rule advocate, became president of the Irish National Land League (1879), and figured prominently in agitation against landlords in Ireland. Though reaction to violent acts by Irish terrorists grew stronger (i.e., Phoenix Park murders), Parnell managed to maintain his position, used his controlling votes to oust and then restore (1886) the Liberals, and forced introduction of the unsuccessful Irish Home Rule Bill (1886). He fell from power after becoming involved in a scandal (1890–91) over an associate's wife.

Parses *See* **Parsis**

Parsifal ⟨Perceval⟩ Knight of Arthurian legend. His search for and discovery of the Holy Grail was a spiritual journey that was portrayed most notably in *Parzival*, a 13th-century poem by Wolfram von Eschenbach.

Parsis ⟨Parses⟩ Followers of Zoroastrianism in India. They migrated to India (*c*8th cent.) from Persia to escape persecution by the Muslims. In modern times they are centered around Bombay.

Parson's Cause Dispute over salaries paid to Anglican ministers in the Virginia colony during the year 1758. In that year, the colony instituted a measure that effectively reduced ministers' pay. It was struck down (1759) by the king, and the ministers subsequently sued for back pay for 1758. In the most famous of these cases, the young lawyer P. Henry defended (1763) Hanover Parish against its minister.

Parthenon Greek temple of the goddess Athena, protectoress of Athens. Built (447–432 BC) during the reign of Pericles, it was one of the greatest works of Greek Doric architecture. The structure was built on the Athenian acropolis by Ictinus and Callicrates, under supervision of the sculptor Phidias. The Parthenon was converted to a Christian church (5th cent. AD) and then to a Muslim mosque (1458). It was damaged (1687) during an attack by the Venetians on the Turks, then in control of the region. Parts of it (the Elgin Marbles) were later removed to the British Museum.

Parthenopean Republic Short-lived Italian republic. The French set up this republic after conquering the kingdom of Naples (Jan. 1799) during the French Revolutionary Wars (1792–1802). It was retaken by the British, under H. Nelson, soon afterward (June, 1799) and the Bourbon rulers were restored.

Parthia Ancient Asian country, located in what is now modern Iran. The territory was part of the Assyrian, Persian, Macedonian, and Seleucid empires before Arsaces founded the Parthian kingdom (247 BC). At its peak (1st cent. BC), the Parthian Empire extended from the Euphrates River to the Indus River and from the Oxus River to the Indian Ocean. Its decline began with defeats by the Romans (39–38 BC). The empire was taken over (AD 226) by Ardashir I, founder of the Sassanidae Empire.

Partisans Yugoslav guerrilla resistance organization that joined the Allies during WW II in fighting the Axis powers. Led by the Yugoslav Communist J. Tito, the Partisans were an effective fighting force and set up an opposition government in Yugoslavia.

Partition(s) of Poland Three successive divisions of Polish territories in the 18th cent. that resulted in complete dismemberment of Poland. **1.** First ~. Russian victories in the Russo-Turkish War of 1768 put it in a position to expand into the region of the Danube, a possibility strongly opposed by Austria. To avert war between Russia and Austria, Prussia proposed that Russia expand into Poland instead. (Poland, torn by a civil war, was unable to resist.) Russia, Austria, and Prussia agreed (Aug. 5, 1772) on the plan and each annexed parts of Poland that together amounted to one-third of Polish domains. **2.** Second ~. Liberal reforms enacted in Poland led to the formation of the Confederation of Targowica (1792) by conservative reactionaries. They asked for help to restore conservative rule, and both the Russians and Prussians invaded Poland. Russia and Prussia then instituted (Jan. 23, 1793) the second partition, leaving only the central part of Poland intact.

3. Third ~. The Poles, led by T. Kosciusko, revolted (1794) against the second partition, and Russia and Prussia put down the rebellion. Austria, Prussia, and Russia thereupon agreed to divide (Oct. 24, 1795) the remaining territory, with the major share going to Russia.

Pascal, Blaise 1623–62. French scientist and philosopher. Pascal invented the syringe, barometer, hydraulic press, and digital calculator. He contributed to the theory of probability, atmospheric pressure, and differential calculus. He converted to Jansenism (c1654).

Paschal II d. 1118. Italian-born pope (1099–1118), successor to Urban II. His reign was marked by continuing struggles over the Investiture Controversy (q.v.), first with Holy Roman Emperor Henry IV, then with Emperor Henry V.

Pashitch, Nikola See **Pašić, Nikola**

Pašić, Nikola ⟨Pashitch, Nikola⟩ 1846–1926. Serbian statesman. He founded and led the Radical party in Serbia and served several times as premier. He was Yugoslavia's first premier (1921–26).

Pasiphae Greek mythical queen, wife of Minos, king of Crete, and mother of both Ariadne and the Minotaur.

Passarowitz, Treaty of Treaty (July 21, 1718) between the Ottoman Empire and Austria and Venice, ending wars (from 1716) with Austria and Venice. Venice ceded its possessions in the Peloponnesus and Crete to the Ottomans. They in turn ceded the Banat of Temesvar, parts of Bosnia and Serbia, and Lesser Walachia to Austria.

Passchendaele, Battle of See **Ypres, Battles of**

Passy, Frédéric 1822–1912. French economist. Passy was a founder of the International League for Permanant Peace (1867). He was co-winner, with J. Dunant, of the first Nobel Peace Prize (1901).

Pasternak, Boris Leonidovich 1890–1960. Russian author. Pasternak's *Doctor Zhivago* won the Nobel Prize for Literature (1958) and the condemnation of Russian Communists. Threatened with exile, he was forced into seclusion.

Pasteur, Louis 1822–95. French chemist whose work led to the germ theory of disease. He discovered the process of pasteurization while studying fermentation in wine, vinegar, and beer. He also found a cure for two kinds of silkworm disease and used vaccination against anthrax in sheep (1881) and against rabies (1885). He headed the French Pasteur Institute for the study of rabies and other diseases.

Paston Letters Correspondence and documents of the English Paston family written during the

15th cent. They are valuable sources of information about English society during that period.

Pastor, Tony (~, Antonio) 1837–1908. American theater impresario. Pastor helped make vaudeville a respectable family entertainment. Among his star performers were Lillian Russell and Weber and Fields.

Pastry War Brief struggle (1838–39) between France and Mexico over the damages suffered by a French pastrycook during Mexico's civil disturbances. Mexico's refusal to make amends resulted in the French blockade of Veracruz and bombardment of San Juan de Ulúa (Oct. 27, 1838). By a treaty (Mar. 9, 1839), Mexico agreed to pay French claims.

Patagonia Located primarily in Argentina, a semi-arid plateau in the southernmost part of South America.

Patay, Battle of Important French victory (June 18, 1429) during the Hundred Years' War (1337–1453). Amid the general French offensive inspired by Joan of Arc, a French force under La Hire surprised and routed some 5,000 English troops under John Talbot, earl of Shrewsbury. This battle, fought at Patay in north-central France, led to the French victory in the north and made possible the crowning of Charles VII at Rheims a month later.

Patel, Vallabhbhai 1875–1950. Indian statesman. A nationalist under M. Gandhi, he took part in organizing the nonviolent demonstrations against British rule and in arranging the independence and partition of British India. He was first deputy minister of independent India (1947–50); his organizational skills were important in molding the diverse elements of India into a unified state.

Pater, Walter Horatio 1839–94. English critic and essayist noted for his devotion to ideal form and beauty, and the technical mastery of his literary style. Among his works are *Studies in the History of the Renaissance*, and *Marius the Epicurean*.

Paterson, William 1658–1719. Scottish financier. He founded and directed the Bank of England (1694–95). He formulated the ill-fated Darien Scheme (*q.v.*).

Pathé, Charles 1863–1957. French film executive. Pathé introduced T. Edison's kinetoscope to French theater audiences and pioneered (1909) the use of newsreels and screen magazines.

Pathet Lao ⟨Lao Country⟩ Laotian Communist political and military organization. Formed in 1950, the group fought the French in the 1950s, later participated in a Laotian coalition government, and, from 1961, fought a bitter civil war against the US-backed Laotian government. With the withdrawal of US forces from Southeast Asia, the Laotian government forces surrendered and the Pathet Lao took control (1975).

Pathfinder, the *See* **Frémont, John Charles**

Paton, Alan Stewart 1903–. South African writer and statesman. He wrote *Cry the Beloved Country* about his country's racial problems and helped organize the Liberal party (1953) to oppose apartheid.

patriarch Religious title. The term first referred to such early Old Testament fathers as Abraham, Isaac, Jacob, etc. The word was later used to denote bishops with jurisdiction over other bishops. The early Christian church recognized three original patriarchates, or administrative divisions: Rome, Antioch, and Alexandria. The patriarchates of Constantinople and Jerusalem were added in the 4th and 5th cents.

patricians Members of the Roman upper class. The patricians represented the wealthy, educated, privileged classes of ancient Rome. For many years only they could hold public office. By the 3rd cent. BC, however, this distinction between the patricians and the plebeians (lower class) was eliminated. Members of the new ruling aristocracy, composed of both patricians and office-holding plebeians, were called nobiles.

Patrick, Saint AD *c*385–461. Christian missionary and saint. Though much of his life is shrouded in legend, Patrick is credited with converting the Irish from paganism to Christianity. Thus he is called the Apostle of Ireland.

Patrimony of St. Peter *See* **Papal States**

Patroclus Greek mythical hero of the Trojan Wars. A friend of Achilles, Patroclus borrowed his armor and, after fighting bravely, was slain by Hector. Achilles returned to battle and avenged his friend's death by slaying Hector.

patronage *See* **spoils system**

Patterson, Eleanor Medill ⟨Gizycka, Eleanor M.⟩ 1884–1948. American editor, newspaper publisher, and writer. Among the newspapers she had an interest in were the *Chicago Tribune*, the *New York Daily News*, and the *Washington Times-Herald*.

Patterson, Joseph Medill 1879–1946. American newspaper publisher. In 1919 Patterson founded the *New York Daily News*, the first successful American tabloid.

Patton, George Smith, Jr. 1885–1945. American general, noted tank corps commander during WW II. A controversial figure, he took part in the North Africa campaign, took Palermo (1943) in the invasion of Sicily, and led his 3d Army across Europe and into Czechoslovakia. He relieved Bastogne during the Battle of the Bulge (*q.v.*).

Paul 1901–64. Greek king (1947–64), successor to his brother, George II. During his reign, Greece maintained a pro-Western stance and resisted Communist attempts to take over the country.

Paul I 1754–1801. Russian emperor (1796–1801), successor to his mother, Catherine II. On gaining the throne, he reversed many of his mother's reforms, alienated the nobility by taking steps to centralize power and, by his inconsistent foreign policy, managed to isolate Russia during the period of the French Revolutionary Wars. He was assassinated Mar. 23, 1801.

Paul II ⟨Barbo, Pietro⟩ 1417–71. Italian-born pope (1464–71), successor to Pius II. He quarreled with French King Louis XI over the Pragmatic Sanction of Bourges *(q.v.)* and vigorously opposed Bohemian King George of Podebrad for his toleration of the Hussites. Paul was also a noted patron of the arts.

Paul III ⟨Farnese, Alessandro⟩ 1468–1549. Italian-born pope (1534–49), successor to Clement VII. He sanctioned (1540) the Society of Jesus (Jesuits), initiated the Catholic Reformation *(q.v.)*, and called the Council of Trent (1545). He was a noted patron of the arts.

Paul IV ⟨Carafa, Gian Pietro⟩ Italian-born pope (1555–59). Though he succeeded in curtailing church corruption, his extreme orthodoxy negated his achievements in the Catholic Reformation. He organized the Roman Inquisition and thereby instituted a reign of terror, provoked war between France and the Spanish Hapsburgs, denounced the religious accommodation of the Peace of Augsburg *(q.v.)*, and instituted the Jewish ghetto in Rome (1555).

Paul V ⟨Borghese, Camillo⟩ 1552–1621. Italian-born pope (1605–21). He put Venice under a papal interdict (1606), though he ultimately lost his attempt to assert papal power there. He also had disputes with the French over Gallicanism *(q.v.)* and the English over King James I's oaths of allegiance to the crown.

Paul VI ⟨Montini, Giovanni Battista⟩ 1897–1978. Italian-born pope (1963–78), successor to John XXIII. Paul continued the Second Vatican Council, begun by John XXIII. But his reaffirmation of the traditional ban on birth control sparked dissension within the church.

Paul, Saint *d.* AD 67. Christian missionary and saint. Originally a Pharisee called Saul of Tarsus, he persecuted Christians until a vision and a miracle converted him. He then became a zealous missionary to the Gentiles and a founder of many churches. His epistles (letters) to his followers are included in the New Testament. He is believed to have been executed in Rome by Nero. His writings greatly influenced subsequent church doctrine.

Paulicians Heretical Christian sect. Centered mostly in Asia Minor (7th–11th cents.), they were gnostic and dualistic in doctrine, and rejected the authority of the Old Testament.

Pauling, Linus Carl 1901–. American biochemist. Pauling won a Nobel Prize in Chemistry (1954) for his theory of chemical bonding and a Nobel Peace Prize (1962) for his opposition to nuclear warfare.

Paullus, Aemilius ⟨Paulus, ~⟩ *c*229–169 BC. Roman general and consul during the Third Macedonian War. Paullus conquered the Inguani people of Liguria and later defeated Perseus of Macedonia (168 BC) at the Battle of Pydna, thereby ending the Macedonian War.

Paul of Aegina 7th cent. AD. Alexandrian physician whose great work was a compilation of the medical knowledge of his day.

Paul of Samosata *fl.* AD 260–272. Christian theologian who evolved a theory of monarchianism. He denied the Trinity and held that Jesus was but a mortal man empowered by God. His teachings were subsequently condemned by the church.

Paul the Deacon *c*725–799? Lombard priest and historian whose history of the Lombards is a valuable source of information about this Germanic people.

Paulus, Aemilius *See* **Paullus, Aemilius**

Pausanias *d. c*466 BC. Spartan general. He was the victorious commander (479) at the Battle of Plataea *(q.v.)* during the Persian Wars. Later charged with aiding Themistocles in a scheme to take power in Sparta, he took sanctuary in the temple of Athena and there starved to death.

Pausanias *fl.* AD 174. Greek geographer. His *Descriptions of Greece* is an important source of information on ancient Greek culture and topography.

Pavia, Battle of **1.** Battle (AD 476) in which the German chieftain Odoacer *(q.v.)* defeated the forces defending the last Western Roman emperor, Romulus Augustus, at Pavia (now in northern Italy). Odoacer subsequently deposed the emperor (Sept. 4, 476) and thus brought the Western Roman Empire to an end. **2.** Siege of the city of Pavia (773–774), then the Lombard capital. Frankish king Charlemagne responded to requests for aid from the pope, then being threatened by the Lombards, and drove the Lombard king Desiderius within the city walls. Desiderius finally surrendered in June, 774, and Charlegmagne made himself king of the Lombards. **3.** Major defeat for the French (Feb. 24, 1525) during the Italian Wars (1494–1559). The French army of 28,000 soldiers, led by King Francis I, was decimated by some 23,000 troops serving Holy Roman Emperor Charles V (of the Spanish Hapsburg line). Francis was captured and later forced to submit to the Treaty of Madrid *(q.v.)*.

Pavlov, Ivan Petrovich 1849–1936. Russian physiologist and psychologist. Pavlov is most famous for his studies on conditioned reflexes. He received a Nobel Prize in Medicine, 1904.

Pavlova, Anna ⟨**Pavlovna**⟩ 1882–1931. Famous Russian ballet dancer. Pavlova danced in the Ballet Russe and later formed her own company. Her great roles were in *Giselle* and *The Dying Swan*.

Pax   Roman goddess of peace. She corresponds to the Greek Irene.

Payne-Aldrich Tariff Act   American protective tariff. This 1909 bill raised some tariffs on foreign imports to protect American industries. Opposition to it by farmers figured in W. Wilson's victory in the presidential election of 1912.

Paz, Octavio 1914–. Mexican poet and diplomat. A major Latin American poet, he has published collected poems, including *La estación violenta*, and essays, including the *The Labyrinth of Solitude*.

Paz Estenssoro, Victor 1907–. Bolivian political leader and president (1952–56, 1960–64). A founder of the National Revolutionary Movement (MNR) in 1941, he became president when the MNR took power (Apr. 1952). During his term, he instituted many sweeping reforms, including granting Indians the vote, expropriation of the tin mines, and redistribution of farmlands. He was overthrown by the military (Nov., 1964).

Pazzi conspiracy   Abortive plot (Apr. 26, 1478) by the Pazzi family to depose Lorenzo de' Medici and family from power in Florence. The plot was backed by Pope Sixtus IV, who wanted to put his nephew in power. The conspirators wounded Lorenzo and killed his brother, Guiliano, but this action provoked a popular uprising against them. Thus the Medicis remained in power.

Peace Commission of 1778   *See* **Carlisle Commission**

Peace of   *See under names inverted, as in* **Pyrenees, Peace of the**

Peachtree Creek, Battle of   *See* **Atlanta Campaign**

Peale, Charles Willson 1741–1827. American painter and naturalist. Peale is best known for his portraits of G. Washington and other Revolutionary era figures.

Pea Ridge, Battle of   *See* **Elkhorn Tavern, Battle of**

Pearl Harbor   Hawaiian harbor and US naval installation, located on the island of Oahu. A treaty (1887) gave the US rights to the harbor as a coaling port and the naval station was established there (1908). The harbor is best remembered, however, for the Japanese sneak attack there Dec. 7, 1941. While US-Japanese negotiations were under way in Washington, over 100 carrier-based Japanese aircraft conducted a devastating surprise attack on the harbor. With nearly the whole US Pacific fleet moored there, Japanese bombers damaged or sank 19 ships, destroyed almost 200 airplanes, and killed over 2,000 servicemen. The raid brought a declaration of war and US entry into WW II the next day.

Pearse, Patrick Henry 1879–1916. Irish writer and patriot. Pearse promoted the use of the Gaelic language. He commanded rebel forces in the Easter Rebellion (1916) and was named president of the provisional rebel government. He was captured and executed by the British.

Pearson, Lester Bowles 1897–1972. Canadian politician. Actively involved with the UN, Pearson won a Nobel Peace Prize (1957) for his mediation of the 1956 Arab-Israeli War. He served as Canada's Liberal party prime minister (1963–68).

Peary, Robert Edwin 1856–1920. American explorer. Peary led the first expedition to reach the North Pole (1909), as well as other earlier expeditions in Greenland. His observations and writings were of considerable scientific importance in the study of arctic regions.

Peasants' Revolt   Popular uprising in England (1381) over a variety of grievances, including the poll tax and the Statute of Labourers (1351), which held down wages of a work force then decimated by the plague. Led by Wat Tyler, the rebels marched on London, took the Tower of London and beheaded the Archbishop of Canterbury. During a meeting (June 14, 1381) at Mile End, the rebels forced King Richard II to make concessions, including an end to serfdom, forced labor, and restrictions on trade. Tyler was killed at London soon afterward, however, and the revolt collapsed. Richard then rescinded the Mile End concessions.

Peasants' War   Revolt (1524–26) by the peasants and townsmen in southern Germany and Austria against the repressive policies of the nobles and clergy. Inspired in part by the Reformation and the teachings of such leaders as M. Luther and H. Zwingli, the peasants and poor townspeople formed armies to force religious and political concessions demanded by such rebel leaders as T. Münzer. Luther denounced the movement, and it was ruthlessly crushed (May 1525) in Germany. In Austria the disorders lasted until 1526.

Pease, Edward   *See* **Fabian Society**

Pecci, Gioacchino   *See* **Leo XIII**

Pedersen, Knut   *See* **Hamsun, Knut**

Pedrarias   *See* **Arias de Ávila, Pedro**

Pedro *See also* **Peter**

Pedro I 1798–1834. First emperor of Brazil (1822–31). Pedro declared Brazilian independence from Portugal (Sept. 7, 1822) and accepted a liberal constitution (1824). Later forced to abdicate to his son, Pedro II, he returned to Portugal, ousted King Miguel and restored his daughter, Maria II.

Pedro II 1825–91. Emperor of Brazil (1831–89), successor to his father, Pedro I. A man of great learning, he worked for reform. The abolition of slavery in Brazil, effected with his support in 1888, was widely opposed by landowners. A republic was declared (Nov. 15, 1889) and he died in exile

Peel, Sir Robert 1788–1850. British statesman, prime minister (1834–35, 1841–46), and founder of the Conservative party *(q.v.)*. A Tory member of Parliament (from 1809) in his early years, he effected a return to the gold standard, instituted criminal law reforms, and established the London police department (called "bobbies" after him). After his first ministry fell, he saw the need for reform, issued his Tamworth Manifesto, and formed the Conservative party. During his second ministry, he introduced an income tax and repealed the Corn Laws *(q.v.)*. The latter action brought down his government (1846).

Pegasus In Greek mythology, a winged horse born from the blood of the slain Medusa. When Bellerophan attempted to ride him to heaven, Pegasus was changed to a constellation.

Péguy, Charles 1873–1914. French poet. A noted Catholic supporter of A. Dreyfus, Péguy combined religious and Socialist thought. Among his works are *Le Mystère de la charité de Jeanne d' Arc* and *Eve*.

Pehlevi *See* **Pahlavi**

Peiping *See* **Peking**

Peipus, Battle of Lake ⟨Battle of Lake Chudskoye⟩ Decisive battle (1242) between the Russians, led by Prince Alexander Nevski of Novgorod, and the Livonian knights. The invading army of Germanic knights, attempting the conquest of Novgorod, were attacked and defeated by Alexander in a battle fought on the ice-covered Lake Peipus.

Peirce, Charles Sanders 1839–1914. American philosopher. Peirce founded the school of Pragmatism *(q.v.)*, later developed by W. James. He regarded logic as the keystone of all philosophy and knowledge.

Peking ⟨Peiping⟩ Capital city (pop. 8,500,000) of the People's Republic of China. The nation's cultural, educational, political, and transportation center, it is located on the site of several earlier cities, dating to the 1st millennium BC. As Cambuluc (Khanbalik), it was Kubla Khan's capital (13th cent.). Renamed Peking, it was China's capital from 1421 to 1912. In 1860 Peking was occupied by British and French troops and in 1900 it was the site of the Boxer Rebellion *(q.v.)*. In 1928 its name was changed to Peiping. Occupied by the Japanese (1937–45) before and during WW II, it was capital of a Japanese puppet government. It was taken by the Communists (1949), who reestablished it as China's capital and renamed it Peking. Under the Communists, Peking was greatly expanded and improved. Located in Peking is the Forbidden City *(q.v.)*, the former imperial residence.

Peking, Treaty of Treaty (Nov. 2, 1860) in which China and Russia settled the frontier border between Sinkiang and Turkestan. China also gave Russia a coastal territory, now the site of Vladivostok.

Pelagianism Christian heresy (5th cent.) as taught by the British monk Pelagius (AD c354–420?). It held that people can choose good over evil and that there is no original sin, which eliminated the need for baptism. This was in opposition to St. Augustine's claims for the necessity of grace for salvation, and Pelagius was excommunicated (418).

Pelagius *See* **Pelagianism**

Pelagius I d. 561. Italian-born pope (556–61), successor to Vigilius. Before becoming pope, he opposed Emperor Justinian's edict (544) against Nestorianism. Reconciled, he became pope and was given temporal control in Rome by Justinian.

Peleus Mythical Greek king of the Myrmidons in Thessaly and the father of Achilles. He took part in the Calydonian hunt.

Pelopidas d. 364 BC. Theban general. Pelopidas recovered Thebes from Spartan control (379 BC), commanded the elite Theban corps, the Sacred Band, at Leuctra and in other battles. He later served under Epaminondas.

Peloponnesian League Confederation of Greek city-states organized and dominated by Sparta (6th cent. BC) as a military alliance.

Peloponnesian War, first *See* **Greece** (460–445 BC)

Peloponnesian War ⟨second ~⟩ ⟨Great ~⟩ War (431–404 BC) between Sparta and Athens (and respective allied city-states) for control of Greece. Before the war Sparta held sway over most of the city-states of inland Greece (through the Peloponnesian League), while Athens controlled the Delian League, a maritime empire extending out over the Aegean. Sparta had a superior land army and Athens had a powerful navy. The two city-states had long been rivals and the intricate system of alliances with other city-states meant that even local conflicts could erupt into a general war. Though Athens entered the war with the riches of the Delian treasury to support its war effort, Sparta ultimately emerged victorious. Athens never regained its former power, and Sparta for a time became the undisputed power in ancient Greece. Key dates in the Peloponnesian War are:

435 BC Dispute between Corcyra and Corinth broke out; Corinthians defeated at the Battle of Leucimne.

433 BC Corcyra formed an alliance with Athens as Corinth, a Spartan ally, prepared to attack.

433 BC Corinthians attacked and Corcyreans were saved from defeat by Athenian intervention; Athenians forced the Corinthians to relinquish control of a colony, Potidaea.

432 BC Revolt by Potidaea put down by Athenians.

432 BC Trade embargo against Megarians further antagonized members of Sparta's Peloponnesian League (432 BC); Athens accused of breaking Thirty Years' Peace; Sparta reluctantly declared war.

431–421 BC Archidamian War, the opening phase of the war; Athenians planned to avoid land war (by remaining inside city walls) while using their navy to disrupt commerce and raid coastal towns of Peloponnesian League; Sparta planned to invade Attica each year to provoke Athenians to land battle.

431 BC Spartans advanced into Attica.

430–428 BC Plague swept Athens, decimating the population and killing the Athenian leader Pericles; Cleon succeeded.

c429 BC Athens attacked and destroyed Potidaea, which had risen against Athenian hegemony.

428 BC Athenians suppressed rebellion on Lesbos.

425 BC Athenians occupied Pylos.

424–422 BC Spartans led by Brasidas conquered Amphipolis and other cities in the north (424 BC); Athens decisively defeated in attempt to regain Amphipolis, and both Cleon and Brasidas died.

421 BC Nicias succeeded as ruler of Athens, secured short-lived truce (Peace of Nicias) marking end of first phase of conflict.

418 BC Battle of Mantineia; Sparta victorious over Mantineia, an Athenian ally.

415 BC Alcibiades contested Nicias' rule in Athens; convinced Athenians to mount campaign against the rich city of Syracuse (in Sicily) to resolve local dispute; massive Athenian fleet assembled, to be led by Alcibiades and Nicias.

415 BC Alcibiades recalled to Athens to answer charges of sacrilege; fled to Sparta and helped them against Athens; Nicias in sole command of expedition against Syracuse.

415–413 BC Syracuse decisively defeated Athenians, led by Nicias; staggering losses seriously weakened Athens.

412 BC Alcibiades took command of Spartan fleet (financed by Persia) and sailed on Athens; led to general uprising against Athens and establishment of the Four Hundred, an oligarchy, in Athens.

410 BC Alcibiades rejoined Athenians; defeated Spartan fleet at Cyzicus.

407 BC Spartan navy, led by Lysander, defeated Athenian fleet at Notium; led to final exile of Alcibiades from Athens.

406 BC Athenian fleet under Conon defeated the Spartans in the Battle of Arginusae.

405 BC Spartans destroyed the Athenian navy at the Battle of Aegospotami, the closing naval battle of the war.

405–404 BC Spartans laid siege to Athens by land and by sea; Athens forced to surrender but was spared destruction by the Spartans; Delian League broken up and government of the Thirty Tyrants imposed on Athens.

Peloponnesus Peninsula of Greece forming the southern part of the country. It is almost completely separated from mainland (central) Greece by the Gulf of Corinth. In ancient times, its major cities included Sparta and Corinth. The region was also called Morea.

Pelops Mythical Greek king. Killed by his father, Tantalus, and served to the gods for their dinner, Pelops was restored to life by the gods when they discovered Tantalus' crime. The Peloponnesus was named for Pelops.

Pemberton, John *See* **Big Black River, Battle of**

Pembroke, William Marshal, 1st earl of *d.* 1219. English nobleman. He served under the English kings Henry II, Richard I, and John. As regent for Henry III, he ended (1217) the barons' revolt begun when King John revoked the Magna Carta.

penal laws General term for the body of English laws promulgated in the 16th and 17th cents. against Roman Catholics in Britain and Ireland. An outgrowth of the English Reformation, penal laws included acts that denied Catholics the right to worship, hold public office, vote, and own land. Many of the acts were passed during the reigns of Henry VIII and Elizabeth I. The laws were overturned by the Catholic Emancipation Act (1829) and other subsequent acts.

penates *See* **lares and penates**

Pendergast, Thomas Joseph 1872–1945. American politician. Pendergast virtually ruled the Democratic party in Missouri and aided the early career of H. Truman. His power was broken by a tax-evasion conviction (1938) and subsequent imprisonment.

Pendleton Civil Service Act US law (Jan. 16, 1883) passed to end political influence and corruption in the hiring of federal government workers. Public pressure for reform had been mounting for some years. After the assassination (1881) of President J. Garfield (by a disgruntled office-seeker), this act, sponsored by Senator George H. Pendleton (1825–89), was passed. The act established civil service exams and hiring by merit and created the Civil Service Commission.

Penelope Mythical Greek matron, wife of Odysseus, mother of Telemachus, and symbol of the faithful wife. During her husband's long absence in the Trojan War, she rejected potential suitors by promising to wed when done with her weaving. She unraveled it each night.

Peninsular campaign Unsuccessful attempt (1862) by Union forces to take Richmond, Virginia, during the American Civil War. Gen. G. McClellan landed his troops on the peninsula between the York and James Rivers (Apr. 1862). McClellan, with about 100,000 men, planned to lay siege to Yorktown, the center of Confederate lines across the peninsula. However, Confederate Gen. J. Johnston withdrew (May 3) toward Richmond, and Union armies advanced to positions around White House Landing (May 16), some twenty miles from Richmond. With his forces occupying both sides of the Chickahominy River, McClellan awaited the arrival of I. McDowell, who was to march south overland from Fredericksburg. But Gen. "Stonewall" Jackson, leading only 18,000 troops, blocked McDowell's forces in the Shenandoah Valley and after defeating them at Winchester, forced McDowell to withdraw back across the Potomac (May 24). On May 31, Gen. Johnston unsuccessfully attacked the south wing of McClellan's forces at Seven Pines (q.v.) and he was seriously wounded. Finally, R.E. Lee launched attacks on Union lines for seven straight days (the Seven Days' Battles), striking at Mechanicsville (June 26), Gaines's Mill (June 27), Savage's Station (June 29), Frayser's Farm (June 30), and Malvern Hill (July 1). McClellan withdrew his forces (July 11) soon after, suffering some 16,000 casualties to almost 21,000 for the Confederates.

Peninsular War Series of military campaigns (1808–14) conducted by British, Portuguese, and Spanish forces against the French in the Iberian Peninsula during the Napoleonic Wars. The Pen-

insular War was prompted by the French invasion of Portugal (Nov., 1807) following Portugal's refusal to join Napoleon's Continental System (q.v.). The French army, under Andoche Junot (1771–1813), forced Portuguese King John VI to flee to Brazil. Meanwhile, French forces under Joachim Murat (1767?–1815) invaded Spain and occupied Madrid (Mar. 23, 1808). Spanish King Charles IV had been deposed, and the new ruler, King Ferdinand VII, was in turn deposed by Napoleon. A rebellion in Madrid (May 2) was ruthlessly crushed by Murat, and Napoleon named his brother J. Bonaparte king of Spain (June 15). In August a British army landed in Portugal. Under A. Wellesley (later duke of Wellington), the British defeated the French at Vimeiro (Aug. 21), forcing Junot to negotiate the convention of Cintra (Aug. 30), by which the French agreed to evacuate Portugal with British assistance. The British then invaded Spain. They were led by Sir John Moore (1761–1809). Napoleon returned to Spain and seized Madrid in December, and the French, under Soult, forced Moore's retreat. The British were evacuated at Coruña (Jan. 16, 1809) after a fierce battle in which Moore fell mortally wounded. Saragossa was taken by the French (Feb. 21, 1809). In April, Wellesley again forced the French out of Portugal and invaded Spain. He defeated the French at Talavera (July 28), but was again forced back into Portugal. The contest continued back and forth until 1812, when Wellesley defeated the French at Salamanca (July 22, 1812) and occupied Madrid for several months. Assuming command of all allied forces in the area, Wellesley again defeated the French at Vitoria (June 21, 1813) and began the invasion of France. The British put Bayonne under siege and defeated the French at Toulouse (Apr. 10, 1814). The Peninsular War came to an end with Napoleon's abdication (Apr., 1814).

Penitent Thief *See* **Good Thief**

Penn, William 1644–1718. English religious leader and founder of Pennsylvania. A Quaker, he obtained rights to Pennsylvania (1681), intending to establish a colony based on religious and political freedom. He planned Philadelphia, visited the area, and established friendly relations with the Indians.

Pennsylvania Middle Atlantic state of the US (pop 11,866,700), the 2nd state. Sweden formed the first settlement on Tinicum Island in 1643, but the Dutch (1655) and then the English (1664) took control of the region. The Quaker W. Penn was granted a royal charter in 1681 and established a liberal government guaranteeing religious freedom. Pennsylvania played an important role in the American Revolution and Philadelphia was the center of the new US government (1790–1800). A boundary dispute with Maryland was settled with agreement on the Mason-Dixon Line (1784). Pennsylvania became a state in 1787 and adopted its constitution in 1873.

Penry, John 1559–93. Welsh Puritan. He was convicted and executed for writing (under the pseudonym Martin Marprelate) Puritan tracts that caused the Marprelate Controversy *(q.v.).*

Pentapolis In ancient times a group of five city-states.

Pentateuch *See* **Moses**

Pentecostal churches Protestant fundamentalist churches that profess baptism with the Holy Spirit, a religious experience that may endow one with the ability to prophesy, speak in tongues, or heal by faith.

People's Budget *See* **Lloyd George, David, 1st earl Lloyd-George of Dwyfor**

People's Charter *See* **Chartism**

People's Council *See* **Volksraad**

People's Republic of China *See* **China**

Pepi I *fl.* c2343?–c2294 BC. Ancient Egyptian ruler of the 6th dynasty. He built many monuments and founded Memphis.

Pepi II *fl.* c2294–c2200 BC. Ancient Egyptian king, successor to his father, Pepi I. His reign, the longest in recorded history, was apparently about 94 years. He built the pyramid at Saqqara, near Cairo.

Pepin I *d.* 838. King of Aquitaine (817–838). The son of Louis the Pious, he joined his brother Charles the Bald in wars against their father.

Pepin of Heristal *d.* 714. Ruler of the Franks (687–714). He became mayor of the palace (680) of the Frankish kingdom of Austrasia and subsequently defeated the mayor of the palace of Neustria (687). Though he kept the Neustrian king on the throne, Pepin was effectively ruler of both states. He was father of Charles Martel and grandfather of Charlemagne.

Pepin of Landen *See* **Carolingians**

Pepin the Short 714?–768. First Carolingian king of the Franks (751–768). He and his brother Carloman succeeded their father, Charles Martel. Pepin ruled Neustria as mayor of the palace under Childeric III, who was then nominal king of all Franks. When Carloman retired to a religious life, Pepin forced Childeric into a monastery, and had himself crowned (751) as king of the Franks. In return for papal consent to his crowning, he protected Rome from the Lombards and turned over conquered Italian territories (including the Exarchate of Ravenna) to the pope in what is called the Donation of Pepin (756). These lands formed the basis for the Papal States.

Pepys, Samuel 1633–1703. English administrator and famous diarist. His diary (1660–69) provided a vivid account of the English Restoration period.

Pequot War War (1636–37) between British colonists and Pequot Indians in Connecticut. Friction between colonists and Indians had been building for some years and the murder (1636) of a colonist on Block Island was blamed on the Indians. In retaliation, the colonial militia and their Indian allies raided and burned the Pequot settlement at Mystic, Connecticut, and slaughtered almost all its 600 inhabitants. The few survivors were hunted down and likewise killed.

Perceval *See* **Parsifal**

Percier, Charles See **Fontaine, Pierre François Leonard**

Percy, Algernon, 10th earl of Northumberland 1602–68. English statesman. Percy attempted to reconcile Charles I with the Parliament. Though he eventually supported Parliament in the English Civil War, he opposed Charles' execution.

Percy, Henry, 1st earl of Northumberland 1342–1408. English nobleman. Percy assisted Henry IV in ousting Richard II. However, he later joined with his son Henry (Hotspur) Percy in an attempt to overthrow Henry (1403).

Percy, Sir Henry ⟨Hotspur⟩ 1366–1402. English nobleman. With his father, Henry Percy, 1st earl of Northumberland, he helped bring Henry IV to power and later distinguished himself in battle against the Scots. He fell out with Henry, however, and joined (1403) with his father and others against Henry. He was killed in battle at Shrewsbury.

Percy, Thomas, earl of Worcester c1344–1403. English nobleman. A son of H. Percy, earl of Northumberland, he helped bring Henry IV to power. He then joined his family in revolt (1403) against Henry and was executed.

Percy, Thomas, 7th earl of Northumberland 1528–72. English nobleman. Percy, a Catholic, plotted (1569) to invade England, rescue the Catholic Mary Queen of Scots, and end the Protestant rule of Elizabeth I. The plan failed and he was beheaded.

Perdiccas *d.* 321 BC. Macedonian general and regent of the empire after the death (323 BC) of Alexander the Great. Perdiccas was killed by his troops while leading a military expedition into Egypt against another of Alexander's generals, Ptolemy. (*See also* Diadochi.)

Pereira, Nuno Alvares 1360–1431. Portuguese general and hero who figured in King John's victory against the Castilians at the Battle of Aljubarrota *(q.v.)*.

Peretti, Felice *See* **Sixtus V**

Pérez, Antonio 1534?–1611. Spanish politician and intriguer, secretary to Spanish King Philip II. He apparently turned Philip against Juan de Escovedo, secretary to the governor of the Spanish Netherlands, and arranged Escovedo's murder. Philip later prosecuted Pérez, who escaped to the Spanish kingdom of Aragón and raised an abortive revolt (1590–91) against Philip.

Pérez de Ayala, Ramón 1880–1962.   Spanish writer, one of the leading Spanish novelists of this century. His works include *Balarmino and Apolonio*, *The Peace of the Path*, and *Tiger Juan*.

Pérez Jiménez, Marcos 1914–. President of Venezuela (1952–58). An army colonel, he took part in the military coup of 1948, was part of the provisional government, and then became president. He ruthlessly suppressed opposition and was later convicted of corrupt practices. He was overthrown (Jan., 1958).

Perga, Apollonius of *See* **Apollonius of Perga**

Pergamum Ancient city in northern Asia Minor, the capital of the kingdom of Mysia and one of the greatest cultural centers of the Hellenistic civilization. Pergamum was governed by the Attalid dynasty and under them became the center of a great empire. The rulers Attalus I (d. 197 BC), Eumanes II (d. 160 BC), and Attalus II (d. 138 BC) allied themselves with Rome against the Seleucids and Syrians and thereby expanded the domains of Mysia to include most of Asia Minor. The city flourished as a cultural and commercial center of Asia, and a great library was founded there. Attalus III, who died (133 BC) without heirs, bequeathed Mysia to the Romans. They subsequently reorganized the kingdom into the province of Asia with Pergamum as its capital.

Peri, Jacopo 1561–c1633. Italian composer. Peri participated in writing what is generally considered the first true opera, *Dafne* (c1597). The work is now lost.

Periander d. 585 BC. Tyrant of Corinth (625–585 BC). His reign was harsh, but Corinth enjoyed commercial prosperity and a cultural flowering under his rule. He is one of the Seven Wise Men of Greece.

Pericles c495–429 BC. Athenian statesman and general, a member of the Alcmaeonidae family. Pericles secured the ostracism of his two chief enemies, Cimon and Thucydides, and thereafter became the leader of Athens. He ended war with Persia (448), asserted Athenian domination over member states of the Delian League, and arranged a truce with Sparta (445). In this period of peace,

Pericles strengthened the Athenian navy and completed fortifications at Athens and Piraeus, instituted reforms that strengthened the Athenian democracy, patronized the arts, and embarked on a great program of building that glorified Athens with such structures as the Parthenon and the Propylaea. He figured in the events that resulted in the Peloponnesian War *(q.v.)*, was ousted from power soon after it began, but was restored shortly before his death.

Perier, Casimir Pierre 1777–1832. French statesman. Perier led the opposition to Charles X, was prime minister (1831–32) to Louis Philippe, and restored order in France following the upheavals of 1830.

Permanent Court of Arbitration *See* **International Court of Justice**

Permanent Court of International Justice *See* **International Court of Justice**

Perón, Juan Domingo 1895–1974.   Argentine president (1946–55, 1973–74) and nationalist. Perón began his career in the army and became minister of war and vice-president (1945). During the early part of his presidency, he and his wife Eva were popular with the workers and were able to make many economic and political changes, in a reform program called the *peronismo*. His regime became increasingly totalitarian and anticlerical, however, and he was deposed (Sept. 1955). He lived in Spain until his brief return to power in 1973.

Perón, María Estela Martínez de ⟨Isabel Perón⟩ 1931–. President of Argentina (1974–76). The second wife (m. 1961) of J. Perón, she was his vice-president (1973–74) and succeeded him after he died in office. She was ousted by a military coup.

Perón, María Eva Duarte de ⟨Evita⟩ 1919–52. Argentine political leader, the wife of President J. Perón (m. 1945). Popular with the masses, she wielded great political power during her husband's first term. She effected many reforms, including voting rights for women.

peronismo *See* **Perón, Juan Domingo**

Perrault, Charles 1628–1703.   French poet whose collection of Mother Goose fairy tales for children is world famous. He also precipitated the great literary dispute (called the "quarrel of the ancients and moderns") with his poem *The Age of Louis the Great* (1687), in which he placed authors of his own age above the great figures of classical times.

Perry, Matthew Calbraith 1794–1858. American naval officer. Perry commanded a US naval mission that forced Japan to accept a treaty opening her ports to Western trade (1854).

Perry, Oliver Hazard 1785–1819.   American naval officer and hero of the War of 1812. He defeated the British at the Battle of Lake Erie and is remembered for reporting his victory with "we have met the enemy and they are ours."

Persephone Greek goddess of fertility, daughter of Zeus and Demeter. Pluto abducted her and confined her to the underworld. She was eventually allowed to return for eight months of each year, spending the other four months (thus winter) in the underworld.

Persepolis Ancient Persian city. Persepolis was a capital of the Achaemenid rulers. It was sacked by Alexander the Great (c330 BC).

Perseus Greek mythical hero who slew the Medusa with weapons given him by the gods. He then rescued and married Andromeda.

Perseus c212–166 BC. Macedonian king (179–168 BC), successor to his father, Philip V. His attempts to restore Macedonian hegemony in Greece led to the Third Macedonian War (q.v.) with Rome and his defeat at the Battle of Pydna (q.v.). He was the last Macedonian king.

Pershing, John Joseph 1860–1948. American general. He won notable victories in the Philippines during the Spanish-American War, led the unsuccessful expedition against F. (Pancho) Villa (1916–17) in Mexico, and commanded the American Expeditionary Force (q.v.) during WW I.

Persia Historic empire of ancient origins centered in modern Iran and at times extending well into southwest Asia. The modern successor state to this empire is Iran. Persia began its rise to prominence in about the 7th cent. BC and by the 6th cent. BC had become the dominant power of the ancient Near Eastern world. After the 5th cent. BC, the power and fortunes of the empire rose and fell. Persia was conquered variously, notably by the Macedonian Greeks and the Muslims, and its vast domains were greatly reduced. Persia nevertheless developed a distinctive culture which drew on Greek, Muslim, and other influences. After a long period of control by Arab Muslims and Turkic peoples, Persia again emerged in the 16th cent. as an independent empire. Modernization began in the early 20th cent., and in 1935 Persia was officially renamed Iran. (For subsequent history, see Iran.) Key dates in the history of Persia include:

c1500 BC Medes and Persians migrated to the Iranian plateau.

c700 BC Achaemenes founded Persian kingdom and the Achaemenid dynasty of Persian kings; kingdom was dominated by Media until 6th cent. BC.

c628–c551 BC Zoroaster lived; founded Zoroastrianism, which became the religion of Persia in following centuries.

c600–559 BC Cambyses I reigned; his son was Cyrus the Great.

558–529 BC Cyrus (the Great) reigned; established Persian dominance over Media and Elam and greatly expanded Persian power and territory; borrowed freely from Assyrian and Babylonian cultures.

546 BC Cyrus conquered Lydia in Asia Minor.

539 BC Cyrus conquered Babylonia; Babylonian captivity of the Jews ended.

529–522 BC Cambyses II reigned; murdered his brother Smerdis to secure his power and then pursued successful campaign to conquer Egypt; a false Smerdis seized throne (522) and Cambyses died on return from Egypt.

522–486 BC Darius I (the Great) reigned after seizing power from the false Smerdis; put down revolts within the empire and reorganized domains into satrapies, or administrative districts; instituted effective communications system using horses; extended empire into northern India and ranged into Europe.

499–479 BC Persian Wars; Darius and his successor Xerxes failed in their attempt to subjugate the Greeks, though Persia continued to influence affairs of Greek city-states in subsequent years.

486–465 BC Xerxes I reigned; lost Persian Wars and fell into dissolute life at Susa; decline of empire began; Xerxes assassinated.

464–425 BC Artaxerxes I reigned; put down revolt in Egypt (460–454 BC), permitted Jews to worship at Judaea, kept Persia out of the Peloponnesian War in Greece.

405 BC Egypt successfully revolted against Persian rule.

404–359 BC Artaxerxes II reigned; rule plagued by many revolts; royal palace at Susa rebuilt.

401 BC Great rebellion by Cyrus the Younger, satrap of Asia Minor; led army against Artaxerxes II; Cyrus defeated and killed at battle of Cunaxa; famous retreat by Greek soldiers (under Xenophon) who had fought for Cyrus.

359–338 BC Artaxerxes III again subjugated Egypt (343 BC) after initial unsuccessful campaigns.

336–330 BC Darius III reigned; failed to halt advance of Alexander the Great.

334 BC Darius defeated by Macedonian Greeks under Alexander at Battle of Granicus.

333 BC Battle of Issus: Alexander again defeated Darius.

331 BC Darius decisively defeated at Battle of Gaugamela; long rule of Achaemenid dynasty ended; Darius fled to Bactria.

330 BC Darius assassinated in Bactria.

323–281 BC Wars of the Diadochi; Alexander's generals warred for control of his empire after his death; most of Persia came under Seleucid rule.

312–64 BC Seleucid dynasty, established by Seleucid I, ruled over much of ancient Persian Empire; at its height it included Babylon, Persia, Syria, Bactria, and part of Asia Minor, though control was weak and domains were gradually reduced to Syria; Seleucids introduced Hellenic (Greek) culture to Persia.

3D CENT. BC Bactria overthrew Seleucid rule; became independent kingdom.

247 BC–AD 224 Parthian Empire founded (south of Caspian Sea) by Arsaces I; after overthrowing Seleucid rule, Parthians dealt with nomadic invasions from northeast and successfully blocked eastward advance of Romans; Parthians pushed their empire westward to Mesopotamia.

64 BC Last of Seleucid domains (Syria) conquered by Romans under Pompey; Persia (proper) under Parthian rule.

AD 224–640 Sassanid dynasty reigned in Persia; empire at its greatest extent reached Indus Valley in east and Mesopotamia in west; Persian culture flourished; many buildings and roads constructed.

AD 226–241 Ardashir I reigned; established Zoroastrianism as state religion; built many cities.

AD 241–272 Shapur I reigned; a successful conqueror, he gained parts of Asia Minor and in wars with Rome took Syria and part of Mesopotamia; captured Emperor Valerian.

AD 293–302 Narses reigned; lost substantial territory to the Roman Empire.

AD 309–379 Shapur II reigned; regained much of the territory lost to the Romans by Narses.

AD 399–420 Yazdegerd I reigned; Christians in Persian domains persecuted.

531–579 Khosru I reigned; Sassanid Empire brought to its greatest extent through successful wars against Byzantines (in time of Justinian and Justin II); reformed administration; literature flourished.

590–628 Khosru II reigned; warred against the Byzantines; initially successful, he occupied Egypt and threatened Constantinople; defeated by the Byzantine Heraclius (622–628).

632–651 Yazdegerd III, last Sassanian ruler, reigned; Persian Empire conquered by the Arabs and absorbed into the Caliphate Empire; Islam introduced into region in place of Zoroastrianism.

819–999 Samanid dynasty in power, native Persian dynasty ruling over Transoxania and Khorasan (in northeast Iran) under nominal control of the Muslim caliphs; Persian culture flourished.

999–1186 Ghaznavid dynasty reigned; this Turkish dynasty took control of much of Samanid Empire (west of river Oxus) and extended empire eastward, eventually embracing Afghanistan and part of India.

11TH–14TH CENT. Seljuks, Muslim Turks, dominated the domains of the Empire of the Caliphate, including Persia.

13TH–16TH CENT. Mongol conquests; Empire of the Caliphate fell to the Mongols (1258); there followed a period of rule by Mongols, Timurs, and Turkmen.

1501–24 Ismail reigned after establishing new Persian Empire; founded Safavid dynasty; established Shi'ite Islam as state religion.

1501–1736 Safavid dynasty in power; engaged in long series of wars with Ottoman Turks and Uzbeks.

1586–1629 Abbas I (the Great) reigned; regained Persian territories lost in wars with Ottoman Turks and Uzbeks; captured Baghdad (1623); encouraged art, trade, and public works.

1722–30 Afghan interlude; Persia under control of Afghans after being defeated by Mir Mahmud.

1724 Russia and Turkey seized portions of Persian Empire.

1730 Nadir Kuli defeated Afghans and forced them from Persia.

1736–47 Nadir Shah reigned; recaptured Persian territories from Russia and Ottoman Empire; invaded India (1738–39).

1794–97 Agha Muhammad reigned as shah; founded Kajar dynasty (ruled 1794–1925); reign noted for its cruelty and repression.

1797–1835 Fath Ali reigned as shah; power of the shah declined as both Russia and Britain sought to dominate Persia; Persia began to lose territories; signed disadvantageous treaty of Gulistan with Russia (1813).

1828 Persia ceded lands in Armenia to Russia by the Treaty of Turkmanchay, following Russo-Turkish War of 1826–28.

1856–57 War with Britain; seizure of Persian lands by Afghanistan provoked war with Afghanistan; Britain interceded, defeated Persia, and forced it to recognize Afghan independence.

1901 Britain was granted oil concession; discovery of oil led to increased rivalry between Britain and Russia over Persia.

1906 Shah Muzaffar-ed-Din established first Persian majlis, or national assembly; liberal constitution drawn up.

1907–09 Muhammad Ali reigned as shah; attempted forcibly to overthrow the constitution (1909) and was deposed.

1909–25 Ahmed Shah reigned; last of the Kajar dynasty.

1914–18 WW I; Persia occupied by British and Russian forces.

1919 Persia signed agreement giving Britain control over Persia while recognizing Persian independence; agreement repudiated in 1921.

1920 Became a member of the League of Nations.

1921 British began withdrawing troops from Persia.

1921 Reza Khan became prime minister by a coup (Feb. 21).

1921 Treaty with the Soviets; Soviets agreed to withdraw from Persia.

1925 Ahmed Shah deposed by majlis (Oct. 31); Prime Minister Reza Khan made shah (Dec. 13).

1925–41 Reza Shah Pahlevi reigned; began modernization and Westernization of Persia.

1935 Persia renamed Iran (Mar. 21).

Persian Wars Series of military campaigns conducted by the Persians against the Greeks, beginning in 499 BC. The wars were sparked by a revolt of the Ionian Greeks against Persian rule (499). The cities of Athens and Eretria aided the Ionian Greeks, but the revolt was crushed (494) by Persian king Darius. Darius then sent a large force to punish Athens and Eretria. The Persians took Macedon and Thrace (492), but their fleet was badly damaged by storms and they were obliged to withdraw. A second expedition occupied Eretria, but while attempting to advance upon Athens, the Persians were defeated at Marathon *(q.v.)* in 490, by an Athenian force led by Miltiades.

Darius gathered a massive third expeditionary force, but died (486) before it could move against Greece. The expedition was conducted by his son and successor, Xerxes I, who landed in Greece in 480. The Persians were delayed at Thermopylae *(q.v.)* by a small Spartan force under Leonidas, and although the Persians took Athens, their navy was destroyed at Salamis *(q.v.)* in 480. Xerxes returned to Persia but left an army in Greece under Mardonius. The Greek victory over Mardonius at Plataea (479) and destruction of the Persian fleet at Mycale that year marked the end of Persia's military campaigns against mainland Greece. After 479, sporadic fighting between the Greeks and Persians continued until a peace was concluded (c449). The wars between Persia and the Greek city-states resulted in the decline of Persian power and the rise of Greek power.

Persius ⟨Flaccus, Aulus Persius⟩ AD 34–62. Roman satirical poet. Persius was a Stoic whose works attacked the loose moral standards of his day. His works, published posthumously, were a great success.

Peru ⟨Republic of Peru⟩ Country located in western South America. Its capital is Lima. Peru was the center of the vast Inca Empire conquered (16th cent.) by the Spanish. From the mid-16th cent. until Peru achieved independence, Lima was the seat of Spanish rule in South America. Peru was also a major source of silver and gold. Since independence, Peru has had a history of political instability. Key dates in Peruvian history include:

12TH CENT. Incas, "people of the sun," settled around Cuzco.

15TH CENT. Extensive empire carved out by the Incas; included most of Peru and Ecuador and parts of neighboring countries; centered in Cuzco.

c1530–32 Civil war between Atahualpa and Huascar, sons of the Inca ruler Huayna Capac (ruled 1487–1525); Huascar defeated and executed by Atahualpa, who became sole ruler.

1532 Spanish conquistador F. Pizarro arrived; seized and imprisoned Atahualpa and collected a huge ransom in gold and silver.

1533 Atahualpa executed by Pizarro; Cuzco captured; Indian peoples subsequently forced to work in mines and on Spanish lands, under system called *encomienda.*

1535 Lima founded by Pizarro.

1536–44 Manco Capac, new Inca emperor, led unsuccessful revolts against the Spanish.

1537–38 Warfare between the Spanish conquerors; Pizarro defeated forces led by P. Alvarado and Diego de Almagro; Almagro executed.

1541 Assassination of Pizarro by supporters of Almagro.

1542 Vaca de Castro, representing the Spanish crown, restored order among the Spanish rulers.

1542 Lima made center of Spanish rule and capital of viceroyalty of Peru, eventually including all of Spanish South America except Venezuela.

1542 "New Laws for the Indies," inspired by B. de las Casas, promulgated; designed to alleviate the hardship of the forced labor imposed on the Indians by the Spanish.

1544–48 Pizarro's brother, Gonzalo, led revolt against the New Laws; though he was defeated, the laws were subsequently not enforced.

1718 Viceroyalty of Peru reduced in size by creation of viceroyalty of New Granada.

1776 Peruvian territory further reduced by creation of the viceroyalty of Rio de la Plata.

1781 Tupac Amuru's Incan revolt against Spain failed; he and his family executed.

1808 Napoleon conquered Spain; led to rise of independence movements throughout South America.

1821 Peruvian independence proclaimed at Lima (July 28), though Spanish royalist forces had not yet been completely defeated.

1822 Guayaquil Conference (July); S. Bolívar took over leadership of South American independence movement from J. San Martín.

1824 Battle of Ayacucho (Dec. 9); Bolívar secured Peruvian independence by decisively defeating Spanish royalists.

1836–39 Peru and Bolivia united in a confederation; opposed by Chile, the confederation was defeated at the Battle of Yungay and broken up.

1844–62 Gen. Ramón Castilla in office as president (except 1850–55); his administration marked by economic development and stability.

1864–66 War with Spain; Spain attacked Peru after Peru failed to meet financial obligations; Spanish driven out.

1860 Republican constitution adopted.

1879 Peru's independence formally recognized by Spain.

1879–84 War of the Pacific; Peru lost valuable mineral-rich lands to Chile; government nearly bankrupt after war.

1883–1929 Tacna-Arica Controversy; prolonged territorial dispute with Chile; ultimately resolved along lines suggested by US president H. Hoover.

1908–30 Augusto Leguía in power as dictator (except 1912–19); promoted further economic development.

1924 V. Haya de la Torre founded the radical APRA party.

1933–39 Gen. Oscar Benavides ruled as dictator.

1939–45 Manuel Prado y Ugarteche in office as president.

1945–48 President José Luís Bustamante y Rivero in office after first free elections in many years; overthrown by military after split with APRA party.

1948–56 Gen. Manual Odría in office.

1963–68 Fernando Belaúnde Terry in office after elections run by military.

1968 Belaúnde Terry ousted; inflation and refusal to take over American-owned oil fields blamed.

1968–75 Gen. Juan Velasco Alvarado in power; head of a revolutionary military government aiming at "democratizing" Peruvian society.

1970 50,000 people killed in earthquake in northern Peru.

1975 Military quelled rioting in Lima (Feb.) that resulted from police strike.

1975 Gen. Francisco Morales Bermuúdez ousted Gen. Juan Velasco Alvarado from presidency in bloodless coup (Aug. 29).

1978 Unrest resulted from sharp rise in food prices after government imposed austerity measures (May).

1979 Peru's financial situation greatly improved by austerity measures and greater returns on exports (including oil); foreign loans repaid.

1980 Fernando Belaúnde Terry installed as president, ending over a decade of military rule.

1981 Cease-fire ended border clashes with Ecuador (Feb.); agreed to international arbitration of dispute.

Perugino c1445–1523. Italian painter. Perugino assisted in the decoration of the Sistine Chapel and was the teacher of Raphael.

Peruzzi, Baldassarre 1481–1536. Italian architect and painter. Peruzzi was appointed an architect of St. Peter's Cathedral after Raphael's death. He was noted for his work on the Palazzo Massini at Rome.

Pestalozzi, Johann Heinrich 1746–1827. Swiss educational reformer. Pestalozzi was concerned with the education of deprived children. His use of concrete experience, as opposed to rote learning, in teaching still influences educational theory today.

Pétain, Henri Philippe 1856–1951. French marshal. Though a hero at Verdun in WW I, Pétain collaborated with the Nazis and became head of the French Vichy government during WW II. He was imprisoned for life after the war.

Peter d. AD 64? Apostle, pope, and saint. According to the Bible Peter, a fisherman of Galilee was originally known as Simon. He was chosen by Jesus to be the first leader (pope) of his disciples. During Jesus' crucifixion, Peter denied knowing him, an act that Jesus had predicted and that Peter bitterly repented. After word of Jesus' ascension to heaven, Peter actively sought converts, and is believed to have been crucified, head downward, in Rome by Nero. In the Roman Catholic church, he is considered the first pope.

Peter I (Peter the Great) 1672–1725. Russian czar (1682–1725), successor to his father, Alexis. Peter's reign was dominated by his efforts to modernize and Westernize Russia. He brought Russia into the European sphere, created the first Russian navy, took measures to control the nobility, improved the position of women, reduced the power of the clergy, and imported Western technology.

Other events of his reign included Russo-Turkish Wars, and the Northern War with Sweden (1700–21). He also created a new capital city, St. Petersburg, on the Baltic.

Peter I 1844–1921. King of Serbia (1903–18) and king of the Serbs, Croats, and Slovenes (1918–21). Peter supported a constitutional monarchy and expanded Serbian domains in the Balkan Wars (q.v.). His son, Alexander, was his regent from 1914.

Peter II 1648–1706. King of Portugal (1683–1706), successor to Alfonso VI. Peter concluded the treaty of Lisbon (Feb., 1683), by which Spain recognized Portugal's independence, and failed in his attempt to keep Portugal out of the War of the Spanish Succession.

Peter II 1715–30. Czar of Russia (1727–30), successor to Catherine I. Only 11 at his accession, he was manipulated by the Dolgoruki family. They arranged the arrest of Catherine's former adviser, A. Menshikov, and moved the capital (1728) to Moscow.

Peter II 1923–70. King of Yugoslavia (1934–45), successor to his father, Alexander, and Yugoslavia's last king. He fled after the Nazi invasion (1941) and while still in exile was deposed (Nov., 1945) in favor of a republic headed by J. Tito.

Peter III 1717–86. King of Portugal (1777–86). He was crowned with his niece, Maria I, and the two ruled jointly. Both were unfit for rule, however, and the government was run by others.

Peter III 1728–62. Czar of Russia (1762), successor to his aunt, Elizabeth. Soon after taking power, Peter removed Russia from the Seven Years' War and alienated both the church and the nobles. His wife thereupon conspired in his overthrow (June 9, 1762) and succeeded him as Catherine II (the Great). Peter was killed a short time later.

Peter IV 1319?–87. King of Aragon (1336–87). He put down a revolt by Aragonese nobles and later revoked the privileges granted to them by Alfonso III.

Peter V 1837–61. King of Portugal (1853–61), successor to Maria II. He ended slavery in Portuguese territories (1858), promoted education and the beginnings of industrialization. His reign was troubled by outbreaks of cholera and yellow fever epidemics.

Peter Lombard c1100–c1160. Italian bishop and theologian. Lombard wrote the *Books of Sentences*, a compilation of early Christian theology that dealt primarily with the nature of the sacraments.

Peterloo massacre Demonstration that was suppressed at St. Peter's field, in England (Aug. 16, 1819). Some 60,000 demonstrators, petitioning for parliamentary reform and repeal of the corn laws (q.v.), were dispersed by a cavalry charge. The action killed six, while injuring more than 400. Popular outrage fueled the drive for reform.

Peters, Carl *See* **Tanganyika**

Petersburg Campaign Concluding action of the American Civil War, fought (June, 1864–Apr., 1865) at Petersburg, Virginia. After the Battle of Cold Harbor, Gen. U. Grant maneuvered around Confederate lines for an attack on Petersburg, which defended the nearby Confederate capital of Richmond. Grant's advance elements were stalled by a small Confederate force under Gen. P. Beauregard, giving Gen. R. Lee time to move up his troops. The battle for Petersburg thereupon degenerated into a long siege and months of grueling trench warfare. Outnumbered, short of supplies, and plagued by desertions, the Confederates held out for ten months before their resistance was broken. After their victory at the Battle of Five Forks (q.v.), the Union armies finally breached Confederate lines the next day (Apr. 2). Gen. Lee began his retreat along the Appomattox River that night and the Union forces took both Petersburg and Richmond (Apr. 3). Lee was forced into final surrender at Appomattox Courthouse (q.v.) on Apr. 9.

Peter the Cruel 1334–69. King of Castile and León (1350–69). Peter was frequently challenged by his illegitimate half-brother Henry of Trastamara, who finally defeated and killed him.

Peter the Great *See* **Peter I**

Peter the Hermit c1050–1115. French religious leader. By his preaching, he won over thousands to the First Crusade (q.v.) and led one of the ill-equipped bands of zealous citizens to Byzantium. His followers were largely wiped out in the early stages of fighting in Asia Minor.

Petite Chouannerie *See* **Chouans**

Petition of Right English parliamentary act (May, 1628), a part of the power struggle between Charles I and Parliament. Prompted by Sir E. Coke, it was intended to stop abuses of power by Charles and included an end to arbitrary arrest and imprisonment, the quartering of soldiers in civilian homes, taxation without parliamentary approval, and the use of martial law in peacetime. Charles agreed to it (June, 1628) in return for money grants he needed to prosecute his foreign wars, then promptly violated it. Nevertheless, the petition is important in English constitutional law.

Petöfi, Sándor 1822–49. Hungarian poet and national hero. Petöfi's many patriotic poems encouraged the Hungarian revolt (1848). He apparently died in battle during the revolt.

Petra Ancient city, located in what is now Jordan. Once the capital of the Nabataeans, it was taken by the Romans in AD 106. The city nevertheless continued as a trade center until the rise of Palmyra displaced it.

Petrarca, Francesco *See* **Petrarch, Francesco**

Petrarch, Francesco ⟨Petrarca, Francesco⟩ 1304–74. Italian Renaissance poet and scholar, Petrarch was one of the greatest scholars and lyric poets of his age and proved to be a major influence in spreading Greek ideals, humanism, and other elements of early Renaissance thought. His sonnets, songs, and madrigals in honor of Laura, his ideal woman, greatly influenced Renaissance poetry.

Petrie, Sir William Matthew Flinders 1853–1942. British archaeologist. Petrie developed many archaeological research techniques and conducted many excavations in Egypt, Palestine, and elsewhere.

Petrograd *See* **Leningrad**

Petronius ⟨Petronius Arbiter⟩ *d.* AD *c*66. Roman satirist. His self-indulgent love of luxury made him social arbiter at Nero's court. He is believed to have written *Satyricon,* which humorously depicted the vulgar sensuality of his times.

Petronius Arbiter *See* **Petronius**

Petrović, George *See* **Karageorge**

Phaedra Mythical Greek princess. Though she was the wife of Theseus, she made advances to his son Hippolytus. Rebuffed, she accused him of rape. He was executed and she committed suicide.

phalanx Greek infantry formation. A phalanx consisted of parallel rows (usually eight) of soldiers in a solid block. It was used with great success for many centuries by the Greeks. The Romans, however, overcame the Greek phalanxes in the Macedonian Wars.

Phansigars *See* **Thugs**

Pharaoh Title of Egyptian kings. The title, meaning "the great house," was bestowed on all kings of ancient Egypt from the time of the New Kingdom.

Pharisees Ancient Jewish religious and political party that began in the 2nd cent. BC. Pharisees emphasized strict observance of the oral as well as the written laws (the Torah), as opposed to their opponents, the Sadducees, who taught only the written law. Reference to them in the New Testament as hypocrites pertains only to those who did not live up to their own strict standards. The Pharisees disappeared after destruction of the Temple (AD 70), but both Orthodox Judaism and Christianity were influenced by their beliefs.

Pharsalus, Battle of Decisive victory (Aug. 9, 48 BC) for J. Caesar over his rival Pompey at this Greek town in Thessaly. Caesar's force of 20,000 was outnumbered more than two to one, but his tactical genius turned the tide. Pompey lost some 15,000 casualties while Caesar's army suffered about 1,200. Pompey fled to Egypt, where he was murdered. This eliminated Caesar's most powerful opponent to his seizing of power in Rome.

Pheidias *See* **Phidias**

phenomenology Philosophical school developed by E. Husserl. Its followers attempted to suspend preconceived notions about the natural world in order to understand and describe events (phenomena) from within the conscious mind. Phenomenology influenced the development of existentialism.

Phidias ⟨Pheidias⟩ *c*500–*c*432 BC. Famed Athenian sculptor. Phidias was in charge of art and public works in Athens under Pericles. Phidias is believed to have been in charge of sculptures for the Parthenon *(q.v.)* and to have executed noted statues of Athena and Zeus.

Philadelphia Historic city (pop. 1,688,200) in Pennsylvania. A major port on the Delaware and Schuylkill rivers, it is a commercial, cultural, and industrial center. It began as a Swedish colony (1640s), becoming a Quaker colony (1681) under William Penn. It grew rapidly and became the dominant cultural center in Colonial times. In Philadelphia the Continental congresses met, the Declaration of Independence was signed in Independence Hall (1776), and the U.S. Constitution was adopted in 1787. It was US capital (1790–1800) and state capital (1790–99).

Philadelphia Convention *See* **Constitutional Convention**

Philadelphus, Ptolemy II *See* **Ptolemy II**

Philaret, Vasily Drosdov *See* **Edict of Emancipation**

Philby, Harold Adrian Russell ⟨Kim Philby⟩ 1912–. British intelligence officer who doubled as a Soviet spy (1933–51). As secretary of the British embassy in Washington (1949–1951) he dispatched vital information concerning the US Central Intelligence Agency. In 1963 he escaped to the Soviet Union.

Philip Name of two saints of the early Christian Church: Philip the Apostle of Jesus, and Philip who was a deacon and evangelist in Samaria and Ethiopia.

Philip ⟨~ the Arabian⟩ AD 204?–249. Roman emperor (244–49). A soldier under Gordian III, Philip executed him, made himself emperor, and ended war with Persia. He presided over the millennial celebration of the founding of Rome. He was overthrown by one of his soldiers, Decius.

Philip ⟨Metacomet⟩ *d.* 1676. The son of Massasoit, he was the leader of Indians in New England during King Philip's War *(q.v.)*. He was killed in battle.

Philip I (of Portugal) *See* **Philip II (of Spain)**

Philip I 1052–1108. Capetian king of France (1060–1108), successor to Henry I. Throughout his reign Philip struggled to prevent the union of England and Normandy, which would overpower France. He was excommunicated by Urban II for disavowing his first marriage and remarrying. His conflict with the church lasted until 1104.

Philip I ⟨Philip the Handsome⟩ 1478–1506. Duke of Burgundy, king of Castile (1506), and founder of the Spanish Hapsburg line. The son of Holy Roman Emperor Maximilian I, he succeeded (1482) as Duke of Burgundy (including The Netherlands) and then married Joanna, daughter of Spanish king Ferdinand II. Later, Philip forced Ferdinand to recognize (1506) his claim to the throne of Castile (as Joanna's husband) but died soon thereafter. Philip's son eventually succeeded in Spain, however, and then became the great Hapsburg Holy Roman Emperor Charles V.

Philip II 382–336 BC. Macedonian king (359–336 BC), whose conquest of Greece laid the foundation for the great Macedonian empire established by his son, Alexander the Great. From 357 BC, Philip embarked on his program of expansion by war and alliances and defeated his last opponents in Greece (Athens and Thebes) in the Battle of Chaeronea (338 BC). He was killed while preparing to invade Persia.

Philip II ⟨Philip Augustus⟩ 1165–1223. French king (1179–1223), successor to his father, Louis VII. Philip was the first powerful Capetian king and more than doubled his domains by conquering parts of Flanders and by taking English possessions on the Continent (Angevin domains). Philip at first involved himself in intrigues between English king Henry II and his sons, Richard and John. Next, he and Richard (then king) embarked on the Third Crusade. They quarreled, and Philip returned and unsuccessfully attempted to take Richard's lands on the Continent. During John's reign, however, Philip finally conquered (1204) Normandy, Brittany, Anjou, Maine, and Touraine. Then, by his victory (1214) at the Battle of Bouvines *(q.v.)*, he established France as a major power. He also instituted administrative reforms and allowed prosecution of the Albigensian Crusade *(q.v.)*.

Philip II 1527–98. King of Spain (1156–98) and Portugal (1580–98, as Philip I). He succeeded his father, Holy Roman Emperor Charles V, to the Spanish throne and had earlier received from him the Spanish Netherlands, Milan, Naples, and Sicily. Philip married English Queen Mary I (1554)

and, after her death (1558), was refused by Elizabeth I. Under Philip, Spain emerged as the dominant power in Italy after the Italian Wars *(q.v.)* and enjoyed victories against the Ottoman Turks, notably the Battle of Lepanto (1571). But Philip's efforts to defend Catholicism (sometimes combined with his political aims) led to trouble at home and abroad. Within the empire, persecutions by the Inquisition were increased, resulting in harsh treatment of the Moriscos *(q.v.)* and a revolt in the Spanish Netherlands. The latter ended in the independence of the United Provinces. Philip's conflicts with Protestants in other countries brought war against England and the disastrous defeat of the Spanish Armada *(q.v.)*, which resulted in the decline of Spain as a military power. He also involved Spain in the French Wars of Religion, which, combined with his other foreign wars, seriously weakened the finances of the empire.

Philip III ⟨Philip the Bold⟩ 1245–85. King of France (1270–85), successor to his father, Louis IX. He died during the retreat from an unsuccessful attack on the Spanish kingdom of Aragon.

Philip III 1578–1621. King of Spain (1598–1621), successor to his father, Philip II. Philip also ruled Naples, Sicily, and Portugal (as Philip II), though he was content to let his favorites do the actual governing. The Moriscos *(q.v.)* were expelled during his reign, in 1609.

Philip IV ⟨Philip the Fair⟩ 1268–1314. Capetian king of France (1285–1314), successor to his father, Philip III. Philip's reign was marked by his successful struggle against the church. Early in his reign, Philip's need for money to prosecute foreign wars caused him to impose a tax on the clergy. Pope Boniface VIII opposed the tax (1296) but was soon forced to concede. Philip next arrested a bishop and thereby renewed the dispute with Boniface. To resolve the matter, Philip convened (1302–03) a council of nobles, clergy, and others (the first French States General). When Boniface answered by threatening Philip with excommunication, Philip had him arrested. Boniface died soon afterward and Philip secured the election of Pope Clement V. Thereafter, Clement cooperated with Philip, moved the papacy to Avignon (1309, *see* Babylonian captivity), and condemned the Knights Templars (whose great wealth Philip confiscated). During his reign Philip engaged in wars with England (1294–1303) and Flanders (1302–04).

Philip IV 1605–65. Spanish king (1621–65), successor to his father, Philip III. His reign was marked by his willingness to let his ministers govern and by Spain's decline as a European power.

Spain's involvement in the Thirty Years' War (1618–48) proved costly. During the war, Portugal won its independence (1640), Catalonia revolted and was occupied by France, and the Union of Utrecht *(q.v.)* won recognition of its independence (1648). Spanish involvement in the French war of the Fronde, ended by the Peace of the Pyrenees *(q.v.)*, cost Spain further losses.

Philip V 238–179 BC. Macedonian king (221–179 BC), successor to Antigonus III. He joined the Achaean League in a successful war against Sparta and the Aetolian League. But his alliance with Hannibal during the Second Punic War against Rome brought Roman retaliation in the First Macedonian War *(q.v.)*. Later efforts to expand his domains provoked renewed Roman military action against him and the Second Macedonian War *(q.v.)* ended in his defeat.

Philip V c1294–1322. French king (1317–22) who succeeded on the death of the infant king, John I. The Salic Law *(q.v.)* was invoked to legitimize Philip's succession over the rightful female heir, an infant named Joan. Philip strengthened local militias and instituted other administrative reforms.

Philip V 1683–1746. Spanish king (1700–46), successor to Charles II, and first Bourbon king of Spain. His succession resulted in the War of the Spanish Succession *(q.v.)* and loss of territories by the Peace of Utrecht *(q.v.)*. Philip's early attempts to retake lost territories in Italy failed when the Quadruple Alliance *(q.v.)* was formed against him. His later involvement in the Wars of the Polish Succession and Austrian Succession, however, won Naples, Sicily, Parma, and Piacenza for Spain.

Philip VI 1293–1350. French king (1328–50), successor to Charles IV, and first king of the Valois line. The Salic Law *(q.v.)* was invoked to allow Philip to succeed over rival claimants. His reign was marked by the beginning of the Hundred Years' War (1337–1453) and the outbreak of the Black Plague (1348–49) in France.

Philip Augustus *See* **Philip II**

Philip of Swabia c1177–1208. German king (1198–1208) of the Hohenstaufen line and successor to Holy Roman Emperor Henry VI. Philip was never crowned emperor and his reign was spent overcoming the opposition of his rival for the crown, the Guelph leader Otto IV. He was murdered soon after the struggle had been resolved.

Philippi, Battle of Victory for the Second Roman Triumvirate of Antony, Lepidus, and Octavian (Augustus) over Brutus and Cassius, assassins of Caesar. The battle began on Oct. 27, 42 BC, near the Macedonian city of Philippi, between forces of around 100,000 on each side. Cassius was defeated by Antony and, believing a rumor that Brutus had also lost, committed suicide. The combined triumvirate force then defeated Brutus' forces on Nov. 16, and he committed suicide. The outcome helped ensure Octavian's accession as emperor.

Philippics Two series of historic orations. Demosthenes denounced Philip II of Macedon as a threat to Athens in a series of orations known as "philippics." The term was later applied to Cicero's denunciation of M. Antony before the Roman Senate.

Philippine Insurrection US-Filipino war (1899–1902), an outgrowth of the Philippine Revolution *(q.v.)* and the Spanish-American War. Filipino leader E. Aguinaldo refused to accept the Treaty of Paris (1898), by which Spain ceded the Philippines to the US, and continued to fight for Filipino independence. Aguinaldo was captured (1901) and the war ended a year later.

Philippine Revolution Filipino war for independence from Spain (1896–98). Sparked by the execution of J. Rizal (Dec. 30, 1896), the war was led by E. Aguinaldo. After the outbreak of the Spanish-American War, Aguinaldo helped US Commodore G. Dewey occupy Manila (1898) and established a provisional government. However, the Treaty of Paris (1898) ceded the Philippines to the US, and Aguinaldo led the Philippine Insurrection *(q.v.)* against US control.

Philippines (Republic of the Philippines) Republic composed of over seven thousand islands in the South Pacific. Its capital is Quezon City. The Philippines were ruled by Spain from the 15th to the late 19th cent. and by the US after the Spanish-American War. The Philippines became fully independent in 1946. Key dates in Philippine history include:

1521 F. Magellan, representing Spain, discovered the Philippines.

1542 Islands named in honor of Prince Philip, later Philip II of Spain.

1564–1571 M. de López de Legaspi completed conquest of islands for Spain.

1571 Manila founded.

1583 Audiencia (colonial supreme court) established.

1600s Wars with the Dutch, then expanding their East Indies holdings.

1600s–1800s Moros (native tribe) active as pirates.

1756–63 Seven Years' War in Europe; Manila occupied by British (1762–63).

19TH CENT. Muslims (Moors) raided the Philippines.

1892 Rise of the nationalist movement; secret society, led by Dr. José Rizal, demanded increased native involvement in government.

1896 Existence of Katipunan, society for complete independence, discovered (Aug.); armed revolt against Spanish began.

1896 Dr. Rizal, not associated with Katipunan, executed (Dec.); became martyr.

1896–98 E. Aguinaldo led revolt against Spain.

1898 Spanish-American War between US and Spain; G. Dewey defeated Spain at Manila Bay (May 1); US gained control of Philippines by Treaty of Paris (Dec. 10), ending the war.

1898 US established military rule (Dec.).

1899–1902 Philippine Insurrection; Aguinaldo fought US, headed short-lived rebel government.

1901 Civilian government authorized by Spooner Amendment.

1902–04 William Howard Taft served as governor-general; Philippine Commission became governing body.

1903 US resolved Friar Lands Question by purchasing church-owned lands for resale to peasants.

1916 Jones Law provided for elected legislature.

1934 Tydings-McDuffie Act, creating transitional commonwealth government leading to Philippine independence.

1935 Constitution approved by Filipinos.

1935–42 Manuel Quezon y Molina in office as first president; commonwealth established (Nov. 15, 1935).

1942–45 WW II; Philippines occupied by Japan after defeating US-Filipino forces at Bataan and Corregidor.

1944 US Gen. D. MacArthur landed (Oct.) at Leyte Gulf.

1945 Manila liberated (Feb.).

1946 Full independence (July 4).

1946–48 Manuel Roxas y Acuna in office as president.

1946–54 Communist-backed Hukbalahap guerrillas, who had fought the Japanese, continued guerrilla warfare; capture of their leader, L. Taruc, broke the rebellion.

1954 Philippines joined Southeast Asia Treaty Organization (SEATO).

1965– Ferdinand Marcos in office as president; his administration continued in power into the 1980s, despite considerable opposition.

1969 Marcos reelected in violent campaign; rioting followed the election.

1972 Martial law instituted (Sept.) to combat terrorism; thousands subsequently killed as government troops attempted to restore order.

1973 Marcos promulgated new constitution; country to be ruled by martial law; Marcos to remain in power indefinitely.

1976 Earthquake hit Mindanao; 8,000 people dead.

1976 Truce reached with Muslim rebels on Mindanao, ending several years of serious rebellion.

1978 Elections for National Assembly held; first since martial law was imposed.

1981 Martial law ended (Jan. 17); many restrictions remained in force.

1981 Plebiscite approved constitutional changes.

1981 Marcos won reelection; opposition refused to take part in the election.

Philippine Sea, Battle of the Major US victory (June 19, 1944) over the Japanese during WW II. Provoked by the US invasion of the Mariana Islands, the Japanese organized a large naval attack force (including nine carriers) to fight against the US task force protecting the Marianas landing operation. Primarily a battle between carrier-based aircraft, it turned into a rout, known as "the Marianas Turkey Shoot." The Japanese lost 400 planes and three aircraft carriers, and the US firmly established naval superiority in the Pacific.

Philip the Arabian *See* **Philip**

Philip the Bold *See* **Philip III; Burgundy**

Philip the Fair *See* **Philip IV**

Philip the Good 1396–1467. Duke of Burgundy (1419–67). By various means, Philip doubled the size of his holdings and established Burgundy as a powerful kingdom. Involved in rivalry with France, he formed an alliance with England against France by the Treaty of Troyes (1420). He eventually made peace with French king Charles VII in the Treaty of Arras (1435). He founded the Order of the Golden Fleece (*q.v.*).

Philip the Handsome *See* **Philip I**

Philip the Magnanimous ⟨~ of Hesse⟩ 1504–67. Landgrave of Hesse and German Protestant leader. He was a leader in the struggle against the Catholic Holy Roman Emperor Charles V and organized the Schmalkaldic League (*q.v.*) of German Protestants (1531).

Philistines Ancient people from the Aegean who settled in Palestine (c12th cent. BC). They were skilled iron workers and frequently fought the Israelites. In modern times, "philistine" means an uncultured person.

Phillips, Wendell 1811–84. American reformer. He was associated with W. Garrison in the crusade for the abolition of slavery, and later campaigned for woman suffrage, labor reform, and prohibition.

Philo ⟨Philo Judaeus⟩ c20 BC–AD 50. Jewish philosopher. Philo was famous for his synthesis of Greek philosophy with biblical theology. He stressed God's perfection and established the concept of Logos (q.v.).

Philoctetes Mythical Greek warrior, the recipient of Hercules' bow and arrows after his death. Philoctetes killed Paris with these weapons and thus helped bring about the fall of Troy.

Philo Judaeus See **Philo**

Philomela Mythical Greek princess. She was raped by her brother-in-law, Tereus, and he cut out her tongue to prevent her from telling. She embroidered the story and sent it to her sister, Procne. In revenge, Procne then killed her son by Tereus and fled with Philomela.

Philometer, Ptolemy VI See **Ptolemy VI**

Philo of Alexandria See **Philo**

Philopater, Ptolemy IV See **Ptolemy IV**

Philostratus ⟨Philostratus the Elder⟩ fl. c217. Greek sophist. He wrote the Life of Apollonius and Lives of the Sophists.

Philostratus the Elder See **Philostratus**

Phinees See **Phinehas**

Phinehas ⟨Phinees⟩ Biblical figure, the grandson of Aaron and his successor as high priest of the Jews.

Phips, Sir William 1651–95. Massachusetts colonial governor (1692–94). Phips commanded New England colonial forces during King William's War (q.v.). He appointed a commission on witchcraft but disbanded it when his own wife was accused. He was recalled to England.

Phnom Penh ⟨Pnom Penh⟩ Cambodian capital city (pop. 300,000?). Believed to have been founded in the 14th cent., it was the Khmer capital after the fall of Angkor and became capital (1867) of French-occupied Cambodia. It was a loyalist stronghold in the civil war (1970–75) with the Khmer Rouge and was almost constantly under siege during that time. After the Khmer victory (Apr. 17, 1975), the city's population was forcibly relocated. The Vietnamese captured the city (Jan. 7, 1979) during its war against the Khmer regime.

Phocas d. 610 Byzantine emperor (602–10), successor to Maurice by his overthrow. He persecuted the Monophysites and Jews and was overthrown (610) by Heraclius.

Phocis Region of ancient Greece, located in central Greece. The Oracle of Delphi and Mount Parnassus were within its boundaries. It was the focus of the three Sacred Wars (q.v.).

Phoebe In Greek mythology, a Titan and the mother of Leto and grandmother of Artemis. She was associated with the moon.

Phoebus Apollo See **Apollo**

Phoenicia Ancient name applied to the narrow coastal region bordering the eastern Mediterranean roughly contiguous with modern Lebanon. The Phoenicians were related to the Canaanites and had established themselves as traders and sailors by the 25th cent. BC. They early came under the influence of the Egyptians, with whom they traded. Although never a unified country, Phoenicia saw the rise of several important cities, notably Byblos, Sidon, Tyre, and Tripoli. Phoenician traders founded settlements throughout the Mediterranean, such as on the islands of Rhodes and Cyprus and at Utica and Carthage. Later, Phoenicia gained independence as Egyptian power began to decline around the 12th cent. BC. During this period Phoenician traders ranged widely through the Mediterranean. It is thought they may have also traveled along the western coast of Africa and possibly as far north as Cornwall. The Phoenicians were known for their metalwork and glasswork, woven cloth, and fabric dyed with a color known as Tyrian purple. Their greatest innovation, however, was their alphabet, which was adopted by the Greeks and eventually replaced the older system of hieroglyphic writing. Phoenicia came under Persian domination in the 6th cent. BC and was conquered by Alexander the Great in the 4th cent. BC. Under Macedonian rule much of the region was hellenized and Phoenician culture underwent a decline. Phoenicia ceased to exist when the area was incorporated into the Roman province of Syria (AD 64).

Phoenix Capital city (pop. 764,900) of Arizona, a resort and manufacturing center. Incorporated in 1881, it became capital of the territory (1889) and then of the state (1912). The Salt River dam (completed 1911) provided electric power and irrigation water for farming. The city underwent a boom during WW II as the site of three military airfields.

Phoenix Park murders Irish terrorist murders. On May 6, 1882, the British secretary of Ireland, Lord Frederick Cavendish, and his undersecretary, Thomas Henry Burke, were stabbed to death in Dublin's Phoenix Park. The Invincibles, a terrorist offshoot of the Fenians, claimed responsibility. Noted Irish leader C. Parnell was cleared of charges that he was involved in the murders.

Photius c820–891. Byzantine scholar and patriarch of Constantinople (858–867, 877–886). Photius rose to prominence when he was chosen to replace St. Ignatius during the iconoclastic controversy. When his election was challenged by Pope

Nicholas I, Photius retaliated by contesting the pope's right to rule in the East. Though Photius was replaced by St. Ignatius, he had already created the beginnings of the schism that was to permanently divide the church. Condemned at the Fourth Council of Constantinople (869), Photius was reconciled with the West and was reinstated as patriarch after St. Ignatius' death. He was, however, forced to resign the office by Byzantine emperor Leo VI.

Phrygia Ancient country of Asia Minor, located in what is now central Turkey. The country prospered from the 8th to 6th cent. BC and two of its kings were supposed to have been the legendary Gordius and Midas. It came under Lydian domination (7th cent.) and thereafter was ruled by various powers.

Phrynichus *fl. c*512–476 BC. Athenian poet and playwright, the first to put women characters in Greek plays. He was fined for writing *Capture of Miletus* because it reminded Athens of the loss of that city.

Phthah *See* **Ptah**

Phyfe, Duncan *c*1768–1854. Scottish-born American furniture maker. His designs were neoclassic (and, later, Empire style) and highly prized for their fine workmanship.

physiocrats French intellectuals (18th cent.) who developed the first complete system of economics. Led by François Quesnay, they emphasized that land was the ultimate source of all wealth, advocated a single tax on it, extolled free trade and laissez-faire, and stressed the importance of natural laws.

Piaget, Jean 1896–1980. Swiss psychologist. Piaget is best known for his studies in child psychology, notably on the sequential stages of a child's intellectual development.

Piast Polish dynasty. The Piasts were Poland's first dynasty, ruling from the 11th cent. to 1370, when they were replaced by the Jagiello line. Branches of the family, however, continued in Bohemia for several more centuries.

Picard, Jean 1620–82. French astronomer. Picard accurately measured the degree of a meridian of the earth. He established the Paris Observatory.

Picasso, Pablo Ruiz 1881–1973. Spanish artist and sculptor, one of the most important artists of this century. His early career is generally divided into periods: blue (from 1901), rose (from 1905), and cubist (from 1907). With G. Braque, Picasso is considered the founder of cubism *(q.v.)* and in 1907 painted his famous early cubist work, *Les Demoiselles d'Avignon*. In the 1920s, some of his works took on a surrealistic tone and foreshadowed the agony portrayed in his *Guernica*,

commemorating the destruction of the town during the Spanish Civil War. Experimenting with various media and styles in his later years, he continued working until his death.

Piccard, Auguste 1884–1962. Swiss-born Belgian physicist. Piccard is noted for both his balloon ascents into the stratosphere and his deep-sea explorations in a bathyscaphe he designed.

Piccolomini, Aeneas Silvius *See* **Pius II**

Pichincha, Battle of Ecuadorian victory (May 24, 1822) over Spanish colonial forces. The Ecuadorians, under A. de Sucre, defeated the Spanish at Pichincha volcano, near Quito, and thereby gained Ecuadorian independence.

Picken, Andrew *See* **Pickens, Andrew**

Pickens, Andrew ⟨Picken, Andrew⟩ 1739–1817. American Revolutionary hero. Pickens served notably in the battles of Cowpens and Eutaw Springs, and captured Augusta, Georgia (1781). He later served in Congress (1793–95).

Pickering, Edward Charles 1846–1919. American astronomer and physicist. Pickering invented the meridian photometer and pioneered stellar photometry and spectroscopy at the Harvard Observatory.

Pickering, Timothy 1745–1829. American politician. Pickering served as G. Washington's adjutant general in the American Revolution and later held Cabinet posts under Washington and J. Adams. A Federalist and a member of the Essex Junto *(q.v.)*, he strongly opposed the War of 1812.

Pickett, George Edward 1825–75. Confederate general in the American Civil War. He is known best for "Pickett's charge" at the Battle of Gettysburg *(q.v.)*, a brave but futile charge on Union forces across a half mile of broken ground.

Pickford, Mary ⟨Smith, Gladys Mary⟩ 1893–1979. American actress, star of silent films such as *Pollyanna*. She was cofounder of the film production company United Artists.

Pico della Mirandola, Giovanni Conte 1463–94. Italian Renaissance philosopher. He published 900 theses that combined Christianity with Platonic thought.

Picquart, Georges 1854–1914. French general. Picquart's ardent defense of Capt. A. Dreyfus in the Dreyfus Affair *(q.v.)* led to his own imprisonment. He was later exonerated and became war minister (1906–09) under G. Clemenceau.

Picquigny, Truce of Agreement signed (1475) at Picquigny, France. By its terms English king Edward IV agreed to withdraw his army from France in return for a cash settlement and an annual pension.

Picts Ancient people of Scotland. They frequently invaded Roman-held Britain and established a kingdom in Scotland that flourished in the 8th cent.

Pied Piper of Hamelin Legendary figure who used his magic pipe, first, to rid the town of Hamelin of rats, and then, when the townspeople refused to pay his fee, to lure away the children. The legend may have been based on the exodus of children during the Children's Crusade *(q.v.)*.

Pierce, Franklin 1804–69. US president (1853–57), the fourteenth, successor to M. Fillmore. A Democrat from New Hampshire, he was a US representative (1833–37) and senator (1837–42) and fought in the Mexican War. In 1852, he was nominated for the presidency by the Democrats to break a deadlock. After defeating Gen. W. Scott, the Whig candidate, he sought to reconcile opposing Democratic factions on the slavery issue by appointing Cabinet officials from both North and South. Pierce adopted a generally unsuccessful policy of foreign expansion, and his request for a program by which the US could acquire Cuba from Spain resulted in the Ostend Manifesto *(q.v.)*. This caused such a furor that his administration disavowed it. During his term of office the US made the Gadsden Purchase *(q.v.)* from Mexico, and the Kansas-Nebraska Act *(q.v.)* was passed (1854). This act, with its doctrine of popular sovereignty, led to Bleeding Kansas *(q.v.)*, which further strained relations between North and South in the years before the Civil War. Pierce's policies made him vastly unpopular, and he retired to New Hampshire at the close of his term.

Pieria Ancient Greek district, located in north Thessaly. The site of Mount Olympus, it was also the legendary birthplace of Orpheus and the Muses.

Piero della Francesca *c*1420–92. Italian Renaissance painter. One of the great Italian Renaissance artists, he is renowned for his religious frescoes, including the series *The Story of the True Cross*.

Pietism Religious movement that began in reaction to the doctrinal orthodoxy of German Lutheranism in the 17th and 18th cents. The leader of this reform was P. Spener, whose book *Pia desideria* encouraged study of the Bible and a spiritual rebirth within the church. Pietism influenced the Moravian and Methodist churches. The movement continued under Spener's successor, August Francke, but declined after Francke's death (1727).

Pietro, Guido di *See* **Angelico, Fra**

Pike, Zebulon Montgomery 1779–1813. American general and explorer. Pike explored much of western America and discovered Pike's Peak, Colorado. He was killed leading a successful attack on York (now Toronto, Canada) during the War of 1812.

Pilgrimage of Grace Uprising (1536–37) in northern England which began (Oct., 1536) in protest against the abolition of papal authority and suppression of the monasteries by King Henry VIII. Some 35,000 Catholic demonstrators were persuaded to disband. Another uprising followed (Jan. 1537), but its leaders were executed and northern England was placed under martial law.

Pilgrims English religious Separatists, and others, who sailed aboard the *Mayflower* to Plymouth Rock (Dec. 21, 1620) and founded the first New England colony. Originally, the Separatists opposed the doctrines of the established Church of England and founded an independent congregation. Around 1607 some of them emigrated to Holland to escape harassment and persecution. The experiment in Holland did not prove satisfactory, and the group then negotiated with a London stock company for a charter that would enable them to go to America. In Sept., 1620, 102 passengers embarked on the *Mayflower* for the voyage. Some of the group, including J. Alden and M. Standish, were non-Separatists (called Strangers), hired to protect the stock company's interests. Before landing they signed the Mayflower Compact *(q.v.)*, which provided for a government by the will of the majority. The name Pilgrim Fathers, as applied to them, comes from an 1820 commemorative speech by D. Webster.

Pillars of Hercules Mythical name given to the promontories at the Mediterranean (eastern) entrance of the Strait of Gibraltar. They are generally identified with the Rock of Gibraltar in Europe and Jebel Musa in Africa.

Pillnitz, Declaration of Statement issued (Aug. 27, 1791) at Pillmitz, now in East Germany, by Austrian emperor Leopold II and Prussian king Frederick William II declaring their willingness to restore French king Louis XVI, provided other European sovereigns agreed. Both monarchs knew that Britain would not agree, so the declaration was empty. However, it caused much resentment in France and helped bring on the French Revolutionary Wars.

Pillow, Gideon Johnson 1806–78. Confederate general in the American Civil War. Pillow's escape from Fort Donelson *(q.v.)* before its surrender to Union forces led to his suspension from command.

Pilsudski, Joseph 1867–1935. Polish general and politician. A lifelong fighter against Russia for Polish independence, he was repeatedly imprisoned and exiled. After declaring Poland a republic (1918) and becoming its first president, he dominated Polish politics, both in and out of office, into the 1930s.

Pincherle, Alberto   *See* **Moravia, Alberto**

Pinckney, Charles   1757–1824. American statesman. As a member of the Constitutional Convention, he submitted a draft of the Constitution, and a number of its elements were incorporated into the final document. He later served in Congress, as governor of South Carolina, and as US minister to Spain.

Pinckney, Charles Cotesworth   1746–1825. American statesman. As special envoy to France (1797) he became involved, with E. Gerry and J. Marshall, in the XYZ Affair *(q.v.)*. He was twice the unsuccessful Federalist candidate for president (1804, 1808).

Pinckney, Thomas   1750–1828. American politician and diplomat. As special envoy to Spain (1794–95) he negotiated a treaty (1795) that established American-Spanish borders in North America and secured American navigation rights on the Mississippi River.

Pindar   522?–443 BC. Greek lyric poet who gave his name to the Pindaric ode of English verse. His major works are the *Epinicia*, odes to the victors of the Olympic, Pythian, Isthmian, and Nemean athletic games. Of these, 44 complete odes survive.

Pinel, Philippe   1745–1826. French physician. Pinel advocated humane treatment of the mentally ill. His views and methods completely changed the long-standing approach to mental illness.

Pinkerton, Allan   1819–84. Scottish-born American detective who formed America's first detective agency (1850). Pinkerton foiled an assassination plot against A. Lincoln (1861) and operated an espionage ring against the Confederates.

Pinochet Ugarte, Augusto   1915– . Chilean military leader and president (1973–). As commander in chief of the army he directed the successful coup against his predecessor, President S. Allende (Sept., 1973).

Pinter, Harold   1930– . English playwright. Pinter's tense, highly personal work includes the plays *The Birthday Party, The Caretaker,* and *The Homecoming.*

Pinzon, Martin Alonso   *d.* 1493. Spanish navigator. Pinzon was co-owner of the ships *Niña* and *Pinta.* He commanded the *Pinta* during Columbus' 1492 expedition.

Pinzon, Vicente Yanez   *fl.* 1492–1509. Spanish explorer and navigator. Pinzon commanded the *Niña* on Columbus' first voyage to America

(1492). He later voyaged to Brazil and the Amazon estuary (early 1500).

Pippi, Giulio   *See* **Romano, Giulio**

piracy   Robbery on the high seas, committed for private gain. In ancient times, Phoenicians preyed on shipping in the Mediterranean. In the Middle Ages, Vikings attacked ships in the Baltic, and Moors also engaged in piracy. The decline of Ottoman power in the Mediterranean led to the rise of the Barbary States *(q.v.)*, whose support of piracy led to conflict with European powers and the US *(see* Tripolitan War) in the 19th cent. The formation of standing navies and international laws has eliminated most piracy.

Piraeus   Athenian seaport. Built (5th cent. BC) by Themistocles, it is the port of Athens and the leading Greek seaport. It was heavily damaged by the Germans during WW II.

Pirandello, Luigi   1867–1936. Italian dramatist. His powerful, realistic plays, among them *Six Characters in Search of an Author,* had a major influence in 20th-cent. drama. He was awarded the Nobel Prize in Literature in 1934.

Pisa, Council of   Roman Catholic church council. It was called (1409) to heal the papal schism that had resulted in the naming of two rival popes, Gregory XII in Rome and Benedict XIII in Avignon. The council deposed both and elected a third pope, Alexander V. Far from ending the schism, the council complicated matters by establishing three papal claimants. The Council of Constance (1414–18) ultimately forced all three to resign and elected Martin V.

Pisa, Leaning Tower of   *See* **Leaning Tower of Pisa**

Pisano, Nicola and **Giovanni**   c1220–84; 1245–1314. Italian sculptors. Nicola founded a school of sculpture at Pisa which influenced later Renaissance art. His son Giovanni perpetuated his work in Siena.

Pisistratus   c605–527 BC. Tyrant of Athens (560–556, 554–527 BC). Pisistratus established Athenian hegemony in Ionia, sponsored extensive public building, passed important land laws, and commissioned a definitive edition of Homer.

Piso, Gaius Calpurnius   *d.* AD 65. Roman politician. A prominent plebeian, he was robbed of his wife by the emperor Caligula. He later plotted against the emperor Nero and killed himself when his plot was discovered.

Piso, Lucius Calpurnius Piso Caesoninus   *d.* after 43 BC. Roman politician, father-in-law of J. Caesar. As consul (58 BC), he took part in the banishment of Cicero, and later attacked him in some of his best-known orations in the Roman Senate.

Pissarro, Camille   1830–1903. French impressionist painter. One of the most influential impressionists, he is noted for his paintings of street scenes.

Pitman, Sir Isaac 1813–97. English inventor of a shorthand system. His phonetic system of shorthand became one of the world's most used and adaptable systems.

Pitt, William (the Younger) 1759–1806. British prime minister (1783–1801, 1804–06), son of W. Pitt the Elder. Pitt led Britain through the French Revolutionary and early Napoleonic Wars. Pitt entered Parliament in 1781 and by 1783 was in effective control of the government as prime minister. He attempted to reorganize government finances in order to reduce the national debt, lowered customs duties, revised the British East India Company's role in India's government (1784), created Upper and Lower Canada by his Constitution Act (1791), and organized Britain (and various foreign coalitions) for war after the start of the French Revolutionary Wars. Seeking a solution to the Irish problem, he sought a union with Ireland and passage of a Catholic Emancipation act. The union was effected (1800), but King George refused to allow passage of the act and Pitt resigned (1801). He returned (1804) to form his second ministry after the outbreak of the Napoleonic Wars and organized the Third Coalition against Napoleon (1805). He died that year. A revived Tory party formed under his leadership.

Pitt, William (the Elder), 1st earl of Chatham 1708–78. British statesman, and noted orator, called "the Great Commoner." His vigorous foreign policies, during the Seven Years' War (1756–63), led to French defeats in India, Africa, and North America, and to Britain's emergence as the world's greatest colonial power. He entered Parliament in 1735 and, called by George II to serve as secretary of state, he effectively became the prime minister (1756–61) for most of the war in which Britain stripped France of most of its colonial empire. He formed a new ministry (1766–68), but was forced to resign because of poor health.

Pitt-Rivers, Augustus Henry Lane-Fox 1827–1900. British pioneer archaeologist. A career army officer, he made extensive excavations on his large estate in Wiltshire, emphasizing total site excavation and careful stratigraphic comparisons.

Pittsburg Landing, Battle of *See* **Shiloh, Battle of**

Pius II ⟨Aeneas Silvius Piccolomini⟩ 1405–64. Pope (1458–64), successor to Calixtus III, a famous Renaissance humanist before becoming a priest. As pope he condemned conciliarism.

Pius IV ⟨Giovanni Angelo de' Medici⟩ 1499–1565. Pope (1559–65), successor to Paul IV. He convened (1562) the third and most important ses-

sion of the Council of Trent, and made permanent the Catholic Reformation by ratifying the council's decrees (1564).

Pius V ⟨Ghislieri, Michele⟩ 1504–72. Pope (1566–72), successor to Pius IV, and saint. As pope he put into effect the decrees of the Council of Trent and encouraged the common defense of Christendom against the Turks.

Pius VI ⟨Giovanni Angelo Braschi⟩ 1717–99. Pope (1775–99), successor to Clement XIV. He opposed the assaults on church authority of both Austrian Josephinism and the French revolutionary Civil Constitution of the Clergy. He was taken as a prisoner to France by Napoleon (1798) after Papal domains were conquered in the French Revolutionary Wars.

Pius VII ⟨Barnaba Gregorio Chiaramonte⟩ 1740–1823. Pope (1800–23), successor to Pius VI. He signed the Concordat of 1801 with Napoleon and took part in his coronation (1804). His later opposition to Napoleon led to French annexation of the Papal States (1809). Pius excommunicated Napoleon but became the emperor's virtual prisoner.

Pius IX ⟨Mastai-Ferretti, Giovanni Maria⟩ 1792–1878. Pope (1846–78), successor to Gregory XVI. His reign was the longest in Catholic history. During his pontificate the Papal States and Rome passed to Italy (1870). He defined the dogma of the Immaculate Conception (1854) and presided over the First Vatican Council (1869–70).

Pius X ⟨Giuseppe Sarto⟩ 1835–1914. Pope (1903–14), successor to Leo XIII, and saint. His pontificate saw the separation of church and state in France and Portugal. He condemned religious Modernism in his encyclical *Pascendi Dominici Gregis*.

Pius XI 1857–1939. Pope (1922–39), successor to Benedict XV. He was noted for his efforts to secure world peace. As pope he negotiated the Lateran Treaty (1929) with B. Mussolini, which made Vatican City an independent state. He denounced fascism, communism, and racism and encouraged missionary work.

Pius XII 1876–1958. Pope (1939–58), successor to Pius XI. Elected pope on the eve of WW II, he worked to relieve the suffering caused by the war. After the Allied victory, however, he was criticized by many for not doing enough to prevent persecution of the Jews. He strongly opposed the rise of communism and excommunicated several East European leaders.

Pizarro, Francisco *c*1476–1541. Spanish conquerer of the Incas of Peru. He first went to the New World in 1509, and accompanied V. de Balboa when the latter discovered the Pacific Ocean (1513). With D. de Almagro, he explored (1522–

26) the west coast of South America, then returned to Spain (1528) to prepare for the conquest of Peru. In 1531, with fewer than 200 men, he enticed the Inca chieftain Atahualpa into his hands by treachery, extracted an enormous ransom from him, and later had him executed (1533). He then captured the city of Cuzco, and the conquest of Peru was completed. Pizarro founded Lima (1535). In 1537–38, he came into conflict with Almagro and his followers, and he ordered Almagro beheaded. Pizarra was later assassinated by Almagro's followers (1541).

Pizarro, Gonzalo c1506–48. Spanish conquistador. He was the half-brother of F. Pizarro and was involved in the conquest of Peru. He became governor of Quito, and later led an unsuccessful revolt against the New Laws protecting the Indians.

Place, Francis 1771–1854. English social reformer. A tailor, he fought successfully against the anti-union Combination Acts. In 1822, he published one of the earliest birth-control tracts.

Plain, the In the French Revolution, the amorphous, moderate party that occupied the lower seats in the National Convention chamber. It was distinguished from the more radical representatives of the Mountain (q.v.), who occupied the higher seats.

Planck, Max 1858–1947. German physicist. He originated (1900) the modern quantum theory (q.v.), which revolutionized modern physics. He was awarded the Nobel Prize in Physics in 1918.

Plan de Iguala (Plan of Three Guarantees) Proclamation issued (Feb. 24, 1821) during the Mexican Revolution by the revolutionary Gen. A. Iturbide. It set forth three fundamental objectives of the drive for independence from Spain and was named for the city in which it was issued. Iturbide ignored the plan after he became emperor of Mexico (1822). The objectives were complete independence from Spain, designation of the Roman Catholic church as the state church, and equal rights for all Mexicans.

Plan of Three Guarantees *See* **Plan de Iguala**

Planudes Maximus c1260–c1330. Byzantine scholar. A learned monk, he was noted for this theological work on the procession of the Holy Spirit and for his editing of the *Greek Anthology* of poetry.

Plataea Ancient city in east-central Greece. It allied itself with Athens against the Persians and was the site of a decisive Greek victory (479 BC) in the Persian Wars (q.v.).

Plato 427?–347 BC. Ancient Greek philosopher, one of the great philosophers of all time. Born to a leading Athenian family, he was originally named Aristocles but was given the name Plato because

of his broad shoulders. Little is known of his life. He became a pupil of Socrates, whose ideas and use of the dialectic (Socratic method) in pursuing truth later played an important role in Plato's writings. After Socrates' trial and execution (399 BC), Plato left Athens and traveled to Megara and, it is thought, to Egypt, Italy, and Syracuse. At Syracuse he was unsuccessful in trying to convert Dionysius the Elder to his idea of a state ruled by a philosopher-king. (He later returned to Syracuse to tutor Dionysius the Younger, but did not succeed in instilling his ideas into the youthful ruler.) Plato returned to Athens (388 BC) and founded the Academy (q.v.), an institution devoted to the investigation of scientific and philosophical truth, which flourished until the 6th cent. AD, when it was closed by Justinian.

Plato taught at the Academy until his death. Among his pupils were Aristotle, and Xenocrates. Plato is known best, however, for his writings, among them the *Republic, Apology, Symposium, Phaedo, Meno,* and the *Laws.* All of his writings take the form of dialogues, and many of them contain the character of Socrates as a leading figure. They are noted for their use of the dialectic, the technique of questioning all beliefs and assumptions in an attempt to come to a larger or more general truth or conception of reality. Plato's system of philosophy was based on the concept of a body of unchangeable and archetypal Ideas, of which the world's objects or appearances are mere approximations. The greatest of these Ideas was the Idea of the Good. The quest for the Good would ultimately lead man to harmony with the state and the universe. Plato's writings had enormous influence in the growth of Western civilization, and his writings retain a position of eminence in both Western philosophy and Western literature. In addition, his writings provide the primary source of knowledge of Socrates' teachings.

Platonism Philosophical school or tradition based on the writings of Plato. Platonism is founded on Plato's concept of reality as a body of eternal and unchangeable Ideas. Objects and other things perceived by the senses are only approximations of the more perfect Ideas and, therefore, approximations of ultimate reality. The primary Idea in the Platonic system is the Idea of the Good. Platonic thought attempted to demonstrate the path by which man could come into moral and esthetic balance with society, the state, and the universe. From Plato's writings numerous philosophical schools developed, and Platonism as a general philosophical movement had a major influence on the development of Western culture. It influenced the early Christian church, played a major role in the intellectual life of the Middle Ages, and also helped shape the intellectual and artistic development of the Renaissance.

Platt, Thomas Collier 1833–1910. US senator (1881) and New York State political boss. He helped T. Roosevelt become governor (1898) and vice-president (1900).

Platt Amendment US legislative provisions concerning Cuba, named for Connecticut senator Orville Platt (1827–1905) and added to the army appropriations bill of Mar. 2, 1901. It attempted to govern US relations with Cuba by forbidding Cuba to make any treaty limiting the island's independence or to incur excessive foreign debt. The US was accorded naval-base rights and the right to intervene. To end US occupation, Cuba agreed to these conditions, but abrogated them in 1934.

Plautus c254–184 BC. Roman writer of comic plays. His comedies, in expressive, idiomatic Latin, greatly influenced later European writers.

plebeians (plebs) In Roman history, the general body of citizens, as opposed to the aristocratic patricians. Originally excluded from all officeholding, by 287 BC (see Rome [287 BC]) they had achieved virtual political equality, although social distinction continued to be maintained.

plebs *See* **plebeians**

Plehve, Vyacheslav Konstantinovich 1846–1904. Czarist Russian official. He pursued forced Russification of minorities, organized pogroms against the Jews, and favored war against Japan to forestall internal tensions. He was finally assassinated.

Pleiad (Pléiade) Name given to several groups of seven poets, including **(1)** the tragic poets who wrote in Alexandria (c280 BC) under Ptolemy II Philadelphus, and **(2)** the 16th-cent. French Renaissance poets led by P. de Ronsard.

Pléiade *See* **Pleiad**

Pleiades In Greek mythology, the seven daughters of Atlas, who were changed into the constellation of the same name.

Plekhanov, Georgi Valentinovich 1857–1918. Russian Marxist theorist and revolutionary leader. A collaborator of N. Lenin up to 1903, Plekhanov later allied himself with the Mensheviks and unsuccessfully attempted reunification with the Bolsheviks.

Plessy vs Ferguson *See* **segregation**

Plimsoll, Samuel 1824–98. British member of Parliament (1868–80) and social reformer. He worked for the welfare of British sailors and inspired maritime regulations and reforms. The Plimsoll line, marking the limit to which a ship may be loaded, is named for him.

Pliny (the Elder) AD 23–79. Roman naturalist. His *Historia naturalis*, an encyclopedic study of plant and animal life, was long a standard authority. He died while investigating the eruption of Mount Vesuvius.

Pliny (the Younger) AD 62?–c113. Roman statesman and author, son of Pliny the Elder. He held various Roman government offices, including that of consul (AD 100), and is noted for a series of letters describing the life of his times.

PLO *See* **Palestine Liberation Organization**

Plotinus AD c205–270. Neoplatonist philosopher. Plotinus formulated an original philosophy that influenced many later systems of thought, including Christian philosophy and 19th-cent. German idealism.

Plutarch AD 46?–c120. Greek biographer and essayist. He was born in Chaeronea, Boeotia, and spent most of his life there, although he visited Rome and also maintained ties with Delphi, where he was a priest of Apollo (after AD c95). He is known best for his series of parallel biographies, *Parallel Lives*. In each book of this series he eulogized the life of a great Greek and that of a comparable Roman figure. Of these paired biographies, 46 survive, and they are an important source for knowledge of the ancient world. They have greatly influenced modern literature.

Pluto Ancient Greek god of the underworld, also known as Hades. The husband of Persephone, he was known by the Romans as Orcus or Dis.

Plymouth Brethren Christian sect. Founded (Dec., 1828) in Dublin and (1830) in Plymouth, England, it has spread especially in English-speaking countries. Congregationally organized, the Brethren hold to fundamental Scripture and recognize no special ministry or priesthood.

Plymouth Colony English colony established (1620) on the coast of Massachusetts by the Pilgrims. Originally granted a patent to settle in Virginia, the colonists, upon arrival in New England, drew up the Mayflower Compact, which formed a government based on majority rule and acknowledged the authority of the English crown. The first Thanksgiving Day (1621) was celebrated by the colony in gratitude for a harvest after a winter of terrible privation. The colony joined (1643) the New England Confederation, and became (1691) part of the colony of Massachusetts.

Pnom Penh *See* **Phnom Penh**

Pobyedonostzev, Konstantin Petrovich 1827–1970. Czarist Russian official. As tutor to czars Alexander III and Nicholas II and as a jurist and official, he promoted autocracy, Russification of minorities, and the supremacy of the Orthodox church.

Pocahontas *c*1595–1617. Indian woman and American folk heroine. The daughter of Indian chief Powhatan, she befriended colonists at the Jamestown, Virginia, settlement and is said to have prevented the Indians from killing Captain J. Smith. Her marriage to settler J. Rolfe helped keep peace between the Indians and Virginia settlers.

Podebrad, George of *See* **George of Podebrad**

Podmore, Frank *See* **Fabian Society**

Poe, Edgar Allan 1809–49. American writer, one of the leading figures of American literature. He was orphaned in childhood, served in the army, and then was enrolled at West Point (1830). Subsequently expelled, he embarked upon his career as a writer. He became a leading critic as editor of the *Southern Literary Messenger* and other publications, and his stories and poems gained wide notice. Poe's life, however, was marked by tragedy and failure, augmented by poverty and drink, and he died (1849) in Baltimore under mysterious circumstances. Many of his works, among them the poems *The Raven* and *Annabel Lee* and the tales *The Fall of the House of Usher* and *The Murders in the Rue Morgue*, have become classics of American literature. His "tales of ratiocination" have been called the origins of the modern mystery story.

Poggio ⟨Bracciolini, Gian Francesco Poggio⟩ 1380–1459. Italian Renaissance humanist and scholar. Poggio rediscovered numerous manuscripts of Roman authors, among them works by Cicero, Lucretius, and Quintilian.

pogrom Attack on minority groups carried out with the connivance or toleration of the authorities. "Pogrom" is derived from the Russian word for riot or devastation. Pogroms against Jews began in Russia in 1881 following the assassination of Czar Alexander II and continued sporadically until the Russian Revolution.

Poincaré, Jules Henri 1854–1912. French mathematician and scientist. His work on the theory of functions made advancements possible in physics. He was also well known for explaining science to the public.

Poincaré, Raymond 1860–1934. French president (1913–20) and three times premier (1912–13, 1922–24, 1926–29). A conservative nationalist, he ordered France's occupation of the Ruhr (1923) after Germany failed to pay war reparations.

Poinsett, Joel Roberts 1779–1851. American diplomat and statesman. He represented the US on missions to Latin America, served in Congress (1821–25), and was secretary of war (1837–41) under President M. Van Buren. He opposed nullification and the growing southern movement toward secession.

Point Four Program US foreign-policy program aimed at providing technical assistance to underdeveloped countries. Named for the fourth point in President H. Truman's 1949 inaugural address, it was eventually integrated into the over-all US foreign-aid program.

Poison Affair French court scandal. In 1679, an investigation revealed that vast segments of the French population patronized female fortunetellers for black masses and poisons as well as for prophecy. Many such fortune-tellers were arrested and executed, among them one Mme. Monvoison, who was burned in 1680. Her daughter charged that King Louis XIV's mistress, Mme. de Montespan, was one of her mother's clients and had obtained potions to secure the king's love and do away with her rivals. Though the charges were never proved, the executions ceased.

Poitiers, battles of Two decisive battles fought near this city in west-central France. **1.** ⟨Tours, Battle of⟩ Important battle (732) that helped end the Muslim invasion of Frankish domains. The Muslims, led by Abdu-r-Rahman, had overrun Aquitaine and were threatening Tours. To protect the city, the Frankish mayor of the palace, Charles Martel, intercepted the Muslim forces near Poitiers, defeated and killed Abdu-r-Rahman, and thereby forced the Muslims to retreat. **2.** Major victory (Sept. 19, 1356) for the English at the close of the first part of the Hundred Years' War (1337–1453). Edward the Black Prince had been conducting a raid into central France when his force of 7,000 men was intercepted near Poitiers by a 16,000-man army under French king John II. In the subsequent battle, English archers and lightly equipped infantrymen outmaneuvered and badly mauled the superior French force. King John was captured and 2,000 French knights were killed. John was ultimately forced to submit to the Treaty of Brétigny *(q.v.)*.

Poitiers, Diane de *See* **Diane de Poitiers**

Poland Republic located in central Europe. Its capital is Warsaw. The kingdom of Poland dates to the late 10th cent. and reached its height of power and prestige in the 16th cent. Dismembered (18th cent.) by Austria, Prussia, and Russia, it was reestablished as a republic (1918) at the end of WW I, but was overrun (1939) by Germany and the Soviets at the opening of WW II. After WW II the reconstituted government of Poland fell under Soviet domination and in 1952 a new constitution established Poland as a people's republic, within the Soviet sphere of influence. Key dates in the history of Poland include:

c840–1370 Piast dynasty ruled in Poland, after gaining control over Slavs in region.

992–1025 Boleslaus reigned; first to designate himself Polish king; negotiated the Peace of Bautzen (1018); established Christianity.

1102–38 Boleslaus III reigned; kingdom divided at his death.

1177–94 Casimir II reigned; reunited most territories; established a senate and advanced peasants' rights.

1200s Mongols invaded Poland (1240) and broke up kingdom; Teutonic Knights moved into the north; Germans and Jews began to colonize Polish domains.

1320–33 Ladislaus I reigned; reestablished Polish kingdom and warred against Teutonic Knights.

1333–70 Casimir III, last Piast ruler, reigned; greatly increased Polish power and prestige in Europe.

1370–82 Polish crown passed to Hungary during reign of Louis I of Hungary.

1386–1434 Ladislaus Jagiello reigned as Ladislaus II; founded Jagiello dynasty.

1386–1572 Jagiello dynasty ruled Poland; greatly expanded Polish domains and fostered a period of great cultural flowering.

1401 Treaty of Vilnius with Lithuania laid basis for union in 1569.

1410 Battle of Tannenberg fought by Poles and Lithuanians against Teutonic Knights; halted Knights' eastern advance.

1434–44 Ladislaus III reigned; died fighting the Ottoman Turks at Battle of Varna (1444).

1447–92 Casimir IV reigned; defeated Teutonic Knights in a long war (1454–66) and gained Pomerania and West Prussia.

1467 Casimir IV convened first Polish Sejm (diet).

1505 Nobles forced Polish monarchy to recognize powers of Sejm to legislate; Sejm composed of aristocrats and clergy.

1548–72 Sigismund II, last Jagiello king, reigned.

1558–82 Livonian War fought; S. Báthory gained several victories over Russia; Poland gained territory in Livonia and forced Russia to renounce its claims.

1565 Catholic Reformation began in Poland.

1569 Union of Lublin; Poland and Lithuania united under a single crown; union remained in effect until 18th cent.

1572 Nobles gained complete control of government on the death of Sigismund II; got power to elect monarch; *liberum veto*, giving any member of Sejm right to veto legislation, later weakened government and was finally abolished (1791).

1575–86 Stephen Báthory reigned; conducted war against Russia.

1587–1632 Sigismund III reigned; briefly held Swedish crown (1592–98) and after being deposed began series of wars between Poland and Sweden.

1587–1668 Vasa dynasty reigned.

c1613 Poles invaded Russia during Time of Troubles; marked new attempt to conquer Russia.

1618 Truce of Deulino halted fighting against Russia; Poles retained conquered lands.

1618–48 Thirty Years' War; Poland joined fighting against the Protestants.

1620–21 Poles victorious over the Ottoman Turks at the Battles of Chocim.

1648–68 John II Casimir reigned; Poland, its power declining, faced a Cossack rebellion in the Ukraine, an invasion by Charles X of Sweden (1655), and invasion by the Russians; Poles, however, managed to stave off total defeat.

1655–60 First Northern War with Sweden; by Peace of Oliva (1660) Polish King John II renounced his claim to the Swedish throne, lost northern Livonia.

1667 Treaty of Andrusov ended Thirteen Years' War with Russia; Poland ceded eastern Ukraine.

1682–99 Poland joined Austria in the Austro-Turkish War; Polish King John III Sobieski defeated the Ottoman Turks at Vienna (1683).

1700–21 Northern War; Poland ravaged during war as Russians and Swedes set up rival kings.

1733–35 War of the Polish Succession fought; led to succession of Augustus III as King of Poland.

1764–95 Stanislaus II elected king with the help of Russia and Prussia; dominated by Catherine II of Russia.

1768 Confederation of Bar formed to oppose Russian domination; defeated in 1772.

1772 First Partition of Poland; one-third of Polish domains annexed by Russia, Austria, and Prussia.

1791 New constitution promulgated as Polish national spirit arose; *liberum veto* abolished.

1792 Confederation of Targowica formed by conservative reactionaries.

1793 Second Partition of Poland; Russia and Prussia invaded Poland to restore conservatives to power; annexed further territories, leaving only central Poland.

1794–95 T. Kosciusko led unsuccessful revolt (1794) against partition; Russia, Prussia, and Austria divided the remaining Polish domains in Third Partition and thus eliminated the Polish state.

1807 Napoleon I established grand duchy of Warsaw by Treaty of Tilsit.

1815 Congress Kingdom of Poland created by Congress of Vienna; Russian czar was king.

1830–31 Russian Czar Nicholas I surpressed November Revolution, Polish uprising.

1863–64 Unsuccessful January Insurrection against Russian domination of Poland; program of Russification and industrialization begun.

1916 Central Powers established (Nov.) an independent kingdom of Poland during WW I.

1918 Republic of Poland proclaimed (Nov.) in wake of Central Powers' defeat in WW I; Joseph Pilsudski named chief of state.

1919 Treaty of Versailles; gave Poland Polish Corridor (strip of land to Baltic) and Polish Prussia; Gdańsk made a free city; border with Russia disputed.

1920 Russo-Polish War fought (Apr.–Oct.); sparked by Polish advances into the Ukraine.

1921 Treaty of Riga; Russia conceded substantial territories in the Ukraine.

1921 Republican constitution promulgated.

1926 Pilsudski seized power in military coup (May 12); became virtual dictator of Poland until his death in 1935.

1939 A. Hitler demanded cession of free city of Gdańsk and concessions in Polish Corridor to Danzig (Mar.); Germany and Poland entered diplomatic crisis that led to opening of WW II.

1939 Germany invaded Poland (Sept. 1), beginning WW II; USSR attacked Poland (Sept. 17); partition accord signed (Sept. 28) between USSR and Germany.

1939–45 German occupation; six million Poles killed in massacres and extermination camps; Jewish population of three million decimated; millions of others consigned to forced labor.

1941 Germany launched invasion of Russia (June); occupied Russian-held Poland.

1943 Katyn Massacre disclosed by Germans; mass grave of 10,000 Polish soldiers (captured by Soviets, 1939) discovered; Germans blamed Soviets; Polish government in exile broke off relations with Soviets.

1944 Warsaw Uprising (Aug.–Oct.); Polish underground captured Warsaw but was finally crushed by Germans, as Soviet forces waited outside Warsaw.

1945 Polish Government of National Unity established (June 28) at Lublin.

1945 Curzon Line recognized as border with Russia.

1945 Potsdam Conference; former German territory to Oder-Neisse Line (including Gdańsk) put under Polish control.

1945 Poland joined the UN.

1946 Unicameral Sejm adopted by referendum.

1947 Communist leader Boleslaw Beirut elected president (Feb. 5) by Polish Sejm.

1949 Soviet field marshal Konstantin Rokossovski made Polish minister of defense (Nov. 7).

1952 New constitution instituted Soviet-style government.

1953 Cardinal Wyszinski, Polish primate, arrested as government opposition to Roman Catholic church mounted.

1955 Poland became a founding member of the Warsaw Pact.

1956 Poznan Riots (June) by industrial workers suppressed; brought Wladyslaw Gomulka to power.

1956–70 Wladyslaw Gomulka (1905–82) in office as head of United Workers (Communist) party; brought end to repression and persecution of Catholics; denounced Stalinist terrorism and halted collectivization of agriculture; by 1960s, however, began reinstituting repression.

1970 Nonaggression treaty with West Germany signed (Dec. 7) by Polish government.

1970 Workers rioted (Dec. 15) in Gdańsk and other cities over announced sharp increases in food prices.

1970–80 Edward Gierek in power (Dec. 20) as Communist party first secretary, following resignation of Wladyslaw Gomulka.

1976 Workers struck (June 25) to protest major increases in food prices.

1979 Pope John Paul II, a native of Poland, visited Poland (June 2–11) on first visit by a pope to Marxist state.

1980 Shipyard strike in Gdańsk quickly spread to other areas in northern Poland (Aug. 14); government reshuffled while negotiations with striking workers continued; government approval of right to strike and right to form unions independent of the Communist party finally ended strike (Aug. 31).

1980 Stanislaw Kania became party secretary, succeeding the ailing Edward Gierek (Sept. 6).

1980 Newly formed independent unions organized into national federation called Solidarity (Sept. 24), led by Lech Walesa.

1981 Strike called by Solidarity for five-day work week ended after government agreed to demands (Jan. 31).

1981   100,000 workers in southern Poland went on a ten-day strike to protest corruption in local government (Feb. 6).

1981   Gen. Wojciech Jaruzelski became chairman of the Council of Ministers (Feb. 9); new strikes broke out.

1981   Millions of workers participated in four-hour general strike over various grievances (Mar. 27).

1981   Polish parliament voted (Apr. 10) to ban strikes for two months; Solidarity vowed to strike if its security was threatened.

1981   Polish government narrowly averted bankruptcy when Western nations made new arrangements for repayment of loans (Apr. 27).

1981   Premier Jaruzelski became leader of Poland's Communist party, replacing S. Kania (Oct. 18).

1981   Government declared a state of emergency (Dec. 13); imposed martial law and began a crackdown against Solidarity which included arrests of thousands of union leaders; Solidarity movement broken and government in firm control by early 1982.

1982   Polish parliament disbanded Solidarity (Oct.), banned future national union federations, and limited right to strike; moves marked effective end of Solidarity movement.

Poland, Congress Kingdom of   *See*   **Congress Kingdom of Poland**

Poland, Partitions of   *See* **Partitions of Poland**

Polano, Pietro Soave   *See* **Sarpi, Paolo**

Pole, Edmund de la, earl of Suffolk   *c*1472–1513. English aristocrat, Yorkist claimant to the throne. He sought Austrian help to make good his claim but was beheaded on the accession of King Henry VIII.

Pole, John de la, earl of Lincoln   *c*1464–87. English aristocrat, Yorkist claimant to the throne. Recognized as heir by his brother-in-law, King Richard III, he led an army from Ireland against Henry VII but was killed.

Pole, Michael de la, 1st earl of Suffolk   *c*1330–89. English chancellor (1383–86). He was a trusted adviser of King Richard II, who advanced his family's fortunes and made him earl of Suffolk. He was finally brought down by his enemies and condemned for treason by Parliament.

Pole, Reginald   1500–58. English Catholic cardinal, archbishop of Canterbury (1556–58). A cousin of the Tudors, he broke with King Henry VIII but returned to help Henry's daughter Queen Mary I (Mary Queen of Scots) in her unsuccessful attempt to restore Catholicism.

Pole, William de la, 4th earl and 1st duke of Suffolk   1396–1450. English political leader. He

became the principal minister to King Henry VI during the Hundred Years' War, and negotiated Henry's marriage (1445) to Margaret of Anjou. His attempts to secure peace with France led to his impeachment, exile, and murder.

Polianov, Treaty of   *See* **Deulino, Truce of**

Polignac, Auguste Jules Armand Marie, prince de   1780–1847.   French royalist statesman. Strongly Catholic in sympathy, he became the principal minister to King Charles X. His ordinances (1830) dissolving the chamber of deputies and muzzling the press led to the July Revolution (*q.v.*) and Charles' downfall.

polis   A Greek city-state (*q.v.*).

Polish Corridor   Territory along the Baltic awarded to Poland by the Treaty of Versailles (1919). Since it divided East Prussia from the rest of Germany, it was the cause of great friction between Poland and Nazi Germany. The dispute led ultimately to the German invasion of Poland and the opening of WW II.

Polish Succession, War of the   War (1733–38) fought to settle the disputed succession to the Polish throne after the death of Polish king Augustus II. Poland, with the support of France, Spain, and Sardinia, sought the succession of Stanislaus I Leszczynski. Russia and Austria supported the accession of Frederick Augustus II, elector of Saxony, as Augustus III. The war ended with the Treaty of Vienna (1735, ratified 1738), by which France acknowledged the accession of Augustus III, and Leszczynski, who abandoned his claim to the throne (1736), received the duchy of Lorraine, which was to revert back to France upon his death. The Spanish ceded Parma and Piacenza to Austria but kept the kingdom of Naples and Sicily.

Politburo   Soviet governmental body. The Politburo is the policy-making and administrative arm of the Communist Party of the USSR and therefore of all Soviet Russia. The first Politburo was created by the Bolsheviks shortly before the 1917 revolution, and included N. Lenin, L. Trotsky, and J. Stalin. After the revolution the Politburo was dissolved, but it was reestablished in 1919. Stalin abolished it in 1952, replacing it with the Presidium. The Politburo was restored in 1966. It generally includes 11 or 12 members, and its meetings are secret.

Politian, Angelo Ambrogini   1454–94. Italian Renaissance humanist. One of the finest classical scholars of the classical revival, he also wrote outstanding vernacular poetry and the first secular play in Italian (1475).

Polk, James Knox   1795–1849.   US president (1845–49), the eleventh, successor to J. Tyler.

During his term of office the US fought the Mexican War *(q.v.)* and thereby greatly expanded its territories in the West and Southwest. A Jacksonian Democrat and staunch supporter of American expansionism, Polk was nominated for president as a "dark horse" candidate to break the deadlocked 1844 Democratic convention. Campaigning on the slogan "Fifty-four Forty or Fight" (the Oregon Territory boundary then being disputed with Britain), he defeated H. Clay in a close election. During his term of office, Polk reestablished an independent Treasury, lowered tariffs through the Walker Tariff Act (1846), successfully negotiated the Oregon Territory boundary dispute, and acquired the Western and Southwestern territories from Mexico.

Polk, Leonides 1806–64. American Episcopal bishop and Confederate general. A graduate (1827) of West Point, he resigned his commission to become a missionary and became first bishop of Louisiana (1841–61). When the American Civil War broke out, he became a Confederate general and was killed in action.

Pollaiuolo, Antonio 1429?–98. Florentine Renaissance artist. Especially noted for his bronze statues, Pollaiuolo also pioneered the study of human anatomy through dissection.

Pollock, Paul Jackson 1912–56. American painter. Viewing art as expression rather than illustration, he became the leading practitioner of abstract expressionism.

Pollux *See* **Castor and Pollux**

Polo, Marco 1254?–1324? Venetian traveler in China. His book known in English as *The Travels of Marco Polo* was one of the earliest and most important sources of Western knowledge of Asia. Born into a Venetian merchant family, he accompanied (1271) his father and uncle on a trip across central Asia. They reached Peking and the court of the Mongol emperor Kublai Khan (1275). Polo became a favorite of the emperor and performed missions for him. He returned to Europe via Persia (1292) and arrived in Venice in 1295. Captured by the Genoese in a sea battle and imprisoned in Genoa, he dictated his fabulous memoirs to a fellow prisoner.

Poltava, Battle of Victory (July 8, 1709) of the forces of Russian czar Peter I over Sweden's king Charles XII, at Poltava, Ukraine during the Northern War. An army of some 50,000 Russians destroyed the entire 20,000-man invading Swedish army, except for some 1,500 who fled south into Turkey with Charles. The battle marked the emergence of Russia as a great European power and ended Sweden's position as a military power.

Polyanov, Peace of Treaty (1634) between Russia and Poland. By its terms Poland received Smolensk in return for Polish recognition of Michael as czar. Michael inaugurated the Romanov dynasty, which ruled Russia until 1917.

Polybius 203?–*c*120 BC. Greek historian. Deported to Rome, he conceived the idea of his great history, relating in 40 books (of which five survive) the conquest of the Mediterranean world by the Romans.

Polycarp, Saint AD *c*70–156? Greek bishop of Smyrna, Asia Minor. A disciple of Saint John the Apostle and the mentor of Saint Irenaeus, he was a leading figure in the establishment of early Christian theology.

Polycrates *d. c*522 BC. Greek tyrant of Samos (*c*535–522 BC). Polycrates gained Samian naval eminence in the Aegean. He sent a fleet of 40 ships commanded by his political foes to aid the Persians against Egypt, but they combined with Spartans in an unsuccessful attempt to depose him. He was eventually lured to the mainland and executed by a Persian satrap.

Polymnia *See* **Muses**

Polyphemus Mythical Greek monster, a cyclops. In Homer's *Odyssey*, he kept Odysseus and his men prisoners in his cave. They got Polyphemus drunk and blinded him, thus securing their escape.

polytheism Belief in many gods, as opposed to the monotheism of Christianity, Judaism, and Islam. In polytheism, each god tends to become identified with a function, such as fire, storm, death, etc., and each tends to become personified.

Pombal, Sebastião José de Carvalho e Mello, marquês de 1699–1782. Portuguese statesman. He organized the reconstruction of Lisbon after the great earthquake of 1755. As chief minister (1756–77) he introduced reforms and reduced the power of the Inquisition, but his harsh, authoritarian, and anticlerical rule earned him great enmity.

Pomerania Historic European region on the Baltic Sea. Originally occupied by Slavs, the area has been overrun, split up, and ruled by several countries, including Prussia, Poland, and Sweden. Many of the leading cities, such as Danzig, were once prominent in the Hanseatic League. Most of Pomerania was restored to Poland after the Potsdam Conference (1945).

Pomerania, Eric of *See* **Eric VII**

Pompadour, Jeanne Antoinette Poisson, marquise de 1721–64. Royal mistress of French king Louis XV. Through her intelligence and beauty she exercised great influence over the king and French policies. She was an outstanding patron of the arts.

Pompeii Ancient Roman city. Situated at the foot of Mount Vesuvius near modern Naples, it was damaged by an earthquake (AD 63), and then completely covered over by the eruption of Vesuvius (AD 79). Rediscovered (1748), it has become a major source of our knowledge of Roman civilization.

Pompeius, Sextus ⟨Pompey the Younger⟩ c75–35 BC. Roman commander. A son of Pompey the Great, he continued to fight against Caesar's forces after Pompey's death (48 BC). He occupied Sicily and attempted to cut off Rome's grain supply. Eventually defeated (36 BC), he fled to Asia Minor but was captured and killed.

Pompey 106–48 BC. Roman general and statesman. Pompey gained important victories in Africa, Italy, Spain, and Gaul, and won for himself the title Magnus ("the Great"). He defeated Lepidus (77 BC), Sertorius (76 BC), and Spartacus (72 BC). In 70 BC he was elected consul along with Marcus Licinius Crassus. Pompey cleared the Mediterranean of pirates and consolidated Rome's Asian possessions. Together with Crassus and J. Caesar, he formed the First Triumvirate (61 BC). The rivalry between Caesar and Pompey remained submerged during Pompey's marriage to Caesar's daughter Julia but intensified after her death (54 BC). In 49 BC, Caesar crossed the Rubicon, invaded Italy, and defeated Pompey at Pharsalus (48 BC). Pompey fled to Egypt, where he was murdered.

Pompey the Younger See **Pompeius, Sextus**

Pompidou, Georges Jean Raymond 1911–74. French premier (1962–68) and president of the Fifth Republic (1969–74). A wartime protégé of C. de Gaulle, he later became prominent as both banker and politician, and helped draft the constitution of the Fifth Republic.

Ponce de León, Juan c1460–1521. Spanish explorer. He founded the oldest settlement in Puerto Rico (1508–09), and discovered Florida (1513), supposedly in quest of a mythical "fountain of youth."

Poncelet, Jean Victor 1788–1867. French mathematician. While a war prisoner in Russia following Napoleon I's campaign, he developed the foundations of modern projective geometry.

Pondicherry Former French colony on the southeast coast of India. Founded in 1674, it was the object of fighting during 18th-cent. colonial wars between Britain and France.

The colony remained in French hands until 1954 (when it was ceded to India), the last remnant of extensive domains lost to the British in the 18th cent.

Poniatowski, Prince Józef Anton 1763–1813. Polish military leader. He fought with distinction against Russia (1792) and took part in the Polish revolt (1794) led by T. Kosciusko. He later became commander in chief of the duchy of Warsaw (1807) under Napoleon, and fought and died during Napoleon's Russian campaign.

Pontiac c1720–69. Ottawa Indian chief who organized the Great Lakes Indian tribes in a nearly successful uprising known as Pontiac's Rebellion (q.v.).

Pontiac's Conspiracy See **Pontiac's Rebellion**

Pontiac's Rebellion ⟨Pontiac's Conspiracy⟩ 1763–66. American Indian uprising against the British after the French and Indian Wars. Pontiac, an Ottawa Indian chief, realized that the British were far less friendly to Indians than the defeated French. He enlisted the support of the tribes of the Great Lakes region and conducted a series of raids on British settlements. Though these attacks were brilliantly planned and executed, superior British weaponry forced Pontiac to sue for peace. The uprising was ended by a treaty of amity (July 25, 1766).

Pontius Pilate fl. AD 26. Roman procurator of Judaea. By "washing his hands" of ultimate responsibility, he allowed the crucifixion of Jesus.

Pontus Ancient country of northeastern Asia Minor, on the Black Sea, in what is now Turkey. It was founded by Mithradates II (c3d cent. BC), and reached its height under the reign of Mithradates VI. The Pontic Empire was not strong enough, however, to withstand the Romans. Pompey occupied Pontus (66 BC), and it was subsequently made a Roman province.

pony express Mail delivery system between St. Joseph, Missouri, and Sacramento, California (inaugurated Apr. 3, 1860). The horse and rider system required more than 150 horse-changing stations to enable relay riders to cover the distance in eight to ten days. The pony express was phased out after the first telegraph service to San Franciso began (Oct. 24, 1861).

Poole, William Frederick 1821–94. American librarian. A director of public libraries in Boston, Cincinnati, and Chicago, he devised (1848) the first periodical index, *Poole's Index to Periodical Literature*.

Pop art Art movement (late 1950s to early 1970s) in which subject matter was taken from the popular culture and included reproductions of such things as comic strips and well-known commercial products. It evolved as a reaction against the cultural pretensions Pop artists saw in other art movements. Andy Warhol (1930–) was one of its leading proponents.

pope *See* **papacy**

Pope, Alexander 1688–1744. English poet and satirist. A master of the heroic couplet and one of the great poets of his age, Pope expressed the ideas of his time in such graceful and polished works as his *Essay on Man*. Among his other works were *Essay on Criticism, The Rape of the Lock,* and *The Dunciad.*

Pope, John 1822–92. Union general in the American Civil War. Pope fought with distinction on the Mississippi but was disastrously defeated at the second Battle of Bull Run (1862).

Popish Plot Fictitious English plot fabricated (1678) by T. Oates. According to Oates, Catholics had formed a conspiracy to assassinate English king Charles II. The wave of hysteria caused by Oates' allegations led to the persecution and killing of many Catholics.

Popol Vuh Quiché Indian (Mayan) manuscript of the 16th cent. Written by a converted Quiché and based on traditional Indian documents and lore, it is an important source for ancient Mayan mythology and culture.

Poppaea Sabina *d.* AD 65. Wife (*m.* AD 62) of the Roman emperor Nero. She is said to have persuaded Nero to kill his former wife, his own mother, and the philosopher Seneca. Nero is said to have kicked her to death.

Popular Front Political coalitions in Europe formed by liberals, moderates, Socialists, and Communists during the 1930s. These coalitions were aimed at blocking the then growing Fascist movement, and Popular Front coalitions gained control of governments in France and Spain during the 1930s. (*See also* France [1936]; Second Republic [Spanish].)

popular sovereignty ⟨squatter sovereignty⟩ Pre-Civil War US political doctrine. It held that the settlers of territories had the right to decide whether they would enter the Union as free or slave states. The doctrine was supported by Sen. S. Douglas and was incorporated into the Compromise of 1850 and the Kansas-Nebraska Act (*q.q.v.*). Opponents of the plan called it "squatter sovereignty," and it proved to be a failure in settling the slavery question. It led to serious conflicts in the territories, notably Bleeding Kansas (*q.v.*).

Populist party American political party that attempted to challenge the major parties during the 1890s by allying an agrarian coalition with labor and other interests. From the 1870s, when farm prices began to decline, American farmers sought to advance their interests through groups such as the Granger movement, the Greenback party, and the Farmers' Alliances. By 1892 the Populist party was formed. It advocated free coinage of silver and expansion of the currency; lowering of transportation costs by nationalization of the railroads; a graduated income tax; direct popular election of senators; and an eight-hour working day. The party nominated J. Weaver for president in 1892, and he received more than a million votes. The party made further gains in the 1894 congressional elections. Because of a convergence of interests in free silver, the party supported the Democratic candidate, W. Bryan, in 1896. After Bryan's defeat, the party rapidly declined as a political force. Some of the elements of its platform were later enacted by the major parties.

Populists *See* **Narodniki**

Poquelin, Jean Baptiste *See* **Molière**

Porphyrogenitus, Constantine *See* **Constantine VII**

Porphyry ⟨Malchus⟩ AD *c*233–*c*304. Greek Neoplatonic philosopher. A disciple and biographer of Plotinus, he also wrote 15 books of anti-Christian polemics, *Adversus Christianos.*

Porson, Richard 1759–1808. English classical scholar. He produced outstanding critical editions of such classical writers as Aeschylus and Euripides.

Port-au-Prince Haitian capital (pop. 745,700). Founded (1749) by French planters, Port-au-Prince has become the chief port as well as the cultural center of Haiti.

Porter, Cole 1893–1964. American composer and lyricist. Porter's lyrics and arresting tunes for such musical shows as *Can Can* and *Kiss Me Kate* made him one of the leading popular composers of his day.

Porter, David 1780–1843. American naval officer. He served in the Tripolitan War, and, as captain of the *Essex* during the War of 1812, captured the *Alert,* the first British warship taken in the war.

Porter, David Dixon 1813–91. American admiral. Son of D. Porter. During the American Civil War, he commanded Union forces on the Mississippi and in the Atlantic blockade, and he contributed to the Union victories at New Orleans (1862) and Vicksburg (1863).

Porter, Horace 1837–1921. American general and diplomat. During the American Civil War, he served as aide-de-camp to Gen. U. Grant (1864–65). He later served as secretary to Pres. Grant (to 1872), US minister to France (1897–1905), and as a US delegate to the Hague Conference (1907).

Porter, Katherina Anne 1890–1980. American writer, considered a master of the short story. She is also the author of an acclaimed novel, *Ship of Fools.*

Porter, William Sydney *See* **Henry, O.**

Portland, William Bentinck, 1st earl of 1649–1709. Dutch-born English statesman. He negotiated the marriage (1677) of William of Orange (King William III) to Mary, daughter of the duke of York (later James II). He accompanied William to England (1688), was created 1st earl of Portland, and fought for William at the Battle of the Boyne (1690). He negotiated the Treaty of Ryswick (1697).

Porto *See* **Oporto**

Porto Rico *See* **Puerto Rico**

Portsmouth, Treaty of Treaty concluded (Sept. 5, 1905) between Russia and Japan at Portsmouth, New Hampshire, ending the Russo-Japanese War. By its terms Russia recognized Japan as the dominant power in Korea and ceded Port Arthur, the Liao-tung Peninsula, and southern Sakhalin Island to Japan. Both powers agreed to restore Manchuria to China.

Portugal (Portuguese Republic) Country located on the west coast of the Iberian peninsula in southern Europe. Its capital is Lisbon. Portugal emerged as an independent state (12th cent.) during the reconquest of the Muslim-held Iberian peninsula by Spanish Christians. From the 15th to 16th cent., the Portuguese created a formidable overseas colonial empire in Asia, Africa, and South America. The Portuguese were soon eclipsed by the other European powers, however. The monarchy was overthrown in 1910. After a period of unstable republican government, A. Salazar came to power (1932) and began his long rule. His death was followed by a period of instability and return to republican government (1976). Key events in Portuguese history include:

5TH–8TH CENT. AD Region, under Roman control (from 1st cent. BC), was later occupied by Visigoths.

711 Moors (Muslims) conquered Visigoths and took control of entire Iberian peninsula.

9TH CENT. Gradual reconquest of region from Muslims begun by Spanish Christians.

1095 County of Portugal given to Count Henry of Burgundy by Alfonso VI of Castile; was dowry of his illegitimate daughter Teresa.

1128 Alfonso I Henriques, son of Henry of Burgundy, seized power in the county; had himself crowned king after defeating the Moors at the Battle of Ourique (1139).

1143 Treaty of Zamora granted Portugal independence from Spain; Alfonso I recognized as king.

1179 Pope Alexander III recognized Portugal as an independent kingdom.

1223–48 Alfonso II reigned; he convened first Cortes.

1248–79 Alfonso III reigned; instituted administrative reforms and promoted commerce.

1250 Algarve in the south finally conquered from the Moors, bringing the Portuguese mainland to its present-day limits.

1256 Lisbon, recaptured from the Moors in 1147, became the Portuguese capital.

1294 King Diniz signed a commercial treaty with Edward I, the first of a long series of English-Portuguese pacts.

1385 Battle of Aljubarrota ended long series of wars with the Spanish kingdom of Castile; Portuguese victory assured Portugal's continued independence.

1385–1433 John I reigned; marked beginning of Portuguese exploration and colonization; wars against the Muslims in North Africa.

1386 Treaty of Windsor allied Portugal permanently with England; John I married to Philippa, daughter of John of Gaunt.

1415 Conquest of Ceuta in Africa from the Moors; Portuguese subsequently expanded control in Morocco.

1418 Prince Henry the Navigator began exploration of the African coast.

1427 Azores discovered and opened to colonization.

1460 Cape Verde Islands and the coast of Guinea became Portuguese colonies; death of Prince Henry the Navigator.

1488 Africa's Cape of Good Hope rounded by Bartholomew Diaz.

1494 Treaty of Tordesillas (June 7) signed with Spain; provided for division of newly discovered lands in Americas, Africa, and Asia.

1496 Jews expelled from Portugal; exodus of middle class and highly educated Jews weakened Portugal.

1497–98 V. da Gama opened up trade route from Portugal to India, providing the foundation for Portuguese Empire.

1500 Brazil claimed by Pedro Alvares Cabral.

1510 A. de Albuquerque occupied Goa, the best port on India's west coast; Goa was a Portuguese colony for over 450 years.

1511 Albuquerque conquered Malacca on Malay peninsula; Portuguese first of European colonial powers to reach China.

1512–13 Occupation of the Moluccas (islands of Indonesia).

1521–57 John III reigned; Portugal reached its height; influence expanded in Brazil, India, Macao, and Moluccas.

1536 Inquisition established.

1578 Battle of Alcazarquivir in Morocco; Sebastian, son of John III, killed with the flower of Portuguese nobility (Aug. 4); kingdom permanently weakened.

1580 Succession disputed after Sebastian's brother, Cardinal Henry, died; Philip II of Spain invaded and conquered Portugal.

1580–1640 Sixty Years' Captivity saw Portugal ruled as Spanish province; Portuguese seaborne empire declined.

1580–98 Spanish King Philip II reigned as Philip I.

c1636 Dutch seized Ceylon and Malacca from the Portuguese; other Asian possessions lost.

1640 Portuguese successfully rebelled against Spanish rule and regained independence.

1640–56 John IV reigned; founded Braganza line; drove Dutch out of Brazil.

1640–1910 Braganca line in power.

1663 Battle of Ameixial (June 8); Portuguese defeated Spanish invaders.

1668 Treaty of Lisbon; Spain recognized Portuguese independence.

1701–14 War of the Spanish Succession; Portugal participated after 1703.

1703 Treaty of Methuen (Dec. 27) gave Portuguese wines preference in England in return for preferential treatment of English textiles.

1750–77 Marquês de Pombal effectively ruled Portugal as minister to Joseph I; introduced Enlightenment ideas, strengthened monarchy at expense of nobles and church, sought to revitalize declining commerce and agriculture.

1755 Lisbon earthquake destroyed the city and killed thousands.

1777–1816 Maria I reigned; Pombal's reforms rescinded, bringing on renewed slow decline of the kingdom.

1801 War of the Oranges; Portugal conquered and divided by France and Spain.

1807 Napoleon's armies marched on Portugal; royal family fled to Brazil; Peninsular War began in following year.

1811 Portugal at last cleared of French troops. Royal family remained in Brazil.

1815 Brazil became a kingdom separate from Portugal, united by the crown.

1816 John VI succeeded to the thrones of both Portugal and Brazil.

1820 Liberal revolution in Portugal created a constitutional monarchy.

1821 John VI returned to Portugal from Brazil; reigned as constitutional monarch (1822–26).

1822 Brazil proclaimed independence; Pedro I established as constitutional monarch there.

1826 Maria II acceded to throne under the regency of Dom Miguel.

1828–33 Civil war; Miguel usurped the throne; Pedro I came to Portugal (1831) and, with the help of European powers, aided the liberals in restoring Maria (1833).

1834–53 Maria II reigned after reaching her majority; struggle between liberals and conservatives during her reign laid basis for later reforms.

1861–89 Louis I reigned; slavery abolished in colonies; legal reforms instituted.

1889–1908 Charles I reigned; assassinated after granting dictatorial powers to his prime minister. João Franco.

1908 Manuel II, last of the Braganzas, succeeded to the throne.

1910 Manuel II deposed by a military coup (Oct. 3–5); republic declared.

1911 Republican constitution instituted; church and state separated.

1911–15 M. de Arriaga in office as first elected president; period of economic problems and political unrest continued into 1920s.

1914–18 Portugal fought with the Allies in WW I.

1926 Military overthrew the government (May).

1926–51 A. Carmona installed as president.

1926 A. Salazar named finance minister; engineered Portugal's economic recovery.

1932–68 Salazar in power as prime minister; thereafter ruled Portugal as dictator.

1933 Salazar-sponsored constitution transformed Portugal into a "corporative state."

1936–39 Salazar supported Gen. F. Franco in the Spanish Civil War.

1939–45 WW II; Portugal remained neutral; from 1943 allowed Allies use of Azores.

1949 Portugal became a founding member of NATO.

1955 Portugal became a member of the UN.

1961 Goa forcibly invaded by the Indian army and annexed to India (Dec. 18).

1962 Revolt by independence fighters in Portuguese Angola broke out.

1968–74 M. Caetano in office as prime minister; replaced the ailing Salazar; opposition to repressive government mounted.

1970 Salazar, long-time head of Portuguese government, died (July 27).

1974 Military coup (Apr. 25) followed government's failure to maintain control over overseas territories in Africa; military junta led by Gen. Antonio de Spinola in power.

1974 Independence granted to Guinea-Bissau (Aug. 26).

1974–76 Gen. Francisco da Costa Gomes in office; replaced De Spinola as president (Sept. 30).

1975 Gen. De Spinola's followers failed in attempted coup (Mar. 11).

1975 Banks and insurance companies nationalized by leftist government (Mar. 14–15).

1975 Agreements reached providing independence to Cape Verde Islands (July 5), Mozambique (June 25), São Tomé and Principe (July 12) and Angola (Nov. 11).

1975 Three-man military junta put in charge of country (July 25).

1975 Communist revolt crushed by government troops (Nov. 25–27).

1976 New constitution adopted.

1976 Moderate Socialist, Gen. Antonio Ramalho Eanes, elected to presidency in first free elections in decades (June 27).

1980 President Ramalho Eanes reelected (Dec. 8) after death of his principal opponent, Francisco Sá Carneiro.

Portuguese East Africa *See* **Mozambique**

Portuguese Guinea *See* **Guinea-Bissau**

Portuguese India Former Portuguese possessions in India. Comprising Goa, Daman, and Diu, they were the remnants of more extensive possessions and were annexed by India (Dec., 1961).

Poseidon Ancient Greek god of the sea. He is identified with the Roman god Neptune.

Poseidonius ⟨Posidonius⟩ *c*135–*c*51 BC. Greek Stoic philosopher. He was very successful in promoting Stoicism among the Romans, but none of his voluminous writings has survived.

Posidonius *See* **Poseidonius**

positivism School of philosophical thought. Positivism holds that all knowledge is based solely on sense experience and denies the possibility of transcendantal or metaphysical knowledge. The origins of both the name and the school are usually ascribed to A. Comte.

Posse. Count Arvid *See* **Agrarian Party**

Post, Emily Price 1873–1960. American writer on manners. Her book *Etiquette* went through some 90 editions, and her newspaper columns, giving commonsense rules for etiquette, ran in some 200 newspapers.

postimpressionism Movement in art dominant in the late 19th and early 20th cents. Going beyond impressionism's preoccupation with light, painters such as P. Cézanne, P. Gauguin, and V. van Gogh combined brilliant colors with studies of angle and form, thus paving the way for the major 20th-cent. movements Cubism and Fauvism.

Potato War *See* **Bavarian Succession, War of the**

Potawatomi Indians North American Indian tribe. First discovered in northern Wisconsin, they moved to occupy both sides of southern Lake Michigan in the 18th cent. In the 1860s, many moved to Kansas and Oklahoma. The Potawatomi took part in Pontiac's Rebellion *(q.v.)* and fought with the British in the War of 1812.

Potemkin, Grigori Aleksandrovich 1739–91. Russian field marshal and statesman. He helped bring Catherine II to the throne (1762) and remained a powerful and influential favorite of hers. He served with distinction in the Russo-Turkish Wars.

Potidaea Ancient Greek city. Colonized *c*600 BC, it led a revolt against Athens (432 BC) that was a cause of the second Peloponnesian War. The city was destroyed (356 BC) by Philip II of Macedon.

Potsdam Conference ⟨Berlin Conference⟩ Allied meeting (July 17–Aug. 2, 1945) at Potsdam, near Berlin, after Germany's surrender in WW II. Present at the conference were US president H. Truman, Russian premier J. Stalin, and Great Britain's prime ministers, first W. Churchill and later (from July 26, after he had succeeded Churchill as prime minister) C. Atlee. The resulting Potsdam Agreement outlawed Nazism in Germany, placed Germany's eastern provinces under the control of Russia and Poland, decentralized the German economy, set terms for reparations, and agreed to try war criminals. The Potsdam Declaration (July 26) called on Japan to surrender unconditionally.

Pottawatomie Massacre Murder of five proslavery settlers on the night of May 24–25, 1856, on Pottawatomie Creek, Kansas. The massacre was carried out by abolitionist J. Brown and his party, and most of the victims were associated with the enforcement of proslavery laws.

Potter, Beatrix 1866–1943. English author of children's stories. She created such classics as the stories of Peter Rabbit and Benjamin Bunny and illustrated them with her own delicate watercolors.

Poulenc, Francis 1899–1963. French composer. A member of Les Six *(q.v.)*, he wrote a variety of sophisticated, often witty songs and is considered a leading composer of this century.

Pound, Ezra Loomis 1885–1972. American poet. A leader in early 20th-cent. modernist literary movements, he created original poetical works, notably his *Cantos*, and was a major influence on US and British literature. His pro-Fascist broadcasts from Italy during WW II led to his incarceration (1946–58) in a mental hospital in Washington, D.C.

Poussin, Nicholas 1594–1665. French painter. Considered the leading 17th-cent. French artist, he painted both religious and mythological scenes in a style that set the standard for French classicism.

Powderly, Terence V   *See* **Knights of Labor**

Powell, John Wesley 1834–1902. American geologist and ethnologist. Surveyor of the Colorado River system, he was the director of the Smithsonian's Bureau of Ethnology (1879–1902) and of the US Geological Survey (1881–94).

Powers, Hiram 1805–73. American sculptor. He worked in Florence in the predominant neoclassical style and became famous for such works as the nude *Greek Slave.*

Powhatan Confederacy League of North American Indian tribes consisting of some 200 settlements in the Virginia tidewater region and on the east shore of the Chesapeake. The confederacy was formed by Chief Wahunsonacock (called Powhatan by settlers) and for a time had friendly relations with the English colonists at Jamestown. The marriage of J. Rolfe to Pocahontas, the chief's daughter, kept the peace until Wahunsonacock's death. Thereafter, Indian resentment over white encroachment on their lands resulted in the Powhatan War *(q.v.)* and defeat of the confederacy.

Powhatan War Intermittent struggle of the tidewater Indian tribes of colonial Virginia and Maryland against encroachment of whites seeking new tobacco lands. The marriage of Pocahontas, daughter of the Indian chief Powhatan (1550?–1618), to J. Rolfe had helped keep peace with the English settlers, but after Powhatan's death his successor led an attack (1622) in which some 350 settlers were killed. Settler reprisal was fierce. The next large-scale Indian attack came in 1644, when some 500 settlers were killed. But the tide soon went against the Indians, eventually resulting in the death of three-quarters of the tribe and the takeover of most of their lands.

Poynings, Sir Edward   *See* **Poynings' Law**

Poynings' Law Acts of the Irish Parliament (1494) secured by the English governor of Ireland, Sir Edward Poynings (1459–1521). The acts sharply limited the power of the Irish Parliament and included statutes putting English laws in force in Ireland and requiring approval of the English king and council for all parliamentary acts.

Poznan Riots Uprising (June, 1956) in the western Polish city of Poznan. Industrial workers staged a general strike demanding bread and freedom. It was suppressed with military force, leaving 53 dead and over 200 wounded, but it led to a change in Polish Communist party leadership.

Pozzo di Borgo, Carlo Andrea 1764–1842. Corsican statesman who served in the Russian diplomatic service. An opponent of the Bonapartes, he worked to promote the alliances that eventually defeated Napoleon I and restored the Bourbon dynasty.

praefect   *See* **prefect**

Praetorian Guard   *See* **Praetorians**

Praetorians ⟨Praetorian Guard⟩ Special military force organized (27 BC) by the Roman emperor Augustus to guard the emperor. As the only military force allowed in Rome, they acquired great power, even making and deposing emperors. Septimius Severus reorganized them (AD 193), and Constantine finally abolished them (AD 312).

Praetorius, Michael 1571–1621. German composer, born Schultheiss. He is remembered for his hundreds of religious choral works as well as for his *Syntagma Musicum*, a history of 17th-cent. music.

pragmatic sanction Royal decree on an issue of major importance to the state. The most famous of these sanctions was that issued by Holy Roman Emperor Charles VI in 1713. Lacking male heirs, Charles decreed that succession to the vast Hapsburg family domains would be continued through his daughter Maria Theresa and not his older brother's daughters. Charles worked tirelessly to secure acceptance of the sanction by European rulers. Nevertheless, Charles' death (1740) marked the beginning of the War of the Spanish Succession *(q.v.)* over Maria Theresa's accession. The Treaty of Aix-la-Chapelle (1748) ending the war confirmed the Pragmatic Sanction of 1713. (*See also* Pragmatic Sanction of Bourges.)

Pragmatic Sanction of Bourges Royal edict issued (July 7, 1438) by French king Charles VII. It supported the Council of Basil, restricted papal authority in France and thus advanced the cause of Gallicanism *(q.v.)*, and extended Charles' control over the French church. Louis XI revoked the pragmatic sanction (1461), and it was finally replaced by the Concordat of Bologna (1516).

Pragmatic Sanction of 1713   *See* **pragmatic sanction**

pragmatism Important 20-cent. philosophical school first articulated by C. Peirce (1878) and developed by W. James and others. It stresses experimentation and practical usefulness as major tests of philosophical truths and places actual experience above speculative doctrines. Other pragmatists include the American J. Dewey and the Europeans F. Schiller and H. Bergson.

Prague Capital city (pop. 1,173,000) of Czechoslovakia; an industrial, commercial, and transportation center. Dating to the 9th cent., it became a leading European city (14th cent.) under Holy Roman Emperor Charles IV. It was a center for the Hussite religious movement (15th cent.). The Hapsburgs came to rule Prague, and it was the scene of the Defenestration of Prague (q.v.) in 1618, which contributed to the Thirty Years' War. In 1918, Prague became the capital of independent Czechoslovakia. It was occupied by the Germans in WW II and was the center of the Prague Spring (q.v.) movement.

Prague, Battle of Prussian victory over Austrian forces before Prague (May 6, 1757) during the Seven Years' War. Prussian forces of some 64,000 under Prussian king Frederick II defeated an Austrian army of comparable size, forcing some Austrian units to retreat and the balance to retire within the city. The Prussians began a siege of the city.

Prague, Defenestration of See **Defenestration of Prague**

Prague, Jerome of See **Jerome of Prague**

Prague, Peace of Treaty (May 30, 1635) ending hostilities between Holy Roman Emperor Ferdinand II, the elector of Saxony, and other German princes. It closed the Swedish phase of the Thirty Years' War.

Prague, Treaty of Agreement (Aug. 23, 1866) ending the Austro-Prussian War. Austria recognized Prussian hegemony over Schleswig-Holstein and was excluded from the North German Confederation, which O. von Bismarck would later form into a modern, unified Germany.

Praguerie Revolt by French noblemen (Feb., 1440) against King Charles VII. Opposed to the king's military reforms and other measures intended to reduce their power, the nobles arose in imitation of a similar revolt in Prague (hence the name). The dauphin (who later became Louis XI) became the figurehead of the revolt, and the nobles continued to resist royal authority until July, 1440.

Prague Spring Abortive attempt to liberalize the Communist regime in Czechoslovakia (Jan.–Aug., 1968). It began with the ouster of the hardline Czech Communist party leader in favor of liberal Communist A. Dubček, and the movement thereafter became a bold attempt to effect democratic and economic reforms within a Communist country. It was an affront to the Russians, how-

ever, and on Aug. 20, 1968, the Russian-dominated Warsaw Pact invaded Czechoslovakia and quickly ended the Prague Spring.

Prairial, coup of 30 See **French Revolution** (1799)

Prajadhipok See **Chakkri dynasty**

Prakrit Family of Indic languages. Developed from the 6th cent. BC as vernacular dialects of Sanskrit, they were rarely literary languages (except the Buddhist sacred language Pali), but they formed the basis of modern Indo-Aryan languages.

Prasad, Rajendra 1884–1963. First president of the republic of India (1950–62). A disciple of M. Gandhi, he was three times president of the Congress party and also presided over the Constituent Assembly that drafted India's constitution (1949).

Pratt, Charles, 1st Earl Camden 1714–94. British jurist, noted for his decision against the legality of general warrants. He was lord chancellor from 1766 to 1770 and was dismissed for opposing taxation of the American colonies.

Praxiteles fl. c370–c330 BC. Ancient Greek sculptor. Considered one of the greatest classical artists, he was famous in antiquity for his nude Aphrodite of Cnidus.

Preble, Edward 1761–1807. American naval officer. He commanded the first American naval force east of the Cape of Good Hope (1799). He also commanded the Constitution in the Tripolitan War.

predestination Theological doctrine holding that God preordains those whom he will save. Some form of the doctrine was developed in the West by Saint Augustine and was further developed by Calvinism.

Preemption Act US statute (1841) by which squatters occupying government lands could purchase 160 acres from the government at nominal cost provided certain conditions were met. The act was repealed Mar. 3, 1891.

prefect ⟨praefect⟩ In ancient Roman government, a class of officers and magistrates to whom authority was delegated. The prefects of the city ruled it in the absence of the consuls, and the Praetorian prefects, commanding the Praetorians, sometimes functioned as virtual prime ministers of the emperors.

Pre-Raphaelites School of English painters and poets, including D.G. Rossetti and J. Millais. The group flourished from 1848 to 1853 and drew its inspiration from the realism of the Italian painters prior to Raphael.

Presbyterianism System of church organization that rose within the Christian church during the Protestant Reformation. It represents a compromise between government by bishops (episcopacy) and congregationalism. Elders assume ministerial and administrative responsibilities within the congregation. Generally Presbyterian churches are governed by a hierarchy of four separate bodies. The session is the governing body of the congregation. Above the session is the presbytery, composed of ministers and elders sent from congregations within a designated area. It is responsible for confirming the congregation's appointment of ministers. Above the presbytery is the synod, which holds some authority over the sessions and presbyteries. The ultimate body is the general assembly, which meets each year to deal with questions involving the entire church. Its head is elected for a term of one year and is the head of the church. Presbyterianism was greatly advanced as a movement by J. Calvin. It spread to the British Isles in the 16th cent. and its doctrinal principles were established by the British Parliament in the 17th cent. Presbyterianism rose in Scotland through the efforts of J. Knox, who founded the Church of Scotland. Other Presbyterian churches included the Presbyterian Church of Ireland and the Calvinistic Methodist Church, in Wales. Presbyterianism also influenced the religious movements in Europe, notably the Huguenots (French Protestants). In America, the Presbyterian Church was founded by the Irish Presbyterian leader, Francis Makemie (1658?–1708). Makemie emigrated to America in 1683 and founded the first presbytery in America in 1706. By the mid-18th cent., disputes arose within the movement over evangelical principles and revivals. Presbyterianism in America later branched into numerous groups. Among the leading Presbyterian bodies today are the United Presbyterian Church in the United States of America, Cumberland Presbyterian Church, and Reformed Presbyterian Church of North America.

Prescott, William Hickling 1796–1859. American historian. His fame rests on the histories *The Conquest of Mexico* and *The Conquest of Peru*, both noted for their distinguished literary style.

president Chief executive officer of a body or state. Most modern republics are headed by presidents, sometimes with extensive powers, as in the US and France, or with restricted powers as in Italy, West Germany, or India. (*See also* Executive Branch; prime minister.)

Presley, Elvis Aron 1935–77. American rock music singer. After his first hit song, *Heartbreak Hotel*, he dominated American rock music until the early 1960s.

pre-Socratics Collective name for those Greek philosophers and schools of philosophy that preceded Socrates. Among the schools are the Ionian, Pythagorean, Eleatic, atomist, and Sophist.

Pressburg, Treaty of Treaty (Dec. 26, 1805) between Napoleon I and Austria during the Napoleonic Wars. It was negotiated after Austria's defeat at the battles of Austerlitz and Ulm and eliminated Austria from the Third Coalition against Napoleon. Austria ceded extensive lands in both Italy and Germany to form new Napoleonic kingdoms and paid a huge indemnity. In return it received Salzburg.

Prester John Legendary Christian ruler. According to 12th cent. accounts originating with the crusaders, Prester John ruled a vast Christian land first thought to be in Asia and later in Africa.

Preston, Battle of Victory (Aug. 17–20, 1648) of O. Cromwell in the English Civil War in which the last of the forces supporting King Charles I were defeated. Some 20,000 Scots invaded England but were decisively defeated by Cromwell's force of 8,500 near Preston, Lancashire.

Pretoria South African capital city (pop. 563,000). Founded in 1855, it became the capital of Transvaal province (1860) and of the Union of South Africa (1910).

Pretoria Convention Agreement (Aug. 3, 1881) between Britain and the Transvaal, amid the continuing conflict with the Boers. The agreement granted the Transvaal self-government subject to British suzerainty and control over foreign relations. It failed to last.

Pretorius, Andries Wilhelmus Jacobus 1799–1853. Boer leader. He was a leader of the Great Trek (*q.v.*) from the British-dominated Cape Colony to Natal. Continuing to oppose the British, he went into the Transvaal (1848) and was instrumental in establishing Transvaal independence.

Pretorius, Martinus Wessel 1819–1901 Boer statesman. Son of A. Pretorius. He was elected (1857) first president of the South African Republic (the Transvaal) and (1859) president of the adjoining Orange Free State, but was unable to unite the two.

Prevost, Sir George 1767–1816. British colonial administrator. As governor general of Canada (1811–15) he followed a policy of conciliation with the French Canadians. His defeats as commander in Canada in the War of 1812 led to his recall.

Priam Legendary last king of Troy. The father of Hector and Paris, he was killed when the Greeks conquered Troy.

Priapus Greek fertility god, god of gardens, cattle, and fishermen. Believed to be a son of Dionysus and Aphrodite, he was represented as a grotesque figure with an immense phallus.

Price, Sterling 1809–67. Confederate general in the American Civil War. Price fought in the Mexican War, served as governor of Missouri (1853–57), and led Confederate forces in the West during the Civil War.

Pride, Thomas *See* **Pride's Purge**

Pride's Purge Incident (Dec. 6, 1648) during the English Civil War, in which some 143 members of the House of Commons were removed by force. The members were mostly Presbyterians, believed to be royalist sympathizers. The purge was carried out by Capt. Thomas Pride (*d.* 1658), who commanded a Parliamentarian military force. Subsequent sessions of Parliament were known as the Rump Parliament (*q.v.*).

Priestley, John Boynton 1894–. British author. A prolific novelist, playwright, and critic, he is especially noted for such expressionist dramas as *Time and the Conways.*

Priestley, Joseph 1733–1804. English scientist and theologian. Priestley conducted important scientific investigations into the nature of electricity and discovered oxygen, calling it "dephlogisticated air."

Prignano, Bartolomeo *See* **Urban VI**

prime minister (premier) The head of government in a parliamentary form of government. He serves under the head of state (king or president). In Britain, the prime minister has broad powers, including responsibility for policy making, administrative functions, and appointment of Cabinet ministers and other lesser government officers. The prime minister is a member of Parliament and usually is the leader of the majority party. He is responsible to Parliament and must resign in the event that his government cannot carry the majority in Parliament. Under other systems of parliamentary government, the president (as head of state) is invested with the real responsibility of governing and the prime minister has only minor functions.

primitivism In art, the work of an artist who has no formal training in art but who nevertheless has developed a talent far beyond that of a novice. Primitives (now more often called "naive painters") have a fresh but unorthodox style. Among the noted painters of this group are H. Rousseau and Grandma Moses.

Primo de Rivera, Jose Antonio *See* **Falange**

Primo de Rivera, Miguel 1879–1930. Spanish general and dictator. After a successful *coup d'état* (Sept., 1923), he became the virtual military dictator of Spain (1923–30). His authoritarian regime provoked widespread opposition and he was forced to resign.

primogeniture In inheritance law, the right of the eldest son to inherit exclusively. In England and Western Europe primogeniture prevented the division of estates and enhanced the power of the landed aristocracy.

Primorski Krai *See* **Maritime Territory**

Prim y Prats, Juan 1814–70. Spanish general and statesman. He helped overthrow (1868) Queen Isabella, the last Spanish Bourbon queen. He also helped install Amadeus of Savoy as king.

Prince Edward Island A Maritime Province of Canada (pop 124,100). Originally inhabited by the Micmac Indians, the island was discovered in 1534 by Jacques Cartier and named Île St. Jean by S. de Champlain (1603). First settled by the French (early 18th cent.), it was ceded to the British in the Treaty of Paris (1763). It became a province (1769), was renamed in honor of Edward, duke of Kent, in 1789, and entered the Canadian confederation in 1873.

Prince of Wales Title traditionally conferred upon the heir apparent to the British throne. It was first given (1303) to Prince Edward, later King Edward II.

Princes, Fronde of the *See* **Fronde**

Princeton, Battle of *See* **Trenton and Princeton, Battles of**

Principality of Antioch One of the most powerful Crusader States (11th–13th cents.). Crusaders conquered the city of Antioch and surrounding territory (located in what is now southeastern Turkey) from the Muslims (1098) during the First Crusade. Bohemond I became its first ruler. It survived until the Mameluke conquest (1268).

Priscian *fl.* AD 500. Latin grammarian. Born in North Africa, he taught at Constantinople. His *Institutiones grammaticae* preserved many otherwise unknown quotations from classical authors and was one of the most popular textbooks of the Middle Ages.

privateering The use of specially commissioned, privately operated ships by belligerents to prey upon enemy shipping in time of war. From the 13th cent. privateering was used to supplement a country's naval strength. The heyday of privateering came in the 16th–17th cents., when such English privateers as J. Hawkins and F. Drake pursued Spanish shipping (late 16th cent.) and the French government commissioned many privateers to prey on English shipping (17th cent.). The US engaged in extensive privateering in the American Revolution and in the War of 1812, and the last letters of marque authorizing privateers to operate were in fact issued by the Confederate States of America. The practice was proscribed by the Declaration of Paris (1856). The Hague Conference (1907) laid down the conditions under which armed merchant vessels are deemed to be warships.

Privy Council In English history, the council of the king's principal advisers. It held executive, legislative, and judicial powers during its heyday. So named during the reign of Henry V (reigned 1413–22), it diminished in importance with the decline of the king's actual political power. Today it remains as a purely formal body.

Probus d. 282. Roman emperor (AD 276–282). He defeated the barbarians in Gaul and Illyria, but by allowing barbarian settlements within the empire he set a dangerous precedent. Eventually he was assassinated by his troops.

Proclamation of 1763 British royal proclamation (Oct. 7, 1763) that attempted to limit further western settlement in North America beyond the Appalachians. Conceived as a measure to conciliate the Indians following Pontiac's Rebellion, it fostered a serious Colonial grievance against the mother country.

Proclus AD c410–485. Greek philosopher. A Neoplatonist, he opposed Christianity and attempted to maintain the prestige of pagan philosophy.

Procne *See* **Philomela**

proconsul In ancient Roman government, originally a consul whose authority was extended to the completion of a commission, such as a military campaign. Later the office was given to the governor of a Roman province.

Procopius *fl.* 6th cent. Byzantine historian. He served as secretary to the military leader Belisarius and wrote volumes that are leading sources for history during the time of Justinian I.

Procopius the Great 1380–1434. Czech Hussite leader. During the Hussite Wars, he inflicted crushing defeats on the Catholic and imperial forces in 1426 and 1431. Embracing the Taborites, or more extreme Hussite faction, he was killed in the Taborite defeat at Lipany (1434).

Procopius the Little d. 1434. Czech Hussite leader. An ally of Procopius the Great, he unsuccessfully commanded the Hussite forces at the siege of Pilsen (1432–34) and died in the battle of Lipany (1434).

Procrustes Legendary Greek robber. He made his victims lie on a bed, stretching the limbs of those too short and cutting off the limbs of those too long. He was finally slain by Theseus.

Progressive Bloc Alliance of Russian liberals and conservatives in the last Russian duma. From Aug., 1915, it urged reforms on the imperial government to restore confidence and improve Russia's performance in WW I. It advocated strict rule of law and political amnesty. After the February Revolution (1917), members of the bloc helped form a committee that appointed the Provisional Government.

Progressive Conservative party ⟨Conservative party⟩ Major Canadian political party. Like its Liberal party counterpart, it is a broad-based coalition rather than an ideologically oriented party. It held power briefly from 1957 to 1963.

Progressive party Name adopted by three US political parties. **1.** Party (also known as Bull Moose party) formed (1912) by Republicans disaffected by the conservative policies of Republican Pres. W. Taft. It arose from the National Republican Progressive League formed (1911) by Sen. R. La Follette, ran T. Roosevelt for president, and split the Republican vote, thereby helping W. Wilson to win the 1912 election. **2.** Party formed (1924) by Sen. R. La Follette in opposition to the conservative policies of both Republican and Democratic parties. La Follette was defeated as its 1924 presidential candidate. **3.** Party formed (1948) by dissident Democrats opposed to the policies of Democratic Pres. H. Truman. It called for a more cooperative policy toward Russia. H. Wallace, its 1948 presidential candidate, received only about 1,000,000 popular votes.

Prohibition In the US, an attempt (1920–33) to legally halt the manufacture, sale, and transportation of alcoholic beverages. The movement for Prohibition grew out of the temperance movements of the 19th and early 20th cents., such as the Prohibition party *(q.v.)* and Anti-Saloon League *(q.v.)*, and was aided by a temporary prohibition law instituted during WW I to conserve grain. Prohibition went into force in many states, but it was adopted nationally with passage (1919) of the Volstead Act *(q.v.)* and ratification (1920) of the 18th Amendment. The program was a failure. Citizens found ways to find and consume liquor, notably in establishments called "speakeasies," and gangsters, among them A. Capone, became involved in the manufacture and sale of illegal liquor. Organized crime in the US flourished in the Prohibition era. Prohibition ended (1933) with ratification of the 21st Amendment, which repealed the 18th Amendment.

Prohibition party Minor US political party, founded (1869) to work for national prohibition of alcoholic beverages. From 1872 it sponsored a presidential candidate in every national election, but its influence actually declined during national prohibition (1920–33).

Prokofiev, Sergei Sergeyevich 1891–1953. Russian composer. He composed a large body of symphonic, operatic, and ballet music, but is probably known best for his orchestration of *Peter and the Wolf.*

Prokopovich, Feofan 1681–1736. Russian Orthodox prelate, theologian, and reformer. Cooperating with Peter the Great, he refashioned Orthodoxy as an arm of the czarist state, which endured until the 1917 Russian revolution.

proletariat The working class, without property and living entirely from the sale of their labor. In Marxist theory, the proletariat is believed to be created by the capitalist system. Marxists further hold that the proletariat would, by historical necessity, eventually resort to revolution to seize power from the capitalists.

Prometheus In Greek mythology, figure who stole fire from heaven and gave it to mankind. For this the gods chained him to a rock where an eagle perpetually fed on his liver. He was released by Hercules.

Propertius, Sextus 50?–15? BC. Roman elegiac poet, a contemporary of Ovid and Vergil. He wrote five books of poems imitating Alexandrian models.

prophet In the Old Testament, a Hebrew spiritual leader who gave guidance to God's people. The role of prophets as moral teachers outweighed their role in foretelling the future. The four major prophets were Isaiah, Jeremiah, Ezekiel, and Daniel. Their writings form a significant part of the Old Testament.

Protagoras c480–410 BC. Greek Sophist philosopher, adversary of Socrates. He promoted the slogan "Man is the measure of all things," i.e., that truth is subjective and relative to the individual.

protectionism System of protecting a nation's domestic industry by levying duty (tariffs) upon competing products imported from abroad. These duties increase the price of the imported goods by comparison with the domestically produced article. They, thus, foster home manufacturers and were imposed in England by Edward III as early as 1337. The first US protective tariff was enacted in 1816 and reached its highest point in US history after WW I. A movement away from protectionism began with British advocacy of free trade in the late 19th cent. and rose as industry in many countries matured. Pres. F. Roosevelt secured from Congress in 1934 the authority to negotiate reciprocal trade agreements lowering tariffs. Protectionism declined after WW II with the formation (1948) of GATT, the General Agreements on Tariffs and Trade, and with the multilateral reductions negotiated in the 1960s, as well as with the creation of the European Common Market (1957).

protectorate In international relations, an arrangement whereby a stronger state undertakes to protect a weaker state, called a protectorate. Theoretically, the protectorate retains its sovereignty, unlike a colony.

Protectorate English government established (1653–59) after the English Civil War and the execution (1649) of Charles I. In 1649 England was declared a commonwealth under the rule of the Rump Parliament, although O. Cromwell, controlling the army, wielded real power. Cromwell dissolved the Rump Parliament (1653) and established the Nominated, or Barebone's, Parliament. After its failure he accepted the Instrument of Government (q.v.), by which he became (1653) lord protector of the commonwealth of England, Scotland, and Ireland. From then until his death Cromwell was virtual dictator in England (ruling through a system of military districts), although he shared nominal power with a council of state and Parliament. In 1657 he accepted the Humble Petition and Advice (q.v.), which allowed him to choose his successor. After his death (1658) his son became lord protector. Cromwell's son resigned in 1659 and the Long Parliament was restored. It in turn brought Charles II (1660) to the throne and thus began the Restoration period.

Protestant Episcopal Church American Protestant denomination, dating from the 17th cent., when the Anglican church was established in America. The American Revolution (1775–83) caused great disorganization among the Anglican churches in the colonies and, after the war, these churches combined (1789) to form the Protestant Episcopal church, a separate entity within the Anglican Communion. It was again divided during the Civil War (1861–65) but reunited upon the cessation of hostilities.

Protestantism One of the three main branches of Christianity, with Roman Catholicism and Eastern Orthodoxy. Protestantism grew out of the Reformation (q.v.) in the 16th cent., and there are numerous Protestant churches that grew out of the reform movement. The two main branches are Lutheranism and Calvinism (qq.v.). The characteristic doctrine of the original Protestant movement was justification by faith alone, not by church dispensations or by good works. Renewed emphasis on the teachings of the Bible and a general movement away from liturgy were also characteristic. Protestantism also evolved new forms of church polity, including Congregationalism, Presbyterianism, and Episcopalianism. In the years after the start of the Reformation, new Protestant churches sprang up and existing ones split into diverse sects. The 20th-cent. ecumenical movement (q.v.), however, has sought to bring about a reunification of churches. (See also Congregationalism, Presbyterianism, Protestant Episcopal church, Church of England, Methodism, Puritanism, Evangelicalism, Great Awakening, Baptists, Anabaptists, Pentecostal Church.)

Protestant Reformation *See* **Reformation**

Protestant Union Association (1608–21) of German Protestant princes. It was formed to prevent an imperial reimposition of Catholicism and went out of existence after the outbreak of the Thirty Years' War.

Proteus Legendary Greek "old man of the sea." He could assume any shape ("protean") but if held fast until he resumed his normal form, he was obliged to answer questions and foretell the future.

Protogenes *fl. c*300 BC. Greek painter, one of the most celebrated of Greek artists of antiquity. None of his paintings has survived.

Proudhon, Pierre Joseph 1809–65. French Socialist and theorist. His theory of "mutualism," in which social groups would bargain within the framework of agreed principles, greatly influenced later radical movements.

Proust, Marcel 1871–1922. French novelist. Author of a vast, panoramic, semi-autobiographical novel, *Remembrance of Things Past*, Proust is considered one of the greatest authors of the 20th cent.

Provençal Dialect of the Romance languages, once spoken in southern France and notable as the literary language of the medieval troubadors. It is also called *langue d'oc.*

Providence American city (pop. 571,300), capital and largest city of Rhode Island. It was founded (1636) by R. Williams.

Provisional Government Russian government formed after the fall of the czar (Mar., 1917). Headed by A. Kerensky, it governed Russia (Mar.–Oct.) until the October Revolution *(q.v.).(See also* Russian Revolution.)

Provisions of Oxford Governmental reforms imposed (1258) on English King Henry III by his barons. In need of money to pay for his unsuccessful foreign ventures, Henry convened the Mad Parliament (June 11, 1258) and was forced to accept reforms. Formulated by a special commission headed by S. de Montfort, the Provisions of Oxford included establishment of a 15-man council to advise the king, and reforms of local administration. These were supplemented by the Provisions of Westminster *(q.v.).* Henry later refused to abide by the provisions, however, and this resulted in the Barons' War *(q.v.).*

Prusa *See* **Bursa**

Prussia Former German state, and one of the most powerful German states, long regarded as the wellspring of German militarism. Its capital

was Berlin. At its height it occupied much of north Germany and extended east into what is now Poland. The Teutonic Knights *(q.v.)* conquered the region (13th cent.), and in the 16th cent. Prussia proper (E. Prussia) passed to the electors of Brandenburg, though it remained under Polish suzerainty. Polish control was ended in 1660, during the time of Frederick William (the Great Elector). In 1701 the Holy Roman Emperor consented to creation of the Kingdom of Prussia, which included lands gained through expansion to the west. Thereafter Prussia continued to enlarge its domains and, under King Frederick William I (reigned 1713–40), important administrative reforms were effected and a strong army was created. The reign (1740–86) of Frederick II (the Great) brought Prussia to a position of power in Europe by victories in the War of the Austrian Succession and the Seven Years' War *(qq.v.).* Prussia also gained additional lands through the Partitions of Poland *(q.v.).* In the post-Napoleonic period in Europe, Prussia and Austria became rivals for control of the German Confederation *(q.v.),* which had been formed from the remnants of the then defunct Holy Roman Empire. Prussia sought to exclude Austria from the confederation and to unite the other states into a German kingdom under its control. This goal was ultimately achieved (1871) through the efforts of Prussian statesman O. von Bismarck and through Prussian victories in two wars that he helped to provoke, the Austro-Prussian War (1866) and the Franco-Prussian War (1871). Prussian king William I was crowned emperor of Germany and in subsequent years Prussia retained control of the empire. Prussia ceased to exist as a political entity in 1934, when A. Hitler formally abolished the German states. (*See also* Germany [1815–71].)

Pruth, Treaty of Agreement (July 23, 1711) between Russian czar Peter the Great and the Ottoman Empire, following Peter's defeat in the third Russo-Turkish War (1710–11). Peter was obliged to relinquish Azov and demilitarize other forts.

Prynne, William 1600–69. English Puritan pamphleteer. His attack on the immorality of the theater led to persecution by the government of King Charles I. An implacable opponent of Archbishop Laud, he came back into favor at the Restoration.

Przhevalsky, Nikolai Mikhailovich 1839–88. Russian explorer. His series of expeditions to Mongolia, Tibet, and Singkiang greatly increased the knowledge of the geography and natural history of these areas.

Psamtik *d.* 609 BC. Egyptian pharaoh, (663–609 BC), founder of the 26th dynasty. He reunited

Egypt, ended Assyrian rule, and opened the country to Greek influence.

Pseudo-Dionysius *See* **Dionysius the Areopagite**

Psyche Mythological Greek maiden loved by Cupid. Psyche was eventually granted immortality as his consort. From the 5th cent. BC, she came to symbolize the soul.

Ptah ⟨Phthah⟩ Ancient Egyptian god. Originally a local god of Memphis, he came to be worshiped as a creator god corresponding to the Greek Hephaestus.

Ptolemaic system Geocentric cosmological system devised (2d cent. AD) by Ptolemy to explain the apparent movement of celestial bodies against the background of the fixed stars. The theory held sway until the development (16th cent.) of the heliocentric system devised by Copernicus.

Ptolemy ⟨Claudius Ptolemaeus⟩ *fl.* 2d cent. AD. Ancient Alexandrian astronomer, mathematician, and geographer. He formulated the geocentric Ptolemaic system. In his *Geography* he erred in calculating the circumference of the earth—a mistake that led C. Columbus to believe he could easily reach Asia by sailing west.

Ptolemy I *d.* 283 BC. Egyptian king (305–285 BC). A Macedonian, Ptolemy was one of Alexander the Great's most successful generals. After Alexander's death (323 BC), he quarreled with other generals (Diadochi, *q.v.*) over the empire's division, and became satrap of Egypt. He engaged in warfare to protect and expand his holdings. Though defeated by Demetrius in a battle at Salamis (306 BC), he named himself Egypt's king and soter (savior) the following year. He established Alexandria as a center of culture and commerce, founded its famed library, planned Egypt's government, and began the Ptolemaic dynasty. He abdicated in favor of his son (285 BC).

Ptolemy II ⟨Philadelphus, Ptolemy II⟩ *c*308–246? BC. Ancient Egyptian king (285–246 BC), successor to his father Ptolemy I. He helped make Alexandria the center of Hellenistic culture, built the city's famous museum, and commissioned the translation of the Hebrew Bible into the Greek Septuagint.

Ptolemy III ⟨Euergetes, Ptolemy III⟩ *d.* 222? BC. Ancient Egyptian king (246–222? BC), successor to his father, Ptolemy II. He reunited Egypt and Cyrenaica, warred with Syria, and established Egyptian naval supremacy in the eastern Mediterranean.

Ptolemy IV ⟨Philopater, Ptolemy IV⟩ *d.* 205 BC. Ancient Egyptian king (221–205 BC), successor to his father, Ptolemy III. Though he defeated the Seleucids in Syria (217 BC), the loss of Syrian lands

and internal rebellions began under his rule. He was a debauched man who ruled through favorites and had many relatives murdered.

Ptolemy V ⟨Epiphanes, Ptolemy V⟩ *d.* 181? BC. Ancient Egyptian king (205–181? BC), successor to his father Ptolemy IV. During his reign Egypt's Levantine possessions were lost in disastrous wars but peace was finally concluded with his marriage to Cleopatra, daughter of Syrian king Antiochus III. The Rosetta Stone concerns his accession to the throne.

Ptolemy VI ⟨Philometer, Ptolemy VI⟩ *d.* 145 BC. Ancient Egyptian king (180–145 BC), successor to his father, Ptolemy V. Obliged to share power with his brother, later Ptolemy VII, he helped bring about the first intervention of Rome in Egyptian affairs.

Ptolemy VII ⟨Physcon, Ptolemy VII⟩ *d.* 116? BC. Ancient Egyptian king (145–116? BC). Usurping the throne from his brother, he ruled with great cruelty, provoking revolts. He drove the scholars from Alexandria.

Ptolemy VIII ⟨Lathyrus, Ptolemy VIII⟩ *d.* 81 BC. Ancient Egyptian king (116–81 BC), successor to his father, Ptolemy VII. He was driven (107) from the throne and returned (88) only after expelling his brother, Ptolemy IX Alexander, whose corule his mother had compelled him to accept.

Ptolemy IX ⟨Alexander, Ptolemy I⟩ *d.* 88 BC. Ancient Egyptian king (107–88 BC). With the help of his mother, he supplanted his brother, Ptolemy VIII, until finally defeated by the latter in a civil war.

Ptolemy X *d.* 80 BC. Ancient Egyptian king (80 BC). He became ruler upon his marriage to the widow of his predecessor, Ptolemy VIII. He murdered her and was in turn murdered by a mob.

Ptolemy XI *d.* 51 BC. Ancient Egyptian king (80–51 BC), an illegitimate son of Ptolemy VIII. His misrule brought about his expulsion and he was restored only by force of Roman arms.

Ptolemy XIII *d.* 44 BC. Last Macedonian king of Egypt (47–44 BC). Married to his sister Cleopatra by J. Caesar, he was murdered at her order in favor of her own son.

Ptolemy XIV 47–30 BC. Ancient Egyptian king (44–30 BC). He was the son of J. Caesar by Cleopatra (daughter of Ptolemy XI), and coruler with his mother until he was killed by Octavian. Following his death, Egypt became a Roman province.

Public Safety, Committee of *See* **Committee of Public Safety**

Public Weal, League of Alliance of French nobles (1465) against French king Louis XI. Led by Duke

Philip the Good of Burgundy, it forced concessions from Louis, but Louis eventually used diplomatic means to overcome the league.

Puccini, Giacomo 1858–1924. Italian operatic composer. His major operas, all tragic love stories centering on feminine protagonists, include *La Bohème, La Tosca,* and *Madama Butterfly.*

Pudovkin, Vsevolod Illarionovich 1893–1953. Russian film director. A pioneer of film techniques in such classic films as *Mother,* he also wrote the books *Film Techniques* and *Film Acting.*

Puebla, Battle and Siege of Two engagements at Puebla, Mexico, during the French campaign to establish Austrian archduke Ferdinand Maximilian as emperor. In the first battle (May 5, 1862), French forces of 7,500 were thrown back with more than 400 casualties by a defending army of 12,000 Mexicans. In the second battle (May 17, 1863), the city surrendered to a larger French force after the French defeated a Mexican relief column.

Pueblo incident Seizure of the US Navy intelligence ship *Pueblo* and 83 crewmen off North Korea (Jan. 23, 1968). The US exerted diplomatic efforts to free the crewmen, contending that the vessel had been in international waters. The crewmen were not released by North Korea until Dec. 23, 1968.

Pueblo Indians American Indian tribes inhabiting compact adobe or stone villages in the southwestern US. Of diverse tribal and linguistic backgrounds, they have similar, settled cultures based on agriculture.

Pueblo Rebellion Pueblo Indian rebellion (1680) against Spanish rule in New Mexico. The Pueblo rose against enforced Christianization (Aug. 10, 1680), expelled the Spaniards, and restored ancestor worship. They retained their independence until reconquered in 1692.

Puerto Rico ⟨Porto Rico⟩ West Indian commonwealth (pop 3,187,600) in union with the US. It was discovered by C. Columbus (1493) and settled by Ponce de León (1508). During the Spanish-American War, American troops occupied Puerto Rico, and it was ceded to the US (1898). The Jones Act (1917) gave the Puerto Ricans US citizenship. A movement for independence led to an assassination attempt on President H. Truman (1950), but a 1967 plebiscite elected to keep commonwealth status.

Pueyrredon, Juan Martin de 1776–1850. Argentine general and statesman. As supreme director of the United Provinces of La Plata (1816–19), he provided key support of J. de San Martín in the conquest of Chile (1817).

Pufendorf, Samuel, Freiherr von 1632–94. German jurist and historian. His work *De Jure Naturae at Gentium* maintained that relations between nations ought to be governed by natural law, not by positive law enacted by man.

Pugachev, Emelian Ivanovich 1726–75. Russian leader of the peasant rebellion of 1773–74. Pretending to be Czar Peter III and to have escaped assassination, he led a formidable but ultimately unsuccessful attempt to abolish serfdom.

Pulaski, Casimir ⟨Pulaski, Kazimierz⟩ c1748–79. Polish aristocrat, patriot, and American Revolutionary leader. Unsuccessful in preventing the First Partition of Poland (1772), he came to America. During the American Revolution he commanded American cavalry with distinction but was killed at Savannah.

Pulaski, Kazimierz *See* **Pulaski, Casimir**

Pulitzer, Joseph 1847–1911. Hungarian-born American newspaper publisher. He revitalized old newspapers, pioneered modern journalism, and endowed both the Columbia University School of Journalism and the Pulitzer prizes.

Pulitzer prizes Annual awards for excellence in American literature, music, and journalism. Endowed by J. Pulitzer, they have been awarded annually since 1917.

Pullman Strike US labor dispute (1894). Workers of the Pullman Palace Car Company in Chicago struck (May 11, 1894) to protest a 25 percent wage cut, brought on by the Panic of 1893. The company refused arbitration and that brought in the national union, the American Railway Union, led by E. Debs. Debs called a nationwide boycott and thereby effectively shut down Chicago's rail traffic. However, Pres. G. Cleveland sent 2,000 federal troops to Chicago and broke the strike after considerable violence.

Punctation of Olmütz *See* **Erfurt Parliament; Revolutions of 1848.**

Punic War Three major wars between Rome and Carthage resulting in the subjugation of Carthage and Rome's acquisition of territories beyond the Italian peninsula. **1.** First ∼. This war (264–241 BC) was brought on by the growing commercial rivalry between Rome and Carthage. Its immediate cause was a conflict between the cities of Messina and Syracuse, on Sicily. Both Carthage and Rome responded to Messina's request for aid, and soon after were at war with one another. The Romans built a great fleet, defeated the Carthaginians at the Battle of Mylae (260), and launched an ill-fated invasion of Africa in which the commander, Regulus, was captured (255) by Greek mercenaries. On Sicily, the Carthaginian commander Hamilcar Barca succeeded in thwarting the Romans' attempt at decisive victory. However, the Roman fleet finally destroyed the Carthaginian fleet in the naval battle of Aegates (241) and thereby forced the Carthaginians to accept peace. Rome gained Carthaginian territories on Sicily. Not long after, Rome also annexed Sardinia and Corsica. **2.** Second ~. War (218–201 BC) between Rome and Carthage, sparked by the Carthaginians' conquest of Saguntum, a Spanish city allied with Rome. In the years after the first war, Carthage had greatly expanded its holdings in Spain. With the outbreak of war, the great Carthaginian general Hannibal led his forces on the now-famous march from Spain, across the Alps, and into north Italy. He won notable victories at Ticinus (218), Trebia (218), Lake Trasimenus (217), and Cannae (216), but failed to take Rome itself. Macedon, a Carthaginian ally, was also defeated in the First Macedonian War *(q.v.).* Although Hannibal gained control of much of southern Italy, Carthage failed to provide him needed support. Finally, the Roman invasion of North Africa by Scipio Africanus Major (204) forced Hannibal to return to Carthage. He was defeated at the Battle of Zama (202), and Carthage itself fell (201). Carthage had to give up its navy and its Spanish territories and never again seriously threatened Roman military superiority. **3.** Third ~. War (149–146 BC) between Rome and Carthage, resulting from continuing commercial rivalry and efforts by the Roman, Cato the Elder, to bring about the complete destruction of Carthage. Rome finally declared war and soon after laid siege to Carthage. The Carthaginians refused to surrender, and the Romans, led by Scipio Africanus Minor, were forced to fight in the streets of the city to gain control of it. They then completely destroyed Carthage and organized Carthaginian domains into the Roman province of Africa.

Punjab Historic region of northwest India whose river-delta areas were sites of prehistoric and early Aryan civilizations, The area was conquered by Alexander the Great, and by the Muslims (8th cent.), who converted western Punjab to Islam. The Punjab flourished under the Mogul empire until the 18th cent., when the Sikhs took control. The British made it a province in 1849. In the 1947 partition of India, western Punjab became part of Pakistan, and eastern Punjab became part of India.

Purandhar, Treaty of Treaty (Mar. 1, 1776) between the Maratha of India and the government of the British East India Company, in Calcutta. The company abandoned support of the Maratha pretender Raghunath Rao (d. 1783) but retained Salsette Island. The company subsequently disavowed the treaty, and the Maratha Wars *(q.v.)* were resumed.

Purcell, Henry 1659–95. English composer and organist. Noted for his opera *Dido and Aeneas* and his fine religious and ceremonial music, he is considered the outstanding influence in English music before Handel.

Pure Land Buddhism School of Mahayana Buddhism, one of the most popular in East Asia. It began in China as early as the 4th cent. and had spread to Japan by the 13th cent.

purge trials Series of political trials (1936–38) in the Soviet Union. The first (Aug., 1936) was held to try several prominent leaders, including G. Zinoviev and L. Kamenev, of complicity in the assassination (Dec., 1934) of S. Kirov, a Communist leader. In fact, it was held to eliminate opponents or potential rivals to the rule of J. Stalin. Subsequent trials (Jan., 1937; Mar., 1938) continued the process, by which Stalin virtually swept away all the old Bolshevik leaders and consolidated his power over every facet of Soviet life, including the Communist party. However, by crippling the party apparatus and eliminating many of Russia's top military leaders, he left Russia vulnerable in the face of the rising power of A. Hitler in Germany. In later years (after Stalin's death) the cases against the trial victims were shown to be complete fabrications.

Puritanism English religious movement (16th and 17th cents.) that sought to reform the Church of England. It arose during the reign of Queen Elizabeth I, and sought to purify (hence its name) the English church of Catholic and political elements. Embracing Calvinism and the authority of the Scriptures, the Puritan movement eventually split into several groups, including the Presbyterians, Congregationalists, Separatists, and Independents. Under King James I, the Presbyterians rose to prominence but were unable to promote changes within the Church of England at the Hampton Court Conference (1604). Repression of the Puritans led to the Pilgrim emigration to America (1620) aboard the *Mayflower (q.v.).* The Puritan movement in England received a further setback with adoption of the repressive Clarendon Code *(q.v.),* aimed at dissenting religious groups. In New England the Puritans established their principles in the Cambridge Platform *(q.v.)* of 1648, and flourished under the leadership of such men as R. Williams, C. Mather, and I. Mather. By the end of the 17th cent. Puritanism had largely ceased to exist as a movement, but its values of hard work, discipline, education, and thrift had an immense and lasting effect on the development of both English and American society.

Puritan Revolution   *See* **English Civil War**

Pusey, Edward Bouverie   1800–82. English theologian and Anglican churchman. With J. Newman he was the principal leader of the Oxford Movement *(q.v.)*.

Pushkin, Aleksandr Sergeyevich   1799–1837. Russian poet. Exemplifying the Romantic writer (he was killed in a duel), he is considered one of the greatest of Russian writers, and is noted for such works as the verse novel *Eugene Onegin.*

Putnam, George Palmer   1814–72. American publisher. He founded (1866) the publishing firm of G.P. Putnam's Sons.

Putnam, Israel   1718–90. American Revolutionary general. During Pontiac's Rebellion *(q.v.)* he relieved Pontiac's siege of Detroit (1764). During the American Revolution he fought at Bunker Hill. He was defeated by the British on Long Island (1776) and on the Hudson (1777).

Putnam, Rufus   1738–1824. American Revolutionary officer, cousin of I. Putnam. He distinguished himself during the American Revolution, helped secure passage of the Northwest Ordinance (1787), and, as a member of the Ohio Company, helped to settle Ohio.

Putney Debates   *See* **Levelers**

Pydna, Battle of   Roman victory (168 BC) over the Macedonians at Pydna, Greece, in the Third Macedonian War. Roman Gen. Lucius Aemilius Paullus routed Macedonian forces and put their king, Perseus, to flight. After the victory, the Romans divided Macedonia into four republics.

Pygmalion   Legendary Greek king. He fell in love with the statue of a woman (which one version says he sculpted). He then prayed to Aphrodite, who brought the statue to life.

Pylos   Harbor in southern Greece. Home of King Nestor, it was the site of an Athenian victory over Sparta (425 BC) and of the Battle of Navarino (1827).

Pym, John   1583?–1643. English statesman. A Puritan, he gave a notable speech (1640) enumerating popular grievances, in the Short Parliament. He was one of the leaders in the Long Parliament whom King Charles I attempted to arrest (1642) in the period leading to the English Civil War.

pyramids   Great stone structures built by various ancient peoples. The best-known pyramids are the Egyptian, especially the three great pyramids at Giza *(q.v.)*, built during the 3d millennium BC (4th–6th dynasties) as the burial places for the pharaohs.

Pyramids, battle of the   Battle fought near Giza (July 21, 1798) between the 36,000-man French

expeditionary force under Napoleon I and a 40,000-man Egyptian army under Murad Bey. The French defeated and dispersed the Egyptians and thus gained access to Cairo.

Pyramus and Thisbe   Legendary Babylonian lovers whose tragic tale was recounted by Ovid in his *Metamorphoses.* Frightened by a lion at a trysting place, Thisbe fled, dropping her veil. The lion seized the veil and covered it with blood from his recent prey. Pyramus, finding the veil, thought Thisbe dead, and mortally wounded himself. Thisbe returned to find Pyramus, and in grief, killed herself.

Pyrenees, Peace of the   Treaty (Nov. 7, 1659) ending hostilities between France and Spain, which had been renewed during the Fronde of the Princes. Spain ceded lands in Flanders, accepted a border with France at the Pyrenees, and betrothed the daughter of King Philip IV to French king Louis XIV. The treaty is generally thought to mark France's rise as Europe's dominant power.

Pyrrho   c360–270 BC. Greek skeptical philosopher. He held that nothing can definitely be known and hence the search for truth is vain. Pyrrhonism, or absolute skepticism, thus derives from him.

Pyrrhus   c318–272 BC. King of Epirus. Pyrrhus was established as coruler of Epirus by Macedonian king Demetrius I. He was overthrown and sent as hostage to Egyptian king Ptolemy I, who befriended him and restored him to his kingdom. Pyrrhus fought costly wars against Macedon and Rome. Although he defeated the Romans at Heraclea (280 BC) and Ausculum (279 BC), the great losses incurred gave rise to the term "Pyrrhic victory." He successfully aided Sicily against Carthage and again defeated Macedonia (273 BC), but his attempts to subdue Sparta led to his defeat. He fled to Argos, where he was pursued by a mob and killed.

Pythagoras   c582–c507 BC. Greek philosopher and mathematician. Little is known of Pythagoras' life, and none of his writings has survived. However, it is ascertained that he founded a combination school and society at Crotona, Italy, that had great influence on Greek and Roman thought. Pythagoras and his school taught that all relationships could be expressed in numbers, and that numbers were the true essence of life. Many theories developed by the Pythagoreans are still employed today in geometry. Philosophically, the Pythagoreans believed in the transmigration of souls, and that the living of a good life would entitle one to a higher rank on the next turn of the "wheel of birth."

Pythagorean school   *See* **Pythagoras**

Pytheas *fl.* 4th cent. BC Greek navigator and geographer who explored the western coastline of Europe, who was the first Greek to visit the British Isles, and who may have sailed as far north as Iceland.

Pythian games Ancient Greek games. They originally featured musical contests in honor of Apollo at Delphi; athletic contests were added in imitation of the Olympic games after 582 BC.

Pythias *See* **Damon and Pythias**

Q

Qaddafi, Muammar al- 1942–. Radical Arab nationalist, Libyan revolutionist and dictator (1969–   ). He led the military coup (Sept., 1969) to overthrow King Idris I, and set himself up as ruler of Libya. His reign has been marked by anti-Western policies, the closing of US bases in Libya (1970), government confiscation of Italian and Jewish property (1970), nationalization of foreign-owned oil facilities (1973), a proposed union with Egypt (1973), and then border wars with Egypt (1977). Qaddafi's support for Arab terrorist groups, such as the PLO (Palestine Liberation Organization), and Muslim revolutionaries, such as Ayatollah Khomeini, has led to the growing isolation of Libya.

Qatar Small oil-rich Arab state on the Persian Gulf, inhabited primarily by Wahabi Muslims. Its capital is Doha. First mentioned in the 10th cent., Qatar was ruled by the Āl-Thānī dynasty from 1868 until the 1970s. Great Britain made Qatar a dependency in 1916. Oil was discovered in the 1940s, and Qatar became independent in 1971.

Quadruple Alliance 1. Alliance (1718) formed by Austria, France, Great Britain, and The Netherlands against Spain. The alliance was established after Spanish king Philip V attempted to overturn the terms of the Peace of Utrecht *(q.v.)* by seizing Sardinia and Sicily. Austrian forces landed in Sicily, and British and French forces advanced into Spain. Philip was forced, by the Treaty of the Hague (1720), to abandon his claims in Italy, and the peace settlements made at Utrecht were renegotiated. **2.** Alliance (Nov. 20, 1815) formed by Austria, Great Britain, Prussia, and Russia after their defeat of Napoleon. The alliance was made to enforce the conditions of the Treaty of Paris of 1815 and to prevent further French military adventures. In 1818 France was admitted to the alliance. Great Britain gradually turned away from continental affairs and participation in the alliance. **3.** Alliance (1834) formed by France, Great Britain, Portugal, and Spain to support the Spanish constitutionalists and Queen Isabella II against the Carlists in the First Carlist War (1833–39).

The alliance was effectively crippled by the Affair of the Spanish Marriages *(q.v.)* in 1846, which led to a serious dispute between France and Great Britain.

Quakers *See* **Society of Friends**

Quantrill, William Clarke 1837–65. Confederate guerrilla leader in the American Civil War. He led a band of marauders in Missouri and Kansas and was responsible for the ruthless pillaging (Aug. 21, 1863) of Lawrence, Kansas, in which some 150 townspeople were killed.

quantum theory In physics, the theory that energy consists of emissions of discrete particles, or quanta. Pioneered by M. Planck and N. Bohr, the theory is used to explain the behavior of particles on the atomic and subatomic levels and is an essential theory of modern physics.

"quarrel of the ancients and the moderns" *See* **Perrault, Charles**

Quartering Act British parliamentary act passed (Mar., 1765) to defray costs of defending the colonies. It forced the American colonials to pay for British troops stationed in the colonies. The law was bitterly resented because it was enacted without approval of the colonial legislatures. It was allowed to lapse in 1770, but another Quartering Act was passed (June 2, 1774) after the Boston Tea Party.

Quasimodo, Salvatore 1901–68. Italian poet and writer, a master of both social and lyrical poetry. He was awarded the Nobel Prize in Literature in 1959.

Quebec Canadian province (pop. 6,325,200). First discovered and explored (1534–41) by J. Cartier, and later by S. de Champlain, the region, named New France, became a French colony (1663). The British gained control of it by the Treaty of Paris (1763), and many Loyalists settled there during and after the American Revolution. In 1791, the area now known as Ontario was made a separate colony called Upper Canada, and Quebec became known as Lower Canada. Although Quebec and Ontario were subsequently reunited (1841), they entered the confederation of Canada as separate provinces (1867).

Quebec Canadian city (pop. 542,000), capital of Quebec province. First settled (1608) by S. de Champlain, it was occupied briefly by the British (1629–32), and became the capital of New France (1663). It was captured by the British (1759) after the historic battle on the Plains of Abraham, and was unsuccessfully attacked (1775) by B. Arnold during the American Revolution. It was the site of the Quebec Conferences (q.v.).

Quebec Act British parliamentary law (June 22, 1774) establishing a permanent government for Canada. The act replaced the temporary administration set up by the Proclamation of 1763, extended Quebec's territory south to the Ohio River, and provided for religious tolerance of Roman Catholics. While the act kept Canada loyal to Britain, it enraged American colonists and contributed to the outbreak of the American Revolution.

Quebec campaign Unsuccessful military expedition (1775–76) by the American colonials against Canada during the American Revolution. Two American contingents were sent against Canada with the ultimate goal of taking Quebec. The force under Gen. B. Montgomery first captured Montreal (Nov., 1775). It later joined a force under Col. B. Arnold in an unsuccessful attack on the strongly fortified Quebec (Dec. 31, 1775). After Montgomery was killed and Arnold was wounded, the Americans broke off the attack. In May, 1776, American forces were withdrawn from Canada.

Quebec Conference **1.** Meeting in Quebec, Canada (Oct. 10–27, 1864) that laid the foundations for an independent dominion of Canada. Thirty-three delegates from the various provinces of British North America drew up a draft constitution called the Quebec Resolutions, or Seventy-two Resolutions. This formed the basis of the 1867 British North America Act (q.v.), creating modern independent Canada. **2.** Conference (Aug. 11–24, 1943) attended by US president F. Roosevelt, British prime minister W. Churchill, Canadian prime minister W. Mackenzie King, and Chinese foreign minister T. Soong. The conference formulated tentative plans for allied landings in Europe. **3.** Meeting between US president F. Roosevelt and British prime minister W. Churchill (Sept. 11–16, 1944) at which strategy for defeating Germany was discussed. It was decided to advance against Germany on two fronts rather than make a single effort to take Berlin.

Queen Anne's War American Colonial war (1702–13) between France and England, the American counterpart of the War of the Spanish Succes-sion. The French and their Indian allies waged a bitter war, but the British emerged victorious. The British captured and burned Spanish-held St. Augustine, Florida (1702), the French massacred townspeople of Deerfield, Massachusetts (1704), the British captured the French colony of Acadia (1710), and then unsuccessfully attempted to take Quebec (1711). The war was ended by the Treaty of Utrecht (q.v.) and Britain gained Newfoundland, Hudson Bay, and Acadia.

Queipo de Llano, Gonzalo See **Fifth column**

Quesnay, François 1694–1774. French economist and physician. A pioneer in the development of economic theory, he was the leader of the physiocrats (q.v.).

Quesnel, Pasquier 1634–1719. French theologian and exponent of Jansenism. One of the principal Jansenist leaders, he was exiled and briefly imprisoned. His teachings were ultimately condemned by Pope Clement XI's papal bull *Unigenitus* (1713).

Quetzalcoatl Ancient Mexican god. Represented as a feathered serpent, he was involved in the cult of human sacrifice. Revered as a god who gave the people corn, weaving, and the calendar, he figured in Aztec and Toltec cultures.

Quevedo y Villegas, Francisco Gómez de 1580–1645. Spanish poet and writer. He was a brilliant satirist as well as a writer of plays and novels.

Quezon City Capital city (pop. 994,700), since 1948, of the Republic of the Philippines. Adjacent to Manila, it was developed as a capital city and named after M. Quezon.

Quezon y Molina, Manuel Luis 1878–1944. First president of the Commonwealth of the Philippines (1935–44). Beginning as a rebel against American rule, he turned to tireless lobbying and was instrumental in obtaining the US legislation establishing the commonwealth.

Quiberon Bay, Battle of British naval victory (Nov. 20, 1759) over the French during the Seven Years' War, at Quiberon Bay, Brittany. The decisive British victory forced the French to abandon their plans to invade Scotland.

quietism Type of religious mysticism based on the belief that total passivity of the soul and suppression of all activity, even prayer, can bring communion with God. This type of mysticism is characteristic of a number of religious traditions, notably Hinduism (q.v.) and Islamic Sufism (q.v.). In the West the doctrine was associated with a Spanish priest, M. de Molinos, and a French mystic, Mme. J. Guyon, both of whom were active in the latter half of the 17th cent.

Quiller-Couch, Sir Arthur Thomas 1863–1944. English man of letters. He edited *The Oxford*

Book of English Verse and other anthologies and wrote novels, criticism, essays, and poetry.

Quimby, Phineas Parkhurst 1802–66. American mental healer. Originally a clockmaker, he possessed hypnotic powers and became prominent as a mental healer. One of his patients was M. Eddy. She later founded Christian Science, but denied that Quimby's ideas influenced its principles.

Quincy, Josiah 1744–75. American pamphleteer. Closely associated with J. Adams, he was influential in rallying the American colonies against British policy. He died at sea after pleading the American case in England.

Quine, Willard Van Orman 1908–. American philosopher and mathematical logician. He refined modern philosophical concepts dealing with language as a logical system.

Quinisext Council ⟨Council in Trullo⟩ Synod of the Orthodox Eastern church convened in Constantinople (692) by Byzantine emperor Justinian II. Pope Sergius I refused to ratify its canons on behalf of the Western church, protesting in particular those allowing clerical marriage below the rank of bishop.

Quintilian ⟨Marcus Fabius Quintilianus⟩ AD c35–c95. Roman writer and rhetorician. A respected teacher of rhetoric, he wrote the *Institutio Oratoria*, a major study of rhetoric. His writings were influential in Renaissance times.

Quirino, Elpidio 1890–1956. Filipino statesman. He served as secretary and aide to M. Quezon, and fought in the underground during WW II. Elected (1946) vice-president under M. Roxas, he succeeded Roxas as president of the Philippines (1948–53).

Quirinus Ancient Roman god. In early times, he was a god of war, but by republican times he had become associated with the legendary founder of Rome, Romulus.

Quisling, Vidkun 1887–1945. Norwegian puppet prime minister (1940–45). A fascist, he served as prime minister under the German occupation of Norway during WW II. His name became a byword for "traitor." He was tried and executed after the war.

Quito Capital city (pop. 742,900) of Ecuador. Conquered by the Spaniards in 1534, Quito is noted for its balmy climate and elevation of nearly 10,000 ft. It is the cultural and educational center of the country.

Quran *See* **Koran**

Qutb ud-Din *See* **Delhi Sultanate**

R

Ra ⟨Re⟩ Egyptian god of the sun and creation. Depicted as sailing across the sky in a celestial barge, he fought the powers of darkness each night.

Rabelais, François c1490–1553. French Renaissance humanist and satirist. A learned monk and physician, he celebrated Renaissance ideals in his great satirical work *Gargantua and Pantagruel*.

Rachel In biblical history one of the four Jewish matriarchs. She was the daughter of Laban. Jacob sought to marry her for seven years, only to be tricked into marriage with her uncomely sister Leah. After another seven years, Jacob finally won Rachel, who bore him Joseph and Benjamin.

Rachmaninov, Sergei Vasilyevich ⟨Rakhmaninov, Sergius Vassilievich⟩ 1873–1943. Russian composer and piano virtuoso. The last great exponent of Russian romanticism, he wrote his best works for the piano. He spent his later life in the US, an expatriate from the Russian Revolution.

Racine, Jean Baptiste 1639–99. French poet and dramatist, considered a master of French classical tragedy. After a bitter rivalry with J. Molière and P. Corneille, he wrote his greatest works, *Britannicus, Bérénice, Bajazet, Iphigénie,* and *Phèdre.* In 1677, he left the theater, married, and became historiographer to Louis XIV. He later wrote two dramas, *Esther* and *Athalie,* at the request of Mme. de Maintenon.

Radcliffe-Brown, Alfred Reginald 1881–1955. British social anthropologist who helped establish a scientific basis for social anthropology. He carried out his major studies on the Andaman Islanders.

Radek, Karl Bernhardovich 1885–1939? Russian Communist politician and journalist. A prominent leader of the Comintern, he was a victim of the Stalinist purge trials *(q.v.).*

Radetzky, Joseph, Count 1766–1858. Austrian field marshal. He served Austria in wars against the Turks during the 1780s and in most all the wars against France during the era of the French Revolution and Empire.

Radhakrishnan, Sarvepalli 1888–1975. Indian philosopher and president of India (1962–67). He

also served as Indian ambassador and vice-president (1952–62). Primarily an academic, he tried to harmonize Hindu philosophy with modern thought.

Radical Republicans Wing of the Republican party during the American Civil War and Reconstruction *(q.v.)* periods. Radicals demanded firm adherence to antislavery doctrines and advocated harsh treatment of the South after the war. Under leaders such as T. Stevens, C. Sumner, and B. Wade in Congress, the Radicals passed much important Reconstruction legislation. At the height of their power, they even tried to impeach President A. Johnson (1868). They have been criticized by historians but were also the only consistent upholders of the rights of blacks. They worked for passage of such key legislation as the 14th Amendment to the Constitution.

Radishchev, Aleksandr Nikolayevich 1749–1802. Russian aristocrat, writer, and liberal. He was exiled to Siberia for denouncing serfdom in what was ostensibly a travel journal, *A Journey from St. Petersburg to Moscow,* published in 1790.

Radom, Confederation of *See* **Confederation of Radom**

Radowitz, Joseph Maria von 1797–1853. Prussian statesman and general. He worked for a German federation under Prussian leadership some 20 years before O. Bismarck brought it into being.

Radzin, Treaty of *See* **Russo-Turkish Wars (1)**

Radziwill Important Polish-Lithuanian princely family that has played a significant role in the history of both countries since the 15th cent. The first prominent Radziwill became palatine of Vilnius (1492), and others followed him in the post. Several Radziwills in the 16th cent. promoted Calvinism in Poland, but their descendants returned to Catholicism during the Catholic Reformation. In the 18th cent., the Radziwills supported the Saxon monarchs in struggles over the Polish crown.

Raetia *See* **Rhaetia**

Raffles, Sir Thomas Stamford 1781–1826. British colonial administrator. He was one of the founders of Britain's empire in the Far East and acquired Singapore for Britain in 1819.

Raghunath Rao *See* **Purandhar, Treaty of**

Rahman, Tunku Abdul *See* **Abdul Rahman, Tunku**

Raid of Ruthven *See* **Ruthven, William, 4th lord of Ruthven**

Raikes, Robert 1735–1811. British philanthropist and newspaper publisher. He started a Sunday school in Gloucester, England, to educate poor children, and sparked a nationwide movement to provide such schooling.

Rainalducci, Pietro ⟨Nicholas V⟩ *d.* 1333. Italian churchman and antipope (1328–30). Holy Roman Emperor Louis IV captured Rome and declared Pope John XXII, residing at Avignon, deposed after John had excommunicated him. Louis then named Rainalducci pope as Nicholas V, but Rainalducci soon submitted to John XXII.

Rainbow Division US 42d Infantry Division. It was the first US combat division to arrive in France in WW I, where it distinguished itself (though with heavy losses).

Rainier III *See* **Monaco**

Rais, Gilles de Laval, seigneur de *See* **Retz, Gilles de Laval, seigneur de**

Rajagopalachari, Chakravarti 1879–1972. Indian political leader and last governor general of India (1948–50). A disciple of M. Gandhi, he cooperated with Britain once Indian independence was assured. He founded the Swatantra (Freedom) party in 1959.

Rajputs People of northwest India who traditionally considered themselves members of the Hindu warrior class. The Rajputs were organized in a clan system and were powerful from the 7th cent. to the early 17th cent., when they became subjects of the Moguls. They rose again briefly (18th cent.) after the fall of the Moguls, only to be subjugated by the Marathas and then the British.

Rakhmaninov, Sergius Vassilievich *See* **Rachmaninov, Sergei Vasilyevich**

Rákóczy, Francis II 1676–1735. Prince of Translyvania and Hungarian nationalist leader. During the War of the Spanish Succession, he led a nearly successful Hungarian rebellion (1703) against the Hapsburg rulers.

Rákóczy, George I 1591–1648. Prince of Transylvania and Hungarian nationalist leader. Pursuing an anti-Hapsburg policy, he successfully invaded Hungary and thereby gained concessions and religious liberty for the Hungarians.

Rákosi, Mátyás 1892–1971. Hungarian Communist leader. He came to Budapest as Communist party secretary with the Soviet army in 1944 and consistently followed a Stalinist line, which

made him unpopular in Hungary. In and out of office as prime minister (1952–56), he fled the country just prior to the Hungarian Revolution of 1956.

Rakovsky, Khristian Georgievich 1873–? Russian Communist leader and diplomat. He was Soviet ambassador in both London and Paris but was ousted from the Communist party (1927) for opposing Stalin. He was tried during the purge trials and was imprisoned.

Ralegh, Sir Walter *See* **Raleigh, Sir Walter**

Raleigh, Sir Walter ⟨Ralegh, ~⟩ 1552?–1618. English courtier, adventurer, and poet. A favorite of Elizabeth I, he organized the ill-fated Roanoke Colony (*q.v.*) and was involved in other unsuccessful colonizing ventures, which nevertheless resulted in the introduction of potatoes and tobacco to Europe. He also led an expedition to South America in search of El Dorado (*q.v.*). He fell out of royal favor on the accession of James I and was eventually beheaded.

Rama *See* **Chakkri dynasty**

Ramakrishna 1836–86. Indian religious seer and mystic, founder of worldwide religious movement based on his belief in a universal religion.

Ramanuja 1017–1137 BC. Hindu religious leader. Rejecting concepts of an exclusive impersonal spirit, he promoted a form of Hinduism emphasizing personal devotion to Vishnu, and was thus influential in the Vaishnava sect.

Ramathibodi I *See* **Rama Tiboti**

Rama Tiboti ⟨Ramathibodi I⟩ 1312–69. Thai warrior-king and lawgiver. In 1350, he established a unified Thai state (Siam), which his descendants, the Ayutthaya dynasty, ruled until 1767. He also drafted a legal code that was not changed significantly until the 19th cent.

Ramayana With the Mahabharata, one of the two most important hundu Sanskrit texts. Written *c*300 BC it chronicles the life of Rama, the ideal man and king.

Rambouillet, Catherine de Vivonne, marquise de 1588–1665. French noblewoman and founder of the first great Parisian literary salon. She received the most distinguished writers and poets of her day and exercised a profound influence on literary taste.

Rameau, Jean Philippe 1683–1764. French composer and music theorist. He wrote influential treatises on harmony and composed harpsichord music, ballets such as *Les Indes Galantes*, and many operas, including *Castor et Pollux*.

Ramée, Pierre de la *See* **Ramus, Petrus**

Rameses *See* **Ramses**

Ramillies, Battle of British allied victory (May 23, 1706) over the French in the War of the Spanish

Succession (1701–14). Fought at Ramillies, in modern Belgium, the battle pitted some 50,000 British, Dutch, and Danish troops under J. Churchill, duke of Marlborough, against an approximately equal French force. The allies won nearly the whole of the Spanish Netherlands (modern Belgium) by this victory.

Ramiro I   *d.* 1063. First king of Aragon (1035–63). He built the kingdom from a base in Navarre, both by appropriating his brother's territories and by conquest of Moorish lands.

Ramsay, Sir William   1852–1916. British scientist. He discovered the entire family of the noble gases: argon, helium, krypton, and xenon. He was awarded the Nobel Prize in Chemistry in 1904.

Ramses I ⟨Rameses⟩ *d.* 1318 BC. Egyptian pharaoh (1320–18 BC), founder of the 19th dynasty. He made his son Seti I co-regent during his brief reign.

Ramses II ⟨Rameses II⟩ *d.* c1237 BC. Egyptian pharaoh (c1304–c1237 BC), named "the Great." His reign was marked by a period of great prosperity, the building of temples at Karnak, Luxor, and Abu Simbel, and increased slavery (possibly including the Hebrews).

Ramses III ⟨Rameses III⟩ *d.* 1167 BC. Egyptian pharaoh (c1198–67 BC). He defended Egypt against invaders from Libya and the "sea peoples," including the original Philistines then colonizing Palestine.

Ramus, Petrus ⟨Ramée, Pierre de la⟩ 1515–72. French humanist and the most eminent logician of his time, born Pierre de la Ramée. His reforms of Aristotelian logic were highly regarded in the 16th and 17th cents. A Protestant, he was murdered during a period of religious persecutions in France.

Ranavalona II   *See* **Malagasy Republic**

Ranavalona III   *See* **Malagasy Republic**

Rand, Ayn   1905–82. Russian-born American novelist. Her books exalt her philosophy, called objectivism, which holds that rational self-seeking is a virtue and altruism is a weakness. *The Fountainhead* and *Atlas Shrugged* are among her works.

Randolph, Asa Philip   1889–1979. American labor leader and pioneer crusader for black civil rights. He organized the Brotherhood of Sleeping Car Porters and helped end job discrimination against blacks in US defense industries. He was a director of the 1963 March on Washington *(q.v.)*.

Randolph, Edmund   1753–1813. American statesman. He formulated the Randolph (Virginia) Plan at the Constitutional Convention and later served as US attorney general (1789–94) and secretary of state (1794–95).

Randolph, John   1773–1833. American political leader. He spent most of his career (1799–1829) in Congress, where he was famous for his wit, eloquence, and stubborn defense of states' rights.

Randolph, Peyton   c1721–75. American Revolutionary leader and first president of the Continental Congress (1774). A longtime member of the Virginia House of Burgesses, he took a leading part in the early events of the American Revolutionary period.

Rangoon   Burmese capital city (pop. 2,276,000), river port, and the country's commercial and industrial center. A small fishing village for many centuries, Rangoon rose to prominence after King Alaungpaya located his capital there (1753). Under British colonial rule from 1852, it was developed into a major port. The Japanese occupied the city (1942–45) during WW II.

Ranjit Singh ⟨Runjeet Singh⟩ 1780–1839. Maharaja of the Punjab. Making himself the principal leader of the Sikhs (from 1801), he founded the Sikh kingdom by conquering Afghan and Pathan territories in northern India.

Ranke, Leopold von   1795–1886. German historian. A votary of carefully researched objective facts, he is considered the father of scientific historiography. He aimed to re-create history as "it actually happened."

Rankin, Jeanette   1880–1973. American congresswoman (1917–19, 1941–43). The first woman member of Congress, she created a furor by casting the only vote against a declaration of war against Japan after Pearl Harbor.

Ranters   English religious sect that flourished during the Commonwealth and Protectorate from 1649 to 1660. Its members believed in pantheism, holding that God is coextensive with nature, and appealed to an inner experience, denying the authority of Scripture. The movement was suppressed by Parliament.

Raoul   *See* **Rudolph**

Rapallo, Treaty of   Two important treaties signed at Rapallo, Italy. **1.** Treaty between Italy and Yugoslavia (Nov. 12, 1920) establishing the Adriatic city of Rijeka (Fiume) as a free city. (It reverted to Yugoslavia after WW II.) **2.** Treaty signed between Germany and the Soviet Union (Apr. 16, 1922) normalizing relations and renouncing mutual war indemnities.

Raphael   In the Bible, the archangel who is represented in the Book of Tobit as the companion of Tobias and the healer of Tobit.

Raphael   1483–1520. Great Italian artist in the High Renaissance style. He studied first with his father, Giovanni Santi, then with Perugino at Perugia, and studied the works of Leonardo da Vinci and Michelangelo. Thereafter, he produced many famous Madonnas and portraits. Summoned to Rome by Pope Julius II (1508), he decorated the Vatican apartment the Stanza della Senatura, and succeeded D. Bramante as chief Vatican architect (1514). His frescoes include the noted *School of Athens* and *Disputa* in the Vatican papal apartment.

Rapp, George *See* **Harmony Society**

Rappites Christian pietistic community that flourished in the 19th cent. It was founded (1803) by George Rapp in Germany, and the Rappites started other such groups in Pennsylvania and Indiana. Membership dwindled because of rules on celibacy, and the community eventually disbanded.

Rask, Rasmus Christian 1787–1832. Danish philologist. He pioneered the study of the relationships between the Indo-European languages and wrote Icelandic and Anglo-Saxon grammars.

Rasmussen, Knud Johan Victor 1879–1933. Danish explorer and ethnologist. Born in Greenland, he conducted many Arctic expeditions. He is noted for his valuable studies of the North American Eskimos.

Rasputin, Grigori Yefimovich 1872–1916. Russian peasant mystic who had great influence in the court of Czar Nicholas II. He gained the favor of Czarina Alexandra because he was able to relieve (1905) the suffering of her hemophiliac son, Alexis. In following years, Rasputin became notorious as a rapacious seducer of women. When Nicholas went to the front during WW I, Rasputin's corrupt influence and scandalous behavior only increased. Thus he hastened the collapse of the czarist government in the months leading up to the Russian Revolution of 1917. A group of noblemen, including Prince Felix Yusupov, plotted his assassination. They poisoned him unsuccessfully, then shot him and drowned him (Dec. 30) in the Neva River.

Ras Tafari *See* **Haile Selassie**

Rastatt and **Baden, treaties of** Treaty signed (Mar., 1714) in Rastatt (now in Germany) by which Holy Roman Emperor Charles VI made his personal peace with France in the War of the Spanish Succession. Some months later, in the Swiss city of Baden, he concluded peace on behalf of the states of the empire. These treaties complemented those signed at the Peace of Utrecht *(q.v.)*.

Rathenau, Walter 1867–1922. German statesman and industrialist. He organized the German economy both for WW I and for reparations payments afterward and ended the postwar German isolation by helping to engineer the Treaty of Ra-

pallo. He was assassinated by nationalist fanatics because he was a Jew.

Rathlin Island *See* **Robert I**

rationalism Philosophical doctrine holding that fundamental truths can be deduced by reason alone. It is opposed to empiricism *(q.v.)*, the doctrine that such knowledge derives from experiences through the senses. R. Descartes articulated the rationalist doctrine in the 17th cent., and it was further developed by B. Spinoza and G. von Leibnitz. I. Kant formulated a modified form of rationalism, called "critical rationalism," in his work *Critique of Pure Reason*. The rationalist doctrine also affected religious thought, giving rise to the deists *(q.v.)*, who denied the truth of religious revelations.

Ravel, Maurice 1875–1937. French composer. An exponent of impressionism, he was both an original composer and a popular one, with such well-known works as *Bolero* and *La Valse*.

Ravenna Historic city (pop. 139,000) in north-central Italy. Founded in early Roman times, it became the capital of the declining Western Roman Empire (402). It was the Ostrogothic capital (5th–6th cents.), then passed to the Byzantines, who created the Exarchate of Ravenna *(q.v.)* as the center of their power in Italy until *c*750. Conquered by the Franks, Ravenna was given to the pope *c*756 (the famous Donation of Pepin), and formed the basis of the Papal States *(q.v.)*. Ravenna became part of Italy during the unification (1860).

Ray, Man 1890–1976. American painter and photographer. One of the chief exponents of the Dada movement after WW I, he created a variety of experimental works of art, some combining photography and painting.

Ram Mohan Roy ⟨Ray, Rammohan⟩ 1774–1833. Indian thinker and reformer. He advocated a reaffirmation of Hindu culture but supported some aspects of Western culture, notably education. He was a scholar in several Oriental languages, translated Sanskrit classics, and was instrumental in abolishing suttee, or sacrifice of a widow on her husband's funeral pyre.

Rayburn, Samuel Taliaferro 1882–1961. Democrat from Texas, Speaker of the US House of Representatives (1940–47, 1949–53, 1955–61). His 48 years in the House set a record, and he was Speaker longer than anyone before him. He generally supported New Deal and Fair Deal legislation.

Raymond IV *d.* 1105. Count of Toulouse (1093–1105). He was one of the principal leaders of the First Crusade *(q.v.)* and was the key figure in organizing it.

Raymond VI 1156–1222. Count of Toulouse, (c1194–1222). Excommunciated for his tolerance toward the Albigenses of southern France, he later fought S. de Montfort during the Albigensian Crusade *(q.v.)*.

Raymond of Tripoli *See* **Baldwin V**

Razin, Stenka *d.* 1671. Cossack leader, head of the propertyless Cossacks of the Don (1670–71). He raided both Russian and Persian settlements, captured or razed several cities, and was finally defeated and captured by Russian troops at Simbirsk. He was taken to Moscow, tortured, and executed.

Re *See* **Ra**

Reagan, Ronald Wilson 1911–. US president (1981–), the 40th, successor to J. Carter. After a long career as a movie actor (from 1937), he entered politics as a conservative Republican in the early 1960s. He served two terms as governor of California (1967–75). Twice defeated in his bid for the Republican presidential nomination (1968, 1976), he won the nomination in 1980. He campaigned on a conservative platform that included tax cuts, reduced federal spending and regulation, and revitalization of the US military. He defeated his Democratic opponent, J. Carter, in a landslide victory. His early administration was marked by the end of the hostage crisis *(q.v.)*, an assassination attempt (by John W. Hinkley, Jr., Mar. 30, 1981) that resulted in the wounding of President Reagan and others, passage of the Reagan budget package for reduced federal spending in all areas except defense, breaking of the nationwide air controllers strike, the successful flight of space shuttle Columbia, successful US efforts in negotiating an end to the Lebanese War, and increased US involvement in the war in El Salvador.

realism In philosophy, the theory that things possess a substantive reality independent of the mind that perceives them. It is opposed to philosophical idealism. In literature and art, it is the school that strives for faithful representation of life as it is really lived, without idealization. It was prominent in literature and art, especially in France, from the mid-19th cent. to the early 20th cent. and was opposed to romanticism.

Rebecca (Rebekah) In the Bible, the wife of the Hebrew patriarch Isaac and the mother of Esau and Jacob.

Rebekah *See* **Rebecca**

reciprocity The principle or policy by which two or more nations grant each other equal treatment, usually in international trade, which usually results in a mutual lowering of import duties.

Reconquista Name for the drive by Spanish Christians to recapture the Iberian peninsula from the Muslims. During the Muslim invasions of the early 8th cent., Christians were only able to maintain control over small kingdoms in northern Spain. By the 11th cent. Spanish Christians began an active campaign to expand these domains and retake the peninsula. They had largely succeeded by the 13th cent. The last Muslim stronghold, Granada, was conquered by King Ferdinand in 1492.

Reconstruction Period in US history (1865–77) that followed the American Civil War. It was marked by the return of Confederate states to the Union, bitter struggles over political and racial differences, and the failure to effect fundamental social and economic reform of Southern society. President A. Lincoln had already adopted a policy of reconciliation toward the South before his assassination, and President A. Johnson generally attempted to continue it. Radical Republicans in Congress, however, wanted harsher treatment for the South. Their Wade-Davis Bill failed in 1864 and they were enraged when provisional state governments, created by Johnson's executive order (1865), enacted Black Codes *(q.v.)* to restrict Negro rights.

Congress responded by passing laws to guarantee Negro rights and to institute harsh reconstruction measures, while the president attempted to veto the legislation. On the national level, the bitter struggle culminated (1868) in the Radical Republicans' (narrowly) unsuccessful attempt to impeach Johnson. The congressional reconstruction program included passage of the 13th Amendment in Dec., 1865, abolishing slavery; the Civil Rights Act (Apr., 1866), countering the Black Codes; the 14th Amendment in June, 1866, guaranteeing Negro rights; legislation sanctioning the Freedmen's Bureau *(q.v.)*; the Reconstruction Act (Mar., 1867), dividing Confederate states (except Tennessee) into five military districts; and the 15th Amendment (1869), guaranteeing Negro voting rights.

Under the military authorities, there came to power Radical Republican governments composed of carpetbaggers (Northern Republicans and opportunists), scalawags (Southern white Republicans), and former Negro slaves. Rebuilding of the war-torn South began, state constitutions were rewritten to conform to standards set by the Republican Congress, and the states were readmitted (six in 1868, the remaining in 1870). The tenure of the pro-Republican carpetbaggers, however, was highly controversial and deeply resented by white Southerners. It was marked by corruption (although apparently no worse than elsewhere in the country), the rise of bitter sectional and racial hatred among Southerners, and the spread of terrorist groups such as the Ku Klux Klan.

Ultimately white Southerners regained control of the state governments, reinstituted discrimination against Negroes, and united to form the one-party, Democratic "solid South." Reconstruction ended with the disputed presidential election of 1876. Republican candidate R. Hayes was awarded the election (which hinged on returns from Louisiana, Florida, and South Carolina), and in 1877 federal troops were withdrawn from the South.

Red Baron *See* **Richthofen, Manfred, baron von**

Red Cambodians *See* **Khmer Rouge**

Red Cross International society, today involved in relief efforts in both wartime and peacetime. It was founded (1863) as a result of J. Dunant's call for establishment of a wartime relief agency to provide wounded with medical aid and was sanctioned by the Geneva Convention of 1864. Its functions were later expanded to include peacetime relief work. The American Red Cross was established (1881) by C. Barton.

Redi, Francesco *c*1626–98. Italian naturalist. A court physician in Tuscany, he proved in one of the first controlled experiments that maggots do not result from spontaneous generation in putrefying meat but come instead from eggs laid by flies.

Red River Settlement British colony in the Red River region of Manitoba, Canada. Settled in 1812, it became the object of rivalry between the Hudson's Bay Company and the North West Company. The Seven Oaks Massacre (1816), in which North West Company agents killed 22 settlers, and other incidents resulted in court battles and the eventual merger of the two companies (1821).

Red Shirt Movement Anti-British movement in the North-West Frontier province of India. It was launched in 1930 by Gaffar Khan (1890–) in support of the Indian National Congress and professed Ghandhian nonviolence.

Reed, John 1887–1920. American writer and radical leader. A wealthy Harvard graduate, he embraced communism, witnessed the Russian Revolution, and wrote a famous account of it, *Ten Days That Shook the World*.

Reed, Walter 1851–1902. American army surgeon and bacteriologist. In controlled experiments using human volunteers, he proved conclusively (1901) that yellow fever was transmitted by mosquitoes.

Reform, Catholic *See* **Catholic Reformation**

Reforma, La Period in Mexican history (1854–76) characterized by liberal reforms directed mainly against special privileges of the army and the church. It began with announcement of the liberals' Plan of Ayutla (Mar. 1, 1854) and the ouster (1855) of the dictator Santa Anna. There followed a succession of liberal presidents (most notably B. Juárez), revolts and civil wars, and the brief restoration of the monarchy under Maximilian. Reform legislation enacted included Ley Juárez (1855), abolishing church and military courts; Ley Lerdo (1856), forcing the sale of church-owned secular lands; a liberal constitution (1857) curtailing military and church power; and Laws of La Reforma (1859), ordering confiscation of church lands.

Reformation Religious reform movement that arose in the 16th cent. It began as a reaction to practices within the Roman Catholic church that some held to be either unsupported by scriptural teaching or simply corrupt and abusive usurpations of authority. The movement ultimately gave rise to the various Protestant churches. Although earlier movements for church reform had arisen in Europe, the Reformation dates from 1517, when Martin Luther issued his Ninety-five Theses. Other religious dissidents, such as John Calvin, also spread the movement for reform, which was fueled by religious zeal, by the new spirit of Renaissance humanism, and by social changes resulting from the growth of a prospering mercantile class. Key dates in the history of the Reformation include:

14TH CENT. John Wyclif led early movement for reform of Roman Catholic church.

1414–18 Council of Constance, unsuccessful attempt to introduce reforms in the Roman Catholic church.

1415 John Huss, Bohemian religious reformer, burned at stake for heresy; death led to outbreak of the Hussite Wars in the Holy Roman Empire.

1517 M. Luther posted his Ninety-five Theses at Wittenberg (Oct. 31) in the Holy Roman Empire; the Reformation began.

1518 In Switzerland, Huldreich Zwingli began campaign against sale of indulgences within the church; led growth of Reformation in Swiss cantons.

1519 Luther defended Protestant doctrine in famous Leipzig Debate (July).

1520 Luther excommunicated from the Roman Catholic church.

1521 Luther refused to recant after being called before the Diet of Worms.

1522–23 Knights' War, unsuccessful rebellion by knights to ensure ancient privileges against the Reformation.

1524–25 Peasant's War; Luther condemned violence of peasants' uprising, which was partly inspired by his teachings; peasants savagely repressed.

1526 First Diet of Speyer convened; decreed that German princes could embrace Lutheran teachings.

1529 Colloquy of Marburg; Luther and Philip Melanchthon debated against John Oecolampadius and Huldreich Zwingli on elements of Reformation doctrine.

1529 Second Diet of Speyer overturned ruling of first diet; Lutheran princes issued a protest against its decrees, thereby becoming known as the Protestants.

1530 Diet of Augsburg convened; Melanchthon drew up the Confession of Augsburg, which became the foundation for Lutheranism.

1531 Protestant nobles in the Holy Roman Empire formed the Schmalkaldic League to oppose Emperor Charles V's threats to use force against Lutheranism.

1534 In England Henry VIII came into conflict with the pope over his attempt to divorce Catherine of Aragon; excommunicated, he secured the Act of Supremacy, establishing the Church of England. Though Henry maintained Catholic character of church, later rulers introduced Protestant liturgy.

1536 John Calvin settled in Geneva and issued *Institutes of the Christian Religion*, foundation for Calvinism.

1539 Lutheranism in England suppressed by issuance of Act of Six Articles.

1545 Council of Trent convened; marked beginning of Catholic Reformation; reforms introduced to counter rising tide of Protestantism.

1546–47 Holy Roman Emperor Charles V defeated the Schmalkaldic League in the Schmalkaldic War.

1547–53 Edward VI reigned in England; began reorganization of Church of England into a Protestant church; secured (1547) repeal of Act of Six Articles and issuance (1549) of Book of Common Prayer.

1555 Peace of Augsburg provided formula for ending conflict between Catholics and Protestants within the Holy Roman Empire.

1559 Synod of French Protestant churches held in Paris; led to organization of Huguenot movement in France.

1560 John Knox secured establishment of Calvinism in Scotland.

1562–98 French Catholics and Huguenots engaged in civil war during Wars of Religion.

1598 French king Henry IV issued the Edict of Nantes, granting religious freedom to the Huguenots.

1618–48 Thirty Years' War; began as a revolt in Bohemia in the Holy Roman Empire and soon became general European war fought between Protestant and Catholic forces.

1648 Peace of Westphalia ended Thirty Years' War and established a measure of religious peace in Europe.

Reformation, Catholic *See* **Catholic Reformation**

Reform Bills Series of laws that enlarged the British electorate and removed voting inequities. A bill in 1832 increased the representation of large towns proportionally and increased the electorate 50 percent by eliminating certain voter qualifications. The 1867 act again redistributed parliamentary seats according to population and again doubled the body of eligible voters. The bill in 1884 enabled nearly all males to vote. In 1918, suffrage was extended to all over the age of 30, regardless of sex, and the voting age was lowered to 21 in 1928.

Reformed Church in America Official name, since 1867, of the Dutch Reformed church in North America. Both its doctrine and system of church government originated in The Netherlands under Calvinist inspiration. It was transplanted to America as the religion of the Dutch colony of New Amsterdam (New York).

Reform Judaism Religious movement that sought to modernize Judaism. Beginning in Germany (19th cent.) under the leadership of such rabbis as A. Geiger, the movement did away with many Orthodox rituals and practices and stressed instead religious faith and ethics. Since the 1930s, Reform congregations have reinstituted some of the traditional practices.

Reform Movement of 1898 Short-lived reform movement in China during the reign of Emperor Kuang Hsü. China's defeat in the Sino-Japanese War (1894–95) and the attempts by Western powers to exploit China gave rise to sentiment for Westernizing Chinese culture. Scholar and reformer K'ang Yu-wei (1858–1927), gained the emperor's confidence and persuaded him to issue sweeping reforms of traditional Chinese society. The movement was cut short, however, by a coup led by the Empress Dowager Tzu Hsi.

Reims *See* **Rheims**

Regency British historical and cultural period (1811–20). It spanned the regency of George, prince of Wales, who came to power as regent after his father, George III, went insane. It was marked by the end of the Napoleonic Wars, dissolute courtly life, an interest in antiquity and Oriental artifacts, and a flowering of the arts. Romantic literature, including the work of J. Keats, G. Byron, P. Shelley, and Sir W. Scott, flourished in this period, which also saw the development of distinctive styles in the decorative arts and architecture.

regicides During the English Civil War period, those who were responsible for the trial and execution of King Charles I (1649). Of those still alive at the Restoration of the monarchy (1660), 15 fled abroad and 29 were convicted of treason. Ten were executed.

Regiomontanus ⟨Müller, Johannes⟩ 1436–76. German mathematician, astronomer, and humanist. Involved in the study of Greek manuscripts, he produced the first systematic modern exposition of trigonometry (c1464).

Régnier, Henri de 1864–1936. French poet and writer. One of the foremost members of the symbolist school, he later wrote in a more classical vein.

Regulating Act British parliamentary legislation passed in 1773 reorganizing the British East India Company. Its object was to improve the government of Bengali domains, and it represented the first British government intervention in the company's administration of India. The British government took over complete administrative control by 1858. (*See also* Government of India acts.)

Regulator movement American Colonial reform society formed in the 1760s. Frontier settlers in western North Carolina formed the group to reform corrupt local government and end oppressive taxation. When the Colonial government failed to act, the Regulators refused to pay taxes and ultimately mounted an insurrection. The Regulators were defeated (1771) by the militia under Gov. W. Tryon. Thereafter, many Regulators fled to Tennessee. A similar group in South Carolina succeeded in effecting reforms during the 1760s, then disbanded without serious incident.

Regulus, Marcus Atilius *d. c*250 BC. Roman general in the First Punic War. Captured by the Carthaginians, he was released on parole to persuade the Senate to make peace. Instead he urged the Romans to persist, and then returned, as agreed, to Carthage, where he is said to have been tortured to death.

Rehoboam *d. c*914 BC. Last king of the united kingdom of Israel (933–914) and first king of Judah. During his reign, the 10 northern Hebrew tribes broke away under the leadership of Jeroboam I to form the kingdom of Judah. Rehoboam then ruled the two southernmost tribes.

Reichstag Legislative assemblies of the Holy Roman Empire and German successor states. The Holy Roman Emperor began to meet with city representatives c1100. The meetings became formal assemblies after 1250 and exerted legislative power until 1648, playing only a ceremonial role after that date. An elected Reichstag was established by the German Empire from 1871 to 1918, and was continued under the Weimar Republic (1919–33). The Reichstag surrendered its power to A. Hitler by the Enabling Act (1933), and was reduced to ceremonial functions during the Third Reich. It was replaced after WW II by the Bundestag in West Germany.

Reichstag fire The burning of the Reichstag building in Berlin on the night of Feb. 27, 1933. A Dutchman, Marinus van der Lubbe, was convicted for setting the fire. A. Hitler blamed the fire on the Communists, however, and used the incident to justify his assumption of dictatorial powers.

Reign of Terror Period during the French Revolution. Instituted Sept. 5, 1793, and directed by the Committee of Public Safety *(q.v.)*, the Terror was intended to crush all opposition to the revolution. Thousands were guillotined or died in prisons. The period also saw the rise of M. Robespierre as virtual dictator of France, enactment of the laws of Maximum (establishing price controls and forbidding hoarding), institution of universal conscription, and reorganization of the army. Toward the end of the Terror, even allies of Robespierre (including followers of J. Hébert and G. Danton) fell victim to the guillotine. Finally, popular reaction against the Terror resulted in the overthrow of Robespierre (July 27, 1794) and the subsequent Thermidorean reaction. (*See also* French Revolution [1793–94].)

Reimarus, Hermann Samuel 1694–1768. German philosopher. A pioneer thinker of the Enlightenment, he denied the supernatural origins of Christianity and advanced the belief in natural religion of the deists.

Reinhardt, Max ⟨Goldmann, Max⟩ 1873–1943. Austrian theater director. He originated many modern dramatic techniques and brought new life to productions of classic Greek and Shakespearean drama.

Reinsurance Treaty Secret treaty (June 18, 1887) between Germany and Russia replacing the Three Emperors' League. It provided that one party would remain neutral if the other became involved in a war, unless Germany attacked France or Russia attacked Austria. Failure to renew the treaty (1890) led to a Franco-Russian alliance.

relativity Physical theory, advanced by A. Einstein and elaborated by Einstein and others, dealing with the nature and relationship of space and time. Toward the end of the 19th cent., certain anomalies in the system of Newtonian mechanics were discovered. In order to explain them, Einstein advanced the special theory of relativity (1905) and the general theory of relativity (1915), which fundamentally altered the perception of the form and structure of the universe. Fundamental to the theory is the concept that all motion is relative and that space and time are not separate and absolute entities. The theory produced a revolution in mathematics and physics that is continuing today. A unified field theory, which seeks to combine the special and general theories of relativity, has yet to be demonstrated.

Religion, Wars of   Series of civil wars (1562–98) in France between the Catholics, led by the powerful Guise family, and the French Protestants, known as Huguenots. The civil wars revolved around religious differences but were further complicated by struggles among the nobility for political power. The wars culminated in the accession of the Huguenot leader, Henry of Navarre (as Henry IV), to the French throne in 1589. In an attempt to resolve the continuing struggle, he converted to Catholicism (1593) and finally ended the wars by the Edict of Nantes (1598), granting religious toleration to the Protestants. Key dates in the history of the wars include:

1560   Conspiracy of Amboise; Huguenots' unsuccessful plot to break influence of Catholic house of Guise over French King Francis II and thereby end persecution of Protestants.

1560–74   Charles IX reigned, following the death of Francis II; a youth at his accession, he was dominated by his mother, Catherine de Medici, throughout his reign.

1562   Massacre of Vassy; Huguenots massacred by troops of François, duke of Guise.

1562–63   First war fought after Huguenots rebelled against persecution.

1567–68   Second war fought.

1568–70   Third war fought; Huguenots led by Louis I de Bourbon and G. de Coligny; war ended by Treaty of St. Germain (1570), which granted some freedoms to the Huguenots.

1572   St. Bartholomew's Day Massacre (Aug. 23); brought on by rising influence of Huguenot leader G. de Coligny; resulted in murder of many Huguenots and sparked fourth war.

1572–73   Fourth war fought; ended by Edict of Bologne.

1574–89   Henry III, another son of Catherine de Medici, reigned; Catherine continued to exercise considerable influence.

1574–76   Fifth war fought; ended by Peace of Monsieur (1576), by which Huguenots received religious freedom everywhere but in Paris.

1576   Holy League formed by Catholics to oppose Protestantism in France; began alliance with Spain.

1577   Sixth war fought; war sparked by Henry III, who revoked toleration of Protestants at the urging of the Catholic Holy League.

1577   Protestants won favorable terms in the Peace of Bergerac (Sept. 17), ending sixth war.

1580   Seventh war fought after persecution of Huguenots continued; concessions to Huguenots confirmed by the Treaty of Fleix, ending the war.

1584   French king Henry III designated Henry of Navarre, a Huguenot, as heir to the French throne; Henry of Guise led Catholic Holy League in opposition, resulting in new war.

1585–89   War of the Three Henrys; Henry of Guise took Paris (1588) and deposed Henry III, who fled; Henry of Guise was murdered (1588); Henry III then turned to Henry of Navarre for support and was murdered (1589), thus ending the war.

1589   Huguenot leader Henry of Navarre became King Henry IV.

1589   Spain invaded France to aid the Catholic Holy League against Henry IV.

1589   Battle of Arques; Henry IV defeated Catholics.

1590   Battle of Ivry; Henry IV again victorious in fighting against Catholics.

1593   Henry IV converted to Catholicism.

1594   Henry IV entered Paris.

1598   Henry issued (Apr. 15) the Edict of Nantes, granting Huguenots religious freedom.

1598   Treaty of Vervins (May 2) ended war with Spain.

religious dualism   *See* **dualism**

Religious Peace of Nürnberg   ⟨Nürnberg Standstill⟩   Truce (July 23, 1532) that for a time ended religious wars between Holy Roman Emperor Charles V (Catholic) and the Schmalkaldic League (Protestant).

relocation centers   WW II internment camps in which Japanese-Americans living in a defined area on the West Coast were forcibly confined between Mar., 1942, and Mar., 1946. Suspected of disloyalty after the Japanese attack on Pearl Harbor, Japanese-Americans were indiscriminately interned in such camps and lost property estimated at some $400 million. This program was later severely criticized and officially deplored by Congress in 1983.

Remarque, Erich Maria   1897–1970.   German novelist, best known for his WW I novel *All Quiet on the Western Front.*

Rembrandt   ⟨Rijn, Harmenszoon van⟩   1606–69. Great Dutch painter, noted for his mastery of technique (especially lighting) and for great depth of understanding of his subjects. He spent many years teaching and enjoyed a wide following until the 1640s, when he lost popularity and began to experience financial problems that continued until his death. He nevertheless produced over 600 paintings, as well as many drawings and etchings, and in the later years of his life created some of his greatest masterpieces. Among his many famous works are *Two Philosophers, The Anatomy Lesson of Dr. Tulip, The Sortie of the Banning Cocq Company, Aristotle Contemplating the Bust of Homer, Bathsheba,* and his series of self-portraits.

Remington, Eliphalet 1793–1861. American arms manufacturer. His firm produced a famous series of rifles and pistols and supplied the US government with small arms from the mid-19th cent.

Remonstrants Dutch Protestants adhering to the liberal Calvinist ideas of J. Arminius. They presented their views to the States General (1610) in a "remonstrance," were condemned by the Protestant Synod of Dort (1618–19), and then were persecuted by the state church until 1625.

Remus Legendary cofounder of Rome (traditionally 753 BC). Remus and his twin brother, Romulus, founded the town that became Rome. After Romulus built a defensive wall around it, Remus jumped over it to prove it ineffective. Enraged, Romulus killed his brother.

Renaissance Transition period in Europe from medieval to modern culture. The Renaissance is generally viewed as a rebirth or reawakening of learning and the arts, which began in Italy in the 1300s and then spread throughout Europe. The Renaissance period may be broadly divided into the Italian Renaissance of the 1300s and 1400s and the Northern Renaissance (centers outside Italy) of the 1400s and 1500s. It may also be divided into Early (*c*1400–*c*1490), High (*c*1490–1520), and Late (1520–1600) periods, though dates of periods vary. Central to the Renaissance period was the rise of Humanism, a movement placing new emphasis on the individual and on the temporal (as opposed to secular) world about him. Man became "the measure of all things" and the "universal man," an individual accomplished in a wide variety of pursuits, became a Renaissance ideal. The intellectual "rebirth" of the Renaissance had wide ramifications. There was a sudden emphasis on education, particularly study of the Greek and Roman classics (the invention of printing helped make this possible). In literature and philosophy, it was man and the world about him that became the center of attention. In the arts, interest shifted from idealized religious themes to more worldly conceptions, and advances were made in areas of technical concern (perspective, use of color, study of human anatomy). In architecture, Renaissance designers adapted earlier classical forms (as in Palladianism) and medieval Gothic styles were gradually abandoned. Advances in science during the Renaissance helped prepare the way for the 17th-cent. revolution in science. The Renaissance in Italy began in Florence, and thereafter spread to Venice, Rome, and other cities. The great cultural flowering in Italy, as elsewhere, was aided by wealthy patrons, including such families as the Medici, Sforza, Este, and Gonzaga, and Roman Catholic popes such as Julius II and Leo X. Leading figures of the Renaissance are listed by country (and then by birth date) below.

Renaissance in Italy

NICOLA PISANO Founded school of sculpture at Pisa and developed style that influenced Renaissance sculpture in Italy. *c*1220–84

GIOTTO Florentine artist and architect; departed from the traditional Byzantine forms and created powerful new style of painting, foreshadowing the Renaissance. 1266–1337

PETRARCH Great Poet, classical scholar, and Humanist; helped spread interest in classical culture by his researches and poems, thereby laying foundations for the early Renaissance. 1304–74

G. BOCCACCIO Poet and storyteller who wrote the *Decameron*, in which the earthly passions of man are portrayed. 1313–75

F. BRUNELLESCHI First great architect of the Renaissance, he developed systematic rules of perspective and designed the celebrated dome of the cathedral in Florence. 1377–1446

L. GHIBERTI Leading 15th-cent. Renaissance sculptor famed for his doors for the baptistry of the cathedral of Florence. *c*1378–1455

DONATELLO Florentine sculptor, among the greatest Renaissance sculptors; he completed such masterpieces as the bronze statue *David* and *Gattamelata*, a prototype of Renaissance equestrian statuary. *c*1386–1466

P. UCCELLO Florentine painter noted for his pioneering use of perspective; masterpiece is cycle of *Noah*, among which is the *Deluge*. 1396–1475

FRA ANGELICO Florentine painter who brought classical stylistic elements to his religious works. *c*1400–55

LUCA DELLA ROBBIA Influential Florentine sculptor who did the marble *cantoria* (singing gallery), famous portrayal of children and innocence;

founded family studio famous for enamelled terracotta works. 1400?–82

MASACCIO Leading Florentine painter; completed fresco *Trinity*, which marked great advance in understanding of perspective; worked on the historic frescoes of the Brancacci Chapel of Santa Maria del Carmine in Florence. 1401–28?

LEON ALBERTI Early example of universal "Renaissance man"; systematized problems of perspective in *Della Pittura*, worked as an architect; wrote poetry; did studies in geography, grammar, and mathematics. 1404–72

FRA FILIPPO LIPPI Florentine painter noted as a great colorist and draftsman; did *Coronation of the Virgin* and other famous works. *c*1406–69

LORENZO VALLA Classical scholar and Humanist; attacked medieval philosophy and did important scholarly and critical works. *c*1407–57

ANTONIO POLLAIUOLO Florentine artist and sculptor, believed first to study human anatomy through dissection. 1429?–98

GIOVANNI BELLINI Venetian painter; helped make Venice a center of Renaissance art; taught Giorgione and Titian. *c*1430–1516

MANTEGNA Noted for his frescoes, especially in the Camera degli Sposi (wedding Chamber) of the Gonzaga palace. 1431–1506

MARSILIO FICINO Philosopher and leading exponent of Platonism in his time, he translated Greek classics into Latin. 1433–99

S. BOTTICELLI Florentine painter; *Birth of Venus* among his famous works. *c*1444–1510

D. BRAMANTE Painter and architect who pioneered the High Renaissance style in architecture. 1444–1514

LEONARDO DA VINCI Archetypal "Renaissance man," who painted masterpiece, *Mona Lisa* and the most famous *Last Supper*; worked as a sculptor, architect, and military engineer; noted also for his scientific studies, especially human anatomy, and for his inventions. 1452–1519

N. MACHIAVELLI Political philosopher and leading Renaissance figure who wrote the classic on political power, *The Prince*. 1469–1527

GIORGIONE Venetian painter; leading figure of the 16th-cent. painting in Venice; works include *The Three Philosophers* and *Tempesta*. 1478–1511

B. PERUZZI Painter and architect who worked in Rome and designed the Palazzo Massini. 1481–1536

ANTONIO DA SANGALLO THE YOUNGER Leading Florentine architect of his time who built the Farnese Palace at Rome; Sangallo's designs greatly influenced later architects. 1483–1546

RAPHAEL A great master of the High Renaissance whose many famous works include series of Madonna altar panels and the frescoes *Disputa* and *School of Athens*. 1483–1564

ANDREA DEL SARTO Noted painter who was influential in Florence and Rome; among his works were frescoes on the life of St. John the Baptist. 1486–1530

TITIAN One of the greatest of Renaissance painters; noted for his religious and mythological paintings; works include *Sacred and Profane Love* and the *Pietà*. 1490–1576

B. CELLINI Sculptured *Perseus with the Head of Medusa* and wrote a famous autobiography; famed as a goldsmith. 1500–71

A. PALLADIO One of the most influential Renaissance architects; developed architectural style (Palladianism) based on classical Roman forms; wrote famous treatise, *Four Books on Architecture*, and designed villas and church facades. 1508–80

TINTORETTO A Venetian, leading painter of Late Renaissance Mannerist school; he painted a *Last Supper* and other famous works. 1518–94

P. VERONESE Great decorative artist of the Venetian school; *Christ in the House of Levi* among his famous paintings. 1528–88

Renaissance in the Low Countries and German States

ROBERT CAMPIN Early Flemish master; taught Van der Weyden; did *Mérode Altarpiece*. *c*1378–1444

J. VAN EYCK Flemish, great Renaissance painter of the 15th cent.; he mastered the technique of painting with oils and made Flanders a center of Renaissance art; his style of realism was widely influential. *c*1390–1441

R. VAN DER WEYDEN Flemish painter noted for his treatment of religious themes; *Christ Descending from the Cross* is one of his masterpieces. *c*1400–64

HANS MEMLING Leading artist of Bruges in his time; painted *Passion Triptych*. *c*1430–94

HUGO VAN DER GOES Greatest Flemish artist of his time; noted for religious works of profound nature; was early influence in northern realism; did masterpiece, *Portinari Altarpiece*. *c*1440–82

M. SCHONGAUER Leading engraver of his time, noted for grace and idealistic beauty of his works; works include *Madonna in a Courtyard* and *St. Sebastian*. *c*1445–91

H. BOSCH Flemish painter; noted for his imaginative, sometimes bizarre works; famous works include *Garden of Earthly Delights. c*1450–1516

J. REUCHLIN German scholar and Humanist; he did important studies of classical Greek and Hebrew writings. 1455–1522

LUCAS CRANACH Leading German painter whose works greatly influenced 16th-cent. German art. 1472–1553

H. HOLBEIN THE YOUNGER German painter; noted for the realism of his portraits; he worked in England from 1532 until his death. 1497–1553

ERASMUS Leading Renaissance Humanist scholar; his works include an edition of the New Testament, of Latin and Greek classics, and critical works; he opposed M. Luther's Protestant reforms. 1466?–1536

A. DÜRER Great German artist of the Renaissance whose famous works include paintings, altarpieces, engravings, and woodcuts. 1471–1528

N. COPERNICUS Polish astronomer; leading scientific figure of the Renaissance, he founded modern astronomy by his theory that the earth and other planets revolve around the sun; paved the way for the scientific revolution of the 17th cent. 1473–1543

MELANCTHON German theologian, scholar, and Humanist; in addition to his major contributions to the Protestant Reformation, Melancthon played a significant role in reforming the German educational system. 1497–1560

M. GRÜNEWALD Great German painter; painted religious, often mystical works, including the *Isenheim Altarpiece. c*1475–1528

P. BRUEGHEL THE ELDER Leading 16th-cent. Flemish painter noted for his landscapes and peasant scenes, including *Peasant Wedding. c*1525–69

O. DI LASSO Among greatest of Renaissance composers; noted for his motets. *c*1530–94

Renaissance in France

GUILLAUME DE MACHAUT Poet and great composer in the 14th cent. Ars Nova musical style. *c*1300–77

J. FOUQUET Leading French painter; famous works include illuminations for the *Book of Hours. c*1415–80

G. BUDÉ Humanist scholar. Major figure of the Renaissance who established study of the classics in France and who helped organize a great library, which became the Bibliothèque Nationale. 1467–1540

JEAN CLOUET A noted portrait painter; he worked in France nearly all his life. *c*1485–*c*1540

F. RABELAIS Scholar, Humanist, and author of classic of satire, *Gargantua and Pantagruel. c*1490–1553

ROSSO FIORENTINO First of several Italians brought to France (1530) by King Francis I and who developed the influential Fontainebleau School of French painting; joined by Primaticcio and others, the school evolved styles of painting and decorative sculpture. 1494–1540

P. DELORME Great Renaissance architect; introduced a classical style to French architecture; did initial design of Tuileries Palace. *c*1510–70

PIERRE LESCOT Architect who developed decorative style; his work contributed to rise of French classicism; with sculptor Jean Goujon designed part of the Louvre. *c*1515–78

P. DE RONSARD Great Renaissance poet; he was a leader of the famous group of French Renaissance poets, the Pléiade; other members were Joachim du Bellay, Antoine de Baïf, Etienne Jodelle, Pontus de Tyard, Jean Dorat, and Rémi Belleau. 1525–85

M. DE MONTAIGNE Great essayist, noted for his three books of essays revealing spirit of Humanism and his mastery of style. 1533–92

Renaissance in England

J. FISHER A noted scholar, Humanist, and theologian, he promoted scholarly study in England; martyred for refusing to yield to King Henry VIII. 1459–1535

J. COLET Was a leading exponent of scholarly studies and of Humanism. 1467?–1519

T. MORE He was an important advocate of Humanism and wrote the classic *Utopia.* 1478–1535

ROGER ASCHAM Scholar, Humanist, and author who promoted the English vernacular. 1515–68

E. SPENSER One of the greatest Elizabethan poets, he wrote the *Faerie Queene* and other works. *c*1552–99

P. SIDNEY Noted Renaissance courtier and poet; wrote the essay *The Defense of Poetry.* 1554–86

F. BACON Philosopher and essayist, author of noted works, including *Novum Organum* and *The New Atlantis*; his work in inductive logic proved important to the later advances in scientific thought. 1561–1626

C. MARLOWE Leading poet and dramatist; introduced use of blank verse and psychological themes in English drama. 1564–93

W. SHAKESPEARE Perhaps the greatest dramatist of all time; his many famous plays mark the culmination of the Elizabethan Age. 1564–1616

I. JONES Architect; he introduced the Renaissance Palladian style in England. 1573–1652

Renaissance in Spain

CARDINAL JIMÉNEZ Promoted classical studies and founded the University of Alcala. 1436–1517

FERNANDO DE HERRERA Humanist and leading neoclassic poet of 16th-cent. Spain. 1534?–97

M. DE CERVANTES Leading figure of the Renaissance in Spain, he wrote the great classic *Don Quixote*. 1547–1616

L. DE VEGA The virtual founder of Spanish drama, he wrote some 1,800 plays; introduced Italian forms to Spanish poetry. 1562–1635

Renan, Ernest 1823–92. French historian, Orientalist, and writer. He left the seminary after a crisis of faith and afterward wrote about religion from a naturalistic point of view.

René 1409–80. King of Naples (1435–80) and duke of Anjou, Bar, and Lorraine. Involved in the dynastic politics of the time, he was driven out of Naples (1442) by his Aragonese rivals and retired to Provence to devote himself to the arts.

Renewed Church of the Brethren *See* **Moravian Church**

Reni, Guido 1575–1642. Italian painter of the Bolognese school. His works include the *Crucifixion of St. Peter* and his masterpiece, *Aurora and the Hours*.

Renner, Karl 1870–1950. First leader of the Austrian republican government, 1918–20, and president of Austria, 1945–50. A socialist, Renner held many key positions in the interwar period and advocated the union of Austria and Germany prior to WW II.

Renoir, Jean 1894–1979. French film director. A son of the painter P. Renoir, he is known for his imaginative cinematic effects. His films include the antiwar masterpiece *La Grande Illusion*.

Renoir, Pierre Auguste 1841–1919. French impressionist painter. He was noted for such effects as light filtering through leaves *(Le Moulin de la Galette)*. Later in his career he returned to more formal techniques *(Bathers)* and then developed a style marked by its sensuousness.

***Renville* Agreement** Truce (Jan. 17, 1948) between the Dutch and the Indonesians, signed on the US Navy ship *Renville*. It marked a lull in the fighting between the Dutch and the Indonesian republicans and remained officially in effect, supplementing the Linggadjati Agreement *(q.v.)*, until Indonesia obtained independence (1949).

reparations Payments required of a defeated nation for war damages, especially those imposed on Germany after WW I and WW II. German WW I reparations set by the Treaty of Versailles amounted to $32 billion, and the Dawes Plan for repayment was formulated (1924). Economic hardship and the worldwide Depression resulted in the Young Plan (1930), but by 1932 Germany had ceased to make further payments. After WW II, German reparations were officially canceled in 1954.

repartimiento Spanish-American colonial system by which colonists were allowed to recruit specified numbers of Indians for forced labor. The system assumed definite form by 1575 and, though progressively modified, continued in some form until the 19th cent.

republic Form of government in which power is vested in officers who represent the public and who govern in accordance with established laws for the sake of the common good. The government of the United States is a federal republic.

Republic, Council of the Preparliament Russian provisional government (Oct.–Nov., 1917), headed by A. Kerensky. Largely ineffective, it was swept away in the Bolshevik seizure of power.

Republic, Roman *See* **Roman Republic; Rome**

Republic of *See names inverted.*

Republican party One of the two major American political parties. Founded (1854) by antislavery Whigs and others who were opposed to the Kansas-Nebraska Act (1854) and the extension of slavery into new US territories, it received support from abolitionists, Free-Soilers, Know-Nothings, and others. Its first presidential candidate, J. Frémont, was defeated in the 1856 election, but its second, A. Lincoln, gained the presidency (1860) and thereby precipitated secession of the southern states and, ultimately, the Civil War. During the war, the party split into moderate and radical factions. The radical Republicans favored harsh Reconstruction measures against the South, and their struggle with Lincoln's successor, A. Johnson, led to impeachment proceedings (1868). Their activities during the administration of U. Grant led to formation of the Liberal Republican party, which unsuccessfully ran H. Greeley against Grant in the 1872 elections.

Other breaks in the Republican party occurred in 1884, when the Mugwumps *(q.v.)* abandoned the party to support Democrat G. Cleveland, and in 1912, when the progressive wing of the party formed the Progressive (Bull Moose) party *(q.v.)*. This Republican split secured the election for the Democrat, W. Wilson. The Republican party, traditionally more conservative than its Democratic counterpart, was hurt in the 20th cent. by corruption in the administration of W. Harding and by the beginning of the Great Depression during the administration of H. Hoover. Hoover was defeated for reelection (1932) by F. Roosevelt, and the Republicans did not regain the presidency until the election (1952) of D. Eisenhower. Subsequent Republican presidents include R. Nixon, G. Ford, and R. Reagan.

Republican People's party   Turkish political party. Formed in 1923 by K. Atatürk, it was Turkey's ruling party until 1950. Since then it has been the leading opposition party (to the Democrat party), with periods of rule. It is republican, secularist, and increasingly leftist in orientation.

Republic of China   *See* **Taiwan**

Resaca de la Palma, Battle of   Second major battle (May 9, 1846) of the Mexican War (1846–48), fought near present-day Brownsville, Texas. An American force, led by Gen. Z. Taylor, intercepted and defeated the Mexican army, under the leadership of Gen. Mariano Arista, then retreating after the Battle of Palo Alto.

Resistance   Underground political and paramilitary forces that grew inside the countries occupied by Germany during WW II. The French Resistance was notable among them. Its network provided intelligence, published clandestine newspapers, and carried out sabotage, especially after the Allied landings (1944) on the Continent. (*See also* Partisans.)

Respighi, Ottorino   1879–1936. Italian composer. His works, such as *The Pines of Rome* and *The Fountain of Rome*, were influenced by the Russian and German Romantics.

Restoration   **1.** Period in English history (1660–88) that included the reigns of Charles II and James II. It began with the restoration of the monarchy under Charles after the experiment in republican government failed (*see* Protectorate). Growing opposition to the Protectorate (now dominated by the military) prompted one of the military leaders, G. Monck, to take control of London (1659). The royalist Convention Parliament (*q.v.*) was convened, and Monck made arrangements for Charles' restoration. Charles then issued the Declaration of Breda (*q.v.*), returned to England (1660), and assumed authority. His subsequent reign was marked by a reaction against Puritans and the policies of austerity they imposed on English life during the Protectorate; enactment of harsh measures by the Cavalier Parliament to ensure religious uniformity with the Church of England (*see* Clarendon Code); the rise of anti-Catholic sentiment; the beginnings of the Whig and Tory parties; and a series of misfortunes, including outbreak of the plague (1665), the

Great Fire of London (1666), and losses in the Second Dutch War (1664–67). Under James II, anti-Catholic sentiment and reaction against his absolutism quickly brought about (1688) the Glorious Revolution (*q.v.*) and the end of the Restoration period. **2.** Period in French history (1814–30) that began with Napoleon's fall from power and restoration of the Bourbon monarchs. Largely through the efforts of C. Talleyrand, Louis XVIII assumed power after Napoleon's first abdication (Apr. 11, 1814), in what is called the First Restoration. His rule was interrupted by Napoleon's Hundred Days (*q.v.*), however, and the Second Restoration began after Napoleon's second abdication (June 22, 1815). The Restoration period included the reigns of Louis and his successor, Charles X. It was marked by France's recovery from its defeat under Napoleon and growing friction between the royalist and republican factions. The Restoration was ended (1830) when these tensions culminated in the July Revolution (*q.v.*).

resurrection   Central Christian doctrine holding that the dead will rise in possession of glorified bodies. This expectation is based on the belief in Christ's resurrection from the dead. Resurrection is a facet of other religions, including Islam.

Retz, Gilles de Laval, seigneur de ⟨Rais, ~, ~⟩ 1404–40. French soldier, nobleman, and marshal of France. A companion of Joan of Arc, he was later convicted of torturing and killing more than 100 children in his castle in Brittany. He thus inspired, it is thought, the Bluebeard legend.

Reuben   Eldest son of the biblical patriarch Jacob. Reuben was ancestor of one of the Twelve Tribes of Israel.

Reuchlin, Johann   1455–1522. German humanist scholar. He was the first Christian to compose a Hebrew grammar, the *Rudimenta Hebraica*, and he defended the study of Hebrew writings before the Inquisition. He also did important studies in classical Greek.

Reuter, Paul Julisu   1816–99. Founder of the first news wire service, Reuters. Born Israel Beer Josaphat, he developed Reuters from a carrier-pigeon service into a worldwide telegraph network transmitting commerical news.

Reuther, Walter Philip   1907–70. American labor leader. He was a president of the United Automobile Workers (UAW) and helped arrange the merger of the CIO (of which he was also president) with the AFL (1955). He broke with AFL-CIO president G. Meany, however, and took the UAW out of the federation in 1969.

Revere, Paul   1735–1818. American Revolutionary hero, immortalized in the poem by H.W. Longfellow. A Boston silversmith, Revere became involved early in the movement for independence and participated (1773) in the Boston Tea Party. A courier for Boston's Committee of Safety, he started out on what became his legendary ride to warn of the coming of British soldiers (Apr. 18, 1775). He was captured by a British patrol, but his two companions, Samuel Prescott (1751–77?) and William Daws (1745–99) escaped. Prescott then went on to complete the mission. The Minutemen were thus prepared for the battles of Lexington and Concord (Apr. 19, 1775), which marked the beginning of the American Revolution.

Reversal of Alliances *See* **Diplomatic Revolution**

reverse lend-lease *See* **lend-lease**

revival Among Protestant churches, a mass reawakening of religious fervor, especially for intense religious experience. Use of the term dates from the rise of Methodism in England and the Great Awakening *(q.v.)* in the US (18th cent.).

Revocation of the Edict of Nantes *See* **Nantes, Edict of**

Revolt of *See names inverted, as in* **Ciompi, Revolt of the**

revolution *See under country names* (i.e., **American, Russian, Chinese**) *and proper names* (i.e., **Glorious Revolution**)

revolution Fundamental change in political institutions, leadership, and social structure, often accompanied by violence. Classic examples are the American, French, Russian, and Chinese revolutions.

Revolution of 1800 *See* **Adams, John**

revolutions of 1848 Revolutions in Europe sparked by the French February Revolution *(q.v.)* of 1848, which overthrew French king Louis Philippe. Soon after the February Revolution, uprisings in Vienna, Prague, Venice, and other cities marked the beginning of a general uprising of national groups within the control of Hapsburg Austria. Austrian emperor Ferdinand was forced to make constitutional concessions in Austria, Hungary, and Bohemia, and was faced with a rising movement for independence in Italy. The revolutions led to Ferdinand's abdication (Dec., 1848) and the accession of his nephew as Francis Joseph I. The uprisings in Bohemia and Italy began to fail in 1848. In Aug. 1849, Francis Joseph, with Russian aid, crushed the revolution in Hungary and forced many of its leaders, including L. Kossuth, to flee. In Germany the uprisings led to establishment (May 18, 1848) of the liberal Frankfurt Parliament, which sought to reform the German Confederation into a unified state. The Parliament, after much deliberation, adopted a new constitution (Mar. 27, 1849) and offered the crown to Prussian king Frederick William IV, who declined.

The Prussians, however, tried to form the Prussian Union, under their domination, but the plan was effectively blocked by Austria by the Punctation of Olmütz (Nov. 29, 1850), which reestablished the old German Confederation. In the meantime, Austria had also reasserted its authority in Italy, Bohemia, and Hungary.

Reyes, Alfonso 1889–1959. Mexican poet, writer, and diplomat, one of the great Spanish literary figures of this century. Among his works are the poem *Visión de Anáhuac* and the essay *Simpatías y diferencias.*

Reyes, Rafael 1850–1921. President of Colombia (1904–09). Elected president, he assumed dictatorial powers and tried to promote the development and modernization of Colombia.

Reykjavik Iceland's capital city (pop. 83,887). It has one-third of the population of Iceland and is the center of the country's extensive cod-fishing industry. It was founded in 874 as the island's first settlement and became the capital in 1904.

Reynaud, Paul 1878–1966. French statesman. A conservative, he held several ministerial posts under the Third and Fourth French republics, and was prime minister when France fell to the Germans (1940) in WW II.

Reynolds, Sir Joshua 1723–92. English portrait painter. He painted in the "grand style" and dominated the artistic life of the mid-18th cent.

Reza Shah Pahlevi 1877–1944. Shah of Iran (1925–41). An army officer, he led a coup (1921) and later became prime minister (1923). He subsequently assumed dictatorial powers, ousted the shah, Ahmed (1925), and began a program of reform and modernization. He changed the name of his country from Persia to Iran (1935).

Rhaetia ⟨Raetia⟩ Ancient Roman province, added to the empire in 15 BC. It occupied an important position in the Alps between the Danube and the Po. Its principal city was the modern Italian city of Trent.

Rhea Greek mother goddess, born of Uranus and Gaea (heaven and earth). She was mother of most of the other major Greek gods, including Zeus, and was worshiped as a fertility goddess.

Rhee, Syngman 1875–1965. First president of South Korea (1948–60). The first Korean to earn an American Ph.D., he worked for Korean independence from Japan. He ruled South Korea as a popular but authoritarian president, until forced from office on election-rigging charges.

Rheims ⟨Reims⟩ City (pop. 183,600) in northern France, site of the Gothic cathedral where French kings were traditionally crowned. Clovis, the king of the Franks, was first crowned there in AD 496, and from the 12th to 19th cents. it was used for royal coronations. The cathedral was heavily damaged in WW I but was restored. In WW II, the German surrender (1945) was signed at Rheims.

Rhine, Confederation of the *See* **Confederation of the Rhine**

Rhineland Region of West Germany west of the Rhine River, and a frequent battleground. After WW I the Treaty of Versailles (1919) provided for occupation of most of it by Allied forces and for its eventual demilitarization (reaffirmed 1925 in the Locarno Pact). The last Allied forces (French) left in 1930. In 1936, Hitler remilitarized the region in clear defiance of the treaty and constructed the Siegfried Line *(q.v.)*.

Rhode Island Northeastern US state (pop. 947,200), the 13th state. The Dutch under Adriaen Block explored the region in 1614 and it was settled by R. Williams (1636) after he was exiled from Massachusetts for religious differences. He was granted a charter (1663) by Charles II to forestall claims by Massachusetts and Connecticut. Rhode Island was one of the first colonies to renounce allegiance to England but refused to ratify the Constitution until 1790. Industrial development began (1790) with S. Slater's textile mill in Pawtucket. Rhode Island's constitution was adopted in 1842 after a rebellion led by T. Dorr.

Rhodes Historic Greek city on the island of Rhodes. It was laid out by Hippodamus in 408 BC and was the site of the Colossus of Rhodes *(q.v.)*, one of the Seven Wonders of the World. Rhodes flourished as a commercial and cultural center until the 2d cent. BC, when competition from Delos resulted in its decline.

Rhodes, Cecil John 1853–1902. British South African statesman and financier. He worked for the extension and consolidation of southern African territories under British domination, made a fortune in diamonds, and endowed the Rhodes scholarships at Oxford.

Rhodes, Colossus of *See* **Colossus of Rhodes**

Rhys, Ernest Percival 1859–1946. Welsh writer and critic. He was best known as the editor of nearly all the 1,000 volumes of the world's great books collected in the Everyman's Library series.

Ribalta, Francisco *c*1555?–1628. Influential Spanish painter, noted for his contrasts of light and dark coloring. His paintings include *Christ Embracing Saint Bernard.*

Ribault, Jean *See* **Ribaut, Jean**

Ribaut, Jean ⟨Ribault, Jean⟩ *c*1520–65. French navigator and explorer. He established French forts and early colonies in South Carolina and Florida in the 1560s. He and the settlers were ultimately killed by the Spaniards.

Ribbentrop, Joachim von 1893–1946. German diplomat and Nazi foreign minister (1938–45). He concluded the Russo-German nonagression pact of Aug., 1939, which paved the way for Hitler's attack on Poland (the immediate cause of WW II). He was executed as a war criminal after the war.

Ricardo, David 1772–1823. English economist. He was a pioneer in the development and systematization of economic theory, especially in such areas as value theory, price levels, and free trade.

Ricci, Matteo 1552–1610. Italian Jesuit missionary in China. By mastering the Chinese language and classics, he was able to interpret Christianity and the West for the Chinese literati and thus introduced them to European culture.

Richard I ⟨Richard Coeur de Lion⟩ ⟨Richard Lion-Heart⟩ 1157–99. King of England (1189–99), successor to his father, Henry II, and hero of popular legends. He became duke of Aquitaine (1172), joined his brothers in a rebellion (1173–74) against their father, and defeated him in another clash (1189). He joined (1190) Philip II of France on the Third Crusade, shortly after becoming king. He conquered Cyprus and with Philip took Acre (1191), but was forced into a treaty with Saladin after failing to take Jerusalem. On his way back to England he was captured in Austria and held for ransom (until 1194) by Holy Roman Emperor Henry VI. He then returned to England, put down a revolt by his brother John, and spent the remainder of his reign fighting Philip II in France.

Richard II 1367–1400. King of England (1377–99), successor to Edward III. Conflicts with his barons eventually led to his overthrow by his cousin, Bolingbroke, duke of Lancaster, who became Henry IV. He was the son of Edward the Black Prince.

Richard III 1452–85. Last Yorkist king of England (1483–85). He took the throne from his brother, Edward IV, eliminating the latter's young sons, until he was defeated and killed in the Battle of Bosworth Field *(q.v.)*, which ended the Wars of the Roses *(q.v.)*.

Richard Coeur de Lion *See* **Richard I**
Richard Lion-Heart *See* **Richard I**
Richardson, Dorothy M. 1882–1957. English novelist. She was a pioneer in the stream-of-consciousness technique, employed in her novel *Pilgrimage.*

Richardson, Henry Hobson 1838–86. American architect. He pioneered the Romanesque revival in America, employing the style in such buildings as Boston's Trinity Church, completed in 1877.

Richardson, Samuel 1689–1761. English novelist. His epistolary novel *Pamela: or Virtue Rewarded* (1740) was one of the first true English novels. Richardson's other works include *Clarissa; or the History of a Young Lady.*

Richelieu, Armand Jean du Plessis, duc de 1585–1642. French cardinal and chief minister (1624–42) to Louis XIII. Made a cardinal in 1622, he rose to power as a favorite of Louis' mother, Marie de Médicis. His domestic policy aimed at weakening the power of the nobility and the Huguenots to establish the central absolute authority of the monarchy. His foreign policy sought to end Hapsburg power. He formed alliances with Protestants during the Thirty Years' War (1618–48) and finally brought France into it (1635) against the Hapsburg powers. The wars wrecked French finances but marked the country's ascendency as a major power.

Richmond Virginia capital city (pop. 219,200), the commercial and cultural center of the region. Settled in 1637, it was made Virginia's capital in 1779 and was incorporated in 1782. It became the capital of the Confederacy in 1861, was burned by the retreating Confederates (1865), and was later rebuilt.

Richter, Hans 1843–1916. Hungarian-born conductor. He was a major orchestra conductor in both Germany and England and a noted authority on the operas of his friend R. Wagner.

Richthofen, Manfred, baron von 1892–1918. German pilot in WW I, known as the "Red Baron." He led the German air group known as Richthofen's Circus and was credited with downing 80 Allied aircraft, a record that made him the principal ace of WW I. He was killed in action on Apr. 21, 1918.

Ricimer d. AD 472. Roman general of Germanic (Suevian) origin. He defeated the Vandals in 456, and then deposed the Western Roman emperor Avitus. While retaining real power, he subsequently installed and ousted a series of emperors (457–472).

Rickenbacker, Edward Vernon 1890–1973. American pilot, WW I ace and industrialist. He downed a record 26 German planes in WW I and later became president and chairman of Eastern Airlines.

Rickover, Hyman George 1900–. American admiral. He directed the planning and building of the world's first atomic-powered submarine, the USS *Nautilus,* launched in 1954.

Ridgway, Matthew Bunker 1895–. American general. He pioneered paratrooper assaults by American forces in Sicily and Normandy during WW II. He later became supreme commander of UN forces in Korea (1951–52) and NATO forces in Europe (1952–53) and served as US chief of staff (1953–55).

Ridley, Nicholas 1500?–55. English bishop, reformer, and Protestant martyr. As bishop of London, he was one of the most effective English reformers. A supporter of the Protestant Lady Jane Grey, he was tried and burned at Oxford with Hugh Latimer after Mary Tudor became queen.

Ridolfi, Roberto 1531–1612. Italian conspirator involved in a plot (1520–71) to restore Catholics to power in England. He planned to murder Queen Elizabeth I and replace her with Mary Queen of Scots, who was to marry the duke of Norfolk. The plan was uncovered when one of the conspirators was captured and confessed. Ridolfi escaped but the duke of Norfolk was beheaded.

Riego y Nuñez, Rafael del 1785–1823. Spanish rebel, a leader in the 1820 liberal revolution.

Riehl, Wilhelm Heinrich 1823–97. German writer. He was a novelist, short-story writer, and a distinguished historian of culture.

Riel's Rebellions Two brief revolts in western Canada against the government. Both were led by Louis Riel (1844–85). In 1869–70, Riel organized the Metis (half European, half Indian) of the Red River area into a provisional government, in order to prevent Canada from taking over the land that until then had been administered by the Hudson's Bay Company. The government crushed the revolt, but gave Red River its own provincial government, and Riel went to America. He led a second revolt (1884–85) on behalf of the Metis of Saskatchewan, but was captured and hanged.

Riemann, Georg Friedrich Bernhard 1826–66. German mathematician. A highly original thinker, he made many contributions to the science of geometry, some of which were later important to the mathematics of the theory of relativity.

Rienzi, Cola di ⟨Rienzo, ~⟩ 1313–54. Popular leader of the medieval city of Rome. He began as an official under authority of the pope (residing at Avignon) and then conceived his grandiose plan of restoring the Roman Empire. He assumed dictatorial powers over the city for a time but was eventually killed by a mob.

Rienzo, Cola di *See* **Rienzi, Cola di**

Riga Russian city (pop. 843,000) in the Soviet Socialist Republic of Latvia. It became a trading settlement and seat of the Livonian Knights *(q.v.)* in the early 13th cent., joined the Hanseatic League *(q.v.)* in 1282, and thereafter became an important commercial center. It came under Polish control (1581) and then was taken by the Russians (1710) during the Northern War. The city became an industrial center in the 19th cent. Then, in the Baltic War of Liberation (1918–20), it became capital of independent Latvia. Taken by the Germans in 1941, it was retaken by the Russians after WW II.

Riga, Treaty of 1. Treaty (Aug. 11, 1920) between Latvia and Russia, at the close of the Baltic War of Liberation (q.v.). By it, Russia recognized Latvia's independence. **2.** Treaty (Mar. 18, 1921) ending the Russo-Polish War (1919–20). By it, Russia ceded parts of the Ukraine and Belorussia to Poland.

Right Opposition Opponents of J. Stalin in the Central Committee of the Soviet Communist party (1928–29). The former "left-wing Bolshevik" N. Bukharin was sometimes considered the leader of this opposition.

Rights and Grievances, Declaration of See **Stamp Act Congress**

Rights of Man, and of the Citizen, Declaration of the French Revolutionary manifesto. Drafted by E. Sieyes and adopted by the French National Assembly on Aug. 26, 1789, this document outlined inalienable rights of individuals. In 1791, it became the preamble to the French constitution, guaranteeing rights of representation, equality before the law, protection of property and from arrest, and freedom of religion, speech, and the press.

Riis, Jacob August 1849–1914. Danish-born American writer and social reformer. He became famous for his book exposing the conditions in New York tenements, *How the Other Half Lives*, published in 1890.

Rijn, Rembrandt Harmenszoon van See **Rembrandt**

Riksdag Swedish parliament. Formed as a two-chamber body in 1866, it was reduced to a single chamber in 1971. The government is responsible to the Riksdag and, since 1975, the Riksdag speaker has had the right to name the premier. From 1435 to 1865, "Riksdag" was the name of Sweden's states general, which included the peasantry as a fourth estate.

Rilke, Rainer Maria 1875–1926. Austrian poet. Considered a major 20th-century literary figure, he is best known for his *Duino Elegies* and *Sonnets to Orpheus*.

Rimbaud, Arthur 1854–91. French poet. He developed a mystical, hallucinatory style in such works as *A Season in Hell* and thereby greatly influenced the later symbolist poets.

Rimini, Golden Bull of See **Golden Bull of Rimini**

Rimsky-Korsakov, Nicolai Andreyevich 1844–1908. Russian composer. One of the Russian nationalist composers, he is best known for such orchestral works as *Scheherezade* and such operas as *The Golden Cockerel*.

Ringling, John ⟨*orig.* Rüngeling, John⟩ 1866–1936. American circus impresario. With five brothers, he organized a circus in 1884, bought out Barnum and Bailey in 1907, and, at his death, had sole control of the extensive Ringling Brothers Circus operation.

Rio de Janeiro Brazilian city (pop. 4,857,700) and major port. It was first settled by the French (1535) but by 1567 it had become a Portuguese possession. It was the capital of Brazil (1763–1960) from colonial times until establishment of the new capital of Brasilia.

Rio de Janeiro, Treaty of Mutual defense treaty (Sept. 2, 1947) between the US and the Latin American republics. It provided for a united response to attack by outside aggressors and for settlement of disputes between signers.

Rio Salado, Battle of Major victory (Oct. 30, 1340) for Christians over the Muslims (Moors) in Spain. Muslims from North Africa launched their last major invasion of Iberia, and Christians thus faced both Spanish and North African Muslims. King Alfonso XI of Castile and Alfonso IV of Portugal joined forces and routed the Muslims at Seville. The victory marked the beginning of the final phase of the Christian takeover in southern Spain.

Ripley, George 1802–80. American reformer and literary critic. He helped establish the utopian Brook Farm (q.v.) experiment and later became an influential book reviewer for the *New York Tribune*.

Risorgimento Italian nationalistic movement resulting in a unified Italian state (1861). In the early 19th cent., during the post-Napoleonic period in Europe, sentiment for unification of Italy, at that time divided and dominated by foreign powers, arose. The Carbonari (q.v.), as well as other secret societies, and G. Mazzini's nationalistic movement (Young Italy) were formed and, by the mid-1800s, the unification movement had gained momentum. Abortive liberal republican revolts failed in 1848–49. The Austrians were driven out of north Italy (1859) and G. Garibaldi's successful military campaign (1860) won much of the rest of Italy for the nationalists. Victor Emmanuel was crowned king of Italy in 1861.

Ristori, Adelaide 1822–1906. Italian tragic actress. She won fame as a child actress in Italy and later became renowned throughout Europe and the Americas.

Rites Controversy Religious dispute (17th–18th cents.) among Catholic missionaries in China about whether Confucian ancestor veneration was compatible with Christian worship. The Jesuits tended to favor the rites, while the Dominicans and Franciscans tended to oppose them. Pope Clement XI banned all ancestral rites in 1704, making further Jesuit missionary work difficult.

Ritschl, Albrecht 1822–89. German Protestant theologian. His work was a reaction against rationalism and stressed the unique revelation contained in the life and teachings of Jesus.

Ritter, Karl 1779–1859. German geographer. One of the founders of modern scientific geography, he was noted for his study of the influence of natural environment on human history.

Rivadavia, Bernardino 1780–1845. Argentine diplomat and statesman, and first president (1826–27) of the United Provinces of La Plata, an Argentine confederation.

Rivera, Diego 1886–1957. Mexican painter. Known for his realistic murals, many on the life and history of Mexico, he identified strongly with populist and leftist causes.

Rivera, José Eustasio 1889–1928. Colombian poet and novelist. He is known for his sonnets and his novel about the rubber gatherers in the Amazon jungle, *The Vortex.*

Rizal, José 1861–96. Philippine writer and nationalist leader. He wrote novels against the Spanish rule in the Philippines. Accused of instigating the revolt against Spain in 1896, he was tried and executed.

Roanoke Colony *See* **Lost Colony**

Robbins, Frederick Chapman 1916–. American physician. A professor of pediatrics, he shared the 1954 Nobel Prize in Medicine with John Enders (1897–) and Thomas Weller (1915–) for discoveries concerning the polio virus.

Robert I *c*865–923. Frankish king (922–23). Ruling the land between the Seine and the Loire, he revolted against Charles III, and was made king of the Franks. He was killed in battle soon after. His grandson was Hugh Capet.

Robert I *d.* 1035. Duke of Normandy (1027–35). A strong ruler, he established order in his domains and aided Henry I of France. By his mistress, he fathered William I ("the Conquerer"), whom he legitimatized and made his heir.

Robert I (Robert the Bruce) 1274–1329. Scottish king (1306–29) and hero of Scottish independence. Following a struggle with John Comyn (*d.* 1306) for leadership of the Scottish nationalists, Robert was crowned king of Scotland (Mar. 27, 1306) in defiance of the English. He was decisively defeated by the English at the Battle of Methven (June 19, 1306) and was driven into hiding on Rathlin Island, off the Irish coast. There, according to tradition, he renewed his determination to free Scotland after watching a spider persevere in making a web. He returned to Scotland (1307),

won new supporters, and ultimately defeated the English at the famous Battle of Bannockburn *(q.v.).* The English recognized Scottish independence by the Treaty of Northampton (1328).

Robert II *c*970–1031. French King (996–1031), successor to his father, Hugh Capet.

Robert II (Robert Curthose) *c*1054–1134. Duke of Normandy (1087–1106). The eldest son of William I ("the Conquerer"), he inherited Normandy, while his brother William II took England. Robert was a leader of the First Crusade.

Robert II 1316–90. King of Scotland (1371–90). He was several times regent during the exiles of his uncle, David II. He eventually succeeded him and thus founded the Stuart line of Scottish (and later British) kings.

Robert III *c*1340–1406. King of Scotland (1390–1406). He ruled (from 1384) for his father, Robert II, until incapacitated by injury in 1388. His brother and his son ruled for him after he became king.

Robert, Henry Martyn 1837–1923. American general and writer. He wrote the famous *Robert's Rules of Order* (1876) for public meetings.

Robert, Saint *See* **Cistercians**

Robert Curthose *See* **Robert II**

Robert Guiscard *c*1015–85. Norman adventurer in Italy and founder of the Kingdom of the Two Sicilies. He was invested by the pope with the rule of southern Italian lands but they remained to be conquered from the Saracens. With his brother Roger I he conquered Sicily, Calabria, Bari, and Salerno. He next took Corfu from the Byzantines (1082). He returned to rescue Pope Gregory VII from Holy Roman Emperor Henry IV, and Robert's troops entered and sacked Rome (1084).

Robert of Courteney *d.* 1228. Latin emperor of Constantinople (1218–28). It was under his ineffective reign that the Latin Empire of Constantinople was reduced to the city and environs.

Robert of Geneva *d.* 1394. Genevan churchman and antipope Clement VII (1378–94). After electing Pope Urban VI, the cardinals reversed themselves and elected Robert, who took up residence at Avignon. This began the Great Schism *(q.v.).*

Roberts, Charles G. D. *See* **Confederation group**

Roberts, Sir Charles George Douglas 1860–1943. Canadian author. He was noted for his stories set in the Canadian wilderness and his popular *History of Canada.*

Roberts, Owen Josephus 1875–1955. American jurist and associate justice of the US Supreme Court (1930–45). He was prosecutor in the Teapot Dome scandal, followed a generally conservative line as justice, and later headed the commission investigating the Pearl Harbor disaster.

Robert the Bruce   *See* **Robert I**

Robert the Strong   *See* **Capetians**

Robespierre, Maximilien François Marie Isidore de   1758–94. French revolutionary. As a lawyer and head of the Jacobins, he was known as "the Incorruptible." He became a member of the National Convention. There, as a leader of the radical Montagnards, he played an important role in ousting (1793) the moderate Girondists from power, and thus in altering the course of the revolution. He next joined (July 27, 1793) and dominated the Committee of Public Safety *(q.v.)* and through it became the leading power behind the Reign of Terror *(q.v.)*, which he ultimately used to eliminate even his former allies. He was finally ousted in the coup of 9 Thermidor (July 27, 1794) and was tried and executed the following day.

Robin Hood   Legendary English hero, whose exploits were the subject of many ballads from the 13th cent. on. He is portrayed as the leader of an outlaw band in Sherwood Forest. He and his men robbed from the rich, gave to the poor, and were always at odds with the hated sheriff of Nottingham.

Robinson, Charles   1818–94. American antislavery leader and first governor of the state of Kansas (1861–63). He was involved in Bleeding Kansas *(q.v.)*, was imprisoned for a time by the proslavery forces in the territory, and assumed the governorship (1861) after Kansas became a state.

Robinson, Edwin Arlington   1869–1935. American poet. He is best known for his series of poems about the common people of the imaginary Tilbury Town. Among them are "Richard Cory," "Miniver Cheevy," and "Luke Havergal."

Rob Roy   1671–1734. Scottish freebooter whose name was Robert MacGregor. As head of the MacGregor clan, he led them in cattle-stealing raids and other ventures. His exploits were celebrated in Sir W. Scott's novel *Rob Roy.*

Robusti, Jacopo   *See* **Tintoretto**

Roca, Julio Argentino   1843–1914. Argentine soldier and president (1880–86, 1896–1904). As an army general he opened up Patagonia for settlement. His term as president was marked by rapid development and increased financial speculation.

Rochambeau, Jean Baptiste Donatien de Vimeur, comte de   1725–1807. French general. Having distinguished himself as a commander in Europe, he was sent (1780) with 6,000 troops to America during the revolution. Accompanying Washington, he was instrumental in winning the Battle of Yorktown *(q.v.)*, which ended the American Revolution.

Rochdale Society of Equitable Pioneers   First successful consumers' cooperative. It was founded in Rochdale, England, in 1844, on the basis of the ideas of R. Owen. The society began with a grocery store and later expanded to include a textile mill and factory on the same cooperative principles.

Rochefort, Victor-Henri, marquis de Rochefort-Lucay   1830–1913. French journalist. He moved from the extreme left to the extreme right, at first opposing Napoleon III and supporting the Paris Commune (1871). He then turned to G. Boulanger and later the nationalists in the Dreyfus Affair.

Rochester, John Wilmot, 2d earl of   1647–80. English courtier and poet. Notoriously dissolute, he nevertheless fought bravely against the Dutch. He was noted for his satiric poems. Among them were *History of Insipids, Maim'd Debauchee,* and *A Satyr Against Mankind.*

Rockefeller, John Davison   1839–1937. American millionaire industrialist and philanthropist. First employed as a bookkeeper, he later organized (with partners) the Standard Oil Company (1870). Thereafter Rockefeller gained control of the oil industry, built Standard Oil into one of the great trusts, and amassed a huge fortune. His company was the object of government antitrust suits in the early 1900s, and after 1911 Rockefeller turned to philanthropy, notably through his Rockefeller Foundation (established 1913).

Rockefeller, John Davison, Jr.   1874–1960. American industrialist and philanthropist. Heir to his father's vast Standard Oil fortune, he was especially noted for his philanthropies, such as funding the restoration of Colonial Williamsburg and donating the land for the United Nations building.

Rockefeller, Nelson Aldrich   1908–79. Forty-first US vice-president (1974–77) and heir to the vast Rockefeller family fortune. A liberal Republican, he served four terms as New York governor (1959–73) and was nominated to the vice-presidency by G. Ford. He was a noted philanthropist and patron of the arts.

Rockefeller, William   1841–1922. American financier. Associated with his brother J. Rockefeller in the oil business, he also had other stock-market, industrial, and banking interests.

Rockingham, Charles Watson-Wentworth, 2d marquess of   1730–82. British prime minister (1765–66, 1782). He attempted to conciliate the American colonies and repealed the Stamp Act during his first ministry. His second ministry, following the collapse of Lord North's government, saw the repeal of Poynings' Law *(q.v.)* but ended before final peace had been made with the American colonials.

Rock of Gibraltar   *See* **Gibraltar**

Rockwell, Norman 1894–1978. American painter and illustrator. Best known for his covers for the *Saturday Evening Post* magazine, he painted scenes typical of American life in a realistic style.

rococo Artistic style that succeeded the baroque in Europe. Originating in 18th-cent. France, the rococo style was characterized by highly ornate and decorative designs and lines.

Rodgers, Richard 1902–79. American composer of musical comedies. He produced many outstanding musical shows in collaboration with L. Hart and O. Hammerstein II, winning Pulitzer prizes with the latter for *Oklahoma* and *South Pacific*.

Rodin, Auguste 1840–1917. Great French sculptor, whose works were executed in a style of Romantic realism. Many of his most famous pieces were studies to be included in the unfinished bronze doors for Paris' Musée des Arts Décoratifs. They include *Adam and Eve, The Thinker,* and *The Kiss.* He is noted also for *The Burghers of Calais.*

Rodney, George Brydges Rodney, 1st baron 1719–92. British admiral, Rodney distinguished himself during the Seven Years' War. He became a national hero by defeating the Spanish, relieving Gibraltar (1780), and the French off Dominica (1782), in fighting related to the American Revolution.

Rodó, José Enrique 1872–1917. Uruguayan writer and philosopher. He upheld spiritual over material values in his most famous essay, *Ariel,* and was considered one of the great Latin American philosophers.

Roebling, John Augustus 1806–69. American civil engineer, born in Germany. He pioneered the use of steel cable in bridge-building, built major suspension bridges at Pittsburgh, Cincinnati, and Niagara, and began the Brooklyn Bridge (completed by his son).

Roebling, Washington Augustus 1837–1926. American civil engineer and bridge builder. The son of J. Roebling, he was associated with his father's firm and completed the building of the Brooklyn Bridge (opened 1883), which had been begun by his father.

Roehm, Ernst *See* **Röhm, Ernst**

Roemer, Olaus *See* **Rømer, Olaus**

Roentgen, Wilhelm Conrad ⟨Röntgen, ~⟩ 1845–1923. German physicist. He discovered X-rays (1895) while serving as director of the Würzburg Physical Institute and thus revolutionized the practice of medicine. He received the Nobel Prize in Physics in 1901.

Roger I c1031–1101. Norman conquerer and count of Sicily. He helped his brother Robert Guiscard conquer southern Italy from the Saracens and Byzantines. He ruled these domains as a papal legate after the death of his brother.

Roger II 1097–1154. Count (1101–30) and then Norman king of Sicily (1130–54). He consolidated the lands conquered by his Norman kinsmen and added Capua, Naples, and the Abruzzi. His rule was one of the most advanced of the times and he brought a period of prosperity. His capital at Palermo became a cultural center.

Roger, Pierre *See* **Clement VI**

Rogers, John 1500?–55. English Protestant reformer and martyr. He published (under the pseudonym Thomas Matthew) the English-language Matthew Bible of 1537, utilizing mostly the translations of William Tyndale and Miles Coverdale. This bible was subsequently revised as the Great Bible, which in turn became the basis for the famous King James Version. Rogers was executed after the accession of Catholic Queen Mary I.

Rogers, William Penn Adair 1879–1935. American humorist, writer, and actor. Beginning with a vaudeville act, he went on to write popular columns and books based on his homespun but shrewd and satirical wit. He also appeared in many movies.

Rogers' Rangers British-American colonial frontier force, composed of some 600 men trained in Indian methods. Commanded by Major Robert Rogers (1731–95), it carried out numerous daring raids during the French and Indian War and Pontiac's Rebellion.

Roget, Peter Mark 1779–1869. English physician and lexicographer. He worked for many years compiling his *Thesaurus of English Words and Phrases* (published in 1852), which has undergone many revisions and remains a standard reference work.

Rohan, Louis René Édouard, prince de 1734–1803. French diplomat and churchman who became a Catholic cardinal. He was French ambassador in Vienna and later was duped into providing security for jewels in the famous Affair of the Diamond Necklace *(q.v.).* He was subsequently banished.

Rohilla War War against the Afghan Rohilla tribe then in India, waged (1774) by the Nawab of Oudh, mainly to recover money owed him by the Rohillas. He crushed the Rohillas with help from a British East India Company brigade provided by W. Hastings, governor of Bengal. The incident later became one of the grounds for Hastings' impeachment.

Röhm, Ernst ⟨Roehm, Ernst⟩ 1887–1934. German National Socialist leader. An early Nazi party member and organizer of the storm troops, he was a potential rival to Hitler. He was executed without trial on Hitler's orders during the Blood Purge (q.v.).

Rojas Pinilla,Gustavo 1900–75. Colombian army leader and president of Colombia (1953–57). He led a coup that ousted the unpopular L. Gómez, but the brutality, ineptitude, and corruption of his own administration led to his ouster by a military junta, backed by both right and left. He was an unsuccessful candidate for president again in 1970.

Roland d. 778. Hero of the great French epic poem *The Song of Roland* in which, as part of Charlemagne's rear guard crossing the Pyrenees, he fought valiantly in a great battle against overwhelming numbers of Saracens. The historical Roland was actually cut off and killed by Basques at the Battle of Roncesvalles (q.v.), a minor engagement.

Roland de la Platière, Jean Marie 1734–93. French Revolutionary leader and minister of the interior (1792). A prominent member of the moderate Girondist faction, he had to flee Paris during the Reign of Terror. He committed suicide after his wife Manon was arrested and guillotined.

Roland de la Platière, Manon Philipon 1754–93. French Revolutionary leader. The wife of Girondist leader J. Roland de la Platière, she maintained a fashionable revolutionary salon. Arrested during the Reign of Terror, she uttered the words "O Liberty, what crimes are committed in thy name!" just before being guillotined.

Rolfe, John 1585–1622. English colonist in Virginia. He introduced the cultivation of tobacco, which became Virginia's staple crop, and married the Indian girl Pocahontas. He took her to England (1616), where she died. He was probably killed in the Indian massacre of 1622 after his return to Virginia.

Rolland, Romain 1866–1944. French novelist, biographer, and musicologist. He exalted art, pacifism, and socialism, especially through his 10-volume novel *Jean Christophe*, about a modern genius. He received the Nobel Prize in Literature in 1915.

Rollo ⟨Rou⟩ ⟨Hrolf⟩ c860–c932. Norman chieftan, founder of the duchy of Normandy. He invaded and conquered the land around the mouth of the Seine (now in France). He was granted rule over it (911) by French King Charles III (the Simple) in return for accepting vassalage and baptism.

Rölvaag, Ole Edvart 1876–1931. Norwegian–American writer. He was noted for his portrayal of immigrants in Minnesota, especially in *Giants in the Earth* and the novels that followed it.

Romagna Historical region of north-central Italy. It was the center of Byzantine domains in Italy (6th–7th cents.) and was later incorporated into the Papal States. Its major city was Ravenna (q.v.).

Romains, Jules ⟨pseud. of Farigoule, Louis⟩ 1885–1972. French writer. He produced a panoramic view of French life in the early 20th cent. in his 27-volume novel, *Men of Good Will*.

Roman Catholic Church One of the three major branches of Christianity (with Protestant and Orthodox Eastern churches). It is a worldwide union of churches recognizing the primacy of Rome. The authority of the popes is traditionally believed to derive from the continuous line of popes (bishops of Rome) succeeding St. Peter. The church claims to be the one true apostolic Christian church, maintaining its supremacy in doctrinal questions that created other branches of Christianity. The early years of the church, following the crucifixion of Jesus Christ, were marked by the rapid spread of Christianity; persecution and then toleration by the Romans; the growing isolation of Rome and the Western church from the Eastern church (centered at Constantinople) after the fall of the Western Roman Empire (AD 476); and finally the alliances between the popes at Rome and the kings of Europe (from the 8th cent.). In following centuries of the Middle Ages, the church became a powerful force in European politics and culture. For a time popes were able to command the submission of the great European monarchs. The struggle between the popes and the Holy Roman emperors, however, gradually eroded that power and, by the 15th–16th cent., papal power was overshadowed by the absolutist monarchs in Europe. Meanwhile the split between the Western and Eastern halves of the Christian world continued to widen, until finally the Schism of 1054 resulted in a complete break and formation of the Orthodox Eastern church (q.v.). A second great division of the Christian world occurred in the 16th cent. The Protestant Reformation (q.v.) resulted in the creation of a host of new Christian sects and forced the Roman Catholic church to institute the sweeping reforms of the Catholic Reformation (q.v.). In modern times the church has been concerned with doctrinal problems raised by modern society and with bridging the divisions within the Christian world. Key events in the history of the church include:

c8–6? BC Jesus born in Bethlehem; worked as a carpenter until around age 30, when he began his public ministry.

AD c30 Jesus Christ crucified in Jerusalem; disciples claimed he rose from the dead, appeared to them, and commissioned them to preach a Gospel (lit. "good news") of eternal salvation through him.

AD c30–44   Disciples of Christ gathered around the Apostle Peter; the nucleus of the new church engaged in preaching the Gospel of Jesus and administering the sacraments.

AD c33   Saul of Tarsus, a Jew, blinded by a vision on the road to Damascus; converted and became St. Paul the Apostle.

AD c43   Apostle St James ("the Greater") became missionary to Spain; martyred.

AD c45   St. Peter moved to Antioch as first bishop of the church there; St. James left as bishop in Jerusalem.

AD c47–49   St. Paul's first missionary journey (with St. Barnabus and St. Mark) to Cyprus and Asia Minor; began to write the letters, or "epistles" that were the earliest New Testament writings.

AD c50   Council of Jerusalem, proto-council of the church; decided that gentiles converting to Christianity need not observe the full ritual Jewish law.

AD c50–53   Second missionary journey of St. Paul; crossed into Europe (Macedonia) where the church later flourished.

AD 53–57   Third missionary journey of St. Paul; wrote great epistles to the Romans and Corinthians.

AD c55   St. Peter left Antioch for Rome, where tradition held he become the first bishop (pope).

AD c59   St. Paul arrested in Jerusalem; sent to Rome for trial.

AC c62   St. James, bishop of Jerusalem, martyred.

AD c67   Persecutions of Christians ordered by Nero; Sts. Peter and Paul martyred, according to tradition.

AD c67–79?   St. Linus, first of the line of successors to St. Peter, became bishop of Rome (pope).

AD c95   St. Clement of Rome (fourth pope) wrote "Epistle to the Corinthians," intervening in affairs of a local Greek church.

AD c107   First mention of the term "Catholic church" (lit. "universal church") in an epistle of St. Ignatius of Antioch.

AD c100–165   St. Justin Martyr, the first Christian apologist; combined Christian belief with Platonic philosophy.

AD 155   Martyrdom of St. Polycarp, Bishop of Smyrna.

AD 177   Large-scale public persecution in the arena at Lyons.

AD c189   St. Irenaeus of Lyons declared in *Adversus Haereses* that "every church must be in harmony" with the Church of Rome.

AD 249–251   Large-scale persecution under the Emperor Decius.

AD 251   St. Cornelius pope (AD 251–253) and martyr; first schism, resulting in the election of an antipope, Novatian.

AD 258   Edict of persecution of the Emperor Valerian; martyrdom of St. Cyprian of Carthage.

AD c275   St. Anthony, pioneer of Christian monasticism, retired into Egyptian desert to pursue the ascetic life.

AD 303   Edict of the Emperor Diocletian unleashed ten-year persecution of Christians.

AD 311   Donatist heresy (holding validity of sacraments depended on sanctity of the minister) in North Africa.

AD 313   Edict of Milan: co-emperors Constantine and Licinius established toleration of Christianity within the Roman Empire.

AD 325   First Council of Nicaea (1st ecumenical council): condemned Arianism and issued creed as official profession of faith.

AD 341   St. Julius pope (AD 337–352); defended Nicaea and claimed Roman primacy based on apostolic tradition stemming from Peter.

AD 356   St. Athanasius, Archbishop of Alexandria (AD 328–373), exiled by the Arian emperor Constantius for his defense of Nicaea.

AD c360   Rise of Macedonianism, the belief that the Holy Spirit was created.

AD 361–363   Emperor Julian ("the Apostate") attempted to reintroduce paganism in the Roman Empire.

AD c370   St. Basil the Great reorganized monasticism in the East.

AD 378   St. Damasus (pope AD 366–384) condemned Apollinarian heresy.

LATE 4TH CENT. AD   Twenty-seven books, constituting the present canon of the New Testament, decreed by Church to be authentic Scripture: Festal Epistle of St. Athanasius of Alexandria (AD 376); Decree of Pope St. Damasus (AD 382); provincial Synod of Carthage (AD 397).

AD 380   Emperor Theodosius the Great decreed Christianity to be the religion of the Roman Empire.

AD 381   First Council of Constantinople (2nd ecumenical council) condemned Macedonianism; issued creed in substantially the form it is recited today as the "Nicene Creed."

AD c400   Pelagianism, heresy denying original sin and affirming humans have perfect freedom of the will, introduced in Rome by British monk Pelagius.

AD **410** St. Augustine of Hippo began writing *The City of God.*

AD **417** St. Innocent I (pope AD 402–417) declared that pronouncements of bishops must be confirmed by the Roman See.

AD **431** Council of Ephesus (3d ecumenical council): condemned Nestorianism, which denied Christ's divinity; declared that the Virgin Mary was "the Mother of God"; provoked centuries-long Nestorian schism.

AD **449** St. Leo the Great (pope AD 440–461) condemned unauthorized "robber council" held at Ephesus and issued his famous *Tome* defining the nature of Christ.

AD **451** Council of Chalcedon (4th ecumenical council): rejected Monophysitism; declared Jesus Christ to be true God and true man at the same time; centuries-long schism of Armenian, Egyptian, Ethiopian, and Syrian Monophysite churches stemmed from council's decree.

AD c**495** Gelasius I (pope AD 492–496) wrote to Byzantine emperor Anastasius I denying the right of the state to interfere in church affairs.

AD c**498** Baptism of Clovis, King of the Franks.

529 Monte Cassino abbey founded in Italy by St. Benedict; became center of Western monasticism.

553 Second Council of Constantinople (5th ecumenical council): reiterated condemnation of Nestorianism.

589 Provincial Synod of Toledo: *Filioque* clause added to the Nicene Creed; provoked long and bitter controversy with the East.

597 St. Gregory the Great (pope 590–604) reformed liturgy; despatched St. Augustine of Canterbury to Christianize England.

610–640 Rise of Monothelite heresy, denying that Christ had both a human and a divine will.

680–681 Third Council of Constantinople (6th ecumenical council): condemned Monothelite heresy.

751 Pepin the Short, King of the Franks, allied Franks with the papacy; marked beginning of Rome's alliance with European powers.

756 "Donation of Pepin"; papal domains constituted as a sovereign entity in central Italy.

768 Accession of Charlemagne as Frankish king.

787 Second Council of Nicaea (7th ecumenical council): convened by Empress Irene to deal with Iconoclasm controversy; last council considered ecumenical by Eastern Orthodox church.

800 Pope St. Leo III (795–816) crowned Charlemagne emperor of the Romans, strengthening ties with Europe's great monarch.

857 Controversy between Ignatius and Photius and at Constantinople over iconoclasm; Photius challenged right of popes to rule in the East; this resulted in breach between Rome and Constantinople, laying basis for future schism of East and West.

865 St. Nicholas the Great (pope 858–867) reaffirmed primacy of Rome.

869–870 Fourth Council of Constantinople (8th ecumenical council): anathematized Photius as a usurper in Constantinople and confirmed decree of Pope Nicholas against him.

910 Cluniac monastic order founded in France.

962 German king Otto I conquered northern Italy and forced the pope to crown him emperor; this marked beginnning of Holy Roman Empire.

11TH CENT. Rise of Scholasticism; appearance of the first great medieval philosophers: P. Abelard, P. Lombard, St. Anselm of Canterbury, etc.

1054 Schism of 1054 between Eastern Orthodox and Roman Catholic churches.

1059 Lateran Synod under Pope Leo IX; established papal election procedure, giving cardinals power to elect pope.

1073–85 St. Gregory VII (Hildebrand) pope; well-known for his reforms and insistence on papal authority.

1077 Holy Roman Emperor Henry IV excommunicated, then pardoned as a penitent at Canossa, Italy, by Pope Gregory VII; great struggle between popes and Holy Roman Emperors continued.

1085 Gregory VII finally driven from Rome by Henry IV; died at Salerno.

1085–1122 Investiture Controversy; power struggle between the papacy and the Holy Roman Empire centering on the question of "lay investiture" (appointment of bishops by secular rulers).

1086 Carthusians, strictest monastic order, founded by St. Bruno of Cologne.

11TH–14TH CENT. The Crusades: medieval holy wars undertaken by European Christians to reconquer the Holy Land from the Muslims.

1098 Cistercian monastic order launched at Cîteaux, France.

1098 Pope Urban II failed to reconcile Eastern and Western churches at the Council of Bari.

1115–35 St. Bernard, Abbott of Clairvaux, France, was principal religious leader in Europe.

1122 Diet of Worms; ended Investiture Controversy.

1123 First Lateran Council (9th ecumenical council) convened; first church council in the West; dealt with church discipline and investiture question, ratifying Diet of Worms.

1139 Second Lateran Council (10th ecumenical council) convened by Innocent II (1130–43); ended schism created by the election of antipope Anacletus II.

1159–81 Alexander III pope; effectively established papal authority over bishops and clergy; excommunicated the Emperor Frederick Barbarossa.

1179 Third Lateran Council (11th ecumenical council): College of Cardinals definitively empowered to elect pope; crusade against Albigenses in southern France proclaimed.

13TH–15TH CENT. Guelphs and Ghibellines were two opposing Italian factions prominent in the struggle for control of Italy; Guelphs usually favored popes, Ghibellines the Holy Roman emperor.

1198–1216 Innocent III pope; height of medieval papacy; preached disastrous Fourth Crusade.

1209 Friars Minor, mendicant order founded by St. Francis of Assisi.

1210 Innocent III excommunicated Holy Roman Emperor Otto IV.

1213 Innocent III forced English King John to acknowledge sovereignty of the pope.

1215 Fourth Lateran Council (12th ecumenical council) convened; doctrine of Transubstantiation defined; Easter duty established.

1216 Dominican Friars, founded as a preaching order, especially to combat heresy.

1225–74 St. Thomas Aquinas, great theologian and philosopher; his adaptation of Aristotle became official Catholic philosophy in 19th cent.

1233 Inquisition (medieval) established by Pope Gregory IX (1227–41) to oppose spread of such heresies as those of Albigenses and Waldenses.

1245 First Council of Lyons (13th ecumenical council): called by Innocent IV (1243–54) during his struggle with the Emperor Frederick II.

1274 Second Council of Lyons (14th ecumenical council): called by Gregory X (1271–76) to act on pledge of Byzantine Emperor Michael VIII to reunite Eastern and Western churches.

1302 Boniface VIII (1294–1303) issued bull *Unam Sanctam* asserting supreme authority over secular state and "every human creature."

1303 Boniface VIII captured and imprisoned by agents of French King Philip IV; died shortly afterward.

1309–77 Babylonian Captivity of the papacy: Clement V (1305–14) brought it about by moving the seat of the papacy to Avignon.

1311–12 Council of Vienne (15th ecumenical council) convened in France; Knights Templar condemned.

1377 Pope Gregory XI (1370–78) moved the papacy back to Rome, ending the captivity.

1378–1415 Great Schism; Urban VI elected pope (1378–84); then abandoned by a faction of cardinals who elected Clement VII antipope (1378–94); both lines perpetuated.

1414–18 Council of Constance (16th ecumenical council): ended Great Schism by electing Martin V (1417–31) as pope; condemned views of J. Wycliffe and burned J. Huss at the stake (1415).

1431–38 Council of Basel; became embroiled in a struggle with Eugenius IV (1431–37) over Conciliarism vs papal authority.

1438–53 Council of Florence (17th ecumenical council); convened to try to end the schism between the Latin and Greek churches.

1483 Spanish Inquisition organized throughout all Spanish possessions.

1492–1503 Alexander VI pope; notoriously corrupt Borgia; successfully resisted invasion of Italy by French King Charles VIII.

1512–17 Fifth Lateran Council (18th ecumenical council) called by Julius II (1503–13) to reform the church; reforms not implemented.

1517 Protestant Reformation: launched by German M. Luther to protest sale of indulgences; nailed 95 theses on Wittenburg church door challenging Catholic doctrine (Oct. 31); he later developed Lutheranism based on principle of justification by faith alone.

1520 Leo X (1513–21) excommunicated Luther (June 15).

1521 Diet of Worms placed Luther under ban of the Holy Roman Empire. (Apr. 17–18).

1523 Adrian VI pope (1522–23); acknowledged guilt of Catholic clergy in helping bring about Protestant Reformation.

1534 Henry VIII secured Act of Supremacy declaring him supreme head of the church in England; Church of England created as organization separate from Rome.

1534–49 Paul III reigned as pope.

1534 Jesuits, or Society of Jesus, founded by St. Ignatius of Loyola; special vow of loyalty to pope taken by Jesuits.

16TH CENT. Catholic Reformation launched in response to Protestant threat.

1545–63 Council of Trent (19th ecumenical council); instituted far-reaching reforms in response to Protestant Reformation; completed comprehensive restatement of Catholic doctrine on the sacraments and instituted radical clerical reforms, including establishment of the modern seminary system for training priests; much important work concluded under Pius IV (1559–65).

1566–72 St. Pius V pope; reformed the missal and promoted the Holy League, which won the victory at sea over the Turks at Lepanto; excommunicated Queen Elizabeth I of England.

1582 Gregorian Calendar instituted (Oct. 15) by Gregory XIII (1572–85).

1621–23 Gregory XV pope; created the Congregation for the Propagation of the Faith to administer church's worldwide missionary effort.

1640 Jansenism, movement emphasizing predestination and denying free will, expounded in *Augustinus*, a book by C. Jansen, Bishop of Ypres.

1643 Bollandists organized: a group of Belgian Jesuits charged with examining and updating lives of the saints.

1653 Five characteristic Jansenist propositions condemned by Innocent X (1644–55).

1713 Clement XI (1700–21) issued Constitution *Unigenitus* against Jansenism.

18TH CENT. Society of Jesus expelled from a number of European countries: Portugal (1759); France (1764); Spain (1767).

1764 Febronianism, belief that all bishops have equal stature, condemned by Clement XIII (1758–69).

1773 Pope Clement XIV (1769–74) dissolved the Jesuit order under pressure from the European Catholic powers.

1790 John Carroll made bishop of Baltimore, first Catholic bishop of the United States.

1790 French Revolution's Civil Constitution of the Clergy subjected the church in France to the National Assembly.

1796 Papal States conquered by Napoleon.

1798 Pius VI taken prisoner by Napoleon.

1809 Napoleon annexed the Papal States to the French Empire and made Pius VII prisoner.

1814 Pius VII restored the Society of Jesus.

1815 Congress of Vienna restored the Papal States to the Pope.

1829 Catholic Emancipation ended persecution of Catholics in Britain.

1846–78 Pius IX pope; defined the dogma of the Immaculate Conception.

1860 Most of Papal States taken from church during the course of Italian unification.

1864 Syllabus of Errors: comprehensive compendium of modern "errors"—"progress, liberalism, and modern civilization"—issued by Pius IX (Dec. 8).

1870 First Vatican Council (20th ecumenical council): declared that God could be known by reason and defined the infallibility of the pope.

1870 German theologian J. Dollinger excommunicated for opposing the doctrine of papal infallibility.

1870 Italian king Victor Emmanuel II seized Rome; pope declared himself a prisoner in the Vatican, marking the beginning of the Roman Question.

1870s *Kulturkampf* of O. von Bismarck directed against Catholicism in Germany.

1878–1903 Leo XIII pope; pope of social justice and opening to modern democracy.

1879 Encyclical *Aeterni Patris* of Leo XIII made the philosophical and theological system of St. Thomas Aquinas church doctrine.

1891 Encyclical *Rerum Novarum* of Leo XIII emphasized rights of the workingman in modern industrial society (May 15).

1903–14 St. Pius X pope; condemned Modernism as "the resumé of all heresies."

1917 Codex juris canonici, revised code of canon law, completed.

1929 Lateran Treaty, agreement between Italy and the papacy settling the Roman Question and establishing the pope as an independent sovereign in Vatican City.

1937 Pope Pius XI (1922–39) condemned Nazism and Communism.

1939–58 Pius XII pope; in Encyclical *Humani Generis* warned that certain modern scientific ideas were incompatible with revealed dogma.

1958–63 John XXIII pope; summoned Vatican Council II (1959).

1962–65 Second Vatican Council (21st ecumenical council) convened by John XXIII; sought to renew spiritual life of all the members of the Church.

1963–78 Paul VI pope; continued Vatican Council II.

1964 Pope Paul VI met Greek Orthodox patriarch Athenagoras in Jerusalem.

1968 Encyclical *Humanae Vitae* of Paul VI reiterating church's traditional condemnation of artificial birth control; caused worldwide controversy and widespread dissent within the church.

1971 International commission of Roman Catholic and Anglican theologians reported agreement on basic teaching concerning the Eucharist (Dec. 30).

1978 John Paul I elected to succeed Paul VI (Aug. 26).

1978 Pope John Paul I died suddenly (Sept. 29); Pole John Paul II elected (Oct. 16); first non-Italian pope in 455 years.

1979 John Paul II began a series of extensive worldwide missionary journeys by visiting the

Dominican Republic, Mexico, US, Poland, Britain, and Spain.

1981   Pope John Paul II seriously wounded by a Turkish terrorist (May 13) in assassination attempt at Vatican City.

1982   Pope John Paul II visited Britain; meetings with Anglican leaders marked a significant step in efforts to reestablish ties between the English church and Rome (May 28).

Romance languages ⟨Romanic languages⟩ Family of European languages descended from Latin. So called because Latin was the language of the Romans, the principal modern Romance languages are French, Italian, Portuguese, Romanian, and Spanish.

Roman Empire   Name of the Roman state after Augustus assumed imperial powers (27 BC) and thus formally ended the republic. The empire was later divided into the Western Roman Empire ⟨Western Empire⟩ and Eastern Roman Empire ⟨Eastern Empire⟩ in AD 286 by Diocletian. Through much of the subsequent period it was governed by co-emperors of the East and West. The death of Theodosius I marked the beginning of the permanent division (AD 395) of the empire. The Western half consisted of Italy, Gaul, western Illyricum, Africa, Spain, and Britain. The Eastern half primarily consisted of the Balkan Peninsula (including the eastern part of Illyricum) and Asia Minor. The Western Roman Empire, unable to withstand the barbarian invasions *(q.v.)*, ceased to exist (AD 476) with the death of Emperor Romulus Augustus. The Eastern Roman Empire survived as the Byzantine Empire, and thus the Carolingian Empire (8th cent.) is sometimes regarded as the successor state to the Western Roman Empire. (*See also* Rome; Byzantine Empire *for detailed history.*)

Romania ⟨Rumania; Socialist Republic of Romania⟩   Republic located in southeastern Europe. Its capital is Bucharest. The area of modern Romania was largely that of the ancient Roman province of Dacia. With the decline of the Roman Empire the region was subsequently invaded numerous times by Goths, Huns, Slavs, and Bulgars. The rise of the principalities of Moldavia and Walachia (14th cent.) was followed by a period of domination (15th–19th cent.) by the Ottoman Empire, and then for a time by the Russian Empire. Proclaimed a kingdom in 1881, Romania became a people's republic in 1947. Key dates in Romania's history include:

1330   John Bassaraba founded the independent principality of Walachia.

1349   Bogdan Voda founded the independent principality of Moldavia

EARLY 15TH CENT.   Walachia became an Ottoman vassal state.

16TH CENT.   Moldavia became an Ottoman vassal state.

1593–1601   Walachian prince Michael the Brave reigned; united Walachia, Moldavia, and Transylvania under his rule (1599–1600); union fell apart after his death.

1711   Moldavia allied with Russia against Ottoman rule; Russian forces sent to region were defeated; Ottomans introduced Phanariot system of rule (rule by governors), generally by Greeks who lived in Constantinople.

1768–74   Russo-Turkish Wars; Ottoman Empire defeated by Russia; Treaty of Kuchuk Kainarji marked rise of Russian influence in Moldavia and Walachia.

1806–12   Russo-Turkish War fought; Russia defeated the Ottomans and gained Bessarabia.

1822   Ottomans consented to make Romanians governors of Moldavia and Walachia.

1828–29   Russo-Turkish War fought; Russians occupied Moldavia and Walachia; Russia gained virtual protectorates over the principalities through the Treaty of Adrianople (1829), ending the war; both remained technically Ottoman holdings.

1848   Romanians staged unsuccessful uprising against foreign domination; defeated by combined Russian and Ottoman intervention.

1854–56   Crimean War; Russian forces withdrew from region and Austrian troops moved in; war ended by Treaty of Paris (1856), which established Moldavia and Walachia as principalities under Ottoman suzerainty; Moldavia awarded southern Bessarabia.

1859   Alexander John Cuza became prince of Moldavia and Walachia.

1862   Moldavia and Walachia joined to form the principality of Romania; capital established at Bucharest.

1866   Cuza deposed; succeeded by Carol I, a member of the house of Hohenzollern-Sigmaringen.

1877–78   Romania allied with Russia in the Russo-Turkish War; war ended by the Treaty of Berlin, by which Romania became independent but ceded southern Bessarabia to Russia.

1881   Romania became a kingdom (1881); Carol I ruled as first king (1881–1914); modernized the country.

1907   Peasant uprising in Moldavia against the Jews and against the landed nobles, the Boyars; uprising crushed, but land reforms were subsequently instituted; conflict marked growth of anti-Semitism in Romania.

1912 First Balkan War against Ottomans; Romania remained neutral.

1913 Second Balkan War; Romania allied with Greece and Serbia against Bulgaria and occupied southern Dobruja.

1914 Carol I died (Oct.); succeeded by his nephew Ferdinand I.

1914–18 WW I; Romania initially remained neutral, then joined (June 1916) the Allies against the Central Powers; after invading Transylvania, the Romanians were driven back and the kingdom occupied by Austro-German troops; Romania withdrew from the war by the Treaty of Bucharest (Feb. 1918) but reentered the war (Nov.) on the eve of its ending.

1918–20 At end of WW I Romania annexed Transylvania, Bessarabia, Bukovina, and part of the Banat; most of its gains were confirmed by the treaties of St. Germain (1919) and Trianon (1920); Russia refused to accept Romanian annexation of Bessarabia.

1919 Romania invaded Hungary and overthrew the Communist government of Bela Kun.

1920–21 Romania joined the Little Entente, an alliance with Czechoslovakia and Yugoslavia.

1922–27 Ion Bratianu, head of the Liberal party, in power; his near-dictatorial authority challenged by both the National Peasants party under Iuliu Maniu and the fascist nationalist organization, the Iron Guard, headed by Corneliu Zelea-Codreanu.

1927 King Ferdinand I died; his grandson Michael was made king under a regency.

1930 Carol, Michael's father, assumed the crown as Carol II.

1938 Carol took control of the government and jailed leaders of the Iron Guard; Zelea-Codreanu and others shot, allegedly while trying to escape.

1939–45 WW II fought.

1940 Romania forced by Germany to cede Bessarabia and Bukovina to Russia, Transylvania to Hungary, and southern Dobruja to Bulgaria (Aug.–Sept., 1940); led to severe unrest in Romania and forced Carol to appoint Ion Antonescu as dictator; Carol then abdicated (Sept. 6).

1939–45 Romania, initially neutral, joined Germany in its invasion (June, 1941) of Russia; later declared war (Dec., 1941) on the US; occupied (1944) by Russian forces; King Michael led overthrow of Antonescu (Aug. 24); Romania signed armistice with Russia (Sept. 12, 1944).

1945 Coalition government dominated by Communists headed by Peter Groza (Mar.).

1947–48 Michael abdicated (Dec. 30, 1947); Romania proclaimed a people's republic; new constitution, modeled on Russian constitution, adopted (Apr. 13, 1948).

1952 New constitution promulgated (July 18), modeled closely on Soviet lines.

1967 Nicolae Ceausescu came to power, marking beginning of long rule in Romania that lasted into the early 1980s.

1968 Warsaw Pact forces invaded Czechoslovakia; Romania did not take part.

1974 Ceausescu became first to hold new office of presidency.

1977 Ceausescu instrumental in preparations for Egyptian president Sadat's visit to Israel.

1980 Ceausescu, continuing his independent foreign policy, condemned the Soviet invasion of Afghanistan.

Romanesque Style of medieval art and architecture that reached its height in the 11th and 12th cents. In architecture it was characterized by the use of rounded arches and massive walls. It gave way to the Gothic style *(q.v.)*. The Romanesque movement in art, centered in France, represented a fusion of Roman, Carolingian, Byzantine, Teutonic, and other influences and was marked by its concern for powerful imagery and grand conception.

Romanic languages *See* **Romance languages**

Roman Inquisition *See* **Inquisition**

Romano, Giulio *(pseud. of* Giulio Pippi) c1492–1546. Italian painter and architect. A favored student of Raphael, he is considered an originator of mannerism *(q.v.)*.

Romanov Russian royal dynasty. The Romanovs ruled Russia from 1613 until the revolutions of 1917. They traced their royal lineage to Anastasia Romanovna, first wife (m. 1547) of Ivan the Terrible. They came to power after the Time of Troubles *(q.v.)* when Michael Romanov became czar. The line ended during the Russian Revolution with the assassinations of Nicholas II and his family, including his son and heir Alexis. Rulers of the Romanov dynasty were:

Michael	1613–45
Alexis	1645–76
Fëdor III	1676–82
Ivan V (with Peter)	1682–96
Peter (the Great)	1682–1725
Catherine I	1725–27
Peter II	1727–30
Anna Ivanova	1730–40
Ivan VI	1740–41
Elizabeth	1741–62
Peter III	1762
Catherine II	1762–96
Paul I	1796–1801
Alexander I	1801–25

Nicholas I	1825–55
Alexander II	1855–81
Alexander III	1881–94
Nicholas II	1894–1917

Roman province of Africa Province created after 146 BC, following conquest of Carthage in the Third Punic War. Initially it consisted of lands once controlled by Carthage, but, by the 1st cent. AD, it had been greatly expanded east and west to include parts of modern Algeria and Libya. Roman Emperor Septimius Severus later created the province of Numidia from its western end. Diocletian created Tripolitania in the east and Byzacena in the south. A commercially prosperous region under the Romans (1st-3d cents. AD), it fell (AD 430) to the Vandals and declined rapidly thereafter.

Roman province of Asia Territory of the Roman Empire in western Asia Minor. It was constituted as a province in 133 BC when Rome gained possession of the Kingdom of Pergamum (q.v.). The importance of the region declined (3d–4th cents. AD) with the rise of Constantinople to the north.

Roman Question See **Lateran Treaty; Law of Guarantees**

Roman Republic **1.** Name of the ancient Roman state from the time the Romans gained independence (c509 BC) from the Etruscan Tarquin kings to the accession of Augustus as Roman emperor (27 BC). (For history, see Rome.) **2.** Republican government established briefly in Rome (1798–99) by the French.

Roman Senate Roman governmental body. Formed in the 6th cent. BC as an advisory council appointed by the kings of Rome, it evolved into a powerful legislative body that lasted until the end of the Roman Empire. Originally composed of patricians, the Senate gradually came to include wealthy plebeians. It wielded great power in financial, administrative, military, and religious affairs until the end of the 2nd cent. BC, when corruption and the rise of two antagonistic political factions within the Senate weakened its ability to govern. The Senate lost much of its power after the assassination (44 BC) of J. Caesar.

romanticism Movement in literature and the arts that arose (18th–19th cents.) as a reaction to the extreme rationalism of the Enlightenment (q.v.) and the strictures of classicism (q.v.) in the arts. The movement began in Germany and England (late 18th cent.) and thereafter spread to other countries. Its aims were various and often conflicting, but generally were characterized by opposition to rationalism and social conventions; belief in the natural man and natural beauty, and in the primacy of human emotions, self-expres-sion, and individualism; and an interest in mystical, medieval, and Oriental themes. The French author and philosopher J. Rousseau is considered an important forerunner of romanticism. The movement gave rise to romantic nationalism and a fondness for experimentation. It declined (from the mid-1800s) and in literature gave way to realism (q.v.). Leading Romantics writers include Sir W. Scott, J. W. von Goethe, and V. Hugo; in music, R. Wagner, R. Schumann, F. Liszt, and F. Chopin; in art, J. Turner and F. Delacroix.

Romanus I d. 948. Byzantine emperor (920–944). He was regent for Constantine VII, but took the throne himself, fought the Bulgars, and clashed with the great landowners of the empire. He was overthrown by his sons, who were then ousted by Constantine VII.

Romanus II 939–963. Byzantine emperor (959–963), successor to Constantine VII. He was an incompetent profligate under whom imperial affairs were in the hands of his wife and favorite eunuchs. However, his military commander, Nicephorus I, won notable victories against the Arabs and eventually succeeded him.

Romanus III ⟨Romanus Argyrus⟩ c968–1034. Byzantine emperor (1028–34). He succeeded to the throne by marrying Empress Zoë, the daughter of Constantine VIII. After an irresponsible rule, he was murdered, probably by Zoë and her husband-to-be, Michael IV.

Romanus IV ⟨Romanus Diogenes⟩ d. 1071. Byzantine emperor (1067–71). He married the widow of his predecessor, Constantine X, and reigned as coregent. He was deposed after his total defeat by the Seljuks at the Battle of Manzikert (q.v.).

Romanus Argyrus See **Romanus III**

Romanus Diogenes See **Romanus IV**

Romany Indo-European language spoken in a number of dialects by the Gypsy peoples. The language is descended from Sanskrit and began evolving toward its modern form about AD 1000, when the Gypsies migrated out of northwestern India. Romany has a rich oral tradition but no written literature.

Rome Historic city (pop. 2,900,000) and capital of Italy, located in central Italy. The Vatican City lies within its borders and Rome has long been the seat of the Roman Catholic church. According to Roman tradition, the city of Rome was founded in 753 BC by Romulus. In subsequent years the city grew and came under the influence of the Etruscans (the Tarquin kings). The Romans drove out the Tarquin kings c509 BC and established the Roman Republic. Rome then became the center of an expanding empire which, by the beginning of the 2d cent. AD, encircled the Mediterranean and included much of Europe as well (*for history during this period see* Rome, *below*). Rome remained the capital of the empire until AD 330 when the capital was moved to Constantinople. By the time of the fall of the (Western) Roman Empire in AD 476, Rome had also been supplanted by Ravenna as chief city of the Italian peninsula. During the following centuries, the bishops of Rome gained temporal authority over the city and, after the 8th cent., Rome became the seat of church-controlled domains in central Italy (known as the Papal States, *q.v.*). The history of Rome during the Middle Ages was chaotic. The struggle for power between the popes and the Holy Roman emperors resulted in numerous attacks on the city. Civil strife resulted from attempts to establish a republic at Rome and from the long struggle between Guelphs and Ghibellines *(q.v.)* in Italy. Finally in the 14th and early 15th cents., during the Babylonian Captivity and the Great Schism, Rome sank into chaos and economic ruin. During the 15th cent., the popes reestablished firm control over Rome (and the Papal States). This time also marked the flowering of the Renaissance in Italy, and the popes commissioned the great artists of their time to adorn Rome with magnificent buildings and works of art. Rome again came under attack during the Italian Wars *(q.v.)* of the 16th cent. But Rome under the popes nevertheless continued its rise as a center of world culture. During the French Revolutionary Wars, Rome was occupied (1798) by Napoleon and a short-lived republic was formed of Italian territories. The popes were restored to control of Rome in 1814, but the seeds of the Italian nationalist movement had been sown. During the Revolutions of 1848, Rome was proclaimed a republic and held out for a short time against the French, who ultimately restored the pope. When the kingdom of Italy was created (1861), its domains did not then include Rome, which remained under papal control. The city was finally occupied in 1870, and in 1871 it was made capital of Italy. The popes, however, refused to recognize the loss of their temporal power and thus began the Roman Question, which was not resolved until 1929. The Fascists came to power through their March on Rome *(q.v.)* in 1922 and the city was captured (1944) by the Allies during WW II. Rome, which remains the spiritual center of the Roman Catholic world today, was the site of a Catholic pilgrimage in 1950. Modern Rome is a commercial and tourist center of Italy. It is the site of many ancient ruins and historic buildings.

Rome (empire)   Great empire of ancient times which for several centuries dominated the Mediterranean world. The history of ancient Rome can be broadly divided into two epochs, the Roman Republic (c509–527 BC) and the Roman Empire (27 BC–AD 476). The rise of Rome began with the subjugation of the Italian peninsula (largely completed in the 3d cent. BC). Acquisition of overseas territories began with the Punic Wars (3d–2d cent. BC) in which the great Carthaginian empire was destroyed and its territories were absorbed by Rome. Thereafter the Romans expanded their domains through various conquests, uniting under their rule an empire that encircled the Mediterranean and extended northward into the British Isles. Roman culture, laws, and customs were spread throughout the empire and greatly influenced the subsequent development of civilization in the West. The decline of the empire began at about the end of the 2d cent. AD and following centuries were marked by the breakdown of authority and political chaos, worsening economic problems, oppressive taxation, and finally the destructive invasions by various barbarian peoples (probably joined by disaffected Roman subjects). The Western Roman Empire collapsed before the barbarian hordes in AD 476, which is traditionally considered the end of the Roman Empire. However, the Eastern Roman Empire continued for many centuries thereafter as the Byzantine Empire *(q.v.)*. (*For history of the Italian peninsula after* 476, *see* Italy. *See also* Rome *(entry above) for history of the city itself.*) Key events in the history of Rome include:

753? BC   Legendary founding of Rome by Romulus.

715?–672 BC   Numa Pompilius, according to tradition, succeeded Romulus as king; established religious and civil law.

c616 BC   Etruscans, a people of northern Italy, gained control of Rome; ruled as the Tarquin kings: Etruscan civilization greatly influenced Roman civilization.

509 BC   Tarquin kings driven out by Romans; uprising caused, according to tradition, by rape of the Roman woman Lucrece; Roman Republic founded.

c509–527 BC   Roman Republic; two consuls elected annually; Senate, established as advisory body to the kings, continued and formalized, and finally dominated government during the republic; government at first controlled by patricians (aristocrats) with plebeians gaining rights and powers over the centuries.

496 BC   Battle of Lake Regillus; Romans defeated neighboring Latins.

c494 BC   Plebes seceded to the Sacred Mount to protest oppression by the patricians; tribunate created.

FROM 471 BC   Tribunes of the plebs elected in the *Councilium Plebis* (assembly).

458 BC   Cincinatus became dictator; defeated the Aequi.

c450 BC   Twelve Tables drawn up as Rome's legal code; plebeian unrest over harsh treatment by patrician magistrates brought about code; became the basis of Roman law until 2d cent. BC.

444 BC   Election of military tribunes begun after plebs agitated for greater powers.

443 BC   Office of censor established; remained part of Roman government until 22 BC.

405–396 BC   Romans put the Veii under siege; the town was finally captured and destroyed.

c391 BC   Augurs (prophets) abolished.

390 BC   Rome sacked by the Gauls; Camillus traditionally believed to have brought about the Gauls' withdrawal.

367 BC   Tribunes C. Licinus and L. Sextus initiated important reforms; plebs, after years of agitation, permitted to name one consul from their ranks; later eligible to hold all other offices, and distinction between patrician and pleb disappeared.

367–345 BC   Romans variously at war with the Gauls, and neighboring Latin tribes; southern Etruria captured; Hernici, Volsci, and others defeated.

343–341 BC   First Samnite War; marked beginning of Rome's move to take control of the Campania.

340–338 BC   Latin Wars; Italian cities rebelled for equal status with Rome but were defeated by Roman armies.

339 BC   Publilian Laws; plebs, or plebeians, gained further power by the reforms of Quintus Publilius Philo.

316–304 BC   Second Samnite War.

312 BC   Construction of Appian Way began.

290 BC   Sabines conquered by Rome.

298–290 BC   Third Samnite War; Romans defeated the rebelling tribes, asserting firm control in central Italy.

287 BC   Reform of the dictator Quintus Hortensius issued after plebeians seceded to the Janiculan hill; *Lex Hortensia* gave plebeians equal status with patricians by making the *plebiscita* (resolutions) of the plebeians binding on all citizens without the approval of the Senate.

282–272 BC   War with the Greek king Pyrrhus, who sought to defend the Greek colony of Tarentum (southern Italy) against the Romans; noted

Battle of Asculum fought (279 BC); Pyrrhus finally withdrew to Greece.

264–241 BC   First Punic War against Carthage; Rome won control of Sicily, a valuable grain-producing region.

238 BC   Romans took control of Sardinia, previously a Carthaginian possession.

229–228, 219 BC   Illyrian Wars conducted on behalf of Greeks against pirates; led to Greek recognition of Roman power.

218–201 BC   Second Punic War against Carthage; Hannibal crossed the Alps into Italy and nearly conquered the Romans; Scipio defeated Hannibal in Africa; Rome gained control of Spain and Carthaginian islands in Mediterranean; Carthaginian power broken.

214–205 BC   First Macedonian War fought with Macedon; Macedonians, in alliance with Carthage, successful against Rome.

c204–149 BC   Cato the Elder flourished; noted statesman who advocated return to the traditional Roman ways; urged destruction of Carthage.

200–196 BC   Second Macedonian War fought; Macedonian power reduced; Roman hegemony in Greece established.

171–168 BC   Third Macedonian War fought; Romans victorious and Macedon divided into four republics.

149–146 BC   Third Punic War against Carthage; Carthage captured and completely destroyed; Carthaginian territories made into Roman province of Africa.

149–148 BC   Fourth Macedonian War fought; led to Roman annexation of Macedon and complete domination of Greece.

143–133 BC   Numantine War; Scipio Africanus the Younger finally defeated the Celtiberians in Spain after long war against them.

c134–132 BC   First Servile War, unsuccessful slave uprising against Romans in Sicily.

133 BC   Tribune T. Gracchus assassinated by opponents of his land reforms, which sought to improve the peasants' lot.

133 BC   Kingdom of Mysia (Pergamum) passed to Rome on the death of its king; Romans organized it as the province of Asia.

121 BC   C. Gracchus killed; as tribune he had instituted radical reforms, including the land reforms of his brother, T. Gracchus, and measure forcing government to supply grain at a fair price; reforms reversed after his tribunate and he was killed in subsequent riots.

111–105 BC   Romans subdued rebellion in Africa led by King Jugurtha; begun by Marius, completed by Sulla.

105 BC Romans defeated by invading Cimbri and Teutones at the Battle of Arausio in Gaul; the tribes then invaded Italy.

104–100 BC Marius reelected consul each year.

102–101 BC Romans, led by Marius, defeated the Cimbri at the Battle of Aquae Sextae (102 BC) and Vercellae (101); Marius hailed as a great hero.

c102–99 BC Second Servile War, unsuccessful slave uprising against Romans in Sicily.

91 BC M. Drusus advanced reforms, including measure granting citizenship to all Italian peoples subject to Rome; Drusus killed.

c90–88 BC Social War, unsuccessful uprising of Italian tribes against Rome; full citizenship granted to all Italian peoples.

88–87 BC Civil war began; Sulla marched his troops into Rome after tribune Publius Sulpicius Rufus tried to impose reforms by force; Marius, a leader of the popular party, fled and Rufus was executed; Sulla, leader of the optimates (aristocrats) became consul (87 BC) and left Rome to lead armies in First Mithridatic War.

88–84 BC First Mithridatic War; Mithridates of Pontus attempted to seize the Roman province of Asia during the Social War; Roman consul Sulla defeated him.

87 BC Cinna, popular party leader, became consul at Rome; attempted to put through Rufus' reforms in Sulla's absence and was driven out of Rome; reentered Rome with Marius' help and massacred many of Sulla's followers.

83–82 BC Sulla, returning from the Mithridatic War, defeated supporters of the popular party; ordered proscription of members of the faction.

83–81 BC Second Mithridatic War; Romans attacked Mithridates; restored conquered territory at the end of the war.

82–79 BC Sulla ruled as dictator; instituted conservative reforms to increase power of the Senate and limit that of the tribunes and judiciary; retired after reforms were enacted.

77 BC Pompey defeated attempt by M. Lepidus to rescind Sulla's reforms by force.

c75–43 BC Cicero flourished; great Roman statesman and orator.

74–63 BC Third Mithridatic War; this war resulted in the complete conquest of Pontus and its annexation to the Roman province of Asia.

73–71 BC Third Servile War, unsuccessful slave uprising in Italy led by Spartacus; slave army defeated by Crassus and Pompey.

70 BC Pompey and Crassus became consuls; rescinded Sulla's reforms, thus restoring power to popular faction.

70–19 BC Vergil lived; considered leading poet of his age.

65–8 BC Horace lived; among the great Latin poets.

64 BC Pompey added domains of Seleucids to the empire as a province; reorganized Rome's province of Asia.

64 BC Palestine brought under Roman control by Pompey.

64–63 BC Conspiracy of Catiline.

60 BC First triumvirate formed by Caesar, Pompey, and Crassus.

59 BC Caesar, as consul, appointed himself to take charge of Gaul for five years (later extended another five years).

59 BC–AD 17 Roman historian, Livy, lived; wrote history of Romans.

58–51 BC Gallic Wars; Caesar's military campaigns led to the conquest of all Gaul and gave him great power and prestige.

53 BC Roman invasion of Parthia halted at Battle of Carrhae; Crassus killed soon after; first triumvirate began to break up.

52 BC Pompey, now leader of the optimates, elected sole consul at Rome; engaged in power struggle with Caesar, leader of the popular party.

49 BC Senate ordered Caesar to disband his army in Gaul.

49 BC Civil war (49–46 BC) began; Caesar, refusing to disband his army, led his soldiers in the famous crossing of the Rubicon (Jan. 10–11); marched into Italy against Pompey.

49 BC Caesar laid siege to Pompey's forces at Brundisium, in Italy; Pompey escaped (Mar.) to Greece.

49 BC Caesar entered Rome; did not institute customary proscription of opponents.

49 BC M. Antony made tribune.

49 BC Caesar successful in fighting against Pompey's supporters in Spain.

49 BC Caesar elected consul after renouncing his election as dictator; returned to pursuit of Pompey.

48 BC Caesar defeated by Pompey at Dyrrhachium (now in Albania).

48 BC Battle of Pharsalus, in Greece; Caesar routed Pompey's forces (Aug. 9); Pompey fled to Eygpt.

48 BC Pompey killed in Egypt by order of King Ptolemy XII.

48–47 BC Alexandrine War; Caesar, pursuing Pompey, had entered Alexandria, Egypt; found himself under siege by Egyptian forces; dallied with Cleopatra; broke siege and subdued Egypt; installed Cleopatra and Ptolemy XIII on the Egyptian throne.

47 BC Caesar defeated Pharnaces II at the Battle of Zela in brief war in Syria and Pontus; Caesar said of the war, "Veni, vidi, vici" (I came, I saw, I conquered); Caesar next went to Africa.

46 BC Caesar victorius against the last of Pompey's forces at the Battle of Thapsus (Feb. 6); Cato the Younger committed suicide; Roman Senate named Caesar dictator for ten years.

46 BC Back in Rome, Caesar pardoned his enemies and began program of reform aimed at improving lot of the populace; then went to Spain to war against Pompey's sons.

46 BC Caesar instituted the Julian Calendar.

45 BC Caesar defeated Pompey's sons at the Battle of Munda, Spain; was made consul for ten years.

44 BC Caesar assassinated (Mar. 15) by opponents who feared his growing power; Cassius, Marcus Brutus, and Decimus Brutus among the assassins; M. Antony rose to power in Rome; began to organize against the assassins, who had fled Rome.

44–43 BC Octavian, Caesar's heir, attempted to claim his rights, but was at first opposed by Antony; the two formed an alliance against Caesar's assassins the next year.

43 BC Second Triumvirate formed (Nov.) by Octavian, Antony, and Lepidus.

43 BC–AD 17 Ovid lived; wrote classics of Latin poetry.

43 BC Cicero executed on orders from Antony, whom he had opposed.

42 BC Forces of Octavian, Antony, and Lepidus won decisive victory at the Battle of Philippi (Oct. 27); Brutus and Cassius committed suicide.

42 BC Marc Antony began his celebrated love affair with Cleopatra.

40 BC Treaty of Brundisium wed Marc Antony to Octavian's sister; Octavian to rule the West, Antony the East; Lepidus to rule Africa.

c39 BC Herod made king of Judea by Marc Antony.

36 BC Octavian defeated Sextus Pompey, a powerful opponent, at the Battle of Mylae.

36 BC Octavian, consolidating his power, deposed Lepidus; Antony, meanwhile, renewed his love affair with Cleopatra (unpopular in Rome) and thus aroused opposition in Rome.

35–33 BC Octavian conquered Illyria.

31–30 BC Final struggle between Octavian and Antony; Antony and Cleopatra defeated at the Battle of Actium (31 BC) and the two lovers committed suicide soon after; Octavian became sole ruler of Rome.

30 BC Egypt made a Roman province after Octavian killed King Ptolemy XIV.

27 BC Octavian accepted imperial title, Augustus; marked beginning of Roman Empire.

27 BC–AD 476 Roman Empire; Roman domains reached their greatest extent during this period; first 200 years marked by peace (Pax Romana) and prosperity.

27 BC–AD 14 Augustus (Octavian) ruled as first Roman emperor; had complete control of the military and the provinces; reformed both the military and provincial administration; undertook building program and patronized the arts, fostering the "Augustan Age."

c8–6 BC Jesus of Nazareth born.

AD 14–c130 Silver Age of Latin literature.

AD 14–37 Tiberius reigned as emperor, following Augustus' death; Tiberius turned over effective rule to the intriguer, Sejanus (AD 23–31), but finally had him executed.

AD 16 Germanicus Caesar suppressed a revolt by Arminius in Germany.

AD 30 Jesus crucified at Jerusalem.

AD 37–41 Caligula reigned; became insane and ruled as a cruel tyrant.

AD 41–54 Claudius I reigned; dominated by his wives; added Mauretania (AD 41–42) to the empire and began final conquest of Britain (AD 43).

AD 54–68 Nero reigned; notorious tyrant.

AD 64 Rome destroyed by great fire; Nero, suspected of having had it set, blamed the Christians and thereupon began persecutions of Christians; Nero rebuilt Rome.

AD 65 Conspiracy to overthrow Nero discovered.

AD 66–73 First Jewish revolt in Judaea; Jerusalem destroyed (AD 70).

AD 68 Nero overthrown; Galba recognized as emperor by Praetorian Guard.

AD 69–79 Vespasian reigned as emperor following a struggle for power; founded Flavian dynasty.

AD 69–82 Colosseum built.

AD 78–84 Agricola conquered much of Britain; served as governor.

AD 79–81 Titus reigned.

AD 79 Pompeii buried under volcanic ash during eruption of Mt. Vesuvius.

AD 81–96 Domitian reigned; bought off the army and the Roman mobs and increased the powers of the emperor; unsuccessful in wars in Dacia; assassinated.

AD 96–98 Nerva reigned; introduced legal and tax reforms.

AD 98–117 Trajan reigned as emperor; warred against Parthia, gaining territories east of the Tigris and Euphrates rivers; empire reached its greatest extent (AD 116).

AD 107 Dacia became a province after a long war against barbarians there (from AD 101).

AD 117–138 Hadrian reigned; undertook considerable building in provinces; imperial edicts became the sole source of Roman law (from AD 131); economic problems, exacerbated by excessive taxation, began to appear.

AD 132–135 Second Jewish revolt; Jews thereafter forbidden to live in Jerusalem.

AD 138–161 Antonius Pius reigned; reign marked by general peace and stability.

AD 161–180 Marcus Aurelius reigned; despite persecution of Christians, his rule considered wise and humane; he was famous exponent of Stoicism.

AD 166–167 Plague throughout the empire; spread by Roman soldiers returning from war with Parthia (AD 162–165).

AD 180–192 Commodius reigned; gave himself up to dissolute life and his reign marked the start of Rome's decline; by arrangement with conspirators, a wrestler named Narcissus strangled Commodius during a match.

AD 193–211 Septimus Severus reigned; his reign began long period of instability in which Praetorian Guard controlled selection of the emperors.

AD 212 Roman citizenship granted to nearly all within the empire by Emperor Caracalla (reigned AD 211–217).

FROM AD c214 Alemanni and Goths began attacks on Roman outposts on the northern frontier in Germany.

AD 250 Decius (reigned AD 249–251); began general persecution of the Christians.

AD 253–270 Barbarians broke through Roman frontier defenses; Alemanni advanced to Milan; Franks passed beyond the Rhine; Goths invaded the Balkans.

AD 260 Emperor Valerian (reigned AD 253–260) captured during wars with Persians.

AD 270 Claudius II (reigned AD 268–270); halted advance of the Goths; allowed them to settle Dacia.

AD 270–275 Aurelian reigned; withdrew from Dacia and drove Alemanni out of Italy.

AD 284–305 Diocletian reigned; instituted wide-ranging administrative, military, and financial reforms; brought measure of stability to the empire, which by this time, however, was crumbling under the weight of costly bureaucracy, excessive taxation, and continuing economic problems.

AD 286 Roman Empire divided into the Western and Eastern empires by Diocletian; named Maximian co-ruler, though by adopting him maintained theoretical unity of the empire.

AD 293 Diocletian divided the empire into four administrative units (two east, two west); each responsible to respective emperor.

AD 306 Constantine began his struggle against rivals for control in the Western Empire.

AD 312 Battle of Milvian Bridge; Constantine defeated his last rival for control of the West; a vision he had before the battle led to his conversion to Christianity.

AD 312 Constantine became emperor in the West, Licinius emperor in the East.

AD 312 Praetorian Guard abolished by Constantine.

AD 313 Edict of Milan issued by Constantine and Licinius; established toleration of Christianity throughout empire.

AD 324 Licinius, emperor of the East, defeated by Constantine.

AD 324–337 Contstantine reigned as sole ruler; Roman Empire reunited under him; he established his capital at Constantinople (AD 330).

AD 325 Constantine called the Council of Nicaea (1st ecumenical) to resolve question of Arianism; established role of emperor in Eastern church.

AD 361–363 Julian the Apostate reigned; tried to reinstate paganism in the empire; Christianity reinstated on his death.

AD 376 Huns conquered Visigoths in region of modern Romania, bringing them into contact with Romans.

AD 378 Visigoths decimated Roman forces at the Battle of Adrianople; Eastern emperor Valens killed; Visigoths swept into Europe.

AD 375–395 Theodosius I the Great reigned as emperor in the East; Valentinian II (AD 375–392) and Gratian (375–383) ruled in West.

AD 383 Gratian killed in revolt by Maximus; Maximus finally killed by Theodosius (AD 388).

AD 390 Theodosius forced to do penance before bishop of Milan for massacring thousands of Greeks; marked victory of church over temporal power of the emperors.

AD 394 Battle of Frigidus; Theodosius defeated Eugenius, who had usurped and killed Valentinian II; Roman Empire united for last time under Theodosius.

AD 395 Roman Empire permanently divided into Eastern and Western Empires on the death of Theodosius I.

AD 395 Honorius became emperor of the West (ruled AD 395–423), Arcadius emperor of the East (ruled AD 395–408).

AD 396–408 Stilicho, a Vandal and commander of Roman troops in the West, successful against invading barbarians; drove Visigoths out of Greece (AD 397), and blocked attempts to invade Italy; Gaul was meanwhile overrun by barbarians (AD 406).

AD c402 Ravenna made capital of the West.

AD 407 Romans withdrew from Britain.

AD 408–450 Theodosius II reigned in the East.

AD 409–410 Visigoths under Alaric invaded Italy; sacked Rome (AD 410); subsequently invaded and conquered Spain.

AD 425–454 Valentinian III reigned in the West.

AD 429–431 Vandals crossed from Spain into Africa; conquered Roman territories in North Africa.

AD 441–443 Attila and his brother Bleda led the Huns in invasion of eastern Roman provinces.

AD 450–452 Attila the Hun invaded Gaul and Italy (AD 452).

AD 455 Valentinian III murdered; succession of rulers set up in the West.

AD 455 Gaiseric, king of the Vandals, sacked Rome.

AD 457–474 Leo I reigned as emperor of the East.

AD 474–491 Zeno reigned as emperor of the East; attempted to win control over the Goths.

AD 475–476 Romulus Augustus reigned as last emperor of the West.

AD 476 Odoacer defeated last Roman forces at Battle of Pavia; deposed Emperor Romulus Augustus (Sept. 4), thus ending Western Roman Empire.

Rome, March on *See* **March on Rome**

Rome, Seven Hills of *See* **Seven Hills of Rome**

Rome, treaties of, Series of agreements signed in Rome (Mar. 25, 1957), between Belgium, France, Italy, Luxemburg, The Netherlands, and West Germany, that established the European Economic Community. The treaties eliminated tariffs, established a ruling council of ministers, and also set up the European Atomic Energy Community (Euratom).

Rømer, Olaus ⟨Römer, Ole⟩ ⟨Roemer, Olaus⟩ 1644–1710. Danish astronomer. By observing the eclipses of Jupiter's satellites, he was able to prove conclusively (1676) that light travels at a definite speed and not instantaneously. He roughly calculated its speed at 140,000 miles per second.

Römer, Ole *See* **Rømer, Olaus**

Rommel, Erwin 1891–1944. German field marshal during WW II. After performing brilliantly in France in 1940, he became the near-legendary German commander of the Afrika Korps in the North Africa Campaign *(q.v.)*. He was commander in northern France when the Allies landed in 1944. Rommel was forced to take poison after discovery of his part in the plot against A. Hitler's life.

Romulus Legendary founder and king of Rome. He and his brother Remus built the town (753 BC). Romulus built a defensive wall around it and, when Remus ridiculed the wall, Romulus killed him. Romulus then populated the town with fugitives, providing them with wives by carrying off the women, the Sabines, of a nearby tribe.

Romulus Augustulus *fl.* 5th cent. AD. Last Roman emperor of the West, (475–476 AD). He was put on the throne by his father, the Roman general Orestes. He was deposed soon after by the German conquerer Odoacer, who sent him into exile.

Roncalli, Angelo Giuseppe *See* **John XXIII**

Roncesvalles, Battle of Ambush of the rear guard of Charlemagne's army (Aug. 15, 778) in the Pyrenees Mountains. This minor engagement took place during Charlemagne's return from a military campaign against the Muslims in Spain and provided the inspiration for the epic poem *The Song of Roland.*

Ronsard, Pierre de 1525–85. French poet. Considered one of the greatest poets of the Renaissance, he was a leader of the Pléiade. His works include *Amours de Cassandre, Hymnes,* and the unfinished *La Franciade.*

Röntgen, Wilhelm Conrad *See* **Roentgen, Wilhelm Conrad**

Roon, Count Albrecht Theodor Emil von 1803–79. Prussian field marshal. As minister of war from 1859, he reorganized the Prussian army and made victories possible in the Austro-Prussian War and in the Franco-Prussian War.

Roosevelt, Anna Eleanor 1884–1962. American political figure, humanitarian, and author. As the wife (*m.* 1905) of Pres. F. Roosevelt, she not only worked with her husband but also pursued her own interests as a newspaper and radio commentator and US representative at the UN (1945–52, 1961).

Roosevelt, Franklin Delano 1882–1945. Thirty-second US president (1933–45), successor to H. Hoover, and the only president to win four consecutive elections (1932, over H. Hoover; 1936, over A. Landon; 1940, over W. Willkie; 1944, over T. Dewey). During his long tenure, Roosevelt saw the country through the Depression *(q.v.)* and most of WW II *(q.v.),* vastly increased the power and prestige of the presidency, and firmly committed the federal government to (then) unprecedented direct involvement in promoting the social and economic well-being of American society. A

New York Democrat, he first served in state and federal posts, was an unsuccessful vice-presidential candidate (1920), and then was partly paralyzed by polio (1921). He nevertheless persevered, became governor of New York (1928–30, 1930–32), and then won the presidency. He took office (1933) during the worst of the Depression and, in his famous first Hundred Days *(q.v.)* in office, he initiated the first wave of his New Deal *(q.v.)* legislation to counter the Depression. His administration during the rest of the 1930s was marked by still more New Deal legislation (though at a slower pace after 1936), the persisting economic stagnation of the Depression, increasing political opposition, and, finally, concern over the menace of war in Europe. By the late 1930s, Roosevelt had already begun to prepare the nation for war and, with W. Churchill, issued the Atlantic Charter *(q.v.)*. After the Pearl Harbor attack (1941) brought the US into the war, he instituted a massive program to put the US economy on a wartime footing and quickly built up American military forces. He then played a prominent role in the Allied wartime conferences (such as Teheran and Yalta) and worked for establishment of the UN. He died shortly before the end of war in the European theater.

Roosevelt, Theodore 1858–1919. Twenty-sixth US president (1901–09), successor to W. McKinley. Roosevelt got his start in politics as a Republican in New York State. After holding both state and federal posts, he became a national hero for his exploits with the Rough Riders *(q.v.)*, notably at the Battle of San Juan Hill during the Spanish-American War (1898). Elected vice-president under W. McKinley (1900), he became president a few months later when McKinley was assassinated. He was subsequently elected to a full term in 1904. Roosevelt's administration was marked by his concerted attacks on the business trusts (trust-busting) and passage of reform legislation, including acts to end railroad rebates (Elkins Act, 1903), to create the Department of Commerce and Labor, and to regulate the quality of food and drugs. Roosevelt also actively involved the US in foreign affairs and he played a role in the Venezuela Claims *(q.v.)* dispute; formulated the Roosevelt corollary to the Monroe Doctrine *(q.v.)*, using it to interfere in Central American affairs; backed Panamanian revolutionaries and, after they set up a rebel government, arranged a treaty for the building of the Panama Canal *(q.v.)*; and mediated at the Portsmouth Conference (1904) to end the Russo-Japanese War. At the end of his term, Roosevelt helped elect his successor, H. Taft, and went abroad for an extended tour. In

1912, after falling out with Taft, he formed the Progressive (Bull Moose) party and attempted to win reelection as president. He lost to W. Wilson. He won the Nobel Peace Prize in 1906.

Roosevelt corollary *See* **Monroe Doctrine**

Root, Elihu 1845–1937. US secretary of war (1899–1904) and secretary of state (1905–09). A dedicated internationalist, he negotiated important treaties with Japan (notably the Root-Takahira Agreement, *q.v.*), Britain, and Latin America and consistently promoted disarmament. He received the Nobel Peace Prize in 1912.

Root, John Wellborn 1850–91. American architect. An associate of D. Burnham and leading architect of the Chicago school, he designed buildings that were important in the development of the modern skyscraper.

Root-Takahira Agreement Executive agreement concluded between the US and Japan (Nov. 30, 1908). By its terms, both countries agreed to support an open-door policy in China, maintain the territorial status quo in East Asia, and work for the continued independence and integrity of China. It was named for US Secretary of State E. Root and the Japanese ambassador to the US, Baron Kogoro Takahira (1854–1926).

Rorschach, Hermann 1884–1922. Swiss psychiatrist and neurologist. He devised the famous Rorschach inkblot test for diagnosing mental disorders.

Rosamond *d.* 1176? Mistress of England's Henry II, known as the "Fair Rosamund." The king acknowledged her (1174) after he had imprisoned his wife, Eleanor of Aquitaine. The many legends about her include one that she was murdered by Eleanor.

Rosas, Juan Manuel de 1793–1877. Dictator of Buenos Aires province and ruler of nearly all Argentina (1835–52). A wealthy rancher, he became governor of Buenos Aires province for the first time from 1828 to 1832. On taking office again (1835), he assumed dictatorial powers and extended his control over most of the other Argentine provinces. Thereafter he instituted a reign of terror; alienated foreign powers and thus provoked French and British blockades of Argentina (1838–40, 1845–50); and became involved in a scheme to take over Uruguay. He was overthrown by J. Urquiza, who, with support from Uruguay and Brazil, defeated Rosas' army at Monte Caseros (Feb. 3, 1852).

Rosecrans, William Starke 1819–98. American Civil War general. A successful commander at Corinth and Murfreesboro, he was relieved of command after his defeat (1863) at the Battle of

Chickamauga Creek *(q.v.)*. He later served as a diplomat and congressman.

Rosenberg, Alfred 1893–1946. German Nazi party leader and ideologist. He began as editor of the Nazi paper and provided the party with its anti-Semitic ideology in his *The Myth of the Twentieth Century*. He was hanged as a war criminal after WW II.

Rosenberg, Julius and **Ethel** First US civilians put to death for espionage. Born in 1918 and 1916 respectively, they were tried, then executed on June 19, 1953. They were convicted of transmitting to the Soviet Union secret information about the atomic bomb (1944–45). The information had allegedly been obtained by Mrs. Rosenberg's brother, army sergeant David Greenglass, who was an employee of the Los Alamos project. Julius, an army signal corps electrical engineer, was an acknowledged Communist. Many unsuccessful efforts were made to obtain clemency for them.

Rose of Lima, Saint 1586–1617. Peruvian religious mystic. A Dominican, she is the patron saint of South America, and the first native-born American to be canonized by the Catholic church.

Roses, Wars of the Dynastic wars (1455–85) in England between the houses of York (white rose insignia) and Lancaster (red rose insignia). They fought over rival claims to the English throne. The claimants in both houses were descendants of Edward III, though the Lancastrians had been in power since 1399. However, the Yorkist position was strengthened by discontent over the ineffective rule of Henry VI and his unpopular queen (Margaret of Anjou), English losses in France during the Hundred Years' War (1337–1453), heavy taxes, and disorders such as Cades' Rebellion *(q.v.)*.

Richard, duke of York, became protector of the kingdom when Henry became temporarily insane (1453–54). The wars began soon after Henry's recovery. Yorkists won the first battle (1455) at St. Albans *(q.v.)*. Fighting ceased until 1459, when Yorkists were beaten at the Battle of Ludford Bridge (Oct. 12). But they were victorious at the Battle of Northampton (July 10, 1460) and forced King Henry to name Richard (and Yorkist heirs) as his successor. This disinherited Queen Margaret's son and she then marched an army against the Yorkists. She won a bloody victory at Wakefield (Dec. 30, 1460), in which Richard was slain. She then won (Feb. 17, 1461) the second Battle of St. Albans *(q.v.)* and marched toward London. However, Richard's son, Edward, had already defeated the Lancastrians (Feb. 2) at the Battle of Mortimer's Cross *(q.v.)* and marched into London first.

Edward was proclaimed King Edward IV (Mar. 4, 1461), routed Margaret's forces at Towton *(q.v.)*, and forced the Lancastrians to flee the country. Edward's reign was undisturbed until 1469, when his brother, George, Yorkist duke of Clarence, and R. Neville, earl of Warwick (a powerful Yorkist) rebelled against him. They were driven out of England (1470) and, in France, formed an alliance with the exiled Lancastrian, Margaret of Anjou, and also won backing from French king Louis XI. They subsequently invaded England (Sept. 1470), briefly restored Henry VI, and put Edward to flight. Edward then formed an alliance with Charles the Bold, duke of Burgundy, and, returning to England (1471), won decisive victories at Barnet *(q.v.)* and Tewkesbury *(q.v.)*. His principal opponents either dead or imprisoned (Henry was apparently murdered), Edward lived out the remainder of his life as king.

The last phase of the wars broke out soon after Edward's death. Edward's brother, Richard III, seized power (1483) from Edward's son. Henry Stafford, 2d duke of Buckingham, raised an unsuccessful revolt and disaffected Yorkists threw their support to the Lancastrian claimant, Henry Tudor. Henry Tudor then defeated and killed (Aug. 22, 1485) Richard at the Battle of Bosworth Field *(q.v.)* and was crowned Henry VII. This ended the wars. Henry further cemented the peace by marrying (1486) Elizabeth of York and by quelling the last Yorkist revolts. The wars decimated the ranks of English nobles and they were subsequently unable to oppose the absolutist powers accumulated by Henry and his Tudor heirs.

Rosetta Stone Inscribed basalt stone that provided the key to deciphering ancient Egyptian hieroglyphics. Found (1799) by Napoleon's troops near Rosetta, Egypt, the stone bore inscriptions in Greek, Egyptian demotic, and hieroglyphics. Preliminary discoveries by Thomas Young (1773–1829) concerning the hieroglyphics were used by J. Champollion to finally decipher the ancient writings (1821).

Rosicrucians International society that claims it has the secret knowledge of the ancients. Its doctrine contains elements of occultism and mysticism. The group was first mentioned in 17th-cent. publications.

Ross, Betsy 1752–1836. American seamstress. Tradition credits her with making the first American flag (adopted by the Continental Congress June 14, 1777).

Ross, Sir John 1777–1856. British admiral and Arctic explorer. His explorations of Arctic waters failed to find a Northwest Passage *(q.v.)*, but the north magnetic pole was located (1831) on one of his expeditions.

Ross, John ⟨Koowescoowe⟩ 1790–1866. American Indian chief of Scottish and Cherokee parentage. He fought valiantly to prevent the expulsion of his people from Georgia but eventually led them on the long journey (from 1835) to the Indian Territory in Oklahoma.

Rossetti, Christina Georgina 1830–94. English poet, sister of D.G. Rossetti. A devout Anglican, she spent her later life as a recluse and wrote religious poems. Her works include *Goblin Market and Other Poems* and *Prince's Progress*.

Rossetti, Dante Gabriel 1828–82. English poet and painter. He was one of the founders of the Pre-Raphaelites, who sought to restore naturalness to painting.

Rossini, Gioacchino Antonio 1792–1868. Italian composer. Best known as an operatic composer, his comic-opera masterpiece is the still popular *The Barber of Seville*. His best-known dramatic opera is *William Tell*.

Rostand, Edmond 1868–1918. French poet and playwright, best known for his famous play *Cyrano de Bergerac*.

Rostovtzeff, Michael Ivanovich 1870–1952. Russian-born American historian and archaeologist. He was noted for his writings on the society and culture of the ancient world, including *Social and Economic History of The Roman Empire* and *A History of the Ancient World*.

Rothko, Mark ⟨Rothkovitch, Marcus⟩ 1903–70. Russian-born American painter. He was a leading exponent of abstract expressionism *(q.v.)*. His later works consisted of rectangles of color painted on large canvases.

Rothkovitch, Marcus *See* **Rothko, Mark**

Rothschild, baron Lionel Nathan de 1808–79. British banker and member of parliament (1858–74). Son of N. Rothschild, he arranged large international loans such as those for the Irish famine (1847) and the Crimean War (1856). He was the first Jewish member of Parliament.

Rothschild, Mayer Amschel 1743–1812. Founder of the Rothschild banking dynasty. Originally a Frankfort money-changer, he capitalized on his position as adviser to the landgrave of Hesse-Kassel and, through his sons, founded Rothschild banks in London, Paris, Vienna, and Naples.

Rothschild, Nathan Meyer 1777–1836. Founder of the London branch of the famous Rothschild banking dynasty. He was noted for helping the British subsidize their allies in the fight against Napoleonic France.

Rou *See* **Rollo**

Rouault, Georges 1871–1958. French expressionist artist. Employing a "stained-glass" style of bold, vivid colors, he is considered one of the foremost religious artists of this century.

Rouget de Lisle, Claude Joseph 1760–1836. French army engineer and writer. He wrote (1792) the French national anthem, *La Marseillaise*.

Rough Riders Popular name for the 1st US Volunteer Cavalry in the Spanish-American War (1898). Largely organized by T. Roosevelt and commanded by L. Wood, they mainly fought on foot in Cuba, having been forced to leave their horses behind in Florida. The Battle of San Juan Hill, fought under Roosevelt's command, was their best-known engagement.

Roundheads Name of the party of Parliamentarians that opposed Charles I in the English Civil War (1642–49). They were so named because of their short haircuts. The Royalists wore their hair long in the then fashionable ringlets.

Round Table In Arthurian legend, the huge table King Arthur had constructed so that no knight could claim precedence over any other. It was first mentioned *c*1155.

Rousseau, Henri 1844–1910. French primitivist painter. He painted exotic scenes of jungles, wild beasts, and strange Gypsies in a naive style. His works include *Monkeys in the Orange Trees*, *Sleeping Gypsy*, and *The Dream*.

Rousseau, Jean Jacques 1712–78. Swiss-born French author and philosopher. A highly controversial figure in his lifetime, he influenced both the development of Romanticism and the political thought of the French Revolution. Rousseau's life was erratic and, after he gained recognition, was marked by bitter quarrels with his friends, flight from one country after another because of hostile reactions to his views, and, finally, at least partial insanity. Among his works were articles for the great French *Encyclopédie*; *Discourse on Arts and Sciences*, which held that civilization corrupted the essential goodness of man; *Discourse on the Origin of Inequality*, which again treated corruption of the natural man by civilization; the famous *Social Contract*, which postulated both subordination of the individual to the general will of society and the common good toward which society must aim; *Émile*, a novel that influenced educational theory; and *Confessions*, his famous autobiography.

Roussel, Albert 1869–1937. French composer. He combined modern experimental techniques with a basic neoclassical style in such well known works as the ballet *Bacchus and Ariane*.

Rowlatt Acts Legislation passed (Feb., 1919) by the British Government of India to extend wartime measures whereby suspected revolutionaries could be tried without juries and even interned without trial. The Indian protests over these measures, led by M. Gandhi, led to the Massacre of Amritsar *(q.v.)*.

Rowley, William 1585?–1642? English Jacobean dramatist. He was both an actor and a collaborator on dozens of plays, most notably *The Changeling*, written with T. Middleton. His own best-known play was *All's Lost by Lust*.

Roxana ⟨Roxane⟩ *d.* 311BC. Wife of Alexander the Great, daughter of a local Bactrian chief. Alexander married her (327 BC) to consolidate his position in Persia and she bore him a posthumous son. Caught in the conflicts between Alexander's generals (Wars of the Diadochi), she and her son were put to death by Cassander.

Roxane *See* **Roxana**

Roxas y Acuna, Manuel 1892–1948. First president of the independent Republic of the Philippines (1946–48). He was Speaker of the House and senator before independence. During WW II he spied for the Allies while serving in the Japanese occupation government in the Philippines.

Royal Academy of Arts Principal British art organization. It was founded in 1768 by George III, with Sir J. Reynolds as its first president. It has 40 academicians and sponsors studies and biennial exhibitions.

Royal Canadian Mounted Police Canadian federal police force. It was founded (1873) as the Northwest Mounted Police with an original force of 300 men to restore order in the frontier provinces. Popularly called the Mounties and long celebrated for its dogged pursuit of criminals, the unit was given federal status in 1920 and now numbers some 14,000 men.

Royal Highlanders *See* **Black Watch**

Royal Society One of the oldest and most prestigious European scientific societies. Founded in London (1660) as the Royal Society of London for the Improvement of Natural Knowledge, it has counted among its members the most distinguished men of science from its founding down to the present.

Royce, Josiah 1855–1916. American philosopher, an exponent of philosophical idealism. In his works he stressed the importance of individuality and will over intellect.

Ruanda *See* **Rwanda**

Ruanda-Urundi Former Belgian colonial territory in central Africa, now divided between the independent states of Rwanda and Burundi. Once a part of German East Africa, the region was taken by Belgium in 1916. It was made a UN trust territory in 1946 and was divided in 1962. The Tutsi and the Hutu are the main peoples inhabiting the area.

Rubens, Peter Paul 1577–1640. Flemish painter, considered the master of baroque art and noted for the sensuousness and use of color in his works. After studying in Italy, he ran a large workshop in Antwerp and used assistants to help with his many commissioned works, including *Descent from the Cross* and the decoration of France's Luxembourg Palace. Later he became a diplomat and was sent on missions to Spain, where he painted the royal family, and to England, where he did the *Allegory of War and Peace*. Among his many other noted works were *Adoration of the Magi*, *The Massacre of the Innocents*, *Venus and Adonis*, and *The Three Graces*.

Rubicon A small stream flowing into the Adriatic. Located in what is now north central Italy, it once marked the border between Cisalpine Gaul and Italy. By crossing the Rubicon with his army (Jan. 10–11, 49 BC), J. Caesar irrevocably committed himself to the civil war with the Roman Senate.

Rubinstein, Anton Grigoryevich 1829–94. Russian pianist, a virtuoso esteemed as a master of technique in his time. He was also a respected composer, though his works are rarely performed today.

Rubinstein, Artur 1886–1982. Polish-born American pianist. Known especially as an interpreter of Chopin, he was one of the most popular of concert pianists for many decades.

Ruby, Jack *See* **Kennedy, John F**

Rudolf 1858–89. Archduke and heir to the Austro-Hungarian empire. His mysterious death (with his mistress) at Mayerling was officially declared a suicide.

Rudolf I ⟨Hapsburg, Rudolf of⟩ 1218–91. German king (1273–91), and first of the Hapsburg line of emperors. His election ended the Interregnum *(q.v.)* in the Holy Roman Empire. His wars against King Ottocar II of Bohemia, a rival for the crown, helped restore eastern German lands, and he consolidated the rule over lands central to his family dynasty (notably Austria). He was never crowned Holy Roman Emperor.

Rudolf II 1552–1612. Holy Roman emperor (1576–1612), successor to his father, Maximilian II. He reversed his father's policy of toleration of Protestantism and openly supported the Catholic Reformation. However, opposition to his policies (notably a revolt by S. Bocskay in Hungary) and Rudolf's mental instability made it increasingly impossible for him to rule. By 1606 his brother Matthias had become actual ruler of the empire.

Rudolph ⟨Raoul⟩ *d.* 936. Duke of Burgundy and king of France (923–36), successor to Robert I. His reign was embroiled in a succession of wars against the Normans and Hungarians, fought to consolidate his position.

Rueil, Peace of *See* **Fronde**

Ruffo, Fabrizio 1744–1827. Roman Catholic cardinal and Neapolitan leader. In 1799 he led a successful insurrection against the Napoleonic regime (Parthenopean Republic) in Naples.

Rufinus *d.* AD 395. Roman statesman. As minister to Theodosius I and his son Arcadius, Rufinus wielded great power in the Eastern Roman empire. He failed in his attempt to marry his daughter to Arcadius and was assassinated by the Goths, probably at the instigation of Stilicho, his rival.

Ruhr District Ruhr River valley (northwest West Germany) and one of the world's leading industrial regions. The presence of high-quality coal ultimately led to the region's development (19th cent.) as a center for steel production and other allied industries. It was important to the German war effort in WW I and was occupied (1923–25) by France and Belgium when Germany failed to meet reparations payments after WW I. In WW II the district again supplied much of Germany's war materials and was heavily bombed (1942–45).

Ruisdael, Jacob van ⟨Ruysdael, Jacob van⟩ *c*1628–82. Dutch painter of the baroque period. Considered one of the greatest landscapists, he influenced the French and English landscapists of the next two centuries. Among his noted works were *Jewish Cemetery* and *Wheatfields.*

Rumania *See* **Romania**

Rumford, Benjamin Thompson, Count 1753–1814. American-born British physicist. He is best-known for his theory that heat is caused by the motion of particles (1798).

Rump Parliament Phase of England's Long Parliament (1640–60) that began following (1648) expulsion of members unacceptable to the rebel army (*see* Pride's Purge). These expelled members were recalled in 1660, restoring the Long Parliament. It voted its own dissolution (Mar. 16, 1660) after providing for the convening of the Convention Parliament (*q.v.*). This paved the way for the English Restoration.

Rundstedt, Gerd von 1875–1953. German field marshal, commander of German forces in Western Europe (1942–45). He was one of the ablest of Hitler's commanders, taking a leading part in the conquest of France, the invasion of Russia, the fortification of Europe, and the Battle of the Bulge.

Runeberg, Johan Ludvig 1804–77. Finnish romantic poet. He wrote verse epics, and the Finnish national anthem, "Our Land," was adapted from one of his poems.

Rungeling, John *See* **Ringling, John**

Runjeet Singh *See* **Ranjit Singh**

Runnimede *See* **Runnymede**

Runnymede ⟨Runnimede⟩ Meadow near the Thames River in Surrey, England, where King John was obliged (1215) by his barons to accept the Magna Carta (*q.v.*).

Rupert 1352–1410. German king (1400–10), successor to Wenceslaus and elector palatine of the Rhine (1398–1410). He unsuccessfully attempted to regain the imperial city of Milan, which had been taken by the Visconti. Rupert was never crowned Holy Roman Emperor.

Rupert, Prince 1619–82. Count palatine of the Rhine and English Royalist general. A grandson of James I, he fought during the Thirty Years' War, and then commanded Royalist forces defending Charles I during the English Civil War. He won notable victories, but was badly defeated at the battles of Marston Moor and Naseby. After the restoration of Charles II, he served as a naval commander in the Dutch Wars and became president of the Hudson's Bay Company.

Rupert's Land Canadian territory held by the Hudson's Bay Company from receipt of its charter in 1670 until it was sold to Canada in 1869. Named after Prince Rupert, the company's first president, it included the vast region constituting the drainage basin of Hudson Bay.

Rurik Dynasty of Russian noblemen and czars that ruled Russia until 1598. The line was founded by Rurik (*d.* 879) and his brothers, Scandinavian adventurers called Varangians, who gained control of Novgorod (*c*862). Rurik's successor later gained control of the Russian princely states, notably Moscow, and thus came to control the empire. Beginning with Ivan III, who ended Tatar control of the region (1480), succeeding members of the line enlarged and consolidated their control over Russian domains. Ivan IV (the Terrible) was the first ruler to proclaim himself czar and Fëdor I was the last ruler of the Rurik family. He was succeeded by B. Godunov, whose reign ended in the Time of Troubles and the rise of the Romanov dynasty.

Rush, Benjamin 1745?–1813. American physician and politician. He served in the Continental Congress (1776–77), signed the Declaration of Independence, was surgeon general of the Continental Army, and finally treasurer of the US mint.

Rush, Richard 1780–1859. American statesman and diplomat. He negotiated the Rush-Bagot Convention *(q.v.)* that demilitarized the Great Lakes and helped establish the 49th parallel as the border between the US and Canada. He also played a role in preliminary talks with the British that led to formulation of the Monroe Doctrine.

Rush-Bagot Convention Agreement signed between the acting US secretary of state R. Rush and the British minister Charles Bagot in 1817. It provided for virtual demilitarization of the US-Canadian border region (notably the Great Lakes) and was the basis of subsequent peaceful border relations between the US and Canada.

Ruskin, John 1819–1900. British art critic and social thinker, the dominant critic of the Victorian period. He promoted the Gothic Revival movement and later took up the cause of improving the condition of the working class. His critical works included *Modern Painters* and *The Stones of Venice.* Among his works on social reform were *Time and Tide* and *Fors Clavigera.*

Russell, Bertrand Arthur William, 3d earl Russell. 1872–1970. British philosopher, one of the most important of this century. He established a considerable reputation prior to WW I, particularly in the field of mathematical logic, with such works as *Principles of Mathematics* (1903) and *Principia Mathematica* (1910–13). From WW I on, however, he became increasingly involved in pacifism, social reform, and nuclear disarmament. Though his outspoken liberal views sometimes resulted in loss of teaching positions and even arrest, he actively pursued such causes until his last days.

Russell, Charles Taze *See* **Jehovah's Witnesses**

Russell, Francis, 2d earl of Bedford *c*1527–85. English courtier and politician. He had to flee the country as a result of his part in the affair of Lady Jane Grey, but returned to hold important posts under Queen Elizabeth I.

Russell, Francis, 4th earl of Bedford 1593–1641. English nobleman who developed the great London market known as Covent Garden.

Russell, Henry Norris 1877–1957. American astronomer. His diagrams showing the relationship between the brightness and spectral class of stars contributed to theories of the evolution of the universe.

Russell, John, 1st earl of Bedford 1486?–1555. English courtier and politician. One of Henry VIII's executors, he was also lord privy seal, and was created early in 1550.

Russell, John, 4th duke of Bedford 1710–71. English politician. An important opponent of Robert Walpole, he was a Whig leader and served in such posts as first lord of the admiralty, lord lieutenant of Ireland, and ambassador to France.

Russell, John, 1st earl Russell 1792–1878. British statesman and twice prime minister (1846–52, 1865–66). As a member of Parliament, he championed such liberal causes as the Catholic Emancipation Act, the Reform Bill of 1832 *(q.v.),* and the repeal of the Corn Laws.

Russell, Lord William 1639–83. English Whig political leader. As a member of Parliament, he opposed Charles II's pro-French policies. Unjustly accused of being involved in the Rye House Plot *(q.v.),* he was executed and later cleared.

Russell, William, 5th earl and 1st duke of Bedford 1613–1700. English nobleman and Civil War leader. He fought variously for both king and Parliament during the English Civil War.

Russia *See* **Union of Soviet Socialist Republics**

Russia, Orthodox Church of *See* **Orthodox Church of Russia**

Russia Company *See* **Muscovy Company**

Russian Civil War War (1918–22) between the Bolshevik Red Army and counterrevolutionary (White Army) forces, variously aided by the Germans, French, British, Japanese, and Americans. The Bolshevik takeover during the Russian Revolution *(q.v.)* coalesced opposition to the Communists (as the Bolsheviks called themselves since 1918) and a number of border territories proclaimed independence. The Red Army, led by L. Trotsky, fought variously in the Ukraine, the Baltic region, northern Russia (against British, French and American forces), the southern Caucasus region, and Siberia (against the Japanese, as well as White Russians). By 1922 most of the former Russian territories had been regained, and with the Communist government in firm control, the Union of Soviet Socialist Republics was proclaimed (Dec. 30). (*See also* Union of Soviet Socialist Republics [1917–22].)

Russian Revolution of 1905 Rebellion in Russia that led to the establishment of a constitutional monarchy and paved the way for the Russian Revolution of 1917. Czar Nicholas II's reign was marked by increased repression and protest against it, calls for reform by the zemstvos *(q.v.),* and widespread discontent over losses in the Russo-Japanese War *(q.v.).* The unrest finally culminated in Bloody Sunday *(q.v.)* in which soldiers fired on a peaceful protest (Jan. 1905). This incident galvanized opposition to the czarist regime and resulted in widespread strikes and uprisings. By October the revolt had reached a fever pitch and Nicholas was forced to issue the October Manifesto *(q.v.),* in which he acceded to rule by a constitution, promised creation of the Duma (a legislative body), and named Count S. Witte prime minister. Order was restored soon after, though the arrest of rebel leaders provoked some further protests.

Russian Revolution of 1917   Name applied to the political uprising in Russia in which the monarchy was overthrown and the Bolsheviks under N. Lenin came to power. The Revolution of 1917, was actually two revolutions: the February Revolution, which led to the overthrow of the czar and end of the Romanov dynasty; and the October Revolution, which brought the Bolsheviks (q.v.) to power in Russia. The revolution had far-reaching consequences. It brought into being the world's first Communist state and resulted in sweeping reform of Russian society. These reforms did not go unopposed, however, and it was not until 1922 that the Communists brought an end to the Russian Civil War (q.v.). (See also Union of Soviet Socialist Republics [1917–22].) Key dates in the history of the revolution include:

1906–11   Nicholas' prime minister Piotr Stolypin attempted unsuccessfully to introduce reforms, while at the same time suppressing the revolutionary movement; assassinated.

1914–18   WW I; severe hardship, failures of Russian government and military reversals contributed to revolutionary movement.

1915   Czar Nicholas took over command of Russian armies at the front (1915); left Czarina Alexandra (dominated by the unpopular Rasputin) in charge of the government; her mismanagement of government only caused further political unrest.

1916   Rasputin assassinated (Dec. 30) by angry noblemen; Rasputin's death failed to ease tensions.

1917   February Revolution (Mar. 8, Feb. 23 Old style); workers in Petrograd (new name of St. Petersburg) went on strike; outbreaks of rioting.

1917   Czar Nicholas attempted to dissolve the Duma (Mar. 11); his order ignored; soldiers in Petrograd joined the workers in the revolt (Mar. 12).

1917   Strikers organized Petrograd Workers' and Soldiers' Soviet (Mar. 12), which began to assume political power in the capital.

1917   Duma established Provisional Government, headed by Prince Georgi Lvov and including Alexander Kerensky; Nicholas abdicated in favor of regency of his brother, Grand Duke Michael (Mar. 15).

1917   Grand Duke Michael abdicated (Mar. 16); Romanov dynasty ended; struggle for power between Petrograd soviet and Provisional Government began.

1917   Provisional Government announced its intention to continue the war against Germany

(Mar. 19); Petrograd soviet gained support among workers and soldiers.

1917   Lenin returned to Russia (Apr.) in "sealed train" provided by Germans. His able supporter, L. Trotsky, arrived in the following month.

1917   Lenin outlined his April theses (Apr., 17) for Bolshevik-dominated government.

1917   Provisional Government foreign minister Pavel Milyukov forced to resign because of his war policies; Kerensky became minister of war (May 18).

1917   First all-Russian Congress of Soviets convened in Petrograd (June 16); delegates largely Mensheviks or Social Revolutionaries; Bolsheviks a minority despite growing support.

1917   Russians launched major military offensive (June 29); its failure (early July) led to growing Bolshevik strength and further weakening of Provisional Government.

1917   Massive demonstrations held in Petrograd (July 16–18); led to resignation of Prince Lvov (July 20); Kerensky became head of Provisional Government.

1917   Provisional Government instituted program of political repression against Bolsheviks and other revolutionary elements (July–Sept.); Lenin forced to flee to Finland.

1917   Gen. Lavr Kornilov led unsuccessful attempt to occupy Petrograd and seize power; arrested (Sept. 14).

1917   Lenin secretly returned to Petrograd (Oct., 20); called for armed insurrection against provisional government.

1917   Provisional government sent troops to close Bolshevik newspapers in Petrograd (Nov., 6), thus sparking revolt.

1917   October Revolution; Bolsheviks seized power in Petrograd (night of Nov. 6–7, Oct. 24–25 Old Style); second all-Russian Congress of Soviets convened (Nov. 7), Bolshevik delegates in majority; most Mensheviks and Social Revolutionaries withdrew; Trotsky announced dissolution of Provisional Government; Kerensky fled; Congress proclaimed Soviets as ruling government bodies throughout Russia; Council of People's Commissars, with Lenin as chairman, created to head government.

1917   Forces of local Soviets fought to take control in ensuing weeks, as Russian civil War began.

Russian Social Democratic Labor party   Russian Marxist political party founded (Mar., 1898) at Minsk by delegates from several revolutionary organizations. Its existence was nominal until its second party congress (1903) in Brussels and London, at which time it divided into two factions, the Bolsheviks *(q.v.)* and the Menshiviks *(q.v.)*.

Russo-Finnish War ⟨Winter War⟩ War between Russia and Finland (Nov., 1939–Mar., 1940). Following the outbreak of WW II, Russia began (Nov. 30, 1939) an undeclared war over demands for certain territorial concessions and demilitarization of Finland's defensive Mannerheim Line. While the Soviets bombed Helsinki and shelled Finnish ports, the Finns, under Field Marshal C. Mannerheim, successfully resisted Soviet attacks on the eastern frontier. In early February, however, superior Russian forces began to break Finnish defenses. Ultimately Finland was forced to sign a peace treaty (Mar. 12, 1940) granting Russia the concessions it sought.

Russo-Japanese War Brief war (1904–05) between Russia and Japan, an outgrowth of rivalry over control of Manchuria and Korea. After negotiations failed (largely because of Russian intransigence) to produce a settlement, Japan launched a surprise attack (Feb. 8, 1904) on the Russian stronghold of Port Arthur, defended by Russian Gen. A. Kuropatkin. The Japanese finally took Port Arthur (Jan. 2, 1905) and inflicted a decisive defeat at the Battle of Mukden (Mar. 10, 1905). The final blow came when Russia's Baltic fleet, attempting to relieve Russian forces in the East, was intercepted and destroyed at Tsushima (May 27, 1905) by a Japanese naval force under Adm. H. Togo. The Treaty of Portsmouth (Aug. 29, 1905) ended the war in a humiliating defeat for Russia. Russia conceded territories (including Port Arthur) to Japan, though it retained control of northern Manchuria. The war marked the emergence of Japan as a major power.

Russo-Polish War War between Russia and Poland (Apr. 25–Oct. 12, 1920) caused by Poland's attempt to seize the Russian Ukraine. Allied with Ukrainian nationalists, the Poles entered the Ukraine and occupied Kiev (May 7, 1920). The Russian counteroffensive began in June and by August the Russians had driven the Poles back to Warsaw. On the verge of total defeat, Poland was saved by the intervention of European powers. A military force under French Gen. M. Weygand aided the Poles and forced the Russians to retreat and finally agree to an armistice. The subsequent Treaty of Riga established the Russo-Polish border until WW II.

Russo-Swedish War War (1741–43) between Russia and Sweden, in which Russia emerged victorious after initial Swedish gains. The war was ended by the Treaty of Åbo *(q.v.)*, by which Sweden ceded territory in Finland to Russia.

Russo-Turkish Wars Wars fought by Russia and the Ottoman Empire (16th–19th cents.) that resulted in Russian conquest of Ottoman domains between the Black Sea and the Balkans. Concern over Russian expansionism and the general decline of the Ottoman Empire eventually brought direct involvement by other European powers in the 19th cent. (*See also* Eastern Question.) **1.** War (1676–81) fought by Czar Fëdor III of Russia against the Ottomans. He gained most of the Turkish Ukraine by the Treaty of Radzin (1681). **2.** War (1695–96) in which Czar Peter I conquered the Ottoman stronghold of Azov on the Black Sea. Though Peter's European allies made peace with the Ottomans in the Treaty of Karlowitz (1699), he continued hostilities until 1702. **3.** War (1710–11) between Peter and the Ottomans, a part of the Northern War (1700–21). Encouraged by France, the Ottomans attacked Russia (1710), defeated Peter's army at Pruth, and by the Treaty of Pruth (1711) regained Azov. **4.** War (1736–39) between the Russians (with their ally, Austria) and the Ottomans, in which the Russians recaptured Azov and overran Moldavia. The Austrians, however, concluded the Treaty of Belgrade (1739), in which Russia acquired only Azov and was forced to agree not to militarize the Black Sea. **5.** War (1768–74) declared by the Ottomans (under Mustafa III) on the Russians, under Catherine II. The Russians conquered Moldavia and Walachia and were victorious in the Crimea. The Treaty of Kuchuk Kainarji *(q.v.)* greatly increased Russian influence in the region and established Russia as the protector of Christians within Ottoman domains. **6.** War (1787–92) between the Russians under Catherine II (with Austria as ally, 1788–91) and the Ottomans. Following Russia's annexation of the Crimea (1783), tensions increased and finally resulted in war, in which Russia and Austria were generally successful. Austria was forced out of the war (1791) by pressure from Prussia. Russia eventually concluded the Treaty of Jassy (1792), by which it extended its boundary to the Dniestr River and gave up Moldavia and Bessarabia. **7.** War (1806–12) between Russia and the Ottomans under Selim III, caused by Selim's removal (1806) of Russian puppet rulers in Moldavia and Walachia. Russian victories in 1811–12 led to the Treaty of Bucharest (1812) and Russia's acquisition of Bessarabia. **8.** War (1828–29) between Russia and the Ottomans, an outgrowth of the Greek War of Independence (1821–30). The Russians were successful on the Asian front and penetrated deep into the Balkans (to Adrianople), but were unable to take Constantinople. By the Treaty of Adrianople *(q.v.)*, Russia won many concessions. **9.** War (1853–56) better known as the Crimean War *(q.v.)*. **10.** War (1877–78) between Russia and the Ottomans, resulting from the Bosnian Rebellion of 1875. Russia actively encouraged the rebels, and Ottoman attempts to suppress the revolt precipitated (1877) a Russian declaration of war (to protect Christians). The Russians decisively defeated the Ottomans, crossed into the Balkans and halted just outside Constantinople. The resulting Treaty of San Stefano gave Russia so much territory that European powers protested and forced Russia to accept modified terms, as set forth at the Congress of Berlin *(q.v.)*.

Ruth In the Bible, Moabite widow who later married Boaz and thereby became an ancestor of David.

Rutherford, Ernest Rutherford, 1st baron 1871–1937. New Zealand-born British physicist, noted for his important studies of radioactivity. He discovered the alpha and beta particles and developed the concept of an atom as a nucleus surrounded by orbiting electrons. He received the Nobel Prize in chemistry in 1908.

Ruthven, William, 4th lord of Ruthven and 1st earl of Gowrie 1541?–1584. Scottish nobleman. An opponent of Mary Queen of Scots, he led (1582) the "Raid of Ruthven," in which the boy king James VI of Scotland (later James I of Great Britain) was kidnapped. Ruthven, pardoned for that conspiracy, was executed after yet another plot.

Rutledge, Ann 1813?–35. Supposed object of A. Lincoln's great love. Lincoln's biographer, William Herndon, created the now discredited story of Lincoln's romance with the girl.

Rutledge, John 1739–1800. American political leader. A member of the Continental Congress and the Constitutional Convention, he was instrumental in drafting and ratifying the Constitution.

Rütli Oath ⟨Grütli ~⟩ Traditionally, an oath sworn by representatives of the Swiss cantons of Uri, Schwyz, and Untenwalden, to join in rebellion against Austria. It is regarded as symbolic of Swiss independence.

Ruysdael, Jacob van *See* **Ruisdael, Jacob van**

Ruyter, Michiel Adriaanszoon de 1607–76. Dutch admiral. He was a lifelong sailor, and his brilliant victories in the Dutch Wars enabled The Netherlands for a time to match British naval power.

Rwanda ⟨Ruanda⟩ East-central African republic. Its capital is Kigali. An agricultural society, Rwanda is the most densely populated nation in Africa. The minority Tutsi tribe dominated the Hutu majority, until the Hutu rebelled (1959), sending thousands of Tutsi into exile. Formed by the division of Ruanda-Urundi, Rwanda became independent in July 1, 1962.

Rye House Plot Failed plot (June 1683) by Whig extremists to assassinate Charles II of England and the duke of York (later James II). It was named for the house where the conspirators met and resulted in the execution of Whig leaders Lord William Russell and Algernon Sidney as suspected conspirators.

Rykov, Aleksey Ivanovich 1881–1938. Russian Bolshevik revolutionary leader. A Politburo member under N. Lenin, he was removed for opposing J. Stalin's collectivization program.

Ryle, Gilbert 1900–74. British philosopher. A leader of the school of rigorous linguistic analysis, he published his noted work, *The Analysis of Mind*, on the mind-body dualism.

Rymer, Thomas 1641–1713. English literary critic. In his *A Short View of Tragedy*, he advocated a return to classicism in drama and attacked such contemporary works as Shakespeare's *Othello*.

Ryswick, Treaty of Treaty (Sept. 27, 1697) between France and the alliance of Britain, The Netherlands, and Spain. It ended the War of the Grand Alliance. France retained Alsace but acknowledged William III as King of England, and the Dutch gained commerical concessions. Conquests in the colonies were restored and France returned captured territories in The Netherlands, Luxembourg, and Catalonia to Spain.

S

Saadi   *See* **Sadi**

Saar   *See* **Saar Territory**

Saarinen, Eero   1910–61. Finnish-born American architect, a pioneer of experimental architecture. His works include St. Louis' Gateway Arch, the Dulles Airport terminal in Washington, D.C., and the US Embassy in London.

Saarinen, Gottlieb Eliel   1873–1950.   Finnish-American architect. A leading practitioner of modern architecture as well as a teacher, he collaborated with his son E. Saarinen on several projects. His works include the music shed for the Berkshire Music Festival at Tanglewood, Massachusetts.

Saarland   *See* **Saar Territory**

Saar Territory   ⟨Saar⟩ German territory now known as the West German state Saarland. A highly industrialized, coal-producing region, it has at various times been ruled by France but became a permanent part of the Federal Republic of Germany in 1957.

Saba   *See* **Sheba**

Sabbatai Zevi   ⟨~ Z'vi⟩ 1626–76. Jewish mystic and sectarian leader. Having proclaimed himself the Messiah, he led an unsuccessful march on Constantinople (1666). Captured, he accepted Islam to save himself.

Sabbatai Z'vi   *See* **Sabbatai Zevi**

Sabbatarians ⟨Southcottians⟩ Christians who advocate strict observance of Sunday as the sabbath. Sabbatarians have frequently promoted blue laws to restrict Sunday activities.

Sabellianism   Christian heresy. Founded by the Roman theologian Sabellius (*fl.* AD *c*220), Sabellianism held that the three persons of the Trinity were not three distinct, independent persons but three manifestations of the one Godhead.

Sabellius   *See* **Sabellianism**

Sabine Crossroads, Battle of   *See* **Taylor, Richard**

Sabines   Ancient people who lived in the Sabine Hills near Rome. According to legend, the Romans, led by Romulus, captured their women and carried them off to provide wives for themselves. The Sabines were conquered by the Romans (290 BC) and became Roman citizens (268 BC).

Sacagawea   *See* **Sacajawea**

Sacajawea   ⟨Sacagawea⟩ ⟨Sakakawea⟩ 1787?–1812. American Indian woman who served as an interpreter on the Lewis and Clark expedition. A Shoshone, she was married to a French Canadian fur trapper hired by Lewis and Clark.

Sac and Fox Indians   ⟨Sauk Indians⟩ Related North American Algonquin Indian tribes. Inhabiting the Great Lakes area, the Sac and Fox tribes provoked the Black Hawk War (*q.v.*). After their defeat they were eventually pushed west across the Mississippi.

Sacco, Nicola   *See* **Sacco-Vanzetti case**

Sacco-Vanzetti case   American criminal trial. On Apr. 15, 1920, a factory paymaster and security guard were robbed and killed at South Braintree, Massachusetts. Two Italian immigrants, Nicola Sacco (1891–1927) and Bartolomeo Vanzetti (1888–1927), were arrested, tried, and convicted (July 14, 1921) of the crime. Critics of the trial pointed to lack of concrete evidence and charged there was prejudice against the defendants because of their ethnic origins and political belief in anarchism. Despite international protests and appeals, both men were executed (1927).

Sackville, Thomas, 1st earl of Dorset   1536–1608. British poet, dramatist, and diplomat in service to Queen Elizabeth I. He is remembered today as the author of the first English tragedy in blank verse, *Gorboduc*, written with Thomas Norton (1532–84).

Sacramento   American city (pop. 275,700), capital of California. First settled in 1839, it grew rapidly after the discovery of gold nearby in 1848 and became California's capital in 1854.

Sacred Band   *See* **Pelopidas**

Sacred War(s)   Wars fought by ancient Greek cities in the Amphictyonic League for protection of the Temple of Apollo at Delphi. **1.** First ~ (*c*596–*c*586 BC). Delphi was located within the territory of the Phocian city of Crisa, and when the city imposed a tax on pilgrims to Delphi, the

Amphictyonic League went to war. Crisa was defeated and destroyed and the league took over administration of Delphi. **2.** Second ~ (*c*448 BC). Fought by Athens against Sparta to restore control of Delphi to Phocis. **3.** Third ~ (355–346 BC). Phocis, fined by the Amphictyonic League for cultivating sacred grounds, seized Delphi and thereupon came under attack. Phocis, supported by Athens and Sparta, successfully resisted until Philip of Macedon joined forces (352) with the Amphicytonic League. Philip concluded the Peace of Philocrates with Athens (346), defeated Phocis, and became chairman of the league. **4.** Fourth ~ (339–338 BC). The league next began a war against Amphissa, which caused Athens to join Thebes against it. Philip of Macedon, leading forces of the league, crushed Athens and Thebes at the Battle of Chaeronea (338) and thereby gained control over Greece.

Sacrosancta *See* **Constance, Council of**

Sadat, Anwar al- 1918–81. Egyptian president (1970–81) and statesman, noted for securing the first Arab peace treaty with Israel. As an Egyptian army officer, Sadat was imprisoned (1942–44) during WW II for aiding the Germans against the British. He was imprisoned again after the war for acts of terrorism but was acquitted and returned to the military. In 1952 he aided his fellow officer and longtime friend G. Nasser in overthrowing King Farouk and served in several posts during Nasser's rule. Made vice-president (1969), he succeeded to the presidency on Nasser's death (1970). He ordered Russian military advisers to leave Egypt and launched the Arab-Israeli War of 1973 (*q.v.*) against Israel. After the war Sadat engaged in a search for a negotiated peace in the Mideast which led eventually to his historic trip to Jerusalem (Nov., 1977) to address the Israeli Knesset. Peace talks between Israel and Egypt, in which the US took part, led to the Israeli-Egyptian Peace Treaty (Mar., 1979). The Arab world vigorously opposed the treaty and instituted a virtual boycott of Egypt. Opposition within Egypt to Sadat's rule culminated in Sadat's assassination (Oct. 6, 1981) by a group of disaffected Muslim fundamentalists within the army.

Sadducees Ancient Jewish sect. Rivals of the Pharisees from *c*200 BC, they held to a strict interpretation of the Torah and centered their worship about the Temple. They disappeared as a group after the destruction of the Temple (AD 70).

Sade, Donatien Alphonse François, comte de 1740–1814. French erotic writer, also known as the marquis de Sade. He was several times confined for his cruel sexual perversions, about which

he wrote in his novels. The word "sadism" was derived from his name.

Sadi ⟨Saadi⟩ 1184–1291. Classical Persian poet. A mystical and lyric poet, he is known best for his poems *Bustan* (Orchard) and *Gulistan* (Rose Garden).

Sad Night, The *See* **Alvarado, Pedro de**

Sadowa, Battle of *See* **Koniggratz, Battle of**

Safavids Persian Muslim dynasty (1501–1736). It was founded by Ismail I, who conquered and subdued large areas of Persia, added several Iraqi territories, and proclaimed Shi'ite Islam as the state religion. Under the military leadership of Abbas I (ruled 1587–1629), the Safavids defeated Turkey, expanded Persia's territories, ended Portuguese encroachment, established trade with the West, and became an international power. The dynasty began a slow decline at the death of Abbas I and ended with the rule (1732–36) of Abbas III, who was overthrown by Nadir Shah.

Sagasta, Práxedes Mateo 1825–1903. Spanish statesman, several times prime minister. He granted autonomy to Cuba (1897) but was blamed for its loss in the Spanish-American War.

Sage, Margaret Olivia Slocum *See* **Sage, Russell**

Sage, Russell 1816–1906. American financier. He amassed an enormous fortune from his holdings in railroads in association with J. Gould. His widow, Margaret Olivia Slocum Sage (1828–1918), made extensive charitable contributions and established the Russell Sage Foundation.

Saigon Vietnamese city, capital of South Vietnam from 1954 until its conquest in 1975 by North Vietnam. Captured by the French (1859), it became a cosmopolitan city under their tutelage. It was the center of the US effort in the Vietnam War, was a center of fighting in the Tet Offensive (*q.v.*), and fell to the Communists at the end of the war (1975).

Saigo Takamori 1828–77. Japanese soldier and statesman. He supported the emperor in the Meiji Restoration but opposed the Westernization of Japan. He eventually led his samurai followers in the unsuccessful Satsuma Revolt (1877), in which he was killed.

saint For names of saints, see under individual names. For places, events, and biographical names beginning with **Saint** or **St.**, *see below.*

Saint Albans, battles of Battles of the English Wars of the Roses. The first (May 22, 1455), a Lancastrian defeat, resulted in the capture of King Henry VI by Richard, duke of York. The second (Feb. 17, 1461) was a Yorkist defeat, inflicted by Queen Margaret.

Saint Albans Raid Confederate attack from Canada (Oct. 19, 1864) on Saint Albans, Vermont, during the American Civil War. Some 25 Confederate raiders robbed three banks, killing one man, and escaped into Canada. Canada refused to return the raiders, but the money they stole was returned.

Saint Augustine City (pop. 12,000) in northeastern Florida, the oldest city in the US. Founded (1565) by P. Menendez de Aviles, it was Spain's northernmost outpost in the New World until Florida was ceded to the US (1821).

Saint Bartholomew's Day, Massacre of See **Massacre of Saint Bartholomew's Day**

St. Clair, Arthur 1734–1818.   Scottish-born American Revolutionary general and first governor of the Northwest Territory (1789–1802). He fought at Princeton and Trenton, and was exonerated from blame for the evacuation of Fort Ticonderoga (1778).

Saint Crispin, Knights of See **Knights of Saint Crispin**

Sainte-Beuve, Charles Augustin 1804–69. French literary critic and historian, considered the greatest literary critic of his day. The extent and quality of his work marked a milestone in French intellectual life.

Saint-Exupéry, Antoine de 1900–1944.   French airman and writer. A pioneer aviator, he celebrated flying in such books as *Night Flight* and *Wind, Sand and Stars*. His fable *The Little Prince* is widely read.

Saint-Gaudens, Augustus 1848–1907.   American sculptor. The leading sculptor of his time, he is noted especially for his statue of Adm. D. Farragut and the memorial in Washington's Rock Creek Cemetery to Mrs. H. Adams.

Saint George's Day Revolt ⟨Estonian Revolt of 1343⟩ Uprising (1343–45) of Estonian peasants against their Danish overlords. Many Danish and German nobles were killed before the Teutonic Knights quelled the rebellion. Denmark sold Estonia to the order (1346), and they in turn placed it under the rule of the Livonian Knights.

Saint-Germain, Treaty of 1. Treaty (1570) between the Huguenots and Catholics during the French Wars of Religion *(q.v.)*. It marked the end of the first phase of the conflict. **2.** Treaty (Sept. 10, 1919) between the Allies and Austria which abolished the Austro-Hungarian monarchy and created the new republic of Austria after WW I. The treaty limited Austria's armed forces and its ability to enter alliances.

St. John, Henry, Viscount Bolingbroke 1678–1751. British statesman. A brilliant Tory leader during the reign of Queen Anne, he was compelled to flee to France (1715) after her death and his implication in a Jacobite plot. Pardoned but banned from politics, he became an influential writer.

Saint John Damascene See **John of Damascus, Saint**

Saint-Just, Louis de 1767–94.   French revolutionary leader. He was an ardent and pitiless ally of M. Robespierre during the Reign of Terror and was eventually guillotined with him.

Saint Laurent, Louis Stephen 1882–1973. Canadian statesman and prime minister (1948–57).

St. Leger, Barry See **Oriskany, Battle of**

Saint Louis American city (pop. 453,100) on the Mississippi. Founded (1763) as a French trading post, it became the major gateway to the West during the 19th cent.

Saint Paul American city (pop. 270,200), capital of Minnesota. First settled in the early 1800s, it became the capital of Minnesota Territory (1849) and the state of Minnesota (1858). A major industrial, rail, and commercial center, it forms, with adjacent Minneapolis, the Twin Cities metropolitan center.

St. Petersburg See **Leningrad**

Saint Peter's church Roman Catholic basilica at the Vatican, Rome. The world's largest church, it was built to replace an earlier (4th-cent.) structure. Work began in 1506, and the church was dedicated in 1626. Many Renaissance artists worked on it, among them D. Bramante, Raphael, and Michelangelo. Beneath the altar is the tomb of Saint Peter.

Saint-Saens, Charles Camille 1835–1921. French composer. A piano and organ virtuoso, he composed symphonies, concerti, and tone poems, but is known best for his opera *Samson and Delilah.*

Saint-Simon, Claude Henri de Rouvro 1760–1825. French social thinker. A great-nephew of L. de Saint-Simon, he formulated an early version of scientific socialism, a precursor of positivism.

Saint-Simon, Louis de Rouvro 1675–1755. French courtier and memorist. An ardent aristocrat, his *Mémoires*, dealing with the court of King Louis XIV, are considered a major contribution to French literature.

Saionji, Kimmochi, Prince 1850–1940. Japanese statesman and prime minister (1906–08, 1911–12). He participated in the Meiji Restoration, traveled in the West, served in many government posts, and tried to moderate his country's turn toward militarism.

Saka Era See **Kaniska Era**

Sakakawea See **Sacajawea**

Saladin 1137?–1193. Muslim sultan and military leader, noted for his chivalry in battle against the Crusaders, founder of the Ayyubid dynasty. An ardent Sunni Muslim, he participated in wars against the Fatimids in Egypt (1164–68), became vizier in Egypt (1169), and formally ended Fatimid control in Egypt (1171). He subsequently extended his control over Damascus, and began to subdue local rulers throughout Syria and Palestine. Saladin then mounted a major campaign against the Latin Kingdom of Jerusalem (q.v.) ruled by the Crusaders. He won a signal victory at the Battle of Hattin (July 4, 1187) in Palestine and went on to take Jerusalem (Oct. 2, 1187), thus effectively ending the Latin Kingdom of Jerusalem. This prompted the unsuccessful Third Crusade (q.v.), after which Saladin permitted Christians access to Jerusalem. Christian domains in the Holy Land, however, were reduced to a small fraction of their former size.

Salamis, Battle of   Naval battle (480 BC) between the Greeks and the Persians during the Persian Wars (q.v.). It was fought in the straits between the island of Salamis and the Greek mainland. The Greeks under Themistocles won the battle, one of the most celebrated encounters of history. Themistocles lured the superior Persian navy (600 ships to over 360 Greek vessels) into the narrow straits, and thus made it impossible for the Persians to maneuver. The Greeks subsequently sank 200-300 Persian ships, losing only about 40.

Salazar, António de Oliveira   1889–1970. Dictator of Portugal (1932–68). As minister of finance (1926, 1928–32), Salazar initiated a number of economic recovery programs. Made premier (1932), he instituted a new constitution (1933) which turned Portugal into a corporate state and gave Salazar dictatorial powers. He also served as minister of war (1936–44) and minister of foreign affairs (1936–47). Although a number of Salazar's reform measures were successful, he was unable to substantially reduce poverty and illiteracy in Portugal. He is credited with making the country financially stable.

Salbai, Treaty of   Treaty (May, 1782) between the British East India Company and the Marathas ending the first of the Maratha Wars. By its terms, similar to those of the earlier Treaty of Purandhar (q.v.), the British withdrew support of the Maratha pretender Ragoba but retained Salsette island.

Salem witch trials   Series of witch trials (May–Oct., 1692) in Salem, Massachusetts. The trials were prompted by three young girls who, having heard tales of voodoo, claimed to be possessed by the devil. Their accusations led to hysteria and further accusations. By the time calm had been restored, 19 persons had been executed for witchcraft.

Sales, Saint Francis of   *See* **Francis of Sales, Saint**

Salian dynasty   Line of German emperors that ruled the Holy Roman Empire from 1024 to 1125. During its tenure, the investiture controversy (q.v.) with the papacy broke out. Its members included:

Conrad II	1024–39
Henry III	1039–56
Henry IV	1056–1106
Henry V	1106–25

Salic law   Rule of succession in some European royal houses forbidding females to succeed to family titles. Supposedly dating to Frankish times, it was invoked by the French, English, and Spanish monarchies.

Salinger, Jerome David   1919–. American writer, known best for his novel *The Catcher in the Rye.*

Salisbury, John of   *See* **John of Salisbury**

Salisbury, Robert Arthur Talbot Gascoyne-Cecil, 3d marquess of   1830–1903. British statesman and prime minister (1885–86, 1886–92, 1895–1902) noted for his advancement of British imperial interests in foreign affairs. Salisbury acted as his own foreign secretary. The Boer War (q.v.) was fought during his third ministry.

Salisbury, Robert Cecil, 1st earl of   1563?–1612. English statesman. He succeeded his father, Lord Burghley, as the principal adviser to Queen Elizabeth I, and negotiated the agreement that allowed the Scottish king to succeed peacefully to the British throne as James I. Cecil also served as James's principal minister.

Sallust ⟨Crispus, Gaius Sallustius⟩ 86–c34 BC. Roman historian. He was expelled from the Senate (50 BC) for immorality and for his support of J. Caesar, and, as governor of Numidia, was accused of extortion. Among his best-known histories is the *Catilina*, concerning the conspiracy of Catiline.

Salome   Stepdaughter of Herod Antipas (d. after AD 40), who was tetrarch of Galilee and Perea. As a reward for dancing before Herod, she demanded the beheading of John the Baptist (q.v.).

Salomon, Haym   1740–1785. American Revolutionary financier and founder of the first Philadelphia synagogue. The principal financial backer of the fledgling American republic, he was impoverished by his loans to the government and to prominent individuals.

Salonica Campaign   WW I Allied military expedition (1915–18), originally intended to aid Serbia, then under attack by Bulgaria. The Allied force of some 40,000 tried (Oct., 1915) to link up with the Serbians but was forced to retreat to Salonica in northeastern Greece. With Salonica as their base, the Allies increased forces there to some 250,000 and launched inconclusive attacks against Bulgarian and German forces. In 1917, the Allies forced the pro-German Greek king, Constantine I, to abdicate. The final Allied offensive from Salonica (from Sept., 1918) resulted in Bulgaria's surrender (Sept. 30), liberation of Serbia (Nov. 1), defeat of the Central Powers in Albania and Montenegro (by Nov. 9), and capture of Romania (Nov. 10). The armistice halted further military action.

Salt Lake City American city (pop. 163,000), capital of Utah. Founded (1847) on Great Salt Lake by B. Young, it is the world center of the church of Jesus Christ of Latter Day Saints (*see* Mormons).

Salvation Army Christian and philanthropic organization founded (1878) in England by W. Booth. Organized with military ranks and uniforms, it emphasizes street-corner evangelism and seeks to help satisfy the spiritual and material needs of the poor.

Salzburg Austrian city (pop. 130,000) noted for its Renaissance architecture and as a center of music and the performing arts. Originally a Celtic settlement, it became an archbishopric (c798) and its archbishops became (13th cent.) powerful princes of the Holy Roman Empire. W. Mozart was born in Salzburg.

Samanids Persian dynasty that ruled (c819–999) after the Arab Muslim conquest of Iran. The dynasty greatly advanced Persian literature, art, and architecture.

Samaritans Ancient Semitic people settled in Samaria, in the former kingdom of Israel, after its conquest by Assyria (c721 BC). Although they adopted Judaism and the Torah, they were shunned by the Jews returning to Judah after their Babylonian exile.

Samarkand One of the world's oldest cities, now in Uzbekistan, south central USSR. Taken by Alexander the Great (329 BC), it was destroyed (AD 1220) by G. Khan, but recovered and became (1370) capital of the empire of Tamerlane. Samarkand came under Soviet control in 1925.

Samnite War(s) Wars between the Romans and the Samnites, tribes of the mountain region of central and southern Italy. The Romans were ultimately victorious and thereby gained control of central and southern Italy. **1.** First ~ (343–341 BC) proved indecisive. **2.** Second ~ (326–304 BC). The Romans, defeated at the Battle of Caudine Forks (321), lost control of Campania (in southern Italy) and in 308, Rome was attacked by various tribes of central Italy. Rome succeeded in gaining the initiative, finally defeated the Samnites, and won firm control of Campania. **3.** Third ~ (298–290 BC). The Samnites united with other tribes (including the Etruscans and Gauls) against the

Romans. Defeated by the Romans at the Battle of Sentinum (295), the tribes were all eventually forced to accept peace.

Samos Greek island near Asia Minor. Colonized (11th cent. BC) by the Ionian Greeks, it became a commercial cultural center. Pythagoras came from Samos. Under various rulers for a millennium, it reverted to Greece in 1913.

Samos, Aristarchus of *See* **Aristarchus of Samos**

Samosata, Paul of *See* **Paul of Samosata**

Samothrace (Samothraki) Greek island in the Aegean, site of the famous statue *Victory (Nike) of Samothrace*, which was found there in 1863. Samothrace had mainly religious importance in antiquity. It has been part of Greece since 1913.

Samothraki *See* **Samothrace**

Sampson, William Thomas *See* **Santiago, Battle of**

Samson Judge of ancient Israel. Tricked by Delilah into revealing his hair was the source of his strength, he was blinded and enslaved when she managed to cut off his hair. He pulled down the Philistine temple when his hair grew back and his strength returned.

Samsonov, Alexander *See* **Tannenburg, Battles of**

Samudra Gupta *d.* AD c380. Indian emperor (AD c330–c380) of the Gupta dynasty, successor to his father, Chandragupta I. He expanded Gupta control over much of northern India. A poet and musician as well as warrior and conqueror, he was considered a model of the ideal Hindu ruler.

Samuel Last of the judges of ancient Israel and first of the prophets after Moses. A legendary Israelite hero, he established the Hebrew monarchy, anointing first Saul and then David.

samurai Japanese warrior class. The samurai rose in the 12th cent. during Japan's feudal period and played a major role in Japanese life. As highly skilled warriors, they were instrumental in establishing the shoguns as real rulers in Japan (12th cent.) and provided the basis for the shoguns' power in subsequent centuries. During the long, peaceful reign of the Tokugawa shoguns (17th–19th cents.), the samurai gradually moved into bureaucratic posts. After the Meiji Restoration (1868), the class was abolished with feudalism, and discontented samurai led several unsuccessful revolts, notably the Satsuma Revolt.

Sancho III ⟨Sancho the Great⟩ c970–1035. King of Navarre (1000–35). He ultimately ruled a unified Spanish state that included Castile, León, Navarre, and Aragon. By his will the kingdom was divided at his death among his four sons.

Sancho the Great *See* **Sancho III**

Sand, George ⟨Dupin, Barrone Dudevant, Amandine Aurore Lucie⟩ 1804–76. French writer. She wrote some 80 novels celebrating women's freedom and the joys of country life and was notorious for her liaisons with famous men of the day.

Sandburg, Carl 1878–1967. American author whose works are noted for their celebration of America and its people. He gained fame with the poem *Chicago*. His six-volume biography of Abraham Lincoln was awarded a Pulitzer Prize in history in 1940. Among his other volumes of poetry are *Smoke and Steel* and *Good Morning, America.* Sandburg's *Complete Poems* received a Pulitzer Prize in poetry in 1951.

Sand Creek Massacre ⟨Chivington Massacre⟩ Massacre of Cheyenne Indians (Nov. 29, 1864) peacefully encamped on the Sand Creek near Fort Lyon, in Colorado. Some 1,000 raiders led by Col. John Chivington ignored the white flag raised by Cheyenne chief Black Kettle and murdered hundreds. The massacre led to fierce conflict with the Plains Indians in the following years.

Sandwich, Edward Montagu, 1st earl of 1625–72. English admiral. He supported Parliament in the English Civil War but escorted King Charles II from Holland back to England at the Restoration. Ennobled by Charles, he later died in battle against the Dutch.

Sandwich, John Montagu, 4th earl of 1718–92. British politician and three-time British lord of the admiralty (1748, 1763, 1771–82). The Sandwich Islands and the sandwich were named after him. He is said to have devised the latter to eat without having to leave the gaming table.

Sandys, Sir Edwin 1561–1629. English Parliamentarian and colonizer. A prominent opponent of absolute monarchy, he advanced constitutional ideas that later contributed to the overthrow of King Charles I. He was a member of both the Virginia Company and the British East India Company.

San Francisco American city (pop. 679,000) on the California coast, one of the leading cities of the US. Founded (1776) as a mission and presidio by the Spanish, it was known as Yerba Buena until after its capture (1846) by the US in the Mexican War. San Francisco grew with the discovery (1848) of gold in California, and a period of lawlessness followed the influx of gold seekers and adventurers. It became the terminus for the first transcontinental railroad (1869) and continued to grow. The earthquake of Apr. 18, 1906, and subsequent fire virtually destroyed the city, but a massive rebuilding effort soon restored it. San Francisco's Golden Gate Bridge was completed in 1937. The UN Charter was drafted here (1945) at the San Francisco Conference *(q.v.).*

San Francisco Conference International conference of 50 nations convened in San Francisco (Apr. 25, 1945) to establish a new international organization following WW II. The conference concluded with the signing of the United Nations Charter (June 26, 1945).

Sanhedrin Ancient Jewish council of elders in Jerusalem which functioned up to the destruction of the Temple (AD 70). According to the Mishna, it had academic functions, but according to the Gospels and Flavius Josephus, it also possessed judicial functions, as in the trial of Jesus.

San Ildefonso, Treaty of **1.** Treaty (1796) between France and Spain concluded at San Ildefonso, Spain. By its terms the two countries became formally allied against Britain in the French Revolutionary Wars. **2.** Secret treaty concluded (1800) between Spain and Napoleon I, confirmed by later treaties of 1801 and 1802. By its terms Spain retroceded Louisiana to France in return for the newly created kingdom of Etruria in Italy. Napoleon subsequently sold Louisiana to the US against the express terms of this treaty.

San Jacinto, Battle of Battle (Apr. 21, 1836) of the Texas war for independence, fought at the San Jacinto River near present-day Houston. Some 800 Texans under S. Houston defeated 1,500 Mexicans under Gen. A. de Santa Anna, thereby ensuring Texas' independence.

San Juan Capital city (pop. 535,000) and main port of Puerto Rico. First settled (1508) by Ponce de León, it was a center of Spanish exploration and colonization and became a leading port in the 18th and 19th cents. It was occupied by US troops (1898) during the Spanish-American War.

San Juan Boundary Dispute Dispute between the US and Great Britain over the northwest boundary between the US and British Columbia. Because of the vague wording of the Oregon Treaty of 1846, both Britain and the US claimed the San Juan Islands in the Gulf of Georgia, southeast of Vancouver. Armed conflict (1859) was avoided when both nations decided on joint occupation. By the Treaty of Washington (1871), German emperor Wilhelm I was chosen as arbitrator and awarded the lands to the US (1872).

San Juan Hill, Battle of US victory over the Spanish (July 1, 1898) at San Juan Hill, in Cuba, during the Spanish-American War. Part of the larger Battle of Santiago *(q.v.),* it is celebrated for the part played in it by T. Roosevelt and the Rough Riders *(qq.v.).*

San Marino ⟨Most Serene Republic of~⟩ Independent republic located in central Italy. Founded in the 4th cent., it is claimed to be the oldest republic in Europe and is the smallest in the world. Its independence was recognized (1631) by the pope, and it secured a treaty of friendship with Italy in 1862.

San Martín, José de 1778–1850. South American revolutionary leader. He played a major part in the liberation of Argentina, Peru, and Chile from Spanish rule. He led an army across the Andes to defeat the Spanish in Chile (1817) and deferred to S. Bolívar (1822), who then became the leader of the South American independence movement.

Sannazaro, Jacopo 1458–1530. Italian poet and humanist. He served as court poet in Naples and is known best for his idyll in prose and verse *Arcadia*.

San Remo, Conference of *See* **Conference of San Remo**

San Salvador Largest city (pop. 400,000) and capital of El Salvador. Established in 1528, it became the Salvadoran capital in 1841. It was heavily damaged by earthquakes in 1854 and 1873.

sans-culotte French term meaning "without knee breeches," applied to the more radical supporters of the French Revolution, especially the lower classes. It derived from the long trousers adopted by the lower classes to replace knee breeches, considered aristocratic. (*See also* Hébert, Jacques René.)

Sanskrit Sacred language of the Hindu religion. Long used by Indian religious scholars and the upper caste, it developed from the earlier Verdic language. Though technically a dead language, it continues to be used in the scholarly and literary fields. The study of Sanskrit in the 18th cent. led to important archaeological discoveries and also to the development of philology as a science.

San Stefano, Treaty of Treaty (Mar. 3, 1878) between Russia and the Ottoman Turks ending the Russo-Turkish War of 1877–78. The defeated Turks agreed to pay a large indemnity; to recognize the independence of Romania, Serbia, and Montenegro; to create an autonomous Bulgaria; and to cede large areas to Russia. This treaty was subsequently altered by the Congress of Berlin (1878).

Santa Anna, Antonio López de 1794–1876. Mexican general and statesman. He fought with A. de Iturbide in securing Mexican independence (1821) but helped to overthrow Iturbide in 1823. He followed a policy of supporting, then helping to overthrow, subsequent leaders. His victory over the Spanish at Tampico (Sept., 1829) gave him the title "Hero of Tampico" and helped him gain the presidency (1833). His ruthless treatment of Texans at the Alamo and Goliad aided the Texan independence movement and contributed to Santa

Anna's defeat by S. Houston at San Jacinto *(q.v.)* and the loss of Texas. Forced from office (1836), Santa Anna returned to power (1839–44, 1846–47) but was again removed from office after his defeats in the Mexican War *(q.v.)*. He returned to power once more in 1853 but was exiled two years later.

Santa Fe American city (pop. 48,900), capital of New Mexico. Founded (1609) by the Spanish, it was a center of trade with Mexico and the terminus of the Santa Fe Trail. It became the territorial capital in 1851.

Santa Fe Trail Wagon route, some 780 miles long, from Independence, Missouri, to Santa Fe, New Mexico. The trail was a major path of westward migration from the 1820s to 1880, when Santa Fe was connected with the transcontinental rail network.

Santander, Francisco de Paula 1792–1840. Colombian revolutionist and statesman. Associated with S. Bolívar, he governed Great Colombia as vice-president during Bolívar's absences from 1821 to 1828. After Bolívar's death, he was president of New Granada (1833–37).

Santa Sophia *See* **Hagia, Sophia**

Santayana, George 1863–1952. Spanish-born American philosopher and writer, known best for his four-volume work *The Life of Reason.*

Santiago Capital (pop 3,449,000) and leading city of Chile. Founded (1541) by P. de Valdivia, it was leveled by an earthquake (1647) but grew into one of South America's largest cities (late 19th cent.).

Santiago, Battle of Battle (July 1–3, 1898) of the Spanish-American War, at Santiago de Cuba. In May, 1898, a Spanish fleet under Admiral Pascual Cervera y Topete (1839–1909) was blockaded in the harbor of Santiago de Cuba by a US fleet under Admiral William Thomas Sampson (1840–1902). On July 1, US ground forces attacked the city's defenses, notably in the Battle of San Juan Hill *(q.v.)*. On July 3, the Spanish fleet attempted to leave the harbor. In Sampson's absence, Commodore W. Schley engaged and destroyed the Spanish squadron, suffering one American dead to Spanish losses of some 600. Santiago de Cuba formally surrendered on July 17. Later a controversy arose as to which US commander achieved the American victory—Schley, who opened the naval engagement, or Sampson, commander of the operation.

Santo Domingo Capital (pop. 673,500) and largest seaport of the Dominican Republic. The oldest continuous settlement in the Western Hemisphere, it was founded (1496) by Bartholomew Columbus (1445?–1514?) and was the seat of Spain's colonial offices in the Americas. Almost destroyed by a hurricane (1930), it was named Ciudad Trujillo, after R. Trujillo, from 1936 to 1961.

Santo Domingo　Former name for the Dominican Republic (q.v.).

Sapir, Edward　1884–1939. Polish-born American linguist and anthropologist. He made major contributions to the study and classification of North American Indian languages.

Sapor I　*See* **Shapur I**

Sapor II　*See* **Shapur II**

Sappho　*fl.* early 6th cent. BC. Ancient Greek lyric poetess of Lesbos. Her lyrics were considered masterly by the ancients, but only a few, mostly fragments, have survived.

Sara　*See* **Sarah**

Saracens　Name applied in the Middle Ages to the Muslim enemies of Christendom. Originally referring to northern Arabian raiders, it eventually was applied to all Muslims, whether Arabs, Moors, or Turks.

Saracoglu, Sukru　1887–1953. Turkish statesman and premier (1942–46). An associate of K. Atatürk in the modernization of Turkey, he served as premier and managed to keep Turkey uninvolved in WW II.

Sarah　⟨Sara⟩ Old Testament matriarch, wife of Abraham and mother of Isaac. Originally childless, she is represented in the Book of Genesis as conceiving in her old age by a special divine favor. Her original name was Sarai.

Saratoga, First Battle of　*See* **Freeman's Farm, Battle of**

Saratoga campaign　American military campaign (Sept.–Oct., 1777) during the American Revolution, near Saratoga, New York. The campaign is considered the turning point of the war. On Sept. 19, 1777, some 6,000 British troops under Gen. J. Burgoyne failed to break through the American defense lines of H. Gates, D. Morgan, and B. Arnold in the Battle of Freeman's Farm (q.v.). This was followed by a decisive American victory over the British (Oct. 7) in the Battle of Bemis Heights. The Americans subsequently surrounded the British and forced Burgoyne's surrender (Oct. 17). This first major American victory heartened the discouraged patriots, encouraged France to aid the American war effort, and ended British plans to isolate the northern colonies from the rest of America.

Sarbinowo, Battle of　⟨Battle of Zorndorf⟩ Prussian victory over Russia (Aug. 25, 1758) in the Seven Years' War. Prussian king Frederick II defeated an invading Russian army and prevented its advance into Brandenburg.

Sardanapalus　Assyrian king identified by some, probably mistakenly, with Ashurbanipal. Sardan-

apalus burned his palace, killing himself and his court, when it appeared Nineveh would be taken.

Sardinia, kingdom of　European kingdom formed (1720) for Duke Victor Amadeus II of Savoy after Sicily passed to Austrian control. The kingdom included Sardinia, Savoy, Piedmont, and Nice, and in the 18th and 19th cents. it grew to include other territories. It became the center of the movement to unify Italy in the 19th cent. and was given control of territories conquered by Garibaldi (q.v.) in 1860. In 1861, Sardinian king Victor Emmanuel II became king of Italy, and the house of Savoy became the ruling house of Italy.

Sardis　Ancient city located near modern Izmir, Turkey. As capital of Lydia, it was the political center of the area and the western terminus for the Persian royal road. It fell to the Ionian Greeks (499 BC) and to the Romans (133 BC), and was finally destroyed by Tamerlane (1402).

Sardou, Victorien　1831–1908. French playwright. Immensely popular in his day, he wrote some 70 plays for famous actors and actresses of the time. For S. Bernhardt he wrote the play *La Tosca*, which formed the basis for the opera by G. Puccini.

Sargent, John Singer　1856–1925. American painter. Most of his work was done in London, where he became the most fashionable portrait painter of the day. He also was noted for his murals and landscapes.

Sargon　d. 705 BC. Ancient Assyrian king (721–705), successor to Tiglath-pileser III. He was also known as Sargon II. He consolidated the Assyrian Empire, defeating and resettling conquered weaker peoples. He conquered Babylon and Samaria and destroyed the northern kingdom of Israel (c721 BC).

Sargon　⟨Sharrukin⟩ *fl.* c2800? BC. Ancient Mesopotamian ruler. From Akkad, he defeated Sumer and established the first great Semitic empire. His empire of Akkad (q.v.) included the area later ruled by Babylonia.

Sarmatia　Ancient territory between the Vistula and the Caspian Sea inhabited (3d cent. BC–3d cent. AD) by the Sarmatians. An ancient Indo-Iranian nomadic people related to the Scythians, they invaded Roman territory and subdued many neighboring tribes. Eventually they were defeated and disappeared.

Sarmiento, Domingo Faustino　1811–88. Argentine educator, writer, and first civilian president of Argentina (1868–74). He became known as a writer and educator in exile until the overthrow of J. de Rosas. His presidency was marked by an expansion of democracy and education.

Sarmiento, Félix Rubén García　*See* **Darío, Rubén**

Sarnoff, David 1891–1971. Russian-born American pioneer in the development of commercial radio and television. Beginning as a wireless telegraph operator, he became famous for his reception of wireless signals from the stricken liner *Titanic* (1912). He later was instrumental in forming both the Radio Corporation of America (RCA) and the National Broadcasting Company (NBC).

Saroyan, William 1908–1981. American writer, noted for his fresh, original novels, plays, and stories celebrating life in America. His play *The Time of Your Life* was awarded the Pulitzer Prize for Drama in 1940, but Saroyan declined the honor.

Sarpi, Paolo ⟨Polano, Pietro Soave⟩ 1552–1623. Venetian theologian and historian. In a dispute between Venice and Pope Paul V over papal jurisdiction, he defended the right of the state to ecclesiastical control. He wrote a history of the Council of Trent, attacking it as an exercise of papal absolutism.

Sarto, Andrea del 1486–1530. Florentine painter during the Renaissance. Noted for his craftmanship, he influenced Florentine painting during the High Renaissance. He painted chiefly religious subjects, including "Madonna in Glory" and "Madonna of the Harpies."

Sarto, Giuseppe   *See* **Pius X**

Sartre, Jean Paul 1905–1980. French philosopher and writer. A major exponent of existentialism, he believed that man is "condemned" to freedom and must rely on his own sense of values and will in life.

Sasbach and Altenheim, Battles of Engagements in the Second Dutch War, fought near the Rhine at Sasbach (July 27, 1675) and Altenheim (Aug. 1, 1675). A French army of some 22,000 initially forced a 20,000-man Austrian force into an untenable position at Sasbach, but the French commander, Marshal H. Turenne, was killed. The Austrians subsequently forced the French to retreat, defeated them at Altenheim (Aug. 1), and forced them to withdraw across the Rhine.

Saskatchewan Province of western Canada (pop. 975,700). Members of the Hudson's Bay Company first explored (1690) then settled the area (1774) and controlled it until 1869, when it became part of Canada's Northwest Territories. Extension of the railroad (1882) into Saskatchewan brought more settlers, and the last Indian rebellion was put down in 1885. Saskatchewan became a province in 1905.

Sassanians   *See* **Sassanidae**

Sassanidae ⟨Sassanids⟩ ⟨Sassanians⟩ Last ancient Persian dynasty to rule before the Arab conquest of Persia (651). The dynasty was founded (AD 226) by Ardashir I. The Sassanidae promoted a revival of native Persian arts and letters and made Zoroastrianism the state religion. The last Sassanidae ruler died in exile in 651.

Sassanids   *See* **Sassanidae**

Satan In Judaeo-Christian teachings, the supernatural figure identified with evil, also known as the devil. Satan originally appeared in Hebrew religion as one of God's angels, and only gradually became a figure of evil, in opposition to God.

Satie, Erik 1866–1925. French composer and leader of the avant-garde. His spare, satirical musical style, a reaction to romanticism, had considerable influence on the development of 20th-cent. music.

Sato, Eisaku 1901–75. Japanese prime minister (1964–72). He held important government posts during Japan's post-war period. As prime minister, he signed a treaty with the US reestablishing Japan's control over Okinawa. He was awarded the Nobel Peace Prize in 1974.

satrap Name given provincial governors of the ancient Persian Empire. In general, a satrap administered the province, collected taxes, and was the supreme judge.

Satsuma Revolt   *See* **Saigo Takamori**

Saturn Ancient Roman god of agriculture, identified with the Greek Cronus. His week-long festival, the Saturnalia, included revelry, temporary equality between slave and citizen, and the exchange of gifts.

satyr Mythological Greek woodland creature usually represented as half man and half goat. Satyrs were boisterous, lusty creatures associated with the cult of Dionysus.

Saud 1902–69. Saudi Arabian king (1953–64), successor to his father, Ibn Saud. Forced to yield some of his powers to an executive council headed by his brother Faisal (1958), he was deposed by Faisal (1964) and died in exile.

Saudi Arabia ⟨Kingdom of Saudi Arabia⟩ Muslim monarchy occupying most of the Arabian peninsula in the Middle East. Its capital is Riyadh. The Muslim holy cities of Mecca and Medina are located in Saudia Arabia, birthplace of Islam. Saudi Arabia is today one of the world's largest oil-producing nations. (*For early history of the region, see* Caliphate, Empire of,) Key dates in Saudi history include:

FROM 16TH CENT. Region under nominal rule of Ottoman Empire.

18TH CENT. Arabia divided into separate principalities.

18TH CENT. Wahabi movement, supported by Saud family and Bedouin tribes, unsuccessfully attempted to unite Arabia.

1811–18 Wahabi movement crushed by Egypt.

1891 Rashid dynasty defeated Wahabi movement.

FROM 1902 Ibn Saud revived the Wahabi movement; seized city of Riyadh; began expanding domains in Arabian peninsula.

1932 Kingdom of Saudi Arabia formed from Ibn Saud's conquests in Nejd and Hejaz.

1932–53 Ibn Saud reigned as king of Saudi Arabia.

1936 Oil discovered.

1938 Large-scale oil exploration began; using revenues, Ibn Saud made massive internal improvements.

1945 Saudis joined UN and Arab League.

1951 New royalty agreement with Aramco, Saudi oil consortium; Saudis receive 50% of net earnings.

1953–64 King Saud reigned, following death of Ibn Saud.

1960 Saudi Arabia became founding member of OPEC; later became leading force in the oil cartel.

1964–75 King Faisal reigned after deposing his brother, Faisal.

1974 Saudis, demanding participation in Aramco, got 60% ownership of company.

1975 Faisal assassinated by nephew (Mar. 25).

1975–82 King Khalid, brother of Faisal, reigned.

1979 Muslim extremists seized the sacred Grand Mosque in Mecca; held it against government troops (Nov. 20–Dec. 4).

1980 Saudi takeover of Aramco completed.

1981 US announced sale of Advance Warning and Command Systems (AWAC) planes to Saudi Arabia; deal linked to Saudi agreement to maintain levels of oil production.

1982 Fahd Bin Abdul-Aziz became king after Khalid died (June 13, 1982).

Sauk Indians *See* **Sac and Fox Indians**

Saul First king (11th cent.?) of the ancient Israelites. In the Bible, he was noted for his prowess in battle and for his jealousy of his successor, David, whom he tried to destroy. He committed suicide to escape capture by the Philistines.

Saussure, Ferdinand de 1857–1913. Swiss Sanskrit scholar and linguistic pioneer. His *Course in General Linguistics* is considered one of the foundations of modern linguistics.

Savelli, Cencio *See* **Honorius III**

Savigny, Friedrich Karl von 1779–1861. German jurist and legal historian. He produced monumental studies of Roman and medieval law and influenced the study of legal history.

Savonarola, Girolamo 1452–98. Italian Dominican religious reformer. He enthralled Florence with his sermons, noted for their moral rigor. He challenged papal authority and later was repudiated and executed by the Florentines.

Savoy, house of European royal dynasty. Founded in the 11th cent. by Humbert I, the White-Handed, it first dominated the French-Swiss-Italian Alpine region, then spread to Piedmont. Made a ducal family of the Holy Roman Empire (1416), it eventually came to rule vast areas of France, Switzerland, and Italy. After receiving the kingdom of Sardinia (1720), their support of Italian unification led to the creation (1861) of the kingdom of Italy, with the house of Savoy as its royal family. The house of Savoy remained the ruling house of Italy until 1946, when a republic was established.

Savoy, Louise of *See* **Louise of Savoy**

Savoy, Prince Eugene of *See* **Eugene of Savoy, Prince**

Savoy Conference English ecclesiastical conference (1661) held at the Savoy Palace in London after the Restoration. Twelve Bishops of the Church of England and twelve Presbyterians failed to reach agreement on worship and a revision of the Book of Common Prayer.

Saxe, Maurice, comte de 1696–1750. French general and marshal of France. An illegitimate son of the elector of Saxony, he rose to supreme command in the War of the Austrian Succession. He led the French victory at Fontenoy (1745).

Saxe-Weimar Former duchy in Thuringia, central Germany. United with Eisenach (1741) to form Saxe-Weimar-Eisenach, it became notable under Duke Charles Augustus for its prosperity and its position as a center of the arts. Its capital, Weimar, became an intellectual capital of Europe.

Saxo Grammaticus *fl.* 1188–1201. Danish medieval chronicler. He wrote a history of early Denmark, *Gesta Danorum*, partly legendary, partly factual. Surviving parts of it inspired W. Shakespeare's *Hamlet* as well as the work of Danish romantic poets.

Saxons Germanic peoples believed to have originated in the area of the Baltic coast that is now Schleswig and the Elbe Valley. First mentioned by Ptolemy (2d cent. AD), their influence grew as the Roman Empire declined. The Saxons conducted numerous raids of piracy along the coasts of northern Germany, Gaul, and Britain, and, with the Angles, many Saxons settled in Britain (5th cent., *see* Anglo-Saxons). On the continent, their constant warfare against the Franks ended with their defeat (9th cent.) and their forced conversion to Christianity by Charlemagne.

Saxony Historic region of northwest Germany once occupied by the Saxons, a Germanic tribe. The Saxons were in firm control of the region by the 5th–6th cent., and in the 5th cent. many of them migrated to Britain. Saxony was conquered by Charlemagne (8th cent.) and incorporated into Frankish domains. It became part of the East Frankish (German) kingdom after 843. Saxony soon became the most powerful of the duchies that emerged during the breakup of the East Frankish kingdom. In 962 the Holy Roman Empire was formed under the leadership of the Saxon duke, Otto (Holy Roman Emperor Otto I).

Saxony, duchy of Medieval German duchy, now located in East Germany, founded by the early 10th cent. Duke Henry I of Saxony was elected German emperor (919), and his line ruled the Holy Roman Empire until 1024. In 1180, Saxony was seized from Henry the Lion by Frederick Barbarossa and was divided. The ducal title passed to one of the fiefs thus created, and its holder became an elector of the Holy Roman Empire (13th cent.).

Saxony, Electoral Historic territory established, along with the title "elector" (13th cent.) after the division (1180) of the duchy of Saxony. Electoral Saxony took part in the Thirty Years' War, first supporting and then opposing the Holy Roman Empire. At the war's end, Saxony emerged as one of the strongest duchies in Germany. In 1697, elector Augustus II became king of Poland. His death led to the War of the Polish Succession (1733–38), after which his son reigned as Polish king Augustus III. During this time Saxony reached its intellectual and cultural golden age, but after the Seven Years' War it began a period of decline. In 1806, it was conquered by Napoleon and made a kingdom.

Saxony, kingdom of Kingdom established (1806) by Napoleon after his conquest of Electoral Saxony. Napoleon raised the electorate to a kingdom and established Frederick Augustus I as its ruler. Saxony's alliance with France contributed to its growth in size and power until Napoleon's downfall. The Congress of Vienna forced Saxony to cede much land to Prussia. In 1830, Saxony was torn by riots, which led to the granting of a constitution the following year. Saxony sided unsuccessfully with Austria during the Austro-Prussian War and entered the German Confederation in 1866. It became part of the German Empire (1871) and after WW I became a state within the Weimar Republic.

Saxony-Anhalt Former state in East Germany, consisting principally of the historical German states of Saxony and Anhalt. It was abolished in 1952.

Sayyid dynasty Dynasty that ruled India's Delhi sultanate from 1414 to 1451. The four sultans of the dynasty were barely able to maintain themselves and eventually gave way to the Lodi dynasty.

Scaevola, Caius Mucius 6th cent.? BC. Legendary Roman hero. Condemned for trying to assassinate Lars Porsena during his siege of Rome (509 BC), he so impressed Porsena by thrusting his hand into flame without flinching that he was ordered released and the siege was lifted.

Scaevola, Quintus Mucius d. 82 BC. Ancient Roman jurist. He served as tribune (106 BC) and as consul (95 BC) and introduced a law limiting Roman citizenship and the right to vote. This contributed to the outbreak of the Social War (q.v.).

Scala, Can Francesco della 〈~, Cane Grande della〉 1291–1329. Medieval Italian lord of Verona and member of the prominent Veronese Ghibelline family. He was appointed the imperial vicar of Verona by Holy Roman Emperor Henry VII. He was a patron of the arts, notably of Dante during his exile from Florence.

Scala, Cane Grande della See **Scala, Can Francesco della**

scalawags Term applied to southern Republicans who supported the federal program of Reconstruction after the American Civil War. A Reconstruction Republican from the North was known as a carpetbagger.

Scaliger, Joseph Justus 1540–1609. Renaissance classical scholar. Son of J. C. Scaliger, he produced prodigious linguistic studies and critical editions of the classics. He founded the modern science of chronology by his comparative study of the calendar, *De Emendatione Temporum*.

Scaliger, Julius Caesar 1484–1558. Italian-born French scholar, physician, and philologist, father of J. J. Scaliger. He produced commentaries on the classics and an early study of Latin grammar as well as polemics against such scholars as Erasmus.

Scanderbeg c1404–68. Albanian national hero. Born an Albanian prince, he became a Turkish hostage in childhood and was raised and educated as a Muslim by Sultan Murad II. When the Turks attacked Albania, he escaped (1443) and formed an alliance of Albanian princes to resist the Turks. As commander of Albanian forces, he repulsed 13 Turkish attacks between 1444 and 1466. Soon after his death, the alliance collapsed and Albania fell to the Turks.

Scandinavia Region of northern Europe consisting primarily of Denmark, Norway, and Sweden. The term is usually extended to include neighboring Finland and also Iceland.

Scannabechi, Lamberto *See* **Honorius II**

Scarlatti, Alessandro 1658/59–1725. Italian composer. Father of D. Scarlatti, he was important in the development of classical harmony and of the opera form. He wrote more than 100 operas, of which the best known is *Il Tigrane*.

Scarlatti, Giuseppe Domenico 1685–1757. Italian composer and virtuoso, son of A. Scarlatti. He is noted for his more than 500 harpsichord sonatas which expanded the sonata form. He composed many while court musician in Madrid.

Scarron, Paul 1610?–60. French writer. He contributed to the development of the drama and the comic burlesque but is remembered for his novel *Le Roman Comique*.

Scaurus, Marcus Aemilius *c*162–*c*89 BC. Ancient Roman official. According to Cicero, he was a powerful conservative leader in the Roman Senate. He conducted successful Alpine campaigns and controlled the grain supply at Ostia. His daughter married Pompey.

Schacht, Hjalmar Horace Greeley 1877–1970. German financial expert. As president of the Reichsbank (1923–30, 1933–39) he helped halt the ruinous inflation in the 1920s, and as minister of economy (1934–37) he achieved economic stabilization and growth in the early years of Nazi Germany.

Schaff, Philip 1819–93. Swiss-born American Protestant theologian and church historian. He was noted for his studies of ecclesiastical history, *History of the Christian Church* and *The Creeds of Christendom*.

Scharnhorst, Gerhard von 1755–1813. Prussian general. In 1807, he began the reorganization of the Prussian army, transforming it from a mercenary force into a citizen army. He introduced the system by which soldiers were trained and served for a short period, then were replaced by new trainees.

Scheidemann, Philipp 1865–1939. German Social Democratic leader. After WW I and the flight of the kaiser, he proclaimed the Weimar Republic and became its first chancellor (1918). He resigned (1919) in protest against the Treaty of Versailles.

Schelling, Friedrich Wilhelm Joseph von 1775–1854. German philosopher. He contributed to the development of the philosophical movement known as idealism.

Schiller, Friedrich von 1759–1805. German poet and dramatist, one of the leading literary figures of his day. His plays include *The Robbers* and *William Tell*. Schiller's poem *Ode to Joy* was used by L. van Beethoven in the last movement of his Ninth Symphony.

Schirra, Walter Marty, Jr. 1923–. US astronaut, one of the seven original astronauts. As commander of Gemini 6 he achieved (Dec. 15, 1965) the first successful space rendezvous by linking his craft with Gemini 7. He also commanded the flight (Oct. 11–12, 1968) of Apollo 7.

Schism 1. Schism of 1054. Final division of the Christian church into the Roman Catholic (Western) church and the Orthodox Eastern church. Doctrinal and other disputes began separating the two churches (as early as the 9th cent.) and included the question of the filioque *(q.v.)* and the controversy over Photius *(q.v.)*. Finally, in 1054, a jurisdictional dispute prompted Pope Leo IX to excommunicate the Patriarch of Constantinople, Michael Cerularius. The patriarch in turn excommunicated the pope and from that point the two churches were considered to be officially separated. 2. Great Schism. Division in the Roman Catholic church (1378–1417) in which two rival lines of popes emerged. Pope Gregory XI died (1378) soon after ending the Babylonian captivity *(q.v.)* and restoring the papacy to Rome. The Romans demanded election of an Italian pope and Pope Urban VI was elected (1378). However, Urban, by his actions, quickly aroused opposition, and within a few months the cardinals declared his election void. They then elected Clement VII as pope. Urban forced Clement out of Rome and Clement subsequently took up residence at Avignon, France. To end the schism, the Council of Pisa was convened (1409) and declared against the then-reigning popes in Rome and France. In 1410 the council installed John XXIII as pope. John succeeded in winning widespread support and then called the Council of Constance (1414). Gregory XII in Rome resigned and the council deposed both John XXIII and Benedict XIII, then reigning in France. Pope Martin V was elected and the schism was ended.

Schleicher, Kurt von 1882–1934. German general and last chancellor (1932–33) of the Weimar Republic. In an attempt to prevent the rise of A. Hitler, he sought unsuccessfully to receive emergency powers from Pres. P. Hindenburg. Schleicher left office Jan. 1933, and Hindenburg made Hitler chancellor soon after.

Schleiermacher, Friedrich Ernst Daniel 1768–1834. German Protestant theologian. He opposed both philosophical rationalism and religious dogma. His writings were a major influence in the development of Protestant theology.

Schlesinger, Arthur Meier 1888–1965. American historian, a pioneer in the study of both social and urban history in America. He emphasized the importance of economics in his best-known work,

The Colonial Merchants and the American Revolution. He edited the notable 13-volume *A History of American Life.*

Schlesinger, Arthur Meier, Jr. 1917–. American historian. His extensive writings on American history include *Age of Jackson* (Pulitzer Prize, 1946), *The Age of Roosevelt, A Thousand Days* (Pulitzer Prize, 1966), and *The Imperial Presidency.*

Schleswig-Holstein Historic region and modern German state located in northwest Germany. Denmark gained control of Schleswig in the 12th cent. and Holstein (in fief to the Holy Roman Empire) in the 14th cent. After the collapse of the Holy Roman Empire (early 19th cent.), the German Confederation gained nominal suzerainty over Holstein, while Denmark retained full sovereignty over Schleswig. The rise of nationalism in Denmark and the German states soon created conflict over Schleswig-Holstein, where there was a considerable native-German population. When Danish king Frederick VII moved to annex Schleswig to Denmark, the War of Schleswig-Holstein (1848–50) broke out between Prussia and Denmark. The status of Schleswig-Holstein was unchanged, however. War again broke out in 1864, Denmark was defeated, and Schleswig-Holstein passed to the joint administration of Austria and Prussia. Prussia, then vying with Austria for domination of the German Confederation, used a dispute over the region to start the Austro-Prussian War (1866). Prussia emerged victorious and annexed Schleswig-Holstein. When the unified German Empire was created (1871), the region passed to Germany.

Schley, Winfield Scott 1839–1911. American naval officer. Second in command of the US fleet at the Battle of Santiago *(q.v.)* during the Spanish-American War, Commodore Schley fought the naval engagement that led to the destruction of the Spanish fleet. Later a controversy arose over whether he or his superior, Admiral William Thomas Sampson (1840–1902), should have received credit for the victory.

Schlick, Moritz 1882–1936. German philosopher. He was a leader of the Vienna Circle, a school of logical positivism.

Schlieffen, Alfred, Graf von 1833–1913. German field marshal. As head of the German general staff (1891–1905) he devised (1895) the Schlieffen plan *(q.v.)*, the strategy later attempted by Germany in WW I.

Schlieffen plan Plan devised by German field marshal A. von Schlieffen to crush French resistance in a war by a massive, lightning attack from the north through Belgian and Dutch territory (ig-

noring their neutrality). The plan also called for an attack by relatively light forces concentrated in the south against France and in the east against Russia. The plan failed during WW I because the forces attacking through Belgium and Holland were not strong enough, but in WW II Germany brilliantly executed the basic plan.

Schliemann, Heinrich 1822–90. German archaeologist who excavated the ruins of ancient Troy. A student of Homer's works, and with independent wealth acquired from business, he devoted himself after early retirement to the search for Troy, and conducted several other excavations, one at Mycenae.

Schmalkaldic League Alliance of Protestant princes and free cities formed at Schmalkalden (1531). Led by Philip of Hesse and John Frederick I of Saxony, it had as its object a common defense against Holy Roman Emperor Charles V's threats to destroy Lutheranism by force. Charles decisively defeated the League at the Battle of Mühlberg (1547).

Schmalkaldic War War (1544–47) waged by Holy Roman Emperor Charles V against the Schmalkaldic League during the Reformation period. Forced to recognize this defensive alliance in 1532, Charles renewed his warfare against it after having made peace with France. He routed the League forces at Mühlberg (1547).

Schmidt, Helmut 1918–. West German chancellor (1974–82). A Social Democrat, he served in the Bundestag from 1953 (except for 1962–65). He served as minister of defense (1969–72) and minister of finance (1972–74) and succeeded W. Brandt as chancellor.

Schoenberg, Arnold *See* **Schönberg, Arnold**

Schofield, John McAllister 1831–1906. Union general in the American Civil War. A successful commander in Tennessee and under W. Sherman in Georgia, he went on to become secretary of war (1868–69) and commander in chief of the US Army (1888–95).

scholasticism Medieval Christian philosophical and theological movement that arose in the 11th cent. It embraced various schools of thought that were in general terms concerned with questions of reconciling faith and reason and it stimulated a renewed interest in ancient Greek philosophy. Earlier Christian thinkers, notably St. Augustine (through his writings on Platonism) helped set the stage for medieval scholasticism. In the 11th cent., St. Anselm founded the movement and in his writings used reason to better understand belief ("faith seeking understanding"). Peter Lombard gave the movement further impetus in the 12th cent. through his work, *The Book of Sen-*

tences, a compilation of the opinions of the church fathers.

The works of Aristotle (translated from Arabic) became available for the first time in Christian Europe by the 13th cent. and had a tremendous impact on medieval scholastic thinkers. Albertus Magnus began the synthesis of Aristotelianism and Christian theology, but St. Thomas Aquinas, one of the greatest thinkers of the Christian church, brought it to full development. Thomism was by no means unopposed, and the theologian Duns Scotus evolved an alternate synthesis. Finally, William of Ockham brought a close to the scholastic tradition (14th cent.) by effectively asserting that there is no rational basis for faith. He thus separated religion and philosophy into two distinct spheres. Thomism, however, experienced a revival in the 15th cent. and in modern times theologians have sought to apply Thomist doctrines to contemporary problems.

Schönberg, Arnold 1874–1951. Austrian-born American composer. He revolutionized modern music through his use of a twelve-tone scale and through his influential writing, teaching, and outstanding compositions.

Schönbrunn, Peace of Treaty signed at Vienna (Oct. 14, 1809) following Austria's defeat by France at the Battle of Wagram *(q.v.)* during the Napoleonic Wars. By its terms Austria lost substantial territories to France, Russia, Bavaria, and the Grand Duchy of Warsaw.

Schoolcraft, Henry Rowe 1793–1864. American explorer and ethnologist. He collected much information and lore about American Indian tribes and was one of the pioneers of Indian studies.

School of Alexandria *See* **Alexandrian School**

Schopenhauer, Arthur 1788–1860. German philosopher. A successor of I. Kant in the idealist school, he saw will rather than mind as the fundamental principle of existence and developed a philosophy based on this idea. His most important work was *World as Will and Idea.*

Schrieffer, John *See* **Bardeen, John**

Schrödinger, Erwin 1887–1961. Austrian physicist. He formulated the basic wave equation, named for him, describing the motion of subatomic particles—the most widely used tool of quantum mechanics. He was awarded the Nobel Prize in physics in 1933.

Schubert, Franz Peter 1797–1828. Austrian composer. He is equally celebrated for his more than 500 lieder (art songs) and for his symphonies, including Symphony in B Flat, Symphony in B Minor, and Symphony in C Major. He is also known for his chamber music, masses, and other compositions. Now considered a musical genius, he achieved little recognition in his lifetime.

Schuman, Robert 1886–1963. French statesman and prime minister (1947–48). As foreign minister (1948–53) he proposed (1950) the Schuman plan for pooling European coal and steel resources. This move toward European cooperation led eventually to the formation of the European Common Market.

Schumann, Robert Alexander 1810–56. German Romantic composer. In his writing and in his compositions he championed the Romantic movement. A versatile composer, he produced both vocal and orchestral pieces. His *Spring* and *Rhenish* symphonies and his Piano Concerto in A minor are considered among his most outstanding works.

Schuman plan *See* **Monnet, Jean**

Schurz, Carl 1829–1906. German-born American statesman, reformer, and journalist. Fleeing Germany after the Revolution of 1848, he distinguished himself in America as politician, diplomat, Civil War general, US senator, and newspaper editor. He was a leader of the mugwumps, opposing J. Blaine in the 1884 presidential campaign.

Schuschnigg, Kurt von 1897–. Austrian statesman. As prime minister (1934–38) he strove to prevent Austria's takeover by Germany (1938). He was a German prisoner until 1945.

Schütz, Heinrich 1585–1672. German baroque composer. He introduced Italian-style music and techniques into German music, wrote many outstanding sacred-music pieces, and composed *Dafne,* considered the first German opera.

Schutzstaffel *See* **Ss**

Schuyler, Philip John 1733–1804. American Revolutionary leader. He served in the Continental Army and was a member of the Continental Congress. As US senator (1789–91, 1797–98) he was a leading Federalist in New York state.

Schwabach, Articles of *See* **Articles of Schwabach**

Schwann, Theodor 1810–82. German physiologist. He isolated the first enzyme (pepsin) from animal tissue, studied muscle contraction, and identified the cell as the basic unit of plant and animal life.

Schwarzenberg, Felix, Fürst zu 1800–52. Austrian statesman. As prime minister (1848–52) he restored the Austrian Hapsburg Empire after its near collapse in the Revolution of 1848. His work was soon eroded by the growth of nationalism.

Schwarzenberg, Karl Philipp, Fürst zu 1771–1820. Austrian field marshal and diplomat. He led the Austrian contingent with Napoleon against Russia (1812) but later commanded the allied forces that defeated Napoleon in 1814.

Schweitzer, Albert 1875–1965. Alsatian theologian, philosopher, and medical missionary in Africa. Renouncing fame as a scholar and musician, he founded (after 1913) a medical mission (Lambaréné Hospital) in Africa, illustrating his philosophical principle of "reverence for life." He was awarded the Nobel Peace Prize in 1952.

Schwenkfeld, Kaspar von 1490–1561. German Protestant religious leader. He tried to chart a middle way between Protestants and Catholics but was persecuted by his fellow Protestants for his views. He founded the sect named for him, the Schwenkfeldians.

Schwerin, Kurt Christoph, Graf von 1684–1757. Prussian field marshal. One of the chief lieutenants of Prussian king Frederick II, he won his greatest victory at the Battle of Mollwitz (1741) in the War of the Austrian Succession.

Scipio Ancient Roman patrician family. They were distinguished by their patronage of Greek culture but even more by family members who were outstanding Roman leaders during the 3d and 2d cents. BC. *(See names below.)*

Scipio, Cneius Cornelius *d.* 211 BC. Roman leader. As consul (222 BC) he completed the subjugation of Cisalpine Gaul, and, with his brother P. Scipio, defeated Hasdrubal in Spain (215).

Scipio, Publius Cornelius *d. c*211 BC. Roman leader and general. He was defeated by Hannibal at the Ticino River (218 BC), but his later campaigns in Spain with his brother C. Scipio significantly hindered the Carthaginian efforts. Both brothers were killed in Spain.

Scipio, Quintus Caecilius Metellus Pius *d.* 46 BC. Roman politician and general. He was consul (52 BC) with Pompey and commanded armies for him in Syria and Egypt. In the struggles for control of the Roman state, he lost to J. Caesar at the Battle of Thapsus, and committed suicide.

Scipio Africanus Major 234?–183 BC. Roman general. Sent as proconsul to Spain (210 BC), he conquered the Carthaginians there during the second Punic War, gained control of the whole country, and pursued the Carthaginians into Africa, where he defeated Hannibal at the Battle of Zama (202 BC). He and his brother Lucius were successful in the war against Syrian king Antiochus III (190 BC).

Scipio Africanus Minor *c*185–129 BC. Roman consul and general, adopted son of P. Scipio. He ended the Third Punic War (149–146 BC) by conquering and destroying Carthage. He was made consul (147 BC) and censor (142). Reelected consul (134), he crushed a revolt in Spain, destroying the

city of Numantia. It is thought that he was murdered by his wife or a member of her family, the Gracchi.

Scipio Nasica Serapio, Publius Cornelius *d. c*132 BC. Ancient Roman politician. He violently opposed the reforms of T. Gracchus and personally led the mob that murdered him.

Scopes trial Celebrated "monkey" trial (July 10–21, 1925) at Dayton, Tennessee. John T. Scopes (1900–70), was charged with violating a 1925 state law by teaching evolution in his high school class. During the trial, C. Darrow, one of Scopes's attorneys, conducted a severe questioning of the fundamentalist beliefs of W. Bryan. Scopes was found guilty and fined. Darrow failed to establish the law's unconstitutionality and it stood until repealed in 1967.

Scotland Former kingdom and now part of Great Britain, located on the island of Great Britain and north of England. Its capital is Edinburgh. Although in union with Britain, Scotland maintains its own system of law and has representation in the British Parliament. Known to the Romans as Caledonia, the region saw the rise (5th–6th cent. AD) of kingdoms established by Picts, Angles, Britons, and Scots; suffered raids (8th–12th cent.) by the Norsemen, and subsequently became embroiled in wars with England, which for centuries sought to establish suzerainty over Scotland. The English and Scottish crowns were joined (1603) under James I, but formal union did not come until 1707. Thereafter the history of Scotland merges with that of Great Britain *(q.v.).* Key dates in the history of Scotland include:

1ST CENT. AD Romans attempted conquest of region, then known as Caledonia.

AD 122 Hadrian ordered construction of military wall to halt continued attacks from Picts in the north (Scotland) on Roman domains in the south.

AD 409 Romans withdrew from Britain.

5th–6th CENT. Britons established kingdom of Strathclyde; Picts established kingdom in northern Scotland; Gaelic Scoti from Ireland established kingdom of Dalriada; Angles established kingdom of Northumbria in southern Caledonia and northern England.

563 St. Columba came to Scotland from Ireland; established monastery and proceeded to spread Christianity.

730 Pictish king Angus MacFergus conquered Dalriada and Strathclyde.

8TH–12TH CENT. Norsemen made continuous raids on the Scottish coast; gained some holdings in Scotland but generally held little more than the Hebrides, Orkney, and Shetland island groups.

844 Dalriada and kingdom of Picts united under Kenneth MacAlpine; new kingdom known as Alban.

1005–34 Malcolm II reigned; defeated Northumbria at Battle of Carham (1018) and extended kingdom at expense of Northumbrians.

1034–40 Duncan reigned; Strathclyde incorporated into kingdom, which became known as Scotland; severe political turmoil culminated in Duncan's murder by Macbeth.

1040–57 Macbeth reigned; killed and succeeded by Duncan's son Malcolm Canmore, who reigned as Malcolm III.

1057–93 Malcolm III reigned; married St. Margaret of Scotland, an English princess (1067); reign marked by increasing influence of English and Roman Catholic ideas and practices in both the kingdom and in the Celtic church.

1093 Malcolm III died; leaders of the Scottish clans forced Margaret and her son Duncan II into exile.

1097–1107 Edgar, son of Malcolm III and Margaret, reigned; began the breakup of traditional Scottish clan society and the introduction of a feudal system, which was continued by his successors.

1124–53 David I reigned; lost Northumbrian possessions to England (1149).

1165–1214 William the Lion reigned; sought to regain Northumbria; captured by the English and forced to sign the Treaty of Falaise (1174), by which he swore fealty to English King Henry II.

1189 English king Richard II renounced provisions of Treaty of Falaise in return for a sum of money.

1249–86 Alexander III reigned; recaptured the Hebrides Islands from the Norsemen (1266); succeeded by his granddaughter, the infant Margaret of Norway.

1290–92 Margaret died (1290), causing struggle for the succession; English king Edward I supported the claims of John de Baliol and invaded Scotland; Baliol made king (Nov. 1292).

1295–96 John de Baliol allied with France (1295) in an attempt to end English suzerainty over Scotland; Baliol defeated (Apr., 1296) at Battle of Dunbar; Edward I annexed Scotland, but the Scots continued to rebel against English rule.

1297 Scottish troops under William Wallace victorious over the English at Battle of Stirling (Sept. 11).

1298 English victorious over the Scots (July 22) at Battle of Falkirk.

1305 Wallace captured and executed by the English; succeeded by Robert the Bruce as leader of Scottish rebellion; Robert was crowned king a year later.

1306–29 Robert the Bruce reigned; established Scottish independence by his victory at the Battle of Bannockburn (June 24, 1314); secured English recognition of Scottish independence by the Treaty of Northampton (1328).

1329–71 David II reigned; rule marked by conflict with Edward de Baliol for the throne and continuing warfare with England.

1346 Invasion of England by David II halted at the Battle of Neville's Cross.

1371–90 Robert II reigned; founded Stuart line in Scotland.

1406–37 James I reigned; held prisoner in England (until 1424); returned to Scotland and attempted to restore order and institute reforms; his rule was resisted by the nobles; he was assassinated.

1488–1513 James IV reigned; married Margaret Tudor, daughter of English king Henry VII, but came into conflict with Henry's son, Henry VIII; led invasion of England but was killed (Sept. 9, 1513) along with many Scottish nobles at Battle of Flodden Field.

1513–42 James V reigned; assumed personal rule in 1528; married Mary of Guise (1538), thereby strengthening the alliance formed with France in 1295 and leading ultimately to war with England (1542); James defeated (Nov., 1542) at Battle of Solway Moss; died soon after.

1542–60 Mary Queen of Scots, daughter of James V, succeeded, under regency of James Hamilton and, later, her mother, Mary of Guise; sent to France (1548), she married the French dauphin (1558), which only fueled resentment against the regency of Mary of Guise; rebellion led by J. Knox (1559–60), aided by English Queen Elizabeth I, led to ouster of Mary of Guise and ascendancy of Scottish Protestants; Scottish Parliament established Presbyterianism as Scottish religion.

1561–67 Mary Queen of Scots returned to Scotland and assumed rule (1561); instituted Counter-Reformation amid complicated political and religious struggle; Mary ultimately deposed (1567) and imprisoned in England, where she was later executed (1587).

1567–1625 Mary succeeded by her son James VI (1567); James assumed rule of Scotland (1583) and established his authority over the Scottish nobles; on death of English Queen Elizabeth I (1603), he became king of both Scotland and England as James I.

1625–49 Charles I reigned in England and Scotland; attempts to introduce Anglican reforms opposed by the Covenanters; Scottish Protestants resisted in the Bishops' Wars (1639–40), which led to the English Civil War.

1642–49 English Civil War; Scottish Covenanters (Presbyterians) had great influence over rebel Parliament until Pride's Purge and ascendancy of the Puritans under O. Cromwell.

1649–60 Scotland ruled under English Commonwealth and Protectorate; rebellions (1649-52) in Scotland in support of royalists put down by Cromwell.

1660–88 Restoration period in England; Presbyterians in Scotland again persecuted by English kings.

1689–1702 Protestants William and Mary reigned after the Glorious Revolution in England; Presbyterianism became Scottish state church.

1702–14 Queen Anne reigned; English and Scottish parliaments passed acts of union that formally united England and Scotland as Great Britain (1707)

Scotland, Church of *See* **Church of Scotland**

Scotland, Saint Margaret of *See* **Margaret of Scotland, Saint**

Scotland Yard Name given the criminal investigation division of the London Metropolitan Police. The name comes from the London street on which the first headquarters of the London police was established (1829).

Scott, Robert Falcon 1868–1912. British naval officer and Antarctic explorer. Scott commanded an expedition to the Antarctic (1901–04). On his second expedition (1910–12), Scott's party of five reached the South Pole one month after R. Amundsen, but all died in bad weather during their journey back.

Scott, Sir Walter 1771–1832. Scottish writer, considered the father of the historical novel. Scott's first major work, the ballad collection *Minstrelsy of the Scottish Border*, appeared in 1802–03, but his great success began with the publication of *Waverley* (1814), the first of a number of historical novels known collectively as the Waverley novels. Scott's novels are set in Scotland, England, and Europe, and their popularity made Scott one of the leading authors of his day. Among them are *Guy Mannering*, *Old Mortality*, *Quentin Durward*, and *Ivanhoe*.

Scott, Winfield 1786–1866. American politician and general who fought with distinction in the War of 1812. Made commanding general of the US army (1841–61), he captured Vera Cruz (1847) during the Mexican War. He was the unsuccessful Whig candidate for president in 1852. He retired shortly after the outbreak of the Civil War.

Scottish Highlands *See* **Highlands, the**

Scottsboro Case Notorious court case (1931) in Scottsboro, Alabama, in which nine blacks were convicted of raping two white girls. The Supreme Court reversed the decision on procedural grounds and one of the girls recanted her testimony at a second trial. The case became famous as an example of racial prejudice affecting a legal verdict.

scribe Ancient Jewish scholar and teacher of the Old Testament and the Law. By the time of Jesus, scribes were the equivalent of doctors of the law, and many conducted classes in the temple precincts for future rabbis. The name was first applied to Ezra.

Scriblerus Club English literary club of the early 18th cent., formed to satirize the literary excesses of the period through the writings of a fictitious person, Martinus Scriblerus. Its members included J. Gay, J. Swift, and A. Pope.

Scribner, Charles 1821–71. American publisher. With Isaac Baker (*d.* 1850), he founded (1846) the publishing company that became (1878) Charles Scribner's Sons.

Scribner, Charles 1854–1930. American publisher. Son of C. Scribner, he became president of Charles Scribner's Sons (1879). During his tenure (1879–1928) the firm published the works of some of the most distinguished writers in America.

Scripps, Edward Wyllis 1854–1926. American newspaper publisher. He organized (1895) the first major newspaper chain and established (1907) the United Press news service.

Scrope, Richard *See* **Neville, Ralph**

scutage Feudal payment to a lord from a vassal in lieu of military service. Scutage existed in Europe, especially in England, but became obsolete by the 14th cent.

Scylla In Greek mythology, a sea monster that lived on the Italian side of the Strait of Messina. She seized and devoured sailors from passing ships. Charybdis, a mythical monster turned into a whirlpool, menaced sailors, among them Odysseus and Jason, from the opposite side of the strait.

Scythia Ancient kingdom of indeterminate boundaries centered in the area north of the Black Sea. The Scythians were nomadic horsemen who made periodic incursions into areas to the south. They flourished from *c*8th cent. BC to the 2d cent. BC, when they were conquered by the Sarmatians.

Seaborg, Glenn Theodore 1912–. American nuclear chemist and chairman of the US Atomic Energy Commission (1961–71). He was the codiscoverer of plutonium and other elements heavier than uranium and was instrumental in the development of the atomic bomb. He was corecipient of the Nobel Prize in chemistry in 1951.

Seale, Bobby *See* **Black Panthers**

"Sealed train"   *See* **Lenin, Nikolai**

sea power   Term used to designate those elements including men, ships, shorelines, and industrial capacity that enable a nation to gain control over a portion of the seas. The term was popularized by the American naval officer and historian Alfred Thayer Mahan (1840–1914), especially in his *The Influence of Sea Power Upon History.*

SEATO   *See* **Southeast Asian Treaty Organization**

Seattle   Capital city (pop. 494,000) of Washington state. First established in the 1850s, it grew slowly until the arrival (late 19th cent.) of the railroad and the advent of the gold rush in Alaska. It has become the commercial and industrial center of the Pacific Northwest.

Sebastian   1554–78. Portuguese king (1557–78), successor to his grandfather, John III. He led the Portuguese army to a disastrous defeat in Morocco at the Battle of the Three Kings (1578). Popular belief refused to accept his death, and various pretenders and rumors of his return long persisted.

Sebastian, Saint   *d.* AD *c*288. Roman Christian martyr. According to tradition, he was a Praetorian Guard under Emperor Diocletian. When Sebastian's Christianity was discovered, Diocletian ordered his death by arrows. Sebastian recovered and returned to confront Diocletian, who ordered him beaten to death. His martyrdom was the subject of numerous Renaissance works of art.

secession   Formal withdrawal of a political entity from a larger entity. The term refers especially to the attempt by 11 southern states to leave the Union (1860–61), thus precipitating the American Civil War.

Second Coalition, War of the   War (1798–1802) conducted by a coalition of European nations against France, the last phase of the French Revolutionary Wars *(q.v.).* On Dec. 24, 1798, the monarchies of Russia and Britain, in agreement with Naples, Portugal, Austria, and the Ottoman Empire, formed the Second Coalition to oppose Napoleon's expansionism. Russia and Britain agreed to drive France from The Netherlands, Austria was to combat Napoleon in Germany, and Switzerland and combined Austro-Russian forces were to expel the French from Italy. The coalition was only partially successful before Russia withdrew (Oct., 1799), and France subsequently regained some of its earlier losses. The conflict was ended by the Treaty of Amiens (Mar. 27, 1802), which also closed the French Revolutionary Wars.

Second Crusade   *See* **Crusade, Second**

Second Empire   French government under the rule of Emperor Napoleon III (1852–70). Originally chosen as president of the Second Republic (1848), Napoleon III declared himself emperor in 1852. He followed Napoleon I's tradition of autocratic rule and expansionism, especially in Asia, Indochina, Mexico, and the Crimea. However, France's humiliation in the Franco-Prussian War (1870) led to his overthrow and declaration of the Third Republic. (*See also* France [1852–70.]

Second Polish Revolution   *See* **January Insurrection**

Second Punic War   *See* **Punic War(s)**

Second Republic   French government (1848–52) formed after the abdication (Feb. 24, 1848) of King Louis Philippe in the February Revolution *(q.v.)* and establishment of the provisional government of L. Blanc. Louis Napoleon, nephew of Emperor Napoleon, was elected president of the republic (Dec. 10). Though the Second Republic had a constitution and a legislature, its rule was brief. Louis Napoleon overthrew his own government, proclaimed himself Emperor Napoleon III (Dec., 1852), and declared the Second Empire.

Second Republic   Spanish republican government (1931–39) formed after the ouster of King Alfonso XIII. A constitution was promulgated and church property was confiscated, but the moderate policies followed by Pres. Niceto Alcalá Zamora (1877–1949) brought attacks from both the right and left. He was ousted in the 1936 elections by the Popular Front (a coalition of republicans, Communists, syndicalists, and Socialistas). Soon after their president, M. Azaña, took office, the Spanish Civil War *(q.v.)* broke out. The Second Republic was replaced by Franco's Nationalist government at the end of the war (1939).

Secret Speech   *See* **destalinization**

secularism   A movement directed toward concern with the sphere of human existence. In most of its manifestations secularism has set itself in conscious opposition to religion, holding that religion is too concerned with an afterlife, even to the detriment of the potentialities of this world.

Sedan, Battle of   Decisive German victory over France (Sept. 1, 1870) during the Franco-Prussian War, at Sedan, France. It resulted in the surrender (Sept. 2) of Napoleon III and the downfall of the French Second Empire.

Sedgemoore, Battle of   Victory (July 16, 1685) of English king James II over the forces of his nephew James Scott, duke of Monmouth, pretender to the throne. The battle, fought at Somerset, resulted in Monmouth's capture and execution.

Sedgwick, John   1813–64. American Civil War general. He fought in the battles of Antietam, Chancellorsville, Fredericksburg, Gettysburg, and in the Wilderness Campaign. He was killed in action at Spotsylvania (May 9, 1864).

Seeckt, Hans von 1866–1936. German general and head of the German army (1920–26). He remolded the limited German army after WW I as a professional force capable of rapid expansion.

Segni, Ugolino di *See* **Gregory IX**

Segovia, Andrés 1894–. Spanish classical guitarist. He revived use of the guitar as a concert instrument through his performances and his transcriptions for guitar from the classical repertory.

segregation Separation of the races (especially in reference to whites and blacks) to maintain the social, economic, and political advantages of one over the other. Though by no means restricted to the US, it has been an important factor in its social history. Segregation of whites and blacks was firmly established in the US South by the end of the post-Civil War Reconstruction *(q.v.)*. The Supreme Court decision in *Plessy* vs *Ferguson* (1896) upheld the legality of separate but equal facilities (such as schools) and thereby ensured continuation of segregation policies. It was not until the late 1930s and 1940s that the trend toward integration began. Antidiscrimination clauses were included in federal contracts (after 1941) under Pres. F. Roosevelt, and Pres. H. Truman ordered integration of the military (1948). The Supreme Court decision in *Brown* vs *Board of Education of Topeka* (1954) began the process of ending school segregation. The 1960s saw the rise of the civil rights movement *(q.v.)* and enactment of landmark civil rights legislation. *See also* apartheid.

Seingalt, Giovanni Giacomo Casanova de *See* **Casanova de Seingalt, Giovanni Giacomo**

seignorial system *See* **Manorial System**

Seisachtheia *See* **Solon**

Sejanus, Lucius Aelius *d.* AD 31. Roman administrator. He was chief adviser for Emperor Tiberius, and may have helped Livilla, wife of the emperor's son Drusus, in Drusus' murder. Tiberius had him executed on suspicion of trying to take power.

Sejm Legislative body of Poland. Polish king Casimir IV summoned the first Polish diet in 1467 and in 1505 the nobles forced the king to recognize the power of the Sejm to legislate. From 1572 until 1791, members of the Sejm had the *liberum veto*, which gave any member the right to veto legislation, and thus weakened the government. In 1919, the Sejm was reorganized into a single, or unicameral, legislature.

Selden, John 1584–1654. English scholar, jurist, and Parliamentarian. A leader in English political life, he was also one of the most erudite scholars of his day. He wrote on the history of English law, religious tithes, and Oriental gods, and in defense of English sovereignty over the seas.

Seleucid Kingdom ⟨Seleucid Empire⟩ Hellenistic empire of Asia Minor. The Seleucid dynasty (312–64 BC) was centered in Syria and ruled over vast areas of Asia Minor which had been captured by Alexander the Great. The dynasty was founded by the Macedonian Seleucus I, one of Alexander's generals, following Alexander's death. In the division of Alexander's empire, Seleucus was given Babylonia. He rapidly added territories that extended from Syria to the Indus River. Subsequent Seleucid rulers were instrumental in spreading Greek culture throughout Asia Minor. However, the empire was gradually reduced and was limited to Syria and Cilicia by the time of its absorption by Rome (64 BC).

Seleucus I *d.* 280 BC. Macedonian general and (from 312 BC) first of the Seleucid rulers of the eastern portions of Alexander the Great's empire. His rule extended over Syria, Asia Minor, Mesopotamia, and Persia. He founded Antioch as his capital.

Selecus II *d.* 226 BC. Syrian king (247–226 BC), successor to his father, Antiochus II. He fought a war with his half brother Ptolemy III of Egypt as well as against his stepmother Berenice, and eventually lost both Parthia and Asia Minor.

Self-Denying Ordinance *See* **New Model Army**

Self-Strengthening movement Chinese movement begun (c1861) to adopt elements of Western civilization in order to strengthen the Ch'ing (Manchu) dynasty against both internal forces and further aggression by Western nations. The movement began to decline in the 1870s.

Selim I 1467–1520. Ottoman Turkish sultan (1512–20). He deposed his father, Bajazet II, and killed all who had claims to the throne. He conquered sections of Persia (1514), added Syria and Egypt to the Ottoman domain, and assumed the spiritual authority of the caliphate.

Selim II c1524–74. Ottoman Turkish sultan (1566–74), successor to his father, Suleiman I. During his reign, Cyprus and Tunisia were added to the empire, but Selim's defeat at the Battle of Lepanto (1571) marked the first major setback to Ottoman expansion.

Selim III 1761–1808. Ottoman Turkish sultan (1789–1807), successor to his uncle Abdu-1-Hamid I. Selim inaugurated a policy of reform and Westernization but was unable to halt the decline in Ottoman power and prestige. Russo-Turkish Wars were fought during his reign. He was overthrown, imprisoned, and murdered.

Seljuks Turkish dynasty that ruled much of western Asia and Asia Minor from the 11th to

13th cents. Originally an Asiatic nomadic people, the Seljuks converted to Islam (11th cent.) and soon created a vast empire after taking power in the Empire of the Caliphate. Rulers of the dynasty included Togrul Beg, grandson of Seljuk, the founder of the dynasty. Leading the Seljuks eastward, Togrul Beg conquered Persia and entered Baghdad (1055), overthrowing the Buyids (Persians who held power under the caliphs). He thus established the Seljuk sultans as effective rulers in the Empire of the Caliphate. He was succeeded (1063) by his son Alp Arslan (1029–72), who conquered Syria and Palestine and defeated and captured Byzantine emperor Romanus IV at the Battle of Manzikert (1071). Alp Arslan was succeeded by his son Malik Shah (ruled 1072–92), who brought the Seljuk Empire to its height. After his death (1092), local rulers took over portions of the empire and the Abbasid caliphs gained control of the central government. Continued Seljuk attacks on the Byzantine Empire led to the Crusades (q.v.). The Seljuk kingdoms were eventually conquered (13th cent.) by Genghis Khan and his successors. The former Seljuk kingdom of Rum became (14th cent.) the nucleus around which the Ottomans formed their great empire.

Selkirk, Thomas Douglas, 5th earl of 1771–1820. Scottish philanthropist and colonizer. To alleviate hardships of Scottish highlanders, he established colonies for them on Prince Edward Island and Manitoba, Canada, notably the Red River Settlement (q.v.).

Sellasia, Battle of See **Antigonus III**; **Cleomenes III**

Semele In Greek mythology, the mother of Dionysus by Zeus. Asking to behold Zeus in his glory, she was killed by his thunderbolts. Zeus rescued Dionysus by placing him in his own thigh, from which he was later born. Zeus ultimately brought Semele out of Hades and made her immortal.

Seminole Indians North American Indian tribe. They formed (18th cent.) from the Creek Indians and settled in Florida. Through the early 19th cent. they resisted European encroachment on their lands, notably in the Seminole Wars (q.v.), until their defeat and removal (1842).

Seminole Wars Series of wars fought between the US and the Seminole Indians in Florida. **1.** The first Seminole War (1817–18) began when Gen. A. Jackson invaded the Spanish-held territory of Florida after a long series of border skirmishes. He defeated the Seminoles and the war encouraged Spain to sell Florida to the US. **2.** The second Seminole War (1835–42) was sparked by attempts of white settlers to remove the Seminoles from their reservation land. The conflict cost 2,000 soldiers and over $20 million and ended only when Seminole leader Osceola (q.v.) was betrayed and killed (1842). Most Seminoles were forced to emigrate westward. Those who refused were tracked down and deported during a third conflict (1855–58).

Semiramis Mythical Assyrian queen, reputed to have founded Babylon and to have married the founder of Nineveh. Eventually she was deified. She came to be identified with the goddess Ishtar.

Semite A member of an ethnic group speaking a Semitic language. As early as 2500 BC the Semites began to migrate from the Arabian Peninsula. Semitic peoples include the ancient Akkadians, Assyrians, Aramaeans, Israelites, and Phoenicians, and the modern Arabs and Jews.

Semmes, Raphael 1809–77. American naval officer. As Confederate commander of the Confederate cruiser *Alabama* (1862–64) during the American Civil War, he was able to inflict extensive damage on Union shipping until the *Alabama* was sunk off Cherbourg, France (June 19, 1864).

Sempach, Battle of Decisive Swiss victory (July 9, 1386) over the Austrians at Sempach, Switzerland. The battle secured the independence of the Swiss Confederation from Austrian Hapsburg rule.

Senate, Roman See **Roman Senate**

Senenayake, Don Stephen 1884–1952. Prime minister of Ceylon (1947–52). After a distinguished political career in Ceylon under British rule, he became (1948) the first prime minister of independent Ceylon and thus is considered the father of his country.

Seneca, Lucius Annaeus ⟨Seneca the Elder⟩ c55 BC–AD 40. Spanish-born Roman rhetorician and writer of influential works on rhetoric. He was the father of the Roman philosopher Seneca.

Seneca, Lucius Annaeus 3 BC–AD 65. ⟨Seneca the Younger⟩ Roman Stoic philosopher, statesman, and dramatist, considered the leading literary figure of his day. Tutor and adviser to Nero, he held great power during Nero's early reign (54–62). Eventually, conflicts with the emperor led to his retirement, and he was finally ordered to commit suicide by Nero. Seneca's writings included moral essays and nine plays. His works had a profound influence on later literature, notably Elizabethan drama.

Seneca the Elder See **Seneca, Lucius Annaeus**

Senegal West African republic (pop. 5,660,000) on the Atlantic Ocean. Its capital is Dakar. First settled by the Portuguese (15th cent.), Senegal was subsequently occupied by the French (17th cent.).

It became a colony (1895), then a member of the French Union (1946). It joined with Mali to form an independent federation (June, 1960) but withdrew from the union two months later. L. Senghor was first president.

Senghor, Leopold Sedar 1906–. African poet, writer, and statesman, and president of Senegal (1960–81). He represented Senegal in the French National Assembly and became the country's first president after its independence, working thereafter for African unity.

Sennacherib d. 681 BC. Ancient Assyrian king (705–681 BC), successor to his father, Sargon II. He is noted for the rebuilding of Nineveh, the destruction of Babylon (689 BC), and the siege of Jerusalem (701 BC).

Sennett, Mack ⟨Sinnott, Michael⟩ 1884–1960. Pioneer American film maker. His best-known comedies involved the misadventures of the Keystone cops.

Sentinum, Battle of Roman victory (295 BC) over the Samnites, Etruscans, and Gauls in the third Samnite War (q.v.), at Sentinum (now Sassoferrato), in central Italy. The battle established Roman preeminence in the region.

Seoul ⟨Kyongsong⟩ Capital of South Korea (pop. 6,879,500) and the commercial, industrial, and political capital of the country. It was capital of the Yi dynasty of Korea from the city's founding (1392) to 1910, when Korea was occupied by the Japanese. Occupied by US forces (1945) after WW II, it became the capital of South Korea in 1948.

Separatists Factions of English Christians who tried to remove themselves from the authority of the Church of England. The principal Separatists were the Brownists (q.v.), Pilgrims, Baptists, and the Society of Friends (qq.v.).

September massacres Series of massacres (Sept. 2–6, 1792) carried out in Paris by French revolutionaries. Some 1,200 jailed prisoners were murdered because of a supposed conspiracy to restore the monarchy.

Septennial Act British parliamentary act (1716) extending the term of a Parliament from three to seven years. It made the dissolution of a Parliament mandatory at the end of seven years. The Whigs secured passage of the act to continue their dominance.

Septimius Severus See **Severus**

Septuagint Oldest existing Greek translation of the Old Testament from the original Hebrew. It was composed in sections from c3d cent. BC to early Christian times. It contains the canonical books of the Bible as well as the Apocryphal or deuterocanonical books. The Septuagint is used by the Greek Orthodox church.

Serbia Constituent republic of Yugoslavia. Settled by Serbs (7th cent.), the region came under Byzantine suzerainty (by 10th cent.). Serbia became the leading kingdom in the Balkan Peninsula under Stephen Dushan (ruled 1331–55). It was a part of the Ottoman Empire from 1459 to 1878 and gained independence (1878) following the Serbo-Turkish War (q.v.). Independent Serbia played a prominent role in the Balkan League and in the Balkan Wars (qq.v.). The assassination of Austrian archduke Francis Ferdinand (1914) by a Serbian nationalist precipitated WW I. After the war, Serbia became part of the united Kingdom of Serbs, Croats, and Slovenes (1918), which formed the basis of modern Yugoslavia. It became a constituent republic of Yugoslavia in 1946.

Serbo-Bulgarian War War (Nov. 13, 1885–Mar. 13, 1886) between Serbia and Bulgaria. After Bulgaria annexed Rumelia, Serbia declared war but was defeated at Slivnitza (Nov. 17–19). Bulgaria was deterred from advancing into Serbia by pressure from the Austro-Hungarian empire, and peace was made on the basis of the status quo.

Serbo-Turkish War of 1876–78 Balkan conflict between Serbia and its ally Montenegro and the Ottoman Empire. In 1875, the Christian peasants of Herzegoina and Bosnia rebelled against their rulers, the Ottoman Turks. Serbia, an independent principality within the Ottoman Empire, sided with Bosnia and declared war on the Ottomans (June, 1876). Though the Serbs technically lost their war by October, they received support from Russia, which tried to pressure the Ottomans into accepting pro-Christian reforms. When they refused, Russia declared war (1877) on the Ottomans (see Russo-Turkish Wars). The Serbs rejoined the conflict and ultimately gained their independence in the Treaty of Berlin (July 13, 1878).

serf In feudalism, a peasant laborer bound to the land owned by a lord. The serf owed payment, usually a portion of crops, and services to the lord in return for protection and use of the land. (See feudalism.)

Serra, Junípero ⟨~, Miguel José⟩ 1713–84. Spanish Franciscan missionary in California. Noted for his austere, virtuous life, he accompanied Spanish expeditions and founded nine missions, some of which were the basis of such California cities as San Diego and San Luis Obispo.

Serra, Miguel José See **Serra, Junípero**

Sertorius, Quintus d. 72 BC. Roman general. He opposed the constitution imposed on Rome by Sulla. From 80 BC he conducted a rebellion in Spain against Rome and was largely successful until his assassination by one of his soldiers.

Servetus, Michael 1511–53. Spanish Reformation theologian and physician. Attacked by both Catholics and Protestants for his speculative books challenging the Trinity and the divinity of Christ, he was finally burned by order of J. Calvin.

Servile Wars Three slave uprisings against Roman rule. **1.** The first Servile War (c134–132 BC) occurred in Sicily. Its leader, Eunus, named himself King Antiochus, and was defeated only with great difficulty. **2.** The second Servile War, also in Sicily, raged from c102 to 99 BC. **3.** The third Servile War (73–71 BC) was led by the gladiator Spartacus. He conquered much of southern Italy before his defeat by Crassus and Pompey.

Sesostris I d. c1926 BC. Ancient Egyptian king of the 12th dynasty (c1970–c1926 BC). Son of Amenemhet I and coregent with him (1980–1970 BC), he led successful expeditions against both Nubia and Libya and brought Egypt to a peak of prosperity.

Sesostris II d. 1878 BC. Ancient Egyptian king (1897–1878 BC) of the 12th dynasty, successor to his father, Amenemhet II, with whom he ruled for a time as coregent. His reign was marked by a growth of mining in Nubia and the development of the Fayyum, a fertile area near Cairo.

Sesostris III d. 1849 BC. Ancient Egyptian king (1878–1849 BC) of the 12th dynasty, successor to his father, Sesostris II. He reestablished Egypt's southern border at the second cataract of the Nile and increased his power at the expense of the nobles.

Sesshu 1420–1506. Japanese landscape painter and Zen Buddhist monk, considered one of the greatest masters of Japanese painting.

Seth In the Bible, the son of Adam and Eve and the father of Enos.

Sethos *See* **Seti**

Seti I ⟨Sethos⟩ d. 1304 BC. Ancient Egyptian king (1318–1304 BC) of the 19th dynasty, successor to his father, Ramses I, and father of Ramses II. He conquered the Libyans, invaded Syria, and built one of the finest tombs in Egypt's Valley of the Kings.

Seti II ⟨Sethos⟩ d. 1210 BC. Ancient Egyptian king (1216–1210 BC), who reigned in the last years of the 19th dynasty. After his brief rule, anarchy reigned in Egypt until the accession of Ramses III.

Seton, Elizabeth Ann Bayley 1774–1821. American Roman Catholic, known as Mother Seton. She founded the Sisters of Charity and was the first native American to be canonized (1974).

Settlement, Act of *See* **Act of Settlement**

Seurat, Georges 1859–91. French neoimpressionist painter. He developed pointillism, a tech-

nique of applying paint in tiny individual dots. With this technique he produced masterpieces such as his *Baignade.*

Seven Against Thebes Seven legendary Greek heroes who fought against King Eteocles of Thebes to restore the throne to his brother Polynices. All but one died. The legend was the basis for *Seven Against Thebes*, by Aeschylus, and *Phoenician Women*, by Euripides.

Seven Churches in Asia Seven early Christian churches to which Saint John the Evangelist addressed the Book of Revelation. These seven churches were in the towns of Ephesus, Smyrna, Pergamum, Thyatira, Sardis, Philadelphia (Lydia), and Laodicea (Phrygia).

Seven Days' Battles Series of battles (June 25–July 1, 1862) during the American Civil War by which Confederate forces led by Gen. R. Lee turned back a Union attempt to capture the Confederate capital of Richmond, Virginia, and ended the Peninsular Campaign (q.v.). The battles were fought against Union troops under Gen. G. McClellan, and occurred at Mechanicsville (June 26), Gaines's Mill (June 27), Savage's Station (June 29), Frayser's Farm (or Glendale, June 30), and Malvern Hill (July 1).

Seven Gods of Luck Group of seven Japanese deities believed to promote happiness and good luck.

Seven Hills of Rome The seven hills upon which the city of Rome was built. The original city of Romulus was built on the Palatine hill. The other hills are: Capitoline (which became the principal one and site of the palaces of the Caesars), Quirinal, Viminal, Esquiline, Caelian, and Aventine.

Seven Oaks Massacre *See* **Red River Settlement**

Seven Pines, Battle of ⟨Fair Oaks, Battle of⟩ Battle (May 31–June 1, 1862) of the American Civil War, near Fair Oaks, Virginia. The battle was part of the Peninsular Campaign (q.v.). Confederate forces under Gen. J. Johnston attacked the Union army, under Gen. G. McClellan, which was advancing toward Richmond. The Confederates inflicted and received heavy losses and were ultimately repulsed. Gen. Johnston was wounded in the battle and was replaced by R.E. Lee soon after.

17th Parallel Name applied to the cease-fire line established by the Geneva Conference of 1954 dividing Vietnam in two parts. The line formed the border between North and South Vietnam until reunification of Vietnam (1976).

Seventh Crusade *See* **Crusade, Seventh**

Seven Weeks' War *See* **Austro-Prussian War**

Seven Wise Men of Greece List of seven great men of ancient Greece. Sources disagree as to which seven should be included, but one list includes Bias, Chilon, Cleobulus, Periander, Pittacus, Solon, and Thales.

Seven Wonders of the World Seven greatest man-made works of the ancient world. Lists varied but usually included the pyramids of Egypt, the Hanging Gardens of Babylon, the Colossus of Rhodes, the statue of Zeus at Olympia, the Temple of Artemis at Ephesus, the Pharos lighthouse of Alexandria, and the Mausoleum at Halicarnassus.

Seven Years' War War fought (1756–63) in Europe and in colonial domains in other parts of the world. The American phase of the war was called the French and Indian War *(q.v.)*. The war evolved from two separate ongoing struggles between European powers: the rivalry between Prussia and Austria (which had been humiliated by Prussia in the War of the Austrian Succession, 1740–48) and the colonial rivalry between Britain and France (in Canada, America, India, and elsewhere). The war itself pitted Prussia, Britain, and Hanover against Austria and France. Austria and France were joined variously by Sweden, Russia, Saxony, and Spain. The war began in 1756 and Prussia and Britain eventually emerged victorious. Prussia was confirmed as a leading European power and Britain became the chief colonial power, having stripped France of nearly all its colonial possessions. Key events in the war include:

1748 Austria, humiliated by loss of Silesia to Prussia in the War of the Austrian Succession (1740–48), formed an alliance with Russia.

1754 French and Indian War; rivalry between French and British in Ohio Valley region flared into armed clashes; war later merged with Seven Years' War.

1756 Treaty of Westminster (Jan.); George II of England allied with Frederick II of Prussia.

1756 Diplomatic revolution; France allied itself with its traditional enemy, Hapsburg Austria, following the pact between Britain and Prussia.

1756 Frederick II of Prussia invaded Saxony (Aug.); the Saxons surrendered (Oct. 15).

1757 Holy Roman Empire (ruled by the Austrian Hapsburgs) declared war on Prussia (Jan.); alliances with France, Russia, and Sweden formed.

1757 Prussia invaded Bohemia; defeated the Austrians at the Battle of Prague (May 6).

1757 In India, British defeated French at the Battle of Plassey (June 23).

1757 French forces occupied Hanover (Sept.) after defeating the British.

1757 Frederick II of Prussia defeated at Kolin by the Austrians (June), and forced to evacuate Bohemia.

1757 Frederick II defeated the Austrians and French at the Battle of Rossbach, in Saxony (Nov. 5).

1757 Battle of Leuthen, in Silesia (Dec. 5); Prussians under Frederick defeated the Austrians.

1758 British and Hanoverians defeated the French and Austrians at Crefeld (June), after driving the French back across the Rhine in the west.

1758 Frederick II defeated the Russians at Zorndorf (Aug.), halting the Russian advance toward Brandenburg.

1758 Prussians defeated by the Austrians at the Battle of Hochkirch (Oct.), but retained possession of Saxony and Silesia.

1759 Battle of Minden (Aug.); British and Hanoverians defeated a new French offensive in the west.

1759 British captured Quebec, in Canada, in a major victory over France (Sept. 13).

1759 Frederick II badly defeated by the Austrians at Kunersdorf (Aug.) and at Maxen (Nov.).

1759 British naval forces defeated French fleet in the Battle of Lagos, off Portugal (Aug. 7–18); headed off French invasion of England.

1759 French abandoned plans to invade Scotland after being defeated in the naval battle of Quiberon Bay, off Brittany (Nov. 20).

1760 British defeated (Jan. 22) French forces in India at the Battle of Wandiwash, Madras; most important battle of the war in India.

1760 Berlin occupied by the Russians (Oct.), but they were soon forced to withdraw.

1760 Prussians victorious (Nov. 3) over Austrians in bloody battle of Torgau; heavy losses ended fighting for the year.

1761 In India, the British were victorious (Jan.) in fighting at Pondicherry, the French stronghold in southern India.

1761 French defeated by the Prussians at Villinghausen (July 15).

1761 British ended aid to Prussia following accession of George III and the fall of W. Pitt (the elder).

1762 Spain entered war on the Austrian-French side, in accordance with the Family Compact.

1762 Czar Peter III succeeded to throne (Jan.) in Russia; an admirer of Prussian king Frederick, he moved to end hostilities with Prussia at a time when Prussia was near defeat.

1762 Treaty of St. Petersburg (May 5); war between Prussia and Russia ended; Sweden made peace with Prussia the same month.

1762 Frederick II defeated the Austrians at Burkersdorf (July 21) and Reichenbach (Aug. 16), recovering Silesia.

1762 British captured Spanish-held Havana, Cuba (Aug. 13), as they continued fighting in the colonies.

1762 Spanish captured fortress of Almeida (Aug. 25) in invasion of Portugal.

1762 Manila, in the Philippines, taken from the Spanish by the British (Oct. 5).

1762 Treaty of Fontainebleau (Nov. 3); preliminary peace between Britain and France.

1763 Treaty of Paris: Britain got French holdings in Canada, America, India, and elsewhere, as well as Spanish Florida; Spain got Cuba and Philippines back from Britain; Spain got Louisiana Territory from France (Feb. 10).

1763 Treaty of Hubertusberg: Prussia, Austria, and Saxony made peace, leaving Silesia in Prussian hands and confirming Prussian preeminence in Germany (Feb. 15).

Severini, Gino 1883–1966. Italian futurist painter. Influenced by both pointillist neoimpressionism and cubism, he was instrumental in gaining acceptance for futurism *(q.v.)* in Italy.

Severus, Flavius Valerius d. AD 307. Roman emperor of the West (AD 306–307). Named Augustus in the west by Galerius. He marched on Rome against Maxentius, whom he failed to defeat. Severus surrendered and later was executed.

Severus, Lucius Septimius (Septimius Severus) AD 146–211. Roman emperor (AD 193–211). Declared emperor by his legions, he successfully fought several rivals, subdued and annexed Mesopotamia, and used the army to increase imperial authority.

Sevier, John 1745–1815. American frontiersman and first governor of Tennessee (1796–1801, 1803–9). He was active in the American Revolution, represented North Carolina in Congress, and served as governor (1785–88) of the temporary western state of Franklin *(q.v.)*.

Seville Spanish city (pop. 588,800) on the Guadalquivir River in southwestern Spain. A prosperous city under the Romans, Vandals, and Visigoths, it became a commercial and intellectual center under Moorish rule (712–1248). It was taken (1248) by Ferdinand III and became (15th–16th cents.) the main port for Spanish trade with the New World. It was superseded by its rival, Cádiz (17th cent.)

Seville, Saint Isidore of *See* **Isidore of Seville, Saint**

Sèvres, Treaty of Treaty (Aug. 10, 1920) between the Allies and the Ottoman Turks, concluded at Sèvres, France, after WW I. By its terms the Ottoman Empire was abolished and Turkey was forced to renounce all non-Turkish possessions. The Dardanelles were internationalized and demilitarized. Palestine and Mesopotamia became British mandates, Syria became a French mandate, and the Hejaz and Armenia became independent kingdoms. The treaty was rejected by the nationalists led by K. Atatürk and was superseded by the Treaty of Lausanne *(q.v.)* in 1923.

Seward, William Henry 1801–72. American Whig and Republican statesman and secretary of state (1861–69). An uncompromising antislavery politician, he failed to gain the 1860 Republican presidential nomination but was Lincoln's first Cabinet officer. He is known best for the purchase of Alaska from Russia (1867).

Seward's Folly *See* **Alaska**

Seychelles Republic (pop. 70,000) in the Indian Ocean consisting of about 85 islands. First settled by the French (18th cent.), the islands were taken by the British (1794), made a crown colony (1903), and became a republic within the British Commonwealth (1976).

Seydlitz, Friedrich Wilhelm, Freiherr von 1721–73. Prussian general. Under Frederick II he reorganized the Prussian cavalry and led it in a series of brilliant victories in the War of the Austrian Succession and the Seven Years' War.

Seymour, Edward, 1st duke of Somerset 1506?–52. Protector of England (1547–50). He was virtual ruler of England during the early minority of Edward VI. His moderate religious and land reforms led to his downfall.

Seymour, Horatio 1810–86. American politician. He was governor of New York (1853–55, 1863–65) and an unsuccessful Democratic candidate for president (1868) against U. Grant. As governor during the New York draft riots (1863) he attempted to conciliate the rioters, which led to his defeat for reelection (1864).

Seymour, Jane 1509?–37. Third queen of English king Henry VIII (m. 1536), former lady-in-waiting to Henry's two previous queens. She gave birth to his only son (who became King Edward VI) and died a few days later.

Seymour, Thomas, Baron Seymour of Sudeley 1508?–1549. English aristocrat. He held high military offices under King Henry VIII after Henry's marriage to his sister Jane Seymour and married (1547) Henry's widow, Catherine Parr. He tried to supplant his brother E. Seymour as protector of Edward VI but was eventually executed for treason.

Sforza, Carlo, Count 1873–1952. Italian diplomat, antifascist leader and minister of foreign affairs (1920–21, 1947–51). He negotiated the Treaty of Rapallo (1922). During B. Mussolini's rule, he lived in exile.

Sforza, Francesco I 1401–66. Italian mercenary. He married (1441) the daughter of F. Visconti, duke of Milan. After Visconti's death (1447), a republic was declared in Milan. Sforza gained control and became duke (1450–66), founding a dynasty that ruled Milan for nearly a century.

Sforza, Francesco II 1495–1535. Last Sforza duke of Milan, son of L. Sforza. He took possession of the duchy (1522) but was deprived of it three years later. Restored as duke (1529), he died without heir.

Sforza, Galeazzo Maria 1444–76. Duke of Milan (1466–76), successor to his father, Francesco I Sforza. He was noted for his cruelty and immorality, and was assassinated.

Sforza, Gian Galeazzo 1469–94. Duke of Milan (1476–80), successor to his father, G. Sforza, under the regency of his mother. The duchy was soon seized from him by his uncle, L. Sforza.

Sforza, Ludovico 1451–1508. Duke of Milan (1494–99), patron of L. da Vinci. Sforza took control of the duchy from his nephew Gian Galeazzo Sforza in 1480 and succeeded officially on his death (1494). He aided French king Charles VIII to invade Naples (1494), then helped to drive him out. He was overthrown by French king Louis XII.

Sforza, Muzio Attendolo 1369–1424. Italian mercenary, founder of the Sforza family. A farmer turned soldier of fortune, he served in the employ of both Naples and Milan. His son Francesco I Sforza became (1450) the first Sforza duke of Milan.

Shackleton, Sir Ernest Henry 1874–1922. English explorer. Shackleton made four record-breaking voyages to the Antarctic. In 1915, after his ship was crushed by ice, he made his way some 800 miles to South Georgia Island to organize a relief expedition for his men.

Shaftesbury, Anthony Ashley Cooper, 1st earl of 1621–83. English statesman. Shaftsbury supported Cromwell but later aided in the restoration of King Charles II. He supported the Test Act and the Popish Plot of T. Oates.

Shaftesbury, Anthony Ashley Cooper, 3d earl of 1671–1713. English philosopher. A pupil of J. Locke, he rejected rationalism and held that humans are endowed with a moral sense. His writings influenced later philosophers.

Shaftesbury, Anthony Ashley Cooper, 7th earl of 1801–85. English social reformer. As a member of the House of Commons (1826–85) he introduced the Coal Mines Act (1842) prohibiting women and children from underground work, sponsored schools and model tenements for the poor, and encouraged the work of F. Nightingale.

Shah Jehan ⟨Shah Jahan⟩ 1592–1666. Fifth Mogul emperor of India (c1628–58). Many great buildings, notably the Taj Mahal, were built during his reign.

Shakers Christian sect founded (c1747) as an offshoot of Quakerism and transplanted to America (1774) by Mother Ann Lee. She claimed to be the incarnation of God's feminine nature. Shakers believed in celibacy and communal sharing of property. More than 20 Shaker communities existed by around 1830, but the movement declined steadily thereafter.

Shakespeare, William ⟨Shakespere, ~⟩ 1564–1616. English poet and playwright, considered the greatest of all dramatists. Few biographical details of his life are certain. He was born in Stratford-upon-Avon; married Anne Hathaway (1582), who gave him three children; went to London, where he gained a reputation as a playwright and actor with the company the Lord Chamberlain's Men (by 1594); enjoyed sufficient prosperity to buy a house in Stratford (1597) and to become a partner in the Globe Theater (1599); and lived out his last years as a country gentleman in Stratford (from 1610). Other details of his life have long been a matter of wide speculation and controversy. Even authorship of the plays attributed to him has been questioned, and a few critics have claimed that Shakespeare's works were actually written by someone else (F. Bacon is often cited). But these issues aside, there is little doubt concerning the depth of understanding, mastery of character, eloquence of language, and dramatic intensity revealed in his plays. Although he is known best for his plays, Shakespeare wrote numerous sonnets, collected and published in 1609; two narrative poems, *Venus and Adonis* (1593) and *The Rape of Lucrece* (1594); and the love poem, *The Phoenix and the Turtle* (1601). Shakespeare enjoyed a wide reputation in his own time, but interest in his works declined in the 17th and 18th cents. The Romantic period (18th–19th cents.), however, marked the beginning of renewed appreciation of Shakespeare. Critical works by G. Lessing, S. Coleridge, W. Hazlitt, and many others helped establish Shakespeare's rightful place in literature. Among Shakespeare's many well-known plays are *Hamlet, Macbeth, Romeo and Juliet, King Lear, The Comedy of Errors, A Midsummer Night's Dream, The Merchant of Venice, Julius Caesar, The Taming of the Shrew, Much Ado About Nothing,* and *All's Well That Ends Well.*

Shakespere, William *See* **Shakespeare, William**

Shalmaneser I *d.* 1290 BC. Assyrian king. He extended Assyria's boundary northward and moved its capital from Assur to Calah, which he had founded.

Shalmaneser II   *See* **Shalmaneser III**

Shalmaneser III ⟨Shalmaneser II⟩ *d.* 825 BC. Assyrian king (860–825 BC). He made war successfully on Babylonia and Israel and received tribute from King Jehu of Israel.

Shalmaneser IV   *See* **Shalmaneser V**

Shalmaneser V ⟨Shalmaneser IV⟩ *d.* 722 BC. Assyrian king (727–722 BC). He fought King Hosea of Israel but died during the siege of the Israelite capital, Samaria. It was finally taken by his successor, Sargon II.

shamanism Ancestral religion of such Central Asian peoples as Mongolians, Kirghiz, Tungus, etc. It is based on belief in the powers of shamans, who heal the sick and are believed to communicate with and appease the gods through incantations, dreams, and visions. Shamanism is also found among the Eskimos and North American Indians.

Shams ud-din Muhammad   *See* **Hafiz**

Shamyl *c*1798–1871. Muslim leader in the Caucasus. He conducted guerrilla warfare against Russian domination and allied himself with England and France in the Crimean War. After the war he was defeated and captured by Russia (1859).

Shang Chinese dynasty, also called the Yin. The Shang ruled northern China from *c*1766 to *c*1122 BC. It is the earliest Chinese dynasty to be historically verified by archaelogical evidence and written inscriptions. The Shang period saw great advances in bronze casting, pottery, weaving, and agriculture. It appears that ancestor worship and human sacrifice were practiced and that Shang rulers had a highly organized system of government.

Shanghai A major seaport and the largest city (pop. 12,000,000) in China. Opened (1842) to the British as one of the first treaty ports accessible to Western nations, it rapidly became a commercial center. Occupied by the Japanese during WW II, it was returned to China (1945), and was occupied by the Communists (1949).

Shapley, Harlow 1885–1972. American astronomer. Shapley determined the size of the Milky Way and the sun's position in it. He also contributed to the fields of photometry and spectroscopy.

Shapur I ⟨Sapor I⟩ *d.* AD 272. Persian king (AD 241–272), successor to his father, Ardashir I. He strengthened the Sassanian Empire founded by his father. He captured Roman emperor Valerian at Edessa (AD 260) and imprisoned him, thereby further weakening the Roman Empire.

Shapur II ⟨Sapor II⟩ AD 309–379. Persian king (AD 309–379) from birth. He waged war against

the Romans and defeated an invasion (AD 363) by Roman emperor Julian, who died in battle. Shapur received an advantageous peace from Julian's successor, Jovian, and gained control of Armenia.

Sharpsburg, Battle of   *See* **Antietam, Battle of**

Sharrukin   *See* **Sargon**

Shaw, George Bernard 1856–1950. Irish playwright, critic, and political pamphleteer, considered one of the great English playwrights. An outspoken Socialist, he revealed his concern for humanity in such plays as *Mrs. Warren's Profession*, *Arms and the Man*, *Major Barbara*, *Pygmalion*, and *Saint Joan*. His plays helped to revolutionize British theater. He was awarded the Nobel Prize in literature in 1925.

Shawano Indians   *See* **Shawnee Indians**

Shawnee Indians ⟨Shawano Indians⟩ North American Indian tribe. Originally inhabiting the Ohio River valley, they migrated to several states before reuniting (18th cent.) in Ohio. Under Tecumseh *(q.v.)*, they rose against encroachment on their lands by settlers, but were defeated at Tippecanoe *(q.v.)* and eventually resettled in Oklahoma.

Shawnee Prophet ⟨Tenskwatawa⟩ 1768–1837. Shawnee Indian mystic and leader, brother of Tecumseh. He led the Shawnee at the Battle of Tippecanoe *(q.v.)* in 1811.

Shay's Rebellion American insurrection (1786–87) led by Daniel Shays (1747?–1825). Massachusetts farmers, suffering because of the financial depression after the American Revolution, rose up in hopes of forcing the government to decrease taxes and issue paper money. The revolt was suppressed. Shays was condemned to death but was pardoned.

Sheba ⟨Saba⟩ Biblical country, located in southern Arabia. Its people, the Sabaeans, colonized Ethiopia (10th cent. BC). According to legend, in the same century, Balkis, queen of Sheba, made a visit to the court of Solomon.

Shechem ⟨Sichem⟩ Biblical city in Palestine, now the town of Nablus. It was the home of Jacob and the site of the tomb of Joseph.

Shelburne, William Petty Fitzmaurice, 2d earl of 1737–1805. English statesman. A supporter of W. Pitt, he attempted unsuccessfully to moderate England's course toward its American colonies. He concluded the Treaty of Paris (1783).

Shelley, Mary Wollstonecraft Godwin 1797–1851. English writer. The daughter of M. Wollstonecraft and wife of P. Shelley, she is known best as author of the classic novel *Frankenstein*.

Shelley, Percy Bysshe 1792–1822. English poet, one of the leading English Romantic poets. Expelled from Oxford for publishing *The Necessity* *of Atheism* (1811), he left his first wife (1814) and ran off to Europe with M. Shelley (née Godwin). There he wrote many of his greatest works, among them *Prometheus Unbound.*

Shenandoah Valley   Valley in northern Virginia, running north to south between the Allegheny and Blue Ridge mountains. It was a strategic Confederate stronghold and source of supplies during the American Civil War (1861–65) and was the scene of many battles. In 1862, Confederate Gen. Stonewall Jackson, operating in the valley, repulsed troops seeking to reinforce Union Gen. McClellan outside Richmond, and thus contributed to the failure of the Union Peninsular Campaign *(q.v.).* Gen. R.E. Lee used the valley as an escape route after offensives against the North failed (notably after Gettysburg, 1863). During 1864, Confederate Gen. J. Early conducted highly successful operations in the valley. Subsequently in that year Union forces under Gen. P. Sheridan began a drive to take control of the valley, completed in 1865.

Shen Nung   Legendary Chinese emperor, believed to have been born in 2800 BC. He was the second of China's mythical great emperors and is said to have taught the Chinese farming skills and to have established an agricultural society.

Shen Yen Huang Ti   *See* **Huang Ti**

Sheraton, Thomas   1751–1806. English furniture maker. Sheraton's graceful furniture designs greatly influenced his age and are still popular today.

Shere Ali   1825–79. Emir of Afghanistan (1863–79). His succession was contested by family members, but he gained control with British assistance. Later he turned away from Britain and was defeated by the British in the second Afghan War *(q.v.)* in 1878.

Sheridan, Philip Henry   1831–88. Union general in the American Civil War. As commander of the Army of the Shenandoah (1864–65), he defeated Confederate Gen. J. Early and laid waste to the Shenandoah Valley. Early later successfully counterattacked, but Sheridan turned a possible Union disaster into a victory. In Apr., 1865, he cut off Gen. R. Lee's retreat at Appomattox, Virginia, forcing Lee to surrender (Apr. 9).

Sheridan, Richard Brinsley   1751–1816. English dramatist. Among his many plays are *The Rivals* and *The School for Scandal.* He entered Parliament (1780) and served in several Cabinet posts.

Sherman, John   1823–1900. American statesman. As US senator (1861–77, 1881–97) he played a role in Reconstruction after the American Civil War and in formulating the Sherman Anti-Trust Act *(q.v.)* and the Sherman Silver Purchase Act

(q.v.). He also served as secretary of the treasury (1877–81) under Pres. R. Hayes.

Sherman, William Tecumseh   1820–91.   Union general in the American Civil War, noted for saying, "War is hell." A West Point graduate (1840), he resigned the army (1853), only to rejoin on the outbreak of the Civil War. He fought at the First Battle of Bull Run and afterward was made a brigadier general of volunteers. Transferred to Tennessee, he fought at Shiloh, in the Vicksburg and Chattanooga campaigns, and other battles (1862–63). Already a brigadier general in the regular army, Sherman became supreme commander in the West (Mar., 1864). He then conducted his successful Atlanta Campaign *(q.v.)* and, after capturing the city, began his devastating "March to the Sea" (Nov. 15).

Sherman Anti-Trust Act   American law (1890), the first designed to prohibit trusts, monopolies, combinations, and restraint of trade on a national and international level. Supreme Court decisions curtailed its effectiveness until Pres. T. Roosevelt actively enforced it. The law was also strengthened by the Clayton Anti-Trust Act (1914).

Sherman Silver Purchase Act   American currency law (1890) requiring the American government to buy set amounts of silver each month to be added to the national currency. The mandatory and excessive purchases of silver soon threatened to drain the nation's gold supply and led to the financial Panic of 1893. The act, and consequently the national policy of bimetalism, was repealed (Nov. 1, 1893) and the gold standard was restored.

Sherman's March to the Sea   *See* **American Civil War** (1864–65)

Sherpas   *See* **Nepal**

Sherwood, Robert Emmet   1896–1955.   American playwright. His plays, among them *The Petrified Forest, Idiot's Delight,* and *There Shall Be No Night,* greatly influenced American drama. Sherwood was awarded four Pulitzer prizes (1936, 1939, 1941, 1949).

Sheshonk I   *d.* c924 BC. Egyptian king (945–924 BC), founder of the 22d dynasty. Originally a mercenary commander, he usurped the throne, and conducted campaigns in Palestine, apparently in support of Jereboam.

Shidehara, Kijuro, Baron   1872–1951.   Japanese diplomat and statesman. As foreign minister (1924–27, 1929–31) he followed a peaceful policy antagonistic to Japanese militarism. After WW II, he served briefly (1945–46) as prime minister.

Shih Huang Ti ⟨Ch'in Shi Huang Ti⟩   255–210 BC. Chinese emperor (247/6–210 BC) who first unified the empire and built the Great Wall of China. Following his accession as king of the Ch'in Kingdom of northwestern China, he annexed six other Chinese kingdoms to create (221 BC) the Ch'in Empire. He thereupon abolished the old feudal order, divided his empire into 36 military districts, established a centralized administration, and instituted uniform standards in weights and measures, laws, and the written language. He was a builder and, in addition to the Great Wall, ordered construction of roads and canals. His struggle with the Confucian scholars (supporters of the old feudal order) led to the Burning of the Books (213 BC) and the eventual rise of the Han dynasty.

Shi'ites   Muslim sect, one of the two major divisions of Islam, the other being the Sunni *(q.v.)*. The Shi'ites originated in Persia as partisans of Ali, son-in-law of Muhammad, after the first Muslim Civil War. They opposed the Ummayad dynasty, supported by the Sunni. The Shi'ites believe that a Mahdi will appear at the millennium. Babism and Bahaism are outgrowths of Shi'ite beliefs. Shi'ism is the official religion of Iran and also has followers in India, Iraq, Yemen, Pakistan, and Oman.

Shiloh   Biblical town in Palestine. It was the home of the prophets Eli, Ahijah, and Samuel; the sanctuary of the Ark of the Covenant; and the meeting place of the Israelites.

Shiloh, Battle of ⟨Pittsburg Landing, Battle of⟩ Battle (Apr. 6–7, 1862) of the American Civil War, near Pittsburg Landing in southwestern Tennessee. The second major battle of the war; it derives its name from Shiloh church nearby. Here Confederate forces under Gen. A. Johnston surprised the Union troops under Gen. U. Grant. Bloody fighting ensued, Johnston was killed, and each side suffered more than 10,000 casualties. Though both sides claimed victory, Confederate failure to completely route the Union has led historians to classify it as a Union victory.

Shimabara Rebellion   Japanese insurrection (1637–38) in which the predominantly Catholic population of Shimabara rose against unjust taxation. More than 100,000 troops failed to quell the rebellion and a Dutch gunship had to be called in. The rebellion caused further Christian persecution and led Japan's leaders to adopt a policy of isolation.

Shimonoseki, Treaty of   Treaty (Apr. 17, 1895) between China and Japan ending the First Sino-Japanese War. By its terms China, who had lost the war, accepted Korean independence and ceded Taiwan, the Pescadores islands, and Port Arthur and the Liaotung Peninsula to Japan. Japan subsequently returned Port Arthur and the Liaotung Peninsula after European protests.

Shinar   Biblical region, located between the Tigris and Euphrates rivers and corresponding to southern Babylonia.

Shinran   1173–1262. Japanese Buddhist philosopher and religious reformer. He founded the True Pure Land sect, the largest Buddhist sect in Japan.

Shinto   Indigenous religion of Japan which is more a way of life than a formal dogma. Its major divinities are Amaterasu, the sun goddess, and her brother Susanowo, the storm god, but all objects contain a holy spirit called kami. Ancestor worship and pilgrimages to shrines are important aspects of Shinto, which literally means "the way of the gods." The Japanese emperor was considered divine as a direct descendent of Amaterasu. This belief was promoted until 1946, when Emperor Hirohito disavowed his divinity.

Shipton, Mother   English prophetess, believed to have been Ursula Southiel Shipton (1488–1561). She allegedly predicted events of King Henry VIII's reign and the date of the Great Fire of London (1666).

Shirpuria   *See* **Lagash**

Shiva ⟨Siva⟩   The four-armed Hindu god of destruction. With Brahma (creation) and Vishnu (preservation), he is one of the three major gods of Hinduism.

Shivaji   *See* **Sivji**

Shockley, William   *See* **Bardeen, John**

shogun   Military leaders who were the effective rulers of Japan from 1192 to 1867. Shogun was the title of the imperial military commander, and in 1192 the emperor appointed Minamoto Yoritomo shogun. Yoritomo gained control over the government, and in subsequent centuries the shoguns, as well as the warrior class they controlled, ruled Japan. The emperor was sovereign in title only. Under the shoguns, Japan remained locked in a rigid feudal system. The emperors did not regain power until the Meiji Restoration (1868), which marked the end of feudalism in Japan and the beginning of the movement toward modernization. The shogunate itself was hereditary and was held successively by the following families:

Kamakura shogunate	
(Minamoto family)	1192–1333
Ashikaga shogunate	1338–1578
Tokugawa shogunate	1603–1867

shogunate   *See also* **Bakufu**

Sholes, Christopher Latham   1819–1890. American journalist and inventor. With Carlos Glidden and Samuel W. Soulé, he invented (1868) the first practical typewriter. The machine, with improvements, became (1874) the Remington typewriter.

Sholokhov, Mikhail Alekansdrovich   1905–. Russian author. He is known best for his trilogy of

Russian life: *The Silent Don, And Quiet Flows the Don,* and *The Don Flows Home to the Sea.* He was awarded a Nobel Prize in literature in 1965.

Shore, Jane *d.* 1527? English mistress to King Edward IV. She had great influence, but after Edward's death, King Richard III forced her into humiliation and poverty.

Short Parliament Fourth English Parliament in the reign of King Charles I. Convened (Apr. 13, 1640) by Charles to provide aid for a war against the Scottish Covenanters, it refused to do so until the king had replied to its grievances. It was dissolved (May 5) and followed (Nov. 3) by the Long Parliament.

Shostakovich, Dmitri 1906–1975. Russian composer. He aroused controversy in Russia by following his own musical values, sometimes in conflict with those of Russian politics. He was renowned for his symphonies and piano and violin concertos.

Shreve, Henry Miller 1785–1851. American steamboat captain who played a major role in the opening of the Mississippi River to commercial trade. Shreveport, Louisiana, is named for him.

Shrewsbury, Charles Talbot, duke of 1660–1718. English statesman. He was one of the seven leaders to sign the paper (1688) inviting William of Orange to become English king in the Glorious Revolution. He also played a major part in securing the succession (1714) of the Hanoverian king George I.

Shrewsbury, John Talbot, 2d earl of *See* **Castillon, Battle of**

Siam *See* **Thailand**

Sian Incident Incident sparked (Dec. 12, 1936) by the arrest of Chinese Nationalist leader Chiang Kai-shek by one of his generals, Chang Hsueh-liang, at Sian, China. Chang demanded that Chiang end his war against the Communists and form a united front to fight the invading Japanese. Chiang agreed and was released (Dec. 25). The incident led to a Communist-Nationalistic coalition that lasted through WW II.

Sibelius, Jean Julius Christian 1865–1957. Finnish composer and nationalist. A Romantic composer, he brought worldwide attention to Scandinavian music with his symphonies and tone poems, among them *Finlandia.*

Siberia Region of the northern Asian USSR stretching from the Urals to the Pacific Ocean and noted for its wealth of natural resources and its harsh climate. It was the site (15th cent.) of the Tatar khanate, which was conquered for Russia (1581) by the Cossacks under Yermak. Russia continued to extend its control over Siberia in the 16th and 17th cents. but relinquished some of its

territory to China by the Treaty of Nerchinsk *(q.v.)* in 1689. Settlement increased after construction (1891–1905) of the Trans-Siberian Railway. Siberia was the center of White Russian resistance (1918–20) to Bolshevik rule after the Russian Revolution. Large petroleum reserves have been found in Siberia and it has been greatly developed in the 20th cent.

Sibyl Mythical ancient Greek prophetess. Sibyls were said to have powers of divination and the ability to intercede with the gods on behalf of humans.

Sichem *See* **Shechem**

Sickingen, Franz von 1481–1523. German knight. A free knight, he aided the election of Charles V as Holy Roman Emperor and protected M. Luther and J. Reuchlin. He died fighting in the Knights' War.

Sickles, Daniel Edgar 1819–1914. American politician and Union general in the American Civil War. He fought in the Peninsular Campaign and at Antietam, Chancellorsville, and Gettysburg. He served in Congress (1857–61, 1893–95).

Sicyon Ancient Greek city in the Peloponnesus northwest of Corinth. It rose to power (6th cent. BC) under Cleisthenes but was later dominated by Corinth or Sparta. It was noted for its artists and art schools.

Sicyon, Butades of *See* **Butades of Sicyon**

Siddons, Sarah Kemble 1755–1831. English actress. A member of the Kemble acting family, she was admired by both audiences and critics for her performances in such roles as Desdemona and Lady Macbeth.

Sidmouth, Henry Addington, 1st Viscount 1757–1844. English statesman. As prime minister (1801–04) he concluded the Treaty of Amiens with Napoleon. As home secretary (1812–21) he persecuted the Luddites and helped to bring about the Peterloo massacre *(q.v.).*

Sidney, Sir Philip ⟨Sydney, ~⟩ 1554–96. English author and courtier. Sidney was influential in the court of Queen Elizabeth I. He is known for his pastoral poems and his prose essay *The Defense of Poetry.*

Siege of *See under names inverted, as in* **Orleans, Siege of**

Siegfried ⟨Sigfrid⟩ ⟨Sigurd⟩ German mythical hero of the Nibelungenlied. He killed the dragon Fafnir and became king of the Nibelungs.

Siegfried Line Line of fortifications built along Germany's western frontier in the 1930s. It corresponded to the French Maginot Line and succeeded in slowing down the Allied offensive in WW II.

Siena Italian city. A great commercial and banking center before the rise of Florence, it was noted for its artistic and architectural influence.

Siena, Saint Catherine of *See* **Catherine of Siena, Saint**

Sierra Leone West African republic (pop. 3,470,000) on the Atlantic Ocean. Its economy is based on agriculture and mining. First explored (15th cent.) by the Portuguese, it was a center for the British slave trade (17th and 18th cents.) until the trade was outlawed by the British (1807). It became a British protectorate (1896) and achieved independence in 1961.

Siete Partidas *See* **Alfonso X**

Sieyes, Emmanuel Joseph 1748–1836. French revolutionary statesman. He played a major role in the early years of the French Revolution, drafted the Declaration of the Rights of Man *(q.v.)*, and later helped organize the *coup d-état* that overthrew the Directory.

Sigebert I *d.* 575. Frankish king of Austrasia (561–575). His reign was marked by nearly constant warfare with his brother Chilperic I. He defeated Chilperic but was assassinated by order of Fredegunde, Chilperic's wife.

Sigel, Franz 1824–1902. German-born American general. A leader of the Baden insurrections of 1848–49, he fled to America after their failure. He served as a Union general during the American Civil War.

Sigfrid *See* **Siegfried**

Sigismund 1368–1437. Holy Roman Emperor (1411–37, crowned 1433), last of the Luxemburg emperors. As Hungarian king (1387–1437) he persuaded Pope John XXIII to convene the Council of Constance (1414–17), which ended the Great Schism *(q.v.)*. He revoked his guarantee of safe passage to J. Huss, who was condemned for heresy and burned. Huss's death led to the Hussite Wars *(q.v.)*.

Sigismund I 1467–1548. Polish king (1506–48), successor to his brother Alexander I. His reign was marked by power struggles with the nobility and warfare with Russia.

Sigismund II ⟨Sigismund Augustus⟩ 1520–72. Polish king (1548–72), successor to his father, Sigismund I. He united Poland with Lithuania and Livonia.

Sigismund III 1566–1632. King of Poland (1587–1632) and Sweden (1592–99). Deposed in Sweden, he engaged in wars to regain his throne. He also invaded Russia and captured Moscow (1610–12).

Sigismund Augustus *See* **Sigismund II**

Sigurd *See* **Siegfried**

Sigurdsson, Jon 1811–79. Icelandic scholar and statesman. He edited many books of Icelandic literature and history. His efforts contributed to Denmark's granting of self-government to Iceland (1874).

Sikhs People of northwest India, followers of a religion founded (15th cent.) by Nanak. Fusing Hindu and Muslim beliefs, the Sikhs worship one God and employ meditation and exercise to attain the realization of God. They revere their guru (teacher) and accept as their only religious text the Adi Granth, largely a collection of hymns by the early gurus. They came to control much of the Punjab (18th cent.) but were defeated by the British in the Sikh Wars *(q.v.)* of the 19th cent.

Sikh Wars Two 19th-cent. wars between the Sikhs and the British. **1.** The first Sikh war (1845–46) was sparked by a Sikh invasion into British India and culminated in the defeat of the Sikhs and British annexation of Kashmir. **2.** The second Sikh war (1848–49) was caused by an uprising and resulted in a British victory and the annexation of the Punjab.

Sikorski, Wladyslaw Eugeniusz 1881–1943. Polish general and statesman. He fought in WW I, commanded in the Russo-Polish War (1920), and served as prime minister (1922–23). He headed (1939–43) the Polish government in exile during WW II.

Sikorsky, Igor Ivan 1889–1972. Ukrainian-born American aircraft engineer. He is noted for the development (1939) of the first successful helicopter.

Silas ⟨Silvanus⟩ Early Christian missionary. He accompanied the Apostle Paul on his second journey.

Silenus Ancient Greek forest god, companion to Dionysus. Part man and part horse, he was said to be often drunk, but was extremely wise.

Silesia European region situated largely in modern Poland but also in Czechoslovakia and East Germany. An industrial and mining center, Silesia was originally part of Poland. It passed to Bohemia (14th cent.), was divided, and was devastated during the Thirty Years' War, after which it passed to Austria (1648). Prussia gained control of much of the region in the Silesian Wars *(q.v.)*. It came under increasing German influence (18th–19th cents.). Partitioned (1921) after WW I, it was seized by Germany in WW II. After the war, most of the region was restored to Poland.

Silesian Wars **1.** The first Silesian War (1740–42) was fought between Prussia and Austria for possession of Silesia. It was begun by the invasion of Silesia by Prussian king Frederick II, in alliance with Bavaria, France, and Saxony. Austria was defeated, and by the Treaty of Breslau (1742) Prussia gained possession of much of Silesia. **2.** The second Silesian War (1744–45) was begun by Frederick II, who crossed Saxony and invaded Bohemia. He captured Prague but was forced back into Saxony. The war was ended by the Treaty of Dresden (1745) between Austria and Prussia, and Frederick retained possession of Silesia. **3.** *See* Seven Years' War.

Silk Road ⟨Silk Route⟩   Ancient trade route across Asia from the Roman Empire to China. Roughly the same route was followed by Marco Polo in his travels.

Silk Route   *See* **Silk Road**

Silla, kingdom of   Ancient kingdom of Korea which arose (1st–2d cent. AD) in southeastern Korea. With the kingdoms of Koguryo and Paekche, it was one of the three early Korean kingdoms and later unified the peninsula under native Korean rule for the first time in 670. An administrative bureaucracy, influenced by Chinese patterns, was set up, and Buddhism flourished. The Silla rulers were supplanted by the Koryo dynasty in 935.

Silvanus   *See* **Silas**

Silva Xavier, José Joaquim da   *See*   **Tiradentes Conspiracy**

Silver Age   Period in Roman literary history (AD 14–c130) following the Golden Age. It was characterized by the writings of Tacitus, Juvenal, Suetonius, Pliny the Elder and Pliny the Younger, and Seneca.

Simcoe, John Graves   1752–1806. British soldier and governor. Simcoe fought in the American Revolution and became (1792) the first lieutenant governor of Upper Canada.

Simeon ⟨Symeon⟩   Biblical patriarch, the second son of Jacob and Leah. He was the ancestor of the southernmost of the Twelve Tribes of Israel.

Simeon I   *d.* 927. Bulgarian prince (893–925) and first czar of Bulgaria (925–927). Simeon warred successfully against the Magyars, Serbs, and the Byzantine Empire. His court became a center of culture.

Simeon II   1937–. Last czar of Bulgaria (1943–46), successor to his father, Boris III. Nominal czar under a regency, he went into exile when the monarchy was abolished.

Simeon Stylites, Saint   *d.* AD 459? Syrian Christian ascetic. Simeon lived for thirty years atop a small, high pillar, from which he preached.

Simms, William Gilmore   1806–70.   American writer, known for his popular historical romances about life in the South.

Simnel, Lambert   1477?–1534? Pretender to the English throne. Yorkists claimed that Simnel was Edward of Warwick and attempted unsuccessfully to overthrow King Henry VII (1487).

Simon, Théodore   *See* **Binet, Alfred**

Simon Bar Cochba   *See* **Bar Kokba, Simon**

Simon Commission   British commission appointed (Nov., 1927) under the chairmanship of Sir John Simon (1873–1954) to study the working of the Indian constitution established in 1919. It was boycotted by the Indian National Congress for its "all white" composition, and its actions and conclusions aroused great hostility among Indian nationalists.

Simonides of Ceos   c556–468? BC. Greek poet, known best for his epitaphs for the dead at Marathon of Thermopylae.

Simon Magus   Biblical Samaritan. A sorcerer, he attempted to buy spiritual powers from the apostles of Jesus. From this comes the word "simony."

Simon of Cyrene   Biblical figure. An onlooker during Jesus' crucifixion, he was obliged to carry the cross of Jesus.

Simon Peter   One of the twelve apostles of Jesus. He was the first bishop of Rome, forerunner of the religious designation "pope." (*See also* Peter.)

Simons, Menno   *See* **Mennonites**

Simpson, Sir George   1792–1860.   Scottish-born Canadian explorer. Simpson explored Canada for the Hudson's Bay Company and made an overland journey (1841–42) across the northern part of the world.

Sims, William Sowden   1858–1936.   American naval officer. He commanded US operations in European waters during WW I. With Burton J. Hendrick (1870–1949) he wrote the Pulitzer Prize-winning *The Victory at Sea.*

sin   Violation of divine law. The concept of sin appears in various forms in several religions but is most highly developed in the Bible and in the teachings of Christianity.

Sin   1. Wilderness in the western Sinai through which the ancient Hebrews wandered. **2.** Ancient Assyro-Babylonian god, father of Ishtar.

Sinai   Peninsula in northeastern Egypt linking Africa with Asia. It was the scene of battles between Israel and Egypt during the Arab-Israeli Wars.

Sinaitic inscriptions   Inscriptions carved on rocks in the Sinai Peninsula. They were discovered (1904–05) by Sir W. Petrie.

Sinan   1489?–1587? Foremost Ottoman architect, who designed and built more than 300 structures. He built the mosques of Suleiman I at Constantinople and Selim II at Adrianople.

Sinatra, Frank ⟨~, Francis Albert⟩ 1915–. American singer and actor. He first gained prominence in the 1930s, and became one of the country's best-known singers in the 1940s. His phenomenal popularity has continued.

Sinclair, Harry F. *See* **Teapot Dome**

Sinclair, Upton Beall 1878–1968. American writer and reformer. One of the muckrakers *(q.v.)*, he is known best for his novel *The Jungle*, an exposé of the meat-packing industry. He was awarded a Pulitzer Prize (1943).

Singapore ⟨Republic of Singapore⟩ Small republic located at the tip of the Malay Peninsula. Originally a Malay city, it was destroyed by the Javanese (14th cent.). Sir T. Raffles refounded (1819) the city and under the British East India Company it became a major world port and naval base in the Straits Settlements. The British surrendered Singapore to the Japanese (1942) during WW II but retook the city (1945). It became self-governing in 1959, briefly joined the Federation of Malaysia (1963–65), and became an independent republic (Sept., 1965).

Singer, Isaac Merrit 1811–75. American inventor. He devised and patented (1851) the first continuous-stitch sewing machine. Although he lost a patent-infringement case (1854) to E. Howe, his company soon became the leading manufacturer of sewing machines.

Sinn Fein Irish Nationalist political party of Ireland, whose name means "We Ourselves." Originally a movement founded (1899) by A. Griffith, it sought to gain independence from England. It gathered momentum after the Easter Rebellion (1916) under the leadership of E. De Valera. After De Valera withdrew (1927) to enter the Dail of the Irish Free State, Sinn Fein declined in importance and eventually became the political arm of the Irish Republican Army (IRA).

Sinnott, Michael *See* **Sennett, Mack**

Sino-French War Undeclared war (1883–85) between France and China arising from French expansion into Vietnam. China claimed Vietnam as a protectorate, and after France declared a protectorate over Annam (1883), China sent troops to Vietnam. Soon defeated, China was forced (1885) to recognize French interests in Annam and Tonkin.

Sino-Japanese War **1.** War (1894–95) between China and Japan over control of Korea. The Japanese, having a modern, well equipped army, easily invaded Shantung and Manchuria and forced the Chinese to sue for peace. By the Treaty of Shimonoseki (1895), the Chinese agreed to pay a large indemnity, to cede vast areas (including Taiwan) to Japan, to grant trade privileges to Japan, and to recognize the nominal independence of Korea. Japan emerged from the conflict as a major international power. **2.** War (1937–45) between China and Japan. Following its occupation of Manchuria (1931–32), Japan pressed the Chinese for further concessions. The ongoing civil war between Chinese nationalists and Communists made it all but impossible to resist the growing threat of an invasion by Japan. By the Sian Incident *(q.v.)* in 1936, Nationalists and Communists agreed to form a common front against the Japanese, and in July 1937 hostilities broke out. Japan quickly occupied Peking and Tientsin, and soon after took Shanghai and the capital of Nanking. The Japanese continued their rapid advance over the eastern portions of China, taking cities and other strategic points while the Chinese pursued a scorched-earth policy and waged a bitter guerrilla war from within. China declared war on the Axis powers in 1941, after the Japanese attack on Pearl Harbor, and the fighting in China thus became part of WW II. In 1942–44, despite an increase in aid from the US and Britain and the diversion of Japanese forces to fighting elsewhere, the Chinese were unable to gain the initiative, though they slowed the Japanese advance and inflicted some serious defeats. In fact, it was not until the spring of 1945, just before the Japanese surrender, that the Chinese were able to mount a successful offensive.

Sinop Turkish seaport on the Black Sea. The destruction of an Ottoman fleet here (1853) by the Russians contributed to the outbreak of the Crimean War (1853–56).

Sino-Soviet Treaty Treaty (Aug. 14, 1945) between China and the USSR. Intended to deter Japanese aggression, it established a joint railway, a joint naval base at Port Arthur, and made Darien a free port.

Sintra, Convention of *See* **Convention of Sintra**

Sion *See* **Zion**

Sioux Indians ⟨Dakota Indians⟩ Confederation of American Indian tribes that inhabited large tracts of the Midwest from Lake Superior to beyond the Dakotas. The Sioux concluded several treaties with the US, but after complications following a treaty (1851) involving US acquisition of much of Minnesota, they rose and massacred settlers. Thus began a series of clashes against further encroachment on tribal lands continuing through the 1860s. In 1867 the Sioux moved to Dakota territory, but discovery of gold in the Black Hills (1867) led to further conflict and the Battle of Little Bighorn *(q.v.)*. The last Sioux uprising ended in the massacre at Wounded Knee *(q.v.)* in 1890.

Siqueiros, David Alfaro 1898–1974. Mexican painter. His murals, such as *March of Humanity* and *Third World*, reflect his ardent socialism and are among Mexico's most celebrated works of art.

Siracusa *See* **Syracuse**

Siren One of several mythological Greek sea nymphs, half woman and half bird, who inhabited an island and lured sailors to destruction on its rocks by their singing. They were outwitted by both Jason and Odysseus.

Sistine Chapel Private papal chapel at the Vatican. Built (1473) by Pope Sixtus IV, it is celebrated for its ceiling paintings by Michelangelo.

Sistova, Peace of Treaty (Aug. 4, 1791) between Austria and Bulgaria, concluded at Sistova, Bulgaria. It adjusted mutual borders and returned Belgrade to Turkey.

Sisyphus Mythical Greek king, founder and ruler of Corinth. He was condemned by Zeus to spend eternity rolling a boulder to the top of a hill in Hades, only to see it roll down again.

Sitter, William de 1872–1934. Dutch astronomer. He advanced the theory of an expanding universe.

Sitting Bull *d.* 1890. American Indian leader. He led the Sioux in the Battle of the Little Bighorn *(q.v.)* in 1876. He surrendered (1881), spent his last years on a reservation, and was killed for allegedly resisting arrest.

Sitwell, Edith 1887–1964. English poet. Her poetry reveals a love of beauty and a sense of humanity's sufferings. Among her works are *Clown's Houses, Street Songs,* and *The Canticle of the Rose.*

Siva *See* **Shiva**

Sivaji ⟨Shivaji⟩ ⟨Grand Rebel⟩ 1627–80. Indian ruler, founder of the Maratha *(q.v.)* kingdom. He expanded his domains at the expense of the Mogul Empire.

Siward ⟨Siward the Strong⟩ *d.* 1055. Danish warrior and earl of Northumbria. He supported Edward the Confessor and later defeated Scottish king Macbeth.

Siward the Strong *See* **Siward**

Six, Les Group of early 20th-cent. composers who opposed the musical traditions of C. Debussy, C. Franck, and others. They were briefly influential.

Six Acts Acts adopted (Dec. 1819) by the British Parliament to suppress the radical movement for parliamentary reform in England. The acts followed the Peterloo massacre and greatly curtailed freedom of speech, press, and assembly.

Six Articles, Act of *See* **Act of Six Articles**

Six-Day War *See* **Arab-Israeli War (Third)**

Six Dynasties Name given to the period in China between the fall of the Han dynasty (AD 220) and the beginning of the Sui (581). The era was marked by political disintegration but such cultural advancements as the introduction of Buddhism and Taoism; medical and scientific study; and the use of coal, tea, and gunpowder. It was named after the six dynasties that ruled during the period: the Wu (AD 222–280), the Eastern Ch'in (317–419), the Liu-Sung (420–479), the Southern Ch'i (479–502), the Liang (502–557), and the Ch'en (557–581).

Sixteen Kingdoms Name applied to a group of dynasties, all but three non-Chinese, that ruled in northern China from AD 304–439.

Sixth Crusade *See* **Crusade, Sixth**

Sixtus IV 1414–84. Pope (1471–84), successor to Paul II. A patron of the arts, he built (1473) the Sistine Chapel. He deeply involved the papacy in political intrigues.

Sixtus V ⟨Peretti, Felice⟩ 1521–90. Italian-born pope (1585–90), successor to Gregory XIII. He made many administrative reforms, restored order in the Papal States, and did much rebuilding in Rome.

Sjahrir, Sutan 1909–66. Indonesian prime minister (1945–47). He negotiated the Linggadjati Agreement with The Netherlands, by which the Indonesian government was recognized and plans were made for a permanent state.

Skagerrak, Battle of *See* **Jutland, Battle of**

Skelton, John 1460?–1529. English satirical poet. Tutor to Henry VIII, he wrote sharp verse satires on the morality and people of his day.

skepticism Philosophical position in which either specific knowledge or the ability to know is called into question. Skepticism has been an important aspect of philosophical thought since ancient times (Democritus and the Sophists). In modern times, D. Hume and I. Kant have advanced such theories.

Skinner, Burrhus Frederick 1904–. American psychologist and noted exponent of behaviorism *(q.v.).*

Skobelev, Mikhail Dmitreyevich 1843–82. Russian general. He fought brilliantly in the Russo-Turkish War (1877–78), figuring in the conquest of Russian Turkistan.

Skriabin, Vyacheslav Mikhailovich *See* **Molotov, Vyacheslav Mikhailovich**

Slater, Samuel 1768–1835. English-born American industrialist. Slater familiarized himself with English cotton-textile machinery and built a similar factory (the first in America) in Rhode Island (1790) from memory.

Slave Coast West African region where European slave traders procured most of their slaves. It includes parts of Nigeria, Dahomey, and Togo.

Slave dynasty First dynasty of the Delhi Sultanate in northern India. It ruled between 1209 and 1290 and was so named because its founder, Qutb-ud-Din Aibak, was once a slave.

slavery Age-old institution of involuntary servitude, now eliminated in nearly every part of the world. Mention of slavery has been found in writings of the Babylonians, Hebrews, Egyptians, and other ancient peoples and it was common among the Greeks and Romans. After the fall of Rome, slavery in the medieval European states was generally replaced by the feudal institution of serfdom. It continued in the Muslim states, however. European involvement in slavery was renewed in the 15th cent. with the beginnings of overseas exploration and colonization, and slaves were used mainly in colonial domains. The Portuguese took the first Negro slaves from West Africa in the 1440s, and in the 16th cent., Spain and England also began trading them (France, Denmark, and American colonials started in the 17th cent.). By the late 17th cent., the English dominated the slave trade. The prime market for slaves was in the New World colonies. The Spanish began importing large numbers of slaves into South America after native Indian slaves proved too rebellious. In North America the first slaves were introduced (1619) at Jamestown, Virginia, and, though slaves were later sent to other British colonies in the Americas, it was in the South that they became an integral part of the plantation economy. Active slave trade by European powers continued throughout the 18th cent. But by the beginning of the 19th cent., abolitionists were already mounting their campaign to bring about its end (see abolition).

Slavonia Region of northern Yugoslavia, historically united with Croatia. In 1918 it became part of Yugoslavia.

Slavophile Russian intellectual movement (mid-19th cent.). Slavophiles held that Russian culture was superior to European civilization. The movement declined after the Crimean War.

Slavs Largest ethnic group in Europe, today divided into three main branches: Western, including Poles, Czechs, Slovaks, and Wends; Southern, including Serbs, Croats, and others; and Eastern, including Great Russians, Ukrainians, and Belorussians. The Slavs are thought to have migrated from Asia to Eastern Europe (3d–2d millennium BC). They were then forced eastward beyond the Oder River to their present homelands (5th–6th cents.) by the expansion of the German states.

Slidell, John 1793–1871. US diplomat. Failure of the "Slidell Mission" in Mexico led to the Mexican War (q.v.). He also figured in the Trent Affair (q.v.).

Slim, William Joseph, 1st viscount 1891–1970. British field marshal. Slim commanded British forces in the reconquest of Burma from the Japanese during WW II.

Sloat, John Drake *See* **Mexican War**

Slovakia Historic region, now a Czechoslovakian constituent republic. Settled by Slovaks (c6th cent.), it became part of the Moravian Empire and was converted to Christianity (9th cent.) by saints Cyril and Methodius. The Magyars conquered Slovakia in 906, and it was ruled by the Hungarians until 1918, when it became part of Czechoslovakia. After the breakup of Czechoslovakia (1938), Slovakia declared its independence (1939) and became allied with Germany for protection. Czechoslovakia was reformed after WW II. The Czech and Slovak republics gained local autonomy under the 1968 constitution.

Sluis, Battle of ⟨Sluys, ~⟩ English naval victory (June 24, 1340) over France at the beginning of the Hundred Years' War. Fought near Bruges, the battle resulted in destruction of the French fleet and gave Edward III command of the English Channel for the next generation.

Sluter, Claus d. c1406. Flemish sculptor, noted for his sculptures on the tomb of Philip the Bold and at the Carthusian monastery of Champmol.

Sluys, Battle of *See* **Sluis, Battle of**

Smetana, Bedřich 1824–84. Czech composer, considered the father of Czech national music. Among his noted works were *The Moldau* and the opera *The Bartered Bride.*

Smith, Adam 1723–90. Scottish economist and philosopher. Smith's famous book, *Wealth of Nations* (1776), greatly influenced economic theory. It argued for laissez-faire doctrines such as free trade and held that the "invisible hand" of individual competition would ultimately work to the public benefit.

Smith, Alfred Emanuel 1873–1944. American politician. The governor of New York (1919–20, 1923–28), he was the first Catholic to become a presidential candidate (1928) of a major party (Democrats). He lost to H. Hoover.

Smith, Edmund Kirby ⟨Kirby-Smith, Edward⟩ 1824–93. Confederate general. Smith fought at Bull Run, headed (from 1863) the Trans-Mississippi Department, and was the last general to surrender (May 26, 1865).

Smith, Gladys Mary *See* **Pickford, Mary**

Smith, Ian Douglas 1919–. Rhodesian politician. A white supremacist, he became prime minister in 1964 and unilaterally declared Rhodesia's independence (1965) from Britain. His white Rhodesian government subsequently resisted international pressures, including economic boycott, and ruled until 1980, when blacks came to power.

Smith, John 1580–1631. English colonist, a founder of Jamestown, Virginia (1607). Probably saved by the intervention of the Indian princess Pocahontas, he later married her and thus established friendly relations with the Indians.

Smith, Joseph 1805–44. American religious leader, founder of the Mormons *(q.v.)*. Some of his religious views, especially those on polygamy, aroused hostility to Mormonism. He was killed by a mob.

Smith, Walter Bedell 1895–1961. American WW II general, Gen. D. Eisenhower's chief of staff (1942–45). He later served as ambassador to the Soviet Union, CIA director, and undersecretary of state.

Smith Act ⟨Alien Registration Act of 1940⟩ US act (June 29, 1940) requiring aliens to register and making it a federal offense to advocate the violent overthrow of the government. This provision was used to prosecute leaders of the American Communist party after WW II.

Smithson, James 1765–1829. English scientist. Smithson bequeathed his fortune to America for the purpose of founding the Smithsonian Institution (established 1846).

Smolensk, Battle of Two battles fought at this western Russian city. **1.** Victory (Aug. 17, 1812) for Napoleon during his invasion of Russia in the Napoleonic Wars. He later vainly tried to rally his troops there during his retreat. **2.** WW II battle (July-Aug. 6, 1941) in which the Germans captured the city during their invasion of the Soviet Union. Russian losses were 100,000 casualties and prisoners.

Smollett, Tobias George 1721–71. Scottish novelist, noted for such comic novels as *The Adventures of Roderick Random, The Adventures of Peregrine Pickle* and *The Expedition of Humphrey Clinker.*

Smoot, Reed 1862–1941. American politician, the first Mormon elected senator (1902). He opposed US entry into the League of Nations and co-authored the Hawley-Smoot Tariff (1930).

Smuts, Jan Christiaan 1870–1950. South African soldier and statesman. He fought the British in the Boer War but later was instrumental in forming the Union of South Africa (1910). He was prime minister (1919–24, 1939–48).

Smyrna Former name for Izmir *(q.v.)*.

Snefru *d c*2589 BC. First Egyptian king (*c*2613–2589) of the 4th dynasty. Under his rule Egyptian mining and trade flourished, and government and administration were refined. The first true pyramid was built at Dahshur during his reign.

Snow, Charles Percy, Baron 1905–80. English author and physicist. As a novelist he is best known for his *Strangers and Brothers* series of novels, including *The Masters* and *The Affair.*

Snowden, Philip, 1st viscount 1864–1937. English statesman, a Laborite, and several times chancellor of the exchequer. He supported free trade and balanced budgets but was ousted with the Labour government (1931) during the Depression.

Sobhuza II *See* **Swaziland**

Sobraon, Battle of British victory in the first of the Sikh Wars in northwestern India. Some 25,000 Sikhs were defeated by a 15,000-man Anglo-Indian force. Sikh losses were 8,000 to 2,300 allied deaths.

Soccer War Brief war (July 14–30, 1969) between El Salvador and Honduras. Supposedly triggered by tensions over soccer matches between the two national teams, it actually resulted from resentment at the expulsion of Salvadoran immigrants from Honduras. About 2,000 soldiers and civilians, mainly Honduran, were killed.

social contract Agreement or bond by which human beings move from a state of nature to form society. This theory was first advanced by T. Hobbes and J. Locke.

Social Credit *See* **Aberhart, William**

social Darwinism Discredited 19th-cent. social philosophy based on the Darwinian theory of evolution. It held that human societies, like animal species, were subject to the law of "survival of the fittest." Chief exponents were British philosopher H. Spencer and American sociologist William Graham Sumner (1840–1910).

Social Democratic Party of Germany German political party. Founded (1863) as a Marxist workers' party, it became a formidable power in Germany during the early 1900s. It was suppressed (1933) by A. Hitler and reorganized after WW II. However, it was unable to successfully challenge the coalition of Christian Democrat and other parties until after 1959, when it eliminated Marxist ideology and broadened its appeal as a people's party. Since the 1970s the party has formed coalition governments in Germany under W. Brandt and H. Schmidt.

Social Gospel Movement in American Protestantism (late 19th–early 20th cent.) that sought to apply the principles of the Gospels to the social questions of the day. It advocated a shorter work week, better working conditions, the right to a living wage, the abolition of child labor, etc. The movement declined when organized labor took up many of its causes.

socialism Politico-economic doctrine. Socialism seeks to replace the competitive capitalist system with a cooperative society, in which means of production and distribution are owned either by the government or collectively by the people. A response to the hardships and social injustice bred by the Industrial Revolution, socialism dates primarily from the works of such thinkers as F. Babeuf, C. de Saint-Simon, C. Fourier, and R. Owen (18th-19th cent.).

Babeuf, sometimes called the first socialist theorist, sought to advance economic egalitarianism during the French Revolution and this gave rise to the revolutionary movement known as Babouvism. Saint-Simon postulated government control of the economy and industry, while Fourier and Owen believed in decentralizing society into small collectives. Experiments in socialism in the early 19th cent. included founding of utopian communes (notably Brook Farm and New Harmony) and L. Blanc's unsuccessful National Workshops (government financed, worker controlled) in France after the 1848 Revolution. New elements of class struggle and the necessity of revolution were added to Socialist thought by way of Marx's and Engels' *Communist Manifesto* (1848).

For the rest of the 19th cent. and into the early 20th, the doctrinal dispute over revolutionary socialism vs evolutionary socialism divided Socialists and ultimately brought about the permanent split between democratic Socialists (advocates of gradual change) and Communists (advocates of revolutionary change). The disputes were evident in the First and Second International *(qq.v.)*, the revolutionary sentiment giving rise to anarchism and syndicalism *(qq.v.)* in the late 19th cent. Gradualists formed the Fabian Society *(q.v.)* in Britain and Social Democratic parties elsewhere in Europe. Though many other issues divided Socialists in the early 1900s, the triumph of the Bolsheviks in the Russian Revolution of 1917 resulted in the complete separation of revolutionaries (now Communists) from the Socialist movement. Thereafter, democratic Socialists gradually gained power in European countries (especially after WW II), notably in Britain (see Labour party), Germany (see Social Democratic party of Germany), and, in the 1980s, France. In the US, the Socialist party *(q.v.)* never managed to gain significant power.

Socialist Labor party American Socialist party established in Philadelphia (1876). Founded on Marxist principles, it opposed simple trade unionism. Under the vigorous leadership of D. De Leon, the party reached its zenith in the 1890s and declined thereafter.

Socialist party Former US political party advocating gradual transformation to a Socialist state in the US. Formed (1901) by a merger of the Social Democratic party and moderate elements of the Socialist Labor party, it reached its zenith in the years between 1910 and 1919, under the leadership of E. Debs. Debs ran for president in 1912 and again in 1920 while in prison for opposing US involvement in WW I. The party was seriously weakened (1919) when the radical wing defected to form the US Communist party. Later, during the 1930s, Pres. F. Roosevelt incorporated many of the party's reforms in the New Deal. Led by N. Thomas from the 1920s, the party declined steadily in subsequent years.

Socialist Revolutionary party Russian political party. Founded (1901) by a Populist coalition, it advocated a classless society and agrarian reform, and carried out political assassinations. It was suppressed (1922) by the Communists.

Social War ⟨Marsic War⟩ Rebellion (90–88 BC) by tribes in central and southern Italy against Roman rule. The tribes, including the Marsians, Samnites, Pelignians, and Lucanians, had been forced into alliance with Rome but did not enjoy the privileges of Roman citizenship. The Roman Marcus Livius Drusus proposed extending citizenship (91 BC), but the move was opposed by the Senate and he was assassinated. The tribes then rose in revolt (90 BC) and attempted to form a confederation (Italia) in opposition to Rome. Roman armies (Sulla was a commander) were unable to break the rebellion. It ended after citizenship was offered to all Roman allies and those tribes that ceased hostilities. Eight new gens (Roman tribes) were created and the new citizens were rapidly assimilated. The Italian peninsula was thus unified under Roman control.

Society of Friends ⟨Quakers⟩ Protestant Christian sect that rejects both formal creed and the need for priests, holding that they interfere with an individual's communion with the Holy Spirit ("inner light"). Established (c1647) in England under the leadership of G. Fox, the Quakers refused to take oaths, to bear arms, to pay religious tithes, or otherwise conform to the English church. They were persecuted until laws regarding religious toleration were passed (late 17th cent.) and, under W. Penn, founded the Quaker colony in Pennsylvania (1681). The Friends were early and zealous supporters of abolition of slavery and actively support pacifism. The American Friends Service Committee (founded 1917) is noted for its support of humanitarian causes.

Society of Jesus ⟨Jesuits⟩ Roman Catholic religious order, founded (1534) by St. Ignatius of Loyola and approved (1540) by Pope Paul III. Missionary work, notably by St. Francis Xavier in the East, began shortly after founding of the order.

The Jesuits played an important role in the Catholic Reformation and also established many schools in Europe. However, they aroused opposition from European monarchs, partly because of their loyalty to the pope, and by 1773 Pope Clement XIV was forced to dissolve the order. Pope Pius VII reinstituted it (1814).

Socinianism Anti-Trinitarian Christian sect founded by Laelius Socinus (1525–62) that flourished in Poland from the 1550s. Socinianists believed Jesus was merely a man, divine only in his function and not his nature. They suffered persecutions and disbanded by the early 17th cent.

Socinus, Laelius *See* **Socinianism**

Socrates 470?–399 BC. Greek philosopher, one of the great philosophers of ancient Greece, whose life and teachings have made a profound impression on Western thought. The son of Sophroniscus, a sculptor, he is thought to have worked in sculpture before turning to philosophy. He fought in the second Peloponnesian War and was noted for his courage and strength. Socrates spent much of his life in the public places of Athens conducting discussions, or dialogues, with his fellow citizens. He developed a mode of inquiry known as the dialectic, or Socratic method, by which the truth of a given statement is tested by a series of questions. His purpose was to gain knowledge, the basis of virtue, or right conduct. He became a well-known figure in Athens and was the subject of mockery in Aristophanes' play *The Clouds.* Eventually he was accused of impiety and corruption of youth and was sentenced to death. With his disciples by his side, he committed suicide by drinking hemlock. Socrates wrote nothing, and our knowledge of his life and teachings comes mainly from the writings of his disciple Plato, notably the *Apology, Crito,* and *Phaedo.*

Sodom ⟨Sodoma⟩ Biblical city. Sodom, along with Gomorrah, was destroyed by God because of its wickedness. Lot and his family were spared.

Sodoma *See* **Sodom**

Sofia Bulgarian capital city (pop. 976,000) and its commercial and cultural center. Founded 2d cent. AD by the Romans, it was ruled by the Byzantines and Ottoman Turks before becoming capital of Bulgaria in 1879.

Soissons, Battle of *See* **Clovis I**

Solemn League and Covenant Agreement (1643) between the Scots and the English Parliamentarians during the English Civil War. By it, the Parliamentarians endorsed Presbyterianism for all of England and Scotland in exchange for Scottish military help against the royalist armies. The agreement was never implemented.

Soleri, Paolo 1919–. Italian-American architect and city planner, known for his futuristic designs of densely populated cities, planned to minimize environmental disturbance.

Solferino, Battle of Bloody battle (June 24, 1859) fought during the Italian Risorgimento *(q.v.),* or war of unification. King Victor Emmanuel II of Piedmont (later of all Italy) and his allied French forces met the Austrian forces in this indecisive battle in northern Italy. The heavy losses (totaling nearly 30,000 dead) moved the French to a settlement, which resulted in Emmanuel's acquisition of Lombardy.

Solidarity *See* **Poland,** 1980–82

Solomon Great king of ancient Israel (973–933 BC), successor to his father, David, and renowned for his wisdom. He encouraged trade and thereby brought on a period of great commercial prosperity. He also built lavish cities, constructed the first Temple at Jerusalem, and (traditionally) was the author of the Song of Solomon, proverbs, and other biblical writings.

Solon c638–c559 BC. Athenian statesman who laid the foundations of democracy in Athens. Elected archon (chief magistrate) (594 BC) amid a social crisis caused by the widespread indebtedness of the populace to the aristocracy, he instituted his economic reforms called Seisachtheia. He ended the practice of securing loans with personal liberty (serfdom resulted from failure to pay), annulled all debts contracted in this manner, restricted exports, and reformed the currency. He also reformed the Athenian constitution, allowing all freemen to participate in the assembly for the first time. The power of the Areopagus *(q.v.)* was limited and a council of Four Hundred was created to represent the propertied class. Solon also introduced a new law code to replace the harsh Draconian Code.

Solzhenitsyn, Aleksandr Isayevich 1918–. Russian writer and a leading dissident against the excesses of the Soviet system. He was exiled to the West in 1974. He received the Nobel Prize in literature, 1970.

Somalia ⟨Somali Democratic Republic⟩ Independent state located on the Horn of Africa and bordering the Gulf of Aden and the Indian Ocean. Its capital is Mogadisho. Key dates in the history of Somalia include:

7TH–10TH CENT. Arab and Persian traders established in region.

16TH CENT. Ottoman Turks ruled north, Sultan of Zanzibar ruled south.

1862 France established coaling station near Djibouti; Italy settled Eritrea.

1870s–84 Egyptian occupation.

1884 British occupied region formerly held by Egyptians.

1887 Britain established protectorate over its territory.

1888 British and French reached agreement on borders of their respective territories in region.

1889 Italy established protectorate in central region.

1936 Italian Somaliland joined to Ethiopian provinces to form Italian East Africa.

1941 WW II; Britain captured and ruled entire area (until 1950).

1950 Italian Somaliland separated from British territory; came under Italian control as UN trust.

1960 Britain and Italy granted their respective sectors independence; regions joined as Republic of Somalia (July 1).

1964–67 Clashes with Ethiopia and Kenya as Somalis sought to unify large Somali populations in those countries with Somalia.

1969 President Abdi Rashid Ali Shermarke assassinated; parliament replaced by Supreme Revolutionary Council.

1969– Maj. Gen. Muhammad Siad Barre in power; he remained in office into the early 1980s.

1976 Barre dissolved council; named Somali Socialist party only legal political party.

1977 Somalia supported Ethiopian rebels in Ogaden region; led to break with Soviets, who supported the Ethiopian central government.

1978 Somalia defeated in war with Ethiopia; US supplied food, relief.

1979 New constitution adopted; People's Assembly elected.

1980 US given bases in Somalia in return for military and economic aid.

Somaliland Region located on the eastern coast of Africa and extending from the equator north to the Gulf of Aden. It is divided between Afars and Issas (*formerly* French Somaliland) and Somalilia (*formerly* British Somaliland and Italian Somaliland).

Somers, John ⟨Sommers, Baron⟩ 1651–1716. English Whig jurist who presided over the framing of the English Bill of Rights (1689) and who was a trusted adviser to William III.

Somerset, Edmund Beaufort, 2d duke of *d.* 1455. English statesman and general. Largely responsible for loss of English territory in France during the Hundred Years' War, he nevertheless held a favored position in Henry VI's government. This provoked the Yorkists and helped precipitate the Wars of the Roses.

Somme, Battle of Two major offensives on the Western Front in northeastern France. **1.** First ~:

Allied French and British offensive (July-Nov., 1916), fought to relieve German pressure on Verdun. Allied generals D. Haig and J. Joffre launched repeated attacks against German defensive positions, commanded by P. Hindenburg and E. Ludendorff, and gained some territory, but at great cost. Losses were 500,000 Allied troops; 450,000 Germans. **2.** Second ~: German offensive (Mar. 21-Apr. 4, 1918) and nearly successful attempt to break through Allied lines. Commanded by Gen. E. Ludendorff, the Germans launched a series of major attacks that ultimately drove Allied troops back some 40 miles. Gen. F. Foch, named Allied commander during the battle, halted the offensive by Apr. 4. Losses, nearly 200,000 Allied troops; 180,000 Germans.

Sommers, Baron *See* **Somers, John**

Somoza, Anastasio 1896–1956. President of Nicaragua (1936–47, 1951–56). As head of the army (from 1933) he ruled the country even when out of office. He established his family's rule in Nicaragua that lasted until 1979.

Sonderbund League (1845) of Catholic cantons of Switzerland. It was formed as a "defense league" against the anti-Catholic movement in the other cantons but was deemed a "separatist league." A brief civil war ensued and ended with the league's defeat in 1847.

Songhai, Empire of Ancient African empire in the Niger valley of the Sudan. Founded by Berbers (c700) and converted to Islam, the empire reached its height under Askia Muhammad I (c1493–1528) with Timbuktu its chief city. The invasion of Moorish troops from Morocco (1591) destroyed the empire.

Songhay *See* **Songhai**

Sonni 'Ali *d.* 1492. Ruler (1464–92) of the Songhai Kingdom. He began the expansion of Songhai domains until he controlled much of the Sudan, including Timbuktu (taken 1468).

Sonnino, Sidney, Baron 1847–1922. Italian diplomat who promoted Italy's entry into WW I and who negotiated the secret Treaty of London (*q.v.*) in 1915.

Sons of Liberty Activist patriotic organizations formed in the American colonies from c1765. They organized protests against unpopular British laws such as the Stamp Act. The same name was adopted (1864) by a Copperhead (*q.v.*) organization seeking a negotiated peace with the Confederacy.

Soong, T. V. 1894–1971. Chinese financier and Kuomintang finance minister (1928–31, 1932–31). He reorganized China's financial systems and renegotiated foreign agreements to restore China's control of its tariff rates.

Soong Ch'ing-ling ⟨Sun Yat-sen, Madame⟩ 1890–. Chinese political leader. The sister of T.V. Soong and wife (*m.* 1914) of Sun Yat-sen, she was active in the Kuomintang until the Communists were expelled.

Soong Mei-ling ⟨Chiang Kai-shek, Madame⟩ 1898–. Chinese political leader. A member of the Soong family, she married Chiang Kai-shek (1927) and helped win Western support for the Kuomintang.

Sophia 1630–1714. Electress of Hanover, and granddaughter of James I of England. Her son became George I of England by the Act of Settlement (*q.v.*).

Sophia Alekseyevna 1657–1704. Regent of Russia (1682–89), daughter of Czar Alexis. She ruled during the minority of her brother Ivan V and half-brother Peter I (Peter the Great).

Sophocles *c*496–*c*406 BC. Greek tragedian who is ranked with his contemporaries Aeschylus and Euripides as one of the greatest tragic poets. Born a patrician, he was a general and statesman. He made several innovations in Greek drama and wrote over 120 plays. His surviving works include *Antigone, Electra, Trachiniate, Philoctetes, Oedipus at Colonus,* and the most famous, *Oedipus Rex.*

Sophists Greek philosophical school that flourished from the 5th cent. BC. Skeptical about the possibility of knowing truth, the Sophists opposed philosophical doctrine and instead taught the art of rhetorical persuasion. Protagoras was the first prominent Sophist.

Soranus *fl.* 1st-2d cent. AD. Ancient Greek physician, an authority on gynecology, obstetrics, and pediatrics. His writings were influential through the 15th cent.

Sorel, Agnes *c*1422–50. French mistress (1444–50) to Charles VII, the first woman to be officially recognized in that capacity in France.

Sorel, Georges 1847–1922. French philosopher, a leading advocate of revolutionary syndicalism (*q.v.*). He wrote *Reflections on Violence.*

Soter ⟨Demetrius⟩ *See* **Demetrius I**

Soubirous, Marie Bernarde *See* **Bernadette, Saint**

soul Spiritual essence or principle that, united with the body, makes up the living human being and, in some beliefs, is part of animals, plants, and even inanimate objects. The nature of the soul and belief in its immortality are major elements in many of the world's religions.

Soulé, Pierre 1801–70. French-born American politician. As US minister to Spain, he joined with J. Buchanan and John Y. Mason (1799–1859) in writing the controversial Ostend Manifesto (*q.v.*).

Soule, Samuel W. *See* **Sholes, Christopher Latham**

Soulouque, Faustin Élie ⟨Faustin I⟩ 1785–1867. Haitian dictator. A former slave and soldier, he was elected to the presidency (1847) and made himself emperor (1849–59).

Soult, Nicolas 1769–1851. French marshal. Under Napoleon, he commanded French forces in the Peninsular Campaign and was chief of staff at Waterloo. He later served royalist governments and brought about the French conquest of Morocco.

Sousa, John Philip 1854–1932. Noted American bandmaster and composer. He conducted the US Marine Band and composed many popular marches, including *Stars and Stripes Forever.*

Sousa, Martim Affonso de 1500?–64. Portuguese admiral. He founded the first Portuguese settlement in Brazil (1532) at São Vincente.

South, the US region, comprising the southeastern and south central states. Traditionally, the Mason-Dixon line has been the dividing line between North and South and until recent times marked political, social, and economic differences; it contributed to friction and divisiveness between the two regions. *See also* individual states; Confederacy; American Civil War.

South Africa, Republic of Republic located at the southern tip of Africa. The national capital is Pretoria; the legislative capital is Cape Town. South Africa was first settled by the Dutch, whose descendants, the Boers, developed the Afrikaner language and culture. British settlement and influence increased from the 17th to 19th cent. As a result, the Boers migrated north and east to found Natal, the Transvaal, and the Orange Free State. All eventually were incorporated, after the Boer War (1899–1902), into the Union of South Africa, which became the independent Republic of South Africa in 1961. Key dates in the history of South Africa include:

1652 Jan van Riebeeck established supply post at Cape of Good Hope for the Dutch East India Company; first permanent European settlement in South Africa.

17TH–18TH CENT. Descendants of Dutch settlers developed Afrikaner society and culture in region; established new farms and settlements inland.

1815 Cape Colony passed to British control by Congress of Vienna.

1835–43 Great Trek, migration of Boers away from British-controlled territory; Piet Retief, Andres Pretorius, and others led the Boers north and east beyond the Orange River.

1843 British annexed Natal, territory settled by Boers (northeast of Cape Colony).

1852 Boers established independent republic of Transvaal.

1854 Boers established independent republic called the Orange Free State.

1856 Transvaal became known as the South African Republic.

1860s–70s Discovery of diamonds (1867) in Orange Free State and gold (1886) in southern Transvaal led to great influx of British to region and resulting friction with Boers; Britain annexed the Transvaal (1877), but restored its independence in 1881.

1886 Johannesburg founded.

1894 British South Africa Company defeated natives in Matabele War.

1895–1896 Leander Starr Jameson led Jameson Raid into Transvaal in attempt to spur uprising of British settlers (Uitlanders) against Boers; raid supported by Cecil Rhodes, prime minister of Cape Colony; raid failed but ultimately contributed to outbreak of Boer (South African) War.

1899–1902 Boer War (South African War) fought between the Boers and British; Boers defeated; Transvaal and Orange Free State made British colonies.

1909 South Africa Act united British colonies into Union of South Africa (Sept. 20).

1910–19 L. Botha in office as first prime minister of the Union of South Africa.

1912 African National Congress Party organized to oppose European domination.

1914–18 Union of South Africa joined Allies in WW I; suppressed revolt (1915) of Boers against support of Britain; occupied (1915) German South-West Africa, which became a League of Nations mandate under South African control after the war.

1919–24 Jan Christiaan Smuts in office as prime minister.

1924–39 J.B.M. Hertzog, leader of the pro-Afrikaner Nationalist party, in office as prime minister; government passed numerous laws advancing segregation of the different racial groups in South Africa.

1939–48 J. Smuts again prime minister; led South Africa into WW II on Allied side despite pro-German sentiment among many Boers; came under fire by Nationalists over his "liberal" policies; UN opposed to South Africa's racial policies.

1945 South Africa joined the UN.

1948–54 D. Malan in office as prime minister; established apartheid policies.

1958–66 H. Verwoerd prime minister.

1966–78 B. Vorster in office as prime minister.

1974 UN declared its authority over South-West Africa, renamed Namibia; South Africa resisted move; unsuccessful attempt made to expel South Africa from the UN.

1974 South Africa suspended from participation in UN General Assembly.

1976 10,000 black students rioted (June) in Soweto, near Johannesburg.

1976 Black homeland of Transkei granted independence by South African government.

1977 Steven Biko, a leading opponent of apartheid, died (Sept. 12) of injuries suffered in prison; death led to renewed protests against South Africa's racial policies.

1977 Government issued (Oct.) new restrictions on political freedoms of blacks; activists arrested and black organizations banned.

1977 Black homeland of Bophuthatswana granted independence by South African government.

1978 Prime Minister B. Vorster resigned; denounced UN plan for independence of Namibia.

1978 Prime Minister Pieter Willem Botha in office; remained in power in the early 1980s.

South Africa Act British act (effective May 31, 1910) that created the Union of South Africa by uniting the British possessions of Cape, Natal, Transvaal, and Orange River. The act also provided a constitution and its provisions established white supremacy there.

South African War *See* **Boer War**

Southampton, Henry Wriothesley, 3d earl of 1573–1624. Soldier and patron of W. Shakespeare, who dedicated *Venus and Adonis* and *The Rape of Lucrece* to him. Southampton participated in Essex's revolt against Elizabeth I (1601).

Southampton, Thomas Wriothesley, 1st earl of 1505–50. English statesman. He negotiated a treaty between Henry VIII and Holy Roman Emperor Charles V, and was made lord chancellor (1544–47). He supported Henry's antipapal measures but remained a Catholic.

Southampton, Thomas Wriothesley, 4th earl of 1606–67. English nobleman. One of Charles I's close advisers during the English Civil War, he became lord high treasurer (1660–67) during the Restoration.

Southampton Insurrection Slave insurrection (Aug., 1831) in Southampton County, Virginia. Led by a rebel slave, N. Turner, who believed he had a divine calling to liberate his brothers, it was quickly suppressed by federal troops.

South Carolina State of southeastern US (pop. 3,119,200), the 8th state. Explored by the Spanish, it was first permanently settled by the French (1562). The English claimed the region in 1629, and Charles II granted it to eight noblemen (1663). North and South Carolina were organized as separate colonies (1713), and in 1729 it became a royal province. During the American Revolution a number of important battles were fought there, and during the American Civil War, South Carolina was the first state to secede (1860). It was readmitted in 1868. The constitution was adopted in 1895.

Southcottians *See* **Sabbatarians**

South Dakota North central state of the US (pop. 690,200), the 40th state. Explored by the French in the mid-18th cent., the area was acquired by the US in the Louisiana Purchase (1803). It was crossed by Lewis and Clark (1804–6). Fur posts were established in spite of trouble with the Sioux Indians, and farmers began to settle the region in the 1850s. It became part of the Dakota Territory in 1861 and the discovery of gold in the Black Hills (c1874) brought a new influx of settlers. South Dakota became a state and adopted its constitution in 1889.

Southeast Asia Treaty Organization ⟨SEATO⟩ Alliance created by a treaty signed (Sept. 8, 1954) by the US, Australia, France, New Zealand, Pakistan, the Philippines, Thailand, and Britain. It was intended to bolster the region's defenses after the French withdrawal from Indochina. The Vietnam War disrupted the alliance and it held its final joint exercises in 1976.

Southern Sung *See* **Sung**

South Sea Bubble Rush of speculative investment (1720) in the South Sea Company, a trading company founded (1711) in England by R. Harley. The end of the War of the Spanish Succession was expected to result in the company's gaining a monopoly on trade with Spain's American colonies, but the treaty of 1713 produced only slightly advantageous terms. With George I as its governor, the company next proposed to take over the British national debt (1720). This brought a rush of speculative investment; company share prices rose from 128.5 to 1,000 pounds in a matter of months. The speculative bubble finally burst in Sept., 1720, bringing the collapse of banks and ruination of thousands of investors.

South-West Africa ⟨Namibia⟩ Mandate of South Africa, located in the extreme southwestern portion of Africa on the Atlantic Coast. Its capital is Windhoek. The area was claimed by the Portuguese, Dutch, and British before becoming a German colony. South Africa gained control of the area in 1915. Key dates in the history of South-West Africa include:

15TH CENT. Portuguese discovered region.

18TH CENT. Portuguese, British, and Dutch explored region.

mid-19TH CENT. British and German missionaries arrived.

1884 Region made a German protectorate.

1904–08 Nama and Herero tribes revolted; Germans put down the revolt, in which thousands were killed.

1908 Diamonds discovered; Europeans began immigrating to South-West Africa.

1915 WW I; South African forces, led by Louis Botha and Jan Christiaan Smuts, captured land from Germany.

1920 Treaty of Versailles made territory a South African League of Nations mandate.

1921–22 South Africa crushed Nama revolt.

1946 UN General Assembly rejected South Africa's application for incorporation of the area; asked to make trusteeship application instead.

1947 Smuts, prime minister of South Africa, announced that South-West Africa would continue to be administered under mandate; refused to make region UN trust territory.

1949 Region granted representation in South African parliament as step toward annexation.

1951 UN-South African negotiations over status of South-West Africa ended in failure.

1951–52 South African delegate boycotted UN General Assembly.

1966 UN General Assembly terminated old League of Nations mandate.

1968 Area renamed Namibia.

1971 International Court ordered South Africa to end its control of South-West Africa; South Africa refused.

1974 UN ordered South Africa to turn South-West Africa's government over to native Namibians.

1975 South Africa proclaimed itself willing to grant Namibian independence, but refused to deal with South-West African People's Organization (SWAPO).

1977 South Africa agreed to negotiate with SWAPO.

1978 South Africa agreed to Namibian independence after period of transition; Marthinus Steyn named to head interim government.

1980 Windheek established as capital.

Soutine, Chaim *See* **expressionism**

Souvanna Phouma 1901–. Laotian statesman. Of royal descent, he was frequently premier during the years of civil war from 1951. Forced to the right by the gains of the Communist Pathet Lao, he relied heavily on US aid during the Vietnam

War years. Nevertheless the Communists took control in 1974–75.

soviet Council and basic elective political unit of the modern Soviet Union's government. Dominated by the Communist party, soviets are arranged in a hierarchy ranging from local to national jurisdiction and are charged with legislative and executive functions. The first soviets were organized by rebels during the 1905 revolution; during the 1917 revolution the soviets, formed in all of Russia's major cities, rivaled the Russian Provisional Government for power. By taking control (1917) of the powerful Petrograd and Moscow soviets, the Bolsheviks took command of the revolution and ultimately all Russia.

Soviet Republic of Hungary Short-lived Communist government of Hungary that ruled after WW I (Mar. 21–Aug. 1, 1919). After initial successes against the invading Czechs and Romanians, Communist premier B. Kun was driven out of Hungary, making way for a counterrevolutionary government.

Soviet Union *See* **Union of Soviet Socialist Republics**

Spaak, Paul Henri 1899–1972. Belgian statesman and Socialist. The Belgian foreign minister at various times from 1938 until his death, he served as premier (1938–39, 1946, 1947–50) and was first UN General Assembly president (1946).

space exploration The age of space exploration began in 1957 with the launching of the first artificial sattelite, Sputnik, by the Soviets. Many other "firsts" were recorded in subsequent years as the US and the Soviets engaged in what became known as the "space race." Both nations struggled to gain the lead (and world prestige) on this new frontier. During the 1960s the race focused on landing a man on the moon and in 1969 the US achieved that goal. Enthusiasm for the space race disappeared in the years following the manned moon missions (partly because of the costs). In the 1970s space exploration was carried forward by unmanned space probes sent to the far planets in the solar system (Mars, Jupiter, Saturn). The major advance of the early 1980s was the successful launch of the US space shuttle Columbia, the first reusable spacecraft. Key events in space exploration include:

1957 Russians launched Sputnik, inaugurating the Space Age (Oct. 4).

1958 US launched Explorer 1, its first satellite (Jan. 31); Van Allen radiation belts discovered.

1959 Soviet Luna 2 became first spacecraft to make hard landing on the moon (Sept. 12).

1959 Luna 3, Soviet space probe, flew around moon and sent back first pictures of the dark side of the moon (Nov.).

1961 Y. Gagarin, a Russian, became the first man to travel in space; orbited earth inside Vostok I for over an hour (Apr. 12).

1961 Alan Shepard, Jr., became first American in space (May 5), aboard Mercury 3.

1961 Vostok 2; Russia's Gherman Titov made the first space flight lasting more than one day (Aug. 6–7).

1962 Mercury 6; John Glenn became first American to orbit the earth (Feb. 20).

1962 Mariner 2, US space probe, passed by Venus (Dec. 14); sent back scientific data.

1962 Communications satellite Telstar launched by US; provided television pictures between Europe and America (July 1).

1963 Vostok 6; Russia's Valentina Tereshkova became first woman in space (June 16–17).

1965 Aleksei Leonov, Soviet cosmonaut aboard Voskhod 2, became first man to "walk" in space (Mar. 18).

1965 Gemini 4; Edward White became first American to "walk" in space (June 3–7).

1966 Luna 9, Soviet space probe, made first soft landing on moon (Jan. 31).

1966 Venera 3, Soviet space probe, reached Venus (Mar. 1).

1966 Gemini 8; first docking of two spacecraft in outer space (Mar. 16–17).

1966 US space probe, Surveyor 1, made soft landing on moon (June 2).

1966 Pioneer 7, US space probe, launched into orbit around the sun (Aug. 17).

1968 Apollo 8; Frank Borman, James Lovell, and William Anders orbited the moon, sending back pictures of the lunar surface (Dec. 21–27).

1969 Venera 5, Soviet space probe, landed on Venus; sent back scientific data (May 16).

1969 Mariner 6, US space probe, passed by Mars (July 31); television pictures and data sent back to earth.

1969 Apollo 11; US astronauts Neil Armstrong, Edwin Aldrin, Jr., and Michael Collins on historic manned moon-landing mission (July 16–24); Armstrong became first man to set foot on the moon (July 20).

1969 Apollo 12; second lunar landing made by Charles Conrad, Richard Gordon, and Alan Bean (Nov. 14–24).

1970 Apollo 13 moon mission (Apr. 11–18) marred by exploding oxygen tank; astronauts returned safely.

1970 Unmanned Soviet moon probe, Luna 16, completed moon landing and return (Sept. 24).

1970 Unmanned Soviet moon probe, Luna 17, landed on moon (Nov 17).

1971 Apollo 14; Alan Shepard, Jr., Stuart Roosa, and Edgar Mitchell made third US moon landing (Jan 31–Feb. 9).

1971 Soyuz 10 mission; Soviet cosmonauts completed in-space docking with space station, Salyut (Apr. 24).

1971 Soyuz 11 successfully completed (June 7) in-space docking with Salyut; three Soviet cosmonauts found dead in capsule after reentry (June 30).

1971 Apollo 15; fourth manned mission to the moon (July 26–Aug. 7); David Scott, Alfred Worden, and James Irwin aboard.

1971 Mariner 9, US space probe, became first to orbit Mars (Nov. 13); sent back close-up pictures of Mars.

1971 Mars 2, Soviet space probe, passed by Mars (Nov. 27); capsule sent down to surface.

1972 Apollo 16 moon mission (Apr. 16–27); US astronauts stayed over 71 hours on moon; Charles Duke, Thomas Mattingly, and John Young aboard.

1972 Apollo 17; Eugene Cernan, Ronald Evans, and Harrison Schmitt made sixth moon mission (Dec. 7–19); stayed 75 hours on last Apollo moon mission.

1973 Soviets landed unmanned moon vehicle, Lunokhod 2, on moon (Jan. 16).

1973 Salyut 2, Soviet orbital workshop in space (Apr. 3–28).

1973 First US orbiting space station, Skylab 2, launched into space; Skylab damaged during flight (May 25–June 22).

1973 US unmanned space probe, Pioneer 10, passed close to Jupiter (Dec. 3); designed to escape solar system (1986).

1973–74 US Skylab 4 mission (Dec. 16–Feb. 8); last of Skylab series.

1974 Mariner 10, US space probe, passed by Venus (Feb. 5); continued to Mercury.

1974 Mariner 10, US space probe, reached Mercury (Mar. 29).

1974 US Pioneer 11 space probe passed by Jupiter en route to Saturn (Dec. 3).

1975 US Apollo 18 and the Soviet Soyuz 19 linked up in orbit around the earth (July 17–19).

1976 US Viking 1 space probe landed on Mars; photos from surface sent back to earth (July 20).

1976 US Viking 2 space probe landed on Mars (Sept. 3).

1977–78 Soviet cosmonauts aboard Soyuz 27 returned to earth after setting 96-day space endurance record (Dec. 10–Mar. 16).

1979 US Voyager 1 space probe passed by Jupiter; photographs of moons sent back to earth (Mar. 5); continued to Saturn.

1979 US Pioneer 11 space probe passed by Saturn; transmitted scientific data on planet (Sept. 1).

1980 US Voyager 1 passed by Saturn (Nov. 12); sent back valuable scientific data and pictures of Saturn's rings; continued to Uranus (1986).

1981 Soyuz 35; Soviet cosmonauts set record of 185 days in space (Apr. 9–Oct. 11).

1981 World's first reusable spacecraft, the US space shuttle Columbia, completed its first flight (Apr. 12–14).

1981 US Voyager 2 passed by Saturn; sent back valuable scientific data (Aug. 25); continued to Uranus (1986).

1981 US space shuttle Columbia returned to earth after completing half of scheduled second mission (Nov. 14).

1982 Columbia successfully completed its third voyage (July 4).

space shuttle *See* **Columbia**

Spain ⟨Spanish State⟩ Country located in Western Europe and occupying the Iberian Peninsula (with Portugal). Its capital is Madrid. The early history of the modern Spanish state begins with the *Reconquista* (reconquest, 11th–15th cent.), in which Spanish Christians drove the Muslims out of the Iberian Peninsula. Spain remained divided between rival kingdoms until the marriage (1469) of King Ferdinand II and Isabella I began the process of unification by bringing together the two largest kingdoms, Aragon and Castile. Ferdinand and Isabella sponsored Columbus' voyage to the New World (1492) and in the next century Spain gained control over most of South America. The vast riches in gold that came out of these colonies helped make Spain the leading European power during the 16th cent. Toward the end of that century, however, Spanish power underwent a decline. By the early 19th cent. its South American colonies were lost in wars for independence. In the 20th cent., Spain was torn by a bloody civil war (1936–39), which brought Gen. F. Franco to power (1939–75). Franco restored order and brought about a measure of economic prosperity. Key events in the history of Spain include:

12TH–11TH CENT. BC Phoenicians established colonies on the peninsula (Cadiz, Tartessus).

11TH–5TH CENT. BC Basques and Iberians occupied Iberian Peninsula.

6TH CENT. BC Celts invaded Iberian Peninsula.

3D CENT. BC Carthaginians, led by Hamilcar Barca, conquered most of the peninsula; established Cartegena as capital.

3D CENT. BC–5TH CENT. AD Roman occupation of Spain; Rome gained control of Spain from Carthage following the Second Punic War.

AD 409 Alans, Suevi, and Vandals invaded Spain.

AD 412–419 Visigoths invaded Spain, forcing out Vandals (who invaded North Africa).

AD 419–711 Visigothic kingdom of Toulouse dominated the Iberian Peninsula; Christianity and Roman culture spread.

711 Muslims, led by Tarik, invaded Spain from North Africa; by 719 conquered all but extreme northern part of Spain, where Christians established kingdom of Asturias (c718).

756 Abd ar-Rahman I established the Umayyad dynasty in Muslim Spain, after the Abbasid line seized power in the Empire of the Caliphate.

778 Spanish March (later called Catalonia) created in northern Spain by Charlemagne out of lands he conquered from Muslims.

866–911 Alfonso III ruled Asturias; greatly extended his domains in wars against Muslims.

905 Independent kingdom of Navarre founded in north.

912–961 Abd ar-Rahman III reigned in Muslim Spain; period marked by cultural flowering; Muslim Spain created a caliphate by Abd ar-Rahman (929).

932 Castile founded as an independent kingdom.

999–1027 Alfonso V gained control of León from the Moors, ruled as king.

1000–35 Sancho III reigned as king of Navarre; briefly united northern Spain under his rule; at his death, Navarre partitioned into kingdoms of Navarre, Aragon, and Castile.

1008–31 Fourth Muslim Civil War; led to elimination of Umayyad caliphate in Spain; Muslim domains broke up into petty kingdoms.

1065–1109 Alfonso VI reigned as king of Castile and León; El Cid active; Alfonso extended Christian domains to Toledo, only to be driven north by Muslim Almoravides.

1086 Muslim Almoravides invaded Spain and seized power; later conquered by Almohades.

1143 Portugal's independence from Spain recognized by Treaty of Zamora.

1145–51 Muslim Almohades invaded Spain and took control over Muslim domains.

1195 Almohades decisively defeated Alfonso VIII of Castile at the Battle of Alarcos.

1212 Alfonso VIII defeated the Muslims in Battle of Navas de Tolosa; Christian reconquest of Spain nearly complete; only Granada remained in Muslim control.

1230 Christian kingdom of Castile united with León; Spain dominated by two great kingdoms, Castile in the west and Aragon in the east.

1238 Kingdom of Granada formed by Muslims.

1340 Battle of Rio Salado, a major victory for Christians over Muslims.

1469 Marriage of Ferdinand II of Aragon and Isabella I of Castile; marked beginning of unification of Spain; though Ferdinand and Isabella each ruled separately, process of centralizing authority begun.

1478 Spanish Inquisition established by King Ferdinand and Queen Isabella; T. de Torquemada, Grand Inquisitor, became notorious for his use of torture and execution.

1492 King Ferdinand and Queen Isabella conquered Granada, last Muslim stronghold; Jews expelled from Spain to promote religious unity.

1492 Columbus discovered the New World for Spain; marked beginning of period of colonialism by European powers.

1494 Treaty of Tordesillas signed (June 7) with Portugal; provided for division of newly discovered lands in Americas, Africa, and Asia.

1494–1559 Italian Wars for control of Italy; Spanish emerged victorious after years of sporadic warfare; gained southern Italy (Kingdom of Naples) and Milan.

16TH CENT. Spanish "Golden Age"; Spain ranked as the leading European power throughout much of the century; expansion of Spanish domains in the New World and tremendous influx of gold provided the base for this power.

1502 Persecution of Muslims in Spain began.

1504 Isabella died; Ferdinand began struggle to gain control of Castile; opposed by Juana (mentally infirm) and her husband Philip.

1506–16 Ferdinand, as regent, gained control of Castile; ruled both kingdoms jointly.

1509–11 Spanish victorious in campaigns against Muslims in North Africa.

1512 Ferdinand acquired southern part of kingdom of Navarre; northern part under French hegemony.

1516–56 Charles I reigned; first of the Hapsburg kings of Spain and first king of united Spain.

1516–1700 Hapsburgs ruled in Spain.

1519–56 Charles I became Holy Roman Emperor Charles V; vast Spanish domains joined with those of Hapsburg Holy Roman Empire; Charles V thus controlled a great and unwieldy family empire.

1519–22 Magellan, in Spanish service, commanded first exploratory voyage around the world; voyage completed by J. Cano, in command after Magellan's death (1521).

1520–21 Revolt of the comuneras; revolt sparked by Charles V's attempts to centralize his authority in Spain.

1556–98 Philip II reigned as king of Spain; inherited Mediterranean territories, Spanish Netherlands, and overseas empire; an absolutist, Philip vigorously supported Catholicism and the Inquisition.

1559 Treaty of Cateau-Cambresis ended Italian Wars to Spain's advantage.

1567 Netherlands rebelled against Philip's attempts to impose royal authority and Inquisition there; in subsequent war for independence, northern part of Spanish Netherlands won independence as United Provinces.

1571 Battle of Lepanto; Spanish forces joined allied fleet that defeated the Ottoman Turks in a signal naval battle.

1580 Portugal united with Spain by Philip following struggle over succession.

1588 Spanish Armada, formed to invade Protestant England, defeated by English and stormy seas; marked beginning of Spain's decline as a European power.

1589–98 Spain interfered in the Wars of Religion in France.

1598–1621 Philip III reigned.

1609 Christian Moors (Moriscos) exiled from Spain.

1618–48 Thirty Years' War in Europe; fighting between Spain and France continued to 1659.

1621–65 Philip IV reigned.

1640 Portugal regained its independence from Spain after a successful revolt.

1640–59 Province of Catalonia rebelled to maintain autonomy.

1659 Peace of the Pyrenees; ended hostilities stemming from the Thirty Years' War; established border.

1665–1700 Charles II reigned as last Spanish Hapsburg king; Spain's power continued to decline.

1667–68 War of Devolution, war with France over the Spanish Netherlands.

1672–78 Third Dutch War; Spain lost Franche-Comte and territories in Flanders to France.

1689–97 War of the Grand Alliance; Spain joined this general war against French king Louis XIV.

1700 Charles II, just before his death, named Philip V, a Frenchman of the House of Bourbon, as his successor.

1700–46 Philip V reigned.

1700–1868 Bourbon line ruled in Spain (except 1808–13).

1701–14 War of the Spanish Succession; Philip successfully defended his succession, though by the Peace of Utrecht the Spanish Netherlands and Spanish Mediterranean domains passed to Austria; Gibraltar, captured (1704) by British, remained in British hands.

1718 Spain joined the Quadruple Alliance.

1733 Family Compact formed between the Bourbon kings of France and Spain.

1733–38 Spain supported Poland in War of the Polish Succession.

1740–48 War of the Austrian Succession.

1756–63 Seven Years' War; by Treaty of Paris ending war, Spain lost Florida and gained Louisiana Territory.

1759–88 Charles III reigned; considered an enlightened despot, he instituted administrative reforms.

1767 Jesuits exiled in attempt to establish state's supremacy over church.

1783 Treaty of Versailles, after the American Revolution; Spain, which had sided with the American colonials against Britain, regained Florida.

1788–1808 Charles IV reigned.

1792–1802 French Revolutionary Wars; Spain at first warred against (1793–95) and was defeated by France; later joined France in War of the Oranges (1801), in which Portugal was conquered.

1800 Spain ceded Louisiana Territory to France.

1803–15 Napoleonic Wars; Spain was invaded (1808) and occupied by French in Peninsular War. Spain's South American colonies used opportunity to begin movement for independence.

1808 Revolt of Aranjuez (Mar.); sparked by Prime Minister M. Godoy's pro-French policies; resulted in King Charles' abdication.

1808 Charles IV abdicated (Mar. 19); Ferdinand VII succeeded him.

1808 Bayonne Conference (Apr. 6); Napoleon forced Ferdinand to abdicate; Napoleon subsequently named his brother Joseph king.

1808–13 Joseph Bonaparte reigned as king; Spanish resisted his rule, aiding British in the Peninsular War.

1810–26 Wars of independence in South America; Spain lost its colonies there as the independence movement spread throughout Spanish New World colonies.

1812 First national Cortes met at Cadiz in unoccupied Spain; liberal constitution drawn up.

1814–33 Ferdinand VII reigned; restored after the French were driven out, he rescinded the liberal constitution and instituted conservative, reactionary policies that bred liberal revolt.

1819 Transcontinental Treaty concluded between Spain and US; Spain ceded Florida and the Oregon country to US; US recognized Spanish sovereignty in Texas.

1820–23 Liberal revolution, led by Col. Rafael Riego, failed; French intervened on behalf of the Spanish monarchy.

1833 Salic Law abolished by Ferdinand VII to allow his daughter Isabella to succeed.

1833–68 Isabella II reigned; her succession marked beginning of dynastic struggle with Carlists.

1834 Estatuto Real, royal charter, granted by Isabella; less liberal than 1812 constitution.

1834–39 First Carlist War.

1868 Military revolt; growing liberal sentiment and disaffection with Isabella led to proclamation of revolution (Sept. 18) by military officers; government forces were defeated soon after and Isabella was deposed (Sept. 29); provisional government set up.

1869 Constitutional monarchy established by the Cortes.

1870–73 Amadeus reigned as king.

1873 Amadeus abdicated in the face of opposition and increasing political problems.

1873 Spanish Republic established; brought down (1874) by Carlist War.

1873–76 Second Carlist War.

1874–85 Alfonso XII reigned, following restoration of the monarchy.

1874–1931 Bourbon line again ruled in Spain.

1876 New constitution adopted; provided for bicameral legislature.

1886–1931 Alfonso XIII reigned; Spain was governed under the regency of his mother, Maria Christina, until the early 1900s.

1898 Spanish-American War; Spain lost Cuba and the Philippines to the US.

1912 Spanish Morocco established as a protectorate after agreement with France defining spheres of influence in Morocco.

1914–18 WW I; Spain remained neutral.

1921 Spanish military defeat (July) at Anul, in Morocco; thousands of Spanish soldiers slaughtered by Moroccan rebel, Abd el-Krim; caused political crisis in Spain.

1923 Military coup (Sept. 13) followed widespread social and political unrest; Primo de Rivera established dictatorship (1923–30).

1930 Rivera forced to resign by mounting opposition to his regime; period of unrest followed his resignation.

1931–1939 Second Spanish Republic, established after Alfonso XIII was deposed.

1931–36 N. Alcala Zamora, leader of provisional republican government, served as first president of the Spanish Republic; term marked by outbreaks by increasingly radical factions on both the conservative and liberal republican sides.

1934 Catalonia proclaimed independence; revolt put down by government.

1934 Unsuccessful uprising by miners.

1936–39 Spanish Civil War; Gen. F. Franco won control of Spain with aid of Italian Fascists and German Nazis.

1939–75 Franco ruled Spain as dictator; opposition suppressed and Falange made only legal political party; church and landed aristocracy restored to favor.

1939–45 WW II; Spain remained nominally neutral.

1942 Cortes reestablished.

1953 Spain signed agreement with US providing for US bases in Spain.

1955 Spain admitted to UN.

1956 Spanish Morocco made part of independent Morocco.

1966 New constitution issued by Franco, following period of mounting unrest; introduced liberal reforms, including relaxed censorship, direct election of some members of the Cortes, and religious freedom.

1968 Spanish Equatorial Guinea granted independence.

1972 Gen. Franco named Prince Juan Carlos as his successor (to become king).

1973 Franco resigned as premier; retained post as head of state.

1973 Premier Carrero assassinated.

1975 Juan Carlos assumed power (Oct. 30) as head of state; Franco seriously ill.

1975 Franco died (Nov. 20).

1975 King Juan Carlos I succeeded Franco as ruler of Spain (Nov. 22).

1976 Political parties legalized.

1977 Diplomatic relations reopened with the Soviets after nearly 40 years.

1977 Communist Party legalized.

1977 First free parliamentary elections held (June) since 1936; Democratic Center coalition victorious.

1978 New constitution providing for constitutional monarchy approved by voters.

1979 Catalonia and Basque provinces granted home rule.

1981 Civil Guardsmen seized the Parliament (Feb. 23) in an abortive coup attempt, which ended the following day.

1982 Socialists won a majority in the elections, bringing them to power in Spain.

1982 Spain became a member of NATO.

Spangenberg, August Gottlieb 1704–92. German-born American religious leader, founder of the Moravian church in America (1740).

Spanish-American War War (Apr.-Dec., 1898) between the US and Spain. Spain's harsh measures against rebels in Cuba became, in the US, the subject of inflammatory newspaper articles, which aroused American public sentiment for war. It reached a fever pitch after the USS *Maine* (Feb. 15, 1898) was sunk in Havana Harbor. Spanish involvement was never proved but relations between the US and Spain broke down. Although Spain called (Apr. 10) for a cessation of hostilities in Cuba, US Pres. W. McKinley asked Congress for and received (Apr. 11) authority to intervene. Spain declared war (Apr. 24) and the US reciprocated (Apr. 25). On May 1, a US fleet under G. Dewey destroyed the Spanish fleet at Manila Bay in the Philippines. In Cuba the major conflict came in the Battle of Santiago *(q.v.)*, in which the Rough Riders under L. Wood and T. Roosevelt fought the Battle of San Juan Hill (July 1) and a US fleet destroyed the Spanish fleet in Santiago Harbor (July 3). In the Philippines, US forces occupied Manila (Aug. 12) a day after signing an armistice. The war was officially ended by the Treaty of Paris (Dec. 10, 1898). By its terms, the US gained control of Cuba, Guam, Puerto Rico, and the Philippines in return for an indemnity of $20,000,000. The war established the US as a world power.

Spanish Armada ⟨Invincible Armada⟩ Great Spanish war fleet, formed (1588) by King Philip II to invade England and put an end to Protestant rule there (under Elizabeth I). The fleet, under command of the Duke of Medina-Sidonia (1550–1615), consisted of about 130 ships. It was anchored at Calais when the English sent fire ships into the anchorage and forced it to scatter. The slow-moving Spanish ships, now out of formation, became easy prey for the English force of 197 smaller and more maneuverable warships and other vessels under the command of C. Howard (of Nottingham). The Armada escaped the English but was further ravaged by storms on the return to Spain. Only half the ships completed the journey and the destruction of the Armada marked Spain's decline as a naval power.

Spanish Civil War War (1936–39) between republican (leftist) and nationalist (rightist) forces in Spain that brought Gen. F. Franco to power in 1939. With the establishment of the Second Spanish Republic in 1931, moderate republicans (liberals, moderate Socialists) gained power. In the first, unsettled years of the republic they were opposed by the nationalists, then consisting of the aristocracy, royalists, the church, military and fascists. However, extremist factions on both sides came to the fore and, after civil war broke out (1936), they played a major role in the continuing struggle. The republican faction was split by conflicts between Communists, anarchists, and radical Socialists. These disputes ultimately contributed to their downfall, despite considerable aid provided by the Soviets. The nationalists, on the other hand, were quickly unified under the leadership of Gen. Franco and were supplied with men and material by Fascist Italy and Nazi Germany. The war devastated Spain, and some 750,000 were killed. Key events in the civil war include:

1931 Monarchy of King Alfonso XIII fell; Second Spanish Republic proclaimed (Apr.).

1931 Republican constitution adopted by the Cortes (legislative assembly) (Dec. 9).

1932 Abortive uprising by royalist faction of the military (Aug. 10); Gen. José Sanjurjo took Seville before rebels were defeated.

1932 Catalonia proclaimed its autonomy (Sept. 25); other local separatist movements arose, weakening republican government.

1933 Nationalists gained majority in elections; liberal reforms negated.

1934 Catalonia unsuccessful in revolt for independence; revolt by Communists put down (Oct.).

1936 Leftist Popular Front won Cortes elections (Feb. 16); nationalists began to consolidate against it.

1936 Spanish Civil War began (July 17–18) when Spanish army, led by Gen. F. Franco, revolted in Morocco; nationalists revolted in Spain.

1936 Nonintervention Pact signed (Aug.) by 27 nations, including Italy, Germany, and Soviets; pact all but ignored by Italy, Germany, and Soviets.

1936 Franco became head of nationalist revolutionary state (Oct. 1), aided by Fascist Italy and Nazi Germany.

1936 Nationalists besieged (Nov.) Madrid; International Brigade (largely Communists) supported republicans.

1937 Málaga fell to Italian troops (Feb. 8).

1937 International Brigade and republicans repulsed nationalists at the Battle of Guadalajara, outside Madrid.

1937 Franco organized (Apr.) fascist Falange and other rightist groups under his command.

1937 German air bombing (Apr.) caused massive destruction and many deaths at Guernica.

1937 Marxists revolted (May) in Barcelona; moderate Socialist premier Largo Caballero ousted; Socialist Juan Negrin led new republican government.

1937 Bilbao, last republican stronghold in the north, fell to the nationalists (June 18).

1937 Republicans won the Battle of Teruel (Dec. 19) during a short-lived offensive; Franco retook Teruel (Feb.).

1938 Nationalist forces split republican territories in two (Mar.–June).

1938 Republicans won Battle of Ebro, but failed to press their advantage (July 24).

1939 Nationalist offensive in Catalonia (Dec.–Jan.); Barcelona fell to Franco (Jan. 26) after heavy fighting; nationalists established control of Catalonia.

1939 Britain and France recognized Franco regime.

1939 Military coup (Mar. 6); Negrin's republican government overthrown; new government sought to end war; Communists rebelled and were defeated; republicans' peace overtures rejected by nationalists.

1939 Nationalists captured Madrid (Mar. 27–28).

1939 Republicans surrendered; civil war ended (Mar. 28).

Spanish Guinea   *See* **Equatorial Africa**

Spanish Inquisition   *See* **Inquisition**

Spanish Main   Name (from the 16th cent.) of the coastal region of northern South America and Central America and adjacent Caribbean waters during Spanish colonial times. This region was famous as a haven for buccaneers who raided Spanish treasure fleets.

Spanish March   Name of the region in northeast Spain established by Charlemagne in 801 after he conquered it during war against the Muslims. It is part of modern Catalonia.

Spanish Marriages, Affair of the   *See* **Affair of the Spanish Marriages**

Spanish Netherlands   *See* **Netherlands, Spanish and Austrian**

Spanish Sahara   Former overseas province of Spain, in northwestern Africa. Spain claimed the region as a protectorate in 1884 and gradually expanded the territory in the 20th cent. It was given up by Spain in 1975 and divided between Mauritania and Morocco.

Spanish Succession, War of the   A war (1701–14) fought in Europe to determine the succession to the Spanish throne on the death of Spanish King Charles II. (Related fighting in the American colonies was known as Queen Anne's War *[q.v.]*.) French king Louis XIV, seeking to greatly enhance French power on the Continent, supported the accession of his grandson Philip of Anjou. This was opposed by England, which feared French political and economic domination of Europe, and by Holy Roman Emperor Leopold I, who championed the claims of his son, Archduke Charles. A third claimant was Bavarian Prince Joseph Ferdinand. Attempts to find a negotiated settlement began after the War of the Grand Alliance (1689–97) with the First and Second Partition treaties. They failed after the death of Charles II and the accession of Philip as Philip V. England then formed the Grand Alliance against France and the war began. Most fighting occurred outside Spain. Key events in the war include:

1698 First Partition Treaty named Bavarian Prince Joseph Ferdinand successor in Spain; France and Holy Roman Empire were to receive territories as compensation; treaty opposed by Spain and nullified by death (1699) of Joseph Ferdinand.

1700 Second Partition Treaty; Austrian archduke Charles (later Holy Roman Emperor Charles VI) named heir in Spain; France would receive Milan, Naples, and Sicily in compensation; opposed by Holy Roman Emperor Leopold I.

1700 Spanish king Charles II named Philip of Anjou as his successor; Charles died; France abrogated the Second Partition Treaty and supported Philip's accession (1700) as Philip V.

1701 Britain, alarmed at the union of the French and Spanish crowns and consequent enormous growth of French power, formed the Grand Alliance with the Holy Roman Empire and The Netherlands; France and Spain allied with Bavaria, Savoy, and Portugal against the Alliance; the war began with fighting in Italy and Bavaria.

1703 Savoy and Portugal joined the Grand Alliance.

1704 British and Imperial forces under the Duke of Marlborough and Prince Eugene of Savoy defeated the French and Bavarians at the Battle of Blenheim (Aug. 13); French forces obliged to withdraw from Bavaria.

1704 Gibraltar fell to British forces.

1705 Holy Roman Emperor Leopold I died; succeeded by Joseph I.

1706 British and allied forces won a major victory over the French at the Battle of Ramillies, Belgium (May 23); took control of most of Spanish Netherlands.

1706 Eugene of Savoy led allied forces to victory over the French in Battle of Turin (Sept. 7); French forced to retreat from Italy.

1707 French victorious at Battle of Almansa (Apr. 25).

1708 British troops won battle of Oudenaarde (July 11); Britain gained initiative in war.

1709 Allied forces under Eugene of Savoy and the Duke of Marlborough defeated the French at Malplaquet (Sept. 11).

1711 Holy Roman Emperor Joseph I died; succeeded by Archduke Charles as Charles VI; Britain withdrew from the alliance because Charles was a claimant to the Spanish throne and an allied victory over France would simply join Spain with the Holy Roman Empire, an equally unacceptable solution to the balance of power in Europe; Charles continued to fight against France.

1713–14 Peace of Utrecht negotiated; series of treaties concluded among European powers ended the war and reorganized European political lines; Philip V's succession confirmed; Britain gained major territorial concessions in Canada from the French.

1714 Treaties of Rastatt and Baden formally ended war between France and Holy Roman Empire.

1720 Treaty of the Hague formally concluded war between Holy Roman Empire and Spain.

Sparta City-state of ancient Greece. Founded c1100 BC by the Dorians, Sparta became, by the 6th cent. BC, one of the most powerful city-states in Greece. Its dominance of the Peloponnesus and support of oligarchies against democracies led to its famous rivalry with Athens. Sparta finally defeated Athens in the Peloponnesian War *(q.v.)* and Sparta became the leading power in Greece. It remained so until its defeat by Thebes at Leuctra (371 BC). Sparta eventually fell under Macedonian, then Roman rule and was destroyed by the Goths (AD 395). In the 18th cent. a new city of Sparta was established near the site of the old one. Key dates in the history of Sparta include:

c11TH CENT. BC Sparta founded by Dorian Greeks.

9TH CENT.? BC Lycurgus created Sparta's militaristic society, aimed at producing fierce warriors.

c800 BC Sparta extended its control over the surrounding region of Laconia.

8TH CENT. BC Earliest known ephors in office; these were Spartan magistrates who served under the Spartan kings and fulfilled executive functions.

735–715 BC First Messenian War; Sparta conquered Messenia, in western Peloponnesus.

c650–c600 BC Sparta put down revolt by Messenians (second Messenian War).

mid-6TH CENT. BC Sparta organized the Peloponnesian League, thereby gaining hegemony over most of the Peloponnesus.

c550 BC Chilon became Spartan ephor; regarded as one of the Seven Wise Men of Greece.

520–490 BC Cleomenes reigned in Sparta; meddled in Athenian politics and maintained Sparta's dominant position in the Peloponnesus.

507 BC Spartans invaded Attica in unsuccessful attempt to oust Cleisthenes and restore aristocracy to power in Athens.

499–479 BC Persian Wars; Sparta joined Athens and other city-states in repulsing invasions of Greece by Persians.

c466 BC Pausanias, Spartan commander accused of treason, took refuge in temple of Athena; Spartans walled him in and left him to starve to death.

464–461 BC Rebellion by helots of Messenia against Sparta.

460–445 BC Sparta fought Athens in the first Peloponnesian War.

431–404 BC Peloponnesian War; Sparta, successful against Athens, emerged as the most powerful city-state in Greece.

c427–400 BC Agis II reigned; led Spartan armies in Peloponnesian War.

395–387 BC Corinthian War; Spartan power in Greece challenged by Athens, Thebes, and other allies; Sparta defeated.

371 BC Sparta defeated by Thebes at the Battle of Leuctra; Sparta's decline began.

338 BC Philip II of Macedonia gained control of Greece.

338–331 BC Agis III reigned; led unsuccessful revolt against Alexander the Great of Macedonia (333–331 BC).

c266–262 BC Chremonidean War; Sparta and Athens fought against Macedonian rule.

222 BC Sparta defeated by Antigonus III of Macedonia.

146 BC Sparta under Roman rule along with the rest of Greece.

AD 395 City destroyed by Goths under Alaric.

Spartacus *d.* 71 BC. Thracian-born Roman gladiator who led the slaves in the Servile War *(q.v.)* in Italy (73–71 BC).

Spartacus League Militant German Socialist organization. Protesting against WW I, the Spartacists split from the German Social Democratic party (1916). They later allied themselves with the

Russian Bolsheviks (1919) and thus became the German Communist party. Party leaders K. Lieb-knecht and R. Luxemburg were murdered after they organized a general strike in Berlin (1919).

Spee, Maximilian, Graf von 1861–1914. German WW I admiral. He routed a British squadron off the coast of Chile in WW I but was defeated and killed soon after at the Battle of Falkland Islands (1914).

Speer, Albert 1905–81. German architect and Nazi official. He organized German war production, bringing it to its peak (1944). Sentenced to 20 years' imprisonment after the war. He wrote *Inside the Third Reich.*

Speke, John Hanning 1827–64. British explorer. He discovered Lake Victoria, one of the sources of the Nile River.

Spencer, Herbert 1820–1903. English philosopher. An early advocate of evolution, he and T. Huxley helped bring about acceptance of Darwin's theory of evolution. His 10-volume *Synthetic Philosophy* covered the principles of various fields of knowledge.

Spener, Philipp Jakob 1635–1705. German theologian, founder of Pietism *(q.v.).*

Spengler, Oswald 1880–1936. German historian and philosopher. Spengler wrote *The Decline of the West,* in which he likened every culture to a personal cycle of birth, growth, maturity, and inevitable decline. The West, he believed, had reached the last phase.

Spenser, Edmund *c*1552–99. English poet, considered one of the finest of Elizabethan England. While in the civil service in Ireland, he published (1590) the first three books of his great unfinished epic peom, *Faerie Queene.* The second three books were published in 1596. He also wrote the love sonnet sequence *Amoretti,* which included the wedding poem *Epithalamion,* celebrating his marriage to Elizabeth Boyle.

Speranski, Mikhail Mikhailovich 1772–1839. Russian statesman and reformer. A trusted adviser to Alexander I, he proposed liberal reforms and a constitution (1809) that angered the nobles and brought about his dismissal. Restored by Nicholas I, he compiled a code of Russian law.

Sperry, Elmer Ambrose 1860–1930. American inventor. Best known as the inventor of the gyroscope, Sperry also devised an arc lamp and a searchlight, improved the dynamo and the Diesel engine, and founded the Sperry Gyroscope Company.

Speusippus *d.* 339 BC. Athenian philosopher. He succeeded his uncle, Plato, as head of the Academy.

sphinx Mythical creature with a human head and the body of a lion (sometimes winged). Although the image was common to many ancient cultures, the best known is the great stone sphinx at Giza, Egypt, dating from *c*2500 BC. In Greek mythology, the sphinx posed a riddle that only Oedipus could answer: What walks on four legs in the morning, two at noon, and three at night? Answer: A human being. He crawls on all fours as a baby, walks on two legs in his prime, and uses a cane in old age.

Spinoza, Baruch 1632–77. Dutch rationalist philosopher. A lens grinder by trade, he developed a monist philosophy that is a noted example of pantheism *(q.v.).* Among his major works were *Treatise on Religion and Political Philosophy,* and *Ethics.*

spiritualism ⟨spiritism⟩ Belief in the existence after death of the human spirit or personality, and its ability to manifest itself. Noted advocates have included Madam Blavatsky and A.C. Doyle.

Spode, Josiah 1754–1827. Famous British pottery manufacturer. He developed a new mixture (adding feldspar and bone ash) for his porcelain and popularized many intricate patterns.

spoils system ⟨patronage⟩ In the US, the practice of awarding government jobs to loyal supporters of the party after an election victory. New York Senator W. Marcy coined the term (1832) when he declared that "to the victor belong the spoils." On the national level, the practice became especially widespread from the first administration of Pres. A. Jackson. It was eventually curbed by the Pendleton Civil Service Act and other such regulations.

Spooner Amendment Amendment to the US Army appropriation bill (Mar. 2, 1901), authorizing the president to abolish the US military government in the Philippines and to establish a civil government.

Spotsylvania Court House, Battle of Bloody Civil War battle fought in May, 1864, in northeastern Virginia, during the Wilderness Campaign.

Spottiswoode, John 1565–1639. Scottish religious leader. He abandoned his Presbyterianism to support James I's plan to introduce episcopacy in Scotland. Named chancellor of Scotland (1635), he fell out of favor and was ousted in 1638.

Spring and Autumn Period *See* Ch'un Chiu

Springfield Capital city (pop. 99,600) of Illinois. Settled in 1818, it became the capital in 1837 and was incorporated in 1840. A. Lincoln lived there (1837–61).

Spurgeon, Charles Haddon 1834–92. English Baptist preacher, noted for his fundamentalist sermons and the wide following he enjoyed during his lifetime.

Spurs, Battle of the ⟨Guinegate, Battle of⟩ English victory (Aug. 16, 1513) over the French during wars of the Holy League. English King Henry VIII, a member of the league, launched an invasion from Calais into northern France. Reinforced with troops sent by Holy Roman Emperor Maximilian I, the English intercepted a French cavalry force at the village of Guinegate. The French, however, retreated suddenly before serious battle had been joined (thus, Battle of the Spurs).

Sputnik The world's first artificial satellite, launched (Oct. 4, 1957) by the Russians as the first of ten satellites in the *Sputnik* series. The second (Nov. 3, 1957) carried a dog, Laika, into earth orbit.

Spyri, Johanna 1827–1901. Swiss writer. The best known of her many children's books is *Heidi*.

Squanto ⟨Tisquantum⟩ *d.* 1622. American Indian. A member of the Pawtuxet tribe, Squanto assisted the Pilgrims at Plymouth Colony, showing them how to plant and fish. He frequently served as guide, interpreter, and mediator.

Sri Lanka ⟨*formerly* Ceylon⟩ Island republic (pop. 14,740,000) in the Indian Ocean southeast of India. Capital is Sri Jayewardenapura Kotte. The island's ancient inhabitants were conquered (6th cent. BC) by the Sinhalese from India. They introduced Buddhism (3d cent. BC) and established a kingdom that reached its peak in the 4th–6th cents. AD. The island was invaded (11th–12th cent.) by the Tamils from India, who established a kingdom in the north. Much of Ceylon's coastal region was conquered (16th cent.) by the Portuguese and their holdings were seized in turn by the Dutch (17th cent.) and the British (1796). The British established a crown colony (1798) and gained control of the entire island (1815) following the overthrow of the kingdom of Kandy, which had ruled the interior. A nationalist movement, originating in the early 20th cent., led to independence (1948) as a dominion within the British Commonwealth. Ceylon was the site in the 1950s of strife between the country's Sinhalese and Tamil populations, and in 1959 its prime minister S.W.R.D. Bandaranaike (1899–1959) was assassinated. His widow, Mrs. Sirimavo Bandaranaike (1916–) became prime minister (1960), began a program of reforms (including nationalization [1962] of British and US businesses) and was voted out of office (1965). A more moderate government lasted until 1970, when Mrs. Bandaranaike again became prime minister as head of a coalition that sought increasingly radical reforms. A Marxist revolt (1971) was crushed in 1972, and that year

Ceylon became a republic under the name Sri Lanka. Mrs. Bandaranaike was voted out of office (1977) and the next year Sri Lanka adopted a presidential form of government. Junius Richard Jayewardene (1906–) became its first president and remained in office into the early 1980s.

SS ⟨Schutzstaffel⟩ ⟨Black Shirts⟩ Nazi military corps (formed 1929). Commanded by H. Himmler, it eventually became the instrument of Nazi party control in Germany and occupied territories. By the end of WW II the SS had grown to 35 divisions responsible for domestic and international security and included the Gestapo, the armed Waffen SS units, and concentration camp guards.

Ssŭ-ma Ch'ien ⟨Si-ma Qien⟩ 145–85 BC. First great historian of China. He wrote the *Shih Chi* (Historical Records), a dynastic history of China down to the end of the 2d cent. BC.

Ssu-ma Kuang 1019–1086. Chinese statesman and historian of the Sung dynasty, compiler of the massive *Comprehensive Mirror for Aid in Government*, a history of China from 403 BC to AD 959.

St. *For names beginning with St., see under* **Saint**

Staël, Germaine de 1766–1817. French writer, considered the greatest French woman of letters. Her book *De l'Allemagne* (1810) was ordered destroyed by Napoleon, and she was exiled. Reprinted later, it introduced German romanticism to France.

Stafford, Henry, 2d duke of Buckingham 1454?–1483. English nobleman, who helped Richard III seize the throne. He later raised an army against Richard, but was captured and beheaded.

Stafford, Humphrey, 1st duke of Buckingham 1402–60. English nobleman. Stafford served in the Hundred Years' War and supported the Lancasters in the War of the Roses. He died at the Battle of Northampton.

Stahl, Georg Ernst 1660–1734. German chemist. Stahl developed both the phlogiston theory of combustion, and the theory of animism—that bodily functions are controlled by the soul.

Stair, James Dalrymple, 1st viscount 1619–95. Scottish judge. A royalist, he was nevertheless appointed judge during the Commonwealth. Ousted during the Restoration he wrote *The Institutions of the Law of Scotland*. He was reappointed under William III.

Stair, John Dalrymple, 1st earl of 1648–1707. Scottish statesman, son of James Stair, lord advocate and secretary of state for William III. His approval of the Glencoe Massacre *(q.v.)* forced his resignation.

Stair, John Dalrymple, 2d earl of 1673–1747. Scottish general and diplomat. He fought for William of Orange (later William III) in Holland and then in England. He served as Ambassador to Paris under George I.

Stakhanovism Movement in the Soviet Union (c1935) to increase industrial workers' output. Aleksey Stakhanov, a coal miner who increased production sevenfold by instituting more efficient techniques, gave his name to the movement. Stakhanovite workers received special pay and privileges.

Stalin, Joseph Vissarionovich 1879–1953. Soviet Communist leader, originally surnamed Dzhugashvili. Stalin joined N. Lenin's Bolshevik faction in 1903 and took part in revolutionary activities. He became (1922) general secretary of the Central Committee after the Bolsheviks came to power in the Revolution of 1917. Shortly before Lenin's death, Stalin and Lenin fell out, but Lenin died before any action was taken. In the ensuing power struggle among Lenin's survivors, Stalin defeated L. Trotsky, G. Zinoviev, L. Kamenev, and N. Bukharin to become virtual dictator of the Soviet Union and the Communist party. In 1928, Stalin instituted a new policy of industrialization and collectivization of agriculture. Resistance by kulaks, or farmers, to collectivization led to untold misery and death. Failures in Stalin's Five Year Plan *(q.v.)* caused further hardship. The 1930s saw the Purge Trials *(q.v.)*, by which Stalin eliminated all potential opponents, and the signing of a nonagression pact (1939) with Germany.

Stalin's hopes of keeping Russia out of WW II ended with the German invasion of the Soviet Union (June 22, 1941), and his inability to deal at first with the invasion contributed to the Red Army's disastrous early losses. He subsequently acted as commander-in-chief of the victorious Soviet forces, although his role as military leader is disputed. Stalin's participation in the Teheran (1943) and Yalta (1945) conferences *(qq.v.)* established the Soviet Union as one of the major world powers, and led to Soviet domination of Eastern Europe after the war. In the late 1940s and early 1950s he became the leading Communist figure in the Cold War *(q.v.)* and further increased his tyrannical rule. After his death (1953), a power struggle led to the rise of N. Khrushchev, who denounced (1956) Stalin's excesses and the personality cult that had formed around him.

Stalingrad ⟨Volgograd⟩ Soviet city (pop. 818,000) now known as Volgograd, capital of Volgograd Oblast. It is a major port on the Volga River and a railroad center. It began as a fort in 1589 for defense against the Cossacks and was conquered by S. Razin in 1670. It was named after Stalin in 1925

but was renamed Volgograd in 1961. (*See also* Stalingrad, Battle of.)

Stalingrad, Battle of Important turning point of WW II during which the Russians gained the offensive against the Germans. More than 500,000 Germans under Gen. von Paulus attacked and largely destroyed Stalingrad in Sept. 1942, but the Russians continued to hold out and by Nov., 1942, Gen. G. Zhukov had surrounded the Germans, who were forced to surrender (Feb. 2, 1943). Hundreds of thousands were killed and wounded on both sides in this bloody battle.

Stalinism Doctrines and policies of Soviet dictator J. Stalin. He advocated a pragmatic rather than an ideological approach to creating the socialist state. He abandoned the idea of spreading revolution throughout the world for the sake of creating "socialism in one country" (the Soviet Union). The results of his programs were far-reaching: he collectivized agriculture, undertook a massive program to industrialize the nation, and suppressed the church. But by far the most prominent aspect of Stalinism was the "cult of personality." His great success in concentrating power in his own hands and his ruthless measures against dissent in any form made him absolute ruler of the Soviet Union and made his dictates the gospel of the Communist party.

Stalin Line Soviet defensive fortifications along the border with Poland. Patterned after the Maginot Line *(q.v.)*, these defenses failed to prevent the German invasion of WW II.

Stalwarts Conservative faction of the US Republican party that vied for power in the 1870s and 1880s. Led by New York Senator Roscoe Conkling and by C. Arthur, the Stalwarts opposed the Half-Breeds *(q.v.)*. Stalwarts fought the civil-service reforms of Pres. R. Hayes and unsuccessfully tried to nominate U. Grant for a third term.

Stambolov, Stefan 1854–95. Bulgarian politician. Stambolov was a regent after the abdication of Prince Alexander (1886–87) and as prime minister (1887–94) dominated Prince Ferdinand. His strong rule led to his forced resignation and assassination.

Stambuliski, Alexander 1879–1923. Bulgarian politician. Stambuliski headed the Peasants' party, became premier (1919) and dictator. In 1923 he was overthrown and executed.

Stamp Act British revenue law (1765) intended to raise funds for the defense of the American colonies by selling stamps that had to be used for all newspapers, legal documents, pamphlets, almanacs, cards, etc. Widespread Colonial opposition (sometimes violent) led to the formation of the Stamp Act Congress *(q.v.)* and the Sons of Liberty *(q.v.).* The British Parliament, which had passed the act without consent of Colonial assemblies, repealed it in Mar., 1766. The Stamp Act was one of the Colonial grievances that resulted in the American Revolution.

Stamp Act Congress Meeting (Oct., 1765) of American colonials to formalize protest against the Stamp Act *(q.v.).* Representatives from New York, New Jersey, Rhode Island, Massachusetts, Pennsylvania, Delaware, South Carolina, Maryland, and Connecticut met in New York City and issued the Declaration of Rights and Grievances, which condemned taxation by the British without Colonial representation in Parliament. Parliament refused to acknowledge the grievances but, under pressure from British merchants, repealed the Stamp Act (Mar., 1766). At the same time Parliament maintained, by the Declaratory Act of 1766, the right to impose taxes within the British Empire.

Standish, Myles *c*1584–1656. English colonist who sailed to America on the Mayflower and served as the military leader and treasurer of Plymouth colony. He is the subject of a famous poem by H. Longfellow about his supposed unsuccessful courtship of Priscilla Mullins.

Stanhope, Charles, 3d earl Stanhope 1753–1816. British politician and inventor. Stanhope was W. Pitt's brother-in-law and urged conciliation toward America. His many inventions include lenses, calculating machines, a printing press, and fireproof stucco.

Stanhope, Lady Hester 1776–1839. English noblewoman and adventuress, secretary to her uncle, W. Pitt. In 1810 she traveled to the Middle East and, living among the natives, was revered by them as a prophetess.

Stanhope, James, 1st earl Stanhope 1673–1721. English general. He fought in the War of the Spanish Succession and, as George I's secretary of state, negotiated the Triple Alliance (1717) and Quadruple Alliance (1718).

Stanhope, Philip 1805–75. English statesman and historian who served as R. Peel's undersecretary for foreign affairs. He wrote *History of England from the Peace of Utrecht to the Peace of Versailles.*

Stanislaus I ⟨Leszczynski, Stanislaus⟩ Polish king (1704–09, 1733–35). Installed (1704) by the Swedes during the Northern War, he fled Poland after their defeat. His return (1733) after the death of King Alexander II precipitated the War of the Polish Succession *(q.v.).*

Stanislaus II ⟨Poniatowski, Stanislaus Augustus⟩ 1732–98. Last king of Poland (1764–95), successor to Alexander III. A lover of Catherine II, he

was installed by her as king of Poland. Though Russia thereafter dominated Poland, Stanislaus attempted to implement reforms. He was unable to prevent the complete dismemberment of the kingdom in the three Partitions of Poland *(q.v.).*

Stanislavsky, Konstantin ⟨Alekseyev, Konstantin Sergeyevich⟩ 1863–1938. Russian actor, director, and teacher. Stanislavsky co-founded the Moscow Art Theater. His "method acting" theories have profoundly influenced modern acting and directing.

Stanley, Sir Henry Morton 1841–1904. British-born American reporter and explorer. Stanley's diverse activities included fighting for both sides in the American Civil War, newspaper reporting, finding the missing Dr. D. Livingstone in Africa, and colonizing the Congo and Uganda.

Stanley, Wendell Meredith 1904–71. American biochemist. He researched the chemical nature of viruses and was cowinner of the 1946 Nobel Prize in Chemistry.

Stanton, Edwin McMasters 1814–69. American statesman. A Radical Republican, he became secretary of war (from 1862) under Pres. A. Lincoln and later under Pres. A. Johnson. However, Johnson's struggle with Radical Republicans, over control of Reconstruction *(q.v.)* policy, resulted in a presidential order discharging Stanton. Soon after radical Republicans in Congress unsuccessfully attempted to impeach Pres. Johnson, saying he had violated the Tenure of Office Act by firing Stanton.

Stanton, Elizabeth Cady 1815–1902. American reformer, a leader of the woman suffrage *(q.v.)* movement. She organized (1848) at Seneca Falls, New York, the first women's rights convention.

Staple, Company of the Merchants of the *See* **Company of the Merchants of the Staple**

Star Chamber English royal court. An outgrowth of the king's council, it eventually included civil and criminal matters in its jurisdiction, and for a time it was a popular expedient to common-law courts. Under the Stuart kings (notably Charles I), however, the court became a device for asserting royal powers. It was abolished (1641) soon after by the Long Parliament.

Starhemberg, Ernst Rüdiger, graf von 1638–1701. Austrian field marshal who successfully defended Vienna against prolonged Turkish attack (1683) during the Austro-Turkish War *(q.v.).*

Starhemberg, Ernst Rüdiger von 1899–1956. Austrian politician. He joined Hitler in the Munich Putsch (1923). Later he formed the Austrian Heimwehr, a fascist group supporting E. Dollfuss.

Stark, John 1728–1822. American Revolutionary general. Stark participated in fighting at

Bunker Hill, Princeton, Trenton, and Saratoga. He defeated Burgoyne at Bennington (1777).

Starr, Belle 1848–89. American frontier figure whose fame as a horse thief and outlaw was spread by exaggerated newspaper accounts of her deeds. She was for a time associated with C. Younger and the James gang and later ran a hideout for outlaws.

state Term applied to the political organization of a society, or the form or institution of government ruling the affairs of a society.

States General ⟨Estates General⟩ Representative assembly. First established in France as an advisory body to King Philip IV *(q.v.)* in the early 14th cent., it was divided into three "estates": the clergy, the nobility, and the people (third estate). Though it acquired jurisdiction over taxes and other powers, it was eclipsed by the growth of royal power. Thus, the States General was seldom convened after 1500 and did not meet at all from 1614 to 1789. Finally, Louis XVI was forced by the chaos of royal finances to convene the body in 1789. The meeting resulted in the union of the clergy and the people, the formation of the National Assembly, and the beginning of the French Revolution. The States General is also the name for the assembly of the Dutch Republic (1579–1795). It was superseded by the National Assembly in 1796.

states' rights Political doctrine prominent in US history. It advocates limitations on federal government powers and is based on the 10th Amendment to the Constitution, which gives the states powers not granted to the federal government or otherwise expressly prohibited. States' rights has figured in many important controversies. The power struggle between Jeffersonian Republicans and the Federalists in the early years of the republic resulted in the drafting of the Kentucky and Virginia Resolutions *(q.v.)*, the first statement of states' rights doctrine. In the 1800s, southern opposition to federal tariff laws fostered the states' rights Nullification Controversy *(q.v.)*, and the determination of southern states to defend slavery led to the bitter American Civil War. This ended the controversy over the states' power to directly oppose federal powers. Nevertheless, states rights became a factor in opposition to desegregation in the South during the 1950s and 1960s. Finally, limitation of federal powers, which have been expanding for decades, was the basis of Pres. R. Reagan's 1980 campaign.

States' Rights Democrats *See* **Dixiecrats**

Statius, Publius Papinius AD c40–c96. Latin poet. The surviving fragments of his work include the *Achilleid*, the *Silvae*, and *Thebaid*.

Statue of Liberty Statue, now a symbol of the American ideal of liberty. A gift from France in memory of the Franco-American alliance during the American Revolution, it was entitled *Liberty Enlightening the World*. The monument was designed by F.A. Bartholdi and was erected on Liberty Island in New York harbor in 1886.

Statute of Wales English law enacted on Mar. 19, 1284, uniting Wales with England after the conquest of Wales by Edward I.

Stavisky Affair French scandal (1934) that for a time threatened to bring down the Third Republic. Serge Alexandre Stavisky had sold great quantities of fraudulent bonds, and discovery of the scandal resulted in his death (1934) by either murder or suicide. Rightists charged that it was murder to protect prominent government officials and began agitating to overthrow the republic. The ministries of C. Chautemps and E. Daladier were forced to resign before calm was finally restored.

Steel, Pact of *See* **Pact of Steel**

Steele, Sir Richard 1672–1729. Noted English writer and dramatist, who wrote essays with J. Addison for the periodicals *Tatler* and *The Spectator*.

Steelyard, Merchants of the *See* **Merchants of the Steelyard**

Steenkirk, Battle of *See* **Grand Alliance, War of the**

Steffens, Joseph Lincoln 1866–1936. American journalist. An editor for such periodicals as *McClure's* and *The American*, he was a leading muckraker *(q.v.)* who exposed business and political corruption.

Steichen, Edward 1879–1973. American photographer. With A. Stieglitz, he founded the Photo-Secession Group (1902) and was among the first to recognize the camera's artistic potential.

Stein, Gertrude 1874–1946. American writer and a leading avante-garde literary figure in the early 1900s. Her works include *The Autobiography of Alice B. Toklas* and *Four Saints in Three Acts*.

Stein, Baron Heinrich Friedrich Karl vom und zum 1757–1831. Prussian statesman and reformer. He was instrumental in abolishing serfdom and effecting other civil, economic, and military reforms.

Steinbeck, John Ernst 1902–68. Noted American novelist. His works include *The Grapes of Wrath, East of Eden, Of Mice and Men*, and *Tortilla Flat*. Nobel Prize in literature (1962).

Steiner, Jakob 1796–1863. Swiss-born German mathematician, a pioneer in the study of synthetic geometry.

Steiner, Rudolf 1861–1925. Austrian-German philosopher. Once a Theosophist, he developed his own philosophy of anthroposophy, which stressed spiritual thought without reliance on the senses or material objects.

Steinmetz, Charles Proteus 1865–1923. German-born American electrical engineer. He made important discoveries concerning alternating current and devised a generator to produce artificial lightning.

Steinway, Henry Englehard 1797–1871. German-born American piano manufacturer, and founder of the famous Steinway and Sons piano company. Steinway introduced many innovations into piano construction.

Stendhal ⟨Marie Henri Beyle⟩ 1783–1842. French writer, one of the great French novelists. His best-known works include the two novels *The Red and the Black* and *The Charterhouse of Parma*.

Stentor In Homer's *Iliad*, a Greek herald with a voice as strong as 50 voices combined. Thus, "stentorian" means "strong-voiced", as applied, for example, to a public speaker.

Stephen, Saint ⟨Stephen I⟩ 969–1038. First king of Hungary (1001–38). Crowned with the blessings of the pope, he Christianized Hungary. He is called the Apostle of Hungary.

Stephen 1097–1154. King of England (1135–54), successor to Henry I. Forced to acknowledge Henry's daughter, Matilda, as legitimate heir, Stephen nevertheless claimed the throne on Henry's death. Matilda invaded England (1139) and, after capturing Stephen at Lincoln (1141), reigned for six months. Stephen regained the throne and drove Matilda out of England (1148), though he was unable to restore order in his domains.

Stephen I *See* **Stephen, Saint**

Stephen II *d.* 757. Italian-born pope (752–757). Threatened by the Lombards, he allied the church with the Franks under Pepin the Short, received the Donation of Pepin from him, and thus became the first pope who was also temporal ruler of the Papal States *(q.v.)*.

Stephen Báthory 1533–86. King of Poland (1575–86). He successfully fought Russian Czar Ivan the Terrible for control of Livonia. His goal, unfulfilled because of his early death, was the unification of Poland, Muscovy, and Transylvania.

Stephen Dushan *c*1308–55. King (1331–46) and czar, (1346–55) of Serbia. One of the notable conquerers of European history, he brought Albania, Bulgaria, and Macedonia into a Serbian empire which, however, did not long survive his death.

Stephens, Alexander Hamilton 1812–83. American politician. Though opposed to secession, Stephens served as Confederate vice-president (1861–65). He continually opposed Pres. J. Davis' policies and sought peace with the Union.

Stephens, Uriah S. *See* **Knights of Labor**

Stephenson, George 1781–1848. English inventor, creator of the first practical railroad locomotive, originally designed for hauling coal in mines. He then built a locomotive for England's first railroad, completed in 1825.

Stepniak, S. 1852–95. Russian revolutionary and author. A Nihilist, he assassinated the czarist chief of police, and defended his actions in *Life for Life*.

Stern, Otto 1888–1969. German-born American physicist. Stern's work with beams of atoms and other discoveries regarding properties of atoms laid the groundwork for atomic science. He received the Nobel Prize in physics, 1943.

Sterne, Laurence 1713–60. British novelist who wrote *A Sentimental Journey* and the famous satirical novel *Tristam Shandy*.

Stesichorus *fl. c*600 BC. Dorian Greek lyric poet. Though only fragments of his work survive, he is thought to have made innovations in Greek poetry and drama.

Steuben, Friedrich Wilhelm, Baron von 1730–94. Prussian general in service of American colonials. From 1778, he was responsible for training the American revolutionary army and organizing it into a conventional military fighting unit. He wrote its first training manual and later was a commander at the Battle of Yorktown.

Stevens, John 1749–1838. American inventor and engineer, a pioneer in steamship design. He built the first American locomotive (1825), and was instrumental in passage of the first US patent laws (1790).

Stevens, Robert Livingston 1787–1856. American engineer and inventor, son of J. Stevens. He invented the T-shape rail and the railroad spike and added the cowcatcher to the front of railroad locomotives.

Stevens, Thaddeus 1792–1868. American statesman. He co-authored the 14th Amendment, was a leader of the Radical Republicans in US Congress during their fight to impose a harsh Reconstruction *(q.v.)* policy, and urged the impeachment of Pres. A. Johnson.

Stevens, Wallace 1879–1955. American poet. An insurance executive, he wrote such poems as *The Man with the Blue Guitar*, and *The Auroras of Autumn*.

Stevenson, Adlai Ewing 1835–1914. American statesman, Stevenson was first assistant postmaster general (1885–89) and vice-president (1893–97) under Pres. G. Cleveland.

Stevenson, Adlai Ewing 1900–65. American statesman. He served as governor of Illinois (1948–52), was twice the unsuccessful Democratic candidate for president (1952, 1956), and was US ambassador to the UN (1961–65).

Stevenson, Robert Louis 1850–94. Scottish author, renowned for such classic novels as *Treasure Island, The Strange Case of Dr. Jekyll and Mr. Hyde,* and *Kidnapped.*

Stewart *See* **Stuart**

Stewart, William Morris 1827–1909. American politician, US senator from Nevada (1864–75, 1887–1905). He wrote the final draft of the 15th Amendment, supported silver coinage and won passage of mining laws.

Stieglitz, Alfred 1864–1946. American photographer. With E. Steichen he founded the Photo-Secession Group (1902) and pioneered the development of photography as an art form. He was noted for his photo studies of his wife, Georgia O'Keefe.

Stilicho, Flavius *d.* AD 408. Roman general. He repulsed invasions by the Vandals (AD 403) and the Goths (AD *c*406). Suspected of plotting against Emperor Honorius, he was beheaded.

Still, Andrew Taylor 1828–1917. American doctor. He founded osteopathy, the theory that diseases can be treated without drugs by massage.

Stilwell, Joseph Warren 1883–1946. American general, commander of US and Nationalist Chinese forces in the Far East during WW II. Forced to retreat during the Japanese invasion of Burma (1942), he led US forces in the reconquest of the region (1943–44).

Stimson, Henry Lewis 1867–1950. American statesman. He was secretary of war (1911–13, 1940–45), serving notably during the WW II years. As secretary of state (1929–33) he formulated the Stimson Doctrine (1932), which proposed the US refuse recognition of territories seized by acts of aggression.

Stimson Doctrine See **Stimson, Henry Lewis**

Stockhausen, Karlheinz 1928–. German composer. Stockhausen's avant-garde techniques include the use of electronic music, improvisation, and simultaneous performances by more than one orchestra.

Stockholm Swedish capital city (pop. 661,300), port, and its largest city. Founded *c*1250, it rose to commercial prosperity as a member of the Hanseatic League. In the 16th cent., it was the focal point of King Gustav's drive for independence. The city became Sweden's capital in 1634 and later became a cultural center. Rapid industrial development occurred in the late 19th cent.

Stockholm, Treaty of Two treaties signed in Stockholm by Sweden during the Great Northern War (1700–21). In Nov., 1719, Sweden ceded Bremen and Verdun to British king George I, in return for financial and military aid against Russia. In the second agreement (Feb., 1720), Sweden sold sections of Pomerania and the port of Stettin to Prussia.

Stockholm Bloodbath Massacre of over 80 Swedish nobles in Stockholm (Nov. 8, 1520), ordered by Danish King Christian II. The incident temporarily prevented break-up of the Kalmar Union *(q.v.)* but ultimately served to unite Sweden for independence. By 1522 Gustavus I had driven the Danes out of Sweden and dissolved the union.

Stockmar, Christian Friedrich, Baron 1787–1863. German physician and diplomat. He helped arrange Prince Albert's marriage to Queen Victoria and later served as his unofficial adviser.

Stoicism Philosophical school founded (*c*300 BC) at Athens by Zeno of Citium. It arose in opposition to Epicureanism *(q.v.)*, spread among the Greeks, and after the 2d cent. BC became influential among the Romans. Stoicism was derived from the teachings of Cynics. Stoics held that all reality is material and that God, or reason, is the universal working force. Thus, living according to nature or reason was to come into harmony with the divine order of the universe. The ideal, virtuous life was to be achieved by exercising wisdom and restraint, by casting off passion and desire, and by right conduct and devotion to duty. Notable adherents of Stoicism include Diogenes of Babylonia, Antipater of Tarsus, Cato the Younger, Seneca, Epictetus, and Emperor Marcus Aurelius.

Stoker, Bram 1847–1912. Irish-born British novelist, best known as the author of *Dracula.*

Stokes, Whitley 1830–1909. Irish jurist. Stokes revised the civil and criminal codes in India.

Stokowski, Leopold 1882–1977. Noted American conductor. Stokowski conducted many contemporary works and unusual orchestrations, and popularized Bach.

Stolypin, Pëter Arkadevich 1863–1911. Russian statesman. As prime minister (1906–11), he attempted to control the revolutionary movement by instituting agrarian land reforms and by ruthless use of secret police.

Stolypin Land Reform *See* **Agrarian Reform Act**

Stone, Harlan Fiske 1872–1946. American jurist, an associate (1925–41) and chief justice (1941–46) of the Supreme Court. He was noted for his dissenting opinions in defense of New Deal legislation.

Stone, Lucy 1818–93. American reformer, a noted public speaker on both abolition and women's rights. With her husband, Henry Blackwell, she helped found the American Woman Suffrage Association.

Stone Age Stage in the development of human culture beginning about 2.5 million years ago and lasting until the beginning of the Bronze Age *(q.v.),* or roughly about 3500 BC (in the Near East). Dating varies widely according to region and particular culture, and an essentially Stone Age culture exists even today among some primitive peoples. The Stone Age is characterized by the use of stone (along with wood and bone) for tools and implements, and is commonly subdivided into the Paleolithic and Neolithic stages. The Paleolithic (Old Stone Age) period is the earliest and lasted until about 8000–6000 BC. The Neolithic (New Stone Age) period is generally taken to begin with the advent of domestication of animals, cultivation of food plants, and development of village culture (although criteria vary). It ends with the appearance of metal weapons and tools. The term Mesolithic (Middle Stone Age) usually refers to a stage of cultural development in northwestern Europe, lasting from about 8000 to 3000 BC.

Stonehenge Famous prehistoric stone structure near Salisbury, in southern England. Built and added to between the 18th and 14th cent. BC, it was apparently used for religious purposes, though not by the Druids, as is popularly believed. The structure is made up of large stones arranged in concentric circles about a central altar stone.

Stones River, Battle of ⟨Battle of Murfreesboro⟩ Battle of the US Civil War, fought (Dec. 31, 1862– Jan. 2, 1863) near Murfreesboro, Tennessee. Union forces under Gen. W. Rosencrans forced the Confederates under B. Bragg to withdraw after a bloody battle.

Storm and Stress *See* **Sturm und Drang**

Storm, Hans Theodor Woldsen 1817–88. German author, best known for the haunting realism of his novellas, especially *The Rider of the White Horse.*

Storting Norwegian parliament (since 1814). It is divided into an upper house (Lagting) and lower house (Odelsting).

Story, Joseph 1779–1845. American jurist, associate justice of the Supreme Court (1811–45). He generally agreed with Chief Justice J. Marshall and wrote the pivotal court opinion in *Martin* vs *Hunter's Lessee* (1816), which established Supreme Court review of state cases involving constitutional law.

Stowe, Harriet Beecher 1811–96. American writer. The sister of H.W. Beecher, her novel

Uncle Tom's Cabin (1852) solidified antislavery sentiment in America.

Strabe 63 BC–after AD 21. Greek geographer and historian. His *Geographica* was a compilation of his own observations and the cumulative knowledge of the geography and history of the ancient world.

Stradivari, Antonio ⟨Stradivarius, Antonius⟩ 1644–1737. Italian violin maker, the acknowledged master of his craft.

Stradivarius, Antonius *See* **Stradivari, Antonio**

Strafford, Thomas Wentworth, 1st earl of 1593– 1641. English statesman. An adviser to Charles I and loyal supporter of his despotic rule, he commanded the king's forces during the second Bishops' War (1640). Following his defeat, Parliamentarians seized the opportunity to eliminate an enemy in their fight with the king. Strafford was impeached and beheaded.

Straits Convention International agreement (July 13, 1840) by which the Ottoman Turks agreed (at the instigation of European powers) to close the Dardanelles to warships during peacetime. The agreement was superseded by the Lausanne Convention (1923), which opened the straits to all warships.

Straits Settlements British colony in the Southeast, including the territories of Singapore, Malacca, Penang, and Labuan. The colony was broken up in 1946.

Stralsund, Treaty of Agreement (May 24, 1370) by which Denmark made extensive commercial concessions to the Hanseatic League. Defeated (1368) by a coalition the league had formed with Sweden and other powers, Danish king Valdemar IV signed the treaty to regain his throne.

Strang, James Jesse 1813–56. Dissident Mormon leader. He failed in his bid to become leader of the Mormons after J. Smith's assassination (1844), formed his own sect (Strangites), and later established a colony on Beaver Island in Lake Michigan.

Strasbourg, Oath of *See* **Oath of Strasbourg**

Strasser, Gregor and **Otto** 1892–1934; 1897– 1974. German Nazi leaders. These brothers were early supporters of A. Hitler. Otto left the party (1930) to join the Socialist Black Front and his brother, a powerful rival of Hitler's within the party, was assassinated (1934).

Strassman, Fritz *See* **Meitner, Lise**

Stratford de Redcliffe, Stratford Canning, Viscount 1786–1880. British diplomat. Stratford served as minister to Ottoman Turkey, and mediated conflicts between that country, Greece, and Russia. He was unable, however, to avert the Crimean War.

Strathclyde Medieval Celtic kingdom in southwestern Scotland, constituted around the 5th cent. Conquered by King Edmund of England in 945, it was annexed by Scotland in 1124.

Strathcona and **Mount Royal, Donald Alexander Smith, 1st baron** 1820–1914. Canadian financier and statesman. Originally a fur trader, he became governor of the Hudson's Bay Company (1889–1914) and was a leading figure in the company that completed the Canadian Pacific Railway.

Straus, Isidor 1845–1912. American merchant. Straus was involved in the family import business, L. Straus and Sons, and, with his brother, N. Straus, took over R.H. Macy and Company. He died aboard the *Titanic.*

Straus, Nathan 1848–1931. American merchant and philanthropist. Straus was associated with the family import business, L. Straus and Sons, and with his brother, I. Straus, took over R.H. Macy and Company. He aided the poor and Zionist charities.

Straus, Oscar Solomon 1850–1926. American diplomat. A member of the wealthy Straus family, Oscar served as minister to Ottoman Turkey under G. Cleveland, W. McKinley and W. Taft.

Strauss, Johann 1825–99. Austrian composer, noted for his waltzes. Strauss ignored his father's opposition and followed him into a musical career. He composed the waltzes *Blue Danube* and *Tales from the Vienna Woods* and the operettas *Die Fledermaus* and *The Gypsy Baron.*

Strauss, Richard Georg 1864–1949. Famous German composer, noted for his romantic operas and symphonic poems. The vast body of his work includes the operas *Elektra, Salome,* and *Der Rosenkavalier,* and the orchestral music *Don Juan, Death and Transfiguration, Thus Spake Zarathustra,* and Till Eulenspiegel's *Merry Pranks.*

Stravinsky, Igor Fëdorovich 1882–1971. Russian-born American composer, one of the great composers of this century. He was best known for his ballets, including *The Firebird, Petrouchka,* and *The Rite of Spring.*

Streicher, Julius 1885–1946. German Nazi leader, a vicious anti-Semite who used his newspaper, *Der Stürmer,* to spread hatred of the Jews. He joined A. Hitler's Nazi party in the early days and was executed as a war criminal after the war.

Stresemann, Gustav 1878–1929. German statesman. As foreign minister of the Weimar Republic, he succeeded in pursuing a policy of conciliation with Germany's former enemies and arranged Germany's admission to the League of Nations. He shared the Nobel Peace Prize (1926).

Strijdom, Johannes Gerhardus 1893–1958. South African politician. A leader of the Nationalist party (from 1929) and supporter of apartheid, he served as prime minister from 1954 to 1958.

strikes Collective work stoppages by employees, usually those who are members of a union seeking higher wages or improved working conditions. Strikes in the US were fairly rare until after the Civil War, when a period of rapid industrialization and the organization of workers began. The late 19th and early 20th cents. witnessed many outbreaks of violence in connection with strikes (notably the Homestead and Pullman strikes, *qq.v.*). Since then, however, violence has steadily played less of a role in labor actions. Though uncommon in the US, strikes in support of political causes are common in Europe. Perhaps the most significant were the widespread strikes (1917) in Russia that helped bring down the czarist government.

Strindberg, Johan August 1849–1912. Swedish playwright and novelist. He is best known for his plays, including *The Father, Miss Julie,* and *The Dance of Death.*

Stroganov Russian merchant family that organized vast colonial enterprises in eastern Russia (16th–17th cents.). They contributed significantly to Russia's expansion into Siberia by organizing entire colonies and military expeditions in pursuit of their commercial expansion. They also provided financial support for czarist governments.

Stroheim, Erich von 1885–1957. Austrian-born American film director and actor. He appeared in such classic films as *The Birth of a Nation, Grand Illusion,* and *Sunset Boulevard,* and directed the critically acclaimed *Greed.*

Strozzi Noble Florentine family that opposed the power of the Medici family in Florence. Its members included Filippo Strozzi the Elder (1426–91), Giambattista Strozzi (1488–1538), and Piero Strozzi (d. 1558).

Struensee, Johann Friedrich 1737–72. German-born Danish politician. As physician to the insane Christian VII, he gained control of the government (1770) and assumed dictatorial powers. He was accused of adultery with Queen Caroline and was beheaded.

Stuart (Stewart) Royal family of Scotland and England (reigned 1603–1714). The family originated in the 11th cent. and from the 12th cent. the Stuarts were hereditary stewards of Scotland. The first Stuart king of Scotland was Robert II (1371–90). The Stuart claim to the English throne stemmed from the marriage of Scottish king James IV to English King Henry VII's daughter, Mary Tudor. Their granddaughter, Mary Queen of Scots, was mother of Scottish king James VI, who became King James I (1603–25), first Stuart king of England. Thereafter the Stuarts reigned (or claimed the throne) during the tumultuous period of the English Civil War, Restoration, and the Glorious Revolution. The Act of Settlement (1701) excluded the Stuarts from the throne, but descendents of the Stuart line ruled until the Hanovers came to power (1714).

Stuart Kings of Scotland

Robert II	1371–90
Robert III	1390–1406
James I	1406–37
James II	1437–60
James III	1460–88
James IV	1488–1513
James V	1513–42
Mary	1542–67
James VI	1567–1625

Stuart Kings of England

| James | 1603–25 |
| Charles I | 1625–49 |

Civil War, Commonwealth, Protectorate

Charles II	1660–85
James II	1685–88
William III	1689–1702
Anne	1702–14

Stuart, Arabella 1575–1615. English noblewoman, a claimant to the throne. Her cousin, King James I, imprisoned her in the Tower of London, where she died.

Stuart, Charles Edward 1720–88. Claimant to the English throne, a grandson of Charles II. The hope of the Jacobites, "Bonnie Prince Charlie," The Young Pretender, led them in an abortive revolt (1745) but was defeated at the Battle of Cullodon (1746). He lived abroad thereafter and died in obscurity.

Stuart, Esme, 1st duke of Lennox c1542–83. Scottish nobleman. A favorite of his cousin King James I of England, he had the Earl of Morton executed for Lord Darnley's murder. He was subsequently driven from Scotland for plotting a Spanish invasion of England to rescue Mary Queen of Scots.

Stuart, Frances Teresa, duchess of Richmond and Lennox 1648–1702. English mistress. A great beauty, she is reputed to be the only woman that Charles II truly loved. She married (1667) Charles Stuart, duke of Richmond, but continued her affair with the king.

Stuart, Gilbert 1755–1828. American portrait painter, noted for his portraits of G. Washington, J. Adams, T. Jefferson, and J. Madison.

Stuart, Henry Benedict Maria (Cardinal York) 1725–1807. Last Stuart to claim the English throne. He became the royal pretender as Henry IX on the death of his brother, Charles Edward Stuart (1788). In return for favors granted by King George III, however, he bequeathed the Stuart family jewels to George IV.

Stuart, James Ewell Brown 1833–64. Confederate cavalry officer in the American Civil War, noted for skillful deployment of his troops in battle and for his daring raids behind Union lines.

Stuart, James Francis Edward (the Old Pretender) 1688–1766. English Prince of Wales, son of King James II and claimant to the English throne as James III. His claim was supported by the Jacobites.

Stuart, Mary *See* **Mary Queen of Scots**

Sture, Sten c1440–1503. Swedish patriot. Sture defeated the Danish king Christian I at Brunkeburg (1471) and unsuccessfully attempted to oppose the union of Sweden with Denmark (Kalmar Union, *q.v.*).

Sturghkh, Karl, graf von 1859–1916. Austrian prime minister (1911–16). He suspended the Parliament (1914) and, an archenemy of liberals and radicals, was assassinated by a Socialist.

Sturm und Drang (Storm and Stress) German literary movement in the 1770s. It developed as a reaction to rationalism and included works of J. Goethe and F. Schiller.

Stuyvesant, Peter 1592–1672. Dutch administrator, governor of New Amsterdam until its capture (1664) by the English, who renamed it New York.

Stymphalian birds (Stymphalides) Man-eating birds in Greek mythology that infested Lake Stymphalus in Arcadia. Hercules killed them as his sixth labor.

Stymphalides *See* **Stymphalian birds**

Styx River in Greek mythology. It was one of the five rivers of Hades, which newly deceased souls crossed. The ferryman Charon provided passage across the river for these souls.

Suárez, Francisco 1548–1617. Spanish Jesuit and prominent Scholastic philosopher. Suarez believed in the equality of souls and disputed the divine right of kings in his *Defensio fidei*.

Suckling, Sir John 1609–42? English poet, one of the Cavalier Poets *(q.v.)*. He was best known for his lyrics.

Sucre, Antonio José de 1795–1830. A South American revolutionary. He was S. Bolívar's chief lieutenant and participated in fighting against the Spanish in Peru, Bolivia, Ecuador, and Colombia and commanded in the Battle of Ayacucho *(q.v.)*. He was first president of Bolivia (1826–28).

Sudan (Republic of the Sudan) Republic located in northeastern Africa. Its capital is Khartoum. Northern Sudan, once part of ancient Nubia, was settled by the Egyptians, who were forced out of the region by the 8th cent. BC. Muslims completed conquest of the region in the 16th cent., and Egypt regained control in the early 19th cent. In 1899 the Anglo-Egyptian Sudan, a condominium under British and Egyptian rule, was established. The Sudan became independent in 1956. Key dates in the history of Sudan include:

c3400–2000 BC Egypt established control over northern Sudan, then part of the ancient region of Nubia.

8TH–4TH CENT. BC Cush kingdom flourished, after Nubians revolted successfully against Egypt.

6TH CENT. AD Christian state of Dongola established; successfully resisted Muslim invasions from Egypt until its fall (15th cent.).

16TH–19TH CENT. Muslim state of Funj flourished in northern Sudan.

1820–22 Region conquered by Egyptians under Muhammad Ali.

1823 Khartoum founded by Egyptians.

1877–80 British officer and administrator C. Gordon served as governor of Egyptian Sudan; streamlined provincial administration and took steps to end the slave trade.

1881–98 Egyptian rule in Sudan challenged by Mahdist revolt led by Muhammad Ahmed, the Mahdi.

1885 Mahdists overran and destroyed Khartoum (Jan.); Gordon killed; Mahdists seized complete control of Egyptian Sudan.

1885 Mahdi died; succeeded by the Khalifa Abdallahi.

1896–98 Joint Anglo-Egyptian expedition to regain Sudan led by British Gen. H. Kitchener; defeated the Khalifa at Omdurman (Sept. 2, 1898).

1899 Anglo-Egyptian Sudan established (Jan. 19); agreement set up joint British and Egyptian rule.

1924 British divided Sudan into separate northern and southern administrative units.

1936 Anglo-Egyptian treaty reaffirmed 1899 agreement for joint rule of Sudan.

1948 Legislative assembly created (June 19); first step in program for Sudanese autonomy.

1953 British and Egyptians signed accord (Feb. 12) calling for Sudanese autonomy within three years.

1955 Predominantly Christian southern Sudanese began revolt against predominantly Muslim northern Sudanese; lasted to 1972.

1956 Sudan became independent (Jan. 1).

1958 Gen. Ibrahim Abboud seized power in military coup.

1964 Parliamentary government restored after Abboud stepped down as military leader.

1969 Col. Gaafar al-Nimeiry seized power; outlawed political parties and proceeded with nationalization of key industries; Nimeiry remained in power into the early 1980s.

1971 Leftist coup by army officers put down (July).

1972 Years of civil war ended (Feb.); southern Sudan granted degree of autonomy by central government.

1973 New constitution adopted; established one-party rule.

1976 Unsuccessful attempt to overthrow Nimeiry; Nimeiry broke diplomatic relations with Libya, suspecting Libyan leader M. Qaddafi of engineering the coup.

Sudetenland *See* **Munich Pact**

Suetonius ⟨Tranquillus, Gaius Suetonius⟩ *fl.* AD c120. Roman biographer. A private secretary to Hadrian, he is chiefly remembered for his *Lives of the Caesars.*

Sudra caste *See* **caste system**

Suez Canal Canal in Eygpt, an important commercial waterway connecting the Mediterranean Sea and the Red Sea. Built by a private French company (1859–69) under the supervision of F. de Lesseps, it passed to the British after they established control over Egypt (1882). After WW II and during the subsequent general withdrawal of the British from Egypt, Britain sought to retain control of the canal. Egyptian leader G. Nasser, however, forced the British to give up the canal (effected June, 1956). He then nationalized the privately-owned canal company (July 26, 1956), when the US refused to go through with a loan to build his coveted Aswan Dam. The resulting Suez Crisis erupted into war when the Israelis, long denied access to the canal, launched the second Arab-Israeli War *(q.v.)* and invaded Egypt. British and French troops entered the fighting (Oct. 31) to retake the canal. They eventually were replaced by UN troops after a cease-fire was arranged (Nov. 6). The canal was completely blocked during the third Arab-Israeli War (1967) and was not reopened until June, 1975, following the fourth Arab-Israeli War (1973).

Suez Crisis *See* **Suez Canal**

Suffolk, Charles Brandon, 1st duke of *d.* 1545. English nobleman. Suffolk was a favorite and brother-in-law of Henry VIII, whom he accompanied to the Field of Cloth of Gold (1520), and for whom he twice invaded France (1523 and 1544).

Suffolk, Henry Grey, duke of *d.* 1554. English nobleman. As father of Lady Jane Grey, he joined Northumberland's plot to make her queen. He was spared execution by Mary Tudor, but later joined the T. Wyatt *(q.v.)* uprising and was beheaded.

Suffolk Resolves Resolutions passed (Sept. 9, 1744) at meetings of American colonists in Suffolk County, Massachusetts, to protest the British Intolerable Acts *(q.v.)*. They called for disobedience to the acts, nonpayment of taxes, the start of regular militia musters, and an end to trade with Britain. The resolves were forwarded to and endorsed by the Continental Congress.

Sufism Muslim mystical, philosophical, and literary movement. An outgrowth of the Shi'ite sect, it stressed the personal union of the soul with God. Sufism flourished especially in Persia in the 11th cent. and produced the best of the Persian poets. Its greatest exponent was Al-Ghazali.

Sugar Act British law (1764) designed to raise revenue for defense of the American colonies and to put an end to smuggling of molasses and sugar from the French and Dutch West Indies to America. New rules regarding shipment and confiscation of illegal cargoes were especially unpopular among colonists and the act helped foment sentiment for revolution.

Suharto (his complete name) 1921–. President of Indonesia (1967–　). A career army officer, he led the army in putting down a Communist-influenced *coup d'état* in 1965. Some 300,000 Indonesian Communists were massacred. From then on he effectively controlled the government, though A. Sukarno remained president. Suharto finally became president in 1967 and was re-elected in 1973.

Sui Chinese dynasty (581–618) that reunited China after the Six Dynasties *(q.v.)* period. The Sui emperors were Yang Chien (541–604) and his son, Yang Kuang (*d.* 618). They began construction of a canal system, called the Grand Canal, and refortified the Great Wall. The dynasty was overthrown and the succeeding T'ang dynasty adopted many of the Sui governmental systems.

Sukarno, Achmed 1901–70. Indonesian statesman, president (1949–67), and leader of the nationalists in the fight for independence from the Dutch (1945–49). After becoming president he consolidated his power, dissolved the assembly (1959), and made himself dictator. At the same time, he sought closer relations with the Communists, particularly the Chinese. An attempted Communist coup, however, resulted in a takeover by the Indonesian army and Sukarno's ouster.

Sulayman *See* **Suleiman**

Suleiman I (Suleiman I) 1494–1566. Sultan of the Ottoman Empire (1520–66), son and successor of Selim I. He was known as "the Magnificent"

and "the Lawgiver" for his expansion of the empire, his patronage of the arts, and his many reforms. His conquests include Belgrade (1521), Rhodes (1522), southern Hungary (at the Battle of Mohács, 1526), and parts of Persia, Iraq, and Tripoli (by 1551). His navy, under the command of Barbarossa, terrorized the Mediterranean. During his reign, Suleiman also formed what became a long-standing alliance with France against the Hapsburg rulers of Europe.

Suleiman II 1642–91. Ottoman sultan (1687–91), successor to his brother, Muhammad IV. Through his minister, Mustafa Kuprili, he introduced liberal reforms. His reign was marked by the Austro-Turkish War (1682–99).

Suleyman I *See* **Suleiman I**

Sulla, Lucius Cornelius 138–78 BC. Roman general and politician. A rivalry with Marius had become a bitter feud and, when Sulla became consul (88 BC), civil war broke out between them. Sulla won that year and then departed for Asia Minor to fight the first Mithradatic War (88–85). Marius subsequently marched on Rome, massacred Sulla's supporters, and took power. Sulla returned to Rome (83), seized power, and defeated Carbo (leader of the Marian party) in the ensuing civil war. He then made himself dictator for life (82) and began the systematic murder of thousands of his opponents. At the same time, he instituted a program of governmental reforms, notably those to restore the power of the Senate. He resigned unexpectedly in 79 BC.

Sullivan, Sir Arthur Seymour 1842–1900. English composer. With lyricist Sir W. Gilbert, Sullivan created such famous operettas as *The Pirates of Penzance, The Mikado,* and *H.M.S. Pinafore.*

Sullivan, John 1740–95. American Revolutionary War general. He saw action at the battles of Long Island, Trenton, Princeton, Brandywine, and Germantown, and fought in the campaign against the Iroquois (1779).

Sullivan, Louis Henry 1856–1924. American architect, considered the "Father of Modernism" for his designs of early skyscrapers, especially the Gage Building and the Chicago Stock Exchange. His pupil was F.L. Wright.

Sully, Maximilien de Béthune, duc de 1560–1641. French financier and statesman. A close friend of Henry IV, he became finance minister (by 1598) and restored the royal treasury, which had been seriously depleted by the Wars of Religion.

Sully-Prudhomme, René François Armand 1839–1907. French poet, one of the Parnassians. His poetry was marked by its philosophical concerns. He won the first Nobel Prize for literature (1901).

sultan Islamic term applied at first to spiritual leaders of the Islamic community and later to Muslim rulers wielding political authority.

Sumatra Treaty *See* **Achinese War**

Sumer Ancient civilization of southern Mesopotamia from roughly the 4th to 3d millennium BC to the beginning of the 2d millennium BC. Though an extensive village culture existed in the region by the 5th millennium BC, the formation of Sumerian cities and the rise of Sumerian culture did not begin until the 4th to 3d millennium. From that time, such cities as Eridu, Erech, Lagash, Larsa, and Ur flourished as commercial and cultural centers and rivaled one another for control of neighboring lands. In the 24th cent. BC, however, the Semitic people of northern Mesopotamia, the Akkadians (*see* Akkad), conquered Sumeria and made it part of their empire. The Akkadians absorbed and thus spread much of the Sumerian culture (including cuneiform writing) before they were in turn conquered (22d cent. BC) by invaders from the north. Thereafter the Sumerians enjoyed a brief resurgence under the leadership of such cities as Lagash and, notably, Ur. But dynastic struggles and invasions by neighboring peoples brought on their final decline in the 20th cent. BC. During their ascendancy, the Sumerians developed the first writing system (cuneiform) in the Near East, the first written civil law code, commercial and banking systems, skills in pottery-making and metal-working and agricultural and military technology. The fall of Sumerian civilization was followed by the rise of Babylonia (*q.v.*).

Summer Offensive *See* **June Offensive**

summit conference Meeting by heads of major powers to discuss fundamental issues of mutual interest. These meetings became a prominent feature of East-West diplomacy after WW II. The first (1955) was attended by US Pres. D. Eisenhower, Soviet leader N. Khrushchev, and British Prime Minister A. Eden and sought to ease Cold War tensions. A 1960 Paris summit between the US, the Soviet Union, and European powers was scuttled by the *U-2* incident (*q.v.*). The 1961 Vienna summit between Pres. J. Kennedy and Khrushchev marked the beginning of further East-West tensions. Pres. R. Nixon's Peking conference (1972) formally began the process of normalizing US-China relations. Nixon's Moscow conference (1972) marked the first visit to Moscow by a US president.

Sumner, Charles 1811–74. US Senator (1851–74) from Massachusetts. A prominent abolitionist, he was attacked and beaten in the Senate by a southern senator, was a leader of Radical Repub-licans demanding a harsh Reconstruction (*q.v.*) policy, and urged the impeachment of Pres. A. Johnson.

Sumter, Thomas 1734–1832. American general. During the American Revolution he commanded (1780) a force of raiders that harassed the British in North and South Carolina. Fort Sumter was named for him.

Sunday, Billy ⟨Ashley, William⟩ 1863–1935. American Christian evangelist and preacher. A former professional baseball player, he gained a wide following (from 1896) for his revival meetings.

Sunday school Program of religious education for the young. The first Sunday school was organized by R. Raikes in England (1780). By 1786 the first one had been organized in Virginia.

Sung Chinese dynasty and historic period (960–1279), which followed the Five Dynasties (*q.v.*) period. One of the great epochs of Chinese history, it was marked by commercial prosperity, a cultural flowering, administrative reforms, and technological innovations. The dynasty was founded by Chao K'uang-yin (reigned 960–976), a general serving the later Chou dynasty ruler. On the emperor's death, Chao took power and by 976 had largely completed reunification of China. With its capital at Kaifeng, the Sung dynasty was not seriously threatened until 1127. At this time, invasions by nomadic Jurchen tribes from the north forced Sung rulers to move their capital to Lin-an (now Hangchow) in the south. Thus the Sung dynasty is usually divided into Northern Sung (960–1127) and Southern Sung (1127–1279). The Sung dynasty was finally conquered (1279) by the invading Mongols under Kublai Khan, who replaced it with the Yüan dynasty. Sung rulers instituted administrative reforms (notably those of Wang An-shih, *q.v.*), many of which were aimed at centralizing power (especially to gain firm control over the military) and also fostered the growth of schools and a great government bureaucracy. Commercial prosperity came as a result of increased trade, notably with India, Persia, and the Arabs. The Sung period was further marked by the increase in printing (with movable type by the 11th cent.); a revival of Confucianism and the writings of Chu Hsi; the compilation of great encyclopedias and histories; and a golden age of Chinese landscape painting and ceramics. It also saw the use of gunpowder and the magnetic compass for navigation.

Sunga Dynasty that ruled North India between *c*185 and *c*73 BC. It succeeded the Maurya Empire. During the rule of this dynasty Brahmanical Hinduism re-emerged as the official state religion, after a temporary eclipse by Buddhism.

Sunnis *See* **Sunnites**

Sunnites ⟨Sunnis⟩ Traditional or orthodox sect of Islam, adhered to by over three-quarters of all Muslims. They accept the actual succession of the early Muslim caliphs, while the other major sect, the Shi'ites *(q.v.)*, say that Ali (the fourth) was the first true successor of Muhammad. The Sunnites also accept the Sunnah as the legitimate body of Muslim traditions.

Sun Yat-sen 1866–1925. Chinese revolutionary, the father of the Chinese republic and leader of the Nationalist Kuomintang until his death. Sun led an abortive revolt at Canton (1895) and for the next 16 years worked in exile to promote revolution in China. He returned to China during the Revolution of 1911 and served for a few months as president of the provisional government (1911–12). Next he led an abortive revolt (1913) against the dictatorial regime of Yüan Shih-k'ai and fled China until 1917. Sun became president of the Nationalist government at Canton (1923), formed an alliance with the Chinese Communists, and reorganized the Nationalist Kuomintang with the help of Russia. He died before being able to launch his planned Northern Expedition *(q.v.)*.

Sun Yat-sen, Madame *See* **Soong Ching-ling**

Suppiluliumas I *See* **Hittite Empire**

Supremacy, Acts of *See* **Acts of Supremacy**

suprematism School of abstract art that began in Russia around 1913. Totally nonrepresentational, it emphasized pure geometric forms. The school was founded by Casimir Malevich (1878–1935) and it influenced modern architecture and industrial design.

Supreme Court Highest court, in the US, empowered to interpret treaties, laws, and the Constitution; mediate disputes between states or citizens of different states; and act as the court of final appeal. The Court was established in 1787 by Article 3 of the Constitution. Originally set at six members, its number stabilized at nine in 1869, despite F.D. Roosevelt's efforts to enlarge it in the 1930s. The justices, including one chief justice and eight associate justices, are appointed for life. Justices have generally fallen into two categories: those who strictly interpret the letter of the law, and those whose looser interpretations allow "implied" governmental powers. The first female justice was appointed to the court in 1981.

Surinam ⟨*formerly* Dutch Guiana⟩ Independent republic located on the northeast coast of South America. Capital is Paramaribo. Settled by the Dutch and the English, Surinam was granted to the Dutch by the Treaty of Breda (1667), in return for abandonment of Dutch claims to New Amsterdam (New York). Surinam became an autonomous state within the kingdom of The Netherlands (1954) and an independent republic (Nov. 25, 1975). In 1980 its government was overthrown by a military *coup d'état*.

Surji-Arjungaon, Treaty of Treaty (Dec. 30, 1803) between the British and the Marathas, concluding the second Maratha War. It virtually ended Maratha independence (they agreed to accept a British resident) and consolidated British rule over northern Indian territory.

Surprise plot *See* **Bye plot**

Surprising Treason *See* **Bye plot**

Surrat, Mary Eugenia 1820–65. American conspirator, who kept the Washington, D.C., boarding house where J. Booth and others planned A. Lincoln's assassination. She was hung, though her actual guilt is still debated.

surrealism Literary and art movement founded in 1924 by A. Breton. An outgrowth of Dada, it focused on the use of unconscious thought processes and their expression.

Suryavarman II *See* **Angkor Wat**

Susanna Biblical matron. She refused seduction by two elders, who in turn vengefully accused her of adultery. Daniel proved their guilt.

Suslov, Mikhail 1902–82. Soviet Communist leader. Suslov held important government positions under J. Stalin, N. Khrushchev, and L. Brezhnev, and was considered a leading spokesman of Soviet Communist ideology. He supported the Russian invasions of Hungary (1956), Czechoslovakia (1968), and Afghanistan (1979), and advocated the imposition of martial law in Poland (1981).

Sussex Incident International incident caused by the sinking of the passenger ship *Sussex* by a German submarine (Mar. 24, 1916). Because two of the 80 casualties were American, the US issued the "Sussex Ultimatum" to Germany (Apr. 18, 1916). Germany initially agreed to give warning and provide for the safety of those aboard ships being torpedoed, but her resumption of unrestricted submarine warfare in (Feb., 1917) helped bring the US into WW I.

Sussex Ultimatum *See* **Sussex Incident**

Sutter, John Augustus 1803–80. German-born American pioneer. Gold found (1848) on Sutter's land in the Sacramento, California, valley set off the Gold Rush (1849). Prospectors overran Sutter's land, killed his cattle, and eventually bankrupted him.

Suttner, Bertha Kinsky, Baroness von 1843–1914. Austrian writer and pacifist. Her pacifist novel *Lay Down Your Arms* profoundly influ-

enced many, including A. Nobel. She was the first
woman awarded the Nobel Peace Prize (1905).

Suvorov, Aleksandr Vasilievich 1729–1800. Russian general who served Russia in many wars, including the Seven Years' War, Russo-Turkish War
(1787–92), and the French Revolutionary Wars.

Sverdrup, Johan 1816–92. Norwegian statesman. A leftist, he was president of the Storting
(1871–84) and prime minister (1884–89). He
helped institute trial by jury, parliamentary and
agrarian reforms, and compulsory military service.

Sverre d. 1202. King of Norway(1184–1202),
considered one of the great Norwegian kings. He
limited the power of the church and aristocracy
and increased the power of the monarchy.

Sviatoslav 920–72. Duke of Kiev (945–72) and
Russian national hero. He spent his entire career
in conquest, expanding Kiev into an empire that
extended from the Volga to the Danube. He was
eventually compelled by his one-time Byzantine
allies to relinquish his Balkan territories.

Svoboda, Ludvik 1895–. Czechoslovakian general and president (1968–75). Svoboda was a military hero in both WW I and WW II. As president,
he obtained the release of the political prisoners
taken in the Russian invasion of 1968.

Swabia Historic region, now in southern West
Germany. Originally settled by the Suevi and Alamanni, it became a duchy in the 9th cent. and
once belonged to the Hohenstaufen family (1105–
1254). Thereafter the duchy was divided into
smaller land holdings. See also Swabian League.

Swabian Leagues Protective associations formed
at various times in the Middle Ages by cities and
other local powers in what is now southern Germany. The most important of them (sometimes
called the Great Swabian League) was formed in
1488 by 22 imperial cities, local leagues, and noblemen. It supported Holy Roman Emperor
Charles V and its army fought the rebels in the
Peasants' War (1524–25). Religious differences
during the reformation forced its dissolution in
1534.

Swahili African Bantu people and language. The
language shows marked Arabic influence and is
spoken in Kenya, Uganda, Tanzania, and Zaire.

Swamp Fox, the See **Marion, Francis**

Swaziland Southeast African kingdom. Capital is
Mbabane. The native Swazis migrated to their
present homeland (early 19th cent.) under pressure from Zulus and soon afterward granted
concessions to European powers. Swaziland became a British territory in 1903, achieved limited
self-government in 1963, and became independent
on Sept. 6, 1968. King Sobhuza II (reigned 1921–

82) dissolved Parliament and assumed personal
control of the kingdom in 1973. A new Parliament, with advisory powers only, was created in
1979. Sobhuza's successor was not named immediately after his death.

sweatshop Term applied to a workplace characterized by unsanitary or dangerous working conditions and by the employment of workers at
extremely low pay. Sweatshops flourished in England, the US, and other nations in the 19th cent.
and contributed to the rise of unions and passage
of labor laws to protect workers.

Sweden ⟨Kingdom of Sweden⟩ Constitutional
monarchy located in northern Europe. Its capital
is Stockholm. United with Norway (1319) and
Denmark (1397), Sweden fell under Danish domination until it gained independence (1523) under
Swedish king Gustavus I. By the 17th cent. Sweden had become the greatest power in the Baltic,
a position it lost in the Great Northern War
(1700–21). During the 19th cent., Norway was
united with Sweden. In the early 20th cent., Sweden began to set up its extensive social welfare
system. Key dates in the history of Sweden include:

993–1024 Olaf Skutkonung reigned; first
Christian king of Sweden.

1150–60 Eric IX reigned; increased Sweden's
military and advanced Christianity; began Swedish conquest of Finland, but was killed by Danish Prince Magnus Henrikson.

1240 Invasion of Novgorod (now Russia)
halted by defeat in the Battle of the Neva.

1319–65 Magnus VII reigned; united (1319)
Norway and Sweden.

1397 Kalmar Union; Queen Margaret joined
Denmark, Norway and Sweden under one crown
at Kalmar, Sweden.

1450 Sten Sture the Elder expelled Danish-
Norwegian king Christian I.

1513–23 Christian II reigned as king of Denmark and Norway (1513–23) and Sweden (1520–
23), successor to his father, King John.

1520 Stockholm Bloodbath (Nov. 8); execution of Swedish nobles by Christian II to prevent
breakup of Kalmar Union.

1521–23 Swedes rebelled against Christian II
and forced Danes from all of Sweden except the
southern tip (1521); made Gustavus Vasa king as
Gustavus I (1523).

1523–60 Gustavus I reigned; made Lutheranism the state religion, established a hereditary
monarchy, and founded the Vasa dynasty.

1560–68 Eric XIV reigned; conquered Estonia
(1561).

1569–92 John III reigned; married the sister of Polish king Sigismund II; succeeded by his son, Polish king Sigismund III.

1592–99 Polish King Sigismund III reigned in Sweden; his rule was opposed by the Swedish Protestants and he was deposed.

1611–32 Gustavus Adolphus reigned as Gustavus II; took Ingermanland and parts of Karelia from Russia (1617); conquered most of Livonia from Poland; led Sweden (1630) into the Thirty Years' War.

1611–13 Sweden defeated by Denmark in Kalmar War.

1618–48 Thirty Years' War.

1632–54 Queen Christina reigned; Peace of Westphalia, ending Thirty Years' War, concluded during her rule; Sweden gained substantial territories and the monarch became a prince of the Holy Roman Empire; Sweden became the dominant Baltic power.

1654–60 Charles X Gustavus reigned following Christina's abdication; waged successful war against Poland (1655–60), the first Northern War; forced Poland to officially cede Livonia by the Treaty of Oliva (May 3, 1660) and won Danish-held territory at southern tip of Sweden.

1660–97 Charles XI reigned; established absolute monarchy.

1697–1718 Charles XII reigned; presided over Sweden's decline during much of the Great Northern War (1700–21).

1700–21 Great Northern War fought by Sweden against coalition of Denmark, Poland, and Russia; defeated, Sweden was forced to sign the treaties of Stockholm (1720) and Nystadt (1721), by which it lost Estonia, Livonia, and most of its German holdings; war marked the decline of Sweden and the rise of Russia as the dominant power in the region.

1718–20 Ulrika Eleanora reigned; acceded to a constitution establishing a constitutional monarchy with authority residing in a Riksdag, or parliament.

1741–43 Sweden defeated in Russo-Swedish War; Finnish Territory ceded to Russia.

c1770–1810 Swedish Enlightenment.

1771–92 Gustavus III reigned; reimposed (Aug. 19, 1772) absolute monarchy; tyrannical rule led to his murder.

1788–89 Nobles and army officers of the Anjala League unsuccessfully attempted to undermine Gustavus III, then at war with Russia.

1792–1809 Gustavus IV reigned; ruled during French Revolutionary and most of the Napoleonic wars; Russia seized Finland from Sweden (1808) and Gustavus was deposed.

1809 Riksdag adopted new constitution (1809) and made Charles XIII king (reigned 1809–18); Charles ceded (1809) Finland to Russia.

1810 French Marshal Jean Baptiste Jules Bernadotte named successor to Charles XIII; Bernadotte soon became leading power in Swedish government.

1814 Sweden and Norway united by Congress of Vienna in Treaty of Kiel.

1818–44 Bernadotte reigned as Charles XIV; established Bernadotte dynasty and began period of peace and liberalization in Sweden.

1905 Union between Norway and Sweden dissolved.

1907–50 Gustavus V reigned; maintained Swedish armed neutrality through both WW I and WW II.

1911 Old-age pension system established; marked beginning of extensive social welfare system set up in Sweden during subsequent years.

1920, 1921–23, 1924–25 H. Branting served as premier; promoted social democracy.

1932–46 Social Democratic leader P. Hansson served as prime minister.

1932–76 Social Democratic party dominant party in Swedish government; shared power with opposing parties during WW II (1939–45) but resumed sole control of the cabinet after the war.

1950–73 Gustavus VI reigned; rule was marked by passage of new laws promoting social welfare in Sweden.

1973 Carl XVI became king (Sept. 15) following death of his father.

1976 Forty-year rule of Social Democrats ended; Thorbjörn Fälldin, coalition government leader, named prime minister.

1978 Prime Minister Ola Ullsten (liberal) in office after struggle over increasing number of nuclear power plants.

1980 Center party leader Fälldin returned to office as head of non-Socialist coalition government.

1980 Voters approved referendum for expansion of nuclear generating system.

1982 Olaf Palme, a Social Democrat, in office as prime minister.

Swedenborg, Emanuel 1688–1772. Swedish scientist and religious leader. Swedenborg devoted himself exclusively to religion after 1734. His writings interpreting the Scriptures became the basis for the Church of New Jerusalem, an organization founded by his followers.

Swedish Enlightenment Literary period (c1770–c1810), the flowering of neoclassicism in Sweden. Sometimes called the Gustavian Enlightenment after Gustavus III, the period saw official encouragement of literature through the royal patronage of Gustavus, as well as the founding of the Swedish Academy (1786).

Sweyn ⟨Sweyn Forkbeard⟩ *d.* 1014. King of Denmark (*c*985–1014). He killed King Olaf I, conquered Norway (1000), and later conquered England (1013). He was the father of Canute.

Sweyn Forkbeard *See* **Sweyn**

Swift, Jonathan 1667–1745. Great English satirist. He wrote social and political satires, including *A Tale of a Tub*, *The Drapier Letters*, *A Modest Proposal*, and the classic *Gulliver's Travels*.

Swinburne, Algernon Charles 1837–1909. English poet. Swinburne at times offended Victorian sensibilities, but his poems were known for their energy, innovativeness, and mastery of the language. His works include *Atalanta in Calydon*, *Poems and Ballads*, and *A Song of Italy*.

Swiss Confederation Union of the 22 Swiss cantons that make up Switzerland. The nucleus of the confederation was formed (1291) by the cantons Uri, Schwyz, and Unterwalden (Forest Cantons) to maintain their liberties against encroachments by the Austrian Hapsburgs. Other cantons joined in the 14th and 15th cents., and the confederation finally won recognition of its independence in 1648. *See also* Switzerland.

Swiss Guards Swiss mercenary soldiers noted for their bravery in the service of European powers, especially France. They were provided (from 1512) by Swiss cantons under agreements called capitulations. The Swiss constitution banned further capitulations (1874).

Swithin, Saint ⟨Swithun, Saint⟩ *fl.* 860. English saint. Swithin was adviser to kings Egbert and Aethelwulf. Traditionally, if there is rain on his feast (July 15), there will be rain for 40 days.

Swithun, Saint *See* **Swithin, Saint**

Switzerland ⟨Swiss Confederation⟩ Country located in central Europe and situated in the mountain ranges of the Alps. Its capital is Bern. The modern state of Switzerland developed from the original "Forest Cantons" that rebelled (13th cent.) against rule of the Austrian Hapsburgs. Switzerland was a center of Calvinism during the 16th-cent. Reformation. The neutrality of Switzerland was guaranteed by the Treaty of Paris in 1815 and the country has maintained a tradition of neutrality since then. Such international conferences as the Geneva Conventions have been held there, and organizations such as the International Red Cross and the International Labor Organization have their headquarters there. Key dates in the history of Switzerland include:

58 BC Helvetii, who inhabited what is now Switzerland, conquered by the Romans.

5TH CENT. AD Territory invaded by Germanic tribes (Alemanni and Burgundii).

6TH CENT. AD Area passed under Frankish control.

1033 Area became part of the Holy Roman Empire.

1276 Rudolf of Hapsburg, Holy Roman Emperor, attempted to assert feudal rights in Switzerland.

1291 Cantons of Uri, Schwyz, and Unterwalden (around Lake Lucerne) formed defensive league against the Hapsburgs; became the basis of the Swiss Confederation.

14TH CENT. Zurich, Glarus, Bern, Lucerne, and Zug joined the Swiss defensive league.

1307 Rutli Oath—traditionally, the alliance of the cantons that became foundation of Swiss independence movement; legend of W. Tell dates from this period.

1315 Austrian invasion repulsed by Swiss Confederation at Battle of Morgarten (Nov. 15).

1386 Swiss routed Austrian Hapsburgs at Battle of Sempach (July 9).

1388 Austrian invaders defeated at the Battle of Nafels, central Switzerland (Apr. 9).

15TH CENT. Fribourg and Solothurn joined the league; Aargau, Thurgau and the valleys of Ticino conquered.

1476 Burgundian invasion repulsed at the Battle of Morat (June 22).

1499 Swiss independence recognized by Emperor Maximilian I in Peace of Basel (Sept. 22).

1513 Basel, Schaffhausen, and Appenzell joined the confederation; confederation now composed of 13 cantons.

1515 Battle of Marignano; the French decisively defeated the Swiss.

1516 Alliance with France formed; Swiss adopted what became traditional policy of neutrality; Swiss mercenaries nevertheless served in European wars.

1519 Swiss Reformation launched by U. Zwingli in Zurich.

1529, 1531 Kappel Wars; religious wars between Protestants and Catholics.

1536 Geneva, under the influence of J. Calvin, revolted against Savoy and its Catholic bishop.

1541 Calvin founded theocratic government at Geneva; made Geneva the center of Calvinism.

1618–48 Switzerland neutral during the Thirty Years' War.

1648 Peace of Westphalia; Switzerland recognized as a completely independent state.

1798 Napoleon conquered Switzerland during the French Revolutionary Wars; established the Helvetic Republic (1798–1803).

1803 Act of Mediation; Napoleon partially restored the traditional Swiss Confederation.

1815 Congress of Vienna; Swiss Confederation restored; nine cantons added.

1815 Treaty of Paris; perpetual Swiss neutrality recognized.

1845 Sonderbund, league of Catholic cantons, established; its existence led to a short civil war and its dissolution (1847).

1848 Constitution adopted; established central federal government, replacing the former confederation.

1864–1949 Geneva Conventions; series of international agreements regulating warfare and treatment of prisoners.

1874 Constitution revised; specified certain federal functions, such as foreign relations and establishing tariffs.

1927 Geneva Conference convened; unsuccessful attempt to reduce naval armaments.

1932–34 Geneva Conference, unsuccessful attempt to reduce armaments, collapsed when A. Hitler withdrew from conference.

1954 Geneva Conference led to armistice in the Korean War.

1958 Geneva Conference held between US, USSR, and Great Britain to discuss nuclear test ban.

1959 Switzerland became a member of the European Free Trade Association.

1971 Woman suffrage approved (Feb. 7).

1972 Switzerland associated with the European Common Market.

1979 Canton Jura created (Jan. 1), bringing total number of cantons to 23 (20 full cantons, 6 half cantons).

1981 Referendum granting women equality with men approved in nationwide vote.

Sybaris Ancient city in what is now southern Italy. Founded by the Achaean Greeks (720 BC), it soon became renown for its wealth and the decadence of its citizens. It was attacked and destroyed (510 BC) by forces from Crotona.

Sybota, Battle of Naval battle (432 BC) during the Peloponnesian War. A combined force from Corcyra and Athens defeated the Corinthian fleet.

Sydenham, Thomas 1624–89. English physician. Called the English Hippocrates, Sydenham observed and described such illnesses as gout, malaria, scarlet fever, and smallpox. He introduced the use of a substance containing quinine to treat malaria and began the practice of using opium medicinally.

Sydney, Philip *See* **Sidney, Sir Philip**

Sykes-Picot Agreement Secret agreement concluded by Britain and France (May 9, 1916), regarding partition of the Ottoman Empire after WW I. Britain was to get direct control of southern Mesopotamia and other territories. France was to get Lebanon and parts of Syria. Additional Arabian territories (to be a federation of states) were designated as within respective spheres of influence.

Sylvester II *d.* 1003. French-born pope (999–1003). The first French pope, Sylvester was renowned for his scientific expertise. He promoted Christianity in Poland and Hungary.

Symbolists French literary school of the late 19th cent. A reaction to naturalism and realism, it sought to express universal truths by subjective or symbolic means. Symbolists were followers of P. Verlaine and S. Mallarmé, and their movement spread to other countries, as well as to other art forms, notably painting and music.

Symeon *See* **Simeon**

Symons, Arthur 1865–1945. British poet and critic. A leading British Symbolist, he helped introduce the movement in Britain.

Symplegades In Greek mythology, two cliffs at the entrance to the Black Sea that moved together to crush any ship passing between them. Jason succeeded in guiding his ship, the Argo, between them and they remained open forever afterward.

syndicalism Theory of government holding that power of the state should be primarily concentrated in the hands of organized labor unions. Influenced by P. Proudhon and G. Sorel, it flourished especially in France, Spain, Italy, and Latin America before WW I. It declined with the spread of Communist-dominated unions.

Synge, John Millington 1871–1909. Irish poet and playwright. Synge is famous for such studies of Irish life as *Riders to the Sun* and *The Playboy of the Western World.*

Synod of *See under names inverted, as in* **Whitby, Synod of**

Syracuse (Siracusa) Historic port city (pop. 108,000) in Sicily, Italy. Founded (734 BC) as a Corinthian colony, it became the most powerful city in Sicily under the tyrant Gelon (5th cent. BC) and a Greek cultural center under Hiero, his successor. Syracuse was the scene of major battles (*see* Syracuse, Battle of) during the Peloponnesian and Punic Wars, and its conquest by the Romans in 212 BC marked the beginning of its decline. Thereafter it was taken by the Byzantines (AD 535), Arabs (AD 878), and the Normans (1085). It later became part of the Kingdom of The Two Sicilies.

Syracuse, Battle of 1. Protracted battle (415–413 BC) during the Peloponnesian War (431–404 BC).

Athens laid siege to the city of Syracuse (now in Sicily) and ultimately committed some 40,000 soldiers and over 200 ships to the action. Syracuse, reinforced by Sparta, eventually killed or captured the entire Athenian force (including the commander Nicias and Demosthenes) and thereby contributed to Athens' defeat in the Peloponnesian War. **2.** Battle (387 BC) in which the Carthaginians suffered a decisive defeat after laying siege to Syracuse. **3.** Battle (214–212 BC) during the Second Punic War (218–201), in which Rome captured the city. A force of 25,000 Romans under Marcellus attacked the city, defended by Hippocrates. After initial defeats brought about in part by defensive weapons devised by Archimedes, the Romans breached the city's defenses and sacked the city.

Syracuse, Dion of *See* **Dion of Syracuse**

Syria (Syrian Arab Republic) Country located at the eastern end of the Mediterranean in the Middle East. Its capital is Damascus. Historically the term "Syria" referred to the region occupied by the modern republic, as well as Jordan, Lebanon, and Palestine. The modern republic was formed in 1944 from territories that once belonged to the Ottoman Empire, which had been acquired by France in the early 1900s during the breakup of the Ottoman Empire. Key events in the history of Syria include:

c2100 BC Amorites (Semites) settled in the area of Syria.

15TH–13TH CENT. BC Syria part of the Hittite Empire, alternating with Egyptian overlordship.

8TH CENT. BC Most of the area conquered and made part of the Assyrian Empire.

538 BC Persia conquered the region.

333–332 BC Alexander the Great made Syria part of his empire.

312–64 BC Seleucid dynasty in power in Syria and environs; established by Seleucus I following breakup of Alexander the Great's empire.

64 BC Domains of Seleucid Empire (greatly reduced) made into a Roman province by Pompey.

4TH CENT. AD Antioch, a principal center of Christianity, was one of the four ancient patriarchates, along with Rome, Alexandria, and, later, Constantinople.

5TH CENT. AD Syria remained part of the Byzantine Empire at the dissolution of the Western Roman Empire.

633–640 Arab Muslim conquest of Syria.

661–750 Damascus served as the seat of the Umayyad caliphate, then the center of the Islamic world.

11TH CENT. Most of Syria under the sway of the Seljuk Turks.

1099 Most of Syria incorporated by the Christian crusaders into the Latin Kingdom of Jerusalem.

1174–87 Saladin, sultan of Egypt, regained Syria for Islam, overthrowing the Latin Kingdom of Jerusalem.

1260 Mongol invasion under Hulagu Khan devastated Syria and almost destroyed Aleppo and Damascus.

1401 The Mongols under Tamerlane again sacked Aleppo and Damascus.

1516 Syria incorporated into the Ottoman Empire for the next four hundred years.

1832–40 Syria annexed to Egypt by Ibrahim Pasha; returned to Ottoman suzerainty (1840).

1920 France granted a League of Nations mandate over Syria, following the breakup of the Ottoman Empire; region included Lebanon.

1926 Lebanon made a separate state by the French.

1936 Syrian autonomy (under the mandate) granted by France; suspended in 1939.

1941 Syria invaded by British and Free French forces, who took it from the Vichy French regime (June).

1941 Syria proclaimed a republic (Sept.).

1943 Rise of Ba'ath party.

1944 Syria became fully independent (Jan. 1); Shukri al-Kuwatli became first president.

1946 French troops finally withdrew, following unrest caused by continued French military presence.

1948–49 Arab-Israeli War; Syria joined in attack on newly created Israeli state.

1949 First of a number of military coups, led by Col. Adib al-Shishakli (Dec.).

1950 Constitution providing for parliamentary government promulgated; lasted less than a year.

FROM 1954 Ba'ath party became a dominant force in Syrian politics.

1958–61 Syria joined with Egypt in the United Arab Republic (UAR).

1961 Army coup in Syria; Syria withdrew from UAR.

1962 Military coup; constitutional government restored.

1963 Coup by Ba'athists; program of nationalization and social reform adopted; split developed in Ba'ath Party.

1966 Coup by radical Ba'athists.

1967 Arab-Israeli War; Israelis victorious in Six-Day War; Golan Heights taken.

1970 Army officers seized power in coup led by Gen. Hafez al-Assad (Nov. 13).

1971 Assad elected president; he remained in office into the early 1980s.

1973 New constitution approved by voters; failure to include provision naming Islam state religion ended in boycott of voting by Sunni Muslims.

1973 First parliamentary elections (May) in over a decade; coalition of Ba'ath, Communist, and Socialist parties secured a substantial majority.

1973 Fourth Arab-Israeli War; Israelis repulsed attacks by Egyptians and Syrians.

1974 Syria signed agreement with Israel (May) whereby the latter returned to 1967 cease-fire line; UN troops in Golan Heights.

1974 Syria introduced UN resolution naming Palestine Liberation Organization (PLO) sole representative of the Palestinians.

1976 30,000 Syrian troops sent into Lebanon to help mediate Lebanese civil war.

1980 Formal agreement signed uniting Libya and Syria (Sept. 10).

1980–82 Syrian troops in Lebanon actively supported Muslim factions in Lebanon; clashes with Israelis developed into heavy fighting during the Lebanese War (1982).

Syrian Orthodox church (Jacobite Church) Christian church founded (6th cent.) as a Monophysite sect. Adherents are sometimes called Jacobites after a principal organizer of the church, Jacob Baradaeus, bishop of Edessa (d. 578).

Syrian Wars 1. First Syrian War (276–272 BC), between Egypt and the Seleucid Empire. It led to the defeat of Seleucid king Antiochus I and the seizure of Phoenicia and much of Anatolia by Egyptian King Ptolemy II. **2.** Second Syrian War (c260–255 BC). It resulted in the defeat of Egypt by Seleucid King Antiochus II, aided by Macedonia. The Seleucids regained much of Phoenicia and Anatolia. **3.** Third Syrian War (c245–241 BC), also known as the Laodicean War. It resulted in the Egyptian defeat of Seleucid king Seleucus II, who lost to Egypt parts of Syria and Asia Minor. **4.** Fourth Syrian War (221–217 BC). It ended in the victory of Egyptian king Ptolemy IV over Seleucid king Antiochus III, who was forced to cede Coele Syria to Egypt. **5.** Fifth Syrian War (c201–195 BC). The Egyptians were defeated by Seleucid king Antiochus III, who regained Coele Syria and parts of southern Asia Minor.

Szold, Henrietta 1860–1945. American Zionist leader. A teacher, she founded (1912) the Jewish women's group Hadassah.

T

Taaffe, Eduard, Graf von 1833–95. Austrian statesman. As premier (1868–70, 1879–93) he attempted to reconcile conflicts between the various national groups comprising the Austro-Hungarian Empire.

Tabari, al- c839–923. Arab historian and writer. He is noted for his commentaries on the Koran and for his *Annals of the Apostles and the Kings*, a compilation of world history from creation to the year 915.

Tabitha *See* **Dorcas**

Table of Abydos Ancient list of kings at the temple of Seti I in Abydos, Egypt. It helped to establish the chronology of the ancient Egyptian kings.

Table of Tanis *See* **Decree Of Canopus**

Taborites Most militant wing of the Bohemian Hussites. Named after their fortified city, Tabor, they founded their own sect but were defeated (1452) by a coalition of Catholics and Hussite Utraquists.

Tacitus AD 55?–c117. Roman historian. Tacitus served in many military and governmental posts before becoming Consul (AD 97). He quickly gained a reputation as an eloquent speaker, then turned to writing. His works include the *Dialogus*, a book on oratory; *Agricola*, a biography of his father-in-law, Agricola; *Germania*, a history of early German tribes; and two major works on Roman history, the *Histories* and the *Annals*.

Tacna-Arica Controversy Prolonged dispute (1883–1929) over the provinces of Arica and Tacna, which Chile had obtained from Peru at the end of the War of the Pacific *(q.v.)*. The dispute was finally resolved by the suggestions of US president H. Hoover that Chile should retain Arica but return Tacna, pay an indemnity, and provide Peru with a free port at Arica.

Tafari Makonnen *See* **Haile Selassie I**

Taft, Robert Alphonso 1889–1953. American statesman, son of W. Taft. As US senator (1939–53) he was cosponsor of the Taft-Hartley Labor Act (1947).

Taft, William Howard 1857–1930. US president (1909–13), the 27th, successor to Pres. T. Roosevelt. Taft became first civil governor of the Philippines (1901–04), and in 1904, he became secretary of war under Roosevelt. Picked by Roosevelt as his successor, Taft became the Republican candidate for president (1908) and defeated W. Bryan in the election. Taft continued Roosevelt's policy of trust-busting, but he modified Roosevelt's Latin American policy into what came to be known as "dollar diplomacy" *(q.v.)*. However, Taft increasingly opposed progressive legislation and policies, and his support of the Payne-Aldrich Tariff (1909) brought much opposition from the progressive wing of the Republican party. He managed to win the 1912 Republican nomination but was now opposed by Roosevelt, who had formed the Progressive (Bull Moose) party *(q.v.)*. This split the Republican party and resulted in the election of the Democratic candidate, W. Wilson. Taft subsequently served as chief justice of the US Supreme Court (1921–30).

Taft-Hartley Labor Act US labor relations act passed (1947) over the veto of Pres. H. Truman. It prohibited the closed shop and jurisdictional and secondary strikes and authorized suits against labor unions and government use of 80-day injunctions against some strikes.

Tagal *See* **Tagalog**

Tagalog ⟨Tagal⟩ Filipino people, second-largest ethnic group in the Philippines. They are largely Christian, and their Malayo-Polynesian language, also called Tagalog, is the official language of the Philippines.

Taginae, Battle of *See* **Busta Gallorum, Battle of**

Tagore, Sir Rabindranath 1861–1941. Indian poet and philosopher. Tagore sought to combine elements of East and West in his works. He was the first Asiatic to win the Nobel Prize in literature (1913).

Taharka *See* **Tirhakah**

Tahmasp I *See* **Ismail I**

Taine, Hippolyte 1828–93. French critic and historian, one of the leading figures in 19th-cent. positivism. He is noted for his applications of scientific principles to the study of history and humanity.

Taiping Rebellion Uprising (1850–64) against the Manchu dynasty of China, a precursor to the Nationalist and Communist movements. Its leader was Hung Hsiu-ch'üan (1814–64) who believed he was the younger brother of Jesus Christ. A new religion was formed around his teachings in the late 1840s and gained support among the peasants and workers in Kwangsi. It was loosely based on Christianity, opposed Confucianism, and advocated (then) radical reforms, such as communal ownership of property and equality of women. Beginning in 1850 with a few thousand followers, the rebels soon gathered support and eventually mustered a highly organized army of a million zealous troops. The rebels succeeded in capturing Nanking in 1853 and made it their capital. The failure of subsequent expeditions and internal dissent weakened the movement, however. An attempt to take Shanghai (1860) was stopped by the "Ever-Victorious Army" organized by Europeans and later led by C. Gordon. A Manchu army under Tseng Kuo-fan beseiged Nanking (1862–64) and finally captured the city (July, 1864). Hung committed suicide and the revolt was broken. Nevertheless, it had seriously weakened the Manchu government and paved the way for later rebellions and the final collapse of the Manchu dynasty.

Taira family Japanese military clan, or family, also called Heike. Founded in the 9th cent., it reached its height in the 12th cent. but was defeated (1185) by the Minamoto clan in the Gempei War (q.v.).

Taira Kiyomori 1118–81. Japanese military leader of the Taira family. He defeated the Minamoto family and led the Taira to high positions in the imperial court.

Taisho ⟨Yoshihito⟩ 1879–1926. Japanese emperor (1912–26). During his reign, Japan joined the Allies in WW I and became firmly established as a great power. His son, the future emperor Hirohito, became regent in 1921.

Taiwan ⟨Republic of China⟩ ⟨Nationalist China⟩ Island republic located off the coast of China. It includes the island of Taiwan (Formosa) and several smaller islands, such as Quemoy and Matsu. Its capital is Taipei. First settled (7th cent.) by the Chinese, the island of Taiwan was visited (1590) by the Portuguese, who named it Formosa. The Dutch established a fort (1624) at what is now Tainan, and the Spanish settled in the north. The Dutch forced the Spanish to give up their holdings (1641), and were in turn forced off Taiwan by the Chinese (1662). Chinese immigration into Taiwan increased, and the island was held by the Manchus

until after the first Sino-Japanese War, when it passed (1895) to Japan. Japan introduced agricultural and industrial improvements. During WW II, Taiwan was bombed by US planes, and after the war it was returned to China. When the Communists came to power on the mainland (1949), Chiang Kai-shek led millions of his Nationalist Chinese followers to the island and established the Kuomintang government there. The Communists planned to invade (1950), but Pres. H. Truman ordered the US Seventh Fleet to the Formosa Strait to deter any Communist attack. When Pres. D. Eisenhower recalled the fleet (1953), the Communists stepped up their attacks on Quemoy and Matsu, leading to a mutual defense agreement (1955) between Taiwan and the US. Despite continued friction between mainland China and Taiwan, the Nationalists secured tremendous advances in agricultural reform and industrialization. But Chiang's plan to topple the People's Republic of China and return to the mainland proved fruitless. In 1971, Taiwan lost its seat in the UN to the People's Republic of China. In 1978, the US recognized the People's Republic and broke diplomatic ties with Taiwan.

Taj Mahal Indian mausoleum in north-central India built (1648) by Shah Jehan in honor of his favorite wife, Mumtaz Maha. It is considered one of the most beautiful buildings in the world.

Takahira, Baron Kogoro See **Root-Takahira Agreement**

Taliesin ⟨Taliessin⟩ fl. 6th cent. Welsh poet, possibly a mythological figure, to whom is attributed authorship of the poems in the Book of Taliesin, a major Welsh work.

Taliessin See **Taliesin**

tallage In feudalism, a tax levied by a lord on his subjects or their property. Tallage evolved in England to be a tax by the king on estates in royal possession and on chartered towns.

Talleyrand, Charles Maurice de ⟨Talleyrand-Périgord, ~⟩ 1754–1838. French statesman and diplomat. Originally a cleric in the court of King Louis XVI, Talleyrand was excommunicated (1791) because of his sympathy for radical church and political reform. His persuasive skills brought him high advisory and diplomatic positions under the Directory, Napoleon, Louis XVIII, and Louis Philippe. He represented France at the Congress of Vienna (1814–15), skillfully limiting the demands of other countries upon France and restoring many European borders to their pre-Napoleonic status.

Tallien, Jean Lambert 1767–1820. French revolutionary. A Jabobin, he supported the Reign of Terror and fell in love with and married (1794) one of his prisoners, T. Tallien. He subsequently led the rebellion of 9 Thermidor which overthrew M. Robespierre.

Tallien, Theresa Cabarrus ⟨Cabarrus, Jeanne Marie Ignace, Theresa de⟩ 1773–1835. French political figure. A prisoner of J. Tallien during the French Revolution, she married him (1794) and greatly influenced his political career.

Talmadge, Eugene 1884–1946. American politician. As governor of Georgia (1933–37, 1941–43) he was noted for his opposition to New Deal policies and for firing several professors from the state university for supporting racial equality.

Talmud Written compilation of the oral laws of the Jews, after the Old Testament, the most important Judaic text. It consists of the Mishna (q.v.), the text of the laws; and the Gemara, commentary. The two versions of the Talmud are the Palestinian (compiled c5th cent. AD) and the Babylonian (compiled c6th cent. AD. The Babylonian Talmud is much longer and is the authoritative work.

Tamerlane ⟨Timur⟩ c1336–1405. Mongol conqueror. A Muslim and self-proclaimed descendent of Genghis Khan, he gained firm control of the throne of Samarkand (in modern Soviet Turkistan) by 1369. Thereafter he led his army of Turks and Mongols in a series of campaigns that vastly expanded his domains. He warred against Persia, and by 1387 had extended his empire to the Euphrates River. Crossing the Euphrates (1392), he advanced northward to conquer the Caucasus region. India was invaded next (1398) and the Delhi Sultanate (q.v.) was ruthlessly destroyed, during which time Tamerlane ordered the massacre of tens of thousands. Turning westward again, Tamerlane captured Baghdad (1401), attacked the Egyptian Mamelukes in Syria, and defeated the Ottoman Turks in Asia Minor (Sultan Bajazet I taken prisoner, 1402). Tamerlane died before launching his planned invasion of China and on his death the empire he had created was divided among his heirs. (*See also* Timurids.)

Tamil Ancient Dravidian dialect, spoken mainly in Madras, India.

Tammany Organization that controlled New York City politics through the Democratic party in the 19th and early 20th cents. Under the leadership of W. Tweed, R. Croker, and others, it gained a national reputation for corruption.

Tammuz Mythical Babylonian god of agriculture and nature. When he died, Ishtar traveled to the underworld to rescue him. His death and resurrection explained the seasonal cycle of nature.

Tanaka Kakuei 1918–. Japanese prime minister (1972–74). He served in the cabinet of E. Sato and succeeded Sato as prime minister. Tanaka opened diplomatic relations with the People's Republic of China but was forced from office under charges of financial improprieties.

Tanaka, Giichi, Baron 1863–1929. Japanese prime minister (1927–29) and general who advocated Japanese expansion. The Tanaka Memorial (1927), a plan for Japanese military conquest attributed to him, is now thought spurious.

Tancred d. 1194. King of Sicily (1190–94). His short reign was marked by a power struggle with his uncle, Holy Roman Emperor Henry VI, who seized Sicily after Tancred's death.

Taney, Roger Brooke 1777–1864. American jurist, fifth chief justice of the US Supreme Court (1836–64). He handed down the landmark court decision in the Dred Scott case (q.v.) of 1857.

T'ang Dynasty of Chinese rulers (618–907). The dynasty was founded after the overthrow of the Sui dynasty by Li Yuan. T'ang rulers greatly expanded the empire, and at its height, under Emperor Hsuan Tsung (ruled 712–756), it included parts of Korea, Manchuria, Mongolia, Tibet, and Turkistan. Trade was stimulated, and in the ensuing period of prosperity the arts, particularly poetry and sculpture, flourished. Such masters as Tu Fu, Wang Wei, Li Po, and Hsüan Tsang lived during this period. Confucianism enjoyed a resurgence and was officially adopted by the state. The civil service system was further refined. However, the empire was weakened by an unsuccessful revolt (755–763) led by An Lu-shan, a Turkish general. In subsequent years, provincial warlords gained power and ultimately overthrew the T'ang rulers.

Tanganyika Former republic in eastern Africa, since 1964 part of the republic of Tanzania (q.v.). Capital was Dar-es-Salaam. Tanganyika was already inhabited by the 9th cent. when Arab and Indian traders established towns along the coast. The region was explored by the Portuguese (15th–16th cents.). German colonists, notably Carl Peters (1856–1918), secured agreements (1884–85) for lands with Tanganyikan natives. The German East Africa Company (formed 1887) then administered the area as German East Africa (q.v.). The company's inadequate rule led to native resistance and ultimate establishment (1891) of a German protectorate. The area was occupied by the British during WW I and in 1920 part of it became a British League of Nations mandate (as Tanganyika). In 1946, it became a UN trust territory, and on Dec. 9, 1961, it achieved independence. J. Nyerere was its first prime minister. When Tanganyika was made a republic (Dec., 1962), Nyerere became its first president. In 1964, Tanganyika merged with Zanzibar to form Tanzania, and its subsequent history is that of Tanzania.

T'ang Hsuan Tsung 685–762. Chinese emperor (712–756), sixth emperor of the T'ang dynasty. During his reign China reached the peak of its power and prosperity, though the T'ang dynasty's decline began soon after.

Tangier Seaport in Morocco on the Strait of Gibraltar, once a Roman city. It passed to the Portuguese (15th cent.), then to England as part of the dowry of Catherine of Braganza on her marriage (1662) to Charles II, then was taken by the Moors (1684). Tangier became an international zone in 1923, and was returned to Morocco in 1956.

T'ang T'ai Tsung 600–649. Chinese emperor (626–649), second emperor of the T'ang dynasty. Considered the founder of the dynasty, he consolidated the empire, drove out the Turks, and encouraged art and literature.

Tannenberg, Battles of 1. Battle (1410) at Tannenberg, Poland, in which the Polish and Lithuanian forces under Polish king Ladislaus II defeated the Teutonic Knights, thus halting their eastward expansion. **2.** Major Russian defeat (Aug. 26–30, 1914) by Germany at Tannenberg, Poland, early in WW I. The Russian forces under Gen. Alexander Samsonov (1859–1914) were surrounded and defeated by German forces under generals P. Hindenburg and E. Ludendorff. Russian casualties were more than 90,000, and Samsonov committed suicide.

Tannhäuser *fl.* 13th cent. German lyric poet and minnesinger celebrated for his wanderings and thought to have taken part in the Sixth Crusade. His legend is the basis for an opera by R. Wagner.

Tantalus Mythical Greek king punished in Hades by the gods. Water receded when he tried to drink and food moved away when he tried to eat, hence the word "tantalize."

Tantras Collection of Hindu and Buddhist holy books that include information on such topics as religious rituals, traditions, and the practice of yoga. They date from the 6th or 7th cent.

Tanzania African republic on the east coast of Africa, formed (1964) by the union of Tanganyika and Zanzibar *(qq.v.)*. Capital is Dar-es-Salaam. Its history prior to 1964 is that of Tanganyika and Zanzibar. In early 1964, a revolution in Zanzibar toppled that country's government. The new government merged Zanzibar with Tanganyika (Apr., 1964) and J. Nyerere became first president of Tanzania. A new constitution was adopted (1965). Although officially united under one government, Tanganyika and Zanzibar have followed somewhat independent courses. In the 1970s, Tanzania came into repeated conflict with Uganda, headed

by I. Amin. In 1979, Tanzanian forces toppled Amin's regime and forced him into exile.

Taoism Major Chinese religious and philosophical system. Taoism was, by tradition, founded by Lao-Tze in the 6th cent. BC. But the book upon which the system is based, *Tao-te-ching,* appears to have been written in the 3d cent. BC. According to Taoism, human beings can find Tao (the Way) by following a policy of nonaction, or passivity. The Way is the natural course of all events in the world, and the human path to happiness is through elimination of desire, ambition, and struggle, which go contrary to all nature. Taoism was in part a reaction to the organized system of ethical conduct advanced by Confucianism. By the 5th cent. AD, it was an organized religion. A hierarchy of gods was developed and ways to increase longevity and achieve immortality were sought. Taoist religion has been an important influence in China, especially in the arts. Although it was suppressed by the Chinese Communist government, Taoism is still practiced in China.

Tappan, Arthur 1786–1865. American merchant and abolitionist, a founder (1833), with W. Garrison, and first president of the American Anti-Slavery Society. In 1840, he broke with Garrison and established the American and Foreign Anti-Slavery Society.

Tarain, Battles of *See* **Taraori, Battles of**

Taraori, Battles of ⟨Tarain, ~⟩ Series of battles (1191–92) resulting in the victory of Muhammad of Ghor (*d.* 1206) over the Rajput raja of Ajmer and Delhi. The victory contributed to the Muslim conquest of northern India.

Tarbell, Ida Minerva 1857–1944. American writer and reformer. One of the muckrakers *(q.v.),* she is known best for her *History of the Standard Oil Company* and *Life of Abraham Lincoln.*

Tardieu, André ⟨Villiers, George⟩ 1876–1945. French statesman and writer. He took part in the Paris Peace Conference *(q.v.)* of 1919 and between the world wars held a number of government posts, including that of premier (1929–30, 1930, 1932). He urged a strong stance against rising German militarism.

Tariff of Abominations US protective tariff passed on May 19, 1828. Originally a political ploy to gain support for A. Jackson's presidential candidacy, the bill was designed to force Pres. J. Q. Adams to defeat it and thereby fall into discredit. It passed, however, and Adams signed it into law. The tariff led J. Calhoun to advocate "nullification" by the states.

tariffs Taxes imposed on imported and sometimes on exported goods, also known as customs duty. Originally used to raise revenue, by the 17th cent. tariffs were used to protect domestic economies. (*See also* protectionism.)

Tarik ⟨~ ibn Ziyad⟩ *fl.* 711. Berber general. Tarik led the first Muslim invasion of Spain (711), conquering much of the Iberian Peninsula and firmly establishing Moorish influence there.

Tarik ibn Ziyad *See* **Tarik**

Tarkington, Newton Booth 1869–1946. American author known for his novels set in small Midwestern towns. His novels included *Penrod, The Magnificent Ambersons,* and *Alice Adams.* The latter two earned him the Pulitzer Prize for the best American novel in 1919 and 1922.

Tarleton, Banastre *See* **Cowpens, Battle of**

Tarpeia Legendary Roman woman who let the Sabines into Rome in return for the bracelets on their left arms. When they entered, they crushed her with their shields, which they carried on their left arms as well.

Tarpeian Rock *See* **Capitoline Hill**

Tarquinius Collatinus *fl.* c509 BC. Legendary Roman. The rape of his wife, Lucrece, by his cousin, Tarquinius Sextus, led to the fall of the last Tarquin king (509 BC) and establishment of the Roman republic.

Tarquinius Priscus, Lucius Roman king (c616–578 BC). He reputedly built the Circus Maximus and the Forum. He was assassinated in a plot to limit the king's power.

Tarquinius, Sextus *fl.* 6th cent. BC. Roman, son of L. Tarquinius Superbus, last king of Rome. Sextus' rape of Lucrece (509 BC) led to the overthrow of the Tarquin line of kings.

Tarquinius Superbus, Lucius Last king of Rome (c534–509 BC). He made Rome powerful and extended its dominions. His cruelty and the rape of Lucrece by his son led to his overthrow.

Tarsus Ancient Asian city, capital of Cilicia, in southern Turkey. It was the birthplace of the Apostle Paul.

Tartars *See* **Tatars**

Tartini, Giuseppe 1692–1770. Italian violinist and composer. Tartini modified the shape of the bow and wrote hundreds of violin pieces, the best-known being *The Devil's Trill.*

Tartu, Treaty of Peace treaty (Feb. 2, 1920) between Estonia and Russia, concluded at Tartu, Estonia, at the end of the Baltic War of Liberation. It established Estonian independence.

Tasman, Abel Janszoon 1603?–59. Dutch navigator. Tasman discovered Tasmania (which he called Van Diemen's Land) and New Zealand (1642).

Tasso, Torquato 1544–95. Italian poet, considered one of the great Renaissance poets. He is known best for *Jerusalem Delivered,* an epic about the First Crusade.

Tatars ⟨Tartars⟩ Turkic-speaking peoples of the USSR living near the Volga River region and numbering some 6,000,000. The name once referred to Mongols and other Asiatic people who invaded Europe, some of whom merged to form the Golden Horde (*q.v.*), a powerful force in Russia. They adopted Islam (14th cent.) and are Sunni Muslims today.

Tate, John Orley Allen 1899–1979. American poet and critic. He was a founder and editor of *The Fugitive* (1922–25) and a member of the southern agrarian literary group known as the Fugitives.

Tauroggen, Convention of *See* **Yorck von Wartenburg, Johann David Ludwig**

Tawney, Richard Henry 1880–1962. British economic historian. Tawney was a leader of numerous social reforms and helped to formulate the Labour party's economic policies. Among his many books is *The Acquisitive Society.*

Taylor, Brook 1685–1731. English mathematician. He formulated Taylor's Theorem, the foundation of differential calculus. He also solved the problem of the center of oscillation.

Taylor, Jeremy 1613–67. English bishop and writer, called the "Shakespeare of the Pulpit" for his moving sermons. They were collected in such volumes as *The Golden Grove.*

Taylor, John 1753–1824. American political philosopher and agriculturalist. Taylor espoused T. Jefferson's contention that democracy was dependent on the farmer. Among his many works are *An Inquiry into the Principles and Policies of the Government of the United States.*

Taylor, Maxwell Davenport 1901–. American general. He commanded the 82d and then the 101st Airborne divisions during WW II and also commanded the Eighth Army during the Korean War. As chairman of the Joint Chiefs of Staff (1962–64) he advocated US involvement in the Vietnam War.

Taylor, Richard 1826–79. Confederate general in the American Civil War, son of Z. Taylor. His defeat of Gen. N. Banks in the Battle of Sabine Crossroads (Apr. 8, 1864) led to the Union withdrawal from Louisiana and failure of the Red River Campaign, an attempt to gain control of the states of Louisiana, Arkansas, and Texas.

Taylor, Zachary 1784–1850. US president (1849–50), the twelfth, successor to J. Polk. Taylor joined the army in 1808 and fought with distinction in the War of 1812 and in the Black Hawk and Seminole wars against the Indians. His military campaigns earned him the nickname "Old Rough-and-Ready." During the Mexican War

(1846–48), he became a national hero by his victories at Palo Alto (q.v.) and Resaca de la Palma (q.v.) and the capture (Sept., 1846) of Monterrey. In the Battle of Buena Vista (q.v.), his decisive victory over a much larger Mexican force ended the war in northern Mexico. Taylor was chosen Whig candidate for president and was elected in 1848. As president he favored the admission of California and New Mexico as states, but his support of the Wilmot Proviso (q.v.), which prohibited the extension of slavery, aroused opposition in the South. Taylor also opposed the key elements of what became the Compromise of 1850 (q.v.). During the last days of his administration he was embroiled in a scandal involving members of his Cabinet. He planned to reorganize the Cabinet but fell ill and died (July 9, 1850).

Tay Son rebellion Vietnamese uprising (1771–88) led by three brothers from Tay Son, Vietnam. They overthrew the ruling dynasties governing Vietnam, defeated the Chinese sent to support the rulers, and unified the country. During their brief rule (1788–93) they attempted to introduce social reforms, and are thus regarded as precursors of the 20th-cent. nationalist movements in Vietnam.

Ta Yü *See* **Yü the Great**

Tchad *See* **Chad**

Tchaikovsky, Piotr Ilich 1840–93. Russian composer, one of the greatest Russian composers. Noted for the melodic and intensely emotional character of his compositions, he is famous for his scores for ballet, including *Swan Lake, The Nutcracker,* and *Sleeping Beauty.* He also composed symphonies, concertos, and other works. Among his best known works are *Fifth Symphony in F Minor, Sixth Symphony in B Minor, Fourth Symphony in F Minor,* and *Violin Concerto in D Major.*

Tea Act British parliamentary act (May 10, 1773) that gave the British East India Company a virtual monopoly on tea trade in the American colonies. American opposition to the act led to the Boston Tea Party (q.v.).

Teach, Edward *See* **Blackbeard**

Teapot Dome Naval oil reserve in Wyoming that gave its name to the Teapot Dome scandal (1922) during the administration of Pres. W. Harding. Secretary of the Interior A. Fall, who held jurisdiction over the oil fields, granted exclusive leases to the fields to Harry F. Sinclair (1876–1956) in apparent consideration of a $200,000 "loan." This and a similar arrangement involving assignment of reserves in California to Edward L. Doheny (1856–1935) caused great embarrassment to the Harding administration and led to Fall's conviction for accepting bribes.

Technocracy American movement, begun in the early 1930s, advocating the reorganization of society through implementation of technological principles. The movement was short-lived, but some of its ideas remain influential.

Tecumseh 1768?–1813. American Indian leader, chief of the Shawnees. His attempt to form a league of Indian tribes against US encroachment on Indian lands ended with the defeat of his brother at Tippecanoe. He fought with the British in the War of 1812 and died at the Battle of the Thames.

Tegucigalpa Capital (pop. 273,900) and largest city of Honduras. Founded in the 16th cent., it became the Honduran capital in 1880.

Teheran ⟨Tehran⟩ Iranian capital (pop. 4,496,200) and largest city of Iran. Founded in the 12th cent., it became Persia's capital (1788). It was the site of the Teheran Conference (1943) during WW II.

Teheran Conference Allied conference (Nov. 28–Dec. 1, 1943) at Teheran, Iran, during WW II. Attended by US president F. Roosevelt, British prime minister W. Churchill, and Soviet premier J. Stalin, it coordinated strategy involving the Allied invasion of Western Europe.

Tehran *See* **Teheran**

Teilhard de Chardin, Pierre 1881–1955. French scientist and Catholic theologian. Teilhard's attempts to reconcile Christianity with what he saw as the ongoing social and mental evolution of man gained many supporters but caused him problems with the church. He put forth his theory in *The Phenomenon of Man.*

Tel Aviv-Jaffa ⟨Tel Aviv-Yafo⟩ Largest city (pop. 343,300) in Israel. Founded in 1909, it was Israel's capital in 1948–49.

Telemachus Greek mythical figure, son of Odysseus and Penelope. Upon Odysseus' return from the Trojan War, Telemachus helped him to slay Penelope's suitors.

Telemann, Georg Philipp 1681–1767. German composer. He was a prolific composer whose large body of works includes operas, chamber music, and oratorios.

Tell, William Legendary Swiss hero. Doubt persists as to Tell's actual existence. He reputedly saved his town of Uri from the Austrians with his bow and arrow, and is credited with shooting an apple from his son's head.

Teller, Edward 1908–. Hungarian-born American physicist. Teller worked with E. Fermi on the atomic bomb and later supported the movement to build the hydrogen bomb.

Tellez, Gabriel *See* **Tirso de Molina**

Temesvar, Battle of Austrian victory (Aug. 9, 1849), with Russian support, over the Hungarians.

By this victory Austria overthrew the Hungarian republic established by the Hungarian Revolution of 1848.

temperance Movement advocating abstinence from alcoholic beverages. The first temperance group was founded (1808) in Saratoga, New York, and others soon appeared in the US, Great Britain, Ireland, and Scandinavia. The movement was led by churches and women's groups and became a major force in the US through the Woman's Christian Temperance Union (founded 1874) and the Anti-Saloon League (founded 1895). A major result of this movement was ratification (1919) of the 18th Amendment to the US Constitution, which secured Prohibition in the US.

Templars See **Knights Templars**

Temple, Sir William 1628–99. English diplomat. He arranged the Triple Alliance (1688) against France and brought about the marriage of William of Orange to Princess Mary of England.

Tempo reforms Japanese reforms implemented (1841–43) by the Tokugawa shogunate in an unsuccessful attempt to restore the financial balance of the shogunate and the political and economic well-being of Japan.

Temujin See **Genghis Khan**

Ten, Council of Venetian tribunal founded (c1310) to investigate plots against the state. It soon gained vast powers in both domestic and foreign matters and existed until abolishment (1797) of the Venetian state by Napoleon.

Tencin, Claudine Alexandrine Guérin de 1685–1749. French writer and literary patron. Her numerous affairs with high political figures brought her wealth and political influence during the reign of King Louis XIV.

Ten Commandments ⟨Decalogue⟩ Ten laws that form the basis of Judaeo-Christian religion. According to the Bible, they were written on two stone tablets and handed down by God to Moses.

Tenentismo Brazilian reform movement of the 1920s. Begun by young army officers seeking social reforms, the movement conducted two revolts (1922, 1924), both of which were quickly crushed. However, it remained an influence into the 1930s.

Teng Hsiao-p'ing ⟨Deng Xiaoping⟩ c1902–. Chinese Communist leader. As general secretary of the Chinese Communist party (1956–67) he worked closely with Mao Tse-tung. Purged (1967) during the Cultural Revolution, he was rehabilitated and became first deputy prime minister (1977–).

Ten Kingdoms Independent kingdoms that rose in southern China in the period (907–960) be-

tween the end of the T'ang and the rise of the Sung dynasties.

Ten Lost Tribes of Israel See **Lost Tribes of Israel**

Tennent, Gilbert 1703–64. American Presbyterian clergyman. A powerful preacher, he was a driving force in the Great Awakening (q.v.).

Tennis Court Oath Oath sworn (June 20, 1789) by members of the Third Estate during the early stages of the French Revolution. The delegates to the Estates General had formed (June 17) the National Assembly, and, finding themselves barred from their meeting place, convened at a tennis court, where they swore not to disband until a constitution had been granted the country. Their determination led King Louis XVI to direct the clergy and nobility to join the National Assembly (June 27).

Tennessee Southeastern US state (pop. 3,835,100), the 16th state. Its capital is Nashville. First claimed by the French, the Tennessee area was ceded to England after the French and Indian Wars (1763). D. Boone explored the region, and Virginians established the first permanent settlement (1769). After the American Revolution, disgruntled settlers formed the independent state of Franklin (1784–88), and in 1796, Tennessee became a state. Tennessee seceded from the Union (1861) during the Civil War and was the locale of several military engagements, notably the Chattanooga Campaign and the battles of Shiloh and Stones River. Tennessee was readmitted to the Union (1866), and its constitution was adopted in 1870.

Tennessee Valley Authority (TVA) US government agency created by Congress in 1933 to manage development of the Tennessee River Basin. The agency oversaw the construction of some 42 dams, achieving both flood control and cheap electric power. The TVA raised much controversy and was regarded by some as an example of government interference with private industry.

Tennyson, Alfred Tennyson, 1st Baron 1809–92. English poet laureate (1850), considered the leading poet of Victorian England. Among his many works are *Idylls of the King, In Memoriam, The Charge of the Light Brigade,* and *Crossing the Bar.*

Tenochtitlán Ancient capital city of the Aztecs, which stood on the site of present-day Mexico City. Founded c1325, it was captured and largely razed (1521) by H. Cortez.

Tenskwatawa See **Shawnee Prophet**

Tenure of Office Act US act passed over a presidential veto (Mar. 2, 1867) forbidding the removal of certain high government officials without the consent of the Senate. President A. Johnson's removal of E. Stanton despite this act led directly to Johnson's impeachment trial.

Ten Years' War Cuban revolt against Spanish rule (1868–78). It was led by Carlos Manuel de Céspedes (1819–74), who called for the gradual emancipation of slaves and universal suffrage. He also favored Cuban independence, although not all the insurrectionists agreed. After 10 years of brutal fighting, which left about 200,000 Cubans and Spanish dead, the insurrection was defeated. The Treaty of El Zanjón (1878) made liberal promises, most of which were not kept.

Tenzing Norgay   *See* **Hillary, Sir Edmund Percival**

Teotihuacán Ancient Mexican city, site of many architectural ruins dating from the Toltec period.

Terence 185–159 BC. Roman playwright known for his comedies adapted from Greek plays. Six of his comedies survive, among them *Andria, Eunuchus,* and *Adelphi.*

Teresa of Avila, Saint 1515–82. Spanish Catholic reformer and mystic who contributed significantly to the Catholic Reformation in Spain. She became the first female Doctor of the Church.

Terman, Lewis Madison 1877–1956. American psychologist. Terman gave the term "IQ" (intelligence quotient) to America with his introduction of the Stanford-Binet intelligence tests for school-children.

Terpsichore   *See* **Muses**

Territory of Orleans Name given to the area forming the state of Louisiana, from its acquisition in the Louisiana Purchase (1804) to statehood (1812).

Tertullian AD c160–c230. Roman theologian. A convert and a strong defender of Christianity, he later became a Montanist, and still later established his own sect, the Tertullians.

Teruel, Battle of Battle (Dec., 1937–Feb., 1938) of the Spanish Civil War, at Teruel, Spain. Republican forces captured Teruel (Dec., 1937) but were unable to hold it. Teruel was recaptured (Feb., 1938) by the forces under Gen. F. Franco.

Teschen, Treaty of Treaty (May 13, 1779) between Austria and Prussia ending the War of the Bavarian Succession. The treaty made territorial adjustments between the two powers and awarded a cash payment to Saxony, Prussia's ally.

Tesla, Nikola 1856–1943. Yugoslavian-born American inventor noted for his contributions to the development of alternating-current electrical technology.

Test Act English statute (1673). It was established to exclude from public office Roman Catholics or those who refused to support the Church of England and the king's supremacy in ecclesiastical affairs.

Tethys   *See* **Titan**

Tet Offensive Major offensive (Feb., 1968) by the Vietcong and North Vietnamese regulars during the Vietnam War. The combined Communist forces staged attacks in more than 100 cities throughout South Vietnam (including Saigon), thus proving their continued strength and embarrassing US military leaders. Fighting lasted a month at the city of Hue and Communist losses were heavy, but the offensive proved a major propaganda victory.

tetrarchy In Roman government, any principality, especially in the East, whose rulers retained a degree of sovereignty but were controlled by the Roman Empire. As Tetrarch of Judaea, Herod the Great was "king" under the Romans. Originally the term came from Macedonia's division of Thessaly into four parts (342 BC).

Tetzel, Johann c1465–1519. German Dominican monk. His granting of indulgences in return for donations to a building fund sparked M. Luther's initial challenge to the Catholic church.

Teutoburg Forest, Battle of the Battle (AD 9) in the Teutoburg Forest, now in West Germany. There the Germans under Arminius defeated the Romany army under Varus, thus halting Roman expansion east of the Rhine.

Teutonic Knights ⟨German Order⟩ Catholic military order founded (1190) at Acre by German nobles during the Third Crusade. In the 13th cent., the order moved to Europe, became a powerful force, and gained control of Prussia. A branch of the order, the Livonian Knights, expanded its rule to the east. Through the 14th cent., the order expanded its holdings and power, and many of its cities became members of the Hanseatic League. Its continued attacks on Poland and Lithuania led to the order's defeat in the Battle of Tannenberg (1410) and its subsequent decline. The order was dissolved (1525) by Grand Master Albert of Brandenburg, who accepted Protestantism and became duke of Prussia under Polish suzerainty.

Tewfik Pasha 1852–92. Khedive of Egypt (1879–92), successor to his father, Ismail Pasha. Egyptian opposition to Western influence during his rule led to military intervention (1882) by the British, who took virtual control of Egypt.

Tewkesbury, Battle of English battle (May 4, 1471), the final battle of the Wars of the Roses. Here the Yorkists under King Edward IV defeated the Lancastrians led by Margaret of Anjou and Prince Edward.

Texas US state in the Southwest (pop. 14,228,400), the 28th state. The Spanish discovered the region (16th cent.), but hostile Indians prevented settlement until the early 18th cent. F. La Salle claimed part of eastern Texas for France (1685), and the French claim was included in the Louisiana Purchase by the US. S. Austin founded the first American settlement in Texas (1821). A province of Mexico, Texas rebelled and declared independence (1836). In the ensuing war, S. Houston defeated the Mexicans at the Battle of San Jacinto (1836), and Texas became an independent republic. US annexation of Texas (1845) led to Texas statehood that year and contributed to the outbreak of the Mexican War. Texas seceded from the Union in 1861 and was readmitted in 1870. The constitution was adopted in 1876.

Texas Rangers Texas military police. They were organized in 1835 to guard the Texas frontier against lawlessness and Indian attacks. In 1935 they became part of the state's highway patrol.

Thackeray, William Makepeace 1811–63. English writer, considered one of the great English novelists. Among his novels are *Vanity Fair, The Paris Sketch-Book,* and *Henry Esmond.*

Thailand (Kingdom of Thailand; *formerly* Siam) Southeast Asian country occupying the western portion of the Indo-Chinese peninsula. Its capital is Bangkok. The Thais are of Indo-Chinese linguistic stock and Thailand was the only Southeast Asian country that maintained its independence throughout the entire period of European colonialism. Thailand has generally been pro-Western in its policies. Key dates in the history of Thailand include:

FROM 6TH CENT. AD   Thai tribes began migrating to the area of modern Thailand.

1253   Mass Thai migration southward into region of present-day boundaries; prompted by destruction of Thai kingdom of Nanchao (in Yunnan, China) by Mongols under Kublai Khan.

1350   Rama Thibodi I established first unified Thai state; founded Ayutthaya dynasty, which ruled until 1767.

1657–88   Narai reigned as king of Siam; established splendid court; preserved freedom from European colonial powers by astute diplomacy.

1688   Antiforeign coup closed Siamese kingdom to most foreigners for over a century.

1782   Gen. Phaya Chakkri founded Chakkri dynasty, which has ruled until present day; he reigned as Rama I; moved capital to Bangkok.

1826   Commercial treaty with Britain.

1833   Commercial treaty with the US.

1851–68   King Mongkut reigned; Westernization began.

1868–1910   Chulalongkorn reigned.

1893   Forced to yield Cambodia and all territory east of the Mekong to France.

1896   Anglo-French accord guaranteed the country's independence.

1917   Siamese government entered WW I on the side of the Allies (July).

1932   Bloodless coup against King Prajadhipok (reigned 1925–35), forcing him to grant a constitution; constitutional monarchy proclaimed (June 27).

1935–46   Rama VIII reigned.

1938–57   Pibul Songgram in power; long tenure began with appointment as premier; eventually became dictator; renamed country Thailand.

1941   Pibul allowed Japanese to enter the country (Dec. 8).

1942   Thailand declared war on the US and Britain (Jan. 25).

1946   Pridi Phanomyang served as leftist premier in postwar government; Pibul held as war criminal.

1946   King Rama VIII died under mysterious circumstances.

1946–   Rama IX reigned; crowned in 1950 after attaining his majority.

1947   Pridi overthrown (Nov. 9) by Pibul as dissatisfaction with Pridi regime was increasing.

1954   Thailand made the headquarters of the Southeast Asia Treaty Organization (SEATO).

1957   Pibul Songgram overthrown in coup led by Marshal Sarit Thanarat; Thanom Kittakachorn made premier.

1958–63   Sarit deposed Thanom and ruled by martial law.

1963   Thanom returned to power; remained in power until 1973.

1968   New constitution restored parliamentary democracy.

1971   Bloodless coup (Nov. 17); Prime Minister Thanom Kittikachorn seized full power.

1972   Interim constitution promulgated; government controls eased (Dec.).

1973   Thanom fled country following student riots (Oct.).

1973   Prime Minister Sanya Thammasak installed; return to civilian government.

1976   Military junta seized power amid political crisis and rioting by leftist students.

1976   US forces ordered out of Thailand (Mar. 20).

1980   Gen. Prem Tinsulanonda in power as premier (Mar.).

1978–80   Massive influx of refugees from Vietnam, Laos, and Cambodia; Vietnamese invasion of Cambodia sent still more refugees into Thailand; hundreds of thousands of Cambodians had returned to their homeland by the end of 1980.

    1981 Attempted military coup failed (Apr. 3).

Thaïs *fl.* 4th cent. BC. Athenian courtesan, mistress to Alexander the Great and later to the king of Egypt. A legend, probably false, holds that she induced Alexander to burn Persepolis.

Thaïs *fl.* 4th cent. AD. Legendary Alexandrian courtesan, said to have been converted to Christianity by St. Paphnutius. Her legend forms the basis for a novel by A. France, which in turn was the basis for the opera *Thaïs* by J. Massenet.

Thakin Shu Maung *See* **Ne Win, U**

Thales c636–c546 BC. Greek philosopher, considered the first Western natural philosopher. One of the Seven Wise Men of Greece, he held that all things were based on one element—water.

Thalia *See* **Muses**

Thames, Battle of the American victory over the British (Oct. 5, 1813) in Ontario, Canada, during the War of 1812. Some 3,000 Americans commanded by W. Harrison defeated 600 British and 1,000 Indian allies under Tecumseh, thereby establishing American control of the Northwest. Tecumseh was killed in this battle.

Thanom Kittikachorn 1911–. Thai army general and prime minister (1963–73). He restored parliamentary democracy under a new constitution (1968), but his seizure of power through a military takeover (1971) led to his ouster (1973).

Thant, U 1909–74. Burmese diplomat. As secretary general of the United Nations (1962–71) he helped find peaceful solutions to the Cuban Missile Crisis (1962) and the conflicts in the Congo (1962) and Cyprus (1964). He was also influential in resolving the India-Pakistan War of 1965.

Thapsus, Battle of Decisive victory (46 BC) for J. Caesar over the remaining supporters of Pompey in North Africa. Thousands were slaughtered, and the opposing commander, M. Scipio, committed suicide. Soon after, Caesar was appointed dictator by the Roman Senate.

Thasos Greek island in the northern Aegean, noted in ancient times for its gold mines.

Thatch, Edward *See* **Blackbeard**

Thatcher, Margaret 1925–. British prime minister (1979–). A Conservative, she was elected amid a worsening economic crisis in Britain and later oversaw the British victory in the Falkland Islands War *(q.v.)*.

Thaw, Harry K. *See* **White, Stanford**

Theatre Guild New York production society formed (1919) to present plays of merit from both America and Europe, regardless of commercial acceptability. Among their many successful productions were *Oklahoma!* and *Porgy and Bess.*

Théâtre-Libre Independent theater founded in Paris (1887) by A. Antoine. An important outlet for new naturalist plays, it had a profound influence on later experimental theaters.

theater of the absurd Movement in the drama of the 1950s and 1960s that depicted the human condition as meaningless and absurd. It was characterized by such plays as S. Beckett's *Waiting for Godot* and E. Ionesco's *The Bald Prima Donna.*

Thebes Ancient Egyptian city. Thebes became the capital of Upper Egypt and rose to prominence with the 11th dynasty (2130–2000 BC), reaching its peak from the 18th to the 20th dynasties. It was the center of worship of the god Amon and the site of Tutankhamen's tomb. It declined as cities on the Nile delta became powerful. Thebes was sacked by Assyrians (661 BC), and Romans (29 BC).

Thebes Greek city, the chief city of ancient Boeotia. Founded by Cadmus and settled by Boeotians before 1500 BC, it was involved in numerous struggles with both Athens and Sparta from the 6th to 4th cents. BC. Thebes allied itself with Athens against Philip II of Macedonia and he defeated them at Chaeronea (338 BC). The city was destroyed by Alexander the Great (336 BC).

Thebes Seven Against *See* **Seven Against Thebes**

Theiler, Max 1899–1972. South African-born American bacteriologist. For his contributions to development of a vaccine for yellow fever, he was awarded a Nobel Prize in physiology and medicine in 1951.

Theia *See* **Titan**

theism In theology, belief in a supreme, personal God who is intimately associated with yet apart from the existence of things. Its opposite is Atheism.

Themis Mythical Greek goddess of wisdom, justice, and order. She was the second wife of Zeus and the mother of Prometheus.

Themistocles c525–c460 BC. Athenian statesman and naval commander. Themistocles urged the strengthening of the Greek navy and defeated the Persians at Salamis (480 BC).

theocracy Form of government in which God is the ultimate authority and laws devolve as from God, through priests or clergy. Thus priests act as both spiritual and secular rulers of the state.

Theocritus *fl.* 3d cent. BC. Greek poet considered the originator of pastoral poetry. He brought pastoral poetry to new heights and influenced such later poets as Vergil and E. Spenser.

Theodora AD c500–548. Byzantine empress (AD 527–548), wife of Emperor Justinian (*m.* AD 523). She had great influence during Justinian's rule and played a key role in saving the throne during the Nika riot (AD 532).

Theodore of Mopsuestia AD c350–428. Greek Christian theologian, bishop of Mopsuestia (AD 392–428). He applied scientific and historical criteria to the study of the Bible. He influenced Nestorius and is sometimes considered the real founder of Nestorianism.

Theodoric I ⟨Thierry I⟩ d. 534. Frankish ruler, a son of Clovis I. On Clovis' death, Theodoric shared the Frankish Kingdom with his brothers Childebert I and Clotaire I.

Theodoric the Great AD c454–526 Ostrogothic king of Italy (493–526). Acting in behalf of Byzantine emperor Zeno, Theodoric led his Gothic army in an invasion of Italy (from 488). By 493 he had captured Ravenna and killed Odoacer, the German chieftain who had overthrown the last Western Roman emperor in 496. He subsequently ruled over Italy as king, though he was nominally in the service of the Byzantines.

Theodosian Code Compilation of Roman laws from the reign of Constantine to that of Theodisius II, under whom it was issued (AD 438). It was later used in compiling the Justinian Code.

Theodosius I ⟨Theodosius the Great⟩ AD 346?–395. Roman emperor of the East (AD 379–395). He defeated the Goths in the East and convened the Second Council of Constantinople (381). He defeated and killed the usurper Maximus (388) and restored Valentinian II to the throne in Italy.

Theodosius II AD 401–450. Roman emperor of the East (AD 408–450), successor to his father, Arcadius. He left the actual ruling to his sister Pulcheria and his wife Eudocia. He authorized the Theodosian Code and negotiated with Attila the Hun.

Theodosius the Great See **Theodosius I**

Theophrastus c372–c287 BC. Greek philosopher. He succeeded Aristotle as head of the Peripatetics. He wrote extensively on plants, nature, and ethics.

Theorell, Axel Hugo Teodor 1903–. Swedish biochemist. He was awarded the Nobel Prize in Physiology and Medicine (in 1955) for his studies of enzyme oxidation.

theosophy Mystical religious philosophy holding that direct knowledge of God is possible and is the means of salvation. Although its concepts date back to early Indian philosophy, modern Theosophy was founded (1875) by H. Blavatsky.

Theresa, Saint 1515–82. Spanish saint, known for her mystical experiences. She founded (1562) the reformed Carmelite order known as the Discalced Carmelites.

Thermidor Eleventh month of the French Revolutionary calendar. The *coup d'état* of 9 Thermidor (July 27, 1794) brought down M. Robespierre and ended the Reign of Terror. The coup was carried out by a hastily organized coalition of factions in the National Convention, following a speech by Robespierre (July 26) in which he denounced certain unnamed enemies. Robespierre and others were guillotined July 28 and the Thermidorian reaction, as it was called, was swift. The machinery of the Reign of Terror was dismantled, the radical Jacobins were suppressed, and the moderates came into control. Radical reforms were rescinded, among them the Law of Maximums, which set controls on wages and prices (in effect 1793–94). The Thermidorian period ended with the establishment of the Directory (*q.v.*) in 1795. (*See also* French Revolution [1794–95].)

Thermopylae Historic Greek pass linking northern and southern Greece. Here a small force of Spartans under Leonidas made a heroic but unsuccessful stand (480 BC) against the vastly superior army of Persian king Xerxes during the Persian Wars.

Thermopylae, Battle of See **Antiochus III**

Theseus Legendary Greek hero, son of Athenian king Aegeus. He killed the Minotaur and defeated the Amazons.

Thespis *fl.* 534 BC. Greek poet, considered the originator of the tragic drama. He was said to have introduced the role of actor to interact with the leader of the chorus, thereby creating dialogue.

Thessaly Ancient Greek region of northern Greece. Surrounded by mountains, Thessaly became a power in Greece (4th cent. BC) but soon declined.

Thetis Mythical Greek figure, the wife of Peleus and mother of Achilles.

Thibault, Jacques Anatole See **France, Anatole**

Thibaw See **Burmese War (Third)**

Thiers, Louis Adolphe 1797–1877. French statesman and historian. Theirs served in several ministerial positions under King Louis Philippe, opposed Emperor Napoleon III and the Franco-Prussian War, and after the war became president of the Third French Republic (1871–73). He suppressed the Commune of Paris (1871).

Thierry I See **Theodoric I**

Third Coalition, War of the (1805) Early phase of the Napoleonic Wars fought by a coalition of England, Austria, Russia, and Sweden against France and Spain. Napoleon defeated the Austrians in the Battle of Ulm (*q.v.*), suffered a naval defeat by the British in the Battle of Trafalgar (*q.v.*), and defeated the Austrians and Russians in the Battle of Austerlitz (*q.v.*), thus crushing the coalition.

Third Crusade   *See* **Crusade, Third**

Third Estate   In prerevolutionary France, one of the three groups represented in the States General, the others being the clergy and the nobility. It was composed largely of townsmen, or burghers. Its establishment (June, 1789) of the National Assembly in France marked the beginning of the French Revolution.

Third Punic War   *See* **Punic War**

Third Reich   Name given the German government (1933–45) under the rule of A. Hitler and the Nazi party. (*See* Germany [1933–45]; Nazi Party.)

Third Republic   Name given the French government established (1870) after the fall of the Second Empire in the Franco-Prussian War. It was succeeded (1940) by the Vichy government during WW II. (*See also* France [1870–1940].)

Third World   Term applied to the less developed and often politically nonaligned countries of Africa, Asia, and Latin Ameria.

Thirteen Colonies, the   Those original British North American colonies which joined in the American Revolution and became the United States. They included Connecticut, Delaware, Georgia, Maryland, Massachusetts, New Hampshire, New Jersey, New York, North Carolina, Pennsylvania, Rhode Island, South Carolina, and Virginia.

38th Parallel   Boundary line adopted at the end of WW II to mark the separate areas in Korea where surrender would be made to American and Soviet forces. After the war, a Communist regime was established in North Korea (Democratic People's Republic of Korea), while the Republic of Korea was established in the south. As a result of the Korean War, South Korea now holds some territory north of the parallel.

Thirty-nine Articles   Articles formulating the official doctrines and beliefs of the Church of England. Officially promulgated by the Canterbury Convocation (1571) and approved by Queen Elizabeth I, they were based on forty-two articles prepared (1553) by Archbishop T. Cranmer.

Thirty-three Immortals   *see* **Lavalleja, Juan Antonio**

Thirty Tyrants   **1.** Name given the group of thirty Athenians who ruled Athens (404–403 BC) under Spartan domination after the Peloponnesian War. They were overthrown by Thrasybulus. **2.** Name given the group of pretenders to the Roman throne who rose during the reigns of emperors Valerian and Gallienus (AD 253–268).

Thirty Years' War   Series of interrelated conflicts (1618–48) that led ultimately to the end of Hapsburg dominance in Europe, the crippling of the Holy Roman Empire, and the emergence of France

as the leading power in Europe. The war, which left Germany devastated, began in Bohemia as a reaction to imperial repression of Protestantism and quickly spread to other Hapsburg domains in the Holy Roman Empire. Denmark and Sweden, each in turn, joined the conflict against the Hapsburgs. In the final phase of the conflict, France entered the war in a successful move to break the power of the Holy Roman Empire. Key dates in the history of the Thirty Years' War include:

1576–1612   Holy Roman Emperor Rudolf II reigned; rule marked by repression of Protestants in Germany, disrupting the uneasy truce established between Protestants and Catholics by the Treaty of Augsburg (1555).

1608–09   Protestant leaders established alliance known as the Evangelical Union (1608); Catholics created the Catholic League (1609); stage set for outbreak of warfare between the factions.

1612–19   Matthias reigned; he failed to win peace between Protestants and Catholics.

1618   Defenestration of Prague; began the Bohemian revolt against Hapsburg rule.

1618–20   Bohemian phase of the war; began with the Protestant revolt throughout Bohemia that spread into other Hapsburg lands.

1619   Bohemians chose Frederick V, elector of the Palatinate, as king; led to split between Lutherans and Calvinists.

1620   Ferdinand II became emperor (Aug.); Catholic League forces under Count Tilly defeated Frederick and the Bohemians at White Mountain (Nov. 8); defeat marked end of Bohemian phase of war; Frederick continued the war in the Palatinate.

1620–25   Palatinate phase of the war; Protestants under Frederick at first successful but ultimately defeated by imperial forces led by Tilly; Palatinate passed to Bavarian Duke Maximilian I.

1622   Imperial forces under Tilly defeated (Apr.) at Weisloch; battle marked high point of Protestant fortunes in the Palatinate.

1622   Tilly defeated the Protestants at Wimpfen (May) and Höchst (June); imperial forces began to crush Protestant resistance in the Palatinate.

1622   Protestants victorious at the Battle of Fleurus (now in Belgium).

1623   Protestants defeated at Stadtlohn (Aug.); battle marked virtual end of the struggle in the Palatinate.

1625–29   Danish phase of the war; Danish king Christian IV entered the conflict partly out of religious motives and partly to oppose growing Hapsburg influence in northern Germany.

1626   Christian IV advanced into Saxony.

1626 Christian IV defeated (Apr.) by imperial forces under Duke Albrecht von Wallenstein at Dessau.

1626 Imperial forces under Tilly inflicted major defeat on Danes (Aug. 27) at Lutter am Barenberge.

1626–27 Imperial forces under Wallenstein and Tilly forced the Danish army north to the Jutland Peninsula.

1629 Emperor Ferdinand II issued the Edict of Restitution (Mar. 6), canceling Protestant titles acquired through the Peace of Augsburg in 1555.

1629 Treaty of Lübeck (May 12); Denmark withdrew from the conflict, thereby ending the Danish phase; Denmark lost territories.

1630–35 Swedish phase of the war; Swedish king Gustavus II (Gustavus Adolphus), enticed by promises of aid from French minister Cardinal Richelieu, entered the war against the Hapsburgs.

1630 Wallenstein dismissed as commander of imperial army; Tilly assumed command.

mid-1630 Gustavus II advanced his Swedish forces into Pomerania.

1631 Tilly captured Magdeburg (May 20) and destroyed the city; severe reprisals taken against the Protestants who had rebelled.

1631 Swedish and Saxon forces victorious over Tilly (Sept.) at Breitenfeld; Protestant forces advanced south.

1632 Tilly defeated and killed (Apr. 14) at the Battle of the Lech; Protestant forces subsequently captured Munich; Wallenstein returned to command imperial army.

1632 Wallenstein engaged Swedes and Saxons at Battle of Lützen (Nov. 16); Wallenstein defeated, but Gustavus II was killed; Gustavus succeeded by Duke Bernhard of Saxe-Weimar, who advanced into Bavaria.

1633 Wallenstein sought unsuccessfully to secure peaceful settlement to the war; was removed from command; continued to seek peace.

1634 Wallenstein assassinated (Feb. 25).

1634 Gen. M. von Matthias replaced Wallenstein as commander of imperial forces.

1634 Imperial forces defeated Protestants, under Bernhard, at Nordlingen (Sept. 6); battle marked virtual end of Protestant alliance with Swedes.

1635 Peace of Prague (May 30) ended Swedish phase of the conflict; its provisions favorable to the Protestants, the treaty formed a groundwork for peace in war-torn Germany.

1635–48 French phase of the war; Cardinal Richelieu, seeking to establish France as leading power in Europe, secured French declaration of war against Hapsburg Spain (May 1635); the war evolved into an international struggle between France (and allies) against the Hapsburgs and the Holy Roman Empire.

1636 Swedes inflicted heavy casualties on imperial armies at the Battle of Wittstock in Germany (Oct. 4); marked recovery from Nordlingen defeat.

1637 Holy Roman Emperor Ferdinand II died; succeeded by his son Ferdinand III.

1638 Duke Bernhard of Saxe-Weimar defeated imperial forces at Rheinfelden (Mar. 3).

1642–45 Swedish forces under Gen. Lennart Torstensson conquered Denmark; advanced south into Austria and Germany, seriously crippling the Hapsburgs' military position.

1642 French minister Cardinal Richelieu died; succeeded by Cardinal Mazarin.

1643 French forces under Prince Louis II de Condé defeated Spanish at Battle of Rocroi (May).

1645 The French under Condé and Viscount Turenne defeated the imperial army at Allersheim (Aug. 3), near Nordlingen.

1645 Matthias ousted as imperial commander.

1647 Treaty of Ulm marked a truce between Bavarian forces and allied French and Swedish armies.

1648 Peace negotiations (1645–48) culminated in the Treaty of Westphalia (Oct. 24), which ended the Thirty Years' War; its terms were favorable to France and Sweden and left the house of Hapsburg and the Holy Roman Empire severely crippled; France became the dominant power in Europe.

Thisbe *See* **Pyramus and Thisbe**

Thistlewood, Arthur 1770–1820. English revolutionary. He organized (1820) the unsuccessful Cato Street Conspiracy to murder R. Castlereagh and other Cabinet members.

Thököly, Emeric ⟨~, Imre⟩ ⟨Tököly, Emeric⟩ 1657–1705. Hungarian patriot. He fought against the Austrian Hapsburgs and in 1678 took command of all rebel Hungarian forces. He was allied with the Turks in their unsuccessful assault on Vienna (1683).

Thököly, Imre *See* **Thököly, Emeric**

Thomas, Dylan Marlais 1914–53. Welsh poet whose work is noted for its originality and brilliant and complicated imagery. Among his writings is the dramatic work *Under Milk Wood*.

Thomas, George Henry 1816–70. Union general in the American Civil War. His actions at the Battle of Chickamauga (1863) saved the Union army from destruction. He later defeated the Confederates at Nashville (1864).

Thomas, John See **Christadelphians**

Thomas, Norman Mattoon 1884–1968. American Socialist leader and Presbyterian minister (1911–31). A leading social reformer, he was six times the Socialist candidate for the presidency from 1928 to 1948.

Thomas, Saint One of the Twelve Apostles of Jesus. His refusal to believe in Jesus' resurrection without evidence led to the term "doubting Thomas." He is thought to have preached in northern Persia and India.

Thomas, Silken See **Fitzgerald, Thomas, 10th earl of Kildare**

Thomas à Becket, Saint 1117–70. English saint, archbishop of Canterbury (1162–70), chancellor of England (1155–62), and onetime friend of King Henry II. Appointed chancellor by Henry and elected archbishop with Henry's aid, Becket infuriated the king by consistently defending church prerogatives and canon law against royal authority. His opposition to the king led to his exile from England (1164–70). Soon after his return, he was murdered by four of the king's knights in Canterbury Cathedral.

Thomas Aquinas, Saint 1225–74. Italian theologian and philosopher whose writings have been officially adopted by the Roman Catholic church. A Dominican, he studied under Albertus Magnus and later taught in Paris and Rome. He successfully opposed the strictly rational interpretation of Aristotelian philosophy advanced by Siger de Brabant (1235?–81?) and the Averroists. He also opposed the teachings of the Augustinians by holding that reason and faith are compatible. His major works are the *Summa Theologica* and *Summa contra Gentiles.*

Thomson, Sir Charles W. See **Challenger Expedition**

Thomson, Sir Joseph John 1856–1940. English physicist noted for his studies of the electrical conductivity of gases and the charge and mass of the electron. He was awarded the Nobel Prize in Physics in 1906.

Thor ⟨Donar⟩ Mythical Norse god of thunder, strength, and war. The patron of peasants, he never hurt humanity. Thursday is named for him.

Thoreau, Henry David 1817–62. American writer and philosopher. Thoreau was an influential transcendentalist. His works include the journal *Walden* and the essay *On Civil Disobedience.*

Thorfinn Karlsefni *fl.* 1002–10. Icelandic navigator. Thorfinn attempted to establish a colony in North America but abandoned the colony after a year.

Thorndike, Edward Lee 1874–1949. American psychologist. Thorndike devised intelligence and learning-ability tests for children. His works include *Mental and Social Measurements* and *The Psychology of Learning.*

Thornton, William 1759–1828. American architect. His plans (submitted 1793) for the proposed Capitol in Washington, D.C., were approved by Pres. G. Washington. Much of the central section of the Capitol follows his design, but other elements of the structure were modified.

Thoth Ancient Egyptian god, identified with the Greek god Hermes. A scribe and messenger, he kept the records of the dead. He was considered the god of learning and was credited with many inventions, among them writing.

Thothmes I See **Thutmose I**

Thothmes II See **Thutmose II**

Thousand, Expedition of the See **Expedition of the Thousand**

Thrace Historical European region in the southeastern part of the Balkan Peninsula. Its inhabitants resisted Greek domination, but the Greeks established several colonies in Thrace, notably Byzantium (6th cent. BC). Thrace was taken by Persia (6th cent. BC) and annexed by Rome (1st cent. BC). It passed to the Byzantine Empire, but by AD 1453 the last of Thrace fell to the Ottoman Turks. Thrace was contested by Bulgaria and Turkey in the Balkan Wars (*q.v.*). After WW I, the region was divided among Greece, Bulgaria, and Turkey by the treaties of Neuilly (1919), Sèvres (1920), and Lausanne (1923).

Thrasybulus *d. c*389 BC. Athenian general and statesman. He was banished by the Thirty Tyrants (404 BC) but overthrew them (403 BC) and reestablished democracy in Athens.

Three-Anti campaign Early campaign (1951–52) by the Chinese Communist party, after its takeover of the Chinese mainland, to eliminate fraud, mismanagement, and corruption.

Three Emperors, Battle of See **Austerlitz, Battle of**

Three Emperors' League Alliance (1873–77, 1881–87) of Germany, Austria-Hungary, and Russia, originated by German chancellor O. von Bismarck, to preserve peace between Russia and Austria-Hungary and to isolate France. It was disrupted by the Russo-Turkish War of 1877–78 but was secretly renewed in 1881.

Three Feudatories, Revolt of the Rebellion (1673–81) against the Ch'ing (Manchu) dynasty by semi-autonomous areas in Yunnan, Kwangtung, and Fukien, headed by former Ming dynasty generals. They attempted to establish a new dynasty but were defeated.

Three Henrys, War of the French civil war (1585–89), one of the French Wars of Religion. It involved the last Valois king, Henry III; Henry, 3d duke of Guise; and the Huguenot Henry of Navarre (later King Henry IV). Navarre's defeat of the Catholic forces of King Henry III at Coutras (Oct. 20, 1587) led the Catholic Henry of Guise to march on Paris to depose Henry III. The king fled to Blois (May, 1588) and subsequently ordered Guise's assassination (Dec., 1588). This led to a revolt of the Catholics and forced the king to seek refuge with Navarre. While in Navarre's camp the king was murdered (July, 1589). Henry of Navarre continued the struggle to gain the throne.

Three Holy Children In the Bible, three Hebrews thrown into a fiery furnace by Nebuchadnezzar. Their faith in God protected them and they escaped unscathed. They were Shadrach, Meshach, and Abednego.

Three Kingdoms Period in Chinese history (AD 220–280) during which three kingdoms ruled China after the fall of the Han dynasty. They were the Wei, which ruled in the north; the Wu, which ruled in the south; and the Shu Han, which ruled in the west. Wei conquered Shu Han (AD 264) and established the Chin dynasty. The dynasty then conquered the Wu (AD 280) and reunited China. The Three Kingdoms has been characterized as a romantic period, notably in the novel *Romance of the Three Kingdoms*.

Three Kings *See* **Magi**

Three Kings, Battle of the ⟨Alcazarquivir, Battle of⟩ Moroccan victory (Aug. 4, 1578) over the Portuguese invasion led by Portuguese king Sebastian I. Sebastian supported the Moorish pretender against the king of Fez and was defeated at Alcazarquivir, Morocco. All three kings died in the battle.

Three Mile Island Nuclear-powered electrical generating plant outside Middletown, Pennsylvania. A nuclear accident at the plant, beginning Mar. 28, 1979, resulted in the venting of radioactive gases. Though a full-scale disaster was averted (by Apr. 9, 1979), the crisis resulted in a major reevaluation of the US nuclear energy program.

Three Principles of the People Ideological goals advanced in China by Sun Yat-sen and later claimed by both the followers of Chiang Kai-shek and the Chinese Communists. They included: Nationalism, freedom from imperialism and imperial rule; Democracy, the ability of the Chinese to govern themselves through a form of democratic structure; and Livelihood, apparently a program to advance land equalization.

Thucydides *c*460–400 BC. Greek historian. He was exiled because of his failure (424) as a leader in the Peloponnesian War and wrote *The History of the Peloponnesian War* during his exile. The work, covering the years 431–411, is noted for its accuracy, impartiality, and (then) novel examination of human character in relation to the events of the war.

Thugs ⟨Phansigars⟩ Indian religious sect. Devoted to the goddess Kali, the Thugs dressed as religious mendicants or merchants and killed their victims, usually travelers, as offerings to her. They were suppressed by the British (19th cent.).

Thule Name given the northernmost known country by the ancient Greeks. The Greek navigator Pytheas (*fl.* 4th cent. BC) reached an island he named Thule. It may have been Iceland, Norway, or one of the Shetland Islands.

Thurber, James Grover 1894–1961. American humorist whose whimsical stories and drawings, which appeared regularly in the magazine *The New Yorker*, were noted for their insight into the human condition.

Thuringia Former German state, now part of East Germany. Taken by the Franks (6th cent.), the region became a march (frontier country) under Charlemagne (804). After 1247, the rule of Thuringia was contested and the land was divided. Most of Thuringia came under the control of Saxony (15th cent.). Its various principalities were reunited (1919) into the state of Thuringia. In WW II, Thuringia was occupied by Russian forces, and in 1952, it was divided among several East German districts.

Thutmose I ⟨Thothmes I⟩ *d. c*1512 BC. Egyptian king (*c*1526–12). He secured control of the Nile Valley as far as its fourth cataract, on whose rocks he inscribed records of his victories. He also sent military expeditions deep into Syria.

Thutmose II ⟨Thothmes II⟩ Ancient Egyptian king (*c*1512–04 BC). He married his half sister Hatshepsut, who quickly overpowered him and ruled in his stead.

Thutmose III *d. c*1450 BC. Egyptian king (*c*1504–*c*1450 BC), successor to his father, Thutmose II. The regency of his aunt, Queen Hatshepsut, ended in *c*1482, and he began the conquests that made Egypt a great power. He added Syria, Kadesh, Mitanni, and part of the Sudan to his empire. He erected many monuments and temples and brought Egypt great wealth and prosperity.

Thutmose IV *d. c*1417 BC. Ancient Egyptian king (*c*1425–17 BC), successor to his father, Amenhotep II. He led successful campaigns in Nubia and Asia Minor. His marriage to the daughter of the Mitanni king in Syria led to a long and advantageous peace.

Thuy, Nguyen Vinh *See* **Bao Dai**

Tiberius 42 BC–AD 37. Second Roman emperor (AD 14–37), successor to his stepfather Augustus. He ruled ably in the early years of his reign but later, under the influence of Sejanus, became a tyrant. He had Sejanus killed (AD 31).

Tibet Autonomous region of China, located in southwestern China. Capital is Lhasa. Tibet was crossed in early times by the trade route from China to India. A Tibetan kingdom rose there (7th cent.) and Buddhism was introduced, which evolved into Tibetan Buddhism (q.v.). Its chief religious leaders, the Dalai Lama and Panchen Lama, became the traditional political leaders (until recent times) of Tibet as well. Tibet came under Mongol domination (12th cent.), and then passed to the Chinese Manchu dynasty (1720). Chinese influence in Tibet waned through the 18th and 19th cents. and Tibet was invaded several times by Gurkhas from Nepal. Tibetan resistance to British attempts to open trade relations led to a British invasion (1904) and subsequent concessions. After the fall of China's Manchu dynasty (1912), Tibet again became independent. China invaded it (1950) and restored Chinese control over the country. A rebellion against Chinese rule (1959) was severely crushed and the Dalai Lama fled to India. The Chinese Communists suppressed Tibetan Buddhism, installed a secular government, and in 1965 the country formally became the Tibetan Autonomous Region.

Tibetan Buddhism (*often incorrectly called* Lamaism) Form of Buddhism found in Tibet, Mongolia, and adjacent regions. It began in Tibet (c7th cent. AD) and is derived from Indian Mahayana Buddhism, though it embodies elements of Tantric Buddhism and the native Tibetan religion, Bon. The important Yellow Hat Sect was begun (15th cent.) by the lama (monk) Tsong-kha-pa (c1357–1419), who introduced many reforms and established rigorous discipline within the monasteries. In 1641, the Mongols came under the influence of the Yellow Hat Sect and gave control of Tibet to the Dalai Lama, who eventually became secular leader of the country. Spiritual control came to reside with the Paschen Lama. The Dalai Lama was exiled (1959) after an abortive revolt against Chinese domination. Since then the Chinese have actively suppressed Tibetan Buddhism.

Tibullus, Albius 54?–18? BC. Roman elegaic poet. Only two works, *Delia* and *Nemesis,* can be definitely ascribed to him. His patron was Messala.

Ticonderoga, Battle of American victory (May 10, 1775) over the British during the American Revolution at Ticonderoga in northeastern New York. E. Allen and the Green Mountain Boys captured Fort Ticonderoga, at the northern end of Lake Champlain. Artillery from the fort was later used to force the British evacuation from Boston (1776).

T'ien-ching *See* **Tientsin**

Tientsin ⟨T'ien-ching⟩ Chinese city (pop. 7,200,000) and major seaport in eastern China. Tientsin was the site of the Treaties of Tientsin (June, 1858), by which the city and 10 other Chinese ports were opened to European trade; and also of the Tientsin Massacre (q.v.). It was a center of fighting during the Boxer Rebellion(q.v.).

Tientsin Massacre Massacre (June 21, 1870) of some 20 French nationals, including the French consul, at Tientsin, China. European warships were sent to Tientsin and war was avoided by Chinese issuance of an official apology.

Tiepolo, Giovanni Battista 1696–1770. Italian artist, considered one of the leading Venetian painters of the 18th cent. His massive frescoes are noted for their use of light and color.

Tiffany, Louis Comfort 1848–1933. American decorative artist. He developed and manufactured a form of colored glass known as Tiffany favrile and produced a great number of works in glass, in the art nouveau style.

Tiglath-pileser I d. c1077 BC. Ancient Assyrian king (c1115–c1077 BC). He conquered parts of the former Hittite empire, invaded Asia Minor and Babylonia, and campaigned west to the Mediterranean.

Tiglath-pileser III d. 728 BC. Ancient Assyrian king (745–728 BC). He conquered Syria and invaded Palestine. He also suppressed a revolt in Babylon (729 BC), thereby becoming titular king of Babylon, and launched campaigns as far east as the Caspian Sea. He brought the Assyrian empire to its greatest extent and also proved an able administrator.

Tigranes I the Great c140–55 BC. Armenian king (c95–55 BC). He conquered northern Mesopotamia, Syria, and Cappodocia, but was defeated (69 and 68 BC) by the Romans under Lucullus. He surrendered (66 BC) to Pompey and subsequently ruled Armenia as a Roman vassal.

Tigris and **Euphrates** Rivers rising in Turkey and flowing through southwestern Asia to join in southern Iraq. The ancient region of Mesopotamia encompassed this river system, and gave rise to such early civilizations as Sumer (q.v.), Akkad (q.v.), Babylonia (q.v.), Assyria (q.v.), and Chaldaea (q.v.).

Tilak, Bal Gangadhar 1856–1920. Indian nationalist leader. He negotiated the Lucknow Pact

(1916), which unified Hindus and Muslims against British rule in India.

Tilden, Samuel Jones 1814–86. American statesman, Democratic presidential candidate (1876) against Republican R. Hayes. Tilden won the popular vote but disputed electoral votes were awarded by a Congressional Commission to Hayes, who won the election.

Tillich, Paul Johannes 1886–1965. German-born American philosopher and theologian. His writings, which sought to blend modern thought with Christianity, include *The Courage to Be* and *My Search for Absolutes*.

Tilly, Johannes Tserklaes, count of 1559–1632. Flemish soldier in Bavarian and imperial service during the Thirty Years' War. As commander of the Catholic League he gained many victories, notably at White Hill *(q.v.)*, in 1620. He seized Magdeburg (1631), which was sacked by his troops. He was defeated and killed at the Battle of Breitenfeld (1632).

Tilsit, Treaties of Two treaties signed (July, 1807) by France during the French Revolutionary Wars. **1.** By the First Treaty of Tilsit (July 7, 1807), France granted Russia freedom to conquer Finland in return for a Russian attempt to mediate between England and France. If England should refuse mediation, Russia was to ally with France. **2.** By the Second Treaty of Tilsit (July 9, 1807), France gained substantial territory from Prussia, and Prussia was obliged to join the Continental System against Britain.

Timbuktu West African city, now in Mali. Founded *c*1000, it rose to become a center of the gold and salt trade and reached its peak (15th cent.) under Songhai rule. Sacked (16th cent.) by the Moroccans, it soon declined.

Time of Troubles Period in Russian history (1604–13) from the rise of the first so-called false Dmitri claimant to the Russian throne to the accession of Czar Michael and establishment of the Romanov dynasty. In 1598, with the death of Czar Fëdor I and the end of the Rurik line, B. Godunov was elected czar. His rule was challenged (1604) by the rise of a pretender in Poland who claimed to be Dmitri, Fëdor's half-brother. He gained much support and at Godunov's death (1605) was made czar. He was murdered (1606) by the Boyars and succeeded by Basil IV Shuisky (ruled 1606–10), who was confronted by peasant revolts and the rise of new pretenders, including a second false Dmitri. The second Dmitri forced Shuisky to seek aid from Sweden, which in turn prompted a Polish invasion (1609) and occupation of Moscow (1610). Polish king Sigismund III sought the Russian throne for himself and pro-

voked increased Russian resistance after the death (1610) of the second Dmitri. Moscow was relieved by Russian forces (1612) and a national assembly elected (1613) Michael Romanov czar, thus establishing the Romanov dynasty.

Timon of Athens *fl.* 5th cent. BC. Athenian misanthrope and recluse. Accounts of his life by Lucian and Plutarch formed the basis for the play *Timon of Athens* by W. Shakespeare.

Timothy, Saint *d.* AD *c*100. Christian disciple, companion to Saint Paul. He is frequently mentioned in the New Testament and two of Paul's letters are addressed to him. According to tradition, he was the first bishop of Ephesus and was martyred there.

Timur *See* **Tamerlane**

Timurids Turkish dynasty (15th cent.) descended from Tamerlane. Upon Tamerlane's death, the empire, comprising domains extending from India to Persia (modern Iran), was divided into eastern and western sections and distributed between his sons. Shah Rokh (ruled 1405–47), given the eastern half of the empire, quickly reunited much of the territory. He sparked a literary and cultural movement, established a library at his capital, Herat, and encouraged trade. After his death, the empire fell into anarchy and eventually disintegrated into local dynasties. Baber, one of these rulers, founded the Mogul *(q.v.)* empire in India.

Tinchebrai, Battle of Battle (Sept. 28, 1106) by which English king Henry I gained control of Normandy.

Tindal, William *See* **Tyndale, William**

Tindale, William *See* **Tyndale, William**

Tintoretto ⟨Robusti, Jacopo⟩ 1518–94. Italian painter, one of the great Venetian Renaissance painters of the 16th cent. A leader of the Mannerist school, he was thought to have been a student of Titian. His many famous works include a *Last Supper, Susanna Bathing, The Golden Calf, The Finding,* and *The Removal of the Body of St. Mark.*

Tippecanoe, Battle of Victory (Nov. 7, 1811) of US forces led by Gen. W. Harrison over the Shawnee Indians led by Tenskwatawa, brother of Tecumseh. The battle, near the Tippecanoe River in Indiana, broke the power of the Indian alliance formed by Tecumseh and also provided Harrison with the slogan "Tippecanoe and Tyler, Too," for his 1840 presidential campaign.

Tipu Sahib 1753–99. Indian Sultan of Mysore (1782–99). He fought against the British and the Marathas in the Mysore Wars. He was killed in the fourth war and his kingdom was divided.

Tiradentes Conspiracy A Brazilian movement against Portuguese rule. It was led by José Joaquim da Silva Xavier (1748–92), also called Tiradentes. He was captured (1789) and executed after a lengthy trial.

Tiresias In Greek mythology, a blind Theban prophet. He prophesied the tragedy of Oedipus.

Tirhakah ⟨Taharka⟩ d. 663 BC. Egyptian pharaoh (689–663 BC). Last king of the 25th (Ethiopian) dynasty in ancient Egypt, he was defeated (671 BC) by the Assyrians in a series of battles and was obliged to abandon Lower Egypt.

Tirpitz, Alfred von 1849–1930. German admiral. As naval secretary from 1897, he built a modern fleet to match the British navy. He retired (1916) during WW I because of opposition to his policy of unrestricted submarine warfare.

Tirso de Molina ⟨Téllez, Gabriel⟩ 1571?–1648. Spanish monk and dramatist. A prolific author of some 400 plays, he provided the first literary treatment of the Don Juan legend in *El Burlador de Sevilla.*

Tisquantum *See* **Squanto**

Tissaphernes d. 395 BC. Persian satrap. He played a major role in Persia's reconquest of the Ionian Greek cities, and in the Battle of Cunaxa (401 BC).

Tisza, Count Stephen 1861–1918. Hungarian premier (1930–05, 1913–17). A strong supporter of the Austro-Hungarian dual monarchy, he favored the alliance with Germany and was assassinated for his support of Hungary's WW I role.

Titans In Greek mythology, the twelve sons and daughters of Uranus, god of heaven, and Gaea, goddess of earth. Led by Cronus, they overthrew their father. They were in turn overthrown by the children of Chronus and Rhea (the Olympians), led by Zeus. The Titans were (sons) Hyperion, Oceanus, Cronus, Iapetus, Coeus, Crius, and (daughters) Phoebe, Rhea, Theia, Themis, Mnemosyne, and Tethys.

Titanic British ocean liner involved in a major seagoing disaster. Believed to be unsinkable, the liner struck an iceberg during the night (Apr. 14, 1912), while on her maiden voyage. It sank the next morning with the loss of more than 1,500 lives.

Tithonus Trojan prince in Greek mythology. Loved by the Goddess Eos, he was granted immortality by Zeus, but not eternal youth. Eos changed him into a grasshopper in his old age.

Titian ⟨*pseud.* of Tiziano Vecellio⟩ 1477–1576. Italian painter, one of the great Renaissance artists. A member of the Venetian school, Titian painted sumptuous religious and mythological paintings, such as the masterpieces *Sacred and Profane Love* and *Rape of Europa.* Among his

many other famous works are *Charles V in Battle, Assumption of the Virgin,* and the *Pietà.*

Tito ⟨Josip Broz⟩ 1892–1980. President of Yugoslavia (1953–80) and Communist leader. A Russian prisoner during WW I, he participated in the 1917 revolution, then returned to Yugoslavia, becoming leader of the Communist party in 1937. During WW II, he led the Partisans (q.v.) in guerrilla fighting and, from 1945, headed the Yugoslav government. He pursued policies independently of the Soviet Union and was expelled from the Cominform (1948). Thereafter he maintained relations with Western and Communist powers, as well as with nonaligned countries. His regime was one of the most liberal in the Communist world.

Titus *fl.* 1st cent. AD. Traditional first bishop of Crete and a disciple of St. Paul. One of Paul's pastoral epistles was addressed to Titus.

Titus AD c39–81. Roman emperor (AD 79–81), successor to his father, Vespasian. As a general he captured (AD 70) and destroyed Jerusalem and the Temple. As emperor, he rebuilt Rome after a great fire (AD 80) and completed the Colosseum.

Titus Flavius Vespasianus *See* **Vespasian**

Titus Lucretius Carus *See* **Lucretius**

Tiw, ⟨Tyr⟩ Ancient Germanic god. One-handed because of a wolf's treacherous bite, Tiw was a god of war that gave his name to Tuesday (Tiw's day).

Tiy *fl.* 1400 BC. Egyptian queen. She was the mother of Ikhnaton, and wife of Amenhotep III, over whom she is thought to have exerted great influence.

Tocqueville, Alexis de 1805–59. French writer and statesman. Tocqueville visited the US in 1831 and wrote the study *Democracy in America,* considered a classic of political literature.

Togliatti, Palmiro 1893–1964. Italian Communist party cofounder and longtime leader. He advocated liberalization of Communist regimes but never broke with Moscow.

Togo, Republic of *See* **Togoland**

Togo, Heihachiro, Count 1847–1934. Japanese admiral. In the Russo-Japanese War, he defeated the Russians at Port Arthur (1904) and at the Battle of Tsuschima in 1905—the first defeat of a European power by Asians.

Togoland Region in West Africa. A former German protectorate, Togo was divided into British and French mandates in 1922. The eastern half became the Republic of Togo in 1960. The rest became part of Ghana in 1957.

Togrul Beg *See* **Seljuks**

Tojo, Hideki 1884–1948. Japanese general and wartime premier (1941–44). Tojo helped instigate the attack on Pearl Harbor (1941) and led Japan's war effort until 1944. He was executed (1945) as a war criminal.

Tokio *See* **Tokyo**

Tököly, Emeric *See* **Thököly, Emeric**

Tokugawa, Iyeyasu *See* **Iyeyasu**

Tokugawa Keiki (Hitotsubashi) 1837–1902. Last Japanese shogun. Made shogun (1867) he surrendered his authority upon the accession (1868) of Mutsuhito as emperor.

Tokugawa Last shogunate of Japan (ruled 1603–1867). Founded by Ieyasu, who came to power (1603) after the death of Hideyoshi, the shogunate ruled by means of a centralized feudal government. The capital was moved from Kyoto to Edo (now Tokyo) and the reign of the Tokugawa family was marked by a period of peace, prosperity, and cultural flowering. Nearly all foreign trade was ended and Confucianism was promoted. The Tokugawa shoguns were ousted from power during the Meiji *(q.v.)* Restoration.

Tokyo ⟨Tokio⟩ ⟨Edo⟩ Japan's capital city (pop. 8,543,800) and its cultural, administrative, and commercial center. Founded in the 15th cent., it became the capital of the Tokugawa shogunate (1603) as the city of Edo. During the Meiji Restoration it was made the imperial capital (1868) as Tokyo. It became an industrial center in the 19th cent. and was severely damaged (1923) in an earthquake. During WW II the city was two-thirds destroyed by Allied bombing.

Toledo Spanish city (pop. 44,000). An important city since Roman times, it was a Visigothic capital (534–712), a Moorish capital (712–1085), and capital of Castile and then of Spain (1087–1560). Under the Spanish it became a center of Christianity, the site of several church councils and seat of the Inquisition.

Toledo, Francisco de *d.* 1584. Spanish colonial administrator and viceroy of Peru (1569–81). He reorganized and stabilized the government of Peru originally set up after the Spanish conquest.

Tolkien, John Ronald Reuel 1892–1973. British author. An Oxford professor, he is best known as the author of the popular trilogy *The Lord of the Rings*.

Tolstoy, Leo 1828–1910. Russian author and philosopher, considered one of the greatest of all novelists. Born into a wealthy family, he attended college for a time and served in the army. He then married (1862) and returned to his country estate, Yasnaya Polyana, where he wrote his masterpieces, *War and Peace* and *Anna Karenina*. He experienced a religious transformation in 1876, and thereafter dedicated himself to social reform and the development of his new religion, which was a form of Christian anarchism.

Toltec Ancient people of Mexico, warriors who dominated central Mexico from *c*900 AD to the rise of the Aztecs (12th–13th cent.). Toltecs were skilled in building, metallurgy, and the arts. They are believed to have worshiped the sun and practiced human sacrifice.

Tombaugh, Clyde William 1906–. American astronomer. He discovered the planet Pluto (1930) after its existence had been predicted by P. Lowell.

Tompkins, Daniel D. 1774–1825. American statesman. He was governor of New York (1807–17) and US vice-president (1817–25) under J. Monroe.

Tone, Theobald Wolfe 1763–98. Irish nationalist leader. Tone worked for legislation to free the Irish from Britain and later joined a French military expedition (1798) to Ireland in support of a rebellion. Captured, he committed suicide.

Tong Wars Violent feuds (1850s–1920s) in US West Coast cities between Chinese immigrants belonging to associations (called tongs) that were dominated by criminal elements.

Toombs, Robert 1810–85. American statesman and Confederate general. He was US senator from Georgia (1853–61) and during the American Civil War he saw action at the second Battle of Bull Run and at Antietam.

Topeka US city (pop. 115,300), capital of Kansas. Founded in 1854 by antislavery activists, Topeka became the capital when Kansas finally became a state in 1861.

Torah Hebrew name for the Pentateuch, the first five books of the Bible. The term is also used more broadly to refer to the entire Hebrew Bible.

Tordesilles, Treaty of Treaty (June 7, 1494) between Spain and Portugal dividing between them the newly discovered lands in the Americas and the East. The treaty generally followed a papal bull, issued by Alexander VI, allotting the Americas to Spain and Africa, and Asia to Portugal. But it fixed the dividing line farther west, giving Portugal a claim to Brazil.

Torgau, Battle of Costly Prussian victory (Nov. 3, 1760) over Austria in the Seven Years' War, fought at Torgau (now in East Germany). Frederick II, leading some 44,000 Prussians, defeated some 65,000 Austrians, commanded by Marshal Count von Daun. Prussian casualties were 13,000.

Tories *See* **Loyalists**

Toronto One of Canada's two largest cities (pop. 2,803,101), capital of Ontario. Located on Lake Ontario, it is a major port. Toronto was the site of a fur-trading post and the French Fort Roille (1749). The British founded the city as York in 1793 and it was damaged in American attacks during the War of 1812. It was renamed Toronto when it was incorporated (1834). Toronto was the scene of W. MacKenzie's uprising (1837), and twice served as Canada's capital (1849–51, 1855–59).

Torquemada, Juan de 1388–1468. Spanish Franciscan monk and cardinal, an uncle of T. de Torquemada. At the Councils of Basel and Constance, he ably defended papal prerogatives against conciliarism.

Torquemada, Tomas de 1420–98. Spanish Dominican monk. An advisor to King Ferdinand and Queen Isabella, he brought about expulsion of the Jews (1492) from Spain and was named grand inquisitor (1493). In this post he promulgated rules for the Inquisition (q.v.) and, by his ruthless enforcement of them, made his name synonymous with cruelty. Some 2,000 persons were condemned while he held office.

Torres Vedras, Lines of *See* **Lines of Torres Vedras**

Torricelli, Evangelista 1608–47. Italian scientist. He was secretary to Galileo and invented the barometer.

Torstensson, Lennart 1603–51. Swedish general. His notable innovations in the use of more mobile field artillery contributed to Swedish success in the Thirty Years' War (1618–48).

Torun, Treaty of Treaty (Oct. 19, 1466) between Poland and the Teutonic Knights. By it Poland obtained the city of Torun and other territories (including Pomerania) from the order and compelled the Teutonic Knights to recognize Polish suzerainty. The treaty restored to Poland lands taken by the order in the 13th cent.

Tory Name of a once-powerful English political party. It was originally applied to Catholic King James II's supporters, who believed in the divine right and absolutist powers of the king. After the Glorious Revolution (1688), the party represented the rural gentry and generally favored a powerful monarchy, religious uniformity, and noninvolvement in foreign wars. The party was powerful under Queen Anne (reigned 1702–14) but was effectively dissolved as a party under George I, because of its ties with the Jacobites (q.v.). A new Tory party formed under the leadership of W. Pitt and remained in power from 1783 to 1830. However, the party's reactionary policies during this period, coupled with passage of the Reform Bill of 1832, resulted in the breakup of the party in the 1830s. Tory factions reemerged in the Conservative party (q.v.).

Toscanini, Arturo 1867–1957. Italian conductor. Considered one of the greatest conductors of all time, he was musical director of La Scala (1898–1907), of the New York Philharmonic (1933–36), and of the NBC Symphony (1937–54).

Tostig d. 1066. Anglo-Saxon earl of Northumbria and brother of England's King Harold II. When his brother sided with Northumbrian rebels against him, Tostig joined Norwegian king Harold III in an unsuccessful invasion of England. Tostig was killed in battle.

totalitarianism Form of authoritarian government in which the state attempts to control every aspect of the life of its citizens. The term was first used to describe the Fascist regime in Italy, the Nazi regime in Germany, and the Communist regime in the Soviet Union.

Totila ⟨Baduila⟩ d. 552. Ostrogothic king. A capable general, he overran most of Italy, briefly reconquering it from the Byzantines (550). He was killed at the Battle of Taginae.

Toulon, Siege of Siege (Aug. 28–Dec. 9, 1793) during the French Revolutionary Wars in which French republican forces succeeded in taking Toulon. Napoleon, then a young artillery officer, first gained notice there.

Toulouse-Lautrec, Henri de 1864–1901. French artist famous for paintings, lithographs, and posters of Parisian night life, such as *Le Moulin de la Galette*.

Toungoo dynasty Burmese ruling dynasty (15th–18th cent.) of a kingdom centered in southern Burma. In the 16th cent. the kingdom was greatly expanded, notably by Bayinnaung, and included all of Burma and parts of neighboring states. Toungoo power began declining after the death (1581) of Bayinnaung.

Tours, Berengar of *See* **Berengar of Tours**

Tours, Saint Gregory of *See* **Gregory of Tours, Saint**

Tours, Truce of Truce concluded on May 28, 1444, between the English and French forces in the Hundred Years' War (1337–1453). It lasted until 1449.

Toussaint L'Ouverture, François Dominique c1744–1803. Haitian revolutionary leader. As the leader of a band of Negro rebels, he sided with the French (c1794) and drove out the British and Spaniards. He fell afoul (1801) of Napoleon, however, when he sought greater independence from France.

Tower of Babel Legendary tower. In the Bible, Noah's descendents attempted to build a tower to heaven. But God caused them to suddenly speak different languages, making them unable to understand each other and complete the tower. Thus it was an early explanation for the diversity of language.

Tower of London Historic British fortress located on the Thames River in London. William the Conqueror was said to have begun fortification of the site (c1066). Construction of the central tower, made of white limestone, was begun (c1078). In succeeding centuries, successive encircling walls were added and the fortress was used variously as a royal palace, a jail, and an arsenal. It was notorious as the place where such historic figures as A. Boleyn, Sir W. Raleigh, and Lady Jane Grey were imprisoned or executed.

Townshend, Charles 1725–67. British chancellor of the Exchequer. A brilliant but unstable politician, he secured passage of the Townshend Acts (q.v.).

Townshend, Charles Townshend, 2d Viscount 1674–1738. English statesman. He was a participant in Whig governments with his brother-in-law, R. Walpole. His major achievement was the conduct of British foreign policy between 1721 and 1730.

Townshend Acts British colonial laws (1767) replacing the Stamp Act. The British Parliament passed these four laws (June 15–July 2, 1767), which were designed to reassert its authority over rebellious American colonists. Named for C. Townshend, British chancellor of the Exchequer, the acts fixed import taxes on glass, lead, paints, papers, and tea; authorized searches to guarantee compliance; and suspended the New York Assembly's powers until that colony complied with the 1765 Quartering Act. These laws stiffened Colonial resistance, and were repealed (1770), except for the tax on tea. This last provision led to the Boston Tea Party (q.v.).

Towton, Battle of Yorkist victory (Mar. 29, 1461) in the English Wars of the Roses (1455–85). Yorkist and Lancastrian forces numbered about 20,000 each and the battle was fought in a blinding snowstorm. The Yorkists gained the upper hand, massacred the Lancastrians and forced King Henry VI to flee England. Yorkist king Edward IV then took the throne.

Toynbee, Arnold 1852–83. English economist and sociologist, noted for pioneering settlement work and his economic history, *The Industrial Revolution in England.*

Toynbee, Arnold Joseph 1889–1975. English historian. He produced a notable theory of the rise and fall of civilizations based on the idea of cultural responses to challenges, in the 12-volume *A Study of History.*

Toyotomi Hideyoshi *See* **Hideyoshi**

trade unions *See* **labor unions**

Trafalgar, Battle of Naval battle (Oct. 21, 1805) between Britain and France, fought during the Napoleonic Wars, off Cape Trafalgar, Spain. It established British naval superiority for the rest of the century and ended Napoleon's plans to invade England. Twenty-seven British ships under Admiral H. Nelson defeated a fleet of 33 French and Spanish ships commanded by P. de Villeneuve. The French lost 20 ships, the British none. But Nelson was killed by a French sniper.

Trail of Tears *See* **Cherokee Indians**

Trajan AD c53–117. Roman emperor (AD 98–117), successor to Nerva. Born in Spain, he was the first non-Italian emperor. He conquered Dacia and much of Parthia in the east. He encouraged building and constructed Trajan's Forum in Rome and Trajan's bridge, the first bridge across the Danube.

Tranquillus, Gaius Suetonius *See* **Suetonius**

Transcendentalism New England literary and philosophical movement (c1835–55). Transcendentalists such as R. Emerson and H. Thoreau believed in the goodness and divinity of man and nature. Their beliefs were marked by an emphasis on individuality and opposition to authority.

Transcontinental Treaty (Adams-Onis Treaty) Treaty between Spain and the US, signed on Feb. 22, 1819. Spain gave up claims to Florida and the Oregon Country in return for US recognition of her sovereignty over Texas.

Transvaal Former independent state and now a South African province, which has the world's richest goldfield. Boers from the Cape Colony began settling there after the Great Trek (q.v.) in the 1830s, gaining independence in 1852. They successfully rebelled against the British annexation (1877), but became outnumbered by foreigners (uitlanders) after the discovery of gold in 1886. During the Boer War (1899–1902) the Transvaal was annexed (1900) by Britain, and it became a province of the Union of South Africa in 1909.

Transylvania Historic region of northwestern and central Romania. Once part of the Roman province of Dacia, it was conquered by Germanic tribes and became part of Hungary under Stephen I (1003). Control of the region was contested between Austria and the Ottoman Empire (15th–18th cents.), though it enjoyed nearly independent status in the 17th cent. Austria finally gained complete control in 1711 and by 1867 it had become part of Hungary. Romanian inhabitants, however, were dissatisfied with Magyar domination and supported the seizure (1918) of Transylvania by Romania. By the Treaty of Trianon (1920), Hungary ceded the territory to Romania.

Trasimene, Battle of Carthaginian victory (217 BC) over the Romans in the Second Punic War, near Lake Trasimene in central Italy. The Carthaginian general Hannibal ambushed and totally destroyed a Roman army led by C. Flaminius, who was killed.

Travis, William Barrett 1811–36. Texas revolutionary hero. He commanded the Texas rebels at the Alamo *(q.v.)* and died in battle there.

Treaty of *See under names inverted, as in* **Paris, Treaty of**

treaty ports Ports specifically designated by treaty as open to trade with foreign nations. In the 19th cent. both China and Japan resisted trade with the West as a matter of policy. To force a change in that policy, Britain precipitated the Opium War *(q.v.)* and, by the resulting Treaty of Nanking (1842), won trading rights in five Chinese treaty ports. In Japan, Commodore M. Perry used the presence of his US naval fleet (1854) to pressure the Japanese into opening their ports to foreign trade, and soon after treaty ports were established there. Other nations followed and eventually there were over 60 treaty ports in China and six in Japan. The system was abolished (1899) in Japan and (1946) in China.

Trebizond, Empire of Kingdom on the south shore of the Black Sea. After the overthrow of the Byzantine Empire (1204) by the Crusaders, two grandsons of Emperor Andronicus I Comnenus founded this successor state in what is now northeastern Turkey. Located on trade routes with the East, it prospered until taken over by the Ottoman Turks in 1461.

Treitschke, Heinrich von 1834–96. German historian. A passionate advocate of German nationalism and power, he expounded his ideas in a major work, *History of Germany in the Nineteenth Century.*

Tremblay, Françoise Leclerc du *See* **Joseph, Father**

Trent, Council of Important council of the Roman Catholic Church (19th ecumenical), held in three sessions (1545–47, 1551–52, 1562–63) under two popes, Paul III and Pius IV. It met in response to the Protestant Reformation, and all doctrinal disputes raised by Protestants were answered. The council's far-reaching results were published in the *Catechism of the Council of Trent* (1566) and included reforms and definitions concerning the sacraments, the Scriptures, church dogma, duties of the clergy, and other subjects. The council marked the beginning of the Catholic Reformation *(q.v.).*

Trent Affair A diplomatic incident during the American Civil War. During the US blockade of the South, the US vessel *San Jacinto*, commanded by Capt. C. Wilkes, seized (Nov. 8, 1861) the British mail steamer *Trent* on the open sea and re-

moved two Confederate commissioners. At the demand of the British, they were released and an international incident was averted.

Trenton US city (pop. 92,100), capital of New Jersey, and a manufacturing and transportation center. First settled by Quakers in 1679, it was a battle site during the American Revolution. It became state capital in 1790.

Trenton and **Princeton, battles of** American Revolutionary War battles, G. Washington's first victories against the British forces of lords Howe and Cornwallis. Washington made his famous crossing of the Delaware River (Dec. 25, 1776) and captured Trenton by taking 918 Hessians prisoner in a surprise attack. He then eluded some 7,000 British soldiers sent to Trenton and routed a British column near Princeton (Jan. 2, 1977) before moving into winter quarters at Morristown.

Trevelyan, George Macaulay 1876–1962. English historian. He was a champion of "literary" historical writing. His works include *History of England* and *English Social History.*

Trianon, Treaty of Treaty signed at Versailles (June 4, 1920) between the victorious WW I Allies and the new state of Hungary that was created out of Austria-Hungary. The new nation ceded territory to Romania (Transylvania and part of Banat), Czechoslovakia (Slovakia and Ruthenia), and the Kingdom of Serbs, Croats, and Slovenes (Croatia, Slavonia, and part of Banat). Its army was also reduced to 35,000.

Tribonian *d.* 545? Roman jurist. He headed the commissions that produced the great compilation of Roman law, the Corpus Juris Civilis *(q.v.)* issued by Emperor Justinian.

tribune Ancient Roman government official. Originally military officers, tribunes by the 5th cent. BC had assumed governmental functions, notably as protectors of the rights of the plebeians. Tribunes were elected by the plebs, were usually 10 in number, and gradually gained control (by their veto power) over the Roman Senate. They had relatively little power during the Roman Empire.

Trident Conference ⟨Anglo-American Conference⟩ Secret wartime conference of WW II in Washington, D.C. (May 12–25, 1943). President F. Roosevelt, Prime Minister W. Churchill, and their combined chiefs of staff planned the opening of a second front in Europe (Normandy invasion).

Trier West German city (pop. 103,400). One of the oldest cities in Germany, it was founded by the Romans in 15 BC and was a Roman provincial capital. During the Middle Ages, its archbishops became the rulers and from the 12th cent. were also electors of the Holy Roman Empire. Trier was incorporated into Prussia in 1815.

Trieste, Free Territory of *See* **Free Territory of Trieste**

Trilling, Lionel 1905–75. American literary critic and essayist. A Columbia University professor, he was noted for his writings on the American liberal tradition (*The Liberal Imagination* and *Middle of the Journey*), as well as for his literary studies.

Trinidad and **Tobago** Independent state composed of two tropical islands off the coast of Venezuela. Capital is Port of Spain. Trinidad was discovered by Columbus (1498), was under British rule from 1803, and was combined with British-ruled Tobago in 1888. It won independence Aug. 31, 1962 and became a republic in 1976. Its prime minister since 1956 has been Eric E. Williams (1911–   ).

Trinity Fundamental Christian doctrine about the nature of God. As defined by several early church councils, God has a single divine essence that subsists in three divine persons: the Father, the Son, and the Holy Ghost.

Tripartite Pact *See* **Axis Powers**

Triple Alliance **1.** Alliance formed (1668) by England, The Netherlands, and Sweden to oppose French aggression during the reign of French king Louis XIV. The alliance was short-lived, as Louis soon secured an agreement (Treaty of Dover) with England. **2.** Alliance formed (1717) by France, Great Britain, and The Netherlands, primarily to oppose Spain and secure the provisions of the Peace of Utrecht. In 1718 the alliance was joined by Austria, and thus became the Quadruple Alliance (*q.v.*). **3.** Alliance formed in the late 19th and early 20th cents. by Germany, Austria-Hungary, and Italy. It was opposed by the Triple Entente. In the late 19th cent. O. von Bismarck sought to strengthen Germany's position against France, following the Franco-Prussian War (1870–71). In 1879, Bismarck secured the defensive Dual Alliance with Austria-Hungary. In 1882, Italy agreed to a defensive alliance with Germany, thus forming the Triple Alliance. The formation of this alliance led first to a series of informal agreements designed to offset the power of the Triple Alliance. By 1891, France had established an informal understanding with Russia. This developed (1893) into a military agreement, which was made public in 1895. In 1898 Théophile Delcassé (1852–1923) became French foreign minister. His policies led to an understanding between France and Great Britain (1904) known as the Entente Cordiale. In 1907 the Anglo-Russian Entente established the set of agreements that completed the Triple En-

tente. The two power blocs—Triple Alliance and Triple Entente—continued to dominate European politics up to the eve of WW I. At that point, Italy was in conflict with Austria-Hungary over the Balkans and refused to enter the war on the side of Germany and Austria-Hungary. This effectively ended the alliance and in 1915, Italy joined the Allies in WW I.

Triple Alliance, War of the War (1865–70) between Paraguay and an alliance formed by Argentina, Brazil, and Uruguay. The war, sparked in part by conflicting interests of Argentina, Brazil, and Paraguay over influence in Uruguay, led to the virtual destruction of Paraguay, the death of a large portion of its population, and loss of much of its territory to Brazil. In 1864–65, Brazil helped establish Venancio Flores (1809–68), a leader of the Colorado faction, as Uruguayan president. Paraguayan president F. López, a supporter of the rival Blanco faction in Uruguay, then declared war on Brazil. He also declared war on Argentina, after it refused to allow Paraguayan forces passage through its territory. Uruguay then joined the alliance with Brazil and Argentina against Paraguay. After initial successes, López withdrew his forces, vastly outnumbered by the Alliance, to Paraguayan territory. By Jan., 1866, the tide had turned against López and, though Paraguayans offered fierce resistance in following years, the Alliance slowly closed in on them. Asunción, the capital, fell in Jan., 1869, and López was captured and executed (Mar. 1, 1870).

Triple Entente *See* **Triple Alliance** (3)

Tripoli Capital of Libya (pop. 551,500). Founded (*c*7th cent. BC) by Phoenicians as Oea, it became one of the three major cities of the region called Tripolitania. Captured by the Romans (1st cent. BC), Tripoli was conquered by various peoples after the 5th cent. AD and was in Muslim hands from the 7th cent. It was a noted haven for pirates during this time and the US fought the Tripolitan War (*q.v.*) to suppress them. Tripoli passed to Italy after the Italo-Turkish War (*q.v.*) and later became capital of Libya.

Tripolitania *See* **Roman Province of Africa**

Tripolitan War Confrontation between the US and the Barbary States (1801–05) resulting from the US refusal to increase payments of tribute to the pasha of Tripoli for his protection from pirate raids. The US blockade of Tripoli (from 1801) was generally unsuccessful against the pirates, and subsequent attempts to negotiate failed. In 1803, the US warship *Philadelphia* was captured by Tripoli and S. Decatur led a famous raiding party that destroyed the ship in the harbor (Feb., 1804). Fighting continued but was unsuccessful until the

US organized a land invasion force against Tripoli in 1805. The Tripolitans agreed to a treaty (June 4, 1805) even before the force, under W. Eaton, reached Tripoli. The agreement ended US payments of tribute but acts of piracy continued in subsequent years.

Tripolitan War *See* **Italo-Turkish War**

Triptolemus In Greek mythology, the inventor of the plow and the teacher of agriculture to the human race. A favorite of the goddess Demeter, from whom he learned, he was symbolized by an ear of wheat.

Trist, Nicholas Philip 1800–74. American diplomat, sent to negotiate an end to the Mexican War. He disregarded orders recalling him and went on to conclude the Treaty of Guadalupe Hidalgo (*q.v.*).

Triton Greek mythological sea creature. Originally a gigantic son of Poseidon, Tritons were later represented as minor gods that were half fish, half man.

triumvirate In ancient Rome, a board of three government officials appointed to carry out a specified task. The term was applied to the alliance (not legally sanctioned by the government) between Caesar, Pompey, and Crassus (formed 60 BC). This was the First Triumvirate. The Second Triumvirate (legally sanctioned) consisted of Octavian (later Augustus), Antony, and Lepidus, and resulted in reforms that gave the triumvirs dictatorial powers. It was organized in 43 BC.

Trojan War Legendary war between the Greeks, led by Agamemnon, and the city of Troy, defended by Hector and others. It is believed to have had its roots in a real conflict that took place c1200 BC. The mythical battle began when the Trojan prince Paris kidnapped Helen, wife of King Menelaus of Sparta. For ten years the Trojans and the invading Greeks fought many heroic but inconclusive battles. Finally the Greeks built a large wooden horse, ostensibly a gift for the Trojans. A number of Greek warriors hid inside it and the Greeks embarked their ships, pretending to sail home. The Trojans wheeled the horse inside the city and that night the warriors opened the gates of Troy for their fellow Greeks, who then conquered the city. The war inspired many poems and stories, most notably Homer's *Iliad* and *Odyssey* (*q.v.*).

Trollope, Anthony 1815–82. Noted English Victorian novelist. A chronicler of the ordinary lives of provincial people, he is famous for his series of novels about the fictional county of Barsetshire. Among these novels were *The Warden* and *Barchester Towers.*

Tromp, Maarten Harpertszoon 1597–1653. Dutch admiral. Given supreme command of the Dutch Navy, he decisively defeated the Spanish in battle (1639) in the English channel. He was killed in the Dutch War (1652–54) with the English.

Troppau, Congress of *See* **Congress of Troppau**

Trotsky, Leon ⟨*pseud. of* Bronstein, Lev Davidovich⟩ 1879–1940. Russian Communist leader. He was a chief theorist, a leader in both the 1905 and 1917 revolutions, and N. Lenin's commissar for foreign affairs. In the latter capacity he arranged the Treaty of Brest-Litovsk with Germany. He next became war commissar, rebuilding the Russian army. Trotsky and his arch-rival, J. Stalin, struggled for power after Lenin's death (1924). Stalin eventually stripped Trotsky of his influence and expelled him from Russia in 1929. Trotsky spent the rest of his life in exile, writing and preaching revolution. Stalin is believed to have masterminded his assassination in Mexico City.

Trotskyism Doctrine of a "permanent revolution" on a worldwide scale advocated by Russian Communist leader L. Trotsky. This doctrine, along with Trotsky's advocacy of a greater role for the working class led to his struggle with J. Stalin, who advocated "socialism in one country." Trotsky was ultimately exiled from Russia and assassinated.

troubadours Medieval lyric poets who composed in the dialect of Provence, *langue d'oc*, in southern France. They flourished between the 11th and the 13th cents. and greatly influenced subsequent European literature.

trouvere Medieval lyric poets and musicians who composed in the *langue d'oc*, the language of northern France and of the French court centered around Paris. They began writing in imitation of the troubadours, and flourished in the 12th and 13th cents.

Troy Ancient city located along the Hellespont in what is now Asian Turkey. Made famous by the legendary Trojan War (*q.v.*), Troy flourished (3d–2d millennium BC) as the center of Troas. Archaeological evidence indicates it was abandoned from 1100 to 700 BC (after the war). New cities were later built on the site until Roman times. The site was identified as the actual location of the legendary Troy by H. Schliemann, who began archaeological digs there in 1870.

Troyes, Chrétien de *See* **Chrétien de Troyes**

Troyes, Treaty of Treaty (May 21, 1420) between England and France, an attempt to settle the Hundred Years' War (1337–1453). English king Henry V was to marry the daughter of Charles VI and thereby become successor to the French throne. But the disinherited French dauphin (later Charles VII) resisted the settlement with the aid of Joan of Arc.

Truce of *See under names inverted, as in Altmark, Truce of*

Trucial Coast *See* **United Arab Emirates**

Trucial Oman *See* **United Arab Emirates**

Trucial States *See* **United Arab Emirates**

Trudeau, Pierre Elliot 1919–. French Canadian Liberal party leader and prime minister (almost continuously since 1968). He has been noted for his championship of liberal domestic programs and for a more independent foreign policy. His administration has been marked in recent years by the rise of French separatism and ongoing attempts at constitutional reform.

Truffaut, François 1932–. French film director and critic. He directed such films as *The 400 Blows* and *Jules and Jim*, considered typical examples of the "new wave" films.

Trujillo Molina, Rafeal Leonidas 1891–1961. General and dictator of the Dominican Republic (1930–61). His rule was marked by ruthless suppression of opposition, which ultimately led to his assassination.

Truman, Harry S. 1884–1972. Thirty-third US president (1945–53), successor to F. Roosevelt. A US senator from Missouri (1935–45), he gained national attention as chairman of a Senate committee investigating defense expenditures. He was elected vice-president under Roosevelt in 1944 and became president on Roosevelt's death (Apr. 12, 1945). Truman participated in the Potsdam Conference *(q.v.)* and ended WW II by ordering the first use of the atomic bombs, dropped on Hiroshima and Nagasaki. Truman's postwar foreign policy was marked by rapidly deteriorating relations with Russia, leading to the Cold War *(q.v.)*. He countered Soviet postwar expansion by issuing the Truman Doctrine *(q.v.)*, which was intended to contain Communism. It was implemented by the Marshall Plan *(q.v.)*, the Point Four Program *(q.v.)*, and establishment of NATO *(q.v.)*. The Berlin blockade and airlift *(q.v.)* of 1948–49 began during this period. At home, much of his domestic legislation was blocked by Congress, which passed the Taft-Hartley Labor Act (1947) over Truman's veto. Truman received the 1948 Democratic presidential nomination and conducted an energetic whistle-stop campaign. He won the election and outwitted the pollsters who predicted that Republican candidate T. Dewey would become president. His second term was marked by continued Congressional resistance to proposed legislation of his Fair Deal *(q.v.)* program and the outbreak of the Korean War *(q.v.)*. During the conflict he aroused a national controversy by dismissing Gen. D. MacArthur from command for insubordination (1951). Truman did not seek reelection in 1952, but supported the candidacy of A. Stevenson.

Truman Doctrine US foreign-policy decision, embodied in a message of President H. Truman of Mar. 12, 1947, calling for military aid to Greece and Turkey to fight Communist rebellions. It signaled US determination to "contain" the further expansion of communism.

Trumbull, John 1756–1843. Early American painter, noted for his Revolutionary War scenes.

Trumbull, Jonathan 1710–85. American patriot. He became governor of Connecticut (1769–84) and during the Revolutionary War supplied G. Washington with war materials and other services.

trust Form of business combine or corporation established to create a monopoly over a particular business or industry. Trusts rose to positions of great power in the US during the late 19th cent. Among the greatest were the oil, steel, sugar, and meat-packing trusts. Their activities led to passage of the Sherman Anti-Trust Act *(q.v.)* of 1890 and they were vigorously prosecuted during the presidency of T. Roosevelt.

trusteeship Method of governing territories. It was established in 1946 by the UN to replace the former League of Nations mandates *(q.v.)*. By the mid-1970s, nearly all the UN trusteeship territories had become independent nations and UN members.

Truth, Sojourner c1797–1883. Former slave and evangelist. Freed in 1827, she embarked on a notable career as a traveling speaker for the Christian Gospels, abolition, and women's rights.

Tryon, William 1729–88. British Colonial governor. As governor of North Carolina, he suppressed the Regulator Movement *(q.v.)*. As Governor of New York during the Revolutionary War period, he was at first forced to govern from a British warship.

Ts'ao Ts'ao AD 155–220. Chinese general. He held real power during the last years of the last Han emperor, Hsien Ti, and set up the new Wei dynasty in 220.

Tseng Kuo-fan 1811–72. Chinese general and government administrator under the Ch'ing dynasty. Tseng was successful in suppressing the Taiping Rebellion and conciliating the Western powers. He gave the declining Chinese imperial government a new lease on life.

Tshombe, Moise Kapenda 1919–69. Congolese leader. Tshombe led Katanga in secession (1960–63) from the newly independent Congo Republic, was said to be implicated in the murder of P. Lumumba, and was finally exiled (1963). He returned to become premier (1964–65) of a reunited Congo

Republic, but soon after was accused of treason and fled.

Tsin *See* **Chin**

Tsong-kha-pa *See* **Tibetan Buddhism**

Tsu Hsi *See* **Tz'u Hsi**

Tubman, Harriet c1820–1913. American abolitionist. An escaped slave, she was a principal figure in the Underground Railroad. She aided the Union army during the Civil War.

Tubman, William Vacanarat Shadrach 1895–1971. Liberian president (1943–71). A descendant of freed American slaves, he filled various governmental posts before becoming president. His long tenure was marked by economic progress and social reforms, including granting to women and native Liberians the right to vote.

Tudor Dynasty of English rulers (reigned 1485–1603). The family was of Welsh origins. Its rise to power began with Owen Tudor (d. 1461), who fought in the service of Henry V, wed Henry's widow (Catherine of Valois), and supported his Lancastrian stepson, Henry VI, in the Wars of the Roses (q.v.). Owen Tudor's grandson (Henry Tudor) became Henry VII after the Lancastrian victory at Bosworth Field (1485) and thus founded the Tudor dynasty. The subsequent Tudor reign saw the rise of England as a naval power, creation of the Church of England, and increased powers of the monarchy. The Tudor sovereigns were:

Henry VII	1485–1509
Henry VIII	1509–47
Edward VI	1547–53
Mary	1553–58
Elizabeth I	1558–1603

Tu Fu 712–770. Chinese poet. Sometimes considered the greatest of all Chinese poets, he wrote pessimistic lyrics attacking court luxury and deploring hardships of the poor.

Tuileries Palace, Storming of the Assault on the French royal palace in Paris (Aug. 10, 1792) during the French Revolution. The attack led to a massacre of the Swiss guards. French king Louis XVI was suspended from all authority by the Legislative Assembly.

Tully *See* **Cicero, Marcus Tullius**

Tulunid dynasty *See* **Egypt** (868)

T'ung Chih 1856–75. Chinese emperor (1862–75) of the Ch'ing dynasty. Most of his reign was spent under the regency of his mother, Tz'ŭ-Hsi. It was a period in which relations with the West were expanded, the Taiping Rebellion was suppressed, and the imperial treasury was restored. T'ung Chih died two years after taking full control of the government.

Tunis Capital (pop. 1,000,000) of Tunisia. Located near ancient Carthage, it was founded in Carthaginian times and rose to prominence under the Muslims (7th cent. AD). It became the capital of Tunisia (9th cent.) and was a commercial center (13th–16th cents.) The Ottoman Turks controlled it from the 16th cent. to the 19th, when the French took control. It was the scene of heavy fighting (1942–43) in WW II.

Tunisia Republic located in northwestern Africa. Capital is Tunis. Once part of Carthage (6th cent. BC), it was conquered (2d cent. BC) by the Romans, then was taken by the Vandals (5th cent. AD), Byzantines (6th cent.), and the Muslims (7th cent.). It thrived under Muslim influence and fell (late 16th cent.) to the Ottoman Turks. Under the rule of Ottoman governors, or beys, Tunisia gained virtual independence within the Ottoman Empire, and became a center for piracy in the 18th and early 19th cents. A French expedition to Tunisia led to establishment (1881) of a French protectorate. During WW II, Tunisia was occupied by German and Italian forces and was the site (1943) of fierce fighting between Allied and Axis armies. Tunisia became independent in 1956. H. Bourguiba became its first prime minister and first president (1957–), when Tunisia became a republic. Bourguiba followed a policy of modernization and agrarian reform and supported a negotiated end to the Middle East crisis between Israel and the Arab nations. During the 1970s his rule was marked by political unrest and by conflict (1980) with Libya.

Tupac Amaru 1742?–81. Peruvian Indian revolutionary. Taking the name of an ancestral Inca leader, he led Peruvian Indians in a revolt (1780–81) to improve their lot. He was captured and executed.

Tupper, Sir Charles 1821–1915. Canadian statesman. As premier of Nova Scotia (1864–67), he helped bring that province into the Dominion. He was instrumental in building the Canadian Pacific Railway and was briefly the federal prime minister (1896).

Turckheim, Battle of French victory (Jan. 5, 1675) over the Austrians in the second Dutch War. French marshal H. Turenne led his forces on a winter march across the Vosges, surprised and routed the Austrians under Count Montecuccoli in the Alsace region. France recovered Alsace by this one battle.

Turenne, Henri de la Tour d'Auvergne, vicomte de 1611–75. Great French military leader. Turenne was created a marshal for his brilliant service in the Thirty Years' War. Though he sided unsuccessfully with Louis II de Bourbon, Prince de Condé in the Fronde of the Parlement (q.v.), Turenne rejoined the government and defeated the

Condé in the Fronde of the Princes *(q.v.)*. He also conducted notable campaigns in the Dutch War (1672–78). He was killed in battle.

Turgenev, Ivan Sergeyevich 1818–83. Russian novelist. Turgenev chronicled the plight of the serfs in *A Sportsman's Sketches* and the conflict with the new, emancipated, nihilistic generation of Russian intelligentsia in *Fathers and Sons*.

Turgot, Anne Robert Jacques 1727–81. French economist and statesman. A Physiocrat *(q.v.)*, he was controller of finance (1774–76) and attempted by drastic reforms to restore the royal treasury. He was opposed by Queen Marie Antoinette, however, and his ouster continued the financial crisis that contributed to the outbreak of the French Revolution.

Turkestan *See* **Turkistan**

Turkey ⟨Republic of Turkey⟩ Republic located in southwestern Asia. Its capital is Ankara. The modern state of Turkey was created by the Treaty of Sèvres (1920), which formally dismantled the Ottoman Empire after WW I. A republic was established (1923) by the Nationalists led by Mustafa Kemal (Kemal Atatürk). Atatürk, as the country's first president, embarked on a program of democratization and industrialization that profoundly changed Turkish life and institutions. For history of the region prior to 1920, *see* Ottoman Empire. Key dates in the history of Turkey include:

1920 Nationalist party, under Mustafa Kemal (later known as Kemal Atatürk), established national government at Ankara (Apr.), in defiance of both the victorious Allied powers and the Turkish Sultan Muhammad VI.

1920 Treaty of Sèvres (Aug. 10) between Allies and Turkish sultan; dismembered the Ottoman Empire and established successor state (Turkey) in northern Anatolia; treaty opposed by Nationalists.

1921 Atatürk and Nationalists entered into treaty of friendship with Soviet Union; continued to resist foreign encroachment in Turkey.

1921–22 Greco-Turkish War fought with Greece after Greek invasion of Anatolia; Atatürk drove the Greeks from Anatolia.

1923 Republican People's party founded by Atatürk; sole Turkish party until 1950.

1922 Turkish sultan deposed (Nov. 1) by Nationalist government; his brother assumed the caliphate, but the sultanate ceased to exist.

1923 Turkish republic proclaimed (Oct. 29); new constitution instituted and Atatürk made first president; government abolished caliphate (1924) and eliminated state support for Islam.

1923 Treaty of Lausanne negotiated with Allies; established borders of modern Turkey, except for contested territory of Alexandretta; Turkey agreed to demilitarization of Dardanelles strait.

1923–38 Atatürk served as president; led successful program of Westernization and industrialization of Turkey; introduced democratic reforms but held great personal power.

1932 Turkey admitted to League of Nations.

1934 Turkey entered Balkan Entente with Greece, Yugoslavia, and Romania.

1936 Montreux Convention signed; military control of the Dardanelles returned to Turkey.

1938–50 Ismet Inönü served as president, following the death of Atatürk; maintained policy of neutrality through most of WW II.

1939 Territory of Alexandretta ceded to Turkey by France.

1945 Turkey declared war (Feb. 23) on Germany and Japan at end of WW II.

1945 Russia renounced friendship treaty with Turkey (Mar.); demanded cession of Kars and Ardelan (in eastern Turkey) and joint military control of Dardanelles; relations between the two countries broken following Turkish refusal.

1945 Turkey became (June 26) a founding member of the UN.

1947 US granted (Mar. 24) military and economic aid to Turkey under Truman Doctrine.

1950 Democratic party victorious in national elections (May 22); Celal Bayar succeeded Inönü as president; Adnan Menderes made prime minister.

1952 Turkey entered NATO.

1960 Increasing economic problems and rising unrest in the 1950s led to passage of increasingly repressive laws; antigovernment demonstrations (Apr.) broke out and a military coup led by Gen. Cemal Gürsel overthrew government (May); Bayar, Menderes and others arrested; Menderes subsequently executed.

1961 New constitution formulated; Gürsel elected president (Oct.); Ismet Inönü made prime minister.

1962 Unsuccessful attempt (Feb.) by military officers to overthrow government.

1965–71 Süleyman Demirel served as prime minister; unable to solve country's growing problems.

1966 Cevdet Sunay became president following death of Cemal Gürsel.

1974 Bülent Ecevit in office as prime minister.

1974 Turkish forces invaded Cyprus (July 20–22) to protect Turkish Cypriots; invasion came after Cypriot leader Archbishop Makarios was ousted by a pro-Greek military coup.

1975 Süleyman Demirel returned to office as prime minister.

1978 Martial law declared (Dec.) in 13 provinces to counter unrest by Muslim sects.

1980 Military coup (Sept. 11) overthrew elected government in wake of growing unrest over economic problems; Gen. Kenan Evren in power; constitution suspended and assembly dissolved.

1981 Government dissolved political parties.

Turkistan ⟨Turkestan⟩ Central Asian region between China, Siberia, and the Caspian Sea. Home of predominantly Turkic peoples, and once dominated by the Mongols, much of it was conquered by the Russians in the 19th cent. It is divided today between the USSR (Western Turkistan) and China (Eastern Turkistan).

Turkmanchay, Treaty of Treaty (Feb. 22, 1828), between Russia and Persia, ending war with Persia (1826–28). Persia had to cede much of Persian Armenia to Russia and grant the latter extensive commercial and extraterritorial rights.

Turks Branch of the Central Asian Turkic people that migrated to the Middle East and Asia Minor between the 11th and the 13th cents. The first wave of Turkish migration was the Seljuks *(q.v.)*, who by 1092 controlled Iran, Mesopotamia, Syria, and Palestine. Beginning from a base in the Seljuk sultanate of Rum, the Osmanli Turks began from the 13th cent. to build what became the Ottoman Empire. This later became the basis of modern Turkey.

Turner, Frederick Jackson 1861–1932. American historian. He virtually founded a school of American historical thought with his theory concerning the effect of the Western frontier on American society and government.

Turner, Joseph Mallord William 1775–1851. British artist. Considered the foremost English landscape and seascape painter, Turner was a Romantic whose works anticipated the impressionists.

Turner, Nat 1800–31. American slave leader. Believing he was called by God to emancipate America's black slaves, he led a rebellion by 60 slaves during Aug., 1831, that terrorized rural Virginia and cost the lives of 51 whites. Turner was captured and executed soon after the revolt broke out, but his revolt gave rise to repressive laws for controlling slaves.

Turpin, Richard 1706–39. English robber whose career as a horse thief and highwayman was much romanticized.

Tuscany Italian province and historic region located in central Italy. It is centered on what was once the ancient Etruscan kingdom of Etruria and was a center of Italian culture in medieval Renaissance times. Florence and Pisa are among its notable cities.

Tutankhamen ⟨Tutenkhamon⟩ *d. c*1352 BC. Egyptian pharaoh (*c*1361–52). He restored the traditional god Amon to prominence after the religious revolution of Ikhnaton. His world-famous tomb was discovered in 1922.

Tutenkhamon *See* **Tutankhamen**

Twain, Mark ⟨*pseud. of* Clemens, Samuel Langhorne⟩ 1835–1910. Noted American author who wrote the classics *The Adventures of Tom Sawyer* and *The Adventures of Huckleberry Finn.*

Tweed, William Marcy 1823–78. American politician and New York City "boss." Gaining control of Democratic party patronage, Tweed and his associates (Tweed Ring) made fortunes through their manipulation of city expenditures.

Tweed Ring Conspiracy of politicians, led by W. Tweed, who defrauded New York City of up to $30 million between 1856 and 1872. They controlled city and even some state offices through the Democratic party's Tammany *(q.v.)* machine. In 1871 they were exposed by *The New York Times* and a reform slate was elected to replace them.

Twelve Conclusions *See* **Lollardry**

Twelve Tables *See* **Rome** (450 BC)

Twelve Tribes of Israel In the Bible, the Hebrew tribes that settled in the Promised Land after the Exodus. The tribes were named after Jacob's offspring. Ten were named after his sons, Reuben, Simeon, Judah, Issachar, Zebulun, Gad, Asher, Dan, Naphtali, and Benjamin. Two were named after his grandsons Ephraim and Manasseh. (*See also* Lost Tribes of Israel.)

Twenty-one Demands List of demands presented to China by Japan (Jan., 1915) and backed by threat of invasion. China submitted May 25. The 21 demands included access to China's harbors and islands, control of mineral deposits, the right to colonize Manchuria and Mongolia, and the territorial exclusion of other world powers. China refused, however, to allow Japan to regulate its military, financial, and trade affairs, as was also demanded.

26th of July Movement Rebel movement organized by F. Castro that overthrew (Jan. 1, 1959) the dictatorship of F. Batista during the Cuban Revolution *(q.v.)*. It began with Castro's abortive attack (July 26, 1953) with 150 rebels on the Santiago army barracks. Imprisoned after the raid (1953–55), Castro organized a new rebel force in

Mexico. He landed in southwestern Cuba (Dec. 2, 1956) with 82 men and was quickly put to flight by government troops. However, he and 11 others managed to establish a base in the Sierra Maestra mountains. With E. Guevara, Castro mounted a guerrilla campaign against Batista that was increasingly successful in the following years. Rebel gains and the withdrawal of US aid to Cuba (1958) finally forced Batista to flee Cuba in 1959.

Two Sicilies, Kingdom of the Name of the kingdoms of Sicily and Naples, which included all of southern Italy below the Papal States and which were variously ruled separately and jointly from the 11th to 19th cents. The Kingdom of Two Sicilies was founded by the Normans, who conquered Sicily and the southern Italian Peninsula (Kingdom of Naples) from the Byzantines, Muslims, and Lombards. The territory passed to the Hohenstaufen Holy Roman emperors (12th cent.). Under them southern Italy became a prosperous commercial center from which Greek and Arab culture spread to Europe. The French nobleman Charles of Anjou conquered Sicily and the Kingdom of Naples (1266) after the Hohenstaufen line died out, but he was driven out of Sicily (1282) after the Revolt of the Sicilian Vespers (q.v.). The Spanish House of Aragon then took control of Sicily (1302), while the Kingdom of Naples remained in the hands of the French Angevin line. A long series of wars between Sicily and Naples ensued, with the Spanish Aragonese finally winning both kingdoms in 1442.

Spanish rule was broken by the War of the Spanish Succession (1701–14) and the brief rule of the Austrian Hapsburgs. By 1735, however, the Spanish Bourbons were again in firm control of both Sicily and Naples. Napoleon gained Italy at the end of the 18th cent. Spanish rule was restored in 1815, and from 1816 the Kingdoms of Sicily and Naples were ruled jointly as the Kingdom of the Two Sicilies. The spread of liberalism and nationalism in the post-Napoleonic period gave rise to revolts by the Carbonari (q.v.) and the movement for unification of Italy. The Kingdom of the Two Sicilies was finally conquered (1860) by the Italian nationalist, G. Garibaldi, and was joined with northern states to form the Kingdom of Italy (1861).

Tyche Greek goddess of chance. She was identified with the Roman Fortuna, and was believed to insure prosperity and good fortune.

Tydings-McDuffie Act US legislation (Mar. 4, 1934) that created a Commonwealth of the Philippines. The Commonwealth (effective July 4, 1936) was to last for ten years. The US continued to control Philippine defense, foreign affairs, and

monetary matters during that period. Philippine independence was granted in 1946.

Tyler, John 1790–1862. Tenth US president (1841–45); successor to W. Harrison. Tyler served as US congressman (1817–21), governor of Virginia (1825–27), and US senator (1827–36). A supporter of states' rights and a follower of the ideas of T. Jefferson, Tyler opposed Pres. A. Jackson. His refusal to help expunge a motion censuring Jackson prompted his resignation from the Senate (1836). Tyler was elected vice-president (1841) under W. Harrison and, after Harrison's death (Apr., 1841), Tyler became the first vice-president to succeed to the presidency. His opposition to reestablishment of a national bank led to Tyler's loss of Whig support and the resignation of his Cabinet, except for D. Webster, who remained to negotiate the Webster-Ashburton Treaty (q.v.) of 1842. Tyler's term of office was also marked by the end of the second Seminole War (1835–43) and by the annexation of Texas (1845). Chosen by a Democratic faction as presidential candidate (1844), Tyler withdrew from the race in favor of J. Polk. In Feb., 1861, Tyler presided over the Washington Peace Conference, an unsuccessful attempt to avoid the Civil War. When the war came, he served in the provisional Confederate Congress.

Tyler, Moses Coit 1835–1900. American literary historian noted for his *A History of American Literature 1607–1765* and *A Literary History of the American Revolution*

Tyler, Wat d. 1381. English rebel leader. He led the Peasants' Revolt (q.v.) in 1381.

Tylor, Sir Edward Burnett 1832–1917. British anthropologist. Often considered the founder of cultural anthropology, Tylor was noted for his theory of cultural evolution.

Tyndale, William ⟨Tindal, ∼⟩ ⟨Tindale, ∼⟩ d. 1536. Pursued by authorities of the English church, he translated the New Testament into English and published (1525) his vernacular edition at Worms. The edition was denounced and Tyndale was captured and burned at the stake some years later. His translation eventually provided the basis for the King James Bible.

Tyndareus In Greek legend, a legendary king of Sparta and husband of Leda (q.v.). He relinquished rule of Sparta to Menelaus after the death of his own sons.

Typhoid Mary ⟨Mallon, Mary⟩ d. 1938. Notorious "carrier" of typhoid fever. She worked as a cook in New York and caused numerous typhoid outbreaks in places where she worked before she was finally arrested (1915).

Tyr *See* **Tiw**

tyrant In Greek history, a ruler who usurped or

acquired power by illegal means. The term was originally not connected with oppressive rule. Tyrants appeared especially during the 7th through 5th cents. BC and often favored the populace against the aristocrats. Instances of their misrule after the 5th cent. gradually gave the term its modern meaning.

Tyrconnel, Richard Talbot, duke and earl of 1630–91. Irish Jacobite leader. Appointed lord deputy of Ireland (1687) by James II, Tyrconnel attempted to continue ruling Ireland after James was deposed (1688) in the Glorious Revolution. He was defeated at the Battle of the Boyne *(q.v.)* and died shortly thereafter.

Tyre Ancient port city on the Mediterranean Sea and located in what is now Lebanon. It was capital of Phoenicia (11th–6th cent. BC) and a famed commercial center for centuries. It was conquered by Alexander the Great (332 BC), by the Romans (64 BC), and by the Muslims (7th cent. AD). It was destroyed when the Muslims retook it from the Crusaders in 1291.

Tyre, William of *See* **William of Tyre**

Tz'ŭ Hsi ⟨Tzu Hsi⟩ 1834–1908. Dowager empress of China (1861–1908) and regent for most of that period. Originally a concubine, she came to power by bearing the emperor's only son, T'ung Chih. As regent for him and his successors, she steadfastly resisted reforms and played a role in the Boxer Rebellion *(q.v.)*.

u

Uccello, Paolo *c*1396–1475. Florentine painter, noted for his pioneering use of perspective and foreshortening in his works.

Uesugi family Japanese clan. Founded during the Kamakura shogunate, it rose (15th cent.) to great power in Japan. It challenged (early 17th cent.) the Tokugawa clan for control in Japan but was defeated. It continued to rule in northern Honshu until the fall of the Tokugawa shogunate (1868).

Uffizi Palace in Florence, Italy. Built in the 16th cent., it is now the site of the Uffizi Gallery, one of the greatest art museums in the world.

Uganda ⟨Republic of Uganda⟩ Independent state located in east-central Africa. Its capital is Kampala. Governed by Britain until 1962, it was under the rule of the notorious dictator Idi Amin during the 1970s. Key dates in Ugandan history include:

AD 1100   Bantu-speaking peoples arrived.

FROM *c*1500   Buganda kingdom established; chief among many kingdoms and tribes occupying present Uganda.

1844   Uganda first visited by Arab traders.

1862   British explorer John Speke was first European in region.

1870s   British and French missionaries arrived.

1880s   Natives slaughtered Christians.

1890   Anglo-German agreement placed Uganda in British sphere of influence.

1894   British protectorate established by British East Africa Company.

1894–1962   British colonial occupation; firm control of countryside established by 1918; small-scale agriculture by native Ugandans developed; Asian immigrants (from Indian subcontinent) controlled commerce.

1962   Uganda became independent (Oct. 9); Mutesa II, king of Buganda, chosen president; Dr. Milton Obote, prime minister.

1963   Uganda became a republic; Mutesa elected president.

1967   New constitution instituted by Prime Minister Obote; abolished traditional kingdoms, notably the still-powerful Buganda, and gave central government more power.

1970   Banks and import-export businesses nationalized as Obote tried to adopt leftist course.

1971   Idi Amin ousted Obote (Jan. 25); established dictatorship.

1971–79   Amin ruled Uganda; his reign marked by charges of ruthless brutality, including reported deaths of some 300,000 of his opponents.

1972   Amin expelled all Asians with British passports and all Israeli advisers.

1975   Amin nationalized all lands without compensation.

1976   Entebbe Raid; Israelis rescued passengers of airliner hijacked by Palestinians; airliner had been held in Uganda with Amin's apparent approval.

1976   Hostilities with Kenya ended by formal agreement.

1978   Border clashes with Tanzania.

1978   Tanzania invaded Uganda (Nov.).

1979   Kampala taken (Apr. 11); Ugandan insurgents aided by Tanzanians deposed Amin, who fled to Libya; provisional government set up.

1980   Military commission under Paulo Muwanga took power.

1980   First elections in years; constitutional government restored; Obote became president.

1981   Antigovernment insurgents reported making frequent terrorist attacks.

Ugolino della Gherardesca *d.* 1289. Italian Guelph nobleman who gained control of Pisa (1284). Political intrigues led to his downfall and to a charge of treason. His brutal death by starvation is related by Dante in the *Inferno*.

Uighurs *See* **Uigurs**

Uigurs ⟨Uighurs⟩ Turkic people of central Asia. They several times achieved political prominence, and an Uigur empire flourished in the 8th and 9th cents. Today they are a Sunni Muslim people living mostly in Chinese Singkiang.

Ukraine ⟨Ukrainian Soviet Socialist Republic⟩ Constituent republic of the European USSR (pop. 49,757,000). Its capital is Kiev, the leading city in

Russia before the invasion of the Golden Horde (13th cent.). In the 14th cent., Lithuania and Poland expanded into the Ukraine, but the harsh Polish rule caused many to flee. The Russians won the eastern Ukraine from Poland (1667) and by 1793 controlled the entire region. The movement for Ukrainian independence flourished through the 19th cent., and after the Russian Revolution the Ukraine declared its independence (1918). The Soviets recognized it by the Treaty of Brest-Litovsk (1918) but later overran it and made it a constituent republic (1923).

Uladislaus II c1456–1516. King of Bohemia (1471–1516) and Hungary (1490–1516). A weak and vacillating ruler, he was notable for signing a treaty (1515) with the Hapsburgs, which, after his son Louis II died without issue, added Bohemia and Hungary to the Hapsburg domains.

Ulbricht, Walter 1893–1973. East German Communist leader. A founder of the German Communist party, he became deputy premier of the German Democratic Republic in 1949 and was secretary general of the Social Unity party (1950–71). He ordered the building of the Berlin Wall (1961).

Ulm, Battle of French victory (Oct. 20, 1805) over the Austrians at Ulm, now in West Germany, during the War of the Third Coalition. By brilliant maneuvering, Napoleon surrounded the Austrian army led by Baron Karl Mack von Leiberich (1752–1828) and compelled Mack to surrender some 20,000 troops.

Ulm, Treaty of Truce (1647) between the French and Swedish forces and Bavaria toward the end of the Thirty Years' War.

Ulpian ⟨Ulpianus, Domitius⟩ d. AD 228. Roman jurist, Praetorian prefect (AD 222–228) under Alexander Severus. His voluminous writings were a major source for the *Digest* of Justinian I.

Ulpianus, Domitius *See* **Ulpian**

Ulster *See* **Northern Ireland**

ultraismo Post–WW I poetic movement in Spain and Spanish America. Influenced by the French symbolist and Parnassian movements, it sought to develop poetry beyond its traditional limits.

ultramontanism In the history of the Roman Catholic Church, the belief that papal jurisdiction is supreme. It opposed Gallicanism and was upheld by the Vatican Council (1869–70), which promulgated the doctrine of papal infallibility.

Ultraroyalists ⟨Ultras⟩ French reactionary royalist faction that advocated increased monarchial powers following the restoration of King Louis XVIII.

Ultras *See* **Ultraroyalists**

Ulysses *See* **Odysseus**

Umar ⟨Omar⟩ 581–644. Second Muslim caliph (634–644). A father-in-law of the prophet Muhammad, he at first opposed Islam, but was converted by 618. He chose Abu Bakr as the first caliph to succeed to the authority of the prophet (632), and succeeded him (634). During his caliphate, Arab armies advanced into Syria, Egypt, and Persia. He established the administration and taxation of the subsequent empire.

Umayyad ⟨Omayyad⟩ Muslim dynasty which ruled (661–750) the empire of the caliphate *(q.v.)*. The Umayyads held power after the first four orthodox caliphs, so-called because the legitimacy of their reigns is unquestioned. The Umayyads, however, took power after Muawiya, founder of the dynasty, deposed the caliph Hasan in 651. The accession of the Umayyads thus gave rise to the split between the majority Sunni Muslim sect (which accepts the Umayyad legitimacy) and the Shi'ite sect (which denies it). The Umayyads established their capital at Damascus, continued the expansion of the empire of the caliphate (Spain was conquered), established effective systems of communication, and instituted administrative reforms. Internal unrest mounted toward the end of their reign and a successful revolt (750) brought the Abbasid dynasty *(q.v.)* to power. Following the revolt, members of the Umayyad family were massacred. Only one is known to have escaped (Abd ar-Rahman I) and he established the Umayyad dynasty in Spain (in power 755–1031). Umayyad caliphs of the caliphate empire are:

Muawiya	661–680
Yazid	680–683
Muawiya II	683
Marwan I	683–685
Abd al-Malik	685–705
Walid I	705–715
Sulayman	715–717
Umar II	717–720
Yazid II	720–724
Hisham	724–743
Walid II	743
Yazid III	743–744
Ibrahim	744
Marwan II	744–750

Umberto I *See* **Humbert I**

Umberto II *See* **Humbert II**

Umbria Mountainous region of central Italy. Conquered by the Romans (3d cent. BC), it was part of the Papal States until incorporated into the kingdom of Italy (1860).

UN *See* **United Nations**

Uncas c1588–c1683. American Indian chief. A Pequot, he broke away and formed the Mohegan

Indian tribe. He fought with the British in the Pequot War *(q.v.)* and waged successful war against the Narragansett Indians.

Underground Railroad Secret system, organized *(c1838)* by abolitionists, Quakers, ex-slaves, and others, to aid southern slaves to escape to freedom in the North or Canada in the years before the American Civil War.

unicorn Mythical creature resembling a horse with a single horn projecting from its forehead. The hunting of the unicorn was the subject of numerous works of art, especially tapestries of the Middle Ages.

uniformitarianism *See* **Lyell, Sir Charles**

Uniformity, Act of *See* **Church of England** (1549)

Union, Acts of *See* **Acts of Union**

union, labor *See* **labor unions**

Union League Clubs Organizations formed in the northern US states during the Civil War to inspire support for the Union. During Reconstruction the clubs raised support for Republican candidates among newly enfranchised blacks and inadvertantly aided the rise of the Ku Klux Klan.

Union of *See also names inverted, as in* **Utrecht, Union of**

Union of October 17 *See* **Octobrists**

Union of Soviet Socialist Republics *(formerly* Russia, *also called* Soviet Union) Country located in Europe and Asia, extending from Eastern Europe across the entire northern part of the Asian continent to the Pacific Ocean. Its capital is Moscow. Traditionally, the history of the Russian state begins in the 9th cent. with Rurik, a Scandinavian invader who established a petty kingdom at Novgorod in northwestern Russia. It was not until the 14th cent., however, that the Duchy of Moscow began its rise as the nucleus of the modern Russian state. The grand dukes of Moscow steadily added to their domains and in the mid-16th cent. Ivan IV the Terrible became the first to call himself "czar" of Russia. Thereafter Russian expansionism pushed the borders eastward into Siberia and southward into Persian and Ottoman domains. By the 19th cent. Russia had become a major European power (especially after repulsing Napoleon's invasion) and had acquired vast territories. But oppressive conditions of the poor and failure to enact reforms led to the spread of radicalism and the Revolution of 1917. The revolution brought the Bolsheviks to power and thereby created the first Communist state. In the years before WW II, Communists sought to consolidate their hold over Russia (renamed Union of Soviet Socialist Republics in 1922) and to rebuild the economy. The Soviets emerged from WW II as a leading world power (with the US). In subsequent

years the Soviets engaged the Western powers in the Cold War, a protracted political rivalry. By the early 1970s the USSR and the US began a rapprochement (détente) aimed at easing Cold War tensions through international cooperation. The program was largely successful in the 1970s and cultural and economic relations between Communist and non-Communist nations were significantly improved. However, the Soviet invasion of Afghanistan (1979) and policies toward Poland in the early 1980s soured US-USSR relations, delivering a setback to the policy of détente. Key events in the history of Russia and the Soviet Union include:

9TH CENT. AD Northwestern Russia occupied by the Eastern Slavs, who had long occupied the region; Khazars, a Turkic people, controlled region to the south (from 7th cent. AD).

9TH–10TH CENT. Varangians, Scandinavian conquerors, invaded Russia.

862 Rurik, a Varangian, established control over Novgorod (near Baltic, in western Russia); founded Rurik dynasty of later Russian rulers.

879–912 Oleg reigned; expanded Varangian domains to include Kiev; moved capital to Kiev (c882); united Eastern Slavs in region and laid foundation of Kievan Russia, which eventually included vast domains lying between the Baltic and Black Seas.

911 Oleg concluded commercial treaty with Byzantine Empire; subsequent contact with Byzantines greatly influenced development of Russian culture.

945–972 Sviatoslav reigned as duke of Kiev; greatly expanded domains and brought duchy to height of its power.

980–1015 Vladimir I reigned; made Christianity (Orthodox Eastern) the state religion (c988).

1019–54 Yaroslav reigned; duchy of Kiev divided among his heirs at his death; control of duchy subsequently rotated among heirs; led to period of wars and collapse of Kievan Russia.

12TH CENT. Autonomous principalities emerged from collapse of Kievan Russia; Novgorod, Vladimir, Suzdal, Smolensk, and (later) Moscow emerged as powerful cities loosely united by common heritage.

c1147 Moscow founded.

1223 First Mongol invasion; armies of Genghis Khan defeated forces of Russian principalities at battle of Kalka River; Mongols withdrew immediately afterward.

1237–40 Second Mongol invasion, led by Batu Khan; Russian cities in south and west (Kiev among them) taken and destroyed; Novgorod in the north bypassed.

1240 Novgorod attacked by invading Swedes; Alexander Nevsky became Russian national hero by defeating Swedes at the Battle of the Neva.

1240s Poland and Duchy of Lithuania expanded into Russian domains, taking control of western parts (what became Belorussia and the Ukraine).

1242 Novgorod attacked by Teutonic Knights; Alexander Nevsky defeated them at the Battle of Lake Peipus.

1242 Empire of the Golden Horde established; dominated Russia from the south until 1480.

1246–63 Alexander Nevski ruled as grand duke of Novgorod; accepted suzerainty of Golden Horde as protection against further invasions.

1300s Rise of Moscow, in the principality of Vladimir, as a powerful city, due partly to its position as a trade center.

1328–41 Ivan I reigned as duke of Moscow; became collector of Russian tribute paid to Mongols and thus gained great wealth; helped make Moscow the residence of the metropolitan see of the Russian church.

1359–89 Demetrius reigned as duke of Moscow; began revolt against Mongol overlords; ceased practice of dividing domains among heirs.

1380 Battle of Kulikovo; Demetrius defeated the Mongols.

1389–1425 Vasily reigned as grand duke of Moscow; struggle for succession broke out on his death.

1392–98 Tamerlane invaded the Empire of the Golden Horde and reached the borders of the Russian principalities; Golden Horde declined steadily thereafter.

1453 Fall of Constantinople to the Ottoman Turks; Moscow proclaimed successor to Roman tradition ("Third Rome") and new center of the Orthodox church.

1462–1505 Ivan III the Great reigned; adopted autocratic style of rule; greatly expanded domains and began drive to unite domains of Eastern Slavs; exploited divisions between Tatar khans.

1472 Ivan married Sophia, niece of the last Byzantine emperor; she is said to have convinced him to adopt Byzantine ways of government.

1474 Rostov captured.

1478 Ivan conquered Novgorod and added its extensive domains to the Grand Duchy of Moscow.

1485 Tver, a powerful rival, was conquered by Ivan.

1497 First code of laws promulgated by Ivan.

1497–1502 Period of civil war over right of succession; Vasily III won.

1505–33 Vasily III reigned as grand duke; greatly strengthened the monarchy; continued expansion, adding Pskov (1510), Smolensk (1514), and Ryazan (1521); emergence of bureaucracy.

1533–84 Ivan IV the Terrible reigned; both cruel and mentally infirm, he became the first to call himself "czar" (1547); greatly expanded Russian domains and consolidated powers of the monarchy at the expense of the boyars (nobles); instituted reign of terror (from c1565).

1552–56 Tatar khanates of Kazan and Astrakhan conquered (1552, 1556), beginning eastward expansion of Russia.

1558–82 Livonian War fought; Russia ultimately forced to renounce claims to Livonia.

1565 Ivan set up *oprichniki* (crown lands) under his direct control.

1566 First national assembly called by Ivan.

1581–82 Conquest of Siberia begun for the czar by the Cossack chief Yermak; eastward expansion at the expense of the Mongols continued.

1584–98 Fedor I reigned as czar; the last of the Rurik dynasty; incompetent and unable to rule; government run by Boris Godunov, his brother-in-law.

1589 Orthodox patriarchate of Moscow given formal status.

1591 Death of Dmitri, heir to the throne; Godunov believed to have arranged murder to secure his succession.

1597 Serfdom established by law.

1598–1605 Boris Godunov reigned as czar; chosen by nobles as czar; successfully concluded brief war with Sweden; popular distrust of him spread, particularly after famine followed crop failures of 1601–02; Time of Troubles began just before his death.

1604–13 Time of Troubles; period of social and political chaos began with revolt led by pretender, Dmitri, who claimed to be heir to Rurik line; Dmitri, made czar (1605) after Godunov's death, was murdered by boyars; ensuing period marked by appearance of new pretenders, peasant revolts, and invasions by Sweden and Poland (Moscow occupied 1610–12); Poles driven out and Michael Romanov elected czar (1613).

1613–45 Michael Romanov reigned; founded Romanov line; on his accession country was in ruins, with many areas still held by Swedes, Poles, and rebels; order gradually restored and agreements concluded with Sweden (1617) and Poland (1618); government bureaucracy, which had survived Time of Troubles, aided recovery.

1613–1917 Romanov dynasty ruled Russia.

1645–76 Alexis reigned as czar; reign marked by promulgation of new law code (1648) that continued serfdom and by acquisition of the eastern Ukraine.

1652–66 Nikon reigned as patriarch of the Russian Orthodox church; introduced reforms to bring Russian rites into conformity with Byzantine rite and thus provoked schism and persecution of Old Believers, who favored Russian tradition; attempts to assert supremacy of church over czar led to his downfall.

1654 Uprising by Zaporozhe Cossacks in Ukraine against Polish rule; Cossacks sought Russian aid.

1654–67 Thirteen Years' War with Poland; Russians, taking advantage of Cossack uprising, gained eastern Ukraine and Kiev.

1656–61 War with Sweden; Russia failed to gain control of Baltic territories.

1670–71 Revolt by Don Cossacks, led by S. Razin; crushed by Czar Alexis' forces.

1676–82 Fedor III reigned; ended system of military and civil appointments on basis of social rank; began wars against Ottoman Turks.

1676–81 Russo-Turkish War; Russians gained most of Turkish Ukraine.

1682–1725 Peter I the Great reigned; made Russia a European power; his reign was dominated by his efforts to modernize and Westernize Russia and by nearly continuous wars; instituted administrative and fiscal reforms; built Russia's first navy.

1689 Peter overthrew the regency of his half-sister Sophia; assumed direct rule.

1695–96 Russo-Turkish War; Peter I captured Azov.

1700–21 Northern War with Sweden; Russia broke Swedish power in the Baltic and gained Livonia, Estonia, Ingermanland, and part of Karelia; victory made Russia a European power.

1703 St. Petersburg, built by Czar Peter, established as Russian capital.

1710–11 Russo-Turkish War; Ottomans attacked Russia, regaining Azov.

1712 Russian Orthodox church put under state control; patriarchate of Moscow abolished.

1721 Czar Peter formally adopted title Emperor of Russia.

1722 Table of ranks issued by Czar Peter; established rigid hierarchy for all government posts; advanced by merit and seniority.

1725–27 Catherine I reigned; the mistress and second wife (m. 1712) of Peter I; A. Menshikov dominated the government.

1727–30 Peter II reigned; manipulated by powerful nobles; A. Menshikov arrested.

1728 Capital moved to Moscow.

1730–40 Anna Ivanovna reigned as czarina; Prussians gained influential posts.

1733–35 Russia allied with Austria against Poland in War of the Polish Succession; gained accession of Frederick Augustus II as Augustus III.

1736–39 Russo-Turkish War; Russians retook Azov.

1740–41 Ivan VI reigned; succeeded as an infant; overthrown in palace conspiracy.

1741–62 Elizabeth reigned as czarina; pursued anti-German policy and allied Russia against Prussia.

1741–43 Russia victorious in Russo-Swedish War; gained Finnish territory.

1756–63 Seven Years' War; Russia allied with other European powers against Prussia for most of war; Elizabeth's death ended Russian participation and saved Prussia from defeat.

1762 Peter III reigned; quickly alienated nobles and the church; his decision to withdraw (1762) from Seven Years' War helped bring about his overthrow.

1762–96 Catherine II the Great; participated in overthrow of her husband; increased Russian power and prestige in Europe; warred against the Ottoman Turks; instituted administrative reforms and patronized the arts.

1764 Stanislaus II installed as Polish king by Catherine; as Catherine's lover he was dominated by her and Russian interests in Poland.

1766 Instruction of Catherine the Great issued.

1768–74 Russo-Turkish War; Russians victorious in Crimea and greatly increased influence in region; Russia established as protector of Christians in Ottoman domains.

1772 First Partition of Poland; Russia gained Polish territories east of the Dnieper and Dvina rivers.

1773–74 Peasant revolt against serfdom led by Pugachev; new, harsher laws on serfdom promulgated after the rebellion was crushed.

1785 Charter to the Nobility issued by Catherine; guaranteed nobles rights and prerogatives.

1787–92 Russo-Turkish War; Russia generally successful in war caused by its annexation of Crimea (1783).

1792–1802 French Revolutionary Wars in Europe.

1793 Second Partition of Poland; Russia gained Lithuanian Belorussia, western Ukraine, and other parts of Poland.

1795 Third Partition of Poland; Russia shared (with Austria and Prussia) remaining central core of Polish kingdom; kingdom ceased to exist.

1796–1801 Paul I reigned; reversed many of Catherine's policies and attempted to limit nobles' powers; his inconsistent foreign policy included brief participation in coalition against France (1798) and alliance against Britain after; assassinated.

1801–25 Alexander I reigned; a liberal ruler early in his reign, he supported the conservative movement of the post-Napoleonic period.

1801 Russia annexed Georgia; Russian possession confirmed (1813) after victory in war with Persia (1804–13).

1803–15 Napoleonic Wars; Alexander, defeated by Napoleon in fighting in Europe, submitted to Napoleon by the Treaty of Tilsit (1807); Napoleon later broke the alliance and launched his ill-fated invasion of Russia (1812); Alexander's rout of the invasion force led to Napoleon's downfall and made Russia a leading European power.

1806–12 Russo-Turkish War; Russia acquired Bessarabia.

1808–09 Russo-Swedish War; Russia gained Finland from Sweden.

1825 Decembrist Conspiracy, abortive revolt (Dec.) by nobles and officers, against accession of Nicholas I.

1825–55 Nicholas I reigned; instituted autocratic, oppressive rule, though he did attempt to improve the lot of the serfs; beginning of spread of revolutionary sentiment; continued Russia's expansionist wars against the Ottoman Empire; Russian literature flourished.

1826–28 War with Persia; Russia gained part of Armenia.

1826 Convention of Akkerman (Oct. 7); Russians forced agreement on Ottoman Empire; Russia to oversee autonomy of Moldavia and Wallachia.

1828–29 Russo-Turkish War; begun in support of Greek independence; Russia penetrated deep into Balkans; Treaty of Adrianople greatly increased Russian influence in region.

1830–31 Polish uprising against Russian rule; revolt crushed and Poland lost measure of autonomy gained in 1815.

1853–56 Crimean War; with the Ottoman Empire on the verge of collapse at the hands of the Russians, other European powers joined Ottomans against Russia; Russia was defeated and in subsequent years the fate of the Ottoman Empire became a major concern of European powers.

1855–81 Alexander II reigned; instituted liberal reforms but failed to prevent rise of populist

Narodniki movement; continued Russian expansion in central Asia and Far East; fostered industrialization.

1860 Treaty of Peking; China ceded Ussuri region (north of Amur River) to Russia; these Far Eastern territories included future site of Vladivostok.

1860 Vladivostok founded; became important Russian naval base in Far East.

1861 Edict of Emancipation freeing the serfs issued by Czar Alexander II; one of various reforms issued by czar.

1863 Polish rebellion suppressed with great brutality.

1864 Zemstvos, local councils, established.

1867 Russia sold Alaska to US.

1871–81 Russia occupied Chinese territory in Ili Crisis.

1872 Three Emperors' League formed with Prussia and Austria-Hungary.

1876 Narodniki, radical populist movement, formed secret Land and Liberty society.

1877–78 Russo-Turkish War; victorious Russians advanced to just outside Constantinople.

1878 Congress of Berlin; European powers forced Russia to accept greatly reduced concessions from Ottoman Empire following war of 1877–78.

1881 Alexander II assassinated by "People's Will," a wing of the Land and Liberty society.

1881–94 Alexander III reigned; instituted reactionary and repressive regime; adopted policies of russification of national minorities by force and persecution of Jews and other religious minority groups; fostered industrialization; miserable conditions of workers helped spread revolutionary movement.

1881 Wave of pogroms conducted against Jews following assassination of Alexander II; continued until Russian Revolution.

1893 Triple Entente formed with France and Britain.

1894–1917 Nicholas II reigned as last czar of Russia; an ineffective ruler, he was unable to stem the rising tide of revolution and was overthrown.

1897 N. Lenin arrested for his radical activities; exiled to Siberia (1897–1900); left Russia for Switzerland (1900).

1898 Russian Social Democratic Labor party, a Marxist group, founded by radicals at Minsk; group was soon after broken up by police and forced to meet in exile in Europe.

1901 Socialist Revolutionary party formed; a leading revolutionary group, it was an ideological outgrowth of the populist Narodniki movement; group conducted terrorist campaign.

1903 Russian Social Democratic Labor party split into two factions, Mensheviks and radical Bolsheviks; Lenin led the Bolsheviks.

1904–05 Russo-Japanese War; Russia suffered a humiliating defeat in the Far East at the hands of the Japanese; helped to further discredit government.

1904 Zemstvo congress (Nov.) convened at St. Petersburg; called for end to government repression and creation of a Duma (representative assembly).

1905 Trans-Siberian railroad completed; fostered colonization of Siberia.

1905 On Bloody Sunday, czar's troops fired (Jan. 22) on protesters in St. Petersburg; Russian Revolution of 1905 began.

1905 Concessions granted (Mar.) by czar, amid wave of strikes and unrest; included creation of advisory assembly and religious toleration; concessions failed to halt spreading unrest.

1905 Treaty of Portsmouth signed, ending Russo-Japanese War (Sept. 5).

1905 Nationwide strike (Oct. 20–30) in protest against czarist government; threat of political collapse forced czar to make concessions.

1905 First soviet (council) formed (Oct. 26) at St. Petersburg.

1905 Czar Nicholas issued October Manifesto (Oct. 30) to liberalize government; constitution granted, civil liberties guaranteed, and Duma (with legislative powers) to be created; Count Witte became first prime minister (dismissed May 1906).

1905 Cadet (Constitutional Democratic party) and Octobrist parties formed as liberal moderates split; Cadet party favored progressive government.

1905 Government arrested (Dec. 16) members of the St. Petersburg soviet.

1905 Uprising by Moscow workers (Dec.) suppressed after hard fighting in the streets.

1906–11 Black Hundreds active against revolutionists in the provinces; carried out pogroms against the Jews.

1906 Fundamental Laws issued (May 6) by czar; limited powers of the Duma and asserted supremacy of czar over Duma.

1906 Duma convened (May 10); dominated by Cadet party; openly critical of czarist government, it was dissolved (July 21).

1906 P. Stolypin named prime minister (June); sought to quench revolutionary ferment by instituting meaningful reforms; supported constitutional government.

1906 Stolypin land reforms instituted (Nov. 22) to distribute land to peasants; ended system of mirs (peasants' communal land-holding system).

1907 New Duma in session (Mar.–June); radical membership increased; dissolved (June 16).

1907–12 New Duma in session; election law favoring conservative elements gave majority of seats to conservatives; order restored in Russia as Prime Minister Stolypin and Duma pressed reform program and suppressed radical unrest.

1907 Anglo-Russian Convention settled disputes with Britain over Persia, Afghanistan, and Tibet; relations strengthened.

1911–12 Scandal over influence of Rasputin in royal court spread; rumors of Rasputin's corrupt and immoral behavior included purported intimate relationship with Czarina Alexandra.

1911 Prime Minister Stolypin assassinated (Sept. 14) by revolutionary.

1912–13 First and Second Balkan Wars; Ottomans driven out of Eastern Europe while tensions between Russia and Austria, over respective interests in region, increased.

1912–17 New Duma in session; conservatives again in the majority.

1914 Assassination of Austrian Archduke Francis Ferdinand by Serbian nationalist (June 28); tensions in Eastern Europe mounted as Germany backed Austria against Serbia; Russia backed its ally, Serbia, and was drawn into WW I.

1914–18 WW I; Russian losses in the war further weakened, then brought down, the czarist government.

1915 Progressive Bloc, alliance of liberals and conservatives in Duma formed (Aug.) to urge reforms; members appointed Provisional Government after fall of imperial government in 1917.

1915 Czar Nicholas took command (Sept.) of the Russian army following the disastrous defeat of Russian forces in the Galicia campaign (May); Czarina Alexandra (dominated by Rasputin) left in charge of government.

1916 Russian government near collapse; mismanagement of government by Alexandra and Rasputin combined with severe economic dislocations, including food shortages, caused by ongoing war.

1916 Rasputin assassinated (Dec. 30) by angry noblemen; Rasputin's death failed to halt collapse of government.

1917 Russian Revolution of 1917; wave of strikes and unrest (Mar.) resulted in creation of Provisional Government and abdication of Czar Nicholas (Mar. 15); Bolsheviks, led by Lenin, seized power (Nov.) and thus established the first Communist state.

1917 Bolshevik government formed (Nov. 7) under Lenin's leadership; L. Trotsky and J. Stalin held high posts; reorganization of Russia along Communist lines begun; banks nationalized and large estates broken up.

1917 Program of establishing worker control of factories begun (Nov. 28); government-controlled unions formed.

1917 Cheka organized to combat counterrevolutionaries (Dec.).

1917 Bolshevik government concluded armistice with Germany (Dec. 5); fighting resumed after Germans demanded Russia cede Poland and other territories in western Russia.

1917 Don Cossacks rebelled against Bolshevik government (Dec. 9); their uprising merged with the other counterrevolutionary warfare of the Russian Civil War.

1917 Church property seized (Dec. 17); suppression of the church begun.

1917 Japanese forces landed at Vladivostok (Dec. 30) and began operations in Far East.

1918–22 Russian Civil War; counterrevolutionary groups, the White Russian Army and foreign troops attempted to topple the Communists; Red Army, organized by L. Trotsky, was ultimately victorious and regained control over nearly all Russian territory.

1918 Constituent Assembly, elected after Bolshevik takeover, convened (Jan. 18); Social Revolutionary party members held clear majority over Bolsheviks; assembly forced to disband by Red Army troops.

1918 Moscow established as Bolshevik capital (Jan.).

1918 Land nationalized (Feb. 19).

1918 Ukraine declared independence from Russia (Jan. 28); one of several border regions to declare independence in the months after the Bolshevik takeover; included Moldavia, Lithuania, and Transcaucasia.

1918 Third International organized (Mar. 2); avowed aim was to spark Communist revolutions in countries throughout the world.

1918 Treaty of Brest-Litovsk concluded (Mar. 3); in the face of a continuing German advance the Bolsheviks agreed to give up Poland, Ukraine, and other territories on the western frontier.

1918 Communist party adopted as name of the Bolshevik party (Mar.).

1918–19 British, later joined by French and US troops, occupied Murmansk and Archangel in extreme northwest Russia; fighting with Bolsheviks began; WW I armistice largely ended US and British support and troops were withdrawn (Oct.).

1918 Constitution adopted (July 10); government run by Politburo and Central Committee of the Communist party (sole legal party); hierarchy of local, provincial, and national (All-Russian) soviets established.

1918 Nicholas and royal family executed by Communists (July 16).

1918 Red Terror instituted by Communists after unsuccessful attempt to assassinate Lenin (Aug. 30); widespread killings of all opponents began; murders of prisoners and enemy suspects by both Reds and Whites numbered perhaps 100,000; some two million of bourgeois class fled Russia.

1918 WW I ended by armistice between Germans and Allies (Nov. 11).

1919–20 White Russian offensives launched against Red Army in western Russia; from Siberia, by Adm. Alexander Kolchak; from the Don region in the south, led by Gen. Anton Denikin; from the Baltic region in the extreme west, led by Gen. Nikolay Yudenich; poor communications and other factors led to the failure of the drives against the Red Army in 1920.

1919 Karakhan Manifesto issued (July 15); offered to renounce Czarist interests in China; contributed to subsequent establishment of Chinese Communist party.

1920 Baltic states of Estonia, Latvia, and Lithunania recognized as independent.

1920 Russo-Polish War fought (Apr.–Oct.); war sparked by Polish advances into the Ukraine.

1920 White Army offensive (June–Nov.) from the Crimea, led by Baron Ferdinand von Wrangel; Red Army drove Wrangel's army into Turkey.

1920 Independence of Finland recognized (Oct. 14).

1920 Food levy instituted (Dec. 14) to help supply the Red Army; peasants, required to give government all surplus food, resisted; peasant uprisings and strikes by workers broke out as Russian economy collapsed (1920–21).

1921 Kronstadt Rebellion was a Russian revolt of sailors at the Kronstadt Naval Base (Feb.–Mar.); capped period of growing unrest at collapse of Russian economy and shortages of food; forced Lenin to institute his New Economic Policy (NEP).

1921 Lenin introduced (Mar. 17) his New Economic Policy to revive the economy; faced with economic collapse and internal unrest, Communist party abandoned "war communism"; food levy abolished and replaced by "tax" which took only part of their surplus; limited capitalism reestablished, though state controlled all major industries; full economic recovery achieved by mid-1920s.

1922 Last elements of White Russian Army driven out of eastern Siberia (into Manchuria) following withdrawal of Japanese from Vladivostok (Oct. 25); Russian Civil War ended.

1922 Treaty of Rapallo signed (Apr. 16) with Germany; this pact for economic cooperation provided Communist Russia with first diplomatic recognition.

1922 Union of Soviet Socialist Republics (USSR) organized (Dec. 30), then including Russia, White Russia, the Ukraine, and Transcaucasia.

1924 Lenin died (Jan. 21).

1924–53 J. Stalin in power; after the first years of vying for power, Stalin gradually increased his power as dictator; established his "personality cult" in the 1930s, which gave him absolute power; promoted industrialization at the expense of Marxist ideals and developed Stalinist line of "socialism in one country."

1924–26 Stalin's struggle for power; opposed chiefly by Trotsky, who wanted to end the New Economic Policy and return to revolutionary economic policies; Trotsky and his allies expelled from party posts (1926), signaling Stalin's victory.

1927 15th All-Union Congress (Dec.); confirmed Stalin's supremacy by condemning opposition to the party line; Trotsky's faction was expelled from the party.

1928 Five-Year Plan instituted by Stalin (Oct. 1) to replace New Economic Policy; stimulated development of heavy industry and reinstituted collectivization of agriculture.

1929 Trotsky exiled from USSR (Jan.).

1930s Collectivization of nearly all farmland completed despite widespread opposition by farmers; some five million peasant farms were forcibly confiscated and owners sent to labor camps in Siberia.

1932–33 Widespread famine resulted partly from government's farm policy.

1933 Communist party purged of about a million members.

1934 USSR joined League of Nations; actively participated in disarmament conferences.

1934 Sergei Kirov, close associate of Stalin, assassinated (Dec. 1); touched off a new round of purges, which reached height in 1936–38.

1935 Alliances with France and Czechoslovakia exacerbated worsening relations with Nazi Germany.

1936–38 Purge Trials; rivals of Stalin eliminated in series of phony trials; led to Stalin's consolidation of power in Russia.

1936–39 Soviets supported loyalists against German-backed nationalists in the Spanish Civil War; relations with Germany worsened.

1936 Anti-Comintern Pact concluded (Nov. 25) between Nazi Germany and Japan; USSR, threatened now in the East, moved closer to alliance with antifascist democracies.

1936 New constitution adopted; supposedly democratic, it maintained the absolute rule of the Communist party; Presidium and two-chamber Supreme Soviet to run government.

1938 Fighting between Soviet and Japanese forces along the Siberian border; Soviets supported the Chinese in the Sino-Japanese War.

1938 German invasion of Czechoslovakia; Soviets unsuccessfully sought firm action from European allies against Germany.

1939 V. Molotov suddenly made commissar of foreign affairs (May); Soviets resisted firm alliance with European allies against Germany.

1939 Non-Aggression Pact signed (Aug. 23) with Nazi Germany, marking sudden reversal in Soviet policy.

1939–45 WW II: Soviets, initially allied with Nazis, joined the Allies when Germany invaded (1941); repulsed German invasion at great cost and participated in "liberation" of Europe; Soviets emerged from the war as a superpower and leading opponent of the US-dominated Western powers.

1939–40 Russo-Finnish War; Russians victorious after hard fighting.

1943 Russian Orthodox church formally restored by Stalin.

1945 Consolidation of Soviet position begun; by war's end Soviets had occupied Eastern Europe and much of Manchuria and Korea; relations with Allies quickly broke down, especially over joint occupation policies in Germany; Soviets moved to gain control over occupied territories; Allies meanwhile resisted expansion of Soviet influence and the Cold War began.

1945 USSR became a charter member of the UN.

1946 Five-year plan announced by Stalin; aimed at economic recovery from war and rebuilding of Soviet industry; industry was quickly restored but agricultural output remained low.

1946–47 Famine resulted from drought in grain-producing regions.

1947 Communists' unsuccessful attempt to seize power in Greece prompted formulation of Truman Doctrine by US; directed at halting Communist expansionism, the doctrine hardened postwar divisions between the East and West.

1947 USSR and satellites refused to take aid under Marshall Plan.

1947 Cominform organized to coordinate Communist parties in various nations.

1948 Break in relations with Yugoslavia; Yugoslav leader Tito established his independent Communist policies.

1948–49 Berlin Blockade and Airlift; friction with former Allies led Soviets to establish unsuccessful blockade of West Berlin.

1949 Soviets exploded their first atomic bomb.

1949 Soviets recognized newly established People's Republic of China.

1950–53 Korean War; relations with US worsened as result of the war.

1952 Stalin issued his "Last Testament," calling for completion of drive against economic problems (Oct.).

1953 Doctors' Plot revealed (Jan. 13) by Stalin.

1953 Soviets exploded their first hydrogen bomb.

1953 Stalin died (Mar. 5); policy of "collective leadership" to replace Stalin's rule was initially adopted by government.

1953 Georgi Malenkov succeeded as premier; N. Khrushchev, as first secretary of the Central Committee, became major rival for power; Malenkov sought increased consumer-goods production and more intensive use of existing agricultural lands; Khrushchev countered by calling for vast expansion of agricultural lands and further development of heavy industry.

1955 Malenkov fell from power (Feb.); replaced by Nikolai Bulganin as premier.

1955 Warsaw Pact formed with satellite nations; created to counter Western NATO alliance.

1955 Soviets adopted policy of giving aid to and forming alliances with non-Communist nations.

1956 Twentieth Party Congress; Khrushchev made his "Secret Speech" (Feb.) denouncing Stalin; destalinization, an easing of restrictions, gave rise to unrest in Poland and Hungary.

1956 Cominform dissolved.

1956 Hungarian Revolution (Oct.–Nov.); Soviet troops used to crush the liberal revolt.

1957 Sweeping reorganization to decentralize economic ministries of government; sparked coalition (Molotov, Malenkov, and Lazar Kaganovich) against Khrushchev; Khrushchev defeated the coalition in a brief power struggle and won their expulsion from party posts.

1957 Soviet satellite Sputnik launched (Oct. 4) as first man-made earth satellite; space race with US began.

1958–64 Khrushchev in office (Jan.) as premier, replacing Bulganin; pursued continuing policy of reform and ongoing Cold War with West; his attempts to stimulate agricultural production failed and the USSR was forced to import grain in 1963.

1959 Premier Khrushchev made historic visit to US (Sept.); marked height of "thaw" in Cold War.

1960 Sino-Soviet split began; Maoist China opposed Soviet "revisionism" of Marxist doctrine; broke with Soviets over implementation of revolutionary Communism; Soviet aid to China ended.

1960–75 Vietnam War; Soviets provided supplies to North Vietnam, but no troops; gained considerable political prestige for Communist movement by the victory over US forces in Vietnam.

1960 U-2 Incident; Soviets downed (May 1) US spy plane over Soviet territory; new round of Cold War tensions began.

1961 Soviets established relations with Cuba following F. Castro's break with US; provided important Communist outpost in Western hemisphere.

1961 Soviet cosmonaut Y. Gagarin became first man to travel in space (Apr. 12).

1961 Berlin Wall erected (Aug.) by East Germans to halt politically embarrassing flow of refugees to West Germany.

1962 Cuban Missile Crisis (Oct.); Soviets forced to withdraw missiles from Cuba after US president J. Kennedy threatened nuclear war.

1963 "Hot-line" telecommunications link between US and USSR installed.

1963 Nuclear Test Ban Treaty signed.

1964 Khrushchev ousted from power (Oct. 14–15); fall caused by failure of his agricultural programs (notably the "virgin lands" scheme), Soviet humiliation in the Cuban Missile Crisis, and the Sino-Soviet split.

1964–82 L. Brezhnev in office as first secretary of the Central Committee; Brezhnev clearly the most powerful member of new government, though "collective leadership" was stressed at first; more orderly course of reform adopted and overt anti-Stalin propaganda halted; by early 1970s, policy of détente with West brought what appeared to be a halt in the Cold War.

1964–80 A. Kosygin in office as premier, replacing Khrushchev in that post.

1965–77 Nikolai Podgorny in office as chairman of the Presidium (president).

1965 Government reestablished 28 economic ministries abolished in Khrushchev era; instituted system whereby individual firms made production decisions on basis of prices and profits; marked radical departure from former close government supervision, though government still controlled basic course of economy; industrial output greatly improved by 1970s.

1968 Five-day, 41-hour work week established for Soviet workers.

1968 Prague Spring; Soviets invaded Czechoslovakia to halt liberalization of government there.

1968 Brezhnev Doctrine issued defending invasion of Czechoslovakia.

1969 Border warfare with Chinese; heavy fighting over Damansky Island in Ussuri River.

1970 Official condemnation of agricultural program approved by Central Committee; increased grain and meat production called for.

1971 Soviets supported India against US-backed Pakistan in war over Bangladesh.

1972 US President R. Nixon visited China (Feb.); marked beginning of US alliance with China, which exploited embarrassing ideological rift in the Communist world.

1972 US President Nixon in USSR on first visit by US president (May 22–June 1); SALT I agreements signed.

1972 Relations with Egypt soured; Soviet personnel asked to leave country in major setback in Soviet Mideast policy.

1972 SALT II talks with US began.

1972 Soviets forced to buy grain from the West following bad harvests.

1973 Shake-up of the Central Committee; Brezhnev's allies, A. Gromyko, Andrei Grechko, and Yuri Andropov installed on the committee.

1973 USSR threatened to intervene in 1973 Arab-Israeli War on behalf of Egyptians; US responded by calling worldwide nuclear alert.

1973 Brezhnev visited US; held talks with US president Nixon.

1974 Trade agreement with US concluded; Soviet emigration policies eased as part of the deal.

1974 Nobel Prize-winning author, A. Solzhenitsyn, forced to leave USSR as a dissident.

1975 New Five-Year Plan announced; called for significant increase in agricultural investment.

1977 New constitution adopted (Oct. 4); Communist party specifically named as ruling party of the Soviet Union.

1977 L. Brezhnev replaced N. Podgorny as chairman of the Presidium (president); first Soviet leader to act as both first secretary of Central Committee and chairman of Presidium.

1979 USSR and US signed SALT II agreement on arms limitation (June); US Senate refused to ratify agreement.

1979 Invasion (Dec.) of Afghanistan by Soviet troops ordered to back puppet regime there; Soviets unable to put an end to guerrilla resistance by Afghans.

1980 US imposed embargo on grain shipments to USSR in response to invasion of Afghanistan (Jan. 4); marked continued deterioration of détente.

1980 US called boycott of Olympic Games to be held at Moscow; boycott only partly successful.

1980–81 Relations with US deteriorated over Solidarity crisis in Poland; USSR backed away from threats of invading Poland.

1980 A. Kosygin resigned (Oct. 23) as premier because of ill health; Nikolay A. Tikhonov succeeded him.

1980 Kosygin died (Dec. 18).

1981 US lifted embargo on Soviet grain purchases (Apr.).

1981 Agreement signed (Nov. 20) for construction of natural gas pipeline from Siberia to Western Europe; US attempted to block pipeline construction for Soviet handling of the Polish crisis.

1982 Strategic Arms Reduction Talks (START) began with US.

1982 Brezhnev died (Nov. 10); Yuri Andropov, former head of the KGB, succeeded Brezhnev as party leader.

unions *See* **labor unions**

Unitarianism Christian denomination. Unitarians deny the doctrine of the Trinity, maintaining that God is one divine, indivisible force. The Unitarian concept has existed under various names since the earliest days of Christianity, but organized Unitarianism had its roots in the Protestant Reformation. Unitarians suffered numerous persecutions, particularly in Poland. They were among America's earliest Colonial settlers and were especially populous in New England and Pennsylvania. The American Unitarian Association was formally established in 1825.

Unitarios One of the two political groups that sought control of Argentina in the early 19th cent. Favoring strong central government, they opposed the Federalists, who favored greater autonomy in the provinces. The Unitarios came to power during the presidency of B. Rivadavia (1826–27).

Unitas Fratrum *See* **Moravian Church**

United Arab Emirates Federation of Arab emirates located on the eastern Arabian Peninsula. The capital is Abu Dhabi. Its members include

Abu Dhabi, Ajman, Dubai, Fujairah, Ras al-Khaimah, Sharjah, and Umm al-Qaiwain. They were formerly called the Trucial States, Trucial Oman, or the Trucial Coast because of the truces signed by each emirate with Great Britain in 1820. In 1892, the states accepted a British protectorate. In the wake of the British withdrawal from the region, the emirates formed the federation in 1971. Ras al-Khaimah chose not to join the federation but reversed its decision in 1972. Oil production among the emirates has made the United Arab Emirates extremely wealthy on a per capita basis. In recent years it has become a major international banking center.

United Arab Republic Name designating the political union between Egypt and Syria (1958–61). Yemen also joined the union (1958). Intended to be the nucleus of the United Arab States, it broke up after a *coup d'état* in Syria and Syria's subsequent withdrawal (1961).

United Empire Loyalists Term applied to those Colonial settlers who supported the British during the American Revolution, especially those who migrated to Canada.

United Front Union formed twice between the Chinese Communist party and the Kuomintang (1924–26, 1936–45). The second alliance was established to achieve a common front against the Japanese invaders.

United Irishmen ⟨United Irish Society⟩ Irish political organization founded (1791) by Wolfe Tone and others to secure legislative reforms. Suppressed by the British, it became an underground movement and played a key role in the Irish rebellion of 1798.

United Irish Society *See* **United Irishmen**

United Kingdom of Great Britain and Northern Ireland Official name of Great Britain since 1921. The United Kingdom includes England, Scotland, Wales, Northern Ireland, and several smaller islands. (*See* Great Britain)

United Malays National Organization Malayan political organization. Founded (1946) to oppose British plans for a Malayan union, it played a key role in establishing (Feb. 1, 1948) the Federation of Malaya and also in securing Malayan independence (Aug. 31, 1957).

United Methodist church ⟨United Methodists⟩ US Protestant denomination formed (1968) by the union of the Methodist and the Evangelical United Brethren churches.

United Nations ⟨UN⟩ International body formed during WW II by the nations allied against the Axis. The term was first used by Pres. F. Roosevelt, and the concept of a permanent body to deal with international problems posing a threat to

world peace gained momentum with the Moscow Declaration (Oct. 30, 1943), the Dumbarton Oaks Conference (Aug.–Oct., 1944), and the Yalta Conference (Feb., 1945). A meeting of the Allied nations at the San Francisco Conference led to signing (June 26) and ratification (Oct. 24) of the United Nations Charter. The charter provided for several structures within the organization, the leading ones being the Secretariat, the Security Council, and the General Assembly.

All members of the UN are represented in the General Assembly, which makes decisions on political, budgetary, trusteeship, and administrative questions. The Security Council includes 15 members, 5 of which—the US, the People's Republic of China, Great Britain, France, and the USSR—are permanent members. The remaining 10 are elected to the council by the General Assembly. The Security Council deals with matters of international security, and in important decisions the affirmative votes of the permanent members are necessary. Hence, frequently UN action has been halted in crises by an effective veto by a member within the Security Council. The Secretariat deals largely with administrative matters involving the UN, but under Secretary General D. Hammarskjold, it gained in importance by adopting measures not specifically called for by the Security Council or General Assembly. From the 1950s, the membership of the UN has grown substantially to more than 150 members.

United Provinces Union of provinces in the Low Countries that had rebelled against Spanish rule (1579). It later became the modern state of The Netherlands (*q.v.*).

United Provinces of Central America *See* **Central American Union**

United States ⟨United States of America⟩ Country located in North America. Its capital is Washington, DC. Originally settled by British colonists (from early 17th cent.), the US achieved independence (18th cent.) by the American Revolution (*q.v.*) and subsequently established a highly successful democratic government under the Constitution. US history in the 19th cent. was marked by the American Civil War (*q.v.*), which threatened to destroy the Union; by westward expansion of US borders to the Pacific Coast; by rapid industrialization after the Civil War; and by the emergence of the US as a world power (late 19th cent.). The US joined the Allies toward the end of WW I and, though it refused to enter the League of Nations, subsequently played an increasingly important role in world affairs. Faced with the crippling Depression at home during the 1930s, the federal government enacted sweeping economic and social reforms that greatly increased its involvement in shaping American society (*see* New Deal). In WW II the US played a leading role in the defeat of the Axis Powers. The US emerged as the leading power in the West following WW II and from the late 1940s to about 1970 engaged in the Cold War *(q.v.)* with the USSR. During this period both the US and the USSR developed massive nuclear arsenals. US involvement in the Vietnam War during the 1960s and early 1970s seriously eroded US prestige and led to widespread internal unrest. The war, and costly social programs undertaken by the federal government during the 1960s, led to economic problems that lasted throughout the 1970s and into the 1980s. Key events in US history include:

c1000   Leif Ericson believed to have landed in North America.

1492   Columbus discovered America (Oct. 12); made first landing in the Bahamas.

1513   Spaniard Ponce de León arrived in Florida; searched for legendary fountain of youth.

1524   G. Verrazano explored east coast, discovered New York Bay for the French.

1529   Cabeza de Vaca explored American Southwest.

1540–42   F. Coronado explored Southwest; traveled north into what is now Kansas.

1542   J. Cabrillo discovered California coast.

1565   St. Augustine, Florida, first permanent settlement in America, established by Spanish.

1587   Lost Colony established on Roanoke Island, North Carolina; founded under charter granted to Sir Walter Raleigh; settlers mysteriously disappeared.

1607   Jamestown (Virginia) established (May 14) as first permanent English settlement in North America.

1607–08   Unsuccessful attempt to establish colony in Maine.

1609–10   H. Hudson explored the Hudson River and Hudson Bay for the Dutch East India Company.

1612   First tobacco cultivated in Virginia.

1614   Capt. J. Smith traveled north from Virginia and explored New England.

1614   Dutch built fort at what is now Albany, New York; explored southern New England coast.

1619   First Negro slaves arrived in Virginia.

1619   Virginia House of Burgesses established.

1620   Pilgrims landed in Massachusetts; established Plymouth Colony.

1622–69   Powhatan War in the South; Virginia and Maryland settlers defeated and killed off most of Powhatan tribe.

1624   Virginia made a royal colony.

1626   P. Minuit of the Dutch New Netherland Company bought Manhattan Island from Indians; established New Amsterdam (later New York City) and settlements in adjacent states.

1630   Massachusetts Bay Colony founded; theocratic government established by the Puritans; thousands of new settlers arrived from England in next decade.

1630s   Colonization of Connecticut begun.

1634   Lord Baltimore (George Calvert) established Maryland Colony as haven for Catholics.

1636   Rhode Island settled by R. Williams.

1636–38   Pequot War in Connecticut; settlers decimated Pequot tribe.

1643   New England Confederation formed; federation of Massachusetts Bay, Plymouth, Connecticut, and New Haven colonies; first such federation in America.

1651–73   Navigation Acts passed by English Parliament; aimed at Dutch, they sought to control trade between England and the colonies.

1663   Royal grant for colonization of the Carolinas.

1664   New Netherland captured by the English, led by the Duke of York; New Amsterdam renamed New York.

1675–76   King Philip's War fought in New England between settlers and Indians.

1676   Bacon's Rebellion by settlers against colonial government.

1677–79   Culpepper's Rebellion; Carolina colonists rebelled against British taxes and regulations.

1682   R. La Salle claimed Mississippi Valley for France; named it Louisiana.

1682   W. Penn established the colony of Pennsylvania; Philadelphia founded.

1684   Massachusetts charter revoked; failure to respect authority of the crown among the charges made against colonists.

1686   Dominion of New England; New England colonies to be united under single colonial government; following Glorious Revolution in England (1688), colonies reverted to separate charter governments.

1689–97   King William's War fought; first of series of wars fought between English, French, and their respective Indian allies for control of colonies in North America.

1691   Plymouth Colony became part of Massachusetts Colony.

1692   Salem witch trials in Massachusetts.

1701   A. Cadillac founded Detroit.

1702–13   Queen Anne's War fought between English and French.

1729 Separate colonies of North and South Carolina established.

1733 Georgia established as the last of the original 13 colonies.

1733 Molasses Act, designed to force American colonists to import more expensive sugar and molasses produced by other British colonies.

1735 P. Zenger acquitted in libel suit; helped establish freedom of press in America.

1737 Walking Purchase, land swindle perpetrated by Pennsylvania officials against the Delaware Indians.

1743–48 King George's War; New England colonials successful in fighting against French in Canada.

1750 British passed Iron Act, which limited American iron industry.

1753 G. Washington sent into Ohio Valley to tell French to withdraw from region.

1754 Contingent of Virginia militia entered Ohio Valley; French forced G. Washington to surrender.

1754 Albany Convention (June 19); called by various colonies for defense against French; B. Franklin's plan for union of colonies rejected.

1754–63 French and Indian War; British gained control of French territory in North America.

1763–66 Pontiac's Rebellion in Great Lakes region; unsuccessful uprising of several Indian tribes led by Pontiac.

1764 Sugar Act passed by British Parliament to raise revenue.

1764–71 Regulator Movement by frontier settlers in western North Carolina; opposed corrupt colonial government.

1765 Stamp Act passed by British Parliament; led to establishment of Stamp Act Congress and Sons of Liberty.

1765 Quartering Act passed by British Parliament; caused great resentment in colonies; was allowed to lapse in 1770.

1765 Stamp Act Congress convened (Oct.) to protest British imposition of Stamp Act and other taxes; issued declaration of grievances.

1766 Stamp Act repealed; British Declaratory Act reasserted Parliament's legislative authority in colonies.

1767 Townshend Acts, four acts passed by the British Parliament to raise revenue and reassert its authority in the colonies; led to increased resistance.

1768 Liberty Affair (June 10); British used troops to quell rioting in Boston caused by Liberty Affair.

1770 Boston Massacre (Mar. 5); British troops, taunted by civilians, fired into a crowd, killing five.

1770 British repealed duties on a number of commodities; tax on tea remained.

1772 British revenue cutter *Gaspee* burned (June) by American colonials in Rhode Island.

1772–74 Committees of Correspondence set up for communications between colonies; figured in spread of independence sentiment for rebellion against British government.

1773 Tea Act passed by British Parliament (May 10).

1773 Boston Tea Party (Dec. 16); colonials dumped shipment of British tea into harbor.

1774 Intolerable Acts passed by Parliament to punish Boston for the Boston Tea Party; increased resentment among colonials and led to convening of First Continental Congress.

1774 Lord Dunmore's War between Virginia militia and Shawnees (Jan.–Oct.).

1774 Suffolk Resolves (Sept.), opposing the Intolerable Acts, passed in Massachusetts; subsequently endorsed by Continental Congress.

1774 First Continental Congress convened (Sept. 5) in Philadelphia.

1775 Virginia Convention (Mar.); P. Henry delivered "give me liberty" speech.

1775–83 American Revolution; colonials, at first fighting for recognition of grievances, soon adopted course for complete independence; under leadership of G. Washington secured defeat of British forces.

1776 Declaration of Independence (July 4) issued by colonials.

1777 Articles of Confederation adopted (Nov. 15); established loose federation of the 13 colonies; name United States of America adopted.

1781 Articles of Confederation in force, following their ratification (Mar. 1).

1783 Treaty of Paris, acknowledging US independence, signed with Britain (Sept. 3).

1786–87 Shays's Rebellion in Massachusetts.

1786 Annapolis Convention (Sept.); by this time weaknesses of government under Articles of Confederation had become apparent; discussion of problems at Annapolis led to convening of the Constitutional Convention.

1787 Northwest Ordinance passed (July) to provide for administration of US territories.

1787 Constitutional Convention (May–Sept.); drafted constitution creating strong federal government.

1787–88 Federalist Papers, series of essays written by A. Hamilton, J. Madison, and J. Hay supporting US Constitution.

1787 Constitution signed (Sept. 17); sent to states for ratification.

1788 Constitution of the United States went into effect (June 21) following ratification by ninth state (New Hampshire); established strong central government with a president and bicameral legislature.

1789 Congress convened for first time under US Constitution (Mar. 4).

1789–93 G. Washington elected first US president; inaugurated (Apr. 30), he guided the US through the crucial early years; attempted unsuccessfully to establish government free of partisan politics.

1789 Bill of Rights passed (Sept. 25) by Congress; guaranteed fundamental liberties.

1790 S. Slater built the first cotton textile factory in the US at Rhode Island.

1791 Bank of the United States created; part of A. Hamilton's aggressive fiscal program as secretary of the treasury.

1791 Vermont admitted as 14th state.

1791 Bill of Rights ratified (Dec. 15).

1792 Republican party, forerunner of the Democratic party, founded by T. Jefferson; opposed Federalist party, led by A. Hamilton and J. Adams.

1792 Kentucky admitted as 15th state.

1792 Tennessee admitted as 16th state.

1793 Washington reelected to second term.

1793 French diplomat E. Genêt asked to leave country after attempting to sway popular opinion in favor of revolutionary France against Britain; US passed Neutrality Act (1794).

1793 Cotton gin invented by E. Whitney.

1794 Whiskey Rebellion broke out; Pennsylvania settlers protest federal tax on whiskey.

1794 Jay's Treaty negotiated; forestalled war with Britain.

1795 Yazoo land claims, land-fraud scheme involving many members of Georgia legislature.

1796 Washington's Farewell Address (Sept. 18).

1797–1801 John Adams, Federalist leader, served as second US president; struggle with Jeffersonian Republicans.

1797 XYZ Affair, attempted bribing of American diplomats by French officials; led to undeclared naval war with France.

1798 Alien and Sedition Acts; notorious acts passed by Federalists and aimed at suppressing the Jeffersonian Republicans.

1798 Virginia and Kentucky Resolutions passed in opposition to Alien and Sedition Acts; hinged on doctrine of states' right to nullify federal law.

1799 Fries' Rebellion in Pennsylvania against federal tax.

1800 Treaty of 1800; ended US alliance with France.

1800 Washington, DC, became US capital, replacing Philadelphia.

1800 Election of 1800 ("Revolution of 1800"); Adams lost but tie between T. Jefferson and A. Burr threw the election into the House, which decided on Jefferson as president and Burr as vice-president.

1801–09 T. Jefferson served as 3d US president; sought economy in government and less interference in states.

1801–05 Tripolitan War against Barbary pirates.

1803 Ohio admitted as 17th state.

1803 *Marbury* vs *Madison*; Supreme Court established judicial review of Congressional legislation.

1803 Louisiana Purchase; US purchased territory from France and thereby doubled size of US.

1804 Vice-Pres. A. Burr killed political rival, A. Hamilton, (July) in duel.

1804–06 Lewis and Clark explored Louisiana territory.

1805 President Jefferson's attempt to have Supreme Court Justice S. Chase impeached failed; helped establish court's independence from political influence.

1807 R. Fulton launched (Aug.) first commercially successful steamboat, the *Clermont*.

1807 Former Vice-President A. Burr tried for treason; acquitted (Sept.).

1807 British ship *Leopard* stopped and searched American frigate *Chesapeake*, removing four crewmen; incident resulted from mutual attempts by Britain and Napoleon of France to blockade shipping; tensions between US and Britain increased.

1807 Embargo Act (Dec.); Jefferson attempted to retaliate against Britain and France for their restrictions, which were hurting US commerce.

1808 American Fur Company incorporated by J. J. Astor; influenced settlement of the Great Lakes region.

1809–17 Pres. James Madison in office.

1809 Embargo Act repealed after proving more harmful to US commerce than to France or Britain; replaced by Non-Intercourse Act.

1810 Macon's Bill No. 2; another attempt at countering French and British blockades.

1811 Battle of Tippecanoe (Nov. 7); W. Harrison victorious in fighting against the Indians in Indiana.

1812 Louisiana admitted as 18th state.

1812–14 War of 1812 fought with Britain.

1813–14 Creek War fought in Alabama and Georgia; Indians, allied with British during War of 1812, defeated by militiamen led by Gen. A. Jackson.

1816 Second Bank of the United States chartered.

1816 American Colonization Society formed to transport freed Negroes to colony in Liberia.

1816 Indiana admitted as 19th state.

1817–25 James Monroe in office as 5th president; his term referred to as "Era of Good Feeling" for relative lack of partisan political struggle.

1817 Rush-Bagot Convention signed with Britain; provided for disarmament of US-Canadian border.

1817–18 First Seminole War; Seminoles in Florida defeated and Spain forced to cede Florida.

1817 Mississippi admitted as 20th state.

1818 Convention of 1818 established western US-Canadian border at 49th parallel.

1818 Illinois admitted as 21st state.

1819 Transcontinental Treaty (Feb. 22) signed between Spain and US; Spain ceded Florida and the Oregon Country; US recognized Spanish sovereignty in Texas.

1819 In *McCulloch* vs *Maryland*, Supreme Court confirmed congressional powers.

1819 Alabama admitted as 22d state.

1820 Missouri Compromise; to maintain the balance between slaveholding and free states (11 each), Missouri to be admitted without restrictions as to slavery, remainder of Louisiana Purchase north of 30° 30' to be free, and Maine to be admitted as free state; marked rise of North-South sectional conflict over slavery.

1820 Maine admitted as 23d state.

1821 Missouri admitted as 24th state.

1823 Monroe Doctrine articulated (Dec. 2) by Pres. Monroe to block attempts to restore colonial control in South America; warned against involvement by European powers in Americas.

1824 American System proposed by H. Clay for American self-sufficiency.

1824 Election of 1824; four-way race finally decided in House in favor of J.Q. Adams, though A. Jackson had won popular vote.

1825–29 J.Q. Adams served as 6th US president; embroiled in bitter feud with Jacksonian Democrats.

1826–34 Rise of the Anti-Masonic party.

1828 Tariff of Abominations, high tariff on imports, designed to protect developing US industries, raised protests, especially in the South; J. Calhoun advanced his theory of nullification.

1829–37 A. Jackson served as 7th US president; spoils system introduced during his administration; Jacksonian democracy ascendant; Jackson's Kitchen Cabinet derided by opposition.

1830 Mormon Church founded in New York.

1830 Indian Removal Act implemented by Pres. Jackson.

1830 Hayne-Webster debate; Sen. D. Webster refuted doctrine of nullification and defended nationalist view of the Union.

1831 Slave revolt, Southampton Insurrection, in Virginia; led by N. Turner.

1831 Eaton Affair; Washington, DC, society snubbed wife of Sec. of War J. Eaton; led to his resignation, despite Pres. Jackson's attempts to intervene.

1832 Tariff of 1832; improved on Tariff of Abominations but failed to quiet opposition in South.

1832–33 Nullification controversy; South Carolina attempted to nullify federal tariffs by state ordinance (1832); Pres. Jackson responded with a Force Bill (1833) to allow use of military to collect tariffs; Tariff of 1833, a compromise advanced by H. Clay, ended the controversy.

1833 Jackson, opposed to "monopolistic" practices of the Bank of United States, transferred federal funds to state banks ("pet banks").

1833 American Anti-Slavery Society founded by W. Garrison; marked rise of abolitionist movement in US.

1834 Whig party organized by H. Clay to oppose politics of A. Jackson.

1834 Indian Territory formally established; originally included lands west of the Mississippi, later reduced to part of present state of Oklahoma; Indians forcibly relocated (by Indian Removal Act of 1830) from east of Mississippi to Indian Territory.

1835 US public debt retired.

1835 Rise of Locofocos, short-lived faction of radical Jacksonian Democrats; advocated end to the national bank and other monopolies.

1835–42 Second Seminole War in Florida sparked by attempts to move Seminoles from their lands; Seminoles defeated and forced to move west.

1836 Texas war for independence; increased settlement of Texas by Americans led to movement to break away from Mexican rule; despite defeat at the famous Battle of the Alamo (Mar. 6), rebels gained independence and formed a republic (1836).

1836 Arkansas became the 25th state.

1836 Specie Circular issued (July) by Pres. Jackson; ordered payment in hard currency for all public lands; designed to halt speculative boom in western real estate; helped precipitate Panic of 1837.

1836–44 Gag rules adopted by US House of Representatives to block antislavery petitions submitted by abolitionists; repealed in 1844.

1837 Michigan became the 26th state.

1837–41 M. Van Buren in office as 8th president; a Democrat, he attempted to continue former Pres. Jackson's policies.

1837 Panic of 1837; financial collapse began in market for western lands and soon spread to commodities markets.

1837 S. Morse successfully demonstrated his telegraph.

1837 *Caroline* Affair, incident between US and Canada.

1838–39 Aroostook War, US-Canadian border incident.

c1838 Underground Railroad formed by abolitionists to help runaway slaves escape to Canada or free states.

1840 Independent Treasury System adopted; won support of Pres. Van Buren after Panic of 1837; had been opposed by Whigs seeking new Bank of the United States.

1840–48 Liberty party formed; first US political party created to promote abolition of slavery.

1841 W. Harrison served (Mar.–Apr.) as 9th US president; first president to die in office (Apr. 4).

1841–45 J. Tyler in office as 10th president, following Harrison's death; first vice-president to succeed to the presidency; opposed Whig effort to establish national bank; his cabinet (except D. Webster) resigned.

1841 Independent Treasury System repealed by Whigs.

1842 Webster-Ashburton Treaty settled Northeast Boundary Dispute.

1845 Florida became the 27th state.

1845–49 J. Polk in office as 11th president; worked vigorously for his programs and supported American expansionism.

1845–48 Mexican War; US, in conflict over territories of the Southwest, invaded and defeated Mexico; Mexico ceded Southwest and California to US by Treaty of Guadalupe Hidalgo.

1845–59 Rise of the Know-Nothing party.

1845 Texas became the 28th state.

1846 Oregon Treaty negotiated between US and England; settled US-Canadian boundary dispute.

1846 Wilmot Proviso (Aug.); measure (never passed) to prohibit slavery in territories acquired in the Mexican War; aroused bitter opposition in South and contributed to growing North-South sectionalism.

1846 Walker Tariff passed; reduced US tariffs.

1846 Independent Treasury System reestablished.

1846 Iowa admitted as 29th state.

1848 California gold rush began; brought great influx of settlers to California.

1848 Wisconsin admitted as 30th state.

1848 Convention at Seneca Falls, New York, marked beginning of modern US feminist movement.

1848 Proslavery Alabama Platform advanced in opposition to the Wilmot Proviso.

1848 Free-Soil party formed by antislavery Whigs and Liberty party members; their presidential candidate, M. Van Buren, split the New York vote (1848) and put Z. Taylor in office.

1849–50 Z. Taylor (Whig) served as 12th president; died in office (July 9).

1850–53 M. Fillmore (Whig) in office as 13th president, succeeding to the presidency after Taylor's death.

1850 Clayton-Bulwer Treaty; US and Britain agreed to refrain from attempts to dominate Central America; provided for joint control of any canal across the Isthmus of Panama.

1850 California admitted as the 31st state.

1850 Compromise of 1850 (Sept. 9–20); ended heated controversy over extension of slavery into new states, raised by impending admission of California as a free state; established doctrine of popular sovereignty, which led to further crises over slavery issue.

1850 Fugitive Slave Act passed; Pres. Fillmore aroused storm of protest from Northern abolitionists by trying to enforce the act, in keeping with the Compromise of 1850.

1853–57 F. Pierce (Democrat) in office as 14th president; pursued expansionist foreign policy; failed to head off growing crisis over slavery.

1853 Gadsden Purchase; US bought strip of territory from Mexico along US-Mexican border.

1854 Commodore M. Perry forced Japan to end isolation and sign Treaty of Kanagawa (Mar.).

1854 Kansas-Nebraska Act (May 30); organized separate territories of Kansas and Nebraska; repealed Missouri Compromise of 1820; substituted doctrine of popular sovereignty; pro- and antislavery elements began to settle region.

1854 Republican party formed (July) at Jackson, Michigan; party formed to oppose slavery.

1854–59 Bleeding Kansas; bitter struggle between pro- and antislavery settlers in Kansas which contributed to the growing national crisis over the slavery issue.

1854 Ostend Manifesto (Oct. 18); called for US to acquire Cuba by purchase or by force; aroused public outcry in North.

1855–58 Third Seminole War; removal of Seminole Indians to the West completed.

1856 Pottawatomie Massacre (May); five pro-slavery settlers murdered by J. Brown and followers in Bleeding Kansas.

1857–61 J. Buchanan (Democrat) in office as 15th president; though opposed to slavery, he sought compromise; his policies failed to prevent the secession of Southern states (1860–61), however.

1857 Dred Scott case; Supreme Court declared Missouri Compromise of 1820 unconstitutional.

1857 Panic of 1857; failure of railroad bonds among causes; many banks failed and widespread unemployment resulted.

1858 Minnesota admitted as the 32d state.

1858 Lincoln-Douglas debates (Aug.–Oct.); seven debates between A. Lincoln and S. Douglas during campaign for Senate; Lincoln won national reputation for opposing slavery as immoral; Douglas reelected to Senate.

1859 Oregon admitted as 33d state.

1859 Harper's Ferry Raid (Oct. 16–18), abortive insurrection led by J. Brown; contributed to outbreak of Civil War.

1859 First American oil well drilled at Titusville, Pennsylvania.

1860s Wars against Indians in the West; various tribes (Sioux, Cheyenne, Apache, Navaho) attempted to resist advance of white settlers and were gradually subdued in bloody wars; Indians resettled on reservations.

1860–61 Pony Express in operation.

1860 Election of 1860; Democrats split over slavery issue, Douglas ran as candidate of Northern Democrats, John Breckinridge as candidate of Southern Democrats; A. Lincoln, Republican candidate, ran as a moderate, opposed to extension of slavery; Lincoln's victory in the election sparked the secessionist movement in the South.

1860 Ordinance of Secession adopted by South Carolina (Dec. 20); other southern states soon followed (from Jan., 1861); President Buchanan refused to use force to prevent secession.

1861 Union supply ship fired on (Jan. 9) while attempting to relieve Ft. Sumter in Charleston, South Carolina, harbor.

1861 Kansas admitted as the 34th state.

1861 Confederate States of America created (Feb. 4) at meeting of seven (four seceded later) secessionist states; provisional government under J. Davis formed; ordered seizure of all federal property within seceded states.

1861 Washington Conference (Feb.); presided over by J. Tyler, it failed to resolve North-South differences and end secessionist movement.

1861 Crittenden Compromise; unsuccessful, last attempt at preventing civil war; defeated in Senate (Mar.).

1861–65 A. Lincoln served as 16th president; he was inaugurated (Mar. 4) and war broke out the following month; Lincoln succeeded ultimately in preserving the Union and in bringing an end to slavery in the US.

1861 Morrill Tariff enacted (Mar.); first of a series of Civil War–period bills that gradually increased tariffs; established high protective tariff structure.

1861 Pres. Lincoln announced (Apr. 6) he would supply Ft. Sumter in Charleston, South Carolina.

1861 Confederates fired (Apr. 12), on Ft. Sumter and thus began hostilities in the war.

1861–65 American Civil War; bloody conflict culminated long North-South sectional struggle over slavery; South, unable to match North's manpower and supplies, was devastated in fighting and finally defeated.

1862 Legal Tender Act passed; first of series passed to help finance war effort.

1862 Homestead Act passed; encouraged settlement of West.

1862 Morrill Act passed; set aside public lands to create land-grant colleges.

1863 Pres. Lincoln issued the Emancipation Proclamation (Jan. 1), freeing slaves in states currently in revolt against union.

1863 West Virginia became 35th state.

1863 Pres. Lincoln delivered his famous Gettysburg Address (Nov. 19).

1864 Nevada admitted as 36th state.

1865 Gen. R. Lee surrendered at Appomattox Court House (Apr. 9), ending Civil War.

1865 Pres. Lincoln assassinated by J. Booth (Apr. 14); died (Apr. 15).

1865–69 A. Johnson in office as 17th president, succeeding on Lincoln's death; attempted to continue Lincoln's policy of reconciliation toward South; engaged in bitter struggle with Radical Republicans in Congress, in attempt to prevent harsh Reconstruction program.

1865 Thirteenth Amendment to the Constitution ratified (Dec. 18); abolished slavery in the US.

1865–77 Reconstruction period; South, ravaged by war, gradually restored; Radical Republicans at first imposed policies designed to guarantee rights of Negroes; but white southerners gained control of state governments, passed laws establishing segregation; segregation was characteristic of southern society until the 1960s.

1867 Nebraska admitted as 37th state.

1867 Tenure of Office Act passed (Mar. 2) by Congress; charges of a violation of its provisions by Pres. A. Johnson were involved in his impeachment (1868).

1867 Alaska territory purchased from Russia.

1867 Grange organized by midwest farmers to counter unfair practices by grain-elevator owners and railroads.

1868 Impeachment proceedings against Pres. Johnson (Feb. 24–May 26), first ever instituted against US president; arose from Johnson's feud with Radical Republicans over Reconstruction policy; Johnson narrowly acquitted.

1868 Burlingame Treaty; treaty of friendship between US and China.

1869–77 U. Grant in office as 18th president; his term marked by continuing problems of Reconstruction, corruption, and various scandals; era known as the Gilded Age.

1869 Union Pacific railway, first transcontinental railway, completed (May 10).

1869 Black Friday financial panic (Sept. 24), caused by speculators' attempt to corner gold market.

1869 Knights of Labor, first major US labor organization, formed.

1870 Fifteenth Amendment ratified; guaranteed Negroes voting rights; along with earlier 14th Amendment and Civil Rights Acts, represented attempts by Republican Congress to guarantee Negroes equal place in post–Civil War society.

1871 Chicago fire (Oct. 8–9); one-third of city destroyed.

1872 Alabama Claims, dispute with Britain, settled by arbitration.

1872 San Juan Boundary Dispute with Great Britain settled; US awarded San Juan Islands southeast of Vancouver.

1873 Crédit Mobilier of America scandal; arose from corrupt practices in financing of Union Pacific Railroad.

1873 Panic of 1873; financial panic caused by speculative boom.

1875 Whiskey Ring scandal.

1876 A. Bell invented the telephone.

1876 Battle of Little Bighorn (June 25); Gen. Custer and his troops massacred in uprising by Sioux and Cheyenne Indians.

1876 Colorado admitted as the 38th state.

1876 Socialist Labor party founded in Philadelphia.

1876 Election of 1876, Hayes vs Tilden; Hayes needed disputed electoral votes from Florida, South Carolina, Louisiana, and Oregon to win; Hayes awarded the election by Congressional commission, after an end to military occupation and Reconstruction in the three Southern states was promised.

1877–81 R. Hayes (Republican) in office as 19th president; ended Reconstruction (1877) by withdrawing last of federal occupation forces in South (Florida, South Carolina, Louisiana); adopted policy of reconciliation toward South.

1878 Bland-Allison Act for free coinage of silver (free-silver movement) passed over President Hayes' veto.

1879 T. Edison invented a commercially practical light bulb.

1881 J. Garfield (Republican) served as 20th president; shot by disgruntled office-seeker (July 2) and died (Sept. 19).

1881 C. Barton founded American Red Cross.

1881–85 C. Arthur (Republican) in office as 21st president, succeeding Garfield on his death; backed civil service reform.

1882–94 Chinese Exclusion Acts passed to prohibit immigration of Chinese (particularly laborers) to US.

1883 Pendleton Civil Service Act passed (Jan. 16); established merit system for hiring government workers and ended long fight over civil service corruption.

1885–89 G. Cleveland (Democrat) in office as the 22d president; a reformer, he fought corruption and political bosses; attempted to lower tariffs and lost reelection.

1886 American Federation of Labor founded; soon eclipsed the Knights of Labor.

1886 Haymarket Square Riot, Chicago (May 4); anarchist bomb killed and injured many.

1886 Statue of Liberty unveiled (Oct. 28) in New York harbor.

1887 Interstate Commerce Commission created to regulate railroads and railroad rates.

1888 Election of 1888; Cleveland won popular vote but lost election to B. Harrison, who won by electoral votes.

1889–93 B. Harrison (Republican) served as 23d US president; administration marked by rising US involvement in international affairs; fiscal policies weakened economy.

1889 North Dakota admitted as 39th state.

1889 South Dakota admitted as 40th state.

1889 Montana admitted as 41st state.

1889 Washington admitted as 42d state.

1890 Sherman Anti-Trust Act passed (July 2); first US law prohibiting trusts.

1890   Idaho admitted as the 43d state.

1890   Wyoming admitted as 44th state.

1890   Sherman Silver Purchase Act passed (July 14); led to financial panic of 1893 and was repealed later that year.

1890   McKinley Tariff passed by Republicans; further increased tariffs.

1890   Sioux Indians massacred at Battle of Wounded Knee (Dec. 29).

1892   Populist party formed; supported free silver and other policies favoring farmers and labor.

1892   Homestead Strike began (June 30); violence between strikers and Pinkerton detectives hired by Carnegie Steel Company.

1893–97   G. Cleveland (Democrat) in office as 24th president (his second term); failed to prevent increase in tariffs and solve continuing economic problems.

1893   Panic of 1893; Pres. Cleveland blamed the Sherman Silver Purchase Act and won its repeal (Oct. 1893).

1894   Coxey's Army of unemployed marched on Washington.

1894   Pullman Strike broken with aid of federal troops.

1894   Wilson-Gorman Tariff passed; continued high protective tariff.

1895–99   Venezuela Boundary Dispute; US, by virtue of Monroe Doctrine, became involved in finding settlement.

1896   Utah admitted as 45th state.

1896   Gold discovered in Klondike, Alaska; gold rush began.

1896   Election of 1896; W. Bryan, Democrat and free-silver advocate, gave famous "Cross of Gold" speech (July 8) attacking Republicans' single gold-standard platform; Bryan won Democratic nomination but lost election to W. McKinley.

1896   *Plessy* vs *Ferguson*; Supreme Court decided in favor of doctrine of "separate but equal" facilities for whites and Negroes; doctrine maintained racial segregation until the 1950–60 period.

1897–1901   W. McKinley (Republican) in office as 25th president; administration marked by period of economic recovery and by expansionism.

1897   Dingley Tariff imposed high protective tariff.

1898   USS *Maine* blown up while in harbor at Havana, Cuba (Feb. 15).

1898   Spanish-American War (Apr.–Dec.); US gained Cuba, Philippines, Guam, and Puerto Rico from Spain.

1898   Hawaii annexed by US.

1899–1902   Philippine Insurrection; began long struggle by Filipino rebels to gain complete independence from US.

1899   US Open Door policy toward China articulated.

1901   Pres. McKinley shot (Sept. 6) by an anarchist; died (Sept. 14).

1901–09   T. Roosevelt (Republican) in office as 26th president, succeeding McKinley; noted for passage of reform legislation, "trust-busting" and other aggressive policies of his administration.

1901   Hay-Pauncefote Treaty with Britain; reversed early Clayton-Bulwer Treaty (1850) and allowed construction of a US-controlled Panama Canal.

1902   Pres. Roosevelt intervened in coal miners' strike.

1902–03   US involved in Venezuela Claims dispute.

1903   US won favorable settlement in the Alaskan Boundary Dispute with Canada.

1903   Elkins Act passed; ended railroad rebates.

1903   Hay-Bunau-Varilla Treaty (concluded with newly independent Panama), granting US rights to the Panama Canal Zone for construction of the Panama Canal; US backed Panamanian independence fighters after Colombia, then in control of Panama, rejected similar treaty for canal.

1903   First powered airplane flight made (Dec. 17) in Wright brothers' plane at Kitty Hawk, North Carolina.

1904   Construction of the Panama Canal begun.

1904   Roosevelt Corollary to the Monroe Doctrine articulated by President Roosevelt; used to justify subsequent intervention by US in affairs of Latin American nations.

1905   Portsmouth Conference; Roosevelt mediated settlement of Russo-Japanese War of 1905.

1906   San Francisco, California, destroyed by earthquake (Apr. 18–19).

1906   Hepburn Act passed; extended jurisdiction of Interstate Commerce Commission to other transport industries besides railroads.

1906   Pure Food and Drug Act passed.

1907   "Gentlemen's agreement" halted Japanese emigration to US.

1907   Oklahoma admitted as 46th state.

1909–13   W. Taft (Republican) in office as 27th president; continued Roosevelt's "trust-busting" policies but came to oppose progressive movement; replaced Roosevelt's aggressive Latin American policy with "Dollar Diplomacy."

1909   National Association for the Advancement of Colored People (NAACP) formed.

1909 Payne-Aldrich Tariff adopted; supported by Taft, it maintained protective tariff.

1910 Mann-Elkins Act passed; further strengthened Interstate Commerce Commission and expanded its jurisdiction.

1912 New Mexico admitted as 47th state.

1912 Arizona admitted as the 48th state.

1912 Election of 1912; Taft, who had lost support of the progressives and was opposed by T. Roosevelt, nevertheless won Republican nomination; Roosevelt formed insurgent Progressive (Bull Moose) party; this split the vote and enabled W. Wilson to win.

1913 Sixteenth Amendment to Constitution ratified; established national income tax.

1913-21 W. Wilson (Democrat) in office as 28th president; administration noted for passage of progressive reform legislation; Wilson guided US through WW I years, vainly attempting to maintain neutrality.

1913 Seventeenth Amendment to Constitution ratified; provided for direct popular election of Senators.

1913 Underwood Tariff enacted, lowering tariffs.

1913 H. Ford developed moving assembly line for mass production of Model T Ford.

1913 Federal Reserve System replaced Independent Treasury System.

1914 US forces landed in Veracruz, Mexico, amid political crisis there.

1914 WW I began in Europe (Aug.); US initially remained neutral.

1914 Panama Canal opened (Aug. 15).

1914 Federal Trade Commission established.

1914 Clayton Antitrust Act passed.

1915 US protested sinking of passenger liner *Lusitania* (May 7) by German submarine.

1916 Punitive raid into Mexico following border raid in US by Mexican rebel P. Villa.

1916 US protested German submarine warfare following sinking of *Sussex* (Mar. 24); Germans halted unrestricted submarine warfare.

1916 Federal Farm Loan Act passed.

1917 US broke relations with Germany (Feb.) after it resumed unrestricted submarine warfare.

1917 Zimmerman Telegram released (Mar. 1).

1917 US declared war on Germany (Apr. 6); participated in war, 1917–18.

1918 W. Wilson announced (Jan. 8) his Fourteen Points, plan to secure lasting peace after WW I. They contained his proposal for League of Nations.

1918-19 President Wilson participated in Paris Peace Conference (Dec.–June); failed to prevent imposition of harsh terms in Versailles treaty, but won establishment of League of Nations.

1919 Eighteenth Amendment to Constitution ratified; instituted Prohibition.

1919-20 US Senate refused to ratify the Versailles treaty; Wilson, seeking popular support for the treaty and the League of Nations, went on nationwide campaign but collapsed (Sept., 1919); Senate formally rejected the treaty (Mar. 1920) and the US never joined the League.

1920 "Red Raids"; Justice Department under A. Mitchell Palmer conducted mass arrests of labor agitators and suspected Communists in wake of Russian Revolution; many deported.

1920 Nineteenth Amendment to Constitution ratified; gave women right to vote.

1920 American Civil Liberties Union founded.

1921-23 W. Harding (Republican) served as 29th US president; administration noted for the corruption of Harding's appointees; Harding died (Aug. 2) at outbreak of Teapot Dome scandal.

1921 Sacco-Vanzetti Case; two Italian immigrants convicted in celebrated case.

1922 Fordney-McCumber Tariff enacted by Republicans; raised tariffs again.

1923-29 C. Coolidge (Republican) in office as 30th president succeeding Harding; restored confidence in government following revelations in Teapot Dome scandal; instituted conservative, pro-business policies and encouraged rampant speculation that led to stock market crash of 1929.

1924 Progressive party formed by R. La Follette to oppose both Republican and Democratic parties in presidential elections.

1925 Scopes trial conducted in Tennessee; C. Darrow defended teacher charged with teaching theory of evolution.

1927 C. Lindbergh completed (May 21) first nonstop, solo transatlantic flight in *Spirit of St. Louis*; became national hero overnight.

1927 Sacco and Vanzetti executed (Aug. 22).

1928 Kellogg-Briand Pact concluded; international agremeent declared end to war as an instrument of national policy.

1929-33 H. Hoover (Republican) served as 31st president; continuation of Coolidge's policies brought on the Depression; Hoover, steadfastly opposed to federal action to restore failing economy, took belated steps toward the end of his administration.

1929 Stock market crash began (Oct. 24), beginning the Depression; stocks continued to fall, bringing on widespread unemployment and business failures.

1929–39 Depression; US phase of the world-wide Great Depression brought on by the collapse of the stock market; economic collapse was halted by the mid-1930s but real economic recovery did not come until the beginning of WW II.

1930 Smoot-Hawley Tariff enacted; imposed highest tariffs ever established.

1932 Reconstruction Finance Corporation established to extend federal credit to banks and other financial institutions (Feb. 2).

1932 Norris-LaGuardia Act passed; contracts forbidding workers to join unions ("yellow dog" contracts) made illegal.

1932 Relief and Construction Act, passed to help states finance relief efforts (July 21).

1932 Federal Home Loan Bank Act passed to halt wave of foreclosures (July 22).

1932 Bonus Army, thousands of war veterans, forcibly expelled from Washington, DC (July).

1933 Twentieth Amendment to Constitution ratified; eliminated lame-duck Congress.

1933–45 F. Roosevelt (Democrat) in office as 32d president; responding to the worsening Depression, he put the federal government squarely behind the effort for economic recovery and put through many relief and reform bills to institute his "New Deal"; the only president elected to four terms, he spent the last years of his administration guiding the US through WW II.

1933–34 First New Deal.

1933 Roosevelt inaugurated (Mar. 4) as wave of bank failures reached crisis point.

1933 President Roosevelt declared bank holiday (Mar. 5).

1933 Special session of Congress convened by Roosevelt (Mar. 9); passage of New Deal legislation begun soon after.

1933 Banking Relief Act passed to prevent collapse of US banking system (Mar. 9).

1933 Civilian Conservation Corps (CCC) established (Mar. 31) to provide 250,000 jobs.

1933 Gold standard abandoned (Apr. 19).

1933 Federal Emergency Relief Act passed (May 12), providing funds for local relief efforts.

1933 Agricultural Adjustment Act (AAA) passed, providing farm subsidies (May 12).

1933 Tennessee Valley Authority created (May 18).

1933 Home Owners Loan Corporation (HOLC) created to help prevent foreclosures (June 13).

1933 Home Owners Refinancing Act passed (June 13).

1933 Glass-Steagall Act passed (June 16), creating the Federal Deposit Insurance Corporation (FDIC).

1933 National Industrial Recovery Act (NIRA) passed (June 16).

1933 Civil Works Administation (CWA) established (Nov. 8); eventually provided jobs for millions of unemployed on government projects.

1933 Twenty-first Amendment to the Constitution ratified; repealed Prohibition (Dec. 5).

1934 Dust storms began in the lower Great Plains region of the Midwest; gave rise to the "Dust Bowl" and the westward migration of thousands of farmers.

1934 Securities and Exchange Commission (SEC) created (June 6).

1934 Reciprocal Tariff Act passed (June 12), giving president power to lower tariffs; brought about end of high protective tariffs.

1934 Federal Communications Commission (FCC) created (June 19) to regulate communications industry.

1934 Federal Housing Authority (FHA) created (June 28).

1935 Committee for Industrial Organization (CIO) founded.

1935–39 Second New Deal.

1935 Works Progress Administration (WPA) created (Apr. 8).

1935 Soil Conservation Service established (Apr. 27).

1935 Supreme Court declared National Industrial Recovery Act (NIRA) unconstitutional (May); struggle between court and Roosevelt reached a climax in 1937.

1935 Rural Electrification Administration (REA) created (May 11).

1935 National Labor Relations Act passed (July 5), granting workers right to organize and bargain collectively.

1935 Social Security Act passed (Aug. 14).

1935 Wheeler-Rayburn Act passed (Aug. 28), putting gas and electricity companies under government control.

1935 Wealth Tax Act passed (Aug. 30) to tax incomes over $50,000 at a higher rate.

1935 Neutrality Act passed (Aug 31); aimed at keeping US out of war.

1936 Supreme Court ruled Agricultural Adjustment Act (AAA) unconstitutional (Jan.).

1936–44 American Labor party active.

1936 Election of 1936; Republican opposition to Roosevelt's New Deal coalesced around charge that free enterprise had been replaced by regulated monopoly; Roosevelt defeated his Republican opponent, A. Landon.

1937 Widespread strikes and labor unrest.

1937 Supreme Court controversy (Feb.–July); Roosevelt, in struggle with court over New Deal legislation, suggested increasing number of justices; plan denounced as scheme to pack the court with supporters and was abandoned.

1937 Hindenburg, a German dirigible, exploded into flames while docking at Lakehurst, New Jersey (May 6); thirty-six persons died.

1937 Neutrality extended (May); arms sales to belligerents prohibited.

1937 Nationwide recession began (Oct.); stock prices declined.

1938 House Un-American Activities Committee formed (May) to investigate Nazis, Communists, and other subversives.

1938 Fair Labor Standards Act passed (June 25), guaranteeing 40-hour work week and minimum wage.

1939 US defense appropriations increased as threat of war in Europe mounted.

1939 WW II broke out in Europe; US proclaimed neutrality (Sept. 5).

1939 Arms embargo established by Neutrality Act repealed to allow France and Britain to purchase munitions.

1940 Smith Act passed; aliens required to register.

1940 Defense appropriation of $18 billion to construct two-ocean navy and raise million-man army (July).

1940 Peacetime draft instituted to raise million-man army (Sept. 14).

1940 Advisory Commission to the Council on National Defense set up to mobilize US industry for possible war effort.

1940 Election of 1940; Roosevelt broke tradition (established by G. Washington) of serving only two terms and ran for third term; overwhelmingly defeated Republican opponent, W. Willkie.

1941 Roosevelt articulates his policy of Four Freedoms.

1941 Lend-Lease program established to supply potential allies (Mar. 1).

1941 Atlantic Charter issued after meeting with British Prime Minister W. Churchill (Aug.).

1941 Pearl Harbor attacked (Dec. 7) by Japanese; US declared war (Dec. 8).

1941–45 US participated in WW II; vast resources of men and matériel available to US, as well as efficient organization of industry gave US the upper hand; with the Allies, fought war in Europe as well as in Pacific Theater against Japanese; the US emerged victorious from the war and with the Soviet Union dominated the postwar world.

1942 War Production Board and Office of Price Administration created to manage wartime economy; rationing system instituted.

1942–45 Manhattan Project, begun by US government to develop atomic bomb; scientists on project achieved first sustained nuclear chain reaction (Dec. 2, 1942) and exploded world's first atomic bomb in test near Los Alamos (July 16, 1945).

1945 Pres. Roosevelt died in office (Apr. 12).

1945–53 H. Truman (Democrat) in office as the 33d president, succeeding Roosevelt; continued many of Roosevelt's policies and brought WW II to a successful conclusion; promoted his Fair Deal domestic policy, instituted programs to rebuild war-torn Europe, and presided over the early phase of the Cold War.

1945 San Francisco Conference held (Apr.–June); UN Charter drafted.

1945 WW II ended with Japan's surrender (Sept. 2).

1945 US joined the newly created UN.

1946 ENIAC, first all-electronic computer, developed.

1946 W. Churchill, former British prime minister, gave famous speech at Fulton, Missouri (Mar. 15); warned of the threat of communism and coined the term "Iron Curtain."

1946 Atomic Energy Commission established.

1947 Taft-Hartley Labor Act passed by Congress.

1947 Truman Doctrine articulated (Mar. 12) by Pres. Truman; responded to Soviet postwar expansionism.

1947 Pres. Truman issued Loyalty Order (Mar. 22) as fears about Communist subversives in government began to spread ("Red Scare").

1947 National Security Act passed to create a Department of Defense and establish the National Security Council.

1948 Marshall Plan; provided massive economic aid for war-torn Europe; brought about rapid economic recovery in Western Europe.

1948–49 US played a leading role in the Berlin Airlift.

1948 Election of 1948; opposed by T. Dewey, Republican, and S. Thurmond, candidate of the Dixiecrats, Truman was expected to lose the election; nevertheless conducted vigorous whistle-stop campaign and won the presidency.

1949 H. Truman announced (Jan. 5) his Fair Deal program.

1949 North Atlantic Treaty Organization (NATO) formed (Apr. 4) by nations of Europe and North America.

1949 A. Hiss, accused of being a Communist, convicted of perjury (Nov. 17, 1950); marked beginning of furor over subversives in government.

1949 Point Four Plan instituted to provide technical aid to underdeveloped nations.

1950–53 Korean War, pitting Communist East and non-Communist West against each other in armed conflict; US played leading role in what was called UN "police action."

1951 Twenty-second Amendment to the Constitution ratified; presidents limited to serving only two terms.

1951 Rosenbergs, accused of stealing atomic secrets, convicted; executed in 1953.

1952 US exploded first hydrogen bomb.

1952 Election of 1952; A. Stevenson ran as Democratic candidate, D. Eisenhower, Republican; vice-presidential candidate R. Nixon, under attack in campaign, gave famous "Checkers" speech (Sept. 23); Eisenhower won election in landslide and Republicans won control of both houses, ending long period of government by Democrats.

1953–61 D. Eisenhower (Republican) in office as 34th president; administration marked by period of general peace and prosperity, conservative domestic policy, and Cold War policies of "containment" of Communism and "massive retaliation" in the event of nuclear war.

1953 Department of Health, Education and Welfare established.

1953–54 McCarthy hearings; marked height of post–WW II "Red Scare"; ended with censure of Sen. J. McCarthy by Senate.

1954 *Brown* vs *Board of Education of Topeka*; Supreme Court reversed long-standing "separate but equal" doctrine and thus began the desegregation of schools.

1954 Southeast Asia Treaty Organization (SEATO) organized.

1955 AFL-CIO, major US labor federation, formed by merger of American Federation of Labor and the Congress of Industrial Organizations.

1955 Civil rights movement began; various civil rights groups sprang up after black woman refused to move to back of a bus (Dec. 5) in Montgomery, Alabama; Rev. M.L. King's Southern Christian Leadership Conference (SCLC) among groups that began nonviolent campaign against racial discrimination.

1956 Federal Aid Highway Act passed; funded construction of interstate highway system.

1957 Eisenhower Doctrine enunciated to halt communism in Mideast.

1957 Civil Rights Act passed; established commission to investigate infringements of Negro voting rights.

1957 Federal troops sent (Sept.) by President Eisenhower to enforce federal court order to desegregate the Little Rock, Arkansas, high school.

1957 Soviets launched (Oct. 4) first earth satellite; US embarrassed by the Soviet "first"; space race began.

1958 Lebanese Crisis; US troops landed in Lebanon.

1959 Alaska became the 49th state.

1959 Hawaii admitted as the 50th state.

1959 Soviet leader N. Khrushchev visited US (Sept.), following visit by US vice-president R. Nixon to the Soviet Union; hopes raised for Cold War "thaw."

1960 US U-2 spy plane shot down (May 1) over Soviet Union.

1961 Diplomatic relations broken (Jan.) with Cuba; marked beginning of troubles between US and Cuba's revolutionary leader, F. Castro.

1961–63 J.F. Kennedy (Democrat) is in office as 35th president; promoted activist and idealistic climate with his New Frontiers program; gave firm federal support to emerging civil rights movement; began limited US involvement in Vietnam; clashed with Communists in continuing Cold War.

1961 Bay of Pigs Invasion (Apr.); unsuccessful, CIA-backed invasion of Cuba; US deeply embarrassed by incident.

1961 Alliance for Progress established to combat communism in South America. US aid reduced after 1971.

1962 J. Glenn became the first American to orbit the earth (Feb. 20).

1962 Federal troops sent by Pres. Kennedy to enforce integration of the University of Mississippi (Sept.–Oct.).

1962 Cuban Missile Crisis (Oct.); Pres. Kennedy forced Soviets to withdraw missiles from Cuba.

1963 US signed Nuclear Test Ban Treaty.

1963 March on Washington, mass demonstration for black civil rights (Aug.).

1963 Pres. Kennedy assassinated (Nov. 22); Warren Commission later investigated shooting to put an end to persistent rumors about various conspiracies.

1963–69 L. Johnson (Democrat) in office as 36th president, succeeding Kennedy; instituted Great Society program and won enactment of legislation for sweeping social reform; made US active participant in Vietnam War; later years of administration marked by widespread antiwar protest and social unrest.

1964 Civil Rights Act of 1964 passed (July 2) to end all discrimination, including religious and sex discrimination.

1964 Gulf of Tonkin Incident; North Vietnam attacked US destroyers (Aug.); Gulf of Tonkin resolution passed by Congress used to justify later massive buildup of US forces in Vietnam.

1964 "War on Poverty" begun by Pres. Johnson with enactment of Economic Opportunity Act (Aug. 30).

1964 Election of 1964; Pres. Johnson ran for first full term against Republican B. Goldwater; Goldwater perceived as dangerously aggressive in foreign-policy thinking; Johnson won landslide victory.

1965–73 US actively involved in Vietnam War; US began bombing North Vietnam (Feb., 1965); sent hundreds of thousands of US troops into battle in unsuccessful effort to block Communist takeover in Vietnam.

1965 Antiwar teach-in held at University of Michigan (Mar.); teach-ins quickly spread to other campuses and thus began the student antiwar movement.

1965 Voting Rights Act of 1965 passed; legislation for Medicare for aged, federal aid to education, and other reform measures passed in this year.

1965 Watts riot (Aug.); first of race riots by blacks that spread to cities across the country; urban unrest among blacks reached a peak by 1968 and tapered off quickly in following years.

1966 Black Panthers, radical-terrorist group, formed; signaled rise of radical militants and end of nonviolent protest in black movement.

1967 Pentagon "siege" by antiwar protesters; marked ascendancy of antiwar protest in US; civil disobedience widespread.

1968 Social unrest reached fever pitch; blacks rioted in cities across the country; rioting by students on various campuses; counterculture, and drug cult within it, widespread among young people.

1968 *Pueblo* Incident (Jan. 23).

1968 Dr. M.L. King, leading figure of civil rights movement, assassinated (Apr. 4).

1968 R.F. Kennedy assassinated (June 5), while campaigning in Democratic primary.

1968 Election of 1968; widespread opposition to Vietnam War forced Johnson out of presidential race; Democratic National Convention (Chicago, Aug.) marred by rioting by antiwar radicals and subsequent "police riot"; H. Humphrey, Democrat, opposed R. Nixon, Republican, in presiden-

tial campaign; G. Wallace made unsuccessful third-party bid; Nixon, campaigning on conservative law-and-order and honorable peace in Vietnam, won election.

1969–74 R. Nixon in office as 37th president; instituted conservative policies, including emphasis on law enforcement and war on widespread drug use; gradually effected US withdrawal from Vietnam; began policy of détente to ease East-West tensions; administration brought down by Watergate scandal.

1969 SALT talks (arms limitation) begun with Soviets.

1969 US landed first man on the moon (July 20).

1969 March on Washington, massive antiwar protest (Nov. 15); demanded immediate, not gradual, withdrawal from Vietnam.

1970 Widespread protest followed US invasion of Cambodia; National guardsmen fired on protesters at Kent State (May 4); 100,000 demonstrated in Washington, DC (May 9).

1970 SST developmental funding bill defeated in Senate.

1971 Equal Rights Amendment passed by Congress; marked rise of women's rights movement that dominated the 1970s; amendment failed to win ratification after long fight (1982).

1971 US Table Tennis team visited China (Apr.); marked start of US efforts to normalize relations with China.

1971 Washington shutdown by antiwar protesters failed (May); 7,000 arrested.

1971 Pentagon Papers leaked to press (June); secret government study revealed US had gradually become entangled in Vietnam War.

1971 Voting age lowered to 18 following ratification of the 26th Amendment.

1971 Draft law expired.

1971 Nixon announced (Aug.) wage and price freeze to combat spiraling inflation; later devalued dollar (1971, 1973, 1974).

1972 Nixon visit to China (Feb. 21–27); process of normalization of relations with China continued.

1972 Pres. Nixon on historic first presidential visit to USSR (May 22–June 1); signed SALT I agreement, limiting antiballistic missile systems and missile launchers for offensive weapons.

1972–74 Watergate Scandal; arrest of Watergate burglars (June, 1972) began scandal, which culminated in Nixon's resignation (Aug. 9, 1974).

1972 SALT II talks began with USSR.

1972 Pres. Nixon signed revenue-sharing bill into law (Oct.).

1972 Election of 1972; Nixon opposed by Sen. G. McGovern; despite recession and continued inflation, Nixon won landslide victory.

1973 Peace agreement "ending" Vietnam War signed at Paris (Jan. 27).

1973 Senate began investigation of emerging Watergate Scandal (Feb.).

1973 Wage and price controls extended (Apr.) to Apr. 30, 1974.

1973 Existence of Nixon tapes revealed (July); long struggle for release of tapes begun by Watergate investigators.

1973 Vice-Pres. Agnew resigned (Oct. 10) under pressure from charges of past corruption; pleaded "no contest" to income tax evasion charge.

1973 Gerald Ford in office as vice-president (Dec. 6).

1974 Supreme Court ordered Pres. Nixon to release tapes sought by Watergate investigators (July 24).

1974 House voted articles of impeachment against President Nixon in Watergate scandal (July 27–30).

1974 Pres. Nixon resigned after admitting involvement in Watergate cover-up; became first president to resign under threat of impeachment (Aug. 9).

1974–76 G. Ford (Republican) in office as 38th president, succeeding Nixon; attempted to restore public confidence in government; recession, inflation, and growing unemployment plagued his administration.

1974 Ford granted Nixon pardon for crimes committed in office (Sept. 8).

1974 N. Rockefeller sworn in as vice-president (Dec. 19).

1975 Last Americans evacuated from South Vietnam (Apr. 29) as North Vietnamese completed successful invasion of South; Vietnam united under Communist rule soon after.

1975 Cambodians captured US cargo ship in *Mayaguez* Incident (May 12).

1976 Pres. Ford ordered sweeping reorganization of US intelligence agencies (Feb. 17).

1976 US Bicentennial celebration (July 4).

1976 Lockheed scandal; firm implicated in payment of bribes to foreign officials to secure contracts.

1976 Election of 1976; Pres. Ford defeated primary challenge by conservative Republican R. Reagan; J. Carter became dark-horse candidate of the Democrats; Carter projected a populist image and, taking advantage of distrust of government, promised sweeping reorganization of executive branch; Carter won election.

1977–81 J. Carter (Democrat) in office as 39th president; his administration marked by growing split with regular Democrats, the energy crisis, and by the success of Camp David negotiations between Egypt and Israel.

1977 House and Senate adopted strict codes of ethics (Mar.–Apr.).

1977 Legislation enacted permitting Pres. Carter to reorganize the executive branch.

1977 Alaska pipeline opened.

1977 US and Panama signed treaty giving Panama eventual control of the Panama Canal; Senate ratified treaty (Apr. 1978).

1978 Camp David accords signed (Sept. 17) by Israeli prime minister M. Begin and Egyptian president A. Sadat; provided a historic "framework for Mideast peace."

1979 Full diplomatic relations with China established (Jan. 1).

1979 Nuclear accident at Three Mile Island power plant in Pennsylvania (Mar. 28).

1979 Pres. Carter began implementation of oil price decontrol (June 1).

1979 US and USSR signed SALT II agreement on arms limitation (June); ratification held up by Senate opposition and Soviet invasion of Afghanistan.

1979–81 Hostage Crisis in Iran; Muslim militants seized US Embassy (Nov. 4) and held 52 Americans hostage; Iranians used incident to humiliate US; finally released hostages (Jan. 20, 1981).

1980 Pres. Carter ordered (Jan. 4) embargo on grain shipments to the Soviet Union in response to the Soviet invasion of Afghanistan.

1980 Influx of Cuban boat people reached major proportions (May–June).

1980 Election of 1980; Pres. Carter won narrow victory in bitter primary race against rival Sen. E. Kennedy; Republican candidate R. Reagan took advantage of growing disaffection with Democrats' liberal policies; campaigned on conservative program of tax cuts, less federal spending and regulation, and strong military; Reagan won landslide victory which swept many Republicans into office.

1980 Prime interest rate rose to 21.5% as effort to stem high inflation rate continued (Dec. 19).

1981– R. Reagan (Republican) in office as 40th president; on taking office began aggressive policy of cutting federal spending (except defense), while cutting taxes; by 1982 Reagan policies had cut inflation and brought down high interest rates, but at the cost of high unemployment.

1981 Americans being held hostage in Iran released (Jan. 20) as Pres. R. Reagan was being sworn in.

1981 Pres. Reagan seriously wounded (Mar. 30) in attempted assassination by John W. Hinckley, Jr.

1981 US launched world's first reusable spacecraft, the space shuttle *Columbia.*

1981 Strike by federal air controllers (Aug.) broken by Pres. Reagan; striking controllers fired.

1981 Sandra D. O'Connor sworn in (Oct. 25) as first woman Supreme Court justice.

1981 Pres. Reagan ordered economic sanctions imposed against the Soviets for their part in the crackdown against Solidarity in Poland.

1982 Demonstration (June 12) in New York City, the largest to-date, in which an estimated 750,000 participated, protesting nuclear arms race.

1982 Provisions of the Civil Rights Act extended for 25 years (June 29).

1982 US successful (Aug.) in its efforts to negotiate withdrawal of PLO guerrillas from Beirut, following Israeli invasion of Lebanon.

Universal Declaration of Human Rights Declaration adopted (Dec. 10, 1948) by the United Nations General Assembly. It proclaimed in general terms the basic social, political, and economic rights that should be accorded to people by governments.

Universalist Church of America American Protestant Christian denomination. Originating in the late 18th cent., it held that everyone will eventually achieve salvation. Holding similar views to those of the Unitarian church, it merged (May, 1961) with the Unitarians to form the Unitarian Universalist Association.

Untouchables *See* **caste system**

Upanishads Philosophical commentaries forming the last section of the Hindu Vedas. The Upanishads are the basis for the Vedanta system of philosophy.

Updike, John Hoyer 1932–. American writer whose novels and stories are noted for their examination and portrayal of modern American life. Among his books are *Rabbit Run, The Centaur,* and *Rabbit Redux.*

Upper Burma Region comprising central and northern Burma, annexed by the British (Jan., 1886) after the third Burmese War. It was occupied by the Japanese (1942–45) during WW II and became part of independent Burma (1948).

Upper Canada Named applied (1791 to 1841) to the Canadian region comprising present-day Ontario. Settled primarily by the British, it was joined with Lower Canada by the Act of Union

(1841) and became known as Canada West. With the confederation of Canada (1867), it became the province of Ontario.

Upper Volta Republic located in West Africa. Its capital is Ouagadougou. Inhabited since Neolithic times, the region was invaded (c12th cent.) by the Mossi, who established several powerful and stable states. France established (1895–96) a protectorate over much of Upper Volta, and in 1919, it was made a separate French colony. In 1947, Upper Volta became a territory within the French Union and then became independent (Aug. 5, 1960). Its government was overthrown (1966) by a military coup. In 1970, a new constitution was adopted, and elections were held in 1978. A coup in 1980 brought another change in leadership.

Ur Ancient Sumerian city once located on the Euphrates River in what is now southern Iraq. One of the earliest cities to rise in Mesopotamia, it was first settled c4000 BC and flourished under the 1st (26th–24th cents. BC) and 3d (22d–21st cents. BC) dynasties. The traditional home of Abraham, it was conquered and destroyed several times. Ur was rebuilt (6th cent. BC) by Nebuchadnezzar II but declined and was abandoned (c4th cent. BC), perhaps because of a change in the Euphrates' course. Excavation of the site (begun 19th cent.) has yielded important discoveries.

Urania *See* **Muses**

Uranus In Greek mythology, the personification of the heavens, born of Gaea (the earth). With Gaea, he fathered the Titans, the Cyclopes, and the Hecatoncheires.

Urartu Ancient kingdom (13th–7th cents. BC) in what is now eastern Turkey (Armenia). Identified as the biblical Ararat, it reached its greatest extent (ruling northern Syria) in the 8th cent. BC. The kingdom was often attacked by the Assyrians and was finally destroyed by invading Scythians and Medes.

Urban II ⟨Eudes of Lagery⟩ ⟨Odo of Lagery⟩ c1042–99. Pope (1088–99), successor to Gregory VII. He continued Gregory's reform movement, strengthened the papacy, and, through his preachings, helped to inspire the First Crusade.

Urban IV ⟨Pantaléon, Jacques⟩ *d.* 1264. Pope (1261–64), successor to Alexander IV. He established the feast of Corpus Christi, opposed the Hohenstaufens, and offered the Sicilian throne to Charles of Anjou

Urban V ⟨Grimoard, Guillaume de⟩ 1310–70. Pope (1632–70), successor to Innocent VI. Elected pope at Avignon, Urban moved the papacy to Rome (1367). Conflict in Rome and continued war between England and France led him to return to Avignon (1370).

Urban VI ⟨Prignano, Bartolomeo⟩ 1318?–89. Pope (1378–89), successor to Gregory XI. His election and subsequent actions alienated the French cardinals. They denied his election and elected Clement VII, thus beginning the Great Schism.

Urban VIII ⟨Barberini, Maffeo⟩ 1568–1644. Pope (1623–44), successor to Gregory XV. Fearing Hapsburg dominance over Rome, he supported the policies of Cardinal Richelieu and the French against Germany in the Thirty Years' War.

Urdu Indo-Iranian language, the official language of Pakistan. Urdu is spoken by more than 25,000,000 people and has a classical literature dating from the 14th cent.

Urey, Harold Clayton 1893–1981. American chemist. He was awarded the Nobel Prize in chemistry in 1934 for his isolation of the heavy-hydrogen isotope deuterium, a major step in the development of nuclear fission.

Urquiza, Justo José de 1801–70. Argentinian soldier and politician. As governor of Entre Rios province he overthrew the Argentine dictator J. de Rosas (1852). He helped to establish and served as president (1854–60) of the Argentine Confederation.

Ursula, Saint *fl.* 4th cent.? AD. Legendary saint said to have been martyred along with 11,000 virgins at Cologne by the Huns. She is the patron saint of the order of the Ursulines.

Uruguay ⟨Oriental Republic of Uruguay⟩ Independent state located on the southeastern coast of South America. Its capital is Montevideo. Uruguay was for a time in the early 20th cent. one of South America's most progressive democracies. Key dates in the history of Uruguay include:

1516 Uruguay discovered by Spaniard Juan Díaz de Solis.

1624 Spain established settlement on Rio Negro.

1680 Portugal established colony at Colonia.

c1777 Spain took complete control of region.

1811–14 Uruguay revolted, gained independence from Spain.

1816–20 Portuguese from Brazil captured Uruguay.

1825 Thirty-Three Immortals, led by J. Lavalleja, declared independence from Brazil; Argentines sent aid.

1827 Rebel forces defeated Brazilian troops at the Battle of Ituzaingó (Feb. 20).

1830 Republic declared; revolts against government began soon after.

1836 Civil war between Blancos (conservatives) and Colorados (liberals) began fifty years of internal disorder.

1865–70 War of the Triple Alliance; Uruguay allied with Brazil and Argentina against Paraguay.

1911–15 J. Batlle y Ordóñez became president; instituted progressive, liberal rule.

1919 New constitution; Ordóñez' liberal principles were included.

1931 Gabriel Terra became president.

1933 Coup by Terra; constitution suspended; Terra ruled until 1938, continuing liberal policies.

1950 Andrés Martínez Trueba elected president.

1952 Presidency abolished by constitutional amendment; Trueba headed nine-member national council.

1958 Colorados, in power for nearly 100 years, overwhelmingly defeated by conservatives (Blancos) in elections.

1966 Alberto Heber became president; urged reforms; constitution revised.

1967 New constitution; executive commission abolished and strong presidential system established as economic problems fomented unrest.

1970 Marxist Tupámaro guerrillas kidnapped and killed US adviser Dan Mitrione.

1972 Tupámaro guerrilla activities provoked government to institute state of internal war.

1972 Tupámaros founder, Raul Sendic, captured.

1972–76 Juan María Bordaberry in office as president.

1973 Military revolted (Feb.) as economic problems worsened; Bordaberry remained in office though military held real power.

1973 Constitutional government dissolved by Bordaberry; political activity banned.

1976 Bordaberry removed by military; Aparicio Méndez installed as president.

1980 Constitution establishing permanent military rule rejected in plebiscite.

1981 Gen. Gregorio Alvarez became president.

Uruk *See* **Erech**

Usher, James *See* **Ussher, James**

Ussher, James ⟨Usher, ~⟩ 1581–1656. Irish scholar and archbishop. He is noted for his biblical chronology, which set the date of Creation at 4004 BC.

Ustinov, Peter Alexander 1921–. English actor, director, and author. He has attained international renown for his books and plays as well as his stage and screen performances.

Utah Western US state (pop. 1,461,000), the 45th state. The capital is Salt Lake City. First explored (1540) by the Spanish, the region was again visited by J. Bridger, who is credited with discovering the Great Salt Lake (1824). The Mormons under B.

Young were the first permanent settlers (1847). The US acquired Utah from Mexico by the Treaty of Guadalupe Hidalgo (1848) at the end of the Mexican War, and Young became governor of Utah Territory (1850). Conflicts between the Mormons and the US government contributed to the Mountain Meadows Massacre *(q.v.)* and led to the Mormon War *(q.v.)* of 1857–58. The Mormon practice of polygamy was a major stumbling block to Utah statehood. Polygamy was abolished (1890), and Utah was admitted as a state in 1896.

Utah War *See* **Mormon War**

Uther Pendragon Legendary British king, thought to be the father of King Arthur.

Uthman ⟨Othman⟩ *d.* 656. Third Muslim caliph (644–56), successor to Omar and son-in-law of Muhammad. He continued Muslim conquest and expanded the power of the caliphate. His establishment of an official version of the Koran led to his assassination and a resulting struggle for leadership.

utilitarianism Ethical theory holding that the goodness of an act may be judged by its usefulness, or utility. The theory was elaborated by such philosophers as J. Bentham, J. Mill, and J.S. Mill. H. Spencer adapted utilitarianism to the scientific principles of evolution.

utopia Term applied to an imaginary ideal state. As such, the term was first used (1516) by T. More in his book *Utopia.* Later utopian societies were described in books by F. Bacon, E. Bellamy, and others.

Utraquists ⟨Calixtines⟩ Bohemian religious sect of the 15th cent. based on the teachings of J. Huss. Its members held that reception of both bread and wine was necessary for the sacrament of communion. They maintained ties with the Catholic church, opposed the more militant Taborites, and disappeared as a movement with the rise of the Reformation.

Utrecht, Peace of Two series of treaties (1713–15), one between France and other European countries and the other between Spain and other European countries, that ended the War of the Spanish Succession. In the first series France concluded treaties (Apr. 11, 1713) with England, The Netherlands, Savoy, Prussia, and Portugal. By these treaties France acknowledged the accession of Queen Anne to the English throne and ceded to England the Hudson Bay territory, Newfoundland,

Nova Scotia, and St. Kitts. The treaties also included French cession of the Spanish Netherlands to Austria by treaty with The Netherlands. France recognized Victor Amadeus II as king of Savoy, recognized the king of Prussia, and signed a peace with Portugal. In the second series of treaties (July, 1713–Feb., 1715), Spain signed treaties with England, Savoy, The Netherlands, and Portugal. Spain ceded Gibraltar and Minorca to England and granted England the right to sell slaves in Spanish America. It ceded Sardinia to Savoy and received acknowledgment of Philip V's succession (the cause of the war); signed a peace with the Dutch; and in 1715 made peace with Portugal. The treaties of Rastatt and Baden *(q.v.)* in 1714, between France and the Holy Roman Empire, completed the settlements.

Utrecht, Union of Union of provinces in the Low Countries that became independent of Spanish rule (1579) and that later became the modern state of The Netherlands *(q.v.).*

Utrillo, Maurice 1883–1955. French painter. A prolific artist noted for his independent style, he was known best for his paintings of street scenes of Paris, especially Montmartre.

U-2 affair Conflict (1960) between US and Russia over the shooting down (May, 1960) of an American U-2 spy plane over the Soviet Union. The affair led to cancellation of a proposed Paris summit meeting between Russia and the Western powers. The U-2 pilot, Francis Gary Powers, was sentenced to prison but was later exchanged for a Russian spy (1962).

Uxmal ⟨Oxmal⟩ Ancient Mayan city in southeastern Mexico, near Merida. It flourished (600–900) during the Mayan late classic period and is known for its excellent examples of Mayan architecture.

Uzbegs *See* **Uzbeks**

Uzbeks ⟨Uzbegs⟩ Turkic people, once a part of the Golden Horde. They occupied parts of Turkistan in central Asia by the 13th cent. and, by the 14th, were ruled by khans of the Golden Horde.

Uzziah ⟨Azariah⟩ *d. c*735 BC. King of Judah (*c*780–740 BC). He defeated the Philistines, rebuilt the walls of Jerusalem, and expanded the territory of the kingdom. He was stricken with leprosy toward the end of his reign, supposedly in punishment for his pride.

V

Vaishnavism Form of Hinduism. Its followers worship Vishnu, especially in his incarnation as Krishna or Rama.

Vaisya caste *See* **caste system**

Valdemar I *See* **Waldemar I**

Valdemar II *See* **Waldemar II**

Valdemar IV *See* **Waldemar IV**

Valdivia, Pedro de *c*1500–54. Spanish conquistador. He conquered Chile (1540s), founded the city of Santiago (1541) during the conquest, and served as governor of Chile.

Valens AD *c*328–378. Roman emperor of the East (AD 364–378), appointed by his brother Valentinian I. Valens defeated the Visigoths, then allowed them to settle in the empire. They rebelled and destroyed the Roman army at the Battle of Adrianople *(q.v.).* There Valens was killed and the eastern empire was rendered defenseless.

Valentine, Saint *d. c*270. Roman Christian priest who was martyred during the reign of Claudius II. His feast day, February 14, is now known as Valentine's Day. He is considered the patron saint of love.

Valentinian I AD 321–375. Roman emperor of the West (AD 364–375), successor to Jovian. He appointed his brother Valens emperor of the East and successfully defended the western frontiers of the empire.

Valentinian II AD 371–392. Roman emperor of the West (AD 375–392), successor to his father Valentinian I. He was deposed (AD 387) by Maximus but restored (AD 388) by Theodosius I. He was murdered, possibly by Arbogast.

Valentinian III AD 419–455. Roman emperor of the West (AD 425–455), appointed by his cousin Theodosius II. He allowed the empire to be ruled by others. During his reign Africa was conquered by the Vandals and Gaul and northern Italy were invaded by the Huns.

Valentinus *See* **Gnosticism**

Valerian *d.* after AD 260. Roman emperor (AD 253–260), successor to Aemilianus. He reimposed persecution of the Christians, appointed his son Gallienus to rule in the West, and was defeated and captured by Persian king Shapur I.

Valéry, Paul 1871–1945. French poet and writer, considered one of the leading French poets of the early 20th cent. His masterpiece is *La Jeune Parque.*

Valla, Lorenzo *c*1407–57. Italian humanist and scholar. He identified the Donation of Constantine as a fraud, and pointed out the failures of the Latin Vulgate to faithfully translate the Greek Bible.

Valley Forge Village in northeastern Pennsylvania, site of the winter encampment (1777–78) of the Continental Army under G. Washington. Here Baron von Steuben drilled the Continental Army into an efficient military unit.

Valmy, Battle of First important battle (Sept. 20, 1792) of the French Revolutionary Wars, at Valmy, France. Some 36,000 French defeated a force of Austrians and Prussians. Both sides suffered casualties of only a few hundred, but the battle showed that the revolutionary forces were capable of defending France.

Valois French royal house, a branch of the Capetians, who ruled France from 1328 to 1589, beginning with Philip VI. The first half of their reign was marked by the Hundred Years' War and by challenges from the nobility. However, the Valois rulers ably met both threats, consolidated their power, and established their sole right of taxation. The direct line ended with the death of Charles VIII (1498). It continued with the houses of Valois-Orléans and Valois-Angoulême until the advent of Henry IV and the Bourbons (1589). Valois kings of France included:

Philip VI	1328–50
John II	1350–64
Charles V	1364–80
Charles VI	1380–1422
Charles VII	1422–61
Louis XI	1461–83
Charles VIII	1483–98
Louis XII	1498–1515
Francis I	1515–47

Henry II	1547–59
Francis II	1559–60
Charles IX	1560–74
Henry III	1574–89

Valois, Catherine of *See* **Catherine of Valois**
Valois, Charles of *See* **Charles of Valois**
Valois, Elizabeth of *See* **Elizabeth of Valois**
Valois, Margaret of *See* **Margaret of Valois**
Valparaiso, Treaty of *See* **Pacific, War of the**
Vanbrugh, Sir John 1664–1726. English dramatist and architect. He established himself as one of the leading Restoration dramatists, then turned to architecture. Among his works is Blenheim Palace in Oxfordshire.
Van Buren, Martin 1782–1862. US president (1837–41), the 8th, successor to A. Jackson. A Democrat, he led the Albany Regency *(q.v.)* and served in the US Senate (1821–28), where he supported the policies of A. Jackson. Elected (1828) governor of New York, he soon resigned to become secretary of state (1829–31). In 1832, Van Buren was elected vice-president under Jackson, and in 1836 he won the presidency. His administration was marked by the financial Panic of 1837, passage of legislation establishing an independent treasury system, US neutrality during the Canadian rebellion of 1837, and the Aroostook War (q.v.), between settlers in Maine and Canada. Van Buren was defeated in the 1840 presidential campaign, and he was a leader of the Barnburners against the Hunkers *(qq.v.)*. In 1848, as the Free-Soil party candidate, he split the Democratic vote and thus helped Z. Taylor win the election.
Vancouver, George 1757–98. English navigator and explorer. He sailed with Captain J. Cook and surveyed the west coast of North America. Vancouver Island and Vancouver, B.C., are named for him.
Vandals Germanic tribe, believed to have originated around Jutland. Fleeing the Huns (early 5th cent. AD), they embarked upon their own campaign of conquest, sweeping through Gaul and into Spain. Led by Gaiseric, they crossed into North Africa (429) and eventually captured Carthage (AD 439). Rome recognized Gaiseric's rule three years later and the Vandals began their pirate attacks upon Mediterranean shipping. From there they raided Sicily and southern Italy, and sacked Rome (AD 455). Arian Christians, they vigorously persecuted other Christian sects. The power of the Vandals declined after Gaiseric's death in the late 5th cent. and was finally broken by the Byzantine general Belisarius (AD 533).
Vandenberg, Arthur Hendrick 1884–1951. American politician. As US senator (1928–51) he moved from a policy of isolationism to support of the foreign policy of Pres. H. Truman and establishment of the United Nations.
Vanderbilt American family. Its wealth and position were secured by Cornelius Vanderbilt (1794–1877), who made an immense fortune in shipping and railroads. He gave $1 million to found Vanderbilt University. His son William Henry Vanderbilt (1821–85) succeeded his father in managing the family railroad interests. William's sons included Cornelius Vanderbilt (1843–99) and George Washington Vanderbilt (1862–1914).
Van Dorn, Earl 1820–63. Confederate general in the American Civil War. Van Dorn received the surrender of Union forces in Texas (1861) and fought at Pea Ridge (Mar., 1862) and Corinth (Oct., 1862). He was murdered in 1863.
Van Dyck, Sir Anthony 1599–1641. Flemish painter. One of the greatest portrait painters of the 17th cent. He developed a characteristic style that lent an air of dignity and elegance to his subjects and made him extremely popular among the European aristocracy. By 1632 he had become court painter to English King Charles I and spent much of the remainder of his life in England. He painted portraits of many of the leading figures of the English court and greatly influenced later English portrait painters. Van Dyck also painted religious subjects and did etchings and drawings.
Vane, Sir Henry 1589–1655. English courtier and Parliamentarian, father of H. Vane. He served in every Parliament from 1614 to 1640 and carried out important diplomatic missions for King Charles I. He lost favor with the king and joined the Parliamentary party.
Vane, Sir Henry 1613–62. English statesman. A Puritan, he served as governor of Massachusetts (1636–37), then returned to England. He attempted to be a moderating influence during and after the English Civil War but was executed for treason after the restoration of King Charles II.
Van Rensselaer, Stephen 1764–1839. American political leader. He took a prominent part in New York politics, serving as lieutenant governor (1795–1801), major general in the War of 1812, and US congressman (1822–29). He was instrumental in building the Erie Canal.
Vanzetti, Bartolomeo *See* **Sacco-Vanzetti case**
Varangians Scandinavian conquerers of Russia in the 9th and 10th cents. Also called "Rus," they thus gave Russia its name. They were gradually absorbed by the Slavs. (*See also* Norsemen.)
Vardhamana *See* **Mahavira**
Vargas, Getulio Dornelles 1883–1954. Brazilian statesman, twice president of Brazil (1930–45, 1951–54). He came to power by revolution. Al-

though he encouraged reform and development in industry and agriculture, his rule was dictatorial.

Varna, battles of 1. Ottoman Turkish victory (Nov. 10, 1444) over the Hungarians at Varna, now in Bulgaria. The Turkish forces defeated the Hungarians under J. Hunyadi and killed Ladislaus, king of Poland and Hungary. Eastern Europe remained in Ottoman control. **2.** Russian victory (Oct. 12, 1828) over the Ottoman Turkish forces of Sultan Mahmud II during the Russo-Turkish War of 1828. After several months of campaigning, the Russians finally forced the Turks, besieged at Varna, to surrender. The Russians were unable to further prosecute the war, however, and soon took up winter quarters.

Varro, Marcus Terentius 116–27? BC. Roman scholar, one of the most versatile, prolific, and brilliant men produced by Rome. His writings filled some 600 books.

Varus, Publius Quintilius d. AD 9. Roman general and consul (13 BC). As commander in Germany (AD 6–9) he was totally defeated by Arminius and committed suicide.

Vasa Swedish family that ruled Sweden (1523–1654) and Poland (1587–1668). Established in Sweden by King Gustavus I, it gained the Polish throne through the marriage of Swedish king John III to the sister of Polish king Sigismund II. Their son, a Catholic, became (1587) Polish king Sigismund III. When he attempted to assume the Swedish throne, however, the Protestant Swedes ousted him and installed his uncle, Charles IX (1599). Thereafter, the two Vasa branches fought frequently for domination. The Protestant Swedish Vasas greatly increased Sweden's Baltic influence. The direct Vasa line in Sweden ended with the abdication of Queen Christina and the crowning of her cousin Charles X (1654). In Poland, the ruling line ended with the abdication (1668) of King John II Casimir.

Vasari, Giorgio 1511–74. Italian architect, painter, and art historian. He is noted for his history of Renaissance art and artists, *Vite de' più eccellenti architetti, pittori e scultori italiani.*

Vasily III 1479–1533. Grand duke of Moscow (1505–33), successor to his father, Ivan III. He continued his father's consolidation of territory by annexing Pskov (1510), Ryazan (1517), and Novgorod-Seversk (1523), and capturing Smolensk (1514).

vassal In feudal society, the holder of a fief, or landed estate granted by an overlord in return for feudal services.

Vassy, massacre of *See* **Guise, François of Lorraine, 2d duke of**

Vatican City Independent city-state located mostly within the city of Rome. It is the official seat of the pope, head of the Roman Catholic church. Vatican City was established by the Lateran Treaty (Feb. 11, 1929) between Italy and Pope Pius XI. The unification of Italy (1870) had deprived the pope of the former Papal States, by which the popes had endeavored to maintain their independence from any secular ruler. The Lateran Treaty guaranteed papal independence.

Vatican Council 1. The First Vatican Council (1869–70), or 20th ecumenical council of the Catholic church, was convened (Dec. 8, 1869) at the Vatican by Pope Pius IX. It was interrupted by the capture of Rome (Oct. 1870) by Italian troops. The council upheld the pope as supreme leader of the Catholic church and promulgated the dogma of papal infallibility when speaking *ex cathedra* on matters of faith or morals. **2.** The Second Vatican Council (1962–65), or 21st ecumenical council of the Catholic church, was convened (Oct. 11, 1962) at the Vatican by Pope John XXIII and continued by Pope Paul VI. The council issued 16 documents through which it sought to promote a spiritual renewal within the Catholic church. It invited representatives from both Protestant and Eastern Orthodox churches to observe the proceedings. Its principal accomplishments included modification of the liturgy of the Mass, support for the spirit of ecumenism, and condemnation of anti-Semitism. Its wide-ranging reforms have had a major impact on the church.

Vauban, Sébastien Le Prestre, marquis de 1633–1707. French military engineer and marshal of France. He developed a series of parallel trenches at the siege of Maastricht (1673) which revolutionized siege warfare. He also invented the socket bayonet.

Vaucreuil-Cavagnal, Pierre François de Rigaud, marquis de 1698–1765. Last French governor of New France (1755–60). After the defeat of Gen. L. Montcalm, he surrendered New France to Britain (1760).

Veblen Thorstein 1857–1929. American economist and social scientist. He is known best for his book *The Theory of the Leisure Class,* which introduced such phrases as "conspicuous consumption."

Vecellio, Tiziano *See* **Titian**

Vedas Sacred Indian texts. Among the oldest examples of ancient Indian literature, the Veda include texts of hymns, poetry, and prose that state the essential beliefs, laws, mythology, prayers, and rituals of Hinduism. They originated with the Aryans, who entered India c1500 BC. The Veda are divided into four primary groupings: the

Samhitas, containing hymns and liturgies; the Brahmanas, prose explanations of sacrificial ceremonies; Aranyakas, instructions for meditations; and the Upanishads, mystical writings.

Vedanta Term used to describe the philosophy on which modern Hinduism is based. Meaning literally "the end of the Veda," it is based on the knowledge of the final Vedic texts, the Upanishads. Vedanta was developed especially by the Hindu sages Sankara and Ramanuja.

Vega Carpio, Lope Félix de 1562–1635. Founder of the Spanish drama. He wrote some 1,800 plays and countless other works in prose and verse. His works included "cloak and sword dramas," "heroic comedies," and dramas of domestic life and were immensely popular.

Vehme *See* **Vehmgericht**

Vehmgericht ⟨Vehme⟩ ⟨vehmic court⟩ Extraordinary criminal tribunal in medieval Germany. These tribunals flourished in the 14th and 15th cents. but declined with the increased authority exerted by the princes.

vehmic court *See* **Vehmgericht**

Velasco, Luis de *d.* 1564. Spanish colonial administrator, second viceroy of New Spain (1550–64). He improved the condition of the Indians and outfitted the expedition that conquered the Philippines.

Velasco, Luis de 1539–1617? Spanish viceroy of Mexico (1590–95, 1607–11) and Peru (1596–1604), son of L. de Velasco.

Velázquez, Diego de 1465?–1522? Spanish soldier and administrator. He sailed with Columbus (1493), was first governor of Cuba (1511–22), and founded Santiago (1514) and Havana (1515).

Velázquez, Diego Rodríguez de Silva y 1599–1660. Spanish painter, one of the great masters of 17th-cent. art. His mature works, which utilized color, perspective, and light to capture a sense of realism, greatly influenced later painters. His works include portraits of Philip IV and Don Carlos, *Surrender of Breda,* and *Borrachos.*

Vellore Mutiny Sepoy uprising against the British (May 10, 1806) at Vellore, India. The Sepoys seized the fortress in which the family of Tipu Sahib lived and killed some 130 British soldiers. The mutiny was soon suppressed and the family of Tipu Sahib was removed to Calcutta.

Vendée, Wars of the French royalist insurrections. From 1793–1832, the French region of the Vendée frequently attempted counterrevolutions to defeat the French Republic and restore the monarchy. The peasants of the Vendée first rebelled against conscription by the French government (Mar., 1793). They were joined by displaced nobles, who spread the revolt throughout the

summer and fall but were defeated at Le Mans (Dec. 12, 1793). The harsh treatment of defeated counterrevolutionaries by the Republicans led to a second Vendée insurrection (1794). Smaller royalist revolts in the Vendée took place in 1799, 1815, and 1832.

Vendôme, César, duc de 1594–1665. French general and politician, a son of French king Henry IV. He participated in conspiracies against King Louis XIII, Cardinal Richelieu, and Cardinal Mazarin.

Vendôme, Louis Joseph, duc de 1654–1712. French general. He fought with distinction in the War of the Grand Alliance and played a major role in the War of the Spanish Succession (1701–14).

Venetia Region of northeastern Italy. Inhabited by the Venetii, it was conquered (2d cent. BC) and made a province by the Romans, ravaged by the Huns (5th cent. AD), and flourished (15th–16th cents.) under the rule of the republic of Venice. Contested by Austria and Italy, it passed to Italy at the close of the Austro-Prussian War (1866) between Austria and Prussia.

Venetian school School of Italian art that flourished in Venice from the 15th through 18th cents. Its artists' works were characterized by their use of color and celebration of light. Among its artists were G. Bellini, Giorgione, Titian, and Tintoretto.

Venezuela ⟨Republic of Venezuela⟩ Independent state located in northern South America on the Caribbean Sea. Its capital is Caracas. Venezuela is one of the world's major oil-producing nations. Key events in Venezuelan history include:

1498 Columbus discovered Venezuela.

1499 Alonas de Ojeda and Amerigo Vespucci explored coast.

1527 First permanent Spanish settlement at Coro.

1567 Caracas founded.

16–18TH CENT. British buccaneers active along coast.

1795 Unsuccessful revolt against Spain.

1810 Revolt against Spain resumed under Francisco Miranda.

1811 Independence declared (July 5).

1821 Independence from Spain established by S. Bolívar's victory at Battle of Carabobo (June 24); Venezuela joined Federation of Greater Colombia.

1830 José Antonio Páez separated Venezuela from federation.

1830–46 Páez in office as first president.

1839–40 British Guiana gained major share of long-disputed territory.

1846–58 José Tadeo Monagas in power.

1864 Short-lived United States of Venezuela formed under Juan Falcon.

1870–88 A. Guzmán Blanco ruled as dictator; overthrown.

1886 British occupied Orinoco River in continuing boundary dispute over British Guiana.

1892–99 Juan Crespo became dictator.

1895 US became involved in ongoing boundary dispute.

1899 Venezuela Boundary Dispute settled in arbitration; most disputed territory awarded to Britain.

1899–1908 Cipriano Castro became president.

1902 Castro's inability to repay long-standing European debts led to Venezuela Claims incident.

1908–35 Dictator J. Gómez in power after deposing Castro; ruled tyrannically; stimulated economic growth.

1935–41 Eleazar López Contrera became president.

1948–58 Military seized power (Nov. 1947) and thereafter installed a series of presidents; military rule ended by popular revolt (1958); democratic government restored.

1958–64 Romulo Betancourt in office as president.

1961 New constitution adopted.

1962 Communist-inspired revolts suppressed as political unrest mounted.

1964–68 Raúl Leoni in power as president.

1966 Leftist terrorists in Caracas suppressed.

1969–74 Rafael Caldera Rodriguez in office as president; legalized Communist Party; established relations with Soviets.

1974–79 Carlos Peréz in office as president.

1976 Nationalization (with compensation) of oil companies.

1978 Oil profits declined; austerity measures instituted.

1979– Luis Herrera Campíns in office as president; remained in office into the early 1980s.

Venezuela Boundary Dispute Prolonged territorial dispute between Great Britain and Venezuela over the boundary between Venezuela and British Guiana. The disagreement continued through much of the 19th cent. but took on added meaning when gold was discovered in the disputed area. In 1887, the nations broke off diplomatic ties. In 1895, US secretary of state R. Olney invoked the Monroe Doctrine and demanded arbitration. Britain at first refused but eventually yielded to avoid conflict with the US. In 1899, an arbitration panel awarded most of the disputed territory to Britain.

Venezuela Claims Financial claims pressed upon Venezuela in the early 20th cent. During the rule of Venezuelan president C. Castro, Venezuela fell into a complicated financial tangle. In Dec., 1902,

France, Great Britain, Germany, and Italy demanded swift repayment of outstanding loans to Venezuela, pressing their claims by sending gunboats to blockade Venezuelan ports. After they bombarded several port cities, the US intervened as unofficial arbitrator. The matter was referred to the Hague Tribunal (1904), which ruled that Venezuela must repay the belligerent countries before settling its debts with neutral nations. Venezuela fulfilled its obligations in 1907.

Venice Italian seaport (pop. 377,600), capital of Venezia province. Venice was first settled (5th cent. AD) by people fleeing from invasions from the north. It elected its first doge in 697, and by the 10th cent., it began its expansion as a commercial and cultural center. It played a major role in the Fourth Crusade, from which it gained numerous colonial holdings in the eastern Mediterranean, among them Crete and the Ionian Islands. Venice became the leading Italian city after its defeat of its rival, Genoa (1381). An uprising in Venice (1310) led to the rule of the Council of Ten *(q.v.)*, which governed Venice until 1797. The rich and powerful Venetian republic in the 15th cent. dominated trade with the East and thus maintained contact between Europe and Asia. With the discovery of the New World and the expansion of the Ottoman Empire (which warred against Venice), Venetian power gradually declined in the 16th and 17th cents. In 1797 the republic of Venice fell and the region passed to Austrian control. Venice became part of Napoleon's kingdom of Venice (1805–15), returned to Austrian control, and became part of Italy (1866) at the end of the Seven Weeks' War between Austria and Prussia.

Venizelos, Eleutherios 1864–1936. Greek statesman. He led the movement in Crete for union with Greece. As Greek prime minister (1910–15, 1917–20) he greatly expanded Greek territory during the Balkan Wars and WW I.

Venus Roman goddess, originally associated with gardens and vegetation. She was later identified with Aphrodite, the Greek goddess of love.

Veracruz Incident US occupation of Vera Cruz, Mexico (Apr.–Nov., 1914) during the Mexican Revolution. The action was prompted by Mexican seizure of a US ship in Tampico Harbor and led to the fall of V. Huerta.

Vercingetorix *d.* 46 BC. Chieftain of the Arverni tribe in Gaul. He led a great revolt against the Romans (52 BC), was defeated by J. Caesar, exhibited in Rome, and executed.

Verdi, Giuseppe 1813–1901. Italian composer, considered the greatest Italian composer of opera in the 19th cent. and perhaps of all time. Among his greatest operas are *Rigoletto*, *Il Trovatore*, and *La Traviata*.

Verdun, Battle of Battle (Feb.-Dec., 1916) fought by French and German forces during WW I for control of the strategic town of Verdun, in northeastern France. The battle began (Feb. 21) when German forces under Crown Prince Wilhelm opened a massive artillery bombardment of French positions around Verdun. The German offensive was calculated to defeat the French army through sheer attrition, as the French were sure to hold Verdun at all costs. After initial German advances, French general H. Pétain assumed command of the Verdun salient, and reinforcements were sent. Through bitter fighting, the Germans continued to advance in the sector but were unable to capture Verdun. Meanwhile the French and British opened the Battle of the Somme (July 1), thus relieving some of the pressure on Verdun. By July 11, the German offensive ground to a halt. The French launched a major counteroffensive (Oct. 24) and by Dec. had regained most of the territory they had lost. The Germans had been unable to crush the French or to break the stalemate on the Western Front. German losses were some 330,000 to French casualties of some 350,000.

Verdun, Treaty of Treaty (843) by which the Carolingian Empire was divided among the three sons and heirs of Emperor Louis I (the Pious). After the death of Louis I (840), the empire was rent by warfare among his sons Louis the German, Charles II (the Bald), and Lothair I. By the treaty, Lothair retained the title of emperor and received much of Italy, Alsace-Lorraine, Burgundy, and the Low Countries. This narrow, middle part of the empire, was called Lotharingia (or Francia Media). Louis the German received territory east of the Rhine, which formed the basis for modern Germany. Charles II received the western territory of the empire, which evolved into modern France.

Vereeniging, Peace of Treaty (May 31, 1902) between Great Britain and the Boers ending the Boer War. By its terms, the Transvaal and the Orange Free State accepted British sovereignty and became crown colonies. Britain paid an indemnity for property destroyed and agreed to establish responsible government as soon as possible.

Vergara, Convention of *See* **Convention of Vergara**

Vergennes, Charles Gravier, comte de 1717–87. French statesman. Appointed foreign minister (1774) by King Louis XVI, he formed the alliance between France and the American colonists during the American Revolution. He negotiated the Treaty of Paris (1783).

Vergil ⟨Virgil⟩ 70–19 BC. Greatest of Latin poets. Born near Mantua, he became a member of the literary circle at the court of Augustus. His works the *Bucolics*, or *Eclogues*, and *Georgics* established him as the foremost poet of his age. His major work, however, remains the *Aeneid*.

Verlaine, Paul 1844–96. French poet, one of the leading poets of the late 19th cent. His works anticipated the poetry of the symbolists.

Vermeer, Jan ⟨Vermeer, Johannes⟩ 1632–75. Dutch painter of the baroque period, noted for his landscapes and domestic interiors. He was a master of light and color and one of the giants of 17th-cent. Dutch painting, though he completed only about 35 paintings. They include *Girl Asleep*, *Young Woman with a Water Jug*, *The Procuress*, and *Soldier and Laughing Girl*.

Vermeer, Johannes *See* **Vermeer, Jan**

Vermont Northeastern US state (pop. 511,500), the 14th state. Its capital is Montpelier. The area was first explored by S. Champlain (1609), who sailed along the lake named after him. The French made several attempts at settlement (17th–18th cents.), but the first permanent settlement was the British Fort Dummer, near present-day Brattleboro, in 1724. The region was claimed by New Hampshire and New York. New Hampshire's issuance of the New Hampshire Grants (*q.v.*) led to conflicts between the two colonies, and E. Allen formed the Green Mountain Boys to resist New York authority. The Green Mountain Boys played a significant role during the American Revolution, notably at the battles of Ticonderoga and Bennington (*qq.v.*). Vermont declared itself an independent state (1777) but was not admitted into the Union until 1791. It took an active role in support of the Union during the American Civil War and was the scene of the St. Albans Raid (1864).

Verne, Jules 1828–1905. French novelist. His extrapolations of contemporary science in fiction had great influence in the development of modern science fiction. Among his works is the classic *Twenty Thousand Leagues Under the Sea*.

Verona Italian city (pop. 264,100), capital of Verona province in northeastern Italy. Ruled by Rome from 89 BC, it was overrun by the Goths (5th–6th cents. AD). Verona reached its zenith (1260–1387) under the rule of the della Scala family but soon declined. It eventually passed into the control of Venice, then (1797) passed to Austria. It became part of the kingdom of Italy (1866) after the Austro-Prussian War.

Verona, Congress of *See* **Congress of Verona**

Veronesa, Paolo 1528–88. Italian painter, considered one of the greatest decorative artists of the

Venetian school. His works are noted for their brilliant use of color.

Verrazano, Giovanni da *See* **New York**

Versailles, Palace of French royal palace at Versailles, southeast of Paris. Begun (17th cent.) under French king Louis XIV, it was the residence of the French kings (1682–1790) and was the site of the early events of the French Revolution. Here Wilhelm I was proclaimed emperor of Germany (1871) and here were signed the treaties of Versailles (1871, 1919).

Versailles, Treaty of Preliminary treaty (1871) ending the Franco-Prussian War, signed at Versailles, France. Negotiators were O. von Bismarck and A. Thiers. France ceded Alsace-Lorraine and agreed to an indemnity of five billion francs.

Versailles, Treaty of Treaty (June 28, 1919) ending WW I. Its provisions, the result of the Paris Peace Conference, were primarily drawn up by US president W. Wilson, British prime minister D. Lloyd-George, French premier G. Clemenceau, and Italian prime minister V. Orlando. Germany was not consulted. The treaty also made provision for establishment of the League of Nations. Germany's colonies became mandates of the League of Nations, and Alsace-Lorraine was returned to France. In addition, Germany was forced to accept responsibility for the war, agreed to huge reparations payment and surrender of equipment, limited its army to 100,000 troops, relinquished vast land holdings to Poland (including the Polish Corridor, *q.v.*), and agreed to demilitarization of the Rhineland. The US did not ratify the treaty, but its provisions were implemented and helped to cause the early rise of A. Hitler and Nazism. Hitler subsequently broke the treaty's provisions.

Verucchio, Malatesta da *See* **Malatesta**

Verus, Lucius Aurelius ⟨Commodus, Lucius Ceionius⟩ AD 130–169. Roman emperor (AD 161–169), coruler with M. Aurelius. Sent to campaign in Parthia (AD 162–165), he spent most of his time in Antioch. He was the first person known to share equally the imperial power.

Vervins, Treaty of Treaty (May 2, 1598) between France and Spain. It helped end the French Wars of Religion by providing for the withdrawal of Spanish support to the Catholic League in France.

Verwoerd, Hendrik Frensch 1901–66. South African political leader. As prime minister of South Africa (1958–66) he led the establishment of apartheid, or separation of the races, in his country.

Vesalius, Andreas 1514–64. Belgian physician whose careful studies of anatomy, made from human cadavers, radically advanced the science of biology and practice of medicine.

Vespasian ⟨Titus Flavius Vespasianus⟩ AD 9–79. Roman emperor (AD 69–79), successor to Vitellius. He restored order to the empire, set an example of simple living, built the Colosseum, and founded the Flavian dynasty.

Vespucci, Amerigo 1454–1512. Italian navigator. He explored the east coast of South America, which he considered to be a new continent. The name "America" is derived from his name.

Vestal Ancient Roman priestess who tended the perpetual fires in the Temple of Vesta, goddess of the hearth. The vestal virgins were chosen from prominent Roman families and were bound by a vow of chastity. They enjoyed great privileges and influence in Roman life.

Veterans of Foreign Wars American veterans' association founded (1899) after the Spanish-American War and chartered by Congress (1936). It is one of the largest veterans' organizations in the US.

veto Power of the executive to invalidate acts by the legislature. Roman tribunes could veto acts of the Roman Senate. In the US, the president may veto acts of Congress, but Congress can override the veto by a two-thirds vote.

viceroy Governor of a province, territory, country by authority of a king or sovereign. Rulers of Spanish territories in the Americas were viceroys, and British viceroys governed Ireland and British India.

Vichy French government headed by Marshal H. Pétain, established during WW II after the French-German armistice (June, 1940). It controlled that part of France not occupied by Germany, and its policies were generally favorable to Germany. The Vichy government lost importance after German occupation (1942) of all France but continued to exist until 1944.

Vicksburg campaign Successful Union campaign (Nov., 1862–July, 1863) to capture Vicksburg, Mississippi, during the American Civil War. Union capture of the city, last Confederate stronghold on the Mississippi, would effectively have divided the Confederacy in two. Confederate forces under Gen. John C. Pemberton (1814–81) fortified the city and for months successfully repelled Union assaults. In Apr. and May, 1863, Union Gen. U. Grant executed a series of maneuvers by which his forces seized key positions south of the city, crossed the Mississippi, and moved east to halt the advance of Gen. J. Johnston, who had sought to link up with Pemberton's forces. Pemberton, who had moved out of Vicksburg to meet Johnston, was forced back to Vicksburg. Grant began a six-week siege that culminated (July 4, 1863) in Pemberton's surrender of Vicksburg. Union losses were about 10,000 to Confederate losses of some 9,000 casualties and 30,000 prisoners. The campaign was a major defeat for the Confederacy and marked Grant's ascendency as the Union's leading commander.

Vico, Giovanni Battista 1668–1744. Italian philosopher and historian. He advanced a theory of the cyclical and evolutionary nature of history and urged scientific methods in historical investigation.

Victor Emmanuel I 1759–1824. King of Sardinia (1802–21), successor to his brother Charles Emmanuel IV. He regained a number of Italian territories after the fall of Napoleon, but his autocratic rule led to an uprising and his abdication (1821).

Victor Emmanuel II 1820–78. King of Sardinia (1849–61) and first king of a united Italy (1861–78). As king of Sardinia he appointed Count C. Cavour prime minister and encouraged the efforts of G. Garibaldi. (*See* Italy [1849–78].)

Victor Emmanuel III 1869–1947. Italian king (1900–46), successor to his father, Humbert I. He brought Italy into WW I on the side of the Allies. He refused to oppose the rise of Fascism and supported the government of B. Mussolini.

Victoria *See* **Nike**

Victoria 1819–1901. Queen of Great Britain and Ireland (1837–1901) and empress of India (1876–1901). Daughter of Edward, duke of Kent, she succeeded her uncle William IV to the English throne, but she was prevented by the Salic law from succeeding to the Hanoverian throne, thus separating the two crowns. Victoria married (1840) her first cousin, Prince Albert of Saxe-Coburg-Gotha, to whom she bore nine children, among them the future Edward VII. Her prime ministers included W. Melbourne, R. Peel, H. Palmerston, B. Disraeli, and W. Gladstone. During her reign, the British Empire reached its peak. Britain established its rule in India, struggled with the question of Home Rule in Ireland, remained neutral during the American Civil War, and fought the Crimean War. Victoria's strict personal moral values greatly enhanced the prestige of the monarchy and gained her enormous popularity. She put her stamp on an entire era of English history, which came to be known as the Victorian Age.

Victorian style Neo-Gothic style of architecture revived in Britain during the reign of Queen Victoria. It began with careful imitation of the Gothic style and gradually developed into a less restricted form. The outstanding buildings designed in the style include the Houses of Parliament and the Manchester Town Hall.

Vidocq, Eugène François 1775–1857. French detective who organized the Police de Sûreté, or security police, during the rule of Napoleon.

Vienna Capital city (pop. 1,592,800) of Austria. Founded by the Celts, it became a Roman military center (1st cent. BC). Vienna was conquered by various groups in subsequent centuries, among them the Franks and Magyars. It was fortified (13th cent.) by Ottocar II and became (1278) the official residence of the Hapsburg rulers. The Hapsburgs held Vienna until 1918, and during their rule the city became one of the leading places of cultural and commercial activity in Europe. The acknowledged music center of Europe, it was the birthplace of L. Beethoven and W. Mozart. After WW I, Vienna became capital of the republic of Austria. Austria was annexed by Germany in 1938, and Vienna remained in German control until after WW II. Vienna and Austria were divided by the Allies into zones of occupation after the war but were reunited in 1955.

Vienna, Congress of *See* **Congress of Vienna**

Vienna, Peace of Treaty (June 23, 1606) that ended the rebellion against the Hapsburgs led by the Hungarian leader S. Bocskay. It secured religious toleration for the Hungarian Protestants within the Austrian Empire.

Vienna, treaties of **1.** Treaty (Nov. 18, 1738) ending the War of the Polish Succession (*q.v.*). **2.** *See* Peace of Schönbrunn. **3.** Treaty (Oct. 30, 1864) by which Denmark ceded Schleswig, Holstein, and Lauenburg to Austria and Prussia. **4.** Treaty (Oct. 3, 1866) between Austria and Italy following the Seven Weeks' War (1866). By its terms Austria ceded Venetia to Italy.

Vienne, Council of Fifteenth ecumenical council of the Catholic church (1311–12), at Vienne, France. Convened by Pope Clement V, it dissolved the order of the Knights Templar and condemned the Beghards.

Vientiane Administrative capital (pop 176,600) and largest city of Laos. Capital of a Laotian kingdom from 1707, it passed under French rule (1893), becoming the capital of the French Laos protectorate (1899–1953).

Vieta, François *See* **Viete, François**

Vietcong ⟨Viet-Nam Cong-San⟩ Communist guerrilla forces that fought in South Vietnam (1954–75) to overthrow the government of South Vietnam and reunify Vietnam under Communist rule. The Vietcong, aided by men and matériel from the North, successfully fought a long and bloody guerrilla campaign against the army of the Republic of South Vietnam and later against the US armed forces sent to aid the South Vietnamese. They formed (1960) the National Liberation Front *(q.v.)*, which in turn joined with other groups to form the Provisional Revolutionary Government (PRG). The PRG took part in the cease-fire negotiations in Paris (1973) but, after US withdrawal from Vietnam, the Vietcong and North Vietnamese regular forces completed the conquest of South Vietnam (1975).

Viète, François ⟨Vieta, ~⟩ 1540–1603. French mathematician noted for his contributions to the development of modern algebra.

Vietminh Popular name for Viet Nam Doc Lap Dong Minh, a coalition of Communist and nationalist groups that fought for Vietnamese independence from French rule. It was formed and led by Ho Chi Minh.

Vietnam Socialist republic located in Southeast Asia. Its capital is Hanoi. Vietnam's history prior to French occupation in the 19th cent. was that of its three kingdoms: Tonkin, in northern Vietnam; Annam, in central Vietnam; and Cochin China in southern Vietnam. The three kingdoms became part of French Indochina (1887). Occupied during WW II by the Japanese, Vietnam was established as an independent state in 1945. Subsequent attempts by the French to regain authority in the region led to the French Indochina War (1946–54) and division of the country into the Democratic Republic of Vietnam in the north and the Republic of Vietnam in the south. The country was reunited under Communist rule in 1976 after the long and bloody Vietnam War *(q.v.)*. Key dates in the history of Vietnam include:

1535 Region first visited by Portuguese; Vietnam then divided into kingdoms of Tonkin, Annam and Cochin China.

1859 Saigon occupied by the French.

1867 France made Cochin China a colony.

1883–85 Sino-French War ended in French control of Vietnam and other Indochina domains.

1884 Annam and Tonkin became French protectorates.

1887 French holdings in Vietnam joined with Cambodia to form French Indochina.

1925–45 Bao Dai reigned as last emperor of Vietnam under French rule.

1940–45 Japanese seized power in Vietnam during WW II.

1945 Japanese made Emperor Bao Dai head of new state of Vietnam (Mar.); Vietnam included Tonkin (in the north), Annam (in central Vietnam), and Cochin China (in the south).

1945 Vietnam occupied by Allied forces at end of WW II; Nationalist Chinese held north and British occupied south.

1945 Ho Chi Minh proclaimed Democratic Republic of Vietnam on withdrawal of Japanese occupation army after WW II.

1946 France reached accord (Mar.) with Ho Chi Minh, recognizing Vietnamese independence within the French Union.

1946 France sought to establish separate state of Cochin China in the south; open warfare erupted in late 1946, marking the beginning of the French Indochina War.

1946–54 French Indochina War; French colonial forces ultimately defeated after protracted struggle with Vietnamese Communists and Nationalists.

1951 Lao-Dong founded by Ho Chi Minh; it replaced the Viet Minh as leading party of the Democratic Republic of Vietnam.

1954 Viet Minh victorious over French (May 5) at Dienbienphu; marked end of French military power in Vietnam.

1954 Geneva Conference divided Vietnam in two along 17th parallel; North Vietnam to be governed by Communists under Ho Chi Minh, south to be governed by Bao Dai regime; elections to be held (July, 1956) to reunify the country.

1955 Bao Dai government removed (Oct.) by referendum; Ngo Dinh Diem made president of new Republic of South Vietnam (proclaimed Oct. 26).

1955–63 Diem ruled as president; instituted increasingly repressive policies to restore order; promoted further unrest and significant gains in rural areas by Vietcong; overthrown and killed (Nov. 1, 1963).

1956 Diem government refused to take part in scheduled elections for reunification of Vietnam.

1960–75 Vietnam War; Vietnam ravaged and ultimately reunited under Communists.

1963 Diem overthrown in military coup; period of great political instability followed (1963–65).

1964 North Vietnamese army began infiltration of South Vietnam; Gulf of Tonkin incident (Aug.), alleged attack on US destroyers by North Vietnamese torpedo boats, led to stepped-up US military intervention in Vietnam War.

1965 Gen. Nguyen Van Thieu became head of South Vietnamese government; Nguyen Cao Ky made prime minister.

1967 New constitution promulgated in South Vietnam (Mar.); Thieu elected president and Ky vice-president in elections (Sept.).

1968 Communists staged massive assault in Tet Offensive, a turning point in the Vietnam War.

1969 Phased withdrawal of US forces began; massive bombing continued.

1969 Ho Chi Minh died (Sept. 3); Ton Duc Thang became president of North Vietnam.

1972 South Vietnamese president Thieu declared martial law (May 10) in the face of Communist advances.

1973 Peace settlement signed (Jan. 27); provided for cessation of all hostilities and withdrawal of all US forces.

1974 Fighting between the South Vietnamese and North Vietnamese intensified in the Central Highlands (Mar.).

1975 North Vietnamese staged massive attack into South Vietnam (Jan.), culminating in toppling of South Vietnamese government.

1975 Evacuation of Americans begun (Apr. 4).

1975 President Thieu resigned (Apr. 21) amid unrest caused by Communist advances in south.

1975 Last Americans evacuated from South Vietnam (Apr. 29); South Vietnam surrendered to Communists (Apr. 30).

1976 North and south formally reunified (July 2).

1977 Vietnam admitted to UN.

FROM **1978** Mass emigration of ethnic Chinese began as Vietnamese government adopted policy to drive them out; China, after accepting hundreds of thousands of refugees, refused to accept more; Vietnamese "boat people" then tried to escape by sea to other Southeast Asian countries.

1978 Treaty of friendship signed with the Soviets.

1978–80 Vietnam invaded Cambodia; overthrew harsh regime of Pol Pot.

1979 China invaded Vietnam's northern border region (Feb. 17–Mar. 15); claimed action was punishment for Vietnam's invasion of Cambodia; withdrew from region.

1981 Truong Chinh became president of Vietnam.

Viet-Nam Cong-San *See* **Vietcong**

Vietnamization US policy during the Vietnam War. Implemented by the Nixon administration (early 1970s), it called for a gradual increase in South Vietnamese participation in the war. US military involvement was to be reduced at the same time, until the South Vietnamese took over all fighting.

Vietnam War War fought (1960–75) by Communist and non-Communist forces for control of South Vietnam. It ended in a Communist victory (and in the reunification of North and South Vietnam), despite heavy involvement by US forces (1965–73). The Vietnam War was an outgrowth of the earlier Indochina War (*q.v.*). At the end of that war, Vietnam was divided into Communist North Vietnam and non-Communist South Vietnam by the Geneva accords of 1954. Elections on the question of reunification were to be held in 1956, but South Vietnamese dictator Diem refused to hold them. As a result, a Communist insurrection broke out in 1957. At the same time, non-Communist opposition to the Diem regime was mounting. Rampant corruption, government repression and persecutions, and favoritism shown Vietnamese Catholics over the majority Buddhists, all contributed to sentiment for rebellion against Diem. Meanwhile, US aid flowed into South Vietnam to support the Diem regime. US involvement between 1954 and 1960, however, was confined to financial aid, military equipment, and a few hundred military advisers. In 1960 guerrilla activity increased markedly and the Communist-dominated National Liberation Front (NLF) was formed by Communist and non-Communist groups in South Vietnam. Open warfare against the South Vietnamese government began. Heavy US involvement in the war started in 1965 and by 1968 over a half million American troops were in Vietnam. In the years of bloody fighting, US troops managed to forestall the collapse of the South Vietnamese government, but they were unable to break the strength of the Vietcong forces (aided by North Vietnam, which was in turn supplied by the USSR). The US government, which had lost considerable prestige both at home and abroad because of US involvement in Vietnam, began withdrawing troops in 1969–70, while at the same time attempting to negotiate a settlement. In 1973 a peace treaty was signed and the last US troops were withdrawn. By 1974, the fighting between Communists and South Vietnamese government forces had increased and in 1975 the Communists mounted their final offensive. South Vietnam surrendered (Apr. 30, 1975), ending the war and setting the stage for reunification of Vietnam. Key events in the history of the Vietnam War include:

1960 Guerrilla forces overran a number of outposts (Jan.) maintained by Vietnamese army regulars (ARVN); marked rise of heavy guerrilla activity in South Vietnam.

1960 National Liberation Front (NLF) formed (Dec. 19–20); composed of both Communists and non-Communists and controlled by Communists; called for overthrow of Diem and reunification with north; thereafter guerrilla activity increased significantly and open war against Diem regime began.

1961 Vietcong strength reached an estimated 15,000; rapid growth in numbers continued in following years.

1961 South Vietnam signed military and economic aid treaty with US.

1961 Diem proclaimed a state of emergency (Oct.) as his political support dwindled.

1961 US president J. F. Kennedy reasserted US commitment to Diem regime (Dec.); sent 1,500 more advisers; US helicopter units began direct involvement in fighting to support South Vietnamese.

1962 US Military Assistance Command formed; US forces in Vietnam reached 10,000 by year's end.

1962 Vietcong continued to make gains in South Vietnam despite increased US assistance; US strategy of "strategic hamlets" failed; Diem failed to enact promised reforms (especially badly needed land reforms) or to end corruption.

1963 Battle of Ap Bac (Jan. 2) in Mekong Delta; 200 Vietcong repulsed attack by 2,000 well-equipped ARVN soldiers.

1963 Buddhists, demonstrating in Hue against persecution by the Diem regime, fired on by police (May 8); seven Buddhists subsequently resorted to protest by self-immolation (from June 11); martial law proclaimed by Diem (Aug. 21).

1963 Diem overthrown and killed in military coup (Nov. 1); period of prolonged political crisis (1963–65) as nine coups were staged and Vietcong guerrillas rapidly expanded their control in South Vietnam.

1963 US troop levels reached 17,000; Vietcong strength put at about 30,000.

1964 US president Johnson reasserted US commitment to South Vietnam (Jan. 1).

1964–68 Gen. W. Westmoreland in command of US troops in Vietnam.

1964 Terrorist bombs exploded (Aug., Dec.) in Saigon hotels where US troops were quartered.

1964 Gulf of Tonkin Incident; US destroyers reported attacks (Aug. 2, 4) by North Vietnamese patrol boats in the Gulf of Tonkin; US bombed North Vietnamese bases.

1964 Gulf of Tonkin resolution passed (Aug. 7) by US Congress; authorized Pres. Johnson to take all steps necessary to protect US forces and prevent further attacks; became important justification for US involvement in war.

1964 Bien Hoa, US air base outside Saigon, attacked by Vietcong (Nov. 1).

1965 US bombing of North Vietnam began (Feb.); attacks on US forces at Pleiku and Quinhon (Feb. 7, 10) first prompted retaliatory bombings of North; Pres. Johnson ordered regular bombing of North Vietnam (Feb. 28) to force negotiations.

1965 First US combat troops sent to Vietnam; 3,500 US Marines landed at Da Nang (Mar. 7–9); Vietcong close to taking complete control of the South as the political crisis continued.

1965 First North Vietnamese regulars (about 400–500 troops) infiltrated into South Vietnam (March–April); US bombing (from 1965) of Ho Chi-minh Trail, major Communist supply line to south, failed to halt flow of men and matériel into South.

1965 Nguyen Cao Ky, military strong man, took control of the government (June); his military dictatorship restored order through harsh repressive measures; broke power of Buddhist resistance (by 1966) and arrested political opponents.

1965 US troops in first major offensive against Vietcong (June 28); in subsequent months began taking over major share of the fighting from the ineffective ARVN regulars.

1965 US troop levels reached 175,000 (Dec.); Vietcong (plus North Vietnamese regulars) reached about 150,000.

1966 Heavy bombing raids conducted throughout North Vietnam; Hanoi and Haiphong bombed for first time (June).

1966 Meeting in Honolulu, Hawaii, between Pres. Johnson, Gen. Ky, and leaders of other countries that sent troops to South Vietnam (including Australia, New Zealand, and South Korea.

1967 New South Vietnamese constitution (Mar.).

1967 Invasion of southern parts of the Demilitarized Zone (DMZ) between North and South Vietnam by US and ARVN troops (May).

1967 Gen. Nguyen Van Thieu elected (Sept.) president, Ky elected vice-president; repressive measures continued.

1968 US troop strength reached about 510,000; Vietcong and North Vietnamese regulars numbered about 230,000.

1968 Siege at Khesanh (Jan.–Apr.); 6,000 US Marines came under heavy attack.

1968 Tet Offensive (Jan. 30–Feb. 25); Vietcong and North Vietnamese launched surprise attacks on more than 100 cities in South Vietnam, including Saigon; the Communists suffered heavy losses; a major propaganda victory for Communists, it forced US president Johnson to halt escalation in Vietnam and begin peace negotiations.

1968 My Lai Massacre (Mar. 16).

1968 Pres. Johnson announced (Mar.) he would not seek reelection as antiwar movement in US reached major proportions.

1968 Communists launched major offensive, hitting points throughout South Vietnam (May 5–13); Saigon under heavy attack.

1968 Paris Peace negotiations began between US and North Vietnam (May 13).

1968 Vietcong and South Vietnam joined Paris Peace talks after UN halted bombing of the north (Nov.).

1969 R. Nixon took office as US president; US began gradual withdrawal of troops from Vietnam; bombing of north continued as peace talks dragged on; US widened war (1970) to Cambodia and Laos.

1970 US carried out bombing raids inside Cambodia (Feb. 11).

1970 Six-month lull in fighting broken by Communist offensive in south (Apr. 1).

1970 US completed withdrawal of 115,000 troops (Apr.); announced plan to withdraw 150,000 more troops by 1971.

1970 South Vietnamese offensive in Cambodia begun with US support (Apr. 29).

1970 Communist offensive near DMZ successfully repulsed (May 8).

1970 Combined US-South Vietnamese naval force moved up Mekong into Cambodia (May).

1970 US bombers hit targets in North Vietnam, Cambodia and Laos (Nov.).

1970 US commando raid (Nov. 21) in North Vietnam unsuccessfully attempted to free US POWs.

1971 South Vietnamese troops, backed by US air support, invaded Laos (Jan. 30).

1971 Fire Base 6 in Central Highlands under siege by Communist forces (Apr.).

1971 DMZ defenses taken over by South Vietnamese (July).

1971 Australian and New Zealand forces withdrawn by year's end.

1971 North Vietnamese offensive along Cambodian border (Sept. 26).

1971 South Vietnamese offensive in eastern Cambodia (Nov.–Dec.).

1972 New US troop withdrawals announced (Jan. 13); US strength to be reduced to 69,000 by May 1.

1972 North Vietnamese offensive (Mar.) across DMZ began; South Vietnamese abandoned northern Quang Tri Province (Apr. 2).

1972 North Vietnamese offensive in South Vietnam cut highway from An Loc to Saigon (Apr. 5).

1972 Central Highlands capital of Hoai An overrun by Communist forces (Apr. 19).

1972 Mining of North Vietnamese ports ordered by US Pres. Nixon (May).

1972 Gen. Frederick C. Weyand replaced Gen. Creighton Abrams as commander of US forces in Vietnam (June).

1972 Heavy US bombing raids over the north marked withdrawal of last US combat troops from South Vietnam (Aug.).

1972 Que Son captured by Communists (Aug. 19).

1972 Quang Tri recaptured by South Vietnamese (Sept. 15).

1972 Heavy bombing of North Vietnam ordered by Pres. Nixon (Dec. 15–30); bombing halted as stalled peace talks resumed.

1973 Peace settlement signed (Jan. 27); provided for end to hostilities and withdrawal of all US forces.

1973 International observers stationed in South Vietnam to monitor truce (Feb. 5).

1974 Heavy fighting between South Vietnamese and Communist forces in the Central Highlands (Mar.).

1975 Final North Vietnamese offensive in South Vietnam began (Jan.).

1975 Evacuation of American personnel in South Vietnam began (Apr. 4).

1975 Pres. Thieu forced to resign (Apr. 21) as Communists advanced in South Vietnam.

1975 Last Americans evacuated from South Vietnam (Apr. 29).

1975 South Vietnam surrendered to Communist forces (Apr. 30), ending the war; formal reunification of North and South Vietnam effected (July 2, 1976).

Vietnam Workers' party *See* **Lao-Dong**

vigilantes American frontiersmen who were members of illegal or extralegal "vigilance committees" formed to establish law in areas where regular judicial systems were lacking or appeared to be inadequate.

Vigilius d. 555. Pope (537–555). He became embroiled in the political and religious struggles over Monophysitism. His policies threatened the canons of the Council of Chalcedon and were bitterly opposed in the West.

Vignoles, Etienne de *See* **La Hire**

Vigny, Alfred Victor, comte de 1797–1863. French poet, dramatist, and novelist, one of France's leading Romantic writers.

Vikings Norse raiders and adventurers who sailed from their homelands in Scandinavia to attack and pillage European coastal settlements (9th–11th cents.). (*See* Norsemen.)

Vikramaditya *See* **Chandragupta II**

Villa, Francisco ⟨Pancho Villa⟩ ⟨Arango, Doroteo⟩ 1877?–1923. Mexican bandit and revolutionary, a leading figure in the revolts against P. Díaz

(1910–11) and V. Huerta (1913–14). Villa's raid on Columbus, New Mexico (Mar. 9, 1916) led to the US punitive expedition into Mexico by Gen. J. Pershing.

Villa, Pancho   *See* **Villa, Francisco**

Villa-Lobos, Heitor   1887–1959. Brazilian composer considered the leading Latin composer of his day. His works are noted for their merging of classical influences with Brazilian folk music.

Villard, Henry ⟨Hilgard, Ferdinand Heinrich Gustav⟩ 1835–1900. American journalist and financier. A leading figure in rail transportation in the Pacific Northwest, he formed (1889) the Edison General Electric Company, serving as its president until 1893.

Villars, Claude Louis Hector, duc de   1653–1734. French soldier and marshal of France. He distinguished himself in the War of the Spanish Succession, negotiated the Treaty of Rastatt (1714), and was supreme commander in the War of the Polish Succession.

Villehardouin, Geoffroi de   *c*1160–*c*1213. French historian and crusader who chronicled the Fourth Crusade in his *Conquête de Constantinople*. He is considered the first French historian.

Villehardouin, Geoffroi I   *d.* 1218. French crusader and adventurer. Nephew of G. Villehardouin, he conquered part of the Peloponnesus, in Greece, and there established a kingdom that was ruled by his family from 1210 to 1278.

villeinage   Aspect of the feudal system by which a villein, or serf, was bound to the land and obliged to perform services to the lord in return for protection and land tenure. The villein was distinguished from the freeholder.

Villèle, Jean Baptiste Séraphin Joseph, comte de   1773–1854. French politician, leader of the French Ultraroyalist faction. As premier (1822–28) he followed conservative policies and stabilized finances.

Villeneuve, Pierre Charles Jean Baptiste Silvestre de   1763–1806. French admiral. He commanded the French fleet and was defeated at the Battle of Trafalgar (1805).

Villeroi, François, duc de   1644–1730. French courtier and marshal of France. A favorite of Louis XIV, he held high military posts in Italy and Flanders but was defeated at the Battle of Ramillies (1706) during the War of the Spanish Succession.

Villiers, George   *See* **Tardieu, André**

Villiers, George William Frederick, 4th earl of Clarendon   1800–70. British statesman, often called the "Great Lord Clarendon." He was three times foreign secretary (1853–58, 1865–66, 1868–70), the first time during the Crimean War (1853–

56). During his third term, he helped pave the way for settlement of the Alabama claims.

Villon, François   1431–1463? One of the greatest French lyric poets. Continually involved in criminal activity, he spent much time in prison and was banished from Paris in 1463.

Vilna dispute   *See* **Vilnius dispute**

Vilnius dispute ⟨Vilna dispute⟩ Conflict between Poland and Lithuania over possession of the city of Vilnius. After WW I, Vilnius was ceded to Lithuania, but during the Russian-Polish War of 1920, it was captured (Sept. 9) by Polish forces, and subsequently was annexed by Poland. Occupied by Russian troops (1939), the city was restored to the Lithuanian SSR in 1944.

Vincent de Paul, Saint   1581?–1660.   French priest known for his charitable work. He founded the Congregation of the Mission (1625), known as Lazarists or Vincentians, as well as other charitable institutions.

Vincent of Beauvais   *c*1190–*c*1264.   French Dominican priest. He wrote the first three volumes of the *Speculum majus*, an encyclopedic summary of all knowledge that remained influential for centuries.

Vinci, Leonardo da   *See* **Leonardo da Vinci**

Vinland ⟨Wineland⟩ Region of North America discovered and named by Leif Ericsson in the 11th cent. Its exact location is not known.

Vinson, Frederick Moore   1890–1953.   American jurist, 13th chief justice of the Supreme Court (1946–53).

Viollet-le-Duc, Eugène Emmanuel   1814–79. French architect and writer, a leader in the Gothic revival movement in France. He restored many medieval structures, including Notre Dame de Paris. His writings stressed the value of function in design.

Virchow, Rudolf   1821–1902.   German pathologist. He contributed to many fields of medical science but is known best as a founder of cellular pathology.

Virgil   *See* **Vergil**

Virginia   Eastern US state (pop. 5,346,300), the 10th state. Its capital is Richmond. The first settlement in Virginia (1587) was backed by Sir W. Raleigh and located on Roanoke Island. The first successful colony was established (1607) at Jamestown. Virginia colony established (1619) the first representative assembly (House of Burgesses) in the New World. The colony thrived as a center of the tobacco trade, but corruption and inability of the governor, W. Berkeley, to protect the colonists from Indian attack led to Bacon's Rebellion *(q.v.)* in 1676. Importation of slaves led to greater prosperity in the colony and the rise of a wealthy class.

Virginia was a leading force in resistance to British authority and played a major role in the American Revolution, which ended with the Yorktown campaign *(q.v.)*. Virginia was admitted to the Union (1788) and seceded (1861) at the opening of the American Civil War. The northwestern portion of the state broke away (1863) to form West Virginia. Virginia was the scene of several major engagements, notably the first and second battles of Bull Run, Chancellorsville, Fredericksburg, and the Wilderness campaign. It was readmitted to the US in 1870.

Virginia and Kentucky Resolutions　Resolutions passed (Nov., 1798) by the Kentucky legislature and (Dec., 1798) the Virginia legislature. Written by T. Jefferson and J. Madison respectively, they defended states' rights and were passed in protest against the Alien and Sedition Acts of the Adams administration. They contributed to the more radical theory of Nullification.

Virginia and New Jersey Plans　In US history, proposed plans for the structure of government offered at the Constitutional Convention *(q.v.)* in 1787. The Virginia Plan, advanced by Edmund Randolph, would have created a strong federal government with a bicameral legislature. The lower house was to be elected by popular vote and would select members of the upper house. The two houses would elect the head of state. The New Jersey Plan, put forward by William Paterson, favored small states and rejected the provision for apportionment by population in both houses. The Connecticut Compromise (adopted July 16) resolved these differences by adopting proportional representation in the lower house and by giving each state an equal vote in the upper house.

Virginia Company　**1.** Virginia Company of London. Joint-stock company chartered (1606) by English king James I for the purpose of colonizing the New World. The company established the first permanent English settlement in Virginia at Jamestown (1607) and administered it until its charter was revoked in 1624. **2.** Virginia Company of Plymouth. Joint-stock company established (1606) by English king James I. It was reorganized (1620) as the Council of New England and established Plymouth colony (1620).

Virginia Convention　American Revolutionary body that met in Virginia (1775, 1776). At the first of these meetings Patrick Henry delivered his "give me liberty or give me death" speech, and at the second he was involved with George Mason in drafting the Virginia Declaration of Rights. This served as a model for the Bill of Rights in the US Constitution.

Virgin Islands　Group of islands in the West Indies including the US Virgin Islands (pop. 95,000), officially the Territory of the Virgin Islands of the United States; and the British Virgin Islands (pop. 10,500). The islands were first discovered (1493) by C. Columbus and subsequently acquired and settled by the English and Danes. The US bought its holdings from Denmark (1917). US Virgin Islanders have held citizenship since 1927, and in 1972 the islands were granted one representative in the US House of Representatives.

Virginius affair　Crisis (1873) arising from the Spanish capture of the US ship *Virginius*, which was caught smuggling guns to Cuba during the Ten Years' War. The executions of 53 people aboard nearly led to war between the US and Spain.

Viriathus　*See* **Viriatus**

Viriatus ⟨Viriathus⟩　*d.* 139 BC. Herdsman of Lusitania who successfully led (*c*147–*c*139 BC) a rebellion against Rome. The rebellion ended shortly after his assassination.

Visconti　Italian family that ruled Milan from the 13th cent. to 1447. The family derived its name from the title viscount. Its members included Giovanni Visconti (*d.* 1354), Gian Galeazzo Visconti (1351–1402), and Filippo Maria Visconti (1392–1447).

Vishnu　One of the three principal gods of Hinduism. He is revered as the preserver of the world and restorer of the moral order.

Visigoths ⟨West Goths⟩　Germanic tribe, the western branch of the Goths. The Visigoths left the Black Sea region (*c*3d cent. AD) and harassed the Roman Empire's border region of Dacia. The Visigoths were allowed to settle in the empire to escape the Huns, but soon rebelled against its excessive taxation. They crushed Emperor Valens at Adrianople (AD 378) and, under Alaric I, sacked Rome (AD 410). They were allowed to rule large areas of Gaul and Spain, and in AD 475, their leader, Euric, declared independence. His son Alaric II was defeated and killed by Clovis (507). The Visigoths then settled around Toledo, and finally capitulated to the invading Muslims (711).

Vitellius, Aulus　AD15–69. Roman emperor (AD 69). Proclaimed emperor at Cologne, he defeated his rival Otho in Italy and ruled briefly before being defeated by Vespasian.

Vitoria, Francisco de　1486–1546. Spanish theologian. He is known best for his ethical opposition to acts of warfare except as matters of defense. He championed the cause of the subjugated peoples of the New World.

Vitruvius ⟨Marcus Vitruvius Pollio⟩　*fl.* 1st cent. BC.　Roman architect, engineer, and writer. He is known for his *De architectura*, a treatise on classical architecture that played a major role in the Classical revival.

Vivaldi, Antonio *c*1675–1741. Italian composer, one of the greatest composers of the Italian Baroque period. A gifted violinist, he is known especially for his instrumental pieces, notably *The Four Seasons*. He also composed operas, cantatas, and other works.

vizier In the Ottoman Empire, the most important minister under the sultan. The term was first adopted in the 14th cent. and was applied to provincial, administrative, and military figures.

Vladimir, Saint *See* **Vladimir I**

Vladimir I ⟨Saint Vladimir⟩ *c*956–1015. Grand duke of Kiev (*c*980–1015) and first Christian ruler of Russia. He consolidated Kiev and Novgorod into a single realm and ordered the conversion of his people to Greek Orthodox Christianity.

Volga Bulgars *See* **Bulgars, Eastern**

Volgograd *See* **Stalingrad**

Volksraad ⟨People's Council⟩ Advisory council established (1916) by the Dutch in Indonesia. It evolved into a genuine legislative body, including both European and Asian members, but was dissolved when the Japanese occupied Indonesia (1942).

Volscians Ancient Italic people known from their wars with the Romans. They participated in the Latin revolt against Rome (340–338 BC) but were conquered by the Romans (late 4th cent. BC).

Volstead Act ⟨National Prohibition Act⟩ Law passed (1919) by the US Congress to enforce the 18th Amendment during Prohibition. It was voided with repeal of the 18th Amendment (1933).

Volta, Alessandro, Conte 1745–1827. Italian physicist, inventor of the voltaic pile, the first electric battery. The volt, the unit of electromotive force, is named after him.

Voltaire, François Marie Arouet de 1694–1778. French author and historian, one of the foremost figures of the Enlightenment. Of middle-class origin, he was educated by the Jesuits and soon made his mark as a poet, playwright, and wit. Imprudent talk and witty lampoons against authority brought him first a stay in the Bastille and then exile in England, prompting his *Letters Concern-*

ing the English, which popularized the ideas of I. Newton and J. Locke. An outstanding historian, he is known best today for such books as *Candide* and his *Philosophical Dictionary*, a forceful work supporting the ideas of the Englightenment.

Vo Nguyen Giap 1912–. Vietnamese general and government minister. A Communist, he became commander of the Vietminh (1946) and defeated the French at Dien Bien Phu (1954). He played a strategic role in the Tet Offensive (1968) during the Vietnam War.

voodooism Religious cult in Caribbean areas, particularly Haiti. Dahomeyan in origin (the word is derived from the West African god *Vodun*), the cult claims to put its adherents in touch with guardian spirits through ritual and magic.

Voroshilov, Kliment Efremovich 1881–1969. Russian military and political leader. As commissar of defense (1925–40) he helped to rebuild the Red Army on the eve of WW II. He also served as president of the Soviet Union (1953–60).

Vorster, Balthazar Johannes 1915–. Prime minister of the Union of South Africa (1966–78).

vorticism Pre-WW I art movement. It sought to simplify forms into an angular, mechanical regularity. Its principal exponents were H. Gaudier-Brzeska and W. Lewis.

Voting Rights Act of 1965 US act passed to ensure the voting rights of blacks previously denied the franchise by literacy and other such tests. The act suspended these tests and empowered federal examiners to certify eligible voters.

Vries, Hugo de 1848–1935. Dutch botanist. He rediscovered the principle of heredity earlier described by G. Mendel and introduced the concept of mutation in plant evolution.

Vuillard, Jean Édouard 1868–1940. French artist, a member of the artistic group known as the Nabis. He is known best for his paintings of domestic interiors.

Vulcan Ancient Roman god of fire, especially destructive fire, as in volcanoes. He later became identified with the Greek god Hephaestus.

Vulgate Latin version of the Bible, completed (AD *c*405) by Saint Jerome and adopted as the standard version by the Roman Catholic church.

W

Wade, Benjamin Franklin 1800–78. US Senator (1851–69). A leader of the Radical Republicans, he was cosponsor of the Wade-Davis Bill *(q.v.)* for Reconstruction, and opposed the policies of A. Lincoln.

Wade-Davis Bill US bill passed (July 2, 1864) before the end of the Civil War, attempting to regulate Reconstruction policies. It never took effect because Pres. A. Lincoln pocket-vetoed it, but it would have required an oath of allegiance to the Union from a majority of a state's citizens; and states would have been required to abolish slavery, repudiate secession, and disqualify from public office anyone who had served the Confederacy. Its principal sponsor was Ohio Senator B. Wade.

Wafd Egyptian nationalist political party founded in 1918. "Wafd" means "delegation," and the name was applied to the party because its founders, including Sa'd Zaghlul, demanded an Egyptian "delegation" (to work for Egyptian independence) in the post-WW I peace process. Although several times declared illegal, the party was Egypt's major organized political force from 1923, and it clashed frequently with King Fuad and his successor, Farouk. Opposed to Germany, it came to power with British support during WW II and returned to power again in 1950, this time agitating for further revisions of Anglo-Egyptian treaties. The Egyptian revolution (1952) and dissolution of the political parties brought an end to the Wafd.

Wages and Hours Act *See* **Fair Labor Standards Act**

Wagner, Richard 1813–83. Famous German composer, whose operas marked the culmination of the German Romantic tradition, and had a great influence on later composers. Among his many works are *The Ring of the Nibelungs, Lohengrin, The Flying Dutchman, Tannhäuser,* and *Tristan und Isolde.*

Wagram, Battle of ⟨Deutsch-Wagram, ~⟩ Battle fought on July 5–6, 1809, near the Austrian village of Wagram. Napoleon, with some 154,000 troops, defeated an army of some 158,000 troops under the Archduke Charles. The battle prevented the formation of a new coalition against Napoleon.

Wahabi Muslim reform movement founded by Muhammad ibn Abd al-wabia (18th cent.). It became the religion of the Saudi rulers and is thus an influential sect in modern Saudi Arabia. It is a puritanical movement which advocates living by the Koran and rejects the excesses of luxury and elaborate worship.

Wahunsonacock *See* **Powhatan Confederacy**

Waiblings *See* **Welfs**

Wainwright, Jonathan Mayhew 1883–1953. American general, who commanded US forces in the Philippines in WW II. Forced to surrender at Corregidor (1942), he and his troops were held as prisoners of war until 1945.

Wairau Affray ⟨Wairau Massacre⟩ Incident (June 17, 1843), in which 22 English settlers were killed by about 90 Maori natives on New Zealand's south island. The settlers had tried to arrest the Maori chiefs for resisting land surveys. The British governor took no action against the Maori but the incident contributed to the outbreak of the Maori Wars.

Wairau Massacre *See* **Wairau Affray**

Waitangi, Treaty of Agreement (Feb. 6, 1840) between the British government and some 500 Maori chiefs. It formed the basis of British annexation and rule of New Zealand. The Maori recognized British sovereignty in return for guarantees of their lands, possessions, and rights as British subjects.

Waite, Morrison Remick 1816–88. American jurist, seventh chief justice of the Supreme Court (1874–88), best known for his influential interpretations of the 14th and 15th Amendments.

Wakefield, Battle of *See* **Roses, Wars of the**

Wake Island, Battle of Japanese attack (Dec. 9, 1941) on the American base situated on Wake Island. A force of 377 US Marines aided by some 1,000 civilian workers held out until Dec. 23 against a massive Japanese assault.

Walachia ⟨Wallachia⟩ Danubian principality. With neighboring Moldavia, it formed (1859) the modern Balkan state of Romania. Its inhabitants preserve the ancient Latin speech of Roman Dacia. Walachia was obliged to acknowledge Turkish suzerainty by 1417, became a virtual Russian protectorate in 1774, and became fully independent as Romania in 1878.

Waldemar I ⟨Valdemar I⟩ ⟨Waldemar the Great⟩ 1131–82. King of Denmark (1157–82). His succession to the Danish throne ended civil war in Denmark. He defeated the Wends, conquered Norwegian lands, and established political ties with Sweden, France, and the Holy Roman Empire.

Waldemar II ⟨Valdemar II⟩ ⟨Waldemar the Victorious⟩ 1170–1241. King of Denmark (1202–41), successor to his brother Canute VI. He conquered a great area in the Baltic but was forced to surrender much of it. He reformed and codified Danish law.

Waldemar IV ⟨Valdemar IV⟩ ⟨Waldemar Atterdag⟩ c1320–75. King of Denmark (1340–75). He regained his kingdom from foreign control and fought against the Hanseatic League. But he was forced to sign the Treaty of Stralsund, which gave the league great influence in Denmark.

Waldemar Atterdag   *See* **Waldemar IV**
Waldemar the Great   *See* **Waldemar I**
Waldemar the Victorious   *See* **Waldemar II**
Waldenses ⟨Waldensians⟩ Religious group centered in Piedmont in Italy and Dauphiné in France from the 12th cent. Founded c1770 by a merchant of Lyons, P. Waldo, the Waldenses sought a life of poverty and gospel simplicity. They eventually drifted into what became heresy to the Roman Catholic church, denying purgatory, the papacy, prayers for the dead, and some of the sacraments. They emphasized a simple biblicism and criticized the ecclesiastical abuses of the day. Often persecuted, they nevertheless continued to survive. Most Waldensians accepted the Reformation and became in effect another Swiss Protestant church (1532). They did not receive full civil and religious rights until 1848.

Waldheim, Kurt 1918–. Fourth secretary general of the UN (1972–82), replacing U Thant of Burma. A career diplomat, he was Austria's UN representative (1965–68), foreign minister (1968–70), and even a presidential candidate (1971).

Waldseemüller, Martin   *See* **America**
Waldstein, Albrecht von   *See* **Wallenstein, Albrecht von**
Wales Historic region of Great Britain, located west of England. The home of Celtic tribes known collectively as the Cymry, Wales was invaded by the Romans and later resisted the Anglo-Saxon invasion of Britain (5th cent. AD). Conquered

(1276–84) by English king Edward I, Wales was formally joined with England in 1536, after which its history merged with that of England. Key dates in the history of Wales include:

55 BC–1ST CENT. AD   Romans advanced into British Isles; occupied areas of Wales, but Welsh tribes contintued to resist Roman rule.

5TH CENT. AD   Celts fled westward in face of Anglo-Saxon invasion, settling in Wales; subsequent centuries saw the rise of several kingdoms in Wales.

MID-10TH CENT.   Hywel Dda reigned in Wales; established unified Welsh legal code.

1062–64   English king Harold led army into Wales (1062–64); defeated Welsh King Gruffydd ap Llewelyn (*d.* 1063).

1136   Welsh forces victorious over English under Henry I.

1158–65   English king Henry II reestablished control in Wales.

1276–84   English king Edward I invaded Wales (1276), defeating Welsh prince Llwewlyn ap Gruffydd; Llewelyn staged unsuccessful revolt (1282) and English established control over all Wales; conquest formalized by Statute of Wales (1284).

1301   Edward I named his son (later Edward II) Prince of Wales; first English heir to be so designated; act helped to appease Welsh toward English rule.

1402–c1415   Owen Glendower staged unsuccessful uprising against English.

1536   Wales formally joined with England through the Act of Union.

18TH CENT.   Welsh nationalism played key role in establishment of Calvinistic Methodist church in Wales.

19TH CENT.   Extensive coal fields opened in the south; Wales became heavily industrialized, but depressed economic conditions in the countryside led to the Rebecca Riots (1843) and mass emigration.

1914   British Parliament ordered disestablishment of Calvinistic Methodist church.

1940s   Welsh nationalism showed marked increase in years following WW II; Welsh language introduced (1944) as working language for primary and secondary schools in Wales.

1979   Welsh voters rejected referendum for home rule.

Wales, Prince of   *See* **Prince of Wales**
Wales, Statute of   *See* **Statute of Wales**
Walewska, Countess Marie 1789–1817. Polish noblewoman, mistress to Napoleon I, and mother of Count A. Walewski.

Walewski, Comte Alexandre Florian Joseph Colonna. 1810–68. French diplomat and a son of Napoleon I and Marie Walewska. He was foreign minister (1855–60) and minister of state (1860–63).

Walker, Robert John 1801–69. American politician. As US Senator (1836–45) he supported westward expansion. He was secretary of the treasury (1845–49) during the Mexican War.

Walker, William 1824–60. American adventurer who led a force to the Mexican state of Lower California (1853–54), briefly establishing a republic. He invaded Nicaragua (1855) and became its president (1856–57).

Walking Purchase Purchase of Delaware Indian lands (1737) in Pennsylvania, in which Pennsylvania Colonial officials cheated the Indians. The Indians determined the size of lands to be sold by the distance a man could walk in a day. Pennsylvania officials, however, cleared a path and secured runners, thereby doubling the size of the tract.

Wallace, Alfred Russel 1823–1913. British naturalist. His studies contributing to the theory of natural selection paralleled, but were independent of, those of C. Darwin.

Wallace, George Corley 1919–. American politician and governor of Alabama (1963–67, 1971–76), noted for resisting school integration in Alabama. A 1968 third-party presidential candidate, he was campaigning for the 1972 Democratic presidential nomination when an assassin's bullet left him partly paralyzed (May 15, 1972).

Wallace, Henry Agard 1888–1965. American agriculturalist, statesman and US vice president (1941–45). A key figure in the New Deal, he was secretary of agriculture (1933–40) before being chosen for the vice-presidency. He was not renominated because of southern opposition.

Wallace, Lewis 1827–1905. American author and soldier, best known as author of the historical novel *Ben Hur.*

Wallace, Sir William c1272–1305. Scottish patriot, a leading figure in the Scottish struggle to win independence from England.

Wallachia *See* **Walachia**

Wallenstein, Albrecht von ⟨Waldstein, Albrecht von⟩ 1583–1634. Bohemian noble who served as the chief general to Holy Roman Emperor Ferdinand II during the Thirty Years' War. One of the most famous military men of his time, he commanded imperial forces twice (1625–30, 1632–34), but lost the emperor's trust and was murdered.

Wallis, John 1616–1703. English mathematician noted for his contributions to the development of calculus. He wrote on many subjects, including conic sections, logic, grammar, and cryptography.

Wall of Antoninus Ancient Roman wall stretching 37 miles across southern Scotland. It was built AD c140 by Antoninus Pius as a defense against attacks from the north.

Walloons French-speaking Belgians. They inhabit mainly the southern provinces of Belgium in contrast to the Dutch-speaking Flemings, who live in the northern provinces.

Walpole, Horace, 4th earl of Orford 1717–97. English author, noted for his Gothic novel *The Castle of Otranto* (1765), and for his many letters, which are an invaluable source for details about life in Georgian England.

Walpole, Robert 1st earl of Orford 1676–1745. British statesman and Whig leader, generally regarded as the first British prime minister. Walpole entered Parliament in 1701 and held ministerial posts (1708–11) until being convicted (1712) on dubious charges of corruption by a Tory administration. He supported the succession of the Hanoverian king George I (1714), which restored the Whigs to power, and thereafter began his ascendancy. In 1720 he was called upon to salvage government finances after the disastrous South Sea Bubble *(q.v.)* incident and in 1721 was appointed first lord of the treasury and chancellor of the exchequer. Thereafter he remained in power until 1742, and by his astute handling of Parliament and skillful distribution of royal patronage helped lay the foundations for the office of prime minister. His purge of opposition elements in his ministry (1733) established his firm control over the Cabinet. Walpole is especially noted for his accomplishments in the area of finance. He also endeavored to promote trade and reduce tariffs, and sought to keep Britain out of war. Unable to escape involvement in the War of the Austrian Succession, Walpole was ousted from power (1742) after reverses in that war.

Walsh, Thomas James 1859–1933. American political leader. As US Senator from Montana (1913–33), he headed the Senate investigation (1922–23) that exposed the Teapot Dome *(q.v.)* oil-reserve scandal.

Walter, Hubert d. 1205. English archbishop and statesman. He accompanied Richard I on the Third Crusade. As archbishop of Canterbury he raised the ransom to free Richard, and in Richard's absence was the effective ruler of England (1194–98).

Walter, Thomas U. *See* **Capitol**

Walter the Penniless d. 1096. French knight, and a leader of a band of soldiers and adventurers known as the Peasants' Crusade. His army plundered eastern Europe in advance of the First Crusade, and was defeated in Asia Minor.

Walther von der Vogelweide c1170–c1230. German minnesinger, considered the greatest lyric poet of medieval Germany.

Walwyn, William *See* **Levelers**

Wanamaker, John 1838–1922. American merchant, who founded (1875) in Philadelphia one of the first department stores, John Wanamaker and Company.

Wandiwash, Battle of British victory over the French (Jan. 22, 1760), near Madras, India. A French force of about 2,000 under the Count de Lally was routed by a British force of about 1,700. The victory was the most significant in India during the Seven Years' War and led to the French withdrawal from India.

Wang An-shih 1021–1086. Chinese poet, Confucian scholar, and government administrator. As chief minister for the Emperor Shen Tsung, he carried out financial reforms, established an agricultural loan program, levied an income tax, and organized a militia.

Wang Ching-wei 1885–1944. Chinese political leader. He was a supporter of Sun Yat-sen and after Sun's death (1925) challenged Chiang Kai-shek for control of the Kuomintang. He served as premier of Japanese-controlled China (1938–44).

Wang Mang 45 BC–AD 23. Chinese Han dynasty official who seized the throne and ruled as emperor (AD 9–23). His many radical governmental and land reforms were opposed by the aristocracy, which rebelled against him and restored the Han dynasty.

Wang Wei 699–759. Chinese poet, painter, and physician of the T'ang dynasty. A leading figure in Chinese cultural history, he is noted for his delicate monochrome landscapes and for his poems depicting pastoral scenes.

Wang Yang-ming 1472–1528. Chinese neo-Confucianist philosopher. He developed a philosophical idealism that conflicted with the realistic Confucianism of the 12th-cent. philosopher Chu Hsi.

Warbeck, Perkin 1474?–99. Flemish impostor and pretender to the English throne. He posed as Richard, the younger brother of Edward V, and sought to usurp the throne of Henry VII. He was defeated, imprisoned, and later executed.

Ward, Artemas 1727–1800. American general, who commanded at the siege of Boston (1775) until G. Washington took over. He later served in the Continental Congress (1780–81) and US Congress (1791–95).

war debts *See* **reparations**

War Hawks Certain southern and western US Congressmen of the 12th Congress (1811–13) who vigorously promoted war with Britain and who were thus largely responsible for the War of 1812. H. Clay and J. Calhoun were among the War Hawks.

Warhol, Andy *See* **Pop art**

warlord Regional military commanders in China who, between 1916 and 1949, often functioned as independent rulers in the areas they controlled. Chinese President Yüan Shi-k'ai had relied on military force to rule and, after his death in 1916, many of his former generals took control of their military territories, especially in the north. In the south, Chiang Kai-shek consolidated Nationalist rule and by his Northern Expedition regained control over warlords. Many warlords retained local control, however, and were not finally eliminated until the Communist victory in 1949.

Warner, Seth 1743–84. American Revolutionary War officer, a leader of the Green Mountain Boys. He played a major role in the capture of Ticonderoga (1775) and Crown Point (1775).

War of *See under names inverted, as in* **Pacific, War of the**

Warren, Earl 1891–1974. Chief justice of the US Supreme Court (1953–69) and three-time governor of California, (1943–53). He presided over many controversial court decisions, notably those outlawing school segregation, establishing the principle of "one man, one vote," and upholding an accused person's rights. He headed the Warren Commission (1963–64), the presidential commission that investigated the assassination of Pres. J. Kennedy.

Warren, Gouverneur Kemble 1830–82. American general in the Civil War. His defense of Little Round Top during the Battle of Gettysburg helped to secure a Union victory.

Warren, Robert Penn 1905–. American novelist, poet, and critic, identified with the group of southern writers known as the Fugitives, who celebrated the southern agrarian traditions. He wrote *All the King's Men.*

Warring States Period (481–221 BC) in Chinese history. This period brought an end to the long reign of the Chou dynasty (ruled 1122–221 BC) and was marked by the rise of a number of petty kingdoms. Corruption was widespread and wars between the states were frequent. Despite the chaotic nature of this period, some of the great thinkers in Chinese history flourished then (notably Mencius) and helped establish doctrines that would later dominate Chinese culture.

Warsaw Poland's capital (pop. 1,474,200), a railroad, industrial, and cultural center. Founded *c*1300, it became capital of the Polish kingdom in 1596. Warsaw was held by the Russians from 1813 until taken by Germany in 1915. In 1918, it became capital of the Polish Republic. During WW II, it was demolished by the Germans, and the Jewish population was decimated, despite a desperate uprising against the Nazis by Jews in the Warsaw ghetto (1943).

Warsaw Pact *See* **Warsaw Treaty Organization**

Warsaw Treaty Organization (Warsaw Pact) Defensive alliance between the USSR and its Eastern European satellites, created by a treaty signed in Warsaw (May 14, 1955) to counterbalance NATO. The Warsaw Pact countries consist of Albania (until 1968), Bulgaria, Czechoslovakia, East Germany, Hungary, Poland, Romania, and the USSR.

Warsaw uprising Rebellion in which the Polish underground army briefly recaptured and held Warsaw against the Germans (Aug.–Oct., 1944). The Poles were defeated by German reinforcements while the Soviet Army remained idle just across the Vistula. Thus any potential Polish military opposition to postwar Soviet domination of Poland was eliminated.

Warwick, Thomas de Beauchamp, earl of *See* **Beauchamp, Thomas de, earl of Warwick**

Washington State of the US Northwest (pop. 4,130,200), the 42nd state. The Spanish, English, and Russians explored the area, but it was American Robert Gray who claimed it for the US (1792). British and US counterclaims were settled in 1846, and Tumwater became the first permanent settlement in 1845. The Washington Territory was created in 1853, and the discovery of gold brought an increase in population. Washington became a state and adopted its constitution in 1889.

Washington, Booker Taliaferro 1856–1915. American black educator. Born a slave, he became the moving force in the establishment of Tuskegee (Alabama) Institute and a spokesman for educational and economic opportunity for blacks.

Washington, D.C. *See* **District of Columbia**

Washington, George 1732–99. First US president (1789–97), known as the Father of His Country. The son of a well-to-do Virginia planter, Washington began his career as a surveyor. He later fought in the French and Indian War (1754–63) and served as commander of the Virginia militia (1755–58). A member of the Virginia House of Burgesses (1759–74), he became a leader of the Colonial movement toward self-government. Washington became a delegate to the first Continental Congress (1774–75), and was named by the second Continental Congress as commander in chief of the Continental Army during the American Revolution *(q.v.)*. Washington remained in command throughout the revolutionary war. He turned a disorganized militia into a well-trained army and, despite severe shortages and chaotic communication between the army and the government, led his forces to ultimate victory at the Battle of Yorktown *(q.v.)* in 1781.

Washington served as president of the Constitutional Convention *(q.v.)* in 1787, and his efforts to secure adoption of the Constitution led to his election as first president of the US. Washington took the oath of office in New York City (Apr. 30, 1789) and appointed such men as T. Jefferson and A. Hamilton to the government, regardless of their political leanings. Later, Washington sought to remain neutral in the growing political struggle between the Republicans and the Federalists. His term as president was marked by the Whiskey Rebellion *(q.v.)* and the conclusion in 1795 of Jay's Treaty *(q.v.)* with Great Britain. Washington was unanimously re-elected (1793), but the bitter political struggle that had developed in the country led him to support the Federalists. His second term was also marked by conflict in the West. Deciding not to accept a third term as president, Washington delivered his celebrated Farewell Address (Sept. 17, 1796), in which he warned against the establishment of permanent alliances. He retired to his estate, Mount Vernon, but returned as commander in chief of the army (1798) when war with France seemed inevitable. War was avoided and Washington died (Dec. 14, 1799) soon after.

Washington, March on *See* **March on Washington**

Washington Peace Conference *See* **Tyler, John**

Washington, Treaty of Agreement (May 8, 1871) between Britain and the US that settled the Alabama claims *(q.v.)* and regulated navigation in the St. Lawrence and the Great Lakes. It was the first treaty in which Canada was recognized as a distinct entity.

Watergate scandal Major US political scandal (1972–74) involving charges of abuse of power, bribery, official misconduct, and attempts to cover up illegal activities. The scandal forced the resignation of President R. Nixon (1974) and resulted in a period of public distrust of government. The scandal began to unfold (June 17, 1972) when five men were arrested for trying to place an illegal wiretap in the Democratic party headquarters at the Watergate apartment complex in Washington, DC. With the two others who were arrested in the case, G. Gordon Liddy and E. Howard Hunt, Jr., the group was linked to the White House but nothing could be proved. In the meantime President Nixon was reelected to a second term and the seven involved in the Watergate incident were tried and convicted (Jan., 1973). A Senate committee was formed (Feb., 1973) to investigate.

The first break in the scandal came in Mar., 1973, when James McCord, one of the seven convicted, charged that the White House had attempted to cover up the incident. By Apr. 30, 1973, President Nixon was forced to dismiss White House advisers H.R. Haldeman, John D. Ehrlichman, and John Dean. Nixon, however, denied he had any involvement in the Watergate burglary or attempts to cover up the incident. Dean later testified that Nixon had approved the cover-up and implicated Haldeman, Ehrlichman, and former attorney general John Mitchell as well. The major break in the scandal came when it was revealed (July, 1973) that Nixon had taped all conversations in his White House office. The struggle for release of the tapes lasted a year and ended when the Supreme Court ruled against the president (July 24, 1974). The House adopted articles of impeachment against President Nixon (July 27–30) and, after publicly admitting he had been involved in the cover-up, Nixon resigned (Aug. 9). He was succeeded by President G. Ford, who later pardoned Nixon for his involvement in Watergate.

Waterloo, Battle of Final battle of the Napoleonic Wars, fought (June 18, 1815) at this Belgian village south of Brussels, and famous as Napoleon's military demise. After the Battle of Ligny, Napoleon sent a third of his 105,000-man army, under Marshal E. de Grouchy, in pursuit of the retreating 45,000-man Prussian army, under G. von Blucher. He then forced the Duke of Wellington's 68,000-man army to withdraw toward Brussels after a battle at Quatre Bras. With the two forces thus separated, Napoleon attacked Wellington at Waterloo at noon on June 18. However, Napoleon's main attack on Wellington's center was stalled by the British. Later that day Blucher arrived with his Prussian force, after having managed to elude Grouchy. These added reinforcements turned the battle into a rout and Napoleon was compelled to retreat with heavy losses (25,000 French casualties plus those taken prisoner; 23,000 allied casualties). Napoleon abdicated for his second and last time June 22.

Waters, Muddy (Morganfield, McKinley) 1915–83. American singer. He was a leading figure in the development of rhythm and blues.

Watling Street Ancient Roman road in England, running from London northwest through St. Al-

bans and other points to Wroxeter. It was built as a military road, and parts of it are still in use.

Watson, James Dewey 1928–. American biologist. He and Sir Francis Harry Compton Crick discovered (1953) the molecular structure of DNA. Co-winner of the Nobel Prize in physiology and medicine in 1962.

Watson John Broadus 1878–1958. American psychologist, the leading figure in the establishment of behaviorism.

Watt, James 1736–1819. Scottish inventor. He devised numerous improvements in and additions to the steam engine of Thomas Newcomen. Watt's improved engine was a milestone in the Industrial Revolution.

Watteau, Jean Antoine 1684–1721. French painter, considered one of the masters of French painting. His works are noted for their use of color and rendering of natural scenes.

Wattignies, Battle of Battle (Oct. 15–16, 1793) during the French Revolutionary Wars in which inexperienced French levies defeated a professional Austrian army. The 50,000-man French force defeated some 30,000 Austrians in this battle in northern France and thus blocked their drive toward Paris.

Waugh, Evelyn Arthur St. John 1903–66. English author, considered the most gifted satirical novelist of his time.

Way of Five Pecks of Rice *See* **Five Pecks of Rice**

Weaver, James Baird 1833–1912. American politician. He supported the policies of the Greenback party, and was its unsuccessful presidential candidate in 1880. He helped to found the Populist party and was its unsuccessful presidential candidate in 1892.

Webb, Sidney James 1858–1947. British social and economic reformer. He and his wife, Beatrice Webb, *née* Potter (1858–1943), were leading figures in the Fabian Society, founded the *New Statesman*, and greatly influenced social reforms in Britain.

Weber, Max 1864–1920. Influential German sociologist and political economist, best known for *The Protestant Ethic and the Spirit of Capitalism*, which explored the role of religious and ethical values in the development of capitalism.

Webster, Daniel 1782–1852. Noted American lawyer and statesman, considered one of the outstanding orators of his day. He was a vigorous supporter of American nationalism but opposed the annexation of Texas and the Mexican War, and sought to preserve the Union even at the cost of continued slavery. He served as senator (1827–41, 1845–50) and twice as secretary of state (1840–43, 1850–52).

Webster, Noah 1758–1843. American lexicographer, best known for his "Blue-backed Speller" (1783) and for his major work, *The American Dictionary of the English Language* (1828).

Webster-Ashburton Treaty Treaty (Aug., 1842) between Great Britain and the US, settling the northeastern boundary between the US and Canada and providing for suppression of the African slave trade. D. Webster represented the US, and Alexander Baring, 1st Baron Ashburton, represented Britain.

Wedgwood, Josiah 1730–95. English pottery manufacturer, whose scientific and practical approach to the production of pottery was matched by his attention to art and beauty. He was a leading figure in the Industrial Revolution.

Wehlau, Treaty of Agreement (Sept. 19, 1657) by which Poland gave up suzerainty over the Duchy of Prussia. The electors of Brandenburg had inherited ducal Prussia from the Teutonic Knights as a Polish fief. Duke Frederick William, however, won full sovereignty by this treaty, in return for providing military aid for Poland's war against Sweden.

Weidman, Charles Edward, Jr. 1901–75. American dancer and choreographer. His dances are noted for their abstract motions and use of pantomime, and have greatly influenced modern dance.

Weil, Simone 1909–43. French philosopher and mystic, whose writings reflect her social activism and attraction to the Roman Catholic faith.

Weill, Kurt 1900–50. German composer, whose operas are noted for their use of social satire. Best known of these is *The Threepenny Opera*, done in collaboration with B. Brecht.

Weimar Republic German republic (1919–33) created after Germany's defeat in WW I. The new government was created (July 31, 1919) amid social unrest (notably uprisings by Communists) and severe economic problems. Subsequent years were characterized by chronic parliamentary instability, a period of inflation, and mass unemployment, all of which eventually led to A. Hitler's rise to power in 1933. (*See also* Germany, 1919–33.)

Weinstein, Nathan *See* **West, Nathanael**

Weismann, August Friedrich Leopold 1834–1914. German biologist. His germ-plasm theory of heredity was a major contribution to the development of modern genetics.

Weiss, Ehrich *See* **Houdini, Harry**

Weizmann, Chaim 1874–1952. Russian-born scientist, Zionist leader, and Israeli statesman. A leader in the Zionist movement, Weizmann helped to negotiate the Balfour declaration *(q.v.)* and was the first president of Israel (1948–52).

Welfs Ruling family in Bavaria and Saxony which clashed (12th cent.) with their kinsmen in the German royal Hohenstaufen family (called Waiblings). The conflict resulted in the exile of Henry the Lion of Bavaria (a Welf) for failing to help the emperor Frederick I Barbarossa in Italy (1176). Thereafter the Welfs managed to get Henry's son, Otto IV, elected as anti-king to Barbarossa's successor, but their line ended with him. The names for the 13th cent. Guelphs and Ghibellines *(q.v.)* in Italy were adopted from this earlier rivalry.

Weller, Thomas *See* **Robbins, Frederick Chapman**

Welles, Gideon 1802–78. American statesman. He served as secretary of the navy under A. Lincoln and A. Johnson. He sided with Johnson against the Radical Republicans in the battle over Reconstruction *(q.v.)* policy.

Welles, Orson 1915–. American actor, director, and producer. His use of innovative techniques in such films as *Citizen Kane* and *The Magnificent Ambersons* greatly influenced film production.

Wellesley, Richard Colley, Marquess 1760–1842. British colonial administrator, brother of Arthur Wellesley, 1st duke of Wellington. As governor general of India (1797–1805) he greatly expanded British rule there.

Wellington Port city (pop. 139,200) and capital of New Zealand. Founded in 1840, it replaced Auckland as the capital in 1865. It is the country's main transportation and communications center, as well as the cultural and financial capital.

Wellington, Arthur Wellesley, 1st duke of 1769–1852. British soldier and statesman. He commanded British, Portuguese, and Spanish forces in the Peninsular War *(q.v.)*, defeated Napoleon in the Battle of Waterloo *(q.v.)*, and served as prime minister of Great Britain (1828–30). During his tenure, the Test Act *(q.v.)* was repealed and Catholic Emancipation *(q.v.)* was enacted.

Wells, Henry 1805–78. American expressman. He established (1848) his own express firm, which he later merged with other companies to form the American Express Company (1850). With W. Fargo he formed Wells, Fargo and Company (1852) to handle express service to California.

Wells, Herbert George 1866–1946. English author and historian. His novels, romances, and stories are marked by his interests in both scientific and social questions. His works include *The War of the Worlds*, *The Time Machine*, *Kipps*, *Tono-Bungay*, and *Outline of History*.

Wem, George Jeffreys, 1st Baron, Jeffreys of *See* **Jeffreys of Wem, George Jeffreys, 1st Baron**

Wenceslaus 1361–1419. King of the Germans (1378–1400), and Bohemia (1378–1419). He was successor to his father, Charles IV. He was an ineffective ruler and his reign was marked by religious and political conflicts and widespread rebellion. Amid a war between German nobles and imperial cities (1380s), he eventually sided with the nobles, only to be deposed as German king by them (in favor of Rupert) in 1400. He also tried and failed to resolve the Great Schism in the Roman Catholic church. After 1400, he retired to his kingdom of Bohemia and was there likewise embroiled in rebellions by nobles who twice imprisoned him (1394, 1402–03). Finally he supported the religious reformer J. Huss against the pope, but was unable to prevent Huss's execution. This led to the Hussite Wars *(q.v.)*, which broke out after Huss's execution.

Wenceslaus I *d.* 1253. King of Bohemia (1230–53), successor to his father Ottocar I. He encouraged Germans to settle in Bohemia, brought Austria under Bohemian control, and was a patron of the arts.

Wenceslaus II 1271–1305. King of Bohemia (1278–1305), successor to his father Ottocar II. He extended Bohemian control into Poland and Hungary, and was made king of Poland (1300–05).

Wenceslaus III *c*1289–1306. King of Hungary (1301–04) and king of Bohemia (1305–06). Son and successor of Wenceslaus II in Bohemia, he renounced his claim to Hungary. He was assassinated after his short reign in Bohemia.

Wenceslaus, Saint *d.* 929. Duke and patron saint of Bohemia. He encouraged Christianity in Bohemia and submitted to the rule of Henry I of Germany. For this he was murdered by his brother, Boleslav I, who succeeded him.

Wends Slavic people inhabiting East Germany. Also called "Sorbs," they are the remnant of a much more extensive Slavic people, whose lands the Germans conquered (6th–12th cents.).

Wentworth, Benning 1696–1770. American Colonial governor of New Hampshire (1741–67), who made the unauthorized New Hampshire Grants *(q.v.)*.

Wentworth, William Charles 1793–1872. Australian statesman. He founded a newspaper, the *Australian* (1824), to advance the cause of self-government and was a leader in the fight for the Australian constitution of 1855.

Wergeland, Henrick 1808–45. Norwegian writer and patriot. The greatest Norwegian writer of his day, Wergeland was a leading figure in the nationalist movement.

Wertheimer, Max 1880–1943. German psychologist whose studies of the perception of motion (1910–12) led to the development of Gestalt psychology.

Wesley, Charles *See* **Methodism**

Wesley, John 1703–91. English evangelist and founder of Methodism *(q.v.)*. He was ordained as a priest of the Church of England (1728). At Oxford, he joined a group (1729) of students, called "methodists," that had been formed by his brother Charles (1707–88) and that included G. Whitefield. John later engaged in missionary work in colonial Georgia (1735–38); when he returned to London, he experienced a religious awakening during a meeting at Aldersgate St. (May 24, 1738). Thereafter he dedicated himself to evangelical work and conducted numerous missions in England, Ireland, and Scotland. He broke with the Calvinists in 1740, and in 1784 issued a declaration formally constituting the Methodist societies.

Wessex Saxon kingdom, once located in southern England, and a part of the Anglo-Saxon Heptarchy. Founded by Saxon invaders in the late 5th cent. AD, it rivaled the other Anglo-Saxon kingdoms for control of territories until the 9th-cent. Danish invasion. Under the leadership of Aethelred I and Alfred the Great, Wessex alone withstood the Danish armies. Then, by reconquering Danish holdings (by 927), the kings of Wessex made themselves masters of all England.

West In American history, the land lying west of the Mississippi River (earlier, west of the original 13 colonies). In the years of westward expansion, the West assumed mythical proportions as the land of unlimited opportunity. (*See also* Manifest Destiny.)

West, Benjamin 1738–1820. American painter of historical scenes. West moved to England in 1763, where George III was his patron. His innovative use of contemporary dress in such paintings as *Death of General Wolfe* influenced later painters.

West, Mae *c*1892–1980. American stage and film actress. Her wit and beauty made her one of the great sex stars of American cinema.

West, Nathanael ⟨Weinstein, Nathan⟩ 1903–40. American novelist. He had a pessimistic but strangely poetic view of American life, which he depicted in such novels as *Miss Lonelyhearts* and *The Day of the Locust*.

West Berlin *See* **Berlin**

Western Chin *See* **Chin**

Western Empire *See* **Roman Empire; Rome**

Western Reserve Tract of land in Ohio on the south shore of Lake Erie which was held by Connecticut, after it surrendered the rest of its western lands to Congress in 1786. Part of it was sold to immigrants whose property was destroyed during the Revolution. It passed to Ohio in 1800.

Western Roman Empire *See* **Roman Empire; Rome**

West Florida Controversy Territorial dispute between Spain and the US over western Florida lands on the Gulf of Mexico, roughly located between the Perdido and Mississippi rivers. America claimed the land as part of the Louisiana Purchase, while Spain claimed it under the 1783 Treaty of Paris. American settlers rebelled (1810) and, reinforced by troops sent by Pres. James Madison, ended effective Spanish control. Spain relinquished its claims to the area (1819) by the Transcontinental Treaty.

West Goths *See* **Visigoths**

West Indies Islands located between North and South America on the eastern edge of the Caribbean Sea. They include the Greater Antilles, the Lesser Antilles, and the Bahamas. First reached by C. Columbus in 1492, the islands were settled by English, French, Dutch, and their imported African slave labor.

Westinghouse, George 1846–1914. American inventor and manufacturer. He invented the railroad air brake, pioneered the development of alternating current electrical systems, and founded the Westinghouse Electric Company.

Westminster, Statute of English laws, the first three of which were enacted under Edward I. **1.** Westminster I (1275) put long-unwritten laws into legal, written forms, most notably equal legal protection for the poor. **2.** Westminster II (1285) concerned land tenure and entailments. **3.** Westminster III (1290) ended the subinfeudation of land by making a new owner responsible to the prime overlord, not the subholder **4.** Statute, passed by Parliament in 1931, recognizing the autonomy of member nations within the United Kingdom. It created the British Commonwealth of Nations *(q.v.)*.

Westminster, Treaties of English treaties signed at Westminster. **1.** Treaty (Apr. 5, 1654) ending the First Dutch War (1652–54), which had been fought primarily on the seas. The Dutch agreed to enter a defensive league with England, pay an indemnity, and exclude the House of Orange from the office of stadtholder. **2.** Treaty (1662) between England's Charles II and Frederick William, elector of Brandenberg. They granted each other most-favored-nation status. **3.** Treaty (Feb. 9, 1674) ending the Third Dutch War (1672–74). The Dutch once again paid an indemnity and returned to England such American Colonial territories as New York, Albany, Long Island, and New Jersey. **4.** Covenant of Westminster (Jan. 1756), which established neutrality between Britain and Frederick the Great of Prussia.

Westminster Abbey Church in Westminster, one of the boroughs of Greater London. A leading example of Gothic architecture in England, the abbey is the burial place of numerous national figures, including many English monarchs, and has been the site of virtually every coronation since William I.

Westminster Assembly ⟨Divines at Westminster, Assembly of⟩ Convocation summoned by the Long Parliament to fix the doctrine and practice of the Church of England. It sat between July 1, 1643, and Feb. 22, 1649. Consisting of some 120 clergy and some 30 lay people, the assembly was entirely Calvinist. Its *Catechisms* and its *Directory of Public Worship* were accepted in Scotland but not in England.

Westminster Conference Meeting held in London (1866–67) to plan the union of Canadian provinces. Resolutions of the conference were incorporated into the British North America Act of 1867.

Westminster Palace ⟨House of Parliament⟩ Complex of buildings built between 1840 and 1860 to house the British Parliament. It was constructed on the site of the former royal palace built in the 11th cent. That building had been used to house Parliament from the 16th cent., but was destroyed by fire in 1834.

Westphalia Historic northwestern German province, most of which is today in the West German state of North Rhine-Westphalia. Once a part of the Duchy of Saxony, it was administered for centuries by the Archbishop of Cologne. Napoleon based a short-lived kingdom for his brother Jerome on part of its territory in 1807. In 1815, after the Congress of Vienna, it became a province of Prussia.

Westphalia, Peace of Treaty (Oct. 24, 1648) ending the Thirty Years' War. The treaty marked the end of the period of religious wars in Europe that arose from the Protestant Reformation. The major participants in the treaty were Sweden and France on the one side and the Holy Roman Empire and Spain on the other. The treaty seriously weakened the Holy Roman Empire by recognizing the sovereignty of the individual German states within its domains. This was an important victory for France, which had sought to break the power of the Hapsburg Holy Roman Emperors. The treaty also recognized the independence of The Netherlands and the Swiss Confederation. Among the various territorial adjustments stipulated in the treaty were those awarding Alsace to France and West Pomerania to Sweden. Other provisions of the treaty related to religious settlements. In general a policy of toleration was instituted in the German states and Calvinism was recognized.

West Virginia   State in the east central US (pop. 1,949,600), the 35th state. Originally an uninhabited part of the state of Virginia, West Virginia was settled by European immigrants who came by way of Pennsylvania. Conflicting claims to the area led to the French and Indian War (1754–63). Sectional differences, including the dispute over slavery, led to conflicts between western Virginians and the rest of the state. Finally they rejected secession in the Civil War and voted instead to form a new state. West Virginia became a state in 1863 and adopted its constitution in 1872.

Weyden, Roger van der   c1400–64.   Flemish painter of religious themes, considered one of the most influential painters of his day.

Weygand, Maxime   1867–1965.   French general, chief of staff to Marshal Foch (1914–23). As French commander in chief (May-June, 1940) during WW II, he was unable to halt the German advance. He later served with the Vichy government.

Weyler y Nicolau, Valeriano   1838–1930.   Spanish general. He was captain-general of Spanish forces in Cuba (1896–97), and his harsh treatment of Cuban rebels caused a wave of protest from America just before the Spanish-American War.

Wharton, Edith Jones   1862–1937.   American novelist, whose works are noted for their insights into the workings of upper class American society. Her works include *Ethan Frome* and *The Age of Innocence*.

Wheatstone, Sir Charles   1802–75. English physicist and inventor. He is credited with the invention of the concertina, the stereoscope, and a device to measure electrical resistance, now known as the Wheatstone bridge. He was co-inventor with W. Cooke of an early telegraph (patented 1837) and inventor of an automatic telegraph transmitter and related devices.

Wheeler, Joseph   1836–1906.   Confederate general in the American Civil War, who opposed William T. Sherman in the Atlanta Campaign. He later served in Congress, and commanded cavalry at Santiago in the Spanish-American War.

Wheeler, William Almon   1819–87.   American politician. He served as US vice-president (1877–81) under R. Hayes, after a contested election.

Wheeler-Howard Act   *See* **Indian Reorganization Act**

Whichcote, Benjamin   *See* **Cambridge Platonists**

Whig   Name used to denote what was variously a political party and a faction in England (17th–early 19th cents.). The Whig faction emerged in 1679 as a group opposing the succession of the Catholic Stuart king James II. James was finally deposed by Whigs and his former Tory supporters in the Glorious Revolution (q.v.) of 1688. Thereafter Whigs became identified with the interests of the landowning aristocracy and the wealthy middle class. Whig leaders, notably Sir R. Walpole, dominated the government during the reigns of George I and George II (1714–60). During the period from 1760 to 1784, Whig and Tory factions ceased to be identifiable as distinct groups and appointments were made on the basis of personal and family influence. In 1784, however, the emergence of a new Tory party (under W. Pitt the Younger) helped coalesce opposition factions into a new Whig party. The Whigs (led by C. Fox) then advanced the interests of industrialists, religious dissenters, and others who favored reforms. The Whig party ceased to exist in the 19th cent. and many of its members joined the emerging Liberal party (q.v.), forming the party's conservative wing.

Whig party   American political party, organized (1834) by H. Clay in reaction to President A. Jackson. They supported internal improvements, the development of western lands, a regulated currency, a system of weights and measures, a national bank, and high protective tariffs. They also supported compromise on the issue of slavery. Both their elected presidents (W. Harrison and Z. Taylor) died in office, however, and the party grew increasingly divided over slavery. After 1854, many Whigs joined the new Republican party.

Whipple, Abraham   1733–1819.   American naval officer. During the American Revolution he captured 11 British merchant ships of the East Indies fleet (1779), one of the greatest captures of the war.

Whiskey Rebellion   Name given to the outbreak of protest west of the Alleghenies against an excise tax imposed (1781) by the newly created US government. The western settlers especially resented the tax on whiskey, the distillation of which was an important economic activity. Pres. G. Washington sent troops, partly to demonstrate the power of the new federal government, and the rebellion was suppressed without bloodshed.

Whisky Ring   Conspiracy by a number of US distillers to deprive the government of tax revenues by bribing officials. The ring was exposed in 1875 and 110 people were convicted. The scandal touched the administration of Pres. U. Grant when his secretary was indicted (though not convicted).

Whistler, James Abbott McNeill   1834–1903. American painter and etcher. Essentially a realist, he pioneered the use of light, form, and color in a way that prefigured abstract art. He is best known for his *Portrait of My Mother*.

Whitby, Synod of Council called by King Oswy of Northumbria (663–664) at Whitby, England, to determine whether the church of Northumbria would follow Celtic or Roman usages. The council's decision to follow Roman usages brought the church closer to European Christian tradition.

White, Edward Douglass 1845–1921. American jurist, associate justice of the Supreme Court (1894–1910) and chief justice (1910–21). He is best known for his "rule of reason" decisions in large antitrust cases, which influenced subsequent antitrust litigation.

White, Elwyn Brooks 1899–. American writer, humorist, and stylist. For many years as a staffer of *The New Yorker* magazine, he distinguished himself for his light, graceful, and witty style. His numerous works include essays, the children's classic *Charlotte's Web*, and his revision of Strunk's *Elements of Style*.

White, Stanford 1853–1906. American architect. His architectural firm designed the original Madison Square Garden in New York City. He was fatally shot (June 25, 1906) by Harry K. Thaw, the outraged husband of the showgirl Evelyn Nesbit, with whom White was having an affair. The murder was one of the most sensationalized cases of the early 1900s.

White, Walter Francis 1893–1955. American civil rights leader and author, who served (1931–55) as secretary of the NAACP.

Whiteboys Peasant associations formed in Ireland around 1760 to harass landlords, tax collectors, and Protestant clergy. They were so named because they wore white clothing during their nightly forays.

Whitefield, George 1714–70. English evangelist, who helped J. Wesley to establish Methodism. He later broke with Wesley and helped to form the Calvinistic Methodist Church. He also preached in America and figured there in the Great Awakening (*q.v.*).

Whitehead, Alfred North 1861–1947. English mathematician and philosopher who collaborated with B. Russell on *Principia Mathematica*, a major study in logic, and who developed a metaphysical theory of reality.

White Hill, Battle of Battle fought on a chalk hill near Prague (Nov. 8, 1620), the first battle of the Thirty Years' War. A German force of some 25,000 under the Count of Tilly defeated a combined Bohemian-Hungarian force of some 15,000 men.

White House Official residence of the president of the US. It is the oldest public building in Washington (the cornerstone was laid in 1792) and was burned by the British (1814). It was rebuilt by James Hoban in 1817 and was restored between 1949 and 1952.

White Lotus Rebellion Chinese rebellion. The White Lotus was a Buddhist cult that opposed domination by the Manchus of the Ch'ing dynasty. From 1796 to 1804, they conducted a guerrilla revolt in the mountains of central China in protest against their poverty and excessive taxation. The imperial forces were hindered for several years by corruption within the army, but they eventually put down the rebellion. However, the revolt revealed the declining power of the Manchus and paved the way for other revolts in the 19th cent. that ended in the overthrow of the Ch'ing dynasty.

White Plains, Battle of Indecisive battle fought (Oct. 28, 1776) near White Plains, New York, during the American Revolution. British Gen. W. Howe, marching with a force of 20,000 men, engaged a Continental brigade of 14,000, led by G. Washington. After the battle, Washington was forced to withdraw.

White Revolution Reform movement in Iran during the 1950s and 1960s, instituted by Mohammed Reza Shah Pahlevi and his advisers. It aimed especially at land reforms, and an Office of Land Reform was established on Aug. 20, 1960. Ultimately, however, the "revolution" failed to gain popular support and the shah was forced to abdicate by the Islamic revolution in 1979.

White Russia *See* **Belorussia**

White Volunteer Army Russian armies formed in the winter of 1917–18 in the peripheral areas of the former Russian Empire to combat the Bolshevik regime established under N. Lenin. Though aided by 14 allied nations, they lacked unified leadership and necessary supplies and were unable to prevail against the Red Army.

Whitgift, John *See* **Marprelate Controversy**

Whitman, Walter 1819–92. American poet, one of the great figures in American literature. His major work, *Leaves of Grass*, is noted for its innovative style.

Whitney, Eli 1765–1825. American inventor of the cotton gin (1793). He also pioneered in the use of interchangeable parts in the manufacture of firearms, a major step in the development of mass production.

Whittier, John Greenleaf 1807–92. American poet and abolitionist, best known for his celebration in verse of his native New England and for his antislavery activities in the years before the Civil War.

Whittington, Richard *d.* 1423. English merchant, lord mayor of London, and subject of a popular English legend. According to the story, he was a poor boy who gave his cat to a merchantman to offer in trade. Ultimately the cat was sold for a fortune to a Moroccan ruler plagued by rats.

Wickliffe, John   *See* **Wycliffe, John**

Wiclif, John   *See* **Wycliffe, John**

Widukind ⟨Wittekind⟩ *d.* c807. Leader of the Saxons against Charlemagne. He raided the Rhineland (778), but later submitted and converted to Christianity (785). He is said to have become duke of the Saxons.

Wiener, Norbert 1894–1964. American mathematician, founder of cybernetics, the science of control and communication in animals and machines.

Wiggin, Kate Douglas Smith 1856–1923. American author and educator, best known for her novel *Rebecca of Sunnybrook Farm.*

Wilberforce, William 1759–1833. English politician, humanitarian, and philanthropist, who led in the movement to abolish slavery and the slave trade within the British Empire.

Wilde, Oscar 1854–1900. Irish poet, dramatist, and wit, and a leader of the Aesthetic movement. His works include the novel *The Picture of Dorian Gray* and the play *The Importance of Being Earnest.*

Wilder, Thornton Niven 1897–1975. American author and playwright, whose plays and novels reflected his belief in the universality of human experience. Wilder received Pulitzer prizes for the novel *The Bridge of San Luis Rey* (1927) and the play *Our Town* (1938).

Wilderness, Battle of the American Civil War battle fought (May 5–6, 1864) in Virginia. Some 100,000 Union troops, commanded by Gen. U. Grant, attacked 60,000 Confederate troops, commanded by Gen. R. Lee, but fighting was indecisive in difficult terrain. Grant lost some 18,000 troops (to Lee's 11,000) before moving on to do battle at Spotsylvania. The battle was part of Grant's drive toward Richmond.

Wilderness Road Route followed by American settlers from Virginia into western Kentucky (1790 to 1840). First blazed as a trail by the frontiersman D. Boone c1775, it led from the Shenandoah Valley through the Cumberland Gap to western Kentucky and the Ohio River region.

Wilfrid, Saint ⟨Wilfrid of York⟩ 634–709? English churchman, Bishop of York (c665), and one of the leading saints of England. He encouraged the adoption of Roman usages at the Synod of Whitby *(q.v.),* bringing the English church closer to the Roman Catholic church.

Wilfrid of York   *See* **Wilfrid, Saint**

Wilhelmina 1880–1962. Queen of The Netherlands (1890–1948), successor to her father William III. Forced into exile in Britain during WW II, she encouraged Dutch resistance to German occupation.

Wilkes, Charles 1798–1877. American naval officer and explorer. He explored the region of Antarctica now called Wilkes Land. In 1861 his actions in the Trent Affair *(q.v.)* nearly led to war with Britain.

Wilkes, John 1727–97. English journalist and politician, several times expelled from Parliament for his outspoken attacks in periodicals. He is noted as a champion of freedom of the press.

Wilkins, Roy 1901–81. American black civil rights leader. Long associated with the NAACP, he served as executive secretary (and later director) from 1955 to 1977. He was a principal organizer of the 1963 March on Washington *(q.v.).*

Wilkinson, James 1757–1825. American general. He served in the Revolutionary War, was a member of the Conway Cabal, and was governor of Louisiana Territory (1805–06). He was implicated in the conspiracy of A. Burr.

William I ⟨William the Conqueror⟩ 1027–87. English king (1066–87) and duke of Normandy (1035–87). The illegitimate son of Robert, duke of Normandy, he succeeded Robert as duke on the latter's death (1035). His early years were marked by continued strife in Normandy. With the help of French king Henry I, he established his rule in Normandy (1047), then later repulsed two French invasions of Normandy (1054, 1058). In 1051, on a visit to his cousin, English king Edward the Confessor, he is thought to have received a promise of the English throne. On Edward's death, however, the crown passed to Harold, earl of Wessex. William secured the pope's support for his claim and raised an army.

Invading England (1066) he defeated and killed Harold in the Battle of Hastings *(q.v.),* marched on London, and was crowned king on Christmas Day. The English resisted his rule and William spent several years crushing rebellions, seizing estates, and redistributing lands to his Norman supporters. He appointed Lanfranc (1005?–89) archbishop of Canterbury, brought the church under his control, and firmly established feudalism in England. In 1072 he forced Scottish king Malcolm to do him homage. William authorized (1085) the compilation of the Domesday Book *(q.v.),* a complete survey of England.

His later years were spent largely in Normandy, while Lanfranc conducted William's affairs in England. William suppressed several rebellions led by his son Robert II, and conducted war against French king Philip I. While campaigning he suffered internal injuries in a fall and died at Rouen. His son Robert succeeded him as duke of Normandy, and his son William as king of England. William the Conqueror was an able administrator, a ruthless and intelligent military commander, and one of the greatest leaders of his time. His conquest of England radically altered the history of England and of Western Europe.

William I ⟨~ the Silent, Prince of Orange⟩ 1533–84. Prince of Orange and Count of Nassau. In 1568 he led the rebellion of The Netherlands against the rule of Philip II of Spain.

William I 1772–1843. First king of The Netherlands (1815–40). Commerce and industry flourished under his rule, but his treatment of Belgium, then part of The Netherlands, led to its secession in 1830.

William I 1797–1888. King of Prussia (1861–88) and first German emperor (1871–88). He appointed O. von Bismarck prime minister of Prussia (1862), and thereafter followed a militaristic policy that finally established Prussian dominance over a unified Germany.

William II ⟨William Rufus⟩ d. 1100. King of England (1087–1100), successor to his father William I the Conqueror. His rule was ruthless and he made many enemies. William appointed Anselm archbishop of Canterbury, and later exiled him. He conducted wars in Scotland, Wales, and Normandy, and maintained Norman rule over England.

William II ⟨William the Good⟩ d. 1189. King of Sicily (1166–89). He allied himself with Frederick I Barbarossa and attempted (1185) unsuccessfully to conquer the Byzantine Empire.

William II 1792–1849. King of The Netherlands (1840–49), successor to his father William I. He restored financial stability to The Netherlands and granted constitutional reforms (1848).

William II 1859–1941. King of Prussia and German emperor (1888–1918). His support of Austria-Hungary against Serbia contributed to the outbreak of WW I and increased military control of the government. With Germany's defeat, he abdicated.

William III ⟨William of Orange⟩ 1650–1702. Stadtholder of the United Provinces of The Netherlands (1672–1702) who became king of England (1689–1702) by the Glorious Revolution (q.v.). He ruled jointly with his wife Queen Mary II, promoted Protestantism, fiscal and parliamentary reform, and led campaigns against Louis XIV in the war of the Grand Alliance. He defeated James II at

the Battle of the Boyne in Ireland, thereby ending James' attempt to retake the English throne.

William III 1817–90. King of The Netherlands (1849–90), and grand duke of Luxembourg, successor to his father William II. During his reign, Luxembourg was granted a parliamentary constitution (1867).

William IV 1765–1837. British king (1830–37), successor to his brother, George IV. He opposed parliamentary reform, but reluctantly accepted passage of the Reform Bill of 1832.

William of Occam   See **Ockham, William of**

William of Ockham   See **Ockham, William of**

William of Orange   See **William I; William III**

William of Tyre c1130–1185. Churchman and historian. He is noted for his *Historia Rerum in Partibus Transmarinis Gestarum*, a history of the Latin kingdom of Jerusalem from 1095–1184.

William Rufus   See **William II**

Williams, Eric E   See **Trinidad and Tobago**

Williams, Roger c1603–83. Colonial religious leader. Banished by the Massachusetts Bay Colony for his religious views, he founded the city of Providence (1636) and the colony of Rhode Island. He encouraged religious toleration.

Williams, Tennessee ⟨b. Thomas Lanier Williams⟩ 1914–83. American playwright, whose works are noted for their insight into the passions and motivations of human beings. Among his many famous plays are *Cat on a Hot Tin Roof, A Streetcar Named Desire*, and *The Night of the Iguana*.

Williams, Thomas Lanier   See **Williams, Tennessee**

Williams, William Carlos 1883–1963. American poet and physician, whose verse is noted for its use of concise language and of everyday objects and experience. His works include *Pictures from Brueghel, and Other Poems* and *In the American Grain*.

William the Conqueror   See **William I**

William the Good   See **William II**

William the Lion 1143–1214. King of Scotland (1165–1214), successor to his brother Malcolm IV. He attempted unsuccessfully to recover Northumbria from England, and extended his control throughout the Scottish kingdom.

Willkie, Wendell Lewis 1892–1944. American industrialist and political leader. A leading critic of the New Deal, he ran unsuccessfully on the Republican presidential ticket in 1940.

Wilmot Proviso Controversial amendment attached to an 1846 bill presented in the US Congress. The bill sought funds to pay for a negotiated settlement of the US and Mexican boundary dispute that had erupted into the Mexican War. The amendment, authored by Pennsylvania Democrat

David Wilmot, contained a ban on extension of slavery into any territories acquired from Mexico. The bill did not pass, but the principle was later adopted by the new Republican party.

Wilson, Charles Thomson Rees 1869–1959. Scottish physicist, inventor of the Wilson cloud chamber. He was awarded, with Arthur C. Compton, the 1927 Nobel Prize for physics.

Wilson, Edmund 1895–1972. American critic and essayist, considered one of the leading American men of letters in the 20th cent. His many works include *The Wound and the Bow* and *To the Finland Station.*

Wilson-Gorman Tariff Act *See* **Cleveland, Stephen Grover**

Wilson, Henry⟨Colbath, Jeremiah Jones⟩ 1812–75. American politician and abolitionist leader. As US senator (1855–72) he was a leader of the Radical Republicans. He served as vice-president (1873–75) under U. Grant.

Wilson, James 1742–98. American jurist. A signer of the Declaration of Independence, he championed the concept of popular sovereignty at the Constitutional Convention of 1787 and served as associate justice of the Supreme Court (1789–98).

Wilson, Sir James Harold 1916–. British statesman. A leader of the Labour party, he served twice as prime minister (1964–70, 1974–76). His government was marked by troubles with white-ruled Rhodesia, serious economic problems, and unrest in Ireland.

Wilson, Woodrow ⟨Thomas Woodrow ~⟩ 1856–1924. Twenty-eighth US president (1913–21), successor to W. Taft. A graduate of Princeton University (1879), Wilson joined the faculty of Princeton (1890) and served as its president (1902–10). He resigned and ran successfully for the governorship of New Jersey (1911–13), during which time he became known for his progressive policies. At the 1912 Democratic convention he was nominated for president on the 46th ballot. A split between the regular Republican party and T. Roosevelt's Progressive party helped Wilson win the election. Wilson's first term was marked by the passage of numerous progressive measures, notably the establishment of the Federal Trade Commission (1914) and passage of the Clayton Antitrust Act (1914) and the Federal Farm Loan Act (1916).

In foreign matters, Wilson opposed the rise of V. Huerta as president of Mexico (1913) and sent US forces to Veracruz (1914). He also authorized the punitive expedition into Mexico (1916) led by Gen. J. Pershing (following P. Villa's raid into the US). Wilson sought to keep the US out of war in Europe. The German sinking (1915) of the liner *Lusitania* aroused sentiment for war in the US. However, following the sinking of the *Sussex,* Wilson secured an agreement from Germany to end its policy of unrestricted submarine warfare. Campaigning on the motto "He kept us out of war," Wilson was reelected (1916). He broke diplomatic relations (Feb., 1917) with Germany after it resumed unrestricted submarine activity, and Congress declared war (Apr. 6).

In 1918, Wilson announced his famous Fourteen Points *(q.v.),* by which he believed the world could be made "safe for democracy" at war's end. In Dec., 1918, he left for France as head of the US delegation to the Paris Peace Conference. He fought unsuccessfully against the harsh terms of the Versailles Treaty but secured a covenant calling for the League of Nations. Returning to America, he found his proposals rejected by Congress. Wilson began a campaign tour across the US to gain popular support, especially for the League, but he suffered a physical collapse (Sept., 1919) and then a stroke (Oct., 1919), from which he never completely recovered. His administration was also marked by passage of the 17th, 18th, and 19th Amendments to the US Constitution. Wilson was awarded the Nobel Peace Prize in 1919.

Wilson's Creek, Battle of Battle of US Civil War, a Confederate victory over Union forces near Springfield, Missouri, on Aug. 10, 1861. A Union force of some 5,400 intercepted an invading force of 11,000 Confederates from Arkansas and after a hard battle was forced to withdraw. The Confederates then took Springfield.

Winckelmann, Johann Joachim 1717–68. German archaeologist, whose *History of the Art of Antiquity* became the basis for modern archaeology.

Winckler, Hugo 1863–1913. German archaeologist and historian whose excavations at Bogazköy, Turkey (1906–12) uncovered the capital of the Hittites and yielded cuneiform tablets that became a main source of information about the Hittite Empire.

Windsor, House of From 1917 the official surname of the royal family of Britain. It replaced the family name of Wettin and dynastic name of Saxe-Coburg-Gotha. This change was effected by George V during WW I.

Windsor, Wallis Warfield, duchess of 1896–. American-born wife of the duke of Windsor. Edward abdicated (1936) his throne (as Edward VIII) in order to marry her.

Windsor Castle Castle in New Windsor, Berkshire, England, which has served as the main residence for English monarchs since William I, the

Conqueror. The castle stands on a site dating from Celtic times.

Wineland *See* **Vinland**

Wingate, Orde Charles 1903–44. British general. During WW II he organized and led the Chindits, or Wingate's Raiders, a guerrilla unit that fought against the Japanese in Burma.

Winkelried, Arnold von *d.* 1386. Swiss hero, whose legendary act of self-sacrifice in battle is said to have led to the Swiss victory over Austria in the Battle of Sempach.

Winnipeg City (pop. 560,800), capital of Canada's Manitoba province. The site of a fur-trading post from 1738, its first settlers were part of the Red River Settlement. Completion of the transcontinental railroad in 1885 enabled it to become one of the world's largest grain-handling centers.

Winslow, Edward 1595–1655. Pilgrim leader, one of the founders of the Plymouth Colony. He served as governor (1633–34, 1636–37, 1644–45).

Winslow, Josiah *c*1629–80. American governor of Plymouth Colony (1673–80), the first native-born Colonial governor in America. He led the colonials in King Philip's War (*q.v.*).

Winter War *See* **Russo-Finnish War**

Winthrop, John 1588–1649. English colonist, governor of the Massachusetts Bay Colony 12 times between 1629 and 1648. He greatly influenced the development of this theocratic community and thus affected the subsequent history of Massachusetts.

Wisconsin North-central state of the US (pop. 4,705,300), the 30th state. Jean Nicolet of France first explored the area (1634), and it was a center of the fur trade in spite of war with the Indians. After 1763, the British took control, then ceded it to the US after the American Revolution (1783). The Black Hawk War (1832) was the last major Indian uprising, and Wisconsin became a territory in 1836. In 1848, it adopted its constitution and was admitted to the Union.

Wise, Isaac Mayer 1819–1900. American rabbi, founder of many of the Reform Jewish institutions in the US. He was the guiding force in founding Hebrew Union College, the Union of American Hebrew Congregations, and the Central Conference of American Rabbis.

Wise Men of the East *See* **Magi**

Wishart, George 1513?–1546. Scottish religious reformer and Protestant martyr. His preaching influenced J. Knox. Wishart was convicted and executed for heresy.

Wissman, Hermann von 1853–1905. German explorer of the Congo region (now Zaire) and German East Africa (now Tanzania). He increased knowledge of the area, established outposts, and served as commissioner and governor of German East Africa.

Witan *See* **Witenagemot**

Witenagemot ⟨Witan⟩ King's council that existed in England in Anglo-Saxon times. It consisted mainly of the nobles and bishops, and advised the king on land grants, taxes, and other matters.

Witherspoon, John 1723–94. Scottish-born American clergyman, president of the College of New Jersey (now Princeton University), and signer of the Declaration of Independence.

Witt, Jan de 1625–72. Dutch statesman and patriot. As grand pensionary, he led Holland in the Dutch Wars and was instrumental in forming the Triple Alliance of 1668 and negotiating the Treaty of Aix-la-Chapelle.

Witte, Count Sergei Yulyevich 1849–1915. Russian statesman. As minister of finance (1892–1903), he helped bring about completion of the Trans-Siberian Railway. He served (1905–06) as prime minister after helping to form the Duma.

Wittekind *See* **Widukind**

Wittelsbach Name of the family dynasty that ruled Bavaria from 1180–1918. In addition to providing Bavarian kings, the line also produced a king of the Germans (Rupert of the Palatinate, 1400–10) and two Holy Roman emperors (Louis IV of Bavaria, 1314–47; Charles VII, 1742–45).

Wittgenstein, Ludwig Josef Johann 1889–1951. Austrian philosopher, one of the major philosophers of the 20th cent. His works deal with the relation of thought and language to the real and metaphysical worlds.

Wittstock, Battle of Swedish victory in the Thirty Years' War. Fought (Oct. 4, 1636) near Berlin, the battle pitted some 22,000 Swedish troops against 30,000 allied troops of the Holy Roman Empire and resulted in imperial losses of 11,000 casualties and 8,000 captured. The Swedes lost about 5,000.

Wobblies *See* **Industrial Workers of the World**

Wodehouse, Pelham Grenville 1881–1975. English author and humorist, best known as creater of Bertie Wooster and his manservant Jeeves in such works as *Much Obliged, Jeeves.*

Wöhler, Friedrich 1800–82. German chemist. His synthesis of urea marked the first time (1828) an organic compound was made artificially from inorganic material.

Wojtyla, Karol *See* **John Paul II**

Wolfe, James 1727–59. British commander in the French and Indian Wars. He led British forces in the capture of Quebec (1759) from the French, thereby ensuring British dominance in Canada.

Wolfe, Thomas Clayton 1900–1938. American novelist, perhaps best known for his semi-autobiographical novel *Look Homeward, Angel*, about a young man's development in a small southern city.

Wolfram von Eschenbach *c*1170–*c*1220. German poet, whose epic poem *Parzifal* is one of the great medieval literary works. Wagner used it as the basis for his opera *Parsifal*.

Wolseley, Garnet Joseph, 1st Viscount 1833–1913. British field marshal. He worked tirelessly to modernize the British army and from 1895 to 1901 he was commander in chief of the British army. He served in many British campaigns, including the Burma War, the Crimean War, and Riel's Rebellion in Canada, and led the attempt to relieve Gordon at Khartoum.

Wolsey, Thomas *c*1475–1530. English statesman and Catholic cardinal. As lord chancellor of England (1515–29), he was the leading force in English politics during the early reign of King Henry VIII.

Woman's Christian Temperance Union Organization founded (1874) in Cleveland, Ohio, to work against the evils of alcoholic beverages. It was instrumental in the adoption of Prohibition *(q.v.)* in the US and now has branches in many countries.

woman suffrage The right of women to the vote. The movement for woman suffrage arose in many countries in the 19th and 20th cents. In the US, woman suffrage began with a declaration of women's rights issued (July 19, 1848) by L. Mott, E. Stanton, and other feminists. The movement gained momentum with the formation (1869) of the National Woman Suffrage Association, which sought woman suffrage through a constitutional amendment; and the American Woman Suffrage Association, which sought it through state legislation. Both factions merged (1890) to form the National American Woman Suffrage Association. A number of states eventually granted woman suffrage and national woman suffrage was established (1920), by the 19th Amendment to the US Constitution. In Great Britain, the movement for woman suffrage began as a part of the Chartist movement, under such leaders as J. Mill and E. Anderson. In the early 20th cent., the movement became more militant under the leadership of E. Pankhurst and others. Women received equal voting rights with men in Britain in 1928.

Wood, Annie *See* **Besant, Annie**

Wood, Leonard 1860–1927. American officer. He helped his friend T. Roosevelt form the Rough Riders *(q.v.)*, served as military governor of Cuba (1899–1902), chief of staff of the US Army (1910–14), and governor general of the Philippines (1921–27).

Woodhull, Victoria Claflin 1838–1927. American journalist and reformer. She supported such controversial causes as woman suffrage, Socialism, and free love, and in 1872 became the first woman candidate for president.

Woodstock US rock music festival (Aug. 16, 1969) held near Bethel, New York. Attended by some 300,000 youths, it marked the high point of the counterculture movement in the US.

Woodville, Elizabeth 1437–92. Wife of King Edward IV of England. After Edward's death, Richard, duke of Gloucester, seized Elizabeth's son, Edward V, and took the throne. Elizabeth's daughter married Henry VII.

Woolf, Virginia 1882–1941. English novelist and critic, whose life and writings had a major impact on 20th-cent. writers. Her home was the center for gatherings of the Bloomsbury Group. Her works include *Mrs. Dalloway* and *To the Lighthouse.*

Woolley, Sir Charles Leonard 1880–1960. English archaeologist. He directed the excavations (1922–34) of the ancient city of Ur, which contributed greatly to knowledge of ancient Mesopotamia.

Worcester, Battle of Rout (Sept. 3, 1651) of the Royalist forces of Charles II by the Parliamentarian forces commanded by O. Cromwell. It was the final victory in the English Civil War (1642–51).

Wordsworth, William 1770–1850. English poet, one of the leading figures of English Romanticism. His works include *Lyrical Ballads, The Prelude,* and *Poems in Two Volumes.*

Works Progress Administration *See* **Work Projects Administration**

Work Projects Administration ⟨*formerly* Works Progress Administration⟩ ⟨WPA⟩ US government agency established in 1935, and originally called the Works Progress Administration (renamed 1939), to create jobs for millions of unemployed during the Great Depression. It operated until 1943.

World Court *See* **International Court of Justice**

World Federation of Trade Unions *See* **labor unions**

World War I Worldwide conflict (1914–18) fought between the Allies (France, Britain, Russia, Italy, US, and others) and the Central Powers (Germany, Austro-Hungarian Empire, Ottoman Empire, and others). The bloodiest, most widespread war the world had known up to that time, WW I resulted in over 30 million casualties, left much of Europe in ruin, and revolutionized modern warfare. Among the causes of WW I were the rise of nationalist movements in Europe (especially in

Serbia); hardening of alliances between various European powers (Triple Alliance and Entente, *q.v.*); colonial rivalries in Africa and elsewhere; the continuing instability of the Balkan Peninsular region (Austrian annexation of Bosnia and Herzegovina, 1908; Balkan Wars, (1912–13); and the gradual collapse of the Ottoman Empire (Eastern Question, *q.v.*). The spark that touched off WW I was the assassination of Austrian Archduke Ferdinand by a Serbian nationalist in 1914. The war quickly spread to many different fronts and eventually involved all the major Western powers. WW I saw the rise of bloody trench warfare (especially on the Western Front), the mechanization of warfare (tanks, planes, and motorized vehicles used), and the advent of chemical warfare. WW I also brought drastic political changes. Russia's staggering losses on the Eastern Front helped bring down the czarist government (1917) and led to creation of the first Communist state. The Ottoman Empire, long in decline, finally collapsed under the strains of war and was dismembered. The war also broke up the Austro-Hungarian Empire, giving rise to the independent states of Austria, Hungary, Czechoslovakia, and Yugoslavia (as it was later called). The German surrender finally ended the war in Nov., 1918. Initially, the tremendous destruction caused by the war gave wide support to the newly created League of Nations and international efforts to end wars. But the war had set in motion great social and economic changes. Coupled with German resentment at the harsh peace terms imposed by the Allies, these changes helped pave the way for the outbreak of WW II.

1914 Austrian Archduke Francis Ferdinand assassinated (June 28) by a Serbian nationalist in Sarajevo, capital of Bosnia; set in motion chain of events that resulted in outbreak of war.

1914 German Emperor William II promised Austria-Hungary its support in any actions taken against Serbia (July 5).

1914 Austria-Hungary sent Serbia an ultimatum (July 23) pressing demands for suppression of Serbian nationalist groups in Serbia (which threatened to incite rebellion in Austria-Hungary).

1914 Serbia acceded to some demands and rejected others (July 25); Austria-Hungary broke relations with Serbia (which had already begun mobilization of forces) and began its own mobilization (July 25).

1914 Russia, Serbia's ally, unsuccessfully attempted to persuade Austria-Hungary to modify terms of its ultimatum and thereby avoid war (July 25); Russia made initial preparations to mobilize in the event of war.

1914 Britain attempted (July 26) to set up negotiations for a settlement; plan rejected by Germany.

1914 Austria declared war on Serbia (July 28).

1914 Russia ordered partial mobilization against Austria-Hungary (July 29); Germany, promising modification of ultimatum to Serbia, warned Russia against continuing mobilization order; Russian Czar Nicholas II hesitated, then ordered full mobilization (July 31).

1914 British requested recognition of Belgian neutrality (July 30); Germany refused.

1914 Germany declared war on Russia (Aug. 1). Russia, meanwhile, had received French commitment of support; French mobilization begun.

1914 German troops marched into Luxembourg (Aug. 1) to begin implementation of Schlieffen Plan; plan called for quick elimination of France from war to allow concentration of forces on Eastern Front; France to be attacked from the north (through Low Countries) and by a second (left) flank farther south.

1914 Germans, commanded by Gen. H. von Moltke, invaded Belgium (Aug. 3) after Belgians refused them right of transit.

1914 Germany declared war on France (Aug. 3).

1914 British, protesting Germany's violation of Belgian neutrality, declared war on Germany (Aug. 4).

1914 Strong fortifications at Liège, Belgium, captured by Germans (Aug. 5–16).

1914 French offensive; French attacks, commanded by Gen. J. Joffre, launched into Alsace (Aug. 7–9), Lorraine (Aug. 14–24), and the Ardennes (Aug. 22–25); all failed.

1914 British Expeditionary Force, commanded by Sir. J. French, landed at Le Havre (from Aug. 7).

1914 Eastern Front, Russian forces launched invasions of East Prussia (Aug. 13) and the Austrian province of Galicia; Russians, defeated at the Battle of Stallupönen (Aug. 17) in East Prussia, repulsed a counterattack at Gumbinnen (Aug. 20); in Galicia, after two inconclusive battles, the Russians won an important victory at the Battle of Gilna Lipa (Aug. 26–Sept. 1) and threw the Austrians into retreat.

1914 Austrians invaded Serbia (Aug. 16); their first invasion was repulsed, as were the second (Sept.) and third (Nov.).

1914 Western Front, Germans continued their drive through Belgium, capturing Namur after five-day siege (Aug. 19–25); Belgian army withdrew to Antwerp and Germans pushed on to take Antwerp (Aug. 20).

1914 Battle of Charleroi (Aug. 22); Germans defeated French and Belgian forces; continued drive through Belgium.

1914 Battle of Mons (Aug. 23–24); Germans defeated the British Expeditionary force; Allied forces in Belgium fell into retreat; Germans meanwhile weakened their right flank by sending troops (Aug. 25) to fight Russians on the Eastern Front; strong right flank was crucial element of Schlieffen Plan.

1914 Japan, as a result of alliances with Britain, declared war on Germany (Aug. 23).

1914 British won Battle of Helgoland Bight (Aug. 27), first major naval engagement.

1914 Eastern Front, German general von Hindenburg took command in Prussia and, with reinforcements from the Western Front, routed and captured the Russian 2d Army at the Battle of Tannenberg (Aug. 26–29); Russian 1st Army, defeated at the Battle of Mazurian Lakes (Sept. 9–14), barely managed to escape German armies.

1914 First Battle of the Marne (Sept. 5–9); Allied forces had taken up defensive positions on the Marne River in France; German attack faltered and after some days of hard fighting the Germans withdrew (Sept. 10–14) northward to defensive positions on the Aisne River in France.

1914 Gen. E. von Falkenhayn replaced Von Moltke as German commander (Sept. 10); opted for victory on Western Front by maintaining defensive positions; opposed efforts for offensives on Eastern Front.

1914 First Battle of the Aisne (Spet. 14–18); Germans held their positions against the British Expeditionary force.

1914 On the Eastern Front in Galicia the Austrians fell into retreat (Sept. 11–28) following Russian victory at Rawa Ruska (Sept. 5–11); retreated some 100 miles before taking up defensive positions.

1914 German campaigns in Poland; first invasion (Sept. 28–Nov. 1) nearly reached Warsaw before the Germans were driven out; second invasion (Nov. 10) culminated in capture of Lodz (Dec. 6) and retreat of Russian forces to defensive positions.

1914 Germans shifted Western Front offensive operations to north with aim of capturing French Channel ports; captured Antwerp, Belgium (Oct. 9).

1914 Ghent and Bruges captured (Oct. 11, 14) by Germans.

1914 Battle of Yser River, Belgium (Oct. 20–27); Germans advanced against Belgian forces; Belgians halted advance by flooding region (Oct. 27).

1914 Battle of Ypres, Belgium (Oct. 30–Nov. 24); Germans attempted to advance farther south but were held up by the British Expeditionary Force.

1914 Turkish Front, Turkey joined Germans (Oct. 29) against Russia; sultan proclaimed a Muslim holy war (Nov. 14); Turks under Enver Pasha launched invasion of Russian Caucasus in which the Turkish 3d Army was decimated (Battle of Sarikamis, Dec.–Jan.); forces from British India meanwhile occupied points in the Persian Gulf region (Oct.–Dec.).

1914 German cruiser squadron, commanded by Admiral von Spee, defeated British naval force (Nov. 1) off Coronel, Chile; British won decisive victory over von Spee at Battle of Falkland Islands (Dec. 8).

1914 Allied offensive along almost entire Western Front (Dec.) failed; war on Western Front shifted to trench warfare and front lines, stretching from Belgian coast to Switzerland, remained largely unchanged until just before war's end.

1915 Abortive Turkish attack on Suez Canal in Egypt (Feb. 3) repulsed by British.

1915 Eastern Front, Second Battle of Mazurian Lakes (Feb. 7–21); Germans inflicted heavy losses on Russians but failed to knock Russia out of the war.

1915–16 Turkish Front, Gallipoli Campaign (Feb. 19–Jan.); Allies, attempting to open supply route to Russia, launched nearly successful naval bombardment on Turkish installations guarding the Dardanelles strait (Feb. 19–Mar. 18); landings at Helles and Ari Burnu (Apr. 25) ended in disaster, as did Suvla Bay landing.

1915 Western Front, Battle of Neuve Chapelle (Mar. 10–13); British offensive made only small gains.

1915 Second Battle of Ypres (Apr. 22–May 15); Germans released chlorine gas (Apr. 22) in first use of poison gas in war.

1915 Battle of Artois (May 9–June 18); combined British and French offensive; French gained some 2½ miles but were unable to break German lines.

1915 In the East, Austro-German offensive in Galicia (May 4–Oct. 1) sent Russians in Austria into desperate retreat; Russians retreated some 300 miles with heavy losses in man and matériel; Czar Nicholas II took command of Russian army (Sept. 8) and by month's end established defensive line between Riga and Carpathian Mts.; much of Poland had been lost.

1915 Passenger liner *Lusitania* sunk by German submarine (May 7), as Germans established (Feb. 17) submarine blockade of Britain; US protested sinking and Germans revised (Sept. 1) submarine policy.

1915 Italy declared war on Austria-Hungary (May 23); ineffective, poorly equipped Italian army, commanded by Count Luigi Cadorna, launched four unsuccessful offensives against the Austrians along the Isonzo River; though Italian front quickly stabilized, it nevertheless tied down Austrian troops.

1915–16 Turkish Front, Armenian massacres; Ottoman government charged ethnic Armenians with aiding Russian forces (June) and ordered them moved away from all strategic points; Armenians subsequently brutalized and marched into desert; some one million killed (1915–16).

1915 On the Western Front, the Battle of Champagne (Sept. 22–Nov. 8); French gained but a few thousand yards in the initial assault; thereafter Gen. Joffre poured more troops into futile effort.

1915 British offensive aimed at Lens (Sept. 25–Oct. 30); British used gas and made more gains but failed to take Lens; British loss heavy, bringing about replacement of Sir French by Sir D. Haig as commander.

1915 Battle of Vimy Ridge (Sept. 25–Oct. 30); French offensive failed to take ridge.

1915 Salonica (Greece) Campaign; French and British landed forces in Greece (Oct. 3–5) in attempt to aid Serbia against impending attack; forces unable to link up with Serbians and retired to positions in Salonica; Allies forced overthrow of pro-German Greek king but otherwise remained inactive until end of war.

1915–16 Serbia and Montenegro conquered (Oct. 6–Jan.); Austro-German forces began invasion of Serbia and were joined by Bulgarian forces (entered war Sept. 22) on Oct. 11; Serbs forced into retreat and were later evacuated to Salonika; Montenegro surrendered (Jan. 17).

1915–16 Turkish Front; Allied forces withdrawn from Gallipoli (Dec. 10–Jan. 9), marking end of disastrous campaign; W. Churchill forced to resign as Lord of the Admiralty because of the failed campaign.

1916 Turkish Front; Russians began slow advance (Jan. 17) in the Caucasus region; captured Turkish stronghold of Trebizond (Apr. 17), repulsed Turkish counterattacks, and continued slow advance to Oct.

1916 On the Western Front, Battle of Verdun (Feb. 21–Dec. 18); Germans, implementing Falkenhayn's planned war of attrition, attacked French fortifications at Verdun; fighting raged almost whole year, with French taking offensive from Aug.; Germans gained little ground and French retained Verdun; of some 750,000 casualties, 350,000 were French.

1916 Italian Front (Mar. 9–Nov. 14); Italians launched unsuccessful offensive (5th Battle of Isonzo, Mar. 9–17); Austrians attacked at Asiago (May 15–July 7) but were driven back in an Italian counterattack (from June 16); Italians made little gain in 6th–9th battles of Isonzo (Aug.–Nov.).

1916 Russian offensive in the east failed (Mar. 18–28); Russian attack at Lake Naroch had been intended to draw German forces from Verdun.

1916 *Sussex* Incident (Mar. 24); passenger ship *Sussex* sunk by German submarine; US ultimatum led Germans to halt unrestricted submarine warfare.

1916 Battle of Jutland (May 31); German High Seas Fleet and British Grand Fleet (under Admiral Jellicoe) engaged in decisive battle; British suffered greater losses but retained control of North Sea.

1916 Arab revolt in the Hejaz (June 5); revolt, encouraged by British, sought to end Ottoman Turk control over Arabia; Mecca captured (June 10) after Arab leader Hussain ibn Ali declared Hejaz independent.

1916 New Russian offensive in the east (June 4–Sept. 20); Russian Gen. Aleksei Brusilov began successful advance from southwest part of front; broke through Austrian lines and pushed whole front westward before drive ended; offensive cost Central Powers heavy losses; Russians lost about one million men, which left army demoralized.

1916 Battle of the Somme (July 1–Nov. 18) in the west; largely British offensive to help relieve pressure on Verdun; limited gains (125 sq. mi. of territory) of little strategic value and achieved at cost of about 600,000 Allied casualties; German losses totalled 450,000; British made first use of tanks (Sept. 15) in battle.

1916 Field Marshal von Hindenburg replaced Falkenhayn as German commander (Aug.).

1916 Romania conquered by Central Powers (Aug. 28–Jan. 7); Romania joined the Allies (Aug. 17) and attacked Austrian Transylvania (Aug. 28); Central Powers invaded Romania (Sept. 1) and by Nov. had turned the tide; Bucharest captured (Dec. 6) and by Jan. 7 Central Powers had all of Romania except northeast.

1916 Peace initiatives by US president W. Wilson; Germans agreed (Dec.) to begin negotiations but British refused because of military situation (Romania had just been lost).

1916 Gen. Robert Nivelle made French commander, replacing Joffre (Dec.).

1917 British campaign in Palestine (Jan.–Dec.); British advance from Egypt toward Ottoman-controlled Palestine began in 1916; British crossed Sinai and fought three battles at Gaza (Mar., Apr., Oct.–Nov.) before dislodging the Turks; crossing into Palestine, they won the Battle of Junction Station (Nov. 13–14) and occupied Jerusalem (Dec. 9).

1917 Germans resumed unrestricted submarine warfare (Feb. 1); expected to be able to win war before US, which sharply opposed unrestricted use of submarines, could enter fighting; US broke diplomatic relations (Feb. 3).

1917 Zimmerman Note released (Mar. 1); secret proposal of alliance between Mexico and Germany aroused US sentiment for entry into war.

1917 British occupied Baghdad (Mar. 11), a strategic city controlling the region of Mesopotamia; thereafter engaged in operations to clear Turkish forces from region; T. E. Lawrence, meanwhile, played an important role in the continuing Arab revolt against the Turks in Arabia.

1917 Russian Revolution of 1917; demoralized by losses in war and years of repressive czarist rule, the Russians rose in revolt; Provisional Government established (Mar.) after the overthrow of Czar Nicholas; Germans transported Bolshevik leader N. Lenin from Switzerland to Russia by famous "sealed train" (Apr.) in hope he would foment new unrest.

1917 US declared war on Germany (Apr. 6), following German submarine attacks on US merchant vessels.

1917 Germans withdrew (Feb.–Apr.) on Western Front to new, stronger defensive positions (the Hindenburg Line).

1917 Allied offensive (Apr.–May) on the Western Front; overall commander was French Gen. Nivelle; began with Battle of Arras (Apr. 9–May 3) in which Canadian forces captured Vimy Ridge (Apr. 12); main attack came in Second Battle of the Aisne (Apr. 16–May 9) in which Germans slaughtered French attackers; exhausted, French army mutinied (May) and many deserted; Gen. H. Pétain replaced Nivelle and restored order (July).

1917 Italian Front (May–Sept.); Italians suffered heavy losses in 10th and 11th battles of Isonzo.

1917 Second Allied Offensive on Western Front (June–Nov.); British captured Messines Ridge (June 7–8) in preliminary battle; British launched main assault in Flanders and Third Battle of Ypres (July 31–Nov. 15); this cost almost 300,000 Allied casualties without achieving breakthrough of German lines; French meanwhile made some gains in fighting at Verdun (Aug. 20–26).

1917 Greece joined Allies (July 2) after Allies forced pro-German King Constantine to abdicate (June 11) in favor of his son, Alexander.

1917 July Offensive on the Eastern Front (July 1–Aug.); provisional government mounted attack on Austrian province of Galicia, led by Gen. Brusilov; German counterattack (from July 19) turned back the Russians and large-scale desertions began; Gen. Kornilov became Russian commander (Aug. 1).

1917 Germans occupied Riga (Sept. 3) at north end of Eastern Front; Germans advanced eastward as Russians retreated, and took much of Latvia (by Oct. 20), as well as Russian islands in eastern Baltic.

1917 American Expeditionary Force, commanded by Gen. Pershing, entered combat on Western Front (Oct.); influx of American combat troops continued, reaching one million by Nov. 1918.

1917 Battle of Caporetto on the Italian Front (Oct. 24–Dec. 26); Austro-German offensive, designed to knock Italy out of the war, sent Italians into retreat from Isonzo River; Italians established new position along Piave River, 70 miles south; Gen. Armando Diaz replaced Gen. Cadorna as Italian commander and Allies sent troops from Western Front.

1917 November Revolution in Russia; Lenin's Bolsheviks seized power (Nov. 7); Lenin soon after sought armistice with Germans; made public secret agreements between Allies at start of war; Russia began negotiations with Central Powers (Dec. 5) for truce.

1917 Battle of Cambrai (Nov. 20–Dec. 3) in the West; British used first massed tank assault but, failing to capitalize on initial gains, were driven back by Germans.

1917 Romania signed truce with Central Powers (Dec. 6); loss of Russian support made further fighting by remnants of Romanian army futile.

1917 Russians concluded armistice (Dec. 15), ending fighting on Eastern Front.

1918 Pres. Wilson announced (Jan. 8) his Fourteen Points, plan to secure lasting peace after war's end.

1918 Treaty of Brest-Litovsk (Mar. 3); Russians, after first refusing harsh German terms, accepted when the German armies advanced into Russian domains in the Baltic and Crimean regions; treaty abrogated when Germany surrendered in Nov.

1918 German spring offensive on the Western Front; hoping to split Allied lines, Germans launched Somme Campaign (Mar. 21–Apr. 8) and gained about 40 miles; French Gen. F. Foch named Allied overall commander (Mar. 26) to at last provide coordination of Allied effort.

1918   Second German offensive at Lys (Apr. 9–29); German drive against British in Flanders advanced 15 miles before being stopped.

1918   Red Baron (M. Richthofen), German ace pilot, killed in action (Apr. 21).

1918   Third German offensive near the Aisne River (May 27–June 6); German surprise attack resulted in advance to the Marne River, near Paris; US troops reinforced French forces at Chateau-Thierry (June 1–4) and halted German advance at the Marne.

1918   Fourth German offensive on the Western Front (June 9–13); Battle of the Metz ended in failure.

1918   Fifth German offensive in the West (July 15–Aug. 6); Second Battle of the Marne began with initial advance by war-weary German troops, who crossed Marne; Gen. Foch turned tide of war with strong counterattack (July 18); Germans, weakened by loss of over three-quarters of a million men in the offensive, withdrew to defensive positions.

1918   Allied offensive in West began (Aug. 8); British broke German lines with surprise attack at Battle of Amiens (Aug. 8–11); Allies won battles of Somme and Arras (Aug. 21–Sept. 3) and Germans retreated behind Hindenburg Line; Americans victorious at the Battle of San Mihiel salient (Sept. 12–13).

1918   Allied offensive from Salonica (Sept. 15–Nov. 10); Bulgaria surrendered (Sept. 29), Serbia liberated (Nov. 1), Albania and Montenegro taken (by Nov. 9) and Romania captured (Nov. 10).

1918   Battle of Megiddo (Sept. 19) in Palestine; British victory marked beginning of northward drive by British and Arab forces; Damascus, Beirut, and Aleppo captured by Allied forces (Oct.); with Allies advancing from Syria and Mesopotamia, Ottoman Turks signed armistice (Oct. 30).

1918   Last Allied offensive in West (Sept.–Nov.); planned two-prong attack began with US Battle of the Argonne Forest (Sept. 26–Oct. 31); British launched attack in north (Sept. 27) and a broad offensive (with Belgians and French) in the north broke the Hindenburg Line in the following days.

1918   German general Ludendorff demanded government begin armistice talks (Sept. 29).

1918   American Army sergeant A. York became a hero after capturing a fortified German position (Oct. 18); took 132 prisoners.

1918   Germans made preliminary contacts with Pres. Wilson to discuss settlement on basis of Fourteen Points (Oct. 4).

1918   Italian Offensive (Oct. 24–Nov. 4); following failure of Austrian attack at Battle of Piave (June 15–24), the Italians mounted an attack (Oct. 24); with the Austro-Hungarian Empire collapsing, the Austrians began to withdraw and by Nov. 3 the Italians had begun attacks on Trieste.

1918   Austria sued for peace (Oct. 27) as the Austro-Hungarian Empire crumbled; Poland declared independence (Oct. 15), followed by Czechs, Yugoslavs, and Hungarians.

1918   Austro-Hungarian Empire signed armistice (Nov. 3); empire broken up into independent republics (Nov.).

1918   First meeting between Gen. Foch and German leaders to discuss terms of armistice (Nov. 8).

1918   Collapse of the German government (Nov. 9); began with mutiny by German sailors at Kiel (Nov. 3); revolt spreading through Germany forced Emperor William to abdicate (Nov. 9); republic was then proclaimed.

1918   Germany concluded armistice (Nov. 11); acceded to harsh terms, including loss of territory, surrender of most of its navy, and loss of military and transportation equipment.

1919   German warships, to be surrendered to Allies, scuttled at Scapa Flow by German crews (June 21).

1919   Treaty of Versailles signed (June 28); imposed harsh terms on Germany, including heavy reparations, strict limit on size of military, loss of all overseas territories, demilitarization of the Rhineland; Germany was stripped of Alsace-Lorraine and other territories, and had formally placed upon it sole responsibility for the war; treaty also set up League of Nations and made other territorial adjustments.

1919–20   Other separate treaties concluded; included Treaty of St. Germain (Sept. 10), signed by Austria; Treaty of Neuilly, signed (Nov. 27) by the Bulgarians; Treaty of Trianon, signed (June 4) by Hungary; and the Treaty of Sèvres, signed by the Ottomans (Aug. 10).

World War II   Worldwide conflict (1939–45) involving all of the great powers and many of the lesser states as well. The combatants were divided into two opposing groups: the Allies (led by Britain, US, France, and [after 1941] the USSR), and the Axis powers (led by Germany, Russia [to 1941], Italy, and Japan). The war resulted in widespread destruction and suffering and cost many millions of lives. In addition, millions of others (notably Jews and Poles) died in Nazi death camps or were made slave laborers. The mechanization of warfare reached new levels in WW II and the airplane emerged as an important weapon in war on land and at sea. Finally, the use of atomic bombs by the US at the end of the war introduced the age of nuclear warfare. The causes of WW II are rooted in the economic, social, and political chaos of Europe following WW I. The economic collapse in Germany after the war and the harsh peace terms imposed by the Allies fostered German resentment and gave birth to A. Hitler's Nazi party. Fascism, under B. Mussolini, was also born of the postwar chaos in Italy. The rise of militaristic, totalitarian regimes was further aided by fear of the Communists and by a new economic collapse in the late 1920s and early 1930s (the Great Depression helped bring Hitler to power in Germany). It was Hitler who, after clearly adopting a militaristic aggressive policy, started WW II by invading Poland (Sept. 1939). Though Hitler quickly conquered Continental Europe, his decision to invade (1941) the USSR (until then an ally) proved to be his undoing. After the Japanese began the war in the Pacific Theater, the US entered the hostilities and Germany was confronted by the combined forces of the US, the USSR, and the British Commonwealth, as well as resistance fighters from conquered nations. From about 1942, the tide of the war turned against the Axis powers and the surrender of Nazi Germay (May, 1945) was closely followed by the Japanese surrender (Sept., 1945). Treaties were signed (1947) at Paris by the Allies and Italy, Romania, Hungary, Bulgaria, and Finland. A peace treaty with Japan was signed (1951). Principal events were:

1938   Germany annexed Austria (Mar.).

1938   Munich Pact signed (Sept.); following policy of appeasement, European powers agreed to formula to allow Germany to take Sudetenland in Czechoslovakia.

1939   Germans occupied all of Czechoslovakia, ignoring terms of Munich Pact.

1939   Italy invaded Albania (Apr.).

1939   Allies abandoned appeasement policy in face of aggression by Germans and Italians; began to build up military forces; formed anti-agression pacts with Turkey, Greece, Romania, and Poland.

1939   Pact of Steel concluded (May 22); confirmed German-Italian alliance.

1939   Nonaggression Pact between Germany and USSR signed (Aug. 24); Germany, no longer threatened with possibility of war on two fronts.

1939   Germany invaded Poland (Sept. 1); WW II began.

1939   Britain and France declared war on Germany (Sept. 3).

1939   German conquest of Poland (Sept. 1–27); Germans demonstrated effectiveness of *Blitzkrieg* using Panzer tanks, highly mobile mechanized infantry units, and strong air cover; two-pronged German attack advanced eastward, while Soviets launched westward attack beginning Sept. 17; Germans captured Warsaw (Sept. 27) and Poland was partitioned between the victorious Germans and Soviets.

1939–40   Russo-Finnish War (Nov. 30–Mar. 12); Soviets invaded Finland and met unexpectedly stiff resistance at Finnish Mannerheim Line; after months of hard fighting, Finland surrendered.

1939   *Admiral Graf Spee,* German pocket battleship, scuttled (Dec. 17) in Montevideo harbor; had been badly damaged in battle with British warships off Uruguayan coast.

1940   Norway conquered by Germans (Apr. 9– June 10); surprise attack began simultaneously in Norway and Denmark; Denmark surrendered (Apr. 9); Norway largely in German hands by mid-May; final victory came with Allied evacuation at Narvik (June 10).

1940   Germans invaded The Netherlands, Luxembourg, and Belgium (May 10).

1940   W. Churchill replaced Chamberlain as British prime minister (May 10).

1940   The Netherlands conquered by Germans (May 10–14); Germans invaded from south and quickly put Dutch forces into retreat to Antwerp (May 13); German bombing attack on Rotterdam (May 14) brought Dutch surrender.

1940   Invasion of Belgium (May 10–28); two German forces advanced, one to the north took Liege (May 12); the other pushed through the Ardennes and broke Allied defenses at Sedan; this force raced to the English Channel (reached May 20); Germans defeated Allied attempt to break out to the south (May 21–23); Belgium surrendered (May 28).

1940   British evacuation at Dunkirk (June 4); encircled by German forces in Belgium, British and other Allied forces withdrew by makeshift flotilla to Britain; supplies and equipment lost.

1940   Battle of France (June 5–22); German offensive began in extreme north, between Abbeville and Sedan and thereby outflanked the French Maginot Line; Germans broke through French defenses at the Aisne and Somme rivers (June 8) and occupied Paris (June 14); defensive fortifications at Verdun captured (June 15) and French sued for peace (June 17); France signed peace terms (June 22); northern France occupied by Germans, southern France run by Vichy government.

1940 Free French army formed (June 23) by C. De Gaulle in London.

1940 French fleet at Oran sunk by British (July 3).

1940 Latvia, Estonia, and Lithuania absorbed by USSR (Aug.).

1940 Italy declared war on Britain and France (June 10).

1940 Italians conquered British Somaliland (Aug. 6–19); marked beginning of war in Africa.

1940 Battle of Britain begun (Aug. 13); fought entirely in the air, the battle began as preparation for German invasion of Britain; German Luftwaffe failed to knock out British RAF and suffered heavy losses; began bombing London (Sept. 7) and abandoned planned invasion; heavy bombing raids on London continued into 1941.

1940 Japan concluded Tripartite Pact with Germany and Italy (Sept. 27).

1940 Italy invaded Egypt (Sept. 13–15) from Libya; British launched counteroffensive (Dec. 8) and drove into Libya; invasions of Italian East Africa begun (Jan. 15, 1941) and completed that year; British advance in Libya continued into Feb., 1941.

1940–41 Axis offensive in the Balkans (Oct.–May); Italian invasion of Greece (Oct. 28) was repulsed and Greeks invaded Albania (Dec. 3); German troops invaded Yugoslavia and Greece (Apr. 6); Yugoslavia surrendered (Apr. 17); captured Athens (Apr. 27), and drove British off Crete (May 31); Hungary, Bulgaria, and Romania meanwhile joined Axis powers.

1940 Submarine warfare in the Atlantic; Germans, unable to match Allied surface fleet; organized submarine wolf packs to sink supply convoys; despite implementation of convoy system, loss of Allied shipping increased steadily until Nov., 1942.

1941 US established Lend-Lease program (Mar. 11) to provide Allies with badly needed supplies; marked increased shift by US from policy of neutrality.

1941 German offensive in North Africa (Apr.–May); Gen. E. Rommel's Afrika Corps launched rapid advance (Apr. 3) against British in Libya; drove British back to Egyptian border by May 29.

1941 R. Hess, close adviser of A. Hitler, flew to Scotland, ostensibly to discuss his plan to end war with British (May 10).

1941 *Bismarck*, German battleship, sunk by British warships while she was on maiden voyage (May 27).

1941 Iraq came under British control (June 4) following brief fight against rebels who had overthrown government there; British and Russian troops later occupied Iran (July 25).

1941 British and Free French occupied Syria, taking control from Vichy French forces. (June 8–14).

1941 USSR invaded by Germans (Operation Barbarossa, June 22); three-pronged attack launched, north toward Leningrad, center toward Smolensk and Moscow, and south toward Kiev; rapid German advance caught hundreds of thousands of Soviet troops, but overall numbers of Soviet troops far greater than Hitler anticipated; Stalin proclaimed "scorched earth" policy as Soviets retreated eastward (July 3).

1941 US occupied Iceland (July 7).

1941 Vichy government of France forced to allow Japan to occupy French Indochina (July 21).

1941 Atlantic Charter signed (Aug. 12) by US and Britain; declaration of common goals for world peace.

1941 Russian Front; Germans, advancing rapidly, surrounded Leningrad (Sept. 8) in north and captured Kiev (Sept. 24) in south; German drive on Moscow began (Oct. 2) and Soviets removed to Kuibyshev (Oct. 19); heavy rains and mud slowed German advance, which reached outskirts of Moscow (Nov. 15); offensive halted (Dec.) by onset of Russian winter before Moscow could be captured.

1941 Soviets signed (Oct. 1) agreements with Britain and US; US to provide supplies under Lend-Lease arrangements; US supply convoys to north Russian ports regularly came under heavy German attacks during war.

1941–42 North Africa campaign; British launched new offensive into Libya (Nov. 18) and drove Germans back to El Agheila (Jan. 18).

1941–42 Russian winter offensive (Dec.–Feb.); Soviet armies attacked Germans around Moscow (Dec. 6); Hitler ordered troops to hold positions and took direct command of army (Dec. 19); Germans. ill-prepared for Russian winter, forced to withdraw (Jan. 15) to west.

1941 Pearl Harbor (Dec. 7); Japanese surprise attack wrecked US Pacific fleet and marked beginning of Japanese offensive in South Pacific.

1941 US declared war (Dec. 8).

1941–42 Japanese offensive in Pacific theater; Bangkok, Thailand occupied (Dec. 8); British battleships *Prince of Wales* and *Repulse* sunk (Dec. 10); Guam captured (Dec. 13); Wake Island captured (Dec. 23); Hong Kong surrendered (Dec. 25); in the Philippines, Manila fell (Jan. 2), Bataan (Apr. 9), and Corregidor (May 6); Singapore fell (Feb. 15); conquest of Dutch East Indies completed (Mar. 9), after victory in Battle of Java Sea (Mar. 1); Burma conquered (Dec.–May).

1941–42 Arcadia Conference (Dec. 22–Jan. 14); Roosevelt and Churchill conferred.

1942 Declaration of the United Nations signed (Jan. 1) by Allied leaders; promised to prosecute war until complete defeat of Axis powers.

1942 Gen. D. MacArthur named supreme commander of Allied forces in Southwest Pacific (Mar. 17), following his withdrawal from the Philippines.

1942 Russian Front; abortive Soviet spring offensive halted after a quarter million soldiers were captured in attack (May 12) on Kharkov, in the south.

1942 Anglo-Soviet Agreement (May 26) united Britain and Russia against Nazi Germany.

1942 British launched air attack on Cologne (May 30–31).

1942 Manhattan Project begun by US (June) to develop atomic bomb.

1942 Pacific theater; US naval and air forces turned back Japanese invasion force heading for New Guinea (Battle of the Coral Sea, May 7–8); Japanese invaded Aleutian Islands (June 3), eventually taking Attu; Battle of Midway (June 4–7), US naval air units heavily damaged Japanese fleet sent to take Midway Island.

1942 Czech village of Lidice destroyed by Germans (June 10) after Czech resistance fighters killed high German SS official, R. Heydrich.

1942 US general D. Eisenhower named commander of US forces in European theater (June 25).

1942 Russian Front; German offensive began (June 28), Stalingrad being among its targets; fighting around the city broke out by Aug. 9, as Germans met stiff Russian resistance; heavy fighting continued into fall, when Soviets launched counterattack.

1942 US offensive in the Pacific; troops landed on Guadalcanal (Aug. 7) beginning of fight in Solomon Islands; Japanese naval force heavily damaged in Battle of Eastern Solomons (Aug. 23–25); Guadalcanal secured by US forces (Feb. 1943).

1942 Dieppe Raid (Aug. 19) failed; Allied (experimental) landing on French coast cost nearly two-thirds of troops.

1942 Allied offensive in New Guinea began (Sept. 25); Japanese had invaded New Guinea (Mar.) in preparation for attack on Australia; US and Australian forces secured Buna and Gona (Dec.); convoy with Japanese reinforcements sunk by Allied aircraft (Mar. 4, 1943).

1942 British counterattacked Japanese in Burma (Oct.); British gains lost in new Japanese attack (Mar.–May, 1943); Allies meanwhile began building (Dec. 1942) the Ledo Road from India, to provide overland supply route to China.

1942 North Africa campaign; following new German offensive by Rommel (Jan.), Germans had pushed British back into Egypt; British Gen. B. Montgomery led his forces in crucial Battle of El Alamein (Oct. 23–Nov. 4), in which Germans were driven back into Libya.

1942 US forces, led by Gen. D. Eisenhower, landed in Algeria (Nov. 8), beginning second front in North Africa; Vichy French forces ceased all resistance (Nov. 10); Allied forces began eastward advance into Tunisia.

1942 Germans extended their zone of occupation in France to include all of France (Nov. 11); French fleet at Toulon scuttled (Nov. 27) by French.

1942–43 Battle of Stalingrad on the Russian Front (Nov.–Feb.); Soviet offensive began (Nov. 19), and soon encircled 22 German divisions around Stalingrad; these forces reduced to about 90,000 men by the time their commander surrendered (Feb. 2); battle turned tide of war against Germans; meanwhile, long German siege of Leningrad was broken (Jan.).

1943 Casablanca Conference held (Jan. 14–24); Roosevelt and Churchill decided to press for complete German surrender; invasion of France put off; invasion of Sicily planned.

1943 Final Allied offensive in North Africa; US forces advancing east through Tunisia, British driving west from Egypt; British captured Tripoli (Jan. 23); Rommel stung US forces at Battle of Kasserine Pass (Feb. 20), but US soon recovered offensive; British broke through German defensive Mareth Line in Tunisia (Mar.) and Allied forces linked up (Apr. 7), securing the North Africa coast; final Allied offensive (May) resulted in capture of remaining Axis troops.

1943 In Russia, German counterattack won Kharkov and Belgorod (Mar. 11, 18) and halted Russian advance after Stalingrad.

1943 Katyn Massacre discovered (Apr. 13).

1943 Warsaw Ghetto uprising (May); some 60,000 Polish Jews rose in desperate and unsuccessful revolt against Nazis; revolt came after Nazis had taken 400,000 to concentration camps.

1943 Trident Conference held (May 12–25); Roosevelt and Churchill planned invasion of Italian peninsula; put off invasion of France to 1944.

1943 Soviets dissolved (May 22) the Comintern, organization for spread of communism; this marked Stalin's policy of appeasing the Allies.

1943 US forces recaptured Attu in the Aleutian Islands (June 3); ended Japanese threat to North American territories.

1943 Allied invasion of Sicily (July 10–Aug. 18); US, British, and Canadian forces, led by Gen. Eisenhower, landed on south coast; Palermo occupied (July 24); Messina captured (Aug. 18), ending the fight for Sicily.

1943 Sustained Russian offensive began (July 11); after a weak German attack, the Russians pushed westward in the region of Orel and Belgorod and by August advance on a broad front was under way; German retreat was confused (by Hitler's intervention) and costly; Soviets crossed Dnieper River in October and recaptured Kiev (Nov. 6); advance continued into 1943.

1943 Allied offensive in the Pacific began (July 1); US and Australian forces advanced in New Guinea, captured Japanese strongholds of Salamaua (July 3) and Lae (Sept. 7); captured New Georgia (Aug. 7), Bougainville (Oct. 31); Gilbert Islands were invaded (Nov. 22).

1943 Fire-bombing of Hamburg (July 24–Aug. 3).

1943 Italy's Fascist leader, B. Mussolini, resigned (July 25) as invasion of Sicily progressed; new government dissolved Fascist party and began peace talks.

1943 Quebec Conference held (Aug. 11–24); Roosevelt and Churchill considered problems related to invasion of France but reached no decisions.

1943 Campaign for Italian mainland; British landed in southern Italy (Sept. 3), US landed at Salerno (Sept. 9); Allies advanced north, taking Naples (Oct. 1); Allies halted by German Gustav Line, south of Cassino, until following spring.

1943 Italy surrendered unconditionally (Sept. 3).

1943 Germans set up Italian puppet state after rescuing the imprisoned Mussolini (Sept. 15); German troops in Italy subsequently put up stiff resistance to Allied forces attempting to take Italian mainland.

1943 Italy declared war on Germany (Oct. 13).

1943 Teheran Conference (Nov. 8–Dec. 1); Roosevelt, Churchill, and Stalin met; Allies to open up second front with invasion of France, in both north and south.

1944 Russian offensive continued; Novgorod captured (Jan. 20) and Soviets reached border of Poland (Feb.); in south, reached Romanian border (Mar. 26); Sevastopol and Crimean region secured (May).

1944 Allied landings at Anzio, Italy (Jan. 22); this attempt to outflank German defensive line failed.

1944 Pacific offensive; US forces invaded Marshall Islands (Feb.), Admiralty Islands (Mar.), and the Marianas (June); US won major victory in Battle of the Philippine Sea (June 1) during Marianas invasion and by it crippled the Japanese navy; Guam secured (Aug.).

1944 Massive bombing raids over Germany (Feb. 20) began.

1944 Allied offensive in Italy; major attack at Cassino (Mar. 15–May 18) finally broke German Gustav Line; Allies pushed north, occupying Rome (June 4) and Florence (Aug. 12); Germans, however, held onto northern Italy until last months of the war.

1944 Normandy invasion; allied landings in France began (June 6) under the command of Gen. Eisenhower; US troops landed at Omaha and Utah beaches, British and Canadian troops at Gold, Juno, and Sword beaches; British reached Caen (July 8) and US forces took St.-Lo (July 18); meanwhile troops and supplies poured in as largest amphibious operation in history progressed.

1944 Russian front; as Normandy invasion progressed, Soviets launched drives in the east; German armies in Poland collapsed (June–July) before Soviet advance; in south, Soviets entered Balkans, capturing Romania (Aug. 24), Bulgaria (Sept. 8), Yugoslavia (Oct. 20); met stiff German resistance in Hungary (Nov.); in the north, Finland surrendered (Sept. 19) and Riga, on the Baltic coast, was taken (Oct. 13).

1944 Hitler narrowly escaped assassination attempt (July 20); Hitler took brutal revenge on all he suspected of complicity.

1944 St.-Lo Breakout in France (July 25–27); US forces broke German lines at St.-Lo, drove southeast to secure Brittany (July–Aug.) and southwest to capture Le Mans (Aug. 8); eastward drive (north of Loire River) next liberated Paris (Aug. 25), which German officers had refused to destroy, and brought the Allies to the Seine River.

1944 Warsaw Uprising (Aug.–Oct.); Polish underground army resistance crushed by Germans; Soviets, meanwhile, halted their advance in Poland just outside Warsaw and refused to aid the pro-West underground army.

1944 Allied landings in southern France, between Marseilles and Nice (Aug. 15); Allied armies moved northward up the Rhone Valley; captured Lyon (Sept. 3) before Germans stalled the advance.

1944 Allied advance eastward; British forces liberated Brussels, Belgium (Sept. 2); Liège captured (Sept. 7), followed by liberation of Luxembourg (Sept. 10) and invasion of German frontier (Sept. 11); Gen. Patton's forces crossed the Moselle River to the south (Sept. 7); airborne assault at Arnheim (to outflank German "West Wall" defenses) failed (Sept. 17–26); Allied supply lines now overextended by rapid pace of advance.

1944 Allied invasion force from southern France linked up with northern invasion force at Dijon (Sept. 15).

1944 Hitler issued call-up of all able-bodied males (Sept. 25) for last-ditch defense of Germany.

1944 V-2 rocket attacks on Britain began (Oct. 7).

1944 British occupied Greece (Oct.), following withdrawal of German forces; revolt by Communists put down.

1944–45 Philippines campaign in the Pacific (Oct. 20–Feb. 23); recapture of the Philippines began with landings on Leyte and naval battle of Leyte Gulf; Leyte secured and Luzon invaded by US (Jan.); Manila taken (Feb. 23); resistance by remnants of Japanese forces continued for duration of the war.

1944 US bombers, flying from air bases on Saipan, began regular bombing raids against Japanese cities (Nov.).

1944 Battle of the Bulge in Western Europe (Dec. 16–Jan. 25); Germans mounted surprise attack aimed at breaking overextended Allied lines and capturing Antwerp, Belgium; was last major German offensive.

1945 Russian advance from the east; Warsaw taken by Soviets (Jan. 17), Krakow (Jan. 19); to south, German resistance in Hungary broken and Budapest finally captured (Feb. 13); Soviet units took Vienna, Austria (Apr. 13) and began fight to take Berlin (Apr. 20).

1945 Yalta Conference held (Feb. 4–11); Roosevelt, Churchill, and Stalin discussed plans for occupation of Germany after war.

1945 Fire-bombing of Dresden (Feb. 13–14).

1945 Battle of Iwo Jima (Feb. 19–Mar. 17) in Pacific; US forces suffered heavy casualties in battle for the strategic island.

1945 Allied offensive into the German Rhineland began (Feb. 23); US forces reached Rhine River (Mar. 2), captured Cologne (Mar. 7); crossed Rhine (Mar. 7) at Remagen; reached Elbe River (Apr. 12). Germans in Ruhr district enveloped (Apr. 1); US forces reached Elbe River (Apr. 12).

1945 Battle of Okinawa (Apr. 1–June 21) fought in Pacific; island provided still closer land base for bombers attacking Japan.

1945 Final Allied offensive in northern Italy (Apr. 9); German resistance broken; last German forces surrendered (May 1).

1945 US president Roosevelt died (Apr. 12).

1945 US and Soviet troops link up at Torgau, along the Elbe River (Apr. 25).

1945 San Fransisco Conference held (Apr.–June); wrote United Nations Charter.

1945 Mussolini captured and killed by anti-Fascists (Apr. 28).

1945 Hitler committed suicide (Apr. 30) as Soviet forces closed in on Berlin; K. Donitz named as his successor.

1945 Berlin capture completed (May 2).

1945 Germany surrendered (May 7); Allied Control Committee formed by Allied military leaders to govern Germany (June 5).

1945 Allies, led by Lord Mountbatten, gained control of Burma (May) after long campaign against Japanese.

1945 Potsdam Conference held (July 17–Aug. 2) by Allies; outlawed Nazism in Germany, established Soviet control of eastern Germany, and called on Japanese to surrender.

1945 Atomic bomb dropped by US on Hiroshima (Aug. 6); city devastated.

1945 Soviet invasion of Japanese-held Manchuria began (Aug. 8).

1945 US dropped second atomic bomb on Nagasaki (Aug. 9).

1945 Japan surrendered (Aug. 14); signed formal surrender (Sept. 2).

1945–46 Nuremberg Trials held to judge leaders of Nazi party for war crimes; twelve sentenced to death, others to prison.

Worms, Concordat of *See* **Concordat of Worms**

Worms, Diet of Imperial diet called (1521) during the Reformation by Holy Roman Emperor Charles V. It was convened at Worms, Germany, to consider action against Protestant reformer M. Luther. Luther had already been condemned by Pope Leo X and was given safe conduct to appear before the diet (Apr. 17, 1521). There Luther was asked to repudiate his teachings; on the following day he refused. The subsequent Edict of Worms (May 25) declared Luther a heretic and outlaw and forced him to go into hiding for some months.

Worms, Synod of **1.** Synod of German Catholic bishops called (1076) at Worms, now in West Germany, by Holy Roman Emperor Henry IV. A high point in Henry's conflict with the pope over lay investiture, the synod declared Pope Gregory VII deposed, in response to Gregory's attempt to impose reforms. Gregory subsequently excommunicated and deposed Henry (1076). **2.** Synod of German bishops called (1122) at Worms to settle the investiture controversy between Holy Roman Emperor Henry V and Pope Calixtus II. The synod formulated the Concordat of Worms (*q.v.*).

Wounded Knee Site on the South Dakota Pine Ridge Indian Reservation where US troops massacred some 200 Sioux Indians (Dec. 29, 1890). After the death of Sitting Bull, some of the Sioux were influenced by a seer and fled the reservation.

They were rounded up at Wounded Knee by US cavalrymen and while the Indians were being disarmed, a fight broke out. The troops opened fire indiscriminately, massacring men, women, and children.

WPA *See* **Works Projects Administration**

Wrangel, Karl Gustaf 1613–76. Swedish general and naval commander. He distinguished himself during the Thirty Years' War, and in 1646 succeeded L. Torstensson as commander in chief. Under Charles X, Wrangel commanded in wars against Poland, Denmark, and Brandenburg.

Wren, Sir Christopher 1632–1723. English architect, astronomer, and mathematician. The greatest architect of his day, he designed more than 50 London churches, including St. Paul's Cathedral.

Wright, Frank Lloyd 1869–1959. American architect whose innovative approach to the design and structure of modern buildings greatly influenced the development of modern architecture.

Wright, Horatio Gouverneur 1820–99. Union general in the American Civil War, who fought at the first Battle of Bull Run, and commanded in the Florida campaign (1862) and in the defense of Washington, D.C. (1864).

Wright, Orville and **Wilbur** 1871–1948; 1867–1912. American inventors. Originally bicycle mechanics, the Wright brothers built a biplane kite (1899). They went on to build the first successful heavier-than-air, powered airplane, which they flew for the first time at Kitty Hawk, North Carolina (Dec. 17, 1903). By 1909, they had won the first contract to construct a military plane for the US Army. Wilbur subsequently ran their airplane-manufacturing company until his death, while Orville devoted himself to research.

Wu Hou 625–705. T'ang empress of China (684–704). She was a concubine of Emperor Kao Tsung who first ruled by her influence and then as empress.

Wundt, Wilhelm 1832–1920. German physiologist and psychologist, considered the father of experimental psychology. He established, at Leipzig, the first laboratory for this discipline.

Wu P'ei-fu 1873–1939. Chinese warlord. He supported Yüan Shih-k'ai and the Chinese republic. From 1916 to 1926 he fought Chang Tso-lin for control of Northern China, but his attempt to unify China failed.

Wu Ti 156–87 BC. Emperor (140–87 BC) of the Chinese Han dynasty. He greatly expanded the empire (into Vietnam, Korea, and the northern and western border regions), instituted administrative reforms to further strengthen imperial authority, set up the Chinese Examination System

(*q.v.*), and established Confucianism as the state religion.

Wyandotte Constitution Antislavery constitution prepared (July, 1859) at Wyandotte, Kansas. It marked the culmination of the struggle between slave and antislave forces known as Bleeding Kansas (*q.v.*). The constitution was approved in a popular referendum (Oct., 1859) and Kansas was finally admitted to the Union (Jan. 29, 1861) as a free state.

Wyatt's Rebellion Unsuccessful rebellion against Queen Mary of England by Sir Thomas Wyatt (*d.* 1554) and others in 1554. The uprising failed to gain popular support and Wyatt surrendered, was tried, and hanged.

Wycherley, William 1640?–1716? English dramatist, whose plays are noted for their satirical wit. Among his best are *The Country Wife* and *The Plain Dealer*.

Wyclif, John *See* **Wycliffe, John**

Wycliffe, John ⟨Wyclif, John⟩ ⟨Wickliffe, John⟩ ⟨Wiclif, John⟩ c1320–84. English reformer and theologian whose attacks on church doctrine anticipated the Protestant Reformation. He began the first English translation of the Bible.

Wyeth, Andrew 1917–. American painter. Noted for his precise technique and subtle use of light and color, he paints rural subjects. His best-known work is *Christina's World*.

Wyoming Western US state (pop. 470,816), the 44th state. The area was held by Spain, France, and England, but by 1846 the US had acquired all of it by purchase or treaty. The fur trade and natural wonders brought explorers, but Indian attacks hindered development until the discovery of gold and the coming of the railroad drew more settlers to the region. The Wyoming Territory was formed in 1868 and was the first to give women the vote. It became a state in 1890 and elected the first US woman governor, Nellie Taylor Ross (1924). Its constitution was adopted in 1890.

Wyoming Massacre Battle (July 3, 1778) between 1,000 British Loyalists (and Iroquois Indians) and some 300 American settlers in the Wyoming valley of Pennsylvania. Most of the settlement men were away with Washington's army. The 300 remaining men and boys ventured out of Forty Fort to meet the British and were massacred by the superior attacking force. The incident outraged American colonials and led to punitive expeditions against the Iroquois Indians.

Wythe, George 1726–1806. American jurist and statesman. A signer of the Declaration of Independence, he was professor of law at the College of William and Mary (1779–90). His teachings influenced T. Jefferson, J. Marshall, and others.

X

Xanthippe ⟨Xantippe⟩ *fl.* 5th cent. BC. Wife of Socrates, proverbial for her troublesome temper and carping disposition.

Xantippe *See* **Xanthippe**

Xavier, Saint Francis 1506–52. Catholic missionary priest, called "the Apostle of the Indies." One of the seven original Jesuits, he converted many thousands in India, Ceylon, the Malay Archipelago, and Japan.

Xenocrates 396–314 BC. Greek philosopher. A disciple of Plato, he succeeded Speusippus as head of the Greek Academy.

Xenophanes *fl* 6th cent. BC. Greek philosopher and poet, a member, and once thought to be the founder of the Eleatic school. He asserted the existence of one God closely identified with the material world.

Xenophon *c*434–*c*355 BC. Greek military leader and historian who commanded Greek forces in the service of Persian King Cyrus the Younger. His best-known work, the *Anabasis*, recounts the retreat of the Ten Thousand Immortals following Cyrus' death at Cunaxa (401 BC).

Xerxes I *c*519–465 BC. Persian king (486–465 BC), successor to his father, Darius I. He prepared a massive force for the conquest of Greece, but was defeated at Salamis (480 BC). His reign marked the beginning of Persia's decline.

XYZ Affair Diplomatic incident (1797) between French and US officials that nearly brought the two nations to war. In 1797, US president J. Adams sent C. Pinckney, J. Marshall, and E. Gerry to France to negotiate an end to French interference with US shipping. The commission was not allowed to meet immediately with French foreign minister C. de Talleyrand, but three agents representing France, called X, Y, and Z later by US officials, approached the three US ministers and suggested that the ministers give them a bribe and guarantee to France a large loan. When the affair was made public, American tempers flared and the US and France began an undeclared naval war. The conflict was ended by negotiation of the Convention of 1800 (Sept., 1800). It was during this affair that Pinckney was thought to have said (but probably did not say), "Millions for defense, sir, but not one cent for tribute."

Y

Yahweh Name of God as revealed to Moses. The name is an extension of the original four-letter name YHWH (the Tetragrammaton). From this also came the name Jehovah.

Yakima Indian Wars Series of wars (1855–59) fought by the Yakima Indians in Washington Territory against US encroachment. The Yakima signed (1855) a treaty and agreed to move to a reservation, but under the leadership of Kamiakin, resisted removal. They were eventually defeated and moved.

Yale, Elihu 1649–1721. American-born official of the British East India Company. Yale College (which later developed into Yale University) was named after him.

Yalta Conference Allied conference (Feb. 4–11, 1945) during WW II, at Yalta in the Crimea. Attended by US president F. Roosevelt, British prime minister W. Churchill, and Russian premier J. Stalin, it restated the Allied determination to receive only unconditional surrender in Germany. The conference planned for the postwar occupation of Germany by the four major Allied powers, discussed the postwar reorganization of Europe, and made plans for the San Francisco Conference (*q.v.*) to establish the United Nations.

Yamagata, Prince Aritomo 1838–1922. Japanese soldier and statesman. He played a major role in the modernization of the Japanese army and establishment of Japan as a world power.

Yamamoto, Isoroku 1884–1943. Japanese admiral. He led the attack on Pearl Harbor, thus precipitating US entry into WW II.

Yamasee War Uprising (1715) of the Yamasee Indians against English settlers in South Carolina. Defeated, the Yamasee fled (1716) to Florida and were assimilated into the Creek and Seminole tribes.

Yamashita, Tomoyuki 1885–1946. Japanese general. During WW II he commanded Japanese forces in the conquest of Singapore, Bataan, and Corregidor, and commanded in the Philippines (1942–45). He was hanged for war crimes committed by his troops.

Yancey, William Lowndes 1814–63. American lawyer and politician. A vigorous supporter of slavery, he sponsored the Alabama Platform (1848) and led in the movement for southern secession.

Yandabo, Treaty of *See* **Burmese War (First)**

Yang Chien *See* **Sui**

Yang Chu 440–360? BC. Chinese philosopher. He opposed the philosophy of Confucianism and was later accused of advocating hedonism.

Yang Kuang *See* **Sui**

Yankee Term applied by Americans to those who live in New England, by Americans from the South to Northerners, and by non-Americans to Americans. It was probably originally applied to Dutch settlers.

Yarmuk River, Battle of the Arab victory (Aug. 20, 636) over the Byzantine army, on a tributary of the Jordan River. An Arab force of some 25,000 decisively defeated 50,000 Byzantines, thereby breaking Byzantine dominance in the region and paving the way for the Arab conquest of Syria.

Yazid I *See* **Caliphate, Empire of** (680–683); **Muslim Civil Wars**

Yazoo land claims Land scheme in which the Georgia state legislature awarded (Jan. 7, 1795) some 35 million acres of land in present-day Mississippi to four land companies for $500,000. Most of the legislators held shares in the land companies. Congress eventually ordered the lands sold and settled all claims at the cost of some $4,000,000.

Yeardley, Sir George c1507–1627. British colonial administrator and three times governor of Virginia (1616–17, 1619–21, 1626–27). During his governorship, the first representative assembly in the English colonies was convened at Jamestown (1619).

Yeats, William Butler 1865–1939. Irish poet and playwright. One of the greatest poets of his day, he was a leading voice in the cause of Irish nationalism. He was awarded the Nobel Prize for literature (1923). Among his best collections of poems were *The Tower* and *The Winding Stair;* he also wrote plays and prose tales.

Yellow-dog contract Contract in which an employer extracts as a condition of employment a promise not to join a labor union. Yellow-dog contracts were declared unenforceable by the Norris-LaGuardia Act (1932).

Yellow Emperor *See* **Huang Ti**

yellow journalism Journalism emphasizing the sensational through the use of bold headlines, scandal stories, exposés, and the like. Its name arose from a comic strip, *The Yellow Kid,* in the New York *World,* and it figured in the circulation wars of the *World* and the New York *Journal* in the 1880s and 1890s. Yellow journalism contributed to the outbreak of the Spanish-American War.

Yellow Turbans Chinese secret society whose members rose against the emperor and his advisers (AD 184–204). Their rebellion contributed to the fall of the Han Dynasty (AD 220).

Yemen (Yemen Arab Republic) Independent state located at the southwestern tip of the Arabian Peninsula on the east coast of the Red Sea. Its capital is San'a. Dominated by Egypt and Turkey into the twentieth century, its recent history has been marked by political unrest and border wars with the People's Democratic Republic of Yemen. Key dates include:

12TH–8TH CENT. BC Minean kingdom ruled Yemen.

8TH–2D CENT. BC Sabaean kingdom ruled.

1ST CENT. BC Roman invasion.

4TH CENT. AD Ethiopian invasions.

6TH–7TH CENT. Persia ruled.

628 Conquered by Muslims; converted to Islam.

10TH CENT. Rassite dynasty of Zaidi sect established in Yemen.

11TH–12TH CENT. Fatimids of Egypt ruled Yemen.

16TH–20TH CENT. Ottoman Empire exercised nominal control over region.

1818–40 Puritanical, nationalistic Wahabi sect briefly took control of Yemen.

1913 Yemen granted autonomy by Ottoman Turks after uprisings against their rule.

1918 Yemen gained independence on collapse of the Ottoman Empire.

1934–35 Boundary dispute with Saudi Arabia; Saudi troops invaded and forced settlement.

1948 Imam Yahaya and two sons assassinated by religious leader Sayyid Abdullah ibn-Ahmad el-Wazir; Emir Seif el-Islam Ahmed crowned as successor after revolt was quashed.

1949–50 50,000 Jews in Yemen evacuated to Israel.

1958–61 Joined with Egypt and Syria to form United Arab States.

1962–67 Junta deposed newly crowned Imam Mansur Billah Muhammad; republic proclaimed.

1962–69 Civil war between forces of new republic and royalist supporters of the imam; Saudi Arabia and Jordan supported royalists; Egypt and Soviets supported republicans.

1967–72 Border war with Southern Yemen (later People's Democratic Republic of Yemen).

1971 Constitution adopted.

1972 Agreement providing for unification with People's Democratic Republic of Yemen signed, but never carried through.

1974 Army took power in bloodless coup; political parties outlawed, constitution suspended.

1974–77 Col. Ibrahim al-Hamidi ruled as head of state; assassinated.

1978 Lt. Col. Ahmed Hussein al-Ghashmi head of Presidential Council; killed by bomb.

1978 Col. Ali Abdullah Saleh chosen president.

1979 Border clash with People's Democratic Republic of Yemen.

Yemen, Southern (People's Democratic Republic of Yemen) This republic is located on the southern Arabian Peninsula in the Middle East. Its capital is Aden. Its early history is closely tied with that of the Yemen Arab Republic *(q.v.).* Key dates in its later history include:

16TH CENT. Became part of the Ottoman Empire; region under control of imams of Yemen.

1839 British East India Company occupied Aden.

1854–1914 Company gradually expanded domains through outright purchase and treaties with local rulers.

1937 Designated Aden Protectorate by Britain.

1963–67 Aden Colony made part of Federation of South Arabia; terrorist campaign against Britain began.

1967 Economy damaged by closing of Suez Canal after the Arab-Israeli War.

1967 Republic established (Nov. 30) after federation collapsed and British withdrew.

1969 President Qahtan Muhammad al Shaabi resigned; replaced by five-man presidential council.

1969–78 Salim Robea Ali chaired presidential council; overthrown and executed; Premier Ali Nasser Muhammad replaced him.

1970 Constitution promulgated; country's name formally changed to People's Democratic Republic of Yemen.

1972 Agreement providing for unification of Yemen Arab Republic and People's Democratic Republic of Yemen signed, but unification was not completed.

1978 Abdul Fattah Ismail elected president; reversed policy of reconciliation with Yemen.

1979 Friendship treaty signed with the Soviets.

1979 Border clashes with Yemen.

1980 Ali Nasir Muhammad al-Hasani became president.

yeoman In English history, a member of a class between the gentry and simple laborers. The term was also applied to servants or retainers of middle rank and to such units as the Yeomen of the Guard, long the personal bodyguard of the king.

Yeomen of the Guard Personal bodyguard of the sovereign of England, established (1485) by Henry VII. They are often called beefeaters.

Yermak Timofeyevich ⟨Ermak Timofeev⟩ d. 1584. Cossack leader. He crossed the Urals, conquered the Tatar khanate of Sibir (1582), and brought Siberia under Russian control

Yersin, Alexandre Émile Jean 1863–1943. Swiss-born French bacteriologist. He discovered, simultaneously with S. Kitasato, the bubonic plague bacillus. He also developed a serum against the disease.

Yggdrasill In Norse mythology, the World Tree that supports the universe. Its branches extend through all lands and into heaven and it roots into the underworld. A squirrel having the run of the branches was thought to breed discord everywhere.

Yiddish Language originally of Central and Eastern European Jews. Developed (12th cent.) from High German and incorporating elements of Hebrew and Slavic, it is celebrated for its rich literature.

Yi dynasty Dynasty of rulers of Korea (1392–1910). The dynasty was founded by Gen. Yi Song-gye, who seized power (1392) with aid from China's Ming rulers. The capital was established at Seoul and Chinese cultural influence was strong (Confucianism was adopted by the state). In subsequent years the dynasty repulsed an invasion by the Japanese (1592) but was forced to recognize the Manchus as their overlords after an invasion in 1627. From the 17th to the 19th cent., the Yi rulers imposed a policy of isolationism and it was not until after the Japanese forced them to accept trade relations (1876) that commerce with Western powers began. Soon after, however, the rise of

Japanese influence on the mainland resulted in the takeover of Korea. In 1910 Japan ended the Yi dynasty reign by annexing the kingdom.

yin-yang In Chinese philosophy, the two opposite but complementary groups of qualities that form the basis of the world. Yin is represented as earth, dark, female, odd, negative, and passive, and Yang is represented as Heaven, light, male, even, positive, and active.

Yoelson, Asa *See* **Jolson, Al**

Yoga System of spiritual control practiced in both Hinduism and Buddhism. By means of the discipline's techniques of breathing and other exercises—control of the senses, meditation, and withdrawal—the subject is led to the blissful union of self with the divine.

Yogacara School of Mahayana Buddhism. Founded in India (4th cent. AD), it flourished especially in the 5th cent. It held that only consciousness was real, not the objects of consciousness.

Yokohama Japan's third largest city (pop. 2,694,000) and leading seaport. Visited (1854) by Commodore M. Perry, it was opened to foreign trade (1859) and soon became a major port. It was severely damaged by earthquake (1923) and by US bombing during WW II.

Yorck von Wartenburg, Johann David Ludwig ⟨York von Wartenburg, ~⟩ 1759–1830. Prussian army officer. He led the Prussian forces in Napoleon's invasion of Russia (1812). Yorck signed the Convention of Tauroggen (Dec. 30, 1812) with Russia, neutralizing his forces and preparing the way for Prussia to join the allies against Napoleon.

Yoritomo 1147–99. Japanese warrior of the Minamoto clan. He became the first Kamakura shogun of Japan (1192).

York, Alvin Cullum 1887–1964. American army sergeant who became one of the most popular heroes of WW I. On Oct. 8, 1918, he advanced on a fortified hill, killing 20 Germans and capturing 132 others, along with 35 machine guns. For this action he won a Croix de Guerre and a Congressional Medal of Honor.

York, Frederick Augustus, duke of 1763–1827. British officer, second son of King George III. He commanded unsuccessful campaigns in The Netherlands during the French Revolutionary Wars. As commander in chief (1798–1809, 1811–27) he helped to modernize the army.

York, house of Royal house of England, a branch of the Plantagenet family. Its members included three kings, Edward IV, Edward V, and Richard III. Its claims to the English throne in opposition to those of the House of Lancaster resulted in the Wars of the Roses *(q.v.)*.

York, Richard Plantagenet, 3d duke of 1411–60. English nobleman and claimant to the throne of England. He served as protector (1454–55 1455–56) during the mental lapses of King Henry IV. His attempts to secure the crown led to the Wars of the Roses *(q.v.)*. He was recognized heir apparent (1460) but was defeated and killed by Margaret of Anjou at the Battle of Wakefield (1460).

Yorktown campaign Final major campaign (Sept. 28–Oct. 19, 1781) of the American Revolution, at Yorktown, Virginia. It resulted in the surrender of the British army under Gen. C. Cornwallis and secured American independence. After the failure of his Carolina campaign *(q.v.)*, Cornwallis moved his army north to Yorktown and fortified it. An American force of some 8,000 under the Marquis de Lafayette then moved into position and bottled up the British. Cornwallis hoped for relief or reinforcement by sea but soon a French fleet under Count F. de Grasse blocked the harbor and began to bombard the British positions. Generals G. Washington and J. Rochambeau marched south and reinforced Lafayette. In New York a British relief expedition was outfitted by Sir H. Clinton but Cornwallis surrendered (Oct. 19) before it could arrive in Virginia.

York von Wartenburg, Johann David Ludwig *See* **Yorck von Wartenburg, Johann David Ludwig**

Yoshida, Shigeru 1878–1967. Japanese statesman. He served as prime minister of Japan five times between 1946 and 1954 and oversaw Japan's recovery from WW II.

Yoshihito *See* **Taisho**

Young, Brigham 1801–77. American Mormon leader. He succeeded J. Smith as president of the Mormon church and led the migration (1846–48) from Illinois to Salt Lake City, Utah.

Young, Thomas *See* **Rosetta Stone**

Young, Whitney Moore, Jr 1921–71. American black civil rights leader. As executive director of the Urban League (1961–71) he led the movement to involve private business and the government in programs to aid America's urban poor.

Younger, Cole 1844–1916. American outlaw. He fought with the Confederate guerrilla band of W. Quantrill during the Civil War and after the war joined the outlaw gang of J. James.

Young Germany ⟨Junges Deutschland⟩ German literary movement of the 1830s and 1840s. The movement was in part a reaction to the nationalism and romanticism as represented by the works of J. Goethe and was influenced by French literature. Among its members was H. Heine.

Younghusband, Sir Francis Edward 1863–1942. British explorer whose travels increased geographical knowledge of central Asia. He secured (1904) a treaty opening Tibet to Western trade.

Young Italy Italian movement that sought establishment of a republic of Italy. Founded (1831) by G. Mazzini, it was instrumental in the Italian Risorgimento, but declined in importance after 1848.

Young Plan Second plan adopted for payment of German reparations after WW I, succeeeding the Dawes Plan. Put into effect in 1930, it was repudiated by A. Hitler.

Young Turks Group of young Turkish revolutionaries who rebelled against Sultan Abdul Hamid II in 1908 and compelled him to restore constitutional government. The term has since been used to designate young factions within larger groups.

Ypres ⟨Ieper⟩ Belgian city located near the border with France. A center of the Flemish cloth industry, it was the scene of several major battles of WW I (*see* Ypres, battles of).

Ypres, battles of 1. The First Battle of Ypres (Oct.–Nov., 1914), between Allied and German forces at Ypres, Belgium during WW I, was largely indecisive. The German advance was halted but the Allies suffered more than 100,000 casualties. **2.** The Second Battle of Ypres (Apr. 22–May 25, 1915) marked the first time the Germans used poison gas. The German assault failed to unseat the Allies and ground to a halt. **3.** The Third Battle of Ypres (July 31–Nov. 10, 1917), also known as the Battle of Passchendaele, began with a massive British artillery bombardment. The Allied advance was crippled by rain and mud, and casualties numbered some 300,000. **4.** The Fourth Battle of Ypres (Apr., 1918) was marked by significant German advances but the Germans were again unable to break the Allied hold on the Ypres salient.

Ypsilanti, Alexander 1792–1828. Greek freedom fighter who led an unsuccessful revolt in Moldavia against Turkish rule (1821).

Ypsilanti, Constantine 1760–1816. Greek hospodar (governor) of Moldavia (1799–1801) and Walachia (1802–07). He encouraged the Serbs to revolt against the Turks. He sought to free Greece but was exiled to Russia.

Ypsilanti, Demetrios 1793–1832. Greek patriot. Son of C. Ypsilanti, he fought in the war for Greek independence (1821) and was commander in chief of Greek forces (1828–30).

Yüan Chinese dynasty (1260–1368) established (1260) by Kublai Khan. The Yüan made their capital at Peking, built the Grand Canal, constructed a road and canal system linking the country, and developed a postal system. They also encouraged trade with the West. Marco Polo lived at their court and took tales of their culture back to Europe. However, the Yüan never established rapport with the Chinese natives and were soon overthrown by the Ming (1368).

Yüan Shih-kai 1859–1916. Chinese imperial official and first president of the Republic of China (1912–16). He ruled harshly and dissolved Parliament in 1914, thus provoking popular revolts. His attempt to establish a new dynasty and restore the empire (1916) led to his downfall.

Yucatan Central American peninsula comprising the southeastern states of Mexico as well as Belize and part of Guatemala. It was the center of Mayan and Toltec civilizations.

Yueh-chih Ancient central Asian people. They ruled a kingdom in Bactria (northern Afghanistan) and northern India (2d cent. BC–5th cent. AD).

Yugoslavia ⟨Socialist Federal Republic of Yugoslavia⟩ Republic located in southeastern Europe. Its capital is Belgrade. Established (1918) at the close of WW I as the Kingdom of Serbs, Croats, and Slovenes, the new nation became known as Yugoslavia in 1929. Yugoslavia was invaded (1941) by German forces during WW II and was partitioned among Germany, Bulgaria, Hungary, and Italy. Yugoslavians conducted a successful guerrilla war under Axis occupation. In 1945 the Communist leader Tito became premier of a new Yugoslav government, and the same year the Federal People's Republic of Yugoslavia was proclaimed. Until his death in 1980 Tito followed an independent program of communism and made Yugoslavia a leading force of the nonaligned nations. Key dates in the history of Yugoslavia include:

1915 Serbia and Montenegro occupied by Central Powers during WW I; Serbian government-in-exile established on Allied-controlled island of Corfu; joined by representatives of other South Slavic territories.

1917 South Slavic Committee for National Unity issued (July 20) the Corfu Declaration, calling for establishment of a pan-Slavic state under a constitutional monarchy.

1918 Representatives of Montenegro voted (Nov. 26) to join Serbia in movement for unification.

1918 Kingdom of Serbs, Croats, and Slovenes proclaimed (Dec. 4); Serbian Prince Alexander became regent for his father, King Peter I; new kingdom included Serbia and Montenegro as well as the former Austro-Hungarian territories of Bosnia and Herzegovina, Croatia, and Slovenia.

1919–20 New kingdom's borders largely settled by post-WW I Paris Peace Conference; con-

tested area of Fiume seized by Italian forces during conference (Sept., 1919).

1920 Treaty of Rapallo signed (Nov. 12) with Italy; Italy received Istria and other territories in return for abandonment of its demand for cession of Dalmatia.

1920–21 Kingdom joined with Czechoslovakia and Romania in defensive pact known as the Little Entente to counter territorial demands by Bulgaria and Hungary.

1921 Peter I died (Aug. 16); Alexander succeeded him as Alexander I.

1928 Stephen Radic, leader of Croatian nationalist movement in the 1920s, assassinated (June 20) by a Serbian representative in the national assembly; Croatian representatives subsequently walked out and established new Croatian parliament in Zagreb.

1929 Alexander I assumed dictatorial powers (Jan. 6); dissolved parliament and proclaimed the Kingdom of Yugoslavia.

1931 Alexander I declared end to his dictatorial rule (Sept. 3); new constitution reestablished parliament but left the king with great power.

1934 Alexander assassinated (Oct. 9) in Marseilles, France; succeeded by his son Prince Peter under regency led by Alexander's cousin, Prince Paul.

1930s Prince Paul forced to establish ever stronger ties with Germany and Italy during the rising political crisis in Europe.

1937 Josip Broz, later known as Tito, became leader of the Yugoslav Communist party.

1939 Yugoslavian government issued (Aug. 26) new program for national government; Croatia received greater autonomy within Yugoslav federation.

1941 Yugoslav government forced (Mar. 22) to join Axis Tripartite Pact; government overthrown (Mar. 24) and Prince Peter acceded to the throne as Peter II; new government proclaimed neutrality.

1941 German forces invaded Yugoslavia (Apr. 6) in cooperation with Bulgarian, Hungarian, and Italian forces; country soon overrun; Yugoslav government evacuated Belgrade (Apr. 12); Yugoslav army disbanded into guerrilla units; Serbia and Croatia were organized as puppet states, with the rest of Yugoslavia divided among Germany, Hungary, Bulgaria, and Italy.

1941–44 Draja Mikhailovich led Chetniks, guerrilla group loyal to government-in-exile; Josip Broz (Tito) led Communist guerrilla forces against both Chetniks and Germans.

1942 Tito established provisional government known as Council for National Liberation.

1944 Yugoslav government-in-exile merged (Nov. 24) with Council for National Liberation.

1945 New government installed (Mar. 7) with Tito as premier and Communists in key positions.

1945–80 Tito in power as head of government.

1945 National elections held (Nov. 11); new assembly proclaimed the Federal People's Republic of Yugoslavia.

1946 New constitution adopted (Jan. 31).

1946 Chetnik leader Mikhailovich captured (Mar. 13); found guilty of treason and collaboration, he was executed (July 17) with several other Chetnik leaders.

1947 Allied-Italian treaty (Feb. 10) restored much of Istria to Yugoslavia; port city of Trieste became international territory under UN administration.

1947–48 Tito conducted extensive purge of opposition and followed program of socialization of economy; programs led to increasing criticism by Soviet Communist party.

1948 Relations between Tito and Soviets reached breaking point; Yugoslav Communist party ousted from Cominform; marked beginning of Tito's independent form of communism.

1953 New constitutional changes introduced (Jan.); office of president established; Tito elected (Jan. 14) first president of Yugoslavia.

1954 Yugoslavia entered defensive alliance with Greece and Turkey.

1954 Trieste partitioned between Italy and Yugoslavia.

1974 Tito elected president for life (May).

1980 President Tito died (May 4); rotating presidency established to prevent unrest among Yugoslavia's various ethnic groups.

1981 Ethnic Albanians in Yugoslavia's Kosovo province rioted (Mar.–Apr.); demanded independence as separate republic.

Yukawa, Hideki 1907–. Japanese physicist. He predicted the existence of the meson (1935) and developed a "nonlocal field" theory for elementary particles. He was awarded the Nobel Prize in physics (1949).

Yukon ⟨Yukon Territory⟩ Canadian territory on the Arctic Ocean noted for its mineral resources. The area was first explored in the 1840s. The region became part of the Northwest Territories (1870) and the Yukon Territory (1898) and was the scene of a major gold rush (1890s).

Yukon Territory *See* **Yukon**

Yü the Great ⟨Ta Yü⟩ *d.* 2197 BC. Semi-legendary Chinese hero, credited with founding the Hsia dynasty, China's first dynasty.

Yung-Lo 1360–1424. Chinese emperor (1403–24), third of the Ming dynasty emperors. He led expeditions against the Mongols, annexed Annam, sent ships as far as East Africa, moved the capital from Nanking to Peking (1421), and brought the Ming Empire to the point of its greatest power and influence.

Z

Zabern Affair Incident (1913) involving the conduct of German army officers in Zabern, now Saverne, in Alsace-Lorraine. The imprudent conduct of a German officer led to riots and arrests and caused a controversy in Germany over German military rule in Alsace-Lorraine.

Zacharias ⟨Zachary⟩ **1.** *fl.* 6th cent. BC. Prophet of the Old Testament. **2.** Book of the Old Testament, also known as Zechariah. **3.** Pope (741–52), known as Saint Zacharias (or Zachary).

Zachary *See* **Zacharias**

Zaghlul Pasha, Saad *c*1860–1927. Egyptian nationalist leader and statesman. As head of the Wafd party he helped lead the movement for Egyptian independence after WW I.

Zaharoff, Sir Basil 1850–1936. International arms dealer and financier. Born in Turkey of Greek parents, he made a fortune selling arms before and during WW I and was suspected of secret political intrigues.

Zahir ud-Din Muhammad *See* **Baber**

zaibatsu Family-owned Japanese financial and economic combines or cartels. They have played an enormous role in Japan's economic development since the Meiji restoration (1868) and control important segments of Japanese commerce, finance, and industry.

Zaimis, Alexander 1855–1936. Greek statesman, seven times premier between 1897 and 1928 and president of Greece from 1929 to 1935. His presidency was marked by clashes between royalists and republicans. He went into exile in Austria after restoration (1935) of the monarchy.

Zaire ⟨Republic of Zaire; *formerly* Belgian Congo⟩ Independent state located in west-central Africa. Its capital is Kinshasa. Since its independence in 1960, Zaire has been shaken by civil war and by Angolan invasions. Key dates in its history include:

1482 Portuguese visited Zaire; established ties with Kongo tribe.

1860s–90s Muhammad bin Hammad, a Swahili, ruled large areas of eastern Zaire.

1878–84 American reporter Henry Stanley explored the Congo region and established control for King Leopold II of Belgium.

1885 King Leopold II obtained personal title to the area at the Berlin Conference; Leopold created independent Congo under his rule.

1890s Control over countryside established; concessions granted to private companies to exploit the colony.

1908 Belgium formally annexed Congo after reports of brutality against blacks by private companies; named region Belgian Congo; exploitation continued, though treatment of native blacks improved.

1960 Congo granted independence (June 30) after rioting by nationalists; called Republic of the Congo.

1960 Joseph Kasavubu became head of state; Patrice Lumumba became prime minister.

1960 Civil war (July); Katanga province seceded (led by Moise Tshombe); South Kasai also seceded.

1960 UN and Belgium sent peace-keeping forces.

1960 Pres. Kasavubu staged army coup (Feb.); former Prime Minister Lumumba killed under suspicious circumstances after his arrest.

1961 UN Secretary General Dag Hammarskjold died (Sept. 17) in plane crash en route to conference with Tshombe.

1962 Tshombe rejected peace plan of new UN Secretary General U Thant.

1962 UN forces in active fighting against Tshombe's rebel troops in Katanga.

1963 Tshombe surrendered (Jan. 14), ending Katanga secession and civil war.

1963 Coalition government formed; Kasavubu made Tshombe premier.

1965 Kasavubu accused Tshombe of treason, dismissed him; was ousted in turn by Gen. Joseph Mobutu.

1965 Mobutu in power; soon after beginning his long rule, he abolished office of prime minister; restored order and initiated his program of

"African Authenticity" by replacing European names of places with African names.

1966 Mobutu nationalized copper mines.

1967 Constitution adopted.

1971 Government changed name from Democratic Republic of the Congo to Zaire.

1974 Constitution amended.

1975 Mobutu nationalized economy; barred religious education in schools; decreed use of African names; changed own name to Mobutu Sese Seko.

1977–78 Two invasions from Angola repulsed with aid from France, Belgium, and US.

Zama, Battle of Decisive Roman victory over Carthage (202 BC) during the Second Punic War, at Zama, southwest of Carthage. There the Romans under Scipio Africanus defeated the Carthaginians led by Hannibal.

Zambia (formerly Northern Rhodesia) Landlocked republic located in south-central Africa. Its capital is Lukasa. Independence was achieved only in 1964. Key dates in its history include:

c1200 Bantu-speaking tribes settled in area.

1851–73 D. Livingstone in Zambia as explorer and missionary.

1855 Livingstone discovered Victoria Falls.

1889–1924 British South Africa Company ruled area; mining operations and European settlement began.

1924 Became a British protectorate; British government thereafter administered region.

1920s Rich copper deposits discovered.

1953–64 Northern Rhodesia made part of the Federation of Rhodesia and Nyasaland.

1959 Kenneth Kaunda, black nationalist, formed United National Independence party.

1962 Widespread protest campaign against white rule.

1964 Northern Rhodesia declared independence (Oct. 24); became Republic of Zambia under black African rule.

1964– K. Kaunda in office as president; Zambia remained in British Commonwealth.

FROM **1965** Zambia's support of UN sanctions against white-ruled (Southern) Rhodesia disrupted Zambia's trade through and with Rhodesia; next years spent developing transport and trade links through other neighboring countries.

1969 Kaunda nationalized (with compensation) foreign copper-mining industry, oil industry.

1972 Kaunda's United National Independence party became only legal party.

1973 New constitution promulgated.

1981 Government forced to impose program of economic austerity as world copper prices fell.

1981 Kaunda reshuffled government in wake of copper miners' strike.

Zamenhof, Ludwig See **Esperanto**

Zamojski, Jan ⟨Zamoyski, ~⟩ 1541–1605. Polish general and statesman. He helped secure the elections of Henry of Anjou, S. Bathory, and Sigismund III as kings of Poland and served as chancellor under each of them. He led Polish forces against the Russians, Turks, and Swedes.

Zamora, Niceto Alcalá See **Second Republic (Spanish)**

Zamora, Treaty of Agreement (1143) between Castile and Portugal by which Portugal became independent of Spain and Alfonso Henriques, count of Portugal, was recognized as King Alfonso I.

Zamoyski, Jan See **Zamojski, Jan**

Zangi 1084–1146. Seljuk ruler. He fought successfully against the crusaders, established the Zangid dynasty (1127–1250), and extended his rule over much of Syria, Palestine, and Iraq.

Zanzibar Island region of Tanzania (q.v.). First explored by the Arabs, it came under Portuguese control (c1505–1698) and then was taken by Arabs from Oman. Under Sayyid Said (1804–56), Zanzibar was a major source for slaves. It became a British protectorate (1890) and joined with Tanganika (1964) to form the United Republic of Tanzania.

Zapata, Emiliano c1879–1919. Mexican revolutionary. An advocate of agrarian reform, he at first supported F. Madero but later opposed Madero and his successors. Zapata's army occupied Mexico City three times in 1914–15.

Zaporozhe Cossacks Ukrainian Cossacks who between the 16th and 18th cents. ruled over a large portion of the Ukraine, defending it against the incursions of Tatars and others. They resisted Polish domination and, in 1654, allied themselves with the Russian czars. After their alliance with the Swedes against the Russians, Peter the Great virtually ended their independence (1709). Their last fortress was destroyed in 1775.

Zapotec Indian people of Mexico inhabiting the eastern and southern regions of Oaxaca. Once an independent nation centered at Monte Albán, they enjoyed an advanced civilization reflecting Mayan and later Toltec influences. Subsequently allied with the Aztecs, they continued to flourish until the Spanish Conquest.

Zara, Siege of Attack (Nov., 1202) by the armies of the Fourth Crusade on Zara, now in Yugoslavia. Zara had placed itself under the protection of Hungary, and the Venetians, anxious to recover it, persuaded the crusaders to attack.

Zarathustra *See* **Zoroaster**

Zealots Jewish sect noted for its extreme opposition to Roman rule in Judea. The Zealots played a leading role in the unsuccessful revolt against Rome (AD 66–70).

Zebulun In the Bible, the son of Jacob and Leah. His name was given to one of the Twelve Tribes of Israel.

Zedekiah ⟨Mattaniah⟩ *fl.* 6th cent. BC. Last king of Judah (597–586 BC). He allied Judah with Egypt and opposed Babylonian rule. Nebuchadnezzar invaded and destroyed the kingdom (586) and initiated the Babylonian Captivity.

Zeeland, Paul van 1893–. Belgian economist and prime minister (1935–37). As prime minister he reaffirmed Belgian neutrality in exchange for German promises of inviolability.

Zelaya, José Santos 1853–1919. President and virtual dictator of Nicaragua (1894–1909). He attempted unsuccessfully to establish by force and revolution the Central American Federation.

Zelle, Margaretha Geertruida *See* **Mata Hari**

zemstvo A local and provincial assembly in czarist Russia. Established (1864) as one of the major reforms of Alexander II, the zemstvos produced numerous reforms and improvements before being superseded (1917) by the Soviets after the Bolshevik revolution.

Zen Buddhism Buddhist sect. It was founded (5th cent. AD) by Bodhidharma, who brought it from India to China. From there it spread to Japan. Zen stresses the awakening (satori) of the wisdom (prajna) that lies dormant within each soul. This wisdom is awakened by meditation and by personal instruction of a master to a pupil. Zen came to be a significant influence in many aspects of Chinese and Japanese life.

Zenger, John Peter 1697–1746. American printer and journalist, publisher of the New York *Weekly Journal*. His trial and acquittal (1735) for libel was a landmark in establishing freedom of the press in America.

Zeno *d.* AD 491. Roman emperor of the East (AD 474–491), successor to his son Leo II. His rule was marked by internal struggle, and his attempt to reconcile orthodox Christians and Monophysites with his *Henotikon* caused further dissension.

Zenobia *d.* after AD 272. Queen of Palmyra. She greatly expanded her realm through conquest in Asia Minor and Egypt before her defeat and capture by the Roman emperor Aurelian (AD 272).

Zeno of Citium *c*336–*c*264 BC. Greek philosopher. Zeno studied under the Cynics before establishing his own school at the Stoa Poikile in Athens, from which evolved the name of his phi-

losophy, Stoicism. Although his writings have not survived, Zeno's teachings were preserved by the philosophical historian Diogenes Laërtius (*fl.* 3d cent. AD).

Zeno of Elea *fl.* 5th cent. BC. Greek philosopher of the Eleatic school. A disciple of Parmenides, he is considered the first to use the dialectical method of reasoning.

Zenta, Battle of Austrian victory (Sept. 11, 1697) over the Ottoman Turks at Zenta, now in Yugoslavia. The Ottoman forces were utterly routed by the Austrians under Prince Eugene of Savoy.

zephyr In Greek mythology, the west wind.

zeppelin Name applied to dirigible balloons, especially German military dirigibles. They were so named after Ferdinand Graf von Zeppelin (1838–1917), the airship's inventor and builder. The German dirigible *Graf Zeppelin* completed an around-the-world flight in 1929.

Zerubbabel *fl.* 520 BC. Governor of Jerusalem at the time of the building of the second Jewish Temple.

Zetkin, Clara 1857–1933. German feminist and Communist leader, one of the founders of the German Communist party.

Zeus Chief ancient Greek god, identified with the Roman god Jupiter. He was the son of Cronus and Rhea and brother and husband of Hera.

Zeuxis *fl.* 5th cent. BC. Ancient Greek painter. His works were noted for their use of shading to produce a sense of realism.

Zhdanov, Andrei Aleksandrovich 1896–1948. Russian Communist leader and general. Made a member of the Politburo (1939), he fought in the Russo-Finnish War and in WW II. A hard-line supporter of J. Stalin, he organized (1947) the Cominform, the Communist Information Bureau.

Zhukov, Georgi Konstantinovich 1896–1974. Russian general and marshal of the Soviet Union. He played a major role in the Russian defeat of the German offensive in WW II.

Ziegfeld, Florenz 1869–1932. American theatrical producer. With the *Ziegfeld Follies* (1907) he introduced the extravagantly staged revue to the American stage.

Zimbabwe ⟨*formerly* Rhodesia; Southern Rhodesia⟩ Independent, landlocked state located in southern Africa. Its capital is Salisbury. In the 1960s and 1970s the white minority government of Rhodesia resisted a UN-backed campaign aimed at ending apartheid policies and bringing black Africans into the government. The struggle lasted until 1980, when black Africans formally took control of the government. Key dates in Zimbabwe's history include:

5TH CENT. AD Bantu peoples arrived.

16TH CENT. Portuguese traders arrived.

1889 Colonized by Cecil Rhodes' British South Africa Company.

1890 Salisbury founded.

1893 Rhodes' company defeated Ndebele tribe.

1896–97 Uprisings by the Ndebele and Shona.

1923 Became self-governing colony of Rhodesia under British crown; white rule established.

1953 Southern part of Rhodesia joined Federation of Rhodesia and Nyasaland.

1963 Federation broke up; Northern Rhodesia and Nyasaland voted for independence; Southern Rhodesia chose to remain a colony.

1964 In Southern Rhodesia conservative Ian Smith became prime minister; restrictions against blacks tightened.

1965 Rhodesia's white minority government declared independence from Britain (Nov. 11); Britain objected.

1967 Became first nation to have mandatory UN sanctions imposed against it.

1970 Rhodesia became republic (Mar. 2); complete segregation of races instituted.

1972 Terrorist activities by black nationalists.

1976 White minority government weakened by economic problems, continuing guerrilla war waged by black nationalists, and end to aid from South Africa; negotiations begun.

1978 Smith agreed to plan for eventual black majority rule.

1978 Smith, Bishop Abel Muzorewa, Ndabingi Sithole and Jeremiah Chirau signed agreement to transfer power to black majority; became executive council.

1979 New constitution enfranchised all blacks; changed name of country to Zimbabwe.

1979 Black majority assumed control (May 31); Muzorewa in office as prime minister; fighting between black nationalist groups.

1979 Britain arranged final agreement between warring factions of black nationalists (Dec.); truce effected pending elections for new black majority government.

1979 Britain's Lord Christopher Soames headed provisional government pending new elections.

1980 Zimbabwe gained formal independence (Apr. 18); Rev. Canaan Banana installed as president, Mugabe as prime minister.

1980 Zimbabwe admitted to UN.

Zimmermann Telegram ⟨Zimmermann Note⟩ Telegram sent (Jan. 16, 1917) by German foreign secretary Arthur Zimmermann to the German ambassador to the US suggesting an alliance with Mexico in the event of US entry into WW I against Germany. The telegram, intercepted and made public, helped arouse American sentiment against Germany.

Zimmerwald Conference Socialist conference (Sept. 4–8, 1915) at Zimmerwald, Switzerland, at which the European Socialist parties attempted to forge a common position on WW I. The conference denounced the war as imperialistic, but a faction led by N. Lenin denounced its resolutions as feeble and tepid.

Zinjanthropus *See* **Leakey, Louis Seymour Bazett**

Zinoviev, Grigori Evseyevich 1883–1936. Russian Communist leader who played a leading role in the Soviet government from 1917 to 1926. With J. Stalin and L. Kamenev he formed the triumvirate that ruled after the death of N. Lenin. He also headed the Comintern (1919–26). He was executed during the Stalinist purges.

Zinoviev letter Letter, probably a forgery, supposedly written (1924) by G. Zinoviev, then head of the Comintern. The letter called on British Communists to begin a revolution. The publication of the letter helped to bring down Britain's first Labour government.

Zinzendorf, Nikolaus Ludwig, Graf von 1700–60. German religious leader who refounded the Moravian church. His religious views greatly influenced 19th-cent. Protestantism.

Zion ⟨Sion⟩ ⟨Mount Sion⟩ Name originally given to a hill in Jerusalem on which stood the Jebusite city conquered by David. Now the word is symbolic of the Promised Land or of heaven.

Zionism Jewish movement for the establishment and preservation of a Jewish national state in Palestine. The first Zionist council was held (1897) in Basel, Switzerland under the leadership of T. Herzl. With the advent of WW I, Great Britain lent its support to the movement through the Balfour Declaration (1917). WW II reemphasized the need for a Jewish homeland. The United Nations plan for the partition of Palestine resulted in the establishment of a Jewish state (May, 1948).

Ziska, John *See* **Zizka, John**

Zita 1892–. Last empress of Austria and queen of Hungary (1916–18), wife of Austrian emperor Charles I (*m.* 1911).

Zizka, John ⟨Ziska, ~⟩ d. 1424. Bohemian military leader. He successfully led the Hussites against Holy Roman Emperor Sigismund in the Hussite Wars and introduced modern tactics of warfare.

Zoar Village in eastern Ohio. Founded (1817) by a group of German Protestant Separatists, it was the site until 1898 of a Separatist experimental communal society.

Zoë *c*978–1050. Byzantine empress (1028–50), daughter of and successor to Constantine VIII. She married Romanus III, but she had him murdered (1034) and made her lover emperor as Michael IV. Michael V, adopted by Zoë, was deposed after a brief reign (1041–42). Zoë next married Constantine IX.

Zog I ⟨Ahmed Bey Zogu⟩ 1895–1961. King of Albania (1928–39). He led Albania into military and financial dependence on Mussolini's Italy and was overthrown after the Italian invasion of Albania.

Zola, Émile 1840–1902. French novelist, a leader of the naturalist movement in France and one of the greatest French writers of the 19th cent. He played a leading role in the Dreyfus Affair.

Zollverein German customs union. Begun (early 19th cent.) by Prussia, it grew through the 19th cent. to include all the German states. Its policies were incorporated (1871) into the German Empire.

Zorndorf, Battle of ⟨Battle of Sarbinowo⟩ Prussian victory (Aug. 25, 1758) over the Russians at Zorndorf (Sarbinowo), Poland. The Russians lost some 24,000 men to the Austrian casualties of 11,000.

Zoroaster ⟨Zarathustra⟩ *c*628–*c*551 BC. Persian religious leader and reformer, founder of Zoroastrianism.

Zoroastrianism Ancient Persian religion founded (6th cent. BC) by Zoroaster. Its teachings center on Ahura Mazda, a god of righteousness, who would battle the evil spirits led by Ahriman until the ultimate victory over evil is achieved. Zoroastrianism was made the state religion of Persia by the Sassanidae (3d cent. AD) and is believed to have influenced both Judaism and Christianity. Its few remaining adherents are known as Parsees.

Zululand Historic region, since 1897 a part of the South African province of Natal. Occupied by the Zulus in the 17th cent., the region was the scene of conflicts, notably the Battle of Blood River *(q.v.)*, between Zulus and the Boers (then on the Great Trek). By 1840, the Boers were in control of Zululand. Thereafter the British, succeeding the Boers, warred against the Zulus, annexed Zululand in 1887, and made it part of Natal (1897).

Zurich Largest Swiss city (pop. 422,640) and one of the world's principal financial centers. Conquered by the Romans (58 BC), the city became a free imperial city (1219) and joined the Swiss Confederation (1351). It was a center of the Swiss Reformation and the home of H. Zwingli.

Zwingli, Huldreich *or* **Ulrich** 1484–1531. Swiss reformer, the leading figure in the Swiss Protestant Reformation. His opposition to M. Luther's views on the nature of the Eucharist led to great dissension within the Protestant church.